A GUIDE BOOK OF
UNITED STATES
COINS
DELUXE EDITION

Washington

From the Original Portrait Painted by Rembrandt Peale.

George Washington was president of the United States when the
first U.S. Mint was established in Philadelphia, Pennsylvania, in 1792.

THE OFFICIAL RED BOOK®

A GUIDE BOOK OF
UNITED STATES
COINS

DELUXE EDITION
1ST EDITION

R.S. YEOMAN

SENIOR EDITOR, KENNETH BRESSETT
WITH Q. DAVID BOWERS AND JEFF GARRETT

A Fully Illustrated Catalog of Useful Information on Colonial and Federal Coinage, 1616 to Date, With Detailed Photographs to Identify Your Coins and Retail Valuation Charts Indicating How Much They're Worth. Plus Illustrated Grading Instructions With Enlarged Images to Determine Your Coins' Conditions. Insider Tips on Treasures Waiting to be Discovered in Your Pocket Change; Advice on Smart Collecting; and More. Based on the Expertise of More Than 100 Professional Coin Dealers and Researchers. Also Featuring Entertaining Stories, Amazing Essays, and Astounding Facts and Figures About All Manner of Rare and Historical Coins of the United States of America.

A Guide Book of United States Coins™, Deluxe Edition
THE OFFICIAL RED BOOK OF UNITED STATES COINS™

THE OFFICIAL RED BOOK and
THE OFFICIAL RED BOOK OF UNITED STATES COINS
are trademarks of Whitman Publishing, LLC.

www.whitman.com

ISBN: 0794843077
Printed in the United States of America.

© 2015 Whitman Publishing, LLC
3101 Clairmont Road, Suite G, Atlanta GA 30329

OCG™ Collecting Guide   WHITMAN™

Collect all the books in the Bowers Series. *A Guide Book of Morgan Silver Dollars* • *A Guide Book of Double Eagle Gold Coins* • *A Guide Book of United States Type Coins* • *A Guide Book of Modern United States Proof Coin Sets* • *A Guide Book of Shield and Liberty Head Nickels* • *A Guide Book of Flying Eagle and Indian Head Cents* • *A Guide Book of Washington and State Quarters* • *A Guide Book of Buffalo and Jefferson Nickels* • *A Guide Book of Lincoln Cents* • *A Guide Book of United States Commemorative Coins* • *A Guide Book of United States Tokens and Medals* • *A Guide Book of Gold Dollars* • *A Guide Book of Peace Dollars* • *A Guide Book of the Official Red Book of United States Coins* • *A Guide Book of Franklin and Kennedy Half Dollars* • *A Guide Book of Civil War Tokens* • *A Guide Book of Hard Times Tokens* • *A Guide Book of Half Cents and Large Cents* • *A Guide Book of Barber Silver Dollars*

For a complete listing of numismatic reference books, supplies, and storage products,
visit Whitman Publishing online at www.whitman.com.

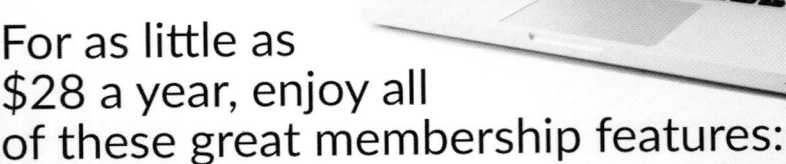

CONTENTS

CONTENTS

CONTENTS

CREDITS AND ACKNOWLEDGMENTS

CONTRIBUTORS TO THE FIRST
DELUXE EDITION RED BOOK

Senior Editor: Kenneth Bressett. Research Editor: Q. David Bowers. Valuations Editor: Jeff Garrett. Special Consultants: Philip Bressett, Robert Rhue, and Ben Todd.

The following coin dealers and collectors have contributed pricing information to this edition:

Gary Adkins	Steve Ellsworth	Jim Koenings	Joel Rettew Jr.
Mark Albarian	Pierre Fricke	John Kraljevich	Joel Rettew Sr.
Dominic Albert	Mike Fuljenz	Richard A. Lecce	Greg Rohan
Buddy Alleva	Dennis M. Gillio	Julian M. Leidman	Maurice Rosen
Richard S. Appel	Ronald J. Gillio	Stuart Levine	Mark Salzberg
Richard M. August	Rusty Goe	Kevin Lipton	Gerald R. Scherer Jr.
Lee J. Bellisario	Ira M. Goldberg	Denis W. Loring	Cherie Schoeps
Mark Borckardt	Lawrence Goldberg	Dwight Manley	Jeff Shevlin
Larry Briggs	Kenneth M. Goldman	David McCarthy	Roger Siboni
H. Robert Campbell	J.R. Grellman	Chris McCawley	James Simek
J.H. Cline	Tom Hallenbeck	Robert T. McIntire	Rick Snow
Elizabeth Coggan	James Halperin	Harry Miller	Scott Sparks
Alan Cohen	Ash Harrison	Lee S. Minshull	David M. Sundman
Gary Cohen	Steven Hayden	Scott P. Mitchell	Anthony J. Swiatek
James H. Cohen	Brian Hendelson	Michael C. Moline	Anthony Terranova
Stephen M. Cohen	John W. Highfill	Paul Montgomery	Troy Thoreson
Steve Contursi	Brian Hodge	Charles Morgan	Frank Van Valen
Marc Crane	John L. Howes	Casey Noxon	Fred Weinberg
Adam Crum	Steve Ivy	Paul Nugget	David Wnuck
Raymond Czahor	Joseph Jones	Mike Orlando	Mark S. Yaffe
John Dannreuther	Donald H. Kagin	Joseph Parrella	
Sheridan Downey	Bradley S. Karoleff	Robert M. Paul	

Special credit is due to the following for contributions to the *Guide Book of United States Coins, Deluxe Edition*: Gary Adkins, David W. Akers, John Albanese, David Allison, Jeff Ambio, the American Numismatic Society, Mitchell Battino, Jack Beymer, Doug Bird, Jon Alan Boka, Mark Borckardt, Q. David Bowers, Kenneth Bressett, Nicholas P. Brown, Roger W. Burdette, David J. Camire, Fonda Chase, Elizabeth Coggan, Greg Cohen, Ray Czahor, John W. Dannreuther, Beth Deisher, Dan Demeo, Cynthia Roden Doty, Richard Doty, Gregory V. DuBay, Bill Eckberg, Michael Fahey, Bill Fivaz, Pierre Fricke, Jeff Garrett, Ira Goldberg, Lawrence Goldberg, Ken Goldman, J.R. Grellman Jr., Ron Guth, James Halperin, Greg Hannigan, Daniel W. Holmes Jr., Gwyn Huston, Walter Husak, Tom Hyland, Wayne Imbrogno, Steve Ivy, R.W. Julian, Brad Karoleff, David W. Lange, Julian Leidman, Jon Lerner, Littleton Coin Company, Denis W. Loring, John Lusk, Ron Manley, J.P. Martin, Jim Matthews, Chris Victor-McCawley, Jim McGuigan, Jack McNamara, Harry Miller, Paul Minshull, Scott Mitchell, Charles Moore, Dan Moore, Jim Neiswinter, Eric P. Newman, Numismatic Guaranty Corporation of America (NGC), Joel J. Orosz, John Pack, Michael Printz, Jim Reardon, Tom Reynolds, Harry Salyards, Thomas Serfass, Neil Shafer, Jeff Shevlin, Craig Sholley, the Smithsonian Institution, Rick Snow, Max

Spiegel, Lawrence R. Stack, Stack's Bowers Galleries, David M. Sundman, James Taylor, Saul Teichman, R. Tettenhorst, Scott Travers, Rich Uhrich, the U.S. Mint (Tom Jurkowsky, director of corporate communications; Michael White; Maria Goodwin, historian; Abby Gilbert, assistant historian), Frank Van Valen, Alan V. Weinberg, Fred Weinberg, Ken and Stephanie Westover, Ray Williams, Doug Winter, and David Wnuck.

Special credit is due to the following for service and data in the 2016 regular edition of the *Guide Book of United States Coins*: Stewart Blay, Roger W. Burdette, Frank J. Colletti, Columbus–America Discovery Group, Charles Davis, Tom DeLorey, David Fanning, Bill Fivaz, Kevin Flynn, Chuck Furjanic, James C. Gray, Charles Hoskins, R.W. Julian, Richard Kelly, George F. Kolbe, David W. Lange, G.J. Lawson, Andy Lustig, J.P. Martin, Syd Martin, Eric P. Newman, John M. Pack, Ken Potter, P. Scott Rubin, Paul Rynearson, Mary Sauvain, Richard J. Schwary, Neil Shafer, Robert W. Shippee, Craig Smith, Jerry Treglia, Mark R. Vitunic, Holland Wallace, Weimar White, John Whitney, Raymond Williams, and John Wright.

Special credit is due to the following for service in past editions of the regular-edition *Guide Book of United States Coins*: David Akers, John Albanese, Lyman Allen, Jeff Ambio, Michael Aron, Mitchell A. Battino, Philip E. Benedetti, Richard A. Bagg, Jack Beymer, George Blenker, Walter Breen, John Burns, Jason Carter, James H. Cohen, Silvano DiGenova, Ken Duncan, Bob Entlich, John Feigenbaum, George Fitzgerald, Dennis Forgue, Harry Forman, George Fuld, Henry Garrett, William Gay, John Gervasoni, Harry Gittelson, Ron Guth, John Hamrick, Gene L. Henry, Karl D. Hirtzinger, Michael Hodder, Jesse Iskowitz, Robert Jacobs, James J. Jelinski, Larry Johnson, A.M. Kagin, Stanley Kesselman, Jerry Kimmel, Mike Kliman, Paul Koppenhaver, Robert B. Lecce, Ed Leventhal, Arnold Margolis, Glenn Miller, Richard Nachbar, William P. Paul, Thomas Payne, Beth Piper, Doug Plasencia, Andrew Pollock III, John Porter, Mike Ringo, J.S. Schreiber, Hugh Sconyers, Robert Shaw, Arlie Slabaugh, Thomas Smith, William Spencer, Paul Spiegel, Lawrence R. Stack, Maurice Storck Sr., Charles Surasky, Steve Tanenbaum, Mark Van Winkle, Russell Vaughn, and Douglas Winter.

Special photo credits are due to the following: Al Adams, the American Numismatic Association, the Architect of the Capitol (Washington, D.C.), Douglas F. Bird, Steve Contursi, Bill Fivaz, Ira & Larry Goldberg Coins & Collectibles, Heritage Auctions, Tom Mulvaney, Numismatic Guaranty Corporation of America (NGC), PCGS, Doug Plasencia, Brent Pogue, Sarasota Rare Coin Gallery, the Smithsonian Institution, Spectrum, Stack's Bowers Galleries, Superior Galleries, and the U.S. Mint.

HOW TO USE THIS BOOK

Numismatics, in its purest sense, is the study of items used as money. Today in the United States, as around the world, the term embraces the activities of a diverse community of hobbyists, historians, researchers, museum curators, and others who collect and study coins, tokens, paper money, and similar objects.

Since 1946 the *Guide Book of United States Coins* has served this community as the preeminent annual reference for coin specifications, mintages, values, photographs, and other information important to collectors and students. With more than 23 million copies in print since the first edition, the *Guide Book* (commonly known as the "Red Book") is well established as the most popular reference in numismatics—not to mention one of the best-selling nonfiction books in the history of American publishing. (In 1964 the 18th edition of the Red Book ranked number 5 on the national sales lists, at 1.2 million copies—higher than Dale Carnegie's *How to Win Friends and Influence People* at number 6, and John F. Kennedy's *Profiles in Courage* at number 9.)

Building on this strong foundation, the Deluxe Edition of the *Guide Book of United States Coins* is an expanded and enlarged volume intended to serve not only beginning collectors, but also intermediate to advanced coin collectors, professional coin dealers and auctioneers, researchers, and investors. It features more photographs, detailed higher-grade valuations, additional listings of die varieties and rare early Proof coins, certified-coin population data, auction records, and other resources that provide a wealth of information on every coin type ever made by the U.S. Mint. The Deluxe Edition also expands on the regular edition's coverage of collectible die varieties, with close-up photographs, valuations, and chart notes. It is a handy single-source guide that educates its users in auction and certification trends, retail valuations, and similar aspects of the marketplace.

Like the regular-edition Red Book, the Deluxe Edition includes information on colonial and early American coins and tokens as well as all federal series (copper half cents through gold double eagles). It also covers private and territorial gold pieces; Hard Times tokens; Civil War tokens; Confederate coins; Hawaiian, Puerto Rican, and Philippine coins; Alaskan tokens; misstrikes and errors; numismatic books; Proof and Mint sets; commemorative coins from 1892 to date; silver, gold, and platinum bullion coins; and other topics.

Readers of the *Guide Book of United States Coins, Deluxe Edition*, benefit from the following useful information.

The "Red Book" has become a popular collectible itself, with fans striving to acquire one of each edition dating back to number 1, published in November 1946 with a 1947 cover date. Rare early volumes can be worth $1,000 or more.

R.S. Yeoman, author of the original *Guide Book of United States Coins*, examining press proofs in 1969.

DENOMINATION INTRODUCTIONS

Each coinage denomination is discussed first in an overview of its history, major design types and sub-types, and general collectability by type. (The dollar denomination is divided into silver dollars, trade dollars, and modern dollars.) A second essay gives collectors a more in-depth analysis of specializing in that denomination. *These sections encapsulate decades of numismatic research and market observation, and they should be read in conjunction with the charts, photographs, and other information that follow.*

TYPE-BY-TYPE STUDIES

Within each denomination, each major coin type is laid out in chronological order. As in the regular-edition Red Book, the type's designer and its specifications (weight, composition, diameter, edge treatment, and production facilities) are given. Coinage designs are pictured at actual size (one Mint State example and one Proof example, when available). Each type section includes summary text on the type's history; aspects of its striking, sharpness, and related characteristics; and its market availability. In-depth grading instructions, with enlarged illustrations, show how to grade each coin type, covering circulation strikes as well as Proofs.

CHARTS

The data charts include these elements:

	Mintage	Cert	Avg	%MS	G-4	VG-8	F-12	VF-20	EF-40	AU-50	MS-60BN / PF-63BN	MS-63BN / PF-64BN	MS-65 / PF-65BN
1863	49,840,000	2,368	61.2	82%	$10	$15	$20	$30	$50	$75	$110	$200	$1,000
	Auctions: $3,055, MS-66, August 2014; $1,998, MS-66, November 2014; $2,820, MS-66, August 2013; $969, MS-65, July 2014												
1863, Doubled-Die Reverse (c)	(d)	2	62.5	100%					$200	$375	$450	$950	$3,000
	Auctions: No auction records available.												
1863, Proof	460	143	64.3								$900	$1,300	$2,500
	Auctions: $9,988, PF-67Cam, September 2014; $1,998, PF-65Cam, July 2014; $1,058, PF-64Cam, November 2014												
1864, Copper-Nickel	13,740,000	1524	58.9	75%	$20	$30	$40	$55	$100	$150	$200	$325	$1,600
	Auctions: $6,463, MS-66, April 2014; $3,055, MS-66, November 2014; $1,351, MS-65, October 2014; $676, MS-64, July 2014												
1864, Copper-Nickel, Proof	370	154	64.3								$900	$1,300	$2,500
	Auctions: $8,813, MS-67Cam, September 2014; $12,925, PF-66DCam, July 2014; $1,880, MS-64Cam, August 2014												

c. Strong doubling is evident on the right leaves of the wreath, and, to a lesser degree, on the upper left leaves. d. Included in circulation-strike 1863 mintage figure.

Mintages. Mintage data is compiled from official Mint records whenever possible, and in other cases from more than 70 years of active numismatic research. In instances where the Mint's early records are in question or have been proven faulty, the official numbers are provided and further information is given in chart notes. For some early Proof coins for which no official mintage records exist, an estimated mintage, or the number of coins known in collections, is given. For modern issues (usually those minted within the past five years), the Mint has released production and/or sales numbers that are not yet officially finalized; these are given in italics.

Note that Mint reports are not always reliable for estimating the rarities of coins. In the early years of the Mint, coinage dies of previous years often were used until they became worn or broken. Certain reported quantities, particularly for gold and silver coins, cover the number of pieces struck and make no indication of the quantity that actually reached circulation. Many issues were deposited in the Treasury as backing for paper currency and later were melted without ever being released to the public.

Gold coins struck before August 1, 1834, are rare today because from 1821 onward (and at times before 1821) the gold in the coins was worth more than their face values, so they were struck as bullion and traded at a premium. Many were exported and melted for their precious-metal value.

Mintage figures shown for 1964 through 1966 are for coins bearing those dates. Some of these coins were struck in more than one year and at various mints, both with and without mintmarks. In recent years, mintage figures reported by the Mint have been revised several times and precise amounts remain uncertain.

Mintage figures shown in italics are estimates based on the most accurate information available. Numismatic research is constantly ongoing, and listed figures are sometimes revised, when new information becomes available.

Certified Populations. For each coin of a particular date and mint, a summary is provided of (1) the number of coins certified, (2) the average grade, on the standard 1–70 scale, of those coins graded, and (3) for circulation-strike coins, the percentage certified in Mint State.

These summaries provide the collector and investor with working data useful in comparing coins offered for sale or bid.

Certified population data is provided courtesy of Numismatic Guaranty Corporation of America (NGC), one of the nation's leading professional third-party grading firms.

It should be noted that for most coins, especially rare dates and varieties, the number certified actually represents the quantity of *submissions*, rather than the number of individual coins submitted. For example, a particular 1801 silver dollar that is submitted for certification five times would be counted the same as five individual coins. Such resubmissions can sometimes result in numbers close to or higher than a coin's entire surviving mintage.

Note, too, that the grade number assigned to a "slabbed" (graded and encapsulated) coin does not tell anything about the strength of that particular coin's strike, the quality of its planchet, whether it has been cleaned or dipped, or its overall eye appeal. Such factors are important to a coin's value. Two rare coins of the same date and variety, each with the same amount of surface wear and graded, for example, MS-63, will find different values in the marketplace if one is eye-pleasing and well struck, and the other is dull and poorly struck.

Valuations. Coin values shown in the Deluxe Edition are retail prices compiled from data and market observations provided by active coin dealers, auctioneers, and other qualified observers, under the direction and analysis of Valuations Editor Jeff Garrett and Senior Editor Kenneth Bressett and their consultants. In this guide book, values from under $1 up to several hundred dollars are for "raw" coins—that is, coins that have *not* been graded and encapsulated by a professional third-party grading service. Values near or above $500 reflect typical auction and retail prices seen for professionally certified coins. The valuations of professionally certified coins often are higher than what collectors normally pay for non-certified ("raw") coins. Values of certified coins may vary widely, depending on the grading service.

The coin market is so active in some categories that values can readily change after publication. Values are shown as a guide and are not intended to serve as a price list for any dealer's stock. A dash appearing in a valuations column indicates that coins in that grade exist even though there are no current retail or auction records for them. The dash does not necessarily mean that such coins are exceedingly rare. Italicized numbers indicate unsettled or speculative (estimated) values. A number of listings of rare coins lack valuations or dashes in certain grades, indicating that they are not available, or not believed to exist, in those grades. Proof coins are not shown with values in circulated grades.

For wholesale pricing, the *Handbook of United States Coins* (popularly called the Blue Book, and published since 1942), by R.S. Yeoman, contains average prices dealers nationwide will pay for U.S. coins. It is obtainable through most coin dealers, hobby shops, bookstores, and the Internet.

Auction Records. Multiple recent auction records are provided for nearly every coin (some exceptions being coins that are too common to sell individually at auction). Each record indicates:

the price paid for the coin (including any fees)

the grade of the coin

the date (month and year) of the auction

This combination of auction data gives valuable market information for each coin. It also serves as a springboard for further research. Many auction firms have online archives of coins sold, or else their auction catalogs can be studied using the information provided.

Chart notes. Additional information is provided for certain coins in chart notes. Historical background, die-variety diagnostics, notable market conditions, and other specific details are intended to further guide the collector and investor.

Abbreviations. These are some of the abbreviations you'll find in the charts.

%MS—Percentage of coins certified in Mint State

Avg—Average grade (on a 1–70 scale)

BN—Brown; descriptive of the coloration or toning on certain copper coins

Cam—Cameo

Cert—Certified population

DblDie—Doubled die

DCam—Deep Cameo

DMPL—Deep Mirror Prooflike

D/S—D Over S; a slash between words or letters represents an overdate or overmintmark

Dt—Date

Ex.—extremely

FB—Full Bands

FBL—Full Bell Lines

FH—Full Head

FS—Full Steps

Horiz—Horizontal

Inv—Inverted

Knbd—Knobbed-Top

Lg—Large

Ltrd—Lettered

Ltrs—Letters

Med—Medium

Mintmk—Mintmark

Obv—Obverse

QuintDie—Quintupled Die

RB—Red and brown; descriptive of the mixture of mint red and brown coloration or toning on a copper coin

RD—Red; descriptive of the mint red color on an untoned copper coin

Rev—Reverse

RPD—Repunched Date

RPM—Repunched Mintmark

Sm—Small

SMS—Special Mint Set

Sq—Square

TransRev—Transitional Reverse

TripDie—Tripled Die

UCam—Ultra Cameo

Var—Variety

COLLECTING U.S. COINS
INVESTING IN RARE COINS

As with the regular edition of the *Guide Book of United States Coins*, those who edit, contribute to, and publish the Deluxe Edition advocate the collecting of coins for pleasure and educational benefits. A secondary consideration is that of investment, the profits of which are usually realized over the long term based on careful purchases. When it comes to investing in rare coins, knowledge is power.

USE COMMON SENSE

The rare-coin market combines some aspects of commodity trading with peculiarities seen more often among markets such as those for fine art, real estate, cut gemstones, and similar investments and collectibles. Armed with knowledge, an investor can have a very rewarding experience buying and selling rare coins. An uneducated investor can just as easily see substantial losses.

The regular edition of the *Guide Book of United States Coins* includes this bit of guidance, which bears repeating here: "The best advice given to anyone considering investing in rare coins is to use common sense." Any collector with common sense would think twice about buying a silver dollar at a flea market for less than its silver value. A common-sense collector who is offered a $1,000 coin from an "unsearched estate," or from a non-specialist who claims to know nothing of its provenance, would refuse it at $500— at least until a diligent examination was possible, and only with an iron-clad return policy and guarantee of authenticity. Profitable investment requires careful selection of qualified dealers (e.g., those professionally credentialed by groups such as the Professional Numismatists Guild [www.pngdealers.com] and the International Association of Professional Numismatists [www.iapn-coins.org]), and educated evaluation of the coins offered for sale.

LEARN ABOUT GRADING

In the past, coin grading was very subjective, and grade descriptions were far from universal. One dealer's "Choice Extremely Fine" might have been another's "About Uncirculated," and adjectives such as *gem* and *brilliant* varied in meaning from collector to collector. Today grading is still a subjective art striving to be an exact science, but progress has been made. The hobby's guidelines have been clearly standardized in systems such as the Official American Numismatic Association Grading Standards for United States Coins, and explored further in illustrated books such as *Grading Coins by Photographs: An Action Guide for the Collector and Investor*.

Today there are professional certification services such as NGC, PCGS, ICG, and ANACS that, for a fee, grade and authenticate coins, encapsulating them in sealed "slabs" with their grades noted. These are third-party firms, so called because they are neither buyer nor seller of the coins graded (which guarantees a professional level of impartiality to the process). Professional grading strives to be completely objective, but coins are graded by humans and not computers. This introduces the subjective element of *art* as opposed to *science*. A coin's grade, even if certified by a leading third-party grader (TPG), can be questioned by any collector or dealer—or even by the TPG that graded it, if the coin is resubmitted for a second look. Furthermore, within a given grade a keen observer will find coins that are low-quality, average, and high-quality for that grade. Such factors as luster, color, strength of strike, and overall eye appeal can make, for example, one MS-65 1914 Barber half dollar more visually attractive than another with the same grade. This gives the smart collector the opportunity to "cherrypick," or examine multiple slabbed coins and

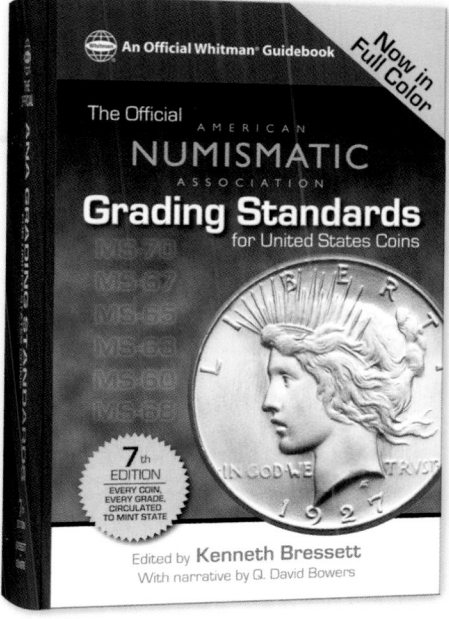

The official coin-grading standards of the American Numismatic Association have been codified in book form. This gives every coin collector and dealer a universal "language"—although grading does remain an art as well as a science.

select the highest-quality example for the desired grade. This process builds a better collection than simply accepting a TPG's assigned grades, and is summed up in the guidance of "Buy the coin, not the slab." (Also, note that a coin certified as, for example, MS-64 might have greater eye appeal—and therefore be more desirable to a greater number of collectors—than a less attractive coin graded MS-65.)

Over the years, collectors have observed a trend nicknamed "gradeflation": the reinterpretation, in practice, of the standards applied to a given grade over time. For example, a coin evaluated by a leading TPG in 1994 as MS-63 might be graded today as MS-65 or even MS-66.

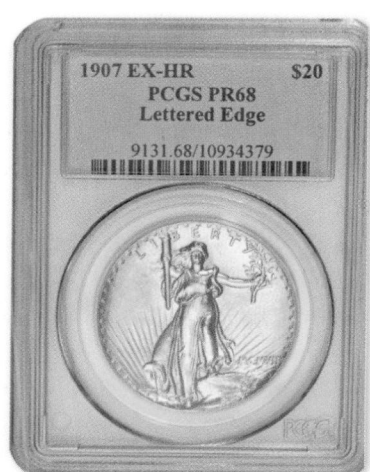

"Slabbed" coins are those that have been professionally graded and encapsulated by a third-party service such as ANACS, NGC, or PCGS.

LEARN ABOUT WHAT YOU'RE BUYING

In addition to carefully vetting professional dealers, examining potential purchases for authenticity (see below for more on this topic), and studying the art and science of grading, an investor can profit by *learning* about coins. Each coin type has a cultural history that provides useful collecting/investing knowledge. For example, the Treasury Department often stored Morgan dollars by the thousands (and millions), so a bag of 1,000 Mint State dollars is not unheard of. On the other hand, the purchaser of a seemingly original bank-wrapped roll of 20 Mint State trade dollars would likely be left holding a pound of counterfeit coins.

Similarly, each coin type has a typical strike, surface quality, and related characteristics; knowledge of these features can help reveal fakes and lower-than-average-quality specimens. The investor who knows that a certain coin type is rarely encountered in a certain high grade is more alert to potential opportunities. Conversely, if a type is common in high grades, the savvy investor will pass on an average or below-average coin and wait for a sharper, more attractive example, knowing that time and the marketplace are on his side.

For these reasons, even if you consider yourself more *investor* than *collector*, it is recommended that you read every section of this Deluxe Edition that covers the coin series in which you are interested. The price and data charts provide one level of information, the denomination introductions another, the type summaries and grading guides yet others; combined, they offer a well-rounded education that prices alone cannot provide.

UNDERSTAND THE GENERAL MARKET

Coin values rise when (1) the economic trend is inflationary and speculators turn to tangible assets as a hedge, or when the number of collectors increases, while coin supplies remain stationary or decrease through attrition or melting; (2) dealers replace their stocks of coins only from collectors or other dealers, who expect a profit over what they originally paid; (3) speculators attempt to influence the market through selective buying; or (4) bullion (gold and silver) prices rise.

Coin values decline when (1) changes in collecting habits or economic conditions alter demand for certain coins; (2) speculators sell in large quantities; (3) hoards or large holdings are suddenly released and cannot be quickly absorbed by the normal market; or (4) bullion (gold and silver) prices decline.

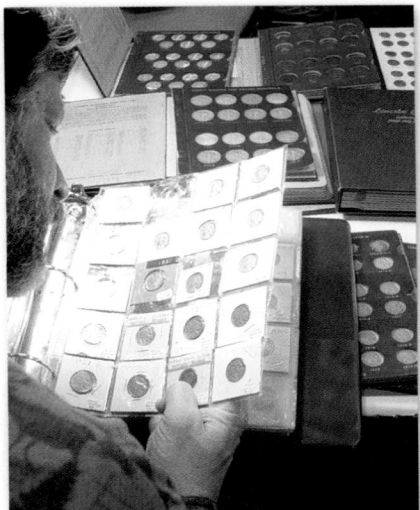

Attending a coin show gives you many opportunities to shop around, examine coins firsthand, talk to experienced collectors and dealers, and learn about the hobby.

LEARN FROM THE EXPERTS

A rich numismatic world is available to the investor and collector who seek to learn. News weeklies such as *Coin World* and *Numismatic News* cover the hobby and its markets from many angles, as do a variety of monthly magazines (like *COINage* and *Coins*) and online blogs. Auction sale results, new U.S. Mint products, convention activities, market reports, and other information await the interested reader.

Web sites such as www.Whitman.com/RedBook, www.NumisMaster.com, and www.CoinFacts.com gather and present information from authoritative sources.

Organizations such as the American Numismatic Association (the ANA, online at www.money.org) and the American Numismatic Society (the ANS, at www.numismatics.org), as well as dozens of specialized groups focused on particular coins or series, offer resources and connections to collectors worldwide.

Every major American city and many smaller cities have coin shops where experienced dealers can be consulted for advice and opinions.

Coin shows are another venue for learning from seasoned collectors and investors. The ANA mounts three popular shows annually, in different cities. Whitman Coin and Collectibles Expo (WhitmanExpo.com) hosts several shows yearly in Baltimore. Florida United Numismatists (FUN) organizes two shows in the winter and summer each year. All of these shows, and dozens of other local and regional conventions, offer opportunities to talk to other collectors and investors, meet market experts, listen to presentations, and examine hundreds of coins, tokens, and medals.

Books are another means of learning from the hobby's experts. Every collector and investor should have at least a basic numismatic library of standard references. (See the bibliography in the back of this volume.) In addition, nearly every specialty in American coins has one or more books devoted to greater in-depth exploration. Numismatic publishing has experienced a renaissance in recent years, making valuable knowledge more affordable and readily available than ever before. One book essential to the investor's understanding of the rare-coin market is a 672-page volume written by the "dean of American numismatics," Q. David Bowers. The *Expert's Guide to Collecting and Investing in Rare Coins* covers topics such as determining coin prices and values; focusing on rarity; quality and value for the smart buyer; coin-market fads, trends, and cycles; making of the modern market for rare coins; predicting the rare-coin market; techniques of smart buying and bidding; protecting your investment; and more. Robert W. Shippee's *Pleasure and Profit: 100 Lessons for Building and Selling a Collection of Rare Coins* offers first-hand insight from an experienced collector. Beth Deisher's *Cash In Your Coins: Selling the Rare Coins You've Inherited* advises on the selling side of the equation. These are just a few examples of the books awaiting today's collector.

In the long run, coin collectors—even those who seek mainly to profit financially from the hobby—are simply custodians of the relics they collect. Again, the regular edition of the *Guide Book of United States Coins* gives sound advice: "Those who treat rare coins with the consideration and respect they deserve will profit in many ways, not the least of which can be in the form of a sound financial return on one's investments of time and money."

SOME ASPECTS OF COLLECTING

The following topics—mints and mintmarks, checking your coins for authenticity, and coins from treasures and hoards as a key to understanding rarity and value—have proven very popular among collectors.

MINTS AND MINTMARKS

Mintmarks are small letters designating where coins were made. Coins struck at Philadelphia before 1979 (except five-cent pieces of 1942 to 1945) do not have mintmarks. Starting in 1979, a letter P was used on the dollar, and thereafter on all other denominations except the cent. The mintmark position is on the reverse of nearly all coins prior to 1965 (the cent is an exception), and on the obverse after 1967.

C—Charlotte, North Carolina (gold coins only; 1838–1861)

CC—Carson City, Nevada (gold and silver coins only; 1870–1893)

D—Dahlonega, Georgia (gold coins only; 1838–1861)

D—Denver, Colorado (1906 to date)

M—Manila (Philippines; 1920–1941; M not used in early years)

O—New Orleans, Louisiana (gold and silver coins only; 1838–1861; 1879–1909)

P—Philadelphia, Pennsylvania (1793 to date; P not used in early years)

S—San Francisco, California (1854 to date)

W—West Point, New York (1984 to date)

| Charlotte, North Carolina | Carson City, Nevada | Dahlonega, Georgia | Denver, Colorado | Manila, Philippines |

| New Orleans, Louisiana | Philadelphia, Pennsylvania | San Francisco, California | West Point, New York |

Prior to 1996 all dies for U.S. coins were made at the Philadelphia Mint. Some dies are now made at the Denver Mint. Dies for use at other mints are made with the appropriate mintmarks before they are shipped to those mints. Because this was a hand operation prior to 1985, the exact positioning and size of the mintmarks may vary slightly, depending on where and how deeply the punches were impressed. (For an example in this book, see the 1975-D Jefferson nickel.) This also accounts for double-punched and superimposed mintmarks such as the 1938 D Over D, and D Over S, Buffalo nickels. Polishing of dies may also alter the apparent size of fine details. Occasionally the mintmark is inadvertently left off a die sent to a branch mint, as was the case with some recent Proof cents, nickels, and dimes. Similarly, some 1982 dimes without mintmarks were made as circulation strikes. The mintmark M was used on coins made in Manila for the Philippines from 1925 through 1941.

Prior to 1900, punches for mintmarks varied greatly in size. This is particularly noticeable in the 1850 to 1880 period, in which the letters range from very small to very large. An attempt to standardize sizes started in 1892 with the Barber series, but exceptions are seen in the 1892-O half dollar and 1905-O dime, both of which have normal and "microscopic" mintmarks. A more or less standard-size, small mintmark was used on all minor coins starting in 1909, and on all dimes, quarters, and halves after the Barber series was replaced in 1916. Slight variations in mintmark size occur through 1945, with notable differences in 1928, when small and large S mintmarks were used.

In recent years a single D or S punch has been used to mark all branch-mint dies. The change to the larger D for Denver coins occurred in 1933. Nickels, dimes, quarter dollars, half dollars, and dollars of 1934 exist with either the old, smaller-size mintmark or the new, larger-size D. All other denominations of 1934 and after are standard. The San Francisco mintmark was changed to a larger size during 1941 and, with the exception of the half dollar, all 1941-S coins are known with either small or large mintmarks. Halves were not changed until 1942, and the 1942-S and 1943-S pieces exist both ways. The

1945-S dime with "microscopic" S is an unexplained use of a punch originally intended for Philippine coins of 1907 through 1920. In 1979, the punches were replaced. Varieties of some 1979 coins appear with either the old- or new-shaped S or D. The S punch was again replaced in 1981 with a punch that yielded a more distinct letter.

The mintmark application technique for Proof coins was changed in 1985, and for circulation-strike production in 1990 and 1991, when the letter was applied directly to the master die rather than being hand punched on each working die. At the same time, all the mintmark letters were made much larger and clearer than those of previous years.

CHECKING YOUR COINS FOR AUTHENTICITY

Coin collectors occasionally encounter counterfeit coins, or coins that have been altered so that they appear to be something other than what they really are. Any coin that does not seem to fit the description of similar pieces listed in this guide book should be looked upon with suspicion. Experienced coin dealers can usually tell quickly whether a coin is genuine, and would never knowingly sell spurious coins to a collector. Rare coins found in circulation or bought from a nonprofessional source should be examined carefully.

The risk of purchasing a spurious coin can be minimized through the use of common sense and an elementary knowledge of the techniques used by counterfeiters. It is well to keep in mind that the more popular a coin is among collectors and the public, the more likely it is that counterfeits and replicas will abound. Until recently, collector coins valued at under $100 were rarely replicated because of the high cost of making such items. The same

These "coins" might appear authentic at first glance, but they're actually modern fakes, made to deceive unwary collectors.

was true of counterfeits made to deceive the public. Few counterfeit coins were made because it was more profitable for the fakers to print paper money. Today, however, counterfeiters in Asia and elsewhere create fakes of a surprising variety of coins, most notably silver dollar types, but also smaller denominations.

The best way to detect counterfeit coins is to compare suspected pieces with others of the same issue. Carefully check size, color, luster, weight, edge devices, and design details. Replicas generally have less detail than their genuine counterparts when studied under magnification. Modern struck counterfeits made to deceive collectors are an exception to this rule. Any questionable gold coin should be referred to an expert for verification.

Cast forgeries are usually poorly made and of incorrect weight. Base metal is often used in place of gold or silver, and the coins are lightweight and often incorrect in color and luster. Deceptive cast pieces have been made using real metal content and modern dental techniques, but these too usually vary in quality and color.

Detection of alterations sometimes involves comparative examination of the suspected areas of a coin (usually mintmarks and date digits) at magnification ranging from 10x to 40x.

Coins of exceptional rarity or value should never be purchased without a written guarantee of authenticity. Professional authentication of rare coins for a fee is available with the services offered by commercial grading services, and by some coin dealers.

Three types of spurious coins you might encounter are replicas, counterfeits, and alterations.

Replicas. Reproductions of famous and historical coins have been distributed for decades by marketing firms and souvenir vendors. These pieces are often tucked away as curios by the original recipients, perhaps in a desk drawer or jewelry box, and later are found by others who believe they have discovered objects of great value. Genuine specimens of extremely rare and/or valuable coins are almost never found in unlikely places.

Most replicas are poorly made, often by the casting method (as opposed to being struck by dies), and are virtually worthless other than as novelties. They can sometimes be identified by a seam that runs around the edge of the piece where the two halves of the casting mold were joined together.

Counterfeits. For many centuries, counterfeiters have produced base-metal forgeries of gold and silver coins to deceive the public in the normal course of trade. These pieces are usually crudely made and easily detected on close examination. Crudely cast counterfeit copies of older coins are the most prevalent. These can usually be detected by the casting bubbles or pimples that can be seen with low-power magnification. Pieces struck from handmade dies are more deceptive, but the engravings do not match those of genuine mint products.

More recently, as coin collecting has gained popularity and rare-coin prices have risen, "numismatic" counterfeits (made not to pass in commerce, but for sale to unsuspecting collectors) have become more common. The majority of these are die-struck counterfeits of gold coins, mass produced overseas since 1950. Forgeries exist of most U.S. gold coins dated between 1870 and 1933, as well as all issues of the gold dollar and three-dollar gold piece. Most of these are very well made, as they were intended to pass the close scrutiny of collectors. Few gold coins of earlier dates have been counterfeited, but false 1799 ten-dollar gold pieces and 1811 five-dollar coins have been made. Gold coins in less than Extremely Fine condition are seldom counterfeited. For more information, including extensive illustrations, consult the *United States Gold Counterfeit Detection Guide*, by Bill Fivaz.

Silver dollars dated 1804, Lafayette commemorative dollars of 1900, several of the low-mintage commemorative half dollars, and 1795 half dimes have been forged in quantity. Minor-coin forgeries made in recent years are the 1909-S V.D.B., 1914-D, and 1955 doubled-die Lincoln cents, 1877 Indian Head cents, 1856 Flying Eagle cents, and, on a much smaller scale, a variety of dates of half cents and large cents. Nineteenth-century copies of colonial coins are also sometimes encountered (see the *Whitman Encyclopedia of Colonial and Early American Coins*).

Commonly seen modern-day counterfeits produced in China include Bust dollars; Liberty Seated dimes, quarters, halves, and dollars; Morgan dollars; and even American Silver Eagles, all of various dates and mintmarks—some fantastical (for example, Morgan dollars dated in the 1700s).

Alterations. Deceivers occasionally alter coins by the addition, removal, or change of a design feature (such as a mintmark or date digit) or by the polishing, sandblasting, acid etching, toning, or plating of the surface of a genuine piece. Among U.S. gold coins, only the 1927-D double eagle is commonly found with a deceptively added mintmark. On $2.50 and $5 gold coins, 1839 through 1856, New Orleans O mintmarks have been altered to C (for Charlotte, North Carolina) in a few instances.

More than a century ago, fraudsters imitated five-dollar gold pieces by gold-plating 1883 Liberty Head five-cent coins of the type without the word CENTS on the reverse. Other coins commonly created fraudulently through alteration include the 1799 large cent and the 1909-S, 1909-S V.D.B., 1914-D, 1922 "plain," and 1943 "copper" cents. The 1913 Liberty Head nickel has been extensively replicated by the alteration of 1903 and 1912 nickels. Scarce, high-grade Denver and San Francisco Buffalo nickels of the 1920s; 1916-D and 1942 Over 1941 dimes; 1918 Over 1917-S quarters; 1932-D and -S quarters; and 1804 silver dollars have all been crafted by the alteration of genuine coins of other dates or mints.

COINS FROM TREASURES AND HOARDS:
A KEY TO UNDERSTANDING RARITY AND VALUE

The following discussion of coin treasures and hoards is derived from the writing of Q. David Bowers.

ELEMENTS OF RARITY

In many instances, the mintage of a coin can be a factor in its present-day rarity and value. However, across American numismatics there are many important exceptions, some very dramatic. As an introduction and example, in this book you will find many listings of Morgan silver dollars of 1878 through 1921 for which the mintage figure does not seem to correlate with the coin's price. For example, among such coins the 1901, of which 6,962,000 were made for circulation, is valued at $475,000 in MS-65. In the same series the 1884-CC, of which only 1,136,000 were struck, is listed at $525, or only a tiny fraction of the value of a 1901.

Why the difference? The explanation is that nearly all of the 6,962,000 dollars of 1901 were either placed into circulation at the time and became worn, or were melted generations ago. Very few were saved by collectors, and today MS-65 coins are extreme rarities. On the other hand, of the 1,166,000 1884-CC silver dollars minted, relatively few went into circulation. Vast quantities were sealed in 1,000-coin cloth bags and put into government storage. Generations later, as coin collecting became popular, thousands were paid out by the Treasury Department. Years after that, in the early 1960s, when silver metal rose in value, there was a "run" on long-stored silver dollars, and it was learned in March 1964 that 962,638 1884-CC dollars—84.7% of the original mintage—were still in the hands of the Treasury Department!

With this information, the price disparities become understandable. Even though the 1901 had a high mintage, few were saved, and although worn coins are common, gem MS-65 coins are rarities. In contrast, nearly all of the low-mintage 1884-CC dollars were stored by the government, and today most of them still exist, including some in MS-65 grade.

There are many other situations in which mintages are not particularly relevant to the availability and prices of coins today. Often a special circumstance will lead to certain coins' being saved in especially large quantities, later dramatically affecting the availability and value of such pieces. The following are some of those circumstances.

Excitement of a New Design. In the panorama of American coinage, some new designs have captured the fancy of the public, who saved them in large quantities when they were released. In many other instances new designs were ignored, and coins slipped into circulation unnoticed.

In 1909 great publicity was given to the new Abraham Lincoln portrait to be used on the one-cent piece, replacing the familiar Indian Head motif. On the reverse in tiny letters were the initials, V.D.B., of the coin's designer, Victor David Brenner. The occasion was the 100th anniversary of Lincoln's birth. Coinage commenced at the Philadelphia and San Francisco mints. In total, 27,995,000 1909 V.D.B. cents were struck and 484,000 of the 1909-S V.D.B.

On August 2, 1909, the new cents were released to the public. A mad scramble ensued, and soon banks had to ration the number paid out to any single individual, this being particularly true in the East. (Interest in the West was less intense, and fewer coins were saved there.) A controversy arose as to the V.D.B. initials, and some newspaper notices complained that as Brenner had been paid for his work, there was no point in giving his initials a prominent place on the coins. Never mind that artists' initials had been used on other coins for a long time. As examples, the M initial of George T. Morgan appeared on both the obverse and reverse of silver dollars from 1878 onward; Chief Engraver Charles E. Barber was memorialized by a B on the neck of Miss Liberty on dimes, quarters, and half dollars from 1892 onward; and the recent (1907 onward) double eagles bore the monogram of Augustus Saint-Gaudens prominently on the obverse. In spite of these precedents, the offending V.D.B. initials were removed, and later 1909 and 1909-S cents were made without them.

Word spread that the cents with V.D.B. would be rare, and people saved even more of them. Today, the 1909 V.D.B. cents are readily available in Mint State. The 1909-S V.D.B., of lower mintage and of which far fewer were saved, lists for $1,950 in MS-63.

Other Popular First-Year Coins. Among other United States coins struck since 1792, these first-year-of-issue varieties (a partial list) were saved in large numbers and are especially plentiful today:

- **1837 Liberty Seated, No Stars, half dime.** Several thousand or more were saved, a large number for a half dime of the era. Apparently, their cameo-like appearance made them attractive curiosities at the time, the same being true of the dimes of the same year.

- **1837 Liberty Seated, No Stars, dime.** Somewhat more than a thousand were saved, a large number for a dime of the era.

- **1883 Liberty Head, Without CENTS, nickel.** The U.S. Mint expressed the value of this new design simply as "V," without mention of cents—not particularly unusual, as three-cent pieces of the era were simply denominated as "III." Certain people gold-plated the new nickels and passed them off as five-dollar gold coins of similar diameter. Soon, the Mint added the word CENTS. News accounts were printed that the "mistake" coins without CENTS would be recalled and would become very rare. Americans saved so many that today this variety is the most plentiful in Mint State of any Liberty Head nickel in the entire series from 1883 to 1913.

- **1892 and 1893 World's Columbian Exposition commemorative half dollars.** These, the first U.S. commemorative half dollars, were widely publicized, and hundreds of thousands were saved. Today they are very common in used condition, because quantities were eventually released into circulation as if they were regular half dollars.

- **MCMVII (1907) High-Relief gold twenty-dollar coin.** Although only about 12,000 were minted, at least 6,000 survive today, mostly in Mint State. Released in December 1907, the coin, by famous sculptor Augustus Saint-Gaudens, created a sensation, and soon examples were selling for $30 each. Today, Mint State coins are plentiful, but as the demand for them is extremely strong, choice specimens sell for strong prices. An MS-63 coin lists for $25,000.

- **1913 Buffalo nickel.** These were saved in large quantities, and today there are more Mint State coins of this year in existence than for any other issue of the next 15 years.

Many coins have been saved as special souvenirs. People often notice a new coinage design and will set examples aside from the first year of issue, making high-grade pieces available for later generations of collectors. Pictured: an 1883 No CENTS Liberty Head nickel; a steel 1943 cent; and a 1999 State quarter.

- **1916 Mercury dime.** In 1916, the Mercury dime's first year of issue, Americans saved many of the new coins from the Philadelphia and San Francisco mints. However, for some reason the low-mintage 1916-D was generally overlooked and today is very rare in Mint State.

- **1932 Washington quarter.** At the Philadelphia Mint, 5,504,000 were minted, and it is likely that several hundred thousand were saved, making them plentiful today. The 1932-D quarter was struck to the extent of 436,800, but for some reason was overlooked by the public, with the result that Mint State coins are rare today. On the other hand, of the 408,000 1932-S quarters struck, thousands were saved. Today, Mint State 1932-S quarters are at least 10 to 20 times more readily available than are equivalent examples of the higher-mintage 1932-D.

- **1943 zinc-coated steel cent.** The novel appearance of this coin resulted in many being saved as curiosities.

- **1964 Kennedy half dollar.** The popularity of the assassinated president was such that many of the hundreds of millions of 1964 half dollars were saved as souvenirs both at home and abroad. This was also the last year the 90% silver half dollar was made for circulation (later versions were 40% silver or copper-nickel), which further increased its popularity.

- **1999–2008 State quarters.** From 1999 to 2008, five different quarter dollar designs were produced each year, with motifs observing the states in the order that they joined the Union. These coins were highly publicized, and hobby companies produced folders, albums, maps, and other holders to store and display them. A Treasury Department study estimated that 98 million Americans saved one or more sets of the coins, starting with the first one issued (Delaware) and continuing to the last (Hawaii).

- **2000 Sacagawea "golden dollar."** These coins, intended to be a popular substitute for paper dollars and to last much longer in circulation, were launched with great fanfare in 2000, and more than just a few were saved by the public. However, the coin did not catch on for general use in commerce. Later issues have been made for sale to collectors, but no quantities have been released for circulation.

COINS FEW PEOPLE NOTICED

In contrast to the examples above, most coins of new designs attracted no particular notice when they were first issued, and were not saved in unusual quantities. In sharp contrast to the highly popular Kennedy half dollar of 1964, its predecessor, the Franklin half dollar (launched in 1948), generated very little interest, and even numismatists generally ignored its debut—perhaps preferring the old Liberty Walking design, which had been a favorite.

Although a long list could be made, here is just a sampling of first-year-of-issue coins that were not noticed in their own time. Few were set aside in like-new condition. Consequently, today they range from scarce to rare in Mint State:

- **1793 cent and half cent.** As popular as these may be today, there is no known instance in which a numismatist or museum in 1793 deliberately saved pieces as souvenirs.

- **1794–1795 Flowing Hair half dime, half dollar, and silver dollar.** The Flowing Hair coins, highly desired today, seem to have attracted little notice in their time, and again there is no record of any having been deliberately saved.

- **1807 and related Capped Bust coinages.** The Capped Bust and related coins of John Reich, assistant engraver at the Mint, were first used in 1807 on the silver half dollar and gold five-dollar piece, and later on certain other denominations. Today these are extremely popular with collectors, but in their time they were not noticed, and few were saved in Mint State.

- **1840 Liberty Seated dollar.** Examples are very scarce in Mint State today and are virtually unknown in gem preservation.

- **1892 Barber dime, quarter dollar, and half dollar.** In 1892 the new Liberty Head design by Charles E. Barber replaced the long-lived Liberty Seated motif. The new coins received bad press notices. Another factor detracting from public interest was the wide attention focused on the forthcoming commemorative half dollars of the World's Columbian Exposition. Not many of the new Barber coins were saved.

- **1938 Jefferson nickel.** Although the numismatic hobby was dynamic at the time, the new nickel design attracted little notice, and no unusual quantities were saved. The market was still reeling from the burst bubble of the 1935 through 1936 commemorative craze, and there was little incentive to save coins for investment.

THE 1962–1964 TREASURY RELEASE

The Bland-Allison Act of February 28, 1878, was a political boondoggle passed to accommodate silver-mining interests in the West. It mandated that the Treasury Department buy millions of ounces of silver each year and convert it to silver dollars. At the time, the world price of silver bullion was dropping, and there were economic difficulties in the Western mining states. From 1878 to 1904 and again in 1921, silver dollars of the Morgan design were minted under Bland-Allison and subsequent acts, to the extent of 656,989,387 pieces. From 1921 to 1928, and in 1934 and 1935, silver dollars of the Peace design were produced in the amount of 190,577,279 pieces.

Although silver dollars were used in commerce in certain areas of the West, paper currency by and large served the needs of trade and exchange. As these hundreds of millions of newly minted dollars were not needed, most were put up in 1,000-coin canvas bags and stored in Treasury vaults. In 1918, under terms of the Pittman Act, 270,232,722 Morgan dollars were melted. At the time, with World War I in its fifth year, the market for silver was temporarily strong, and there was a call for bullion to ship to India to shore up confidence in Britain's wartime government. No accounting was kept of the dates and mints involved in the destruction. Only the quantities were recorded (this procedure being typical when the Treasury melted old coins). However, hundreds of millions remained. Now and again there was a call for silver dollars for circulation, especially in the West; and in the East and Midwest there was a modest demand for pieces for use as holiday and other gifts; in such instances many were paid out. The example of the high-mintage 1901

Typical silver mining scene, late 1880s.

THE CARSON CITY SILVER DOLLARS
THE LAST OF A LEGACY

The cover to a GSA flyer advertising the Treasury's hoard of Carson City silver dollars for sale.

dollar being rare in Mint State, as most were circulated, is reflective of this. Other coins were stored, such as the low-mintage 1884-CC, of which 84.7% were still in the hands of the Treasury as late as 1964! At this time the Treasury decided to hold back bags that were marked as having Carson City dollars, although in records of storage no account was made of them earlier.

A Carson City Morgan dollar from the Treasury release.

Beginning in a significant way in the 1950s, silver dollars became very popular with numismatists. The rarest of all Morgan silver dollars by 1962 was considered to be the 1903-O. In the *Guide Book of United States Coins*, an Uncirculated coin listed for $1,500, the highest price for any variety. Experts estimated that fewer than a dozen Mint State coins existed in all of numismatics. It was presumed that most had been melted in 1918 under the Pittman Act.

Then, in November 1962, during the normal payout of silver dollars as gifts for the holiday season, some long-sealed bags of coins were taken from a Philadelphia Mint vault that had remained under seal since 1929. It was soon found that brilliant 1903-O dollars were among these! A treasure hunt ensued, and hundreds of thousands of these former rarities were found. The rush was on!

From then until March 1964, hundreds of millions of Morgan and Peace dollars were emptied from government and bank storage. At one time a long line of people, some with wheelbarrows, formed outside of the Treasury Building in Washington, D.C., to obtain bags of dollars. Finally only about three million coins remained, mostly the aforementioned Carson City issues, which the Treasury decided to hold back. These were later sold at strong premiums in a series of auctions held by the General Services Administration (GSA). In the meantime, Morgan and Peace dollars became very large and important sections of the coin hobby, as they remain today. However, as can be seen, the combined elements of some coins' having been melted in 1918, others having been placed into circulation generations ago, and still others existing in Mint State from long-stored hoards, results in silver dollar prices that often bear little relation to mintage figures.

OTHER FAMOUS HOARDS

While the great Treasury release of 1962 through 1964 is the most famous of all hoards, quite a few others have attracted interest and attention over the years.

- **The Castine Hoard of Early Silver Coins (discovered in the 1840s).** From November 1840 through April 1841, Captain Stephen Grindle and his son Samuel unearthed many silver coins on their farm on the Bagaduce River about six miles from the harbor of Castine, Maine. The number of pieces found was not recorded, but is believed to have been between 500 and 2,000, buried in 1690 (the latest date observed) or soon afterward. Most pieces were foreign silver coins, but dozens of Massachusetts Pine Tree shillings and related silver coins were found. This hoard stands today as one of the most famous in American history.

- **The Bank of New York Hoard (1856).** Around 1856 a keg containing several thousand 1787 Fugio copper cents was found at the Bank of New York at 44 Wall Street. Each was in Mint State, most with brown toning. For many years these were given out as souvenirs and keepsakes to clients. By 1948, when numismatist Damon G. Douglas examined them, there were 1,641 remaining. Today, many remain at the bank and are appreciated for their history and value.

- **The Nichols Find of Copper Cents (by 1859).** In the annals of American numismatics, one of the most famous hoards is the so-called Nichols Find, consisting of 1796 and 1797 copper cents, Mint State, perhaps about 1,000 in total. These were distributed in the late 1850s by David Nichols. All were absorbed into the hobby community as of 1863, by which time they were worth $3 to $4 each, or less than a thousandth of their present-day value.

- **The Randall Hoard of Copper Cents (1860s).** Sometime soon after the Civil War, a wooden keg filled with as-new copper cents was located, said to have been beneath an old railroad platform in Georgia. Revealed were thousands of coins dated 1816 to 1820, with the 1818 and 1820 being the most numerous. Today, the Randall hoard accounts for most known Mint State examples of these particular dates.

- **The Colonel Cohen Hoard of 1773 Virginia Halfpennies (by the 1870s).** Sometime in the 1870s or earlier, Colonel Mendes I. Cohen, a Baltimore numismatist, obtained a cache of at least 2,200 Uncirculated 1773 Virginia halfpennies. These passed through several hands, and many individual pieces were dispersed along the way. As a result, today they are the only colonial (pre-1776) American coins that can be easily obtained in Mint State.

- **The Exeter Hoard of Massachusetts Silver (1876).** During the excavation of a cellar near the railroad station in Exeter, New Hampshire, a group of 30 to 40 Massachusetts silver shillings was found in the sand, amid the remains of what seemed to be a wooden box. All bore the date 1652 and were of the Pine Tree and Oak Tree types, plus, possibly, a rare Willow Tree shilling.

- **The Economite Treasure (1878).** In 1878 a remarkable hoard of silver coins was found in a subterranean storage area at Economy, Pennsylvania, in a building erected years earlier by the Harmony Society, a utopian work-share community. The March 1881 issue of the *Coin Collector's Journal* gave this inventory: Quarter dollars: 1818 through 1828, 400 pieces. Half dollars: 1794, 150; 1795, 650; 1796, 2; 1797, 1; 1801, 300; 1802, 200; 1803, 300; 1805 Over 04, 25; 1805, 600; 1806, 1,500; 1807, 2,000; 1815, 100. Common half dollars: 1808 through 1836, 111,356. Silver dollars: 1794, 1; 1795, 800; 1796, 125; 1797, 80; 1798 Small Eagle reverse, 30; 1798 Large Eagle reverse, 560; 1799 5 stars facing, 12; 1799, 1,250; 1800, 250; 1801, 1802, and 1803, 600. Foreign silver (French, Spanish, and Spanish-American), total face value: $12,600. Total face value of the hoard: $75,000. Other information indicates that most of the coins had been taken from circulation and showed different degrees of wear.

- **The Hoard of Miser Aaron White (before 1888).** Aaron White, a Connecticut attorney, distrusted paper money and even went so far as to issue his own token with the legend NEVER KEEP A PAPER DOLLAR IN YOUR POCKET TILL TOMORROW. He had a passion for saving coins and accumulated more than 100,000 pieces. After his death the coins were removed to a warehouse. Later, they were placed in the hands of dealer Édouard Frossard, who sold most of them privately and others by auction on July 20, 1888, billing them as "18,000 American and foreign copper coins and tokens selected from the Aaron White hoard." An overall estimate of the White hoard, as it existed before it was given to Frossard, was made by Benjamin P. Wright, and included these: "250 colonial and state copper coins, 60,000 copper large cents (which were mainly 'rusted' and spotted; 5,000 of the nicest ones were picked out and sold for 2¢ each), 60,000 copper-nickel Flying Eagle and Indian cents (apparently most dated 1862 and 1863), 5,000 bronze two-cent pieces, 200 half dollars, 100 silver dollars, 350 gold dollars, and 20,000 to 30,000 foreign copper coins."

- **The Collins Find of 1828 Half Cents (1894).** Circa 1894, Benjamin H. Collins, a Washington, D.C., numismatist, acquired a bag of half cents dated 1828, of the 13-stars variety. Historians believe that about 1,000 coins were involved, all bright Uncirculated. By the early 1950s all but a few hundred had been distributed in the marketplace, and by now it is likely that all have individual owners.

- **The Chapman Hoard of 1806 Half Cents (1906).** About 1906, Philadelphia dealer Henry Chapman acquired a hoard of 1806 half cents. Although no figure was given at the time, it is estimated that a couple hundred or so coins were involved. Most or all had much of their original mint red color, toning to brown, and with light striking at the upper part of the wreath.

- **The Baltimore Find (1934).** One of the most storied hoards in American numismatics is the Baltimore Find, a cache of at least 3,558 gold coins, all dated before 1857. On August 31, 1934, two young boys were playing in the cellar of a rented house at 132 South Eden Street, Baltimore, and found these coins hidden in a wall. Later, more were found in the same location. On May 2, 1935, many of the coins were sold at auction, by which time others had been sold quietly, some unofficially. This hoard included many choice and gem coins dated in the 1850s. Leonard Augsburger's award-winning *Treasure in the Cellar* tells the complete tale.

- **The New Orleans Bank Find (1982).** A few minutes past noon, on October 29, 1982, a bulldozer unearthed a cache of long-hidden silver coins, believed to have been stored in three wooden boxes in the early 1840s. They were mostly Spanish-American issues, but hundreds of United States coins, including 1840-O and 1841-O Liberty Seated quarters, were also found. Men in business suits, ladies in dresses, and others scrambled in the dirt and mud to find treasure. The latest-dated coin found was from 1842. This must have been a secret reserve of some long-forgotten merchant or bank.

- **Wells Fargo Hoard of 1908 $20 (1990s).** In the 1990s, dealer Ron Gillio purchased a hoard of 19,900 examples of the 1908 No Motto double eagle. For a time these were stored in a Wells Fargo Bank branch, giving the name to the cache. All were Mint State, and many were of choice and gem quality. Offered in the market, these were dispersed over a period of several years.

- **Gold coins from abroad (turn of the 21st century).** In the late 20th and early 21st centuries, some exciting finds of Mint State double eagles were located in foreign banks. Involved were high-grade examples of some Carson City issues in the Liberty Head series and hundreds of scarce-mintmark varieties dated after 1923. As is often the case when hoards are discovered, pieces were filtered into the market without any publicity or an accounting of varieties found.

SUNKEN TREASURE

Throughout American history, tens of thousands of ships have been lost at sea and on inland waters. Only a handful of these vessels were reported as having had significant quantities of coins aboard. In recent decades, numismatists have been front-row center as wrecks from several sidewheel steamers lost in the 1850s and 1860s have yielded rare coins.

The SS *New York* was launched in 1837, carrying passengers between New York City and Charleston, South Carolina. The steamer was carrying $30,000 or more in money when she encountered an unexpected hurricane in the Gulf of Mexico on September 5, 1846. Captain John D. Phillips ordered the anchor dropped, hoping to ride out the storm. The wind and waves increased, however, and for two days those aboard watched as the rigging and other parts of the ship were torn apart. On September 7 the storm prevailed and the *New York* was overwhelmed, sinking into water 60 feet deep. An estimated 17 people—about one third of the passengers and crew—lost their lives. Decades later, in 2006 and 2007, treasure seekers recovered more than 2,000 silver coins and several hundred gold coins from the shipwreck. Most of the silver was heavily etched from exposure to the salt water, but certain of the gold coins were in high grades, including some of the finest known examples of their date and mint.

Eight years after the loss of the *New York*, the SS *Yankee Blade* was off the coast of Santa Barbara, California, steaming at full speed in a heavy fog. Captain Henry T. Randall believed the ship was in deep water far out to sea, and he was trying to establish a speed record—certain to be beneficial in advertising. In fact the steamer was amid the rockbound Channel Islands, and in the fog she smashed onto a rock and got hung up. The date was October 1, 1854. On board was some $152,000 in coins consigned by a banking house, plus other gold, and about 900 passengers and crew. Most of them escaped, but in the ensuing confusion before the *Yankee Blade* sank, between 17 and 50 lost their lives. Over the years most of the coins appear to have been recovered, under circumstances largely unknown. In 1948 the hull was found again and divers visited the wreck. Around 1977 more recoveries were yielded, including 200 to 250 1854-S double eagles. All showed microscopic granularity, possibly from the action of sea-bottom sand, and all had die cracks on the reverse. Little in the way of hard facts has ever reached print.

The wreck and recovery of the SS *Central America* was much better documented. The steamer was lost on September 12, 1857, carrying about $2.6 million in gold treasure, heading from Havana, Cuba, to New York City. A monster hurricane engulfed the ship on the 10th and 11th; Captain William Lewis Herndon enlisted the aid of male passengers to form a bucket brigade to bail water, but their efforts proved futile. The ship was swamped, and the captain ordered the American flag be flown upside-down, a signal of distress. The nearby brig *Marine* approached and nearly all of the *Central America*'s women and children were transferred over, along with some crew members, before the *Central America* was overwhelmed by the waves and went down, with Captain Herndon standing on the paddle box. The steamer ultimately settled 7,200 feet deep, and some 435 lives were lost. The wreck was found in 1987 and over time more than $100 million worth of treasure was brought to the surface. This included more than 5,400 mint-fresh 1857-S double eagles, hundreds of gold ingots (including one weighing 80 pounds), and other coins.

In the 1990s another sidewheel steamer was found: the SS *Brother Jonathan*, lost with few survivors as she attempted to return to safe harbor in Crescent City, California, after hitting stormy weather on her way north to Oregon (January 30, 1865). More than 1,000 gold coins were recovered from the wreck, including many Mint State 1865-S double eagles. Detailed files and photographs recorded every step of the recovery.

In 2003 another 1865 shipwreck was located: that of the SS *Republic*, lost off the coast of Georgia while en route from New York City to New Orleans on October 25, just months after the Civil War ended. The steamer sank in a hurricane along with a reported $400,000 in silver and gold. Recovery efforts brought up 51,000 coins and 14,000 other artifacts (bottles, ceramics, personal items, etc.). The coins included 1,400 double eagles dating from 1838 to 1858, and thousands from the 1850s and 1860s; plus more than 180 different examples of Liberty Seated half dollars, including five 1861-O die combinations attributed to Confederate control of the New Orleans mint. The most valuable single coin was a Mint State 1854-O $20, then valued at more than $500,000.

Shipwrecks continue to be found even today, and the hobby community eagerly awaits news of coins and treasure found amidst their watery resting places.

THE STORY OF AMERICAN MONEY

This introduction to U.S. coins is based on the work of the late Dr. Richard G. Doty,
senior curator of numismatics at the Smithsonian Institution.

Much of the early story of American coins focuses on the importation, adaptation, manufacture, and spread of a variety of monetary forms by the European colonizers of America and their descendants. To set the stage, though, we must first render an accounting of earlier peoples—Native Americans—and the monies they created.

Native Americans were more practical than Europeans—their monies were rooted in their immediate experience, in their proximate environment. While Europeans remained wedded to one particular monetary form, coinage, native peoples used what was there and did quite well.

But before we examine any examples in particular, we should realize that, regardless of time or place, any exchange medium must satisfy a number of requirements. If it does so, it will stand as viable money, likely to remain in fashion; if it does not, it will soon be replaced by something else. To be money, objects with *durability* have distinct advantages over their competitors. The aspiring monetary form should be *practical*, either directly or indirectly. It must be *easily quantifiable*. It must be of *moderate scarcity*, rare enough to possess an aura of desirability, plentiful enough so that everyone can see it and have at least a minimal chance of obtaining it. Finally, *beauty*, either for display or for other purposes, gives some potential trading objects an advantage over others (without being an absolute requirement for any of them). With these conditions met, nearly anything, either natural or manufactured, can become money.

Just what media the Native Americans used depended on their location, at least to a degree. Peoples occupying an area rich in fur-bearing animals would probably incorporate pelts into their monetary-exchange practices. But so might adjacent peoples who occupied areas where game was scarce. And while shells might form trading objects for coastal tribes, they might be known and used in the interior as well—at least in areas connected with the seacoast by reasonably easy communication.

THE EARLY AMERICAN "MONEY"

Hides and shells became the foundation of native monetary systems in the lands that would become the United States and Canada. In time, particular types of pelts and particular varieties of shells came to hold a special regard and became units or standards of value. The beaver's skin gained such a role, perhaps because the animal was regarded as sacred by many peoples. Skins of other animals were traded as multiples and fractions of one beaver, and when European commodities came to the tribes, the new goods too were tariffed in terms of so many to one "made" beaver (that is, a properly skinned and tanned pelt).

Elsewhere, shells, clams, and conchs were extremely important, for they were the raw materials behind the most important single type of native currency in all of North America. This was wanpanpiage, wampumpeage, or wampum.

Wampum is an old Algonquian word meaning "a string of white beads." Another term, *suckauhock*, was used for strings fashioned from purple beads, but the earliest European settlers tended to use the shortened term *wampum* indiscriminately, and their practice survives. Wampum consisted of short beads, cut from the shells of clams and conchs, drilled by hand, and strung. This means of trade appears to have originally seen employment when woven into patterned belts, for telling stories and conveying messages. It only gradually came into use as a display of wealth and, finally, as a unit of wealth. We know that it had achieved this final, crucial stage and was an accepted form of money before European settlement, for the explorer Jacques Cartier found it so employed in the mid-1530s. We believe we understand why it achieved popularity as a monetary form: under pre-industrial conditions, wampum was difficult to manufacture. It served as a unit of value because of the work and skill required to make it.

Wampum was popular on the Atlantic seaboard of North America, among both Native Americans and European newcomers. There was a parallel monetary form on the Pacific seaboard, based on the shell of a different sea creature, the dentalium (or tooth shell), but it never captured the attention of the European newcomers in the way that wampum did, and it played little role in post-contact economies.

To the south, other trading objects held sway. In Mexico, copper axe-shaped objects called *siccapili* (in modern Spanish *tajaderas*, "chopping knives") found popularity among Aztecs and their contemporaries—so much so that the earth is still yielding large numbers of them to the plows of modern farmers. Cacao beans were mainstays of the Aztec monetary system, and they illustrate one of the earliest instances of the debasement of a non-coin monetary form: the delicious contents of the cacao bean were sometimes scooped out and substituted with earth, the skin carefully replaced, and the extraction cleverly hidden.

Corn was also used as a trade commodity, and so was gold, either cast into bars or traded in transparent quills so that its purity could be seen by all. Hernán Cortés found tin circulating as money in several of the provinces through which he and his tiny band marched on their way to glory, but his compatriot Francisco Pizarro found much less to the south. The economy of the Inca Empire was paternalistic, socialistic—so planned, in fact, that commercial transactions (and thus the employment of money) were largely unnecessary. But it has been suggested that leaves of the coca plant—the source of a modern, international commodity called cocaine—may have enjoyed a limited monetary function prior to the Spanish conquest.

Elsewhere in the Americas, tribes in what became Venezuela appear to have used strings of shells, a form of money similar to wampum although probably not inspired by it. Some of the Brazilian peoples used arrows; others used stringed beads of snail shells. The latter practice persisted in Mato Grosso, Brazil, well into the 20th century.

The longevity of this particular form of money should alert us to an important fact about "primitive" monetary forms: they did not all obligingly disappear when the first Europeans arrived on American shores. While few of them displayed the persistence seen with the shell money of Mato Grosso (in part because few places in the Americas were as impenetrable as this jungle area in western Brazil), many of them were found as useful by new settlers as old, and they formed essential links between old economies and new.

Indeed, it is difficult to see how the numismatic history of the United States could have been written in the absence of the skins of fur-bearing animals and the shells of creatures of the sea. Along with commodities known to and developed by Native Americans (but not generally used by them for trade) and scant supplies of coinage and other trading objects brought from Europe, furs and shells would form most of the basis of our early money—but not all. A final ingredient was being created to the south, one whose influence would be so persistent and ultimately so potent that it would shape the very way we reckoned and fashioned our symbols of wealth.

Aztec siccapili or tajadera, an axe-shaped object used as money in Mexico; one was worth 8,000 cacao beans (like those pictured).

THE SPANISH CENTURIES

This final ingredient was the Spanish conquest of most of the Western Hemisphere. It began with Columbus's first voyage in 1492, and in some ways it is still going on, as the spread of Spanish language and culture across today's United States suggests. But it was far more active, and far less peaceful, five centuries ago.

At that time, nothing less than the wholesale exportation of one way of life (and a snuffing-out or radical transmutation of many others) was occurring. We have no idea how many millions died in the process—from new diseases, from new and merciless labor systems—but the event certainly stands as the greatest of all holocausts, the most massive population revolution in all of human history.

While it was running its course, a hybrid society was being created, and in it the Spanish worldview would predominate, first by force, later by tradition. Of course, one of the key elements in the Spanish world was the *coin*—and attached to it was the belief that this small metallic object and wealth were essentially interchangeable, simultaneous concepts. The idea did not originate in Spain, but when Spaniards carried it to the Americas, a number of interesting events took place. All of them stemmed from a central fact: the new lands contained vast quantities of silver and gold.

These metals were, of course, one of the primary reasons Spanish colonization began and was maintained. At first the newcomers were happy merely to appropriate what had been collected by someone else. These metals were sent back to the homeland and were quickly turned into coinage there.

Then, just as they were running through the last of the precious metals they had appropriated, Spain's people soon began finding new, raw sources of American gold and silver. At first this metal was simply refined on the spot and sent in ingot form to Sevilla, where it was turned into coinage and would soon benefit commerce in Spain and eventually all of Europe.

But metal in ingot form would be of no particular use to those who had actually found it. These people, in the Caribbean islands, Mexico, Peru, and Bolivia, were developing expanding consumer economies by the middle years of the 16th century—economies that needed coinage if they were to continue to expand.

And so an obvious though era-defining solution was devised: let the locals make their own coinage, following Spanish forms, denominations, and designs. It was obvious in part because of the primitive minting technology then in force: virtually anybody could make a creditable coin, provided the metal was at hand. But it defined the era because this was the first time anyone had ever done so in the Western Hemisphere. For the first time in human history, the concept and the making of coins spread beyond Europe and Asia, the lands of their birth.

THE EMERGENCE OF A STAPLE

By 1625 no fewer than eight mints had been established in Spanish America. Of them, several didn't last long (those at Santo Domingo, La Plata, Panama, and Cartagena), and two were sporadic (Bogotá and Lima). Two other mints were unqualified successes from the beginning: those of Mexico City, which struck its first coins in 1536, and Potosí, which entered production about four decades later. No final reckoning of the production of these facilities can ever be made, but the combined output of Mexico City and Potosí alone was several billion pieces.

Coins from these mints made their way into the pockets of local burghers, paused there only momentarily, then made their journey to Spain and flowed out of that country almost as soon as they entered it. They paid for wars; they furnished luxuries and even necessities that a local population—enamored of the instant wealth and good life promised by the coins—either could not or would not create at home. Those coins traveled in odd directions and found strange resting places: hordes of them have been discovered along the coast of China, suggesting that the commerce of the 17th century was far more complex than we had previously imagined.

We call these crude coins "cobs," the name perhaps derived from *cabo de barra*, "end of a bar." The name provides a clue to their manufacture. A rough ingot was cast, then crudely sliced into coin-size planchets or blanks. The blanks could be adjusted down to their desired weight by means of a file, after which they were struck by hand. Cobs were struck in both gold and silver, but silver predominated at most mints. Within the coinage of that metal, one denomination in particular came to overshadow all the others. This was the piece of eight, and it would finally become the most successful, longest-lived trade coin in all of human history.

Between its introduction (probably in the 1530s, though possibly somewhat earlier) and its demise, some 400 years would elapse. The piece of eight would be struck at half a dozen mints in Spain, and in more than two dozen mints in Spanish America and the independent successor states. The final examples would appear in 1949, when the failing Nationalist government of Chiang Kai-shek asked the Mexico City mint to strike several million pieces on its behalf as an alternative to its own inflated currency.

The piece of eight's brothers were the Joachimsthaler and its descendants: the Danish daler, the French écu, the British crown, and others, all of which came into being because of a greater abundance of silver during late-medieval and early-modern times. But the piece of eight overshadowed them all because it was able to draw on a larger source of metal than any of its competitors. Its persistence, and that of the other members of the series, surprises us when we least expect it. Consider, for example, that the New York Stock Exchange quoted securities in terms of an eighth of a point until 1997 because the *real*—the eighth of a piece of eight—was the lowest increment allowed on the Wall Street bourse!

Typical "cob" coins of the early 1600s.

INTERLOPERS!

The Spanish conquest did not occur in a vacuum. In Europe, honest amazement over Columbus's success turned quickly to envy, denial, and determined attempts to match it. When the interlopers were done, the map of the Spanish Empire would be greatly altered, and the seeds of a new country would be planted. In time, those seeds would grow into the United States of America.

An unusual Mexican cob, pre-1700. Despite its bizarre shape, the coin was of good Mexican silver, and that was what mattered to those who spent it.

The people who planted those particular seeds were Britons, but they were not the first to dispute Spanish exclusivity in the Americas. The first non-Spaniards to do something about the new transatlantic possibility were Spain's neighbors on the Iberian Peninsula, the Portuguese. Lisbon had been sending explorers down and around the African coast since the mid-1480s; in 1500, one of its captains, Pedro Álvares Cabral, just happened to get blown so far off course that he arrived at a new land altogether, on the far side of the Atlantic. This was named after a rosy-red dyewood found there—Brazil. By the 1530s the Portuguese were making a determined attempt to settle the vast new land that their captain had discovered.

Other Europeans soon entered the fray, first biting off bits of Spanish and Portuguese wealth; they would soon be biting off bits of Spanish and Portuguese *land*, as well. The wealth was appropriated first probably because it involved less of an outlay on the part of national governments. The original Iberian conquests had largely been affairs of private enterprise for public gain; so were many of the early efforts to redistribute the loot.

The first targets of attack were those Spanish vessels carrying home the rich American cargos of silver, gold, and other commodities. By the 1520s these vessels were being attacked and captured, their contents triumphantly carried into French harbors. The Spanish retaliated as best they could, arming their merchantmen and soon creating a convoy system featuring two main arrangements. In the first, vessels brought Spanish (and, increasingly, other European) goods one way, and carried gold, silver, and other American materials the other. In the second, convoys crossed the Pacific, voyaging all the way from Acapulco to the Philippines, carrying pieces of eight to Manila where they were traded for Chinese products, especially spices and silks.

This *flota* system made transport much safer, and it also made matters easier for royal bookkeepers back home because all legal trade was conducted and controlled through a single channel. However, raids on outlying vessels were common, especially when the scourge of hurricanes scattered members of the convoy. Indeed, the weather sent more vessels to the bottom than did Spain's enemies.

There were other ways of capitalizing on Spanish good fortune. A series of increasingly audacious captains, ranging from Hawkins to Drake to Morgan to Anson, conducted raids on Spanish-American cities. These were coastal sites, where rich cargos were gathered prior to shipment to Spain. One could move in quickly, pick up anything of value, and then decamp before the Spanish navy arrived on the scene. To this day, we are impressed by the massive walls of Campeche in Mexico and Cartagena in Colombia—those walls had to be thick if they were to keep out the likes of Sir Francis Drake and company!

Eventually they began doing more than simply raiding: they began wintering over, and what had been targets for looting became places for permanent settlement. As peoples from Scandinavia had with the rich towns on the coasts and rivers of England, Ireland, and France centuries earlier, Britons, French, Danes, Dutchmen, and Swedes began nibbling away at lands that their controllers were unable or unwilling to defend.

The enemies of Spain and Portugal turned up in the strangest places. We most certainly would not expect to see the enterprising Dutch in Brazil. But they were there, nevertheless, occupying the area around Recife for nearly a quarter of a century—and for the record, they were striking the first true Brazilian coins there in 1645, precisely half a century before the Portuguese got around to setting up their first mint at Rio. The French had been in Brazil nearly a hundred years before, but had minted no coins to mark the occasion.

So the islands and bits of the mainland were eaten away. In time, the useful theory of "no peace beyond the line" was proclaimed by Spain and its enemies. It was a way of ensuring that, regardless of peace treaties in Europe, warfare might continue in the Indies as Spain's competitors attempted to take—and Spain attempted to defend and retake—lands and property as the opportunity appeared.

Of course, we are especially interested in the fortunes of one particular group of interlopers, the English. To understand the coins of the United States, we must explore what the English and those who followed managed to do with their particular share of New World treasure.

THE THIRTEEN COLONIES AND THEIR MONIES

British colonization of the future United States began in earnest shortly after 1600. It was carried forward in a number of ways, by diverse peoples, and from a variety of motives. In Virginia, whose first settlement was loyally named *Jamestown* after the reigning British monarch, economic profit was the primary motive. In Massachusetts, a religious motive—the desire to commune with the Deity in a particular, though officially frowned-upon, fashion—led to the Pilgrim settlement at inhospitable Plymouth. A few miles to the north, a second settlement was established some 10 years later, in 1630. Unlike Plymouth, Boston was a going concern from the very beginning, perhaps because its founders were both people of conscience and people of business. Merchants of the town would soon be trading in a number of places where they had no business operating—with interesting effects upon America's money.

The economic and religious motives behind the founding of these colonies and others often were intertwined so completely that neither original colonizers nor subsequent historians could separate them. But this simple fact should not blind us to the complex nature of the fabric of America's early culture. The identity, color, and weave of that fabric would shift over time, as they still do today.

For example, dissenting Protestants were hardly the only sects represented in the new settlements. Maryland, which was first colonized at St. Mary's City in 1634, was meant as a haven for English Catholics. Other non-Anglican peoples came over too: Jews were represented by the 1640s at the latest, while Lutherans would be found here as early as the 1630s.

What's more, the fabric did in fact contain bold colors other than British red, as there was more than one colonizing country along the Eastern seaboard. Swedes penetrated the future Delaware, building Fort Christina (the future Wilmington—loyally named after their current monarch) in 1638, holding power there and along the adjacent rivers until 1655. The Dutch ejected them from that region and nearby settlements in New Jersey in 1655, leaving behind an architectural legacy in the form of the New World's first log cabins.

The Dutch remained the main players in the Middle Colonies, as well as Manhattan Island, until 1664, when Britons swept the Hollanders. Still, those areas long retained a determinedly non-English flavor, including a splendid, distinctly unusual tolerance for non-Christians. The Dutch also left another legacy to those who would follow: they had become accustomed to trading in the Native American monetary medium called wampum, to which they were introducing their English neighbors by the end of the 1620s.

By the mid-1600s, the British and their competitors were moving into new places ranging from Maine to Virginia. Settlers looking for economic opportunity and political liberty were advancing along the Connecticut River by the early and middle 1630s. Other pioneers in search of religious toleration were settling that smallest and quirkiest of British colonies, Rhode Island, just a few years later.

South of Virginia, colonization generally came later. South Carolina was set up as a proprietary colony, an arrangement tending to result in closer ties with the mother country than was usually the case elsewhere. North Carolina, home of the first and failed English colonial experiment at Roanoke in the 1580s, was one of the last places to be settled. The combination of coastal swamps and hostile Native Americans would long act to deter full European colonization of this area, and the European population of North Carolina would long remain modest.

English Catholics, under the protection of King Charles, colonized the region that would become Maryland. Here, they bargain with Native Americans.

That left Pennsylvania and Georgia. Both were "planned" settlements; unlike many other places, these two areas of British colonization were deliberately organized and selected, and they were brought into existence from a mixture of public and private goals. Pennsylvania was intended in part as a home for adherents of another non-Anglican religious sect facing difficulties at home, the Society of Friends (or Quakers). Though the Swedes and Dutch were there first, the pious Quakers had the better of the argument: in 1681, William Penn (to whose father King Charles II of England owed a good deal of money) accepted a royal grant to a vast new domain. This area was named after him—Pennsylvania, or "Penn's Woods."

The motives for founding Georgia were no less laudable. Led by James Oglethorpe, a number of British philanthropists were interested in establishing a haven where debtors might go to get a second chance in life. They shared their aspirations with the British government, which was interested in setting up a buffer zone between its established colonies to the north and Spanish Florida to the south. The goals of both groups coalesced in the founding of Savannah in 1733.

CHALLENGES—AND INNOVATIONS—FOR NEW ENGLAND

By the early years of the 18th century, British colonization had been underway for five generations. What had resulted was not one single, uninterrupted stretch of British red from Maine to Georgia, but a number of nuclei of varying sizes and fortunes, rather like beads on a string—with large spaces between one bead and another.

Despite extensive searching, these colonizers found no gold, no silver, and precious little copper. Indeed, nothing much would be found for more than 200 years. No metal meant no local coins. Combined with two other factors, this metallic dearth would ensure that the monetary development of the future United States could not and would not proceed on a "normal" and preferred path.

The European contribution to the monetary problem was a politico-economic theory of national wealth and power called *mercantilism*. Simply stated, mercantilism viewed a colony and its mother country in a fixed, monopolistic trading relationship, in which almost everything of value found in the ground or grown on the land was sent home. Furthermore, anything needed by the colonists that they could not produce themselves had to be sent from the mother country and paid for in the currency of the mother country. In other words, any coins that the colonies managed to accumulate should be remitted to the metropolis in payment for goods received under the closed economic arrangement.

If we apply the theory of mercantilism to the metal-poor British colonies along the Atlantic coast, logic tells us that the British government would hardly make an effort to export coinage to these shores when it was seeking to extract wealth from them. Furthermore, because trading was legally circumscribed, logic also suggests that the British colonies would remain coin-poor if the British metropolis remained true to the mercantilist idea. And this, of course, it did: hadn't mercantilism enriched the Spanish and the Portuguese?

The American contribution to the monetary crisis was a failure to satisfy the two conditions absolutely necessary for the functioning of a cashless economy: limited trading and a stable population. Had these two conditions been in force, all might have been well—but they weren't.

Almost from the beginning, these British colonies were economic and demographic successes, so that the monetary supply never had a chance of catching up with, much less surpassing, the monetary demand. Far from easily sending coinage back to Britain, people here could have used every spare piece of change that Britain could send. Along with the shortage of native precious metals, this inability of supply to ever meet demand would shape the story of American numismatics for a quarter of a millennium. It was even more important than the influence of mercantilism, as it continued to mold America's money long after the British and their theory had departed its shores.

Faced with perpetual lack and growing need, confronted with the very results of their success, the men and women of New England and the other colonies would replicate, create, try, reject, and redesign every monetary form ever invented anywhere else throughout the entire story of numismatics.

AMERICAN SOLUTIONS TO AMERICAN PROBLEMS

Their first investigations involved barter: if you don't have something, trade something else to get it. While theory tells us that anything can be swapped for anything else, logic tells us that some commodities have a better chance than others of becoming trading goods. The criteria mentioned earlier (durability, utility, scarcity, etc.) held true for the first colonists as they did for the Native Americans who witnessed their arrival.

The Europeans' list of preferred items included shot and powder, which were obviously useful in their new circumstances. It also contained nails, which may seem odd until we stop to think about it. Nails were obviously easily quantifiable, they were durable, they had utility, and they were very scarce in the beginning days of European settlement because they had to be imported from the old country. As such, nails were traded against British currency—a hundred of one size equal to six pence, a hundred of a larger size equal to ten pence, and so forth.

Other trade goods had a more direct connection with the land. In 1612 John Rolfe (who is perhaps better known as the husband of Pocahontas) saved the starving Virginia colony by putting in his first crop of tobacco, which could be traded for necessary supplies. The plant had come to Europe by the beginning of the 1560s, and by the late 1500s and early 1600s it was set to become Europe's latest craze. Consequently, Virginia's first legislature granted tobacco a monetary status in 1619, fixing its value at three shillings per pound for the best grade, half that for the lower grade.

Over the years, though, that high value descended precipitously. Bear in mind two of the primary conditions for the suitability of a commodity as money: it must be kept in short supply, and it must be durable. Tobacco proved to have neither property, as many residents of the Virginia colony soon began growing their own and thereby flooded the market. Also, the product itself was very susceptible to drying out or rotting. That, in turn, led to the development of "tobacco notes"—paper certificates issued against the value of the crop—which hinted at the direction American money would finally take.

Like the cultivation of tobacco, the trapping of wild animals for their pelts was adopted from Native Americans, and this would give colonists another form of commodity money—or rather several forms. While beaver was always the most popular pelt, and was the yardstick against which other pelts (and other goods, ranging from yards of cloth to thread, hats, shirts, and axes) were measured, otter skins were also popular, as were those of foxes and other animals. Furs were more popular in frontier areas than elsewhere, but their usage finally extended from the Atlantic to the Pacific, matching and anticipating the march of European settlement itself.

One more commodity traded in the British colonies was the aforementioned wampum. Among the new arrivals to what would become the United States, the Dutch appear to have taken it up first: they would have obtained it from tribes on Long Island, a major center of wampum production for many years. In 1627 they carried it to Plymouth Colony, from whence it spread across New England and eventually to the South, where it was known as "roanoke."

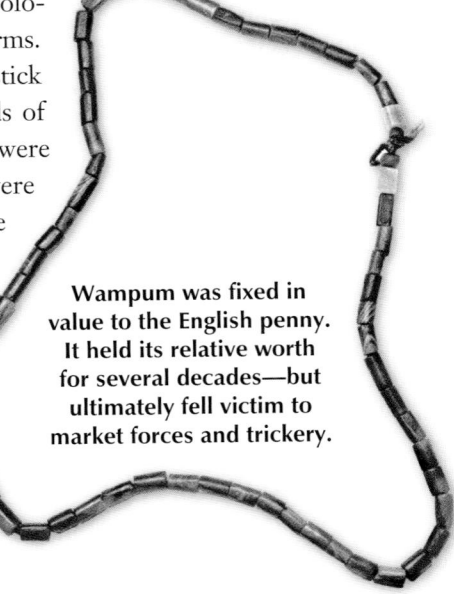

Wampum was fixed in value to the English penny. It held its relative worth for several decades—but ultimately fell victim to market forces and trickery.

As the incoming colonists happily embraced the medium as another partial solution to their chronic lack of cash, the established tribes began viewing it with increased favor as well, in part because their new neighbors seemed to take it so seriously. The growing popularity of this exchange medium led to two results that we might have anticipated: Wampum was overproduced, and it was adulterated.

When first introduced among European Americans, wampum was tariffed at so many beads to one English penny, in much the same manner as tobacco or nails. These fixed valuations began fraying in the late 1650s, however, as Native Americans—and enterprising Europeans as well—expanded production. Inevitably, wampum's value descended, and the last official use of the medium among Europeans appears to have taken place in the early 1690s. By then other monetary expedients were being pressed into service.

The counterfeiting of wampum, meanwhile, was achieved in Europe by the middle years of the 17th century and was sent to the New World along with other trading goods. A family of immigrants named Campbell began producing ceramic wampum later in the colonial period, and their operation continued until the closing years of the 19th century—which must represent a record of sorts for counterfeit money! Finally, other settlers discovered that the lower-valued white beads could be dyed to look like the more valuable purple variety; native tribes rarely fell for the adulteration, but it did gull the newcomers often enough.

EARLY AMERICAN COINAGE: MASSACHUSETTS

That grown men were playing childish tricks on each other suggests the monetary desperation in which they found themselves. Pelts, nails, tobacco, and wampum of varying plausibility—all would have been gladly cast aside at the sight of a coin. But no metal for such a coin existed. Even if it had, it would have to have been remitted to England, not retained in America. But one spot in the new lands was about to find a way around both limitations. That place was the town of Boston, and what Boston did must not only rank as a benchmark in the story of numismatics, but in that of the human spirit as well.

In 1652 the colonists of Massachusetts Bay began producing crude coins bearing a fancy NE (for "New England") on the obverse and the Roman numerals III, VI, or XII (for three, six, or twelve pence) on the reverse. They received the silver from illegal trade with the sugar islands of the Caribbean. The good people of Boston sent down rum, timber, and grain, and the good people of the Antilles sent back sugar and coins, mostly pieces of eight. These coins should have been sent on to England, but many of them were retained in Massachusetts, especially if they were lightweight or of poor silver quality (and, in fact, the mint at Potosí was then in the midst of a major scandal, corruptible minters having adulterated the silver coinage there).

In order to make the new coins unattractive to Britons and thereby keep them in circulation in the New World, local coiners deliberately made their new coins lightweight (compared to their British counterparts), while still expressing their denominations in British currency. This way, no London merchant would touch the coins (for he would have to go to the trouble of melting them down and selling them as bullion), but a Boston merchant would embrace them, for they would form part of a closed monetary system based on the familiar coins of the mother country.

Boston silversmith John Hull and his partner Robert Saunderson minted these coins between June and October 1652. Minting was stopped when it was realized that the tiny devices were easy targets for the clipper and the forger. The NE coins were soon followed by pieces of a more elaborate design, named after the type of tree occupying the central space on their obverses.

We call the earliest of these tree series "Willow Tree" pieces. They were made in tiny numbers between 1654 and 1660, double- and triple-struck, very rarely showing all of the designs on either side. They were followed by Oak Tree shillings and subdivisions (including a tiny twopence), and the Pine

Tree coins. The Pine Tree shilling is perhaps the most readily available of our early colonial issues; it is also among the most famous of all American coins and will repay a closer look.

On the obverse stands a pine tree. This tree may be an oblique reference to one of New England's few truly valuable exports at the time: timber for masts for the Royal Navy. Around the tree is the name of the colony, rendered as MASATHVSETS, a spelling that supposedly mimicked the sound of the original Native American name for the region. On the reverse, the remainder of the mint name is spelled out, along with the denomination XII, for twelve pence or one shilling, and the date.

It is this date that adds the final element of ingenuity to the Massachusetts silver coinage. With one exception, it is always rendered as 1652 (the exception is the Oak Tree twopence, dated 1662). This was the case for one of two reasons. First, the mint was founded in 1652. However, the second possibility is far more likely: the coins were deliberately and consistently dated 1652 to evade English law.

Under that law, the king enjoyed sole right of coinage. But in 1652, there was no king: Royal Charles's head had been separated from his body some three years earlier, and Cromwell's Commonwealth of England ruled in royalty's place. Surely regicides would scarcely look askance at a Massachusetts coinage.

In 1660 the English monarchy was restored, and there was an even greater reason to retain the old date on the coinage, as an issue dated 1652 could pass for an old coin struck when there was no king. As it turns out, King Charles had more important matters on his mind anyway, and he left the upstart coinage alone for the first two decades of his reign. During those years, the Oak Tree pieces were struck (down to 1667), as well as two issues of Pine Tree coins (between 1667 and 1674, and 1675 and 1682).

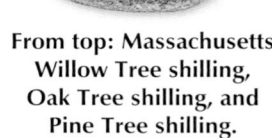

From top: Massachusetts Willow Tree shilling, Oak Tree shilling, and Pine Tree shilling.

Hull and Saunderson's contract with the Massachusetts General Court expired in 1682, and there seems to have been no talk about a renewal of the agreement. The tiny mint appears to have been working full bore for the last two years of its existence, as colonial authorities began receiving indications that the Crown was finally about to resume its prerogatives; they accordingly hurried their local coiners along. London did reassert its monopoly over the coinage, and soon enough Sir Edmund Andros was appointed as the new governor of a centralized, dictatorial administration embracing all of New England. Andros had instructions to bring the region to heel; they may have included a forced resumption of barter.

OTHER EARLY AMERICAN COINAGE

While Massachusetts was producing its own coinage, others were coping as best they could. Maryland had coinage produced *for* it; the Catholic noblemen who founded the colony wished to provide convenient money for their co-religionists, and Cecil Calvert, second Lord Baltimore, had been granted the right to coin.

Although none of it is dated, we know that this issue was minted during the winter of 1658–1659, but we have no idea by whom it was struck. It is commonly suggested that these coins were made at the Tower of London, but the members of the series—silver shillings, sixpence, fourpence or "groats," threepence, and a "denarium" or copper penny, of which fewer than ten are known—are well struck and far superior to most British coinage of the period.

The possible connection to the Tower Mint is even less plausible, as Calvert was not convicted of a crime when arrested and questioned in a London court about his coinage. For these reasons and others, Richard Doty, senior curator of numismatics for the Smithsonian Institution, suggested Ireland as a possible site for the Calvert mint: "The fabric of these pieces does not suggest the Tower Mint to me, and a Catholic island would have been a logical and sympathetic place to coin for a Catholic nobleman."

Interestingly, Ireland is linked to a second series circulating in the early colonies, although that link is anything but direct. A Quaker named Mark Newbie (or Newby) led a number of the faithful to settle in the vicinity of the modern city of Camden, New Jersey, and brought with him a cask containing £30 worth of coppers to distribute. These pieces—farthings and halfpennies—are named after him ("Newbie coppers"); they are alternately known as St. Patrick coppers, for that saint adorns their reverses. And that brings us back to Ireland.

The coppers weren't struck there—they had an English origin—but they *were* coined for Irish consumption. They were originally intended to pay Charles I's Catholic troops, who were engaged in fighting Cromwell's people in the Ulster Rebellion. The pieces were made sometime in 1641 or 1642, disappeared from trade once Charles I was beheaded, resurfaced with the Restoration of 1660, and were finally demonetized by the end of the 1670s. That was when Newbie came across these pieces and gave them a new lease on life.

The St. Patrick coinage's attractive appearance is augmented by a bit of yellow metal (brass, meant to resemble gold), splashed onto the copper during the minting process and positioned so that the king would appear to be receiving a golden crown. This care suggests a limited mintage, a suggestion belied by the known number of die combinations—more than 120 for the farthings alone. They may have been created by Nicholas Briot, using the roller method, but we know far less about these pieces than we would like.

The designs of the so-called St. Patrick coppers were similar for both the farthing- and halfpenny-sized coins. On the halfpenny, the saint is shown blessing the faithful, with the legend ECCE GREX—"Behold the Flock."

The same may be said for a curious issue featuring an elephant on its obverse, intended for British settlement in the Carolinas. We know that much because the reverse of this copper halfpenny token says GOD: PRESERVE: CAROLINA: AND THE: LORDS: PROPRIETORS. It is clearly related to another, much rarer issue with a reference to the northern colonies, whose reverse inscription reads GOD: PRESERVE: NEW: ENGLAND. Both pieces are dated 1694, and both pieces are connected to a third—which is where our mystery begins.

This third token has the arms of London, along with the legend GOD: PRESERVE: LONDON, but no date. Many believe this coin was struck prior to the others, the reverse legend perhaps referring to the plague and Great Fire besetting the English capital in 1665–1666. Others believe that the London token was struck at the same time as the two others, in the mid-1690s, although they are unable to explain the legend.

As for the elephant, it has been suggested the beast was put on the obverse by order of the Royal African Company, which had gotten the copper for the issue from West Africa. Consider, also, that golden guineas from the reign of Charles II and his immediate successors bore a tiny elephant to suggest the origins of the metal they contained.

We know a bit more about one last piece, a fleeting reminder of the attempt by James II to achieve control over the inhabitants of British North America. The issue would be made from tin—a most unstable coining material if used alone, but a sop to the miners of tin-rich Cornwall—and bear an equestrian portrait of the king. They were shipped across the Atlantic, but in the inhospitable climate of the New World, they deteriorated rapidly. Today an unblemished piece is a major rarity. We know why these pieces were made, under whose franchise (Richard Holt's, granted by the king), who designed them (the artist John Croker), and where they were struck (at the Royal Mint, in the Tower of London), but we are somewhat confused as to their denomination. The pieces bear the legend VAL. 24. PART. REAL. (value 1/24-real), suggesting they were to be tied to a Spanish or Spanish-American monetary system rather than a British or British-American one. But this denomination cannot be equated with anything in common use in Spain, Great Britain, or their colonies. Pieces of a similar size were struck at the Tower by James II and circulated as halfpence, and generations of collectors have assumed that these American coins had the same value, regardless of denomination. But it *would* be satisfying to know what James and his coiners had intended.

Paper Money on the American Scene

With James's successors, the story of America's money would take an essential new path, one it would follow for the next two centuries. The new monarchs, King William III and Queen Mary, promptly became involved in a war with the French in Canada. This struggle for control of North America would persist through most of the ensuing three-quarters of a century, and it would eventually leave the English victorious, even as the seeds were being planted for their most resounding defeat.

For us, the essential fact is this: English colonists were expected to do their bit for a war effort that was being waged at least partly for their benefit. The first time they were asked to contribute was in 1690, when Massachusetts was asked to pay expenses for a military action by the British against the French in Canada. The request put the colony in a quandary, for there was a scarcity of cash with which to meet it.

Someone in the colonial government hit upon an interesting idea: why not issue official paper certificates to hire the troops and purchase the supplies? This scheme would work because the colony and its citizens knew that they would be reimbursed by the Crown at the end of the war. But because that was the case, the scheme was carried forward another crucial step: because reimbursement had been promised and everyone knew it, and because the paper would therefore circulate as readily as coinage, why not leave it in circulation rather than redeem it at the end of the war, in the process augmenting cash in a cash-strapped economy?

It was done. In 1690 and 1691, two issues with an aggregate face value of £40,000 were printed and circulated. The notes were receivable by the colonial treasurer in payment of taxes at a 5 percent premium, which was another way of ensuring their popularity and use. The paper-money practice soon spread elsewhere, and a new chapter in the global story of numismatics was under way.

The next half-century would see numerous notable developments in paper money, from the public note-issuing bank to engraving, typesetting, and Benjamin Franklin's nature prints.

A Snapshot at Mid-Century: 1750

The year 1750 is a good time to pause for a moment, to review the nature of America's money during the best years of the colonial period. Paper had come to lie at its heart. By that year, 12 of the 13 colonies either had issued paper or were currently doing so, and the 13th, Virginia, would join the parade in 1755. An amazing amount of bartering still occurred as well, and not all of it in the backcountry. However, as this volume is concerned primarily with coins, that is where we will focus.

SUPPLIES FROM THE MOTHERLAND

Great Britain occasionally sent over coins as payment for American participation in its ongoing saga with the French. A large number of halfpennies and farthings arrived on these shores in that very manner in 1749, part of a remittance to Massachusetts for the colony's expedition to capture Cape Breton from the French. Much of the rest of the remittance was made up of silver coin, which likely flowed back to England in short order; but the coppers did stay in America.

The colonists also used coins struck in England but without official British designs. For example, William Wood was contracted by King George I to produce two issues—one for use in Ireland and one for use in the colonies, both of which eventually came to circulate in the latter. The Irish coins featured a seated figure of Hibernia, the American coins a splendid open rose; their common obverse was a right-facing portrait of the king. They were well struck in a handsome alloy invented by Wood, one he called "Bath metal," consisting of three-quarters copper, slightly less than one-quarter zinc, and a tiny amount of silver—though not nearly enough to make the coins struck from it circulate at their stipulated value.

William Wood's Rosa Americana design declared the American Rose to be UTILE DULCI—"Useful and Pleasant." Despite the sweet words, his shortweight coins were a flop.

After the Irish pieces were violently rejected by their intended users out of a combination of outraged nationalism and anger over their short weight, some of the "Hibernia" pieces were later foisted on the colonies, where they met with a somewhat better reception than did Wood's coins specifically struck for American consumption.

Those pieces—issued in twopenny, penny, and halfpenny denominations and known as the "Rosa Americana" coinage—were less than half the weight they theoretically should have been. But more to the point, the Crown had not bothered to consult local assemblies before shipping the coins to New England and New York. Colonials refused to accept them, and the Massachusetts legislature issued emergency parchment money for one penny, twopence, and threepence even *before* Wood's coinage arrived. As a result, the Rosa Americana coinage was never effectively put into circulation in the North (although it did enter commerce in the South somewhat later), and its poor reception persuaded Wood to suspend production early in 1724.

OTHER EXTRANATIONAL ALTERNATIVES

British mints were not the only source of coins used in the British colonies. Regardless of theory and legality, reality found Americans trading all over the world, bringing back foreign coinage as they did so. Provided the coinage was of good gold or silver, it circulated in the colonies by weight, and elaborate tables were prepared and published that enabled businessmen to calculate what a certain coin should weigh and how much it was worth against another.

Thus, pieces from silver French écus to Turkish golden zeri mahbubs were traded. That being said, Americans did come to prefer one issue in particular over others (including anything British): this was the piece of eight. By now, they knew it as the "Mexican dollar" (because most of those coming their way originated at the busy mint at Mexico City) or the "Spanish milled dollar" (because Spain had introduced coining machinery to the Americas by this time, using it to strike the piece of eight). The coins that were struck, and which Americans used, were now indistinguishable from other 18th-century issues, save for one thing: their marvelous, evocative designs.

The obverse of the new piece of eight featured a splendid baroque crowned shield, along with the name and titles of the king of Spain, but it is the reverse that claims our attention. There, the Pillars of Hercules—which had been appearing on Spanish-American coins since the 1530s, a proclamation of the New World origins of the silver they contained—are wrapped by ribbons. It has been suggested that the dollar sign ($) was inspired by the right-hand ribbon.

Here and there, people were beginning to reckon their money in terms of Mexican dollars instead of English sterling. We should not be surprised; the American colonists had been using the piece of eight since the very beginning, and they were now more familiar with it than with several members of the British system, including that nation's closest equivalent, the crown. We know of the change from one system to another by the fact that various colonies begin printing paper

Did the American dollar sign ($) come from the reverse of the Spanish-American piece of eight? Notice the column at the right on this 1732 coin of King Philip V, struck in Mexico City.

money denominated in dollars rather than pounds. Massachusetts led the way in 1750, its notes backed by a deposit of pieces of eight it had recently received. Other colonies would eventually follow, in part because the denomination would soon have a new appeal—that of nationalism.

DOMESTIC EFFORTS

In addition to foreign coins, paper money, and "country pay" or barter, there were several issues of domestic coins: one in Virginia, another in Connecticut, and a third in Pennsylvania. The Virginia issue is known from precisely two examples, brass shilling tokens from the town of Gloucester, dated 1714. We know nothing about the reasons for the issue, beyond the fact that it seems to have been the idea of two local landowners, Christopher Righault and Samuel Dawson.

We know a bit more about the second issue, from Granby, Connecticut. In 1737 an enterprising owner of a copper mine in the region named Samuel Higley issued tokens denominated THE VALUE OF THREE PENCE. When his neighbors complained that his tokens were overvalued, he changed his obverse legend to VALUE ME AS YOU PLEASE, but still retained the III for three pence!

Samuel's brother John took over the mint upon the death of the former, striking undated pieces and a few more dated 1739. We have no idea of the original extent of the Higley issues, but eight obverse dies and five reverses are known. Because most show no signs of breakage, the mint's output could have been fairly extensive. Yet its tokens remain excessively rare today, for Higley's copper was so pure that it was frequently recycled into other uses.

The Pennsylvania issue came about in 1766, a product of the furor over the Stamp Act. James Smithers, a British gunsmith who had just immigrated to Philadelphia, poured all of the frustration felt by the colonials into his "halfpennies" and "farthings," pieces that may have begun as commemorative medalets but which ended up as part of the monetary supply. The portrait on the obverse is of William Pitt the Elder, one of the voices of reason on the British side during the Stamp

This William Pitt halfpenny token refers to the British politician's efforts to have the hated Stamp Act repealed: NO STAMPS.

Act crisis. His more famous son would eventually become prime minister in the 1780s, just in time to deal with an infant United States, created in part by those very policies of coercion that his father had deplored.

Added to these American tokens was an import, one that began with one message and ended with another. In 1760 an Irish buttonmaker named Roche struck halfpenny- and farthing-size copper tokens with the words VOCE POPULI surrounding the head on the obverse, and the word HIBERNIA surrounding a representation of Ireland on the reverse. He probably intended the obverse to remind Dubliners of the deposed Catholic Stuart regime or the virtues of home rule, for the portrait has been identified with the two Jacobite pretenders, while the legend surrounding it is Latin for "By the Voice of the People." But Roche's tokens were eventually shipped to America in large numbers, and colonists there embraced them because their obverse sentiment now seemed an appropriate commemoration of their own struggles against Mad King George.

Regardless of such odds and ends, the primary circulating medium in America was now paper money. Americans had used it to pay for wars on behalf of England; they were about to use it to fight a war *against* England. And when they did so, that previously trustworthy medium would betray their confidence.

THE WAR OF INDEPENDENCE AND ITS AFTERMATH

Of all of the world's wars for national sovereignty, that which created the United States of America is among the most confusing and complex. It has been said that a third of the American people were ardent patriots, another third remained loyal to the mother country, and the final third had no opinion but scrambled to get out of the way of the other two. This observation oversimplifies matters, but there is a grain of truth to it.

The war was generally more popular in New England than it was in the South—but the new nation's greatest general was a Virginian. And the war was fought to free a people. But which one? Certainly not Native Americans. Certainly not African-Americans. And certainly not women—although they might partake of the banquet as guests of their husbands and do the washing-up. Indeed, this was a most confusing war.

We do not even know when the complaining—the perennial practice and right of any colonial people—reached a point that might finally yield a bid for independence. We think it began to accelerate after the final victory against the French in 1763, when Britons and Americans fell to quarreling over the spoils of the war. In this way of thinking, the opening salvo was the Proclamation Act of 1763, wherein King George III drew a line from one end of the Appalachian chain to the other and forbade settlers to cross it. Americans were angered, but the crisis over the Sugar Act in 1764 and the much greater furor over the Stamp Act in 1765—both of which were seen by Britons as revenue-raising measures, and by Americans as intolerable affronts—kept the pot at a boil.

Still, all this doesn't tell us when, or why, the mutual estrangement began. It is obvious this falling-out had deep roots indeed, going back to when the first colonists left one world for another. The earliest settlers found that English habits and customs did not always work in an American setting; they discovered that makeshift, local expedients might actually serve better than orthodox, imported ones, and were branded hayseeds and hicks by their English cousins for doing so.

Through our numismatic examinations, we have already seen the slow process by which transplanted Englishmen were becoming Americans. We have seen it with the Pine Tree shilling, and we have especially seen it with paper money. Give the people who devised such clever monetary schemes a century and a half to evolve in new directions, and there was virtually no chance that they would *not* strike out on their own at one point or another.

But they would still do so with mixed feelings when that time finally came. The estrangement reached its flashpoint in the spring of 1775, when royalist governor Thomas Gage of Massachusetts sent British regulars to Concord to seize military supplies stored there by Americans. Alerted by Paul Revere and William Dawes, Americans assembled on the morning of April 19 on Lexington Green and fired the "shot heard round the world." Not all of their fellow colonists agreed with their stance, nor did all Britons agree with the response of the Redcoats who opposed them. On both sides of the Atlantic, war fever would take some time to build up, clarify, and capture the popular imagination. And it would never monopolize thinking in either place.

FINANCING THE WAR OF INDEPENDENCE

While military aid might in time be forthcoming from Britain's enemies, France and Spain—and golden onzas and silvery écus might come to America along with the soldiers and arms—the insurgents would first have to prove that their unaided cause was a going concern and that they had a chance of defeating England (or were at least capable of holding on until that country gave way). This caution on the part of Britain's former and potential enemies meant that American money would have to pay for an American war, and the form that money would take must be paper, for there was really no other possibility. After all, hadn't that same approach worked during the conflict between the English and the French in Canada?

What Americans failed to realize was that paper money had worked during earlier campaigns because Great Britain had directly or indirectly stood behind the currency being issued. The mother country was scarcely likely to do so in this case unless Americans succeeded in invading, defeating, and occupying it, and extracting such payment by force. Not even the most ardent patriot could have expected this scenario to take place.

Another reason why paper money had worked was that earlier American participation in wars had been limited and short lived. But this conflict would be different: it would go on year after year, and would involve enemy occupation of many of the most productive portions of the upstart nation, including several of its largest cities.

That being said, the revolutionaries did well enough for the first year or two. They had caught the British by surprise and had soon taken most of New England. But they failed in a bid to bring the blessings of liberty to the remainder of British North America, and despite the urgings of Benjamin Franklin and other leaders, Canada would remain in British hands.

Elsewhere, the tide began to move against them. They lost New York City in 1776, General George Washington being defeated at the Battle of Long Island that August. Sir William Howe took the national capital of Philadelphia a year later. A striking American victory at Saratoga in October 1777 would eventually mean a favorable turning for the war, because it would embolden France and Spain to enter the conflict on America's behalf. But it produced little of concrete benefit just yet, and Washington had his hands full simply keeping his army alive through the winter of 1777–1778 at Valley Forge.

America's money reflected all this. In the spring of 1775, the colonies (or "states," as they soon began calling themselves) began the issue of paper currency to pay for their portions of the fighting. So did a new, ad hoc national government, whose modest, temporary powers would eventually be made law under the Articles of Confederation. This central government issued what it called Continental Currency: Benjamin Franklin's old firm (he had taken on a partner named Hall before selling out entirely, and Hall had engaged a partner of his own named Sellers) printed the notes, which were denominated in terms of Spanish milled dollars.

The Continental Congress also had hopes of issuing a coinage, a symbol of its sovereignty, as a bolster to local morale, and as a backing for Continental Currency. When it came time to print the fifth issue of national paper, the dollar note was deliberately omitted, and was replaced with a Continental

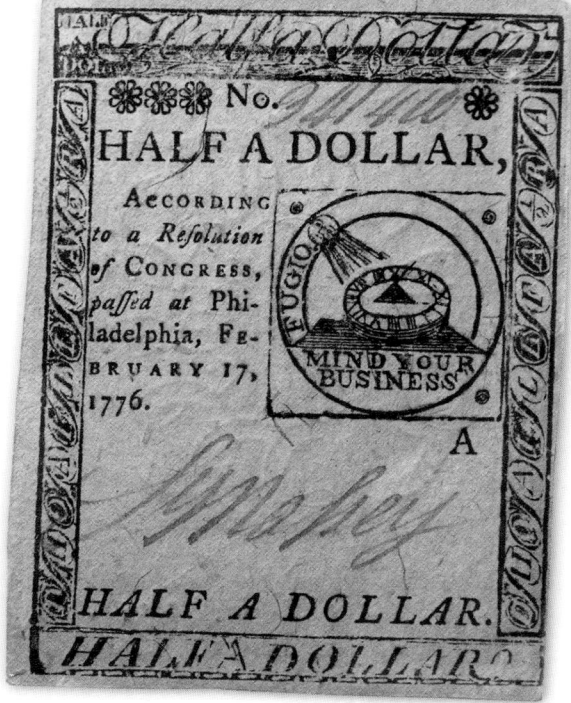 

The notes issued by the Continental Congress were denominated in Spanish dollars.

dollar coin, struck from silver provided by the French. Elisha Gallaudet prepared dies for the new issue. He used the motifs—the sundial and the linked rings—from his earlier fractional paper currency.

The national government had no mint at this time, so Gallaudet set up his own facility, either in his hometown of Freehold, New Jersey, or in nearby Philadelphia. He made a few patterns in silver, a few more in brass, and more still in pewter. The latter alloy looked enough like silver to give a good idea of the appearance of the future coinage, but was at the same time soft enough not to damage his dies. Then the project ground to a halt. No French silver was forthcoming, and it soon became impractical to issue a dollar coin in any metal.

Some final observations about Continental Currency may be made. This money was issued from a number of places, reflecting the shifting fortunes of the patriot cause. While the first and last series were from Philadelphia—the original site of the national government—one in 1777 was circulated from Baltimore, while another in 1778 came from York, Pennsylvania—places to which the government had been forced to flee ahead of British troops. The York issue is particularly interesting, because it leads us to a major problem with Continental Currency: it was extensively counterfeited. It was forged by Americans, and there was nothing particularly new about that. But it was also forged by Britons; that *was* new, and contributed to the currency's problems.

THE DECLINE OF AMERICA'S NEW CURRENCY

If we assume that, at the time of the first issue of federal and state paper in the spring of 1775, $1.00 in national or, for example, Maryland-issued paper could purchase one Mexican piece of eight, we see matters as they were for the first 20 months of the war. By the beginning of 1777, Continental Currency was still standing firm, but that of several states was slipping: it then took $1.50 in Maryland notes to purchase that same Mexican dollar.

The autumn of that same year was the crucial point: in October, issues of the states ranged from a ratio of 1.09:1 to 3:1, and the value of Continental Currency had descended as well, down to 1.10:1. This was worrisome, but hardly fatal if it stopped there.

But it did not stop there. By March 1779, even though French and Spanish aid was coming in, state and federal currency alike had slipped to around 10:1 against the piece of eight. By then, the Continental Congress was printing the new, safer, bicolor notes, but it was increasingly unable to persuade anyone to accept them, other than the soldiers who received them as pay. The states had no better luck with their issues, and paper continued to slide. By April 1780, the ratio of Continental Currency to the Spanish dollar was 40:1, and the national government had decided not to issue any more. This was just as well, because by that time, it had circulated nearly a quarter-billion dollars' worth of paper. The states that continued to print money (and most did; what other choice had they?) saw its real value fall to a hundredth, and finally a thousandth, of its stated specie value. By then, they had printed as much money as the federal government, meaning that there was enough paper in circulation to purchase every house, factory, and farm in the new republic several times over—if there were anyone foolish enough to take this currency seriously.

So great was this problem that Congress and the states finally decided to do something about it. By a resolution passed on March 18, 1780, a new issue of paper was authorized, but it was one with a difference. This issue would consist of bills circulated by the states, exchangeable for Continental Currency at 40 to 1, the same value ratio that Continental notes now had against the Mexican dollar. The states of Maryland, Massachusetts, New Hampshire, New Jersey, New York, Pennsylvania, Rhode Island, and Virginia participated in the plan; the other states were either unwilling or unable to do so, or they were still occupied by British troops. In this way, more than $111,000,000 in Continental Currency was removed from circulation; a goodly amount of state paper was also lured in by the same law and destroyed.

In time, much of the remaining federal and state paper of the Revolutionary era was presented and redeemed for federal bonds under the funding plans of Alexander Hamilton and other Federalists. Some of the state issues stayed in circulation for some years, rendering continued (if suspect) service on the local economic scene. Other notes made their way into cupboards and jars, awaiting a redemption that never took place. And a new phrase entered into American English usage: "not worth a Continental," meaning worthless and useless. Americans had been badly mauled by their previously trustworthy exchange medium, and on the national level at least they would not soon forget the experience.

The Americans' war would eventually end, despite the collapse of the medium they had chosen to pay for it. Hoping to reverse the trend symbolized by the surrender of Philadelphia and the loss of the West, Great Britain had struck south, capturing the capitals of Georgia and South Carolina. Troops under Lord Cornwallis then swung north, hoping to roll up the American war effort before France and Spain could make a difference. Eventually, a siege resulted at Yorktown, and when Cornwallis surrendered his forces on October 19, 1781, the war was effectively over—although it would take two years of the canniest American diplomatic efforts to negotiate the peace, with the Treaty of Paris of 1783.

New Coins During a Critical Transition

After Yorktown, Americans were granted an opportunity they had never had before and would never have again. They had defeated an enemy and were therefore free to reject its monetary system as well. Additionally, because their own, makeshift monetary system had buckled, they were enabled and forced to reject it, too. What would they seek to erect in the places of these failed and rejected precursors? Would it work any better?

Americans kept some kinds of paper money, but not all. The states could and did issue such paper (normally expressed in dollar denominations, though not always) because they were sovereign entities. The large amounts of Spanish pieces of eight and French écus that had come in during the final stages of the war enabled states to back some of their notes with promises of specie payment—although this hard money soon left their treasuries and the states continued to print.

Several of the states also espoused a coinage of sorts. The only one to set up its own mint was Massachusetts. It had made a previous attempt to coin back in 1776, as had its neighbor New Hampshire, but the urgent demands of war and a shortage of copper had stopped both projects in the very beginning of the pattern stage. Now Massachusetts made a second, more successful attempt, and its coppers (which contained a generous amount of that metal) made numismatic history: they were the first American coins to bear the denominations CENT and HALF CENT.

The mint that struck the Massachusetts half cents and cents was shut down in early 1789, in compliance with the newly ratified Constitution— and because each coin cost more to produce than its face value.

Other states allowed private mints to produce their coinage, resulting in generally lighter pieces and less artistic imagery. Between late 1785 and early 1789, several firms in Connecticut struck more than 340 varieties of halfpenny-size coppers. New York never got around to formally authorizing coinage, but a number of private mints would create money for it anyway. Their designs sometimes resembled English halfpennies, and sometimes incorporated elements from the state's coat of arms. New Jersey also contracted for its money, and the result was a copious coinage, struck at Rahway Mills, Elizabeth-town, Morristown, New York City, and possibly on Staten Island. These coins—dated 1786, 1787, and 1788, but likely struck into 1789 and deliberately back-dated—are also of historical significance, as they were the first circulating American coins to bear the national shield (seen on many later federal issues) and the motto E PLURIBUS UNUM (seen on virtually all later federal issues).

None of the other states circulated its own coinage, although one of them, Virginia, saw the circulation of copper halfpence it had ordered in the final days of the colonial period. Virginia's royal charter of 1609 had given it the right to mint its own coins—the only one of the 13 colonies to enjoy this privilege. It had never set up its own mint due to lack of metal, but its Assembly authorized the Tower Mint to strike a copper coinage for it in May 1773. Some five tons' worth of coins were accordingly prepared and sent across the Atlantic.

By the time they arrived in Virginia, the first acts of the American Revolution were taking place. Thus, most of those Virginia halfpennies that had gotten into trade were soon pulled out, and hoarded for the duration of the war. After Yorktown, however, many did go into trade, where they passed from hand to hand in company with counterfeit and genuine British and Irish halfpence and the sponsored and unsponsored issues of several states—and of an adjacent, independent country: Vermont.

THE UNION GROWS

One of the last areas to be colonized, the Vermont Republic had sided with the Revolution, but it had also become involved in an acrimonious land dispute with its giant neighbor, New York. Until that dispute was settled, it would remain resolutely out of the Union. During that time, the country produced both notes and coins.

Reuben Harmon Jr. was chosen by the Vermont legislature to strike its copper coinage. His diemaker, William Coley of New York, incorporated the idea of the 14th entity into the reverse design of his coppers: here was an all-seeing eye (adapted from a contemporaneous British import, the Nova Constellatio copper), surrounded by 13 stars. The 14th star would be Vermont, and the region's aspirations of becoming a part of the new United States—as soon as those annoying New Yorkers saw matters its way—formed the basis of the reverse legend: STELLA. QUARTA. DECIMA., "The Fourteenth Star."

This reverse was close enough to those on the well-known Nova Constellatio coppers to encourage acceptance, but the landscape obverse Coley chose (or had chosen for him by the lawmakers) met with local resistance. As such, the design was changed, and Harmon and other coiners struck coppers until mid-1789 with a male head on the obverse and a seated female on the reverse.

Thus far, we have been talking mostly about copper coins, and with good reason: the great majority of coinages proposed and circulated during those years *were* copper—in part because of a scarcity of silver and gold. But there was one silver issue that managed to get into circulation, as well as one gold coin.

The circulating issue came from Annapolis, Maryland, and was the product of John Chalmers and Thomas Sparrow, who also engraved Maryland's paper money designs. The most common member of the series was the shilling, whose obverse bears clasped hands, an age-old symbol of amity. Meanwhile the reverse depicts the danger that can follow when friends have a falling-out. Here are two birds squabbling over a worm, oblivious to a serpent ready to attack them at any time. The message is clear enough in the light of current politics: if the states continue to squabble with each other—as they were indeed doing during the period of the Confederation—a greater enemy might destroy them.

Finally, we come to one of the most famous coins in American history, the gold Brasher doubloon. The coin's namesake, Ephraim Brasher of New York, may have struck coppers on a speculative basis. It has been suggested that the Brasher doubloons were patterns for a new copper coinage, struck in gold by way of a *douceur* or bribe to state legislators to secure the contract. If so, the ploy failed, but precisely seven doubloons with one design and an eighth and ninth with another design have survived.

Ephraim Brasher was a New York goldsmith and jeweler. He was also a neighbor and friend of George Washington's. In the late 1780s Brasher struck gold coins about equal in weight to the Spanish doubloon, equivalent to $16. The coins are punched with his initials, EB.

THE RISE OF A NEW CONSTELLATION

In 1783 Robert Morris, superintendent of finance under the Confederation, proposed an ambitious federal coinage. Had it been implemented, it would have meant a completely new direction for American numismatics: it would be fully decimal, with pieces ranging from 5 to 1,000 "units," the latter a silver coin weighing about two-thirds as much as the Mexican dollar. A handful of patterns were struck in Philadelphia, their simple designs featuring an all-seeing eye for the obverse, surrounded by 13 rays and stars, with the legend NOVA CONSTELLATIO, a "New Constellation" in the firmament of nations.

These coins never got beyond the pattern stage because their coiners never secured enough silver for more than a few trial pieces. But they did inspire Morris's assistant, Gouverneur Morris (no relation), to secure another coinage from another source. Gouverneur Morris went to England and partnered with coiner George Wyon to strike undenominated coppers very similar to the ill-fated Philadelphia patterns.

These pieces—dated 1783 and 1785 but apparently struck in 1785 and 1786—found a ready circulation in the United States, for their metal was good and their designs patriotic.

The Nova Constellatio coppers were hardly the only halfpenny-size imports at this time. Thomas Jefferson conceived of a new decimal coinage system based on an old coin, the Spanish or Mexican dollar, to be divided into hundredths. Someone in Congress suggested the name "decad" for the large copper piece that would sit on the bottom rung of the new monetary arrangement.

The name of this coin would eventually be changed to cent, but Thomas Wyon was asked to produce patterns in line with Congress's current idea. What resulted was perhaps the most iconographically loaded coin in early American history—and, ironically, it was struck by an Englishman. On the obverse, the goddess Diana leans against an altar while trampling on a crown. On the altar is a helmet, closely and deliberately resembling a liberty cap. Around her, we see the legend, INIMICA TYRANNIS AMERICANA—"America, Enemy of Tyrants."

There is one more message-bearing copper coin of the period worth mentioning: the "Georgius Triumpho" copper of 1783. The obverse head was probably intended to represent General Washington. The reverse introduces us to the subtleties of the 18th-century mind: a female, presumably representing liberty and independence, is enclosed in a framework with 13 vertical bars, and there are 4 fleurs-de-lis at the corners of the frame. The complete image probably means that American freedom is protected and secured through joint action of the states (the 13 bars), supported on all sides by aid from the French monarchy (the fleurs-de-lis).

Thus, by 1787 the nation's small change was composed of a confusing mixture of state coppers, British and Irish halfpennies, Morris's Nova Constellatio and other British speculative pieces—as well as large numbers of counterfeits manufactured on both sides of the Atlantic. Congress became convinced that a national standard must be issued under its aegis, a full-weight coin of good copper, against which everyone else's issues might be judged.

FLEDGLING ATTEMPTS

Not possessing a mint of its own, Congress had to contract for its money along with everyone else. It picked a Connecticut coiner named James Jarvis to do the work, and it picked the designs—Franklin's old sundial / linked rings concept, seen earlier on fractional notes and the Continental dollar in 1776.

Jarvis had been recommended by his friend Colonel William Duer, to whom he had paid a bribe of $10,000 for the contract. The obliging colonel helped him on his way, giving Jarvis more than 70,000 pounds of federally owned copper with which to begin work. This was a small fraction of what his contract called for, however, and he sailed for Europe in search of more metal.

He failed in his attempt, his somewhat shady reputation making industrialists wary of dealing with him. He finally returned home without his copper.

Meanwhile Jarvis's coining cronies had gotten the federal metal, and they were busily using it to coin lighter-weight Connecticut coppers! To minimize federal suspicion, they did strike some "Fugio" coppers on the federal pattern (their name comes from the obverse legend, the Latin for "I Fly," referring to time on the sundial; they are also known as "Franklin cents"), but fewer than 400,000 pieces were shipped to the treasurer of the United States on May 21, 1788, and Jarvis and his partners fled the country.

Fugio coppers are sometimes called "Franklin cents" because of their legends, attributed to Benjamin Franklin.

Fugio coppers proved unpopular with both the federal government (they were slightly under their legal weight and therefore useless if the federal government were serious about its reform) and with the people (who by this time were unfamiliar with the design). Very few went into circulation, and the government eventually sold what was left of the Fugio coins to a contractor with the unlikely name of Royal Flint.

As it would turn out, Flint was a friend of Colonel Duer's, and so we have come full circle. Flint went bankrupt before he could pay the government and was hauled off to jail. Duer joined him there a few years later; the Fugio story has no heroes.

But it did serve to symbolize what a growing number of people were saying: the government that had sponsored the coins must be strengthened, either reformed or scrapped altogether in favor of a more plausible, dignified, centralized government that would be taken seriously at home and abroad. The current central government could not tax, and it could not keep the peace. It was also incapable of being taken seriously by Europeans, as Britons moved against its newly won territories in the northwest, and Spaniards and others snubbed its diplomats in Europe.

A gathering had been held at Annapolis in September 1786 in the hopes of strengthening the Articles of Confederation. Few states bothered to send delegations, and the meeting broke up without concrete result—except for a promise to hold a second convention in Philadelphia the following spring. Then farmer and Revolutionary War veteran Daniel Shays and his disaffected peers (sinking in debt because they were not paid for their war service) swung into action, terrorizing parts of Massachusetts until dispersed by state militiamen in early 1787.

Shays' Rebellion turned the tide. It sent a shiver of horror through every merchant and creditor in the Republic, for if debtors could revolt in western Massachusetts, they could make trouble anywhere. That spring meeting at Philadelphia would be well attended indeed: out of its deliberations would come a new government, and a new chapter in the story of American numismatics. Most importantly, it would establish for the ages who could make money—and who could not.

"HARD MONEY" AND THE YOUNG REPUBLIC, 1789–1830

The 56 delegates who came to Philadelphia in May 1787 were entrusted with debating and enacting improvements to the Articles of Confederation—most notably, granting the national government the power of direct taxation. The hand of this group of "Federalist" debaters, led by Alexander Hamilton, was first seen in the decision to scrap the old edifice instead of tinkering with it. They wished the new nation to be taken seriously by the other members of the constellation of independent states, and they felt there were no means by which this might be accomplished if the current balance between state and national authority in America were to remain where it was. What's more, the Articles of Confederation, with their weak central control and strong local power (a balance that seemed to be increasingly favoring debtor farmers), were simply bad for business.

Joined to this was a certain snobbery on the part of Alexander Hamilton and many of his fellow delegates. It seemed undeniable that a government of the better sorts of people (or one made up of the rich, the well-born, and the able, in one Federalist's revealing words) was desirable and would be easier to achieve under a new political compact than under the current one. The members of this convention were in basic agreement on what they wanted, and they therefore managed to achieve it in the form of a written document, the Constitution of 1787.

The hands of the propertied delegates were visible throughout the document. States were expressly forbidden to interfere with contracts. The debt of the federal government was expressly recognized, its payment guaranteed. The central government was authorized to put down domestic uprisings. Federal judges were appointed for life, senators would be elected by state legislatures rather than by the people, and the president would receive a relatively long term—four years—and be chosen not by the people, but by an electoral college.

This national conservative trend would continue into the monetary arena. The uncontrolled emission of state and federal paper had threatened ruin to the mercantile classes along the Atlantic seaboard, so when it came time to discuss what sorts of money would be allowed and be created, and by whom, a permanent change was made. The Constitution's framers made their points most explicitly in two clauses of the first section of the new document.

Henceforth, states could not "coin Money; emit Bills of Credit [paper money]; [or] make any Thing but gold and silver Coin a Tender in Payment of Debts" (Article I, Section 10, paragraph 1). From then on, only the national government would have the authority to "coin Money, regulate the Value thereof, and of foreign Coin, and fix the Standard of Weights and Measures" (Article I, Section 8, paragraph 5). The Constitution did not state that the new central government could circulate paper money, and that vagueness was deliberate: Hamilton and his fellow framers were dedicated to the dream of making the United States a "hard money" country (based on specie—gold and silver coins) if this were humanly possible, but they also wanted the escape hatch of federal paper in case of extreme circumstances.

The new basic accord had to be ratified before its shortcomings could become manifest. The delegates to the Constitutional Convention finished their labors on September 8, 1787, sparking more than a year's worth of sincere debate. The tiny state of Delaware was first to swing into position behind the new compact (December 7, 1787) and within a month or so was joined by Pennsylvania, New Jersey, Georgia, and Connecticut. The ninth and crucial state, New Hampshire, ratified the Constitution on June 21, 1788.

Proving that governments can function without unanimity, George Washington was elected the first president by acclamation and got down to business with his new administration in New York City in April 1789, before both North Carolina, in November 1789, and Rhode Island, in May 1790, officially embraced the new system.

The Constitution laid the foundation for the new nation's money.

URGENT MATTERS FOR THE NEW NATION

Among the earliest concerns were finance and money. Alexander Hamilton had persuasively argued that the new government must be a model of fiscal honesty from the outset, and Article VI of the Constitution was sheer genius on the part of the young financier and his adherents. It recognized and assumed the debts of the states and former national government under the Articles of Confederation. This article did *not* specify payment in full—and the amount actually received, in the guise of long-term bonds, was not unduly generous—but the agreement to pay *anything* on notes already widely seen as worthless was a brilliant stroke and shifted loyalty on the part of the business community—which held most of the depreciated paper—away from the local and toward the new national government.

Because Hamilton and his colleagues distrusted paper, and because they were sincerely interested in underscoring the majesty and sovereignty of their new country and creation, they would have to do something about the coinage, and in fairly short order. State issues came to a halt in the spring of 1789, and a copper panic the following July drove both good coins and bad from circulation. A number of public and private groups and merchants took up the slack on the local level, and issues of small-change notes began appearing in commerce that summer. The bills were almost always denominated in pence, although those of the Bank of North America also proclaimed that they were worth one-ninetieth or three-ninetieths of a dollar, an attempt to express their value according to an old system, even as their issuers were moving toward a new.

As for the larger denominations, foreign gold and silver coinage would still be used when available. But the other earlier commercial mainstay was out: the states were no longer able to issue paper money, and the federal power was disinclined to do so. By 1790 there seemed a very real prospect that American business transactions would have to once again be carried on by barter and with Spanish-American currency.

At least the preliminary question of the identity of the American currency unit, and the relation of subordinate and multiple denominations to that unit and to each other, had effectively been answered by the end of the 1780s. In 1792 the law passed: the new American unit would be an old coin, the Spanish-American piece of eight, called by an old name, the dollar, but divided in a new fashion, decimally into dimes and cents.

Americans like to believe that they were the first to devise the concept of a stable, orderly arrangement of monetary denominations based on the number ten, but they were not. The ancient Greeks of Syracuse and other areas had dekadrachms, huge silver pieces equal to ten drachms. And that workhorse of the later Roman Republic and early Roman Empire, the silver denarius, was originally equal to ten copper asses. Neither ancient precursor left an indelible mark on the world's later money, and it would be another millennium and a half before the decimal monetary concept came to stay—this time in Russia, introduced in 1700 by Peter the Great.

That being said, Americans did not base their coinage arrangements on the Russian precedent, nor that of anyone else. On the contrary, the inhabitants of the fledgling United States would see their decimal coinage arrangement adopted around the world—first by Revolutionary France, then by Latin Europe and Latin America, and finally by the erstwhile enemy herself, when British coinage became decimal in 1971.

THE MINT ACT OF 1792

The United States enacted its decimal idea into law with the Mint Act of 1792. Passed on April 2, the law first proclaimed the establishment of a United States mint in the current national capital, Philadelphia, and determined the types of employees for the new facility and their salaries. Second, it established a decimal relationship between the members of the new coinage system and set down what those members would be, what quality and quantity of metal they would contain, and what images they might display.

Finally, the Mint Act guaranteed that the new coining facility would strike gold and silver for the public free of charge—an absolute necessity were the new operation to get the raw materials needed for coinage. What would the new coins be? As we might expect, they would center on the dollar, but the following chart shows all members of the proposed new system.

Metal	Name	Value ($)	Weight	Fineness
Gold	Eagle	10.00	270 grains (17.496 grams)	0.917
Gold	Half eagle	5.00	135 grains (8.748 grams)	0.917
Gold	Quarter eagle	2.50	67.5 grains (4.374 grams)	0.917
Silver	Dollar	1.00	416 grains (26.956 grams)	0.892
Silver	Half dollar	0.50	208 grains (13.478 grams)	0.892
Silver	Quarter dollar	0.25	104 grains (6.739 grams)	0.892
Silver	Disme	0.10	41.6 grains (2.696 grams)	0.892
Silver	Half disme	0.05	20.8 grains (1.348 grams)	0.892
Copper	Cent	0.01	264 grains (17.107 grams)	1.000
Copper	Half cent	0.005	132 grains (8.533 grams)	1.000

A few observations are in order. The word *disme* was shortened rather quickly to *dime*, which was how the word would be pronounced in any case. The copper cents and half cents had their weights reduced before coining began in earnest, as the price of copper had meanwhile risen. And the inclusion of a half cent brings a reminder that this was a hybrid system that treated an old coin in a new way.

That old coin, of course, was the piece of eight, which had always been divided into eight reales. It would continue to circulate beside its new American cousin—indeed it would *need* to continue to do so: it would be decades before there were enough American dollars in circulation to render Spanish-American coins unnecessary. Any American needing change for a real would also need a half cent, since the Spanish-American coin was worth 12-1/2 cents in the new reckoning.

Eight reales, four reales, two reales, and one real, all of the late 1700s.

Similarly, the quarter dollar would find a place in the new system, even though common sense tells us that one-fourth is not really part of a decimal arrangement. But the quarter would equal a coin with which all Americans had long been familiar, the two-real piece. And the quarter eagle ($2.50 gold piece), one suspects, was introduced because it expressed a decimal concept of sorts, equaling ten quarter dollars. In sum, this system was not completely decimal; rather, it contained comfortingly familiar elements in addition to those that were new, which is probably why it became so successful.

The Mint Act of 1792 set down designs for the new coinage in a fairly detailed fashion. Although there was a groundswell of sentiment in favor of depicting the president on the obverses of the new coins, Washington objected, saying it reminded him too much of monarchical practice. And so the Mint Act stipulated that one side of each coin be devoted to "an impression emblematic of liberty," with an inscription to that effect. Gold and silver coins were to incorporate an eagle, the national bird, onto their reverse designs, while reverses for cents and half cents were simply required to express the denomination.

The Mint Act and American coinage were not guaranteed or inevitable. In the years between 1789 and 1792, there was a good deal of talk about outsourcing the coinage to any of several private moneyers in Great Britain, Matthew Boulton's Soho Mint being the leading contender. Congress mulled over the idea of a foreign coiner, but while Boulton sent no samples, another British firm did. This was William and Alexander Walker, who commissioned John G. Hancock Sr. to prepare a handsome series of copper pattern cents as well as rarer pieces without denomination. The national legislature was impressed, but it was finally swayed by the arguments of Thomas Paine and Thomas Jefferson, who believed it simply made no sense to hold American coinage hostage to a European source in dangerous times.

LAYING THE MINT'S FOUNDATION

One of the prime movers in favor of a new coinage was Robert Morris, who had been behind the ill-fated trials of 1783. He found a temporary mint site in the cellar of a coach house belonging to a saw-maker named John Harper, who hired a self-taught diesinker, goldsmith, and silversmith named Peter Getz to cut the dies. Getz made strikings in copper and silver, presumably intended to represent cents and half dollars. Though Congress was not particularly taken with his artistry, Getz's efforts may have nudged Congress in the direction of passing the Mint Act.

Going forward, the government continued to use the coach house for minting purposes. Using dies engraved by Robert Birch, Harper's press struck the first American coin legally authorized by the new government, a half disme with a chubby portrait of Liberty on the obverse, and a scrawny eagle on the reverse. Some 1,500 of these pieces were struck on July 13, 1792.

At this point, the Mint Act was law, but the coining facility it had called into being had not yet opened. It would shortly do so, however: a site at Seventh Street and Sugar Alley was purchased for a trifle more than $4,000; the Republic received the deed on July 18 and the cornerstone was laid July 31. Now the mint proper could be erected.

As the walls were going up, designers and coiners began their work. Between September and December 1792 they experimented with three denominations. Someone contributed an obverse die for a disme companion to Birch's earlier half disme; it was married to a reverse by Birch, and the new chief coiner, Henry Voigt, struck a half dozen or so of the new coins in copper and in silver. Voigt's colleague, Joseph Wright, created a quarter dollar pattern with a charming young head of Liberty obverse and a standing eagle reverse. Two examples

About 1,500
half dismes
were struck.

have survived in copper as well as an equal number in "white metal," a soft coining alloy composed mostly of tin.

Chief Coiner Voigt contributed a pattern himself, the "silver center" cent. This represented an attempt to create a coin worth a cent in a size more convenient than one made of pure copper. We do not know precisely how Voigt positioned the plug in the center of the planchet, and the difficulty he encountered appears to have tempted him to strike other patterns from the same dies wherein the silver was either mixed with the copper or was absent altogether. Fewer than 20 pieces of all types are known.

Finally, the man who had designed the half disme struck at one mint designed a cent struck at another. Robert Birch recycled his head from the silver half disme, turned it the other way, and struck a few cent trials in copper and one in white metal. The latter is particularly interesting because of a brief reverse legend, G*W Pt—for "George Washington President," the final gasp of the movement to honor the nation's chief executive on its coins.

These early pieces are among the most revered members of American numismatics, but with the exception of the Birch half disme, none would have been seen by the average citizen of the day. Still, that citizen was beginning to see the first "real" U.S. coins within a few months. In March 1793, the first issues—copper cents designed by Henry Voigt—began trickling from the new mint. For the obverse, Voigt employed a wild-haired, right-facing head of Liberty design that drew some criticism in the print media of the day. But the real adverse comment was reserved for his reverse, where Voigt reintroduced a design idea that had been in existence since 1776—linked rings, which began as a symbol of national unity but now appeared uncomfortably similar to a chain of slavery.

Mint director David Rittenhouse thus suggested a new design, and cents of this second type were struck through the summer of 1793. They were followed that September by a third attempt, the final contribution of the gifted Joseph Wright. Wright's Liberty borrowed heavily from Augustin Dupré's Libertas Americana medal of 1783, down to the Phrygian cap, an ancient symbol of the newly freed slave, behind her head. That motif, which also appeared on Wright's copper half cents struck between July and September 1793, would be incorporated into the designs of Wright's successors for a century after the engraver's untimely death in late 1793.

All told, the new mint struck 111,512 cents and 35,334 half cents that first year—not bad for a first effort, but scarcely guaranteed to alleviate American monetary difficulties on the lower end of the coinage scale. The new national coiners expanded their copper output the following year, and the year after that, but their fellow citizens still had recourse to more traditional sources for most of their small change. They kept those small-denomination, local notes in commerce, and they printed even more (sometimes denominated in cents, sometimes in pence). They also imported cent-sized tokens from Great Britain.

TOKEN COINAGE FOR CHANGING TIMES

By the beginning of the 1790s, Britons were experiencing a scarcity of official small change, making that which was suffered by Americans pale in comparison. The last time England had had legal copper money placed into circulation was two decades earlier, but as the country entered the beginning stages of the Industrial Revolution, vast amounts of low-value coinage would be needed to pay the new, salaried workers.

The Royal Mint was reluctant to provide public copper coins, and so private copper would fill in. Their issue began in North Wales in 1787, and by the middle of the next decade hundreds of merchants and firms across England, Scotland, Wales, and Ireland were busily providing the coppers that the Royal Mint would not. By that time, members of the upper and middle classes were beginning to treasure them for their collector interest as well as for their economic utility.

The collector coppers celebrated popular places, called attention to noteworthy historical events, and paid homage to the famous people of the day. It was probably inevitable that American personas and motifs would make their appearance, and while British collectors snapped up the more artistic creations featuring George Washington, the less popular appear to have been sent over to the United States to circulate there beside the new national cents.

The 1790s also saw British presses strike two types of copper tokens specifically intended for circulation among Americans—not simply sent there when rejected at home. The first of these was the Talbot, Allum & Lee cents of 1794–1795, ordered by a merchant house in New York City. These tokens found instant favor as cents—even though they were slightly lighter than the official issue—and the fledgling U.S. Mint found these coppers appealing as well. Needing rolled copper for half-cent planchets in the spring of 1795, Director Rittenhouse bought some 1,076 pounds of the tokens (around 52,000 of them) from William Talbot and recycled them into the national coining process.

The second made-for-America piece was created by Matthew Boulton for Philip Parry Price Myddelton in 1796. Myddelton had come into possession of a huge tract of land in Kentucky, and as part of his efforts to persuade impoverished British farmers and laborers to immigrate to the land, he enlisted Boulton to employ the talented Conrad Heinrich Küchler to design copper tokens for the project. However, these never got beyond the pattern stage, as in 1796 Myddelton was thrown into prison for his ambitious plan—to encourage the departure of British artisans was illegal.

Successes, Challenges, and Innovations

By the time of the Myddelton fiasco, the federal mint had managed to expand its production into metals other than copper. In October 1794, the first silver half dollars were coined, and on the 15th of that month the first representatives of the new American dollar also left the coining press. Of the latter, some 1,758 suitable for circulation were struck on that single day; no more were made until the following year.

Those dollars have much to say about the fledgling Mint and its first products. They were designed by Robert Scot, who would be responsible for most of America's coin designs over the next decade and a half. His dollar's Liberty head and eagle were criticized for their delicacy of execution, but that was hardly his fault: the new mint had no press strong enough to give its dollars a sharp impression, nor would it have until the following year—after which Scot's designs were seen to have improved.

The new dollars would serve as the flagship for American silver coins: any design changes adopted there were usually extended to lower denominations a year or two later. For example, when Scot abandoned his simple eagle for a heraldic one on the dollar, smaller silver coins replicated this substitution as well—as would gold coinage, which was first struck by the Mint in 1795 as eagles and their halves, designed once more by Robert Scot.

By the time the last of the legally mandated denominations—the quarter eagle, which appeared in mid-1796—was being coined, it was becoming apparent that at least a portion of the Mint's production could not be achieved in the ordinary

The first U.S. silver dollar was of the
Flowing Hair type, designed by Robert Scot.

way. The difficulty stemmed from two considerations: the low value of cents and half cents, and the time and trouble it took to make them.

Consider for a moment. If you were a Mint director in the late 1790s, and you had a set amount of money to produce during a given term, would you not prefer to meet it by striking eagles rather than cents? Those cents took as much labor to make as did the $10 pieces—more, in fact, because copper was harder to roll and strike than gold. And yet when you were finished, you had a cent instead of an eagle, and you still had virtually all of your coining left to do.

Rolling sheets was not the only problem; as far as anyone knew, the United States was still short of native coining metals. The simple winning of independence had done nothing to alleviate the shortage. Americans had little domestic gold or silver—or copper—which meant that their coiners had to scrounge for it. A 1798 cent exists overstruck on a halfpenny token from Anglesey, North Wales. One wonders whether this was accidental.

SEEKING ASSISTANCE

Of course, there *was* an area blessed with much copper and the technological wherewithal to turn it into blanks: Great Britain. By early 1796 the new U.S. Mint director, Elias Boudinot, was preparing to hold his nose and ask the old enemy for help.

Britain responded. Between 1796 and 1837, Cornish and Welsh copper was made into planchets of two sizes, then sent across the Atlantic to be elaborated into half cents and cents at Philadelphia. While two other firms participated, the favored agency was Boulton, Watt & Company—one more instance of the enterprising Matthew Boulton capitalizing on his ties with America. Boulton's planchets were made from the best copper, of the correct weight, and carefully finished, but they were not always available when needed.

On two occasions, their tardy delivery helped change the course of American numismatic history. The first was in the late 1790s, when Boulton delayed so long in sending copper that the U.S. Mint virtually ceased production in that metal, striking only a few thousand cents in 1799 and no half cents whatsoever between 1797 and 1800. The second occasion took place about 15 years later, but it was scarcely Soho's fault: the United States declared war on Great Britain in the spring of 1812, and the two countries remained hostile for nearly three years. During those years, the Mint struck no half cents and a dwindling number of cents, until it halted production altogether with the last of the 1814-dated coins. Cent coinage resumed in 1816 with the end of the war, and it steadily expanded through the 1820s.

By then, Americans were essentially doing business with only three of the ten denominations stipulated in the Mint Act: cents, half dollars, and half eagles. The cent was becoming essential on the lower end of the monetary scale, especially as the supply of genuine and counterfeit British and Irish halfpennies dwindled through attrition. The half dollar represented a handy amount of money in the United States, and the half eagle was popular because its gold value was conveniently close to other gold coins that Americans were using: the British guinea, the French louis d'or, and the Spanish-American double escudo.

But what about the other seven stars in the American monetary constellation? Several were unpopular and rarely produced because there existed better-known foreign coins that were preferred in trade. Thus, the half dime and dime yielded place to the half real and real, while the quarter dollar was rarely struck because people found it essentially duplicated the Latin American double real.

Other members could not be kept in circulation, most notably the silver dollar. This coin had been overvalued in relation to the piece of eight—it was slightly lighter and composed of slightly less-pure silver—and was thus swapped for pieces of eight in the West Indies, where it passed for par. The gold eagle suffered from similar problems; in 1803, France adopted a new silver-to-gold ratio of 15-1/2 to 1, and it became profitable to ship American gold coins to France for melting.

Seeking to end these evils, in 1804 an irate Boudinot suspended coinage of both eagles and dollars, a suspension that would hold for nearly four decades. The Mint director might have been relieved, for the policy meant that he had two fewer denominations to produce.

And this was a material consideration: the early U.S. Mint was a very inefficient coiner. Its equipment was ancient, made up of the castoffs and hand-me-downs of other countries and other coiners, as well as creaking machinery originally intended for other purposes. Its coiners were not masters of the craft, nor were its designers. The political climate was hostile, to say the least; the Mint regularly came up for review and could have been voted out of existence whenever such examination was made. It indeed came close to being abolished in 1800 and again in 1802; only an 11th-hour decision kept the facility open in the latter instance.

Not until May 19, 1828, would the U.S. Mint be authorized to remain "in force and operation, unless otherwise provided by law." But even by that period, its production had come nowhere close to meeting the demands of the people it attempted to serve.

FOREIGN COINS IN THE UNITED STATES

The same two conditions we saw at the beginning of America's story still held true. The country was metal-poor, and even with materials the Mint had no chance whatsoever of matching the needs of a population which was doubling every two decades. Thus, Americans would do as they had done since the beginning: they would turn to other people's coiners for help.

That being said, the Constitution granted the government the ability to ensure that their new federal creation played a key role in circulation regardless—Article I, Section 8, gave Congress the power to "regulate the Value . . . of foreign Coin." They exercised this power on February 9, 1793, when "an act regulating foreign coins, and for other purposes" was passed. The new law, which went into effect on the following first of

Various successors to the Spanish American piece of eight, such as this Peruvian 8 reales, were widely accepted in U.S. commerce.

July, demonetized all foreign coinage *except* the gold coins of Great Britain, Portugal, France, Spain, and Spanish America, and the silver coins of France and Spain. It also established values at which those coins were to circulate: for example, the Spanish dollar would be worth 100 cents, and its French equivalent 110.

The new law was intended as a stopgap. It stipulated that three years from the beginning of American silver and gold coinage, everything foreign except the Spanish and Spanish-American piece of eight would be demonetized. The reality was that the U.S. Mint simply could not make enough domestic coins to replace foreign ones, so Congress climbed down from its lofty but unattainable position of self-sufficiency, renewing the act in 1798, 1802, and 1806. The act was then allowed to expire, but foreign coins were allowed to circulate anyway. By 1816 an act renewing the circulation of foreign gold and silver coins was back on the books, and the provision was renewed periodically until the Act of 1857.

Which foreign coins circulated here? The Spanish and Spanish-American piece of eight led the way in silver, although coins like the Brazilian 960 reis (often a recycled Spanish-American peso, restruck at Bahia or Rio de Janeiro) gave it much competition in the 1810s and 1820s, as did the French five-franc piece, or piastre, in the 1830s.

In gold, British, French, Spanish-American, and Brazilian pieces held sway. The British guinea was important, but the last representatives of this denomination were struck in 1813. Four years later, its successor, the sovereign, emerged as a dominant player in international and intra-American commerce. In terms of sheer popularity, the sovereign would have frequently yielded place to the Spanish and Spanish-American onza or doubloon, particularly in border areas of the Old Southwest.

Aided by recurrent infusions of fresh foreign coinage, the American monetary system limped along. Had Americans had enough coinage of any kind for commercial use, they would have been satisfied; but even with the piece of eight, the sovereign, the gold of Brazil, and the silver of France, they were not receiving all the hard money they needed to keep up with their present and prospective rates of economic development.

What had been true before still held true now: America was a demographic and commercial success, but with an economy that constantly outpaced the orthodox money supply, they replied with an unorthodox one. Just as the Constitution was taking force, just as it was seeking to channel America's money in a particular direction, the prospective users of that money were cutting a path of their own with the paper note from the private bank. Between the years 1790 and 1865, private paper currency would reign.

GOLD!

The era of "rag" money—called "broken-bank notes" by the disrespectful and "obsolete notes" by the serious—lasted from approximately 1782 to 1866, coinciding rather nicely with the antebellum "first American republic." During this period, printers such as Jacob Perkins; Murray, Draper, Fairman & Company; and, later, the American Bank Note Company and National Bank Note Company would combat counterfeiting with ingenious new technologies and create numismatic works of art with their private bank currency. The miracle of 19th-century American growth simply could not have occurred without those paper notes, but the "rag" times would eventually end.

A combination of factors would soon ensure that the paper-money system that had taken three-quarters of a century to construct would only take a few years to demolish. One of these factors was the Civil War (see the following section). But earlier, the inevitability of the private note was challenged by a second, even more surprising event. For the first time in their history, Americans were getting enough precious metal, and enough expertise in coining it, to reduce their age-old dependence on paper.

The big discovery occurred approximately one week after the signing of the Treaty of Guadalupe Hidalgo, which ended the Mexican-American War and granted the United States title to Texas, New Mexico, Arizona, Nevada, Utah, part of Colorado, and California. A Mormon recent arrival to the West named James Marshall observed a glint of bright yellow—gold!—in the tailrace at a sawmill on the American River, near Sacramento. Nothing happened for several weeks because John Augustus Sutter (who owned the mill where the gold was found) did all he could to keep the discovery hidden.

But another Mormon named Sam Brannan wandered by, found out what had happened, and promptly rode back to San Francisco yelling, "Gold! Gold! Gold on the American River!" at the top of his lungs. And, as the saying goes, there went the neighborhood.

Within the next 18 months, some 75,000 gold seekers arrived from the East Coast, Europe, and even Australia. The effects of the California gold rush are almost too enormous to calculate. The discovery upset the old financial ratio between gold and silver, helping to precipitate a monetary instability that would last until both metals were removed from coinage more than 100 years later. It also inflamed tensions between North and South, as it became clear that California was bound to join the Union as a "free" state, therefore aligned with the North in foreign and domestic policy.

Thus, the California gold rush was one of the events leading to the American Civil War—and it would also help to ensure that the North would have the means with which to pursue it. For those interested in the story of America's money, the era has a double significance. First, it brought about a fascinating series of locally made coins, among the most interesting and historic issues in all of American numismatics. Second, the gold rush and related strikes elsewhere would mean that, combined with better coining technology, Americans would for the first time have enough domestic coinage for their monetary needs.

THE SMALLER SOUTHERN STRIKE

These were the great days of private gold coinage. Between 1848 and 1861, makeshift mints were established in California, Utah, Oregon, and Colorado to take advantage of the newly available precious metal, making it useful for local commerce and sending it back East for reworking there. In this, the private Western mints were similar to Spanish-American producers of pieces of eight. In both instances, the idea was to create a useful, feasible coinage *now*; those with artistic sensibilities could improve upon it later. Consequently we should not look for great artwork on these private issues.

Nor should we look for the first of them in California. We should look instead to an isolated area where North Carolina, South Carolina, and Georgia come together. Gold was found in that part of the world shortly before 1800, and, while it sparked nothing quite comparable with the California Gold Rush, there was enough precious metal in those layers and folds of the land to inspire a sizable mining scramble in the late 1820s, the eviction of Native Americans and their replacement by white settlers, and the appearance of private coiners by the early 1830s.

Templeton Reid—a sometime jeweler, gunsmith, watchmaker, and general handyman—was the first, setting up a mint in Milledgeville, Georgia, in 1830 and turning about $1,500 worth of metal into $2.50, $5, and $10 gold pieces. He soon packed up for Gainesville, where he struck a few hundred more coins between August and October 1830, but afterwards he seems to have abandoned coinage for nearly 20 years, relocating to Columbus, Georgia, where he engaged in creating and marketing new and better types of cotton gins.

Reid's coins were simple affairs, featuring his name and the denomination on one side, the origins of the precious metal and (usually) the date on the other. While he was criticized for creating lightweight coins, he made his money from pure gold, and so his coins were worth slightly more than their face value as bullion. This goes far toward explaining their extreme rarity today: most of them were melted down and recoined in Philadelphia.

You may be wondering how Templeton Reid managed to keep from being arrested: after all, if states could not coin money, how could an individual? The answer is that the framers of the Constitution apparently never anticipated that a private citizen would *want* to coin money, assuming instead that federal facilities would provide plentiful coinage for everyone. As we have seen, this did not occur. Private bank notes were one result. Private gold coinage was another.

Reid eventually struck one more coinage, this time shortly after the beginning of the rush to California. Numismatists long assumed that the coiner had followed the lure of metal west, as the coin is a $10 piece designated CALIFORNIA GOLD. But it

When the federal government failed to meet local coinage needs, enterprising Americans struck their own private money. Templeton Reid was one such entrepreneur—a jeweler, gunsmith, and inventor who turned his creativity to coins, including this $10 "Georgia Gold" piece.

now appears more likely that this coin (and a companion $25 piece that was stolen from the U.S. Mint Collection in 1858 and never recovered) was struck in Columbus. The elderly coiner was in no condition to travel and in fact died within a few months of his final foray into private moneying.

Not long after Reid's first issues, a family of German extraction named Bechtler set up shop near Rutherfordton, North Carolina—a few miles southeast of Asheville, a few miles northwest of the South Carolina and Georgia lines, and a local center for the gold trade. The family patriarch, Alt Christoph, soon made himself indispensable as the town's only jeweler and watchmaker. Meanwhile the locals petitioned Congress for a mint to turn their gold nuggets and dust into federal coinage. When they were ignored, they turned to the Bechtlers for help. Thus, the head of the clan was striking quarter and half eagles by July 1831, and by the end of the year, he had created an altogether new American coin: the gold dollar.

In time, the gold region got its mint—or rather two mints, one in Charlotte, North Carolina, and the other in Dahlonega, Georgia. Neither was an unqualified success, but they were enjoying enough trade by the end of the 1830s to persuade Alt Christoph to get out of the private minting business. In 1840 he transferred it to his son August, who moved the mint into the center of town and began striking gold dollars sometime in 1842, minting them in large numbers until his death in July 1846.

This brought a nephew into the trade: Christoph Jr. He continued to coin dollars and $5 pieces until the end of 1849 or the beginning of 1850. By then, the family's gold dollars were facing competition from official coins of the same denomination (first struck in Philadelphia in 1849), and this younger Christoph Bechtler seems to have given up the coining trade to concentrate on the family's earlier profession as a jeweler. Bechtler dollars and other coins continued to circulate alongside ordinary, federal products for many years; most of the surviving examples show evidence of a lengthy life in circulation.

CALIFORNIA GOLD: A DRAMA IN THREE ACTS

Numismatist Walter Breen divided California private gold coinage into three main stages. The first began in the winter of 1848–1849 and continued through April 1850. A number of individuals and firms struck $5 and $10 coins at that time, and they created a number of circulating ingots as well. This first stage came to an end after the public learned that several of these issues were debased or contained less than their stated value in gold.

Local authorities then enacted legislation clamping down on private issues, but the laws were not enforceable, and another spate of private issues soon entered commerce. This second stage lasted until March 1851, and it was brought to a close by rumors that the new wave of private issues was also short-weight. No further private coins appeared during the remainder of 1851.

The third and final stage of California private coinage began in January 1852 and continued through 1856. While some new moneyers entered the field and placed their names on issues ranging up to $50, the most interesting event during this stage occurred on the lower end of the scale, as "fractional" gold coins—tariffed at 25¢ and 50¢, plus a related issue of dollars—entered commerce.

In the earliest stage, one of the first firms to strike coins was the Cincinnati Mining & Trading Company, which in 1849 struck a few different coins bearing a distinctive Liberty head with a feather head-dress on the obverse and a unique left-facing eagle with a shield on the reverse. Both $5 and $10 coins were made, but their gold content was rumored to be low, and consequently almost all of the firm's products were soon pulled out of circulation and melted down. So were the issues of the Pacific Company, which were also struck in 1849, likely by hand with a sledgehammer.

One of the few firms to make a lasting contribution in this early period was Moffat & Company, which began issuing rectangular ingots in July 1849, graduating to normal coinage later that year. The concern's $5 and $10 gold pieces bore a deliberate similarity to ordinary U.S. gold coins.

The second stage of the California coinage saw the production of excessively rare rectangular ingots at a state assay office, but these soon yielded to orthodox coins: $5, $10, and, for the first time in California, $20 pieces. Two firms stood out here. Baldwin & Company was one, and their $10 gold piece depicting a *vaquero*, or Mexican cowboy, is among the most famous of all private gold issues. Schultz & Company, which set up shop behind the Baldwin mint and struck $5 pieces in 1851, was the other.

The third and final stage lasted for four years, and it saw a new player enter the field: the national government. In the autumn of 1850, a federal assay office of gold was created in San Francisco. It was granted the right to make ingots of refined gold, worth $50 each. A New York watchmaker named Augustus Humbert was appointed to assay the metal, and he, in turn, subcontracted the actual coining of it to Moffat & Company.

Whether or not anyone had so intended, Humbert's octagonal ingots (also called "slugs," or "Californians") entered circulation as ordinary coins—indeed, they were the principal accepted currency in California between 1851 and 1853. By 1852 Humbert was producing $10 as well as $50 ingots, and he added the double-eagle denomination in 1853. Humbert's ingots, with their distinctive eagle-and-shield obverses and engine-turned reverses, were better than anyone else's coins. They led naturally to an even more official coinage, as the assay office closed its doors in late 1853, and four months later a new branch of the U.S. Mint opened in its place.

But even after the establishment of the San Francisco Mint, private coining did not disappear; it persisted for some years. Kellogg & Company alone produced more $20 gold pieces in 1854 than the new federal facility, and those coins filled cashiers' tills in the mid-1850s, as did gigantic round $50 coins struck by two Hungarian veterans of the failed European revolutions of 1848, Count Samuel C. Wass and Agoston P. Molitor. Wass, Molitor & Company produced smaller coins as well, but they achieved immortality with those huge slugs, each of which contained more than a quarter of a troy pound of pure gold.

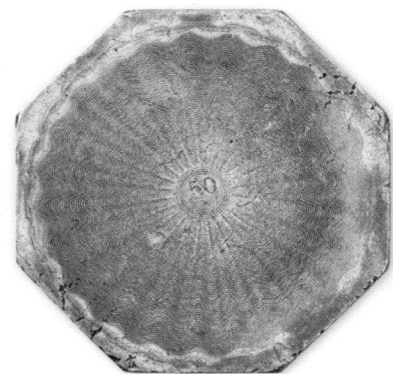

At the other end of the spectrum stood a motley assemblage of jewelers and dentists, people skilled at working with gold in small quantities. They now proceeded to create California "fractional" coins—tiny octagonal and round half dollars and quarters, as well as dollars. Most of the makers are anonymous, and their designs were simple. One thing is certain: coiners of fractional pieces had nothing whatsoever to do with makers of larger-denomination coins; the two groups were entirely separate.

This 1851 $50 gold piece was struck by Moffat & Co. for Augustus Humbert, United States assayer of gold. These heavy coins were called "slugs" because they could knock a man out in a fight—or so the Wild West legend goes.

OTHER REGIONS TAKE THE STAGE

The California gold rush had a ripple effect on the rest of the country. It influenced the tensions between North and South, but it was also responsible for smaller events of numismatic importance in Utah, Oregon, and Colorado. Neither of the first two areas had abundant gold of their own, but both had personal connections with California; many Oregon farmers had abandoned their plows and headed south at the first rumors of the gold strike, and recent migrants from Joseph Smith's peaceable Mormon kingdom near the Great Salt Lake (including the aforementioned Marshall and Brannan) accounted for many of the first prospectors to arrive in the Sacramento Valley.

UTAH: THE LAND OF THE HONEYBEE

Utah was settled in 1847 by followers of Joseph Smith, the martyred prophet of the Latter Day Saints. Led by Brigham Young, the faithful had trekked across the "Great American Desert" in search of a land so remote and so unpromising that other Americans would leave it (and them) alone. Their leader chose a site by the Great Salt Lake, and here the Mormons settled in July 1847.

They had only a limited and brief success in keeping other Americans out of Utah, however. Soon, victory in the Mexican War would grant the United States title to the American West—including the very area where Smith's disciples were building their theocratic state—and the California gold rush would result in thousands of "forty-niners" passing through the region. But the Mormons would stay where they were, and they would soon find that interlopers offered opportunities as well as threats.

Those heading west needed goods of all sorts and were prepared to pay high prices, and Mormon miners and others returning east bore gold, much of which was left behind in Utah. Thus, money could be made, and within a few months of the California strike, authorities in Utah were preparing to make it quite literally; Young enlisted the services of a British convert named John Mobourn Kay to make a distinctive local coinage, and a makeshift mint was in operation by the end of 1848.

The first coins struck were $10 pieces, some 46 of them, produced during the last month of 1848 but dated 1849. Production problems delayed an extension of the coinage until the following September, but from then through 1851, half eagles and quarter eagles were struck in some quantity, and a new denomination also entered American numismatic history: the double eagle, or $20 gold piece.

All of these coins used the same distinctive design, incorporating a three-pointed Phrygian crown—the emblem of the Mormon priesthood—and an abbreviated legend, G.S.L.C.P.G. ("Great Salt Lake City Pure Gold"). However, the gold in the Mormons' coins was *not* pure, and each denomination was only worth about 85 percent of its face value. In consequence, several thousand of the pieces were melted down in San Francisco, victims of the same backlash that was making instant rarities of the Pacific Company's coinage and other suspect issues.

At the end of the 1850s, the Mormon mint tried again, issuing half eagles notable for their incorporation of phonetic alphabet characters and the Mormon name for Utah, *Deseret*. By that time, it had a new source of gold—the region known as Colorado, where the yellow metal had been discovered in 1858. Alfred Cummings, governor of Utah Territory, finally quashed this coinage, but Colorado and its gold would soon write its own chapter in the story of private gold coinage.

This $5 gold piece shows a lion (hearkening to one of Brigham Young's nicknames, "Lion of the Lord"), an eagle, and a beehive. Deseret, Young's proposed named for the state of Utah, was the word for "honeybee" in the Book of Mormon.

OREGON: THE LAND OF "BEAVER MONEY"

The land of Oregon, occupied jointly by Americans and British for approximately three decades in the early 1800s, became sole property of the United States in 1846 and was formally organized as the Oregon Territory in 1848. Within a year, its citizens would be striking coinage from California gold.

The implements used to create this coinage still exist, housed at the Oregon Historical Society in Portland. Inspecting them makes one thing immediately apparent: the Oregon pioneers struck their eagles and half eagles *by hand*, using a sledgehammer instead of an orthodox coining press. Such a primitive way to coin money worked well enough in this instance for two reasons: Oregonian coiners were only making a few thousand pieces, and they were making them from a soft metal—pure gold from California.

The Oregon coinage was privately struck, but it had nearly begun as an official issue of the territory. Disputes over the value and measuring of gold dust led to a push for a territorial mint, but incoming governor Joseph Lane blocked the bill, arguing that such issues by a territory were illegal under the U.S. Constitution. Lane was on shaky ground; the Constitution indeed forbade coinage by states, but it said nothing about territories. He was the governor, though, and his word prevailed; if there was to be Oregon coinage, it would not be official, but private.

Soon, eight prominent businessmen founded the Oregon Exchange Company to strike those private coins. Their first issue, a $5 gold piece, bears on its obverse a beaver, whose valuable fur had inspired some of the earliest exploration and settlement of the region, and the initials T.O. (for "Territory of Oregon"). The reverse bears the denomination, the amount of gold, and the name of the issuer. Not long after, $10 pieces appeared, following the general designs of the $5 coins.

There was no attempt at assaying or standardization with this "beaver money," but to be on the safe side, the Oregonians made their coins' weights well *above* federal standards: when assayed at Philadelphia, the fives were found to be worth $5.50 and the tens $11. California bankers nevertheless valued them much lower, and they quickly melted down the great majority of the Oregon pieces to make a profit—perhaps 50 coins survive today. Actual coining came to a stop around September 1, 1849. By 1850 gold coins from California were arriving in Oregon in fair numbers, thus ending the monetary emergency that had led to the beaver money.

COLORADO: POLITICS, PIKES PEAK, AND PARSONS

Settlement of Colorado—acquired piecemeal between 1803, with the Louisiana Purchase, and 1848, with Mexico's official cession—began in earnest only after the discovery of gold on the South Platte River in July 1858. That summer brought a scramble comparable to the one in California a decade earlier. In this instance, conditions were even harsher: food was scarce, housing minimal, theft and violence rampant, and law enforcement nonexistent. The nearest secure source of many essential supplies was either Omaha, Nebraska, or St. Joseph, Missouri, and the neighboring Kansas Territory was in the midst of a bloody internal conflict.

Given their conditions, in 1859 Coloradans took the only logical step: they organized their own government, calling the region the "Territory of Jefferson," telling the federal government about it after the fact. By that time, gold dust and nuggets had become the universal media of exchange, and the inconveniences of such a system led to agitation for a local coinage. In 1860 it would be met by a firm calling itself Clark, Gruber & Company.

This concern was already doing business as a bank and assay office, but late in 1859, one of the principals made an arduous trip back East to purchase dies, presses, and the other necessities for a mint. In mid-January 1860, three lots were acquired in Denver City to house the new enterprise, and by early July the mint was ready to strike its first coinage. This was an up-to-date facility, and its output was impressive; between July and October 1860, some $120,000 of quarter eagles, half eagles, eagles, and double eagles was produced. The two lower denominations copied ordinary federal designs (Liberty's head for the obverse, and an eagle with a shield for the reverse), while the $10 and $20 pieces proudly displayed a romantic, if inaccurate, depiction of Pikes Peak on the obverse.

The "Pikes Peak" gold coins of Clark, Gruber & Company show a fanciful view of the famous landmark. The company also made coins with a traditional Liberty-head design.

After a temporary break during a harsh winter, Clark, Gruber & Company replaced Pikes Peak with Liberty on all denominations and struck approximately $240,000 in the next year, followed by $223,000 in 1862. Sadly, only a tiny percentage of these coins have survived, and this mint's days were soon numbered. The federal government never recognized the Jefferson Territory and instead organized the region as the Territory of Colorado in February 1861. Under national control, local enterprises such as private mints would face an uncertain future.

Indeed, the national government forced the sale of the mint in April 1863 on the pretext that the facility would be wanted for a federal facility in Denver. A national branch mint would indeed come into production on the site—but not until 1906. During its first 43 years, the facility would function only as an assay office.

Clark, Gruber & Company was by far the most prolific of the Colorado coiners, but there were two others, located elsewhere in the region. One of these was John J. Conway & Company, which set up shop in August 1861 at Georgia Gulch and made undated quarter eagles, half eagles, and eagles for a brief time. The other coiner was Dr. John D. Parsons, who set up a coining operation at Tarryall Mines, and in 1861 struck a few quarter eagles and half eagles with a most distinctive obverse design—it showed a quartz-reduction mill, used for separating gold from its rocky matrix. The operation came to an abrupt halt when Dr. Parsons ran out of gold, and today no more than half a dozen of his quarter eagles and three of his half eagles are known.

PRIVATE GOLD COINAGE DRAWS TO A CLOSE

The Colorado issues round out the period of private precious-metal coinage in the United States. There would be other strikes of gold and silver, but none of them produced a distinctive coinage. Why did they not? For one, private precious-metal coinage ceased because Congress declared it illegal in 1864. More importantly, though, times had changed.

The American Civil War was approaching its crescendo. The war would bring to a close the supremacy of local power and authority over national. The ending of that old tradition would inevitably have an effect on money; in the new climate, the private, local coin was an anachronism.

At the same time, the underpinnings that could bind the nation's disparate parts were expanding and improving. By 1864 the North was building a transcontinental railroad. Telegraphic communications were expanding as well, fostered by the war effort. What was emerging was the potential for a new, national economy, stretching from one coast to the other. The system would experience growing pains for the remainder of the century, but it would eventually mean that Americans would spend *national* coins when they used metallic money for trade.

And finally, the public coiner—the U.S. Mint—was getting better at the production of money, and was finally able to drive its competitors—the private coiners—from the field. Improvements at the main Philadelphia facility were underway by 1816; a fire at the beginning of the year had destroyed its old wooden millhouse, and Mint director Robert Maskell Patterson used the fire as an opportunity to incorporate a steam engine into the coining process. This engine powered the rolling operation—which at last gave this crucial step the power and precision it required—as well as the planchet-cutter, resulting in an increase in the Mint's productivity.

Mint personnel got better at their craft as well. They were asking Great Britain's Boulton, Watt & Company for technical advice in the mid-1820s, centering on the production of specimen strikes, or Proofs. By 1828 the minters were cautiously experimenting with restraining collars, which kept coins more consistent in shape and quality, and therefore more difficult to counterfeit.

By the end of the 1820s, congressional agitation to close the U.S. Mint had abated, and the institution faced an altogether different problem: space. Thus, the cornerstone for a new mint was laid by 1829, and the facility opened in January 1833. Next on the docket was to upgrade the old machinery; the key player here would be Franklin Peale, employed as all-purpose fact finder by Mint director Samuel Moore.

In this capacity Peale visited the more modern mints in Europe between 1833 and 1835. He investigated the facilities of the British Royal Mint, which used a type of coining press that Boulton had patented in 1790—essentially the traditional screw press, strengthened for connection to a new motive force, the steam engine. Peale also explored the mint in Karlsruhe, in the German grand duchy of Baden. Both there and in Paris he saw a different apparatus, one patented by Diedrich Uhlhorn in 1817 and lately improved upon by M. Thonnelier, which featured a toggle action and was more efficient with the steam power it received. What's more, since it did not coin by means of a screw—the most vulnerable and difficult-to-replace part of the Boulton apparatus—this machine was far more durable.

Peale was sold on the new press, and although he did not purchase one (not being empowered to in any case), he did manage to draw and memorize its essentials. He replicated them once he returned home in mid-1835, and by March 1836, a new press powered by the Mint's steam engine had been built and was striking its first coins. The improvement was clear from the outset: the new machinery could make twice or thrice as many coins as the old methods, and the resulting coins were also much more consistent in strike and finish.

Old ways and new: a half dollar struck in the traditional method (top), and another struck in a new way, by the power of steam (bottom); both were made in 1836.

THE MINT RISES TO PROMINENCE

Meanwhile more coinage metal was discovered. By 1837 a domestic source of copper had been found, breaking the Mint's 40-year dependence on planchets from Boulton, Watt & Company. Soon the Mint would find native suppliers of gold—in North Carolina and Georgia, mentioned earlier—and finally silver.

Just as significantly, Congress passed an Act in 1835 authorizing the establishment of branches of the U.S. Mint at Charlotte, North Carolina; Dahlonega, Georgia; and New Orleans, Louisiana. The first two towns were in convenient proximity to the mines that supplied Reid and the Bechtlers with bullion; and New Orleans was a convenient locale for a supply of precious metal too, in the form of coins from Mexico and elsewhere in Latin America. The Crescent City's economy was booming by the mid-1830s; why not help it along (and bolster local and national pride) by setting up a branch mint there as well?

Thus, by the spring of 1838, the United States had not one official coiner but four, all equipped with steam power and modern coining machinery. While the facilities at Dahlonega and Charlotte never reached expectations and were closed for good at the beginning of the Civil War, the mint in New Orleans was a success from the beginning, coining gold and silver on a regular basis until the outbreak of the conflict, and reopening in 1879 to remain in business for another 30 years.

As we have seen, a Western branch mint was opened in San Francisco in 1854. All the new mints (and the greater productivity of their parent at Philadelphia) led to a momentous decision some three years later, when Congress passed the Coinage Act of 1857, repealing "all former acts authorizing the currency of foreign gold and silver coins, and declaring the same a legal tender in payment for debts." For the first time in their history, the inhabitants of the United States felt confident enough about their own money to prohibit the use of other people's coins. And so all those pieces of eight, sovereigns, louis d'ors, thalers, and onzas assumed their present roles as parts of the nation's numismatic legacy—remembered with thanks, but no longer an active part of an ongoing story.

Ironically, the U.S. Mint would find itself unable to keep its own coins in circulation just four years later, when the quarreling between North and South deepened into a shooting war. In both places, uncertainty drove coinage into hiding and turned the American people back to their traditional expedient, the paper note, just as the potential seemed to have been achieved for banishing it once and for all.

FROM A CIVIL WAR TO A GILDED AGE

The Civil War meant and still means many things to Americans. It has produced feelings that have clarified, deepened, and changed over the past century and a half since the guns fell silent. But for all the complexity, the greatest lesson of the conflict is obvious: Americans would have to pay for the fine words enshrined in the Declaration of Independence with lives lived in a new way. They would have to actually take seriously the stirring phrase about the equality of *all* men.

The tremendously eventful 50 years that followed—called the "Gilded Age" after Mark Twain and Charles Dudley Warner's on-point satirical novel of the era—would see the nation struggle with that idea, all the while undergoing massive expansion and political change. The moniker could not be more apt; was not a *golden* age a period when humankind was at its best, transcending limitations of class, race, sex, and worldview? In reality, this was an age that posed as something solid and worthy, but whose gold plating was thin and easily worn away to reveal the bigotry and brass beneath.

Consider all that occurred between 1865 and 1914. The nation assumed its present borders when Alaska was added in 1867 and Hawaii in 1898, and it gained temporary and sometimes permanent control over other areas, too: the Philippines, Puerto Rico, Guam, the Canal Zone, and Guantánamo Bay. Meanwhile the continental states filled up thanks to increased immigration, improving transportation and communication, and advancing industry. The frontier finally disappeared.

These changes were for the better, or at least neutral, but they inevitably influenced some groups more than others, and caused immense friction and unrest virtually everywhere. Farmers lost their position at the head of the table, and Native Americans got shoved away altogether, locked up on reservations. African Americans saw most of what little they had won taken back in the South with the ending of Reconstruction; those who voyaged north found a scarcely more hospitable reception there. The organized labor movement experienced several sputtering beginnings, and though its days of success lay far distant in the next century, it was becoming increasingly apparent that those who owned the factories and firms owned a good deal more—including major portions of the state and federal governments.

The issue of tariffs and regional grudges caused tension between Democrats and Republicans, but the lasting truth was that the major parties both had an agenda that suited them and the economic elite while generally ignoring the real and worsening problems of the average citizen. As a result, the middle and late portions of the Gilded Age would see two movements for reform, speaking to the needs of the "forgotten man": the Populist and Progressive fronts, the latter of which would make more headway and help eradicate some of the worst social and industrial evils by the end of the period.

At bottom, all of this activity was tending in one direction: the country and its people were becoming ever more interconnected.

CURRENCY DURING THE CIVIL WAR

The Civil War was the defining experience of U.S. history—a true "watershed," to use a word ordinarily reserved by historians for far lesser events. The war split the country's story neatly down the middle;

in four short years the United States became a completely different country. And all this we have been saying about the country's history might be equally applied to its money.

In the four years of the Civil War, America's money would begin in familiar forms, then be constantly altered under pressure, and finally emerge with fundamentally new identities which remain today with minor modifications. Put most simply, the national government would be forced to acquire the same monopolistic powers over bills and notes that it had claimed over coins with the Coinage Act of 1857, as it became clear within six months of its start that the war must be fought and paid for by both sides with the time-honored expedient of paper money.

This money would take different forms, from the familiar private bank note to state notes and federal bills both Union and Confederate. All would be printed in mass quantities, whether by means of engraving, typesetting, or lithography. New media would emerge, including postage currency and bronze Civil War tokens.

Coinage, meanwhile, would be scarce, as gold and silver began disappearing from circulation in both the North and South shortly after the beginning of hostilities (thanks to the hoarding public). The mints at Charlotte, Dahlonega, and New Orleans all closed down in the spring of 1861. But coins would not disappear altogether. With the small number of coins it did produce during the period, the U.S. Mint concentrated on the lower end of the scale: cents bearing the new Indian Head design; a new two-cent piece introduced in 1864 (the first American coin to bear the motto "In God We Trust"); and a second three-cent piece to augment unwanted supplies of the first.

The two-cent coin was one of the shortest-lived series in U.S. coinage, being struck in a ten-year period that ended in 1873.

The three-cent piece takes a bit of explaining. The original version was introduced in 1851, when the postal rate for a first-class letter was lowered to 3¢, and was struck in quantity between then and 1853, first in silver, whose fineness was deliberately low, and later in the fineness current for all other American silver coins, 90 percent. The coiners at the U.S. Mint found their new, tiny coin so unpopular that production was drastically decreased and then ceased altogether in 1873; but early in 1865, they decided to try again—this time with a slightly larger coin struck in copper-nickel. They made a good many of the new pieces that first year, and the coins did in fact perform a modest service on the lower end of the monetary scale, but this version eventually proved as unpopular as the silver examples, and production stopped in 1889.

For what limited success federal coiners enjoyed on the base-metal end of the monetary column, they found even less when they turned to precious metals. Silver coins of the period—which bore Christian Gobrecht's Liberty Seated design, introduced in the late 1830s—were struck in very small number in the early 1860s, and most of them came from the branch mint at San Francisco rather than the parent facility at Philadelphia. In fact, the main U.S. mint virtually closed down at the end of 1861, and only half dollars were produced in a quantity comparable to that of pre-war years.

A similar pattern held for gold coins, most of which bore a rather pedestrian Liberty head with coronet, again designed by Gobrecht. The major exception was the slightly more attractive double eagle, designed by the man responsible for the current cent, the two-cent piece, and both three-cent pieces: James Barton Longacre. Whereas other gold denominations were struck in minuscule quantities after 1861, production of double eagles actually *ascended* through the war.

Virtually all of it, however, was accounted for by the San Francisco Mint, where the large gold coins were quickly struck and shipped east to bolster banking and the war effort. It would take the end of the armed conflict for America's metallic money to truly reemerge; meanwhile Reconstruction and new political ideas were shaping a distinctly new nation.

MONEY IN THE GILDED AGE

The shift from the local to the national, from the particular to the universal, was implicit in the Northern victory of 1865; for the next half century, Americans would have civic calm at home, and thus they had the time and concentration necessary to determine where their new interconnections might lead. Part of the evidence that they were doing so comes from the money they were producing during the Gilded Age.

What do we see when we take a closer look? First, there is a return to coinage with the end of the Civil War. The uncertainty was over: once put in circulation, specie would remain there. Therefore, production of most denominations expanded, at least until the harsh economic times of the middle and later 1870s. The exceptions to this rule were those coins on the lower end of the scale, as issues of cents, two-cent pieces, and three-cent pieces were decreasing by the late 1860s.

On the upper end, the production of gold double eagles continued to rise through the 1870s. The production of these massive capstones increased because there seemed to be an endless supply of gold in the West, and the double eagle was the most efficient way to turn that resource into something use-ful. The great majority were struck at the San Francisco branch mint, assisted after 1870 by a new federal facility at Carson City, Nevada. This facility was erected primarily in response to the massive Comstock silver strike, but it was also a source of gold coinage until its closing in 1893.

While many of the new double eagles were sent back East, many more stayed near their point of ori-gin—so many, in fact, that Congress had to alleviate the resultant banking nightmare with a new type of paper money, the National Gold Bank Note. Thus, while the national banking system and its notes proliferated throughout the country and homogenized currency, the federal government of the day might indeed respond to local monetary differences and act on behalf of influential interests on the state or regional level. Another example is the story of Western silver and the Morgan dollar.

A QUESTION OF METALS

The United States had long had a "bimetallic" monetary system, one based on two precious metals that were interchangeable with each other at a fixed ratio. This ratio had been established in 1834 at 16:1 (meaning that weight for weight, gold was worth 16 times as much as silver), and the system functioned adequately until the California Gold Rush upset the silver-to-gold ratio in favor of silver coinage. Con-gress responded to the subsequent melting and exportation of silver by reducing the precious-metal content of the half dollar, quarter, dime, and half dime, a measure that helped get silver coinage back into commerce until the emergency of the Civil War.

Not long before that crisis began, silver had been found near Virginia City, in the Nevada Territory (recently separated from the Utah Territory), and so much of it was shortly being taken from the ground there that the Union soon made Nevada into its own state. The nation's monetary system meanwhile acquired a headache of monumental size and duration, as the 16:1 ratio was again being upset—but this time in favor of gold. Matters worsened still in 1871, when the new German Empire adopted a strict gold standard, exporting nearly two-thirds of its silver stock, and adding more than $200 million of the metal to a market already glutted.

Mine owners and their congressional representatives were vocal in their distress, and the official reply was the Mint Act of February 12, 1873. The act gave with one hand and took away with the other: it put a slightly greater amount of silver in the half dollar, quarter, and dime, and it also created the silver trade dollar, which was intended to compete with the piece of eight in Far Eastern trade; but it halted production of the half dime, three-cent piece, and two-cent piece, and it closed out coinage of the normal silver dollar.

This was the famous "Crime of '73," which would soon become a rallying point for Western silver and Midwestern agrarian interests against the "goldbugs" of the East. Never mind that virtually no silver dollars had been struck during the 1860s and that no one wanted the three million or so that had been struck since 1870; for Western miners, the Mint Act of 1873 was outrage pure and simple, and they spent the next five years fighting to get it repealed. They would see success in 1878 with the passage of the Bland-Allison Act.

The act restored unlimited legal-tender status to silver dollars on the traditional standard, and it committed the U.S. Treasury to purchasing between two and four million dollars' worth of silver bullion each month for production of the new coins. The pieces were to have new designs by George T. Mor-gan, and his left-facing-portrait head of Liberty and more naturalistic reverse eagle represented a cautious attempt to bring more artistry to American coinage, a movement which gathered force as other denominations were redesigned after 1891. But for now, the dollar's new look was the last thing on most people's minds.

The Morgan silver dollar was struck by the millions starting in 1878.

The reception and significance of the Morgan dollar varied wildly from place to place. The West was partially assuaged, because the region's silver production now had an outlet, and the new dollars were a circulating mainstay there for many years to come. They were also popular in the South, and millions were struck in New Orleans after the reopening of the federal branch mint there in 1879.

THE ISSUE COMES TO A HEAD—AND THEN FADES

As the years went on, other groups grew progressively fonder of the Morgan dollar: medium and small farmers of the Midwest, West, and South, robbed of purchasing power in the 1880s and 1890s by a persistent agricultural depression, began to see the new silver dollars as a possible salvation. If the U.S. Mint coined them in unlimited numbers, then so much money would flood into the economy that the price of farm products would rise, and farmers could thus pay off their debts more easily than before.

But fortunately for the moneyed interests—who had a dislike and distrust of silver and rallied around gold—the Bland-Allison Act had stopped short of giving silver full bimetallic parity with gold at the old 16:1 ratio; it had also offered something less than completely "free" (unlimited) silver coinage. Both of these points would soon become rallying cries for miners and farmers. The Act did, however, allow for a massive coinage of cheap silver at inflated prices, a value-to-denomination ratio that became increasingly unrealistic as yet more silver poured from the mines and mints.

Along with the Morgan dollars, the Bland-Allison Act created a new type of paper currency, the Silver Certificate. This specialized note, originally intended to redeem the new dollars and later extended to the redemption of Legal Tender Notes issued during the Civil War, could not be exchanged for Gold Certificates. Nor would it remotely resemble any other type of federal paper money (the words "silver" and "silver dollars" dominating the designs), so anyone handed a Silver Certificate could immediately spot it and refuse it, demanding payment in a gold-based medium instead. But despite these measures and East Coast opposition, the new currency type gradually assumed a larger role in the national economy, as it was considerably easier to handle than the cumbrous coins it represented.

Today the debate over a gold standard versus a gold-and-silver standard may strike us as academic, but it had real and immediate connotations for those alive during the closing years of the 19th century. When miners and small farmers clamored for "the free and unlimited coinage of silver at the rate of sixteen to one," they were demanding recognition and respect for old ways of life that were now at risk. The fact that they could view endless coinage of a whitish metal with few nonmonetary applications as a panacea suggests that they were not being particularly realistic; but then, the same might be said for the opposition, who viewed the gold standard as sacred and any attempt to add silver as profane.

The issue came to a head in the presidential campaign of 1896, fought out against the backdrop of a miserable, three-year-long depression that had left factory workers unemployed and farmers and miners even worse off than before. Democratic candidate William Jennings Bryan hammered away at the Free Silver idea while Republican William McKinley's adherents spoke for gold coinage and a higher tariff. The latter—called "Big Bill McKinley, Advance Agent of Prosperity"—was elected, and sure enough, prosperity followed.

From this point, the issue of bimetallism faded in importance. When the Republic officially went on a gold standard in March 1900, Bryan and the Democrats railed and ran against it that fall—but no one cared and McKinley was reelected. He had more than prosperity on his side by that time; since he had taken office in March 1897, the United States had acquired an overseas empire. In the broader view of history, the new domains (and the fact that McKinley was reelected in part because of them) represented a historic shift in emphasis on the part of America's people; they were ready to look outward, and what they saw and how they reacted would amend the nature of their numismatic history in some very surprising ways.

NEW EMPIRE, NEW MONEY

Change was in the air by the early 1870s. That the United States was looking abroad for economic gain was suggested by the new trade dollar; why mint such a coin for the Far Eastern trade if you were not interested in that trade yourself? And while the coin may not have lived up to expectations, Chinese merchants accepted it readily enough, until a fall in silver prices in 1876 resulted in millions of the coins recrossing the Pacific.

Another change: Prior to 1857, foreign coins were legal and common in circulation in the United States. By 1876 the Mint was actually beginning to coin for other countries—first for Venezuela, and later for other small nations in the Western Hemisphere, including the Dominican Republic in 1897, El Salvador in 1904, and Costa Rica in 1905. By 1906 it was supplying Mexico (in an interesting case of historical reciprocity), and the Mint would continue to extend its coinage production across Latin America during the first half of the 20th century.

In the 1880s, the U.S. Mint extended its attentions in another overseas direction—to Hawaii. The islands formed an independent kingdom in those days, but American missionaries had been preaching there since 1820, shortly followed by Yankee traders and businessmen. In 1847 an issue of copper keneta (cents) had been prepared for King Kamehameha III by a private mint in Attleboro, Massachusetts, but the issue was poorly received as the monarch's portrait was almost unrecognizable and the reverse denomination was misspelled.

American penetration of the islands increased its pace after 1849. In the early 1880s, King Kalākaua I desired another issue of Hawaiian coinage. His representative, sugar baron Claus Spreckels, approached the U.S. Mint with preliminary designs and a proposal for coining a million dollars' worth of silver into coinage for the island chain. The issue would consist of dala (dollars, on an exact par with the U.S. coin), hapalua (half dollars), hapaha (quarters), and umi keneta (ten-cent pieces)—making it possible to strike the entire issue on planchets left over from regular American coining—all of which were dated 1883.

Of course, Hawaii would eventually be annexed by the United States (1898) and later admitted to the Union, but this Pacific interest was an exception for the period as most of the U.S. Mint's foreign coining adventures were pursued in Spanish America. Two of the nations there for which the United States shortly would coin were Cuba and Panama, and there was a very good reason: the United States had helped create both countries in their modern forms.

In the case of Cuba, it was the Spanish-American War—that is, the U.S. military intervention in the Cuban War of Independence—that sparked the connection. From the time the war was won until 1902, the United States would occupy the island, and from then until 1915 American money would continue to circulate in the newly independent nation. After that, the Philadelphia Mint struck a new, distinctly Cuban coinage until the rise of Fidel Castro.

In the case of Panama, American desire for an interoceanic canal would prompt President Theodore Roosevelt to not only support a Panamanian revolt against controlling Colombia but also to act as midwife to the resultant new country. In this role the United States would strike no fewer than 6 new coins—based on a new coinage unit named for Vasco Núñez de Balboa— ranging from 1/2 to 50 centesimos. Interestingly, however, the mintages of those first issues of 1904 and most succeeding coinages were minuscule, as for the majority of business the country has preferred to use American coinage and American paper currency.

Charles Barber of the U.S. Mint designed this Hawaiian issue featuring King Kalākaua.

Finally, relevant to the topic of American imperialism and its numismatic importance, there was an outcome of the Spanish-American War that was just as important as Cuban independence: the American acquisition of Puerto Rico, Guam, and the Philippine Islands. The first two remain under U.S. control and still use U.S. coinage, and while the third is now independent and uses its own monetary system, the United States did strike coins for the Philippines for some time.

During the Philippines' days as a colony (1899–1935) and a commonwealth (1935–1946), Filipino coins were struck at every current American mint except New Orleans, and starting in 1920 at a new, special facility set up in Manila. The anomalous nature of the islands' status was demonstrated by the designs seen on their coinage: for obverses, a seated Filipino or a standing Filipina, for reverses, an American eagle surmounting an American shield. The coins were created by a local artist named Melecio Figueroa, and they were denominated in centavos and pesos.

A RENAISSANCE IN AMERICAN MONEY

Theodore Roosevelt may be said to be the father of Panamanian numismatics, but numismatists know him far better in an American capacity: more than any other person, he was responsible for an artistic awakening in early 20th-century U.S. coinage. Once reelected in 1904, the energetic leader swung into action.

Roosevelt became involved in numismatics because he was deeply disgusted with the appearance of the American coins then in circulation. The old Gobrecht silver designs had been abandoned in 1891 in favor of new images for the dime, quarter, and half dollar, but these did not represent much of an improvement. Designer Charles E. Barber's Liberty head was acceptable, but his eagle was completely heraldic and appeared outdated even at the time it was introduced.

When it came to minor coinage, James B. Longacre's Indian Princess still graced the cent, more than 40 years after she had first appeared there. A copper-nickel five-cent piece, or "nickel," had been introduced in 1866, but its designs similarly failed to inspire. These included a fancy obverse shield and a reverse numeral by Longacre (used until 1883), and a trite obverse Liberty head and a large reverse "V" by Barber (used thereafter).

The designs of the gold coins annoyed President Roosevelt most of all. Ideas introduced by Gobrecht in 1838 and by Longacre in 1850 were still present on coins ranging from the quarter eagle to the double eagle. Surely, reasoned the president, the nation could do better than *that!*

He knew a gifted sculptor and medalist named Augustus Saint-Gaudens, who had been responsible for an attractive medal in a modern style portraying Christopher Columbus, created in conjunction with the 400th anniversary of the discovery of America. The politician and the artist had maintained contact over the years, and the latter responded magnificently to the former's call for help.

Saint-Gaudens's $10 gold piece featured a simple, left-facing Liberty with a feathered warbonnet (headgear added at the insistence of the president) and a naturalistic eagle inspired by an ancient Egyptian silver coin. His double eagle was still more ambitious, and it is arguably the most beautiful American coin. We see a figure of Liberty on the obverse, striding toward us in the dawn, holding the torch of freedom and the olive branch of peace. On the reverse, we see another eagle, this time soaring above the sun.

Augustus Saint-Gaudens's gold double eagle is considered by many to be the most beautiful U.S. coin ever designed.

Saint-Gaudens would unfortunately die in the summer of 1907, and he never saw the completion of his project. Luckily, though, Barber would succeed in reducing the high relief of his prototypes, making them more practical for striking. This may have robbed the actual coins of a portion of their artistry, but even amended for the worse they were splendid coins.

Roosevelt left office at the beginning of March 1909, also having secured the redesign of the quarter eagle and half eagle before he departed. These coins featured designs somewhat reminiscent of those on Saint-Gaudens's $10 piece, but struck *into* rather than *onto* the planchets, so that the fields of the new coins became their highest points. The innovative treatment engendered criticism (largely because it was assumed it would trap dirt and spread disease), but like the designs by Saint-Gaudens, these by Bela Lyon Pratt would serve on America's gold coinage until the final years of the medium itself.

Roosevelt's successor, William Howard Taft, continued the drive for greater numismatic artistry. A redesigned cent appeared during his first year in office, when Lithuanian immigrant Victor David Brenner created a new design to help the country mark the centenary of the birth of Abraham Lincoln. Slightly amended, Brenner's obverse portrait of "Honest Abe" is still in use; the reverse has changed from the original Wheat Ears, to the Lincoln Memorial (1959), to a set of four different reverses (2009 only, for the 200-year anniversary of Lincoln's birth), to the current Union Shield.

But back to the beginning of the 20th century: numismatic redesign continued after the Democratic Party regained national office in the election of 1912, and the five-cent piece was modified the following year. America's most artistic minor coin resulted: the Indian Head, or Buffalo, nickel showed what a gifted designer (in this case James Earle Fraser) could do with a humble coin in a base metal.

COMMEMORATIVES AND TOKENS

Another event in American numismatics during the Gilded Age was the creation of a coin for celebration rather than for commerce: the commemorative. Its origins in the United States date to 1892. The concept has much deeper roots elsewhere—coinage celebratory of a particular event or personage was known to the ancient Greeks, and was revived here and there in the Renaissance—but commemoratives truly gained popularity in Europe during the 19th century and their attraction eventually extended to the Americas as well.

While some earlier issues (such as the 1848 CAL. quarter eagle) could be considered commemorative coins, collectors begin the American series with a half dollar and quarter issued in conjunction with the World's Columbian Exposition in 1893. Half dollars with a head of Columbus on the obverse and a representation of the *Santa Maria* on the reverse—a collaborative effort between Charles Barber and George Morgan—were produced for sale in 1892 and 1893, while a quarter with Queen Isabella on the obverse and a female figure with a distaff and spindle on the reverse—the work of Barber alone—appeared in 1893. Some 5,000,000 of the half dollars were minted in Philadelphia, along with about 24,000 of the quarters.

From these modest beginnings, a numismatic industry would grow. Barber was responsible for a silver dollar celebrating George Washington and the Marquis de Lafayette dated 1900. The busy designer also tried his hand at a series of tiny commemorative gold dollars made for the Louisiana Purchase Exposition, dated 1903, and the Lewis and Clark Exposition, dated 1904 and 1905.

Meanwhile the career of another American monetary form, the token, was in decline. Like the celebratory coin, the private substitute for the regular coin had roots in the classical world, and we have seen this monetary form during the colonial period and the Civil War. During the Gilded Age, the locus of the token shifted West, as that region was chronically short of small change.

There were silver dollars and gold coins aplenty, but the mints at San Francisco, Carson City, and Denver (which began striking money in 1906) made far fewer small coins than large; they struck no cents until 1908 and no five-cent pieces until 1912. Furthermore, what smaller members of the silver series were struck tended to stay in large Western cities, to the detriment of merchants in small Western towns.

The latter responded as Americans had always addressed a monetary shortage: they obtained and circulated alternative money. Across the region, thousands of types of tokens, struck in brass, copper, zinc, aluminum, and even hard rubber, were called into service to expand the money supply. Because of the federal law of 1864 (which made private coinage illegal), these merchants' tokens generally promised payment in a specific article (a five-cent cigar, for instance) or "in trade," meaning that the customer might use the token as he pleased for the amount indicated on the piece.

These pieces formed a vital part of numismatic Americana during the Gilded Age, but their localism was more apparent than real. A handful of firms in New York and Chicago struck the majority of them. Here as elsewhere, diversity was yielding place to uniformity in the matter of America's money, a trend accelerated in the 20th century.

Tokens struck by merchants were one way to alleviate
the shortage of small-change coins in circulation.

ISOLATION, DEPRESSION, AND INTERVENTION: AMERICA, 1914–1945

Prior to 1940, a combination of distance, nationalism, and problems and prospects at home kept American attention firmly fixed on domestic affairs rather than foreign ones. This national tendency was never more evident than in the summer of 1914; when citizens of the New World heard that a conflagration had once more erupted in the Old, they heartily congratulated themselves on staying clear of it. They had problems enough at home.

Trusts were everywhere—those faceless octopi that restricted trade, held down wages, and squeezed the "little guy" to death. And along with the oil trust, sugar trust, steel trust, and the like, there was, it appeared, a "money trust." By the time President Woodrow Wilson was inaugurated on March 4, 1913, public opinion was demanding a dismantling of that beast, or at least its containment by the federal government. One way to keep it within bounds might be by exerting a greater federal control over the sinews of the banking system and the paper money employed in its operations. Thus the Federal Reserve Act of 1913 was born, and, in the following year, a new type of currency: the Federal Reserve Note.

The Federal Reserve Act divided the nation into 12 districts, each with a Federal Reserve Bank at its heart. The 12 districts, their cities, and the symbols that each must employ on the notes they issue are as follows:

District	City of Issue	Identification Symbol
1	Boston	1 or A
2	New York City	2 or B
3	Philadelphia	3 or C
4	Cleveland	4 or D
5	Richmond	5 or E
6	Atlanta	6 or F
7	Chicago	7 or G
8	St. Louis	8 or H
9	Minneapolis	9 or I
10	Kansas City, MO	10 or J
11	Dallas	11 or K
12	San Francisco	12 or L

Working in tandem with the Federal Reserve Board in Washington, each of the member banks had the theoretical power and obligation to advise on and act as a watchdog over banking activity within its district.

The Federal Reserve Notes of 1914 and later may have appeared to be local (or at least regional), but they were undeniably products of the national government. All were printed in Washington at the Bureau of Engraving and Printing. Among all the types of federal, state, and local currency issued in America over the past three centuries, this is the only one that has survived to the present.

FROM WORLD WAR I TO THE CRASH

American participation in the Great War (renamed the "First World War" when it became apparent that it would not be the last of its kind) was limited; the Yanks were not there for the first, and worst, of the fighting, and their vision of the conflict was therefore tinged with an aura of romance. This idealism was extremely significant for what happened next: there would be a paradigm shift, from concentration on domestic problems to a crusade to save Europe from itself, "to make the world safe for democracy," in the words of the American leader.

But when U.S. optimism collided with European reality (the Allies' desire to turn their victory in 1918 into a settling of old scores), the outcome was the worst of several possible combinations. Disillusioned, Americans would reject any substantive role in the new, postwar world order. Their disillusionment would extend to matters domestic as well, and the zeal for public reform would be replaced by one for private gain. Thus the Roaring Twenties, a supposedly golden age of unparalleled industrial growth, personal liberation, and new social, economic, and cultural icons: the automobile, the radio, and the flapper.

It was quite an era, but the golden dust of this new age was not scattered equally across the Republic, enriching all of its people. Accustomed to high commodity prices during the war, Midwestern and Southern farmers saw their incomes shrink and their debts rise after the beginning of the 1920s. Factory workers did poorly too, their wages held down by a new, anti-labor stance on the part of public officials. A determined managerial attempt to sell the concepts of the company union and the open shop kept wages depressed as well.

African Americans did still worse. Those who had migrated to the North before and during the war found that they were no more welcome there than they had been in the South. Women did slightly better; at least they now had the vote, and they could exert some influence on the national scene. But all in all, as the 1920s roared on, a disturbing fact became slowly apparent to those who wished to see it: much of the economic boom was based on hot air. All those new buildings, automobiles, radios, and other accessories of the New Era might someday disappear, when everyone's credit, and hence their ability to purchase them, ran out. If that ever happened, matters would become very interesting indeed.

And it happened, of course. In 1928 Herbert Hoover—a former secretary of commerce and one of the architects of the prosperous 1920s—was elected president of the United States. He was inaugurated in March 1929, and some seven months later, the house of cards tumbled down.

A DECLINE IN COINAGE AND PAPER MONEY

The hard times of the Great Depression had a variety of effects on American numismatics. For coinage, the years between 1929 and 1933 saw a decline in production, for those out of work would hardly need an abundance of new coins for their diminishing purchases. In the year of the stock-market crash, no fewer than eight coinage denominations were in current production at the U.S. Mint; the only American denominations not struck that year were dollars and eagles. In 1930 the total was six, and in 1931, four, where it remained in 1932 and 1933. Additionally, two of those four denominations were gold, which was of no earthly value to the average citizen, whose weekly wages were probably less than the value of the smaller denomination (the eagle), if they were being received at all. Only in 1934 did the quantity of denominations struck and coins minted begin rising.

Paper money was still being printed, but currency was now made in a new, smaller model. The types of notes in circulation remained what they had been prior to the crash—Federal Reserve bills, Silver Certificates, Legal Tender Notes, and the rest—but a standardization of design, if not of type, now set in. Of course, the nation's people were far more concerned about the soundness of their currency than the sameness of its designs; worry centered on locally issued National Bank Notes, as banks began failing immediately after the Wall Street crash in the autumn of 1929.

Despite President Hoover's optimism, the number of failures grew. Soon average citizens were taking their savings (if they had any) out of the bank and stuffing them under the mattress, where they could at least keep an eye on them. By late 1932, a crisis was reached; that November, Hoover lost his bid for reelection to Franklin Delano Roosevelt, but the nation would have to wait until the following March (when the new president was inaugurated) for any significant federal intervention.

Meanwhile governors began doing their bit on the state level to stop the hemorrhaging of the banking system by proclaiming "banking holidays," periods during which every bank within their jurisdiction would be forced to close its doors. The first state to take this action was Nevada. The closure was only supposed to last for 12 days, but it was extended indefinitely. By February 1933, other states were following in Nevada's wake, and by the time Hoover finally left the White House and Roosevelt moved in, virtually every bank in the country had shut down or was operating under extreme difficulties.

Once again faced with a shortage of "normal" money, Americans were forced to make money of their own beginning in 1931. In places, these efforts extended until 1939, but the core period coincided with the banking crisis of late 1932 and early 1933. During those few months, Americans gave their money a vitality and variety it had rarely enjoyed before and has never enjoyed since.

They constructed their makeshift money from a variety of materials, including paper, wood (there really were "wooden nickels" during these days), base metal, leather, fish skin, vulcanite, and—in a marvelous instance of history repeating itself—clamshells. A bewildering number of authorities stood behind those issues—large cities, small towns, companies and firms within those cities and towns, and mutual aid associations. This "Depression scrip" appeared in all 48 of the current states, as well as the Alaskan Territory. In short, there was a period of localism in currency fully comparable with that of the 19th century, if of shorter duration.

A citizen of Pismo Beach, California, could reimburse this clamshell for $1 at the Harter Drug Company.

Roosevelt and a New Deal

The incoming Roosevelt administration would take very determined steps to end the banking crisis that had inspired the locally issued scrip. The president proclaimed a national bank holiday on March 6, 1933, that would allow for careful examination of each bank's finances. Solvent banks gradually reopened their doors between the 13th and 15th of March, and those found unsound would stay closed.

This bold stroke, as well as Roosevelt's programs for other aspects of the economy and his self-assured attitude, brought a return of confidence to the nation and a return of normal money to the channels of commerce. It was originally thought that even *more* money in circulation would be necessary, and thus the Federal Reserve *Bank* Note (as opposed to the Federal Reserve Note) was formed as an interim national currency—but normal currency came back into circulation more quickly than anticipated, and the new notes were curtailed later in 1933.

Other types of money were being curtailed as well. Between 1933 and 1935, competing types of national paper currency were eclipsed by the Federal Reserve Note, and the Roosevelt administration concluded that National Banks' right to issue currency should be revoked. Other forms of currency fared scarcely better. The president also demonetized gold coinage (and Gold Certificates, the currency redeemable in gold coin), a policy he and a Democratic Congress would accomplish with successive laws passed in 1933 and 1934.

Under the new philosophy, the printing of the venerable National Bank Note came to a close in 1935; production of Silver Certificates was restricted to lower denominations; and most U.S. currency was made "redeemable in lawful money" rather than spelling out precisely what sort of coin might be received for each note. What Roosevelt and his advisors sought was a plausible currency that was also manageable, manipulable, and capable of expansion in times of depression and of contraction in times of inflation.

They found their solution in the Federal Reserve System with the Federal Reserve Note. Henceforth, this type of currency would reign supreme, and America's paper money would lose most of its individuality and localism. The state-chartered banks of the 1700s and 1800s, and the National Banks that succeeded them and continued the custom of locally issued currency, were history.

AN EXPLOSION OF COMMEMORATIVES

Even as economic and social pressures and prospects (as well as Roosevelt's policies) were increasing "sameness" in American money, the federal government showed itself partial to celebrating the diversity and richness of American history. Beside the state guides produced by the Federal Writers' Workshops in the 1930s and 1940s, it found one of its most lasting expressions on the commemorative coin.

Commemorative coinage came to the United States with the Columbian Exposition celebrations of 1892–1893, and it took root in America by the first years of the new century. Commemoratives were issued from time to time during the 1910s and 1920s. Some of the most notable issues of the period would be the huge round and octagonal $50 pieces produced for the Panama-Pacific Exposition in 1915, as well as the new Peace silver dollar introduced at the end of 1921.

Commemorative coinage continued through the administrations of Harding and Coolidge, ordinarily restricted to a single denomination, the half dollar. Issues of that period tended to focus on events rather than places—battles of the American Revolution, the sesquicentennial of Independence, the centenary of the Monroe Doctrine—but the most successful of them celebrated a place as well as an epoch: the Oregon Trail.

The Oregon Trail half dollar is considered by many to have one of the most artful of U.S. commemorative designs.

The collapse of 1929 brought celebratory coinage to an abrupt end for four years. True, a commemorative was introduced for the bicentennial of George Washington's birth in 1932, but it soon transmogrified into that most pedestrian of 20th-century American circulating coins: the Washington quarter, which is still in production today. The real resumption of commemorative coinage began in 1934, accelerated in 1935, crested in 1936, and continued to enliven America's money through 1939, after which concern with overproduction and possible warfare put a damper on such numismatic enthusiasm.

But while it lasted, what a time it was! A fundamental shift had taken place, and while events would still receive their commemorative due, the real emphasis was now on the places where the events had occurred. Such celebration of local themes was underscored by the employment of local artists to create the designs for the new issues, and while some of the artistic attempts were more successful than others, the overall effect of the multiplicity of commemorative coins was a positive one. American collectors now look back to those days as a golden age of numismatics, even though their parents and grandparents may have thought that the spate of commemoratives was getting out of hand.

FRESH NEW CIRCULATING COINS

The period of the American commemorative coincided with one of the high points of American numismatic artistry on circulating coinage. True, the daring and beautiful designs of Pratt and Saint-Gaudens passed from the scene when gold coinage stopped in 1933, but these were great days indeed for silver and base-metal coinage.

John Flanagan's portrait of George Washington on the quarter dollar may have been a step down, artistically, compared to its dramatic predecessor by Hermon MacNeil. For other circulating denominations during the 1930s, the artistic flowering that Theodore Roosevelt had begun still held sway. Brenner's cent and Fraser's five-cent piece were in everyday use. The dime and half dollar were both redesigned in 1916, and Charles Barber's trite renditions were replaced by magnificent, authentically "patriotic" images by Adolph Alexander Weinman.

As with MacNeil's quarter, Weinman's dime and half dollar were designed just prior to American entry into the First World War, and the themes they incorporated suggested as much. For the dime, a realistic, left-facing head of Liberty imparted a new freshness to American numismatic design, although the wings on the goddess's cap, placed there to symbolize liberty of thought, were mistaken for the attributes of a god and the coin became known as the "Mercury" dime. Weinman's reverse brought an altogether new concept to American coinage: the fasces, emblem of unity, something obviously desired in the face of international danger.

Attractive as was his dime, this artist's half dollar was his greater contribution to U.S. numismatics, and it stands as the most beautiful circulating design ever created for that denomination. On the obverse, we see Liberty wearing an American flag and striding toward the dawn with a bundle of oak and laurel branches in the crook of her left arm; on the reverse is the American eagle, a splendidly naturalistic depiction of the bird.

By the time Weinman's dime and half dollar were replaced in the 1940s, James Earle Fraser's Buffalo nickel had passed from the scene as well, supplanted by Felix Schlag's design honoring Thomas Jefferson. The new coin marked a deepening of the trend away from symbolic representations and toward real people, a move already seen with the Lincoln cent of 1909 and the Washington quarter of 1932. This nickel is still in production today, although it has seen modifications in design over the years, some of them dramatic.

Weinman's Liberty Walking half dollar, like his dime, debuted in 1916 and was part of the U.S. Mint's lineup into the 1940s.

NEW STRUGGLES BRING NEW MONEY

After an uneasy armed truce lasting 21 years, the old adversaries of 1914 squared off once again; war broke out in September 1939, as expansionist Germany attempted one final bluff and found at last that there was a point beyond which the other side (Great Britain and France) would not retreat.

In the beginning, most Americans were quite happy to stay out of the conflict, as they had been in 1914. For the first two-thirds of a year, the war seemed to involve little more than politics, as Hitler absorbed Poland without opposition from his theoretical adversaries. But then came *Blitzkrieg*, as Germany overran Norway, Denmark, the Low Countries, and finally France itself, making the war look very real indeed.

Thus, as the 1940s began, the United States was uncertain. It did not want Germany and its allies to win the war, but getting deeply involved might be the only way to avoid that outcome. Then, as all eyes were on Europe, the event that would tip the scales occurred at a venue Americans regarded as a side-show, if they thought about it at all: on December 7, 1941, Japan attacked the United States at that splendid base the Navy had acquired from the Hawaiian monarchy back in 1887, Pearl Harbor.

Americans would henceforth be as deeply involved in the world conflict as anyone else, declaring war on the Japanese as well as their allies, Hitler's Germany and Mussolini's Italy. U.S. participation in the Second World War lasted some 45 months and left 292,131 dead and 671,801 wounded of the 16,353,659 men and women who served in its armed forces. It would also permanently change America's conduct abroad, as the nation embraced its larger role on the international scene.

But American participation in the Second World War changed even more at home than it did abroad. It planted seeds for future movements, including the empowerment of women and African Americans, groups that played key roles in the war efforts. The conflict was also a hotbed for technological development, resulting in new innovations both good (such as plastics, synthetic fibers centering on nylon, artificial lubricants, and new food products) and controversial (the Bomb).

Of course, the nationwide change also extended to coins and currency. In the case of the former, copper was removed from the cent at the end of 1942. Its alloy was changed to zinc-plated steel in 1943, and melted-down gun-shell casings in 1944, 1945, and 1946. Nickel was deemed a critical war material, too, and so a concoction of copper (56 percent), silver (35 percent), and manganese (9 percent) was introduced in October 1942 and used in the five-cent coin through 1945. More than half a billion coins were made from the threefold alloy, distinguished by their slightly different color and a large mintmark (including a new "P" for Philadelphia) over the dome of Monticello rather than a small one at its right side.

Changes in paper currency occurred more in peripheral areas. The new Hawaiian issues were simply ordinary Silver Certificates upon which a brown seal was substituted for the blue one appropriate to that type of currency. Additionally, the word HAWAII was overprinted twice in small letters on the face and once in gigantic letters on the back. The idea was that the distinctive notes, printed for circulation in Hawaii, could be declared irredeemable if the Japanese occupied the islands and seized the local banks. Notes were also issued for use of American troops in Europe and North Africa; some of this "Allied Military Currency" was denominated in dollars and some was denominated in the currencies of those countries in which U.S. soldiers served, but none was truly American currency.

Meanwhile the U.S. Mint's early activities in providing Latin American countries with coins were expanded dramatically during the war. The Mint continued to supply a number of old customers, and it also created "liberation" issues of several types. For the Philippines (which had had its own mint in Manila since 1920, but which had fallen to Japan early in the war), massive coin issues of the prewar types were prepared in Denver and San Francisco in 1944 and 1945, and placed in Philippine commerce as the islands were liberated by U.S. and local troops.

The U.S. Mint also served as temporary coiner for the Netherlands, supplying its possessions with money of the prewar type when the mother country was unable to do so. Finally, coins were prepared for liberated France and Belgium. Their extreme simplicity of design illustrates the urgency of the times. A two-franc coin was struck in brass for France, while the Mint found a handy way of recycling the unwanted steel-cent planchets of 1943, turning them into the Belgian double francs of 1944.

Thus the coinage and currency of an America at war. For all of the diversity of metals and types, and for all of the interesting experiments, the numismatic expedients of the Second World War left no permanent imprint on the story of the nation's money. When the fighting had ended, reality snapped back into its earlier, prewar mold: normal alloys returned and commemorative issues soon resumed. But an unintended and doleful new coin entered the monetary spectrum as well, and it might serve to symbolize the war and the events that had led up to it.

The coin was a dime, approved late in 1945, introduced early in 1946. The nation's new dime bore the head of the man who had dominated the American war effort and who had died in its pursuit: Franklin Delano Roosevelt. The coin is still in circulation today, linking Americans, many several generations removed from the war, with the man and the events.

COLD WAR AND BEYOND: 1946 TO THE PRESENT

The years since the end of the Second World War have been among the most eventful in American, and indeed human, history. The conflict convinced us that we must look outside our walls, and take larger responsibility for international affairs. Our new relationship meant hot wars in Korea and Vietnam, Kuwait, Afghanistan, and Iraq; a cold war with Russia; and an inability to enjoy the promised fruits of our earlier victory in 1945.

Meanwhile, on a domestic level we have seen several recessions; the longest economic boom in American history; the rise of the suburb and the decline of the central city; multiple cultural and technological revolutions; and a doubling of our population. Changes indeed, changes everywhere, except one place: until very recently, America's money scarcely changed at all.

Throughout history there was a dynamism at work in the coinage and currency of the United States, a dynamism spurred by and reflective of the larger events of the period. Yet here, against a background of some of the greatest alterations ever seen in ways of life, we still use American coinage and paper currency that would be recognizable to the average man and woman of 1946.

What happened? Why did the money become fixed in a single, virtually changeless pattern? And what does this say about larger issues?

The postwar decades of national stress played a major role in the unusual continuity of America's money. When people are constantly bombarded with threats and turmoil, they tend to take what comfort they can in prosaic objects that have "always" been with them in the same reliable form. Coins and paper money can fall into this category.

Between 1989 and 1991, the United States' major perceived foreign threat—the Soviet Union—removed itself from contention, and, for the first time since 1945, a real debate arose and still goes on about the designs on American coinage and paper currency, not only on the part of collectors but on the part of the wider public. Put most simply, America had more important matters on its mind until fairly recently; changes are taking place now that the nation has the leisure to look at its coins and notes with a more critical eye.

Of course, other forces have been at work, too. For example, when it comes to coinage, contemporary minters are mainly concerned with technological considerations; designs are adopted or rejected not primarily because of their looks, but because they will or will not translate well to an easy-to-mass-produce piece of metal. The arrangements that grace American circulating coinage are relatively successful from that standpoint. They are well balanced, obverse to reverse, so that designs on each side come up reasonably well in a single, quick blow of the press. And to the cry of the artist for reform of design comes the response of the minter: if it works, leave it alone. This is one reason for continuity on American coinage.

A new dime in 1946 would honor the fallen president who had rallied the United States throughout the war.

Another is the amount of verbiage that must, either by force of law or by force of tradition, be placed on the coinage. The elements that each coin must bear include the name of the country, a national motto ("E Pluribus Unum"), a second national motto ("In God We Trust"), a *third* national motto ("Liberty"), the denomination, the date, and the place of mintage, symbolized by a mintmark. Once you get all that onto a coin, you have precious little room for anything else, and if a design manages to cram everything in and still proves easy to coin, you will hold onto it very tightly.

AMERICAN MONEY IN STAGNATION

In 1959 the cent was changed in commemoration of Lincoln's 150th birthday and the half-century mark of the Lincoln cent itself. The martyred president continued to form the obverse design. But on the reverse, the "wheat ears" gave way to an attempt to depict the entire Lincoln Memorial—an attempt which found some success from a technological perspective, perhaps less from an artistic one.

Its comrades, the Washington quarter and the Jefferson nickel, seemingly have been in circulation forever. The quarter's basic designs date from 1932, and those of the nickel date from 1938. Both the dime and the half dollar were redesigned shortly after the end of the Second World War. Franklin Delano Roosevelt was placed on the obverse of the dime in 1946. The new dime's design was neat and compact.

In 1947 the last coins using the Weinman designs were struck, replaced by John R. Sinnock's less artistic designs featuring Benjamin Franklin on the obverse and the Liberty Bell on the reverse. In order to comply with the Mint Act of 1792, Sinnock added a tiny eagle to the right of the bell. This odd placement neatly summarizes the somewhat ungainly concept of the entire design, which came to an abrupt end in 1963. The next year saw another new design, this one by Gilroy Roberts and Frank Gasparro, paying homage to the martyred president, John Fitzgerald Kennedy. These designs still appear on half dollars, although the coins themselves are no longer released to banks for general distribution, and rarely appear in circulation.

Another coin that has seen its usage progressively restricted is the metallic dollar. Production for circulation was halted in 1935, and did not resume until 1971, when Frank Gasparro's new dollar appeared featuring a rendition of the *Apollo 11* insignia on the reverse and a left-facing head of President Dwight David Eisenhower on the obverse. The coin was struck only intermittently through 1978.

By that time, the dollar was not circulating except in certain areas of the West, such as the casinos of Las Vegas. In an attempt to increase the coin's convenience and appeal, and to create a more durable dollar than the paper one, the U.S. Mint reduced the coin's size, bringing out a smaller version in the spring of 1979 that replaced Eisenhower with groundbreaking feminist Susan B. Anthony. The Mint made more than 750 million dollars of this version in 1979, but the public was lukewarm about the new entry, and output shrank to less than 100 million in 1980 and less than 14 million in 1981.

The Susan B. Anthony dollar (1979–1999) continued with the reverse design of the earlier Eisenhower dollar.

The Mint then gave up and the coins were put in storage, where most of them still remain. A second release took place in 1999, but it proved no more successful than the first. Of course, no American coin actually contained silver by that point, and virtually none had since the mid-1960s; the United States removed silver from most of its coinage by the Act of July 23, 1965. The value of the precious metal had risen to the point where it eventually was worth the effort to melt down American coins for their silver. Since 1970, when the last of the half dollar's silver was removed, nearly every circulating American coin above five cents has consisted of the same metallic composition, with outer layers of 75 percent copper and 25 percent nickel bonded to cores of pure copper.

But the dime, quarter, and half dollar owed some of their continuing acceptance to their continuity of size and design—plus the fact that they were the *only* dimes, quarters, and halves provided by the government for public use. At the time of the introduction of the Anthony coin, the public already had a paper dollar, as well as a coin of a "real" dollar size: the Eisenhower dollar, which was reassuringly heavy, if not silver.

All of these changes—the elimination of precious metal, the melting of earlier issues, reductions in size (in the case of the dollar), and the freezing of designs—contributed to a curious fact in American numismatics. Fewer and fewer young people became interested in the hobby, for there was less and less to attract them to the coinage of their own country.

Collecting might be said to hinge upon the availability of objects with discernible differences, combined with the attractions of rarity and age. When the oldest coin one is likely to see in circulation is dated 1965; when it looks like every other coin in one's pocket and elsewhere; and when its numbers are counted in the billions, there is little reason to look at pocket change, little reason to collect it, little reason to venture into numismatics.

AN INJECTION OF CREATIVE CHANGE

The commemorative coin served as a partial solution to the dilemma. Three such issues were struck shortly after 1945, celebrating the centenary of the state of Iowa (issues of 1946); paying homage to the educator Booker T. Washington (issues of 1946 through 1951); and granting recognition to Booker T. Washington again, in conjunction with the scientist George Washington Carver (issues of 1951 through 1954). These two individuals were African Americans, and the commemoratives bearing their portraits suggested that members of this race were at least beginning to receive a measure of their due on American coins, anticipating their progress in wider matters.

But there was rather more to the Washington/Carver coin than appeared at first glance. It was promoted by one S.J. Phillips to provide funds "to oppose the spread of communism among Negroes in the interest of National Defense"; the coin appeared at the height of the Cold War, and the government was concerned about subversion in all aspects of society at the time. Phillips was deeply in debt from promoting the earlier half dollar for Booker T. Washington and needed money to pay off creditors and avoid lawsuits. In time, the real purpose of the Washington/Carver coin became common knowledge in Congress, and it cast a pall over the American commemorative lasting for a quarter of a century. Commemorative coinage came to a halt.

In 1975 and 1976, the reverses of the quarter dollar, half dollar, and dollar were redesigned to celebrate the bicentennial of the declaration of American independence. Of the three designs chosen (a Revolutionary War drummer for the quarter, Independence Hall for the half, and the Liberty Bell superimposed on the moon for the dollar), only the quarter design represented a real success; its artist, Jack L. Ahr, took the pains necessary to fit his concept into the circular constraints of a coin. Significantly, all three coins were released into commerce as normal issues, even though special presentation pieces could be purchased if desired.

The commemorative coin had been fully rehabilitated by the early 1980s. In 1982 the 250th anniversary of George Washington's birth was recorded on a new silver half dollar, struck only for collectors and not for circulation. That forecast the future. Since then, a large number of commemoratives have been struck in silver, and there has been a resumption of gold commemorative coinage as well.

It is worth noting that while most of the issues of the 1930s paid homage to places as well as people and events, therefore injecting a note of localism into a national coinage, the issues of the 1980s and later have swung away from localism and toward events, places, and persons of national significance. Their subject matter proclaims as much: the Olympic Games, American immigration, the Korean War, the bicentennial of Congress, the National Baseball Hall of Fame, to name just a few recent topics.

A New Renaissance of American Money

In recent years, nothing less than a renaissance has taken place in America's coinage and currency. Hobbyists have made a determined effort to bring experimentation and localism back to these media and have found congressmen, senators, and numismatic writers sympathetic to the cause. It was slow going at the outset, but the rebirth is well under way.

The State quarters program is a case in point. Writers and hobby representatives such as Kenneth Bressett, Art Kagin, David Ganz, and Harvey Stack were hard at work promoting the idea as early as the beginning of the 1990s, but the first State quarters only came from the presses in 1999. A tremendous amount of pushing, shoving, and dedication had filled the intervening years, but all the effort was worth it; the State quarters did more to increase the ranks of casual and dedicated coin collectors than has any other program, or any other type of coinage, in all American history.

The idea for the program was to gain new collectors and retain old ones by putting coins with obvious differences into circulation. Contests were held in each state to select a unique reverse design, and the coins were issued at a rate of five per year in the same order that the states came into the Union. By doing all this, a sense of *history*, *place*, and *time* was distilled into a small, attractive object that everyone saw and all could afford.

While the quality of the designs varies, each of the coins does what it was intended to do: educate the public; show something of the variety of America; and function as solid, dependable money. The success of the program spawned a similar series of five-cent pieces, coins whose reverses allude to various aspects of the Lewis and Clark expedition while their obverses present us with various portraits of Thomas Jefferson, the president under whose aegis the historic trek took place. The idea was extended to include quarters for the District of Columbia and the five U.S. territories in 2009, followed by a series of National Park quarters starting in 2010. Even the lowly cent was refurbished, in 2009: celebrating Abraham Lincoln's 200th birthday, four new reverse designs were released, each emblematic of a major period in the martyred leader's life. Starting in 2010, the cent has featured a shield design, representing Lincoln's preservation of the Union.

In every case, the goal has been to produce money that everyone can afford to collect from circulation. For those so inclined, the Mint also strikes and sells Proof versions of these coins, along with a sizable run of other commemoratives and bullion coins in precious metals. One of the most successful of these ventures featured James Earle Fraser's designs for the nickel, successfully transferred to silver (in 2001) and gold (in 2006); here, the desire to commemorate merged with the desire to make something that would compete with other countries' bullion coins.

Finally, the past few years have witnessed other attempts at producing a small-sized circulating dollar coin. The first attempt featured Sacagawea on the obverse and a bald eagle in flight on the reverse, the latter standing as perhaps the most beautiful rendition of our national symbol to ever grace a base-metal coin. Struck in an alloy of copper, zinc, manganese, and nickel, the "golden" dollar was introduced in 2000 was struck until 2008.

And even while acceptance of the first golden dollar coin was in question, the popularity of the State quarters program emboldened the collecting fraternity to request a *second* dollar coin—or rather, a series. These coins (the same size as the first at 26.5 mm, a trifle larger than the quarter) celebrate the administration of every deceased American president from George Washington onward. These coins, which are currently being introduced at the rate of four per year, represent innovation: many of the presidential portraits face the viewer rather than appearing in profile; some mandatory wording (IN GOD WE TRUST and E PLURIBUS UNUM, as well as the actual year of issue) was for a time moved to the

Two new lines of "golden dollars" (the Sacagawea and the Presidential series) are among the U.S. Mint's innovations in recent years.

edge; and a depiction of the Statue of Liberty on the reverse stands in place of the word LIBERTY. Taking the place of the Sacagawea dollar, and running alongside the Presidential dollars, is the series of Native American dollars (2009 to date). These feature an annually changing design that honors the important contributions made by Indian tribes and individual Native Americans to the development and history of the United States.

Looking Forward

Will any of these new dollars be able to oust that traditional workhorse, the dollar bill? This seems unlikely unless special steps are taken. People are conservative when it comes to what they deem "normal" money, and they are likely to stick with what they know.

What about the survival of the one-cent piece? The 2009 Lincoln commemoratives are about the only pieces of good news for this most humble member of our monetary system. The price of copper rose in the early 1980s, so zinc was substituted for it, but recently the price of zinc has risen too. About the only remaining cheap metallic candidate is aluminum, but public opposition would be expected: we have come to regard aluminum as nearly worthless.

And there's still a larger problem: people simply don't use the cent as they once did. The coin's purchasing power has essentially disappeared. So the previously unmentionable is now being discussed: if we were to do away with the cent, would the Republic survive? Groups have sprung up to defend this hallowed member of the monetary system. Some are composed of traditionalists, who feel the cent must be saved, if only for its symbolic value; others represent the zinc industry, for which the billions of cents struck each year represent a significant profit.

And there is the question of what to do with all those unwanted cents. If we want to save the denomination, how do we get these billions of coins out of dresser drawers and piggy banks and back into trade? The simplest, most elegant solution might involve a permanent halt in production but continuing legality for those coins already struck. Since new cents would not be added to commerce, old ones would come out of hiding, perform at least a part of the role for which they had been created, become worn out, and quietly disappear.

The trials of the dollar and the eclipse of the cent should not cause alarm. At bottom, the American monetary system is always a work in progress. Change is inevitable, and if one world seems to be ending, another is beginning. Here and abroad, money is the product of *people*. And where there are people, there is always movement.

These developments are exciting for the hobbyist, but they are perhaps more important for the historian and student of numismatics: among other things, they proclaim that the exceptional, the unusual, and the local have by no means disappeared from America's media of exchange, and that what appeared at first glance to be a closing door is also an open one, welcoming, beckoning. Who knows where it may lead our people—and our money?

Colonial Issues

BRITISH NEW WORLD ISSUES

SOMMER ISLANDS (BERMUDA)

This coinage, the first struck for the English colonies in the New World, was issued circa 1616. The coins were known as *Hogge Money* or *Hoggies*, from the wild hogs depicted on their obverses.

The Sommer Islands, as Bermuda was known at the time, were under the jurisdiction of the Virginia Company, a joint-stock mercantile venture formed under a British royal patent and headquartered in London. (This venture was actually undertaken by two companies: the Virginia Company of Plymouth, for what is now New England; and the Virginia Company of London, for the American South.)

English government of the islands had started a few years before the coins were issued—by accident! In 1609 Admiral Sir George Somers led a fleet bound from England to the New World, laden with relief supplies for the Virginia settlement of Jamestown. Somers and his ship were separated from the rest of the fleet in a strong storm, and they ran onto the reefs of the Bermuda Islands, some 700 miles from Virginia. (The islands were named for Juan de Bermúdez, who is believed to have stopped there some hundred years earlier.) For ten months Somers and his party were able to live on wild hogs and birds, local plants, and fish, building houses and a church. During this time they also constructed two small ships, in which, in May 1610, most of the shipwrecked colonists continued their interrupted journey to Virginia.

Bermuda became a separate entity of the Virginia Company of London, from November 1612 until June 29, 1615, when "the Governour and Company of the City of London for the Plantacon of the Somer Islands" (often called the Bermuda Company by historians) was officially incorporated under royal charter. This incorporation granted the right of coinage. The coins did not arrive in the islands until May 16, 1616, at the earliest, a year after Bermuda was under its new charter.

The pieces were struck on thin planchets of brass or copper, lightly silvered, in four denominations: shilling, sixpence, threepence, and twopence, each indicated by Roman numerals. A wild hog is the main device and appears on the obverse side of each coin. SOMMER ISLANDS is inscribed (misspelling both the English admiral's name and the corporation's) within beaded circles on the larger denominations. The reverse shows a full-rigged galleon, or carrack, with the flag of St. George on each of four masts.

"In an era when British silver shillings and fractions traded in commerce based on their intrinsic value," writes Q. David Bowers, "the Bermuda pieces were tokens of little value, a fiat currency that circulated in the manner that paper money would later be used worldwide—good as long as both parties had confidence in the value. As might be expected, these coins had little or no trade value other than within the islands, where they were mostly used at the company storehouse, exchanged for supplies" (*Whitman Encyclopedia of Colonial and Early American Coins*).

These coins of Bermuda did not circulate in North America, but they have traditionally been considered part of early "American" coinage. Sylvester S. Crosby, writing in his 1875 masterwork *Early Coins of America*, insisted that the Bermuda coins laid claim to being "the first ever struck for the English colonies in America," this despite the fact that the islands were not a part of the Virginia colony proper. The regular edition of the *Guide Book of United States Coins* has included them in its pre-federal coverage since the first edition, published in 1946.

	Twopence		Threepence		
	Sixpence Obverse	Large Portholes Reverse	Small Portholes Reverse		
	Shilling Obverse	Small Sail Reverse	Large Sail Reverse		

	AG	G	VG	F	VF	EF
Twopence, Large Star Between Legs	$4,250	$6,500	$9,000	$18,000	$45,000	$75,000
Twopence, Small Star Between Legs	$4,250	$6,500	$9,000	$18,000	$45,000	$75,000
Threepence	—	—	$75,000	$125,000	$175,000	—
Sixpence, Small Portholes	$3,500	$4,500	$7,500	$15,000	$50,000	$70,000
Sixpence, Large Portholes	$3,750	$4,750	$8,000	$16,000	$60,000	$90,000
Shilling, Small Sail	$4,750	$6,500	$11,000	$35,000	$65,000	$95,000
Shilling, Large Sail	$6,000	$10,000	$35,000	$65,000	$90,000	—

MASSACHUSETTS
"NEW ENGLAND" COINAGE (1652)

The earliest authorized medium of exchange in the New England settlements was wampum. The General Court of Massachusetts in 1637 ordered "that wampamege should passe at 6 a penny for any sume under 12 d." Wampum consisted of shells of various colors, ground to the size of kernels of corn. A hole was drilled through each piece so it could be strung on a leather thong for convenience and adornment.

Corn, pelts, and bullets were frequently used in lieu of coins, which were rarely available. Silver and gold coins brought over from England, Holland, and other countries tended to flow back across the Atlantic to purchase needed supplies. The colonists, thus left to their own resources, traded with the friendly Native Americans in kind. In 1661 the law making wampum legal tender was repealed.

Agitation for a standard coinage reached its height in 1651. England, recovering from a civil war between the Puritans and Royalists, ignored the colonists, who took matters into their own hands in 1652.

The Massachusetts General Court in 1652 ordered the first metallic currency—the New England silver threepence, sixpence, and shilling—to be struck in the English Americas (the Spaniards had established a mint in Mexico City in 1535). Silver bullion was procured principally in the form of mixed coinage from the West Indies. The mint was located in Boston, and John Hull was appointed mintmaster; his assistant was Robert Sanderson (or Saunderson). At first, Hull received as compensation one shilling threepence for every 20 shillings coined. This fee was adjusted several times during his term as mintmaster.

The planchets of the New England coins were struck with prepared punches twice (once for the obverse, and once for the reverse). First the letters NE were stamped, and then on the other side the numerical denomination of III, VI, or XII was added.

These are called "NE coins" today.

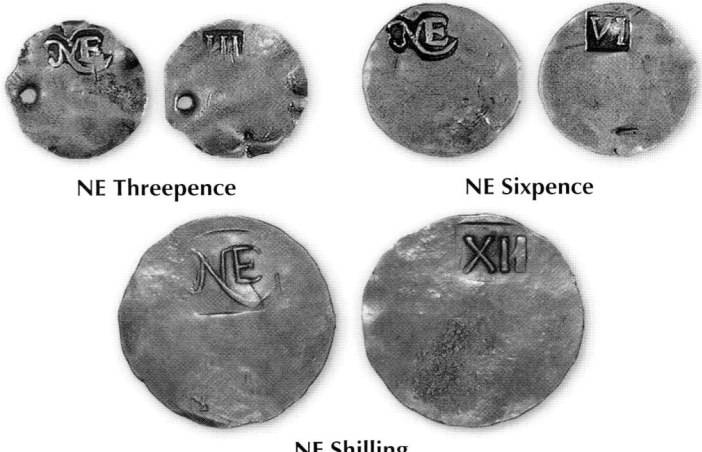

NE Threepence NE Sixpence

NE Shilling

Early American coins in conditions better than those listed are rare and are consequently valued much higher.

	G	VG	F	VF	EF	AU
NE Threepence (a)				—		
NE Sixpence (b)	$45,000	$90,000	$175,000	$285,000		
NE Shilling	$55,000	$100,000	$150,000	$250,000	$300,000	$400,000

a. Unique. b. 8 examples are known.

WILLOW TREE COINAGE (1653–1660)

The simplicity of the designs on the NE coins invited counterfeiting, and clipping or shaving of the edges by charlatans who sought to snip a little bit of metal from a lot of coins and thereby accumulate a pile of silver. Therefore, they were soon replaced by the Willow Tree series.

All of the Willow Tree coins bore the date 1652, when Oliver Cromwell was in power in Britain, after the English civil war and during the Interregnum government. In fact they were minted from 1653 to 1660. The date 1652 may have been used simply because this was the year the coinage was authorized. Output increased over the years, and the coins were plentiful in circulation.

These pieces, like all early American coins, were produced from handmade dies that are often individually distinctive. The tree in the design is known as a "willow" not from any official legislative records, and certainly not from lifelike resemblance to an actual willow tree, but from terminology dating from 1867 in an auction catalog of the Joseph Mickley Collection. To make the coins, a worker likely placed a silver planchet into a rocker press, which forced a curved upper die against a curved or flat bottom die. This would explain the slight elongation and gentle bend of many Willow Tree coins.

NEW ENGLAND is spelled out, instead of being abbreviated, as on the earlier NE coinage.

Among the four classes of Massachusetts silver coins—NE, Willow Tree, Oak Tree, and Pine Tree—the Willow Tree pieces are far and away the rarest today. The die varieties that can be found and identified are of interest to collectors who value each according to individual rarity. Values shown for type coins are for the most frequently seen die variety.

Threepence   **Sixpence**

Shilling

	G	VG	F	VF	EF
1652 Willow Tree Threepence (a)		—	—	—	
	Auctions: $632,000, VF, October 2005				
1652 Willow Tree Sixpence (b)	$20,000	$35,000	$70,000	$160,000	$250,000
	Auctions: $253,000, Unc., November 2005				
1652 Willow Tree Shilling	$21,000	$37,000	$90,000	$200,000	$295,000
	Auctions: $276,000, EF, November 2005				

a. 3 examples are known. **b.** 14 examples are known.

OAK TREE COINAGE (1660–1667)

The Oak Tree coins of Massachusetts were struck from 1660 to 1667, following the Willow Tree coinage. The 1662-dated twopence of this type was the only coin of the Willow Tree, Oak Tree, and Pine Tree series that did not bear the date 1652. Numismatists are divided on whether the twopence date of 1662 is an error, or a deliberate use of the year that the new denomination was authorized.

The obverse of these coins features a tree traditionally described by numismatists as an oak tree. Although it is deciduous, it does not closely resemble a specific species. On the reverse, NEW ENGLAND is spelled out, surrounding the date and denomination.

In 1660 the Commonwealth of England was dissolved and the British monarchy was restored under King Charles II. At the time, following longstanding tradition and law, the right to produce coins was considered to be a royal sovereign prerogative. Sylvester Crosby in *Early Coins of America* suggested that during the Massachusetts silver coinage period, numerous tributes—including ship masts, 3,000 codfish, and other material items—were sent to the king to placate him and postpone any action on the Massachusetts coinage question. As with many situations involving early American coinage, facts are scarce.

As with other types of Massachusetts silver, a number of die varieties of Oak Tree coinage can be collected and studied. In the marketplace they are seen far more often than are the two earlier types. They are valued according to their individual rarity. Values shown here are for the most frequently seen die varieties.

Twopence

Threepence

Sixpence

Shilling

	G	VG	F	VF	EF	AU	Unc.
1662 Oak Tree Twopence, Small 2	$600	$1,000	$2,000	$4,000	$6,500	$8,500	$13,000
1662 Oak Tree Twopence, Large 2	$600	$1,000	$2,000	$4,000	$6,500	$8,500	$13,000
1652 Oak Tree Threepence, No IN on Obverse	$725	$1,250	$3,000	$6,500	$11,000	$17,000	—
1652 Oak Tree Threepence, IN on Obverse	$725	$1,350	$3,250	$7,000	$13,000	$21,000	$50,000
1652 Oak Tree Sixpence, IN on Reverse	$800	$1,300	$3,200	$7,500	$16,000	$21,000	$40,000
1652 Oak Tree Sixpence, IN on Obverse	$800	$1,300	$3,200	$7,500	$14,000	$19,000	$35,000
1652 Oak Tree Shilling, IN at Left	$750	$1,250	$3,000	$7,000	$10,500	$16,000	$28,000
1652 Oak Tree Shilling, IN at Bottom	$750	$1,250	$3,000	$6,500	$10,000	$14,500	$26,000
1652 Oak Tree Shilling, ANDO	$900	$1,900	$4,000	$8,500	$15,000	$20,000	$34,000
1652 Oak Tree Shilling, Spiny Tree	$750	$1,250	$3,250	$7,000	$12,000	$17,000	$31,000

PINE TREE COINAGE (1667–1682)

The first Pine Tree coins were minted on the same-size planchets as the Oak Tree pieces, in denominations of threepence, sixpence, and shilling. Subsequent issues of the shilling were narrower in diameter and thicker. Large Planchet shillings ranged from 27 to 31 mm in diameter; Small Planchet shillings ranged from 22 to 26 mm in diameter.

The design of the Pine Tree coins borrowed from the flag of the Massachusetts Bay Colony, which featured a pine tree. On the reverse, NEW ENGLAND is spelled out, surrounding the date and a Roman numeral indicating the denomination (III, VI, or XII).

Large quantities of Pine Tree coins were minted. The coinage was abandoned in 1682. A proposal to renew coinage in 1686 was rejected by the General Court of Massachusetts.

As with other types of Massachusetts silver, a number of die varieties of Pine Tree coins are available for collecting and study. In the marketplace, they are valued according to their individual rarity. Values shown here are for the most often seen die varieties.

Threepence   **Sixpence**

Shilling, Large Planchet (1667–1674)   **Shilling, Small Planchet (1675–1682)**

	G	VG	F	VF	EF	AU	Unc.
1652 Threepence, Pellets at Trunk	$550	$800	$1,600	$3,200	$6,000	$9,000	$19,000
1652 Threepence, Without Pellets	$550	$800	$1,600	$3,250	$6,000	$9,000	$19,000
1652 Sixpence, Pellets at Trunk	$600	$925	$1,800	$3,600	$6,250	$10,000	$20,000
1652 Sixpence, Without Pellets	$600	$950	$1,900	$3,800	$6,750	$11,000	$21,000
1652 Shilling, Large Planchet (27–31 mm)							
Pellets at Trunk	$700	$1,100	$2,400	$5,000	$8,750	$14,000	$26,000
Without Pellets at Trunk	$700	$1,000	$2,300	$4,750	$8,500	$13,000	$25,000
No H in MASATUSETS	$800	$1,400	$3,000	$7,500	$13,500	$20,000	—
Ligatured NE in Legend	$700	$1,100	$2,400	$5,000	$8,750	$14,000	$26,000
1652 Shilling, Small Planchet (22–26 mm)	$600	$925	$2,200	$4,000	$6,800	$11,000	$25,000

MARYLAND

LORD BALTIMORE COINAGE

Cecil Calvert, the second Lord Baltimore, inherited from his father nearly absolute control over Maryland. Calvert believed he had the right to coin money for the colony, and in 1659 he ordered shillings, sixpences, and groats (four-penny pieces) from the Royal Mint in London and shipped samples to Maryland, to his brother Philip, who was then his secretary for the colony. Calvert's right to strike coins was upheld by Oliver Cromwell's government. The whole issue was small, and while his coins did circulate in Maryland at first, by 1700 they had largely disappeared from commerce.

Calvert's coins bear his portrait on the obverse, with a Latin legend calling him "Lord of Mary's Land." The reverses of the larger denominations bear his family coat of arms and the denomination in Roman numerals. There are several die varieties of each. Some of these coins are found holed and repaired. The copper penny, or denarium, is the rarest denomination, with only nine reported specimens, including some found in recent times by detectorists using electronic devices.

The silver groats (fourpence), sixpence, and shillings were used extensively in commerce, and today most examples show considerable wear. Typical grades include VG, Fine, and VF, often with surface marks or damage. Those graded AU or higher are major rarities. The silver pieces have an engrailed edge.

Penny (Denarium) Fourpence (Groat)

Sixpence Shilling

	G	VG	F	VF	EF	AU
Denarium copper (a)	—	—	$75,000	$125,000	—	—
	Auctions: $241,500, AU, May 2004					
Fourpence	$3,500	$6,000	$12,000	$25,000	$35,000	$50,000
Sixpence	$1,700	$2,500	$5,000	$10,000	$14,000	$18,500
Shilling	$2,100	$3,500	$6,500	$14,000	$20,000	$35,000

a. Extremely rare.

NEW JERSEY
ST. PATRICK OR MARK NEWBY COINAGE

Mark Newby was a shopkeeper in Dublin, Ireland, in the 1670s and came to America in November 1681, settling in West Jersey (today's New Jersey). He brought with him a quantity of copper pieces, of two sizes, believed by numismatists to have been struck in Dublin circa 1663 to 1672. These are known as *St. Patrick coppers.* (Alternatively, they may have been struck for circulation in Ireland by Pierre Blondeau to fill an order made by the duke of Ormonde, but this has not been confirmed.) The larger-sized piece, called by collectors a *halfpenny*, bears the arms of the City of Dublin on the shield on the reverse. The smaller-sized piece, called a *farthing*, does not. Although neither bears a denomination, these are designations traditionally assigned by numismatists. Both sizes have reeded edges.

Newby became a member of the legislature of West Jersey, and under his influence the St. Patrick coinage was made legal tender by the General Assembly of New Jersey in May 1682. The legislature did not specify which size piece could circulate, only that the coin was to be worth a halfpenny in trade and that no one would be obliged to accept more than five shillings' worth (120 coins) in one payment. Some numismatists believe the larger-size coin was intended. However, many more farthing-size pieces are known than halfpennies, and numerous coins of the farthing size have been excavated by detectorists in New Jersey, while none of the larger coins have been found this way. Most numismatists believe that the smaller-sized piece was the one authorized as legal tender. Copper coins often circulated in the colonies at twice what they would have been worth in England.

The obverses show King David crowned, kneeling and playing a harp. The legend FLOREAT REX ("May the King Prosper") is separated by a crown. The reverse side of the halfpence shows St. Patrick with a crozier in his left hand and a trefoil in his right, and surrounded by people. At his left side is a shield. The legend is ECCE GREX ("Behold the Flock"). The farthing reverse shows St. Patrick driving away reptiles and serpents as he holds a metropolitan cross in his left hand. The legend reads QUIESCAT PLEBS ("May the People Be at Ease").

The decorative brass insert found on the coinage, usually over the crown on the obverse, was put there to make counterfeiting more difficult. On some pieces this decoration has been removed or does not show. Numerous die variations exist (more than 140 of the smaller coins, and 9 of the larger). The silver strikings, and a unique gold piece, were not authorized as legal tender, although many of the silver coins are heavily worn, suggesting that they were passed many times from hand to hand in commerce, perhaps at the value of a shilling.

St. Patrick "Farthing" St. Patrick "Halfpenny"

	G	VG	F	VF	EF	AU
St. Patrick "Farthing"	$125	$325	$900	$2,750	$7,500	$17,000
Similar, Halo Around Saint's Head	$750	$2,000	$7,000	$17,000	$45,000	—
Similar, No C in QUIESCAT	$1,000	$4,500	$10,000	$20,000	—	—
St. Patrick "Farthing," Silver	$1,800	$3,500	$10,000	$20,000	$30,000	$50,000
St. Patrick "Farthing," Gold (a)						—
	Auctions: $184,000, AU, January 2005					
St. Patrick "Halfpenny"	$350	$800	$1,200	$3,000	$12,000	$20,000

a. Unique.

COINAGE AUTHORIZED BY BRITISH ROYAL PATENT

AMERICAN PLANTATIONS COINS (1688)

These tokens, struck in nearly pure tin, were the first royally authorized coinage for the British colonies in America. They were made under a franchise granted in August 1688 to Richard Holt, an agent for the owners of several tin mines. Holt proposed that the new issues be made with a Spanish monetary designation to increase their acceptance in the channels of American commerce, where Spanish-American coins were often seen. Thus the tokens are denominated as 1/24 part of a Spanish real.

The obverse shows an equestrian portrait of King James II in armor and flowing garments. The reverse features four heraldic shields (English, Scottish, French, and Irish) connected by chains. The edge is decorated with dots.

Numismatist Eric P. Newman has identified seven different obverse dies and an equal number of reverse dies. Most American Plantation tokens show black oxidation of the tin. Bright, unblemished original specimens are more valuable. (Around 1828 a London coin dealer acquired the original dies and arranged for restrikes to be made for sale. In high grades these pieces are seen more frequently in the marketplace than are originals. They are valuable but worth less than original strikes.)

(1688) James II Plantation 1/24 Real coinage	G	VG	F	VF	EF	AU	Unc.
1/24 Part Real	$225	$300	$500	$1,000	$1,750	$4,000	$7,000
1/24 Part Real, ET. HB. REX	$275	$400	$900	$2,000	$3,200	$8,500	$12,000
1/24 Part Real, Sidewise 4 in 24	$425	$1,000	$1,900	$4,500	$6,500	$10,000	$20,000
1/24 Part Real, Arms Transposed	$675	$1,500	$2,500	$6,500	$9,000	$13,000	—
1/24 Part Real, Restrike	$100	$150	$250	$450	$600	$900	$2,200

COINAGE OF WILLIAM WOOD (1722–1733)

William Wood, an English metallurgist, experimented with the production of several pattern coins (of halfpenny, penny, and twopence size) in 1717. In 1722 he was granted royal patents to mint coins for America and Ireland. At the time his productions were largely unpopular as money, but later generations of coin collectors have sought his Rosa Americana coins for their connections to colonial America. The Hibernia coins are similar in some respects; they have no connection with America but are sought as companion pieces.

ROSA AMERICANA COINS (1722–1723, 1733)

On July 12, 1722, William Wood obtained a patent from King George I to make coins for the American colonies. At the time the colonies were facing a serious shortage of circulating coins.

The first pieces Wood struck were undated. Later issues bear the dates 1722, 1723, 1724, and 1733. The Rosa Americana pieces were issued in three denominations—half penny, penny, and twopence—and were intended for America. This type had a fully bloomed rose on the reverse with the words ROSA AMERICANA UTILE DULCI ("American Rose—Useful and Sweet").

The obverse, common to both Rosa Americana and Hibernia pieces, shows the head of George I and the legend GEORGIUS D:G MAG: BRI: FRA: ET. HIB: REX ("George, by the Grace of God, King of Great Britain, France, and Ireland") or abbreviations thereof.

Despite Wood's best efforts, these Rosa Americana coins circulated in the colonies only to a limited extent. They eventually did see use as money, but it was back in England, and likely at values lower than their assigned denominations. (Each was about half the weight of its English counterpart coin.)

The 1733 twopence is a pattern that bears the bust of King George II facing to the left. It was issued by the successors to the original coinage patent, as William Wood had died in 1730.

The coins are made of a brass composition of copper and zinc (sometimes mistakenly referred to as *Bath metal*, an alloy proposed by Wood that would have also included a minute portion of silver). Planchet quality is often rough and porous because the blanks were heated prior to striking. Edges often show file marks.

	VG	F	VF	EF	AU	Unc.
(No date) Twopence, Motto in Ribbon *(illustrated)*	$200	$400	$700	$1,300	$3,200	$6,000
(No date) Twopence, Motto Without Ribbon (a)		—	—	—		

a. 3 examples are known.

	VG	F	VF	EF	AU	Unc.
1722 Halfpenny, VTILE DVLCI	$925	$2,250	$3,800	$6,750	$9,750	
1722 Halfpenny, D.G.REX ROSA AMERI. UTILE DULCI	$150	$200	$400	$950	$1,500	$3,500
1722 Halfpenny, DEI GRATIA REX UTILE DULCI	$150	$200	$400	$950	$1,500	$3,200

	VG	F	VF	EF	AU	Unc.
1722 Penny, GEORGIVS			$12,000	$17,500	$25,000	$30,000
1722 Penny, VTILE DVLCI	$170	$300	$700	$1,300	$2,750	$6,000
1722 Penny, UTILE DULCI	$150	$200	$400	$700	$1,300	$3,200

	VG	F	VF	EF	AU	Unc.
1722 Twopence, Period After REX	$150	$275	$600	$1,200	$2,500	$4,500
1722 Twopence, No Period After REX	$150	$275	$600	$1,200	$2,500	$4,500

	VG	F	VF	EF	AU	Unc.
1723 Halfpenny, Uncrowned Rose	$900	$1,750	$3,500	$5,000	$8,000	$10,000
1723 Halfpenny, Crowned Rose	$110	$170	$350	$750	$1,600	$3,900

	VG	F	VF	EF	AU	Unc.
1723 Penny *(illustrated)*	$100	$150	$350	$600	$1,000	$2,500
1723 Twopence	$150	$275	$400	$800	$1,300	$2,700

	EF	AU	Unc.
1724, 4 Over 3 Penny (pattern), DEI GRATIA	$7,500	$15,000	$22,000
1724, 4 Over 3 Penny (pattern), D GRATIA	$8,750	$20,000	$34,000
(Undated) (1724) Penny, ROSA: SINE: SPINA. (a)	$35,000	$45,000	—

a. 5 examples are known.

1724 Twopence (pattern)		
	Auctions: $25,300, Choice AU, May 2005	

1733 Twopence (pattern), Proof

Auctions: $63,250, Gem PF, May 2005

WOOD'S HIBERNIA COINAGE (1722–1724)

Around the same time that his royal patent was granted to strike the Rosa Americana coins for the American colonies, William Wood received a franchise to produce copper coins for circulation in Ireland. This was ratified on July 22, 1722. The resulting coins, likely struck in Bristol, England, featured a portrait of King George and, on the reverse, a seated figure with a harp and the word HIBERNIA. Their edges are plain. Denominations struck were farthing and halfpenny, with dates of 1722, 1723, and 1724. These Hibernia coins were unpopular in Ireland and faced vocal public criticism, including from satirist Jonathan Swift. "It was asserted that the issues for Ireland were produced without Irish advice or consent, that the arrangements were made in secret and for the private profit of Wood, and that the pieces were seriously underweight" (*Whitman Encyclopedia of Colonial and Early American Coins*). As a result, King George reduced the number of coins allowed by Wood's patent, and the franchise was retired completely in 1725 in exchange for Wood receiving a £24,000 pension over eight years. Some of the unpopular Hibernia coins, meanwhile, may have been sent to the American colonies to circulate as small change. Their popularity with American numismatists stems from the similarity of their obverses to those in the Rosa Americana series.

Numerous varieties exist.

| 1722, Hibernia Farthing | 1722, Hibernia Halfpenny, First Type | 1722, Hibernia Halfpenny, Ssecond Type | 1723, 3 Over 2 |

1724, Hibernia Farthing   1724, Hibernia Halfpenny

	G	VG	F	VF	EF	AU	Unc.
1722 Farthing, D: G: REX		$500	$750	$2,200	$3,500	$7,500	$14,000
1722 Halfpenny, D: G: REX, Rocks at Right (pattern)		—	—	$8,000	$12,000	$20,000	$40,000
1722 Halfpenny, First Type, Harp at Left		$100	$150	$300	$600	$900	$1,600
1722 Halfpenny, Second Type, Harp at Right		$70	$100	$200	$550	$1,100	$2,000
1722 Halfpenny, Second Type, DEII (blunder)		$150	$350	$800	$1,500	$2,000	$3,200
1723 Farthing, D.G.REX		$100	$125	$250	$400	$550	$1,000
1723 Farthing, DEI. GRATIA. REX		$50	$80	$125	$225	$400	$600
1723 Farthing (silver pattern)		$1,800	$2,500	$4,500	$6,000	$8,500	$15,000
1723 Halfpenny, 3 Over 2 (a)	$45	$75	$150	$450	$850	$1,300	$2,400
1723 Halfpenny	$30	$45	$75	$125	$275	$400	$775
1723 Halfpenny (silver pattern)			—	—	—	—	—
1724 Farthing	$55	$125	$225	$750	$1,600	$2,250	$4,000
1724 Halfpenny	$50	$100	$150	$350	$700	$1,100	$2,200
1724 Halfpenny, DEI Above Head					—	—	—

a. Varieties exist.

VIRGINIA HALFPENNIES (1773–1774)

In 1773 the British Crown authorized coinage of copper halfpennies for the colony of Virginia, not to exceed 25 tons' weight. "This was the first and only colonial coinage authorized and produced in Britain for use in an American colony, thereby giving the Virginia pieces the unique claim of being the only true American colonial coinage" (*Whitman Encyclopedia of Colonial and Early American Coins*). The designs included a laurelled portrait of King George III and the royal coat of arms of the House of Hanover. The coins were struck at the Tower Mint in London. Their edges are plain.

Most Mint State pieces available to collectors today are from a hoard of some 5,000 or more of the halfpennies held by Colonel Mendes I. Cohen of Baltimore, Maryland, in the 1800s. Cohen came from a prominent banking family. His cache was dispersed slowly and carefully from 1875 until 1929, as the coins passed from his estate to his nieces and nephews. Eventually the remaining coins, numbering approximately 2,200, the property of Bertha Cohen, were dispersed in one lot in Baltimore. These pieces gradually filtered out, in groups and individually, into the wider numismatic marketplace.

The Proof patterns that were struck on a large planchet with a wide milled border are often referred to as pennies. The silver pieces dated 1774 are referred to as shillings, but they may have been patterns or trials for a halfpenny or a guinea.

Red Uncirculated pieces without spots are worth considerably more.

	G	VG	F	VF	EF	AU	Unc.
1773 Halfpenny, Period After GEORGIVS	$25	$50	$100	$150	$350	$500	$900
1773 Halfpenny, No Period After GEORGIVS	$35	$75	$140	$200	$400	$600	$1,200

1773, "Penny"   1774, "Shilling"

	PF
1773 "Penny"	$25,000
1774 "Shilling" (a)	*$130,000*

a. 6 examples are known.

EARLY AMERICAN AND RELATED TOKENS

ELEPHANT TOKENS (CA. 1672–1694)

LONDON ELEPHANT TOKENS

The London Elephant tokens were struck in London circa 1672 to 1694. Although they were undated, two examples are known to have been struck over 1672 British halfpennies. Most were struck in copper, but one was made of brass. Their legend, GOD PRESERVE LONDON, may have been a general plea for divine aid and not a specific reference to the outbreak of plague in 1665 or the great fire of 1666.

These pieces were not struck for the colonies, and they probably did not circulate widely in America, although a few may have been carried there by colonists. They are associated, through a shared obverse die, with the 1694 Carolina and New England Elephant tokens. They have a plain edge but often show the cutting marks from planchet preparation.

	VG	F	VF	EF	AU	Unc.
(1694) Halfpenny, GOD PRESERVE LONDON, Thick Planchet	$300	$550	$900	$1,500	$2,500	$4,200
(1694) Halfpenny, GOD PRESERVE LONDON, Thin Planchet	$500	$1,000	$3,250	$4,750	$7,250	$12,000
Similar, Brass (a)				—		
(1694) Halfpenny, GOD PRESERVE LONDON, Diagonals in Center of Shield	$700	$2,500	$7,000	$9,500	$17,000	$38,000
(1694) Halfpenny, Similar, Sword in Second Quarter of Shield	—	—	$20,000	—	—	—
(1694) Halfpenny, LON DON	$1,100	$2,500	$5,000	$8,500	$15,000	$24,000

a. Unique.

CAROLINA ELEPHANT TOKENS

Although no law is known authorizing coinage for Carolina, two very interesting pieces known as Elephant tokens were made with the date 1694. These copper tokens are of halfpenny denomination. The reverse reads GOD PRESERVE CAROLINA AND THE LORDS PROPRIETERS 1694.

The second and more readily available variety has the last word spelled PROPRIETORS. The correction was made on the original die, for the E shows plainly beneath the O. On the second variety the elephant's tusks nearly touch the milling.

The Carolina pieces were probably struck in England and perhaps intended as advertising to heighten interest in the Carolina Plantation. Another theory suggests they may have been related to or made for the Carolina coffee house in London.

	VG	F	VF	EF	AU	Unc.
1694 PROPRIETERS	$4,500	$6,000	$13,000	$22,000	$40,000	$75,000
1694 PROPRIETERS, O Over E	$4,250	$5,800	$12,500	$20,000	$37,500	$70,000

NEW ENGLAND ELEPHANT TOKENS

Like the Carolina tokens, the New England Elephant tokens are believed to have been struck in England, possibly as promotional pieces to increase interest in the American colonies, or perhaps related to the New England coffee house in London

	VG	F	VF	EF	AU
1694 NEW ENGLAND		$100,000	$135,000	$160,000	—

NEW YORKE IN AMERICA TOKENS (1660S OR 1670S)

The New Yorke in America tokens are farthing or halfpenny tokens intended for New York, issued by Francis Lovelace, who was governor from 1668 until 1673. The tokens use the older spelling with a final "e" (YORKE), which predominated before 1710. The obverse shows Cupid pursuing the loveless butterfly-winged Psyche—a rebus on the name Lovelace. The reverse shows a heraldic eagle, identical to the one displayed in fesse, raguly (i.e., on a crenellated bar) on the Lovelace coat of arms. In weight, fabric, and die axis the tokens are similar to certain 1670 farthing tokens of Bristol, England, where they may have been struck. There is no evidence that any of these pieces ever circulated in America. Fewer than two dozen are believed to now exist.

	VG	F	VF	EF
(Undated) Brass or Copper	$7,500	$18,000	$30,000	$60,000
(Undated) Pewter	$7,000	$23,000	$33,000	$72,500

GLOUCESTER TOKENS (1714)

Sylvester S. Crosby, in his book *The Early Coins of America*, stated that these tokens appear to have been intended as a pattern for a shilling—a private coinage by Richard Dawson of Gloucester (county), Virginia. The only specimens known are struck in brass, although the denomination XII indicates that a silver coinage (one shilling) may have been planned. The building depicted on the obverse may represent some public building, possibly the courthouse.

Although neither of the two known examples shows the full legends, combining the pieces shows GLOVCESTER COVRTHOVSE VIRGINIA / RIGHAVLT DAWSON. ANNO.DOM. 1714. This recent discovery has provided a new interpretation of the legends, as a Righault family once owned land near the Gloucester courthouse. A similar, but somewhat smaller, piece possibly dated 1715 exists. The condition of this unique piece is too poor for positive attribution.

	F
1714 Shilling, brass (a)	$120,000

a. 2 examples are known.

HIGLEY OR GRANBY COPPERS (1737–1739)

Dr. Samuel Higley owned a private copper mine near Granby, Connecticut, in an area known for many such operations. Higley was a medical doctor, with a degree from Yale College, who also practiced blacksmithing and experimented in metallurgy. He worked his mine as a private individual, extracting particularly rich copper, smelting it, and shipping much of it to England. He also made his own dies for plain-edged pure-copper "coins" that he issued.

Legend has it that a drink in the local tavern cost three pence, and that Higley paid his bar tabs with his own privately minted coins, denominated as they were with the legend THE VALUE OF THREEPENCE. When his supply of such coppers exceeded the local demand, neighbors complained that they were not worth the denomination stated, and Higley changed the legends to read VALUE ME AS YOU PLEASE and I AM GOOD COPPER (but kept the Roman numeral III on the obverse).

After Samuel Higley's death in May 1737 his older brother John continued his coinage.

The Higley coppers were never officially authorized. There were seven obverse and four reverse dies. All are rare. Electrotypes and cast copies exist.

	AG	G	VG	F	VF
1737 THE VALVE OF THREE PENCE, CONNECTICVT, 3 Hammers	$5,800	$11,000	$20,000	$38,000	$84,000
1737 THE VALVE OF THREE PENCE, I AM GOOD COPPER, 3 Hammers (a)	$6,300	$12,500	$25,000	$50,000	$100,000
1737 VALUE ME AS YOU PLEASE, I AM GOOD COPPER, 3 Hammers	$5,800	$11,000	$20,000	$38,000	$88,000
1737 VALVE • ME • AS • YOU • PLEASE, I • AM • GOOD • COPPER, 3 Hammers (a)				—	
(1737) VALUE • ME • AS • YOU • PLEASE, J • CUT • MY • WAY • THROUGH, Broad Axe	$5,500	$10,000	$19,000	$37,000	$82,000
(1737) THE • WHEELE • GOES • ROUND, Reverse as Above (b)				*$150,000*	
1739 VALUE • ME • AS • YOU • PLEASE, J • CUT • MY • WAY • THROUGH, Broad Axe	$8,000	$20,000	$27,500	$60,000	$135,000

a. 3 examples are known. **b.** Unique.

HIBERNIA–VOCE POPULI COINS

These coins, struck in the year 1760, were prepared by Roche, of King Street, Dublin, who was at that time engaged in the manufacture of buttons for the army. Like other Irish tokens, some could have found their way to colonial America and possibly circulated in the colonies with numerous other counterfeit halfpence and "bungtown tokens." There is no evidence to prove that Voce Populi pieces, which bear the legend HIBERNIA (Ireland) on the reverse, ever circulated in North America. Sylvester S. Crosby did not include them in *The Early Coins of America*, 1875. Nor were they covered in Wayte Raymond's *Standard Catalogue of United States Coins* (until Walter Breen revised the section on colonial coins in 1954, after which they were "adopted" by mainstream collectors). Various theories exist regarding the identity of the bust portrait on the obverse, ranging from kings and pretenders to the British throne, to the provost of Dublin College.

There are two distinct issues. Coins from the first, with a "short bust" on the obverse, range in weight from 87 to 120 grains. Those from the second, with a "long bust" on the obverse, range in weight from 129 to 154 grains. Most of the "long bust" varieties have the letter P on the obverse. None of the "short bust" varieties bear the letter P, and, judging from their weight, they may have been contemporary counterfeits.

Large-Letter Variety Farthing

Halfpenny

Halfpenny, "P" Before Face

VOOE POPULI

	G	VG	F	VF	EF	AU	Unc.
1760 Farthing, Large Letters	$235	$400	$600	$1,750	$3,000	$5,750	$10,000
1760 Farthing, Small Letters			$6,000	$22,000	$60,000	—	—
1760 Halfpenny	$70	$100	$170	$300	$525	$850	$1,700
1760 Halfpenny, VOOE POPULI	$100	$150	$225	$500	$650	$1,250	$3,750
1760 Halfpenny, P Below Bust	$125	$200	$300	$700	$1,100	$2,400	$6,500
1760 Halfpenny, P in Front of Face	$100	$175	$250	$600	$1,000	$1,800	$5,500

PITT TOKENS (CA. 1769)

William Pitt the Elder, the British statesman who endeared himself to America, is the subject of these brass or copper pieces, probably intended as commemorative medalets. The so-called halfpenny (the larger of the type's two sizes) served as currency during a shortage of regular coinage. The farthing-size tokens are rare.

The reverse legend (THANKS TO THE FRIENDS OF LIBERTY AND TRADE) refers to Pitt's criticism of the Crown's taxation of the American colonies, and his efforts to have the Stamp Act of March 22, 1765, repealed in 1766. The obverse bears a portrait and the legends THE RESTORER OF COMMERCE and NO STAMPS.

"Little is known concerning the circumstances of issue. Robert Vlack suggests that the pieces may have been designed by Paul Revere. Striking may have been accomplished around 1769 by James Smither (or Smithers) of Philadelphia" (*Whitman Encyclopedia of Colonial and Early American Coins*).

Farthing   Halfpenny

	G	VG	F	VF	EF	AU	Unc.
1766 Farthing	$3,500	$6,000	$12,000	$30,000	$42,000	—	
1766 Halfpenny		$500	$600	$1,350	$2,500	$3,600	$9,500
1766 Halfpenny, silvered				$2,000	$4,250	$6,000	$13,000

RHODE ISLAND SHIP MEDALS (CA. 1779)

The circumstances of the issue of these medals (or tokens) are mysterious. They were largely unknown to American coin collectors until 1864, when a specimen was offered in W. Elliot Woodward's sale of the Seavey Collection. It sold for $40—a remarkable price at the time.

The obverse shows the flagship of British admiral Lord Richard Howe at anchor, while the reverse depicts the retreat of American forces from Rhode Island in 1778. The inscriptions show that the coin was meant for a Dutch-speaking audience. The word *vlugtende* ("fleeing") appears on the earlier issues below Howe's flagship—an engraving error. After a limited number of pieces were struck with this word, it was removed on most coins. A wreath was added, eliminating the word *vlugtende*, after which the final coinage took place. It is believed the medal was struck in England circa 1779 or 1780 for the Dutch market, as propaganda to influence Dutch opinion against the American cause. Specimens are known in pinchbeck, copper, and pewter.

Rhode Island Ship Medal (1778–1779)   Legend "vlugtende" Below Ship   Wreath Below Ship

	VF	EF	AU	Unc.
With "vlugtende" (fleeing) Below Ship, Brass or copper		—		
Wreath Below Ship, Brass or copper	$1,100	$1,900	$3,500	$6,000
Without Wreath Below Ship, Brass or copper	$1,000	$1,800	$2,900	$5,200
Similar, Pewter	$4,500	$7,500	$11,500	$17,000

JOHN CHALMERS ISSUES (1783)

John Chalmers, a Maryland goldsmith and silversmith, struck a series of silver tokens of his own design in Annapolis in 1783. The dies were by Thomas Sparrow, another silversmith in the town. The shortage of change in circulation and the refusal of the American people to use underweight cut Spanish coins prompted the issuance of these pieces. (Fraudsters would attempt to cut five "quarters" or nine or ten "eighths" out of one Spanish silver dollar, thereby realizing a proportional profit when they were all spent.)

On the Chalmers threepence and shilling obverses, two clasped hands are shown, perhaps symbolizing unity of the several states; the reverse of the threepence has a branch encircled by a wreath. A star within a wreath is on the obverse of the sixpence, with hands clasped upon a cross utilized as the reverse type. On this denomination, the designer's initials TS (for Thomas Sparrow) can be found in the crescents that terminate the horizontal arms of the cross. The reverse of the more common shilling varieties displays two doves competing for a worm underneath a hedge and a snake. The symbolic message is thought to have been against the danger of squabbling with brethren over low-value stakes while a dangerous mutual enemy lurked nearby. The edges of these tokens are crudely reeded. There are only a few known examples of the shilling type with 13 interlinked rings, from which a liberty cap on a pole arises.

Threepence	Sixpence, Small Date	Sixpence, Large Date

Shilling, Birds, Long Worm   **Shilling, Rings**

	VG	F	VF	EF	AU
1783 Threepence	$2,200	$4,400	$9,000	$20,000	$37,500
1783 Sixpence, Small Date	$3,200	$7,000	$18,000	$30,000	$55,000
1783 Sixpence, Large Date	$2,600	$6,000	$15,000	$30,000	$55,000
1783 Shilling, Birds, Long Worm *(illustrated)*	$1,250	$2,500	$7,500	$14,000	$25,000
1783 Shilling, Birds, Short Worm	$1,200	$2,200	$6,500	$12,000	$22,500
1783 Shilling, Rings (a)	$50,000	$100,000	$200,000	—	—

a. 5 examples are known.

FRENCH NEW WORLD ISSUES

None of the coins of the French regime relate specifically to territories that later became part of the United States. They were all general issues for the French colonies of the New World. The coinage of 1670 was authorized by an edict of King Louis XIV dated February 19, 1670, for use in New France,

Acadia, the French settlements in Newfoundland, and the French West Indies. The copper coinage of 1717 to 1722 was authorized by edicts of 1716 and 1721 for use in New France, Louisiana, and the French West Indies.

COINAGE OF 1670

The coinage of 1670 consisted of silver 5 and 15 sols and copper 2 deniers (or "doubles"). A total of 200,000 of the 5 sols and 40,000 of the 15 sols was struck at Paris. Nantes was to have coined the copper, but did not; the reasons for this may never be known, since the archives of the Nantes Mint before 1700 were destroyed. The only known specimen is a pattern struck at Paris. The silver coins were raised in value by a third in 1672 to keep them circulating, but in vain. They rapidly disappeared, and by 1680 none were to be seen. Later they were restored to their original values. This rare issue should not be confused with the common 1670-A 1/12 ecu with reverse legend SIT. NOMEN. DOMINI. BENEDICTUM.

The 1670-A double de l'Amerique Françoise was struck at the Paris Mint along with the 5- and 15-sols denominations of the same date. All three were intended to circulate in France's North American colonies. Probably due to an engraving error, very few 1670-A doubles were actually struck. Today, only one is known to survive.

Copper Double   **Silver 5 Sols**

	VG	F	VF	EF	Unc.
1670-A Copper Double (a)			$225,000		
1670-A 5 Sols	$1,000	$2,000	$5,000	$7,000	$18,000
1670-A 15 Sols	$13,000	$32,000	$75,000	$125,000	—

a. Unique.

COINAGE OF 1717–1720

The copper 6 and 12 deniers of 1717 were authorized by an edict of King Louis XV (by order of the six-year-old king's regent, the duke of Orléans) dated December 1716, to be struck at Perpignan (mint-mark Q). The order could not be carried out, for the supply of copper was too brassy, and only a few pieces were coined. A second attempt in 1720 also failed, probably for the same reason. As a result all issues of these two years are rare.

1720 20 Sols

1717-Q 12 Deniers

1720 6 Deniers

	F	VF	EF
1717-Q 6 Deniers, No Crowned Arms on Reverse (a)			
1717-Q 12 Deniers, No Crowned Arms on Reverse			—
1720 6 Deniers, Crowned Arms on Reverse, Copper	$550	$900	$1,750
1720 20 Sols, Silver	$375	$700	$1,500

a. Extremely rare.

BILLON COINAGE OF 1709–1760

The French colonial coins of 30 deniers were called *mousquetaires* because of the outlined cross on their reverse, evocative of the design on the short coats worn by French musketeers. These coins were produced at Metz and Lyon. The 15 deniers was coined only at Metz. The sou marque and the half sou were coined at almost every French mint, those of Paris being most common. The half sou of 1740 is the only commonly available date. Specimens of the sou marque dated after 1760 were not used in North America. A unique specimen of the 1712-AA 30 deniers is known in the size and weight of the 15-denier coins.

30 Deniers "Mousquetaire"

Sou Marque (24 Deniers)

	VG	F	VF	EF	AU	Unc.
1711–1713-AA 15 Deniers	$150	$300	$500	$1,000	$1,750	$4,000
1709–1713-AA 30 Deniers	$75	$100	$250	$400	$675	$1,500
1709–1713-D 30 Deniers	$75	$100	$250	$400	$675	$1,500
1738–1748 Half Sou Marque, various mints	$60	$100	$200	$350	$575	$1,200
1738–1760 Sou Marque, various mints	$50	$80	$125	$175	$300	$500

COINAGE OF 1721–1722

The copper coinage of 1721 and 1722 was authorized by an edict of King Louis XV dated June 1721. The coins were struck on copper blanks imported from Sweden. Rouen and La Rochelle struck pieces of nine deniers (one sou) in 1721 and 1722. New France received 534,000 pieces, mostly from the mint of La Rochelle, but only 8,180 were put into circulation, as the colonists disliked copper. In 1726 the rest of the issue was sent back to France.

In American coin catalogs of the 1800s, these coins were often called "Louisiana coppers."

	VG	F	VF	EF
1721-B (Rouen)	$500	$1,000	$3,500	$10,000
1721-H (La Rochelle)	$100	$175	$1,000	$2,500
1722-H	$100	$175	$1,000	$2,500
1722-H, 2 Over 1	$175	$275	$1,200	$4,000

FRENCH COLONIES IN GENERAL (1767)

These copper coins were produced for use in the French colonies and only unofficially circulated in Louisiana along with other foreign coins and tokens. Most were counterstamped RF (République Française) for use in the West Indies. The mintmark A signifies the Paris Mint. The edge is decorated with a double row of dots.

	VG	VF	EF	AU
1767 French Colonies, Sou	$120	$250	$800	$1,600
1767 French Colonies, Sou, counterstamped RF	$100	$200	$300	$600
1722-H	$100	$175	$1,000	$2,500
1722-H, 2 Over 1	$175	$275	$1,200	$4,000

Post-Colonial Issues

The coins explored in this section are classified as "post-colonial" because they came after the colonial period (some during the early months of rebellion; most after the official declaration of independence) but before the first federal Mint was established in Philadelphia in 1792.

Early American coins were produced from hand-engraved dies, which are often individually distinctive. For many types, the great number of die varieties that can be found and identified are of interest to collectors who value each according to its individual rarity. Values shown for type coins in this section are for the most common die variety of each.

SPECULATIVE ISSUES, TOKENS, AND PATTERNS

NOVA CONSTELLATIO COPPERS (1783–1786)

The Nova Constellatio coppers, dated 1783 and 1785 and without denomination, were struck in fairly large quantities in Birmingham, England, and were shipped to New York where they entered circulation. Apparently they resulted from a private coinage venture undertaken by Constable, Rucker & Co., a trading business formed by William Constable, John Rucker, Robert Morris, and Gouverneur Morris as equal partners. The designs and legends were copied from the denominated patterns dated 1783 made in Philadelphia (see page 147). A few additional coppers dated 1786 were made by an inferior diesinker.

"The Nova Constellatio coppers were well received and saw extensive use in commerce, as evidenced by the wear seen on typically specimens today," writes Q. David Bowers in the *Whitman Encyclopedia of Colonial and Early American Coins*. "Later, they were devalued, and many were used as undertypes (planchets) for Connecticut and, to a lesser extent, New Jersey and Vermont coppers."

1783, Pointed Rays, Small U.S., CONSTELLATIO		1783, Pointed Rays, Large U.S., CONSTELLATIO	

	VG	F	VF	EF	AU	Unc.
1783, CONSTELLATIO, Pointed Rays, Small U.S.	$100	$200	$350	$700	$1,250	$2,750
1783, CONSTELLATIO, Pointed Rays, Large U.S.	$100	$225	$650	$1,100	$2,500	$6,750

1783, Blunt Rays, CONSTELATIO

1785, Blunt Rays, CONSTELATIO   1785, Pointed Rays, CONSTELLATIO

	VG	F	VF	EF	AU	Unc.
1783, CONSTELATIO, Blunt Rays	$100	$225	$550	$1,050	$1,800	$5,750
1785, CONSTELATIO, Blunt Rays	$100	$225	$550	$1,200	$3,000	$7,200
1785, CONSTELLATIO, Pointed Rays	$100	$200	$375	$750	$1,200	$2,750
1785, Similar, Small, Close Date	$300	$600	$2,500	$4,500	$6,500	$15,000
1786, Similar, Small Date	$4,200	$7,000	$12,500	$20,000		
1783, CONSTELLATIO, Pointed Rays, Small U.S.	$100	$200	$350	$700	$1,250	$2,750
1783, CONSTELLATIO, Pointed Rays, Large U.S.	$100	$225	$650	$1,100	$2,500	$6,750
1783, CONSTELATIO, Blunt Rays	$100	$225	$550	$1,050	$1,800	$5,750
1785, CONSTELATIO, Blunt Rays	$100	$225	$550	$1,200	$3,000	$7,200
1785, CONSTELLATIO, Pointed Rays	$100	$200	$375	$750	$1,200	$2,750
1785, Similar, Small, Close Date	$300	$600	$2,500	$4,500	$6,500	$15,000
1786, Similar, Small Date	$4,200	$7,000	$12,500	$20,000		

IMMUNE COLUMBIA PIECES (1785)

These pieces are considered private or unofficial coins. No laws describing them are known. There are several types bearing the seated figure of Justice. These pieces are stylistically related to the Nova Constellatio coppers, with the Immune Columbia motif with liberty cap and scale replacing the LIBERTAS and JUSTITIA design.

1785, Silver, 13 Stars   1785, Pointed Rays, CONSTELLATIO

	F	VF	EF
1785, Copper, 13 Stars	$15,000	$27,000	$40,000
1785, Silver, 13 Stars	$22,000	$45,000	$60,000
1785, Pointed Rays, CONSTELLATIO, Extra Star in Reverse Legend, Copper	$15,000	$27,000	$40,000
1785, Pointed Rays, CONSTELLATIO, Gold (a)			—
1785, Blunt Rays, CONSTELATIO, Copper (b)		—	—

Note: The gold specimen in the National Numismatic Collection (now maintained by the Smithsonian) was acquired in 1843 from collector Matthew A. Stickney in exchange for an 1804 dollar. **a.** Unique. **b.** 2 examples are known.

1785, George III Obverse

	G	VG	F	VF
1785, George III Obverse	$5,500	$8,500	$11,000	$16,000
1785, VERMON AUCTORI Obverse, IMMUNE COLUMBIA	$6,250	$10,000	$14,000	$35,000

1787, IMMUNIS COLUMBIA, Eagle Reverse

	VG	F	VF	EF	AU	Unc.
1787, IMMUNIS COLUMBIA, Eagle Reverse	$600	$1,000	$3,000	$4,500	$6,500	$11,000

Note: Believed to be a prototype for federal coinage; some were coined after 1787.

CONFEDERATIO AND OTHER SPECULATIVE PATTERNS

The Confederatio and associated coins are believed by some numismatists to be private proposals for patterns for America's early federal coinage. The 1785, Inimica Tyrannis America, variety may owe its design to a sketch by Thomas Jefferson. In all, 10 dies were presumed to have been used to strike coins in 11 combinations. No one knows for certain who made these coins, but some speculate the dies were produced by a combination of Walter Mould, John Bailey, and James Atlee in this country in connection with securing a federal-coinage contract. No documentation has been found. The pattern shield reverse ultimately found its way to the New Jersey state coinage.

America   Americana   Washington

Immunis   Eagle   Libertas et Justitia

Large Circle   Small Circle   Pattern Shield

The 1786, Immunis Columbia, with scrawny-eagle reverse is a related piece probably made by a different engraver or mint.

	VG	F	VF	EF	AU
1785 Inimica Tyrannis America, Large Circle (a,b)	$40,000	$70,000	$100,000	$175,000	$275,000
1785 Inimica Tyrannis Americana, Small Circle (c,d)	$30,000	$40,000	$60,000	$150,000	$250,000
1785 Inimica Tyrannis Americana, Large Circle, Silver (b,e)		$35,000 **(f)**			
1785 Gen. Washington, Large Circle (g,h)	$50,000	$75,000	$125,000	$250,000	
1786 Gen. Washington, Eagle (i,j)		$40,000			
(No Date) Gen. Washington, Pattern Shield (k,l)		$75,000	$100,000 **(f)**		$350,000
1786 Immunis, Pattern Shield (m,n)		$25,000	$50,000	$100,000	$125,000
1786 Immunis, 1785 Large Circle (o,j)	$30,000				$100,000
1786 Eagle, Pattern Shield (p,e)					$200,000
1786 Eagle, 1785 Large Circle (q,j)		$35,000	$50,000		
1785 Libertas et Justitia, 1785 Large Circle (r,e)	$25,000				
1785 Small Circle, 1787 Excelsior Eagle (s,j)		$35,000			
1786 Immunis Columbia, Scrawny Eagle (l)			$50,000	$90,000	

a. America obverse, Large Circle reverse. b. 7 examples are known. c. Americana obverse, Small Circle reverse. d. 9 examples are known. e. 1 example is known. f. Damaged. g. Washington obverse, Large Circle reverse. h. 6 examples are known. i. Washington obverse, Eagle reverse. j. 2 examples are known. k. Washington obverse, Pattern Shield reverse. l. 3 examples are known. m. Immunis obverse, Pattern Shield reverse. n. 17 examples are known. o. Immunis obverse, Large Circle reverse. p. Eagle obverse, Pattern Shield reverse. q. Eagle obverse, Large Circle reverse. r. Libertas et Justitia obverse, Large Circle reverse. s. Small Circle obverse, 1787 Excelsior Eagle reverse. Image of the 1787 Excelsior eagle (facing right) is on page 122.

COINAGE OF THE STATES

NEW HAMPSHIRE (1776)

New Hampshire was the first of the states to consider the subject of coinage following the Declaration of Independence. On March 13, 1776, by which time the colonies were in rebellion but had not yet formally declared their independence, the New Hampshire House of Representatives established a committee to consider the minting of copper coins. The committee recommended such coinage as a way to facilitate small commercial transactions.

William Moulton was empowered to make a limited quantity of coins of pure copper authorized by the State House of Representatives in 1776. Although cast patterns were prepared, it is believed that they were not approved. Little of the proposed coinage was ever actually circulated.

Other purported patterns are of doubtful origin. These include a unique engraved piece and a rare struck piece with large initials WM on the reverse.

		G
1776 New Hampshire Copper		$100,000
	Auctions: $172,500, VG-10, March 2012	

MASSACHUSETTS

MASSACHUSETTS UNOFFICIAL COPPERS (1776)

Presumably, in 1776, the year the colonies proclaimed their independence from Britain, three types of Massachusetts coppers were created. Very little is known about their origins or the circumstances of their production. Numismatic historians deduced them to be patterns until recent scholarship cast doubt on their authenticity as coppers of the Revolutionary War era.

The obverse of one of these coppers has a crude pine tree with "1d LM" at its base and the legend MASSACHUSETTS STATE. The reverse has a figure probably intended to represent the Goddess of Liberty, seated on a globe and holding a liberty cap and staff. A dog sits at her feet. The legend LIBERTY AND VIRTUE surrounds the figure, and the date 1776 is situated beneath.

Sylvester S. Crosby, writing in 1875 in *The Early Coins of America*, traced the provenance of this unique copper back to a grocer who sold it to a schoolboy around 1852. The grocer was from "the northerly part" of Boston, and he had "found it many years before while excavating on his premises, in the vicinity of Hull or Charter Street."

	VF
1776 Pine Tree Copper (a)	—

a. Unique, in the Massachusetts Historical Society collection.

A similar piece, probably from the same source as the Pine Tree copper, features a Native American standing with a bow on the obverse, with a worn legend that may read PROVINCE OF MASSA or similar. On the reverse is a seated figure and globe, visible partially visible legend (LIBERTATIS), and the date 1776 at bottom. The only known example was overstruck on a 1747 English halfpenny, and is holed.

	VG
1776 Indian Copper (a)	—

a. Unique.

A third Massachusetts piece is sometimes called the *Janus copper*. On the obverse are three heads, facing left, front, and right, with the legend STATE OF MASSA. 1/2 D. The reverse shows the Goddess of Liberty facing right, resting against a globe. The legend is GODDESS LIBERTY 1776.

	F
1776 Halfpenny, 3 Heads on Obverse (a)	—
Auctions: $44,650, Fine, January 2015; $40,000, Fine, November 1979	

a. Unique.

MASSACHUSETTS AUTHORIZED ISSUES (1787–1788)

An "Act for establishing a mint for the coinage of gold, silver and copper" was passed by the Massachusetts General Court on October 17, 1786. The next year, the council directed that the design of the copper coins should incorporate ". . . the figure of an indian with a bow & arrow & a star on one side, with the word 'Commonwealth,' the reverse a spread eagle with the words—'of Massachusetts A. D. 1787'—" (this wording would be slightly different in the final product).

The coinage of Massachusetts copper cents and half cents in 1787 and 1788 was under the direction of Captain Joshua Witherle of Boston. These were the first coins bearing the denomination *cent* as established by Congress. They were produced in large quantities and are fairly plentiful today. The wear seen on many of the Massachusetts cents and half cents indicates that they enjoyed long circulation in commerce. Many varieties exist, the most valuable being that with arrows in the eagle's right talon.

Most of the dies for these coppers were made by Joseph Callender. Jacob Perkins of Newburyport also engraved some of the 1788 dies.

The mint was abandoned early in 1789, in compliance with the newly ratified U.S. Constitution, and because its production was unprofitable.

1787 Half Cent

1787 Cent, Obverse

Arrows in
Right Talon

Arrows in Left Talon

	G	VG	F	VF	EF	AU	Unc.
1787 Half Cent	$100	$125	$225	$500	$750	$1,200	$2,800
1787 Cent, Arrows in Right Talon	$10,000	$16,000	$25,000	$50,000	$75,000	$100,000	$180,000
1787 Cent, Arrows in Left Talon	$100	$110	$200	$600	$1,250	$2,500	$6,000
1787 Cent, "Horned Eagle" (die break)	$110	$120	$225	$650	$1,300	$2,800	$7,000

1788 Half Cent

1788 Cent, Period After MASSACHUSETTS

	G	VG	F	VF	EF	AU	Unc.
1788 Half Cent	$100	$125	$215	$550	$1,000	$1,500	$3,200
1788 Cent, Period After MASSACHUSETTS	$100	$110	$200	$500	$800	$1,750	$4,750
1788 Cent, No Period After MASSACHUSETTS	$115	$120	$250	$675	$1,500	$2,800	$6,000

CONNECTICUT (1785–1788)

Authority for establishing a mint near New Haven was granted by the state of Connecticut to Samuel Bishop, Joseph Hopkins, James Hillhouse, and John Goodrich in October 1785. They had petitioned the state's General Assembly for this right, noting the public need—small coins were scarce in circulation and many of those seen were counterfeits. Under the Assembly's grant, the four minters would pay the state's treasury an amount equal to 5 percent of the copper coins they produced. To make a profit, the minters would deduct this royalty, plus their other expenses (including materials, labor, and distribution), from the face value of the coins they struck.

Available records indicate that most of the Connecticut coppers were coined under a subcontract, by Samuel Broome and Jeremiah Platt, former New York merchants. Abel Buell was probably the principal diesinker. Many others were struck by Machin's Mills in Newburgh, New York, and were not authorized by Connecticut. These are as highly prized by collectors as are regular issues.

The Connecticut coppers were often struck crudely and on imperfect planchets. Numerous die varieties exist; over the years, collectors have given many of them distinctive nicknames.

1785 Copper, Bust Facing Left

1785 Copper, Bust Facing Right

1785 Copper, African Head

	G	VG	F	VF	EF	AU
1785 Copper, Bust Facing Left	$150	$250	$500	$1,500	$3,600	$8,000
1785 Copper, Bust Facing Right	$40	$70	$150	$500	$1,400	$3,500
1785 Copper, African Head	$70	$120	$400	$1,250	$3,500	$8,000

1786 Copper, ETLIB INDE

1786 Copper, Large Head Facing Right

1786 Copper, Mailed Bust Facing Left

1786 Copper, Draped Bust

1786 Copper, Mailed Bust Facing Left, Hercules Head

	G	VG	F	VF	EF	AU
1786 Copper, ETLIB INDE	$75	$140	$325	$850	$2,500	$7,000
1786 Copper, Large Head Facing Right	$250	$500	$1,500	$4,600	$10,000	
1786 Copper, Mailed Bust Facing Left	$45	$75	$140	$450	$1,100	$2,800
1786 Copper, Draped Bust	$80	$150	$400	$1,100	$2,750	$6,700
1786 Copper, Mailed Bust Facing Left, Hercules Head	$110	$200	$500	$2,000	$4,750	

1787 Copper, Small Head Facing Right, ETLIB INDE

1787 Copper, Muttonhead Variety

	G	VG	F	VF	EF	AU
1787 Copper, Small Head Facing Right, ETLIB INDE	$100	$170	$300	$1,600	$4,200	$8,500
1787 Copper, Liberty Seated Facing Right (a)		—				
1787, Mailed Bust Facing Right, INDE ET LIB	$100	$180	$400	$2,200	$5,000	
1787 Copper, Muttonhead	$100	$180	$400	$2,200	$5,000	$9,000

a. 2 examples are known.

1787 Copper, Mailed Bust Facing Left

1787 Copper, Laughing Head

1787 Copper, Reverse

	G	VG	F	VF	EF	AU
1787 Copper, Mailed Bust Facing Left	$45	$70	$120	$400	$1,100	$2,800
1787 Copper, Mailed Bust Facing Left, Laughing Head	$55	$100	$200	$500	$1,100	$2,300

**1787 Copper,
Horned Bust**

	G	VG	F	VF	EF	AU
1787 Copper, Mailed Bust Facing Left, Horned Bust	$45	$70	$125	$400	$750	$1,800
1787 Copper, Mailed Bust Facing Left, Hercules Head *(see 1786 for illustration)*	$400	$800	$2,000	$4,250	$8,000	—
1787 Copper, Mailed Bust Facing Left, Dated 1787 Over 1877	$90	$180	$600	$1,600	$4,750	—
1787 Copper, Mailed Bust Facing Left, 1787 Over 88	$180	$235	$700	$1,800	$5,000	—
1787 Copper, Mailed Bust Facing Left, CONNECT, INDE	$55	$125	$200	$600	$1,500	$3,000
1787 Copper, Mailed Bust Facing Left, CONNECT, INDL	$375	$700	$1,500	$3,200	$7,000	

1787 Copper, Draped Bust Facing Left

	G	VG	F	VF	EF	AU
1787 Copper, Draped Bust Facing Left	$35	$60	$90	$250	$600	$1,050
1787 Copper, Draped Bust Facing Left, AUCIORI	$45	$70	$100	$350	$900	$1,500
1787 Copper, Draped Bust Facing Left, AUCTOPI	$50	$75	$140	$500	$1,200	$2,200
1787 Copper, Draped Bust Facing Left, AUCTOBI	$50	$75	$140	$500	$1,200	$2,000
1787 Copper, Draped Bust Facing Left, CONNFC	$45	$65	$110	$400	$900	$1,500
1787 Copper, Draped Bust Facing Left, CONNLC	$75	$150	$250	$800	$3,000	—
1787 Copper, Draped Bust Facing Left, FNDE	$45	$70	$150	$400	$1,300	$2,400
1787 Copper, Draped Bust Facing Left, ETLIR	$45	$65	$125	$350	$1,000	$1,700
1787 Copper, Draped Bust Facing Left, ETIIB	$45	$65	$125	$350	$1,000	$1,800
1787 Copper, GEORGIVS III Obverse, INDE•ET Reverse	$1,500	$3,250	$3,500	—	—	—

1788 Copper, Mailed Bust Facing Right

	G	VG	F	VF	EF	AU
1788 Copper, Mailed Bust Facing Right	$45	$80	$150	$500	$1,300	$2,500
1788 Copper, GEORGIVS III Obverse *(Reverse as Above)*	$110	$210	$550	$1,550	$3,250	—
1788 Copper, Small Head *(see 1787 for illustration)*	$1,750	$4,000	$5,000	$12,000	$22,000	—

1788 Copper, Mailed Bust Facing Left   1788 Copper, Draped Bust Facing Left

	G	VG	F	VF	EF	AU
1788 Copper, Mailed Bust Facing Left	$50	$75	$175	$400	$1,100	$2,200
1788 Copper, Mailed Bust Facing Left, CONNLC	$60	$130	$250	$600	$1,800	$3,200
1788 Copper, Draped Bust Facing Left	$50	$75	$175	$400	$1,100	$2,200
1788 Copper, Draped Bust Facing Left, CONNLC	$85	$200	$450	$1,100	$2,500	$4,000
1788 Copper, Draped Bust Facing Left, INDL ET LIB	$80	$140	$300	$800	$2,000	$3,800

NEW YORK AND RELATED ISSUES (1780S)

No official state coinage for New York is known to have been authorized. However, a number of issues in copper and gold were made relating to the state, by a variety of different issuers.

BRASHER DOUBLOONS (1786–1787)

Among the most famous early American pieces coined before establishment of the U.S. Mint at Philadelphia were those produced by the well-known New York City silversmith, goldsmith, and jeweler Ephraim Brasher, who was a neighbor and friend of George Washington's when that city was the seat of the federal government.

The gold pieces Brasher made weighed about 408 grains and were valued at $15 in New York currency. They were approximately equal to the Spanish doubloon, which was equal to 16 Spanish dollars.

Pieces known as *Lima Style doubloons* were dated 1742, but it is almost certain that they were produced in 1786, and were the first efforts of Brasher to make a circulating coin for regional use. Neither of the two known specimens shows the full legends; but weight, gold content, and hallmark are all identical to those for the 1787-dated Brasher coins. An analogous cast imitation Lima style doubloon dated 1735 bears a hallmark attributed to Standish Barry of Baltimore, Maryland, circa 1787.

The design used on the 1787 Brasher doubloon features an eagle on one side and the arms of New York on the other. In addition to his impressed hallmark, Brasher's name appears in small letters on each of his coins. The unique 1787 gold half doubloon is struck from doubloon dies on an undersized planchet that weighs half as much as the larger coins. It is in the National Numismatic Collection in the Smithsonian Institution.

It is uncertain why Brasher produced these pieces. He may have produced them for his own account, charging a nominal fee to convert metal into coin. He was later commissioned by the government to test and verify other gold coins then in circulation. His hallmark EB was punched on each coin as evidence of his testing and its value. In some cases the foreign coins were weight-adjusted by clipping.

"1742" (1786) Lima Style gold doubloon (a)		$700,000
	Auctions: $690,000, EF-40, January 2005	

a. 2 examples are known.

		EF
1787 New York gold doubloon, EB on Breast		*$5,000,000*
	Auctions: $2,990,000, EF-45, January 2005	
1787 New York gold doubloon, EB on Wing		*$4,000,000*
	Auctions: $4,582,500, MS-63, January 2014	
1787 New York gold half doubloon (a)		—
Various foreign gold coins with Brasher's EB hallmark		*$5,000–$16,000*

a. Unique, in the Smithsonian Collection.

NEW YORK COPPER COINAGE

Several individuals petitioned the New York Legislature in early 1787 for the right to coin copper for the state, but a coinage was never authorized. Instead, a law was passed to regulate the copper coins already in use. Nevertheless, various unauthorized copper pieces were made privately and issued within the state.

One private mint known as Machin's Mills was organized by Captain Thomas Machin, a distinguished veteran of the Revolutionary War, and situated at the outlet of Orange Pond near Newburgh, New York. Shortly after this mint was formed, on April 18, 1787, it was merged with the Rupert, Vermont, mint operated by Reuben Harmon Jr., who held a coinage grant from the Republic of Vermont. The combined partnership agreed to conduct their business in New York, Vermont, Connecticut, or elsewhere if they could benefit by it (though their only known operation was the one at Newburgh).

The operations at Machin's Mills were conducted in secret and were looked upon with suspicion by the local residents. They minted several varieties of imitation George III halfpence, as well as counterfeit coppers of Connecticut and New Jersey. Only their Vermont coppers had official status.

Mints located in or near New York City were operated by John Bailey and Ephraim Brasher. They had petitioned the legislature on February 12, 1787, for a franchise to coin copper. The extent of their partnership, if any, and details of their operation are unknown. Studies of the state coinage show that they produced primarily the EXCELSIOR and NOVA EBORAC pieces of New York, and possibly the "running fox" New Jersey coppers.

*Believed to be the bust
of George Washington.*

	G	VG	F	VF	EF	AU
1786, NON VI VIRTUTE VICI	$6,000	$10,000	$20,000	$40,000	$60,000	$90,000

**1787 EXCELSIOR Copper,
Eagle on Globe Facing Left**

**1787 EXCELSIOR Copper,
Large Eagle on Obverse**

	G	VG	F	VF	EF
1787 EXCELSIOR Copper, Eagle on Globe Facing Right	$2,750	$4,000	$8,500	$22,000	$40,000
1787 EXCELSIOR Copper, Eagle on Globe Facing Left	$2,750	$3,500	$8,000	$18,000	$37,500
1787 EXCELSIOR Copper, Large Eagle on Obverse, Arrows and Branch Transposed	$4,000	$6,500	$16,000	$33,000	$55,000

1787, George Clinton

1787, Indian and New York Arms

1787, Indian and Eagle on Globe

1787, Indian and George III Reverse

	G	VG	F	VF	EF
1787, George Clinton	$10,000	$20,000	$50,000	$100,000	$250,000
1787, Indian and New York Arms	$8,000	$14,000	$35,000	$75,000	$125,000
1787, Indian and Eagle on Globe	$12,000	$20,000	$50,000	$85,000	$125,000
1787, Indian and George III Reverse (a)	—				

a. 3 examples are known.

BRITISH COPPER COINS AND THEIR IMITATIONS
(INCLUDING MACHIN'S MILLS AND OTHER UNDERWEIGHT COINAGE OF 1786–1789)

The most common copper coin used for small transactions in early America was the British halfpenny. Wide acceptance and the non–legal-tender status of these copper coins made them a prime choice for unauthorized reproduction by private individuals.

Many such counterfeits were created in America by striking from locally made dies, or by casting or other crude methods. Some were made in England and imported into this country. Pieces dated 1781 and 1785 seem to have been made specifically for this purpose, while others were circulated in both countries.

Genuine regal British halfpence and farthings minted in London and dated 1749 are of special interest to collectors because they were specifically sent to the North American colonies as reimbursement for participation in the expedition against Cape Breton, and circulated extensively throughout New England.

Genuine British halfpenny coppers of both George II (dated 1729–1754) and George III (dated 1770–1775) show finely detailed features within a border of close denticles; the 1 in the date looks like a J. They are boldly struck on good-quality planchets. Their weight is approximately 9.5 grams; their diameter, 29 mm.

British-made lightweight imitation halfpence are generally smaller in diameter and thickness, and weigh less than genuine pieces. Details are crudely engraved or sometimes incomplete. Inscriptions may be misspelled. Planchet quality may be poor.

	G	F	VF	EF	AU
1749, George II British farthing	$15	$35	$75	$175	$250
1749, George II British halfpenny	$20	$50	$100	$200	$300
1770–1775, George III British halfpenny (a)	$10	$20	$50	$100	$250
1770–1775, British imitation halfpenny (a)	$8	$15	$20	$100	$250

a. Values shown are for the most common variety. Rare pieces are sometimes worth significantly more.

During the era of American state coinage, New York diemaker James F. Atlee and/or other coiners minted unauthorized, lightweight, imitation British halfpence. These American-made false coins have the same or similar devices, legends, and, in some cases, dates as genuine regal halfpence, but they contain less copper. Their details are often poorly rendered or missing. Identification of American-made imitations has been confirmed by identifying certain punch marks (such as letters and numerals) and matching them to the distinct punch marks of known engravers.

There are four distinct groups of these halfpence, all linked to the regular state coinage. The first group was probably struck in New York City prior to 1786. The second group was minted in New York City in association with John Bailey and Ephraim Brasher during the first half of 1787. The third group was struck at Machin's Mills during the second half of 1787 and into 1788 or later. A fourth group, made by the Machin's Mills coiners, consists of pieces made from dies that were muled with false dies of the state coinages of Connecticut, Vermont, and New York. Pieces with very crude designs and other dates are believed to have been struck elsewhere in New England.

GEORGIVS/BRITANNIA
"MACHIN'S MILLS" COPPER HALFPENNIES MADE IN AMERICA

Dates used on these pieces were often "evasive," as numismatists describe them today. They include dates not used on genuine pieces and, sometimes, variations in spelling. They are as follows: 1771, 1772, 1774, 1775, and 1776 for the first group; 1747 and 1787 for the second group; and 1776, 1778, 1787, and 1788 for the third group. Pieces generally attributed to James Atlee can be identified by a single outline in the crosses (British Union) of Britannia's shield and large triangular denticles along the coin circumference. The more-valuable American-made pieces are not to be confused with the similar English-made George III counterfeits (some of which have identical dates), or with genuine British half-pence dated 1770 to 1775.

Group I coins dated 1771, 1772, 1774, 1775, and 1776 have distinctive bold designs but lack the fine details of the original coins. Planchets are generally of high quality.

Group II coins dated 1747 and 1787 are generally poorly made. The 1 in the date is not J-shaped, and the denticles are of various sizes. There are no outlines to the stripes in the shield.

Group III coins dated 1776, 1778, 1787, and 1788, struck at Machin's Mills in Newburgh, New York, are similar to coins of Group II, with their triangular-shaped denticles. Most have large dates and berries in the obverse wreath.

	AG	G	VG	F	VF	EF	AU
1747, GEORGIVS II. Group II	$150	$325	$450	$1,000	$4,500	$10,000	$20,000
1771, GEORGIVS III. Group I	$70	$110	$250	$400	$1,500	$3,300	$6,000
1772, GEORGIVS III. Group I	$80	$150	$275	$600	$2,000	$3,750	$8,000
1772, GEORGIUS III. Group I	$85	$200	$375	$900	$2,800	$5,500	—
1774, GEORGIVS III. Group I	$40	$80	$125	$300	$900	$2,750	$5,000
1774, GEORGIUS III. Group I	$80	$150	$250	$500	$2,000	$4,500	—
1775, GEORGIVS III. Group I	$35	$75	$125	$300	$800	$2,200	$4,750
1776, GEORGIVS III. Group III	$175	$325	$500	$1,000	$3,000	$7,000	—
1776, GEORCIVS III, Small Date	$1,000	$2,000	$4,500	$9,000	$18,000	—	—
1778, GEORGIVS III. Group III	$40	$90	$150	$350	$900	$2,500	$4,000
1784, GEORGIVS III	$200	$400	$900	$1,750	$3,500	$5,000	$7,500
1787, GEORGIVS III. Group II	$30	$75	$125	$250	$750	$1,500	$3,250
1787, GEORGIVS III. Group III	$30	$75	$125	$250	$750	$1,500	$3,250
1788, GEORGIVS III. Group III	$35	$80	$150	$300	$800	$1,750	$3,500

Note: Values shown are for the most common varieties in each category. Rare pieces can be worth significantly more. Also see related George III combinations under Connecticut, Vermont, and New York.

The muled coins of Group IV are listed separately with the Immune Columbia pieces and with the coins of Connecticut, Vermont, and New York. Other imitation coppers made by unidentified American makers are generally very crude and exceedingly rare. Cast copies of British coins probably circulated along with the imitations without being questioned. Counterfeits of silver Spanish-American coins and Massachusetts tree coins may have also been coined by American minters.

NOVA EBORAC COINAGE FOR NEW YORK

An extensive issue of 1787-dated copper coins appeared, each with a bust on the obverse surrounded by NOVA EBORAC ("New York"). The reverse showed a seated goddess with a sprig in one hand and a liberty cap on a pole in the other hand, with the legend VIRT. ET. LIB. ("Virtue and Liberty") surrounding, and the date 1787 below. The letter punches used on this issue are identical to those used on the Brasher doubloon die. It is likely that John Bailey and Ephraim Brasher operated a minting shop in New York City and produced these and possibly other issues.

1787, NOVA EBORAC, Reverse:
Seated Figure Facing Right

1787, NOVA EBORAC, Reverse:
Seated Figure Facing Left

1787, NOVA EBORAC, Small Head

1787, NOVA EBORAC, Large Head

	AG	G	F	VF	EF	AU
1787, NOVA EBORAC, Seated Figure Facing Right	$50	$110	$225	$800	$1,500	$3,250
1787, NOVA EBORAC, Seated Figure Facing Left	$50	$90	$200	$600	$1,000	$2,000
1787, NOVA EBORAC, Small Head	$1,700	$4,000	$10,000	$20,000		
1787, NOVA EBORAC, Large Head	$500	$900	$2,000	$5,000		

NEW JERSEY (1786–1788)

On June 1, 1786, the New Jersey General Assembly granted to businessman and investor Thomas Goadsby, silversmith and assayer Albion Cox, and minter Walter Mould authority to coin three million coppers weighing six pennyweight and six grains (150 grains total, or 9.72 grams) apiece, to be completed by June 1788, on condition that they deliver to the state treasurer "one Tenth Part of the full Sum they shall strike." These coppers were to pass current at 15 to the shilling. Revolutionary War hero and New Jersey state legislator Matthias Ogden also played a significant financial and political role in the operation.

In an undertaking of this kind, the contractors purchased the metal and assumed all expenses of coining. The difference between these expenses and the total face value of the coins issued represented their profit.

Later, Goadsby and Cox asked authority to coin two-thirds of the total independently of Mould. Their petition was granted November 22, 1786. Mould was known to have produced his coins at Morristown, while Cox and Goadsby operated in Rahway. Coins with a diameter of 30 mm or more are generally considered Morristown products. Coins were also minted in Elizabethtown by Ogden and, without authority, by Machin's Mills.

The obverse shows design elements of the state seal, a horse's head with plow, and the legend NOVA CÆSAREA (New Jersey). The reverse has a United States shield and, for the first time on a coin, the legend E PLURIBUS UNUM (One Composed of Many). More than 140 varieties exist. The majority have the horse's head facing to the right; however, three of the 1788 date show the head facing left. Other variations have a sprig beneath the head, branches below the shield, stars, cinquefoils, a running fox, and other ornaments.

1786, Date Under Plow Beam

1786 and 1787, Pattern Shield

1786, Date Under Plow, No Coulter

	AG	G	F	VF	EF
1786, Date Under Plow Beam			$85,000	$125,000	$200,000
1786, Date Under Plow, No Coulter	$500	$900	$3,000	$7,000	$10,000
1787, Pattern Shield (a)	$400	$700	$1,750	$3,000	$5,000

a. The so-called Pattern Shield reverse was also used on several speculative patterns. See page 113.

1786, Straight Plow Beam, Protruding Tongue

1786, Wide Shield

1786, Curved Plow Beam, Bridle Variety

	AG	G	F	VF	EF	AU
1786, Straight Plow Beam (common varieties)	$25	$55	$200	$575	$1,000	$1,500
1786, Curved Plow Beam (common varieties)	$25	$55	$200	$575	$1,100	$1,700
1786, Protruding Tongue	$30	$70	$235	$600	$1,850	$4,500
1786, Wide Shield	$30	$75	$240	$650	$2,000	$5,000
1786, Bridle variety	$30	$75	$240	$650	$2,000	$5,000

1787, PLURIBS Error   **1787, U Over S in PLURIBUS**   **1787, PLURIRUS Error**

	AG	G	F	VF	EF	AU
1786, PLUKIBUS error	$30	$75	$250	$450	$1,700	$4,500
1787, PLURIBS error	$40	$125	$500	$1,600	$3,500	$7,500
1787, Second U Over S in PLURIBUS	$40	$160	$470	$1,100	$3,200	$5,000
1787, PLURIRUS error	$40	$160	$470	$1,100	$3,200	$5,500

1787, Sprig   **1787, WM**   **1787, Hidden WM**
Above Plow   **Above Plow**

	AG	G	F	VF	EF	AU
1787, Sprig Above Plow (common varieties)	$25	$65	$220	$650	$1,200	$2,500
1787, No Sprig Above Plow (common varieties)	$25	$65	$220	$550	$900	$1,600
1787, WM Above Plow (a)				—		
1787, Hidden WM in Sprig	$35	$75	$225	$675	$1,800	$3,500

a. Unique.

1787 Over 1887   **1787, Camel Head**   **1787, Serpent Head**

	AG	G	F	VF	EF	AU
1787, Date Over 1887	$200	$600	$3,000	$6,000	$15,000	—
1787, Camel Head (snout in high relief)	$30	$60	$200	$650	$900	$1,750
1787, Serpent Head	$35	$85	$400	$1,700	$4,000	$6,500
1787, Goiter Variety	$40	$75	$250	$700	$2,500	$5,000

1788, Fox Before Legend	1788, Indistinct Coulter	1788, Fox After Legend

1788, Braided Mane	1788, Head Facing Left

	AG	G	F	VF	EF	AU
1788, Horse's Head Facing Right, several varieties	$25	$60	$175	$550	$900	$1,600
1788, Horse's Head Facing Right, Running Fox Before Legend	$75	$150	$550	$2,000	$4,500	$9,000
1788, Similar, Indistinct Coulter	$150	$650	$2,500	$6,500	$15,000	—
1788, Horse's Head Facing Right, Running Fox After Legend	$9,000	$25,000	$75,000	$100,000	—	
1788, Braided Mane	$50	$300	$1,200	$3,500	$6,000	$12,000
1788, Horse's Head Facing Left	$175	$450	$1,750	$4,750	$12,000	—

REPUBLIC OF VERMONT (1785–1788)

The Republic of Vermont was not formally part of the Union in the 1780s. However, it considered itself American and allied with the original 13 colonies, having declared independence from Britain in January 1777 and having fought in the Revolutionary War. After the war Vermont sought political connection with the United States. Territorial disagreements with New York delayed its entry into the Union, but this was finally accomplished in 1791, when it was admitted as the 14th state. In the meantime, Vermont had already embarked on its own experiments in local coinage.

Reuben Harmon Jr., a storekeeper and entrepreneur of Rupert, Vermont, was granted permission by the Vermont House of Representatives to coin copper pieces for a period of two years beginning July 1, 1785. The well-known Vermont "Landscape" coppers were first produced in that year. The franchise was extended for eight years in 1786.

Harmon's mint was located in the northeast corner of Rupert near a stream known as Millbrook. Colonel William Coley, a New York goldsmith, made the first dies. Some of the late issues were made near Newburgh, New York, by the Machin's Mills coiners.

Most coppers made in Vermont were struck on poor and defective planchets. These included the landscape and Draped Bust Left varieties. Well-struck coins on smooth, full planchets command higher prices. Later pieces made at Machin's Mills are on high-quality planchets but usually have areas of weak striking.

1785, IMMUNE COLUMBIA

| 1785, VERMONTS | 1785, Reverse | 1785, VERMONTIS |

1786, VERMONTENSIUM   **1786, Baby Head**

1786, Bust Left   **1786, Reverse**   **1787, Reverse**

	AG	G	VG	F	VF	EF	AU
1785, IMMUNE COLUMBIA	$4,250	$6,250	$10,000	$14,000	$35,000	—	—
1785, VERMONTS	$150	$275	$500	$750	$2,500	$4,250	$9,000
1785, VERMONTIS	$175	$325	$650	$1,400	$4,250	$10,000	$19,500
1786, VERMONTENSIUM	$110	$200	$350	$550	$1,350	$3,000	$5,500
1786, Baby Head	$200	$275	$400	$1,250	$4,000	$10,500	—
1786, Bust Left	$80	$125	$250	$650	$2,400	$4,000	—
1787, Bust Left	$3,000	$4,500	$10,500	$27,000	$42,000	—	

1787, BRITANNIA

	AG	G	VG	F	VF	EF	AU
1787, BRITANNIA (a)	$45	$90	$120	$200	$450	$1,000	$2,200

a. The reverse of this coin is always weak.

1787, 1788, Bust Right (Several Varieties)

	AG	G	VG	F	VF	EF	AU
1787, Bust Right, several varieties	$60	$110	$150	$250	$900	$2,250	$4,000
1788, Bust Right, several varieties	$50	$90	$120	$225	$600	$1,400	$3,250
1788, Backward C in AUCTORI	$3,000	$4,500	$7,500	$17,500	$37,500	$75,000	
1788, *ET LIB* *INDE	$175	$300	$550	$1,250	$4,000	$10,000	—

1788, GEORGIVS III REX/ET•LIB+INDE+

	AG	G	VG	F	VF	EF	AU
1788, GEORGIVS III REX (a)	$300	$500	$900	$2,200	$4,500	$11,000	

a. This piece should not be confused with the common English halfpence with similar design and reverse legend BRITANNIA.

PRIVATE TOKENS AFTER CONFEDERATION

The formal ratification of the Articles of Confederation—the document signed amongst the original 13 colonies, which established the United States of America as a confederation of sovereign states and served as its first constitution—was accomplished in early 1781. A number of private coinages sprang up after confederation, intended to facilitate local commerce. These were not the products of the federal government, but were tokens issued by businesses and other private concerns.

NORTH AMERICAN TOKENS (DATED 1781)

These tokens were struck in Dublin, Ireland. The obverse shows the seated figure of Hibernia, the personification of Ireland, facing left. The date of issue is believed to have been much later than that shown on the token (1781). Like many Irish tokens, this issue found its way to America in limited quantities and was accepted in commerce near the Canadian border.

	VG	F	VF	EF	AU
1781, Copper or Brass	$60	$100	$200	$650	$1,300

Bar Coppers (ca. 1785)

The Bar coppers are undated and of uncertain origin. They have 13 parallel and unconnected bars on one side. On the other side is the large roman-letter USA monogram. The design is virtually identical to that used on a Continental Army uniform button.

The significance of the design is clearly defined by its extreme simplicity. The separate 13 states (bars) unite into a single entity as symbolized by the interlocking letters (USA).

These pieces are believed to have first circulated in New York during November 1785, as mentioned in a report in the *New Jersey Gazette* of November 12, 1785. They may have been made in England. Although they are scarce, examples enter the marketplace with regularity, and nearly all are in higher grades.

John Adams Bolen (1826–1907), a numismatist and a master diesinker in Springfield, Massachusetts, struck copies of the Bar copper around 1862. On these copies, the letter A passes under, instead of over, the S. Bolen's intent was not to deceive, and he advertised his copies plainly as reproductions. But his skills were such that W. Elliot Woodward, a leading auctioneer of tokens and medals in the 1860s, vacillated between selling Bolen's copies and describing them as "dangerous counterfeits." Bolen copies of the Bar copper are highly collectible in their own right, but they are less valuable than the originals.

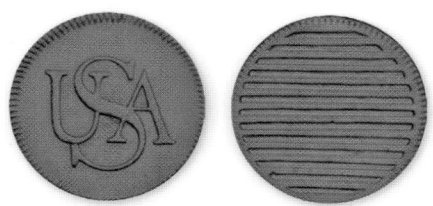

	G	VG	F	VF	EF	AU	Unc.
(Undated) (Circa 1785) Bar Copper	$500	$1,900	$3,250	$6,500	$10,000	$14,000	$23,000

Auctori Plebis Tokens (1787)

These tokens are sometimes included with the coins of Connecticut, as they greatly resemble issues of that state. (The obverse features a draped male bust, possibly King George II, wearing laurels and facing left.) They were struck in England by an unknown maker, possibly for use in America.

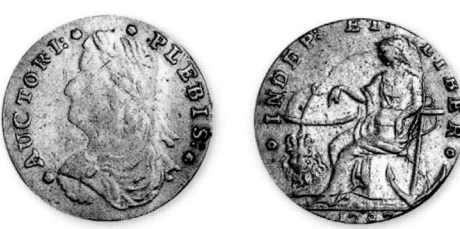

	G	VG	F	VF	EF	AU	Unc.
1787, AUCTORI PLEBIS	$90	$110	$225	$450	$900	$1,600	$7,500

Mott Store Cards (Dated 1789)

These 19th-century store cards have long been included in Early American coin collections because of the date they bear (1789). Most scholars believe these were produced no earlier than 1807 (and possibly in the Hard Times era of the late 1830s) as commemoratives of the founding of the Mott Company, and served as business cards. The firm, operated by Jordan Mott, was located at 240 Water Street, a fashionable section of New York at that time.

The obverse of the token features an eagle with wings spread and an American shield as a breastplate. The eagle holds an olive branch and arrows in his talons. Above is the date 1789, and around the rim is the legend CLOCKS, WATCHES, JEWELRY, SILVERWARE, CHRONOMETERS. The reverse of the token features a regulator clock with the legend MOTT'S N.Y. IMPORTERS, DEALERS, MANUFACTURERS OF GOLD & SILVER WARES.

	VG	F	VF	EF	AU	Unc.
"1789," Mott Token, Thick Planchet	$80	$175	$300	$450	$600	$1,200
"1789," Mott Token, Thin Planchet	$80	$200	$350	$800	$1,400	$2,500
"1789," Mott Token, Entire Edge Engrailed	$80	$300	$450	$1,000	$1,800	$3,200

STANDISH BARRY THREEPENCE (1790)

Standish Barry, of Baltimore, was a watch- and clockmaker, an engraver, and, later, a silversmith. In 1790 he circulated a silver threepence of his own fabrication. The tokens are believed to have been an advertising venture at a time when small change was scarce. The precise date on this piece may indicate that Barry intended to commemorate Independence Day, but there are no records to prove this. The head on the obverse is probably that of James Calhoun, who was active in Baltimore politics in the 1790s. The legend BALTIMORE TOWN JULY 4, 90, appears in the border. An enigmatic gold doubloon is also attributed to Barry (see page 121).

Nearly all examples of the silver threepence show significant wear, suggesting that they circulated for a long time.

	VG	F	VF	EF	AU
1790 Threepence	$10,000	$22,500	$50,000	$100,000	$160,000

ALBANY CHURCH PENNIES (1790)

The First Presbyterian Church of Albany, New York, authorized an issue of 1,000 copper uniface tokens in 1790. These passed at 12 to a shilling. They were used to encourage parishioner donations (at that time, there was a scarcity of small change in circulation). They were also intended to stop contributions of worn and counterfeit coppers (in the words of the church elders' resolution, "in order to add respect to the weekly collections"). Two varieties were made, one with the addition of a large D (the abbreviation for *denarium*, or penny, in the British monetary system) above the word CHURCH. All are rare, with fewer than a dozen of each variety known.

	VG	F	VF	EF
(Undated) (1790) Without D	$12,500	$22,500	$40,000	$60,000
(Undated) (1790) With D Added	$12,500	$22,500	$40,000	$60,000

KENTUCKY TOKENS (CA. 1792–1794)

These tokens were struck in England circa 1792 to 1794. Their obverse legend reads UNANIMITY IS THE STRENGTH OF SOCIETY; the central motif is a hand holding a scroll with the inscription OUR CAUSE IS JUST. The reverse shows a pyramid of 15 starbursts surrounded by rays. Each star in the triangle represents a state, identified by its initial letter. These pieces are usually called *Kentucky cents* or *Kentucky tokens* because the letter K (for Kentucky) happens to be at the top. Some of the edges are plain; others are milled with a diagonal reeding; and some have edge lettering that reads PAYABLE IN LANCASTER LONDON OR BRISTOL, PAYABLE AT BEDWORTH NUNEATON OR HINKLEY, or PAYABLE AT I. FIELDING, etc.

These are not known to have circulated in America. Rather, they were made as produced as collectibles, popular among English numismatists and others at the time. Likely more than 1,000 Kentucky tokens are in the hands of numismatists today.

	VF	EF	AU	Unc.
(1792–1794) Copper, Plain Edge	$185	$275	$450	$850
(1792–1794) Copper, Engrailed Edge	$500	$900	$1,350	$2,800
(1792–1794) Copper, Lettered Edge, PAYABLE AT BEDWORTH, etc.	—	—	—	—
(1792–1794) Copper, Lettered Edge, PAYABLE IN LANCASTER, etc.	$200	$300	$475	$950
(1792–1794) Copper, Lettered Edge, PAYABLE AT I. FIELDING, etc.	—	—	—	—

FRANKLIN PRESS TOKENS (1794)

These were English tradesman's tokens of the kind collected by English numismatists in the late 1700s and early 1800s. (As a group, they were popularly called Conder tokens, after James Conder, the man who first cataloged them for collectors.) The Franklin Press tokens did not circulate as money in America, but, being associated with a London shop where Benjamin Franklin once worked, they have long been included in American coin collections.

The obverse features a wood-frame printing press of the style that Benjamin Franklin would have operated by hand as a printer in England in 1725. He had left Philadelphia at the age of 18 to buy printing supplies in London and look for work. Around the central design is the legend SIC ORITOR DOCTRINA SURGETQUE LIBERTAS ("Thus Learning Advances and Liberty Grows"), and below is the date, 1794. The reverse legend reads PAYABLE AT THE FRANKLIN PRESS LONDON.

Most are plain-edged, but rare lettered-edge varieties exist, as well as a unique piece with a diagonally reeded edge.

	VG	VF	EF	AU	Unc.
1794 Franklin Press Token	$100	$250	$350	$550	$900
Similar, Edge Reads AN ASYLUM FOR THE OPPRESS'D OF ALL NATIONS			*(unique)*		
Similar, Edge Diagonally Reeded			*(unique)*		

TALBOT, ALLUM & LEE CENTS (1794–1795)

Talbot, Allum & Lee was a firm of importers engaged in the India trade and located at 241 Pearl Street, New York. It placed a large quantity of English-made coppers in circulation during 1794 and 1795.

ONE CENT appears on the 1794 issue, and the legend PAYABLE AT THE STORE OF on the edge. The denomination is not found on the 1795 reverse but the edge legend was changed to read WE PROMISE TO PAY THE BEARER ONE CENT. Rare plain-edged specimens of both dates exist. Exceptional pieces have edges ornamented or with lettering CAMBRIDGE BEDFORD AND HUNTINGDON.X.X.

It is estimated that more than 200,000 of these tokens were minted, though no original records have been located. Varieties and mulings are known; the values shown here are for the most common types.

Many undistributed tokens were sold to the Philadelphia Mint in a time of copper shortage. These were cut down and used by the Mint as planchets for coining 1795 and 1797 half cents.

1794 Cent, With NEW YORK   **1795 Cent**

	VG	F	VF	EF	AU	Unc.
1794 Cent, With NEW YORK	$65	$80	$225	$350	$550	$1,350
1794 Cent, Without NEW YORK	$500	$850	$2,750	$5,000	$7,500	$16,000
1795 Cent	$60	$80	$200	$300	$400	$800

MYDDELTON TOKENS (1796)

Philip Parry Price Myddelton was an Englishman who bought land in America after the Revolutionary War. He hoped to begin a vibrant farming community along the Ohio River and entice English crafts-men and workers to move there. To this end he contracted the design of a promotional token and had examples made in copper and silver. These tokens were struck at the Soho Mint of Boulton and Watt near Birmingham, England. Although their obverse legend reads BRITISH SETTLEMENT KENTUCKY, and Myddelton planned to order large quantities of the copper version for shipment to the United States, they were never actually issued for circulation in Kentucky. The entrepreneur was arrested in August 1796 and convicted in London for the crime of convincing hundreds of workers to leave England for America. He was jailed in Newgate prison for three and a half years, which ended his Kentucky plans.

The obverse of Myddelton's token shows Hope presenting two "little genii" (his description) to the goddess Liberty. She welcomes them with an open hand. At her feet is a flourishing sapling and a cornucopia representing America's bounty, and she holds a pole with a liberty cap. On the reverse, seated Britannia leans wearily on a downward-pointing spear, looking at the broken scale and fasces—symbols of unity, justice, and liberty—scattered at her feet.

Sylvester S. Crosby, in *The Early Coins of America*, remarked that "In beauty of design and execution, the tokens are unsurpassed by any piece issued for American circulation."

	PF
1796, Proof, Copper	$20,000
1796, Proof, Silver	$25,000

COPPER COMPANY OF UPPER CANADA TOKENS (EARLY 1800S)

These pieces were struck some time in the early 1800s. The obverse is the same as that of the Myddelton token. The new reverse refers to a Canadian firm, the Copper Company of Upper Canada, with the denomination ONE HALF PENNY. These tokens may have been made for numismatic purposes (for sale to collectors), or as part of the coiner's samples. Their maker is unknown. Restrikes were made in England in the 1890s.

	PF
1796, Proof, Copper	$7,500

CASTORLAND MEDALS (1796)

These medals, or "jetons," are dated 1796 and allude to a proposed French settlement known as Castorland. This was to be located on the Black River, in northern New York, not far from the Canadian border. Peter Chassanis of Paris had acquired land that he and others intended to parcel into large farms, with Chassanis heading the settlement's government, two commissaries residing at its seat, Castorville, and four commissaries headquartered in Paris. The medals were to be given as payment ("in recognition of the care which they may bestow upon the common concerns") to the Parisian directors of the colonizing company for their attendance at board meetings.

Some 20 French families, many of them aristocratic refugees from the French Revolution, moved to the settlement between 1796 and 1800. Challenges including sickness, harsh northern New York winters, loss of livestock, and theft of finances proved too much for the company, and Castorland was dissolved in 1814. Many of the surviving settlers moved to more prosperous American communities or returned to Europe.

The obverse of the Castorland medal features a profile portrait of the ancient goddess Sybele, associated with mountains, town and city walls, fertile nature, and wild animals. She wears a *corona muralis* ("walled crown"), laurels, and a draped head covering. The legend reads FRANCO-AMERICANA COLONIA, with CASTORLAND 1796 below. On the reverse the goddess Ceres, patroness of agriculture, stands at a maple with a sap drill while the tree's bounty flows into a waiting bucket. Ceres holds a cornucopia; at her feet are a sickle and a sheaf of wheat. A beaver at the bottom of the reverse further symbolizes Castorland and its resources (*castor* is French for "beaver," an animal crucial to the very profitable North American fur trade in the early 1800s). The legend, in Latin, is SALVE MAGNA PARENS FRUGUM—"Hail, Great Mother of Crops" (from Virgil).

Copy dies of the Castorland medal are still available and have been used at the Paris Mint for restriking throughout the years. Restrikes have a more modern look than originals; their metallic content (in French) is impressed on the edge: ARGENT (silver), CUIVRE (copper), or OR (gold).

	EF	AU	Unc.
1796, Original, Silver (reeded edge, unbroken dies)	$3,000	$4,400	$7,200
1796, Original, Silver (reverse rusted and broken)	$300	$600	$1,500
1796, Original, Bronze (reverse rusted and broken)	$200	$300	$700
(1796) Undated, Restrike, Silver (Paris Mint edge marks)		$30	$70
(1796) Undated, Restrike, Bronze (Paris Mint edge marks)		$20	$40

THEATRE AT NEW YORK TOKENS (CA. 1798)

These penny tokens were issued by Skidmore of London and illustrate the New Theatre (later known as the Park Theatre) in Manhattan, as it appeared circa 1797. The theater was New York City's attempt at a prestigious new level of entertainment, as the famous John Street Theatre (the "Birthplace of American Theater") was suffering from poor management and physical decay in the 1790s. The building's cornerstone was laid on May 5, 1795, and the theater opened on January 29, 1798, with a presentation of entertainments including Shakespeare's *As You Like It*.

The obverse of this copper token features a view of the playhouse building with the legend THE THEATRE AT NEW YORK AMERICA. The reverse shows an allegorical scene of a cornucopia on a dock, with bales, an anchor, and sailing ships. The legend reads MAY COMMERCE FLOURISH. The edge is marked I PROMISE TO PAY ON DEMAND THE BEARER ONE PENNY.

All known examples are struck in copper and have a Proof finish. They were made for collectors, not for use as advertising. Today examples are scarce, with about 20 known.

	EF
	PF
Penny, THE THEATRE AT NEW YORK AMERICA	—
Penny, THE THEATRE AT NEW YORK AMERICA, Proof	$26,000

NEW SPAIN (TEXAS) JOLA TOKENS (1817–1818)

In 1817 the Spanish governor of Texas, Colonel Manuel Pardo, authorized Manuel Barrera to produce 8,000 copper coins known as jolas. These crudely made pieces show the denomination ½ (real), the maker's initials and the date on the obverse, and a five-pointed star on the reverse.

The 1817 coins were withdrawn from circulation the following year and replaced by a similar issue of 8,000 pieces. These bear the date 1818 and the initials, JAG, of the maker, José Antonio de la Garza. Several varieties of each issue are known. All are rare.

	F	VF	EF
1817 1/2 Real	$40,000	$50,000	$70,000
1818 1/2 Real, Large or Small Size	$10,000	$15,000	$20,000

NORTH WEST COMPANY TOKENS (1820)

These tokens were probably valued at one beaver skin and struck in Birmingham, England, in 1820 by John Walker & Co. All but two known specimens are holed. Most have been found in Oregon in the region of the Columbia and Umpqua river valleys. They feature a portrait of King George IV on the obverse, with the legend TOKEN and the date 1820. The reverse shows a beaver in the wild, with the legend NORTH WEST COMPANY.

James A. Haxby, in the *Guide Book of Canadian Coins and Tokens*, writes, "The pieces actually issued for circulation were pierced at the top for suspension or stringing. Unholed copper strikes are known with plain or engrailed edge and are very rare. A number of pieces have been found buried in western Canada and as far south as central Oregon."

Holed Brass Token   **Unholed Copper Token**

	AG	G	VG	F	VF
1820, Copper or Brass (with hole)	$375	$800	$2,250	$4,250	$8,500
1820, Copper, unholed, plain or engrailed edge	—	—	—	—	—

WASHINGTON PIECES

Medals, tokens, and coinage proposals in this interesting series dated from 1783 to 1795 bear the portrait of George Washington. The likenesses in most instances were faithfully reproduced and were designed to honor the first president. Many of these pieces were of English origin and, although dated 1783, probably were made in the 1820s or later.

The legends generally signify a strong unity among the states and the marked display of patriotism that pervaded the new nation during that period. We find among some of these tokens an employment of what were soon to become the nation's official coin devices, namely, the American eagle, the United States shield, and stars. The denomination ONE CENT is used in several instances, while on some of the English pieces HALFPENNY will be found. Several of these pieces were private patterns for proposed coinage contracts.

GEORGIVS TRIUMPHO TOKENS

Although the head shown on these tokens bears a strong resemblance to that on some coins of King George III, many collectors consider the Georgivs Triumpho ("Triumphant George") tokens a commemorative of America's victory in the Revolutionary War.

The reverse side shows the Goddess of Liberty behind a framework of 13 bars and fleurs-de-lis. Holding an olive branch in her right hand and staff of liberty in her left, she is partially encircled by the words VOCE POPOLI ("By the Voice of the People") 1783.

	VG	F	VF	EF	AU	Unc.
1783, GEORGIVS TRIUMPHO	$110	$225	$500	$700	$1,200	$6,000

WASHINGTON PORTRAIT PIECES (1780s TO EARLY 1800s)

Military Bust. "The 1783-dated Washington Military Bust coppers bear a portrait, adapted (with a different perspective on the coin and a wreath added to the head) from a painting by Edward Savage," writes Q. David Bowers in the *Whitman Encyclopedia of Colonial and Early American Coins*. "These seem to have circulated in England as well as America. . . . Many varieties exist, but they are not well known outside of a circle of specialists. Accordingly, the opportunity exists to acquire rare die combinations for little premium over a regular issue."

The reverse features a seated female figure holding an olive branch and a pole topped by a liberty cap. Values shown are for the most common varieties.

1783, Large Military Bust, Point of Bust Close to W

1783, Small Military Bust

	F	VF	EF	AU	Unc.
1783, Large Military Bust	$75	$160	$350	$500	$1,750
1783, Small Military Bust, Plain Edge	$80	$175	$400	$750	$2,500
1783, Small Military Bust, Engrailed Edge	$100	$200	$550	$1,100	$3,000

Draped Bust. Draped Bust coppers dated 1783 depict Washington with the top of a toga draped over his shoulder. One variety includes a button at the folds in front of the toga. Another variety has no button, and has the initial "I" (for Ingram) in the toga, above the right side of the numeral 3 in the date. Both varieties feature a similar reverse design with a female figure seated on a rock, holding an olive branch and a pole surmounted by a liberty cap.

1783, Draped Bust, No Button   **With Button**

	F	VF	EF	AU	Unc.
1783, Draped Bust, No Button *(illustrated)*	$80	$160	$300	$500	$1,600
1783, Draped Bust, With Button (on Drapery at Neck)	$125	$225	$350	$700	$3,200
1783, Draped Bust, Copper Restrike, Plain Edge, Proof	$125	$225	$350	$700	$900
1783, Draped Bust, Copper Restrike, Engrailed Edge, Proof					$750
1783, Draped Bust, Silver Restrike, Engrailed Edge, Proof					$1,800

Unity States. The 1783-dated coppers with the legend UNITY STATES OF AMERICA were likely coined in the early 1800s at the Soho Mint in Birmingham, England. The obverse features a portrait of Washington in a toga and wearing laurels. The reverse is a copy of the wreath design on the copper cent produced by the Philadelphia Mint from 1796 to 1807, with UNITED spelled UNITY, perhaps as a way to evade charges of counterfeiting.

Despite the American denomination of this piece, they likely circulated in England (at the value of a halfpenny), as reflected by examples being found there in quantity in later years. They were imported into the United States as well, for use as a cent, and are mentioned in several counterfeit-detector publications in the 1850s.

1783, Unity States

	VG	VF	EF	AU	Unc.
1783, UNITY STATES	$100	$200	$325	$550	$1,400

Double Head. Although the Washington Double Head cents are undated, some numismatists assign them a date of 1783, given their resemblance to the Military Bust coppers that bear that date (even though those were probably struck years later). They were likely struck in Birmingham, England, by Edward Thomason sometime in the 1820s or later. They were made in England, as evidenced by many having been found there, but long after the Conder token era. They are denominated ONE CENT and, when exported to the United States, circulated along with Hard Times tokens of the 1830s.

Undated Double-Head Cent

	F	VF	EF	AU	Unc.
(Undated) Double-Head Cent	$100	$250	$425	$725	$2,400

Ugly Head. The so-called Ugly Head token is a medalet struck in copper and white-metal varieties, possibly satirical, and presumably of American origin. The token's legend reads WASHINGTON THE GREAT D.G. The abbreviation "D.G." on English coins stands for Dei Gratia ("By the Grace of God"), and the portrait appears to be wigless and possibly toothless, leading some numismatists to opine that the token is a satire on George Washington. Bowers notes that the token's date, 1784, has no particular significance in Washington's life. By that year the American Revolution was over and the general had retired his commission as commander-in-chief of the Continental Army. He would not assume the presidency until 1789. The reverse of the token features a design of linked rings with abbreviations for the British colonies, reminiscent of the 1776 Continental dollar.

1784, Ugly Head

		G
1784, Ugly Head, Copper		$100,000
	Auctions: $20,000, Crude Good, December 1983	
1784, Ugly Head, Pewter		(unique)

Large and Small Eagle. Large Eagle and Small Eagle one-cent tokens dated 1791 were made in Birmingham, England, sponsored by merchants W. and Alex Walker of that city as proposals for official American coinage. Bowers writes in the *Whitman Encyclopedia of Colonial and Early American Coins* that the Walker firm "shipped a cask filled with these cents, estimated to be about 2,500 Large Eagle and 1,500 Small Eagle coins, to Thomas Ketland & Sons, a Philadelphia contact, to be distributed to legislators. The depiction of Washington was contrary to the president's own desires, who felt that having his image on coins would appear to have the 'stamp of royalty.'"

1791 Cent, Small Eagle Reverse, Edge Lettered UNITED STATES OF AMERICA

1791 Cent, Large Eagle Reverse

	VG	F	VF	EF	AU	Unc.
1791 Cent, Small Eagle (Date on Reverse)		$475	$650	$800	$1,200	$2,750
1791 Cent, Large Eagle (Date on Obverse)	$150	$350	$550	$750	$1,100	$2,400

Liverpool. The Liverpool Halfpenny tokens were most likely made around 1793. They were intended for circulation as small change in England, although numismatists of the time also sought them for their collections. The obverse shows a uniformed bust of George Washington, as used on the Large Eagle one-cent tokens of 1791. The reverse features a sailing ship and the legend LIVERPOOL HALF-PENNY, a design used on various English Conder tokens.

1791 Liverpool Halfpenny

	VG	F	VF	EF	AU	Unc.
1791 Liverpool Halfpenny, Lettered Edge	$850	$1,250	$2,000	$3,250	$6,500	—

1792. An extensive series of 1792-dated Washington pieces was produced in many varieties, bearing no denomination. These apparently were made in England, and were collected by numismatists in addition to circulating as coinage substitutes in America.

1792 Cent, Small Eagle Reverse,
Edge Lettered UNITED STATES OF AMERICA

	VG	F	VF	EF
1792, WASHINGTON PRESIDENT, Eagle With 13 Stars Reverse				
PRESIDENT at Side of Bust, Copper				—
PRESIDENT, Silver			$125,000	—
PRESIDENT, Gold (a)			—	
PRESIDENT Extends Below Bust, Copper (a)				—

a. Unique.

1792, WASHINGTON PRESIDENT   **Legend Reverse**

	VG	F	VF	EF
1792, WASHINGTON PRESIDENT, Legend on Reverse				
Plain Edge, Copper		$2,750	$7,500	$18,000	$50,000
Lettered Edge, Copper		—	—	—	—

(1792) Undated,
**WASHINGTON
BORN VIRGINIA**

	VG	F	VF	EF
(1792) Undated, WASHINGTON BORN VIRGINIA, Eagle With 13 Stars Reverse *(reverse illustrated on previous page)*, Copper (a)		—		
(1792) Undated, WASHINGTON BORN VIRGINIA, Legend on Reverse				
Copper	$1,250	$2,250	$4,500	$8,000
Silver	—	—	—	—

a. 3 examples are known.

Peter Getz. Dies engraved by silversmith, mechanic, and inventor Peter Getz of Lancaster, Pennsylvania, are believed to have been made to produce a half dollar and a cent as a proposal to Congress for a private contract coinage before the Philadelphia Mint became a reality. These feature George Washington, in a military bust portrait, and a heraldic eagle.

1792, Small Eagle

Large Eagle Reverse

	VG	F	VF	EF	AU	Unc.
1792, Small Eagle, Silver	—	—	—	$300,000		
Auctions: $241,500, AU, May 2004						
1792, Small Eagle, Copper	$6,000	$12,000	$27,500	$45,000	$65,000	$90,000
Auctions: $299,000, MS-64 BN, November 2006						
1792, Small Eagle, Ornamented Edge (Circles and Squares), Copper	—	—	—	$175,000		
Auctions: $207,000, AU, November 2006						
1792, Small Eagle, Ornamented Edge, Silver (a)	—	—	$125,000	$200,000		
Auctions: $391,000, Gem BU PL, May 2004						
1792, Large Eagle, Silver			—	—		
Auctions: $34,500, EF, May 2004						

a. 4 examples are known.

Roman Head. The 1792-dated Roman Head cents show Washington in the style of an ancient Roman dignitary. These copper pieces were struck in England for collectors, as opposed to being intended for circulation. Their edge is lettered UNITED STATES OF AMERICA.

1792 Cent, Roman Head

			PF
1792 Cent, Roman Head, Lettered Edge UNITED STATES OF AMERICA, Proof			$90,000

Ship Halfpenny. The 1793 Ship Halfpenny tokens were struck from an overdated (3 Over 2) reverse die. These copper pieces were intended for collectors, but nearly all of them ended up in circulation in England. The more common lettered-edge variety reads PAYABLE IN ANGLESEY LONDON OR LIVERPOOL.

1793 Ship Halfpenny

	VG	F	VF	EF	AU	Unc.
1793 Ship Halfpenny, Lettered Edge	$100	$200	$400	$600	$850	$3,250
1793 Ship Halfpenny, Plain Edge (a)			—	—		

a. Rare.

1795 Copper. Copper tokens dated 1795 were made in large quantities as promotional pieces for the London firm of Clark & Harris, dealers in stoves and fireplace grates. The die work is attributed to Thomas Wyon, and numismatists believe the pieces were struck in Birmingham, England, for circulation in the British Isles (although collectors saved them as well).

The obverse features a right-facing portrait of George Washington in military uniform. Two varieties exist, Small Buttons and Large Buttons (describing the coats on his frock). The legend reads G. WASHINGTON: THE FIRM FRIEND TO PEACE & HUMANITY.

The reverse shows a fireplace with a coal grate, with legends PAYABLE BY CLARK & HARRIS 13. WORMWOOD St. BISHOPSGATE and LONDON 1795.

Most have a diagonally reeded edge, although some are edge-lettered as PAYABLE AT LONDON LIVERPOOL OR BRISTOL.

1795, Small Buttons   **1795, Large Buttons**

	F	VF	EF	AU	Unc.
1795, Large Buttons, Lettered Edge	$180	$350	$700	$1,500	$2,200
1795, Large Buttons, Reeded Edge	$80	$175	$300	$400	$700
1795, Small Buttons, Reeded Edge	$80	$200	$400	$725	$1,750

Liberty and Security. The Liberty and Security halfpenny and penny tokens were made in England in 1795 as collectibles, although the halfpence also circulated widely there as small change. Their designs consist of a portrait of George Washington, identified by name, and a heraldic eagle surmounting a stylized American shield, holding a sprig of olive and several arrows. Some of their edges are plain, and some are lettered with various phrases such as AN ASYLUM FOR THE OPPRESS'D OF ALL NATIONS and BIRMINGHAM REDRUTH & SWANSEA.

Varieties exist in copper and white metal, and with mulings of different reverses.

The common name of this series derives from the reverse legend, LIBERTY AND SECURITY.

1795, Liberty and Security Halfpenny

	F	VF	EF	AU	Unc.
1795 Halfpenny, Plain Edge	$110	$200	$500	$950	$2,650
1795 Halfpenny, LONDON Edge	$100	$210	$525	$750	$2,500
1795 Halfpenny, BIRMINGHAM Edge	$125	$250	$550	$1,100	$2,800
1795 Halfpenny, ASYLUM Edge	$200	$400	$1,100	$2,000	$5,500
1795 Penny, ASYLUM Edge	$2,500	$8,500	$12,500	$18,000	$32,500

(1795) Undated, Liberty and Security Penny, ASYLUM Edge

	F	VF	EF	AU	Unc.
(1795) Undated, Liberty and Security Penny	$275	$450	$650	$1,150	$2,250
Same, Corded Outer Rims	$600	$1,000	$2,000	$3,250	$5,750

North Wales. "The undated North Wales halfpenny issues, believed to have been struck in England in the early 1790s (usually listed as 1795, although this may be two or three years after they were coined), are part of the 'evasion halfpence' series. Accordingly, unlike Conder tokens, they were not created for collectors. None are known to have survived with sharp features and in high grades, as is characteristic of cabinet pieces" (*Whitman Encyclopedia of Colonial and Early American Coins*).

(1795) Undated, NORTH WALES Halfpenny

	G	F	VF	EF	AU
(1795) Undated, NORTH WALES Halfpenny	$90	$200	$500	$1,400	$2,800
(1795) Undated, Lettered Edge	$450	$1,450	$5,000	$8,000	—
(1795) Undated, Two Stars at Each Side of Harp	$2,200	$7,500	$13,500		

Success Tokens. Small and large types exist of these mysterious pieces of unknown date and purpose. Today known as Success tokens, they may have been souvenirs, perhaps struck to commemorate George Washington's second inauguration (March 1793), or 19th-century gaming tokens. They were struck in copper or brass and most likely were made in the mid-1800s. Specimens with original silvering are rare and are valued 20% to 50% higher than others. Varieties exist.

(Undated) Large Success Token

(Undated) Small Success Token

	F	VF	EF	AU	Unc.
(Undated) SUCCESS Token, Large, Plain or Reeded Edge	$250	$450	$750	$1,400	$2,750
(Undated) SUCCESS Token, Small, Plain or Reeded Edge	$300	$500	$800	$1,600	$3,000

Contract Issues and Patterns

CONTINENTAL CURRENCY (1776)

The Continental Currency dollars (as they are known to numismatists) were made to serve in lieu of a paper dollar, but the exact nature of their monetary role is still unclear. They were the first dollar-sized coins ever attributed to the United States. One obverse die was engraved by someone whose initials were E.G. (thought to be Elisha Gallaudet) and is marked EG FECIT ("EG Made It"). Studies of the coinage show that there may have been two separate emissions made at different mints, one in New York City. The link design on the reverse was suggested by Benjamin Franklin and represents the former colonies.

Varieties result from differences in the spelling of the word CURRENCY and the addition of EG FECIT on the obverse. These coins were struck in pewter, brass, and silver. Pewter pieces served as a dollar, taking the place of a Continental Currency paper note. Brass and silver pieces may have been experimental or patterns. The typical grade encountered for a pewter coin is VF to AU. Examples in original bright Uncirculated condition are worth a strong premium.

Numerous copies and replicas of these coins have been made over the years. Authentication is recommended for all pieces.

	CURRENCY	CURENCY

	G	F	VF	EF	AU	Unc.
1776 CURENCY, Pewter (a)	$7,750	$12,000	$24,000	$36,000	$50,000	$70,000
1776 CURENCY, Brass (a)	$25,000	$40,000	$75,000	$135,000	$220,000	—
Auctions: $299,000, MS-63, July 2009						
1776 CURENCY, Silver (b)		$275,000	$400,000			
Auctions: $1,410,000, MS-63, May 2014; $1,527,500, MS-62, January 2015; $1,527,500, EF-40, January 2015						
1776 CURRENCY, Pewter	$8,000	$13,000	$25,000	$37,500	$52,500	$75,000
1776 CURRENCY, EG FECIT, Pewter	$8,500	$15,000	$27,000	$40,000	$55,000	$77,500
Auctions: $546,250, MS-67, January 2012						

a. 2 varieties. b. 2 examples are known.

	G	F	VF	EF	AU	Unc.
1776 CURRENCY, EG FECIT, Silver (b)	—	—	—	$850,000	—	—
Auctions: $1,410,000, MS-63, May 2014						
1776 CURRENCEY, Pewter	—	—	—		$175,000	—
1776 CURRENCY, Pewter, Ornamented Date (c)				—		
Auctions: $276,000, EF-45, July 2009						

b. 2 examples are known. **c.** 3 examples are known.

NOVA CONSTELLATIO PATTERNS (1783)

These Nova Constellatio pieces represent the first official patterns for a coinage of the United States. They were designed by Benjamin Dudley for Gouverneur Morris to carry out his ideas for a decimal coinage system. The 1,000-unit coin is a mark, the 500 a quint. These denominations, together with the small 100-unit piece, were designed to fit in with the many different values for foreign coins that constituted money in America at the time. These pattern pieces represent the first attempt at a decimal ratio, and were the forerunners of our present system of money values. Neither the proposed denominations nor the coins advanced beyond the pattern stage. These unique pieces are all dated 1783. There are two types of the quint. The copper "five" was first brought to the attention of collectors in 1980. Electrotype and cast copies exist.

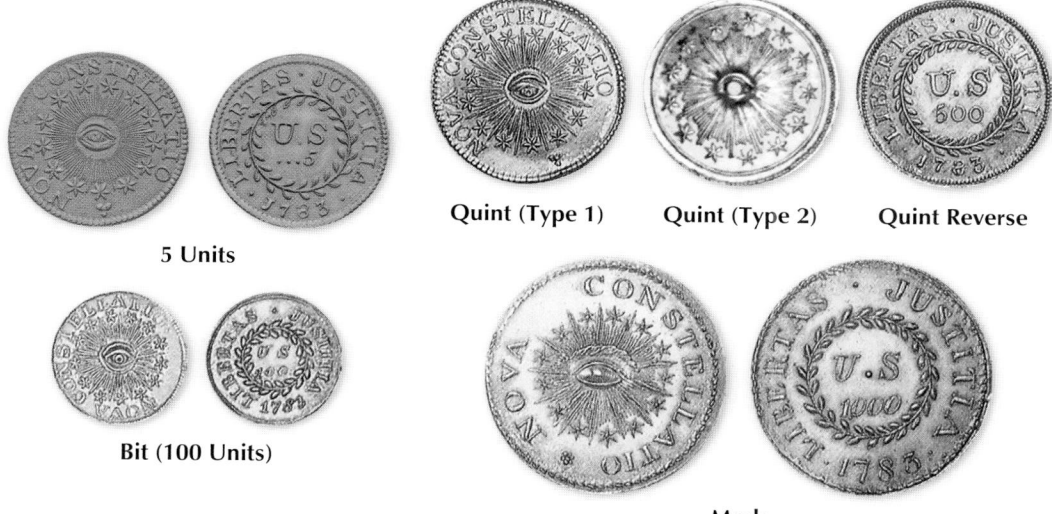

5 Units

Quint (Type 1)   Quint (Type 2)   Quint Reverse

Bit (100 Units)

Mark

1783 (Five) "5," Copper		*(unique)*
1783 (Bit) "100," Silver, Decorated Edge		*(2 known)*
	Auctions: $97,500, Unc., November 1979	
1783 (Bit) "100," Silver, Plain Edge		*(unique)*
	Auctions: $705,000, AU-55, May 2014	
1783 (Quint) "500," Silver, Type 1		*(unique)*
	Auctions: $165,000, Unc., November 1979	
1783 (Quint) "500," Silver, Type 2		*(unique)*
	Auctions: $1,175,000, AU-53, April 2013	
1783 (Mark) "1000," Silver		*(unique)*
	Auctions: $190,000, Unc., November 1979	

FUGIO COPPERS (1787)

The first coins issued by authority of the United States for which contract information is known today were the "Fugio" pieces. Entries in the *Journal of Congress* supply interesting information about proceedings relating to this coinage. For example, the entry of Saturday, April 21, 1787, reads as follows: "That the board of treasury be authorized to contract for three hundred tons of copper coin of the federal standard, agreeable to the proposition of Mr. James Jarvis. . . . That it be coined at the expense of the contractor, etc."

On Friday, July 6, 1787, it was "[r]esolved, that the board of treasury direct the contractor for the copper coinage to stamp on one side of each piece the following device, viz: thirteen circles linked together, a small circle in the middle, with the words 'United States,' around it; and in the centre, the words 'We are one'; on the other side of the same piece the following device, viz: a dial with the hours expressed on the face of it; a meridian sun above on one side of which is the word 'Fugio,' [the intended meaning is *time flies*] and on the other the year in figures '1787,' below the dial, the words 'Mind Your Business.'"

The legends have been credited to Benjamin Franklin and are similar in some respects to the 1776 Continental Currency pewter and other coins.

These pieces were coined in New Haven, Connecticut. Most of the copper used in their coinage came from military stores or salvaged metal. The dies were made by Abel Buell of New Haven.

1787, WITH POINTED RAYS

The 1787, With Pointed Rays, was later replaced by the With Club Rays variety.

American Congress Pattern   Cross After Date   Label With Raised Rims

	G	VG	F	VF	EF	AU	Unc.
Obverse Cross After Date, No Cinquefoils							
Reverse Rays and AMERICAN CONGRESS				—	$250,000	$350,000	
Reverse Label with Raised Rims (a)					$27,000		
Reverse STATES UNITED	$300	$650	$1,150	$3,000	$5,800	$12,500	—
Reverse UNITED STATES	$275	$600	$950	$2,750	$5,500	$11,000	—

a. Extremely rare.

Cinquefoil After Date
These types, with pointed rays, have regular obverses punctuated with four cinquefoils (five-leafed ornaments).

	G	VG	F	VF	EF	AU	Unc.
STATES UNITED at Sides of Circle, Cinquefoils on Label	$150	$300	$600	$1,000	$1,500	$2,100	$4,000
STATES UNITED, 1 Over Horizontal 1	$225	$450	$1,000	$4,000	$8,500		
UNITED STATES, 1 Over Horizontal 1	$200	$400	$900	$3,500	$7,500		
UNITED STATES at Sides of Circle	$150	$300	$600	$1,000	$1,750	$2,200	$4,500
STATES UNITED, Label With Raised Rims, Large Letters in WE ARE ONE	$250	$500	$800	$2,500	$5,500	$11,000	$20,000
STATES UNITED, 8-Pointed Star on Label	$200	$500	$700	$1,150	$2,500	$5,000	$10,000
UNITED Above, STATES Below	$600	$1,350	$3,000	$7,500	$10,000	$13,500	—

1787, WITH CLUB RAYS

The 1787, With Club Rays, is differentiated between concave and convex ends.

Rounded Ends   **Concave Ends**

	G	VG	F	VF	EF	AU
Club Rays, Rounded Ends	$250	$450	$900	$1,750	$3,500	$7,000
Club Rays, Concave Ends to Rays, FUCIO (C instead of G) (a)	$1,400	$3,250	$7,500	$20,000	$33,000	
Club Rays, Concave Ends, FUGIO, UNITED STATES	$1,900	$3,800	$8,000	$22,000	—	—
Club Rays, Similar, STATES UNITED Reverse	—	—	—	—	—	—

a. Extremely rare.

The so-called New Haven "restrikes" were made for Horatio N. Rust from dies recreated in 1859. These are distinguished by narrow rings on the reverse. At the time the fanciful story was given that teenaged C. Wyllys Betts discovered original dies in 1858 on the site of the Broome & Platt store in New Haven, where the original coins had been made.

New Haven Restrike.
Note narrow rings.

	EF	AU	Unc.
Gold (a)		—	—
Silver	$3,000	$4,250	$6,500
Copper or Brass	$400	$500	$800

a. 2 examples are known.

1792 PROPOSED COINAGE

Some members of the House of Representatives favored a depiction of the president's head on the obverse of each federal coin; others considered the idea an inappropriately monarchical practice. George Washington himself is believed to have expressed disapproval of the use of his portrait on American coins. The majority considered a figure emblematic of Liberty more appropriate, and the Senate finally concurred in this opinion. Robert Birch was an engraver employed to design proposed devices for American coins. He, perhaps together with others, engraved the dies for the disme and half disme. He also cut the dies for the large copper patterns known today as *Birch cents*. Most 1792 half dismes circulated and were considered to be official coinage, rather than patterns; they are summarized here and discussed in more detail under "Half Dismes."

1792 SILVER CENTER CENT

The dies for the 1792 cent with a silver center may have been cut by Henry Voigt. The coins are copper with a silver plug in the center. The idea was to create a coin with an intrinsic or melt-down value of a cent, but of smaller diameter than if it were made entirely of copper. On the obverse is a right-facing portrait of Miss Liberty, the legend LIBERTY PARENT OF SCIENCE & INDUSTRY, and the date 1792.

	F	VF	EF	AU
Cent, Silver Center (a)	$250,000	$450,000	$550,000	$650,000
Auctions: $1,997,500, MS-64, August 2014; $1,410,000, MS-63BN+, May 2014; $705,000, MS-61+, September 2014				
Cent, Without Silver Center (b)	$275,000	$400,000	$600,000	—
Auctions: $603,750, VF-30, January 2008				

a. 14 examples are known, including one unique specimen without plug. **b.** 9 examples are known.

1792 BIRCH CENT

On the large-diameter copper Birch cent, the portrait of Miss Liberty is "bright-eyed and almost smiling," as described in *United States Pattern Coins*. The legend LIBERTY PARENT OF SCIENCE & INDUSTRY surrounds the portrait. BIRCH is lettered on the truncation of her neck, for the engraver. On the reverse is a ribbon-tied wreath with the legend UNITED STATES OF AMERICA and the denomination in fractional terms of a dollar: 1/100. The edge of some examples is lettered TO BE ESTEEMED BE USEFUL (with punctuating stars).

G★W.Pt.

	F	VF	EF
Copper, Lettered Edge, TO BE ESTEEMED * BE USEFUL* (a)	$250,000	$650,000	$750,000
Auctions: $564,000, MS-61, January 2015			
Copper, Plain Edge (b)		$700,000	
Copper, Lettered Edge, TO BE ESTEEMED BE USEFUL * (b)		—	
Auctions: $2,585,000, MS-65★, January 2015			
White Metal, G*W.Pt. (George Washington President) Below Wreath (c)			—

a. 8 examples are known. **b.** 2 examples are known. **c.** Unique.

1792 HALF DISME

About 1,500 silver half dismes were struck in mid-August 1792 in the shop of John Harper, using equipment ordered for the Philadelphia Mint (the foundation stones of which would be laid on July 31). Nearly all were placed into circulation. In his annual address that autumn, President George Washington noted that these had been so distributed. Their obverse design is a portrait of Miss Liberty similar to the Birch cent's, but facing left. Its legend is abbreviated as LIB. PAR. OF SCIENCE & INDUSTRY. The reverse shows an eagle in flight, with UNI. STATES OF AMERICA around the top, and HALF DISME below.

	Mintage	AG	G	VG	F	VF	EF	AU	Unc.
Silver	1,500	$8,500	$20,000	$27,500	$40,000	$75,000	$110,000	$175,000	$325,000
	Auctions: $1,292,500, SP-67, August 2014								

1792 DISME

The 1792 pattern disme occurs in one silver variety and two copper varieties (plain-edged and the more readily available reeded-edge). The obverse legend is abbreviated as LIBERTY PARENT OF SCIENCE & INDUST., with the date 1792 below Miss Liberty's neck. The reverse features an eagle in flight, different in design from that of the half disme, with UNITED STATES OF AMERICA around the top of the coin and the denomination, DISME, below.

	VF	EF	Unc.
Silver (a)	$750,000	$1,000,000	$2,000,000
Auctions: $998,750, AU-50, January 2015			
Copper *(illustrated)* (b)	$135,000	$225,000	$500,000
Auctions: $1,057,500, MS-64, January 2015			

a. 3 examples are known. b. Approximately 15 examples are known.

1792 QUARTER DOLLAR

Joseph Wright, an accomplished artist in the private sector, designed this pattern, thought to have been intended for a quarter dollar. Wright was George Washington's choice for the position of first chief engraver of the Mint, and he later designed the 1793, Liberty Cap, cent in that capacity, but died of yellow fever before being confirmed by Congress. Unique uniface trials of the obverse and reverse also exist.

	EF
1792, Copper (*illustrated*) (a)	$750,000
Auctions: $2,232,500, MS-63, January 2015	
1792, White Metal (b)	$325,000

a. 2 examples are known. **b.** 4 examples are known.

THE LIBERTAS AMERICANA MEDAL (1782)

The Liberty Cap coinage of the fledgling United States was inspired by the famous Libertas Americana medal, whose dies were engraved by Augustin Dupré in Paris in 1782 from a concept and mottoes proposed by Benjamin Franklin. To Franklin (then U.S. minister to France), the infant Hercules symbolized America, strangling two serpents representing the British armies at Saratoga and Yorktown. Minerva, with shield and spear, symbolized France as America's ally, keeping the British Lion at bay. Franklin presented gold examples of the medal to the French king and queen and silver strikings to their ministers, "as a monumental acknowledgment, which may go down to future ages, of the obligations we are under to this nation."

Between 100 and 125 original copper medals exist, and two dozen or more silver; the location of the two gold medals is unknown. Over the years the Paris Mint has issued restrikes that are appreciated and collected at a fraction of the cost for originals.

	PF-50	PF-60	PF-63	PF-65
Libertas Americana medal, Proof, Copper (a)	$8,000	$12,500	$18,000	$45,000
Libertas Americana medal, Proof, Silver (b)	$40,000	$80,000	$120,000	$150,000

a. 100 to 125 examples are known. **b.** At least 24 examples are known.

Half Cents
1793–1857

This survey of U.S. half cents is based on the work of Q. David Bowers, a numismatic professional, and author in the field, for more than 60 years.

COLLECTING HALF CENTS

THE SMALLEST U.S. DENOMINATION

Copper half cents, the smallest denomination ever made in the United States, were first struck in the summer of 1793, under the provisions of the Mint Act of April 2, 1792. For the first several years, production was extensive—as the Treasury department envisioned that the half cent would become a very useful coin on the American scene. However, demand proved to be less than was anticipated, and after 1795 production fell off sharply. The production of copper coins was a profitable operation for the Mint, unlike silver and gold coinage, which was mainly an accommodation to depositors. In making coppers for its own account, striking a single cent instead of two half cents represented an efficiency. Until 1857 the half cent remained part of the American coinage scene, but production was intermittent, and today many varieties are very scarce.

Indeed, there were many dates that never appeared on half cents: 1798, 1799, 1801, 1812 to 1824, 1827, 1830, and 1837 to 1839. Sometimes, half cents were coined in calendar years, such as a delivery of 12,170 in 1799, but from dies bearing earlier dates.[1] The mintage was limited solely to Proofs for collectors in the years 1836, 1840 to 1848, and 1852. Only 2,200 half cents dated 1831 were struck; all of them seem to have mirrored surfaces but were not specifically intended for numismatists, who in any event were small in number at that early time.

LIMITED USE IN COMMERCE

During the era that half cents were coined, many products and services were priced in figures that ended in a half cent, such as 12-1/2¢, or 37-1/2¢. This was not due to the availability of half cent coins but, instead, was a result of the *silver* coinage of the era: the Spanish-American real or *bit*, valued at 12-1/2¢, was a popular coinage unit, and the quarter dollar or *two-bits* (which became a nickname for the federal quarter dollar as well) was seen more often than were Uncle Sam's 25¢ pieces. A storefront museum in New York City charging 12-1/2¢ admission expected patrons to tender a silver bit worth that amount, not, for example, a United States dime, two copper cents, and a half cent.

Now and again the Mint would get special requests for half cents, most notably an order on May 11, 1832, by Washington Cilley, of New York City, for the immense quantity of 400,000.[2] It could be that this spurred additional coinages for the next several years, but if that order was filled, a large inventory remained.

As was true of most other federal coins, half cents were familiar to citizens in their time of production (1793 to 1857) and were so ordinary that few people stopped to record them. Accordingly, you can read hundreds if not thousands of newspaper articles, scenes of everyday American life, and more, and not come across a single mention of a half cent coin being in a change drawer or purse, or being spent in circulation. What was everybody's business in, say, 1804, is nobody's business now, for contemporary writers ignored the commonplace.

Examples of half cents in existence today tell us that these pieces were indeed used, and used intensely, especially for pieces dated from 1793 through 1811 (after which there was a long gap in which none were made), as today grades such as Good, Very Good, and Fine are normal for such years. However, in comparison to cents, mintages were small.

Half cents of later decades (starting with 1825, when coinage resumed) tended to circulate very little, and today examples dated from the 1820s are most often seen in grades such as Extremely Fine or About Uncirculated. Finally, in January 1857, half cents were produced for the last time. However, James Ross Snowden, the director of the Mint, noted a few years later in his book *A Description of Ancient and Modern Coins in the Cabinet of the Mint of the United States* that most 1857-dated coins were held back at the Mint and melted.[3]

DESIGNS OF HALF CENTS

Half cents were produced in a variety of designs, more or less following those used on large copper cents (except for the first year, 1793) and often lagging behind the year in which a given motif was first used on the cent. For example, the Draped Bust obverse made its debut on cent pieces in 1796, but it was not until 1800 that this style of half cent appeared. On the half cent the Classic Head motif was used as late as 1836, but in the cent series the last year it was employed was 1814.

Here is an example of the half cent's predecessor, the British halfpenny. Whereas this coin features a portrait of King George III, every United States half cent bears an allegorical portrait of Liberty.

The designs of half cents included these, listed here with a comparison of their dates of use on cent pieces:

1793: Liberty Cap, Head Facing Left (not used on cents)

1794: Liberty Cap, Head Facing Right, Large Head (used on cents from 1793 to 1796)

1795–1797: Liberty Cap, Head Facing Right, Small Head (similar in style to cents of 1795)

1800–1808: Draped Bust (used on cents from 1796 to 1807)

1809–1836: Classic Head (used on cents from 1808 to 1814)

1840–1857: Braided Hair (used on cents from 1839 to 1857)

WAYS TO COLLECT

While over the years the half cent has been a focus of attention for many serious numismatists, the denomination has never been in the mainstream of popularity. The main reason is probably the presence of many formidable rarities, including the famous 1796 half cent (which exists in two die varieties—with pole to the liberty cap and without pole, the latter an engraving error), the 1831 and 1836 half cents, and the string of Proofs produced from 1840 through 1848 and again in 1852, with no related circulation strikes. The passion of American numismatists to acquire long sequences of dates is thwarted by the many interruptions in the series. The unintended benefit for numismatists is that in many instances high-grade and very rare half cents can be purchased today at prices much lower than those for copper cents of comparable rarity or, for that matter, for contemporary silver coins.

Today, the main market of half cents is from collectors who desire one nice example of each major *design type*. This is a very doable challenge, as all are readily available except for the 1793 half cent, which stands alone as the only year of its design and is somewhat scarce and expensive.

Beyond that, other numismatists aspire to collect half cents by basic dates and major varieties, such as those listed in the regular edition of *A Guide Book of United States Coins* (the Red Book). Still beyond that, specialists endeavor to collect by die varieties as listed by Roger S. Cohen Jr. and Walter Breen in their texts. Some collectors concentrate on a specific era of coinage, such as early issues, or, in some instances, on a particular year—1804, for example, which yields a dozen die combinations and many die states (showing development and progression of cracks, breaks, relapping, and die deterioration). In addition, there are a few collectors who specialize in collecting error half cents or even varieties by different die rotation positions or die states—1804, Crosslet 4 "Spiked Chin," Stems to Wreath (BW-4), has a nearly unlimited number of die states, for example. Misstruck coins and other mint errors are widely desired.

BOOKS ABOUT HALF CENTS

The die varieties and characteristics of half cents have commanded the attention of several scholars and writers who have published articles and a handful of books about them. In the latter category is Édouard Frossard's *United States Cents and Half Cents Issued Between the Years of 1793 and 1857*, published in 1879. The next notable comprehensive study of die varieties was Ebenezer Gilbert's 1916 book *United States Half Cents*, which was used by several generations of numismatists, who attributed varieties by "G" numbers, such as 1793 G-2, for a particular die variety struck during the first year of issue, G-2 being one of four varieties known of that date. Some old-time collectors still use Gilbert numbers today.

Quietly, a Maryland accountant named Roger S. Cohen Jr. enjoyed collecting and studying this denomination over a long period of years. In 1971 his book *American Half Cents: "The Little Half Sisters"* reached print to the extent of about 2,000 copies, followed by a second edition in 1982.[4] Cohen concentrated mainly on issues made for circulation, although he gave light treatment to the large panorama of Proofs produced for collectors, most notably for the dates 1831, 1836, 1840 to 1848, and 1852. These are classified in the back of the book under "Other Half Cents." Moreover, Cohen sought to illustrate his study with worn examples, often lacking detail, with the rationale that these were what the typical person might collect. This, in effect, was an everyman's guide to half cents. Cohen designations or "C" numbers began to be used, often supplanting the Gilbert numbers that had been popular for such a long time, as the Gilbert book was long out of print. Today, the Gilbert numbers have all but disappeared in use, although sometimes they are cross-referenced.

Jack H. Robinson's popular *Copper Quotes by Robinson*, launched in 1982, and now in its 19th edition, does not list Proofs. The rationale for this is that Proof-only half cents are all very rare, and a nice collection can be formed by concentrating on circulation issues. As Proofs represent a different method of manufacture, this can be an additional rationale. However, in other series, Proof-only dates are collected as part of a complete set. One of many examples is the Shield nickel type from 1866 to 1883, in which the 1877 and 1878 were made only in Proof format.

After losing his original manuscript, Walter Breen was forced to start over from scratch and eventually compiled a masterpiece published in 1983 under the direction of Jack Collins and with the help of Alan Meghrig: *Walter Breen's Encyclopedia of United States Half Cents 1793–1857*. For this book—a magnificent tome of more than 500 pages in length, with superb illustrations and on coated paper—Breen outdid himself, including more minutiae than most readers thought existed! Breen's text introduced "B" numbers.

Almost immediately after Breen's book was produced, many collectors felt compelled to declare their allegiance to either the older Cohen text, viewed as very easy to use, or the almost overwhelming new effort by Breen. Some dealers and collectors refused to use the new Breen numbers. However, in time these feelings faded, and today most people who are deeply involved in the half cent series find both books to be very useful. For the specialist interested in such arcane but interesting byways as striking methods, planchet sources and characteristics, and extensive descriptions of particularly notable individual examples, the Breen book is foundational. The politics of the matter are beyond the purview of the present book.

A later addition to the literature is the grand opus of Ronald P. Manley, *The Half Cent Die State Book 1793–1857*, published in 1998. This text goes beyond Breen and Cohen and concentrates on the various *states* of the dies, including cracks, buckling, breakage, and more, with sage comments on what the author observed. The entire work is illustrated with enlarged photographs. Circulation strikes, not Proofs, are discussed, and for this reason the Cohen numbers are given precedence in the text, with Breen numbers mentioned in a subsidiary role. This essential book was meant to be used with the Cohen and Breen books, not to supersede them.

EARLY AMERICAN COPPERS AND FELLOWSHIP

The bimonthly journal *Penny-Wise*, published by the numismatic society Early American Coppers, serves as a forum for critiques of past studies (the Breen book in particular), announcements of new discoveries, market updates, and various commentaries and articles on half cents, including much information not available elsewhere. In recent years the editor has been Harry E. Salyards, a man who combines intellectual depth with an appreciation for what the public enjoys to create an editorial mix somewhat reminiscent of another physician, George F. Heath, who founded *The Numismatist* in 1888 and remained with the journal through his death in 1908.

The pleasure of collecting is always enhanced by having good friends engaged in the same pursuit. Although the number of half cent specialists is small in comparison to those collecting large copper cents, there are still enough enthusiasts that there is no lack of opportunity to share a prized new acquisition, inquire about a die variety, or simply "talk coins."

HOW TO USE THIS SECTION

The coins in this study are organized by year of issue. However, within each year-by-year section, the die varieties are not listed chronologically. The use of Bowers-Whitman or "BW" numbers is a convenience to readers in cross-referencing half cents within each year-by-year section of the text, as these numbers begin anew in each section.

Charts giving typical values for the half cents of one year may appear at the beginning of the catalog for that year. Some coins are priced individually in charts following their catalog entries.

LIBERTY CAP, HEAD FACING LEFT (1793)

Designer: *Henry Voigt.* **Weight:** *104 grains (6.74 grams).* **Composition:** *Copper.*
Diameter: *21.2 to 24.6 mm.* **Edge:** *Lettered TWO HUNDRED FOR A DOLLAR.*

1793 (Bowers-Whitman–4,
Cohen-4, Breen-4).

The 1793 half cent, the key issue of the six major half cent types, is the only year of its design, with Miss Liberty facing left and a liberty cap on a pole behind her head, this cap being the ancient *pilaeus*, or symbol of freedom. The motif was adapted from Augustin Dupré's Libertas Americana medal, created in Paris in 1782 by commission from Benjamin Franklin. Soon after these half cents were struck, with the first delivery being on July 20, the Liberty Cap design was employed on the large copper cent, but with Miss Liberty facing to the right.

Augustin Dupré's famous Libertas Americana struck in France under a commission given by Benjamin Franklin. This inspired the Liberty Cap motif used on half cents and cents beginning in 1793. This impression is in silver.

The Liberté Françoise medal by Andre Galle, struck in bell metal and issued in 1792 for a reunion of French artists held in Lyon, has a similar motif, obviously adapted from the preceding, on which Miss Liberty faces to the left (as on the half cent).

Coiner Henry Voigt cut the dies for the 1793 half cents. The same motif, but slightly differently styled and with the head facing the other way, is thought to have been used by Joseph Wright for the 1793 Liberty Cap cents.

Not only is the 1793 half cent one of a kind as a design type, but it has the further cachet of being the first year of the denomination and a key date as well—it is elusive in all grades. Accordingly, the possession of an attractive 1793 half cent has been a badge of distinction for many accomplished numismatists.

Design Details

As noted, the obverse features the head of Miss Liberty, facing left, with a liberty cap on a pole behind her head. LIBERTY is above, curved along the border. The date 1793 is between the neck truncation and the border. A circle of raised beads is around the border on both sides a short distance in from the rim. Such beads were not used on half cents of later years.

The reverse displays a wreath open at the top and tied with a ribbon bow below. Among the wreath leaves are *sprays of berries*, the only use of this feature in the series. Around the border is the inscription UNITED STATES OF AMERICA. At the center in two lines is HALF / CENT. The fraction 1/200 is below the ribbon bow.

The 1793 half cent gives the denomination *three times:* as HALF / CENT and 1/200 on the reverse and as TWO HUNDRED FOR A DOLLAR on the edge. The same triple denomination feature is found on several other early copper types. Interestingly, during this decade no mark of value at all is found on certain other denominations—such as the silver half dime, dime, and quarter, and all gold coins!

GRADING STANDARDS

MS-60 to 65 (Mint State). *Obverse:* In the lower ranges, MS-60 and 61, some light abrasions can be seen on the higher areas of the portrait. Luster in the field is incomplete, particularly in the center of the open areas. At the MS-63 level, luster should be complete, with no abrasions evident. In higher levels, the luster is deeper, and some original mint color may be seen. *Reverse:* In the lower ranges some

1793; Bowers-Whitman–3, Cohen-3, Breen-3. Graded MS-60BN.

abrasions are seen on the higher areas of the leaves. Generally, luster is complete in all ranges, as the open areas are protected by the lettering and wreath. Otherwise, the same comments apply as for the obverse.

Illustrated coin: Well struck and nicely centered on the planchet, this example shows no sign of wear. Its color is a rich orange-brown overall, with a bit of darker gray-brown on the lower-right edge and field of the obverse. The faint roughness on the obverse is a flaw of the original planchet, and is not related to wear.

AU-50, 53, 55, 58 (About Uncirculated).
Obverse: Friction is seen on the higher parts, particularly on the rounded cheek and on the higher strands of the hair. Friction and scattered marks are in the field, ranging from extensive at AU-50 to minimal at AU-58. Luster may be seen in protected areas, minimal at AU-50, but sometimes extensive on an AU-58 coin. Border beads, if well struck, are separate and boldly defined. *Reverse:* Friction

1793; BW-3, C-3, B-3. Graded AU-50.

is seen on the higher wreath leaves and (not as easy to discern) on the letters. The fields, protected by the designs, show friction, but not as noticeably as on the obverse. At AU-55 and 58 little if any friction is seen. The reverse may have original luster, toned brown, minimal on lower About Uncirculated grades, sometimes extensive at AU-58. Border beads, if well struck, are separate and boldly defined. Grading at the About Uncirculated level is mainly done by viewing the obverse.

Illustrated coin: This grade would probably be viewed as conservative by many. A well-struck coin with excellent detail in most areas, but with the beads light on the right obverse rim. Light wear is seen on the higher areas.

EF-40, 45 (Extremely Fine). *Obverse:* Wear is seen on the portrait overall, with reduction or elimination of some separation of hair strands on the highest part. The cheek is ever so slightly flat on the highest part. Some leaves will retain some detail, especially where they join the stems. Luster is minimal or non-existent at EF-40 and may survive in traces in protected areas at EF-45. *Reverse:* Wear is seen on the highest wreath and rib-

1793; BW-2, C-2, B-2. Graded EF-40, perhaps conservatively.

bon areas and the letters. Luster is minimal, but likely more noticeable than on the obverse, as the fields are protected by the designs and lettering.

Illustrated coin: The coin has decent strike on both sides except for some blending of border beads, not unusual at this level.

VF-20, 30 (Very Fine). *Obverse:* Wear on the portrait has reduced the hair detail to indistinct or flat at the center on a VF-20 coin, with slightly more detail at VF-30. The thin, horizontal (more or less) ribbon near the top of the hair is distinct. The border beads are blended together, with many blurred or missing. No luster is seen. *Reverse:* The leaf details are nearly completely worn away at VF-20, and with slight detail at VF-30. The

1793; BW-1, C-1, B-1. Graded VF-30.

border beads are blended together, with many indistinct. Some berries in the sprays may be worn away, depending on the strike (on strong strikes they can be seen down into Very Good and Good grades). No luster is seen. HALF CENT may be weak, but is fully readable, on certain coins (such as BW-1, C-1, B-1) in which this feature was shallowly cut into the dies.

Illustrated coin: A sharp coin, with lightly granular surfaces. HALF CENT is weak on the reverse due to striking, not to wear.

F-12, 15 (Fine). *Obverse:* The hair details are mostly worn away, with about one-third visible, mainly at the edges. Border beads are weak or worn away in areas. F-15 shows slightly more detail. *Reverse:* The wreath leaves are worn flat, but their edges are distinct. HALF CENT may be missing on 1793 (Bowers-Whitman–1)—also true of lower grades given below. Border beads are weak or worn away in areas. F-15 shows slightly more detail.

1793; BW-2, C-2, B-2. Graded F-15.

Illustrated coin: Scattered planchet flaws from the strip-rolling process are not unusual, but must be mentioned. The reverse, if graded alone, might be considered a VF.

VG-8, 10 (Very Good). *Obverse:* The portrait is well worn, although the eye can be seen, and the hair tips at the right show separation. Border beads are worn away, and the border blends into the field in most if not all of the periphery. LIBERTY and 1793 are bold. VG-10, not an official ANA grading designation, is sometimes applied to especially nice Very Good coins. *Reverse:* The wreath, bow, and lettering are seen in outline

1793; BW-2, C-2, B-2. Graded VG-8.

form, and some leaves and letters may be indistinct in parts. Border beads are worn away, and the border blends into the field in most if not all of the periphery.

Illustrated coin: Raised rim beads are gone, and rim blends into the field in areas. The outside areas of the letters are worn.

G-4, 6 (Good). *Obverse:* The portrait is worn smooth and is seen only in outline form, although the eye position can be discerned. LIBERTY and 1793 are complete, although the date may be weak. *Reverse:* Extensive wear is seen overall. From half to two-thirds of the letters in UNITED STATES OF AMERICA and the fraction numerals are worn away. The reverse shows more evidence of wear than does the obverse,

1793; BW-3, C-3, B-3. Graded G-6.

and is key in assigning this grade. G-6 is often assigned to finer examples in this category.

Illustrated coin: A well-worn example, but one showing the portrait, LIBERTY, and date very clearly. The reverse shows fewer details.

AG-3 (About Good). *Obverse:* Wear is more extensive than on the preceding. The portrait is visible only in outline. LIBERTY is weak but usually fully discernible. 1793 is weak, and the bottoms of the digits may be worn away. *Reverse:* Parts of the wreath are visible in outline form, and all but a few letters are gone. Grading of AG-3 is usually done by the reverse.

1793; BW-2, C-2, B-2. Graded AG-3.

Illustrated coin: This is a well-worn and somewhat porous example.

Fair-2 (Fair). *Obverse:* Worn nearly smooth. Date is partly visible, not necessarily clearly. Head of Miss Liberty is in outline form. Some letters of LIBERTY are discernible. *Reverse:* Worn nearly smooth. Peripheral letters are nearly all gone, with only vestiges remaining. Wreath is in outline form. HALF CENT ranges from readable to missing (the latter on certain die varieties as struck).

1793. Graded Fair-2.

Illustrated coin: This coin is well worn and granular, but identifiable as to date and distinctive type.

1793, Liberty Cap, Head Facing Left

Mintage (per *Mint Report*): 35,334.

The 1793 half cent is among the most famous of United States design types, as the Liberty Cap, Head Facing Left motif was made only in this year. Accordingly, there has always been a strong demand for them. The appearance of a high-grade example is always a notable occasion.

Most 1793 half cents are fairly decent in appearance, although some, particularly of Bowers-Whitman–1, have light striking, due to the die, of the words HALF / CENT on the reverse. For BW-1 it is not unusual for a piece to be in, say, Fine grade with all features distinct, except with scarcely a trace of the denomination. Such pieces should be avoided if you are seeking a single coin for type, as enough examples of other varieties occur with full lettering. Planchet quality is another aspect, and sometimes rifts and fissures are encountered. Other half cents may have rim bruises. The use of "BW" numbers is a convenience to readers in cross-referencing half cents within each year-by-year section of the text, as they do not run in continuous order throughout the text.

Somewhat more than 1,000 1793 half cents are estimated to exist, most of which are in grades from AG-3 to F-12. At these levels, many are dark and porous. Cherrypicking of quality is advised. At the VF and EF levels the 1793 is scarce, but enough exist that market appearances occur often. Eye appeal tends to be higher, but there are many exceptions. True AU and Mint State coins range from scarce to very rare. Most of these are very attractive.

The copper for the 1793 half cent was of good quality, giving a pleasing, light-brown, smooth planchet to nearly all examples (in sharp contrast with the next year). Over the years a number of pieces have been variously described as AU or Uncirculated, and some of these are truly beautiful to behold and, better yet, to own. As a general rule, high-grade pieces typically have lustrous light-brown surfaces but little if anything in way of *original* mint red.

There are four die combinations of the 1793 half cent which are of interest to dedicated specialists. These combine two different obverse dies with three different reverses. All are collectible and of about the same rarity and market value, although availability varies in certain grades.

Typical values for 1793 half cents.

	Cert	Avg	%MS	AG-3	G-4	VG-8	F-12	VF-20	EF-40	AU-50	MS-60BN	MS-63BN
1793	162	32.9	9%	$1,250	$3,000	$5,750	$9,500	$14,000	$25,500	$40,000	$67,500	$100,000

1793 • Bowers-Whitman–1, Cohen-1, Breen-1 *Breen dies:* 1-A. **Estimated population:** 250 to 300.

Obverse: L in LIBERTY on same level as I; L over forehead. Bottom of 7 closer to rim than bottom of 9. No center dot. The bottom edge of the bust is smoothly curved on this variety. *Points of distinction:* The obverse develops rust streaks, but no cracks or breaks.

Reverse: *Left branch:* 15 leaves, 10 sprays of berries. *Right branch:* 16 leaves, 10 sprays of berries. Period after AMERICA. The center of the reverse was cut shallowly in the die, with the result that even high-grade examples are apt to show HALF / CENT lightly defined, and once wear took place, the inscription often partially or completely disappeared. *Points of distinction:* The reverse in its latest and very rare state has a rim cud over F AME extending only into the denticles.

1793 (Bowers-Whitman–1, Cohen-1, Breen-1).

Detail of period after AMERICA.

Notes: This variety exists in Mint State, but it is very rare as such. *Gilbert* (1916) G-4 "Letter L entirely over forehead / 15 leaves on left branch, 16 leaves on right." This is considered by some to be the rarest of the four varieties of the year. However, Bill Eckberg and Tom Reynolds studied the matter and found all four varieties of the year to be about the same rarity, averaging an estimated 300 or so of each.[5] Usually seen in lower grades, although a few EF and AU coins appear now and again. This is the first 1793 half cent variety struck, a variety desired by type collectors who seek first-year-of-issue pieces.

1793 • BW-2, C-2, B-2. *Breen dies:* 1-B. *Estimated population:* 275 to 350.

Obverse: Same die as preceding. *Points of distinction:* A little spur or die defect develops at the upper left of the 9.

Reverse: *Left branch:* 15 leaves, 8 sprays of berries. *Right branch:* 15 leaves, 9 sprays of berries. Heavy center dot above left upright of N in CENT. Ribbon ends crowd fraction;

1793 (BW-2, C-2, B-2).

bar curved downward; 2 high. Ribbon ends crowd fraction; bar curved downward; 2 high.

Notes: This variety exists in Mint State, but it is very rare as such. *Gilbert* (1916) G-3 "Letter L entirely over forehead / 15 leaves on each branch." The dies are often misaligned.

1793 • BW-3, C-3, B-3. *Breen dies:* 2-B. *Estimated population:* 275 to 350.

Obverse: L lower than I; L over junction of forehead and hair. Bottom of 9 closer to rim than bottom of 7. The bottom edge of the bust is sharply "hooked."

Reverse: Same die as preceding.

Notes: This variety exists in Mint State, but it is rare as such. *Gilbert* (1916) G-1 "Low L partly over hair / 15 leaves on each branch of wreath."

1793 (BW-3, C-3, B-3).

1793 • BW-4, C-4, B-4. *Breen dies:* 2-C. *Estimated population:* 275 to 350.

Obverse: Same die as preceding. *Points of distinction:* Clash marks develop as the die is used.

Reverse: *Left branch:* 13 leaves, 9 sprays of berries. *Right branch:* 14 leaves, 10 sprays of berries. Light center dot above upper left of N. *Points of distinction:* Light clash marks develop.

1793 (BW-4, C-4, B-4).

Notes: This variety exists in Mint State, but it is rare as such. *Gilbert* (1916) G-2 "Low L partly over hair / 13 leaves on left branch, 14 on right." This is the most often seen die combination and also the variety most often seen in grades of AU and above. Sometimes on planchets that are slightly wider than normal. Walter Breen writes of "presentation pieces," but elsewhere no information is found about this.

LIBERTY CAP, HEAD FACING RIGHT (1794–1797)

Designer: *Robert Scot.* **Weight:** *104 grains (6.74 grams) for thick planchet, lettered edge varieties (including all of 1794 and two of 1795); variable weights for other examples struck on planchets cut down from misstruck large cents or Talbot, Allum & Lee tokens (each bearing the denomination states as "one cent"); 84 grains (5.44 grams) for plain edge varieties as well as the lettered edge 1797 variety. The figures given are statutory weights. Actual weights usually vary.* **Composition:** *Copper.* **Diameter:** *23.5 mm.* **Edge:** *Lettered TWO HUNDRED FOR A DOLLAR on all of 1794, some of 1795, and one variety of 1797; plain edge on some of 1795, all of 1796, and most of 1797. One variety of 1797 has a gripped edge with indentations.*

1794, High Relief Head
(BW-9, C-9, B-9).

Half cents of this type are remarkably diverse. The portraits are in two distinctive sizes, and planchets are of two different formats, plus some variations. As a general type such coins are readily available, the most often seen being pieces dated 1795. The quality of striking and the appearance of surviving pieces is subject to wide variation. Overall, these factors create a very interesting section within the half cent denomination.

TALBOT, ALLUM & LEE

In 1795 the Mint experienced a shortage of copper, and to satisfy the demand the Mint purchased many thousands of undistributed cent-size advertising tokens minted by Peter Kempson & Co., Birmingham, England, and imported them into America by the New York City firm of Talbot, Allum & Lee. Dated 1794 and 1795, these bore the image of the standing goddess of Commerce on the obverse and a fully rigged sailing ship on the reverse. Each was denominated "ONE CENT."

At the Mint, half cent planchets were cut from them, much as a cookie cutter might take a circle of dough from a larger piece. Fed into the coining press, the planchets became half cents, but in many instances the parts of the original design of the token can still be seen in the fields or even on the edges, creating interesting undertypes for collectors. Some half cents of 1795 and 1797 show this feature.

DESIGN DETAILS

The type of 1794 with *Large* Liberty Head Facing Right, Liberty Cap behind head, is very distinctive. As to whether it should be considered as a basic type, or simply as a sub-type to be included with the issues from 1795 to 1797, as here, is a matter of opinion, and you can make your own decision.

The obverse of the 1794 half cent features Miss Liberty with a *large* Liberty Head facing right, with a liberty cap on a pole behind her head. LIBERTY is above, curved along the border. The date is between the neck truncation and the border. Portrait styles vary, and the regular-edition *Guide Book of United States Coins* lists a "High Relief" head and a "Normal Head" for 1794. These are considered distinctive styles within the present type. It is thought that Robert Scot was the engraver of the portrait and wreath hubs.

The half cents 1795 to 1797 have a *small* Liberty Head facing right, but are otherwise similar in general style to the 1794. Unlike the type of 1794, half cents of the years 1795 to 1797, with small head, have a cameo-like appearance, with the portrait surrounded by an especially large area of open field. On certain varieties, the denticles are especially large and prominent, nicely framing the interior features. Engraving may have been by John Smith Gardner, an assistant to Robert Scot, or may have been by or shared with Scot.

GRADING STANDARDS

MS-60 to 70 (Mint State). *Obverse:* On MS-60 and 61 coins there are some traces of abrasion on the higher areas of the portrait. Luster in the field is incomplete, particularly in the center of the open areas. At MS-63, luster should be complete, and no abrasion is evident. At higher levels, the luster is deeper, and some original mint color may be seen. At MS-65 there are some scattered contact marks and possibly some traces of finger-

1794; BW-9, C-9, B-9. Graded MS-65.

prints or discoloration, but these should be minimal and not at all distracting. Above MS-65, a coin should approach perfection. *Reverse:* In the lower ranges some abrasions are seen on the higher areas of the leaves. Generally, luster is complete in all ranges, as the open areas are protected by the lettering and wreath. Otherwise, the same comments apply as for the obverse.

    Illustrated coin: A spectacular coin of a year seldom seen in Mint State. Both sides have rich, brown surfaces. On the obverse the luster is light, while on the reverse it is not as noticeable. Note that the obverse die is in very high relief and of the Large Head style, while the reverse is in shallower relief.

AU-50, 53, 55, 58 (About Uncirculated). *Obverse:* Friction is seen on the higher parts, particularly the center of the portrait. Friction and scattered marks are in the field, ranging from extensive at AU-50 to minimal at AU-58. To reiterate: knowledge of the die variety is important. For certain shallow-relief dies (such as those of 1797) an About Uncirculated coin may appear to be in a lower grade. Luster may be seen in protected

1797, 1 Over 1; BW-1, C-1, B-1. Graded AU-58.

areas, minimal at AU-50, but sometimes extensive on an AU-58 coin. *Reverse:* Friction is seen on the higher wreath leaves and (not as easy to discern) on the letters. The fields, protected by the designs, show friction, but not as noticeably as on the obverse. At AU-55 and 58 little if any friction is seen. The reverse may have original luster, toned brown, minimal on lower About Uncirculated grades, sometimes extensive on higher. Grading at the About Uncirculated level is mainly done by viewing the obverse.

    Illustrated coin: This coin has lustrous light-brown surfaces. It was struck from a buckled and cracked obverse die. A decent strike overall, with excellent eye appeal—rare for this date, although this particular variety is often seen nicer than most others of the year.

EF-40, 45 (Extremely Fine). *Obverse:* Wear is seen on the portrait overall, with some reduction or elimination of the separation of hair strands on the highest part. This varies by die variety, as some are better delineated than others. The cheek shows light wear. Luster is minimal or nonexistent at EF-40, and may survive in traces in protected areas (such as between the letters) at EF-45. *Reverse:* Wear is seen on the highest wreath

1794; BW-1a, C-1a, B-1a. Graded EF-45.

and ribbon areas and the letters. Luster is minimal, but likely more noticeable than on the obverse, as the fields are protected by the designs and lettering. Sharpness will vary depending on the die variety. Expect certain issues of 1794 and 1797 to be lighter.

Illustrated coin: This coin's dies were cut in shallow relief and with low rims. This makes the coin much less sharp overall than the one illustrated for Mint State.

VF-20, 30 (Very Fine). *Obverse:* Wear on the portrait has reduced the hair detail to indistinct or flat at the center. The border denticles are blended together, with many indistinct. No luster is seen. Again, knowing details of the die variety is important. A VF-20 or 30 1797 is very different in appearance from a 1794, Large Head, in the same grade. *Reverse:* The leaf details are nearly completely worn away at VF-20, with slight

1795; BW-5, C-4, B-4; date punctuated as "1,795" due to a die flaw; plain edge. Graded VF-20.

detail at VF-30. The border denticles are blended together, with many indistinct. No luster is seen. The sharpness of details depends on the die variety. Half cents of 1797 require special care in their study.

Illustrated coin: The denticles are prominent on the left side of the obverse, from light to missing at the right side. The center of HALF CENT is slightly light due to the die, not to wear. The die is sunken at ER of AMERICA, as made.

F-12, 15 (Fine). *Obverse:* The hair details are mostly worn away, with about one-third visible, mainly at the edges. Border denticles are weak or worn away in areas. F-15 shows slightly more detail. *Reverse:* The wreath leaves are worn flat, but their edges are distinct. Border denticles are weak or worn away in areas. F-15 shows slightly more detail.

1795; BW-4, C-3, B-3; date punctuated as "1,795" due to a die flaw. Graded F-15.

VG-8, 10 (Very Good). *Obverse:* The portrait is well worn, although the eye can be seen, and the hair tips at the left show separation. Border denticles are worn away on some issues (not as much for 1795 coins), and the border blends into the field in most if not all of the periphery. LIBERTY and the date are bold. VG-10, not an official ANA grading designation, is sometimes applied to especially nice Very Good coins. *Reverse:* The

1794; BW-2, C-2b, B-2a. Graded VG-10.

wreath, bow, and lettering are seen in outline form, and some leaves and letters may be indistinct in parts. Border denticles are worn away, and the border blends into the field in most if not all of the periphery. In certain die varieties and die states, especially of 1797, some letters may be very weak or missing.

Illustrated coin: This coin has fairly strong features overall for the grade, and some granularity.

G-4, 6 (Good). *Obverse:* The portrait is worn smooth and is seen only in outline form, although the eye position can be discerned. LIBERTY and the date are complete, although the date may be weak. Denticles are gone on some, but not all, die varieties. *Reverse:* Extensive wear is seen overall. From half to two-thirds of the letters in UNITED STATES OF AMERICA, and the fraction numerals, are worn away. Certain shallow-

1795; BW-1, C-1, B-1. Graded G-4.

relief dies may have letters missing. G-6 is often assigned to finer examples in this category.

Illustrated coin: This coin shows smooth, even wear. It was struck on a dark planchet. HALF CENT is light due to being shallowly cut in the die.

AG-3 (About Good). *Obverse:* Wear is more extensive than on the preceding. The portrait is visible only in outline. LIBERTY is weak but usually fully discernible. The date is weak, and the bottoms of the digits may be worn away. *Reverse:* Parts of the wreath are visible in outline form, and all but a few letters are gone. Grading of AG-3 is usually done by the reverse, as the obverse typically appears to be in a slightly higher grade. If

1795; BW-5, C-4, B-4; date punctuated as "1,795" due to a die flaw. Graded AG-3.

split grading were used, more than just a few half cents of this type could be designated as G-4 / AG-3 or even G-6 / AG-3.

Illustrated coin: The obverse, if graded separately, would be a clear G-4 or even G-6, but with some light scratches. The reverse is worn down to AG-3.

1794, Liberty Cap, Large Head Facing Right

Mintage (per *Mint Report*): 81,600.

Half cents of this date are a distinct type, Liberty Cap, Large Head Facing Right. The key is *Large*, as the later years of this general style (1795 to 1797) all have a Small Head. Five different obverse dies and a like number of reverse dies were made, yielding nine different combinations. The obverse dies can vary widely in their appearance, some with the head in high relief, others with a low-relief portrait. The use of hub punches was in its beginning stages. The boldness of the letters and numerals can vary as well.

The reverse wreaths fall into two main categories: What Walter Breen calls the Heavy Wreath is the earlier style and is more "solid" in its appearance. The Cent Type Wreath is lighter and somewhat delicate; berries and stems were added by hand, as were some leaves, giving differences in placement among the various dies. Lettering was punched in by hand as well, as were the fraction details.

Certain varieties exist with both large and small edge letters, designated respectively as "a" and "b" in the text below, following the method of Roger S. Cohen Jr. This does not necessarily reflect the order in which they were struck.

Half cents of 1794 have a personality all of their own. Generally, they were struck on rough planchets, granular, and—if not dark and spotted at the time of use—certainly with enough metallic imperfections that such pieces quickly toned to gray or even black. Although there are some exceptions, the typical half cent of 1794 is rather rustic in its appearance, not particularly well struck, and somewhat porous. Finding one with nice eye appeal can be a challenge—much more so than for the 1793.

Not many 1794 half cents have survived in higher grades. Typically encountered are pieces in Good, VG, and Fine, not often VF, and hardly ever EF or finer. No matter what the grade, aesthetic appeal is apt to be low—a factor that numismatists have to live with, although some examples are nicer than others. However, you do have the market advantage that not everyone considers the 1794 to be a separate type, and, beyond that, relatively few non-specialists are aware of the rarity of pieces with good eye appeal.

Mint State coins are exceedingly rare—far rarer than the famous 1793, although this is not well known. Grading is apt to be liberal.

Typical values for 1794 half cents. Rare varieties may be worth more.

	Cert	Avg	%MS	AG-3	G-4	VG-8	F-12	VF-20	EF-40	AU-50	MS-60BN	MS-63BN
1794	195	34.4	10%	$300	$500	$825	$1,550	$2,750	$6,100	$14,250	$24,000	$46,250

1794 • BW-1a and b, C-1a and b, B-1a and b. *Breen dies:* 1-A. **Estimated population:** BW-1a: 350 to 500; BW-1b: 23 to 30.

Obverse: Date low, double punched, and very widely spaced, far below neck, giving this die a very distinctive appearance. The 4 much closer to denticles than to portrait. The pole is weak and is distant from denticles. Head high in field, especially the bottom of the hair.

Reverse: Heavy Wreath. 15 leaves on each branch. 4 berries on left branch and 4 on the right. *Points of distinction:* On a few pieces swelling is seen at the top of the wreath.

1794 (BW-1a, C-1a, B-1a).

Detail of widely spaced date.

Notes: BW-1a occurs in Mint State, and is rare as such. VF or so is the highest grade known for BW-1b. *Gilbert* (1916) G-9 (without reference to edge lettering) "Head large and high—date very low / 8 berry reverse. . . . In Dr. Maris' description of half cents of this year he includes one variety that would be a combination of my Obverse No. 6 with Reverse of No. 9. Neither Steigerwalt nor Frossard mention this variety, and it is unknown to me." Large or small edge letters, designated a or b. R. Tettenhorst found that the space between the R and E of HUNDRED is much greater on the small letters issues than on the large.[6] It is not unusual for this variety to be dark or to be slightly greenish. Most are in lower grades.

1794 • BW-2a and b, C-2a and b, B-2a and b. *Breen dies:* 2-B. *Estimated population:* BW-2a: 16 to 20; BW-2b: 400 to 700.

1794 (BW-2, C-2, B-2).

Obverse: Date low and closely spaced with 94 closer than the other numerals; 1 below neck (on all other dies it is below hair); 4 slightly closer to denticles than to portrait. Pole bold and nearly touches a denticle. Portrait centered in the field. *Points of distinction:* A faint crack is seen at the tops of ERTY. Clash marks later develop, then multiply as their intensity increases.

Reverse: Heavy Wreath. 15 leaves on each branch, or 16 if you include the merest trace of leaves at each side of HALF. 5 berries on left branch and 4 on the right, or 5 if you include the merest trace of one protruding slightly from a leaf below the first A of AMERICA.

Notes: VF and EF are the highest grades known for BW-2a, and rare so fine. EF and AU are the highest grades known for BW-2b. *Gilbert* (1916) G-5 (without reference to edge lettering) "Large head, 7 of date low / 9 berry reverse." Large or small edge letters, designated a or b. This variety has a bold, pleasing portrait, well placed in the field. On later die states (Manley 2.0 and 3.0) prominent clash marks are seen in the field in front of the portrait, showing leaves from the wreath on the reverse.

1794 • BW-3a and b, C-5, B-3a and b. *Breen dies:* 3-C. *Estimated population:* BW-3a: 6 to 10;[7] BW-3b: 110 to 140.

1794 (BW-3b, C-5, B-3b).

Obverse: Date distinctively spaced as 1 79 4; low and closely spaced with 79 closer than the other numerals; 4 slightly closer to denticles than to portrait. Pole bold and nearly touches a denticle. Portrait centered in the field. (Compare to BW-1). *Points of distinction:* Perfect die examples are followed by examples with clash marks beneath the chin and in front of the throat.

Reverse: Heavy Wreath. 16 leaves on each branch. 5 berries on left branch (including one hardly visible at the first T in STATES) and 6 on the right.

Notes: Fine or so is the highest grade known for BW-3a. AU is the highest grade known for BW-3b. *Gilbert* (1916) G-8 (without reference to edge lettering) "Large head, 79 about level at top and close together / 11 berries." Large or small edge letters, designated a or b. On this variety the portrait is in especially high relief with luxuriant waves of hair and a rounded cheek, very attractive. The reverse is equally nicely styled, with a bold wreath enclosing and also within delicate letters.

1794 • BW-4a and b, C-6, B-4a and b. *Breen dies:* 3-D. *Recorded population:* BW-4a: 1. *Estimated population:* BW-4b: 30 to 40.

Obverse: Same die as preceding. *Points of distinction:* Clash marks are present, as with the earlier use.

Reverse: Cent Type Wreath. 14 leaves on left branch, 18 on the right. Leaves at apex of wreath are distant from each other. Tip of second highest leaf on left is under A.

1794 (BW-4b, C-6, B-4b).

Notes: *Gilbert* (1916) G-6 (without reference to edge lettering) "Large head, 79 about level at top and close together / 12 berries, leaf touching left stand of H." Large or small edge letters, designated a or b. The only known example of BW-4a has been graded from VG cleaned to simply Fine. It is believed to have first appeared in Abe Kosoff's sale of the Lehrman Collection, 1963, Lot 50. In the sale of the Roger S. Cohen, Jr. Collection by Superior, 1992, it was graded VG-8. The piece has been cleaned and shows extensive friction marks.[8] The highest grade known for BW-4b is EF.

1794 • BW-5a and b, C-3a and b, B-5a and b. *Breen dies:* 3-E. *Estimated population:* BW-5a: 5 to 8; BW-5b: 55 to 70.

Obverse: Same die as preceding.

Reverse: Cent Type Wreath. 14 leaves on left branch, 18 on the right. Leaves at apex of wreath touch or nearly touch. Second-highest leaf on left is under T. *Points of distinction:* The obverse is first seen with clash marks around the portrait, most notably in front of the neck. Later, mounding is seen to the right of 4.

1794 (BW-5a, C-3a, B-5a).

Notes: AU is the highest grade known for BW-5a. VF is the highest grade known for BW-5b. *Gilbert* (1916) G-7 (without reference to edge lettering) "Large head, 79 about level at top and close together / 12 berries— Leaf nearly touching top of H and another the top of T." Large or small edge letters, designated a or b.

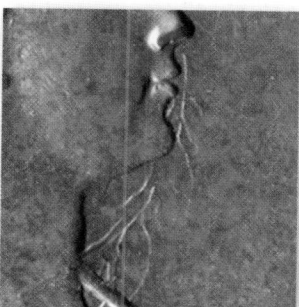

Detail of clash marks in front of the neck and mouth, showing outlined leaves from the wreath on the reverse.

1794 • BW-6a and b, C-4a and b, B-6a and b. *Breen dies:* 4-E. ***Estimated population:*** BW-6a: 10 to 12; BW-6b: 900 to 1,100.

1794 (BW-6b, C-4b, B-6b).

Obverse: Date high and heavy, 9 low and leans left, 4 close to neck. Cap very close to denticles. Pole heavy and touches denticles. ***Points of distinction:*** Clash marks are seen below the chin and in front of the neck. Later, mounding begins from the left of the date.

Reverse: Same die as preceding. ***Points of distinction:*** There is a crack from the denticles between TE of UNITED and to the leaves. Later, another crack is seen through M of AMERICA.

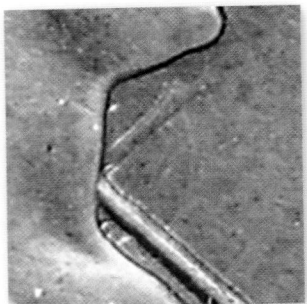

Detail of clash marks below the chin and in front of the neck.

Notes: Fine is the highest grade known for BW-6a. BW-6b exists in Mint State, but is very rare as such. *Gilbert* (1916) G-4 (without reference to edge lettering) "Large head—9 low / 12 berries with a leaf nearly touching top of H." Large or small edge letters, designated a or b. Concerning the "a" variety: eight are known to Ronald P. Manley. This variety was discovered by Commodore W.C. Eaton in 1921, after which the next was publicized by W.K. Raymond in 1973.[9] The finest is Fine. BW-6b is considered the second most common variety of the year.[10]

1794, High Relief Head • BW-7, C-7, B-7. *Breen dies:* 5-D. ***Estimated population:*** 35 to 50.

1794, High Relief Head (BW-7, C-7, B-7).

Obverse: Head in high relief, more so than for any other obverse die. This is Breen's *High Relief Head.* The cap is spaced away from the denticles. The 4 very nearly touches the neck. The pole is distant from denticles and terminates about even with the neck tip. ***Points of distinction:*** Because of the high relief, the highest details are sometimes weakly struck. Light clash marks are seen.

Detail of the date.

Reverse: Same as reverse of BW-4. ***Points of distinction:*** A crack is seen from the denticles through the right side of E of UNITED into the wreaths, causing a bulging at the same time.

Notes: Two are in Mint State, one of which is in the British Museum. *Gilbert* (1916) G-2 (without reference to edge lettering) "Small head, 4 nearly touching bust / 12 berries—Leaf touches left stand of H." Small edge letters. Most are in lower grades.

1794, High Relief Head • BW-8, C-8, B-8. *Breen dies:* 5-C. *Estimated population:* 45 to 60.

Obverse: Same die as preceding. *Points of distinction:* Delicate clash marks can be seen, mainly between the Liberty Cap and the hair.

Reverse: Same as reverse of BW-3. *Points of distinction:* Clash marks at the left. Later, on the reverse a crack develops from the denticles through the second T of STATES to the wreath, later still going farther to the right.

1794, High Relief Head (BW-8, C-8, B-8).

Notes: EF is the highest grade known, but examples are very rare at this level. *Gilbert* (1916) G-3 "Small head, 4 nearly touching bust / 11 berry reverse." Small edge letters. Most are in lower grades. An EF coin is exceptional.

1794, High Relief Head • BW-9, C-9, B-9. *Breen dies:* 5-B. *Estimated population:* 700 to 900.

Obverse: Same die as preceding. *Points of distinction:* The pole is usually rather light. First seen with no crack, but with light clash marks. In a slightly later state a crack is seen through the top of IBERTY. Another crack develops from the rim at the lower left, extending to the hair.

1794, High Relief Head (BW-9, C-9, B-9).

Reverse: Same as reverse of BW-4. *Points of distinction:* On the reverse a rim cud affecting only the denticles is to the lower left of the fraction.

Notes: Rare in Mint State, but among 1794 half cents this is the variety most often seen at this level. *Gilbert* (1916) G-1 "Small head—4 nearly touches bust / 9 berry reverse." Small edge letters. Comment from R. Tettenhorst: "Among the 1794, High Relief Head (BW-9), and 1795, Pole to Cap, Lettered Edge (BW-1), and "Punctuated Date" (1,795), Lettered Edge (BW-2), half cents there exist a few thin-planchet lettered-edge specimens. I have a speculation that these may have been test strikings to see if the appearance of the new thinner coins was satisfactory. What led to my thought was the observation that these thinner-planchet lettered-edge specimens exist only on the varieties struck after Congress approved the reduction in weight. Some 1794 BW-9s are believed to have been struck in 1795, after the approval. I do not know of any thin-planchet specimens of other 1794-dated varieties. This likely led to the Mint finding that the obverse and reverse impressions were quite acceptable, but the edge was too thin to support the lettering without running into the top and bottom of the rim to create unsightly nicks."[11] BW-9 is the most often seen variety of the year. The high relief of the head has made this an especially popular coin. Most are in lower grades. Any coin AU or finer is a rarity.

1795, Liberty Cap, Small Head Facing Right

Mintage (per *Mint Report*): 139,690.

Half cents of 1795 feature the new small Liberty Head. The engraver is unknown. It may have been Robert Scot, or there is the possibility (per Walter Breen) that an assistant, John Smith Gardner, did the work. The result was very pleasing, yielding a small portrait surrounded by a wide field and framed by prominent denticles. This style was continued through 1797.

The reported circulation-strike mintage of 139,690 for *all* 1795 half cents (lettered and plain edge varieties) may include some coins of earlier dates. It is thought that the mintage of the lettered edge pieces was 25,600. The numismatic availability of the 1795 Lettered Edge half cents is probably about a third of the total, with the Plain Edge varieties accounting for the remaining two-thirds.

The first half cents of this year were struck on thick planchets, with lettered a edge, and an authorized weight of 104 grains. Soon, the standard was changed to 84 grains, resulting in a thinner planchet, now with plain edge. However, some plain-edge half cents were struck on thick, heavy planchets cut down from misstruck large cents. Accordingly, 1795-dated half cents can be quickly grouped into two major categories: Lettered Edge and Plain Edge. Within these categories are die varieties including the popular "Punctuated Date," which has a small, comma-like die flaw after the 1, giving the fanciful appearance of 1,795.

As a rule of thumb, the Lettered Edge half cents, the rarer of the two styles, are much harder to find well struck and on smooth planchets. Many are porous and rough. In contrast, the Pole to Cap and Punctuated Date varieties of Plain Edge are often seen with superb eye appeal. The No Pole to Cap variety is from a ground-down or resurfaced die that originally had a pole. These are often poorly struck regarding details of the design or have other problems, including off-center and double impressions.

Finding a high quality 1795, Lettered Edge, will be a challenge. In contrast, enough high-grade Plain Edge examples have survived that EF, AU, or even Mint State pieces can be found with some looking.

1795, Pole to Cap, Lettered Edge •

BW-1, C-1, B-1. *Breen dies:* 1-A. *Estimated population:* 1,000 to 1,500.

Obverse: Date as I795 with I instead of 1 punch used for date, an engraving error unique among early copper coins.

Reverse: 17 leaves on left branch, 16 on the right. 4 berries on left branch, 4 on the right, with berries to each side of the ribbon bow. Tip of lowest outside-left leaf opposite bottom of U of UNITED. Leaf tip under upright of second T in STATES. *Points of distinction:* On later states there is slight mounding at AME.

1795, Pole to Cap, Lettered Edge (BW-1, C-1, B-1).

Detail of erroneous I in date.

Notes: This variety exists in Mint State, but is very rare at this level. *Gilbert* (1916) G-1 "Lettered edge with pole / 8 berries, 4 on each branch" Gilbert inadvertently lists the same variety as G-2, as preceding, but with a *plain* edge. Comment by R. Tettenhorst: "He is wrong about this, since all examples are simply specimens of BW-1 with the edge lettering ground off, outside of the Mint, possibly to be passed off as specimens of G-2."[12] Regarding thick (usual) and thin planchets for BW-1, see commentary by R. Tettenhorst under 1794, High Relief Head (BW-9). This variety is usually seen in lower grades, but AU and Mint State coins are occasionally offered.

	Cert	Avg	%MS	AG-3	G-4	VG-8	F-12	VF-20	EF-40	AU-50	MS-60BN	MS-63BN
1795, Pole to Cap, Lettered Edge	56	32.7	13%	$290	$490	$800	$1,500	$2,750	$6,000	$12,000	$17,000	$24,000

1795, "Punctuated Date" (1,795), Lettered Edge • BW-2a and b, C-2a, B-2a. *Breen dies:* 2-A. *Estimated population:* 400 to 600.

Obverse: Die flaw between 1 and 9 gives the appearance of 1,795. *Points of distinction:* A slight mounding is seen.

Reverse: Same die as preceding. *Points of distinction:* A slight mounding at AME is present. Later mounding occurs at ER of AMERICA, and clash marks are added near the top.

1795, "Punctuated Date" (1,795),
Lettered Edge (BW-2, C-2a, B-2a).

Notes: This variety exists in Mint State, but is extremely rare at this level. *Gilbert* (1916) G-3 "Lettered edge with pole, punctuated date / 8 berry reverse." Large (a) and small (b) edge lettering. Regarding thick (usual) and thin planchets for BW-2, see commentary by R. Tettenhorst under 1794, High Relief Head, (BW-9). Most are in lower grades. A true Mint State coin is a great rarity.

	Cert	Avg	%MS	AG-3	G-4	VG-8	F-12	VF-20	EF-40	AU-50	MS-60BN
1795, "Punctuated Date" (1,795), Lettered Edge	5	19.2	0%	$360	$540	$800	$1,500	$3,000	$6,500	$12,000	$25,000

1795, "Punctuated Date" (1,795), Plain Edge • BW-3, C-2b, B-2b. *Breen dies:* 2-A. *Estimated population:* 18 to 24.

Obverse: Same die as preceding.

Reverse: Same die as preceding.

Notes: This variety exists in AU and Mint State, though both are exceedingly rare. *Gilbert* (1916) G-8 "Plain edge with pole, punctuated date / 8 berry reverse. . . . Struck on thin planchet with *plain* edge. It is believed to be excessively rare as but one specimen is known." Typical grades are About Good to Very Good. Priced after BW-5.

1795, "Punctuated Date" (1,795), Plain Edge • BW-4, C-3, B-3. *Breen dies:* 2-B. *Estimated population:* 40 to 55.

Obverse: Same die as preceding.

Reverse: 17 leaves on left branch, 16 on the right. 5 berries on left branch, 4 on the right, with berries to each side of the ribbon bow. Tip of lowest outside-left leaf opposite bottom of U of UNITED. No leaf tip under upright of second T of STATES. *Points of distinction:* This variety can be found with a perfect die, but mounding develops at the center, causing the letters AL and EN to become weak.

Notes: VF and EF are the highest grades known, the latter extremely rare. *Gilbert*

1795, "Punctuated Date" (1,795),
Plain Edge (BW-4, C-3, B-3).

Detail of the comma-like flaw in the date.
Also note that the 5 is from a much smaller font. Often, matching the sizes of numerals was overlooked in making dies for early half cents.

(1916) G-7 "Plain edge with pole, punctuated date / 2 leaves and 2 berries under first A in AMERICA. . . . Excessively rare variety, but two specimens actually known." Walter Breen observed that "Gilbert's description was confusing." Low grades are par for this variety, About Good to Fine, although a few exist in higher grades. Priced after BW-5.

1795, "Punctuated Date" (1,795), Plain Edge (1,795),

Plain Edge • BW-5, C-4, B-4. *Breen dies:* 2-C. *Estimated population:* 300 to 500.

Obverse: Same die as preceding. *Points of distinction:* There is a slight mounding in the right field. This increases as the die continues in use.

Reverse: 17 leaves on left branch, 16 on the right. 3 berries on left branch, 4 on the right, none to each side of the ribbon bow. Tip of lowest outside-left leaf opposite center of N of UNITED. Lowest outside leaf on right is opposite C of AMERICA. *Points of distinction:* At first the die is bulged, then a diagonal crack develops. Usually weakly struck at the center.

1795, "Punctuated Date" (1,795), Plain Edge (BW-5, C-4, B-4). Overly long denticles are a characteristic of certain half cent dies of 1795 to 1797. On this example, HALF CENT is lightly struck due to the requirement for metal flow to fill the obverse portrait.

Notes: This variety exists in Mint State, but is very rare at this level. *Gilbert* (1916) G-4 "Plain edge with pole—punctuated dates / 7 berry reverse." This variety exists across the board grade-wise. AU and Mint State coins are usually very attractive.

	Cert	Avg	%MS	AG-3	G-4	VG-8	F-12	VF-20	EF-40	AU-50	MS-60BN	MS-63BN
1795, "Punctuated Date" (1,795), Plain Edge	6	32.2	17%	$250	$400	$625	$1,200	$1,900	$4,800	$9,500	$14,000	$23,000

1795, No Pole to Cap, Plain Edge •

BW-6a and b, C-5a and b, B-5a and b (thin and thick planchets). *Breen dies:* 3-C. *Estimated population:* BW-6a: 500 to 800; BW-6b: 80 to 120.

Obverse: Obverse of BW-1, but ground down so as to remove the pole.

Reverse: Same die as preceding. Advanced state with diagonal crack and some bulging. *Points of distinction:* In its final state, cracks are major, causing the die to fail, resulting in somewhat lower relief of the lower two-thirds of the coin, as compared to the upper third.

1795, No Pole to Cap, Plain Edge (BW-6a, C-5a, B-5a).

Notes: This variety exists in Mint State, but is very rare at this level. *Gilbert* (1916) G-6 "Plain edge without pole / 7 berry reverse, 3 on left branch and 4 on right. . . . Sometimes found struck on a thick planchet." Valued slightly higher if significant traces of a Talbot, Allum & Lee undertype can be seen. Some on thick planchets cut down from misstruck large cents; worth a

1795, No Pole to Cap, Plain Edge (BW-6a, C-5a, B-5a), detail of another coin with part of a Talbot, Allum & Lee token inscription visible in an inverted position at the left of and below the date.

strong premium if significant traces of the cent are still discernible. On thick planchet examples the date can be weak on the obverse, and the denomination can be weak at the center of the reverse. Priced after BW-7.

1795, No Pole to Cap, Plain Edge •

BW-7; C-6a and b; B-6a, 6b, and 6c. *Breen dies:* 3-D. **Estimated population:** Thin (normal) planchet: 1,000 to 1,500; thick planchet: 500 to 750.

Obverse: Obverse of BW-1, but ground down so as to remove the pole, in this state also used for BW-6. **Points of distinction:** Early impressions are from a perfect die. Later there is a slight mounding to the right of Y.

1795, No Pole to Cap, Plain Edge (BW-7, C-6a, B-6a).

Reverse: 18 leaves on left branch, 16 on the right. 3 berries on left branch, 6 on the right. Tip of lowest outside-left leaf opposite left part of N of UNITED. Lowest outside leaf on right opposite second A of AMERICA.

Notes: Mint State is seen. Examples are rare so fine, but this is the 1795 variety most often seen at this level. *Gilbert* (1916) G-5 "Plain edge without pole / Triple leaf under IT. 3 berries on left branch and 6 on right. . . . This variety is often found struck over Talbot, Allum & Lee cents of 1794." Valued considerably higher if inscriptions from an undertype large cent are legible. Valued slightly higher if significant traces of the Talbot, Allum & Lee undertype can be seen. On a few there are some traces of the original T.A.&L. edge lettering; these are worth even more. Three examples are known struck on planchets cut out from copper trial pieces for half dollars, including 1794 Overton-104 and 105 and 1795 Overton-117, according to Manley (*Half Cent Die States*, page 63). These are of exceptional value. R. Tettenhorst: "There is an unusually large number of double strikes, including flip-over double strikes, for this particular variety. What was going on at the Mint to create these anomalies is unknown."[13] The date is usually weak on thick-planchet half cents.

	Cert	Avg	%MS	AG-3	G-4	VG-8	F-12	VF-20	EF-40	AU-50	MS-60BN	MS-63BN
1795, No Pole to Cap, Plain Edge	32	27.4	0%	$250	$400	$625	$1,200	$1,900	$4,800	$9,500	$14,000	$23,000

1796, Liberty Cap, Small Head Facing Right

Circulation mintage (popular estimate): 1,390.

The 1796 half cent is one of America's "trophy" rarities, a classic. For this coinage two obverse dies were prepared. The first lacked the pole to the cap, not because of grinding (as with 1795), but due to forgetfulness on the part of the die cutter, a true engraving error. This die developed a horizontal crack at an early stage, and relatively few were made.

In the *American Numismatical Manual*, 1859, Montroville W. Dickeson commented about the 1796 half cents:

> In our very extensive researches, though were 115,480 pieces of this design and denomination issued in this year, we have only been able to find 10 pieces in the whole; and our investigations have resulted in but one type and two varieties. There may be more, but we have not been able to discover them.
>
> Taking into view the number coined, it is difficult to account for this scarcity. But, probably being defective, from the imperfect tempering of the dies, as the greater number of the very few pieces we have found indicate, they may have been deemed unworthy of care or preservation. But three cabinets in Philadelphia contain a specimen of this coin; they are consequently both rare and valuable.

The Dickeson text, the first comprehensive book on American rare coins, necessarily had many errors, as the author had little to draw upon in this early era. However, the account is reflective of the rarity of the date. That there was another variety, the No Pole variety, was not known at the time. Walter Breen writes that the first publication of the No Pole was by David Proskey in 1880.

Modern standard references usually state the total production of 1796-dated half cents to have been 1,390, the figure quoted above, but this is a guess, representing the smallest of several deliveries of half cents this year. Moreover, even for this delivery there is no evidence that the coins were from 1796-dated dies. The truth is that except for calendar year 1793, when all half cents in the first year necessarily bore that date, we have no precise figures for *any* mintage of early half cents bearing a particular date. Even for 1793-dated half cents, some may have been made in 1794, adding to the 1793 calendar-year figure.

In his Mint history, Stewart wrote, "For 1796 half cents, in calendar year 1796, 60,000 were delivered on March 12, 49,000 on March 31st, then 5,090 in the second quarter, and 1,390 in the third and fourth quarters combined."

Stewart contemplated the situation and continued, "It is probable that the half cents delivered in March were dated 1796, which, if true, should make the half cents of 1796 common, but the fact remains they are very rare. If the half cents of March were dated 1795 this would account for the rarity of the 1796 half cent."

This open conjecture by Stewart was later translated into *fact*, and today the figure of 1,390 1796 half cents is usually given without question. In actuality, no one knows how many were made. It is possible that some but not all were made earlier than the third and fourth quarters. It is also possible that some were made in 1797.[14]

Certainly, the production of 1796 half cents was low, whatever the figure. In proportion to surviving examples the popular estimate given above is probably in the right ballpark. Likely, about 20 percent of these were of the No Pole variety.

In *The Numismatist*, July 1916, Commodore W.C. Eaton, an early student of die varieties in several series, including current Lincoln cents, suggested that the publication

> [s]tart an investigation as to how many collectors have specimens of the 1796 half cent? In my belief, considering the prices even poor copies bring, this is one of the most overrated coins in the whole United States series. I have nearly a dozen half cents in my collection that I consider rarer than the 1796, bought at prices very far less than that half cent brings, though, to be sure, there are only types that are rare and not the entire date, as in the case of the 1796.
>
> But the securing of a 1796 is only a question of money, for they appear in auctions every little while, when an unlimited bid will secure them, while those I have in mind, money could not buy, because they could not be found. I venture to say that if collectors will come forward and own up to the possession of a 1796, the number found will surprise one who judges only by the price they bring. To be sure, the fear of lessening the value of the coin in their possession may deter collectors from so coming forward, but we must depend on their interest in true numismatic knowledge to urge them on.

Nothing worthwhile came of the proposal, although a few responses were received.

The second variety of 1796 half cent is from a different die, with prominent pole, and is that most often seen, although on an absolute basis it is also rare. Today, perhaps as many as two dozen of the 1796, No Pole, half cents exist, mostly in low grades in about Good to Fine, often porous, but with several high-grade and notable examples to delight connoisseurs who can afford them. For the 1796, With Pole, the population is likely in the range of 100 to 120 or so pieces, again mostly in lower grades, although the number of pieces in AU or Mint State is around a dozen.

Some of the highest-grade half cents of both types for 1796 were located in England, where in the late 1700s such pieces were collected, during an era in which numismatics had not yet become popular in the United States. Thomas L. Elder, leading New York City coin dealer and auctioneer, reminisced about an English find by well-known numismatist Henry C. Miller.

> He sold out his fine cent collection and some other items in 1916, I think it was, and we got fine results for him. Sometime prior to that he had secured a pair of Proof 1796 half cents from a dealer in London for something less than $50 for the two. As he collected no half cents, he turned them over to me, and in a sale on East 23rd Street we got $300 for one of the half cents, which to that time seemed a world's record. In the cent sale just mentioned, however the second half cent made the great record of over $700, going into the cabinet of a leading Detroit collector, now retired.[15]

Today the 1796 is recognized as a formidable rarity, and either of the 1796 half cent varieties in *any* grade at all can be called a landmark and causes a ripple of excitement when appearing in an auction presentation.

1796, No Pole to Cap • BW-1, C-1, B-1a.

Breen dies: 1-A. **Estimated population:** 20 to 24, although estimates vary, some as low as 17.

Obverse: No pole to cap, an engraving error.

Reverse: Continuing the style of the preceding year. On this die, 4 berries on the left side, 3 on the right.

Notes: *Gilbert* (1916) G-2 "Plain edge without pole."All known examples have a nearly horizontal die crack bisecting the obverse, no

1796, No Pole to Cap (BW-1, C-1, B-1a). This is the most famous rarity in the half cent series. All known examples have a die crack bisecting the obverse.

doubt accounting for the short use of this die and the consequent rarity of coins today. Some pieces have reflective surfaces and have been cataloged as *Proof* in the past. Examples of the 1796, No Pole, change hands infrequently, and thus the market value is subject to differing opinions.

About four are known in Mint State. The finest two are believed to be one in a Missouri collection (illustrated here; ex John Murdoch Collection, London, 1904) and the Louis E. Eliasberg Collection example (ex Richard Winsor Collection, 1895), the latter certified as MS-67, which is perhaps generous, but the coin is wonderful.[16]

Numismatic Notes: *A Proof 1796, No Pole, half cent?:* The Louis E. Eliasberg Collection sale in 1996 offered a remarkable example of this rarity (one of three there), cataloged as, "MS-65 or better, red and brown. Superb, sharp strike and well centered with excellent definition of all denticles. Square edge. Fully prooflike and most probably a presentation or specimen coin; just as easily called Proof-65 or finer. Mirrorlike characteristics in every aspect of obverse and reverse. Mostly light brown with significant areas of original mint red, especially in protected areas such as the date numerals, LIBERTY, and, on the reverse, within the wreath and letters," followed by extensive additional information.

The pedigree was given as:

> Richard B. Winsor; S.H. and Henry Chapman, December 16–17, 1895, Lot 1012 $300; George H. Earle, Jr.; Henry Chapman, June 25–29, 1912, Lot 3609 $400; Col. James W. Ellsworth; Wayte Raymond, privately; William Cutler Atwater, Sr.; Atwater Estate; B. Max Mehl, June 11, 1946, Lot 129 $1,125; Louis E. Eliasberg, Sr.

In his 1946 offering of the Atwater coin, B. Max Mehl called this a "Brilliant semi-Proof," and went on to say:

> I really believe the coin is and was struck as a Proof. It has a brilliant light olive surface with traces of the original mint red nicely blended in. It is magnificently struck and centered with deep milled borders and sharp edge. While I am endeavoring to be conservative in both my description of condition of these coins, and also the use of superlative adjectives, but this gem is simply too much for me to overcome.

Indeed, Henry Chapman described this coin as a "Proof" while cataloging the Earle Collection in 1912. It is sometimes fashionable to call early prooflike coins "Proofs," and in some instances they may have been intended as presentation pieces in this regard. However, there is no documentation of any Proofs in any series being made by a special proofing process prior the early 1820s (the Smithsonian Institution has a full 1821 Proof set, ex the Mint Cabinet, the earliest such set). Even after the early 1820s there are few records available until the late 1850s. Should a coin be called a Proof because it looks like one, or should there be surrounding evidence or documentation or at least long-standing tradition that it was made as a Proof? This point has not been completely resolved.

	Cert	Avg	%MS	AG-3	G-4	VG-8	F-12	VF-20	EF-40	AU-50	MS-60BN
1796, No Pole to Cap	1	62.0	100%	$18,750	$42,500	$65,000	$125,000	$180,000	—	—	$500,000

1796, With Pole to Cap • BW-2, C-2, B-2a and b. *Breen dies: 2-A.* **Estimated population:** 100 to 120.

Obverse: With pole to cap. LIBERTY positioned slightly more to the right than on BW-1.

Reverse: Same die as preceding.

Notes: *Gilbert* (1916) G-1 "Plain edge with pole." Despite the absolute rarity of this issue, nearly 10 different examples have been

1796, With Pole to Cap (BW-2, C-2, B-2). A famous rarity.

graded as Mint State, with Europe as the main source (see BW-1 and also Numismatic Notes). R. Tettenhorst note: "It is interesting that more Mint States or nearly Mint State specimens of 1796 exist than for any other Liberty Cap half cent, despite the overall rarity of these two varieties. This would seem to indicate that there was some early activity by collectors who recognized the rarity of the date."[17] About 10 to 12 are known in Mint State.[18]

Numismatic Notes: *Edwards copies:* Sometime before 1866, Francis S. Edwards issued a copy of the 1796, With Pole, half cent from new dies. The copy has many minute differences from the original. On the copy the leaf below O in OF extends significantly to its left; on the original the leaf ends below the left edge of the O. Both dies were rusted. Reportedly, after his death the dies were destroyed as were all but 12 remaining coins.

The Edwards 1796 half cent copy.

The number actually struck is not known. These are collectible in their own right today.

Such a coin was mentioned in a January 5, 1866, address by Dr. Winslow Lewis to the Boston Numismatic Society.

As an association we have endeavored to caution collectors against the unjustifiable practice, now too palpably restored to, of issuing facsimiles of rare coins and medals. Of the funeral gold medal of Washington, we are cognizant of at least two struck recently in New York, and we know, also, that the rare half cent, which has brought $96, has been imitated and the counterfeits circulated.[19]

On November 7, 1907, H.O. Granberg, of Oshkosh, Wisconsin, a wealthy collector and coin trader of the era, made an offer to Theophile E. Leon, of Chicago, who was the main buying agent for Virgil M. Brand: "Smith's re-strike half cents $100.00." It is not known if Granberg had more than one.

As to Dr. Edwards, he is famous, or perhaps notorious, as an issuer of copies that seemed to have been marketed without disclosing their true nature. This included the Charles Carroll of Carrollton medal (the original was from dies by Christian Gobrecht), gold Washington funeral medals (in imitation of the Jacob Perkins dies), reissues of Bolen copies from dies acquired from Bolen (these are widely chronicled in specialized numismatic literature), and unknown others.

His collection was cataloged by Edward D. Cogan at the sale room of Bangs, Merwin & Co., New York City, on October 16–20, 1865, under the title of *Catalogue of a Very Extensive and Valuable Collection of American and Foreign Gold, Silver, Copper Coins and Medals, also Colonial, Pattern, Washington, and Presidential and Political Pieces. The property of the late Dr. F.S. Edwards of New York*. Emmanuel Attinelli commented:

> Dr. Francis S. Edwards, whose decease brought his large and valuable collection under the hammer, was an Englishman by birth, by profession a physician. To him was attributed the appearance of several counterfeit pieces of rare American coins and medals, which, though extremely well executed, were quickly detected.[20]

R. Tettenhorst comments:

> An interesting fact about the Edwards copy is the enormous variation in weight. I have a specimen weighing 59.4 grains and another weighing 91.8 grains, and have seen others with in-between weights, for example, 63.3 grains and 73.8 grains. No two seem to have the same weight.[21]

	Cert	Avg	%MS	AG-3	G-4	VG-8	F-12	VF-20	EF-40	AU-50	MS-60BN	MS-63BN
1796, With Pole to Cap	22	38.3	45%	$14,000	$21,500	$27,500	$37,500	$60,000	$85,000	$110,000	$200,000	$362,500

	Cert	Avg	%MS	MS-60BN	MS-63BN	MS-63RB	MS-65BN	MS-65RB
Edwards Copy	0	n/a		$16,250	$20,000	$31,250	$37,500	$45,000

1797, Liberty Cap, Small Head Facing Right

Mintage (per *Mint Report*): 27,525.

Half cents of 1797 continue the small portrait style initiated in 1795, but are apt to be casually struck, sometimes on rough planchets, and sometimes lacking detail in certain areas. The planchets for some of these are believed to have been cut from misstruck cents. Of course, this is part of the charm and fascination of early coppers—the numismatic equivalent of being *rustic* or *naïve*, to pick up terms from folk art. Perhaps the most rustic is the so called Low Head, in which the portrait of Miss Liberty is quite low on the die, with the date crowded below it. Some of the Low Head half cents have lettered edges, incompletely fitting on the thin planchet, with the result that the letters are not fully visible. Why these were made is anyone's guess. Nearly all examples in existence today are in low grades. Planchets cut from Talbot, Allum & Lee cents were extensively used this year. Many surviving coins show traces of the T.A.&L. lettering or motifs.

Half cents of 1797 were extensively used in circulation, to which the abundance of worn examples attests. After 1797 there was no call for the denomination, and none were struck with the dates 1798 or 1799.

1797, 1 Above 1 in Date • BW-1; C-1; B-1a, 1b, and 1c. *Breen dies:* 1-A. ***Estimated population:*** Thin planchet: 400 to 600; thick planchet: 900 to 1,200.

Obverse: Erroneous 1 over regular 1 in date. The engraver started the date too high, abandoned the 1, and punched 1797 below it. Slight traces of other earlier digits can be seen above the date on high-grade examples. Bottom of 9 with knob. ***Points of distinction:*** Perfect die in early impressions. Then a crack develops at the rim by the end of the pole, followed by a mounding at L of LIBERTY, other bulges, and more cracks, culminating in a shattered die (Manley State 5.0).

1797, 1 Above 1 in Date (BW-1, C-1, B-1).

Detail of 1 above 1.

Reverse: 5 berries to the left, 3 to the right. Pair of leaves under ME of AMERICA. ***Points of distinction:*** In late states a crack starts below the 2 in the fraction, and later mounding develops, actually a result of metal displacement due to problems on the obverse, resulting in ICA being indistinct or absent.

Notes: Perhaps 10 to 12 exist in Mint State. *Gilbert* (1916) G-4 "Plain edge with pole, 1 over date." Breen's a, b, and c are for thin planchets, thick planchets cut down from large cents, and thick planchets cut down from T.A.&L. cents. If with significant traces of a T.A.&L. undertype this variety is worth a slight premium. This is a very popular and widely available variety. Quite a few are in grades of EF or finer, usually showing die cracks.

	Cert	Avg	%MS	AG-3	G-4	VG-8	F-12	VF-20	EF-40	AU-50	MS-60BN	MS-63BN
1797, 1 Above 1 in Date	60	31.7	0%	$190	$375	$650	$1,100	$1,800	$4,100	$7,200	$16,000	$32,500

1797, Regular Head, Plain Edge • BW-2; C-2; B-2a, 2b, and 2c. *Breen dies:* 2-A. ***Estimated population:*** Thin planchet: 250 to 400; thick planchet with traces of cent undertype: 8 to 12; thick planchet with no traces of undertype: 50 to 75.

Obverse: Head centered on the die. Date low. Bottom of 9 with knob. ***Points of distinction:*** Perfect die.

Reverse: Same die as preceding.

Notes: 8 to 10 are in Mint State. *Gilbert* (1916) G-3 "Plain edge with pole, date distant from bust." Breen's a, b, and c are for thin planchets, thick planchets cut down from large cents, and thick planchets cut down from T.A.&L. cents. If with significant traces of a T.A.&L. undertype this variety is worth a slight premium. Most are in lower grades.

1797, Regular Head, Plain Edge (BW-2, C-2, B-2).

Detail of knobbed nine.

	Cert	Avg	%MS	AG-3	G-4	VG-8	F-12	VF-20	EF-40	AU-50	MS-60BN
1797, Regular Head, Plain Edge	59	24.2	7%	$200	$425	$700	$1,250	$3,000	$6,000	$8,100	$16,000

1797, Low Head, Lettered Edge •

BW-3, C-3b, B-3a. *Breen dies: 3-B.* ***Estimated population:*** 75 to 100.

Obverse: Head very low. 1 of 1797 nearly touches hair. Bottom of 9 sharply pointed. ***Points of distinction:*** A light crack develops in the right obverse field, with accompanying mounding. This becomes larger as the use of the die continues.

1797, Low Head, Lettered Edge (BW-3, C-3b, B-3a).

Reverse: 4 berries to the left, 3 to the right. Cluster of three leaves under ME of AMERICA. ***Points of distinction:*** There is a crack from the denticles through E of UNITED into the interior of the wreath.

Notes: EF is the highest grade known. *Gilbert* (1916) G-1 "Lettered edge with pole." The Low Head varieties are presented here in the same order that they appeared in Breen: Lettered Edge, Gripped Edge, and Plain edge. Ronald P. Manley studied the die states and came to the same conclusion as Breen, writing "it appears to me that most (or perhaps all) 1797 C-3c specimens were minted after the lettered edge coins, but before the plain edge coins."[22] All are on thick planchets, presumably from cut-down large cents. Often seen on a dark and porous planchet and with extensive wear. With its unusual obverse die and the anachronistic edge lettering, this is one of the great curiosities among early American copper coins. Demand is insatiable, and the typical coin in Good or VG grade with surfaces as mentioned will inevitably draw many bids at an auction.

	Cert	Avg	%MS	AG-3	G-4	VG-8	F-12	VF-20	EF-40
1797, Low Head, Lettered Edge	4	14.3	0%	$1,200	$1,875	$2,950	$6,000	$15,000	$30,000

1797, Low Head, Gripped Edge • BW-4, C-3c, B-3b. *Breen dies: 3-B.* ***Estimated population:*** 12 to 15.

Obverse: Same die as preceding.

Reverse: Same die as preceding.

Notes: VG is the highest grade known. Edge with widely and irregularly incised vertical and curved lines, the "gripped" edge.[23] All known are in low grades.

	Cert	Avg	%MS	AG-3	G-4	VG-8
1797, Low Head, Gripped Edge	0	n/a		$32,500	$48,750	$65,000

1797, Low Head, Plain Edge • BW-5,

C-3a, B-3c. *Breen dies: 3-B.* ***Estimated population:*** 400 to 600.

Obverse: Same die as preceding.

Reverse: Same die as preceding.

Notes: EF and AU are the highest grades known, and examples are rare as such. *Gilbert* (1916) G-2 "Plain edge with pole, date close to bust." Thick and thin planchet varieties.

1797, Low Head, Plain Edge (BW-5, C-3a, B-3c).

Low grades are the rule, but the Plain Edge is found in higher average grades, by far, than the Lettered Edge variety from the same dies.

	Cert	Avg	%MS	AG-3	G-4	VG-8	F-12	VF-20	EF-40
1797, Low Head, Plain Edge	6	11.7	0%	$300	$625	$975	$2,250	$4,500	$13,500

DRAPED BUST (1800–1808)

Designer: *Robert Scot.* **Weight:** *84 grains (5.44 grams).* **Composition:** *Copper. Most planchets were imported from Boulton & Watt of Birmingham, England. These were of exceptionally high quality, in contrast to the variable stock made at the Mint from scrap copper and other sources. There were exceptions, and it is thought that the half cents of 1802 were made from domestic sources.* **Diameter:** *23.5 mm.* **Edge:** *Plain.*

**1806, Small 6, Stems to Wreath
(BW-1, C-2, B-1); a well-known rarity.**

For purposes of finding a nice example to include in a type set, Draped Bust half cents are readily available in most any desired grade, up through and including Mint State, the latter being somewhat elusive in proportion to the demand for them. Many pieces have a generous measure of eye appeal. Examples from old-time hoards are sometimes available for the 1800 and 1806 varieties, especially the latter date. These are usually highly lustrous, attractive, and have original mint orange blended with natural light-brown toning. The reverses typically have areas of light striking, particularly on the upper leaves.

Within this type the 1802, 2 Over 0, is an exception to the above rule, is scarce, and is often seen in low grades or with rough surfaces. Those dated 1804 exist in a wide and fascinating panorama of obverses with Plain 4 and Crosslet 4, and reverses With Stem to Wreath and Without Stem, in various combinations. The half cents of 1808, 8 Over 7, and 1808 are rare in high grades.

DESIGN DETAILS

On the obverse the head of Miss Liberty faces to the right, her hair behind, some tied with a ribbon at the back and with other tresses falling to her shoulder. Her bosom at the lower right is draped in cloth. The letters of LIBERTY are above her head, and the date is between the bust and the bottom border. The image was from a drawing by Gilbert Stuart, said to have been of a society lady. John Eckstein was paid $30 on September 9, 1795, to take the Stuart image and make a model from it, from which a punch or hub could be made for coinage. The dies were made by Robert Scot, chief engraver at the Mint. The Draped Bust motif was first used on certain silver dollars of 1795, then on copper cents and silver half dimes, dimes, quarter dollars, and half dollars of 1796.

The reverse is of the same general style as the 1794 through 1797 type, but more carefully executed in the dies and, accordingly, more standardized. The wreath is open at the top and tied with a ribbon bow below. Around the border is the inscription UNITED STATES OF AMERICA. At the center in two lines is HALF / CENT. The fraction 1/200 is below the ribbon bow. All half cents of 1800 and some of 1802 have a single leaf at each side of the wreath apex. This style is called the Reverse of 1800. Most of the 1802 half cents and all later coins through 1808 have one leaf at the top left and a pair of leaves at the top right, called the Reverse of 1802. The left side of the wreath has 16 leaves and the right has 19 leaves. The berries and stems were added by hand, as was the lettering, resulting in discernible variations.

GRADING STANDARDS

MS-60 to 70 (Mint State). *Obverse:* In the lower grades, MS-60 and 61, some slight abrasions can be seen on the higher areas of the portrait. Luster in the field is incomplete, particularly in the center of the open areas, which on this type are very extensive. At the MS-63 level, luster should be nearly complete, and no abrasions evident. In higher levels, the luster is complete and deeper and some original mint color may be seen. MS-64 coins may have

1804, Crosslet 4, Stems to Wreath;
BW-9, C-10, B-9. Graded MS-63RB.

some slight discoloration or scattered contact marks. A well-graded MS-65 or higher coin has full, rich luster; no marks visible except under magnification; and a blend of brown toning or nicely mixed (not stained or blotchy) mint color and natural brown toning. *Reverse:* In the lower Mint State ranges some abrasions are seen on the higher areas of the leaves. Generally, luster is complete in all ranges, as the open areas are protected by the lettering and wreath. Sharpness of the leaves can vary by die variety, so check this aspect. Otherwise, the same comments apply as for the obverse.

Illustrated coin: This is a nice example, with a generous amount of mint red on the obverse and traces of red on the reverse. There is a spot in the area below the chin and in front of neck.

AU-50, 53, 55, 58 (About Uncirculated). *Obverse:* Friction is seen on the higher parts, particularly the hair of Miss Liberty. Friction and scattered marks are in the field, ranging from extensive at AU-50 to minimal at AU-58. Luster may be seen in protected areas, minimal at AU-50, with more at AU-58. At AU-58 the field may retain some luster, as well. In all instances, the luster is lesser in area and in "depth" than on the reverse of this type.

1806, Large 6, Stems to Wreath;
BW-4, C-4, B-4. Graded AU-58.

Reverse: Friction is evident on the higher wreath leaves and (not as easy to discern) on the letters. Again, the die variety should be checked. The fields, protected by the designs, show friction, but not as noticeably as on the obverse. At AU-55 and 58, little if any friction is seen. The reverse may have original luster, toned brown, minimal on lower About Uncirculated grades, often extensive at AU-58.

EF-40, 45 (Extremely Fine). *Obverse:* Wear is seen on the portrait overall, with reduction or elimination of some separation of hair strands on the highest part. The cheek shows light wear. Luster is minimal or nonexistent at EF-40, and may survive among the letters of LIBERTY at EF-45. *Reverse:* Wear is seen on the highest wreath and ribbon areas, and the letters. Luster is minimal, but likely more noticeable than on the obverse, as the fields are protected by the designs and lettering.

1804, Plain 4, Stems to Wreath;
BW-12, C-11, B-12. Graded EF-45.

Illustrated coin: Probably lightly cleaned years ago, this coin's obverse has a slightly orange hue.

VF-20, 30 (Very Fine). *Obverse:* Wear on the portrait has reduced the hair detail to indistinct or flat at the center. The border denticles are blended together, with many indistinct. No luster is seen. *Reverse:* The leaf details are nearly completely worn away at VF-20, and with slight detail at VF-30. The border denticles are blended together, with many indistinct. No luster is seen.

1804; BW-5, C-8, B-7. Graded VF-20.

F-12, 15 (Fine). *Obverse:* The hair details are mostly worn away, with about one-third visible, mainly at the edges. Border denticles are weak or worn away in areas. F-15 shows slightly more detail. *Reverse:* The wreath leaves are worn flat, but their edges are distinct. HALF CENT may be missing on weakly struck varieties (also true of lower grades given below). Border denticles are weak or worn away in areas. F-15 shows slightly more detail.

1804, Crosslet 4, "Spiked Chin"; BW-3, C-7, B-5. Graded F-15.

Illustrated coin: This is the "Spiked Chin" variety, so called because of a thornlike projection from the chin. The variety does not affect the grade.

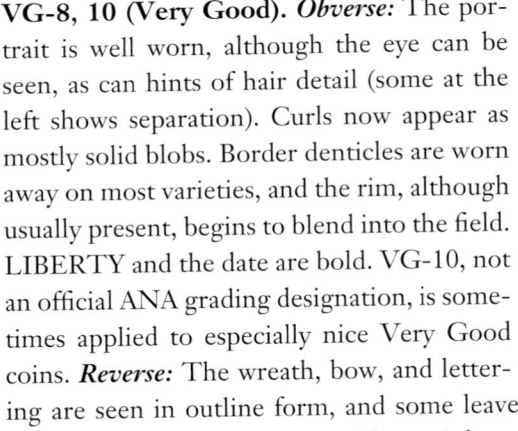

VG-8, 10 (Very Good). *Obverse:* The portrait is well worn, although the eye can be seen, as can hints of hair detail (some at the left shows separation). Curls now appear as mostly solid blobs. Border denticles are worn away on most varieties, and the rim, although usually present, begins to blend into the field. LIBERTY and the date are bold. VG-10, not an official ANA grading designation, is sometimes applied to especially nice Very Good coins. *Reverse:* The wreath, bow, and lettering are seen in outline form, and some leaves and letters may be indistinct in parts. The border may blend into the field on some of the periphery.

1805, Small 5, Stems to Wreath; BW-3, C-3, B-3. Graded VG-8.

Illustrated coin: This coin has smooth, even wear. The obverse die has the usual bulge in the right field seen on this variety.

G-4, 6 (Good). *Obverse:* The portrait is worn smooth and is seen only in outline form, although the eye position can be discerned. LIBERTY and the date are complete, although the date may be weak. The border blends into the field more extensively than on the preceding, but significant areas are still seen. *Reverse:* Extensive wear is seen overall. From half to two-thirds of the letters in UNITED STATES OF AMERICA and the fraction numerals are worn away. G-6 is often assigned to finer examples in this category.

1805, Small 5, Stems to Wreath; BW-2, C-2, B-2. Graded G-4 (NCS).

Illustrated coin: The coin shows much wear, but the key features for G-4 are present. The surfaces are dark and lightly porous and should be described as such in a listing.

AG-3 (About Good). *Obverse:* Wear is more extensive than on the preceding. The portrait is visible only in outline. LIBERTY is weak but usually discernible. The date is weak, and the bottoms of the digits may be worn away, but must be identifiable. *Reverse:* Parts of the wreath are visible in outline form, and all but a few letters are gone.

1802, 2 Over 0; BW-2, C-2, B-2. Graded AG-3.

Illustrated coin: The obverse is clearly G-4 or so, but the overall grade is defined by the reverse, which is AG-3.

1800, Draped Bust

Mintage (per *Mint Report*): 202,908.

Half cents dated 1800, known from just a single pair of dies, are from a mintage reported to be 202,908 pieces. This high figure probably represents the use of improved-quality steel in the dies, although some coins of earlier dates could have been included in the figure. Proportionally, the mintage seems reasonable in relation to surviving examples of the year.

Most 1800-dated half cents are fairly well struck on pleasing, smooth planchets. Today, examples are apt to be very attractive in appearance. Examples are readily available in just about any desired grade.

In the 1930s a hoard of several dozen or more 1800 half cents was discovered in Boston. Examples from this holding display mint red, but are usually spotted. Estimates that the hoard was of 30 to 100 pieces have reached print. Other 1800-dated half cents of the same variety, typically with lustrous brown surfaces, are said to have come from another hoard discovered in New England. This other cache is believed to have been found before 1910 and to have contained "hundreds of pieces."[24] These no doubt account for the Mint State coins seen with some frequency in the marketplace today.

Typical values for 1800 half cents.

	Cert	Avg	%MS	G-4	VG-8	F-12	VF-20	EF-40	AU-50	MS-60BN	MS-63BN	MS-63RB	MS-65BN
1800	195	46.0	31%	$55	$100	$190	$300	$700	$1,000	$2,100	$4,050	$6,750	$14,000

1800 • BW-1, C-1, B-1a and b. *Breen dies:* 1-A. **Estimated population:** 1,200 to 1,600.

Obverse: Draped Bust type, 1800 date.

Reverse: Reverse of 1800 with a single leaf at each side of the wreath apex. **Points of distinction:** The die goes through several states, from perfect to relapped. Perfect die specimens are relatively rare and usually command a premium. In late impressions a crack is seen through at the tops of NITE, expanding slightly on very late impressions.

1800 (BW-1, C-1, B-1).

Notes: Some were struck on planchets made from cut-down large cents. Light striking at the top of the wreath is typical. Early die state pieces with complete and bold obverse and reverse border dentilation are extremely rare and highly prized among specialists. Mint State coins are plentiful. Pristine (untreated and with original surfaces) coins are usually a glossy red-and-brown color.

Numismatic Notes: Walter Breen, in his *Encyclopedia*, states that 20,978 of the 1800-dated half cents were from planchets made at the Mint, and that 190,552, representing higher quality, were imported. In actuality, there is no way of knowing this. R.W. Julian suggests that the 20,978 figure probably includes coins dated 1797.[25]

1802, 2 Over 0, Draped Bust

Mintage (per *Mint Report*): 14,366.

The 1802 half cents are quite curious. The die was overdated from an unused 1800 die, creating 1802, 2 Over 0. Two reverse varieties are known, the extremely rare early style with one leaf at each side of the wreath apex (Reverse of 1800), and the scarce but available second reverse with one leaf at the left of the wreath and two leaves at the upper right (Reverse of 1802).

As to whether the *Mint Report* coinage figure of 14,366 is correct, this cannot be determined. In any event, half cents dated 1802 are sufficiently rare to support a figure in this range. If so, an estimate might be 500 of the Reverse of 1800 style and 13,866 of the Reverse of 1802.

Most half cents of 1802, 2 Over 0, were struck on poor planchets and when seen today are apt to be porous and rough. All or nearly all were struck on planchets cut down from misstruck large cents. Any example showing significant traces of the undertype lettering or other features is worth a sharp premium.

Nearly all are in low grades, with Good and VG being about normal; some are even lower quality, and only a few can be legitimately called Fine. At the VF level the 1802, 2 Over 0, is rare. Any coin that can reasonably be designated EF is an extreme rarity. No AU or Mint State examples are known of either variety.

The 1802, 2 Over 0, with Reverse of 1800 is more than just a rare die variety of interest to advanced specialists. It is rare as a *basic* variety, listed in the regular edition of the *Guide Book of United States Coins*, and widely desired. All known examples show extensive wear. The auction offering of an example in any grade is traditionally the cause for a lot of excitement.

1802, 2 Over 0, Reverse of 1800, 1 Leaf Each Side of Wreath Apex •

BW-1, C-1, B-1. *Breen dies: 1-A.* **Estimated population: 20 to 25.**[26]

Obverse: 1802 Over 0 die.

Reverse: Reverse of 1800.

Notes: Fine is the highest grade known, to the extent of just 3 or 4 coins. *Gilbert* (1916) G-2 "This combination is exceedingly rare." All known pieces are in low grades, and a nice VG would be a prize. Most were struck after the coins of the BW-2, C-2, variety were coined.

1802, 2 Over 0, Reverse of 1800, 1 Leaf Each Side of Wreath Apex (BW-1, C-1, B-1); a classic rarity.

	Cert	Avg	%MS	AG-3	G-4	VG-8	F-12
1802, 2 Over 0, Reverse of 1800	2	0.0	0%	$13,750	$24,500	$35,000	$50,000

1802, 2 Over 0, Reverse of 1802, 1 Leaf Left, 2 Leaves Right at Wreath Apex •

BW-2, C-2, B-2. *Breen dies: 1-B.* **Estimated population: 500 to 800.**

Obverse: Same die as preceding.

Reverse: Reverse of 1802.

Notes: Two EF coins are the highest-graded examples known, followed by several VF coins. *Gilbert* (1916) G-1 "This reverse is usually found in poor condition, and sometimes with slight die breaks from end of stems extending toward A and U." Nearly all are in low grades with dark or porous surfaces.

1802, 2 Over 0, Reverse of 1802, 1 Leaf Left, 2 Leaves Right at Wreath Apex (BW-2, C-2, B-2). Rare in any grade.

Detail of overdate.

Numismatic Notes: *Mintage figures:* The original mintage of 1802 half cents is subject to debate. The regular edition of the *Guide Book of United States Coins* reports a total of 20,266 coins, this being the total of deliveries dated August 8, 1802; October 4, 1802; and August 8, 1803. Others believe the mintage should be recorded as just 14,366 coins, with the 5,900 of August 1803 being coins actually dated 1803.

Contemporary records state that those of August 1803 were struck on planchets made from *spoiled cents* or *mint errors*, using today's terminology. The reason for assuming these to be dated 1802 is simple: a few 1802 half cents show traces of undertype from large cents, while not a single example dated 1803 shows any undertype.

An early comment: In the *American Numismatical Manual*, 1859, Montroville W. Dickeson commented about the 1802 half cents:

> [There are but] one type and three varieties, and the number coined very small, being but 14,366, which has rendered them very rare. One of the varieties is from the die of 1800 altered, and portions of the naught are perceptible around the figure 2, which is smaller than the other figures. They command a good price when perfect, which is rarely the case.

As noted earlier (under 1796), Dickeson's comments are often inaccurate, but are interesting to read today. Only two varieties are known to modern numismatists.

	Cert	Avg	%MS	AG-3	G-4	VG-8	F-12	VF-20	EF-40
1802, 2 Over 0, Reverse of 1802	47	9.0	0%	$475	$850	$2,000	$4,500	$14,000	$35,000

1803, *Draped Bust*

Mintage (per *Mint Report*): 97,000.

Although the number of 1803-dated half cents is not known for certain, as Mint records reflect quantities minted during a *calendar year*, which can be quite different from the *dates on the dies actually used*, the figure 97,200 appears in the regular edition of the *Guide Book of United States Coins* and other places. Most likely, the actual mintage of pieces dated 1803 was several times that figure, from coins struck in 1804 and 1805, but with the 1803 date.

Most pieces are quite attractive, are on nice planchets, and are seen in grades from Good to VF, although occasional EF or finer pieces are encountered. Any true Uncirculated coin is a first-class rarity. It is not unusual for there to be some light striking at the center of the reverse, particularly at the A of HALF and the E of CENT.

This particular year did not turn up in hoards, and thus Mint State coins are very rare. The typical showing for a high-grade collection of half cents is AU.

Two obverse dies and four reverse dies were combined to create four different varieties. All are collectible, but BW-2 and BW-3 are scarcer than the others, with BW-2 being the scarcest.

Typical values for 1803 half cents. Rare varieties may be worth more.

	Cert	Avg	%MS	G-4	VG-8	F-12	VF-20	EF-40	AU-50	MS-60BN	MS-63BN
1803	197	32.7	11%	$38	$75	$190	$300	$800	$1,300	$3,200	$6,500

1803 • BW-1, C-1, B-1. *Breen dies:* 1-A. *Estimated population:* 3,000 to 4,000.

Obverse: 03 very close. TY of LIBERTY close. 3 close to drapery.

Reverse: 5 berries at left and right. A bold engraver's scratch in the form of a line joins the right side of the fraction bar to the ribbon. An artifact from an earlier punch is seen as a raised area at the top inside of U of UNITED.

Notes: This variety exists in Mint State, but is scarce at this level. *Gilbert* (1916) G-2 "Large 1/200 with imperfect regula." A *regula* is a fraction bar. This is the most available variety of the year.

1803 (BW-1, C-1, B-1).

Detail of the engraver's scratch joining the fraction bar to the right ribbon.

1803 • BW-2, C-2, B-2. *Breen dies:* 1-B. *Estimated population:* 80 to 120.

Obverse: Same die as preceding.

Reverse: 5 berries at left and right. No artifact inside of U of UNITED. No engraver's scratch at fraction bar. In denominator, 200 properly spaced. ***Points of distinction:*** At a late state there is a rim cud over TAT on the reverse. This expands to cover STAT.

1803 (**BW-2, C-2, B-2**).

Notes: EF examples occur, but the variety is very rare at this level. *Gilbert* (1916) G-4 "Large 1/200 variety with no imperfection in the regula." This is the most elusive variety of the year, and by a wide margin. Choice examples are particularly desirable. The highest grade known to Walter Breen was EF, with the next finest being VF.

1803 • BW-3, C-4, B-4. *Breen dies:* 1-D. *Estimated population:* 250 to 300.

Obverse: Same die as preceding.

Reverse: 6 berries to the left, 5 to the right (only reverse with this count). F of HALF leans right and touches L at left and berry at right. This die was probably made in 1805 and combined with an 1803 obverse still on hand to strike coins. ***Points of distinction:*** This die was used to coin 1803 (BW-3); 1805,

1803 (**BW-3, C-4, B-4**).

Small 5, Stems to Wreath (BW-2); 1805, Small 5, Stems to Wreath (BW-3); and 1805, Large 5, Stems to Wreath (BW-4).

Notes: Mint State is known in this variety, but AU is a more practical objective. *Gilbert* (1916) G-1 "The only 11 berry variety." This variety was actually struck in 1805. Accordingly, a listing by emission sequence (which this is not) would have this as the last variety of the year.

1803 • BW-4, C-3, B-3. *Breen dies:* 2-C. *Estimated population:* 1,250 to 1,750.

Obverse: 0 and 3 distant from each other, as 180 3. TY of LIBERTY wide. 3 not close to drapery.

Reverse: 5 berries at left and right. No artifact inside of U of UNITED. No engraver's scratch at fraction bar. In denominator 200 the 2 and 0 are properly spaced, but 00 almost touch; fraction bar is long and extends to nearly halfway over the top of 2. Berry under left upright of M of AMERICA, point of leaf under right upright of M. ***Points of distinction:*** This die was used to coin 1803 (BW-4) and 1804, Crosslet 4, Stems to Wreath (BW-1).

1803 (**BW-4, C-3, B-3**).

Notes: Mint State is known for this variety, but examples are very scarce as such. However, among the Mint State 1803 half cents that exist, nearly all with lustrous brown surfaces, most are of the BW-4 variety. *Gilbert* (1916) G-3 "Figure 3 in date distant from 0 / Ciphers in denominator nearly connect." [Ciphers = 00] "But few coins of this variety are without die imperfections."

1804, Draped Bust

Mintage (per *Mint Report*): 1,055,312.

The *Mint Report* gives 1,055,312 as the coinage for this calendar year. It is likely that 200,000 or more were from 1803-dated dies. Still, if 800,000 dated 1804 were struck, this is still the most generous figure of the half cent denomination up to this point in time, a figure later exceeded only by the 1809 half cent. Interestingly, these year-date productions are the converse of the total production quantities of cents of these two years, which were made in relatively low quantities. Further, certain 1804-dated half cents are believed to have been struck in calendar year 1805.

Such a large production necessarily called for many half-cent dies to be made. The result created a playground for numismatists of a later era. Walter Breen states it well: "The date 1804 is the commonest of all the Draped Bust half cents. It is also the date with the largest number of varieties, and it is rich in rare dies and bizarre or extreme die breaks; dies were used long after they would otherwise have been discarded."[27]

Popular varieties exist of various combinations of the obverse with Plain 4 in date, with Crosslet (Serif) at the right side of the 4, With Stems in the reverse wreath (normal), and Stemless (an engraving error). In addition, certain 1804 half cents have a so-called "Spiked Chin," a little thorn protruding from Miss Liberty's chin, and a series of fingerprint-like lines in the right field. These are marks from a piece of a screw that fell into the press after the die had been used to strike "perfect" coins. It became trapped between a planchet and the obverse die, leaving telltale marks on the die.[28] Mint errors such as double strikes are rare for the earlier varieties of 1804, but become fairly plentiful among the later ones, extending to 1805, Medium 5, Stemless Wreath (BW-1).[29]

Adding to the collecting possibilities in the field of 1804 half cents, many coins show varying degrees of die cracks, and some have "cud" breaks from a piece falling out of the die at the rim. As if this were not enough, some coins were struck with dies aligned other than the normal 180 degrees apart. *The Half Cent Die State Book 1792–1857*, by Ronald P. Manley, is the definitive guide to these specialties.

As a general rule, half cents of 1804 are usually found on attractive planchets, with nice surfaces, often medium to dark brown, sometimes lighter. AU coins are seen with frequency, although Mint State pieces are very scarce. There were no hoards found of this date, as were found for half cents of 1800 and 1806.

1804, Crosslet 4, Stems to Wreath •

BW-1, C-1, B-1. *Breen dies:* 1-A. **Estimated population:** 250 to 400.

Obverse: 4 high; crossbar points to center of 0. 1 slightly nearer to denticles than is the 4.

Reverse: 5 berries at left and right. In denominator 200 the 2 and 0 are properly spaced, but 00 almost touch; fraction bar long and extends to nearly halfway over the top of 2. Berry under left upright of M of AMERICA, point

1804, Crosslet 4, Stems to Wreath (BW-1, C-1, B-1).

of leaf under right upright of M. **Points of distinction:** This die was used to coin 1803 (BW-4) and 1804, Crosslet 4, Stems to Wreath (BW-1). A crack develops at the right side of the second T of STATES.

Notes: Mint State is known, but examples are exceedingly rare at this level. This variety is also rare in AU. *Gilbert* (1916) G-6 "Figure 4 of date touches bust / Ciphers of denominator nearly touch each other." Nearly all of this variety are found in worn grades, with Very Fine being about the best that normally can be obtained.

	Cert	Avg	%MS	AG-3	G-4	VG-8	F-12	VF-20
1804, Crosslet 4, Stems to Wreath (BW-1)	(a)			$45	$85	$110	$225	$900

a. Included in certified population for 1804, Crosslet 4, Stems to Wreath (BW-6 to BW-9).

1804, Crosslet 4, Stems to Wreath • BW-2a, C-delisted, B-4. *Breen dies:* 1-B. *Estimated population:* 12 to 14.

Obverse: Same die as preceding.

Reverse: 5 berries at left and right. Berry slightly right of the middle of M of AMERICA. No leaf point under F in OF.

Notes: Not known to Gilbert. This variety is an earlier state of the following and struck from the same die pair.[30] VG is the highest grade known.

1804, Crosslet 4 "Spiked Chin," Stems to Wreath (Later die state of the preceding) • BW-2b, C-5, B-4a. *Breen dies:* 1a-B. *Estimated population:* 150 to 250.

1804, Crosslet 4 "Spiked Chin,"
Stems to Wreath (BW-2b, C-5, B-4a).

Obverse: Same as obverse of BW-1 and BW-2, but die now injured, with a thorn or "spike" protruding to the right from the chin and grooves (threads from a bolt segment that was mistakenly left in the press) in the field below the chin.

Reverse: Same die as preceding.

Notes: *Gilbert* (1916) G-11 "Spiked chin / Outer figures of the denominator under ribbon ends." Later state of the BW-2 die combination. Two or three Mint State examples have been reported. Most are VF or graded lower. Priced after BW-5.

1804, Crosslet 4 "Spiked Chin," Stems to Wreath • BW-3, C-7, B-5. *Breen dies:* 1a-C. *Estimated total population:* 125 to 175.

1804, Crosslet 4 "Spiked Chin,"
Stems to Wreath (BW-3, C-7, B-5).

Obverse: Same die and state as preceding. *Points of distinction:* The die in this combination always has a light crack through the top of LIBERTY. In its latest state a spectacular die cud exists from 1 o'clock clockwise to 4 o'clock.

Reverse: 5 berries at left and right. Berry slightly right of the middle of M of AMERICA. Point of a leaf ends below bottom-left serif of F in OF. *Points of distinction:* In its latest state there is a die cud from 1 o'clock clockwise to 4 o'clock, and another over TES of STATES.

Notes: AU examples exist, but are rare so fine. *Gilbert* (1916) G-9 "Spiked chin / With triple leaves under the left stand of F in OF. . . . Excessively rare—but two specimens now known." Priced after BW-5.

1804, Crosslet 4 "Spiked Chin," Stems to Wreath • BW-4, C-6, B-6.

Breen dies: 1a-D. **Estimated total population:** 1,200 to 1,500.

Obverse: Same die and state as preceding.

1804, Crosslet 4 "Spiked Chin," Stems to Wreath (BW-4, C-6, B-6).

Detail of "spiked" chin.

Reverse: 5 berries at left and right. Fraction bar long and extends to nearly halfway over the top of 2. Berry nearly opposite center of M of AMERICA. *Points of distinction:* Cracks develop, and in the latest state the reverse has spectacular rim cuds comprising most of the area from half past 2 o'clock at the right, continuing clockwise until about 8 o'clock on the left. The Manley text gives illustrations of the die as it deteriorates.

Notes: *Gilbert* (1916) G-8 "Spiked chin / With slight break from right stem end." According to Ronald P. Manley, fewer than six Mint State examples are known. Priced after BW-5.

1804, Crosslet 4 "Spiked Chin," Stems to Wreath • BW-5, C-8, B-7.

Breen dies: 1a-E. **Estimated population:** 2,200 to 3,000.

Obverse: Same die and state as preceding. *Points of distinction:* The die crack at the top of LIBERTY expands. This develops into what is called a "retained cud" above LIBE, a broken section of the die at a different level, but still in the coining press, therefore not creating a cud.

1804, Crosslet 4 "Spiked Chin," Stems to Wreath (BW-5, C-8, B-7).

Reverse: 5 berries at left and right. Second A of AMERICA very close to and nearly touches ribbon; tip of outermost leaf in pair is below right upright of M.

Notes: *Gilbert* (1916) G-7 "Spiked chin and protruding tongue / Crack connects R in AMERICA to border." Known in Mint State.

Typical values for 1804, "Spiked Chin". Rare varieties may be worth more.

	Cert	Avg	%MS	G-4	VG-8	F-12	VF-20	EF-40	AU-50	MS-60BN	MS-63BN
1804, Crosslet 4 "Spiked Chin," Stems to Wreath	368	43.9	14%	$45	$85	$110	$250	$425	$800	$1,700	$3,200

1804, Crosslet 4, Stems to Wreath •

BW-6, C-4, B-2. *Breen dies:* 2-B. *Estimated population:* 40 to 70.

Obverse: 4 of 1804 slightly closer to the rim than to the drapery.

Reverse: Same as reverse of BW-2.

Notes: AU is the highest grade known. *Gilbert* (1916) G-10 "4 of date low / Outer figures of denominator under ribbon ends."

1804, Crosslet 4, Stems to Wreath (BW-6, C-4, B-2).

Cracks develop in both obverse and reverse in a later state. Ronald P. Manley believes this to be the first variety issued among half cents dated 1804. Most are in lower grades. Priced after BW-9.

1804, Crosslet 4, Stems to Wreath •

BW-7, C-2, B-3. *Breen dies:* 2-A. *Estimated population:* 15 to 20.

Obverse: Same die as preceding. *Points of distinction:* A crack develops into a rim cud over RTY.

Reverse: Same as reverse of BW-1.

Notes: Not known to Gilbert. The finest recorded is Fine-15. Priced after BW-9.

1804, Crosslet 4, Stems to Wreath (BW-7, C-2, B-3).

1804, Crosslet 4, Stems to Wreath •

BW-8, C-9, B-8. *Breen dies:* 3-E. *Estimated population:* 1,200 to 1,700.

Obverse: Date widely spaced. Crossbar of 4 points to below center of 0. 4 with ample space separating it from the drapery and the denticles, but slightly closer to the drapery. *Points of distinction:* In its latest state there is a heavy die crack through IBER and a cud above RTY.

1804, Crosslet 4, Stems to Wreath (BW-8, C-9, B-8).

Reverse: Same as reverse of BW-6.

Notes: *Gilbert* (1916) G-5 "Crosslet 4 With Stems, 4 distant from 0 in date." Most examples are VF or lower. A few Mint State coins have been reported. Priced after BW-9.

1804, Crosslet 4, Stems to Wreath •

BW-9, C-10, B-9. *Breen dies:* 4-E. *Estimated population:* 2,000 to 3,500.

Obverse: 4 high; crossbar points to slightly below center of 0. 1 and 4 about the same distance above the denticles.

Reverse: Same die as preceding. Die crack through R is heavier.

1804, Crosslet 4, Stems to Wreath (BW-9, C-10, B-9).

Notes: *Gilbert* (1916) G-4 "Crosslet 4 nearly touching 0 in date / With stems." Mint State examples appear regularly, one of relatively few of 1804 for which this can be said.

Typical values for 1804, Crosslet 4, Stems to Wreath. Rare varieties may be worth more.

	Cert	Avg	%MS	G-4	VG-8	F-12	VF-20	EF-40	AU-50	MS-60BN	MS-63BN
1804, Crosslet 4, Stems to Wreath (BW-6 to BW-9)	113	45.9	18%	$40	$75	$100	$200	$375	$675	$1,300	$2,800

1804, Crosslet 4, Stemless Wreath •

BW-10, C-12, B-11. *Breen dies: 4-F. Estimated population:* 1,600 to 2,000.

Obverse: Same die as preceding.

Reverse: Stemless Wreath. 6 berries on left branch, 5 on the right. *Points of distinction:* This durable die was used to coin 1804, Crosslet 4, Stemless Wreath (BW-10); 1804, Plain 4, Stemless Wreath (BW-11); 1805, Medium 5, Stemless Wreath (BW-1); and 1806, Small 6, Stemless Wreath (BW-3).

1804, Crosslet 4, Stemless Wreath (BW-10, C-12, B-11).

Notes: *Gilbert* (1916) G-3 "Crosslet 4 nearly touching 0 of date / With stemless wreath." Walter Breen wrote: "Prior to about 1965 this was a rarity in Mint State. Since then, many have turned up, mostly brown or strangely mottled, possibly representing a hoard. Weak, uneven strikings are common."[31]

	Cert	Avg	%MS	AG-3	G-4	VG-8	F-12	VF-20	EF-40	AU-50	MS-60BN	MS-63BN	MS-65BN
1804, Crosslet 4, Stemless Wreath	54	54.9	46%	$45	$85	$110	$200	$365	$675	$1,300	$2,800	$4,000	$9,000

1804, Plain 4, Stemless Wreath •

BW-11, C-13, B-10. *Breen dies: 5-F. Estimated population:* 6,000 to 9,000.

Obverse: Plain 4 (without crosslet), unique for this year.

Reverse: Same die as preceding. *Points of distinction:* In later stages a rim cud develops in the denticles over MER.

Notes: *Gilbert* (1916) G-2 "Plain 4 / Without stems." Readily available in Mint State, usually with attractive brown surfaces.

1804, Plain 4, Stemless Wreath (BW-11, C-13, B-10).

	Cert	Avg	%MS	AG-3	G-4	VG-8	F-12	VF-20	EF-40	AU-50	MS-60BN	MS-63BN	MS-65BN
1804, Plain 4, Stemless Wreath	187	44.2	18%	$40	$75	$100	$200	$350	$650	$1,300	$2,800	—	$8,500

1804, Plain 4, Stems to Wreath •

BW-12, C-11, B-12. *Breen dies: 5-G. Estimated population:* 500 to 750.

Obverse: Same die as preceding.

Reverse: Stems to Wreath. 6 berries on left branch, 5 on the right. *Points of distinction:* On the latest state the reverse die sinks, creating bulges in coins struck, essentially obliterating the center of the coins on examples that survive today in worn grades.

1804, Plain 4, Stems to Wreath (BW-12, C-11, B-12).

Notes: *Gilbert* (1916) G-1 "Plain 4 / With stems." Although this variety is not at all hard to find, lower grades are the rule. Walter Breen commented, "Very rare above Very Fine." Known in Mint State, but rare so fine.

	Cert	Avg	%MS	G-4	VG-8	F-12	VF-20	EF-40
1804, Plain 4, Stems to Wreath	11	31.4	0%	$50	$100	$150	$475	$1,250

1805, Draped Bust

Mintage (per *Mint Report*): 814,464.

Although the reported coinage for the calendar year 1805 is generous, it is likely that many within that figure were from earlier-dated dies, specifically 1804.

Half cents of 1805 fall neatly into two major categories (with four die combinations): Small 5 with Stemless Wreath (with two die varieties) and Large 5 with Stems to Wreath. The four die combinations are Medium 5 with Stemless Wreath, Small 5 with Stems to Wreath (with two Small 5 die varieties), and Large 5 with Stems to Wreath. Two of these varieties are readily available, the other two are elusive. Although the sizes of the 5 numeral are popularly called Small, Medium, and Large, the difference is not great and is sometimes difficult to tell if a reference coin or photograph is not handy. However, as the Medium 5 obverse is only combined with the Stemless Wreath reverse (the same die used in 1804), this makes identification of the Stems to Wreath coins easier.

Generally, half cents of this date are attractive and on nice planchets, somewhat similar to 1804 in this regard. In the absence of any known hoards, high-grade examples of BW-1 and BW-4, the usually seen varieties, are very scarce. The Small 5, Stems to Wreath, varieties—BW-2 and BW-3—are found only in lower grades. These are very well known, due to wide listings, such as in the regular edition of the *Guide Book of United States Coins.*

1805, Medium 5, Stemless Wreath •

BW-1, C-1, B-1. *Breen dies:* 1-A. **Estimated population:** 1,600 to 1,900.

Obverse: Medium 5 closer to the drapery than to the denticles; top of 5 double punched. The vertical stroke of the 5 is longer than the flag at the top.

Reverse: Stemless Wreath, the die used in 1804. **Points of distinction:** This durable die was used to coin 1804, Crosslet 4, Stemless Wreath (BW-10); 1804, Plain 4, Stemless Wreath (BW-11); 1805, Medium 5, Stemless Wreath (BW-1); and 1806, Small 6, Stemless Wreath (BW-3). Most are in worn grades. Mint State coins occasionally come on the market, but these cannot be traced to any particular hoard.

1805, Medium 5, Stemless Wreath (BW-1, C-1, B-1).

Notes: *Gilbert* (1916) G-1 "Small 5 / Stemless wreath." Known in Mint State, but uncommon at this grade.

	Cert	Avg	%MS	AG-3	G-4	VG-8	F-12	VF-20	EF-40	AU-50	MS-60BN	MS-63BN
1805, Medium 5, Stemless Wreath	43	39.7	12%	$45	$75	$135	$200	$400	$750	$1,350	$3,000	$4,000

1805, Small 5, Stems to Wreath •

BW-2, C-2, B-2. *Breen dies:* 2-B. **Estimated population:** 35 to 50.

Obverse: 5 small and about equidistant from the denticles and the drapery. The vertical stroke of the 5 is shorter than the flag at the top.

Reverse: Top of T of CENT clearly separated from leaf; tip of lower-right serif in leaf. Tip of leaf between A and T of STATES. Tip of rightmost leaf in cluster under center of O in OF. *Points of distinction:* This die was used to coin 1803 (BW-3); 1805, Small 5, Stems to Wreath (BW-2); 1805, Small 5, Stems to Wreath (BW-3); and 1805, Large 5, Stems to Wreath (BW-4).

1805, Small 5, Stems to Wreath (BW-2, C-2, B-2); a classic rarity.

Notes: *Gilbert* (1916) G-4 "Small 5 / With stems; with a berry touching F. . . . Excessively rare—but two specimens now known." *Points of distinction:* Nearly all are in very weak or low grades. On most, HALF / CENT is very weak. EF is the highest grade known, but examples are seldom seen at this level. VF coins are very rare as well.

	Cert	Avg	%MS	AG-3	G-4	VG-8	F-12	VF-20
1805, Small 5, Stems to Wreath (BW-2)	(a)			$3,750	$6,500	$10,000	$20,000	$50,000

a. Included in certified population for 1805, Small 5, Stems to Wreath (BW-3).

1805, Small 5, Stems to Wreath •

BW-3, C-3, B-3. *Breen dies:* 2-C. **Estimated population:** 140 to 180.

Obverse: As preceding. Later use of the die, now with a prominent bulge before the face.

Reverse: Same 5 berries to the left, 6 to the right. F of HALF leans right and touches L at left and berry at right. *Points of distinction:* This die was used to coin 1803 (BW-3); 1805, Small 5, Stems to Wreath (BW-2); 1805, Small 5, Stems to Wreath (BW-3); and 1805, Large 5, Stems to Wreath (BW-4).

1805, Small 5, Stems to Wreath (BW-3, C-3, B-3).

Notes: *Gilbert* (1916) G-3 "Small 5 / With stems; a berry above F in HALF. . . . Very rare." Usually found in lower grades. EF is the highest grade known, but examples are very rare at this level.

	Cert	Avg	%MS	AG-3	G-4	VG-8	F-12	VF-20
1805, Small 5, Stems to Wreath (BW-3)	7	13.9	0%	$250	$525	$1,000	$3,875	$14,000

1805, Large 5, Stems to Wreath •

BW-4, C-4, B-4. *Breen dies:* 3-C. **Estimated population:** 1,300 to 1,600.

Obverse: 5 large and touches the drapery. The vertical strike of the 5 is about the same length as the flag at the top.

Reverse: Same die as preceding, but a later state. *Points of distinction:* This die was used to coin 1803 (BW-3); 1805, Small 5, Stems to Wreath (BW-2); 1805, Small 5, Stems to

1805, Large 5, Stems to Wreath (BW-4, C-4, B-4).

Wreath (BW-3); and 1805, Large 5, Stems to Wreath (BW-4). Light cracks develop on the obverse. Ronald P. Manley reports that, comments in the Breen *Encyclopedia* notwithstanding, no examples have been found without cracks. It could be that the cracks were created during the hardening of the die, which would mean that all states have this characteristic.

Notes: *Gilbert* (1916) G-2 "Large 5 / With stems." Despite a relatively high population, this variety is nearly always seen in lower grades. Mint State is known, but examples are rare at this level.

	Cert	Avg	%MS	G-4	VG-8	F-12	VF-20	EF-40	AU-50
1805, Large 5, Stems to Wreath	27	33.4	0%	$55	$85	$150	$225	$415	$850

1806, Draped Bust

Mintage (per *Mint Report*): 356,000.

The mintage figure of 356,000 for the calendar year was probably augmented greatly by additional production of 1806-dated half cents in calendar years 1807 and 1808. Today the date is easily available, although one of the four die varieties is scarce and another is rare.

Half cents of 1806 are popularly classified as 1806, Small 6, Stems to Wreath (a rarity); 1806, Small 6, Stemless Wreath; and 1806, Large 6, Stems to Wreath. The later two are readily available in high grades, this being especially true for 1806, Large 6, Stems to Wreath (BW-4).

It is said that sometime around 1906 Philadelphia dealer Henry Chapman found a hoard of 1806 half cents (BW-4) variously estimated to contain from about 200 pieces up to "many hundreds." Certainly, the latter comment is closer to the truth, as these are seen with some frequency today. Many of these have generous areas of original mint red, but are spotted. They are almost always weakly struck at the drapery and the upper part of the wreath.[32]

1806, Small 6, Stems to Wreath •

BW-1, C-2, B-1. *Breen dies:* 1-A. **Estimated population:** 175 to 225.

Obverse: Small 6, positioned lower than the following; bottom about level with bases of 180. **Points of distinction:** Light clash marks are always seen.

Reverse: 6 berries left (lowest outside berry has no stem and is attached to a leaf point), 5 to the right. Lowest outside berry on left has no stem and is at the point of a leaf. Fraction bar short.

1806, Small 6, Stems to Wreath (BW-1, C-2, B-1); a well-known rarity.

Notes: *Gilbert* (1916) G-2 "Small 6 / With stems. R and I in AMERICA connect. . . . A rare variety." Several AU pieces are known, but only one Mint State. The die faces do not seem to have been parallel with each other, with the result that the left side is often lighter in detail than the right.

	Cert	Avg	%MS	G-4	VG-8	F-12	VF-20	EF-40	AU-50
1806, Small 6, Stems to Wreath (BW-1)	19	29.1	0%	$240	$390	$775	$1,450	$3,375	$7,750

1806, Small 6, Stems to Wreath •

BW-2, C-3, B-2. *Breen dies:* 2-A. **Estimated total population:** 20 to 30.

Obverse: Small 6, higher than the previous; bottom higher than bases of 180.

Reverse: Same die as preceding. *Points of distinction:* Late die states have a rim cud over ICA.

Notes: This is a very famous and highly desired rarity. Unknown to Gilbert. Ronald P. Manley: "The rarest variety for the date. Unknown in grades higher than Fine. Almost always found with the obverse die misaligned–off center, with an unusually broad rim at 6 o'clock. The reverse is typically well centered."

1806, Small 6, Stems to Wreath
(BW-2, C-3, B-2); the key variety of this year.

Detail of the date.

	Cert	Avg	%MS	AG-3	G-4	VG-8	F-12
1806, Small 6, Stems to Wreath (BW-2)	(a)			$3,750	$7,750	$19,000	$35,000

a. Included in certified population for 1806, Small 6, Stems to Wreath (BW-1).

1806, Small 6, Stemless Wreath •

BW-3, C-1, B-3. *Breen dies:* 2-B. **Estimated population:** 4,500 to 6,000.

Obverse: Same die as preceding.

Reverse: Stemless wreath. *Points of distinction:* This durable die was used to coin 1804, Crosslet 4, Stemless Wreath (BW-10); 1804, Plain 4, Stemless Wreath (BW-11); 1805, Medium 5, Stemless Wreath (BW-1); and 1806, Small 6, Stemless Wreath (BW-3).

1806, Small 6, Stemless Wreath (BW-3, C-1, B-3).

Notes: *Gilbert* (1916) G-1 "Small 6 / Without stems." This variety exists in Mint State.

	Cert	Avg	%MS	G-4	VG-8	F-12	VF-20	EF-40	AU-50	MS-60BN	MS-63BN	MS-63RB
1806, Small 6, Stemless Wreath	115	46.3	20%	$40	$75	$100	$175	$300	$675	$1,200	$2,900	$3,800

1806, Large 6, Stems to Wreath •

BW-4, C-4, B-4. *Breen dies:* 3-C. **Estimated population:** 2,000 to 3,000.

Obverse: Large 6 with tip into the drapery. *Points of distinction:* Early impressions show repunching at the top of the 6, which is thin; later impressions show the 6 heavier and without traces of repunching.

Reverse: 5 berries left, 5 berries right. Fraction bar lengthened with a spine to the right that ends close to the ribbon. *Points of distinction:* This die was also used to coin 1807 (BW-1).

1806, Large 6, Stems to Wreath (BW-4, C-4, B-4).

Notes: Mint State is known for this variety. *Gilbert* (1916) G-3 "Large 6 with 6 touching bust / With stems." Many Uncirculated coins exist from the hoard described above. Most have a generous amount of original mint red-orange. Usually lightly struck at the top of the wreath.

	Cert	Avg	%MS	G-4	VG-8	F-12	VF-20	EF-40	AU-50	MS-60BN	MS-63BN	MS-63RB
1806, Large 6, Stems to Wreath	80	51.6	45%	$40	$80	$125	$180	$325	$675	$1,100	$2,750	$3,600

1807, Draped Bust

Mintage (per *Mint Report*): 476,000.

The number of 1807-dated half cents is not known, but the figure 476,000 represents the number of coins struck during the calendar year, probably with many from earlier-dated dies. There is only one die variety of the 1807. Many of the 1807-dated coins were likely struck in 1808.

No hoards contained 1807 half cents to any degree, and today most pieces are encountered in worn grades, mostly VG to EF, with AU or better falling into the scarce category. A true Mint State 1807 is *very* rare. Surfaces are often dark and/or porous, as is also the case for 1808 half cents.

Typical values for 1807 half cents.

	Cert	Avg	%MS	G-4	VG-8	F-12	VF-20	EF-40	AU-50	MS-60BN	MS-63BN
1807	258	38.0	7%	$45	$95	$145	$200	$500	$1,000	$2,000	$3,750

1807 • BW-1, C-1, B-1. *Breen dies:* 1-A. **Estimated population:** 4,000 to 5,000.

Obverse: 180 close to border, 7 overly large and close to border and to drapery. The only die of the year.

Reverse: The same die used to coin 1806, Large 6, Stems to Wreath (BW-4). Now the die is relapped, removing many denticles.

1807 (BW-1, C-1, B-1).

Notes: Mint State is known, but examples are very rare at this level. *Gilbert* (1916) G-1 "Many specimens of this date have the entire border on both obverse and reverse milled [with denticles prominent], while on others the milling is on a portion of the circumference only, or entirely absent." Early die state pieces with full obverse and reverse border denticles exist, but they are extremely rare. These are highly prized by specialists.

1808, 8 Over 7, Draped Bust

Circulation mintage (estimate): Fewer than 50,000.

The *Mint Report* of 400,000 half cents struck in calendar year 1808 may have comprised some half cents of earlier dates, most likely 1804 to 1806. Half cents dated 1808, 8 Over 7, as here, and 1808 are quite scarce in comparison to these earlier dates.

One overdated obverse die was combined with two reverses, creating two varieties for the year. BW-1, discovered by Roger S. Cohen Jr. in 1952, is sufficiently rare that Walter Breen knew of only four by the time he created his work on half cents in 1983. Today there are perhaps a dozen known, the finest VF. Surfaces are often dark and/or porous, similar to 1807.

As for BW-2, examples are scarce in any grade. Breen knew of only one Uncirculated coin, in a Missouri collection, tracing its pedigree to Philadelphia pharmacist Robert Coulton Davis. The Eliasberg specimen of BW-2, graded EF-40, was accompanied by the note, "Fewer than ten examples are known in grades equal or better than this."[33]

1808, 8 Over 7 • BW-1, C-1, B-1. *Breen dies:* 1-A. **Estimated population:** 12 to 15.

Obverse: Overdated die, 1808 Over 7.

Reverse: Berry opposite and slightly higher than center of T of CENT. In fraction, 20 closer than 00. Stem tip is distant from base of second A of AMERICA. **Points of distinction:** In late states a die crack develops through the tops of STATES, and others are seen as well.

1808, 8 Over 7 (BW-1, C-1, B-1); a classic rarity.

Notes: This variety is a major rarity. Nearly all are in low grades, an exception being a VF coin. VG and Fine are about the highest grades available from a practical viewpoint. Unknown to Gilbert. This variety was discovered in 1952 by Roger S. Cohen Jr. A Good-4 coin in Superior's February 1992 sale of the Cohen Collection brought $18,150.

	Cert	Avg	%MS	G-4	VG-8	F-12	VF-20
1808, 8 Over 7 (BW-1)	(a)			$38,750	$52,500	$100,000	$157,500

a. Included in certified population for 1808, 8 Over 7 (BW-2).

1808, 8 Over 7 • BW-2, C-2, B-2. *Breen dies:* 1-B. **Estimated population:** 600 to 900.

Obverse: Same die as preceding.

Reverse: Berry opposite upper serif of T of CENT. In fraction, 20 wider than 00. Stem tip has thorn-like projection extending to nearly touch the base of second A of AMER-ICA. **Points of distinction:** This die was used to coin 1808, 8 Over 7 (BW-2), and 1808 (BW-1). On later states a rim cud is seen

1808, 8 Over 7 (BW-2, C-2, B-2).

above TY, extending to the right. Still later, another cud over BE develops, then in the latest stages, the cud is continuous from BE to the right, past the final Y.

Notes: *Gilbert* (1916) G-1 "Small 8 over 7." Rare VF or better, very rare at any higher level. Unique in Mint State. AU coins are extremely rare.

	Cert	Avg	%MS	G-4	VG-8	F-12	VF-20	EF-40	AU-50
1808, 8 Over 7 (BW-2)	44	21.0	0%	$240	$390	$725	$2,000	$5,000	$11,750

1808, Draped Bust

Mintage (per *Mint Report*): 400,000.

The 1808 regular half cents, not overdated, are somewhat scarce. Very curiously, the *second* 8, but not the first, was made by taking the small 0 punch used to create the fraction 1/200 and punching it twice, one impression over the other![34] This would likely indicate that the die was first made with a partial date, and with a regular 8 punch, reading 180, but when completed an 8 punch was not readily at hand.

Typical grades range from Good to VF, with anything higher ranging from scarce to rare. Surfaces are often dark and/or porous, similar to 1807.

Similar to the comment for 1807, the mintage figure has no real meaning. The actual production of the 1808 perfect date half cents was probably less than 100,000.

Typical values for 1808 half cents.

	Cert	Avg	%MS	G-4	VG-8	F-12	VF-20	EF-40	AU-50	MS-60BN	MS-63BN
1808	119	30.8	2%	$45	$85	$145	$220	$525	$1,300	$2,500	$5,000

1808 • BW-1, C-3, B-3. *Breen dies:* 2-B. *Estimated population:* 3,000 to 4,000.

Obverse: 1808 die with curious second 8 made by using a small 0 punch twice (the same punch that made the 00 in the fraction denominator).

Reverse: Berry opposite center of T of CENT. In fraction, 20 wider than 00. Stem tip has thorn-like projection extending to nearly touch the base of second A of AMERICA. *Points of distinction:* This die was used to coin 1808, 8 Over 7 (BW-2), and 1808 (BW-1).

Notes: *Gilbert* (1916) G-2 "High 8 touching bust." Gilbert also listed his No. 3, with relapped obverse "to eliminate a slight accidental defect at the top of the head." Very rare in Mint State with slightly more than a half dozen reported, mostly at lower levels. AU coins are rare.

1808 (BW-1, C-3, B-3).

Detail of the date showing the second 8 improvised by using a small 0 punch twice.

CLASSIC HEAD (1809–1836)

Designer: *John Reich.* **Weight:** *84 grains (5.44 grams).*
Composition: *Copper.* **Diameter:** *23.5 mm.* **Edge:** *Plain.*

1835 (BW-1, C-1, B-1).

The Classic Head half cent design was first used in 1809 and was continued intermittently until 1836. Large quantities were struck of certain years (especially 1809) and for certain dates in the 1820s and 1830s. This type is quite unusual within American numismatics, as there was a flurry of coinage activity from 1809 to 1811, and after that, nothing until 1825. The final shipment of copper planchets prior to the War of 1812 arrived from Boulton & Watt on April 15, 1812, and contained cents only, as the Mint had not ordered any for half cents. On April 27, 1829, Director Moore wrote to Senator Sanford of New York stating that half cents were not popular, and banks, post offices, and others did not order them often. If half cents were shipped in lieu of cents, complaints arose.[35] Once the Mint resumed making half cents in 1825, demand remained erratic. By 1829, coinage outstripped demand to the point that a large surplus was built up, and remained in the vaults until 1833. In addition, as copper coins were a profit center for the Mint, it was inefficient to coin copper into half cents instead of cents, as it took twice as much effort.

The worn appearance of most early half cents is testimony that they found extensive use in commerce, in spite of their unpopularity. Typical grades seen today in the marketplace range from Good to VF, but with enough EF and AU coins that finding one will not be a problem. Most of the higher-grade coins of the first three years are of the 1809 date. Occasional coins of Mint State are encountered for the early dates, again nearly always of 1809, and never with significant original orange-red mint color.

After 1811 there was a long span in which no half cents were coined, until 1825, when production recommenced with 63,000 in that calendar year; followed by 234,000 in 1826; none in 1827; 606,000 in 1828; and 487,000 in 1829. Again these are calendar-year figures. Actual dating of the coins may have varied. One curious variety among 1828 half cents is the variety with 12 instead of 13 stars on the obverse, an engraving error. This variety is scarcer than the 13-star issue, particularly in higher grades. Most examples show signs of wear. Ronald P. Manley in his essential *Half Cent Die State Book* comments that the obverse die for Classic Head half cents of 1825 to 1836 was made from a new hub created from the master hub of 1809. The new dies lacked the crack-like defect across Miss Liberty's neck and the hair that was so characteristic of early Classic Head dies. Deterioration resulted in a defective L in LIBERTY.

After 1829 there was again a gap in coinage, until 1831, when Mint records suggest that just 2,200 were struck, creating a great rarity. Today, very few are known. However, at a later time the Mint stepped into the breach and supplied collectors by creating restrikes, not carefully matching the dies, with the result that among restrikes, one variety has a die originally used in 1836, and another 1831-dated restrike has a die from the era of 1840 to 1857. Such technical niceties were not widely known when such pieces were restruck, but later generations of collectors used them as forensic evidence to endeavor to decipher what happened.

Although the term *restrike* has a negative connotation, in the half cent series this has had little effect on the demand for the rare issues. These commence with the curious 1811 restrike and continue into the 1850s. Many are the instances in which restrikes of certain dates have brought far more money than have originals. Walter Breen's 1983 text on half cents devotes many pages to the technical aspects of restrikes of various sorts, and the present reader is referred to that text for additional data.

From 1832 through 1835, more half cents were struck. It is not known if the dates on the coins matched the calendar years, and some questions have been raised. Half cents of this era were not popular with the public. Many were stored by banks and others, and some coins found their way into hoards that were later distributed into numismatic circles. Today, half cents of this era are available in Mint State with some frequency, often with significant amounts of mint red (actually orange), but usually with flecks or spots. Half cents of the year 1833 are sometimes highly prooflike, and now and again they are listed as Proofs in catalogs, this being more the policy of generations ago than of collectors today.

The Classic Head half cent rounded out its existence with those dated 1836, struck only in Proof format for cabinet or collecting purposes, with none made for general circulation. Today, only a few dozen 1836-dated half cents are known, the so-called originals, with the correct reverse of the year; restrikes with the correct reverse; and restrikes with a mismatched reverse of the general style used from 1840 to 1857 (and lacking the line under the word CENT).

While rarities such as 1831 and 1836 are highly admired by those who can afford them, the elite and generally unavailable status of these has turned some away from collecting half cents in general. Roger Cohen, in the first edition of his book, elected not to study them, preferring to concentrate only on pieces made for general circulation. Proofs were given light treatment in his second edition. Note that the Cohen or "C" cross references for Proofs are cumbersome and hardly ever cited today.

There were no half cents struck in 1837, 1838, or 1839. Sometimes a popular Hard Times Token with the inscription HALF CENT WORTH OF PURE COPPER, of a completely different design, has been collected along with the half cent series, simply because in the 1930s Wayte Raymond—realizing there were no federal half cents of this date—included a space for the token in his "National" brand albums. A tradition was created, and today such pieces jump out from a page of the *Guide Book of United States Coins*. Properly the piece belongs in the Hard Times tokens series.

Half cents of 1825 and later are available in higher average grades such as EF and AU, as these did not circulate widely. Mint State coins from old-time hoards are available of certain dates in the 1820s and 1830s, particularly 1828, 1833, and 1835. Such coins may have generous amounts of original mint-orange color (incorrectly called "red"), but usually with flecks or spots. There are *many* retoned and artificially colored pieces on the market, including in certified holders. Cherrypicking is strongly recommended, and you may have to consider several or more possibilities before finding one with excellent aesthetic appeal. A trustworthy dealer can be a good counsel in your search, until you gain sufficient knowledge.

Proofs were struck of various years in the 1820s per "conventional wisdom," but this is open to serious question. Ronald P. Manley states, "No unequivocal Proof half-cent from the 1820s is known to me."[36] PCGS has certified no Proof half cent dated before 1831.[37] Q. David Bowers and several half cent and large cent experts have agreed that no Proofs of the 1820s, at least through and including 1828, can be confirmed to be true mirror Proofs, sharply struck, and with mirror edges (when viewed edge-on). This is in contravention to Walter Breen's texts, which list *many* Proofs from that decade.

Proofs were definitely made in the 1830s, with the well-known 1831 and 1836 being great rarities (these dates were also restruck at the Mint circa 1859 and later). Some prooflike coins (especially of the 1833 date) have been sold as Proofs. Finding a choice Proof with excellent appeal is a daunting task.

Design Details

The Classic Head design was created by John Reich, a German immigrant who worked as an assistant engraver at the Mint. The motif was created in 1808 for the large copper cent, but first used in the half cent series in 1809.

On the obverse the head of Miss Liberty faces to the left, her hair in curls close to her head and secured by a band on which is lettered LIBERTY. The date is below the head. Seven stars are at the left border and six are to the right. All numerals were entered individually into the die by separate punches. This design was essentially swiped by Chief Engraver William Kneass in 1834 for use on the Classic Head $2.50 gold coins and $5 gold pieces.

In 1809 a crack developed in the obverse hub midway between the bottom of the ear and the top of the curl that rests completely on the neck. This crack is seen on all dies of 1810 and 1811. In 1825 a new hub was introduced with some slight differences in the hair and ribbon ends to the right.

The wreath is a departure from earlier times and now features a continuous wreath of leaves and berries decorated with a ribbon bow at the bottom. Within is the denomination HALF / CENT. Around the border is UNITED STATES OF AMERICA.

Grading Standards

MS-60 to 70 (Mint State). *Obverse:* In the lower grades, MS-60 and 61, some slight abrasions can be seen on the portrait, most evident on the cheek, as the hair details are complex on this type. Luster in the field is complete or nearly complete. At MS-63, luster should be complete, and no abrasions are evident. In higher levels, the luster is complete and deeper, and some original mint color may be seen. MS-64 coins may have

1835; BW-1, C-1, B-1. Graded MS-63BN.

some slight discoloration or scattered contact marks. A well-graded MS-65 or higher coin has full, rich luster, with no marks visible except under magnification, and has a nice blend of brown toning or nicely mixed (not stained or blotchy) mint color and natural brown toning. Coins dated 1809 to 1811 may exhibit significant weakness of details due to striking (and/or, in the case of most 1811s, porous planchet stock). *Reverse:* In the lower Mint State grades, some abrasions are seen on the higher areas of the leaves. Mint luster is complete in all Mint State grades, as the open areas are protected by the lettering and wreath. Sharpness of the leaves can vary by die variety, so check this aspect. Otherwise, the same comments apply as for the obverse. Coins dated 1809 to 1811 may exhibit significant weakness of details due to striking (and/or, in the case of most 1811s, porous planchet stock).

Illustrated coin: This example has lustrous brown surfaces and nice eye appeal.

AU-50, 53, 55, 58 (About Uncirculated).

Obverse: Friction is seen on the higher parts, particularly the cheek and hair (under magnification) of Miss Liberty. Friction and scattered marks are in the field, ranging from extensive at AU-50 to minimal at AU-58. Luster may be seen in protected areas, minimal at the AU-50 level, with more showing at AU-58. At AU-58 the field may retain some luster as well. *Reverse:* Friction is seen on the

1809; BW-4, C-6, B-6. Graded AU-58.

higher wreath leaves and (not as easy to discern) on the letters. Again, half cents of 1809 to 1811 require special attention. The fields, protected by the designs, show friction, but not as noticeably as on the obverse. At AU-55 and 58, little if any friction is seen. The reverse may have original luster, toned brown, minimal on lower About Uncirculated grades, often extensive at AU-58.

Illustrated coin: Here is a lovely example with rich, brown luster. Stars 1 to 5 on the left are weak, as struck, and the denticles are light in that area (not mentioned on third-party grading labels; such distinctions are up to the buyer to discover and evaluate). Otherwise, the striking is sharp.

EF-40, 45 (Extremely Fine). *Obverse:* Wear

is seen on the portrait overall, with reduction or elimination of some separation of hair strands. The cheek shows light wear. Luster is minimal or nonexistent at EF-40 but may survive among the letters of LIBERTY at EF-45. *Reverse:* Wear is seen on the highest wreath and ribbon areas and the letters. Luster is minimal, but likely more noticeable than on the obverse, as the fields are protected by the designs and lettering.

1811; BW-2, C-2, B-2. Graded EF-40.

Illustrated coin: This coin is of about typical strike, with some lightness at the star centers, although wear caused some of the lightness. The surfaces are lightly granular.

VF-20, 30 (Very Fine). *Obverse:* Wear on the portrait has reduced the hair detail, but much can still be seen (in this respect the present type differs dramatically from earlier types). *Reverse:* The wreath details, except for the edges of the leaves, are worn away at VF-20, and have slightly more detail at VF-30.

Illustrated coin: This coin has gray-brown surfaces. At this level and lower, sharpness of the original strike diminishes in importance, as star centers, hair, leaves, and so on show significant wear.

1811; BW-2, C-2, B-2. Graded VF-20.

F-12, 15 (Fine). *Obverse:* The hair details are fewer than on the preceding, but many are still present. Stars have flat centers. F-15 shows slightly more detail. *Reverse:* The wreath leaves are worn flat, but their edges are distinct. F-15 shows slightly more detail.

Illustrated coin: Smooth, even wear characterizes this example of the scarce 1811 half cent. Some light porosity or granularity is normal at this grade level.

1811; BW-2, C-2, B-2. Graded F-15.

VG-8, 10 (Very Good). *Obverse:* The portrait is well worn, although the eye and ear can be seen, as can some hair detail. The border is well defined in most areas. *Reverse:* The wreath, bow, and lettering are seen in outline form, and some leaves and letters may be indistinct in parts. The border is well defined in most areas.

Illustrated coin: Here is a "poster example" of this grade—smooth, with even wear, a nice planchet, and overall attractive appearance.

1811; BW-1, C-1, B-1. Graded VG-8.

G-4, 6 (Good). *Obverse:* The portrait is worn smooth and is seen only in outline form. Much of LIBERTY on the headband is readable, but the letters are weak. The stars are bold in outline. Much of the rim can be discerned. *Reverse:* Extensive wear is seen overall. Lettering in UNITED STATES OF AMERICA ranges from weak but complete (although the ANA grading guidelines allow for only half to be readable; the ANA text illustrates the words in full) to having perhaps a third of the letters missing. HALF CENT is usually bold.

1811; BW-2, C-2, B-2. Graded G-4.

AG-3 (About Good). *Obverse:* Wear is more extensive than on the preceding. The portrait is visible only in outline. A few letters of LIBERTY are discernible in the headband. The stars are weak or worn away on their outer edges. The date is light. *Reverse:* The wreath is visible in outline form. Most or even all of UNITED STATES OF AMERICA is worn away. HALF CENT is usually readable.

1828. Graded AG-3.

PF-60 to 70 (Proof). Proofs were struck of various years in the 1820s and 1830s, with 1831 and 1836 being great rarities (these dates were also restruck at the Mint circa 1859 and later). Some prooflike circulation strikes (especially of the 1833 date) have been certified as Proofs. Except for the years 1831 and 1836, for which Proofs are unequivocal, careful study is advised when contemplating the purchase of a coin described as Proof.

1831, First Restrike; BW-1a, C-PR-2, B-2. Graded PF-66RB.

Blotchy and recolored Proofs are often seen, but hardly ever described as such. Probably fewer than 25 of the Proofs of this type are truly pristine—without one problem or another. *Obverse and Reverse:* Proofs that are extensively hairlined or have dull surfaces, this being characteristic of many issues (1831 and 1836 usually excepted), are graded PF-60 to 62 or 63. This includes artificially toned and recolored coins, a secret that isn't really secret among knowledgeable collectors and dealers, but is rarely described in print. To qualify as PF-65 or higher, hairlines should be microscopic, and there should be no trace of friction. Surfaces should be prooflike or, better, fully mirrored, without dullness.

1809, Classic Head

Mintage (per *Mint Report*): 1,154,572.

The production of the first year, 1809 was very generous at 1,154,572, presumably all from 1809-dated dies, based on the ratio of surviving examples. This production figure takes its place as the highest quantity produced for any half cent from 1793 to 1857.

Today, half cents of 1809 are among the more plentiful in the marketplace. Several die varieties exist of 1809, including one with a small 0 figure inside the larger regular 0 and the 1809, Triple Punched 9 (earlier called 1809 over inverted 6, but now with that status debunked).

Half cents dated 1809 are seen in a wide variety of grades, including more than a few in EF, AU, or even in lustrous brown Mint State. Planchets tend to be somewhat on the dark side.

Typical values for 1809, Normal Date, half cents. Rare varieties may be worth more.

	Cert	Avg	%MS	G-4	VG-8	F-12	VF-20	EF-40	AU-50	MS-60BN	MS-63BN	MS-63RB
1809, Normal Date	379	45.8	26%	$30	$60	$100	$150	$375	$750	$1,300	$2,200	$3,500

1809, Normal Date • BW-1, C-1, B-2.

Breen dies: 2-B. ***Estimated population:*** 50 to 100.

Obverse: Left edge of curl is slightly to the left of the center of the 0. ***Points of distinction:*** In its latest state in the present combination a faint crack connects stars 11 and 12.

Reverse: Tip of highest leaf directly below right edge of second S of STATES. Berry directly opposite upright of T of UNITED.

1809, Normal Date (BW-1, C-1, B-2).

Berry directly opposite right foot of R of AMERICA. ***Points of distinction:*** A rim cud is seen from M through slightly past I of AMERICA.

Notes: This variety, unknown to Gilbert, was discovered by Richard Picker in 1954. That several dozen have been found since that time is testimony to the popularity of Roger S. Cohen Jr.'s book, which came into wide use in an era in which very few collectors had a copy of the Gilbert text. EF is the highest grade known.

1809, Normal Date • BW-2, C-2, B-3.

Breen dies: 2-C. ***Estimated population:*** 200 to 350.

Obverse: Same die as preceding. ***Points of distinction:*** The tiny crack at stars 11 and 12 expands.

Reverse: Tip of highest leaf slightly past right edge of second S of STATES. Berry slightly to the right of the upright of T of UNITED. Tip of leaf opposite tip of lower-

1809, Normal Date (BW-2, C-2, B-3).

right serif of F in OF. ***Points of distinction:*** In time a tiny cud break appears above the space between D and S.

Notes: *Gilbert* (1916) G-3 "The cipher of date without the inner circle / High leaf ending before the front of S." Known in Mint State, but very rare as such.

1809, Normal Date • BW-3, C-3, B-4.

Breen dies: 3-C. ***Estimated population:*** 800 to 1,200.

Obverse: Star 13 close to 9 of 1809. Left edge of curl is above center of 0. ***Points of distinction:*** Cracks are seen at the stars.

Reverse: Same die as preceding. ***Points of distinction:*** The die in a late state shows deterioration of the denticles.

1809, Normal Date (BW-3, C-3, B-4).

Notes: Known in Mint State. *Gilbert* (1916) G-4 "Close star variety / High leaf below front of S and another below right stand of F in OF. . . . First star to the right is but 1-1/4 mm from the 9."

1809, Normal Date • BW-4, C-6, B-6.

Breen dies: 5-E. **Estimated population:** 3,000 to 5,000.

Obverse: Star 13 distant from 9 of 1809; the 9 is about the same distance from the 8 in the date as from Star 13. Star 1 is closer to the denticles than to the bust. Left edge of curl is above and slightly to the right of the center of 0.

Reverse: Tip of highest leaf far past right edge of second S of STATES, but not quite halfway to O in OF.

1809, Normal Date (BW-4, C-6, B-6).

Notes: This variety exists in Mint State. *Gilbert* (1916) G-2 "Perfect date variety / High leaf ending midway between S and O." The dies deteriorate with use, with rim breaks developing on the obverse, and with relapping and deterioration of the reverse.

1809, Small o Within 0 of Date •

BW-5, C-4, B-1. *Breen dies:* 1-A. **Estimated population:** 700 to 1,000.

Obverse: 0 in date punched over earlier smaller 0 digit.

Reverse: Tip of highest leaf below left edge of O in OF.

Notes: Mint State is known, but examples are seldom seen at this level. *Gilbert* (1916) G-1 "In date the cipher has an inner circle / High leaf ending near letter O." Most show extensive circulation. The obverse and reverse dies seem to have been relapped (details in Ronald P. Manley, *The Half Cent Die State Book 1793–1857*, a source generally valuable for all of the half cent varieties).

1809, Small o Within 0 of Date (BW-5, C-4, B-1).

Detail showing a large 0 punched over a smaller o.

	Cert	Avg	%MS	G-4	VG-8	F-12	VF-20	EF-40	AU-50
1809, Small o Within 0 of Date	16	36.8	0%	$45	$70	$120	$275	$650	$1,350

1809, Repunched 9 • BW-6, C-5, B-5.

Breen dies: 4-D. **Estimated population:** 2,000 to 3,000.

Obverse: With repunched date, formerly called "9 over inverted 9," but now known not to have an inverted digit.[38]

Reverse: Tip of highest leaf slightly past right edge of second S of STATES. Berry slightly to the right of the upright of T of UNITED. Tip of leaf past tip of lower-right serif of F in OF.

Notes: This variety exists in Mint State. *Gilbert* (1916) G-5 "Very close star variety /

1809, Repunched 9 (BW-6, C-5, B-5).

Detail of the date showing the repunched 9.

High leaf past front of S and another ending to the right of F. . . . Date measures 7-1/2 mm wide, with first star to the right 1 mm. distant." Gilbert made no mention of any date punch anomaly. Both dies deteriorate with use, mainly affecting the denticles, which become increasingly blurry. Relapping removes some low relief details.

	Cert	Avg	%MS	G-4	VG-8	F-12	VF-20	EF-40	AU-50	MS-60BN	MS-63BN	MS-63RB	MS-65BN	MS-65RB
1809, Repunched 9	214	49.8	18%	$37	$70	$100	$150	$375	$750	$1,300	$2,200	$3,250	$10,000	$20,000

1810, Classic Head

Mintage (per *Mint Report*): 215,000.

Among early Classic Head half cents the 1810 is considered to be slightly scarce, but not quite in the same league of scarcity as the 1811. Only one pair of dies was used. Most are seen with extensive wear. Always seen with some areas of light striking on the obverse stars on the right, as the die faces were not parallel. Mint State examples are rare and are unknown with significant original red-orange mint color.

Typical values for 1810 half cents.

	Cert	Avg	%MS	G-4	VG-8	F-12	VF-20	EF-40	AU-50	MS-60BN	MS-63BN	MS-63RB
1810	94	41.6	19%	$40	$75	$125	$260	$540	$1,000	$2,000	$3,200	$6,750

1810 • BW-1, C-1, B-1. *Breen dies:* 1-A. *Estimated population:* 2,000 to 3,000.

Obverse: 0 of 1810 slightly repunched. *Points of distinction:* A crack is seen through stars 5 to 7, continuing to the top of the hair.

Reverse: Standard design of the type.

Notes: Mint State is known for this variety. Examples grading better than EF are scarce.

1810 (BW-1, C-1, B-1).

1811, Classic Head

Mintage (per *Mint Report*): 63,140.

The 1811 is the key date among early half cents of the Classic Head type. The mintage is given as 63,140, which is likely in the ballpark, at least. Two different die varieties are known, sometimes called Wide Date and Close Date, although the difference is not particularly noticeable. In the marketplace, VF is a high grade for either of the two varieties, and a sharp EF is exceptional. True Mint State coins are rare, with perhaps a half dozen or so different examples known, with maybe the finest being the BW-2 in the Eliasberg Collection, 1996, graded as MS-63.

The so-called 1811 restrike, actually a numismatic fantasy or novodel (as the die combination was never originally struck, so it cannot be restruck), is an interesting addition to the coinage of this year. These are very rare and always attract attention when offered.

1811 • BW-1, C-1, B-1. *Breen dies:* 1-A. *Estimated population:* 150 to 225.

Obverse: Wide Date. Spaced as 1 81 1 with 81 closer than 18 or 11. Star 1 about equidistant from denticles and neck. Star 13 is equidistant between the curl and border (a quick reference point). *Points of distinction:* The die developed a crack to the left of the date, which progressively enlarges, eventually resulting in a large piece falling from the left obverse rim, extending to include part of two

1811 (BW-1, C-1, B-1); this is by far the rarer of two varieties of this year.

stars, and later consuming part of four stars. Examples with the break involving two stars are extremely rare, with only a half dozen known, and those always in low grades. Those showing the break through all four stars are rare, although much more available than the two-star break pieces.

Reverse: Only one die. Berry opposite upright of R of AMERICA, unlike any other dies to this point in time. *Points of distinction:* The die develops a light crack which expands along the rim.

Notes: *Gilbert* (1916) G-2 "Distant 18 in date." Mint State is known, and examples are rare so fine. AU coins occasionally come on the market and are also rare.

	Cert	Avg	%MS	G-4	VG-8	F-12	VF-20	EF-40
1811 (BW-1)	3	18.3	0%	$390	$875	$1,650	$2,750	$6,500

1811 • BW-2, C-2, B-2. *Breen dies:* 2-A. *Estimated population:* 1,000 to 1,400.

Obverse: Close Date. Spaced as 181 1 with second 1 farther away. Star 1 much closer to denticles than to neck. Star 13 nearly touches the border (a quick reference point).

Reverse: Same die as preceding.

Notes: *Gilbert* (1916) G-1 "Close 18 in date." Mint State is known for this variety, and examples are very rare as such. AU and EF are practical goals.

1811 (BW-2, C-2, B-2).

Detail of star 13, nearly touching the border.

	Cert	Avg	%MS	G-4	VG-8	F-12	VF-20	EF-40	AU-50
1811 (BW-2)	5	23.4	0%	$375	$850	$1,550	$2,500	$6,000	$7,500

1811, "Restrike" with Reverse of 1802, Mismatched Dies • BW-3. *Breen dies: 1811, 2-1802, B.* **Estimated population:** 10 to 12.

Obverse: Same as BW-2.

Reverse: Die used to coin 1802 Over 0, Reverse of 1802, 1 Leaf Left, 2 Leaves Right at Wreath Apex (BW-2), open wreath.

1811, "Restrike" with Reverse of 1802, Mismatched Dies (BW-3).

Notes: Exists in Mint State. All such examples are about the same, although some have mint color. A numismatic fantasy or novodel pairing two dies never originally used together. All are in Mint State, usually brown with some traces of red-orange, from rusted dies yielding rough surfaces. Walter Breen in his 1983 work listed 10 "demonstrably different" specimens.

Numismatic Notes: *The 1811 restrike:* This curious coin was privately struck in the mid-1800s using dies discarded as scrap iron by the Mint. The obverse is that of 1811 (BW-2), and the reverse is a mismatched type used to coin 1802 Over 0, Reverse of 1802, 1 Leaf Left, 2 Leaves Right at Wreath Apex (BW-2). This is popularly known as the "Mickley Restrike," but evidence specifically linking the *production* to that old-time Philadelphia collector is circumstantial at best, seemingly based on this posthumous listing by Édouard Frossard in his 16th Sale:

> Lot 1246: 1811 Very fine impression; struck from the dies while in the possession of the late Mr. Mickley. It will be remembered that the reverse of this half cent is the same as reverse of a 'draped bust' half cent, and that both obverse and reverse dies have since been destroyed. Extremely rare.

However, Mickley did own the obverse die at one time, as it was included in the catalog of his estate.

The first auction appearance was likely in a sale by Edward Cogan in 1859, when an 1811 half cent was described as having a "Different reverse, very rare type." Later, it became popular to state that 12 specimens were coined, but there seems to be no documentation at all as to when it was struck, or by whom, or how many were made.

	Cert	Avg	%MS	MS-60BN	MS-63BN	MS-63RB	MS-64BN	MS-64RB
1811, "Restrike" with Reverse of 1802, Mismatched Dies	5	63.8	100%	$18,750	$24,500	$30,000	$37,500	$50,000

QUALITY AMONG LATER-DATE HALF CENTS

Half cents from 1825 onward are generally found with good eye appeal and on good planchets. Striking is usually quite good. Prices listed are for such coins. Examples with flat stars, mushy denticles, or other problems should be worth slightly less, but the market hardly notices. Among Mint State coins, recolored, stained, or blotchy coins are worth less (again, in the marketplace such coins are usually not identified as such). There are opportunities for cherrypicking for quality, but not to the extent found on earlier half cent issues.

1825, Classic Head

Mintage (per *Mint Report*): 63,000.

The idea of resuming coinage of half cents occurred by August 10, 1824, when Mint Director Samuel Moore wrote to Matthew Boulton on August 10, to ask about prices of half cent planchets. None had been struck for many years. Planchets were obtained from Boulton, who was supplying *cent* planchets to the Mint at the time. John Reich's Classic Head motif was dusted off for the new coinage.

Mintage began in December 1825 in response to a significant order placed in November by Jonathan Elliott & Sons of Baltimore. The Mint Treasurer informed the Elliott company on November 23 that no half cents were on hand at the time, but they perhaps would be in January. Mint records, however, indicate that none were paid out until the second quarter of 1826.[39] By that time, the Classic Head motif had been discontinued years earlier on the *cent* pieces and had been replaced in 1816 with what Ken Bressett designated in modern times (for use in the regular edition of the *Guide Book of United States Coins*) as the Matron Head.

Half cents were not called for in commerce, and none had been made for a long period of time. In 1859 Dr. Montroville W. Dickeson noted that by 1825 "people had acquired the habit of disregarding fractions, and had no disposition to renew them for making change. We can recollect, however, when in some portions of our country the half cent was rigidly exacted, and where many a war of words, and sometimes of fists, grew out of such a controversy."[40]

The mintage figure is for the calendar year. The availability of this date suggests that additional coins were struck in 1826 and recorded in that calendar year.

Examples are easy enough to find, and are usually in higher grades, VF upward. Mint State coins appear with frequency, but are usually in lower MS ranges.

Proofs: None.

1825 • BW-1, C-1, B-1. *Breen dies:* 1-A. *Estimated population:* 300 to 500.

Obverse: Center of curl over the center of the 5. Stars 4 and 5, 8 and 9, and 11 and 12 are more widely spaced than the others. *Points of distinction:* The die develops light cracks in its latest state.

Reverse: Only one die. Standard type of the period.

1825 (BW-1, C-1, B-1).

Notes: *Gilbert* (1916) G-2 "Curl over 5 of date." Examples exist in Mint State, typically brown.

1825 • BW-2, C-2, B-2. *Breen dies:* 2-A. *Estimated population:* 3,500 to 4,500.

Obverse: Center of the curl over the left edge of the 5. Stars 1 through 3 and 11 to 12 more widely spaced than are the others.

Reverse: Same die as preceding.

Notes: *Gilbert* (1916) G-1 "Curl over 25 of date." Some coins have prooflike surfaces. Examples exist in Mint State, typically brown.

1825 (BW-2, C-2, B-2).

Typical values for BW-2. BW-1 is worth more.

	Cert	Avg	%MS	G-4	VG-8	F-12	VF-20	EF-40	AU-50	MS-60BN	MS-63BN	MS-63RB	MS-65BN	MS-65RB
1825 (BW-2)	262	49.7	26%	$600	$55	$75	$100	$200	$325	$800	$1,750	$3,000	$6,000	$15,000

1826, Classic Head

Mintage (per *Mint Report*): 234,000.

It is likely that the mintage figure for calendar year 1826 included many from 1825-dated dies. Half cents of 1826 are characteristically lightly struck at the highest stars on each side of the head. Examples are easy enough to find in circulated grades, VF and upward, with EF and AU being typical. Mint State coins are fairly scarce and are usually in lower MS ranges.

Proofs: None.

1826 • BW-1, C-1, B-1. *Breen dies:* 1-A. *Estimated population:* 3,500 to 4,500.

Obverse: Stars 1 and 2 are widely separated in comparison to stars 2 and 3, which are closer together. Star 13 points to a denticle slightly below its center. Cross-hatching of raised file marks to the right of the 6. *Points of distinction:* Light cracks develop on later states.

1826 (BW-1, C-1, B-1).

Reverse: Leaf tip ends far past second S of STATES. Stray part of serif between tops of E and D of UNITED.

Notes: *Gilbert* (1916) G-1 "High leaf past S." Examples exist in Mint State, typically brown.

Typical values for BW-1. BW-2 is worth more.

	Cert	Avg	%MS	G-4	VG-8	F-12	VF-20	EF-40	AU-50	MS-60BN	MS-63BN	MS-63RB	MS-65BN	MS-65RB
1826 (BW-1)	344	50.0	32%	$30	$50	$75	$90	$150	$300	$600	$1,000	$1,500	$2,875	$5,000

1826 • BW-2, C-2, B-2. *Breen dies:* 2-B. *Estimated population:* 200 to 275.

Obverse: Stars 1 and 2 are close together in comparison to stars 2 and 3, which are more widely separated. Star 13 points to a space between denticles. *Points of distinction:* At the date tiny remnants of a horizontal 6 are visible. Lower-grade examples do not show this. In the extreme-latest state there is a rim cud on the left, consuming parts of stars 4 and

1826 (BW-2, C-2, B-2).

5, creating a much-sought variety. Just seven are known according to Ronald P. Manley.

Reverse: Leaf tip ends under second S of STATES, slightly to the right of its center. *Points of distinction:* This die was also used to coin 1828, 13 Stars, (BW-1). Was it also used for 1828, 12 Stars (BW-3)? (See that listing for Gilbert comment.)

Notes: *Gilbert* (1916) G-2 "High leaf under S." Mint State is known, and examples are very rare as such.

1828, Classic Head

Mintage (per *Mint Report*): 606,000.

The 1828 half cent is found with three die varieties. Two of these have the normal 13 stars on the obverse, but the third has just 12. Interestingly, coins of this date consist of three different obverses combined with three different reverses, with no overlapping. As the dies do not show signs of significant breakage, dies in each pair must have been retired from the press at the same time.

The 12-star variety is a remarkable die-cutting error with relatively few equivalents in American coinage (others include the 1817 cent with 15 instead of 13 stars and the 1832 half eagle with only 12 stars). It is likely that many coins from the large mintage of 606,000 were never released.

Today, the 13-star coins, which exist in two die varieties, are plentiful in the marketplace. The typical coin is EF or AU with light-brown surfaces. Mint State coins are easily found, most no doubt from the Collins Find (see page 215). These hoard coins are often seen with much or most original orange-red mint color, but nearly always with flecks or spots. Cherrypicking will yield a very eye-pleasing coin.

The 12-star variety is readily found, usually at the VF or EF level. AU coins are scarce, and true Mint State coins are slightly rare. None were in the Collins Find. These typically have lustrous brown surfaces. The Eliasberg coin, a notable specimen, was graded MS-63 with about 10 percent original mint red. We have never seen one with full *original* mint color. The demand for this variety, in any and all grades, has always been very strong. This is a "must have!" coin for many buyers who do not otherwise seek die varieties, with the listing in the perennially popular *Guide Book of United States Coins* making it known to millions of readers.

Proofs: None.

1828, 13 Stars • BW-1, C-1, B-1. *Breen dies:* 1-A. **Estimated population:** 1,000 to 1,500.[41]

Obverse: 13 stars. Rays of Star 7 point to slightly above and slightly below the outline of the ribbon. Star 13 points to between two denticles.

Reverse: Berry under upright of T of UNITED just slightly above its center. Tip of leaf under second S of STATES slightly right of its center. **Points of distinction:** This die was also used to coin 1826 (BW-2).

1828, 13 Stars (BW-1, C-1, B-1).

Notes: *Gilbert* (1916) G-2 "High leaf under S." There is not much price differentiation in the marketplace between BW-1 and BW-2. In Mint State the BW-1 is *far rarer* than BW-2. Mint State examples are typically brown. Priced after BW-2.

1828, 13 Stars • BW-2, C-3, B-2. *Breen dies:* 2-B. **Estimated population:** 5,000 to 7,000.

Obverse: 13 stars. Rays of Star 7 point to the top corner of the ribbon frame and to the curl on the forehead. 2 of 1828 leans forward so that the lower left is out of alignment with the first 8. Star 13 points to a denticle.

Reverse: Berry under upright of lower-left serif of E of UNITED just slightly above its center. Tip of leaf past right edge of second S of STATES. Tip of leaf under C of AMERICA just slightly right of its center.

1828, 13 Stars (BW-2, C-3, B-2).

Detail of date with 2 slightly out of alignment.

Notes: *Gilbert* (1916) G-1 "High leaf extending beyond S." This is the variety found in the Collins Hoard. Such coins are plentiful in the marketplace today. As such, Mint State is known, often with significant original color.

Typical values for 1828, 13 Stars. BW-1 is worth slightly more, and BW-2, slightly less.

	Cert	Avg	%MS	VG-8	F-12	VF-20	EF-40	AU-50	MS-60BN	MS-63BN	MS-63RB	MS-65BN	MS-65RB	MS-65RD
1828, 13 Stars	132	49.0	38%	$50	$70	$95	$125	$225	$350	$600	$1,000	$1,875	$3,500	$6,000

1828, 12 Stars • BW-3, C-2, B-3. *Breen dies:* 3-C. **Estimated population:** 3,000 to 4,000.

Obverse: 12 stars. The date is farther to the right than usual for the type.

Reverse: Berry under lower-right serif of upright of T of UNITED just slightly above its center. Tip of leaf slightly farther past second S of STATES than on BW-2. Tip of leaf under right edge of C of AMERICA.

1828, 12 Stars (BW-3, C-2, B-3); the curious variety with 12 obverse stars.

Notes: Mint State exists in this variety, typically brown. *Gilbert* (1916) G-3 "12 star variety." Gilbert also noted—upon close examination of the die state of "a coin struck from practically a perfect die"—that *in a later state* this reverse was combined with an 1826 obverse die. However, this 1828 reverse die does not match that used on either of the 1826 half cents described here or in the Breen *Encyclopedia*. Meanwhile, *another* 1828 reverse (BW-1) was combined with 1826 (BW-2). This 1828 use seems to have occurred later.

Numismatic Notes: *The 1828 with 12 stars:* In the *Historical Magazine*, May 1860, a reader's query was published from W. West, of Haverford, Pennsylvania: "Half cent of 1828. Can you, or any of the knowing ones among your correspondents, tell why there are only twelve, instead of thirteen, stars on the half cents of 1828? I have often asked coin collectors, but they professed ignorance."

	Cert	Avg	%MS	G-4	VG-8	F-12	VF-20	EF-40	AU-50	MS-60BN	MS-63BN	MS-63RB
1828, 12 Stars	213	50.8	25%	$35	$55	$75	$120	$250	$425	$1,300	$1,850	$3,500

THE COLLINS FIND OF *1828 HALF CENTS* (WITH *13 STARS*)

In his catalog of the Allison W. Jackman Collection, June 28–29, 1918, Philadelphia dealer Henry Chapman inserted this commentary after lot 879, a rare *1811* half cent, to shed light on the ready availability in Uncirculated grade of 1828-dated half cents, the variety with 13 obverse stars:

> This [1811] coin was discovered in 1884, being brought by an old colored woman of Alexandria, Va., to Mr. Benjamin H. Collins of Washington, to whom she stated she had a bag of them! He, thinking there was not any mistake about the hoard, sold it [*i.e.*, the 1811] to S.H. & H. Chapman for $3! With the remark, 'How many more will you take?'
>
> We said the lot.
>
> The woman subsequently brought him the bag, but to his astonishment they were all 1828 13 stars! And it has always been a mystery to me that an 1811 equally fine as the 1828s should have been in with the later date, and that her pick at random should have alighted on the only 1811 in the bag! It was subsequently sold in the Warner Sale, $67, and there bought by Mr. Jackman.

The preceding account has a number of inaccuracies and requires some amplification and modification including the following information:

B.H. Collins of Washington, D.C., specialized in early copper coins, especially cents, and was known for the fine specimens he handled, including several notable pieces imported from Europe. However, in 1884 he was an employee of the Treasury department. It was not until the 1890s that he became a rare-coin dealer. Thus, the date of the hoard is moved up a decade to 1894. The 1811 half cent was sold by Collins to Chapman for $18, not $3. Further, the Warner and Jackman specimens were two different coins. The number of 1828 half cents in the hoard was stated to be 50 by Collins in a conversation with John F. Jones in December 1899.

It is not known how many 1828 13-stars half cents were in the Collins Find, and the figure of 50 may be correct, but probably it is not. Many more than that are known today. In 1988 Walter Breen commented that the hoard "apparently originally numbered 1,000; as late as 1955 a remnant containing several hundred pieces was in the holdings of F.C.C. Boyd."[42]

In confirmation of the preceding, in 1996 John J. Ford Jr. stated that many of these pieces were owned by David U. Proskey, who sold them to Boyd along with other material. In the early 1950s about 200 to 300 bright red coins were sold by Boyd to New Netherlands Coin Co.[43]

Fact-finding concerning hoards is never an easy task, and absolute definition is often impossible. The typical Collins Find specimen seen today is bright orange-red with spotting.[44]

1829, Classic Head

Mintage (per *Mint Report*): 487,000.

The reported coinage of 487,000 for the calendar year probably includes some of earlier dates. There is only one die pair known for the 1829 half cents. Alternatively, more than one pair of dies may have been used, but production from the other dies was never released. Mintage figures for half cents of this era do not usually correlate with the availability of coins in the marketplace today.

On December 31, 1829, the Mint had 43 kegs of half cents on hand, comprising 848,000 coins—including the undistributed production of that year plus many from the year previous; this represents an average of 19,721 coins per keg.[45] The Mint shipped coins in wooden kegs as a heavy keg could be rolled easily, whereas if the coins had been boxed, a wheeled cart would have been required.

Today, the 1829 half cent is common in grades such as EF or AU. As to Mint State coins, they are scarce, but enough exist that finding one will be no problem. Most are lustrous brown or with some tinges of mint red (orange-red)—scarcely ever with much original mint red.

Proofs: A few meeting the qualification for this attribution exist, including the Philip Showers coin now in a Missouri collection.

	Cert	Avg	%MS	G-4	VG-8	F-12	VF-20	EF-40	AU-50	MS-60BN	MS-63BN	MS-63RB	MS-65BN	MS-65RB
1829	335	51.9	47%	$30	$50	$70	$100	$140	$235	$400	$700	$1,175	$2,000	$3,750

1829 • BW-1, C-1, B-1. *Breen dies:* 1-A. *Estimated population:* 3,000 to 5,000.

Obverse: Date low and close to border, 1 and 2 slightly high. Stars 1 and 2 and 11 and 12 closely spaced.

Reverse: Berry opposite lower-left serif of E of UNITED. Tip of leaf ends slightly past second S of STATES.

Notes: None known to have been in any hoard. Mint State exists in this variety, typically brown.

1829 (BW-1, C-1, B-1).

1831, Classic Head

Mintage (per *Mint Report*): 2,200.

This year introduced a modification of the rims. The denticles are in the form of beads set inside a flat rim, the equivalent of what has been called a "closed collar" in the new style of certain silver coins of the era, beginning in 1828.

Although hundreds of thousands of undistributed half cents of earlier years were in storage at the Mint, coinage in 1831 was reported as 2,200 pieces. No examples are known with mint luster or frost. Whether the circulated coins that are recorded are circulation strikes or Proofs that were spent has been a matter of debate in the pages of *Penny-Wise*. Ronald P. Manley, for instance, took up the subject in "A Case for Proof-Only 1831 Half Cents," May 15, 1996. Just one obverse die was made, and this was used to coin Proofs as well as circulation strikes. R.W. Julian cites convincing evidence that 2,200 half cents were struck in this year, although the documents do not mention the date(s) on the coins. It is Q. David Bowers's view that 2,200 1831-dated half cents were struck as representatives of the new technology. These seem to have been struck from a single die pair that had prooflike or full Proof surfaces. Whether all were released is an open question, as the coins today are even rarer than a typical surviving percentage of the mintage might suggest.

Regarding the surface, an analogy can be drawn to the 1836-dated Gobrecht silver dollars struck at the Mint in 1836 and early 1837 to the extent of 1,600 pieces—all with mirrored surfaces. Nearly all of these dollars were simply listed as coinage in the *Mint Reports* (no mention of mirror surfaces), and nearly all were placed into circulation for face value at the time. Thus, the answer seems to be: all were Proofs or had mirrored surfaces.

Original 1831 half cents were made in the year indicated, in small numbers for inclusion in Proof sets as well as for any interested numismatists (the Mint was very accommodating for such requests, but the population of collectors was very small), as well as in larger amounts for circulation (but from the same dies). Sometime after 1836, the so-called First Restrikes were coined, combining the single obverse die with a Proof die used to make 1836-dated Proof half cents. Still later, Second Restrikes were made, with the new reverse style (probably not before spring 1859, smaller wreath, no line below CENT) introduced in 1840, but on a Proof die with parallel die scratches over RICA (the "Second Restrike" reverse, used with dies 1840 through 1849 and again in 1852).

1831, Original • BW-1, C-1 (for Proof, C-1, B-1)

1831, Original • BW-1, C-1 (for Proof, C-EO-5), B-1. *Breen dies:* 1-A. ***Estimated population:*** Circulated Proofs: 20 to 30; Proof-60 and upward: 10 to 15.

Obverse: Small date placed low on the coin. 8 smaller and with base higher than other numerals.

1831, Original (BW-1, C-1, B-1).

Reverse: Large Berries. Tip of leaf under right edge of second S of STATES. Tiny artifact remainder of an accidental stray serif at inside leaf and field below E of STATES. *Points of distinction:* Also used to coin 1832 (BW-1).

Notes: Proofs for numismatic purposes were made in two styles: with bright, mirrorlike surface and with matte-like bronzed surface. Today, perhaps two-thirds or so of the known pieces are mirrorlike and one-third are bronzed. The bronzed Proofs were made by a special process involving bronzing powder, a popular format for Mint *medals*, but not often employed for coins. Otherwise, all had mirrored surfaces.

	Cert	Avg	%MS	PF-40	PF-50	PF-60	PF-63BN	PF-63RB
1831, Original (Proofs and circulated coins)	6	54.7		$50,000	$60,000	$77,500	$150,000	$200,000

1831, Restrike From the Same Obverse Die, Reverse of 1836 •

BW-1a, C-PR-2, B-2. *Breen dies:* 1-B. *Estimated population:* Proofs: 35 to 50.

Obverse: Same die as preceding. Now repolished.

Reverse: Large Berries. Tip of leaf under lower-left serif of second S of STATES. *Later use* of the reverse of 1836, Proof (BW-1). Cracks eventually develop.

1831, Restrike From the Same Obverse Die, Reverse of 1836 (BW-1a, C-PR-2, B-2).

Notes: Breen's "First Restrike," but not called that here, to avoid confusion—as elsewhere, that nomenclature refers to a style of 1840 die with Small Berries.

	Cert	Avg	%MS	PF-60	PF-63BN	PF-63RB	PF-65BN	PF-65RB
1831, Restrike From the Same Dies	(a)			$10,000	$15,000	$20,000	$23,000	$37,500

a. Included in certified population for 1831, Original.

1831, Second Restrike Die, Reverse of 1840 •

BW-2, C-SR-25, B-3. *Breen dies:* 1-C. *Estimated population:* Proofs: 7 to 11.

Obverse: Same die as preceding. Further polished, now with slight bulging in field.

Reverse: Small Berries. Wreath type by Christian Gobrecht, introduced in 1840; later Proof die with diagonal raised lines over RICA ("Second Restrike" die).

1831, Second Restrike Die, Reverse of 1840 (BW-2, C-SR-25, B-3).

Notes: Usually well struck, but at least one is known with flat striking.[46]

Numismatic Notes: *Levick commentary (1866):* J.N.T. Levick, in his copy of W. Elliot Woodward's auction catalog of the Francis S. Hoffman Collection, offered in April 1866, provided a marginal note helping to pinpoint the time of issue. For an 1831, Large Berries, Proof, half cent Levick noted, "These were restruck at the Mint in quantity in 1860."

This was probably a reference to restriking 1831 half cents in general, not to the specific example being sold in the Hoffman sale. Levick's comment is one of the earliest to address restrikes of the 1831 year. The Second Restrikes were known at the time and were called "Small Berries."

Frossard commentary (1879): Édouard Frossard, in his 1879 *Monograph of United States Cents and Half Cents issued between the years 1793 and 1857,* stated:

> The obverse dies of 1831 and 1836 were at some subsequent date combined with the reverse of probably the 1856 half cent, forming a combination known among collectors as the 1831 and 1836 Mint Restrikes. Only 12 of the 1831 and possibly less of the 1836 are said to have been issued.

However, the Mint did not release production figures for such restrikes, which are thought to have been a private venture to enrich Mint personnel, and thus Frossard's estimate is a guess. The reverse of 1856—small berries and with doubling of NT of CENT and of the wreath ribbon, as used on restrikes of half cents dated in the 1840s—is a different die.

	Cert	Avg	%MS	PF-60	PF-63BN	PF-63RB	PF-65BN	PF-65RB
1831, Second Restrike Die	10	65.6		$14,500	$22,000	$33,750	$45,000	$65,000

1832, Classic Head

Circulation mintage (estimate): 51,000.

The *Mint Report* data for 1832 to 1835 are patently incorrect and, in any event are given for *1833 to 1836* (in fact, there were no circulation strikes *dated* 1836). The estimated figures given here are moved back a year, to reflect 1832 to 1835, and are still probably off the mark. These are calendar-year production numbers and do not necessarily reflect the dates on the coins.

Half cents of this year are readily available. Most are well struck. Typical grades are EF and AU. Mint State coins are scarcer. These are generally seen in grades from MS-60 to MS-63 with brown color.

Typical values for 1832 half cents.

	Cert	Avg	%MS	F-12	VF-20	EF-40	AU-50	MS-60BN	MS-63BN	MS-63RB	MS-65BN	MS-65RB
1832	397	53.3	39%	$70	$100	$140	$200	$325	$475	$875	$1,450	$4,000

	Cert	Avg	%MS	PF-60	PF-63BN	PF-63RB	PF-65BN	PF-65RB
1832, Proof	1	64.0	100%	$7,000	$10,000	$13,500	$20,000	$32,500

1832 • BW-1, C-1, B-1. *Breen dies:* 1-A. *Estimated population:* Circulation strikes: 1,250 to 1,750; Proofs: 4 to 8.

Obverse: Small date close to border. 1 slightly high.

Reverse: Tip of leaf under right edge of second S of STATES. Tiny artifact remainder of an accidental stray serif at inside leaf and field below E of STATES. Berry opposite space between T and E of UNITED.

1832 (BW-1, C-1, B-1).

Notes: *Gilbert* (1916) G-2 "High leaves terminate at end of S and under upright of F." Many Mint State examples are known, usually with brown surfaces, rarely with some mint color.

1832 • BW-2, C-2, B-2. *Breen dies:* 1-B. *Estimated population:* 1,250 to 1,750.

Obverse: Same die as preceding. *Points of distinction:* A light crack develops in later states.

Reverse: Tip of leaf under E of STATES. Berry opposite lower-left serif of T of UNITED. *Points of distinction:* A light crack develops into a heavy crack.

1832 (BW-2, C-2, B-2).

Notes: *Gilbert* (1916) G-1 "High leaves end under E and F." Proofs were struck from these dies. Mint State is known, brown being usual, occasionally with some mint color.

1832 • BW-3, C-3, B-3. *Breen dies:* 1-C.
Estimated population: 1,250 to 1,750.

Obverse: Same die as preceding.

Reverse: Tip of leaf under right edge of second S of STATES. Berry opposite upright of T of UNITED. Tip of leaf slightly past C of AMERICA.

Notes: *Gilbert* (1916) G-3 "High leaves terminate at ends of S and F." Walter Breen states a few Proofs were struck of this variety.

1832 (BW-3, C-3, B-3).

Mint State is known, brown being usual, occasionally with some mint color.

1833, *Classic Head*

Circulation mintage (estimate): 103,000.

Only one die pair is known for the 1833 half cents. The number of coins minted with the date 1833 is not known, but the production must have been into six figures. Today, most pieces in the marketplace are EF or AU. Mint State coins are plentiful. These are often highly prooflike, thus making the differentiation between a prooflike Mint State coin and a full Proof coin controversial and very difficult to determine. Many of these are hoard coins (see Numismatic Notes below). As late as the mid-1950s, it was not unusual for old-time dealers to have a nice supply of these in stock. Today, they are widely dispersed. Many have been cleaned and recolored, giving them an orangish hue. Undipped coins are *light* yellow-orange with some black toning flecks. Most are well struck.

Half cents had piled up in storage at the Mint after coinage of the denomination resumed in the 1820s (see information under 1829). Between 1829 and a report of June 19, 1833, 12 kegs with $1,170 face value, or 234,000 half cents, had been melted for use as alloy in the silver and copper coinage. Nine kegs (141,000 coins) were still at the Mint as of June 19.[47]

Proofs: Many if not *most* 1833 "Proof" half cents are really prooflike circulation strikes, in Q. David Bowers's opinion. This yields a large population far exceeding any true Proof mintage of the era, and far exceeding the number of numismatists interested in such pieces at that time.

Typical values for 1833 half cents.

	Cert	Avg	%MS	F-12	VF-20	EF-40	AU-50	MS-60BN	MS-63BN	MS-63RB	MS-65BN	MS-65RB	MS-65RD
1833	588	58.6	68%	$70	$100	$140	$200	$325	$450	$750	$1,250	$3,500	$7,250

	Cert	Avg	%MS	PF-60	PF-63BN	PF-63RB	PF-65BN	PF-65RB
1833, Proof	15	64.1		$4,750	$5,750	$8,500	$10,500	$13,000

1833 • BW-1, C-1, B-1. *Breen dies:* 1-A.
Estimated population: Circulation strikes: 3,500 to 5,000; Proofs: 25 to 50.

Obverse: Only one die. Date widely spaced, 83 closer than are the other numerals.

Reverse: Only one die. *Points of distinction:* Also used to coin all half cents of 1834 and some of 1835.

Notes: *Gilbert* (1916) B G-1 "High leaves

1833 (BW-1, C-1, B-1).

terminate under S and upright of F." Mint State exists with much original color, usually with flecks.

Numismatic Notes: *The Guttag Hoard:* In the 1930s the Guttag Brothers, New York City securities brokers and rare-coin dealers, discovered a large hoard of 1833 half cents.[48] The number was never published, but likely was well over 1,000 pieces, perhaps over 2,000. Most were bright red, usually with some tiny black flecks. During the 1930s, these sold for about 25¢ each on the market. In the mid-1950s the remainder coins were distributed in New York and sold for several dollars apiece. Many of the 1833 half cents were prooflike and more than just a few were offered as Proofs.[49]

1834, Classic Head

Circulation mintage (estimate): 141,000.

The 1834 half cent is similar to the 1833 in several ways. There is only one die pair this year. The actual coinage of pieces bearing this date is not known, but must have been generous. Circulated examples are plentiful and are typically EF or AU. Mint State coins are easy to find as well, but they are not nearly as plentiful as those of 1833 and 1835. Relatively few display original mint color.

    Proofs: Proofs were struck from this die pair. Some prooflike circulation strikes have been classified as Proofs, but the problem is not nearly as acute as for 1833.

Typical values for 1834 half cents.

	Cert	Avg	%MS	F-12	VF-20	EF-40	AU-50	MS-60BN	MS-63BN	MS-63RB	MS-65BN	MS-65RB	MS-65RD
1834	603	56.4	53%	$70	$100	$140	$200	$325	$450	$750	$1,250	$3,500	$5,250

	Cert	Avg	%MS	PF-60	PF-63BN	PF-63RB	PF-65BN	PF-65RB
1834, Proof	13	65.0		$5,000	$6,000	$9,000	$13,750	$17,500

1834 • BW-1, C-1, B-1. *Breen dies:* 1-A. *Estimated population:* Circulation strikes: 3,500 to 5,000; Proofs: 20 to 30.

Obverse: Only one die. Date widely spaced, 8 slightly high, 4 larger than the other numerals.

Reverse: Only one die. *Points of distinction:* Also used to coin half cents of 1833 and 1835.

Notes: Mint State with brown surfaces can be found, sometimes with a small amount of original color.

1834 (BW-1, C-1, B-1).

1835, Classic Head

Circulation mintage (estimate): 398,000.

Why the Mint struck more half cents in 1835—when several hundred thousand were still on hand from earlier years—is a mystery. Today, the 1835, known in two varieties, is a common date. Most in the marketplace are EF or AU, although many Mint State coins exist, mostly from the Elmer Sears hoard (see Numismatic Notes for BW-2).

    Proofs: Proofs were struck from the BW-2 die combination and are rare today.

Typical values for 1835 half cents.

	Cert	Avg	%MS	F-12	VF-20	EF-40	AU-50	MS-60BN	MS-63BN	MS-63RB	MS-65BN	MS-65RB
1835	1126	56.1	56%	$70	$100	$140	$200	$325	$450	$750	$1,250	$3,500

	Cert	Avg	%MS	PF-60	PF-63BN	PF-63RB	PF-65BN	PF-65RB
1835, Proof	2	64.0		$5,000	$6,000	$8,500	$10,500	$13,000

1835 • BW-1, C-1, B-1. *Breen dies:* 1-A. *Estimated population:* 4,500 to 6,000.

Obverse: Small date placed well above the border. The 3 is slightly smaller than the other numerals.

Reverse: Berry opposite lower-right serif of T of UNITED. ST of STATES widely spaced. *Points of distinction:* This die was also used to coin half cents of 1833 and 1834.

Notes: *Gilbert* (1916) G-2 "A wide space between S and T in STATES." Mint State with red and brown surfaces can be found.

Numismatic Notes: See BW-2.

1835 (BW-1, C-1, B-1).

Detail of wide ST of STATES.

1835 • BW-2, C-2, B-2. *Breen dies:* 1-B. *Estimated population:* Circulation strikes: 4,000 to 5,000. Proofs: 15 to 20.

Obverse: Same die as preceding.

Reverse: Berry opposite upright of T of UNITED. ST of STATES closely spaced. *Points of distinction:* Cracks develop in the later state.

Notes: *Gilbert* (1916) G-1 "Little space between S and T in STATES." Proofs were struck from this die combination. Mint State with red and brown surfaces can be found.

1835 (BW-2, C-2, B-2).

Numismatic Notes: *The Sears Hoard:* In the 1930s dealer Elmer Sears is said to have found a hoard of 1835 half cents, "probably a bag of 1,000 pieces, possibly more than that. They were in spotty mint red Uncirculated state."[50] It was not unusual to see groups of these coins as late as the 1950s.[51]

1836, *Classic Head*

Proof mintage (estimate): 140 to 240.

As there was no need for more half cents in 1836, no circulation strikes were made. Proofs were struck in small numbers for inclusion in sets and for anyone else interested. The *original* coinage was very small, probably fewer than 50.

Sometime later, this same die pair was taken out of a vault, repolished, and used to strike more 1836-dated Proofs. These are designated as "First Restrikes." These tend to have squarer rims and edges than do originals. It is not known when these restrikes were made, but it may have been in the 1840s and 1850s, when the 1836 was found to be rare as a date by numismatists, and requests for more were made. The curators of the Mint Cabinet (established in June 1838), Jacob Reese Eckfeldt and William E. DuBois, were very interested in numismatics and were accommodating to collectors.

At a later date, possibly beginning in the spring of 1859, the Second Restrike coins were made, perhaps initiating a production that extended over the next decade or so. These have the style introduced in 1840, with smaller wreath and other modifications. This particular die is distinguished by having four diagonal die lines over RICA. The same die was paired with other Proof obverses of various dates from 1840 onward as well as the earlier 1831 obverse.

1836, Early Die State, Original, Proof • BW-1, C-EO-12, B-1. *Estimated population:* Proofs: 30 to 40.

Obverse: Small date fairly high from the border. 3 low.

Reverse: Large Berries. Tip of leaf under lower-left serif of second S of STATES.

Notes: Compare to the following.

1836, Early Die State, Original, Proof (BW-1, C-EO-12, B-1).

	Cert	Avg	%MS	PF-60	PF-63BN	PF-63RB	PF-65BN	PF-65RB
1836, Early Die State, Original, Proof	13	63.8		$6,000	$8,000	$10,000	$12,500	$17,500

1836, Later Die State, Restrike from the Same Dies, Proof • BW-1a, C-PR-1, B-1a. *Estimated population:* Proofs: 10 to 15.

Obverse: Same die as preceding. Slightly bulged or buckled at the center.

Reverse: Same die as preceding. Now repolished.

Notes: Walter Breen gives these separate numbers, but as the dies are identical, the BW-1 designation covers both here, with the additional notation.

1836, Later Die State, Restrike, Proof (BW-1a, C-PR-1, B-1a).

	Cert	Avg	%MS	PF-60	PF-63BN	PF-63RB	PF-65BN	PF-65RB
1836, Later Die State, First Restrike, Proof	(a)			$5,000	$7,000	$10,500	$13,500	$17,500

a. Included in certified population for 1836, Early Die State, Original, Proof.

1836, Second Restrike, Proof • BW-2, C-SR-16, B-2. *Breen dies:* 1-C. *Estimated population:* Proofs: 6 to 10.

Obverse: Same die as preceding. Further bulging, especially in the right field, causing some weakness to the stars.

Reverse: Small Berries. Wreath type by Christian Gobrecht, introduced in 1840s; later Proof die with diagonal raised lines over RICA ("Second Restrike" die).

1836, Second Restrike, Proof (BW-2, C-SR-16, B-2).

Notes: Wide rims on both sides. The illustrated coin, from a Missouri collection, is struck off center. This is a late restrike, probably from the 1860s or perhaps early 1870s. This issue is a classic rarity.

	Cert	Avg	%MS	PF-60	PF-63BN	PF-63RB	PF-65BN	PF-65RB
1836, Second Restrike, Proof	2	64.5		$15,000	$20,000	$26,250	$32,500	$42,500

The 1837 Half Cent Token (Not a Mint Issue)

No half cents were struck with the date of 1837. After 1836, the next circulation-strike mintage was in 1849. In the meantime, Proofs were struck for each year from 1840 onward. During the Hard Times era, which began in 1837, several hundred different varieties of copper cent-sized tokens were issued. Some bore political or satirical devices and inscriptions, while others advertised merchants or products.

Among all of these was a single variety of the *half cent* denomination. Struck from dies believed to have been made by New York City engraver Edward Hulseman, the token bears on the obverse a perched eagle, copied from the motif used on contemporary quarter dollars, with the inscription STANDARD WEIGHT AND VALUE, 1837. The reverse has a wreath enclosing the inscription HALF / CENT / WORTH / OF with the additional inscription PURE COPPER and stars on the outside of the wreath.

An early mention of it by J.N.T. Levick was published in the *American Journal of Numismatics*, April 1870, as part of "Description of the 'Hard Times Tokens' of '37": "Many collectors regard this piece as a pattern; but why, I can not explain. I should more readily assume it to be a satirical piece. Other collectors place it among their half cents of that year, there being no half cents issued in 1837, '8, and '9."

Likely, the dies made by Hulseman at his shop at 80 Nassau Street were for the account of one of the token manufacturers in New England. Cent-sized tokens were typically wholesaled at $6 per thousand to merchants and others, who gave them out in change at the value of a cent. Perhaps these half-cent tokens wholesaled for $3 per thousand.

Later, this token became well known and was listed in Lyman H. Low's definitive text, *Hard Times Tokens*, and still later elsewhere, as in Russell Rulau's *Standard Catalog of United States Tokens 1700–1900*. Wayte Raymond's "National" album for half cents included a space for it.

Examples are readily collectible today. Typical grades are VF and EF, with AU being scarcer. Mint State coins are scarcer yet and invariably are lustrous brown.

	Cert	Avg	%MS	VF-20	EF-40	AU-50	MS-60BN	MS-63BN
1837 "Hard Times" Token	0	n/a		$145	$250	$350	$725	$1,250

1837, Half Cent Token (Hard Times Token) • *Estimated Population:* 400 to 600.

Notes: Mint State with brown surfaces can be found.

1837, Half Cent Token (Hard Times Token).

BRAIDED HAIR (1840–1857)

Designer: *Christian Gobrecht.* **Weight:** *84 grains (5.44 grams).*
Composition: *Copper.* **Diameter:** *23.5 mm.* **Edge:** *Plain.*

1853 (BW-1, C-1, B-1).

The Braided Hair half cent type was introduced in 1840, a year after it was inaugurated in the copper cent series. At the time there was little market demand for the denomination, and quantities of earlier dates were on hand at banks and at the Mint. Accordingly, the half cents of the years 1840 through 1848 were made only in small numbers, in Proof format, for sale to collectors and for inclusion in Proof sets.

To be specific, Mint inventory figures show these earlier-dated half cents on hand:

December 31, 1840: 402,200 • September 22, 1841: 371,710 • December 31, 1842: 330,400 • September 30, 1843: 267,100 • December 31, 1844: 174,952 • December 31, 1845: 149,594 • June 30, 1846: 135,560 • September 30, 1847: 102,956 • March 31, 1848: 95,844 • June 30, 1848: 88,848 • September 30, 1848: 7,258.[52]

As the inventory was depleted, circulation strikes of the Braided Hair design were first made in 1849 (of the Large Date variety first) and were produced through 1857, with the exception of 1852 (for which only Proofs were made). These circulation issues are easily enough collected today.

The 1840 to 1848; 1849, Small Date; and 1852 issues are referred to as "Proof only" in listings. Proofs of the years 1854 to 1857 can be found with some searching, as they appear on the market with regularity. For these dates, circulation strikes are plentiful. Some earlier Proofs were made, including for the 1849, Large Date, and are extremely rare.

Philadelphia dealer E.B. Mason Jr. contributed this to the *American Journal of Numismatics* in January 1871:

> *Re-Struck Half Cents Distinguishable from Originals, Hub of 1841.* Scarcer half cents, comprising amongst others, those from 1840 to 1849 inclusive, were re-struck at the U.S. Mint some years subsequently to the date of their issue. By one formerly employed in the Mint I have been told that all these dates were re-coined excepting two, the dies of which he understood could not be found.
>
> He apprehended there was no way by which they could be distinguished from originals, unless the latter could be traced to a time prior to the year of re-coinage. Another person who had, as I supposed, unusual facilities for acquaintance with the subject, stated that there were re-strikes of all the forties, but not more to the best of his knowledge than three complete sets.
>
> These representations not being satisfactory to my mind, I have endeavored to find out what I could learn from a careful examination of the coins themselves. In the effort to obtain a complete set of the Half Cents, a '46 and a '43 came into my hands. I found they had reverses that were not products of the same die. The former had ten large round berries, prominently adorning its wreath. The other had eleven berries of much smaller size, some of them even rudimentary, and mostly rather elongated. They also differed in the arrangement of the ribbon which fastens the ends of the wreath. On the '46, it was turned, at the upper part, *behind the first leaf* to the observer's left. On the '43, it was turned back upon itself at an acute angle, *leaving the corresponding leaf in its entirety* resting upon the field.
>
> Further investigation showed there was a '46, having a like reverse with my '43, and a '43 with a reverse like my '46; and not only so, but eventually I found half cents from 1840 to 1849, inclusive, having each of the reverses. The small berry and sharp-angled-ribbon reverse, proved to be precisely that of all the common halves of '49, and later dates.
>
> The inference was irresistible, either that two dies were employed each year during the decade under consideration—which is highly improbable, considering the exceedingly limited number coined—or else that those with a reverse like that of the late dates, were made with one or more of the late dies. This last supposition has been confirmed by an inspection of the Mint Cabinet, an opportunity for which was recently given me by the Director, where I found all these halves to be products of what is concluded by considerations presented above, to have been original dies.
>
> The reader may be assured that more than three complete sets were made, true though it be that they, as well as the originals, on account of the chain of which they form an important part, as well as their great scarcity, will always be desirable, and only to be obtained at a large premium.
>
> It may be interesting to mention a slight accidental depression which can be traced on all half cents of the '40s and '50s, excepting 1840. This depression runs across the hair, below the ear, in the direction of the

fourth star to the right of the date. It shows that the hub of 1841 was ever after employed on the half cents, and is another instance of the light which minute examination throws upon the science of numismatics.

E.M., Philadelphia, October 1870.

In *Numisma*, in January 1883, Édouard Frossard included this under "Numismatic Correspondence":

We lay no claim to the discovery of differences in half cents. These have always been known and recognized among well posted coin dealers and collectors. The greater part of the half cents were restruck at the Mint at a time when the governing officers desired to increase the collection of Washington medals at the Mint by exchange, and were coined with that object in view, not as is generally supposed for speculative purposes.

It was not until Breen's monograph, *Proof Coins Struck by the United States Mint*, was published by Wayte Raymond in 1953, that the "First Restrike" and "Second Restrike" terms were used by specialists, and even then the interest was not widespread. New Netherlands Coin Company catalogs that were written in that decade by Breen and John J. Ford Jr. used the nomenclature. Since then, such listings have been widespread. Earlier, they were typically called Originals and Restrikes, or Large Berries and Small Berries.

Although there are no records of coinage, as the rarity of various First Restrike and Second Restrike half cents can vary widely, it may be that the Mint kept a small stock of originals (possibly) and restrikes on hand (not differentiating the two reverse varieties of the restrikes), and from time to time struck more as needed. Certainly, they were never made in sets.

As to Proofs in the marketplace today, the traditional way to collect them—for collectors desiring more than one of each date—is to acquire them by Large Berries (Original) and Small Berries (Restrike) varieties, often ignoring that within the restrikes there are two reverse dies. The first person to collect all three reverses was probably Emery May Holden Norweb, who sought them as early as the mid-1950s.[53] Somewhat later, R. Tettenhorst collected these three, plus a later-identified fourth variant, the Second Restrike on 96.1 grain planchets—struck after the regular Second Restrikes.

Today, most Proofs are in grades from Proof-60 to 63 or 64. True Proof-65 and higher coins are rare. Many have been cleaned and later retoned (any coin with hairlines has been dipped or cleaned at one time). This is not necessarily important, as it is the overall eye appeal that counts the most.

As to circulation strikes, most Braided Hair half cents on the market are well struck and of pleasing appearance. Grades range from VF to AU for most seen, although Mint State coins appear with frequency. Full or nearly full-bright mint-orange examples can be found for 1854 and 1855. The 1849, Large Date, 1850, and the 1853 are usually seen toned. Half cents of 1850, 1856, and 1857 are usually brown or, sometimes, red and brown. Many recolored pieces are on the market, and others have spots, etc. Connoisseurship is needed to acquire choice examples, and it is worthwhile to pay a premium for such.

DESIGN DETAILS

Christian Gobrecht, a highly accomplished artist and engraver, created the motif. The head of Miss Liberty is compact, faces left, with a tiara or diadem inscribed LIBERTY, and with her hair in a knot at the back, circled with beads. Thirteen stars surround most of the periphery. The date is below. In 1840 the half cent series began entering the date into the die by a four-digit logotype. Throughout the rest of the design's tenure, which continued to 1857, the same date logotype was used on all dies made for a given year, with the solitary exception of 1849, which occurs in Large Date and Small Date styles.

The reverse design of the 1840 to 1857 half cents is somewhat similar to the preceding type, except no line appears under CENT, the wreath is smaller, and the rim is flat and more prominent.

Originals among the Proof-only dates have Large Berries in the wreath. This is the style used to strike half cents in the year indicated on the dies, for inclusion in Proof sets or for sale to numismatists. Until

First Restrikes were made, circa 1856 (see below), Original die pairs for some dates were used to make a small number of restrikes. Some of these probably cannot be differentiated today from Original strikings.

First Restrike half cents among the Proof-only dates have Small Berries, and the NT of CENT is slightly doubled, and there is also doubling of the wreath ribbon. This was the die used to strike Proof 1856 half cents for inclusion in sets of that year. Accordingly, it is sometimes called the Reverse of 1856.

Second Restrike half cents among the Proof-only dates have Small Berries, and diagonal file marks over RICA of AMERICA. Likely, these were made from about the spring of 1859, or later, and continued in production in occasional batches for a decade or more. These are on planchets that are more or less within range of the normal weight of 84 grains.

Second Restrike half cents on heavy planchets, averaging 96.1 grains, are known for all dates from 1840 to 1848 and are very rare as a class. The collection of R. Tettenhorst includes one of each of these.

As *Walter Breen's Encyclopedia of United States Half Cents 1793–1857* delineates, there are occasional exceptions, such as Large Berry pieces being made as restrikes, etc., such technicalities being beyond the scope of the discussion here.

GRADING STANDARDS

MS-60 to 70 (Mint State). *Obverse:* In the lower Mint State grades, MS-60 and 61, some slight abrasion can be seen on the portrait, most evidently on the cheek. Check the tip of the coronet as well. Luster in the field is complete, or nearly so. At MS-63, luster should be complete, and no abrasions evident. At higher levels, the luster is complete and deeper, and some original mint color may be seen. Mint frost on this type is usually deep,

1855; BW-1, C-1, B-1. Graded MS-64RB.

sometimes satiny, but hardly ever prooflike. MS-64 coins may have some slight discoloration or scattered contact marks. A well-graded MS-65 or higher coin has full, rich luster; no contact marks visible except under magnification; and a nice blend of brown toning or nicely mixed (not stained or blotchy) mint color and natural brown toning. The late Walter Breen stated that he had never seen an 1853 (common date) half cent with extensive original mint color, but these are plentiful with brown-toned surfaces. *Reverse:* In the lower Mint State grades some abrasions are seen on the higher areas of the leaves. Mint luster is complete in all Mint State grades, as the open areas are protected by the lettering and wreath.

Illustrated coin: Red and brown on the obverse, this example is mostly brown on the reverse.

AU-50, 53, 55, 58 (About Uncirculated). *Obverse:* Wear is evident on the cheek, the hair above the forehead, and the tip of the coronet. Friction is evident in the field. At AU-58, luster may be present except in the center of the fields. As the grades go down to AU-50, wear is more evident on the portrait. Wear is seen on the stars, but is not as easy to discern as it is elsewhere. At AU-50 there is either no luster or only traces of luster close to the letters and devices. *Reverse:* Wear is most evident on the highest areas of the leaves and the ribbon bow.

1851; BW-1, C-1, B-1. Graded AU-58.

Luster is present in the fields. As the grades go downward from AU-58 to 50, wear increases and luster decreases. At the AU-50 level there is either no luster or traces of luster close to the letters and devices.

Illustrated coin: This coin shows Full Details on both sides, and has eye-pleasing light-brown surfaces.

EF-40, 45 (Extremely Fine). *Obverse:* Wear is more extensive on the portrait, including the cheek, hair, and coronet. The star centers are worn down slightly. Traces of luster are minimal, if at all existent. *Reverse:* The centers of the leaves are well worn, with detail visible only near the edges of the leaves and nearby, with the higher parts worn flat. Letters show significant wear. Luster, if present, is minimal.

1854; BW-1, C-1, B-1. Graded EF-40.

VF-20, 30 (Very Fine). *Obverse:* Wear is more extensive than on the foregoing. Some of the strands of hair are fused together. The center radials of the stars are worn nearly completely away. *Reverse:* The leaves show more extensive wear, with details visible at the edges, and only minimally and not on all leaves. The lettering shows smooth, even wear.

The Braided Hair half cent is seldom collected in grades lower than VF-20.

1855; BW-1, C-1, B-1. Graded VF-20.

PF-60 to 70 (Proof). For the issues of 1840 to 1848, 1849, Small Date, and 1852, only Proofs were made, without related examples for circulation. All were restruck at the Mint. Generally, the quality of these Proofs is very good, with excellent striking of details and nice planchet quality. *Obverse and Reverse:* Superb gems at PF-65 and 66 show hairlines only under high magnification, and at PF-67 none are seen. The fields are deeply mirror-

1852, First Restrike; BW-2, C-SR-12, B-2. PF-64RB.

like. There is no evidence of friction. At lower levels, hairlines increase, with a profusion at PF-60 to 62 (and also a general dullness of the fields). Typical color for an undipped coin ranges from light or iridescent brown to brown with some traces of mint color. Except for issues in the 1850s, Proofs are nearly always BN or, less often, RB. The rare Proofs of the 1840s are sometimes seen with light wear and can be classified according to the About Uncirculated and Extremely Fine comments above, except in place of "luster" read "Proof surface."

Illustrated coin: A high-quality coin with a generous amount of original mint color, this piece could just as easily be designated PF-64RD, for some "RD" coins do not have this much color. Some light hairlines keep it from a higher grade. Excellent eye appeal.

1840, Braided Hair

Proof mintage (estimate): 125 to 200.

Production was limited only to Proofs. Originals struck for inclusion in sets this year and for sale to numismatists have large berries. First Restrikes were coined beginning in 1856 or later, and Second Restrikes were likely coined commencing in or after the spring of 1859, as noted in the overview of this type.

1840, Original, Large Berries, Proof

• BW-1, C-PO-1, B-1a. *Breen dies:* 1-A. *Estimated population:* Proof: 20 to 25.

Obverse: 1840, only die of the year.

Reverse: Large Berries in wreath.

Notes: Some show traces of flattened reeding or reeding-like vertical lines. According to Walter Breen, "Blanks were experimentally reeded, then coined in a plain collar, obliterating the reeding, but leaving a knurled effect

1840, Original, Large Berries, Proof (BW-1, C-PO-1, B-1a).

at the junction between outer rim and edge. Reason unknown." Robert Schonwalter suggested that the Mint used an old collar for the half eagle denomination which was 22.5 mm diameter.[54] He continues on to theorize that they reamed out the collar to the proper 23 mm diameter, leaving only traces of the edge reeding. Some 1840 half cents were made from these dies at a slightly later date (Breen-1b).

	Cert	Avg	%MS	PF-60	PF-63BN	PF-63RB	PF-65BN	PF-65RB
1840, Original, Large Berries, Proof	11	63.8		$5,500	$6,500	$8,000	$10,000	$15,000

1840, First Restrike, Small Berries, Proof

• BW-2, C-SR-2, B-2. *Breen dies:* 1-B. *Estimated population:* Proof: 7 to 9.

Obverse: Same die as preceding.

Reverse: Small Berries in wreath. Slight doubling at NT of CENT and wreath ribbon.

1840, First Restrike, Small Berries, Proof (BW-2, C-SR-2, B-2).

	Cert	Avg	%MS	PF-60	PF-63BN	PF-63RB	PF-65BN	PF-65RB
1840, First Restrike, Small Berries, Proof	(a)			$4,750	$5,750	$7,500	$10,500	$15,000

a. Included in certified population for 1840, Second Restrike, Small Berries, Proof.

1840, Second Restrike, Small Berries, Proof

• BW-3, C-SR-17, B-3. *Breen dies:* 1-C. *Estimated population:* Proof: 14 to 17.

Obverse: Same die as preceding.

Reverse: Small Berries in wreath. Diagonal die lines over RICA.

1840, Second Restrike, Small Berries, Proof (BW-3, C-SR-17, B-3).

Notes: Some have high wire rims. Some were restruck on heavy (96.1 grains average) planchets and are exceedingly rare (the suffix "a" can be added after the BW number to describe these).

	Cert	Avg	%MS	PF-60	PF-63BN	PF-63RB	PF-65BN	PF-65RB
1840, Second Restrike, Small Berries, Proof	8	64.5		$5,300	$6,375	$7,500	$9,375	$14,000

1841, Braided Hair

Proof mintage (estimate): 150 to 250.

Production was limited only to Proofs. Originals struck for inclusion in sets this year and for sale to numismatists have Large Berries. First Restrikes were coined beginning in 1856 or later, and Second Restrikes were likely coined commencing in or after the spring of 1859, as noted in the overview of this type.

The 1841 seems to be the most available of all the Original-Proof half cents of the years 1840 to 1849; Proof *cents* of this year are also plentiful in comparison to others of the era. Remarkably, six were in the Chapman brothers' sale of the George Eavenson Collection, April 16–17, 1903.[55]

The color is sometimes an especially bright orange-red. All examples seen by Q. David Bowers have a die crack beginning at the rim, extending close to—but not touching—star 7, through stars 3 to 5, to the border. This crack occurred at a very early time. (Breen notes one perfect die piece was reported to him, though he did not see it.) The Eliasberg coin and a number of others have what can be called a crushed reeded edge (alternatively, reamed collar) similar to the 1840, Original.

This year the obverse hub sustained a dent or injury to the thick strand of hair that extends from under the back of the earlobe downward. Now, there is a gap in the strand, which is seen on all 1841 and later obverses of the Braided Hair type.

1841, Original, Large Berries, Proof

• BW-1, C-PO-2, B-1. *Breen dies: 1-A. Estimated population:* Proof: 35 to 50.

Obverse: 1841, only die of the year.

Reverse: Large Berries in wreath.

Notes: Some have crushed "reeding" on the edge (as viewed edge-on). All seen have a cracked obverse die.

1841, Original, Large Berries, Proof (BW-1, C-PO-2, B-1).

	Cert	Avg	%MS	PF-60	PF-63BN	PF-63RB	PF-65BN	PF-65RB
1841, Original, Large Berries, Proof	18	64.2		$4,350	$5,500	$7,500	$8,750	$13,000

1841, First Restrike, Small Berries, Proof

• BW-2, C-SR-3, B-2. *Breen dies: 1-B. Estimated population:* Proof: 5 to 7.

Obverse: Same die as preceding.

Reverse: Small Berries in wreath. Slight doubling at NT of CENT and wreath ribbon.

1841, First Restrike, Small Berries, Proof (BW-2, C-SR-3, B-2).

	Cert	Avg	%MS	PF-60	PF-63BN	PF-63RB	PF-65BN	PF-65RB
1841, First Restrike, Small Berries, Proof	(a)			$5,500	$6,500	$8,000	$11,000	$15,000

a. Included in certified population for 1841, Second Restrike, Small Berries, Proof.

1841, Second Restrike, Small Berries, Proof • BW-3, C-SR-18, B-3. *Breen dies:* 1-C. **Estimated population:** Proof: 10 to 12.

Obverse: Same die as preceding.

Reverse: Small Berries in wreath. Diagonal die lines over RICA.

1841, Second Restrike, Small Berries, Proof (BW-3, C-SR-18, B-3).

Notes: Most advanced stage of the obverse crack, heavier at and near stars 2 and 3. Sometimes seen with a high wire rim. Some were restruck on heavy planchets (96.1 grains average) and are exceedingly rare (the suffix "a" can be added after the BW number to describe these).

	Cert	Avg	%MS	PF-60	PF-63BN	PF-63RB	PF-65BN	PF-65RB
1841, Second Restrike, Small Berries, Proof	8	64.6		$4,500	$5,500	$7,500	$9,000	$13,000

1842, Braided Hair

Proof mintage (estimate): 120 to 180.

Similar to other half cents of the era, production of the 1842 was limited only to Proofs. Originals struck for inclusion in sets this year and for sale to numismatists have large berries. First Restrikes were coined beginning in 1856 or later, and Second Restrikes were likely coined commencing in or after the spring of 1859, as noted in the overview of this type.

The 1842 is one of the rarest Originals of the decade. Examples come on the market at widely spaced intervals, and usually only when advanced collections of half cents are sold—although, in the market since the 1990s, some have been bought by "trophy coin" enthusiasts, who are not otherwise interested in half cents. It is difficult to determine the population of *any* half cent, except for a handful of famous pedigreed rarities. Often, the same coin will appear in multiple catalog listings or be represented more than once in certification service reports. Some of these were distributed as part of full 1842 Proof sets, which contained the famous 1842, Small Date, quarter dollar.

1842, Original, Large Berries, Proof • BW-1, C-PO-3, B-1. *Breen dies:* 1-A. **Estimated population:** Proof: 15 to 20.

Obverse: 1842, only die of the year.

Reverse: Large Berries in wreath.

1842, Original, Large Berries, Proof (BW-1, C-PO-3, B-1).

	Cert	Avg	%MS	PF-60	PF-63BN	PF-63RB	PF-65BN	PF-65RB
1842, Original, Large Berries, Proof	5	63.4		$5,925	$7,000	$9,000	$10,000	$15,000

1842, First Restrike, Small Berries, Proof • BW-2, C-SR-4, B-2. *Breen dies:* 1-B. *Estimated population:* Proof: 15 to 20.

Obverse: Same die as preceding.

Reverse: Small Berries in wreath. Slight doubling at NT of CENT and wreath ribbon.

Notes: Often seen with a high wire rim.

1842, First Restrike, Small Berries, Proof (BW-2, C-SR-4, B-2).

	Cert	Avg	%MS	PF-60	PF-63BN	PF-63RB	PF-65BN	PF-65RB
1842, First Restrike, Small Berries, Proof	(a)			$5,000	$6,000	$7,500	$9,000	$13,000

a. Included in certified population for 1842, Second Restrike, Small Berries, Proof.

1842, Second Restrike, Small Berries, Proof • BW-3, C-SR-19, B-3. *Breen dies:* 1-C. *Estimated population:* Proof: 20 to 25.

Obverse: Same die as preceding.

Reverse: Small Berries in wreath. Diagonal die lines over RICA.

Notes: Some were restruck on heavy planchets (96.1 grains average) and are exceedingly rare (the suffix "a" can be added after the BW number to describe these).

1842, Second Restrike, Small Berries, Proof (BW-3, C-SR-19, B-3).

	Cert	Avg	%MS	PF-60	PF-63BN	PF-63RB	PF-65BN	PF-65RB
1842, Second Restrike, Small Berries, Proof	10	64.7		$5,500	$6,500	$8,000	$10,000	$14,000

1843, Braided Hair

Proof mintage (estimate): 125 to 200.

The story of the 1843 half cent is similar to that of the other Proof-only issues of the decade. Originals struck for inclusion in sets this year and for sale to numismatists have large berries. First Restrikes were coined beginning in 1856 or later, and Second Restrikes were likely coined commencing in or after the spring of 1859, as noted in the overview of this type.

In the midst of this listing of the "rarest of the rare" in the half cent series it is easy to lose sight of the absolute rarity of these pieces—an experience similar to being in the room full of Rembrandt oils at the Metropolitan Museum. However, *any single specimen* from the lineup of 1840 to 1849 Proofs, originals as well as restrikes, can be incredibly difficult to find in the first place, and even more so for an eye-appealing example.

The 1843, Second Restrike, is one of the great rarities of the decade, with fewer than a dozen estimated to exist, perhaps only slightly more than a half dozen. As First Restrikes exist in much larger numbers, this may reinforce the idea of the Mint keeping an inventory of restrikes, and making only a few Second Restrikes, as the supply of First Restrikes was generous. However, it is often unwise to theorize.

1843, Original, Large Berries, Proof

• BW-1, C-PO-4, B-1a. *Breen dies:* 1-A. **Estimated population:** Proof: 25 to 35.

Obverse: 1843, only die of the year.

Reverse: Large Berries in wreath.

1843, Original, Large Berries, Proof (BW-1, C-PO-4, B-1a).

	Cert	Avg	%MS	PF-60	PF-63BN	PF-63RB	PF-65BN	PF-65RB
1843, Original, Large Berries, Proof	6	62.7		$5,175	$6,250	$8,250	$9,375	$14,000

1843, First Restrike, Small Berries, Proof

• BW-2, C-SR-5, B-2. *Breen dies:* 1-B. **Estimated population:** Proof: 30 to 35.

Obverse: Same die as preceding.

Reverse: Small Berries in wreath. Slight doubling at NT of CENT and wreath ribbon.

Notes: Some have high wire rims. Sometimes with striking weakness at the center of the reverse.

1843, First Restrike, Small Berries, Proof (BW-2, C-SR-5, B-2).

	Cert	Avg	%MS	PF-60	PF-63BN	PF-63RB	PF-65BN	PF-65RB
1843, First Restrike, Small Berries, Proof	(a)			$5,000	$6,500	$7,750	$9,500	$14,000

a. Included in certified population for 1843, Second Restrike, Small Berries, Proof.

1843, Second Restrike, Small Berries, Proof

• BW-3, C-SR-20, B-3. *Breen dies:* 1-C. **Estimated population:** Proof: 7 to 9.

Obverse: Same die as preceding.

Reverse: Small Berries in wreath. Diagonal die lines over RICA.

Notes: Some were restruck on heavy planchets (96.1 grains average) and are exceedingly rare (the suffix "a" can be added after the BW number to describe these).

1843, Second Restrike, Small Berries, Proof (BW-3, C-SR-20, B-3).

	Cert	Avg	%MS	PF-60	PF-63BN	PF-63RB	PF-65BN	PF-65RB
1843, Second Restrike, Small Berries, Proof	7	64.7		$5,250	$6,750	$8,000	$9,750	$14,500

1844, Braided Hair

Proof mintage (estimate): 120 to 180.

Half cents of 1844 continue the pace of Proof-only dates. Originals struck for inclusion in sets this year and for sale to numismatists have large berries. First Restrikes were coined beginning in 1856 or later, and Second Restrikes were likely coined commencing in or after the spring of 1859, as noted in the overview of this type.

The 1844, First Restrike, is a prime rarity for the specialist, possibly because the Mint had a supply of Originals on hand to satisfy the numismatic demand. Often a span of many years will elapse between auction appearances for the First Restrike. It should be noted that for nearly all auction appearances before 1950 there is no way to determine whether a given "Small Berries" half cent is a First Restrike or a Second Restrike, unless its later pedigree can be traced. The differences are too minute to show up in halftone photographs, and collectors and dealers were not aware of such distinctions.

1844, Original, Large Berries, Proof

- BW-1, C-PO-5, B-1. *Breen dies:* 1-A. *Estimated population:* Proof: 19 to 24.

Obverse: 1844, only die of the year.

Reverse: Large Berries in wreath.

1844, Original, Large Berries, Proof (BW-1, C-PO-5, B-1).

	Cert	Avg	%MS	PF-60	PF-63BN	PF-63RB	PF-65BN	PF-65RB
1844, Original, Large Berries, Proof	9	62.9		$5,550	$6,500	$8,750	$9,500	$14,750

1844, First Restrike, Small Berries, Proof

- BW-2, C-SR-6, B-2. *Breen dies:* 1-B. *Estimated population:* Proof: 7 to 9.

Obverse: Same die as preceding.

Reverse: Small Berries in wreath. Slight doubling at NT of CENT and wreath ribbon.

Notes: Most are toned brown with little or no orange-red mint color.

1844, First Restrike, Small Berries, Proof (BW-2, C-SR-6, B-2).

	Cert	Avg	%MS	PF-60	PF-63BN	PF-63RB	PF-65BN	PF-65RB
1844, First Restrike, Small Berries, Proof	(a)			$5,750	$6,750	$8,500	$10,000	$17,500

a. Included in certified population for 1844, Second Restrike, Small Berries, Proof.

1844, Second Restrike, Small Berries, Proof

- BW-3, C-SR-21, B-3. *Breen dies:* 1-C. *Estimated population:* Proof: 14 to 17.

Obverse: Same die as preceding.

Reverse: Small Berries in wreath. Diagonal die lines over RICA.

Notes: Some have high wire rims. Some were restruck on heavy planchets (96.1 grains average) and are exceedingly rare (the suffix "a" can be added after the BW number to describe these).

1844, Second Restrike, Small Berries, Proof (BW-3, C-SR-21, B-3).

	Cert	Avg	%MS	PF-60	PF-63BN	PF-63RB	PF-65BN	PF-65RB
1844, Second Restrike, Small Berries, Proof	2	65.5		$5,000	$6,000	$7,500	$9,000	$14,000

1845, Braided Hair

Proof mintage (estimate): 110 to 170.

Half cents of 1845 are next in the lineup of Proof-only dates. Originals struck for inclusion in sets this year and for sale to numismatists have large berries. First Restrikes were coined beginning in 1856 or later, and Second Restrikes were likely coined commencing in or after the spring of 1859, as noted in the overview of this type.

Original 1845 half cents have been cataloged in the past as the rarest date among the Proof-only dates in the 1840s. However, it is likely that the 1842 and the 1849, Small Date, are rarer. The distinction is largely academic, for rarity-wise each of these three Proofs is more or less in the league of such classics as the 1876-CC twenty-cent piece, 1838-O half dollar, and 1804 silver dollar.

1845, Original, Large Berries, Proof

• BW-1, C-PO-6, B-1a. *Breen dies:* 1-A. ***Estimated population:*** Proof: 16 to 20.

Obverse: 1845, only die of the year.

Reverse: Large Berries in wreath.

Notes: Walter Breen reported one example from this die pair from dies later repolished.

1845, Original, Large Berries, Proof (BW-1, C-PO-6, B-1a).

	Cert	Avg	%MS	PF-60	PF-63BN	PF-63RB	PF-65BN	PF-65RB
1845, Original, Large Berries, Proof	3	65.0		$5,425	$6,500	$8,750	$11,000	$17,500

1845, First Restrike, Small Berries, Proof

• BW-2, C-SR-7, B-2. *Breen dies:* 1-B. ***Estimated population:*** Proof: 8 to 10.

Obverse: Same die as preceding.

Reverse: Small Berries in wreath. Slight doubling at NT of CENT and wreath ribbon.

1845, First Restrike, Small Berries, Proof (BW-2, C-SR-7, B-2).

	Cert	Avg	%MS	PF-60	PF-63BN	PF-63RB	PF-65BN	PF-65RB
1845, First Restrike, Small Berries, Proof	(a)			$5,750	$6,750	$8,500	$10,000	$16,000

a. Included in certified population for 1845, Second Restrike, Small Berries, Proof.

1845, Second Restrike, Small Berries, Proof

• BW-3, C-SR-22, B-3. *Breen dies:* 1-C. ***Estimated population:*** Proof: 12 to 14.

Obverse: Same die as preceding.

Reverse: Small Berries in wreath. Diagonal die lines over RICA.

1845, Second Restrike, Small Berries, Proof (BW-3, C-SR-22, B-3).

Notes: Some were restruck on heavy planchets (96.1 grains average) and are exceedingly rare (the suffix "a" can be added after the BW number to describe these).

	Cert	Avg	%MS	PF-60	PF-63BN	PF-63RB	PF-65BN	PF-65RB
1845, Second Restrike, Small Berries, Proof	9	64.4		$5,000	$6,000	$8,000	$9,000	$14,000

1846, Braided Hair

Proof mintage (estimate): 125 to 200.

Half cents of 1846 are similar in concept to other Proof-only issues of the era. Originals struck for inclusion in sets this year and for sale to numismatists have large berries. First Restrikes were coined beginning in 1856 or later, and Second Restrikes were likely coined commencing in or after the spring of 1859, as noted in the overview of this type.

Curiously, the numerals in the date of the 1846 die are very rustic and not from normal punches of the era. This anomaly, vividly evident when the digits are viewed under magnification, is unexplained. Perhaps an amateur cut certain of the punches, with the "8" in particular being crude in comparison to other "8" digits of the era and also in the "script" style (as opposed to the "block" style used elsewhere on coppers of the decade).

Detail of the 1846 date with script-style 8.

The First Restrike is one of the great rarities of the series. Walter Breen knew of only six examples.

1846, Original, Large Berries, Proof

• BW-1, C-PO-7, B-1. *Breen dies:* 1-A. *Estimated population:* Proof: 20 to 25.

Obverse: 1846, only die of the year.

Reverse: Large Berries in wreath.

1846, Original, Large Berries, Proof (BW-1, C-PO-7, B-1).

	Cert	Avg	%MS	PF-60	PF-63BN	PF-63RB	PF-65BN	PF-65RB
1846, Original, Large Berries, Proof	8	64.0		$5,550	$6,500	$8,500	$9,500	$14,750

1846, First Restrike, Small Berries, Proof

• BW-2, C-SR-8, B-2. *Breen dies:* 1-B. *Estimated population:* Proof: 5 to 7.

Obverse: Same die as preceding.

Reverse: Small Berries in wreath. Slight doubling at NT of CENT and wreath ribbon.

Notes: A great rarity.

1846, First Restrike, Small Berries, Proof (BW-2, C-SR-8, B-2).

	Cert	Avg	%MS	PF-60	PF-63BN	PF-63RB	PF-65BN	PF-65RB
1846, First Restrike, Small Berries, Proof	(a)			$8,000	$10,000	$12,500	$15,000	$20,000

a. Included in certified population for 1846, Second Restrike, Small Berries, Proof.

1846, Second Restrike, Small Berries, Proof • BW-3, C-SR-23, B-3. *Breen dies:* 1-C. ***Estimated population:*** Proof: 14 to 17.

Obverse: Same die as preceding.

Reverse: Small Berries in wreath. Diagonal die lines over RICA.

Notes: Some were restruck on heavy planchets (96.1 grains average) and are exceedingly rare (the suffix "a" can be added after the BW number to describe these).

1846, Second Restrike, Small Berries, Proof (BW-3, C-SR-23, B-3).

	Cert	Avg	%MS	PF-60	PF-63BN	PF-63RB	PF-65BN	PF-65RB
1846, Second Restrike, Small Berries, Proof	7	65.1		$5,000	$6,000	$8,000	$9,000	$14,000

1847, *Braided Hair*

Proof mintage (estimate): 200 to 300.

The Proof-only half cents of 1847 mirror the other issues of the era. Originals struck for inclusion in sets this year and for sale to numismatists have large berries. First Restrikes were coined beginning in 1856 or later, and Second Restrikes were likely coined commencing in or after the spring of 1859, as noted in the overview of this type.

The date logotype of this year is large in relation to the space provided for it, this also being true for 1848. The First Restrike is one of the great rarities in the series. Walter Breen knew of three pieces and commented, "It is still the rarest of all die combinations among the Proof-only dates, being rarer than the 1831 or 1836 with Small Berries or the 1852 with Large Berries." This probably precipitated a generous production of Second Restrikes, which today are among the most available Proofs of the era.

1847, Original, Large Berries, Proof
• BW-1, C-PO-8, B-1a. *Breen dies:* 1-A. ***Estimated population:*** Proof: 20 to 25.

Obverse: 1847, only die of the year.

Reverse: Large Berries in wreath.

Notes: Some seem to have been restruck from this die pair, but probably sparingly.

1847, Original, Large Berries, Proof (BW-1, C-PO-8, B-1a).

	Cert	Avg	%MS	PF-60	PF-63BN	PF-63RB	PF-65BN	PF-65RB
1847, Original, Large Berries, Proof	10	64.4		$10,000	$12,500	$17,500	$25,000	$40,000

1847, First Restrike, Small Berries, Proof • BW-2, C-SR-9, B-2. *Breen dies:* 1-B. *Estimated population:* Proof: 3 or 4.

Obverse: Same die as preceding.

Reverse: Small Berries in wreath. Slight doubling at NT of CENT and wreath ribbon.

1847, First Restrike, Small Berries, Proof (BW-2, C-SR-9, B-2).

	Cert	Avg	%MS	PF-60	PF-63BN	PF-63RB	PF-65BN	PF-65RB
1847, First Restrike, Small Berries, Proof	(a)			$40,000	$50,000	$77,500	$97,500	$110,000

a. Included in certified population for 1847, Second Restrike, Small Berries, Proof.

1847, Second Restrike, Small Berries, Proof • BW-3, C-SR-24, B-3. *Breen dies:* 1-C. *Estimated population:* Proof: 30 to 40.

Obverse: Same die as preceding.

Reverse: Small Berries in wreath. Diagonal die lines over RICA.

Notes: Some were restruck on heavy planchets (96.1 grains average) and are exceedingly rare (the suffix "a" can be added after the BW number to describe these).

1847, Second Restrike, Small Berries, Proof (BW-3, C-SR-24, B-3).

	Cert	Avg	%MS	PF-60	PF-63BN	PF-63RB	PF-65BN	PF-65RB
1847, Second Restrike, Small Berries, Proof	15	64.7		$5,000	$6,000	$8,000	$9,000	$14,000

1848, Braided Hair

Proof mintage (estimate): 150 to 225.

The 1848 winds down the Proof-only run of this decade, as the next year, 1849, did include circulation strikes in addition to Proofs. Originals struck for inclusion in sets in 1848 and for sale to numismatists have large berries. First Restrikes were coined beginning in 1856 or later, and Second Restrikes were likely coined commencing in or after the spring of 1859, as noted in the overview of this type.

The date is too large for the space provided and crowds the base of the portrait of Miss Liberty. The Mint had a similar problem with the overly large dates on certain 1848 half dimes. Originals are on the rare side. In contrast, in the context of Proof-only half cents the First Restrike is plentiful.

1848, Original, Large Berries, Proof • BW-1, C-PO-9, B-1a. *Breen dies:* 1-A. *Estimated population:* Proof: 15 to 20.

Obverse: 1848, only die of the year.

Reverse: Large Berries in wreath.

Notes: Several known examples seem to have been restruck at a later date (see Breen).

1848, Original, Large Berries, Proof (BW-1, C-PO-9, B-1a).

1848, Original, Large Berries, Proof	Cert	Avg	%MS	PF-60	PF-63BN	PF-63RB	PF-65BN	PF-65RB
1848, Original, Large Berries, Proof	4	64.0		$6,000	$7,000	$9,000	$10,000	$14,000

1848, First Restrike, Small Berries, Proof • BW-2, C-SR-10, B-2. *Breen dies: 1-B.* **Estimated population:** Proof: 30 to 35.

Obverse: Same die as preceding.

Reverse: Small Berries in wreath. Slight doubling at NT of CENT and wreath ribbon.

Notes: Walter Breen considered this to be the most available of all First Restrike dates.

1848, First Restrike, Small Berries, Proof (BW-2, C-SR-10, B-2).

	Cert	Avg	%MS	PF-60	PF-63BN	PF-63RB	PF-65BN	PF-65RB
1848, First Restrike, Small Berries, Proof	(a)			$5,000	$6,000	$8,000	$9,000	$14,000

a. Included in certified population for 1848, Second Restrike, Small Berries, Proof.

1848, Second Restrike, Small Berries, Proof • BW-3, C-SR-25, B-3. *Breen dies: 1-C.* **Estimated population:** Proof: 10 to 12.

Obverse: Same die as preceding.

Reverse: Small Berries in wreath. Diagonal die lines over RICA.

Notes: Some were restruck on heavy planchets (96.1 grains average) and are exceedingly rare (the suffix "a" can be added after the BW number to describe these).

1848, Second Restrike, Small Berries, Proof (BW-3, C-SR-25, B-3).

	Cert	Avg	%MS	PF-60	PF-63BN	PF-63RB	PF-65BN	PF-65RB
1848, Second Restrike, Small Berries, Proof	12	64.5		$6,000	$7,500	$9,500	$11,000	$15,500

1849, Braided Hair

Proof mintage, Small Date (estimate): 70 to 90.
Circulation mintage, Large Date: 39,864.

Half cents of 1849 are classified by two major varieties: Small Date, made early in the year and only in Proof format, and Large Date, made for circulation, with a few Proofs.

The Proof 1849, Small Date, was made for sets of this year and to supply numismatists who desired a Proof of the date. The estimated Proof mintage for this date size reflects its scarcity. Probably, some collectors of the 1850s and 1860s who had a Large Date did not desire a Small Date, as the year 1849 was already represented.

Originals of the Small Date variety have large berries. This is the rarest of the Proof-only Original half cents of the 1840s. In 1879 in his *Monograph of United States Cents and Half Cents Issued Between the Years 1793 and 1857*, Édouard Frossard stated that he had never seen the one that Dr. Edward Maris had. For many years the Chapman brothers stated that only five were known. In recent decades the census has expanded, but any larger figure probably contains some duplication. In the era of the Chapmans—roughly from the late 1870s to the late 1920s—only a few dealers handled most of the major rarities, and it was easier to keep track of them. Today, in the early 21st century, coins are much more widespread in their distribution, and there are probably a couple hundred dealers or more who handle American rarities, most of whom keep little record of pedigrees.

First Restrikes of the Small Date variety were coined beginning in 1856 or later. The production seems to have been modest, no doubt as circulation-strike Large Date coins filled the demand for half cents of the 1849 year. No Second Restrikes have been reported for this issue. The Small Date is from a small logotype punch similar to that used for half cents prior to 1847.

In summary, the Proof 1849, Small Date, half cent with large berries may be rarer than presently thought, and more in line with the Chapmans' account than later tabulations. Breen forthrightly states, "12 known." The status of the 1849, Large Berries, half cent as "Original" or "Restrike" has been debated over the years, although the "large berries = original" rule of thumb is usually applied for half cents of the 1840s, never mind that there are occasional exceptions.

You may want to review Breen's comments on pages 426 and 427 of his *Encyclopedia of United States Half Cents 1793–1857*. In brief, 1849, Small Date, half cents with the large berries reverse style have long been called originals. As there is only one variety and one die state of the 1849, Small Date, half cent with Large Berries reverse, it is presumed that they were all made at the same time. It is not known for certain whether that time was 1849, or whether it was later. Further, as Breen states, "Should it later prove that all of them were made in 1859 or 1860, their status would not affect their rarity and should not affect their value."

Another obverse die was made with a Large Date logotype and used to produce circulation strikes, the first in this format since 1835. Such format is exceedingly rare. Demand for the denomination remained low, and the mintage was modest. The reverse is of the Small Berries style. Only one die variety is known. Examples are fairly scarce, but are easily obtainable in relation to the demand for them. EF and AU are typical grades. Mint State coins are seen now and again, and usually are well struck with lustrous brown surfaces. One Proof is reported by R. Tettenhorst.

1849, Small Date, Original, Large Berries, Proof • BW-1, C-PO-10, B-1.

Breen dies: 1-A. **Estimated population:** Proof: 12 to 14.

Obverse: 1849, small numerals in date.

Reverse: Large Berries in wreath.

1849, Small Date, Original, Large Berries, Proof (BW-1, C-PO-10, B-1).

	Cert	Avg	%MS	PF-60	PF-63BN	PF-63RB	PF-65BN	PF-65RB
1849, Small Date, Original, Large Berries, Proof	4	59.0		$4,700	$6,000	$7,750	$10,500	$22,500

1849, Small Date, First Restrike, Small Berries, Proof • BW-2, C-SR-11,

B-2. *Breen dies:* 1-B. **Estimated population:** Proof: 18 to 22.

Obverse: Same die as preceding.

Reverse: Small Berries in wreath. Slight doubling at NT of CENT and wreath ribbon.

1849, Small Date, First Restrike, Small Berries, Proof (BW-2, C-SR-11, B-2).

	Cert	Avg	%MS	PF-60	PF-63BN	PF-63RB	PF-65BN	PF-65RB
1849, Small Date, First Restrike, Small Berries, Proof	5	64.4		$4,850	$5,750	$9,250	$9,750	$15,000

1849, Large Date • BW-3, C-1 (Proof,

PO-11), B-4. *Breen dies:* 2-D. **Estimated population:** Circulation strikes: 1,750 to 2,250; Proofs: 2 to 4.

Obverse: Date in large numerals.

Reverse: Small berries in wreath.

Notes: Mint State is the highest grade for this variety, usually brown, sometimes with partial original color. One Proof was reported by R. Tettenhorst. Jim McGuigan suggests a population of 2 to 4 Proofs.

1849, Large Date (BW-3, C-1, B-4).

	Cert	Avg	%MS	VF-20	EF-40	AU-50	MS-60BN	MS-63BN	MS-63RB	MS-65BN	MS-65RB
1849, Large Date	276	58.4	63%	$100	$150	$240	$500	$700	$1,500	$2,550	$3,500

1850, Braided Hair

Circulation mintage: 39,812.

The 1850 is the scarcest date of the 1849 to 1857 circulating issues, but enough exist that finding one will be no problem. EF and AU grades are the rule. Mint State coins are scarce. When seen, they typically have lustrous brown surfaces. Coins with significant original color are rare.

Proofs: Proofs were struck from the same die pair used for circulation, which always causes problems in attribution. The numismatic tradition on what is an early Proof and what is a prooflike circulation strike still is not definitive or complete, and thus population estimates, which are based on the literature (in combination with personal experience), must be taken with a grain of salt. In general, for all 1850 denominations, few Proofs were struck.

Typical values for 1850 half cents.

	Cert	Avg	%MS	VF-20	EF-40	AU-50	MS-60BN	MS-63BN	MS-63RB	MS-65BN	MS-65RB
1850	226	57.8	60%	$100	$150	$240	$500	$750	$1,425	$2,400	$3,500

	Cert	Avg	%MS	PF-60	PF-63BN	PF-63RB	PF-65BN	PF-65RB
1850, Proof	8	62.8	88%	$5,000	$7,000	$10,000	$13,000	$17,000

1850 • BW-1, C-1 (Proof, PO-12), B-1. *Breen dies:* 1-A. **Estimated population:** Circulation strikes: 1,750 to 2,250; Proofs: 10 to 12.

Obverse: Four-digit 1850 logotype impressed shallowly into the single working die, thus the date is never bold. This die was used to make circulation strikes as well as Proofs.

Reverse: Small Berries. Tiny line connects bases of A and T of STATES.

1850 (BW-1, C-1, B-1).

Notes: This variety exists in Mint State, usually with brown surfaces, and is elusive as such.

1851, Braided Hair

Circulation mintage: 147,672.

Mint records note that two obverse dies were prepared for the 1851 half cent, but a second has never been identified. Circulated coins are plentiful in the context of the series. EF and AU are typical grades. Uncirculated coins are plentiful in the marketplace, many with some pale mint red. Luster is usually "shallow," rather than deep and frosty.

Proofs: Although Walter Breen has stated that "at least 20 exist," the attribution of prooflike circulation strikes vis-à-vis Proofs is not always certain. True Proofs are very rare.

Typical values for 1851 half cents.

	Cert	Avg	%MS	VF-20	EF-40	AU-50	MS-60BN	MS-63BN	MS-63RB	MS-65BN	MS-65RB	MS-65RD
1851	754	58.5	64%	$80	$100	$175	$275	$550	$650	$1,000	$2,000	$3,500

	Cert	Avg	%MS	PF-60	PF-63BN	PF-63RB	PF-65BN	PF-65RB
1851, Proof	0	n/a		$7,000	$8,000	$15,000	$20,000	$25,000

1851 • BW-1, C-1 (Proof, PO-13), B-1. *Breen dies:* 1-A. **Estimated population:** Circulation strikes: 5,500 to 7,500. Proofs: 3 to 5.

Obverse: Four-digit 1851 logotype in small digits, well placed between the portrait and the denticles, and deeply punched into the die. Traces of an earlier 1 to the right of the final digit. *Points of distinction:* Only one die this year—used to make circulation strikes as well as Proofs.

1851 (BW-1, C-1, B-1).

Reverse: Small Berries. Top of crosslet of E of CENT joined to top of letter. Tiny line connects bases of A and T of STATES.

Notes: Mint State can be found, brown or with some original color.

1852, Braided Hair

Proof mintage (estimate): 225 to 325.

The 1852 half cent was made only in Proof format. These can be classified as Originals with Large Berries accompanied by First Restrikes and Second Restrikes with small berries.

The situation, however, is more complex, especially if the extensive commentary in Walter Breen's 1983 *Encyclopedia of United States Half Cents 1793–1857* is followed. He suggests that Large Berries coins are restrikes, devoting nearly three pages to his discussion (hinting that he could have spent more: "There is no point in devoting 20-odd pages...."), concluding that the 1852 B-4 is struck from the Large Berries reverse used on Originals of the 1840s, but with the 1852 obverse die repolished and *in a later state than 1852 B-2* (First Restrike die), which, if characteristic of all Large Berries examples, would seem to support his restrike view. As to what constituted an Original, Breen suggested that a Small Berries die, but not either of the First Restrike or Second Restrike dies, was likely, but he had never encountered one.

This view seems more likely: Richard T. Coleman Jr., in "Series VII Restrikes: The Breen Effect," *Penny-Wise*, November 15, 1998, states, "The entire concept of Series VII restrikes seems to have been fabricated by Mr. Breen in order to support his theory that 1852 Large Berry reverse half cents are 'restrikes' not originals."

In the present text we list the Large Berries first, then the two restrikes, following the order of 1840 to 1848 and 1849, Small Date, Proofs.

1852, Original, Large Berries, Proof

• BW-1, C-SR-1, B-4. *Breen dies:* 1-A. **Population:** Proof: 5 recorded (see Eliasberg Collection, 1996).

Obverse: 1852, only die of the year.

Reverse: Large Berries in wreath.

Notes: Called a restrike by Walter Breen and Roger Cohen Jr. (who listed this variety as Original in the first edition of his book, but a Restrike in the second edition). Emery May Holden Norweb spent several decades in the search for one.

1852, Original, Large Berries, Proof (BW-1, C-SR-1, B-4).

	Cert	Avg	%MS	PF-60	PF-63BN	PF-63RB	PF-65BN	PF-65RB
1852, Original, Large Berries, Proof	1	65.0		$200,000	$200,000	$200,000	$400,000	$400,000

1852, First Restrike, Small Berries, Proof

• BW-2, C-SR-12, B-2. *Breen dies:* 1-B. **Estimated population:** Proof: 100 to 125.

Obverse: Same die as preceding.

Reverse: Small Berries in wreath. Slight doubling at NT of CENT and wreath ribbon.

Notes: This is the variety usually seen.

1852, First Restrike, Small Berries, Proof (BW-2, C-SR-12, B-2).

	Cert	Avg	%MS	PF-60	PF-63BN	PF-63RB	PF-65BN	PF-65RB
1852, First Restrike, Small Berries, Proof	(a)			$4,000	$5,875	$8,750	$10,000	$15,000

a. Included in certified population for 1852, Second Restrike, Small Berries, Proof.

1852, Second Restrike, Small Berries, Proof • BW-3 C-SR-26, B-3. *Breen dies:* 1-C. **Estimated population:** Proof: 10 to 15.

Obverse: Same die as preceding.

Reverse: Small Berries in wreath. Diagonal die lines over RICA.

Notes: The Small Berries half cents of this year have been described by die varieties only rarely, and thus estimates are more tentative than among other Proof-only years.

1852, Second Restrike, Small Berries, Proof (BW-3, C-SR-26, B-3).

	Cert	Avg	%MS	PF-60	PF-63BN	PF-63RB	PF-65BN	PF-65RB
1852, Second Restrike, Small Berries, Proof	34	64.3		$5,000	$7,250	$12,000	$15,000	$20,000

1853, Braided Hair

Circulation mintage: 129,694.

The 1853 half cent is available in high grades. All Mint State coins are brown or, less often, brown with traces of red. No full orange-red example is known, except for cleaned pieces. No Proofs are known. Circulated coins are typically EF or AU.

Typical values for 1853 half cents.

	Cert	Avg	%MS	VF-20	EF-40	AU-50	MS-60BN	MS-63BN	MS-63RB	MS-65BN	MS-65RB
1853	947	61.0	80%	$80	$100	$175	$275	$550	$650	$1,000	$1,700

1853 • BW-1, C-1, B-1. *Breen dies:* 1-A. **Estimated population:** 5,500 to 7,500.

Obverse: Date in a large logotype is boldly impressed into the die. It is too large for the allotted space and appears crowded.

Reverse: Small Berries.

Notes: Mint State with brown surfaces or some mint color are common.

1853 (BW-1, C-1, B-1).

Detail of crowded date.

1854, Braided Hair

Circulation mintage: 55,358.
Proof mintage (estimate): 40 to 60.

A single obverse and two reverse dies were used to coin 1854 half cents. Circulation strikes are fairly scarce and are typically in grades of EF or AU. Hundreds of Mint State coins exist, mostly from the A.C. Gies hoard (see Numismatic Notes on page 245).

   Proofs: Proofs are very rare in proportion to later half cent Proofs of the decade.

Typical values for 1854 half cents.

	Cert	Avg	%MS	VF-20	EF-40	AU-50	MS-60BN	MS-63BN	MS-63RB	MS-65BN	MS-65RB	MS-65RD
1854	698	61.6	84%	$90	$105	$175	$290	$560	$675	$1,050	$1,750	$3,000

	Cert	Avg	%MS	PF-60	PF-63BN	PF-63RB	PF-65BN	PF-65RB
1854, Proof	4	64.3		$3,825	$4,750	$7,500	$7,750	$12,000

1854 • BW-1a and b, C-1 (Proof, C-PO-14), B-1 and 2. *Breen dies:* 1-A and B. ***Estimated population:*** Circulation strikes: 2,500 to 3,500. Proofs: 25 to 30.

Obverse: Medium-size logotype positioned slightly high in the die. ***Points of distinction:*** Only one die this year—used to make circulation strikes as well as Proofs.

Reverse: The Breen text describes these two dies, here with Bowers-Whitman numbers assigned:

1854 (BW-1a, C-1, B-1).

> BW-1a: Heavily impressed; no rust pit on I of United; Stem right of T forms a loop, though it is very thin; both A's in AMERICA closed; base arc line joins AT in STATES.

> BW-1b: Rust pit on I in UNITED at top and extending down a little into upright; steams right of T in CENT do not form a loop; A's in AMERICA open at their bases. The scarcer of the two varieties by far, although most in the marketplace have not been attributed. Mirror Proofs were also struck from this die pair.

Notes: This variety exists in Mint State.

Numismatic Notes: ***The A.C. Gies hoard:*** August C. Gies, a jeweler and numismatist of Pittsburgh, Pennsylvania, was said to be a hoarder par excellence, and it is has been related that he had bank-wrapped rolls of most bronze, nickel, and silver coins after about 1900. Apparently he did have some, but they were nearly all of smaller denominations. An example of a story that grew in the telling, he is traditionally assigned the ownership of one roll each of such rarities as the 1901-S and 1913-S quarter dollars. After a few more retellings he was said to have quantities of just about everything.[56]

Circa 1935 Gies happened upon a marvelous group of 1,000 half cents dated 1854, each coin being a bright orange-red, typically with some minor spotting. The 1930s seemed to be a good decade for finding such things, as other half cents came to light elsewhere. These 1854 half cents were distributed in numismatic channels in due course and provide the source for most pieces seen today.

In 1941, as his first job when working for Joe and Morton Stack, young John J. Ford Jr. had to catalog cents and other coins from the Gies holdings. Thomas L. Elder may have been involved in the transaction as well. At the time Ford was given the opportunity to buy some bright red 1854 half cents for $1 each, which he did. Ford later stated that accounts of Gies putting away rare rolls of higher denominations were "pure hogwash."[57]

Gies was born on January 29, 1855, and spent his life in the Pittsburgh area. In 1879 he moved to East Liberty and gained employment with a jeweler. In 1883 he opened his own jewelry business, and remained active in the trade until 1941. Along the way he collected coins and saved bank-wrapped rolls of coins of smaller denominations. He died in 1944.

1855, Braided Hair

Circulation mintage: 56,500.
Proof mintage (estimate): 90 to 110.

Half cents of 1855 were struck from a single die pair. Circulated examples are slightly scarce and are usually EF or AU. Mint State coins are seen often and are mostly from hoards (see Numismatic Notes below). These usually have some light spotting.

Proofs: Proofs were made from the same die pair, for inclusion in sets as well as single sales.

Typical values for 1855 half cents.

	Cert	Avg	%MS	VF-20	EF-40	AU-50	MS-60BN	MS-63BN	MS-63RB	MS-65BN	MS-65RB	MS-65RD
1855	1007	62.1	87%	$80	$100	$170	$275	$550	$650	$1,000	$1,600	$3,000

	Cert	Avg	%MS	PF-60	PF-63BN	PF-63RB	PF-65BN	PF-65RB
1855, Proof	19	64.3		$3,500	$4,500	$7,500	$7,500	$10,000

1855 • BW-1, C-1 (Proof, SO-1), B-1. *Breen dies:* 1-A. *Estimated population:* Circulation strikes: 4,000 to 5,000; Proofs: 40 to 60.

Obverse: Date small logotype with italic 5s. *Points of distinction:* Only one die this year— used to make circulation strikes as well as Proofs.

Reverse: Small Berries. Raised line from denticle above E of AMERICA.

1855 (BW-1, C-1, B-1).

Notes: Very common in Mint State with much original color. There are more "RD" half cents of this date than for all others combined.[58]

Numismatic Notes: *The Judge Putnam hoard:* In 1864 and again in 1868, 1871, and 1877, Judge J.P. Putnam of Boston journeyed to Philadelphia to participate in the annual Assay Commission ritual. Putnam was a numismatist and a personal friend of Roxbury, Massachusetts, dealer W. Elliot Woodward.[59] Under the Assay Commission procedure, the various mints (at the time these being Philadelphia, Carson City,[60] and San Francisco) set aside samples of coins struck from silver and gold (but not copper). These were sent to the Philadelphia Mint and reserved for the Assay Commission, which met early the following year to review the preceding year's precious-metal coinage. Thus, on Monday, February 8, 1864, the commission members gathered to review coins bearing the date 1863.[61]

Undoubtedly, Judge Putnam enjoyed being a part of the 1864 ceremony, for it was considered an honor to be named to the select group. Apparently, while he was there he sought to acquire some souvenirs of his visit, and obtained a few bright Uncirculated copper half cents bearing the date 1855, which were left over from that year. Coins of this denomination had not been made at the Mint since early 1857, and almost all supplies on hand had been melted shortly afterward.[62] Nearly 20 years later, on December 16–18, 1885, W. Elliot Woodward offered for sale the A.W. Matthews Collection and other properties, to which certain coins from the former holdings of Putnam, now deceased, had been consigned.[63] Lot 1761 was described as:

> 1855 [half cents] Bright red Uncirculated. In 1855 Judge J.P. Putnam, of Boston, was a member of the Mint Assay Commission; he bought these half cents from the Mint, and parted with them only just

before his death. All are perfect, and nearly all are selected for fineness of impression, as well as other qualities. Another lot so fine probably does not exist. 10 pieces.

A further 18 pieces were described as being from the same source and of the same quality, followed by 47 more with no attribution, but likely from the same group. The same sale continued with quantities of 1856 and 1857 half cents, including 19 Uncirculated examples of the last date of the denomination.

The Charles French hoard: In the 1940s Charles French (born Lehrenkraus), a hobby-shop operator and rare-coin dealer in Troy, New York, purchased a small cloth bag containing 500 bright-red half cents, each bearing the date 1855. The coins had been found in a small metal safe, of the type painted black with a scene on the front, as were commonly used in the late 1800s and early 1900s.

Fearing a reduction in their numismatic market value, French said little about the coins at the time, but parceled them out to clients and in small groups to dealers. By about 1960 most or all were gone.[64]

1856, Braided Hair

Circulation mintage: 40,230.
Proof mintage (estimate): 110 to 130.

One obverse die and three reverse dies were used to coin 1856 half cents. Circulation strikes are fairly scarce and are usually EF or AU.[65] Mint State examples are scarcer yet. Most are brown or have some tinges of red. Full original mint red coins, uncleaned and unspotted, are exceedingly rare.

Proofs: These were made in fair quantity and are mostly from the die with doubling at NT and the ribbon, used to make First Restrike Proofs of earlier dates. Some copper-nickel strikings were made from Proof dies (Judd-177), as patterns to test alloy variations.

Typical values for 1856 half cents.

	Cert	Avg	%MS	VF-20	EF-40	AU-50	MS-60BN	MS-63BN	MS-63RB	MS-65BN	MS-65RB	MS-65RD
1856	368	60.3	74%	$100	$125	$185	$325	$575	$690	$1,250	$2,000	$3,750

	Cert	Avg	%MS	PF-60	PF-63BN	PF-63RB	PF-65BN	PF-65RB
1856, Proof	24	64.2		$3,500	$4,500	$7,500	$7,500	$11,500

1856 • BW-1a, b, and c; C-1 (Proof, C-SO-2 from BW-1a, C-SR-13 for BW-1c); B-1 to 3. *Breen dies:* 1-A, B, and C. **Estimated population:** Circulation strikes: 1,400 to 1,800; Proofs: 70 to 90 (typically Breen dies 1-C).

Obverse: Medium logotype punched deeply into the die, a bit deeper on the right, giving the 56 digits a bolder appearance. **Points of distinction:** Only one die this year—used to make circulation strikes as well as Proofs.

1856 (BW-1c, C-1, B-3).

Reverse: The Breen text describes these three dies, here with Bowers-Whitman numbers assigned. **BW-1a:** Rust pit on I in UNITED. **BW-1b:** No rust pit on I in UNITED. Only used to strike *patterns*, Judd-177. Fewer than 25 known. **BW-1c:** Doubled NT in CENT, this being the same die used to make First Restrike half cents of the 1840s. So called "Reverse of 1856," the regular reverse thought to have been first used this year (earlier-dated half cents from this die are considered to be restrikes).

Notes: Mint State, brown, can be found—sometimes with hints of red.

1857, Braided Hair

Circulation mintage: 35,180.
Proof mintage (estimate): 170 to 220.

Although 35,180 half cents were struck in 1857 (delivered on January 14), Mint records seem to indicate that only 10,000 were shipped. It is not known if all were dated 1857. Requests for coins, including from collectors, were honored by the director until February 28, 1857, after which the remaining coins were melted.[66]

Today, examples of the 1857 half cent are scarce. Most are EF or AU, but probably as many as 500 Mint State coins exist, most of which are brown, sometimes with tinges of red, often mottled. Full-red pieces exist and are usually a pale hue. There are two die varieties, but in the marketplace little notice is taken of the differences.[67]

Proofs: Proofs are known from two die pairs, most being of the BW-2 variety. This is the most available Proof year in the half cent series.

1857 • BW-1, C-1 (Proof, SO-3 for BW-1a, SR-14 for BW-1b), B-1. *Breen dies:* 1-A. ***Estimated population:*** Circulation strikes: 1,600 to 3,200; Proofs: 5 to 7.

Obverse: Standard design.

Reverse: Breen: "Plain dot on right side of first A in AMERICA, about mid-high, noticeable even on worn examples."

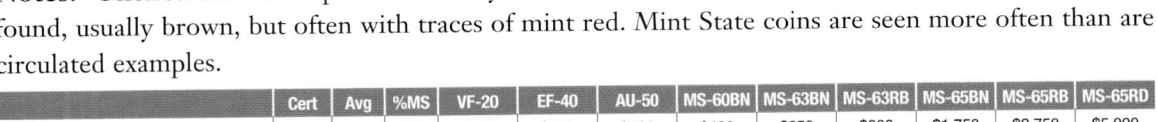

1857 (BW-1, C-1, B-1).

Notes: Uncirculated examples are easily found, usually brown, but often with traces of mint red. Mint State coins are seen more often than are circulated examples.

	Cert	Avg	%MS	VF-20	EF-40	AU-50	MS-60BN	MS-63BN	MS-63RB	MS-65BN	MS-65RB	MS-65RD
1857 (BW-1)	567	61.0	81%	$140	$180	$260	$400	$650	$800	$1,750	$2,750	$5,000

1857 • BW-2, C-1, B-2. *Breen dies:* 1-B. ***Estimated population:*** Circulation strikes: 50 to 80. Proofs: 120 to 150.

Obverse: Same as preceding.

Reverse: With doubling at NT of CENT and wreath ribbon. The "First Restrike" die.

Notes: This variety exists in Mint State, usually brown.

1857 (BW-2, C-1, B-2).

	Cert	Avg	%MS	PF-60	PF-63BN	PF-63RB	PF-65BN	PF-65RB
1857, Proof	39	63.9		$3,400	$4,500	$7,500	$7,500	$12,000

Large Cents
1793–1857

This survey of U.S. large cents is based on the work of Q. David Bowers,
a numismatic professional, and author in the field, for more than 60 years.

COLLECTING LARGE CENTS

THE MOST POPULAR AMERICAN DENOMINATION

Large copper cents were made in larger quantities than any other denomination during their era, from 1793 to 1857. Produced under the provisions of the Mint Act of April 2, 1792, the first coins were delivered in March 1792. Excepting 1,500 silver half dismes struck in July 1792, before the Mint was built, these were the first federal coins coined for general circulation under that legislation.

Cents and half cents were struck for the Mint's own account. Any difference between the cost of copper and the production of the coins went to the bottom line. In contrast, silver coins and gold coins, first made in 1794 and 1795, respectively, were produced as an accommodation to depositors of those metals, and the Mint's service charge yielded a negligible return. This profit policy translated into a desire for the Mint to produce copper coins year in and year out, resulting in a fairly steady output of copper cents.

The *Annual Report of the Director of the Mint* stated that copper cents were delivered from the coiner to the treasurer for every calendar year except 1815 and 1823. However, in the waning days of 1815 some cents were indeed struck, but from dies dated 1816, as evidenced by a January 1, 1816, report that coinage was already underway. Regarding 1823-dated cents, examples exist, but are scarce, of 1823, 3 Over 2, and 1823—no doubt struck in calendar year 1824. Until Robert Maskell Patterson became Mint director in July 1835, it seems to have been standard practice to use dies until they were well worn or cracked, even after the expiration of the date on the die. There were exceptions, such as when existing dies were overdated, including 1799, 9 Over 8; 1800, 180 Over 179; 1800, 1800 Over 1798; 1810, 10 Over 09; 1811, 1 Over 0; 1823, 3 Over 2; 1824, 4 Over 2; 1826, 6 Over 5; and 1839, 9 Over 6.

USE IN COMMERCE

During the era that large cents were coined, they were widely used, but only in certain regions. Reports reveal that they were very popular in the Northeast, continuing down to about Virginia, but were not as often seen south of that point. To the west, they were in wide use to the western border of Pennsylvania in the early years; then they came into use in certain of the prairie states. Otherwise, the lowest-value coins in circulation in the deep South and the West were the silver half dime and the Spanish-American half real, or *medio*, worth 6-1/4¢. Cents were often shipped in wooden kegs, some with an estimated 14,000 coins. Kegs were easier to handle than crates, as they could be rolled on the ground or floor. At least two accounts tell of unopened kegs of cents being shipped back to the North years after they had come to the South: one, of 1811-dated cents, sent back to the Mint; another, of mixed-date 1816 to 1820 coins, shipped from Georgia to New York City after the Civil War.

In the areas of their popularity, cents circulated actively, as evidenced by the worn condition of early dates surviving today. These were everybody's coins. A pocketful of "pennies" would buy breakfast, lunch, or dinner; a glass of beer; permission to use a turnpike; or admission to a museum.

More than a few were counterstamped as advertisements or souvenirs by merchants and others. In Pittsfield, New Hampshire, dentist and saloon operator Dr. G.G. Wilkins stamped his name on thousands of large cents. When the Marquis de LaFayette revisited America in 1824 and 1825, many copper cents were stamped with his portrait on one side and Washington's on the other. Federal cents were not alone in circulation, as cent-sized copper coins dating back to the 1780s, Hard Times tokens, and various foreign coppers were plentiful as well.

A 1793, Wreath, cent, a numismatic classic in its own right, counterstamped "BRADBURY" in a hallmark punch, by Theophilus Bradbury, a Newburyport, Massachusetts, silversmith and jeweler. The coin is also stamped with a punch depicting an eagle in a vertical oval.

An 1825 cent advertising MESCHUTT'S / METROPOLITAN / COFFEE ROOM / 433. BdWAY. The stamper, proprietor Frederick Meschutt, found that the logotype punch was best impressed upon well-worn large cents with fairly smooth surfaces. Most coins observed have the counterstamp sharp, but the host coin worn nearly smooth, indicating that the stamp was applied to a well-worn coin.

An 1841 cent stamped VOTE THE LAND FREE, for use in the presidential campaign of 1844.

A counterstamp of an 1851 cent advertising Goodwin's Grand Greasejuice (G.G.G.) and Goodwin's Grand Glittering Globules (G.G.G.G.)—products of Charles H. Goodwin of Exeter, New Hampshire.

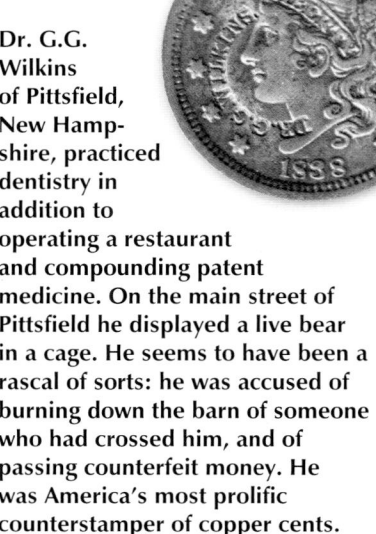

Dr. G.G. Wilkins of Pittsfield, New Hampshire, practiced dentistry in addition to operating a restaurant and compounding patent medicine. On the main street of Pittsfield he displayed a live bear in a cage. He seems to have been a rascal of sorts: he was accused of burning down the barn of someone who had crossed him, and of passing counterfeit money. He was America's most prolific counterstamper of copper cents.

CHARLES H. GOODWIN,
DRUGGIST & MANUFACTURING CHEMIST,
DEALER IN
Drugs, Medicines, Dye Stuffs, Perfumery and Fancy Goods.
Inventor, Manufacturer, and Proprietor of the following Preparations:
G. G. G., or Q. of F., GOODWIN'S GRAND GREASEJUICE, OR QUINTESSENCE OF FAT,
The great AMERICAN Compound for the embellishment, preservation, growth, and beauty of the Human Hair.
The unrivalled Breath Perfume,
G. G. G. G., GOODWIN'S GRAND GLITTERING GLOBULES, or AMBROSIAL AROMATIC YANKEE CACHOUS.
G. G. T., and Q. of Q., Goodwin's Grand Tobaccojuice, and Quintessence of Quicksilver,
The great American Remedy for the *Cimex Lectularius*, or common Bed Bug.
Also of Goodwin's Flavoring Extracts, and Madame Delectable's Handkerchief Perfume.
All orders to be addressed to CHARLES H. GOODWIN, Chemist, at
GOODWIN'S GRAND GREASEJUICE DEPOT,
No. 49 Water Street, Exeter, N. H.

A Charles H. Goodwin directory advertisement featuring the G.G.G.G. and related products. (*New England Business Directory*, 1856).

Large cents remained in use until after the passage of the Act of February 21, 1857, which changed the standard to the small copper-nickel cent. A two-year period was allowed to exchange Spanish-American silver coins for the new cents, followed by an extension of six months. Millions of copper cents were exchanged at the same time. Early in the Civil War, all coins disappeared from circulation. However, in Canada these coins remained in wide use throughout the 1860s (Canada did not mint its own cents until 1858).

IF A CENT COULD SPEAK

In 1861 Harper & Brothers published W.C. Prime's guide to numismatics, *Coins, Medals, and Seals, Ancient and Modern*, which was copyrighted 1860. Prime included this contemplation, relevant to early coppers:

> It is a trite, but by no means a worn-out idea, that a coin, could it speak, would be able to relate a stranger story than any other article to which imagination might give a voice. Such a thought can never be worn out, for it is inexhaustible in its richness. Human fancy fails utterly to trace the possible adventures of a copper that was coined even last year; and for every month that a coin has been in circulation a lifetime must needs be added to the years that would be required to sum up the incidents in which one can conjecture that coin as an actor.

The idea that a copper's own story could be interesting was hardly new, and seems to have been included as a writing exercise in formal instruction in English composition, as in this paper written by a student at a Massachusetts preparatory school in 1858:

Autobiography of a Cent

I am one of the humblest of a large class of beings who have made some stir in the world.

There are others that can boast of far greater value and higher pretentions. I have not the brilliancy of an eagle nor yet the lustre of the dollar, all we lay claim to as a race is good common sense. I do not wish to boast but in my sphere, I am as useful as those who take a higher rank in society.

I was born in the year 1800 in the city of Philadelphia, when with thousands of others I was cast-forth upon the tender mercies of this selfish world. Then I had not the sad and dull aspect I now wear but was bright and cheerful. The world was all before me and on my mission for good or for evil I went forth. I would here say that I have always been the slave of others to come and to go at their bidding.

My pleasing looks caught the notice of a lovely boy and I was laid aside as a keepsake, but my beauty soon faded. I became dim and it was not long before I passed into the possession of the confectioner where I met many of my companions. With the candy merchants I have always been a great favorite, but my stay here was short.

I cannot now give a detailed account of my life and adventures but it must be reserved for another time. Mine has been an active life. I have done some good in my day, have been the humble instrument of feeding the hungry and clothing the naked. To man I have been a friend indeed.

I have mingled in all kinds of society, have been in the mansion of the sick and the cottage of the poor and everywhere have I been welcomed as a friend. I have grasped the hand of the miser and pressed the trembling finger of the beggar. With children I have ever been deemed a great favorite.

I have resided for the most of my life in the New England states; have made occasional visits to the middle states; and have been over as far as the Mississippi River; and I once went down to New Orleans. We meet with but little favor in the South, and my owner could not dispose of me until his return to the North.

About a year since an event took place which I fear will prove fatal to many of my companions if not to myself. Another race has taken our good name with no more merit and even less show but the public are always caught with new things and they are now the favorites.[1]

I am at present now quietly resting from my labors, what is before me I cannot tell. Like the race of the red man we may be destined to become extinct and be found only here and there wanderers on the earth or carefully preserved on the shelves of the museum.

A.A. Ingersoll.
Merrimac Academy
June 14, 1858.
Composition No. 4.[2]

DESIGNS OF LARGE COPPER CENTS

Cents were produced in a variety of designs, mostly of distinctive motifs used only on this denomination and the copper half cent. Exceptions were the obverse designs of Draped Bust coins, which were also used on silver issues, and Braided Hair cents, which were also used on gold. In both instances, their appearance on higher denomination coins antedated their use on copper.

The designs of cents included these, listed here with a comparison of their dates of use on half cents and higher-denomination coins:

1793: Flowing Hair obverse, Chain reverse (not used on other coins)

1793: Flowing Hair obverse, Wreath reverse (not used on other coins)

1793–1796: Liberty Cap, Head Facing Right (used on half cents 1794–1797)

1796–1807: Draped Bust (used on half cents 1800–1808, silver coins 1795–1807)

1808–1814: Classic Head (used on half cents 1809–1836)

1816–1839: Matron Head and variations (not used on other coins)

1839–1857: Braided Hair (used on half cents 1840–1857, gold coins 1838–1908)

WAYS TO COLLECT

Large copper cents have been a foundation stone of American numismatics ever since the 1850s. The completion of a date set from 1793 to 1857 (except 1815) with one of each, plus important varieties, has been a goal of thousands of collectors, from the casual to those serious enough to make it a lifetime pursuit. Fortunately, all are available in the marketplace, although 1793, 1799 in particular, and 1804 are rare. Among later dates, the 1823 is the key issue, although thousands exist.

Collecting cents by basic design types, rather than by years, is a popular pursuit, often done in connection with obtaining one of each motif in other series from half cents to gold double eagles. Those who concentrate on cents usually desire not just dates, but major varieties, such as those listed in the regular edition of *A Guide Book of United States Coins*. Still beyond that, specialists endeavor to collect these cents by die varieties as listed in the book on cents of 1793 to 1814 by Dr. William H. Sheldon and the later cents of 1816 to 1857 in Howard R. Newcomb's study. For certain years, such as 1794 and some of the later Braided Hair dates, there are dozens of varieties. Other years, such as 1806 and 1809, have just one die combination.

To know large cents is to love them, it has been said. They possess a quintessence that is elusive of definition. In *Early American Cents*, Dr. William H. Sheldon discussed their appeal, including this:

Old copper, like beauty, appears to possess a certain intrinsic quality or charm which for many people is irresistible. An experienced dealer in American numismatic materials recently wrote as follows: "Sooner or later, if a collector stays at the business long enough, it is three to one his interest in all the other series will flag and he will focus his attention on the early cents."

Gold, silver, and even bronze appear to be very much the same wherever you see them. Coins made of these metals become "old money" and "interesting," like the stuff seen in museums, but copper seems to possess an almost living warmth and a personality not encountered in any other metal. The big cent is something more than old money. Look at a handful of the cents dated before 1815, when they contained relatively pure copper. You see rich shades of green, red, brown, yellow, and even deep ebony; together with blendings of these not elsewhere matched in nature save perhaps in autumn leaves. If the light is good (direct sunlight is preferable) you will possibly observe that no two of the coins are of quite the same color.

Copper oxidizes differently in different atmospheres, and the way it colors and weathers depends also upon the impurities and traces of other metals which it may contain. The copper that went into the early cents must have been of highly variable assay, recruited as it was from almost every possible source. Some came from Sweden, some from England, some was obtained by melting up copper nails, spikes, and copper finishings from wrecked ships (including both British and American men-of-war). Some of it came from kitchen and other household utensils donated or sold to the Mint in response to urgent appeals. George Washington is said to have donated 'an excellent copper tea-kettle as well as two pairs of tongs early in 1793 for the first cents. It is not surprising, therefore, that to some extent the different early die varieties are recognizable by characteristic color and surface texture, as well as by die breaks, peculiarities of the planchets, and so on. Every early cent has a character of its own.

This is, indeed, the quintessential part. It has no equivalent in the collecting of contemporary gold and silver coins. A VF-20 example of scarce die variety of a 1795 half eagle, a date made in many different obverse and reverse combinations, would stir very little interest even at a gathering of gold specialists. A VF-20 copper cent of 1795, a variety of equal rarity, would be a pass-around-and-examine coin at a meeting of cent enthusiasts.

Another appeal of large cents is that the market for large copper cents is remarkably steady over the years. In *Early American Cents*, Dr. William H. Sheldon singled out a particular date, 1794, as being a bellwether of the coin market as a whole, and this is not inaccurate. Beyond that, a newcomer to large cents may wish to take a quick glance at several large copper cents, listed common to rare, by dates, but not die varieties—such as those listed in the regular edition of the *Guide Book of United States Coins*—and note the prices over a period of years. From the first edition of the *Guide Book of United States Coins*, which was published in 1946 (with a cover date of 1947) down to the latest, the "profit march" for these coins has been upward. Few people seeking to buy rare coins as an investment would investigate large copper cents, as "investment quality" coins are supposed to be in silver or gold and in grades of MS-65 and higher. However, a well-worn 1793, Chain, cent, or a Mint State 1820 from the Randall Hoard, or the curious 1839, 9 Over 6, in Fine-12 grade have all done very well over the years, as have most others.

Books About Cents

Today, varieties of the 1793 to 1814 cents are generally collected by the Sheldon numbers (S-1, S-2, etc.) first given in *Early American Cents*, 1949, and its revision, *Penny Whimsy*, 1958. Building upon this foundation, *Walter Breen's Encyclopedia of Early United States Cents 1793–1814*, edited by Mark Borckardt, gives more information than available in any other single source, along with Breen numbers (B-1, B-2, etc.).[3]

For later issues, *United States Copper Cents 1816–1857*, by Howard R. Newcomb, 1944, remains the standard reference, with Newcomb numbers (N-1, N-2, etc.), which include numerous additions by later scholars. *United States Large Cents 1816–1839*, by William C. Noyes, 1991, and *The Cent Book, 1816–1839*, by John D. Wright, 1992, each offer large illustrations of varieties in combination with useful information. The *Attribution Guide for United States Large Cents 1840–1857*, by J.R. (Bob) Grellman Jr., 1987, is useful for these later issues, for which die-variety differences are often very tiny.

Studies of the availability of various cents in different grades include the popular *Copper Quotes by Robinson* (Jack H. Robinson) and various censuses created by EAC members Del Bland, William C. Noyes, and others. Population reports published by the Numismatic Guaranty Corporation of America (NGC) and the Professional Coin Grading Service (PCGS) are useful for general information, but are usually organized by dates and/or (use is inconsistent) the major varieties listed in the regular edition of the *Guide Book of United States Coins*. Sheldon and Newcomb–listed die combinations are not treated.

In addition to the preceding works, much pleasure can be derived from collecting older texts on cents by Sylvester S. Crosby, Edward Maris, Édouard Frossard, Frank D. Andrews, George Clapp, and others. Auction catalogs with descriptions and illustrations of important collections of large cents furnish a challenge to collect, with certain early sales—such as those by the Chapman brothers and issued with photograph plates—rare and in strong demand. In modern times, many fine collections have been brought to market by auction companies via memorable catalogs.

Two books by John W. Adams, *United States Numismatic Literature. Volume I. Nineteenth Century Auction Catalogues* (1982) and *United States Numismatic Literature. Volume II. Twentieth Century Auction Catalogues* (1990), listed catalogs and rated them by content on an alphabetical scale. Those with large copper cents earning an A+ rating are especially important.

Early American Coppers and Fellowship

The bimonthly journal *Penny-Wise*, published by Early American Coppers, serves as a forum for critiques of past studies, the announcement of new discoveries, market updates, and various commentaries and articles on cents as well. The group is dynamic and has sustained and developed interest in copper cents for more than 40 years. It has attracted the "brightest and the best" of the numismatic community. Many are the Ph.D. and M.D. degrees attached to members' names.

The basic appeal of EAC is that, while a checkbook and a good bank account are nice to have, neither is at all essential to the enjoyment of EAC membership, and the possession of such is not even a consideration of camaraderie. To enjoy copper cents it is necessary to add investigation, study, and connoisseurship to the equation. The field is always changing, new ideas and theories are constantly presented, and new discoveries made. Thanks to this dynamism, facilitated in part by EAC, copper cents remain as appealing to collect today as they were in the 1850s.

How to Use This Section

The coins in this study are organized by year of issue. However, within each year-by-year section, the die varieties are not listed chronologically. The use of "BW" numbers is a convenience to readers in cross-referencing half cents within each year-by-year section of the text, as these numbers begin anew in each section.

Charts giving typical values for the cents of one year may appear at the beginning of the catalog for that year. Some coins are priced individually in charts following their catalog entries.

FLOWING HAIR, CHAIN REVERSE (1793)

Designer: *Henry Voigt.* **Weight:** *208 grains (13.48 grams).*
Composition: *Copper.* **Diameter:** *Average 26 to 27 mm.* **Edge:** *Vine and bars design.*

**1793, Chain AMERICA (Bowers-Whitman–4;
Sheldon-3; Breen-4).**

The first federal cents for circulation were struck at the Mint from February 27 through March 12, 1793. These were of the Chain motif and were made to the extent of 36,103 pieces. The first of these issues bore the abbreviated inscription UNITED STATES OF AMERI. Perhaps 5,000 to 10,000 were made of this style, judging from the ratio of surviving examples. The rest of the 36,103 pieces of the Chain type were of the AMERICA type.

Today Chain AMERI. cents are scarce in all grades. These can be considered a separate type, but most collectors opt to acquire just one Chain cent, with either the AMERI. or AMERICA spelling.

DESIGN DETAILS

The obverse depicts the head of Miss Liberty facing right, her hair loosely arranged. LIBERTY is lettered at the border above. The date 1793 is between the head and the bottom border.

On the reverse a chain of 15 elongated links forms a circle enclosing ONE / CENT and the fraction 1/100. At the time there were 15 states in the Union (the most recent additions being Vermont in 1791 and Kentucky in 1792). The links were intended to symbolize unity, a similar gesture to the interlocked rings that appeared on the 1776, Continental Currency, pewter dollar and certain paper money. As noted, around the outer border is the inscription UNITED STATES OF AMERI. On the second type the inscription is spelled out fully as UNITED STATES OF AMERICA.

Both obverse and reverse borders are plain (without beads or denticles). The edges have a design of vines and vertical bars.

Historical Magazine, founded in 1857, was the first American periodical to regularly include numismatic items. The February 1859 issue included a submission by L.C. of Hartford, Connecticut, who sent in a notice from the *Argus*, which had been published in Boston on March 26, 1793. This quoted an account from Newark, New Jersey, criticizing America's first cent from the Philadelphia Mint:

> The American *cents* (says a letter from Newark) do not answer our expectations. The chain on the reverse is but a bad omen for liberty, and liberty herself appears to be in a fright. May she not justly cry out in the words of the apostle, *"Alexander the coppersmith has done me much harm; the Lord reward him according to his works!"*

It will be remembered that *Alexander* Hamilton was at that time secretary of the Treasury. At the time newspapers often acquired information by clipping items from other periodicals. Earlier, on March 18, essentially the same observation had been printed in Philadelphia in the *Mail, or Claypoole's Daily Advertiser.*

Comments such as this were undoubtedly responsible for the motifs being changed to a fuller portrait of Miss Liberty on the obverse and a wreath design in place of the chain motif on the reverse.

GRADING STANDARDS

MS-60 to 70 (Mint State). *Obverse:* In the lower–Mint State grades, MS-60 and 61, some slight abrasions can be seen on the higher areas of the portrait. The large open field shows light contact marks and perhaps a few nicks. At MS-63 the luster should be complete, although some very light abrasions or contact marks may be seen on the portrait. At MS-64 or higher—a nearly impossible level for a Chain cent—there is no sign of abrasion anywhere. Mint color is not exten-

1793; Bowers-Whitman–5, Sheldon-4, Breen-5. Graded MS-65BN.

sive on any known Mint State coin, but traces of red-orange are sometimes seen around the rim and devices on both sides. *Reverse:* In the lower–Mint State grades some abrasions are seen on the chain links. There is some abrasion in the field. At MS-63, luster should be unbroken. Some abrasion and minor contact marks may be evident. In still higher grades, luster is deep and there is no sign of abrasion.

Illustrated coin: This variety has a distinctive obverse with a period after the date and LIBERTY.

AU-50, 53, 55, 58 (About Uncirculated). *Obverse:* Light wear is seen on the highest areas of the portrait. Some luster is seen in the large open fields at the AU-58 level, less at 55, and little if any for 53 and 50. Scattered marks are normal and are most evident in the field. At higher levels, some vestiges of luster may be seen among the letters, numerals, and between the hair tips. *Reverse:* Light wear is most evi-dent on the chain, as this is the most prominent

1793; BW-1, S-1, B-1. Graded AU-50.

feature. The letters show wear, but not as extensive. Luster may be seen at the 58 and 55 levels, usually slightly more on the reverse than on the obverse. Generally, the reverse grades higher than the obverse, usually by a step, such as a 50 obverse and a 53 reverse (such a coin would be listed as the lower of the two, or AU-50).

Illustrated coin: Described by an auction cataloger: "Very well defined, some softness on the usually weak highest point of the hair, other fine details well delineated. Some very faint planchet granularity is seen, and a few short parallel fissures are noted around the central reverse. Some scattered nicks, old thin curved scratch from nose through chin and below, another pin scratch on the high forehead."

EF-40, 45 (Extremely Fine). *Obverse:* The center of the portrait is well worn, with the hair visible only in thick strands, although extensive detail remains in the hair tips at the left. No luster is seen. Contact marks are nor-mal in the large expanse of open field, but should be mentioned if they are distracting. *Reverse:* The chain is bold and shows light wear. Other features show wear, as well— more extensive in appearance, as the relief is

1793; BW-2, S-2, B-2. Graded EF-40.

lower. The fields show some friction, but not as much as on the obverse.

Illustrated coin: A cut or void is seen in Miss Liberty's hair, as are some pinpricks and marks. Light scratches are seen at the top of the head. The reverse is especially bold. Surfaces are microscopically granular on both sides.

VF-20, 30 (Very Fine). *Obverse:* More wear is seen on the portrait, with perhaps half or slightly more of the hair detail showing, mostly near the left edge of the hair. The ear usually is visible (but might not be, depending on the sharpness of strike). The letters in LIBERTY show wear. The rim remains bold (more so than on the reverse). *Reverse:* The chain shows more wear than on the preceding, but is still bold. Other features show more wear and may be weak in areas. The rim may be weak in areas.

1793; BW-4, S-3, B-4. Graded VF-20.

Illustrated coin: Nice detail is seen in the hair strands at the left. There are some marks near the neck and in the right field, not unusual for this grade. The reverse has a dig below the T in CENT.

F-12, 15 (Fine). *Obverse:* The hair details are mostly worn away, with about one-third visible, that being on the left. The rim is distinct on most examples. The bottoms of the date digits are weak or possibly worn away. *Reverse:* The chain is bold, as is the lettering within the chain. Lettering around the border shows extensive wear, but is complete. The rim may be flat in areas.

1793; BW-1, S-1, B-1. Graded F-15.

Illustrated coin: This coin has a planchet flaw and many tiny pin scratches, with a few heavier scratches above the portrait. Overall, this coin is better than F-15, but the grade compensates for the scratches. This points to the necessity for astute buyers to go beyond an alphanumeric grading number and study the coin itself. The same can be said for most early copper cents.

VG-8, 10 (Very Good). *Obverse:* The portrait is well worn, although Miss Liberty's eye remains bold. Hair detail is gone at the center, but is evident at the left edge of the portrait. LIBERTY is always readable, but may be faded or partly missing on shallow strikes. The date is well worn, with the bottom of the numerals missing (published standards vary on this point, and it used to be the case that a full date was mandatory). *Reverse:* The chain remains bold, and the center letters are all readable. Border letters may be weak or incomplete. The rim is smooth in most areas.

1793; BW-5, S-4, B-5. Certified as F-12, but more closely fitting, perhaps, VG-10, if one deducts for overall porosity.

Illustrated coin: Sometimes, early copper cents cannot be neatly pigeonholed into grade categories.

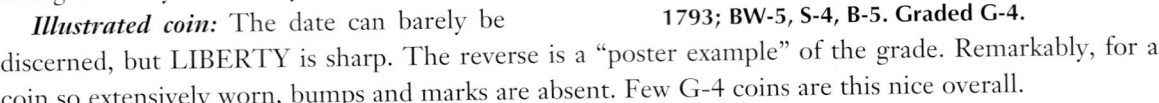

G-4, 6 (Good). *Obverse:* The portrait is worn smooth and is seen only in outline form, although the eye position can be discerned. LIBERTY may be weak. The date is weak, but the tops of the numerals can be discerned. *Reverse:* The chain is fully visible in outline form. Central lettering is mostly or completely readable, but light. Peripheral lettering is mostly worn away.

1793; BW-5, S-4, B-5. Graded G-4.

Illustrated coin: The date can barely be discerned, but LIBERTY is sharp. The reverse is a "poster example" of the grade. Remarkably, for a coin so extensively worn, bumps and marks are absent. Few G-4 coins are this nice overall.

AG-3 (About Good). *Obverse:* The portrait is visible as an outline. LIBERTY and the date are mostly or even completely worn away. Contact marks may be extensive. *Reverse:* The chain is fully visible in outline form. Traces of the central letters—or, on better strikes, nearly all of the letters—can be seen. Around the border all letters are worn away.

1793; BW-4, S-3, B-4. Graded AG-3.

Illustrated coin: The date is completely worn away, but most of LIBERTY is readable. Two edge bumps on the left are unusual for this low grade. The reverse is quite bold, and some peripheral lettering can be seen.

1793, Chain Reverse

Circulation mintage (assumed): 36,103.

The first delivery of cents from the coiner (Henry Voigt) to the Mint treasurer was on March 1, 1793, and consisted of 11,178 pieces—these representing the first copper coins of the new Mint.[4] Frank H. Stewart, in *History of the First United States Mint, Its People and Its Operations*, suggested that the 110,512 cents struck during calendar year 1793 included 36,103 of the Chain type, made from March 1 to 12; 63,353 Wreath cents, struck from April 9 to July 17; and 11,056 Liberty Cap cents, delivered from the coiner to the treasurer on September 18. While the delivery figures are correct, there are no hard facts to back up the assignment of specific designs to the deliveries. It is not necessarily true that different deliveries represent abandonment of earlier dies—in fact it is improbable! This is a *very important* concept as it applies across the board to all early delivery figures for half cents and large cents.

Perhaps the September 18 shipment included some of the Wreath type? In such situations, certain figures can be no more than estimates. Nevertheless, they can be useful, if backed up by surveys of existing coins, to determine relative population. At least with the 1793 cents we know they were all dated that year. It would not be surprising if certain 1793 cents (of the later Liberty Cap type) were also struck in calendar year 1794, but we will never know.

There were four different obverse dies cut for the Chain cents, one of them having a period after LIBERTY and another after the date. Just two reverses were made, one with AMERI. and the other with AMERICA. R.W. Julian has provided a Mint record stating that coiner Henry Voigt cut the dies.[5]

The details of Miss Liberty's hair are often indistinct or missing, even on many higher-grade examples. For all grades, the reverse is often sharper than the obverse. Hence, if split grading were popular today (as it once was), a Chain AMERI. cent might be correctly graded as VG-8/F-12, or similarly.

The Chain cents remained in circulation for many years. In 1859 Dr. Montroville W. Dickeson wrote in the *American Numismatical Manual* that he had found several different varieties by pulling them from circulation. In the cradle days of numismatic popularity, beginning in a large way in 1858 and 1859, any 1793 cent attracted attention, and a particularly nice one was apt to cost several dollars.

Most 1793, Chain, cents known today are well worn, as might be expected from their first having attracted widespread notice in the 1850s. Today, even in Fair-2 or About Good-3 grades, they are collectible and in strong demand. Some of the lowest grades have nearly everything worn away except a shadow or outline of the chain—enough to identify the type, but not to reveal much else. Such a coin is still very desirable as a filler and will find many buyers in the marketplace.

Grades from G-4 through F-12 constitute most of the Chain cents in the marketplace. VF coins are scarcer, and EF scarcer yet. Offerings at the AU level, punctuated by the occasional Mint State example, draw a lot of attention and are usually showcased as prime attractions when offered at auction.

Scratches, edge bumps, and porosity are common among 1793 cents. The answer is to cherrypick for quality.

Several collectors have found cents of the 1793 year (all three types) to be an interesting specialty, none more so than Charles Ruby, a California college professor who was prominent in the large cent field for many years. Kenneth Rendell and Q. David Bowers were overnight guests at his home in 1958, and were treated to seeing multiple custom plastic holders filled with 1793 cents, most of which were in low grades, but each with its own charm.

1793, Chain AMERI. • Bowers-Whitman–1, Sheldon-1, Breen-1. Crosby 1-A.[6] *Breen dies: 1-A.* **Estimated population: 120 to 160.**

Obverse: Y of LIBERTY opposite lower forehead. Date widely spaced with widest space between 7 and 9. ***Points of distinction:*** Clash marks develop from the chain on the reverse, and can be seen near the center of the coin. On most examples there is a bulge under the 1 of the date. The obverse die was slightly misaligned in the coin press. This causes the date to be weak and LIBERTY to be strong. This is especially noticeable on lower-grade examples on which the date can be completely worn away. This also happens on the BW-24 obverse.

Reverse: AMERI. abbreviation. ***Points of distinction:*** The reverse is found either perfect or with a bulge under the U of UNITED.

1793, Chain AMERI. (Bowers-Whitman–1, Sheldon-1, Breen-1).

Detail of the finely delineated hair strands and widely spaced date.

AMERI. abbreviation and part of chain.

The next die state has a crack over TAT of STATES. The rarest die state is terminal because this crack has become a heavy cud that extends to the rim. It is the failure of this die that is the cause of the creation of the next variety that now spells AMERICA in full.

Notes: Mintage estimated as 4,500.[7] This variety occurs in Mint State occasionally. EF and AU are more practical possibilities for collectors.

Numismatic Notes: *1889 comment on the desirability of BW-1, suggesting this variety had been popular since about 1839:* W.E. Woodward's January 21–22, 1889, sale of the Charles Stetson Collection included lot 4: "1793 Reverse has the abbreviated legend 'Ameri.' this cent is Uncirculated and almost bright; it is the finest cent of this kind known, except that of Mr. Mickley's, which is a brilliant Proof, and has sold several times for about $175. . . . As collectors have been looking for this cent for about 50 years, that another perfect specimen should turn up is hardly to be expected."[8]

	Cert	Avg	%MS	AG-3	G-4	VG-8	F-12	VF-20	EF-40	AU-50	MS-60BN
1793, Chain AMERI.	36	23.9	8%	$6,300	$11,250	$17,625	$28,500	$49,250	$87,500	$200,000	$318,750

1793, Chain AMERICA • BW-2, S-2, B-2. Crosby 1-C. *Breen dies:* 1-B. *Estimated population:* 75 to 120.

Obverse: Same die as preceding. *Points of distinction:* Clash marks develop near the center. There is a bulging beneath the last three date numerals.

Reverse: AMERICA spelled out in full.

Notes: Mintage estimated as 6,500. This variety can be found in Mint State, but it is very rare as such. AU coins appear now and again.

1793, Chain AMERICA (BW-2, S-2, B-2).

	Cert	Avg	%MS	AG-3	G-4	VG-8	F-12	VF-20	EF-40	AU-50
1793, Chain AMERICA (BW-2)	(a)			$4,650	$7,750	$13,625	$19,250	$36,125	$61,500	$111,000

a. Included in certified population for 1793, Chain AMERICA (BW-4).

1793, Chain AMERICA • BW-3, S-NC-1, B-3. Crosby 2-C. *Breen dies:* 2-B. *Recorded population:* 2.

Obverse: Widest LIBERTY, with the Y opposite the eye. LIBERTY is also farther away from the rim than on any other Chain variety. *Points of distinction:* A crack develops at the rim below 7, continuing up to the left. This probably happened very early in the life of the die, accounting for the extreme rarity of impressions today.

Reverse: Same die as preceding.

Notes: Mintage estimated as 100. Two known: EF-45, American Numismatic Society; and Poor-1, found in 1967, in the Daniel W. Holmes Jr. Collection 1996–2008. The EF coin shows a small crack from the border through 1 of 1793, which may have quickly developed so as to render the die useless, accounting for the rarity.

1793, Chain AMERICA • BW-4, S-3, B-4. Crosby 3-C. *Breen dies:* 3-B. *Estimated population:* 400 to 500.

Obverse: Y of LIBERTY opposite eyebrow. 179 spaced about the same distance apart; 93 very close, 3 slightly low. The R is overly large and tilts to the right. Clash marks from the reverse often seen in front of the mouth and throat and under the neck. *Points of distinction:* The planchets used for this variety are approximately 1 mm larger than those used on the other Chain cents.

1793, Chain AMERICA (BW-4, S-3, B-4).

Reverse: Same die as preceding. *Points of distinction:* The late die state exhibits a crack through the bottom of UNITED.

Notes: Mintage estimated as 16,000. This variety is available in Mint State, but it is exceedingly rare as such. EF and AU coins are more practical possibilities.

	Cert	Avg	%MS	AG-3	G-4	VG-8	F-12	VF-20	EF-40	AU-50	MS-60BN
1793, Chain AMERICA (BW-4)	113	24.0	6%	$4,650	$7,750	$13,625	$19,250	$36,125	$61,500	$111,000	$250,000

1793, Chain AMERICA, Period After LIBERTY and Date • BW-5, S-4, B-5.

Crosby 4-C. *Breen dies:* 4-B. *Estimated population:* 200 to 300.

Obverse: With a period after LIBERTY and another after the date. The hair detail is more attractive than on the preceding dies and somewhat differently styled. *Points of distinction:* Early-die-state coins usually have a bulge between the lower hair and the rim. This bulge develops into a tiny crack, which

1793, Chain AMERICA, Period After LIBERTY and Date (BW-5, S-4, B-5).

is joined by a second crack that goes toward the date. There is also a small rim break at 8 o'clock.

Reverse: Same die as preceding.

Notes: Mintage estimated as 9,000. This variety can be found in Mint State, but it is exceedingly rare as such. EF and AU coins are more practical possibilities. An MS-66BN example of this coin sold at auction for $2,350,000 in January 2015.

	Cert	Avg	%MS	AG-3	G-4	VG-8	F-12	VF-20	EF-40	AU-50
1793, Chain AMERICA, Period After LIBERTY and Date	13	26.6	0%	$5,075	$8,125	$14,500	$20,500	$38,750	$66,250	$123,750

FLOWING HAIR, WREATH REVERSE (1793)

Designer: *Henry Voigt.* **Weight:** *208 grains (13.48 grams).*
Composition: *Copper.* **Diameter:** *26 to 28 mm.*
Edge: *Vine and Bars design, or lettered ONE HUNDRED FOR A DOLLAR. The varieties with lettered edge give the denomination three times: as ONE / CENT and 1/100 on the reverse and as ONE HUNDRED FOR A DOLLAR on the edge. The same triple denomination feature is found on several other early copper types.*

1793, Sprung Die, Wreath Type, Vine and Bars Edge (BW-12, S-6, B-7).

Mint records (from coiner Voigt's account book) show that coining of the Wreath cents commenced on April 4. Between April 9 and July 17, 1793, there were 63,353 large copper cents delivered. Conventional wisdom is that all of these were of the Wreath type, although whether the division is clear cut between the ending of the Chain type and the beginning of the Wreath type is subject to question, as noted above in the narrative concerning Chain cents.

The Wreath cent, named for the reverse, reflected a great change in the cent motif—now with a restyled portrait in high relief and with the reverse chain eliminated. Both obverse and reverse were given a beaded border, at once protective and attractive. Q. David Bowers has said that the elegance of this issue has no equivalents earlier or later in the large cent series.

Eleven different die combinations were used to accomplish the coinage. All but the final combination has the vine and bars edge treatment. The BW-21 and BW-22 edge devices are split between the vine and bars (scarcer) and those lettered ONE HUNDRED FOR A DOLLAR.

Today, Wreath cents are at once rare and popular, serving as foundation stones in American numismatics. Such coins are in continual demand, and there has never been a time in which the market for them has been slow. Typical grades range from Good to Fine, or so. Many pieces have problems, and cherrypicking is needed to find one that is just right.

DESIGN DETAILS

As with the Chain cents, R.W. Julian has located documentation that the dies of the Wreath cents were cut by coiner Voigt.[9] On the obverse the head of Miss Liberty faces to the right, in bold relief, with prominent hair tresses flowing back. Above, is LIBERTY; below, a three-leaf sprig, and below that the date 1793. The border is beaded. The entire arrangement is very elegant. The botanical nature of the sprig and its variations have furnished the subject for many numismatic commentaries. For the usually seen sprig, laurel has been suggested. Writing in the *New-York Dispatch*, April 19, 1857, Augustus B. Sage offered this possibility. "The palm leaf cent of 1793 [has] the addition of three small palm leaves under the bust, and the olive wreath, taking the place of the chain around 'one cent, 1-100.'" Although palm leaves may have been used on other coins (most notably the $5 and $10 issues of 1795), they do not seem to be a candidate for the foliage on the 1793 cent.

The most famous sprig is that of the 1793, Strawberry Leaf, cent, as it has been called by generations of numismatists. This motif has been called a *pattern* by some, but there seems to be little support for that, as all examples show evidence of circulation. John Kleeberg suggested it may be a contemporary counterfeit.[10] Walter Breen in his *Encyclopedia* discussed such theories and concluded, "What punches are clear enough for certainty leave no doubt of its Mint origin, and the edge ornamentation is as on the other genuine 1793 cents." As this variety is front-row center in the numismatic annals of 1793 cents, it is worthwhile to devote space here for a detailed discussion.

Sylvester Sage Crosby included this in *The United States Coinage of 1793—Cents and Half Cents*, 1897:

> This is the obverse . . . having been first known as the "Clover leaf" Cent, but which I think may properly be called the Cotton leaf Cent, and is the greatest rarity of its class, only three specimens being known to collectors, one having reverse D, and two, reverse E. It bears upon a stem rising from near the angle of the 7, three trefoil leaves and a blossom, or boll of cotton.
>
> The legend and date are in small characters, the R larger and higher than the other letters and placed over the hair, close above the forehead. The date is less than two millimeters from the hair at the left, and more than four from the point of the bust, which is longer and more rounded at its tip than in any other known die. The double curl under the neck is rather heavy.
>
> It is difficult to account for the scarcity of specimens from this die, as it appears to have been thought worthy of two reverse dies, neither it, or either of its reverses showing any signs of deterioration, and neither reverse being known to have been used with any other obverse. It is hoped that better specimens of these may yet be discovered.

In *The Numismatist*, May 1912, Edgar H. Adams in his "Live American Numismatic Items" column, included mention of the auction offering of such a cent, when Lyman H. Low called the cataloger of the coin, Édouard Frossard, a "liar":

At one of Frossard's sales at Kennedy's Fifth Avenue Auction Rooms, on December 20th, 1894 a specimen described as "Very Fair" for $120. It was this cent that incidentally caused the historic fight when Frossard and another prominent dealer, both veterans, rolled around the floor of the auction room, trying to kick each other, and the late H.P. Smith lost a diamond pin in the confusion incidental to separating them.

Adams went on to discuss the "rare variety of the clover, strawberry, or whatever kind of leaf one may choose," noting that an article in the current issue of *Steigerwalt's Messenger* was confused and contained several errors.

Jim Neiswinter, well-known specialist in the study of cents of the 1793 year, provided this comment in connection with the present book:

In December 2004 Bob Grellman, Dan Holmes, John Kleeberg, Bob Hoge, and I met at the American Numismatic Society. Dan brought his two Strawberry Leafs plus some of his other Wreath cents. We spent the day comparing them to the ANS Strawberry and Wreath cents. At the end of the day we all agreed that the Strawberries were all Mint products. This was later delineated in the *Penny Whimsy* article of March 2005. We also discovered that there are two varieties of the Vine and Bars edge device—the first is on all the Chains, plus the Sheldon-8 and 9.[11]

In *Coin World*, January 17, 2005, this commentary by Andrew W. Pollock III appeared, and is probably the last word on the subject:

The 1793 Flowing Hair, Wreath, "Strawberry Leaf" cent has been one of the most celebrated varieties in American numismatics since the 19th century. Although the "Strawberry leaf" moniker has been a popular designation for many decades, some numismatists over the years have conjectured that the intended design of the sprig beneath Miss Liberty's head is either from a cotton plant or clover plant.

The suggestion that the design represents cotton is supported not only by the shape of the leaves, which is very similar to the shape of the leaves of certain varieties of cotton plants that can be found illustrated on the Internet and in agricultural textbooks, but also from the fact that Eli Whitney's cotton gin was invented in 1793, something brought to my attention by John Pack.

The recent auction of the finest known example of the "Strawberry Leaf" cent (American Numismatic Rarities, Nov. 30, Lot 130) resulted in my having an opportunity to examine the coin, whereupon I suspected that the sprig was actually intended to be that of a grape plant, having three leaves; a poorly defined cluster of grapes; and possibly a vestigial tendril. It could be argued that the "cluster" element might have been intended as a cotton boll. However, I'm inclined to the view that an open cotton boll would have been depicted as having a more uniform periphery and perhaps with the open boll projecting upward as is represented in drawings and photographs of cotton plants having ripe cotton ready to be harvested. I have found an example of a grape ornamentation on a piece of silverware made in Great Britain in the first quarter of the 19th century. The ornamentation depicts grape leaves, grape clusters and tendrils. The similarity of the grape leaves depicted in the ornamentation with the leaves featured on the 1793 Flowing Hair cent is striking. It is also worth mentioning that the grape clusters in the ornamentation are not all of a uniform inverted pear shape, which seems to be characteristic of modern depictions seen in still life paintings and advertisements.

I also found at chartingnature.com another rendering of a grape leaf that is similar titled *Wine-Grape-Raisin Precoce de Montreuil.* The Internet has provided numismatists and other students of the humanities with vast resources by which they can pursue their scholarly investigations. In connection with the inquiry to ascertain if the 1793 Flowing Hair, "Strawberry Leaf" cent may have actually been intended as a "Grape Leaves and Cluster" cent, I conducted a Google search to determine if any events occurred in America in 1793 pertaining to grapes or vineyards.

I learned that according to some unattributed lecture notes posted on the Purdue University website pertaining to the topic of "Wine Appreciation" that "America's first commercial winery, the Pennsylvania Vine Company, [was] founded in 1793 near Philadelphia by Pierre Legaux." At the web site of the American Philosophical Society in Philadelphia, an archival finding aid presents the background story of Peter Legaux and the Pennsylvania Vine Co.:

"In January 1793, Peter Legaux submitted a plan to the American Philosophical Society for 'the establishment of the Vine culture in Pennsylvania by means of public subscription, authorized and protected by Government.'"

Following Legaux's proposal to the APS, the Pennsylvania Legislature passed an act authorizing the incorporation of a company for promoting culture of the vine. A subscription was raised and shares issued to some of Philadelphia's most important merchants and friends of improvement. . . . It should be noted that the president of the American Philosophical Society at the time of Legaux's proposal was David Rittenhouse, who also at that time was the director of the Mint. Production of the coin variety may have simply been intended to signify Rittenhouse's approbation of the project. Although this evidence in no way constitutes proof that the 1793 Flowing Hair, "Strawberry Leaf" cent is indeed a Pennsylvania vineyard commemorative, nonetheless, the information provides what seems to be a plausible context for the creation of a fascinating and enigmatic variety.

The reverse displays an open wreath with sprays of berries among the leaves (the only year with this feature), tied with a single ribbon bow at the bottom, enclosing the two-line inscription, ONE / CENT. Around the border is UNITED STATES OF AMERICA. Below the bow is 1/100. The border is beaded. The wreath is *extremely curious* from a botanical viewpoint, and what the engraver had in mind is anybody's guess. The sprays of berries are among olive or, most likely, laurel leaves, or whatever (the same type of leaves had different berries on later reverses), with the same branches also yielding *tiny maple leaves*. The reverse is very attractive and closely matches the style used on all half cents of the 1793 year.

GRADING STANDARDS

MS-60 to 70 (Mint State). *Obverse:* On MS-60 and 61 coins there are some traces of abrasion on the higher areas of the portrait, most particularly the hair. As this area can be lightly struck, careful inspection is needed for evaluation, not as much in Mint State (as other features come into play), but in higher circulated grades. Luster in the field is incomplete at lower–Mint State levels, but should be in generous quantity. At MS-63, luster

1793; BW-18, S-8, B-13. Graded MS-64BN.

should be complete, and no abrasion evident. At higher levels, the luster is deeper, and some original mint color may be seen. At MS-65 there might be some scattered contact marks and possibly bare traces of fingerprints or discoloration. Above MS-65, a coin should approach perfection. A Mint State 1793, Wreath, cent is an object of rare beauty. *Reverse:* In the lower–Mint State grades some abrasion is seen on the higher areas of the leaves. Generally, luster is complete in all grades, as the open areas are protected by the lettering and wreath. In many ways, the grading guidelines for this type follow those of the 1793 half cent—also with sprays of berries (not seen elsewhere in the series).

Illustrated coin: This near-gem Wreath cent is well struck, with full separation on Liberty's curls. The planchet is of unusually high quality, lacking the usual streaks and pits common to early cents. The fields and devices are smooth and unblemished, and the color is a rich chocolate brown, with no specks or carbon spots. In addition to being in a high numerical grade, this coin has exceptional eye appeal.

AU-50, 53, 55, 58 (About Uncirculated). *Obverse:* Friction is seen on the highest areas of the hair (which may also be lightly struck) and the cheek. Some scattered marks are normal in the field, ranging from more extensive at AU-50 to minimal at AU-58. *Reverse:* Friction is seen on the higher wreath leaves and (not as easy to discern) on the letters. The fields, protected by the designs (including sprays of berries at the center), show fric-

1793; BW-18, S-8, B-13. Graded AU-50.

tion, but not as noticeably as on the obverse. At AU-55 and 58, little if any friction is seen. Border beads, if well struck, are separate and boldly defined.

Illustrated coin: Offered at auction with this description: "Glossy dark steel brown with appealing surface quality. Under a strong glass, the surfaces show extremely fine granularity . . . only really notable near the borders. A natural planchet flaw at the rim above O in OF is a reminder of the tribulations the Mint endured in its first year of full operations. The marks that are present are utterly inoffensive, with just a dull scrape under 17 of the date and a minor old scratch under the last S of STATES. . . . The overall eye appeal, both in hand and under careful scrutiny, is very nice."

EF-40, 45 (Extremely Fine). *Obverse:* More extensive wear is seen on the high parts of the hair, creating mostly a solid mass (without detail of strands) of varying width in the area immediately to the left of the face. The cheek shows light wear. Luster is minimal or non-existent at EF-40, and may survive in traces in protected areas (such as between the letters) at EF-45. *Reverse:* Wear is seen on the highest wreath and ribbon areas, and the let-

1793; BW-17, S-9, B-12. Graded EF-40.

ters. Luster is minimal, but likely more noticeable than on the obverse, as the fields are protected by the designs and lettering. Some of the beads blend together.

Illustrated coin: This coin shows some granularity and contact marks, with lighter brown color than usual.

VF-20, 30 (Very Fine). *Obverse:* Wear on the hair is more extensive, and varies depending on the die variety and sharpness of strike. The ANA grading standards suggest that two-thirds of the hair is visible, which in practice can be said to be "more or less." More beads are blended together, but the extent of this blending depends on the striking and variety. Certain parts of the rim are smooth, with beads scarcely visible at all. No

1793; BW-17, S-9, B-12. Graded VF-25.

luster is seen. The date, LIBERTY, and hair ends are bold. *Reverse:* The leaf details are nearly completely worn away at VF-20, with slight detail at VF-30. The border beads are blended together, with many indistinct. Some berries in the sprays are light, but nearly all remain distinct. No luster is seen.

Illustrated coin: Note some tiny pin scratches, and overall planchet granularity. The sharpness is better than usually seen at this grade.

F-12, 15 (Fine). *Obverse:* The hair details are mostly worn away, with about one-third visible, mainly at the edges. The ANA grading standards suggest that half of the details are visible, seemingly applying to the total area of the hair. However, the visible part, at the left, also includes intermittent areas of the field. Beads are weak or worn away in areas. F-15 shows slightly more detail. By this grade, scattered light scratches, noticeable contact

1793; BW-17, S-9, B-12. Graded F-12.

marks, and the like are the rule, not the exception. These are not mentioned at all on holders and are often overlooked elsewhere, except in some auction catalogs and price lists. Such marks are implicit for coins in lower grades, and light porosity or granularity is common as well. *Reverse:* The wreath leaves are worn flat, but their edges are distinct. Border beads are weak or worn away in areas. F-15 shows slightly more detail.

Illustrated coin: This is a sharp coin, but it shows some minor (non-distracting) pits near the base of the obverse. It has even color, superb visual appeal, and a mostly smooth surface.

VG-8, 10 (Very Good). *Obverse:* The hair is well worn toward the face. Details at the left are mostly blended together in thick strands. The eye, nose, and lips often remain well defined. Border beads are completely gone, or just seen in traces, and part of the rim blends into the field. LIBERTY may be slightly weak. The 1793 date is fully visible, although there may be some lightness. Scattered marks are more common than on

1793; BW-17, S-9, B-12. Graded VG-8.

higher grades. *Reverse:* The wreath, bow, and lettering are seen in outline form, and some leaves and letters may be indistinct in parts. Most of the berries remain visible, but weak. Border beads are worn away, and the border blends into the field in most if not all of the periphery.

Illustrated coin: This is an attractive example for the grade, with just one tiny pit near the top of the 3 and some minor granularity.

G-4, 6 (Good). *Obverse:* The hair is worn smooth except for the thick tresses at the left. The eye, nose, and lips show some detail. LIBERTY is weak, with some letters missing. The date is discernible, although partially worn away. The sprig above the date is usually prominent. The border completely blends into the field. *Reverse:* Extensive overall wear. The wreath is seen in outline form, with some areas weak. Usually ONE CENT

1793; BW-17, S-9, B-12. Graded G-4.

remains readable at the center. The border letters and fraction show extensive wear, with some letters very weak or even missing, although most should be discernible. Dark or porous coins may have more details on both sides in an effort to compensate for the roughness. Marks, edge bumps, and so on are normal.

Illustrated coin: This coin's certified-grade holder noted that the surfaces are "corroded," a rather harsh term (oxidized or deeply oxidized might be gentler). At G-4, problems are expected. The date is weak, but most other features are discernible.

AG-3 (About Good). *Obverse:* Wear is more extensive than on the preceding. The eye, nose, and lips may still be discernible, and the sprig above the date can usually be seen. LIBERTY may be very weak or even missing. The date is gone, or just a trace will remain. *Reverse:* Parts of the wreath are visible in outline form. ONE CENT might be readable, but this is not a requirement. Most border letters are gone. If a coin is dark or

1793; BW-12, S-6, B-7. Graded AG-3.

porous it may be graded AG-3 and may be sharper than just described, with the porosity accounting for the lower grade.

Illustrated coin: This piece is toned gray overall, and with porous surfaces. The date is gone, but other features on both sides are discernible, making for easy attribution as to die variety.

1793, Wreath Reverse

Circulation mintage (assumed): 63,353.

Cents of the Wreath design are often acquired singly for inclusion in a type set. Collecting by varieties has also been popular, this including varieties created by the two edge types. The final die pair, which created BW-21, with Vine and Bars edge, was the only pair used for Lettered Edge coins, with either two leaves or one on the edge, as on BW-22 and BW-23.

The most famous of all Wreath cents is the so-called Strawberry Leaf, as discussed in the introductory material for this type. These are very rare and are always seen with extensive wear. There are two varieties, with one obverse die combined with two reverses.

Extensive wear is the rule for all varieties. Similar to the situation for Chain cents, the Wreath cents did not attract much attention until the rise of numismatics as a popular hobby in the 1850s, by which time the typical coin had spent many decades in commercial use.

Grades of surviving coins ranging from About Good-3 upward are collectible and highly prized. Most in the marketplace range from G-4 to Fine-12 or so, although Very Fine and Extremely Fine coins cross the auction block with regularity. Mint State examples exist for the Vine and Bars edge type, some of which are rather liberally graded, and these always attract a lot of attention. The Lettered Edge type is exceedingly rare if better than AU.

The dies were cut by hand and have many distinctive differences from one to another. The descriptions given below can be used quickly and simply. Other features can be discerned from the photographs.

Every 1793, Wreath, cent has its own personality. Use the grading number as a start, and then seek a coin with minimal or no edge bumps, planchet rifts, porosity, or heavy marks. Choice-appearing cents may be more expensive, and it may be necessary to view several coins to find one that is just right, but the search will be worth it. A smooth, attractive 1793, Wreath, cent is an item of rare beauty in any grade.

Most 1793, Wreath, cents are fairly well struck, although high-grade pieces may exhibit some weakness on the highest hair tresses and on the leaf details. On lower-grade pieces these areas are worn, so the point is moot.

It has been estimated that more than 2,000 1793, Wreath, cents with Vine and Bars edge exist and 500 or so of the Lettered Edge. As is true of many other American coins with interesting or unusual edge devices, the encasing of examples in certain types of certified holders prevents study and numismatic enjoyment of this feature.

1793, Wreath Type, Vine and Bars Edge • BW-11, S-5, B-6. Crosby 6-F. *Breen dies: 5-C. Estimated population: 120 to 160.*

Obverse: Stem slanted, distant from 9, points to upper right of 7 and is about on the same slant as the upright of the 7. The date and LIBERTY are larger on this die than on any other of the type. The sizes of LIBERTY and the date are the same size as those found on all the Chain varieties. That is why this is considered the first Wreath variety. Found perfect and also in a very rare late state with the die broken over LI and BER.

Reverse: Outside maple leaves (a.k.a. trefoils) under N and D of UNITED. Bow small and heavy. *Points of distinction:* A couple of tiny bulges are seen on later states.

Notes: This variety is available in Mint State, but rare so fine. Several exist. EF and AU pieces are seen with some regularity and are highly prized.

1793, Wreath Type, Vine and Bars Edge (BW-11, S-5, B-6).

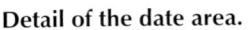

Detail of the date area.

Detail of part of the wreath, including sprays of berries, beaded border, tiny maple leaves ("trefoils").

	Cert	Avg	%MS	AG-3	G-4	VG-8	F-12	VF-20	EF-40	AU-50	MS-60BN	MS-63BN
1793, Wreath Type, Vine and Bars Edge (BW-11)	(a)			$700	$2,380	$4,700	$7,400	$14,500	$28,000	$40,625	$65,000	$117,500

a. Included in certified population for 1793, Wreath Type, Vine and Bars Edge (BW-17).

1793, Sprung Die, Wreath Type, Vine and Bars Edge • BW-12, S-6, B-7.

Crosby 7-F. *Breen dies: 6-C.* ***Estimated population:*** *300 to 400.*

1793, Sprung Die, Wreath Type, Vine and Bars Edge (BW-12, S-6, B-7).

Obverse: Leaves meet above 9, stem is close to 9 and points at upper right of 7. Rightmost leaf extends far beyond 3 and points to the tip of the neck. Leftmost leaf ends below curl. B of LIBERTY low. ***Points of distinction:*** First called the "Sprung Die" by Sylvester Crosby because there is always a bulge or convexity on the obverse running from the back of the hair to the rim. The latest die state has a crack from the lower lip to the right rim, and another short horizontal crack hidden in the hair below the bulge.

Reverse: Same die as preceding. ***Points of distinction:*** On some examples, on the back there is a short crack through TE of UNITED.

Notes: This coin can be found in Mint State, but is very rare as such.

	Cert	Avg	%MS	AG-3	G-4	VG-8	F-12	VF-20	EF-40	AU-50
1793, Sprung Die, Wreath Type, Vine and Bars Edge	(a)			$675	$2,200	$4,370	$6,930	$13,500	$24,670	$36,170

a. Included in certified population for 1793, Wreath Type, Vine and Bars Edge (BW-17).

1793, Wreath Type, Vine and Bars Edge • BW-13, S-7, B-8. Crosby 8-F. *Breen dies: 7-C.* ***Estimated population:*** *25 to 30.*

1793, Wreath Type, Vine and Bars Edge (BW-13, S-7, B-8).

Obverse: Stem ends above left edge of 9 and not close to it; right leaf very small. ***Points of distinction:*** Charles Ruby's famous double dot cent is considered by some to be the only known example of the earliest die state. This coin has two beads, one on top of the other, above the I of LIBERTY and does not exhibit any die sinking at the date. On most other examples there is some degree of die sinking at 1793 that leaves a swelling or raised area which tends to weaken the last three figures. In the latest state there is a crack from the top

Detail of LIBERTY with dots above I.

border from above R, through the base of T, to the front part of the hair, and the swelling at the date has developed into a crack from the rim, through the 9, and to the top part of the 7.

Reverse: Same die as preceding. There is usually a light crack through TE of UNITED. See notes below concerning the discovery of this variety.

Notes: Only two examples are known above VF, one of which is held by the American Numismatic Society.

Numismatic Notes: From Sylvester Sage Crosby, *The United States Coinage of 1793—Cents and Half Cents,* 1897:

> The discovery of this obverse was a curious instance of the appearance of a new die after a search of many years over a large field. Nearly ten years after the publication of the article on these cents in the

Journal of Numismatics, in 1869, when we had most of the important collections at our service, and a thorough search had been made in all directions, a lot of about seventy-five worn-out 1793 Cents was sent to me from Philadelphia, for examination. Among these I found two pieces from a die hitherto unnoticed, the only feature sufficiently preserved to distinguish them being the sprig under the bust.

I learned of no similar pieces for another ten years, when a better specimen was shown to me, belonging to Mr. Henry Phelps, of Worcester, Mass.; but in the Winsor sale of 1895, a fine and well-preserved specimen was discovered and purchased by its present owner, Dr. Thomas Hall, of Boston, and was by him alone recognized as from this rare die. This is the piece represented upon the plate. The two worn pieces first found are still in my possession, but are in so poor condition that they should not be considered as affecting its rarity, which should be estimated as only short of unique.

[This variety was discovered in 1878, just in time to be noted in Édouard Frossard's 1879 *Monograph of United States Cents and Half Cents*.]

	Cert	Avg	%MS	AG-3	G-4	VG-8	F-12	VF-20
1793, Wreath Type, Vine and Bars Edge (BW-13)	(a)			$7,125	$10,250	$19,000	$33,750	$50,000

a. Included in certified population for 1793, Wreath Type, Vine and Bars Edge (BW-17).

1793, Wreath Type, Vine and Bars Edge • BW-14, S-NC-5, B-9. Crosby 10-F.

Breen dies: 8-C. ***Recorded population:*** 1.

Obverse: Stem end is thick, points down past the right side of 7 and ends near the upper right of 7.

Reverse: Same die as preceding. ***Points of distinction:*** On the only known example there is a short break through TE of STATES, more advanced than on any other use of this reverse.

1793, Wreath Type, Vine and Bars Edge (BW-14, S-NC-5, B-9).

Notes: Unique. In the collection of the American Numismatic Society. EF-45.

1793, Wreath Type, Vine and Bars Edge, "Injured Rim" • BW-15, S-10, B-10. Crosby 10-I. *Breen dies:* 8-D. ***Estimated population:*** 120 to 160.

Obverse: Same die as preceding. ***Points of distinction:*** Known as the "Injured Rim" variety because the obverse die has been injured at the 3 o'clock position on the coin, opposite Liberty's nose. This has caused the edge of the die to become slightly indented, which causes the beads on the coin to become somewhat raised and form a straight line for about 6 mm.

Reverse: Outside maple leaf under E of UNITED. Between S and the O in OF one spray of berries, ends below left side of O. ***Points of distinction:*** Early die state coins have a rim crack or break over NIT in UNITED. On the latest state this break extends from the end of the U to the beginning of the E.

1793, Wreath Type, Vine and Bars Edge, "Injured Rim" (BW-15, S-10, B-10).

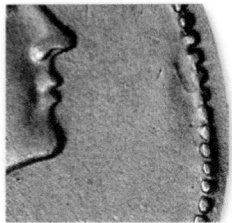

Detail of the injured rim.

Notes: This variety appears in Mint State, but is rare at this level. The finest is held by the ANS.

	Cert	Avg	%MS	AG-3	G-4	VG-8	F-12	VF-20	EF-40	AU-50
1793, Wreath Type, Vine and Bars Edge (BW-15)	(a)			$675	$2,430	$4,675	$7,350	$14,625	$28,250	$42,500

a. Included in certified population for 1793, Wreath Type, Vine and Bars Edge (BW-17).

1793, Wreath Type, Vine and Bars Edge • BW-16, S-NC-4, B-11. Crosby 9-I.

Breen dies: 9-D. **Recorded population:** 5.

Obverse: Horizontal stem over 79, only die with this feature.

Reverse: Same die as preceding. *Points of distinction:* The rim break now extends from the middle of the U to the end of E of UNITED.

1793, Wreath Type, Vine and Bars Edge (BW-16, S-NC-4, B-11).

Notes: Of the five recorded examples, the most recent was discovered by Chris Young in 2000. The highest-graded pieces are G-4 to VG-8. The finest is owned by Yale University.

1793, Wreath type, Vine and Bars Edge, Widest Ribbon Bow • BW-17, S-9, B-12. Crosby 9-H. *Breen dies:* 9-E. **Estimated population:** 750 to 1,000.

Obverse: Same die as preceding. *Points of distinction:* Eventually cracks develop on the portrait.

Reverse: Widest ribbon bow extends from C to T of CENT. Outside maple leaf under E of UNITED. Between S and O in OF two

1793, Wreath Type, Vine and Bars Edge, Widest Ribbon Bow (BW-17, S-9, B-12).

sprays of berries end, each at a different angle. *Points of distinction:* The reverse is sometimes found perfect but also with several progressions of short cracks. One starts at the top of C in AMERICA and crosses the second A and the ends of the ribbon. Another runs from R of AMERICA to the lower leaves on the right. A light crack is sometimes found running through UNITED. The latest die state has severe die failure between CA of AMERICA and the right ribbon. An MS-66+BN example of this coin sold at auction for $528,750 in August 2014.

Notes: The most often encountered 1793 variety. Mint State examples come on the market now and again and are the Wreath cents most often seen at this level.

	Cert	Avg	%MS	AG-3	G-4	VG-8	F-12	VF-20	EF-40	AU-50	MS-60BN	MS-63BN
1793, Wreath Type, Vine and Bars Edge (BW-17)	186	33.0	12%	$675	$2,300	$4,460	$7,075	$13,875	$25,375	$36,170	$59,375	$106,250

1793, Wreath Type, Vine and Bars Edge, Triangular Ribbon Bow, ONE / CENT High • BW-18, S-8, B-13. Crosby

9-G. *Breen dies:* 9-F. *Estimated population:* 400 to 500.

1793, Wreath Type, Vine and Bars Edge, Triangular Ribbon Bow, ONE / CENT High (BW-18, S-8, B-13).

Obverse: Same die as preceding. ***Points of distinction:*** A faint die crack is usually seen from the point of the bust to the border. Sometimes a short crack runs from the left top of the Y to the border, another from the top of the R, and still another from the top of the B to the border. The 9 and the 3 are sometimes poorly formed due to clash marks.

Reverse: The ribbon bow is triangular and ONE / CENT is high. Outside maple leaf under T of UNITED. ***Points of distinction:*** The reverse is always found with a delicate break and sometimes a sort of bulge extending almost straight across the coin from the first T of STATES to the second A of AMERICA, running through the center dot.

Notes: This variety can be found in Mint State, but it is quite rare as such.

	Cert	Avg	%MS	AG-3	G-4	VG-8	F-12	VF-20	EF-40	AU-50
1793, Wreath Type, Vine and Bars Edge (BW-18)	(a)			$675	$2,300	$4,460	$7,075	$13,875	$25,375	$36,170

a. Included in certified population for 1793, Wreath Type, Vine and Bars Edge (BW-17).

1793, Wreath Type, Strawberry Leaf, Vine and Bars Edge • BW-19, S-NC-2,

B-14. Crosby 5-D. *Breen dies:* 10-G. ***Recorded population:*** 1.

Obverse: "Strawberry" or other variant twig.

Reverse: ONE / CENT is centered in the wreath. Second A of AMERICA very close to ribbon.

1793, Wreath Type, Strawberry Leaf, Vine and Bars Edge (BW-19, S-NC-2, B-14). Detail of "Strawberry" leaf at BW-20.

Notes: The only recorded example of this variety has been graded as Fair-2 or finer. One expert suggested VG-8. It is in the Daniel W. Holmes Jr. Collection. It was found in circulation in 1845 by John Meader, a grocer in Providence, Rhode Island.

1793, Wreath Type. Strawberry Leaf, Vine and Bars Edge • BW-20, S-NC-3, B-15. Crosby 5-E. *Breen dies: 10-H.* **Recorded population:** 3.

Obverse: Same die as preceding.

Reverse: ONE / CENT high in wreath. Second A of AMERICA distant from ribbon.

Notes: The finest example is VG-7 by conservative grading (or VG-10 or F-12, opinions vary). It was housed in the Lorin G. Parmelee Collection (1890), years later in an old-time Maine estate, then with Republic Jewelry and Coins, and subsequently it was auctioned by American Numismatic Rarities, then by Stack's in January 2009 for $862,500. The other two examples are AG-3.

1793, Wreath Type, Strawberry Leaf, Vine and Bars Edge (BW-20, S-NC-3, B-15). This is the Parmelee coin, the finest known.

Detail of strawberry leaf.

Numismatic Notes: *An early auction offering:* On October 23–24, 1877, J.W. Scott & Co. held its first auction. The venue was the sale room of Bangs & Co. This 62-page offering, *Catalogue of a Fine Collection of Gold, Silver & Copper Coins and a Very Complete Collection of Centennial Medals*, included publicity about the curious and rare 1793, Strawberry Leaf, large cent. Cataloged by Scott himself according to some accounts (alternatively, David Proskey may have done the work), the effort was later criticized by Scott's jealous competitor and former employee, Édouard Frossard, in *Numisma*, who wrote that he expected better of Scott. Frossard called the sale an event of little numismatic importance and for good measure noted:

> There is no method in the arrangement, the descriptions are for the better part crude, and mostly faulty, especially in the estimates of degree of preservation, most of the silver looking as if it had been polished or burnished. . . . The work of a numismatist is the result of close and undisturbed application, attention, and training; it can never be satisfactorily accomplished by hurried consultations with chance visitors during the bustle and hurry incidental to a miscellaneous publishing business and the retailing of postage stamps.[12]

1793, Wreath Type, Vine and Bars Edge • BW-21, S-11a, B-16a. Crosby 11-J Vine and Bars. *Breen dies: 11-I.* **Estimated population:** 75 to 120.

Obverse: Stem points to, and ends above, the top of 9. First leaf points straight up, next two point right. *Points of distinction:* Clash marks from the wreath are usually seen below the chin.

Reverse: Outside maple leaf under IT of UNITED. *Points of distinction:* A faint crack is often seen crossing the left ribbon and stem, the bottom of the numerator, and the fraction bar, reaching the end of the right ribbon.

Notes: This variety can be found in Mint State, but is exceedingly rare as such.

	Cert	Avg	%MS	AG-3	G-4	VG-8	F-12	VF-20	EF-40	AU-50
1793, Wreath Type, Vine and Bars Edge (BW-21)	(a)			$775	$2,850	$5,375	$8,440	$16,875	$35,000	$48,330

a. Included in certified population for 1793, Wreath Type, Vine and Bars Edge (BW-17).

1793, Wreath Type, Lettered Edge With 2 Leaves • BW-22, S-11b, B-16b. Crosby 11-A

Lettered Edge, 2 Leaves. *Breen dies:* 11-I. ***Estimated population:*** 120 to 160.

Obverse: Same die as preceding. ***Points of distinction:*** Clash marks develop, including AMERICA incused in front of Liberty's face, then are removed from the die.

Reverse: Same die as preceding.

Notes: The highest-known grade for a piece of this variety is AU.

	Cert	Avg	%MS	AG-3	G-4	VG-8	F-12	VF-20	EF-40
1793, Wreath Type, Lettered Edge With 2 Leaves	(a)			$875	$3,100	$5,625	$8,940	$18,750	$37,500

a. Included in certified population for 1793, Wreath Type, Lettered Edge With 1 Leaf.

1793, Wreath Type, Lettered Edge With 1 Leaf • BW-23, S-11c, B-16c.

Crosby 11-J Lettered Edge, 1 Leaf. *Breen dies:* 11-I. ***Estimated population:*** 400 to 500.

Obverse: Same die as preceding.

Reverse: Same die as preceding.

Notes: These Lettered Edge cents are often seen on defective planchets. This variety exists in Mint State, but for all practical purposes is unobtainable. AU coins come on the market now and then.

1793, Wreath Type, Lettered Edge With 1 Leaf (BW-23, S-11c, B-16c).

	Cert	Avg	%MS	AG-3	G-4	VG-8	F-12	VF-20	EF-40	AU-50
1793, Wreath Type, Lettered Edge With 1 Leaf	36	26.5	6%	$775	$2,680	$4,940	$7,940	$15,625	$30,875	$48,250

LIBERTY CAP (1793–1796)

Designer: *Probably Joseph Wright.* **Weight:** *208 grains (13.48 grams) for the thick planchet, 168 grains (10.89 grams) for the thin planchet.* **Composition:** *Copper.* **Diameter:** *Average 29 mm.* **Edge:** *Early pieces lettered ONE HUNDRED FOR A DOLLAR; the later pieces have plain edges.*

1794, Buckled Obverse, No Protruding Leaf Under I of AMERICA (BW-17, S-27, B-9).

The Liberty Cap cent was created in the summer of 1793, probably by Joseph Wright, whom the Mint had intended to be staff engraver. The records show that Wright unfortunately fell ill from yellow fever before he could officially take office, and he passed away sometime in mid-September, although the exact death date has not been found. An accomplished portrait artist, he had earlier engraved some dies for the Mint, including the 1792 eagle-on-globe pattern quarter dollar.

The motif of the Liberty Cap cent followed the obverse design of Augustin Dupré's Libertas Americana medal—which was produced in Paris in 1782 at the suggestion of Benjamin Franklin—except that on the cent the head faces to the right rather than to the left. This was the second use of the motif at the Mint, as, in July, half cents were made of the Liberty Cap design (with Miss Liberty facing to the left, as on Dupré's original).

After Wright's passing, the duty of making new dies fell to Robert Scot. This he did in fine style, although he lowered the relief of the Liberty Cap motif in 1794, after which the design lost some of its charm. Walter Breen, seemingly acting on presumption rather than facts, specifically attributed various Liberty Cap obverse portraits and reverse wreath styles to John Smith Gardner, who was hired as an assistant to Scot in November of that year. In 1795 Gardner's annual salary was $936. Gardner, a seal engraver by profession, left the Mint in early 1796, but returned for a time that summer. It is likely that various people, ranging from talented engravers such as Gardner to mechanics and other employees, made certain dies using portrait punches created by Scot. Although the die sinking was well done, the workmanship of the *finish punching* (alignment of separately entered letters and numerals) of the dies of 1794 cents ranges from expert, these being the majority, to amateur. The Liberty Cap cents of 1795 and 1796 are more uniform in their appearance.

While Liberty Cap cents dated 1793 are major rarities, during 1794, 1795, and part of 1796, far more than a million were made, offering an example of an affordable type set. Those of 1794 and some of 1795 have the edge lettered ONE HUNDRED FOR A DOLLAR, while those made later in 1795 and in 1796 are on thinner planchets and have a plain edge.

Cents of this type are from hand-made dies and have many interesting variations. On the obverse the letters in LIBERTY and the numerals in the date vary in their placement. On the reverse the letters, fraction details, and berries were added by hand, creating many differences. Denticles range from short to long, closely or widely spaced, and with rounded or pointed tips.

As a basic type, the Liberty Cap cent is sufficiently plentiful that there is a wide selection in the marketplace for almost any grade desired up to VF, although offerings are scarce in higher grades. Liberty Cap cents of 1793 are rare in any grade, but especially so if VF and EF, and of pleasing appearance. Cents of 1794 can be found in grades from well worn to EF and AU, with occasional appearances of Mint State coins. Cents of 1795 of the Plain Edge type are readily available in all grades, including AU and, to a lesser extent, Mint State, although there are not many Mint State coins in existence. Cents of 1796 are elusive in high grades, although some Mint State coins come on the market now and again.

While there are many variations, in general the Liberty Cap cents of 1793 are found with dark surfaces and in lower grades. High quality is elusory. Cents of 1794 vary widely, but most are one or another shade of brown. The cents of 1795 and 1796 are more uniform in appearance and are found in higher average grades. Striking varies depending upon the die combination.

As is true of other early coppers, many Liberty Cap cents have scratches, edge bumps, discoloration, porosity, and other detriments. The manner of describing these varies widely. For certified coins, a number such as VF-20 is all the information given. Specialists, the better auction houses, and others sophisticated in the field usually describe the appearance and any negatives with an accompanying narrative.

Dr. Sheldon particularly enjoyed the Liberty Cap issues, and in *Penny Whimsy* wrote this:

> Considered as a whole, the Liberty Cap cents possess a charm not often exceeded among the things made by man. To no small degree the charm inheres in the great variability and individuality of these dies, of which there are no less than 105 [*sic*, should be 106]—53 obverses and 52 [*sic*, should be 53] reverses (in 1793, 3 obverses and 2 reverses; in 1794, 39 obverses and 38 reverses; in 1795, 5 obverses and 6 reverses; in 1796, 6 obverses and 7 reverses).
>
> About three-fourths of the Liberty Caps are dated 1794, and among these nearly all of the variation occurs, since the first of the 1794s are practically duplicates of the 1793s, and the last of them are virtually duplicates of the 1795s and 1796s. A collection of 1794 cents reflects much of the story of one

of the most pioneering and romantic struggles in American history. In the little Mint building on 7th Street in Philadelphia, during the middle of the last decade of the 18th century, history seems to have almost held her breath for a time, and we find the marks of her desperately clenched teeth engraved deeply on the soft copper pennies of those years. . . .

DESIGN DETAILS

The obverse features the head of Miss Liberty facing right, her hair flowing downward in tresses behind. A liberty cap is behind her head, and the pole to the cap is partially visible behind her head and above her neck to the right. LIBERTY is above. The date is below her neck. Issues of 1793 have a beaded border on both sides, adding a special elegance. Issues of 1794 to 1796 have denticles around the border of the obverse and reverse.

The portrait was modified slightly during this span, with the Head of 1793 (used on some 1794 cents as well) being more delicate, the Head of 1794 describing most for that year, and the Head of 1795 describing the final issues.

The reverse features an open wreath of olive (presumably) leaves, tied with a ribbon bow (that now has two loops) at the bottom and enclosing ONE / CENT. It is somewhat similar to the reverse used on 1793, Wreath, cents, except no longer with sprays of berries or maple leaves (trefoils). Numismatists usually refer to *berries* on Wreath cents, not to *olives*. Around the border is UNITED STATES OF AMERICA. The fraction 1/100 is below the bow.

The earlier varieties, those minted in 1794 and in early 1795, with lettered edge give the denomination *three times:* as ONE / CENT and 1/100 on the reverse and as ONE HUNDRED FOR A DOLLAR on the edge. The same triple denomination feature is found on several other early copper types.

GRADING STANDARDS

MS-60 to 70 (Mint State). *Obverse:* On MS-60 and 61 coins there are some traces of abrasion on the higher areas of the portrait. Luster is incomplete, particularly in the field. At MS-63, luster should be complete, and no abrasion evident. At higher levels, the luster is deeper, and some original mint color may be seen on some examples. At the MS-65 level there may be some scattered contact marks and possibly some traces of finger-

1794; BW-22, S-30, B-12. Graded MS-66BN.

prints or discoloration, but these should be very minimal and not at all distracting. Generally, Liberty Cap cents of 1793 (in particular) and 1794 are harder to find with strong eye appeal than are those of 1795 and 1796. Mint State coins of 1795 often have satiny luster. Above MS-65, a coin should approach perfection, especially if dated 1795 or 1796. Certified Mint State cents can vary in their strictness of interpretation. *Reverse:* In the lower–Mint State grades some abrasion is seen on the higher areas of the leaves. Generally, luster is complete in all grades, as the open areas are protected by the lettering and wreath. Often on this type the reverse is shallower than the obverse and has a lower rim.

Illustrated coin: This light brown example is sharply struck and shows no trace of wear. The planchet has mildly grainy areas, but the overall texture is glossy. The blemish in the left obverse field is due to a chip in the die rather than damage to the coin. Despite a few minor spots on the reverse, this coin would be the centerpiece of an advanced collection.

AU-50, 53, 55, 58 (About Uncirculated).

Obverse: Very light wear is evident on the highest parts of the hair above and to the left of the ear. Friction is seen on the cheek and the liberty cap. Coins at this level are usually on smooth planchets and have nice eye appeal. Color is very important. Dark and porous coins are relegated to lower grades, even if AU-level sharpness is present. *Reverse:* Very light wear is evident on the higher parts

1794; BW-97, S-70, B-62. Graded AU-55.

of the leaves and the ribbon, and, to a lesser extent, on the lettering. The reverse may have original luster, toned brown, varying from minimal (at lower About Uncirculated grades) to extensive. Grading at the About Uncirculated level is mainly done by viewing the obverse, as many reverses are inherently shallow due to lower-relief dies.

Illustrated coin: On this particular die variety the obverse rim denticles are particularly bold, helping to shield the field from wear. The motifs and inscriptions on both sides are cut deeply into the dies. Some porosity can be seen in the denticles above the I of LIBERTY. Excellent eye appeal overall.

EF-40, 45 (Extremely Fine).

Obverse: The center of the coin shows wear or a small, flat area, for most dies. Other hair details are strong. Luster is minimal or nonexistent at EF-40, and may survive in traces in protected areas (such as between the letters) at EF-45. *Reverse:* Wear is seen on the highest wreath and ribbon areas and the letters. Luster is minimal, but likely more noticeable than on the obverse, as the fields are protected by the

1794; BW-98, S-71, B-63. Graded EF-40.

designs and lettering. Sharpness varies depending on the die variety but is generally shallower than on the obverse, this being particularly true for many 1795 cents.

Illustrated coin: This coin has attractive light-brown surfaces. The flatness at the center of the obverse is partly from striking, not entirely from wear. Marks are evident, and on the reverse there is a rim bruise opposite the U in UNITED.

VF-20, 30 (Very Fine).

Obverse: Wear on the portrait has reduced the hair detail to indistinct or flat at the center, and on most varieties the individual strands at the left edge are blended together. One rule does not fit all. The ANA grading standards suggest that 75% of the hair shows, while PCGS suggests 30% to 70% on varieties struck from higher-relief dies, and less than 50% for others. Examples such as this reflect the artistic,

1793; BW-27, S-13, B-20. Graded VF-20.

rather than scientific, nature of grading. *Reverse:* The leaf details are nearly completely worn away at VF-20, and with slight detail at VF-30. Some border letters may be weak, and ditto for the central letters (on later varieties of this type). The border denticles are blended together with many indistinct. No luster is seen. The sharpness of details depends on the die variety.

Illustrated coin: This is the rarest of the three major types of 1793—eagerly sought in all grades. Unlike later Liberty Cap cents, those of 1793 have raised beads instead of denticles at the border. This one has a dark planchet with some scattered marks, not unusual for the date and type.

F-12, 15 (Fine). *Obverse:* The hair details are mostly worn away, with about one-third visible, mainly at the lower edges. Border denticles are weak or worn away in areas, depending on the height of the rim when the coin was struck. F-15 shows slightly more detail. *Reverse:* The wreath leaves are worn flat, but their edges are distinct. Border denticles are weak or worn away in areas. F-15 shows slightly more detail. At this level and lower, planchet darkness and light porosity are common, as are scattered marks.

1794; BW-101, S-72, B-65. Graded F-12.

Illustrated coin: Some lines and contact marks, as is expected for the grade.

VG-8, 10 (Very Good). *Obverse:* The hair is more worn than on the preceding, with detail present only in the lower areas. Detail can differ, and widely, depending on the dies. Border denticles are worn away on some issues (not as much for 1793 and 1794 coins), and the border will blend into the field in areas in which the rim was low to begin with, or in areas struck slightly off center. LIBERTY and the date are bold. VG-10 is

1794; BW-61, S-49, B-41. Graded VG-10.

sometimes applied to especially nice Very Good coins. *Reverse:* The wreath, bow, and lettering are seen in outline form, and some leaves and letters may be indistinct in parts. Border denticles are worn away, and the border blends into the field in most if not all of the periphery. In certain die varieties and die states, especially of 1797, some letters may be very weak, or missing.

Illustrated coin: This coin is sharp in some areas, and lightly struck at the upper-right border and on the corresponding part of the reverse, probably from the die faces not being parallel in the coining press. Note scattered light pitting and marks.

G-4, 6 (Good). *Obverse:* The portrait is worn smooth and is seen only in outline form, although the eye and nose can be discerned. LIBERTY and the date are complete, although the date may be weak. Denticles are gone on varieties struck with low or shallow rims. *Reverse:* Extensive wear is seen overall. From half to two-thirds of the letters in UNITED STATES OF AMERICA and the fraction numerals are worn away. Certain

1796; BW-5, S-84, B-5. Graded G-4.

shallow-relief dies may have letters missing. G-6 is often assigned to finer examples in this category. Darkness, porosity, and marks characterize many coins.

Illustrated coin: Note the dark and lightly porous planchet. ONE CENT not visible on the reverse due to the shallow die and striking (such situations can vary from one die to another). Otherwise, this coin is close to VG-8.

AG-3 (About Good). ***Obverse:*** Wear is more extensive than on the preceding. The portrait is visible only in outline. LIBERTY will typically have some letters worn away. The date is weak, but discernible. ***Reverse:*** Parts of the wreath are visible in outline form, and all but a few letters are gone. Grading of AG-3 is usually done by the reverse, as the obverse typically appears to be in a slightly higher grade.

1794; BW-95, S-68, B-60. Graded AG-3.

Illustrated coin: This coin is fully G-4 on the obverse, but weak on the reverse, prompting a more conservative grade. It has no serious marks or edge bumps (somewhat unusual for an AG-3).

1793, Liberty Cap

Circulation mintage (assumed): 11,056.

In terms of artistic beauty, many numismatists agree that the 1793, Liberty Cap, cents represent the best vintage for the design, being more attractive than the cents of late 1794 continuing through 1796. The 1793 cents were struck on broad planchets, providing ample field area between the border of raised beads and the rim and highlighting the beads, which seem to have been fully struck on all examples. It is thought that 1793-dated Liberty Cap cents were made from September 1793 to January 1794, although no specific records exist. Beads were not used on later cents of this design.

1793, Liberty Cap, cents are usually seen in low grades, Good or Very Good, often with dark and porous surfaces. Smooth, evenly worn pieces with attractive surfaces are in the distinct minority, probably on the order of about one coin in five. Thus, cherrypicking is essential to achieve quality—this being more true for the 1793, Liberty Cap, than for any other single cent type. If offered two examples, each Fine-15, one ordinary (dark and/or porous) coin priced at "market" per listings in standard guides, and the other with a pleasing surface and offered at 50% over market, it would be best, according to the advice of Q. David Bowers, to buy the more expensive one. Similarly, a smooth, pleasing VG-8 coin would be better to own than a dark and porous VF-20.

An estimated several hundred exist today, all save a handful being in lower grades as noted above. AU examples are exceedingly rare, and anything higher is in the "impossible" category.

The finest known example is the piece, BW-27, described as MS-64 or finer by Mark Borckardt in the sale of the Louis E. Eliasberg Sr. Collection, 1996, which is also the only known 1793, Liberty Cap, cent of any variety in Mint State. It now reposes in a fine Southern collection. Here is the pedigree chain, along with excerpts from certain of the descriptions:

> Édouard Frossard sale #21, May 1882, lot 627 $181.

> William H. Cottier; S.H. and H. Chapman, June 1885, lot 655 $90. "Uncirculated. Magnificent, strong even impression. Brilliant light olive, partly red color. The finest example known of this, the rarest U.S. cent."

Thomas Cleneay; S.H. and H. Chapman, December 1890, lot 1800 $200, to Peter Mougey.

Thomas L. Elder sale #43, Mougey Collection, September 1910, lot 1 $340 to Clarence S. Bement: 1793 Liberty Cap variety. Crosby 12-L. Perfectly centered, even impression, sharp, Uncirculated, and partly red. From the Cleneay Sale, Lot No. 1800. Mr. Mougey journeyed from Cincinnati to Philadelphia for the sole purpose of securing this prize, which is the finest known specimen of this variety, and as such, its actual value is practically unlimited.

Henry Chapman, Bement Collection, May 1916, lot 291 $720, to Col. James W. Ellsworth: Uncirculated, and might easily be called a Proof. Superb, even, sharp impression. Most beautiful light olive with traces of the original color, and acknowledged by everyone to be the finest example known to exist. It is a gem of the highest class, and unique in this state of preservation. This cent cost Mr. Bement $500, the greatest price a U.S. cent has ever sold for, and I predict that it will now bring a greater sum.

Wayte Raymond and John Work Garrett, 1923, as part of their purchase for $100,000 of the Ellsworth Collection. The collection was divided, Raymond got the cent, and in the same year sold it to William Cutler Atwater.

B. Max Mehl, June 11, 1946, Atwater Collection, lot 14 $2,000, to Louis E. Eliasberg Sr.: Truly the possession of this cent will pay great dividends not only in dollars and cents, but in the satisfaction, joy and pride of ownership. I do not recall during my forty-five years of numismatic experience, during which time I have handled a very goodly portion of the finest collections of American coins offered, of having pass through my hands such a thrilling coin!

Bowers and Merena Galleries, May 1996, Eliasberg Collection. $319,000 to a Southern numismatist: 1793 Liberty Cap. S-13. High Rarity-3. MS-64 or finer, brown. *Strike:* On a broad planchet thus providing field area between the beads and the rim, showcasing the beads, which in all instances are sharply struck. An early striking and quite possibly a presentation or specimen striking as indicated by Walter Breen in his *Encyclopedia of United States and Colonial Proof Coins.* The edge is lettered ONE HUNDRED FOR A DOLLAR with this lettering boldly defined. *Surfaces:* Light brown with ample tinges of red mint color. Very faint planchet roughness is noted inside the wreath. *Narrative:* An American numismatic landmark, and certainly one of the foremost highlights in the entire field of extant large cents 1793 to 1857. The only fully Mint State example of 1793 Liberty Cap coinage known—of any die variety. . . .

1793, Bisecting Obverse Crack, Liberty Cap • BW-24, S-14, B-17. Crosby 13-L. *Breen dies:* 12-J. **Estimated population: 60 to 75.**

Obverse: Space between two beads is over upright of I of LIBERTY; ample space between top of L and bead. The border has 95 beads. **Points of distinction:** All known examples have a prominent die crack vertically bisecting the die. The obverse die was slightly misaligned in the coin press.

**1793, Bisecting Obverse Crack,
Liberty Cap (BW-24, S-14, B-17).**

This caused the date to be weak and LIBERTY to be strong. This is especially noticeable on lower-grade examples. This also happened on the 1793, Chain AMERI. (BW-1).

Reverse: Upper-left leaf at wreath top nearly touches bottom leaf in pair to the right. Heavy cluster of three leaves below O in OF. The leaf opposite the M of AMERICA points towards the first A. The right ribbon is squared off and ends just below the fraction bar, which it touches. *Points of distinction:* Die used on BW-26, BW-27, BW-29, BW-30. This reverse die was reworked to create 1794, Fallen 4 in Date (Also with Button on Cap) (BW-84).[13]

Notes: The highest-graded examples of this variety are AU. More practically, a collector should seek EF and VF examples.

	Cert	Avg	%MS	AG-3	G-4	VG-8	F-12	VF-20	EF-40
1793, Bisecting Obverse Crack, Liberty Cap	(a)			$6,330	$10,500	$14,500	$29,500	$49,375	$90,000

a. Included in certified population for 1793, Liberty Cap (BW-27).

1793, Liberty Cap • BW-25, S-NC-6, B-18. Crosby unlisted. *Breen dies:* 13-J. *Recorded population:* 2.

Obverse: One bead is centered above R of LIBERTY, both pole and bottom of 7 point directly at a bead. There is a space between the 2 beads over the upright of T. *Points of distinction:* A bulging develops at the left side of the obverse, apparently causing failure and quick retirement of this die, explaining its rarity.

1793, Liberty Cap (BW-25, S-NC-6, B-18).

Reverse: Same die as preceding.

Notes: The known examples grade VG-8 and G-4. Discovered by R.E. Naftzger Jr. in February 1978.

1793, Liberty Cap • BW-26, S-16, B-19. Crosby 14-L. *Breen dies:* 14-J. *Estimated population:* 20 to 25.

Obverse: Bead over upright of I of LIBERTY; bead over upright of T. The lowest lock of hair has a short, heavy hook at the end in contrast with its delicate termination on the other two obverses. The border has 97 beads. *Points of distinction:* A faint crack is seen from the rim, through Y, and to the forehead. Another crack develops at the lower left and extends to the lowest curl. The obverse, plated by Sheldon—listed as S-16 by Sheldon—in *Early American Cents* and *Penny Whimsy*, is described as having a "heavy die break." This break has proven to be a lamination defect in the planchet.[14] Also used on BW-28.

1793, Liberty Cap (BW-26, S-16, B-19).

Reverse: Same die as preceding.

Notes: The reverse is usually rotated 135° instead of the normal 180°. The highest-graded examples are Fine and VF.

	Cert	Avg	%MS	AG-3	G-4	VG-8	F-12
1793, Liberty Cap (BW-26)	(a)			$11,000	$16,660	$28,125	$52,500

a. Included in certified population for 1793, Liberty Cap (BW-27).

1793, Liberty Cap • BW-27, S-13, B-20.

Crosby 12-L. *Breen dies:* 15-J. **Estimated population:** 160 to 200.

Obverse: Space between two beads is over upright of I of LIBERTY; L extremely close to bead. The border has 95 beads. Also used on BW-29.

Reverse: Same die as preceding. **Points of distinction:** A slight bulge develops at the center.

1793, Liberty Cap (BW-27, S-13, B-20).

Notes: The finest example is the spectacular Atwater-Eliasberg Mint State coin, unique at that level. Several AU examples exist.

	Cert	Avg	%MS	AG-3	G-4	VG-8	F-12	VF-20	EF-40	AU-50
1793, Liberty Cap (BW-27)	21	13.2	0%	$5,830	$9,670	$13,375	$25,750	$45,500	$85,000	$200,000

1793, Liberty Cap • BW-28, S-15, B-22.

Crosby 14-K. *Breen dies:* 14-K. **Recorded population:** 12.

Obverse: Same as used for BW-26, except for the top of the L of LIBERTY not being fully struck up. This is probably due to that part of the die being filled. This does not occur on the BW-26.

Reverse: One leaf under O in OF. Another

1793, Liberty Cap (BW-28, S-15, B-22).

leaf points directly at, and almost touches, the center stem of the M of AMERICA. The right ribbon is pointed and ends below the fraction bar next to the denominator.

Notes: The highest-graded example is Fine.

1793, Liberty Cap • BW-29, S-12, B-21.

Crosby 12-K. *Breen dies:* 15-K. **Estimated population:** 25 to 30.

Obverse: Same die as used for BW-27. *Points of distinction:* A slight bulge develops in the left field.

Reverse: Same as the preceding. **Points of distinction:** The die sunk at the center, causing the coins to bulge and the central features to wear away quickly.

1793, Liberty Cap (BW-29, S-12, B-21).

Notes: The highest-graded example is VF.

Numismatic Notes: Sylvester Crosby discovered this variety in the collection of William Fewsmith of Camden, New Jersey, in October 1869. This was just six months after J.N.T. Levick's plate of 1793 cents was published in the *American Journal of Numismatics*. Remarkably, Levick and Crosby missed only two collectable varieties of 1793—this one and the BW-13.

	Cert	Avg	%MS	AG-3	G-4	VG-8	F-12	VF-20
1793, Liberty Cap (BW-29)	(a)			$9,500	$14,330	$20,375	$40,000	$61,670

a. Included in certified population for 1793, Liberty Cap (BW-27).

1794, Liberty Cap

Circulation mintage (assumed): 918,521.

Among all early American coins there is no numismatic panorama of die varieties more interesting and extensive than the copper cents of 1794. These have been a specialty for many collectors over the years, forming collections exemplified most notably, in recent generations, by the John W. Adams Collection (sold by Bowers and Merena Galleries, 1982), a 1794 copper cent exhibit that took the Best of Show award at the ANA convention in the summer of 1982, and the Walter Husak Collection (auctioned by Heritage, 2008).[15] Cents of this date display many interesting differences in die arrangement and are particularly fascinating to collect. Within EAC, the "Boys of '94" take special interest in these issues. Jon Alan Boka treated the topic in his 2005 book, *Provenance Gallery of the Year 1794, United States Large Cents.*

The appeal of cents of this date has a particularly rich numismatic history, beginning in a significant way with the monograph, *Varieties of the Copper Issues of the United States Mint in the Year 1794,* published by Dr. Edward E. Maris in 1869, with a second edition in 1870. By any account, Maris was one of the greats in the early years of the hobby. He is still remembered for his attribution of New Jersey state coppers of the years 1786 through 1788, for which numismatists still use the Maris variety designations today. In the early 1870s he seems to have been the discoverer of the hitherto numismatically unknown 1861, Confederate States of America, cent, which was struck from dies by Robert Lovett Jr. To tell all about Maris would require many pages and would still be abbreviated.

His 1869 work and the 1870 second edition described the dies and assigned names for the cents, some of which were derived from medicine and mythology. Examples include varieties such as *Double Chin, Sans Milling, Tilted 4, Young Head, The Coquette, Crooked 7, Pyramidal Head, Mint Marked Head, Scarred Head, Standless 4, Abrupt Hair, Severed Hairs, The Ornate, Venus Marina, Fallen 4, Short Bust, Patagonian, Nondescript, Amatory Face, Large Planchet, Marred Field, Distant 1, Shielded Hair, Separated Date, The Plicae* (for a group of varieties), *Roman Plica* and *'95 Head,* among a few others. His preface included this:

> As far as our means of information enable us to arrive at a conclusion, the only copper coins made at our Mint in 1794, were of the denomination of Cent and Half Cent. Of the former, the record says 918,521 were issued, and 81,600 of the latter.
>
> The interest excited in the minds of collectors by their variety—a consequence probably of the breakage of dies—is shared by the writer, and has resulted in this attempt to describe the most noticeable peculiarity of each with sufficient accuracy to enable the careful examiner to recognize any given specimen, in a condition not below fair.
>
> This has been no easy work, as the close general resemblance which many of them bear to each other, makes it difficult to convey by the pen, points of difference readily detected by the eye. It is not claimed that every existing variety has come under examination. A pioneer work should not be expected to be thorough. On the other hand, the descriptions given were made from personal inspection of pieces now in his cabinet.

Significantly, Maris observed that cents of this year are so diverse they can be attributed in any condition "not below fair." This probably translates to Good-4 today. The point remains well taken, as today as in 1869, a nice collection of this year can be assembled in lower grades without losing any of the coins' numismatic desirability and significance.

Modern numismatists with a sense of tradition and history occasionally use Maris's designations in catalog descriptions. Later students of the series, including Dr. William H. Sheldon, added more nicknames, including *Apple Cheek, Wheel Spoke Reverse,* etc. Beyond these, such appellations as *Starred Reverse* and *Missing Fraction Bar* are self-explanatory.

Édouard Frossard, W.W. Hays, Francis Worcester Doughty, and others studied cents of this year and wrote about them, occasionally adding new varieties and redescribing previously known ones.

In 1923 S. Hudson Chapman published *United States Cents of the Year 1794.* In 1982 John W. Adams, specialist in cents of that year, wrote:

> Chapman added two more 1794 varieties which had been discovered in the interim, thus raising the number to 59. He also rearranged the listing of the varieties, substituting new numbers for the Hays numbers. The Chapman monograph is illustrated by excellent plates, and it is perhaps the most generally adequate presentation of the subject. However, the older Hays numbers seem to have taken deep root in the affections of coin collectors and it now appears likely that the name Hays will long be associated with this, the most extensive one-date series of American coins.[16]

Curiously, Chapman had some difficulty photographing the cents, and one of his experiments involved placing the coins underwater in front of a camera lens peering downward.

Other studies could be mentioned, but the most comprehensive was that created by Dr. William H. Sheldon for *Early American Cents,* 1949, followed by the updated *Penny Whimsy* in 1958. *United States Large Cents 1793–1814,* by William C. Noyes, is particularly valuable for its photographs. The last word in terms of detail is provided by *Walter Breen's Encyclopedia of Early United States Cents 1793–1814,* 2000. Much in terms of the spirit and enjoyment of these cents can be found in various issues of *Penny-Wise,* a journal of Early American Coppers.

Amidst everyday cares, 1794 large cents remain an island of refuge—an escape perhaps from present-day reality to the times of long ago when, at least in retrospect, the surroundings were incredibly nostalgic and romantic.

The appeal that 1794 cents possess has prompted hours of discussion among collectors of the series and has motivated otherwise busy individuals to travel tens of thousands of miles, write innumerable letters, and spend tens of thousands of dollars in their quest for needed varieties. What is the quintessence that has caused the owners of such coins to experience a deep joy unsurpassed elsewhere in American numismatics?

In addition to the obvious characteristics—rich surface coloration, interesting and varied dies, curious and unexplained varieties, elusive rarities, and the like—there seems to be a special aura surrounding the pieces, a quality which has aroused a fierce desire on the part of those who lack certain varieties and a pride of possession for those who own them. Dr. Sheldon has touched upon this in his writings, as have John Adams and others. As you review the variety descriptions and illustrations to follow, perhaps you will capture some of the spirit. It can be said that to know 1794 cents is to love them.

Thousands of cents of this date exist, and appearances in the marketplace are frequent. While specialists have attributed them by die varieties for many years, especially since the appearance of Sheldon's *Early American Cents,* most collectors and dealers have simply called them 1794 cents, or used one of the several styles listed in the regular edition of the *Guide Book of United States Coins.* For many years neither PCGS nor NGC cited variety attributions, but this has changed in recent times. The result is that today there is ample opportunity to examine "generic" 1794 cents and find scarce or even rare die combinations. This has been a sport for users of eBay, where photographs permit identification while sitting in a comfortable chair and browsing on a laptop computer.

Per *Penny Whimsy,* there are 58 collectible varieties for cents of this year, plus Dr. Sheldon's noncollectibles. The pursuit of a complete set of the "collectibles" is both possible and relatively affordable, though the fugitive element of timing has a role in the accomplishment. The acquisition of certain rare varieties may involve waiting until a desirable one appears on the market and being the highest bidder. Throughout numismatic history, approximately 30 individuals have been able to assemble all 58, two of them doing it twice (Robinson S. Brown Jr. and Denis W. Loring). One collector, George H. Clapp, donated his complete set to the American Numismatic Society. Daniel W. Holmes Jr. did the "impossible" by obtaining all of the non-collectible varieties as well!

Most 1794 cents show extensive wear, with typical grades ranging from Good to Fine. In proportion to demand, VF examples are scarce, EF coins are rare, and AU cents are rarer yet. Mint State coins are encountered only infrequently, such as when notable collections cross the auction block. While the planchet quality for 1794 cents is generally good, the experience of circulation in commerce has resulted in many receiving rim bumps, nicks, scratches, corrosion, and other problems. Accordingly, cherrypicking is a very worthwhile pursuit. Striking sharpness ranges from weak to strong, and generally is dependent on the die variety. A given variety usually has the same striking characteristics.

Although much ink is usually spent when a high-grade or rare 1794 cent crosses the auction block for tens of thousands of dollars, a very nice set with most of the varieties can be assembled in lesser grades. These are sharp enough to reveal enough detail needed to identify the varieties, and for the most part they may be quite affordable.

Today, building a representative collection of 1794-dated cents is an enjoyable pursuit. Within such grades as Good to Fine, most of the varieties can be acquired, and for a modest cost. Even the famous Starred Reverse, with slightly more than 60 examples known, comes on the market regularly, usually in lower grades, but with a number of the definitive stars visible around the border on the opposite side.

1794, HEAD STYLE OF 1793

BW-1 to BW-4 are in the style Early Head, or Head of 1793. Hair is heavy, particularly behind the ear. The lowest lock ends in a short, small hook (except BW-1). These are from the same obverse portrait punch cut by Joseph Wright for the 1793, Liberty Cap, cents. Hair details were modified by hand, resulting in some differences, especially in their tips to the lower left.

There are three obverse dies. Check the thickness of the hair and lower lock first to be sure that a coin is a member of this class. Then check the obverse features, then verify by checking the reverse possibilities, for which there are only two.

There are two edge styles, the "a" having the point and stem of the leaf after DOLLAR pointing down, and "b" with these features pointing up.

1794, Head of 1793, Wide Straight Date

• BW-1a and b, S17a and b, B-1a and b. *Breen dies:* 1-A. **Estimated population:** BW-1a: 60 to 75; BW-1b: 2 known.

Obverse: *Date:* In line rather than curved; 9 high. **Tip of pole points to:** Denticle, slightly right of its center. Pole heavy. **LIBERTY:** B slightly low; I opposite denticle. **Points of distinction:** Hook on lowest curl not fully formed. Many show a swelling and a tiny crack from L to the head and a small crack from the end of the pole to the border. In the very rare latest stage a crack bisects the die. *Maris designation:* Tilted 4. **Sheldon designation:** Wide Straight Date.

1794, Head of 1793, Wide Straight Date (BW-1a, S-17a, B-1a).

Detail of the "Wide Straight Date" and surrounding area.

Reverse: *Berries left and right:* 8-7. Berries are small. **Upright of second T of STATES opposite:** Denticle. *Fraction:* Numerator high and truncated at lower left. Bar slightly curved, extends from upper left of 1 to slightly past center of second 0. *Points of distinction:* UNITED STATES distant from denticles. TE of STATES wide. Stem is boldly visible below the ribbon knot, between the sides of the ribbon. Branch on left is out of alignment with its continuation as the stem to lower right. N of CENT first punched upside down, then corrected, leaving an irrelevant serif visible at lower right. Denticles smaller than on next reverse.

Notes: The highest grades that BW-1a—point and stem of leaf after DOLLAR point downward—is known in are EF and AU. For BW-1b—point and stem of leaf after DOLLAR point upward—the highest-known grade is AG-3.

1794, Head of 1793, Double Chin •

BW-2a and b, S-18a and b, B-2a and b. *Breen dies:* 2-A. *Estimated population:* BW-2a: 15 to 20; BW-2b: 120 to 160.

Obverse: *Date:* Date curved along border with each digit being about the same distance from the border. 1 centered. 4 slightly low. *Tip of pole points to:* Denticle, slightly right of its center. Pole lighter toward its end. *LIBERTY:* LIB and TY wide; I opposite denticle.

1794, Head of 1793, Double Chin (BW-2b, S-18b, B-2b).

Points of distinction: Slight double chin. A tiny crack is usually seen on the 12th denticle to the left of the 1 in the date. *Sheldon designation:* Double Chin.

Reverse: Same die as preceding. *Points of distinction:* The die is lightly lapped or polished to remove clash marks. The die was polished again, after which there were more clash marks—one of many dies that were subjected to repeated abuse through operator carelessness. On about half the examples there is a bulge at and near TED of UNITED.

Notes: The highest grade that BW-2a—point and stem of leaf after DOLLAR point downward—is known in is VF. Mint State examples exist for BW-2b—point and stem of leaf after DOLLAR point upward.

Typical values for BW-2b only. BW-2a is worth much more.

	Cert	Avg	%MS	AG-3	G-4	VG-8	F-12	VF-20	EF-40	AU-50	MS-60BN
1794, Head of 1793, Double Chin (BW-2b)	17	13.5	6%	$900	$1,630	$2,800	$5,250	$13,125	$29,750	$58,125	$128,330

1794, Head of 1793, Double Chin, Reverse Letters Close to Denticles •

BW-3a and b, S-19a and b, B-3a and b. *Breen dies:* 2-B. *Estimated population:* BW-3a: 30 to 45; BW-3b: 120 to 160.

Obverse: Same die as preceding. *Points of distinction:* Bulge from below the cap to a curl. All have a tiny crack at the 12th denticle to the left of the first digit of the date.

Reverse: *Berries left and right:* 8-7. One

1794, Head of 1793, Double Chin, Reverse Letters Close to Denticles (BW-3a, S-19a, B-3a).

berry detached in field beyond fourth berry on right. *Upright of second T of STATES opposite:* Denticle. *Fraction:* Numerator right of center and leans left. Bar slightly curved; extends from near upper left of 1 to center of second 0; 1 slightly low. *Points of distinction:* UNITED STATES very close to denticles. Right stem ends near rightmost serif of A. No stems between ribbon ends below knot. Denticles heavy and pointed.

Notes: The highest grade that BW-3a—point and stem of leaf after DOLLAR point downward—is found in is VF. BW-3b—point and stem of leaf after DOLLAR point upward—can be found in EF.

Typical values for BW-3b only. BW-3a is worth more.

	Cert	Avg	%MS	AG-3	G-4	VG-8	F-12	VF-20	EF-40
1794, Head of 1793, Double Chin (BW-3b)	(a)			$950	$1,920	$3,360	$6,375	$16,875	$43,330

a. Included in certified population for 1794, Head of 1793, Double Chin (BW-2b).

1794, Head of 1793, Close Straight Date, Reverse Letters Close to Denticles

• BW-4a and b, S-20, and B-4a and b. *Breen dies:* 3-B. ***Estimated population:*** BW-4a: 1 known; BW-4b: 75 to 120.

1794, Head of 1793, Close Straight Date, Reverse Letters Close to Denticles (BW-4b, S-20b, B-4b).

Obverse: *Date:* In line rather than curved; 94 slightly low; 94 wide. ***Tip of pole points to:*** Space between denticles. *LIBERTY:* RT slightly wide; I opposite space between denticles. *Maris designation:* Exact Head of 1793. *Sheldon designation:* Close Straight Date.

Reverse: Same die as preceding.

Notes: George Clapp considered his example of this variety to be the very finest coin he owned (see Sheldon). With the "a" edge—

Detail of the "Close Straight Date" and surrounding area.

point and stem of leaf after DOLLAR point downward—the highest-known grade is Good. With "b" edge—point and stem of leaf after DOLLAR point upward—the highest-known grade is AU (American Numismatic Society), but VF is a more realistic objective for collectors.

Typical values for BW-4b only. BW-4a is unique.

	Cert	Avg	%MS	AG-3	G-4	VG-8	F-12	VF-20
1794, Head of 1793, Close Straight Date (BW-4b)	(a)			$1,430	$2,580	$4,420	$9,750	$24,250

a. Included in certified population for 1794, Head of 1793, Double Chin (BW-2b).

1794, HEAD STYLE OF 1794

For all varieties listed in this style (except BW-45 to BW-48) the tip of the lower lock forms a hook.

Typical values for 1794, Head of 1794. Rare varieties may be worth more. Some varieties are priced individually, as follows.

	Cert	Avg	%MS	AG-3	G-4	VG-8	F-12	VF-20	EF-40	AU-50	MS-60BN	MS-63BN
1794, Head of 1794	264	32.1	4%	$275	$410	$600	$950	$1,925	$4,625	$7,150	$15,750	$34,625

1794, Flat Pole, Reverse Letters Close to Denticles • BW-10, S-21, B-5.

Breen dies: 4-B. **Estimated population:** 300 to 400.

Obverse: *Date:* 1 centered. 4 slightly low. *Tip of pole points to:* Space between denticles; recut and broad and flat at its end (very distinctive). **LIBERTY:** RTY wide; I opposite denticle slightly to right of its center. *Points of distinction:* Sixth lock (counting from bottom) bent downward and nearly touching the fifth. Most have a tiny crack from the border to the top of the cap. Some have other cracks at and near the cap. *Maris designation:* Sans Milling. *Sheldon designation:* Flat Pole.

Reverse: Same die as preceding. Usually with two tiny cracks at the border at the second S of STATES and left of E of AMERICA.

1794, Flat Pole, Reverse Letters Close to Denticles (BW-10, S-21, B-5).

Detail of the date and flat pole. Note the hook at the bottom of the lowest lock, characteristic of most of the Head of 1794 cents. The missing denticles at the right are due to a planchet clip.

Notes: Édouard Frossard's description (*Monograph*, 1879): "Date wide. Liberty staff expanded and flattened at the end. There is not the slightest trace of milling on obverse, thus contrasting with the reverse, which is protected by a bold and serrated elevation around the edge." This variety occurs in Mint State, but it is very rare as such.

1794, Bent Hair Lock, Mounded Reverse • BW-12, S-22, B-6. *Breen dies:* 5-C. **Estimated population:** Thousands.

Obverse: *Date:* 1 centered. 4 centered. *Tip of pole points to:* Space between denticles. **LIBERTY:** LI closer than other letters; I opposite space between two denticles. *Points of distinction:* Sixth lock (counting from bottom) bent downward and nearly touching the fifth. Clash marks develop as do mounding and eventually, cracks. *Maris designation:* Large Planchet. *Sheldon designation:* Bent Hair Lock.

Reverse: *Berries left and right:* 8-7. Two top left berries and one top-right berry very small. Lowest berry near bow larger than higher berry. *Upright of second T of STATES opposite:* Denticle, slightly right of its center. *Fraction:* Bar very close to second 0. *Points of distinction:* Left ribbon not connected to knot. With swellings ("mounds") at the upper part of the right wreath and on the lower half of the wreath on both sides. *Sheldon designation:* Mounded Reverse.

1794, Bent Hair Lock, Mounded Reverse (BW-12, S-22, B-6), die cracks from B to head, from Y to head, and to the right of the pole.

Detail showing the Bent Hair Lock, the sixth lock up from the bottom.

Notes: Sheldon believed this to be the second most common 1794 variety. The highest-known grade is AU.

1794, "Shattered Obverse" (usually)

• *BW-14, S-23, B-7. Breen dies:* 6-D. *Estimated population:* 75 to 120.

1794, "Shattered Obverse" (usually) (BW-14, S-23, B-7).

Obverse: *Date:* 1 centered, bottom serifs minimal or absent. 4 centered, bottom serifs minimal. *Tip of pole points to:* Denticle; pole becomes thicker toward its end. *LIBERTY:* IB closest, I opposite denticle, ERT wide. *Points of distinction:* Top of seventh (counting from bottom) thick. Usually seen with die cracks, although some are from perfect dies. *Maris designation:* Standless 4. *Sheldon designation:* Shattered Obverse.

Reverse: *Berries left and right:* 6-7. All berries large; later, after relapping for use on BW-16, they are small. *Upright of second T of STATES opposite:* Denticle, slightly left of its center. *Fraction:* Bar wide, covers top of 1 to left and extends beyond second 0 to right. *Points of distinction:* Lower-right pair of leaves have tips close together.

Notes: This variety can be found in AU, but is very rare at this level.

1794, Scarred Head, Full Cheeks •

BW-16, S-24, B-8. *Breen dies:* 7-D. *Estimated population:* 1,250 to 1,500.

1794, Scarred Head, Full Cheeks (BW-16, S-24, B-8), with delicate die crack from the border through the neck.

Obverse: *Date:* 1 high. 4 high. *Tip of pole points to:* Denticle, and is close to it. *LIBERTY:* LIBE wide; I opposite left side of denticle. *Points of distinction:* Hair ends in seven very thin locks. Cheek especially rounded, hollow area in hair to left of neck, this being the "scar." Cracks develop, one, then two, which join, and become heavy. There is usually some roughness in the die at the lower region of the neck and between the date and the neck. *Maris designation:* Scarred Head. *Sheldon designation:* Scarred Head, Full Cheeks—Sheldon's father called it the "Apple Cheek" variety.

Reverse: Same die as preceding. *Points of distinction:* A bulge develops and weakens the central inscriptions.

Notes: This variety occurs in Mint State.

1794, Buckled Obverse, No Protruding Leaf Under I of AMERICA •

BW-17, S-27, B-9. *Breen dies:* 8-E. *Estimated population:* 45 to 60.

1794, Buckled Obverse, No Protruding Leaf Under I of AMERICA (BW-17, S-27, B-9).

Obverse: *Date:* 1 centered. 4 slightly high. *Tip of pole points to:* Denticle, and is close to it. LIBERTY: BE and TY wide, I opposite left side of denticle. *Points of distinction:* Third lock long, sixth lock short. Die bulged horizontally at center, later develops into a crack. *Maris designation:* Egeria (elusive lady). *Sheldon designation:* Buckled Obverse.

Reverse: *Berries left and right:* 5-6. So tiny as to be an unreliable guide for attribution. *Upright of second T of STATES opposite:* Denticle. *Fraction:* Bar slightly curved down to left. 10 wide, 00 slightly closer to each other. *Points of distinction:* No protruding leaf under I of AMERICA, the leaf is centered on top of the branch. Right branch does not connect to knot, but resumes at knot and continues down to the left.

Notes: Highest-known grades are EF and AU.

1794, No Protruding Leaf Under I of AMERICA • BW-18, S-28, B-10. *Breen dies:* 9-E. *Estimated population:* 500 to 750.

1794, No Protruding Leaf Under I of AMERICA (BW-18, S-28, B-10).

Obverse: *Date:* 1 centered. 4 low. *Tip of pole points to:* Denticle, slightly right of its center. *LIBERTY:* IB and ERT wide, I opposite denticle. *Points of distinction:* Top two locks the same curved shape, heavy, and close to each other. Sheldon says: "The cheek is full, exuberant looking." Relapping causes some weakness. Cracks develop. *Maris designation:* Ornate.

Reverse: Same die as preceding. *Points of distinction:* Faint cracks are seen at the left branch. Clash marks as a triple outline from the top of the head on the obverse are seen in late states.

Notes: This variety occurs in Mint State.

1794, Long Tail on Right Ribbon • BW-20, S-29, B-11. *Breen dies:* 9-F. *Estimated population:* 750 to 1,000.

1794, Long Tail on Right Ribbon (BW-20, S-29, B-11).

Obverse: Same die as preceding. *Points of distinction:* Die state further advanced. *Sheldon designation:* Tailed Reverse.

Reverse: *Berries left and right:* 10-8. Three topmost berries at left are stemless. Berry under left upright of M of AMERICA has another berry, disconnected, beyond it; Sheldon considered this to be a berry (giving a count of 8 on the right), Breen did not. *Upright of second T of STATES opposite:* Left part of bold, sharp denticle. *Fraction:* 1 heavy, misshapen, and slightly low. *Points of*

The curiously long right ribbon and the long tail to the R.

distinction: Lettering very close to denticles, especially on the left. Leaf immediately above E of ONE is hollow. Sheldon: "The right ribbon end and the R of AMERICA have long tails, and this is one of the most easily recognized reverses of the series." The ribbon end is particularly distinct and nearly reaches the denticles. A crack is often seen from the border through R of AMERICA to the wreath. Bulges develop.

Notes: This variety occurs in Mint State, and it is a rarity so fine.

1794, Marred Field, Long Tail on Right Ribbon • BW-22, S-30, B-12.
Breen dies: 10-F. *Estimated population:* 1,250 to 1,500.

Obverse: Early die state. *Date:* 1 very high; barely touches hair. 4 high. ***Tip of pole points to:*** Space between denticles. *LIBERTY:* all letters close; TY slightly less close than others, I opposite denticle. ***Points of distinction:*** Lowest lock with thin C-shaped curl below it. Small raised island in field opposite locks 4 and 5, giving the name *Marred Field*. Some examples are without clash marks. Later impressions are with prominent clash marks between cap and top of head. Sheldon: "The hair is luxuriant, and the cheeks are full. Miss Liberty seems to smile." Also used on BW-24, BW-39, BW-40, BW-41, and BW-42. ***Maris designation:*** *Amatory Face* in the 1869 (first) edition; changed in the second edition to *Amiable Face*—seemingly a change from love to friendship. ***Sheldon designation:*** First Marred Field.

1794, Marred Field, Long Tail on Right Ribbon (BW-22, S-30, B-12). Early (but not earliest) state of the obverse die with tiny island to left of locks 4 and 5, and with clash marks between cap and top of hair. For later die combinations, the obverse was reground. Reverse with distinctively long right ribbon, now well worn and with granularity and bulges, especially near the top.

Detail of island between fourth and fifth locks.

Reverse: Same die as preceding. Well worn by this time. Slightly buckled. Faint clash marks are seen at the upper part of the wreath.

Notes: This variety occurs in Mint State, and is very rare as such.

1794, Marred Field, Long Fraction Bar • BW-24, S-31, B-13. *Breen dies:* 10-G. *Estimated population:* Thousands.

Obverse: Same die as preceding, but a slightly later die state, with clash marks below LIB ground away. Additional flaws ("mars") in left field. ***Sheldon designation:*** Second Marred Field. He thought this to be an entirely different die. The use of the same obverse die is continued with BW-39, BW-40, BW-41, and BW-42.

1794, Marred Field, Long Fraction Bar (BW-24, S-31, B-13).

Reverse: *Berries left and right:* 6-6. Fourth berry on the left is partly covered by a leaf. ***Upright of second T of STATES opposite:*** Denticle. *Fraction:* Very wide fraction bar extending to left and right beyond denominator, the longest on any die of this year. ***Points of distinction:*** Some leaves on inside of wreath are incomplete. ***Sheldon designation:*** Long Fraction Bar Reverse.

Notes: Can be found in Mint State.

1794, Dot Between L and I, 7 9 Wide, Four Berries Opposite R •

BW-25, S-NC-8, B-14. *Breen dies:* 11-H. *Recorded population:* 3.

1794, Dot Between L and I, 7 9 Wide, Four Berries Opposite R (BW-25, S-NC-8, B-14). Detail of dot between L and I at BW-26.

Obverse: *Date:* 1 slightly low. 7 and 9 widely spaced, 9 leans left, 94 close. 4 centered. *Tip of pole points to:* Space between denticles, and is close to it. *LIBERTY:* Dot between bases of L and I (only die with this feature), other letters widely spaced, I opposite space between denticles. *Points of distinction:* Locks of hair except lowest are thin. *Maris designation:* Separated Date.

Reverse: *Berries left and right:* 6-8. 4 berries close to each other, with 2 on each side of stem, below R of AMERICA. *Upright of second T of STATES opposite:* Space between denticles. *Fraction:* Numerator close to bar, 1 in denominator close to bar. *Points of distinction:* A crack is seen at the upper left.

Notes: Discovered by Willard C. Blaisdell in December 1965. The highest-graded example of this variety is Fine.

1794, Dot Between L and I, 7 9 Wide, Short, Thick Fraction Bar •

BW-26, S-25, B-15.[17] *Breen dies:* 11-I. *Estimated population:* 300 to 400.

1794, Dot Between L and I, 7 9 Wide, Short, Thick Fraction Bar (BW-26, S-25, B-15).

Obverse: Same die as preceding. *Points of distinction:* Clash marks develop.

Reverse: *Berries left and right:* 8-7. On the left there are 6 large berries and 2 tiny high berries. *Upright of second T of STATES opposite:* Space between denticles. *Fraction:* Bar thick and very short, ends at right edge of 1 and to the left of the center of the second 0. *Points of distinction:* Center dot partly embedded in left upright of N of CENT. Faint clash marks from the obverse are seen

Detail of dot between L and I.

at the top of the reverse. Some have a tiny crack from D of UNITED to the wreath.

Notes: This variety occurs in Mint State, but is a great rarity as such. Several AU coins exist.

1794, Dot Between L and I, 7 9 Wide, Wide Fraction Bar With Thin Ends

• BW-27, S-26, B-16. *Breen dies:* 11-J. *Estimated population:* 750 to 1,000.

Obverse: Same die as preceding. Die relapped, causing dramatic weakness in the hair to the lower left. Multiple clash marks develop later.

Reverse: *Berries left and right:* 5-6. All are large. *Upright of second T of STATES opposite:* Denticle. *Fraction:* Very wide due to thin lines extending to left and right; extends far beyond Denominator. 1 slightly low.

1794, Dot Between L and I, 7 9 Wide, Wide Fraction Bar With Thin Ends (BW-27, S-26, B-16). Obverse die relapped, creating weakness in the form of open areas at the lower left of the hair. Parts of the lower right of the Liberty Cap are ground away. The dot between L and I is now very small.

Points of distinction: Raised die flaw on left part of O in OF is always present. A crack develops from the rim through E of STATES to the wreath, later joined by another crack from the first S to the wreath.

Notes: This variety can be found in Mint State.

1794, Dot Between L and I, 7 9 Wide

• BW-29, S-NC-11, B-17. *Breen dies:* 11-K. *Recorded population:* 4.

Obverse: Same die as preceding. *Points of distinction:* Late state of the die with certain details weakened by relapping.

Reverse: *Berries left and right:* 6-6. Top-left berries sometimes obscured. Inside berry to right of E of ONE is tiny. *Upright of second T of STATES opposite:* Denticle. *Fraction:*

1794, Dot Between L and I, 7 9 Wide (BW-29, S-NC-11, B-17).

Numerator close to bar and over right part of first 0. Left edge of bar at edge of 1.

Notes: The highest-graded example is VG-8.

1794, Up-turned Locks • BW-30, S-32, B-18.

Breen dies: 12-K. **Estimated population:** 400 to 500.

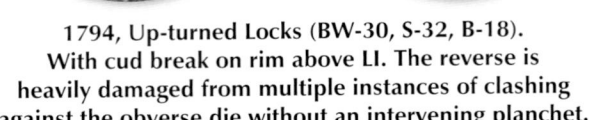

Obverse: *Date:* 1 very low. 4 very low. *Tip of pole points to:* Left part of denticle, and is close to it. *LIBERTY:* Letters widely spaced, BE widest but only slightly, I opposite denticle. *Points of distinction:* Fourth and sixth locks (counting up from the bottom) have tips turned upward. Some incomplete areas of hair opposite neck and also in another area opposite cap. Sometimes seen with a short rim crack over LI. *Maris designation:* Venus Marina. *Sheldon designation:* Up-turned Locks.

1794, Up-turned Locks (BW-30, S-32, B-18). With cud break on rim above LI. The reverse is heavily damaged from multiple instances of clashing against the obverse die without an intervening planchet.

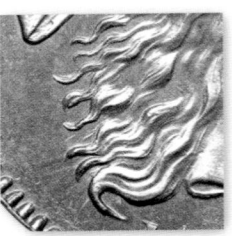

Detail showing the upturned ends to the locks.

Reverse: Same die as preceding. *Points of distinction:* Now heavily damaged from multiple clashing. Usually seen with a heavy crack from the border through the first S of STATES through the wreath and slightly into the interior.

Notes: Mint State, and a rarity as such.

1794, Up-turned Locks, "Wheel Spoke" Breaks on Reverse • BW-31, S-33, B-19.

Breen dies: 12-L. **Estimated population:** 20 to 25.

Obverse: Same die as preceding. *Points of distinction:* Cud break over LI always present, as on the late state of the preceding use. A crack develops from this break down to the cap.

1794, Up-turned Locks, "Wheel Spoke" Breaks on Reverse (BW-31, S-33, B-19).

Reverse: *Berries left and right:* 6-6. *Upright of second T of STATES opposite:* Denticle. *Fraction:* Bar is closer to the right ribbon than the left; partially covers 1 and extends to half over the second 0. Numerator is left of center on the bar and is over the first 0. *Points of distinction:* "Wheel Spoke" reverse, from buckling (actually, sinking of the center of the die) and cracks at several places around the rim. On worn coins the buckling results in ONE / CENT being worn away quickly. *Sheldon designation:* Six "Wheel Spoke" Breaks.

Notes: The highest-grade examples are VF. In 1958, when *Penny Whimsy* was published, Dr. Sheldon noted this: "Nine examples of this famous rarity are now known to us, but unfortunately, three of them are impounded in the American Numismatic Society, and two of the remaining six are injured or burnished coins." It is testimony to the interest in varieties that since 1958 the population has about doubled. Numismatists like nicknames, and "Wheel Spoke" has helped make this variety very popular.

1794, Single Berry Left of Bow •

BW-32, S-34, B-20. *Breen dies:* 12-M. *Estimated population:* 30 to 45.

Obverse: Same die as preceding. *Points of distinction:* The crack from the cud break to the cap expanded as the die was used.

Reverse: *Berries left and right:* 5-6. Most berries small. Only a single berry (instead of two) near left ribbon bow; this and the next

1794, Single Berry Left of Bow (BW-32, S-34, B-20).

die are the only ones with this feature. *Upright of second T of STATES opposite:* Space between denticles, but closer to denticle on the left. *Fraction:* Numerator high. Bar thick and barely covers all of the denominator. 1 high, first 0 low and leans right. *Points of distinction:* Lowest leaf on left points to the left foot of the second A of AMERICA. Berry to left of C of CENT also near a leaf tip.

Notes: The highest grades for this variety are VF (most practically) and EF. Dr. Sheldon (1958): "Ten now known to us, eight of them in collectors' hands. . . . Four examples new to the present writer have appeared since *Early American Cents* was written. Still a great rarity, most fervently desired by collectors who are dangerously sick with the cent disease."

1794, 9 in Denticle, Single Berry Left of Bow •

BW-34, S-35, B-21. *Breen dies:* 13-M. *Estimated population:* 45 to 60.

Obverse: *Date:* 1 very low, close to or touches denticle. 9 embedded in denticle. 4 very low. *Tip of pole points to:* Space between denticles and is close to it. *LIBERTY:* Irregularly spaced, high, and close to denticles; ER widest, R nearly touches denticles, and I opposite left part of denticle. *Points of distinction:* Lowest lock is thinner than normal, higher locks are medium size and all well defined. Rounded cheek on Miss Liberty. Most (but not all) have a crack beginning at the border between E and R extending down through the portrait, and another from the border through the lower part of the cap to the hair, and sometimes other progressions as well. *Sheldon designation:* Delicate Lower Lock.

1794, 9 in Denticle, Single Berry Left of Bow (BW-34, S-35, B-21).

Date showing 9 embedded in a denticle, unique among 1794 dies.

Detail of the ribbon bow with a single berry (instead of the usual two) at the left, similar to the reverse of BW-37.

Reverse: Same die as preceding.

Notes: The highest grades for this variety are VF (most practically) and EF.

1794, Low Head, Single Berry Left of Bow • BW-36, S-NC-1, B-22. *Breen dies:* 14-M. *Recorded population:* 4.

Obverse: *Date:* 1 low. 4 centered, very close to neck and to denticles. *Tip of pole points to:* Denticle, and is close to it; pole is thick and wide. *LIBERTY:* LI close, others widely spaced, RT widest. I close to and opposite denticle. *Sheldon designation:* Low Head.

1794, Low Head, Single Berry
Left of Bow (BW-36, S-NC-1, B-22).

Reverse: Same die as preceding. *Points of distinction:* A bulge and then a heavy break develop.

Notes: The highest-graded piece is G-4.

1794, Low Head, Single Berry Left of Bow (but different die) • BW-37, S-36, B-23. *Breen dies:* 14-N. *Estimated population:* 45 to 60.

Obverse: Same die as preceding. *Points of distinction:* Clash marks are seen on later states as is a faint crack.

1794, Low Head, Single Berry Left of Bow
(but different die) (BW-37, S-36, B-23).

Reverse: *Berries left and right:* 6-7. Fourth berry on right is tiny. Only a single berry is near the left ribbon bow; this and the preceding die are the only ones with this feature. *Upright of second T of STATES opposite:* Space between denticles, but closer to denticle on the right. *Fraction:* Numerator high. Bar very thin, barely covers 1, extends to slightly more than halfway over second 0.

Detail of the ribbon bow with a single berry (instead of
the usual two) at the left, similar to the reverse of BW-34.

Second 0 high. *Points of distinction:* Lowest leaf on right points to C of AMERICA. No leaf tip near berry to left of C of CENT. Cracks develop.

Notes: The highest-known grade for this variety is AU.

1794, Distant 1, Single Berry Left of Bow (die as preceding) • BW-38, S-37, B-24. *Breen dies:* 15-N. *Estimated population:* 13 to 19.

Obverse: *Date:* 1 low and distant from 7. 79 close. 4 low. *Tip of pole points to:* Denticle. *LIBERTY:* IBE wide, 1 opposite denticle just left of its center. *Points of distinction:* In the later state the die is relapped, causing some lightness of detail at the back of the hair. *Sheldon designation:* Distant 1.

1794, Distant 1, Single Berry Left of Bow
(die as preceding) (BW-38, S-37, B-24).

Reverse: Same die as preceding.

Notes: The highest grades this variety is known in are VF and EF, and it is very rare in either grade. This is among the more famous varieties of 1794, and it is readily distinguishable at sight. Unknown to Maris, Frossard, and other students of the series, the first example was located by Lancaster, Pennsylvania, dealer Charles Steigerwalt in the spring of 1900. Though it was unknown to W.W. Hays in his 1893 work, it was included in a New York sale as a "Hays-44" and returned as misattributed. Steigerwalt recognized it as new, and in the 1910 reprint of the Hays text it was added as No. 59. Some old-timers have referred to this as the "Steigerwalt variety."[18]

Numismatic Notes: *Regarding Steigerwalt:* The June 1900 issue of *The Numismatist* noted this:

> Charles Steigerwalt [the Lancaster, Pennsylvania dealer] has recently bought the collection of the late Mr. Hays, the most valuable part of which was the series of many varieties of the 1794 cent which he had long made an object of study, and which is well known by the late Ed. Frossard's illustrated monograph upon them. The collection was also rich in New Jersey and Connecticut series. But Dr. Hall, of Boston, has the finest collection of these latter in existence, probably as fine a collection of the 1794 varieties and very probably the finest collection of the U.S. cents known.

In the August issue Steigerwalt invited inquiries concerning the purchase of the Hays Collection of 1794 cents, which he held at $1,000, but would entertain a slightly lower offer. "Further details will be given to any person who really means business and does not inquire out of idle curiosity only."

1794, Marred Field, Single Berry Left of Bow (die as preceding) •

BW-39, S-38, B-25. *Breen dies:* 10-N. *Estimated population:* 45 to 60.

Obverse: Later die state, reworked and strengthened. Dr. Sheldon considered the reworked obverse die to be a different die. See *Walter Breen's Encyclopedia of Early United States Cents 1793–1814* for details. *Date:* The 1 is centered on BW-39, BW-41, and BW-42 after more regrinding. 4 centered and

1794, Marred Field, Single Berry Left of Bow (die as preceding) (BW-39, S-38, B-25).

close to both neck and denticles. *Tip of pole points to:* Between denticles. *LIBERTY:* All letters close; TY slightly less close than others, I opposite denticle, some letters weak at top due to regrinding. *Points of distinction:* Prominent raised island in field opposite locks 4 to 6. *Maris designation:* Amiable Face. *Sheldon designation:* Third Marred Field.

Reverse: Same die as preceding.

Notes: The highest grade this variety is found in is AU.

1794, Marred Field, Fatal [Reverse] Break Variety •

BW-40, S-NC-2, B-26. *Breen dies:* 10-O. *Recorded population:* 2.

Obverse: Same die as preceding. *Points of distinction:* Cracks develop near the left border, followed by additional cracks. In the late state much of the detail is missing at D and ST at the upper left.

Reverse: *Berries left and right:* 7-6. Berry under left upright of M of AMERICA.

1794, Marred Field, Fatal [Reverse] Break Variety (BW-40, S-NC-2, B-26).

Upright of second T of STATES opposite: Denticle. *Fraction:* Bar extends from right edge of 1 to halfway over second 0. 1 over first 0. *Points of distinction:* Pair of leaves above E of ONE complete. Leaf points to the right of the bottom-right serif of T of CENT. Ribbons widely spread and not near fraction. Right ribbon bow touches stem of leaves. Denticles large and pointed. The die is broken from the border above E of UNITED through the D, and in this general area, raising the relief of the field, probably ending its service. *Sheldon designation:* Fatal Break Variety.

Notes: The two examples are graded Mint State (the example held by the ANS) and VG-10.

1794, Marred Field, "Sprawled Ribbon Ends" • BW-41, S-39, B-27. *Breen dies:* 10-P. *Estimated population:* 20 to 25.

1794, Marred Field, "Sprawled Ribbon Ends" (BW-41, S-39, B-27).

Obverse: Same die as preceding. Some later impressions with light clash marks between top of cap and hair. Cracks are more prominent than earlier.

Reverse: *Berries left and right:* 7-6. Berry under center of M of AMERICA. *Upright of second T of STATES opposite:* Denticle. *Fraction:* Bar extends from right edge of 1 to left of center of second 0. 1 over first 0. *Points of distinction:* Pair of leaves above E of ONE has bottom leaf with only the tip. Leaf points to the bottom-right serif of T of CENT. Ribbons widely spread and not near fraction. Right ribbon bow nearly touches stem of leaves. Denticles large and pointed, the largest on any 1794 cent reverse. Found with a crack from the rim near the 1 of the denominator, across the ribbon and into I of UNITED. Dr. Sheldon knew of only one coin lacking this crack. In the late state the center sinks, causing a buckling on the coin and weakness at the lettering. *Sheldon designation:* Sprawled Ribbon Ends.

Notes: The highest grades for this variety are EF and AU, and it is rare at either level.

1794, Marred Field • BW-42, S-40, B-28. *Breen dies:* 10-Q. *Estimated population:* 30 to 45.

1794, Marred Field (BW-42, S-40, B-28).

Obverse: Same die as preceding. *Points of distinction:* Cracks are even more prominent in this stage of the die.

Reverse: *Berries left and right:* 7-7. *Upright of second T of STATES opposite:* Denticle, slightly right of its center. *Fraction:* Bar extends from right edge of 1 to slightly past center of second 0. 1 over first 0. First 0 low, and second 0 high. *Points of distinction:* Ribbon bow is high above knot. Denticles have rounded ends. Light cracks develop.

Notes: The highest-graded examples are AU and Mint State (exceedingly rare).

1794, Truncated Hair Locks, Most Berries Are Tiny • BW-44, S-41, B-30.

Breen dies: 16-S. *Estimated population:* 300 to 400.

Obverse: *Date:* 1 low. 7 and 9 close, 9 almost touches denticle. 4 very low. *Tip of pole points to:* Space between denticles. *LIBERTY:* Close to denticles, widely spaced, ER closest, 1 opposite left part of denticle. *Points of distinction:* "Between the cap and the head,

1794, Truncated Hair Locks, Most Berries Are Tiny (BW-44, S-41, B-30). Late state of the reverse die.

two short locks terminate abruptly, one above the pole and one below it." Sometimes with a crack from the border between 7 and 9. Clash marks are removed by light relapping. Further clash marks develop, as do cracks. *Maris designation:* Abrupt Hair. *Sheldon designation:* Truncated Hair Locks.

Reverse: *Berries left and right:* 7-7. 4 inner berries on left are large, all others are tiny. *Upright of second T of STATES opposite:* Denticle. *Fraction:* Bar from about halfway over the 1 to halfway over the second 0. First 0 low. *Points of distinction:* Denticles short and rounded. The reverse is sometimes perfect, but most often with crack from the border through D, along the top of CE, to N, then into N of ONE, continuing. Various stages of this crack are known.

Notes: The highest-obtainable grade is EF. There is one example in Mint State (held by the ANS).

1794, Truncated Hair Locks, Weak "OF" • BW-45, S-42, B-29. *Breen dies:* 16-R. *Estimated population:* 160 to 200.

Obverse: Same die as preceding. *Points of distinction:* Light clash marks develop.

Reverse: *Berries left and right:* 6-6. *Upright of second T of STATES opposite:* Space between two denticles and slightly closer to the left one. *Fraction:* Bar covers most of 1 and about two-thirds of the second 0. Numerator over first 0. All digits in denominator lean slightly right. *Points of distinction:* A thin spine extends from the tip of the left stem. OF always light. AM of AMERICA wide. Denticles rounded.

1794, Truncated Hair Locks, Weak "OF" (BW-45, S-42, B-29).

Detail of weak OF and wide A and M of AMERICA.

Notes: The highest grades for this variety are AU and Mint State (unique).

1794, Lowest Lock Clipped, No Hook, Weak "OF" • BW-46, S-43, B-32. *Breen dies:* 17-R. *Estimated population:* 750 to 1,000.

1794, Lowest Lock Clipped, No Hook, Weak "OF" (BW-46, S-43, B-32).

Obverse: *Date:* 1 very high and over space between denticles. 4 touches neck. *Tip of pole points to:* Denticle, just right of its center. *LIBERTY:* Letters fairly evenly spaced; I opposite space between denticles. *Points of distinction:* Lowest lock clipped at its end, eliminating the hook, tip points downward to the left. No loop under left side of neck. Sheldon: "Here for the first time we see a new set of figures with larger and taller 7, pointed 4, taller, more pointed 1, and a slightly taller 9. This is the beginning of Chapman's Style 3, and in this group [through S-51] the busts are a little smaller and narrower, with the hair in rolled locks over the ear, and the lowest curl

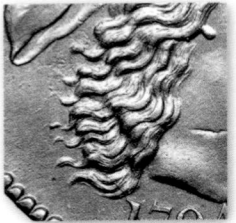

Detail showing the lowest lock of hair without a hook at the end.

only about the same thickness as those above it. The hair is treated in more minute detail, as if to try to delineate the separate hairs. The faces have full, plump cheeks." The die is found perfect or with a crack from the border behind the cap, and sometimes another crack from the border through 7 and 1 to the hair. *Maris designation:* Short Bust.

Reverse: Same die as preceding. *Points of distinction:* Usually seen with a crack from the border through U and the wreath, to C of CENT.

Notes: The highest grades for this variety are AU and Mint State (held by the ANS).

1794, Lowest Lock Clipped, No Hook • BW-48, S-NC-10, B-31. *Breen dies:* 17-T. *Recorded population:* 1.

Obverse: Same die as preceding.

Reverse: *Berries left and right:* 6-6. *Upright of second T of STATES opposite:* Denticle, slightly to left of its center. *Fraction:* Bar slants slightly down to left; barely covers 1 and extends most of the way above second 0. 10 wide, 00 closer.

1794, Lowest Lock Clipped, No Hook (BW-48, S-NC-10, B-31).

Notes: This example is VG-10. Discovered by Christopher B. Young at the ANA convention, July 27, 1994. The only unique 1794 cent variety. Daniel W. Holmes Jr. Collection.

1794, Lowest Lock Clipped, No Hook, Right Ribbon End Weak •

BW-49, S-44, B-33. *Breen dies:* 17-U. *Estimated population:* 1,250 to 1,500.

Obverse: Same die as preceding. *Points of distinction:* Obverse always seen with crack from the rim through 17, extending left, and always with clash marks. Later cracks develop.

Reverse: *Berries left and right:* 7-6. Berry under left upright of M of AMERICA. Large

1794, Lowest Lock Clipped, No Hook, Right Ribbon End Weak (BW-49, S-44, B-33).

berry centered left of C of CENT. *Upright of second T of STATES opposite:* Denticle. *Fraction:* Bar slants, covers 1, and extends most of the way above second 0. 1 high and leans right, 1 and 0 wide, 00 closer. Second 0 weak. *Points of distinction:* Right ribbon end weak. Sometimes with a perfect die, but usually with a crack from the border near O, down to the N of ONE, and sometimes continuing.

Notes: The highest grades for this variety are AU and Mint State (unique).

1794, Lowest Lock Clipped, No Hook •

BW-51, S-NC-5, B-34. *Breen dies:* 17-V. *Recorded population:* 2.

Obverse: Same die as preceding. *Points of distinction:* Die cracks as on preceding use, now with a bulge.

Reverse: *Berries left and right:* 7-6. *Upright of second T of STATES opposite:* Denticle. *Fraction:* Bar extends from right edge of 1 to slightly past center of second 0. 1 leans right,

1794, Lowest Lock Clipped, No Hook (BW-51, S-NC-5, B-34).

first 0 low. *Points of distinction:* Center dot within left upright of N of CENT near its top. A crack develops and expands. The die was laminated at the center, causing streaks and rough spots.

Notes: Discovered by John Pawling in 1951, thus not included in *Early American Cents* (1949). The two examples are graded, respectively, AG-3 and Fair-2.

1794, Braided Hair • BW-52, S-45,

B-35. *Breen dies:* 18-V. **Estimated population:** 30 to 45.

Obverse: *Date:* 1 very high and over denticle. 4 touches neck. **Tip of pole points to:** Denticle, just right of its center. **LIBERTY:** LI and ER close, I opposite space between denticles. **Points of distinction:** Locks 2 to 6 have delicate points, 2 and 3 are similar to an open claw, and there is a large space between 4 and 5 extending well into the main part of the hair. **Maris designation:** The Plicae. Sheldon: "Called by Maris *The Plicae,* referring to the fact that the hair is partially twisted or coiled into heavy, separate braids which point out behind in quite a novel manner." Whether a modern observer would call the hair *braided* is questionable. The tresses

1794, Braided Hair (BW-52, S-45, B-35).

Hair with heavy tresses.

are heavy and bold, however. **Sheldon designation:** Braided Hair.

Reverse: Same die as preceding. **Points of distinction:** Always with die damage in the form of ridges diagonally down to the right from TA of STATES. Sometimes with a tiny crack from the border, to IC, to the nearest leaf, and continuing onward.

Notes: The highest grades for this variety are AU and Mint State (unique).

1794, Braided Hair, Ridge at E of

CENT • BW-54, S-46, B-36. *Breen dies:* 18-W. **Estimated population:** 300 to 400.

Obverse: Same die as preceding. **Points of distinction:** Die crack upward from border beyond the date. Sometimes with another crack beginning at the border below C and continuing upward. Many different die states are known.

Reverse: *Berries left and right:* 6-6. 2 berries near bow are stemless. Upper-left berry very small. **Upright of second T of STATES opposite:** Space between denticles. **Fraction:** Bar extends from center of 1 to near center of second 0. 1 leans right, first 0 low. **Points of distinction:** Die defect caused a prominent ridge at E of CENT.

Notes: The highest grades for this variety are AU and Mint State.

1794, Braided Hair, Ridge at E of CENT (BW-54, S-46, B-36).

Detail showing the die defect at E of CENT and nearby; this permits instant recognition of the variety.

1794, Left Edge of Neck Ends in Sharp Tip • BW-58, S-47, B-39. *Breen dies:* 20-Z. *Estimated population:* 120 to 160.

1794, Left Edge of Neck Ends in Sharp Tip (BW-58, S-47, B-39).

Obverse: *Date:* 1 high, doubled denticle to left of its base. 94 close. 4 very high, almost touches neck. *Tip of pole points to:* Slightly right of center of rounded denticle. *LIBERTY:* Left base of R slightly low; I opposite denticle. *Points of distinction:* Left part of neck ends in a sharp tip instead of blending into the hair, with no loop. Cracks develop. *Maris designation:* Young Head. *Sheldon designation:* Braided Upper Locks.

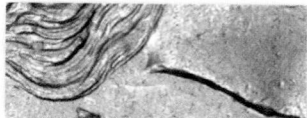

Detail of neck ending in sharp tip.

Reverse: *Berries left and right:* 6-6. Arranged 2 outside and 4 inside on each branch. *Upright of second T of STATES opposite:* Space between denticles. *Fraction:* Bar extends from right edge of 1 to center of second 0. 10 wider than 00; second 0 slightly low. *Points of distinction:* Small piece or notch out of the bottom of the ribbon bow at left. On most (but not all) a tiny crack begins at the border past the first A of AMERICA to a leaf.

Notes: The highest grades for this variety are VF and EF (exceedingly rare).

1794, Left Edge of Neck Ends in Sharp Tip, Starred Reverse • BW-59, S-48, B-38. *Breen dies:* 20-Y. *Estimated population:* 50 to 60.

1794, Left Edge of Neck Ends in Sharp Tip, Starred Reverse (BW-59, S-48, B-38). Around the reverse border are 94 tiny five-pointed stars. The Adams-Husak coin, the finest known.

Obverse: Same die as preceding. *Points of distinction:* Light clash marks are seen, then removed by lapping.

Reverse: Unique Starred Reverse die. Apparently, 94 tiny five-pointed stars were first placed around the border of the die, for a reason unknown today. Later, the die was completed with normal features, including cutting denticles around the border, some of which took away certain star elements, though most remain and are bold when viewed under magnification. The most famous of all 1794 cent

Detail of certain of the stars (Holmes coin).

dies. Dr. Sheldon: "Collectors mention it with religious awe." The BW-59 and BW-84 reverses are the only ones of the year with smaller letters than the others. *Points of distinction:* The die buckles and eventually fails.

Notes: The highest grades for this variety are VF and EF (unique).

Numismatic Notes: This variety has attracted continuing excitement ever since its discovery, said to have been by the teenaged Henry Chapman in the year before he went into business with S. Hudson

Chapman to form the Chapman brothers partnership (which endured until 1906). The description of the coin and the scenario of its finding as related by S.H. here:

> Reverse. A circle of 94 minute, 5 pointed stars inside the deeply serrated border with some of the stars between or under the points of the serrature. It seems as if the engraver had at first attempted to use this circle of stars as a border, and then, not approving of it, engraved the serrated border to and over them. The stars and points are not equally spaced and the serrature points, therefore, cover some of the stars. At first glance they appear as if they were merely marks dividing the spaces for the serrature points, but each is a perfectly formed, minute, 5 pointed star. . . .
>
> This die was discovered by Henry Chapman during 1877. Dr. Maris, the first man to make a study of the series, was standing between him and the author whilst we were examining a lot of 1794 Cents, when H.C., picking up a specimen and examining it, exclaimed, 'Here is a die with minute stars around the reverse.' Dr. Maris confirmed the discovery and said, 'It was previously unknown.'[19]

The discovery coin was sold to large cent specialist Samuel Bispham. On February 11–12, 1880, his collection was sold by the Chapmans.

On April 6, Joseph Chandler Roach wrote to New York dealer Édouard Frossard about the variety, stating that he owned one and Lorin G. Parmelee of Boston owned another (acquired from Maris). Frossard looked through his inventory and promptly found a fourth.

Soon afterward, E.B. Mason Jr., in his *Numismatic Visitor*, printed this, without bothering to mention the Chapmans, who were competitors in Philadelphia:

> For the first time, in any journal we present a description of the new and important discovery of the new and beautiful 'Starred' variety of the U.S. cent of 1794. This coin made its debut at a coin sale in New York last February, and was purchased by a lucky dealer for four dollars and twenty-five cents! A duplicate of this rare piece was picked up in this city in March, and is now for sale at this office. The 'starred' variety differs from the common pieces only on the reverse. Eighty-nine [sic] small, fine pointed stars circle around the serrated, or milled border, just between the points, giving to the cent a really handsome appearance. The above pieces are from original dies, and give evidence of considerable circulation and abrasions. . . .
>
> R.C. Davis, the well known numismatist, has after considerable investigation discovered that the starred variety of the 1794 U.S. cent derives its origin from the experimental piece of 1792, known as the 'Eagle on a Rock,' which can only be seen in the Mint Cabinet of coins, this city. Around the edge of the latter are eighty-seven [sic] small five pointed stars, bearing an exact resemblance to the stars on the 1794 starred cent. This fact leads to the conclusion that some of the planchets bearing only the stars, were used when the Mint authorities were coining the 1794 cents. This explanation enhances the fictitious value of the three known specimens of the 'Starred 94' now owned by Haseltine, Roach and Mason of this city.

Likely the Haseltine coin was actually owned by J. Colvin Randall, a local dealer and investor who often worked in Haseltine's office. S.K. Harzfeld's auction of November 26–27, 1880, included such a cent, consigned by Randall. Édouard Frossard, in his magazine, *Numisma*, publicized the discovery. It was certainly the item of the year in 1880.

In *Numisma*, that same month, Frossard printed a poem submitted by Thomas S. Collier, entitled, "On the Star-Circled Cent of 1794."

In the almost century-and-a-half since 1880, the Starred Reverse has been the subject of many mentions, articles, and comments. Dr. Sheldon thought the variety was "the whim of an idle hour at the Mint." Don Taxay, in *U.S. Mint and Coinage*, viewed it as a pattern. Q. David Bowers added comments in the 1982 offering of the John W. Adams Collection of 1794 cents, to this effect: the die was certainly made for a special purpose, whether for a pattern or a proposed regular issue, but, after the tiny five-pointed stars were punched around the periphery, the die was set aside. Rather than waste it, the die was made into a cent reverse.

What really happened may never be known. This unique variety keeps its secret well!

Most 1794, Starred Reverse, cents are in lower grades. Any example in any grade has significant value if some of the stars can be discerned. The finest is the S.S. Forrest Jr. coin, obtained from Spink & Son, London, later found in the John W. Adams Collection, and sold in 2008 as part of the Walter Husak Collection. Q. David Bowers owned this coin for a time in the 1970s.

In lower grades the date and several stars must be discernible.

	Cert	Avg	%MS	Fair-2	AG-3	G-4	VG-8	F-12	VF-20
1794, Starred Reverse	7	13.7	0%	$9,830	$14,500	$21,330	$29,375	$51,750	$115,000

1794, Left Edge of Neck Ends in Sharp Tip • BW-60, S-NC-9, B-40. *Breen dies:* 20-AA. *Recorded population:* 2.

Obverse: Same die as preceding. *Points of distinction:* A crack develops and becomes heavy, through the center, to the rim at the upper right.

Reverse: *Berries left and right:* 5-6. *Upright of second T of STATES opposite:* Highest outside leaf on left. *Fraction:* Bar short. Second 0 very close to ribbon. Numerator slightly right of center of first 0. *Points of distinction:* Leaves very close at wreath apex. In its late state the die develops a vertical, bisecting crack. Probably, this occurred soon after it was first used, accounting for its rarity today.

Notes: The two examples, graded VG-7 and AG-3, are both in the Daniel W. Holmes Jr. Collection.

1794, Left Edge of Neck Ends in Sharp Tip (BW-60, S-NC-9, B-40), early reverse die state.

1794, Left Edge of Neck Ends in Sharp Tip (BW-60, S-NC-9, B-40), late reverse die state.

1794, Left Edge of Neck Ends in Sharp Tip, Closed Wreath

• BW-61, S-49, B-41. *Breen dies:* 20-BB. *Estimated population:* 750 to 1,000.

Obverse: Same die as preceding. During this mating, a large, vertical die crack develops from the border through the left side of E to the hair.

1794, Left Edge of Neck Ends in Sharp Tip, Closed Wreath (BW-61, S-49, B-41).

Reverse: *Berries left and right:* 9-6. Largest is under the left upright of M of AMERICA. *Upright of second T of STATES opposite:* Denticle. *Fraction:* Numerator leans right and is close to bar. Bar almost covers 1, extends to slightly past center of second 0, and ends at ribbon. In the denominator 1 is distant and leans right. *Points of distinction:* Leaf tips touch at wreath apex. First S of STATES high; TA close. This is the most extensively mated reverse die of the 1794 year. *Sheldon designation:* Closed Wreath.

Detail from another coin showing the late-state obverse die crack.

The fraction is crowded to the right, and the digits are irregularly aligned.

Notes: Found in AU and Mint State; both grades are very rare.

1794, Left Edge of Neck Ends in Sharp Tip (different die), Closed Wreath

• BW-63, S-50, B-43. *Breen dies:* 22-BB. *Estimated population:* 45 to 60.

Obverse: *Date:* 1 very high, almost touches hair. Double denticle below 7. 4 very high, barely touches neck. *Tip of pole points to:* Left part of triangular denticle. *LIBERTY:* Closely spaced, I opposite denticle slightly left of its center. *Points of distinction:* Left

1794, Left Edge of Neck Ends in Sharp Tip (different die), Closed Wreath (BW-63, S-50, B-43).

part of neck ends in a sharp tip instead of blending into the hair; slight trace of loop above top right of 7. Lowest lock severed behind neck, with space before it resumes. In a later state there is relapping, probably to remove clash marks. In the latest state a crack develops from the 4, extending right, to the tip of the bust, and through the pole. *Sheldon designation:* Short Bust, Detached Lower Lock.

Reverse: Same die as preceding.

Notes: The highest grade this variety is found in is AU.

1794, Second and Fourth Locks Long, Left Edge of Neck Ends in Sharp Tip (different die), Closed Wreath • BW-65, S-51, B-42. *Breen dies:* 21-BB. *Estimated population:* 60 to 75.

Obverse: *Date:* 1 very high, almost touches hair. 4 very high, barely touches neck. *Tip of pole points to:* Space between denticles. *LIBERTY:* IB and TY wide, I opposite denticle slightly left of its center. *Points of distinction:* Left part of neck ends in a sharp tip instead of blending into the hair, with no loop. Second and fourth locks long and with brush-like ends. The obverse is usually perfect, but some have a crack beginning between 1 and 7, going across the top of the 7 to the neck, and curving down to the end of the pole. Sometimes with an additional crack extending from the left border. *Sheldon designation:* Long Locks.

1794, Second and Fourth Locks Long, Left Edge of Neck Ends in Sharp Tip (different die), Closed Wreath (BW-65, S-51, B-42).

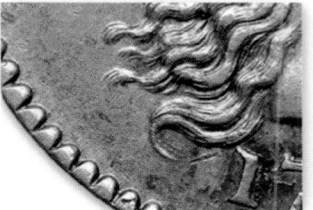

Detail showing the long second and fourth locks with brush-like ends.

The leaves touch at the top of the wreath, unique among 1794 cent dies.

Reverse: Same die as preceding.

Notes: The highest grade this variety is found in is EF.

1794, Date spaced 1 79 4, Closed Wreath • BW-67, S-52, B-44. *Breen dies:* 23-BB. *Estimated population:* 25 to 30.

Obverse: *Date:* 1 very high, almost touches hair. 4 very high, barely touches neck. Pole points to right part of rounded denticle. 94 close, date spaced as 1 79 4. *Tip of pole points to:* Right part of denticle, and is close to it. *LIBERTY:* L close to cap, LI close, I opposite denticle. *Points of distinction:* Hair strands

1794, Date Spaced 1 79 4, Closed Wreath (BW-67, S-52, B-44).

bold and coarse. Usually with a crack below the top of the cap to the hair, but a few are from a perfect die. Tom Morley called it the "Bully Head," from its strong, tough-appearing visage.[20] *Sheldon designation:* 1 and 7 Distant.

Reverse: Same die as preceding.

Notes: The highest grade this variety is found in is VF, and it is very rare as such.

1794, Severed Sixth Lock, Closed Wreath • BW-69, S-53, B-45. *Breen dies: 24-BB. Estimated population:* 20 to 25.

Obverse: *Date:* 1 very high, almost touches hair. 4 very high, almost touches neck. *Tip of pole points to:* Center of triangular denticle. *LIBERTY:* L close to cap, RT close, I opposite space between denticles. *Points of distinction:* Hair strands bold and coarse. Tip of sixth lock detached. *Sheldon designation:* Severed Sixth Lock.

1794, Severed Sixth Lock,
Closed Wreath (BW-69, S-53, B-45).

Reverse: Same die as preceding.

Notes: The highest grade this variety is found in is EF.

Detail of the severed lock.

1794, 7 Tilts to Right, Closed Wreath • BW-70, S-54, B-46. *Breen dies: 25-BB. Estimated population:* 300 to 400.

Obverse: *Date:* 1 very high. 7 tilted to the right. 4 very high. *Tip of pole points to:* Space between denticles, slightly closer to denticle on the right. *LIBERTY:* RT close, I opposite left part of denticle. *Points of distinction:* Hair strands bold and coarse. Sixth lock (counting up from the bottom) detached and forms a small island. Bottom lock ends in a chisel-like point and has a very small hook. Clash marks develop, and in the late state there is a delicate crack from the left border to the hair. *Maris designation:* Crooked 7. *Sheldon designation:* Slanting 7.

1794, 7 Tilts to Right, Closed Wreath (BW-70, S-54, B-46).

Date showing the slanting or tilted 7.

Reverse: Same die as preceding.

Notes: The highest grades this variety is found in are EF and AU.

1794, 7 Tilts to Right, Ribbon Bow With Two Knots, "Crazy A" in STATES • BW-71, S-55, B-47. *Breen dies:* 25-CC. *Estimated population:* 500 to 750.

1794, Tilts to Right, Ribbon Bow With Two Knots, "Crazy A" in STATES (BW-71, S-55, B-47).

Obverse: Same die as preceding. *Points of distinction:* The obverse continues with the crack from the preceding use of the die, now sometimes with an additional crack branching off from the first and going down through the hair.

Reverse: *Berries left and right:* 6-5. All large except for the fourth on the left. *Upright of second T of STATES opposite:* Denticle, slightly to right of its center. *Fraction:* Numerator heavy, close to or touching bar,

Detail showing the "Crazy A" (from another coin).

and slightly right of the center of the second 0. Bar extends from left side of 1 to halfway over second 0. First 0 low. *Points of distinction:* "Crazy A" in STATES is high and leans left. Two ribbon knots, one above the other. Leaves are very close at wreath apex. Amateur workmanship. On some coins there is a die crack in the left obverse field. *Sheldon designation:* Big Berries Variety.

Notes: The highest grades this variety is found in are AU and Mint State, very rare at either level.

1794, 7 Tilts to Right, "Office Boy" Reverse • BW-72, S-56, B-48. *Breen dies:* 25-DD. *Estimated population:* 300 to 400.

1794, 7 Tilts to Right, "Office Boy" Reverse (BW-72, S-56, B-48).

Obverse: Same die as preceding. *Points of distinction:* Cracks as preceding, but now more prominent. In a late state the obverse is relapped, removing the clash marks.

Reverse: *Berries left and right:* 8-7. Breen counted 6-7, perhaps overlooking two tiny ones near the branch at top left. *Upright of second T of STATES opposite:* Denticle. *Fraction:* Numerator leans right and touches bar. Bar extends from over 1 to near top center of second 0. *Points of distinction:* Irregular spacing of some letters; TA of STATES connected, T high, etc. Leaf pair with points opposite second A of AMERICA. Lower-right ribbon end partly detached. Two ribbon knots, one high and detached. Dr. Sheldon: "Highly defective reverse. In addition to the nine defective leaves, the bow is incomplete, Amateur workmanship, probably from the same hand as the preceding reverse." Called the "Office Boy" Reverse by John Clapp.

Notes: The highest grades this variety is found in are AU and Mint State, very rare at either level.

	Cert	Avg	%MS	AG-3	G-4	VG-8	F-12	VF-20	EF-40
1794, 7 Tilts to Right, "Office Boy" Reverse	(a)			$310	$460	$640	$900	$2,580	$7,000

a. Included in certified population for 1794, Head of 1794.

1794, "Pyramidal Head," Button on Cap • BW-74, S-57, B-55. *Breen dies:* 29-JJ. *Estimated population:* Thousands.

Obverse: *Date:* 1 very high. 4 slightly high. *Tip of pole points to:* Denticle, and is close to it. *LIBERTY:* IB wide, I opposite denticle. *Points of distinction:* Hair strands are bold and coarse and are fairly straight in a line slanting down to the left, evocative of the edge of a pyramid. Tiny dot ("button") on outside of lower left of cap—as also seen on BW-84—is really much ado about nothing on examination. Perfect die state or with light parallel cracks from the nose and lower lip to the border, increasing in visibility with die use. *Maris designation:* Pyramidal Head. *Sheldon designation:* Button Variety.

1794, "Pyramidal Head," Button on Cap (BW-74, S-57, B-55).

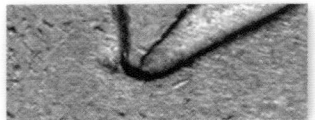

Small "button" or die defect on outside of lower left of the cap.

Reverse: *Berries left and right:* 7-7. *Upright of second T of STATES opposite:* Denticle, slightly to left of its center. *Fraction:* Bar extends from close to upper left of 1 to past center of second 0. 1 in numerator very high. *Points of distinction:* ICA of AMERICA close to denticles. Lowest berry on inside left touches ribbon. Leaves close at wreath apex. An injury to the die is seen over CA. In its late state, die sunk at the center, producing a prominent bulge nearly obliterating the lettering.

Notes: This variety is known in Mint State.

1794, Thick Hair, Wide Date • BW-76, S-58, B-56. *Breen dies:* 30-KK. *Estimated population:* 300 to 400.

Obverse: *Date:* 1 very high. 4 low. *Tip of pole points to:* Denticle, and is close to or touches it. *LIBERTY:* LIBE wide, B slightly low, I opposite space between denticles and slightly closer to denticle on the right. *Points of distinction:* Hair strands bold and coarse. *Maris designation:* Many Haired. *Sheldon designation:* Thick Hair, Wide Date.

1794, Thick Hair, Wide Date (BW-76, S-58, B-56).

Detail showing the thick hair strands.

Reverse: *Berries left and right:* 6-7. *Upright of second T of STATES opposite:* Space between denticles. *Fraction:* Numerator leans slightly right. Bar curved; extends from upper right of 1 to right edge of second 0. First 0 low and near end of denticle. *Points of distinction:* Right stem close to ribbon and points past A. RICA close to denticles. Some have a crack through UNIT, these being in the minority. Clash marks develop, and a crack becomes prominent, eventually generating a rim cud. This last state is very rare.

Notes: The highest grades this variety is found in are EF and AU (exceedingly rare).

1794, Thick Hair, Wide Date, Left Ribbon Bow Double Cut • BW-77, S-59, B-57. *Breen dies: 30-LL.* **Estimated population:** 300 to 400.

Obverse: Same die as preceding. *Points of distinction:* The obverse is found perfect, but also is found with a small crack from between the 9 and the 4 to the neck.

1794, Thick Hair, Wide Date, Left Ribbon Bow Double Cut (BW-77, S-59, B-57).

Reverse: *Berries left and right:* 7-7. *Upright of second T of STATES opposite:* Denticle, slightly to left of its center. *Fraction:* Leans sharply to the right. Numerator to the left of center of bar and over second 0. Bar extends from center of 1 to past center of second 0. 1 high. Second 0 near denticle. *Points of dis-*

The tilted fraction and the reverse die crack.

tinction: Letters on right are close to denticles. Left stem short. Left ribbon bow is double cut at top. Many denticles blended are together except for their tips. The reverse can be found perfect, but often has a crack starting at the border beneath the end of the left ribbon. This continues to expand, eventually becoming heavy.

Notes: This variety is known in Mint State.

1794, Thick Hair, Close Date • BW-79, S-60, B-52. *Breen dies: 27-HH.* **Estimated population:** 200 to 300.

Obverse: *Date:* 1 very high, close to or barely touches hair. 4 close to or barely touches neck. *Tip of pole points to:* Left part of denticle and nearly touches it. *LIBERTY:* RT close, R close to hair, I opposite right part of denticle. *Points of distinction:* Hair strands bold and coarse. Lock 5, small, and with tip

1794, Thick Hair, Close Date (BW-79, S-60, B-52).

disconnected. There are often clash marks between the hair and LIB, sometimes dramatic. Some coins have a faint crack in the same area. *Maris designation:* Patagonian. *Sheldon designation:* Thick Hair, Close Date.

Reverse: *Berries left and right:* 6-5. *Upright of second T of STATES opposite:* Denticle, slightly to left of its center. *Fraction:* Bar extends from upper left of 1 to past center of second 0. First 0 low. *Points of distinction:* The right leaf of the lowest-inside pair on the right is a simple line and seems to be edgewise. The ribbon bow comes from the knot on the left, and the right ribbon end is high above the knot and does not connect to anything. Denticles heavy and pointed. Light clash marks are seen.

Notes: The highest grades this variety is found in are AU and Mint State (exceedingly rare). Édouard Frossard's 1879 description: "The head large, the ear nearly square. The legend LIBERTY near milling, with the R close to head. In the date, 1 touches the hair, and 4 the bust. The cap and staff touch the milling."

1794, Thick Hair, Close Date, Short Right Stem • BW-80, S-61, B-53.

Breen dies: 27-II. *Estimated population:* 120 to 160.

Obverse: Same die as preceding. *Points of distinction:* A faint crack on the preceding use of this die can be more developed but still is not strong. The incuse marks are still present. An additional mark or crack can sometimes be seen from the rim to the hair left of the 1 in the date.

1794, Thick Hair, Close Date, Short Right Stem (BW-80, S-61, B-53).

Reverse: *Berries left and right:* 7-7. *Upright of second T of STATES opposite:* Denticle, slightly to left of its center. *Fraction:* Bar extends from upper right of 1 to center of second 0. First 0 low. *Points of distinction:* Short right stem. Denticles heavy and pointed. Multiple clash marks are seen, most

Detail of the reverse showing clash marks in the form of denticles from the obverse die. These are most prominent to the left and right of the end of the left ribbon.

prominently along the bottom border. The obverse die became loose in the press and fell on the reverse die, impressing the denticles into the steel.

Notes: The highest grades this variety is found in are AU and Mint State. Sheldon notes that all of this variety are on planchets that are thicker than usual.

1794, Heavy, Stubby Lower Lock, Short Right Stem • BW-82, S-62, B-54.

Breen dies: 28-II. *Estimated population:* 75 to 120.

Obverse: *Date:* 1 very high. 4 high. *Tip of pole points to:* Denticle. *LIBERTY:* IBE wide, I opposite denticle. *Points of distinction:* Hair strands bold and coarse. Lowest lock especially heavy. Locks 4 to 6 weak or incomplete at tips. Usually (but not always) with a large cud break at left border. The obverse is rarely found perfect, but is most often seen with a large "cud" rim break behind the neck, the most dramatic on any 1794 obverse die. *Maris designation:* Trephined Head. *Sheldon designation:* Heavy, Stubby Lower Lock.

1794, Heavy, Stubby Lower Lock, Short Right Stem (BW-82, S-62, B-54). The obverse has the usually-seen dramatic break at the left border.

Detail of trephined head.

Reverse: Same die as preceding.

Notes: This variety is known from EF to Mint State, but is a rarity at any high level. Trephined Head refers to the marked depression in the hair above the highest lock, suggesting that Miss Liberty's skull had been drilled with a saw to remove a circular disc of bone, thus relieving pressure on the brain, from a blood clot, for example.[21]

1794, Fallen 4 in Date (also With Button on Cap) • BW-84, S-63, B-37.

Breen dies: 19-X. *Estimated population:* 500 to 750.

Obverse: *Date:* 1 very high. 9 very high, creating illusion of "Fallen 4." The 17 and 4 are about on the same level. *Tip of pole points to:* Space between denticles, and nearly touches denticles. *LIBERTY:* L distant from cap, by the width of the letter L, doubled denticle opposite upper left of I, T over forehead, only die with this characteristic. *Points of distinction:* Tiny dot ("button") on outside of lower left of cap—as also seen on BW-74—but in the present instance the button is often overlooked. Some denticles crude and irregular.

1794, Fallen 4 in Date (also With Button on Cap) (BW-84, S-63, B-37).

Detail showing the "Fallen 4," more properly designated as "High 9."

Some light clash marks are seen. Probably the most distinctive of the 1794 obverse dies, perhaps cut by a mechanic rather than an engraver. George Clapp called this the Drunken Diecutter's Obverse.

Reverse: *Berries left and right:* 6-5. Berries near bow are tiny. *Upright of second T of STATES opposite:* Denticle, slightly left of its center. *Fraction:* Bar wide and extends beyond denominator; touches ribbon on right. Numerator very low with 00 running into border. *Points of distinction:* Lettering extremely close to denticles all around. The BW-59 and BW-84 reverses are the only ones of the year with smaller letters than the others. Denticles heavy and crude. Amateurish workmanship overall, matching the only obverse die mated with this reverse. Some light clash marks are seen.[22] Remarkably, this reverse die is a reworking of 1793, Bisecting Obverse Crack, Liberty Cap (BW-27), and other combinations of this die employed in 1793.[23]

Notes: The highest grades this variety is found in are AU and Mint State (unique).

	Cert	Avg	%MS	AG-3	G-4	VG-8	F-12	VF-20	EF-40	AU-50
1794, Fallen 4 in Date (also With Button on Cap)	(a)			$330	$510	$730	$1,120	$2,420	$6,330	$12,250

a. Included in certified population for 1794, Head of 1794.

1794, Shielded Hair • BW-86, S-NC-6, B-49.

Breen dies: 26-EE. *Recorded population:* 2.

Obverse: *Date:* 1 very high, barely touches hair. 4 high. *Tip of pole points to:* Denticle. *LIBERTY:* BER slightly wide, R leans right, I opposite left part of denticle. *Points of distinction:* Denticles deep and heavy at lower left, in effect protecting the hair. Strands of hair are bold and coarse. Tips of third to seventh locks in nearly a straight line. *Maris designation:* Shielded Hair (Maris knew this die from the variety next described).

1794, Shielded Hair (BW-86, S-NC-6, B-49).

Reverse: *Berries left and right:* 5-7 (per Breen). *Upright of second T of STATES opposite:* Denticle, slightly to left of its center. *Fraction:* Numerator tilts right and does not touch bar. Bar from right edge of 1 to nearly center of second 0. Second 0 low. *Points of distinction:* The die is sunken at the center, causing the coin to be raised and the raised part to wear very quickly. There is a crack from the border between D of UNITED and S, extending into the field.

Notes: Both examples are Fine. Discovered by Walter Breen in August 1957, at which time he was the main staff cataloger for the New Netherlands Coin Company.

1794, Shielded Hair, Missing Fraction Bar • BW-87, S-64, B-50. *Breen dies: 26-FF. Estimated population:* 60 to 75.

Obverse: Same die as preceding.

Reverse: *Berries left and right: 7-7. Upright of second T of STATES opposite:* Denticle, slightly to right of its center. *Fraction:* No fraction bar, one of the most famous reverse dies of the era. *Points of distinction:* Denticles heavy and somewhat pointed. In its late state, the die is bulged at the center and a crack extends from the border through the D of UNITED, continuing inward.

1794, Shielded Hair, Missing Fraction Bar (BW-87, S-64, B-50).

Detail of fraction with missing horizontal bar.

Notes: This variety occurs in Mint State, but is exceedingly rare as such. This variety is widely listed, including in the regular edition of the *Guide Book of United States Coins*, and is one of the most desired rarities of 1794.

	Cert	Avg	%MS	AG-3	G-4	VG-8	F-12	VF-20	EF-40	AU-50
1794, Shielded Hair, Missing Fraction Bar	(a)			$420	$670	$925	$2,070	$4,580	$9,330	$23,330

a. Included in certified population for 1794, Head of 1794.

1794, Shielded Hair, Short Stems to Wreath • BW-88, S-65, B-51. *Breen dies: 26-GG. Estimated population:* Thousands.

Obverse: Same die as preceding. *Points of distinction:* Clash marks and cracks develop.

Reverse: *Berries left and right: 7-6.* Berries are large except for tiny fifth and small seventh on left; fifth berry easy to miss. *Upright of second T of STATES opposite:* Denticle. *Fraction:* Numerator close to bar. Bar extends from center of 1 to past center of second 0. First 0 low. *Points of distinction:* Short stems to wreath. Found perfect or with light cracks.

1794, Shielded Hair, Short Stems to Wreath (BW-88, S-65, B-51).

Detail of numerator touching fraction bar.

Notes: The highest grades this variety is found in are AU and MS-60 (exceedingly rare). This is the commonest of all 1794 cents and by far the most often seen of the Shielded Hair varieties. The name is derived "from the deeply-impressed denticles on the left side which give the variety its name, and in effect 'shield' the hair from wear—making the variety fertile ground for overgrading!

The *whole coin's* appearance must be assessed in determining grade. In the case of this particular variety, to fail to do so could leave the buyer the 'proud' owner of a F-15 coin in an EF-40 holder!"[24]

1794, Distant 1, Heavy Figures, Split Pole (on most) • BW-90, S-66, B-58.

Breen dies: 31-MM. **Estimated population:** 30 to 45.

Obverse: *Date:* 1 low. 4 slightly low. **Tip of pole points to:** Left side of denticle and is distant from it. **LIBERTY:** L close to cap, Y completely over forehead (very unusual), and I opposite left part of denticle. **Points of distinction:** Hair strands bold and coarse. Found with a perfect die, or with a crack across the neck to the hair, and also from the bottom of the neck across the lowest lock and into the field. Other cracks later develop. **Sheldon designation:** Split Pole Variety, as most (but not all) have a die crack paralleling the pole, making it appear split or doubled. Also, according to Sheldon, Distant 1, Heavy Figures.

1794, Distant 1, Heavy Figures, Split Pole (on most) (BW-90, S-66, B-58).

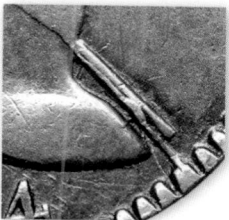

"Split Pole" caused by a die crack.

Reverse: *Berries left and right:* 6-7. Most berries are very small. **Upright of second T of STATES opposite:** Denticle. **Fraction:** Bar extends from center of 1 to center of second 0. 1 in denominator high. **Points of distinction:** No trace of stems in the unusually narrow space between the ribbon knot and numerator. Clash marks are seen above the wreath and below the ribbon knot.

Notes: VF is the highest grade known for this variety.

1794, MODIFIED HEAD STYLE

BW-94 to BW-99 are in this style. The tip of the lowest lock almost forms a circle, and the tip points upward. The portrait is also in lower relief. Walter Breen attributes this portrait and the finished dies to John Smith Gardner, although there is no documentary support of this. Gardner worked as "acting assistant engraver," later as assistant engraver, until March 31, 1796. Craig Sholley suggests that Robert Scot created all of the portrait hubs, and the modified head dies are those finished by John Smith Gardner with the "circle lock" being his signature. Again, there is no proof of this, but the style change and timing (Scot being involved with silver coinage) are curious.

According to Sheldon, "The heads are a little larger, border, and the whole design is executed in a 'hard, inartistic style, as continued in 1795.' The relief is now almost entirely flat, the hair is braided into five heavy coarse locks, there is little evidence of fine engraving, the features suggest no expression other than a grim stare, or as Maris put it, a Roman stare. He called these the *Roman Plicae.*"

The preceding may be a bit harsh, as these cents—as well as those of 1795 and 1796, continuing the slightly modified design—are highly appreciated. However, the character is changed somewhat, as continued to happen with still later designs, as die making became more routine and less individually artistic.

There are five obverse dies. Check the lower lock first to be sure that a coin is a member of this class. Then check the obverse features, then verify by checking the reverse possibilities, for which there are three dies.

1794, "Marred Hair and Cheek," Lowest Lock Nearly a Circle • BW-94, S-67, B-59. *Breen dies:* 32-MM. *Estimated population:* 300 to 400.

Obverse: *Date:* 1 closer to curl than to 7. 4 centered. Date widely spaced. *Tip of pole points to:* Denticle, and is not close to it. *LIBERTY:* L separated from cap by about the same distance that the bases of I and B are separated. *Points of distinction:* Marks on portrait from contact with the reverse die.

1794, "Marred Hair and Cheek," Lowest Lock Nearly a Circle (BW-94, S-67, B-59).

End of lower lock nearly a circle, but incomplete. Found perfect or with three faint die cracks. *Maris designation:* Roman Plica. *Sheldon designation:* Marred Hair and Cheek.

Reverse: Same die as preceding.

Notes: This variety is known in Mint State.

1794, Bisecting Obverse Die Crack • BW-95, S-68, B-60. *Breen dies:* 33-MM. *Estimated population:* 45 to 60.

Obverse: *Date:* 1 much closer to 7 than to curl. Tip of 7 low and above denticle. 4 high. *Pole points to:* Left side of denticle. *LIBERTY:* L close to cap. IB wide. *Points of distinction:* Lower lock forms a nearly complete loop ("circle" so called). Appears with a bisecting crack from 8 o'clock to 2 o'clock that varies from very light to heavy.

1794, Bisecting Obverse Die Crack (BW-95, S-68, B-60). The bisecting obverse crack is light on this example.

Reverse: Same die as preceding. *Points of distinction:* Light clash marks are seen.

Notes: The highest grades this variety is known in are EF and AU, and it is rare at either level. Unknown to Maris. First publicized in Édouard Frossard's 23rd Sale, August 3, 1882, lot 548.

1794, Lower Lock a Circle • BW-96, S-69, B-61. *Breen dies:* 34-MM. *Estimated population:* 300 to 400.

Obverse: *Date:* 1 about equidistant from curl and 7. 4 slightly high. 1 was first punched in an inverted position, then corrected (trace of serif as tiny spine at upper-right side of final 1 is sometimes visible). *Pole points to:* Space between denticles. *LIBERTY:* L separated from cap slightly more than the same distance that the bases of I and B are separated. IBER wide. *Points of distinction:* Lower lock forms a complete loop ("circle" so called) by virtue of a tiny spine connecting it to the main lock.

1794, Lower Lock a Circle (BW-96, S-69, B-61).

A complete "circle" is formed at the end of the lower lock.

Reverse: Same die as preceding. ***Points of distinction:*** Dr. Sheldon knew of a single example with a horizontal, bisecting die crack across the reverse, passing through the first T of STATES, the E of CENT, and the second A of AMERICA.

Notes: This variety is known in Mint State.

1794, Lower Lock a Circle • BW-97,
S-70, B-62. *Breen dies:* 34-NN. ***Estimated population:*** 750 to 1,000.

Obverse: Same die as preceding. Lower lock forms a complete loop ("circle" so called). ***Points of distinction:*** The die develops crack from denticle down to between TY, eventually to the face.

Reverse: ***Berries left and right:*** 6-7. ***Upright of second T of STATES opposite:*** Denticle, slightly to the left of its center. ***Fraction:*** Bar extends from center of 1 to center of second 0. 1 in denominator high. Denominator close to denticles. ***Points of distinction:*** Three leaves (the center one a protruding tip) under D of UNITED. C of AMERICA tilted right. Some injury is seen at the lower right of the wreath. First and last part of border inscription closer to denticles than other lettering.

1794, Lower Lock a Circle (BW-97, S-70, B-62).

Notes: This variety is known in Mint State.

1794 • BW-98, S-71, B-63. *Breen dies:*
35-NN. ***Estimated population:*** 750 to 1,000.

Obverse: ***Date:*** 1 closer to curl than to 7. 94 close. 4 slightly high. ***Pole points to:*** Denticle. ***LIBERTY:*** L close to cap. LI closer than are other letters. ***Points of distinction:*** Raised parallel die lines at nose and eyebrow (best seen on high-grade coins). The obverse is found perfect and also with a light crack from the border through the tip of the cap and the top of LIBE. Some later coins have other cracks as well. Clash marks are seen in front of the chin and neck, with some traces of AMERICA in the upper field of the obverse on some.

1794 (BW-98, S-71, B-63).

Reverse: Same die as preceding. ***Points of distinction:*** Clash marks are seen.

Notes: This variety is known Mint State, and is rare as such.

Detail showing the curious raised lines on the eyebrow and nose.

1794 • BW-99, S-NC-3, B-64. *Breen dies:* 36-OO. *Recorded population:* 2.

Obverse: *Date:* 1 high under lowest lock and closer to curl than to 7. 4 high. *Pole points to:* Space between denticles. *LIBERTY:* L about as close to cap as it is to I. IBE very wide. *Points of distinction:* Tips of four upper locks of hair are in a straight line. Top of 1 very close to hair above it.

1794 (**BW-99, S-NC-3, B-64**).

Reverse: *Berries left and right:* 6-7. *Upright of second T of STATES opposite:* Denticle, slightly to the left of its center. *Fraction:* Bar extends from upper right of 1 to near center of second 0. In the denominator, 10 widely spaced, 0's lean slightly right. *Points of distinction:* Some letters in AMERICA very close to denticles. Two leaves under D of UNITED. Tip of highest leaf on left points to highest leaf on right, slightly below its tip. Short stem on berry under left upright of M of AMERICA. A light crack is seen from the D of UNITED extending upward to the wreath.

Notes: The two pieces are Fine-12, per conservative grading, (Daniel W. Holmes Jr. Collection) and G-6 (American Numismatic Society). Unknown to Maris. Discovered by Ebenezer Gilbert in the early 1900s.

1794, WITH HEAD STYLE OF 1795

BW-101 is the only 1794 issue with this style. The tip of the lowest lock is short and points downward. This design is continued in 1795, earning it the designation *Head of 1795*.

Typical values for 1794, Exact Head of 1795, cents.

	Cert	Avg	%MS	AG-3	G-4	VG-8	F-12	VF-20	EF-40	AU-50
1794, Exact Head of 1795	45	31.9	11%	$300	$450	$660	$850	$2,375	$4,800	$8,500

1794, Exact Head of 1795, Tip of Lowest Lock Points Downward • BW-101, S-72, B-65. *Breen dies:* 37-OO. *Estimated population:* 500 to 750.

Obverse: *Date:* 179 widely spaced, 94 close. 17 very close to border. *Pole points to:* Denticle. *LIBERTY:* L nearly touches cap. LI and ER close. *Points of distinction:* Tip of lowest lock points downward; no curl. Only 1794 die with this feature. Most show a die

1794, Exact Head of 1795, Tip of Lowest Lock Points Downward (**BW-101, S-72, B-65**).

crack from the rim to upper left of Y, to lower right of T, to hair. *Maris designation:* '95 Head.

Reverse: Same die as preceding. *Points of distinction:* Found perfect or with a crack from the border diagonally through D of UNITED to the wreath stem.

Notes: The highest grades this variety is known in are AU and Mint State, and it is rare so fine. Walter Breen suggests that these were delivered on December 30, 1794, along with some examples of the preceding variety. This makes the assumption that this, the most modern of 1794 dies, was part of the last pair used, a theory not necessarily consistent with Mint practice of the era.

Numismatic Notes: *Dickeson's 1859 comments about 1794 cents:* Montroville W. Dickeson's *American Numismatical Manual*, 1859, included this about the cents dated 1794:

Of this emission we have discovered but one type; of which 26 varieties have come under our notice, which may be determined mainly by reference to the variations of those of 1793. These cents are somewhat thicker than those that preceded them, the weight of each being increased by about 17 grains;[25] the hair of the goddess, also, does not recede so much from the forehead. The planchets from which they were struck were of good copper, and the milling of the edges being more prominent has protected them from the effect of abrasion, and hence they are frequently found in a fine state of preservation. They are quite plenty, the number issued by the Mint amounted, according to the official statement, to 12,513,300;[26] and the number of dies in a single year excites surprise, the preparation of each die involving much expense.

1795, Liberty Cap

Circulation mintage, Lettered Edge (estimated): 37,000.
Circulation mintage, Plain Edge (estimated): 501,500.

The cents of 1795 are an interesting study in that they comprise several widely differing varieties, but the number of die combinations is small compared to the year before or the year after. All are of the Liberty Cap design with a wreath reverse, similar to the general style of 1794. R.W. Julian and Craig Sholley suggest that the portrait and wreath hubs were likely made by Mint engraver Robert Scot. Some of, or perhaps all of, the working dies were finished by assistant engraver John Smith Gardner, as Scot—as the chief engraver—would have been addressing the silver and gold coinage, which was politically more urgent, himself. The historical records, along with the fact that the dies appear to be hand cut and quite different in design from other Mint products, strongly suggest that the Jefferson Head cents were made outside of the Mint by a man named John Harper.

In this year, the Mint had been busy with silver and gold coin production and with problems arising from the making of dies. The first shipment of cents of this date, amounting to 37,000 coins, was made on December 1, 1795. This is widely given as the entire mintage figure for the lettered edge type, but there is no way to know if it is accurate, as the present-day rarity of lettered-edge coins suggests a higher figure.

Early issues are on thick planchets with lettered edges and a statutory weight of 208 grains, The price of copper was rising in the market, and the direction was given by President Washington on December 27 that henceforth the weight should be reduced to 168 grains. The new coins were made on thinner planchets with plain edges. From December 28 to 31, some 45,000 cents were struck of the new standard. These were delivered on January 1, 1796. From January 16 to March 31, 1796, five more deliveries took place, presumably of 1795-dated coins, amounting to 456,500 cents, giving a total of 501,500 thin-planchet coins of 1795 in all. Afterward there was a long interval before more coins were struck. Dr. Sheldon suggests that this was because new dies were being engraved for the 1796 cents. Julian and Sholley state that Mint records show that the facility was very busy with silver and gold coinage at this time.

The cents of 1795 were sent to banks throughout the country. Prior to this all the United States Mint coins, according to Frank H. Stewart, had been issued only locally in Philadelphia.

One of the thin-planchet varieties was made with a completely reeded edge, as on gold coins of the era, the only large copper cent of this format. The reason it was made is unknown.

The most curious cents of the year are the so-called Jefferson Heads. George H. Clapp and Howard R. Newcomb, in *The United States Cents of the Years 1795, 1796, 1797, and 1800,* discussed the Jefferson Head cents at some length, noting that "the late David Proskey was one of our best-informed students of the large cents of the United States," referencing Proskey's comment from the *Coin Collector's Journal,* March 1880:

This so-called "Jefferson Head" cent was probably named for the same reason as the Guinea pigs (because they did not come from Guinea, and they are not pigs); the portrait on the piece does not resemble that of Jefferson, nor did he have aught to do with the issue, and last, but not least, *it is not a cent;* but is undoubtedly a counterfeit of the cent of 1795, and was struck somewhere about 1803. The workmanship and style of every portion of the piece show that the dies were never executed at the U.S. Mint; the hair alone would be sufficient to condemn it, no artist employed in the mint since its establishment would have engraved such a stiff unnatural mass after having for models the beautiful wavy locks which adorn the earlier coins; the figures and letters are totally unlike any used on the cents; the fraction 1/100 is of the size figures found on the issue of 1803; the wreath with its lobster claw leaves and three-looped bow furnishes more evidence of the inexpert tool of an imitator who had before him different types of cents and engraved the least difficult part of each; the short and narrow serrated border on the reverse is unlike any used in 1795, while the absence of the border ornamentation on the obverse, even on the best of them, would indicate that a worn cent was copied. . . .

Dr. Sheldon noted,

By some the *Jefferson* cents have been regarded as contemporary counterfeits, but others have thought it more likely that these coins were the result of a sort of whimsical experiment on the part of some Mint employee who may have been caricaturing, or merely have been "idly trying his hand." I am inclined to this latter view. At any rate the coins are of entirely different design from any of the regular cents, and they possess quite a personality of their own. Moreover, they certainly circulated as cents, for many of the specimens are in well worn condition, and for a long time the Jefferson has been looked upon with favor by cent collectors—at least as a mystery and a curiosity. . . .

Walter Breen, largely drawing upon information unearthed by R.W. Julian, created a chapter on them for his *Encyclopedia of Early United States Cents 1793–1814:* "Harper's 'Jefferson' Cents."[27] It was revealed that John Harper, a mechanic and saw maker with a factory near Trenton, New Jersey, had visited the Mint during a time when the institution was having problems and Congress had mounted an inquiry into its operations.[28] He sought to obtain a private contract to produce coins.

At his own expense, Harper prepared a coining press and had cent dies cut to produce a quantity of copper coins, examples of which were given to the Congressional committee. Mint Director Elias Boudinot confiscated Harper's dies, but offered him the position of assistant coiner, which the latter declined. By inference, Breen suggests that what were later called Jefferson Head cents were the samples prepared by Harper. Necessarily, they were of different workmanship than the Mint products. As to whether Harper's proposal coins and the Jefferson Heads are one and the same, this can only be assumed, as there is no specific documentation.

While the panorama of 1795 cent varieties is small and the varieties quite diverse, among these are several major rarities, including the Reeded Edge and Jefferson Head issues. Accordingly, most collectors will be content with the less expensive and more available issues.

Typical grades for the Lettered Edge or early issues tend to be low, and the coins are often dark or porous. In contrast, most Plain Edge cents of the typically seen varieties are on smooth planchets of high quality, although relatively few are perfectly centered. The Reeded Edge and Jefferson Head coins exist only in lower grades.

LETTERED EDGE VARIETIES

Typical values for 1795, Lettered Edge. Rare varieties may be worth more.

	Cert	Avg	%MS	AG-3	G-4	VG-8	F-12	VF-20	EF-40	AU-50	MS-60BN	MS-63BN
1795, Lettered Edge	48	33.4	15%	$275	$410	$625	$1,290	$2,290	$6,330	$9,580	$19,170	$39,000

1795, LIBER-TY Hyphenated, 5 Does Not Touch Neck, ONE / CENT High, Lettered Edge • BW-1, S-73, B-1.

Breen dies: 1-A. *Estimated population:* 60 to 75.

1795, LIBER-TY Hyphenated, 5 Does Not Touch Neck, ONE / CENT High, Lettered Edge (BW-1, S-73, B-1).

Obverse: *Date:* Serif of 1 close to hair, upper right of 5 close to but distinctly separated from the neck. Base of 5 centered over a denticle. Date distant from border. *Pole points to:* Denticle, slightly left of its center. *LIBERTY:* Always found with the hyphen-like die crack of LIBER-TY, the other parts of which are within the base of the R and extend to the T. BE and RT wide. Upright of T over junction of hair and forehead.

Detail showing the die crack appearing as a hyphen in LIBER-TY.

Reverse: ONE / CENT high in wreath. Single leaf to each side of wreath apex. Two leaves opposite D of UNITED. Leaf slightly more than half over E of ONE. Found perfect and later with a crack from the top of U to N to the base of I to below TE to D and beyond. Another delicate crack is sometimes seen from the center of F in OF to the first A of AMERICA to the base of ME to R to the top of I to the rim over C.

Notes: The highest grades this variety is found in are VF and EF, and it is a rarity at either level. First identified by Sylvester S. Crosby and published in J.W. Haseltine's catalog of Crosby's collection, June 1883. Usually seen in low grades.

1795, Top of 5 Overlaying the Neck, ONE / CENT High, Lettered Edge • BW-2, S-74, B-2.

Breen dies: 2-A. *Estimated population:* 160 to 200.

1795, Top of 5 Overlaying the Neck, ONE / CENT High, Lettered Edge (BW-2, S-74, B-2).

Obverse: *Date:* Top of 1 close to hair, but serif distant from curl to the left. Top of 5 high and into the neck, showing flag of 5 overlaying the neck (not buried in it). *Pole points to:* Denticle, slightly right of its center. Tip of pole shallow. *LIBERTY:* Widely spaced. B leans right. Upright of T above junction of hair and forehead. *Points of distinction:* Found perfect and with a crack from the rim below 95, to the top of the 9, and to the neck.

Detail of the date. Note the top of the 5 showing its overlay on the bottom edge of the neck.

Reverse: Same as preceding. Now, the cracks are more advanced, and on some coins a new crack is seen across TES and beyond. Sometimes cracks are nearly all around the border.

Notes: This variety is known in Mint State. Lot 500 of the Eliasberg Collection Sale, 1996, offered an example of this variety (cataloged by Mark Borckardt) described as:

1795 Lettered Edge. S-74. Low Rarity-4. VF-35. Sharpness of AU-50. Strike: Well centered and sharply detailed. Surfaces: Olive brown obverse with lighter tan reverse. Lightly porous and burnished with the appearance of having been lightly etched. Pedigree: William Cutler Atwater, B. Max Mehl, June 11, 1946, Lot 18 $57.50; Louis E. Eliasberg, Sr.

The original Mehl commentary is illustrative of why it is exceedingly difficult to make modern conclusions about the grade of a coin based on an old-time listing, this from the Atwater catalog:

Extremely fine, although I doubt if the coin has ever been in circulation. Was purchased as an Uncirculated specimen. Just the barest touch of cabinet friction with unusually sharp impression. Medium olive surface on obverse and very light brown on reverse. Very rare so choice.

1795, 3 Leaves at Apex, ONE / CENT Slightly High, Lettered Edge • BW-3,

S-75, B-3. *Breen dies: 2-B. **Estimated population:** 300 to 400.*

Obverse: Same as preceding. ***Points of distinction:*** Cracks as on the preceding, and with a delicate crack across the tops of RITE to the rim opposite the mouth.

Reverse: ONE / CENT fairly high. At the apex, single leaf left and double to the right,

1795, 3 Leaves at Apex, ONE / CENT Slightly High, Lettered Edge (BW-3, S-75, B-3).

this being definitive for Lettered Edge cents of this date. ***Points of distinction:*** There is a crack from the rim at the left through the top of ME of AMERICA. Buckling is later seen at this point.

Notes: This variety is known in Mint State. This variety is often granular or on defective planchets. The National Numismatic Collection in the Smithsonian has a Mint State coin overstruck on a Talbot, Allum & Lee token, plain edge except for OF showing from the original T.A.&L. cent.

1795, LIBERTY Not Hyphenated, 5 Touches Neck, 2 Leaves at Apex, ONE / CENT High, Lettered Edge •

BW-4, S-76a, B-4a. *Breen dies: 3-C. **Estimated population:** 45 to 60.*

Obverse: *Date:* Serif of 1 close to hair, upper right of 5 touches the neck. Base of 5 centered over a denticle, slightly to the left of its center. Date distant from border. ***Pole points to:*** Denticle, slightly left of its center. *LIBERTY:* L almost touches cap. LI close. Upright of T over hair to left of forehead. ***Points of distinction:*** Multiple clash marks develop.

1795, LIBERTY Not Hyphenated, 5 Touches Neck, 2 Leaves at Apex, ONE / CENT High, Lettered Edge (BW-4, S-76a, B-4a).

Reverse: ONE / CENT high in wreath.

Detail of date. The top of 5 touches the neck.

Single leaf to each side of wreath apex. Three leaves opposite D of UNITED. Leaf completely over E of ONE ending above right upright of N. ***Points of distinction:*** Multiple clash marks develop.

Notes: The variety is known in EF to Mint State, and is exceedingly rare at these levels. Some are struck on thin planchets; one of these was graded MS-70 by Dr. Sheldon, but now is graded MS-63.[29]

PLAIN EDGE VARIETIES

Typical values for 1795, Plain Edge. Rare varieties may be worth more.

	Cert	Avg	%MS	AG-3	G-4	VG-8	F-12	VF-20	EF-40	AU-50	MS-60BN	MS-63BN
1795, Plain Edge	209	28.7	11%	$190	$320	$480	$960	$1,490	$4,250	$7,000	$10,170	$24,000

1795, RTY Widely Spaced, ONE / CENT High, Plain Edge • BW-5, S-NC-2, B-5. *Breen dies: 4-C. Recorded population: 2.*

1795, RTY Widely Spaced, ONE / CENT High, Plain Edge (BW-5, S-NC-2, B-5).

Obverse: *Date:* 1 close to hair, tip of 5 pierces neck. 79 very close, 17 slightly less close, 95 widest in date. *Pole points to:* Space between denticles. *LIBERTY:* Not easily discernible. Breen says RTY widely spaced.

Reverse: Same as preceding.

Notes: Discovered by Walter Breen in a consignment for Lester Merkin's sale of March 1969; AG-3. A second example was found in 1993; Fair-2. Both are struck over Talbot, Allum & Lee cents.

Detail showing part of the word "YORK" and other lettering from the Talbot, Allum & Lee undertype.

1795, LIBERTY Not Hyphenated, 5 Touches Neck, 2 Leaves at Apex, ONE / CENT High, Plain Edge • BW-8, S-76b, B-4b. *Breen dies: 3-C. Estimated population: Thousands.*

Obverse: Same as preceding. *Points of distinction:* Found perfect, as on the Lettered Edges, and also in a later state with a fine crack from the rim at the left of the 1, to the tip of the second hair lock, to the cap, and back to the rim. Sometimes swellings are seen in the left and right field.

Reverse: Same as preceding. *Points of distinction:* Found perfect on early impressions, later with the die crumbling at OF and at the N of ONE and the back of CENT. On some rare examples, a rim break obliterates part of R and all of IC. After most of these had been struck, "the obverse was reground, leaving the pole weaker and severing the second lock from the hair, together with the upper half of the third lock" (Sheldon's comment).

Notes: This variety is known in Mint State. Misstruck, off-center, etc., coins are not rare. Walter Breen calls it the commonest of the Liberty Cap cents.

1795, 5 Touches Neck, ONE / CENT Centered, Dot Within First A of AMERICA, Plain Edge • BW-9, S-77, B-6. *Breen dies:* 3-D. *Estimated population:* 300 to 400.

1795, 5 Touches Neck, ONE / CENT Centered, Dot Within First A of AMERICA, Plain Edge (BW-9, S-77, B-6).

Obverse: Same as described under BW-4. *Points of distinction:* Found perfect and also with swelling in the left and right fields, later with a crack extending from the shoulder above the date to the cap and border.

Reverse: Two leaves at wreath apex. ONE / CENT centered within wreath; C low. Five groups of three leaves in the left branch, four groups in the right. Raised dot within upper space of first A of AMERICA. *Points of distinction:* Found perfect and also with many

Detail showing the tiny raised dot in the first A of AMERICA.

delicate cracks, also with weakening at OF, at NI, and at CENTS, and flattening of most of the leaves in the wreath. This die must have been injured severely by contact with some hard object.

Notes: The highest grades this variety occurs in are AU and Mint State (unique).

1795, ONE / CENT Centered, Dot Within First A of AMERICA, Plain Edge • BW-10, S-NC-3, B-7. *Breen dies:* 3-E. *Recorded population:* 4.

1795, ONE / CENT Centered, Dot Within First A of AMERICA, Plain Edge (BW-10, S-NC-3, B-7).

Obverse: Same as preceding. Now relapped so as to remove many details.

Reverse: Leaf tip under lower-left serif of T of STATES. Rightmost leaf tip of pair to left of O of ON is about halfway up the O. Pair of leaves to left of C of CENT extend nearly to its top; berry above leftmost leaf in pair. *Points of distinction:* A bulge develops at the top, probably early in the life of the die, accounting for the rarity of the variety.

Notes: Grades are Poor-1 to AG-3. Discovered by Jack H. Beymer in July 1979 and published in April 1980.

1795, Pole Connected to Denticle, ONE / CENT Centered, Plain Edge •

BW-11, S-78, B-8. *Breen dies: 5-F.* ***Estimated population:*** Thousands.

Obverse: *Date:* Serif of 1 close to hair, upper right of 5 touches the neck. Base of 5 centered over a denticle left of its center. Date distant from border. Compare to BW-4. *Pole points to:* Denticle, and runs into it, a definitive feature. *LIBERTY:* L distant from cap. All letters close. T well over hair to left of forehead. *Points of distinction:* Found perfect and with a faint crack under the jaw near the neck. On some examples the die is slightly eroded at the top of the 5, connecting that digit to the neck.

1795, Pole Connected to Denticle, ONE / CENT Centered, Plain Edge (BW-11, S-78, B-8).

Detail showing date and the pole connecting to a denticle.

Reverse: Leaf tip under upright of T of STATES. Rightmost leaf tip of pair to left of O of ON is about even with the base of the O. Pair of leaves to left of C of CENT extend about halfway up the letter; no berry above leftmost leaf in pair. *Points of distinction:* Multiple clash marks are seen.

Notes: This variety is known in Mint State.

1795, Date Spaced 1 79 5, Reeded Edge •

BW-13, S-79, B-9. *Breen dies: 6-G.* ***Recorded population:*** 5.

Obverse: *Date:* Spaced as 1 79 5 with 79 close. 1 close to hair and 5 close to neck. *Pole points to:* Left side of denticle. *LIBERTY:* BE wide. Top of T low. Bottom of Y low. *Points of distinction:* Upright of Y over junction between hair and forehead.

Reverse: Three leaves at apex. 14 leaves to

1795, Date Spaced 1 79 5, Reeded Edge (BW-13, S-79, B-9), a rarity. The finest known example.

the left, 18 to the right. 7 berries on each branch. Triple leaf below OF. This die was also used to coin 1796, Three Leaves Opposite OF, Single Leaf Over O of ONE, Reverse of 1794 (BW-43), and 1796, Three Leaves Opposite OF, Reverse of 1794 (BW-44, BW-45, BW-46, BW-47, and BW-48).

Notes: The finest is the Daniel W. Holmes Jr. coin variously graded as VG-8 and 10, other examples are Good and VG. With a fully reeded edge, unique among early cents, but similar to the edge of gold coins of the era. Struck in a collar, for reasons unknown. The reeding is not entirely regular (based on an examination by Jack Robinson in January 1989). Today this is one of the most "celebrated" varieties among early cents, in terms of collector comment. An example in any grade, if shown at an EAC meeting, is bound to attract interest. One example is a holed brockage, ex Homer K. Downing and Charles Ruby.

Numismatic Notes: The first publication of this variety seems to have been in the W.A. Lilliendahl Collection that was cataloged by William Harvey Strobridge with assistance from Edward Cogan, which was sold in 1,232 lots from May 26 to 28, 1862, in one of the most popular auction venues of the time: Bangs, Merwin & Co., Irving Building, 594–596 Broadway, New York. The cent was described as, "1795 Thick die, milled edge, in excellent preservation, and excessively rare." This coin is not traced today, as evidenced by all known examples being in very low grades.[30]

THE JEFFERSON HEADS

1795, Jefferson Head, Lettered Edge • BW-15a and b, S-NC-1, B-10a and b. *Breen dies:* 7-H. *Recorded population:* 3.

1795, Jefferson Head, Lettered Edge (BW-15a, S-NC-1, B-10a).

Obverse: "Jefferson Head" portrait of Miss Liberty. No ribbon. Small date. Only the one die for the various Jefferson Head varieties.

Reverse: Highest leaf pair on the left at apex is mostly over the lower leaf pair on right side of apex. Leaf above O of ONE points to the left, past the tops of the letters. *Points of distinction:* In the late state, two cracks at the left.

Notes: Two minor edge variations: BW-15a (1 known) with FOR in large letters and leaf after DOLLAR pointing downward. Discovered in June 1974 by Anthony Terranova and Joseph Rose. Fine-12 with obverse scratch. BW-15b (2 known), occurring in VF-20 and Fair-2.

1795, Jefferson Head, Lettered Edge • BW-16a, S-NC-4, B-11a. *Breen dies:* 7-I. *Recorded population:* 2.

1795, Jefferson Head, Lettered Edge (BW-16a, S-NC-4, B-11a).

Obverse: Same as preceding.

Reverse: Highest leaf pair on left at apex is slightly over a leaf on the right side of the apex. Leaf above O of ONE points to N.

Notes: Lettered edge. Leaf after DOLLAR points upward. Discovered by Curtis Ray Whitson in August 1991. G-5 (Daniel W. Holmes Jr. Collection) and Poor, holed.

1795, Jefferson Head, Plain Edge • BW-16b, S-80, B-11b. *Breen dies:* 7-I. *Estimated population:* 45 to 60.

1795, Jefferson Head, Plain Edge (BW-16b, S-80, B-11b).

Obverse: Same as preceding.

Reverse: Same as preceding.

Notes: VF is the highest grade known. This is the plain-edged version and the only readily collectible example of the Jefferson Head, although it is rare. Beware of electrotypes (see Numismatic Notes). The finest is VF-35 (per Breen). One example is known struck over a Liberty

Cap cent with Lettered Edge, earlier in the Homer K. Downing Collection, later in the Daniel W. Holmes Jr. Collection.

Numismatic Notes: W.E. Woodward in his sale of the Levick, Emery, Ilsley, and Abbey Collections, October 18 through 22, 1864, offered lot 671, "1795 Sometimes called the 'Jefferson Head,'" an early use of this term.

Édouard Frossard's description (*Monograph*, 1879):

> Jefferson Head. The head is entirely different from any variety of this or other dates. The profile is in a nearly straight line from the hair to the point of nose; the lips pouting, the chin pointed, the hair straight, with a few thin locks at the end, one of which forms a long double curl under the bust, and points at 1 in date. There is no band around the hair. The legend LIBERTY in large letters, widely spaced, is equally distant from cap, head and edge. The date between 179 wide, the 5 a little nearer 9. *Reverse:* ONE CENT in centre large; the legend and the fractional denominator also large. The wreath bears large elongated leaves, nearly all double and forked, pointing in every direction, with apparently eleven berries on the left, and twelve on right branch. Struck on a thick planchet; only traces of milling are discernable on the obverse, and but little on reverse. Edge plain; diameter 29 mm.

Mention of an example was printed under "Replies to Correspondents," in *Mason's Coin Collectors' Herald*, March 1880, in answer to a query from A.C.L. of Hartford:

> We sold the celebrated 'Jefferson Head' cent 1795 some years ago to the late A.S. Robinson for $90. It has a queer history. Bought by us for one dollar and a half in 1868, sold to [J. Colvin] Randall for $10, sold by Mr. R. at auction to Mr. Haseltine for $145, thence to Mr. Fewsmith for about the same amount; thence transferred to us in 1872, with the above result. Now owned by a large manufacturer in Massachusetts and valued at $300. We have had three specimens, all poor—besides the latter which is the finest known of the 'Jefferson Head' variety.

Mason had electrotypes made of a coin owned by J. Colvin Randall and offered them for sale for 50¢ each. In that era electrotypes were widely bought and sold as "fillers." The British Museum supplied electrotypes of its coins on special order, and in the early 1900s the American Numismatic Society did the same (without reference here to Jefferson Head cents). Some of Mason's electrotypes survived to the modern era and are occasionally confused with originals.

	Cert	Avg	%MS	AG-3	G-4	VG-8	F-12	VF-20
1795, Jefferson Head, Plain Edge	1	10.0	0%	$13,750	$23,750	$33,330	$56,670	$121,250

1796, Liberty Cap

Circulation mintage (assumed): 109,825.

This was a year of change. It seems that early in 1796 the Mint was busy striking cents from 1795-dated dies. Then came the production of 1796, Liberty Cap, cents, with deliveries extending from May 12 to June 8. These were ostensibly comprised of 109,825 coins—a figure which is per a comment in *Mason's Coin and Stamp Collectors' Magazine*, December 1867. Though *Mason's* is not necessarily a reliable source, in this instance the periodical quoted a Mint officer. The change to the Draped Bust motif began afterward, with the first deliveries of the new design on October 12.

The heads on 1796, Liberty Cap, cents are in slightly higher relief than are those of 1795, in some instances resulting in the reverses being more shallowly defined, as more copper had to flow into the deep obverse die in the coining press. This also had the effect of the reverses wearing down more quickly once the coins were placed into circulation. On many lower-grade 1796 cents in existence today, the obverse is a grade or two higher than the reverse. On the obverse of coins from certain dies, if Miss Liberty is oriented with the profile of her face more or less vertical, the date can be off center to the left. On the same coins, if the date is centered at the bottom, the profile is tilted back.

The reverses are subtly different from earlier Liberty Caps in that the denticles are smaller and the leaves are thinner. All have a single leaf at each side of the wreath apex, the so-called Reverse of 1795. Certain 1796 reverses were later used in 1797 and 1798.

Director Boudinot, on December 22, 1795, suggested to the Secretary of State that planchets be imported, and on March 1, 1796, he ordered ten tons of copper, with the planchets to weigh seven pennyweights, from William L. Coltman of London. In the following October he wrote to Coltman that the planchets had arrived on the *Rebecca* under Captain James Hughes, and were badly executed—having been cut from coarse rolled sheet copper almost as rough as cast iron—and were not clean.[31]

As a class, the 1796, Liberty Cap, cents are scarcer than those of the year before. The quality of the planchets varies, due no doubt to the acquisition of copper from diverse sources. Examples are available in all grades from well worn to the very occasional Mint State. Apart from the basic type, there are no particular varieties that have attracted attention beyond specialists. Among the varieties, some are quite scarce, but none are impossibly rare or expensive. Thus, this is the first year for which the completion of a full set of Liberty Cap die combinations is a possibility.

Typical values for 1796, Liberty Cap. Rare varieties may be worth more.

	Cert	Avg	%MS	G-4	VG-8	F-12	VF-20	EF-40	AU-50	MS-60BN
1796, Liberty Cap	141	25.7	11%	$430	$640	$1,375	$2,725	$6,000	$13,500	$27,830

1796, No Triple Leaves on Outside of Right Branch • BW-1, S-91, B-1.
Breen dies: 1-A. *Estimated population:* 400 to 500.

Obverse: *Date:* 1 below hair. Numerals widely and about evenly spaced, but 96 slightly closer. 6 below neck. *Pole points to:* Space between denticles. *LIBERTY:* L close to cap. Fairly closely spaced. *Points of distinction:* There is a die bulge from the rim to the nose and in the left field, the intensity of which increases with subsequent strikes. Sometimes there is a crack from the back of the lower hair and another through the center of 6 in the date.

1796, No Triple Leaves on Outside of Right Branch (BW-1, S-91, B-1).

Reverse: Outside triple leaves opposite IT and ED. C of CENT distant and leans right. *Points of distinction:* This variety exists from a perfect die and also with a crack through the second S of STATES and from the rim to I of AMERICA. Similarities between this reverse die and that used to coin BW-2 indicate that BW-1 may have been the first 1796, Liberty Cap, struck, rather than the last, as is often thought.[32]

Notes: This variety is known in Mint State.

1796, Closest Date, Pole Very Close to Bust

• BW-2, S-81, B-2. *Breen dies:* 2-B. *Estimated population:* 300 to 400.

Obverse: *Date:* 1 barely touches hair. 17 very wide, 79 closer, 96 closest. 6 close to neck. *Pole points to:* Space between denticles, and is very close to the bust. *LIBERTY:* L barely touches the cap. BER wide. *Points of distinction:* Typically seen with a rough area from the left rim to the cap. Sometimes with a light

1796, Closest Date, Pole Very Close to Bust (BW-2, S-81, B-2).

crack from below the nose to the rim, and another from the rim, past the right of Y, and to the nose.

Reverse: Outside triple leaves opposite IT, ED, and CA. *Points of distinction:* This die was used to coin BW-2 and 1798, Style 2 Hair, Small 8, Style 2 Letters, Reverse of 1795 (BW-3). Relapped in a later state.

Notes: The highest grades for this variety are AU and Mint State (unique). Dr. Sheldon observed diameters from 28 mm to 30.5 mm for this variety.

1796, Closest Date, Pole Very Close to Bust, Triple Leaf Opposite AM

• BW-3, S-82, B-3. *Breen dies:* 2-C. *Estimated population:* 75 to 120.

Obverse: Same as preceding. *Points of distinction:* A faint bulge develops in the field. Some die chips are seen.

Reverse: Outside triple leaves opposite IT, ED, AM, and CA. *Points of distinction:* This die was used to coin BW-3, BW-4, BW-5,

1796, Closest Date, Pole Very Close to Bust, Triple Leaf Opposite AM (BW-3, S-82, B-3).

and 1798, Style 1 Hair, Large 8, Style 1 Letters, Reverse of 1795 (BW-2). A small crack is from the base of E of AMERICA to the adjacent R.

Notes: The highest grades for this variety are EF and AU. This variety is difficult to find with good eye appeal.

1796, Triple Leaf Opposite AM

• BW-4, S-83, B-4. *Breen dies:* 3-C. *Estimated population:* 120 to 160.

Obverse: *Date:* 1 below hair. 17 very wide, 79 closer, 96 closest. 6 close to neck. *Pole points to:* Denticle. *LIBERTY:* L close to but does not touch the cap. IB wide. Base of Y low. *Points of distinction:* Breen reports only two examples of this variety without the break between the end of the pole and the

1796, Triple Leaf Opposite AM (BW-4, S-83, B-4).

bust. Examples are known with a rim break from the left of B, along the top of RTY, and to the rim. Die scaling is seen across the lower edge of the cap and in front of the mouth.

Reverse: Same as preceding. This die was used to coin BW-3, BW-4, BW-5, and 1798, Style 1 Hair, Large 8, Style 1 Letters, Reverse of 1795 (BW-2).

Notes: AU is the highest grade known. This variety is difficult to find with good eye appeal.

1796, Date Slopes Down to the Right • BW-5, S-84, B-5. *Breen dies:* 4-C. *Estimated population:* 300 to 400.

Obverse: *Date:* 1 close to hair. Date slopes down to the right so that the 6 is slightly closer to the denticles than to the neck. Definitive. *Pole points to:* Denticle, and is distant from neck. *LIBERTY:* LIBER wide. T partly over junction between hair and forehead (also definitive). *Points of distinction:* Liberty's mouth is slightly open. Denticles are thin and widely spaced. A sinking of the die caused a swelling at 6. This is the most distinctive die among the 1796 obverses.

1796, Date Slopes Down to the Right (BW-5, S-84, B-5).

Detail showing date sloping down to the right and becoming closer to the denticles.

Reverse: Same as preceding. This die was used to coin BW-3, BW-4, BW-5, and 1798, Style 1 Hair, Large 8, Style 1 Letters, Reverse of 1795 (BW-2). *Points of distinction:* Sometimes with a crack through the top of the letters in OF.

Notes: This variety is known in Mint State.

1796, Date Slopes Down to the Right • BW-6, S-85, B-6. *Breen dies:* 4-D. *Estimated population:* 60 to 75.

Obverse: Same as the preceding.

Reverse: Outside triple leaves opposite UN, IT, ED, and CA. Segment of a leaf covers branch below center of M. Three leaves opposite O of ONE; two leaves near T of CENT; leaf tip under left edge of O in OF. Numerator is too far right above the bar; bar is closer to left ribbon than to the right. Denticles opposite CA and lower are irregular in size and spacing. *Points of distinction:* On a later state the die is relapped, removing some of the lower-relief features.

1796, Date Slopes Down to the Right (BW-6, S-85, B-6).

Detail of the reverse showing irregularity of the denticles.

Notes: This variety can be found in VF to AU, the latter unique. This variety is difficult to find with good eye appeal.

1796, Date Slopes Down to the Right • BW-7, S-86, B-7. *Breen dies:* 4-E. *Estimated population:* 45 to 60.

Obverse: Same as the preceding.

Reverse: Outside triple leaves opposite UN, ED, RI, and CA. Three leaves opposite O of ONE; two leaves near T of CENT; leaf tip far past left edge of O in OF and closer to S.

1796, Date Slopes Down to the Right (BW-7, S-86, B-7).

Notes: The highest grades this variety is found in are EF and AU, extremely rare at either level. This variety is difficult to find with good eye appeal.

1796, Date Slopes Down to the Right • BW-8, S-87, B-8. *Breen dies:* 4-F. *Estimated population:* 300 to 400.

Obverse: Same as the preceding. *Points of distinction:* Some later impressions have a light crack from the denticles under 7, across the bust and the end of the pole, in an arc to the border above.

Reverse: Outside triple leaves opposite UN,

1796, Date Slopes Down to the Right (BW-8, S-87, B-8).

IT, ED, and A. Two leaves opposite O of ONE; three leaves below T of CENT. *Points of distinction:* This die was used to coin BW-8, BW-9, BW-10, and 1798, Style 1 Hair, Large 8, Style 2 Letter, Reverse of 1795 (BW-1). Multiple clash marks are seen.

Notes: The highest grades this variety is found in are AU and Mint State (unique).

1796, Club Pole • BW-9, S-88, B-9. *Breen dies:* 5-F. *Estimated population:* 120 to 160.

Obverse: *Date:* About evenly spaced, but 96 slightly closer. 1 near hair, 6 near neck. *Pole points to:* Space between denticles. "Club Pole" variety, with pole thicker at the end, somewhat like a baseball bat. *LIBERTY:* L touches cap. BE wide. *Points of distinction:* Sometimes with a small crack from the denticles through the right side of 7 to the neck.

1796, Club Pole (BW-9, S-88, B-9).

Reverse: Same as the preceding. This die was used to coin BW-8, BW-9, BW-10, and 1798, Style 1 Hair, Large 8, Style 2 Letter, Reverse of 1795 (BW-1).

Notes: The variety can be found in are VF to AU, the latter exceedingly rare.

1796 • BW-10, S-89, B-10. *Breen dies:* 6-F. *Estimated population:* 300 to 400.

Obverse: *Date:* 1 close to hair. Widely spaced, but 96 slightly closer. 6 barely touches neck. *Pole points to:* Space between denticles and is distant from them. *LIBERTY:* IBERT wide. *Points of distinction:* Denticles are large and some are irregular. Clash marks develop and a bulge is seen at the bottom border.

Reverse: Same as the preceding. This die was used to coin BW-8, BW-9, BW-10, and 1798, Style 1 Hair, Large 8, Style 2 Letter, Reverse of 1795 (BW-1). *Points of distinction:* Clash marks develop.

1796 (BW-10, S-89, B-10).

Detail of 6 touching neck.

Notes: The finest example of this variety is a unique EF-40. Despite the large population, the finest attainable is only VF or so. Eye appeal is a problem on most examples.

1796 • BW-11, S-90, B-11. *Breen dies:* 6-G. *Estimated population:* 30 to 45.

Obverse: Same as the preceding. *Points of distinction:* A rare late state has a crack through the top of LIBER.

Reverse: Outside triple leaves opposite UN, ED, and C. Two leaves opposite O of ONE; two leaves below T of CENT. Numerator 1 is too far right above the bar. Denticles are

1796 (BW-11, S-90, B-11).

heavy and closely spaced. *Points of distinction:* This die was used to coin BW-11 and 1797, Reverse of 1795 (BW-1); 1797, Plain Edge, Wide 1 7 97 Date, Reverse of 1795 (BW-2a); 1797, Gripped Edge, Wide 1 7 97 Date, Reverse of 1795 (BW-2b); 1797, Reverse of 1795, Plain Edges (BW-3a); and 1797, Reverse of 1795, Gripped Edge (BW-3b). This variety exists from a perfect die and also with a short crack above N of ONE. The dies are usually oriented in the same direction.

Notes: This variety can be found in Mint State, and it is extremely rare as such. This is the most difficult 1796, Liberty Cap, to locate in any grade, and as most lack good eye appeal, the challenge is even greater in this respect.

DRAPED BUST (1796–1807)

Designer: *Robert Scot.* **Weight:** *168 grains (10.89 grams).*
Composition: *Copper.* **Diameter:** *Average 29 mm.* **Edge:** *Plain.*

**1796, 6 Berries Left and Right, Leaf Tip
Opposite D, Reverse of 1797, Large
Fraction (BW-65, S-119, B-40).**

The Draped Bust cent made its debut in 1796, following a coinage of Liberty Cap cents the same year. The motif, from a drawing by Gilbert Stuart, was first employed on certain silver dollars of 1795.

The new design proved to be very durable and was used through and including 1807. While the 1799 is a classic rarity and the 1804 is elusive, enough exist of most other dates that finding a choice one will be no problem. As a rule, the earlier dates are scarcer than the later ones. Generally, they are struck on high-quality planchets, many of which were imported from Boulton & Watt, of Birmingham, England.

Most cents of this type are well worn, some nearly smooth. Such levels as Fine and Very Fine are readily available and form the basis of many collections. At the EF and AU levels the coins are progressively scarcer. Mint State coins are rare for most varieties, except for some that were part of the famous Nichols Find (described below).

Striking can vary in quality. Some areas of the denticles are apt to be weak, and on the reverse the higher leaves in the wreath are often lightly defined. This is apt to vary from one variety to another. Though the planchet quality is generally good, many dark and porous coins are in the marketplace. Except for rare die varieties, one can be choosy and cherrypick for quality.

THE NICHOLS FIND

Chances are excellent that if you encounter a Mint State 1796 or 1797 copper large cent, it will be linked by pedigree to the famous Nichols Find (also known as the Goodhue-Nichols Find).

According to numismatic tradition, these pieces came from an original bag of cents obtained in late 1797 or early 1798 by Benjamin Goodhue, who was born in Salem, Massachusetts, in 1748 and died there in 1814. Goodhue, a Federalist, was a representative to Congress from 1789 to 1796 and a senator from 1796 to 1800. He is said to have been the grandfather of Mrs. Nichols.

If Goodhue obtained the pieces at the Mint, it would probably have been after November 21, 1797, for during 1797 coins were only delivered by the coiner to the treasurer from November 22 to December 18. Blank planchets had been imported recently from Matthew Boulton of Birmingham, England, such planchets being remarkable for their high quality (in sharp contrast to those made within the Mint, often from copper of uncertain purity and often irregular). As a result, coins in collections today, and attributed to this hoard, are apt to have particularly smooth and glossy surfaces.

It is believed that Goodhue gave the coins to his daughters, who continued to pass them down in the family. Eventually, they were distributed from the Salem area.

One account quotes a rumor that the coins came from Major C.P. Nichols of Springfield, Massachusetts.[33]

In any event, by 1858 or 1859, the numismatic community was aware of the coins, at which time they traded for about $1 each. By 1863 all of the pieces had been dispersed—apparently by David Nichols—by which time they had a market value of about $3 to $4 apiece.

Another story suggests, citing an erroneous date, that they were dispersed to collectors, "perhaps just prior to 1863," and that "David Nichols of Gallows Hill, near Salem, passed them out at face value."[34]

The assigning of the quantity of 1,000 pieces to the hoard is assumed from Mint records that show in 1797 that the Mint regularly issued cents in bags of 1,000 and boxes of 5,000 coins. As at least several hundred examples are known to exist today, the estimate of 1,000 may be reasonable.

This first-person account by John Robinson, of Salem, Massachusetts, sheds further light on the quantity in this statement, although by the time he saw the coins it is probable that some had already been paid out:

> I began in 1857 with a bright copper cent of that year I found in my mother's purse, and a handful of coins from the Far East from an old sea chest of my father's. Additions were gained by looking over the coins in the tills of the Salem shopkeepers who allowed me to poke over their silver and copper coins unrestricted. The old tollhouse on Beverly Bridge furnished an almost Uncirculated cent of 1823, and a beautiful cent of 1800 over 1799 came from a Salem shoe shop. These were obtained at one cent each.
>
> The older collectors helped us, too, and David Nichols, living near Gallows Hill, would occasionally open the bag of mint-bright cents of 1796 and 1797 and give us one of each. The lot came, it was said, from the Hon. Benjamin Goodhue, who received them in part pay for his services in the U.S. Senate. As I remember them at the time there were about 50 or 60 of each date in the bag.[35]

Today, the typical Nichols Find cent is apt to be glossy brown with somewhat prooflike fields, toned a medium brown. Varieties attributable to this source include 1796, 6 Berries Left and Right, Leaf Tip Opposite D, Reverse of 1797, Large Fraction (BW-65); 1797, Berries: 6-6 (BW-13); and 1797, Closest Date, Berries 6-6 (BW-21).

Examples of 1798, Style 1 Hair, Large 8 Embedded in Drapery (BW-15), which was not in the Nichols Find, appear to have been struck on planchets from the same Boulton lot and were probably made very early in 1798.[36]

DESIGN DETAILS

On the obverse the head of Miss Liberty faces to the right, her hair behind, some tied with a ribbon at the back, and other tresses falling to her shoulder. Her bosom at the lower right is draped in cloth. The letters of LIBERTY are above her head, and the date is between the bust and the bottom border. Denticles are around the border. The same design was used on half cents from 1800 to 1808, as described earlier.

The reverse is of the same general style as that used on the Liberty Cap cents, but somewhat more standardized—this increasingly being the case for most coinage designs as the years progressed and technology became more advanced.

The wreath is open at the top and tied with a ribbon bow below. Some early dies have one leaf to each side of the wreath apex, the so-called Reverse of 1795, but most in this series have one leaf at the upper left and two at the upper right.

Around the outside of the wreath is the inscription UNITED STATES OF AMERICA. At the center in two lines is ONE CENT. The fraction 1/100 is below the ribbon bow. Denticles are around the border.

The portrait and wreath hubs were made by Robert Scot, chief engraver at the Mint, from a drawing by Gilbert Stuart. It appears that various Mint employees assisted in the making of the working dies—apparently including at least one mechanic or other person not skilled as a die sinker, as evidenced by

---

the glaring errors on several different 1802 reverses. Craig Sholley, in his studies of contemporary Mint records, found them incomplete for this period. Accordingly, it is not known if an apprentice or laborer was assigned to the chief coiner's department.

GRADING STANDARDS

MS-60 to 70 (Mint State). *Obverse:* In the lower–Mint State grades, MS-60 and 61, some slight abrasion can be seen on the higher areas of the portrait, especially the cheek, and the hair behind the forehead. Luster in the field is incomplete, particularly in the center of the open areas, which on this type are very open, especially at the right. At MS-63, luster should be nearly complete, and no abrasions evident. In higher levels, the lus-

1797, Reverse of 1797, Stems; BW-21, S-123, B-12. Graded MS-62BN.

ter is complete and deeper, and some original mint color should be seen. MS-64 coins may have some slight discoloration or scattered contact marks. A well-graded MS-65 or higher coin will have full, rich luster; no marks visible except under magnification; and a nice blend of brown toning or nicely mixed (not stained or blotchy) mint color and natural brown toning. *Reverse:* In the lower–Mint State ranges some abrasions are seen on the higher areas of the leaves. Generally, luster is complete in all Mint State ranges, as the open areas are protected by the lettering and wreath. Sharpness of the leaves can vary by die variety, so check this aspect. Otherwise, the same comments apply as for the obverse.

Illustrated coin: This handsome crimson-brown example is well struck, especially on the obverse. The tiny divot in the field in front of Liberty's throat is a planchet flaw, rather than damage. The coin has no significant blemishes on either side. (Note on the reverse what appears to be a scratch across the two Ns in ONE and CENT. This is actually a scratch on the plastic slab, not on the coin; if one were to examine the coin in person and tilt the slab, the scratch would appear to move in relation to the coin.)

AU-50, 53, 55, 58 (About Uncirculated). *Obverse:* Friction is seen on the higher parts, particularly the hair of Miss Liberty and the cheek. Friction and scattered marks are in the field, ranging from more extensive at AU-50 to minimal at AU-58. Luster may be seen in protected areas, minimal at AU-50, more visible at AU-58. At AU-58 the field may retain some luster, as well. In many instances, the luster is smaller in area and lesser in "depth"

1803, Small Date, Small Fraction; BW-29, S-247, B-5. Graded AU-50.

than on the reverse of this type. Cents of this type can be very beautiful in About Uncirculated. *Reverse:* Friction is seen on the higher wreath leaves and (not as easy to discern) on the letters. Again, the die variety should be checked. The fields, protected by the designs, show friction, but not as noticeably as on the obverse. At AU-55 and 58, little if any friction is seen. The reverse may have original luster, toned brown, minimal on lower About Uncirculated grades, often extensive at the AU-58 level. General rules for cents follow the half cents of the same type.

Illustrated coin: This is the popular "Mumps" variety, with a bulge below the chin. The coin has many tiny scattered marks, but is pleasing overall.

EF-40, 45 (Extremely Fine). *Obverse:* Wear is seen on the portrait overall, with reduction or elimination of some separation of hair strands on the highest part. By the standards of the Early American Coppers society, if the "spit curl" in front of Liberty's ear is missing, the coin is not EF. The cheek shows more wear than on higher grades, and the drapery covering the bosom is lightly worn on the higher areas. Often weakness in the separa-

1803; BW-24, S-256, B-15. Graded EF-45.

tion of the drapery lines can be attributed to weakness in striking. Luster is minimal or nonexistent at EF-40, and may survive in amongst the letters of LIBERTY at EF-45. *Reverse:* Wear is seen on the highest wreath and ribbon areas, and on the letters. Luster is minimal, but likely more noticeable than on the obverse, as the fields are protected by the designs and lettering. The ANA grading standards state that at EF-45 nearly all of the "ribbing" (veins) in the leaves is visible, and that at EF-40 about 75% is sharp. In practice, striking plays a part as well, and some leaves may be weak even in higher grades.

Illustrated coin: This is a high-level coin from the aspect of sharpness, with details perhaps befitting AU-50, but reduced slightly due to some planchet porosity. Nice eye appeal overall.

VF-20, 30 (Very Fine). *Obverse:* Wear on the portrait has reduced the hair detail further, especially to the left of the forehead. The rolling curls are solid or flat on their highest areas, as well as by the ribbon behind the hair. The border denticles are blended together, with many indistinct. No luster is seen. *Reverse:* The leaf details are nearly completely worn away at VF-20, and with slight detail at VF-30. The ANA grading standards are a bit stricter:

1803; BW-14, S-260, B-19. Graded VF-20.

30% remaining at VF-20 and 50% at VF-30. In the marketplace, fewer details can be seen on most certified coins at these levels. The border denticles are blended together with many indistinct. No luster is seen.

Illustrated coin: The wreath is bold, but most leaves are worn flat on their high parts.

F-12, 15 (Fine). *Obverse:* Many hair details are worn away, with perhaps one-half to one-third visible, mainly at the edges and behind the shoulder. Border denticles are weak or worn away in areas. F-15 shows slightly more detail. Porosity and scattered marks become increasingly common at this level and lower. *Reverse:* The wreath leaves are worn flat, but their edges are distinct. Little if anything remains of leaf vein details. Border denticles

1799, 9 Over 8; BW-2, S-188, B-2. Graded F-12.

are weak or worn away in areas. F-15 shows slightly more detail.

Illustrated coin: Note the gray, toned surfaces, with very light porosity and some scattered marks. The date is full and clear (sometimes a challenge). Cents of 1799, 9 Over 8, and 1799 are the keys to the series and often are graded liberally.

VG-8, 10 (Very Good). *Obverse:* The portrait is well worn, although the eye can be seen, as can hints of hair detail. Some hair at the left shows separation. Curls now appear as mostly solid blobs. Border denticles are worn away on most varieties, and the rim, although usually present, begins to blend into the field. LIBERTY and the date are bold in most areas, with some lightness toward the rim. VG-10 is sometimes applied to especially nice Very Good coins. *Reverse:* The

1803, Small Date, Small Fraction; BW-6, S-245, B-2. Graded VG-8.

wreath, bow, and lettering are seen in outline form, and some leaves and letters may be indistinct in parts. The border may blend into the field on some of the periphery. The strength of the letters is dependent to an extent on the specific die variety.

Illustrated coin: This is a late die state with a massive "cud" break on the lower-right reverse rim.

G-4, 6 (Good). *Obverse:* The portrait is worn smooth and is seen only in outline form, although the eye position can be discerned and some curls can be made out. LIBERTY is readable, but the tops of the letters may fade away. The date is clearly readable, but the lower part of the numerals may be very weak or worn away. The border will blend into the field more extensively than on the preceding, but significant areas will still be seen. *Reverse:*

1799; BW-1, S-189, B-3. Graded G-4.

Extensive wear is seen overall. From one-half to two-thirds of the letters in UNITED STATES OF AMERICA and the fraction numerals are worn away. On most varieties, ONE CENT is fairly strong. G-6 is often assigned to finer examples in this category.

Illustrated coin: Note the dark planchet, as typical, and some light porosity.

AG-3 (About Good). *Obverse:* Wear is more extensive than on the preceding. The portrait is visible only in outline. LIBERTY is weak, partially worn away, but usually discernible. The date is weak, and the bottoms of the digits may be worn away, but must be identifiable. *Reverse:* Parts of the wreath are visible in outline form, and all but a few letters are gone. ONE CENT is usually mostly or completely discernible, depending on the variety.

1799, 9 Over 8; BW-2, S-188, B-2. Graded AG-3.

Illustrated coin: The obverse, if graded separately, would qualify as G-4, but the reverse does not come up to that level.

1796, Draped Bust

Circulation mintage (assumed): 363,375.

The first delivery of Draped Bust cents took place in October 1796, according to figures supplied to *Mason's Coin and Stamp Collectors' Magazine*, December 1867, by a Mint official. William E. DuBois and some others at the Mint were interested in the history of the institution at that time, but certain of the information Mint people supplied was not reliable. That said, we can only assume that these figures may be correct, but acknowledge that we have no way of verification. The annual *Report of the Director of the Mint* gave calendar-year figures which often, including for 1796, were not relevant to the actual number of coins struck bearing that date.

Prior to 1836, the Mint often reused serviceable dies (including obverses) from prior years. Also, the Mint would occasionally hold over coins struck at the very end of a year and deliver them in early January of the next. The figures in the *Annual Report of the Director of the Mint* are thus merely the number of coins *delivered* during that year and have little relevance to the actual number of coins bearing any given date. As noted earlier, this created many "mintages" for coins that did not bear the calendar-year date, such as 12,170 half cents struck in 1799 from earlier dies.

Mint Director Robert Maskell Patterson, who served from 1835 to 1851, disliked this practice, feeling that the official figures should represent the date on the coins. He essentially put an end to this arrangement, and (with some exceptions) the figures from 1836 on (especially for copper) do represent the coins struck for that date.

The 1867 account noted that 363,375 Draped Bust (presumably) cents were delivered through and including November 24, 1796. Craig Sholley found that the treasurer's account book corroborates the figure, but gives December 31 as the final delivery date. However, this is an accounting date and not necessarily the exact date the coiner delivered the coins to the treasurer. Also, as Dr. Sheldon pointed out, additional 1796-dated coins were struck in 1797, as evidenced by the fact that their reverses were also used—in an earlier die state—on some cents with 1797 obverses.[37]

Draped Bust cents of this date come in two easily discernible reverse styles: with one leaf at each side of the wreath apex—Reverse of 1795—and with one leaf on the left and two on the right—Reverse of 1794, and also the Reverse of 1797. In the following listing the Reverse of 1795 varieties are listed first, for ease of attribution. The Sheldon and Breen texts comingle them. Certain obverse dies mated with Reverse of 1795 dies were also mated with Reverse of 1797 dies and are listed in the Reverse of 1797 section. As a general rule, denticles on 1796, Draped Bust, cents are not prominent, and some show hardly any denticles at all, this being particularly true of obverses. Obverse denticles tend to be long and thin, while those on the reverse are variously long and thin or short and somewhat pointed.

Cents of this type and date are usually seen in circulated grades, from well worn upward. At the EF level most are rare, and AU and Mint State coins range from very rare to extremely rare. Exceptions are provided by Nichols Find varieties, often seen in Mint State. However the demand for them by seekers of "trophy coins," who are usually not interested in other varieties in lesser grades, has always furnished a strong market when they cross the auction block.

Cents of this date and type are generally rare. Unlike the situation for collectors a generation ago, nearly all are expensive, even at the Good and VG levels. As always, cherrypicking for quality is advised.

ONE LEAF EACH SIDE OF WREATH APEX—1796 WITH REVERSE STYLE OF 1795

The nearly dozen different varieties can be easily distinguished by checking the obverse first and then the three-leaf clusters on the reverse. Remarkably, each of the different reverses has a different cluster arrangement.

Typical values for 1796, Draped Bust, cents with the Reverse of 1795. Rare varieties may be worth more.

	Cert	Avg	%MS	G-4	VG-8	F-12	VF-20	EF-40	AU-50	MS-60BN	MS-63BN
1796, Draped Bust, Reverse of 1795	19	23.6	5%	$490	$850	$1,580	$2,940	$6,375	$12,875	$19,500	$28,830

1796, Numerals 796 Equidistant From Border, Reverse of 1795 •

BW-15, S-97, B-20. *Breen dies:* 13-J. *Estimated population:* 300 to 400.

Obverse: Bases of 796 each about the same distance from the border, which is definitive for an obverse mated with a Reverse of 1795. *Points of distinction:* From a perfect die, but also seen with a crack over TY developing into a rim break and a break at the right rim.

1796, Numerals 796 Equidistant From Border, Reverse of 1795 (BW-15, S-97, B-20).

Reverse: Outside triple leaves opposite UN, IT, ED, and CA. Only Style of 1795 reverse with this configuration among 1796 cents. Four berries on each branch. In fraction, first 0 leans right and is distant from 1.

Notes: The highest-known grades for this variety are EF and AU, and it is very rare at these levels.

1796, 96 Close, 6 Does Not Lean Sharply Right, Reverse of 1795 •

BW-16, S-98, B-21. *Breen dies:* 14-J. *Estimated population:* 120 to 160.

Obverse: 179 wide, 96 close, 6 does not lean sharply right; knob of 6 is just slightly farther right than the curve below it; bottom of 9 only slightly higher than bottom of 7 (Compare to BW-32). *Points of distinction:* There is a crack from the rim to the upper right of Y.

1796, 96 Close, 6 Does Not Lean Sharply Right, Reverse of 1795 (BW-16, S-98, B-21).

Reverse: Same as preceding. *Points of distinction:* Seen with a perfect die and also with a crack at the first A of AMERICA.

Notes: This variety can be found in Mint State, and is very rare so fine.

1796, 96 Close, 6 Does Not Lean Sharply Right, Reverse of 1795 •

BW-17, S-99, B-22. *Breen dies:* 14-K. *Estimated population:* 45 to 60.

Obverse: Same as preceding. *Points of distinction:* Some die deterioration is seen at the throat. There is a crack from the rim to the upper right of Y. Sometimes seen with a crack from the rim behind the shoulder, up through the ribbon to B to the rim.

1796, 96 Close, 6 Does Not Lean Sharply Right, Reverse of 1795 (BW-17, S-99, B-22).

Reverse: Triple leaf cluster opposite D and ER. Only Style of 1795 reverse with this configuration among 1796 cents.

Notes: VF is the highest grade known. This variety is difficult to find with good eye appeal.

1796, T Over Junction of Hair and Forehead, Reverse of 1795 • BW-20, S-NC-4, B-23. *Breen dies:* 15-K. *Estimated population:* 30 to 45.

Obverse: T over junction of hair and forehead, the only obverse die with this feature mated with a Reverse of 1795, and thus definitive. 17 very close; 796 evenly spaced and slightly wider. *Points of distinction:* This die was used to coin BW-20, BW-40, and BW-53.

1796, T Over Junction of Hair and Forehead, Reverse of 1795 (BW-20, S-NC-4, B-23).

Reverse: Same as preceding. *Points of distinction:* On a rare late state there is a crack from the rim to the top of TES.

Notes: VG is the highest grade known.

1796, Date Hyphenated 17-96, Reverse of 1795 • BW-24, S-NC-2, B-31. *Breen dies:* 19-Q. *Reported population:* 11.

Obverse: Date with hyphen-like flaw causing it to read 17-96. Date widely spaced. 6 close to drapery. Rough patch in the field below the ribbon knot. *Points of distinction:* This die was used to coin BW-24, BW-25, BW-26, BW-27, BW-55, and BW-56.

1796, Date Hyphenated 17-96, Reverse of 1795 (BW-24, S-NC-2, B-31). For detail of hyphen, see BW-26.

Reverse: Outside triple leaves opposite UN, D, ME, and CA. Only Style of 1795 reverse with this configuration among 1796 cents. O in OF slightly low and leans right. Lowest leaf in cluster of three close to junction of AM. 1 of denominator far left and touches or nearly touches ribbon. T of CENT leans slightly to the right.

Notes: The highest grade known is EF (unique), followed by Fine, then VG.

1796, Date Hyphenated 17-96, Reverse of 1795 • BW-25, S-96, B-32. *Breen dies:* 19-R. *Estimated population:* 20 to 25.

Obverse: Same as preceding. *Points of distinction:* This die was used to coin BW-24, BW-25, BW-26, BW-27, BW-55, and BW-56.

1796, Date Hyphenated 17-96, Reverse of 1795 (BW-25, S-96, B-32). For detail of hyphen, see BW-26.

Reverse: Outside triple leaves opposite IT, D, and AM. Only Style of 1795 reverse with this configuration among 1796 cents. *Points of distinction:* From a perfect die and also with a crack across the die from T of UNITED, to M of AMERICA, and to the rim.

Notes: VG and Fine are the highest grades. Most range from Poor to AG-3. Walter Breen: "20 currently known."

1796, Date Hyphenated 17-96, Reverse of 1795 • BW-26, S-93, B-34.

Breen dies: 19-T. *Estimated population:* 300 to 400.

Obverse: Same as preceding. *Points of distinction:* A rough area in the left field below the ribbon knot is always present. Some have a light crack through the date. This die was used to coin BW-24, BW-25, BW-26, BW-27, BW-55, and BW-56.

1796, Date Hyphenated 17-96, Reverse of 1795 (BW-26, S-93, B-34).

Detail showing the hyphenated date.

Reverse: Outside triple leaves opposite IT, ED, M, and ER. Only Style of 1795 reverse with this configuration among 1796 cents. Five berries on the left branch, four on the right. Fraction bar tilts to the right. Second 0 high. *Points of distinction:* Early impressions are from a perfect die, after which cracks develop at AMERICA and expand to include the lower-right ribbon and fraction.

Notes: This variety is known in Mint State.

1796, Date Hyphenated 17-96, Reverse of 1795 • BW-27, S-95, B-35.

Breen dies: 19-U. *Estimated population:* 30 to 45.

Obverse: Same as preceding. *Points of distinction:* With cracks and also with die deterioration at ER. This die was used to coin BW-24, BW-25, BW-26, BW-27, BW-55, and BW-56.

1796, Date Hyphenated 17-96, Reverse of 1795 (BW-27, S-95, B-35).

Reverse: Outside triple leaves opposite UN, ED, and RI. Only Style of 1795 reverse with this configuration among 1796 cents. The leftmost leaf in the pair opposite C of CENT is skeletal and overlaps the stem. Fraction well centered and spaced; first 0 slightly low.

Notes: EF and AU are the highest grades known, and examples are exceedingly rare at those levels.

1796, 6 Leans Sharply Left, Reverse of 1795 • BW-30, S-116, B-36. *Breen dies: 20-V.* **Estimated population:** 60 to 75.

Obverse: 6 leans sharply left so that the knob is about centered over the rest of the digit; knob very close to drapery; definitive for an obverse die mated with a Reverse of 1795. Die used with BW-30 and BW-68.

Reverse: Outside triple leaves opposite UN, ED, and ER. Only reverse with this configuration. NITE wide, ST wide. Numerator close to or touches fraction bar; bar nearly touches the left ribbon.

Notes: VF is the highest grade known. This variety is difficult to find with good eye appeal.

1796, 6 Leans Sharply Left, Reverse of 1795 (BW-30, S-116, B-36).

Detail of leaning 6 in date.

1796, 96 Close, 6 Leans Sharply Right, Reverse of 1795 • BW-32, S-92, B-28. *Breen dies: 18-N.* **Estimated population:** 300 to 400.

Obverse: 6 leans so far right that the knob at the top is farther to the right than is the curve below it; bottom of 9 much higher than bottom of 7; definitive for an obverse die mated with a Reverse of 1795 die (compare to BW-16). **Points of distinction:** This die was used to coin both BW-32 and BW-54. Seen from a perfect die and also with cracks, including at the base of RTY nearly to the rim and another in front of the face. Later, more cracks develop, and the die shatters.

1796, 96 Close, 6 Leans Sharply Right, Reverse of 1795 (BW-32, S-92, B-28).

Detail of leaning 6 in date.

Reverse: Outside triple leaves opposite N, D, and CA. Only Style of 1795 reverse with this configuration among 1796 cents. First T of STATES leans slightly right. Lowest leaf of group of three points to the left foot of the second A of AMERICA; stem points to right foot of the same letter. Fraction well spaced and somewhat delicate; first 0 slightly low. **Points of distinction:** Seen from a perfect die and also with a rim break at the end of the right ribbon.

Notes: This variety is known in Mint State, and it is very rare as such.

ONE LEAF LEFT AND TWO LEAVES RIGHT AT APEX—1796 WITH REVERSE STYLE OF 1794

This arrangement is adapted from that given in *Walter Breen's Encyclopedia of Early United States Cents 1793–1814.* The reverse configuration is the key to identifying the varieties easily. The Style of 1794 coins have leaf clusters modified by hand, there being only three dies used. One reverse has no three-leaf clusters on the reverse and is identifiable by a two-leaf cluster below OF. The other two have a three-leaf cluster below OF (as do Reverse Style of 1797 coins, with the position varying slightly). These other two dies have other differences, as described, differentiating them from the Style of 1797.

In contrast, the Style of 1797 coins which were made with a punch with all of the leaves in place and with only *one* three-leaf cluster in the wreath (the cluster at the outside top of the right-hand wreath).

Typical values for 1796, Draped Bust, cents with the Reverse of 1794. Rare varieties may be worth more. Some varieties are priced individually, as follows.

	Cert	Avg	%MS	G-4	VG-8	F-12	VF-20	EF-40	AU-50	MS-60BN
1796, Draped Bust, Reverse of 1794	30	14.1	0%	$410	$875	$1,680	$2,750	$6,250	$12,625	$19,000

1796, Leaf Pair Opposite OF, Numerator Merged Into Fraction Bar, Reverse of 1794 • BW-40, S-101, B-25. *Breen dies:* 15-M. *Estimated population:* 60 to 75.

Obverse: Correct LIBERTY spelling. Upright of T over junction of hair and forehead. Definitive in combination with this reverse. *Points of distinction:* This die was used to coin BW-20, BW-40, and BW-53. Clash marks develop, then a crack through ERTY.

1796, Leaf Pair Opposite OF, Numerator Merged Into Fraction Bar, Reverse of 1794 (BW-40, S-101, B-25).

Reverse: Leaf pair (instead of cluster of three) opposite OF, definitive for a Reverse of 1794 die. Denticles have rounded ends. Numerator merged into the fraction bar; first 0 low. Single leaf below C of CENT.

Detail of numerator merging into fraction bar.

Notes: There is a Mint State (ANS) example, then grades drop down to EF.

1796, Leaf Pair Opposite OF, Numerator Merged Into Fraction Bar, Reverse of 1794 • BW-41, S-102, B-26. *Breen dies:* 16-M. *Estimated population:* 120 to 160.

Obverse: Correct LIBERTY spelling. Upright of T over hair. Definitive in combination with this reverse. *Points of distinction:* From a perfect die and also with a crack from the rim through BE to the hair.

1796, Leaf Pair Opposite OF, Numerator Merged Into Fraction Bar, Reverse of 1794 (BW-41, S-102, B-26).

Reverse: Same as preceding. *Points of distinction:* From a perfect die and also with a crack at the top of AMERI.

Notes: EF is the highest grade known.

1796, "LIHERTY", Leaf Pair Opposite OF, Numerator Merged Into Fraction Bar, Reverse of 1794 •

BW-42, S-103, B-27. *Breen dies:* 17-M. *Estimated population:* 120 to 160.

Obverse: The intended B in LIBERTY appears as an H, the result of the B being punched backwards and then corrected. Definitive in combination with the Reverse of 1794. This die was used for both BW-42 and BW-70.

1796, "LIHERTY", Leaf Pair Opposite OF, Numerator Merged Into Fraction Bar, Reverse of 1794 (BW-42, S-103, B-27).

Reverse: Same as preceding. *Points of distinction:* A crack develops at the top of AMERI.

Notes: Exists in AU and Mint State (unique). This distinctive error is one of the most popular of the era.

	Cert	Avg	%MS	G-4	VG-8	F-12	VF-20	EF-40	AU-50
1796, "LIHERTY", Leaf Pair Opposite OF, Reverse of 1794	(a)			$750	$2,250	$4,670	$8,000	$19,625	$40,000

a. Included in certified population for 1796, "LIHERTY", Reverse of 1797, Large Fraction.

1796, Three Leaves Opposite OF, Single Leaf Over O of ONE, Reverse of 1794 •

BW-43, S-108, B-12. *Breen dies:* 7-H. *Estimated population:* 120 to 160.

Obverse: *Date:* Widely spaced and close to denticles. 7 very close to denticle. 6 touches denticle. Knobs of 9 and 6 half cut off from defective punch. *LIBERTY:* LIB widely spaced. *Points of distinction:* Denticles wide and closely spaced. Some are from a perfect die, and others display light cracks.

1796, Three Leaves Opposite OF, Single Leaf Over O of ONE, Reverse of 1794 (BW-43, S-108, B-12).

Reverse: Three leaves opposite OF. Seven berries in left branch with *just one* near the ribbon bow. Leaf points to inside of right foot of second A of AMERICA. Single leaf over O and another over N of ONE. Leaf below C of CENT distant from berry to left of C. *Points of distinction:* This die was used to coin BW-43, BW-44, BW-45, BW-46, BW-47, BW-48, and 1795, Date Spaced 1 79 5, Reeded Edge (BW-13). Seen with the right ribbon attached, or in a later state, disconnected.

Notes: The highest grades known for this variety are EF and AU; it is very rare at these levels.

1796, Three Leaves Opposite OF, Reverse of 1794 • BW-44, S-107, B-13.[38]

Breen dies: 8-H. *Estimated population:* 45 to 60.

Obverse: *Date:* Positioned low, with 7 lowest. Knobs of 9 and 6 half cut off from defective punch. 6 closer to denticles than to drapery. *LIBERTY:* LI slightly wider than IB. RT wide. Base of Y low. Tip of lower-right serif of T above junction of hair and

1796, Three Leaves Opposite OF, Reverse of 1794 (BW-44, S-107, B-13).

forehead. *Points of distinction:* A massive cud break develops at the rim at top of Y and extends to the right. Coins with this break are especially rare.

Reverse: Same as preceding. *Points of distinction:* The die has been relapped to remove clash marks.

Notes: The highest grades known for this variety are Fine and VF (very rare). This variety is difficult to find with good eye appeal.

1796, Three Leaves Opposite OF, Reverse of 1794 • BW-45, S-106, B-14.
Breen dies: 9-H. **Estimated population:** 75 to 120.

Obverse: *Date:* 1 and 96 distant from denticles, 7 close. Knobs of 9 and 6 half cut off due to the same defective punch. 6 leans slightly to the right. *LIBERTY:* IBE wide. ER closest. Tip of lower-right serif of T above junction of hair and forehead. *Points of distinction:* From a perfect die, or with light cracks.

1796, Three Leaves Opposite OF,
Reverse of 1794 (BW-45, S-106, B-14).

Reverse: Same as preceding. *Points of distinction:* Cracks develop in later states.

Notes: AU is the highest grade known.

1796, Three Leaves Opposite OF, Reverse of 1794 • BW-46, S-109, B-15.
Breen dies: 10-H. **Estimated population:** 200 to 300.

Obverse: *Date:* Fairly evenly spaced. Curved along and not close to denticles, except for base of 7. Knob of 9 half cut off, from a defective punch. 6, using the same punch but inverted, has the knob patched. *LIBERTY:* Letters fairly evenly spaced. IB slightly closer

1796, Three Leaves Opposite OF,
Reverse of 1794 (BW-46, S-109, B-15).

than are any others. Tip of lower-right serif of T very slightly to the right of the junction of the hair and forehead. *Points of distinction:* A crack develops from the lowest curl through the top of 1796, and later a crack extends from the rim through T to the hair.

Reverse: Same as preceding. *Points of distinction:* Seen with the right ribbon attached, or in a later state, disconnected. On a late state, part of right stem is missing near bow knot.

Notes: VF and EF are the highest known grades.

1796, Three Leaves Opposite OF, Reverse of 1794 • BW-47, S-110, B-16.
Breen dies: 11-H. **Estimated population:** 500 to 750.

Obverse: *Date:* 6 in date is much closer to denticles than is any other digit (compare to the next). 179 wide, 96 close; knobs on 9 and 6 half cut off. 6 leans right with the knob beyond the curve below. *LIBERTY:* Repunched left uprights of L and I. Base of T

1796, Three Leaves Opposite OF,
Reverse of 1794 (BW-47, S-110, B-16).

above bases of R and Y. ***Points of distinction:*** On all examples a die crack connects 96 at their centers. Also used for BW-50.

Reverse: Same as preceding. ***Points of distinction:*** Late die state with part of stem missing. Cracks develop.

Notes: This variety is known in Mint State. According to Walter Breen, the most available cent variety among 1796 issues of both types.

1796, Three Leaves Opposite OF, Reverse of 1794 • BW-48, S-111, B-17.

Breen dies: 12-H. ***Estimated population:*** 60 to 75.

Obverse: *Date:* 1 farther from hair than on the preceding variety. 6 in date is much closer to denticles than is any other digit (compare to the preceding, which is similar). 179 wide, 96 close; knobs on 9 and 6 half cut off. 6 leans slightly right with the knob about even with

1796, Three Leaves Opposite OF,
Reverse of 1794 (BW-48, S-111, B-17).

the curve below. ***LIBERTY:*** LI close, other letters wide. Tip of lower-right serif on T over junction of hair and forehead. ***Points of distinction:*** Usually seen with light cracks.

Reverse: Same as preceding. ***Points of distinction:*** Seen with the right ribbon attached, or in a later state, disconnected. Cracks develop in later states.

Notes: The highest grades are VF to AU (unique). This variety is difficult to find with good eye appeal.

1796, Three Leaves Opposite OF, Leaf Pair Over O of ONE, Reverse of 1794 • BW-49, S-NC-5, B-18. *Breen dies:* 12-I. ***Reported population:*** 8.

Obverse: Same as preceding.

Reverse: Three leaves opposite OF. Seven berries in left branch with *two* near the ribbon bow. No leaf under second A of AMERICA. Leaf pair over O and another over N of ONE. Leaf below C of CENT very close to berry to left of C.

1796, Three Leaves Opposite OF, Leaf Pair Over
O of ONE, Reverse of 1794 (BW-49, S-NC-5, B-18).

Notes: The highest grade reported by Walter Breen is Fine-15. This variety was discovered by Howard R. Newcomb and published by George H. Clapp in "New Varieties of 1796 Cents," *The Numismatist*, January 1934.

1796, Three Leaves Opposite OF, Reverse of 1794 • BW-50, S-112, B-19.

Breen dies: 11-I. **Estimates population:** 75 to 120.

Obverse: Same as BW-47. ***Points of distinction:*** Always with light die cracks.

Reverse: Same as preceding. ***Points of distinction:*** Most have a light crack from the rim to the second T of STATES to a leaf tip. In its latest state the die sinks at the center, and coins are bulged in this area.

1796, Three Leaves Opposite OF, Reverse of 1794 (BW-50, S-112, B-19).

Notes: EF to AU (exceedingly rare) are the highest grades for this variety. This variety is difficult to find with good eye appeal.

ONE LEAF LEFT AND TWO LEAVES RIGHT AT APEX—1796 WITH REVERSE STYLE OF 1797

The Style of 1797 coins were made with a punch with all of the leaves. There is just one three-leaf cluster in the wreath, and it is at the upper outside of the right-hand wreath. The berries, stems, lettering, and fraction were added by hand, providing differences that can aid in attribution.

The fractions on the Reverse Style of 1797 coins come in two sizes: small and large. Walter Breen used this as a convenient way to separate four of the die varieties, a method continued here.

Typical values for 1796, Draped Bust, cents with the Reverse of 1797. Rare varieties may be worth more. Some varieties are priced individually, as follows.

	Cert	Avg	%MS	AG-3	G-4	VG-8	F-12	VF-20	EF-40	AU-50	MS-60BN	MS-63BN	MS-63RB	MS-65BN
1796, Draped Bust, Reverse of 1797	23	19.8	13%	$250	$440	$810	$1,520	$2,500	$4,690	$6,500	$11,250	$17,625	$28,250	$60,000

1796 WITH REVERSE STYLE OF 1797—SMALL FRACTION

There are only four combinations under this heading. By checking the obverse and reverse they can be identified easily enough, although as two of them are very rare, those are not likely to be encountered.

1796, T Over Junction of Hair and Forehead, Reverse of 1797, Small Fraction • BW-53, S-100, B-24. *Breen dies:* 15-L. **Estimated population:** 45 to 60.

Obverse: T over junction of hair and forehead. Definitive in combination with this reverse. ***Points of distinction:*** This die was used to coin BW-20, BW-40, and BW-53.

Reverse: Five berries to the left and five to the right. Outside berry opposite left upright

1796, T Over Junction of Hair and Forehead, Reverse of 1797, Small Fraction (BW-53, S-100, B-24).

of M of AMERICA, definitive for use with this reverse. CENT is very low. Fraction too far right, with bar close to ribbon. ***Points of distinction:*** Usually from a perfect die, but the ANS has one with a significant crack at STATES.

Notes: EF is the highest grade known. This variety is difficult to find with good eye appeal.

1796, Reverse of 1797, Small Fraction • BW-54, S-NC-1, B-29. *Breen dies:* 18-O. *Estimated population:* 20 to 25.

Obverse: 6 leans so far right that the knob at the top is farther to the right than is the curve below it; bottom of 9 much higher than bottom of 7; definitive for an obverse die mated with a Reverse of 1797, Small Fraction, die. *Points of distinction:* This die was used to coin both BW-32 and BW-54. Always with light cracks.

1796, Reverse of 1797, Small Fraction (BW-54, S-NC-1, B-29).

Reverse: Five berries on the left branch, four on the right. No outside berry below first A of AMERICA.

Notes: F and VF are the highest grades known, and examples are rare as such; usually VG or so is the highest grade seen. Once Non-Collectible, changed to *Now-Collectible.*

1796, Date Hyphenated 17-96, Reverse of 1797, Small Fraction • BW-55, S-94, B-30. *Breen dies:* 19-P. *Estimated population:* 30 to 45.

Obverse: Date with hyphen-like flaw causing it to read 17-96. Date widely spaced. 6 close to drapery. Rough patch in the field below the ribbon knot. *Points of distinction:* This die was used to coin BW-24, BW-25, BW-26, BW-27, BW-55, and BW-56. Clash marks are seen near the portrait. A light crack develops at and near the rim including ER.

1796, Date Hyphenated 17-96, Reverse of 1797, Small Fraction (BW-55, S-94, B-30).

Reverse: Five berries on each branch. Leaf touches left serif of left foot of second A of AMERICA, definitive in combination with this obverse. Fraction low; first 0 low.

Detail of low fraction, with low first 0.

Notes: VF and EF are the highest grades, the latter exceedingly rare. This variety is extremely hard to find with good eye appeal.

1796, Date Hyphenated 17-96, Reverse of 1797, Small Fraction • BW-56, S-NC-3, B-33. *Breen dies:* 19-S. *Estimated population:* 20 to 25.

Obverse: Same as preceding. *Points of distinction:* A weakness develops at ER. This die was used to coin BW-24, BW-25, BW-26, BW-27, BW-55, and BW-56.

Reverse: Six berries in the left branch, five in the right, diagnostic in combination with this

1796, Date Hyphenated 17-96, Reverse of 1797, Small Fraction (BW-56, S-NC-3, B-33).

obverse. Tip of top leaf on the right ends between S and O in OF. Left stem thicker than the right stem. CENT low, T tilts to the right. *Points of distinction:* In later die states there is a rim break at TE of UNITED.

Notes: Fine and VF are the highest grades, the latter exceedingly rare.

1796 WITH REVERSE STYLE OF 1797—LARGE FRACTION

The Stemless Wreath variety, BW-60 is immediately distinguishable. This die was also used in 1797. Walter Breen groups the others, With Stems, into two categories: Wide Date and Close Curved Date. These are not immediately distinguishable by sight, except by experts. Accordingly, the other guidelines must be used, in combination in all instances with pictures.

1796, Stemless Wreath, Reverse of 1797, Large Fraction • BW-60, S-NC-7, B-46. *Breen dies:* 26-BB. *Recorded population:* 3 known.

Obverse: *Date:* 7 low. 9 high, 6 highest and touching drapery. *LIBERTY:* IBER wide.

Reverse: Stemless Wreath.

Notes: 3 are known, not counting a partial impression of the dies on a previously struck *half cent.* One is in the ANS, another was

1796, Stemless Wreath, Reverse of 1797, Large Fraction (BW-60, S-NC-7, B-46).

found by Rod Burress in 1999, and the third was bought on the Internet by Dan Demeo in 2007. The curious half cent was identified in 1994 by Mark Borckardt.[39] The highest grades are Fine (half cent overstrike), Good, and AG-3. This variety is now known as Sheldon NC-7, though earlier listed in *Early American Cents* as NC-6. This listing was canceled, as it was thought that the only known example, in the American Numismatic Society, was altered from a 1797, Stemless Wreath, cent. In November 1994, Mark Borckardt met with Denis Loring and John Kleeberg at the ANS, and Loring confirmed that the Borckardt coin was indeed what had earlier been called NC-6. That number now being occupied by another variety, the new designation NC-7 was given.[40]

1796, No Ribbon Knot, Reverse of 1797, Large Fraction • BW-62, S-117, B-37. *Breen dies:* 21-W. *Estimated population:* 30 to 45.

Obverse: *Date:* Widely spaced. 9 distant from denticles. 6 closest to denticles and centered over two of them. *LIBERTY:* B leans right. BE and RT wide. *Points of distinction:* Clash marks and cracks develop.

Reverse: No ribbon knot, an engraving

1796, No Ribbon Knot, Reverse of 1797, Large Fraction (BW-62, S-117, B-37).

error; definitive. Five berries on each side of the wreath. Tip of highest-right leaf between ES of STATES, seen only on this and BW-64 within this style. *Points of distinction:* Some have a crack from the rim to the right side of the D.

Notes: The highest-graded examples are EF and AU, and very rare as such. This variety is difficult to find with good eye appeal.

1796, Top of 6 Overlays Drapery, Reverse of 1797, Large Fraction •

BW-63, S-NC-6, B-38. *Breen dies: 22-W. Recorded population:* 3.

Obverse: *Date:* 1 close to or touches hair. 6 overlays drapery. Compare to BW-67. 179 close, 96 wider. *LIBERTY:* Upright of T over forehead. *Points of distinction:* Crack at D of UNITED.

Reverse: Same as preceding.

1796, Top of 6 Overlays Drapery, Reverse of 1797, Large Fraction (BW-63, S-NC-6, B-38).

Notes: Discovered by Denis Loring at the 1970 ANA Convention. Both examples are AG-3.

1796, 6 Berries Left and Right, Berry Opposite D, Reverse of 1797, Large Fraction •

BW-64, S-118, B-39. *Breen dies:* 22-X. *Estimated population:* 30 to 45.

Obverse: Same as preceding.

Reverse: Tip of highest-right leaf between ES of STATES, seen only on this and BW-62 within this style. Six berries on each branch; berry opposite D of UNITED, this definitive within the style. Denominator widely spaced, with 10 especially so. *Points of distinction:* Most are struck from a perfect die, but some have a crack from under the end of the left ribbon to below 1 of 100, which develops into a break.

1796, 6 Berries Left and Right, Berry Opposite D, Reverse of 1797, Large Fraction (BW-64, S-118, B-39).

Notes: VF and EF are the highest grades known, the latter exceedingly rare. This variety is almost impossible to find with "nice" surfaces.

1796, 6 Berries Left and Right, Leaf Tip Opposite D, Reverse of 1797, Large Fraction •

BW-65, S-119, B-40. *Breen dies:* 22-Y. *Estimated population:* 300 to 400.

Obverse: Same as preceding. *Points of distinction:* All have a crack from the denticles, to the lower curl, to the bases of 17, and then back to the rim; also a crack from the denticles below the 6 to the bust and into the field.

1796, 6 Berries Left and Right, Leaf Tip Opposite D, Reverse of 1797, Large Fraction (BW-65, S-119, B-40).

Reverse: Six berries left and six right. Leaf tip opposite D of UNITED; definitive within the style. Fraction wide, with 1 in denominator near ribbon. *Points of distinction:* Two denticles over TA of STATES are connected. A crack is sometimes seen over AT, and other minor cracks can be in evidence.

Detail of two connected denticles over TA of STATES.

Notes: The Nichols Find contained many Mint State coins of this variety. Surfaces are often prooflike. Walter Breen estimated that "several hundred" of this die combination were found. *However,* in grades such as VG to VF this variety is a significant rarity.

1796, Reverse of 1797, Large Fraction, 1 of 100 Too Far Left • BW-66, S-113, B-41. *Breen dies:* 23-Z. *Estimated population:* 45 to 60.

1796, Reverse of 1797, Large Fraction, 1 of 100 Too Far Left (BW-66, S-113, B-41).

Obverse: *Date:* Close to denticles, 6 closest and over a pointed denticle. Knob on 9 half cut off, knob on top of 6 patched with a blob. *LIBERTY:* LIBE wide. L leans left. *Points of distinction:* Die cracks are in the date area.

Reverse: Six berries left and five right. Denominator too far left, with 1 near ribbon. Left ribbon recut on its right side. *Points of distinction:* This die was used to coin BW-66, BW-67, BW-68, and 1797, Berries: 6-5 (BW-22).

Notes: VF is the highest grade known. This variety is difficult to find with good eye appeal.

1796, Top of 6 Overlays Drapery, Reverse of 1797, Large Fraction, 1 of 100 Too Far Left • BW-67, S-114, B-42. *Breen dies:* 24-Z. *Estimated population:* 60 to 75.

1796, Top of 6 Overlays Drapery, Reverse of 1797, Large Fraction, 1 of 100 Too Far Left (BW-67, S-114, B-42).

Obverse: *Date:* Fairly evenly spaced. Tip of 1 very close to hair. 96 high, top of 6 overlays drapery. Compare to BW-63. Knobs on 9 and 6 half cut off. *LIBERTY:* Fairly evenly spaced. ER very close to hair. Upright of T over junction of hair and forehead, unusual on dies of this date. *Points of distinction:* This variety is found from a perfect die and also with cracks at TY, later a rim break in that area.

Reverse: Same as preceding. *Points of distinction:* There is always a crack from the rim to the second T of STATES. Later impressions have a crack at adjacent A, which expands to become a small break at the rim. This die was used to coin BW-66, BW-67, BW-68, and 1797, Berries: 6-5 (BW-22).

Notes: VF and EF are the highest grades known.

1796, 6 Leans Sharply Left, Reverse of 1797, Large Fraction, 1 of 100 Too Far Left • BW-68, S-115, B-43. *Breen dies:* 20-Z. *Estimated population:* 300 to 400.

1796, 6 Leans Sharply Left, Reverse of 1797, Large Fraction, 1 of 100 Too Far Left (BW-68, S-115, B-43).

Obverse: 6 leans sharply left so that the knob is about centered over the rest of the digit; knob very close to drapery; definitive for an obverse die mated with a Reverse of 1795. *Points of distinction:* Perfect-die impressions exist, after which the die developed many cracks and, eventually, a break at the rim at TY. Die used with BW-30 and BW-68.

Reverse: Same as preceding. *Points of distinction:* Some clash marks are seen in the field. This die was used to coin BW-66, BW-67, BW-68, and 1797, Berries: 6-5 (BW-22). BW-68 was struck *after* 1797, Berries: 6-5 (BW-22).

Notes: VF and EF are the highest grades known. This variety is difficult to find with good eye appeal.

1796, Reverse of 1797, Large Fraction, 1 of 100 Nearly Touches Ribbon • BW-69, S-105, B-44. *Breen dies:* 25-AA. *Estimated population:* 45 to 60.

Obverse: *Date:* 17 wide, 79 slightly closer, 96 close. 6 first punched low, then repunched in present position. *LIBERTY:* LI and BER wide. *Points of distinction:* Clash marks are seen, later multiple. Cracks develop.

1796, Reverse of 1797, Large Fraction, 1 of 100 Nearly Touches Ribbon (BW-69, S-105, B-44).

Reverse: Six berries left and five right. Second A of AMERICA close to side of ribbon. 1 in denominator too far left and nearly touches the ribbon.

Notes: VF or so is the highest grade for this variety, but mention has been made of a unique Mint State coin.

1796, "LIHERTY", Reverse of 1797, Large Fraction, 1 of 100 Nearly Touches Ribbon • BW-70, S-104, B-45. *Breen dies:* 17-AA. *Estimated population:* 200 to 300.

Obverse: Intended B in LIBERTY appears as an H, the result of the B being punched backwards and then corrected. Definitive in combination with the Reverse of 1797. This die was used for BW-42 and BW-70. *Points of distinction:* From a perfect die, or with a crack at the drapery at the right. In a late state a cud break is seen over TY.

1796, "LIHERTY", Reverse of 1797, Large Fraction, 1 of 100 Nearly Touches Ribbon (BW-70, S-104, B-45).

Detail showing the "H" in LIHERTY.

Reverse: Same as preceding. *Points of distinction:* From a perfect die or with several cracks.

Notes: EF is the highest grade known.

	Cert	Avg	%MS	G-4	VG-8	F-12	VF-20	EF-40	AU-50	MS-60BN	MS-63BN
1796, "LIHERTY", Reverse of 1797, Large Fraction	13	26.5	8%	$710	$2,080	$4,750	$5,930	$17,500	$30,000	$70,000	$125,000

1797, Draped Bust

Mintage (per *Mint Report*): 897,510.

Cents of 1797 were made in many different varieties. The earliest ones were probably from a Reverse of 1795 style die with a single leaf at the top of the wreath apex. This die was mated with three obverses. The Gripped Edge variety, discussed below, was part of that series.

Other 1797 cents have the later reverse style with one leaf at the upper left and two at the upper right. These were made with punches incorporating the wreath and its leaves, with berries, stems, lettering, and the fraction added by hand, creating many variations.

In addition to the Gripped Edge, many other varieties have faint lines on the edges, prompting this comment in *Penny Whimsy:*

> Many of the varieties are more or less marked or "milled" on the edges, with faint diagonal lines in patches, but never evenly, and never entirely around the edge. Since the process probably had to do with the preparation of the planchets, and not with the striking of the coins themselves, the presence or absence of traces of milling is a condition of no great concern to the student of die variation.

On April 26, 1797, Director Boudinot ordered 15 tons of planchets from Boulton & Watt, which arrived on the *Adriana* and were quite satisfactory. In contrast, when 9,296 pounds weight of planchets arrived from the Governor & Company of copper mines on the *William Penn* they proved to be a bad lot. These cost £11 a ton more than those from Boulton & Watt. "They were concave and convex and had to be cleaned and milled before being struck. These were the second lot of inferior planchets from the same concern resulting in nearly everything else being ordered from Boulton & Watt."[41]

Some coins from the Boulton & Watt planchets were included in the famous Nichols Find (see details under the introduction for 1796 cents).

Among the varieties of this year the several Stemless Wreath coins from two different reverse dies have always been popular. This type of error is also found among cents of other dates, as well as in some half cent varieties. Otherwise, the field of varieties is standard to the casual observer, but can be differentiated by berry counts, letter positions, and other usual methods. LIBERTY is slightly farther to the right on the typical 1797 coin, with the T over or close to the junction of the hair and forehead. Walter Breen notes that some varieties have the B from a punch with the upper-left serif too short or completely missing. Sometimes this defect was repaired by hand.

Most 1797 cents in the marketplace are in worn grades. AU and higher coins range from scarce to rare, except for certain Nichols Find pieces in Mint State, often with prooflike surfaces.

The following listing begins with Reverse of 1795 coins, then Reverse of 1797 with Stemless Wreath, then the others.

One Leaf Each Side of Wreath Apex—1797 With Reverse Style of 1795

The varieties under this listing are from a single reverse die combined with three different obverses.

1797, Reverse of 1795 • BW-1, S-NC-1, B-1. *Breen dies:* 1-A. *Reported population:* 9.

Obverse: *Date:* About evenly spaced. 7 close to drapery. *LIBERTY:* The most widely spaced of any 1797 die. T is mostly over the forehead. *Points of distinction:* The ANS example has a crack at BERT.

Reverse: Outside triple leaves opposite UN, ED, and C. Two leaves opposite O of ONE;

1797, Reverse of 1795 (BW-1, S-NC-1, B-1).

two leaves below T of CENT. Numerator 1 is too far right above the bar. Denticles are heavy and closely spaced. *Points of distinction:* This die was used to coin 1797 BW-1, BW-2a, BW-2b, BW-3a, BW-3b, and 1796 (BW-11).

Notes: Walter Breen enumerates six coins, the finest VF-25, the others AG-3 to VG-8.

1797, Plain Edge, Wide 1 7 97 Date, Reverse of 1795 • BW-2a, S-120a, B-2a.

Breen dies: 2-A. *Estimated population:* 200 to 300.

Obverse: *Date:* First three digits of the date are spaced widely as 1 7 97. Definitive with this reverse. 7 close to drapery. *LIBERTY:* IB and TY close. Upright of T over hair. *Points of distinction:* The die deteriorated from "perfect" to rough. A crack develops at the left and continues through the date.

1797, Plain Edge, Wide 1 7 97 Date, Reverse of 1795 (BW-2a, S-120a, B-2a).

Reverse: Same as preceding. *Points of distinction:* Some are from a perfect die, and the others have a crack from the denticles past the left of U of UNITED.

Notes: AU and Mint State (unique) are the highest grades known.

	Cert	Avg	%MS	G-4	VG-8	F-12	VF-20	EF-40	AU-50
1797, Plain Edge, Wide 1 7 97 Date, Reverse of 1795	8	16.6	0%	$225	$410	$875	$2,250	$6,625	$22,500

1797, Gripped Edge, Wide 1 7 97 Date, Reverse of 1795 • BW-2b, S-120b, B-2b.

Breen dies: 2-A. *Estimated population:* 750 to 1,000.

Obverse: Same as preceding.

Reverse: Same as preceding.

Notes: AU and Mint State (unique) are the highest grades known. This variety is "Gripped Edge" in the form of irregularly spaced notches on the edge. The purpose of this is unknown. Enough of these exist that they are plentiful in the marketplace.

Numismatic Notes: *Early mentions of what is called the Gripped Edge today:*

Mason's Coin Collectors' Herald, June 1880:

Another Rare Variety of U.S. Cents. For the first time we make public the discovery of a 1797 cent with an indented periphery, resembling a lettered edge, caused by the clamps holding the planchets to prevent turning in the dies.

Mason's Coin Collector's Magazine and Coin Price Current, December, 1890:

The Indented Edge 1797 Cent. A collector in San Francisco has forwarded a very fine 1797 U.S. cent, with indented edge, and wishes to dispose of it, unless he can learn its true history. We would be pleased to have an article from any of the experts in the U.S. Mint or elsewhere, concerning the origin of the Indented Edge 1797 Cent. That it was a Mint issue, with its peculiar irregular reeded edge, we have no doubt, and it may be true that owing to the planchets moving or jumping during coinage that clamps with teeth were used to hold the planchets in position. Who knows? The Editor.

	Cert	Avg	%MS	G-4	VG-8	F-12	VF-20	EF-40	AU-50
1797, Gripped Edge, Wide 1 7 97 Date, Reverse of 1795	12	26.6	0%	$240	$450	$925	$2,250	$7,500	$20,000

1797, Reverse of 1795, Plain Edge •

BW-3a, S-121a, B-3a. *Breen dies: 3-A. Estimated population:* 10 to 15.

Obverse: *Date:* Date compact. 17 closer than are the other numerals. Base of 7 over denticle. *LIBERTY:* Closely spaced. LI slightly wider than IB. Upper left of B defective. Upright of T over junction of hair and forehead. *Points of distinction:* The die states range from perfect through various progressions of die cracks.

1797, Reverse of 1795, Plain Edge (BW-3a, S-121a, B-3a).

Reverse: Same as preceding. *Points of distinction:* With a die crack from the denticles past the left of U of UNITED and some other tiny cracks.

Notes: The highest grades for this variety are VG (exceedingly rare), then Good. *Copper Quotes by Robinson* advises that there are many low-grade fakes of this variety.

	Cert	Avg	%MS	AG-3	G-4
1797, Reverse of 1795, Plain Edge	(a)			$2,250	$4,830

a. Included in certified population for 1797, Plain Edge, Wide 1 7 97 Date, Reverse of 1795.

1797, Reverse of 1795, Gripped Edge •

BW-3b, S-121b, B-3b. *Breen dies: 3-A. Estimated population:* 300 to 400.

Obverse: Same as preceding.

Reverse: Same as preceding.

Notes: With Gripped Edge. This variety exists in Mint State, and is exceedingly rare as such.

1797, Reverse of 1795, Gripped Edge (BW-3b, S-121b, B-3b).

	Cert	Avg	%MS	G-4	VG-8	F-12	VF-20	EF-40	AU-50	MS-60BN
1797, Reverse of 1795, Gripped Edge	(a)			$275	$520	$1,320	$3,250	$11,500	$25,000	$50,000

a. Included in certified population for 1797, Gripped Edge, Wide 1 7 97 Date, Reverse of 1795.

ONE LEAF LEFT AND TWO LEAVES RIGHT AT APEX—ONLY ONE THREE-LEAF CLUSTER IN WREATH —1797 WITH REVERSE STYLE OF 1797

The Style of 1797 coins were made with a punch with all of the leaves. There is just one three-leaf cluster in the wreath, and it is at the upper outside of the right-hand wreath. The berries, stems, lettering, and fraction were added by hand, providing differences that can aid in attribution. Cents of this style comprise the vast majority of issues of the year.

The Stemless Wreath varieties are listed first, as attribution is simplified, thereby reducing the number of "regular" coins following.

STEMLESS WREATH VARIETIES

1797, Stemless Wreath • BW-6,

S-NC-8, B-26. *Breen dies:* 18-R. *Recorded population:* 1.

Obverse: *Date:* Medium width. 79 wide. Base of each digit is over a denticle. *LIBERTY:* Defective B. LI slightly wider than IB. LI closest to denticles. T mostly over hair, partly over forehead. *Points of distinction:* Die break (piece removed from the die) "hangs down" from the denticles far to the

1797, Stemless Wreath (BW-6, S-NC-8, B-26).

left of L, and extends to opposite the second ribbon. This die was used to coin BW-6, BW-7, BW-34, and BW-35. A die break becomes even more prominent.

Reverse: Stemless Wreath, first die. Tip of leaf under right part of D of UNITED. Outside leaf of pair under center of M of AMERICA. Leaf close to but does not touch C of CENT. *Points of distinction:* This die was used to coin BW-6 and BW-10.

Notes: This coin is VF-25 with the sharpness of a higher grade. It resides in the Daniel W. Holmes Jr. Collection. This variety, unknown when *Early American Cents* and *Penny Whimsy* were compiled, was found by Ed Kucia in 1980 and confirmed as a new variety at the Early American Coppers convention in 1985.[42]

1797, Stemless Wreath • BW-7, S-131,

B-27. *Breen dies:* 18-S. *Estimated population:* 500 to 750.

Obverse: Same as preceding. *Points of distinction:* Often with a small crack below the right of the R and a tiny crack from the end of the nose. This die was used to coin BW-6, BW-7, BW-34, and BW-35.

1797, Stemless Wreath (BW-7, S-131, B-27).

Reverse: Stemless Wreath, second die. Tip of leaf under center of D of UNITED. Outside leaf of pair under right upright of M of AMERICA. Leaf connected to C of CENT.

Notes: EF is the highest grade known.

	Cert	Avg	%MS	G-4	VG-8	F-12	VF-20	EF-40
1797, Stemless Wreath (BW-7)	23	24.8	4%	$250	$530	$1,180	$2,500	$8,875

1797, 17 Wide, Stemless Wreath •

BW-8, S-132, B-28. *Breen dies:* 19-S. *Estimated population:* 45 to 60.

Obverse: *Date:* 1 heavy, other numerals lighter. Second 7 lowest at its base, but is centered between a denticle and the drapery. *LIBERTY:* BE very wide, TY slightly wide. B defective. E over low area of hair wave.

1797, 17 Wide, Stemless Wreath (BW-8, S-132, B-28).

Upright of T over junction of hair and forehead. *Points of distinction:* A slight bulge develops in the right field.

Reverse: Same as preceding. *Points of distinction:* Some have a rim break opposite IC of AMERICA.

Notes: This coin can be found in Mint State (unique), then VF is the next-highest grade. Usually seen in low grades.

	Cert	Avg	%MS	G-4	VG-8	F-12	VF-20
1797, 17 Wide, Stemless Wreath (BW-8)	(a)			$440	$940	$2,750	$4,750

a. Included in certified population for 1797, Stemless Wreath (BW-7).

1797, Second 7 Nearly Touches Short Denticle, Stemless Wreath •

BW-9, S-133, B-29. *Breen dies:* 20-S. *Estimated population:* 60 to 75.

Obverse: *Date:* Low. First 7 over denticle. Second 7 lower and nearly touches a *shorter* denticle; the next two denticles to the right are fused together. *LIBERTY:* I leans right. B leans right and is not defective. E over low area of hair wave. Upright of T over junction of hair and forehead. *Points of distinction:* Lower-right part of the drapery is usually weakly struck. This die was used to coin both BW-9 and BW-36. Incuse marks from wreath are in front of throat, with traces elsewhere. V-shaped break from rim to top of RT.

1797, Second 7 Nearly Touches Short Denticle, Stemless Wreath (BW-9, S-133, B-29).

Detail of low second 7 and fused denticles.

Reverse: Same as preceding. *Points of distinction:* Often with a crack at the top of STATE and a light rim break over IC.

Notes: VF is seen occasionally, there is one EF (ANS).

	Cert	Avg	%MS	G-4	VG-8	F-12	VF-20
1797, 2nd 7 Nearly Touches Short Denticle, Stemless Wreath (BW-9)	(a)			$440	$940	$2,750	$4,690

a. Included in certified population for 1797, Stemless Wreath (BW-7).

1797, 7 Embedded in Drapery, Stemless Wreath •

BW-10, S-143, B-31. *Breen dies:* 21-R. *Estimated population:* 45 to 60.

Obverse: *Date:* Second 7 close to shortened denticle and, at the top, is embedded in the drapery. *LIBERTY:* IB and ER close. B leans right. R has tiny right serif extension, Breen's "Style II, curled tail to R," the only 1797 obverse die with this feature. Upright of T over hair. *Points of distinction:* This die also used to strike BW-37.

1797, 7 Embedded in Drapery, Stemless Wreath (BW-10, S-143, B-31).

Reverse: Stemless Wreath, first die (also see BW-6 above). Tip of leaf under right part of D of UNITED. Outside leaf of pair under center of M of AMERICA. Leaf close to but does not touch C of

CENT. *Points of distinction:* This die was used to coin both BW-6 and BW-10. Clash marks are seen and there is a light crack near D of UNITED.

Notes: EF is the highest grade known.

	Cert	Avg	%MS	G-4	VG-8	F-12	VF-20	EF-40
1797, 7 Embedded in Drapery, Stemless Wreath (BW-10)	(a)			$440	$940	$2,670	$4,560	$10,170

a. Included in certified population for 1797, Stemless Wreath (BW-7).

WREATH WITH STEMS VARIETIES

For this extensive series of reverse dies, the distribution of berries left and right furnishes a quick guide to differentiating varieties prior to checking other features. The Breen chronology, less the varieties earlier described, is followed.

Typical values for 1797 cents With Stems. Rare varieties may be worth more.

	Cert	Avg	%MS	G-4	VG-8	F-12	VF-20	EF-40	AU-50	MS-60BN	MS-63BN
1797, With Stems	179	34.2	20%	$200	$350	$530	$1,160	$2,260	$3,750	$6,560	$12,560

1797, "Island" in Field Before Throat, Berries: 5-5, Left Bow and Ribbon Disconnected From Knot, Small Fraction • BW-12, S-134, B-4.

Breen dies: 4-B. **Estimated population:** 120 to 160.

1797, "Island" in Field Before Throat, Berries: 5-5, Left Bow and Ribbon Disconnected From Knot, Small Fraction (BW-12, S-134, B-4).

Obverse: *Date:* High above denticles. 1 barely touches hair. 7's are lowest and each is over a denticle. 97 close. Second 7 barely touches drapery. *LIBERTY:* LI wider than IB. BER wide. B defective. E touches hair. T mostly over forehead. *Points of distinction:* Prominent raised "island" in field before throat, from a chip out of the die; definitive. Swelling behind the lower curls and neck. Die scratch connects 97.

Reverse: *Berries left and right:* 5-5. *Fraction:* First 0 is very low. Bar extends from over left edge of 1 to just past center of second 0. Small Fraction, the only such size among

Detail of the reverse, showing amateurish die punching at the center, hardly the work of an experienced die sinker.

1797 cents. *Points of distinction:* Lowest leaves on right are incomplete. Bottom of left bow and top of ribbon are very weak or not attached to knot. Letters in ONE / CENT are amateurishly punched and poorly aligned. Occurs in early state with perfect die (rare) and later with a crack from E of AMERICA to the wreath. Cracks develop and a bulge renders indistinct the letters NE of ONE.

Notes: EF and AU are the highest grades known, the latter exceedingly rare. Some have raised beads on the edge, an aspect not publicized in earlier generations and not well studied today.

1797, Berries: 6-6 • BW-13, S-135, B-5.

Breen dies: 5-C. **Estimated population:** 300 to 400.

Obverse: *Date:* Base of both 7's low, and each over a space between denticles. Upper right of second 7 barely touches drapery. *LIBERTY:* LI very close, B defective. Upright of T over junction of hair and forehead. **Points of distinction:** Crack from C of AMERICA to the rim; some have a light crack from I to nearby leaf.

1797, Berries: 6-6 (BW-13, S-135, B-5).

Reverse: *Berries left and right:* 6-6; one of two dies with this arrangement. See BW-21 for the other. **Points of distinction:** Lowest berry on right partly overlaps stem. Leaf slightly separated from C of CENT. In denominator, 10 wider than 00.

Notes: Mint State coins are seen with frequency, from the Nichols Find, this also being true for the other 6-6 berries variety. However, the demand for them is so strong that there is always a lot of attention in the auction room when one is offered. Some show original mint color, more than any other from this source. The passion for "trophy coins" has led to a "push" toward liberal grading of this variety.[43]

1797, Berries: 5-4 (only die) • BW-14, S-NC-6, B-6.

Breen dies: 5-D. **Recorded population:** 2.

Obverse: Same as preceding. **Points of distinction:** A bulge develops across the lower left, near the center.

Reverse: *Berries left and right:* 5-4; definitive.

Notes: AG-3 and G-4. This variety was discovered by Ray Chatham in 1958.

1797, Berries: 5-4 (only die) (BW-14, S-NC-6, B-6).

1797, Berries: 5-4 (only die) • BW-15, S-136, B-7.

Breen dies: 6-D. **Estimated population:** 300 to 400.

Obverse: *Date:* 1 and first 7 lean right. 17 wide, 79 wider, 97 close. First 7 very close to denticle; second very close to or touches denticle. *LIBERTY:* L closest to denticles. LI and ER close. B not defective. Upright of T over hair.

1797, Berries: 5-4 (only die) (BW-15, S-136, B-7).

Reverse: Same as preceding. **Points of distinction:** Perfect die or with a light crack from the rim, through U to the wreath, and then back to the rim. Crack from left of E of AMERICA to the wreath, continuing back to the C and to the rim.

Notes: AU is the highest grade known.

1797, Berries: 6-5 • BW-16, S-137, B-8. *Breen dies:* 6-E. **Estimated population:** 500 to 750.

Obverse: Same as preceding. *Points of distinction:* A crack develops on the rim at the lower left.

Reverse: *Berries left and right:* 6-5. *Fraction:* Numerator is directly over first 0. Fraction bar ends at edge of 1. *Points of distinction:* Tip of leftmost leaf in pair opposite space between E and D of UNITED. Right foot of second A of AMERICA touches ribbon. One of two reverse 6-5 dies used to coin 1797 cents. See BW-22 for the other. Some have swelling at UNI and RICA, leading to obliterating IC and part of the adjacent A. Crack from rim below 00 through ribbon and stem.

Notes: AU is the highest grade known.

1797, Berries: 6-5 (BW-16, S-137, B-8).

Detail of second A of AMERICA and ribbon.

1797, Closest Date, Berries: 5-5, Incomplete Leaf Opposite T of UNITED, Spine From Bar to Left Ribbon, 1 of 100 Nearly Touches Ribbon • BW-17, S-122, B-9. *Breen dies:* 7-F. **Estimated population:** 30 to 45.

Obverse: *Date:* Base of both 7's low and each over a denticle. Upper right of second 7 nearly touches drapery. *LIBERTY:* LIB close. B not defective. Upright of T over junction of hair and forehead. *Points of distinction:*

1797, Closest Date, Berries: 5-5, Incomplete Leaf Opposite T of UNITED, Spine From Bar to Left Ribbon, 1 of 100 Nearly Touches Ribbon (BW-17, S-122, B-9).

Die states range from perfect to with cracks at AMERICA. Sheldon's "Closest Date."

Reverse: *Berries left and right:* 5-5. *Fraction:* Spine on fraction bar to or near left ribbon. 1 in denominator leans right, is distant from 0, and almost touches the ribbon. *Points of distinction:* Outside leaf opposite T of UNITED is incomplete (compare to BW-28). Leaf left of C of CENT is simply an arc. Cracks develop.

Notes: Fine and VF are the highest grades known, the latter exceedingly rare. This variety is usually found with a dark, porous surface.

1797, Closest Date, Berries: 5-5, Short Fraction Bar • BW-18, S-NC-2, B-10.

Breen dies: 7-G. *Estimated population:* 20 to 25.

1797, Closest Date, Berries: 5-5, Short Fraction Bar (BW-18, S-NC-2, B-10).

Obverse: Same as preceding.

Reverse: *Berries left and right:* 5-5. Four berries are without stems. *Fraction:* Fraction bar very short and covers neither the 1 or the second 0. *Points of distinction:* A light crack through the top of ED of UNITED is seen, as is a break in the denticles over D ST, later expanding.

Notes: Discovered by Howard R. Newcomb in 1944 (the same year his book on 1816 to 1857 cents was published). VG and Fine are the highest grades known, the latter being very rare.

1797, Closest Date, Berries: 5-5, Short Fraction Bar With Spine to Right, Distant 1 in Fraction • BW-20, S-NC-3, B-11.

Breen dies: 7-H. *Estimated population:* 25 to 30.

1797, Closest Date, Berries: 5-5, Short Fraction Bar With Spine to Right, Distant 1 in Fraction (BW-20, S-NC-3, B-11).

Obverse: Same as preceding.

Reverse: *Berries left and right:* 5-5. *Fraction:* 1 in the denominator is far to the left. Fraction bar short, but does extend halfway over second 0 (compare to the preceding), this not including a tiny engraver's scratch or spine extending to the right. *Points of distinction:* Eventually, a heavy rim cud is seen over TES.

Notes: Discovered by Henry C. Hines in 1944. Known only in grades of Fine (very rare) and below.

1797, Closest Date, Berries: 6-6 • BW-21, S-123, B-12.

Breen dies: 7-I. *Estimated population:* 120 to 160.

1797, Closest Date, Berries: 6-6 (BW-21, S-123, B-12).

Obverse: Same as preceding.

Reverse: *Berries left and right:* 6-6; one of two dies with this arrangement. See BW-13 for the other. *Fraction:* In denominator 10 closer than 00. *Points of distinction:* Lowest berry on right adjacent to stem. Fused denticle pair above space between TA. Leaf solidly touches C of CENT. Seen without and later with minor cracks.

Detail of fused denticle pair over TA of STATES.

Notes: This variety is usually seen in Mint State from the Nichols Find, this also being true for the other 6-6 variety. The present variety is the least often encountered from that source.[44]

1797, Berries: 6-5 • BW-22, S-NC-5, B-13.

Breen dies: 8-J. **Estimated population:** 20 to 25.

Obverse: *Date:* 179 evenly spaced, 97 close. Upper right of second 7 barely touches drapery. *LIBERTY:* B defective. TY farther below denticles than are other letters. T very slightly right of junction of hair and forehead. **Points of distinction:** The die develops a crack through ERTY, then a rim break.

Reverse: *Berries left and right:* 6-5. *Fraction:* Numerator is right of center of first 0. Fraction bar ends between 1 and 0. **Points of distinction:** Tip of leftmost leaf in pair opposite center of D of UNITED. Right foot of

1797, Berries: 6-5 (BW-22, S-NC-5, B-13).

Detail of short fraction bar.

second A of AMERICA is separated from ribbon. One of two reverse 6-5 dies used to coin 1797 cents. See BW-16 for the other. This die was also used to coin 1796, Reverse of 1797, Large Fraction, 1 of 100 Too Far Left (BW-66); 1796, Top of 6 Overlays Drapery, Reverse of 1797, Large Fraction, 1 of 100 Too Far Left (BW-67); and 1796, 6 Leans Sharply Left, Reverse of 1797, Large Fraction, 1 of 100 Too Far Left (BW-68).

Notes: Discovered by Pittsburgh dealer A.C. Gies in 1935. VF and EF are the highest grades known, the latter very rare.

1797, Berries: 5-5, E of AMERICA Over M, Right Ribbon Hollow, Denominator Spaced Widely •

BW-23, S-124, B-14. *Breen dies:* 9-K. **Estimated population:** 30 to 45.

Obverse: *Date:* 17 very slightly wider than 797. *LIBERTY:* LIB close. B without defect. R touches hair. Upright of T over junction of hair and forehead. **Points of distinction:** Obverse swellings are more extensive than on the previous use of this die.

1797, Berries: 5-5, E of AMERICA Over M, Right Ribbon Hollow, Denominator Spaced Widely (BW-23, S-124, B-14).

Reverse: *Berries left and right:* 5-5. *Fraction:* Fraction bar short and closer to right ribbon. Denominator digits very wide, with first 0 low. **Points of distinction:** E of AMERICA over *faint* traces of an erroneous M. Leaf point under slightly left of center of M. Level point of right ribbon is weak. With swelling at OF.

Notes: F to VF are the highest grades known, the latter being especially rare. Nearly always seen in lower grades. BW-23 is easily confused with BW-31, so check both descriptions.

1797, Swelling at 97 and Drapery, Berries: 5-5, E of ONE Directly Over
T • BW-24, S-125, B-15. *Breen dies:* 9-L. *Estimated population:* 45 to 60.

Obverse: Same as preceding. ***Points of distinction:*** Now with swelling at 97 and drapery, extending into right field. In late states the swelling obliterates the entire date.

Reverse: *Berries left and right:* 5-5. *Fraction:* Small fraction bar far from denominator

1797, Swelling at 97 and Drapery, Berries: 5-5, E of ONE Directly Over T (BW-24, S-125, B-15).

1 and ends over left part of second 0; 1 much closer to left ribbon than 0 is to right. ***Points of distinction:*** E of ONE directly over T. F in OF and second A are light, as copper went to create the swelling opposite this point in the coining press.

Notes: VF is the highest grade known. Usually found in low grades.

1797, Fused Denticles at 4 O'clock, Berries: 5-5, E of ONE Directly Over
T • BW-25, S-126, B-16. *Breen dies:* 10-L. *Estimated population:* 300 to 400.

Obverse: *Date:* Second 7 over a denticle; left top very close to drapery, right top touches drapery. *LIBERTY:* LIB close. B defective. Upright of T over junction of hair and forehead. ***Points of distinction:*** Defect joins denticles at 4 o'clock on rim; expands to become

1797, Fused Denticles at 4 O'clock, Berries: 5-5, E of ONE Directly Over T (BW-25, S-126, B-16).

a large crack and break. This die state, impressive to view, is not particularly rare.

Reverse: Same as preceding. ***Points of distinction:*** Found from a perfect die and also with light cracks.

Notes: AU is the highest known grade.

1797, Deep Dip in Wave Under E, Berries: 5-5, E of ONE Directly Over T • BW-26, S-127, B-17. *Breen dies:*
11-L. *Estimated population:* 120 to 160.

Obverse: *Date:* Fairly evenly spaced. Second 7 about equidistant from denticles and drapery, and visibly separated from each. *LIBERTY:* LI close. B not defective. Under the upright of E the hair wave is "angular," per the literature—actually a deeper dip or trough between two waves—as compared to all other dies of the year. Upright of T over junction of hair and forehead. ***Points of distinction:*** Some are from a perfect die, and others have a crack beginning at the denticles opposite the ribbon knot.

1797, Deep Dip in Wave Under E, Berries: 5-5, E of ONE Directly Over T (BW-26, S-127, B-17).

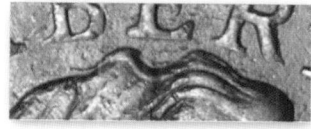

Detail showing deep dip between hair waves.

Reverse: Same as preceding. *Points of distinction:* Always with two light cracks.

Notes: VF and EF are the highest grades known, the latter extremely rare.

1797, Berries: 5-5, Spine on Fraction Bar to Right • BW-27, S-141, B-18.
Breen dies: 12-M. *Estimated population:* 120 to 160.

Obverse: *Date:* 17 wide, 97 close. Second 7 distant from drapery. Sometimes the knob on the 9 is weak. *LIBERTY:* BE wide. B defective, but later patched. Upright of T over junction of hair and forehead.

1797, Berries: 5-5, Spine on Fraction Bar to Right (BW-27, S-141, B-18).

Reverse: *Berries left and right:* 5-5. *Fraction:* Small fraction bar ends over left side of first 0. Spine extends from fraction bar to right ribbon. *Points of distinction:* F in OF repunched. AM touches. C of CENT attached to leaf. Some die injury around the wreath. Often seen with one or more cracks on the lower part of the coin.

Notes: VF is a reasonable objective, but an EF and an AU are recorded.

1797, 7 Distant From Drapery, Berries: 5-5, Incomplete Leaf Opposite T of UNITED • BW-28, S-NC-4, B-19. *Breen dies:* 13-N. *Reported population:* 3.

Obverse: *Date:* Second 7 distant from drapery. *LIBERTY:* BE and RTY wide. BER higher above the hair than usual. B not defective. Upright of T over junction of hair and forehead. *Points of distinction:* A crack is in the right field.

1797, 7 Distant From Drapery, Berries: 5-5, Incomplete Leaf Opposite T of UNITED (BW-28, S-NC-4, B-19).

Reverse: *Berries left and right:* 5-5. *Fraction:* Short fraction bar ends between 1 and 0 and halfway over second 0. *Points of distinction:* Leaf opposite T of UNITED incomplete. Leaf left of C of CENT skeletal (compare to BW-17).

Notes: Discovered by Dr. Sheldon in 1934, early in his interest in the subject. Fine is the highest grade known.

1797, R on Head, Berries: 5-5 • BW-30, S-138, B-20. *Breen dies:* 14-N. *Estimated population:* Thousands.

Obverse: *Date:* 179 about evenly spaced, 97 slightly closer. Bases of 7's each over a denticle. Second 7 very close to drapery. *LIBERTY:* LIB closer to denticles. B without imperfection; sharp curl point under upright. Left of R barely touches head. Upright of T over junction of hair and forehead. *Points of distinction:* Sometimes with a light crack from Y into the field.

1797, R on Head, Berries: 5-5 (BW-30, S-138, B-20).

Reverse: Same as preceding. *Points of distinction:* Some have light cracks at STATES. Usually swollen at OF in this state.

Notes: This variety exists in Mint State.

1797, Berries: 5-5, Spine From Stem to U, Line to Right of Fraction Bar •

BW-31, S-139, B-21. *Breen dies:* 15-O. *Estimated population:* Thousands.

1797, Berries: 5-5, Spine From Stem to U, Line to Right of Fraction Bar (BW-31, S-139, B-21).

Obverse: *Date:* Ends of 7's point to spaces between denticles. Second 7 about equidistant from drapery and denticles, and visibly separated from each. *LIBERTY:* IB close. B without imperfection. R close to hair. Upright of T over junction of hair and forehead. *Points of distinction:* Sometimes from a perfect die, but usually with extensive cracks, these very interesting to view.

Detail of line between the fraction bar and right ribbon.

Reverse: *Berries left and right:* 5-5. *Fraction:* Short fraction bar begins to right of 1 and ends over left part of second 0. *Points of distinction:* Spine from left stem to U. Line past bar to right, to ribbon, but not connected to it.

Notes: BW-23 is easily confused with BW-31, so check both descriptions. This variety exists in Mint State. This is far and away the most often seen of the 1797 cent varieties.[45]

1797, Broken T Obverse, Berries: 5-5, Spine From Stem to U, Line to Right of Fraction • BW-32, S-140, B-22.

Breen dies: 16-O. *Estimated population:* Thousands.

1797, Broken T Obverse, Berries: 5-5, Spine From Stem to U, Line to Right of Fraction (BW-32, S-140, B-22).

Obverse: *Date:* 17 wide. Second 7 close to drapery. *LIBERTY:* ER wide. B defective. Top bar of T broken. Upright of T over junction of hair and forehead, but mostly over hair. *Points of distinction:* Typically seen with a light crack from the denticles up to the left. A later state has a crack downward from Y, and still later with swelling at the date.

Detail showing broken T.

Reverse: Same as preceding. *Points of distinction:* Bulges and cracks develop.

Notes: Though thousands exist, this variety is scarcer than BW-31. This variety exists in Mint State.

1797, R on Head, Berries: 5-5, M Over E • BW-33, S-128, B-23. *Breen dies:* 17-P. *Estimated population:* 300 to 400.

Obverse: *Date:* 1 over denticle; touches hair. Upper-left serif and upper-right corner of second 7 touch drapery; bottom opposite space between denticles. *LIBERTY:* BER wide. B without defect. R touches hair. Upright of T over junction of hair and forehead. *Points of distinction:* Examples can be found from a perfect die as well as with cracks that become extensive.

1797, R on Head, Berries: 5-5,
M Over E (BW-33, S-128, B-23).

Detail of M over erroneous E.

Reverse: *Berries left and right:* 5-5. *Points of distinction:* M of AMERICA over erroneous E. Many denticles are fused at the bottom border. Multiple clash marks, mostly light, are seen. Walter Breen says at least 12 sets can be discerned, indicating very careless press operation. Cracks develop.

Notes: AU is the highest grade known.

1797, Berries: 5-5, M Over E • BW-34, S-129, B-24. *Breen dies:* 18-P. *Estimated population:* 45 to 60.

Obverse: See description under BW-6. *Points of distinction:* This die was used to coin BW-6, BW-7, BW-34, and BW-35. On most examples a crack begins at the denticles above the ribbon, extends into the field and then back to the rim. Walter Breen knew of only two without this feature.

1797, Berries: 5-5, M Over E (BW-34, S-129, B-24).

Reverse: Same as preceding.

Notes: VF and EF are the highest grades known. Most examples are in lower grades.

1797, Berries: 5-5 • BW-35, S-130, B-25. *Breen dies:* 18-Q. *Estimated population:* 750 to 1,000.

Obverse: Same as preceding. *Points of distinction:* The crack behind ribbon is advanced on this use of the die. Often with a tiny crack at the upright of R. This die was used to coin BW-6, BW-7, BW-34, and BW-35.

Reverse: *Berries left and right:* 5-5. *Points of distinction:* Die ground down too far, fragmenting the leaf nearest to T of UNITED and severing the tip of the left ribbon.

Notes: AU and low-range Mint State are the highest grades known.

1797, Berries: 5-5 (BW-35, S-130, B-25).

Detail of severed ribbon ends.

1797, 7 Embedded in Drapery, Berries: 5-5, Spine From Bar to Right Ribbon • BW-36, S-NC-7, B-30.
Breen dies: 20-T. *Recorded population:* 1.

Obverse: See description under BW-9. *Points of distinction:* This die was used to coin BW-9 and BW-36. Now a large crack extends from the rim, above the end of the drapery, to the bottom of the throat.

Reverse: Thin spine extends from fraction bar to near right ribbon (compare to BW-20). Upper-left serif of D partly missing.

Notes: Unique. VG-7. Daniel Holmes Jr. Collection. Discovered by Julius Reiver in October 1968.[46]

1797, 7 Embedded in Drapery, Berries: 5-5, Spine From Bar to Right Ribbon (BW-36, S-NC-7, B-30).

1797, 7 Embedded in Drapery, Berries: 5-5, Spine From Bar to Right Ribbon • BW-37, S-142, B-32. *Breen dies:* 21-T. *Estimated population:* 30 to 45.

Obverse: This die was also used to strike BW-10, see for description.

Reverse: Same as preceding.

Notes: VF is the highest grade known.

1797, 7 Embedded in Drapery, Berries: 5-5, Spine From Bar to Right Ribbon (BW-37, S-142, B-32).

1798, 8 Over 7, Draped Bust

Mintage (per *Mint Report*): **Part of the total for 1798.**

There are two overdated obverse dies and two reverse dies that combine to create a total of three varieties. The most often seen is BW-3. All are collectible, although, except for specialists, most buyers opt for a single example. The typical coin is apt to be in a grade from Good to Fine or VF. Walter Breen knew of no Mint State examples, but William C. Noyes reports an MS-60 coin of BW-3.

Both Sheldon and Breen mix the 1798, 8 Over 7, overdate among regular dates. However, it is thought that most readers consider the overdate to merit a special listing of its own.

1798, 8 Over 7, Closely Spaced Overdate, 8 Touches Drapery • BW-1, S-150, B-6. *Breen dies:* 4-E. *Estimated population:* 50 to 70.

Obverse: *Date:* Date spaced closely. Upper right of 8 touches drapery; definitive. *LIBERTY:* ER wide. Center of E over highest wave of hair. T mostly over hair and only slightly over forehead. *Points of distinction:* Very thin, long denticles.

1798, 8 Over 7, Closely Spaced Overdate, 8 Touches Drapery (BW-1, S-150, B-6).

Reverse: Left stem points to center of U. Fraction bar ends over upper right of 1 in denominator. Leaf edge is noticeably into the bottom-right part of T of CENT. *Points of distinction:* This die was used to coin BW-1 and 1798, Style 1 Hair, Large 8, 8 Very Low (BW-11). Some are bulged at S OF A.

Notes: In his census William C. Noyes lists the R.E. Naftzger Jr. coin as EF-45, the finest recorded. VF is a more achievable objective.

	Cert	Avg	%MS	G-4	VG-8	F-12	VF-20
1798, 8 Over 7, Closely Spaced Overdate, 8 Touches Drapery (BW-1)	(a)			$510	$1,875	$4,500	$8,330

a. Included in certified population for 1798, 8 Over 7, Widely Spaced Overdate, 8 Distant from Drapery (BW-3).

1798, 8 Over 7, Closely Spaced Overdate, 8 Touches Drapery •

BW-2, S-151, B-7. *Breen dies:* 4-F. *Estimated population:* 200 to 300.

Obverse: Same as preceding. *Points of distinction:* In this use a bulge develops in the left field. Eventually, cracks develop, and a rim break is seen at the lower right.

Reverse: Left stem points to lower left of U. Fraction bar ends over space between 1 and 0 in denominator; closer to 1 than to 0. Leaf edge barely overlaps the outer part of the lower-right serif of T of CENT. *Points of distinction:* Some are from a perfect die, others have light cracks.

Notes: EF and AU are the highest grades known, the latter extremely rare.

1798, 8 Over 7, Closely Spaced Overdate,
8 Touches Drapery (BW-2, S-151, B-7).

Detail showing the overdate and long, thin denticles.

	Cert	Avg	%MS	G-4	VG-8	F-12	VF-20	EF-40
1798, 8 Over 7, Closely Spaced Overdate, 8 Touches Drapery (BW-2)	(a)			$360	$800	$3,000	$7,500	$17,500

a. Included in certified population for 1798, 8 Over 7, Widely Spaced Overdate, 8 Distant from Drapery (BW-3).

1798, 8 Over 7, Widely Spaced Overdate, 8 Distant From Drapery

• BW-3, S-152, B-13. *Breen dies:* 10-K. *Estimated population:* 500 to 750.

Obverse: *Date:* Date spaced widely. Upper right of 8 distant from drapery; definitive. *LIBERTY:* ER close. Lower left of E over highest wave of hair. Upright of T over junction of hair and forehead. *Points of distinction:* Short, thick denticles. There is a light

1798, 8 Over 7, Widely Spaced Overdate,
8 Distant From Drapery (BW-3, S-152, B-13).

crack from the denticles to the hair, and on some there is another crack to the ends of the knot.

Reverse: Top-right leaf tip below right edge of S. Crossbar of E of AMERICA connected to serif above. Left stem is very thick at the end and points past U to lower left of N. Fraction bar closer to left ribbon. Denominator widely spaced and with the tops of the digits all on about the same level (unusual, as the first 0 is often lower); 1 leans right. *Points of distinction:* This die was used to coin BW-3 and 1798, Style 1 Hair, Small 8, Leaf Tip Below Right Edge of S (BW-18).

Notes: EF and AU are the highest grades known, the latter extremely rare. Walter Breen notes that the only AU coin known to him, now graded AU-55, had been graded MS-70 in 1966. This is the overdate most often seen, an ideal choice for those who collect one of each major variety listed in the regular edition of the *Guide Book of United States Coins.*

	Cert	Avg	%MS	G-4	VG-8	F-12	VF-20	EF-40	AU-50
1798, 8 Over 7, Widely Spaced Overdate, 8 Distant from Drapery (BW-3)	20	25.7	5%	$240	$470	$1,120	$3,125	$9,250	$18,000

1798, Draped Bust

Mintage (per *Mint Report*): 841,745.

The Sheldon text (and others) suggests points for differentiating the dies of this year, the most difficult assignment up to this point in time, as the dies become more stereotyped. These obverse distinctions are:

Large 8 and Small 8: The Large 8 is about 20 percent taller than the adjacent 9. The bottom center is more nearly round than the following. The Small 8 is about the same size as the adjacent 9. The bottom center is elliptical.

Large 8 in date.   Small 8 in date.

Style 1 Hair and Style 2 Hair: The Style 2 has an extra curl on the interior between the outer curl and the drapery. Generally, Style 1 Hair dies also have very long denticles.

Style 1 Hair.   Style 2 Hair.

Style 1 and Style 2 letters in LIBERTY: Style 1 letters display an R with the lower right delicate, thinner at the bottom, with a serif extending to the right. Style 2 letters display an R with the lower right thicker at the bottom, plus a serif extending to the right. Harry E. Salyards offers this: "I think the best way to differentiate these is to think of the Style 1 'R' as a *gentle slope*, almost like an italic lower case *l* rotated 90 degrees counterclockwise; whereas the Style 2 'R' looks like a *boot*, with the 'heel' almost closing the space toward the upright of the letter."[47]

Style 1 Letters.   Style 2 Letters.

Reverse distinctions include the Type of 1795 with just two leaves at the wreath apex and the type of 1797 with one leaf on the left and two on the right. The latter reverses can be found with Style 1 "R" or Style 2 "R" in AMERICA.

In the present listing the distinctive Reverse of 1795 varieties are listed first. These are followed by the 1797 Style 1 Hair and Style 2 Hair issues, under which Large 8 and Small 8 varieties are noted as is the letter "R" style.

ONE LEAF EACH SIDE OF WREATH APEX—1798 WITH REVERSE STYLE OF 1795

The varieties under this listing are from two reverse dies (both used earlier in 1796) combined with three different obverses. Interestingly, once you check the reverse, simply checking the *style* of the obverse will permit quick attribution as each die is different. Sometimes called Reverse of 1796.

1798, Style 1 Hair, Large 8, Style 2 Letters, Reverse of 1795 • BW-1, S-155, B-9. *Breen dies:* 6-H. *Estimated population:* 300 to 400.

Obverse: *Date:* Very widely spaced. Tip of 7 points between two denticles. 8 high and close to or touches drapery. *LIBERTY:* Widely and fairly evenly spaced. Upright of T over forehead just past hair. *Points of distinction:* Exceptionally long and spike-like denticles. Some are from a perfect die, while others have one or more cracks.

1798, Style 1 Hair, Large 8, Style 2 Letters, Reverse of 1795 (BW-1, S-155, B-9).

Reverse: Outside triple leaves opposite UN, IT, ED, and A. Two leaves opposite O of ONE; three leaves below T of CENT. *Points of distinction:* A light crack is from N to above E of ONE. This die was also used to coin 1796, Date Slopes Down to Right (BW-8); 1796, Club Pole (BW-9); and 1796 (BW-10).

Notes: A popular variety usually seen in lower grades, but many EF and finer coins exist, into the Mint State category—which is itself quite rare.

	Cert	Avg	%MS	G-4	VG-8	F-12	VF-20	EF-40	AU-50
1798, Style 1 Hair, Large 8, Style 2 Letters, Reverse of 1795	(a)			$320	$650	$1,400	$2,625	$7,125	$12,375

a. Included in certified population for 1798, Style 1 Hair, Reverse of 1797.

1798, Style 1 Hair, Large 8, Style 1 Letters, Reverse of 1795 • BW-2, S-156, B-10. *Breen dies:* 7-I. *Estimated population:* 30 to 45.

Obverse: *Date:* 1 close to or touches hair. 17 close. 8 high and touches drapery. *LIBERTY:* Closely spaced. E between two hair high points. Upright of T over junction of hair and forehead. *Points of distinction:* Long spike-like denticles. Some are from a perfect die, and others have a crack starting at the denticles at the lower right.

1798, Style 1 Hair, Large 8, Style 1 Letters, Reverse of 1795 (BW-2, S-156, B-10).

Reverse: Outside triple leaves opposite IT, ED, A, and CA. *Points of distinction:* This die was also used to coin 1796, Closest Date, Pole Very Close to Bust, Triple Leaf Opposite AM (BW-3); 1796, Triple Leaf Opposite AM (BW-4); and 1796, Date Slopes Down to the Right (BW-5). Always with a light crack at the top from OF at the top extended to the left.

Notes: VF is the highest grade known.

	Cert	Avg	%MS	G-4	VG-8	F-12	VF-20
1798, Style 1 Hair, Large 8, Style 1 Letters, Reverse of 1795	(a)			$2,330	$5,330	$8,500	$16,875

a. Included in certified population for 1798, Style 1 Hair, Reverse of 1797.

1798, Style 2 Hair, Small 8, Style 2 Letters, Reverse of 1795 • BW-3, S-178, B-26. *Breen dies:* 19-S. *Estimated population:* 30 to 45.

1798, Style 2 Hair, Small 8, Style 2 Letters, Reverse of 1795 (BW-3, S-178, B-26).

Obverse: *Date:* About evenly spaced. 1 distant from hair. 8 distant from portrait. *LIB-ERTY:* Fairly evenly spaced and high above head. Upright of T over junction of hair and forehead. *Points of distinction:* Denticles small. Crack in the right field becomes more prominent, and another crack develops through the date.

Reverse: Outside triple leaves opposite IT, ED, and CA. *Points of distinction:* This die was also used to coin 1796, Closest Date, Pole Very Close to Bust (BW-2). Multiple cracks develop.

Notes: Fine and VF are the highest grades known.

	Cert	Avg	%MS	G-4	VG-8	F-12	VF-20
1798, Style 2 Hair, Small 8, Style 2 Letters, Reverse of 1795	(a)			$2,950	$5,750	$9,670	$23,330

a. Included in certified population for 1798, Style 2 Hair, Reverse of 1797.

ONE LEAF LEFT AND TWO LEAVES RIGHT AT APEX— *1798 WITH REVERSE STYLE OF 1797*

Typical values for 1798, Style 1 Hair, cents with the Reverse of 1797. Rare varieties may be worth more.

	Cert	Avg	%MS	G-4	VG-8	F-12	VF-20	EF-40	AU-50	MS-60BN	MS-63BN	MS-63RB
1798, Style 1 Hair, Reverse of 1797	76	24.6	1%	$110	$180	$250	$750	$2,470	$5,330	$10,000	$18,750	$29,000

STYLE 1 HAIR, LARGE 8, STYLE 1 LETTERS

There are six varieties within this group. The obverses and reverses are described in a manner in which each obverse and reverse combination is unique.

1798, Style 1 Hair, Large 8, Leaf Tip Between S and O, Buckled Reverse Die • BW-6, S-144, B-1. *Breen dies:* 1-A. *Estimated population:* 30 to 45.

1798, Style 1 Hair, Large 8, Leaf Tip Between S and O, Buckled Reverse Die (BW-6, S-144, B-1).

Obverse: *Date:* Closely spaced, Sheldon's "Large Close Date," Breen's "Closest Date." 17 slightly wider than 798. 1 and 8 each about centered between bust and denticles. Tip of 7 points to denticle. *LIBERTY:* LIB close. E over space between two high waves. R close to hair. Upright of T over junction of hair and forehead. *Points of distinction:* Denticles long, thin, and widely spaced. Closely spaced over the space between R and T.

Detail of close date.

Reverse: Top-right leaf tip below space between S and O. Long fraction bar with spine *tilting slightly upward* at right end. 10 slightly closer than

00. *Points of distinction:* A bulge extends from A of STATES across the die to near R of AMERICA. On later impressions, cracks are seen here and there.

Notes: Typically VG is highest in the marketplace, but one each VF and EF have been reported.

1798, Style 1 Hair, Large 8, Spine Connects Bar to Right Ribbon •
BW-7, S-145, B-2. *Breen dies:* 1-B. *Estimated population:* 300 to 400.

1798, Style 1 Hair, Large 8, Spine Connects Bar to Right Ribbon (BW-7, S-145, B-2).

Obverse: As preceding. *Points of distinction:* From a perfect die or with a crack, in from the neck, extending to the denticles.

Reverse: Top-right leaf tip below S slightly right of its center. Leaf below left side of C of CENT is skeletal. Fraction bar connects with right ribbon via a spine; definitive. Small, raised die chip directly below ribbon knot (weak on some). Three denticles are heavy and close over second S of STATES. All denticles are bold. *Points of distinction:* Die

Detail of three heavy denticles over second S of STATES.

states vary from perfect to with a bulge at the upper right, later with a crack over OF and with minor cracks elsewhere.

Notes: EF is the highest grade known.

1798, Style 1 Hair, Large 8, Spine From Stem to U •
BW-8, S-146, B-3. *Breen dies:* 2-C. *Estimated population:* 45 to 60.

Obverse: *Date:* Fairly evenly spaced. 1 closer to hair than to denticles. 8 closer to denticles than to drapery. *LIBERTY:* IB and RTY close. Hair under R unfinished. Upright of T over junction between hair and forehead, more over forehead. *Points of distinction:* This is a very curious die, that underwent various relapping and strengthening, also used on BW-9.

1798, Style 1 Hair, Large 8, Spine From Stem to U (BW-8, S-146, B-3).

Reverse: Top-right leaf tip below space between E and S. Left stem has a spine projecting from its end; on high-grade examples this connects to U. In the denominator the 1 is to the left of the end of the bar.

Notes: VF is typical highest, but single EF (ANS) and Mint State coins have been reported.

1798, Style 1 Hair, Large 8, 1 Lower Than First 0 in Fraction, Second 0 Almost Touches Ribbon • BW-9, S-147, B-4. *Breen dies:* 2-D. *Estimated population:* 60 to 75.

Obverse: Same as preceding, but reworked, with loop added below drapery, hair strengthened under R (R now touches hair).

Reverse: A of STATES slightly low and leans right. Top-right leaf tip below right corner of E. C of CENT low, T high. Tiny fraction bar. 1 lower than adjacent 0 (definitive); second 0 far right and nearly touches ribbon. *Points of distinction:* Light cracks develop.

1798, Style 1 Hair, Large 8, 1 Lower Than First 0 in Fraction, Second 0 Almost Touches Ribbon (BW-9, S-147, B-4).

Detail of low 1 in denominator.

Notes: VF and EF are the highest grades known, and examples are very rare as such.

1798, Style 1 Hair, Large 8, Hollow Area in Lower Curls • BW-10, S-148, B-11. *Breen dies:* 8-J. *Estimated population:* 750 to 1,000.

Obverse: *Date:* 1 closer to hair than to denticles. 98 slightly close. 8 almost touches denticles and is distant from drapery. *LIBERTY:* BE slightly wide. B leans slightly right. R close to hair. Upright of T over junction of hair and forehead. *Points of distinction:* Hollow or flat area at inside outer edge of lower curls from excess relapping of the die. Die states vary from perfect to later states with light cracks, then heavy cracks and a cud break over ERT.

1798, Style 1 Hair, Large 8, Hollow Area in Lower Curls (BW-10, S-148, B-11).

Detail showing hollow or flat area in lower curls.

Reverse: Berry below left side of E of UNITED has a long stem and does not touch leaves. Top-right leaf tip below S slightly left of its center. ONE / CENT irregularly aligned. *Points of distinction:* There is a light crack at the top of UNITED and extending to the right. Later states have a crack at the top of AMERICA. This die was used to coin BW-10 and BW-14.

Notes: This variety exists in Mint State.

1798, Style 1 Hair, Large 8, 8 Very Low • BW-11, S-149, B-5. *Breen dies:* 3-E. *Estimated population:* 60 to 75.

Obverse: *Date:* 179 close. 1 and 8 closer to denticles than to bust. *LIBERTY:* LIB close. Prominent curl between B and E. R lower than E and close to head. Upright of T over junction of hair and forehead, closer to forehead. *Points of distinction:* Defects develop in the right obverse field.

1798, Style 1 Hair, Large 8, 8 Very Low (BW-11, S-149, B-5).

Reverse: Berry below left side of E of UNITED has a long stem and does not touch leaves. Top-right leaf tip below S slightly left of its center. Small spine from left of fraction bar (not visible on all examples). Bar slants

Detail of slanted fraction bar.

down to right; covers about half of 1 and left part of second 0. *Points of distinction:* This die was also used to coin 1798, 8 Over 7, Closely Spaced Overdate, 8 Touches Drapery (BW-1). Some are bulged at S OF A.

Notes: This variety has a very low top range, with the finest variously graded as net F-12 and F-15, and the next dozen no better than VG.[48]

STYLE 1 HAIR, LARGE 8, STYLE 2 LETTERS
There are only two varieties in this category, making their attribution easy.

1798, Style 1 Hair, Large 8, 7 Almost Touches Denticle • BW-14, S-153, B-12. *Breen dies:* 9-J. *Estimated population:* 300 to 400.

Obverse: *Date:* 179 close, 98 wide. 7 almost touches a denticle. 8 about halfway between denticles and drapery. *LIBERTY:* I leans slightly right. ERT close. T mostly over hair. *Points of distinction:* Fused denticles over space between B and E. Some are from a per-

1798, Style 1 Hair, Large 8, 7 Almost Touches Denticle (BW-14, S-153, B-12).

fect die, and others have one or more cracks. In its latest state there is a break connecting the rim to the bust.

Reverse: Berry below left side of E of UNITED has a long stem and does not touch leaves. Top-right leaf tip below S slightly left of its center. ONE about evenly spaced. *Points of distinction:* This die was used to coin BW-10 and BW-14. Peripheral cracks expand as the die is used.

Notes: Known only in circulated grades. EF is the highest-known grade.

1798, Style 1 Hair, Large 8 Embedded in Drapery • BW-15,

S-154, B-8. *Breen dies:* 5-G. *Estimated population:* 75 to 120.

Obverse: *Date:* 1 about equidistant from hair and denticles. 17 wide. 8 high and into the drapery. *LIBERTY:* IBE wide. R close to hair. T mostly over hair. *Points of distinction:* Denticles long and spike-like. Some are from a perfect die, and others have a crack from the drapery to the denticles.

1798, Style 1 Hair, Large 8 Embedded in Drapery (BW-15, S-154, B-8).

Reverse: Top-right leaf tip below S slightly right of its center. O of ONE distant from N; N close to E. Berry left of bow has its own stem. *Points of distinction:* A swelling can be seen among certain of the peripheral letters.

Notes: EF plus a single Mint State are the highest grades recorded.

STYLE 1 HAIR, SMALL 8, STYLE 2 LETTERS

This format includes 10 different die varieties, two of which Dr. Sheldon rated as Non Collectible, the only such rarities among 1798 issues. Careful examination of both sides will permit identification.

1798, Style 1 Hair, Small 8, Leaf Tip Below Right Edge of S • BW-18,

S-NC-1, B-14. *Breen dies:* 11-K. *Recorded population:* 6.

Obverse: *Date:* 79 close. 8 slightly closer to denticles than to drapery. *LIBERTY:* I leans slightly right. RTY slightly wide. T mostly over hair. *Points of distinction:* A crack develops at the upper right, eventually connecting to the hair.

1798, Style 1 Hair, Small 8, Leaf Tip Below Right Edge of S (BW-18, S-NC-1, B-14).

Reverse: Top-right leaf tip below right edge of S; definitive. Crossbar of E of AMERICA connected to serif above. Left stem is very thick at the end and points past U to lower left of N. Fraction bar closer to left ribbon. Denominator widely spaced and with the tops of the digits all on about the same level (unusual, as the first 0 is often lower); 1 leans right. *Points of distinction:* This die was also used to coin 1798, 8 Over 7, Widely Spaced Overdate, 8 Distant from Drapery (BW-3).

Notes: The "best" coin has EF sharpness, *but* with a deep scratch in the right obverse field, suggesting various "net" grades ranging from F-12 to VF-20.[49]

1798, Style 1 Hair, Small 8, Three Fused Denticles Below 9 • BW-19, S-157, B-15. *Breen dies:* 12-L. ***Estimated population:*** 750 to 1,000.

Obverse: *Date:* 98 very slightly wide. Three fused denticles below 9; definitive. 8 about equidistant from denticles and drapery. *LIBERTY:* High above head. Fairly closely spaced. B leans right. E centered over high wave. Upright of T over hair. *Points of dis-*

1798, Style 1 Hair, Small 8, Three Fused Denticles Below 9 (BW-19, S-157, B-15).

tinction: Sometimes from a perfect die, but more often with die crumbling and, in a later state, a crack through 798.

Reverse: Top-right leaf tip below center edge of S. Raised area within C of AMERICA; Breen suggests that it is the remnant of an erroneous T. Ribbon segments are weak. Numerator 1 is left of center above bar. Bar extends from upper right of 1 to about halfway over second 0. 10 wide, 00 closest. *Points of distinction:* Some are from a perfect die, and others have one or two light cracks among the border letters. Rust developed on the die in later use.

Notes: This variety is known in Mint State.

1798, Style 1 Hair, Small 8, Rim Break Over RTY, Leaf Tip Between S and O, Left Stem Too Short • BW-20, S-NC-2, B-16. *Breen dies:* 13-M. ***Recorded population:*** 6.

Obverse: *Date:* 79 wide. *LIBERTY:* Very widely spaced. T mostly over forehead. *Points of distinction:* On all a large rim cud is seen at RTY and to the left and right, indicating this die must have had a problem very early.

1798, Style 1 Hair, Small 8, Rim Break Over RTY, Leaf Tip Between S and O, Left Stem Too Short (BW-20, S-NC-2, B-16).

Reverse: Top-right leaf tip below space between S and O; definitive. AMERICA widely spaced (normally the spacing is close and AME in particular are tight or touching at their bases). C of CENT separated from leaf. Left stem too short. 6 berries left, 5 right.

Notes: The highest-graded example is VG-8.

1798, Style 1 Hair, Small 8, Left Stem Too Short • BW-21, S-158, B-17. *Breen dies:* 14-M. ***Estimated population:*** 120 to 160.

Obverse: *Date:* 17 close, 98 wide. 17 closest to denticles. 8 slightly closer to drapery than to denticles. *LIBERTY:* LI close. E and R each over a wave. Upright of T over hair. Y slightly low. *Points of distinction:* Center curl behind shoulder is a flat area at its center. Loop under drapery incomplete at left. In its

1798, Style 1 Hair, Small 8, Left Stem Too Short (BW-21, S-158, B-17).

late state there are three nearly vertical, nearly parallel die cracks in the left field.

Reverse: Same as preceding. ***Points of distinction:*** Some are from a perfect die, and others show cracks around the border letters.

Notes: EF to AU are the highest grades known, the latter extremely rare.

1798, Style 1 Hair, Small 8, Three Vertical Cracks in Left Field, 1 of 100 Distant to Left

• BW-22, S-159, B-18. *Breen dies:* 14-N. ***Estimated population:*** 200 to 300.

1798, Style 1 Hair, Small 8, Three Vertical Cracks in Left Field, 1 of 100 Distant to Left (BW-22, S-159, B-18).

Obverse: Same as preceding. ***Points of distinction:*** Always with three nearly vertical, nearly parallel die cracks in the left field (but compare to BW-21, sometimes seen in this state).

Reverse: Top-right leaf tip below S very slightly to the right of its center. Right stem very close to leaf and points to left foot of A. Fraction bar with thin spine at right. 10 widely separated with 1 left of the bar. ***Points***

Detail of distant 1 in denominator.

of distinction: With cracks among the letters around the border. This die was used to coin both BW-22 and BW-26.

Notes: There is a coin of Mint State in the ANS, otherwise EF and AU are the highest grades available.

1798, Style 1 Hair, Small 8, Lines From Denticles to ER of AMERICA

• BW-23, S-160, B-21. *Breen dies:* 17-P. ***Estimated population:*** 30 to 40.

1798, Style 1 Hair, Small 8, Lines From Denticles to ER of AMERICA (BW-23, S-160, B-21).

Obverse: *Date:* 1 slightly closer to hair than to denticles. 98 wide. 8 about centered between drapery and the top of a denticle. *LIBERTY:* Widely spaced, ERT closest. Lower-left serif of E over high wave of hair. T over junction between hair and forehead. ***Points of distinction:*** Some are from a perfect die, and others have a light crack from the denticles, extending to the neck, upper drapery, and hair.

Reverse: Top-right leaf tip below S very slightly to the left of its center. Lower-left serifs of E of STATES and F are mostly missing. Lines from denticles to ER of AMER-

Detail showing crude alignment of letters. Likely, workmen who had little artistic skill prepared certain dies in this era.

ICA. ***Points of distinction:*** This die was used to coin BW-23, BW-25, and BW-43. This is an earlier *stage* of the die, later reworked, used to coin BW-24.[50] Some are from a perfect die, while others have cracks among the border letters.

Notes: This variety exists in Mint State, and is rare so fine.

1798, Style 1 Hair, Small 8, Large Berries, Serif of C of CENT a Tiny Spine • BW-24, S-161, B-22. *Breen dies:* 17-Q. *Estimated population:* Thousands.

1798, Style 1 Hair, Small 8, Large Berries, Serif of C of CENT a Tiny Spine (BW-24, S-161, B-22).

Obverse: Same as preceding. *Points of distinction:* Cracks develop and expand.

Reverse: Top-right leaf tip below S very slightly to the left of its center. Top serif of C of CENT is a tiny downward spine. Berries are very large. Numerator centered over bar and high above it. Fraction bar centered between ribbons and extends from right side of 1 to near center of second 0. Compare to BW-27. *Points of distinction:* This die in an earlier *stage* was used to coin BW-23, BW-25, and BW-43. Afterward it was reworked to coin the presently described BW-24.[51] Cracks and bulges develop over the life of the die, and there is a large rim break at the upper left.

Notes: Readily available in EF or slightly finer grades. However, AU and Mint State are both very rare.

1798, Style 1 Hair, Small 8, Incomplete Hair Below ER, Full Knob on 9, Lines From Denticles to ER of AMERICA • BW-25, S-162, B-23. *Breen dies:* 18-P. *Estimated population:* 120 to 160.

1798, Style 1 Hair, Small 8, Incomplete Hair Below ER, Full Knob on 9, Lines From Denticles to ER of AMERICA (BW-25, S-162, B-23).

Obverse: *Date:* 1 without upper-left serif. Full knob on 9. 8 centered between denticles and drapery. *LIBERTY:* ERT wide. Upright of T over hair. *Points of distinction:* Highest waves of hair below ER are low and incomplete (compare to the next). Clash marks develop. A crack extends from the rim to the ribbon.

Reverse: See BW-23. *Points of distinction:* This die was used to coin BW-23, BW-25, and BW-43. This is an earlier *stage* of the die, later reworked, used to coin BW-24.[52] Some are from a perfect die, and others have a light crack beginning in the denticles between S of STATES and O. Clash marks are at the top of the die.

Notes: There is one example of Mint State (ANS), otherwise VF is the highest grade.

1798, Style 1 Hair, Small 8, Incomplete Hair Below ER, Knob on 9 Incomplete • BW-26, S-163, B-19. *Breen dies:* 15-N. *Estimated population:* 120 to 160.

1798, Style 1 Hair, Small 8, Incomplete Hair Below ER, Knob on 9 Incomplete (BW-26, S-163, B-19).

Obverse: *Date:* 1 about equidistant from hair and denticles. Partial knob on 9. 8 twice as close to denticles than to drapery. *LIBERTY:* IB closest. Upright of T over hair. *Points of distinction:* Highest waves of hair below ER are low and incomplete (compare to the preceding). The die began to crack apart, with cracks increasing in heaviness with later impressions.

Reverse: See BW-22. *Points of distinction:* This die was used to coin BW-22 and BW-26. The die, already with cracks, is now seen with more, most heavy.

Notes: VF is the highest grade known.

1798, Style 1 Hair, Small 8, Large Berries, Serif of C of CENT Normal

• BW-27, S-164, B-20. *Breen dies:* 16-O. *Estimated population:* 120 to 160.

Obverse: *Date:* 1 close to and almost touches hair. 79 close. 8 closer to drapery than to denticles. *LIBERTY:* LIB close. I leans right. E and R over high hair waves. Upright of T over hair. *Points of distinction:* A few were struck from a perfect die, but most have swelling, sometimes extensive, near the bottom border.

1798, Style 1 Hair, Small 8, Large Berries, Serif of C of CENT Normal (BW-27, S-164, B-20).

Reverse: Top-right leaf tip below S is left of S's center, but not quite below serif. E of STATES and F have short left serifs. Lowest leaf on the right is incomplete. C of CENT has normal serif. Left branch thick at end. Right ribbon bow weak on its right side. Large berries. Numerator centered over bar and high above it. Bar centered between ribbons and extends from right side of 1 to left side of second 0. 10 very slightly closer than 00. Compare to BW-24.

Notes: AU is the highest grade known.

Typical values for 1798, Style 2 Hair, cents with the Reverse of 1797. Rare varieties may be worth more.

	Cert	Avg	%MS	G-4	VG-8	F-12	VF-20	EF-40	AU-50	MS-60BN	MS-63BN	MS-63RB
1798, Style 2 Hair, Reverse of 1797	198	31.0	4%	$90	$160	$300	$640	$2,050	$3,600	$8,070	$16,500	$26,670

STYLE 2 HAIR, LARGE 8, STYLE 2 LETTERS

This format includes just three varieties, all of which share the same obverse. Accordingly, attribution is by the reverse die. The features at and near CENT are definitive.

1798, Style 2 Hair, Large 8

• BW-29, S-165, B-31. *Breen dies:* 23-U. *Estimated population:* 120 to 160.

Obverse: *Date:* Date low. 79 close. *LIBERTY:* High above head. LIB and ER slightly close. TY unusually wide. Upright of T over hair. *Points of distinction:* Highest hair waves under ER are shallow. Die chip gives Miss Liberty a little wart below her chin.

1798, Style 2 Hair, Large 8 (BW-29, S-165, B-31).

Reverse: Prominent stem on leaf pair below T of CENT; serif on C is light (but not a spine); berry opposite C touches branch. *Points of distinction:* Some are from a perfect die, and others have a crack from the denticles, to between I and C, and to a berry.

Notes: VF and EF are the highest grades known, the latter being extremely rare.

1798, Style 2 Hair, Large 8 • BW-30, S-166, B-32. *Breen dies:* 23-V. **Estimated population:** Thousands.

Obverse: Same as preceding.

Reverse: Little or no stem on leaf pair below T of CENT; serif on C is a spine; berry opposite C touches branch. **Points of distinction:** All display a crack from the denticles, through E of UNITED, to the leaves and other lower areas, and to the second 0 to the rim. Some others have additional cracks.

1798, Style 2 Hair, Large 8 (BW-30, S-166, B-32).

Notes: Available in Mint State. One of the most often seen varieties of 1798. Years ago this was a popular variety to alter to "1799," but the reverse crack serves to quickly identify such deceptions. "This is a very difficult coin to find with nice surfaces. There are probably only 30 to 40 that are truly choice." [53]

1798, Style 2 Hair, Large 8 • BW-31, S-167, B-33. *Breen dies:* 23-W. **Estimated population:** Thousands.

Obverse: Same as preceding. **Points of distinction:** The crack present on the previous use has expanded, and on some coins there are additional cracks. The die was worn far past what would have been a normal useful life.

Reverse: Little or no stem on leaf pair below T of CENT; serif on C is normal; berry opposite C is on a stem and does not touch the branch. **Points of distinction:** Multiple cracks occur, and a rim cud develops at the top of the first T of STATES.

1798, Style 2 Hair, Large 8 (BW-31, S-167, B-33).

Detail showing flow marks in the field from an extremely worn die.

Notes: Another readily available variety. AU and a couple of Mint State exist. As AU coins exist in fair numbers, some will probably "graduate" to become Mint State. There is a difference of opinion among experts as to the actual grades of the finest pieces. Walter Breen lists more than a dozen AU and MS examples, while some others suggest the actual population is no more than half that many.[54]

STYLE 2 HAIR, SMALL 8, STYLE 2 LETTERS

This format is the most extensive within the 1798 year and thus provides the greatest challenge for distinction. Attention to details on both sides, including comparing with the photographs, will result in the correct die-variety attribution.

1798, Style 2 Hair, Small 8, Leaf Tip Under Center of D of UNITED •

BW-34, S-168, B-27. *Breen dies:* 20-J. *Estimated population:* 300 to 400.

1798, Style 2 Hair, Small 8, Leaf Tip Under Center of D of UNITED (BW-34, S-168, B-27).

Obverse: *Date:* Fairly evenly spaced, 98 very slightly wider. 1 slightly closer to hair than to denticles. Tip of 7 opposite space between denticles. 8 significantly closer to drapery than to denticles. *LIBERTY:* IB closest. B leans slightly right. E and R over waves of hair. Upright of T over hair. *Points of distinction:* Multiple clash marks are seen in the latest state.

Reverse: Style 2 letters. Top-right leaf tip below center of S. Very long stem to the berry right of T of CENT. Fraction bar closer to left ribbon. 10 closer than 00. *Points of distinction:* Cracks are present on all examples.

Notes: AU is the highest grade except for one Mint State.

1798, Style 2 Hair, Small 8 • BW-35,

S-169, B-28. *Breen dies:* 20-T. *Estimated population:* 300 to 400.

1798, Style 2 Hair, Small 8 (BW-35, S-169, B-28).

Obverse: Same as preceding. *Points of distinction:* A small rim break develops between 9 and 8. Bulges develop.

Reverse: Style 2 letters. Top-right leaf tip slightly left of center of S. Left stem slightly shorter than right. Fraction bar is heavy and slopes down to the right slightly. 1 in denominator high. *Points of distinction:* Light clash marks are on all.

Notes: AU is the highest grade known.

1798, Style 2 Hair, Small 8 • BW-36,

S-170, B-29. *Breen dies:* 21-T. *Estimated population:* 300 to 400.

1798, Style 2 Hair, Small 8 (BW-36, S-170, B-29).

Obverse: *Date:* Fairly evenly spaced. 1 and 8 distant from bust. *LIBERTY:* Fairly evenly spaced, including ERT (compare to next). E over wave. T mostly over hair. *Points of distinction:* Some are from a perfect die, but most have a crack from the denticles through the ribbon ends, ending at the denticles behind the lowest curl. A crack develops from the rim, through T, and to the hair.

Reverse: Same as preceding.

Notes: The base of the date is into the border on many pieces. Several EF examples and one Mint State example exist.

1798, Style 2 Hair, Small 8 • BW-37,
S-171, B-30. *Breen dies:* 22-T. **Estimated population:** 120 to 160.

Obverse: *Date:* Fairly evenly spaced. 1 is slightly closer to hair than to denticles. 8 is closer to drapery than to denticles. *LIBERTY:* E over wave. ER closer than RT. Upright of T over hair. **Points of distinction:** A close copy of the preceding die. A rim cud is to the left of L. On some there is a crack from the rim over T, through Y, and to the denticles on the right edge.

Reverse: Same as preceding.

Notes: EF and AU are the highest grades known, the latter very rare.

1798, Style 2 Hair, Small 8 (BW-37, S-171, B-30).

Detail of rim cud to the left of L.

1798, Style 2 Hair, Small 8 • BW-38,
S-172, B-34. *Breen dies:* 24-X. **Estimated population:** 750 to 1,000.

Obverse: *Date:* Serif of 1 is closer to hair than base is to denticles. Base of 7 over denticle. 98 slightly wide. 8 closer to denticles than drapery, and over a denticle. *LIBERTY:* High above head. IB close; both letters lean slightly right. T mostly over hair. **Points of distinction:** Some are from a perfect die, but

1798, Style 2 Hair, Small 8 (BW-38, S-172, B-34).

most have denticle clash marks at the upper rim. On later strikings the die deteriorates further.

Reverse: Style 2 letters. Top-right leaf tip under serif of S. Left stem slightly shorter than right. Fraction bar slopes down to the right slightly. 1 in denominator high. **Points of distinction:** Some are from a perfect die, others have a light crack from the left ribbon to A of AMERICA, and in a later state some appear with a heavy break over ICA.

Notes: AU and lower-range Mint State are the highest grades known, and all examples are rare at these levels.

1798, Style 2 Hair, Small 8 • BW-40,

S-173, B-38. *Breen dies:* 27-BB. ***Estimated population:*** 300 to 400.

Obverse: *Date:* Fairly evenly spaced. Serif of 1 closer to hair than base is to denticles. 7 points to space between denticles. 8 closer to denticles than to drapery. *LIBERTY:* LI close. I leans slightly right. BER wide. E and R over waves. Upright of T over hair. Base of Y low and with patched lower-left serif. *Points of distinction:* Some are from a perfect die, but most have a cud over RTY, and on the latest impression this expands to the left.

1798, Style 2 Hair, Small 8 (BW-40, S-173, B-38).

Detail of cud over RTY.

Reverse: Style 2 letters. Top-right leaf tip under serif of S. Lower-left serif of E of STATES incomplete. Left stem slightly shorter than right. Berry left of bow touches the stem. Pair of leaves opposite RI touch the stem. Numerals in denominator evenly spaced. *Points of distinction:* This die was also used to coin 1799, 9 Over 8 (BW-1). Most are from a perfect die, but some have a crack at the top of NITE. In the latest state, quite rare, there is a rim break at CA.

Notes: This variety exists in Mint State, and is elusive as such.

1798, Style 2 Hair, Small 8, Spine on Top of 1 of 1798, Raised Chips Below Ribbon • BW-41, S-174, B-35.

Breen dies: 25-Y. ***Estimated population:*** 750 to 1,000.

Obverse: *Date:* Tiny spine extends upward from top of 1. 17 close. 8 closer to drapery than to denticles. *LIBERTY:* High over head. BERT wide. E and left upright of R over waves. T mostly over hair. Left-bottom serif

1798, Style 2 Hair, Small 8, Spine on Top of 1 of 1798, Raised Chips Below Ribbon (BW-41, S-174, B-35).

of Y patched. *Points of distinction:* Problems develop, including a short crack at the lower left. The die is relapped to remove multiple clash marks.

Reverse: Style 2 letters. Top-right leaf tip under serif of S. A of STATES leans slightly right; lower-left serif of E incomplete. Numerator 1 leans slightly left. 1 in denominator closer to bar than other numerals. *Points of distinction:* There is a light crack near the fraction, and on some later impressions there are clash marks in that area.

Notes: AU is the highest grade known.

1798, Style 2 Hair, Small 8 • BW-42,
S-175, B-36. *Breen dies: 25-Z.* **Estimated population:** 200 to 300.

Obverse: Same as preceding. *Points of distinction:* The die in this use, relapped, develops a small rim crack at the lower-left rim.

Reverse: Style 2 letters. Top-right leaf tip under serif of S. Lower-left serif of E incomplete. Left stem slightly shorter. *Points of*

1798, Style 2 Hair, Small 8 (BW-42, S-175, B-36).

distinction: On this later state other cracks eventually develop, some so light as to be seen only on high-grade examples. Eventually there is a rim break engulfing the top of the U.

Notes: EF, or slightly finer, is the highest grade available.

1798, Style 2 Hair, Small 8, Lines From Denticles to ER of AMERICA •
BW-43, S-176, B-24. *Breen dies: 19-P.* **Estimated population:** 120 to 160.

Obverse: *Date:* Low and fairly evenly spaced. *LIBERTY:* LIB slightly closer than other letters. T mostly over hair. Not often found from a perfect die. Most have a crack which starts at the lower right and extends upward. On later strikings this expands, such as in the next use of the die, for BW-44.

1798, Style 2 Hair, Small 8, Lines From Denticles to ER of AMERICA (BW-43, S-176, B-24).

Reverse: See BW-23. Style 2 letters. *Points of distinction:* With two or more cracks. This die was used to coin BW-23, BW-25, and BW-43. This is an earlier *stage* of the die, later reworked, used to coin BW-24.[55]

Notes: EF and AU are the highest grades known, and examples are very rare as such. One EF coin in the ANS is struck over a British Conder token with "N ANGLE" visible on the edge, from part of a longer inscription.[56]

1798, Style 2 Hair, Small 8, Style 1 Reverse Letters, Parts of Ribbon Missing • BW-44, S-177, B-25. *Breen dies:*
19-R. **Estimated population:** 75 to 120.

Obverse: Same as preceding. *Points of distinction:* Now always with vertical die crack in right field, as is already seen in late states of BW-43.

Reverse: Style 1 letters (thinner lower right of R). Top-right leaf tip under center of S.

1798, Style 2 Hair, Small 8, Style 1 Reverse Letters, Parts of Ribbon Missing (BW-44, S-177, B-25).

Berry opposite upright of E of UNITED fused into leaf. IC widely spaced. Berry to right of T of CENT has long stem. Parts of both ribbons are missing, most dramatically leaving a raised "island" past A. Numerator to slight right of center above fraction bar.

Notes: VF is the highest grade known.

1798, Style 2 Hair, Small 8 • BW-45, S-179, B-37.[57] *Breen dies:* 26-AA. ***Estimated population:*** 750 to 1,000.

Obverse: *Date:* Low. 98 slightly wide and about on the same level. *LIBERTY:* Widely spaced. E and R over high waves of hair. Serifs at base of Y are mostly gone. T mostly over hair. *Points of distinction:* Clash marks develop, and are removed by relapping, after which additional clash marks are sustained.

1798, Style 2 Hair, Small 8 (BW-45, S-179, B-37).

Reverse: Style 2 letters. Top-right leaf tip under serif of S. E of AMERICA first punched upside down, then corrected. CE slightly wider than usual. *Points of distinction:* Clash marks develop, and are removed by relapping.

Notes: This variety exists in Mint State.

1798, Style 2 Hair, Small 8, Patch of Hair Missing Below Ear • BW-46, S-180, B-41. *Breen dies:* 29-EE. ***Estimated population:*** 40 to 55.

Obverse: *Date:* Low. 79 slightly closer. 8 higher than other numerals. *LIBERTY:* IB close. Both letters lean slightly right. Upright of T over hair. *Points of distinction:* Patch of hair missing below ear to the left. Nearly horizontal crack in the left field and a light crack at the top of ER.

1798, Style 2 Hair, Small 8, Patch of Hair Missing Below Ear (BW-46, S-180, B-41).

Reverse: Style 2 letters. Top-right leaf tip under serif of S. Leaf opposite T of UNITED weak. R of AMERICA has a straight tail from reworking (not Style 1). Left stem shorter and thinner than right. *Points of distinction:* As the die deteriorates, a large rim cud is seen above TATE.

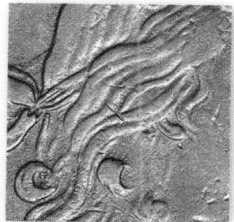

Detail of missing hair.

Notes: VF is the highest grade known.

1798, Style 2 Hair, Small 8, Berries 6 Left and 5 Right, Large Heavy Fraction • BW-47, S-181, B-42. *Breen dies:* 29-FF. *Estimated population:* 300 to 400.

1798, Style 2 Hair, Small 8, Berries 6 Left and 5 Right, Large Heavy Fraction (BW-47, S-181, B-42).

Obverse: Same as preceding. *Points of distinction:* The crack at the left expands, and there is an additional crack.

Reverse: Style 2 letters. Top-right leaf tip under serif of S. Large fraction with heavy features. The denominator of the fraction shows 00 over a previous smaller 00.

Detail of the fraction showing 00 over smaller 00 in the denominator.

Notes: AU and Mint State are the highest-known grades, and examples are rare as such.

1798, Style 2 Hair, Small 8, Style 1 Reverse Letters, Line Connects Right Ribbon and A • BW-48, S-182, B-43. *Breen dies:* 30-GG. *Estimated population:* 160 to 200.

1798, Style 2 Hair, Small 8, Style 1 Reverse Letters, Line Connects Right Ribbon and A (BW-48, S-182, B-43).

Obverse: *Date:* 79 slightly closer. 8 closer to drapery than to denticles. *LIBERTY:* BE and RT slightly wide. T above hair but close to junction. *Points of distinction:* Flat area in hair above first hair strand over 1.

Reverse: Style 1 letters. Top-right leaf tip slightly left of center of S. CENT low. A die scratch forms a ridge from the right ribbon to A; definitive.

Detail of line between second A of AMERICA and ribbon.

Notes: Singles are AU and Mint State, otherwise grades are EF and lower.

1798, Style 2 Hair, Small 8, High Top Serif on 7 • BW-50, S-183, B-44. *Breen dies:* 31-GG. *Estimated population:* 45 to 60.

1798, Style 2 Hair, Small 8, High Top Serif on 7 (BW-50, S-183, B-44).

Obverse: *Date:* Low and evenly spaced. High top serif on 7. *LIBERTY:* LIB close, IB closest. E and R over high waves. Upright of T over hair but close to junction. *Points of distinction:* Compare to the following, especially LIBERTY.

Reverse: Same as preceding.

Notes: VF and EF are the highest-known grades. Comment from Harry E. Salyards: "This is an excellent variety to illustrate the perils of assigning a high rarity rating to a not-particularly-distinctive variety, which looks very similar to . . . a very common variety—in this case, the S-184 that follows. Sheldon called the S-183 an R-8 in *Early American Cents*, having seen all of *two* examples. By the time of publication of *Penny Whimsy* it was down to an R-7; by the revised EAC rarity ratings in the early 1980s, it was down to R-6; and now it's considered no better than an R-5."[58]

1798, Style 2 Hair, Small 8, High Top Serif on 7 • BW-51, S-184, B-45.

Breen dies: 32-GG. **Estimated population:** 1,250 to 1,500.

Obverse: *Date:* Low and about evenly spaced. High top serif on 7. *LIBERTY:* Widely spaced. Uprights of E and R over high waves. Upright of T over junction of hair and forehead, but slightly more over hair. **Points of distinction:** Compare to the preceding, especially LIBERTY.

Reverse: Same as preceding.

Notes: This variety exists in Mint State, and is rare so fine.

1798, Style 2 Hair, Small 8, High Top Serif on 7 (BW-51, S-184, B-45).

1798, Style 2 Hair, Small 8, Thick Fraction Bar Slopes Down to Right • BW-52, S-185, B-46. *Breen dies:* 32-HH. **Estimated population:** 500 to 750.

Obverse: Same as preceding. **Points of distinction:** Multiple cracks are seen on all.

Reverse: Style 2 letters. Highest-right leaf below serif of S (slightly more left than usual). Fraction bar overly thick and sloped down to right. Numerator over 0, but left of center of the bar. **Points of distinction:** On early impressions a clash mark with denticles is above ERICA. This fades, but other clashes appear. In a late state there is a rim cud over IC.

Notes: EF is the highest-known grade.

1798, Style 2 Hair, Small 8, Thick Fraction Bar Slopes Down to Right (BW-52, S-185, B-46).

Detail of fraction with thick, sloping bar.

1798, Style 2 Hair, Small 8, Style 1 Reverse Letters, Crack From Fraction to ME • BW-53, S-186, B-39. *Breen dies:* 28-CC. **Estimated population:** 750 to 1,000.

Obverse: *Date:* Low. 79 slightly close. *LIBERTY:* LIB and ER close. E and R over high waves. Upright of T over hair. Lower-right serif of Y short. **Points of distinction:** Always with a light crack at TY to the right rim.

1798, Style 2 Hair, Small 8, Style 1 Reverse Letters, Crack From Fraction to ME (BW-53, S-186, B-39).

Reverse: Berry left of bow is distant from the stem. Pair of leaves opposite RI overlap and hide the stem. *Points of distinction:* Crack from rim beginning below the fraction, continuing through the lower right of the fraction and the leaf tips, and curving up to the right through ME is always present on the 1798 coins. This die was also used to coin 1799, 9 Over 8 (BW-2). The 1799, 9 Over 8, overdate was struck first. The rim cud over IC has expanded, and other cracks appear.

Notes: A single example in Mint State is reported, otherwise grades are EF and lower.

1798, Style 2 Hair, Small 8 • BW-54, S-187, B-40. *Breen dies:* 28-DD. *Estimated population:* Thousands.

Obverse: Same as preceding. *Points of distinction:* The crack has expanded, and other cracks eventually develop.

Reverse: Style 2 letters. Top-right leaf tip under serif of S. Left branch short. Top-left berry droops. Fraction bar short. *Points of distinction:* Some coins are from a perfect die, and others have one or more cracks.

1798, Style 2 Hair, Small 8 (BW-54, S-187, B-40).

Notes: This variety exists in Mint State. Breen believes this is the commonest variety of 1798.

1799, 9 Over 8, Draped Bust

Mintage (per *Mint Report*): Unknown.

The production of 1799-dated cents is unknown but was smaller than any other year in the series; most of the cents in the 1799 Mint Report were from dies dated 1798. The 1799, 9 Over 8, overdate cent, nearly always seen in lower grades, is usually lumped with the 1799 perfect date in terms of publicity and respect among non-specialists. The 1799 date, while not the most famous of the large cents (that honor probably goes to the 1793 issues), is far and away the rarest. Generally, a collector of cents by date will opt to acquire just a "1799," whether it is an overdate, as here, or the more available perfect date.

The overdate exists in two varieties, sharing a common obverse die. Both reverse dies are very well made and resemble each other very closely, except for very minor details as described. Both were also used to coin 1798-dated cents.

The 1799, 9 Over 8, is highly prized by specialists, and a great deal of attention accompanies the auction offering of an example in, say, Very Fine.

The *Mint Report* for calendar year 1799 gives a delivery figure of 904,585. However, virtually all of these cents were dated 1798. No one knows why the Mint bothered preparing just two 1799-dated dies, with one being an overdate of 1798, but it seems likely that the Mint simply did not wish to go a full year without issuing any coins with the 1799 date. This odd turn of events thus lead to the single scarcest date in the large cent series. This theme was repeated in 1803, when the Mint again over-estimated the number of dies needed (albeit for a different reason) leading to the next scarcest date, the 1804.[59]

1799, 9 Over 8 • BW-1, S-NC-1, B-1.

Breen dies: 1-A. *Recorded population:* 8.

Obverse: *Date:* About evenly spaced, but 99 is slightly wider. The 9 Over 8 overdate figure is very clear, with the under 8 bold, and is distant from the drapery. *LIBERTY:* IB close. E and R over high waves of hair. Upright of T over hair.

Reverse: Berry left of bow touches the stem. Pair of leaves opposite RI touch the prominently raised stem. *Points of distinction:* This die was also used to coin 1798, Style 2 Hair, Small 8 (BW-40).

**1799, 9 Over 8 (BW-1, S-NC-1, B-1).
For detail of overdate, see BW-2.**

Notes: Breen records the best as the Fine-12 Geiss coin (this grade being per Breen), listed in *Penny Whimsy* as VF-20. Others are VG-7 and lower. This variety was discovered by Dr. Sheldon in B. Max Mehl's Frederic W. Geiss Collection sale, February 18, 1947, lot 48.

1799, 9 Over 8 • BW-2, S-188, B-2. *Breen dies:* 1-B. *Estimated population:* 175 to 225.

Obverse: Same as preceding. *Points of distinction:* The die fails with a curving break at the right side of LIBERTY. A rare late die state shows triple cracks at LIBERTY. At this time the average life for a coining die was about 40,000 impressions.

Reverse: Berry left of bow is distant from the stem. Pair of leaves opposite RI overlap and hide the stem. *Points of distinction:* This die was also used to coin 1798, Style 2 Hair, Small 8, Style 1 Reverse Letters, Crack From Fraction to ME (BW-53). The 1798 was struck first. A very rare late die state shows a crack from the rim to the second 0, up through three leaf tips to ME, and to the rim.

1799, 9 Over 8 (BW-2, S-188, B-2).

Detail of the overdate.

Notes: A single AU example is followed by several grades of VF. Examples are mostly in low grades and are often porous or corroded. This variety is rare in grades of VG and upward, with pleasing, smooth surfaces.

	Cert	Avg	%MS	AG-3	G-4	VG-8	F-12	VF-20
1799, 9 Over 8 (BW-2)	7	8.4	0%	$3,630	$5,670	$13,500	$20,330	$32,000

1799, Draped Bust

Mintage (per *Mint Report*): Unknown.

The production of 1799-dated cents is unknown but was smaller than any other year in the series; most of the cents in the 1799 Mint Report were from dies dated 1798. The 1799 cent, sharing honors with the 1799, 9 Over 8, overdate, has been the most famous date in the series, ever since numismatics became a popular hobby in the 1850s. Nearly all are well worn, in grades such as About Good to VG, usually porous, corroded, or with other detractions—what Jack Robinson, William C. Noyes, and others might call "scudzy." Properly graded VG, Fine, and VF coins, if on smooth planchets and with excellent eye appeal, are very highly prized.

Over the years there has been much speculation as to why most examples show extensive wear, including the theory that the copper was especially soft. However, tests on the cents using the Mohs scale of hardness (devised to test minerals) have shown that the copper does not measurably differ from other cents of the era. Probably, the mintage quantity was very small, and it was only by chance that no Mint State examples were saved.

In the 19th century, a time when it was not generally realized in numismatic circles that calendar-year mintage figures were not necessarily relevant to the number of coins struck with that *date*, several theories arose as to why the 1799 cent was so rare, when the mintage was liberal. See Numismatic Notes for BW-1.

There is only one die variety of the perfect date 1799 cent.

Typical values for 1799 cents.

	Cert	Avg	%MS	AG-3	G-4	VG-8	F-12	VF-20
1799	42	11.8	2%	$3,170	$4,750	$9,100	$15,330	$27,000

1799 • BW-1, S-189, B-3. *Breen dies:* 2-C. *Estimated population:* 800 to 1,000.

Obverse: *Date:* Perfect (not overdated) second 9. 99 close. Second 9 distant from drapery. *LIBERTY:* High above head. LIB and ER slightly close. E and R over high waves of hair. Upright of T over hair.

Reverse: Tip of highest outside leaf under serif of S. Berries very large. Figures in the denominator are heavy and closely spaced, 00 being slightly closer. Bar extends from upper left of 1 to left side of second 0. *Points of distinction:* On the latest state, two small rim breaks occur at the upper right.

1799 (BW-1, S-189, B-3). This is the Henry C. Hines Collection example, AU, considered to be the finest known.

Notes: The finest by a good measure is the AU-50 coin commonly referred to as the "Hines cent." The coin turned up in England in the 1920s and was sold by A.H. Baldwin & Sons, Ltd. Later owners included Frank H. Shumate, Elmer Sears, and Wayte Raymond, the last selling it to Henry Hines for a reported $2,500.[60] From Hines it went to Robert Henderson, founder of the Sheraton Hotel chain. In 1947 it crossed the block in Numismatic Gallery's ANA Convention sale and sold below market value at $1,500. In September 1958 it was the star attraction, or should have been, at Abe Kosoff's sale of the Dr. James O. Sloss Collection. There was not as much "buzz" as was hoped for (Q. David Bowers, who was present, noted), and it went quietly to R.E. Naftzger Jr., in whose collection it remained until 1992. The cent went through several hands, into the Daniel Holmes Collection, auctioned by Ira and Larry Goldberg in 2009. For that offering the catalogers, Bob Grellman and Chris Victor-McCawley, called it AU-55, but NGC raised the bar by many numbers and certified it as MS-62. Another high-grade (for a 1799) cent was also owned by Hines, and was sold in 1952 by New Netherlands Coin Co. as part of the Homer K. Downing Collection. This sale provided the first deeply researched and extensively annotated catalog by that company, starting a tradition that quickly became famous.

Most coins of this variety are low grade and with problems, as noted above. It is a possibility that some of the nicer examples of this and other scarce varieties owe their survival to J.N.T. Levick and others who were allowed to enter the Mint circa 1857 to search through the old coppers that had been redeemed for the new small cents.[61] As Dr. Sheldon and others point out, overgrading is rampant for coins of this date. For the typically available well-worn coin it is difficult to find an example with a nice balance, having both LIBERTY and the date well defined.[62]

Numismatic Notes: Édouard Frossard, *Monograph of United States Cents and Half Cents Issued Between the Years 1793 and 1857,* 1879:

> In nearly every 1799 cent we have examined, the legend or date was weak. From the fact that the two last numbers of the date appear weak and even indistinct, collectors should not hastily reject the piece as spurious; the impression itself may have been light, and the indistinct date may be caused by a softness in the metal, the lack of a properly milled border, or the closeness of the curls of the 9 to the rim, causing the date to be easily abraded or worn by friction while in circulation. Nevertheless, the boasted rarity of this piece has undoubtedly acted as an incentive to dishonest practices on the part of numismatic tinkers and others, who wished (and still wish) to produce specimens that can pass as genuine among credulous or inexperienced collectors. We therefore caution those collectors in whose eyes an altered or forged coin is an abomination, and who want none but genuine specimens in their cabinets, to closely examine by means of a lens, or to submit to those more experienced than they, before purchasing, any specimen on which rests the slightest shadow of doubt.

> One thing is certain, either the 1799 cents change ownership with amazing rapidity, or the number available to collectors has vastly increased. At any rate, the difficulty experienced by Mr. Mickley, when first in search of a specimen of this date to complete his set of cents, no longer exists, and fair to good specimens can easily be obtained when wanted. We have had as many as seven 1799 cents, from which to make a selection, when desiring to purchase a fine specimen for a private collection. In condition there was but little difference between them, they ranking at what may be called "very good for date," but in price they ranged all the way from $20 to $100—the last by no means the best.

On the rarity of the 1799 cent: From the *American Journal of Numismatics,* October 1882:

> A Very Scarce Penny: A good story is told by numismatists regarding the big pennies of the year 1799, and was originated by the late Dr. M.W. Dickeson, who had a sly method of creating a market for his goods. The tale was to the effect that some years ago in Salem, Mass., someone conceived the idea that it would be a good thing to send all the pennies they could get to Africa; so a ship was loaded up after the coin had been secured, and in due course of time it arrived in that very warm country. Here the work of trading began, and the bright and shining coppers were traded off with the female natives for oils and other merchantable articles. The African bored holes in the coins and used them for necklaces, ear-rings, nose-rings and other ornaments. The result of this was that the pennies were very scarce. The story is generally believed by coin collectors, and as a result a good penny of the year 1799 commands all the way from $15 to $25, according to the degree of perfection.

> Mr. E. Mason, Jr., the numismatist, has another version to give regarding the scarcity of this coin. He said that the records of the Mint for the years 1798–99 show that over 700,000 pennies were coined, but that on account of the method of keeping the accounts, it was impossible to tell just how many there were each year.

> "The cause of the scarcity," Mr. Mason said, "lies in the fact that the coins were imperfectly struck off. The date on the bottom seemed to be very soft, and it readily wore off. I have had some three or four thousand of these pennies, and I believe I have seen as many more with the date completely obliterated. There are pennies of other years that are more difficult to obtain than those of 1799, and if there were so many of them in Africa, it would pay to send an agent there to hunt them up, and we would have had a man there long ago. Some time ago it was said that the pennies of 1812 were

commanding large figures, and that only a few were in existence. They can be had readily for three or four cents apiece."—*Philadelphia Record*.

Mehl's Numismatic Monthly, February 1908:

Rare Copper Cents. Coin Collector's Theory to Account for Their Scarcity.

That some of the rarest and most valuable of the United States cents, particularly those dated 1799 and 1804, owe their scarcity to the fact that Fulton built the steamboat *Clermont* is the theory held by some coin collectors. They believe that thousands of the old time large copper cents went toward making the copper boiler for the pioneer steamboat.

This theory would explain the mystery that has long puzzled coin collectors as to the reason for the almost total disappearance of the cents of the dates mentioned. The first cents struck at the United States Mint at Philadelphia were of large size. The copper blanks, or planchets, were imported from England, being sent over in kegs. Copper at this period was a scarce article in this country, with the exception of the small quantity produced at the only copper mines then known in the United States, those at Granby, Conn., nearly all the metal used here came from England.

Builders of steam engines in those days were of the opinion that boilers constructed of iron were unsafe and impracticable and as a consequence boilers were made of copper, all the boilers that came from England being, it is said, constructed of that metal. Fulton was likewise of the belief that copper was the only fit metal to be used in boilers. It is likewise possible that, finding a scarcity of metal with which to construct the boiler of the *Clermont*, he finally resorted to the most convenient source of supply, which happened to be the large United States copper cents.

Of course, the cost of such a boiler would represent a large sum, but it is on the records that the steam frigate *Fulton*, another ship, launched in 1815, the year of the inventor's death, had a boiler entirely constructed of copper which alone cost the large sum of $23,000. That the supply of cents of this period was large enough to meet such a demand is also likely enough. From 1793 to and including 1795, 1,066,033 cents were coined and in 1796, 974,000 were struck.[63]

Joseph Mickley and the 1799 cent: One of numismatics's favorite twice-told tales involved Joseph J. Mickley, early numismatist in Philadelphia. He was a repairer of violins, pianos, and other instruments. His home was open to fellow collectors, who enjoyed many evenings of camaraderie there. Today he is remembered as one of the most famous people in the hobby.

Edward Groh, another early collector—and, at the age of 20, one of five founders of the American Numismatic Society, in March 1858—outlived most of his peers. On October 20, 1901, an interview with him was printed in the *New York Times*. Groh told the reporter about the coin collecting scene of 30 or 40 years earlier. The veteran numismatist lamented that in early times it was possible to track down rare issues and find bargains among coins in circulation, but now it had become a "very matter-of-fact science and study." Further:

The story of Mickley's chase after the 1799 cent illustrates the difference of methods then and now. Mr. Mickley wasn't a collector when he started to hunt for that cent, but he had been born in the year 1799, and wanted the coin for a pocket piece. Nowadays he would have found out the whereabouts of every cent of that mintage simply by consulting any dealer in town. As it was, he had to go about it in the old way. Now it happens that the 1799 cent is the rarest known, and it was years before Mr. Mickley had his ambition to possess one fulfilled. By that time he had become so interested in examining coins and consulting with collectors all over the country that he had become quite an enthusiast on the subject himself. When he died a few years ago he left one of the finest private coin collections in the country.

Actually, Mickley, who began collecting coins by 1817, sold most of his collection to W. Elliot Woodward in 1867.[64] Mickley died on February 15, 1878.

The Abbey 1799 cent: The name of pioneer numismatist Lorenzo Abbey is remembered today through the so-called "Abbey cent," a particularly nice example of the rare 1799 year. On September 8, 1863, his collection was auctioned by Henry Leeds & Co., New York City. In 1996 this was cataloged by Mark Borckardt as part of the Eliasberg Collection sale.

Abbey is said by some to have bought the 1799 cent circa 1844, but accounts vary. Historian E.J. Attinelli recalled the collector and his holdings, but described his entry into coins as a transaction involving Augustus B. Sage, which would have taken place circa 1858:[65]

> This was a coin sale, succeeding one of furniture, etc. The owner of the coins was the gentleman whose name is perpetuated in the celebrated 'Abbey Cent' of 1799, which, notwithstanding so many years have elapsed, since it was brought to the notice of the numismatic public, still maintains its position as one of the finest known. Mr. Abbey is a native of [New York state], having been born in Herkimer County, on the 14th of January, 1823. He has long been a resident of [New York City], carrying on an extensive business in needles, fishing-hooks, and tackle.
>
> His introduction to numismatology occurred through the following incident: Mr. John Martense, a friend of his and a numismatist, having a duplicate Unc. cent of 1826, presented it to Mr. Abbey, stating that it was worth about $5; being somewhat incredulous, he took it to Mr. [Augustus B.] Sage, who at once offered Mr. Abbey $7 for the cent. Somewhat astonished by finding fine coins to have such a value, he at once applied himself in diligent search for others, and with some considerable success. The very next day he procured from a grocer's till the rare 'large head Nova Eborac.' The 1799 cent above alluded to, he bought for $25 from Mr. Rogers in Fulton St., who had bought it from a countryman for $2. Among other pieces he thus brought to the knowledge of numismatists, were the 'Washington half dollars' in copper, the 1802 half dime, subsequently sold in Mr. Lilliendahl's sale for $380, and other fine or rare pieces.[66]

Samuel Abbott Green: Samuel Abbott Green began collecting coins when he found a rare 1799 cent in circulation, sometime around 1846.[67] His interest grew, and in time he became prominent in the Boston Numismatic Society. He eventually served on the 1870 and 1872 Assay Commissions and as a co-editor of the *American Journal of Numismatics*.

Where is this coin today?: In the June 1917 issue of *The Numismatist*, Dr. Robert Cornell Jr. of Philadelphia, paid for a half-page notice that stated:

> I think I am correct in assuming that there has never yet been discovered a 1799 cent Uncirculated, but the foremost dealers and many prominent collectors have assured me that my specimen, almost Uncirculated, is the finest known. I cannot compete with the unlimited bids which have recently been the rule in sales where coins that I would consider fit associates for the 1799 have been sold. If I can get a suitable offer for my small collection of choice cents, many having original red, some brilliant, I will sell it.

1800, 1800 Over 1798, Draped Bust

Mintage (per *Mint Report*): A small part of the 1800 figure.

It seems that, in 1800, unfinished dies were held in the engraver's department, including a 1798 die and several in which all digits except the last had been entered, as 179. Each of these was overdated to read 1800. The supply arose from the Mint having overestimated the coinage for 1798, believing that planchet shipments from Boulton & Watt would arrive on a routine basis. Delays were experienced, and problems resulted.

Today there are a remarkable 11 different die combinations of overdates for this year. The 1800, 1800 Over 1798, varieties are listed here, all from the single obverse die (with Style 1 Hair), followed by the 1800, 180 Over 179, varieties in a separate section. Among the 1800, 1800 Over 1798, two are rare, the first with only three known and the second with slightly more than a dozen. The remaining two are obtainable easily enough.

1800, 1800 Over 1798, 1 Right of Center of Small Fraction Bar •

BW-1, S-NC-5, B-3. *Breen dies:* 2-B. **Recorded population:** 3.

1800, 1800 Over 1798, 1 Right of Center of Small Fraction Bar (BW-1, S-NC-5, B-3).

Obverse: *Date:* Very compact. 7 bold under the 8. Loop of 9 visible within first 0; part of the top of the 9 visible above it. Traces of the center of the 8 within the second 0, and a small trace above it. 1 and second 0 about equidistant from bust and denticles. *LIBERTY:* ER slightly wide. E over wave, R almost touching wave. Upright of T over hair.

Reverse: Numerator, 1, far to the right of the center of the very small bar. Bar extends from upper right of 1 to above left side of second 0; definitive. Bar much closer to the left ribbon than to the right ribbon. *Points of distinction:* A heavy rim cud is seen at the upper right, extending well into AME.

Notes: Discovered by D. Stanley Q. West in 1965 and published in 1968, thus not included in *Penny Whimsy* or other early references.[68] The three examples are VG-10 (discovery coin), AG-3, and AG-3.

1800, 1800 Over 1798 • BW-2,

S-NC-6, B-4. *Breen dies:* 2-C. **Recorded population:** 13.

Obverse: Same as preceding.

Reverse: Numerator, 1, centered above fraction bar. Bar extends from above center of 1 to above center of second 0. Bar equidistant between the two ribbons.

1800, 1800 Over 1798 (BW-2, S-NC-6, B-4).

Notes: Walter Breen records the highest as "VF-25, sharpness of EF-40, but repaired at D ST." At one earlier time it was auctioned as AU.

1800, 1800 Over 1798 • BW-3, S-190,

B-5. *Breen dies:* 2-D. **Estimated population:** 300 to 400.

Obverse: Same as preceding. *Points of distinction:* Some are from a perfect die, and others have one or two cracks.

Reverse: First S of STATES low. Numerator, 1, is very slightly left of center above fraction bar. Bar extends from upper right of 1 to slightly past center of second 0.

1800, 1800 Over 1798 (BW-3, S-190, B-5).

Notes: This variety exists in Mint State, and is rare as such. Priced after BW-4.

1800, 1800 Over 1798, 1 in Numerator Too High • BW-4, S-191, B-2. *Breen dies:* 2-A. **Estimated population:** 300 to 400.

Obverse: Same as preceding.

Reverse: Numerator, 1, is very slightly left of center above the short fraction bar. Bar extends from upper right of 1 to slightly past center of second 0. In denominator the 1 is very high. Bar is closer to right ribbon than to left. *Points of distinction:* With a clash mark over STAT and a prominent mounding at the fraction, as well as various cracks. This die was also used to coin 1800, 180 Over 179, Serif of 7 at Upper Left of 8 (BW-6). Comment by Harry E. Salyards: "Sheldon, of

1800, 1800 Over 1798, 1 in Numerator Too High (BW-4, S-191, B-2).

Detail of overdate.

course, considered the NC-1 [1800, 180 Over 179, Serif of 7 at Upper Left of 8 (BW-6), in this text] a different reverse die. Much of the difficulty comes from having to compare two almost-completely hubbed reverse dies, as seen on two traditional die varieties—one of which, the NC-1, shows no distinguishing cracks, and is known by only three examples; the other of which is available by the hundreds, and is full of cracks and clashes!"[69]

Notes: EF and AU are the highest grades known.

	Cert	Avg	%MS	G-4	VG-8	F-12	VF-20	EF-40	AU-50
1800, 1800 Over 1798 (BW-3 and BW-4)	21	27.7	5%	$225	$650	$1,750	$3,000	$7,250	$17,000

1800, 180 Over 179, Draped Bust

Mintage (per *Mint Report*): Part of the total for 1800.

Among the unused dies on hand in 1800 were five that were partially completed as 179. The 7 and 9 were overpunched with an 8 and 0, and in the empty space a final 0 was added.

All have Style 2 Hair (interior curl left of drapery). Check the fraction on each reverse die, as this feature has more idiosyncrasies than any other part of the die.

Typical values for 1800, 180 Over 179, cents. Rare varieties may be worth more.

	Cert	Avg	%MS	G-4	VG-8	F-12	VF-20	EF-40	AU-50	MS-60BN
1800, 180 Over 179	58	24.0	7%	$120	$220	$410	$775	$2,600	$4,830	$9,375

1800, 180 Over 179, Serif of 7 at Upper Left of 8 • BW-6, S-NC-1, B-1.

Breen dies: 1-A. *Recorded population:* 3.

Obverse: *Date:* 180 closer than 00. 1 closer to hair than to denticles. Upper-left serif of 7 at upper left of 8, but a different die from the somewhat similar BW-9; top of 8 higher than other numerals. Traces of 9 within first 0. Second 0 about equidistant between denticles and drapery. *LIBERTY:* IB slightly close. Left of E and left of R each over high wave. Upright of T over hair.

1800, 180 Over 179, Serif of 7 at Upper Left of 8 (BW-6, S-NC-1, B-1).

Detail of overdate.

Reverse: Numerator, 1, is very slightly to the left of center above short fraction bar. Bar extends from upper right of 1 to slightly past center of second 0. In denominator the 1 is very high. Bar is closer to right ribbon than to left. *Points of distinction:* This die was also used to coin 1800, 1800 Over 1798, 1 in Numerator Too High (BW-4). See note under 1800, 1800 Over 1798, 1 in Numerator Too High (BW-4).

Notes: The three examples are F-12, VG-8, and G-6.

1800, 180 Over 179, "Horned 8", Fraction Bar Tilts Down to Right •

BW-7, S-192, B-6. *Breen dies:* 3-E. *Estimated population:* 300 to 400.

Obverse: *Date:* 18 close. 1 closer to hair than to denticles. Top serif and upper right of 7 visible above 8, creating a "Horned 8." Upper loop of 9 and ball of 9 bold within first 0. Second 0 closer to denticles than to drapery. *LIBERTY:* IB close. ER wide. Left of E and left of R each over high wave. T mostly over hair, slight part over forehead. Base of Y slightly low.

1800, 180 Over 179, "Horned 8", Fraction Bar Tilts Down to Right (BW-7, S-192, B-6).

Detail of overdate.

Reverse: Lower-left serif of E of STATES missing. Fraction bar tilts down to right and is distant from 10, but close to second 0. Closer to the left ribbon than to the right. Numerator, 1, is very slightly left of the center above short fraction bar. Bar extends from upper right of 1 to slightly past center of second 0. In denominator the 1 is very high. Bar is closer to right ribbon than to left. *Points of distinction:* Always with an arc-like crack from the rim through the fraction, up to the right to the rim at I. Later, other cracks appear.

Notes: A single example in Mint State is followed by an AU, then at least two EF.

1800, 180 Over 179, "Horned 8", Square Left End, Pointed Right End to Fraction Bar • BW-8, S-193, B-7.

Breen dies: 3-F. **Estimated population:** 120 to 160.

Obverse: Same as preceding.

Reverse: Stemless leaf pair below T of CENT. Fraction bar square at left end, pointed at right. Numerator centered over it. Bar extends from upper right of 1 to center of second 0. **Points of distinction:** Most often with a crack at the fraction bar and to the left. Another at E of AMERICA. Sometimes with cud break at the rim below the fraction.

1800, 180 Over 179, "Horned 8", Square Left End, Pointed Right End to Fraction Bar (BW-8, S-193, B-7).

Detail of overdate.

Notes: A single Mint State is followed by an EF, then multiple graded at the VF level. Dr. Sheldon knew of no more than a dozen when *Early American Cents* was published in 1949. Since then many have been found—testimony to the appeal and effective use of Sheldon's text.

1800, 180 Over 179, Serif of 7 at Upper Left of 8, Horizontal Top of 7 in Upper Loop • BW-9, S-194, B-8.

Breen dies: 4-G. **Estimated population:** 400 to 500.

Obverse: *Date:* 1 closer to hair than to denticles. 18 slightly wide. Serif of 7 protrudes from upper left of 7, but a different die than BW-6, described earlier; horizontal element of 7 prominent within upper loop. 9 and ball prominent within first 0, and outline of top of 9 protrudes above it. *LIBERTY:* Base of L slightly low. RTY wide. E and R over high waves of hair. T above hair. **Points of distinction:** Often with rim deterioration above RTY.

1800, 180 Over 179, Serif of 7 at Upper Left of 8, Horizontal Top of 7 in Upper Loop (BW-9, S-194, B-8).

Detail of overdate.

Reverse: First S of STATES slightly low. In fraction, numerator 1 is closer to bar than any denominator figures and is slightly to the left of center. 1 in denominator is closer to bar than either 0. **Points of distinction:** With crack from the second 0 to A at the right. Additional cracks appear, eventually resulting in a prominent rim cud below the fraction.

Notes: This variety exists in Mint State.

1800, 180 Over 179 • BW-10, S-195, B-9. *Breen dies:* 4-H. *Estimated population:* 40 to 60.

Obverse: Same as preceding. *Points of distinction:* With a rim cud at right of T and all of Y.

Reverse: CE extremely close, ENT separated. Thin fraction bar. Numerator, 1, centered over bar. Both 1's about the same distance from the bar. *Points of distinction:*

1800, 180 Over 179 (BW-10, S-195, B-9).

With a crack from the denticles to the second 0 into ICA. Some mounding in the same area.

Notes: A single AU (ANS) is followed by several of grade VF.

1800, 180 Over 179, Top of 7 Above 8 • BW-11, S-196, B-10. *Breen dies:* 5-I. *Estimated population:* Thousands.

Obverse: *Date:* 180 close, 00 very slightly wider. Top of 7 protrudes above 8; definitive. Upper loop of 9 and ball prominent in first 0. *LIBERTY:* IB close. E and R over high waves of hair. TY slightly low. Upright of T over hair.

Reverse: First S of STATES quite low. Numerator, 1, slightly to left of center of bar, and is slightly closer to the left ribbon. Bar from upper right of 1 to slightly left of the center of second 0. *Points of distinction:* A light crack is at ES of STATES.

1800, 180 Over 179, Top of 7 Above 8 (BW-11, S-196, B-10).

Detail of overdate.

Notes: AU is the highest grade known.

1800, 180 Over 179, "Horned 8", "Hook" Below Second S • BW-12, S-NC-2, B-11. *Breen dies:* 6-J. *Estimated population:* 12 to 20.

Obverse: *Date:* 180 close. Serif and upper right of 7 visible above 8; "Horned 8," but a different die from that described earlier. *LIBERTY:* LI close. Upright of T over hair. *Points of distinction:* A crack extends from the rim opposite the bust, up to the right, and

1800, 180 Over 179, "Horned 8", "Hook" Below Second S (BW-12, S-NC-2, B-11).

a short distance into the field. This develops into a cud in the latest stages.

Reverse: "Hook" below second S of STATES, the trace of an earlier-punched letter. In fraction, numerator 1 centered. Both 1's about the same distance from the bar. Bar extends from upper right of 1 to above center of the second 0, and is closer to right ribbon. *Points of distinction:* This die was also used to coin 1800, "Q" Variety (Triangle Past First 0), Right Serif of T Over Forehead, "Hook Below Second S" (BW-20).

Notes: VG and Fine are the highest grades known, the latter very rare.

1800, Draped Bust

Mintage (per *Mint Report*): 2,822,175.

The cents of 1800 (perfect date) are all with Style 2 Hair. The die varieties are often quite similar, making close attention to the descriptions—and especially the photographs—very important. Checking the spacing of LIBERTY, the date numerals, and the layout of the fraction on the reverse can be especially useful. On BW-20 the right serif of the T is over the forehead; on all other dies in this group the T is completely over the hair, though sometimes barely.

Save for two rarities, the varieties are collectible, although several are elusive in high grades. Most cents of this year are found well worn, leading some to suggest that the copper used was especially soft, but there is no proof of this.

Typical values for 1800 cents. Rare varieties may be worth more.

	Cert	Avg	%MS	AG-3	G-4	VG-8	F-12	VF-20	EF-40	AU-50	MS-60BN	MS-63BN	MS-65BN
1800	134	25.7	10%	$45	$90	$165	$340	$550	$2,270	$3,750	$6,250	$13,625	$17,500

1800, "Q" Variety (Triangle Past First 0), Right Serif of T Over Forehead, "Hook Below Second S" •

BW-20, S-197, B-12. *Breen dies:* 7-J. *Estimated population:* Thousands.

Obverse: *Date:* 18 close. Die defect within first 0 and a triangular defect far past its lower right (in fact, next to the second 0), giving rise to the somewhat far-fetched nickname of "Q" variety or "18Q0." A useful guide for quick identification as all have this feature. *LIBERTY:* IB close. Lower-left serif of Y defective. Right serif of T over forehead, but the rest of the letter is over the hair (only such die in this group). *Points of distinction:* All have a V-shaped break from the border to between I and B.

1800, "Q" Variety (Triangle Past First 0),
Right Serif of T Over Forehead, "Hook
Below Second S" (BW-20, S-197, B-12).

Detail of fanciful "Q."

Reverse: "Hook" below second S of STATES, the trace of an earlier-punched letter. In fraction, numerator, 1, centered. Both 1's about the same distance from the bar. Bar extends from upper right of 1 to above center of the second 0, and is closer to right ribbon. *Points of distinction:* This die was also used to coin 1800, 180 Over 179, "Horned 8", "Hook" Below Second S (BW-12). Usually with one or two small cracks, later a rim break over AT of STATES.

Notes: This variety exists in Mint State.

1800 • BW-21, S-198, B-19. *Breen dies:* 10-Q. *Estimated population:* 30 to 45.

Obverse: *Date:* Fairly evenly spaced. Serif of 1 very close to curl, base distant from denticles. Second 0 closer to drapery than to denticles, and centered over a denticle. *LIBERTY:* Letters close, IB perhaps closest. E and R over high waves. Lower-left serif of Y weak. *Points of distinction:* Typically with clash marks above and near TY.

1800 (BW-21, S-198, B-19).

Reverse: Numerator, 1, slightly right of the center of bar. Bar from upper right of 1 to just before center of the second 0, and slants down slightly to the left. Denominator 1 much closer to the bar than is second 0. Both 0's about the same distance below the bar. *Points of distinction:* Crack from ribbon to top of 1. Light crack at ICA to past the end of the right ribbon.

Notes: VG is the highest-known grade. This has the lowest top grade of *any* Sheldon-numbered 1800 variety.[70]

1800 • BW-22, S-199, B-14. *Breen dies:* 9-L. *Estimated population:* 120 to 160.

Obverse: *Date:* Widely and fairly evenly spaced. Serif of 1 prominent and very close to curl, base distant from denticles. Second 0 closer to denticles than to drapery. Both 0's light at their bases. *LIBERTY:* LIB close. E and R over high waves.

1800 (BW-22, S-199, B-14).

Reverse: Berry opposite E of UNITED has no stem and is wedged between leaf point below and leaf stem above. Numerator, 1, very slightly right of the center of bar. Bar begins over upper right of 1 and ends slightly before center of second 0. First 0 low. *Points of distinction:* Some are from a perfect die, but more often this variety appears with cracks, the die finally failing in the upper section.

Notes: There is one example of grade AU (ANS), followed by several VF pieces.

1800 • BW-23, S-200, B-15. *Breen dies:* 9-M. *Estimated population:* 300 to 400.

Obverse: *Date:* Widely and fairly evenly spaced. Serif of 1 small and very close to curl, base distant from denticles. Second 0 closer to denticles than to drapery. *LIBERTY:* LIB close, IB closest. E and R are each slightly right of the center of a hair wave. *Points of distinction:* Typically struck so that the denticles are short at the upper left and larger at the lower right. Bulges develop, as do cracks.

1800 (BW-23, S-200, B-15).

Reverse: Serif on C of CENT a tiny spine. Numerator, 1, slightly left of the center of bar and leans slightly left; slightly closer to left ribbon than to the right ribbon. Bar begins over right corner of 1 and ends just before center of second 0. Bar is slightly closer to left ribbon. First 0 low. *Points of distinction:* Nearly always with one or more cracks. This die was first used to coin BW-33, then reworked to coin BW-23.[71]

Notes: VF is the highest grade known.

1800 • BW-24, S-NC-3, B-16. *Breen dies:* 9-N. *Estimated population:* 25 to 30.

Obverse: Same as preceding.

Reverse: Serif on C of CENT a tiny spine. Spike at top of I of AMERICA. Numerator, 1, close to and centered over bar; closer to left ribbon. Bar begins over right corner of 1 and ends just before center of second 0. First 0 low.

Notes: Single examples of EF and VF are followed by multiple at the VG level.

1800 (BW-24, S-NC-3, B-16).

1800 • BW-25, S-201, B-17. *Breen dies:* 9-O. *Estimated population:* 75 to 120.

Obverse: Same as preceding. *Points of distinction:* A crack is seen at the left of 1 of 1800.

Reverse: No stems to leaves left of O of ONE. Numerator, 1, close to and centered over bar. Bar begins over right corner of 1 and ends over center of second 0. Both 0's low. *Points of distinction:* Multiple cracks develop.

Notes: VF is the highest grade known.

1800 (BW-25, S-201, B-17).

1800, Spike on Right Side of Right Ribbon • BW-26, S-202, B-18. *Breen dies:* 9-P. *Estimated population:* 75 to 120.

Obverse: Same as preceding. *Points of distinction:* Now with much heavier cracks through the lower-left obverse. These probably caused the die to fail, accounting for the elusive nature of this variety today.

Reverse: Raised projection or spike on outside of right ribbon about one-third up from its tip. Numerator, 1, very slightly left of center. Bar thickest about one-third of the distance from its right edge, and tapers to become thinner to the left and right. Bar begins over right corner of 1 and ends just before center of second 0. All denominator numerals are low and closer to being on the same level than usually seen. Denticles thin and closely spaced. *Points of distinction:* This die was first used to coin

1800, Spike on Right Side of
Right Ribbon (BW-26, S-202, B-18).

Detail showing spike on right ribbon.

BW-26, then reworked to coin BW-27 and 1801 (BW-4).[72] Multiple cracks develop. Some have swelling that consumes TATE and extends to other areas.

Notes: EF and AU (especially rare) are the highest grades known.

1800, Die Chips in Field Opposite Nose • BW-27, S-203, B-29. *Breen dies:* 19-V. *Estimated population:* 300 to 400.

Obverse: *Date:* Evenly spaced. Tiny serif of 1 very close to curl; base of 1 distant from denticles. Second 0 closer to drapery than to denticles. *LIBERTY:* ER wide. E mostly over wave, left upright of R over wave. *Points of distinction:* Connected string of die chips in field past nose, closer to denticles. This die was continued in use far beyond retirement age.

1800, Die Chips in Field Opposite Nose (BW-27, S-203, B-29).

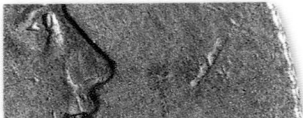

Detail showing a string of die chips in the field beyond the nose.

Reverse: AM slightly separated, ME touch. Numerator, 1, high and slightly left of the center of bar. Bar begins part-way over the 1 and ends slightly past center of second 0. Denominator 1 particularly heavy. First 0 low. *Points of distinction:* This die was first used to coin BW-26, then reworked to coin BW-27 and 1801 (BW-4).[73]

Notes: This variety exists in Mint State, and is very rare as such.

1800 • BW-28, S-204, B-25. *Breen dies:* 16-T. *Estimated population:* 120 to 160.

Obverse: *Date:* Serif of 1 almost touches hair above it but is spaced from curl. 18 close, 00 widest. Second 0 is about centered between the denticles and drapery and is over a space between denticles. *LIBERTY:* LIB close, BE slightly wide. Left of E and R over waves. *Points of distinction:* Always with clash marks and sometimes with a crack in the right field. Late die states have a rim break at the right.

1800 (BW-28, S-204, B-25).

Reverse: C of CENT barely touches leaf. Left wreath stem short. Numerator, 1, fairly close to bar and centered over it, also centered over the 0 below. Bar begins part-way over 1 and ends over center of the second 0. First 0 low. 1 and second 0 are about equidistant from the bar. Bar closer to right ribbon. Otherwise, quite similar to BW-28.

Notes: AU is the highest grade known.

1800, Flat Spot in Hair Above 1 •

BW-29, S-205, B-26. *Breen dies:* 17-T. **Estimated population:** 120 to 160.

Obverse: *Date:* 18 wide, 80 close, 00 closest. 1 and 8 closer to bust than to denticles. *LIBERTY:* Uprights of E and R over high waves. ER and TY wide. Upright of T over hair but barely. Y slightly low. ***Points of distinction:*** Above the hair strand above the 1 is a flat or "bald" spot with no hair; definitive. Most have a horizontal crack at the left, from the hair toward the rim.

Reverse: Same as preceding.

Notes: This variety exists in Mint State.

1800, Flat Spot in Hair Above 1 (BW-29, S-205, B-26).

Detail of bald spot in hair.

1800 • BW-30, S-206, B-27. *Breen dies:* 17-U. **Estimated population:** 300 to 400.

Obverse: Same as preceding, but flat spot has been repaired by adding hair. ***Points of distinction:*** The horizontal crack in the left field is slightly larger as it extends toward the left rim.

Reverse: C of CENT barely touches leaf. Left wreath stem short. Numerator, 1, fairly close to bar and centered over it, also cen-

1800 (BW-30, S-206, B-27).

tered over the 0 below. Bar begins part-way over 1 and ends slightly before center of the second 0. First 0 low. 1 much closer to bar than is second 0. Bar closer to left ribbon. Otherwise, it is quite similar to BW-28 and BW-29. ***Points of distinction:*** On most, a triangular rim cud below the first 0 is seen, with various cracks.

Notes: EF is the highest grade known.

1800, Low L, Rim Break at Fraction •

BW-31, S-207, B-28. *Breen dies:* 18-U. **Estimated population:** 300 to 400.

Obverse: *Date:* 1 much closer to hair than to denticles. 00 wide. Second 0 about equidistant from denticles and drapery and is centered over a space between denticles. *LIBERTY:* L low (unusual). LIB close, LI closest. Uprights of E and R over waves. Upright of T over hair but barely. ***Points of distinction:***

1800, Low L, Rim Break at Fraction (BW-31, S-207, B-28).

distinction: Some have a small crack from the hair to T.

Reverse: Same as preceding. ***Points of distinction:*** The state is advanced, still with the prominent rim cud at the bottom, but with additional development.

Notes: VF and EF are the highest grades known, the latter quite rare.

1800, Die Failure Above TY • BW-32,
S-208, B-21. *Breen dies:* 12-S. *Estimated population:* 300 to 400.

Obverse: *Date:* Serif of 1 almost touches curl. 00 slightly close. Second 0 much closer to denticles than to drapery. *LIBERTY:* LIB slightly close. Uprights of E and R over waves. RTY wide. Upright of T over hair, but barely. *Points of distinction:* Most, but not all, have die failure at the rim over TY.

1800, Die Failure Above TY (BW-32, S-208, B-21).

Reverse: Numerator, 1, slightly left of center of bar and about the same distance from it as is the 1 in the denominator. 1 in denominator closer to bar than second 0 (which leans left). Bar slightly closer to right ribbon than to the left.

Notes: VF is the highest grade known.

1800 • BW-33, S-NC-4, B-22. *Breen dies:*
13-S. *Reported population:* 9.

Obverse: *Date:* 1 close to hair and distant from denticles. 00 slightly close. *LIBERTY:* LIB close. E and R over waves of hair. Y slightly low. *Points of distinction:* This die was first used to coin BW-33, then reworked to coin BW-23.[74] Cracks develop, resulting in die damage, including a very large cud break at the left rim.

1800 (BW-33, S-NC-4, B-22).

Reverse: Same as preceding.

Notes: There is a single example of AU, VG is the next-highest grade.

1800 • BW-34, S-209, B-23. *Breen dies:*
14-S. *Estimated population:* 300 to 400.

Obverse: *Date:* 1 much closer to hair than to denticles. 18 wide. Second 0 about equidistant from denticles and drapery, and centered over a denticle. *LIBERTY:* Very closely spaced, especially LIB and ERT. E and upright of R over waves. Y slightly low. *Points of distinction:* Prominent clash marks are seen near the portrait. The die fails, causing indistinct areas.

1800 (BW-34, S-209, B-23).

Reverse: Same as preceding. *Points of distinction:* Found perfect and later with very light rim break under 00 to right ribbon end; also, light crack from rim to top of AM, through center of ER, near the bottom of ICA, and from right foot of A to ribbon end. This develops into rim cud below the fraction, extending to the right.

Notes: There is a single example of Mint State, then several occur in AU.

1800 • BW-35, S-210, B-24. *Breen dies:* 15-S. *Estimated population:* 30 to 45.

Obverse: *Date:* Closely spaced, 18 closest. 1 close to hair. Denticles often off the planchet. *LIBERTY:* IB close. Uprights of E and R over waves. Y slightly low. *Points of distinction:* Early impressions have a crack at ER, continuing past the hair to near the right rim. The die fails further with continued use.

1800 (BW-35, S-210, B-24).

Reverse: Same as preceding. *Points of distinction:* The die deteriorates, cracks are seen, and a rim break is over M of AMERICA and another over the space between I and C.

Notes: EF and AU are the highest grades known, and the variety is very rare as such.

1800 • BW-36, S-211, B-13. *Breen dies:* 8-K. *Estimated population:* 400 to 500.

Obverse: *Date:* Evenly spaced. 1 and second 0 closer to bust than to denticles. *LIBERTY:* Closely spaced. E and R over hair waves. Base of Y slightly low. *Points of distinction:* Swelling and die failure continue. In its late state, the die has a crack at the bottom of 18.

1800 (BW-36, S-211, B-13).

Reverse: Numerator, 1, slightly to left of the center of heavy bar and spaced from it the same distance as the 1 in the denominator; numerator, 1, is slightly closer to the left ribbon than to the right. Bar extends from upper right of 1 to center of second 0. 1 and second 0 about the same distance from bar. Bar is slightly closer to the right ribbon. *Points of distinction:* Some have a light crack from E to S of STATES.

Notes: This variety exists in Mint State, and is very rare at this level.

1800, Tiny Spike at Center Inside of C of CENT • BW-37, S-212, B-20.

Breen dies: 11-R. *Estimated population:* 300 to 400.

Obverse: *Date:* 1 much closer to hair than to denticles. 18 wide. Second 0 closer to denticles than to drapery. *LIBERTY:* IBE wide. E and upright of R over hair curls. TY low. Lower-left serif of Y defective. *Points of distinction:* A crack is seen on many, from the denticles to the hair, and another is from the denticles to the forehead, continuing into the portrait.

1800, Tiny Spike at Center Inside of C of CENT (BW-37, S-212, B-20).

Detail of spike on C in CENT.

Reverse: Tiny spike at center inside of C of CENT. Right stem slightly heavier than the left stem and diagonally tapered to a point at lower right. Numerator, 1, centered over bar, and it and bar about equidistant between the ribbons. Bar begins left of the center of denominator 1, above the vertical left edge of 1, and ends over center of second 0. First 0 slightly low. Second 0 leans left.

Notes: AU is the highest grade known.

1801, Draped Bust

Mintage (per *Mint Report*): 1,362,837.

The cents of 1801 can be divided into two groups, as Dr. William H. Sheldon and Walter Breen divided them in the past. The first group has the first 1 in the date with a serif, while the second 1 in the date lacks this feature. As the 1 with serif is the style of 1800, and as the second 1 in all instances is blunt, it can be assumed that the Serif 1's were made as incomplete dies with the date as 180, probably in 1800, when the Serif 1 was still in use. In 1801 the dies were completed using the Blunt 1 punch whose use was initiated that year. The second group comprises dies with both 1's blunt, which were created entirely in 1801.

Spice is added to the 1801 cent roster by egregious blunders among the reverse dies. *Three* dies have 1/000 instead of the correct 1/100; another is similar, but with the erroneous first 0 in the denominator overpunched with a 1 (one of the first-mentioned dies corrected); and the third blunder is the most famous of all errors in the large cent series: in addition to the fraction appearing as 1/000, the left stem of the wreath is missing and UNITED appears as IINITED. A mechanic or other workman—not an engraver!—probably made these curious dies. Luckily, all three error types exist in sufficient numbers that they are readily collectible. What a numismatic playground!

As with 1800-dated cents, apart from the error varieties, the details of the fraction are perhaps the best guide to attributing the reverses in your first run-through.

Typical values for 1801 cents. Rare varieties may be worth more. Some varieties are priced individually, as follows.

	Cert	Avg	%MS	AG-3	G-4	VG-8	F-12	VF-20	EF-40	AU-50	MS-60BN	MS-63BN
1801	120	25.1	7%	$40	$70	$175	$375	$600	$1,930	$4,050	$8,500	$17,375

1801 WITH FIRST 1 IN DATE WITH POINTED TOP SERIF

1801 • BW-1, S-213, B-1. *Breen dies:* 1-A.
Estimated population: 600 to 800.

Obverse: *Date:* First 1 with serif near curl, base distant from denticles. 80 low; 01 slightly wide. Second 1 closer to denticles than to drapery. *LIBERTY:* LI and RT close. Uprights of E and R over hair waves. T mostly over hair, but with tip of lower-right serif barely over forehead. Y slightly low. *Points of distinction:* Four wavy cracks are

1801 (BW-1, S-213, B-1).

always seen in the field, an indication of improperly tempered die steel that caused the die surface to sink and coins to have mounding.[75]

Reverse: Left stem shorter than the right. Numerator, 1, is centered on fraction bar and close to it. Both the numerator and the bar are about centered between the ribbons. Bar begins over upper right of 1 and ends near center of second 0. 100 is distant from bar; numerals evenly spaced; first 0 slightly low. *Points of distinction:* A crack extends from the numerator upward, through E of AMERICA to the denticles. More cracks develop, and in a late state there is a rim cud in the denticles left of the fraction (not clear on all examples).

Notes: This variety exists in AU and Mint State, and is very rare at either level.

1801 • BW-2, S-214, B-2. *Breen dies:* 2-A. *Estimated population:* 300 to 400.

Obverse: First 1 with serif near curl, base distant from denticles and over a space between denticles. 80 close. Second 1 closer to denticles than to drapery and over a space between denticles. *LIBERTY:* LIB close. E and upright of R over hair waves. Upright of T over hair. *Points of distinction:* The rim fails at RTY, and later a cud develops in that area.

1801 (BW-2, S-214, B-2).

Reverse: Same as preceding. *Points of distinction:* Cracks expand, including two diagonal cracks that are more or less parallel at the lower right. The rim break is slightly larger.

Notes: This variety exists in Mint State.

1801 • BW-3, S-215, B-4. *Breen dies:* 3-A. *Estimated population:* 75 to 120.

Obverse: First 1 with serif near curl. 180 close. Numeral 0 much closer to denticles than to drapery. *LIBERTY:* LIB close. E and upright of R over hair waves. Upright of T over hair. *Points of distinction:* Cracks develop below the ribbon, close to the hair. In a late state, the die fails above TY, and bulges are seen. Used first on BW-4.

1801 (BW-3, S-215, B-4).

Reverse: Same as preceding. *Points of distinction:* The die fails, causing mounding, clash marks are seen in areas, and cracks develop.

Notes: This variety exists in AU and Mint State (unique).

1801 • BW-4, S-NC-1, B-3. *Breen dies:* 3-B. *Estimated population:* 20 to 25.

Obverse: Same as preceding. *Points of distinction:* Coined before BW-3, and with the obverse in an earlier die state.

Reverse: AM slightly separated, ME touch. Numerator, 1, high, and slightly left of the center of bar. Bar begins part-way over the 1 and ends slightly past center of second 0.

1801 (BW-4, S-NC-1, B-3).

Denominator 1 particularly heavy. First 0 low. *Points of distinction:* Clash marks are seen at the top border. This die was first used to coin 1800, Spike on Right Side of Right Ribbon (BW-26), then reworked to coin BW-4 and 1800, Die Chips in Field Opposite Nose (BW-27).[76] On this mating there are die incusations and problems at the top and upper-right border and nearby letters.

Notes: High grades are Mint State (unique) followed by VF and multiple Fine examples.

1801 • BW-5, S-NC-5, B-9. *Breen dies:* 6-F. *Recorded population:* 4.

Obverse: *Date:* First 1 slightly closer to hair than to denticles, centered over a denticle. 01 slightly wide. Second 1 over a denticle and slightly closer to drapery than to denticle. *LIBERTY:* LIB and RT close. E and upright of R over hair waves. Upright of T, over hair and has a shortened bottom-right serif. *Points of distinction:* This was a very durable obverse in terms of mating with multiple reverses.

1801 (BW-5, S-NC-5, B-9).

Reverse: Berry to the upper left of O of ONE has stem downward, unlike any of the other three reverses mated with this obverse. Numerator 1 close to bar. Bar begins over right side of 1 and ends over center of 0. First 0 slightly low. *Points of distinction:* The known examples have a retained cud at the upper left, encompassing most of STATES, where the die had cracked and sunk, effectively raising the field on the struck coin in this area. Note that "ATES" is visible within this umbrella-shaped area, even on the Fair-2 coin.

Notes: Grades are Fair-2 and Poor-1.While the details of the obverse die can be gained from its later use on other varieties, the reverse information is incomplete.

1801, Fraction Bar Connected to Right Ribbon • BW-6, S-NC-2, B-10.
Breen dies: 6-G. *Reported population:* 9.

Obverse: Same as preceding.

Reverse: Scratch from right side of fraction bar goes to right ribbon. Numerator, 1, slightly closer to the left ribbon than to the right. Bar begins slightly right of center of denominator 1. First 0 slightly low.

1801, Fraction Bar Connected to Right Ribbon (BW-6, S-NC-2, B-10).

Notes: VG is the highest grade known.

1801, Three Errors Reverse • BW-7,
S-219, B-11. *Breen dies:* 6-E. *Estimated population:* 750 to 1,000.

Obverse: Same as preceding. *Points of distinction:* Some have ERTY indistinct due to die deterioration.

Reverse: The famous Three Errors Reverse. The fraction appears as the mathematically meaningless 1/000, the left stem to the

1801, Three Errors Reverse (BW-7, S-219, B-11).

wreath is missing, and UNITED appears as IINITED. The latter was caused by first punching the U upside down, then correcting it. This die is also somewhat unusual in that there is a tiny space between C of CENT and the leaf, whereas they are usually connected. *Points of distinction:* This die, first used on BW-7, was also used to coin BW-14. Cracks develop and a cud is seen at the lower left, the final

iteration of a prominent crack in this area. Likely, this die was made by a mechanic, not a skilled engraver.

Notes: This variety exists in AU and Mint State. It is fortunate that this popular variety is readily obtainable in the marketplace, although most are well worn.

Detail showing the three errors: the meaningless fraction 1/000, left wreath stem missing, and IINITED instead of UNITED.

In lower grades the three errors must all be discernible.

	Cert	Avg	%MS	AG-3	G-4	VG-8	F-12	VF-20	EF-40	AU-50
1801, Three Errors Reverse (BW-7)	20	20.6	10%	$110	$275	$700	$1,750	$4,250	$12,750	$28,750

1801, 1/000 Error, Berry Directly Right of Top of E of ONE • BW-8, S-220, B-12. *Breen dies:* 6-H. *Estimated population:* 300 to 400.

Obverse: Same as preceding. *Points of distinction:* A crack extends from the lower rim upward, forming an arc to the right, then traveling to the second 1, and on to the denticles. The rim deteriorates, causing cuds below the date and to the left and right. Clash marks are near the portrait.

1801, 1/000 Error, Berry Directly Right of Top of E of ONE (BW-8, S-220, B-12).

Reverse: Error fraction 1/000. One of three 1801 dies—also see BW-16 and BW-17—with this feature. Left foot of A of STATES slightly high. ONE in normal position; E distant from leaf pair above it; berry horizontally

Detail showing the 1/000 error fraction, one of several different dies with this mistake.

opposite upper right of E. Highest leaf tip on right under right part of S. No thorn from lower-left wreath stem. *Points of distinction:* Cracks develop and expand. A cud is seen above AM.

Notes: EF is the highest grade known.

In lower grades the error fraction must be visible.

	Cert	Avg	%MS	AG-3	G-4	VG-8	F-12	VF-20	EF-40
1801, 1/000 Error, Berry Directly Right of Top of E of ONE (BW-8)	(a)			$120	$220	$410	$1,050	$2,250	$4,375

a. Included in certified population for 1801, 1/000 Error, Thorn on Stem at Left (BW-17).

1801, Highest Right Leaf Tip Right of S, Fraction Spaced as 1 00 • BW-9, S-NC-4, B-14. *Breen dies:* 8-J. *Recorded population:* 9.

Obverse: *Date:* Serif of first 1 points to top part of curl. 80 close. 1 distant from drapery. *LIBERTY:* LIBE slightly close. Uprights of E and R over hair waves. Upright of T over hair, but close to forehead.

1801, Highest Right Leaf Tip Right of S, Fraction Spaced as 1 00 (BW-9, S-NC-4, B-14).

Reverse: Highest-right leaf tip is to the right of the S, the only die of this class (with first 1 having serif) with this feature. Numerator, 1, right of the center of bar. Bar starts over center of denominator 1 and ends over left edge of second 0. 10 very wide—compare to BW-18. *Points of distinction:* This die was used to coin BW-9 and BW-15.

Notes: VG is the highest grade known.

1801 WITH FIRST 1 IN DATE WITH BLUNT TOP (NO POINTED SERIF)

1801, Corrected Fraction • BW-11, S-221, B-5. *Breen dies:* 4-C. **Estimated population:** 750 to 1,000.

1801, Corrected Fraction (BW-11, S-221, B-5).

Obverse: *Date:* First 1 about equidistant from curl and denticles. 01 slightly wide. Second 1 closer to drapery than to denticles. *LIBERTY:* LIB close. Uprights of E and R over high hair waves. Upright of T over hair. Lower-left serif of Y long. Compare to BW-12—the same die in a later state.

Detail showing the corrected fraction.

Reverse: Erroneous 1/000 die with first 0 overpunched with the correct 1. Space between C of CENT and leaf (usually these touch); T high. Perhaps cut by a mechanic. This is a different die from the Corrected Fraction of 1803. *Points of distinction:* A rim cud is at the top right and another is over STA.

Notes: A very popular variety that is readily available in the marketplace. This variety exists in Mint State.

	Cert	Avg	%MS	AG-3	G-4	VG-8	F-12	VF-20	EF-40	AU-50	MS-60BN	MS-63BN
1801, Corrected Fraction	4	26.5	25%	$120	$310	$600	$1,200	$2,330	$5,330	$7,250	$16,670	$30,830

1801 • BW-12, S-216, B-6. *Breen dies:* 4-D. **Estimated population:** Thousands.

1801 (BW-12, S-216, B-6).

Obverse: Same as preceding. *Points of distinction:* Certain features, such as LIBERTY, can be indistinct due to die damage. Indeed, even high-grade coins are notoriously mushy looking. Compare the obverse of this variety with that of the same die earlier, as it appears on BW-11.

Reverse: N of CENT leans right. 1 is centered over bar. Bar begins left of the center of 1 and continues to above the center of the second 0. Bar leans slightly down to the right and is closer to right ribbon. 100 fairly evenly spaced. First 0 very slightly low. *Points of distinction:* OF is often indistinct. A rim break is seen over STA.

Detail showing N leaning in CENT.

Notes: This variety exists in Mint State.

1801, T Over Forehead • BW-13,
S-217, B-7. *Breen dies:* 5-D. **Estimated population:** 15 to 20.

Obverse: *Date:* Upright of first 1 closer to
denticles than to hair. 80 close. Second 1 closer
to denticles than to hair. *LIBERTY:* Positioned far right. LIB close. B and E over high
waves of hair. T completely over forehead;
only die in this category with this feature.

1801, T Over Forehead (BW-13, S-217, B-7).

Reverse: Same as preceding. **Points of distinction:** Most show evidence of die failure near the bottom
border.

Notes: EF and AU are the highest grades known for this variety, and it is very rare as such.

1801, Three Errors Reverse • BW-14,
S-218, B-8. *Breen dies:* 5-E. **Estimated population:** 30 to 45.

Obverse: Same as preceding. **Points of distinction:** In the late state a bulge is at ERTY
and a slight bulge at the left of the lowest curl.
This state is rare.

Reverse: This die was also used to coin
BW-7, see entry for details.

1801, Three Errors Reverse (BW-14, S-218, B-8).

Notes: Far the rarer of the two matings with
the Three Errors Reverse. Fine and VF are the highest grades known.

In lower grades the three errors must all be visible.

	Cert	Avg	%MS	AG-3	G-4	VG-8	F-12	VF-20
1801, Three Errors Reverse (BW-14)	(a)			$675	$1,375	$2,375	$9,000	$19,000

a. Included in certified population for 1801, Three Errors Reverse (BW-7).

1801 • BW-15, S-222, B-16. *Breen dies:* 9-J.
Estimated population: 1,250 to 1,500.

Obverse: *Date:* 1's each equidistant from
denticles and bust. 80 close. *LIBERTY:* LIB
close. Uprights of E and R over hair waves.
Upright of T over hair. **Points of distinction:**
A cud is over IB. Clash marks through LIB-
ERTY are on some coins.

Reverse: See BW-9. **Points of distinction:**
This die was used to coin BW-9 and BW-15.
In its latest use, examples of which are very
rare, there is a large rim break over NITE.

Notes: This variety exists in Mint State. One
of the more plentiful varieties of the era.

1801 (BW-15, S-222, B-16).

Detail of rim cud at IB in LIBERTY.

1801, 1/000 Error, Berry Opposite Center of E of ONE • BW-16, S-NC-3, B-15. *Breen dies: 9-K. Estimated population: 25 to 30.*

1801, 1/000 Error, Berry Opposite Center of E of ONE (BW-16, S-NC-3, B-15).

Obverse: Same as preceding.

Reverse: Error fraction 1/000. One of three dies—also see BW-8 and BW-17—with this feature. Highest leaf tip on right slightly right of S. ONE too high, E close to leaf pair above it; berry opposite center of E. No thorn at end of stem at the left. This die was later altered to create the Corrected Fraction die of 1803: 1803, Lump Under Chin, Corrected Fraction 1/100 Over 1/000 (BW-5).[77]

Notes: VG is the highest grade known.

Detail showing error fraction. Detail of the injured rim.

In lower grades the 1/000 error must be visible.

	Cert	Avg	%MS	Fair-2	AG-3	G-4	VG-8
1801, 1/000 Error, Berry Opposite Center of E of ONE (BW-16)	(a)			$550	$1,225	$3,250	$8,500

a. Included in certified population for 1801, 1/000 Error, Thorn on Stem at Left (BW-17).

1801, 1/000 Error, Thorn on Stem at Left • BW-17, S-223, B-17. *Breen dies: 9-L. Estimated population:* Thousands.

1801, 1/000 Error, Thorn on Stem at Left (BW-17, S-223, B-17).

Obverse: Same as preceding. *Points of distinction:* The rim break on the earlier use is expanded here, and on a later state another is seen at the lower right.

Reverse: Error fraction 1/000. One of three dies—also see BW-8 and BW-16—with this feature. Highest leaf tip on right under right part of S. ONE in normal position; E distant from leaf pair above it; berry above and right of upper right of E. Thorn at the end of the stem at the left. *Points of distinction:* A light crack from the denticles to the right side of D of UNITED is seen on most coins. This die was also used to coin 1802, 1/000 Error Fraction (BW-1).

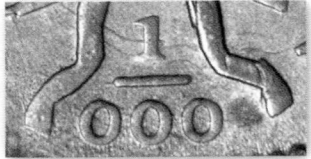

Detail showing the 1/000 error fraction, one of several different dies with this mistake.

Notes: This variety exists in Mint State. This variety is one of the most often seen of this year.

In lower grades the 1/000 error must be visible.

	Cert	Avg	%MS	AG-3	G-4	VG-8	F-12	VF-20	EF-40	AU-50
1801, 1/000 Error, Thorn on Stem at Left (BW-17)	37	24.6	5%	$115	$230	$410	$780	$1,680	$2,925	$6,940

1801, Fraction Spaced as 1 00 •

BW-18, S-224, B-13. *Breen dies:* 7-I. **Esti-mated population:** Thousands.

Obverse: *Date:* About evenly spaced numerals. First 1 slightly closer to hair than to denticles. Second 1 is slightly closer to denticles than to drapery. *LIBERTY:* LIB close and higher than adjacent E. Uprights of E and R over high waves of hair. Upright of T over hair. Y low and has lower-left serif missing.

1801, Fraction Spaced as 1 00 (BW-18, S-224, B-13).

Reverse: Highest-right leaf tip under center of S. Numerator, 1, very high, slightly right of the center of bar, and much closer to ribbon knot than to bar. Denominator spaced as 1 00—compare to BW-9; 1 closer to bar than 00. *Points of distinction:* Clash marks are seen. Cracks develop, and in the latest state there is a rim break above F in OF.

Notes: This variety is one of the most often seen of this year. AU is the highest grade known.

1802, Draped Bust

Mintage (per *Mint Report*): 3,435,100.

There are 20 die combinations of the 1802 cent, 11 of which have engraving errors! In April 1802, the second bill to abolish the Philadelphia Mint was introduced in Congress. Although change was made, uncertainty as to the future may have affected the quality of work.[78]

The normal wreath of the year has 5 berries to the left and 5 to the right. Error dies omit one berry on the right, either opposite E of ONE or T of CENT. A T of LIBERTY, punched over a previous erroneous Y, accounts for another erring die. Missing stems and wrong fractions make up the other error dies. These distinctive errors are an advantage for attribution. Remarkably, the error coins all have generous populations, and some are common. In the following listing the error varieties are listed first, leaving only nine to be deciphered by other means.

Penny Whimsy notes:

> Taken as a whole, the cents of this year are commoner, probably, than those of any other date before 1816. Among the twenty known varieties there are only two unobtainable rarities (NC-1 and NC-2), and these two involve but a single die which is not duplicated on commoner coins. Yet the 1802's have been largely neglected by collectors, perhaps because they contain only three varieties which may be said to possess dramatic peculiarities—the 000 denominator, which is a carry-over from 1801; the stemless wreath; and the stemless wreath with extra "S" and extra fraction bar. According to Mint records, 3,435,100 cents were coined during the calendar year 1802, a record not broken until 1817.

The key word in the above is *dramatic*, as there certainly is no lack of interesting varieties with less obvious peculiarities.

The typical 1802 cent shows extensive wear, although many EF and AU coins can be found, as can scattered Mint State examples. All of the planchets were imported from Boulton & Watt of Birmingham, England and were of good quality.

Check for an error die first, then if a coin does not match, continue in the following section.

Typical values for 1802 cents not from error dies. Rare varieties may be worth more. Some varieties are priced individually, as follows.

	Cert	Avg	%MS	G-4	VG-8	F-12	VF-20	EF-40	AU-50	MS-60BN	MS-63BN	MS-63RB	MS-65BN	MS-65RB
1802	385	30.4	3%	$35	$65	$140	$300	$500	$1,200	$2,200	$4,750	$12,000	$23,000	$43,750

1802, ERROR DIE, VARIETIES

1802, 1/000 Error Fraction

• BW-1, S-228, B-4. *Breen dies:* 3-C. *Estimated population:* 750 to 1,000.

Obverse: *Date:* Fairly evenly spaced. 1 close to hair and distant from denticles; centered over space between denticles. 2 closer to drapery than to denticles. *LIBERTY:* BE slightly wide. E and upright of R over hair waves. Upright of T over hair. Lower-left serif of Y defective. *Points of distinction:* Loop under drapery is above 80 and curved downward. This die was also used to coin BW-17.

1802, 1/000 Error Fraction (BW-1, S-228, B-4).

Reverse: Error fraction 1/000. Highest leaf tip on right is under right part of S. ONE in normal position; E distant from leaf pair above it; berry above and right of upper right of E. Thorn at the end of the stem at the left.

Detail showing the 1/000 error fraction, one of several different dies with this mistake.

Points of distinction: This die was also used to coin 1801, 1/000 Error, Thorn on Stem at Left (BW-17). Several cracks are seen. Eventually, severe sinking of the die obliterates ATES.

Notes: This variety exists in Mint State. As there is only one 1802 reverse die with the 000 feature, the other descriptions can be ignored if a coin meets this criterion.

In lower grades the error fraction must be visible.

	Cert	Avg	%MS	AG-3	G-4	VG-8	F-12	VF-20	EF-40	AU-50	MS-60BN	MS-63BN	MS-65BN
1802, 1/000 Error Fraction	20	39.6	20%	$80	$200	$325	$575	$950	$1,970	$3,330	$8,130	$15,500	$25,000

1802, Stemless Wreath, Single Fraction Bar

• BW-2, S-231, B-9. *Breen dies:* 6-E. *Estimated population:* Thousands.

Obverse: *Date:* Fairly evenly spaced; 2 very slightly wider. 1 close to hair, distant from denticle, and centered over denticle. 2 much closer to drapery than to denticles. *LIBERTY:* LIB close. E and R over waves of hair. Y slightly low. Upright of T over hair. *Points of distinction:* Typically with a crack at the bottom of 802 and

1802, Stemless Wreath, Single Fraction Bar (BW-2, S-231, B-9).

from the rim through R, the base of T, and under Y, passing through the field in front of the nose and branching opposite the mouth into two finer cracks, which pass to the rim opposite the chin and the neck.

Reverse: No stems to wreath; single fraction bar; definitive for attribution. *Points of distinction:* Clash marks and light cracks are usual for this variety. In the final stage, quite rare, a piece fell out of the die between two long cracks at the top of the wreath.

Notes: This variety exists in Mint State. As there is only one reverse die with stemless wreath and single fraction bar, the other descriptions can be ignored if a coin meets these criteria.

In lower grades both errors must be visible.

	Cert	Avg	%MS	AG-3	G-4	VG-8	F-12	VF-20	EF-40	AU-50	MS-60BN
1802, Stemless Wreath, Single Fraction Bar	44	30.9	5%	$60	$110	$200	$425	$850	$2,250	$3,380	$7,670

1802, E Close Over Dip Between Waves, T Mostly Over Forehead, Three Errors: Stemless Wreath, Double Fraction Bar, Extra Earlier S

• BW-3, S-241, B-20. *Breen dies:* 14-M. *Estimated population:* 1,250 to 1,500.

Obverse: *Date:* 1 is slightly closer to hair than to the denticle below it; base of 1 is triangular or pyramidal, rather than left and right serifs being horizontal. 18 wide. 2 slightly closer to drapery than to denticles. *LIBERTY:* IB close. E over dip between two waves of hair; unusual. *Points of distinction:* T mostly over forehead; unusual.

1802, E Close Over Dip Between Waves, T Mostly Over Forehead, Three Errors: Stemless Wreath, Double Fraction Bar, Extra Earlier S (BW-3, S-241, B-20).

Reverse: No stems to wreath; double fraction bar; definitive. Second S of STATES blundered with bold traces of an extra earlier S below it. ONE is too high. *Points of distinction:* This die was also used to coin 1803, Three Errors: Stemless Wreath, Double

Detail showing stemless wreath and double fraction bar.

Detail showing extra second S of STATES.

Fraction Bar, Extra Earlier S (BW-1). The 1803 coin was minted first. A light crack from F in OF to the nearby A expands and eventually develops into a rim cud. Another rim crack above TATE eventually develops into a rim cud over AT.

Notes: AU and Mint State are the highest grades, the later being particularly rare. As there is only one reverse die with stemless wreath and double fraction bar, the other descriptions can be ignored. In a way this is a "Three Errors" reverse! This seems to be yet another example of a mechanic (not engraver) sinking a die.

Lower grades must have the Stemless Wreath and Double Fraction Bar visible, but not necessarily the Extra S.

	Cert	Avg	%MS	AG-3	G-4	VG-8	F-12	VF-20	EF-40	AU-50
1802, Three Errors: Stemless Wreath, Double Fraction Bar, Extra Earlier S	(a)			$60	$115	$205	$440	$900	$2,375	$4,070

a. Included in certified population for 1802, Stemless Wreath, Single Fraction Bar.

OTHER 1802 VARIETIES

1802, Berries: 5 Left, 4 Right. No Berry Opposite E of ONE

• BW-4, S-238, B-11. *Breen dies:* 7-G. *Estimated population:* 120 to 160.

Obverse: *Date:* 1 closer to hair than to the denticle over which it is centered. 18 slightly wide. 2 closer to drapery than to denticles. *LIBERTY:* IB closest. Uprights of E and R over hair waves. Lower-right serif of T is barely over forehead. Y slightly low and with lower-

1802, Berries: 5 Left, 4 Right. No Berry Opposite E of ONE (BW-4, S-238, B-11).

left serif defective. *Points of distinction:* Denticles typically weak or missing on lower part of the coin. This die was used to coin both BW-4 and BW-12. Clashing has further injured the die on this combination.

Reverse: No berry opposite E of ONE. Denticles short and with rounded ends. *Points of distinction:* Cracks appear, and a rim break to the left pendant of T, across the tops of ATE, and back to the rim over S is seen in the latest state.

Notes: VF is the highest grade known.

1802, T Over Junction of Hair and Forehead, Berries: 5 Left, 4 Right, No Berry Opposite T of CENT, Bar Tilts Down to the Left • BW-5, S-234, B-14. *Breen dies:* 9-J. *Estimated population:* 200 to 300.

1802, T Over Junction of Hair and Forehead, Berries: 5 Left, 4 Right, No Berry Opposite T of CENT, Bar Tilts Down to the Left (BW-5, S-234, B-14).

Obverse: *Date:* 1 very close to hair and distant from denticles. 2 closer to drapery than to denticles. *LIBERTY:* BE and RTY wide. E centered over dip between two waves of hair. Upright of T over junction of hair and forehead. *Points of distinction:* An early die clash led to a rim break over B. This progresses to cover much of BERT, the so-called "dripping paint" break.

Detail showing fraction bar sloping down to the left.

Reverse: No berry opposite T of CENT. Fraction bar tilts slightly down to the left, and is closer to the denominator 1 than to the second 0. Bar is much closer to the right ribbon than to the left. *Points of distinction:* Found with crumbling of the die along the lower edges of bottom pair of leaves on right branch, and along right stem.

Notes: This variety exists in Mint State. As there are three obverses mated to this reverse, and as there is another reverse without a berry to the right of T, the details need to be studied closely when attributing a coin to this variety.

1802, Left of E Over Wave of Hair, Berries: 5 Left, 4 Right, No Berry Opposite T of CENT, Bar Tilts Down to the Left • BW-6, S-235, B-15. *Breen dies:* 10-J. *Estimated population:* 300 to 400.

1802, Left of E Over Wave of Hair, Berries: 5 Left, 4 Right, No Berry Opposite T of CENT, Bar Tilts Down to the Left (BW-6, S-235, B-15).

Obverse: *Date:* 1 and 2 are each about equidistant between the denticles and the bust. *LIBERTY:* Left uprights of E and R over waves of hair. Upright of T over hair. *Points of distinction:* A rim break develops at TY and expands. On the latest state, there is a heavy arc-like die crack from the rim into the field at the right, extending into the neck, and continuing behind the head to the left.

Reverse: Same as preceding. *Points of distinction:* Seen with a crack from rim between E and S, through right branch and I, and to rim.

Notes: This variety exists in AU and Mint State.

1802, E Centered Over Wave of Hair, Berries: 5 Left, 4 Right, No Berry Opposite T of CENT, Bar Tilts Down to the Left • BW-7, S-236, B-16. *Breen dies:* 11-J. *Estimated population:* Thousands.

Obverse: *Date:* 1 and 2 each closer to the bust than to the denticles. 02 close. *LIBERTY:* E and R centered over waves of hair. Lower-right serif of T defective; T over hair. *Points of distinction:* A light crack extends from below 1, upward, and then into the field at the left.

1802, E Centered Over Wave of Hair, Berries: 5 Left, 4 Right, No Berry Opposite T of CENT, Bar Tilts Down to the Left (BW-7, S-236, B-16).

Reverse: Same as preceding. *Points of distinction:* In this pairing, the last use of the die, additional cracks are seen. The upper reverse demonstrates a latticework of cracks, with a rim cud ultimately developing over ST.

Notes: This variety exists in Mint State.

1802, T Over Hair, Berries: 5 Left, 4 Right, No Berry Opposite T of CENT, Bar Tilts Up to the Left • BW-8, S-239, B-17. *Breen dies:* 12-K. *Estimated population:* 300 to 400.

Obverse: *Date:* 1 much closer to hair than to denticles. 2 slightly closer to drapery than to denticles. *LIBERTY:* LIB and ER close. Uprights of E and R over waves of hair. Upright of T over hair. *Points of distinction:* Crack off forelock and through the field in front of the nose becomes progressively heavier, extending to the rim, opposite the mouth. Another crack develops off the underside of the nose, joining the former crack at the rim. The die sinks between these cracks, forming an "elephant trunk" off Liberty's face.

1802, T Over Hair, Berries: 5 Left, 4 Right, No Berry Opposite T of CENT, Bar Tilts Up to the Left (BW-8, S-239, B-17).

Detail showing fraction bar sloping up to the left.

Reverse: No berry opposite T of CENT. Fraction bar tilts sharply up to the left, and is much farther from denominator 1 than from the second 0. Bar is slightly closer to the left ribbon than to the right. *Points of distinction:* Clash marks are seen at RICA, and later elsewhere. A crack develops across the die above its center.

Notes: AU is the highest grade known. As there are three obverses mated to this reverse, and as there is another reverse without a berry to the right of T, the details need to be studied closely when attributing a coin to this variety.

1802, T Over Junction of Hair and Forehead, Berries: 5 Left, 4 Right, No Berry Opposite T of CENT, Bar Tilts Up to the Left • BW-9, S-240, B-18. *Breen dies: 13-K. Estimated population:* 200 to 300.

1802, T Over Junction of Hair and Forehead, Berries: 5 Left, 4 Right, No Berry Opposite T of CENT, Bar Tilts Up to the Left (BW-9, S-240, B-18).

Obverse: *Date:* 1 slightly closer to hair than to denticles. 2 equidistant between drapery and denticles. *LIBERTY:* LIB close. E over dip between waves of hair. Upright of T over junction of hair and forehead. *Points of distinction:* Typically (but not always) with a crack upward from the lower rim, through the drapery, and through the bust to in front of the eye. Clash marks are the norm.

Reverse: Same as preceding. *Points of distinction:* Cracks are more extensive than on the previous use.

Notes: This variety exists in EF and AU, and is rare as such. Multiple VF coins exist.

1802, T in LIBERTY Punched Over Y, Highest Right Leaf Over Right Edge of S • BW-10, S-232, B-12. *Breen dies: 8-H. Estimated population:* Thousands.

1802, T in LIBERTY Punched Over Y, Highest Right Leaf Over Right Edge of S (BW-10, S-232, B-12).

Obverse: *Date:* 1 very high, nearly touching hair, and distant from denticles. 2 slightly closer to drapery than to denticles. *LIBERTY:* IBE close, E leans right. Uprights of E and R over high waves of hair. T cut over an erroneous Y. Parts of the arms of the Y can be seen to each side of the upper part of the upright of the T, especially on the right; definitive. Y mostly over hair, but slightly over forehead. *Points of distinction:* Light clash marks are often seen at the top. Many have a break in the denticles below 18, which eventually extends to involve five denticles, centered under the 1.

Detail of T over Y.

Reverse: Highest leaf on right under right edge of S; definitive. Outer leaf tip under first T of STATES. Medium-size berries. Fraction bar nearly touches left ribbon. Nearly always with clash marks between denticles and AMERICA. *Points of distinction:* Several cracks can be seen, the extent of which expanded as the coinage progressed. A rim break forms at the left above ATE.

Notes: This variety exists in Mint State.

1802, T in LIBERTY Over Y, Highest Right Leaf Over Lower-Left Serif of S • BW-11, S-233, B-13. *Breen dies:* 8-I. *Estimated population:* 500 to 750.

Obverse: Same as preceding. *Points of distinction:* On this use a further three-denticle rim break develops.

Reverse: Highest leaf on right under lower-left serif of S; definitive. Outer leaf tip under right edge of first S of STATES. Large berries. Space between fraction bar and left ribbon. *Points of distinction:* Several cracks are usually seen.

1802, T in LIBERTY Over Y, Highest Right Leaf Over Lower-Left Serif of S (BW-11, S-233, B-13).

Notes: AU is the highest grade known.

1802, Lower-Right Serif of T Is Slightly Over Forehead, Berry Directly Right of Top Serif of O of ONE • BW-12, S-237, B-10. *Breen dies:* 7-F. *Estimated population:* 750 to 1,000.

Obverse: See BW-4. *Points of distinction:* Usually seen with a crack through ERTY. This die was also used to coin BW-4.

Reverse: Highest-right leaf tip under lower-left serif of S. Berry directly right of top serif of E of ONE. Fraction bar extends from

1802, Lower-Right Serif of T Is Slightly Over Forehead, Berry Directly Right of Top Serif of O of ONE (BW-12, S-237, B-10).

upper right of 1 to *past center* of second 0. Bar is much closer to the right ribbon than to the left. *Points of distinction:* Multiple light cracks are the rule.

Notes: This variety exists in Mint State.

1802, E Close Over Dip Between Waves, T Mostly Over Forehead, Thorn From Left Stem to U • BW-13, S-242, B-19. *Breen dies:* 14-L. *Estimated population:* 750 to 1,000.

Obverse: See BW-3. *Points of distinction:* Some, but not all, clash marks seen on the previous use of the die have been removed.

Reverse: Highest-right leaf tip under center of S. Thorn from left stem to U; definitive. Bold center dot over left upright of N. Numerator, 1, centered high above bar. Bar begins at the upper right of 1 and extends to just short of the center of the second 0. 100 very widely spaced. *Points of distinction:* This die was also used to strike 1803, "Unicorn Variety," 3 Embedded in Drapery (BW-6) and 1803, Unfinished Hair Below E (BW-28). A crack is seen at the left over part of UNITED.

1802, E Close Over Dip Between Waves, T Mostly Over Forehead, Thorn From Left Stem to U (BW-13, S-242, B-19).

Detail showing thorn from stem to U.
Detail of the injured rim.

Notes: AU is the highest grade known. Walter Breen notes that it is likely that this variety was struck in 1803 and was delivered by the coiner on February 22 of that year.

1802, 1 Touches Hair, Highest-Right Leaf Tip Right of S, Berry Opposite Upper Right of E of ONE • BW-14, S-225, B-1. *Breen dies:* 1-A. *Estimated population:* 400 to 500.

1802, 1 Touches Hair, Highest-Right Leaf Tip Right of S, Berry Opposite Upper Right of E of ONE (BW-14, S-225, B-1).

Obverse: *Date:* 1 touches hair; definitive. 2 much closer to drapery than to denticles. *LIBERTY:* IB close. E and R over waves of hair. Upright of T over hair. Y slightly low. *Points of distinction:* Multiple die clashes across the end of the bust, and across and below 802, lead to a typical rim break below 802. Unclashed early state coins are rare.

Reverse: Highest-right leaf tip to right of S; definitive. Berry opposite the upper-right tip of E of ONE; only die with berry in this position. *Points of distinction:* Cracks develop, and eventually a cud eliminates most of E of STATES.

Notes: This variety exists in Mint State.

1802, 1 Touches Hair, Highest-Right Leaf Tip Left of Center of S • BW-15, S-226, B-2. *Breen dies:* 1-B. *Estimated population:* 400 to 500.

1802, 1 Touches Hair, Highest-Right Leaf Tip Left of Center of S (BW-15, S-226, B-2).

Obverse: Same as preceding. *Points of distinction:* In this usage there is always a rim break below 802. Additionally, a crack develops, curving from the right rim to the end of the nose, eventually extending up along it to the forehead and the upper rim above B.

Reverse: Highest-right leaf tip left of the center of S. Medial side of both bow loops incomplete. Right foot of A lower than adjacent left foot of M and right lower foot of M below adjacent left foot of E. Compare to BW-19, where ME join at base. Left, club-like stem shorter than the right stem. Fraction bar heavy and closer to the right ribbon than to the left. Numbers distant from it. Bar begins over the space between 1 and 0 and ends just short of the center of the second 0. 10 closer than 00. *Points of distinction:* A light crack is at the top of the letters at the upper right.

Notes: This variety exists in Mint State.

1802, 1 Does Not Touch Hair, Highest-Right Leaf Tip Left of Center of S • BW-16, S-NC-1, B-3. *Breen dies:* 2-B. *Estimated population:* 35 to 50.

1802, 1 Does Not Touch Hair, Highest-Right Leaf Tip Left of Center of S (BW-16, S-NC-1, B-3).

Obverse: *Date:* 1 and 2 are closer to bust than to denticles. *LIBERTY:* R over wave of hair. Upright of T over hair. Lower-left serif of Y defective. *Points of distinction:* Loop under drapery is above 802 and is *straight* except at its leftmost part. Most commonly seen with a bisecting crack from the border, through the right of B, into Liberty's hair, curving in front of the ear to cross the neck and drapery, and continuing to the rim to the right of 2—this being light on early impressions, heavier on later ones. Still later, another crack develops.

Reverse: Same as preceding. *Points of distinction:* Clash marks are seen. A light crack is through AMERI.

Notes: VF and EF are the highest grades known, and example are rare as such. This variety was Non-Collectible when *Early American Cents* was published in 1949.

1802 • BW-17, S-227, B-5. *Breen dies:* 3-B. *Estimated population:* 750 to 1,000.

1802 (BW-17, S-227, B-5).

Obverse: See BW-1. *Points of distinction:* This die was also used to coin BW-1.

Reverse: Same as preceding. *Points of distinction:* Multiple clash marks are seen. The crack described earlier now extends farther to the left to F in OF.

Notes: This combination is often seen with prominent clash marks on the obverse from the wreath, seen behind the hair and under the hair ribbon—as well as, most prominently, in front of the forehead and under the chin—prompting Dr. Sheldon to call it the Cobweb Variety. This variety exists in AU and Mint State, the latter being very rare.

1802 • BW-18, S-229, B-6. *Breen dies:* 4-B. *Estimated population:* 500 to 750.

1802 (BW-18, S-229, B-6).

Obverse: *Date:* 1 slightly closer to hair than to denticles. 18 wide. 8 low and leans right. 2 about centered between denticles and drapery. LIBERTY: L lower than I. IB much closer than LI. E and R over waves of hair. Upright of T over hair. Lower-left serif of Y longer than right. *Points of distinction:* Usually with cracks near the top border.

Reverse: Same as preceding. *Points of distinction:* Here, in its last use, cracks develop into cud breaks, first over TES and then over AME as well.

Notes: This variety exists in Mint State.

1802, Highest-Right Leaf Tip Under Left Edge of S, Left Stem Short •

BW-19, S-NC-2, B-7. *Breen dies:* 4-D. *Estimated population:* 18 to 22.

Obverse: Same as preceding. *Points of distinction:* With a crack through BERTY, as in the latest state of the preceding use.

Reverse: Highest-right leaf tip under left edge of S. ME joined at base. Compare to BW-15, BW-16, BW-17, and BW-18, where right lower foot of M is below the adjacent left foot of E. Left stem short. Fraction bar closer to left ribbon than to right. Bar begins over upper right of 1 and extends to above center of second 0. 10 wider than 00.

1802, Highest-Right Leaf Tip Under Left Edge of S, Left Stem Short (BW-19, S-NC-2, B-7).

Detail showing bottom-right serif of M under bottom-left serif of E. Detail of the injured rim.

Notes: VF and EF are the highest grades known, but examples are very rare so fine. Most are VG or lower. Walter Breen notes that only one was known to Dr. Sheldon when *Early American Cents* was published in 1949. When *Penny Whimsy* came out in 1958 the population was three, which increased to at least 15 when Breen's *Encyclopedia* was released in 2000. As has often happened, Sheldon's NC for Non-Collectible can be called *Now*-Collectible.

1802 • BW-20, S-230, B-8. *Breen dies:* 5-D. *Estimated population:* Thousands.

Obverse: *Date:* 1 and 2 are closer to the bust than to the denticles. 1, 8, and 0 are each centered over a denticle and are level with one another. 80 close. *LIBERTY:* LIB very close. L slightly lower than I. Uprights of E and R over hair waves. Upright of T over hair. Y slightly low. *Points of distinction:* In this use, another crack is seen at the lower right.

1802 (BW-20, S-230, B-8).

Reverse: Same as preceding. *Points of distinction:* Multiple horizontal cracks develop through the upper reverse, with die sinking eventually obliterating TES.

Notes: This variety exists in AU and Mint State, especially rare in the latter category.

Numismatic Notes: *The Hidden Find:* The Charles Stetson Collection, cataloged by W. Elliot Woodward, was auctioned on January 21 and 22, 1889. Stetson lived in Quincy, Massachusetts, and was born in 1832. Lot 26, an 1802 cent, was described as, "Nearly red, Uncirculated; extremely fine, in almost Proof condition; one of the few known as the Hidden Find, discovered many years ago in R.I.; very rare."[79] As Arthur Conan Doyle did in his Sherlock Holmes detective stories—with mysterious references such as the "giant rat of Sumatra"—Woodward and his contemporaries printed many asides in their catalogs, some of which were probably recognized at the time by the knowing ones, but which left most readers clueless. A certain William E. Hidden was a well-known antiquarian and numismatist around the turn of the 20th century (his collection was sold by Thomas Elder in 1916); could he have been associated with the Hidden Find?

1803, *Draped Bust*

Mintage (per *Mint Report*): 3,131,691.

The year 1803 saw an unprecedented production of cents. Struck on high-quality planchets imported from Boulton & Watt, the coins were attractive and problem free. Many were struck from 1802-dated dies.

Today, cents of this year, comprising two dozen different die combinations, are, for the most part, readily collectible.

There are two obverse styles, the Small Date and the Large Date. Reverses come with Small Fraction and Large Fraction. Errors are plentiful, as was the situation in 1802. These errors include a stemless wreath, also with a double fraction bar; two dies with the 1 in the numerator way too high; another with double fraction bar (but with the correct two stems to the wreath); a corrected error fraction; and one with the top of the 3 in the date embedded in the drapery. In many cases, dies were likely made by a workman from the coining department.[80]

These errors are listed first below (Group 1), then the Large Dates as there are just two of them (Group 2), then the remaining Large Fractions in combination with Small Dates (Group 3), and finally the remaining Small Date, Small Fraction varieties. In this way the last category can be studied on its own.

Within the Small Fraction varieties there are many dies that are quite similar. These have been divided into: Coins with unusual features as headlined (Group 4). Coins with 3 (1803) touching or nearly touching the drapery (Group 5). Remaining Small Date, Small Fraction varieties not yet classified (Group 6).

To follow this method, start at the beginning of the 1803 varieties and go downward until your coin is identified. This method does not reflect the order in which the coins were struck and, in some instances the use of the same die on two varieties may not have adjacent Bowers-Whitman numbers (but such dies are cross-referenced).

Typical values for 1803 cents. Rare varieties may be worth more. Some varieties are priced individually, as follows.

	Cert	Avg	%MS	AG-3	G-4	VG-8	F-12	VF-20	EF-40	AU-50	MS-60BN	MS-63BN
1803	253	31.4	7%	$65	$140	$300	$600	$1,400	$2,500	$5,000	$15,000	$30,000

Group 1: 1803, Error Dies

1803, Three Errors: Stemless Wreath, Double Fraction Bar, Extra Earlier S •
BW-1, S-243, B-1. *Breen dies:* 1-A. *Estimated population:* 750 to 1,000.

Obverse: *Date:* Small Date with blunt 1. 1 closer to hair than to denticles and is centered over the space between two denticles. 18 slightly close. 3 very close to, but does not touch, drapery. *LIBERTY:* IB very close. Uprights of E and R over hair waves. Upright of T over hair. Y slightly low; lower-left serif repaired. *Points of distinction:* Early in the life of the die a crack develops from the curl on the neck, across the throat, and slightly

1803, Three Errors: Stemless Wreath, Double Fraction Bar, Extra Earlier S (BW-1, S-243, B-1). Earlier S (below second S in STATES). Die also used *later* to coin 1802, E Close Over Dip Between Waves, T Mostly Over Forehead, Three Errors: Stemless Wreath, Double Fraction Bar, Extra Earlier S (BW-3)—see enlarged illustrations there.

into the right field. Later, a rim break develops opposite nose and forehead, eventually extending upward through the denticles above, and down to the tops of TY.

Reverse: No stems to wreath; double fraction bar; definitive. Second S of STATES blundered with bold traces of an earlier S below it. ONE is too high. In a way this a "Three Errors" reverse! *Points of distinction:* Usually with clash marks at ERICA, later removed. Crack from rim, to 3, and on to drapery. Die possibly made by a mechanic. This die was used to coin both 1802, E Close Over Dip Between Waves, T Mostly Over Forehead, Three Errors: Stemless Wreath, Double Fraction Bar, Extra Earlier S (BW-3) and 1803 (BW-1). The 1803 coin was minted *first.*

Notes: There is only one 1803 variety with this reverse. This is one of the most popular varieties of the year. Examples are readily available, and a few are known in Mint State. Quoting *Penny Whimsy:* "In this marriage, the reverse is always found *without* the cracks noted for the 1802 marriage, demonstrating, as Newcomb points out, that this particular 1803 cent must have been struck before some of the 1802 cents were struck. The same thing is encountered four or five times among the early cents, and probably indicates that when a number of dies were still in good condition and not worn out, the transition from one date to the next was sometimes accomplished more or less gradually, with occasional returning to a die of the earlier date, perhaps in order to 'use it up.' They had to be thrifty at the Mint, especially with Congress in session almost next door, and many a congressman looking for something to 'correct.'"[81]

In lower grades all three errors must be visible.

	Cert	Avg	%MS	AG-3	G-4	VG-8	F-12	VF-20	EF-40	AU-50	MS-60BN	MS-63BN
1803, Stemless Wreath, Double Fraction Bar, Extra Earlier S	12	32.8	17%	$75	$160	$300	$570	$970	$2,250	$4,500	$10,000	$17,000

1803, Lump Under Chin (on most), 1 of Numerator Far Too High, Tip of Highest Outside-Right Leaf Under S • BW-2, S-246, B-4. *Breen dies:* 3-D. *Estimated population:* 200 to 300.

Obverse: Date high, with 1 and 3 close to bust. Fairly evenly spaced. *LIBERTY:* IB closest. E and R over waves of hair. Upright of T over hair. *Points of distinction:* Top of hair unfinished just below highest horizontal strand, from relapping of the die. This die was used to coin BW-2, BW-4, BW-5, and BW-29. Lump under chin on all except early strikes. This combination was the *first* use of the obverse die.

1803, Lump Under Chin (on most), 1 of Numerator Far Too High, Tip of Highest Outside-Right Leaf Under S (BW-2, S-246, B-4).

Detail showing carelessly punched fraction with numerator too high, bar tilting slightly down to the left, and 1 punched more deeply and much closer to the bar than the other two digits.

Reverse: Numerator, 1, far too high, close to the ribbon knot, and distant from the fraction bar; bar over 1 of denominator; definitive. Compare to BW-3. Tip of highest outside-right leaf under S of STATES. *Points of distinction:* Found perfect, and with crack from rim to left of first S through tops of STA. Later, the rim becomes heavily broken over STA.

Notes: Most (but not all) have a lump under the chin, Sheldon's "Mumps Obverse." EF and AU are the highest grades known, and examples are very rare in the latter category.

1803, 1 of Numerator Far Too High, Tip of Highest Outside-Right Leaf Between E and S • BW-3, S-NC-1, B-9. *Breen dies: 4-I.* **Estimated population:** 30 to 45.

Obverse: *Date:* 1 slightly farther from hair than 3 is to drapery; centered over a denticle. 18 close. *LIBERTY:* LIB close. Uprights of E and R over waves of hair. Upright of T over hair. Lower-left serif of Y repaired. *Points of distinction:* This die was used to coin BW-3, BW-30, and BW-31. In this use the die was reground to remove clash marks, after which, seemingly per the usual, more are sustained.

1803, 1 of Numerator Far Too High, Tip of Highest Outside-Right Leaf Between E and S (BW-3, S-NC-1, B-9).

Reverse: Numerator, 1, far too high, close to the ribbon knot and distant from the fraction bar; bar *not* over 1 of denominator; definitive. Compare to BW-2. Tip of highest outside-right leaf between E and S of STATES; definitive. *Points of distinction:* Of those seen by Walter Breen, just one had a crack at NITED.

Detail showing high 1 in numerator.

Notes: VF and EF are the highest grades known, and examples are very rare as such. Most are Fine or lower.

1803, Lump Under Chin, Double Fraction Bar • BW-4, S-248, B-6. *Breen dies: 3-F.* **Estimated population:** 120 to 160.

Obverse: Same as BW-2. Lump under chin. "Mumps Obverse." *Points of distinction:* This die was used to coin BW-2, BW-4, BW-5, and BW-29. In this use the lump remains prominent, and a slight bulging is seen at the lower right.

1803, Lump Under Chin, Double Fraction Bar (BW-4, S-248, B-6).

Reverse: Double fraction bar, the first light and above the other; definitive. *Points of distinction:* A crack is over MERI.

Notes: This variety exists in AU and Mint State, the latter being extremely rare. Most are in lower grades.

Detail showing double fraction bar, the first faint above the second.

In lower grades the Double Fraction Bar must be visible.

	Cert	Avg	%MS	AG-3	G-4	VG-8	F-12	VF-20	EF-40	AU-50
1803, Lump Under Chin, Double Fraction Bar	(a)			$120	$230	$520	$1,150	$2,350	$6,000	$11,000

a. Included in certified population for 1803.

1803, Lump Under Chin, Corrected Fraction 1/100 Over 1/000 • BW-5, S-249, B-7. *Breen dies:* 3-G. *Estimated population:* 750 to 1,000.

1803, Lump Under Chin, Corrected Fraction 1/100 Over 1/000 (BW-5, S-249, B-7).

Obverse: Same as preceding. Lump under chin. "Mumps Obverse." *Points of distinction:* This die was used to coin BW-2, BW-4, BW-5, and BW-29. With a crack at the right of the date, which expands and ends in a rim break.

Reverse: This die was first employed as the 1801, 1/000 Error, Berry Opposite Center of E of ONE (BW-16) die, then was corrected later to its present form.[82] *Points of distinction:* A crack at ERIC expands, eventually resulting in a rim cud over RIC.

Detail showing corrected fraction, an alteration of the die used to coin 1801, 1/000 Error, Berry Opposite Center of E of ONE (BW-16).

Notes: This variety exists in Mint State. There is only one 1803 variety with this reverse. An eagerly sought and quite available variety.

In lower grades the fraction must be clear.

	Cert	Avg	%MS	AG-3	G-4	VG-8	F-12	VF-20	EF-40	AU-50	MS-60BN	MS-63BN
1803, Lump Under Chin, Corrected Fraction 1/100 Over 1/000	14	30.6	7%	$85	$170	$370	$630	$1,010	$2,350	$4,830	$10,500	$18,000

1803, "Unicorn Variety," 3 Embedded in Drapery • BW-6, S-245, B-2. *Breen dies:* 2-B. *Estimated population:* 300 to 400.

1803, "Unicorn Variety," 3 Embedded in Drapery (BW-6, S-245, B-2).

Obverse: *Date:* 3 embedded into drapery; definitive. Fairly evenly spaced. 1 closer to hair than to denticles. *LIBERTY:* L slightly low. LIB close, IB closest. Uprights of E and R over hair waves. Upright of T over hair. Y slightly low. *Points of distinction:* Clash marks are in the field. One of these protrudes from the forehead, giving rise to the designation, "Unicorn Variety."

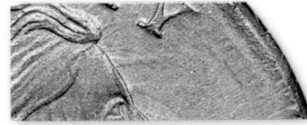

Detail of clash mark protruding from forehead.

Reverse: ONE high; berry to right and slightly higher than center of crossbar. Tiny die scratch connects left stem with U. Numerator over first 0, and about the same distance from the bar. Bar begins slightly right of 1 and ends left of the center of second 0. 100 spaced widely. *Points of distinction:* This die was used to strike BW-6, BW-28, and 1802, E Close Over Dip Between Waves, T Mostly Over Forehead, Thorn From Left Stem to U (BW-13). With extensive cracks and a rim break over N of UNITED. Later the rim breaks at RICA.

Notes: This variety exists in Mint State.

GROUP 2: 1803, LARGE DATES (TWO SIZES OF FRACTIONS)

1803, Large Date (Pointed 1), Large Fraction • BW-8, S-265, B-23. *Breen dies:* 14-S. *Estimated population:* 120 to 160.

Obverse: *Date:* Large Date with pointed 1; definitive. 1 and 3 both touch bust. 03 close. *LIBERTY:* LIB close, ER slightly close. Uprights of E and R over hair waves. Upright of T over hair. *Points of distinction:* Arc-like raised lines are to the right of the drapery, probably from a lathe. Seen with a perfect die and also with cracks. Also see BW-9.

Reverse: Large Fraction; definitive in combination with this obverse. Slightly larger letters than the following—BW-9. OF and AMERICA closer than on BW-9. *Points of distinction:* Occasionally from a perfect die in its early use, but often with a network of cracks.

1803, Large Date (Pointed 1),
Large Fraction (BW-8, S-265, B-23).

Large Date.

Notes: EF and AU are the highest grades known. It is thought that the Large Dates were among the last cents struck with the 1803 date. Just one obverse die was made with this style. This variety and the next, listed in the regular edition of the *Guide Book of United States Coins*, are in very strong demand.

	Cert	Avg	%MS	AG-3	G-4	VG-8	F-12	VF-20	EF-40
1803, Large Date (Pointed 1), Large Fraction	(a)			$125	$260	$550	$1,200	$2,000	$6,500

a. Included in certified population for 1803.

1803, Large Date (Pointed 1), Small Fraction • BW-9, S-264, B-24. *Breen dies:* 14-R. *Estimated population:* 60 to 75.

Obverse: Same as preceding. *Points of distinction:* With a crack through the right of 1, upward, then curving back to the rim. Another crack forms later.

Reverse: Small Fraction; definitive in combination with this obverse. Smaller letters than on the preceding—BW-8. OF and AMER-

1803, Large Date (Pointed 1),
Small Fraction (BW-9, S-264, B-24).

ICA much farther apart than on BW-8. Extra berry below first T of STATES. *Points of distinction:* This die was used to coin BW-9 and BW-19. The cracks are more extensive on this use, and die failure eventually blanks out STA.

Notes: VF is the highest grade known. This variety is in great demand, due in part to its listing in the regular edition of the *Guide Book of United States Coins*.

GROUP 3: 1803, SMALL DATE, LARGE FRACTIONS

This group combines three obverse dies with three reverses to create five different varieties. The reverses all have Large Letters, with OF and AMERICA spaced closer than on the Small Fraction varieties.

1803, Small Date, Large Fraction, Outside Berry Below T of STATES, Short Fraction Bar • BW-11, S-257, B-16. *Breen dies:* **10-N.** *Estimated population:* 750 to 1,000.

1803, Small Date, Large Fraction, Outside Berry Below T of STATES, Short Fraction Bar (BW-11, S-257, B-16).

Obverse: *Date:* 1 and 3 closer to bust than to denticles. 1 is very far from the curl and is over a denticle. *LIBERTY:* LIB close; IB closest. ER close. E and R over waves of hair. T is repunched low on the left and is thicker than normal at that point; T is over hair. *Points of distinction:* High-grade impressions show raised arcs on the bust, from a lathe during the die-finishing process.

Reverse: Outside berry below T of STATES; definitive within this group. Short fraction bar starts over left part of first 0 (definitive within this group), ends left of center of second 0. *Points of distinction:* Multiple cracks develop, and eventually severe die sinking

Detail of the obverse, showing arcs from lathe work.

Detail of the late state of the reverse, showing mounding at STATES from the sinking of the die surface.

develops, obliterating STATES—as well as much of the date in the corresponding spot on the obverse, due to insufficient metal flow to fill the corresponding part of the obverse die.

Notes: Readily available in the marketplace, including a handful of Mint State.

1803, Small Date, Large Fraction, Leaf Tip Under Left Serif of E of UNITED • BW-12, S-258, B-17. *Breen dies:* 10-O. *Estimated population:* Thousands.

1803, Small Date, Large Fraction, Leaf Tip Under Left Serif of E of UNITED (BW-12, S-258, B-17).

Obverse: Same as preceding. *Points of distinction:* In this use the die is relapped to remove clash marks, after which more appear. A bulge develops to the left of the lowest curl. Usually with a crack from the rim, through the 1, to curls, back to rim. Lathe lines are still visible on high-grade examples.

Reverse: Leaf tip under left serif of E of UNITED; definitive within this group. T of CENT close to, but does not touch, leaf; definitive within this group. Fraction bar

Detail of line through D.

starts above right side of 1 and ends close to center of second 0. Bar is closer to the right ribbon than to the left. A diagonal die line, apparently the slip of an engraving tool, causes a raised line from the rim diagonally through the upper right of the D of UNITED. *Points of distinction:* Clash marks develop.

Notes: Plentiful in Mint State (in the context of early cents) and thus an ideal candidate for a type set.

1803, Small Date, Large Fraction •

BW-13, S-259, B-18. *Breen dies:* 11-O. *Estimated population:* 120 to 160.

Obverse: *Date:* 1 and 3 closer to bust than to denticles. 1 over space between denticles. Ball on 3 weak. *LIBERTY:* LI wide. IB and ER slightly close. Uprights of E and R over waves of hair. Lower-left serif of T long; right serif short, and while over the hair, is closer to the forehead than on any die of this group. *Points of distinction:* Extensive clash marks develop.

1803, Small Date, Large Fraction (BW-13, S-259, B-18).

Reverse: Same as preceding. *Points of distinction:* A very few have a crack from the rim left of the first S, connecting the tops of TAT, and back to the rim over the left edge of E. In the latest state there is a rim break over TAT.

Notes: This variety exists in AU and Mint State, and examples are very rare at these levels. Nearly all are in lower grades. Dr. Sheldon called this the "Ghost 3" variety due to the weak ball at the bottom.

1803, Small Date, Large Fraction, Fraction Bar Closer to Left Ribbon •

BW-14, S-260, B-19. *Breen dies:* 11-P. *Estimated population:* Thousands.

Obverse: Same as preceding. *Points of distinction:* Except for a rare early state of this use, the die has been relapped to remove clash marks, and certain features were strengthened, including the bottom of the 3, which had become weak. Additional clash marks develop. A crack develops from T to the hair.

1803, Small Date, Large Fraction, Fraction Bar Closer to Left Ribbon (BW-14, S-260, B-19).

Reverse: Fraction bar starts above right side of 1 and ends close to center of second 0. Bar is longer than the preceding. Bar is closer to the left ribbon than to the right; definitive within this group. *Points of distinction:* A small rim break is seen over the space above the second S of STATES and the O in OF. This was struck after some examples of BW-15 had been struck. After BW-14 was struck, BW-15 was continued in production. Multiple clash marks.

Notes: This variety exists in Mint State.

1803, Small Date, Large Fraction, Corner of 3 in Drapery • BW-15,

S-261, B-20. *Breen dies:* 12-P. *Estimated population:* 500 to 750.

Obverse: *Date:* Corner of 3 in drapery; definitive in this group. *LIBERTY:* LIBE close; LI closest. E and R over waves of hair. Upright of T over hair. *Points of distinction:* A small die defect or "spur" extends to the right at the bottom of the forehead. Most

1803, Small Date, Large Fraction, Corner of 3 in Drapery (BW-15, S-261, B-20).

have an arc-like crack from between 8 and 0, upward through Liberty's shoulder and hair, and then down to the rim at the left. This expands on late states, and mounding is also seen. Altered to create the spurious 1804, "Restrike" from mismatched dies.

Reverse: Same as preceding. *Points of distinction:* Many clash marks are seen.

Notes: This variety exists in AU and Mint State, and examples are very rare in the latter category. This obverse die was discarded as scrap metal by the Mint. Years later it was altered outside of the Mint to read "1804" and was used to make the so-called 1804 "restrikes."

GROUP 4: 1803, SMALL DATE, SMALL FRACTIONS, WITH UNUSUAL FEATURES AS HEADLINED

This group comprises two varieties with characteristics that are unusual among the remaining coins. Each boldface headline is definitive.

1803, T Over Junction of Hair and Forehead • BW-18, S-252, B-11. *Breen dies:* 5-J. *Estimated population:* 750 to 1,000.

Obverse: *Date:* Spaced as 1 8 03. 1 and 3 closer to bust than to denticles. *LIBERTY:* LIB close. E over dip between two hair waves. Upright of T over junction of hair and forehead; definitive. *Points of distinction:* Usually (but not always) with a crack at the base of the date. This enlarges and other problems occur, including a rim cud.

1803, T Over Junction of Hair and Forehead (BW-18, S-252, B-11).

Reverse: Numerator, 1, high and centered over first 0. Bar begins at upper left of 1 and ends slightly before center of second 0. Bar closer to right ribbon than to left. *Points of distinction:* This die was used to coin both BW-18 and BW-30, with BW-18 being struck second. Crack through E of UNITED continues to wreath, then expands to near O in OF, and on to rim. Clash marks are seen.

Notes: This variety exists in Mint State, and examples are extremely rare as such.

1803, Outside Berry Below First T of STATES • BW-19, S-263, B-22. *Breen dies:* 13-R. *Estimated population:* 300 to 400.

Obverse: *Date:* 18 slightly close, 80 wider, 03 closest. Top of 3 touches or almost touches drapery. *LIBERTY:* IB closest. E and R over hair waves. Upright of T over hair. *Points of distinction:* This die was used to coin BW-19 and BW-25. Die flaws as in the preceding use of the die. Now with a crack at the base of the date, which expands to form a cud.

1803, Outside Berry Below First T of STATES (BW-19, S-263, B-22).

Reverse: Extra berry below first T of STATES; definitive within this group. *Points of distinction:* This die was used to coin BW-9 and BW-19. Cracks develop, most notably one at the upper left, beginning past D of UNITED, extending to the wreath, and exiting through the left side of the O in OF.

Notes: This variety exists in AU and Mint State, and it is especially rare in the latter category.

GROUP 5: 1803, SMALL DATE, SMALL FRACTIONS, WITH 3 OF 1803 TOUCHING OR NEARLY TOUCHING DRAPERY

1803, 3 Touches Drapery • BW-21, S-253, B-12. *Breen dies:* 6-K. **Estimated population:** 500 to 750.

1803, 3 Touches Drapery (BW-21, S-253, B-12).

Obverse: *Date:* 1 closer to hair than to denticle; centered over a denticle. 803 closer to denticles than is the 1. 03 close. *LIBERTY:* LIB close. E and upright of R over hair waves. Upright of T over hair. Y slightly low. *Points of distinction:* Usually with a crack to the right of date, which later expands. In the latest state there is a rim break at 180. Eventually a break develops in the denticles and extends from below the 0 in the date, to the left, and past the lateral margin of Liberty's lowest curl.

Detail showing die chip in denominator.

Reverse: Dash (chip) after second 0 in denominator; definitive within the group. Berry centered opposite top edge of E of ONE. Bottom serifs of T's complete. *Points of distinction:* Usually with one or more cracks, although perfect die impressions exist.

Notes: This variety exists in AU and Mint State, the latter being extremely rare.

1803, 3 Touches Drapery • BW-22, S-254, B-13. *Breen dies:* 7-L. **Estimated population:** 1,250 to 1,500.

1803, 3 Touches Drapery (BW-22, S-254, B-13).

Obverse: *Date:* 1 closer to hair than to denticle; centered over a denticle. 03 close. 3 closer to denticles than any other numeral. *LIBERTY:* LIB close. I leans right, with lower-left serif above adjacent serif of L. E and upright of R over hair waves. Upright of T over hair. Y slightly low. *Points of distinction:* Perfect die, or with a crack from the right of 3 to drapery, augmented by other breaks, and culminating in a rim cud at the lower right.

Detail showing missing serif on T's.

Reverse: Fraction bar covers second 0; definitive within the group. Numerator is twice as close to the bar as it is to the ribbon knot. The bottom-right serifs on all T's are missing.

Notes: Although this is in the same population range as the preceding, the present coin is fairly plentiful in Mint State, no doubt the result of some undocumented hoard. EF and AU coins are likewise easy to find.

1803, 3 Touches Drapery • BW-23,

S-255, B-14. *Breen dies:* 8-L. **Estimated population:** Thousands.

Obverse: *Date:* 1 very close to hair, and is centered over a denticle. 03 close. 3 much closer to denticles than is any other numeral. *LIBERTY:* LIB close; IB closest. E and R over waves of hair. Upright of T over hair; lower-right serif defective. Y slightly low, and with bottom serifs defective. **Points of distinction:** Clash marks are seen, and increase as the die continues in use.

1803, 3 Touches Drapery (BW-23, S-255, B-14).

Reverse: Same as preceding. **Points of distinction:** A crack at ST becomes a rim cud over STAT. A light crack is at the right.

Notes: This variety exists in Mint State.

1803, 3 Touches Drapery • BW-24,

S-256, B-15. *Breen dies:* 9-M. **Estimated population:** 300 to 400.

Obverse: *Date:* 1 closer to hair than to denticles; centered over space between two denticles. 03 close. All numerals about the same distance from denticles. *LIBERTY:* IB closest. LI and ERT slightly close. E and R over waves of hair. Upright of T over hair; lower-left serif long. Y slightly low. **Points of distinction:**

1803, 3 Touches Drapery (BW-24, S-256, B-15).

tinction: The die deteriorates, and a crack develops from the rim, upward through the 8, into the bust, curving to the right, and exiting through the end of the drapery. Bulges develop.

Reverse: Fraction bar too far left: begins over the center of 1, ends over the left side of the second 0. Lower-right serif on second T of STATES missing; present on other T's. **Points of distinction:** With multiple cracks.

Notes: This variety exists in AU and Mint State.

1803, 3 Nearly Touches Drapery •

BW-25, S-262, B-21. *Breen dies:* 13-Q. *Estimated population:* 200 to 300.

Obverse: *Date:* Spaced as 18 04. 1 closer to hair than to denticles; centered over denticle. All numerals about the same distance from denticles. *LIBERTY:* Letters close; IB closest. E and left upright of R over waves of hair. Upright of T over hair. Lower-right serif of Y defective. **Points of distinction:** This die

1803, 3 Nearly Touches Drapery (BW-25, S-262, B-21).

was used to coin both BW-19 and BW-25. With linear ridges caused by die cuts or flaws in the right field and on the bosom.

Reverse: Leaf point under upright of D; definitive within the group. Berry nearly opposite center of E of ONE. Both stems short. Bottom serifs of T's complete. ***Points of distinction:*** Almost all are from a perfect die state. Later, there is a crack at STATES.

Notes: VF is the highest grade known.

GROUP 6: REMAINING *1803, SMALL DATE, SMALL FRACTIONS*

1803, Unfinished Hair Below E •

BW-28, S-244, B-3. *Breen dies:* 2-C. **Estimated population:** 120 to 160.

Obverse: Same as BW-6. For its present use, it has been relapped, giving an unfinished or plain area below the strand beneath E. ***Points of distinction:*** Clash marks are seen in front of the neck and throat.

1803, Unfinished Hair Below E (BW-28, S-244, B-3).

Reverse: Numerator about centered between ribbon knot and the fraction bar below. Bar extends from upper right of 1 to center of second 0. ***Points of distinction:*** This die was used to strike BW-6, BW-28, and 1802, E Close Over Dip Between Waves, T Mostly Over Forehead, Thorn From Left Stem to U (BW-13).

Notes: EF and AU are the highest grades known.

1803, Lump Under Chin, Point on Left Wreath Stem, Short Fraction Bar •

BW-29, S-247, B-5. *Breen dies:* 3-E. *Estimated population:* 300 to 400.

Obverse: See BW-2. Here in its later state with a lump under the chin, the "Mumps Obverse." ***Points of distinction:*** This die was used to coin BW-2, BW-4, BW-5, and BW-29.

1803, Lump Under Chin, Point on Left Wreath Stem, Short Fraction Bar (BW-29, S-247, B-5).

Reverse: A point or thorn is at the end of the left stem. Numerator about centered between ribbon knot and the very short bar below. ***Points of distinction:*** With cracks at UNITED.

Notes: This variety exists in AU and Mint State, the latter being extremely rare.

1803, Loop Under Drapery Very Faint or Missing, Fraction Bar Close to Second 0 •

BW-30, S-250, B-10. *Breen dies:* 4-J. **Estimated population:** 300 to 400.

Obverse: *Date:* See BW-3. ***Points of distinction:*** This die was used to coin BW-3, BW-30, and BW-31. Multiple clash marks develop, nearly a dozen totally.

1803, Loop Under Drapery Very Faint or Missing, Fraction Bar Close to Second 0 (BW-30, S-250, B-10).

Reverse: See BW-18. ***Points of distinction:*** This die was used to coin BW-18 and BW-30, with BW-30 being its earliest use.

Notes: This variety exists in Mint State.

1803, Loop Under Drapery Very Faint or Missing, Fraction Bar Distant From Second 0 • BW-31, S-251,

B-8. *Breen dies:* 4-H. *Estimated population:* 750 to 1,000.

Obverse: Same as preceding. Drapery loop weak. *Points of distinction:* Various cracks are seen. This die was used to coin BW-3, BW-30, and BW-31, here in its final use.

Reverse: E of ONE leans right. NT of CENT low. Fraction bar is very short and is about centered between the numerator and the denominator.

Notes: This variety exists in Mint State.

1803, Loop Under Drapery Very Faint or Missing, Fraction Bar Distant From Second 0 (BW-31, S-251, B-8).

Detail showing distant second 0.

1804, Draped Bust

Circulation mintage: 200,000 (estimated).

The 1804 is the most famous cent rarity after 1799. The published mintage of 756,838, without question, was mostly composed of earlier dates. A modern population of about 1,200 1804-dated coins has been suggested, as has a survival rate of two percent. This formula would project an original mintage of about 60,000 for 1804-dated cents. The Mint used a more durable die steel beginning in the 1800 to 1802 years. As Adam Eckfeldt became accustomed to the forging requirements, the new steel dramatically increased the die life. This caused some problems with overestimating the number of dies to be prepared. Accordingly, in 1804 the calendar-year coinage was mostly from earlier dated dies on hand.[83] Facts are scarce.

In 1859, in his *American Numismatical Manual*, Dr. Montroville W. Dickeson noted that, in circulation, one 1804-dated cent could be found for every 30 cents of 1805. The author had been acquainted with cents for quite some time and also wrote of finding 1793 issues at face value.

Only one die variety is known, BW-1, which exists in three die states: S-266a from unbroken dies; S-266b with break (which begins as a crack) at ERT at the top of the obverse die; and S-266c, with obverse break, and with a reverse break connecting the top of MERIC. As most cents have these cuds, the dies must have been employed for a significant time with these breaks. Elsewhere among early coppers, large cud breaks on both sides would usually flag a die pair for removal, making such coins a scarcer die state.

No fully Mint State 1804 cents exist today by the standards generally used up until a few years ago. Recently some of these cents have been graded Mint State, despite the fact that this represents a lowering of standards.[84] As often, opinions are aplenty, and buyers can form their own. 1,200 or so exist in circulated grades. "Gradeflation" is probably here to stay, as grades go up, and up some more, although the coins themselves do not change. No doubt, "Uncirculated" examples will become more available as old-time conservative grading fades from view.

Grades are typically Good to Fine, although quite a few VF pieces exist. EF and AU coins are very elusive. Many retooled and burnished coins are in numismatic circulation.

The so-called "restrike" of this date is actually a spurious concoction, as neither the obverse nor the reverse die was ever used in 1804. Sometime in the 1860s an unknown person took a rusted, broken obverse die of 1803, Small Date, Large Fraction, Corner of 3 in Drapery (BW-15); tooled and lapped it and amateurishly changed the last digit from a 3 to a 4; and combined it with a reverse of 1820 (Newcomb-12), the latter being a different design (with continuous wreath) than that employed in 1804. Apparently, the intent was to create a "filler" for cent collectors, and not to deceive. Multiple examples of this curious cent began to appear on the market in 1868 and attracted notice at the time.[85] In the years since then, the 1804 "restrike" has been popular in its own right, and many numismatists aspire to have an example of this and also the 1823 "restrike" in their collections. Most are in Mint State with brown toning, often with some traces of lighter color. The dies were used for restriking multiple times over the years and are still in existence today.

1804, Original • BW-1a, b, and c; S-266a, b, and c; B-1. *Breen dies:* 1-A. **Estimated population:** 750 to 1,000.

Obverse: *Date:* Blunt 1, crosslet 4. Numerals about equally spaced and distant from denticles. *LIBERTY:* IB close. Uprights of E and R over hair waves. Upright of T over hair. *Points of distinction:* This variety exists from a perfect die and also with a light crack, then, later, a rim cud break over RTY.

Reverse: Large letters. Large fraction. E of CENT leans right. Long stems to all berries except the two lowest on outside left. *Points of distinction:* Early impressions developed a crack over MERIC that developed into a cud break.

1804, Original (BW-1c, S-266c, B-1). A high-grade 1804 cent in the latest die state with cud breaks on obverse and reverse rims. This is the rarest cent date of the 19th century.

Notes: AU is the highest grade known, although some have been called Mint State (see overview). With perfect obverse this is known as BW-1a. With cud break on obverse and no break on reverse this is BW-1b. With cud breaks on both sides this is BW-1c. On all the 0 of 1804 is opposite O in OF, reflecting slight rotation of the dies. The population and mintage estimates are from Craig Sholley. Many collectors endeavor to obtain each of the three die states.

	Cert	Avg	%MS	AG-3	G-4	VG-8	F-12	VF-20	EF-40	AU-50	MS-60BN
1804, Original	86	17.4	1%	$1,375	$2,250	$3,800	$5,500	$8,830	$17,330	$44,670	$133,330

1804, "Restrike" From Mismatched Dies • BW-3, S-unlisted, B–un-numbered. *Estimated population:* 400 to 700.

Obverse: 1803, Small Date, Large Fraction, Corner of 3 in Drapery (BW-15) obverse die, rusted and cracked, altered to read "1804."

Reverse: 1820, Large Date (N-12), reverse die, rusted, worn, and relapped, thus removing detail. New denticles added around the border. Originally, this die was paired with a 1820, Matron Head.

1804, "Restrike" From Mismatched Dies (BW-3, S-unlisted, B–un-numbered).

Notes: Fantasy "restrike," so called, from two dies, neither of which was used in 1804. This variety is known in Mint State.

Numismatic Notes: *Reminiscence by Edward Groh (1901):* Edward Groh, born in New York City on June 2, 1837, became interested in numismatics about 1855. In 1858 he was a founder of the American Numismatic Society. On October 20, 1901, the *New York Times* printed an interview with him, which included this:

> Generally speaking, all the money that has become worth more than face value has been absorbed by amateurs, or has fallen into the hands of dealers. The only way to gather rare pieces is to buy of dealers or to attend auction sales of private collections. When I was a young fellow, things were different. Take the 1804 cent for instance. One was sold in this city not many months ago for $200. I remember finding a half dozen of those very coins when I was a boy, simply by examining the change that passed through my hands. It paid one to examine change then. I never let a single piece slip by unnoticed.

Commentary concerning the "Restrike" (1907): Lancaster, Pennsylvania dealer Charles Steigerwalt commented in *The Numismatist*, February 1907, about the "restrikes" of the 1804 and 1823 cents. Concerning the 1804:

> It was supposed that the 1804 came from the same source as the 1823, but the originator of those disclaimed any knowledge of the 1804. An effort was made in a recent sale catalogue to throw an air of mystery around this 1804. That is simply ridiculous. The obverse has been identified as an 1803, but if that date was too common, a crude 4 was cut over the 3 and a reverse of the period after the fraction was omitted, probably of about 1816 or later, was used in striking these abominations. By whom struck is unknown, but it was at a period long after, when the dies were rusty, and certainly not at the Mint.

	Cert	Avg	%MS	AU-50	MS-60BN	MS-63BN	MS-63RB
1804, "Restrike" From Mismatched Dies	176	49.6	48%	$980	$1,230	$1,620	$2,580

1805, Draped Bust

Mintage (per *Mint Report*): 941,116.

There are three die varieties of this year, two of which are common and the third slightly scarce. Two obverse and two reverse dies were used. The mintage figure for this calendar year undoubtedly includes many coins of earlier dates, particularly 1803.

In his *Encyclopedia*, Walter Breen commented, "Between December 1950 and December 1953 I attributed over 30,000 unpicked large cents. This 'observation series' became the basis for the rarity ratings in *Penny Whimsy*. In his 1879 *Monograph*, Édouard Frossard gave this comment, "The 1805 cents are rare in very fine or uncirculated condition, [and in other states are also] not very common."

Cents of this date tend to have relatively few problems. Most are light or medium brown.

Typical values for 1805 cents. In Mint State, BW-2 and BW-3 are worth more.

	Cert	Avg	%MS	G-4	VG-8	F-12	VF-20	EF-40	AU-50	MS-60BN
1805	49	39.4	18%	$60	$125	$290	$530	$1,300	$2,500	$5,670

1805, Blunt 1, Outside Leaf Under O in OF • BW-1, S-267, B-1. *Breen dies:* 1-A. *Estimated population:* Thousands.

Obverse: *Date:* Blunt 1; definitive. 5 much closer to drapery than 1 is to hair. 05 close. *LIBERTY:* All letters fairly close, IB closest. Uprights of R and E over waves of hair. Upright of T over hair. Y low and with defective bottom serifs. *Points of distinction:* Later reground to remove clash marks.

Reverse: Tip of highest-left leaf under left serif of S. Outside leaf tip under O in OF. T of CENT touches leaf. Numerator high. Bar much closer to right ribbon than to left. *Points of distinction:* Some have a crack over AM and a crack from the first S of STATES to T and to the wreath.

1805, Blunt 1, Outside Leaf Under O in OF (BW-1, S-267, B-1).

Detail showing blunt 1 in date.

Notes: Three times more populous than BW-3 (according to Breen). This variety exists in Mint State. Some high-quality fakes by the "Bay Area counterfeiter," made in the 1970s, exist. Authentication or certification (by a leading service) is recommended.[86] As to genuine coins, they are very plentiful in the marketplace, including in EF, AU, and the lower Mint-State ranges. This is the only variety for which Mint State coins are occasionally seen, but at low levels.

1805, Blunt 1, Outside Leaf Under F in OF • BW-2, S-268, B-2. *Breen dies:* 1-B. *Estimated population:* 300 to 400.

Obverse: Same as preceding. *Points of distinction:* Additional clash marks develop, and mounding or bulging is seen in the left and right fields.

Reverse: Tip of highest-left leaf past right side of S. Outside leaf tip under F in OF. T of CENT does not touch leaf. Numerator

1805, Blunt 1, Outside Leaf Under F in OF (BW-2, S-268, B-2).

high. Bar about equidistant from left and right ribbons. 00 close. *Points of distinction:* This die was used on BW-2 and BW-3 and 1806 (BW-1).

Notes: This is the scarcest by far of the three varieties of the year. Exists in AU and is rare as such. Most are VF or lower. The highest recorded by Walter Breen is AU-50.

1805, Pointed 1, Outside Leaf Under F in OF • BW-3, S-269, B-3. *Breen dies:* 2-B. *Estimated population:* Thousands.

Obverse: *Date:* Pointed 1; definitive. 1 touches hair. 80 wide. 5 touches, or nearly touches, drapery. *LIBERTY:* IB very close. E and upright of R over wave of hair. Upright of T over hair; bottom serifs heavy. *Points of distinction:* A crack develops through the base of 180. Clash marks occur and are most obvious on later impressions.

Reverse: Same as preceding.

Notes: This variety exists in AU and Mint State, the latter quite rare.

1805, Pointed 1, Outside Leaf Under F in OF (BW-3, S-269, B-3).

Detail showing pointed 1 in date.

1806, *Draped Bust*

Mintage (per *Mint Report*): 941,116.

The 1806 cent has always been viewed as a slightly scarce date. However, examples are easy to find, including in EF, AU, and low Mint State grades. Most are attractive and are one or another shade of brown. The reported mintage figure seems overly generous and must include cents of some earlier date(s). Only one die variety is known.

In his *American Numismatical Manual*, 1859, Dr. Montroville W. Dickeson described two varieties that are not known today: "We have seen one variety of this cent which was struck from the altered die of 1805, which must have been broken or discarded, as it is the only specimen we have met with. We have also seen another variety on which 1/000 occurs."

	Cert	Avg	%MS	G-4	VG-8	F-12	VF-20	EF-40	AU-50	MS-60BN
1806	78	32.0	10%	$150	$325	$520	$1,030	$2,500	$4,500	$9,500

1806 • BW-1, S-270, B-1. *Breen dies:* 1-A. *Estimated population:* Thousands.

Obverse: *Date:* Pointed 1 is very slightly closer to hair than to the denticle over which it is positioned. 80 slightly wide. 6 barely touches drapery; left side of top of inner curve irregular. *LIBERTY:* L slightly low. IB very close. E and R over hair waves. Upright of T over hair. *Points of distinction:* Perfect

1806 (BW-1, S-270, B-1).

die impressions exist, followed by those with a crack at the lowest curl and partially to the denticles, with a raised area to the left of the lowest curl, and also extending to the right of the date.

Reverse: Tip of highest-left leaf just past right of S. Numerator slightly closer to ribbon knot than to fraction bar. 00 close. *Points of distinction:* This die was also used on 1805, Blunt 1, Outside Leaf Under F in OF (BW-2) and 1805, Pointed 1, Outside Leaf Under F in OF (BW-3).

Notes: Exists in Mint State. Walter Breen quotes Benjamin H. Collins's description of an 1806 cent with Pointed 6, unknown today, stating that its possible existence is logical as the 1807, 7 Over 6, over-dates possibly (but not certainly) have the 6's pointed.

1807, 7 Over 6, Draped Bust

Circulation mintage (per *Mint Report*): Part of the total for 1807.

The 1807, 7 Over 6, overdate exists in two varieties, both of which are avidly sought. The first listed is by far the rarer and is in exceptional demand, as it is listed in the regular edition of the *Guide Book of United States Coins.*

Examples of either variety are usually attractive and problem-free.

1807, 7 Over 6, Small 7 Over 6, Blunt 1 • BW-1, S-272, B-2. *Breen dies:* 2-A. *Estimated population:* 60 to 75.

Obverse: *Date:* Blunt 1 (definitive) high above denticles and very close to hair. 7 punched over a (possible) Pointed 6, which is still mostly visible, and boldly. Upper right and left of 7 touch drapery. *LIBERTY:* Widely spaced. IB slightly close. Uprights of E and R over hair waves. Upright of T over hair, but with lower-right serif close to forehead. Y slightly low. *Points of distinction:* In the latest state, rare, a crack develops from the rim, through R, and to the eyebrow.

1807, 7 Over 6, Small 7 Over 6, Blunt 1 (BW-1, S-272, B-2).

Detail of overdate.

Reverse: Tip of highest-left leaf slightly left of S. Numerator centered over fraction bar and slightly closer to bar than to ribbon knot. 00 close. *Points of distinction:* This die was used to coin BW-1, BW-2, and 1807, "Comet" Variety (For Most), Small Fraction, Bar Not Connected to Ribbon (BW-1).

Notes: EF and AU are the highest grades known, and examples are very rare as such.

	Cert	Avg	%MS	AG-3	G-4	VG-8	F-12	VF-20
1807, 7 Over 6, Small 7 Over 6, Blunt 1	4	16.5	0%	$1,750	$3,250	$8,000	$17,000	$24,330

1807, 7 Over 6, Large 7 Over 6, Pointed 1 • BW-2, S-273, B-3. *Breen dies:* 3-A. *Estimated population:* Thousands.

Obverse: *Date:* Pointed 1 (definitive) centered over denticle and closer to hair. 18 closer to denticles than are other numerals. 80 close. Large, very heavy 7, with thick base, over Pointed 6. 7 very close to drapery. *LIBERTY:* LIB slightly close. E and R over hair waves. Upright of T over hair. *Points of distinction:* A tiny horizontal crack begins at the rim at about 7 o'clock. Bulges become prominent.

1807, 7 Over 6, Large 7 Over 6, Pointed 1 (BW-2, S-273, B-3).

Detail of overdate.

Reverse: Same as preceding. *Points of distinction:* Perfect die impressions exist. Later states transition to having a crack from the rim, through C of AMERICA, and to the opposite leaf, indicating this was the last combination using this die.

Notes: Exists in Mint State. This is a very popular and easily collectible variety.

	Cert	Avg	%MS	G-4	VG-8	F-12	VF-20	EF-40	AU-50	MS-60BN
1807, 7 Over 6, Large 7 Over 6, Pointed 1	71	26.7	10%	$110	$210	$375	$630	$1,430	$2,630	$6,900

1807, *Draped Bust*

Mintage (per *Mint Report*): 829,221.

The perfect date, or non-overdated, 1807 is known in four die varieties, two of which are common. Most famous is the "Comet Variety," number BW-1. Most cents of this date are attractive and range from light to dark brown.

1807, "Comet" Variety (for most), Small Fraction, Bar Not Connected to Ribbon • BW-1, S-271, B-1. *Breen dies:* 1-A. *Estimated population:* Thousands.

1807, "Comet" Variety (for most), Small Fraction, Bar Not Connected to Ribbon (BW-1, S-271, B-1).

Obverse: *Date:* High above denticles. 1 nearer hair than denticles. 18 slightly wide. Upper right of 7 close to drapery. *LIBERTY:* ERT slightly wide. Uprights of E and R over waves of hair. Upright of T over hair, but right serif is close to the forehead; right serif is short. *Points of distinction:* When seen with the die flaw behind the head, this is known as the "Comet Variety." Later, the "comet" becomes heavier, and clash marks are seen. In the final state, there is a bulge at 7, rendering the digit indistinct.

Reverse: See 1807, 7 Over 6, Small 7 Over 6, Blunt 1 (BW-1). Bar not connected to ribbon and A. C of CENT touches leaf. *Points of distinction:* This die was also used to coin 1807, 7 Over 6, Small 7 Over 6, Blunt 1 (BW-1), and 1807, 7 Over 6, Large 7 Over 6, Pointed 1 (BW-2).

Notes: Exists in Mint State. The "Comet Variety" is among the best known of the Draped Bust cents. The appellation lends itself well to coin sale descriptions, such as "Great Comet Appears." Indeed, the early die state without the "comet" (the die sank slightly in this position) attracts little interest, making the "Comet" a member of that curious category in which a damaged, worn, or broken die can be more valuable that a perfect one.[87] In the 1895 catalog of the Winsor Collection, the Chapman brothers described a coin as "1807 Comet variety." Earlier, in the June 1890 offering of the Parmelee Collection, David U. Proskey and Harlan P. Smith simply noted that the variety has a "bar-like defect in die from hair to border." S.H. Chapman noted this is "commonly called the Comet variety" in his April 1923 catalog of the Beckwith Collection.[88]

"Comet" must be visible.

	Cert	Avg	%MS	G-4	VG-8	F-12	VF-20	EF-40	AU-50	MS-60BN	MS-63BN
1807, "Comet" Variety	26	32.4	19%	$130	$290	$600	$1,070	$3,280	$4,250	$12,000	$28,670

1807, Small Fraction, Connected By Line to Ribbon and A • BW-2, S-274, B-4. *Breen dies:* 4-B. *Estimated population:* 500 to 750.

1807, Small Fraction, Connected By Line to Ribbon and A (BW-2, S-274, B-4).

Obverse: *Date:* Lower than the preceding. 1 much closer to the hair than to the denticles. 80 slightly wide. 7 about centered between drapery and denticles. *LIBERTY:* IB close; lower right of I slightly lower than nearby left serif of B. E and R over waves of hair. Upright of T over hair, but right serif is close to forehead. Y slightly low and with lower-right serif pointed.

Reverse: A die scratch connects the right side of the bar with the ribbon and the A; definitive. C of CENT is close to, but does not touch, the leaf. *Points of distinction:* Die failure has caused mounding and weakness. Several cracks are seen.

Notes: EF and AU are the highest grades known, and examples are quite rare as such. Worth more than BW-4, especially in high grades.

1807, Base of B Level With E, Large Fraction • BW-3, S-275, B-5. *Breen dies:* 4-C. *Estimated population:* 400 to 500.

1807, Base of B Level With E, Large Fraction (BW-3, S-275, B-5).

Obverse: Same as preceding. *Points of distinction:* In a late state, a crack is through the top of LIBERTY.

Reverse: Left stem short and stubby. Tip of highest-left leaf under S and slightly left of its center. Fraction large. Bar begins over center of 1 and continues to left of the center of second 0. 00 close. Second 0 leans left.

Notes: EF and AU are the highest grades known. Worth more than BW-4, especially in high grades.

1807, Base of B Above E, Large Fraction • BW-4, S-276, B-6. *Breen dies:* 5-C. *Estimated population:* Thousands.

1807, Base of B Above E, Large Fraction (BW-4, S-276, B-6).

Obverse: *Date:* Low, similar to the preceding. Fairly evenly spaced. 7 about centered between drapery and denticles. *LIBERTY:* L slightly low. B higher than E. ERT wide. E and R over waves of hair. Upright of T over hair. Y slightly low. *Points of distinction:* With a swelling at the rim below the lowest curl. In a later state there are rim breaks in the denticles above LIBE.

Reverse: Same as preceding.

Notes: Exists in Mint State. The dies are often rotated. Walter Breen: "Arguably the commonest of all Draped Bust cents."

	Cert	Avg	%MS	G-4	VG-8	F-12	VF-20	EF-40	AU-50	MS-60BN
1807, Base of B Above E, Large Fraction	23	20.6	0%	$110	$220	$410	$620	$1,400	$3,000	$5,230

CLASSIC HEAD (1808–1814)

Designer: *John Reich.* **Weight:** *168 grains (10.89 grams).*
Composition: *Copper.* **Diameter:** *Average 29 mm.* **Edge:** *Plain.*

1810, 10 Over 09 (BW-1, S-281, B-1).

The Classic Head design by John Reich, assistant engraver at the Mint, was introduced in 1808 and was continued through 1814. Today, all dates are available, with no major rarities, although those of 1809 are considered to be scarcer than the others. Generally, the earlier dates are seen on light-brown planchets and are somewhat casually struck, with many design details weak or absent. Cents of 1814 are often dark and porous.

Finding a sharply struck Classic Head cent, with smooth, attractive fields, and of a brown (rather than gray or black) color, will be a great challenge, involving the inspection of many coins. Lightness of striking is the rule for the vast majority of cents of this type. On the obverse the points to look for include sharpness of the denticles, star centers, hair details, and leaf details. On the reverse, the high parts of the leaves and the denticles are checkpoints. The center lettering is usually quite sharp.

When found, an ideal piece will probably not cost much more than an average example of its date and grade, for most buyers are not oriented toward seeking quality. Grading numbers alone suffice for all but dedicated specialists.

Most examples are well worn, in grades from Good to VF or so. EF coins are scarce by comparison, and AU pieces are scarcer yet. Mint State coins are quite rare and tend to be at lower levels such as MS-60 or MS-61. Any coin conservatively graded as MS-63 or higher is very rare.

All planchets for these cents were imported from Boulton & Watt of Birmingham, England, a firm well known for the excellent quality of its products. The last shipment recorded from that source arrived on April 15, 1812, on the eve of the War of 1812, after which business was not recommenced with this British supplier until after the conflict. Afterward, supplies on hand were used until they were exhausted. As noted in chapter 1, in 1814 the price of copper metal had risen to the point that many cents were melted by speculators. This wholesale destruction no doubt made earlier cent issues rarer than the mintage figures indicate.

Craig Sholley suggests that either the Mint or Boulton & Watt may have begun adding a lubricant to the planchet, or that the British supplier may have begun utilizing a different source, or different ore base, that contained impurities. Whatever the reason, extant coins from later Classic Head years tend to be dark, porous, or both—quite unlike the Draped Bust issues.

The Classic Head series seems to have instituted a Mint policy whereby obverse and reverse dies were replaced at the same time. Earlier, the procedure had been for the pressman to examine the dies as they were being used, then if one die or another became unfit, to remove it and replace it with another. Accordingly, in earlier times, the same obverse die could be mated with two or more reverses, and vice versa. From 1808 through 1814, each obverse is matched with a single distinctive reverse not used elsewhere within that year.

No cents were struck with the date 1815, due to the unavailability of planchets; Mint records show that the supply was exhausted as of October 27, 1814. Mintage resumed late in 1815, using dies dated 1816, of the Matron Head design.

DESIGN DETAILS

The Classic Head, by assistant engraver John Reich, features Miss Liberty facing to the left, with a band in her hair inscribed LIBERTY. Years ago, this was sometimes called the Turban Head, although no turban is present. In 1879, Édouard Frossard, in *Monograph of United States Cents and Half Cents Issued Between the Years 1793 and 1857*, used this nomenclature.

Seven stars are at the border to the left, and six stars are to the right. The date is between the head and the bottom border.

The obverse die was created with a hub punch with the portrait of Miss Liberty. Details of the LIBERTY word were punched by hand into the headband. Seven stars to the left and six to the right were added by individual punches; thus, they vary slightly in their spacing. The dates were added by single punches, one at a time.

The term *Classic Head* seems to have originated with E.D. Mason Jr. in *Mason's Coin and Stamp Collector's Magazine*, February 1868. The design is distinctive, and was also used on half cents (beginning in 1809). Years later, in 1834, it was revived by chief engraver William Kneass and used, with slight modifications, on $2.50 and $5 gold coins.

The reverse, also probably by Reich, is a departure from the previous style. A continuous wreath tied with a ribbon bow at the bottom encloses the inscription ONE / CENT. Around the border is UNITED STATES OF AMERICA. The reverse is from a punch including the wreath and berries, ONE / CENT, and the line under the last word. Accordingly, there are no variations in count or position among any of these features. The letters around the periphery were added by hand, and provide the opportunity to identify die varieties. The position of certain leaf tips in relation to the letters, particularly the second S in STATES, is a handy guide.

GRADING STANDARDS

MS-60 to 70 (Mint State). *Obverse:* In the lower-Mint State grades, MS-60 and 61, some slight abrasions can be seen on the portrait, most evidently on the cheek, as the hair details are complex on this type. Luster in the field is complete or nearly complete; the field is not as open on this type as on the Draped Bust issues. At 63, luster should be complete, and no abrasion evident. In higher levels, the luster is complete and deeper, and some original

1814; BW-2, S-295, B-2. Graded MS-64BN.

mint color may be seen. MS-64 coins may have some slight discoloration or scattered contact marks. A well-graded MS-65 or higher coin will have full, rich luster; no marks visible except under magnification; and a nice blend of brown toning or nicely mixed (not stained or blotchy) mint color and natural brown toning. Incomplete striking of some details, especially the obverse stars, is the rule. *Reverse:* In the lower-Mint State grades, some abrasion is seen on the higher areas of the leaves. Mint luster is complete in all Mint State grades, as the open areas are protected by the lettering and wreath. Sharpness of the leaves can vary by die variety, so check this aspect. Otherwise, the same comments apply as for the obverse.

Illustrated coin: This example is sharply struck and generally well centered. Medium-brown and golden-brown in color, the surface has a trace of original Mint luster in protected areas. The only notable blemish is a tiny vertical nick in the obverse field in front of Liberty's throat, which on a coin of this caliber has no particular market effect. Even the finest of early coppers are apt to show some tiny normal marks.

AU-50, 53, 55, 58 (About Uncirculated). *Obverse:* Friction is seen on the higher parts, particularly the cheek. The hair will have friction and light wear, but will not be as obvious. Friction and scattered marks are in the field, ranging from more extensive at AU-50 to minimal at AU-58. Luster may be seen in protected areas, minimal at AU-50, but more visible at AU-58. At AU-58 the open field may retain some luster, as well.

1813; BW-1, S-292, B-2. Graded AU-50.

Reverse: Friction is seen on the higher wreath leaves and on the letters. Fields, protected by the designs, show less friction. At the AU-55 and 58 levels little if any friction is seen. The reverse may have original luster, toned brown, minimal on lower About Uncirculated grades, often extensive at AU-58.

Illustrated coin: Note the dark planchet, typical due to the copper stock used this year. The light striking at the star centers is normal, and some lightness of strike is seen on the hair, especially above LIBERTY. The denticles on Classic Head cents are nearly always off center on one side or the other—here on the reverse.

EF-40, 45 (Extremely Fine). *Obverse:* Wear is seen on the portrait overall, but most hair detail will still be present. The cheek shows light wear. Luster is minimal or nonexistent at EF-40, and may survive in among the letters of LIBERTY at EF-45. *Reverse:* Wear is seen on the highest wreath and ribbon areas and the letters. Leaf veins are visible except in the highest areas. Luster is minimal, but likely more noticeable than on the obverse, as

1814, Plain 4; BW-2, S-295, B-2. Graded EF-45.

the fields are protected by the designs and lettering.

Illustrated coin: A very attractive coin, far above average in sharpness, but with some "old oxidation" seen around certain of the elements.

VF-20, 30 (Very Fine). *Obverse:* Wear on the portrait has reduced the hair detail, especially on the area to the right of the cheek and neck, but much can still be seen. *Reverse:* The wreath details, except for the edges of the leaves and certain of the tips (on leaves in lower relief), are worn away at VF-20, and with slightly more detail at VF-30.

Illustrated coin: This is an attractive example, conservatively graded. The VF-35 grade is not "official" but is widely used.

1810, 10 Over 09; BW-1, S-281, B-1. Graded VF-35.

F-12, 15 (Fine). *Obverse:* The hair details are fewer than on the preceding, but many are still present. The central hair curl is visible. Stars have flat centers. F-15 shows slightly more detail. The portrait on this type held up well to wear. *Reverse:* The higher areas of wreath leaves are worn flat, but their edges are distinct. F-15 shows slightly more detail.

Illustrated coin: Note the planchet—dark and lightly porous, as is often seen on cents of this type.

1812, Small Date; BW-3, S-290, B-2. Graded F-12.

VG-8, 10 (Very Good). *Obverse:* The portrait is well worn, although the eye and ear can be seen clearly. The hair is mostly blended, but some slight separation can be seen in areas. The border is raised in most or all areas. *Reverse:* The wreath is more worn than on the preceding grade, but there will still be some detail on the leaves. On most coins, ONE CENT is bold. Border letters are light or weak but are fully readable. The border is well defined in most areas.

1809; BW-1, S-280, B-1. Graded VG-8.

Illustrated coin: This is a dark and somewhat porous example of what is considered to be the key issue of the Classic Head type.

G-4, 6 (Good). *Obverse:* The portrait is worn smooth and is seen only in outline form. Much or even all of LIBERTY on the headband is readable, but the letters are weak. The stars are weak, only in outline form, and several may scarcely be discerned. *Reverse:* Extensive wear is seen overall. Lettering in UNITED STATES OF AMERICA is weak, but completely discernible. The wreath is in outline, but still fairly bold, and ONE CENT is usually strong.

1814; BW-2, S-295, B-2. Graded G-4.

AG-3 (About Good). *Obverse:* Wear is more extensive than on the preceding. The portrait is visible only in outline. Most letters of LIBERTY are discernible, as this feature is in low relief. The stars are weak or worn away on their outer edges, and the date is light. *Reverse:* The wreath is visible in outline form but remains fairly strong. Most or even all of UNITED STATES OF AMERICA is worn away. ONE CENT is usually easily readable.

1808; BW-2, S-278, B-2. Graded AG-3.

1808, Classic Head

Mintage (per *Mint Report*): 1,009,000.

There are three varieties of the 1808, each struck from a separate die pair. The typical BW-1 and BW-2 have light striking in areas, usually the stars, while BW-3 is sharper on average.

Most 1808 cents show extensive wear, but attractive AU and (usually lower) Mint State grades come on the market now and again, particularly when fine collections cross the auction block.

Typical values for 1808 cents. Rare varieties may be worth more.

	Cert	Avg	%MS	G-4	VG-8	F-12	VF-20	EF-40	AU-50	MS-60BN	MS-63BN
1808	97	35.0	18%	$110	$275	$500	$920	$2,620	$5,500	$8,000	$15,670

1808 • BW-1, S-277, B-1. *Breen dies:* 1-A. *Estimated population:* 750 to 1,000.

Obverse: Frame line in front of L of LIBERTY bulges outward to the left. Rim and denticles at the bottom of the border are weak.

Reverse: Leaf tip under second S of STATES slightly right of its center. Leaf tip under the beginning of the serif to the right of the center of upright of F in OF. *Points of distinction:*

1808 (BW-1, S-277, B-1).

Sometimes the die is perfect, but more often there are cracks.

Notes: The bottom of the obverse is usually weak, as is the corresponding area of the reverse (the top left, at STATES). Sometimes Star 1 is very weak, giving rise to the nickname of "12 Stars" variety. This variety exists in Mint State and is rare as such.

1808 • BW-2, S-278, B-2. *Breen dies:* 2-B. *Estimated population:* 300 to 500.

Obverse: Frame line straight. All stars on the right are about evenly spaced. *Points of distinction:* On the late state there are rim breaks, including near stars 8, 10, and 11.

Reverse: Leaf tip is under right edge of second S of STATES on sharp impressions; otherwise very slightly left of the right edge. Leaf tip under center of upright of F in OF.

1808 (BW-2, S-278, B-2).

Notes: This variety exists in Mint State and rare as such. It is by far the scarcest variety of the year.

1808 • BW-3, S-279, B-3. *Breen dies:* 3-C. *Estimated population:* Several thousand.

Obverse: Frame line straight. Stars 9 and 10 are more closely spaced than are any other stars on the right. *Points of distinction:* This variety occurs with a perfect die and also injured, with the stars on the right blended into the rim and other distortions. Dr. Sheldon: "This die must have come into violent

1808 (BW-3, S-279, B-3).

contact with something hard." A light crack develops from the rim, to star 3, and to the chin. On the latest state there is a rim break at 10 o'clock.

Reverse: Leaf tip under second S of STATES very slightly to the right of its center. Leaf tip under center of upright of F in OF.

Notes: This variety exists in Mint State and is rare as such.

1809, Classic Head

Mintage (per *Mint Report*): 222,867.

For many years the 1809 has been considered the key date of the Classic Head type. In actuality, cents of this date are fairly plentiful, and in worn grades they are not difficult to find. There is only one die pair.

The obverse is usually flatly struck in some areas, with indistinct star centers and a thin or incomplete border, although there are exceptions. The reverse is usually sharper. The color can vary from light brown to quite dark. Most examples show wear, often extensive. At the EF and AU levels the 1809 *is* somewhat scarce. Well over a dozen examples have been graded Mint State over the years, though usually in lower ranges. Presumably, the Mansion House find (see Numismatic Notes) had higher-level Mint State coins that were secreted about the time of their coinage.

In his 1879 *Monograph*, Édouard Frossard noted: "This date is very scarce, and seldom found in fine condition. The impression of the obverse is light, the milling slight and low; hence specimens which have been in circulation are generally much worn about the edge."

	Cert	Avg	%MS	G-4	VG-8	F-12	VF-20	EF-40	AU-50	MS-60BN
1809	61	31.2	8%	$275	$450	$775	$1,630	$4,500	$8,570	$13,830

1809 • BW-1, S-280, B-1. *Breen dies:* 1-A. *Estimated population:* 750 to 1,000.

Obverse: Only die of the year. Star 13 close to date. *Points of distinction:* Some are from a perfect die state, but most are usually cracked from star 11 to near the point of the upper ribbon. Extensive clash marks are seen on later states.

1809 (BW-1, S-280, B-1). An example
with a remarkably sharp strike.

Reverse: Berry under upright of T of UNITED. Leaf tip under center of second S of STATES. *Points of distinction:* Some are from a perfect die, but usually this variety is seen with one or more cracks. The reverse is nearly always sharper than the obverse. Later, small cracks develop, and in its late state the die loses a small piece below E of STATES.

Notes: This variety exists in Mint State.

Numismatic Notes: *A cornerstone find:* Thomas Birch & Sons' June 21, 1871, sale of the M.W. Nickerson consignment offered as Lot 183 an 1809 large cent, "One of nine taken from the cornerstone of the Mansion House, Philadelphia; extremely rare."[89]

Years earlier the Mansion House, located at 122 South Third Street, was considered to be one of the leading stopping places in the city, with its well-known contemporaries including the U.S. Hotel (opposite the Bank of the United States), City Hotel, National Hotel, Washington Hotel, and Congress Hall.[90]

1810, 10 Over 09, Classic Head

Mintage (per *Mint Report*): Part of the total for 1810.

There is just one die pair for the 1810, 10 Over 09, overdate, making classification easy. An 1809 die, different from the one actually used for coinage in 1809, was overpunched with 1 and 0 digits. Some lightness of striking at the star centers is usual, but there are many exceptions.

The typically found coin shows extensive wear. At the AU level this variety is rare, and in Mint State few are found.

	Cert	Avg	%MS	G-4	VG-8	F-12	VF-20	EF-40	AU-50	MS-60BN	MS-63BN
1810, 10 Over 09	43	30.5	12%	$110	$225	$500	$900	$2,230	$3,750	$9,000	$18,330

1810, 10 Over 09 • BW-1, S-281, B-1.

Breen dies: 1-A. ***Estimated population:*** Thousands.

Obverse: Overdate. Just one die.

Reverse: Tip of leaf under second S of STATES.

Notes: In their late state the dies became worn and grainy, resulting in flow lines in the fields, particularly on the obverse, and distending of the outermost star points. This variety exists in Mint State.

1810, 10 Over 09 (BW-1, S-281, B-1).

Detail of overdate.

1810, Classic Head

Mintage (per *Mint Report*): 1,458,500.

On each of the four obverse dies the highest tuft of hair, on the outside about B of LIBERTY, was finished by hand, resulting in some slight differences. Cents of this date are much better struck than those of the year preceding, but some lightness of the stars is normal. The color tends to be a pleasing light brown.

Typical values for 1810 cents. Rare varieties may be worth more.

	Cert	Avg	%MS	G-4	VG-8	F-12	VF-20	EF-40	AU-50	MS-60BN	MS-63BN
1810	118	33.9	14%	$100	$200	$450	$850	$1,700	$3,570	$8,170	$17,000

1810 • BW-1, S-282, B-3. *Breen dies:* 3-C.

Estimated population: 750 to 1,000.

Obverse: Star 1 closer to denticle than to bust. Stars 5 and 6 closer than are stars 6 and 7. ***Points of distinction:*** Cracks develop through certain of the stars.

Reverse: Tip of leaf at right edge of second S of STATES. Tip of leaf opposite right edge of N of UNITED.

1810 (BW-1, S-282, B-3).

Notes: This variety exists in Mint State.

1810 • BW-2, S-283, B-4. *Breen dies:* 4-D. *Estimated population:* 750 to 1,000.

Obverse: Star 1 close to denticle and distant from bust. Left top of T of LIBERTY at same level as top of adjacent R.

Reverse: Tip of leaf slightly past second S of STATES.

Notes: This variety exists in Mint State.

1810 (BW-2, S-283, B-4).

1810 • BW-3, S-284, B-5. *Breen dies:* 5-E. *Estimated population:* 400 to 500.

Obverse: Star 1 close to denticle and distant from bust; innermost point repunched. Left top of T of LIBERTY lower than top of adjacent R.

Reverse: Tip of leaf far past second S of STATES. Bottom of EN of CENT close; top of NT more widely spaced. Tops of UNI touch or nearly touch.

Notes: This variety exists in Mint State.

1810 (BW-3, S-284, B-5).

1810 • BW-4, S-285, B-2. *Breen dies:* 2-B. *Estimated population:* 750 to 1,000.

Obverse: Star 1 slightly closer to denticle than to bust, and well separated from each. Stars 3 and 4 are more widely spaced than are any others on the left. *Points of distinction:* A crack develops through the base of 10 and connects the stars at the right.

Reverse: Tip of leaf at right edge of second S of STATES. Tip of leaf opposite left serif of I of UNITED. Bottom of EN of CENT and top of NT about equally spaced.

1810 (BW-4, S-285, B-2).

Notes: This variety exists in Mint State.

Numismatic Notes: A fantasy "restrike" of the 1810 cent was made sometime around the 1850s. The obverse die is the same as used on BW-4, but rusted and cracked. The reverse die is the same as used on the fantasy "restrike" 1804—1804, "Restrike" From Mismatched Dies (BW-3)—originally used on the 1820, Large Date (N-12). Only two examples are known, both struck in tin.

1811, 1 Over 0, Classic Head

Mintage (per *Mint Report*): Part of the total for 1811.

This variety, from a single pair of dies, usually comes on a dark planchet, somewhat rough, perhaps due to a lubricant on the Boulton & Watt planchets or the use of a different source of metal by that firm.

The striking is usually fairly good, save for some slight lightness at the star centers, particularly toward the bottom. Nearly all examples show extensive wear. In his *Encyclopedia*, Walter Breen knew of no example better than AU-55, this being the only Classic Head cent variety for which Mint State coins are not recorded—at least per conservative grading practice.

However, in his *American Numismatical Manual*, 1859, Dr. Montroville W. Dickeson states this: "We are indebted for ours to an unopened keg returned to the Mint from Charleston, South Carolina." We can only read this and weep. Probably, this was years prior to 1859 and the pivotal 1855 Kline sale (see chapter 4), and Mint officials considered the cents to be of no special value.

	Cert	Avg	%MS	G-4	VG-8	F-12	VF-20	EF-40	AU-50
1811, 1 Over 0	23	28.9	13%	$200	$425	$950	$2,170	$5,920	$14,170

1811, 1 Over 0 • BW-1, S-286, B-2.
Breen dies: 2-B. **Estimated population:** 300 to 400.

Obverse: Overdate with 0 boldly visible under final 1.

Reverse: Point of leaf under second S of STATES. Raised dash under upright of E of ONE.

Notes: A previously unused 1810 die was overdated. AU is the highest grade known.

1811, 1 Over 0 (BW-1, S-286, B-2).

Detail of overdate.

1811, *Classic Head*

Mintage (per *Mint Report*): 218,025.

Similar to the overdate, the "normal" or "perfect" 1811 date is often found dark and porous. Other examples are a light brown.

Striking varies, but some light striking at certain star centers and high areas of the leaves is the rule, not the exception. The typical coin shows extensive wear, but VF and EF examples are not hard to find. Mint State coins are very elusive and are usually in lower ranges of that classification.

	Cert	Avg	%MS	G-4	VG-8	F-12	VF-20	EF-40	AU-50	MS-60BN	MS-63BN
1811	69	31.8	16%	$175	$325	$650	$1,330	$3,070	$7,330	$13,330	$20,000

1811 • BW-1, S-287, B-1. *Breen dies:* 1-A.
Estimated population: 750 to 1,000.

Obverse: Normal or perfect date (not over-date). **Points of distinction:** Rim breaks develop opposite stars 2 to 4. In the final state, rare, there is a rim break near the star 9.

Reverse: Point of leaf slightly past second S of STATES.

Notes: This variety exists in Mint State.

1811 (BW-1, S-287, B-1).

1812, Classic Head

Mintage (per *Mint Report*): 1,075,500.

The difference between a Large Date and a Small Date 1812 cent is not obvious at a quick glance. A comparison of the two will show a taller 1 in the Large Date. In the Small Date the 1 is shorter than the 2; in the Large Date they are about the same height. There are four die combinations this year—in each case, a unique use of an obverse matching a unique use of a reverse. The sharpness of strike varies, but usually some of the obverse stars are flat at their centers.

Most cents of this date are well worn, although perhaps 25 or so Mint State examples exist per conservative grading, significantly more if graded liberally. Higher-grade coins are often of the BW-3 variety. Surfaces are often dark and somewhat granular. As is true of all Classic Head cents, cherrypicking within a given grade can yield dividends.

Typical values for 1812 cents. Rare varieties may be worth more.

	Cert	Avg	%MS	VF-20	EF-40	AU-50	MS-60BN	MS-63BN
1812	59	33.7	8%	$1,000	$2,000	$4,000	$10,000	$20,000

1812, Large Date • BW-1, S-288, B-3.
Breen dies: **3-C**. *Estimated population:* 750 to 1,000.

Obverse: Large Date.

Reverse: Berry under lower-left serif of first T of STATES. Tip of leaf past second S of STATES.

Notes: This variety exists in Mint State.

1812, Large Date (BW-1, S-288, B-3).

1812, Large Date • BW-2, S-289, B-4.
Breen dies: **4-D**. *Estimated population:* Thousands.

Obverse: Large Date.

Reverse: Berry directly under upright of first T of UNITED, the only reverse with this feature.

Notes: This variety exists in Mint State.

1812, Large Date (BW-2, S-289, B-4).

1812, Small Date • BW-3, S-290, B-2.
Breen dies: **2-B**. *Estimated population:* Thousands.

Obverse: Small Date. Star 1 closer to denticles than to bust; points to slightly left of the center of a denticle. *Points of distinction:* Breen notes that "there is a small hoard of Mint State specimens," but no other information is given.

1812, Small Date (BW-3, S-290, B-2).

Reverse: Berry under lower-left serif of first T of STATES; tip of leaf under second S. Berry under space between A and M of AMERICA.

Notes: This variety occurs in Mint State.

1812, Small Date • BW-4, S-291, B-1. *Breen dies:* 1-A. ***Estimated population:*** 750 to 1,000.

Obverse: Small Date. Star 1 is about equidistant from the bust and the denticles and points to the space between denticles. ***Points of distinction:*** A crack develops and expands, in the latest state through the entire base of the date and connecting through all of the stars.

1812, Small Date (BW-4, S-291, B-1).

Reverse: Berry under lower-left serif of first T of STATES; tip of leaf under second S. Berry under right foot of first A of AMERICA.

Notes: This variety exists in AU and Mint State, the latter being very rare.

1813, Classic Head

Mintage (per *Mint Report*): 418,000.

Cents of 1813 follow the general rule for classic head cents, particularly the later ones: the surfaces are often granular and the color dark. These variations may suggest different sources for the copper.

Typical values for 1813 cents. Rare varieties may be worth more.

	Cert	Avg	%MS	VF-20	EF-40	AU-50	MS-60BN	MS-63BN
1813	150	38.8	12%	$925	$1,875	$3,400	$8,500	$16,250

1813 • BW-1, S-292, B-2. *Breen dies:* 2-B. ***Estimated population:*** 1,000 to 1,250.

Obverse: Stars 6 and 7 and stars 12 and 13 close.

Reverse: Berry under space between S and T of STATES. ***Points of distinction:*** Cracks developed as the die was used.

Notes: This variety exists in Mint State.

1813 (BW-1, S-292, B-2).

1813 • BW-2, S-293, B-1. *Breen dies:* 1-A. ***Estimated population:*** 750 to 1,000.

Obverse: Stars 6 and 7 widely apart; stars 12 and 13 close. Star 13 closer to date than on BW-1.

Reverse: Berry under upright of first T of STATES. ***Points of distinction:*** This die, by that time very rusted, was combined in the 1860s with a damaged 1823 obverse and was used to make 1823 "restrike" cents (see 1823 Cents).

1813 (BW-2, S-293, B-1).

Notes: This variety exists in Mint State. It is called 1813/12, an overdate, by Walter Breen, such feature being noticeable only on very high-grade pieces of the earliest die state. This nomenclature is hardly ever used, and it is generally considered to be a regular date.

1814, Classic Head

Mintage (per *Mint Report*): 357,830.

R.W. Julian suggests that the cents of this date, delivered from the coiner to the Mint treasurer on October 27, were deposited at face value in the Bank of Pennsylvania in December. By that time, the treasurer of the United States had advised against paying out cents, possibly as the market price for copper was at a high level. At that time, and in other times when copper was scarce or expensive, industrial concerns would buy kegs of copper cents and melt them to secure a supply of the metal.[91] Further coinage was suspended, as the supply of planchets had been exhausted.

Cents of 1814 are easily enough collected today. Of all Classic Head cents, the two die varieties of 1814 are best known for being dark and porous. Although occasional examples are seen at the Mint State level, none have been observed with original mint color.

1814, Crosslet 4 • BW-1, S-294, B-1.

Breen dies: 1-A. ***Estimated population:*** Thousands.

Obverse: Crosslet 4. Base of 4 higher than the base of adjacent 1.

Reverse: Tip of leaf slightly past second S of STATES.

Notes: This variety is found in Mint State.

1814, Crosslet 4 (BW-1, S-294, B-1).

	Cert	Avg	%MS	G-4	VG-8	F-12	VF-20	EF-40	AU-50	MS-60BN	MS-63BN
1814, Crosslet 4	69	29.8	13%	$80	$200	$400	$875	$1,800	$3,200	$6,500	$12,750

1814, Plain 4 • BW-2, S-295, B-2. *Breen dies:* 2-B. ***Estimated population:*** Thousands.

Obverse: Plain 4. Base of 4 on about the same level as the base of adjacent 1. ***Points of distinction:*** Die deterioration at the throat continues to the chin and the mouth, creating the "Bearded Variety." A crack develops from the rim to the 11th star, continuing to the curl, later becoming heavy and joining the rim.

1814, Plain 4 (BW-2, S-295, B-2).

Reverse: Tip of leaf under second S of STATES. ***Points of distinction:*** A rim break is above D of UNITED and on the latest state also above TA of STATES.

Notes: This variety exists in Mint State.

Numismatic Notes: *Gold in 1814 cents:* The May 1858 issue of *Historical Magazine* included these replies to a question about 1814 cents:

> United States Cent, 1814: Cents coined in 1814 may be occasionally met with, though I think them quite rare. I have several in my possession. On looking over large quantities at various times, I have never met with a single genuine one of 1815. The records of the Mint state that the amount of copper

coinage for 1814 was $3,578.30, but none was coined the succeeding year, according to the records, though I have no doubt some few were struck off.

Madison
Baltimore, March 6, 1858.

Another Reply.—Cents of the coinage of 1814 are occasionally met with in circulation. I have a number of them in my possession. A reference to the tables of the Mint, containing a statement of its operations in different years, shows that in 1814 $3,578.30 worth of copper was coined, and that no cents were minted in 1815 or 1828.

I have heard it stated that the scarcity of copper, incident to the war of 1812, was the reason that so few cents were coined in 1813 and 1814, and that none were coined in 1815.

How the absurd story that the cents of 1814 contained gold originated, I am unable to explain. Chemical tests have, in several instances, been applied to the cents of that year, but the presence of gold has never yet been detected.

B.H.H. Troy, N.Y., March 5, 1858.

B.H.H. was B.H. Hall, a numismatist and researcher in the 1850s. Little is known today about Hall. However, he was an active correspondent with Charles I. Bushnell about both Vermont copper coinage (dated 1785–1788) and Fugio cents (dated 1787). In 1858 he provided information to John Hickcox for use in his book.

In the *American Numismatical Manual*, 1859, Dr. Montroville W. Dickeson partially explained the gold rumor: "Additional value has been attached to the issue of this year in consequence of the rumor that it contained gold lost at the Mint at that time. Many cling to them with much tenacity on that account—the slightest basis for credulity being ardently responded to."

The Fulton rumor: The July 1872 issue of the *Journal of Numismatics* noted that in 1814 Robert Fulton built a steamship for the United States called the SS *Fulton.* "One rule he uniformly observed was to have in use copper and not iron boilers; the latter, he thought, were too liable to explosion, and the explosion of iron he believed, would be very disastrous. Wherefore, the boiler of the *Fulton,* which vessel was built in the time of the last British war with the United States, when copper was very scarce and dear, was composed in part of the copper coined cents."

There seems to be no reason to give credence to this comment.

	Cert	Avg	%MS	G-4	VG-8	F-12	VF-20	EF-40	AU-50	MS-60BN	MS-63BN
1814, Plain 4	79	27.6	11%	$80	$200	$400	$875	$1,800	$3,200	$6,500	$12,500

MATRON HEAD (1816–1839)

Designer: *Robert Scot. Later modifications made by Christian Gobrecht.*
Weight: *168 grains (10.89 grams).* **Composition:** *Copper.*
Diameter: *27.5 mm.* **Edge:** *Plain.*

1829, Large Letters (N-1). Mint State with a generous amount of original color, rare and remarkable for any variety of this date.

The Matron Head cent, first coined in 1816, has variously been described as numismatically beautiful or artistically ugly—displaying beauty strictly in the eyes of the beholder. Without doubt, the earlier-discussed 1793 Chain, with Miss Liberty appearing to be in a "fright," is exceedingly delightful to numismatists today, never mind that Miss Liberty may not have won a beauty contest. So it may be with the Matron Head cent—the design is what it is, we are used to it, and in its own way it is quite appealing to many specialists. Indeed, it is one of the most numismatically popular motifs in early-1800s coinage, with coins issued from 1816 until 1839, familiarly called the "middle dates."

The basic obverse and reverse designs remained the same until 1835, when modifications were made by Christian Gobrecht, who had been signed as a staff engraver in September of that year. Slightly different styles were continued through 1839, including such curiously named varieties as the *Silly Head* and *Booby Head*. The culmination was the Braided Hair type of late 1839, inaugurating the next major type in the series.

Alexander Vattemare, a Frenchman who visited the United States at least twice in the period from the late 1830s to the 1850s in promotion of a literary and cultural exchange program, visited the Mint and collectors, conducted interviews, and wrote a book, *Collection de Monnaies et Médailles de l'Amérique du Nord de 1652 à 1858*, which was published in Paris in 1861.[92] He claimed that the model for Scot's Liberty head of 1816 was the wife of Director Patterson, but no verification of this has been found.[93]

As noted, from late 1835 through 1839, a number of distinctly different portraits were created in the copper cent series, no doubt by Christian Gobrecht. Perhaps he used the cent series as an experimental ground for ideas that might later be adopted to higher denominations. In the spring of 1836, steam presses were used for the first time at the Philadelphia Mint to strike cents, and perhaps the advent of this power provided a reason for modifying designs. This change may have affected size, relief, or other aspects of the coins, the details of which are now forgotten, and are known to us only by the study of the coins themselves.

There are many die varieties across the series that range from common to unique, according to Howard R. Newcomb's *United States Copper Cents 1816–1857*. The interest in these varieties is extensive, due in no small part to specialist works written about them by John D. Wright and William C. Noyes, plus discussions in *Penny-Wise*. Individual treatment of those varieties, which often differ only by minor details, is beyond the scope of the present text. Many dates and varieties apart from the Newcomb varieties beckon, and such obvious and popular differences as Small Letters and Large Letters and different portrait styles are enumerated below.

Circulated examples of Matron Head cents and the later revisions of the design exist in approximate relationship to their mintages. Generally, fewer of the early dates are found, and the average grade is lower. Coins from 1816 through the 1820s are common in grades such as Good and VG, although many Fine and VF pieces exist. For the 1830s, Fine to Very Fine is typical, plus many EF and AU coins.

Those of 1816 to 1820 (particularly 1818 and 1820) are readily available in Mint State from the famous Randall Hoard. Otherwise, Mint State coins are generally scarce in the type, although those of the 1830s are more available than those of the 1820s. Those of the 1830s are seen with the most frequency, especially for the years 1836 to 1839.

In general, copper cents of this era are fairly well struck *except* for the stars. And, of course, this is a big exception. Relatively few of the earlier years have full centers on all of the stars, and in many instances they are quite flat. While 1816, 1817, and 1821 do 1823 tend to be darkly hued, sometimes even close to black, most other dates are a pleasing brown. Of course, even in the problem years there are many examples where the color is brown. Surface quality is usually good, with the result that coins in grades as low as Very Good and Fine can be a delight to the eye and pleasing to own. This statement would be difficult for a specialist in silver or gold coins to understand, but show a copper specialist a smooth VG 1823 or 1839, 9 Over 6, cent and you'll likely receive a compliment.

Regarding striking, such as on the stars, denticles, and higher areas of the hair on the obverse and wreath leaves on the reverse, this differs from one die variety to another. Specialized texts such as the William C. Noyes and John D. Wright books mentioned below are a guide to such. This is important, as there is no sense chasing a perfect strike if one does not exist for a given variety.

A set of the different *major* varieties we list can be acquired for very reasonable cost in grades from VF to AU, excepting a handful of scarce issues—and even these, such as 1823, 1824, 4 Over 2, and 1839, 9 Over 6, in particular, are not impossible—and can always be represented by lower-grade coins. In Mint State there is a lot of value in the marketplace at the MS-60 to MS-63 level, cherrypicked for quality. Mint State cents with significant mint red attract a lot of attention and usually cost much more. There is unlimited opportunity for cherrypicking, for some MS-60 coins are finer than those graded MS-63. The opposite is true, of course, and such are the pieces to avoid. As in other series, certain dates have "personalities" all their own. As an example, an 1823, 3 Over 2, cent is apt to be quite dark, even black. In contrast, nearly all 1836 cents are light brown.

While some usable obverse dies were probably held over and used later, from 1816 onward the calendar-year mintages are a much more reliable indicator of year-date production than Mint figures were for cents dated earlier. What seems to be the major exception to this rule is 1823, for which no mintage figure is known. Probably, the cents from this year were included in the 1824 accounting.

For all Matron Head dies, the dates were punched into dies one digit at a time. The use of a four-digit logotype or *gang punch* was not initiated until 1840, this being in the second year of the Braided Hair series.

Proof cents were made in small quantities and are very rare for all dates. This is a highly technical area, and careful study is recommended. In the opinion of Q. David Bowers, many "Proofs," including certified examples, are not true Proofs at all.

The middle-date cents are fascinating to explore, indeed one of the most interesting areas in early-1800s numismatics. A great *advantage* for you is that striking and die quality is not mentioned at all on certified holders and is not often noted in descriptions of coins for sale. Accordingly, cherrypicking for quality offers many opportunities, as *most* of these cents either have some weakness of striking (most notably at the star centers), or are struck from tired dies with grainy surfaces, or both.

The following listings from 1816 to the end of the series do not include Whitman numbers as we do not treat all of the many die varieties. Instead, we highlight the "at sight" varieties that are the most popular as does, for example, the regular edition of the *Guide Book of United States Coins*. If you are interested in all the die varieties, these books are your passport: *United States Copper Cents 1816–1857*, by Howard R. Newcomb, 1944, remains the standard reference, with Newcomb numbers (N-1, N-2, etc.), which received numerous additions from later scholars. *United States Large Cents 1816–1839*, by William C. Noyes, 1991, and *The Cent Book, 1816–1839*, by John D. Wright, 1992, both offer large illustrations of varieties in combination with useful information.

THE RANDALL HOARD

Among United States large cents of the early years of the Matron Head design (sometimes referred to as the Coronet design), nearly all are very elusive in Mint State, except for 1816 through 1820. Today, many of these exist, with 1818 and 1820 being by far the most numerous. Such coins are commonly attributed to the Randall Hoard. Cents dated 1816 are in the minority in this regard and are not even mentioned in some historical accounts of the hoard and may be from another source.[94] The number of coins involved is not known, but it seems likely that about 5,000 to 10,000 were found in a small keg.

It seems that these came to light in the 1860s. John Swan Randall, of Norwich, New York, wrote the details to Edward D. Cogan on January 7, 1870, by which time such coins had attracted attention in the numismatic marketplace. E.B. Mason Jr. had called them *restrikes*, because of their brightness:

I should not sell coin that I knew or believed to be re-strikes without letting it be known. The bright, Uncirculated cents I have sold of 1817, 1818, 1819, 1820, and 1825, I am very sure *are not re-strikes*. I bought them of Wm. H. Chapman & Co., dry goods merchants of this village, and the head of the firm, W.H.C., informed me that he got them of a wholesale merchant in New York, who informed him that he got them from a merchant in Georgia; that he took them as a payment on a debt, and that the Georgia merchant wrote him that they were found since the war in Georgia buried in the earth.

Mr. Chapman said to me that he was in New York about the time the cents were received there, and that the merchant who had (ditto) thought they were too large to use, and did not know what to do with them; and that he (Chapman) thinking that his customers here would be pleased with bright cents, offered ninety cents a hundred for them, which was immediately taken. Chapman & Co. commenced paying them out here, and their bright appearance and old dates made many think they were counterfeits, and they were called 'Chapman's counterfeits,' and the firm stopped paying them out.

I then went to the store and asked W.H. Chapman if he had disposed of many of his bright cents. He replied, 'No. I made a bad bargain,' and laughed about their being regarded as his counterfeits. I then offered to take them at the price he paid—ninety cents a hundred—and he was very willing to let me have them. They were loose together in a small keg, and the great mass of them were of 1818; and a great many, though apparently Uncirculated, were more or less corroded or discolored. I enclose herewith one of the 1817 and 1818, discolored on one side and bright on the other, From this statement, you will see that there can be very little doubt about their being the genuine issues of the United States Mint of their respective dates.

Very respectfully, John Swan Randall

The typical example seen today with a Randall Hoard pedigree is a mixture of bright original red with flecks and stains of deep brown or black. Few if any are pristine (uncleaned, undipped) full mint red. As late as the 1950s it was not unusual to see groups of Randall Hoard coins in dealers' stocks. By the 1990s the supply had become widely dispersed, and when seen such coins were apt to be as isolated examples. It is a matter of debate today whether the hoard contained significant coins dated 1825, as this year is hardly ever seen with a brightness and flecks similar to that of the earlier hoard coins.

DESIGN DETAILS

On the obverse the head of Miss Liberty faces to the left, her face having a serious or even severe aspect. On most dies her hair is tied with *plain* hair cords in a bun behind her head, and additional tresses fall behind her neck. Above her forehead a tiara or diadem is lettered LIBERTY. Beginning in 1835, modifications were made, including the adoption of *beaded* hair cords in 1837. On all, the date digits were punched individually, as were the stars, creating variations that are easily observed today.

The reverse motif is similar to that used from 1808 to 1814. A continuous wreath tied with a ribbon bow at the bottom encloses the inscription ONE / CENT, with a line under the latter word (except for certain varieties of 1839). Around the border is UNITED STATES OF AMERICA. There are variations in the size of the lettering.

The 1816 design is attributed to Robert Scot. Modifications from 1835 to 1839 are attributed to Christian Gobrecht.

GRADING STANDARDS

MS-60 to 70 (Mint State). *Obverse:* In the lower-Mint State grades, MS-60 and 61, some slight abrasions can be seen on the portrait, most evidently on the cheek, which on this type is very prominent. Higher areas of the hair can be checked, particularly the top and back of Liberty's head, but do not confuse with lightness of strike. Luster in the field is complete or nearly complete. At MS-63, luster

1826. Graded MS-63BN.

should be complete, and no abrasion is evident. In higher levels, the luster is complete and deeper, and some original mint color may be seen. MS-64 coins may have some minimal discoloration or scattered contact marks. A well-graded MS-65 or higher coin will have full, rich luster; no marks visible except under magnification; and a nice blend of brown toning or nicely mixed mint color and natural brown toning. Randall Hoard coins of the 1816 to 1820 years usually have much mint red and some black spotting. *Reverse:* In the lower-Mint State grades some abrasion is seen on the higher areas of the leaves. Mint luster is complete in all Mint State grades, as the open areas are protected by the lettering and wreath. Sharpness of the leaves can vary by die variety, so check this aspect. Otherwise, the same comments apply as for the obverse.

Illustrated coin: This 1826 cent is lovely to look at—and would be still nicer to own. Early copper cents have a wide appeal.

AU-50, 53, 55, 58 (About Uncirculated). *Obverse:* Friction is seen on the higher parts, particularly the cheek. The hair has friction and light wear, usually most notable in the general area above BER of LIBERTY. Friction and scattered marks are in the field, ranging from extensive at AU-50 to minimal at AU-58. Luster may be seen in protected areas, minimal at the AU-50 level, more visible at AU-58. At AU-58 the field may retain some

1828. Graded AU-55BN.

luster as well. *Reverse:* Friction is seen on the higher wreath leaves and on the letters. Fields, protected by the designs, show friction. At the AU-55 and 58 levels little if any friction is seen. The reverse may have original luster, toned brown, minimal on lower About Uncirculated grades, often extensive at AU-58.

Illustrated coin: This example has rich brown surfaces. Among early copper cents, selected About Uncirculated coins such as this one can have eye appeal matching that of lower-level Mint State pieces.

EF-40, 45 (Extremely Fine). *Obverse:* Wear is seen on the portrait overall, but most hair detail is still present, except in higher areas. The cheek shows light wear. Luster is minimal or nonexistent at EF-40, and may survive in among the letters of LIBERTY at EF-45. *Reverse:* Wear is seen on the highest wreath and ribbon areas, and on the letters. Leaf veins are visible except in the highest areas.

1829; N-6. Graded EF-40.

Luster is minimal, but likely more noticeable than on the obverse, as the fields are protected by the designs and lettering.

Illustrated coin: Here is a well-centered coin. On this variety the obverse denticles are larger (reducing the area of the field somewhat) than those on the reverse.

VF-20, 30 (Very Fine). *Obverse:* Wear on the portrait has reduced the hair detail, especially on the area to the right of the cheek and neck, but much can still be seen. *Reverse:* The wreath details, except for the edges of the leaves and certain of the tips (on leaves in lower relief), are worn away at VF-20, and with slightly more detail at VF-30.

Illustrated coin: Some light granularity is most noticeable on the reverse.

1839, 9 Over 6; N-1. Graded VF-20.

F-12, 15 (Fine). *Obverse:* The hair details are fewer than on the preceding, but still many are present. Wear is extensive above and below the LIBERTY coronet, with the area from the forehead to the coronet worn flat. Stars have flat centers. F-15 shows slightly more detail. *Reverse:* The higher areas of wreath leaves are worn flat, but their edges are distinct. F-15 shows slightly more detail.

1823; N-2. Graded F-15.

VG-8, 10 (Very Good). *Obverse:* The portrait is well worn, although the eye and ear can be seen clearly. The hair is mostly blended, but some slight separation can be seen in lower areas. The border is raised in most or all areas. *Reverse:* The wreath is more worn than on the preceding, but still there is some detail on the leaves. On most coins, ONE CENT is bold. Border letters are light or weak but are fully readable. The border is well defined in most areas.

1823, 3 Over 2; N-1. Graded VG-8.

Illustrated coin: Note the tiny scratches on the cheek, and many tiny marks in the field. This coin has a pleasing light-brown color, and overall good eye appeal.

G-4, 6 (Good). *Obverse:* The portrait is worn smooth and is seen only in outline form. Much or even all of LIBERTY on the headband is readable, but the letters are weak, and L may be missing. The stars are weak. The rim is usually discernible all around. *Reverse:* Extensive wear is seen overall. Lettering in UNITED STATES OF AMERICA is weak, but completely discernible. The wreath is in outline, but still fairly bold, and

1831; N-12. Graded G-6.

ONE CENT is usually strong. The rim is usually faded into the field in many areas (depending on the die variety).

Illustrated coin: Here is an advanced die state with a cud break at the lower right of the obverse, and with cracks connecting most of the stars. Note the double profile to the portrait, caused by die "chatter" during the coining process.

AG-3 (About Good). *Obverse:* Wear is more extensive than on the preceding. The portrait is visible only in outline. Most letters of LIBERTY remain discernible in the headband, as this feature is in low relief. The stars are weak or worn away on their outer edges, and the date is light. *Reverse:* The wreath is visible in outline form, but remains fairly strong. Most of UNITED STATES OF AMERICA is worn away. ONE CENT is usually readable, but light.

1818; N-6. Graded AG-3.

PF-60 to 70 (Proof). Proofs were made for cents from 1817 onward. Often, what are called "Proofs" are only partially mirrorlike, and sometimes the striking is casual, e.g., with weakness on certain of the stars. Complicating the situation is the fact that all but one of the same die pairs were also used to make circulation strikes. Many misattributions were made generations ago, some of which have been perpetuated. Except among large-cent

1838; N-11. Graded PF-64BN.

specialists, debate is effectively ended when a certification service seals a coin as a Proof (logic aside). True Proofs with deeply mirrored surfaces are in the small minority. *Obverse and Reverse:* Proofs that are extensively hairlined or have dull surfaces, this being characteristic of many issues (exceptions, when found, are usually dated in the 1830s) are graded PF-60 to 62 or 63. Artificially toned and recolored coins may be graded lower. To qualify as PF-65 or higher, hairlines should be microscopic, and there should be no trace of friction. Surfaces should be prooflike or, better, fully mirrored and without dullness.

Illustrated coin: Note some light striking of the stars, and excellent centering.

1816, Matron Head

Mintage (per *Mint Report*): 2,820,982.

There are nine known die combinations among 1816, Newcomb-1 to Newcomb-9. Seven different obverse dies were used. Assuming that the mintage figure for this year includes only Matron Head cents and none from the earlier type, this yields an average mintage per die of 402,000 coins.

All but one are hard to find in Mint State and when seen are usually in lower ranges, this comment being generally true of other Matron Head cents of this decade, except for Randall Hoard coins. N-1 and N-3 are rare. The solitary exception for the 1816 date is provided by N-2, of which William C. Noyes comments, "Major part of Randall Hoard with thousands of spotty Mint State examples. However, few, if any, true MS-65s can be found."

Cents of 1816 are easily available as a date in nearly any grade desired, although examples at the EF and AU levels are scarcer than lower grades and are also scarcer than Mint State. Many are dark in color, this being true of 1817-dated cents, as well, and for the later dates in the Classic Head series. Mint State coins are rare except for N-2, as noted above.

Typical values for 1816 cents. Rare varieties may be worth more. Mint State values are for N-2 only.

	Cert	Avg	%MS	G-4	VG-8	F-12	VF-20	EF-40	AU-50	MS-60BN	MS-63BN	MS-63RB	MS-65BN	MS-65RB
1816	309	54.1	57%	$25	$50	$75	$150	$220	$350	$650	$850	$1,600	$2,400	$3,600

1816 • Newcomb-1 to Newcomb-9. ***Estimated population:*** Many thousands.

Notes: This is the first of the Randall Hoard dates. Randall Hoard coins tend to average around MS-63 and MS-64, with spotting. Some have been stripped down and recolored a glossy brown (a color never present when the hoard was found). Certified coins for this or any other Matron Head date represent the tiniest fraction of the population in collectors' hands. The highest certified are four MS-66BN, four MS-65RB, and two MS-65RD. Probably, several thousand Mint State coins exist, but 1816 is far scarcer date than are 1818 and 1820.

A high-grade example of 1816 (N-2), probably from the Randall Hoard. The color is original, and spotting is considerably less than usually seen. Some lightness of strike and erosion of the denticles is normal for N-2. Overall, it is a remarkable coin.

Numismatic Notes: The new design and working dies were probably ready by August 1815 because Patterson thought that the planchets might arrive from England as early as September.[95] However, it was not until about November 20 that the *Coromandel*, carrying the invoice from Boulton, actually docked at Philadelphia. The kegs of blanks were in the hold (as ballast) and thus were unloaded last, or nearly so. All were in the Mint by December 11. As Boulton promised in his letter of May 1815, costs of the copper planchets were down significantly from 1812. The average planchets in 1815 cost 8.057 mills while the corresponding cost in 1812 had been 9.057 mills. The profit to the government was thereby much higher, offsetting other Mint expenses. The cost was lower for other reasons than merely the price of raw copper. The end of the war in early 1815 had reduced insurance rates as well as the special dockage fees charged by the British government as part of a series of wartime taxes.

Patterson ordered that coinage begin as soon as possible, and it is known that several thousand pieces had been struck by December 31, when the annual report of the director noted that cent coinage had resumed. Almost certainly Scot had dated the dies with the year 1816, probably because it was expected that nothing would be released to the public until after January 1. For reasons that are not quite clear at present, the coinage of cents was very slow in late December and early January. It is known, from a letter of Patterson to Boulton, dated December 27, that Mint officials were not completely pleased with the quality of the 1815 planchet delivery. According to Patterson, the blanks were "not quite round" and not sufficiently "milled up" on the edges. This may have required slight modifications to the dies or coin press. There is a second possibility for delay of coinage. On December 30, 1815, John White was paid $53.50 by Mint Treasurer James Rush for cutting a screw. The accounts do not say that this was for a coining press or, if so, which one, but almost certainly it was for a damaged coining press, likely the cent press. The repair could also have been for the half dollar press; coinage was also delayed here, inexplicably, until after January 1.

Copper coinage resumed within a few days of the January 11, 1816, fire and was strong for the next several weeks. On February 3, several kegs, which contained 183,500 coins, were sent to the Bank of Pennsylvania. The rest were all forwarded to the same bank by February 26, for a total coinage of 465,500 from the 1815 Boulton planchet shipment. Only one press was used at this time, as there was no urgency to the coinage. With the delivery, on February 26, of 89,000 cents to the Bank of Pennsylvania, the Mint was once more out of planchets. However, in the latter part of 1815, Patterson had managed to persuade the Treasury that sufficient funds were on hand for the additional needed 20 tons of copper, and that amount had been ordered. This shipment was not received until late May 1816.

1817, Matron Head

Mintage (per *Mint Report*): 3,948,400.

There are 17 different die combinations of 1817 cents, N-1 to N-17. N-16 is the unique 15-Star variety described separately below, leaving 16 varieties with the normal 13 stars.

Mint State examples of this year are easy to find, with N-3, N-6, N-8, N-13, and N-14 (in particular) being those most often seen in this grade, nearly all attributable to the Randall Hoard. N-10 is likewise available in Mint State, but is much scarcer. Circulated examples are mostly Good to Fine and are often dark in color, this also being true for 1816 and the later dates in the Classic Head series. EF and AU coins are on the scarcer side, and for some varieties AU and Mint State pieces are rare.

A die state of N-9 develops a lump at the top of the head opposite star 9. This has been called the "Mouse Variety" or "Mouse Top Variety" and is popular for that reason (see Numismatic Notes). These are easily enough obtained, except at the Mint State level.[96]

Detail of the "mouse" on N-9, sometimes called a "crown" or "royal crown" in numismatic folklore.

Typical values for 1817 cents. Rare varieties may be worth more.

	Cert	Avg	%MS	G-4	VG-8	F-12	VF-20	EF-40	AU-50	MS-60BN	MS-63BN	MS-63RB	MS-65BN	MS-65RB
1817	434	53.4	56%	$25	$40	$70	$150	$195	$290	$525	$800	$1,200	$1,775	$2,700

1817 • N-1 to N-15, N-17. *Estimated population:* Many thousands.

Notes: This is a very common date among early Matron Head cents. Except for Randall Hoard coins, Mint State coins range from scarce to rare. The typical grade encountered is Good to Fine. Choice EF and AU coins are much scarcer. Many circulated coins tend to be on the dark side.

A high-grade Mint State example of N-9, the "Mouse Variety." This die break has been the subject of fanciful tales over the years.

Numismatic Notes: *Mouse Variety:* The Portsmouth (New Hampshire) *Daily Chronicle,* Tuesday, February 15, 1887, included what was likely a reference to what we call the "Mouse Variety" today:

> No Great of a Lion: 'Two big copper cents, issued in 1817,' says the Philadelphia *Call,* 'are among the rarest in the coin collection of the Philadelphia Mint. These have the Liberty head well defined, but on the top of the head, over the liberty cap, is a small protuberance, which, under the microscope, appears as a crown. This was cut in the die by an English engraver, who thus set the British crown over the American liberty head.'
>
> It is more commonly known that the back hair of the maiden who represents Liberty on our standard silver dollars is done up in semblance of a lion's head when viewed upside down. As it is also the work of an English artist, the lion may be taken for a British lion. The engraver, however, was considerate enough to put the animal under Liberty's cap, which acts in a measure as a cage or an extinguisher, although the fierce creature shows a disposition and an ability to get out and roar at almost any time, the maiden's attention being attracted in another direction. . . .

Similarly, but a few years later, in *The Numismatist,* December 1891, in a column of queries:

> R.A., Dublin. encloses the following from his scrapbook, and desires to know whether it is true or not. Will some of our correspondents give us light on the subject? 'Two big copper cents issued in 1817 are among the rarest in the coin collection of the Philadelphia Mint. These have the Liberty Head well defined, but on top of the head over the cap is a small protuberance which, under a microscope, appears as a crown. This was cut in the die by an English engraver, who thus covertly set the British Crown over the American Liberty Head.'

1817, 15 Obverse Stars • N-16. *Estimated population:* 1,250 to 1,500.

Notes: Newcomb-16 has 15 stars on the obverse instead of the usual 13, the only instance of such an error in the series. The reason for this is unknown. For many years this has been a "must have" coin for even casual collectors of cents. As if the uniqueness of the stars were not enough, the 1 in the date is blunt instead of having a pointed top serif,

1817, 15 Obverse Stars (N-16). The famous 15-Star variety. Nearly all known examples are in circulated grades.

the only such cent of the era with a blunt 1. As there is only one die combination for the 15-Stars, the obverse is unique and definitive. The reverse, however, which has no unusual features, was also mated to create the normal star-count N-1. All seen of N-16 have been struck from what seem to be non-parallel die faces in the coining press, resulting in deep boldness of the denticles at the lower left of the reverse and lightness in some other areas of both sides.

This variety is quite scarce in the context of 1817-dated cents overall, but enough exist that an example can be found without difficulty. Nearly all show extensive wear. Attractive EF and AU coins are rare, and Mint State coins are even more so. Some years ago Q. David Bowers was offered two "MS-65" coins by a leading cent expert. Upon examination, they were found to be MS-60 at best. "You need to be liberal for the 15-Star," he was told, "for there are none finer than this." An estimated 15 to 25 true Mint State coins are known, most around the MS-60 level.

A related scenario is implied in the McCawley-Grellman description of a coin (illustrated above) offered in 2009 in Larry and Ira Goldberg's sale of the Ted Naftzger Collection of Middle Dates, lot 47. Graded MS-65BN by PCGS, the catalogers added their own opinion, "Del Bland says MS-60+. Our grade is MS-63." This is one of many examples, in the Naftzger catalog as well as in offerings by others, in which grade opinions can vary widely.

	Cert	Avg	%MS	G-4	VG-8	F-12	VF-20	EF-40	AU-50	MS-60BN	MS-63BN
1817, 15 Obverse Stars	45	50.2	24%	$35	$50	$150	$350	$675	$1,075	$3,150	$4,500

1818, Matron Head

Mintage (per *Mint Report*): 3,167,000.

Cents of the year 1818 comprise 10 different die varieties, N-1 to N-10, none of which is an instant-eye or regular-edition *Guide Book of United States Coins* variety.

Randall Hoard cents come to the fore in 1818 and in 1820, these being the two most encountered years from that hoard. For 1818 the hoard varieties are N-1, N-7, and N-10, with N-10 being one of the two most plentiful die combinations in this hoard. William C. Noyes suggests that thousands exist of this coin alone. This particular variety is nearly always found with a die crack connecting all of the stars and the date. Very curiously, 1820, Large Date (N-13), the other very common hoard coin, has a similar encircling crack.

Apart from hoard coins, Mint State examples are generally scarce, and for some varieties are rare. The typical 1818 is apt to be Good to Fine and of a brown color.

Detail of 1818 (N-3), showing star 1 low and opposite the tip of the neck.

Detail of 1818 (N-10), showing star 1 significantly to the left of the tip of the neck. Most die varieties among early Matron Head cent dates can be easily identified, after some practice.

Typical values for 1818 cents. Rare varieties may be worth more.

	Cert	Avg	%MS	G-4	VG-8	F-12	VF-20	EF-40	AU-50	MS-60BN	MS-63BN	MS-63RB	MS-65BN	MS-65RB
1818	728	58.4	76%	$25	$40	$70	$150	$190	$290	$475	$675	$960	$1,800	$2,800

1818 • N-1 to N-10. *Estimated population:* Many thousands.

Notes: The rarest die variety is N-4, nearly all of which are in circulated grades. The hand-punched date numerals and stars of this and other cents of the era make them fairly easy to differentiate using the Newcomb, Wright, or Noyes texts. Certain Randall Hoard coins are plentiful, with N-10 being especially so, and thus ideal for anyone selecting an example of the date. Most have abundant original mint red, usually with some spotting.

An exceptionally high quality 1818 (N-10) Mint State cent from the Randall Hoard, with characteristic encircling die cracks caused by improper annealing of the steel die (not from extensive use of the die).

1819, 9 Over 8, Matron Head

Circulation mintage (estimate): Several hundred thousand.

A single 1819, 9 Over 8, die is known. The production probably ran to several hundred thousand coins, creating a variety that is easily collectible today. The overdate feature is easily discerned. Most are in circulated grades, although enough Mint State coins exist that finding one will not be a problem. Gems are rare, however.

	Cert	Avg	%MS	G-4	VG-8	F-12	VF-20	EF-40	AU-50	MS-60BN	MS-63BN
1819, 9 Over 8	111	51.0	41%	$30	$50	$150	$250	$360	$560	$1,125	$1,900

1819, 9 Over 8 • N-1. *Estimated population:* Several thousand.

Notes: Stars 2 and 4 are repunched. Common in all circulated grades. Scarce in Mint State, but enough are around that finding one will be no problem. A typical conservative (EAC) grade is MS-60, translating to two or three points higher in the popular marketplace.

1819, 9 Over 8 (N-1).

Detail of the overdate.

1819, Matron Head

Mintage (per *Mint Report*): 2,671,000.

Known to the extent of nine varieties, N-2 to N-10, this date can be compared to others of its era, except that for 1819 there are far fewer Randall Hoard coins, these being N-8 and N-9. Less often seen in Mint State are N-2 and N-6. All nine varieties are readily collectible, with several being scarce, N-7 the scarcest, and a rarity in Mint State. Most examples are in worn grades, VG to Fine being common, probably as retrieved from circulation by enthusiasts in the 1850s. At the EF and AU level the 1819 is quite a bit scarcer.

Typical values for 1819 cents. Rare varieties may be worth more.

	Cert	Avg	%MS	G-4	VG-8	F-12	VF-20	EF-40	AU-50	MS-60BN	MS-63BN	MS-63RB	MS-65BN
1819	341	53.5	58%	$25	$45	$110	$175	$325	$475	$875	$1,250	$1,750	$2,000

1819 • N-2 to N-10. *Estimated population:* Many thousands.

Notes: An estimated 500 to 800 examples each are known of N-8 and N-9, from the Randall Hoard. These usually have generous mint color with some spotting.

1819 (N-8). Some stars are flat at the center, this being true of the vast majority of Matron Head cents of all years.

1820, 20 Over 19, Matron Head

Mintage (per *Mint Report*): Part of the total of 1820.

The Mint must have been overoptimistic in 1819, for it seems that early in 1820 at least three unused obverse dies were on hand. Two of these, N-2 and N-3, were overdated by punching 20 separately over the last two digits, from a 2 punch and a small 0 punch. The other, N-1, may be 1820, 182 Over 181, as there is no trace of a final 9. This die has a large 0. William C. Noyes calls these the Large Overdate (N-1) and Small Overdate (N-2 and N-3) varieties respectively.

The position of the under-digit 1 beneath the 2 provides identification of each variety. The N-1 variety has the 1 centered under the 2, N-2 has the 1 under the left part of the 2, and N-3 has the 1 under the right part of the 2. All three dates are illustrated here.

As a standard variety the 1820, 20 Over 19, overdate is readily collectible, most being N-1, of which multiple thousands are estimated to exist. N-2 and N-3 are scarcer, although there are enough in the marketplace that specialists can find them. Curiously, N-3 is the variety most often seen at the gem level. Otherwise, typical grades are VG and Fine. EF and AU coins are slightly scarce.

Detail of 1820, 20 Over 19, Large Overdate (N-1). 1 centered under the 2. The 0 is very large, in curious contrast to the adjacent small 2. No clear trace of a 9 can be seen under the final figure.

Detail of 1820, 20 Over 19, Small Overdate (N-2). 1 under left part of 2. All digits are about the same size. The 1 is distant from the 8. Traces of the knob of the 9 can be seen protruding from the lower left of the 0, and traces of the loop of the 9 can be seen within it.

Detail of 1820, 20 Over 19, Small Overdate (N-3). 1 under right part of 2. All digits are about the same size. The 1 is distant from the 8. Traces of the inner loop of the 9 are prominent within the 0.

Typical values for 1820, 20 Over 19, cents. Rare varieties may be worth more.

	Cert	Avg	%MS	G-4	VG-8	F-12	VF-20	EF-40	AU-50	MS-60BN	MS-63BN	MS-63RB	MS-65BN	MS-65RB
1820, 20 Over 19	55	43.4	33%	$30	$60	$150	$300	$420	$775	$1,500	$2,300	$3,375	$5,250	$10,500

1820, 20 Over 19 • N-1 to N-3. *Estimated population:* Many thousands.

Notes: These three overdate varieties are interesting, available, and easy to identify, suggesting the possibility for a small specialized collection. Each of the overdates has a "personality" of its own. Most examples are of the 1820, 20 Over 19, Large Overdate (N-1) variety. Mint State coins seem to be scarcest for N-1, although this is the most available variety in circulated grades.

1820, 20 Over 19, Small Overdate (N-3).

1820, *Matron Head*

Mintage (per *Mint Report*): 4,407,550.

There are 15 die combinations of the 1820 cent, (with large 0) and Small Date (small 0). In addition there are two styles of the digit 2. These are described in the Notes below.

This is a very common date, as the mintage suggests. There are, however, three very scarce varieties (N-4, N-6, and N-14) and several others that are slightly scarce. Randall Hoard coins are very common for N-13, seen with a distinctive series of cracks connecting the stars and the date—a cousin to

Detail of 1820, Small Date (N-8), showing detail of the date with inner curl on 2. This strike shows blank planchet area beyond the denticles, revealing that the denticles on this die were added in the form of pellets.

Detail of 1820, Large Date (N-13), showing detail of the date with knob on 2. Although this is called a "knob," it is simply a thicker area.

1818 (N-10) in this regard. The N-13 is one of the better struck of the hoard varieties and is a good candidate for a type set. Less often seen from the same source, but plentiful, are N-10 and N-12 to N-15. Mint State examples of other varieties range from very scarce to rare. Circulated coins are aplenty, typically in VG or Fine. EF and AU coins are scarce in comparison. Most have a medium-brown color.

1820, Small Date • N-4 to N-8, N-14. *Estimated population:* Together with Large Date, many thousands.

Notes: Small 0 of 1820. There are two types of 2 digits, one with a delicate inner curl and one with a heavy end of irregular shape sometimes called a "knob," as follows: N-4: 2 with inner curl; N-5: inner curl; N-6: inner curl; N-7: inner curl; N-8: inner curl; N-14: 2 knob.

Together with 1820, Large Date, common in all grades including Mint State, although certain varieties are rare, as noted above.

1820, Small Date (N-4).

Numismatic Notes: See next entry.

Typical values for 1820, Small Date. Rare varieties may be worth more.

	Cert	Avg	%MS	EF-40	AU-50	MS-60BN	MS-63BN	MS-63RB	MS-65BN	MS-65RB
1820, Small Date	35	52.4	54%	$300	$500	$950	$1,350	$2,250	$2,900	$4,200

1820, Large Date • N-9 to N-13 and N-15. *Estimated population:* Together with Small Date, many thousands.

Notes: Large 0 of 1820. There are two types of 2 digits, one with a delicate inner curl and one with a heavy end of irregular shape sometimes called a "knob," as follows: N-9: 2 with inner curl; N-10: knob; N-11: knob; N-12: knob; N-13: knob; N-15: inner curl.

Together with Small Date, common in all grades including Mint State, although certain varieties are rare, as noted above.

1820, Large Date (N-13). This is the most plentiful of the Randall Hoard coins. It is instantly identifiable by the signature die cracks linking the stars and the date. Although not sharp in all details, the N-13 is one of the better-struck varieties of the year. The uniformity of mint color on the obverse, without flecks or stains, is remarkable.

Numismatic Notes: *Excess supply of copper cents:* From *Niles' Register*, November 18, 1820: "Mint of the United States. Philadelphia Nov. 1820. The public are informed that the coinage of copper will be discontinued, for some time, at the Mint of the United States. A large supply of cents, however, is now ready for distribution; and, on application, will be furnished, to any reasonable amount, in exchange for an equal amount in specie, or paper (notes or drafts) receivable in any of the banks in Philadelphia; or on evidence of credit being entered in favor of the Treasury of the United States, in the Bank of the United States, or any of its branches. Shipments will be made agreeable to order; insurance effected and paid, and an adequate allowance made for freight to any port in the United States, to which vessels are cleared out from Philadelphia. Application to be made to the treasurer of the Mint. James Rush. Nov. 10."

High-grade examples elusive: In 1859, in his *American Numismatical Manual*, Dr. Montroville W. Dickeson wrote: "The slight milling of the edges of these coins render good specimens difficult to be obtained." Milling is a correct (but, today, largely forgotten) term describing the raised rims. They are low on many 1820 cents, making the coins more susceptible to wear, and making high-grade examples rarer than would otherwise be the case.

Typical values for 1820, Large Date. Rare varieties may be worth more.

	Cert	Avg	%MS	EF-40	AU-50	MS-60BN	MS-63BN	MS-63RB	MS-65BN	MS-65RB
1820, Large Date	99	58.2	74%	$210	$325	$450	$600	$825	$1,250	$2,000

1821, Matron Head

Mintage (per *Mint Report*): 389,000.

The 1821 cent has the lowest mintage of any Matron Head up to this point in time. The actual coinage of 1821-dated coins is not known, but it probably approximated the *Mint Report* figure. There are two die varieties, each fairly common, but the N-1 is slightly less plentiful than the N-2. This fits in well with the mintage figure, as the average life for a die was about 400,000 impressions at the time, but with wide variations. We have no way of knowing if the calendar-year mintage was all dated 1821, but if it was, considering that there were two obverse dies, the production per die was far less than typical. R.W. Julian suggests that it was not until about 1836 that calendar-year figures accurately represented coins dated with the same year.[97] Even then, there were occasional exceptions. Reverses tended to outlive obverses; both reverse dies were reused in 1822.

As a *date* the 1821 is a key issue, not in a class with the 1823, but one of the scarcest years in the Matron Head series. Typical grades are VG to Fine or so. EF and AU coins are scarce. Many coins of this year and the next two are on the dark side. Mint State coins are rarities, and were it not for the Boston find (see Numismatic Notes for N-1 and N-2), they would be extreme rarities. In any market season a nice high-grade 1821 cent at auction attracts a lot of attention.

Typical values for 1821 cents.

	Cert	Avg	%MS	G-4	VG-8	F-12	VF-20	EF-40	AU-50	MS-60BN	MS-63BN	MS-63RB
1821	119	33.2	9%	$100	$200	$450	$900	$1,650	$3,150	$8,875	$15,500	$28,500

1821 • N-1 and N-2. *Estimated population:* 3,000 to 4,500.

Notes: On N-1 star 13 points to a denticle; on N-2 it points to the space between denticles. There is no significant price difference between the varieties in circulated grades. Estimated 5 to 7 Mint State known of N-1, 15 to 20 of N-2 (in *The Cent Book,* John D. Wright suggests as many as 27). At the AU level fewer than 80 are estimated to exist.

From a small group found in Boston a generation ago, this N-2 is one of only a handful of 1821 circulation-strike cents with original mint color. In the field inside the denticles the original compass scribe line is seen, used during the die preparation process to help position the elements.

Numismatic Notes: *A significant find:* In 1821 a particular building was constructed in Boston, and to memorialize the event at least seven new copper cents were placed in its cornerstone. In 1981 the structure was razed, and the long-forgotten pieces came to light. These coins were attributed as two examples of N-1 and five of N-2. Both N-1 coins were called Mint State-63 by the cataloger, while four of the five examples of N-2 were graded MS-63 and the fifth MS-60. These were sold at auction by New England Rare Coin Galleries in 1981, six of the pieces went to Garry Fitzgerald and one to R.E. Naftzger Jr.[98]

1822, Matron Head

Mintage (per *Mint Report*): 2,072,339.

As a date, the 1822 is slightly scarce. Across the 14 known die combinations, none is really common, and several are rare, with the laurels going to N-14, of which just six are known—the best in Fine grade. Mint State coins come on the market with regularity, but for certain varieties are unknown. The average coin in numismatic hands is probably VG or fine. Quite a few exist at the EF level, somewhat fewer for AU. Generally, these are fairly well struck, on smooth planchets, and possessing excellent eye appeal. The hue is often dark.

Typical values for 1822 cents. Rare varieties may be worth more.

	Cert	Avg	%MS	G-4	VG-8	F-12	VF-20	EF-40	AU-50	MS-60BN	MS-63BN	MS-63RB	MS-65BN	MS-65RB
1822	201	45.5	27%	$30	$50	$100	$200	$425	$700	$1,200	$1,800	$3,000	$4,900	$12,000

1822 • N-1 to N-14. *Estimated population:* Many thousands.

Notes: On average, cents of this date are fairly well struck. Possibly 100 to 200 Uncirculated coins are known, mainly in lower levels and hardly ever with a trace of mint red. In the AU range there are probably fewer than 1,000. Estimates vary widely among specialists.

A gem 1822 (N-2) with a significant amount of original mint red. Very few cents of any variety of this year have any mint color. Most are quite dark. The stars are very sharp, except for a few with slight weakness at the centers.

1823, 3 Over 2, Matron Head

Mintage (per *Mint Report*): Included in the *1824* report.

The mintage of the 1823, 3 Over 2 is unknown, but it was likely very small. No cents were struck in calendar year 1823, leading to the conclusion that dies (this and the "perfect date") of this year were used later, probably in 1824. The overdate is scarce as a basic "date," actually an overdate, but the only variety, N-1, would not otherwise attract much notice on its own. In Mint State the variety is a great rarity, and at the AU level they are seldom seen. Some are slightly prooflike. Most are VG to Fine or so. Usually well-struck, and sometimes even needle-sharp, pieces are the rule. Nearly all are dark, and the surface is often unsatisfactory. Cherrypicking is needed to acquire one with good eye appeal within any given grade.

	Cert	Avg	%MS	G-4	VG-8	F-12	VF-20	EF-40	AU-50	MS-60BN
1823, 3 Over 2	78	23.5	0%	$200	$400	$1,000	$2,000	$3,100	$5,750	$13,750

1823, 3 Over 2 • N-1. *Estimated population:* 1,000 to 1,250.

Notes: Difficult to find with good eye appeal. Mint State coins by typical market grading probably number 5 to 7, or, per EAC strict grading, about half of that. Probably 10 to 15 can be called AU.

1823, 3 Over 2 (N-1).

1823, Matron Head

Mintage (per *Mint Report*): None.
Mintage (estimate): 20,000 to 40,000.

There is no specific mintage record for the 1823 "perfect date" (non-overdate), as no cents were coined in this calendar year. There is just one variety, N-2. The production was no doubt small, probably only in the tens of thousands. The reverse die was reused in 1824. In the *American Numismatical Manual*, 1859, Dr. Montroville W. Dickeson gave this mintage:

> The number coined—obtained through letters from Washington—was 12,250.* This coinage is not acknowledged in the Mint report, it being, from that authority, one of the years of non-coinage. The copper of this emission is pure and soft, hence the cents are much worn, and can be rarely found in a condition worthy of preservation. They command a premium. (*See *State Papers*, first Session, 18th Congress, vol. ii. Doc. 152.)

While this figure is probably far too low, it reflects that in the cradle days of numismatics the 1823 was considered to be rare. Today the 1823 remains the rarest by far of all dates from 1816 to 1857.

The fact that numismatists were allowed to sort through cents that were shipped to the Mint for redemption after the large coppers were discontinued is very significant. Likely, 1823 cents were picked out, while most—if not all—other dates from 1816 onward were ignored unless they were in high grades. Accordingly, if this is true, the survival rate of 1823 cents is much higher than other years of the era, pointing to a very low mintage. If, say, 1,000 cents of this date exist today, and the survival rate was just two percent or three percent of the mintage—a figure that Walter Breen and some others have used for certain early coins—this would indicate a mintage of 33,000 to 50,000 or so. If the survival rate was higher due to numismatists picking these coins out from shipments, and was five percent or so, that would indicate a mintage of just 20,000. These can only be guesses, but the mintage of 1823-dated cents must have been very small.

On the obverse the stars are lightly or flatly struck, most noticeably at the left, although the denticles are usually well defined. Similar to the 1823, 3 Over 2, most coins are somewhat dark, but the average surface quality is better on N-2. The typical coin is VG or Fine. VF pieces are scarce in the context of dates of the era, and EF and AU examples are rare. The reverse die was later used to coin 1824, 4 Over 2 (N-5).

So-called "restrikes" were made with this date, first appearing in 1867. These are fantasy combinations of the 1823 obverse, now rusted and damaged, with an irrelevant reverse from 1813. All are in Mint State, or close, today. See details below, including in Numismatic Notes.

1823 • N-2. *Estimated population:* 800 to 1,200.

Notes: Probably 8 to 12 Mint State coins exist, the finest being the Naftzger coin (illustrated here). At the AU level an estimated 25 to 40 exist. Estimates vary widely. As no mintage figure has been published, the 1823 is one of the most unappreciated coins of its era. "Restrikes" were made in copper (see below), but some were struck in silver—these off-metal pieces are beyond the scope of the present listings.

1823 (N-2). Of all dates in the Matron Head series, the 1823 is by far the rarest. The illustrated coin is one of few high-level Mint State coins known.

Numismatic Notes: *The 1823 "restrike":* In the *American Numismatical Manual*, 1859, Dr. Montroville W. Dickeson did not mention this coin, suggesting that it was unknown at the time. It is likely that, similar to the "restrike" half cent of 1811 and cent of 1804, someone used dies discarded by the Mint as "scrap iron." Many various dies were owned by Joseph J. Mickley (although this pair seems to have taken a different path; see below), and other were held past 1950 by Wayte Raymond.[99] The 1823 restrikes began appearing in quantity in 1867. Before then, $3 each was asked for an 1823-dated cent.[100] Early restrikes are from an uncracked obverse die. Later, a bisecting crack extends from 10 o'clock down to the right to 4 o'clock, and another crack extends from between 7 and 8 o'clock into the portrait. The dies were used at later times, in the meantime deteriorating

1823, "Restrike" later die state. These were made over a long period of time from the 1860s onward. The dies still exist today.

further. They were still in existence in the 1950s when C. Douglas Smith offered them to Q. David Bowers, and they are probably held by a collector today. As these were struck over a long period of time, there are multiple states of die cracks, rim erosion, and other deterioration. Some in Mint State have traces of mint red or yellowish red.

In February 1907 in *The Numismatist*, Lancaster, Pennsylvania, dealer Charles Steigerwalt told of the "restrikes" of the 1804 and 1823 cents. Concerning the latter: "While at a recent sale, information regarding the 1823 was given by an aged collector, who told how, years ago, he had found the dies in New York, probably sold with old iron from the Mint, brought them to Philadelphia, had a collar made, which was lacking, and the coins struck by a man named Miller in 7th Street, that city. Later the dies came into possession of a then leading dealer there and, when his store was sold out in 1885, the writer finding them among a lot of old dies purchased, they were at once destroyed so effectually that no more will ever come from that source. These coins never saw the Mint and are counterfeits pure and simple."

	Cert	Avg	%MS	G-4	VG-8	F-12	VF-20	EF-40	AU-50	MS-60BN
1823, Original	43	23.8	5%	$250	$500	$1,500	$3,000	$4,375	$8,750	$19,250

	Cert	Avg	%MS	AU-50	MS-60BN	MS-63BN
1823, "Restrike"	61	63.3	97%	$925	$1,250	$1,500

1824, 4 Over 2, Matron Head

Mintage (per *Mint Report*): Part of the 1824 total.

In terms of basic overdates, the 1824, 4 Over 2, is one of the most desired in the later series. The overdate feature is very bold and can be seen with the naked eye. One obverse die was mated with two reverses to create the only two varieties, N-1 and N-5—the second being especially elusive today. Nearly all of both varieties are in lower grades. A handful of Mint State N-1 coins exist (for N-5, see Numismatic Notes), but an EF or an AU is a very respectable high grade for this variety. The Eliasberg Collection N-1 was AU.

Light striking is seen on the obverse stars on N-1, with N-5 on average being slightly sharper. Typical grades are VG to Fine or Very Fine. Most have a brown color and nice eye appeal.

Typical values for N-1. N-5 in any grade is worth much more.

	Cert	Avg	%MS	G-4	VG-8	F-12	VF-20	EF-40	AU-50	MS-60BN
1824, 4 Over 2	40	38.1	13%	$60	$100	$300	$750	$1,500	$2,500	$6,000

1824, 4 Over 2 • N-1 and N-5. *Estimated population:* 1,500 to 2,000.

Notes: Two unused 1822 obverse dies were overdated, this and the 1823, 3 Over 2. An estimated 4 to 6 Mint State coins exist and perhaps 15 to 25 AU examples. EF coins are scarce. N-5 is rarer in all grades.

Numismatic Notes: *More about the N-5:* As for high-level examples of the N-5, the Naftzger Collection, generally featuring choice and gem middle-date cents, checked in with a Very Fine example. With wide variables in reported grades, it is difficult to know "who's on first," so to speak. A coin owned by

1824, 4 Over 2 (N-1).

Detail of the date on 1824, 4 Over 2 (N-1).

the late Garry Fitzgerald has been reported as MS-65 in William C. Noyes' *United States Large Cents 1816–1839* (1991) and as AU-55 in *The Official Condition Census for U.S. Large Cents 1793–1839* (1995) by Noyes, Del Bland, and Dan Demeo. It is generally agreed that the American Numismatic Society has a Mint State coin, but if any others exist, their status is not universally agreed upon. The reverse die for 1824, 4 Over 2 (N-5) is the same as used for the 1823 (N-2).

1824, Matron Head

Mintage (per *Mint Report*): 1,262,000.

The 1824 cent is one of the scarcer dates among early Matron Head issues, but it is generally not recognized as such. Three obverse dies were used, each varying slightly in their spacing left to right, in combination with three different reverses, as N-1 to N-4. N-1 is quite common, the other three are slightly scarce.

The typical coin is lightly struck on some of the stars, but is generally sharp in most other details. Most are in grades from VG to VF, but enough EF and AU coins exist that finding one will be no problem. Mint State coins are scarce, and choice and gem pieces are especially so. Few have even a tinge of mint color. In all grades the usual 1824 cent is brown and with nice eye appeal.

Typical values for 1824 cents. Rare varieties may be worth more.

	Cert	Avg	%MS	G-4	VG-8	F-12	VF-20	EF-40	AU-50	MS-60BN	MS-63BN	MS-63RB	MS-65BN
1824	123	44.7	20%	$40	$75	$150	$300	$500	$850	$2,400	$4,000	$5,000	$8,000

1824 • N-1 to N-4. *Estimated population:* Many thousands.

Notes: 150 to 250 Mint State coins (estimates vary widely). 500 to 1,000 AU.

1824 (N-2).

1825, Matron Head

Mintage (per *Mint Report*): 1,461,100.

Cents of 1825 are slightly scarce in higher grades. This year and others of the era, except for the enigmatic 1823, seem to survive approximately in proportion to their mintages. Accordingly, 1824 is slightly scarcer than 1825, and 1825 is slightly scarcer than 1826. Also, as the years pass, the survival rate is higher. For instance, of any given 100,000 cents struck during 1816 and the same number made in 1825, more 1825s survive.

There are 10 varieties among 1825 cents, N-1 to N-10, none of which is really common. They range from slightly scarce to rare. In the aggregate there are enough that as a *date*, 1825 is common. Grades range from well worn to Mint State. Striking is usually typical for the era: sharp except for some of the stars, especially those on the left. Most have a brown color.

Typical values for 1825 cents. Rare varieties may be worth more.

	Cert	Avg	%MS	G-4	VG-8	F-12	VF-20	EF-40	AU-50	MS-60BN	MS-63BN	MS-63RB	MS-65BN
1825	154	44.9	29%	$30	$50	$100	$150	$340	$650	$1,850	$2,750	$4,700	$7,500

1825 • N-1 to N-10. *Estimated total population:* Thousands.

Notes: The die varieties are all collectible and often have significant differences in the spacing of the date numerals and the positions of the stars. Extant are 180 to 280 Mint State coins (estimates vary widely) and 600 to 1,100 AU.

1825 (N-7). This example displays well-struck stars, including at the centers. As a class such coins are rare among Matron Head cents of the era. Many of the denticles on both sides are indistinct, not unusual for the type.

1826, 6 Over 5, Matron Head

Circulation mintage (estimated): 200,000.

The 1826, 6 Over 5, overdate is one of the least easily discerned major varieties listed in the regular edition of the *Guide Book of United States Coins*. It cannot be quickly identified by examining the date, and only high-grade examples show traces of this feature. Designated as N-8, the 1826, 6 Over 5, is priced only as a generic 1826 when the overdate cannot be discerned. As has been pointed out many times, including by Chris Victor-McCawley and J.R. (Bob) Grellman Jr. in the offering of the Naftzger Collection, "there is some discussion whether or not this is a true overdate." At the upper inside of the 6 there is an artifact that might be the flag of a 5, and at the lower-outside-left of the 6 is a slight extra curve that might be from an earlier 5. Under high magnification on a high-grade example the overdate seems to be convincing. On lower-grade coins,the answer seems to be no.

An 1826, 6 Over 5, in *any* grade can be identified by die characteristics. The date is spaced as 1 8 26, with the first three digits widely spaced and the last two very close—unique among 1826 obverse dies. The innermost point of star 6 points *below* the top edge of the coronet—also distinctive among 1826 dies. Even for high grades of this date, some which are not identified as such in the marketplace, this is a handy guide for cherrypicking overdates rather than perfect dates!

The usual coin has some lightness on the stars, but they are sharper than on many other varieties of the era. Denticles are weak or incomplete in areas. Most are brown color and have nice eye appeal.

The overdate must be visible under magnification.

	Cert	Avg	%MS	EF-40	AU-50	MS-60BN	MS-63BN	MS-63RB	MS-65BN
1826, 6 Over 5	17	55.2	53%	$1,240	$2,000	$3,900	$7,750	$11,375	$22,000

1826, 6 Over 5 • N-8. *Estimated population:* 1,000 to 1,250.

Notes: Only a tiny percentage show the overdate feature. Readily available in higher grades, which are often found not identified as N-8, but rather as a perfect-date variety.

1826, 6 Over 5 (N-8). The overdate feature on this variety is very subtle.

Detail of the 1826, 6 Over 5 (N-8), showing the distinctive spacing of the date numerals as 1 8 26.

Closer view, showing the overdate features.

1826, Matron Head

Mintage (per *Mint Report*): 1,517,425.
Circulation mintage (estimated): 1,300,000.

The 1826 is the date in the 1821 to 1829 range that is most often seen in high grades. There are seven varieties: N-1, N-3 to N-7, and N-9. N-8 is the earlier discussed 1826, 6 Over 5, and N-2, listed by Newcomb in 1944, is no longer recognized. A collection of varieties is easily enough assembled. Although some are scarce, specialists are scarcer yet, making them relatively inexpensive. All are available in Mint State, to varying degrees. N-7 is rated as the most common.

The typical 1826 is likely VG to Fine or so. VF coins are plentiful, as are EF pieces, and AU examples are not hard to find. Mint State coins are usually brown, sometimes with a trace of mint color. Most have some lightness on the stars and some incomplete denticles, although occasional exceptions are found.

Typical values for 1826 cents. Rare varieties may be worth more.

	Cert	Avg	%MS	G-4	VG-8	F-12	VF-20	EF-40	AU-50	MS-60BN	MS-63BN	MS-63RB	MS-65BN
1826	241	50.2	37%	$25	$40	$75	$150	$250	$450	$900	$1,500	$2,650	$3,100

1826 • N-1, N-3 to N-7, and N-9. *Estimated population:* Thousands.

Notes: For reasons unknown today, the 1826 is seen more often in Mint State than the 1824 and 1825. EF and AU coins are readily available as well. In the context of Matron Head cents from 1821 to 1829, this is the most frequently encountered. 300 to 500 Mint State coins (estimates vary widely) exist, along with 800 to 1,400 AU.

1826 (N-3). The obverse of this example retains most of the original compass scribe line, used for positioning the stars.

Numismatic Notes: *A hoard in Boston:* In the 1940s a man doing some work in the Boston harbor area made a remarkable discovery. The man was working in what was left of an old building that had been the office of a customs agent or toll-taker of some kind in the early 1800s. Cemented into the floor of the structure was a little metal vault or strongbox. The top was pried off, revealing an old-time version of a piggy bank. All in a heap were dozens of large cents dated 1826, and no others. Grades ranged from worn nearly smooth up to lustrous Uncirculated, or close to it. Apparently, some long-forgotten person took a fancy to this particular date and each time an 1826 cent was found in the course of commerce it was dropped through a slot in the floor into this tiny chamber. This must have gone on for many years, judging from the wide variation in grades.

As large cents did not circulate much after 1857 and not at all after the summer of 1862, presumably this cache was formed in the 1840s or 1850s, after which it was untouched for the best part of a century. Perhaps the original depositor passed away and never told anyone about the cents, or perhaps he realized that their value was insufficient to warrant tearing up the floor. The hoard was acquired by Oscar G. Schilke, well-known Connecticut numismatist and one-time president of the New York Coin Club. For several years afterward, he had a good trading stock of cents of this date![101]

1827, Matron Head

Mintage (per *Mint Report*): 2,357,732.

There are 12 die combinations of the 1827 cent, an average of about 200,000 per die pair. However, some are scarce to rare (N-12 being especially so), and others are common, so usage must have varied. It is Q. David Bowers's experience that this date is common in worn grades, but in Mint State is slightly scarcer than the lower-mintage 1826. Hard facts are elusive, and those who have studied market appearances closely have varied opinions.

As the stars were punched by hand, as were the date digits, there are many variations. Likely, the typical method for the engraver was to put the first star near the tip of the coronet, then add stars to the left and right around the border. As spacing varied, this resulted in many observable differences of star 1 in relation to the neck tip and the date. Similarly, the date digits can be widely or compactly spaced.

The usual 1827 is in a grade from VG to Fine or VF, although EF coins are plentiful. At the Mint-State level this date is scarce, and for some of the die varieties, extremely rare or even unknown. The strike, with respect to the stars and denticles, usually has some weakness, but it is better on average than for the several preceding dates. Planchet quality and eye appeal are usually good.

Typical values for 1827 cents. Rare varieties may be worth more.

	Cert	Avg	%MS	EF-40	AU-50	MS-60BN	MS-63BN	MS-63RB	MS-65BN
1827	207	47.0	31%	$225	$425	$775	$1,400	$2,500	$3,250

1827 • N-1 to N-12. *Estimated population:* Many thousands.

Notes: This variety is available in Mint State.

1827 (N-5).

1828, Matron Head

Mintage (per *Mint Report*): 2,260,624.

Cents of 1828 are popularly collected by two major varieties, Small Date and Large Date, each from a different font of punches. 8 in the Small Date is what is called the *Script 8* in some other series, and has a heavy diagonal down stroke at the center, from the upper left to the lower right. The 8 in the

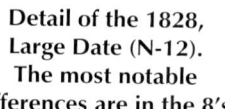

Detail of the 1828, Large Date (N-12). The most notable differences are in the 8's.

Detail of the 1828, Small Date (N-10).

Large Date is sometimes called a *Block 8* and has top and bottom sections separated by a thin horizontal element. As there is not much difference with the 1's and 2's, it would be better to call these varieties Large 8's and Small 8's, from a technical viewpoint.

As the large digits are necessarily more closely spaced, these varieties are often called Small Wide Date and Large Narrow Date, as they have been in the regular edition of the *Guide Book of United States Coins*. Of the 12 varieties, 11 are the Large Date and N-10 is the only Small Date.

Of the Large Date varieties, all are collectible, but several are scarce. N-4 is found only in lower grades, and N-12, save for the Naftzger gem (illustrated), is impossible to find in Mint State. The 1828s usually have some areas of light striking on the stars, but the typical coin is much sharper than are those of the early 1820s. The denticles are usually complete, or nearly so, and on some dies they are very bold. The usual 1828 is VG to Fine or a bit better. EF and AU coins are plentiful. Most are of a brown color and have good eye appeal. Mint State coins are easily found, but they hardly ever appear with significant mint red.

The 1828, Small Date (N-10) is quite common, but as this is the only die variety with that feature, and there are multiples with the Large Date, the Small Date is several times scarcer than the other. The price difference is modest as there are still plenty to go around. Most have some flatness of the stars. The denticles are usually complete, but not bold.

1828, Large Date • N-1 to N-9, N-11, and N-12. *Estimated population:* Many thousands.

Notes: An estimated 400 to 700 Mint State coins exist, few of which show any mint color. There are many choice and gem examples. EF and AU coins are common.

1828, Large Date (N-12), one of 11 Large Date varieties.

Typical values for 1828, Large Date. Rare varieties may be worth more.

	Cert	Avg	%MS	G-4	VG-8	F-12	VF-20	EF-40	AU-50	MS-60BN	MS-63BN	MS-63RB	MS-65BN	MS-65RB
1828, Large Date	73	51.2	32%	$25	$50	$75	$150	$230	$400	$1,250	$1,750	$2,800	$4,250	$10,000

1828, Small Date • N-10. *Estimated population:* Several thousand.

Notes: An estimated 30 to 50 Mint State coins exist, including in the choice and gem categories. EF and AU coins are plentiful.

1828, Small Date (N-10), the only such variety.

	Cert	Avg	%MS	G-4	VG-8	F-12	VF-20	EF-40	AU-50	MS-60BN	MS-63BN	MS-63RB	MS-65BN
1828, Small Date	19	49.3	42%	$30	$70	$100	$200	$310	$650	$1,950	$3,500	$5,500	$20,000

1829, Matron Head

Mintage (per *Mint Report*): 1,414,500.

Cents of 1829 are usually classified in two categories: Large Letters (on the reverse) and Medium Letters, the latter sometimes called Small Letters. The Medium Letters coins (N-3, N-5, and N-9) all share the same reverse. Large Letters coins (N-1, N-2, N-4, and N-6 to N-8) combine several obverses and reverses. There are two sizes of 1's, although these are not often noticed. All have Large 1's, except N-7 to N-9, which have Small 1's.

The Large Letters coins are readily available in all grades, including choice and gem Mint State. Striking varies, and usually there is some flatness at certain star centers and, often, on the hair. This particular date is well known in this regard. Denticles, depending on the variety, range from small to prominent, but are usually full.

Medium Letters coins are scarce across the board for the three varieties, with N-9 being rare, with only one reported in Mint State. While the striking is not quite as flat as a pancake, in numismatic equivalents it comes close. Light areas are prominent on both sides, due to spacing the dies too far apart in the coining press. Most are VG to Fine or so. At the EF level they are rare, and AU coins are rarer yet. Mint State coins are very rare. The eye appeal of both styles of 1829 cents is usually very good.

Cents of 1829 are the last of the years that can be called slightly scarce. After this time, all are more plentiful. The average grade of surviving pieces rises as well.

1829, Large Letters • N-1, N-2, N-4, and N-6 to N-8. *Estimated population:* Many thousands.

Notes: Per general market grading, Mint State coins are estimated to be around 125 to 250, few with mint red, and most in lower levels. EF and AU coins are easy to find.

1829, Large Letters (N-1). Mint State with a generous amount of original color, rare and remarkable for any variety of this date.

Typical values for 1829, Large Letters. Rare varieties may be worth more.

	Cert	Avg	%MS	G-4	VG-8	F-12	VF-20	EF-40	AU-50	MS-60BN	MS-63BN	MS-63RB
1829, Large Letters	39	48.0	38%	$25	$40	$90	$175	$250	$440	$825	$1,500	$3,000

1829, Medium Letters • N-3, N-5, and N-9. *Estimated population:* 750 to 1,000.

Notes: Mint State coins are very rare. Per conservative EAC grading, only a handful exist. Per grading used elsewhere, perhaps 10 to 20 survive. Grading in coppers is, of course, the eternal question and will never be resolved to everyone's satisfaction. AU examples are rare.

1829, Medium Letters (N-5). Areas of light striking are seen on both sides. This is the Naftzger coin graded MS-64 by PCGS.

Typical values for 1829, Medium Letters. Rare varieties may be worth more.

	Cert	Avg	%MS	G-4	VG-8	F-12	VF-20	EF-40	AU-50	MS-60BN	MS-63BN
1829, Medium Letters	15	43.0	20%	$50	$150	$350	$500	$1,150	$2,500	$7,000	$10,500

1830, Matron Head

Mintage (per *Mint Report*): 1,711,500.

Similar to the cents of the preceding year, the 1830 cents are found with Large Letters and Medium Letters on the reverse. The first are common as a class and are readily available in all grades. This is comprised of N-1 to N-5 and N-7 to N-11. The Medium Letters cents, N-6, are rare in any grade and very rare in AU.

Among 1830 Large Letters cents the 10 varieties range from common to very rare, the latter being the case for N-9. Striking varies, but usually there is some lightness, particularly on the stars, and the denticles can be light. Mint State coins are often seen, usually a lustrous brown and with good eye appeal, among the common varieties. For some others, no Mint State coins have been recorded. The average grades of coins in the marketplace is Fine or better, although VG coins can be found as well. EF and AU coins are plentiful. Nearly all have good eye appeal.

The finest known, the Naftzger Collection coin, has been graded 60+ and 63 in specialized references—this being EAC grading—and MS-67 by PCGS. This is one of the very rarest of the major cent varieties listed in the regular edition of the *Guide Book of United States Coins*.

1830, Large Letters • N-1 to N-5 and N-7 to N-11. *Estimated population:* Many thousands.

Notes: Per general market grading, Mint State coins are estimated to be around 125 to 250, few with mint red, and most in lower levels. EF and AU coins are easy to find.

1830, Large Letters (N-1). The compass scribe line inside the denticles is often called the "inner ring."

Typical values for 1830, Large Letters. Rare varieties may be worth more.

	Cert	Avg	%MS	G-4	VG-8	F-12	VF-20	EF-40	AU-50	MS-60BN	MS-63BN	MS-63RB	MS-65BN	MS-65RB
1830, Large Letters	87	48.0	37%	$30	$50	$90	$125	$210	$325	$550	$1,000	$1,900	$2,700	$3,600

1830, Medium Letters • N-6. *Estimated population:* 250 to 400.

Notes: Only one Mint State coin has been recorded. EF and AU coins are collectible, but are very rare, with a population of perhaps 20 to 30 combined.

1830, Medium Letters (N-6), the finest known example, and a major rarity as such. The sharpness is outstanding on both sides, save for a trivial lightness on the hair.

	Cert	Avg	%MS	G-4	VG-8	F-12	VF-20	EF-40	AU-50
1830, Medium Letters	7	36.0	14%	$100	$350	$750	$1,500	$2,000	$4,100

1831, Matron Head

Mintage (per *Mint Report*): 3,359,260.

The cents of 1831 and 1832 are in many ways comparable. Both have very large mintages, both have Large Letters and Medium Letters styles, and both are common in all grades.

For the 1831 the Large Letters varieties are N-1, N-6 to N-10, and N-14, and the Medium Letters are N-2 to N-5 and N-11. N-13 isn't used and does not exist. The Large Letters coins are much more numerous, but enough exist of both the Large Letters and Medium Letters to fill the demand. Some varieties are scarce. Striking is usually good, with stars full or nearly so, but there are some flat exceptions. Denticles are usually bold, again with some exceptions. The average grade is perhaps Fine or a bit better. Planchet quality is excellent, and across the various grades most have good eye appeal.

1831, Large Letters • N-1, N-6 to N-10, and N-14. *Estimated population:* Many thousands.

Notes: This variety exists in Mint State.

1831, Large Letters (N-6).

Typical values for 1831, Large Letters. Rare varieties may be worth more.

	Cert	Avg	%MS	EF-40	AU-50	MS-60BN	MS-63BN	MS-63RB	MS-65BN	MS-65RB
1831, Large Letters	84	53.3	54%	$150	$250	$400	$700	$1,150	$1,800	$3,500

1831, Medium Letters • N-2 to N-5 and N-11. *Estimated population:* Many thousands.

Notes: Perhaps about one-third to half as many examples exist for this variety as for the Large Letters. This variety exists in Mint State.

1831, Medium Letters (N-3).

Typical values for 1831, Medium Letters. Rare varieties may be worth more.

	Cert	Avg	%MS	EF-40	AU-50	MS-60BN	MS-63BN	MS-63RB	MS-65BN	MS-65RB
1831, Medium Letters	42	51.7	43%	$200	$350	$750	$1,600	$2,750	$2,300	$3,700

1832, Matron Head

Mintage (per *Mint Report*): 2,362,000.

There are only three die varieties for this date, and two of them are slightly scarce. This calls into question the published mintage figure, which would imply that well over a million would have been struck of the common N-3. The only explanation is that in calendar year 1832 the Mint used earlier-dated dies. R.W. Julian has suggested that figures are incorrect for certain *half cents* of the era, and it seems they are for cents as well. A more reasonable estimated output is about 200,000 or so coins for N-3 and fewer for N-1 and N-2, perhaps yielding 300,000 or so cents actually *dated* 1832.

These are found in the Large Letters style, this being the common N-3, and two of the Medium Letters style, N-1 and N-2. Most have lightness at the star centers. Other details, including the denticles, are often bold, but there are exceptions. Both styles are common in all grades, but the Medium Letters coins are less so. Nearly all have nice eye appeal.

1832, Large Letters • N-3. *Estimated population:* Many thousands.

Notes: This variety exists in Mint State.

1832, Large Letters (N-3).

	Cert	Avg	%MS	EF-40	AU-50	MS-60BN	MS-63BN	MS-63RB	MS-65BN	MS-65RB
1832, Large Letters	29	56.4	59%	$150	$250	$375	$650	$1,000	$2,300	$3,300

1832, Medium Letters • N-1 and N-2.

Estimated population: Many thousands.

Notes: Perhaps only half as many examples as for the Large Letters variety. This variety exists in Mint State.

1832, Medium Letters (N-1).

Typical values for 1832, Medium Letters.

	Cert	Avg	%MS	EF-40	AU-50	MS-60BN	MS-63BN	MS-63RB	MS-65BN	MS-65RB
1832, Medium Letters	27	59.6	63%	$200	$550	$900	$1,200	$2,250	$2,900	$4,500

1833, Matron Head

Mintage (per *Mint Report*): 2,739,000.

There are six die combinations this year, N-1 to N-6, again casting suspicion that in calendar year 1833, as in 1832, earlier-dated dies were used for part of the production. On the other hand, certain of the dies show *extreme wear* as evidenced by grainy fields and indistinct denticles. Perhaps the die steel was very strong and resisted cracking. The answer may await further study. All have Large Letters on the reverse, seemingly illogical, as smaller letters would have reduced metal flow, permitting the stars to be sharper. Indeed, slightly later in this series, Small Letters would become standard. Very early die states of N-4 show traces of a 2 under the 3—an overdate.

While N-4 is slightly scarce, the other of the five varieties are in generous supply, and there are far more than enough to fill the needs of specialists. All are readily available in Mint State, to varying degrees of availability. These include many at the choice and gem levels. Striking varies. Those from tired dies (such as the Naftzger coin above, which is certified as PCGS MS-66) are apt to be weak and grainy. Those from fresh dies are typically very lustrous. These would seem to furnish ample opportunity for cherrypicking, as most buyers in the marketplace don't seem to care. Most coins have brown surfaces and nice eye appeal. Significant mint color is rare.

1833 • N-1 to N-6. *Estimated population:* Many thousands.

Notes: Well over 1,000 Mint State coins are estimated, and far more than that exist at the EF and AU levels.

1833 (N-3), an impression from an extensively worn obverse die.

Typical values for 1833 cents. Rare varieties may be worth more.

	Cert	Avg	%MS	EF-40	AU-50	MS-60BN	MS-63BN	MS-63RB	MS-65BN	MS-65RB
1833	252	52.6	46%	$150	$250	$375	$750	$1,500	$2,600	$3,700

1834, Matron Head

Mintage (per *Mint Report*): 1,855,100.

Cents of 1834 are known to exist in seven die combinations. Variables include large or small 8 in the date, large or small stars, and—on the reverse—large or medium letters. These variables can be organized into four classes, each of which are listed in the regular edition of the *Guide Book of United States Coins* and are avidly collected:

1834, Large 8, Large Stars, Large Letters: N-6 (quite scarce) and N-7 (Proofs only). Circulation strikes of this variety are usually seen in lower grades. They are in strong demand.

1834, Large 8, Large Stars, Large Letters (N-6). Second scarcest of the 1834 die combinations, and the only variety with these features.

1834, Large 8, Large Stars, Medium Letters: N-5 (the rarity of the year). This variety is in extreme demand due to its listing in popular references beyond the large cent specialty. The illustrated coin is from the Naftzger Collection and was graded MS-60 by William C. Noyes, a grade which was confirmed independently by Chris Victor-McCawley and J.R. (Bob) Grellman Jr. PCGS certified the coin as MS-65.[102]

1834, Large 8, Large Stars, Medium Letters (N-5). Far and away the rarest combination of the year and the only combination with these features.

1834, Large 8, Small Stars, Medium Letters: N-3 (common) and N-4 (slightly scarce).

1834, Large 8, Small Stars, Medium Letters (N-3). One of two die combinations with these features. Common. This particular example has a so-called "Double Profile," or doubled outline to the face, from die "chatter," the result of a loosely fitted obverse die in the coining press.

1834, Small 8, Large Stars, Medium Letters: N-1 (very common) and N-2 (very common).

1834, Small 8, Large Stars, Medium Letters (N-1). One of two die combinations with these features. The commonest of the styles.

Striking varies, but most have lightness among the stars. Denticles are usually complete, but can be weak. Some are struck from tired dies. Most are in lower grades, VG to Fine and VF being typical. The commoner die combinations are likewise the ones easiest to find in Mint State. This year is a delight for cherrypickers, for coins graded high can have low eye appeal and vice versa.

Proofs: N-7 was made only in Proof format. This is the only Proof in the Matron Head series made from dies which were not also used to coin circulation strikes.

1834, Large 8, Large Stars, Large Letters • N-6. *Estimated population:* 300 to 500.

Notes: Very rare in Mint State, with possibly 10 to 20 extant per general market grading, fewer than 5 by EAC grading. Many exist at the EF and AU levels although most are well worn.

Numismatic Notes: See 1834, Small 8, Large Stars, Medium Letters.

1834, Large 8, Large Stars, Large Letters (N-6).

	Cert	Avg	%MS	VG-8	F-12	VF-20	EF-40	AU-50	MS-60BN	MS-63BN
1834, Large 8, Large Stars, Large Letters	13	45.2	8%	$150	$300	$400	$575	$1,300	$2,625	$4,000

1834, Large 8, Large Stars, Medium Letters • N-5. *Estimated population:* 100 to 150.

Notes: Extremely rare in Mint State, with possibly 7 to 12 extant per general market grading, fewer than 4 by EAC grading.

Numismatic Notes: See 1834, Small 8, Large Stars, Medium Letters.

1834, Large 8, Large Stars, Medium Letters (N-5).

	Cert	Avg	%MS	VG-8	F-12	VF-20	EF-40	AU-50	MS-60BN
1834, Large 8, Large Stars, Medium Letters	5	50.2	20%	$750	$1,500	$2,500	$3,700	$6,500	$10,250

1834, Large 8, Small Stars, Medium Letters • N-3 and N-4. *Estimated population:* Many thousands.

Notes: Easily available from low grades to Mint State.

Numismatic Notes: See 1834, Small 8, Large Stars, Medium Letters.

1834, Large 8, Small Stars, Medium Letters (N-3).

Typical values for 1834, Large 8, Small Stars, Medium Letters.

	Cert	Avg	%MS	EF-40	AU-50	MS-60BN	MS-63BN	MS-63RB	MS-65BN	MS-65RB
1834, Large 8, Small Stars, Medium Letters	32	50.0	34%	$140	$240	$350	$625	$925	$1,400	$3,000

1834, Small 8, Large Stars, Medium Letters • N-1 and N-2. *Estimated population:* Many thousands.

Notes: Easily available from low grades to Mint State.

Numismatic Notes: Late in 1834 the government of Venezuela ordered 100,000 cents, and these were shipped. In 1835 the Venezuelan government ordered a million more cents. It is

1834, Small 8, Large Stars, Medium Letters (N-1).

not known how many, *if any*, were shipped of the 1835 coins.[103] If any were, likely they consisted of, say, up to a half dozen different die varieties, perhaps accounting for the rarity of certain of these today.

Typical values for 1834, Large 8, Small Stars, Medium Letters.

	Cert	Avg	%MS	EF-40	AU-50	MS-60BN	MS-63BN	MS-63RB	MS-65BN	MS-65RB
1834, Small 8, Large Stars, Medium Letters	74	54.5	50%	$140	$240	$350	$625	$925	$1,400	$3,000

1835, Matron Head and Matron Head Modified

Mintage (per *Mint Report*): 3,878,400.

The mintage of this year is very generous, touching a new high. There are 18 different die combinations, N-1 to N-19, with N-7 found to be the same as N-17 and thus now just a single variety.

The cents of 1835 are found in three styles. It seems likely that the first two were made under the engravership of William Kneass. Christian Gobrecht, hired in September, would be a logical choice as the author of the new Head of 1836 motif (a slight revision of the earlier style) as well as various other portrait changes through the end of the middle date series. All cents of this year have Medium Letters on the reverse.

The die varieties that are common are also easy to find in Mint State, after which there are challenges. For N-18, a grade of Very Fine would be a notable example. The Naftzger coin was graded EF-40 by McCawley and Grellman, and PCGS designated it as AU-58.

Many coins of this year, including surviving Mint State examples, are struck from tired dies showing graininess and deterioration. Eye appeal is often lacking. It would seem that an MS-60 coin, sharply struck and from fresh dies, would be a better buy (and at a fraction of the price) than an MS-65, weakly struck and from tired dies. For this date there is ample opportunity for cherrypicking for quality.

The styles and the relevant Newcomb numbers:

1835, Large 8, Large Stars: N-1 (common) and N-9 (slightly scarce).

1835, Small 8, Small Stars: N-2 (very scarce), N-3 (very scarce), N-4 (rare), N-5 (slightly scarce), N-6 (very common), N-10 (rare), N-11 (rare), N-12 (rare), N-13 (very scarce), N-18 (very rare), and N-19 (very rare).

1835, Head of 1836: N-7 (incorporating N-17, a later die state; very common), N-8 (very common), N-14 (scarce), N-15 (scarce), and N-16 (scarce). The new head is more petite-appearing, has the cheek more rounded, and as a quick point of identification, the bust is slightly longer and thus extends slightly farther to the left. The stars are small.

1835, Large 8, Large Stars • N-1 and
N-9. *Estimated population:* Many thousands.

Notes: Fewer examples exist than for the next two styles. Many Mint State coins exist, and they are easy to acquire. Striking and die quality can be low.

1835, Large 8, Large Stars (N-1).

Typical values for 1835, Large 8, Large Stars.

	Cert	Avg	%MS	VG-8	F-12	VF-20	EF-40	AU-50	MS-60BN	MS-63BN	MS-63RB	MS-65BN	MS-65RB
1835, Large 8, Large Stars	13	53.7	46%	$100	$150	$250	$360	$700	$1,125	$1,700	$2,375	$2,550	$4,600

1835, Small 8, Small Stars • N-2 to
N-6, N-10 to N-13, N-18, and N-19. *Estimated population:* Many thousands.

Notes: Mint State coins of the common varieties are easy to find, but often these are from tired dies or have striking problems.

1835, Small 8, Small Stars (N-6).

Typical values for 1835, Small 8, Small Stars. Rare varieties may be worth more.

	Cert	Avg	%MS	VF-20	EF-40	AU-50	MS-60BN	MS-63BN	MS-63RB	MS-65BN	MS-65RB
1835, Small 8, Small Stars	47	46.9	30%	$150	$190	$375	$475	$675	$1,400	$1,750	$3,750

1835, Head of 1836 • N-7 (N-17), N-8,
and N-14 to N-16. *Estimated population:* Many thousands.

Notes: Mint State coins of the common varieties are easy to find, but often these are from tired dies or have striking problems.

1835, Head of 1836 (N-8), with modified portrait.

Typical values for 1835, Head of 1836. Rare varieties may be worth more.

	Cert	Avg	%MS	VF-20	EF-40	AU-50	MS-60BN	MS-63BN	MS-63RB	MS-65BN	MS-65RB
1835, Head of 1836	94	53.5	40%	$100	$150	$250	$350	$550	$900	$1,300	$2,000

1836, Matron Head Modified

Mintage (per *Mint Report*): 2,111,000.

In March 1836, following the ceremonial striking of medalets, a steam press was first employed for the coinage of the cent denomination. Seven die combinations are known for this date, N-1 to N-7. The most often seen is N-3, usually with a rim cud at the sixth star, making it instantly identifiable. This may well be the most common Matron Head cent of the decade.[104] Certain die varieties range from scarce to rare.

Continuing the trend of the time, the Mint used dies over an extended life span, creating many coins with grainy fields and mushy denticles. Weakly struck stars are the rule. Even the more available varieties are hard to find with a combination of decent (never mind needle-sharp) strike, frosty surfaces (from fresh dies), and good eye appeal. In this context this "common" date is actually rare if well-struck coins are desired, again yielding many opportunities for cherrypicking.

Typical values for 1836 cents. Rare varieties may be worth more.

	Cert	Avg	%MS	EF-40	AU-50	MS-60BN	MS-63BN	MS-63RB	MS-65BN	MS-65RB
1836	213	53.1	48%	$125	$250	$350	$550	$900	$1,300	$2,000

1836 • N-1 to N-7. ***Estimated population:*** Many tens of thousands.

Notes: Common in all grades, including Mint State, but certain die varieties are rare.

1836 (N-3) with distinctive rim cud at star 6.
This is one of the more plentiful varieties of the era.

1837, Matron Head Modified

Mintage (per *Mint Report*): 5,558,300.

The mintage this year hit a new record. There are 16 known die varieties, reflecting extended average use of die pair. More telling is the number of *different* dies. In this year 12 obverses turned out an average of 436,000 coins each! This "economy" is vividly evident in the quality of the coins struck, which, once again, are often from tired dies, sometimes relapped. Striking was done casually, and many coins have weak stars or denticles or both. These shortcomings are typically more evident on the obverse than the reverse. Once again, this year is a cherrypicker's delight.

In this year a new portrait was introduced, attributed to Christian Gobrecht. Instead of having Plain Hair Cords as before, and dating back to 1816, Miss Liberty now has Beaded Hair Cords, which were continued for the rest of the type. The Plain Hair Cord coins come with Medium Letters and Small Letters on the reverse. These styles yield the following combinations:

1837, Plain Hair Cords, Medium Letters: N-1 to N-4, N-6, N-7 (combined with N-8, same pair, N-8 the *earlier* die states), and N-13 to N-17.

1837, Plain Hair Cords, Small Letters: N-5. Scarce, and the key to this trio of styles. This coin is always a classic, due to its listing in the regular edition of the *Guide Book of United States Coins*.

1837, Beaded Hair Cords: N-9 to N-12.

1837, Plain Hair Cords, Medium Letters • N-1 to N-4, N-6, N-7 (N-8), and N-13 to N-17. *Estimated population:* Many thousands.

Notes: Common in Mint State, scarcer with significant original mint color.

1837, Plain Hair Cords, Medium Letters (N-1). The obverse die was well used by this point, with a grainy rather than lustrous surface. Lightly struck stars. Remarkable original mint color.

Typical values for 1837, Plain Hair Cords, Medium Letters. Rare varieties may be worth more.

	Cert	Avg	%MS	EF-40	AU-50	MS-60BN	MS-63BN	MS-63RB	MS-65BN	MS-65RB
1837, Plain Hair Cords, Medium Letters	149	59.0	66%	$125	$250	$350	$550	$775	$1,200	$2,300

1837, Plain Hair Cords, Small Letters • N-5. *Estimated population:* 750 to 1,000.

Notes: Estimated 100 to 200 Mint State coins known (or 25 to 50 by EAC grading). Many EF and AU coins exist.

1837, Plain Hair Cords, Small Letters (N-5). This is the key issue among the three styles of the year. Only one die variety combined these features.

	Cert	Avg	%MS	EF-40	AU-50	MS-60BN	MS-63BN	MS-63RB	MS-65BN	MS-65RB
1837, Plain Hair Cords, Small Letters	24	55.0	50%	$125	$250	$375	$600	$825	$1,500	$2,600

1837, Beaded Hair Cords • N-9 to N-12. *Estimated population:* Many thousands.

Notes: Common in Mint State, scarcer with significant original mint color.

1837, Beaded Hair Cords (N-11).

Typical values for 1837, Beaded Hair Cords.

	Cert	Avg	%MS	EF-40	AU-50	MS-60BN	MS-63BN	MS-63RB	MS-65BN	MS-65RB
1837, Beaded Hair Cords	75	58.8	61%	$110	$200	$325	$500	$775	$1,200	$1,900

1838, Matron Head Modified

Mintage (per *Mint Report*): 6,370,000.

This mintage and part of the 1837 mintage combine to break all coinage records to this point. The Panic of 1837, which had its roots in late 1836 and early 1837, became a reality on May 10, 1837, when banks stopped paying out silver and gold coins. There arose a strong demand for copper coins, and the Mint rushed to fill it, being joined by private manufacturers who issued millions of "Hard Times tokens."

Cent coinage for 1838 was comprised of 15 different varieties, N-1 to N-16, with N-11 and N-13 being different die states of the same combination. As 11 obverse dies were involved, this indicates an average coinage of 579,000 coins per die! Quality is all over the map—from very sharp and from fresh dies, to pieces from tired dies, with mushy denticles and flat stars. This is yet another cherrypicker's playground.

Typical values for 1838 cents. Rare varieties may be worth more.

	Cert	Avg	%MS	EF-40	AU-50	MS-60BN	MS-63BN	MS-63RB	MS-65BN	MS-65RB
1838	815	56.2	60%	$120	$225	$335	$575	$925	$1,325	$2,150

1838 • N-1 to N-11 (N-13), N-12, and N-14 to N-16. ***Estimated population:*** Many tens of thousands.

Notes: The commonest Matron Head cent. Common in all grades. Mint State coins tend to be brown or with partial mint color, rarely full "red."

1838 (N-4).

1839, 9 Over 6, Matron Head Modified

Circulation mintage (estimated): 20,000 to 40,000.

The 1839, 9 Over 6, is one of the most interesting overdates in the series. In 1839 a die of 1836 with Plain Hair Cords was overdated with a 9, creating an 1839 cent with Plain Hair Cords—a style that had been discontinued two years earlier. Inexplicably, Howard Newcomb thought the overdate to be a die break, apparently not noticing the Plain Hair Cords feature. 1839 was a time of transition (see next listing), and the Matron Head was discontinued late in the year. It is easy to envision that a survey was taken of the Matron Head dies on hand, so as to use them up, and this one from several years earlier was found. In later states a horizontal crack developed across the obverse, expanded, and led to the retirement of the die. The mintage must have been very small. The reverse die was used on 1839, Silly Head (N-4 and N-9).

Today this overdate is nearly always seen in lower grades, with VG to Fine or the occasional VF being usual. Any higher grade is a rarity. The illustrated coin has been variously graded by EACers as MS-60 (William C. Noyes) and 63 (McCawley and Grellman), and by PCGS as MS-65.

	Cert	Avg	%MS	VG-8	F-12	VF-20	EF-40
1839, 9 Over 6	48	14.0	0%	$1,500	$3,000	$5,000	$9,000

1839, 9 Over 6 • N-1. *Estimated population:* 200 to 350.

Notes: Only one Mint State coin is known, perhaps 3 to 5 AU, and 15 to 20 EF. Most of the others are Fine or Very Fine.

1839, 9 Over 6 (N-1), the overdate with anachronistic Plain Hair Cords.

Detail of the overdate.

1839, *Matron Head Modified*

Mintage (per *Mint Report*): 3,128,661.

Of all dates in the Matron Head series, cents of 1839 are the most diverse and, because of that, likely the most interesting. It seems that in 1839 Christian Gobrecht was contemplating many changes. Already, in 1838, the Braided Hair design was adopted on the $10 eagle, in 1839 it would be employed on the $5 half eagle, and then, in 1840, on the $2.50 quarter eagle—these being all of the gold denominations at the time. The silver series had been revised recently, beginning with the Gobrecht dollar in 1836 and the use of the Liberty Seated motif in the other denominations, including the half dime (1837), dime (1837), quarter dollar (1838), and half dollar (1839).

In 1839 the engraver experimented with some new portraits, including those we know as the Silly Head and the Booby Head. Problems of striking had been endemic to the Matron Head series since day one, with the obverse stars in particular causing problems. By 1839, the Small Letters style of reverse had helped solve that, as less metal flow was needed in the press in the area of the reverse die opposite the stars on the obverse.

Toward the end of the 1839 year, the Braided Hair design—an adaptation of that used on the gold coins—was made standard for the cent. The 1839, 9 Over 6, is discussed in the preceding section, and the 1839, Braided Hair, is in the following section. That leaves these three main styles of Matron Head cents, all of which are with Beaded Hair Cords:

1839, Head of 1838: This is the style of the preceding year (and also late 1837) without a "browlock" or protruding wave of hair above the forehead, and with the back of the shoulder covered by hair. There is a line under CENT on the reverse. Varieties N-2 (slightly scarce) and N-3 (very common) comprise this style. *Quick identification:* No browlock.

1839, Silly Head: This variety appears with prominent browlock (curl of hair projecting to the left at the top of the forehead). Hair surrounds the back of the shoulder and base of T of LIBERTY, with the serifs of T touching the hair. There is a line under CENT on the reverse. Varieties N-4 (very common) and N-9 (slightly scarce) comprise this style. *Quick identification:* With browlock, line under CENT.

1839, Booby Head: This variety appears with prominent browlock. Hair surrounds the back of the shoulder, and T of LIBERTY is embedded in the hair, with no serifs visible. There is no line under CENT on the reverse. Varieties N-5 (quite scarce), N-6 (scarce), N-7 (slightly scarce), N-10 (quite scarce), N-11 (very common), N-12 (very scarce), N-13 (slightly scarce), N-14 (quite scarce), and N-15 (rare) comprise this style. *Quick identification:* With browlock, no line under CENT.

Striking quality varies, and some are from tired dies. Mint State coins are readily available for the common die varieties. Circulated coins average Fine or Very Fine, with EF and AU coins being abundant. Most are a brown color and have nice eye appeal.

1839, Head of 1838 • N-2 and N-3.
Estimated population: Thousands.

Notes: This variety exists in Mint State.

1839, Head of 1838 (N-2).

Typical values for 1839, Head of 1838.

	Cert	Avg	%MS	VG-8	F-12	VF-20	EF-40	AU-50	MS-60BN	MS-63BN	MS-63RB	MS-65BN	MS-65RB
1839, Head of 1838	93	56.0	46%	$40	$65	$100	$130	$240	$340	$550	$1,000	$1,450	$2,000

1839, Silly Head • N-4 and N-9. *Estimated population:* Many thousands.

Notes: This variety exists in Mint State.

1839, Silly Head (N-9). Prominent browlock
on forehead. Right side of neck truncation
blends into hair. Line under CENT. This is an
extraordinary coin with nearly full original mint red.
The stars are quite sharp, but the denticles are mushy.

Typical values for 1839, Silly Head.

	Cert	Avg	%MS	VG-8	F-12	VF-20	EF-40	AU-50	MS-60BN	MS-63BN	MS-63RB	MS-65BN	MS-65RB
1839, Silly Head	126	51.6	48%	$50	$100	$150	$225	$400	$850	$1,200	$2,200	$2,850	$3,900

1839, Booby Head • N-5 to N-7 and N-10 to N-15. *Estimated population:* Many thousands.

Notes: This variety exists in Mint State.

1839, Booby Head (N-11). Prominent browlock on forehead. Right side of neck truncation ends in a square with point or corner visible. No line under CENT. Full original mint red. Sharp stars. Obverse denticles weak.

Typical values for 1839, Booby Head.

	Cert	Avg	%MS	VG-8	F-12	VF-20	EF-40	AU-50	MS-60BN	MS-63BN	MS-63RB	MS-65BN	MS-65RB
1839, Booby Head	209	53.4	52%	$50	$100	$150	$200	$350	$740	$1,300	$2,325	$2,925	$4,100

BRAIDED HAIR (1839–1857)

Designer: *Christian Gobrecht.* **Weight:** *168 grains (10.89 grams).*
Composition: *Copper.* **Diameter:** *27.5 mm.* **Edge:** *Plain.*

1856, Upright 5 in Date (N-8).

The Braided Hair type, introduced in 1839, continued uninterrupted until 1857. The coins of the earlier years in this date range are referred to as the Petite Head type, while later issues are referred to as the Mature Head—although they both have braided hair. Production was generous, with the result that a set of dates is easily enough collected today, although there are many rare die varieties. The earlier dates, as well as 1857, are not seen as often as the others.

Of special interest are two well-known die blunders in which the four-digit logotype, introduced in 1840, was entered in the die at least partially upside down and then corrected. Thus, we have 1844 over 81, and 1851 over 81. In both instances, the full inverted date is not visible, but just traces of it are. Beyond these are hundreds of die varieties with minute differences, the later ones differentiated mainly by small differences in the date logotype positions. *United States Copper Cents 1816–1857,* by Howard R. Newcomb, 1944, is the standard reference for the Braided Hair cent, but it requires a great deal of patience to use. There are no photographs, and "stock" line drawings plus adjectives are used instead. Essential, and more convenient, is the *Attribution Guide for United States Large Cents 1840–1857,* by J.R. (Bob) Grellman Jr. Before the listing for each year, there is a guide to basic characteristics. Such extra study is worthwhile, because, if the discipline of large copper cents appeals to you, there is the added allure that exceedingly rare varieties are often available for the price of "regular" examples of any given date. Even if they are classified properly, these rare varieties are often reasonably priced—as collector demand is not great—creating a heaven for cherrypicking.

The striking quality of cents of the 1839 to 1857 era varies from issue to issue. Generally, the earlier dates are better struck, but even these are apt to have some weakness. Points to check are star centers (in particular), denticles, and then the hair and leaf details. Generally, the denticles on coins of the 1850s range from weak in areas to "mushy" or indistinct. Some cents of the 1850s have rough patches in the fields from lamination or from grease or debris adhering to the dies. Planchet quality is usually good. Many dies were used beyond their normal life, and these became rough and granular, giving streaky and grainy effects ("flow lines" if radial) to the fields of such pieces.

Among Mint State coins, most from 1839 through and including 1849 are generally seen with brown surfaces or brown with tinges of red. Only rarely are any seen with full *original mint red*, although the deficiency of retained brightness has been made up in spades by large numbers of pieces being dipped. It is buyer beware, and even among certified coins there are many recolored, processed, etc, pieces. These are not necessarily undesirable to own, providing you know what they are and do not pay "original mint color" price for them. Again, great care should be taken either by you, an experienced friend, or a dealer/advisor. Certain die varieties from 1850 to 1856 are frequently seen in Mint State with nearly full original color, usually with some flecks, and are mostly from small hoards. Cents of 1857 are nearly always brown or with some tinges of mint color, scarcely ever with full *original* color. Again, cherrypicking opportunities abound.

Circulated coins exist in approximate proportion to their mintages; although, note that the saving percentage is higher for the later dates. Likely, two percent to three percent of the original mintages survive today. Grades of Fine and Very Fine are about par for the 1840s; Very Fine and Extremely Fine, for the 1850s. For 1857, EF and AU are typical.

Proofs were made in small quantities of certain of the earlier years. In 1856 and 1857, production of Proofs increased, with the result that these dates, while scarce today, do come on the market with some frequency. Certain Proofs of the 1844 to 1849 era—namely 1844 (N-8), 1845 (N-14), 1846, Small Date (N-22 and N-24), 1847 (N-42), 1848 (N-19), and 1849 (N-18)—share a common reverse die. Some, or all, may be restrikes made in the late 1850s and later.[105]

The curtain came down on the large copper cent after the coinage of January 1857, and the abolition of the denomination under the Act of February 21 of that year. However, in 1868, during a period when the Mint was making all sorts of rare patterns, restrikes, and delicacies for collectors, some imaginative person, identity unknown, produced perhaps a dozen or so 1868 large copper cents—identical in design and appearance to those of the 1850s, but bearing the 1868 date.

DESIGN DETAILS

Christian Gobrecht created this new portrait. This being part of a redesign of the copper and gold series—commencing with the 1838 $10 gold and completed with the half cent and $2.50 gold in 1840—the design is not a modification of anything done earlier. The head of Miss Liberty is compact, facing left with a tiara or diadem inscribed LIBERTY and her hair, circled with beads, in a knot at the back of her head. Thirteen stars surround most of the periphery, and the date is below.

Cents of 1839 and 1840 have the head tilted forward in relation to the date, the 1841 and 1842 cents are also tilted, but less so, and this is also true of the 1843 cents of the earlier type. The earlier heads are more delicate, leading Kenneth Bressett, editor of the *Guide Book of United States Coins*, to designate these as *Petite Heads*, a nomenclature we follow here. In 1843 the transition was made to an upright portrait, the *Mature Head*. Most cents after 1843 are less delicate in appearance than are those of earlier dates, and the dies are more stereotyped.

Numerals were punched individually into the 1839 die and the 1840 Large Date dies, after which four-digit logotypes came into use.

The reverse design of cents from 1839 to early 1843 is similar to that used on later Matron Heads, with a continuous wreath with a ribbon below, ONE / CENT within, and around the border in small letters, UNITED STATES OF AMERICA. In 1843 a transition was made to a heavier wreath and larger letters, a style continued through to the end of the series.

GRADING STANDARDS

MS-60 to 70 (Mint State). *Obverse:* In the lower-Mint State grades, MS-60 and 61, some slight abrasions can be seen on the portrait, most evidently on the cheek. Check the tip of the coronet and the hair above the ear, as well. Luster in the field is complete or nearly so. At MS-63, luster should be complete, and no abrasion evident. If there is weakness on the hair it is due to light striking, not to wear; this also applies for the stars. In

1845. Graded MS-63RB.

higher levels, the luster is complete and deeper, and some original mint color may be seen. Mint frost on this type is usually deep, sometimes satiny, but hardly ever prooflike. MS-64 coins may have some slight discoloration or scattered contact marks. A well-graded MS-65 or higher coin will have full, rich luster; no marks visible except under magnification; and a nice blend of brown toning or nicely mixed (not stained or blotchy) mint color and natural brown toning. MS-64RD or higher coins with original color range from scarce to very rare for dates prior to 1850, but those of the 1850s are seen regularly (except for 1857). *Reverse:* In the lower-Mint State grades some abrasion is seen on the higher areas of the leaves. Mint luster is complete in all Mint State ranges, as the open areas are protected by the lettering and wreath. The quality of the luster is the best way to grade both sides of this type.

Illustrated coin: This attractive coin has mixed mint red and brown coloring.

AU-50, 53, 55, 58 (About Uncirculated). *Obverse:* Wear is evident on the cheek, the hair above the ear, and the tip of the coronet. Friction is evident in the field. At AU-58, luster may be present except in the center of the fields. As the grade goes down to AU-50, wear becomes more evident on the cheek. Wear is seen on the stars, but is not as easy to discern as it is elsewhere and, in any event, many stars are weakly struck. At AU-50 there

1849. Graded AU-58.

will be either no luster or only traces of luster close to the letters and devices. *Reverse:* Wear is most evident on the highest areas of the leaves and the ribbon bow. Luster is present in the fields. As grade goes down from AU-58 to 50, wear increases and luster decreases. At AU-50 there will be either no luster or just traces close to the letters and devices.

Illustrated coin: Some friction is present, but the coin has nearly full luster and outstanding eye appeal. Note some lightness of strike on the stars, as usual (and not reflective of the grade).

EF-40, 45 (Extremely Fine). *Obverse:* Wear is more extensive on the portrait, including the cheek, the hair above the ear, and the coronet. The star centers are worn down slightly (if they were sharply struck to begin with). Traces of luster are minimal, if at all existent. *Reverse:* The centers of the leaves are well worn, with detail visible only near the edges of the leaves and nearby, with the higher parts worn flat. Letters show significant wear. Luster, if present, is minimal.

1856, Slanting 5. Graded EF-40.

Illustrated coin: Note the light wear on the higher areas; and lightly struck stars, as is typical. This coin has attractive light-brown surfaces.

VF-20, 30 (Very Fine). *Obverse:* Wear is more extensive than on the preceding. Some of the strands of hair are fused together at the top of the head, above the ear, and on the shoulder. The center radials of the stars are nearly completely worn away. *Reverse:* The leaves show more extensive wear. Details are visible at the leaves' edges only minimally and not on all the leaves. The lettering shows smooth, even wear.

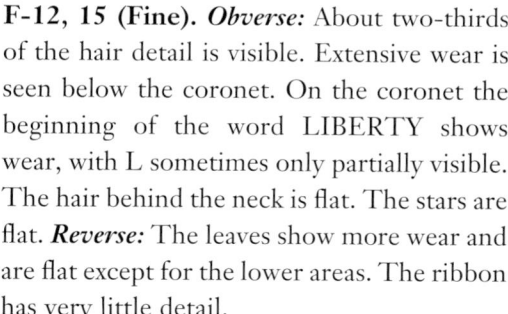

1855, Upright 5's. Graded VF-20.

F-12, 15 (Fine). *Obverse:* About two-thirds of the hair detail is visible. Extensive wear is seen below the coronet. On the coronet the beginning of the word LIBERTY shows wear, with L sometimes only partially visible. The hair behind the neck is flat. The stars are flat. *Reverse:* The leaves show more wear and are flat except for the lower areas. The ribbon has very little detail.

The Braided Hair large cent is seldom collected in grades lower than F-12.

1857, Large Date. Graded F-12.

PF-60 to 70 (Proof). Except for 1841, Proof Braided Hair cents before 1855 range from rare to very rare. Those from 1855 to 1857 are seen with some frequency. Most later Proofs are well struck and of nice quality, but there are exceptions. Most pieces from this era that have been attributed as Proofs really are such, but beware of deeply toned "Proofs" that are actually prooflike, or circulation strikes with polished fields, and recolored.

1857; N-3. Graded PF-63BN.

Obverse and Reverse: Superb gems PF-65 and 66 show hairlines only under high magnification, and at PF-67 none are seen. The fields usually are deeply mirrorlike on issues after 1843, sometimes less so on earlier dates of this type. Striking should be sharp, including the stars (unlike the situation for many Proofs of the Matron Head type). There is no evidence of friction. In lower grades, hairlines are more numerous, with a profusion of them at the PF-60 to 62 levels, and there is also a general dullness of the fields. Typical color for an undipped coin ranges from light or iridescent brown to brown with some traces of mint color. Except for issues after 1854, Proofs are nearly always BN or, less often, RB. Proof-like pieces are sometimes offered as Proofs. Beware deeply toned "Proofs" and those that do not have full mirrorlike fields.

Illustrated coin: Early Proofs from this period are scarce to extremely rare. This example is well struck (the reverse is slightly off-center), with a generally light-brown color except for a few darker areas on the reverse, not unusual for a coin with the BN designation.

1839, Braided Hair

Circulation mintage (estimated): 200,000 to 300,000.

Just one die pair, N-8, was used to coin the 1839, Braided Hair. The number struck is not known, but was likely 200,000 to 300,000, considering that 13 obverse dies were used this year (12 of the earlier type) to strike 3,128,661 coins, averaging about 240,000 coins per obverse die. In the context of cents of that date, N-8 is common. If star 1, star 13, and the date are aligned horizontally, the portrait leans forward. This orientation was adjusted in later years.

Striking varies from weak to sharp, but it is usually quite good. Examples are available in all grades from VG to Mint State. In this last category, choice and gem coins with excellent eye appeal are available. As the first year of the type, this variety has always drawn a lot of attention, and offerings of high-grade examples always meet with an enthusiastic reception.

Proofs: None.

	Cert	Avg	%MS	VG-8	F-12	VF-20	EF-40	AU-50	MS-60BN	MS-63BN	MS-63RB	MS-65BN	MS-65RB
1839, Braided Hair	66	54.7	55%	$50	$75	$150	$205	$430	$700	$1,075	$1,425	$3,625	$7,250

1839, Braided Hair • *N-8. Estimated population:* 4,000 to 6,000.

Notes: An estimated 40 to 50 are known in Mint State. In *The Cent Book,* 1991, John D. Wright estimated equal to or more than 30, stating "it is amazing how many really choice examples are around," and called the variety "mega-common" across all grades.

1839, Braided Hair (N-8), the first variety in the Braided Hair series.

1840, Braided Hair

Mintage (per *Mint Report*): 2,462,700.

Cents of 1840 are found in Large Date and Small Date varieties. This was a year of transition, and the Large Dates were punched in by hand, one digit at a time. The Small Date coins, made later, represent the first use of a four-digit logotype, in which all digits were punched into a die at once. Accordingly, the Large Date obverses vary in the alignment of the digits, whereas the dates on the Small Date obverses are all identical.

Certain of the portraits have a "hole in the ear," a round depression immediately above the earlobe.[106] This is seen on some other dies of this era. These are not delineated here, but are treated in detail in the Grellman text.

In one variety of 1840, Small Date Over Large 18 (N-2), 1840 is punched over the large digits 18, which were punched into the die by hand in 1839 and never finished. Rather than make the die a Large Date 1840 by punching in two more individual numbers, the four-digit Small Date logotype punch was used, creating one of the most unusual varieties in the series.

The varieties listed here are these:

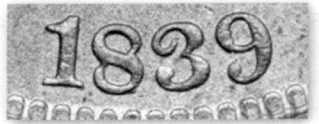

Detail of the 1839, Braided Hair, with individual digits punched into the die. A partially completed die with 18 only was used to create the 1840, Small Date Over Large 18 (N-2).

Detail 1840, Small Date Over Large 18 (N-2), with undertype hand-punched 18 figures at left, under the 18 of the logotype.

1840, Small Date Over Large 18: N-2 only. In 1839 this die was prepared as 18, with the last two spaces left blank, to be filled in when the die was used. The 8 is of the *script* type. All figures were punched by hand. As the third digit was not added, this allowed the die to be used for 1839, if needed, or the new decade, 1840. In 1840 the four-digit logotype was used for the first time. In this instance the logotype is applied with a straight orientation, rather than the curved style used with singly-applied digits in 1839. The logotype also uses a *block* 8 instead of script. The die was punched with the 1840 date, leaving abundant traces of the earlier 18. In addition to producing a large quantity of circulation strikes, this die pair was also given a mirror finish and used to strike Proofs.

1840, Large Date: N-5 to N-10. The digits were punched individually into each die and thus vary in alignment. The figures are large and are arranged in a gentle curve. These were the first 1840 dies made.

1840, Small Date: N-1, N-3, N-4, and N-12. These varieties are punched with the four-digit logotype, comprised of small figures about evenly spaced; the top of the block-type 8 is smaller than the bottom; there is a plain (not crosslet) 4. These were the last dies made.

For each of the above styles, typical grades range from VG upward, with VF being about the median. Mint State coins are scarce, and choice and gem pieces are rare. Only a few have significant original mint color.

Proofs: Mirror Proofs were struck of N-2, in addition to circulation strikes.

1840, Large Date • N-5 to N-10. *Estimated population:* More than 30,000.

Notes: This variety occurs in Mint State.

1840, Large Date (N-6).

Typical values for 1840, Large Date.

	Cert	Avg	%MS	EF-40	AU-50	MS-60BN	MS-63BN	MS-63RB	MS-65BN	MS-65RB
1840, Large Date	91	56.7	55%	$85	$200	$300	$500	$1,150	$1,200	$2,500

1840, Small Date Over Large 18 •

N-2. *Estimated population:* More than 5,000.

Notes: This variety occurs in Mint State.

1840, Small Date Over Large 18 (N-2).

	Cert	Avg	%MS	EF-40	AU-50	MS-60BN	MS-63BN	MS-63RB	MS-65BN	MS-65RB
1840, Small Date Over Large 18	8	43.6	38%	$300	$450	$950	$1,800	$2,250	$2,675	$5,000

	Cert	Avg	%MS	PF-60	PF-63BN	PF-63RB	PF-65BN
1840, Small Date Over Large 18, Proof	8	56.3		$4,500	$7,000	$10,500	$20,000

1840, Small Date • N-1, N-3, N-4, and N-12. *Estimated population:* More than 22,000.

Notes: This variety is available in Mint State.

1840, Small Date (N-3).

Typical values for 1840, Small Date.

	Cert	Avg	%MS	EF-40	AU-50	MS-60BN	MS-63BN	MS-63RB	MS-65BN	MS-65RB
1840, Small Date	83	50.0	39%	$85	$200	$300	$500	$1,150	$1,200	$2,500

1841, Braided Hair

Mintage (per *Mint Report*): 1,597,367.

Cents of the year 1841 are all of the same standard appearance—the dies possess no significant blunders or date-size variations, yielding simplicity in the resulting coins, so to speak—not that this is desirable! The varieties run from N-1 to N-7, with N-1 known only in Proof format. Circulation strikes are plentiful and can be obtained in nearly any grade desired. Typical examples range from VG to VF. Mint State coins are easy enough to find and usually are lustrous brown or brown with some traces of original color. As always, coins from worn-out dies, with weak stars, or with weak denticles are abundant in the marketplace. Choice coins are easy enough to find within the date (but vary with certain die varieties) and cost no more than coins of average quality.

Proofs: All are of the N-1 variety, a combination used only for Proofs. While hardly common overall, this date is the most available Proof cent of this era, until the coins of the mid-1850s. The reason for this surplus is unknown, although it was an inaugural year (for William Henry Harrison, who caught cold at the swearing-in event and died within the month), and there may have been some ceremony attached to this happenstance.

Typical values for 1841 cents.

	Cert	Avg	%MS	VG-8	F-12	VF-20	EF-40	AU-50	MS-60BN	MS-63BN	MS-63RB	MS-65BN	MS-65RB
1841	141	54.8	51%	$40	$50	$100	$160	$275	$525	$1,100	$1,350	$1,825	$3,000

1841, Proof • N-1. *Estimated population:* 45 to 60.

	Cert	Avg	%MS	PF-60	PF-63BN	PF-63RB	PF-65BN
1841, Proof	20	64.3		$4,000	$6,000	$9,500	$16,000

1841 • N-2 to N-7. *Estimated population:* More than 35,000.

Notes: This variety occurs in Mint State.

1841 (N-5). Extensive die cracks are seen through the date and stars.

1842, Braided Hair

Mintage (per *Mint Report*): 2,383,390.

Cents of this date can be found in two styles, Small Date (N-1 and N-2) and Large Date (N-3 to N-9, but N-3 and N-8 being different states of the same dies). Although both the Small Date and Large Date are common overall, there are more of the Small Dates.

Typical examples of either date size range from VG to VF or so, but higher grades are plentiful as well. Mint State coins have brown surfaces or are brown with some mint color. Occasionally a "RD" Large Date comes on the market. For any high-grade examples, cherrypicking for fresh dies and a sharp strike will pay dividends. Check the star centers. Coins from tired dies will be grainy, rather than lustrous, and may have flow lines.

Proofs: N-1 (Small Date) Proofs were made. These combinations were also used to make circulation strikes.

1842, Small Date • N-1 and N-2. *Estimated population:* More than 12,000.

Notes: This variety exists in Mint State.

1842, Small Date (N-2).

Typical values for 1842, Small Date.

	Cert	Avg	%MS	EF-40	AU-50	MS-60BN	MS-63BN	MS-63RB	MS-65BN
1842, Small Date	47	53.6	49%	$90	$220	$375	$650	$1,300	$2,200

	Cert	Avg	%MS	PF-60	PF-63BN	PF-63RB	PF-65BN
1842, Small Date, Proof	6	64.4		$4,500	$7,000	$11,000	$20,000

1842, Large Date • N-3 (N-8) to N-7 and N-9. *Estimated population:* More than 35,000.

Notes: This variety is available in Mint State.

1842, Large Date (N-3).

Typical values for 1842, Large Date. Rare varieties may be worth more.

	Cert	Avg	%MS	EF-40	AU-50	MS-60BN	MS-63BN	MS-63RB	MS-65BN	MS-65RB
1842, Large Date	121	53.6	50%	$85	$150	$300	$500	$850	$1,800	$3,000

1843, Braided Hair

Mintage (per *Mint Report*): 2,425,342.

This was a year of transition, yielding three main styles that have been avidly collected for a long time. The change was made from the Petite Head, leaning forward, to the Mature Head. In the second, Miss Liberty is positioned upright and is less delicate in her features. Large Letters were used on the reverse for this year, replacing the Small Letters in use since 1839. Changes of this nature were also made on other denominations. Why the Small Letters were discontinued is not known. In fact this change is surprising, as the smaller font facilitated sharpness of strike by decreasing the necessary amount of metal flow. Furthermore, many numismatists of today find the Small Letters more attractive.

Sharpness varies, but in general the Petite Head type is better than the Mature Head varieties. As usual, check the star centers and denticles first, and then check for graininess in the field from tired dies. There are many sharp, attractive coins in the marketplace, but overall they are in the minority.

The three styles for this year:

1843, Obverse and Reverse of 1842: N-2, N-3, N-8 through N-12, and N-14—N-10 being a die state of N-15. Petite Head obverse, Small Letters reverse. This is the most often seen style of the year.

1843, Obverse of 1842 and Reverse of 1844: N-4. Petite Head obverse, Large Letters reverse. This is the key issue of the year, with just one die combination. Although it is common—several thousand exist—it is seen much less often than the two other styles.

1843, Obverse and Reverse of 1844: N-5, N-6, N-16, and N-17. Mature Head obverse and Large Letters reverse, the style used from this point through 1857.

Proofs: Proofs were struck of N-12 (used for circulation strikes as well) and N-14 (used only for Proofs).

1843, Obverse and Reverse of 1842 • N-2, N-3, N-8 to N-10 (N-15), N-11, N-12, and N-14. *Estimated population:* More than 25,000.

Notes: This variety is known in Mint State.

1843, Obverse and Reverse of 1842 (N-8). Petite Head. Small Letters.

Typical values for 1843, Obverse and Reverse of 1842. Rare varieties may be worth more.

	Cert	Avg	%MS	EF-40	AU-50	MS-60BN	MS-63BN	MS-63RB	MS-65BN	MS-65RB
1843, Obverse and Reverse of 1842	153	56.4	63%	$85	$160	$300	$450	$875	$1,750	$2,750

1843, Obverse of 1842, Reverse of 1844 • N-4. *Estimated population:* More than 3,500.

Notes: This variety exists in Mint state.

1843, Obverse of 1842 and Reverse of 1844 (N-4). Petite Head. Large Letters.

	Cert	Avg	%MS	EF-40	AU-50	MS-60BN	MS-63BN	MS-63RB	MS-65BN	MS-65RB
1843, Obverse of 1842, Reverse of 1844	53	53.2	47%	$210	$320	$825	$1,500	$1,850	$2,300	$4,000

1843, Obverse and Reverse of 1844 • N-5, N-6, N-16, and N-17. *Estimated population:* More than 12,000.

Notes: This variety exists in Mint State.

1843, Obverse and Reverse of 1844 (N-6). Mature Head. Large Letters. This is the style used for the rest of the series.

Typical values for 1843, Obverse and Reverse of 1844. Rare varieties may be worth more.

	Cert	Avg	%MS	EF-40	AU-50	MS-60BN	MS-63BN	MS-63RB	MS-65BN	MS-65RB
1843, Obverse and Reverse of 1844	43	48.2	42%	$150	$275	$550	$900	$1,500	$2,100	$3,500

	Cert	Avg	%MS	PF-60	PF-63BN	PF-63RB	PF-65BN
1843, Proof	9	64.4		$4,500	$7,000	$11,000	$20,000

1844, Braided Hair

Mintage (per *Mint Report*): 2,398,752.

Cents of this year are numbered from N-1 to N-8, with N-6 and N-7 being different states of the same combination. Most numismatists, except for dedicated collectors of Newcomb varieties, seek a regular 1844 and an example of N-2, the last being a blunder. The 1844 logotype was first punched in an inverted position, heavier on one side, with the number 184 impressed into the die. It was then corrected by overpunching 1844 in the correct orientation. This variety is commonly called 1844 over 81, the *81* being the upside-down 18. This error variety is somewhat scarce in relation to 1844 cents overall.

The typical 1844, including the error die, is about as expected: there is some lightness of the stars, often from overused dies. Mint State coins can be blotchy if with partial mint color, suggesting that the best choice is a consistent brown.

Proofs: N-8 was used to strike Proofs only.

Typical values for 1844 cents. Rare varieties may be worth more. Some varieties are priced individually, as follows.

	Cert	Avg	%MS	VG-8	F-12	VF-20	EF-40	AU-50	MS-60BN	MS-63BN	MS-63RB	MS-65BN	MS-65RB
1844	183	54.2	49%	$40	$50	$100	$140	$255	$450	$750	$1,225	$1,750	$2,800

1844 • N-1 and N-3 to N-7. *Estimated population:* More than 45,000.

Notes: This variety exists in Mint State.

1844, Proof • N-8. *Estimated population:* 12 to 20.

	Cert	Avg	%MS	PF-60	PF-63BN	PF-63RB	PF-65BN
1844, Proof	7	64.4		$6,000	$13,000	$20,000	$30,000

1844, 1844 Over 81 • N-2. *Estimated population:* More than 6,000.

Notes: In 1883, Frank Andrews, in *An Arrangement of United States Copper Cents*, gave this: "A curved line from near right top of first 4, defects, or outlines also seen at top of 8 and final 4." This variety occurs in Mint State.

1844, 1844 Over 81 (N-2).

Detail of overdate.

	Cert	Avg	%MS	VG-8	F-12	VF-20	EF-40	AU-50	MS-60BN	MS-63BN	MS-63RB	MS-65BN
1844, 1844 Over 81	31	47.5	32%	$65	$100	$200	$325	$650	$1,350	$2,750	$4,000	$5,500

1845, Braided Hair

Mintage (per *Mint Report*): 3,894,804.

Similar to those of 1841, the cents of 1845 are all similar at first glance, with no die blunders or specific varieties that attract interest other than by specialists. There are 11 die combinations listed by J.R. (Bob) Grellman Jr., being N-1 to N-15, with some former stand-alone Newcomb numbers now realized as die states of other numbers within that series.

The quality is about the same as other cents of this era: often with flat star centers and lightness elsewhere or from dies that were used beyond retirement age. Mint State coins are usually brown or brown with a tinge of mint color (often not well blended). Most "brilliant" coins which appear for this year through 1849 are only brilliant by virtue of dipping. There are many cherrypicking opportunities.

Proofs: N-14 was only coined in Proof format. This is the only unquestioned Proof variety.[107]

Typical values for 1845 cents. Rare varieties may be worth more.

	Cert	Avg	%MS	EF-40	AU-50	MS-60BN	MS-63BN	MS-63RB	MS-65BN	MS-65RB
1845	303	56.0	61%	$75	$135	$225	$375	$800	$1,200	$2,500

1845 • N-1 to N-13, N-15. *Estimated population:* More than 90,000.

Notes: This variety exists in Mint State.

1845, Proof • N-14. *Estimated population:* 12 to 15.

1845 (N-11).

	Cert	Avg	%MS	PF-60	PF-63BN	PF-63RB	PF-65BN
1845, Proof	5	63.8		$4,250	$8,000	$15,000	$23,000

1846, Braided Hair

Mintage (per *Mint Report*): 4,120,800.

The 1846 cents can be divided into Small Date, Medium Date, and Tall Date varieties. A summary of the sizes:

1846, Small Date: N-1 to N-10, N-15, and N-18 to N-22. These comprise 14 different obverse dies, as two inadvertent double listings occur.

Detail of 1846, Small Date (N-3). Deep impression of the four-digit logotype. The thick or lumpy 1 has a thick lower-left serif and a thin lower-right serif; the lower-right outside curve of 8 is cut off; 4 is misshapen with the left point cut off, the serif at right irregular, and the lower-left serif too small; 6 with area of left side of the digit flat. The 1 in the date is only lumpy on deep impressions of the logotype. On deep impressions the upper part of the 6 is closer to the top curve of the lower part of the digit.

Detail of 1846, Small Date, Proof (N-22), with digits more lightly impressed into the die, plus some reduction of the size of the numerals due to polishing to create a Proof surface. Accordingly, the digits appear slightly smaller and more widely spaced.

Detail of 1846, Small Date (N-4). Logotype as preceding, but here with all four digits double punched.

1846, Medium Date: N-11, the only variety.

Detail of 1846, Medium Date (N-11). Base of 1 high, base of 6 low, 4 somewhat misshapen.

1846, Tall Date: N-12, N-13 (same dies as N-23 and N-26 in different states), N-14, and N-16. Four different obverse dies.

Detail of 1846, Tall Date (N-12).

Of the preceding, the Small Date is most often seen in the marketplace, with the Tall Date being quite a bit scarcer, and the Medium Date being scarcest of all. However, on an absolute basis at least several thousand Medium-Date cents exist, so they are readily collectible, though at a premium in comparison to the others.

The same careless striking and use of dies until they wore out yields another year for which cherry-picking can pay great dividends. Obtaining one of each of the three date styles can be done as quickly as a wink, including in Mint State, if you do not care about sharpness of strike and freshness of dies. If you do, set aside several *months*—or perhaps longer!—to complete the trio. Mint State coins are typically brown or brown with some traces of red. Very few have full original mint color.

Proofs: N-22 (Small Date) and N-24 (Tall Date) are known only in Proof format, with no related circulation strikes.[108] A few examples of N-1 (Small Date) are also considered to be Proof, but this variety is usually seen as a circulation strike.[109]

1846, Small Date • N-1 to N-10, N-15, and N-18 to N-22. *Estimated population:* More than 70,000.

Notes: This variety is known in Mint State.

1846, Small Date, Proof (N-22).

Typical values for 1846, Small Date. Rare varieties may be worth more.

	Cert	Avg	%MS	EF-40	AU-50	MS-60BN	MS-63BN	MS-63RB	MS-65BN	MS-65RB
1846, Small Date	254	55.3	62%	$75	$135	$225	$350	$750	$1,200	$2,000

1846, Medium Date • N-11. *Estimated population:* More than 4,000.

Notes: This is the key to the date-size series this year. Known in Mint State.

	Cert	Avg	%MS	EF-40	AU-50	MS-60BN	MS-63BN	MS-63RB	MS-65BN	MS-65RB
1846, Medium Date	31	57.6	71%	$90	$175	$275	$450	$950	$1,425	$2,850

1846, Tall Date • N-12 to N-14 and N-16. *Estimated population:* More than 15,000.

Notes: This variety is known in Mint State.

Typical values for 1846, Tall Date. Rare varieties may be worth more.

	Cert	Avg	%MS	VG-8	F-12	VF-20	EF-40	AU-50	MS-60BN	MS-63BN	MS-63RB	MS-65BN	MS-65RB
1846, Tall Date	50	49.7	46%	$50	$60	$100	$200	$360	$750	$1,225	$1,700	$2,150	$4,250

1846, Proof • *Estimated population:* 15 to 20.

	Cert	Avg	%MS	PF-60	PF-63BN	PF-63RB	PF-65BN
1846, Proof	2	66.0		$4,250	$8,250	$15,500	$24,000

1847, Braided Hair

Mintage (per *Mint Report*): 6,183,669.

Cents of 1847 follow suit with those of 1846 in that, under careful study, the appearance of the date digits can be very curious. In several instances a smaller 7 is seen protruding from under the large or final 7, and sometimes traces of other digits are seen as well.

All 1847 cents are of the same "Large Date" size. Varieties are numbered N-1 to N-43, but—allowing for several delistings and several combinations of die states—the ultimate number of die pairs, as listed in the Grellman text, is 31. In addition to the curious "Large over Small 7" varieties, there are other repunchings not listed here.

Dies with Large 7 over Small 7, sometimes showing other digits as well, include:

N-1: N-1 shows the entire date repunched, with evidence of earlier figures at the bottom.

Detail of 1847 (N-1).

N-2 (and 31, the same in a later state) and N-18: Top of small 7 protrudes above top of final 7. These are two different dies, each with the small 7 in a slightly different position. The

Detail of 1847, Large 7 With Small 7 Above (N-2).

N-18 also has clear repunching at the top of the 8 and is the rarer of the two varieties.

N-3 (and N-33, same dies): Upper-left part of small 7 in front of upper left of final 7. Delicate traces of other numerals are seen as well.

Detail of 1847, Large 7 With Small 7 to Left (N-3).

For nearly all of the 1847 varieties, cherry-picking will pay rich dividends, as many coins have weak stars and other areas, or they are from dies that were kept in the press too long.

Proofs: N-42 was struck only in Proof format and is the only unquestioned Proof of this year. Other supposed "Proofs," including varieties listed in the Breen text and some by Newcomb, are merely proof-like circulation strikes.[110]

Typical values for 1847 cents. Rare varieties may be worth more. Some varieties are priced individually, as follows.

	Cert	Avg	%MS	EF-40	AU-50	MS-60BN	MS-63BN	MS-63RB	MS-65BN	MS-65RB
1847	673	57.5	65%	$75	$135	$225	$350	$600	$950	$1,900

1847 • N-1 to N-43, except the following. *Estimated total population:* More than 120,000.

Notes: This variety is known in Mint State.

1847, Large 7 With Small 7 Above •

N-2 (N-31) and N-18. *Estimated population:* More than 9,000 as a group.

Notes: This variety exists in Mint State.

1847, Large 7 With Small 7 Above (N-2).

Typical values for 1847, Large 7 With Small 7 Above. N-18 is worth more.

	Cert	Avg	%MS	VG-8	F-12	VF-20	EF-40	AU-50	MS-60BN
1847, Large 7 With Small 7 Above	30	53.8	50%	$75	$100	$200	$400	$750	$1,000

1847, Large 7 With Small 7 to Left • N-3 (N-33). *Estimated population:* More than 3,000.

Notes: This variety is known in Mint State.

Typical values for 1847, Large 7 With Small 7 to Left.

	Cert	Avg	%MS	VG-8	F-12	VF-20	EF-40	AU-50	MS-60BN	MS-63BN	MS-63RB
1847, Large 7 With Small 7 to Left	(a)			$50	$75	$100	$200	$400	$600	$750	$1,000

a. Included in certified population for 1847, Large 7 with Small 7 Above.

1847, Proof • N-42. *Estimated population:* 12 to 15.

	Cert	Avg	%MS	PF-60	PF-63BN	PF-63RB	PF-65BN
1847, Proof	1	64.0		$4,250	$8,000	$15,000	$23,000

1848, Braided Hair

Mintage (per *Mint Report*): 6,415,799.

There are 32 different die combinations this year, intermittently numbered from N-1 to N-46. Beyond these 32, there are different die states of the same pair, which were given different numbers, and two varieties which have been delisted. The date numerals seem to be from a single four-digit logotype, but spacing can vary depending upon the depth of the punch into the die and the polishing or lapping done to the completed die.

The same suggestions apply as for earlier years: cherrypicking can pay great dividends as there is a wide variation in sharpness and quality among coins in the marketplace.

For the really dedicated specialist there is a monograph on this particular date, *Major Die States of 1848 Large Cents,* by Daniel Argyro (1995). Using the standard line drawing from the Newcomb 1944 book he added lines and indications to point out die cracks, die lines, and date alignments.

The 1848, Small Date, is a contemporary *counterfeit* made in large quantities. Examples are highly prized today.

Proofs: N-19 is found only in Proof format, the only unquestioned Proof die combination of this year.

Typical values for 1848 cents. Rare varieties may be worth more.

	Cert	Avg	%MS	EF-40	AU-50	MS-60BN	MS-63BN	MS-63RB	MS-65BN	MS-65RB
1848	714	56.3	59%	$75	$130	$225	$350	$600	$925	$1,850

1848 • N-1 to N-18 and N-20 to N-46. *Estimated population:* More than 140,000.

Notes: This variety is known in Mint State.

1848, Proof • *N-19. Estimated population:* 20 to 30.

1848, Proof (N-19).

	Cert	Avg	%MS	PF-60	PF-63BN	PF-63RB	PF-65BN
1848, Proof	10	64.7		$5,000	$9,500	$15,000	$23,000

1848, Braided Hair, Small Date (Counterfeit)

The 1848, Small Date, cent, a contemporary counterfeit, has attracted the interest of numismatists for a long time, especially after its listing by Wayte Raymond in the *Standard Catalogue of United States Coins*. Examples are struck from dies that imitated the federal design. Production must have been from somewhat crude facilities, for double and slightly off-center striking is typical.

Various Mint correspondence addresses counterfeit copper cents, though mostly in connection with giving this designation to what we know today as Hard Times tokens. In 1849 an investigator, F.C. Treadwell, was put on the trail of the flood of counterfeit 1848 cents. He enlisted the help of James Paar, of 77 Mott Street, who turned in this report to Treadwell:

> New York, November 12, 1849
>
> Dear Sir:
>
> Yours came duly to hand and I have taken some pains and believe I have succeeded in finding the location of our New York Mints. I am certain that large quantities of cents are made here and put into circulation. We have now hundreds of thousands of dollars [worth of cents] and the stock daily increasing. The cent makers are in companies . . . who get them into circulation amongst their brethren, the pawnbrokers. Some of these pawnbrokers use from $200 to $500 worth of cents weekly and pay them out at 96 to the dollar to people who are necessitated to come within their grasp. . . .
>
> About a month since a man hired a room in the Congress Mills, 172 Forsythe street, from John Coull, for the purposes, as he stated, to manufacture cents for the Mint. Instead of commencing to manufacture, he brought in about 30 kegs of planchets which he said that the Mint had refused to stamp on account of their being tarnished. He brightened them up by a chemical process which took him nearly a month to do and when finished put them up into kegs again and sent them out to one of our Mints. This was last week. I have no doubt but that they are in the act of being stamped at this time. Mr. Coull had the curiosity to follow them to the supposed Mint and was admitted through the front premises with the exception of one room, which was kept private. There are those other places in the same neighborhood where the business is transacted but perhaps the same commission. There are others out of this state, but not far from New York. I have the houses and locations of these manufacturers and can furnish them to any officer who may call on me if the United States Mint thinks my statements sufficient to warrant proceedings against the parties.
>
> On Friday evening last a girl called at a grocery in the Bowery for [illegible] and paid 18 cents in new bright cents of 1849. She was asked where she got so many new pennies. She said 'I got them out of the keg.' 'Well, where did the keg come from?' 'Oh, why we make them.' 'Who makes them?' She tells the name of the parties and leaves her own name and address.

One of the parties named has been selling cents for a long time at from 2-1/2 to 15 per cent off the price (face value). I have more information but consider this enough to trouble you as the US Mint [illegible]. I have sent a few specimens. The five bright ones are what the girl paid at the grocery, which you may exhibit if you think proper.

I am, dear sir, yours,

James Paar.

At the Mint the coins were examined by chief engraver James B. Longacre and chief coiner Franklin Peale and found to be counterfeit.[111]

1848, Small Date (Counterfeit) • *Estimated population:* 12 to 15.

Notes: VF or so is the highest known grade.

1848, Small Date (Counterfeit).

	Cert	Avg	%MS	VG-8	F-12	VF-20
1848, Small Date (Counterfeit)	0	n/a		$6,000	$7,000	$10,000

1849, Braided Hair

Mintage (per *Mint Report*): 4,178,500.

For 1849 there are 20 different die combinations recorded. These are listed from N-1 to N-30, including some that are die states of others and three that have been delisted. The 1849 date seems to have been applied with a four-digit logotype. An early state of N-8 has a line outside of the lower right of the 9 and has been called an "overdate" by some. However, this is not convincing when viewed under high magnification, and there are no specific traces of an undertype 8 in the open bottom center or the left of the 9.

Most have light striking in areas, usually most notably on the obverse stars or denticles. Quality and cherrypicking opportunities are similar to the preceding date. This is the last year in which Mint State coins are very rare with much original color. From 1850 to 1856 they are easily found.

Proofs: N-18 occurs only in Proof format. Other alleged "Proofs" are prooflike circulation strikes according to Grellman.[112] Per contra, Denis Loring considers some strikings of N-30 to be Proofs.[113]

Typical values for 1849 cents. Rare varieties may be worth more.

	Cert	Avg	%MS	EF-40	AU-50	MS-60BN	MS-63BN	MS-63RB	MS-65BN	MS-65RB
1849	417	55.8	55%	$120	$200	$325	$525	$1,000	$1,350	$2,475

1849 • N-1 to N-17 and N-19 to N-30.
Estimated population: More than 100,000.

Notes: This variety is known in Mint State.

1849 (N-22, late die state of N-6).

1849, Proof • N-18. *Estimated population:* 20 to 25.

	Cert	Avg	%MS	PF-60	PF-63BN	PF-63RB	PF-65BN
1849, Proof	3	64.3		$4,250	$8,500	$16,000	$25,000

1850, Braided Hair

Mintage (per *Mint Report*): 4,426,844.

Cents of 1850 comprise 20 different die combinations, given as most of the numbers in the range from N-1 to N-28. A single four-digit logotype seems to have been used. Differentiating styles of this year, the date was heavier if the logotype was punched deeply into the die, and in such instances the ball of the 5 is close to the vertical line above it. On lightly punched dies there is a significant space between the 5 and the vertical line.

As cents of this date, indeed of the decade, were in circulation for just a short time, nearly all grade Fine or higher, most VF or higher. EF and AU coins are common, as are Mint State examples. Among the last category, there are many examples from old-time hoards with extensive original color and brilliance, but coins with brown surfaces or brown with partial mint color are much more common. N-7 is the hoard variety most often seen. Striking and die quality varies, again furnishing ample opportunity for cherrypicking.

Proofs: About 10 Proofs are known of N-11, struck before the same combination was used to make circulation issues.

Typical values for 1850 cents. Rare varieties are worth more.

	Cert	Avg	%MS	EF-40	AU-50	MS-60BN	MS-63BN	MS-63RB	MS-65BN	MS-65RB
1850	934	60.4	79%	$80	$160	$240	$290	$400	$700	$1,225

1850 • N-1 to N-28. *Estimated population:* More than 100,000.

Notes: This variety is known in Mint State.

1850 (N-15).

1851, Braided Hair

Mintage (per *Mint Report*): 9,889,707.

Coinage this year hit a record high, producing a mintage figure not closely approached by any other year. As a result, cents of 1851 comprise a record 42 different die combinations. These have been assigned most numbers in the range from N-1 to N-45. N-11, N-28, and N-32 have been delisted. N-42 is uncertain and is under study. A single four-digit logotype seems to have been used.

N-3 is the most important of these varieties—a blundered die, called "1851 Over 81." This blunder was caused by a logotype being first punched in an inverted position, then corrected with a regularly oriented logotype—an error related to the 1844/81 coin. The sharpness of the 1851/81—never strong to begin with—fades with die use, and later impressions hardly show the blunder. Accordingly, the only N-3 cents with a premium value are those with the error distinct. These are common on an absolute basis, but

**Detail of 1851,
1851 Over 81 (N-3).**

they form only a tiny fraction of the extant 1851 cents. Mint State coins with significant original color are very rare.

Usual grades for an 1851 cent range from Fine or higher, and most are VF or higher. EF and AU coins are common, as are Mint State examples. Among the last category are many examples from old-time hoards with extensive original color and brilliance, although these bright examples are a small minority of the Mint-State population overall. Most are brown or brown with partial mint color. Striking and die quality varies, again furnishing ample opportunity for cherrypicking.

Proofs: None.

Typical values for 1851 cents. Rare varieties may be worth more. Some varieties are priced individually, as follows.

	Cert	Avg	%MS	EF-40	AU-50	MS-60BN	MS-63BN	MS-63RB	MS-65BN	MS-65RB
1851	1345	58.8	70%	$60	$125	$180	$230	$350	$650	$1,200

1851 • N-1, N-2, and N-4 to N-45. *Estimated population:* More than 225,000.

Notes: This variety occurs in Mint State.

1851, 1851 Over 81 • N-3. *Estimated population:* Thousands exist.

Notes: This variety is known in Mint State.

1851, 1851 Over 81 (N-3).

	Cert	Avg	%MS	F-12	VF-20	EF-40	AU-50	MS-60BN	MS-63BN	MS-63RB	MS-65BN
1851, 1851 Over 81	89	57.9	69%	$100	$200	$275	$375	$750	$1,250	$1,650	$2,700

1852, Braided Hair

Mintage (per *Mint Report*): 5,063,094.

Cents of 1852 are found in 19 different die combinations, an impressive panorama. These have been assigned continuous numbers from N-1 to N-23, with N-2, N-9, N-13, and N-19 delisted. A single four-digit logotype seems to have been used.

Similar to other cents of the era, those dated 1852 were in circulation for just a short time, nearly all grade Fine or higher, most VF or higher. EF and AU coins are common, as are Mint State examples. Among the last category are many examples from old-time hoards with extensive original color and brilliance. Most of these are the N-8 variety. Among the entire population of Mint State coins, most are brown or red and brown. Once again, striking and die quality varies, furnishing ample opportunity for cherrypicking.

Proofs: A few Proofs were struck of N-24. Three examples are known today.[114]

Typical values for 1852 cents. Rare varieties may be worth more.

	Cert	Avg	%MS	EF-40	AU-50	MS-60BN	MS-63BN	MS-63RB	MS-65BN	MS-65RB
1852	1271	60.3	75%	$60	$125	$180	$230	$350	$635	$1,150

1852 • N-1 to N-33. *Estimated population:* More than 120,000.

Notes: This variety is known in Mint State.

1852 (N-16).

1853, Braided Hair

Mintage (per *Mint Report*): 6,641,131.

Cents of 1853 are found in 33 different die combinations, an impressive panorama. These have been assigned continuous numbers from N-1 to N-33, with no sharing of a number and no deletions. A single four-digit logotype seems to have been used.

Most are in grades of VF upward, with EF and AU examples being common. Mint State coins are plentiful as well, but, similar to other dates of the decade, are only a tiny fraction of the entire population. Many have significant red, most are brown or red and brown. The brilliant cents most often seen are those of the N-25 variety. Light strikes are common, as are impressions from tired dies. Specialists consider the striking of cents of this date to be among the poorest of the era. Again, cherrypicking will pay dividends, as certified holders make no mention of these problems.

Proofs: None.

Typical values for 1853 cents. Rare varieties may be worth more.

	Cert	Avg	%MS	EF-40	AU-50	MS-60BN	MS-63BN	MS-63RB	MS-65BN	MS-65RB
1853	2016	60.2	75%	$60	$125	$180	$230	$350	$635	$1,150

1853 • N-1 to N-33. *Estimated population:* More than 140,000.

Notes: This variety occurs in Mint State.

Numismatic Notes: *Hoard notes:* In August 1891 this notice appeared in *The Numismatist:* "In the vaults of the Central National Bank of Lynn, Massachusetts, are a lot of 1853 cents that have remained there since they came from the Mint in that year, and are

1853 (N-10).

perfect and Uncirculated. Charles G. Bailey of 134 Chestnut Street, Lynn, an official of the bank, has them for disposal at reasonable prices."

In addition to the preceding, Walter Breen said quantities of Mint State examples of 1853 N-25 were from caches discovered in the 1930s, possibly from bank reserves. "There may have been a full keg or more of 1853 cents, which would mean at least a ballpark figure of about 14,000 coins." [115] Q. David Bowers has found no verification of this or any other huge hoard of Mint State large cents being discovered in the early 1930s, but they may have been. It is said that dealer Elmer Sears found 1,000 or so Mint State coins. In any event, it is highly unlikely that any quantity even remotely reaching 14,000 Mint State coins exists. Breen "facts" are sometimes questionable.

1854, *Braided Hair*

Mintage (per *Mint Report*): 4,236,156.

For 1854 there are 29 die combinations, numbered from N-1 to N-30, with N-15 delisted. There are logotype and punch variations.

Quality varies, as expected, for less care was spent on coining cents than for any other denomination. As with other cents of the era, this circumstance pays nice dividends for cherrypickers. The typical grade is VF upward, with EF and AU being common. Most Mint State coins are red or red and brown, but brilliant examples are often met with.

Proofs: Beginning with this year, Proofs were made in more significant quantities, perhaps a couple dozen all told. These are of the N-12 variety, a combination also used to make circulation strikes. "There is very little difference between the final Proofs struck and the first circulation strikes from these dies."[116]

Typical values for 1854 cents. Rare varieties may be worth more.

	Cert	Avg	%MS	EF-40	AU-50	MS-60BN	MS-63BN	MS-63RB	MS-65BN	MS-65RB
1854	1072	58.9	67%	$60	$125	$180	$230	$350	$650	$1,200

1854 • N-1 to N-30. *Estimated population:* More than 100,000.

Notes: This variety exists in Mint State.

1854, Proofs • N-12. *Estimated population:* 20 to 25.

1854 (N-25).

	Cert	Avg	%MS	PF-60	PF-63BN	PF-63RB	PF-65BN
1854, Proof	5	64.6		$4,750	$8,500	$10,000	$14,000

1855, *Braided Hair*

Mintage (per *Mint Report*): 1,574,829.

The mintage dropped sharply this year, probably due to the rising cost of copper. Patterns of lighter weight and smaller diameter were made, continuing a program launched in 1850. Cents (and half cents) were a profit center at the Mint, and profits were being diminished.

Cents of 1855 were made in two main styles:

Upright 55 in date: N-1 to N-8, and N-12. N-13 has been assigned, but is a different die state of N-5. The net is 10 different die combinations.

Detail of 1855, Upright 55 (N-4).

Slanting (italic) 55 in date: N-9 to N-11, or three die combinations. Later states of N-9 are of the famous *Knob on Ear* variety. The die deteriorated at the center and pieces fell out, causing a prominent lump on the coins. These command a premium and are listed separately here and in various popular guides. N-11 was made only in Proof format.

Detail of 1855, Slanting 55 (N-9).

Detail of 1855, Slanting 55, Knob on Ear (N-9 in a later state).

Both of these styles are very common (N-9 and N-10 are each common in their own right), but there are more of the Upright 55. Typical grades are VF upward. High-level examples are plentiful. The 1855 N-4 with Upright 55 is easy to find with nearly full mint red, and N-5 is seen in this condition with some frequency as well. Otherwise, most Mint State coins are brown or brown with traces of red. As there is no hoard variety among the Slanting 55 coins, these are much harder to find with full original color.

Proofs: Proofs are of the N-10 and N-11 (Slanting 5's) varieties. N-11 was made only in Proof format.

1855, Upright 55 • N-1 to N-8 and N-12. *Estimated population:* More than 30,000.

Notes: This variety exists in Mint State.

1855, Upright 55 (N-4).

Typical values for 1855, Upright 55. Rare varieties may be worth more.

	Cert	Avg	%MS	EF-40	AU-50	MS-60BN	MS-63BN	MS-63RB	MS-65BN	MS-65RB
1855, Upright 55	335	58.8	65%	$60	$125	$180	$230	$350	$635	$1,150

1855, Slanting 55 • N-9 to N-11. *Estimated population:* More than 7,000.

Notes: This variety exists in Mint State.

Typical values for 1855, Slanting 55. Rare varieties may be worth more.

	Cert	Avg	%MS	EF-40	AU-50	MS-60BN	MS-63BN	MS-63RB	MS-65BN	MS-65RB
1855, Slanting 55	88	59.0	61%	$65	$130	$200	$275	$650	$1,250	$2,000

1855, Slanting 55, Proof • N-10 and N-11. *Estimated population:* 50 to 65.

Notes: Examples are about equally divided between N-10 and N-11.

	Cert	Avg	%MS	PF-60	PF-63BN	PF-63RB	PF-65BN
1855, Slanting 55, Proof	10	64.5		$4,500	$6,000	$8,750	$12,000

1855, Slanting 55, Knob on Ear • N-9. *Estimated population:* Several thousand.

Notes: This variety is known in Mint State.

The knob must be prominent to merit these prices. Otherwise, regular 1855, Slanting 55, values apply.

	Cert	Avg	%MS	VF-20	EF-40	AU-50	MS-60BN	MS-63BN	MS-63RB	MS-65BN
1855, Slanting 55, Knob on Ear	128	56.7	50%	$150	$180	$310	$455	$760	$1,375	$2,325

1856, Braided Hair

Mintage (per *Mint Report*): 2,690,463.

The mintage was modest this year, again in view of the high prevailing copper prices. Cents of 1856 are usually collected by the two major styles, Upright 5 and Slanting or Italic 5:

1856, Upright 5: N-6 to N-12, or seven die combinations. N-20 is of this style, but is a state of N-8.

Detail of 1856, Upright 5 (N-8).

1856, Slanting or Italic 5: N-1 to N-5, N-13, N-14, N-16 to N-19, N-21, and N-22, or 15 die combinations. Examples of N-14 are said to exist in large quantities from bank hoards of the 1930s, per Breen's 1988 *Encyclopedia*, but such coins are not common today.

Detail of 1856, Slanting 5 (N-21).

Both styles are very common in all grades from VF or so to Mint State. Most Mint State coins are brown or brown with some original color. Full original color coins are scarcer than for the immediately preceding years. The striking is usually quite good *except* for the star centers. Coins with sharp stars are in the minority. Cherry picking will pay dividends, but not as richly as for earlier years.

Proofs: N-5 (Slanting 5) was struck in Proof format only. Likely, more than 100 were made.

1856, Upright 5 • N-6 to N-12. *Estimated population:* More than 20,000.

Notes: This variety occurs in Mint State.

1856, Upright 5 (N-8).

Typical values for 1856, Upright 5. Rare varieties may be worth more.

	Cert	Avg	%MS	EF-40	AU-50	MS-60BN	MS-63BN	MS-63RB	MS-65BN	MS-65RB
1856, Upright 5	220	59.2	64%	$65	$130	$200	$270	$365	$675	$1,200

1856, Slanting 5 • N-1 to N-5, N-13, N-14, N-16 to N-19, and N-22. *Estimated population:* More than 45,000.

Notes: This variety occurs in Mint State.

Typical values for 1856, Slanting 5. Rare varieties may be worth more.

	Cert	Avg	%MS	EF-40	AU-50	MS-60BN	MS-63BN	MS-63RB	MS-65BN	MS-65RB
1856, Slanting 5	333	57.7	62%	$65	$130	$200	$270	$365	$675	$1,200

1856, Slanting 5, Proof • N-5. *Estimated population:* 65 to 80.

	Cert	Avg	%MS	PF-60	PF-63BN	PF-63RB	PF-65BN
1856, Slanting 5, Proof	21	64.8		$4,000	$5,000	$7,000	$12,500

1857, Braided Hair

Mintage (per *Mint Report*): 333,456.

The last year of issue, 1857, is an interesting study in itself. Struck only in January of that year, and to the extent of 333,456 pieces, the 1857 cent comes in Large Date and Small Date varieties, and is scarcer than even the low mintage figure would indicate. Many, probably most, were held back at the mint and melted. It is unlikely that even half the mintage was released. Craig Sholley suggests that the Mint released 140,000 cents.[117] However, the Mint supplied anyone who asked for cents of this date, as part of the above 140,000. Assuming that perhaps 10,000 to 20,000 exist today—strictly a guess—many of these probably were acquired by curio dealers and others at the time to be sold to collectors.

Interestingly, the 1857 cent is hardly ever seen with much original mint brilliance. The typical Mint State coin is apt to be lustrous brown or brown with some minor evidences of lighter color. A coin with *original* surfaces and full color would be a rarity. Most such pieces have been dipped.

There is just one die combination of the Large Date, N-1, but it is common enough that examples can be easily found. It is much more often seen than the Small Date.

The Small Date is found in four combinations, these being N-3 and N-5, used only for Proofs, and N-2 and N-4, used for circulation strikes. As a class, the Small Dates are common, but N-2 is less often seen than N-4. As these coins circulated for only a short time, typical grades are EF upward. The date is common, and there are enough to supply numismatic needs, but they are not often seen in comparison to earlier dates of the decade. Flat stars are the rule. Otherwise, the eye appeal of an 1857 cent is usually quite good.

Proofs: Proofs were made of N-3 and N-5, both of the Small Date variety. These die pairs were only used to make Proofs. Likely the mintage close to 200 to 300. This is the most readily available Proof large cent as a *date*, but as a *variety* the 1856, Slanting 5 (N-5), is most often seen.

1857, Large Date • N-1. *Estimated population:* 7,000 to 14,000.

Notes: This variety is known in Mint State.

1857, Large Date (N-1). An exceptional example with full, original color. Most of this variety and date are brown or brown with slight tinges of mint color.

	Cert	Avg	%MS	EF-40	AU-50	MS-60BN	MS-63BN	MS-63RB	MS-65BN	MS-65RB
1857, Large Date	572	58.2	63%	$250	$375	$500	$825	$1,000	$1,350	$2,225

1857, Small Date • N-2 and N-4. *Estimated population:* 3,000 to 6,000.

Notes: This variety is known in Mint State.

1857, Small Date (N-4). An exceptional example with full original color.

Typical values for 1857, Small Date.

	Cert	Avg	%MS	EF-40	AU-50	MS-60BN	MS-63BN	MS-63RB	MS-65BN	MS-65RB
1857, Small Date	205	56.1	48%	$250	$380	$515	$850	$1,050	$1,625	$2,450

1857, Small Date, Proof • N-3 and N-5. *Estimated population:* 100 to 125.

Notes: N-3 is slightly more available than N-5.

	Cert	Avg	%MS	PF-60	PF-63BN	PF-63RB	PF-65BN
1857, Small Date, Proof	8	65.1	100%	$4,750	$5,500	$8,000	$13,000

1868, Braided Hair

Proof mintage (estimate): 12 to 15.

In 1868—by which time the Mint had been creating rare patterns, restrikes, and other issues, secretly filtering them into the numismatic market—a large copper cent was created of the exact Braided Hair type, last regularly issued in 1857. At the time, the same obverse was paired with a new reverse of the three-cent denomination (not relevant to the listing here).

The 1868 large cent is similar on both sides to the 1843 to 1857 Mature Head type. The number struck was not recorded, nor was any information entered into Mint records. Today, it is estimated that 12 to 15 were struck in copper, plus some in copper-nickel (not relevant to the copper version discussed here). *United States Patterns* lists this as Judd-611, although it is not really a pattern.

Today the 1868 large copper cent is a member of that small but highly publicized (except for this cent) and extremely expensive class of "numismatic delicacies" struck after their regular series had ended, with examples having been distributed privately. Others include the 1913 Liberty Head nickel, the 1804 silver dollar, the 1884 trade dollar, and the1885 trade dollar.

Most examples of the 1868 large cent are attractive and with brown surfaces.

	Cert	Avg	%MS	PF-60	PF-63BN	PF-63RB	PF-65BN	PF-65RB
1868, Proof	0	n/a		$11,250	$14,750	$15,980	$18,440	$20,000

1868, Proof • *Estimated population:* 15 to 18.

Notes: Proof-65 and 66 are the highest grades known. Nearly all are "nice" Proofs, though one lightly circulated example exists.[118]

The 1868, Proof, a numismatic delicacy.

Small Cents
1857 to Date

AN OVERVIEW OF SMALL CENTS

On May 25, 1857, the U.S. Mint debuted its new small-diameter Flying Eagle cent. Designed by Chief Engraver James B. Longacre, the obverse featured a flying eagle, copied after Christian Gobrecht's silver dollar of 1836. The reverse showed an agricultural wreath enclosing the denomination. Problems developed with striking the pieces up properly, and in 1859 a new type, the Indian Head cent, was introduced. With several variations this design was continued through 1909. In that year the Lincoln cent with Wheat Ears reverse was introduced. The series was continued for many years, until 1959, when the Memorial Reverse type was introduced, continuing the same Lincoln portrait on the obverse. Then in 2009 four different reverses were introduced to commemorate the 200th anniversary of the birth of Abraham Lincoln. In 2010 a new reverse symbolized President Lincoln's preservation of the Union.

Forming a type set of small cents is done easily enough, although the first two issues, the 1857–1858 Flying Eagle cent and the 1859 Indian Head with laurel wreath reverse, can be expensive in higher grades. Striking quality is a consideration for all small cents from 1857 to the end of the Indian Head series in 1909, but enough exist that finding a needle-sharp piece is simply a matter of time. Lincoln cents are easy enough to find sharply struck, though some varieties are more difficult to find this way than others.

FOR THE COLLECTOR AND INVESTOR: SMALL CENTS AS A SPECIALTY

Flying Eagle and Indian Head cents often are collected together by specialists, who usually aspire to add the pattern 1856 Flying Eagle to the series. Proof Flying Eagle and Indian Head cents form a separate specialty and are widely collected. The Flying Eagle and Indian Cent Collectors Society (www.fly-inclub.org) welcomes aficionados of these series. Its journal, *Longacre's Ledger*, serves as a forum for new discoveries, market information, and the exchange of ideas and research.

One of the foundations of modern American numismatics is the collecting of Lincoln cents, 1909 to date. Collectors have a wide variety of folders, albums, and holders to choose from; these have a tradition dating back to the

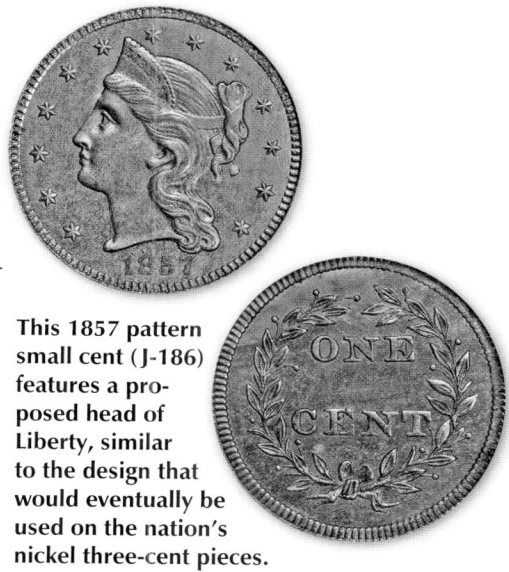

This 1857 pattern small cent (J-186) features a proposed head of Liberty, similar to the design that would eventually be used on the nation's nickel three-cent pieces.

1930s, when R.K. Post of Neenah, Wisconsin, launched his "penny boards" (made for him by Whitman Publishing Co., which later acquired the rights), and Wayte Raymond marketed a series of "National" album pages. Today, a search through pocket change might yield coins dating back to 1959, the first year of the Lincoln Memorial reverse, before which date even high-mintage issues are hardly ever seen. A generation ago it was possible to find cents from 1909 onward. However, key issues such as 1909-S V.D.B. (the most famous of all "popular rarities" in the U.S. series), 1914-D, 1924-D, 1926-S, 1931-S, and 1955 Doubled Die eluded most enthusiasts.

Lincoln cents can be collected casually, or a specialty can be made of them. A dedicated enthusiast may want to secure one each in a grade such as MS-65, also taking care that each is sharply struck. There are quite a few issues, including Denver and San Francisco varieties from about 1916 to the late 1920s, that are plentiful *except* if sharply struck (with full hair detail on the Lincoln portrait, no tiny marks on Lincoln's shoulder, and sharp details and a smooth field on the reverse). Die-variety specialists have dozens of popular doubled dies, overmintmarks, and other varieties to hunt down, using the *Cherrypickers' Guide* as their standard reference. With the Mint's rollout of four new reverse designs in 2009, and another in 2010, the Lincoln cent promises to intrigue another generation of Americans and continue to bring new collectors to the hobby.

FLYING EAGLE (1857–1858)

Designer: *James B. Longacre.* **Weight:** *4.67 grams.* **Composition:** *.880 copper, .120 nickel.*
Diameter: *19 mm.* **Edge:** *Plain.* **Mint:** *Philadelphia.*

Circulation Strike Proof

History. The nation's large copper cents became increasingly expensive to produce, leading the U.S. Mint to experiment with smaller versions during the 1850s. Finally a new design and format were chosen: the Flying Eagle cent, of smaller diameter and 4.67 grams' weight (compared to nearly 11). Many patterns were made of this design in 1856 (for distribution to interested congressmen), and later restrikes (bearing that same date) were extensive, with the result that many numismatists collect the 1856 cent along with the regular series. Distribution of the new 1857, Flying Eagle, cents for circulation commenced on May 25 of that year. Problems resulted from striking the design properly, and the motif was discontinued in 1858. Although attempts were made to create a modified, thinner eagle, the unattractive results were scrapped in favor of an entirely new design. The coins remained in circulation until the early 1900s, by which time any found in pocket change were well worn.

Striking and Sharpness. The heavy wreath on the reverse was opposite in the dies (while in the press) from the head and tail of the eagle on the obverse, and, accordingly, many Flying Eagle cents were weakly struck in these areas. Today, this lightness of strike is most visible at each end of the eagle and on the wreath, particularly the higher areas, and on the vertical separation at the middle of the ribbon knot. Striking weakness is most obvious (especially for novice collectors) on the eagle's tail feathers. Many Flying Eagle cents, however, are quite well struck. A first-class Proof should have a fully and deeply mirrored field on both sides, except for those of 1856, which are usually a combination of mirrorlike and grainy in character.

Availability. As a type the Flying Eagle cent is easy to find, although some varieties, such as 1856 and 1858, 8 Over 7, range from scarce to rare. Most are seen in worn grades. In MS, many are in the marketplace, although dipping, cleaning, and recoloring (causing staining and spotting) have eliminated the majority from consideration by connoisseurs. Proof Flying Eagle cents dated 1856 are plentiful, surviving from the quantity of perhaps 2,000 to 2,500 or more restruck in 1859 and later. (Today's collectors do not distinguish, price-wise, between the 1856 originals and restrikes dated 1856.) Proofs of 1857 are very rare. Proofs of 1858 are rare, but are significantly more readily available than for 1857. Some prooflike Mint State coins have been called Proofs. Quality is a challenge for Proofs, and problem-free examples are in the minority.

GRADING STANDARDS

MS-60 to 70 (Mint State). *Obverse:* Contact marks, most obvious in the field, are evident at MS-60, diminishing at MS-61, 62, and higher. The eagle, the feathers of which usually hide marks, shows some evidence as well. At Gem MS-65 or finer there is no trace of friction or rubbing. A few tiny nicks or marks may be seen, but none are obvious. At MS-67 and higher levels the coin will approach perfection. A theoretically perfect MS-70 will

1857, Snow-2. Graded MS-65.

have no marks at all evident, even under a strong magnifier. Although in practice this is not always consistent, at MS-66 and higher there should be no staining or other problems, and the coin should have good eye appeal overall. *Reverse:* Check the higher parts of the wreath for slight abrasions at MS-60 to 62. Otherwise, the above guidelines apply.

Illustrated coin: Both sides of this coin exhibit crisp striking detail and smooth, satiny luster. Pinkish-rose in general, it has a splash of light red tinting on the obverse over the eagle's right wing.

AU-50, 53, 55, 58 (About Uncirculated). *Obverse:* At AU-50, light wear is seen on the breast of the eagle, the top edge of the closest wing, and, less so, on the head. As both the head and tail tip can be lightly struck, these are not reliable indicators of grade. Luster is present in traces among the letters. At higher About Uncirculated levels the evidence of wear diminishes. An AU-58 coin will have nearly full luster, but friction is seen in the

1856. Graded AU-50.

fields, as are some marks. *Reverse:* At AU-50, light wear is seen on the ribbon bow and the highest areas of the leaves. Some luster is seen (more than on the obverse). Friction is evident, as are some marks, but these will not be as distracting as those on the obverse, as the heavy wreath and lettering are more protective of the reverse field. In higher grades, wear is less, and at AU-58 nearly full—or even completely full—luster is seen.

Illustrated coin: This is a well-struck example of this rate date. Some slightly mottled toning is on the obverse.

EF-40, 45 (Extremely Fine). *Obverse:* Wear is more extensive, especially on the eagle's breast and the top of the closest wing. Wear will also show on the other wing in the area below OF. Marks may be more extensive in the field. The wear is slightly greater at EF-40 than at EF-45, although in the marketplace these two grades are not clearly differentiated. *Reverse:* More wear shows on the higher areas of the wreath, but most detail

1856. Graded EF-40.

will still be present. There may be tinges of luster in protected areas, more likely at EF-45 than at 40.

VF-20, 30 (Very Fine). *Obverse:* Wear is appreciable, with the breast feathers gone over a larger area and with more wear on the wings. The tail shows significant wear, negating the aspect as to whether it was well struck originally. Marks are more extensive, although across all grades the durable copper-nickel metal resisted heavy marks and cuts; any such should be separately described. Staining and spotting, not related to grade, is common.

1858, Small Letters. Graded VF-20.

Cherrypicking (examining multiple coins, all slabbed at the same grade level, and selecting the finest of them) at this and lower grades will yield nice coins in any given category. *Reverse:* The wreath is worn flat in the higher and medium-relief areas, although some detail is seen in the lower areas close to the field. ONE / CENT may be slightly weak, depending on the quality of original strike. Marks are fewer than on the obverse.

F-12, 15 (Fine). *Obverse:* The eagle shows extensive wear, with about half of the feathers gone. Some detail is still seen, especially on the underside of the closest wing, above the breast. *Reverse:* Wear is even more extensive, with the wreath nearing flatness, but still with some detail in the lower areas.

1857. Graded F-12.

VG-8, 10 (Very Good). *Obverse:* On the obverse the eagle is clear in outline form, but only a small number of feathers can be discerned, mostly above the breast. Letters and the date show extensive wear but are complete and clear. *Reverse:* The wreath is now mostly an outline, although some lower-relief features can be differentiated. ONE / CENT may be weak (depending on the strike).

1858, Large Letters. Graded VG-8.

G-4, 6 (Good). *Obverse:* The eagle is nearly completely flat, with just a few feathers, if any, discernible. The rim is worn down, making the outer parts of the letters and the lower part of the date slightly weak, but all are readable. *Reverse:* The wreath is basically in outline form, with hardly any detail. ONE / CENT is weak, usually with CENT weakest. The rim is worn down.

1858, Large Letters. Graded G-6.

AG-3 (About Good). *Obverse:* Wear is extensive, but most of the eagle is visible in outline form. The letters are mostly worn away, with vestiges remaining here and there. The date is partially worn away at the bottom, but is distinct and readable. *Reverse:* The wreath is so worn that it cannot be distinguished from the field in areas, usually toward the top. ONE / CENT is mostly gone, but much of CENT can be discerned (unless the coin was a weak strike to begin with).

1856. Graded AG-3.

PF-60 to 70 (Proof). *Obverse and Reverse:* Gem PF-65 coins have very few hairlines, and these are visible only under a strong magnifying glass. At the PF-67 level or higher there should be no evidence of hairlines or friction at all. PF-60 coins can be dull from repeated dipping and cleaning (remember, hairlines on any Proof were caused by cleaning with an abrasive agent; they had no hairlines when struck). At PF-63 the mirrorlike fields should

1858, Large Letters. Graded PF-66 Cameo.

be attractive, and hairlines should be minimal, best seen when the coin is held at an angle to the light. No rubbing is seen. PF-64 coins are even nicer.

1857, Reverse 25¢ Clash
FS-01-1857-901.

1857, Obverse $20 Clash
FS-01-1857-403.

1858, Large Letters **1858, Small Letters**

1858, 8 Over 7
FS-01-1858-301.

	Mintage	Cert	Avg	%MS	G-4	VG-8	F-12	VF-20	EF-40	AU-50	MS-60BN PF-60	MS-63BN PF-63BN	MS-65 PF-65BN
1856 † (a)	2,000	0	n/a		$6,500	$7,500	$9,000	$11,000	$12,500	$14,500	$16,500	$20,000	$55,000
Auctions: $32,900, MS-64, April 2013													
1856, Proof	1,500	403	58.8								$14,000	$18,500	$28,000
Auctions: $38,188, PF-65, January 2014; $14,100, PF-63, August 2014													
1857	17,450,000	3,424	53.7	61%	$30	$40	$50	$60	$150	$225	$380	$900	$4,000
Auctions: $21,150, MS-66, June 2014; $4,113, MS-65, November 2014; $2,468, MS-64+, November 2014; $2,350, MS-64, July 2014													
1857, Obverse 50¢ Clash (b)	(c)	119	34.7	26%					$250	$450	$800	$1,250	
Auctions: $3,525, MS-65, October 2014; $5,816, MS-65, October 2013													
1857, Reverse 25¢ Clash (d)	(c)	37	44.2	35%					$200	$400	$850	$2,750	
Auctions: $223, EF-40, July 2014													
1857, Obverse $20 Clash (e)	(c)	18	20.0	0%					$2,500	$6,000	$15,000		
Auctions: $242, F-12, March 2011													
1857, Proof	100	35	63.9								$5,000	$8,500	$25,000
Auctions: $34,075, PF-65, October 2014; $8,813, PF-64, October 2014													
1858, All kinds	24,600,000												
1858, Large Letters		1,523	49.2	49%	$30	$40	$50	$60	$150	$225	$375	$900	$4,000
Auctions: $9,988, MS-66, October 2014; $17,625, MS-66, June 2013; $3,290, MS-65, November 2014; $1,645, MS-64, October 2014													
1858, 8 Over 7 (f)		171	53.2	53%	$75	$100	$200	$400	$850	$1,500	$3,500	$8,500	$50,000
Auctions: $74,025, MS-65, October 2014; $70,500, MS-65, April 2013; $764, AU-55, July 2014; $317, VF-25, August 2014													
1858, Small Letters		1,721	47.1	43%	$30	$40	$50	$60	$150	$225	$400	$950	$4,000
Auctions: $24,675, MS-66, October 2014; $16,450, MS-66, August 2013; $3,525, MS-65, August 2014; $2,233, MS-64, November 2014													
1858, Large Letters, Proof	100	35	64.7								$5,000	$8,500	$25,000
Auctions: $20,563, PF-65, October 2014; $8,225, PF-64, October 2014													
1858, Small Letters, Proof	200	25	64.2								$5,000	$8,500	$25,000
Auctions: $32,900, PF-66, January 2014; $14,100, PF-64, October 2014; $7,638, PF-64, October 2014													

† Ranked in the *100 Greatest U.S. Coins* (fourth edition). **a.** Actually a pattern, but collected along with the regular issue since it shares the same design. See *United States Pattern Coins*, tenth edition. **b.** The obverse die was clashed with the obverse die of a Liberty Seated half dollar. This is most evident through AMERICA. **c.** Included in circulation-strike 1857 mintage figure. **d.** The reverse die was clashed with the reverse die of a Liberty Seated quarter dollar. The outline of the eagle's head is evident above ONE. **e.** The obverse die was clashed with the obverse die of a Liberty Head double eagle. **f.** The flag of the upper-right corner of a 7 can be seen above the second 8 in the date. There is a raised triangular dot in the field above the first 8. Late-die-state specimens are worth considerably less than the values listed, which are for early die states.

INDIAN HEAD (1859–1909)

Variety 1 (Copper-Nickel, Laurel Wreath Reverse, 1859):
Designer: *James B. Longacre.* **Weight:** *4.67 grams.* **Composition:** *.880 copper, .120 nickel.*
Diameter: *19 mm.* **Edge:** *Plain.* **Mint:** *Philadelphia.*

Copper-Nickel,
Laurel Wreath Reverse,
Without Shield (1859)

Copper-Nickel,
Laurel Wreath Reverse,
Without Shield, Proof

Variety 2 (Copper-Nickel, Oak Wreath With Shield, 1860–1864):
Designer: *James B. Longacre.* **Weight:** *4.67 grams.* **Composition:** *.880 copper, .120 nickel.*
Diameter: *19 mm.* **Edge:** *Plain.* **Mint:** *Philadelphia.*

Copper-Nickel,
Oak Wreath Reverse,
With Shield (1860–1864)

Copper-Nickel,
Oak Wreath Reverse,
With Shield, Proof

Variety 3 (Bronze, 1864–1909): **Designer:** *James B. Longacre.*
Weight: *3.11 grams.* **Composition:** *.950 copper, .050 tin and zinc.*
Diameter: *19 mm.* **Edge:** *Plain.* **Mints:** *Philadelphia, San Francisco.*

Bronze, Oak Wreath Reverse,
With Shield (1864–1909)

Bronze, Oak Wreath Reverse,
With Shield, Proof

History. After nearly a dozen varieties of patterns were made in 1858, in 1859 the Indian Head was adopted as the new motif for the cent. Observers of the time noted the incongruity of placing a Native American war bonnet on a bust which was meant to be both female and classically Greek; designer James B. Longacre's earlier use of a feathered tiara on the Indian Head three-dollar gold piece had been viewed as less strange. The reverse of the 1859 coin illustrates an olive (or laurel) wreath. In 1860 this was changed to a wreath of oak and other leaves with a shield at the apex, a design continued through the end of the series in 1909. From 1859 through spring 1864 cents were struck in copper-nickel, the alloy used earlier for Flying Eagle cents. In 1864 a new bronze alloy was adopted.

Indian Head cents remained in circulation through the 1940s, but by the early 1950s were rarely seen. In the 1930s, when Whitman and other coin boards and folders became widely available, collectors picked many key dates out of circulation. The typical grade for the scarce issues of the 1870s was Good or so, and the 1908-S and 1909-S could be found in VF.

Striking and Sharpness. The strike on Indian Head cents can vary widely. On the obverse the points to check include the details at the tips of the feathers and the diamonds on the ribbon. The diamonds *cannot* be used as a grading marker, and the feather tips can be used only if you have familiarity with how sharp the coin was struck to begin with. In general, the reverse is usually sharper, but check the leaf and shield details. On many bronze cents beginning in the 1870s the bottom of the N of ONE and the tops of the EN of CENT are light, as they were in the dies (this is not factored when grading). Check the denticles on both sides. Generally, copper-nickel cents of the early 1860s are candidates for light striking as are later issues in the bronze format, of the 1890s onward.

Availability. In worn grades Indian Head cents are available in proportion to their mintages, in combination with survival rates being higher for the later issues. (The low-mintage 1909-S was saved in larger quantities than the higher-mintage 1877, as an example.) MS coins survive as a matter of chance, with those of 1878 and before being much scarcer than those of 1879 and later, and some of the 1900s being readily available. Many if not most higher-grade MS coins have been dipped or recolored, unless they are a warm orange-red color with traces of natural brown. The search for quality among bronze cents is particularly challenging. Some tiny toning flecks are to be expected on many coins, and as long as they are microscopic they can often be ignored (except in grades on the far side of MS-65). A set of MS-65 coins in RB or RD can be formed quickly, but a collection with *original* color, sharp strike, and excellent eye appeal may take several years.

During the years these coins were in production, collectors who wanted single pieces each year often bought Proofs. In the late 1930s, many 1878–1909 Proof Indian Head cents began to be released from several estate hoards. These had vivid violet and blue iridescent toning from being stored for decades in tissue paper. They are highly sought-after today.

Proofs. Proof Indian Head cents were made of all dates 1859 to 1909. The 1864 bronze variety with a tiny L (for designer James B. Longacre) on the ribbon is a rarity, with only about two dozen known. Generally, Proofs are sharp strikes until the 1890s, when some can be weak. On bronze coins tiny carbon flecks are typical, but should be microscopic. If larger, avoid, and at PF-65 or higher, avoid as well. The majority of Proofs have been dipped, and many bronze pieces have been retoned. Most undipped coins are either rich brown (can be very attractive) or red and brown. The late John J. Pittman spent 50 years trying to find a Gem Proof 1907 Indian Head cent with brilliant original color! Cherrypicking is the order of the day. Extra value can be found in BN and RB, simply because investors won't buy them; instead, they are drawn to RD coins, most of which have been "improved" (dipped and retoned).

Proofs are generally designated BN if the surfaces are mainly brown or iridescent, or have up to perhaps 30% original mint red-orange color (there is little consistency, within the hobby community, in this determination). RB is the designation if the surface is a mixture of red-orange and brown, best if blended together nicely, but often with patches of mint color among brown areas. RD designates a coin with original (in theory) mint-red orange, always blending to slight natural brown toning unless the coin has been dipped. Likely, any RD coin with even a few hairlines has been cleaned (or at least mishandled) at one time; in most such cases, what appears to be mint-red color is not original. Certification services take no notice of this. For this reason, a connoisseur will prefer a gem BN coin with no hairlines to a PF-65 or 66 RD coin with some hairlines. Proof copper-nickel Indian Head cents of 1859 to 1864 need no letter to indicate color, as their hue derives more from the nickel than the copper. As a general rule, these survive in higher grades and with greater eye appeal, as they stayed "brilliant" (the watchword for most collectors until recent decades) and did not need dipping. Moreover, when such pieces were cleaned and acquired hairlines, they tended to be fewer than on a bronze coin, due to the very hard nature of the copper-nickel alloy.

GRADING STANDARDS

MS-60 to 70 (Mint State). *Obverse:* Contact marks, most obvious in the field, are evident at MS-60, diminishing at MS-61, 62, and higher. This abrasion is most noticeable on copper-nickel cents, for it blends in with the background on bronze issues. The cheek of the Indian and the field show some evidence as well. Typical color is BN, occasionally RB at MS-63 and 64, unless dipped to be RD. At gem MS-65 or finer there is no trace of abra-

1894. Graded MS-66+RD.

sion. A few tiny nicks or marks may be seen, but none are obvious. At MS-67 and finer the coin will approach perfection. Check "RD" coins for originality. A theoretically perfect MS-70 will have no marks at all, even under a strong magnifier. Although in practice this is not always consistent, at MS-66 and higher there should be no staining or other problems, and the coin should have good eye appeal overall. *Reverse:* Check the high parts of the wreath for abrasion. Otherwise the above comments apply.

Illustrated coin: Absolutely unblemished, this lovely gem retains every bit of its original, reddish-orange mint color and frosty texture.

AU-50, 53, 55, 58 (About Uncirculated). *Obverse:* At AU-50, wear is most noticeable on the hair above the ear, on the central portion of the ribbon, on the curl to the right of the ribbon, and near the feather tips, although the last is not a reliable indicator due to strik-ing. Luster is present, but mostly in protected areas. At AU-53 and 55, wear is less. At AU-58 friction is evident, rather than actual wear. Luster, toned brown, is nearly com-

1873, Close 3, with doubled LIBERTY. Graded AU-50.

plete at AU-58, but may be incomplete in the field. *Reverse:* At AU-50, light wear is seen on the ribbon and the higher-relief areas of the leaves, while the lower areas retain their detail. Some luster may be present in protected areas. At AU-53 and 55, wear is less and luster is more extensive. An AU-58 coin will have nearly full luster and show only light friction.

Illustrated coin: This is a coin with excellent eye appeal. Its glossy brown surfaces retain some luster.

EF-40, 45 (Extremely Fine). *Obverse:* Wear is more extensive, but all of LIBERTY is very clear. Wear is seen on the hair above and below the ear, on the central portion of the ribbon, and on the feather tips. Overall the coin is bold. Scattered marks are normal for this and lower grades, most often seen on the cheek and in the field. *Reverse:* The higher-relief parts of the leaves and ribbon bow show light wear, but details are sharp in lower

1869. Graded EF-45.

areas. Some tiny lines in the vertical stripes in the shield may be blended. Scattered marks may be pres-ent, but on all grades they are usually fewer on the reverse than on the obverse.

VF-20, 30 (Very Fine). *Obverse:* Wear is more extensive. LIBERTY shows significant wear on BE but is sharp overall. Most hair detail is gone. The feather tips show greater wear (the extent of which will depend on the original strike). The ribbon and hair no longer show separation. *Reverse:* Wear is more extensive than on the preceding, and many tiny vertical lines are fused together. Detail is still good on lower levels of the leaves.

1877. Graded VF-30.

   Illustrated coin: Note the slight granularity to the surfaces.

F-12, 15 (Fine). *Obverse:* By tradition the word LIBERTY should be fully readable, but weak on the higher letters of LIB. PCGS suggests this is true except if a coin was lightly struck. Full or incomplete, well struck or lightly struck, no matter what the coin, most buyers still want the word to be discernible. Other areas have correspondingly more wear than on the next-higher grade. *Reverse:* The higher areas of the leaves and the bow show

1909-S. Graded F-12.

wear. The shield shows greater wear than on the preceding. Overall, the reverse appears to be less worn than the obverse, this being generally true of all circulated grades.

VG-8, 10 (Very Good). *Obverse:* A total of at least three letters in LIBERTY must be visible. This can be a combination of several partial letters. PCGS does not adhere to this rule and suggests that wear on the feathers is a better indicator. The rim may blend into the field in areas, depending on striking. *Reverse:* Wear is even more extensive. Leaves on the left have hardly any detail, while those on the right may have limited detail. The rim is complete.

1877. Graded VG-8.

   Illustrated coin: The weakness at the base of the N of ONE is due to the nature of the dies, not to wear.

G-4, 6 (Good). *Obverse:* The coin is worn flat, with the portrait visible mostly in outline form, with only slight indication of feathers. Lettering and date are complete. Part of the rim is usually gone. At G-6, the rim is clearer. *Reverse:* The wreath is nearly flat, although some hints of detail may be seen on the right side. All letters are readable, although the inscription is light at the center (on issues from the 1870s onward). The rim is discernible all around, but is light in areas. At G-6 the rim is clearly delineated.

1877. Graded G-4 or slightly better.

Illustrated coin: This is a "strong" Good, a candidate for G-6 (not an official ANA grade, but widely used), with excellent definition within that grade. The weakness at the base of the N of ONE is due to the nature of the dies, not to wear.

AG-3 (About Good). *Obverse:* Most letters are worn away, as is the rim. The portrait is in outline form. The date is clearly readable, but may be weak or missing at the bottom. *Reverse:* Extensive wear prevails, although the rim will usually be more discernible than on the obverse. Most lettering, or sometimes all, is readable.

Illustrated coin: As is often the case, the reverse, if evaluated separately, could be graded G-4. Some light spotting is acceptable.

1877. Graded AG-3.

PF-60 to 70 (Proof). *Obverse and Reverse:* Gem PF-65 coins will have very few hairlines, and these are visible only under a strong magnifying glass. At any level and color, a Proof with hairlines likely (though not necessarily) has been cleaned. At PF-67 or higher there should be no evidence of hairlines or friction at all. Such a coin is fully original. PF-60 coins can be dull from repeated dipping and cleaning and are often toned iridescent colors. At

1864, Copper-Nickel. Graded PF-66.

PF-63 the mirrorlike fields should be attractive, and hairlines should be minimal. These are easiest to see when the coin is held at an angle to the light. No rubbing is seen. PF-64 coins are even nicer.

COPPER-NICKEL COINAGE

| **1860, Rounded Bust** | | **1860, Pointed Bust** |

	Mintage	Cert	Avg	%MS	G-4	VG-8	F-12	VF-20	EF-40	AU-50	MS-60BN PF-63BN	MS-63BN PF-64BN	MS-65 PF-65BN
1859	36,400,000	2,032	57.4	65%	$15	$20	$25	$55	$110	$200	$285	$600	$3,500
	Auctions: $23,500, MS-66+, November 2014; $11,750, MS-66, April 2013; $3,966, MS-65, September 2014												
1859, Proof	*800*	196	64.4								$1,600	$3,000	$5,000
	Auctions: $13,513, PF-66Cam, June 2014; $4,700, PF-66, September 2014; $3,173, PF-64, October 2014												
1859, Oak Wreath With Shield, experimental reverse (a)		0	n/a									$2,000	
	Auctions: No auction records available.												
1860, Rounded Bust	20,566,000	1,180	59.8	75%	$10	$15	$20	$35	$65	$100	$185	$250	$1,200
	Auctions: $8,813, MS-66, January 2014; $3,290, MS-66, October 2014; $2,938, MS-66, October 2014; $764, MS-64, December 2014												
1860, Pointed Bust	**(b)**	154	58.9	73%	$20	$25	$30	$50	$100	$165	$300	$575	$3,500
	Auctions: $32,900, MS-67, February 2014; $7,931, MS-66, October 2014; $2,409, MS-65, August 2014; $1,469, MS-64, July 2014												
1860, Rounded Bust, Proof	*1,000*	56	64.8								$1,000	$2,200	$3,500
	Auctions: $9,989, PF-66, April 2014; $5,875, PF-66, August 2014; $8,813, PF-66, October 2014; $4,137, PF-66, October 2014												

a. 1,000 pieces were made but never released for circulation. b. Included in circulation-strike 1860, Rounded Bust, mintage figure.

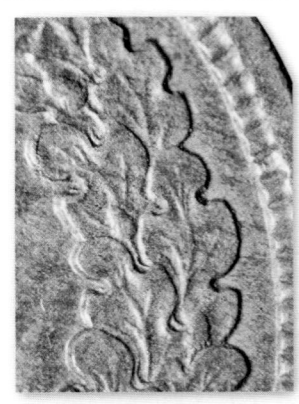

1863, Doubled-Die Reverse
FS-01-1863-801.

	Mintage	Cert	Avg	%MS	G-4	VG-8	F-12	VF-20	EF-40	AU-50	MS-60BN PF-63BN	MS-63BN PF-64BN	MS-65 PF-65BN
1861	10,100,000	1,124	56.7	67%	$25	$35	$45	$60	$110	$175	$225	$325	$1,100
	Auctions: $14,100, MS-67, October 2014; $4,113, MS-66, February 2014; $2,820, MS-66, September 2014												
1861, Proof	*1,000*	84	64.2								$1,500	$3,400	$7,750
	Auctions: $24,675, PF-66, September 2013; $2,585, PF-64, October 2014; $1,763, PF-64, October 2014												
1862	28,075,000	1,774	61.3	83%	$10	$15	$20	$30	$50	$75	$110	$200	$1,000
	Auctions: $15,275, MS-67, February 2013; $11,163, MS-67, October 2014; $8,813, MS-67, November 2014												
1862, Proof	*550*	308	64.7								$900	$1,300	$2,500
	Auctions: $11,750, PF-67Cam, September 2014; $2,468, PF-66Cam, November 2014; $4,113, PF-66, June 2014												
1863	49,840,000	2,368	61.2	82%	$10	$15	$20	$30	$50	$75	$110	$200	$1,000
	Auctions: $3,055, MS-66, August 2014; $1,998, MS-66, November 2014; $2,820, MS-66, August 2013; $969, MS-65, July 2014												
1863, Doubled-Die Reverse (c)	**(d)**	2	62.5	100%					$200	$375	$450	$950	$3,000
	Auctions: No auction records available.												
1863, Proof	*460*	143	64.3								$900	$1,300	$2,500
	Auctions: $9,988, PF-67Cam, September 2014; $1,998, PF-65Cam, July 2014; $1,058, PF-64Cam, November 2014												
1864, Copper-Nickel	13,740,000	1,524	58.9	75%	$20	$30	$40	$55	$100	$150	$200	$325	$1,600
	Auctions: $6,463, MS-66, April 2014; $3,055, MS-66, November 2014; $1,351, MS-65, October 2014; $676, MS-64, July 2014												
1864, Copper-Nickel, Proof	*370*	154	64.3								$900	$1,300	$2,500
	Auctions: $12,925, PF-66DCam, July 2014												

c. Strong doubling is evident on the right leaves of the wreath, and, to a lesser degree, on the upper left leaves. **d.** Included in circulation-strike 1863 mintage figure.

Bronze Coinage

   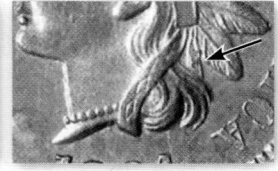

1864, No L   **1864, With L**

	Mintage	Cert	Avg	%MS	G-4	VG-8	F-12	VF-20	EF-40	AU-50	MS-60BN PF-63BN	MS-63BN PF-64RB	MS-65RB PF-65RD	MS-65RD
1864, Bronze, All kinds	39,233,714													
1864, No L		1,278	60.5	86%	$15	$20	$25	$45	$70	$90	$115	$150	$400	$1,000
	Auctions: $764, MS-66RB, September 2014; $881, MS-65RD, August 2014; $306, MS-64RB, October 2014													
1864, With L		1,380	52.4	52%	$55	$80	$150	$200	$275	$350	$450	$600	$1,800	$5,000
	Auctions: $2,115, MS-65RB, May 2013; $1,469, MS-64RD, November 2014; $1,293, MS-64RB, July 2014; $646, MS-62RB, September 2014													
1864, No L, Proof	*150+*	122	64.7								$500	$1,750	$9,000	
	Auctions: $17,625, PF-67RB, April 2013; $2,585, PF-65RB, November 2014; $2,129, PF-65RB, October 2014													
1864, With L, Proof	*20+*	6	64.5								$12,500	$45,000		
	Auctions: $141,000, PF-65RD, September 2013													

**1865, Die Gouge
in Headdress**
FS-01-1865-1401.

1865, Doubled-Die Reverse
FS-01-1865-1801.

1869, 9 Over 9
FS-01-1869-301.

Shallow N

Bold N

	Mintage	Cert	Avg	%MS	G-4	VG-8	F-12	VF-20	EF-40	AU-50	MS-60BN	MS-63BN / PF-63BN	MS-65RB / PF-64RB	MS-65RD / PF-65RD
1865	35,429,286	917	61.3	85%	$15	$20	$25	$30	$45	$65	$90	$150	$600	$1,750
Auctions: $1,998, MS-66RB, October 2014; $1,998, MS-65RD, March 2013; $270, MS-64BN, October 2014; $165, MS-64BN, September 2014														
1865, Die Gouge in Headdress (a)	(b)	0	n/a							$500	$750	$1,200	
Auctions: No auction records available.														
1865, Doubled-Die Reverse	(b)	10	41.6	40%					$800	$1,100	$2,200	$5,500		
Auctions: $1,175, AU-55, April 2013														
1865, Proof	500+	140	64.3									$375	$850	$7,500
Auctions: $14,100, PF-65Cam, August 2014; $15,275, PF-66RD, October 2014; $12,925, PF-65RD, June 2014; $3,055, PF-64RD, October 2014														
1866	9,826,500	959	55.5	62%	$50	$65	$80	$100	$190	$250	$290	$380	$1,500	$4,000
Auctions: $1,087, MS-66BN, September 2014; $3,290, MS-65RD, June 2014; $499, MS-63RB, August 2014; $212, MS-62BN, October 2014														
1866, Proof	725+	123	64.5									$400	$750	$5,000
Auctions: $21,150, PF-66Cam, June 2014; $2,820, PF-65Cam, October 2014; $999, PF-65RB, July 2014; $529, PF-64BN, November 2014														
1867	9,821,000	926	54.8	63%	$50	$70	$90	$135	$230	$275	$300	$400	$1,600	$6,000
Auctions: $6,463, MS-65RD, February 2014; $1,293, MS-65RB, October 2014; $6,756, MS-65RD, October 2014														
1867, Proof	625+	188	64.4									$400	$750	$5,000
Auctions: $3,525, PF-66RB, July 2014; $6,463, PF-66RD, March 2014; $705, PF-64RB, August 2014; $306, PF-63BN, October 2014														
1868	10,266,500	906	54.9	63%	$40	$50	$70	$125	$170	$220	$250	$360	$925	$4,000
Auctions: $1,880, MS-66RB, September 2014; $29,375, MS-66RD, April 2014; $3,525, MS-65RD, October 2014														
1868, Proof	600+	127	64.4									$375	$600	$5,000
Auctions: $17,625, PF-66RD, June 2014; $6,756, PF-65RD, September 2014; $588, PF-63BN, October 2014														
1869	6,420,000	956	48.1	51%	$85	$120	$235	$335	$445	$550	$600	$700	$1,800	$4,750
Auctions: $3,290, MS-66RB, August 2013; $1,763, MS-64RB, October 2014; $499, MS-61BN, November 2014; $1,175, MS-60BN, July 2014														
1869, 9 Over 9	(c)	341	43.7	40%	$125	$225	$450	$575	$725	$825	$975	$1,200	$2,400	
Auctions: $1,645, MS-64RB, November 2014; $3,055, MS-64RD, August 2014; $1,410, MS-63RB, September 2014														
1869, Proof	600+	170	64.4									$380	$650	$3,000
Auctions: $4,847, PF-66Cam, June 2014; $11,750, PF-66RD, October 2014; $1,528, PF-65RB, October 2014; $558, PF-64RB, November 2014														
1870, Shallow N	5,275,000	3	38.7	33%	$80	$100	$220	$320	$400	$500	$550	$900	$1,500	
Auctions: $1,265, MS-64RB, March 2012														
1870, Bold N	(d)	861	49.3	51%	$55	$75	$200	$280	$375	$450	$500	$850	$1,300	$4,200
Auctions: $23,500, MS-66RD, May 2013; $3,819, MS-65RD, October 2014; $1,880, MS-65RB, November 2014; $705, MS-65BN, July 2014														

Note: Cents dated 1869 and earlier have a shallow N in ONE. Those dated 1870, 1871, or 1872 have either shallow N or bold N, except Proofs of 1872, which were struck only with the bold N, not the shallow N. Those dated 1873 to 1876 all have the bold N. Circulation strikes of 1877 have the shallow N, while Proofs have the bold N. **a.** Currently described as a die gouge in the *Cherrypickers' Guide to Rare Die Varieties*, sixth edition, volume I, the curved "gouge" is a mark from the Janvier reducing lathe. **b.** Included in circulation-strike 1865 mintage figure. **c.** Included in circulation-strike 1869 mintage figure. **d.** Included in circulation-strike 1870, Shallow N, mintage figure.

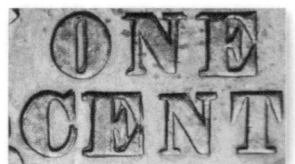

1870, Doubled-Die Reverse
FS-01-1870-801.

1873, Close 3

1873, Open 3

1873, Doubled LIBERTY
FS-01-1873-101.

	Mintage	Cert	Avg	%MS	G-4	VG-8	F-12	VF-20	EF-40	AU-50	MS-60BN	MS-63BN / PF-63BN	MS-65RB / PF-64RB	MS-65RD / PF-65RD
1870, Doubled-Die Reverse	(d)	10	56.3	80%					$575	$750	$850	$1,000	$2,500	$4,150
Auctions: $1,035, MS-64RB, January 2012														
1870, Shallow N, Proof	1,000+	175	64.3									$325	$525	$1,900
Auctions: $1,380, PF-65RB, April 2012														
1870, Bold N, Proof	(e)	(f)										$325	$750	$2,500
Auctions: $3,173, PF-67RB, August 2014; $10,575, PF-66RD, January 2014; $9,988, PF-66RD, July 2014; $1,528, PF-64RD, November 2014														
1871, Shallow N	3,929,500	2	54.0	0%	$130	$180	$325	$450	$575	$650	$775	$950	$2,600	
Auctions: $2,585, MS-63RB, February 2013														
1871, Bold N	(g)	955	47.4	47%	$70	$85	$250	$350	$475	$525	$550	$800	$2,350	$7,000
Auctions: $44,063, MS-66RD, January 2014; $999, MS-64BN, November 2014; $999, MS-62BN, October 2014														
1871, Shallow N, Proof	960+	199	64.2									$500	$875	$2,350
Auctions: $7,344, PF-65RD, January 2013														
1871, Bold N, Proof	(h)	(i)										$325	$600	$2,150
Auctions: $2,350, PF-65RD, June 2014; $499, PF-65BN, October 2014; $294, PF-62BN, November 2014; $282, PF-60BN, November 2014														
1872, Shallow N	4,042,000	3	34.7	0%	$100	$170	$370	$425	$575	$700	$950	$1,250	$4,500	
Auctions: $881, AU-55, April 2013														
1872, Bold N	(j)	1,107	45.1	41%	$90	$140	$300	$375	$500	$650	$785	$1,150	$4,000	$17,000
Auctions: $28,200, MS-65RD, June 2014; $3,819, MS-65RB, August 2014; $5,581, MS-64RD, October 2014; $588, AU-58BN, July 2014														
1872, Bold N, Proof (k)	950+	222	64.3									$400	$700	$4,300
Auctions: $7,050, PF-66RD, October 2014; $705, PF-65BN, November 2014; $705, PF-64RB, November 2014														
1873, All kinds	11,676,500													
1873, Close 3		273	55.2	60%	$25	$35	$65	$125	$185	$235	$410	$550	$2,500	$10,000
Auctions: $6,463, MS-65RD, October 2014; $2,820, MS-65RB, December 2013; $1,293, MS-64RB, October 2014; $793, MS-63RB, July 2014														
1873, Doubled LIBERTY		94	43.2	29%	$200	$350	$825	$1,750	$2,500	$4,500	$6,500	$10,000	$57,500	
Auctions: $9,988, MS-63RB, October 2014; $7,050, MS-63BN, September 2014; $7,638, MS-63BN, June 2013														
1873, Open 3		504	54.1	56%	$20	$30	$50	$85	$160	$190	$250	$325	$1,250	$7,500
Auctions: $4,406, MS-65RD, April 2014; $3,819, MS-65RD, October 2014; $470, MS-64RB, November 2014; $470, MS-63RB, July 2014														
1873, Close 3, Proof	1,100+	235	64.3									$275	$550	$2,000
Auctions: $1,293, PF-65RB, April 2013; $589, PF-64RD, October 2014; $470, PF-64RB, October 2014														
1874	14,187,500	870	57.9	70%	$20	$25	$45	$65	$100	$150	$225	$250	$725	$3,500
Auctions: $1,880, MS-65RD, October 2014; $2,820, MS-65RD, April 2013; $1,116, MS-65RB, October 2014														
1874, Proof	700	163	64.4									$250	$400	$2,000
Auctions: $823, PF-66BN, July 2014; $1,175, PF-65RB, June 2013; $617, PF-64RD, October 2014; $470, PF-64RB, July 2014														

Note: Cents dated 1869 and earlier have a shallow N in ONE. Those dated 1870, 1871, or 1872 have either shallow N or bold N, except Proofs of 1872, which were struck only with the bold N, not the shallow N. Those dated 1873 to 1876 all have the bold N. Circulation strikes of 1877 have the shallow N, while Proofs have the bold N. **d.** Included in circulation-strike 1870, Shallow N, mintage figure. **e.** Included in 1870, Shallow N, Proof, mintage figure. **f.** Included in certified population for 1870, Shallow N, Proof. **g.** Included in circulation-strike 1871, Shallow N, mintage figure. **h.** Included in 1871, Shallow N, Proof, mintage figure. **i.** Included in certified population for 1871, Shallow N, Proof. **j.** Included in 1872, Shallow N, mintage figure. **k.** Proofs of 1872 were struck only with the bold N, not the shallow N.

1875, Dot Reverse
FS-01-1875-801.

1880, Doubled-
Die Obverse,
Reverse Clash
FS-01-1880-101.

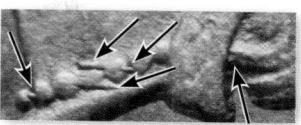

1882, Misplaced Date
FS-01-1882-401.

	Mintage	Cert	Avg	%MS	G-4	VG-8	F-12	VF-20	EF-40	AU-50	MS-60BN	MS-63BN	MS-65RB	MS-65RD
												PF-63BN	PF-64RB	PF-65RD
1875	13,528,000	812	57.3	72%	$20	$35	$60	$75	$120	$160	$235	$265	$900	$3,750
	Auctions: $1,763, MS-66RB, July 2014; $5,581, MS-65RD, December 2013; $881, MS-65RB, August 2014; $646, MS-64RB, August 2014													
1875, Dot Reverse (l)	(m)	0	n/a								—			
	Auctions: $700, AU-50BN, April 2012													
1875, Proof	700	179	64.2									$250	$500	$4,000
	Auctions: $8,813, PF-65RD, June 2014; $306, PF-63RB, October 2014													
1876	7,944,000	779	54.7	64%	$35	$40	$70	$135	$225	$240	$300	$390	$1,000	$3,000
	Auctions: $1,998, MS-65RD, October 2014; $1,880, MS-65RD, October 2013; $1,293, MS-65RB, November 2014; $270, MS-62RB, November 2014													
1876, Proof	1,150	208	64.5									$250	$450	$2,000
	Auctions: $15,275, PF-66Cam, January 2014; $2,585, PF-66RD, October 2014; $646, PF-64RD, October 2014; $823, PF-64BN, November 2014													
1877 (n)	852,500	2,822	23.8	12%	$900	$1,100	$1,550	$2,000	$2,500	$3,000	$3,800	$4,500	$13,500	$25,000
	Auctions: $32,900, MS-65RD, August 2014; $14,100, MS-65RB, January 2014; $9,518, MS-64RB, August 2014; $3,525, AU-58BN, August 2014													
1877, Proof	900	264	63.8									$2,750	$4,500	$15,000
	Auctions: $9,988, PF-66RD, October 2014; $14,100, PF-66RD, June 2013; $3,525, PF-64RB, October 2014; $3,819, PF-63RB, November 2014													
1878	5,797,500	742	56.0	70%	$35	$45	$60	$110	$200	$275	$325	$380	$950	$2,500
	Auctions: $8,813, MS-66RD, September 2014; $1,645, MS-65RD, October 2013; $881, MS-65RB, August 2014; $388, MS-63RB, October 2014													
1878, Proof	2,350	322	64.3									$235	$450	$1,500
	Auctions: $7,638, PF-66Cam, June 2014; $1,763, PF-65Cam, August 2014; $1,116, PF-65Cam, November 2014; $588, PF-64RD, October 2014													
1879	16,228,000	807	61.4	86%	$8	$12	$20	$40	$70	$80	$90	$140	$425	$1,400
	Auctions: $2,233, MS-65RD, June 2014; $470, MS-65RB, November 2014; $259, MS-64RB, July 2014; $247, MS-63RB, August 2014													
1879, Proof	3,200	378	64.5									$150	$325	$1,350
	Auctions: $11,163, PF-67RD, July 2014; $2,115, PF-66Cam, August 2014; $1,645, PF-66RD, October 2014; $217, PF-64BN, November 2014													
1880	38,961,000	703	62.7	93%	$5	$7	$9	$12	$30	$60	$80	$130	$400	$1,300
	Auctions: $5,288, MS-66RD, June 2014; $940, MS-65RD, September 2014; $441, MS-65RB, November 2014; $129, MS-64BN, November 2014													
1880, Doubled-Die Obverse, Reverse Clash (o)	(p)	9	55.3	78%					$390	$750	$1,500	$2,000	$2,900	
	Auctions: $2,070, MS-65BN, June 2009													
1880, Proof	3,955	386	64.4									$150	$325	$1,350
	Auctions: $8,813, PF-67RD, June 2014; $969, PF-66RB, August 2014; $705, PF-65RD, July 2014; $646, PF-65RB+, July 2014													

Note: Cents dated 1869 and earlier have a shallow N in ONE. Those dated 1870, 1871, or 1872 have either shallow N or bold N, except Proofs of 1872, which were struck only with the bold N, not the shallow N. Those dated 1873 to 1876 all have the bold N. Circulation strikes of 1877 have the shallow N, while Proofs have the bold N. **l.** In 1875 Mint officials suspected a longtime employee was stealing Indian Head cents. They secretly modified a reverse die by making a small gouge in the N in ONE, and then put the die into production one morning. Later that morning the suspect employee was called aside. He was asked to empty his pockets, revealing 33 of the marked cents. At first he insisted his son gave him this pocket change, but when confronted with the secretly marked die, he admitted his guilt. He tendered his resignation, disgraced, after more than 50 years of service to the Mint. The market value for this variety is not yet reliably established. **m.** Included in circulation-strike 1875 mintage figure. **n.** Beware the numerous counterfeits and altered-date 1877 cents. The latter typically are altered from 1875- or 1879-dated cents. **o.** Doubling is visible on the obverse in higher grades, as a very close spread on LIBERTY. The primary diagnostic, though, is the misaligned die clash evident on the reverse, with obvious reeding running from the upper-right leaf tip, through the E of ONE, and down to the very top of the N of CENT. **p.** Included in circulation-strike 1880 mintage figure.

1886, Variety 1
The last feather points between the I and the C in AMERICA.

1886, Variety 2
The last feather points between the C and the A in AMERICA.

1887, Doubled-Die Obverse
FS-01-1887-101.

	Mintage	Cert	Avg	%MS	G-4	VG-8	F-12	VF-20	EF-40	AU-50	MS-60BN	MS-63BN	MS-65RB	MS-65RD
												PF-63BN	PF-64RB	PF-65RD
1881	39,208,000	729	62.7	94%	$5	$6	$8	$10	$25	$35	$60	$90	$315	$1,350
Auctions: $1,645, MS-67RB, October 2014; $6,463, MS-66RD, October 2014; $1,528, MS-66RB, August 2014														
1881, Proof	3,575	385	64.6									$150	$325	$1,350
Auctions: $2,115, PF-66RB, November 2014; $1,880, PF-66RD, June 2013; $1,234, PF-65Cam, July 2014; $881, PF-65RB, August 2014														
1882	38,578,000	743	63.1	94%	$5	$6	$8	$10	$25	$35	$60	$90	$315	$1,350
Auctions: $294, MS-64RB, July 2014; $247, MS-64RB, October 2014; $3,525, EF-40, April 2013; $66, AU-55BN, October 2014														
1882, Misplaced Date (q)	(r)	4	64.5	100%						$450	$875	$1,700	$6,000	
Auctions: $220, EF-45, February 2007														
1882, Proof	3,100	386	64.7									$150	$325	$1,000
Auctions: $823, PF-66RB, September 2014; $734, PF-66BN, November 2014; $2,703, PF-65RD, January 2014; $323, PF-65BN, July 2014														
1883	45,591,500	724	62.9	93%	$5	$6	$8	$10	$25	$35	$60	$90	$315	$1,350
Auctions: $2,585, MS-66RD, February 2014; $499, MS-65RB, July 2014; $241, MS-65BN, July 2014; $217, MS-64RB, October 2014														
1883, Proof	6,609	564	64.6									$150	$325	$1,350
Auctions: $5,581, PF-67RB, August 2014; $2,938, PF-66RD, March 2013; $646, PF-66BN, November 2014; $441, PF-65RB, November 2014														
1884	23,257,800	678	63.0	93%	$5	$7	$10	$14	$27	$40	$75	$120	$450	$1,650
Auctions: $4,994, MS-66RD, June 2014; $1,645, MS-65RD, September 2014; $257, MS-64RB, August 2014														
1884, Proof	3,942	489	64.8									$150	$325	$1,350
Auctions: $7,050, PF-67Cam, June 2013; $4,113, PF-67RD, September 2014; $1,880, PF-66RD, July 2014; $306, PF-64RD, October 2014														
1885	11,761,594	649	62.3	88%	$8	$9	$15	$30	$65	$80	$110	$200	$650	$2,100
Auctions: $12,925, MS-66RD, April 2013; $1,528, MS-66RB, November 2014; $1,645, MS-65RD, October 2014														
1885, Proof	3,790	459	64.9									$150	$325	$1,350
Auctions: $4,994, PF-68BN, September 2013; $1,528, PF-66RB, July 2014; $2,115, PF-65RD, October 2014; $529, PF-65RB, October 2014														
1886, All kinds	17,650,000													
1886, Variety 1		368	57.1	61%	$6	$8	$20	$50	$140	$175	$200	$250	$975	$4,000
Auctions: $8,813, MS-66RB, June 2013; $1,410, MS-64RD, July 2014; $764, MS-64RB, November 2014; $235, MS-63BN, September 2014														
1886, Variety 2		457	57.8	69%	$7	$12	$25	$75	$175	$220	$325	$500	$2,900	$14,000
Auctions: $9,400, MS-65RD, January 2013; $2,115, MS-65RB, August 2014; $482, MS-60RB, July 2014; $247, AU-58BN, October 2014														
1886, All kinds, Proof	4,290													
1886, Variety 1, Proof		117	64.6									$150	$325	$1,800
Auctions: $3,819, PF-66RD, June 2014; $1,880, PF-66RB, October 2014; $1,763, PF-65RD, October 2014; $558, PF-64RB, August 2014														
1886, Variety 2, Proof		70	64.5									$350	$750	
Auctions: $1,116, PF-66BN, April 2013; $1,763, PF-64RB+, November 2014; $306, PF-64BN, November 2014														
1887	45,223,523	581	62.2	92%	$3	$4	$5	$8	$18	$28	$55	$80	$575	$1,700
Auctions: $4,700, MS-66RD, November 2014; $8,813, MS-66RD, February 2013; $382, MS-65RD, November 2014														
1887, DblDie Obverse	(s)	28	41.4	18%					$250	$490	$800	$1,650	$8,000	
Auctions: $881, MS-62BN, October 2013; $176, VF-25BN, October 2014														
1887, Proof	2,960	315	64.4									$150	$300	$3,500
Auctions: $16,450, PF-66RD, June 2014; $823, PF-66BN, November 2014; $382, PF-64RB, October 2014														

q. The bases of at least four 1s are evident within the beads of the necklace. **r.** Included in circulation-strike 1882 mintage figure.
s. Included in circulation-strike 1887 mintage figure.

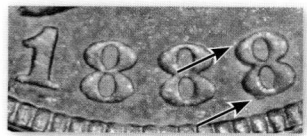

1888, Last 8 Over 7
FS-01-1888-301.

1891, Doubled-Die Obverse
FS-01-1891-101.

1894, Doubled Date
FS-01-1894-301.

	Mintage	Cert	Avg	%MS	G-4	VG-8	F-12	VF-20	EF-40	AU-50	MS-60BN	MS-63BN PF-63BN	MS-65RB PF-64RB	MS-65RD PF-65RD
1888	37,489,832	721	60.2	87%	$3	$4	$5	$8	$22	$27	$65	$130	$725	$2,250
	Auctions: $11,750, MS-66RD, June 2014; $1,704, MS-65RD, July 2014; $1,880, MS-65RD, September 2014; $529, MS-64RD, October 2014													
1888, Last 8 Over 7	(t)	10	41.8	20%	$1,200	$1,500	$2,000	$3,500	$7,500	$15,000	$25,000	$35,000		
	Auctions: $23,500, AU-58, April 2013													
1888, Proof	4,582	265	64.2									$150	$315	$3,500
	Auctions: $15,275, PF-66RD, October 2014; $382, PF-64RB, August 2014; $2,585, PF, February 2013; $294, PF-64BN, December 2014													
1889	48,866,025	733	62.5	93%	$3	$4	$5	$7	$18	$30	$60	$80	$400	$2,000
	Auctions: $13,513, MS-66RD, October 2014; $10,575, MS-66RD, October 2014; $4,113, MS-65RD, April 2014; $1,880, MS-65RD, October 2014													
1889, Proof	3,336	269	64.3									$150	$315	$1,750
	Auctions: $4,113, PF-66RD, February 2013; $499, PF-65RB, July 2014; $341, PF-64RB, July 2014; $282, PF-64BN, November 2014													
1890	57,180,114	670	62.9	95%	$3	$4	$5	$7	$16	$30	$60	$80	$450	$1,150
	Auctions: $4,113, MS-66RB, March 2014; $470, MS-64RD, July 2014; $170, MS-64RB, August 2014; $170, MS-63BN, July 2014													
1890, Proof	2,740	258	64.1									$150	$315	$1,650
	Auctions: $1,058, PF-65RD, October 2014; $1,293, PF-65RD, August 2013; $1,293, PF-64Cam, September 2014; $470, PF-64RD, November 2014													
1891	47,070,000	789	62.7	94%	$3	$4	$5	$7	$15	$30	$60	$80	$400	$1,100
	Auctions: $9,106, MS-66RD, November 2014; $1,528, MS-65RD, July 2014; $1,293, MS-65RD, August 2014; $135, MS-64RB, August 2014													
1891, Doubled-Die Obverse	(u)	12	45.9	25%					$250	$450	$750	$1,150		
	Auctions: $138, VF-35, December 2011													
1891, Proof	2,350	278	64.2									$150	$315	$1,375
	Auctions: $18,213, PF-65DCam, July 2014; $911, PF-64Cam, September 2014; $558, PF-64RB, November 2014; $176, PF-62RB, November 2014													
1892	37,647,087	704	63.0	95%	$3	$4	$5	$8	$20	$30	$60	$80	$375	$1,100
	Auctions: $8,813, MS-66RD, August 2013; $3,055, MS-65RD, October 2014; $1,293, MS-65RD, October 2014; $306, MS-64RD, October 2014													
1892, Proof	2,745	296	64.4									$150	$315	$1,200
	Auctions: $3,525, PF-67RD, November 2013; $2,585, PF-66Cam, November 2014; $2,233, PF-65RD, October 2014; $1,175, PF-64Cam, July 2014													
1893	46,640,000	839	63.1	95%	$3	$4	$5	$8	$20	$30	$60	$80	$350	$900
	Auctions: $6,463, MS-67RD, April 2013; $282, MS-64RD, October 2014; $176, MS-64RB, November 2014; $135, MS-63RB, November 2014													
1893, Proof	2,195	259	64.2									$150	$315	$1,300
	Auctions: $823, PF-65RB, November 2014; $499, PF-64RD, April 2013; $284, PF-64RB, October 2014; $247, PF-63RB, November 2014													
1894	16,749,500	733	61.7	89%	$5	$6	$15	$20	$50	$70	$85	$115	$385	$1,100
	Auctions: $3,290, MS-66RD, January 2014; $2,585, MS-66RD, October 2014; $2,174, MS-66RD, November 2014; $414, MS-64RB, July 2014													
1894, Doubled Date	(v)	88	51.0	60%	$30	$40	$65	$130	$225	$385	$675	$1,200	$4,000	$9,000
	Auctions: $5,875, MS-64RD, January 2013; $4,113, MS-64RB, September 2014; $296, VF-30BN, August 2014; $300, VF-30BN, October 2014													
1894, Proof	2,632	287	64.1									$150	$315	$1,200
	Auctions: $5,581, PF-66RD, September 2013; $1,351, PF-65Cam, November 2014; $558, PF-65RB, November 2014													

t. Included in circulation-strike 1888 mintage figure. **u.** Included in circulation-strike 1891 mintage figure. **v.** Included in circulation-strike 1894 mintage figure.

	Mintage	Cert	Avg	%MS	G-4	VG-8	F-12	VF-20	EF-40	AU-50	MS-60BN	MS-63BN	MS-65RB	MS-65RD
												PF-63BN	PF-64RB	PF-65RD
1895	38,341,574	851	62.9	95%	$3	$4	$5	$8	$15	$25	$40	$65	$200	$800
	Auctions: $23,500, MS-67RD, November 2014; $7,050, MS-66RD, January 2014; $1,880, MS-66RD, October 2014; $206, MS-64RB, October 2014													
1895, Proof	2,062	263	64.5									$160	$315	$1,200
	Auctions: $9,988, PF-66Cam, June 2014; $1,880, PF-66RB, November 2014; $823, PF-64RB, November 2014; $260, PF-62RB, November 2014													
1896	39,055,431	638	62.7	94%	$3	$4	$5	$8	$15	$25	$40	$65	$220	$925
	Auctions: $1,528, MS-65RD, July 2014; $259, MS-64RD, July 2014; $182, MS-64RB, August 2014; $59, MS-63BN, October 2014													
1896, Proof	1,862	224	64.3									$150	$300	$1,350
	Auctions: $5,875, PF-65Cam, June 2014; $646, PF-65BN, November 2014; $295, PF-64RB, September 2014; $194, PF-64BN, November 2014													
1897	50,464,392	777	62.9	94%	$3	$4	$5	$8	$15	$25	$40	$65	$200	$925
	Auctions: $31,725, MS-67RD, August 2014; $7,050, MS-66RD, January 2014; $529, MS-64RD, September 2014; $118, MS-64RD, October 2014													
1897, Proof	1,938	246	64.5									$150	$300	$1,200
	Auctions: $6,169, PF-67RD, October 2014; $588, PF-65RB, July 2014; $411, PF-63RB, November 2014													
1898	49,821,284	861	62.9	94%	$3	$4	$5	$8	$15	$25	$40	$65	$195	$575
	Auctions: $2,820, MS-66RD, April 2013; $368, MS-65RB+, November 2014; $458, MS-64RD+, October 2014; $212, MS-64RD, October 2014													
1898, Proof	1,795	253	64.8									$150	$300	$1,200
	Auctions: $7,931, PF-66Cam, June 2014; $27,025, PF-66RB, August 2014; $2,233, PF-66RD, August 2014; $353, PF-64RB, November 2014													
1899	53,598,000	1,412	63.5	95%	$3	$4	$5	$8	$15	$25	$40	$65	$195	$460
	Auctions: $3,525, MS-66RD, January 2014; $2,233, MS-66RD, September 2014; $1,351, MS-66RD, October 2014; $558, MS-65RD, October 2014													
1899, Proof	2,031	253	64.7									$150	$300	$1,200
	Auctions: $5,875, PF-67RD, June 2014; $764, PF-64Cam, November 2014; $823, PF-66RB, November 2014; $478, PF-65RB, October 2014													
1900	66,831,502	909	62.9	94%	$2	$3	$5	$6	$10	$20	$35	$60	$170	$460
	Auctions: $9,988, MS-67RD, December 2013; $2,115, MS-66RD+, July 2014; $1,998, MS-66RD, October 2014; $529, MS-65RD, December 2014													
1900, Proof	2,262	246	64.7									$140	$300	$1,200
	Auctions: $2,350, PF-66RB+, August 2014; $2,115, PF-66RD, October 2014; $5,581, PF-66RD, April 2013; $411, PF-64RD, October 2014													
1901	79,609,158	1,608	63.3	96%	$2	$3	$5	$6	$10	$20	$35	$60	$170	$440
	Auctions: $2,115, MS-67RB, November 2013; $1,293, MS-66RD, August 2014; $588, MS-65RD, August 2014; $194, MS-64RD, July 2014													
1901, Proof	1,985	276	64.8									$150	$300	$1,200
	Auctions: $2,500, PF-67RB, July 2014; $1,528, PF-66RD, October 2014; $999, PF-66RB, August 2014													
1902	87,374,704	1,554	62.8	95%	$2	$3	$5	$6	$10	$20	$35	$55	$170	$485
	Auctions: $1,998, MS-66RD, July 2014; $2,585, MS-66RD, December 2013; $705, MS-65RD, November 2014; $165, MS-64RD, July 2014													
1902, Proof	2,018	285	64.6									$150	$300	$1,200
	Auctions: $7,344, PF-67RD, June 2014; $823, PF-66RB, November 2014; $1,146, PF-65RD, October 2014; $341, PF-64RB, July 2014													
1903	85,092,703	1,434	62.7	94%	$2	$3	$5	$6	$10	$20	$35	$60	$170	$440
	Auctions: $4,406, MS-67RD, July 2014; $1,998, MS-66RD, October 2014; $1,528, MS-66RD, November 2014; $411, MS-65RD, August 2014													
1903, Proof	1,790	245	64.6									$150	$300	$1,200
	Auctions: $2,820, PF-66RD, October 2014; $1,763, PF-66RB, November 2014; $499, PF-64RD, July 2014													
1904	61,326,198	1,226	62.8	94%	$2	$3	$5	$6	$10	$20	$40	$60	$170	$460
	Auctions: $2,585, MS-66RD, June 2014; $441, MS-65RD, November 2014; $183, MS-65RB, July 2014; $59, MS-63RB, November 2014													
1904, Proof	1,817	233	64.2									$150	$300	$1,200
	Auctions: $6,463, PF-67RB, October 2014; $4,994, PF-66Cam, June 2014; $2,585, PF-65Cam, October 2014; $7,931, PF-65RB, July 2014													
1905	80,717,011	1,446	62.9	94%	$2	$3	$5	$6	$10	$20	$35	$60	$170	$490
	Auctions: $19,975, MS-67RD, April 2013; $6,169, MS-66RD+, September 2014; $2,115, MS-66RD, September 2014; $456, MS-65RD, August 2014													
1905, Proof	2,152	245	64.5									$140	$300	$1,200
	Auctions: $411, PF-64RD, October 2014; $529, PF-64RB, November 2014; $8,225, PF, March 2014; $223, PF-63RB, October 2014													
1906	96,020,530	1,646	62.5	92%	$2	$3	$5	$6	$10	$20	$35	$55	$170	$440
	Auctions: $23,500, MS-67RD, June 2014; $2,585, MS-66RD, August 2014; $617, MS-65RD, September 2014; $247, MS-62BN, July 2014													
1906, Proof	1,725	218	64.5									$150	$300	$1,200
	Auctions: $21,150, PF-67Cam, June 2014; $2,820, PF-66RB+, November 2014; $1,704, PF-66RB, November 2014; $2,939, PF-64RB, July 2014													
1907	108,137,143	1,778	62.3	93%	$2	$3	$5	$6	$10	$20	$40	$60	$170	$440
	Auctions: $23,500, MS-67RD, December 2013; $364, MS-65RD, October 2014; $329, MS-65RB, October 2014; $247, MS-64RD, October 2014													
1907, Proof	1,475	205	64.4									$150	$300	$1,250
	Auctions: $4,113, PF-66RD, April 2014; $764, PF-65RD, October 2014; $306, PF-64RB, October 2014; $382, PF-62BN, November 2014													

	Mintage	Cert	Avg	%MS	G-4	VG-8	F-12	VF-20	EF-40	AU-50	MS-60BN	MS-63BN / PF-63BN	MS-65RB / PF-64RB	MS-65RD / PF-65RD
1908	32,326,367	1,549	63.1	95%	$2	$3	$5	$6	$10	$20	$40	$60	$170	$440
Auctions: $19,975, MS-67RD, February 2013; $3,525, MS-66RD, August 2014; $4,113, MS-66RD+, October 2014; $1,293, MS-65RD, August 2014														
1908, Proof	1,620	277	64.7									$150	$300	$1,200
Auctions: $1,293, PF-66RB, November 2014; $1,175, PF-65RD, January 2014; $382, PF-64RD, October 2014; $2,585, PF-62RB, July 2014														
1908S	1,115,000	2,764	45.7	37%	$90	$100	$125	$145	$175	$250	$290	$400	$850	$2,300
Auctions: $4,882, MS-66RD, August 2014; $3,290, MS-65RD, January 2014; $1,763, MS-65RD, October 2014; $1,146, MS-64RD, October 2014														
1909	14,368,470	2,074	62.5	95%	$12	$15	$17	$20	$25	$30	$45	$65	$175	$440
Auctions: $3,819, MS-67RD, January 2014; $11,163, MS-67RD, August 2014; $4,113, MS-66RD+, September 2014														
1909, Proof	2,175	254	64.6									$150	$300	$1,300
Auctions: $12,925, PF-67RD, June 2014; $1,645, PF-66RD, August 2014; $1,645, PF-64Cam, November 2014; $206, PF-63RB, July 2014														
1909S	309,000	2,971	40.3	30%	$450	$500	$600	$700	$750	$850	$1,000	$1,200	$2,000	$5,000
Auctions: $9,989, MS-66RD, June 2014; $5,875, MS-65RD, August 2014; $2,585, MS-64RD, October 2014; $1,786, MS-63RD, August 2014														

LINCOLN, WHEAT EARS REVERSE (1909–1958)

Variety 1 (Bronze, 1909–1942): **Designer:** *Victor D. Brenner.* **Weight:** *3.11 grams.* **Composition:** *.950 copper, .050 tin and zinc.* **Diameter:** *19 mm.* **Edge:** *Plain.* **Mints:** *Philadelphia, Denver, San Francisco.*

Variety 1, Bronze
(1909–1942)

Mintmark location, all varieties 1909 to date, is on the obverse below the date.

Variety 1, Bronze,
Matte Proof

Variety 2 (Steel, 1943): **Weight:** *2.70 grams.* **Composition:** *Steel, coated with zinc.* **Diameter:** *19 mm.* **Edge:** *Plain.*

Variety 2, Steel (1943)

Variety 1 Resumed (1944–1958): **Weight:** *3.11 grams.* **Composition:** *1944–1946—.950 copper and .050 zinc; 1947–1958—.950 copper and .050 tin and zinc.* **Diameter:** *19 mm.* **Edge:** *Plain.*

Variety 1 Resumed, Bronze
(1944–1958)

Variety 1 Resumed, Bronze,
Mirror Proof

History. The Lincoln cent debuted in 1909 in honor of the hundredth anniversary of the birth of Abraham Lincoln. Sculptor and engraver Victor David had been chosen to design the new cent because the artistry of Chief Engraver Charles Barber was under heavy criticism at the time. The new cent was released on August 2, 1909, and the earliest coins of the year's issue had Brenner's initials (V.D.B.) on the reverse; this was soon discontinued. (His initials would be restored in 1918, on the obverse, on Lincoln's shoulder.) This was the first U.S. cent to feature the motto IN GOD WE TRUST.

From 1909 to 1942 the coins were struck in bronze. In 1943, during World War II, zinc-coated steel was used for their planchets, as a way to reserve copper for the war effort. The bronze alloy would be resumed in 1944. (Although no bronze cents were officially issued in 1943, a few pieces struck on bronze or silver planchets are known to exist for that year; bronze examples have recently sold for more than $200,000. Such errors presumably occur when an older planchet is mixed in with the normal supply of planchets and goes through the minting process. Through a similar production error, a few 1944 cents were struck on steel planchets. Beware the many regular steel cents of 1943 that were later plated with copper, either as novelties or to deceive collectors; a magnet will reveal their true nature.) In 1944, 1945, and 1946, the Mint used salvaged gun-cartridge cases as its source metal for coining cents. In Mint State, the color of cents of these years can appear slightly different from other bronze Wheat Ear cents.

The Philadelphia, Denver, and San Francisco mints all produced Lincoln Wheat Ear cents, but not in all years. The Wheat Ears reverse design was used from 1909 until the coin's 50th anniversary in 1959, at which time it was replaced with a view of the Lincoln Memorial.

Striking and Sharpness. As a rule, Lincoln cents of 1909 through 1914 are fairly well struck. From 1915 through the end of the 1920s, many are weak, with Denver Mint coins particularly so. Issues of the 1930s onward are mostly well struck. With many different die pairs used over a long period of time, striking quality varies. On the obverse, check for details in Lincoln's hair and beard. Also check the lettering and the inner edge of the rim. Tiny marks on the shoulder of Lincoln indicate a weak strike there; this area cannot be used to determine wear on high-grade coins. (During striking, there was not enough die pressure to fill this, the deepest point of the obverse die; therefore, stray marks on the raw planchet remain evident in this spot.) On the reverse check the wheat stalks, letters, and inner rim. A weak strike will usually manifest itself on the O of ONE (the area directly opposite Lincoln's shoulder). Coins struck from overused or "tired" dies can have grainy or even slightly wavy fields on either side.

Availability. Of the earlier Lincoln Wheat Ears cents, those of 1909 are easily found in MS; later early dates are scarcer, although Philadelphia varieties were made in higher quantities and are more often seen. Beginning in the early 1930s, collectors saved bank-wrapped rolls of Mint State cents in large quantities (starting mainly in 1934, though the low-mintage 1931-S was also hoarded). Dates after this time all are plentiful, although some more so than others, and there are a number of scarce and rare varieties. The collector demand for scarcer Lincoln cents and higher-grade issues is intense, resulting in a strong market. Many Mint State coins before the 1930s have been dipped and recolored, this being particularly true of pieces listed as RD. Others are stained and blotchy.

Proofs. Matte Proof Lincoln cents of a new style were made from 1909 to 1916. These have minutely matte or pebbled surfaces caused by special treatment of the dies. The rims are square and sharp. Such pieces cannot easily be told from certain circulation strikes with similar borders. Certified holders usually list these simply as "Proof," not "Matte Proof." Buy only coins that have been verified by an expert. Most are brown, or brown with tinges of red. Nearly all full "red" coins have been dipped or recolored.

Exceptional specimens dated 1917 are reported to exist, although no records exist to indicate they are true Proofs.

Mirror-finish Proofs were made from 1936 to 1942 and again from 1950 to 1958. Proofs of this era are mostly from dies polished overall (including the portrait), although some later issues have frosted ("cameo") portraits. Quality can be a problem for the 1936 to 1942 issues. Check for carbon spots and recoloring. Proofs of later dates are easy to find.

Generally, Proofs below 63 are unattractive and are not desired by most collectors.

GRADING STANDARDS

MS-60 to 70 (Mint State).

Obverse and Reverse: At MS-65 and higher, the luster is rich on all areas, except perhaps the shoulder (which may be grainy and show original planchet surface). There is no rubbing, and no contact marks are visible except under magnification. Coins with full or nearly full mint orange-red color can be designated RD; those with full or nearly full brown-toned surfaces can be designated BN; and

1943. Graded MS-68.

those with a substantial percentage of red-orange and of brown can be called RB. Ideally, MS-65 or finer coins should have good eye appeal, which in the RB category means nicely blended colors, not stained or blotched. Below MS-65, full RD coins become scarce, and at MS-60 to 62 are virtually non-existent, unless they have been dipped. Copper is a very active metal, and influences such as slight abrasions, contact marks, and so on that define the grade also affect the color. The ANA grading standards allow for "dull" and/or "spotted" coins at MS-60 and 61, as well as incomplete luster. In the marketplace, interpretations often vary widely. BN and RB coins at MS-60 and 61 are apt to be more attractive than (dipped) RD coins.

Illustrated coin: This zinc-coated steel cent is an ultra gem in quality.

AU-50, 53, 55, 58 (About Uncirculated).

Obverse: Slight wear shows on Lincoln's cheekbone to the left of his nose, and also on his beard. At AU-55 or 58 there may be some hints of mint red-orange. Most coins in About Uncirculated are BN, but are often not designated by color. *Reverse:* Slight wear is evident on the stalks of wheat to the left and right. Otherwise, the same standards apply as for the obverse.

1909-S, V.D.B. Graded AU-50BN.

Illustrated coin: This is a sharp example of the most famous Lincoln cent issue.

EF-40, 45 (Extremely Fine). *Obverse:* Light

wear is seen on Lincoln's portrait, and hair detail is gone on the higher areas, especially above the ear. *Reverse:* Light wear is seen overall, but the parallel lines in the wheat stalks are clearly separated.

1909, No V.D.B. Graded EF-45.

VF-20, 30 (Very Fine). *Obverse:* Lincoln's portrait is worn all over, with most hair detail gone at the center. Hair separation is seen at the back and the top of the head, but hairs are blended together. The jaw outline is clear. The center of the ear is defined and the bowtie is clear. The date and lettering is sharp. *Reverse:* More wear is seen, but still the lines in the wheat stalks are separated. Lettering shows wear but is very clear.

1909-S, V.D.B. Graded VF-20.

    Illustrated coin: Some gray discoloration is hardly noticeable near the rims.

F-12, 15 (Fine). *Obverse:* More wear is seen overall. Hair definition is less. The center of the ear is partially visible. The jaw outline and bowtie are clear. *Reverse:* Most lines in the wheat stalks are either weak or blended with others, but more than half of the separating lines are clear.

1914-D. Graded F-12.

VG-8, 10 (Very Good). *Obverse:* The portrait is more worn, with only slight hair strands visible (thick strands blended). The ear opening is visible. The bowtie and jacket show fewer details. *Reverse:* The lines in the wheat stalks are blended together in flat areas. Perhaps 40% to 50% of the separating lines can be seen. The rim may be weak in areas.

1910-S. Graded VG-8.

G-4, 6 (Good). *Obverse:* The portrait is well worn. Some slight details are seen at the top of the head and the bottom of the coat. LIBERTY is weak. The rim may touch or blend with the tops of the letters forming IN GOD WE TRUST. The date and mintmark (if any) are very clear. *Reverse:* The wheat stalks are flat, with just a few scattered details visible.

1911. Graded G-4.

AG-3 (About Good). *Obverse:* Wear is extensive. The portrait is mostly in outline form, with only scattered details visible. LIBERTY is weak and perhaps with some letters missing. IN GOD WE TRUST blends in with the rim, and several letters are very weak or missing. *Reverse:* The rim is worn down to blend with the outside of the wheat stalks in some areas, although some hints of the edge of the stalks can be seen. Lettering is weak, with up to several letters missing.

1913-D. Graded AG-3.

PF-60 to 70 (Matte Proof). *Obverse and Reverse:* At the Matte PF-65 level or higher there are no traces of abrasion or contact marks. Color will range from brown (BN)—the most common—to brown with significant tinges of mint red-orange (RB), or with much mint color (RD). Most RD coins have been dipped. Some tiny flecks are normal on coins certified as PF-65 but should be microscopic or absent above that. Coins in the PF-60 to

1912, Matte Proof. Graded PF-64RD.

63 range are BN or sometimes RB—almost impossible to be RD unless dipped. Lower-grade Proofs usually have poor eye appeal.

Illustrated coin: This lovely coin has above-average eye appeal.

PF-60 to 70 (Mirror Proof). *Obverse and Reverse:* PF-65 and higher coins are usually RB (colors should be nicely blended) or RD, the latter with bright red-orange fading slightly to hints of brown. Some tiny flecks are normal on coins certified as PF-65 but should be microscopic or absent above that. PF-60 and 61 coins can be dull, stained, or spotted but still have some original mint color. Coins with fingerprints must be given

1936, Mirror Proof. Graded PF-65RD.

a low numerical grade. Lower-grade Proofs usually have poor eye appeal.

Illustrated coin: A few flecks are seen here and there.

Designer's initials, V.D.B.
(1909 Reverse Only)

No V.D.B. on Reverse
(1909–1958)

V.D.B. on Shoulder
(Starting 1918)

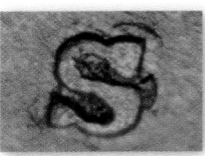

1909-S, S Over
Horizontal S
FS-01-1909S-1502.

	Mintage	Cert	Avg	%MS	G-4	VG-8	F-12	VF-20	EF-40	AU-50	MS-60BN	MS-63BN	MS-65RD
											PF-63RB	PF-64RB	PF-65RD
1909, V.D.B.	27,995,000	10,438	63.3	96%	$15	$16	$17	$18	$19	$20	$25	$30	$175
	Auctions: $881, MS-67RD, July 2014; $823, MS-67RD, September 2014; $1,763, MS-67RD, June 2013; $499, MS-66RD+, August 2014												
1909, V.D.B., Proof (a)	1,194	56	65.0									$3,500	$5,000
	Auctions: $258,500, PF-67RB+, August 2014; $55,813, PF-66RB, June 2014												
1909S, V.D.B. † (b)	484,000	8,002	45.2	42%	$700	$800	$900	$1,000	$1,150	$1,250	$1,500	$1,950	$5,500
	Auctions: $117,500, MS-67RD, February 2014; $17,625, MS-66RD, August 2014; $11,163, MS-66RD, October 2014												
1909	72,702,618	1,514	63.4	97%	$4	$5	$6	$7	$8	$12	$17	$20	$160
	Auctions: $1,880, MS-67RD, August 2014; $1,763, MS-67RD, November 2014; $4,406, MS-67RD, April 2013; $670, MS-66RD+, October 2014												
1909, Proof	2,618	237	64.6								$700	$1,150	$2,700
	Auctions: $6,463, PF-66RB+, August 2014; $5,875, PF-66RD, April 2013; $1,782, PF-65RD, August 2014; $1,657, PF-64RD, August 2014												
1909S	1,825,000	3,098	40.6	40%	$100	$110	$125	$150	$225	$275	$325	$365	$1,050
	Auctions: $10,281, MS-67RD, February 2013; $4,700, MS-66RD, November 2014; $881, MS-65RD, October 2014; $411, MS-64RB, October 2014												
1909S, S Over Horizontal S	(c)	516	50.6	65%	$110	$115	$135	$160	$235	$285	$340	$370	$1,250
	Auctions: $1,880, MS-66RD, September 2014; $1,998, MS-66RD, January 2014; $969, MS-65RD, July 2014; $353, MS-64BN, July 2014												
1910	146,801,218	1,152	63.5	95%	$0.35	$0.50	$1	$1.50	$4	$10	$18	$25	$230
	Auctions: $4,406, MS-67RD, June 2014; $3,055, MS-67RD, September 2014; $2,938, MS-67RD, November 2014												
1910, Proof	4,118	245	64.2								$600	$1,100	$2,500
	Auctions: $7,638, PF-67RB, August 2014; $1,764, PF-65RB, July 2014; $470, PF-63RB, August 2014												
1910S	6,045,000	1,193	57.1	77%	$17	$20	$22	$25	$45	$80	$100	$120	$635
	Auctions: $15,275, MS-66RD, June 2014; $1,880, MS-66RD, August 2014; $1,998, MS-66RD, October 2014; $206, MS-64RB, November 2014												
1911	101,177,787	634	63.5	97%	$0.45	$0.65	$1.50	$2.50	$6	$11	$21	$50	$400
	Auctions: $7,050, MS-67RD, April 2014; $1,645, MS-66RD, October 2014; $441, MS-65RD, August 2014; $165, MS-64RD, August 2014												
1911, Proof	1,725	201	64.3								$600	$1,050	$3,400
	Auctions: $9,400, PF-66RD, June 2014; $14,688, PF-66RB, August 2014; $853, PF-65BN, October 2014; $705, PF-64RB, August 2014												
1911D	12,672,000	774	58.7	78%	$6	$7	$10	$20	$50	$75	$95	$125	$1,400
	Auctions: $8,225, MS-66RD, April 2014; $7,050, MS-66RD, October 2014; $6,169, MS-66RD, October 2014; $3,819, MS-65RD, September 2014												
1911S	4,026,000	893	49.7	52%	$50	$55	$60	$65	$85	$110	$185	$235	$2,750
	Auctions: $14,100, MS-66RD, October 2014; $881, MS-65RB, November 2014; $2,820, MS-65RD, August 2013; $505, MS-64RD, October 2014												
1912	68,153,060	620	63.1	95%	$1.25	$1.65	$2.25	$5.50	$13	$25	$35	$50	$385
	Auctions: $18,800, MS-67RD, April 2013; $499, MS-65RD, December 2014; $441, MS-65RD, October 2014; $118, MS-64RD, July 2014												
1912, Proof	2,172	214	64.3								$600	$1,050	$6,250
	Auctions: $3,966, PF-66RB, February 2014; $14,100, PF-66RB+, August 2014; $999, PF-65RB, October 2014; $940, PF-64RB, July 2014												
1912D	10,411,000	586	57.9	72%	$7	$8	$10	$25	$65	$100	$170	$240	$1,850
	Auctions: $8,238, MS-66RD, September 2014; $1,998, MS-65RD+, November 2014; $7,050, MS-65RD, February 2013; $823, MS-64RD, July 2014												
1912S	4,431,000	778	50.6	59%	$24	$26	$29	$40	$75	$110	$180	$255	$3,500
	Auctions: $2,820, MS-65RD, October 2014; $4,406, MS-65RD, November 2013; $1,410, MS-64RD, August 2014; $783, MS-64RD, November 2014												

† Ranked in the *100 Greatest U.S. Coins* (fourth edition). *Note:* No early references (pre-1960s), Mint records, or reliable market listings have been found to confirm the existence of true 1917 Proofs. "Examples seen have had nice matte-like surfaces, sometimes on just one side, but have lacked the vital combination of broad, flat rims on both sides and a mirror Proof edge (when viewed edge-on from the side)" (*A Guide Book of Lincoln Cents*). The leading certification services do not recognize Proofs of this year. The editors of this book also do not believe that true Proofs of 1917 exist. **a.** Of the 1,194 coins reported struck, an estimated 400 to 600 were issued. **b.** Many counterfeits exist—some die struck, some made by adding an "S" to a Philadelphia coin. **c.** Included in 1909-S mintage figure.

1917, Doubled-Die
Obverse
FS-01-1917-101.

	Mintage	Cert	Avg	%MS	G-4	VG-8	F-12	VF-20	EF-40	AU-50	MS-60BN / PF-63RB	MS-63BN / PF-64RB	MS-65RD / PF-65RD
1913	76,532,352	639	62.7	94%	$0.85	$1	$2	$4	$18	$27	$35	$55	$420
	Auctions: $19,975, MS-67RD, January 2013; $1,410, MS-66RD, July 2014; $529, MS-65RD, July 2014; $470, MS-65RD, August 2014												
1913, Proof	2,983	313	64.5								$600	$1,050	$2,500
	Auctions: $25,850, PF-67RD, January 2014; $8,225, PF-67RB, August 2014; $1,410, PF-65RB, November 2014; $1,058, PF-64RD, October 2014												
1913D	15,804,000	572	58.3	77%	$3	$3.50	$4.50	$10	$50	$70	$110	$175	$2,200
	Auctions: $10,575, MS-66RD, January 2014; $8,225, MS-66RD, October 2014; $881, MS-64RD, August 2014; $705, MS-64RD, September 2014												
1913S	6,101,000	698	49.3	57%	$14	$17	$20	$31	$60	$100	$175	$225	$5,300
	Auctions: $4,406, MS-65RD, June 2014; $676, MS-64RD, July 2014; $388, MS-63RD, September 2014; $823, MS-61BN, October 2014												
1914	75,238,432	673	60.8	88%	$0.75	$1	$2	$6	$20	$40	$55	$70	$450
	Auctions: $28,200, MS-67RD, August 2013; $2,585, MS-66RD, November 2014; $499, MS-65RD, July 2014; $270, MS-64RD, September 2014												
1914, Proof	1,365	158	64.7								$600	$1,100	$2,500
	Auctions: $3,525, PF-66BN, June 2014; $8,226, PF-66RB+, August 2014; $4,406, PF-66RB, October 2014; $1,410, PF-65RB, July 2014												
1914D (d)	1,193,000	4,316	25.7	10%	$200	$250	$300	$425	$875	$1,500	$2,000	$3,300	$18,000
	Auctions: $18,800, MS-65RD, January 2014; $28,200, MS-65RD+, October 2014; $4,406, MS-64RD, October 2014; $3,290, MS-62BN, October 2014												
1914S	4,137,000	684	45.2	38%	$24	$28	$30	$40	$85	$175	$325	$460	$8,150
	Auctions: $5,875, MS-65RD, September 2014; $6,463, MS-65RD, September 2013; $1,528, MS-64RD, July 2014; $793, MS-64BN, October 2014												
1915	29,092,120	569	60.6	86%	$1.75	$2.50	$5	$18	$60	$70	$90	$105	$875
	Auctions: $10,575, MS-67RD, September 2014; $3,525, MS-66RD, January 2014; $1,293, MS-66RD, November 2014; $1,116, MS-65RD, August 2014												
1915, Proof	1,150	122	64.7								$750	$1,200	$3,500
	Auctions: $4,406, PF-66RB, July 2014; $22,325, PF-66RB+, August 2014; $17,625, PF-65RD, January 2014; $801, PF-64BN, October 2014												
1915D	22,050,000	854	57.8	80%	$2	$3	$4	$7	$22	$45	$85	$120	$1,100
	Auctions: $4,465, MS-66RD, October 2014; $7,638, MS-66RD, June 2013; $1,063, MS-65RD, September 2014; $940, MS-65RD, November 2014												
1915S	4,833,000	603	47.8	50%	$20	$25	$30	$35	$70	$135	$200	$235	$5,000
	Auctions: $23,500, MS-66RD, September 2013; $7,638, MS-65RD, November 2014; $3,055, MS-64RD, October 2014; $852, MS-63RB, July 2014												
1916	131,833,677	789	63.2	96%	$0.30	$0.50	$0.75	$2	$8	$13	$18	$35	$300
	Auctions: $2,350, MS-67RD, March 2014; $1,880, MS-67RD, August 2014; $2,820, MS-67RD, October 2014; $505, MS-66RD, July 2014												
1916, Proof	1,050	95	64.8								$1,500	$2,500	$12,000
	Auctions: $30,550, PF-66RB+, August 2014; $1,880, PF-64RB, October 2014; $7,931, PF-64RB, June 2014; $4,700, PF-63RB, July 2014												
1916D	35,956,000	734	60.8	85%	$1	$1.75	$3	$6	$15	$35	$75	$150	$2,850
	Auctions: $17,625, MS-66RD, June 2014; $282, MS-65RB, August 2014; $823, MS-64RD+, July 2014; $441, MS-64RD, October 2014												
1916S	22,510,000	719	58.9	77%	$1.75	$2.25	$3.50	$8	$25	$50	$105	$175	$7,500
	Auctions: $911, MS-65RB, July 2014; $7,638, MS-65RD, August 2013; $1,183, MS-64RD, October 2014; $1,410, MS-64RD, November 2014												
1917	196,429,785	714	60.9	91%	$0.30	$0.40	$0.50	$2	$4	$10	$16	$32	$425
	Auctions: $823, MS-66RD, September 2014; $1,586, MS-66RD+, November 2014; $2,585, MS-66RD, January 2013; $145, MS-64RD, September 2014												
1917, Doubled-Die Obverse	(e)	65	36.0	18%	$85	$145	$225	$450	$1,000	$1,600	$2,750	$6,000	$20,000
	Auctions: $499, MS-65RB, October 2014; $541, MS-64RD, October 2014; $329, MS-64RB, July 2014; $5,875, MS-63BN, August 2013												
1917D	55,120,000	600	60.2	83%	$0.80	$1	$1.75	$4.50	$35	$50	$80	$125	$2,750
	Auctions: $9,400, MS-65RD, August 2014; $2,350, MS-65RD, August 2013; $1,116, MS-64RD, August 2014; $2,703, MS-64RD, November 2014												
1917S	32,620,000	441	59.6	81%	$0.50	$0.65	$1	$2.50	$10	$25	$75	$160	$13,000
	Auctions: $11,750, MS-67RD, August 2014; $17,625, MS-67RD, November 2014; $881, MS-66RD, November 2014; $4,113, MS-65RD, December 2013												

d. Many counterfeits exist, including crude fakes, sophisticated die-struck forgeries, and altered 1944-D cents (the latter, unlike an authentic 1914-D cent, will have the designer's initials, V.D.B., on the shoulder). **e.** Included in 1917 mintage figure.

1922, No D
FS-01-1922-401.

1922, Weak D

	Mintage	Cert	Avg	%MS	G-4	VG-8	F-12	VF-20	EF-40	AU-50	MS-60BN / PF-63RB	MS-63BN / PF-64RB	MS-65RD / PF-65RD
1918	288,104,634	553	63.3	95%	$0.20	$0.30	$0.50	$1.50	$3	$8	$16	$27	$330
	Auctions: $423, MS-64BN, September 2014; $200, MS-63RB, August 2014; $74, MS-62BN, November 2014												
1918D	47,830,000	459	59.2	76%	$0.75	$1.25	$2.50	$4	$12	$35	$80	$140	$3,500
	Auctions: $25,850, MS-66RD, August 2013; $11,163, MS-65RD, October 2014; $1,528, MS-64RD, November 2014; $764, MS-64RB, August 2014												
1918S	34,680,000	522	60.0	78%	$0.50	$1	$2	$3	$11	$32	$80	$185	$9,500
	Auctions: $823, MS-67RD, August 2014; $1,058, MS-67RD, October 2014; $499, MS-66RD, August 2014; $3,525, MS-64RD, February 2014												
1919	392,021,000	758	63.4	95%	$0.20	$0.30	$0.40	$1	$3.25	$5	$14	$28	$230
	Auctions: $8,225, MS-68RD, April 2014; $1,058, MS-67RD, October 2014; $499, MS-66RD, August 2014; $182, MS-65RD, September 2014												
1919D	57,154,000	561	62.0	90%	$0.50	$0.75	$1	$4	$10	$32	$65	$110	$2,400
	Auctions: $1,763, MS-65RD, January 2014; $1,410, MS-65RD, October 2014; $353, MS-64RB, July 2014; $311, MS-64RB, August 2014												
1919S	139,760,000	620	60.8	84%	$0.20	$0.40	$1	$2	$6	$18	$50	$115	$6,000
	Auctions: $7,638, MS-65RD, April 2014; $482, MS-64RB, July 2014; $259, MS-64RB, November 2014; $123, MS-63BN, December 2014												
1920	310,165,000	675	63.4	96%	$0.20	$0.30	$0.35	$0.50	$2.25	$4	$15	$28	$220
	Auctions: $940, MS-66RD, January 2013; $881, MS-66RD+, September 2014; $705, MS-66RD, September 2014; $200, MS-65RD, November 2014												
1920D	49,280,000	485	60.7	84%	$1	$2	$3	$6.50	$19	$40	$80	$110	$2,050
	Auctions: $22,325, MS-66RD, June 2014; $283, MS-64RB, November 2014; $182, MS-63RB, October 2014; $45, MS-60BN, November 2014												
1920S	46,220,000	489	59.9	77%	$0.50	$0.65	$1.50	$2.25	$10	$35	$110	$185	$12,500
	Auctions: $3,173, MS-64RD, October 2014; $2,115, MS-64RD, February 2013; $259, MS-63RB, November 2014; $79, MS-62BN, November 2014												
1921	39,157,000	528	63.0	95%	$0.50	$0.60	$1.30	$2.10	$9	$22	$50	$80	$345
	Auctions: $3,290, MS-66RD, January 2014; $411, MS-65RD, September 2014; $112, MS-64RD, October 2014; $16, MS-60RD, November 2014												
1921S	15,274,000	649	57.8	66%	$1.50	$2.25	$3.50	$7	$35	$75	$135	$190	$11,500
	Auctions: $1,293, MS-65RB, September 2014; $499, MS-64RB, July 2014; $1,880, MS-64RD, August 2013; $282, MS-63RB, November 2014												
1922D	7,160,000	1,501	41.7	45%	$20	$21	$25	$27	$40	$75	$110	$165	$2,000
	Auctions: $2,585, MS-65RD, August 2013; $499, MS-64RD, November 2014; $229, MS-63RD, July 2014; $106, MS-62RB, November 2014												
1922, No D (f)	(g)	2,932	21.6	2%	$600	$750	$1,000	$1,250	$2,500	$4,500	$10,000	$25,000	
	Auctions: $82,250, MS-65BN, April 2013; $3,819, AU-55BN, August 2014; $1,768, EF-45BN, October 2014; $893, EF-40BN, August 2014												
1922, Weak D (f)	(g)	443	15.8	2%	$25	$35	$50	$70	$160	$200	$350	$1,000	
	Auctions: $2,174, MS, April 2014; $376, AU-58BN, October 2014; $329, AU-58BN, October 2014; $153, AU-55BN, October 2014												
1923	74,723,000	543	63.5	98%	$0.35	$0.45	$0.65	$1	$5	$9.50	$15	$30	$360
	Auctions: $4,700, MS-67RD, June 2013; $1,645, MS-66RD+, September 2014; $247, MS-64RD+, July 2014; $84, MS-64RD, November 2014												
1923S	8,700,000	393	57.2	64%	$4	$6	$7	$10	$40	$90	$220	$390	$17,000
	Auctions: $2,350, MS-65RB, June 2014; $3,055, MS-64RB, October 2014; $823, MS-64RB, November 2014; $353, MS-62RB, August 2014												
1924	75,178,000	384	63.4	96%	$0.20	$0.30	$0.40	$0.85	$5	$10	$24	$50	$375
	Auctions: $16,450, MS-67RD, April 2013; $12,925, MS-67RD, July 2014; $470, MS-65RD, November 2014; $259, MS-64RD, November 2014												
1924D	2,520,000	1,083	44.5	39%	$40	$45	$50	$60	$125	$175	$300	$375	$10,000
	Auctions: $9,400, MS-65RD, January 2014; $2,820, MS-64RD, November 2014; $705, MS-64RB, November 2014; $470, MS-63BN, July 2014												
1924S	11,696,000	455	56.2	65%	$1.30	$1.50	$2.75	$5.50	$20	$75	$125	$225	
	Auctions: $9,400, MS-64RD, January 2014; $764, MS-64RB, November 2014; $529, MS-63RB, October 2014; $88, MS-60BN, November 2014												

f. 1922 cents with a weak or completely missing mintmark were made from extremely worn dies that originally struck normal 1922-D cents. Three different die pairs were involved; two of them produced "Weak D" coins. One die pair (no. 2, identified by a "strong reverse") is acknowledged as having struck "No D" coins. Weak D cents are worth considerably less. Beware of fraudulently removed mintmark.
g. Included in 1922-D mintage figure.

	Mintage	Cert	Avg	%MS	G-4	VG-8	F-12	VF-20	EF-40	AU-50	MS-60BN	MS-63BN	MS-65RD
											PF-63RB	PF-64RB	PF-65RD
1925	139,949,000	788	64.3	98%	$0.20	$0.25	$0.35	$0.60	$3	$6.50	$10	$20	$135
	Auctions: $1,410, MS-67RD, August 2014; $2,115, MS-67RD, September 2013; $110, MS-65RD, December 2014; $44, MS-64RD, September 2014												
1925D	22,580,000	604	61.5	88%	$0.85	$1.30	$2.45	$4	$13	$30	$75	$90	$3,750
	Auctions: $4,113, MS-65RD, January 2014; $764, MS-64RD+, July 2014; $382, MS-64RD, September 2014; $129, MS-63RB, October 2014												
1925S	26,380,000	468	60.0	80%	$0.75	$1	$1.85	$2.75	$12	$30	$90	$200	$18,000
	Auctions: $4,700, MS-65RB, February 2014; $852, MS-64RB, July 2014; $259, MS-63RB, October 2014; $200, MS-62BN, November 2014												
1926	157,088,000	982	64.7	99%	$0.20	$0.25	$0.30	$0.50	$2	$4	$8	$18	$110
	Auctions: $1,116, MS-67RD, January 2014; $353, MS-66RD, July 2014; $259, MS-65RD, October 2014; $84, MS-65RD, November 2014												
1926D	28,020,000	467	60.0	82%	$1.35	$1.75	$3.50	$5.25	$14	$32	$85	$125	$3,550
	Auctions: $4,700, MS-65RD, February 2013; $353, MS-64RB, November 2014; $353, MS-64RB, December 2014; $364, MS-63RB, July 2014												
1926S	4,550,000	796	55.1	54%	$9	$10	$13	$17	$35	$75	$155	$325	$100,000
	Auctions: $9,988, MS-65RB, October 2013; $1,058, MS-64RB, November 2014; $1,058, MS-63RB, August 2014; $259, MS-62BN, November 2014												
1927	144,440,000	737	63.8	97%	$0.20	$0.25	$0.30	$0.60	$2	$3.50	$10	$20	$135
	Auctions: $7,638, MS-67RD, February 2014; $1,880, MS-67RD, October 2014; $368, MS-66RD, September 2014; $115, MS-65RD, August 2014												
1927D	27,170,000	540	61.5	87%	$1.25	$1.75	$2.75	$3.75	$7.50	$25	$62	$85	$2,100
	Auctions: $2,233, MS-65RD, January 2014; $617, MS-65RB, July 2014; $159, MS-64RB, September 2014; $212, MS-64RB, December 2014												
1927S	14,276,000	394	60.9	83%	$1.50	$2	$3	$5	$15	$40	$85	$140	$7,500
	Auctions: $529, MS-64RB, July 2014; $1,763, MS-64RD, June 2013; $535, MS-63RD, November 2014; $86, MS-62BN, November 2014												
1928	134,116,000	815	64.0	98%	$0.20	$0.25	$0.30	$0.60	$2	$3	$9	$13	$120
	Auctions: $1,058, MS-67RD, September 2014; $3,408, MS-67RD, April 2013; $499, MS-66RD, July 2014; $120, MS-65RD, October 2014												
1928D	31,170,000	495	62.0	87%	$0.75	$1	$1.75	$3	$5.50	$17	$37	$80	$1,200
	Auctions: $7,050, MS-66RD, November 2014; $1,410, MS-65RD, June 2014; $141, MS-64RD, September 2014; $51, MS-63RB, November 2014												
1928S	17,266,000	325	61.0	86%	$1	$1.60	$2.75	$3.75	$9.50	$30	$75	$100	$4,250
	Auctions: $4,406, MS-65RD, September 2013; $764, MS-64RB, October 2014; $470, MS-64RB, November 2014; $382, MS-63RB, November 2014												
1929	185,262,000	929	64.5	98%	$0.20	$0.25	$0.30	$0.75	$2	$4	$8	$14	$105
	Auctions: $5,581, MS-67RD, April 2014; $1,528, MS-67RD, August 2014; $705, MS-67RD, September 2014; $382, MS-66RD+, August 2014												
1929D	41,730,000	409	63.0	94%	$0.40	$0.85	$1.25	$2.25	$5.50	$13	$25	$37	$550
	Auctions: $4,113, MS-66RD, January 2014; $2,585, MS-66RD, August 2014; $1,645, MS-66RD, October 2014; $458, MS-65RD, July 2014												
1929S	50,148,000	658	63.5	96%	$0.50	$0.90	$1.65	$2.35	$5.80	$14	$21	$29	$475
	Auctions: $4,700, MS-66RD, October 2014; $4,113, MS-66RD, March 2013; $411, MS-65RD, October 2014; $65, MS-64RD, October 2014												
1930	157,415,000	3,280	65.3	100%	$0.15	$0.20	$0.25	$0.50	$1.25	$2	$6	$10	$43
	Auctions: $3,525, MS-67RD, February 2014; $823, MS-67RD, August 2014; $108, MS-66RD, October 2014; $40, MS-65RD, October 2014												
1930D	40,100,000	627	64.3	98%	$0.20	$0.25	$0.30	$0.55	$2.50	$4	$12	$28	$115
	Auctions: $1,645, MS-66RD, June 2014; $441, MS-66RD, October 2014; $142, MS-65RD, August 2014; $141, MS-65RD, September 2014												
1930S	24,286,000	1,494	64.8	99%	$0.20	$0.25	$0.30	$0.60	$1.75	$6	$10	$12	$90
	Auctions: $6,463, MS-66RD, April 2014; $2,377, MS-66RD, August 2014; $499, MS-66RD, October 2014; $84, MS-65RD, November 2014												
1931	19,396,000	627	64.1	97%	$0.50	$0.75	$1	$1.50	$4	$9	$20	$35	$125
	Auctions: $5,288, MS-67RD, August 2013; $999, MS-66RD, August 2014; $153, MS-65RD, July 2014; $42, MS-64RB, October 2014												
1931D	4,480,000	716	60.4	73%	$5	$6	$7	$8.50	$13.50	$37	$60	$70	$875
	Auctions: $4,113, MS-66RD, April 2013; $1,528, MS-65RD, August 2014; $270, MS-65RB, October 2014; $165, MS-64RB, July 2014												
1931S	866,000	4,360	55.2	62%	$60	$75	$85	$100	$125	$150	$175	$195	$550
	Auctions: $2,350, MS-66RD, January 2014; $646, MS-65RD, October 2014; $558, MS-64RD, July 2014; $141, MS-63RB, November 2014												
1932	9,062,000	693	64.6	98%	$1.50	$1.75	$2	$2.50	$4.50	$12	$20	$28	$115
	Auctions: $259, MS-66RD, November 2014; $940, MS-66RD, September 2013; $95, MS-65RD, October 2014; $34, MS-64RB, October 2014												
1932D	10,500,000	415	63.9	94%	$1.50	$1.75	$2.50	$2.75	$4.50	$11	$19	$28	$155
	Auctions: $8,519, MS-67RD, November 2013; $206, MS-65RD, August 2014; $56, MS-64RD, September 2014; $49, MS-64RD, October 2014												
1933	14,360,000	654	64.8	98%	$1.50	$1.75	$2.50	$3	$6.25	$13	$20	$30	$115
	Auctions: $2,115, MS-67RD, October 2014; $3,557, MS-67RD, August 2013; $112, MS-65RD, July 2014; $32, MS-64RB, July 2014												
1933D	6,200,000	1,016	64.4	97%	$3.50	$3.75	$5.50	$7.25	$12	$19	$26	$25	$135
	Auctions: $5,581, MS-67RD, February 2014; $764, MS-67RD, October 2014; $558, MS-66RD+, November 2014; $141, MS-65RD, August 2014												

1934, Doubled-Die Obverse
FS-01-1934-101.

1936, Doubled-Die Obverse
FS-01-1936-101.

	Mintage	Cert	Avg	%MS	G-4	VG-8	F-12	VF-20	EF-40	AU-50	MS-60BN / PF-63RB	MS-63BN / PF-64RB	MS-65RD / PF-65RD
1934	219,080,000	1,864	65.8	100%	$0.15	$0.18	$0.20	$0.30	$1	$4	$10	$7	$37
	Auctions: $1,058, MS-67RD, September 2014; $1,058, MS-67RD+, November 2014; $764, MS-67RD, December 2013; $33, MS-66RD, November 2014												
1934, Doubled-Die Obverse (h)	(i)	3	58.0	67%									$250
	Auctions: $1,600, MS-64RB, October 2011												
1934D	28,446,000	866	64.8	99%	$0.20	$0.25	$0.50	$0.75	$2.25	$7.50	$22	$40	$62
	Auctions: $11,163, MS-67RD, April 2014; $229, MS-66RD, July 2014; $123, MS-66RD, October 2014; $223, MS-66RD, December 2014												
1935	245,388,000	1,870	65.7	99%	$0.15	$0.18	$0.20	$0.25	$0.50	$1	$3	$5	$33
	Auctions: $1,293, MS-67RD, March 2014; $106, MS-67RD, October 2014; $92, MS-67RD, November 2014; $106, MS-64RB, November 2014												
1935D	47,000,000	1,321	65.8	100%	$0.15	$0.18	$0.20	$0.25	$0.50	$2	$5	$6	$39
	Auctions: $823, MS-67RD, February 2014; $153, MS-67RD, August 2014; $141, MS-67RD, October 2014; $588, MS-67RD, November 2014												
1935S	38,702,000	780	64.9	99%	$0.15	$0.18	$0.25	$0.50	$2	$5	$12	$17	$60
	Auctions: $1,469, MS-67RD, October 2014; $3,055, MS-66RD+, July 2014; $1,175, MS-66RD, October 2014; $106, MS-65RD, December 2014												
1936	309,632,000	2,615	65.6	99%	$0.15	$0.18	$0.25	$0.50	$1.50	$2.60	$5	$10	$30
	Auctions: $705, MS-67RD, February 2014; $353, MS-67RD, July 2014; $2,820, MS-67RD+, September 2014; $306, MS-67RD, October 2014												
1936, Doubled-Die Obverse (j)	(k)	52	43.6	23%			$72.50	$120	$200	$350	$485	$300	
	Auctions: $646, MS-62BN, August 2014; $259, AU-50, April 2014; $80, VF-30BN, November 2014; $76, VF-30BN, November 2014												
1936, Proof	5,569	710	64.0								$200	$485	$2,750
	Auctions: $21,150, PF-66Cam, June 2013; $3,525, PF-66RD, October 2014; $2,585, PF-65RD, October 2014; $823, PF-64RD, October 2014												
1936D	40,620,000	1,611	66.0	100%	$0.15	$0.20	$0.30	$0.50	$1	$2	$4	$5	$21
	Auctions: $646, MS-67RD, August 2013; $411, MS-67RD, October 2014; $145, MS-67RD, October 2014; $79, MS-67RD, December 2014												
1936S	29,130,000	1,174	65.6	100%	$0.15	$0.25	$0.40	$0.55	$1	$3	$5	$6	$25
	Auctions: $4,259, MS-67RD, February 2014; $2,703, MS-67RD, September 2014; $2,585, MS-67RD, November 2014; $881, MS-66RD+, October 2014												
1937	309,170,000	3,794	66.1	100%	$0.15	$0.20	$0.30	$0.50	$1	$2	$3	$4	$15
	Auctions: $90, MS-67RD, August 2014; $94, MS-67RD, October 2014; $2,233, MS-67RD+, November 2013; $35, MS-66RD, November 2014												
1937, Proof	9,320	826	64.4								$75	$90	$350
	Auctions: $21,150, PF-67Cam, September 2013; $5,288, PF-66Cam, August 2014; $1,763, PF-65Cam, October 2014; $3,643, PF-64RD, July 2014												
1937D	50,430,000	2,509	66.2	100%	$0.15	$0.20	$0.25	$0.40	$1	$3	$5	$6	$17
	Auctions: $135, MS-67RD, January 2014; $123, MS-67RD, August 2014; $106, MS-67RD, August 2014; $40, MS-66RD, August 2014												
1937S	34,500,000	1,471	66.0	100%	$0.15	$0.20	$0.30	$0.40	$1	$3	$5	$8	$22
	Auctions: $1,998, MS-67RD, January 2014; $881, MS-67RD+, July 2014; $764, MS-67RD+, July 2014; $55, MS-66RD, July 2014												
1938	156,682,000	2,011	66.1	100%	$0.15	$0.20	$0.30	$0.40	$1	$2	$4	$7	$16
	Auctions: $2,585, MS-67RD+, September 2014; $106, MS-67RD, October 2014; $2,820, MS-67RD, November 2013; $27, MS-66RD, November 2014												
1938, Proof	14,734	963	64.5								$65	$80	$200
	Auctions: $2,585, PF-66Cam, January 2014; $1,058, PF-66Cam, September 2014; $1,469, PF-66Cam, November 2014; $881, PF-65Cam, October 2014												
1938D	20,010,000	2,005	66.1	100%	$0.20	$0.30	$0.50	$0.80	$1.25	$3	$4	$7	$17
	Auctions: $3,055, MS-67RD, January 2014; $3,290, MS-67RD, August 2014; $100, MS-67RD, November 2014; $89, MS-67RD, December 2014												
1938S	15,180,000	2,474	66.1	100%	$0.40	$0.50	$0.60	$0.75	$1.10	$3	$4	$6	$21
	Auctions: $2,115, MS-67RD+, July 2014; $118, MS-67RD, July 2014; $92, MS-67RD, August 2014; $40, MS-66RD, August 2014												

h. The remains of a secondary 3 and 4 are evident below the primary digits. **i.** Included in 1934 mintage figure. **j.** FS-01-1936-101. **k.** Included in circulation-strike 1936 mintage figure.

	Mintage	Cert	Avg	%MS	G-4	VG-8	F-12	VF-20	EF-40	AU-50	MS-60BN	MS-63BN	MS-65RD
											PF-63RB	PF-64RB	PF-65RD
1939	316,466,000	2,874	66.1	100%	$0.15	$0.18	$0.20	$0.25	$0.50	$1	$2	$3	$14
	Auctions: $108, MS-67RD, August 2014; $106, MS-67RD, October 2014; $705, MS-67RD, June 2013; $38, MS-66RD, December 2014												
1939, Proof	13,520	967	64.6								$60	$70	$180
	Auctions: $2,820, PF-67RD, January 2014; $1,410, PF-67RD, October 2014; $270, PF-66RD, November 2014; $212, PF-65RD, September 2014												
1939D	15,160,000	1,588	66.1	100%	$0.50	$0.60	$0.65	$0.85	$1.25	$3	$4	$10	$18
	Auctions: $529, MS-67RD, April 2014; $86, MS-67RD, October 2014; $100, MS-67RD, November 2014; $69, MS-67RD, December 2014												
1939S	52,070,000	3,155	66.0	100%	$0.15	$0.20	$0.30	$0.75	$1	$2.50	$3	$9	$16
	Auctions: $1,175, MS-67RD+, July 2014; $1,116, MS-67RD+, August 2014; $3,966, MS-67RD, August 2013; $24, MS-66RD, November 2014												
1940	586,810,000	2,226	66.1	100%	$0.15	$0.18	$0.20	$0.40	$0.60	$1	$2	$8	$14
	Auctions: $3,819, MS-67RD, January 2014; $212, MS-67RD, July 2014; $147, MS-67RD, September 2014; $74, MS-65RD, November 2014												
1940, Proof	15,872	953	64.5								$50	$60	$170
	Auctions: $7,931, PF-67RD, June 2013; $4,700, PF-67RD, August 2014; $6,463, PF-67RD, October 2014; $764, PF-66RD, July 2014												
1940D	81,390,000	1,409	66.2	100%	$0.15	$0.18	$0.25	$0.60	$0.75	$2	$3	$9	$15
	Auctions: $94, MS-67RD, August 2014; $68, MS-67RD, November 2014; $119, MS-67RD, December 2014; $159, MS-67RD, January 2013												
1940S	112,940,000	2,512	66.1	100%	$0.15	$0.18	$0.20	$0.50	$1	$1.75	$3	$5	$15
	Auctions: $999, MS-67RD+, November 2014; $100, MS-67RD, November 2014; $79, MS-67RD, December 2014; $306, MS-67RD, June 2013												
1941	887,018,000	2,671	66.0	99%	$0.15	$0.18	$0.20	$0.30	$0.60	$1.50	$2	$8	$14
	Auctions: $147, MS-67RD, July 2014; $212, MS-67RD, August 2014; $259, MS-67RD, October 2014												
1941, Proof	21,100	1,032	64.4								$45	$55	$165
	Auctions: $28,200, PF-67RD, November 2013; $705, PF-66RD, August 2014; $382, PF-66RD, October 2014; $705, PF-64RD, July 2014												
1941D	128,700,000	1,760	66.4	100%	$0.15	$0.18	$0.20	$0.50	$1	$3	$4	$6	$15
	Auctions: $2,115, MS-67RD+, August 2014; $165, MS-67RD, August 2014; $63, MS-67RD, August 2014; $441, MS-67RD, August 2013												
1941S	92,360,000	2,433	66.2	100%	$0.15	$0.18	$0.30	$0.50	$1	$3	$4	$9	$15
	Auctions: $646, MS-67RD, August 2014; $306, MS-67RD, October 2014; $119, MS-67RD, December 2014; $1,880, MS-67RD, November 2013												
1942	657,796,000	2,427	65.9	100%	$0.15	$0.18	$0.20	$0.25	$0.50	$0.75	$1	$7	$14
	Auctions: $3,290, MS-67RD+, July 2014; $112, MS-63RB, November 2014; $14,100, AU-58, November 2013; $282, Fair-2BN, November 2014												
1942, Proof	32,600	1,537	64.0								$45	$58	$150
	Auctions: $1,880, PF-66Cam, November 2014; $2,115, PF-66Cam, June 2013; $999, PF-65Cam, July 2014												
1942D	206,698,000	3,040	66.1	100%	$0.15	$0.18	$0.20	$0.25	$0.50	$0.85	$1	$7	$14
	Auctions: $170, MS-67RD, August 2014; $141, MS-67RD, December 2014; $3,055, MS-67RD, November 2013; $20, MS-65RD, November 2014												
1942S	85,590,000	1,929	66.0	99%	$0.20	$0.25	$0.30	$0.85	$1.25	$5.50	$7	$11	$17
	Auctions: $3,290, MS-67RD, February 2014; $2,350, MS-67RD+, September 2014												

	Mintage	Cert	Avg	%MS	F-12	VF-20	EF-40	AU-50	MS-63BN	MS-65	MS-66	MS-67	MS-68
1943	684,628,670	8,175	66.0	100%	$0.30	$0.35	$0.40	$0.50	$2.50	$8	$35	$90	$1,200
	Auctions: $382, MS-67, July 2014; $182, MS-67, November 2014												
1943, Bronze † (a)	(b)	8	56.6	25%				$200,000					
	Auctions: $218,500, AU-58, January 2010												
1943, Silver (a)	(b)	0	n/a				$3,000	$4,500					
	Auctions: $4,313, AU-58, March 2010												
1943D	217,660,000	5,987	66.4	100%	$0.35	$0.40	$0.45	$0.75	$3	$10	$35	$90	$1,300
	Auctions: $1,175, MS-68, July 2014; $705, MS-68, July 2014; $2,820, MS-68, April 2013; $209, MS-67, October 2014												

† Ranked in the *100 Greatest U.S. Coins* (fourth edition). **a.** In 1943 a handful of cents were accidentally struck on old bronze and silver planchets, instead of the intended steel planchets. Today about a dozen are known to exist. Numerous regular steel cents have been plated with copper as novelties or with intent to deceive; their true nature is easily revealed with a magnet. **b.** Included in 1943 mintage figure.

1943-D, Boldly Doubled Mintmark
FS-01-1943D-501.

	Mintage	Cert	Avg	%MS	F-12	VF-20	EF-40	AU-50	MS-63BN	MS-65	MS-66	MS-67	MS-68
1943D, Boldly Doubled Mintmark (c)	(d)	28	64.0	100%	$40	$50	$60	$80	$100	$1,400	$2,500	$10,000	
	Auctions: $1,116, MS-65, December 2013; $441, MS-64, July 2014; $353, MS-63, November 2014; $505, MS-62, November 2014												
1943S	191,550,000	6,519	66.1	100%	$0.40	$0.65	$0.75	$1	$6	$20	$50	$135	$2,000
	Auctions: $306, MS-67, August 2014; $153, MS-67, November 2014; $135, MS-67, December 2014; $165, MS-66, October 2014												

c. FS-01-1943D-501. **d.** Included in 1943-D mintage figure.

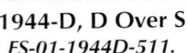

1944-D, D Over S
FS-01-1944D-511.

1946-S, S Over D
FS-01-1946S-511.

	Mintage	Cert	Avg	%MS	VF-20	EF-40	AU-50	MS-63RB	MS-65RB / PF-65RD	MS-65RD / PF-66RD	MS-67RD / PF-67RD
1944	1,435,400,000	3,191	65.9	100%	$0.10	$0.20	$0.35	$1	$5	$12	$65
	Auctions: $2,233, MS-67RD+, September 2014; $79, MS-67RD, November 2014										
1944D	430,578,000	3,567	65.7	98%	$0.10	$0.20	$0.35	$0.85	$4	$14	$85
	Auctions: $141, MS-67RD, July 2014; $119, MS-67RD, September 2014; $58, MS-67RD, August 2014										
1944D, D Over S	(a)	96	53.8	52%	$125	$175	$235	$450	$700	$2,500	
	Auctions: $1,116, MS-64RD, January 2014; $470, MS-64RB, September 2014; $646, MS-64RD, October 2014; $419, MS-64RB, October 2014										
1944S	282,760,000	4,593	66.1	100%	$0.15	$0.20	$0.35	$0.85	$4	$13	$110
	Auctions: $141, MS-67RD, May 2014; $101, MS-67RD, July 2014; $96, MS-67RD, July 2014										
1945	1,040,515,000	2,465	65.7	100%	$0.10	$0.20	$0.35	$0.85	$2	$10	
	Auctions: $764, MS-67RD, November 2014; $41, MS-66RD, August 2014; $36, MS-66RD, August 2014; $3,819, MS-68RD, November 2013										
1945D	266,268,000	3,930	66.0	100%	$0.10	$0.20	$0.35	$0.85	$2	$10	$140
	Auctions: $2,115, MS-67RD, June 2014; $165, MS-67RD, July 2014; $2,585, MS-67RD, September 2014; $99, MS-67RD, October 2014										
1945S	181,770,000	3,576	66.3	100%	$0.15	$0.20	$0.35	$0.85	$2	$10	$95
	Auctions: $106, MS-67RD, September 2014; $89, MS-67RD, December 2014; $84, MS-67RD, October 2014										
1946	991,655,000	1,420	65.5	100%	$0.10	$0.20	$0.35	$0.60	$2	$14	
	Auctions: $7,168, MS-67RD, January 2014; $2,585, MS-67RD, October 2014; $2,585, MS-67RD, November 2014; $470, MS-66RD+, August 2014										
1946D	315,690,000	2,270	66.0	100%	$0.10	$0.20	$0.35	$0.60	$2	$10	$300
	Auctions: $2,115, MS-67RD, March 2014; $176, MS-67RD, August 2014; $129, MS-67RD, November 2014; $182, MS-67RD, December 2014										
1946S	198,100,000	3,660	66.0	100%	$0.15	$0.20	$0.35	$0.60	$2	$10	$135
	Auctions: $470, MS-67RD, July 2014; $470, MS-67RD, December 2014; $940, MS-67RD, September 2013; $20, MS-66RD, November 2014										
1946S, S Over D	(b)	20	62.1	85%	$35	$75	$125	$240		$575	
	Auctions: $1,998, MS-66RD, June 2014										
1947	190,555,000	1,249	65.6	100%	$0.10	$0.20	$0.40	$1	$3	$15	
	Auctions: $3,525, MS-67RD, July 2014; $4,113, MS-67RD, April 2013; $294, MS-66RD+, August 2014; $106, MS-66RD, November 2014										
1947D	194,750,000	1,851	65.9	100%	$0.10	$0.20	$0.40	$0.60	$2	$10	$650
	Auctions: $176, MS-67RD, October 2014; $764, MS-67RD, February 2013										
1947S	99,000,000	2,585	66.0	100%	$0.20	$0.25	$0.50	$0.85	$2	$10	$175
	Auctions: $1,704, MS-67RD, February 2014; $1,998, MS-67RD+, August 2014; $1,293, MS-67RD+, August 2014; $153, MS-67RD, November 2014										

a. Included in 1944-D mintage figure. **b.** Included in 1946-S mintage figure.

1951-D, D Over S
FS-01-1951D-512.

	Mintage	Cert	Avg	%MS	VF-20	EF-40	AU-50	MS-63RB	MS-65RB / PF-65RD	MS-65RD / PF-66RD	MS-67RD / PF-67RD
1948	317,570,000	1,166	65.6	100%	$0.10	$0.20	$0.35	$0.85	$2	$15	
	Auctions: $7,168, MS-67RD, January 2014; $441, MS-66RD+, September 2014; $135, MS-66RD, October 2014; $153, MS-66RD, November 2014										
1948D	172,637,500	1,657	65.7	100%	$0.10	$0.20	$0.35	$0.60	$2	$10	$900
	Auctions: $353, MS-67RD, October 2014; $259, MS-67RD, November 2014; $188, MS-67RD, November 2014; $999, MS-67RD, August 2013										
1948S	81,735,000	2,460	66.1	100%	$0.20	$0.30	$0.35	$1	$3	$10	$150
	Auctions: $1,998, MS-67RD+, August 2014; $212, MS-67RD, August 2014; $101, MS-67RD, August 2014; $306, MS-67RD, June 2013										
1949	217,775,000	1,016	65.7	100%	$0.10	$0.20	$0.35	$1	$3	$20	
	Auctions: $3,055, MS-67RD, July 2014; $247, MS-66RD, October 2014; $159, MS-66RD, October 2014										
1949D	153,132,500	1,416	65.8	100%	$0.10	$0.20	$0.35	$1	$3	$10	
	Auctions: $1,058, MS-67RD, October 2014; $1,164, MS-67RD, November 2014; $353, MS-67RD, December 2014; $1,763, MS-67RD, June 2013										
1949S	64,290,000	2,894	66.1	100%	$0.25	$0.30	$0.35	$2	$4	$15	$200
	Auctions: $3,173, MS-67RD, March 2014; $247, MS-67RD, August 2014; $153, MS-67RD, September 2014; $41, MS-66RD, August 2014										
1950	272,635,000	954	65.7	100%	$0.10	$0.20	$0.35	$0.85	$2	$20	$1,500
	Auctions: $1,410, MS-67RD, August 2014; $1,293, MS-67RD, September 2014; $3,055, MS-67RD, August 2013; $96, MS-66RD, August 2014										
1950, Proof	51,386	1,312	65.3						$70	$90	$750
	Auctions: $5,141, PF-67DCam, January 2014; $12,925, PF-66DCam+, September 2014; $482, PF-66Cam, July 2014; $306, PF-65Cam, November 2014										
1950D	334,950,000	1,667	65.7	100%	$0.10	$0.20	$0.35	$0.60	$2	$15	
	Auctions: $353, MS-67RD, November 2014; $282, MS-67RD, December 2014; $212, MS-67RD, December 2014										
1950S	118,505,000	1,817	66.0	100%	$0.15	$0.25	$0.35	$0.85	$2	$15	
	Auctions: $9,400, MS-67RD+, September 2014; $588, MS-67RD, October 2014; $529, MS-67RD, December 2014; $1,293, MS-67RD, June 2013										
1951	284,576,000	827	65.7	100%	$0.10	$0.25	$0.35	$0.70	$2	$18	
	Auctions: $2,291, MS-67RD, July 2014; $5,288, MS-67RD, August 2013; $353, MS-66RD+, August 2014; $411, MS-66RD+, October 2014										
1951, Proof	57,500	1,236	65.6						$65	$85	$225
	Auctions: $1,763, PF-67Cam, April 2013; $376, PF-67RB, September 2014; $206, PF-67RB, November 2014; $90, PF-66RB, September 2014										
1951D	625,355,000	2,213	65.7	100%	$0.10	$0.12	$0.35	$0.60	$2	$9	$750
	Auctions: $282, MS-67RD, September 2014; $94, MS-67RD, November 2014; $1,410, MS-67RD, June 2013										
1951D, D Over S	(c)	31	63.6	94%							
	Auctions: $2,350, MS-67RD, April 2014; $82, MS-65RD, August 2014										
1951S	136,010,000	1,359	65.9	100%	$0.25	$0.30	$0.50	$1	$3	$11	$550
	Auctions: $823, MS-67RD, January 2014; $170, MS-67RD, August 2014; $529, MS-67RD, September 2014; $617, MS-67RD, November 2014										
1952	186,775,000	1,007	65.8	100%	$0.10	$0.15	$0.35	$1	$3	$16	$4,500
	Auctions: $4,994, MS-67RD, April 2014; $2,350, MS-67RD, July 2014; $270, MS-66RD, August 2014; $135, MS-66RD, December 2014										
1952, Proof	81,980	1,241	65.9						$50	$75	$125
	Auctions: $1,528, PF-67Cam, April 2013; $306, PF-66Cam, July 2014; $646, PF-66Cam, October 2014; $646, PF-66RB, September 2014										
1952D	746,130,000	2,202	65.8	100%	$0.10	$0.15	$0.25	$0.75	$2	$9	
	Auctions: $823, MS-67RD, September 2014; $646, MS-67RD, September 2014; $411, MS-67RD, November 2014; $1,058, MS-67RD, December 2013										
1952S	137,800,004	1,640	66.0	100%	$0.15	$0.20	$0.35	$2	$4	$13	$490
	Auctions: $4,113, MS-67RD+, November 2014; $123, MS-67RD, November 2014; $999, MS-67RD, June 2013										

c. Included in 1951-D mintage figure.

1955, Doubled-Die Obverse
FS-01-1955-101.

1955, Doubled-Die Obverse, Closeup of Date

1956-D, D Above Shadow D
FS-01-1956D-508.

	Mintage	Cert	Avg	%MS	VF-20	EF-40	AU-50	MS-63RB	MS-65RB / PF-65RD	MS-65RD / PF-66RD	MS-67RD / PF-67RD
1953	256,755,000	1,076	65.6	100%	$0.10	$0.15	$0.20	$0.50	$1	$18	
Auctions: $14,100, MS-67RD, January 2014; $8,813, MS-67RD, August 2014; $5,889, MS-67RD, August 2014; $4,700, MS-67RD, October 2014											
1953, Proof	128,800	1,717	66.3						$30	$40	$100
Auctions: $2,585, PF-67Cam, February 2014; $499, PF-67Cam, July 2014; $1,293, PF-66DCam, October 2014; $223, PF-66Cam, November 2014											
1953D	700,515,000	2,129	65.7	100%	$0.10	$0.15	$0.20	$0.50	$1	$11	
Auctions: $2,115, MS-67RD, July 2014; $1,998, MS-67RD, November 2014; $3,525, MS-67RD, August 2013; $100, MS-66RD+, October 2014											
1953S	181,835,000	2,002	65.9	100%	$0.10	$0.15	$0.20	$0.60	$2	$12	$300
Auctions: $3,055, MS-67RD, March 2014; $306, MS-67RD, July 2014; $153, MS-67RD, November 2014; $69, MS-67RD, December 2014											
1954	71,640,050	1,100	65.4	100%	$0.25	$0.35	$0.45	$0.60	$2	$27	
Auctions: $23,500, MS-67RD, March 2014; $1,175, MS-66RD+, July 2014; $1,645, MS-66RD+, August 2014; $881, MS-66RD+, October 2014											
1954, Proof	233,300	1,851	66.4						$20	$30	$60
Auctions: $2,820, PF-68Cam, April 2013; $115, PF-66Cam, September 2014; $129, PF-66Cam, November 2014; $112, PF-66Cam, November 2014											
1954D	251,552,500	2,845	65.9	100%	$0.10	$0.12	$0.20	$0.50	$1	$10	
Auctions: $141, MS-67RD, October 2014; $123, MS-67RD, December 2014; $1,293, MS-67RD, June 2013; $36, MS-66RD+, October 2014											
1954S	96,190,000	5,945	66.0	100%	$0.10	$0.12	$0.20	$0.50	$1	$8	
Auctions: $70, MS-67RD, August 2014; $119, MS-67RD, December 2014; $1,880, MS-67RD, August 2013											
1955	330,958,200	1,604	65.0	97%	$0.10	$0.12	$0.15	$0.35	$1	$19	
Auctions: $1,998, MS-67RD, September 2014; $3,819, MS-67RD, December 2013; $49, MS-66RD, July 2014; $60, MS-66RD, October 2014											
1955, Doubled-Die Obverse †	(d)	3,252	58.9	49%	$1,650	$1,850	$2,000	$3,750 (e)	$15,000	$35,500	
Auctions: $25,850, MS-64RD, January 2014; $19,975, MS-64RD, August 2014; $4,994, MS-64RB, August 2014; $3,525, MS-63RB, August 2014											
1955, Proof	378,200	3,080	67.1						$18	$30	$50
Auctions: $7,638, PF-68DCam, April 2013; $940, PF-67DCam, July 2014; $74, PF-67Cam, September 2014; $135, PF-67Cam, November 2014											
1955D	563,257,500	3,432	65.7	100%	$0.10	$0.12	$0.15	$0.35	$1	$10	
Auctions: $7,050, MS-67RD, April 2013; $165, MS-66RD+, September 2014; $130, MS-66RD+, October 2014											
1955S	44,610,000	11,070	66.1	100%	$0.20	$0.30	$0.40	$0.85	$3	$8	$145
Auctions: $2,115, MS-67RD, February 2014; $470, MS-67RD, July 2014; $270, MS-67RD, August 2014; $170, MS-67RD, October 2014											
1956	420,745,000	1,932	65.7	100%	$0.10	$0.12	$0.15	$0.35	$1	$13	
Auctions: $3,819, MS-67RD, August 2013; $823, MS-67RD, September 2014; $823, MS-67RD, September 2014; $588, MS-67RD, November 2014											
1956, Proof	669,384	2,942	67.2						$10	$25	$30
Auctions: $7,638, PF-68DCam, June 2013; $705, PF-67DCam, July 2014; $247, PF-66DCam, October 2014; $341, PF-68RD, July 2014											
1956D	1,098,201,100	3,599	65.6	99%	$0.10	$0.12	$0.15	$0.30	$1	$9	$2,750
Auctions: $589, MS-67RD, July 2014; $705, MS-67RD, August 2014; $3,525, MS-67RD+, November 2014; $1,175, MS-67RD, November 2013											
1956D, D Above Shadow D (f)	(g)	99	63.3	90%	$10	$25	$30	$35		$170	
Auctions: $1,293, MS-67RD, February 2014											

† Ranked in the *100 Greatest U.S. Coins* (fourth edition). **d.** Included in circulation-strike 1955 mintage figure. **e.** Value in MS-60BN, $2,350; in MS-63BN, $3,500; in MS-65BN, $12,000. Varieties exist with doubling that, while still strong, is weaker than that pictured; these command premiums, but are not nearly as valuable. Note that many counterfeit 1955 Doubled Die cents exist. On authentic pieces, there is a faint die scratch under the left horizontal bar of the T in CENT. **f.** The remains of a totally separated D mintmark are evident in the field below the primary D. **g.** Included in 1956-D mintage figure.

1958, Doubled-Die Obverse
FS-01-1958-101.

	Mintage	Cert	Avg	%MS	VF-20	EF-40	AU-50	MS-63RB	MS-65RB	MS-65RD	MS-67RD
									PF-65RD	PF-66RD	PF-67RD
1957	282,540,000	2,089	65.7	100%	$0.10	$0.12	$0.15	$0.30	$1	$15	$1,350
	Auctions: $515, MS-67RD, September 2014										
1957, Proof	1,247,952	3,331	67.1						$17	$25	$30
	Auctions: $1,028, PF-68Cam, July 2014; $1,058, PF-68Cam, April 2013; $282, PF-67Cam, November 2014; $84, PF-67Cam, November 2014										
1957D	1,051,342,000	4,309	65.7	99%	$0.10	$0.12	$0.15	$0.30	$1	$9	
	Auctions: $705, MS-67RD, August 2014; $558, MS-67RD, October 2014; $2,115, MS-67RD, June 2013										
1958	252,525,000	2,768	65.7	100%	$0.10	$0.12	$0.15	$0.30	$1	$9	$450
	Auctions: $194, MS-67RD, August 2014; $881, MS-67RD, October 2014; $1,528, MS-67RD, June 2013										
1958, Doubled-Die Obverse (h,i)	(j)	0	n/a						—		
	Auctions: No auction records available.										
1958, Proof	875,652	3,084	67.1						$15	$20	$30
	Auctions: $1,293, PF-67DCam, June 2013; $1,293, PF-68Cam, July 2014; $74, PF-67Cam, November 2014; $62, PF-67Cam, November 2014										
1958D	800,953,300	5,293	65.8	100%	$0.10	$0.12	$0.15	$0.30	$1	$8	$425
	Auctions: $1,939, MS-67RD, January 2014; $106, MS-67RD, August 2014; $2,585, MS-67RD+, September 2014; $212, MS-67RD, September 2014										

h. 3 examples are known. **i.** No specimens have been reported being found in circulation, Wheat cent bags, Uncirculated rolls, "or other means that would lead to credibility of a true accidental release from the mint" (*Cherrypickers' Guide to Rare Die Varieties*, sixth edition, volume I). **j.** Included in circulation-strike 1958 mintage figure.

LINCOLN, MEMORIAL REVERSE (1959–2008)

Copper Alloy (1959–1982): **Designer:** *Victor D. Brenner (obverse), Frank Gasparro (reverse).* **Weight:** *3.11 grams.* **Composition:** *1959–1962—.950 copper, .050 tin and zinc; 1962–1982— .950 copper, .050 zinc.* **Diameter:** *19 mm.* **Edge:** *Plain.* **Mints:** *Philadelphia, Denver, San Francisco.*

Copper Alloy (1959–1982)

Copper Alloy, Proof

Copper-Plated Zinc (1982 to date): **Designer:** *Victor D. Brenner (obverse), Frank Gasparro (reverse).* **Weight:** *2.5 grams.* **Composition:** *copper-plated zinc (core: .992 zinc, .008 copper, with a plating of pure copper; total content .975 zinc, .025 copper).* **Diameter:** *19 mm.* **Edge:** *Plain.*

Copper-Plated Zinc (1982–2008)

Copper-Plated Zinc, Proof

History. In 1959 a new cent design, by Frank Gasparro, was introduced to mark the 150th anniversary of Abraham Lincoln's birth. Victor Brenner's portrait of Lincoln was maintained on the obverse. The new reverse featured a view of the Lincoln Memorial in Washington, D.C., with Daniel Chester French's massive statue of the president faintly visible within. In 1969 the dies were modified to strengthen the design, and Lincoln's head on the obverse was made slightly smaller. In 1973 the dies were further modified, and the engraver's initials (FG) were enlarged. In 1974 the initials were reduced slightly. During 1982 the dies were modified again and the bust, lettering, and date were made slightly smaller. The Lincoln Memorial reverse was used until 2009, when a switch was made to four new reverse designs honoring the bicentennial of Lincoln's birth. Lincoln Memorial cents were struck for circulation at the Philadelphia, Denver, and San Francisco mints, with the latter in smaller numbers. Partway through 1982 the bronze alloy was discontinued in favor of copper-coated zinc.

Striking and Sharpness. Striking varies and can range from "sloppy" to needle sharp. On the obverse, check Lincoln's hair and beard (although the sharpness of this feature varied in the dies; for more information see *A Guide Book of Lincoln Cents* [Bowers]). Tiny marks on the shoulder of Lincoln indicate a weak strike there. On the reverse the sharpness can vary, including on the tiny statue of Lincoln and the shrubbery. On the reverse there can be light striking on the steps of the Memorial, and at IBU and M of E PLURIBUS UNUM. The quality of the fields can vary, as well. Some early copper-coated zinc cents, particularly of 1982 and 1983, can have planchet blisters or other problems. All Proof Lincoln Memorial cents are of the mirror type, usually with cameo or frosted contrast between the devices and the fields. High quality is common. Special Mint Set (SMS) coins were struck in lieu of Proofs from 1965 to 1967, and in some instances these closely resemble Proofs.

Availability. Coins in this series are plentiful for standard dates and mintmarks. Collectible varieties exist, and are eagerly sought by specialists, who use the *Cherrypickers' Guide to Rare Die Varieties* as their standard reference. Some of the more popular varieties are illustrated and listed herein.

GRADING STANDARDS

MS-60 to 70 (Mint State). *Obverse and Reverse:* At MS-65 and higher, the luster is rich on all areas, except perhaps the shoulder (which may be grainy and show original planchet surface). There is no rubbing, and no contact marks are visible except under magnification. Coins with full or nearly full mint orange-red color can be designated RD; those with full or nearly full brown-toned surfaces can be designated BN; and those

1970-S, Large Date. Graded MS-65RD.

with a substantial percentage of red-orange and of brown can be called RB. Ideally, MS-65 or finer coins should have good eye appeal, which in the RB category means nicely blended colors, not stained or blotched. Below MS-65, full RD coins become scarce, and at MS-60 to 62 are virtually non-existent, unless they have been dipped. Copper is a very active metal, and influences such as slight abrasions, contact marks, and so on that define the grade also affect the color. The ANA grading standards allow for "dull" and/or "spotted" coins at MS-60 and 61, as well as incomplete luster. In the marketplace, interpretations often vary widely. BN and RB coins at MS-60 and 61 are apt to be more attractive than (dipped) RD coins.

Illustrated coin: Note this coin has a few flecks.

AU-50, 53, 55, 58 (About Uncirculated). *Obverse:* Same guidelines as for the preceding type except that tinges of original mint-red are sometimes seen on coins that have not been cleaned. *Reverse:* Slight wear is seen on the Lincoln Memorial, particularly on the steps, the columns, and the horizontal architectural elements above.

1996-D. Graded AU-50.

EF-40, 45 (Extremely Fine). *Obverse:* Light wear is seen on Lincoln's portrait, and hair detail is gone on the higher areas, especially above the ear. *Reverse:* Most detail is gone from the steps of the Lincoln Memorial, and the columns and other higher-relief architectural elements show wear.

The Lincoln cent with Memorial reverse is seldom collected in grades lower than EF-40.

1962-D. Graded EF-40.

PF-60 to 70 (Proof). *Obverse and Reverse:* PF-65 and higher coins are usually RB (colors should be nicely blended) or RD, the latter with bright red-orange fading slightly to hints of brown. Some tiny flecks are normal on coins certified as PF-65 but should be microscopic or absent above that. PF-60 and 61 coins can be dull, stained, or spotted and still have some original mint color. Coins with fingerprints must be given a low numerical grade. Lower-grade Proofs usually have poor eye appeal. Generally, Proofs below PF-64 are not desired by most collectors.

1979-S, Type 2. Graded PF-68RD Cameo.

Illustrated coin: A hint of toning is on Lincoln's jacket. Note the deep cameo contrast.

	Mintage	Cert	Avg	%MS	MS-63RB	MS-65RD	MS-66RD	MS-67RD
					PF-65RD	PF-67RD	PF-67Cam	PF-68DCam
1959	609,715,000	1,364	65.7	100%	$0.20	$0.30	$40	$550
	Auctions: $1,528, MS-67RD, April 2014; $2,233, MS-67RD, September 2014; $106, MS-66RD, July 2014; $118, MS-65RD, July 2014							
1959, Proof	1,149,291	2,809	67.2		$3	$20	$55	$865
	Auctions: $1,528, PF-68DCam, January 2014; $494, PF-67DCam, November 2014; $212, PF-67DCam, November 2014; $106, PF-68Cam, November 2014							
1959D	1,279,760,000	1,062	65.8	100%	$0.50	$0.55	$25	$475
	Auctions: $470, MS-67RD, July 2014; $441, MS-67RD, October 2014; $259, MS-67RD, November 2014; $646, MS-67RD, September 2013							

1960, Large Date

1960, Small Date

**1960-D, D Over D,
Large Over Small Date**
FS-01-1960D-101.

	Mintage	Cert	Avg	%MS	MS-63RB / PF-65RD	MS-65RD / PF-67RD	MS-66RD / PF-67Cam	MS-67RD / PF-68DCam
1960, Large Date (a)	586,405,000	1,581	65.5	100%	$0.20	$0.30	$30	
Auctions: $3,819, MS-67RD, December 2013; $70, MS-66RD, September 2014; $3,290, MS-64RD, October 2014									
1960, Small Date (a)	(b)	1,143	65.5	100%	$3	$7	$40	
Auctions: $3,349, MS-67RD, November 2013									
1960, Large Date, Proof	1,691,602	2,605	67.3		$2	$25	$45	$375
Auctions: $2,585, PF-69DCam, April 2013; $427, PF-68DCam, September 2014; $306, PF-68DCam, December 2014									
1960, Small Date, Proof	(c)	1,776	67.1		$22	$40	$75	$2,300
Auctions: $823, PF-68DCam, November 2014; $212, PF-67DCam, September 2014; $1,659, PF-68DCam, April 2013									
1960D, Large Date (a,d)	1,580,884,000	1,026	65.4	98%	$0.20	$0.30	$30	
Auctions: $306, MS-67RD, July 2014; $3,055, MS-67RD, September 2013									
1960D, Small Date (a)	(e)	1,352	65.6	99%	$0.20	$0.30	$30	$1,850
Auctions: $734, MS-67RD, July 2014; $825, MS-67RD, August 2014; $588, MS-67RD, November 2014; $1,880, MS-67RD, April 2013									
1960, D Over D, Small Over Large Date	(e)	262	64.2	98%	$200	$400	$2,000	
Auctions: $1,998, MS-66RD, June 2013; $153, MS-65RD, September 2014; $153, MS-65RD, November 2014									
1961	753,345,000	738	65.1	99%	$0.15	$0.30	$50	
Auctions: $176, MS-67RD, December 2013; $94, MS-63RB, July 2014									
1961, Proof	3,028,244	3,275	67.2		$1.50	$23	$40	$375
Auctions: $3,055, PF-69DCam, June 2013; $294, PF-68DCam, November 2014; $229, PF-68DCam, December 2014									
1961D	1,753,266,700	942	65.4	99%	$0.15	$0.30	$70	$100
Auctions: $4,406, MS-67RD, June 2014; $58, MS-66RD, September 2014									
1962	606,045,000	976	65.5	100%	$0.15	$0.30	$50	
Auctions: $8,813, MS-67RD, February 2014; $329, MS-67RD, July 2014; $2,350, MS-67RD, October 2014									
1962, Proof	3,218,019	3,589	67.3		$1.50	$10	$15	$100
Auctions: $1,058, PF-69DCam, June 2014; $764, PF-69DCam, November 2014; $123, PF-68DCam, August 2014									
1962D	1,793,148,140	824	65.4	99%	$0.15	$0.30	$75	$250
Auctions: $4,994, MS-67RD, January 2014; $3,290, MS-67RD, September 2014; $46, MS-66RD, August 2014									
1963	754,110,000	1,427	65.3	100%	$0.15	$0.30	$60	
Auctions: $3,173, MS-67RD, January 2014									
1963, Proof	3,075,645	3,995	67.4		$1.50	$10	$15	$55
Auctions: $499, PF-69DCam, February 2014; $441, PF-69DCam, November 2014; $153, PF-69DCam, December 2014									
1963D	1,774,020,400	591	65.4	100%	$0.15	$0.30	$100	$475
Auctions: $2,820, MS-67RD, September 2013; $66, MS-66RD, August 2014; $259, MS-66RD, October 2014									

a. The alignment of the 1 and 9 in the date can be used for a quick determination of Large versus Small Date. *Large Date:* the top of the 1 is significantly lower than the top of the 9. *Small Date:* the tops of the 1 and 9 are at the same level. b. Included in circulation-strike 1960, Large Date, mintage figure. c. Included in 1960, Large Date, Proof, mintage figure. d. A variety once called 1960-D, Large Date, D Over Horizontal D, has been disproved as such, and is now considered simply a triple-punched D. e. Included in 1960-D, Large Date, mintage figure.

1969-S, Doubled-Die Obverse
FS-01-1969S-101.

	Mintage	Cert	Avg	%MS	MS-63RB / PF-65RD	MS-65RD / PF-67RD	MS-66RD / PF-67Cam	MS-67RD / PF-68DCam
1964	2,648,575,000	683	65.2	100%	$0.15	$0.30	$65	
	Auctions: $3,525, MS-66RD+, October 2014; $441, MS-63RB, November 2014; $2,585, MS-61RD, April 2013							
1964, Proof	3,950,762	6,991	67.8		$1.50	$10	$15	$25
	Auctions: $217, PF-69DCam, June 2014; $188, PF-69DCam, November 2014; $141, PF-69DCam, December 2014; $470, PF-69RD, July 2014							
1964D	3,799,071,500	443	65.5	99%	$0.15	$0.30	$42	
	Auctions: $2,350, MS-67RD, July 2014; $3,173, MS-67RD, September 2014; $2,820, MS-67RD, November 2013; $176, MS-66RD+, November 2014							
1965	1,497,224,900	395	65.9	100%	$0.20	$0.50	$27	
	Auctions: $7,638, MS-67RD, January 2014; $353, MS-67RD, November 2014; $217, MS-67RD, December 2014; $176, MS-64RD, July 2014							
1965, Special Mint Set	2,360,000	1,444	66.3	100%	$11	$55		
	Auctions: $441, PF-65Cam, June 2013; $259, PF-65Cam, September 2014; $282, PF-65Cam, October 2014; $170, PF-65Cam, November 2014							
1966	2,188,147,783	275	65.5	99%	$0.20	$0.50	$60	
	Auctions: $382, MS-65RD, November 2013							
1966, Special Mint Set	2,261,583	1,861	66.7	100%	$10	$25		
	Auctions: $2,585, PF-67Cam, June 2014; $223, PF-67Cam, September 2014; $188, PF-66Cam, October 2014; $206, PF-68RD, September 2014							
1967	3,048,667,100	187	65.5	99%	$0.20	$0.50	$90	
	Auctions: $2,350, MS-67RD, January 2014; $358, MS-67RD, August 2014; $646, MS-67RD, September 2014; $529, MS-67RD, September 2014							
1967, Special Mint Set	1,863,344	1,906	66.8	100%	$11	$42		
	Auctions: $5,581, PF-68Cam, June 2014; $823, PF-67Cam, October 2014; $206, PF-66Cam, September 2014; $182, PF-66Cam, September 2014							
1968	1,707,880,970	312	65.5	100%	$0.25	$0.60	$35	
	Auctions: $1,293, MS-67RD, March 2013							
1968D	2,886,269,600	500	65.4	99%	$0.15	$0.40	$27	
	Auctions: $1,116, MS-67RD, April 2013							
1968S	258,270,001	683	65.4	100%	$0.15	$0.40	$30	
	Auctions: $529, MS-67RD, June 2013							
1968S, Proof	3,041,506	913	67.2		$1	$15	$20	$50
	Auctions: $764, PF-69DCam, June 2014							
1969	1,136,910,000	401	65.7	100%	$0.35	$0.70	$55	
	Auctions: $3,819, MS-62RD, June 2014							
1969D	4,002,832,200	476	65.4	99%	$0.15	$0.30	$30	
	Auctions: $1,234, MS-64RD, January 2014							
1969S	544,375,000	741	64.3	94%	$0.15	$0.50	$65	
	Auctions: $4,406, MS-67RD, January 2014; $64, MS-66RD, September 2014; $59, MS-66RD, November 2014; $53, MS-66RD, November 2014							
1969S, Doubled-Die Obverse ‡ (f)	(g)	12	57.7	33%	$75,000			
	Auctions: $21,150, AU-55, June 2014							
1969S, Proof	2,934,631	1,092	67.2		$1	$10	$15	$35
	Auctions: $1,009, PF-69DCam, June 2014; $852, PF-69DCam, November 2014							

‡ Ranked in the *100 Greatest U.S. Modern Coins.* **f.** Beware of specimens that exhibit only strike doubling, as opposed to a true doubled die; these are worth only face value. See Appendix A of the *Cherrypickers' Guide to Rare Die Varieties,* sixth edition, volume I. **g.** Included in circulation-strike 1969-S mintage figure.

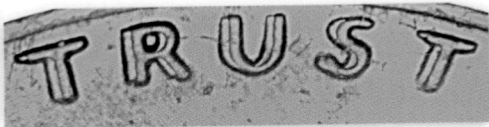

1970-S, Small Date (High 7)	1970-S, Large Date (Low 7)	1970-S, Doubled-Die Obverse FS-01-1970S-101.

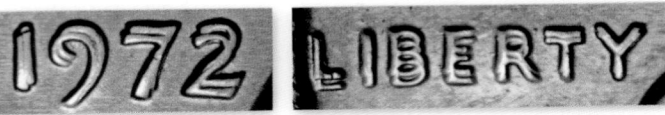

1972, Doubled-Die Obverse
FS-01-1972-101.

	Mintage	Cert	Avg	%MS	MS-63RB / PF-65RD	MS-65RD / PF-67RD	MS-66RD / PF-67Cam	MS-67RD / PF-68DCam
1970	1,898,315,000	365	65.5	99%	$0.30	$0.65	$25	$250
Auctions: $4,406, MS-67RD, March 2014								
1970D	2,891,438,900	307	65.3	100%	$0.15	$0.30	$70	$900
Auctions: $45, MS-66RD, June 2013								
1970S, All kinds	690,560,004							
1970S, Small Date (High 7)		744	64.4	100%	$25	$55	$240	
Auctions: $499, MS-66RD, June 2013								
1970S, Large Date (Low 7)		1,291	64.8	98%	$0.20	$0.50	$30	$950
Auctions: $382, MS-67RD, August 2014; $1,410, MS-67RD, April 2013; $70, Fair-2BN, August 2014								
1970S, Doubled-Die Obverse		12	63.1	83%				
Auctions: $10,350, MS-64RD, December 2008								
1970S, All kinds, Proof	2,632,810							
1970S, Small Date (High 7), Proof		425	66.6		$40	$65	$150	
Auctions: $4,994, PF-69DCam, December 2013; $96, PF-67Cam, September 2014; $66, PF-67Cam, October 2014								
1970S, Large Date (Low 7), Proof		1,011	67.0		$1	$15	$25	$65
Auctions: $764, PF-69DCam, November 2014; $1,058, PF-69DCam, December 2013; $50, PF-68RD, November 2014								
1971	1,919,490,000	614	65.4	99%	$0.25	$0.60	$25	
Auctions: $4,406, MS-67RD, June 2014; $217, MS-67RD, August 2014								
1971, Doubled-Die Obverse	(h)	26	63.2	92%		$50		
Auctions: $82, AU-58, December 2013; $56, AU-50BN, November 2014								
1971D	2,911,045,600	237	65.4	100%	$0.20	$0.50	$24	$850
Auctions: $329, MS-62BN, September 2013								
1971S	525,133,459	396	65.4	98%	$0.20	$0.50	$50	
Auctions: $3,290, MS-67RD, June 2014; $411, MS-67RD, September 2014								
1971S, Proof	3,220,733	1,144	67.3		$1	$18	$30	$120
Auctions: $764, PF-68RD, June 2014								
1971S, Doubled-Die Obverse, Proof	(i)	90	66.5		$40	$150	$200	
Auctions: $718, PF-67RD, April 2013								
1972	2,933,255,000	575	65.1	96%	$0.15	$0.30	$32	
Auctions: $3,290, MS-67RD, December 2013; $66, MS-60BN, August 2014								
1972, Doubled-Die Obverse (j)	(k)	2,180	64.3	99%	$400	$650	$1,050	$5,800
Auctions: $12,925, MS-67RD, March 2014; $1,880, MS-66RD, July 2014; $987, MS-66RD, July 2014								
1972D	2,665,071,400	213	65.1	97%	$0.15	$0.30	$30	
Auctions: $2,820, MS-67RD, June 2013								
1972S	376,939,108	269	64.9	98%	$0.25	$0.75	$75	$1,000
Auctions: $1,410, MS-67RD, June 2013								
1972S, Proof	3,260,996	658	67.3		$1	$15	$20	$35
Auctions: $499, PF-69DCam, June 2013								

h. Included in 1971 mintage figure. **i.** Included in 1971-S, Proof, mintage figure. **j.** Several less dramatically doubled varieties exist; these command premiums over the normal coin but are worth considerably less than the variety pictured. Counterfeits of the 1972 doubled die are frequently encountered. **k.** Included in 1972 mintage figure.

	Mintage	Cert	Avg	%MS	MS-63RB / PF-65RD	MS-65RD / PF-67RD	MS-66RD / PF-67Cam	MS-67RD / PF-68DCam
1973	3,728,245,000	407	65.7	100%	$0.15	$0.30	$35	$600
	Auctions: $470, MS-67RB, August 2013							
1973D	3,549,576,588	416	65.6	100%	$0.15	$0.30	$35	
	Auctions: $4,994, MS-67RD, February 2014							
1973S	317,177,295	233	65.1	99%	$0.25	$0.85	$200	
	Auctions: $558, MS-66RD, December 2013							
1973S, Proof	2,760,339	240	67.5		$1	$13	$16	$30
	Auctions: $235, PF-69DCam, November 2014; $61, PF-69DCam, May 2013							
1974	4,232,140,523	281	65.9	100%	$0.15	$0.30	$25	$175
	Auctions: $382, MS-66RD, November 2013							
1974D	4,235,098,000	312	65.6	100%	$0.15	$0.30	$25	$100
	Auctions: $206, MS-67RD, July 2013							
1974S	409,426,660	144	65.1	100%	$0.25	$0.75	$100	$900
	Auctions: $1,998, MS-67RD, September 2013							
1974S, Proof	2,612,568	270	67.3		$1	$13	$16	$30
	Auctions: $45, PF-69DCam, May 2013							
1975	5,451,476,142	322	65.8	100%	$0.15	$0.30	$30	$150
	Auctions: $6,463, MS-62RD, January 2014							
1975D	4,505,275,300	193	65.7	100%	$0.15	$0.30	$25	$350
	Auctions: $4,113, MS-67RD, March 2014							
1975S, Proof	2,845,450	474	67.2		$3.50	$13	$16	$30
	Auctions: $109, PF-69DCam, August 2009							
1976	4,674,292,426	172	65.9	99%	$0.15	$0.30	$25	$55
	Auctions: $7,931, MS-68RD, January 2014							
1976D	4,221,592,455	112	65.3	100%	$0.15	$0.30	$35	$750
	Auctions: $529, MS-67RD, June 2013							
1976S, Proof	4,149,730	740	67.2		$3.20	$13	$16	$30
	Auctions: $153, PF-69DCam, June 2013							
1977	4,469,930,000	250	66.1	100%	$0.15	$0.30	$55	$130
	Auctions: $529, MS-67RD+, September 2014; $113, MS-67RD, June 2013; $306, MS-63RD, October 2014							
1977D	4,194,062,300	405	65.2	100%	$0.15	$0.30	$90	$650
	Auctions: $1,175, MS-67RD, June 2013; $153, MS-64RD, July 2014							
1977S, Proof	3,251,152	405	68.2		$2.50	$13	$16	$30
	Auctions: $42, PF-69DCam, September 2009							
1978	5,558,605,000	153	65.5	99%	$0.15	$0.30	$80	$625
	Auctions: $4,259, MS-67RD+, September 2014; $3,819, MS-67RD, September 2013							
1978D	4,280,233,400	174	65.5	100%	$0.15	$0.30	$75	$425
	Auctions: $259, MS-67RD, June 2013							
1978S, Proof	3,127,781	430	67.5		$2.50	$13	$16	$30
	Auctions: $75, PF-69DCam, May 2009							
1979	6,018,515,000	613	66.6	100%	$0.15	$0.30	$20	$70
	Auctions: $23, MS-67RD, November 2009							
1979D	4,139,357,254	276	65.5	100%	$0.15	$0.30	$60	
	Auctions: $764, MS-67RD, June 2014; $306, MS-64RD, July 2014							
1979S, Type 1, Proof	3,677,175	549	68.3		$5	$11	$13	$20
	Auctions: $920, PF-70DCam, January 2010							
1979S, Type 2, Proof	(l)	641	68.0		$6	$17	$20	$30
	Auctions: $3,819, PF-70DCam, August 2013							

l. Included in 1979-S, Type 1, Proof, mintage figure.

1980, Doubled-Die Obverse
FS-01-1980-101.

1982, Large Date   **1982, Small Date**

	Mintage	Cert	Avg	%MS	MS-63RB / PF-65RD	MS-65RD / PF-67RD	MS-66RD / PF-67Cam	MS-67RD / PF-68DCam
1980	7,414,705,000	176	65.3	100%	$0.15	$0.30	$25	$125
	Auctions: $212, MS-67RD, June 2013; $764, MS-64RD, September 2014; $823, MS-64RD, November 2014							
1980, Doubled-Die Obverse	(m)	231	61.7	79%	$225	$350		
	Auctions: $253, MS-65RD, September 2008							
1980D (n)	5,140,098,660	257	65.3	100%	$0.15	$0.30	$40	$400
	Auctions: $499, MS-67RD, March 2013; $59, MS-65RD, July 2014							
1980S, Proof	3,554,806	861	68.4		$2.50	$10	$11	$15
	Auctions: $94, PF-70DCam, October 2009							
1981	7,491,750,000	150	65.3	99%	$0.15	$0.30	$35	$125
	Auctions: $1,058, MS-66BN, September 2013							
1981D	5,373,235,677	181	65.5	99%	$0.15	$0.30	$40	$225
	Auctions: $823, MS-63RD, June 2013							
1981S, Type 1, Proof	4,063,083	987	68.3		$3	$10	$11	$15
	Auctions: $4,113, PF-70DCam, August 2013							
1981S, Type 2, Proof	(o)	597	67.9		$20	$30	$40	$55
	Auctions: $123, PF-69DCam, July 2014; $76, PF-69DCam, November 2014							
1982, Large Date	10,712,525,000	114	64.9	100%	$0.20	$0.35	$25	$55
	Auctions: $55, MS-67RD, October 2013							
1982, Small Date	(p)	134	65.3	100%	$0.30	$0.50	$45	$125
	Auctions: $92, MS-67RD, May 2014							
1982D	6,012,979,368	136	65.3	99%	$0.15	$0.30	$25	$35
	Auctions: $764, MS-68RD, June 2013							
1982, Zinc, Large Date	(p)	368	66.3	100%	$0.35	$0.50	$35	$60
	Auctions: $646, MS-68RD, June 2013; $31, MS-66RD, September 2014							
1982, Zinc, Small Date	(p)	383	66.5	100%	$0.50	$0.85	$37	
	Auctions: $299, MS-66RD, December 2009							
1982D, Zinc, Large Date	(q)	244	66.4	100%	$0.20	$0.40	$25	$45
	Auctions: $27, MS-66RD, April 2009							
1982D, Zinc, Small Date	(q)	236	66.2	100%	$0.15	$0.30	$15	$275
	Auctions: $27, MS-66RD, April 2009							
1982S, Proof	3,857,479	456	68.1		$2.50	$10	$11	$15
	Auctions: No auction records available.							

m. Included in 1980 mintage figure. **n.** A variety previously listed in the *Cherrypickers' Guide* as a 1980-D, D Over S, has since been delisted from that catalog. It should command no premium. **o.** Included in 1981-S, Type 1, Proof, mintage figure. **p.** Included in 1982, Large Date, mintage figure. **q.** Included in 1982-D mintage figure.

  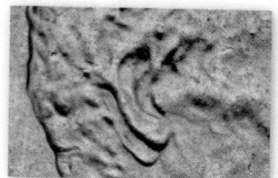

1983, Doubled-Die Reverse
FS-01-1983-801.

1984, Doubled Ear
FS-01-1984-101.

	Mintage	Cert	Avg	%MS	MS-63RB / PF-65RD	MS-65RD / PF-67RD	MS-66RD / PF-67Cam	MS-67RD / PF-68DCam
1983	7,752,355,000	222	65.4	97%	$0.15	$0.30	$18	$45
	Auctions: $282, MS-66RB, July 2014; $23,500, MS-62RB, December 2013							
1983, Doubled-Die Reverse (r)	(s) 936		64.9	98%	$250	$385	$550	$1,200
	Auctions: $1,763, MS-67RD, March 2014; $558, MS-66RD, July 2014; $411, MS-66RD, November 2014							
1983D	6,467,199,428	219	66.6	100%	$0.15	$0.30	$15	$30
	Auctions: $646, MS-68RD, March 2013							
1983S, Proof	3,279,126	552	68.4		$3	$10	$11	$15
	Auctions: $115, PF-70DCam, October 2009							
1984	8,151,079,000	186	65.7	99%	$0.15	$0.30	$15	$35
	Auctions: $734, MS-64RD, September 2013							
1984, Doubled Ear (t)	(u) 546		65.5	99%	$175	$230	$350	$425
	Auctions: $411, MS-67RD, September 2014; $382, MS-67RD, November 2014; $1,528, MS-67RD, December 2013							
1984D	5,569,238,906	197	66.1	99%	$0.15	$0.30	$15	$35
	Auctions: $1,410, MS-68RD, June 2013; $141, MS-64RD, July 2014							
1984S, Proof	3,065,110	480	68.9		$4	$10	$11	$15
	Auctions: $544, PF-70DCam, June 2013							
1985	5,648,489,887	519	66.4	100%	$0.15	$0.30	$15	$35
	Auctions: $5,875, MS-68RD, February 2014; $764, MS-65RD, October 2014							
1985D	5,287,339,926	357	66.8	99%	$0.15	$0.30	$15	$30
	Auctions: $44, MS-68RD, August 2009							
1985S, Proof	3,362,821	538	68.9		$5	$11	$12	$15
	Auctions: $881, PF-70DCam, June 2013							
1986	4,491,395,493	253	66.6	100%	$0.15	$0.30	$15	$35
	Auctions: $881, MS-66BN, February 2014							
1986D	4,442,866,698	284	66.8	100%	$0.15	$0.30	$15	$35
	Auctions: $107, MS-68RD, June 2013							
1986S, Proof	3,010,497	490	68.9		$7	$11	$12	$15
	Auctions: $558, PF-70DCam, June 2013							
1987	4,682,466,931	340	66.8	100%	$0.15	$0.30	$14	$30
	Auctions: $170, MS-68RD, June 2013							
1987D	4,879,389,514	469	66.6	100%	$0.15	$0.30	$15	$30
	Auctions: $529, MS-68RD, June 2013							
1987S, Proof	4,227,728	718	68.9		$5	$10	$11	$15
	Auctions: $353, PF-70DCam, June 2013							
1988	6,092,810,000	196	66.4	99%	$0.15	$0.30	$20	$40
	Auctions: $683, MS-68RD, June 2014; $881, MS-68RD, September 2014							
1988D	5,253,740,443	260	66.6	100%	$0.15	$0.30	$14	$25
	Auctions: $683, MS-68RD, June 2014; $881, MS-68RD, September 2014							
1988S, Proof	3,262,948	442	68.9		$9	$11	$12	$15
	Auctions: $115, PF-70DCam, May 2013							

r. All reverse lettering is strongly doubled, as are the designer's initials and portions of the Lincoln Memorial. **s.** Included in 1983 mintage figure. **t.** Values are for coins certified as the Doubled Ear variety (FS-101). More than 1,500 certifications exist for all 1984 doubled-die varieties; this number certainly includes FS-101, but it is unknown how many. **u.** Included in 1984 mintage figure.

1992, Normal **1992, Close AM**

	Mintage	Cert	Avg	%MS	MS-63RB / PF-65RD	MS-65RD / PF-67RD	MS-66RD / PF-67Cam	MS-67RD / PF-68DCam
1989	7,261,535,000	325	66.5	100%	$0.15	$0.30	$14	$25
	Auctions: $4,113, MS-68RD, June 2013							
1989D	5,345,467,111	323	66.4	100%	$0.15	$0.30	$14	$30
	Auctions: $247, MS-68RD, June 2014							
1989S, Proof	3,220,194	571	68.9		$9	$11	$12	$15
	Auctions: $86, PF-70DCam, August 2013							
1990	6,851,765,000	204	66.6	100%	$0.15	$0.30	$19	$35
	Auctions: $705, MS-62BN, February 2014							
1990D	4,922,894,533	293	66.8	100%	$0.15	$0.30	$14	$25
	Auctions: $118, MS-64RD, July 2014							
1990S, Proof	3,299,559	812	69.0		$5	$10	$11	$15
	Auctions: $529, PF-67RD, September 2013							
1990, No S, Proof	(v)	61	67.9		$4,500	$6,500	—	
	Auctions: $19,975, PF-69DCam, January 2014							
1991	5,165,940,000	199	66.7	100%	$0.15	$0.30	$14	$25
	Auctions: $353, MS-68RD, July 2014; $585, MS-68RD, September 2013							
1991D	4,158,446,076	340	66.9	100%	$0.15	$0.30	$14	$25
	Auctions: $135, MS-68RD, June 2013							
1991S, Proof	2,867,787	807	69.1		$12	$13	$14	$16
	Auctions: $84, PF-70DCam, May 2013							
1992	4,648,905,000	514	67.0	100%	$0.15	$0.30	$14	$25
	Auctions: $482, MS-68RD, February 2013							
1992, Close AM ‡ (w)	(x)	5	60.0	60%	—	—		
	Auctions: No auction records available.							
1992D	4,448,673,300	283	66.7	99%	$0.15	$0.30	$14	$25
	Auctions: $58, MS-68RD, June 2013							
1992D, Close AM ‡ (w)	(y)	14	60.4	64%	—	—		
	Auctions: No auction records available.							
1992S, Proof	4,176,560	1,728	69.0		$5	$10	$11	$12
	Auctions: $66, PF-70DCam, May 2013							
1993	5,684,705,000	260	66.9	100%	$0.15	$0.30	$14	$25
	Auctions: $188, MS-65RD, July 2014							
1993D	6,426,650,571	405	66.9	100%	$0.15	$0.30	$14	$25
	Auctions: $40, MS-68RD, June 2013							
1993S, Proof	3,394,792	1,672	68.8		$9	$10	$11	$12
	Auctions: $84, PF-70DCam, November 2014; $55, PF-70DCam, May 2013							

‡ Ranked in the *100 Greatest U.S. Modern Coins*. **v.** An estimated 100 to 250 Proofs of 1990 were struck without the S mintmark (apparently from a circulation-strike die, without a mintmark, which had been given a mirror finish). This error escaped the notice of at least 14 people during die preparation and coining. **w.** The reverse hub used for cents from 1974 to 1992 had the AM of AMERICA separated. A new reverse hub with the AM close together was used for all cents in 1993. At least one new reverse die of each type was used for 1992-P and -D cents made for circulation but it is not known if this usage was deliberate or accidental. Proof coinage reverted to the wide-AM design in 1994. In subsequent years a few dies from the circulation-strike hub were used for making Proof coins. **x.** Included in 1992 mintage figure. **y.** Included in 1992-D mintage figure.

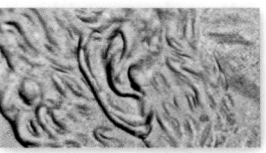

1995, Doubled-Die Obverse
FS-01-1995-101.

1997, Doubled Ear
FS-01-1997-101.

	Mintage	Cert	Avg	%MS	MS-63RB / PF-65RD	MS-65RD / PF-67RD	MS-66RD / PF-67Cam	MS-67RD / PF-68DCam
1994	6,500,850,000	188	66.7	99%	$0.15	$0.30	$14	$25
Auctions: $881, MS-65RD, September 2013								
1994D	7,131,765,000	271	66.8	99%	$0.15	$0.30	$15	$25
Auctions: $176, MS-68RD, March 2013								
1994S, Proof	3,269,923	1,427	68.9		$9	$11	$12	$13
Auctions: $66, PF-70DCam, May 2013								
1995	6,411,440,000	316	66.6	100%	$0.15	$0.30	$15	$30
Auctions: $149, MS-68RD, June 2014								
1995, Doubled-Die Obverse ‡	(z)	18,053	67.2	100%	$35	$50	$90	$220
Auctions: $206, MS-68RD, December 2014; $317, MS-68RD, May 2013; $72, MS-67RD, August 2014; $66, MS-67RD, August 2014								
1995D	7,128,560,000	270	66.9	99%	$0.15	$0.30	$15	$35
Auctions: $82, MS-68RD, August 2014; $764, MS-68RD, September 2014; $223, MS-68RD, September 2014								
1995S, Proof	2,797,481	1,432	69.0		$9	$11	$12	$13
Auctions: No auction records available.								
1996	6,612,465,000	292	66.8	100%	$0.15	$0.30	$12	$20
Auctions: $188, MS-68RD, June 2013; $51, MS-65RD, December 2014								
1996, Wide AM (w)	(aa)	(bb)			—	—		
Auctions: No auction records available.								
1996D	6,510,795,000	417	66.9	100%	$0.15	$0.30	$12	$20
Auctions: $3,525, MS-65RD, September 2013; $129, MS-64RD, November 2014; $153, MS-62RD, July 2014								
1996S, Proof	2,525,265	1,297	69.0		$4.50	$9	$10	$12
Auctions: $76, PF-70DCam, November 2014; $92, PF-70DCam, May 2013								
1997	4,622,800,000	168	66.4	100%	$0.15	$0.30	$15	$42
Auctions: $1,998, MS-68RD, June 2013; $764, MS-66RD, October 2014; $66, MS-64RD, November 2014								
1997, Doubled Ear	(cc)	11	64.5	100%	$275	$500		
Auctions: $153, MS-65RD, February 2014; $82, MS-64RD, July 2014								
1997D	4,576,555,000	222	66.7	100%	$0.15	$0.30	$14	$30
Auctions: $585, MS-68RD, September 2013								
1997S, Proof	2,796,678	1,228	69.0		$10	$12	$13	$14
Auctions: No auction records available.								
1998	5,032,155,000	165	66.3	98%	$0.15	$0.30	$12	$18
Auctions: $705, MS-68RD, September 2014; $600, MS-68RD, October 2014; $940, MS-67RD, April 2013; $223, MS-66RD, July 2014								
1998, Wide AM ‡ (w)	(dd)	294	65.0	97%	$15	$25	$40	$600
Auctions: $84, MS-66RD, November 2014; $84, MS-66RD, November 2014; $72, MS-65RD, June 2014								
1998D	5,225,353,500	199	66.8	100%	$0.15	$0.30	$17	$57
Auctions: $235, MS-68RD, June 2013; $59, MS-67RD, July 2014								
1998S, Proof	2,086,507	1,428	68.9		$9	$10	$11	$12
Auctions: $115, PF-70DCam, December 2009								
1998S, Close AM, Proof (ee)	(ff)	73	68.8		$475	$525	$575	$700
Auctions: $7,475, PF-70DCam, April 2012								

‡ Ranked in the *100 Greatest U.S. Modern Coins*. **w.** The reverse hub used for cents from 1974 to 1992 had the AM of AMERICA separated. A new reverse hub with the AM close together was used for all cents in 1993. At least one new reverse die of each type was used for 1992-P and -D cents made for circulation but it is not known if this usage was deliberate or accidental. Proof coinage reverted to the wide-AM design in 1994. In subsequent years a few dies from the circulation-strike hub were used for making Proof coins. **z.** Included in 1995 mintage figure. **aa.** Included in 1996 mintage figure. **bb.** Included in certified population for 1996. **cc.** Included in 1997 mintage figure. **dd.** Included in 1998 mintage figure. **ee.** Varieties were made in the circulation-strike style, with the A and the M in AMERICA nearly touching each other. On normal Proofs the two letters have a wide space between them. **ff.** Included 1998-S, Proof, mintage figure.

1999, Normal	1999, Wide AM	1999-S, Normal, Proof	1999-S, Close AM, Proof

	Mintage	Cert	Avg	%MS	MS-63RB / PF-65RD	MS-65RD / PF-67RD	MS-66RD / PF-67Cam	MS-67RD / PF-68DCam
1999	5,237,600,000	229	65.5	100%	$0.15	$0.30	$13	$30
	Auctions: $940, MS-67RD, October 2014; $368, MS-67RD, October 2014; $1,410, MS-66RD, July 2014							
1999, Wide AM ‡ (w)	(gg)	171	64.4	95%		$500		$1,500
	Auctions: $470, MS-66RD, October 2014; $764, MS-65RD, June 2014; $259, MS-65RD, October 2014							
1999D	6,360,065,000	233	66.9	100%	$0.15	$0.30	$12	$25
	Auctions: $1,293, MS-69RD, June 2013							
1999S, Proof	3,347,966	5,812	69.1		$6	$9	$10	$12
	Auctions: $62, PF-70DCam, January 2013							
1999S, Close AM, Proof (ee)	(hh)	294	68.3		$80	$100	$125	$190
	Auctions: $212, PF-69DCam, May 2013; $96, PF-67DCam, September 2014; $74, PF-67DCam, November 2014							
2000	5,503,200,000	849	65.8	100%	$0.15	$0.30	$12	$25
	Auctions: $852, MS-68RD, November 2014; $62, MS-66RD, December 2014; $764, MS-66RD, April 2013; $223, MS-65RD, July 2014							
2000, Wide AM (w)	(ii)	874	65.6	100%	$10	$20	$35	$55
	Auctions: $40, MS-66RD, November 2014; $30, MS-66RD, November 2014; $28, MS-66RD, November 2014							
2000D	8,774,220,000	192	66.7	100%	$0.15	$0.30	$12	$25
	Auctions: $118, MS-64RD, July 2014; $31, MS-63RD, November 2014; $141, MS-62RD, April 2014							
2000S, Proof	4,047,993	5,527	69.1		$4	$7	$8	$10
	Auctions: $55, PF-70DCam, May 2013							
2001	4,959,600,000	96	66.8	100%	$0.15	$0.30	$11	$18
	Auctions: $103, MS-65RD, November 2014; $74, MS-65RD, November 2014; $59, MS-65RD, November 2014							
2001D	5,374,990,000	180	66.9	100%	$0.15	$0.30	$11	$18
	Auctions: $441, MS-69RD, June 2013							
2001S, Proof	3,184,606	4,280	69.1		$4	$7	$8	$10
	Auctions: $64, PF-70DCam, May 2013							
2002	3,260,800,000	110	67.3	100%	$0.15	$0.30	$11	$16
	Auctions: $123, MS-69RD, June 2014							
2002D	4,028,055,000	134	67.2	100%	$0.15	$0.30	$12	$19
	Auctions: $213, MS-69RD, June 2013							
2002S, Proof	3,211,995	4,707	69.1		$4	$7	$8	$10
	Auctions: $79, PF-70DCam, June 2013							
2003	3,300,000,000	256	67.0	100%	$0.15	$0.30	$11	$16
	Auctions: $66, MS-69RD, June 2013							
2003D	3,548,000,000	149	66.3	100%	$0.15	$0.30	$10	$15
	Auctions: $141, MS-69RD, July 2013							
2003S, Proof	3,298,439	7,801	69.1		$4	$7	$8	$10
	Auctions: $229, PF-70DCam, November 2014; $60, PF-70DCam, May 2013							
2004	3,379,600,000	149	66.8	100%	$0.15	$0.30	$10	$20
	Auctions: $353, MS-69RD, June 2013							
2004D	3,456,400,000	124	66.5	100%	$0.15	$0.30	$10	$18
	Auctions: $49, MS-68RD, June 2013							

‡ Ranked in the *100 Greatest U.S. Modern Coins*. **w.** The reverse hub used for cents from 1974 to 1992 had the AM of AMERICA separated. A new reverse hub with the AM close together was used for all cents in 1993. At least one new reverse die of each type was used for 1992-P and -D cents made for circulation but it is not known if this usage was deliberate or accidental. Proof coinage reverted to the wide-AM design in 1994. In subsequent years a few dies from the circulation-strike hub were used for making Proof coins. **ee.** Varieties were made in the circulation-strike style, with the A and the M in AMERICA nearly touching each other. On normal Proofs the two letters have a wide space between them. **gg.** Included in 1999 mintage figure. **hh.** Included in 1999-S, Proof, mintage figure. **ii.** Included in 2000 mintage figure.

| | Mintage | Cert | Avg | %MS | MS-63RB | MS-65RD | MS-66RD | MS-67RD |
					PF-65RD	PF-67RD	PF-67Cam	PF-68DCam
2004S, Proof	2,965,422	5,239	69.1		$4	$7	$8	$10
	Auctions: $59, PF-70DCam, May 2013							
2005	3,935,600,000	2,564	67.3	100%	$0.15	$0.30	$10	$25
	Auctions: $53, MS-69RD, June 2009							
2005D	3,764,450,500	2,478	66.9	100%	$0.15	$0.30	$20	$40
	Auctions: $42, MS-67RD, May 2009							
2005S, Proof	3,344,679	10,764	69.1		$4	$7	$8	$10
	Auctions: $51, PF-70DCam, May 2013							
2006	4,290,000,000	1,424	67.0	100%	$0.15	$0.30	$10	$18
	Auctions: $23, MS-67RD, May 2009							
2006D	3,944,000,000	1,195	66.7	100%	$0.15	$0.30	$13	$25
	Auctions: $21, MS-67RD, May 2009							
2006S, Proof	3,054,436	5,061	69.2		$4	$7	$8	$10
	Auctions: $58, PF-70DCam, May 2013							
2007	3,762,400,000	528	67.0	100%	$0.15	$0.30	$16	$30
	Auctions: $39, MS-67RD, May 2009							
2007D	3,638,800,000	319	66.1	100%	$0.15	$0.30	$16	$33
	Auctions: $646, MS-65RD, August 2013							
2007S, Proof	2,577,166	4,616	69.1		$4	$7	$8	$10
	Auctions: $59, PF-70DCam, May 2013							
2008	2,558,800,000	208	67.3	100%	$0.15	$0.30	$12	$18
	Auctions: $21, MS-67RD, May 2009							
2008D	2,849,600,000	189	66.7	100%	$0.15	$0.30	$15	$31
	Auctions: $247, MS-68RD, March 2013							
2008S, Proof	2,169,561	3,636	69.1		$4	$7	$8	$10
	Auctions: $60, PF-70DCam, May 2013							

LINCOLN BICENTENNIAL (2009)

Designer: *Victor D. Brenner (obverse), Richard Masters (Birth and Early Childhood reverse); Charles Vickers (Formative Years reverse); Joel Iskowitz (Professional Life reverse); and Susan Gamble (Presidency reverse).*
Weight: *Regular-issue coins—2.5 grams; special coins included in collector sets—3.1 grams.*
Composition: *Regular-issue coins—copper-plated zinc (core: .992 zinc, .008 copper, with a plating of pure copper; total content .975 zinc, .025 copper); special coins included in collector sets—.950 copper, .005 tin and zinc.* **Diameter:** *19 mm.* **Edge:** *Plain.* **Mints:** *Philadelphia, Denver, San Francisco.*

Birth and Early Childhood

Formative Years

Birth and Early Childhood, Proof

Formative Years, Proof

Circulation Strike

Proof

Professional Life

Presidency

Professional Life, Proof

Presidency, Proof

History. The one-cent coins issued during 2009 pay unique tribute to President Abraham Lincoln, commemorating the bicentennial of his birth and the 100th anniversary of the first issuance of the Lincoln cent. Four different reverse designs were issued by the U.S. Mint, each representing a major aspect of Lincoln's life. The obverse retained the traditional profile portrait of previous years.

The reverse designs, released quarterly throughout 2009, are:

- Birth and Early Childhood (designer, Richard Masters; sculptor, Jim Licaretz), depicting a small log cabin like the one in which Lincoln was born in Kentucky.

- Formative Years (designer and sculptor, Charles Vickers), showing a youthful Abe Lincoln taking a break from rail-splitting to read a book, in Indiana.

- Professional Life (designer, Joel Iskowitz; sculptor, Don Everhart), with Lincoln standing in front of the Illinois state capitol in Springfield, symbolic of his pre-presidential career in law and politics.

- Presidency (designer, Susan Gamble; sculptor, Joseph Menna), depicting the partially completed U.S. Capitol dome in Washington, D.C., as it appeared when Lincoln held office.

The coins issued for general circulation were made of the exact same copper-plated composition used in the cent since 1982. Special versions struck for inclusion in collector sets were made of the same alloy as the first Lincoln cents of 1909—95 parts copper and 5 parts tin and zinc—and with a Satin finish.

Several die varieties (both circulation-strike and Proof) exist with minor doubling in the Formative Years reverse. Their values, which vary generally according to the severity of the doubling, are not yet firmly established with an active buy-and-sell market. These and other Lincoln cent die varieties are studied in greater depth in the *Cherrypickers' Guide to Rare Die Varieties.*

Striking and Sharpness. Striking is generally sharp. The quality of the fields can vary. Some 2009 cents, even from original rolls and bags, have surface marks that look like water spots. All Proof Lincoln Bicentennial cents are mirror Proofs, usually with cameo or frosted contrast between the devices and the fields.

Availability. Cents of this year were minted in quantities that, while large, were much smaller than for previous years (in the hundreds of millions, rather than multiple billions), if each of the four designs is considered individually. They are readily available in the numismatic marketplace, and are starting to be seen more frequently in circulation. High-quality Proofs (PF-69 and 70) are common in the secondary market.

GRADING STANDARDS

MS-60 to 70 (Mint State). *Obverse and Reverse:* At MS-65 and higher, luster is rich on all areas; there is no rubbing, and no contact marks are visible except under magnification. Coins with full or nearly full mint orange-red color can be designated RD; those with a substantial percentage of red-orange and of brown can be called RB; and those with full (or nearly full) brown-toned surfaces can be designated BN. Some 2009

2009, Formative Years. Graded MS-63.

cents, even from original rolls and bags, have surface marks that look like water spots.

The Lincoln Bicentennial cent is seldom collected in grades lower than MS-60.

PF-60 to 70 (Proof). *Obverse and Reverse:* PF-65 and higher coins are RB (with colors nicely blended) or RD, the latter with bright red-orange color sometimes fading to hints of brown. Some tiny flecks are normal on coins certified as PF-65 but should be microscopic or absent above that level. PF-60 and 61 coins can be dull, stained, or spotted and still have some original mint luster. Proof coins with fingerprints are impaired and must

2009-S, Presidency. Graded PF-70RD Deep Cameo.

be given a lower numerical grade. Lower-grade Proofs usually have poor eye appeal. Generally, Proofs of these types below PF-65 are not desired by most collectors.

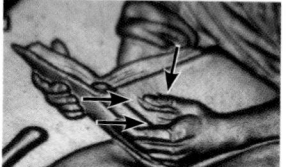

2009, Formative Years, Seven Fingers
FS-01-2009-801.
Other varieties exist.

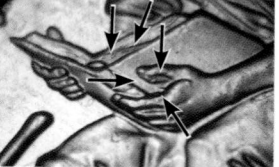

2009, Formative Years, Seven Fingers
FS-01-2009-802.
Other varieties exist.

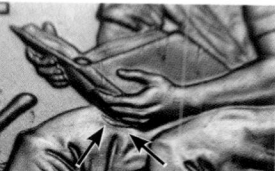

2009, Formative Years, Doubled Pinky
FS-01-2009-805.
Other varieties exist.

2009, Formative Years, Skeleton Finger
FS-01-2009-808.
Other varieties exist.

	Mintage	Cert	Avg	%MS	MS-63RB	MS-65RD	MS-66RD / PF-65RD	MS-67RD / PF-67RD	MS-68RD / PF-67Cam	MS-69RD / PF-68DCam
2009, Birth and Early Childhood	284,400,000	13,751	65.8	100%	$0.15	$0.30	$12	$20		
Auctions: $4, MS-66RD, June 2013										
2009, Birth and Early Childhood, copper, Satin Finish	784,614	1,579	67.7	100%					$15	$45
Auctions: No auction records available.										
2009D, Birth and Early Childhood	350,400,000	4,949	65.9	100%	$0.15	$0.30	$12	$20		
Auctions: No auction records available.										
2009D, Birth and Early Childhood, copper, Satin Finish	784,614	1,663	67.7	100%					$17	$95
Auctions: No auction records available.										
2009S, Birth and Early Childhood, Proof	2,995,615	14,333	69.1				$4	$7	$8	$10
Auctions: $86, PF-70DCam, May 2013										
2009, Formative Years (a)	376,000,000	27,030	65.9	100%	$0.15	$0.30	$12	$20		
Auctions: $16, MS-66RD, March 2013										
2009, Formative Years, copper, Satin Finish	784,614	1,481	67.6	100%					$15	$45
Auctions: No auction records available.										
2009D, Formative Years (a)	363,600,000	2,640	65.9	100%	$0.15	$0.30	$12	$20		
Auctions: No auction records available.										
2009D, Formative Years, copper, Satin Finish	784,614	1,516	67.5	100%					$20	$250
Auctions: No auction records available.										
2009S, Formative Years, Proof	2,995,615	14,222	69.1				$4	$7	$8	$10
Auctions: $96, PF-70DCam, June 2013										

a. Several varieties exist with minor die doubling. Their values vary and their market is not yet firmly established.

	Mintage	Cert	Avg	%MS	MS-63RB	MS-65RD	MS-66RD	MS-67RD	MS-68RD	MS-69RD
							PF-65RD	PF-67RD	PF-67Cam	PF-68DCam
2009, Professional Life	316,000,000	17,267	66.0	100%	$0.15	$0.30	$12	$20		
	Auctions: $4, MS-66RD, June 2013									
2009, Professional Life, copper, Satin Finish	784,614	1,828	67.8	100%					$15	$45
	Auctions: No auction records available.									
2009D, Professional Life	336,000,000	1,943	66.0	100%	$0.15	$0.30	$12	$20		
	Auctions: No auction records available.									
2009D, Professional Life, copper, Satin Finish	784,614	1,474	67.6	100%					$15	$210
	Auctions: No auction records available.									
2009S, Professional Life, Proof	2,995,615	14,279	69.1				$4	$7	$8	$10
	Auctions: $90, PF-70DCam, May 2013									
2009, Presidency	129,600,000	4,454	65.9	100%	$0.15	$0.30	$12	$20		
	Auctions: $3, MS-65RD, August 2011									
2009, Presidency, copper, Satin Finish	784,614	1,479	67.6	100%					$15	$45
	Auctions: No auction records available.									
2009D, Presidency	198,000,000	1,365	65.9	100%	$0.15	$0.30	$12	$20		
	Auctions: No auction records available.									
2009D, Presidency, copper, Satin Finish	784,614	1,583	67.6	100%					$15	$200
	Auctions: No auction records available.									
2009S, Presidency, Proof	2,995,615	14,494	69.1				$4	$7	$8	$10
	Auctions: $66, PF-70DCam, June 2013									

LINCOLN, SHIELD REVERSE (2010 TO DATE)

Designer: *Victor D. Brenner (obverse) and Lyndall Bass (reverse).*
Weight: *2.5 grams.* **Composition:** *Copper-plated zinc (core: .992 zinc, .008 copper, with a plating of pure copper; total content .975 zinc, .025 copper).*
Diameter: *19 mm.* **Edge:** *Plain.* **Mints:** *Philadelphia, Denver, San Francisco.*

Circulation Strike

Proof

History. Symbolically capping the life story told by the Lincoln Bicentennial cents of 2009, today's cents feature a reverse design "emblematic of President Lincoln's preservation of the United States as a single and united country." This is the seventh reverse used on the Lincoln type since 1909.

The shield motif was designed by U.S. Mint Artistic Infusion Program Associate Designer Lyndall Bass, and engraved by Mint Sculptor-Engraver Joseph Menna. It was unveiled during the launch ceremony for the fourth and final 2009 Bicentennial cent, held at the Ulysses S. Grant Memorial at the Capitol Building in Washington, DC, November 12, 2009.

In addition to a new reverse design, the Shield Reverse cents feature a modern update of Victor David Brenner's original portrait for the 1909 Lincoln cent.

Striking and Sharpness. Striking is generally sharp. All Proof Lincoln, Shield Reverse, cents are mirror Proofs, usually with cameo or frosted contrast between the devices and the fields.

Availability. Cents of this design are minted in large quantities. They are readily available in the numismatic marketplace, and have successfully entered circulation through normal distribution channels. High-quality Proofs (PF-69 and 70) are common in the secondary market.

GRADING STANDARDS

MS-60 to 70 (Mint State). *Obverse and Reverse:* At MS-65 and higher, luster is rich on all areas; there is no rubbing, and no contact marks are visible except under magnification. Coins with full or nearly full mint orange-red color can be designated RD; those with a substantial percentage of red-orange and of brown can be called RB; and those with full (or nearly full) brown-toned surfaces can be designated BN. Some 2009 cents, even from original rolls and bags, have surface marks that look like water spots.

2010-D. Graded MS-67RD.

The Lincoln, Shield Reverse, cent is seldom collected in grades lower than MS-60.

PF-60 to 70 (Proof). *Obverse and Reverse:* PF-65 and higher coins are RB (with colors nicely blended) or RD, the latter with bright red-orange color sometimes fading to hints of brown. Some tiny flecks are normal on coins certified as PF-65 but should be microscopic or absent above that level. PF-60 and 61 coins can be dull, stained, or spotted and still have some original mint luster. Proof coins with fingerprints are impaired and must

2010-S. Graded PF-70RD Deep Cameo.

be given a lower numerical grade. Lower-grade Proofs usually have poor eye appeal. Generally, Proofs of this type below PF-65 are not desired by most collectors.

	Mintage	Cert	Avg	%MS	MS-63RB / PF-65RD	MS-65RD / PF-67RD	MS-66RD / PF-67Cam	MS-67RD / PF-68DCam
2010	1,963,630,000	6,837	65.5	100%	$0.15	$0.30	$10	$15
	Auctions: $50, MS-66RD, May 2014							
2010D	2,047,200,000	2,308	65.9	100%	$0.15	$0.30	$10	$15
	Auctions: $823, MS-67RD, November 2014; $4,994, MS-67RD, April 2013							
2010S, Proof	1,689,364	5,575	69.1		$4	$7	$8	$10
	Auctions: No auction records available.							
2011	2,402,400,000	275	67.1	100%	$0.15	$0.30	$10	$15
	Auctions: $39, MS-67RD, June 2013							
2011D	2,536,140,000	266	66.8	100%	$0.15	$0.30	$10	$15
	Auctions: $23, MS-67RD, June 2013							
2011S, Proof	1,673,010	6,205	69.1		$7	$7.50	$8	$10
	Auctions: $76, PF-70DCam, May 2014							

	Mintage	Cert	Avg	%MS	MS-63RB PF-65RD	MS-65RD PF-67RD	MS-66RD PF-67Cam	MS-67RD PF-68DCam
2012	3,132,000,000	274	67.0	100%	$0.15	$0.30	$10	$15
	Auctions: No auction records available.							
2012D	2,883,200,000	168	66.9	100%	$0.15	$0.30	$10	$15
	Auctions: No auction records available.							
2012S, Proof	*1,237,415*	2,016	69.1		$7	$7.50	$8	$10
	Auctions: $74, PF-70DCam, May 2013							
2013	3,750,400,000	551	66.2	100%	$0.15	$0.30	$10	$15
	Auctions: No auction records available.							
2013D	3,319,600,000	354	66.8	100%	$0.15	$0.30	$10	$15
	Auctions: No auction records available.							
2013S, Proof	*1,237,976*	2,419	69.2		$7	$7.50	$8	$10
	Auctions: No auction records available.							
2014	3,990,800,000	568	66.8	100%	$0.15	$0.30	$10	$15
	Auctions: No auction records available.							
2014D	4,155,600,000	574	66.7	100%	$0.15	$0.30	$10	$15
	Auctions: No auction records available.							
2014S, Proof	*670,425*	3,446	69.3		$7	$7.50	$8	$10
	Auctions: No auction records available.							
2015		0	n/a		$0.15	$0.30	$10	$15
	Auctions: No auction records available.							
2015D		0	n/a		$0.15	$0.30	$10	$15
	Auctions: No auction records available.							
2015S, Proof		0	n/a		$7	$7.50	$8	$10
	Auctions: No auction records available.							

Two-Cent Pieces
1864–1873

AN OVERVIEW OF TWO-CENT PIECES

The two-cent piece was introduced in 1864. Made of bronze, it was designed by U.S. Mint chief engraver James B. Longacre, and was the first circulating U.S. coin to bear the motto IN GOD WE TRUST. At the time, coins were scarce in circulation because of the ongoing Civil War and the public's tendency to hoard hard currency, and silver and gold issues were entirely absent. Treasury officials felt that the two-cent piece would prove to be very popular as a companion to the Indian Head cent. However, the introduction of the nickel three-cent piece in 1865 negated much of this advantage, the production of two-cent pieces declined, and by 1873, when the denomination was discontinued, its only coinage consisted of Proofs for collectors.

A full "type set" of the two-cent piece consists of but a single coin. Most available in Mint State are the issues of 1864 and 1865, often seen with original mint orange color fading to natural brown. Proofs are available for all years.

An 1864 two-cent piece with the first appearance of the motto IN GOD WE TRUST, compared to its intended "companion," the Indian Head cent.

FOR THE COLLECTOR AND INVESTOR: TWO-CENT PIECES AS A SPECIALTY

Two-cent pieces can be collected by date and variety. A basic display consists of an 1864, Large Motto; 1864, Small Motto (rare); 1873, Close 3; and 1873, Open 3, the latter two being available only in Proof format. Some specialists opt to include just one of the 1873 varieties.

Collectors should select both circulation strikes and Proofs with care, for the number of truly choice *original* (unprocessed, undipped, not retoned) coins is but a small percentage of the whole. As a type, though, the two-cent piece is readily available for collecting.

Several specialized studies of two-cent pieces have been published over a long span of years, the first of significance being "Two-Cent Pieces of the United States," by S.W. Freeman, published in the *Numismatist*, June 1954.

TWO-CENT PIECES (1864–1873)

Designer: *James B. Longacre.* Weight: *6.22 grams.*
Composition: *.950 copper, .050 tin and zinc.* Diameter: *23 mm.*
Edge: *Plain.* Mint: *Philadelphia.*

Circulation Strike   Proof

History. The two-cent piece, struck in bronze like the new Indian Head cents, made its debut under the Mint Act of April 22, 1864. Coins of all kinds were scarce in circulation at the time, due to hoarding. The outcome of the Civil War was uncertain, and Americans desired "hard money." Many millions of two-cent pieces were struck in 1864, after which the mintage declined, due to once-hoarded Indian Head cents becoming available again and to the new nickel three-cent coins being introduced in 1865. Continually decreasing quantities were made through 1872, and only Proofs were struck in the coin's final year, 1873.

Striking and Sharpness. Points to check for sharpness on the obverse include WE in the motto, the leaves, and the horizontal shield lines. On the reverse check the wreath details and the border letters. Check the denticles on both sides. Most coins are quite well struck.

Availability. Most MS coins are dated 1864 or 1865, after which the availability declines sharply, especially for the issue of 1872. Among 1864 coins most seen are of the Large Motto variety. Small Motto coins are elusive. Coins with much or nearly all *original* mint red-orange color are rare for the later years, with most in the marketplace being recolored. The 1864, Small Motto, Proof, is a great rarity, with fewer than two dozen estimated to exist. Coins of 1873 were made only in Proof format, of the Close 3 and Open 3 styles. Proofs of most dates are easily enough acquired. Very few have original color. Do not overlook the many nice brown and red-and-brown pieces on the market (some investors acquire only "red" copper coins, leaving many great values among others). Refer to the comments under Proof Indian Head cents.

GRADING STANDARDS

MS-60 to 70 (Mint State). *Obverse and Reverse:* At MS-65 and higher, the luster is rich on all areas. There is no rubbing, and no contact marks are visible except under magnification. Coins with full or nearly full mint orange-red color can be designated RD (the color on this is often more orange than red), those with full or nearly full brown-toned surfaces can be designated BN, and those with a substantial percentage of red-orange

1872. Graded MS-65RD.

and of brown can be called RB. Ideally, MS-65 or finer coins should have good eye appeal, which in the RB category means nicely blended colors, not stained or blotched, the latter problem mostly with dipped and irregularly retoned coins. Below MS-65, full RD coins become scarce, although MS-64RD coins can be attractive. These usually have more flecks and tiny spots, while the color remains bright. At MS-60 to 62, RD coins are virtually nonexistent, unless they have been dipped. The ANA standards allow for "dull" and/or "spotted" coins at MS-60 and 61 as well as incomplete luster. As a rule, MS-60 to 63BN coins can be fairly attractive if not spotted or blotched, but those with hints of color usually lack eye appeal.

Illustrated coin: This exceptional example is of a date that is rarely found at this grade level.

AU-50, 53, 55, 58 (About Uncirculated).

Obverse: WE shows light wear, this being the prime place to check. The arrowheads and leaves also show light wear. At AU-50, level wear is more noticeable. At AU-53 and 55, wear is less. At AU-58, friction is evident, rather than actual wear. Luster, toned brown, is nearly complete at AU-58, but may be incomplete in the field. *Reverse:* At AU-50, light wear is seen on the ribbon and the higher-

1871. Graded AU-55.

relief areas of the leaves and grains, while the lower areas retain their detail. Some luster may be present in protected areas. At AU-53 and 55, wear is lesser and luster is more extensive. An AU-58 coin will have nearly full luster and show only light friction.

EF-40, 45 (Extremely Fine).

Obverse: Wear is more extensive. WE shows wear extensively, but still is clear. The leaves lack detail on their highest points. Some scattered marks are normal at this and lower grades. *Reverse:* The higher-relief parts of the leaves and ribbon bow show further wear, as do other areas.

1864, Small Motto. Graded EF-45.

VF-20, 30 (Very Fine).

Obverse: WE is clear, but not strong. Leaves show more wear, as do all other areas. *Reverse:* Still more wear is seen, but the leaves still are separately defined. The wheat grains are very clear.

1867. Graded VF-20.

F-12, 15 (Fine). *Obverse:* WE is the defining factor and is very weak, but readable, if only barely. Other areas show more wear. The edges of some leaves are gone, blending them into adjacent leaves. *Reverse:* Wear is more extensive. Near the apex of the wreath the edges of some leaves are gone, blending them into adjacent leaves. The grains of wheat are clear, but some are slightly weak.

Illustrated coin: WE is very weak. Some scratches on the shield should be separately described.

1864, Small Motto. Graded F-12.

VG-8, 10 (Very Good). *Obverse:* WE is gone, although the ANA grading standards and *Photograde* suggest "very weak." IN GOD and TRUST are readable, but some areas may be weak. The inner edges of most leaves are gone. *Reverse:* The wear appears to be less extensive than on the obverse. All lettering is bold. A few grains of wheat may be well worn or even missing.

1864, Large Motto. Graded VG-8.

G-4, 6 (Good). *Obverse:* Wear is more extensive, and the leaf bunches are in flat clumps. IN GOD and TRUST are very worn, with a letter or two not visible. *Reverse:* All letters are clear. The wreath is mostly in outline on G-4. On G-6, perhaps half the grains are visible.

1872. Graded G-6.

AG-3 (About Good). *Obverse:* The motto shows only a few letters. The leaves are flat. Only a few horizontal shield stripes can be seen. *Reverse:* The wreath is in outline form. The letters are weak, with 20% to 40% worn away entirely.

1865. Graded AG-3.

PF-60 to 70 (Proof). *Obverse and Reverse:* Gem PF-65 two-cent pieces will have very few hairlines, and these visible only under a strong magnifying glass. At any level and color, a Proof with hairlines has likely been cleaned, a fact usually overlooked. At PF-67 or higher there should be no evidence of hairlines or friction at all. Such a coin is fully original. PF-60 coins can be dull from repeated dipping and cleaning and are often

1873, Close 3. Graded PF-67RD.

toned iridescent colors or have mottled surfaces. At PF-63, the mirrorlike fields should be attractive, and hairlines should be minimal, most easily seen when the coin is held at an angle to the light. No rubbing is seen. PF-64 coins are even nicer. As a general rule, Proofs of 1873 are of very high quality but, unless dipped or cleaned, are nearly always toned light brown.

Illustrated coin: This superb, fully red Gem is one of the finest known. The strike is razor sharp, and the only irregularity is a hint of pale lilac toning at the lower edge of the reverse.

1864, Small Motto   1864, Large Motto

1865, Plain 5   1865, Fancy 5

	Mintage	Cert	Avg	%MS	G-4	F-12	VF-20	EF-40	AU-50	MS-60BN	MS-63BN / PF-63BN	MS-64BN / PF-64BN	MS-65RD / PF-65RB
1864, Small Motto (a)	(b)	578	53.3	67%	$225	$400	$600	$850	$1,000	$1,500	$1,750	$2,000	$7,200
Auctions: $22,325, MS-66RD, August 2013; $12,338, MS-65RD, August 2014; $2,585, MS-65BN, August 2014; $705, EF-45BN, October 2014													
1864, Large Motto (c)	19,822,500	3,669	61.3	87%	$15	$25	$30	$50	$80	$110	$175	$200	$1,600
Auctions: $7,344, MS-67BN, January 2014; $2,844, MS-66RD, July 2014; $1,410, MS-65RD, July 2014; $106, AU-58BN, December 2014													
1864, Small Motto † (d)	(e)	8	64.8								$20,000	$25,000	$75,000
Auctions: $105,750, PF-66RD, June 2014													
1864, Large Motto, Proof	100+	131	64.6								$550	$800	$2,500
Auctions: $14,100, PF-67RB, August 2013; $2,820, PF-66RB, October 2014; $2,585, PF-65BN, November 2014; $999, PF-64BN, August 2014													
1865 (f)	13,640,000	2,390	61.0	84%	$15	$25	$30	$50	$80	$110	$175	$200	$1,600
Auctions: $2,820, MS-66RD, October 2014; $4,113, MS-66RD, March 2014; $1,355, MS-65RD, July 2014; $96, AU-58BN, December 2014													
1865, Proof	500+	155	64.7								$450	$500	$1,200
Auctions: $6,463, PF-66Cam, October 2014; $15,275, PF-66RD, April 2013; $4,847, PF-65Cam, October 2014; $3,819, PF-64RB, August 2014													

† Ranked in the *100 Greatest U.S. Coins* (fourth edition). **a.** The circulated Small Motto is distinguished by a wider D in GOD, and the first T in TRUST nearly touching the ribbon crease at left. **b.** Included in circulation-strike 1864, Large Motto, mintage figure. **c.** The circulated Large Motto is distinguished by a narrow D in GOD, and a 1 mm gap between the first T in TRUST and the ribbon crease. **d.** 20 to 30 examples are known. **e.** Included in 1864, Large Motto, Proof, mintage figure. **f.** Circulated varieties show the tip of the 5 either plain or fancy (curved).

1867, Doubled-Die Obverse
FS-02-1867-101.

1869, Doubled-Die Obverse
FS-02-1869-101.

	Mintage	Cert	Avg	%MS	G-4	F-12	VF-20	EF-40	AU-50	MS-60BN	MS-63BN / PF-63BN	MS-64BN / PF-64BN	MS-65RD / PF-65RB
1867	2,938,750	548	60.1	82%	$20	$30	$35	$50	$80	$125	$175	$225	$2,450
Auctions: $12,925, MS-66RD, April 2014; $2,180, MS-66RB, October 2014; $793, MS-65RB, August 2014; $106, AU-55BN, October 2014													
1867, Doubled-Die Obverse (g)	(h)	57	43.4	35%	$100	$200	$300	$600	$850	$1,500	$2,750	$3,200	
Auctions: $22,325, MS-65RD, January 2014													
1867, Proof	625+	204	64.7								$450	$500	$1,200
Auctions: $1,763, PF-66RB, August 2014; $3,525, PF-65RD, January 2014; $999, PF-65RB, October 2014; $382, PF-60BN, August 2014													
1868	2,803,750	544	60.2	81%	$20	$36	$50	$75	$110	$150	$225	$375	$4,000
Auctions: $9,400, MS-66RD, January 2014; $15,275, MS-65RD, October 2014; $1,410, MS-65RB, August 2014; $212, AU-58BN, October 2014													
1868, Proof	600+	187	64.4								$450	$500	$1,200
Auctions: $9,400, PF-67RD, October 2014; $16,450, PF-66Cam, June 2014; $7,344, PF-65Cam, August 2014; $282, PF-60BN, September 2014													
1869	1,546,500	476	59.8	78%	$25	$40	$55	$80	$125	$160	$225	$375	$3,500
Auctions: $15,275, MS-66RD, January 2014; $11,163, MS-65RD, October 2014; $212, MS-62BN, July 2014; $141, AU-55BN, December 2014													
1869, Double-Die Obverse	(i)	0	n/a							$600	$900	$1,250	
Auctions: No auction records available.													
1869, Proof	600+	224	64.6								$450	$500	$1,250
Auctions: $8,225, PF-66RD, June 2014; $823, PF-65RB, November 2014; $1,645, PF-64RD, September 2014; $329, PF-62RB, November 2014													
1870	861,250	370	58.1	75%	$35	$55	$85	$135	$200	$275	$300	$575	$4,500
Auctions: $11,163, MS-65RD, June 2014; $2,350, MS-65RB, August 2014; $705, MS-64RB, September 2014; $129, VF-25BN, October 2014													
1870, Proof	1,000+	269	64.5								$450	$550	$1,275
Auctions: $17,038, PF-67RD, August 2014; $41,125, PF-67RD, February 2014; $5,581, PF-67BN, August 2014; $9,988, PF-66RD, September 2014													
1871	721,250	515	58.5	73%	$40	$85	$110	$150	$225	$300	$375	$800	$5,500
Auctions: $28,200, MS-66RD, April 2013; $4,700, MS-65RD, October 2014; $1,528, MS-65RB, October 2014; $182, MS-61BN, October 2014													
1871, Proof	960+	270	64.6								$450	$550	$1,275
Auctions: $8,813, PF-66RD, October 2014; $6,169, PF-66RD, February 2014; $7,638, PF-65Cam, October 2014; $200, PF-65BN, October 2014													
1872	65,000	290	36.3	30%	$400	$600	$800	$1,050	$1,650	$2,800	$3,600	$3,900	$25,000
Auctions: $34,075, MS-66RD, October 2014; $39,950, MS-66RD, January 2014; $16,450, MS-66RB, October 2014; $4,700, MS-64RB, September 2014													
1872, Proof	950+	342	64.6								$900	$950	$1,300
Auctions: $11,163, PF-66RD, April 2014; $3,290, PF-65RB, August 2014; $1,410, PF-65BN, August 2014													
1873, Close 3, Proof	400	273	64.0								$3,200	$3,500	$4,500
Auctions: $4,406, PF-66RB, August 2014; $12,925, PF-66RB, November 2013; $4,700, PF-66BN, August 2014; $3,525, PF-65RB, October 2014													
1873, Open 3, Proof (Alleged Restrike)	200	123	63.6								$3,000	$3,250	$4,000
Auctions: $11,750, PF-66RB, June 2014; $2,703, PF-65BN, October 2014; $3,290, PF-64RB, August 2014													

g. This variety is somewhat common in low-end circulated grades, but is considered rare in EF and AU, and very rare in MS. **h.** Included in circulation-strike 1867 mintage figure. **i.** Included in circulation-strike 1869 mintage figure.

Three-Cent Pieces
1851–1889

AN OVERVIEW OF THREE-CENT PIECES

SILVER THREE-CENT PIECES

The silver three-cent piece or *trime* is one of the more curious coins in American numismatics. The rising price of silver in 1850 created a situation in which silver coins cost more to produce than their face value. Mintages dropped sharply and older pieces disappeared from circulation. In 1851 a solution was provided by the three-cent piece. Instead of being made with 90% silver content, the fineness was set at 75%. Accordingly, the coins were worth less intrinsically, and there was no advantage in melting them. Large quantities were made through 1853. In that year, the standards for regular silver coins were changed, and other denominations reappeared on the marketplace, making the trime unnecessary. Mintages dropped beginning in 1854, until 1873, when production amounted to just 600 Proofs for collectors.

Of the three varieties of trimes, Variety 2 (1854–1858) is at once the scarcest and, by far, the most difficult to find with a sharp strike. In fact, not one in fifty Variety 2 coins is needle sharp. Curiously, when such pieces are found they are likely to be dated 1855, the lowest-mintage issue of the type. Trimes of the Variety 1 design (1851–1853) vary widely in striking, but can be found sharp. Variety 3 coins (1859–1873) often are sharp.

Mint State coins are readily found for Variety 1 and are usually in grades from MS-60 to 63 or so, although quite a few gems are around with attractive luster. Sharply struck gems are another matter and require some searching to find. Mint State Variety 2 trimes are all rare, and when seen are apt to be miserably struck and in lower grades. Variety 3 coins are readily found in Mint State, including in MS-65 and higher grades.

The New Orleans Mint struck some $21,600 face value of silver trimes in 1851, the first year of issue.

Proofs were made of all years, but not in quantity until 1858, when an estimated 210 were struck. For all dates after 1862, high-grade Proofs are much more readily available today than are Mint State coins. Circulated examples are available of all three varieties. While extensively worn coins of Variety 1 are available, most Variety 2 coins are Fine or better and most Variety 3 pieces are VF or better.

FOR THE COLLECTOR AND INVESTOR: SILVER THREE-CENT PIECES AS A SPECIALTY

Trimes cover a fairly long span of years and embrace several design types, but comprise no "impossible" rarities. Accordingly, it is realistic to collect one of each Philadelphia Mint coin from 1851 to 1873 plus the 1851-O. There are two overdates in the series, 1862, 2 Over 1 (which is distinct and occurs only in circulation-strike format), and 1863, 3 Over 2 (only Proofs, and not boldly defined), which some specialists collect and others ignore. A curious variety of 1852 has the first digit of the date over an inverted 2.

Typically, a high-grade set includes Mint State examples of all issues 1851 through 1857 and Proofs after that date. As noted, Variety 2 trimes usually are very poorly struck, save the occasionally encountered sharp 1855. As an example, a specialist in the series who found an 1856 with needle-sharp details, at three times the regular market price, might be well advised to buy it. After 1862, Mint State coins are rare for most dates. The formation of a choice Mint State set 1851 through 1872 plus a Proof 1873 would be a formidable challenge.

A set of circulated coins can be gathered through and including 1862, after which such pieces become very rare. Most later dates will have to be acquired on a catch-as-catch-can basis, perhaps by acquiring impaired Proofs for certain of the years.

NICKEL THREE-CENT PIECES

Nickel three-cent pieces were introduced in 1865 to help fill the need for coins in circulation. At the time, silver and gold issues were hoarded, and were available only at a premium. The nickel three-cent piece joined the Indian Head cent and the new (as of 1864) two-cent piece. The coin proved to be very popular in its time, and millions were struck. In 1866 the nickel five-cent piece was introduced, after which time the demand for the nickel three-cent piece diminished somewhat. However, pieces were made in quantity until 1876. In that year silver coins again returned to circulation, and mintages for the nickel three-cent piece dropped sharply. Only Proofs were made in 1877 and 1878. In later years, mintages ranged from small to modest, except for 1881.

Mint State coins are readily available for the early years, although many if not most have weak striking in areas or are from clashed dies. Pristine, sharp Mint State coins on the market are mostly of later years, in the 1880s, where such pieces are the rule, not the exception.

FOR THE COLLECTOR AND INVESTOR: NICKEL THREE-CENT PIECES AS A SPECIALTY

Nickel three-cent coins are interesting to collect by date sequence from 1865 to 1889. Varieties are provided by the 1873, Close 3, and 1873, Open 3, and the 1887, 7 Over 6, overdate. A set of Mint State coins is considerably more difficult to form than a run of Proofs. A hand-selected set of well-struck coins MS-65 or finer could take several years to complete.

Among Proofs, the rarest year is 1865, probably followed by the "perfect date" (not overdate) 1887. Proofs of the 1860s and early 1870s are scarce in PF-65 with excellent strike and eye appeal. Proofs of the latter decade of coinage are much more readily available and usually are choice.

SILVER THREE-CENT PIECES (TRIMES) (1851–1873)

Variety 1 (1851–1853): **Designer:** *James B. Longacre.* **Weight:** *0.80 gram.*
Composition: *.750 silver, .250 copper.* **Diameter:** *14 mm.*
Edge: *Plain.* **Mints:** *Philadelphia, New Orleans.*

Variety 1 (1851–1853)   **Variety 1, Proof**

Variety 2 (1854–1858): **Designer:** *James B. Longacre.* **Weight:** *0.75 gram.*
Composition: *.900 silver, .100 copper.* **Diameter:** *14 mm.* **Edge:** *Plain.* **Mint:** *Philadelphia.*

Variety 2 (1854–1858)   **Variety 2, Proof**

Variety 3 (1859–1873): **Designer:** *James B. Longacre.* **Weight:** *0.75 gram.*
Composition: *.900 silver, .100 copper.* **Diameter:** *14 mm.* **Edge:** *Plain.* **Mint:** *Philadelphia.*

Variety 3 (1859–1873)   **Variety 3, Proof**

History. In 1850 Americans began hoarding their silver coins, as the flood of gold from California made silver disproportionately valuable. To provide a small coin for commerce, the Mint introduced the silver three-cent piece, or *trime.* These were .750 fine (as opposed to the standard .900 fineness), and contained less than 3¢ of metal, so there was no incentive to hoard or melt them. Three different designs were made, Variety 1 of which was struck from 1851 to 1853. These coins were popular in their time and circulated widely. These are distinguished from the other two designs by having no outline or frame around the obverse star. The Act of February 21, 1853, reduced the amount of silver in other denominations (from the half dime to the half dollar, but not the dollar), which discouraged people from hoarding them. The tiny trime lost the public's favor, and mintages decreased.

In 1854 the design was changed considerably, creating Variety 2, which was made through 1858. The alloy was modified to the standard for other issues and the weight was lightened. A raised border was added to the obverse star plus two line frames around it. On the reverse an olive branch was placed above the III and a bundle of arrows below it. This new motif proved to be very difficult to strike up properly.

In 1859 the design was modified again, creating Variety 3. Demand for the denomination continued to be small, and after 1862 very few were made for circulation, as silver coins were hoarded by the war-weary public and began to trade at a premium. Under the Coinage Act of 1873 the trime was discontinued, and that year only Proofs were struck. Also in that year, nearly the entire production of non-Proof coins of 1863 to 1872 was melted.

Striking and Sharpness. On the Variety 1 obverse the tiny shield at the center of the star often lacks certain details. On the reverse check the details and strength of the III. On both sides check the rims. Needle-sharp coins are in the minority. Sharpness of strike has been nearly completely overlooked in the marketplace.

Trimes of Variety 2 are usually poorly struck, with some or all of these characteristics: obverse lettering weak in places; frames around the star of inconsistent strength or missing in certain areas; shield weak in places; reverse stars irregular and poorly formed; olive branch and arrows weak in areas; weak or irregular rims. Now and then a sharp 1855 is found.

Most Variety 3 trimes are sharply struck. Points to look for include full outlines around the star, full shield on the star, and full leaf details and sharp stars.

Most Proofs are needle sharp and have mirrored surfaces, although some of the late 1860s and early 1870s can have slightly grainy or satiny lustrous surfaces. Striking quality varies. Lint marks and surface problems are not unusual. Careful examination is recommended.

Availability. Circulated examples of the Variety 1 trimes are plentiful. MS coins are often seen, although the 1851-O is scarce in MS and high circulated grades. Most MS coins are lustrous and attractive, especially at 63 and above. Circulated Variety 2 coins are scarce in all grades, particularly so at MS-64 and higher. With a needle-sharp strike, MS-65 and higher are *rarities*. Among Variety 3 trimes, circulated coins of the years 1859 to 1862 are easy to find. All later dates range from scarce to rare in circulation-strike format. MS-63 and better coins 1865 and later are very rare. A few Proofs were made in the early 1850s and are great rarities today. After 1857, production increased to an estimated 210 or so in 1858, through 500 to 700 or so as a yearly average in the 1860s to 1873.

GRADING STANDARDS

MS-60 to 70 (Mint State). *Obverse and Reverse:* At MS-60, some abrasion and very minor contact marks are evident, most noticeably on the obverse star and the C ornament on the reverse. At MS-63, abrasion is hard to detect except under magnification. An MS-65 coin will have no abrasion. Luster should be full and rich (not grainy). Grades above MS-65 are defined by having fewer marks as perfection is approached. Most high-grade Mint State coins are of the Variety 3 design.

1851-O, Variety 1. Graded MS-66.

Illustrated coin: This is an exceptional example of the only branch-mint coin in the trime series.

AU-50, 53, 55, 58 (About Uncirculated). *Obverse:* Light wear is most obvious on the star arms and shield on Variety 1, and on the points of the frames on Variety 2 and Variety 3. At AU-50, luster is evident, but only on part of the field. At AU-58 luster is nearly complete. *Reverse:* Light wear is seen on the C ornament and III. On Variety 2 and 3, light wear is seen on the leaves and arrows.

1868, Variety 3. Graded AU-50.

Illustrated coin: Overall this is a decent strike, but with some reverse stars flat at their centers.

EF-40, 45 (Extremely Fine). *Obverse:* More wear is seen, most noticeable on the ridges of the star arms, this in addition to more wear on the frames (Variety 2 and Variety 3). Luster is absent, or seen only in traces. *Reverse:* More wear is seen on the C ornament and III. On Variety 2 and Variety 3 more wear is seen on the leaves and arrows.

　　Illustrated coin: This is sharply struck, as are most Variety 3 trimes.

1863, Variety 3. Graded EF-45.

VF-20, 30 (Very Fine). *Obverse:* Further wear reduced the relief of the star. On Variety 2 and Variety 3 the frames show further wear and begin to blend together. The center shield shows wear, and its border is indistinct in areas, but its horizontal and vertical stripes are fully delineated (unless the coin was weakly struck). *Reverse:* Still more wear is seen on the C ornament and III. On Variety 2 and Variety 3 the high-relief areas of the

1869, Variety 3. Graded VF-20.

leaves and the feathers of the arrow are partially worn away. Stars are flat at their centers (on sharply struck coins in addition to, as expected, on weak strikes).

F-12, 15 (Fine). *Obverse:* The star is worn so as to have lost most of its relief. On Variety 2 and Variety 3 the frames are mostly blended together. The center shield shows wear, and its border is flat (or else showing only slight separation of its two outlines), but its horizontal and vertical stripes still are delineated (unless the coin was weakly struck). *Reverse:* Still more wear is seen on the C ornament and III. On Variety 2 and Variety 3 the

1851, Variety 1. Graded F-12.

high-relief areas of the leaves, and the feathers of the arrow, have slight if any detail. Stars are flat. The designs within the C ornament are missing much detail.

VG-8, 10 (Very Good). *Obverse:* The border is incomplete in places, but all lettering is bold. The horizontal and vertical stripes within the shield begin to blend together, but most remain well delineated. *Reverse:* Still more wear is seen on all areas. The designs within the C ornament have more detail gone.

1852, Variety 1. Graded VG-10.

G-4, 6 (Good). *Obverse:* The border is worn into the tops of the letters and the bottom of the date. The shield is blended into the star, and only traces of the shield outline remain. In this grade most coins seen are Variety 1. *Reverse:* The border is worn into the outer parts of the stars. Additional wear is seen in all other areas.

1853, Variety 1. Graded G-4.

AG-3 (About Good). *Obverse:* The star is flat. Strong elements of the shield are seen, but the tiny lines are mostly or completely blended together. Lettering and date are weak and partially missing, but the date must be identifiable. In this grade most coins seen are Variety 1. *Reverse:* The border is worn into the stars, with outer elements of the stars now gone. Additional wear is seen in all other areas. The designs within the C ornament are only in outline form.

1851, Variety 1. Graded AG-3.

PF-60 to 70 (Proof). *Obverse and Reverse:* Proofs that are extensively cleaned and have many hairlines, or that are dull and grainy, are lower level, such as PF-60 to 62. These are difficult to verify as Proofs. For a trime with medium hairlines and good reflectivity, an assigned grade of PF-64 is indicated, and with relatively few hairlines, gem PF-65. PF-66 should have hairlines so delicate that magnification is needed to see them. Above that, a Proof should be free of such lines.

1873, Variety 3. Graded PF-61.

Illustrated coin: Many hairlines are mostly masked by attractive toning, yielding a highly collectible coin at this lower Proof grade level.

	Mintage	Cert	Avg	%MS	G-4	VG-8	F-12	VF-20	EF-40	AU-50	MS-60	MS-63	MS-65
											PF-63	PF-64	PF-65
1851	5,447,400	1,236	61.1	88%	$25	$45	$50	$70	$80	$150	$200	$275	$850
	Auctions: $4,113, MS-67, November 2014; $4,700, MS-67, March 2013; $1,586, MS-66, July 2014; $147, AU-55, September 2014												
1851, **Proof** (a)		0	n/a								—		
	Auctions: No auction records available.												
1851O	720,000	462	58.9	75%	$40	$60	$75	$100	$175	$250	$450	$700	$3,000
	Auctions: $11,163, MS-67, July 2014; $12,925, MS-66, December 2013; $793, MS-62, October 2014; $317, AU-55, October 2014												

a. 1 or 2 examples are known.

1852, 1 Over Inverted 2
FS-3S-1852-301.

1853, Repunched Date
FS-3S-1853-301.

1854, Repunched Date
FS-3S-1854-301.

	Mintage	Cert	Avg	%MS	G-4	VG-8	F-12	VF-20	EF-40	AU-50	MS-60	MS-63	MS-65
											PF-63	PF-64	PF-65
1852, 1 Over Inverted 2 (b)	(c)	1	61.0	100%					$775	$950	$1,150	$1,425	$1,950
Auctions: No auction records available.													
1852	18,663,500	1,566	58.4	81%	$25	$45	$50	$70	$80	$150	$200	$275	$850
Auctions: $4,113, MS-67, November 2014; $8,225, MS-67, September 2014; $1,175, MS-66, November 2014													
1852, Proof (d)		0	n/a								—		
Auctions: No auction records available.													
1853	11,400,000	837	55.0	70%	$25	$45	$50	$60	$80	$150	$180	$275	$950
Auctions: $4,994, MS-67, October 2014; $7,638, MS-67, April 2014; $353, MS-64, July 2014													
1853, Repunched Date (e)	(f)	0	n/a						$100	$200	$260	$300	$1,000
Auctions: No auction records available.													
1854	671,000	367	59.5	75%	$40	$55	$60	$70	$120	$225	$350	$700	$3,000
Auctions: $64,625, MS-68, June 2014; $1,880, MS-65, August 2014; $441, MS-62, July 2014; $129, AU-58, September 2014													
1854, Repunched Date (g)	(h)	0	n/a						$185	$325	$500	$800	$3,500
Auctions: No auction records available.													
1854, Proof	25–35	9	64.0								$13,000	$16,000	$35,000
Auctions: $41,125, PF-65, June 2014; $14,688, PF-64, October 2014													
1855	139,000	144	54.3	56%	$40	$65	$75	$125	$200	$350	$600	$1,100	$7,500
Auctions: $22,325, MS-66, October 2014; $12,925, MS-66, October 2014; $9,400, MS-65, January 2014; $229, EF-45, November 2014													
1855, Proof	30–40	24	64.8								$5,000	$8,500	$15,000
Auctions: $21,150, PF-66Cam, October 2014; $8,225, PF-64, October 2014													
1856	1,458,000	341	58.2	70%	$40	$45	$50	$70	$120	$235	$360	$700	$3,200
Auctions: $2,585, MS-65, November 2014; $4,553, MS-65, August 2013; $456, MS-62, November 2014; $170, AU-55, October 2014													
1856, Proof	40–50	34	64.4								$4,300	$6,500	$17,000
Auctions: $21,738, PF-66, January 2014													
1857	1,042,000	347	58.6	78%	$40	$45	$50	$70	$120	$235	$360	$700	$2,750
Auctions: $11,750, MS-67, June 2014; $3,408, MS-65, August 2014; $306, AU-58, November 2014; $21, VF-35, November 2014													
1857, Proof	60–80	40	64.6								$3,750	$5,000	$12,500
Auctions: $15,863, PF-66, June 2014													
1858	1,603,700	619	57.9	70%	$40	$45	$50	$70	$120	$235	$360	$700	$2,750
Auctions: $21,738, MS-67, October 2014; $3,819, MS-66, October 2014; $247, AU-58, November 2014													
1858, Proof	210	108	64.6								$2,750	$4,500	$7,500
Auctions: $35,250, PF-67, October 2014; $16,450, PF-67, December 2013; $13,513, PF-66, September 2014													
1859	364,200	329	61.0	81%	$40	$45	$50	$60	$100	$175	$215	$300	$1,000
Auctions: $3,055, MS-66, October 2014; $441, MS-64, December 2014; $165, AU-58, December 2014													
1859, Proof	800	110	64.1								$750	$1,100	$2,000
Auctions: $10,575, PF-66Cam, October 2014; $4,406, PF-66, October 2014; $1,528, PF-64Cam, July 2014; $617, PF-63, October 2014													
1860	286,000	326	58.6	66%	$40	$45	$50	$60	$100	$175	$215	$300	$1,000
Auctions: $4,406, MS-67, June 2014; $411, MS-64, October 2014; $176, AU-58, November 2014													
1860, Proof	1,000	78	63.9								$750	$1,200	$4,500
Auctions: $705, PF-63, November 2014													

b. An inverted 2 is visible beneath the primary 1. "A secondary date punch was obviously punched into the die in an inverted orientation and then corrected after some effacing of the die" (*Cherrypickers' Guide to Rare Die Varieties,* sixth edition, volume I). **c.** Included in circulation-strike 1852 mintage figure. **d.** 1 example is known. **e.** Secondary digits are visible to the north of the primary 1 and 8. This repunched date can be detected on lower-grade coins. **f.** Included in 1853 mintage figure. **g.** Secondary digits are visible to the west of the primary digits on the 8 and 5. **h.** Included in circulation-strike 1854 mintage figure.

1862, 2 Over 1
FS-3S-1862-301.

	Mintage	Cert	Avg	%MS	G-4	VG-8	F-12	VF-20	EF-40	AU-50	MS-60 / PF-63	MS-63 / PF-64	MS-65 / PF-65
1861	497,000	831	60.9	78%	$40	$45	$50	$60	$100	$175	$215	$285	$1,000
Auctions: $7,050, MS-67, October 2014; $4,113, MS-67, June 2013; $282, MS-62, December 2014; $165, AU-55, December 2014													
1861, Proof	1,000	95	64.2								$750	$1,000	$2,000
Auctions: $13,513, PF-68, October 2014; $2,115, PF-66, October 2014													
1862, 2 Over 1 (i)	(j)	327	63.6	91%	$40	$45	$50	$60	$100	$200	$250	$350	$1,200
Auctions: $8,225, MS-67, December 2013; $3,643, MS-66, September 2014; $353, AU-58, September 2014; $212, AU-55, November 2014													
1862	343,000	1,121	62.8	89%	$40	$45	$50	$60	$100	$175	$215	$285	$1,000
Auctions: $3,819, MS-67, March 2013; $1,410, MS-66, November 2014; $212, MS-62, October 2014; $176, AU-55, October 2014													
1862, Proof	550	147	64.1								$750	$1,000	$2,000
Auctions: $30,550, PF-67Cam, October 2014; $14,100, PF-66Cam, June 2014; $2,375, PF-66, July 2014; $940, PF-64, November 2014													
1863	21,000	91	64.3	97%	$300	$325	$350	$375	$435	$550	$800	$1,100	$2,100
Auctions: $7,050, MS-67, October 2014; $6,463, MS-66, October 2014; $23,500, MS-65, June 2014													
1863, So-Called 3 Over 2, Proof	(k)	0	n/a								$1,800	$3,600	$6,250
Auctions: $47,000, PF-66Cam, June 2014; $2,350, PF-64, October 2014													
1863, Proof	460	135	64.3								$650	$1,000	$1,500
Auctions: $11,750, PF-68, June 2014; $21,150, PF-67Cam, October 2014; $5,581, PF-66Cam, August 2014													
1864	12,000	92	63.4	91%	$300	$325	$350	$375	$435	$550	$650	$1,000	$2,100
Auctions: $13,513, MS-68, October 2014; $2,233, MS-65, October 2014; $5,288, MS-65, August 2013													
1864, Proof	470	171	64.6								$750	$1,000	$1,500
Auctions: $14,100, PF-67Cam, October 2014; $5,875, PF-67, October 2014; $10,281, PF-66Cam, April 2014													
1865	8,000	103	62.5	87%	$325	$350	$425	$450	$475	$575	$675	$1,100	$2,200
Auctions: $3,525, MS-65, August 2014; $9,400, MS-65, August 2013; $2,115, MS-64, November 2014													
1865, Proof	500	153	64.4								$750	$1,000	$1,500
Auctions: $2,585, PF-66, November 2014													
1866	22,000	82	62.8	88%	$300	$325	$350	$400	$425	$500	$630	$1,000	$2,100
Auctions: $23,500, MS-67, November 2013; $2,468, MS-64, August 2014													
1866, Proof	725	202	64.2								$650	$1,000	$1,500
Auctions: $23,500, PF-67Cam, April 2013; $588, PF-60, August 2014													
1867	4,000	42	62.2	86%	$325	$350	$425	$450	$475	$525	$675	$1,300	$3,500
Auctions: $20,563, MS-66, October 2014; $16,450, MS-66, August 2013; $4,113, MS-63, August 2014; $3,525, MS-63, August 2014													
1867, Proof	625	268	64.4								$750	$1,000	$1,500
Auctions: $11,817, PF-67Cam, August 2014; $29,375, PF-67Cam, November 2013; $6,463, PF-67, October 2014; $1,531, PF-65Cam, September 2014													

i. A secondary 1 is evident beneath the 2 of the date. "This overdate is believed to be due more to economy (the Mint having used a good die another year) than to error. Circulated examples are about as common as the regular-dated coin" (*Cherrypickers' Guide to Rare Die Varieties*, sixth edition, volume I). **j.** Included in circulation-strike 1862 mintage figure. **k.** Included in 1863, Proof, mintage figure.

	Mintage	Cert	Avg	%MS	F-12	VF-20	EF-40	AU-50	MS-60	MS-63	MS-64	MS-65	MS-66
											PF-63	PF-64	PF-65
1868	3,500	33	60.3	82%	$425	$450	$475	$550	$690	$1,400	$2,300	$6,250	$11,000
Auctions: $16,450, MS-66, October 2014; $5,288, MS-63, August 2014; $3,525, MS-63, April 2013													
1868, Proof	600	270	64.1								$650	$1,000	$1,500
Auctions: $13,513, PF-67Cam, October 2014; $4,438, PF-67, September 2013; $999, PF-63, August 2014													
1869	4,500	49	62.4	86%	$425	$475	$525	$600	$700	$1,400	$2,100	$3,200	$5,750
Auctions: $15,863, MS-67, August 2013; $7,638, MS-66, October 2014; $1,645, MS-63, August 2014													
1869, Proof	600	180	64.4								$750	$1,000	$1,500
Auctions: $11,456, PF-68Cam, October 2014; $18,800, PF-67Cam, October 2014; $15,275, PF-67Cam, August 2013; $558, PF-55, August 2014													
1869, So-Called 9 Over 8, Proof (a)	(b)	0	n/a								$2,000	$3,000	$5,750
Auctions: $18,800, PF-66Cam, August 2014; $16,450, PF-66Cam, August 2013													
1870	3,000	88	61.6	80%	$425	$450	$475	$550	$675	$1,300	$1,850	$4,800	$6,250
Auctions: $30,550, MS-67, January 2014; $4,406, MS-66, October 2014													
1870, Proof	1,000	245	64.1								$750	$1,000	$1,500
Auctions: $21,738, PF-68Cam, April 2014; $7,638, PF-67Cam, August 2014; $8,225, PF-67, October 2014; $3,525, PF-66, October 2014													
1871	3,400	146	63.7	91%	$425	$450	$475	$500	$650	$1,000	$1,400	$2,000	$3,000
Auctions: $4,994, MS-66, March 2013; $1,528, MS-65, November 2014; $1,657, MS-65, August 2014													
1871, Proof	960	223	64.1								$650	$1,000	$1,500
Auctions: $5,581, PF-67Cam, August 2014; $10,575, PF-67, October 2014; $12,339, PF-67, April 2013; $4,113, PF-66Cam, July 2014													
1872	1,000	46	61.6	87%	$450	$475	$500	$600	$1,000	$1,800	$2,500	$5,500	$10,000
Auctions: $18,800, MS-67, October 2014; $7,050, MS-66, October 2014; $9,400, MS-66, June 2014; $11,163, MS-65, October 2014													
1872, Proof	950	233	64.2								$750	$1,000	$1,500
Auctions: $11,750, PF-67Cam, October 2014; $16,450, PF-66DCam, April 2014; $3,819, PF-66Cam, August 2014; $1,880, PF-65Cam, November 2014													
1873, Close 3, Proof (a)	600	379	64.0								$2,000	$2,500	$2,800
Auctions: $14,100, PF-67DCam, January 2014; $8,225, PF-67, October 2014; $3,819, PF-66Cam, August 2014; $1,058, PF-60, July 2014													

a. Proof only. **b.** Included in 1869, Proof, mintage figure.

NICKEL THREE-CENT PIECES (1865–1889)

Designer: *James B. Longacre.* **Weight:** *1.94 grams.* **Composition:** *.750 copper, .250 nickel.* **Diameter:** *17.9 mm.* **Edge:** *Plain.* **Mint:** *Philadelphia.*

Circulation Strike

Proof

History. The copper-nickel three-cent coin debuted in the final year of the Civil War, 1865. The American public was still hoarding silver coins (a situation that would continue until 1876), including the silver three-cent piece. The highest-denomination coin remaining in circulation at the time was the recently introduced two-cent piece. After 1875, when silver coins circulated once again, the three-cent denomination became redundant and mintages dropped. The last pieces were coined in 1889.

Striking and Sharpness. On the obverse check the hair and other portrait details. On the reverse the tiny vertical lines in the Roman numeral III can be weak. Check the denticles on both sides of the coin. Among circulation strikes, clashed dies are common, particularly for the earlier high-mintage years. Generally, coins of the 1860s and 1870s have weakness in one area or another. Many if not most of the 1880s are well struck. Proofs from 1878 onward often have satiny or frosty fields, rather than mirrored surfaces, and resemble circulation strikes.

Availability. Circulated examples of dates from 1865 to the mid-1870s are readily available. MS coins, particularly from the 1860s, are easily found, but often have areas of weakness or lack aesthetic appeal. MS coins of the 1880s are readily found for most dates (except for 1883, 1884, 1885, and 1887), some of them probably sold as Proofs. Many Proofs of the era had slight to extensive mint luster. Proofs were struck of all dates and can be found easily enough in the marketplace. The rarest is the first year of issue, 1865, of which only an estimated 500 or so were made. The vast majority of 1865s have a repunched date. Second rarest (not counting PF-only date of 1877) is the 1887 (perfect date, not the overdate) with a production of about 1,000 coins. Proofs of the years 1865 to 1876 can be difficult to find as true gems, while later Proofs are nearly all gems.

GRADING STANDARDS

MS-60 to 70 (Mint State). *Obverse and Reverse:* Mint luster is complete in the obverse and reverse fields. Lower grades such as MS-60, 61, and 62 can show some evidence of abrasion. This is usually on the area of the hair to the right of the face (on the obverse), and on the highest parts of the wreath (on the reverse). Abrasion can appear as scattered contact marks elsewhere. At MS-63, these marks are few, and on MS-65 they are fewer yet. In grades above MS-65, marks can only be seen under magnification.

1870. Graded MS-65.

Illustrated coin: This example is lightly toned.

AU-50, 53, 55, 58 (About Uncirculated). *Obverse:* Light wear is seen on the portrait, most notably on the upper cheek and on the hair to the right of the face. Mint luster is present in the fields, ranging from partial at AU-50 to nearly complete at AU-58. All details are sharp, unless lightly struck. *Reverse:* Light wear is seen on the top and bottom horizontal edges of the III and the wreath. Luster is partial at AU-50, increasing to nearly full at AU-58. All details are sharp, unless lightly struck.

1868. Graded AU-50.

EF-40, 45 (Extremely Fine). *Obverse:* More wear is seen on the cheek and the hair to the right of the face and neck. The hair to the right of the coronet beads shows light wear. *Reverse:* The wreath still shows most detail on the leaves. Some wear is seen on the vertical lines within III (but striking can also cause weakness). Overall the reverse appears to be very bold.

1881. Graded EF-40.

VF-20, 30 (Very Fine). *Obverse:* Most hair detail is gone, with a continuous flat area to the right of the face and neck, where the higher hair strands have blended together. The hair to the right of the coronet beads shows about half of the strands. *Reverse:* Higher details of the leaves are worn away; the central ridges are seen on some. Wear on the vertical lines in III has caused some to merge, but most are separate.

1873, Open 3. Graded VF-20.

F-12, 15 (Fine). *Obverse:* Wear is more extensive. The forehead blends into the hair above it. About 10% to 29% of the hair detail to the right of the coronet remains, and much detail is seen lower, at the right edge opposite the ear and neck. Denticles are distinct. *Reverse:* The top (highest-relief) part of most leaves is flat. Many vertical lines in III are fused. Denticles are distinct.

1874. Graded F-12.

VG-8, 10 (Very Good). *Obverse:* Less hair detail shows. Denticles all are clear. *Reverse:* The leaves show more wear. The inner edges of some leaves are worn away, causing leaves to merge. Only about half, or slightly fewer, of the lines in III are discernible.

1865. Graded VG-10.

G-4, 6 (Good). *Obverse:* Most hair details are gone, but some remain at the lower right. The rim is worn smooth in areas, and many denticles are missing. The lettering is weak, but readable. *Reverse:* The leaves mostly are worn flat. Very few lines remain in III. The rim is worn smooth in areas, and many denticles are missing.

1867. Graded G-4.

AG-3 (About Good). *Obverse:* The rim is worn away and into the tops of most of the letters. The date remains bold. *Reverse:* The rim is worn away and into some of the leaves.

1867. Graded AG-3.

PF-60 to 70 (Proof). *Obverse and Reverse:* PF-60, 61, and 62 coins show varying amounts of hairlines in the field, decreasing as the grade increases. Fields may be dull or cloudy on lower-level pieces. At PF-65, hairlines are visible only under magnification and are very light; the cheek of Miss Liberty does not show any friction or "album slide marks." Above PF-65, hairlines become fewer, and in ultra-high grades are nonexistent, this mean-

1884. Graded PF-67.

ing that the coins have never been subject to wiping or abrasive cleaning. At PF-65 or better, expect excellent aesthetic appeal. Blotched, deeply toned, or recolored coins are sometimes seen at Proof levels from PF-60 through 65 or even 66 and should be avoided, but these are less often seen than on contemporary Proof nickel five-cent pieces.

Illustrated coin: This superb gem, with delicate toning, is a connoisseur's delight.

1866, Doubled-Die Obverse
FS-3N-1866-101.

	Mintage	Cert	Avg	%MS	G-4	VG-8	VF-20	EF-40	AU-50	MS-60	MS-63 / PF-63	MS-65 / PF-65	MS-66 / PF-66
1865	11,382,000	1,915	60.0	79%	$15	$20	$30	$40	$65	$120	$160	$600	$1,200
	Auctions: $734, MS-66, October 2014; $1,175, MS-66, February 2013; $200, MS-64, September 2014; $44, F-12, November 2014												
1865, Proof	500+	202	64.8								$1,650	$3,000	$8,000
	Auctions: $3,819, PF-66Cam, November 2014; $1,410, PF-63, November 2014												
1866	4,801,000	763	60.3	83%	$18	$20	$28	$40	$65		$160	$600	$1,500
	Auctions: $9,989, MS-67, August 2014; $3,819, MS-66, September 2013; $499, MS-65, November 2014; $106, MS-62, November 2014												
1866, Doubled-Die Obverse (a)	(b)	5	48.4	20%				$150	$250		$450	$900	
	Auctions: No auction records available.												
1866, Proof	725+	303	64.4								$350	$1,500	$2,000
	Auctions: $2,715, PF-66DCam, October 2014; $4,113, PF-66DCam, July 2014; $470, PF-64Cam, November 2014												

a. Moderate doubling is visible on AMERICA and on portions of the hair. "The dies clashed midway through the obverse's life. Mid– and late–die-state coins exhibit the clash marks and die cracks as progression occurs. This variety has proven extremely scarce" (*Cherrypickers' Guide to Rare Die Varieties*, sixth edition, volume I). b. Included in circulation-strike 1866 mintage figure.

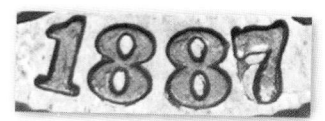

1887, 7 Over 6, Proof
FS-3N-1887-302.

	Mintage	Cert	Avg	%MS	G-4	VG-8	VF-20	EF-40	AU-50	MS-60	MS-63	MS-65	MS-66
											PF-63	PF-65	PF-66
1867	3,915,000	580	59.6	76%	$15	$20	$30	$40	$65	$120	$160	$700	$1,900
	Auctions: $1,410, MS-66, January 2014; $206, MS-64, October 2014; $247, MS-64, August 2014; $112, MS-62, September 2014												
1867, Proof	*625+*	340	64.8								$350	$1,500	$2,000
	Auctions: $6,463, PF-66DCam, July 2014; $2,475, PF-66Cam, August 2014; $1,116, PF-65Cam, August 2014; $705, PF-65Cam, August 2014												
1868	3,252,000	548	60.5	81%	$15	$20	$30	$40	$65	$120	$160	$600	$1,200
	Auctions: $1,116, MS-66, October 2014; $1,058, MS-66, September 2014; $115, MS-62, November 2014; $80, AU-58, August 2014												
1868, Proof	*600+*	289	64.8								$350	$1,500	$2,000
	Auctions: $4,704, PF-67DCam, September 2014; $4,406, PF-66DCam, April 2013; $1,763, PF-66Cam, November 2014; $388, PF-64, July 2014												
1869	1,604,000	383	61.1	83%	$15	$20	$30	$40	$65	$135	$185	$750	$1,500
	Auctions: $617, MS-65, September 2014; $823, MS-65, July 2014; $129, MS-63, October 2014; $41, MS-60, November 2014												
1869, Proof	*600+*	375	64.7								$350	$950	$1,500
	Auctions: $9,173, PF-67DCam, January 2014; $3,819, PF-66DCam, September 2014; $382, PF-64Cam, November 2014												
1870	1,335,000	408	61.1	82%	$20	$25	$30	$40	$65	$140	$195	$725	$1,450
	Auctions: $4,406, MS-66, September 2014; $3,525, MS-66, January 2014; $588, MS-65, July 2014; $94, MS-61, November 2014												
1870, Proof	*1,000+*	345	64.5								$350	$950	$1,500
	Auctions: $13,513, PF-66DCam, November 2014; $1,763, PF-66Cam, November 2014; $3,055, PF-66Cam, August 2013; $382, PF-64Cam, October 2014												
1871	604,000	226	61.4	86%	$20	$25	$30	$40	$65	$140	$195	$750	$1,500
	Auctions: $2,174, MS-66, October 2014; $2,585, MS-66, November 2013; $129, MS-62, November 2014; $223, AU-58, December 2014												
1871, Proof	*960+*	369	64.5								$350	$1,000	$1,500
	Auctions: $6,756, PF-67Cam, August 2014; $1,528, PF-66Cam, December 2013; $999, PF-66, September 2014; $382, PF-64, November 2014												
1872	862,000	181	60.5	80%	$20	$25	$30	$40	$65	$150	$210	$1,200	$2,200
	Auctions: $1,880, MS-66, October 2014; $2,115, MS-66, April 2013; $282, MS-64, October 2014; $153, MS-62, November 2014												
1872, Proof	*950+*	431	64.5								$350	$950	$1,400
	Auctions: $3,055, PF-67, June 2014; $1,528, PF-66Cam, October 2014; $940, PF-66, November 2014; $353, PF-64, October 2014												
1873, Close 3	390,000	102	57.4	70%	$20	$25	$30	$40	$65	$150	$210	$1,400	$2,750
	Auctions: $2,820, MS-66, April 2013; $505, MS-64, October 2014; $470, MS-64, September 2014; $64, MS-60, September 2014												
1873, Open 3	783,000	88	57.6	76%	$20	$25	$30	$40	$70	$160	$350	$5,000	
	Auctions: $6,463, MS-66, November 2014; $10,575, MS-66, April 2013; $2,952, MS-65, October 2014; $705, MS-64, July 2014												
1873, Close 3, Proof	*1,100+*	440	64.4								$350	$1,000	$1,500
	Auctions: $7,050, PF-67, September 2013; $1,116, PF-66Cam, November 2014; $1,410, PF-66, November 2014; $558, PF-65Cam, July 2014												
1874	790,000	179	59.7	77%	$20	$25	$30	$40	$65	$150	$210	$1,000	$2,100
	Auctions: $3,525, MS-66, October 2014; $2,585, MS-66, March 2013												
1874, Proof	*700+*	337	64.7								$350	$900	$1,300
	Auctions: $8,519, PF-67, August 2013; $1,175, PF-66Cam, November 2014; $1,058, PF-66, October 2014; $411, PF-64, September 2014												
1875	228,000	229	62.9	91%	$20	$25	$35	$45	$80	$175	$225	$750	$1,500
	Auctions: $1,645, MS-66, April 2013; $353, MS-64, October 2014; $323, MS-64, October 2014; $235, MS-64, October 2014												
1875, Proof	*700+*	252	64.4								$350	$1,300	$2,000
	Auctions: $7,638, PF-66Cam, July 2014; $8,225, PF-66Cam, February 2014; $1,175, PF-66, September 2014; $1,414, PF-65Cam, September 2014												
1876	162,000	114	59.1	77%	$20	$25	$35	$50	$110	$200	$260	$1,600	$2,500
	Auctions: $6,463, MS-66, January 2014; $1,410, MS-65, November 2014; $1,469, MS-65, October 2014; $229, MS-63, July 2014												
1876, Proof	*1,150+*	394	64.5								$350	$900	$1,300
	Auctions: $4,994, PF-67Cam, August 2014; $1,175, PF-66Cam, November 2014; $2,233, PF-66Cam, February 2013; $646, PF-64, September 2014												
1877, Proof (c)	900	482	64.9								$2,000	$4,400	$5,500
	Auctions: $11,163, PF-67Cam, January 2014; $5,581, PF-66Cam, September 2014; $3,819, PF-65DCam, November 2014; $3,055, PF-64, October 2014												
1878, Proof (c)	2,350	686	65.0								$1,000	$1,100	$1,450
	Auctions: $8,225, PF-68Cam, January 2014; $1,645, PF-67Cam, October 2014; $1,880, PF-67, November 2014; $940, PF-66Cam, September 2014												

c. Proof only.

	Mintage	Cert	Avg	%MS	G-4	VG-8	VF-20	EF-40	AU-50	MS-60	MS-63 / PF-63	MS-65 / PF-65	MS-66 / PF-66
1879	38,000	175	57.9	73%	$60	$70	$90	$125	$175	$300	$400	$850	$1,200
Auctions: $4,113, MS-67, February 2014; $589, MS-65, July 2014; $84, EF-40, November 2014; $100, VF-30, September 2014													
1879, Proof	3,200	941	65.1								$450	$700	$850
Auctions: $14,100, PF-67DCam, April 2013; $1,006, PF-67Cam, November 2014; $1,175, PF-67, November 2014; $259, PF-62, November 2014													
1880	21,000	198	59.3	80%	$90	$110	$150	$200	$220	$350	$410	$850	$1,350
Auctions: $3,290, MS-67, July 2014; $1,175, MS-66, July 2014; $1,116, MS-66, August 2014													
1880, Proof	3,955	954	65.0								$450	$700	$850
Auctions: $9,400, PF-67Cam, June 2014; $940, PF-67, November 2014; $734, PF-66Cam, July 2014; $532, PF-66, October 2014													
1881	1,077,000	575	59.7	74%	$20	$25	$30	$40	$65	$125	$185	$650	$1,000
Auctions: $999, MS-66, April 2014; $382, MS-65, November 2014; $206, MS-64, November 2014; $92, AU-58, August 2014													
1881, Proof	3,575	1,005	65.2								$350	$600	$850
Auctions: $11,163, PF-67DCam, February 2014; $1,116, PF-67Cam, November 2014; $588, PF-66, July 2014; $141, PF-60, November 2014													
1882	22,200	111	50.3	44%	$110	$125	$180	$225	$275	$400	$500	$1,200	$3,000
Auctions: $823, MS-64, August 2014; $593, MS-63, December 2013; $153, F-15, July 2014													
1882, Proof	3,100	1,031	65.2								$400	$600	$850
Auctions: $4,406, PF-68, October 2014; $5,875, PF-68, January 2014; $1,175, PF-67, October 2014; $529, PF-66, October 2014													
1883	4,000	47	54.1	51%	$175	$190	$275	$350	$400	$550	$900	$5,200	$15,000
Auctions: $25,850, MS-67, October 2014; $3,966, MS-64, August 2014; $1,880, MS-62, October 2014; $823, AU-50, September 2014													
1883, Proof	6,609	1,512	64.8								$400	$600	$850
Auctions: $1,116, PF-67Cam, September 2014; $1,763, PF-67, November 2014; $881, PF-66, September 2014; $300, PF-64, November 2014													
1884	1,700	31	52.4	42%	$350	$375	$510	$600	$650	$900	$1,100	$10,000	$16,000
Auctions: $4,700, AU-55, January 2014; $4,847, AU-53, August 2014; $1,998, EF-45, November 2014; $1,410, VF-20, September 2014													
1884, Proof	3,942	1,158	64.8								$400	$600	$850
Auctions: $9,400, PF-68Cam, June 2014; $2,233, PF-67Cam, November 2014; $341, PF-64, November 2014; $223, PF-60, November 2014													
1885	1,000	37	57.3	68%	$410	$435	$575	$700	$800	$950	$1,200	$12,500	$18,000
Auctions: $22,325, MS-66, June 2014; $423, MS-64, October 2014; $3,055, AU-50, August 2014													
1885, Proof	3,790	989	64.7								$500	$600	$850
Auctions: $1,367, PF-67, September 2014; $3,760, PF-67Cam, June 2014; $617, PF-66, July 2014; $306, PF-60, November 2014													
1886, Proof (c)	4,290	1,039	64.7								$500	$650	$875
Auctions: $1,058, PF-67Cam, November 2014; $1,351, PF-67Cam, July 2014; $529, PF-66, October 2014; $294, PF-60, November 2014													
1887	5,001	111	55.8	61%	$275	$325	$350	$400	$500	$550	$675	$1,500	$2,250
Auctions: $2,350, MS-66, June 2013; $1,058, MS-65, August 2014; $309, AU-58, October 2014; $441, VF-35, October 2014													
1887, Proof	2,960	348	64.2								$500	$900	$1,200
Auctions: $2,115, PF-67, January 2014; $1,998, PF-66, July 2014; $646, PF-65, October 2014; $212, PF-62, November 2014													
1887, 7 Over 6, Proof (d)	(e)	471	64.9								$575	$800	$1,100
Auctions: $7,638, PF-67Cam, April 2014; $1,058, PF-66Cam, July 2014; $588, PF-65, October 2014; $382, PF-62, July 2014													
1888	36,501	302	59.4	69%	$50	$65	$75	$100	$150	$300	$400	$850	$1,350
Auctions: $2,115, MS-67, October 2014; $999, MS-66, October 2014; $188, AU-58, September 2014; $94, VF-35, November 2014													
1888, Proof	4,582	1,061	64.8								$400	$600	$850
Auctions: $1,763, PF-67Cam, October 2014; $1,058, PF-67, July 2014; $2,350, PF-66DCam, March 2014; $112, PF-60, November 2014													
1889	18,125	235	60.0	69%	$80	$100	$135	$220	$250	$350	$450	$850	$1,350
Auctions: $2,820, MS-67, October 2014; $2,585, MS-67, June 2014; $1,116, MS-66, October 2014; $329, MS-62, November 2014													
1889, Proof	3,436	1,075	65.0								$400	$600	$850
Auctions: $6,463, PF-68, August 2014; $1,234, PF-67Cam, November 2014; $529, PF-66, November 2014; $212, PF-62, November 2014													

c. Proof only. d. Strong remnants of the underlying 6 are evident on either side of the lower portion of the 7, with the 1 and both 8's clearly repunched. This Proof overdate is relatively common; note that the regular date can be valued higher than the variety. e. Included in 1887, Proof, mintage figure.

Nickel Five-Cent Pieces
1866 to Date

AN OVERVIEW OF NICKEL FIVE-CENT PIECES

Five-cent pieces made of nickel were introduced in 1866, in an era in which the silver half dime as well as other silver denominations were not seen in circulation. More than a dozen designs and their variations have graced the "nickel" in the past 140-plus years.

While Shield nickels of both varieties are slightly scarce in upper Mint State levels, they are within the financial reach of most collectors. Proofs are available of each variety, but the 1866–1867 With Rays and the 1913, Buffalo, Variety 1, issues are rare.

The quality of strike presents a challenge across the various types of nickel five-cent pieces, most particularly with the 1866–1867, With Rays, for there are fewer possibilities from which to choose. Although 1913–1938, Buffalo, Variety 2, nickels are often poorly struck, there are enough sharp ones that finding a choice example should present no great challenge for the collector.

FOR THE COLLECTOR AND INVESTOR: FIVE-CENT PIECES AS A SPECIALTY

Shield nickels of the 1866–1883 era are often collected by date sequence. A full set includes 1866 and 1867, With Rays, plus 1867 to 1883, Without Rays. In addition, there is the 1879, 9 Over 8, overdate, which is found only in Proof format but is readily available (constituting perhaps a third or so of the Proof mintage of 3,200 for the 1879 year) and the 1883, 3 Over 2 (scarce, and available only as a circulation strike).

Circulation strikes are available of all Shield nickel dates, 1866 to 1883, except 1877 and 1878, which were made only in Proof format. A set of Proofs can be completed except for the 1867, With Rays, which is exceedingly rare in Proof, with an estimated population of fewer than two dozen coins. Most 1878 Proofs are frosty and appear not much different from Mint State, but only Proofs were made this year.

In circulated grades, Shield nickels are available in proportion to their mintage figures. The dates 1879 to 1881 had high Proof mintages (in the context of Proof figures), but low circulation-strike mintages, and thus they are key dates in the latter format. In other words, a gem MS-65 1880, Shield, nickel (16,000 coined, but few were saved, as collectors acquired Proofs instead) is exceedingly rare today. In the same year 3,955 Proofs were struck, all were preserved by collectors and dealers, and today the Proof 1880 is one of the most plentiful dates.

Liberty Head nickels of the 1883, Without CENTS (or "No CENTS"), variety are plentiful in Mint State and also in Proof. Later dates With CENTS, through 1912, are generally available in proportion to their mintages. The 1885 and 1886 are considered to be key dates. Proofs are readily collectible, although pristine high-quality examples can be hard to find. The 1912-D and 1912-S are scarce. In 1913 an estimated five Liberty Head nickels were privately made, and today stand as famous rarities.

Among Buffalo nickels, 1913 to 1938, the different dates and mints can be collected easily enough in circulated grades, although certain issues such as 1913-S, Variety 2; 1921-S; and 1926-S are on the scarce side. An overdate, 1918-D, 8 Over 7, is a rarity at all grade levels. Curious varieties are provided by the very rare 1916, Doubled Date; the scarce 1937-D, 3-Legged (the die was heavily polished, resulting in some loss of detail); and the fascinating and readily available 1938-D, D Over S, overmintmark.

While likely never a serious option to become circulating coinage, Eastman Johnson's "holey" design for a five-cent piece, struck in 1884, is an interesting example of a numismatic "what-if." Shown (enlarged) is Judd-1724, struck in nickel. Other examples were struck in aluminum and white metal.

In choice or gem Mint State most branch-mint Buffalo nickels, 1914–1927, are fairly scarce, and some are quite rare. Most branch-mint coins of the 1920s are lightly struck in one area or another, with the 1926-D being particularly infamous in this regard. Sharply struck examples of such varieties are worth much more than lightly struck ones, although the grading services take no particular note of such differences. Matte Proofs of dates 1913 to 1916 were struck, and mirror-finish Proofs were made in 1936 and 1937. These exist today in proportion to their mintages.

Jefferson nickels from 1938 to date are readily collectible in Mint State and Proof format. Many otherwise common varieties can be very rare if sharply struck.

SHIELD (1866–1883)

Designer: *James B. Longacre.* **Weight:** *5 grams.* **Composition:** *.750 copper, .250 nickel.*
Diameter: *20.5 mm.* **Edge:** *Plain.* **Mint:** *Philadelphia.*

Variety 1, Rays Between Stars
(1866–1867)

Variety 1, Rays Between Stars,
Proof

 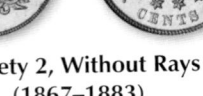

Variety 2, Without Rays
(1867–1883)

Variety 2, Without Rays, Proof

History. The nickel five-cent piece was introduced in 1866. At the time, silver coins (except the trime) did not circulate in the East or Midwest. The new denomination proved popular, and "nickels" of the Shield variety were made continuously from 1866 to 1883. All 1866 nickels have rays between the stars on the reverse, as do a minority of 1867 issues, after which this feature was dropped. In 1877 and 1878 only Proofs were made, with no circulation strikes. The design, by Chief Engraver James B. Longacre, is somewhat similar to the obverse of the two-cent piece. Some Shield nickels were still seen in circulation in the 1930s, by which time most had been worn nearly smooth.

Striking and Sharpness. Sharpness can be a problem for Shield nickels in the 1860s through 1876, much less so for later years. On the obverse the horizontal shield stripes, vertical stripes, and leaves should be checked. The horizontal stripes in particular can be blended together. On the reverse the star centers can be weak. Check all other areas as well. Die cracks are seen on *most* circulation-strike Shield nickels, and do not affect value. Proof Shield nickels were struck of all dates 1866 to 1883, including two varieties of 1867 (With Rays, a great rarity, and the usually seen Without Rays). Fields range from deeply mirrorlike to somewhat grainy in character to mirror-surface, depending on a given year. Many of 1878, a date struck only in Proof format, have *lustrous* surfaces or prooflike surfaces combined with some luster, resembling a circulation strike. While most Proofs are sharp, some have weakness on the shield on the obverse and/or the star centers on the reverse. Lint marks or tiny recessed marks from scattered debris on the die faces are sometimes encountered, especially on issues of the 1870s, but not factored into the grade in commercial certification unless excessive.

Availability. Circulated coins generally are available in proportion to their mintage quantities (exceptions being the 1873, Open 3, and 1873, Close 3, varieties, which tend to be elusive in all grades despite their relatively high mintage). MS coins are similarly available, except that 1880 is a rarity. Those dated 1882 and 1883 are plentiful.

GRADING STANDARDS

MS-60 to 70 (Mint State). *Obverse and Reverse:* At MS-60 some abrasion and very minor contact marks are evident, most noticeably on high points of the shield on the obverse and the field on the reverse. Sometimes light striking on the shield and stars can be mistaken for light wear, and marks on the numeral 5 on the reverse can be from the original planchet surface not struck up fully. At MS-63 abrasions are hard to detect except

1872. Graded MS-66.

under magnification. An MS-65 coin will have no abrasion. Luster should be full and rich (not grainy). Grades above MS-65 are defined by having no marks that can be seen by the naked eye. Higher-grade coins display deeper luster or virtually perfect prooflike surfaces, depending on the dies used.

Illustrated coin: This is a gem with rich luster, light golden toning, and great eye appeal.

AU-50, 53, 55, 58 (About Uncirculated).
Obverse: Light wear is on the outside edges of the leaves, the frame of the shield, and the horizontal stripes (although the stripes can also be weakly struck). Mint luster is present in the fields, ranging from partial at AU-50 to nearly complete at AU-58. All details are sharp, unless lightly struck. *Reverse:* Light wear is seen on the numeral 5, and friction is seen in the field, identifiable as a change of color (loss of luster). Luster is partial at AU-50, increasing to nearly full at AU-58. All details are sharp, unless lightly struck.

1881. Graded AU-50.

EF-40, 45 (Extremely Fine). *Obverse:* Nearly all shield border and leaf detail is visible. Light wear is seen on the shield stripes (but the horizontal stripes can be weakly struck). *Reverse:* More wear is seen on the numeral 5. The radial lines in the stars (if sharply struck to begin with) show slight wear. The field shows more wear.

1881. Graded EF-40.

VF-20, 30 (Very Fine). *Obverse:* The frame details and leaves show more wear, with much leaf detail gone. The shield stripes show more wear, and some of the vertical lines will begin to blend together. *Reverse:* More wear is seen overall, but some radial detail can still be seen on the stars.

1868. Graded VF-20.

F-12, 15 (Fine). *Obverse:* Most leaves are flat and have little detail, but will remain outlined. The shield frame is mostly flat. Most horizontal lines are blended together, regardless of original strike. Many vertical lines in the stripes are blended together. IN GOD WE TRUST is slightly weak. *Reverse:* All areas are in outline form except for slight traces of the star radials. Lettering is bold.

1867, Without Rays. Graded F-12.

VG-8, 10 (Very Good). *Obverse:* Many leaves are flat and blended with adjacent leaves. The frame is blended and has no details. Only a few horizontal lines may show. Vertical lines in the stripes are mostly blended. IN GOD WE TRUST is weak. *Reverse:* All elements are visible only in outline form. The rim is complete.

1866. Graded VG-8.

G-4, 6 (Good). *Obverse:* The shield and elements are seen in outline form except the vertical stripe separations. IN GOD WE TRUST is weak, and a few letters may be missing. *Reverse:* The rim is mostly if not completely worn away and into the tops of the letters.

   Illustrated coin: Overall this coin is slightly better than G-4, but the 5 in the date is weak, making G-4 an appropriate attribution.

1866. Graded G-4.

AG-3 (About Good). *Obverse:* The rim is worn down and blended with the wreath. Only traces of IN GOD WE TRUST can be seen. The date is fully readable. *Reverse:* The rim is worn down and blended with the letters, some of which may be missing.

1868. Graded AG-3.

PF-60 to 70 (Proof). *Obverse and Reverse:* PF-60, 61, and 62 coins show varying amounts of hairlines in the reverse field in particular, decreasing as the grade increases. Fields may be dull or cloudy on lower-level pieces. At PF-65, hairlines are visible only under magnification and are very light and usually only on the reverse. Above PF-65, hairlines become fewer, and in ultra-high grades are nonexistent, this meaning that the coins have never been subject to wiping or abrasive cleaning. At PF-65 or better, expect excellent aesthetic appeal.

1877. Graded PF-67 Cameo.

1866, Repunched Date
Several varieties exist.

	Mintage	Cert	Avg	%MS	G-4	VG-8	F-12	VF-20	EF-40	AU-50	MS-60 / PF-63	MS-63 / PF-65	MS-65 / PF-66
1866, Rays	14,742,500	1,616	60.2	78%	$30	$45	$50	$100	$150	$250	$300	$450	$2,500
	Auctions: $2,585, MS-66, August 2014; $11,163, MS-66, October 2013; $353, AU-58, October 2014; $282, Fair-2, July 2014												
1866, Repunched Date (a)	**(b)**	26	50.3	42%	$60	$75	$150	$200	$250	$375	$575	$950	
	Auctions: $8,813, MS-64, October 2014; $12,925, MS-64, August 2014; $1,175, AU-50, August 2014; $1,293, AU-50, March 2013												
1866, Rays, Proof	*600+*	268	64.8								$1,750	$3,250	$5,000
	Auctions: $4,115, PF-66Cam, September 2014; $2,585, PF-65Cam, August 2014; $1,234, PF-62, September 2014												

a. There are at least five similar, very strong repunched dates for 1866; the values shown are typical for each. **b.** Included in circulation-strike 1866, Rays, mintage figure.

1873, Close 3   1873, Open 3   1873, Close 3, Doubled-Die Obverse

Several varieties exist. Pictured are
FS-05-1873-101 (left) and FS-05-1873-102 (right).

	Mintage	Cert	Avg	%MS	G-4	VG-8	F-12	VF-20	EF-40	AU-50	MS-60 / PF-63	MS-63 / PF-65	MS-65 / PF-66
1867, Rays	2,019,000	560	58.9	71%	$35	$50	$65	$130	$200	$300	$375	$500	$3,500
	Auctions: $41,125, MS-67, October 2013; $8,225, MS-66, July 2014; $353, AU-58, December 2014; $223, AU-53, September 2014												
1867, Rays, Proof †	25+	31	64.5								$35,000	$60,000	$85,000
	Auctions: $55,813, PF-66, August 2014; $44,063, PF-65Cam, October 2014												
1867, No Rays	28,890,500	866	60.5	77%	$25	$30	$35	$50	$65	$110	$150	$225	$800
	Auctions: $2,233, MS-66, October 2014; $2,585, MS-66, August 2014; $353, MS-64, November 2014; $141, AU-58, December 2014												
1867, No Rays, Proof	600+	266	64.3								$475	$2,250	$4,000
	Auctions: $6,463, PF-67Cam, September 2014; $4,994, PF-66Cam, October 2014; $2,820, PF-66, October 2014; $411, PF-62, October 2014												
1867, No Rays, Pattern Reverse, Proof (c)	(d)	2	65.5								$6,500	$9,000	
	Auctions: No auction records available.												
1868	28,817,000	838	60.4	78%	$25	$30	$35	$50	$65	$110	$150	$225	$800
	Auctions: $1,763, MS-66, November 2014; $2,233, MS-66, October 2014; $86, AU-58, October 2014; $112, AU-55, September 2014												
1868, Proof	600+	209	64.7								$350	$1,000	$1,250
	Auctions: $9,400, PF-66DCam, August 2013; $1,528, PF-65Cam, November 2014; $282, PF-62, November 2014; $259, PF-62, August 2014												
1869	16,395,000	502	60.4	82%	$25	$30	$35	$50	$65	$110	$140	$225	$800
	Auctions: $1,058, MS-66, September 2014; $11,750, MS-66, October 2013; $141, MS-62, August 2014; $153, MS-61, September 2014												
1869, Proof	600+	356	64.4								$350	$800	$1,400
	Auctions: $646, PF-65, September 2014; $329, PF-64, October 2014												
1870	4,806,000	215	58.5	77%	$30	$35	$60	$80	$100	$150	$250	$300	$1,750
	Auctions: $4,994, MS-66, June 2014; $1,293, MS-65, October 2014; $1,763, MS-65, September 2014; $84, EF-45, October 2014												
1870, Proof	1,000+	317	64.3								$350	$800	$1,400
	Auctions: $8,225, PF-67Cam, July 2014; $1,175, PF-66Cam, September 2014; $1,586, PF-66, October 2014; $881, PF-64, October 2014												
1871	561,000	105	56.3	70%	$80	$100	$150	$215	$280	$350	$450	$625	$2,250
	Auctions: $4,113, MS-66, October 2014; $5,875, MS-66, February 2014; $1,821, MS-65, September 2014; $188, VF-30, July 2014												
1871, Proof	960+	322	64.5								$350	$825	$1,400
	Auctions: $3,525, PF-66Cam, October 2014; $1,351, PF-66Cam, July 2014; $764, PF-64Cam, November 2014												
1872	6,036,000	265	58.9	72%	$35	$45	$75	$100	$125	$175	$235	$300	$1,500
	Auctions: $25,850, MS-67, October 2013; $1,998, MS-66, November 2014; $1,645, MS-65, September 2014; $112, AU-55, October 2014												
1872, Proof	950+	356	64.8								$350	$700	$1,000
	Auctions: $1,528, PF-66, November 2014; $499, PF-64Cam, October 2014; $646, PF-64, October 2014												
1873, Close 3	436,050	64	60.1	78%	$30	$40	$60	$100	$140	$200	$325	$585	$2,750
	Auctions: $2,703, MS-65, August 2014; $3,525, MS-65, October 2013; $170, MS-60, September 2014												
1873, Close 3, Doubled-Die Obverse (e)	(f)	15	56.9	60%							$425	$675	$900 / $1,500 / $3,500
	Auctions: $881, MS-63, September 2014; $499, MS-62, June 2013												
1873, Open 3	4,113,950	79	59.3	80%	$30	$35	$60	$80	$100	$140	$210	$300	$2,000
	Auctions: $2,468, MS-66, September 2014; $10,575, MS-66, March 2013; $1,293, MS-64, August 2014; $84, EF-45, September 2014												
1873, Close 3, Proof	1,100+	358	64.5								$350	$700	$1,000
	Auctions: $4,700, PF-67, October 2014; $5,875, PF-67, August 2014; $1,763, PF-66Cam, November 2014												

† Ranked in the *100 Greatest U.S. Coins* (fourth edition). **c.** These were made from a pattern (Judd-573) reverse die that is slightly different than the regular Without Rays design. **d.** 21 to 30 examples are known. **e.** There are several varieties of 1873, Close 3, Doubled-Die Obverse. The values shown are representative of the more avidly sought varieties; others command smaller premiums. **f.** Included in circulation-strike 1873, Close 3, mintage figure.

1883, 3 Over 2
Several varieties exist, as well as pieces with a recut 3. Pictured are FS-05-1883-301 (left) and FS-05-1883-305 (right).

	Mintage	Cert	Avg	%MS	G-4	VG-8	F-12	VF-20	EF-40	AU-50	MS-60	MS-63	MS-65
											PF-63	PF-65	PF-66
1874	3,538,000	158	60.6	78%	$30	$40	$65	$80	$125	$170	$250	$325	$1,500
	Auctions: $3,525, MS-66, November 2014; $165, MS-62, October 2014; $11,163, MS, February 2014; $147, AU-55, September 2014												
1874, Proof	700+	300	64.6								$350	$750	$1,100
	Auctions: $1,116, PF-66, September 2014; $646, PF-65, November 2014; $353, PF-64, September 2014												
1875	2,097,000	150	59.7	81%	$45	$60	$100	$130	$160	$220	$275	$360	$1,700
	Auctions: $4,113, MS-66, July 2014; $4,406, MS-66, June 2014; $2,820, MS-65, September 2014; $558, MS-64, November 2014												
1875, Proof	700+	290	64.4								$350	$1,150	$2,000
	Auctions: $2,233, PF-66Cam, November 2014; $3,055, PF-66Cam, October 2014; $881, PF-65Cam, November 2014												
1876	2,530,000	257	61.5	86%	$40	$55	$80	$115	$150	$200	$250	$325	$1,250
	Auctions: $3,768, MS-66, September 2014; $4,406, MS-66, August 2014; $5,875, MS-66, October 2013; $165, AU-53, September 2014												
1876, Proof	1,150+	394	64.6								$350	$800	$1,100
	Auctions: $3,055, PF-67Cam, $5,581, PF-66DCam, September 2014; November 2014; $1,880, PF-66Cam, September 2014												
1877, Proof (g)	900	442	64.6								$3,250	$4,800	$5,000
	Auctions: $7,344, PF-66Cam, September 2014; $8,225, PF-66Cam, August 2014; $4,700, PF-66, November 2014												
1878, Proof (g)	2,350	602	64.6								$1,600	$1,850	$3,500
	Auctions: $1,546, PF-66, November 2014; $1,645, PF-66, September 2014; $1,528, PF-65Cam, September 2014												
1879	25,900	81	57.0	72%	$375	$475	$600	$660	$725	$750	$900	$1,000	$2,000
	Auctions: $4,994, MS-66, October 2014; $7,638, MS-66, June 2013; $3,819, MS-64, August 2014; $823, EF-45, August 2014												
1879, Proof	3,200	561	64.7								$400	$775	$1,000
	Auctions: $1,764, PF-67, October 2014; $999, PF-66Cam, October 2014; $1,058, PF-66, October 2014												
1879, 9 Over 8, Proof (h)	(i)	0	n/a								$425	$800	$1,000
	Auctions: $8,813, PF-68, October 2014; $15,275, PF-67Cam, February 2014; $1,410, PF-66Cam, July 2014; $1,410, PF-66, October 2014												
1880	16,000	37	46.0	24%	$475	$560	$675	$980	$1,300	$1,850	$4,000	$7,500	$47,500
	Auctions: $88,125, MS-65, August 2014; $193,875, MS, February 2014; $5,288, AU-55, August 2014; $2,938, VF-35, August 2014												
1880, Proof	3,955	886	64.5								$400	$650	$900
	Auctions: $1,880, PF-67Cam, September 2014; $3,173, PF-67Cam, February 2013; $1,381, PF-67, July 2014												
1881	68,800	150	49.3	53%	$250	$300	$425	$510	$600	$775	$850	$1,000	$1,950
	Auctions: $8,519, MS-67, October 2013; $2,115, MS-65, September 2014; $2,115, MS-64, August 2014; $206, G-4, November 2014												
1881, Proof	3,575	818	64.9								$400	$650	$900
	Auctions: $1,998, PF-67Cam, August 2014; $1,175, PF-67, October 2014; $646, PF-66Cam, October 2014												
1882	11,472,900	1,026	59.2	82%	$25	$30	$35	$50	$65	$110	$150	$225	$725
	Auctions: $6,170, MS-67, September 2014; $1,116, MS-66, November 2014; $170, MS-62, November 2014; $8,519, AU-55, April 2014												
1882, Proof	3,100	912	65.1								$350	$650	$900
	Auctions: $1,351, PF-67, October 2014; $3,055, PF-66DCam, October 2014; $200, PF-61, September 2014												
1883	1,451,500	1,697	61.9	83%	$25	$30	$35	$50	$65	$110	$150	$225	$725
	Auctions: $3,525, MS-67, January 2014; $823, MS-66, October 2014; $1,116, MS-66, August 2014; $94, AU-58, October 2014												
1883, 3 Over 2 (j)	(k)	38	58.2	63%	$250	$325	$650	$950	$1,250	$1,750	$2,100	$2,750	$5,000
	Auctions: $15,275, MS-67, December 2013												
1883, Proof	5,419	1,146	64.8								$350	$650	$900
	Auctions: $1,410, PF-67, September 2014; $705, PF-66, November 2014; $145, PF-60, July 2014												

g. Proof only. **h.** This variety is confirmed only with Proof finish, although Breen mentions two circulation strikes and further mentions that there are "at least two varieties" (*Walter Breen's Complete Encyclopedia of U.S. and Colonial Coins*). In the *Guide Book of Shield and Liberty Head Nickels*, Bowers discusses research and theories from Breen, DeLorey, Spindel, and Julian, noting that the variety's overdate status is "not determined." **i.** Included in 1879, Proof, mintage figure. **j.** Several varieties exist. For more information, see the *Cherrypickers' Guide to Rare Die Varieties*, sixth edition, volume I. "Beware of 1882 Shield nickels with a filled-in, blobby 2, as these are very frequently offered as 1883, 3 Over 2. This is possibly the single most misunderstood coin in all U.S. coinage." (Howard Spindel, communication to Q. David Bowers, quoted in *A Guide Book of Shield and Liberty Head Nickels*.) **k.** Included in circulation-strike 1883 mintage figure.

LIBERTY HEAD (1883–1912)

Designer: *Charles E. Barber.* **Weight:** *5 grams.* **Composition:** *.750 copper, .250 nickel.*
Diameter: *21.2 mm.* **Edge:** *Plain.* **Mints:** *Philadelphia, Denver, San Francisco.*

Variety 1, Without CENTS   Variety 1, Without CENTS, Proof
(1883)

Variety 2, With CENTS   *Mintmark locations is on the*   Variety 2, With CENTS, Proof
(1883–1912)   *reverse, to the left of CENTS.*

History. Liberty Head nickels were popular in their time, minted in large quantities most years, and remained in circulation through the 1940s, by which time most were worn down to grades such as AG-3 and G-4. Stray coins could still be found in the early 1950s. Serious numismatic interest in circulated examples began in the 1930s with the popularity of Whitman and other coin boards, folders, and albums. Many of the scarcer dates were picked from circulation at that time. The five known 1913, Liberty Head, nickels were not an authorized Mint issue, and were never placed into circulation.

Striking and Sharpness. Many Liberty Head nickels have areas of light striking. On the obverse, this is often seen at the star centers, particularly near the top border. The hair above the forehead can be light as well, and always is thus on 1912-S (the obverse die on this San Francisco issue is slightly bulged). On the reverse, E PLURIBUS UNUM can vary in sharpness of strike. Weakness is often seen at the wreath bow and on the ear of corn to the left (the kernels in the ear can range from indistinct to bold). Even Proofs can be weakly struck in areas. Mint luster can range from minutely pebbly or grainy (but still attractive) to a deep, rich frost. Some later Philadelphia coins show stress marks in the field, particularly the obverse, from the use of "tired" dies. This can be determined only by observation, as "slabbed" grades for MS coins do not indicate the quality of the luster or surfaces. Proof Liberty Head nickels were struck of all dates 1883 to 1912, plus both varieties of 1883 (with and without CENTS). The fields range from deeply mirrorlike to somewhat grainy character to mirror-surface, depending on a given year. While most Proofs are sharp, some have weakness at the star centers and/or the kernels on the ear of corn to the left of the ribbon bow. These weaknesses are overlooked by the certification services. Generally, later issues are more deeply mirrored than are earlier ones. Some years in the 1880s and 1890s can show graininess, a combination of mint luster and mirror quality. Lint marks or tiny recessed marks from scattered debris on the die faces are sometimes encountered, but not factored into third-party–certified grades unless excessive.

Availability. All issues from 1883 to 1912 are readily collectible, although the 1885 (in particular), 1886, and 1912-S are considered to be key dates. Most readily available are well-worn coins in AG-3 and G-4. As a class, VF, EF, and AU pieces are very scarce in relation to demand. MS coins are generally scarce in the 1880s, except for the 1883, Without CENTS, which is plentiful in all grades. MS pieces are less scarce in the 1890s and are easily found for most 20th-century years, save for 1909, 1912-D, and 1912-S, all of which are elusive.

GRADING STANDARDS

MS-60 to 70 (Mint State). *Obverse and Reverse:* Mint luster is complete in the obverse and reverse fields. Lower grades such as MS-60, 61, and 62 can show some evidence of abrasion, usually on the portrait on the obverse and highest parts of the wreath on the reverse, and scattered contact marks elsewhere. At MS-63 these marks are few, and at MS-65 they are fewer yet. In grades above MS-65, marks can only be seen under magnification.

Illustrated coin: This MS coin is lightly toned and lustrous.

1900. Graded MS-64.

AU-50, 53, 55, 58 (About Uncirculated).
Obverse: Light wear is seen on the portrait and on the hair under LIB. Mint luster is present in the fields, ranging from partial at AU-50 to nearly complete at AU-58. All details are sharp, unless lightly struck. *Reverse:* Light wear is seen on the V, the other letters, and the wreath. Luster is partial at AU-50, increasing to nearly full at AU-58. All details are sharp, unless lightly struck.

Illustrated coin: E PLURIBUS UNUM shows some light striking.

1887. Graded AU-50.

EF-40, 45 (Extremely Fine). *Obverse:*
Nearly all hair detail is visible, save for some lightness above the forehead. Stars show radial lines (except for those that may have been lightly struck). Overall bold appearance. *Reverse:* The wreath still shows most detail on the leaves. Denticles are bold inside the rim.

Illustrated coin: This coin shows some light striking at the bottom of the wreath, especially to the left of the ribbon bow.

1883, Without CENTS. Graded EF-40.

VF-20, 30 (Very Fine). *Obverse:* Letters in
LIBERTY are all well defined. Hair detail is seen on the back of the head and some between the ear and the coronet. Denticles are bold. Some stars show radial lines. *Reverse:* Detail is seen in the wreath leaves. Lettering and denticles are bold, although E PLURI-BUS UNUM may range from medium-light to bold (depending on the strike).

Illustrated coin: The hair detail on this date and mint is usually not as well defined as on Philadelphia issues.

1912-S. Graded VF-20.

F-12, 15 (Fine). *Obverse:* All of the letters in LIBERTY are readable, although the I may be weak. The detail beginning at the front of hair is visible. Denticles are well defined. *Reverse:* Detail of the leaves begins to fade in the wreath. Denticles are well defined all around the border. E PLURIBUS UNUM has medium definition, and is complete.

1912-S. Graded F-12.

VG-8, 10 (Very Good). *Obverse:* Three or more letters in LIBERTY can be discerned. This can be a combination of two full letters and two or more partial letters. Some hair detail shows at the back of the head. The rim is well outlined and shows traces of most or even all denticles. *Reverse:* The wreath and lettering are bold, but in outline form. E PLURIBUS UNUM is readable, but may be weak. The rim is complete all around, with traces of most denticles present.

1885. Graded VG-8.

G-4, 6 (Good). *Obverse:* The rim is complete all around. Some denticles show on the inside of the rim. The date, Liberty head, and stars are in outline form. No letters of LIBERTY are visible in the coronet. *Reverse:* V and the wreath are visible in outline form. Most letters are complete, but may be faint. E PLURIBUS UNUM is very weak (this feature can vary, and on some G-4 coins it is better defined). The rim is complete in most areas, but may blend with the field in some parts.

1885. Graded G-4.

AG-3 (About Good). *Obverse:* The head is outlined, with only the ear hole as a detail. The date is well worn; the bottom of the digits can be weak or incomplete. The stars are solid, without detail; some may be incomplete. The rim is indistinct or incomplete in some areas. *Reverse:* Details are nearly all worn away, showing greater effects of wear than does the obverse. V is in outline form. The wreath is in outline form, and may be indistinct in areas. Lettering ranges from faint to missing, but with some letters readable. The rim is

1891. Graded AG-3.

usually worn down into the letters.

PF-60 to 70 (Proof). *Obverse and Reverse:* PF-60, 61, and 62 coins show varying amounts of hairlines in the field, decreasing as the grade increases. Fields may be dull or cloudy on lower-level pieces. At PF-65, hairlines are visible only under magnification and are very light; the cheek of Miss Liberty does not show any abrasion or "album slide marks." Above PF-65, hairlines become fewer, and in ultra-high grades are nonexistent, this mean-

1911. Graded PF-66.

ing that the coins have never been subject to wiping or abrasive cleaning. At PF-65 or better, expect excellent aesthetic appeal. Blotched, deeply toned, or recolored coins can be found at most Proof levels from PF-60 through 65 or even 66, and should be avoided. Watch for artificially toned lower-grade Proofs colored to mask the true nature of the fields.

Illustrated coin: This Proof shows medium-toned surfaces.

	Mintage	Cert	Avg	%MS	G-4	VG-8	F-12	VF-20	EF-40	AU-50	MS-60 / PF-63	MS-63 / PF-64	MS-65 / PF-65
1883, Without CENTS	5,474,300	6,999	63.3	93%	$7	$8	$9	$11	$15	$18	$35	$50	$225
Auctions: $2,233, MS-67, October 2014; $280, MS-66, November 2014; $94, MS-64, November 2014; $235, AU-53, October 2014													
1883, Without CENTS, Proof	5,219	1,002	64.7								$300	$450	$700
Auctions: $16,450, PF-67DCam, June 2014; $2,585, PF-67Cam, October 2014; $2,350, PF-66DCam, October 2014													
1883, With CENTS	16,026,200	988	61.6	85%	$20	$30	$35	$55	$85	$120	$150	$200	$650
Auctions: $3,819, MS-66, September 2014; $9,694, MS-66, April 2014; $270, MS-64, September 2014; $100, AU-55, November 2014													
1883, With CENTS, Proof	6,783	722	64.5								$275	$400	$600
Auctions: $10,575, PF-67Cam, June 2014; $1,293, PF-67, August 2014; $6,463, PF-66DCam, October 2014; $470, PF-65Cam, October 2014													
1884	11,270,000	456	59.6	81%	$20	$30	$35	$55	$85	$130	$190	$300	$1,800
Auctions: $2,115, MS-66, November 2014; $8,225, MS-66, February 2014; $382, MS-64, August 2014; $212, MS-62, November 2014													
1884, Proof	3,942	800	64.5								$250	$375	$600
Auctions: $5,581, PF-68, October 2014; $14,100, PF-67DCam, September 2014; $2,938, PF-66DCam, August 2014; $617, PF-66, July 2014													
1885	1,472,700	779	27.6	27%	$550	$600	$850	$1,000	$1,350	$1,700	$2,000	$3,400	$10,000
Auctions: $14,100, MS-66, October 2014; $4,406, MS-64, November 2014; $1,528, AU-58, November 2014; $141, Fair-2, November 2014													
1885, Proof	3,790	801	64.7								$1,300	$1,400	$1,500
Auctions: $3,966, PF-67Cam, November 2014; $7,344, PF-67, February 2014; $1,998, PF-66Cam, November 2014													
1886	3,326,000	715	30.7	31%	$275	$320	$425	$500	$700	$825	$1,000	$2,600	$7,000
Auctions: $5,875, MS-65, April 2013; $3,055, MS-64, October 2014; $1,880, MS-62, October 2014; $405, VF-25, November 2014													
1886, Proof	4,290	800	64.6								$650	$675	$1,000
Auctions: $3,525, PF-67Cam, October 2014; $8,225, PF-67, June 2014; $384, PF-62, August 2014; $382, PF-60, September 2014													
1887	15,260,692	454	62.3	89%	$15	$20	$35	$50	$75	$110	$140	$195	$950
Auctions: $11,163, MS-66, August 2013; $1,293, MS-65, November 2014; $235, MS-64, November 2014; $159, MS-62, November 2014													
1887, Proof	2,960	570	64.4								$250	$375	$600
Auctions: $4,113, PF-67Cam, August 2014; $3,819, PF-67, October 2014; $7,050, PF-66Cam, March 2014; $441, PF-65, October 2014													
1888	10,167,901	369	58.7	82%	$30	$40	$60	$120	$175	$220	$275	$340	$1,200
Auctions: $3,819, MS-66, August 2014; $7,638, MS-66, April 2013; $823, MS-65, July 2014; $499, MS-64, November 2014													
1888, Proof	4,582	771	64.5								$250	$375	$600
Auctions: $1,586, PF-67, August 2014; $2,585, PF-66Cam, November 2014; $6,463, PF-66Cam, July 2014; $176, PF-62, November 2014													
1889	15,878,025	567	63.3	95%	$15	$20	$30	$50	$75	$120	$140	$175	$800
Auctions: $1,175, MS-66, November 2014; $3,819, MS-66, April 2013; $247, MS-64, November 2014; $129, MS-62, July 2014													
1889, Proof	3,336	619	64.6								$250	$375	$600
Auctions: $3,819, PF-68, August 2014; $2,585, PF-67, October 2014; $6,463, PF-67, February 2014; $247, PF-64, November 2014													

1899, Repunched Date, Early Die State

1899, Repunched Date, Late Die State

FS-05-1899-301.

	Mintage	Cert	Avg	%MS	G-4	VG-8	F-12	VF-20	EF-40	AU-50	MS-60 / PF-63	MS-63 / PF-64	MS-65 / PF-65
1890	16,256,532	330	62.1	90%	$10	$20	$25	$40	$65	$110	$160	$200	$1,000
	Auctions: $2,468, MS-66, November 2014; $2,585, MS-66, October 2014; $9,988, MS-66, November 2013; $16, F-15, September 2014												
1890, Proof	2,740	469	64.1								$250	$375	$600
	Auctions: $7,050, PF-67Cam, October 2014; $5,581, PF-66DCam, June 2013; $259, PF-64, July 2014; $165, PF-62, November 2014												
1891	16,832,000	419	62.8	93%	$7	$12	$25	$45	$70	$125	$160	$200	$950
	Auctions: $2,585, MS-66, April 2013; $646, MS-65, November 2014; $282, MS-64, October 2014; $129, MS-62, October 2014												
1891, Proof	2,350	468	64.2								$250	$375	$600
	Auctions: $9,400, PF-67Cam, November 2014; $6,169, PF-66DCam, April 2014; $1,528, PF-66Cam, November 2014												
1892	11,696,897	433	62.5	93%	$6	$10	$20	$40	$65	$110	$140	$160	$1,200
	Auctions: $2,115, MS-66, October 2014; $7,050, MS-66, November 2013; $259, MS-64, October 2014; $129, MS-61, September 2014												
1892, Proof	2,745	515	64.4								$250	$375	$600
	Auctions: $8,225, PF-67Cam, November 2014; $11,163, PF-66DCam, January 2014; $1,060, PF-66Cam, October 2014												
1893	13,368,000	466	63.0	95%	$6	$10	$20	$40	$65	$110	$140	$160	$1,000
	Auctions: $1,880, MS-66, October 2014; $9,694, MS-66, November 2013; $646, MS-65, November 2014; $106, AU-58, September 2014												
1893, Proof	2,195	470	64.6								$250	$375	$600
	Auctions: $3,525, PF-67Cam, November 2014; $1,175, PF-66Cam, November 2014; $247, PF-64, November 2014												
1894	5,410,500	329	59.2	80%	$20	$35	$100	$165	$240	$300	$350	$425	$1,350
	Auctions: $4,700, MS-67, June 2014; $1,528, MS-66, November 2014; $617, MS-64, October 2014; $317, MS-62, July 2014												
1894, Proof	2,632	460	64.3	99%							$250	$375	$600
	Auctions: $5,581, PF-67Cam, October 2014; $9,988, PF-67Cam, April 2014; $2,115, PF-66Cam, October 2014												
1895	9,977,822	342	62.4	93%	$6	$8	$22	$45	$70	$115	$140	$200	$2,000
	Auctions: $3,290, MS-66, October 2014; $5,288, MS-66, November 2013; $382, MS-64, October 2014; $129, AU-58, August 2014												
1895, Proof	2,062	431	64.2								$250	$375	$600
	Auctions: $5,875, PF-67, April 2014; $1,645, PF-67, August 2014; $3,055, PF-66Cam, October 2014; $646, PF-65, October 2014												
1896	8,841,058	309	61.8	90%	$9	$18	$35	$65	$90	$150	$190	$265	$2,100
	Auctions: $9,988, MS-66, November 2014; $4,700, MS-66, October 2014; $129, MS-60, November 2014												
1896, Proof	1,862	418	64.4								$250	$375	$600
	Auctions: $9,988, PF-67DCam, October 2014; $1,410, PF-66Cam, November 2014; $7,050, PF-66Cam, April 2014												
1897	20,426,797	444	62.5	94%	$4	$5	$12	$27	$45	$70	$100	$160	$900
	Auctions: $4,406, MS-66, September 2014; $4,113, MS-66, January 2014; $194, MS-64, October 2014; $129, MS-62, September 2014												
1897, Proof	1,938	461	64.7								$250	$375	$600
	Auctions: $4,700, PF-68Cam, August 2014; $3,055, PF-67Cam, November 2014; $1,763, PF-66Cam, November 2014												
1898	12,530,292	406	62.7	94%	$4	$5	$12	$27	$45	$75	$150	$185	$950
	Auctions: $999, MS-66, November 2014; $1,175, MS-66, October 2014; $2,350, MS-66, March 2013; $823, MS-65, November 2014												
1898, Proof	1,795	429	64.6								$250	$375	$600
	Auctions: $2,585, PF-67Cam, August 2014; $5,006, PF-67Cam, June 2014; $2,820, PF-66DCam, August 2014												
1899	26,027,000	731	62.8	95%	$2	$3	$8	$20	$30	$60	$90	$130	$600
	Auctions: $940, MS-66, November 2014; $3,525, MS-66, January 2014; $382, MS-65, November 2014; $68, AU-58, September 2014												
1899, Repunched Date (a)	(b)	0	n/a						$85	$150	$190	$240	$800
	Auctions: No auction records available.												
1899, Proof	2,031	455	64.7								$250	$375	$600
	Auctions: $2,115, PF-67Cam, August 2014; $1,410, PF-67, October 2014; $2,585, PF-66Cam, April 2014; $259, PF-64Cam, October 2014												

a. "The loop of a 9, or possibly (but unlikely) an 8, is evident within the lower loop of the second 9. Some specialists believe this to be an 1899/8 overdate. However, we feel it is simply a repunched date, with the secondary 9 far to the south of the primary 9 at the last digit" (*Cherrypickers' Guide to Rare Die Varieties*, sixth edition, volume I). **b.** Included in circulation-strike 1899 mintage figure.

1900, Doubled-Die Reverse
FS-05-1900-801.

	Mintage	Cert	Avg	%MS	G-4	VG-8	F-12	VF-20	EF-40	AU-50	MS-60	MS-63	MS-65
											PF-63	PF-64	PF-65
1900	27,253,733	812	63.3	95%	$2	$3	$8	$15	$30	$65	$90	$140	$525
Auctions: $1,410, MS-66, November 2014; $3,290, MS-66, January 2014; $358, MS-65, November 2014; $176, MS-64, November 2014
1900, Doubled-Die Reverse (c)	**(d)**	4	61.5	75%					$110	$160	$235	$310	$875
Auctions: No auction records available.
1900, Proof	2,262	471	64.8								$250	$375	$600
Auctions: $1,645, PF-67Cam, August 2014; $1,058, PF-66Cam, October 2014; $2,585, PF-66Cam, November 2013; $329, PF-64, July 2014
1901	26,478,228	739	63.1	96%	$2	$3	$5	$13	$30	$60	$85	$135	$500
Auctions: $28,200, MS-67, August 2013; $823, MS-66, October 2014; $153, MS-64, September 2014; $92, MS-61, November 2014
1901, Proof	1,985	515	64.9								$250	$375	$600
Auctions: $1,763, PF-67Cam, August 2014; $4,700, PF-67Cam, July 2014; $1,410, PF-66Cam, October 2014; $247, PF-64, November 2014
1902	31,487,561	732	62.8	94%	$2	$3	$4	$13	$30	$60	$85	$135	$500
Auctions: $28,200, MS-67, September 2013; $2,820, MS-66, November 2014; $1,351, MS-66, November 2014; $100, MS-62, November 2014
1902, Proof	2,018	472	64.7								$250	$375	$600
Auctions: $4,259, PF-67Cam, August 2014; $7,050, PF-67Cam, June 2013; $1,234, PF-67, October 2014; $764, PF-66, October 2014
1903	28,004,935	813	63.0	95%	$2	$3	$4	$13	$30	$60	$85	$135	$500
Auctions: $588, MS-66, November 2014; $2,233, MS-66, July 2014; $471, MS-65, November 2014; $80, MS-61, November 2014
1903, Proof	1,790	545	64.9								$250	$375	$600
Auctions: $4,113, PF-68Cam, August 2014; $19,975, PF-68Cam, January 2014; $4,700, PF-67, September 2014; $881, PF-66Cam, October 2014
1904	21,403,167	688	63.2	95%	$2	$3	$4	$13	$30	$60	$85	$135	$500
Auctions: $4,113, MS-67, April 2013; $1,763, MS-66, October 2014; $188, MS-64, December 2014; $69, AU-58, September 2014
1904, Proof	1,817	463	64.3								$250	$375	$600
Auctions: $6,463, PF-67Cam, August 2014; $1,410, PF-67, October 2014; $4,113, PF-65Cam, August 2013; $329, PF-64, October 2014
1905	29,825,124	834	62.8	94%	$2	$3	$4	$13	$30	$60	$85	$135	$500
Auctions: $7,050, MS-66, July 2014; $940, MS-66, November 2014; $148, MS-64, December 2014; $76, MS-61, November 2014
1905, Proof	2,152	457	64.6								$250	$375	$600
Auctions: $4,994, PF-68, October 2014; $2,820, PF-67Cam, August 2014; $4,994, PF-66Cam, April 2013; $397, PF-65Cam, October 2014
1906	38,612,000	620	61.9	89%	$2	$3	$4	$13	$30	$60	$75	$125	$700
Auctions: $4,113, MS-66, November 2013; $4,700, MS-65, August 2014; $382, MS-65, November 2014; $558, MS-64, August 2014
1906, Proof	1,725	444	64.6								$250	$375	$600
Auctions: $2,532, PF-67Cam, November 2014; $4,113, PF-67Cam, April 2013; $1,175, PF-66Cam, September 2014; $617, PF-66, July 2014
1907	39,213,325	604	61.8	90%	$2	$3	$4	$13	$30	$60	$85	$135	$800
Auctions: $1,439, MS-66, October 2014; $1,528, MS-66, July 2014; $153, MS-64, October 2014; $82, MS-62, November 2014
1907, Proof	1,475	367	64.3								$250	$375	$600
Auctions: $2,350, PF-67Cam, August 2014; $7,344, PF-67Cam, March 2013; $1,645, PF-67, August 2014; $1,528, PF-66Cam, October 2014
1908	22,684,557	536	62.0	90%	$2	$3	$4	$13	$30	$60	$85	$135	$825
Auctions: $1,058, MS-66, November 2014; $2,585, MS-66, August 2014; $670, MS-65, September 2014; $170, MS-64, July 2014
1908, Proof	1,620	446	64.6								$250	$375	$600
Auctions: $4,553, PF-67Cam, October 2014; $5,581, PF-67Cam, April 2014; $1,058, PF-66Cam, September 2014; $106, PF-60, November 2014

c. Doubling on this very popular variety is evident on all reverse design elements, including the V, with a stronger spread on the lower quadrant of the reverse. d. Included in circulation-strike 1900 mintage figure.

1913, Liberty Head

	Mintage	Cert	Avg	%MS	G-4	VG-8	F-12	VF-20	EF-40	AU-50	MS-60 / PF-63	MS-63 / PF-64	MS-65 / PF-65
1909	11,585,763	417	60.7	86%	$3	$4	$5	$15	$32	$70	$95	$140	$975
	Auctions: $1,763, MS-66, November 2014; $2,115, MS-66, September 2013; $881, MS-65, November 2014; $217, MS-64, October 2014												
1909, Proof	4,763	1,335	65.0								$250	$375	$600
	Auctions: $4,994, PF-68Cam, November 2014; $1,880, PF-67Cam, October 2014; $470, PF-66, October 2014; $1,058, PF-65DCam, October 2014												
1910	30,166,948	630	62.0	88%	$2	$3	$4	$13	$30	$60	$85	$135	$525
	Auctions: $2,820, MS-66, October 2014; $8,225, MS-66, August 2013; $441, MS-65, November 2014; $153, MS-64, December 2014												
1910, Proof	2,405	712	65.0								$250	$375	$600
	Auctions: $12,399, PF-68Cam, August 2014; $2,820, PF-67Cam, November 2014; $4,994, PF-67, June 2013; $558, PF-66, October 2014												
1911	39,557,639	1,232	62.6	93%	$2	$3	$4	$13	$30	$60	$75	$125	$525
	Auctions: $1,058, MS-66, November 2014; $2,350, MS-66, December 2013; $153, MS-64, October 2014; $80, AU-58, September 2014												
1911, Proof	1,733	584	64.7								$250	$375	$600
	Auctions: $3,055, PF-67Cam, October 2014; $764, PF-66Cam, October 2014; $4,700, PF-66Cam, August 2013; $499, PF-65Cam, November 2014												
1912	26,234,569	1,086	62.0	92%	$2	$3	$4	$13	$30	$60	$85	$135	$500
	Auctions: $1,028, MS-66, November 2014; $881, MS-66, October 2014; $153, MS-64, July 2014; $77, MS-62, November 2014												
1912, Proof	2,145	580	64.5								$250	$375	$600
	Auctions: $3,055, PF-67Cam, August 2014; $4,994, PF-67Cam, June 2014; $823, PF-66Cam, October 2014; $166, PF-62, July 2014												
1912D	8,474,000	765	60.5	89%	$3	$4	$10	$38	$85	$175	$300	$400	$1,900
	Auctions: $14,100, MS-67, June 2014; $2,938, MS-66, November 2014; $270, MS-61, July 2014; $217, AU-58, September 2014												
1912S	238,000	1,245	34.3	43%	$175	$240	$285	$500	$850	$1,400	$1,750	$2,000	$5,500
	Auctions: $3,878, MS-65, November 2014; $2,056, MS-64, November 2014; $30,550, MS, February 2014; $382, VF-25, July 2014												
1913 † (e)		0	n/a									$3,750,000	
	Auctions: No auction records available.												
1913, Proof † (e)		2	47.5								$3,500,000	$3,750,000	
	Auctions: $3,290,000, PF-64, January 2014; $3,172,500, PF-63, April 2013												

† Ranked in the *100 Greatest U.S. Coins* (fourth edition). **e.** An estimated five 1913, Liberty Head, nickels (four circulation-strike and one Proof) were struck under irregular circumstances at the Mint. Some researchers consider them all to be Proofs. They were dispersed and are now held in various public and private collections.

INDIAN HEAD OR BUFFALO (1913–1938)

Designer: *James Earle Fraser.* **Weight:** *5 grams.* **Composition:** *.750 copper, .250 nickel.*
Diameter: *21.2 mm.* **Edge:** *Plain.* **Mints:** *Philadelphia, Denver, San Francisco.*

**Variety 1, FIVE CENTS
on Raised Ground (1913)**

Mintmark location for all
varieties is on the reverse,
below FIVE CENTS.

**Variety 1, FIVE CENTS
on Raised Ground, Proof**

**Variety 2, FIVE CENTS
in Recess (1913–1938)**

**Variety 2, FIVE CENTS in Recess,
Matte Proof (1913–1916)**

**Variety 2, FIVE CENTS in
Recess, Satin Proof (1936)**

**Variety 2, FIVE CENTS in Recess,
Mirror Proof (1936–1937)**

History. The Indian Head nickel five-cent piece today is almost universally known as the "Buffalo" nickel, after the American bison on the reverse. The design made its debut in 1913. James Earle Fraser, a sculptor well known in the private sector, was its creator. The obverse features an authentic portrait of a Native American, modeled as a composite from life, with three subjects posing. Unlike any preceding coin made for circulation, the Buffalo nickel had little in the way of open, smooth field surfaces. Instead, most areas on the obverse and reverse were filled with design elements or, especially on the reverse, an irregular background, as on a bas-relief plaque. Soon after the first coins were released, it was thought that the inscription FIVE CENTS, on a high area of the motif, would wear too quickly. The Mint modified the design to lower the ground under the bison, which had been arranged in the form of a mound (on what became known as Variety 1). The flat-ground design is called Variety 2.

Striking and Sharpness. Most circulation-strike Buffalo nickels are poorly struck in one or more areas, and for many Denver and San Francisco issues of the 1920s the striking is very poor. However, enough sharp strikes exist among common dates of the 1930s that one can be found with some patience. Certification services do not reflect the quality of strike on their labels, so examine carefully. The matter of striking sharpness on Buffalo nickels is an exceedingly important aspect for the connoisseur (who might prefer, for example, a sharply struck coin in AU-58 over a fully lustrous MS example with much shallower detail). Points to check on the obverse include the center of the coin, especially the area immediately above the tie on the braid. On the reverse check the fur on the head of the bison, and the fur "line" above the bison's shoulder on its back. On both sides, examine the overall striking of letters and other details.

Availability. Among circulated varieties of standard dates and mintmarks, availability is in proportion to their mintages. Among early issues the 1913-S, Variety 2, is the scarcest. The date wore away more quickly on the Variety 1 coins than on the modified design used from later 1913 through the end of the series. In the 1920s the 1926-S is the hardest to find. Collectors sought Buffalo nickels from circulation until the 1960s, after which most were gone. By that time the dates in the teens were apt to have their dates completely worn away, or be AG-3 or G-4. Among MS nickels, the issues of 1913 were saved in quantity as novelties, although 1913-S, Variety 2, is slightly scarce. Philadelphia Mint issues are readily available through the 1920s, while MS-63 and finer mintmarked issues from 1914 to 1927 can range from scarce to rare. From 1931 to 1938, all dates and mintmarks were saved in roll quantities, and all are plentiful today. Many Buffalo nickels in MS are very rare if with Full Details, this being especially true for mintmarked issues after 1913, into the early 1930s. Sharpness of strike is not noted on certification holders, but a connoisseur would probably rather own a Full Details coin in MS-65 than an MS-66 or higher with a flat strike.

Proofs. Proof Buffalo nickels are of two main styles. Matte Proofs were made from 1913 to 1916 and are rare. These have minutely granular or matte surfaces, are sharply struck with Full Details of the design on both sides, and have edges (as viewed edge-on) that are mirrored, a distinctive figure. These are easily confused with circulation strikes except for the features noted. Certified holders usually list these simply as "Proof," not "Matte Proof." Some early Proofs of 1936 have satiny rather than mirror-like fields. Later Proofs of 1936 and all of 1937 have a mirror surface in the fields. The motifs of the 1936 and 1937 mirror Proofs are lightly polished in the die (not frosty or matte).

GRADING STANDARDS

MS-60 to 70 (Mint State). *Obverse and Reverse:* Mint luster is complete in the obverse and reverse fields, except in areas not fully struck up, in which graininess or marks from the *original planchet surface* can be seen. Lower grades such as MS-60, 61, and 62 can show some evidence of abrasion, usually on the center of the obverse above the braid, and on the reverse at the highest parts of the bison. These two checkpoints are often areas of light

1937-D, 3-Legged. Graded MS-65.

striking, so abrasion must be differentiated from original planchet marks. At MS-63 evidences of abrasion are few, and at MS-65 they are fewer yet. In grades above MS-65, a Buffalo nickel should be mark-free.

Illustrated coin: A gem example with exceptional eye appeal, this coin has smooth, satiny surfaces free of toning or notable detractions. An uncommonly sharp strike is also notable, especially on the reverse.

AU-50, 53, 55, 58 (About Uncirculated).
Obverse: Light wear is seen on the highest area of the cheek, to the left of the nose, this being the most obvious checkpoint. Light wear is also seen on the highest-relief areas of the hair. Luster is less extensive, and wear more extensive, at AU-50 than at higher grades. An AU-58 coin will have only slight wear and will retain the majority of luster.
Reverse: Light wear is seen on the shoulder

1918-D, 8 Over 7. Graded AU-58.

and hip, these being the key checkpoints. Light wear is also seen on the flank of the bison and on the horn and top of the head. Luster is less extensive, and wear more extensive, at AU-50 than at higher grades. An AU-58 coin will have only slight wear and will retain the majority of luster.

Illustrated coin: This lovely example has sharply defined details, though it is slightly light at the centers. This is an exceptional grade for this very rare overdate variety.

EF-40, 45 (Extremely Fine). *Obverse:* More wear is seen on the cheek (in particular) and the rest of the face. The center of the coin above the braid is mostly smooth. Other details are sharp. *Reverse:* More wear is evident. The tip of the horn is well defined on better strikes. The shoulder, flank, and hip show more wear. The tip of the tail may be discernible, but is mostly worn away.

1937-D. Graded EF-40.

VF-20, 30 (Very Fine). *Obverse:* The hair above the braid is mostly flat, but with some details visible. The braid is discernible. The feathers lack most details. On Variety 1 coins the date is light. *Reverse:* Wear is more extensive, with most fur detail on the high area of the shoulder gone, the tip of the tail gone, and the horn flat. Ideally the tip of the horn should show, but in the marketplace many certified coins do not show this. On some coins this is due to a shallow strike.

1937-D. Graded VF-20.

F-12, 15 (Fine). *Obverse:* Only slight detail remains in the hair above the braid. Some of the braid twists are blended together. LIBERTY is weak, and on some coins the upper part of the letters is faint. The rim still is separate. On all coins, the date shows extensive wear. On Variety 1 coins it is weak. *Reverse:* The horn is half to two-thirds visible. Fur details are gone except on the neck at the highest part of the back.

1918-D, 8 Over 7. Graded F-12.

VG-8, 10 (Very Good). *Obverse:* Hair details above the braid are further worn, as is the hair at the top of the head. Most braid twists are blended together. The rim is worn down to the tops of the letters in LIBERTY. The date is light on all coins and very weak on those of Variety 1. *Reverse:* The base of the horn is slightly visible. Fur details are worn more, but details can still be seen on the neck and top of the back. The hip and flank beneath are worn flat.

1918-D, 8 Over 7. Graded VG-8.

G-4, 6 (Good). *Obverse:* Scarcely any hair details are seen at the center, and the braid is flat. The rim and tops of the letters in LIBERTY are blended. The date is weak but readable, with at least the last two numerals showing on earlier issues. *Reverse:* The rim is worn to blend into the tops of some or all letters in UNITED STATES OF AMERICA (except for Variety 1). E PLURIBUS UNUM and FIVE CENTS are full, and the mintmark, if any, is clear. The front part of the bison's head blends into the rim.

1918-D, 8 Over 7. Graded G-4.

AG-3 (About Good). *Obverse:* The head is mostly flat, but the facial features remain clear. LIBERTY is weak and partly missing. The date may be incomplete but must be identifiable. *Reverse:* Further wear is seen. On Variety 1 coins, UNITED STATES OF AMERICA is full and readable. On the Variety 2 the rim is worn further into the letters. The reverse of the Variety 1 nickels is bolder as the overall grade is defined by the date, which wore away more quickly than on the Variety 2.

1913-S, Variety 2. Graded AG-3.

Illustrated coin: This coin is barely identifiable as to date but with its mintmark clear.

PF-60 to 70 (Matte Proof). *Obverse and Reverse:* Most Matte Proofs are in higher grades. Those with abrasion or contact marks can be graded PF-60 to 62; these are not widely desired. PF-64 can have some abrasion. Tiny flecks are not common, but are sometimes seen. At the Matte PF-65 level or higher there will no traces of abrasion or flecks. Differences between higher-grade Proofs are highly subjective, and one certified at PF-65 can be similar to another at PF-67, and vice-versa.

1914. Graded Matte PF-67.

PF-60 to 70 (Mirror Proof). *Obverse and Reverse:* Most mirror Proofs are in higher grades. PF-60 to 62 coins can have abrasion or minor handling marks, but are usually assigned such grades because of staining or blotches resulting from poor cleaning. PF-63 and 64 can have minor abrasion and staining. Tiny flecks are not common, but are sometimes seen, as are dark stripe lines from the glued seams in the cellophane envelopes used by the Mint. PF-65 and higher coins should be free of stains, flecks, and abrasion of any kind. Differences

1916. Graded Mirror PF-67.

between higher-grade Proofs are highly subjective, and one certified PF-65 can be similar to another at PF-67, and vice-versa.

Illustrated coin: This fully struck Matte Proof example has a satiny sheen and no detracting blemishes. The obverse has a delicate, champagne-gold toning, while the reverse is an attractive silver-blue with pale rose highlights.

**1913, Variety 1,
3-1/2 Legged**
FS-05-1913-901.

1914, 4 Over 3
FS-05-1914-101.

	Mintage	Cert	Avg	%MS	G-4	VG-8	F-12	VF-20	EF-40	AU-50	MS-60 / PF-63	MS-63 / PF-64	MS-65 / PF-65
1913, Variety 1	30,992,000	7,661	64.2	96%	$12	$15	$16	$20	$25	$35	$45	$60	$170
Auctions: $9,400, MS-68, October 2014; $22,325, MS-68, April 2014; $1,234, MS-67, October 2014; $368, MS-66, July 2014													
1913, Variety 1, 3-1/2 Legged (a)	**(b)**	0	n/a						$420	$540	$720	$1,200	$10,800
Auctions: $10,350, MS-64, April 2009													
1913, Variety 1, Proof	1,520	308	65.4								$1,200	$1,800	$3,250
Auctions: $9,400, PF-67, July 2014; $9,988, PF-67, April 2014; $3,525, PF-66, July 2014; $3,819, PF-65, October 2014													
1913D, Variety 1	5,337,000	2,143	62.8	90%	$15	$20	$24	$34	$42	$60	$75	$80	$300
Auctions: $1,998, MS-67, November 2014; $3,055, MS-67, August 2014; $705, MS-66, October 2014; $118, MS-64, November 2014													
1913S, Variety 1	2,105,000	1,491	60.6	82%	$45	$50	$60	$70	$90	$110	$130	$180	$650
Auctions: $3,672, MS-67, November 2014; $8,813, MS-67, August 2013; $1,058, MS-66, July 2014; $112, MS-62, November 2014													
1913, Variety 2	29,857,186	1,891	62.9	91%	$10	$12	$14	$17	$22	$30	$40	$80	$320
Auctions: $7,050, MS-67, August 2014; $4,583, MS-67, August 2014; $881, MS-66, November 2014; $66, MS-64, November 2014													
1913, Variety 2, Proof	1,514	246	65.1								$1,000	$1,600	$2,250
Auctions: $6,463, PF-67, July 2014; $4,994, PF-67, July 2014; $1,998, PF-66, August 2014													
1913D, Variety 2	4,156,000	1,185	52.8	57%	$120	$150	$175	$200	$235	$260	$300	$400	$1,150
Auctions: $17,625, MS-67, August 2013; $2,115, MS-66, July 2014; $482, MS-64, December 2014; $212, AU-55, July 2014													
1913S, Variety 2	1,209,000	1,620	48.2	47%	$340	$400	$450	$500	$600	$750	$900	$1,100	$3,600
Auctions: $28,200, MS-67, April 2014; $1,058, MS-62, October 2014; $494, AU-55, October 2014; $296, Fair-2, October 2014													
1914	20,664,463	1,495	58.6	80%	$20	$22	$25	$30	$35	$45	$60	$85	$420
Auctions: $7,638, MS-67, April 2014; $646, MS-66, November 2014; $1,645, MS-66, August 2014; $141, MS-64, October 2014													
1914, 4 Over 3 (c)	**(d)**	0	n/a		$200	$250	$325	$525	$1,000	$1,500	$2,800	$6,250	$22,500
Auctions: $8,338, MS-64, April 2012													
1914, Proof	1,275	416	65.4								$1,000	$1,500	$2,200
Auctions: $5,581, PF-67, November 2014; $9,400, PF-67, July 2014; $1,880, PF-66, November 2014; $2,820, PF-66, October 2014													
1914D	3,912,000	1,157	51.9	55%	$90	$125	$160	$220	$325	$400	$450	$550	$1,300
Auctions: $4,700, MS-66, July 2014; $529, MS-64, November 2014; $376, AU-58, July 2014; $223, EF-45, July 2014													
1914S	3,470,000	1,429	57.9	71%	$26	$38	$45	$65	$90	$160	$200	$425	$1,800
Auctions: $7,638, MS-66, August 2014; $679, MS-64, November 2014; $282, MS-62, November 2014; $135, AU-58, November 2014													

a. The reverse die was heavily polished, possibly to remove clash marks, resulting in a die with most of the bison's front leg missing. **b.** Included in circulation-strike 1913, Variety 1, mintage figure. **c.** The straight top bar of the underlying 3 is visible at the top of the 4. The start of the 3's diagonal is seen on the upper right, outside of the 4. On some coins, a hint of the curve of the lower portion of the 3 shows just above the crossbar of the 4. **d.** Included in circulation-strike 1914 mintage figure.

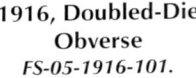

1916, Doubled-Die Obverse FS-05-1916-101.	1916, Missing Designer's Initial FS-05-1916-401.	1918, Doubled-Die Reverse FS-05-1918-801.	1918-D, 8 Over 7 FS-05-1918D-101.

	Mintage	Cert	Avg	%MS	G-4	VG-8	F-12	VF-20	EF-40	AU-50	MS-60 PF-63	MS-63 PF-64	MS-65 PF-65
1915	20,986,220	1,398	62.4	90%	$6	$8	$9	$15	$25	$45	$60	$90	$300
Auctions: $4,113, MS-67, October 2014; $4,994, MS-67, July 2014; $600, MS-66, November 2014; $153, MS-64, September 2014												
1915, Proof	1,050	338	65.2								$1,000	$1,600	$2,250
Auctions: $5,288, PF-67, October 2014; $4,847, PF-67, July 2014; $1,880, PF-66, September 2014; $1,645, PF-66, July 2014												
1915D	7,569,000	944	58.2	63%	$20	$35	$40	$70	$130	$160	$270	$350	$1,700
Auctions: $4,406, MS-66, August 2014; $7,050, MS-66, April 2014; $200, MS-62, November 2014; $96, AU-55, October 2014												
1915S	1,505,000	754	49.1	54%	$50	$75	$115	$200	$400	$500	$650	$1,000	$3,000
Auctions: $3,819, MS-66, October 2014; $2,115, MS-65, November 2014; $646, AU-58, September 2014; $123, VF-25, November 2014												
1916	63,497,466	2,002	61.9	89%	$6	$7	$8	$10	$15	$25	$50	$85	$300
Auctions: $5,288, MS-67, October 2014; $5,581, MS-67, August 2014; $558, MS-66, November 2014; $80, MS-64, November 2014												
1916, DblDie Obverse (e)	(f)	99	39.5	11%	$2,200	$4,000	$7,750	$11,000	$18,500	$32,000	$60,000	$140,000	$325,000
Auctions: $28,200, AU-55, August 2014; $30,550, AU-55, January 2014												
1916, Missing Initial (g)	(f)	0	n/a					$135	$200	$280	$375	$600	
Auctions: $341, AU-55, February 2014												
1916, Proof	600	175	65.0								$1,200	$2,000	$3,500
Auctions: $8,813, PF-67, July 2014; $10,869, PF-67, June 2014; $3,819, PF-66, October 2014												
1916D	13,333,000	1,165	59.7	75%	$16	$28	$30	$45	$90	$120	$175	$260	$1,750
Auctions: $6,463, MS-66, August 2014; $24,675, MS-66, January 2014; $588, MS-64, October 2014; $74, MS-61, November 2014												
1916S	11,860,000	897	59.3	71%	$10	$15	$20	$40	$90	$125	$190	$275	$1,800
Auctions: $4,406, MS-66, November 2014; $470, MS-64, November 2014; $176, MS-62, August 2014; $129, AU-58, October 2014												
1917	51,424,019	945	61.8	88%	$8	$9	$10	$12	$16	$35	$60	$150	$485
Auctions: $4,847, MS-67, August 2014; $764, MS-66, September 2014; $182, MS-64, November 2014; $72, MS-62, November 2014												
1917D	9,910,000	861	54.3	60%	$18	$30	$50	$85	$150	$275	$350	$750	$2,400
Auctions: $7,050, MS-66, July 2014; $11,163, MS-66, August 2013; $707, MS-64, September 2014; $470, MS-61, December 2014												
1917S	4,193,000	706	49.4	50%	$22	$40	$75	$115	$200	$375	$450	$1,200	$3,750
Auctions: $16,450, MS-66, September 2014; $9,988, MS-66, April 2013; $1,058, MS-64, August 2014; $341, AU-58, November 2014												
1918	32,086,314	586	60.8	85%	$6	$7	$8	$16	$32	$50	$125	$325	$1,275
Auctions: $2,468, MS-66, September 2014; $4,406, MS-66, January 2014; $499, MS-64, November 2014; $270, MS-62, December 2014												
1918, DblDie Reverse (h)	(i)	3	49.2	33%	$190	$260	$375	$525	$1,450	$2,300	$3,500	$7,000	
Auctions: $170, VF-20, August 2013												
1918D, 8 Over 7 † (j)	(k)	742	20.2	6%	$1,000	$1,500	$2,700	$5,500	$8,500	$12,000	$34,000	$57,500	$285,000
Auctions: $258,500, MS-65, August 2013; $1,498, VF-20, July 2014; $1,175, VG-8, October 2014; $764, G-4, September 2014												
1918D	8,362,000	685	47.5	47%	$22	$40	$65	$135	$225	$350	$450	$1,050	$3,600
Auctions: $8,813, MS-66, August 2014; $9,518, MS-66, March 2014; $1,528, MS-64, September 2014; $558, AU-58, November 2014												
1918S	4,882,000	654	54.9	66%	$14	$27	$55	$110	$200	$325	$585	$2,750	$22,000
Auctions: $8,225, MS-65, September 2014; $22,325, MS-65, April 2014; $4,994, MS-64, November 2014; $499, MS-61, November 2014												

† Ranked in the *100 Greatest U.S. Coins* (fourth edition). **e.** The date, chin, throat, feathers, and the tie on the braid are all doubled. "Beware of 1916 nickels with strike doubling on the date offered as this variety. . . . The true doubled die must look like the coin shown here" (*Cherrypickers' Guide to Rare Die Varieties*, sixth edition, volume I). **f.** Included in circulation-strike 1916 mintage figure. **g.** The initial F, for Fraser—normally below the date—is clearly absent. Some dies exist with a partially missing or weak initial; these do not command the premium of the variety with a completely missing initial. **h.** Doubling is most obvious to the north on E PLURIBUS UNUM. Some coins show a die crack from the rim to the bison's rump, just below the tail. **i.** Included in 1918 mintage figure. **j.** "Look for the small die crack immediately above the tie on the braid, leading slightly downward to the Indian's jaw. The beginning of this die break can usually be seen even on lower-grade coins" (*Cherrypickers' Guide to Rare Die Varieties*, sixth edition, volume I). **k.** Included in 1918-D mintage figure.

	Mintage	Cert	Avg	%MS	G-4	VG-8	F-12	VF-20	EF-40	AU-50	MS-60	MS-63	MS-65
											PF-63	PF-64	PF-65
1919	60,868,000	1,124	62.3	90%	$2.25	$3	$3.50	$8	$15	$32	$55	$125	$485
	Auctions: $6,756, MS-67, October 2014; $13,513, MS-67, August 2013; $1,528, MS-66, September 2014; $170, MS-64, October 2014												
1919D	8,006,000	670	48.5	42%	$15	$30	$75	$135	$260	$350	$600	$1,500	$6,500
	Auctions: $11,163, MS-66, June 2013; $8,519, MS-65, July 2014; $1,880, MS-64, August 2014; $382, AU-55, October 2014												
1919S	7,521,000	745	50.1	46%	$9	$20	$50	$125	$260	$375	$625	$1,800	$14,000
	Auctions: $89,300, MS-66, January 2013; $11,750, MS-65, July 2014; $2,938, MS-64, November 2014; $764, MS-62, November 2014												
1920	63,093,000	849	62.3	91%	$1.50	$2.50	$3	$7	$14	$30	$65	$145	$625
	Auctions: $10,575, MS-67, April 2013; $2,233, MS-66, October 2014; $194, MS-64, November 2014; $94, MS-62, November 2014												
1920D	9,418,000	708	52.6	59%	$8	$15	$32	$115	$275	$325	$585	$1,400	$5,000
	Auctions: $20,563, MS-65, April 2014; $5,288, MS-65, July 2014; $2,585, MS-64, July 2014; $646, EF-45, September 2014												
1920S	9,689,000	729	53.8	58%	$4.50	$12	$28	$100	$200	$300	$575	$1,850	$25,000
	Auctions: $8,813, MS-65, October 2014; $16,450, MS-65, July 2014; $2,820, MS-64, October 2014; $470, MS-61, November 2014												
1921	10,663,000	739	60.4	82%	$4	$6	$8	$24	$50	$75	$150	$320	$700
	Auctions: $4,700, MS-67, October 2014; $9,988, MS-67, January 2014; $1,645, MS-66, September 2014; $200, MS-62, September 2014												
1921S	1,557,000	1,063	32.9	23%	$75	$125	$200	$550	$950	$1,200	$1,600	$2,100	$7,250
	Auctions: $11,750, MS-66, September 2013; $8,813, MS-65, August 2014; $676, EF-45, October 2014; $247, VF-25, September 2014												
1923	35,715,000	922	62.6	90%	$2	$3	$4	$6	$13	$35	$65	$160	$575
	Auctions: $1,116, MS-66, October 2014; $4,700, MS-66, February 2014; $441, MS-65, November 2014; $174, MS-64, December 2014												
1923S	6,142,000	1,145	51.6	59%	$8	$10	$30	$135	$300	$400	$600	$900	$8,500
	Auctions: $8,225, MS-66, August 2014; $67,563, MS-66, June 2013; $2,350, MS-64, November 2014; $382, AU-58, October 2014												
1924	21,620,000	652	62.4	90%	$1.50	$2	$5	$10	$24	$42	$75	$160	$700
	Auctions: $28,200, MS-67, April 2013; $1,821, MS-66, August 2014; $295, MS-64, August 2014; $84, MS-62, November 2014												
1924D	5,258,000	773	48.7	54%	$8.50	$12	$30	$85	$235	$325	$390	$765	$3,850
	Auctions: $23,500, MS-66, August 2014; $44,063, MS-66, June 2013; $4,700, MS-65, November 2014; $470, AU-55, September 2014												
1924S	1,437,000	990	29.5	18%	$15	$32	$110	$475	$1,150	$1,700	$2,300	$3,700	$12,000
	Auctions: $8,225, MS-65, July 2014; $18,800, MS-65, April 2014; $2,703, MS-62, November 2014; $1,351, EF-45, August 2014												
1925	35,565,100	954	63.5	95%	$3	$3.50	$4	$8	$15	$32	$42	$100	$390
	Auctions: $8,813, MS-67, August 2013; $558, MS-66, November 2014; $141, MS-64, August 2014; $63, MS-62, October 2014												
1925D	4,450,000	778	53.6	66%	$10	$20	$40	$95	$185	$265	$400	$750	$4,750
	Auctions: $6,463, MS-66, November 2014; $19,975, MS-66, January 2013; $7,050, MS-65, September 2014; $170, EF-45, September 2014												
1925S	6,256,000	851	49.7	50%	$5	$9	$18	$90	$180	$250	$475	$1,850	$27,500
	Auctions: $23,999, MS-66, October 2014; $16,450, MS-65, September 2014; $28,200, MS-65, September 2013; $558, MS-62, November 2014												
1926	44,693,000	1,418	63.7	96%	$1.25	$1.75	$2.50	$5	$10	$20	$32	$75	$190
	Auctions: $2,585, MS-67, October 2014; $4,406, MS-67, January 2014; $411, MS-66, October 2014; $72, MS-64, November 2014												
1926D	5,638,000	842	54.3	69%	$10	$18	$28	$110	$185	$300	$350	$500	$4,600
	Auctions: $8,519, MS-66, September 2014; $15,275, MS-66, April 2013; $306, MS-62, September 2014; $306, AU-55, November 2014												
1926S	970,000	1,686	30.0	12%	$25	$45	$100	$375	$900	$2,650	$4,500	$9,200	$95,000
	Auctions: $105,750, MS-65, September 2013; $4,259, MS-61, August 2014; $2,115, AU-55, November 2014; $705, EF-45, August 2014												
1927	37,981,000	1,015	63.5	94%	$1.25	$1.75	$2.50	$4	$12	$21	$35	$80	$245
	Auctions: $999, MS-66, November 2014; $1,998, MS-66, April 2013; $194, MS-65, October 2014; $106, MS-64, November 2014												
1927, Presentation Strike, Proof (l)	(m)	5	65.0									$30,000	$48,000
	Auctions: $43,125, SP-65, January 2012												
1927D	5,730,000	777	60.1	84%	$2.50	$6	$7	$32	$80	$135	$180	$310	$7,000
	Auctions: $23,500, MS-66, September 2014; $705, MS-64, September 2014; $184, MS-62, November 2014; $100, EF-45, November 2014												
1927S	3,430,000	615	55.4	56%	$1.50	$3	$5	$34	$95	$185	$550	$2,000	$16,000
	Auctions: $14,100, MS-65, July 2014; $2,233, MS-63, September 2014; $940, MS-61, November 2014; $182, AU-50, November 2014												

l. Some experts believe that certain 1927 nickels were carefully made circulation strikes; such pieces are sometimes certified as "Examples" or "Presentation Strikes." Professional numismatic opinions vary. See Bowers, *A Guide Book of Buffalo and Jefferson Nickels.* **m.** The mintage figure is unknown.

  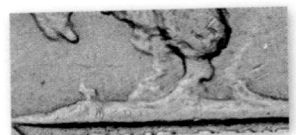

1935, Doubled-Die Reverse
FS-05-1935-801.

1936-D, 3-1/2 Legged
FS-05-1936D-901.

	Mintage	Cert	Avg	%MS	G-4	VG-8	F-12	VF-20	EF-40	AU-50	MS-60 / PF-63	MS-63 / PF-64	MS-65 / PF-65
1928	23,411,000	876	63.3	92%	$1.25	$1.75	$2.50	$5	$13	$23	$32	$80	$280
	Auctions: $646, MS-66, November 2014; $2,585, MS-66, July 2014; $159, MS-65, November 2014; $94, MS-64, November 2014;												
1928D	6,436,000	1,541	63.1	97%	$1.50	$2.50	$5	$15	$45	$50	$60	$110	$600
	Auctions: $2,350, MS-66, November 2014; $4,700, MS-66, February 2014; $485, MS-65, September 2014;												
1928S	6,936,000	717	60.5	81%	$1.75	$2	$2.50	$11	$26	$110	$260	$550	$3,500
	Auctions: $19,975, MS-66, August 2013; $2,820, MS-65, August 2014; $705, MS-64, October 2014; $147, AU-55, November 2014												
1929	36,446,000	1,170	63.1	94%	$1.25	$1.50	$2.50	$4	$12	$20	$40	$75	$315
	Auctions: $9,988, MS-67, September 2014; $23,500, MS-67, January 2014; $558, MS-66, November 2014												
1929D	8,370,000	727	62.7	93%	$1.25	$2	$2.50	$7	$32	$45	$60	$130	$1,175
	Auctions: $2,174, MS-66, October 2014; $15,275, MS-66, February 2014; $259, MS-64, October 2014; $129, MS-62, November 2014												
1929S	7,754,000	887	63.0	92%	$1.25	$1.50	$2	$4	$12	$25	$55	$80	$390
	Auctions: $11,750, MS-67, February 2014; $573, MS-66, October 2014; $110, MS-64, November 2014; $56, MS-62, October 2014												
1930	22,849,000	1,396	63.3	94%	$1.25	$1.50	$2.50	$4	$11	$20	$35	$75	$220
	Auctions: $3,173, MS-67, July 2014; $353, MS-66, November 2014; $588, MS-66, July 2014; $95, MS-64, November 2014												
1930S	5,435,000	726	62.6	92%	$1.25	$1.50	$2.50	$4	$14	$35	$65	$120	$385
	Auctions: $881, MS-66, November 2014; $3,055, MS-66, October 2014; $294, MS-65, November 2014; $353, MS-64, November 2014												
1931S	1,200,000	1,957	62.5	92%	$15	$16	$20	$25	$35	$55	$65	$100	$275
	Auctions: $38,188, MS-67, April 2013; $1,293, MS-66, October 2014; $4,994, MS-66, July 2014; $141, MS-64, December 2014												
1934	20,213,003	1,097	63.4	92%	$1.25	$1.50	$2.50	$4	$10	$18	$50	$65	$250
	Auctions: $4,847, MS-67, September 2014; $8,521, MS-67, July 2014; $558, MS-66, September 2014; $90, MS-64, November 2014												
1934D	7,480,000	1,176	63.1	95%	$1.50	$2.50	$4	$9	$20	$45	$80	$125	$550
	Auctions: $2,644, MS-66, November 2014; $16,450, MS-66, September 2014; $529, MS-65, July 2014; $147, MS-64, November 2014												
1935	58,264,000	1,555	63.4	92%	$1	$1.50	$1.75	$2	$3	$10	$22	$45	$120
	Auctions: $5,288, MS-67, September 2014; $1,528, MS-67, August 2014; $329, MS-66, November 2014; $42, MS-64, December 2014												
1935, DblDie Reverse (n)	(o)	165	30.6	6%	$45	$55	$100	$160	$500	$1,300	$5,250	$6,500	$25,000
	Auctions: $4,994, MS-63, August 2013; $999, AU-50, October 2014; $353, EF-40, December 2014; $223, VF-25, November 2014												
1935D	12,092,000	1,256	63.5	96%	$1	$1.50	$2.50	$6	$18	$42	$75	$85	$400
	Auctions: $8,813, MS-67, August 2014; $1,293, MS-66, July 2014; $2,350, MS-66, June 2014; $129, MS-64, November 2014												
1935S	10,300,000	1,348	63.6	96%	$1	$1.50	$2	$2.50	$4	$18	$55	$70	$210
	Auctions: $2,585, MS-67, July 2014; $4,994, MS-67, June 2014; $441, MS-66, October 2014; $94, MS-64, October 2014												
1936	118,997,000	3,129	64.1	92%	$1	$1.50	$1.75	$2	$3	$9	$22	$40	$80
	Auctions: $482, MS-67, November 2014; $3,819, MS-67, April 2014; $89, MS-66, November 2014; $70, MS-64, October 2014												
1936, Proof, Both kinds	4,420										$1,150	$1,250	$1,500
1936, Satin Finish, Proof		636	65.8										
	Auctions: $9,400, PF-68, November 2014, $16,450, PF-68, February 2013; $1,827, PF-67, November 2014												
1936, Brilliant Finish, Proof		562	65.5								$1,250	$1,500	$1,750
	Auctions: $12,925, PF-68, September 2013; $2,350, PF-67, July 2014; $2,115, PF-66, October 2014; $1,528, PF-65, October 2014												
1936D	24,814,000	2,257	64.1	97%	$1	$1.50	$1.75	$2	$4	$12	$38	$45	$100
	Auctions: $1,087, MS-67, October 2014; $999, MS-67, July 2014; $118, MS-66, November 2014; $91, MS-66, November 2014												
1936D, 3-1/2 Legged (p)	(q)	0	n/a		$850	$1,500	$2,500	$8,000	$9,000	$18,000			
	Auctions: $3,290, AU-50, January 2014												
1936S	14,930,000	1,585	64.4	97%	$1	$1.50	$1.75	$2	$4	$12	$38	$45	$95
	Auctions: $2,409, MS-67, September 2014; $1,645, MS-67, July 2014; $165, MS-66, November 2014; $176, MS-66, October 2014												

n. Strong doubling is evident on FIVE CENTS, E PLURIBUS UNUM, and the eye, horn, and mane of the bison. This variety (FS-05-1935-801) is extremely rare above VF, and fewer than a dozen are known in MS. Do not mistake it for the more moderately doubled FS-05-1935-803, which commands much lower premiums. **o.** Included in 1935 mintage figure. **p.** The right front leg has been partially polished off the die—similar to the 1937-D, 3-Legged, variety, but not as severe. (This variety is not from the same die as the 1937-D.) Fewer than 40 are known in all grades. Incorrectly listed by Breen as 1936-P.

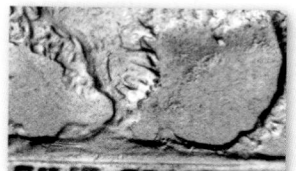

1937-D, 3-Legged
FS-05-1937D-901.

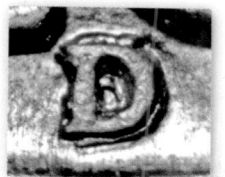

1938-D, D Over S
FS-05-1938D-511.

	Mintage	Cert	Avg	%MS	G-4	VG-8	F-12	VF-20	EF-40	AU-50	MS-60	MS-63	MS-65
											PF-63	PF-64	PF-65
1937	79,480,000	7,596	65.3	98%	$1	$1.50	$1.75	$2	$3	$9	$22	$40	$60
	Auctions: $6,756, MS-68, January 2014; $499, MS-67, November 2014; $329, MS-67, November 2014; $86, MS-66, October 2014												
1937, Proof	5,769	1,581	65.7	100%							$1,250	$1,500	$1,750
	Auctions: $16,450, PF-68, January 2014; $1,821, PF-67, November 2014; $2,585, PF-67, September 2014; $1,293, PF-66, October 2014												
1937D	17,826,000	4,120	64.9	97%	$1	$1.50	$1.75	$3	$4	$10	$32	$42	$60
	Auctions: $411, MS-67, August 2014; $3,819, MS-67, January 2014; $70, MS-66, November 2014; $119, MS-64, August 2014												
1937D, 3-Legged (r)	(s)	6,181	50.0	28%	$550	$600	$650	$750	$900	$1,000	$2,250	$4,500	$35,000
	Auctions: $52,875, MS-66, February 2013; $3,819, MS-63, October 2014; $881, AU-55, November 2014; $705, EF-45, September 2014												
1937S	5,635,000	3,455	65.0	99%	$1	$1.50	$1.75	$3	$5	$9	$32	$42	$65
	Auctions: $411, MS-67, October 2014; $8,813, MS-67, April 2013; $1,293, MS-66, October 2014; $69, MS-66, November 2014												
1938D	7,020,000	31,104	65.7	100%	$3.50	$4	$4.50	$4.75	$5	$8	$22	$36	$60
	Auctions: $16,450, MS-68, June 2014; $259, MS-67, December 2014; $940, MS-67, September 2014; $177, MS-66, October 2014												
1938D, D Over D	(t)	2,484	65.6	100%	$4.50	$6.50	$9	$11	$20	$25	$45	$50	$75
	Auctions: $7,050, MS-68, October 2013; $2,820, MS-67, October 2014; $78, MS-66, November 2014; $86, MS-66, October 2014												
1938D, D Over S (u)	(t)	2,057	65.2	99%	$5.50	$8	$10	$14	$20	$32	$55	$80	$160
	Auctions: $3,290, MS-67, September 2014; $7,638, MS-67, August 2013; $259, MS-66, November 2014; $159, MS-66, October 2014												

r. The reverse die was polished heavily, perhaps to remove clash marks, resulting in the shaft of the bison's right front leg missing. Beware altered examples fraudulently passed as genuine. "Look for a line of raised dots from the middle of the bison's belly to the ground as one of the diagnostics on the genuine specimen" (*Cherrypickers' Guide to Rare Die Varieties*, sixth edition, volume I). **s.** Included in 1937-D mintage figure. **t.** Included in 1938-D mintage figure. **u.** There are five different D Over S dies for this date. Varieties other than the one listed here (FS-05-1938D-511) command smaller premiums.

JEFFERSON (1938 TO DATE)

Designer: *1938–2003—Felix Schlag; 2004— Felix Schlag (obverse), Norman E. Nemeth (Peace Medal reverse), and Al Maletsky (Keelboat reverse); 2005—Joe Fitzgerald (obverse), Jamie Franki (American Bison reverse), and Joe Fitzgerald (Ocean in View reverse); 2006 to date—Jamie Franki (obverse) and Felix Schlag (reverse).* **Weight:** *5 grams.* **Composition:** *1938–1942, 1946 to date—.750 copper, .250 nickel; 1942–1945—.560 copper, .350 silver, .090 manganese, with net weight .05626 oz. pure silver.* **Diameter:** *21.2 mm.* **Edge:** *Plain.* **Mints:** *Philadelphia, Denver, San Francisco.*

Monticello Reverse (1938–2003)

Wartime Silver Alloy (1942–1945)

Mintmark location, 1938–1941 and 1946–1964, is on the reverse, to the right of Monticello.

Mintmark location, 1968 to date, is on the obverse, near the date (exact location varies with changes in portrait style).

Mintmark location, 1942–1945, is on the reverse, above Monticello.

Monticello Reverse, Proof

Wartime Silver Alloy, Proof

Westward Journey, Obverse (2004)

Peace Medal Reverse (2004)

Keelboat Reverse (2004)

Westward Journey, Obverse, Proof

Peace Medal Reverse, Proof

Keelboat Reverse, Proof

Westward Journey, Obverse (2005)

American Bison Reverse (2005)

Ocean in View Reverse (2005)

Westward Journey, Obverse, Proof

American Bison Reverse, Proof

Ocean in View Reverse, Proof

Jefferson Modified (2006 to Date)

Jefferson Modified, Proof

History. The Jefferson nickel, designed by Felix Schlag in a public competition, made its debut in 1938, and has been a numismatic favorite since. The obverse for many years featured a portrait of Thomas Jefferson after the famous bust by Jean Antoine Houdon, and the reverse a front view of Jefferson's home, Monticello. From partway through 1942 to the end of 1945 a copper-silver-manganese alloy replaced the traditional 75% copper and 25% nickel composition. This was to help save nickel for the war effort. These silver-content coins bear a distinctive P, D, or S mintmark above the dome of Monticello. Starting in 1966, Felix Schlag's initials, FS, were added below the presidential bust; this continued through 2004, after which the obverse portrait changed. The coinage dies were remodeled to strengthen the design in 1971, 1972, 1977, and 1982. The mintmark position, originally on the reverse to the right of Monticello, was moved to the obverse starting in 1968. In 2004 special designs commemorating the Westward Journey (Lewis and Clark expedition) were introduced; the program continued through 2005. In 2006 a new obverse portrait debuted, along with a return to Monticello on the reverse.

Striking and Sharpness. On the obverse, check for weakness on the portrait, especially in the lower jaw area. On the reverse, most circulation strikes have weak details on the six steps of Monticello, especially under the third pillar from the left, as this section on the reverse was opposite in the dies (in the press) from the high parts of the Jefferson portrait, and metal could not effectively flow in both directions at once. Planchet weight allowance was another cause, the dies being spaced slightly too far apart. Jefferson nickels can be classified as "Full Steps" (FS) if either five or six of Monticello's porch steps (with the top step counting as one) are clear. Notations of 5FS or 6FS can indicate the number of visible steps. It is easier to count the incuse lines than the raised steps. If there are four complete, unbroken lines, the coin qualifies as Full Steps (with five steps); five complete, unbroken lines indicate six full steps. There must be no nicks, cuts, or scratches interrupting the incuse lines. It is difficult to determine a full five-step count on the 1938 and some 1939 issues, as the steps are wavy and ill-defined; a great deal of subjectivity is common for these dates. Even if the steps are mostly or fully defined, check other areas to determine if a coin has Full Details overall. Interestingly, nickels of the 1950s and 1960s are among the most weakly struck. The silver-content coins of the 1940s usually are well struck. Some nickels of the 1950s to 1970s discolored easily, perhaps due to some impurities in the alloy. Proofs were struck from 1938 to 1942, 1950 to 1964, and 1968 to date. All have mirror fields. Striking is usually with Full Details, although there are scattered exceptions. Most survivors are in high grade, PF-64 and upward. Most since the 1970s have frosted or cameo contrast on the higher features. Special Mint Set (SMS) coins were struck in lieu of Proofs from 1965 to 1967; these in some instances closely resemble Proofs.

Availability. All basic dates and mintmarks were saved in roll quantities. Scarce issues in MS include 1939-D and 1942-D. The low-mintage 1950-D was a popular speculation in its time, and most of the mintage went into numismatic hands, making MS coins common today. Many different dates and mints are rare if with 5FS or 6FS; consult *A Guide Book of Buffalo and Jefferson Nickels* for details.

GRADING STANDARDS

MS-60 to 70 (Mint State). *Obverse and Reverse:* Mint luster is complete in the obverse and reverse fields, except in areas not fully struck up, in which graininess or marks from the *original planchet surface* can be seen. This may include the jaw, the back of Jefferson's head, and the higher-relief central features of Monticello. The highest parts of the design may have evidence of abrasion and/or contact marks in lower MS grades. Lower grades such as MS-60, 61, and 62 can show some evidence of abrasion, usually on the same areas that display weak striking. At MS-63, evidences of abrasion are few, and at MS-65 they are fewer yet. In grades above MS-65, a Jefferson nickel should be mark-free.

1939. Graded MS-67.

Note: For modern issues of 2003 to date, check the higher parts of the obverse and reverse for abrasion and contact marks. Otherwise the same rules apply.

2004-D, Peace Medal. Graded MS-66.

The Westward Journey / Jefferson Modified nickel is seldom collected in grades lower than MS-60.

Illustrated coin (1939): A brilliant and attractive example, this coin displays a hint of toning.

AU-50, 53, 55, 58 (About Uncirculated). *Obverse:* The cheekbone and the higher points of the hair show light wear, more at AU-50 than at AU-58. Some mint luster will remain on some AU-55 and most AU-58 coins. *Reverse:* The central part of Monticello shows light wear, but is difficult to evaluate as this area often shows weakness of strike. Some mint luster will remain on some AU-55 and most AU-58 coins.

1942-P. Graded AU-50.

EF-40, 45 (Extremely Fine). *Obverse:* More wear is evident on the cheekbone. The higher parts of the hair are without detail. *Reverse:* Monticello shows wear overall. The bottom edge of the triangular area above the columns at the center are worn away.

1938-S. Graded EF-40.

VF-20, 30 (Very Fine). *Obverse:* Most hair detail is lost, except for the back of the head and lower area. The cheekbone is flat and mostly blended into the hair at the right. *Reverse:* Many shallow-relief architectural features are worn away. The windows remain clear and the four columns are distinct.

The Jefferson nickel is seldom collected in grades lower than VF-20.

1938-S. Graded VF-20.

PF-60 to 70 (Proof). *Obverse and Reverse:* Most Proof Jefferson nickels are in higher grades. Those with abrasion or contact marks can be graded PF-60 to 62 or even 63; these are not widely desired by collectors. PF-64 can have some abrasion. Tiny flecks are sometimes seen on coins of 1938 to 1942, as are discolorations (even to the extent of black streaks); these flaws are from cellophane holders. You should avoid such coins. Undipped Proofs of the early era often have a slight bluish or yellowish tint. At PF-65 or higher there are no traces of abrasion or flecks. Evaluation of differences between higher-grade Jefferson Proofs is highly subjective; one certified at PF-65 might be similar to another at PF-67, and vice-versa. All Proof Westward Journey and Jefferson Modified nickels have mirror fields. Striking is typically with full details, although there are

1939. Graded PF-68.

2005-S Bison. Graded PF-70 Ultra Cameo.

scattered exceptions. At PF-69 and 70 there are no traces of abrasion, contact marks, or other flaws.

Illustrated coin (1939): This example has a uniformly mirrored finish. Its smooth, unblemished surfaces have a silver-rose, powder-blue, and pale gold iridescence. The higher parts of the portrait are lightly struck.

Illustrated coin (2005): The example shown exhibits PF-70 characteristics. Nearly all Westward Journey and Jefferson Modified nickel Proofs are as issued, in PF-69 or 70.

Five Steps

Six Steps

1939, Doubled-Die
Reverse
FS-05-1939-801.

	Mintage	Cert	Avg	%MS	VF-20	EF-40	AU-50	MS-60	MS-63	MS-65	MS-65FS	MS-67
										PF-65	PF-66	PF-67
1938	19,496,000	860	65.5	98%	$0.50	$1	$1.50	$3	$4	$16	$150	$200
Auctions: $2,218, MS-67FS, September 2014; $188, MS-66FS, October 2014; $165, MS-66, October 2014; $112, MS-65, July 2014
1938, Proof	19,365	1,224	65.5							$125	$175	$400
Auctions: $1,880, PF-68, June 2013; $353, PF-67, July 2014; $118, PF-66, November 2014; $84, PF-66, October 2014
1938D	5,376,000	2,261	66.2	100%	$1.50	$2	$3	$7	$9	$14	$125	$150
Auctions: $3,525, MS-67FS, November 2014; $89, MS-67, December 2014; $100, MS-66FS, November 2014; $79, MS-66, October 2014
1938S	4,105,000	1,101	65.9	99%	$2.50	$3	$3.50	$4.50	$8	$16	$270	$600
Auctions: $4,259, MS-67FS, February 2014; $84, MS-67, October 2014; $306, MS-67, September 2014; $212, MS-65FS, November 2014
1939	120,615,000	1,212	65.1	93%	$0.25	$0.50	$1	$2	$2.50	$12	$47	$225
Auctions: $999, MS-67FS, October 2014; $5,288, MS-67FS, February 2014; $94, MS-67, December 2014; $35, MS-66, August 2014
1939, Doubled-Die Reverse (a)	(b)	258	55.0	55%	$80	$110	$150	$200	$375	$1,000	$2,400	$4,500
Auctions: $89, EF-40, November 2014; $86, EF-40, November 2014; $70, EF-40, November 2014; $7,050, EF-40, August 2013
1939, Proof	12,535	868	65.4							$125	$175	$400
Auctions: $11,163, PF-68, January 2014; $382, PF-67, October 2014; $159, PF-66, November 2014; $34, PF-62, September 2014
1939D	3,514,000	1,264	65.5	97%	$10	$13	$30	$60	$90	$120	$500	$450
Auctions: $259, MS-67, September 2014; $2,115, MS-67, February 2014; $88, MS-66, September 2014; $84, MS-66, August 2014
1939S	6,630,000	680	65.1	96%	$2	$5	$10	$18	$35	$70	$400	$450
Auctions: $1,528, MS-67, November 2013; $247, MS-65FS, November 2014; $229, MS-65FS, September 2014
1940	176,485,000	634	65.8	97%	$0.25	$0.40	$0.75	$1	$1.50	$15	$45	$250
Auctions: $306, MS-67FS, October 2014; $294, MS-67FS, July 2014; $1,293, MS-67FS, June 2014; $129, MS-67, December 2014
1940, Proof	14,158	871	65.4							$125	$160	$600
Auctions: $12,925, PF-68, June 2013; $1,116, PF-67, November 2014; $135, PF-66, November 2014; $100, PF-66, December 2014
1940D	43,540,000	1,304	66.0	99%	$0.35	$0.50	$1	$2	$2.50	$10	$45	$150
Auctions: $229, MS-67FS, November 2013
1940S	39,690,000	394	65.6	99%	$0.35	$0.50	$1	$2.25	$3	$12	$70	$350
Auctions: $94, MS-67, December 2014; $165, MS-66FS, November 2014; $306, MS-66FS, March 2014
1941	203,265,000	629	65.8	99%	$0.20	$0.30	$0.50	$0.75	$1.50	$12	$65	$250
Auctions: $1,528, MS-68, September 2013; $940, VF-20, October 2014
1941, Proof	18,720	1,038	65.3							$95	$150	$600
Auctions: $18,800, PF-68, June 2013; $3,055, PF-67, October 2014; $141, PF-66, November 2014; $76, PF-66, August 2014
1941D	53,432,000	1,314	66.0	99%	$0.25	$0.40	$1.50	$2.50	$3.50	$10	$45	$75
Auctions: $200, MS-67FS, August 2014; $1,410, MS-67FS, April 2014; $94, MS-67, December 2014; $70, MS-67, August 2014
1941S (c)	43,445,000	280	65.4	97%	$0.30	$0.50	$1.50	$3	$4	$12	$80	$625
Auctions: $282, MS-66FS, November 2014; $2,585, MS-66FS, April 2014

a. Very strong doubling is evident to the east of the primary letters, most noticeably on MONTICELLO and FIVE CENTS. Lesser doubling is also visible on UNITED STATES OF AMERICA and the right side of the building. **b.** Included in circulation-strike 1939 mintage figure. **c.** Large and small mintmark varieties exist.

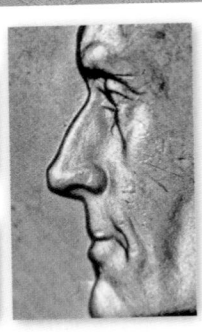

1942-D, D Over Horizontal D
FS-05-1942D-501.

1943-P, 3 Over 2
FS-05-1943P-101.

1943-P, Doubled-Die Obverse
The "Doubled Eye" variety. FS-05-1943P-106.

	Mintage	Cert	Avg	%MS	VF-20	EF-40	AU-50	MS-60	MS-63	MS-65 / PF-65	MS-65FS / PF-66	MS-67 / PF-67
1942	49,789,000	616	65.3	99%	$0.30	$0.45	$1.25	$4	$6	$15	$85	$250
Auctions: $823, MS-66FS, November 2014; $159, MS-66FS, October 2014; $235, MS-66FS, July 2014; $940, MS-66FS, April 2014												
1942, Proof	29,600	1,751	65.7							$90	$130	$200
Auctions: $1,234, PF-68, November 2014; $11,750, PF-68, June 2013; $101, PF-67, November 2014; $75, PF-66, November 2014												
1942D	13,938,000	1,204	65.7	99%	$1	$2	$5	$28	$38	$60	$80	$380
Auctions: $663, MS-67FS, September 2014; $823, MS-67FS, March 2014; $141, MS-67, November 2014; $84, MS-66FS, November 2014												
1942D, D Over Horizontal D (d)	(e)	73	48.8	27%	$75	$200	$500	$1,500	$3,000	*$10,000*		
Auctions: $15,275, MS-66, April 2013; $764, AU-58, October 2014; $329, AU-50, August 2014; $44, F-12, September 2014												
1942P, Silver	57,873,000	4,311	66.3	100%	$2	$2.50	$3.25	$7	$12	$20	$75	$50
Auctions: $4,113, MS-68, June 2014; $106, MS-67, December 2014; $259, MS-66FS, October 2014; $235, MS-66, November 2014												
1942P, Proof, Silver	27,600	2,672	65.5							$180	$250	$275
Auctions: $3,055, PF-67Cam, August 2014; $14,100, PF-67Cam, April 2014; $247, PF-67, December 2014; $123, PF-66, November 2014												
1942S	32,900,000	3,987	66.2	100%	$2	$2.50	$3.25	$7	$12	$25	$200	$100
Auctions: $3,055, MS-67FS, September 2014; $1,645, MS-67FS, September 2014; $3,525, MS-67FS, November 2013												
1943P, 3 Over 2 (f)	(g)	300	55.2	64%	$50	$100	$165	$225	$260	$700	$1,100	$2,750
Auctions: $8,813, MS-67FS, March 2014; $3,819, MS-66FS, August 2014; $1,880, MS-66, August 2014; $764, MS-65FS, August 2014												
1943P	271,165,000	4,810	65.9	98%	$2	$2.50	$3	$5	$8	$20	$40	$65
Auctions: $306, MS-67FS, September 2014; $823, MS-67FS, August 2014; $69, MS-66FS, November 2014												
1943P, Doubled-Die Obverse (h)	(g)	126	62.2	82%	$25	$40	$60	$90	$160	$650	$1,000	$2,200
Auctions: $1,293, MS-67, July 2014; $1,116, MS-66FS, August 2014; $1,998, MS-66FS, March 2014; $588, MS-66, August 2014												
1943D	15,294,000	7,722	66.3	100%	$2	$3.50	$4	$6	$12	$20	$45	$55
Auctions: $141, MS-67FS, December 2014; $89, MS-67FS, November 2014; $1,528, MS-67FS, September 2014												
1943S	104,060,000	4,839	66.2	100%	$2	$2.50	$3	$5	$8	$20	$50	$70
Auctions: $1,116, MS-67FS, July 2014; $341, MS-67, October 2014; $84, MS-66FS, November 2014; $4,113, AU-55, November 2013												
1944P (i)	119,150,000	3,164	66.0	100%	$2	$2.50	$3.25	$7	$12	$30	$80	$125
Auctions: $9,400, MS-67FS, March 2014; $235, MS-67, December 2014												
1944D	32,309,000	5,271	66.3	100%	$2	$2.50	$3	$6	$12	$25	$35	$70
Auctions: $10,575, MS-68FS, February 2014; $159, MS-67FS, October 2014; $235, MS-67, December 2014; $101, MS-66FS, August 2014												
1944S	21,640,000	4,895	66.3	100%	$2	$2.50	$3	$5	$10	$20	$160	$80
Auctions: $1,998, MS-67FS, March 2014; $382, MS-66FS, November 2014; $212, MS-65FS, November 2014												

Note: Genuine examples of some wartime dates were struck in nickel, in error. **d.** The initial D mintmark was punched into the die horizontally, then corrected. "This is the rarest of the major Jefferson nickel varieties in Mint State" (*Cherrypickers' Guide to Rare Die Varieties*, sixth edition, volume I). **e.** Included in 1942-D mintage figure. **f.** "This popular variety was created when the die was first hubbed with a 1942-dated hub, then subsequently hubbed with a 1943-dated hub. The diagonal of the 2 is visible within the lower opening of the 3. Doubling is also visible on LIBERTY and IN GOD WE TRUST. . . . There is at least one 1943-P five-cent piece that has a faint, short die gouge extending upward from the lower ball of the 3; this is often mistaken for the overdate" (*Cherrypickers' Guide to Rare Die Varieties*, sixth edition, volume I). **g.** Included in 1943-P mintage figure. **h.** This variety is nicknamed the "Doubled Eye." Doubling is visible on the date, LIBERTY, the motto, and, most noticeably, Jefferson's eye. **i.** 1944 nickels without mintmarks are counterfeit.

1945-P, Doubled-Die Reverse
FS-05-1945P-803.

	Mintage	Cert	Avg	%MS	VF-20	EF-40	AU-50	MS-60	MS-63	MS-65	MS-65FS	MS-67
										PF-65	PF-66	PF-67
1945P	119,408,100	3,322	65.8	100%	$2	$2.50	$3	$5	$8	$20	$125	$750
Auctions: $8,813, MS-67FS, April 2014; $353, MS-66FS, December 2014; $382, MS-66FS, November 2014											
1945P, DblDie Reverse (j)	(k)	209	63.9	95%	$20	$30	$50	$75	$130	$800	$7,000	
Auctions: $14,100, MS-66FS, March 2014; $441, MS-65, October 2014											
1945D	37,158,000	5,468	66.3	100%	$2	$2.50	$3	$5	$8	$20	$40	$125
Auctions: $4,847, MS-68, July 2014; $2,703, MS-67FS, July 2014; $141, MS-67, December 2014; $100, MS-66FS, December 2014											
1945S	58,939,000	5,579	66.2	100%	$2	$2.50	$3	$5	$8	$20	$200	$150
Auctions: $4,700, MS-67FS, July 2014; $84, MS-67, September 2014; $999, MS-66FS, October 2014; $2,350, MS-64, November 2013											
1946	161,116,000	248	64.9	98%	$0.25	$0.30	$0.35	$0.75	$2.50	$15	$200	
Auctions: $1,763, MS-67, December 2013; $259, MS-65FS, December 2014; $382, MS-65FS, November 2014											
1946D	45,292,200	746	65.5	99%	$0.35	$0.40	$0.45	$1	$2.50	$12	$35	$500
Auctions: $1,528, MS-67FS, September 2014; $2,938, MS-67FS, August 2014; $353, MS-67FS, July 2014											
1946S	13,560,000	665	65.7	99%	$0.40	$0.45	$0.50	$1	$2	$11	$125	$130
Auctions: $353, MS-66FS, December 2014; $223, MS-66FS, October 2014; $529, MS-66FS, April 2014											
1947	95,000,000	382	65.4	99%	$0.25	$0.30	$0.35	$0.75	$1.75	$12	$65	$135
Auctions: $4,113, MS-67FS, June 2014; $212, MS-66FS, August 2014											
1947D	37,822,000	687	65.8	100%	$0.30	$0.35	$0.40	$0.90	$1.75	$11	$30	$150
Auctions: $646, MS-67FS, November 2014; $940, MS-67FS, July 2014; $1,586, MS-67FS, February 2014											
1947S	24,720,000	328	65.2	98%	$0.40	$0.45	$0.50	$1	$1.75	$12	$50	$750
Auctions: $2,056, MS-66FS, June 2014											

Note: Genuine examples of some wartime dates were struck in nickel, in error. **j.** There are several collectible doubled-die reverses for this date. Values are for the variety pictured (FS-05-1945P-801), with a strongly doubled reverse. The doubling spread increases from left to right. **k.** Included in 1945-P mintage figure.

1949-D, D Over S
FS-05-1949D-501.

	Mintage	Cert	Avg	%MS	MS-60	MS-63	MS-65	MS-65FS	MS-66	MS-66FS	MS-67	MS-67FS
										PF-65	PF-66	PF-67
1948	89,348,000	204	65.2	99%	$1	$1.50	$10	$200	$75	$1,750		
Auctions: $53, MS-66, December 2014; $129, MS-65FS, October 2014; $100, MS-64FS, November 2014; $62, MS-64FS, November 2014											
1948D	44,734,000	570	65.7	100%	$1.60	$4	$10	$30	$45	$90	$150	
Auctions: $1,528, MS-67FS, October 2014; $1,763, MS-67FS, July 2014; $2,115, MS-67FS, April 2013; $42, MS-66FS, July 2014											
1948S	11,300,000	690	66.0	100%	$1.50	$2.50	$9	$45	$40	$250	$175	
Auctions: $705, MS-67, October 2014; $223, MS-66FS, December 2014; $411, MS-66FS, June 2013											
1949	60,652,000	254	65.2	99%	$2.50	$9	$12	$1,750	$35			
Auctions: $1,553, MS-65FS, February 2010											
1949D	36,498,000	644	65.5	99%	$1.50	$6	$10	$50	$25	$185	$225	
Auctions: $84, MS-67, December 2014; $411, MS-67, July 2014											
1949D, D Over S (a)	(b)	58	62.6	95%	$150	$200	$500	$1,800	$1,200			
Auctions: $646, MS-66, August 2014; $1,293, MS-66, July 2014; $1,763, MS-65, April 2013; $200, MS-64, October 2014											
1949S	9,716,000	304	65.4	99%	$1.75	$5	$10	$275	$50	$1,500		
Auctions: $15,275, MS-67FS, January 2014; $235, MS-65FS, November 2014; $188, MS-65FS, November 2014											

a. The top serif of the S is visible to the north of the D, with the upper left loop of the S visible to the west of the D. "This variety is quite rare in Mint State and highly sought after. Some may still be found in circulated grades. Some examples have been located in original Mint sets" (*Cherrypickers' Guide to Rare Die Varieties*, sixth edition, volume I). **b.** Included in 1949-D mintage figure.

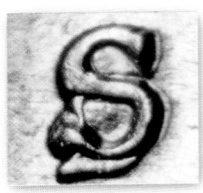

1954-S, S Over D
FS-05-1954S-501.

	Mintage	Cert	Avg	%MS	MS-60	MS-63	MS-65	MS-65FS	MS-66	MS-66FS	MS-67	MS-67FS
										PF-65	PF-66	PF-67
1950	9,796,000	462	65.8	100%	$2	$3.25	$8	$175	$60	$500		
Auctions: $4,994, MS-67FS, April 2014; $94, MS-67, December 2014; $106, MS-65FS, November 2014												
1950, Proof	51,386	1,294	66.1							$75	$85	$125
Auctions: $9,988, PF-68Cam, April 2014; $201, PF-68, October 2014; $72, PF-67, October 2014; $165, PF-66Cam, November 2014												
1950D	2,630,030	3,788	65.5	100%	$14	$16	$20	$60	$70	$150	$275	$3,000
Auctions: $1,939, MS-67FS, August 2014; $1,528, MS-67FS, July 2014; $388, MS-67, December 2014; $411, MS-66FS, November 2014												
1951	28,552,000	273	65.4	100%	$3	$6.50	$15	$425	$80	$2,000		
Auctions: $16,450, MS-67FS, February 2014; $306, MS-66FS, November 2014; $940, MS-66FS, October 2014; $306, MS-66FS, July 2014												
1951, Proof	57,500	1,585	66.7							$65	$75	$120
Auctions: $103, PF-68, December 2014; $4,700, PF-67DCam, April 2014; $200, PF-67Cam, December 2014; $76, PF-66, November 2014												
1951D	20,460,000	558	65.7	100%	$4	$7	$11	$80	$30	$300	$575	
Auctions: $2,820, MS-66FS, June 2013												
1951S	7,776,000	441	65.7	100%	$1.50	$2	$12	$200	$55	$1,000		
Auctions: $940, MS-67, November 2014; $881, MS-66FS, February 2013; $170, MS-65FS, August 2014												
1952	63,988,000	242	65.5	100%	$1	$4	$9	$950	$175	$2,000	$400	
Auctions: $259, MS-66FS, July 2014; $259, MS-64FS, November 2014; $476, AU-55, April 2014												
1952, Proof	81,980	1,570	66.9							$45	$60	$75
Auctions: $235, PF-69, July 2014; $14,100, PF-68DCam, April 2013; $823, PF-68Cam, October 2014; $135, PF-67Cam, November 2014												
1952D	30,638,000	386	65.7	100%	$3.50	$6.25	$15	$200	$35	$600	$650	
Auctions: $15,275, MS-67FS, April 2014; $141, MS-65FS, November 2014												
1952S	20,572,000	550	65.7	100%	$1	$1.50	$12	$300	$35	$2,500		
Auctions: $8,813, MS-66FS, April 2014; $282, MS-65FS, November 2014												
1953	46,644,000	251	65.4	100%	$0.25	$0.75	$8	$3,000	$80	$4,000		
Auctions: $123, MS-66, June 2014												
1953, Proof	128,800	1,995	67.1							$45	$50	$65
Auctions: $15,275, PF-68DCam, April 2013; $65, PF-68, September 2014; $135, PF-67Cam, November 2014; $35, PF-67, July 2014												
1953D	59,878,600	557	65.6	99%	$0.25	$0.75	$9	$225	$40	$900	$650	
Auctions: $123, MS-67, October 2014; $135, MS-66FS, October 2014; $206, MS-65FS, October 2014; $329, MS-65FS, February 2013												
1953S	19,210,900	451	65.3	100%	$0.75	$1	$10	$5,000	$100			
Auctions: $1,293, MS-64FS, June 2013												
1954	47,684,050	288	65.0	100%	$1	$1.50	$15	$375	$25	$2,000	$250	
Auctions: $999, MS-66FS, November 2014; $207, MS-65FS, February 2010												
1954, Proof	233,300	2,225	67.3							$22	$40	$55
Auctions: $5,875, PF-68DCam, March 2013												
1954D	117,183,060	261	64.2	98%	$0.60	$1	$30	$700	$100	$250		
Auctions: $294, MS-65FS, November 2014; $329, MS-65FS, July 2014; $3,055, MS-65FS, April 2014												
1954S	29,384,000	665	64.7	99%	$1.75	$2	$15	$4,000	$165			
Auctions: $558, MS-64FS, November 2014; $1,645, MS-64FS, October 2013												
1954S, S Over D (c)	(d)	173	63.2	95%	$26	$40	$160	$500	$1,000			
Auctions: $558, MS-66, June 2014; $123, MS-65, November 2014; $147, MS-65, August 2014; $80, MS-64, November 2014												

c. The overall strength of the strike is the important factor in this overmintmark's value. **d.** Included in 1954-S mintage figure.

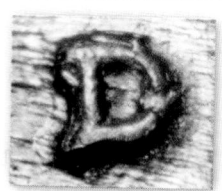

1955-D, D Over S
FS-05-1955D-501.

	Mintage	Cert	Avg	%MS	MS-60	MS-63	MS-65	MS-65FS	MS-66	MS-66FS / PF-65	MS-67 / PF-66	MS-67FS / PF-67
1955	7,888,000	365	65.0	100%	$0.75	$1	$15	$900	$100			
Auctions: $382, MS-65FS, April 2014												
1955, Proof	378,200	3,777	67.6							$18	$30	$45
Auctions: $3,231, PF-69DCam, September 2013; $123, PF-66DCam, November 2014												
1955D	74,464,100	389	64.4	98%	$0.50	$0.75	$20	$4,500	$150			
Auctions: $165, MS-66, August 2014; $999, MS-64FS, February 2013												
1955D, D Over S (e)	(f)	139	64.0	96%	$36	$57.50	$175	$500	$1,000			
Auctions: $2,820, MS-66, February 2013; $96, MS-65, November 2014; $141, MS-65, October 2014												
1956	35,216,000	631	65.4	100%	$0.50	$0.75	$20	$80	$45	$275		$5,000
Auctions: $588, MS-66FS, June 2014												
1956, Proof	669,384	3,029	67.5							$4	$25	$40
Auctions: $47, PF-69, October 2014; $5,581, PF-68DCam, June 2013												
1956D	67,222,940	420	65.5	100%	$0.50	$0.75	$20	$675	$35	$3,000	$500	
Auctions: $911, MS-65FS, February 2013												
1957	38,408,000	377	65.0	100%	$0.50	$0.75	$15	$125	$80	$2,600		
Auctions: $441, MS-66FS, April 2014												
1957, Proof	1,247,952	3,152	67.3							$3	$12	$20
Auctions: $881, PF-68Cam, June 2013												
1957D	136,828,900	564	65.4	100%	$0.50	$0.70	$15	$150	$35	$2,750		
Auctions: $2,115, MS-67FS, November 2014; $141, MS-67, October 2014; $206, MS-66FS, October 2014; $208, MS-62, August 2013												
1958	17,088,000	245	64.3	100%	$0.60	$0.80	$12	$700				
Auctions: $1,116, MS-66FS, November 2014; $764, MS-65, January 2014												
1958, Proof	875,652	2,889	67.3							$8	$12	$20
Auctions: $7,050, PF-68DCam, April 2013												
1958D	168,249,120	672	65.4	99%	$0.40	$0.50	$12	$50	$75	$100		$3,500
Auctions: $1,763, MS-67FS, December 2013												
1959	27,248,000	505	65.3	99%	$0.25	$0.50	$10	$80	$125	$1,000		
Auctions: $212, MS-66FS, November 2014; $176, MS-66FS, November 2014; $306, MS-66FS, July 2014; $719, MS-66FS, October 2013												
1959, Proof	1,149,291	2,523	67.3							$3	$10	$20
Auctions: $7,050, PF-69DCam, April 2013; $1,293, PF-68DCam, September 2014												
1959D	160,738,240	442	65.4	99%	$0.25	$0.50	$8	$250	$50	$2,250		
Auctions: $1,293, MS-67FS, April 2014; $1,175, MS-66FS, November 2014; $411, MS-66FS, October 2014; $106, MS-65FS, November 2014												
1960	55,416,000	327	65.2	99%	$0.25	$0.50	$8	$1,750	$70			
Auctions: $1,495, MS-65FS, February 2010												
1960, Proof	1,691,602	2,952	67.3							$3	$10	$18
Auctions: $6,463, PF-69DCam, March 2013; $229, PF-69Cam, September 2014												
1960D	192,582,180	355	65.4	99%	$0.25	$0.50	$10		$100		$500	
Auctions: $223, MS-66, February 2013												

e. There are 10 or more different D Over S varieties for 1955. Values shown are for the strongest (FS-05-1955D-501); others command smaller premiums. **f.** Included in 1955-D mintage figure.

	Mintage	Cert	Avg	%MS	MS-60	MS-63	MS-65	MS-65FS	MS-66	MS-66FS / PF-65	MS-67 / PF-66	MS-67FS / PF-67
1961	73,640,100	330	65.5	100%	$0.25	$0.50	$20	$2,500	$60	$3,500		
Auctions: $2,530, MS-65FS, February 2010												
1961, Proof	3,028,144	3,247	67.2							$3	$10	$18
Auctions: $1,763, PF-69DCam, April 2013												
1961D	229,342,760	260	65.0	100%	$0.25	$0.50	$20	$6,000	$200		$2,000	
Auctions: $11,163, MS-64FS, February 2013												
1962	97,384,000	338	65.2	99%	$0.25	$0.50	$10	$50	$30	$600	$425	
Auctions: $21,150, MS-67FS, August 2013												
1962, Proof	3,218,019	3,822	67.3							$3	$10	$18
Auctions: $823, PF-69DCam, September 2013												
1962D	280,195,720	177	64.5	98%	$0.25	$0.50	$30					
Auctions: $89, MS-63FS, November 2014; $118, MS-63FS, June 2013												
1963	175,776,000	597	65.4	100%	$0.25	$0.50	$10	$150	$40	$1,200		
Auctions: $247, MS-66FS, March 2014; $72, MS-65FS, November 2014												
1963, Proof	3,075,645	4,339	67.4							$3	$10	$18
Auctions: $317, PF-69DCam, December 2014; $823, PF-69DCam, September 2013												
1963D	276,829,460	115	63.9	96%	$0.25	$0.50	$30	$7,500				
Auctions: $7,475, MS-65FS, February 2010												
1964	1,024,672,000	306	65.2	99%	$0.25	$0.50	$8	$325	$60	$2,000		
Auctions: $14,100, MS-67FS, September 2014; $1,763, MS-66FS, September 2014; $1,058, MS-66FS, September 2013												
1964, Proof	3,950,762	7,047	68.1							$3	$10	$18
Auctions: $129, PF-69DCam, December 2014; $108, PF-69DCam, September 2014; $194, PF-69DCam, March 2013												
1964D	1,787,297,160	401	65.0	99%	$0.25	$0.50	$5	$750	$55	$4,000		
Auctions: $1,175, MS-65FS, September 2014; $1,175, MS-65FS, April 2014												
1965	136,131,380	328	65.8	99%	$0.25	$0.50	$5	$50	$25	$250	$200	
Auctions: $165, MS-67, December 2014; $646, MS-66, August 2013												
1965, Special Mint Set ‡	2,360,000	2,028	66.6	100%						$5 (g)	$20	$45
Auctions: $5,288, PF-67DCam, July 2014; $123, PF-67Cam, September 2014												
1966	156,208,283	101	65.0	97%		$0.25	$5	$50	$25	$250	$200	
Auctions: $56, MS-66, July 2014; $322, MS-65DCam, February 2010												
1966, Special Mint Set ‡	2,261,583	1,939	66.8	100%						$5 (h)	$20	$35
Auctions: $282, PF-68Cam, September 2014; $94, PF-67Cam, November 2014												
1967	107,325,800	186	65.6	99%		$0.25	$5	$50	$25	$250	$200	
Auctions: $132, MS-66, February 2013												
1967, Special Mint Set ‡	1,863,344	2,099	66.8	100%						$5 (i)	$20	$30
Auctions: $1,058, PF-69Cam, July 2014; $705, PF-67DCam, October 2014; $30, PF-66Cam, October 2014												

‡ Ranked in the *100 Greatest U.S. Modern Coins*. **g.** Value in PF-64FS is $10; in PF-65FS, $55. **h.** Value in PF-64FS is $10; in PF-65FS, $65. **i.** Value in PF-64FS is $10; in PF-65FS, $60.

	Mintage	Cert	Avg	%MS	MS-63	MS-64FS	MS-65	MS-65FS	MS-66	MS-66FS / PF-66	MS-67 / PF-67Cam	MS-67FS / PF-69DC
1968D	91,227,880	386	65.7	100%	$0.25		$4		$35			
Auctions: No auction records available.												
1968S	100,396,004	291	65.6	100%	$0.25	$475	$5	$1,350	$35	$4,000	$275	
Auctions: No auction records available.												
1968S, Proof	3,041,506	1,093	67.8							$4	$16	$115
Auctions: $4,406, PF-65, August 2013												
1969D	202,807,500	264	65.8	100%	$0.25	$10	$4		$115			
Auctions: $94, MS-66, February 2013												
1969S	120,165,000	124	64.9	100%	$0.25		$2		$350			
Auctions: No auction records available.												
1969S, Proof	2,934,631	1,096	67.8							$4	$10	$400
Auctions: $282, PF-69DCam, November 2014; $1,116, PF-69DCam, June 2013												

	Mintage	Cert	Avg	%MS	MS-63	MS-64FS	MS-65	MS-65FS	MS-66	MS-66FS	MS-67	MS-67FS
										PF-66	PF-67Cam	PF-69DC
1970D	515,485,380	202	65.3	100%	$0.25		$10			$180		
	Auctions: $200, MS-63, August 2013; $200, MS-62, July 2014											
1970S	238,832,004	1,344	67.3	100%	$0.25	$225	$8	$400	$225	$650		
	Auctions: $999, MS-66FS, December 2013; $89, MS-64FS, November 2014											
1970S, Proof	2,632,810	1,146	67.7							$4	$15	$300
	Auctions: $411, PF-69DCam, September 2014; $499, PF-69DCam, September 2013											

	Mintage	Cert	Avg	%MS	MS-63	MS-64FS	MS-65	MS-65FS	MS-66	MS-66FS	MS-67	MS-67FS	MS-69FS
											PF-66	PF-67Cam	PF-69DC
1971	106,884,000	245	64.8	99%	$0.75	$10	$3	$30	$50	$130			
	Auctions: $127, MS-66FS, February 2010												
1971D	316,144,800	646	66.0	100%	$0.30	$10	$3	$20	$30	$60		$875	
	Auctions: $646, MS-67FS, August 2013												
1971, No S, Proof ‡ (a)	1,655	92	67.6								$1,250	$1,500	$8,000
	Auctions: $5,875, PF-69DCam, March 2013; $1,058, PF-68Cam, October 2014; $1,175, PF-67Cam, July 2014; $999, PF-66, September 2014												
1971S, Proof	3,220,733	1,179	67.8								$8	$20	$600
	Auctions: $1,528, PF-69DCam, June 2013												
1972	202,036,000	115	65.3	99%	$0.25	$10	$3	$40	$60	$300			
	Auctions: $141, MS-66FS, November 2014; $276, MS-66FS, March 2012												
1972D	351,694,600	137	64.9	99%	$0.25	$10	$3	$40	$75	$350			
	Auctions: $212, MS-63, November 2014; $823, MS-63, August 2013												
1972S, Proof	3,260,996	788	67.7								$8	$20	$120
	Auctions: $79, PF-69DCam, November 2014; $89, PF-69DCam, September 2014; $74, PF-69DCam, September 2014												
1973	384,396,000	187	65.1	100%	$0.25	$10	$3	$30	$45	$150	$110		
	Auctions: $103, MS-66FS, February 2013												
1973D	261,405,000	216	65.4	100%	$0.25	$10	$3	$25	$30	$60	$90		
	Auctions: $353, MS-65, February 2014												
1973S, Proof	2,760,339	285	67.9								$7	$15	$30
	Auctions: $44, PF-69DCam, September 2009												
1974	601,752,000	219	64.9	100%	$0.25	$40	$3	$175	$35	$900			
	Auctions: $46, MS-65FS, November 2014; $110, MS-65FS, March 2014												
1974D	277,373,000	149	65.2	99%	$0.25	$15	$3	$40	$45	$150		$1,750	
	Auctions: $34, MS-66FS, November 2014; $200, MS-62, April 2013												
1974S, Proof	2,612,568	370	67.1								$8	$12	$20
	Auctions: $25, PF-69DCam, March 2008												
1975	181,772,000	216	65.5	100%	$0.50	$20	$3	$50	$50	$300			
	Auctions: $2,115, MS-67FS, September 2014; $118, MS-66FS, November 2014; $259, MS-62, August 2013												
1975D	401,875,300	145	65.3	100%	$0.25	$15	$3	$60	$55	$300			
	Auctions: $165, MS-66FS, November 2014; $299, MS-66FS, February 2010												
1975S, Proof	2,845,450	509	67.9								$8	$12	$20
	Auctions: $42, PF-68Cam, August 2013												
1976	367,124,000	67	64.8	100%	$0.45	$30	$3	$175	$37	$675		$3,600	
	Auctions: $1,265, MS-66FS, February 2012												
1976D	563,964,147	208	65.0	100%	$0.45	$10	$3	$30	$40	$300			
	Auctions: $235, MS-65, February 2014; $94, MS-64, July 2014												
1976S, Proof	4,149,730	787	67.8								$8	$12	$20
	Auctions: $36, PF-70DCam, January 2010												

‡ Ranked in the *100 Greatest U.S. Modern Coins*. **a.** 1971, Proof, nickels without the S mintmark were made in error after an assistant engraver forgot to punch a mintmark into a die. The U.S. Mint estimates that 1,655 such error coins were struck.

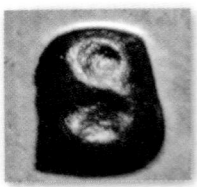
1979-S, Filled S (Type 1), Proof

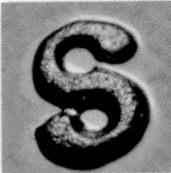
1979-S, Clear S (Type 2), Proof

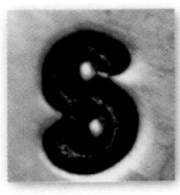
1981-S, Rounded S (Type 1), Proof

1981-S, Flat S (Type 2), Proof

	Mintage	Cert	Avg	%MS	MS-63	MS-64FS	MS-65	MS-65FS	MS-66	MS-66FS	MS-67	MS-67FS	MS-69FS
											PF-66	PF-67Cam	PF-69DC
1977	585,376,000	139	65.4	100%	$0.25	$70	$3	$150	$48	$1,000			
Auctions: $881, MS-64, October 2014; $329, MS-63, September 2013													
1977D	297,313,422	109	65.1	100%	$0.50	$10	$3	$35	$40	$275			
Auctions: $940, MS-68, August 2013													
1977S, Proof	3,251,152	712	68.3								$7	$12	$20
Auctions: $1,116, PF-70DCam, April 2013													
1978	391,308,000	122	65.4	100%	$0.25	$35	$3	$175	$55	$900			
Auctions: $43, MS-64, July 2014; $259, MS-64, September 2013; $282, MS-63, October 2014													
1978D	313,092,780	119	65.2	100%	$0.25	$15	$3	$40	$55	$100			
Auctions: $104, MS-66FS, February 2010													
1978S, Proof	3,127,781	663	68.6								$7	$12	$20
Auctions: $294, PF-70DCam, December 2014; $282, PF-70DCam, November 2014; $170, PF-70DCam, November 2014													
1979	463,188,000	95	65.2	99%	$0.25	$40	$3	$300	$50	$1,000			
Auctions: $1,116, MS-64, September 2014; $499, MS-62, December 2013													
1979D	325,867,672	282	64.8	99%	$0.25	$10	$4	$30	$37	$150			
Auctions: $182, MS-66FS, February 2013													
1979S, Proof, Both kinds	3,677,175												
1979S, Type 1, Proof		753	68.6								$7	$12	$22
Auctions: $1,763, PF-70DCam, June 2013													
1979S, Type 2, Proof		789	68.8								$7	$12	$20
Auctions: $646, PF-70DCam, June 2013													
1980P	593,004,000	144	65.5	100%	$0.25	$10	$4	$45	$30	$250			
Auctions: $5,875, MS-66, August 2014; $259, MS-64, October 2014; $646, MS-64, August 2014; $194, MS-63, November 2014													
1980D	502,323,448	145	65.1	100%	$0.25	$10	$3	$20	$60	$250			
Auctions: $217, MS-66FS, February 2013													
1980S, Proof	3,554,806	933	68.6								$7	$12	$20
Auctions: No auction records available.													
1981P	657,504,000	191	65.6	99%	$0.25	$100	$3	$500	$50	$3,500			
Auctions: $259, MS-66FS, November 2014; $188, MS-64, February 2014; $499, MS-63, October 2014													
1981D	364,801,843	163	65.0	100%	$0.25	$10	$3	$30	$35	$180			
Auctions: $206, MS-66FS, June 2014													
1981S, Proof, Both kinds	4,063,083												
1981S, Type 1, Proof		1,097	68.6								$7	$12	$20
Auctions: $1,528, PF-70DCam, June 2013													
1981S, Type 2, Proof		922	68.8								$10	$13	$30
Auctions: $3,525, PF-70DCam, April 2013													
1982P	292,355,000	34	64.7	94%	$5	$12	$10	$50	$35	$325			
Auctions: $881, MS-67, February 2014; $2,350, MS-62, September 2014													
1982D	373,726,544	66	65.0	97%	$2	$25	$6	$55	$30	$400			
Auctions: $374, MS-66FS, February 2010													
1982S, Proof	3,857,479	806	68.7								$8	$12	$20
Auctions: No auction records available.													

	Mintage	Cert	Avg	%MS	MS-63	MS-64FS	MS-65	MS-65FS	MS-66	MS-66FS	MS-67	MS-67FS	MS-69FS
											PF-66	PF-67Cam	PF-69DC
1983P	561,615,000	34	63.9	91%	$2	$60	$9	$400	$60	$1,500			
	Auctions: $41, MS-65, July 2014; $558, MS-65, August 2013												
1983D	536,726,276	37	64.4	95%	$1.50	$15	$4	$175	$35	$875			
	Auctions: $863, MS-66FS, June 2010; $112, MS-65FS, November 2014												
1983S, Proof	3,279,126	758	68.8								$8	$12	$20
	Auctions: $1,528, PF-70DCam, June 2013												
1984P	746,769,000	139	65.4	100%	$1	$10	$3	$25	$40	$100			
	Auctions: $66, MS-66FS, February 2013												
1984D	517,675,146	130	65.1	99%	$0.25	$10	$3	$30	$65	$275			
	Auctions: $36, MS-65FS, February 2013												
1984S, Proof	3,065,110	584	68.6								$10	$12	$20
	Auctions: $705, PF-70DCam, June 2013												
1985P	647,114,962	130	65.5	100%	$0.50	$25	$3	$50	$60	$400			
	Auctions: $89, MS-66FS, November 2014; $70, MS-66FS, November 2014; $259, MS-62, November 2013												
1985D	459,747,446	111	65.3	100%	$0.50	$10	$3	$40	$45	$225		$2,000	
	Auctions: $196, MS-66FS, June 2010												
1985S, Proof	3,362,821	614	68.9								$8	$12	$20
	Auctions: $1,528, PF-70DCam, June 2013												
1986P	536,883,483	129	65.7	100%	$0.50	$10	$3	$50	$35	$200			
	Auctions: $47, MS-66FS, November 2014; $99, MS-66FS, February 2013												
1986D	361,819,140	108	65.4	100%	$1	$10	$2.75	$35	$50	$275			
	Auctions: $253, MS-66FS, February 2010												
1986S, Proof	3,010,497	473	68.9								$9	$13	$20
	Auctions: $3,525, PF-70DCam, April 2013												
1987P	371,499,481	343	66.0	100%	$0.25	$10	$2.75	$15	$60	$65		$250	
	Auctions: $329, MS-67FS, June 2014												
1987D	410,590,604	338	65.6	100%	$0.25	$10	$3.50	$20	$30	$150			
	Auctions: $173, MS-67FS, April 2008												
1987S, Proof	4,227,728	603	68.9								$8	$12	$20
	Auctions: $558, PF-70DCam, June 2013												
1988P	771,360,000	108	65.9	100%	$0.25	$12	$3	$30	$35	$140			
	Auctions: $329, MS-67, August 2013; $69, MS-64, July 2014												
1988D	663,771,652	169	65.3	99%	$0.25	$10	$3	$35	$32	$125			
	Auctions: $165, MS-67, June 2014												
1988S, Proof	3,262,948	522	68.7								$9	$13	$25
	Auctions: $823, PF-70DCam, June 2013												
1989P	898,812,000	207	65.9	100%	$0.25	$10	$2.75	$20	$25	$35		$700	
	Auctions: $18, AU-50, August 2013												
1989D	570,842,474	133	65.1	100%	$0.25	$12	$2.75	$40	$35	$180			
	Auctions: $188, MS-66FS, February 2013												
1989S, Proof	3,220,194	574	69.0								$8	$12	$20
	Auctions: $82, PF-70DCam, May 2013												
1990P	661,636,000	146	65.9	99%	$0.25	$10	$2.75	$20	$25	$40			
	Auctions: $24, MS-66FS, October 2009												
1990D	663,938,503	123	65.0	99%	$0.25	$9	$2.75	$30	$45	$200			
	Auctions: $129, MS-67FS, June 2014												
1990S, Proof	3,299,559	834	69.1								$8	$12	$20
	Auctions: $441, PF-69DCam, June 2014												

	Mintage	Cert	Avg	%MS	MS-63	MS-64FS	MS-65	MS-65FS	MS-66	MS-66FS	MS-67 / PF-66	MS-67FS / PF-67Cam	MS-69FS / PF-69DC
1991P	614,104,000	93	65.6	100%	$0.30	$10	$2.75	$45	$35	$190			
Auctions: $90, MS-66FS, February 2013													
1991D	436,496,678	97	65.4	100%	$0.30	$10	$2.75	$25	$35	$160			
Auctions: $76, MS-66FS, February 2013													
1991S, Proof	2,867,787	751	69.1								$10	$12	$20
Auctions: $64, PF-70DCam, August 2013													
1992P	399,552,000	138	65.8	100%	$1.50	$10	$3	$20	$28	$50		$2,000	
Auctions: $88, MS-67FS, August 2013													
1992D	450,565,113	114	65.2	100%	$0.25	$10	$2.75	$30	$30	$160			
Auctions: $72, MS-66FS, February 2013													
1992S, Proof	4,176,560	1,486	69.1								$8	$12	$20
Auctions: $45, PF-70DCam, May 2013													
1993P	412,076,000	128	65.8	100%	$0.25	$10	$1	$30	$35	$75			
Auctions: $68, MS-66FS, February 2013													
1993D	406,084,135	171	65.4	100%	$0.25	$10	$1	$20	$20	$40	$100	$400	
Auctions: $374, MS-67FS, February 2010													
1993S, Proof	3,394,792	1,536	69.0								$8	$12	$20
Auctions: $47, PF-70DCam, October 2009													
1994P	722,160,000	151	65.9	100%	$0.25	$10	$2	$25	$25	$100	$35		
Auctions: $881, MS-63, April 2013													
1994P, Special Uncirculated ‡ (b)	167,703	1,585	68.9	100%	$50	$75	$75	$125	$125	$150	$250	$500	
Auctions: $123, MS-70, November 2014; $66, MS-69FS, March 2013; $40, MS-69, September 2014; $38, MS-69, November 2014													
1994D	715,762,110	100	64.8	99%	$0.25	$10	$1	$30	$35	$100	$50		
Auctions: $92, MS-66FS, February 2013													
1994S, Proof	3,269,923	1,373	69.1								$8	$12	$20
Auctions: $33, PF-70DCam, April 2013													
1995P	774,156,000	155	66.2	100%	$0.25	$20	$1	$40	$20	$90	$25	$250	
Auctions: $499, MS-65, August 2013; $141, MS-63, July 2014													
1995D	888,112,000	56	65.0	98%	$0.50	$10	$1	$25	$25	$200	$35	$1,200	
Auctions: $940, MS-67FS, April 2014													
1995S, Proof	2,797,481	1,338	69.1								$10	$13	$20
Auctions: $79, PF-70DCam, February 2010													
1996P	829,332,000	186	65.7	100%	$0.25	$18	$1	$20	$25	$30	$35	$350	
Auctions: $41, MS-65, July 2014; $282, MS-63, July 2014													
1996D	817,736,000	218	65.2	100%	$0.25	$20	$1	$22	$25	$35	$35	$200	
Auctions: $161, MS-67FS, February 2010													
1996S, Proof	2,525,265	1,363	69.1								$8	$12	$25
Auctions: $56, PF-70DCam, February 2010													
1997P	470,972,000	75	65.9	100%	$0.50	$10	$2	$45	$25	$175	$50	$350	
Auctions: $66, MS-66FS, August 2013													
1997P, Special Uncirculated ‡ (b)	25,000	853	69.3	100%	$200	$100	$225	$300	$300	$375	$450	$800	
Auctions: $200, MS-70FS, October 2014; $499, MS-70FS, June 2014; $223, MS-69FS, November 2014; $118, MS-69FS, November 2014													
1997D	466,640,000	90	65.1	99%	$1	$15	$2	$50	$20	$100	$25	$500	
Auctions: $33, MS-66FS, June 2014													
1997S, Proof	2,796,678	1,333	69.2								$8	$12	$25
Auctions: $36, PF-70DCam, December 2009													

‡ Ranked in the *100 Greatest U.S. Modern Coins*. **b.** Special "frosted" Uncirculated nickels were included in the 1993, Thomas Jefferson, commemorative dollar packaging (sold in 1994) and in the 1997, Botanic Garden, sets. They resemble Matte Proof coins.

	Mintage	Cert	Avg	%MS	MS-63	MS-64FS	MS-65	MS-65FS	MS-66	MS-66FS	MS-67 / PF-66	MS-67FS / PF-67Cam	MS-69FS / PF-69DC
1998P	688,272,000	86	65.2	100%	$0.35	$8	$1	$35	$45	$125	$110	$400	
Auctions: $176, MS-65, July 2014; $940, MS-64, August 2014; $42, MS-62, November 2014													
1998D	635,360,000	97	64.1	97%	$0.35	$10	$1	$100	$60	$450	$150		
Auctions: $66, MS-65FS, November 2014; $90, MS-65FS, June 2014													
1998S, Proof	2,086,507	1,550	69.3								$8	$12	$25
Auctions: $47, PF-70DCam, November 2009													
1999P	1,212,000,000	175	65.3	97%	$0.25	$10	$1	$20	$25	$75	$35	$250	
Auctions: $141, MS-65FS, July 2014; $84, MS-64FS, July 2014; $282, MS-64, October 2014													
1999D	1,066,720,000	154	65.5	99%	$0.25	$8	$1	$15	$30	$300	$50		
Auctions: $32, MS-64, November 2014; $26, MS-63, November 2014; $21, MS-64, November 2014; $100, MS-64, July 2014													
1999S, Proof	3,347,966	6,086	69.1								$9	$12	$25
Auctions: $42, PF-70DCam, September 2009													
2000P	846,240,000	113	65.6	100%	$0.25	$10	$2	$12	$18	$35	$25	$500	
Auctions: $470, MS-67FS, August 2013													
2000D	1,509,520,000	171	65.9	99%	$0.25	$10	$1	$12	$18	$50	$25	$500	
Auctions: $47, MS-64FS, July 2014; $881, MS-64, October 2014; $94, MS-63, July 2014; $92, MS-64, July 2014													
2000S, Proof	4,047,993	6,352	69.1								$7	$12	$25
Auctions: $17, PF-69DCam, March 2014													
2001P	675,704,000	86	65.8	99%	$0.25	$8	$1	$10	$12	$20	$25	$40	
Auctions: $50, MS-67FS, June 2013													
2001D	627,680,000	64	65.5	98%	$0.25	$8	$1	$10	$12	$20	$25	$130	
Auctions: $138, MS-67FS, February 2010													
2001S, Proof	3,184,606	4,790	69.2								$7	$12	$25
Auctions: $17, PF-69DCam, March 2014													
2002P	539,280,000	72	65.5	100%	$0.25	$8	$2	$10	$12	$20	$30	$75	
Auctions: $72, MS-67FS, June 2014													
2002D	691,200,000	56	65.3	95%	$0.25	$8	$1	$10	$12	$90			
Auctions: $74, MS-66FS, February 2013													
2002S, Proof	3,211,995	5,305	69.1								$7	$12	$25
Auctions: $15, PF-69DCam, February 2013													
2003P	441,840,000	177	65.8	99%	$0.25	$8	$1	$10	$12	$20	$22	$50	
Auctions: $1,058, MS-68FS, November 2013													
2003D	383,040,000	126	65.1	100%	$0.25	$8	$1	$15	$12	$80			
Auctions: $86, MS-66FS, February 2013													
2003S, Proof	3,298,439	9,088	69.2								$7	$12	$25
Auctions: $15, PF-69DCam, March 2014													

	Mintage	Cert	Avg	%MS	MS-63	MS-65	MS-65FS	MS-66	MS-66FS	MS-67	MS-67FS / PF-65	MS-68FS / PF-67	MS-69FS / PF-69DC
2004P, Peace Medal	361,440,000	2,111	63.7	97%	$0.25	$0.75		$8		$50			
Auctions: $200, MS-67, February 2013													
2004D, Peace Medal	372,000,000	509	65.7	100%	$0.25	$0.75		$5		$30			
Auctions: $374, MS-68, February 2010													
2004S, Peace Medal, Proof	2,992,069	11,823	69.2								$8	$12	$25
Auctions: $15, PF-69DCam, March 2014													
2004P, Keelboat	366,720,000	266	65.6	100%	$0.25	$0.75		$5		$20			
Auctions: $299, MS-68, February 2010													
2004D, Keelboat	344,880,000	321	65.9	100%	$0.25	$0.75		$5		$20			
Auctions: No auction records available.													
2004S, Keelboat, Proof	2,965,422	11,831	69.2								$8	$12	$25
Auctions: $31, PF-70DCam, November 2013													

	Mintage	Cert	Avg	%MS	MS-63	MS-65	MS-65FS	MS-66	MS-66FS	MS-67	MS-67FS	MS-68FS	MS-69FS
											PF-65	PF-67	PF-69DC
2005P, American Bison	448,320,000	4,176	66.7	100%	$0.35	$1.25		$8		$30			
	Auctions: $28, MS-69, January 2010												
2005D, American Bison	487,680,000	4,493	66.1	100%	$0.35	$1.25		$8		$25			
	Auctions: $388, MS-66, June 2014; $170, MS-64, November 2014; $26, MS-64, November 2014; $84, MS-64, November 2014												
2005S, American Bison, Proof	3,344,679	19,080	69.2								$10	$15	$30
	Auctions: $34, PF-70DCam, July 2013												
2005P, Ocean in View	394,080,000	3,204	66.5	100%	$0.25	$0.75		$6		$25			
	Auctions: $19, MS-66, February 2010												
2005D, Ocean in View	411,120,000	3,400	66.5	100%	$0.25	$0.75		$5		$22			
	Auctions: $15, MS-65, August 2009												
2005S, Ocean in View, Proof	3,344,679	18,785	69.2								$8	$12	$25
	Auctions: $21, PF-70DCam, November 2013												
2006P, Monticello	693,120,000	278	65.3	100%	$0.25	$0.75	$4	$3	$5	$8	$10	$20	$30
	Auctions: $705, MS-67FS, July 2014; $19, MS-64FS, January 2013												
2006D, Monticello	809,280,000	318	65.7	100%	$0.25	$0.75	$5	$4	$6	$9	$22	$30	$50
	Auctions: $11, MS-67, July 2008												
2006S, Monticello, Proof	3,054,436	7,203	69.3								$5	$12	$25
	Auctions: $32, PF-70DCam, April 2013												
2007P	571,680,000	45	65.1	100%	$0.25	$0.50	$4	$3	$5	$8	$10	$20	$30
	Auctions: $11, MS-68FS, July 2008												
2007D	626,160,000	27	64.8	100%	$0.25	$0.50	$5	$4	$6	$9	$22	$30	$50
	Auctions: $14, MS-68FS, July 2008												
2007S, Proof	2,577,166	5,513	69.3								$4	$12	$30
	Auctions: $15, PF-69DCam, May 2013												
2008P	279,840,000	93	65.5	100%	$0.25	$0.50	$4	$3	$5	$8	$10	$20	$30
	Auctions: No auction records available.												
2008D	345,600,000	59	64.9	100%	$0.25	$0.50	$5	$4	$6	$9	$22	$30	$50
	Auctions: No auction records available.												
2008S, Proof	2,169,561	4,069	69.5								$4	$12	$30
	Auctions: $56, PF-70DCam, June 2009												
2009P	39,840,000	209	65.3	100%	$0.30	$0.70	$4	$3	$5	$8	$10	$20	$30
	Auctions: No auction records available.												
2009D	46,800,000	160	65.1	100%	$0.30	$0.70	$5	$4	$6	$9	$22	$30	$50
	Auctions: No auction records available.												
2009S, Proof	2,179,867	6,184	69.3								$4	$12	$30
	Auctions: $79, PF-70UCam, November 2009												
2010P	260,640,000	72	65.8	100%	$0.25	$0.50	$4	$3	$5	$8	$10	$20	$30
	Auctions: $15, MS-67FS, June 2013												
2010D	229,920,000	108	65.9	100%	$0.25	$0.50	$5	$4	$6	$9	$22	$30	$50
	Auctions: No auction records available.												
2010S, Proof	1,689,216	4,200	69.3								$4	$12	$30
	Auctions: $62, PF-70DCam, June 2013												
2011P	450,000,000	180	66.5	100%	$0.25	$0.50	$4	$3	$5	$8	$10	$20	$30
	Auctions: No auction records available.												
2011D	540,240,000	231	66.6	100%	$0.25	$0.50	$5	$4	$6	$9	$22	$30	$50
	Auctions: No auction records available.												
2011S, Proof	1,453,276	5,703	69.3								$4	$12	$30
	Auctions: $35, PF-70DCam, June 2013												

	Mintage	Cert	Avg	%MS	MS-63	MS-65	MS-65FS	MS-66	MS-66FS	MS-67	MS-67FS	MS-68FS	MS-69FS
											PF-65	PF-67	PF-69DC
2012P	464,640,000	113	66.7	100%	$0.25	$0.50	$4	$3	$5	$8	$10	$20	$30
	Auctions: No auction records available.												
2012D	558,960,000	113	66.7	100%	$0.25	$0.50	$5	$4	$6	$9	$20	$27	$40
	Auctions: No auction records available.												
2012S, Proof	*1,237,415*	2,186	69.5								$4	$12	$30
	Auctions: No auction records available.												
2013P	607,440,000	98	66.4	100%	$0.25	$0.50	$4	$3	$5	$8	$10	$20	$30
	Auctions: No auction records available.												
2013D	615,600,000	92	66.6	100%	$0.25	$0.50	$5	$4	$6	$9	$20	$27	$40
	Auctions: No auction records available.												
2013S, Proof	*802,460*	2,284	69.4								$4	$12	$30
	Auctions: No auction records available.												
2014P	635,520,000	137	67.0	100%	$0.25	$0.50	$4	$3	$5	$8	$10	$20	$30
	Auctions: No auction records available.												
2014D	*570,720,000*	147	67.1	100%	$0.25	$0.50	$5	$4	$6	$9	$20	$27	$40
	Auctions: No auction records available.												
2014S, Proof	*665,100*	2,330	69.4								$4	$12	$30
	Auctions: No auction records available.												
2015P		0	n/a		$0.25	$0.50	$4	$3	$5	$8	$10	$20	$30
	Auctions: No auction records available.												
2015D		0	n/a		$0.25	$0.50	$5	$4	$6	$9	$20	$27	$40
	Auctions: No auction records available.												
2015S, Proof		0	n/a								$4	$12	$30
	Auctions: No auction records available.												

Half Dismes
1792

AN OVERVIEW OF HALF DISMES

Half dimes or five-cent silver coins were provided for in the Mint Act of April 2, 1792. The spelling was stated as *half disme*. The latter word (likely pronounced "dime," as in modern usage, but perhaps in some places as "deem," in the French mode) was used intermittently in government correspondence for years afterward, but on coins dated 1794 and beyond it appeared only as *dime*.

President George Washington, in his fourth annual message to the House of Representatives, November 6, 1792, referred to the half disme:

> In execution of the authority given by the Legislature, measures have been taken for engaging some artists from abroad to aid in the establishment of our Mint; others have been employed at home. Provision has been made of the requisite buildings, and these are now putting into proper condition for the purposes of the establishment.
>
> There has also been a small beginning in the coinage of half-dismes; the want of small coins in circulation calling the first attention to them. The regulation of foreign coins, in correspondence with the principles of our national Coinage, as being essential to their due operation, and to order in our money-concerns, will, I doubt not, be resumed and completed.

The 1792 half dismes are studied in *United States Pattern Coins* (the hobby's standard reference on pattern coins and experimental and trial pieces), and some numismatists have traditionally referred to them as patterns. It is true that they were struck at a private shop in Philadelphia while the official Mint buildings were still in planning. However, several factors point to their status as regular circulating coins. The half disme was authorized as a federal issue by congressional legislation. Its mintage was considerable—some 1,500 or so pieces—and, as noted by President Washington, the coins were meant to alleviate the national need for small change. Furthermore, nearly all surviving examples show signs of extensive wear.

The 1792 half dismes are not commonly collected, simply because they are not common coins; only 200 to 300 are estimated to still exist. However, their rarity, the romance of their connection to the nation's founding, and the mysteries and legends surrounding their creation make them a perennial favorite among numismatists.

Legend has it that George and Martha Washington contributed the silver used to mint the first half dismes. (Portrait of Mrs. Washington by John Chester Buttre, after Gilbert Stuart.)

HALF DISME (1792)

Designer: *Unknown (possibly Robert Birch).* **Weight:** *1.35 grams.*
Composition: *.8924 silver, .1076 copper.* **Diameter:** *16.5 mm.*
Edge: *Reeded.* **Mint:** *John Harper's shop, Philadelphia.*

Judd-7, Pollock-7,
Logan-McCloskey–1.

History. Rumors and legends are par for the course with the 1792 half disme. Martha Washington is sometimes said to have posed for the portrait of Miss Liberty, despite the profile's dissimilarity to life images of the first lady. Longstanding numismatic tradition says that President George Washington had his own silver tableware taken to the mint factory to be melted down, with these little coins being the result. Whether these Washingtonian connections are true or not, other facts are certain: while the Philadelphia Mint was in the planning stage (its cornerstone would be laid on July 31, 1792), dies were being cut for the first federal coinage of that year. The designer may have been Robert Birch, a Mint engraver who created (or helped create) the dies for the half disme, the disme, and other coins. The half dismes were struck in a private facility owned by saw-maker John Harper, in mid-July. It is believed, from Thomas Jefferson's records, that 1,500 were made. Most were placed into circulation. The coin's designs, with a unique head of Miss Liberty and an outstretched eagle, would not be revived when normal production of the half dime denomination started at the Mint's official facilities in 1795.

Striking and Sharpness. These coins usually are fairly well struck, but with some lightness on Miss Liberty's hair above her ear, and on the eagle's breast. Some examples have adjustment marks from the planchet being filed to adjust the weight prior to striking.

Availability. Most of the estimated 200 to 300 surviving coins show extensive wear. Some AU and MS coins exist, several in choice and gem state, perhaps from among the four examples that Mint Director David Rittenhouse is said to have reserved for himself.

GRADING STANDARDS

MS-60 to 70 (Mint State). *Obverse:* No wear is visible. Luster ranges from nearly full at MS-60 to frosty at MS-65 or higher. Toning often masks the surface, so careful inspection is required. *Reverse:* No wear is visible. The field around the eagle is lustrous, ranging from not completely full at MS-60 to deep and frosty at MS-65 and higher.

1792. Graded MS-64.

AU-50, 53, 55, 58 (About Uncirculated). *Obverse:* Light wear is seen on the cheek and on the hair (not as easily observable, as certain areas of the hair may be lightly struck). Luster ranges from light and mostly in protected areas at AU-50, to extensive at AU-58. Friction is evident in the field, less so in the higher ranges. *Reverse:* Light wear is seen on the eagle, but is less noticeable on the letters. Luster ranges from light and mostly in pro-

1792. Graded AU-58.

tected areas at AU-50, to extensive at AU-58. Friction is evident in the field, less in the higher ranges.

Illustrated coin: This is a problem-free example with nice definition, save for some normal lightness of strike at the centers.

EF-40, 45 (Extremely Fine). *Obverse:* The hair shows medium wear to the right of the face and on the bust end. The fields have no luster. Some luster may be seen among the hair strands and letters. *Reverse:* The eagle shows medium wear on its breast and the right wing, less so on the left wing. HALF DISME shows wear. The fields have no luster. Some luster may be seen among the design elements and letters.

1792. Graded EF-40.

VF-20, 30 (Very Fine). *Obverse:* More wear is seen on the hair, including to the right of the forehead and face, where only a few strands may be seen. The hair tips at the right are well detailed. The bust end is flat on its high area. Letters all show light wear. *Reverse:* The eagle displays significant wear, with its central part flat and most of the detail missing from the right wing. Letters all show light wear.

1792. Graded VF-35.

Illustrated coin: Note the medium wear on both sides. The coin has a scratch on the obverse from P (in PAR) to near the center of the head. Scattered marks of a minor nature are evident; these are not unexpected at this grade.

F-12, 15 (Fine). *Obverse:* The portrait, above the neck, is essentially flat, but details of the eye, the nose, and, to a lesser extent, the lips can be seen. The bust end and neck truncation are flat. Some hair detail can be seen to the right of the neck and behind the head, with individual strands blended into heavy groups. Both obverse and reverse at this grade and lower are apt to show marks, minor digs, and other evidence of handling.

1792. Graded F-12.

Reverse: Wear is more advanced than on a Very Fine coin, with significant reduction of the height of the lettering, and with some letters weak in areas, especially if the rim nearby is flat.

VG-8, 10 (Very Good). *Obverse:* The head has less detail than a Fine coin and is essentially flat except at the neck. Some hair, in thick strands, can be seen. The letters show extensive wear, but are readable. *Reverse:* The eagle is mostly flat, and the letters are well worn, some of them incomplete at the borders. Detail overall is weaker than on the obverse.

1792. Graded VG-8.

G-4, 6 (Good). *Obverse:* There is hardly any detail on the portrait, except that the eye can be seen, as well as some thick hair tips. The date is clear. Around the border the edges of the letters are worn away, and some are weak overall. *Reverse:* The eagle is only in outline form. The letters are very worn, with some missing.

1792. Graded G-4.

AG-3 (About Good). *Obverse:* Extreme wear has reduced the portrait to an even shallower state. Around the border some letters are worn away completely, some partially. The 1792 date can be seen but is weak and may be partly missing. *Reverse:* Traces of the eagle will remain and there are scattered letters and fragments of letters. Most of the coin is worn flat.

Illustrated coin: The scratches on the obverse should be noted.

1792. Graded AG-3.

	Mintage	Cert	Avg	%MS	AG-3	G-4	VG-8	F-12	VF-20	EF-40	AU-50	MS-60	MS-62
1792 †	1,500	43	49.1	42%	$8,500	$20,000	$27,500	$40,000	$75,000	$110,000	$175,000	$325,000	$400,000
	Auctions: $212,750, AU-58, March 2012												

† Ranked in the *100 Greatest U.S. Coins* (fourth edition).

Half Dimes
1794–1873

AN OVERVIEW OF HALF DIMES

The first half dimes, dated 1794 and of the Flowing Hair type, were not actually struck until 1795. In that year additional half dimes with the 1795 date were made. In 1796 and 1797 the short-lived Draped Bust obverse combined with the Small Eagle reverse was used, after which no half dimes were struck until 1801. From that year through 1805, excepting 1804, the Draped Bust obverse was used in combination with the Heraldic Eagle reverse. Then followed a long span of years without any coinage of the denomination. In 1829 the laying of the cornerstone for the second Philadelphia Mint precipitated a new issue, the Capped Bust design, some examples of which were made for the ceremony. Production was resumed for circulation, and half dimes of this motif were made through 1837. In that year the Liberty Seated motif, by Christian Gobrecht, was introduced, to be continued without interruption through 1873, although there were a number of design modifications and changes during that span.

Assembling a set of the different half-dime types is a challenge for the collector. The 1794 and 1795, Flowing Hair, half dimes are fairly scarce at all levels and are quite rare in choice Mint State. Then come the Draped Bust obverse, Small Eagle reverse half dimes of 1796 and 1797. In the late 1960s, researcher Jim Ruddy found that of the various silver types (including the more famous 1796–1797 half dollars), half dimes of this type were the hardest to complete a photographic set of, from the lowest grades to the highest.

Draped Bust obverse, Heraldic Eagle reverse half dimes of the 1800–1805 years are scarce in all grades, more so than generally realized. In Mint State they are very rare, although on occasion some dated 1800 turn up (not often for the others). Finding a *sharply struck* example is next to impossible, and a collector may have to give up on this aspect and settle for one that has some weakness in areas.

Capped Bust half dimes and the several variations of Liberty Seated half dimes will pose no problem at all, and with some small amount of patience a collector will be able to find a sharply struck example in nearly any grade desired.

FOR THE COLLECTOR AND INVESTOR: HALF DIMES AS A SPECIALTY

Collecting half dimes by early die varieties of 1794–1837, and/or by dates and mintmarks (beginning with the 1838-O), has captured the fancy of many numismatists over the years. As these coins are so small it is necessary to have a magnifying glass when studying the series—something the collector of silver dollars and double eagles does not need.

One of the earlier enthusiasts in the field was Philadelphia attorney and numismatist Harold P. Newlin, who in 1883 issued *A Classification of the Early Half Dimes of the United States*. Newlin's two

favorite varieties were the 1792 half disme and the rare 1802, and after reading his enticing prose about the desirability of each, no doubt some collectors in 1883 put both coins on their "must have" lists.

Among early half dimes the rarest and most expensive is the 1802. In 1883 Newlin listed just 16 examples known to him. Although no one has compiled an up-to-date registry, it is likely that fewer than 30 exist. Most are well worn. Other early half dimes range from rare to very rare.

Capped Bust half dimes of the 1829–1837 years are all easily available as dates, but some of the die varieties are very rare. Today, most half dimes on the market are not attributed by varieties, making the search for such things rewarding when a rarity is found for the price of a regular coin.

In 1978 the numismatic world was startled to learn that Chicago dealer Edward Milas had located an 1870-S half dime, a variety not earlier known to exist and not listed in

The Draped Bust, Small Eagle, reverse bears 15 stars, representing the states in the Union that existed at that time. In 1797 a 16-star variety was also produced to acknowledge Tennessee, which had just joined the Union.

the annual Mint reports. Other than this coin, still unique today, the dates and mints in the Liberty Seated series 1837 to 1873-S are readily collectible by date and mint, with no great rarities. There are several very curious varieties within that span, the most interesting of which may be the 1858, Over Inverted Date. The date was first punched into the die upside down, the error was noted, and then it was corrected.

FLOWING HAIR (1794–1795)

Designer: *Unknown*. **Engraver:** *Robert Scot*.
Weight: *1.35 grams*. **Composition:** *.8924 silver, .1076 copper*.
Diameter: *Approximately 16.5 mm*. **Edge:** *Reeded*. **Mint:** *Philadelphia*.

Logan-McCloskey–3.

History. Half dimes dated 1794 and 1795, of the Flowing Hair type, were all struck in the calendar year 1795, although dies were ready by the end of 1794. The Flowing Hair motif was also used on half dollars and silver dollars of the same years, but not on other denominations.

Striking and Sharpness. Many Flowing Hair half dimes have problems of one sort or another, including adjustment marks (from the planchet being filed down to proper weight) and/or light striking in some areas. On the obverse, check the hair and stars, and on the reverse the breast of the eagle. It may not be possible to find a *needle-sharp* example, but with some extensive searching a fairly decent strike can be obtained. Sharp striking and excellent eye appeal add dramatically to the value.

Availability. Examples appear on the market with frequency, typically in lower circulated grades. Probably 250 to 500 could be classified as MS, most of these dated 1795. Some searching is needed to locate choice examples in any grade. As a rule, half dimes are more readily available than are half dollars and dollars of the same design, and when found are usually more attractive and have fewer problems.

GRADING STANDARDS

MS-60 to 70 (Mint State). *Obverse:* At MS-60 some abrasion and contact marks are evident, most noticeably on the cheek and in the fields. Luster is present, but may be dull or lifeless, and interrupted in patches. At MS-63, contact marks are very few, and abrasion is hard to detect except under magnification. An MS-65 coin has no abrasion, and contact marks are so minute as to require magnification. Luster should be full and rich. Coins

1794; LM-2. Graded MS-62.

graded above MS-65 are more theoretical than actual for this type—but they do exist, and are defined by having fewer marks as perfection is approached. *Reverse:* Comments apply as for the obverse, except that abrasion and contact marks are most noticeable on the eagle at the center. The field area is small and is protected by lettering and the wreath, and in any given grade shows fewer marks than on the obverse.

Illustrated coin: Through the olive-charcoal patina, one can see that this satiny example is free of distracting abrasions.

AU-50, 53, 55, 58 (About Uncirculated). *Obverse:* Light wear is seen on the hair area immediately to the left of the face and neck, on the cheek, and on the top of the neck truncation, more so at AU-50 than at 53 or 55. An AU-58 coin will have minimal traces of wear. An AU-50 will have luster in protected areas among the stars and letters, with little in the open fields or on the portrait. At AU-58, most luster is present in the fields, but is worn away

1795; LM-10. Graded AU-50.

on the highest parts of the motifs. *Reverse:* Light wear is seen on the eagle's body and right wing. At AU-50, detail is lost in most feathers in this area. However, striking can play a part, and some coins are weak to begin with. Light wear is seen on the wreath and lettering. Luster is the best key to actual wear. This will range from perhaps 20% remaining in protected areas at AU-50 to nearly full mint bloom at AU-58.

Illustrated coin: Note the toned surfaces. Lightness at the bottom of the obverse and on the eagle's breast and right wing is more from strike than wear. Scattered tiny marks and thin scratches are evident, but there are no severe dents or adjustment marks.

EF-40, 45 (Extremely Fine). *Obverse:* More wear is evident on the portrait, especially on the hair to the left of the face and neck; the cheek; and the tip of the neck truncation. Excellent detail remains in low-relief areas of the hair. The stars show wear, as do the date and letters. Luster, if present at all, is minimal and in protected areas. *Reverse:* The eagle, this being the focal point to check, shows more wear. Observe in combination with a

1795; LM-8. Graded EF-40.

knowledge of the die variety, to determine the sharpness of the coin when it was first struck. Some were flat at the center at the time they were made. Additional wear is on the wreath and letters, but many details are present. Some luster may be seen in protected areas, and if present is slightly more abundant than on the obverse.

Illustrated coin: Extensive adjustment marks on Miss Liberty's hair, forehead, nose, and eye prompt a grade slightly lower than might otherwise be the case. Note the light strike on the eagle.

VF-20, 30 (Very Fine). *Obverse:* The hair is well worn at the VF-20 level, less so at VF-30. The strands are blended so as to be heavy. The cheek shows only slight relief, and the tip of the neck truncation is flat. The stars have more wear, making them appear larger (an optical illusion). *Reverse:* The body of the eagle shows few if any feathers, while the wings have about half of the feathers visible, depending on the strike. The leaves lack

1795; LM-3. Graded VF-20.

detail and are in outline form. Scattered, non-disfiguring marks are normal for this and lower grades. Any major defects should be noted separately.

Illustrated coin: Here is a pleasing example with smooth, even wear. At this level any lightness of strike is moot, as overall wear is present.

F-12, 15 (Fine). *Obverse:* Wear is more extensive than on a Very Fine coin, reducing the definition of the thick strands of hair. The cheek has less detail, and the stars appear larger. The rim is distinct and many denticles remain visible. *Reverse:* Wear is more extensive. Now, feather details are reduced, mostly remaining on the right wing. The wreath and lettering are more worn, and the rim is usually weak in areas, although some denticles can be seen.

1795; LM-8. Graded F-12.

Illustrated coin: This is an "as you like it" coin—ostensibly a nice example of the grade, problem-free at quick glance, but with a slight planchet bend and some hairlines.

VG-8, 10 (Very Good). *Obverse:* The portrait is mostly seen in outline form, with most hair strands gone, although the tips at the lower left are clear. The ear is discernible, as is the eye. The stars appear larger still, again an illusion. The rim is weak in areas. LIBERTY and the date are readable and usually full, although some letters may be weak at their tops. *Reverse:* The eagle is mostly an outline, although some traces of feathers may be seen

1795; LM-8. Graded VG-8.

in the tail and the lower part of the inside of the right wing. The rim is worn, as are the letters, with some weak, but the motto is readable.

Illustrated coin: This is a well-circulated example with no problems worthy of mention.

G-4, 6 (Good). *Obverse:* Wear is more extensive, and some stars may be missing or only partially visible. The head is an outline, although a few elements of thick hair strands may be seen. The eye is visible only in outline form. The rim is well worn or even missing. LIBERTY is worn, and parts of some letters may be missing, but elements of all are readable. The date is readable, but worn. *Reverse:* The eagle is flat and discernible in outline

1795; LM-8. Graded G-4.

form. The wreath is well worn. Some of the letters may be partly missing. At this level some "averaging" can be done. If the letters are stronger than usual in one area, but some are missing in another area, the coin can still qualify as G-4.

Illustrated coin: This coin has slightly stronger detail on the reverse than on the obverse. Scattered marks are normal for the grade.

AG-3 (About Good). *Obverse:* Wear is so extensive that the coin is barely identifiable. The head is in outline form, LIBERTY is mostly gone, and the date, while readable, may be partially missing. *Reverse:* The reverse is well worn with parts of the wreath and lettering missing.

Illustrated coin: This is a late state of the dies with a rim cut at upper right obverse. The coin has been through the mill, but is suitable as a filler for the type.

1795; LM-10. Graded AG-3.

	Mintage	Cert	Avg	%MS	AG-3	G-4	VG-8	F-12	VF-20	EF-40	AU-50	MS-60	MS-63
1794	(a)	64	64.8	98%	$850	$1,500	$1,800	$2,400	$3,750	$7,500	$11,000	$18,000	$35,000
	Auctions: $129,250, MS-65, August 2014; $6,463, EF-40, August 2014; $4,313, VF-30, April 2012; $764, Fair-2, October 2014												
1795	86,416	1,007	62.8	95%	$550	$1,350	$1,600	$1,850	$3,250	$6,500	$8,000	$13,500	$20,000
	Auctions: $94,000, MS-67, April 2013; $5,288, AU-50, August 2014; $646, Fair-2, November 2014; $552, Fair-2, October 2014												

a. Included in 1795 mintage figure.

DRAPED BUST,
SMALL EAGLE REVERSE (1796–1797)

Designer: *Probably Gilbert Stuart.* **Engraver:** *Robert Scot.*
Weight: *1.35 grams.* **Composition:** *.900 silver, .100 copper.*
Diameter: *Approximately 16.5 mm.* **Edge:** *Reeded.* **Mint:** *Philadelphia.*

LM-2.

History. Although the Draped Bust obverse design was used on various copper and silver coins circa 1795 to 1808, it was employed in combination with the *Small Eagle* reverse only on silver coins of 1795 to 1798—for the half dime series, only in 1796 and 1797.

Striking and Sharpness. Most 1796–1797 half dimes are weak in at least one area. Points to check for sharpness include the hair of Miss Liberty, the centers of the stars, the bust line, and, on the reverse, the center of the eagle. Check for planchet adjustment marks (these are infrequent). Denticles around the border are usually decent, but may vary in strength from one part of the border to another. Sharp striking and excellent eye appeal add to the value dramatically.

Availability. This type is fairly scarce in *any* grade; in MS-63 and finer, no more than a few dozen examples have been traced. As is advisable for other early silver types, beware of deeply toned or vividly iridescent-toned pieces whose flawed surface characters are obscured by the toning, but which are offered as MS; in truth some of these are barely better than EF.

GRADING STANDARDS

MS-60 to 70 (Mint State). *Obverse:* At MS-60 some abrasion and contact marks are evident, most noticeably on the cheek, on the drapery, and in the right field. Luster is present, but may be dull or lifeless, and interrupted in patches. At MS-63, contact marks are very few, and abrasion is hard to detect except under magnification, although this type is sometimes graded liberally due to its rarity. An MS-65 coin has no abrasion, and contact

1797; LM-1, Valentine-2. Graded MS-62.

marks are so minute as to require magnification. Luster should be full and rich. Coins graded above MS-65 are more theoretical than actual for this type—but they do exist, and are defined by having fewer marks as perfection is approached. *Reverse:* Comments apply as for the obverse, except that abrasion and marks are most noticeable on the eagle at the center, a situation complicated by the fact that this area was often flatly struck. Grading is best done by the obverse, then verified by the reverse. The field area is small and is protected by lettering and the wreath, and in any given grade shows fewer marks than on the obverse.

Illustrated coin: The bold cracks visible on the obverse of this bright, brilliant-white example were caused by the state of the obverse die, which was in an advanced stage of breakup when the coin was struck. The strike, although a bit soft at the center of the reverse, is quite bold by the standards of this early half-dime series. The surface on both sides has a nice, satiny texture.

AU-50, 53, 55, 58 (About Uncirculated).
Obverse: Light wear is seen on the hair area above the ear and extending to left of the forehead, on the ribbon, and on the bosom—more so at AU-50 than at 53 or 55. An AU-58 coin has minimal traces of wear. An AU-50 coin has luster in protected areas among the stars and letters, with little in the open fields or on the portrait. At AU-58, most luster is present in the fields, but is worn away on the highest parts

1797, 16 Stars; LM-3. Graded AU-50.

of the motifs. *Reverse:* Light wear is seen on the eagle's body (keep in mind this area might be lightly struck) and edges of the wings. Light wear is seen on the wreath and lettering. Luster is the best key to actual wear. This ranges from perhaps 20% remaining in protected areas at AU-50 to nearly full mint bloom at AU-58.

Illustrated coin: This coin has typical strike on both sides, with lightness on the higher areas. The eagle's wing feathers are well defined, but the head is missing. Attractive iridescent toning is visible.

EF-40, 45 (Extremely Fine). *Obverse:* More wear is evident on the upper hair area and the ribbon and on the drapery and bosom. Excellent detail will remain in low relief areas of the hair. The stars show wear as will the date and letters. Luster, if present at all, is minimal and in protected areas. *Reverse:* The eagle shows more wear, this being the focal point to check. On most examples, many feathers remain on the interior areas of the wings.

1796; LM-1. Graded EF-45.

Check the eagle in combination with a knowledge of the die variety to determine the sharpness of the coin when it was first struck. Additional wear is evident on the wreath and letters, but many details are present. Some luster may be seen in protected areas and, if present, is slightly more abundant than on the obverse.

Illustrated coin: This is the LIKERTY variety, its fanciful name derived from the top and bottom lines of the B being defective. The strike is above average, indeed outstanding, at the center and elsewhere. Note the scrape in the right obverse field. The coin has peripheral "halo" toning, perhaps from being housed in a National (Raymond) holder for many years.

VF-20, 30 (Very Fine). *Obverse:* The higher-relief areas of hair are well worn at VF-20, less so at VF-30. The drapery and bosom show extensive wear. The stars have more wear, making them appear larger (an optical illusion seen on most worn silver coins of this era). *Reverse:* The body of the eagle shows few if any feathers, while the wings have about half of the feathers visible, depending on the strike. The leaves lack most detail

1796; LM-1. Graded VF-30.

and are in outline form. Scattered, non-disfiguring marks are normal for this and lower grades; any major distractions should be noted separately.

Illustrated coin: This coin is nice overall, with good detail for the grade. At this grade lightness of strike is not very important, as wear prevails.

F-12, 15 (Fine). *Obverse:* Wear is more extensive than on a Very Fine coin. Wear is particularly noticeable on the hair, face, and bosom, and the stars appear larger. About half the hair detail remains, most noticeably behind the neck and shoulder. The rim may be partially worn away and may blend into the field. *Reverse:* Wear is more extensive. Feather details are diminished, with fewer than half remaining on the wings. The wreath

1797, 15 Stars; LM-1. Graded F-15.

and lettering are worn further, and the rim is usually weak in areas, although some denticles can be seen.

Illustrated coin: This is a lovely coin with excellent eye appeal; certainly a high-end or conservatively graded example.

VG-8, 10 (Very Good). *Obverse:* The portrait is mostly seen in outline form, with most hair strands gone, although there is some definition at the back of the hair and behind the shoulder. The ear is discernible, as is the eye. The stars appear larger still, again an illusion. The rim is weak in areas. LIBERTY and the date are readable and usually full, although some letters may be weak at their tops. *Reverse:* The eagle is mostly an outline,

1797, 15 Stars; LM-1. Graded VG-8.

with parts blending into the field (on lighter strikes). The rim is worn, as are the letters, with some weak, but the motto is readable.

Illustrated coin: Scattered marks, particularly on the obverse, are more plentiful than regularly seen at this level.

G-4, 6 (Good). *Obverse:* Wear is more extensive, and some stars may be partly missing. The head is an outline. The eye is visible only in outline form. The rim is well worn or even missing in areas. LIBERTY is worn, and parts of some letters may be missing, but elements of all should be readable. The date is readable, but worn. *Reverse:* The eagle is flat and discernible in outline form, and may be blending into the field. The wreath is well

1796. Graded G-4.

worn. Some of the letters may be partly missing. At this level some "averaging" can be done. If the letters are stronger than usual in one area, but some are missing in another area, the coin can still qualify as G-4.

AG-3 (About Good). *Obverse:* Wear is so extensive that the coin is barely identifiable. The head is in outline form. LIBERTY is mostly gone, as are some of the stars. The date, while readable, may be partially worn away. *Reverse:* The reverse is well worn, with parts of the wreath and lettering missing.

Illustrated coin: Note the significant scratches on the obverse. While problems are expected at this low grade, prominent defects should be mentioned.

1796; LM-1. Graded AG-3.

1796, 6 Over 5

1796, LIKERTY

1797, 15 Stars

1797, 16 Stars

1797, 13 Stars

	Mintage	Cert	Avg	%MS	AG-3	G-4	VG-8	F-12	VF-20	EF-40	AU-50	MS-60	MS-63
1796, 6 Over 5	10,230	14	55.1	71%	$700	$1,500	$1,800	$3,500	$5,000	$9,500	$15,000	$26,000	$43,000
	Auctions: $31,725, MS-63, August 2013												
1796, LIKERTY (a)	**(b)**	52	48.3	29%	$700	$1,500	$1,800	$3,450	$4,750	$8,750	$12,500	$16,000	$35,000
	Auctions: $17,625, MS-61, September 2013; $1,586, Fair-2, October 2014; $676, Fair-2, October 2014												
1797, 15 Stars	44,527	32	49.8	22%	$700	$1,500	$1,800	$3,450	$4,750	$8,750	$12,500	$16,000	$25,000
	Auctions: $70,500, MS-64, June 2014; $7,638, AU-55, October 2014; $2,820, Fair-2, October 2014; $1,175, Fair-2, October 2014												
1797, 16 Stars	**(c)**	23	46.6	39%	$700	$1,500	$1,800	$3,450	$4,750	$8,750	$12,500	$16,000	$25,000
	Auctions: $54,344, MS-65, June 2014; $734, Fair-2, October 2014; $1,763, Fair-2, August 2014												
1797, 13 Stars	**(c)**	5	48.2	0%	$750	$2,000	$3,500	$4,500	$6,500	$13,500	$25,000	$40,000	$60,000
	Auctions: $25,850, AU-55, February 2013												

a. A die imperfection makes the B in LIKERTY somewhat resemble a K. **b.** Included in 1796, 6 Over 5, mintage figure. **c.** Included in 1797, 15 Stars, mintage figure.

DRAPED BUST,
HERALDIC EAGLE REVERSE (1800–1805)

Designer: *Robert Scot.* **Weight:** *1.35 grams.* **Composition:** *.8924 silver, .1076 copper.*
Diameter: *Approximately 16.5 mm.* **Edge:** *Reeded.* **Mint:** *Philadelphia.*

LM-1.

History. The combination of Draped Bust obverse / Heraldic Eagle reverse was used in the silver half dime series from 1800 to 1805. The obverse style, standardized with 13 stars, is the same as used in 1796 and 1797. During this span the rare 1802 was produced, and none were minted with the date 1804.

Striking and Sharpness. Most 1800–1805 half dimes are lightly struck in one area or another. The obverse stars usually show some weakness. On many coins the central details of Miss Liberty are not sharp. On the reverse the upper right of the shield and the adjacent part of the eagle's wing are often soft, and several or even most stars may be lightly defined (sharp stars show sharply peaked centers); high parts of the clouds are often weak. The area on the reverse opposite the bosom of Miss Liberty may be flat or weak, due to the metal having to flow in both directions when the coins were struck. (The area curving obliquely up and to the right of the eagle's head—exactly mirroring the curvature of the bust on the obverse—is especially prone to weakness of strike.) Denticles are likely to be weak or missing in areas. Many have Mint-caused adjustment marks, from overweight planchets being filed down to proper specifications. In summary, *a sharply struck coin is a goal, not necessarily a reality*. In this series, sharp striking and excellent eye appeal will add to a coin's value dramatically, this being particularly true for all issues from 1801 to 1805.

Availability. This is a challenging type to find with nice eye appeal. Many toned pieces have been recolored to hide flaws or to improve eye appeal. Some are porous or have other problems. The majority of pieces surviving today are dated 1800, and nearly all of the AU or finer coins are of this date.

GRADING STANDARDS

MS-60 to 70 (Mint State). *Obverse:* At MS-60 some abrasion and contact marks are evident, most noticeably on the cheek, on the drapery, and in the right field. Luster is present, but may be dull or lifeless, and interrupted in patches. At MS-63, contact marks are very few, and abrasion is hard to detect except under magnification, although this type is sometimes graded liberally due to its rarity. An MS-65 coin will have no abrasion,

1800; LM-1, V-1. Graded MS-63.

and contact marks are so minute as to require magnification. Luster should be full and rich. Coins graded above MS-65 are more theoretical than actual for this type—but they do exist, and are defined by having fewer marks as perfection is approached. *Reverse:* Comments apply as for the obverse, except that abrasion and contact marks are most noticeable on the eagle's neck, the tips of the wing, and the tail. The field area is complex—with stars above the eagle, the arrows and olive branch, and other features, there is not much open space. Accordingly, marks will not be as noticeable as on the obverse.

Illustrated coin: Both sides of this example are suitably well struck, with surfaces free of outwardly distracting abrasions. The obverse has a rich antique-copper patina, with hints of pale gold and rose. The reverse is lighter in color, with cobalt-blue and champagne-pink highlights around a pinkish-silver center.

AU-50, 53, 55, 58 (About Uncirculated). *Obverse:* Light wear is seen on the hair area above the ear and extending to left of the forehead, on the ribbon, and on the bosom, more so at AU-50 than at AU-53 or 55. An AU-58 coin will have minimal traces of wear. An AU-50 coin will have luster in protected areas among the stars and letters, with little in the open fields or on the portrait. At AU-58, most luster is present in the fields,

1800; LM-3. Graded AU-58.

but is worn away on the highest parts of the motifs. *Reverse:* Comments as for Mint State coins, except that the eagle's neck, the tips and top of the wings, the clouds, and the tail show noticeable wear, as do other features. Luster ranges from perhaps 20% remaining in protected areas at AU-50 to nearly full mint bloom at AU-58. Often the reverse of this type retains much more luster than the obverse.

Illustrated coin: Note the lightness of strike at the center obverse and stars, and on the reverse the upper left of the shield. This coin has light iridescent toning.

EF-40, 45 (Extremely Fine). *Obverse:* More wear is evident on the upper hair area and the ribbon, and on the drapery and bosom. Excellent detail remains in low-relief areas of the hair. The stars show wear, as do the date and letters. Luster, if present at all, is minimal and only in protected areas. *Reverse:* Wear is greater than on an About Uncirculated coin, overall. The neck lacks feather detail on its highest points. Feathers lose some detail near the edges of the wings, and some areas of the horizontal lines in the shield may be blended together. Some traces of luster may be seen, more so at EF-45 than at EF-40.

1805; LM-1. Graded EF-40.

Illustrated coin: Note the lightness of strike on the bust at the right, and, on the reverse, on the eagle at the right.

VF-20, 30 (Very Fine). *Obverse:* The higher-relief areas of hair are well worn at VF-20, less so at VF-30. The drapery and bosom show extensive wear. The stars have more wear, making them appear larger (an optical illusion seen on most worn silver coins of this era). *Reverse:* Wear is greater, including on the shield and wing feathers. Star centers are flat. Other areas have lost detail as well.

1805; LM-1. Graded VF-30.

Illustrated coin: This is a very acceptable example of this scarce date. It has light striking in the same areas as the EF-40 coin above.

F-12, 15 (Fine). *Obverse:* Wear is more extensive than on a Very Fine coin, particularly noticeable on the hair, face, and bosom, and the stars appear larger. About half the hair detail remains, most noticeably behind the neck and shoulder. The rim may be partially worn away and may blend into the field. *Reverse:* Wear is even more extensive, with the shield and wing feathers being points to observe. The incuse E PLURIBUS UNUM

1800; LM-1. Graded F-12.

may have a few letters worn away. The clouds all seem to be connected. The stars are weak. Parts of the border and lettering may be weak.

Illustrated coin: This coin has smooth, even wear—a nice example of the grade.

VG-8, 10 (Very Good). *Obverse:* The portrait is mostly seen in outline form, with most hair strands gone, although there is some definition at the back of the hair and behind the shoulder. The ear is discernible, as is the eye. The stars appear larger still, again an illusion. The rim is weak in areas. LIBERTY and the date are readable and usually full, although some letters may be weak at their tops. *Reverse:* Half or so of the letters in the

1800; LM-3. Graded VG-8.

motto are worn away. Most feathers are worn away, although separation of some of the lower feathers may be seen. Some stars are faint. The border blends into the field in areas, and some letters are weak.

G-4, 6 (Good). *Obverse:* Some stars may be partly missing. The head is an outline. The eye is visible only in outline form. The rim is well worn or even missing in areas. LIBERTY is worn, and parts of some letters may be missing, but elements of all should be readable. The date is readable, but worn. *Reverse:* The upper part of the eagle is flat, and feathers are noticeable only at the lower edge of the wings and do not have detail. The upper part of the

1805. Graded G-4.

shield is flat. Only a few letters of the motto can be seen. The rim is worn extensively, and a few letters may be missing.

AG-3 (About Good). *Obverse:* Wear is so extensive that the coin is barely identifiable. The head is in outline form. LIBERTY is mostly gone; same for the stars. The date, while readable, may be partially worn away. *Reverse:* Extensive wear is seen overall, with the rim worn away and some areas worn smooth. The eagle can be discerned in outline form, but not necessarily completely. A few stray motto letters may remain.

1803; LM-2. Graded AG-3.

Illustrated coin: This coin is extensively worn, but defect free.

1800, LIBEKTY

	Mintage	Cert	Avg	%MS	AG-3	G-4	VG-8	F-12	VF-20	EF-40	AU-50	MS-60	MS-63
1800	24,000	132	64.5	96%	$450	$1,000	$1,500	$2,000	$3,000	$6,000	$8,500	$12,500	$21,500
	Auctions: $25,850, MS-64, August 2014; $4,994, AU-50, October 2014; $2,350, EF-40, November 2014												
1800, LIBEKTY (a)	16,000	44	45.0	30%	$450	$1,200	$1,750	$2,500	$3,250	$6,500	$8,500	$13,000	$22,000
	Auctions: $31,725, MS-64, April 2014; $3,086, VF-25, October 2014; $617, Fair-2, October 2014												

a. A defective die punch gives the R in LIBERTY the appearance of a K.

1803, Large 8   **1803, Small 8**

	Mintage	Cert	Avg	%MS	AG-3	G-4	VG-8	F-12	VF-20	EF-40	AU-50	MS-60	MS-63
1801	27,760	1,933	63.0	96%	$450	$1,500	$2,000	$3,000	$4,000	$6,500	$10,000	$16,000	$27,500
	Auctions: $5,581, EF-40, February 2014												
1802 †	3,060	2	50.0	0%	$20,000	$33,000	$44,000	$60,000	$125,000	$200,000	$250,000		
	Auctions: $352,500, AU-50, June 2014												
1803, Large 8	37,850	10	38.0	30%	$450	$1,000	$1,300	$2,000	$3,000	$6,500	$9,000	$14,000	$22,500
	Auctions: $7,050, AU-50, February 2014												
1803, Small 8	(b)	2	58.0	50%	$450	$1,000	$1,400	$2,500	$3,250	$6,500	$10,000	$20,000	$35,000
	Auctions: $5,922, EF-35, April 2013; $999, Fair-2, October 2014												
1805	15,600	3,359	63.0	97%	$450	$1,000	$1,300	$2,750	$3,500	$9,000	$20,000	$40,000	
	Auctions: $9,400, EF-45, August 2013; $729, AG-3, August 2014; $793, Fair-2, October 2014												

† Ranked in the *100 Greatest U.S. Coins* (fourth edition). **b.** Included in 1803, Large 8, mintage figure.

CAPPED BUST (1829–1837)

Engraver: *William Kneass, after a design by John Reich.* **Weight:** *1.35 grams (changed to 1.34 grams in 1837).*
Composition: *.8924 silver, .1076 copper (changed to .900 silver, .100 copper in 1837).*
Diameter: *Approximately 15.5 mm.* **Edge:** *Reeded.* **Mint:** *Philadelphia.*

Circulation Strike   **Proof**
LM-7.   *LM-4.*

History. Half dimes of the Capped Bust design were first struck the morning of July 4, 1829, to be included in the cornerstone time capsule of the new (second) Philadelphia Mint building and, presumably, to have some inexpensive coins on hand for distribution as souvenirs. Engraver John Reich's design was not new; it had been used on half dollars as early as 1807. It was logical to employ it on the new half dime, a coin that had not been made since 1805. The new half dimes proved popular and remained in circulation for many years.

Striking and Sharpness. Striking varies among Capped Bust half dimes, and most show lightness in one area or another. On the obverse, check the hair details to the left of the eye, as well as the star centers. On the reverse, check the eagle's feathers and neck. The motto, which can be a problem on certain other coins of this design (notably half dollars), is usually bold on the half dimes. Denticles range from well defined to somewhat indistinct, and, in general, are sharper on the obverse than on the reverse.

Proofs. Proofs were struck in small quantities, generally as part of silver Proof sets, although perhaps some were made to mark the Mint cornerstone event mentioned above; facts are scarce. True Proofs have fully mirrored fields. Scrutinize deeply toned pieces (deep toning often masks the true nature of a coin, e.g., if it is not a true Proof, or if it has been cleaned or repaired). Some pieces attributed as "Proofs" are not Proofs. This advice applies across the entire Capped Bust silver series.

Availability. Finding an example in any desired grade should not be a challenge. Finding one with Full Details will take more time. Connoisseurship is required at the MS level, given the high value of these coins.

GRADING STANDARDS

MS-60 to 70 (Mint State). *Obverse:* At MS-60 some abrasion and contact marks are evident, most noticeably on the cheek, on the hair below the left part of LIBERTY, and on the area near the drapery clasp. Luster is present, but may be dull or lifeless, and interrupted in patches. At MS-63, contact marks are very few, and abrasion is hard to detect except under magnification. An MS-65 coin

1831; LM-4, V-4. Graded MS-67.

has no abrasion, and has contact marks so minute as to require magnification. Luster should be full and rich, usually more so on half dimes than larger coins of the Capped Bust type. Grades above MS-65 are seen now and again, and are defined by having fewer marks as perfection is approached. *Reverse:* Comments apply as for the obverse, except that abrasion and contact marks are most noticeable on the eagle's neck, the top of the wings, the claws, and the flat band that surrounds the incuse motto. The field is mainly protected by design elements and does not show abrasion as much as does the obverse.

Illustrated coin: This example is nearly pristine. Rich with original mint luster, the softly frosted surfaces thin to hints of reflectivity in the fields. The strike is strong from rim to center, delineating the intricate design elements clearly. Brilliant, save for a faint champagne-colored iridescence, the coin has no distracting abrasions.

AU-50, 53, 55, 58 (About Uncirculated). *Obverse:* Light wear is seen on the cap, the hair below LIBERTY, the hair near the clasp, and the drapery at the bosom. At AU-58, the luster is extensive except in the open area of the field, especially to the right. At AU-50 and 53, luster remains only in protected areas. *Reverse:* Wear is visible on the eagle's neck, the top of the wings, the claws, and the flat band above the eagle. An AU-58 coin will

1835, Small Date, Large 5 C.; LM-9.1. Graded AU-53.

have nearly full luster. At AU-50 and 53, there will still be significant luster, more than on the obverse.

Illustrated coin: Vivid iridescent toning is evident, perhaps as acquired from longtime storage in a cardboard album. The light areas on the obverse coincidentally showcase the points of wear to be observed at this level. Some lightness of strike is seen at the centers and at the eagle's neck.

EF-40, 45 (Extremely Fine). *Obverse:* Wear is most noticeable on the higher areas of the hair. The cap shows more wear, as does the cheek. Stars, usually protected by the rim, still show their centers (unless lightly struck). Luster, if present, is in protected areas among the star points and close to the portrait. *Reverse:* The wings show wear on the higher areas of the feathers, and some details are lost. Feathers in the neck are light. The eagle's claws and the

1835, Small Date and 5 C.; LM-10. Graded EF-45.

leaves show wear. Luster may be present in protected areas, even if there is little or none on the obverse.

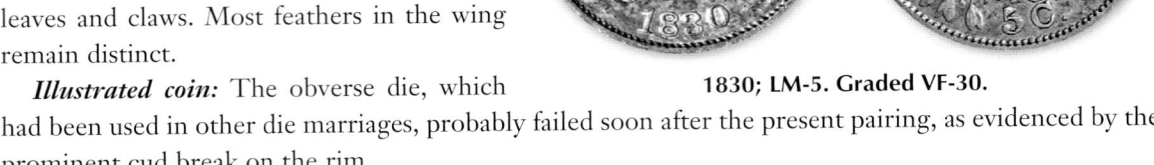

VF-20, 30 (Very Fine). *Obverse:* Wear has caused most of the hair to be combined into thick tresses without delicate features. The curl on the neck is flat. Most stars, unless they were weakly struck, retain their interior lines. *Reverse:* Wear is most evident on the eagle's neck, to the left of the shield, and on the leaves and claws. Most feathers in the wing remain distinct.

1830; LM-5. Graded VF-30.

 Illustrated coin: The obverse die, which had been used in other die marriages, probably failed soon after the present pairing, as evidenced by the prominent cud break on the rim.

F-12, 15 (Fine). *Obverse:* Wear is more extensive, with much of the hair blended together. The drapery is indistinct at its upper edge. Stars have lost some detail at the centers, but still have relief (are not flat). *Reverse:* Wear is more extensive, now with only about half of the feathers remaining on the wings. Some of the horizontal lines in the shield may be worn away.

1837, Small 5 C. Graded F-12.

VG-8, 10 (Very Good). *Obverse:* The hair is less distinct, with the area surrounding the face blended into the facial features. LIBERTY is complete, but weak in areas. The stars are nearly flat, although some interior detail can be seen on certain strikings. *Reverse:* Feathers are fewer and mostly appear on the right wing. Other details are weaker. All lettering remains easily visible.

1829. Graded VG-8.

G-4, 6 (Good). *Obverse:* The portrait is mostly in outline, with few interior details discernible. LIBERTY may still be readable or may be partially worn away, depending on the variety. Stars are flat at their centers. *Reverse:* The eagle mostly is in outline form, although some feathers can be seen in the right wing. All letters around the border are clear. E PLURIBUS UNUM may be weak, sometimes with a few letters worn away.

1837, Small 5 C. Graded G-6.

AG-3 (About Good). *Obverse:* The portrait is an outline, although traces of LIBERTY can still be seen. The rim is worn down, and some stars are weak. The date remains clear. *Reverse:* The reverse shows more wear overall than the obverse, with the rim indistinct in areas and many letters worn away.

1835, Small Date, Large 5 C. Graded AG-3.

PF-60 to 70 (Proof). *Obverse and Reverse:* Proofs that are extensively cleaned and have many hairlines, or that are dull and grainy, are lower level, such as PF-60 to 62. These are not of great interest to specialists unless they are of rare die varieties (such as 1829, LM-1 to 3, described in the image caption). With medium hairlines, an assigned grade of PF-64 may be in order, and with relatively few hairlines, gem PF-65. PF-66 should have

1829; LM-2, V-3. Graded PF-64.

hairlines so delicate that magnification is needed to see them. Above that, a Proof should be free of such lines. Grading is highly subjective with early Proofs, and eye appeal also is a factor.

Illustrated coin: Both sides of this Proof example are fully defined, even at the denticles. The fields have a glittering reflectivity, while the devices have a satin texture, providing for a cameo-like appearance overall. There are no detracting blemishes, and only a hint of light olive-russet toning.

	Mintage	Cert	Avg	%MS	G-4	VG-8	F-12	VF-20	EF-40	AU-50	MS-60	MS-63	MS-65
											PF-60	PF-63	PF-65
1829	1,230,000	712	58.1	65%	$75	$90	$135	$190	$250	$375	$525	$1,300	$4,500
Auctions: $999, MS-63, October 2014; $705, MS-62, November 2014; $11,750, AU-58, April 2013; $259, AU-55, July 2014													
1829, Proof	20–30	8	64.4								$4,500	$10,000	$35,000
Auctions: $36,719, PF-65Cam, January 2014													
1830	1,240,000	600	58.5	69%	$55	$75	$80	$125	$185	$250	$375	$850	$3,000
Auctions: $9,400, MS-66, February 2014; $2,115, MS-65, October 2014; $423, AU-58, October 2014; $153, AU-50, September 2014													
1830, Proof	10–15	3	64.8								$4,500	$12,500	$37,000
Auctions: $49,938, PF-66, September 2013; $30,550, PF-64, August 2014													
1831	1,242,700	760	60.1	73%	$55	$75	$80	$125	$185	$250	$375	$850	$3,000
Auctions: $7,050, MS-67, April 2014; $541, MS-62, October 2014; $270, AU-58, October 2014; $135, AU-55, November 2014													
1831, Proof	20–30	1	67.0								$4,500	$12,500	$38,000
Auctions: $73,438, PF-67, January 2014													
1832	965,000	945	59.5	71%	$55	$75	$80	$125	$185	$250	$375	$850	$3,000
Auctions: $14,100, MS-67, June 2014; $1,058, MS-64, October 2014; $447, MS-62, October 2014; $200, AU-55, September 2014													
1832, Proof	5–10	2	64.0								$5,000	$13,000	$40,000
Auctions: $19,550, PF-64, March 2004													
1833	1,370,000	607	58.8	68%	$55	$75	$80	$125	$185	$250	$375	$850	$3,000
Auctions: $21,150, MS-67, April 2014; $456, MS-62, October 2014; $235, AU-55, September 2014; $176, EF-45, October 2014													

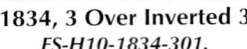

1834, 3 Over Inverted 3
FS-H10-1834-301.

1835, Small Date

1835, Large Date

Small 5 C.

Large 5 C.

	Mintage	Cert	Avg	%MS	G-4	VG-8	F-12	VF-20	EF-40	AU-50	MS-60 / PF-60	MS-63 / PF-63	MS-65 / PF-65
1834	1,480,000	592	59.4	68%	$55	$75	$80	$125	$185	$250	$375	$850	$3,000
Auctions: $7,050, MS-67, November 2013; $1,659, MS-65, August 2014; $306, AU-58, November 2014; $90, VF-35, December 2014													
1834, 3 Over Inverted 3	(a)	20	53.7	45%	$55	$80	$100	$150	$250	$500	$600	$1,200	$4,500
Auctions: $1,351, MS-64, October 2014; $881, AU-58, November 2014; $1,645, AU-58, April 2013; $106, EF-45, September 2014													
1834, Proof	25–35	13	65.1								$4,500	$10,000	$35,000
Auctions: $32,900, PF-66, November 2013; $12,925, PF-64, October 2014; $14,100, PF-64, August 2014													
1835, All kinds	2,760,000												
1835, Large Date and 5 C.		49	56.0	61%	$55	$75	$80	$125	$185	$250	$375	$850	$3,000
Auctions: $8,813, MS-66, November 2013; $646, MS-61, October 2014; $247, AU-55, August 2014; $153, VF-35, July 2014													
1835, Large Date, Small 5 C.		22	57.9	50%	$55	$75	$80	$125	$185	$250	$375	$850	$3,000
Auctions: $1,293, MS-64, August 2014; $1,880, MS-64, March 2013; $153, AU-50, November 2014													
1835, Small Date, Large 5 C.		28	55.1	64%	$55	$75	$80	$125	$185	$250	$375	$850	$3,000
Auctions: $7,638, MS-67, April 2013; $141, AU-50, November 2014; $106, EF-40, November 2014; $76, Fair-2, October 2014													
1835, Small Date and 5 C.		41	56.6	63%	$55	$75	$80	$125	$185	$250	$375	$850	$3,000
Auctions: $17,625, MS-67, March 2013; $223, MS-60, November 2014; $306, AU-55, July 2014; $69, AU-50, November 2014													
1835, Proof	0	n/a									$5,000	$13,000	
Auctions: No auction records available.													
1836, Small 5 C.	1,900,000	37	54.2	49%	$55	$75	$80	$125	$185	$250	$375	$850	$3,000
Auctions: $3,173, MS-66, August 2013; $3,290, MS-65, August 2014; $123, AU-55, October 2014; $84, VF-35, September 2014													
1836, Large 5 C.	(b)	26	56.5	69%	$55	$75	$80	$125	$185	$250	$375	$850	$3,000
Auctions: $3,055, MS-64, February 2014; $515, AU-58, October 2014; $705, AU-55, July 2014; $147, EF-45, October 2014													
1836, 3 Over Inverted 3	(b)	31	54.8	52%	$65	$85	$100	$150	$250	$475	$675	$1,200	$3,750
Auctions: $12,925, MS-66, October 2014; $940, MS-63, June 2013													
1836, Proof	5–10	2	65.5								$4,500	$10,000	$35,000
Auctions: $47,000, PF-66, February 2014													
1837, Small 5 C.	871,000	33	58.6	67%	$65	$85	$100	$185	$300	$500	$975	$2,100	$10,000
Auctions: $1,880, MS-63, June 2013													
1837, Large 5 C.	(c)	27	51.1	48%	$55	$75	$80	$125	$185	$250	$400	$850	$3,500
Auctions: $22,325, MS-66, November 2013; $435, MS-62, October 2014; $112, EF-45, November 2014; $59, VF-35, November 2014													
1837, Proof (d)	5–10	0	n/a								$6,500	$14,000	$37,500
Auctions: No auction records available.													

a. Included in circulation-strike 1834 mintage figure. **b.** Included in 1836, Small 5 C., mintage figure. **c.** Included in 1837, Small 5 C., mintage figure. **d.** The 1837, Proof, coin is untraced.

LIBERTY SEATED (1837–1873)

Variety 1, No Stars on Obverse (1837–1838): **Designer:** *Christian Gobrecht.*
Weight: *1.34 grams.* **Composition:** *.900 silver, .100 copper.*
Diameter: *15.5 mm.* **Edge:** *Reeded.* **Mints:** *Philadelphia, New Orleans.*

**Variety 1, No Stars
on Obverse (1837–1838)**   **Variety 1, No Stars
on Obverse, Proof**

Variety 2, Stars on Obverse (1838–1853): **Designer:** *Christian Gobrecht.*
Weight: *1.34 grams.* **Composition:** *.900 silver, .100 copper.* **Diameter:** *15.5 mm.*
Edge: *Reeded.* **Mints:** *Philadelphia, New Orleans.*

**Variety 2, Stars on
Obverse (1838–1853)**   **Variety 2, Stars
on Obverse, Proof**

Variety 3, Arrows at Date, Reduced Weight (1853–1855):
Designer: *Christian Gobrecht.* **Weight:** *1.24 grams.* **Composition:** *.900 silver, .100 copper.*
Diameter: *15.5 mm.* **Edge:** *Reeded.* **Mints:** *Philadelphia, New Orleans.*

**Variety 3, Arrows at Date,
Reduced Weight (1853–1855)**   **Variety 3, Arrows at Date,
Reduced Weight, Proof**

Variety 2 Resumed, With Weight Standard of Variety 3 (1856–1859):
Designer: *Christian Gobrecht.* **Weight:** *1.24 grams.* **Composition:** *.900 silver, .100 copper.*
Diameter: *15.5 mm.* **Edge:** *Reeded.* **Mints:** *Philadelphia, New Orleans.*

**Variety 2 Resumed, Weight
Standard of Variety 3 (1856–1859)**   **Variety 2 Resumed, Weight
Standard of Variety 3, Proof**

Variety 4, Legend on Obverse (1860–1873): **Designer:** *Christian Gobrecht.*
Weight: *1.24 grams.* **Composition:** *.900 silver, .100 copper.* **Diameter:** *15.5 mm.*
Edge: *Reeded.* **Mints:** *Philadelphia, New Orleans, San Francisco.*

**Variety 4, Legend on
Obverse (1860–1873)**   *Mintmark location,
1860–1869 and
1872–1873, is on the
reverse, below the bow.*   *Mintmark location,
1870–1872, is on the
reverse, above the bow.*   **Variety 4, Legend
on Obverse, Proof**

History. The Liberty Seated design without obverse stars, known as Variety 1, was used in the half dime and dime series only at the Philadelphia Mint in 1837 and the New Orleans Mint in 1838 (1838-O). The motif, by Christian Gobrecht, follows the obverse inaugurated on the 1836 silver dollar. Miss Liberty has no drapery at her elbow. In 1838 13 obverse stars were added, and in 1840 a restyling (drapery added to the elbow) by Robert Ball Hughes appeared. Arrows were added to the sides of the date starting in 1853, through 1855; these denoted the reduction of weight under the terms of the Act of February 21, 1853. The earlier design resumed in 1856. The reverse design stayed the same during these changes. In 1860 on the half dime the legend UNITED STATES OF AMERICA was moved to the obverse, in place of the stars. The reverse displayed a "cereal wreath" (as it was called in Mint records) enclosing the words HALF DIME.

Striking and Sharpness. For half dimes dated 1837 to 1838, check the highest parts of the Liberty Seated figure (especially the head and horizontal shield stripes) and, on the reverse, the leaves. Check the denticles on both sides. These coins are very attractive, and the starless obverse gives them a cameo-like appearance. For half dimes dated 1838 to 1859, strike quality varies widely. Most from 1838 to 1852 are sharper than later ones, but there are exceptions. (Coins with "mushy" details are especially common among the high-mintage dates of the mid- to late 1850s.) On the obverse, check the star centers, the head and center of Miss Liberty, and the denticles. On the reverse, check the wreath leaves and denticles. Excellent strike and deeply mirrored fields characterized nearly all Proofs. Points to check on coins dated 1860 to 1873 include the head of Miss Liberty on the obverse, the wreath details on the reverse (particularly at the inside upper left, above H of HALF) and the denticles on both sides. Generally, MS coins have excellent luster, although some struck from relapped dies tend to be prooflike and with many striae. The word LIBERTY is not an infallible guide to grading at lower levels, as on some dies the shield was in lower relief, and the letters wore away less quickly. This guideline should be used in combination with other features. Generally, Proofs are well made, with deeply mirrored fields, although some of the late 1860s and early 1870s can have weak areas. Average quality in the marketplace is higher than for larger Liberty Seated denominations.

Availability. Liberty Seated half dimes are easily available as a type, but with many scarce varieties. The Philadelphia coins are easily available in all grades. The 1838-O is a rarity in true Mint State, often is over-graded, and typically has low eye appeal. Such issues as 1849-O and 1846 are extreme rarities at the true MS level. San Francisco coins, first made in 1863, are rare in MS for the first several years. Grades above MS-65 are seen with regularity, more often than the related No Stars dimes. Quality varies widely, and many MS coins are artificially toned.

Proofs. It is likely that at least several dozen Proofs were made of the 1837 half dime, although perhaps more were made of the related dime. Today, attractive examples exist and are rare. Nearly all designated as Proofs are, indeed, Proofs. If you aspire to acquire one, select an example with deep mirror surfaces. 1858 was the first year Proofs were widely sold to collectors, and an estimated 210 silver sets were distributed. (Proofs were made of earlier dates, but in much smaller numbers.) It is believed that 800 Proofs were struck of 1859, of which slightly more than 400 found buyers. From 1860 to 1873, Proof coins were made in fair quantities each year and are readily available today. The quality of Proofs on the market varies widely, mainly due to cleaning and dipping. Patience and care are needed to find a choice example.

GRADING STANDARDS

MS-60 to 70 (Mint State). *Obverse:* At MS-60 some abrasion and contact marks are evident, most noticeably on the bosom, thighs, and knees. Luster is present, but may be dull or lifeless, and interrupted in patches in the large open field. At MS-63, contact marks are very few, and abrasion is hard to detect except under magnification. An MS-65 coin has no abrasion, and contact marks are so minute as to require magnification. Luster

1837, Small Date. Graded MS-62.

should be full and rich, except for Philadelphia (but not San Francisco) half dimes of the early and mid-1860s. Most Mint State coins of 1861 to 1865, Philadelphia issues, will have extensive die striae (from the dies being incompletely finished). Some low-mintage Philadelphia issues may be prooflike (and some may even be mislabeled as Proofs). Clashmarks are common in this era. Half dimes of this type can be very beautiful at this level. *Reverse:* Comments apply as for the obverse except that in lower Mint State grades abrasion and contact marks are most noticeable on the highest parts of the leaves and the ribbon, less so on HALF DIME. The field is mainly protected by design elements and does not show abrasion as much as does the open-field obverse on a given coin.

Illustrated coin: This is an attractive example with a hint of toning.

AU-50, 53, 55, 58 (About Uncirculated).
Obverse: Light wear is seen on the thighs and knees, bosom, and head. At AU-58, the luster is extensive, but incomplete. Friction is seen in the large open field. At AU-50 and 53, luster is less. *Reverse:* Wear is noticeable on the leaves and ribbon. An AU-58 coin has nearly full luster—more so than on the obverse, as the design elements protect the small field areas. At AU-50 and 53, there still is significant luster, more than on the obverse.

1837, Large Date. Graded AU-58.

EF-40, 45 (Extremely Fine). *Obverse:* Further wear is seen on all areas, especially the thighs and knees, bosom, and head. Little or no luster is seen. *Reverse:* Further wear is seen on all areas, most noticeably at the leaves to each side of the wreath apex, and on the ribbon bow knot. Leaves retain details except on the higher areas.

1838-O. Graded EF-40.

VF-20, 30 (Very Fine). *Obverse:* Further wear is seen. Most details of the gown are worn away, except in the lower-relief areas above and to the right of the shield. Hair detail is gone on the higher points. *Reverse:* Wear is more extensive. The highest leaves are flat, particularly the larger leaves at the top of the wreath.

1837, Small Date. Graded VF-25.

F-12, 15 (Fine). *Obverse:* The seated figure is well worn, but with some detail above and to the right of the shield. LIBERTY on the shield is fully readable, but weak in areas. *Reverse:* Most detail of the leaves is gone. The rim is worn but remains bold, and most if not all denticles are visible.

1837, Small Date. Graded F-12.

VG-8, 10 (Very Good). *Obverse:* The seated figure is more worn, but some detail can be seen above and to the right of the shield. The shield is discernible. In LIBERTY at least three letters are readable but very weak at VG-8; a few more appear at VG-10. *Reverse:* Further wear has combined the details of most leaves. The rim is complete, but weak in areas. On most coins the reverse appears to be in a slightly higher grade than the obverse.

1837, Large Date. Graded VG-8.

G-4, 6 (Good). *Obverse:* The seated figure is worn smooth. At G-4 there are no letters in LIBERTY remaining. At G-6, traces of one or two can be seen. *Reverse:* Wear is more extensive. The leaves are all combined and in outline form. The rim is clear but well worn and missing in some areas, causing the outer parts of the peripheral letters to be worn away in some instances. On most coins the reverse appears to be in a slightly higher grade than the obverse.

1837, Small Date. Graded G-4.

AG-3 (About Good). *Obverse:* The seated figure is mostly visible in outline form, with no detail. The rim is worn away. The date remains clear. *Reverse:* Many if not most letters are worn away, as are parts of the wreath, though this and the interior letters are discernible. The rim can usually be seen, but is weak.

1837, Small Date. Graded AG-3.

PF-60 to 70 (Proof). *Obverse and Reverse:* Proofs that are extensively cleaned and have many hairlines, or that are dull and grainy, are lower level, such as PF-60 to 62. These are not widely desired, save for the rare (in any grade) date of 1846. Both the half dime and dime Proofs of 1837 were often cleaned, resulting in coins which have lost much of their mirror surface. With medium hairlines and good reflectivity, a grade of PF-64 is

1837, Large Date. Graded PF-67.

assigned, and with relatively few hairlines, gem PF-65. In various grades hairlines are most easily seen in the obverse field. PF-66 should have hairlines so delicate that magnification is needed to see them. Above that, a Proof should be free of such lines.

Illustrated coin: Note the brown tone. Fully mirrored fields are seen when the coin is held at an angle to the light.

1837, Small Date *Note the flat-topped 1.*	**1837, Large Date** *Note the pointed-top 1.*	**No Drapery From Elbow** (1837–1840)	**Drapery From Elbow** (Starting 1840)

	Mintage	Cert	Avg	%MS	G-4	VG-8	F-12	VF-20	EF-40	AU-50	MS-60 PF-60	MS-63 PF-63	MS-65 PF-65
1837, Small Date	1,405,000	49	58.7	69%	$40	$55	$80	$145	$235	$500	$725	$1,100	$3,400
	Auctions: $22,325, MS-67, June 2014; $1,200, MS-64, July 2014; $447, AU-58, October 2014; $120, VF-25, July 2014												
1837, Large Date	(a)	28	63.0	82%	$40	$55	$80	$145	$235	$450	$700	$1,100	$3,000
	Auctions: $12,925, MS-67, October 2014; $19,975, MS-67, November 2013; $4,406, MS-66, August 2014; $400, AU-53, October 2014												
1837, Proof	15–20	10	64.3								$6,500	$14,000	$37,500
	Auctions: $105,750, PF-67, June 2014												
1838O, No Stars	70,000	37	48.5	35%	$90	$150	$235	$550	$850	$1,350	$2,500	$8,500	$30,000
	Auctions: $49,938, MS-66, October 2014; $11,750, MS-64, February 2014; $6,169, MS-63, October 2014; $147, Fair-2, October 2014												

a. Included in 1837, Small Date, mintage figure.

1838, Normal Stars

1838, Small Stars

1840-O, No Drapery,
Normal Reverse
*Note four-leaf cluster
next to DIME.*

1840-O, No Drapery,
Transitional Reverse
*Note three-leaf cluster
next to DIME.*

	Mintage	Cert	Avg	%MS	G-4	VG-8	F-12	VF-20	EF-40	AU-50	MS-60 PF-60	MS-63 PF-63	MS-65 PF-65
1838, No Drapery, Large Stars	2,225,000	716	61.2	78%	$18	$21	$28	$35	$75	$175	$250	$420	$1,700
Auctions: $16,450, MS-68, October 2014; $30,550, MS-68, November 2013; $558, MS-64, October 2014; $176, AU-55, October 2014													
1838, No Drapery, Small Stars	(a)	43	59.0	70%	$22	$30	$55	$100	$185	$360	$560	$1,100	$3,750
Auctions: $3,290, MS-65, October 2014; $3,408, MS-65, March 2013; $764, MS-63, July 2014; $529, AU-55, October 2014													
1838, Proof	4–5	2	64.8								$10,000	$12,500	$50,000
Auctions: $129,250, PF-67, October 2014; $182,125, PF-66, January 2014													
1839, No Drapery	1,069,150	309	60.9	77%	$20	$25	$30	$40	$75	$160	$260	$420	$2,000
Auctions: $4,700, MS-67, April 2013; $4,700, MS-66, July 2014; $881, MS-64, September 2014; $182, AU-55, October 2014													
1839, Proof	5–10	4	64.5								$10,000	$12,500	$37,500
Auctions: $27,600, PF-65Cam, April 2008													
1839O, No Drapery	1,060,000	72	53.1	44%	$20	$25	$30	$40	$80	$170	$525	$1,850	$6,250
Auctions: $2,820, MS-64, June 2014; $317, AU-53, July 2014; $176, AU-50, September 2014; $235, EF-40, October 2014													
1840, No Drapery	1,034,000	298	60.7	78%	$20	$25	$30	$35	$70	$150	$260	$420	$2,000
Auctions: $7,638, MS-67, June 2014; $5,581, MS-66, September 2014; $423, MS-64, October 2014; $118, AU-53, September 2014													
1840, No Drapery, Proof	5–10	3	65.7								$10,000	$12,500	$37,500
Auctions: $30,550, PF-64, April 2014													
1840O, No Drapery	695,000	49	53.4	27%	$20	$23	$30	$40	$85	$285	$725	$2,250	$15,000
Auctions: $18,213, MS-66, June 2014; $141, EF-45, July 2014; $80, VF-25, September 2014													
1840O, No Drapery, Transitional Reverse (b)	100	0	n/a						$800	$1,250	$1,600		
Auctions: $431, F-15, November 2011													
1840, Drapery	310,085	62	59.2	76%	$25	$40	$55	$120	$210	$360	$460	$825	$2,700
Auctions: $19,975, MS-67, June 2014; $411, MS-62, October 2014; $165, AU-50, October 2014; $141, EF-40, July 2014													
1840, Drapery, Proof	(c)	0	n/a										
Auctions: No auction records available.													
1840O, Drapery	240,000	39	47.5	13%	$30	$55	$110	$160	$425	$1,250	$3,100	$8,200	
Auctions: $30,550, MS-63, June 2014; $911, AU-50, July 2014; $734, EF-45, July 2014; $411, VF-35, July 2014													
1841	1,150,000	173	61.3	82%	$16	$20	$30	$35	$75	$160	$210	$325	$1,300
Auctions: $5,434, MS-67, October 2014; $1,177, MS-66, August 2014; $1,998, MS-66, June 2014; $123, AU-53, October 2014													
1841, Proof	10–20	4	64.3								$10,000	$15,000	$45,000
Auctions: $28,200, PF-65, October 2014; $46,000, PF-65, January 2008													
1841O	815,000	52	51.5	29%	$20	$24	$35	$50	$110	$300	$665	$1,525	$6,000
Auctions: $14,688, MS-67, October 2014; $881, AU-53, January 2014; $112, AU-50, September 2014; $358, EF-45, November 2014													

a. Included in 1838, No Drapery, Large Stars, mintage figure. **b.** "This rare transitional variety exhibits large letters and open or split buds on the reverse die, along with a small O mintmark. The key diagnostic of the variety is three-leaf clusters on either side of the word DIME, while the common reverse has four-leaf clusters" (*Cherrypickers' Guide to Rare Die Varieties*, sixth edition, volume II). **c.** The mintage figure is unknown.

1848, Medium Date

1848, Large Date

1849, So-Called 9 Over 6
FS-H10-1849-302.

1849, 9 Over 8
FS-H10-1849-301.

	Mintage	Cert	Avg	%MS	G-4	VG-8	F-12	VF-20	EF-40	AU-50	MS-60	MS-63	MS-65
											PF-60	PF-63	PF-65
1842	815,000	173	60.0	71%	$16	$20	$27	$35	$70	$150	$200	$325	$1,250
Auctions: $940, MS-66, October 2014; $1,293, MS-66, July 2014; $69, AU-55, November 2014; $123, AU-55, September 2014													
1842, Proof	*10–20*	5	65.5								$8,000	$12,000	$26,000
Auctions: $12,075, PF-64, January 2010													
1842O	350,000	36	47.3	25%	$30	$40	$65	$185	$525	$825	$1,275	$2,250	$12,500
Auctions: $588, EF-45, October 2014; $176, EF-45, September 2014; $219, VF-30, December 2011													
1843	1,165,000	225	60.0	72%	$16	$20	$27	$35	$75	$160	$210	$325	$1,400
Auctions: $3,819, MS-67, June 2014; $558, MS-64, August 2014; $188, AU-58, October 2014; $130, AU-55, October 2014													
1843, 1843 Over 1843, Proof	*10–20*	1	67.5								$8,000	$12,000	$26,000
Auctions: $55,813, PF-67, January 2014													
1844	430,000	164	61.8	86%	$16	$20	$27	$35	$75	$160	$210	$325	$1,400
Auctions: $3,055, MS-67, November 2014; $3,525, MS-67, October 2014; $4,113, MS-67, February 2014; $1,116, MS-66, October 2014													
1844, Proof	*15–25*	7	64.4	100%							$8,000	$12,000	$26,000
Auctions: $35,250, PF-67, February 2014; $12,925, PF-64, October 2014													
1844O	220,000	33	39.5	12%	$80	$115	$200	$550	$1,000	$3,000	$5,500	$13,000	$25,000
Auctions: $21,150, MS-65, October 2014; $1,704, AU-50, July 2014; $212, VF-20, October 2014; $94, G-6, September 2014													
1845	1,564,000	209	59.8	71%	$16	$20	$27	$35	$70	$150	$200	$325	$1,250
Auctions: $1,528, MS-66, February 2013; $911, MS-65, October 2014; $282, MS-61, December 2014; $74, AU-55, September 2014													
1845, Proof	*10–15*	6	65.3								$9,000	$14,000	$30,000
Auctions: $64,625, PF-68, January 2014													
1846	27,000	51	31.6	2%	$350	$525	$900	$1,250	$2,750	$4,500	$10,000	$25,000	
Auctions: $23,501, MS-63, June 2014; $32,900, MS-62, October 2014; $3,055, EF-40, July 2014; $2,585, VF-35, October 2014													
1846, Proof	*10–20*	7	65.3								$8,000	$12,000	$26,000
Auctions: $35,250, PF-66, June 2014													
1847	1,274,000	195	59.5	71%	$16	$20	$27	$35	$75	$160	$225	$500	$1,250
Auctions: $3,290, MS-67, October 2014; $7,050, MS-66, November 2013; $219, MS-62, November 2014; $123, AU-53, October 2014													
1847, Proof	*8–12*	3	64.7								$8,000	$12,000	$26,000
Auctions: $38,188, PF-67, October 2014; $36,719, PF-66Cam, April 2014													
1848, Medium Date	668,000	97	57.7	57%	$16	$20	$27	$35	$75	$160	$250	$500	$2,750
Auctions: $3,055, MS-65, June 2013; $182, AU-50, September 2014													
1848, Large Date	**(d)**	34	57.5	53%	$22	$32	$45	$65	$130	$285	$575	$1,600	$3,500
Auctions: $558, MS-61, August 2014; $368, AU-55, December 2013													
1848, Proof	*6–8*	2	65.0								$9,000	$14,000	$45,000
Auctions: $63,250, PF-66, July 2008													
1848O	600,000	75	62.7	87%	$22	$25	$35	$60	$120	$250	$410	$720	$2,200
Auctions: $12,338, MS-67, January 2014													
1849, All kinds	1,309,000												
1849, 9 Over 6 (e)		37	56.3	65%	$25	$35	$40	$60	$125	$225	$500	$1,200	$2,250
Auctions: $2,585, MS-65, June 2014; $200, MS-60, September 2014													
1849, 9 Over Widely Placed 6 (f)		21	54.5	48%	$30	$40	$60	$100	$175	$260	$620	$1,400	$2,750
Auctions: $7,050, MS-67, June 2014; $470, AU-55, August 2014													

d. Included in 1848, Medium Date, mintage figure. **e.** Fivaz and Stanton contend that this is actually a 9 Over 8 overdate (*Cherrypickers' Guide to Rare Die Varieties*, sixth edition, volume II). **f.** The 4 of the date is at least triple punched, with one secondary 4 south and one east of the primary 4. There is also a secondary numeral east of the lower portion of the 9.

	Mintage	Cert	Avg	%MS	G-4	VG-8	F-12	VF-20	EF-40	AU-50	MS-60	MS-63	MS-65
											PF-60	PF-63	PF-65
1849, Normal Date		133	59.0	60%	$20	$25	$30	$40	$75	$160	$235	$520	$1,600
	Auctions: $4,406, MS-67, June 2014; $270, MS-61, November 2014; $188, AU-58, November 2014												
1849, Proof	*8–12*	3	64.7								$8,000	$12,000	$26,000
	Auctions: $22,325, PF-65, June 2014												
1849O	140,000	52	50.3	37%	$30	$40	$85	$220	$475	$1,200	$2,500	$4,200	$12,000
	Auctions: $6,756, MS-65, November 2014; $7,638, MS-65, June 2014; $529, EF-40, October 2014; $212, VF-20, September 2014												
1850	955,000	223	61.8	84%	$18	$22	$28	$40	$70	$160	$220	$350	$1,200
	Auctions: $12,925, MS-68, October 2014; $881, MS-65, October 2014; $427, MS-64, November 2014; $188, AU-58, October 2014												
1850, Proof	*8–12*	4	64.0								$12,000	$20,000	$50,000
	Auctions: $57,500, PF-65, January 2008												
1850O	690,000	65	55.9	54%	$25	$30	$40	$65	$120	$310	$750	$1,650	$4,000
	Auctions: $14,100, MS-66, October 2014; $411, AU-58, July 2014; $341, AU-55, October 2014; $100, AU-53, September 2014												
1851	781,000	156	59.1	75%	$18	$22	$28	$40	$70	$160	$200	$325	$1,200
	Auctions: $9,400, MS-68, April 2013; $823, MS-65, July 2014; $129, AU-55, October 2014												
1851O	860,000	116	57.0	58%	$25	$30	$35	$50	$110	$235	$525	$850	$3,850
	Auctions: $2,644, MS-65, June 2013; $89, AU-55, September 2014; $200, AU-55, July 2014; $94, AU-50, November 2014												
1852	1,000,500	184	62.0	85%	$18	$22	$28	$40	$75	$160	$210	$325	$1,200
	Auctions: $7,050, MS-67, April 2013; $147, AU-55, September 2014												
1852, Proof	*10–15*	8	64.3								$8,000	$12,000	$30,000
	Auctions: $30,550, PF-65, January 2014; $14,100, PF-64, October 2014												
1852O	260,000	52	51.7	38%	$30	$40	$75	$135	$260	$525	$865	$2,000	$8,250
	Auctions: $8,813, MS-66, June 2014; $206, EF-40, October 2014												
1853, No Arrows	135,000	136	60.1	80%	$35	$45	$75	$135	$260	$500	$750	$1,200	$2,500
	Auctions: $12,925, MS-68, October 2014; $2,820, MS-66, October 2013; $1,410, MS-64, October 2014; $470, AU-58, October 2014												
1853O, No Arrows	160,000	31	34.9	6%	$200	$300	$425	$750	$2,250	$3,500	$6,200	$12,500	
	Auctions: $32,900, MS-65, October 2014; $25,850, MS-65, October 2014; $3,819, AU-55, April 2013; $999, VF-25, July 2014												
1853, With Arrows	13,210,020	1,195	58.3	63%	$20	$25	$30	$35	$70	$140	$200	$310	$1,450
	Auctions: $18,800, MS-67, October 2014; $5,728, MS-67, October 2014; $411, MS-64, September 2014; $217, AU-58, November 2014												
1853, With Arrows, Proof (g)	*3–5*	1	64.0								$20,000	$25,000	
	Auctions: No auction records available.												
1853O, With Arrows	2,200,000	95	53.5	47%	$20	$25	$35	$50	$70	$160	$275	$925	$3,500
	Auctions: $16,450, MS-67, October 2014; $27,025, MS-67, April 2014; $7,638, MS-66, October 2014												
1854	5,740,000	613	59.0	72%	$20	$25	$30	$35	$65	$140	$230	$325	$1,500
	Auctions: $9,988, MS-67, August 2013; $1,645, MS-66, September 2014; $411, MS-64, October 2014; $106, AU-58, October 2014												
1854, Proof	*15–25*	10	64.6	100%							$4,750	$8,500	$15,000
	Auctions: $9,694, PF-65, August 2013												
1854O	1,560,000	95	58.5	64%	$20	$24	$35	$45	$75	$155	$285	$775	$3,500
	Auctions: $2,350, MS-65, August 2014; $3,290, MS-65, August 2013; $170, AU-53, December 2014; $94, AU-50, November 2014												
1855	1,750,000	245	60.7	76%	$20	$25	$30	$35	$65	$130	$210	$350	$2,000
	Auctions: $9,400, MS-67, June 2014; $3,819, MS-66, July 2014; $141, AU-53, September 2014; $123, AU-53, November 2014												
1855, Proof	*15–25*	19	65.1								$4,750	$8,500	$15,000
	Auctions: $21,150, PF-66, June 2014; $11,750, PF-65, October 2014												
1855O	600,000	93	59.8	72%	$20	$25	$35	$55	$175	$200	$560	$1,100	$4,200
	Auctions: $25,850, MS-68, June 2014; $3,819, MS-65, July 2014; $558, MS-62, October 2014; $188, EF-45, September 2014												
1856	4,880,000	451	60.3	75%	$18	$22	$25	$35	$65	$130	$185	$320	$1,200
	Auctions: $14,100, MS-68, October 2014; $1,880, MS-66, January 2014; $382, MS-64, September 2014; $153, AU-55, December 2014												
1856, Proof	*40–60*	25	64.7								$2,500	$4,500	$10,000
	Auctions: $9,400, PF-66, October 2014; $10,869, PF-65Cam, June 2013												
1856O	1,100,000	93	56.3	35%	$18	$22	$25	$55	$110	$265	$575	$1,000	$2,350
	Auctions: $5,875, MS-66, October 2014; $1,410, MS-64, August 2014; $558, MS-62, September 2014; $194, AU-50, October 2014												

g. This coin is extremely rare.

1858, Repunched High Date
FS-H10-1858-301.

1858, Over Inverted Date
FS-H10-1858-302.

1860, Obverse of 1859, Reverse of 1860
Transitional pattern, with stars (Judd-247).

	Mintage	Cert	Avg	%MS	G-4	VG-8	F-12	VF-20	EF-40	AU-50	MS-60 / PF-60	MS-63 / PF-63	MS-65 / PF-65
1857	7,280,000	820	60.6	79%	$18	$22	$25	$35	$65	$130	$185	$320	$1,100
Auctions: $3,055, MS-67, October 2014; $5,288, MS-67, September 2014; $188, MS-62, September 2014; $129, AU-55, November 2014													
1857, Proof	*40–60*	29	65.0								$2,200	$3,000	$5,500
Auctions: $21,738, PF-67Cam, January 2014; $7,050, PF-66, August 2014													
1857O	1,380,000	232	58.4	65%	$18	$22	$25	$45	$70	$200	$350	$500	$1,600
Auctions: $4,113, MS-67, April 2014; $1,410, MS-66, September 2014; $456, MS-64, October 2014; $212, AU-58, September 2014													
1858	3,500,000	707	61.4	82%	$18	$22	$25	$35	$65	$130	$185	$320	$1,100
Auctions: $940, MS-66, November 2014; $7,638, MS-66, August 2013; $411, MS-64, July 2014; $91, AU-55, September 2014													
1858, Repunched High Date (h)	(i)	6	43.2	17%	$40	$60	$100	$150	$235	$350	$650	$1,200	$3,000
Auctions: $135, AU-50, November 2014; $65, VF-30, July 2011													
1858, Over Inverted Date (j)	(i)	28	55.9	50%	$40	$60	$100	$150	$220	$325	$625	$1,100	$2,750
Auctions: $7,638, MS-65, February 2014													
1858, Proof	*300*	84	64.1								$850	$1,400	$4,500
Auctions: $4,994, PF-66Cam, October 2014; $6,169, PF-66, June 2014; $2,585, PF-65, October 2014													
1858O	1,660,000	233	60.4	78%	$18	$22	$30	$50	$80	$155	$265	$450	$1,450
Auctions: $11,163, MS-67, June 2014; $1,293, MS-66, October 2014; $441, MS-64, October 2014; $282, MS-63, October 2014													
1859	340,000	248	62.3	86%	$18	$22	$30	$45	$80	$130	$220	$425	$1,250
Auctions: $14,100, MS-68, October 2014; $3,819, MS-67, July 2014; $129, AU-50, October 2014													
1859, Proof	*800*	229	64.1								$550	$1,250	$4,000
Auctions: $10,575, PF-67Cam, October 2014; $12,925, PF-67, March 2013; $7,638, PF-67, October 2014; $1,293, PF-64, November 2014													
1859, Obverse of 1859 (With Stars), Reverse of 1860, Proof (k)	*20*	6	63.5								$19,000	$35,000	$55,000
Auctions: $34,500, PF-63, August 2010													
1859O	560,000	119	61.2	77%	$20	$25	$35	$50	$130	$210	$285	$375	$1,950
Auctions: $2,233, MS-66, October 2014; $2,585, MS-66, July 2014; $165, AU-53, October 2014; $176, AU-53, September 2014													
1860, Obverse of 1859 (With Stars), Reverse of 1860 (l)	*100*	55	64.4	100%							$2,500 / $3,750	$3,000 / $6,000	
Auctions: $5,750, MS-66, February 2012													
1860, Legend on Obverse	798,000	522	62.6	87%	$16	$20	$25	$30	$50	$80	$160	$250	$800
Auctions: $7,050, MS-68, September 2014; $8,225, MS-68, April 2013; $2,820, MS-67, September 2014; $353, MS-64, July 2014													
1860, Proof	1,000	112	64.3								$350	$575	$1,650
Auctions: $2,115, PF-66Cam, July 2014; $$3,290, PF-66Cam, April 2014; 1,528, PF-65Cam, July 2014													
1860O	1,060,000	235	60.4	75%	$16	$20	$25	$30	$50	$100	$200	$320	$950
Auctions: $823, MS-65, November 2014; $382, MS-64, July 2014; $411, MS-63, July 2014; $176, AU-55, October 2014													

h. The date was first punched into the die very high, then corrected and punched into its normal location. The original high-date punch is clearly visible within the upper portions of the primary date. **i.** Included in circulation-strike 1858 mintage figure. **j.** The date was first punched into the die in an inverted orientation, and then corrected. The bases of the secondary digits are evident above the primary digits. **k.** This transitional issue, made surreptitiously at the Mint for a private collector, has the new Liberty Seated die made in the old style of 1859, but with the date of 1860. The reverse is the regular die of 1860, with a cereal wreath. Classified as Judd-267 (*United States Pattern Coins,* tenth edition). **l.** Classified as Judd-232 (*United States Pattern Coins,* tenth edition), this features the obverse design of 1859 and the reverse of 1860.

1861, So-Called 1 Over 0
FS-H10-1861-301.

	Mintage	Cert	Avg	%MS	G-4	VG-8	F-12	VF-20	EF-40	AU-50	MS-60	MS-63	MS-65
											PF-60	PF-63	PF-65
1861	3,360,000	612	59.8	73%	$16	$20	$25	$30	$50	$85	$160	$260	$800
Auctions: $2,350, MS-67, September 2014; $5,875, MS-67, June 2014; $1,763, MS-66, September 2014; $94, AU-55, November 2014													
1861, So-Called 1 Over 0	(m)	0	n/a		$35	$45	$50	$90	$250	$375	$600	$900	$3,000
Auctions: $11,750, MS-67, June 2014; $3,290, MS-66, July 2014; $1,293, MS-64, August 2014; $188, EF-45, November 2014													
1861, Proof	1,000	95	64.4								$350	$575	$1,650
Auctions: $6,169, PF-67, June 2014													
1862	1,492,000	668	62.4	87%	$25	$30	$45	$55	$65	$110	$180	$260	$800
Auctions: $8,813, MS-68, October 2014; $11,163, MS-68, June 2014; $2,233, MS-67, November 2014; $223, MS-61, November 2014													
1862, Proof	550	182	64.4								$350	$575	$1,650
Auctions: $44,063, PF-68Cam, November 2013; $3,966, PF-67Cam, October 2014; $1,528, PF-66Cam, October 2014; $1,410, PF-66, October 2014													
1863	18,000	116	62.0	89%	$160	$185	$235	$300	$475	$625	$725	$950	$1,600
Auctions: $4,406, MS-67, February 2013; $317, VF-30, October 2014; $282, VF-30, July 2014; $217, F-12, July 2014													
1863, Proof	460	182	64.1								$350	$575	$1,650
Auctions: $3,290, PF-67, June 2014; $1,763, PF-66, November 2014; $1,763, PF-65Cam, July 2014													
1863S	100,000	91	60.0	75%	$30	$40	$45	$55	$160	$320	$750	$1,000	$3,000
Auctions: $7,638, MS-65, August 2013; $306, EF-45, October 2014; $400, EF-45, July 2014; $129, VF-35, July 2014													
1864	48,000	46	59.4	80%	$325	$440	$500	$725	$925	$1,100	$1,200	$1,350	$2,450
Auctions: $7,344, MS-67, June 2014; $1,528, EF-40, October 2014; $558, VF-20, August 2014													
1864, Proof	470	142	64.2								$350	$575	$1,650
Auctions: $4,700, PF-67, August 2014; $4,259, PF-67, June 2014													
1864S	90,000	57	54.5	53%	$45	$55	$100	$135	$285	$440	$725	$1,400	$3,750
Auctions: $7,931, MS-67, June 2014; $1,998, MS-64, August 2014; $646, AU-53, October 2014; $206, VF-35, July 2014													
1865	13,000	51	59.1	76%	$275	$340	$425	$550	$675	$750	$850	$1,250	$2,000
Auctions: $8,813, MS-67, October 2014; $2,585, MS-66, August 2014; $1,116, MS-63, December 2013; $852, AU-53, October 2014													
1865, Proof	500	160	64.2								$350	$575	$1,650
Auctions: $9,400, PF-67Cam, March 2014; $3,055, PF-67, October 2014; $3,408, PF-66Cam, October 2014; $541, PF-63, July 2014													
1865S	120,000	51	53.0	39%	$30	$40	$50	$75	$175	$550	$950	$2,100	$4,750
Auctions: $16,450, MS-66, October 2014; $6,463, MS-65, October 2014; $4,406, MS-65, October 2014; $382, EF-45, October 2014													
1866	10,000	61	60.0	82%	$325	$375	$425	$550	$650	$700	$825	$1,200	$2,500
Auctions: $734, AU-55, October 2014; $823, AU-55, August 2014; $1,116, AU-50, December 2013													
1866, Proof	725	165	64.0								$350	$575	$1,650
Auctions: $7,050, PF-67DCam, October 2014; $6,169, PF-66DCam, August 2014; $1,410, PF-65, August 2014; $411, PF-55, October 2014													
1866S	120,000	73	59.2	64%	$30	$40	$50	$65	$160	$375	$475	$950	$3,500
Auctions: $441, AU-55, November 2013; $282, AU-50, October 2014; $170, EF-45, October 2014; $141, EF-40, July 2014													
1867	8,000	86	60.4	85%	$450	$525	$625	$750	$850	$925	$1,100	$1,400	$2,000
Auctions: $14,100, MS-67, June 2014; $2,350, MS-65, July 2014; $940, AU-53, October 2014; $505, VG-8, July 2014													
1867, Proof	625	221	64.5								$350	$575	$1,650
Auctions: $8,813, PF-68, January 2014; $4,406, PF-67Cam, October 2014; $1,880, PF-66Cam, August 2014; $793, PF-64, October 2014													
1867S	120,000	64	58.0	59%	$25	$35	$50	$65	$160	$325	$575	$1,200	$3,200
Auctions: $8,225, MS-66, June 2014; $382, AU-55, October 2014; $100, EF-40, September 2014													

m. Included in circulation-strike 1861 mintage figure.

1872, Doubled-Die Obverse
FS-H10-1872-101.

	Mintage	Cert	Avg	%MS	G-4	VG-8	F-12	VF-20	EF-40	AU-50	MS-60	MS-63	MS-65
											PF-60	PF-63	PF-65
1868	88,600	76	61.6	87%	$55	$65	$120	$185	$325	$475	$675	$900	$1,700
Auctions: $7,051, MS-67, October 2014; $4,406, MS-67, June 2014; $940, MS-64, August 2014; $441, AU-58, October 2014													
1868, Proof	600	172	64.1								$350	$575	$1,650
Auctions: $11,163, PF-67DCam, April 2014; $4,818, PF-67Cam, November 2014; $3,819, PF-67, October 2014; $2,350, PF-66Cam, October 2014													
1868S	280,000	140	61.3	71%	$16	$20	$30	$35	$45	$130	$320	$600	$2,200
Auctions: $6,464, MS-66, October 2014; $441, MS-63, November 2014; $353, AU-58, July 2014; $200, AU-55, October 2014													
1869	208,000	104	62.8	87%	$16	$20	$30	$35	$45	$160	$260	$400	$1,100
Auctions: $2,950, MS-67, October 2014; $1,763, MS-66, February 2013; $1,410, MS-65, August 2014; $188, MS-60, December 2014													
1869, Proof	600	215	64.3								$350	$575	$1,650
Auctions: $2,820, PF-67Cam, October 2014; $2,585, PF-67, September 2014; $1,293, PF-65, July 2014; $470, PF-60, November 2014													
1869S	230,000	85	61.9	84%	$16	$20	$30	$35	$45	$130	$320	$800	$3,750
Auctions: $1,528, MS-64, October 2014; $1,763, MS-64, March 2014; $295, AU-55, October 2014													
1870	535,000	276	60.9	81%	$16	$20	$25	$30	$45	$80	$150	$275	$900
Auctions: $5,288, MS-67, July 2014; $10,575, MS-67, June 2014; $646, MS-64, August 2014; $112, AU-58, October 2014													
1870, Proof	1,000	182	64.3								$350	$575	$1,650
Auctions: $7,050, PF-68, June 2014; $2,115, PF-66Cam, September 2014; $2,350, PF-66Cam, July 2014; $1,528, PF-66, November 2014													
1870S † (n)		1	63.0	100%								$1,250,000	
Auctions: $661,250, MS-63, July 2004													
1871	1,873,000	460	61.2	77%	$16	$20	$25	$30	$45	$80	$150	$275	$900
Auctions: $4,553, MS-67, October 2014; $1,998, MS-66, June 2013; $159, MS-62, October 2014; $129, AU-58, July 2014													
1871, Proof	960	203	63.6								$350	$575	$1,650
Auctions: $2,820, PF-67Cam, October 2014; $4,406, PF-67, October 2014; $646, PF-64, July 2014; $403, PF-63, April 2012													
1871S	161,000	115	60.8	69%	$18	$22	$32	$65	$80	$180	$310	$500	$2,200
Auctions: $3,055, MS-66, October 2014; $170, AU-58, August 2014; $99, AU-50, October 2014; $141, AU-50, July 2014													
1872	2,947,000	395	60.7	76%	$16	$20	$25	$30	$45	$80	$150	$275	$900
Auctions: $1,880, MS-67, September 2014; $2,585, MS-66, February 2013; $135, MS-62, July 2014; $94, AU-58, September 2014													
1872, DblDie Obv (o)	(p)	9	43.2	0%					$200	$300	$550	$800	
Auctions: $89, EF-45, August 2011													
1872, Proof	950	175	64.2								$350	$575	$1,650
Auctions: $3,819, PF-67Cam, July 2014; $4,313, PF-67, December 2011; $1,528, PF-66Cam, October 2014; $1,175, PF-65Cam, July 2014													
1872S, All kinds	837,000												
1872S, Mintmark above bow		163	61.9	82%	$20	$25	$30	$45	$60	$80	$150	$275	$800
Auctions: $3,055, MS-67, November 2013; $1,058, MS-66, October 2014; $200, AU-58, October 2014; $95, AU-55, October 2014													
1872S, Mintmark below bow		149	62.0	81%	$20	$25	$30	$45	$60	$80	$150	$275	$800
Auctions: $2,820, MS-67, October 2014; $1,763, MS-66, April 2013; $188, MS-62, October 2014; $159, AU-58, September 2014													
1873, Close 3 (q)	712,000	137	59.8	75%	$16	$20	$25	$30	$45	$80	$150	$275	$900
Auctions: $8,225, MS-67, June 2014; $881, MS-66, November 2014; $270, MS-63, October 2014; $94, AU-55, September 2014													
1873, Proof	600	239	64.3								$350	$575	$1,650
Auctions: $11,163, PF-67DCam, January 2014; $558, PF-64, October 2014													
1873S Close 3 (q)	324,000	251	62.6	87%	$16	$20	$25	$30	$45	$80	$150	$275	$800
Auctions: $5,875, MS-67, June 2014; $646, MS-65, October 2014; $382, MS-64, July 2014; $129, AU-58, October 2014													

† Ranked in the *100 Greatest U.S. Coins* (fourth edition). **n.** The 1870-S coin is unique. **o.** "Doubling is evident on UNITED STATES OF AMERICA and on most elements of Miss Liberty. AMERICA is the strongest point" (*Cherrypickers' Guide to Rare Die Varieties*, sixth edition, volume II). **p.** Included in circulation-strike 1872 mintage figure. **q.** Close 3 only.

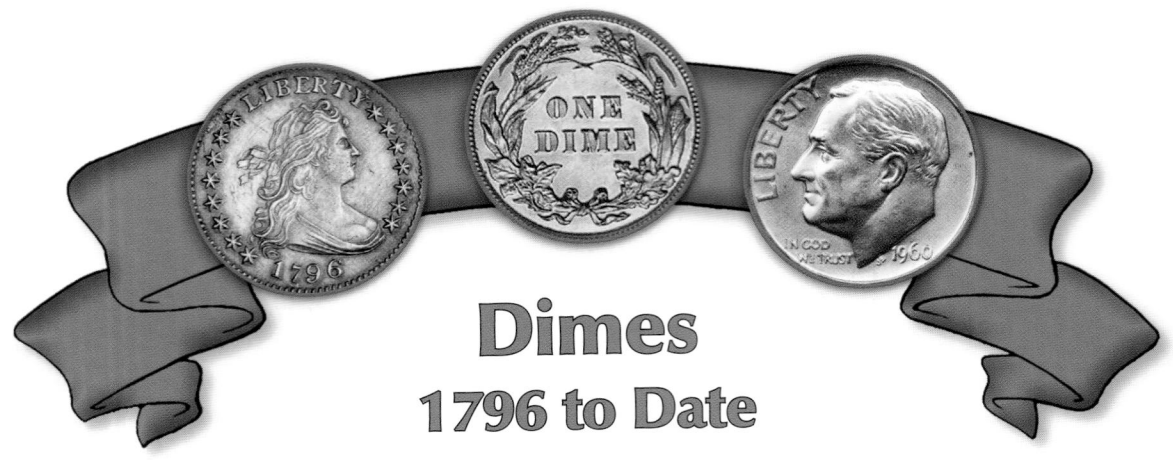

Dimes
1796 to Date

AN OVERVIEW OF DIMES

A collection of dimes ranging from 1796 to date includes many interesting issues. As a type, none are super-rare, but earlier types, combining low mintages with commonly weak striking, can be a challenge for the collector.

The 1796–1797 dime with Draped Bust obverse, Small Eagle reverse, is the rarest of the dime types by far, with fewer than 50,000 pieces minted. These hail from an era in which there was no numismatic interest in saving such coins. Finding a choice example in whatever grade desired will require time and effort.

Then comes the Draped Bust obverse, Heraldic Eagle reverse type, made from 1798 through 1807 (except for 1799). Today these are available easily enough in circulated grades, but are elusive in Mint State. Nearly all are lightly struck—another challenge. Capped Bust dimes of the 1809–1828 years also require connoisseurship to locate a sharply struck specimen. For all of these early types some compromise with perfection is required.

Later Capped Bust dimes of 1828 to 1837 can be found well struck, as can be the later variations within the Liberty Seated type. Barber, Mercury, and Roosevelt dimes are easy to find in just about any grade desired.

Proofs are most readily available from the Liberty Seated era to the present and are sometimes included in type sets, usually answering the call for sharply struck pieces, as most (but not all) were made with care.

FOR THE COLLECTOR AND INVESTOR: DIMES AS A SPECIALTY

Dimes have been a very popular denomination to collect on a systematic basis. Generally, interest is separated into different eras. Those of the early years, the Draped Bust and Capped Bust issues, 1796 to 1837, are enthusiastically sought not only for dates and major varieties (as, for example, those listed in the charts to follow), but also by more rarefied die varieties. Aficionados use the book *Early United States Dimes, 1796–1837*, whose listings are by JR numbers, for John Reich, the

Chief Engraver John R. Sinnock's first design for the Roosevelt dime was turned down, but his subsequent engraving was accepted. The dime was chosen to honor Franklin D. Roosevelt shortly after his death.

designer of the Capped Bust silver issues. The John Reich Collectors Society (www.jrcs.org), publisher of the *John Reich Journal*, serves as a forum for the exchange of ideas and new information.

Among early varieties, the 1796; 1797, 16 Stars; and 1797, 13 Stars, are each rare in all grades. Dimes with the Heraldic Eagle reverse, 1798–1807, are generally scarce, but not prohibitively rare, although Mint State coins are elusive. Among the reverse dies some were shared with contemporary quarter eagles of like design and diameter—feasible as there is no indication of denomination on them. Indeed, there was no mark of value on any dime until 1809.

Among Classic Head dimes of the 1809–1828 years, the 1822 is the key date and is especially rare in high grades. Among the modified Classic Head dimes of 1829–1837, all varieties listed in this book are available without difficulty. An example of how a newly discovered variety can be considered unique or exceedingly rare, and later be recognized as plentiful, is provided by the 1830, 30 Over 29, overdate, first publicized by Don Taxay in 1970 in *Scott's Comprehensive Catalogue of United States Coinage* (cover-dated 1971). The overdate was then considered one of a kind, but since then dozens more have been identified.

Liberty Seated dimes of the various varieties have been a popular specialty over a long period of time. There are no impossible rarities except for the unique 1873-CC, Without Arrows, but certain other varieties are very hard to find, including the Carson City issues of the early 1870s.

Barber dimes can be collected by date and mint from 1892 to 1916, except for the 1894-S, of which only 24 are believed to have been struck, with only about 10 accounted for today. The other Barber varieties range from common to scarce. Mercury dimes, 1916–1945, have an enthusiastic following. The key issues are 1916-D (in particular); 1921; 1921-D; 1942, 2 Over 1; and 1942-D, 2 Over 1. Roosevelt dimes from 1946 to date can easily be collected by date and mint and are very popular.

DRAPED BUST, SMALL EAGLE REVERSE (1796–1797)

Designer: *Probably Gilbert Stuart.* **Engraver:** *Robert Scot.*
Weight: *2.70 grams.* **Composition:** *.8924 silver, .1076 copper.*
Diameter: *Approximately 19 mm.* **Edge:** *Reeded.* **Mint:** *Philadelphia.*

John Reich-2.

History. Dimes were first minted for circulation in 1796. There are no records of publicity surrounding their debut. The coins featured the Draped Bust obverse, as used on cents and other silver coins, combined with the Small Eagle reverse. Some 1796 dimes exhibit prooflike surfaces, suggesting that they may have been "presentation pieces," but no records exist to confirm this possibility.

Striking and Sharpness. Most dimes of this type have weakness or problems in one area or another, usually more so on those dated 1797. Points to check for sharpness include the hair of Miss Liberty, the drapery lines on the bust, the centers of the stars, and, on the reverse, the breast and wing feathers of the eagle. Also check for adjustment marks. A sharply struck coin is a goal, not necessarily a reality. Sharp striking and excellent eye appeal add dramatically to the value.

Availability. This is the rarest and most expensive type in the dime series. Within any desired grade, examples should be selected with great care, as many have problems of one sort or another. MS coins are especially rare; when seen they are usually dated 1796. Dimes of 1797 are much rarer in all grades, and nearly impossible to find in MS-63 or finer.

GRADING STANDARDS

MS-60 to 70 (Mint State). *Obverse:* At MS-60, some abrasion and contact marks are evident, most noticeably on the cheek, the drapery, and the right field. Luster is present, but may be dull or lifeless, and interrupted in patches. At MS-63, contact marks are very few, and abrasion is hard to detect except under magnification, although this type is sometimes graded liberally due to its rarity. An MS-65 coin has no abrasion, and contact

1796; JR-4. Graded MS-61.

marks are so minute as to require magnification. Luster should be full and rich. Coins graded above MS-65 are more theoretical than actual for this type—but they do exist, and are defined by having fewer marks as perfection is approached. *Reverse:* Comments apply as for the obverse, except that abrasion and marks are most noticeable on the eagle at the center, a situation complicated by the fact that this area was sometimes lightly struck. The field area is small and is protected by lettering and the wreath, and in any given grade shows fewer marks than on the obverse.

Illustrated coin: This coin is significantly above average in strike, but shows numerous contact marks in the right obverse field. The luster is especially rich on the reverse.

AU-50, 53, 55, 58 (About Uncirculated). *Obverse:* Light wear is seen on the hair area above the ear and extending to left of the forehead, on the ribbon, and on the bosom, more so at AU-50 than at 53 or 55. An AU-58 coin has minimal traces of wear. An AU-50 coin has luster in protected areas among the stars and letters, with little in the open fields or on the portrait. At AU-58, most luster is present in the fields, but is worn away on the

1796; JR-4. Graded AU-50.

highest parts of the motifs. Generally, grading guidelines for this dime type follow those of the related half dimes. *Reverse:* Light wear is seen on the eagle's body (keep in mind that the higher parts of this area might be lightly struck) and the edges of the wings. Light wear is seen on the wreath and lettering. Luster is the best key to actual wear. This ranges from perhaps 20% remaining in protected areas (at AU-50) to nearly full mint bloom (at AU-58).

Illustrated coin: This coin is attractive overall. Some scattered marks are evident, and it possibly was cleaned long ago and retoned.

EF-40, 45 (Extremely Fine). *Obverse:* More wear is evident on the upper hair area and the ribbon, and on the drapery and bosom. Excellent detail remains in low-relief areas of the hair. The stars show wear as do the date and letters. Luster, if present at all, is minimal and in protected areas. *Reverse:* The eagle shows more wear, this being the focal point to check. Many feathers remain on the

1797, 16 Stars; JR-1. Graded EF-40.

interior areas of the wings. Additional wear is on the wreath and letters, but many details are present. Some luster may be seen in protected areas, and if present is slightly more abundant than on the obverse.

Illustrated coin: Note some adjustment marks in and behind the hair.

VF-20, 30 (Very Fine). *Obverse:* The higher-relief areas of hair are well worn at VF-20, less so at VF-30. The drapery and bosom show extensive wear. The stars have more wear, making them appear larger (an optical illusion seen on most worn silver coins of this era). *Reverse:* The body of the eagle shows few if any feathers, while the wings have about half of the feathers visible, depending on the strike. At VF-30 more than half of the

1796; JR-1. Graded VF-20.

feathers may show. The leaves lack most detail and are in outline form. Scattered, non-disfiguring marks are normal for this and lower grades. Any major defects should be noted separately.

Illustrated coin: Note the thin scratch from star 5 to the back of the head, and a tiny planchet flaw in front of the forehead. This is a late state of the obverse die, with a large cud break at lower left.

F-12, 15 (Fine). *Obverse:* Wear is more extensive than on a Very Fine coin, particularly noticeable on the hair, face, and bosom, and the stars appear larger. About half the hair detail remains, most noticeably behind the neck and shoulder. The rim may be partially worn away and blend into the field. *Reverse:* Wear is more extensive. Now, feather details are diminished, with fewer than half remaining on the wings. The wreath

1797, 16 Stars. Graded F-12.

and lettering are worn further, and the rim is usually weak in areas, although some denticles can be seen.

VG-8, 10 (Very Good). *Obverse:* The portrait is mostly seen in outline form, with most hair strands gone, although there is some definition at the back of the hair and behind the shoulder. The ear is discernible, as is the eye. The stars appear larger still, again an illusion. The rim is weak in areas. LIBERTY and the date are readable and usually full, although some letters may be weak at their tops. *Reverse:* The eagle is mostly an outline

1797, 13 Stars. Graded VG-10.

with parts blending into the field (on lighter strikes). The rim is worn, as are the letters, with some weak, but the motto is readable.

G-4, 6 (Good). *Obverse:* Wear is more extensive, and some stars may be partly missing. The head is an outline. The eye is visible only in outline form. The rim is well worn or even missing in areas. LIBERTY is worn, and parts of some letters may be missing, but elements of all should be readable. The date is readable, but worn. *Reverse:* The eagle is flat and discernible in outline form, and may be blending into the field. The wreath is well worn. Some of the letters may be partly missing. At this level some "averaging" can be done. If the letters are stronger than usual in one area, but some are missing in another area, the coin can still qualify as G-4.

Illustrated coin: This is a late die state, with a cud break at lower-left obverse. The reverse, if graded alone, would be higher than G-6.

1796; JR-1. Graded G-6.

AG-3 (About Good). *Obverse:* Wear is so extensive that the coin is barely identifiable. The head is in outline form. LIBERTY is mostly gone, same for the stars. The date, while readable, may be partially worn away. *Reverse:* The reverse is well worn with parts of the wreath and lettering missing.

Illustrated coin: This is a late die state, with a cud break at lower-left obverse.

1796; JR-1. Graded AG-3.

| | | | | **1797, 16 Stars** | | **1797, 13 Stars** | | | | | | |

	Mintage	Cert	Avg	%MS	AG-3	G-4	VG-8	F-12	VF-20	EF-40	AU-50	MS-60	MS-63
1796	22,135	253	50.0	42%	$1,000	$2,200	$3,400	$4,800	$7,000	$11,500	$15,000	$25,000	$40,000 (a)
	Auctions: $793,125, MS-68, August 2014; $881,250, MS-67, June 2014; $617, Fair-2, October 2014; $529, Fair-1, July 2014												
1797, All kinds	25,261												
1797, 16 Stars		19	45.1	37%	$1,100	$2,500	$3,750	$5,250	$7,500	$12,000	$18,000	$35,000	$47,500
	Auctions: $35,250, MS-62, April 2014												
1797, 13 Stars		20	29.9	5%	$1,200	$2,800	$4,000	$5,500	$8,000	$13,500	$20,000	$55,000	$80,000
	Auctions: $38,188, AU-58, April 2014												

a. Value in MS-65 is $85,000.

DRAPED BUST, HERALDIC EAGLE REVERSE (1798–1807)

Designer: *Robert Scot.* **Weight:** *2.70 grams.* **Composition:** *.8924 silver, .1076 copper.*
Diameter: *Approximately 19 mm.* **Edge:** *Reeded.* **Mint:** *Philadelphia.*

JR-3.

History. Dimes of this style were minted each year from 1798 to 1807 (with the exception of 1799 and 1805). The designs follow those of other silver coins of the era.

Striking and Sharpness. Nearly all have one area or another of light striking. On the obverse, check the hair details and drapery lines, and the star centers. On the reverse, the upper right of the shield and the adjacent part of the eagle's wing often are soft, and several or even most stars may be lightly defined (sharp stars show sharply peaked centers); high parts of the clouds are often weak. Denticles are likely to be weak or missing in areas on either side. Expect to compromise on the strike; a sharply struck coin is a goal, not necessarily a reality. Certain reverse dies of this type were also used to coin quarter eagles. Sharp striking and excellent eye appeal dramatically add to a Draped Bust dime's value, this being particularly true for the dates most often seen in MS: 1805 and 1807 (which are usually weakly struck, especially 1807).

Availability. Although certain die varieties are rare, the basic years are available, with 1805 and 1807 being the most often seen. As a class, MS coins are rare. Again, when seen they are usually dated 1805 or 1807, and have areas of striking weakness. Coins of 1801 through 1804 are scarce in VF and higher grades, very scarce in AU and better.

GRADING STANDARDS

MS-60 to 70 (Mint State). *Obverse:* At MS-60 some abrasion and contact marks are evident, most noticeably on the cheek, the drapery at the shoulder, and the right field. Luster is present, but may be dull or lifeless, and interrupted in patches. At MS-63, contact marks are very few, and abrasion is hard to detect except under magnification. An MS-65 coin has no abrasion, and contact marks are so minute as to require magnifica-

1805, 4 Berries in Branch; JR-2. Graded MS-66.

tion. Luster should be full and rich. Coins graded above MS-65 are more theoretical than actual for this type—but they do exist, and are defined by having fewer marks as perfection is approached. *Reverse:* Comments apply as for the obverse, except that abrasion and marks are most noticeable on the eagle's neck, the tips of the wing, and the tail. The field area is complex, without much open space, given the stars above the eagle, the arrows and olive branch, and other features. Accordingly, marks are not as noticeable as on the obverse.

Illustrated coin: Some planchet adjustment marks at the left obverse are not particularly noticeable at a casual glance. The reverse shows some strike weakness on the stars above and to the left of the eagle's beak and on the horizontal stripes on the shield, particularly to the right. For an 1805 dime this is an above-average strike.

AU-50, 53, 55, 58 (About Uncirculated).
Obverse: Light wear is seen on the hair area above the ear and extending to left of the forehead, on the ribbon, and on the drapery at the shoulder, more so at AU-50 than at 53 or 55. An AU-58 coin has minimal traces of wear. An AU-50 coin has luster in protected areas among the stars and letters, with little in the open fields or on the portrait. At AU-58, most luster is present in the fields,

1802; JR-2. Graded AU-50.

but is worn away on the highest parts of the motifs. *Reverse:* Comments as preceding, except that the eagle's neck, the tips and top of the wings, the clouds, and the tail now show noticeable wear, as do other features. As always, a familiarity with a given die variety will help differentiate striking weakness from actual wear. Luster ranges from perhaps 20% remaining in protected areas (at AU-50) to nearly full mint bloom (at AU-58). Often the reverse of this type will retain much more luster than the obverse.

Illustrated coin: Note some marks below the Y in LIBERTY.

EF-40, 45 (Extremely Fine). *Obverse:* More wear is evident on the upper hair area and the ribbon and on the drapery and bosom. Excellent detail remains in low-relief areas of the hair. The stars show wear, as do the date and letters. Luster, if present at all, is minimal and in protected areas. *Reverse:* The neck lacks feather detail on its highest points. Feathers have lost some detail near the edges of the wings, and some areas of the horizontal lines

1800; JR-2. Graded EF-40.

in the shield may be blended together, particularly at the right (an area that is also susceptible to weak striking). Some traces of luster may be seen, more so at EF-45 than at EF-40.

Illustrated coin: Note two small digs on the bosom and scattered other marks.

VF-20, 30 (Very Fine). *Obverse:* The higher-relief areas of hair are well worn at VF-20, less so at VF-30. The drapery and bosom show extensive wear. The stars have more wear, making them appear larger (an optical illusion seen on most worn silver coins of this era). *Reverse:* Wear is greater, including on the shield and wing feathers. Star centers are flat. Other areas have lost detail, as well. E PLURIBUS UNUM is complete (this incuse feature tended to wear away slowly).

1801; JR-1. Graded VF-20.

Illustrated coin: Here is a problem-free example with normal wear for this grade.

F-12, 15 (Fine). *Obverse:* Wear is more extensive than on a Very Fine coin, particularly noticeable on the hair, face, and bosom, and the stars appear larger. About half the hair detail remains, most noticeably behind the neck and shoulder. The rim may be partially worn away and blend into the field. *Reverse:* Wear is even more extensive, with the shield and wing feathers being points to observe. About half of the feathers are visible

1807; JR-1. Graded F-12.

(depending on striking). E PLURIBUS UNUM may have a few letters worn away. The clouds all seem to be connected. The stars are weak. Parts of the border and lettering may be weak.

   Illustrated coin: This is one of the more readily available die varieties of the type; nearly always weakly struck, but at F-12 this is not as important as it would be in higher grades.

VG-8, 10 (Very Good). *Obverse:* The portrait is mostly seen in outline form, with most hair strands gone, although there is some definition at the back of the hair and behind the shoulder. The ear may be discernible. The eye is evident. The stars appear larger still, again an illusion. The rim is weak in areas. LIBERTY and the date are readable and usually full, although some letters may be weak at their tops. *Reverse:* Half or so of the

1802; JR-4. Graded VG-10.

letters in the motto are worn away. Most feathers are worn away, although separation of some may be seen. Some stars are faint. The border blends into the field in areas, and some letters are weak. Sharpness can vary widely depending on the die variety. At this level, grading by the obverse first, then checking the reverse, is recommended.

   Illustrated coin: This coin has a dig on the obverse near star 2, a few other marks (not unusual for the grade), and attractive iridescent toning.

G-4, 6 (Good). *Obverse:* Some stars may be partly missing. The head is an outline. The eye is visible only in outline form. The rim is well worn or even missing in areas. LIBERTY is worn, and parts of some letters may be missing, but elements of all should be readable. The date is readable, but worn. *Reverse:* The upper part of the eagle is flat, and feathers are noticeable at the lower edge of the wing. Some scattered feather detail may or may not be seen. The

1798, Large 8; JR-4. Graded G-4.

upper part of the shield is flat or nearly so, depending on the variety. Only a few letters of the motto can be seen, although this depends on the variety. The rim is worn extensively, and a few letters may be missing.

   Illustrated coin: This is a late state of the obverse die, with cracks in the right field. Due to the original relief of the dies of this particular specimen, the reverse is better defined than the obverse and is a candidate for VG. On some other dimes the opposite can be true.

AG-3 (About Good). *Obverse:* Wear is very extensive, and some stars and letters are extremely weak or missing entirely. The date is readable. *Reverse:* Extensive wear is seen overall, with the rim worn away and some areas worn smooth. The eagle can be discerned in outline form, but not necessarily completely. A few stray motto letters may remain. Sometimes the obverse can be exceedingly worn (but the date must be readable) and the reverse with more detail, or vice-versa.

1805, 4 Berries in Branch; JR-2. Graded AG-3.

Illustrated coin: This coin has extensive wear overall, but is remarkably free of marks and problems for this low grade.

1798, 8 Over 7

1798, 8 Over 7, 16 Stars on Reverse

1798, 8 Over 7, 13 Stars on Reverse

1798, Large 8

1798, Small 8

	Mintage	Cert	Avg	%MS	AG-3	G-4	VG-8	F-12	VF-20	EF-40	AU-50	MS-60	MS-63
1798, All kinds	27,550												
1798, 8 Over 7, 16 Stars on Reverse		51	53.3	61%	$350	$800	$1,200	$1,500	$2,500	$3,500	$5,250	$9,000	$20,000
	Auctions: $88,125, MS-65, November 2013												
1798, 8 Over 7, 13 Stars on Reverse		7	44.9	43%	$350	$1,000	$2,200	$4,250	$7,000	$10,000	$20,000	$55,000	
	Auctions: $58,750, MS-62, January 2014												
1798, Large 8		23	47.5	30%	$325	$750	$1,000	$1,500	$2,500	$3,750	$4,750	$8,000	$20,000 **(a)**
	Auctions: $70,500, MS-63, June 2014; $499, AG-3, August 2014												
1798, Small 8		4	33.3	25%	$350	$800	$1,100	$1,750	$3,500	$5,500	$12,500	$25,000	$40,000
	Auctions: $103,500, MS-64, January 2012												
1800	21,760	51	41.2	14%	$325	$750	$1,000	$1,500	$3,000	$4,000	$8,000	$22,500	$42,000
	Auctions: $352,500, MS-66, June 2014; $259, Fair-2, October 2014												
1801	34,640	36	32.7	17%	$325	$750	$1,100	$2,000	$3,750	$6,000	$11,000	$30,000	$48,500
	Auctions: $4,406, VF-25, February 2014; $411, Fair-2, August 2014												
1802	10,975	38	33.5	16%	$500	$1,500	$2,000	$3,000	$5,000	$10,000	$17,500	$35,000	
	Auctions: $67,563, MS-62, September 2013												
1803	33,040	33	30.1	12%	$350	$800	$1,250	$1,800	$3,200	$6,000	$11,500	$48,000	
	Auctions: $35,250, AU-53, August 2013; $823, Fair-2, November 2014												

a. Value in MS-65 is $50,000.

1804, 13 Stars on Reverse

1804, 14 Stars on Reverse

1805, 4 Berries

1805, 5 Berries

	Mintage	Cert	Avg	%MS	AG-3	G-4	VG-8	F-12	VF-20	EF-40	AU-50	MS-60	MS-63
1804, All kinds	8,265												
1804, 13 Stars on Reverse		2	55.0	0%	$750	$2,000	$4,000	$8,500	$15,000	$30,000	$60,000		
Auctions: $48,175, EF-45, April 2013													
1804, 14 Stars on Reverse		7	34.7	14%	$800	$2,250	$4,250	$9,000	$20,000	$50,000	$100,000		
Auctions: $367,188, MS-63, April 2013													
1805, All kinds	120,780												
1805, 4 Berries		269	42.2	39%	$250	$600	$900	$1,400	$2,000	$3,000	$4,000	$7,500	$14,000 (b)
Auctions: $49,938, MS-66, April 2014													
1805, 5 Berries		38	36.6	26%	$250	$600	$900	$1,400	$2,200	$3,400	$4,500	$9,000	$20,000
Auctions: $1,998, VF-20, June 2013													
1807	165,000	269	45.1	38%	$250	$550	$850	$1,300	$2,000	$2,750	$3,800	$6,500	$12,500 (c)
Auctions: $55,813, MS-65, June 2014; $2,587, AU-53, August 2014; $317, G-4, October 2014													

b. Value in MS-65 is $40,000. **c.** Value in MS-65 is $38,500.

CAPPED BUST (1809–1837)

Variety 1, Wide Border (1809–1828): **Designer:** *John Reich.*
Weight: *2.70 grams.* **Composition:** *.8924 silver, .1076 copper.*
Diameter: *Approximately 18.8 mm.* **Edge:** *Reeded.* **Mint:** *Philadelphia.*

Variety 1, Wide Border (1809–1828)
JR-1.

Variety 1, Wide Border, Proof
JR-12.

Variety 2, Modified Design (1828–1837): **Designer:** *John Reich.*
Weight: *2.70 grams (changed to 2.67 grams, .900 fine in 1837).*
Composition: *.8924 silver, .1076 copper.*
Diameter: *Approximately 18.5 mm.* **Edge:** *Reeded.* **Mint:** *Philadelphia.*

Variety 2, Modified Design (1828–1837)
JR-7.

Variety 2, Modified Design, Proof
JR-4.

History. The wide-border dimes were struck intermittently from 1809 to 1828. The design, by John Reich, closely follows that inaugurated with the Capped Bust half dollars of 1807. New equipment at the U.S. Mint was used to make the 1828, Small Date, dimes, and those subsequent. The slightly modified design includes smaller denticles or beads in the border and other minor differences, and they are of uniform diameter. The 2 in the 1828, Small Date, dime has a square (not curled) base.

Striking and Sharpness. Many if not most Wide Border dimes have areas of light striking. On the obverse, check the star centers, the hair details, and the drapery at the bosom. On the reverse, check the eagle, especially the area in and around the upper right of the shield. Denticles are sometimes weak, but are usually better defined on the reverse than on the obverse. The height of the rims on both sides can vary, and coins with a low rim or rims tend to show wear more quickly. Most dimes of the modified design (Variety 2) are fairly well struck, with fewer irregularities of strike than those of 1809 to 1828. On the obverse, check the hair and the brooch. The stars usually are sharp, but don't overlook them. On the reverse, check the details of the eagle. The denticles usually are sharp.

Availability. There are no extremely rare dates in this series, so all are available to collectors, but certain die varieties range from rare to extremely rare. In MS, most are scarce and some rare. The dates of the early 1830s to 1835 are the most readily available. Those exhibiting a strong strike, with Full Details, command a premium, especially the earlier dates. Most have nice eye appeal.

Proofs. Proof Capped Bust dimes of 1809 to 1828 were struck in small numbers, likely mostly as part of presentation sets. As is the case with any and all early Proofs, you should insist on a coin with deeply and fully (not partially) mirrored surfaces, well struck, and with good contrast. Carefully examine deeply toned pieces (deep toning can mask the true nature of a coin, e.g., if it is not a true Proof, or if it has been cleaned or repaired). More than just a few pieces attributed as "Proofs" are not Proofs at all. Proofs were made of each year from 1828 to 1837 and are rare. Beware of "Proofs" that have deeply toned surfaces or fields that show patches of mint frost. Buy slowly and carefully.

GRADING STANDARDS

MS-60 to 70 (Mint State). *Obverse:* The rims are more uniform for the 1828–1837 variety than for the 1809–1828 variety, striking is usually very sharp, and any abrasion occurs evenly on both sides. At MS-60 some abrasion and contact marks are evident, most noticeably on the cheek and on the area near the drapery clasp. Luster is present, but may be dull or lifeless, and interrupted in patches. At MS-63, contact marks are very few, and

1814, Small Date; JR-1. Graded MS-66.

abrasion is hard to detect except under magnification. An MS-65 coin has no abrasion, and contact marks are so minute as to require magnification. Luster should be full and rich. Grades above MS-65 are seen now and again, and are defined by having fewer marks as perfection is approached. *Reverse:* Comments apply as for the obverse, except that abrasion and contact marks are most noticeable on the eagle's neck, the top of the wings, the claws, and the flat band that surrounds the incuse motto. The field is mainly protected by design elements and does not show abrasion as much as does the obverse.

Illustrated coin: This coin is sharply struck at the centers, and lightly struck on some stars, border areas, and denticles. It has deep, rich mint luster.

AU-50, 53, 55, 58 (About Uncirculated). *Obverse:* The rims are more uniform for the 1828–1837 variety than for the 1809–1828 variety, striking is usually very sharp, and any abrasion occurs evenly on both sides. Light wear is seen on the cap, the hair below LIBERTY, the hair near the clasp, and the drapery at the bosom. At AU-58, the luster is extensive except in the open area of the field, especially to the right. At AU-50 and 53, lus-

1823, 3 Over 2, Small E's in Legend; JR-1. Graded AU-50.

ter remains only in protected areas. As is true of all high grades, sharpness of strike can affect the perception of wear. *Reverse:* Wear is evident on the eagle's neck, the top of the wings, and the claws. An AU-58 has nearly full luster. At AU-50 and 53, there still is significant luster, more than on the obverse.

Illustrated coin: This coin shows some tiny adjustment marks (scarcely visible). It is lightly struck at the center, and grading was mostly done by observing the luster.

EF-40, 45 (Extremely Fine). *Obverse:* The rims are more uniform for the 1828–1837 variety than for the 1809–1828 variety, striking is usually very sharp, and the wear occurs evenly on both sides. Wear is more extensive, most noticeable on the higher areas of the hair. The cap shows more wear, as does the cheek. Stars still show their centers (unless lightly struck, and *many* are). Luster, if present, is in protected areas among the star

1827, Pointed Top 1 in 10 C.; JR-7. Graded EF-45.

points and close to the portrait. *Reverse:* The wings show wear on the higher areas of the feathers (particularly on the right wing), and some details are lost. Feathers in the neck are light. The eagle's claws show wear. Luster may be present in protected areas, even if there is little or none on the obverse.

Illustrated coin: This coin is lightly struck on some stars, but fairly well struck at the center. It may be useful to compare the detail with that on the lightly struck coin used to illustrate the About Uncirculated level, a reminder that multiple factors need to be considered when grading early coins. Overall, a nice example of the grade.

VF-20, 30 (Very Fine). *Obverse:* The rims are more uniform for the 1828–1837 variety than for the 1809–1828 variety, striking is usually very sharp, and wear occurs evenly on both sides. Wear is more extensive, and most of the hair is combined into thick tresses without delicate features. The curl on the neck is flat. Unless they were weakly struck to begin with, most stars retain their interior lines. *Reverse:* Wear is most evident on the eagle's

1811, 11 Over 09; JR-1. Graded VF-20.

neck, to the left of the shield, and on the leaves and claws. Most feathers in the wing remain distinct.

Illustrated coin: The reverse has multiple die cracks (but not as many as on later states of this die). It is a wonder how the reverse die held together.

F-12, 15 (Fine). *Obverse:* The rims are more uniform for the 1828–1837 variety than for the 1809–1828 variety, striking is usually very sharp, and wear occurs evenly on both sides. (For both varieties the striking is not as important at this and lower grades.) Wear is more extensive, with much of the hair blended together. The drapery is indistinct along part of its upper edge. Stars have lost detail at the center and some may be flat. The height of

1821, Large Date; JR-2. Graded F-12.

obverse rim is important in the amount of wear the coin has received. *Reverse:* Wear is more extensive, now with only about a third to half of the feathers remaining on the wings, more on the wing to the left. Some of the horizontal lines in the shield may be worn away.

 Illustrated coin: Some pin scratches are evident. This is a rare die variety; slightly more than a dozen are known. The die failed at stars 1 to 3, soon ending its life. Traces of a resultant bulge can be seen.

VG-8, 10 (Very Good). *Obverse:* The hair is less distinct, with the area surrounding the face blended into the facial features. LIBERTY is complete, but weak in areas. Stars are nearly flat. *Reverse:* Feathers are fewer and mostly visible on the eagle's left wing. Other details are weaker. All lettering remains easily readable, although some letters may be faint.

 Illustrated coin: Here is a mint error double struck while in the press, with some of the first-strike features still visible.

1827, Pointed Top 1 in 10 C.; JR-1. Graded VG-8.

G-4, 6 (Good). *Obverse:* The portrait is mostly in outline, with few interior details discernible. LIBERTY may still be readable or may be partially worn away, depending on the variety (this varies due to the strike characteristics of some die marriages). Stars are flat at their centers. *Reverse:* The eagle is mostly in outline form, although some feathers can be seen in the right wing. All letters around the border are clear on a sharp strike;

1820, Large 0. Graded G-4.

some letters are light or missing on a coin with low rims. E PLURIBUS UNUM may be weak, often with some letters worn away.

 Illustrated coin: This is an attractive, problem-free coin at this grade.

AG-3 (About Good). *Obverse:* The portrait is an outline, although traces of LIBERTY can still be seen. The rim is worn down, and some stars are weak. The date remains clear although weak toward the rim. *Reverse:* The reverse shows more wear overall than the obverse, with the rim indistinct in areas and many if not most letters worn away.

Illustrated coin: This is a well-worn but still attractive example.

1822; JR-1. Graded AG-3.

PF-60 to 70 (Proof). *Obverse and Reverse:* Generally, Proof dimes of the 1828–1837 variety are of better quality than the 1809–1828 variety and have Full Details in almost all areas. Proofs of this type can have areas of light striking, such as at the star centers. Proofs that are extensively cleaned and have many hairlines, or that are dull and grainy, are lower level, such as PF-60 to 62. These are not of great interest to specialists unless they

1825; JR-2. Graded PF-66.

are of rare die varieties. A PF-64 has fewer hairlines, but they are obvious, perhaps slightly distracting. A Gem PF-65 should have fewer still and full mirrored surfaces (no trace of cloudiness or dullness). PF-66 should have hairlines so delicate that magnification is needed to see them. Above that, a Proof should be free of such lines. Grading is highly subjective with early Proofs, and eye appeal also is a major factor.

Illustrated coin: Note some lightness of strike left of the neck on the obverse and at the upper right of the shield on the reverse.

1811, 11 Over 09

1814, Small Date

1814, Large Date

1814, STATESOFAMERICA

| | Mintage | Cert | Avg | %MS | G-4 | VG-8 | F-12 | VF-20 | EF-40 | AU-50 | MS-60 | MS-63 | MS-65 |
											PF-60	PF-63	PF-65
1809	51,065	45	39.8	40%	$200	$300	$550	$900	$1,800	$2,500	$4,500	$7,200	$25,000
Auctions: $31,725, MS-64, June 2014													
1811, 11 Over 09	65,180	59	42.5	31%	$120	$200	$300	$625	$1,700	$2,200	$4,000	$6,500	$32,500
Auctions: $8,225, MS-64, February 2014													
1814, All kinds	421,500												
1814, Small Date		33	55.4	58%	$55	$85	$125	$275	$725	$1,200	$2,500	$5,000	$15,000
Auctions: $5,875, MS-64, January 2014; $259, EF-40, October 2014													
1814, Large Date		29	50.3	52%	$40	$50	$75	$185	$600	$1,000	$2,000	$4,000	$12,500
Auctions: $14,100, MS-65, November 2013; $2,820, MS-64, October 2014													
1814, STATESOFAMERICA		14	45.5	43%	$60	$90	$120	$300	$900	$1,500	$3,000	$5,000	$13,000
Auctions: $374, VG-10, February 2012													

1820, Large 0   1820, Small 0   1820, STATESOFAMERICA

1821, Large Date   1821, Small Date

1823, 3 Over 2   1823, 3 Over 2, Small E's   1823, 3 Over 2, Large E's

1824, 4 Over 2   1824 and 1827, Flat Top 1   1824 and 1827, Pointed Top 1

	Mintage	Cert	Avg	%MS	G-4	VG-8	F-12	VF-20	EF-40	AU-50	MS-60 PF-60	MS-63 PF-63	MS-65 PF-65
1820, All kinds	942,587												
1820, Large 0		9	41.7	33%	$40	$45	$60	$125	$500	$675	$1,400	$2,750	$12,500
	Auctions: $1,704, MS-62, December 2013; $1,058, AU-55, July 2014; $881, AU-53, August 2014; $212, F-12, September 2014												
1820, Small 0		42	40.1	21%	$40	$45	$60	$150	$600	$700	$1,500	$3,500	$13,000
	Auctions: $1,293, MS-60, February 2014												
1820, STATESOFAMERICA		13	47.4	46%	$50	$75	$150	$250	$750	$1,250	$3,000	$5,000	$15,000
	Auctions: $67,563, MS-66, June 2014; $441, F-12, August 2014												
1820, Proof	2–5	1	66.0								$12,000	$20,000	$65,000
	Auctions: $80,500, PF-66, February 2008												
1821, All kinds	1,186,512												
1821, Small Date		59	47.6	49%	$35	$50	$75	$150	$525	$850	$1,750	$3,500	$14,000
	Auctions: $5,581, MS-64, March 2013; $1,175, MS-60, August 2014												
1821, Large Date		84	38.9	23%	$35	$50	$60	$135	$500	$800	$1,700	$3,250	$13,500
	Auctions: $19,975, MS-65, April 2014; $1,528, AU-58, October 2014												
1821, Proof	5–8	4	64.5								$10,000	$18,000	$45,000
	Auctions: $55,200, PF-65, April 2005												
1822	100,000	42	32.7	31%	$1,200	$2,100	$3,200	$4,800	$8,000	$11,000	$15,000	$26,000	
	Auctions: $70,500, MS-66, February 2013												
1822, Proof (a)	2–5	0	n/a								$15,000	$25,000	$70,000
	Auctions: $440,625, PF-66Cam, June 2014												
1823, 3 Over 2, All kinds	440,000												
1823, 3 Over 2, Small E's		8	38.1	25%	$35	$50	$60	$120	$450	$800	$1,500	$3,000	$14,000
	Auctions: $8,813, MS-65, June 2014												
1823, 3 Over 2, Large E's		15	36.9	40%	$35	$50	$60	$120	$450	$700	$1,400	$3,000	$15,000
	Auctions: $7,050, MS-65, April 2013												

a. This coin is extremely rare.

| 1828, Large Date, Curl Base 2 (Variety 1) | 1828, Small Date, Square Base 2 (Variety 2) | 1829, Curl Base 2 |

| 1829, Small 10 C. | 1829, Medium 10 C. | 1829, Large 10 C. |

	Mintage	Cert	Avg	%MS	G-4	VG-8	F-12	VF-20	EF-40	AU-50	MS-60 PF-60	MS-63 PF-63	MS-65 PF-65
1824, 4 Over 2, Flat Top 1 in 10 C.	100,000	9	31.8	0%	$40	$65	$110	$375	$800	$1,500	$2,250	$4,000	$17,500
Auctions: No auction records available.													
1824, 4 Over 2, Pointed Top 1 in 10 C.	(b)	2	14.5	0%	$300	$700	$1,200	$2,500	$4,250				
Auctions: No auction records available.													
1824, 4 Over 2, Proof	4–6	4	66.0								$10,000	$18,000	$45,000
Auctions: $42,550, PF-65, July 2005													
1825	410,000	112	49.5	45%	$35	$50	$75	$150	$500	$900	$2,000	$3,500	$12,000
Auctions: $4,700, MS-64, June 2013; $411, EF-40, August 2014; $247, EF-40, August 2014													
1825, Proof	4–6	3	65.0								$10,000	$18,000	$40,000
Auctions: $18,400, PF-63, June 2011													
1827, Flat Top 1 in 10 C.	1,215,000	2	10.0	0%	$225	$375	$900	$1,250	$1,800	$3,000			
Auctions: No auction records available.													
1827, Pointed Top 1 in 10 C.	(c)	0	n/a		$35	$50	$65	$125	$450	$700	$1,500	$3,000	$13,500
Auctions: $28,200, MS-66, June 2014; $588, AU-58, August 2014; $397, EF-40, July 2014; $212, VF-30, August 2014													
1827, Proof	10–15	7	65.5								$10,000	$18,000	$40,000
Auctions: $120,750, PF-67, February 2008													
1828, Variety 1, Large Date, Curl Base 2	(d)	28	45.3	29%	$50	$80	$130	$300	$625	$1,200	$2,250	$5,500	$18,000
Auctions: $4,113, AU-58, November 2013													
1828, Variety 2, Small Date, Square Base 2	(e)	50	49.5	44%	$40	$50	$75	$150	$400	$750	$1,300	$2,500	$10,000
Auctions: $2,820, MS-63, April 2013													
1828, Proof	4–6	2	62.5								$10,000	$15,000	$35,000
Auctions: $29,900, PF-65, February 2008													
1829, All kinds	770,000												
1829, Curl Base 2 (f)		9	6.2	0%	$7,000	$10,000	$15,000	$25,000					
Auctions: $7,638, VG-8, June 2014													
1829, Small 10 C.		54	41.6	33%	$32	$40	$45	$100	$375	$475	$1,000	$2,000	$8,000
Auctions: $16,450, MS-66, November 2013; $458, AU-55, October 2014; $247, EF-40, August 2014; $259, EF-40, November 2014													
1829, Medium 10 C.		8	37.5	38%	$35	$40	$45	$100	$400	$600	$1,700	$3,200	$8,500
Auctions: $717, AU-55, August 2013													
1829, Large 10 C.		15	43.1	27%	$35	$45	$60	$125	$425	$750	$2,000	$4,000	$12,000
Auctions: $259, F-12, November 2013													
1829, Proof	6–10	4	63.5								$8,500	$15,000	$30,000
Auctions: $37,375, PF-66, June 2002													

b. Included in 1824, 4 Over 2, Flat Top 1 in 10 C., mintage figure. c. Included in 1827, Flat Top 1 in 10 C., mintage figure. d. 1828, Variety 1 and Variety 2, have a combined mintage of 125,000. e. 1828, Variety 1 and Variety 2, have a combined mintage of 125,000. f. Only one working die for the 1829 dime coinage featured a curled 2, rather than the normal square-based 2. Nearly all known examples are in low grades.

1830, 30 Over 29   1830, Large 10 C.   1830, Small 10 C.

1833, Last 3 Normal   1833, Last 3 High

1834, Small 4   1834, Large 4

	Mintage	Cert	Avg	%MS	G-4	VG-8	F-12	VF-20	EF-40	AU-50	MS-60 PF-60	MS-63 PF-63	MS-65 PF-65
1830, All kinds	510,000												
1830, 30 Over 29 (g)		40	53.4	45%	$40	$60	$110	$200	$450	$650	$1,300	$4,000	$10,000
Auctions: $23,500, MS-66, June 2014; $270, VF-35, December 2014													
1830, Large 10 C.		0	n/a		$35	$40	$45	$80	$325	$500	$1,200	$2,500	$9,000
Auctions: $35,250, MS-65, June 2014; $707, AU-58, July 2014; $170, AU-50, August 2014; $382, AU-50, October 2014													
1830, Small 10 C.		6	40.3	50%	$35	$40	$45	$80	$375	$650	$1,200	$2,500	$9,000
Auctions: $1,221, MS-63, January 2012													
1830, Proof (h)	5–8	3	64.0								$8,500	$15,000	$30,000
Auctions: $18,800, PF-63, April 2014													
1831	771,350	353	53.5	53%	$35	$40	$45	$80	$300	$450	$1,000	$2,000	$7,500
Auctions: $8,225, MS-65, January 2014; $5,581, MS-65, August 2014; $1,058, AU-55, August 2014; $482, AU-55, October 2014													
1831, Proof	15–25	10	64.8								$8,500	$15,000	$30,000
Auctions: $58,750, PF-66Cam, January 2014													
1832	522,500	330	52.0	51%	$35	$40	$45	$80	$300	$450	$1,000	$2,000	$7,500
Auctions: $3,819, MS-64, March 2013; $441, AU-53, September 2014; $329, AU-50, July 2014; $88, Fair-2, July 2014													
1832, Proof (i)	2–5	0	n/a								—		
Auctions: No auction records available.													
1833, All kinds	485,000												
1833		358	51.0	50%	$35	$40	$45	$80	$300	$450	$1,000	$2,000	$7,500
Auctions: $18,800, MS-67, October 2013; $1,528, MS-63, October 2014; $740, AU-58, September 2014; $1,058, AU-50, July 2014													
1833, Last 3 High		30	47.4	40%	$35	$40	$45	$80	$300	$450	$1,000	$2,000	$7,500
Auctions: $17,625, MS-66, April 2013													
1833, Proof	5–10	5	65.6								$9,000	$17,000	$40,000
Auctions: $13,800, PF-64, January 2009													
1834, All kinds	635,000												
1834, Small 4		12	33.9	25%	$35	$40	$45	$80	$300	$450	$1,500	$2,250	$9,000
Auctions: $2,101, MS-63, October 2013; $529, AU-55, November 2014													
1834, Large 4		62	42.1	31%	$35	$40	$45	$80	$300	$450	$1,000	$1,850	$7,500
Auctions: $28,200, MS-68, August 2013; $411, AU-53, October 2014													
1834, Proof	5–10	3	65.7								$8,500	$15,000	$30,000
Auctions: $35,250, PF-65, October 2014													

g. The tail of the 2 is evident to the right of the lower curve of the 3. The very top of the 9 is evident below the 0. Surface doubling from the initial 1829 punch is also evident on the 8. There are three of four known dies of this overdate; all are similar and command similar values. Today the variety is known to be more common than thought in the early 1970s, when it was first publicized. **h.** Values are for JR-6. A very few Proof versions of the 1830, 30 Over 29, dime are known. A PF-60, JR-4, sold at auction in January 2012 for $5,750. **i.** This coin is extremely rare.

	Mintage	Cert	Avg	%MS	G-4	VG-8	F-12	VF-20	EF-40	AU-50	MS-60	MS-63	MS-65
											PF-60	PF-63	PF-65
1835	1,410,000	580	49.6	45%	$35	$40	$45	$80	$300	$450	$1,000	$2,000	$7,500
	Auctions: $12,925, MS-66, March 2013; $529, MS-60, November 2014; $341, AU-53, October 2014; $529, AU-50, July 2014												
1835, Proof	5–10	7	64.6								$8,500	$15,000	$30,000
	Auctions: $41,125, PF-65Cam, April 2014												
1836	1,190,000	262	50.5	43%	$35	$40	$45	$80	$300	$450	$1,000	$2,000	$7,500
	Auctions: $44,063, MS-67, December 2013; $353, AU-50, October 2014												
1836, Proof	2–5	3	63.8								$8,500	$15,000	$35,000
	Auctions: $6,900, PF-66, September 1998												
1837	359,500	160	49.3	54%	$35	$40	$45	$80	$300	$450	$1,000	$2,000	$7,500
	Auctions: $30,550, MS-66, November 2013; $705, AU-58, September 2014												
1837, Proof	2–5	1	64.0								$8,500	$15,000	$40,000
	Auctions: $23,000, MS-64 Specimen, April 2010												

LIBERTY SEATED (1837–1891)

Variety 1, No Stars on Obverse (1837–1838): **Designer:** *Christian Gobrecht.*
Weight: *2.67 grams.* **Composition:** *.900 silver, .100 copper.* **Diameter:** *17.9 mm.*
Edge: *Reeded.* **Mints:** *Philadelphia, New Orleans.*

**Variety 1, No Stars on Obverse
(1837–1838)**

**Variety 1, No Stars on Obverse,
Proof**

Variety 2, Stars on Obverse (1838–1853): **Designer:** *Christian Gobrecht.*
Weight: *2.67 grams.* **Composition:** *.900 silver, .100 copper.* **Diameter:** *17.9 mm.*
Edge: *Reeded.* **Mints:** *Philadelphia, New Orleans, San Francisco.*

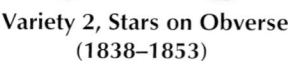

**Variety 2, Stars on Obverse
(1838–1853)**

*Mintmark location,
1837–1860 (Variety 2),
is on the reverse,
above the bow.*

**Variety 2, Stars on Obverse,
Proof**

Variety 3, Stars on Obverse, Arrows at Date, Reduced Weight (1853–1855):
Designer: *Christian Gobrecht.* **Weight:** *2.49 grams.* **Composition:** *.900 silver, .100 copper.*
Diameter: *17.9 mm.* **Edge:** *Reeded.* **Mints:** *Philadelphia, New Orleans, San Francisco.*

**Variety 3, Stars on Obverse,
Arrows at Date, Reduced
Weight (1853–1855)**

**Variety 3, Stars on Obverse,
Arrows at Date, Reduced
Weight, Proof**

Variety 2 Resumed, With Weight Standard of Variety 3 (1856–1860):
Designer: *Christian Gobrecht.* **Weight:** *2.49 grams.* **Composition:** *.900 silver, .100 copper.*
Diameter: *17.9 mm.* **Edge:** *Reeded.* **Mints:** *Philadelphia, New Orleans, San Francisco.*

Variety 2 Resumed,
Weight Standard of Variety 3
(1856–1860)

Variety 2 Resumed, Weight
Standard of Variety 3, Proof

Variety 4, Legend on Obverse (1860–1873): **Designer:** *Christian Gobrecht.*
Weight: *2.49 grams.* **Composition:** *.900 silver, .100 copper.* **Diameter:** *17.9 mm.*
Edge: *Reeded.* **Mints:** *Philadelphia, New Orleans, San Francisco, Carson City.*

Variety 4, Legend on Obverse
(1860–1873)

Mintmark location,
1860 (Variety 4)–1891,
is on the reverse,
below the bow.

Variety 4, Legend
on Obverse, Proof

Variety 5, Legend on Obverse, Arrows at Date, Increased Weight (1873–1874):
Designer: *Christian Gobrecht.* **Weight:** *2.50 grams.* **Composition:** *.900 silver, .100 copper.*
Diameter: *17.9 mm.* **Edge:** *Reeded.* **Mints:** *Philadelphia, New Orleans, San Francisco, Carson City.*

Variety 5, Legend on Obverse,
Arrows at Date, Increased
Weight (1873–1874)

Variety 5, Legend on Obverse,
Increased Weight, Proof

Variety 4 Resumed, With Weight Standard Variety of 5 (1875–1891):
Designer: *Christian Gobrecht.* **Weight:** *2.50 grams.* **Composition:** *.900 silver, .100 copper.*
Diameter: *17.9 mm.* **Edge:** *Reeded.* **Mints:** *Philadelphia, New Orleans, San Francisco, Carson City.*

Variety 4 Resumed,
Weight Standard Variety of 5
(1875–1891)

Variety 4 Resumed, Weight
Standard Variety of 5, Proof

History. The first of the Liberty Seated designs, with no stars on the obverse, was inspired by Christian Gobrecht's silver dollar of 1836. The reverse features a different motif, with a wreath and inscription. This variety was made only at the Philadelphia Mint in 1837 and at the New Orleans Mint in 1838. Liberty Seated dimes of the Stars on Obverse varieties were first made without drapery at Miss Liberty's elbow. These early issues have the shield tilted sharply to the left. Drapery was added in 1840, and the shield reoriented, this being the style of the 1840s onward. Variety 3 coins (minted in part of 1853, and all of

1854 and 1855) have arrows at the date, signifying the reduction in weight brought on by the Coinage Act of February 21, 1853. The earlier design resumed in 1856 at the new weight standard. Liberty Seated dimes were made in large quantities, and circulated widely. In 1860 the Liberty Seated design continued with UNITED STATES OF AMERICA replacing the stars on the obverse. A new reverse featured what the Mint called a "cereal wreath," encircling ONE DIME in two lines. In 1873 the dime was increased in weight to 2.50 grams (from 2.49); arrows at the date in 1873 and 1874 indicate this change, making Variety 5. Variety 4 (without the arrows) resumed from 1875 and continued to the end of the series in 1891.

Striking and Sharpness. Coins of these varieties usually are fairly well struck for the earlier years, somewhat erratic in the 1870s, and better from the 1880s to 1891. Many Civil War dimes of Philadelphia, 1861 to 1865, have parallel die striae from the dies not being finished (this being so for virtually all silver and gold issues of that period). Some dimes, especially dates from 1879 to 1881, are found prooflike. Check the highest parts of the Liberty Seated figure (especially the head and horizontal shield stripes), the star centers, and, on the reverse, the leaves. Check the denticles on both sides. Avoid coins struck from "tired" or overused dies, as evidenced by grainy rather than lustrous fields (on higher-grade coins). Issues of the Carson City Mint in the early 1870s, particularly 1873-CC, With Arrows, are often seen with porous surfaces (a post-striking effect).

Note that the word LIBERTY on the shield is not an infallible key to attributing lower grades. On some dies such as those of the early 1870s the shield was in low relief on the coins and wore away slowly, with the result that part or all of the word can be readable in grades below F-12.

Availability. The 1837 is readily available in all grades, including MS-65 and higher. The 1838-O is usually seen with wear and is a rarity if truly MS-63 or above. Beware coins with deep or vivid iridescent toning, which often masks friction or evidence of wear. Coins with uniformly grainy etching on both sides have been processed and should be avoided. The 1838 to 1860 dimes are plentiful as a rule, although certain dates and varieties are rare. Most MS coins on the market are dated in the 1850s and are often found MS-63 to MS-65. While certain issues of the 1860s through 1881 range from scarce to very rare, those from 1882 to 1891 are for the most part very common, even in MS-63 and finer.

Proofs. Examples of Proofs have deep-mirror surfaces and are mostly quite attractive. Proofs of 1837 (but not 1838-O) were struck in an unknown small quantity, but seemingly more than the related 1837 half dime. Proofs were made of most years and are mostly available from 1854 onward, with 1858 and especially 1859 being those often seen. Some Proofs of the 1860s and early 1870s can be carelessly struck, with areas of lightness and sometimes with lint marks. Those of the mid-1870s onward are usually sharply struck and without problems. Proof Liberty Seated dimes of this variety were made continuously from 1860 to 1891. They exist today in proportion to their mintages. Carefully examine deeply toned pieces to ensure the toning does not hide flaws.

GRADING STANDARDS

MS-60 to 70 (Mint State). *Obverse:* At MS-60, some abrasion and contact marks are evident, most noticeably on the bosom and thighs and knees. Luster is present, but may be dull or lifeless, and interrupted in patches in the large open field. At MS-63, contact marks are very few, and abrasion is hard to detect except under magnification. An MS-65 coin has no abrasion, and contact marks are so minute as to require magnification. Luster

1837, Large Date. Graded MS-65.

should be full and rich, except for Philadelphia (but not San Francisco) dimes of the early and mid-1860s. Most Mint State coins of the 1861 to 1865 years, Philadelphia issues, have extensive die striae (from not completely finishing the die). Some low-mintage Philadelphia issues may be prooflike. Clashmarks are common in this era. This is true of contemporary half dimes as well. Half dimes of this type can be very beautiful at this level. Grades above MS-65 are seen with regularity, more so than for the related No Stars dimes. *Reverse:* Comments apply as for the obverse, except that in lower Mint State grades abrasion and contact marks are most noticeable on the highest parts of the leaves and the ribbon, less so on ONE DIME. At MS-65 or higher there are no marks visible to the unaided eye. The field is mainly protected by design elements and does not show abrasion as much as does the open-field obverse on a given coin.

Illustrated coin: This coin is brilliant, with areas of toning.

AU-50, 53, 55, 58 (About Uncirculated).

Obverse: Light wear is seen on the thighs and knees, bosom, and head. At AU-58, the luster is extensive, but incomplete. Friction is seen in the large open field. At AU-50 and 53, luster is less. *Reverse:* Wear is evident on the leaves (especially at the top of the wreath) and ribbon. An AU-58 coin has nearly full luster, more so than on the obverse, as the design elements protect the small field areas. At

1838-O. Graded AU-55.

AU-50 and 53, there still is significant luster, more than on the obverse.

Illustrated coin: Lustrous and lightly toned, this is an exceptional example of this scarce New Orleans dime.

EF-40, 45 (Extremely Fine). *Obverse:* Further wear is seen on all areas, especially the thighs and knees, bosom, and head. Little or no luster is seen. *Reverse:* Further wear is seen on all areas, most noticeably at the leaves to each side of the wreath apex and on the ribbon bow knot. Leaves retain details except on the higher areas.

1837, Large Date. Graded EF-40.

VF-20, 30 (Very Fine). *Obverse:* Further wear is seen. Most details of the gown are worn away, except in the lower-relief areas above and to the right of the shield. Hair detail is mostly or completely gone. *Reverse:* Wear is more extensive. The highest leaves are flat.

1837, Small Date. Graded VF-30.

F-12, 15 (Fine). *Obverse:* The seated figure is well worn, with little detail remaining. LIBERTY on the shield is fully readable but weak in areas. On the 1838–1840 subtype Without Drapery, LIBERTY is in higher relief and will wear more quickly; ER may be missing, but other details are at the Fine level. *Reverse:* Most detail of the leaves is gone. The rim is worn but bold, and most if not all denticles are visible.

1838-O. Graded F-12.

    Illustrated coin: The word LIBERTY is full but is weak at ER.

VG-8, 10 (Very Good). *Obverse:* The seated figure is more worn, but some detail can be seen above and to the right of the shield. The shield is discernible. In LIBERTY at least three letters are readable but very weak at VG-8; a few more visible at VG-10. On the 1838–1840 subtype Without Drapery, LIBERTY is in higher relief, and at Very Good only one or two letters may be readable. However, LIBERTY is not an infallible

1838-O. Graded VG-8.

way to grade this type, as some varieties have the word in low relief on the die, so it wore away slowly. *Reverse:* Further wear has combined the details of most leaves. The rim is complete, but weak in areas. The reverse appears to be in a slightly higher grade than the obverse.

G-4, 6 (Good). *Obverse:* The seated figure is worn smooth. At G-4 there are no letters in LIBERTY remaining on most (but not all) coins. At G-6, traces of one or two can be seen (except on the early No Drapery coins). *Reverse:* Wear is more extensive. The leaves are all combined and in outline form. The rim is well worn and missing in some areas, causing the outer parts of the peripheral letters to be worn away in some instances. On

1837, Small Date. Graded G-4.

most coins the reverse appears to be in a slightly higher grade than the obverse.

AG-3 (About Good). *Obverse:* The seated figure is mostly visible in outline form, with no detail. The rim is worn away. The date remains clear. *Reverse:* Many if not most letters are worn away, at least in part. The wreath and interior letters are discernible. The rim is weak.

1838. Graded AG-3.

PF-60 to 70 (Proof). *Obverse and Reverse:* Proofs that are extensively cleaned and have many hairlines, or that are dull and grainy, are lower level, such as PF-60 to 62. These command less attention than more visually appealing pieces, save for the scarce (in any grade) dates of 1844 and 1846, and 1863 through 1867. Both the half dime and dime Proofs of 1837 were often cleaned, resulting in coins that have lost much of their mirror surface. With

1837. Graded PF-65.

medium hairlines and good reflectivity, an assigned grade of PF-64 is indicated, and with relatively few hairlines, Gem PF-65. In various grades hairlines are most easily seen in the obverse field. PF-66 should have hairlines so delicate that magnification is needed to see them. Above that, a Proof should be free of such lines.

1837, Large Date   **1837, Small Date**   **No Drapery From Elbow, Tilted Shield (1838–1840)**   **Drapery From Elbow, Upright Shield (1840–1891)**

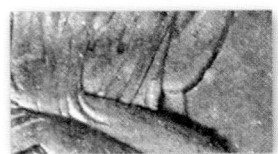

1838, Small Stars   **1838, Large Stars**   **1838, So-Called Partial Drapery**

| | Mintage | Cert | Avg | %MS | G-4 | F-12 | VF-20 | EF-40 | AU-50 | MS-60 | MS-63 | MS-64 | MS-65 |
											PF-60	PF-63	PF-65
1837, All kinds	682,500												
1837, Large Date		34	51.4	44%	$45	$100	$300	$500	$700	$1,100	$1,800	$4,000	$7,750
Auctions: $44,063, MS-68, June 2014; $6,463, MS-66, October 2014; $676, AU-55, October 2014; $411, EF-40, November 2014													
1837, Small Date		34	53.3	44%	$50	$120	$325	$525	$725	$1,200	$2,000	$4,500	$8,500
Auctions: $36,719, MS-67, November 2013; $6,463, MS-64, July 2014; $353, AU-50, November 2014													
1837, Proof	25–35	26	63.9								$8,500	$15,000	$40,000
Auctions: $41,125, PF-65, June 2014; $13,513, PF-64, October 2014													
1838O, Variety 1	406,034	160	43.0	19%	$60	$140	$400	$750	$1,200	$3,000	$6,750	$11,000	$18,000
Auctions: $28,200, MS-65, October 2014; $10,575, MS-64, November 2013; $1,880, AU-55, July 2014; $823, EF-45, November 2014													
1838, Variety 2, All kinds	1,992,500												
1838, Small Stars		72	58.6	71%	$30	$55	$80	$175	$400	$700	$1,350	$2,000	$4,000
Auctions: $25,850, MS-68, October 2014; $3,290, MS-65, August 2014; $3,966, MS, March 2014; $382, AU-58, November 2014													
1838, Large Stars		380	60.0	71%	$25	$30	$40	$120	$250	$350	$850	$1,100	$3,000
Auctions: $8,225, MS-67, October 2014; $11,163, MS-67, August 2013; $1,998, MS-65, October 2014; $1,058, MS-64, October 2014													
1838, Partial Drapery (a)		22	62.0	77%	$30	$60	$100	$200	$500	$850	$2,000		
Auctions: $23,500, MS-67, October 2014; $329, AU-53, October 2014													
1838, Proof (b)	2–3	0	n/a										
Auctions: $161,000, PF-67Cam, January 2008													

a. The so-called "partial drapery" is not a design variation; rather, it is evidence of die clashing from the E in DIME on the reverse. **b.** The 1838 and 1841, Proof, dimes may be unique.

| **1839-O, Repunched Mintmark** | **1841-O, Transitional Reverse, Small O** | **1841-O, Transitional Reverse, Large O** | **Regular Reverse Style of 1841-O** |

	Mintage	Cert	Avg	%MS	G-4	F-12	VF-20	EF-40	AU-50	MS-60	MS-63	MS-64	MS-65
											PF-60	PF-63	PF-65
1839	1,053,115	228	61.0	72%	$20	$30	$40	$135	$250	$400	$850	$1,100	$3,000
Auctions: $14,100, MS-68, August 2013; $3,525, MS-66+, August 2014; $940, MS-64, November 2014; $159, EF-45, July 2014													
1839, Proof	4–5	3	64.3								$7,000	$10,000	$45,000
Auctions: $36,719, PF-66, April 2013													
1839O	1,291,600	83	54.0	47%	$25	$40	$45	$135	$275	$450	$1,400	$2,400	$6,000
Auctions: $6,463, MS-64, June 2014; $135, VF-35, December 2014													
1839O, Repunched Mintmark	(c)	1	30.0	0%				$150	$325	$750	$1,500		
Auctions: $13,800, MS-66+, February 2012													
1839O, Proof	2–3	1	65.0									$25,000	$75,000
Auctions: $74,750, PF-65, October 2008													
1840, No Drapery	981,500	132	56.9	60%	$20	$25	$40	$135	$250	$400	$850	$1,200	$4,000
Auctions: $11,163, MS-67, June 2014; $368, AU-58, October 2014													
1840, No Drapery, Proof	4–5	5	65.0								$10,000	$15,000	$30,000
Auctions: $27,600, PF-65Cam, August 2007													
1840O, No Drapery	1,175,000	27	44.7	22%	$25	$40	$55	$230	$800	$2,500	$6,000	$12,000	
Auctions: $38,188, MS-65, June 2014; $485, AU-50, October 2014; $112, Fair-2, October 2014													
1840, Drapery	377,500	21	48.6	33%	$35	$90	$175	$300	$450	$1,200	$5,500	$10,000	
Auctions: $38,188, MS-64, November 2013; $499, EF-40, November 2014													
1841 (d)	1,622,500	80	59.0	68%	$20	$30	$35	$60	$140	$350	$650	$1,200	$3,250
Auctions: $4,700, MS-65, October 2014; $4,700, MS-65, June 2013; $69, EF-45, November 2014													
1841, Proof (d)	2–3	1	63.0									$65,000	
Auctions: $41,125, PF-63Cam, October 2014													
1841, No Drapery, Proof	2–3	2	60.3									$75,000	
Auctions: $305,500, PF-67, November 2013													
1841O	2,007,500	78	49.5	27%	$25	$35	$50	$85	$225	$900	$1,800	$2,750	$5,000
Auctions: $8,225, MS-65, October 2014; $5,288, MS-64, October 2014; $1,175, MS-63, October 2014; $19,975, AU-58, April 2014													
1841O, Transitional Reverse, Small O (e)	(f)	3	11.3	0%									
Auctions: $940, G-6, June 2013													
1841O, Transitional Reverse, Large O (e)	(f)	3	8.3	0%									
Auctions: $2,611, F-12, January 2014													
1842	1,887,500	169	51.8	48%	$20	$30	$35	$50	$125	$400	$650	$1,100	$3,250
Auctions: $4,113, MS-66, August 2014; $4,113, MS-65, April 2014; $2,585, MS-65, October 2014; $206, AU-58, November 2014													
1842, Proof	6–10	4	63.8								$10,000	$15,000	$40,000
Auctions: $37,375, PF-65Cam, April 2008													
1842O	2,020,000	77	46.8	25%	$25	$35	$70	$265	$1,300	$2,500	$5,500	$7,500	
Auctions: $9,106, MS-65, October 2013; $4,289, MS-63, July 2014; $470, EF-45, August 2014; $382, EF-45, October 2014													

c. Included in circulation-strike 1839-O mintage figure. **d.** Two examples are known of 1841, No Drapery, Small Stars, Upright Shield. One is a Proof and the other is a circulation strike in VF. **e.** The 1841-O, Transitional Reverse, varieties were struck with a reverse die that was supposed to have been discontinued in 1840, but saw limited use into 1841. Note the closed buds (not open, as in the regular reverse die of 1841); also note that the second leaf from the left (in the group of four leaves to the left of the bow knot) reaches only halfway across the bottom of the U in UNITED. **f.** Included in 1841-O mintage figure.

	Mintage	Cert	Avg	%MS	G-4	F-12	VF-20	EF-40	AU-50	MS-60	MS-63	MS-64	MS-65
											PF-60	PF-63	PF-65
1843	1,370,000	114	46.1	37%	$20	$30	$35	$50	$125	$400	$800	$1,250	$3,500
	Auctions: $8,225, MS-66, June 2014												
1843, Proof	10–15	11	64.5								$5,000	$10,000	$25,000
	Auctions: $25,850, PF-66, June 2014												
1843O	150,000	40	38.3	5%	$85	$350	$800	$1,900	$6,500	$18,000			
	Auctions: $141,000, MS-62, June 2014; $1,293, VF-35, October 2014; $1,058, VF-30, July 2014; $734, VF-25, October 2014												
1844	72,500	94	24.2	10%	$200	$450	$700	$1,200	$1,800	$4,000	$12,000	$20,000	$35,000
	Auctions: $30,550, MS-65, October 2013; $11,750, MS-64, October 2014; $3,290, MS-61, August 2014; $499, VF-35, August 2014												
1844, Proof	4–8	2	64.0								$18,000	$32,500	$75,000
	Auctions: $44,063, PF-65, October 2014												
1845	1,755,000	195	53.7	57%	$20	$30	$35	$50	$125	$400	$800	$1,250	$3,000
	Auctions: $2,056, MS-65, April 2014; $1,880, MS-65, October 2014; $1,645, MS-65, July 2014; $153, AU-50, November 2014												
1845, Proof	6–10	5	64.8								$7,500	$10,000	$25,000
	Auctions: $19,975, PF-65, April 2013												
1845O	230,000	42	46.5	14%	$25	$75	$200	$550	$1,200	$3,500			
	Auctions: $16,450, MS-62, August 2013; $2,174, AU-50, October 2014; $1,998, AU-50, October 2014												
1846	31,300	54	25.9	2%	$200	$475	$900	$2,400	$8,500	$15,000	$38,000		
	Auctions: $47,000, MS-63, June 2014; $1,175, VF-35, October 2014; $1,175, VF-30, July 2014; $1,293, VF-30, August 2014												
1846, Proof	8–12	6	63.7								$10,000	$15,000	$40,000
	Auctions: $31,725, PF-65, March 2013												
1847	245,000	36	52.6	36%	$20	$40	$70	$125	$350	$950	$2,500	$4,500	$9,500
	Auctions: $5,581, MS-63, February 2014; $4,700, MS-63, October 2014; $229, EF-45, November 2014												
1847, Proof	3–5	1	66.0								$8,000	$13,000	$40,000
	Auctions: $35,250, PF-66Cam, March 2013; $44,063, PF-66, October 2014												
1848	451,500	64	57.1	61%	$20	$32	$50	$85	$150	$550	$850	$1,500	$6,500
	Auctions: $1,410, MS-64, October 2014; $823, MS-63, February 2014; $57, EF-40, November 2014												
1848, Proof	10–15	10	64.7								$5,000	$10,000	$25,000
	Auctions: $27,025, PF-66, February 2013												
1849	839,000	74	56.6	59%	$20	$30	$40	$60	$125	$300	$900	$1,750	$4,000
	Auctions: $14,100, MS-66, June 2014; $353, MS-62, October 2014; $80, EF-40, November 2014												
1849, Proof	4–6	3	65.3								$10,000	$15,000	$40,000
	Auctions: $35,250, PF-65, August 2013												
1849O	300,000	76	45.9	25%	$25	$50	$125	$300	$750	$2,500	$6,000		
	Auctions: $6,463, MS-64, June 2014; $3,819, MS-63, August 2014; $1,706, AU-58, August 2014; $646, AU-55, September 2014												
1850	1,931,500	137	57.0	65%	$20	$30	$40	$60	$125	$300	$700	$1,200	$5,500
	Auctions: $999, MS-64, October 2014; $529, MS-63, January 2014; $259, MS-60, December 2014; $36, EF-40, October 2014												
1850, Proof	4–6	4	64.6								$10,000	$15,000	$40,000
	Auctions: $44,063, PF-66, October 2014												
1850O	510,000	22	44.9	27%	$25	$40	$90	$175	$375	$1,200	$2,600	$4,500	$6,500
	Auctions: $30,550, MS-67, October 2014; $14,100, MS-66, October 2014; $7,344, MS-65, October 2014; $3,672, MS-63, October 2013												
1851	1,026,500	73	56.6	60%	$20	$30	$40	$60	$125	$350	$850	$1,400	$5,000
	Auctions: $20,563, MS-67, June 2013; $170, AU-53, October 2014												
1851O	400,000	35	50.7	17%	$25	$40	$80	$175	$450	$2,000	$3,750	$6,500	
	Auctions: $2,115, MS-60, February 2013; $1,880, AU-53, October 2014; $206, EF-40, October 2014												
1852	1,535,500	95	58.2	65%	$20	$30	$40	$60	$125	$300	$700	$1,200	$3,250
	Auctions: $6,463, MS-67, June 2014; $4,700, MS-67, November 2014												
1852, Proof	5–10	8	64.4								$5,000	$10,000	$25,000
	Auctions: $8,225, PF-62, January 2014												
1852O	430,000	50	55.2	54%	$30	$50	$140	$250	$350	$1,600	$2,500	$3,500	
	Auctions: $11,163, MS-65, June 2014; $306, EF-40, July 2014; $270, EF-45, October 2014; $194, VF-35, July 2014												

	Mintage	Cert	Avg	%MS	G-4	F-12	VF-20	EF-40	AU-50	MS-60	MS-63	MS-64	MS-65
											PF-60	PF-63	PF-65
1853, No Arrows	95,000	105	55.5	73%	$100	$275	$475	$625	$725	$900	$1,500	$2,500	$3,500
	Auctions: $18,800, MS-68, October 2014; $6,463, MS-67, November 2013; $4,113, MS-66, October 2014; $558, EF-45, October 2014												
1853, With Arrows	12,078,010	847	59.1	69%	$20	$25	$30	$50	$175	$300	$675	$1,000	$2,000
	Auctions: $22,913, MS-68, October 2014; $8,813, MS-67, October 2014; $2,585, MS-66, November 2014; $3,819, MS-66, November 2013												
1853, Proof	5–10	6	64.8								$12,500	$30,000	$75,000
	Auctions: $52,875, PF-66, June 2014; $34,075, PF-65, October 2014; $14,100, PF-62, October 2014												
1853O	1,100,000	35	46.8	17%	$25	$50	$100	$275	$500	$1,750	$3,250	$5,000	$8,500
	Auctions: $10,575, MS-65, October 2014; $6,463, MS-64, October 2014; $5,288, MS-64, August 2013; $123, VF-30, July 2014												
1854	4,470,000	233	58.6	64%	$20	$25	$30	$50	$175	$300	$675	$1,000	$2,000
	Auctions: $5,288, MS-67, June 2014; $4,994, MS-67, August 2014; $1,410, MS-65, September 2014; $1,293, MS-65, November 2014												
1854, Proof	8–12	9	65.0								$8,000	$15,000	$40,000
	Auctions: $25,850, PF-65Cam, April 2013; $19,975, PF-65, October 2014												
1854O	1,770,000	84	59.9	79%	$20	$25	$45	$85	$200	$400	$1,100	$1,500	$3,500
	Auctions: $3,055, MS-66, August 2014; $7,638, MS-65, August 2013; $165, AU-50, August 2014												
1855	2,075,000	104	61.5	81%	$20	$25	$30	$60	$185	$325	$900	$1,400	$3,500
	Auctions: $18,800, MS-67, June 2014; $1,293, MS-64, July 2014; $253, AU-58, July 2014; $53, EF-40, October 2014												
1855, Proof	8–12	15	65.0								$8,000	$15,000	$30,000
	Auctions: $38,188, PF-67Cam, March 2013												
1856, All kinds	5,780,000												
1856, Large Date		24	47.1	21%	$18	$22	$36	$60	$160	$400	$850	$2,000	
	Auctions: $9,400, MS-66, October 2014; $16,450, MS-65, August 2013; $306, AU-58, October 2014												
1856, Small Date		80	53.5	53%	$16	$20	$30	$50	$130	$300	$650	$1,250	$2,750
	Auctions: $10,575, MS-67, April 2014; $8,813, MS-67, October 2014; $411, MS-61, November 2014; $66, AU-50, July 2014												
1856, Proof	40–50	26	64.4								$2,500	$4,500	$13,000
	Auctions: $25,850, PF-67, June 2014												
1856O	1,180,000	55	54.3	51%	$18	$25	$35	$65	$250	$800	$1,500		$6,000
	Auctions: $3,672, MS-65, October 2014; $1,469, MS-63, November 2013; $147, EF-45, November 2014												
1856S	70,000	23	42.8	9%	$120	$375	$600	$1,250	$1,700	$3,800	$15,000	$20,000	$45,000
	Auctions: $19,975, MS-64, October 2014; $15,210, MS-63, September 2013; $705, AU-50, November 2014; $1,410, EF-40, October 2014												
1857	5,580,000	492	59.8	72%	$16	$20	$30	$50	$130	$300	$700	$1,000	$2,000
	Auctions: $5,875, MS-66, January 2014; $3,290, MS-66, October 2014; $3,055, MS-65, August 2014; $1,528, MS-65, August 2014												
1857, Proof	45–60	36	64.6								$2,000	$3,750	$6,000
	Auctions: $9,988, PF-67, October 2014; $7,344, PF-66, October 2014; $8,813, PF-66, April 2013												
1857O	1,540,000	181	61.4	86%	$18	$25	$35	$70	$200	$425	$750	$1,100	$2,500
	Auctions: $3,525, MS-66, July 2014; $4,994, MS-66, November 2013; $2,350, MS-65, August 2014; $441, MS-62+, July 2014												
1858	1,540,000	133	60.4	74%	$16	$20	$30	$50	$130	$300	$700	$1,000	$2,000
	Auctions: $6,463, MS-67, June 2014; $823, MS-64, November 2014												
1858, Proof	(g)	78	64.5								$1,000	$1,500	$4,500
	Auctions: $5,581, PF-66, October 2014; $7,344, PF-66, September 2013												
1858O	290,000	47	55.3	38%	$25	$40	$85	$135	$300	$600	$1,000	$2,500	$6,000
	Auctions: $21,150, MS-66, June 2014; $306, AU-50, November 2014; $200, EF-40, October 2014												
1858S	60,000	29	37.6	10%	$100	$225	$450	$900	$1,600	$3,800	$16,000	$25,000	
	Auctions: $88,125, MS-66, June 2014; $940, EF-45, October 2014; $1,968, EF-45, November 2014; $1,058, VF-35, October 2014												
1859	429,200	145	62.4	86%	$20	$22	$32	$60	$140	$300	$700	$1,000	$2,500
	Auctions: $7,638, MS-67, October 2014; $8,225, MS-65, November 2013; $141, AU-55, July 2014; $88, EF-45, July 2014												
1859, Proof	(g)	210	64.6								$950	$1,500	$4,000
	Auctions: $22,325, PF-68DCam, September 2013												

g. The mintage figure is unknown.

1859 Pattern Dime: Obverse of 1859,
Reverse of 1860, Proof
Judd-233

1861, Six Vertical
Shield Lines

	Mintage	Cert	Avg	%MS	G-4	F-12	VF-20	EF-40	AU-50	MS-60	MS-63	MS-64	MS-65
											PF-60	PF-63	PF-65
1859, Obverse of 1859, Reverse of 1860, Proof (h)	(i)	13	64.8								$10,000	$18,500	$25,000
Auctions: $5,875, PF-67Cam, October 2014; $4,113, PF-66Cam, July 2014; $3,672, PF-66Cam, October 2014; $2,585, PF-65, July 2014													
1859O	480,000	116	59.6	71%	$20	$25	$60	$95	$275	$400	$900	$1,100	$2,750
Auctions: $6,463, MS-67, October 2014; $4,113, MS-66, October 2014; $6,756, MS-66, August 2013; $1,998, MS-65, October 2014													
1859S	60,000	19	28.2	11%	$100	$300	$650	$1,500	$4,000	$11,000	$26,000		
Auctions: $25,850, MS-63, October 2014; $1,175, EF-45, January 2014; $1,410, VF-30, August 2014; $881, VF-20, July 2014													
1860S, Variety 2	140,000	40	53.9	45%	$35	$60	$150	$400	$950	$2,500	$5,000	$8,500	$15,000
Auctions: $1,998, MS-61, April 2014; $206, EF-40, November 2014; $200, F-15, July 2014													
1860, Variety 4	606,000	117	63.1	91%	$16	$20	$32	$40	$100	$200	$325	$425	$1,350
Auctions: $3,055, MS-67, June 2013; $940, MS-65, July 2014; $517, MS-64+, October 2014; $165, MS-61, October 2014													
1860, Variety 4, Proof	1,000	158	64.5								$325	$750	$1,850
Auctions: $6,463, PF-67, October 2014; $1,646, PF-65+, September 2014; $734, PF-64, July 2014; $411, PF-62, September 2014													
1860O, Variety 4	40,000	44	29.2	7%	$325	$850	$1,800	$4,000	$8,000	$15,000			
Auctions: $7,638, AU-53, August 2014; $5,581, EF-45, December 2013; $1,528, EF-40, November 2014; $1,116, EF-40, October 2014													
1861 (j)	1,883,000	139	59.0	77%	$16	$22	$30	$40	$100	$200	$325	$425	$1,350
Auctions: $1,763, MS-66, June 2014; $382, MS-64, November 2014													
1861, Proof	1,000	101	64.0								$350	$750	$2,000
Auctions: $8,225, PF-67Cam, December 2013; $2,943, PF-65Cam, July 2014; $764, PF-63Cam, August 2014; $652, PF-64, November 2014													
1861S	172,500	25	46.0	32%	$40	$110	$200	$450	$1,000	$2,100	$5,500		
Auctions: $49,938, MS-66, June 2014; $2,585, AU-58, October 2014; $1,293, AU-53, November 2014; $588, EF-40, August 2014													
1862	847,000	173	62.6	91%	$16	$25	$30	$40	$100	$185	$350	$500	$1,500
Auctions: $2,585, MS-66, April 2014; $2,438, MS-66, August 2014; $1,763, MS-66, October 2014; $2,468, MS-66, November 2014													
1862, Proof	550	104	63.8								$350	$750	$2,000
Auctions: $2,351, PF-66Cam, February 2013; $940, PF-64Cam, September 2014													
1862S	180,750	17	43.3	35%	$45	$90	$200	$675	$900	$1,800	$4,000	$7,000	
Auctions: $35,250, MS-65, October 2014; $646, AU-50, October 2014; $646, VF-30, April 2014; $388, VF-25, July 2014													
1863	14,000	42	57.4	83%	$310	$600	$750	$900	$1,100	$1,300	$1,750	$2,750	$3,750
Auctions: $6,463, MS-67, August 2013; $7,638, MS-65, August 2014; $1,116, MS-60, August 2014													
1863, Proof	460	159	64.6								$325	$700	$1,850
Auctions: $11,163, PF-67Cam, October 2014; $15,863, PF-66DCam, April 2014; $2,820, PF-65DCam, November 2014; $1,763, PF-66, August 2014													
1863S	157,500	30	52.2	33%	$40	$60	$120	$350	$700	$1,500	$4,500	$9,000	$26,000
Auctions: $1,586, AU-58, February 2014; $940, AU-50, October 2014													

h. In 1859 the Mint made a dime pattern, of which some 13 to 20 examples are known. These "coins without a country" do not bear the nation's identity (UNITED STATES OF AMERICA). They are transitional pieces, not made for circulation, but struck at the time that the dime's legend was being transferred from the reverse to the obverse (see Variety 4). For more information, consult *United States Pattern Coins*, 10th edition (Judd). **i.** The mintage figure is unknown. **j.** The dime's dies were modified slightly in 1861. The first (scarcer) variety has only five vertical lines in the top part of the shield.

	Mintage	Cert	Avg	%MS	G-4	F-12	VF-20	EF-40	AU-50	MS-60	MS-63	MS-64	MS-65
											PF-60	PF-63	PF-65
1864	11,000	41	56.7	76%	$225	$425	$575	$875	$1,100	$1,200	$1,750	$2,250	$4,000
	Auctions: $17,625, MS-66, June 2014; $2,233, VF-30, September 2014; $529, VF-20, August 2014
1864, Proof	470	163	64.4								$325	$700	$1,850
	Auctions: $5,581, PF-66Cam, September 2013; $564, PF-63, October 2014; $499, PF-62, October 2014
1864S	230,000	34	50.5	47%	$55	$120	$210	$375	$600	$1,500	$1,900	$3,500	$6,000
	Auctions: $25,850, MS-67, June 2014; $382, EF-40, October 2014
1865	10,000	52	56.4	73%	$250	$550	$700	$800	$950	$1,200	$2,000	$2,500	$3,500
	Auctions: $14,688, MS-67, October 2014; $9,988, MS-67, November 2013; $1,528, EF-40, October 2014; $1,528, VF-20, August 2014
1865, Proof	500	113	64.1								$350	$750	$2,000
	Auctions: $5,053, PF-66Cam, October 2014; $881, PF-64Cam, August 2014; $4,700, PF-67, June 2014; $3,408, PF-66, November 2014
1865S	175,000	25	40.3	16%	$65	$275	$475	$750	$2,200	$6,750	$12,000		
	Auctions: $41,125, MS-65, October 2014; $1,175, VF-35, October 2014; $600, VF-30, July 2014; $458, VF-30, July 2014
1866	8,000	42	57.0	79%	$450	$1,200	$1,500	$2,000	$2,100	$2,200	$2,600	$2,800	$3,500
	Auctions: $12,925, MS-66, April 2013; $1,645, EF-40, July 2014; $423, VF-20, August 2014
1866, Proof	725	168	64.4								$325	$700	$1,850
	Auctions: $1,293, PF-65Cam, September 2014; $8,225, PF-68, October 2014; $470, PF-62, October 2014
1866S	135,000	31	41.0	35%	$40	$75	$135	$350	$600	$1,150	$4,500	$6,500	$17,500
	Auctions: $1,880, AU-53, February 2014; $1,293, AU-50, September 2014; $441, VF-30, September 2014
1867	6,000	46	60.8	85%	$400	$750	$950	$1,100	$1,300	$1,500	$2,500	$3,250	$4,000
	Auctions: $11,163, MS-68, June 2014; $2,468, MS-64, July 2014
1867, Proof	625	128	64.2								$300	$700	$1,650
	Auctions: $1,528, PF-65Cam, October 2014; $2,585, PF-64DCam, June 2014; $1,763, PF-66, August 2014; $1,058, PF-65, October 2014
1867S	140,000	27	51.6	52%	$32	$100	$170	$425	$700	$1,250	$2,500	$4,000	$7,500
	Auctions: $8,225, MS-65, June 2014; $7,344, MS-65, October 2014; $217, VF-20, July 2014; $176, VF-20, November 2014
1868	464,000	39	59.2	82%	$18	$30	$40	$65	$150	$300	$850	$1,250	$3,500
	Auctions: $2,820, MS-65, October 2014
1868, Proof	600	149	63.9								$325	$700	$1,650
	Auctions: $5,875, PF-66Cam+, July 2014; $2,116, PF-66Cam, November 2014; $7,050, PF-66Cam, September 2013; $1,175, PF-65, July 2014
1868S	260,000	19	54.3	63%	$20	$35	$70	$125	$225	$400	$1,000	$2,000	$5,000
	Auctions: $14,100, MS-66, October 2014; $541, AU-50, October 2014; $212, AU-50, December 2013; $308, EF-40, November 2014
1869	256,000	25	55.0	60%	$18	$30	$65	$100	$200	$400	$900	$1,850	$3,500
	Auctions: $4,553, MS, March 2014; $294, AU-50, October 2014; $222, AU-50, November 2014
1869, Proof	600	172	64.1								$325	$700	$1,650
	Auctions: $4,553, PF-66Cam, September 2014; $1,586, PF-66Cam, September 2014; $3,173, PF-67, October 2014; $1,528, PF-66, November 2014
1869S	450,000	61	61.5	84%	$18	$25	$50	$150	$250	$400	$800	$1,500	$3,400
	Auctions: $5,875, MS-66, September 2014; $1,293, MS-62, April 2014; $223, EF-45, November 2014; $223, EF-45, October 2014
1870	470,500	68	61.0	82%	$16	$25	$30	$50	$100	$200	$450	$950	$1,850
	Auctions: $9,988, MS-66, June 2014; $79, AU-50, October 2014
1870, Proof	1,000	155	64.1								$325	$700	$1,650
	Auctions: $7,050, PF-67, January 2014
1870S	50,000	33	42.1	39%	$250	$400	$475	$600	$850	$1,800	$2,750	$3,500	$6,000
	Auctions: $22,325, MS-66, January 2014; $1,175, AU-53, October 2014; $705, VF-35, November 2014; $793, VF-30, July 2014
1871	906,750	68	59.7	68%	$16	$25	$30	$50	$150	$250	$425	$900	$2,000
	Auctions: $7,050, MS-66, November 2014; $5,581, MS-66, October 2014; $2,233, MS-65, April 2013; $617, MS-64, October 2014
1871, Proof	960	149	64.1								$325	$700	$1,650
	Auctions: $14,100, PF-67Cam, September 2013; $1,410, PF-65Cam, August 2014; $1,880, PF-66, November 2014
1871CC	20,100	22	37.4	27%	$2,500	$5,200	$8,000	$12,500	$25,000	$50,000	$100,000		
	Auctions: $270,250, MS-65, October 2014; $27,025, AU-55, May 2013; $6,463, AU-50, July 2014; $5,288, EF-40, November 2014
1871S	320,000	28	55.6	46%	$25	$80	$140	$225	$300	$550	$1,200	$2,500	$7,000
	Auctions: $11,750, MS-65, October 2014; $588, AU-58, July 2014; $558, EF-45, October 2014; $212, VF-30, October 2014

1872, Doubled-Die Reverse
FS-10-1872-801.

1873, With Arrows,
Doubled-Die Obverse
FS-10-1873-101.

1873, Close 3   **1873, Open 3**

	Mintage	Cert	Avg	%MS	G-4	F-12	VF-20	EF-40	AU-50	MS-60	MS-63 / PF-60	MS-64 / PF-63	MS-65 / PF-65
1872	2,395,500	82	58.8	73%	$18	$25	$30	$40	$90	$175	$300	$750	$1,350
	Auctions: $1,439, MS-65, March 2014; $529, MS-64, October 2014												
1872, Doubled-Die Reverse (k,l)	(m)	2	37.5	0%	$50	$75	$150	$250	$350	$750			
	Auctions: $425, VF-20, May 2008												
1872, Proof	950	138	63.9								$325	$700	$1,650
	Auctions: $4,700, PF-67Cam, November 2014; $3,290, PF-66Cam, March 2013; $1,175, PF-66, October 2014; $382, PF-62, August 2014												
1872CC	35,480	39	25.7	0%	$500	$2,000	$4,000	$10,000	$18,500	$50,000	$200,000		
	Auctions: $15,275, AU-50, November 2014; $8,225, EF-45, March 2014; $8,225, EF-45, October 2014; $4,994, VF-35, July 2014												
1872S	190,000	22	54.6	50%	$25	$85	$140	$225	$400	$1,200	$2,500	$4,000	$15,000
	Auctions: $7,638, MS-64, April 2013; $2,820, MS-63, September 2014; $353, EF-45, October 2014												
1873, No Arrows, Close 3	1,506,800	41	58.0	63%	$16	$22	$25	$40	$90	$150	$250	$650	$1,500
	Auctions: $6,463, MS-67, June 2014; $259, AU-58, October 2014												
1873, No Arrows, Open 3	60,000	34	50.7	38%	$20	$50	$75	$130	$200	$600	$1,500	$3,000	$9,000
	Auctions: $9,400, MS-64, August 2013; $353, AU-55, October 2014; $259, AU-55, October 2014												
1873, No Arrows, Close 3, Proof	600	174	64.3								$325	$700	$1,650
	Auctions: $16,450, PF-68Cam, November 2013; $423, PF-62Cam, December 2014												
1873CC, No Arrows † (n,o)	12,400	0	n/a							*$2,000,000*			
	Auctions: $7,475, VF-20, January 2012												
1873, With Arrows	2,378,000	180	57.6	66%	$18	$26	$55	$150	$300	$550	$900	$1,650	$4,000
	Auctions: $1,528, MS-64, July 2014; $1,294, MS-64, August 2014; $23,500, AU-58, June 2014; $282, AU-55, October 2014												
1873, With Arrows, Doubled-Die Obverse (p)	(q)	4	27.8	25%	$65	$200	$500	$1,000	$1,500				
	Auctions: $3,220, VF-25, October 2011												
1873, With Arrows, Proof	500	104	64.2								$750	$1,500	$5,500
	Auctions: $9,988, PF-67Cam, September 2014; $9,988, PF-66Cam, September 2014; $16,450, PF-67, November 2013												
1873CC, With Arrows	18,791	39	16.8	3%	$2,700	$5,000	$8,500	$17,000	$40,000	$50,000	$65,000		$275,000
	Auctions: $199,750, MS-65, June 2014; $7,638, AU-50, November 2014; $9,400, VF-35, August 2014; $8,225, VF-35, August 2014												
1873S	455,000	66	63.1	92%	$22	$35	$60	$175	$450	$1,000	$2,100	$3,750	$6,500
	Auctions: $24,675, MS-67, June 2014; $1,116, MS-63, September 2014; $364, AU-53, July 2014; $329, AU-50, October 2014												

† Ranked in the *100 Greatest U.S. Coins* (fourth edition). **k.** The first die hubbing was almost completely obliterated by the second, which was rotated about 170 degrees from the first. The key indicators of this variety are inside the opening of the D, and near the center arm of the E in ONE. **l.** This coin is considered rare. **m.** Included in circulation-strike 1872 mintage figure. **n.** Most of the mintage of 1873-CC (Without Arrows) was melted after the law of 1873, affecting the statuses and physical properties of U.S. coinage, was passed. **o.** This coin is considered unique. **p.** Doubling is evident on the shield and on the banner across the shield. Although well known for decades, very few examples of this variety have been reported. **q.** Included in circulation-strike 1873, With Arrows, mintage figure.

1875-CC, Mintmark Above Bow

1875-CC, Mintmark Below Bow

1876-CC, Variety 1 Reverse

1876-CC, Variety 2 Reverse
FS-10-1876CC-901.

	Mintage	Cert	Avg	%MS	G-4	F-12	VF-20	EF-40	AU-50	MS-60	MS-63	MS-64	MS-65
											PF-60	PF-63	PF-65
1874	2,939,300	258	58.3	67%	$18	$25	$55	$150	$310	$600	$1,000	$1,750	$4,000
	Auctions: $67,563, MS-68, August 2013; $19,975, MS-67, October 2014; $705, MS-63, July 2014; $341, AU-58, December 2014												
1874, Proof	700	191	63.8								$750	$1,500	$5,500
	Auctions: $3,819, PF-65Cam, September 2014; $27,025, PF-67, June 2014; $5,288, PF-66, September 2014; $1,234, PF-64, November 2014												
1874CC	10,817	12	34.9	8%	$4,500	$12,500	$18,000	$28,000	$48,000	$65,000	$175,000		
	Auctions: $152,750, MS-63, October 2014; $41,125, AU-53, April 2014; $25,850, EF-45, July 2014; $9,694, VG-8, July 2014												
1874S	240,000	61	59.5	77%	$25	$65	$110	$225	$500	$900	$2,000	$4,000	$8,500
	Auctions: $12,925, MS-66, October 2014; $3,055, MS-64, April 2013; $123, VF-20, November 2014												
1875	10,350,000	393	61.7	88%	$15	$20	$25	$35	$80	$150	$250	$450	$1,000
	Auctions: $7,639, MS-67, September 2013; $599, MS-65, November 2014; $247, MS-64, October 2014; $170, MS-62, December 2014												
1875, Proof	700	158	64.4								$300	$650	$1,650
	Auctions: $3,819, PF-66Cam, February 2014; $1,821, PF-66Cam, August 2014; $1,645, PF-66Cam, September 2014												
1875CC, All kinds	4,645,000												
1875CC, Above Bow		136	54.3	61%	$28	$35	$50	$70	$150	$325	$500	$1,250	$2,750
	Auctions: $3,525, MS-66, April 2014; $764, MS-64, October 2014; $470, MS-61, July 2014; $170, AU-53, November 2014												
1875CC, Below Bow		64	55.8	69%	$28	$35	$50	$70	$125	$350	$550	$1,400	$3,000
	Auctions: $2,938, MS-65, October 2014; $4,994, MS-65, September 2013												
1875S, All kinds	9,070,000												
1875S, Below Bow		63	57.9	73%	$15	$20	$25	$35	$85	$160	$250	$450	$1,200
	Auctions: $881, MS-65, June 2013; $911, MS-64, October 2014; $353, MS-64+, November 2014												
1875S, Above Bow		30	62.6	80%	$15	$20	$25	$35	$85	$160	$250	$450	$1,200
	Auctions: $1,880, MS-66, August 2014; $1,998, MS-65, April 2014; $235, MS-62, October 2014												
1876	11,450,000	331	61.7	88%	$15	$20	$25	$35	$80	$150	$250	$450	$1,000
	Auctions: $2,589, MS-67, September 2013; $705, MS-65, July 2014; $646, MS-65, July 2014; $153, MS-62, August 2014												
1876, Proof	1,150	155	63.7								$300	$650	$1,750
	Auctions: $7,331, PF-67★, April 2012												
1876CC	8,270,000	350	56.3	69%	$27	$32	$45	$65	$100	$230	$450	$550	$1,500
	Auctions: $12,338, MS-67, September 2014; $14,100, MS-67, February 2013; $441, MS-63, September 2014; $306, AU-58, September 2014												
1876CC, Variety 2 Reverse (r)	(s)	2	55.8	50%				$250	$350	$600	$1,250		
	Auctions: $3,738, MS-64, February 2012												
1876CC, Proof	3–4	5	65.5								—		$55,000
	Auctions: $38,188, PF-65, October 2014												
1876S	10,420,000	99	59.2	75%	$15	$20	$25	$35	$80	$150	$250	$450	$1,750
	Auctions: $3,819, MS-66, April 2014; $1,763, MS-66, August 2014; $1,116, MS-65+, August 2014; $382, MS-64, November 2014												
1877	7,310,000	156	62.2	89%	$15	$20	$25	$35	$80	$150	$250	$450	$900
	Auctions: $4,113, MS-67, October 2014; $5,581, MS-67, November 2013; $229, MS-62, July 2014; $106, AU-58, October 2014												
1877, Proof	510	118	63.9								$300	$650	$1,750
	Auctions: $9,400, PF-67, June 2014; $999, PF-65, September 2014; $617, PF-64, November 2014; $670, PF-64, December 2014												
1877CC	7,700,000	415	59.3	80%	$27	$32	$45	$65	$100	$230	$400	$600	$1,350
	Auctions: $7,050, MS-67, April 2014; $7,931, MS-67, October 2014; $7,638, MS-67, November 2014; $1,998, MS-65, August 2014												
1877S	2,340,000	87	61.7	86%	$15	$20	$25	$35	$80	$150	$250	$450	$1,000
	Auctions: $18,800, MS-67, October 2014; $2,820, MS-65, June 2013; $212, MS-63, October 2014; $165, AU-58, October 2014												

r. The scarce Variety 2 reverse exhibits a single point to the end of the left ribbon; the common Variety 1 reverse has a split at the ribbon's end. **s.** Included in circulation-strike 1876-CC mintage figure.

	Mintage	Cert	Avg	%MS	G-4	F-12	VF-20	EF-40	AU-50	MS-60	MS-63	MS-64	MS-65
											PF-60	PF-63	PF-65
1878	1,677,200	83	62.1	92%	$15	$20	$25	$35	$80	$150	$250	$450	$900
	Auctions: $8,225, MS-67, September 2013; $170, MS-63, October 2014												
1878, Proof	800	167	64.0								$300	$650	$1,750
	Auctions: $388, PF-62Cam, November 2014; $3,055, PF-67, October 2014; $2,820, PF-66, September 2013												
1878CC	200,000	69	52.8	68%	$150	$250	$350	$420	$625	$1,200	$1,850	$3,000	$4,000
	Auctions: $13,513, MS-66, August 2013; $2,938, MS-65, August 2014; $705, EF-45, October 2014; $223, VG-10, July 2014												
1879	14,000	201	63.6	94%	$200	$325	$400	$500	$550	$625	$750	$950	$1,250
	Auctions: $3,525, MS-67, August 2014; $4,113, MS-67, April 2013; $646, MS-64, October 2014; $588, MS-63+, October 2014												
1879, Proof	1,100	303	64.3								$275	$650	$1,750
	Auctions: $1,175, PF-65Cam, July 2014; $1,058, PF-65Cam, November 2014; $470, PF-63Cam, November 2014; $4,406, PF-67, November 2013												
1880	36,000	149	61.9	87%	$150	$250	$350	$400	$500	$650	$750	$950	$1,250
	Auctions: $6,463, MS-68, October 2014; $4,113, MS-67, January 2014; $2,706, MS-67, July 2014; $3,290, MS-67, August 2014												
1880, Proof	1,355	314	64.5								$300	$650	$1,750
	Auctions: $793, PF-64Cam+, October 2014; $646, PF-64Cam, September 2014; $470, PF-62Cam, November 2014; $8,813, PF-68, November 2014												
1881	24,000	85	57.2	75%	$160	$260	$375	$425	$525	$675	$775	$975	$1,350
	Auctions: $4,994, MS-67, August 2013; $499, MS-62, November 2014; $499, AU-53, October 2014; $217, VG-10, October 2014												
1881, Proof	975	254	64.6								$275	$650	$1,750
	Auctions: $6,463, PF-68Cam, April 2014; $4,113, PF-67Cam, September 2014; $1,528, PF-66Cam, July 2014; $1,293, PF-66Cam, October 2014												
1882	3,910,000	377	63.2	93%	$15	$20	$25	$35	$80	$150	$250	$450	$800
	Auctions: $3,672, MS-67, June 2014; $4,113, MS-67, September 2014; $2,938, MS-67, October 2014; $1,058, MS-65, July 2014												
1882, Proof	1,100	339	64.5								$300	$650	$1,750
	Auctions: $7,638, PF-67Cam, March 2013; $1,351, PF-66Cam, September 2014; $3,290, PF-67, August 2014; $3,290, PF-67, September 2014												
1883	7,674,673	469	61.7	88%	$15	$20	$25	$35	$80	$150	$250	$450	$800
	Auctions: $9,400, MS-68, July 2014; $7,344, MS-68, October 2014; $170, MS-62, July 2014; $141, MS-62, September 2014												
1883, Proof	1,039	303	64.3								$300	$650	$1,750
	Auctions: $8,225, PF-68, July 2014; $8,813, PF-68, September 2014; $1,307, PF-66, November 2014; $881, PF-64, November 2014												
1884	3,365,505	388	63.2	91%	$15	$20	$25	$35	$80	$150	$250	$450	$800
	Auctions: $7,344, MS-68, June 2013; $705, MS-66, November 2014; $535, MS-65, October 2014; $53, AU-50, October 2014												
1884, Proof	875	312	65.0								$300	$650	$1,750
	Auctions: $6,463, PF-68Cam, March 2013; $1,410, PF-66Cam, July 2014; $1,116, PF-65Cam, July 2014; $1,058, PF-65Cam, November 2014												
1884S	564,969	58	59.8	72%	$20	$32	$60	$100	$300	$750	$1,200	$1,850	$5,000
	Auctions: $1,149, MS-64, June 2014; $1,116, MS-64, November 2014; $229, AU-50, November 2014												
1885	2,532,497	341	63.1	92%	$15	$20	$25	$35	$80	$150	$250	$450	$800
	Auctions: $3,173, MS-67, June 2014; $558, MS-65, November 2014; $141, MS-62, September 2014												
1885, Proof	930	291	64.8								$300	$650	$1,750
	Auctions: $6,463, PF-68Cam, April 2013; $2,585, PF-67Cam, August 2014; $1,410, PF-66+, October 2014												
1885S	43,690	56	34.9	25%	$400	$800	$1,400	$2,200	$4,000	$5,500	$9,000	$16,000	$27,500
	Auctions: $49,938, MS-66, June 2014; $1,645, VF-30, October 2014; $999, VF-20, October 2014; $999, F-12, August 2014												
1886	6,376,684	574	62.6	90%	$15	$20	$25	$35	$80	$150	$250	$450	$800
	Auctions: $1,880, MS-67, October 2014; $881, MS-66, October 2014; $1,116, MS-66, February 2013; $793, MS-65, August 2014												
1886, Proof	886	289	64.4								$300	$650	$1,750
	Auctions: $12,925, PF-68Cam, June 2014; $2,350, PF-66, September 2014; $1,116, PF-65, August 2014												
1886S	206,524	63	61.9	87%	$30	$50	$75	$135	$200	$600	$1,200	$2,000	$4,500
	Auctions: $8,813, MS-67, October 2014; $4,700, MS-66, September 2014; $6,463, MS-66, June 2013; $2,585, MS-65, October 2014												
1887	11,283,229	543	61.5	86%	$15	$20	$25	$35	$80	$150	$250	$450	$800
	Auctions: $2,115, MS-66+, July 2014; $2,820, MS-65, February 2013; $456, MS-64, July 2014; $329, MS-64, September 2014												
1887, Proof	710	207	64.5								$300	$650	$1,750
	Auctions: $6,463, PF-67Cam, February 2014; $4,406, PF-67Cam, September 2014; $3,819, PF-67Cam, October 2014; $646, PF-64Cam, August 2014												
1887S	4,454,450	288	61.3	85%	$15	$20	$25	$35	$80	$150	$250	$450	$1,200
	Auctions: $805, MS-65, November 2013; $470, AU-53, September 2014; $69, AU-50, October 2014												

1891-O, O Over Horizontal O
FS-10-1891o-501.

1891-S, Repunched Mintmark
FS-10-1891S-501.

	Mintage	Cert	Avg	%MS	G-4	F-12	VF-20	EF-40	AU-50	MS-60	MS-63	MS-64	MS-65
											PF-60	PF-63	PF-65
1888	5,495,655	304	61.6	87%	$15	$20	$25	$35	$80	$150	$250	$450	$800
Auctions: $9,988, MS-67, June 2014; $382, MS-64, October 2014; $123, MS-62, November 2014													
1888, Proof	832	220	64.6								$300	$650	$1,750
Auctions: $1,410, PF-66Cam, November 2014; $2,585, PF-67, August 2014; $2,115, PF-66, February 2014; $852, PF-65, July 2014													
1888S	1,720,000	66	59.2	67%	$15	$20	$25	$35	$100	$250	$650	$1,000	$2,750
Auctions: $10,575, MS-66, June 2014; $940, MS-63, July 2014; $112, AU-53, October 2014													
1889	7,380,000	329	61.7	87%	$15	$20	$25	$35	$80	$150	$250	$450	$800
Auctions: $4,700, MS-67, January 2014; $3,819, MS-67, July 2014; $3,819, MS-67, October 2014; $2,585, MS-66+, October 2014													
1889, Proof	711	173	64.6								$300	$650	$1,750
Auctions: $2,820, PF-67Cam, August 2014; $8,519, PF-68, June 2014; $2,585, PF-67, August 2014; $1,293, PF-66, September 2014													
1889S	972,678	83	60.5	66%	$20	$30	$50	$80	$150	$450	$900	$1,200	$4,500
Auctions: $4,113, MS-66, April 2014; $4,847, MS-66, October 2014													
1890	9,910,951	552	61.9	87%	$15	$20	$25	$35	$80	$150	$250	$450	$800
Auctions: $4,113, MS-67, January 2014; $618, MS-65, July 2014; $294, MS-64, October 2014; $212, MS-63, October 2014													
1890, Proof	590	206	64.5								$300	$650	$1,750
Auctions: $12,103, PF-68DCam, June 2014; $2,820, PF-66DCam, August 2014; $3,055, PF-67, October 2014; $1,528, PF-66, October 2014													
1890S, Large S	1,423,076	106	60.3	78%	$18	$25	$55	$85	$150	$350	$700	$1,000	$1,750
Auctions: $1,645, MS-65, October 2014; $2,233, MS-65, August 2013; $212, MS-61, September 2014; $129, AU-53, July 2014													
1890S, Small S (t)	(u)	(v)											
Auctions: $1,208, MS-65, February 2006													
1891	15,310,000	947	62.1	88%	$15	$20	$25	$35	$80	$150	$250	$450	$800
Auctions: $3,819, MS-67, June 2014; $2,938, MS-67, September 2014; $707, MS-66, October 2014; $535, MS-65, November 2014													
1891, Proof	600	222	64.9								$300	$650	$1,750
Auctions: $6,463, PF-67Cam, November 2013													
1891O	4,540,000	203	60.7	85%	$15	$20	$30	$50	$100	$175	$375	$600	$1,350
Auctions: $7,638, MS-67, August 2013; $353, MS-64, October 2014; $823, MS-64, November 2014; $259, MS-63, October 2014													
1891O, O Over Horizontal O (w)	(x)	2	51.5	0%	$60	$120	$150	$225	—	—			
Auctions: $253, AU-58, May 2010													
1891O, Proof (y)	2–3	2	66.0										
Auctions: No auction records available.													
1891S	3,196,116	161	62.4	89%	$15	$20	$25	$35	$80	$175	$325	$500	$1,100
Auctions: $7,638, MS-67, June 2014; $1,998, MS-66, November 2014; $190, MS-62, July 2014; $59, AU-50, October 2014													
1891S, Repunched Mintmark (z)	(aa)	0	n/a						$200	$225	$500		
Auctions: $5,750, MS-66, September 2010													

t. This coin is considered rare. **u.** Included in 1890-S, Large S, mintage figure. **v.** Included in certified population for 1890-S, Large S. **w.** The primary O mintmark was punched over a previously punched horizontal O. **x.** Included in circulation-strike 1891-O mintage figure. **y.** This coin is considered extremely rare. **z.** The larger primary S mintmark (known as the medium S) was punched squarely over the smaller S, which is evident within both loops. **aa.** Included in 1891-S mintage figure.

BARBER OR LIBERTY HEAD (1892–1916)

Designer: *Charles E. Barber.* **Weight:** *2.50 grams.* **Composition:** *.900 silver, .100 copper (net weight: .07234 oz. pure silver).* **Diameter:** *17.9 mm.* **Edge:** *Reeded.*
Mints: *Philadelphia, Denver, New Orleans, San Francisco.*

Circulation Strike

Mintmark location is on the reverse, below the bow.

Proof

History. This dime belongs to a suite of silver coins (including the quarter and half dollar) designed by U.S. Mint chief engraver Charles E. Barber. It features a large Liberty Head styled similarly to contemporary French coinage. The reverse of the dime continues the "cereal wreath" motif of the late Liberty Seated era.

Striking and Sharpness. Check the details of the hair on the obverse. The reverse usually is sharp. If weakness is seen, it is typically in the wreath details. The denticles usually are sharp on the obverse and reverse. The Proofs of 1892 to 1901 usually have cameo contrast between the designs and the mirror fields. Later Proofs vary in contrast.

Availability. With the exception of the rare 1894-S, of which fewer than a dozen are known, all dates and mintmarks are collectible. Probably 90% or more of the survivors are in lower grades such as AG-3 and G-4. The word LIBERTY in the headband, a key to grading, tended to wear away quickly. Relatively few are in grades from Fine upward. MS coins are somewhat scarce, this being especially true of the branch-mint issues. MS-63 and finer Barber dimes usually are from the Philadelphia Mint or, if from a branch mint, are dated after 1905. Proof Barber dimes survive in proportion to their mintages. Choice and Gem examples are more easily found among dimes than among quarters and half dollars of this type. All were originally sold in silver-coin sets.

GRADING STANDARDS

MS-60 to 70 (Mint State). *Obverse:* At MS-60, some abrasion and contact marks are evident, most noticeably on the cheek and the obverse field to the right. Luster is present, but may be dull or lifeless. Many Barber coins have been cleaned, especially of the earlier dates. At MS-63, contact marks are very few; abrasion still is evident, but less than at lower levels. An MS-65 coin may have minor abrasion on the cheek, but contact marks are so

1897-O. Graded MS-65.

minute as to require magnification. Luster should be full and rich. *Reverse:* Comments apply as for the obverse, except that in lower Mint State grades abrasion and contact marks are most noticeable on the highest parts of the leaves and the ribbon, less so on ONE DIME. At MS-65 or higher, there are no marks visible to the unaided eye. The field is mainly protected by design elements and does not show abrasion as much as does the obverse on a given coin.

Illustrated coin: This is a lustrous coin, with scattered areas of toning.

AU-50, 53, 55, 58 (About Uncirculated).
Obverse: Light wear is seen on the head, especially on the forward hair under LIBERTY. At AU-58, the luster is extensive, but incomplete, especially on the higher parts and in the right field. At AU-50 and 53, luster is less. *Reverse:* Wear is seen on the leaves and ribbon. An AU-58 coin will have nearly full luster, more so than on the obverse, as the design elements protect the small field areas. At AU-50 and 53, there still is significant luster.

1907-S. Graded AU-50.

EF-40, 45 (Extremely Fine). *Obverse:* Further wear is seen on the head. The hair above the forehead lacks most detail. LIBERTY shows wear but still is strong. *Reverse:* Further wear is seen on all areas, most noticeably at the wreath and ribbon. Leaves retain excellent details except on the higher areas.

1895-O. Graded EF-40.

VF-20, 30 (Very Fine). *Obverse:* The head shows more wear, now with nearly all detail gone in the hair above the forehead. LIBERTY shows wear, but is complete. The leaves on the head all show wear, as does the upper part of the cap. *Reverse:* Wear is more extensive. The details in the highest leaves are weak or missing, but in lower levels the leaf details remain strong.

1914-S. Graded VF-30.

F-12, 15 (Fine). *Obverse:* The head shows extensive wear. LIBERTY, the key place to check, is weak, especially at ER, but is fully readable. The ANA grading standards and *Photograde* adhere to this. PCGS suggests that lightly struck coins "may have letters partially missing." Traditionally, collectors insist on full LIBERTY. *Reverse:* Much detail of the leaves in the higher areas is gone. The rim remains bold.

1901-S. Graded F-12.

 Illustrated coin: LIBERTY is readable, but letters ER are light.

VG-8, 10 (Very Good). *Obverse:* A net of three letters in LIBERTY must be readable. Traditionally LI is clear, and after that there is a partial letter or two. *Reverse:* Further wear has made the wreath flat; now only in outline form with only a few traces of details. The rim is complete.

1895-O. Graded VG-8.

G-4, 6 (Good). *Obverse:* The head is in outline form, with the center flat. Most of the rim is there. All letters and the date are full. *Reverse:* The leaves are all combined and in outline form. The rim is weak in areas.

1892. Graded G-4.

AG-3 (About Good). *Obverse:* The lettering is readable, but the parts near the border may be worn away. The date is clear. *Reverse:* The wreath and interior letters are partially worn away. The rim is weak.

1908-S. Graded AG-3.

PF-60 to 70 (Proof). *Obverse and Reverse:* Proofs that are extensively cleaned and have many hairlines, or that are dull and grainy, are lower level, such as PF-60 to 62. These are not widely desired, save for the rare (in any grade) year of 1895, and even so most collectors would rather have a lustrous MS-60 than a dull PF-60. With medium hairlines and good reflectivity, an assigned grade of PF-64 is indicated. Tiny horizontal lines on Miss Liberty's cheek, known

1911. Graded PF-67 Deep Cameo.

as *slide marks*, from National and other album slides scuffing the relief of the cheek, are endemic among Barber silver coins. With noticeable marks of this type, the highest grade assignable is PF-64. With relatively few hairlines, a rating of PF-65 can be given. PF-66 should have hairlines so delicate that magnification is needed to see them. Above that, a Proof should be free of any hairlines or other problems.

    Illustrated coin: Proof dimes of 1911 are rare (only 543 minted), but one with a Deep Cameo finish, as displayed by this coin, is *extremely* rare. The coin is fully struck on both sides, and has neither a blemish nor a trace of toning.

1893, 3 Over 2

1897, Repunched Date
FS-10-1897-301.

	Mintage	Cert	Avg	%MS	G-4	VG-8	F-12	VF-20	EF-40	AU-50	MS-60 / PF-60	MS-63 / PF-63	MS-65 / PF-65
1892	12,120,000	1,272	62.1	86%	$7	$7.50	$18	$25	$30	$80	$135	$240	$650
	Auctions: $3,525, MS-67, June 2014; $2,851, MS-67, August 2014; $517, MS-65, November 2014; $470, MS-65, November 2014												
1892, Proof	1,245	294	64.4								$275	$575	$1,500
	Auctions: $17,625, PF-68Cam, April 2013; $4,406, PF-67Cam, July 2014; $646, PF-64Cam, October 2014; $705, PF-64Cam, November 2014												
1892O	3,841,700	237	58.9	76%	$12	$15	$35	$50	$75	$95	$175	$300	$1,250
	Auctions: $4,994, MS-66, February 2013												
1892S	990,710	149	50.7	60%	$65	$120	$190	$240	$280	$330	$425	$775	$3,500
	Auctions: $10,575, MS-66, October 2014; $7,050, MS-65, June 2014; $1,175, MS-64, July 2014; $353, AU-50, August 2014												
1893, 3 Over 2 (a)	(b)	0	n/a		$140	$150	$160	$175	$200	$300	$700	$1,800	$5,500
	Auctions: $8,225, MS-66, October 2014												
1893	3,339,940	286	59.8	83%	$8	$12	$20	$30	$45	$75	$150	$250	$950
	Auctions: $4,700, MS-67, October 2014; $15,275, MS-67, August 2013; $529, MS-64, July 2014; $229, MS-63, August 2014												
1893, Proof	792	269	65.0								$275	$575	$1,500
	Auctions: $8,225, PF-67Cam, January 2014; $1,528, PF-67, October 2014												
1893O	1,760,000	166	53.4	66%	$30	$45	$120	$150	$190	$230	$325	$650	$2,250
	Auctions: $9,988, MS-67, October 2014; $2,115, MS-65, February 2013; $940, MS-64, September 2014; $382, MS-63, December 2014												
1893S (c)	2,491,401	142	54.8	67%	$15	$25	$37	$60	$85	$150	$290	$700	$3,000
	Auctions: $4,847, MS-66, October 2014; $2,350, MS-65, July 2013												
1894	1,330,000	203	51.5	63%	$30	$45	$120	$160	$180	$220	$325	$500	$1,200
	Auctions: $1,645, MS-66, September 2014; $485, MS-64, September 2014; $2,233, MS-66, June 2013; $200, MS-60, November 2014												
1894, Proof	972	319	64.9								$275	$575	$1,500
	Auctions: $4,994, PF-68, October 2014; $5,699, PF-68, July 2013; $1,194, PF-66, September 2014; $676, PF-64, July 2014												
1894O	720,000	124	29.5	19%	$70	$95	$200	$275	$425	$600	$1,450	$2,500	$12,500
	Auctions: $16,450, MS-65, August 2014; $17,121, MS-65, October 2014; $10,575, MS-65, August 2013; $382, EF-40, September 2014												
1894S, Proof † (d)	24	6	64.5									*$1,750,000*	
	Auctions: $1,552,500, PF-64, October 2007												
1895	690,000	166	44.5	49%	$80	$160	$325	$475	$550	$625	$725	$1,000	$2,500
	Auctions: $5,500, MS-66, June 2014; $940, MS-64, October 2014; $1,116, MS-64, November 2014												
1895, Proof	880	317	64.9								$275	$575	$1,600
	Auctions: $5,875, PF-68Cam, April 2013; $1,410, PF-66Cam, August 2014; $1,293, PF-66, August 2014; $705, PF-64, July 2014												
1895O	440,000	262	20.3	10%	$375	$550	$850	$1,250	$2,400	$3,400	$6,000	$10,000	$25,000
	Auctions: $34,075, MS-65, January 2014; $1,116, VF-20, August 2014; $435, VG-8, October 2014; $382, G-6, September 2014												
1895S	1,120,000	209	48.6	57%	$42	$60	$135	$190	$240	$310	$500	$1,100	$6,000
	Auctions: $15,863, MS-66, June 2014; $4,113, MS-65+, October 2014; $1,410, MS-64, October 2014; $1,293, MS-64, October 2014												
1896	2,000,000	135	56.0	74%	$10	$22	$50	$75	$100	$120	$175	$500	$1,150
	Auctions: $8,225, MS-66, October 2014; $1,058, MS-65, July 2014; $881, MS-65, October 2014												
1896, Proof	762	254	64.7								$275	$575	$1,500
	Auctions: $15,275, PF-68Cam, June 2014; $676, PF-64, July 2014; $588, PF-64, July 2014												
1896O	610,000	111	31.0	23%	$80	$160	$290	$350	$450	$650	$1,000	$2,400	$7,500
	Auctions: $12,925, MS-67, October 2014; $15,275, MS-66, January 2014; $33, AG-3, November 2014												
1896S	575,056	147	41.7	51%	$80	$150	$280	$335	$400	$550	$850	$1,500	$4,500
	Auctions: $9,400, MS-66, June 2014; $6,463, MS-66, October 2014; $441, AU-50, December 2014; $499, EF-40, August 2014												

† Ranked in the *100 Greatest U.S. Coins* (fourth edition). **a.** Overlaid photographs indicate this is not a true overdate. **b.** Included in circulation-strike 1893 mintage figure. **c.** Boldly doubled mintmark. **d.** The reason for the low mintage of the Proof 1894-S dime is unknown. Popular theories, among others, include a rounding out of the Mint's record books, or a special presentation to bankers visiting the San Francisco Mint. Fewer than a dozen examples are known to exist.

	Mintage	Cert	Avg	%MS	G-4	VG-8	F-12	VF-20	EF-40	AU-50	MS-60 PF-60	MS-63 PF-63	MS-65 PF-65
1897	10,868,533	440	61.7	86%	$4	$5	$8	$15	$32	$75	$135	$240	$625
	Auctions: $3,055, MS-67, June 2014; $2,585, MS-67, October 2014; $470, MS-65, July 2014; $588, MS-65, October 2014
1897, Repunched Date (e)	(f)	1	63.0	100%					$80	$120	$200		
	Auctions: No auction records available.
1897, Proof	731	248	64.8								$275	$575	$1,500
	Auctions: $7,638, PF-68Cam, August 2014; $14,100, PF-68Cam, October 2014; $7,638, PF-68Cam, August 2013
1897O	666,000	119	39.0	42%	$65	$115	$280	$375	$475	$600	$900	$1,700	$4,000
	Auctions: $7,638, MS-64, September 2013; $329, VF-35, September 2014; $282, VF-35, November 2014; $247, F-15, November 2014
1897S	1,342,844	100	49.9	52%	$18	$35	$90	$120	$175	$260	$450	$1,000	$3,750
	Auctions: $1,528, MS-64, August 2014; $1,880, MS-64, September 2013; $176, EF-40, October 2014
1898	16,320,000	465	61.9	84%	$4	$5	$8	$12	$26	$75	$115	$220	$675
	Auctions: $2,233, MS-66, April 2014; $1,293, MS-66, July 2014; $1,058, MS-66, September 2014; $1,528, MS-66, October 2014
1898, Proof	735	290	65.2								$275	$575	$1,500
	Auctions: $9,988, PF-68Cam, August 2013; $1,175, PF-64DCam, July 2014; $1,175, PF-65Cam, September 2014; $794, PF-64+, September 2014
1898O	2,130,000	86	52.5	60%	$12	$26	$85	$140	$190	$280	$450	$1,200	$3,000
	Auctions: $9,400, MS-66, June 2014; $881, MS-63, August 2014; $38, EF-40, November 2014
1898S	1,702,507	60	54.3	58%	$8	$15	$32	$45	$80	$150	$375	$1,200	$3,500
	Auctions: $10,281, MS-66, June 2014; $206, AU-55, December 2014
1899	19,580,000	339	60.5	80%	$4	$5	$8	$12	$25	$75	$130	$240	$650
	Auctions: $4,113, MS-67, October 2014; $1,116, MS-65, August 2014; $188, MS-63, July 2013
1899, Proof	846	240	64.8								$275	$575	$1,500
	Auctions: $16,450, PF-68, June 2014; $617, PF-64, July 2014; $212, PF-60, November 2014
1899O	2,650,000	114	48.5	52%	$10	$18	$65	$95	$140	$225	$400	$1,150	$4,000
	Auctions: $7,050, MS-66, October 2014; $4,406, MS-65, November 2013; $2,585, MS-64, August 2014; $705, MS-63, July 2014
1899S	1,867,493	102	58.2	72%	$8.50	$16	$32	$35	$45	$110	$300	$750	$2,750
	Auctions: $7,050, MS-67, October 2014; $5,875, MS-67, December 2013; $2,820, MS-66, September 2014; $1,893, MS-65, July 2014
1900	17,600,000	250	60.9	81%	$4	$5	$8	$12	$25	$75	$125	$240	$850
	Auctions: $6,463, MS-67, August 2013; $1,998, MS-66, August 2014; $558, MS-65, July 2014; $229, MS-63, October 2014
1900, Proof	912	230	64.8								$275	$575	$1,500
	Auctions: $7,050, PF-67Cam, August 2013; $1,424, PF-66Cam+, October 2014; $1,234, PF-66Cam, November 2014; $5,581, PF-68, October 2014
1900O	2,010,000	101	46.5	45%	$18	$38	$110	$160	$220	$360	$650	$1,150	$5,000
	Auctions: $4,994, MS-66, October 2014; $5,640, MS-66, September 2013
1900S	5,168,270	153	57.1	55%	$5	$6	$12	$20	$30	$75	$175	$425	$1,800
	Auctions: $1,293, MS-65, November 2014; $881, MS-64, July 2014; $1,116, MS-64, February 2013
1901	18,859,665	299	61.7	82%	$4	$5	$7	$10	$26	$75	$125	$240	$625
	Auctions: $1,410, MS-66, September 2014; $1,058, MS-66, October 2014; $1,763, MS-66, April 2013; $558, MS-65, August 2014
1901, Proof	813	246	64.4								$275	$575	$1,500
	Auctions: $4,113, PF-67Cam, October 2014; $1,763, PF-66Cam, August 2014; $2,585, PF-67, June 2014; $1,481, PF-66, October 2014
1901O	5,620,000	113	54.6	54%	$4	$5.50	$16	$28	$75	$180	$450	$950	$3,800
	Auctions: $3,966, MS-66, April 2013; $470, MS-62, November 2014; $411, MS-62, December 2014; $200, G-4, November 2014
1901S	593,022	131	35.2	26%	$80	$150	$350	$450	$550	$675	$1,050	$1,800	$5,500
	Auctions: $6,463, MS-66, June 2013; $1,293, AU-58, August 2014; $470, VF-30, August 2014; $148, F-12, November 2014
1902	21,380,000	223	58.1	70%	$4	$5	$6	$8	$25	$75	$125	$240	$660
	Auctions: $1,116, MS-66, January 2014; $1,645, MS-66, October 2014; $441, MS-62, August 2014
1902, Proof	777	203	64.2								$275	$575	$1,500
	Auctions: $4,700, PF-67, February 2013; $1,250, PF-66, August 2014; $1,175, PF-66, October 2014; $1,116, PF-66, October 2014
1902O	4,500,000	128	55.8	62%	$4	$6	$15	$32	$65	$150	$400	$1,000	$4,000
	Auctions: $9,400, MS-67, October 2014; $3,290, MS-65, June 2014
1902S	2,070,000	90	50.6	56%	$9	$20	$55	$80	$140	$200	$400	$1,000	$4,000
	Auctions: $3,290, MS-66, October 2014; $2,820, MS-65, June 2014; $1,442, MS-64, October 2014; $270, MS-61, August 2014

e. More than one repunched date exists for 1897. This listing is for FS-10-1897-301 (see the *Cherrypickers' Guide to Rare Die Varieties*, sixth edition, volume II), one of the most dramatic RPDs of the series. The secondary digits of the date are evident west of the primary digits.
f. Included in circulation-strike 1897 mintage figure.

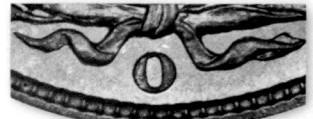

1905-O, Normal O   **1905-O, Micro O**

	Mintage	Cert	Avg	%MS	G-4	VG-8	F-12	VF-20	EF-40	AU-50	MS-60 PF-60	MS-63 PF-63	MS-65 PF-65
1903	19,500,000	163	58.4	72%	$4	$5	$6	$8	$25	$75	$125	$240	$1,000
	Auctions: $1,763, MS-66, October 2014; $1,175, MS-65, June 2014; $153, MS-62, July 2014												
1903, Proof	755	213	64.4								$275	$575	$1,500
	Auctions: $12,925, PF-68, October 2014; $14,100, PF-68, August 2013; $3,290, PF-67, August 2014; $1,183, PF-66, July 2014												
1903O	8,180,000	167	56.3	48%	$5	$6	$14	$25	$55	$110	$275	$550	$4,500
	Auctions: $7,638, MS-66, April 2013; $2,585, MS-65, July 2014												
1903S	613,300	117	34.9	26%	$85	$130	$350	$475	$700	$850	$1,200	$1,800	$3,500
	Auctions: $3,525, MS-66, March 2013; $2,350, MS-63, August 2014; $881, AU-50, July 2014; $734, EF-45, September 2014												
1904	14,600,357	187	61.0	83%	$4	$5	$6	$9	$25	$70	$110	$240	$1,400
	Auctions: $2,938, MS-66, June 2014; $999, MS-65+, November 2014												
1904, Proof	670	221	64.3								$275	$575	$1,500
	Auctions: $4,994, PF-67Cam, April 2013; $1,175, PF-65Cam, September 2014; $1,087, PF-65, August 2014; $705, PF-64, October 2014												
1904S	800,000	129	41.8	40%	$45	$75	$160	$235	$325	$475	$800	$1,500	$4,000
	Auctions: $11,163, MS-66, June 2014; $1,410, MS-63, September 2014; $558, AU-55, July 2014; $476, AU-53, July 2014												
1905	14,551,623	188	59.4	74%	$4	$5	$6	$10	$25	$75	$125	$240	$660
	Auctions: $4,406, MS-67, October 2014; $3,525, MS-66, January 2014; $1,645, MS-66, July 2014; $247, MS-64, July 2014												
1905, Proof	727	215	64.7								$275	$575	$1,500
	Auctions: $646, PF-64Cam, November 2014; $693, PF-64Cam, December 2014; $7,638, PF-68, June 2014; $1,175, PF-65, October 2014												
1905O	3,400,000	165	56.0	73%	$5	$10	$35	$60	$100	$150	$300	$500	$1,350
	Auctions: $5,434, MS-67, October 2014; $1,792, MS-66, January 2014; $999, MS-65, October 2014; $341, AU-50, August 2014												
1905O, Micro O	(g)	34	34.0	15%	$25	$50	$110	$160	$175	$275	$600	$3,500	
	Auctions: $4,113, MS-62, June 2014; $282, VF-25, August 2014; $223, VF-25, October 2014												
1905S	6,855,199	182	57.2	62%	$4	$6	$9	$20	$40	$95	$250	$325	$950
	Auctions: $4,553, MS-67, October 2014; $1,410, MS-66, October 2014; $646, MS-64, September 2013												
1906	19,957,731	356	60.2	79%	$4	$5	$6	$10	$25	$75	$125	$240	$625
	Auctions: $1,175, MS-66, June 2014; $499, MS-65, July 2014; $452, MS-65, August 2014; $165, MS-63, October 2014												
1906, Proof	675	189	64.6								$275	$575	$1,500
	Auctions: $2,115, PF-67, August 2014; $4,113, PF-67, October 2014; $1,763, PF-66, October 2014; $646, PF-64, November 2014												
1906D	4,060,000	107	57.1	77%	$4	$5	$8	$15	$35	$80	$175	$400	$1,500
	Auctions: $11,750, MS-67, April 2013; $1,058, MS-65, September 2014												
1906O	2,610,000	141	59.3	84%	$6	$14	$45	$75	$110	$130	$200	$325	$1,100
	Auctions: $14,100, MS-67, November 2013; $881, MS-66, July 2014; $1,586, MS-65, July 2014; $38, F-12, November 2014												
1906S	3,136,640	121	58.4	76%	$4	$6	$13	$25	$45	$110	$275	$550	$1,250
	Auctions: $1,998, MS-66, October 2014; $881, MS-65, July 2014; $529, MS-64, September 2014; $247, MS-62, December 2014												
1907	22,220,000	437	60.5	81%	$4	$5	$6	$10	$25	$75	$125	$240	$625
	Auctions: $1,058, MS-66, June 2014; $1,469, MS-66, August 2014; $969, MS-66, November 2014; $470, MS-65, July 2014												
1907, Proof	575	187	64.7								$275	$575	$1,500
	Auctions: $823, PF-64Cam, July 2014; $7,638, PF-68, December 2013; $1,179, PF-66, August 2014; $423, PF-63, July 2014												
1907D	4,080,000	81	58.9	73%	$4	$5	$10	$20	$45	$110	$300	$900	$2,250
	Auctions: $8,519, MS-67, February 2013; $3,055, MS-66, October 2014; $1,645, MS-65, November 2014; $84, AU-50, December 2014												
1907O	5,058,000	164	58.7	77%	$4	$7	$30	$45	$70	$110	$200	$375	$1,200
	Auctions: $15,863, MS-67, November 2013; $1,645, MS-66, September 2014; $1,763, MS-66, November 2014; $971, MS-65, July 2014												
1907S	3,178,470	98	55.6	54%	$4	$6	$15	$27	$75	$150	$400	$750	$2,500
	Auctions: $5,288, MS-66, September 2013; $1,651, MS-65, September 2014												

g. Included in 1905-O mintage figure.

1912-S, Doubled-Die Obverse
FS-10-1912S-101.

	Mintage	Cert	Avg	%MS	G-4	VG-8	F-12	VF-20	EF-40	AU-50	MS-60 / PF-60	MS-63 / PF-63	MS-65 / PF-65
1908	10,600,000	318	60.5	85%	$4	$5	$6	$10	$25	$75	$125	$240	$625
Auctions: $5,581, MS-67, October 2014; $705, MS-66, June 2014; $499, MS-65, July 2014; $470, MS-65, August 2014													
1908, Proof	545	190	64.7								$275	$575	$1,500
Auctions: $8,225, PF-68, June 2014; $2,468, PF-67, July 2014; $1,175, PF-66, November 2014; $364, PF-62, July 2014													
1908D	7,490,000	192	56.8	65%	$4	$5	$6	$10	$28	$75	$130	$300	$1,000
Auctions: $4,406, MS-67, October 2014; $3,055, MS-67, October 2014; $1,175, MS-66, October 2014; $1,116, MS-65, November 2013													
1908O	1,789,000	111	57.9	74%	$6	$12	$45	$65	$95	$150	$300	$600	$1,250
Auctions: $4,406, MS-67, July 2014; $4,406, MS-67, October 2014; $3,966, MS-67, November 2014; $7,638, MS-67, November 2013													
1908S	3,220,000	93	56.6	59%	$4	$6	$15	$25	$45	$170	$350	$800	$1,500
Auctions: $2,820, MS-66, June 2014; $3,584, MS-66, October 2014; $1,234, MS-65, July 2014													
1909	10,240,000	286	60.7	84%	$4	$5	$6	$10	$25	$75	$125	$240	$625
Auctions: $881, MS-66, November 2014; $881, MS-66, July 2014; $499, MS-65, July 2014; $135, MS-62, July 2014													
1909, Proof	650	256	64.6								$275	$575	$1,500
Auctions: $2,350, PF-66Cam, July 2014; $4,994, PF-68, October 2014; $7,638, PF-68, December 2013; $458, PF-63, July 2014													
1909D	954,000	112	55.1	69%	$8	$20	$60	$90	$140	$225	$500	$1,000	$2,500
Auctions: $3,525, MS-66, June 2014; $123, EF-45, December 2014													
1909O	2,287,000	109	56.9	71%	$5	$8	$13	$25	$70	$150	$250	$575	$1,500
Auctions: $3,055, MS-66, June 2014; $4,406, MS-66+, November 2014; $1,116, MS-63, July 2014; $411, MS-62, October 2014													
1909S	1,000,000	102	53.1	68%	$9	$20	$80	$130	$180	$310	$550	$1,400	$2,800
Auctions: $2,350, MS-65, June 2014; $2,174, MS-65, October 2014; $2,056, MS-65, October 2014													
1910	11,520,000	458	61.6	87%	$4	$5	$6	$10	$25	$75	$125	$240	$625
Auctions: $5,170, MS-67, January 2014; $470, MS-65, July 2014; $388, MS-65, October 2014; $329, MS-64, September 2014													
1910, Proof	551	218	64.7								$275	$575	$1,500
Auctions: $4,994, PF-66DCam, August 2013; $999, PF-65Cam, November 2014; $2,133, PF-67, September 2014; $884, PF-64, July 2014													
1910D	3,490,000	89	57.7	74%	$4	$5	$10	$20	$48	$95	$220	$450	$1,500
Auctions: $2,115, MS-66, June 2014													
1910S	1,240,000	67	53.3	61%	$6	$9	$50	$70	$110	$180	$425	$700	$2,250
Auctions: $7,344, MS-67, June 2014; $2,820, MS-66, July 2014; $411, MS-62, July 2014													
1911	18,870,000	925	61.4	86%	$4	$5	$6	$10	$25	$75	$125	$240	$625
Auctions: $3,055, MS-67, October 2014; $3,525, MS-67, June 2013; $764, MS-66, September 2014; $646, MS-66, November 2014													
1911, Proof	543	234	64.9								$275	$575	$1,500
Auctions: $1,528, PF-66Cam, August 2014; $764, PF-64Cam, August 2014; $19,975, PF-69, April 2013; $2,376, PF-67, July 2014													
1911D	11,209,000	260	59.8	77%	$4	$5	$6	$10	$25	$75	$125	$240	$625
Auctions: $4,113, MS-67, July 2014; $3,525, MS-67, September 2014; $529, MS-65, July 2014; $676, MS-65, August 2014													
1911S	3,520,000	185	61.6	84%	$4	$5	$10	$20	$40	$100	$200	$400	$1,000
Auctions: $881, MS-66, October 2014; $999, MS-66, November 2014; $852, MS-65, July 2014; $558, MS-64, August 2014													
1912	19,349,300	954	61.5	85%	$4	$5	$6	$10	$25	$75	$110	$220	$600
Auctions: $1,410, MS-66, December 2013; $470, MS-65, July 2014; $294, MS-64, December 2014; $84, MS-60, November 2014													
1912, Proof	700	183	64.5								$275	$575	$1,500
Auctions: $12,925, PF-67Cam, April 2013; $11,163, PF-68, October 2014; $1,653, PF-66, August 2014; $1,175, PF-65, August 2014													
1912D	11,760,000	336	56.6	68%	$4	$5	$6	$10	$25	$75	$125	$240	$625
Auctions: $1,058, MS-66, September 2014; $3,819, MS-66, November 2013; $588, MS-65, August 2014; $79, AU-58, September 2014													
1912S	3,420,000	176	60.4	76%	$4	$5	$6	$12	$35	$90	$170	$300	$850
Auctions: $1,293, MS-66, June 2013; $206, MS-62, July 2014; $206, MS-62, August 2014													
1912S, DblDie Obv (h)	(i)	0	n/a						$100	$180	$425		
Auctions: No auction records available.													

h. The doubling is most evident on UNITED. i. Included in 1912-S mintage figure.

	Mintage	Cert	Avg	%MS	G-4	VG-8	F-12	VF-20	EF-40	AU-50	MS-60	MS-63	MS-65
											PF-60	PF-63	PF-65
1913	19,760,000	789	60.7	82%	$4	$5	$6	$10	$25	$75	$125	$240	$625
Auctions: $881, MS-66, August 2014; $846, MS-66, September 2014; $1,763, MS-66, April 2013; $499, MS-65, July 2014													
1913, Proof	622	196	64.1								$275	$575	$1,500
Auctions: $1,528, PF-66Cam, November 2014; $2,233, PF-66Cam, August 2013; $1,124, PF-65Cam, July 2014; $705, PF-64Cam, October 2014													
1913S	510,000	209	38.3	41%	$35	$55	$125	$190	$250	$320	$500	$800	$1,500
Auctions: $4,113, MS-66, June 2014; $2,820, MS-66, November 2014; $170, EF-45, November 2014; $153, VF-20, September 2014													
1914	17,360,230	832	61.2	85%	$4	$5	$6	$10	$25	$75	$125	$240	$625
Auctions: $911, MS-66, July 2014; $999, MS-66, October 2014; $517, MS-65, July 2014; $529, MS-65, August 2014													
1914, Proof	425	167	64.5								$275	$575	$1,500
Auctions: $11,751, PF-68, June 2014; $3,525, PF-67, October 2014; $1,676, PF-66, August 2014; $423, PF-63, July 2014													
1914D	11,908,000	515	58.6	74%	$4	$5	$6	$10	$20	$75	$110	$220	$600
Auctions: $1,939, MS-66+, November 2014; $1,028, MS-66, November 2014; $705, MS-65, July 2014; $276, MS-64, November 2014													
1914S	2,100,000	162	58.7	78%	$4	$5	$10	$18	$40	$80	$175	$350	$1,400
Auctions: $2,115, MS-66, October 2014; $1,880, MS-66, February 2013; $153, MS-61, July 2014													
1915	5,620,000	326	61.3	84%	$4	$5	$6	$10	$25	$75	$125	$240	$625
Auctions: $1,028, MS-66, January 2014; $734, MS-66, July 2014; $456, MS-65, July 2014; $353, MS-64, November 2014													
1915, Proof	450	143	64.4								$275	$575	$1,500
Auctions: $4,406, PF-66Cam, June 2014; $2,820, PF-67, October 2014; $646, PF-64, October 2014; $646, PF-64, November 2014													
1915S	960,000	145	57.9	69%	$7	$12	$35	$50	$70	$140	$275	$475	$1,400
Auctions: $1,410, MS-65, February 2014; $999, MS-65, October 2014; $588, MS-64, November 2014; $176, AU-58, September 2014													
1916	18,490,000	1249	60.7	83%	$4	$5	$6	$10	$25	$75	$125	$240	$625
Auctions: $3,819, MS-67, June 2014; $470, MS-65, July 2014; $470, MS-65, August 2014; $295, MS-64, August 2014													
1916S	5,820,000	321	60.9	79%	$4	$5	$6	$10	$25	$75	$125	$240	$650
Auctions: $3,525, MS-66, June 2014; $1,058, MS-66, September 2014; $2,585, MS-66, November 2014; $456, MS-65, July 2014													

WINGED LIBERTY HEAD OR "MERCURY" (1916–1945)

Designer: *Adolph A. Weinman.* **Weight:** *2.50 grams.* **Composition:** *.900 silver, .100 copper (net weight .07234 oz. pure silver).* **Diameter:** *17.9 mm.* **Edge:** *Reeded.* **Mints:** *Philadelphia, Denver, San Francisco.*

Circulation Strike

Mintmark location is
on the reverse, at the
base of the branch.

Proof

History. In 1916 a new dime, designed by sculptor Adolph A. Weinman (who also created the half dollar that debuted that year), replaced Charles Barber's Liberty Head type. Officially Weinman's design was known as the Winged Liberty Head, but numismatists commonly call the coin the *Mercury* dime, from Miss Liberty's wing-capped resemblance to the Roman god. The reverse depicts a fasces (symbolic of strength in unity) and an olive branch (symbolic of peaceful intentions). Production was continuous from 1916 to 1945, except for 1922, 1932, and 1933.

Striking and Sharpness. Many Mercury dimes exhibit areas of light striking, most notably in the center horizontal band across the fasces, less so in the lower horizontal band. The bands are composed of two parallel lines with a separation or "split" between. The term Full Bands, abbreviated FB, describes coins with both parallel lines in the center band distinctly separated. *In addition*, some dimes may display weak striking in other areas (not noted by certification services or others), including at areas of Liberty's hair, the rim, and the date. Dimes of 1921 in particular can have FB but poorly struck dates. Proof dies were completely polished, including the portrait.

Availability. Certain coins, such as 1916-D; 1921-P; 1921-D; 1942, 2 Over 1; and 1942-D, 2 Over 1, are elusive in any grade. Others are generally available in lower circulated grades, although some are scarce. In MS many of the issues before 1931 range from scarce to rare. If with FB and also sharply struck in other areas, some are rare. MS coins usually are very lustrous. In the marketplace certain scarce early issues such as 1916-D, 1921, and 1921-D are often graded slightly more liberally than are later varieties. Proofs were minted from 1936 to 1942 and are available in proportion to their mintages.

GRADING STANDARDS

MS-60 to 70 (Mint State). *Obverse:* At MS-60, some abrasion and contact marks are evident on the highest part of the portrait, including the hair immediately to the right of the face and the upper left part of the wing. At MS-63, abrasion is slight at best, less so for 64. Album slide marks on the cheek, if present, should not be at any grade above MS-64. An MS-65 coin should display no abrasion or contact marks except under magnification, and

1919-S. Graded MS-65.

MS-66 and higher coins should have none at all. Luster should be full and rich. *Reverse:* Comments apply as for the obverse, except that the highest parts of the fasces, these being the horizontal bands, are the places to check. The field is mainly protected by design elements and does not show contact marks readily.

Illustrated coin: This lustrous example is lightly toned.

AU-50, 53, 55, 58 (About Uncirculated). *Obverse:* Light wear is seen on the cheek, the hair immediately to the right of the face, the left edge of the wing, and the upper right of the wing. At AU-58, the luster is extensive, but incomplete, especially on the higher parts and in the field. At AU-50 and 53, luster is less. *Reverse:* Light wear is seen on the higher parts of the fasces. An AU-58 coin has nearly full luster, more so than on the obverse, as the

1942, 2 Over 1. Graded AU-55.

design elements protect the field areas. At AU-50 and 53, there still is significant luster. Generally, the reverse appears to be in a slightly higher grade than the obverse.

EF-40, 45 (Extremely Fine). *Obverse:* Further wear is seen on the head. Many of the hair details are blended together, as are some feather details at the left side of the wing. *Reverse:* The horizontal bands on the fasces may be fused together. The diagonal bands remain in slight relief against the vertical lines (sticks).

1921. Graded EF-40.

VF-20, 30 (Very Fine). *Obverse:* The head shows more wear, now with the forehead and cheek mostly blending into the hair. More feather details are gone. *Reverse:* Wear is more extensive, but the diagonal and horizontal bands on the fasces still are separated from the thin vertical sticks.

1942, 2 Over 1. Graded VF-20.

F-12, 15 (Fine). *Obverse:* The head shows more wear, the hair has only slight detail, and most of the feathers are gone. In the marketplace a coin in F-12 grade usually has slightly less detail than stated by the ANA grading standards or *Photograde*, from modern interpretations. *Reverse:* Many of the tiny vertical sticks in the fasces are blended together. The bands can be barely discerned and may be worn away at the highest-relief parts.

1916-D. Graded F-12.

VG-8, 10 (Very Good). *Obverse:* Wear is more extensive on the portrait, and only a few feathers are seen on the wing. The outlines between the hair and cap and of the wing are distinct. Lettering is clear, but light in areas. *Reverse:* The rim is complete, or it may be slightly worn away in areas. Only a few traces of the vertical sticks remain in the fasces. Current interpretations in the marketplace are given here and are less strict than those

1916-D. Graded VG-8.

listed by the ANA grading standards and *Photograde*. Often, earlier issues are graded more liberally than are later dates.

G-4, 6 (Good). *Obverse:* Wear is more extensive, with not all of the outline between the hair and the wing visible. The rim is worn into the edges of the letters and often into the bottom of the last numeral in the date. *Reverse:* The rim is worn away, as are the outer parts of the letters. The fasces is flat or may show a hint of a vertical stick or two. The leaves are thick from wear. The mintmark, if any, is easily seen.

1916-D. Graded G-4.

AG-3 (About Good). *Obverse:* The rim is worn further into the letters. The head is mostly outline all over, except for a few indicates of edges. Folds remain at the top of the cap. The date is clearly visible. *Reverse:* The rim is worn further into the letters. The mintmark, if any, is clear but may be worn away slightly at the bottom. The apparent wear is slightly greater on the reverse than on the obverse.

1916-D. Graded AG-3.

PF-60 to 70 (Proof). *Obverse and Reverse:* Proofs that are extensively cleaned and have many hairlines, or that are dull and grainy, are lower level, such as PF-60 to 62. These are not widely desired, and represent coins that have been mistreated. With medium hairlines and good reflectivity, assigned grades of PF-63 or 64 are appropriate. Tiny horizontal lines on Miss Liberty's cheek, known as *slide marks*, from National and

1939. Graded PF-67.

other album slides scuffing the relief of the cheek, are common; coins with such marks should not be graded higher than PF-64, but sometimes are. With relatively few hairlines and no noticeable slide marks, a rating of PF-65 can be given. PF-66 should have hairlines so delicate that magnification is needed to see them. Above that, a Proof should be free of any hairlines or other problems.

Full Bands

	Mintage	Cert	Avg	%MS	G-4	VG-8	F-12	VF-20	EF-40	AU-50	MS-60	MS-63	MS-65
1916	22,180,080	2,664	62.8	94%	$4	$5	$7	$8	$15	$25	$35	$48	$120
	Auctions: $4,406, MS-68FB, September 2014; $1,880, MS-67FB, October 2014; $1,293, MS-67FB, October 2014; $388, MS-66FB, October 2014												
1916D † (a)	264,000	3,848	10.7	6%	$1,000	$1,500	$2,600	$4,200	$6,000	$9,000	$13,500	$17,000	$28,000
	Auctions: $58,750, MS-66FB, August 2014; $9,496, MS-60, November 2014; $3,672, VF-30, September 2014; $2,350, VF-20, July 2014												
1916S	10,450,000	940	58.9	87%	$4	$6	$9	$12	$20	$25	$42	$65	$215
	Auctions: $5,581, MS-67FB, August 2014; $588, MS-65FB, October 2014; $170, MS-64FB, July 2014; $165, MS-64FB, December 2014												
1917	55,230,000	799	62.3	89%	$3	$3.25	$3.50	$6	$8	$12	$30	$60	$170
	Auctions: $7,050, MS-67FB, November 2013; $823, MS-66FB, August 2014; $259, MS-65FB, July 2014; $764, MS-65FB, October 2014												
1917D	9,402,000	551	61.1	82%	$4.50	$6	$11	$22	$45	$95	$145	$350	$1,050
	Auctions: $7,638, MS-65FB, June 2014; $4,125, MS-65FB, September 2014; $4,700, MS-65FB, November 2014; $611, MS-64FB, October 2014												
1917S	27,330,000	561	61.7	85%	$3	$3.25	$4	$7	$12	$30	$60	$180	$500
	Auctions: $1,645, MS-66FB, August 2014; $411, MS-64FB, July 2014; $282, MS-63FB, November 2014; $3,055, MS-67, July 2014												

† Ranked in the *100 Greatest U.S. Coins* (fourth edition). **a.** Beware of altered or otherwise spurious mintmarks.

	Mintage	Cert	Avg	%MS	G-4	VG-8	F-12	VF-20	EF-40	AU-50	MS-60	MS-63	MS-65
1918	26,680,000	425	62.4	88%	$3	$4	$6	$12	$25	$40	$70	$125	$425
	Auctions: $2,233, MS-66FB, January 2014; $1,528, MS-66FB, October 2014; $1,116, MS-65FB, July 2014; $294, MS-64FB, September 2014												
1918D	22,674,800	523	61.2	85%	$3	$4	$6	$12	$24	$50	$125	$250	$600
	Auctions: $88,125, MS-66FB, June 2014; $16,450, MS-65FB, August 2014; $10,575, MS-65FB, November 2014; $852, MS-66, July 2014												
1918S	19,300,000	386	61.9	87%	$3	$3.25	$5	$10	$18	$40	$120	$275	$725
	Auctions: $16,450, MS-66FB, August 2013; $411, MS-61FB, August 2014; $764, MS-65, August 2014; $259, MS-63, August 2014												
1919	35,740,000	473	62.1	87%	$3	$3.25	$4	$6	$10	$30	$45	$150	$375
	Auctions: $8,813, MS-67FB, March 2013; $1,116, MS-65FB, July 2014; $282, MS-64FB, September 2014; $153, MS-63FB, December 2014												
1919D	9,939,000	379	60.8	84%	$4	$7	$12	$24	$35	$75	$200	$450	$1,800
	Auctions: $2,468, MS-64FB, November 2014; $1,880, MS-62FB, September 2014; $5,288, MS-66, February 2014; $793, MS-65, November 2014												
1919S	8,850,000	260	59.3	67%	$3.50	$4	$8	$16	$35	$75	$200	$450	$1,200
	Auctions: $7,050, MS-64FB, December 2013; $141, AU-58, November 2014												
1920	59,030,000	722	63.2	95%	$3	$3.25	$3.50	$5	$8	$15	$35	$75	$260
	Auctions: $881, MS-66FB, August 2014; $1,410, MS-66FB, August 2013; $499, MS-65FB, July 2014; $119, MS-64FB, October 2014												
1920D	19,171,000	412	61.5	84%	$3	$3.50	$4.50	$8	$20	$45	$145	$350	$775
	Auctions: $44,063, MS-67FB+, July 2014; $2,350, MS-64FB, August 2014; $1,116, MS-64FB, August 2014; $1,528, MS-66, October 2014												
1920S	13,820,000	279	61.8	82%	$3.25	$4	$5	$8	$18	$45	$145	$325	$1,450
	Auctions: $11,750, MS-66FB, February 2014; $14,100, MS-66FB+, September 2014; $4,700, MS-65FB, October 2014; $4,113, MS-65FB, August 2014												
1921	1,230,000	1,140	27.1	21%	$65	$80	$130	$320	$600	$925	$1,200	$2,200	$3,500
	Auctions: $18,800, MS-67FB, June 2013; $7,050, MS-65FB, October 2014; $1,175, AU-58, September 2014; $823, AU-55, July 2014												
1921D	1,080,000	1,167	27.0	21%	$80	$130	$210	$420	$775	$1,250	$1,500	$2,600	$3,500
	Auctions: $9,400, MS-66FB, January 2014; $9,400, MS-66FB, July 2014; $2,468, MS-64FB, August 2014; $2,820, MS-64, November 2014												
1923 (b)	50,130,000	888	63.1	93%	$3	$3.25	$3.50	$5	$7	$16	$30	$45	$130
	Auctions: $4,406, MS-67FB, October 2013; $470, MS-66FB, November 2014; $223, MS-65FB, September 2014; $112, MS-64FB, October 2014												
1923S	6,440,000	326	60.0	77%	$3	$4	$8	$18	$65	$105	$160	$400	$1,250
	Auctions: $4,406, MS-65FB, October 2014; $4,406, MS-65FB, August 2013; $2,585, MS-64FB, August 2014; $329, MS-61, July 2014												
1924	24,010,000	527	63.9	96%	$3	$3.25	$4	$6	$15	$30	$45	$100	$210
	Auctions: $1,880, MS-67FB, August 2014; $4,113, MS-67FB, September 2014; $4,406, MS-67FB, March 2013; $764, MS-66FB, October 2014												
1924D	6,810,000	421	61.2	85%	$3.50	$4.50	$8	$24	$70	$110	$175	$500	$950
	Auctions: $1,058, MS-65FB, August 2014; $1,058, MS-65FB, July 2014; $1,116, MS-65FB, August 2013; $705, MS-64FB, August 2014												
1924S	7,120,000	330	60.4	79%	$3.50	$4	$6	$10	$60	$110	$200	$500	$1,250
	Auctions: $7,050, MS-65FB, June 2014; $3,290, MS-64FB, October 2014; $499, MS-64, November 2014												
1925	25,610,000	329	62.8	89%	$3	$3.25	$4	$5	$10	$20	$30	$85	$225
	Auctions: $1,880, MS-67FB, August 2013; $1,423, MS-66FB+, November 2014; $147, MS-62FB, September 2014; $89, MS-64, September 2014												
1925D	5,117,000	288	59.5	70%	$4	$5	$12	$45	$120	$200	$375	$800	$1,700
	Auctions: $10,575, MS-66FB, April 2014; $9,400, MS-66FB, July 2014; $9,400, MS-66FB, October 2014; $2,820, MS-65FB, October 2014												
1925S	5,850,000	241	61.2	80%	$3.25	$4	$8	$18	$70	$110	$180	$500	$1,400
	Auctions: $9,694, MS-66FB, April 2013; $611, MS-62FB, December 2014; $353, MS-62, July 2014; $78, AU-50, September 2014												
1926	32,160,000	689	63.3	94%	$3	$3.25	$3.50	$5	$7	$16	$25	$65	$250
	Auctions: $3,290, MS-67FB, July 2014; $6,463, MS-67FB, August 2013; $294, MS-65FB, December 2014; $129, MS-64FB, September 2014												
1926D	6,828,000	446	61.7	87%	$3.25	$4.50	$6	$10	$28	$50	$125	$275	$600
	Auctions: $4,406, MS-66FB, July 2014; $5,875, MS-66FB, February 2013; $1,821, MS-65FB, November 2014; $705, MS-64FB, October 2014												
1926S	1,520,000	357	47.3	35%	$13	$15	$26	$60	$250	$450	$825	$1,500	$2,850
	Auctions: $3,525, MS-64FB, July 2014; $9,400, MS-67, August 2013; $2,233, MS-64, November 2014; $764, MS-60, July 2014												
1927	28,080,000	515	62.6	92%	$3	$3.25	$3.50	$5	$7	$15	$30	$60	$150
	Auctions: $2,115, MS-67FB, June 2014; $764, MS-66FB, July 2014; $247, MS-65FB, September 2014; $306, MS-65FB, November 2014												
1927D	4,812,000	263	59.6	71%	$3.50	$5.50	$8	$25	$80	$100	$200	$400	$1,200
	Auctions: $8,813, MS-65FB, August 2013; $1,116, MS-64, November 2014; $159, AU-58, September 2014; $100, AU-55, November 2014												
1927S	4,770,000	216	60.8	81%	$3.25	$4	$6	$12	$28	$50	$275	$550	$1,400
	Auctions: $7,050, MS-65FB, June 2014; $1,528, MS-65, November 2014; $588, MS-62, July 2014; $129, MS-60, September 2014												

b. Dimes dated 1923-D or 1930-D are counterfeit.

1928-S, Small S

1928-S, Large S
FS-10-1928S-501.

1929-S, Doubled-Die Obverse
FS-10-1929S-101.

	Mintage	Cert	Avg	%MS	G-4	VG-8	F-12	VF-20	EF-40	AU-50	MS-60	MS-63	MS-65
1928	19,480,000	432	63.7	95%	$3	$3.25	$3.50	$5	$7	$18	$30	$55	$130
	Auctions: $1,880, MS-67FB, August 2013; $646, MS-66FB, July 2014; $470, MS-66FB, October 2014; $441, MS-66FB, August 2014												
1928D	4,161,000	269	60.5	81%	$4	$5	$8	$20	$50	$95	$175	$360	$850
	Auctions: $4,259, MS-65FB, June 2014; $1,175, MS-64FB, August 2014; $1,293, MS-64FB, November 2014; $823, MS-62FB, November 2014												
1928S (c)	7,400,000	9	58.1	56%	$3	$3.25	$4	$6	$16	$45	$150	$320	$400
	Auctions: $4,406, MS-66FB, January 2014; $764, MS-64FB, July 2014; $329, MS-63FB, September 2014; $382, MS-65, November 2014												
1929	25,970,000	833	64.3	97%	$3	$3.25	$3.50	$5	$6	$12	$22	$35	$75
	Auctions: $2,056, MS-67FB, September 2014; $999, MS-67FB, November 2014; $6,463, MS-67FB, August 2013; $212, MS-65FB, December 2014												
1929D	5,034,000	1,171	64.3	99%	$3	$3.50	$5	$8	$15	$24	$30	$36	$75
	Auctions: $11,163, MS-68FB, July 2014; $3,819, MS-67FB+, August 2014; $1,998, MS-67FB, August 2014; $558, MS-66FB, November 2014												
1929S	4,730,000	375	63.6	93%	$3	$3.25	$3.75	$5	$10	$20	$35	$45	$125
	Auctions: $3,290, MS-67FB, August 2014; $2,820, MS-67FB, September 2014; $5,288, MS-67FB, March 2013; $1,146, MS-66FB, November 2014												
1929S, Doubled-Die Obverse (d)	(e)	5	59.0	60%								$150	$200
	Auctions: $170, AU-58, December 2009												
1930 (b)	6,770,000	406	63.6	93%	$3	$3.25	$3.50	$5	$8	$16	$30	$50	$125
	Auctions: $1,058, MS-66FB, October 2014; $999, MS-66FB, November 2014; $1,528, MS-66FB, August 2013; $317, MS-64FB, October 2014												
1930S	1,843,000	280	63.4	92%	$3	$4	$5	$7	$15	$45	$80	$150	$210
	Auctions: $11,163, MS-67FB, February 2013; $1,645, MS-66FB, July 2014; $764, MS-67, November 2014; $411, MS-66, September 2014												
1931	3,150,000	443	63.5	93%	$3	$3.10	$4	$6	$10	$22	$35	$70	$150
	Auctions: $9,988, MS-67FB, July 2014; $12,338, MS-67FB, September 2013; $740, MS-65FB, November 2014; $411, MS-66, December 2014												
1931D	1,260,000	543	62.5	91%	$8	$9	$12	$20	$35	$60	$90	$140	$280
	Auctions: $1,293, MS-67FB, October 2014; $2,350, MS-67FB, August 2013; $1,175, MS-66FB, July 2014; $940, MS-66FB, August 2014												
1931S	1,800,000	396	60.6	85%	$4	$5	$6	$10	$16	$45	$90	$150	$300
	Auctions: $28,200, MS-67FB, November 2013; $6,463, MS-66FB+, July 2014; $5,288, MS-66FB, September 2014; $2,585, MS-65FB, October 2014												

b. Dimes dated 1923-D or 1930-D are counterfeit. **c.** Two mintmark styles exist: Large S (scarce) and Small S (common). About 80% of 1928-S dimes are of the Small S style. The scarcer Large S is worth about two to three times the values listed (which are for the Small S). **d.** Moderate doubling is evident on the date and IN GOD WE TRUST. **e.** Included in 1929-S mintage figure.

	Mintage	Cert	Avg	%MS	F-12	VF-20	EF-40	AU-50	MS-60	MS-63	MS-65 / PF-65	MS-65FB / PF-66	MS-66 / PF-67
1934	24,080,000	896	64.5	97%	$3	$3.10	$3.50	$16	$25	$35	$50	$140	$65
	Auctions: $7,050, MS-68FB, February 2014; $3,290, MS-68FB, September 2014; $441, MS-67FB, November 2014; $90, MS-65FB, November 2014												
1934D	6,772,000	655	64.3	96%	$3	$3.10	$8	$33	$50	$60	$85	$325	$230
	Auctions: $1,528, MS-67FB, November 2014; $4,406, MS-67FB, August 2013; $646, MS-66FB, July 2014; $499, MS-66FB, August 2014												
1935	58,830,000	1,386	65.1	97%	$3	$3.10	$3.25	$7	$10	$15	$35	$75	$60
	Auctions: $7,638, MS-68FB, March 2013; $411, MS-67FB, July 2014; $294, MS-67FB, August 2014; $411, MS-67FB, September 2014												
1935D	10,477,000	472	63.9	94%	$3	$3.10	$8	$26	$35	$50	$90	$525	$325
	Auctions: $3,525, MS-67FB, June 2014; $3,819, MS-67FB, November 2014; $764, MS-66FB, September 2014; $470, MS-65FB, August 2014												
1935S	15,840,000	589	65.0	98%	$3	$3.10	$5	$16	$22	$30	$40	$350	$80
	Auctions: $270, MS-65FB, August 2014; $141, MS-64FB, October 2014; $3,819, MS-68, June 2014												

1936-S, Possible Overdate
FS-10-1936S-110.

	Mintage	Cert	Avg	%MS	F-12	VF-20	EF-40	AU-50	MS-60	MS-63	MS-65	MS-65FB	MS-66
											PF-65	PF-66	PF-67
1936	87,500,000	1736	65.1	97%	$3	$3.10	$3.50	$7	$10	$18	$30	$90	$48
Auctions: $5,289, MS-68FB, June 2014; $499, MS-67FB, August 2014; $74, MS-66FB, December 2014													
1936, Proof	4,130	1,071	65.0								$1,200	$1,750	$4,500
Auctions: $1,880, PF-67, August 2014; $3,826, PF-67, April 2013; $1,234, PF-66, July 2014; $1,704, PF-66, November 2014													
1936D	16,132,000	561	64.2	93%	$3	$3.60	$6	$16	$25	$40	$55	$275	$80
Auctions: $5,581, MS-68FB, August 2013; $364, MS-66FB, August 2014; $182, MS-65FB, August 2014; $129, MS-64FB, July 2014													
1936S	9,210,000	963	65.4	99%	$3	$3.10	$3.50	$13	$23	$30	$35	$95	$55
Auctions: $764, MS-67FB, July 2014; $1,857, MS-67FB+, September 2014; $1,763, MS-67FB, February 2013													
1936S, Possible Overdate (a)	**(b)**	0	n/a										
Auctions: $1,500, MS-65FB, November 2011													
1937	56,860,000	3,852	65.7	99%	$3	$3.10	$3.25	$7	$10	$15	$30	$60	$40
Auctions: $2,820, MS-68FB, February 2013; $588, MS-67FB, July 2014; $206, MS-67FB, August 2014													
1937, Proof	5,756	1,228	65.4								$600	$950	$1,400
Auctions: $3,525, PF-68, October 2014; $3,055, PF-68, October 2014; $4,259, PF-68, June 2013; $705, PF-67, October 2014													
1937D	14,146,000	956	65.3	98%	$3	$3.10	$4	$12	$21	$30	$45	$100	$85
Auctions: $1,763, MS-68FB, July 2014; $5,581, MS-68FB, August 2013; $123, MS-66FB, November 2014													
1937S	9,740,000	920	65.5	98%	$3	$3.10	$3.50	$12	$20	$30	$40	$185	$80
Auctions: $1,998, MS-67FB, April 2014; $823, MS-67FB, July 2014; $676, MS-67FB, November 2014; $247, MS-66FB, October 2014													
1938	22,190,000	1527	65.5	99%	$3	$3.10	$3.25	$7	$10	$15	$30	$85	$55
Auctions: $6,463, MS-68FB, February 2013; $212, MS-67FB, October 2014; $235, MS-66FB, October 2014													
1938, Proof	8,728	1,777	65.4								$550	$750	$1,100
Auctions: $1,880, PF-68, October 2014; $9,988, PF-68, June 2013; $447, PF-67, July 2014; $282, PF-66, August 2014													
1938D	5,537,000	1,675	65.5	99%	$3	$3.20	$4	$11	$18	$25	$35	$65	$75
Auctions: $3,995, MS-68FB, August 2013; $382, MS-67FB, July 2014; $70, MS-65FB, August 2014													
1938S	8,090,000	944	65.2	97%	$3	$3.10	$3.50	$12	$20	$28	$42	$160	$80
Auctions: $3,819, MS-68FB, August 2013; $881, MS-67FB, August 2014; $764, MS-67FB, August 2014													
1939	67,740,000	3,078	65.9	98%	$3	$3.10	$3.25	$6	$8	$12	$26	$180	$40
Auctions: $9,400, MS-68FB, October 2014; $10,281, MS-68FB, December 2013; $1,998, MS-67FB+, July 2014													
1939, Proof	9,321	1,960	65.9								$275	$600	$750
Auctions: $2,233, PF-67Cam, November 2014; $1,469, PF-68, August 2014; $1,175, PF-68, September 2014; $4,994, PF-68, June 2013													
1939D	24,394,000	3,267	65.8	99%	$3	$3.10	$3.25	$6	$8	$12	$32	$55	$60
Auctions: $8,225, MS-69FB, September 2014; $1,645, MS-68FB, July 2014; $1,880, MS-68FB, November 2013													
1939S	10,540,000	764	65.1	98%	$3	$3.10	$4	$13	$23	$30	$42	$725	$110
Auctions: $3,819, MS-67FB, January 2014; $999, MS-66FB, October 2014; $112, MS-67, July 2014													
1940	65,350,000	3,120	65.7	98%	$3	$3.10	$3.25	$5	$7	$12	$30	$50	$45
Auctions: $9,988, MS-68FB, August 2013; $165, MS-67FB, October 2014; $153, MS-67FB, December 2014													
1940, Proof	11,827	2,152	65.6								$250	$350	$600
Auctions: $11,750, PF-69, January 2014; $3,055, PF-68, August 2014; $2,585, PF-68, October 2014; $1,586, PF-68, November 2014													
1940D	21,198,000	2,298	65.6	99%	$3	$3.10	$3.25	$5	$7	$14	$35	$50	$50
Auctions: $1,998, MS-68FB, August 2013; $194, MS-67FB, August 2014; $182, MS-67FB, September 2014													
1940S	21,560,000	2,305	65.7	99%	$3	$3.10	$3.25	$6	$8	$15	$35	$100	$40
Auctions: $6,463, MS-68FB, July 2014; $529, MS-67FB, July 2014; $881, MS-67FB, September 2014; $529, MS-67FB, November 2014													

a. "The secondary image of a 2 is evident beneath the 3 of the date. Most evident is the flat portion of the base of the underlying 2. Remains of what is likely a secondary 9 are evident to the left of the primary 9. Many die polish marks are also evident throughout the surface of the obverse. No doubling is evident on other elements. . . . The length of time between the striking of the last 1929-dated coins and this 1936 coin would seem to eliminate the possibility of a 2 underlying the 3. However, examination has matched the shapes on the image under the 3 to that of the 2 on 1929-dated dimes. Stranger things have happened. Keep in mind that 1936 was during the Great Depression, when Mint personnel wanted to save money whenever possible." (*Cherrypickers' Guide to Rare Die Varieties*, sixth edition, volume II) **b.** Included in 1936-S mintage figure.

1941-S, Small S

1941-S, Large S
FS-10-1941S-511.

1942, 42 Over 41
FS-10-1942-101.

1942-D, 42 Over 41, Repunched Mintmark
FS-10-1942D-101.

1943-S, Trumpet Tail Mintmark
FS-10-1943S-511.

	Mintage	Cert	Avg	%MS	F-12	VF-20	EF-40	AU-50	MS-60	MS-63	MS-65 / PF-65	MS-65FB / PF-66	MS-66 / PF-67
1941	175,090,000	4,111	65.3	97%	$3	$3.10	$3.25	$5	$7	$12	$30	$50	$45
	Auctions: $5,288, MS-68FB, November 2013; $270, MS-67FB, August 2014; $4,113, MS-67FB, October 2014; $182, MS-67FB, November 2014												
1941, Proof	16,557	2,743	65.5								$225	$350	$575
	Auctions: $7,050, PF-68, June 2013; $617, PF-67+, July 2014; $353, PF-67+, September 2014; $306, PF-67+, November 2014												
1941D	45,634,000	3,074	65.4	98%	$3	$3.10	$3.25	$6	$8	$14	$25	$50	$32
	Auctions: $1,880, MS-68FB, November 2013; $427, MS-67FB+, August 2014; $153, MS-67FB, September 2014												
1941S	43,090,000	4,278	65.6	99%	$3	$3.10	$3.25	$5	$7	$12	$30	$50	$38
	Auctions: $8,225, MS-68FB, June 2013; $470, MS-67FB+, September 2014; $353, MS-67FB, November 2014; $499, MS-67, November 2014												
1941S, Large S (c)	(d)	30	54.8	63%							$325		
	Auctions: $120, MS-63, June 2010												
1942, 42 Over 41 (e)	(f)	1,584	40.8	7%	$625	$800	$1,000	$1,750	$2,500	$4,500 (g)	$15,000	$37,500	$20,000
	Auctions: $6,463, MS-68FB, November 2014; $5,288, MS-68FB, November 2013; $364, MS-67FB, August 2014												
1942	205,410,000	4,725	65.2	97%	$2.25	$3.10	$3.25	$4.50	$6	$12	$30	$50	$45
	Auctions: $49,350, MS-65FB, August 2014; $8,225, MS-64, February 2014; $1,410, AU-58, July 2014; $940, AU-53, September 2014												
1942, Proof	22,329	4,055	65.7								$225	$350	$575
	Auctions: $15,275, PF-69, November 2013; $1,645, PF-68, August 2014; $1,704, PF-68, September 2014; $1,528, PF-68, November 2014												
1942D, 42 Over 41 (h)	(i)	923	38.7	10%	$675	$850	$1,100	$1,850	$2,600	$4,750 (j)	$9,500	$30,000	$12,000
	Auctions: $49,938, MS-66FB, June 2013; $2,115, AU-55, September 2014; $823, AU-50, August 2014; $558, AU-50, October 2014												
1942D	60,740,000	4,990	59.7	80%	$3	$3.10	$3.25	$4.50	$6	$12	$28	$48	$45
	Auctions: $1,410, MS-68FB, August 2014; $1,293, MS-68FB, August 2014; $2,115, MS-68FB, November 2013												
1942S	49,300,000	1,674	65.2	97%	$3	$3.10	$3.25	$6	$8	$20	$35	$150	$50
	Auctions: $10,575, MS-68FB, January 2013; $1,410, MS-67FB+, October 2014; $705, MS-67FB, October 2014												
1943	191,710,000	4,625	65.4	98%	$3	$3.10	$3.25	$4.50	$6	$12	$27	$55	$35
	Auctions: $17,625, MS-68FB, November 2013; $529, MS-67FB, September 2014; $499, MS-67FB, October 2014												
1943D	71,949,000	5,365	65.5	99%	$3	$3.10	$3.25	$4.50	$6	$15	$30	$50	$45
	Auctions: $6,463, MS-68FB, January 2014; $2,585, MS-67FB, August 2014; $74, MS-66FB, October 2014; $170, MS-65FB, August 2014												
1943S	60,400,000	3,172	65.8	99%	$3	$3.10	$3.25	$5	$7	$16	$30	$70	$40
	Auctions: $3,055, MS-68FB, January 2014; $2,820, MS-68FB, October 2014; $411, MS-67FB, July 2014; $159, MS-67FB, October 2014												
1943S, Trumpet Tail Mintmark (k)	(l)	7	62.6	71%							$450	$750	$500
	Auctions: $130, MS-62, December 2011												

c. This is the "Trumpet Tail" S mintmark, which is rare for this date. The upper serif points downward and the lower serif is rounded, like the bell of a trumpet. There are several dies known for the Large S dime, including one that is repunched. For more information, see the *Cherrypickers' Guide*. **d.** Included in 1941-S mintage figure. **e.** Doubling is evident in the 42 over 41 overdate, and slightly evident on IN GOD WE TRUST. Values for this variety fluctuate. **f.** Included in circulation-strike 1942 mintage figure. **g.** Value in MS-64 is $7,200. **h.** Doubling is evident in the 42 over 41 overdate, slightly evident on IN GOD WE TRUST, and as a D over D repunched mintmark (slanted west). Values for this variety fluctuate. **i.** Included in 1942-D mintage figure. **j.** Value in MS-64 is $7,200. **k.** This variety is considerably rarer than the 1941-S, Large S, which also features a Trumpet S mintmark. It is extremely rare in MS, and examples with FB command a significant premium. The top serif of the S points downward, with the lower serif rounded, much like the bell of a trumpet. **l.** Included in 1943-S mintage figure.

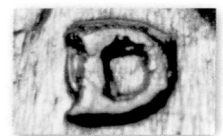   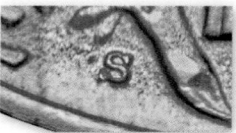

1945-D, D Over Horizontal D
FS-10-1945D-506.
 1945-S, S Over Horizontal S
FS-10-1945S-503.
 1945-S, Normal S
 1945-S, Micro S
FS-10-1945S-512.

	Mintage	Cert	Avg	%MS	F-12	VF-20	EF-40	AU-50	MS-60	MS-63	MS-65 / PF-65	MS-65FB / PF-66	MS-66 / PF-67
1944	231,410,000	5,401	65.4	98%	$3	$3.10	$3.25	$4.50	$6	$12	$25	$80	$45
	Auctions: $15,275, MS-68FB, November 2014; $9,400, MS-67FB, January 2014; $1,763, MS-67FB, September 2014												
1944D	62,224,000	7,023	65.8	99%	$3	$3.10	$3.25	$5	$7	$15	$30	$50	$48
	Auctions: $3,290, MS-68FB, April 2013; $259, MS-67FB+, July 2014; $147, MS-67FB, August 2014; $353, MS-67FB, October 2014												
1944S	49,490,000	5,088	65.8	99%	$3	$3.10	$3.25	$5	$7	$15	$30	$55	$50
	Auctions: $11,750, MS-68FB, November 2013; $45, MS-65FB, September 2014; $74, MS-67, October 2014; $129, MS-66, July 2014												
1945	159,130,000	5,960	65.5	99%	$3	$3.10	$3.25	$4.50	$6	$12	$28	$10,000	$45
	Auctions: $14,100, MS-65FB, November 2013; $188, MS-67, July 2014; $96, MS-67, July 2014												
1945D	40,245,000	6,621	65.7	100%	$3	$3.10	$3.25	$4.50	$6	$12	$26	$45	$50
	Auctions: $9,988, MS-68FB, November 2013; $306, MS-67FB, August 2014; $881, MS-67FB+, October 2014; $188, MS-67FB, December 2014												
1945D, D Over Horizontal D (m)	(n)	5	50.2	0%							$950		
	Auctions: No auction records available.												
1945S	41,920,000	5,772	66.0	99%	$3	$3.10	$3.25	$4.50	$6	$12	$30	$125	$40
	Auctions: $11,750, MS-68FB, November 2013; $1,293, MS-67FB, July 2014; $411, MS-67FB, August 2014; $499, MS-67FB, November 2014												
1945S, S Over Horizontal S (o)	(p)	0	n/a								$950		
	Auctions: No auction records available.												
1945S, Micro S (q)	(p)	1,084	65.3	98%	$3.25	$3.50	$6	$18	$30	$40	$100	$650	$120
	Auctions: $7,638, MS-67FB, June 2014; $6,463, MS-67FB, August 2014; $5,875, MS-67FB, August 2014; $529, MS-67, July 2014												

m. The first D mintmark was punched into the die horizontally and then corrected. **n.** Included in 1945-D mintage figure. **o.** The first S mintmark was punched into the die horizontally and then corrected. **p.** Included in 1945-S mintage figure. **q.** The S mintmark is significantly smaller than that of the normal S punch. This variety has the only mintmark punch of this type and size known to have been used during the 1940s. It was originally used for Philippine coins of 1907 through 1920.

ROOSEVELT (1946 TO DATE)

Silver (1946–1964, and some modern Proofs): **Designer:** *John R. Sinnock.*
Weight: *2.50 grams.* **Composition:** *.900 silver, .100 copper (net weight: .07234 oz. pure silver).*
Diameter: *17.9 mm.* **Edge:** *Reeded.* **Mints:** *Philadelphia, Denver, San Francisco.*

Silver, Circulation Strike
Mintmark location is on the reverse, to the left of the fasces.
Silver, Proof

Clad (1965 to date): **Designer:** *John R. Sinnock.* **Weight:** *2.27 grams.*
Composition: *Outer layers of copper-nickel (.750 copper, .250 nickel) bonded to inner core of pure copper.*
Diameter: *17.9 mm.* **Edge:** *Reeded.* **Mints:** *Philadelphia, Denver, San Francisco, West Point.*

Clad, Circulation Strike
Mintmark location is on the obverse, above the date.
Clad, Proof

History. After President Franklin D. Roosevelt died in 1945, the Treasury rushed to create a coin in his honor. The ten-cent denomination was particularly appropriate, given the president's active support of the March of Dimes' fundraising efforts to cure polio. The obverse of the coin bears Roosevelt's profile portrait, while the reverse features a torch flanked by branches of olive and oak.

Striking and Sharpness. Compared to earlier coinage series, collectors and dealers have paid relatively little attention to the sharpness of Roosevelt dimes. The obverse portrait is such that lightness of strike on the higher points is difficult to detect. On the reverse, check the leaves and the details of the torch. Some with complete separation on the lower two bands have been called Full Torch (FT) or Full Bands (FB), but interest in this distinction seems to be minimal in today's marketplace.

Availability. All are common, although some are more common than others. MS coins in higher grades are usually very lustrous.

Note: Values of common-date silver coins have been based on a silver current bullion price of $20 per ounce, and may vary with the prevailing spot price.

GRADING STANDARDS

MS-60 to 70 (Mint State). *Obverse:* At MS-60, some abrasion and contact marks are evident on the cheek, the hair above the ear, and the neck. At MS-63, abrasion is slight at best, less so for MS-64. An MS-65 coin should display no abrasion or contact marks except under magnification, and MS-66 and higher coins should have none at all. Luster should be full and rich. *Reverse:* Comments

1960-D. Graded MS-67FB.

apply as for the obverse, except that the highest parts of the torch, flame, and leaves are the places to check. On both sides the fields are protected by design elements and do not show contact marks readily.

AU-50, 53, 55, 58 (About Uncirculated). *Obverse:* Light wear is seen on the cheek and higher-relief part of the hair. At AU-58, the luster is extensive, but incomplete, especially on the higher parts and in the field. At AU-50 and 53, luster is less. *Reverse:* Light wear is seen on the higher parts of the torch and leaves. An AU-58 coin has nearly full luster. At AU-50 and 53, there still is significant luster.

1955. Graded AU-50.

EF-40, 45 (Extremely Fine). *Obverse:* Further wear is seen on the head. Some details are gone in the hair to the right of the forehead. *Reverse:* Further wear is seen on the torch, but the vertical lines are visible, some just barely. The higher-relief details in the leaves, never strong to begin with, are worn away.

The Roosevelt dime is seldom collected in grades lower than EF-40.

1950-S. Graded EF-40.

PF-60 to 70 (Proof). *Obverse and Reverse:* Proofs that are extensively cleaned and have many hairlines, or that are dull and grainy, are lower level, such as PF-60 to 62. These are not widely desired, and represent coins that have been mistreated. Fortunately, only a few Proof Roosevelt dimes are in this category. With medium hairlines and good reflectivity, assigned grades of PF-63 or 64 are appropriate. PF-65 may have hairlines so delicate that magnification is needed to see them. Above that, a Proof should be free of any hairlines or other problems.

1964. Graded PF-69 Deep Cameo.

	Mintage	Cert	Avg	%MS	EF-40	MS-63	MS-65	MS-66 / PF-65	MS-67 / PF-66	MS-67FB / PF-67
1946	255,250,000	1,603	66.1	100%	$2	$4.25	$12	$28	$110	$850
	Auctions: $2,820, MS-68FB, June 2014; $293, MS-67FB, August 2014; $1,880, MS-68, October 2014; $79, MS-65, July 2014									
1946D	61,043,500	2,069	66.2	100%	$2	$4.25	$14	$30	$100	$300
	Auctions: $3,525, MS-68FB, June 2014; $129, MS-67FB, August 2014; $194, MS-67FB, September 2014; $135, MS-67FB, September 2014									
1946S	27,900,000	2,522	66.3	100%	$2	$4.50	$20	$32	$90	$245
	Auctions: $3,819, MS-68FB, February 2014; $705, MS-67FB, July 2014; $148, MS-67FB, August 2014; $499, MS-67FB, September 2014									
1947	121,520,000	1,200	65.7	97%	$2	$6	$12	$24	$55	$2,000
	Auctions: $353, MS-67FB, April 2014; $259, MS-67FB, September 2014; $69, MS-67, November 2014									
1947D	46,835,000	1,146	66.2	100%	$2	$6.50	$12	$24	$30	$750
	Auctions: $270, MS-67FB, August 2014; $1,763, MS-67FB, November 2013									
1947S	34,840,000	2,021	66.4	100%	$2	$6	$12	$30	$110	$500
	Auctions: $5,288, MS-68FB, November 2013; $165, MS-67FB, September 2014; $175, MS-67FB, November 2014; $1,116, MS-68, September 2014									
1948	74,950,000	1,021	66.1	100%	$2	$4	$12	$30	$85	$500
	Auctions: $881, MS-67FB, April 2014; $153, MS-67FB, September 2014; $353, MS-67FB, October 2014; $112, MS-67FB, December 2014									
1948D	52,841,000	1,238	66.2	100%	$2	$6	$12	$30	$85	$225
	Auctions: $89, MS-67FB, December 2014; $141, MS-67FB, August 2013; $764, MS-68, September 2014									
1948S	35,520,000	1,521	66.3	100%	$2	$5.50	$12	$32	$100	$225
	Auctions: $96, MS-67FB, June 2014; $76, MS-67FB, August 2014; $705, MS-67FB+, September 2014; $141, MS-67FB, September 2014									
1949	30,940,000	1,122	65.9	99%	$3.75	$26	$32	$70	$125	$825
	Auctions: $1,293, MS-67FB, February 2014; $165, MS-66FB, November 2014; $29, MS-66, July 2014; $46, MS-66, November 2014									
1949D	26,034,000	1,663	66.2	100%	$2.75	$12	$20	$35	$105	$300
	Auctions: $4,113, MS-68FB, February 2013; $470, MS-67FB, September 2014; $112, MS-67FB, September 2014									
1949S	13,510,000	2,274	66.3	99%	$5	$45	$55	$75	$190	$2,500
	Auctions: $940, MS-67FB, July 2014; $999, MS-67FB, November 2014; $3,290, MS-67FB, June 2013									
1950	50,130,114	1,350	65.9	99%	$3	$13	$16	$35	$135	$600
	Auctions: $8,813, MS-68FB, April 2014; $153, MS-67FB, September 2014									
1950, Proof	51,386	1,271	66.3					$50	$65	$120
	Auctions: $18,800, PF-68DCam, March 2014; $329, PF-67Cam, November 2014; $50, PF-67, November 2014									
1950D	46,803,000	1,627	66.3	100%	$2	$6	$12	$28	$90	$200
	Auctions: $1,410, MS-68FB, June 2014; $86, MS-67, July 2014; $165, MS-67+, November 2014; $123, MS-67, November 2014									

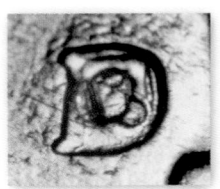
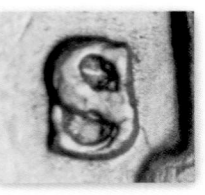

1950-D, D Over S
FS-10-1950D-501.

1950-S, S Over D
FS-10-1950S-501.

	Mintage	Cert	Avg	%MS	EF-40	MS-63	MS-65	MS-66	MS-67	MS-67FB
								PF-65	PF-66	PF-67
1950D, D Over S (a)	(b)	0	n/a			$400	$650	$825	$1,100	
	Auctions: No auction records available.									
1950S	20,440,000	1,447	66.2	99%	$5	$38	$55	$75	$135	$600
	Auctions: $1,528, MS-68FB, July 2014; $1,763, MS-67FB, March 2014; $90, MS-66FB, November 2014; $101, MS-67, August 2014									
1950S, S Over D (c)	(d)	0	n/a			$250	$400	$750	$1,000	$1,675
	Auctions: $159, MS-66, August 2014; $84, MS-65, June 2014; $57, MS-64, November 2014									
1951	103,880,102	1,479	66.1	100%	$2	$4.25	$10	$30	$110	$450
	Auctions: $2,585, MS-67FB, February 2014; $176, MS-67FB, October 2014; $153, MS-67FB, October 2014; $94, MS-67FB, December 2014									
1951, Proof	57,500	1,616	66.7					$50	$65	$100
	Auctions: $23,500, PF-68DCam, January 2014; $123, PF-67Cam, September 2014; $125, PF-67Cam, November 2014; $411, PF-69, July 2014									
1951D	56,529,000	907	66.2	100%	$2	$4	$10	$28	$130	$550
	Auctions: $3,525, MS-68FB, July 2014; $646, MS-67FB+, December 2014									
1951S	31,630,000	1,540	66.4	100%	$3.50	$14	$25	$45	$110	$450
	Auctions: $3,055, MS-68FB, April 2013; $382, MS-67FB+, July 2014; $734, MS-67FB+, August 2014; $165, MS-67FB, August 2014									
1952	99,040,093	1,006	66.0	100%	$2	$4.25	$10	$30	$85	$1,200
	Auctions: $141, MS-67FB, September 2014; $176, MS-67FB, November 2014; $617, MS-67FB, August 2013; $42, MS-66FB, September 2014									
1952, Proof	81,980	1,260	66.7					$35	$50	$85
	Auctions: $881, PF-68Cam, November 2014; $1,116, PF-68Cam, April 2013; $165, PF-66Cam, November 2014									
1952D	122,100,000	1,130	66.1	100%	$2	$4.25	$9	$25	$30	$500
	Auctions: $118, MS-67FB, September 2014; $2,115, MS-67FB, August 2013									
1952S	44,419,500	1,633	66.3	100%	$3	$8	$12	$35	$75	$750
	Auctions: $3,290, MS-68FB, October 2014; $940, MS-67FB+, November 2014; $3,966, MS-69, January 2014; $76, MS-67, July 2014									
1953	53,490,120	793	66.0	100%	$2	$4	$8	$15	$90	$225
	Auctions: $411, MS-67FB, June 2014; $529, MS-67FB, December 2014; $558, MS-67+, August 2014; $98, MS-67, September 2014									
1953, Proof	128,800	1,738	66.8					$38	$55	$80
	Auctions: $999, PF-68Cam, June 2013; $106, PF-67Cam, November 2014									
1953D	136,433,000	1,106	66.1	100%	$2	$3.50	$8	$20	$45	$500
	Auctions: $259, MS-67FB, July 2014; $259, MS-67FB, November 2014; $411, MS-67FB, September 2013									
1953S	39,180,000	2,300	66.3	100%	$3	$4	$9	$25	$65	$875
	Auctions: $823, MS-67FB, April 2014; $470, MS-67FB, September 2014; $881, MS-68, September 2014									
1954	114,010,203	1,259	65.9	100%	$2	$4	$8	$20	$32	$1,000
	Auctions: $165, MS-67FB, September 2014; $129, MS-67FB, November 2014; $83, MS-66FB, August 2014									
1954, Proof	233,300	2,098	67.0					$18	$25	$30
	Auctions: $9,400, PF-68DCam, April 2014; $84, PF-67Cam, November 2014; $358, PF-69, July 2014; $141, PF-69, October 2014									
1954D	106,397,000	949	66.0	100%	$2	$4	$9	$14	$30	$750
	Auctions: $112, MS-67FB, September 2014; $100, MS-67, December 2014; $43, MS-67, November 2014; $141, MS-67, October 2013									
1954S	22,860,000	2,034	66.2	100%	$2	$4	$9	$16	$40	$750
	Auctions: $212, MS-67FB, December 2014; $1,116, MS-67FB, August 2013; $79, MS-67, August 2014									

a. The diagonal stroke of the initially punched S mintmark is visible within the opening of the primary D mintmark. The lower curve of the S is evident on the lower right curve of the D. **b.** Included in 1950-D mintage figure. **c.** The S mintmark is punched squarely over a previously punched D. CONECA lists this coin as an S Over Inverted S, indicating that the line enclosing the lower loop is that of the long upper serif on an inverted S. However, Fivaz and Stanton, in the *Cherrypickers' Guide to Rare Die Varieties*, sixth edition, volume II, "believe this to be an [overmintmark] (actually S/S/D) because the long upper serif of an S would not enclose the lower opening. In addition, the curve of the face of a D is clearly evident in the upper opening." **d.** Included in 1950-S mintage figure.

1960, Doubled-Die Obverse, Proof
FS-10-1960-102. Various die states exist.

	Mintage	Cert	Avg	%MS	EF-40	MS-63	MS-65	MS-66	MS-67	MS-67FB
								PF-65	PF-66	PF-67
1955	12,450,181	2,070	66.0	100%	$2	$4	$8	$16	$25	$1,000
	Auctions: $1,528, MS-67FB, September 2013; $999, MS-67+, July 2014									
1955, Proof	378,200	3,370	67.4					$15	$20	$25
	Auctions: $881, PF-68DCam, April 2013; $28, PF-67, November 2014									
1955D	13,959,000	1,387	65.6	100%	$2	$4	$8	$15	$24	$650
	Auctions: $123, MS-67FB, September 2014; $165, MS-67FB, December 2014; $88, MS-67, March 2014									
1955S	18,510,000	2,956	66.0	100%	$2	$4	$8	$15	$60	$2,300
	Auctions: $235, MS-67FB, September 2014; $200, MS-67FB, December 2014; $2,350, MS-67FB, August 2013									
1956	108,640,000	2,064	66.2	100%	$2	$3	$6	$14	$45	$1,000
	Auctions: $9,988, MS-68FB, December 2013; $764, MS-67FB, October 2014; $98, MS-66FB, August 2014; $129, MS-66FB, November 2014									
1956, Proof	669,384	2,910	67.5					$8	$10	$18
	Auctions: $646, PF-68DCam, June 2013; $65, PF-68Cam, October 2014; $94, PF-68Cam, December 2014; $58, PF-69, October 2014									
1956D	108,015,100	982	66.1	100%	$2	$3	$6	$15	$35	$800
	Auctions: $153, MS-67FB, September 2014; $217, MS-67FB, July 2013									
1957	160,160,000	2,129	66.2	100%	$2	$3	$6	$14	$65	$2,000
	Auctions: $1,998, MS-67FB, April 2014; $21, MS-67, November 2014									
1957, Proof	1,247,952	3,663	67.5					$5	$8	$25
	Auctions: $4,113, PF-69DCam, January 2014									
1957D	113,354,330	1,482	66.1	100%	$2	$3	$6	$14	$20	$2,000
	Auctions: $2,233, MS-68FB, September 2014; $1,763, MS-67FB, February 2014; $411, MS-67FB, September 2014									
1958	31,910,000	2,124	66.3	100%	$2	$3	$7	$15	$55	$2,000
	Auctions: $2,585, MS-67FB, June 2014; $1,998, MS-67FB, November 2014									
1958, Proof	875,652	2,786	67.3					$5	$8	$15
	Auctions: $2,585, PF-69DCam, April 2013									
1958D	136,564,600	1,618	66.2	100%	$2	$3	$7	$14	$45	$300
	Auctions: $2,115, MS-68FB, January 2014; $1,163, MS-68FB, October 2014; $100, MS-67FB, November 2014									
1959	85,780,000	1,424	66.0	100%	$2	$3	$6	$15	$35	$700
	Auctions: $1,528, MS-67FB, June 2014									
1959, Proof	1,149,291	2,540	67.4					$6	$8	$15
	Auctions: $165, PF-69Cam, November 2014; $940, PF-68DCam, April 2014									
1959D	164,919,790	1,040	66.1	100%	$2	$3	$6	$14	$25	$150
	Auctions: $118, MS-67FB, August 2014; $79, MS-67FB, September 2014; $165, MS-67FB, October 2013									
1960	70,390,000	1,174	65.9	100%	$2	$3	$6	$14	$25	$800
	Auctions: $2,938, MS-67FB, June 2014; $705, MS-67FB, August 2014; $470, MS-67FB, August 2014; $80, MS-66FB, October 2014									
1960, Proof	1,691,602	3,758	67.4					$6	$10	$20
	Auctions: $153, PF-69DCam, December 2014; $499, PF-69DCam, November 2013; $76, PF-65, July 2014; $40, PF-64, November 2014									
1960, Doubled-Die Obverse, Proof	(e)	64	66.4					$150	$250	
	Auctions: $106, PF-67, November 2014; $129, PF-67, June 2013; $127, PF-67, March 2012									

e. Included in 1960, Proof, mintage figure.

1963, Doubled-Die Reverse
FS-10-1963-805.

1963-D, Doubled-Die Reverse
FS-10-1963D-801.

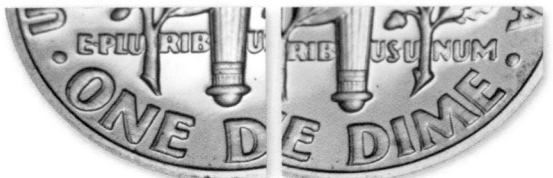

1963, Doubled-Die Reverse, Proof
FS-10-1963-802. Other varieties exist

	Mintage	Cert	Avg	%MS	EF-40	MS-63	MS-65	MS-66	MS-67	MS-67FB
								PF-65	PF-66	PF-67
1961	93,730,000	1,153	65.9	100%	$2	$3	$5	$12	$35	$1,500
Auctions: $1,880, MS-67FB, February 2014; $470, MS-67FB, December 2014										
1961, Proof	3,028,244	4,016	67.3					$5	$8	$15
Auctions: $329, PF-69DCam, November 2014; $223, PF-69DCam, December 2014										
1961D	209,146,550	841	65.9	100%	$2	$3	$5	$12	$25	$700
Auctions: $411, MS-67FB, November 2014; $259, MS-67FB, December 2014; $306, MS-67FB, October 2013										
1962	72,450,000	1,318	65.9	100%	$2	$3	$5	$12	$40	$500
Auctions: $112, MS-67FB, September 2014; $106, MS-67FB, December 2014; $30, MS-66FB, March 2013										
1962, Proof	3,218,019	3,932	67.3					$5	$8	$15
Auctions: $282, PF-69DCam, December 2014; $74, PF-70, December 2014										
1962D	334,948,380	987	66.1	99%	$2	$3	$5	$12	$30	$350
Auctions: $294, MS-67FB, March 2014; $84, MS-67FB, September 2014; $999, MS-67FB+, October 2014; $119, MS-67FB, December 2014										
1963	123,650,000	1,083	65.9	100%	$2	$3	$5	$12	$30	$300
Auctions: $5,581, MS-67FB, February 2014										
1963, Doubled-Die Reverse (f)	(g)	11	63.3	91%		$25	$38	$90		
Auctions: No auction records available.										
1963, Proof	3,075,645	5,321	67.4					$5	$8	$15
Auctions: $165, PF-69DCam, December 2014; $113, PF-69DCam, November 2014; $147, PF-69DCam, May 2013; $92, PF-68DCam, August 2014										
1963, Doubled-Die Reverse, Proof (h)	(i)	521	66.9					$150	$250	
Auctions: $129, PF-67DCam, December 2014; $100, PF-68, December 2014										
1963D	421,476,530	1,053	65.8	99%	$2	$3	$5	$12	$30	$2,000
Auctions: $382, MS-67FB, December 2014; $2,115, MS-67FB, September 2013; $115, MS-66FB, November 2014										
1963D, Doubled-Die Reverse (j)	(k)	14	63.6	93%		$120	$200	$275		
Auctions: $94, MS-66, September 2014										

f. Doubling is evident on UNITED, E PLURIBUS, the olive branch, and the stem. Lesser doubling is also visible on ONE DIME. **g.** Included in circulation-strike 1963 mintage figure. **h.** Several less-valuable 1963, Proof, DDRs exist. Values shown are for FS-10-1963-802. **i.** Included in 1963, Proof, mintage figure. **j.** Doubling is evident on all reverse lettering, with the most obvious doubling on AMERICA and on the top of the flame. Most MS examples are MS-63 and lower. **k.** Included in 1963-D mintage figure.

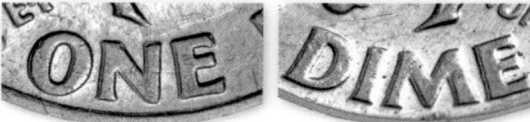

1964-D, Doubled-Die Reverse
FS-10-1964D-801. Other varieties exist.

1967, Doubled-Die Obverse
FS-10-1967-101.

1968-S, Doubled-Die Obverse, Proof
FS-10-1968S-102.

1968-S, No Mintmark, Proof
FS-10-1968S-501.

	Mintage	Cert	Avg	%MS	EF-40	MS-63	MS-65	MS-66 / PF-65	MS-67 / PF-66	MS-67FB / PF-67
1964 (l)	929,360,000	1,358	65.7	99%	$2	$3	$5	$12	$30	$500
	Auctions: $1,058, MS-67FB, June 2014; $470, MS-67FB, September 2014; $82, MS-67, August 2014									
1964, Proof	3,950,762	9,883	67.8					$5	$8	$15
	Auctions: $84, PF-69DCam, September 2014; $84, PF-69DCam, September 2014; $329, PF-70, June 2014									
1964D (l)	1,357,517,180	1,538	65.7	98%	$2	$3	$5	$12	$50	$400
	Auctions: $270, MS-67FB, September 2014; $235, MS-67FB, September 2014; $940, MS-67+, July 2014									
1964D, Doubled-Die Reverse (m)	(n)	17	56.8	18%	$35	$100	$160	$235	$450	—
	Auctions: $165, MS-64, November 2014; $62, EF-45, November 2014									
1965	1,652,140,570	102	65.8	98%			$2.50	$6	$25	$1,000
	Auctions: $3,819, MS-68FB, March 2013; $64, MS-66FB, November 2014; $47, MS-61, July 2014									
1965, Special Mint Set ‡	2,360,000	1,809	67.1	100%				$11	$13	$17
	Auctions: $176, PF-67Cam, November 2014									
1966	1,382,734,540	173	66.2	97%			$2.25	$6	$30	$1,000
	Auctions: $2,820, MS-68FB, November 2013; $153, MS-68, July 2014; $141, MS-68, July 2014									
1966, Special Mint Set ‡	2,261,583	1,780	67.2	100%				$11	$13	$20
	Auctions: $176, PF-68Cam, October 2014									
1967	2,244,007,320	161	64.6	84%			$2	$5	$25	$750
	Auctions: No auction records available.									
1967, Doubled-Die Obverse (o)	(p)	0	n/a			$400	$600	$850		
	Auctions: No auction records available.									
1967, Special Mint Set ‡	1,863,344	1,939	67.2	100%				$12	$14	$18
	Auctions: $2,300, MS-69Cam, March 2010									
1968	424,470,400	183	65.9	99%			$2	$5	$25	$900
	Auctions: $382, MS-67FB, September 2014; $236, MS-67FB, December 2014; $1,116, MS-67FB, December 2013									
1968D	480,748,280	394	66.4	99%			$2	$5	$20	$125
	Auctions: $141, AU-58, November 2013									
1968S, Proof	3,041,506	900	68.0					$2	$4	$6
	Auctions: $13, PF-70Cam, March 2009									
1968S, Doubled-Die Obverse, Proof (q)	(r)	12	67.0					$350	$500	$750
	Auctions: $74, PF-67, March 2012									
1968S, No Mintmark, Proof ‡ (s)	(r)	10	68.0					$12,000	$15,000	$20,000
	Auctions: $22,325, PF-68, November 2014									

‡ Ranked in the *100 Greatest U.S. Modern Coins*. **l.** The 9 in the date has either a pointed tail or a straight tail. **m.** There are several varieties of 1964-D with a doubled-die reverse. The variety pictured and valued here is FS-10-1964D-801. For more information, see the *Cherrypickers' Guide to Rare Die Varieties*, sixth edition, volume II. **n.** Included in 1964-D mintage figure. **o.** This is a very rare doubled die. Its doubling is evident on IN GOD WE TRUST, the date, and the designer's initials. **p.** Included in circulation-strike 1967 mintage figure. **q.** There are several 1968-S, Proof, doubled-die obverse varieties. The one listed here is FS-10-1968S-102 (see the *Cherrypickers' Guide to Rare Die Varieties*, sixth edition, volume II). **r.** Included in 1968-S, Proof, mintage figure. **s.** The S mintmark was inadvertently left off the coinage die; this defect was probably discovered before the end of the die's life.

1970, Doubled-Die Reverse
FS-10-1970-801.

	Mintage	Cert	Avg	%MS	EF-40	MS-63	MS-65	MS-66	MS-67	MS-67FB
								PF-65	PF-66	PF-67
1969	145,790,000	90	65.1	99%			$3	$6	$30	
Auctions: $176, MS-66FB, December 2014; $470, MS-67, April 2014										
1969D	563,323,870	480	66.2	100%			$2	$6	$25	$1,000
Auctions: $17, MS-64, August 2013										
1969S, Proof	2,394,631	794	68.2					$2	$4	$6
Auctions: $206, PF-69DCam, October 2009										
1970	345,570,000	140	64.4	96%			$2	$6	$35	
Auctions: $52, MS-67, October 2014; $55, MS-66, June 2014										
1970, Doubled-Die Reverse (t)	(u)	4	62.3	75%			$300	$650	—	
Auctions: $56, MS-65, June 2009										
1970D	754,942,100	233	65.0	97%			$2	$5	$35	
Auctions: $16, MS-65FB, November 2014; $200, MS-61, January 2014										
1970S, Proof	2,632,810	895	67.7					$2	$4	$6
Auctions: $17, PF-70DCam, August 2009										
1970S, No Mintmark, Proof ‡ (s)	(v)	159	67.6					$800	$900	$1,000
Auctions: $2,585, PF-69Cam, October 2014; $646, PF-68, November 2014; $501, PF-67, November 2014										
1971	162,690,000	64	64.9	100%			$2.50	$6	$40	
Auctions: $276, MS-66FB, January 2012										
1971D	377,914,240	136	65.7	100%			$2.25	$6	$40	$700
Auctions: $109, MS-67FB, April 2012										
1971S, Proof	3,220,733	1,167	68.2					$2	$4	$6
Auctions: $15, PF-68DCam, August 2009										
1972	431,540,000	89	65.0	99%			$2	$6	$60	
Auctions: $79, MS-67, November 2014										
1972D	330,290,000	168	65.7	100%			$2	$6	$40	$800
Auctions: $141, MS-67FB, December 2014										
1972S, Proof	3,260,996	963	68.0					$2	$4	$6
Auctions: $127, PF-70DCam, October 2009										
1973	315,670,000	83	65.2	100%			$2	$5	$70	$1,200
Auctions: $59, MS-67, November 2014										
1973D	455,032,426	131	65.4	100%			$2	$6	$50	$500
Auctions: $84, MS-67FB, December 2014										
1973S, Proof	2,760,339	399	67.7					$2	$4	$6
Auctions: $489, PF-70DCam, October 2009										
1974	470,248,000	50	65.0	100%			$2	$5	$25	
Auctions: $52, MS-67, March 2004										
1974D	571,083,000	100	65.5	100%			$2	$5	$25	$1,000
Auctions: $51, MS-67, October 2007										
1974S, Proof	2,612,568	343	67.9					$2	$4	$6
Auctions: $69, PF-70DCam, October 2009										

‡ Ranked in the *100 Greatest U.S. Modern Coins*. **s.** The S mintmark was inadvertently left off the coinage die; this defect was probably discovered before the end of the die's life. **t.** Doubling on this extremely rare variety is evident on all reverse lettering, especially on UNITED STATES OF AMERICA, with slightly weaker doubling on ONE DIME. **u.** Included in circulation-strike 1970 mintage figure. **v.** Included in 1970-S, Proof, mintage figure.

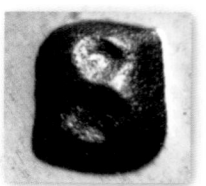

**1979-S, Filled S
(Type 1), Proof**

**1979-S, Clear S
(Type 2), Proof**

	Mintage	Cert	Avg	%MS	EF-40	MS-63	MS-65	MS-66	MS-67	MS-67FB
								PF-65	PF-66	PF-67
1975	585,673,900	110	65.3	99%			$2	$4	$25	$1,000
Auctions: $112, MS-66FB, November 2014										
1975D	313,705,300	183	66.2	99%			$2	$5	$30	$600
Auctions: $84, MS-67FB, December 2014; $270, MS-68, July 2014										
1975S, Proof	2,845,450	490	68.0					$2.50	$4	$6
Auctions: $1,610, PF-70DCam, January 2010										
1975S, No Mintmark, Proof (s)	(w)	0	n/a					$38,000	$40,000	$50,000
Auctions: $349,600, PF-68, August 2011										
1976	568,760,000	125	66.1	100%			$2	$5	$25	$1,200
Auctions: $1,035, MS-68, January 2012										
1976D	695,222,774	125	65.7	97%			$2	$5	$45	$1,200
Auctions: $100, MS-67FB, December 2014										
1976S, Proof	4,149,730	820	68.1					$2.75	$4	$6
Auctions: $30, PF-70Dcam, December 2009										
1977	796,930,000	175	65.9	100%			$2	$5	$25	$1,200
Auctions: $64, MS-66FB, October 2008										
1977D	376,607,228	103	65.6	100%			$2	$5	$25	$1,200
Auctions: $64, MS-65FB, December 2007										
1977S, Proof	3,251,152	763	68.5					$2.50	$4	$6
Auctions: $69, PF-70DCam, January 2010										
1978	663,980,000	78	65.7	99%			$2	$5	$30	$1,200
Auctions: $17, MS-65, August 2008										
1978D	282,847,540	71	65.8	100%			$2	$5	$25	
Auctions: $100, MS-66FB, December 2014										
1978S, Proof	3,127,781	649	68.8					$2.50	$4	$6
Auctions: $104, PF-70DCam, February 2010										
1979	315,440,000	135	65.8	100%			$2	$5	$30	
Auctions: $21, MS-66, December 2007										
1979D	390,921,184	112	65.7	100%			$2	$5	$30	
Auctions: $28, MS-67, December 2004										
1979S, Type 1, Proof	3,677,175	818	69.0					$2.50	$4	$6
Auctions: $74, PF-70DCam, January 2010										
1979S, Type 2, Proof	(x)	875	69.1					$5	$6	$8
Auctions: $58, PF-70DCam, August 2014										
1980P	735,170,000	91	65.6	99%			$2	$5	$25	
Auctions: $26, MS-67, March 2004										
1980D	719,354,321	83	65.8	100%			$2	$4	$30	
Auctions: $13, MS-66, February 2008										
1980S, Proof	3,554,806	1,054	68.5					$2.50	$4	$6
Auctions: $40, PF-70DCam, October 2009										

s. The S mintmark was inadvertently left off the coinage die; this defect was probably discovered before the end of the die's life. **w.** Included in 1975-S, Proof, mintage figure. **x.** Included in 1979-S, Type 1, Proof, mintage figure.

1981-S, Rounded S
(Type 1), Proof

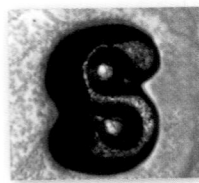
1981-S, Flat S
(Type 2), Proof

1982, No Mintmark,
Strong Strike
FS-10-1982-501.

1982, No Mintmark,
Weak Strike
FS-10-1982-502.

| | Mintage | Cert | Avg | %MS | EF-40 | MS-63 | MS-65 | MS-66 | MS-67 | MS-67FB |
								PF-65	PF-66	PF-67
1981P	676,650,000	183	66.1	100%			$2	$5	$40	$70
Auctions: $329, MS-68FB, December 2014; $129, MS-65, January 2013										
1981D	712,284,143	288	66.5	100%			$2	$4	$20	$80
Auctions: $123, MS-68FB, December 2014										
1981S, Type 1, Proof	4,063,083	1,181	68.8					$2.50	$4	$6
Auctions: $56, PF-70DCam, December 2009										
1981S, Type 2, Proof	(y)	516	69.0					$2.50	$6	$8
Auctions: $159, PF-70DCam, August 2014										
1982, No Mintmark, Strong Strike ‡ (z)	(aa)	430	64.2	93%			$225	$300	$650	$1,800
Auctions: $705, MS-67, June 2013; $441, MS-66FB, July 2014; $329, MS-66, July 2014; $282, MS-65, August 2014										
1982, No Mintmark, Weak Strike ‡ (z)	(aa)	445	64.4	93%			$85	$120	$300	
Auctions: No auction records available.										
1982P	519,475,000	185	66.2	98%			$7.50	$18	$50	$1,000
Auctions: $153, MS-67FB, December 2014; $56, MS-67, November 2014										
1982D	542,713,584	114	65.8	98%			$2.50	$6	$25	$700
Auctions: $1,410, MS-67FB, April 2014; $118, MS-67FB, December 2014										
1982S, Proof	3,857,479	718	69.0					$2.50	$4	$6
Auctions: $74, PF-70DCam, December 2009										
1983P	647,025,000	108	65.7	96%			$7	$15	$30	$250
Auctions: $489, MS-68, April 2012										
1983D	730,129,224	48	65.8	96%			$3.25	$8.50	$25	$200
Auctions: $223, MS-68, November 2014; $188, MS-68, December 2013										
1983S, Proof	3,279,126	803	69.2					$3	$4	$6
Auctions: $150, PF-70DCam, December 2009										
1983S, No Mintmark, Proof (s) ‡	(bb)	129	68.7					$750	$850	$1,000
Auctions: $600, PF-69DCam, November 2014; $588, PF-69DCam, November 2014; $647, PF-68DCam, October 2014										
1984P	856,669,000	142	66.5	100%			$2	$5	$20	$100
Auctions: $212, MS-68FB, December 2014										
1984D	704,803,976	103	65.4	100%			$2.25	$5	$20	$150
Auctions: $94, MS-67FB, May 2012										
1984S, Proof	3,065,110	543	69.1					$2.50	$4	$6
Auctions: $106, PF-70DCam, March 2013										
1985P	705,200,962	109	66.5	100%			$2.25	$5	$25	$150
Auctions: $66, MS-67FB, November 2014										
1985D	587,979,970	172	66.8	100%			$2.25	$5	$30	$100
Auctions: $129, MS-68FB, December 2014										
1985S, Proof	3,362,821	608	69.1					$3	$4	$6
Auctions: $16, PF-69DCam, August 2009										

‡ Ranked in the *100 Greatest U.S. Modern Coins*. **s.** The S mintmark was inadvertently left off the coinage die; this defect was probably discovered before the end of the die's life. **y.** Included in 1981-S, Type 1, Proof, mintage figure. **z.** The P mintmark was omitted from this working die. There are two versions of this variety: one with a strong strike, and one with a weak strike. The strong strike is far more valuable and in demand than the weak. **aa.** Included in 1982-P mintage figure. **bb.** Included in 1983-S, Proof, mintage figure.

	Mintage	Cert	Avg	%MS	EF-40	MS-63	MS-65	MS-66	MS-67	MS-67FB
								PF-65	PF-66	PF-67
1986P	682,649,693	154	65.9	99%			$2.50	$5	$20	$800
	Auctions: $89, MS-67FB, December 2014									
1986D	473,326,970	101	66.0	99%			$2.50	$4	$20	$700
	Auctions: $123, MS-67FB, December 2014									
1986S, Proof	3,010,497	454	69.1					$4	$5	$7
	Auctions: $48, PF-70DCam, April 2013									
1987P	762,709,481	89	66.1	99%			$2	$5	$25	$800
	Auctions: $259, MS-67FB, December 2014									
1987D	653,203,402	118	66.1	98%			$2.50	$4	$20	$200
	Auctions: $382, MS-67FB, December 2014									
1987S, Proof	4,227,728	603	69.1					$3	$4	$6
	Auctions: $15, PF-69DCam, August 2009									
1988P	1,030,550,000	115	65.8	97%			$2	$5	$35	$225
	Auctions: $103, MS-64, July 2014									
1988D	962,385,489	125	66.2	99%			$2.75	$4	$40	$100
	Auctions: $165, MS-68FB, December 2014									
1988S, Proof	3,262,948	409	69.1					$4	$5	$7
	Auctions: $60, PF-70DCam, May 2013									
1989P	1,298,400,000	120	66.3	100%			$2.25	$5	$20	$100
	Auctions: $106, MS-68FB, December 2014; $45, MS-65, July 2014									
1989D	896,535,597	170	66.4	99%			$2	$6	$20	$75
	Auctions: $242, MS-68FB, April 2012									
1989S, Proof	3,220,194	447	69.1					$4	$5	$6
	Auctions: $15, PF-69DCam, August 2009									
1990P	1,034,340,000	55	66.3	98%			$2.50	$6	$20	$1,000
	Auctions: $27, MS-67, March 2004									
1990D	839,995,824	81	66.1	98%			$2	$4	$25	$1,100
	Auctions: $12, MS-67, March 2004									
1990S, Proof	3,299,559	630	69.3					$2.50	$4	$6
	Auctions: $56, PF-70DCam, December 2009									
1991P	927,220,000	55	66.3	98%			$2	$4	$20	$100
	Auctions: $27, MS-67, March 2004									
1991D	601,241,114	41	65.3	100%			$2	$4	$20	$200
	Auctions: $127, MS-67, May 2012									
1991S, Proof	2,867,787	646	69.4					$4	$5	$7
	Auctions: $31, PF-70DCam, June 2014									
1992P	593,500,000	71	67.0	100%			$2	$5	$35	$150
	Auctions: $322, MS-67FB, May 2010									
1992D	616,273,932	54	66.3	100%			$2	$4	$30	$200
	Auctions: $99, MS-67FB, April 2012									
1992S, Proof	2,858,981	476	69.5					$3	$4	$6
	Auctions: $53, PF-70DCam, December 2009									
1992S, Proof, Silver	1,317,579	1,266	69.2					$6	$7	$8
	Auctions: $36, PF-70DCam, October 2014									
1993P	766,180,000	110	66.4	97%			$2	$4	$30	$250
	Auctions: $53, MS-67FB, April 2012									
1993D	750,110,166	75	65.9	100%			$2	$4	$25	$500
	Auctions: $15, MS-66FB, October 2008									
1993S, Proof	2,633,439	504	69.4					$5	$6	$7
	Auctions: $62, PF-70DCam, December 2009									
1993S, Proof, Silver	761,353	1,006	69.1					$7	$8	$9
	Auctions: $94, PF-70DCam, February 2010									

	Mintage	Cert	Avg	%MS	EF-40	MS-63	MS-65	MS-66 PF-65	MS-67 PF-66	MS-67FB PF-67
1994P	1,189,000,000	97	66.4	97%			$2	$4	$25	$200
Auctions: $76, MS-67FB, June 2014										
1994D	1,303,268,110	56	65.6	100%			$2	$4	$25	$300
Auctions: $130, MS-64, July 2014										
1994S, Proof	2,484,594	597	69.5					$5	$6	$8
Auctions: $59, PF-70DCam, October 2009										
1994S, Proof, Silver	785,329	948	69.2					$8	$9	$10
Auctions: $96, PF-70DCam, May 2013										
1995P	1,125,500,000	60	66.9	100%			$2	$4	$30	$500
Auctions: $21, MS-66FB, August 2009										
1995D	1,274,890,000	73	66.0	97%			$2.25	$5	$35	$425
Auctions: $259, MS-67FB, December 2014; $18, MS-65FB, November 2014										
1995S, Proof	2,117,496	406	69.5					$10	$16	$20
Auctions: $84, PF-70DCam, December 2009										
1995S, Proof, Silver	679,985	1,061	69.1					$14	$23	$30
Auctions: $100, PF-70DCam, May 2013										
1996P	1,421,163,000	148	66.7	98%			$2	$4	$25	$30
Auctions: $165, MS-68FB, December 2014; $40, MS-64, November 2014										
1996D	1,400,300,000	184	66.2	99%			$2	$4	$20	$75
Auctions: $11, MS-67FB, October 2008										
1996W ‡ (cc)	1,457,000	4,373	66.5	100%			$20	$30	$50	$100
Auctions: $282, MS-68FB, April 2014; $42, MS-67, October 2014										
1996S, Proof	1,750,244	413	69.4					$3	$6	$8
Auctions: $42, PF-70DCam, February 2010										
1996S, Proof, Silver	775,021	979	69.1					$8	$10	$15
Auctions: $88, PF-70DCam, May 2013										
1997P	991,640,000	61	66.6	98%			$2	$6	$60	$100
Auctions: $26, MS-67FB, November 2014										
1997D	979,810,000	67	66.1	99%			$2	$6	$65	$100
Auctions: $11, MS-65FB, October 2008										
1997S, Proof	2,055,000	319	69.6					$8	$10	$15
Auctions: $69, PF-70DCam, December 2009										
1997S, Proof, Silver	741,678	1,062	69.2					$12	$18	$22
Auctions: $46, PF-70DCam, May 2013										
1998P	1,163,000,000	83	66.8	99%			$2	$3	$18	$100
Auctions: $11, MS-66FB, September 2008										
1998D	1,172,250,000	68	66.0	99%			$2	$3	$15	$100
Auctions: $118, MS-67FB, December 2014										
1998S, Proof	2,086,507	316	69.5					$4	$6	$8
Auctions: $17, PF-69DCam, August 2009										
1998S, Proof, Silver	878,792	1,168	69.3					$6	$8	$10
Auctions: $79, PF-70DCam, February 2010										
1999P	2,164,000,000	117	66.8	97%			$2	$3	$15	$30
Auctions: $3,055, MS-64, January 2014; $36, MS-64, July 2014; $38, MS-63, November 2014										
1999D	1,397,750,000	108	66.4	99%			$2	$3	$15	$40
Auctions: $1,610, MS-69FB, April 2010										
1999S, Proof	2,543,401	2,366	69.2					$4	$6	$8
Auctions: $67, PF-70DCam, January 2010										
1999S, Proof, Silver	804,565	3,670	69.2					$7	$8	$12
Auctions: $76, PF-70DCam, May 2013										

‡ Ranked in the *100 Greatest U.S. Modern Coins*. **cc.** Issued in Mint sets only, to mark the 50th anniversary of the design.

	Mintage	Cert	Avg	%MS	EF-40	MS-63	MS-65	MS-66	MS-67	MS-67FB
								PF-65	PF-66	PF-67
2000P	1,842,500,000	56	65.3	88%			$2	$3	$15	$30
Auctions: $66, MS-65, July 2014; $26, MS-64, July 2014; $823, MS-64, June 2013; $45, MS-63, July 2014										
2000D	1,818,700,000	74	66.4	96%			$2	$3	$15	$30
Auctions: $11, MS-68FB, September 2008										
2000S, Proof	3,082,572	1,310	69.3					$2.50	$4	$7
Auctions: $59, PF-70DCam, December 2009										
2000S, Proof, Silver	965,421	4,279	69.3					$5	$6	$8
Auctions: $28, PF-70DCam, April 2013										
2001P	1,369,590,000	56	66.5	100%			$2	$3	$12	$30
Auctions: $79, MS-64, November 2014										
2001D	1,412,800,000	69	66.2	94%			$2	$3	$12	$30
Auctions: No auction records available.										
2001S, Proof	2,294,909	1,016	69.4					$2.50	$4	$7
Auctions: $50, PF-70DCam, December 2009										
2001S, Proof, Silver	889,697	3,685	69.4					$5	$6	$8
Auctions: $36, PF-70UCam, February 2010										
2002P	1,187,500,000	32	66.6	97%			$2	$3	$12	$30
Auctions: $11, MS-68FB, September 2008										
2002D	1,379,500,000	39	66.4	97%			$2	$3	$12	$30
Auctions: $14, MS-68FB, October 2008										
2002S, Proof	2,319,766	1,482	69.3					$2.50	$4	$7
Auctions: $44, PF-70DCam, December 2009										
2002S, Proof, Silver	892,229	3,532	69.4					$5	$6	$8
Auctions: $42, PF-70UCam, March 2010										
2003P	1,085,500,000	139	66.0	100%			$2	$3	$10	$30
Auctions: $11, MS-68FB, October 2008										
2003D	986,500,000	98	65.7	100%			$2	$3	$10	$30
Auctions: $11, MS-68FB, September 2008										
2003S, Proof	2,172,684	3,458	69.3					$2.50	$4	$7
Auctions: $52, PF-70DCam, March 2010										
2003S, Proof, Silver	1,125,755	4,500	69.3					$4.50	$5	$8
Auctions: $38, PF-70UCam, March 2010										
2004P	1,328,000,000	75	66.8	100%			$2	$3	$8	$30
Auctions: $94, MS-68FB, December 2014										
2004D	1,159,500,000	72	66.8	100%			$2	$3	$8	$35
Auctions: $21, MS-68FB, October 2008										
2004S, Proof	1,789,488	1,357	69.3					$3	$5	$7
Auctions: $69, PF-70DCam, October 2009										
2004S, Proof, Silver	1,175,934	4,423	69.5					$5	$6	$8
Auctions: $40, PF-70DCam, November 2013										
2005P	1,412,000,000	32	67.1	100%			$2	$3	$8	$65
Auctions: $129, MS-67FB, December 2014; $74, MS-67FB, November 2014										
2005D	1,423,500,000	30	66.2	97%			$2	$3	$8	$80
Auctions: $47, MS-67FB, November 2014; $106, MS-67FB, December 2014										
2005S, Proof	2,275,000	6,049	69.3					$2.50	$4	$7
Auctions: $40, PF-70DCam, December 2009										
2005S, Proof, Silver	1,069,679	5,440	69.5					$5	$6	$8
Auctions: $40, PF-70DCam, November 2013										

	Mintage	Cert	Avg	%MS	EF-40	MS-63	MS-65	MS-66 PF-65	MS-67 PF-66	MS-67FB PF-67
2006P	1,381,000,000	45	65.8	98%			$2	$3	$6	$22
	Auctions: $94, MS-67FB, December 2014									
2006D	1,447,000,000	37	66.4	100%			$2	$3	$6	$22
	Auctions: $16, MS-69FB Satin, September 2008									
2006S, Proof	2,000,428	1,851	69.4					$2.50	$4	$7
	Auctions: $69, PF-70DCam, October 2009									
2006S, Proof, Silver	1,054,008	2,960	69.5					$5	$6	$8
	Auctions: $56, PF-70UCam, February 2010									
2007P	1,047,500,000	19	66.2	100%			$2	$3	$6	$22
	Auctions: $59, MS-67FB, December 2014; $223, MS-64, June 2013									
2007D	1,042,000,000	22	66.5	100%			$2	$3	$6	$22
	Auctions: $53, MS-67FB, December 2014									
2007S, Proof	1,702,116	1,662	69.6					$2.50	$4	$7
	Auctions: $40, PF-70DCam, December 2009									
2007S, Proof, Silver	875,050	3,436	69.6					$5	$6	$8
	Auctions: $26, PF-69DCam, February 2013									
2008P	391,000,000	20	66.0	100%			$2	$3	$5	$22
	Auctions: $188, MS-67FB, December 2014; $100, MS-66FB, November 2014									
2008D	624,500,000	51	66.4	100%			$2	$3	$4	$20
	Auctions: No auction records available.									
2008S, Proof	1,405,674	1,298	69.7					$2.50	$4	$7
	Auctions: $56, PF-70DCam, October 2009									
2008S, Proof, Silver	763,887	3,695	69.8					$5	$6	$8
	Auctions: $36, PF-70UCam, March 2010									
2009P	96,500,000	252	65.7	100%			$2	$3	$4	$20
	Auctions: No auction records available.									
2009D	49,500,000	155	66.1	100%			$2	$3	$5	$20
	Auctions: No auction records available.									
2009S, Proof	1,482,502	3,337	69.6					$2.50	$4	$7
	Auctions: $23, PF-69DCam, February 2013									
2009S, Proof, Silver	697,365	3,875	69.7					$5	$6	$8
	Auctions: $40, PF-70UCam, March 2010									
2010P	557,000,000	127	66.6	100%			$2	$3	$4	$20
	Auctions: $65, MS-68FB, December 2014									
2010D	562,000,000	104	66.2	100%			$2	$3	$4	$20
	Auctions: $44, MS-67FB, December 2014									
2010S, Proof	1,103,815	1,356	69.5					$2.50	$4	$7
	Auctions: No auction records available.									
2010S, Proof, Silver	585,401	3,746	69.7					$5	$6	$8
	Auctions: No auction records available.									
2011P	748,000,000	197	67.3	100%			$2	$3	$4	$20
	Auctions: $84, MS-69FB, December 2014									
2011D	754,000,000	197	67.1	100%			$2	$3	$4	$20
	Auctions: No auction records available.									
2011S, Proof	1,098,835	2,326	69.5					$2.50	$4	$7
	Auctions: No auction records available.									
2011S, Proof, Silver	574,175	4,676	69.7					$5	$6	$8
	Auctions: No auction records available.									

	Mintage	Cert	Avg	%MS	EF-40	MS-63	MS-65	MS-66 / PF-65	MS-67 / PF-66	MS-67FB / PF-67
2012P	808,000,000	93	67.0	100%			$2	$3	$4	$20
Auctions: $499, MS-69FB, December 2014										
2012D	868,000,000	96	66.9	100%			$2	$3	$4	$20
Auctions: No auction records available.										
2012S, Proof	841,972	1,386	69.5					$2.50	$4	$7
Auctions: No auction records available.										
2012S, Proof, Silver	395,443	1,526	69.8					$5	$6	$8
Auctions: No auction records available.										
2013P	1,086,500,000	76	66.8	100%			$2	$3	$4	$20
Auctions: No auction records available.										
2013D	1,025,500,000	116	67.2	100%			$2	$3	$4	$20
Auctions: No auction records available.										
2013S, Proof	802,460	1,738	69.6					$2.50	$4	$7
Auctions: No auction records available.										
2013S, Proof, Silver	419,719	0	n/a					$5	$6	$8
Auctions: No auction records available.										
2014P	1,125,500,000	131	67.4	100%			$2	$3	$4	$20
Auctions: No auction records available.										
2014D	1,177,000,000	0	n/a				$2	$3	$4	$20
Auctions: No auction records available.										
2014S, Proof	665,100	1,167	69.6					$2.50	$4	$7
Auctions: No auction records available.										
2014S, Proof, Silver	393,037	2,639	69.9					$5	$6	$8
Auctions: No auction records available.										
2015P							$2	$3	$4	$20
Auctions: No auction records available.										
2015D							$2	$3	$4	$20
Auctions: No auction records available.										
2015S, Proof								$2.50	$4	$7
Auctions: No auction records available.										
2015S, Proof, Silver								$5	$6	$8
Auctions: No auction records available.										

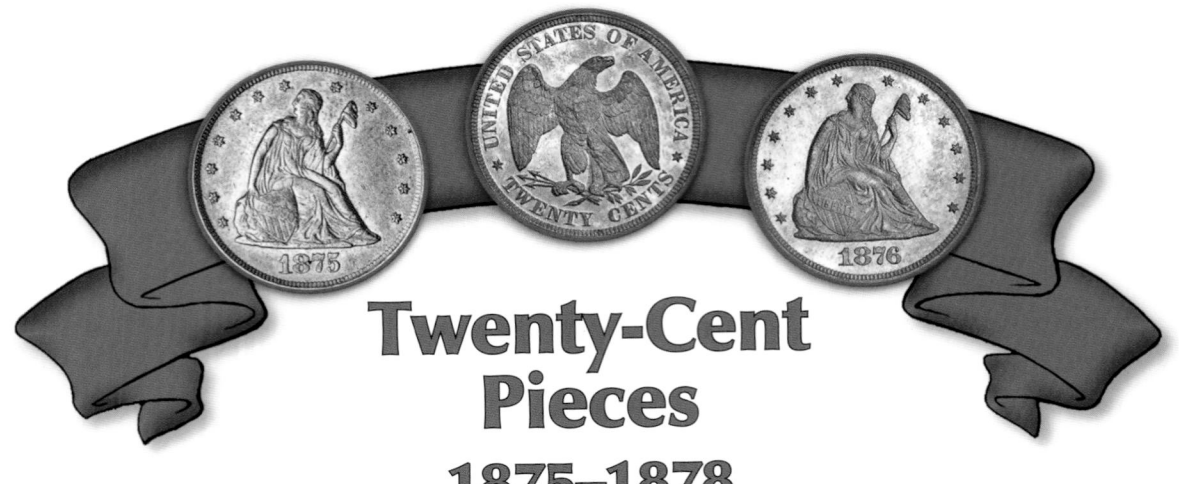

Twenty-Cent Pieces
1875–1878

AN OVERVIEW OF TWENTY-CENT PIECES

The twenty-cent piece, made in silver, proved to be the shortest-lived denomination in American coinage history. The coins were struck in quantity in their first year of issue, 1875, after which it was learned that the public confused them with quarter dollars. Mintages dropped sharply, and in 1877 and 1878 coinage was limited to just Proofs for collectors.

Both sides of the twenty-cent piece were designed by U.S. Mint chief engraver William Barber. The obverse is simply an adaptation of the Liberty Seated motif earlier used on other denominations. The reverse is new and depicts a perched eagle (of the same general appearance as introduced by Barber on the 1873 silver trade dollar).

Only one twenty-cent piece is needed for inclusion in a type set. By far the most readily available in Mint State is the 1875-S, followed by the 1875-CC. These are often somewhat lightly struck on the reverse, particularly near the top of the eagle's wings. The 1875 and 1876 Philadelphia coins are occasionally encountered in Mint State and are usually well struck.

Proofs are readily available for all years, 1875 through 1878.

Chief Engraver William Barber merged the beloved Liberty Seated motif with the perched eagle when he designed the twenty-cent piece.

FOR THE COLLECTOR AND INVESTOR: TWENTY-CENT PIECES AS A SPECIALTY

A full date-and-mintmark set of twenty-cent pieces consists of the 1875, 1875-CC, 1875-S, 1876, 1876-CC, 1877, and 1878, the latter two years being available only in Proof format. The great challenge in forming a set is the 1876-CC, of which 10,000 were minted, but, seemingly, all but about two dozen were melted. Those that do survive are typically encountered in Mint State and are widely heralded when they are offered at auction.

LIBERTY SEATED (1875–1878)

Designer: *William Barber.* **Weight:** *5 grams.* **Composition:** *.900 silver, .100 copper.* **Diameter:** *22 mm.* **Edge:** *Plain.* **Mints:** *Philadelphia, Carson City, San Francisco.*

Circulation Strike

Mintmark location is on the reverse, below the eagle.

Proof

History. The twenty-cent coin debuted in 1875 as a convenient denomination to make change in the West (at the time silver coins did not circulate in the East or Midwest). The coins sometimes were confused with quarter dollars, given their similar Liberty Seated design on the obverse, and their similar size. The quantity minted dropped considerably in 1876, and in 1877 and 1878 only Proofs were struck. Despite the brief time of their production, these coins were still seen in circulation through the early 1900s, by which time they were often casually used as quarters. Proof coins were made of all years 1875 to 1878.

Striking and Sharpness. Areas of weakness are common. On the obverse, check the head of Miss Liberty and the stars. The word LIBERTY is *raised* on this coin, a curious departure from other Liberty Seated coins of the era, on which it is recessed or incuse (the Gobrecht silver dollars of 1836 and 1839 being exceptions). On the reverse, check the eagle's feathers, especially the top of the wing on the left, but other areas can be weak as well. Some 1875-S coins are highly prooflike. The 1877 and 1878 are Proof-only issues with no related circulation strikes. Most have been cleaned or even lightly polished. Many Proofs in the marketplace have been convincingly retoned to mask problems. Proofs are usually well struck, but more than just a few are somewhat flat on the hair details of Miss Liberty.

Availability. Most often seen is the high-mintage 1875-S, although the 1875 and 1875-CC are encountered with frequency. The 1876 is quite scarce and when seen is usually in high grades and well struck. The 1876-CC is a rarity, and only about two dozen are known, nearly all of which are MS. The eye appeal of MS coins can vary widely. The number of letters in LIBERTY on certain coins graded from VG through VF can vary widely in the marketplace. Proofs most often seen are those of 1875 and 1876. For some unexplained reason, high-quality Proofs of the series' final two years are very hard to find.

GRADING STANDARDS

MS-60 to 70 (Mint State). *Obverse:* At MS-60, some abrasion and contact marks are evident, most noticeably on the bosom and thighs and knees. Luster is present, but may be dull or lifeless. At MS-63, contact marks are very few, and abrasion is hard to detect except under magnification. An MS-65 coin has no abrasion, and contact marks are sufficiently minute as to require magnification. Check the knees of Liberty and the right field.

1875-S, S Over S. Graded MS-61.

Luster should be full and rich. *Reverse:* Comments apply as for the obverse, except that in lower–Mint State grades abrasion and contact marks are most noticeable on the eagle's breast and the top of the wing to the left. At MS-65 or higher, there are no marks visible to the unaided eye. The field is mainly protected by design elements and does not show abrasion as much as does the obverse on a given coin.

AU-50, 53, 55, 58 (About Uncirculated). *Obverse:* Light wear is seen on the thighs and knees, bosom, and head. At AU-58, the luster is extensive but incomplete, especially in the right field. At AU-50 and 53, luster is less. *Reverse:* Wear is evident on the eagle's breast (the prime focal point) and the top of the wings. An AU-58 coin will have nearly full luster, more so than on the obverse, as the design elements protect the small field areas. At AU-50 and 53, there still are traces of luster.

1875-CC. Graded AU-50.

EF-40, 45 (Extremely Fine). *Obverse:* Further wear is seen on all areas, especially the thighs and knees, bosom, and head. Little or no luster is seen on most coins. From this grade downward, sharpness of strike of the stars and the head does not matter to connoisseurs. *Reverse:* Further wear is evident on the eagle's breast and wings. Some feathers may be blended together.

1875. Graded EF-40.

VF-20, 30 (Very Fine). *Obverse:* Further wear is seen. Most details of the gown are worn away, except in the lower-relief areas above and to the right of the shield. Hair detail is mostly or completely gone. As to whether LIBERTY should be completely readable, this seems to be a matter of debate. On many coins in the marketplace the word is weak or missing on one to several letters. ANA grading standards and PCGS require full LIBERTY. *Reverse:* Wear is more extensive, with more feathers blended together, especially in the right wing. The area below the shield shows more wear.

1875-S. Graded VF-20.

AG-3 (About Good). *Obverse:* The seated figure is mostly visible in outline form, with only a hint of detail. Much of the rim is worn away. The date remains clear. *Reverse:* The border letters are partially worn away. The eagle is mostly in outline form, but with a few details discernible. The rim is weak or missing.

1875. Graded AG-3.

PF-60 to 70 (Proof). *Obverse and Reverse:* Proofs that are extensively cleaned and have many hairlines, or that are dull and grainy, are lower level, such as PF-60 to 62. These are not widely desired. With medium hairlines and good reflectivity, an assigned grade of PF-64 is indicated, and with relatively few hairlines, Gem PF-65. In various grades hairlines are most easily seen in the obverse field. PF-66 should have hairlines so delicate that magnification is needed to see them. Above that, a Proof should be free of such lines.

1876. Graded PF-64.

	Mintage	Cert	Avg	%MS	G-4	VG-8	F-12	VF-20	EF-40	AU-50	MS-60 / PF-60	MS-63 / PF-63	MS-65 / PF-65
1875	38,500	455	54.1	51%	$235	$270	$350	$420	$550	$710	$925	$1,600	$6,000
Auctions: $22,325, MS-67, June 2014; $2,233, MS-64, July 2014; $1,880, MS-64, October 2014; $1,763, MS-64, November 2014													
1875, Proof	1,200	248	63.6								$1,500	$3,000	$8,500
Auctions: $18,800, PF-67Cam, September 2014; $6,169, PF-65Cam, October 2014; $28,200, PF-67, June 2014; $1,528, PF-62, October 2014													
1875CC	133,290	903	40.5	34%	$400	$450	$550	$750	$1,100	$1,800	$2,300	$4,500	$12,500
Auctions: $49,938, MS-66, June 2014; $15,275, MS-65, August 2014; $3,525, MS-64, October 2014; $3,290, MS-63, October 2014													
1875S (a)	1,155,000	2,990	50.3	49%	$110	$120	$150	$175	$250	$400	$650	$1,400	$4,500
Auctions: $19,975, MS-67, June 2014; $9,400, MS-66, July 2014; $3,055, MS-65, July 2014; $3,525, MS-65, August 2014													
1875S, Proof	10–20	2	63.0								$15,000	$25,000	$75,000
Auctions: No auction records available.													
1876	14,400	430	58.4	66%	$210	$275	$350	$420	$500	$650	$950	$1,500	$6,000
Auctions: $55,813, MS-67, June 2014; $10,869, MS-66, October 2014; $16,450, MS-66, November 2014; $2,350, MS-64+, August 2014													
1876, Proof	1,500	300	63.5								$1,500	$3,000	$8,500
Auctions: $21,150, PF-67Cam, October 2014; $18,800, PF-66Cam, June 2013; $28,200, PF-65DCam, August 2014; $6,463, PF-64DCam+, October 2014													
1876CC †	10,000	7	64.6	100%							$175,000	$250,000	$375,000	$550,000
Auctions: $564,000, MS-65, January 2013													
1877, Proof	510	260	63.8								$4,500	$5,750	$12,500
Auctions: $27,025, PF-66Cam, November 2013; $5,288, PF-63Cam, August 2014; $8,225, PF-65, August 2014													
1878, Proof	600	314	63.6								$4,250	$5,250	$12,000
Auctions: $4,700, PF-64Cam, September 2014; $12,925, PF-65, April 2013; $4,700, PF-63, July 2014; $3,290, PF-63, August 2014													

† Ranked in the *100 Greatest U.S. Coins* (fourth edition). **a.** There are at least two misplaced-date die varieties of the 1875-S twenty-cent piece. These do not command a premium in the marketplace. A repunched mintmark is likewise common.

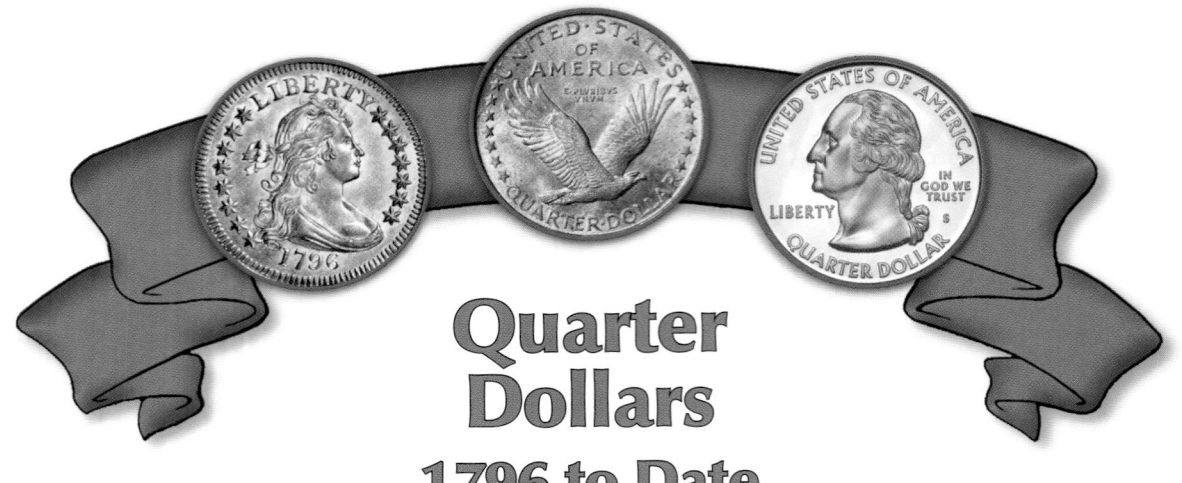

Quarter Dollars

1796 to Date

AN OVERVIEW OF QUARTER DOLLARS

In 1796 the first silver quarters were struck at the Philadelphia Mint. The Draped Bust obverse in combination with the Small Eagle reverse was produced only in this year, after which no pieces of this denomination were produced until 1804. At that time the Draped Bust obverse was continued, but now with the Heraldic Eagle reverse. The coinage proved to be brief and lasted only through 1807, after which no quarters were struck until 1815. The new quarters dated 1815 were of the Capped Bust style, by John Reich. These were produced intermittently through 1838. The Liberty Seated motif, by Christian Gobrecht, made its debut in 1838 and was produced continuously through 1891, with several modifications in design and metallic content over the years. The Liberty Head quarter, today called the Barber quarter after its designer, was introduced in 1892 and minted continuously through 1916. The obverse features the head of Miss Liberty, and the reverse a heraldic eagle. In late 1916 the Standing Liberty by Hermon A. MacNeil became the new design. This was produced through 1930, except for 1922. Some changes to both the obverse and reverse were made partway through 1917.

The Washington quarter dollar was struck in 1932 to observe the 200th anniversary of the birth of our first president. Washington quarters have been struck continuously since then, except for 1933, and with none dated 1975. In 1976 a special Bicentennial motif was introduced. Beginning in 1999 the State quarters were launched, issued at the rate of five per year, covering all 50 states, each coin having its own distinctive design. After this successful and popular program came quarter dollars with motifs celebrating the District of Columbia and U.S. territories. A similar program commemorating national parks started in 2010 and is slated to run through 2021.

While there are no super-rarities among the different *types* of quarter dollars, the first one, the 1796 with Draped Bust obverse and Small Eagle reverse, is hard to find and expensive in all grades. The values are, of course, justified by the great demand for this single-year type.

Two famous quarter-dollar designers:
Charles Barber and Christian Gobrecht.

The collector's greatest challenge in finding a decent strike is in the short-lived 1804–1807 type with the Heraldic Eagle reverse. Sufficient quantities were made that examples from these years are not rarities, but nearly all are weakly struck. Quarters of the 1815–1828 Capped Bust, large planchet, type are available easily enough in worn grades but are scarce to rare in Mint State. Some cherrypicking (close examination for high quality within a given grade) is needed to find a sharp strike.

Respite from the sharp-strike difficulty is at last found with the 1831–1838 type, Capped Bust, small diameter, and without E PLURIBUS UNUM. Most are quite nicely struck. Also, for the first time Mint State coins are generally available with frequency in the marketplace, although those with good eye appeal are in the distinct minority.

The Liberty Seated quarters of the several types made from 1838 to 1891 are generally available in proportion to their mintages, with an allowance for the earlier dates being scarcer than the later ones—as they had a longer time to become worn or lost. Many quarters of earlier dates were melted circa 1850 to 1853, when the price of silver rose on international markets, making such coins worth slightly more than 25 cents in melt-down value.

Barber quarters, 1892–1916, present no difficulty for the collector, except that there is a challenge to find an example with sharp striking overall, including in the telltale area on the reverse at and near the eagle's leg to the right. MS-65 and better Barber quarters are scarcer than generally known (the same can be said for Barber half dollars). Proofs were sold to collectors and saved, and thus they are available in proportion to their mintages, with probably 70% to 80% surviving today.

The Variety 1 Standing Liberty quarter is a rarity if dated 1916, for only 52,000 were struck, and not many were saved. The feasible alternative is the 1917, Variety 1, which is often seen in Mint State, sharply struck, and very beautiful. Standing Liberty quarters of the Variety 2 design, minted from partway through 1917 to 1930, often are weakly struck on the head of Miss Liberty and on the shield rivets, and sometimes other places as well. Diligent searching is needed to locate a nice example.

Washington quarters also present no difficulty for collectors. The State, D.C./Territorial, and America the Beautiful (National Park) reverses are appealing in their diversity and make a fascinating study in themselves.

FOR THE COLLECTOR AND INVESTOR: QUARTER DOLLARS AS A SPECIALTY

The formation of a specialized collection of quarter dollars from 1796 to date, by dates, mints, and major varieties, is a considerable challenge. As a class, quarters are considerably more difficult to acquire than are either dimes or half dollars. Relatively few numismatists have ever concentrated on the entire series.

The 1796 is rare and popular both as a date and a type. The 1804, although elusive in worn grades, is of commanding importance if in AU or Mint State. The 1823, 3 Over 2, is a classic rarity and is nearly always encountered well worn. From the same decade the 1827 is famous. Although Mint records indicate that 4,000 circulation strikes were produced in calendar-year 1827, they were probably struck from 1825-dated or earlier dies, as no unequivocal circulation strike has ever been located. There are, however, a dozen or so Proofs. Originals are distinguished by the 2 (in the 25 C. denomination) having a curved base, while restrikes, also very rare, have a square-base 2.

One of the unsolved mysteries in numismatics involves certain quarter dollars dated 1815 (the die variety known as Browning-1) and 1825, 5 Over 3 (Browning-2), which are often seen counterstamped, above the cap, with either an E or an L. Hundreds exist. As other quarter-dollar die varieties were made during this period, but only these two bear counterstamps, it may be that this was done either at the Mint or elsewhere before they were generally distributed.

Ard W. Browning's 1925 text, *The Early Quarters of the United States, 1796–1838*, remains the standard reference on the series, together with new information added here and there, including in issues of the *John*

Reich Journal, the magazine of the John Reich Collectors Society, and in more recently published books.

The panorama of Liberty Seated quarters from 1838 to 1891 is highlighted by several rarities, notably the 1842, Small Date (known only in Proof format), and the 1873-CC, Without Arrows (of which only five are known, at least three being Mint State). The others are generally available, but some can be almost impossible to find in Mint State, the 1849-O, certain early San Francisco issues, and Carson City coins of the early 1870s being well known in this regard. From the mid-1870s onward Mint State coins are generally available, including choice and gem pieces. Proofs from 1858 onward can be found in proportion to their mintages, with later dates often being seen with higher numerical designations than are earlier ones.

Jean Antoine Houdon's famous bust of George Washington was the inspiration for the obverse design of the Washington quarter.

Barber quarters are collectible by date and mint, although the "big three" rarities, the 1896-S, 1901-S, and 1913-S, are expensive and hard to find.

Standing Liberty quarters, 1916–1930, represent a short-lived series, one easy enough to collect in grades up to MS-63, except for the rare 1918-S, 8 Over 7, overdate. Finding higher-grade coins that are sharply struck is another matter entirely, and over the years few sets of this nature have been assembled.

Washington quarters are all collectible, with no great rarities. However, in relation to the demand for them, certain early issues are elusive, the 1932-D being a well-known example. Modern issues, including the Bicentennial, State, D.C./Territorial, and National Park coins, are at once plentiful, inexpensive, and interesting.

DRAPED BUST, SMALL EAGLE REVERSE (1796)

Designer: *Probably Gilbert Stuart.* **Engraver:** *Robert Scot.*
Weight: *6.74 grams.* **Composition:** *.8924 silver, .1076 copper.*
Diameter: *Approximately 27.5 mm.* **Edge:** *Reeded.* **Mint:** *Philadelphia.*

Browning-2.

History. The Philadelphia Mint coined its first quarter dollar in 1796. Its design followed that of other silver U.S. coins. Only 6,146 were made, followed by a production hiatus until 1804, by which time a new reverse was used. Thus the 1796 was isolated as a single-year type.

Striking and Sharpness. On the obverse, check the hair details and the star centers. Most are well struck. On the reverse, most are well struck except for the head of the eagle, which can be shallow or flat, especially on the Browning-2 variety (there are two known die varieties for this year, Browning-1 being the rarer). Rarely is a Full Details coin encountered. The denticles are unusually bold and serve to frame the motifs. Check for planchet adjustment marks (from overweight planchets being filed down at the Mint to achieve proper weight). A few pieces have carbon streaks, which lower their value. Sharp striking (as on Browning-2) will add to the value. Most MS examples have excellent eye appeal.

Availability. Examples are available in all grades from well worn to superb MS. Nearly all of the latter are highly prooflike, but there are some exceptions. Although hundreds of circulated examples exist, demand for this famous coin exceeds supply in the marketplace, making public offerings a scene of excitement and strong bidding. Hundreds of higher-grade examples also survive, many of them prooflike and attractive. They attract great attention when offered for sale.

GRADING STANDARDS

MS-60 to 70 (Mint State). *Obverse:* At MS-60, some abrasion and contact marks are evident, most noticeably on the cheek, the drapery, and the right field. Luster is present, but may be dull or lifeless, and interrupted in patches. On prooflike coins the contact marks are more prominent. At MS-63, contact marks are very few, and abrasion is hard to detect except under magnification, although this type is sometimes graded liberally due to

1796; Browning-2. Graded MS-65.

its rarity. An MS-65 coin has no abrasion, and contact marks are so minute as to require magnification. Luster should be full and rich. Grades above MS-65 are defined by having fewer marks as perfection is approached. *Reverse:* Comments apply as for the obverse, except that abrasion and contact marks are most noticeable on the eagle at the center, a situation complicated by the fact that this area is typically flatly struck (except on the Browning-2 variety). Grading is best done by the obverse, then verified by the reverse. The field area is small and is protected by lettering and the wreath and in any given grade shows fewer marks than on the obverse.

Illustrated coin: This is well struck except on the eagle's breast and, especially, the eagle's head.

AU-50, 53, 55, 58 (About Uncirculated).
Obverse: Light wear is seen on the hair area above the ear and extending to left of the forehead, on the ribbon, on the drapery at the shoulder, and on the high points of the bust line, more so at AU-50 than at 53 or 55. An AU-58 coin has minimal traces of wear. An AU-50 coin has luster in protected areas among the stars and letters, with little in the open fields or on the portrait. At AU-58,

1796; Browning-2. Graded AU-53.

most luster remains in the fields, but is worn away on the highest parts of the motifs. *Reverse:* Light wear is seen on the eagle's body (keep in mind this area is nearly always lightly struck) and the edges of the wings. Light wear is seen on the wreath and lettering. Luster is the best key to actual wear. This ranges from perhaps 20% remaining in protected areas (at AU-50) to nearly full mint bloom (at AU-58).

Illustrated coin: This coin has rich iridescent toning. A few minor marks are not worthy of special notice.

EF-40, 45 (Extremely Fine). *Obverse:* More wear is evident on the upper hair area and the ribbon, and on the drapery and bosom. Excellent detail remains in low-relief areas of the hair. The stars show wear as do the date and letters. Luster, if present at all, is minimal and in protected areas. *Reverse:* The eagle shows more wear, this being the focal point to check. Most feathers remain on the interior areas of the wings. Additional wear is on

1796; Browning-2. Graded EF-40.

the wreath and letters, but many details are present. Some luster may be seen in protected areas and if present is slightly more abundant than on the obverse.

Illustrated coin: Here is an attractive, problem-free coin.

VF-20, 30 (Very Fine). *Obverse:* The higher-relief areas of hair are well worn at VF-20, less so at VF-30, although much detail remains on the areas below the ear. The drapery and bosom show extensive wear. The stars have more wear, making them appear larger (an optical illusion seen on most worn silver coins of this era). *Reverse:* The body of the eagle shows few if any feathers, while the wings have about half of the feath-

1796; Browning-2. Graded VF-20.

ers visible, mostly on the right wing, depending on the strike. The leaves lack most detail and are in outline form. Scattered, non-disfiguring marks are normal for this and lower grades. Any major defects should be noted separately.

Illustrated coin: A few faint scratches are not unusual for coins in this grade.

F-12, 15 (Fine). *Obverse:* Wear is more extensive than on a Very Fine coin, particularly noticeable on the hair, face, and bosom. The stars appear larger. About half the hair detail remains, most noticeably behind the neck and shoulder. The denticles remain strong (while on most other silver denominations of this design they become weak at this grade level). *Reverse:* Wear is more extensive. Now feather details are diminished, with

1796; Browning-2. Graded F-15.

fewer than half remaining on the wings. The wreath and lettering are worn further, and the rim is slightly weak in areas, although most denticles can be seen.

VG-8, 10 (Very Good). *Obverse:* The portrait is mostly seen in outline form, with most hair strands gone, although there is some definition at the back of the hair and behind the shoulder. The ear is discernible, as is the eye. The stars appear larger still, again an illusion. The rim is weak in areas. Most denticles are seen, some of them even bold. LIBERTY and the date are readable and usually full, although some letters may be weak

1796; Browning-2. Graded VG-8.

at their tops (the high rim and denticles protect the design more on the quarter dollar than on other silver coins of this type). *Reverse:* The eagle is mostly an outline, with parts blending into the field (on lighter strikes), although some slight feather detail can be seen on the right wing. The rim is worn, as are the letters, with some weak, but the motto is readable. Most denticles remain clear.

Illustrated coin: Some granularity is not unusual for the grade.

G-4, 6 (Good). *Obverse:* Wear is more extensive. The head is an outline. The rim still is present, as are most of the denticles, most well defined. LIBERTY is worn, but complete. The date is bold. *Reverse:* The eagle is flat and discernible in outline form, blending into the field in areas. The wreath is well worn. Some of the letters may be partly missing. Some rim areas and denticles are discernible. At this level some "averaging" can

1796; Browning-2. Graded G-4.

be done. If the letters are stronger than usual in one area, but some are missing in another area, the coin can still qualify as G-4.

Illustrated coin: Overall this is a nice coin showing extensive wear. It has some pin scratches above the eagle.

AG-3 (About Good). *Obverse:* Wear is so extensive that the coin is barely identifiable. The head is in outline form, LIBERTY is mostly gone, same for the stars, and the date, while readable, may be partially worn away. *Reverse:* The reverse is well worn, with parts of the wreath and lettering missing.

1796. Graded AG-3.

	Mintage	Cert	Avg	%MS	AG-3	G-4	VG-8	F-12	VF-20	EF-40	AU-50	MS-60	MS-63
1796 †	6,146	176	34.6	22%	$7,000	$12,000	$17,000	$26,000	$35,000	$45,000	$50,000	$75,000	$160,000
	Auctions: $881,250, SP-66, August 2014; $1,527,500, MS-67, November 2013; $52,875, AU-58, August 2014; $64,625, AU-55, August 2014												

† Ranked in the *100 Greatest U.S. Coins* (fourth edition).

DRAPED BUST, HERALDIC EAGLE REVERSE (1804–1807)

Designer: *Robert Scot.* **Weight:** *6.74 grams.* **Composition:** *.8924 silver, .1076 copper.*
Diameter: *Approximately 27.5 mm.* **Edge:** *Reeded.* **Mint:** *Philadelphia.*

Browning-4.

History. Early on, the U.S. Mint's production of silver coins in any given year depended on requests made by depositors of silver; they were not made for the Mint's own account. After 1796 no quarters were struck until 1804. When production started up again, the Draped Bust obverse was used, but with the new Heraldic Eagle reverse—similar to that on other silver (and gold) denominations of the time. The Heraldic Eagle design was patterned after the Great Seal of the United States.

Striking and Sharpness. Virtually all examples are lightly struck in one area or another. On the obverse, check the hair details and the star centers. On the reverse, check the shield, stars, feathers, and other design elements. The denticles and rims on both sides often have problems. Quarters of 1807 are usually the lightest struck. Also check for planchet adjustment marks (where an overweight planchet was filed down by a Mint worker to reach acceptable standards). Sharp striking and excellent eye appeal add to a coin's value. This series often is misgraded due to lack of understanding of its strike anomalies.

Availability. All dates are collectible, with 1804 being scarcer than the others and a rarity in MS. Those of 1805, 1806, and 1807 are readily available in the marketplace, usually in circulated grades although MS examples are sometimes seen. Some die varieties are rare. High-grade coins with Full Details are very rare.

GRADING STANDARDS

MS-60 to 70 (Mint State). *Obverse:* At MS-60, some abrasion and contact marks are evident, most noticeably on the cheek, the drapery, and the right field. Luster is present, but may be dull or lifeless, and interrupted in patches. At MS-63, contact marks are very few, and abrasion is hard to detect except under magnification. An MS-65 coin will have no abrasion, and contact marks are so minute as to require magnification. Luster

1806; Browning-9. Graded MS-66.

should be full and rich. Coins graded above MS-65 are more theoretical than actual for this type—but they do exist, and are defined by having fewer marks as perfection is approached. As noted in the introduction, expect weakness in some areas. *Reverse:* Comments apply as for the obverse, except that abrasion and contact marks are most noticeable on the eagle's neck, the tips of the wing, and the tail. The field area is complex, without much open space, given the stars above the eagle, the arrows and olive branch, and other features. Accordingly, marks are not as noticeable as on the obverse.

Illustrated coin: This coin is lightly struck on the right obverse stars and at the center of the reverse. Some planchet adjustment marks are mostly hidden. Some tiny carbon streaks are on the obverse (seemingly typical for Browning-9).

AU-50, 53, 55, 58 (About Uncirculated).
Obverse: Light wear is seen on the hair area above the ear and extending to left of the forehead, on the ribbon, and on the drapery at the shoulder, more so at AU-50 than at 53 or 55. An AU-58 coin has minimal traces of wear. An AU-50 coin has luster in protected areas among the stars and letters, with little in the open fields or on the portrait. At AU-58, most luster is present in the fields,

1804; Browning-1. Graded AU-58.

but is worn away on the highest parts of the motifs. *Reverse:* Comments as preceding, except that the eagle's neck, the tips and top of the wings, the clouds, and the tail now show noticeable wear, as do other features. Luster ranges from perhaps 20% remaining in protected areas (at AU-50) to nearly full mint bloom (at AU-58). Often the reverse retains much more luster than the obverse, more so on quarter dollars than on other denominations of this design.

Illustrated coin: Lightly struck on the obverse stars. The reverse has some light areas but is sharp overall. A few planchet adjustment marks are visible. Abundant luster and good eye appeal rank this as an exceptional example of this date, the most difficult of the type to find in high grades.

EF-40, 45 (Extremely Fine). *Obverse:* More wear is evident on the upper hair area and the ribbon, and on the drapery at the shoulder and the bosom. Excellent detail remains in low-relief areas of the hair. The stars show wear, as do the date and letters (note: on most coins of this type the stars are softly struck). Luster, if present at all, is minimal and in protected areas. *Reverse:* Wear is greater than on an About Uncirculated coin, overall. The

1804; Browning-1. Graded EF-45.

neck lacks feather detail on its highest points. Feathers have lost some detail near the edges of the wings, and some areas of the horizontal lines in the shield may be blended together. Some traces of luster may be seen, more so at EF-45 than at EF-40.

VF-20, 30 (Very Fine). *Obverse:* The higher-relief areas of hair are well worn at VF-20, less so at VF-30. The drapery and bosom show extensive wear. The stars have more wear, making them appear larger (an optical illusion seen on most worn silver coins of this era). *Reverse:* Wear is greater, including on the shield and wing feathers, although more than half of the feathers are defined. Star centers are flat. Other areas have lost

1807; Browning-2. Graded VF-25.

detail as well. Some letters in the motto may be missing, depending on the strike.

Illustrated coin: Note some scattered marks and granularity. This date is notoriously weakly struck, but at Very Fine this is not as noticeable as in higher grades.

F-12, 15 (Fine). *Obverse:* Wear is more extensive than on a Very Fine coin, particularly noticeable on the hair, face, and bosom. The stars appear larger. About half the hair detail remains with the tresses fused so as to appear thick, most noticeably behind the neck and shoulder. The rim may be partially worn away and blend into the field. *Reverse:* Wear is even more extensive, with the shield and wing feathers being points to observe.

1805; Browning-1. Graded F-12.

About half of the feathers can be seen. The incuse E PLURIBUS UNUM may have a few letters worn away. The clouds all seem to be connected. The stars are weak. Parts of the border and lettering may be weak. As with most quarters of this type, peculiarities of striking can account for some weakness.

Illustrated coin: Note some scratches on the shield.

VG-8, 10 (Very Good). *Obverse:* The portrait is mostly seen in outline form, with most hair strands gone, although there is slight definition at the back of the hair and behind the shoulder. The ear is discernible, as is the eye. The stars appear larger still, again an illusion. The rim is weak in areas. LIBERTY and the date are readable and usually full, although some letters may be weak at their tops. *Reverse:* Wear is more extensive. Half

1805; Browning-4. Graded VG-8.

or so of the letters in the motto are worn away. Most feathers are worn away, although separation of some of the lower feathers may be seen. Some stars are faint. The border blends into the field in areas (depending on striking), and some letters are weak.

G-4, 6 (Good). *Obverse:* Wear is more extensive, and some stars may be partly missing. The head is an outline. The eye is visible only in outline form. The rim is well worn or even missing in areas. LIBERTY is worn, and parts of some letters may be missing, but elements of all should be readable. The date is readable, but worn. *Reverse:* Wear is more extensive. The upper part of the eagle is flat, and feathers are noticeable only at some (but

1805; Browning-1. Graded G-4.

not necessarily all) of the lower edge of the wings, and do not have detail. The shield lacks most of its detail. Only a few letters of the motto can be seen (depending on striking). The rim is worn extensively, and a few letters may be missing.

Illustrated coin: Note the small edge cut near the first star.

AG-3 (About Good). *Obverse:* Wear is so extensive that the coin is barely identifiable. The head is in outline form, LIBERTY is mostly gone. Same for the stars. The date, while readable, may be partially worn away. *Reverse:* Extensive wear is seen overall, with the rim worn away and some areas worn smooth. The eagle can be discerned in outline form, but not necessarily completely. A few stray motto letters may remain. Some-times the obverse appears to be more worn than the reverse, or vice-versa.

1807; Browning-1. Graded AG-3.

Illustrated coin: This coin is slightly finer than AG-3 overall, but is reduced in grade due to a circular scratch at the center of the reverse.

1806, 6 Over 5

	Mintage	Cert	Avg	%MS	AG-3	G-4	VG-8	F-12	VF-20	EF-40	AU-50	MS-60	MS-63
1804	6,738	122	17.8	4%	$2,200	$4,250	$6,000	$8,500	$13,000	$28,500	$50,000	$80,000	$170,000
Auctions: $82,250, AU-55, November 2013													
1805	121,394	316	24.1	5%	$200	$475	$600	$1,000	$1,800	$3,750	$5,250	$10,000	$20,000
Auctions: $49,938, MS-64, November 2013; $823, F-12, July 2014; $499, VG-8, November 2014													
1806, All kinds	206,124												
1806, 6 Over 5		123	27.5	9%	$250	$600	$750	$1,100	$1,725	$4,000	$6,000	$11,000	$28,000
Auctions: $152,750, MS-66, November 2013; $1,116, VG-10, October 2014													
1806		471	24.8	10%	$225	$500	$650	$950	$1,600	$3,600	$5,000	$10,000	$16,000
Auctions: $94,000, MS-65, November 2013; $1,880, VF-30, October 2014; $529, VG-10, July 2014; $306, VG-8, November 2014													
1807	220,643	248	24.7	13%	$225	$500	$650	$950	$1,600	$3,600	$5,250	$10,000	$16,000
Auctions: $411,250, MS-66, November 2013; $646, F-15, November 2014; $306, G-4, November 2014; $112, Fair-2, October 2014													

CAPPED BUST (1815–1838)

Variety 1, Large Diameter (1815–1828): **Designer:** *John Reich.*
Weight: *6.74 grams.* **Composition:** *.8924 silver, .1076 copper.*
Diameter: *Approximately 27 mm.* **Edge:** *Reeded.* **Mint:** *Philadelphia.*

Variety 1, Large Diameter (1815–1828)
Browning-1.

Variety 1, Large Diameter, Proof
Browning-4.

Variety 2, Reduced Diameter, Motto Removed (1831–1838):
Designer: *William Kneass.* Weight: *6.74 grams (changed to 6.68 grams, .900 fine, in 1837).*
Composition: *.8924 silver, .1076 copper.* Diameter: *24.3 mm.* Edge: *Reeded.* Mint: *Philadelphia.*

Variety 2, Reduced Diameter,
Motto Removed (1831–1838)
Browning-1.

Variety 2, Reduced Diameter,
Motto Removed, Proof

History. The Capped Bust design, by John Reich, was introduced on the half dollar of 1807 but was not used on the quarter until 1815. The difference between the Large Diameter and the Small Diameter types resulted from the introduction of the close collar in 1828. Capped Bust, Reduced Diameter, quarter dollars are similar in overall appearance to the preceding type, but with important differences. The diameter is smaller, E PLURIBUS UNUM no longer appears on the reverse, and the denticles are smaller and restyled using a close collar.

Striking and Sharpness. Striking sharpness of Capped Bust, Large Diameter, quarters varies. On the obverse, check the hair of Miss Liberty, the broach clasp (a particular point of observation), and the star centers. On this type the stars are often well defined (in contrast with half dollars of the same design). On the reverse, check the neck of the eagle and its wings, and the letters. The details of the eagle often are superbly defined. Check the scroll or ribbon above the eagle's head for weak or light areas. Examine the denticles on both sides. When weakness occurs it is usually in the center. Proofs were struck for inclusion in sets and for numismatists. Some deeply toned coins, and coins with patches of mint luster, have been described as Proofs but are mostly impostors, some of which have been certified or have "papers" signed by Walter Breen. Be careful! Nearly all coins of the Capped Bust, Reduced Diameter, Motto Removed, variety are very well struck. Check all areas for sharpness. Some quarters of 1833 and 1834 are struck from rusted or otherwise imperfect dies and can be less attractive than coins from undamaged dies. Avoid any Proofs that show patches of mint frost or that are darkly toned.

Availability. Most quarters of the Large Diameter variety range from slightly scarce to rare, with the 1823, 3 Over 2, and the 1827 being famous rarities. Typical coins range from well worn to Fine and VF. AU and MS coins are elusive (and are usually dated before the 1820s), and gems are particularly rare. All authentic Proofs are rarities. Examples of the Reduced Diameter, Motto Removed, variety are readily available of all dates, including many of the first year of issue. Mint frost ranges from satiny (usual) to deeply frosty. Proofs were struck of all dates for inclusion in sets and for sale or trade to numismatists; avoid deeply toned pieces, and seek those with deep and full (not partial) mirror surfaces and good contrast.

GRADING STANDARDS

MS-60 to 70 (Mint State). *Obverse:* At MS-60, some abrasion and contact marks are evident, most noticeably on the cheek, the hair below LIBERTY, and the area near the drapery clasp. Luster is present, but may be dull or lifeless, and interrupted in patches. At MS-63, contact marks are very few, and abrasion is hard to detect except under magnification. An

1818, 8 Over 5; Browning-1. Graded MS-65.

MS-65 coin has no abrasion, and contact marks are so minute as to require magnification. Luster should be full and rich. Grades above MS-65 are seen now and again and are defined by having fewer marks as perfection is approached. Grading for Reduced Diameter, Motto Removed, examples is similar, except the rims are more uniform, striking is usually very sharp, and the wear occurs evenly on both sides. *Reverse:* Comments apply as for the obverse, except that abrasion and contact marks are most noticeable on the eagle's neck, the top of the wings, the claws, and the flat band that surrounds the incuse motto. The field is mainly protected by design elements and does not show abrasion as much as does the obverse on a given coin.

Illustrated coin: Note some lightness of strike on the lower curls on the obverse and the eagle's neck on the reverse.

AU-50, 53, 55, 58 (About Uncirculated).

Obverse: Light wear is seen on the cap, the hair below LIBERTY, the curl on the neck, the hair near the clasp, and the drapery. At AU-58, the luster is extensive except in the open area of the field, especially to the right. At AU-50 and 53, luster remains only in protected areas. Grading for Reduced Diameter, Motto Removed, examples is similar, except the rims are more uniform, striking is usually

1815. Graded AU-50.

very sharp, and the wear occurs evenly on both sides. *Reverse:* Wear is evident on the eagle's neck, the top of the wings, the claws, and the flat band above the eagle. An AU-58 coin has nearly full luster. At AU-50 and 53, there still is significant luster, more than on the obverse. Generally, light wear is most obvious on the obverse.

Illustrated coin: This About Uncirculated example has gray and light lilac toning.

EF-40, 45 (Extremely Fine). *Obverse:* Wear

is more extensive, most noticeably on the higher areas of the hair. The cap shows more wear, as does the cheek. Most or all stars have some radial lines visible (unless lightly struck, as many are). Luster, if present, is in protected areas among the star points and close to the portrait. Grading for Reduced Diameter, Motto Removed, examples is similar, except the rims are more uniform, striking is

1818; Browning-2. Graded EF-40.

usually very sharp, and the wear occurs evenly on both sides. *Reverse:* The wings show wear on the higher areas of the feathers, and some details are lost. Feathers in the neck are light on some (but not on especially sharp strikes). The eagle's claws and the leaves show wear. Luster may be present in protected areas, even if there is little or none on the obverse.

Illustrated coin: This coin was lightly cleaned long ago and has nicely retoned, although most graders would probably simply call it EF-40. It is attractive for the grade.

VF-20, 30 (Very Fine). *Obverse:* Wear is more extensive, and most of the hair is combined into thick tresses without delicate features. The curl on the neck is flat. Details of the drapery are well defined at the lower edge. Unless they were weakly struck, the stars are mostly flat although a few may retain radial lines. Grading for Reduced Diameter, Motto Removed, examples is similar, except the rims are more uniform, striking is usually

1825, 5 Over 4; Browning-2. Graded VF-20.

very sharp, and the wear occurs evenly on both sides. *Reverse:* Wear is most evident on the eagle's neck, to the left of the shield, and on the leaves and claws. Most feathers in the wing remain distinct, but some show light wear. Overall, the reverse on most quarters at this level shows less wear than the obverse.

Illustrated coin: Overall this is a pleasing coin. A few tiny scratches are masked by the toning; as with any accurate description, these should be noted.

F-12, 15 (Fine). *Obverse:* Wear is more extensive, with much of the hair blended together. The drapery is indistinct at its upper edge. The stars are flat. Grading for Reduced Diameter, Motto Removed, examples is similar, except the rims are more uniform, striking is usually very sharp, and the wear occurs evenly on both sides. *Reverse:* Wear is more extensive, now with only about half of the feathers remaining on the wings. The claws on the right are fused at their upper parts.

1821; Browning-5. Graded F-12 or slightly finer.

Illustrated coin: Note that some light scratches are mostly covered by toning.

VG-8, 10 (Very Good). *Obverse:* The hair is less distinct, with the area above the face blended into the facial features. LIBERTY is complete, but can be weak in areas. At the left the drapery and bosom are blended together in a flat area. The rim is worn away in areas, and blends into the field. *Reverse:* Feathers are fewer and mostly on the eagle's wing to the left. Other details are weaker. E PLURIBUS UNUM is weak, perhaps with some letters missing. All border lettering remains easily readable.

1815; Browning-1. Graded VG-8.

Illustrated coin: This is a well worn, problem-free example from the inaugural year of this type.

G-4, 6 (Good). *Obverse:* The portrait is mostly in outline, with few interior details discernible. LIBERTY may still be readable or may be partially worn away, depending on the variety. Most or all of the border is worn away, and the outer parts of the stars are weak. *Reverse:* The eagle mostly is in outline form, although some feathers can be seen in the wing to the left. All letters around the border are clear. E PLURIBUS UNUM is mostly or completely worn away.

1822, 25 Over 50 C.; Browning-2. Graded G-4.

AG-3 (About Good). *Obverse:* The portrait is an outline. Most of LIBERTY can still be seen. Stars are weak or missing toward what used to be the rim. The date remains clear, but may be weak at the bottom. *Reverse:* The reverse shows more wear than at G-4, but parts of the rim may remain clear.

Illustrated coin: Note the planchet laminations on the reverse.

1835. Graded AG-3.

PF-60 to 70 (Proof). *Obverse and Reverse:* Proofs that are extensively cleaned and have many hairlines, or that are dull and grainy, are lower level, such as PF-60 to 62. While any early Proof coin will attract attention, lower-level examples are not of great interest to specialists unless they are of rare die varieties. With medium hairlines, an assigned grade of PF-64 may be in order and with relatively few, Gem PF-65. PF-66 should have

1835; Browning-7. Graded PF-63.

hairlines so delicate that magnification is needed to see them. Above that, a Proof should be free of such lines. Grading is highly subjective with early Proofs, and eye appeal also is a factor.

Illustrated coin: Some scattered marks in the obverse field are mostly masked by toning.

1818, 8 Over 5

1818, Normal Date

	Mintage	Cert	Avg	%MS	AG-3	G-4	VG-8	F-12	VF-20	EF-40	AU-50	MS-60	MS-63
											PF-60	PF-63	PF-65
1815	89,235	157	44.5	38%	$75	$135	$200	$300	$550	$1,600	$2,200	$3,500	$7,000
	Auctions: $282,000, MS-67, November 2013; $999, VF-30, October 2014; $635, F-15, September 2014; $499, VG-8, September 2014												
1818, 8 Over 5	361,174	104	52.7	60%	$40	$100	$175	$225	$450	$1,500	$2,000	$3,200	$6,500
	Auctions: $176,250, MS-67, November 2013; $270, F-15, July 2014; $259, F-12, October 2014; $88, G-6, July 2014												
1818, Normal Date	(a)	487	41.2	30%	$40	$100	$150	$200	$425	$1,450	$2,200	$3,500	$6,500
	Auctions: $67,563, MS-66, December 2013; $1,410, EF-45, October 2014; $282, VF-20, September 2014; $76, G-6, July 2014												

a. Included in 1818, 8 Over 5, mintage figure.

1819, Small 9

1819, Large 9

1820, Small 0

1820, Large 0

1822, 25 Over 50 C.

1823, 3 Over 2

1824, 4 Over 2

1825, 5 Over 2

1825, 5 Over 4

	Mintage	Cert	Avg	%MS	AG-3	G-4	VG-8	F-12	VF-20	EF-40	AU-50 / PF-60	MS-60 / PF-63	MS-63 / PF-65
1819, Small 9	144,000	39	22.3	10%	$40	$100	$150	$200	$425	$1,450	$2,200	$3,500	$7,500
Auctions: $30,550, MS-64, November 2013; $646, EF-45, September 2014; $353, VF-20, September 2014; $106, VG-10, July 2014
1819, Large 9	(b)	25	36.4	12%	$40	$100	$150	$200	$425	$1,450	$2,200	$3,500	$11,000
Auctions: $23,501, MS-64, November 2013; $764, VF-25, July 2014; $282, VG-10, October 2014
1820, Small 0	127,444	18	38.9	22%	$40	$100	$150	$200	$425	$1,450	$2,200	$3,500	$6,500
Auctions: $3,055, AU-55, February 2014; $441, VF-20, September 2014; $176, G-6, July 2014; $94, G-6, July 2014
1820, Large 0	(c)	26	39.8	19%	$40	$100	$170	$225	$500	$1,550	$2,500	$3,500	$10,000
Auctions: $41,125, MS-66, November 2013
1820, Proof	6–10	2	65.5									$50,000	$130,000
Auctions: $97,750, PF-64, May 2008
1821	216,851	253	39.8	24%	$40	$100	$150	$200	$425	$1,450	$2,200	$3,500	$6,500
Auctions: $30,550, MS-65, November 2013; $235, F-12, July 2014; $141, VG-10, July 2014; $112, G-6, November 2014
1821, Proof	6–10	4	65.1									$40,000	$100,000
Auctions: $94,000, PF-65, October 2014; $51,750, PF-64, April 2009
1822	64,080	114	39.3	18%	$55	$110	$190	$265	$500	$1,550	$2,600	$3,850	$9,000
Auctions: $25,850, MS-64, November 2013
1822, 25 Over 50 C.	(d)	14	35.3	21%	$825	$2,100	$4,750	$6,000	$8,500	$15,000	$24,000	$40,000	$75,000
Auctions: No auction records available.
1822, Proof	6–10	2	65.5									$40,000	$100,000
Auctions: $229,125, PF-65, January 2014
1823, 3 Over 2	17,800	8	45.0	25%	$20,000	$32,000	$38,000	$50,000	$65,000	$80,000	$100,000	—	
Auctions: $17,625, G-4, February 2014
1823, 3 Over 2, Proof	2–4	0	n/a									$100,000	
Auctions: $396,563, PF-64, June 2014
1824, 4 Over 2	168,000	74	26.6	4%	$300	$650	$1,000	$1,700	$3,000	$5,000	$5,500	$25,000	$50,000
Auctions: $35,250, MS-62, June 2014; $999, VG-8, August 2014
1824, 4 Over 2, Proof	2–4	1	63.0									$50,000	
Auctions: No auction records available.
1825, 5 Over 2	(e)	16	36.8	0%	$85	$175	$200	$300	$750	$2,500	$8,000	$16,000	$27,500
Auctions: $3,290, VF-30, February 2014; $159, G-6, July 2014; $94, G-4, July 2014
1825, 5 Over 4	(e)	142	43.7	20%	$50	$100	$150	$200	$450	$1,500	$2,200	$3,500	$6,500
Auctions: $1,495, EF-45, April 2012
1825, 5 Over 4 Over 3, Proof	6–10	0	n/a									$40,000	
Auctions: $4,313, PF-63, January 2010

b. Included in 1819, Small 9, mintage figure. **c.** Included in circulation-strike 1820, Small 0, mintage figure. **d.** Included in circulation-strike 1822 mintage figure. **e.** Included in circulation-strike 1824, 4 Over 2, mintage figure.

1827, Original, Proof
Curl-Base 2 in 25 C.

1827, Restrike, Proof
Square-Base 2 in 25 C.

1828, 25 Over 50 C.

	Mintage	Cert	Avg	%MS	AG-3	G-4	VG-8	F-12	VF-20	EF-40	AU-50	MS-60	MS-63
											PF-60	PF-63	PF-65
1827, 7 Over 3, Original, Proof †	20–30	4	52.5								$85,000	$135,000	$300,000
Auctions: $411,250, PF-64, June 2014													
1827, 7 Over 3, Restrike, Proof	20–30	10	64.2									$50,000	$115,000
Auctions: $69,000, PF-66, July 2009													
1828	102,000	173	42.1	27%	$40	$100	$150	$200	$425	$1,450	$2,200	$3,500	$8,000
Auctions: $49,938, MS-65, February 2013; $153, VG-10, July 2014; $135, VG-8, July 2014; $94, G-6, July 2014													
1828, 25 Over 50 C.	(f)	18	39.4	17%	$100	$200	$350	$700	$1,600	$3,000	$4,000	$13,000	$22,000
Auctions: $352,500, MS-67, November 2013; $117,500, MS-63, August 2014													
1828, Proof	8–12	6	64.2								$15,000	$40,000	$100,000
Auctions: $82,250, PF-65, June 2014													

† Ranked in the *100 Greatest U.S. Coins* (fourth edition). *Note:* Although 4,000 1827 quarters were reported to have been made for circulation, their rarity today (only one worn piece is known, and it could be a circulated Proof) suggests that this quantity was for coins struck in calendar-year 1827 but bearing an earlier date, probably 1825. **f.** Included in circulation-strike 1828 mintage figure.

1831, Small Letters
Browning-2.

1831, Large Letters
Browning-6.

	Mintage	Cert	Avg	%MS	G-4	VG-8	F-12	VF-20	EF-40	AU-50	MS-60	MS-63	MS-65
											PF-60	PF-63	PF-65
1831, Small Letters	398,000	63	49.6	24%	$70	$100	$125	$150	$400	$750	$1,250	$4,500	$27,500
Auctions: $117,500, MS-67, November 2013; $1,311, AU-58, August 2014; $382, EF-45, November 2014; $188, VF-25, October 2014													
1831, Large Letters	(a)	41	49.1	27%	$70	$100	$125	$150	$400	$750	$1,300	$4,500	$30,000
Auctions: $32,900, MS-65, November 2013; $1,528, MS-60, November 2014; $294, AU-50, September 2014; $88, VF-20, October 2014													
1831, Large Letters, Proof	20–25	1	65.0								$15,000	$22,500	$75,000
Auctions: $141,000, PF-66, January 2014													
1832	320,000	159	47.0	30%	$70	$100	$125	$150	$425	$750	$1,400	$4,500	$25,000
Auctions: $18,800, MS-65, November 2013; $1,645, AU-55, July 2014; $353, EF-40, November 2014; $341, VF-35, August 2014													

a. Included in 1831, Small Letters, mintage figure.

1834, O Over F in OF
FS-25-1834-901.

	Mintage	Cert	Avg	%MS	G-4	VG-8	F-12	VF-20	EF-40	AU-50	MS-60 PF-60	MS-63 PF-63	MS-65 PF-65
1833	156,000	180	47.9	29%	$80	$110	$135	$200	$475	$850	$1,600	$4,500	$25,000
Auctions: $76,375, MS-66, November 2013; $1,116, AU-55, September 2014; $270, EF-40, September 2014; $113, F-15, September 2014													
1833, O Over F in OF (b)	(c)	62	46.3	16%	$85	$120	$165	$235	$500	$900	$1,700	$6,000	$30,000
Auctions: No auction records available.													
1833, Proof	10–15	5	64.9								$15,000	$25,000	$90,000
Auctions: $46,000, PF-65Cam, April 2009													
1834	286,000	550	46.9	31%	$70	$100	$125	$150	$400	$750	$1,400	$4,500	$24,000
Auctions: $70,500, MS-67, April 2014; $764, AU-53, September 2014; $382, EF-45, September 2014; $212, VF-35, November 2014													
1834, O Over F in OF (b)	(d)	53	47.8	17%	$80	$110	$150	$200	$450	$850	$1,600	$5,700	$30,000
Auctions: $1,116, AU-58, November 2014; $588, AU-50, October 2014													
1834, Proof	20–25	8	64.9								$15,000	$22,500	$75,000
Auctions: $235,000, PF-66, November 2013													
1835	1,952,000	540	44.1	16%	$70	$100	$125	$150	$400	$750	$1,400	$4,500	$25,000
Auctions: $58,750, MS-67, November 2013; $1,116, AU-55, October 2014; $361, EF-45, November 2014; $123, VF-25, October 2014													
1835, Proof	10–15	5	64.2								$15,000	$25,000	$90,000
Auctions: $25,850, PF-63, August 2013													
1836	472,000	207	39.6	17%	$70	$100	$125	$150	$400	$750	$1,400	$4,700	$27,500
Auctions: $99,875, MS-67, November 2013; $705, AU-50, August 2014; $558, EF-45, November 2014; $165, VF-30, November 2014													
1836, Proof	8–12	2	65.5								$15,000	$25,000	$100,000
Auctions: $97,750, PF-67, January 2006													
1837	252,400	268	49.5	35%	$70	$100	$125	$150	$400	$750	$1,400	$4,500	$25,000
Auctions: $76,375, MS-66, June 2014; $646, AU-55, November 2014; $306, EF-40, November 2014; $100, VF-25, October 2014													
1837, Proof	8–12	2	66.0								$15,000	$25,000	$90,000
Auctions: $132,250, PF-67, August 2006													
1838	366,000	254	47.0	29%	$70	$100	$125	$150	$400	$750	$1,400	$4,500	$25,000
Auctions: $25,850, MS-65, April 2013; $646, AU-50, October 2014; $282, VF-35, October 2014; $147, VF-30, October 2014													
1838, Proof	8–12	2	66.3								$25,000	$35,000	$100,000
Auctions: $48,875, PF-64, July 2011													

b. The OF is re-engraved with the letters connected at the top, and the first A in AMERICA is also re-engraved. Other identifying characteristics: there is no period after the C in the denomination, and the 5 and C are further apart than normal. **c.** Included in circulation-strike 1833 mintage figure. **d.** Included in circulation-strike 1834 mintage figure.

LIBERTY SEATED (1838–1891)

Variety 1, No Motto Above Eagle (1838–1853): **Designer:** *Christian Gobrecht.*
Weight: *6.68 grams.* **Composition:** *.900 silver, .100 copper.* **Diameter:** *24.3 mm.*
Edge: *Reeded.* **Mints:** *Philadelphia, New Orleans.*

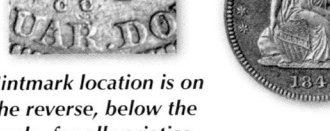

Variety 1 (1838–1853)

Mintmark location is on the reverse, below the eagle, for all varieties.

Variety 1, Proof

Variety 2, Arrows at Date, Rays Around Eagle (1853): **Designer:** *Christian Gobrecht.*
Weight: *6.22 grams.* **Composition:** *.900 silver, .100 copper.* **Diameter:** *24.3 mm.*
Edge: *Reeded.* **Mints:** *Philadelphia, New Orleans.*

Variety 2 (1853)   Variety 2, Proof

Variety 3, Arrows at Date, No Rays (1854–1855): **Designer:** *Christian Gobrecht.*
Weight: *6.22 grams.* **Composition:** *.900 silver, .100 copper.* **Diameter:** *24.3 mm.*
Edge: *Reeded.* **Mints:** *Philadelphia, New Orleans, San Francisco.*

Variety 3 (1854–1855)   Variety 3, Proof

Variety 1 Resumed, With Weight Standard of Variety 2 (1856–1865):
Designer: *Christian Gobrecht.* **Weight:** *6.22 grams.* **Composition:** *.900 silver, .100 copper.*
Diameter: *24.3 mm.* **Edge:** *Reeded.* **Mints:** *Philadelphia, New Orleans, San Francisco.*

Variety 1 Resumed, Weight   Variety 1 Resumed, Weight
Standard of Variety 2 (1856–1865)   Standard of Variety 2, Proof

Variety 4, Motto Above Eagle (1866–1873): **Designer:** *Christian Gobrecht.*
Weight: *6.22 grams.* **Composition:** *.900 silver, .100 copper.* **Diameter:** *24.3 mm.*
Edge: *Reeded.* **Mints:** *Philadelphia, San Francisco, Carson City.*

Variety 4 (1866–1873)   Variety 4, Proof

Variety 5, Arrows at Date (1873–1874): **Designer:** *Christian Gobrecht.*
Weight: *6.25 grams.* **Composition:** *.900 silver, .100 copper.* **Diameter:** *24.3 mm.*
Edge: *Reeded.* **Mints:** *Philadelphia, San Francisco, Carson City.*

Variety 5 (1873–1874) Variety 5, Proof

Variety 4 Resumed, With Weight Standard of Variety 5 (1875–1891):
Designer: *Christian Gobrecht.* **Weight:** *6.25 grams.* **Composition:** *.900 silver, .100 copper.*
Diameter: *24.3 mm.* **Edge:** *Reeded.* **Mints:** *Philadelphia, New Orleans, San Francisco.*

Variety 4 Resumed, Weight Variety 4 Resumed, Weight
Standard of Variety 5 (1875–1891) Standard of Variety 5, Proof

History. The long-running Liberty Seated design was introduced on the quarter dollar in 1838. Early issues lack drapery at Miss Liberty's elbow and have small lettering on the reverse. Drapery was added in 1840 and continued afterward. In 1853 a reduction in the coin's weight was indicated with the addition of arrows at the date and rays on the reverse (in the field around the eagle). The rays were omitted after 1853, but the arrows were retained through 1855. The motto IN GOD WE TRUST was added to the reverse in 1866. Arrows were placed at the date in the years 1873 and 1874 to denote the change of weight from 6.22 to 6.25 grams. The new weight, without the arrows, continued through 1891.

Striking and Sharpness. On the obverse, check the head of Miss Liberty and the star centers. If these are sharp, then check the central part of the seated figure. On the reverse, check the eagle, particularly the area to the lower left of the shield. Check the denticles on both sides. Generally, the earliest issues are well struck, as are those of the 1880s onward. The word LIBERTY is not an infallible guide to grading at lower levels, as on some dies the shield was in lower relief, and the letters wore away less quickly. This guideline should be used in combination with examining other features. Some Proofs (1858 is an example) have lint marks, and others can have light striking (particularly in the 1870s and 1880s). Avoid "problem" coins and those with deep or artificial (and often colorful) toning.

Availability. Coins of this type are available in proportion to their mintages. MS coins can range from rare to exceedingly rare, as they were mostly ignored by numismatists until the series ended. Quality can vary widely, especially among branch-mint coins. Proofs of the earlier years are very rare. Beginning with 1856, they were made in larger numbers, and from 1859 onward the yearly production was in the multiple hundreds. Proofs of the later era are readily available today; truly choice and gem pieces with no distracting hairlines are in the minority and will require diligent searching.

GRADING STANDARDS

MS-60 to 70 (Mint State). *Obverse:* At MS-60, some abrasion and contact marks are evident, most noticeably on the bosom and thighs and knees. Luster is present, but may be dull or lifeless. At MS-63, contact marks are very few, and abrasion is hard to detect except under magnification. An MS-65 coin has no abrasion, and contact marks are sufficiently minute as to require magnification. Check the knees of Liberty and the right

1853, With Arrows. Graded MS-66.

field. Luster should be full and rich. Most Mint State coins of the 1861 to 1865 years, Philadelphia issues, have extensive die striae (from not completely finishing the die). *Reverse:* Comments apply as for the obverse, except that in lower Mint State grades abrasion and contact marks are most noticeable on the eagle's neck, the claws, and the top of the wings (harder to see there, however). At MS-65 or higher there are no marks visible to the unaided eye. The field is mainly protected by design elements and does not show abrasion as much as does the obverse on a given coin.

Illustrated coin: This coin is an ultra gem.

AU-50, 53, 55, 58 (About Uncirculated). *Obverse:* Light wear is seen on the thighs and knees, bosom, and head. At AU-58, the luster is extensive, but incomplete, especially in the right field. At AU-50 and 53, luster is less. *Reverse:* Wear is evident on the eagle's neck, claws, and top of the wings. An AU-58 coin has nearly full luster, more so than on the obverse, as the design elements protect the small field areas. At AU-50 and 53, there still are traces of luster.

1874-S. Graded AU-50.

Illustrated coin: Light wear is evident, and faintly toned luster can be seen on both sides.

EF-40, 45 (Extremely Fine). *Obverse:* Further wear is seen on all areas, especially the thighs and knees, bosom, and head. Little or no luster is seen on most coins. From this grade downward, sharpness of strike of the stars and the head does not matter to connoisseurs. *Reverse:* Further wear is evident on the eagle's neck, claws, and wings. Some feathers in the right wing may be blended together.

1851-O. Graded EF-40.

VF-20, 30 (Very Fine). *Obverse:* Further wear is seen. Most details of the gown are worn away, except in the lower-relief areas above and to the right of the shield. Hair detail is mostly or completely gone. *Reverse:* Wear is more extensive, with more feathers blended together, especially in the right wing. The area below the shield shows more wear.

1870-CC. Graded VF-20.

F-12, 15 (Fine). *Obverse:* The seated figure is well worn, but with some detail above and to the right of the shield. LIBERTY is readable but weak in areas. *Reverse:* Wear is extensive, with about half of the feathers flat or blended with others.

1864-S. Graded F-12.

VG-8, 10 (Very Good). *Obverse:* The seated figure is more worn, but some detail can be seen above and to the right of the shield. The shield is discernible. In LIBERTY at least the equivalent of two or three letters (can be a combination of partial letters) must be readable but can be very weak at VG-8, with a few more visible at VG-10. However, LIBERTY is not an infallible guide to grade this type, as some varieties had the word in

1849-O. Graded VG-8.

low relief on the die, so it wore away slowly. *Reverse:* Further wear has flattened all but a few feathers, and the horizontal lines of the shield are indistinct. The leaves are only in outline form. The rim is visible all around, as are the ends of most denticles.

G-4, 6 (Good). *Obverse:* The seated figure is worn smooth. At G-4 there are no letters in LIBERTY remaining on most (but not all) coins; some coins, especially of the early 1870s, are exceptions. At G-6, traces of one or two can barely be seen. *Reverse:* The designs are only in outline form, although some vertical shield stripes can be seen on some. The rim is worn down, and tops of the border letters are weak or worn away, although the inscription can still be read.

1872-CC. Graded G-4.

 Illustrated coin: Assigned this grade by a third-party certification service, the reverse of this coin is slightly more worn than usual for G-4—probably the result of a bit of optimism in view of the rarity of this issue.

AG-3 (About Good). *Obverse:* The seated figure is mostly visible in outline form, with only a hint of detail. Much of the rim is worn away. The date remains clear. *Reverse:* The border letters are partially worn away. The eagle is mostly in outline form, but with a few details discernible. The rim is weak or missing.

1856-O. Graded AG-3.

PF-60 to 70 (Proof). *Obverse and Reverse:* Proofs that are extensively cleaned and have many hairlines, or that are dull and grainy, are lower level, such as PF-60 to 62. These are not widely desired by connoisseurs. With medium hairlines and good reflectivity, an assigned grade of PF-64 is appropriate and with relatively few hairlines, Gem PF-65. In various grades hairlines are most easily seen in the obverse field. PF-66 should have hairlines so delicate that magnification is needed to see them. Above that, a Proof should be free of such lines.

1867. Graded PF-65.

| 1839, No Drapery | 1840-O, Drapery | 1840-O, Drapery, Normal O | 1840-O, Drapery, Large O |

Coins designated Deep Cameo or Ultra Cameo bring a premium of 50% to 100% above listed values.

	Mintage	Cert	Avg	%MS	G-4	VG-8	F-12	VF-20	EF-40	AU-50	MS-60 PF-60	MS-63 PF-63	MS-65 PF-65
1838, No Drapery	466,000	174	54.7	47%	$35	$40	$60	$100	$375	$750	$2,000	$6,750	$30,000
	Auctions: $141,000, MS-66, November 2013; $5,875, MS-64, November 2014; $999, AU-55, September 2014											
1838, Proof	2–3	0	n/a		*(extremely rare)*								
	Auctions: No auction records available.											
1839, No Drapery	491,146	137	51.6	28%	$35	$40	$60	$100	$375	$750	$1,850	$5,500	$40,000
	Auctions: $52,875, MS-67, October 2014; $8,813, MS-64, July 2014; $2,585, MS-62, August 2014; $382, EF-45, October 2014											
1839, Proof (a)	2–3	1	65.0										$450,000
	Auctions: $270,250, PF-65, October 2014; $411,250, PF-65, April 2013											
1840O, No Drapery	382,200	137	49.3	29%	$40	$45	$70	$120	$400	$800	$1,900	$8,200	$30,000
	Auctions: $329,000, MS-67, November 2013; $1,880, MS-62, October 2014; $353, EF-40, October 2014; $26, VG-10, October 2014											
1840, Drapery	188,127	39	52.5	33%	$25	$30	$55	$100	$180	$300	$950	$4,500	$25,000
	Auctions: $35,250, MS-66, November 2013; $1,657, MS-62, November 2014; $415, AU-55, October 2014; $74, VF-35, November 2014											
1840, Drapery, Proof	5–8	3	64.7										$125,000
	Auctions: $99,889, PF-65, August 2013											
1840O, Drapery	43,000	75	51.1	36%	$30	$50	$70	$110	$210	$500	$1,300	$3,900	$25,000
	Auctions: $7,050, MS-64, November 2014; $35,250, MS-64, April 2014; $999, MS-62, August 2014; $588, AU-55+, August 2014											
1840O, Drapery, Large O (b)	(c)	0	n/a							$4,750	$9,000		
	Auctions: $3,220, MS-63, December 2010											

a. This piece is unique. **b.** The O mintmark punch is about 25% larger than normal. There are two known reverse dies for this variety, with one showing doubled denticles. **c.** Included in 1840-O, Drapery, mintage figure.

1842, Small Date
Philadelphia Small Date is Proof only.

1842, Large Date

1842-O, Small Date

1842-O, Large Date

	Mintage	Cert	Avg	%MS	G-4	VG-8	F-12	VF-20	EF-40	AU-50	MS-60 / PF-60	MS-63 / PF-63	MS-65 / PF-65
1841	120,000	67	57.6	64%	$45	$70	$100	$150	$250	$325	$900	$2,300	$12,000
Auctions: $41,125, MS-66, November 2013; $2,585, MS-64, November 2014; $141, EF-40, September 2014													
1841, Proof	3–5	1	66.0								$75,000	$115,000	$200,000
Auctions: $235,000, PF-66, April 2013													
1841O	452,000	56	54.7	50%	$30	$45	$60	$80	$175	$320	$800	$1,900	$14,000
Auctions: $55,813, MS-67, June 2014; $1,122, MS-63, November 2014; $411, AU-50, July 2014													
1842, Large Date (d)	88,000	42	52.2	33%	$75	$100	$160	$250	$350	$650	$1,750	$4,500	$13,000
Auctions: $8,813, MS-65, October 2014; $6,169, MS-64, August 2013; $329, EF-40, October 2014													
1842, Small Date, Proof † (e)	3–5	2	65.0									$60,000	$125,000
Auctions: $282,000, PF-65, October 2014; $258,500, PF-65, August 2013													
1842O, All kinds	769,000												
1842O, Small Date	16	26.7	6%	$350	$550	$1,000	$1,900	$3,750	$7,500	$18,000	$75,000		
Auctions: $55,813, MS-63, October 2014; $32,900, AU-58, December 2013; $470, G-6, November 2014													
1842O, Large Date	59	42.1	39%	$30	$50	$70	$110	$220	$600	$1,750	$4,800		
Auctions: $6,463, MS-64, October 2014; $7,050, MS-64, April 2013; $3,290, MS-63, November 2014; $306, AU-53, November 2014													
1843	645,600	97	58.5	59%	$25	$30	$35	$45	$85	$175	$450	$1,250	$8,000
Auctions: $3,290, MS-64, November 2013; $1,058, MS-62, October 2014; $100, EF-40, September 2014													
1843, Proof	10–15	4	61.0								$12,500	$20,000	$50,000
Auctions: $64,625, PF-66, April 2013													
1843O	968,000	50	45.1	16%	$30	$45	$60	$125	$250	$800	$2,000	$7,000	$15,000
Auctions: $7,344, MS-63, November 2014; $2,585, AU-58, November 2014; $544, EF-45, July 2014; $153, F-15, July 2014													
1844	421,200	83	55.6	46%	$25	$30	$35	$45	$85	$175	$525	$1,500	$9,000
Auctions: $17,625, MS-65, November 2013; $1,880, MS-64, November 2014; $2,115, MS-64, July 2014; $100, AU-50, November 2014													
1844, Proof (f)	3–5	1	66.0										
Auctions: $276,000, PF-66, July 2009													
1844O	740,000	49	50.2	31%	$30	$45	$60	$85	$200	$360	$1,400	$3,500	$10,000
Auctions: $12,925, MS-65, June 2014; $382, AU-53, October 2014; $188, AU-50, September 2014; $69, VF-20, November 2014													
1845	922,000	121	56.8	50%	$25	$30	$35	$45	$80	$160	$550	$1,400	$6,000
Auctions: $4,847, MS-65, October 2014; $7,638, MS-65, November 2013; $1,821, MS-64, November 2014; $705, MS-62, October 2014													
1846	510,000	75	56.0	45%	$25	$30	$35	$50	$85	$180	$600	$1,500	$12,000
Auctions: $22,325, MS-66, January 2014													
1846, Proof	15–20	9	64.3								$5,000	$10,000	$30,000
Auctions: $25,850, PF-65, April 2013													
1847	734,000	66	55.8	48%	$25	$30	$35	$45	$80	$160	$575	$1,200	$9,000
Auctions: $14,100, MS-65, November 2013; $1,763, MS-64, November 2014; $705, MS-62, November 2014; $176, EF-45, July 2014													
1847, Proof	6–8	4	65.3								$5,000	$10,000	$30,000
Auctions: $28,200, PF-65, November 2013; $14,688, PF-64, July 2014													
1847O	368,000	34	45.4	18%	$35	$50	$75	$150	$800	$2,500	$4,500	$12,000	
Auctions: $12,925, MS-63, June 2014; $8,225, AU-58, August 2014; $3,055, AU-53, July 2014; $1,116, EF-45, November 2014													

† Ranked in the *100 Greatest U.S. Coins* (fourth edition). **d.** The Large Date was used on the Philadelphia Mint's 1842 coins struck for circulation. **e.** For the Philadelphia Mint's quarters of 1842, the Small Date was used on Proofs only. **f.** 2 examples are known.

1853, Repunched Date, No Arrows or Rays
FS-25-1853-301.

**1853, 3 Over 4 (Arrows at
Date, Rays Around Eagle)**
FS-25-1853-1301.

	Mintage	Cert	Avg	%MS	G-4	VG-8	F-12	VF-20	EF-40	AU-50	MS-60	MS-63	MS-65
											PF-60	PF-63	PF-65
1848	146,000	35	50.3	37%	$25	$35	$60	$100	$175	$300	$1,150	$4,000	$15,000
Auctions: $21,150, MS-67, November 2013; $11,750, MS-66, October 2014; $4,259, MS-64, November 2014; $259, EF-40, October 2014													
1848, Proof	5–8	2	65.0								$5,000	$10,000	$35,000
Auctions: $64,625, PF-66, October 2014; $55,813, PF-66, August 2013													
1849	340,000	84	54.8	35%	$25	$30	$45	$75	$160	$250	$800	$1,900	$12,500
Auctions: $10,575, MS-65, November 2013; $1,175, MS-63, August 2014; $259, AU-50, October 2014; $76, VF-35, July 2014													
1849, Proof	5–8	3	64.3								$5,000	$10,000	$35,000
Auctions: $32,900, PF-65, January 2014													
1849O	(g)	40	34.3	15%	$450	$600	$1,100	$2,400	$6,000	$7,750	$15,000	$20,000	
Auctions: $14,100, AU-58, August 2014; $7,050, AU-55, November 2014; $7,638, AU-53, February 2013; $3,055, VF-25, July 2014													
1850	190,800	34	57.7	56%	$30	$45	$65	$95	$175	$240	$1,000	$2,800	$11,000
Auctions: $38,188, MS-67, June 2014; $3,055, MS-64, November 2014; $1,293, MS-60, November 2014; $544, AU-50, September 2014													
1850, Proof	5–8	3	65.0										
Auctions: $258,500, PF-68, August 2013													
1850O	412,000	68	54.6	49%	$30	$45	$65	$95	$175	$475	$1,600	$3,500	$20,000
Auctions: $11,163, MS-65, June 2014; $306, VF-35, October 2014; $94, VF-20, September 2014; $188, F-12, November 2014													
1851	160,000	36	51.7	36%	$35	$50	$75	$125	$200	$300	$1,000	$2,000	$9,500
Auctions: $25,850, MS-67, November 2013; $3,290, MS-64, November 2014; $646, AU-53, November 2014; $617, EF-45, October 2014													
1851O	88,000	35	27.3	9%	$150	$275	$475	$850	$1,500	$3,000	$8,000	$32,500	
Auctions: $28,200, MS-63, October 2014; $15,275, MS-62, July 2014; $2,938, AU-50, November 2014; $1,058, VF-35, November 2014													
1852	177,060	51	56.3	59%	$45	$55	$95	$135	$225	$300	$675	$1,500	$7,000
Auctions: $105,750, MS-68, November 2013; $1,528, AU-55, September 2014; $588, AU-50, November 2014; $282, AU-50, November 2014													
1852, Proof	5–8	1	65.0										$125,000
Auctions: $105,750, PF-65, April 2013													
1852O	96,000	25	31.7	8%	$175	$250	$400	$1,000	$2,250	$4,500	$9,000	$42,500	
Auctions: $3,819, MS-60, November 2014; $1,821, EF-40, November 2014; $1,293, VF-25, October 2014; $306, AG-3, November 2014													
1853, Repunched Date, No Arrows or Rays (h)	44,200	41	49.2	49%	$300	$400	$625	$800	$1,500	$3,000	$4,000	$7,800	$10,000
Auctions: $38,188, MS-68, June 2014; $32,900, MS-67, October 2014													
1853, Variety 2	15,210,020	1182	51.3	38%	$25	$30	$35	$50	$175	$300	$900	$2,250	$15,000
Auctions: $67,563, MS-67, September 2013; $22,325, MS-66, October 2014; $1,528, MS-62, October 2014; $411, AU-55, October 2014													
1853, Variety 2, 3 Over 4 (i)	(j)	47	42.7	21%	$35	$70	$110	$225	$350	$675	$2,000	$5,500	$40,000
Auctions: $9,988, MS-64, October 2014; $12,925, MS-64, June 2014													
1853, Variety 2, Proof	10–15	5	65.2								$30,000	$50,000	$125,000
Auctions: $141,000, PF-66Cam, August 2013; $64,625, PF-64, October 2014													
1853O, Variety 2	1,332,000	85	46.0	16%	$25	$45	$60	$75	$250	$1,100	$3,250	$11,000	$30,000
Auctions: $28,200, MS-66, October 2014; $15,275, MS-64, June 2014; $2,115, AU-58, November 2014; $89, VF-25, November 2014													

g. Included in 1850-O mintage figure. **h.** The secondary 5 and 3 are evident south of the primary digits. In the past, this variety was erroneously attributed as a 53 Over 2 overdate. This is the only die known for 1853 that lacks the arrows and rays. **i.** In addition to the 3 punched over a 4, there is also evidence of the repunched 8 and 5 (weaker images slightly north and west of the primary digits). The right arrow shaft is also doubled, north of the primary. "On well-worn or late-die-state specimens, the doubling of the arrow shaft may be the only evidence of the overdate. This is the only quarter dollar date known to be punched over the *following* year!" (*Cherrypickers' Guide to Rare Die Varieties*, sixth edition, volume II). **j.** Included in 1853, Variety 2, mintage figure.

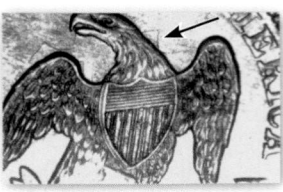

| 1854-O, Normal O | 1854-O, Huge O | 1856-S,
S Over Small S
FS-25-1856S-501. | 1857, Clashed
Reverse Die
FS-25-1857-901. |

	Mintage	Cert	Avg	%MS	G-4	VG-8	F-12	VF-20	EF-40	AU-50	MS-60 / PF-60	MS-63 / PF-63	MS-65 / PF-65
1854	12,380,000	610	53.1	39%	$25	$30	$35	$45	$75	$225	$500	$1,100	$8,000
	Auctions: $45,531, MS-67, October 2014; $3,819, MS-65, August 2014; $646, MS-61, November 2014; $259, AU-53, November 2014												
1854, Proof	20–30	10	64.3								$10,000	$17,500	$30,000
	Auctions: $30,550, PF-66, April 2013												
1854O, Normal O	1,484,000	94	46.3	37%	$30	$35	$45	$55	$100	$275	$1,200	$2,500	$15,000
	Auctions: $2,820, MS-64, November 2014; $1,293, MS-62, August 2014; $353, AU-55, September 2013; $141, EF-45, October 2014												
1854O, Huge O (k)	(l)	58	20.4	0%	$900	$1,250	$2,500	$4,250	$7,000	$8,500			
	Auctions: $4,994, EF-45, February 2013; $705, G-6, August 2014; $558, AG-3, July 2014												
1855	2,857,000	163	55.0	41%	$25	$30	$35	$45	$85	$225	$575	$1,450	$9,500
	Auctions: $41,125, MS-67, November 2013; $951, MS-63+, November 2014; $588, MS-62, July 2014; $282, AU-53, November 2014												
1855, Proof	20–30	10	64.6								$10,000	$17,500	$30,000
	Auctions: $28,200, PF-66, October 2014; $21,150, PF-65Cam, April 2013												
1855O	176,000	29	45.5	38%	$40	$65	$110	$275	$400	$2,000	$5,000	$12,000	
	Auctions: $1,058, VF-35, July 2014; $1,528, VF-35, April 2013; $235, VF-20, September 2014												
1855S	396,400	28	43.5	18%	$40	$60	$85	$175	$350	$1,100	$3,000	$8,500	$30,000
	Auctions: $5,875, MS-63, August 2014; $1,410, AU-55, August 2013; $1,001, EF-45, July 2014; $423, VF-25, July 2014												
1855S, Proof	1–2	1	64.0					*(unique)*					
	Auctions: $176,250, PF-64, August 2013												
1856	7,264,000	238	54.4	48%	$25	$30	$35	$45	$75	$175	$350	$600	$4,000
	Auctions: $10,575, MS-66, June 2014; $764, MS-64, July 2014; $92, EF-45, November 2014; $89, VF-20, July 2014												
1856, Proof	40–50	28	64.0								$3,500	$6,500	$20,000
	Auctions: $12,959, PF-66, August 2014; $5,875, PF-63, August 2014												
1856O	968,000	70	48.8	26%	$25	$45	$55	$65	$80	$250	$1,100	$2,500	$10,000
	Auctions: $11,163, MS-65, November 2014; $11,750, MS-65, June 2014; $259, EF-45, September 2014; $86, VF-35, November 2014												
1856S, All kinds	286,000												
1856S		23	40.8	22%	$40	$60	$100	$200	$1,500	$2,250	$6,500	$20,000	$40,000
	Auctions: $18,800, MS-64, June 2014; $705, AU-50, October 2014; $129, VF-20, September 2014; $84, VG-8, November 2014												
1856S, S Over Small S (m)		5	19.0	0%	$200	$325	$750	$1,500	$2,500	$6,000	—		
	Auctions: $28,200, AU-58, June 2014												
1857	9,644,000	518	55.7	58%	$25	$30	$35	$45	$75	$160	$325	$575	$3,250
	Auctions: $35,250, MS-68, November 2013; $7,050, MS-67, October 2014; $764, MS-64, November 2014; $247, AU-58, October 2014												
1857, Clashed Rev Die (n)	(o)	5	50.2	40%					$500	$750			
	Auctions: No auction records available.												
1857, Proof	40–50	42	63.9								$3,250	$4,750	$10,000
	Auctions: $7,931, PF-66, November 2014; $15,275, PF-65Cam, June 2013												
1857O	1,180,000	82	52.8	29%	$30	$40	$50	$60	$150	$400	$1,200	$4,000	
	Auctions: $5,875, MS-64, October 2014; $1,439, MS-61, December 2013; $235, EF-45, September 2014; $106, VF-25, July 2014												
1857S	82,000	41	50.0	24%	$60	$110	$200	$375	$600	$1,200	$4,000	$8,750	
	Auctions: $7,344, MS-64, October 2014; $3,525, MS-62, November 2014; $4,847, AU-58, March 2014; $1,763, AU-55, July 2014												

k. The Huge O mintmark is very large, extremely thick on the left side, and irregular, suggesting that it was punched into the die by hand. **l.** Included in 1854-O mintage figure. **m.** A larger S mintmark was punched over a much smaller S mintmark, the latter probably intended for half-dime production. **n.** The reverse clashed with the reverse die of an 1857 Flying Eagle cent. Images of the cent reverse die are easily visible on either side of the eagle's neck, within the shield, and below the eagle's left wing. **o.** Included in circulation-strike 1857 mintage figure.

	Mintage	Cert	Avg	%MS	G-4	VG-8	F-12	VF-20	EF-40	AU-50	MS-60 / PF-60	MS-63 / PF-63	MS-65 / PF-65
1858	7,368,000	397	55.0	54%	$25	$30	$35	$45	$75	$175	$350	$600	$3,000
	Auctions: $25,850, MS-67, November 2013; $7,050, MS-66, July 2014; $170, AU-55, October 2014; $76, EF-45, August 2014													
1858, Proof	300	68	63.4								$1,300	$2,250	$7,500
	Auctions: $44,063, PF-67, April 2013; $9,400, PF-66, October 2014; $9,694, PF-66, September 2014													
1858O	520,000	41	49.6	15%	$30	$40	$45	$65	$125	$350	$1,800	$7,500	$25,000
	Auctions: $705, AU-55, August 2013; $94, EF-45, September 2014													
1858S	121,000	38	39.2	3%	$50	$75	$250	$650	$2,000	$5,250	$15,000	—	
	Auctions: $7,050, AU-58, November 2014; $11,163, AU-58, March 2014; $1,763, EF-40, November 2014; $1,528, VF-35, November 2014													
1859	1,343,200	127	55.2	49%	$25	$30	$35	$45	$80	$175	$400	$1,100	$6,000
	Auctions: $4,406, MS-65, June 2014; $1,411, MS-64, November 2014; $223, AU-55, September 2014; $100, AU-50, November 2014													
1859, Proof	800	154	64.1								$1,050	$1,650	$5,500
	Auctions: $19,975, PF-67, November 2013; $3,525, PF-65, October 2014; $2,350, PF-64Cam, August 2014; $999, PF-63, November 2014													
1859O	260,000	41	52.4	27%	$25	$40	$50	$65	$135	$400	$1,250	$4,000	$12,000
	Auctions: $25,263, MS-65, April 2013; $646, AU-53, November 2014; $129, AU-50, September 2014; $72, VF-20, November 2014													
1859S	80,000	20	31.5	0%	$100	$200	$350	$650	$4,200	$12,500	$45,000		
	Auctions: $30,550, AU-58, June 2014; $1,410, VF-30, November 2014; $881, VF-25, November 2014; $141, G-4, November 2014													
1860	804,400	117	55.9	44%	$25	$30	$35	$45	$80	$175	$400	$975	$5,500
	Auctions: $14,100, MS-66, October 2014; $4,994, MS-65, February 2014; $1,175, MS-64, November 2014; $247, AU-55, October 2014													
1860, Proof	1,000	109	64.0								$750	$1,100	$5,000
	Auctions: $44,063, PF-68, November 2013; $3,672, PF-65+, October 2014; $3,525, PF-65, September 2014													
1860O	388,000	72	54.9	39%	$30	$45	$55	$65	$95	$375	$1,000	$2,400	$15,000
	Auctions: $20,563, MS-66, October 2014; $4,994, MS-64, September 2013; $1,528, MS-63, November 2014; $676, AU-58, July 2014													
1860S	56,000	22	28.7	5%	$600	$1,000	$2,000	$5,750	$12,500	$20,000	$50,000		
	Auctions: $55,813, MS-61, October 2014; $30,550, AU-55, March 2014; $3,819, VF-25, November 2014; $3,055, F-15, July 2014													
1861	4,853,600	580	58.0	58%	$25	$30	$33	$45	$80	$175	$350	$750	$3,500
	Auctions: $3,819, MS-66, October 2014; $823, MS-64, November 2014; $388, MS-62, December 2014; $217, AU-55, October 2014													
1861, Proof	1,000	97	63.5								$750	$1,200	$5,000
	Auctions: $188,000, PF-68Cam, November 2013; $2,820, PF-64, August 2014; $941, PF-63, November 2014													
1861S	96,000	27	30.5	0%	$150	$235	$500	$1,500	$2,500	$10,000			
	Auctions: $3,173, EF-40, June 2013; $123, Fair-2, October 2014													
1862	932,000	157	58.3	65%	$25	$30	$33	$50	$85	$175	$350	$750	$3,750
	Auctions: $25,850, MS-67, June 2014; $411, AU-58, November 2014; $217, AU-55, July 2014; $100, EF-40, October 2014													
1862, Proof	550	136	63.7								$750	$1,100	$5,000
	Auctions: $55,813, PF-68Cam, November 2013; $9,400, PF-67Cam, September 2014; $764, PF-62, November 2014													
1862S	67,000	45	44.9	24%	$55	$85	$150	$325	$800	$1,800	$3,800	$9,000	
	Auctions: $44,063, MS-64, June 2014; $7,050, MS-63, November 2014; $3,525, AU-58, October 2014; $353, EF-40, October 2014													
1863	191,600	62	56.6	65%	$40	$50	$75	$130	$240	$375	$625	$1,100	$4,500
	Auctions: $6,463, MS-66, October 2014; $3,819, MS-65, August 2014; $2,820, MS-64, August 2014; $588, EF-40, October 2014													
1863, Proof	460	153	63.6								$750	$1,200	$5,000
	Auctions: $19,975, PF-67Cam, November 2013; $4,113, PF-65, August 2014; $1,763, PF-64, September 2014; $617, PF-62, July 2014													
1864	93,600	58	54.3	60%	$75	$85	$120	$175	$275	$425	$625	$1,700	$5,500
	Auctions: $2,585, MS-64, June 2013; $470, EF-45, October 2014													
1864, Proof	470	199	63.9								$750	$1,200	$5,000
	Auctions: $141,000, PF-68Cam, November 2013; $11,750, PF-67, July 2014; $3,525, PF-65Cam, September 2014; $881, PF-62Cam, September 2014													
1864S	20,000	41	30.9	15%	$275	$400	$800	$1,250	$3,800	$5,500	$12,000	$30,000	
	Auctions: $28,200, MS-64, June 2014; $617, EF-40, November 2014; $3,290, VF-25, July 2014; $1,410, VF-20, October 2014													
1865	58,800	47	48.3	34%	$75	$85	$130	$200	$275	$500	$800	$1,400	$8,000
	Auctions: $41,125, MS-66, June 2014; $705, AU-50, October 2014; $459, EF-40, November 2014													
1865, Proof	500	173	64.0								$750	$1,200	$5,000
	Auctions: $58,750, PF-68Cam, November 2013; $7,931, PF-66, July 2014; $3,819, PF-65Cam, August 2014; $1,410, PF-64, August 2014													
1865S	41,000	38	49.6	42%	$85	$125	$175	$450	$1,000	$1,500	$3,000	$6,000	$15,000
	Auctions: $64,625, MS-66, February 2014; $999, EF-40, October 2014; $200, G-4, September 2014													

	Mintage	Cert	Avg	%MS	G-4	VG-8	F-12	VF-20	EF-40	AU-50	MS-60 / PF-60	MS-63 / PF-63	MS-65 / PF-65
1866	16,800	42	54.2	69%	$350	$500	$625	$950	$1,600	$1,850	$2,200	$2,600	$6,250
	Auctions: $13,513, MS-66, October 2014; $8,225, MS-65, January 2014; $2,351, MS-64, November 2014; $1,175, EF-45, October 2014												
1866, No Motto, Proof † (p)	1	0	n/a						*(unique)*				
	Auctions: No auction records available.												
1866, Proof	725	154	64.1								$500	$950	$2,750
	Auctions: $19,975, PF-68, November 2013												
1866S	28,000	23	32.2	22%	$200	$300	$575	$1,000	$2,500	$3,000	$4,500	$10,000	$40,000
	Auctions: $25,263, MS-65, October 2014; $18,800, MS-63, November 2013; $1,293, VF-30, September 2014; $1,175, VF-20, October 2014												
1867	20,000	29	45.8	41%	$200	$300	$450	$650	$1,350	$1,650	$2,600	$8,500	
	Auctions: $14,100, MS-64, June 2014; $8,225, MS-63, October 2014; $2,820, MS-62, September 2014; $1,528, AU-55, November 2014												
1867, Proof	625	169	64.1								$500	$1,000	$2,750
	Auctions: $8,225, PF-67Cam, November 2013; $10,575, PF-67, October 2014; $2,585, PF-65Cam, August 2014; $881, PF-62, October 2014												
1867S	48,000	15	27.8	13%	$200	$310	$525	$1,000	$4,500	$8,400	$18,000	$35,000	
	Auctions: $3,055, EF-45, November 2014; $3,525, EF-40, September 2013; $282, Fair-2, September 2014												
1868	29,400	32	52.3	56%	$120	$150	$200	$300	$525	$625	$1,200	$2,200	$7,500
	Auctions: $61,688, MS-66, June 2014; $411, VF-35, October 2014												
1868, Proof	600	154	63.5								$500	$1,000	$2,750
	Auctions: $47,000, PF-68Cam, November 2013; $3,525, PF-66+, September 2014; $2,820, PF-65, October 2014												
1868S	96,000	37	43.6	30%	$80	$100	$170	$300	$900	$1,500	$3,500	$7,750	$25,000
	Auctions: $17,625, MS-66, June 2014; $881, EF-40, October 2014; $646, VF-20, August 2014; $118, F-12, September 2014												
1869	16,000	24	46.0	50%	$250	$300	$425	$550	$900	$1,100	$1,900	$3,000	$12,000
	Auctions: $25,850, MS-66, October 2014; $6,463, MS-65, November 2014; $1,175, EF-35, March 2013												
1869, Proof	600	175	63.5								$500	$1,000	$2,750
	Auctions: $18,800, PF-67Cam, November 2013; $445, PF-53, September 2014												
1869S	76,000	29	40.1	17%	$80	$120	$190	$325	$1,000	$1,600	$4,000	$6,500	$17,500
	Auctions: $10,869, MS-64, October 2014; $19,975, MS-64, August 2013; $999, AU-50, November 2014; $1,410, EF-45, November 2014												
1870	86,400	31	51.5	39%	$50	$60	$110	$175	$275	$450	$800	$2,200	$8,750
	Auctions: $9,400, MS-66, September 2014; $11,163, MS-66, January 2014; $382, EF-45, November 2014; $353, EF-45, November 2014												
1870, Proof	1,000	155	63.6								$500	$975	$2,500
	Auctions: $23,500, PF-67Cam, November 2013; $6,169, PF-67, October 2014; $1,880, PF-66, August 2014; $881, PF-64, October 2014												
1870CC	8,340	26	27.4	4%	$10,000	$14,000	$18,500	$25,000	$35,000	$65,000			
	Auctions: $70,500, AU-53, January 2014												
1871	118,200	43	54.5	60%	$30	$40	$60	$115	$225	$350	$600	$1,500	$8,000
	Auctions: $32,900, MS-67, June 2014												
1871, Proof	960	142	63.6								$500	$950	$2,500
	Auctions: $5,141, PF-67Cam, July 2014; $9,988, PF-67Cam, November 2013; $2,820, PF-65DCam, September 2014; $928, PF-64, December 2014												
1871CC	10,890	13	25.0	8%	$2,500	$5,000	$9,500	$17,000	$25,000	$45,000	$75,000		$350,000
	Auctions: $352,500, MS-65, June 2014												
1871S	30,900	26	51.7	54%	$325	$500	$1,500	$2,000	$1,500	$4,500	$6,750	$10,000	$17,500
	Auctions: $30,550, MS-66, June 2014; $2,115, VF-30, October 2014; $2,350, VF-25, November 2014; $1,176, G-6, July 2014												
1872	182,000	59	52.9	47%	$30	$40	$60	$115	$200	$300	$650	$2,000	$7,500
	Auctions: $14,100, MS-67, October 2014; $8,550, MS-66, April 2013; $3,525, MS-64, November 2014; $235, EF-40, October 2014												
1872, Proof	950	174	64.0								$500	$950	$2,400
	Auctions: $22,325, PF-68, August 2013; $3,055, PF-66, August 2014; $2,115, PF-65Cam, October 2014; $329, PF-55, July 2014												
1872CC	22,850	26	21.5	4%	$1,200	$1,800	$2,400	$3,800	$12,000	$20,000	$40,000		
	Auctions: $82,250, MS-62, October 2014; $17,625, AU-53, August 2013; $4,406, F-15, August 2014; $1,645, G-6, October 2014												
1872S	83,000	19	45.4	47%	$750	$1,000	$1,400	$3,000	$6,000	$8,000	$15,000	$25,000	$50,000
	Auctions: $44,063, MS-66, October 2014; $12,338, AU-55, January 2014; $5,288, AU-50, August 2014; $4,406, EF-40, November 2014												

† Ranked in the *100 Greatest U.S. Coins* (fourth edition). **p.** The unique 1866, Proof, quarter dollar without motto (as well as the half dollar and dollar of the same design) is not mentioned in the Mint director's report. "Not a pattern, but a muling created at a later date as a numismatic rarity" (*United States Pattern Coins*, tenth edition). Saul Teichman dates its creation to the 1870s. It is classified as Judd-536.

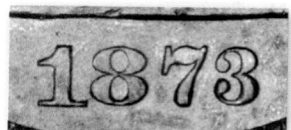 

1873, Close 3   1873, Open 3

	Mintage	Cert	Avg	%MS	G-4	VG-8	F-12	VF-20	EF-40	AU-50	MS-60 / PF-60	MS-63 / PF-63	MS-65 / PF-65
1873, Variety 4, Close 3	40,000	12	31.3	25%	$125	$225	$300	$700	$1,500	$2,500	$18,000	$40,000	
Auctions: $9,988, AU-58, April 2014													
1873, Variety 4, Open 3	172,000	33	56.7	61%	$30	$45	$65	$125	$200	$300	$500	$1,100	$5,500
Auctions: $8,225, MS-65, November 2013; $1,763, MS-63, July 2014													
1873, Variety 4, Proof	600	171	63.5								$500	$950	$2,400
Auctions: $44,063, PF-68Cam, November 2013; $5,875, PF-67, October 2014; $2,350, PF-66Cam, August 2014; $1,116, PF-64Cam, November 2014													
1873CC, Variety 4 † (q)	4,000	3	58.3	67%				—	$115,000	$125,000	$150,000	$400,000	
Auctions: $431,250, MS-63, January 2009													
1873, Variety 5	1,271,160	245	55.8	51%	$25	$30	$40	$60	$225	$425	$850	$1,650	$4,000
Auctions: $1,188, MS-63, September 2013													
1873, Variety 5, Proof	540	154	63.7								$900	$1,450	$7,200
Auctions: $41,125, PF-68Cam, October 2014; $52,875, PF-68Cam, November 2013; $3,055, PF-64Cam, August 2014; $2,820, PF-64, July 2014													
1873CC, Variety 5	12,462	24	26.4	13%	$3,500	$6,000	$11,500	$17,000	$25,000	$35,000	$75,000	$95,000	
Auctions: $9,988, VG-8, June 2014													
1873S, Variety 5	156,000	54	51.9	37%	$35	$40	$65	$125	$350	$750	$2,000	$6,000	$20,000
Auctions: $259, AU-50, October 2014; $159, VF-25, July 2014													
1874	471,200	95	57.6	57%	$25	$30	$40	$65	$200	$450	$900	$1,550	$5,000
Auctions: $5,875, MS-66, November 2014; $5,288, MS-65, January 2014; $1,528, MS-63, August 2014; $76, VF-30, July 2014													
1874, Proof	700	263	64.0								$900	$1,450	$7,200
Auctions: $22,325, PF-67, April 2014; $8,519, PF-66Cam, September 2014; $14,100, PF-66Cam, July 2014; $823, PF-62, October 2014													
1874S	392,000	153	60.8	80%	$25	$35	$65	$115	$265	$485	$950	$1,450	$3,750
Auctions: $19,975, MS-67, July 2014; $23,501, MS-67, June 2014; $4,113, MS-66, August 2014; $1,116, MS-62, August 2014													
1875	4,292,800	317	59.3	70%	$25	$30	$35	$45	$65	$160	$275	$550	$1,800
Auctions: $8,813, MS-67, October 2014; $4,113, MS-67, October 2014; $1,763, MS-66, July 2014; $329, AU-58, October 2014													
1875, Proof	700	164	63.9								$500	$950	$2,400
Auctions: $16,450, PF-67Cam, November 2013; $7,050, PF-66Cam, July 2014; $2,115, PF-65Cam, September 2014													
1875CC	140,000	50	50.2	36%	$80	$140	$200	$350	$650	$1,200	$3,000	$6,750	$30,000
Auctions: $28,200, MS-65, October 2014; $2,820, AU-55, February 2014; $2,233, AU-53, September 2014; $1,293, EF-45, November 2014													
1875S	680,000	100	56.0	60%	$35	$45	$70	$115	$200	$300	$600	$1,400	$3,750
Auctions: $3,055, MS-65, October 2014; $4,113, MS-65, August 2013; $68, EF-40, November 2014													
1876	17,816,000	551	57.2	65%	$25	$30	$35	$45	$65	$160	$275	$550	$1,650
Auctions: $7,050, MS-67, June 2014; $2,849, MS-66, August 2014; $229, MS-61, November 2014; $159, AU-55, October 2014													
1876, Proof	1,150	216	63.9								$500	$950	$2,400
Auctions: $47,000, PF-68, November 2013; $4,700, PF-67, August 2014; $2,350, PF-66, November 2014; $646, PF-62Cam, September 2014													
1876CC	4,944,000	341	51.1	49%	$45	$65	$75	$85	$120	$250	$600	$1,250	$4,000
Auctions: $4,137, MS-66, April 2014; $223, AU-55, July 2014; $212, EF-45, August 2014; $129, VF-30, July 2014													
1876S	8,596,000	296	59.8	73%	$25	$30	$35	$45	$65	$160	$275	$550	$2,250
Auctions: $1,528, MS-65, August 2014; $505, MS-64, July 2014; $1,293, MS-64, November 2013; $329, AU-58, November 2014													

† Ranked in the *100 Greatest U.S. Coins* (fourth edition). **q.** 6 examples are known.

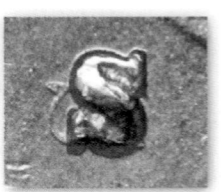

**1877-S, S Over
Horizontal S**
FS-25-1877S-501.

	Mintage	Cert	Avg	%MS	G-4	VG-8	F-12	VF-20	EF-40	AU-50	MS-60	MS-63	MS-65
											PF-60	PF-63	PF-65
1877	10,911,200	408	60.3	77%	$25	$30	$35	$45	$65	$160	$275	$550	$1,650
Auctions: $7,638, MS-68, September 2014; $14,100, MS-68, June 2014; $3,055, MS-67, November 2014; $705, MS-64, September 2014													
1877, Proof	510	145	63.5								$500	$950	$2,400
Auctions: $22,325, PF-68Cam, November 2013; $2,585, PF-66Cam, November 2014; $1,880, PF-65Cam, July 2014; $911, PF-64, October 2014													
1877CC (r)	4,192,000	471	57.0	70%	$45	$65	$75	$85	$120	$220	$475	$900	$2,250
Auctions: $9,988, MS-67, October 2014; $38,188, MS-67, June 2014; $4,113, MS-66, October 2014; $1,293, MS-64, August 2014													
1877S	8,996,000	358	59.5	75%	$25	$30	$35	$45	$65	$160	$275	$550	$1,850
Auctions: $10,810, MS-67, June 2014; $764, MS-64, July 2014; $329, MS-62, November 2014; $223, AU-58, November 2014													
1877S, S Over Horizontal S (s)	(t)	52	59.3	63%	$30	$45	$85	$150	$250	$400	$800	$2,000	$4,500
Auctions: $23,500, MS-66, June 2014; $1,645, MS-63, July 2014; $217, EF-45, November 2014													
1878	2,260,000	108	58.8	72%	$25	$30	$35	$45	$65	$160	$260	$550	$2,900
Auctions: $7,050, MS-66, October 2014; $3,290, MS-66, September 2014; $529, MS-63, August 2013													
1878, Proof	800	199	63.7								$500	$950	$2,400
Auctions: $25,850, PF-68, November 2013; $999, PF-64, November 2014; $529, PF-62Cam, November 2014													
1878CC	996,000	256	56.1	64%	$55	$70	$85	$120	$200	$300	$700	$1,500	$4,000
Auctions: $10,575, MS-66, October 2014; $18,800, MS-66, April 2013; $1,528, MS-64, September 2014; $411, AU-53, November 2014													
1878S	140,000	31	53.9	61%	$125	$230	$360	$525	$700	$1,300	$2,250	$4,000	$20,000
Auctions: $19,975, MS-66, October 2014; $9,400, MS-64, July 2014; $7,050, MS-63, July 2014; $3,819, MS-62, October 2014													
1879	13,600	212	63.6	92%	$120	$140	$200	$250	$325	$400	$575	$800	$2,000
Auctions: $28,200, MS-68, August 2013; $5,581, MS-67, September 2014; $4,994, MS-66, August 2014; $411, EF-45, October 2014													
1879, Proof	1,100	302	63.9								$500	$950	$2,400
Auctions: $3,819, PF-67, October 2014; $7,638, PF-67, November 2013; $2,585, PF-66, November 2014; $1,645, PF-65, November 2014													
1880	13,600	132	62.3	88%	$120	$140	$200	$250	$325	$400	$575	$800	$2,000
Auctions: $21,150, MS-68, April 2014; $3,055, MS-66, October 2014; $705, MS-62, October 2014; $423, VF-35, August 2014													
1880, Proof	1,355	375	64.4								$500	$950	$2,400
Auctions: $28,200, PF-68, November 2013; $3,408, PF-67Cam, September 2014; $1,880, PF-65Cam, October 2014; $294, PF-55, November 2014													
1881	12,000	104	60.1	83%	$160	$180	$250	$300	$375	$425	$625	$850	$2,100
Auctions: $4,700, MS-67, October 2014; $2,115, MS-66, November 2014; $10,575, MS-66, April 2013; $1,528, MS-64, September 2014													
1881, Proof	975	297	64.3								$500	$950	$2,400
Auctions: $44,063, PF-68Cam, November 2013; $4,406, PF-67Cam, October 2014; $3,290, PF-66Cam+, October 2014; $364, PF-61, October 2014													
1882	15,200	74	60.5	82%	$130	$160	$210	$265	$325	$425	$625	$900	$2,000
Auctions: $3,525, MS-67, August 2014; $2,585, MS-66+, November 2014; $482, AU-53, October 2014; $382, EF-45, November 2014													
1882, Proof	1,100	305	64.3								$500	$950	$2,400
Auctions: $21,150, PF-68Cam, November 2013; $8,225, PF-67DCam, September 2014; $4,553, PF-67, November 2014; $1,763, PF-66, October 2014													
1883	14,400	84	60.7	87%	$130	$160	$210	$265	$325	$425	$625	$900	$2,250
Auctions: $9,988, MS-67, June 2014; $4,406, MS-66, November 2014													
1883, Proof	1,039	348	64.3								$500	$950	$2,400
Auctions: $47,000, PF-69Cam, November 2013; $4,553, PF-65DCam+, November 2014; $646, PF-62Cam, November 2014													

r. The 1877-CC quarter with fine edge-reeding is scarcer than that with normally spaced reeding; in the marketplace, there is no price differential. **s.** This variety, known since the 1950s, was caused by an initial S mintmark being punched into the die horizontally, and then corrected with an upright S mintmark. **t.** Included in 1877-S mintage figure.

	Mintage	Cert	Avg	%MS	G-4	VG-8	F-12	VF-20	EF-40	AU-50	MS-60 / PF-60	MS-63 / PF-63	MS-65 / PF-65
1884	8,000	97	56.5	77%	$225	$275	$350	$425	$550	$600	$700	$900	$2,100
	Auctions: $8,225, MS-67, October 2014; $3,819, MS-66, December 2013; $1,058, MS-64, August 2014; $646, AU-55, August 2014												
1884, Proof	875	283	64.5								$500	$950	$2,400
	Auctions: $70,500, PF-69Cam, November 2013; $2,115, PF-66, September 2014; $1,645, PF-65, September 2014												
1885	13,600	82	60.7	80%	$130	$160	$225	$275	$325	$400	$675	$1,100	$2,750
	Auctions: $3,408, MS-66, November 2013; $999, AU-58, September 2014; $259, F-12, November 2014; $341, VG-10, October 2014												
1885, Proof	930	263	64.1								$500	$950	$2,400
	Auctions: $9,400, PF-68Cam, October 2014; $47,000, PF-68Cam, November 2013; $2,585, PF-66Cam, August 2014; $1,410, PF-65+, August 2014												
1886	5,000	39	60.7	85%	$300	$375	$475	$575	$675	$750	$1,000	$1,400	$3,500
	Auctions: $18,800, MS-67, June 2014; $3,525, MS-66, November 2014; $2,233, MS-65, November 2014; $564, G-6, October 2014												
1886, Proof	886	292	64.4								$500	$950	$2,400
	Auctions: $5,288, PF-67Cam, September 2014; $17,625, PF-67Cam, November 2013; $1,880, PF-66, September 2014; $529, PF-62, August 2014												
1887	10,000	96	62.1	85%	$225	$250	$325	$385	$475	$525	$750	$1,100	$2,200
	Auctions: $5,875, MS-67, October 2014; $6,463, MS-67, September 2013; $705, MS-61, October 2014; $705, AU-58, October 2014												
1887, Proof	710	230	64.4								$500	$950	$2,400
	Auctions: $41,125, PF-68Cam, November 2013; $4,994, PF-66Cam+, September 2014; $1,880, PF-66, November 2014												
1888	10,001	142	63.3	94%	$200	$245	$325	$425	$500	$650	$700	$1,000	$2,100
	Auctions: $5,581, MS-67, January 2014; $881, MS-64, September 2014; $764, MS-63, October 2014; $341, F-12, October 2014												
1888, Proof	832	223	64.2								$500	$950	$2,400
	Auctions: $11,899, PF-68Cam, April 2013; $6,756, PF-67, October 2014; $1,645, PF-65Cam, September 2014												
1888S	1,216,000	144	57.2	70%	$25	$30	$35	$45	$70	$160	$300	$850	$3,000
	Auctions: $9,988, MS-66, January 2014; $1,116, MS-64, November 2014; $176, AU-53, October 2014; $129, AU-53, July 2014												
1889	12,000	179	63.5	91%	$150	$175	$225	$275	$325	$450	$600	$750	$1,800
	Auctions: $4,994, MS-67+, November 2014; $5,434, MS-67, June 2014; $999, MS-64, October 2014; $517, AU-53, October 2014												
1889, Proof	711	186	64.5								$500	$950	$2,400
	Auctions: $19,975, PF-68DCam, August 2013; $9,989, PF-68, September 2014; $4,113, PF-67Cam, September 2014; $1,586, PF-65, July 2014												
1890	80,000	185	62.9	88%	$60	$75	$100	$125	$175	$300	$525	$775	$1,850
	Auctions: $11,750, MS-68, October 2014; $6,463, MS-67+, November 2014; $8,813, MS-67, April 2014; $1,821, MS-66, September 2014												
1890, Proof	590	231	64.8								$500	$950	$2,400
	Auctions: $9,106, PF-68Cam, September 2014; $18,213, PF-68, June 2014; $4,406, PF-67, August 2014; $589, PF-61, November 2014												
1891	3,920,000	651	60.9	79%	$25	$30	$35	$45	$65	$160	$260	$550	$1,800
	Auctions: $3,055, MS-67, August 2014; $6,527, MS-67, January 2014; $1,880, MS-66, November 2014; $734, MS-64, October 2014												
1891, Proof	600	237	64.6								$500	$950	$2,400
	Auctions: $9,988, PF-68, October 2014; $9,400, PF-67DCam, September 2014; $16,450, PF-67Cam, November 2013; $353, PF-61, December 2014												
1891O	68,000	38	40.7	39%	$200	$350	$600	$1,300	$2,250	$3,200	$4,400	$8,500	$27,000
	Auctions: $129,250, MS-66, August 2013; $341, G-6, October 2014												
1891S	2,216,000	188	59.7	74%	$25	$30	$35	$45	$70	$160	$260	$550	$2,000
	Auctions: $705, MS-64, December 2013; $259, AU-58, October 2014; $165, AU-53, October 2014												

BARBER OR LIBERTY HEAD (1892–1916)

Designer: *Charles E. Barber.* **Weight:** *6.25 grams.*
Composition: *.900 silver, .100 copper (net weight .18084 oz. pure silver).*
Diameter: *24.3 mm.* **Edge:** *Reeded.* **Mints:** *Philadelphia, Denver, New Orleans, San Francisco.*

   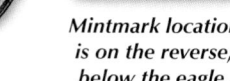  

Circulation Strike

Mintmark location is on the reverse, below the eagle.

Proof

History. The Liberty Head design was by Charles E. Barber, chief engraver of the U.S. Mint. Barber quarters feature the same obverse motif used on dimes and half dollars of the era, with the designer's initial, B, found at the truncation of the neck of Miss Liberty. The reverse depicts a heraldic eagle holding an olive branch in one talon and arrows in the other, along with a ribbon reading E PLURIBUS UNUM.

Striking and Sharpness. On the obverse, check the hair details and other features. On the reverse, the eagle's leg at the lower right and the arrows can be weak. Also check the upper–right portion of the shield and the nearby wing. Once these coins entered circulation and acquired wear, the word LIBERTY on the headband tended to disappear quickly. Most Proofs are sharply struck, although more than just a few are weak on the eagle's leg at the lower right and on certain parts of the arrows. The Proofs of 1892 to 1901 usually have cameo contrast between the designs and the mirror fields. Later Proofs vary in their contrast.

Availability. Barber quarters in Fine or better grade are scarce. Today, among circulation strikes, 90% or more in existence are G-4 or below. MS coins are available of all dates and mints, but some are very elusive. The 1896-S, 1901-S, and 1913-S are the key dates in all grades. Proofs exist in proportion to their mintages. Choicer examples tend to be of later dates.

GRADING STANDARDS

MS-60 to 70 (Mint State). *Obverse:* At MS-60, some abrasion and contact marks are evident, most noticeably on the cheek and the obverse field to the right. Luster is present, but may be dull or lifeless. Many Barber coins have been cleaned, especially of the earlier dates. At MS-63, contact marks are very few. Abrasion still is evident, but less than at lower levels. Indeed, the cheek of Miss Liberty virtually showcases abrasion. An MS-65 coin

1913. Graded MS-62.

may have minor abrasion, but contact marks are so minute as to require magnification. Luster should be full and rich. *Reverse:* Comments apply as for the obverse, except that in lower Mint State grades abrasion and contact marks are most noticeable on the head and tail of the eagle and on the tips of the wings. At MS-65 or higher, there are no marks visible to the unaided eye. The field is mainly protected by design elements, and often appears to grade a point or two higher than the obverse.

   Illustrated coin: This is an attractive, lightly toned example.

AU-50, 53, 55, 58 (About Uncirculated). *Obverse:* Light wear is seen on the head, especially on the forward hair under LIBERTY. At AU-58, the luster is extensive but incomplete, especially on the higher parts and in the right field. At AU-50 and 53, luster is less. *Reverse:* Wear is evident on the head and tail of the eagle and on the tips of the wings. At AU-50 and 53, there still is significant luster. An AU-58 coin (as determined by the obverse) can have the reverse appear to be full Mint State.

1915-S. Graded AU-50.

   Illustrated coin: Note the typical light striking on the eagle's talons and arrows at lower right. This coin has some lightness at the upper right of the shield.

EF-40, 45 (Extremely Fine). *Obverse:* Further wear is seen on the head. The hair above the forehead lacks most detail. LIBERTY shows wear, but still is strong. *Reverse:* Further wear is seen on the head and tail of the eagle and on the tips of the wings, most evident at the left and right extremes of the wings. At this level and below, sharpness of strike on the reverse is not important.

1916. Graded EF-40.

VF-20, 30 (Very Fine). *Obverse:* The head shows more wear, now with nearly all detail gone in the hair above the forehead. LIBERTY shows wear, but is complete. The leaves on the head all show wear, as does the upper part of the cap. *Reverse:* Wear is more extensive, particularly noticeable on the outer parts of the wings, the head, the shield, and the tail.

1913-S. Graded VF-30.

F-12, 15 (Fine). *Obverse:* The head shows extensive wear. LIBERTY, the key place to check, is weak, especially at ER, but is fully readable. The ANA grading standards and *Photograde* adhere to this. PCGS suggests that lightly struck coins "may have letters partially missing." Traditionally, collectors insist on full LIBERTY. *Reverse:* More wear is seen on the reverse in the places as above. E PLURIBUS UNUM is light, with one to several letters worn away.

1907. Graded F-12.

VG-8, 10 (Very Good). *Obverse:* A net of three letters in LIBERTY must be readable. Traditionally, LI is clear, and after that there is a partial letter or two. *Reverse:* Further wear has smoothed more than half of the feathers in the wing. The shield is indistinct except for a few traces of interior lines. The motto is partially worn away. The rim is full, and many if not most denticles can be seen.

1901-S. Graded VG-8.

G-4, 6 (Good). *Obverse:* The head is in outline form, with the center flat. Most of the rim is there. All letters and the date are full. *Reverse:* The eagle shows only a few feathers, and only a few scattered letters remain in the motto. The rim may be worn flat in some or all of the area, but the peripheral lettering is clear.

1913-S. Graded G-4.

AG-3 (About Good). *Obverse:* The stars and motto are worn, and the border may be indistinct. Distinctness varies at this level. The date is clear. Grading is usually determined by the reverse. *Reverse:* The rim is gone and the letters are partially worn away. The eagle is mostly flat, perhaps with a few hints of feathers.

   Illustrated coin: This is a pleasing example of the grade, with bold date and mintmark and no problems.

1901-S. Graded AG-3.

PF-60 to 70 (Proof). *Obverse and Reverse:* Proofs that are extensively cleaned and have many hairlines, or that are dull and grainy, are lower level, such as PF-60 to 62. These are not widely desired by collectors. With medium hairlines and good reflectivity, an assigned grade of PF-64 is appropriate. Tiny horizontal lines on Miss Liberty's cheek, known as slide marks, from National and other album slides scuffing the relief of the cheek, are endemic on all Barber silver coins. With noticeable marks of this type, the highest grade assignable is PF-64. With relatively few hairlines, a rating of PF-65 can be given. PF-66 should have hairlines so delicate that magnification is needed to see them. Above that, a Proof should be free of any hairlines or other problems.

1894. Graded PF-63.

   Illustrated coin: Light gray and lilac toning combine to create a beautiful coin.

1892, Variety 1 Reverse   **1892, Variety 2 Reverse**
Note position of wing tip relative to E in UNITED.

Coins designated Deep Cameo or Ultra Cameo bring a premium of 50% to 100% above listed values.

	Mintage	Cert	Avg	%MS	G-4	VG-8	F-12	VF-20	EF-40	AU-50	MS-60	MS-63	MS-65
											PF-60	PF-63	PF-65
1892 (a)	8,236,000	1,659	60.9	75%	$9	$10	$26	$45	$75	$130	$235	$440	$1,100
Auctions: $11,456, MS-68, October 2014; $3,672, MS-67, November 2014; $1,058, MS-66, August 2014; $441, MS-64, December 2014
1892, Proof	1,245	385	64.7								$450	$800	$1,900
Auctions: $14,100, PF-68DCam, September 2014; $15,864, PF-68, February 2013; $2,350, PF-66Cam, July 2014; $1,645, PF-65Cam+, October 2014
1892O	2,460,000	422	59.8	68%	$15	$20	$45	$60	$95	$160	$300	$475	$1,550
Auctions: $17,625, MS-68, June 2014; $2,703, MS-66, August 2014; $1,528, MS-64, August 2014; $329, MS-62, November 2014
1892S	964,079	122	50.0	54%	$30	$50	$80	$130	$200	$300	$475	$1,050	$4,000
Auctions: $35,250, MS-67, June 2014; $7,638, MS-66, August 2014; $3,525, MS-65, August 2014; $705, MS-62, October 2014
1893	5,444,023	305	58.7	70%	$9	$10	$26	$45	$75	$130	$235	$440	$1,400
Auctions: $22,325, MS-67, April 2013; $4,994, MS-66, October 2014; $1,058, MS-65, September 2014
1893, Proof	792	311	65.1								$450	$775	$1,900
Auctions: $11,163, PF-68, October 2014; $4,406, PF-67Cam, August 2014; $3,672, PF-66DCam, July 2014
1893O	3,396,000	204	57.7	65%	$10	$14	$30	$60	$110	$170	$275	$500	$2,000
Auctions: $23,500, MS-68, October 2014; $4,113, MS-66, August 2013; $558, MS-64, August 2014; $294, AU-58, December 2014
1893S	1,454,535	109	51.0	61%	$20	$35	$60	$110	$175	$300	$425	$1,000	$6,000
Auctions: $15,275, MS-67, October 2014; $4,553, MS-65, August 2014; $705, AU-58, July 2014; $188, EF-45, September 2014
1894	3,432,000	172	59.3	76%	$9	$10	$26	$35	$50	$95	$150	$240	$450	$1,200
Auctions: $2,233, MS-66, October 2014; $1,645, MS-65, June 2014
1894, Proof	972	340	64.8								$450	$800	$1,900
Auctions: $9,400, PF-68+, October 2014; $4,406, PF-67Cam, October 2014; $2,820, PF-66Cam, October 2014; $499, PF-62, October 2014
1894O	2,852,000	149	55.9	66%	$10	$20	$45	$70	$130	$230	$325	$725	$2,000
Auctions: $1,293, MS-64, February 2014; $200, AU-55, July 2014
1894S	2,648,821	202	59.2	74%	$10	$15	$40	$60	$120	$210	$325	$725	$2,500
Auctions: $1,469, MS-65, November 2014; $2,468, MS-65, November 2013; $734, MS-64, July 2014; $223, MS-60, November 2014
1895	4,440,000	221	57.6	72%	$10	$14	$30	$45	$80	$140	$250	$500	$1,600
Auctions: $8,813, MS-67, June 2014; $1,645, MS-65, July 2014; $470, MS-63, October 2014; $282, AU-58, October 2014
1895, Proof	880	273	64.9								$450	$800	$1,900
Auctions: $15,716, PF-68Cam, August 2014; $22,325, PF-68Cam, November 2013; $3,055, PF-66Cam, October 2014; $1,058, PF-64, September 2014
1895O	2,816,000	116	54.0	59%	$12	$20	$50	$70	$140	$230	$400	$900	$2,600
Auctions: $49,938, MS-68, June 2014; $5,875, MS-66, August 2014; $940, MS-63, October 2014; $600, MS-62, August 2014
1895S	1,764,681	112	49.0	50%	$20	$32	$70	$120	$170	$275	$420	$1,050	$3,500
Auctions: $12,925, MS-67, August 2013; $1,880, MS-64, July 2014; $329, MS-60, November 2014
1896	3,874,000	191	58.8	80%	$10	$14	$30	$45	$80	$135	$250	$425	$1,250
Auctions: $11,750, MS-67, October 2014; $999, MS-65, September 2013
1896, Proof	762	322	65.4								$450	$800	$1,900
Auctions: $23,500, PF-68Cam, November 2013; $10,575, PF-68, October 2014; $4,700, PF-67Cam, October 2014; $1,293, PF-66, October 2014
1896O	1,484,000	152	41.0	41%	$55	$85	$200	$320	$550	$800	$1,000	$2,000	$6,500
Auctions: $22,325, MS-67, October 2014; $8,813, MS-65, August 2013; $1,175, AU-58, July 2014; $1,116, AU-55, September 2014
1896S	188,039	437	12.5	8%	$900	$1,500	$2,400	$3,800	$5,000	$7,000	$10,000	$17,500	$50,000
Auctions: $76,375, MS-67, October 2014; $52,875, MS-65, August 2014; $7,638, AU-53, November 2014; $3,290, VF-30, August 2014

a. There are two varieties of the 1892 reverse. Variety 1: the eagle's wing covers only half of the E in UNITED; Variety 2: the eagle's wing covers most of the E. Coins of Variety 1 are somewhat scarcer.

	Mintage	Cert	Avg	%MS	G-4	VG-8	F-12	VF-20	EF-40	AU-50	MS-60	MS-63	MS-65
											PF-60	PF-63	PF-65
1897	8,140,000	274	58.2	72%	$9	$14	$26	$40	$70	$120	$240	$450	$1,400
	Auctions: $4,113, MS-67, November 2014; $16,450, MS-66, February 2013; $617, MS-64+, July 2014; $244, MS-62, October 2014												
1897, Proof	731	273	64.8								$450	$800	$1,900
	Auctions: $7,050, PF-68, October 2014; $6,463, PF-67DCam, August 2014; $2,115, PF-66Cam, November 2014; $1,116, PF-66, October 2014												
1897O	1,414,800	117	39.2	36%	$40	$65	$180	$340	$385	$600	$850	$1,800	$3,250
	Auctions: $23,500, MS-67, October 2013; $2,233, MS-64, August 2014												
1897S	542,229	151	32.1	30%	$120	$150	$300	$550	$825	$1,000	$1,600	$1,900	$6,000
	Auctions: $15,275, MS-66, September 2013; $4,994, MS-65, July 2014; $1,410, AU-53, August 2014; $764, EF-40, September 2014												
1898	11,100,000	336	57.8	68%	$9	$10	$26	$45	$70	$125	$225	$425	$1,200
	Auctions: $364, MS-64, July 2014; $353, MS-63, November 2014; $153, AU-58, September 2014												
1898, Proof	735	328	65.6								$450	$775	$1,900
	Auctions: $27,025, PF-69, June 2014; $5,728, PF-68, October 2014; $4,113, PF-67DCam, September 2014; $2,291, PF-66Cam, November 2014												
1898O	1,868,000	84	48.5	50%	$15	$28	$70	$140	$300	$390	$625	$1,500	$8,750
	Auctions: $58,750, MS-68, June 2014; $11,779, MS-66, September 2014; $2,470, MS-64, August 2014; $62, VF-30, September 2014												
1898S	1,020,592	71	51.4	52%	$11	$25	$40	$55	$100	$200	$400	$1,400	$7,500
	Auctions: $18,800, MS-67, June 2014; $7,638, MS-66, August 2014; $200, AU-58, September 2014; $170, EF-45, October 2014												
1899	12,624,000	341	56.6	67%	$9	$10	$26	$45	$75	$125	$225	$400	$1,100
	Auctions: $3,819, MS-66, October 2014; $911, MS-65, October 2014; $2,820, MS-65, August 2013; $259, MS-62, December 2014												
1899, Proof	846	201	64.9								$450	$800	$1,900
	Auctions: $8,813, PF-68Cam, October 2014; $12,338, PF-67DCam+, November 2014; $999, PF-64Cam, November 2014; $529, PF-62, November 2014												
1899O	2,644,000	101	56.1	63%	$11	$18	$35	$70	$120	$260	$400	$800	$2,500
	Auctions: $9,988, MS-67, October 2014; $4,700, MS-65, August 2013; $2,820, MS-65, August 2014; $79, VF-30, October 2014												
1899S	708,000	57	56.6	51%	$27	$40	$95	$110	$140	$270	$425	$1,400	$3,500
	Auctions: $8,225, MS-67, October 2014; $4,406, MS-66, March 2014; $1,998, MS-63, October 2014; $1,058, MS-61, July 2014												
1900	10,016,000	287	59.3	76%	$9	$10	$26	$45	$75	$125	$240	$425	$1,250
	Auctions: $3,409, MS-66, October 2013; $999, MS-65, September 2014; $141, AU-55, September 2014; $129, AU-50, August 2014												
1900, Proof	912	269	64.9								$450	$800	$1,900
	Auctions: $14,100, PF-68Cam, April 2013; $3,290, PF-67Cam, October 2014; $3,000, PF-67, August 2014; $2,585, PF-66Cam, October 2014												
1900O	3,416,000	114	53.6	61%	$12	$26	$65	$110	$150	$310	$525	$850	$3,500
	Auctions: $1,998, MS-64, October 2013; $411, AU-58, December 2014; $382, AU-53, August 2014; $212, EF-45, October 2014												
1900S	1,858,585	122	52.7	33%	$10	$15	$35	$55	$80	$130	$350	$1,000	$4,500
	Auctions: $6,463, MS-66, April 2014; $1,645, MS-64, October 2014; $411, MS-62, July 2014; $356, AU-58, September 2014												
1901	8,892,000	278	52.6	64%	$9	$10	$26	$45	$80	$135	$240	$425	$1,350
	Auctions: $15,275, MS-67, June 2014; $410, MS-64, November 2014; $315, MS-63, July 2014; $247, AU-58, October 2014												
1901, Proof	813	250	64.8								$450	$800	$1,900
	Auctions: $8,813, PF-68, August 2014; $2,820, PF-67Cam, October 2014; $8,813, PF-67Cam, November 2013; $1,194, PF-65Cam, October 2014												
1901O	1,612,000	76	32.8	24%	$40	$60	$140	$275	$550	$750	$950	$1,850	$5,500
	Auctions: $22,325, MS-67, June 2014; $3,819, MS-64, October 2014; $940, EF-40, August 2014; $165, F-12, September 2014												
1901S	72,664	308	8.3	4%	$5,250	$10,000	$16,500	$23,000	$30,000	$32,500	$37,500	$45,000	$75,000
	Auctions: $258,500, MS-67, June 2014; $18,800, VF-25, July 2014; $6,463, VG-8, November 2014; $1,880, AG-3, October 2014												
1902	12,196,967	294	56.1	61%	$9	$10	$26	$45	$65	$120	$240	$425	$1,200
	Auctions: $940, MS-65, July 2014; $1,351, MS-65, August 2013; $499, MS-64, August 2014; $74, AU-55, September 2014												
1902, Proof	777	227	64.3								$450	$800	$1,900
	Auctions: $8,225, PF-68, October 2014; $5,288, PF-67Cam, November 2014; $11,163, PF-67, June 2013; $2,234, PF-66, October 2014												
1902O	4,748,000	107	50.7	47%	$10	$16	$50	$85	$140	$225	$475	$1,300	$3,750
	Auctions: $4,994, MS-66, September 2013; $135, AU-50, September 2014												
1902S	1,524,612	107	54.8	58%	$14	$22	$55	$90	$160	$240	$500	$950	$3,200
	Auctions: $18,213, MS-68, October 2014; $19,975, MS-67, April 2013; $499, AU-58, November 2014; $56, F-15, September 2014												

	Mintage	Cert	Avg	%MS	G-4	VG-8	F-12	VF-20	EF-40	AU-50	MS-60 PF-60	MS-63 PF-63	MS-65 PF-65
1903	9,759,309	128	55.1	57%	$9	$10	$26	$45	$65	$120	$240	$450	$2,000
	Auctions: $5,875, MS-66, September 2013; $76, AU-58, September 2014												
1903, Proof	755	288	65.2								$450	$775	$1,900
	Auctions: $13,055, PF-68Cam, August 2013; $2,703, PF-67, November 2014; $1,293, PF-65, August 2014; $940, PF-64, July 2014												
1903O	3,500,000	90	52.3	43%	$10	$12	$40	$60	$120	$275	$425	$1,200	$4,500
	Auctions: $6,463, MS-66, November 2014; $5,288, MS-66, August 2014; $259, AU-55, October 2014; $101, EF-45, November 2014												
1903S	1,036,000	87	56.8	71%	$15	$25	$45	$85	$150	$275	$425	$850	$2,200
	Auctions: $4,259, MS-66, August 2013; $1,763, MS-65, August 2014; $141, AU-53, September 2014; $118, VF-35, December 2014												
1904	9,588,143	162	57.0	61%	$9	$10	$26	$45	$70	$120	$225	$400	$1,200
	Auctions: $7,344, MS-67, June 2014; $306, MS-63, November 2014; $135, AU-50, August 2014; $38, VF-35, November 2014												
1904, Proof	670	264	64.8								$450	$800	$1,900
	Auctions: $4,250, PF-67, August 2014; $1,821, PF-66, October 2014; $1,089, PF-64Cam, September 2014												
1904O	2,456,000	124	50.1	46%	$30	$40	$85	$150	$240	$450	$800	$1,300	$3,000
	Auctions: $41,125, MS-67, June 2014												
1905	4,967,523	187	53.1	62%	$30	$35	$50	$65	$70	$120	$240	$440	$1,300
	Auctions: $4,124, MS-66, October 2014; $558, MS-64, November 2014; $204, MS-61, November 2014; $135, AU-55, November 2014												
1905, Proof	727	247	64.6								$450	$800	$1,900
	Auctions: $7,931, PF-68, October 2014; $4,406, PF-67, August 2014; $1,410, PF-65, November 2014; $383, PF-61, September 2014												
1905O	1,230,000	80	47.1	50%	$40	$60	$120	$220	$260	$350	$475	$1,250	$5,500
	Auctions: $16,450, MS-67, October 2014; $5,288, MS-65, June 2013; $824, AU-53, September 2014; $200, VF-30, November 2014												
1905S	1,884,000	105	50.9	50%	$30	$40	$75	$100	$105	$225	$350	$1,000	$3,500
	Auctions: $10,575, MS-67, October 2014; $2,174, MS-65, October 2014; $1,645, MS-64, August 2013; $153, EF-45, December 2014												
1906	3,655,760	202	60.0	81%	$9	$10	$26	$45	$70	$120	$240	$425	$1,100
	Auctions: $2,820, MS-66, June 2014												
1906, Proof	675	205	65.0								$450	$800	$1,900
	Auctions: $14,100, PF-68, November 2013; $1,645, PF-66, October 2014; $2,820, PF-66+, August 2014; $969, PF-64, July 2014												
1906D	3,280,000	121	59.6	78%	$9	$10	$30	$50	$70	$145	$250	$450	$1,450
	Auctions: $1,293, MS-65, November 2014; $1,175, MS-65, August 2013; $84, EF-45, September 2014												
1906O	2,056,000	139	60.2	78%	$9	$10	$40	$60	$100	$200	$300	$550	$1,450
	Auctions: $2,585, MS-66, June 2014; $1,058, MS-64, October 2014; $482, AU-50, November 2014												
1907	7,132,000	363	58.7	70%	$9	$10	$26	$40	$65	$120	$225	$400	$1,100
	Auctions: $8,225, MS-68, November 2014; $823, MS-65, November 2014; $1,528, MS-65, July 2014; $709, MS-64, September 2014												
1907, Proof	575	310	65.0								$450	$800	$1,900
	Auctions: $9,106, PF-68Cam, November 2014; $11,750, PF-68Cam, November 2013; $3,408, PF-67Cam, July 2014; $882, PF-64, November 2014												
1907D	2,484,000	106	55.8	70%	$9	$10	$26	$48	$70	$175	$250	$650	$2,250
	Auctions: $7,050, MS-66, June 2014; $823, MS-64, August 2014; $165, AU-55, September 2014												
1907O	4,560,000	182	57.3	70%	$9	$10	$26	$45	$70	$135	$275	$500	$1,850
	Auctions: $9,988, MS-68, June 2014; $3,055, MS-66, October 2014; $259, MS-62, October 2014; $101, AU-55, September 2014												
1907S	1,360,000	75	55.3	73%	$10	$18	$45	$70	$140	$280	$475	$1,200	$5,000
	Auctions: $15,275, MS-67, June 2014; $212, AU-58, September 2014; $147, EF-45, December 2014												
1908	4,232,000	233	59.7	75%	$9	$10	$26	$45	$70	$120	$240	$425	$1,100
	Auctions: $10,575, MS-67, October 2014; $1,645, MS-66, April 2013; $388, MS-64, October 2014; $176, AU-58, August 2014												
1908, Proof	545	189	64.8								$450	$775	$1,900
	Auctions: $8,813, PF-68, October 2014; $7,344, PF-68, September 2013; $3,055, PF-67, August 2014; $1,410, PF-66, October 2014												
1908D	5,788,000	245	54.1	60%	$9	$10	$26	$45	$70	$120	$240	$425	$1,250
	Auctions: $12,925, MS-68, October 2014; $2,350, MS-66, August 2014; $341, MS-62, September 2014; $103, AU-53, September 2014												
1908O	6,244,000	232	56.5	72%	$9	$10	$26	$45	$65	$120	$240	$425	$1,200
	Auctions: $4,259, MS-66, October 2014; $529, MS-64, October 2014; $223, MS-62, November 2014; $176, AU-58, November 2014												
1908S	784,000	117	50.5	62%	$18	$38	$85	$165	$325	$465	$750	$1,200	$4,500
	Auctions: $12,925, MS-67, October 2014; $2,585, MS-65, November 2014; $2,056, MS-64+, August 2014; $470, EF-45, October 2014												

	Mintage	Cert	Avg	%MS	G-4	VG-8	F-12	VF-20	EF-40	AU-50	MS-60 / PF-60	MS-63 / PF-63	MS-65 / PF-65
1909	9,268,000	494	57.8	70%	$9	$10	$26	$45	$65	$120	$240	$425	$1,100
	Auctions: $2,585, MS-66, April 2013; $499, MS-64, August 2014; $177, AU-58, October 2014												
1909, Proof	650	272	64.8								$450	$800	$1,900
	Auctions: $18,800, PF-68, November 2013; $4,113, PF-67, November 2014; $1,763, PF-66Cam, November 2014; $2,115, PF-66, September 2014												
1909D	5,114,000	281	53.0	57%	$9	$10	$26	$45	$85	$150	$240	$425	$1,100
	Auctions: $2,585, MS-66, November 2013; $767, MS-65, November 2014; $364, MS-64, October 2014; $147, AU-53, August 2014												
1909O	712,000	75	42.8	53%	$42	$100	$400	$650	$1,000	$1,800	$3,000	$4,000	$10,000
	Auctions: $14,100, MS-65, August 2013; $3,525, AU-50, September 2014; $823, VF-20, November 2014												
1909S	1,348,000	107	52.2	67%	$9	$10	$35	$55	$90	$185	$285	$750	$2,000
	Auctions: $3,055, MS-66, June 2014; $1,704, MS-65, September 2014; $1,410, MS-64, August 2014												
1910	2,244,000	184	58.6	79%	$9	$10	$26	$45	$80	$140	$240	$425	$1,100
	Auctions: $4,700, MS-67, June 2014; $823, MS-65, September 2014; $499, MS-64, October 2014; $106, AU-53, September 2014												
1910, Proof	551	270	65.1								$450	$800	$1,900
	Auctions: $38,188, PF-69Cam, August 2014; $7,344, PF-68Cam, July 2014; $15,275, PF-68Cam, November 2013; $2,941, PF-67, August 2014												
1910D	1,500,000	122	54.7	64%	$10	$11	$45	$70	$125	$240	$350	$900	$1,600
	Auctions: $9,400, MS-67, June 2014; $823, MS-64, August 2014; $505, MS-62, July 2014												
1911	3,720,000	279	59.6	74%	$9	$10	$26	$45	$70	$125	$240	$425	$1,100
	Auctions: $7,931, MS-67, October 2014; $2,115, MS-66, August 2014; $499, MS-64, October 2014; $123, AU-53, November 2014												
1911, Proof	543	241	65.3								$450	$800	$1,900
	Auctions: $7,050, PF-68Cam, November 2014; $17,038, PF-68Cam, November 2013; $9,694, PF-68, October 2014; $2,233, PF-66Cam, July 2014												
1911D	933,600	107	45.8	47%	$30	$40	$150	$300	$400	$600	$850	$1,300	$5,500
	Auctions: $21,150, MS-67, October 2014; $4,994, MS-65, August 2013; $1,645, MS-64, August 2014; $259, VF-30, August 2014												
1911S	988,000	193	60.2	81%	$9	$10	$55	$85	$165	$280	$375	$750	$1,500
	Auctions: $11,750, MS-68, October 2014; $7,050, MS-67, April 2014; $2,350, MS-66, October 2014; $529, AU-58, September 2014												
1912	4,400,000	424	59.4	79%	$9	$10	$26	$45	$70	$120	$240	$425	$1,100
	Auctions: $2,115, MS-66, January 2013; $881, MS-65, September 2014; $558, MS-64, August 2014; $247, MS-62, October 2014												
1912, Proof	700	218	64.6								$450	$800	$1,900
	Auctions: $14,100, PF-68, August 2013; $2,820, PF-67Cam, November 2014; $3,173, PF-66Cam+, November 2014; $1,175, PF-66, October 2014												
1912S	708,000	98	55.3	67%	$20	$30	$65	$90	$125	$220	$400	$900	$1,500
	Auctions: $2,938, MS-66, August 2014; $1,234, MS-65, July 2014; $1,116, MS-64, August 2013												
1913	484,000	139	51.2	56%	$22	$35	$100	$180	$400	$525	$900	$1,200	$4,000
	Auctions: $4,700, MS-66, September 2014; $2,820, MS-65, August 2014; $499, EF-45, August 2014; $282, VF-35, September 2014												
1913, Proof	613	244	64.5								$450	$850	$1,900
	Auctions: $8,225, PF-67, February 2013; $1,410, PF-65Cam, October 2014; $1,410, PF-65, November 2014; $1,116, PF-64Cam, September 2014												
1913D	1,450,800	177	54.9	64%	$12	$15	$35	$60	$85	$175	$275	$450	$1,150
	Auctions: $7,050, MS-67, September 2014; $8,813, MS-67, June 2014; $353, MS-63, August 2014; $136, AU-53, November 2014												
1913S	40,000	454	10.9	9%	$1,650	$2,200	$5,000	$7,500	$10,000	$12,750	$15,000	$20,000	$30,000
	Auctions: $70,500, MS-67, June 2014; $6,463, VF-30, November 2014; $1,998, VG-10, November 2014; $1,293, G-6, October 2014												
1914	6,244,230	618	58.0	72%	$9	$10	$22	$40	$65	$115	$225	$400	$1,100
	Auctions: $4,113, MS-67, October 2014; $1,422, MS-66, July 2014; $470, MS-64, November 2014; $106, AU-55, July 2014												
1914, Proof	380	203	64.8								$450	$950	$2,100
	Auctions: $7,050, PF-68, October 2014; $14,100, PF-67Cam, April 2013; $2,938, PF-67, November 2014; $1,293, PF-65, August 2014												
1914D	3,046,000	327	58.0	73%	$9	$10	$22	$40	$65	$120	$240	$425	$1,100
	Auctions: $6,463, MS-67, October 2014; $410, MS-64, November 2014; $204, MS-61, November 2014; $165, AU-58, September 2014												
1914S	264,000	333	17.6	14%	$125	$180	$375	$550	$825	$975	$1,400	$1,650	$3,500
	Auctions: $19,975, MS-67, October 2014; $6,463, MS-65, August 2014; $1,645, EF-45, October 2014; $165, VG-8, November 2014												

	Mintage	Cert	Avg	%MS	G-4	VG-8	F-12	VF-20	EF-40	AU-50	MS-60	MS-63	MS-65
											PF-60	PF-63	PF-65
1915	3,480,000	452	58.9	77%	$9	$10	$22	$40	$65	$120	$240	$425	$1,200
	Auctions: $6,169, MS-67, July 2013; $1,240, MS-66, July 2014; $764, MS-65, October 2014; $470, MS-64, October 2014												
1915, Proof	450	174	64.3								$450	$1,000	$2,200
	Auctions: $19,975, PF-68, November 2013; $1,410, PF-65, September 2014; $617, PF-63, November 2014; $353, PF-60, November 2014												
1915D	3,694,000	619	59.4	77%	$9	$10	$22	$40	$70	$120	$240	$425	$1,100
	Auctions: $2,820, MS-67, November 2013; $470, MS-64+, November 2014; $159, AU-58, October 2014; $118, AU-50, November 2014												
1915S	704,000	192	54.1	63%	$25	$40	$60	$85	$115	$200	$285	$475	$1,300
	Auctions: $6,463, MS-66+, July 2014; $353, MS-63, November 2014; $62, VF-20, September 2014												
1916	1,788,000	415	59.7	75%	$9	$10	$22	$40	$70	$120	$240	$425	$1,000
	Auctions: $3,819, MS-67, October 2014; $7,638, MS-67, June 2014; $1,293, MS-66, November 2014; $76, AU-55, October 2014												
1916D	6,540,800	1,457	60.3	79%	$9	$10	$22	$40	$70	$120	$240	$425	$1,000
	Auctions: $9,400, MS-68, November 2013; $4,113, MS-67, November 2014; $1,469, MS-66, November 2014; $270, MS-61, September 2014												

STANDING LIBERTY (1916–1930)

Variety 1, No Stars Below Eagle (1916–1917): **Designer:** *Hermon A. MacNeil.*
Weight: *6.25 grams.* **Composition:** *.900 silver, .100 copper (net weight .18084 oz. pure silver).*
Diameter: *24.3 mm.* **Edge:** *Reeded.* **Mints:** *Philadelphia, Denver, San Francisco.*

**Variety 1, No Stars Below Eagle
(1916–1917)**

*Mintmark location is on the
obverse, at the top left of
the date, for both varieties.*

Variety 2, Stars Below Eagle (1917–1930): **Designer:** *Hermon A. MacNeil.*
Weight: *6.25 grams.* **Composition:** *.900 silver, .100 copper (net weight .18084 oz. pure silver).*
Diameter: *24.3 mm.* **Edge:** *Reeded.* **Mints:** *Philadelphia, Denver, San Francisco.*

**Variety 2, Stars Below Eagle
(1917–1930)**

History. The Standing Liberty quarter dollar, designed by sculptor Hermon A. MacNeil (whose initial, M, is located above and to the right of the date), was greeted with wide acclaimed from its first appearance. All of 1916 and many of 1917 are of the Variety 1 design, with the right breast of Miss Liberty exposed on the obverse and with no stars below the eagle on the reverse. Variety 2 of the Standing Liberty design was introduced in 1917 and continued to the end of the series. Miss Liberty is clothed in a jacket of chainmail armor, and the reverse is slightly redesigned, with stars below the eagle. These changes came at the suggestion of the designer, Hermon A. MacNeil.

Striking and Sharpness. Many if not most 1916 quarters are somewhat lightly struck on the head and body of Miss Liberty. The 1917, Variety 1, quarters usually are quite well struck. When light striking is found, it is usually on the higher-relief parts of the head, the right knee (not as obvious), and the rivets on the left side of the shield. The 1917 Philadelphia Mint coins are usually sharper than the other varieties of this type. Most coins of the Variety 2 design have areas of light striking. On the obverse these are most notable on the head of Miss Liberty and on the shield, the latter often with the two lower-left rivets weak or missing and with the center emblem on the shield weak. The center of the standing figure can be weak as well, as can the upper-left area at and near the date. After 1924 the date was slightly recessed, eliminating that problem. On the reverse, check the eagle's breast. A misleading term, Full Head (FH), is widely used to describe quarters that have only *partial* head details; such coins often actually have the two lower-left shield rivets poorly struck or not visible at all. Most third-party grading services define these criteria for "Full Head" designation (in order of importance): a full, unbroken hairline from Liberty's brow down to the jawline; all three leaves on the head showing; and a visible ear hole.

Availability. The 1916 quarter is the key to the series. Examples tend to be liberally graded in the real-life marketplace, especially in EF and AU, this in contrast to more careful grading for the less valuable 1917 issues. Circulated coins of 1916 and 1917 often have the date worn partly away, due to the high position of this feature in the design. Among Variety 2 coins, the 1918-S, 8 Over 7, is recognized as the key issue, and the 1919-D, 1921, 1923-S, and 1927-S as quite scarce. MS coins are readily available for most issues, but Full Details coins can be *extreme* rarities. Circulated coins dated from 1917 through 1924 often have the date worn partly away, due to the high position of this feature in the design. On MS coins the luster usually is rich and attractive. No Proof coins of this type were officially issued, but specimen strikings dated 1917 are known to exist.

GRADING STANDARDS

MS-60 to 70 (Mint State). *Obverse:* At MS-60 some abrasion and contact marks are evident on the higher areas, which are also the areas most likely to be weakly struck. This includes the rivets on the shield to the left and the central escutcheon on the shield, the head, and the right leg of Miss Liberty. The luster may not be complete in those areas on weakly struck coins, even those certified above MS-65—the *original planchet surface*

1917, No Stars. Graded MS-67.

may be revealed as it was not smoothed out by striking. Accordingly, grading is best done by evaluating abrasion and mint luster as it is observed. Luster may be dull or lifeless at MS-60 to 62 but should have deep frost at MS-63 or better, particularly in the lower-relief areas. At MS-65 or better, it should be full and rich. *Reverse:* Striking is usually quite good, permitting observation of luster in all areas. Check the eagle's breast and the surface of the right wing. Luster may be dull or lifeless at MS-60 to 62 but should have deep frost at MS-63 or better, particularly in the lower-relief areas. At MS-65 or better, it should be full and rich.

Illustrated coin: This gorgeous coin has sharply struck details and full luster.

AU-50, 53, 55, 58 (About Uncirculated).
Obverse: Light wear is seen on the figure of Miss Liberty, especially noticeable around her midriff and right knee. The shield shows wear, as does the highest part of the sash where it crosses Miss Liberty's waist. At AU-58 the luster is extensive, but incomplete on the higher areas, although it should be nearly full in the panels of the parapet to the left and right, and in the upper field. At AU-50 and 53, luster is

1916. Graded AU-55.

less. *Reverse:* Wear is most evident on the eagle's breast, the edges of both wings, and the interior area of the right wing. Luster is nearly complete at AU-58, but at AU-50, half or more is gone.

Illustrated coin: The original luster is still present in some areas of this lightly struck coin.

EF-40, 45 (Extremely Fine). *Obverse:* Wear is more extensive, with the higher parts of Miss Liberty now without detail and the front of the right leg flat. The shield is worn. On coins dated from 1917 to 1924 the date shows wear at the top (on those of 1925 to 1930, with the date recessed, the numbers are bold). Little or no luster is seen, except perhaps among the letters. *Reverse:* The eagle shows more wear, with the surface of the right wing being mostly flat. Little or no luster is evident.

1927-S. Graded EF-40.

VF-20, 30 (Very Fine). *Obverse:* Wear is more extensive. The higher-relief areas of Miss Liberty are flat, and the sash crossing her waist is mostly blended into it (some sharply struck pieces being exceptions). The left side of the shield is mostly flat, although its outline can be seen. On quarters dated 1917 to 1924 the top of the date shows more wear. *Reverse:* The eagle shows further wear, with the body blending into the wing above

1927-S. Graded VF-20.

it. Much feather detail is gone from the wing to the left (on quarters dated 1925 to 1930; less so for those dated 1917 to 1924). Most detail is gone from the right wing.

F-12, 15 (Fine). *Obverse:* Miss Liberty is worn nearly flat. Most detail in her gown is gone, except to the left of her leg and below her knee to the right. The stars on the parapet are well worn, with some indistinct. The top of the date is weak. Quarters of the rare 1916 date are slightly weaker than those of 1917 in this and lower grades. On quarters of 1917 to 1924 the top of the date is weak. On those dated 1925 to 1930 the date remains strong.

1916. Graded F-12.

Reverse: The eagle shows further wear, this being greater on 1925 to 1930 issues than on the earlier dates.

VG-8, 10 (Very Good). *Obverse:* The obverse is worn further, with fewer details in the skirt, and part of the shield border to the left blended into the standing figure. The date is partially worn away at the top, and quarters from 1917 to 1924 have less detail. Those from 1925 to 1930 retain more detail, and the date is full. *Reverse:* The eagle is worn further, with only about a third of the feathers now discernible, these mostly on the wing to the left.

1917, No Stars. Graded VG-8.

G-4, 6 (Good). *Obverse:* The wear is more extensive. Most coins have the stars missing, the standing figure flat, and much of the date worn away, although still clearly identifiable. Quarters of 1925 to 1930 show more detail and the date is clear. *Reverse:* The eagle is mostly in outline form, with only a few feather details visible. The rim is worn into the letters, and on quarters of 1916 to 1924, E PLURIBUS UNUM is very faint; it is clear on quarters of later dates.

1927. Graded G-6.

AG-3 (About Good). *Obverse:* The obverse is worn nearly smooth, and the date is mostly gone. On some coins just one or two digits are seen. Fortunately, those digits are usually on the right, such as a trace of just a 6, which will identify the coin as a 1916. On quarters of 1925 to 1930 the wear is more extensive than for G-4, but most features are discernible and the date is clear. *Reverse:* The eagle is flat, and the border is worn down further.

1927. Graded AG-3.

On quarters of 1916 to 1924, E PLURIBUS UNUM is extremely faint or even missing in areas; it remains readable on quarters of later dates.

Full Head Details, Variety 1
Note the excellently defined cheek, facial features, and wreath.

Full Head Details, Variety 2
Note the full unbroken hairline from brow to neck, all three leaves clearly visible in Liberty's cap, and a visible ear hole.

Pedestal Date
(1917–1924)

Recessed Date
(1925–1930)

1918-S, 8 Over 7
FS-25-1918S-101.

	Mintage	Cert	Avg	%MS	G-4	VG-8	F-12	VF-20	EF-40	AU-50	MS-60	MS-63	MS-65FH
1916 †	52,000	855	45.2	49%	$9	$10	$22	$40	$70	$120	$240	$425	
	Auctions: $49,938, MS-66FH, June 2014; $41,125, MS-66FH, November 2014; $18,800, MS-63FH, September 2014												
1917, Variety 1	8,740,000	6,253	60.5	81%	$25	$45	$65	$90	$110	$200	$250	$350	$1,100
	Auctions: $4,406, MS-67FH, July 2014; $4,553, MS-67FH, September 2014; $25,850, MS-67FH, August 2013; $1,645, MS-66FH, October 2014												
1917D, Variety 1	1,509,200	1,803	59.8	76%	$30	$55	$80	$120	$200	$250	$325	$425	$2,000
	Auctions: $5,581, MS-67FH, August 2014; $4,994, MS-67FH, September 2013; $2,585, MS-66FH, September 2014; $3,525, MS-66FH, October 2014												
1917S, Variety 1	1,952,000	1,116	56.5	69%	$40	$70	$110	$150	$210	$285	$350	$475	$3,200
	Auctions: $9,400, MS-67FH, September 2013; $5,288, MS-66FH, August 2014; $3,055, MS-66FH, October 2014; $2,415, MS-65FH, July 2014												
1917, Variety 2	13,880,000	1,498	60.9	79%	$25	$40	$55	$70	$100	$150	$210	$275	$900
	Auctions: $9,988, MS-67FH, August 2014; $7,638, MS-67FH, September 2013; $2,115, MS-66FH, October 2014; $1,586, MS-66FH, November 2014												
1917D, Variety 2	6,224,400	806	59.1	69%	$45	$55	$85	$110	$150	$210	$260	$350	$3,000
	Auctions: $8,519, MS-66FH, October 2014; $7,931, MS-66FH, June 2013; $1,528, MS-66, August 2014; $1,058, MS-65, October 2014												
1917S, Variety 2	5,552,000	758	59.9	72%	$45	$60	$90	$120	$160	$225	$260	$350	$3,250
	Auctions: $45,825, MS-67FH, January 2013; $8,519, MS-66FH, October 2014; $2,833, MS-65FH, July 2014; $3,055, MS-65FH, October 2014												
1918	14,240,000	848	61.1	77%	$20	$25	$30	$35	$55	$90	$140	$225	$1,650
	Auctions: $58,750, MS-68FH, February 2013; $4,700, MS-66FH, July 2014; $3,966, MS-66FH, October 2014; $558, MS-64FH+, October 2014												
1918D	7,380,000	695	58.6	64%	$25	$40	$75	$90	$145	$200	$275	$400	$4,000
	Auctions: $32,900, MS-67FH, May 2013; $2,827, MS-65FH, October 2014; $1,528, MS-64FH, August 2014; $940, MS-64FH, August 2014												
1918S	11,072,000	925	56.9	65%	$20	$25	$35	$45	$60	$120	$200	$300	$12,000
	Auctions: $58,750, MS-66FH, October 2014; $35,250, MS-66FH, February 2013; $5,875, MS-65FH, November 2014												
1918S, 8 Over 7 † (a)	(b)	336	41.0	20%	$1,600	$2,200	$3,600	$5,000	$8,000	$13,000	$19,000	$32,500	$250,000
	Auctions: $188,000, MS-64FH, June 2014; $24,675, AU-58FH, July 2014; $3,819, VF-20, October 2014												
1919	11,324,000	1,074	61.1	79%	$35	$45	$60	$80	$100	$135	$185	$250	$1,500
	Auctions: $36,719, MS-69, April 2013; $8,225, MS-67FH, August 2014; $3,819, MS-66FH+, October 2014; $2,233, MS-65FH, July 2014												
1919D	1,944,000	450	48.5	40%	$85	$120	$200	$400	$600	$800	$950	$1,500	$35,000
	Auctions: $42,594, MS-65FH, June 2014; $19,975, MS-64FH+, August 2014; $2,350, MS-64, November 2014; $4,406, AU-58FH, August 2014												
1919S	1,836,000	470	49.0	37%	$80	$110	$175	$350	$550	$750	$900	$1,500	$30,000
	Auctions: $258,500, MS-67FH, April 2014; $16,450, MS-64FH, September 2014; $6,463, MS-63FH, August 2014; $2,585, MS-60, August 2014												

† Ranked in the *100 Greatest U.S. Coins* (fourth edition). **a.** This clear overdate was caused by the use of two differently dated hubs when the die was made. "Because of the boldness of the 7, this variety can be confirmed easily in low grades. . . . This variety is extremely rare in high grades. We recommend authentication because alterations do exist. Genuine specimens have a small die chip above the pedestal, just to the left of the lowest star on the right" (*Cherrypickers' Guide to Rare Die Varieties*, sixth edition, volume II). **b.** Included in 1918-S mintage figure.

	Mintage	Cert	Avg	%MS	G-4	VG-8	F-12	VF-20	EF-40	AU-50	MS-60	MS-63	MS-65FH
1920	27,860,000	1,681	61.4	79%	$15	$20	$30	$35	$55	$100	$160	$230	$1,500
	Auctions: $29,375, 67FH, August 2014; $11,163, MS-67, February 2014; $3,819, MS-66FH, September 2014; $4,113, MS-66FH, October 2014												
1920D	3,586,400	383	54.4	58%	$50	$60	$80	$120	$165	$225	$350	$800	$6,500
	Auctions: $19,975, MS-66FH, October 2014; $16,450, MS-66FH, April 2013; $1,116, MS-63, July 2014; $705, AU-58, September 2014												
1920S	6,380,000	553	58.2	65%	$20	$25	$35	$50	$65	$140	$270	$750	$20,000
	Auctions: $99,875, MS-66FH, October 2014; $17,625, MS-65FH, June 2013; $2,468, MS-63FH, September 2014; $588, MS-63, October 2014												
1921	1,916,000	1,001	45.5	45%	$175	$225	$475	$700	$800	$1,150	$1,600	$2,200	$5,500
	Auctions: $52,875, MS-67FH, November 2013; $2,820, MS-63FH, August 2014; $1,293, AU-58, October 2014; $999, AU-58, November 2014												
1923	9,716,000	1,496	61.7	84%	$15	$20	$30	$38	$55	$100	$170	$240	$4,000
	Auctions: $19,975, MS-67FH, August 2014; $29,375, MS-67FH, February 2013; $353, MS-62FH, July 2014; $676, MS-66, November 2014												
1923S	1,360,000	764	49.6	46%	$280	$425	$740	$1,100	$1,500	$2,000	$2,600	$3,400	$6,500
	Auctions: $21,150, MS-66FH, February 2013; $4,406, MS-66, October 2014; $4,113, MS-66, November 2014; $3,055, MS-64, November 2014												
1924	10,920,000	1,079	61.2	82%	$15	$20	$25	$35	$55	$110	$185	$275	$1,500
	Auctions: $16,450, MS-68, May 2013; $4,847, MS-67FH, July 2014; $2,820, MS-66FH, August 2014; $4,700, MS-66FH, October 2014												
1924D	3,112,000	1,511	62.7	90%	$55	$70	$100	$140	$195	$230	$325	$375	$4,500
	Auctions: $35,250, MS-67FH, February 2013; $11,163, MS-66FH, October 2014; $10,869, MS-66FH, November 2014; $3,055, MS-65FH, October 2014												
1924S	2,860,000	574	59.4	71%	$26	$33	$45	$65	$130	$250	$350	$900	$5,500
	Auctions: $12,925, MS-65FH, January 2014; $8,813, MS-65FH, October 2014; $6,463, MS-65FH, November 2014; $2,820, MS-64FH, October 2014												
1925	12,280,000	1,178	61.4	83%	$7.50	$8	$10	$20	$45	$100	$160	$250	$1,000
	Auctions: $8,519, MS-67FH, November 2014; $12,925, MS-67FH, September 2013; $341, MS-63FH, September 2014; $306, MS-63FH, December 2014												
1926	11,316,000	1,208	61.5	81%	$7.50	$8	$9	$20	$45	$90	$150	$250	$2,000
	Auctions: $27,025, MS-67FH, November 2013; $1,175, MS-65FH, November 2014; $353, MS-65, November 2014; $588, MS-65, December 2014												
1926D	1,716,000	2,181	63.1	97%	$7.50	$10	$22	$40	$80	$140	$180	$250	$24,000
	Auctions: $105,750, MS-67FH, April 2014; $646, MS-66, July 2014; $364, MS-64, July 2014; $282, MS-64, July 2014												
1926S	2,700,000	416	56.3	61%	$7.50	$10	$15	$28	$110	$225	$350	$775	$25,000
	Auctions: $48,175, MS-66FH, February 2013; $17,038, MS-65FH, September 2014; $911, MS-63, September 2014; $764, AU-58, July 2014												
1927	11,912,000	1,416	60.6	78%	$7.50	$8	$9	$17	$35	$80	$140	$225	$1,100
	Auctions: $15,275, MS-67FH, February 2013; $2,585, MS-66FH, October 2014; $558, MS-64FH, October 2014; $364, MS-64FH, November 2014												
1927D	976,000	953	60.6	88%	$15	$20	$30	$75	$150	$220	$270	$310	$3,000
	Auctions: $16,450, MS-67FH, October 2014; $764, MS-66, September 2014; $882, MS-66, November 2014												
1927S	396,000	1,086	28.6	14%	$40	$50	$130	$350	$1,100	$2,800	$5,000	$7,000	$150,000
	Auctions: $258,500, MS-66FH, August 2014; $94,000, MS-65FH, April 2014; $176,250, MS-65FH, October 2014; $11,750, MS-66, July 2014												
1928	6,336,000	929	61.3	80%	$7.50	$8	$9	$17	$40	$80	$140	$225	$1,750
	Auctions: $5,875, MS-67FH, November 2013; $3,290, MS-66FH, August 2014; $441, MS-64FH, October 2014; $259, MS-62FH, August 2014												
1928D	1,627,600	1,437	63.2	93%	$7.50	$8	$9	$17	$35	$80	$150	$235	$5,000
	Auctions: $4,113, MS-67, February 2014; $529, MS-66, July 2014; $517, MS-66, October 2014; $411, MS-65, September 2014												
1928S (c)	2,644,000	1,361	63.1	91%	$7.50	$8	$9	$22	$40	$90	$140	$235	$900
	Auctions: $2,350, MS-67FH, August 2014; $3,525, MS-67FH, April 2013; $823, MS-65FH, November 2014; $678, MS-64FH, October 2014												
1929	11,140,000	1,798	61.6	82%	$7.50	$8	$9	$17	$35	$80	$140	$225	$800
	Auctions: $1,528, MS-66, November 2013; $676, MS-65FH, July 2014; $630, MS-65FH, October 2014; $623, MS-65FH, December 2014												
1929D	1,358,000	969	60.9	77%	$7.50	$8	$9	$17	$40	$80	$140	$230	$5,000
	Auctions: $7,050, MS-65FH, April 2013; $646, MS-66, July 2014; $646, MS-66, November 2014; $411, MS-65, July 2014												
1929S	1,764,000	1,364	61.8	84%	$7.50	$8	$9	$17	$35	$80	$140	$225	$850
	Auctions: $7,050, MS-67FH, April 2013; $3,055, MS-67FH, July 2014; $4,994, MS-66FH, October 2014; $558, MS-64FH, October 2014												
1930	5,632,000	3,410	61.9	80%	$7.50	$8	$9	$17	$35	$80	$140	$225	$800
	Auctions: $5,288, MS-67FH, July 2014; $4,406, MS-67FH, October 2014; $3,055, MS-67FH, November 2014; $1,175, MS-66FH+, August 2014												
1930S	1,556,000	1,042	62.0	85%	$7.50	$8	$9	$17	$35	$80	$140	$225	$800
	Auctions: $10,575, MS-68FH, August 2014; $2,375, MS-67FH, July 2014; $3,819, MS-67FH, November 2013; $2,585, MS-66FH, November 2014												

c. Large and small mintmarks exist; their values are the same.

WASHINGTON, EAGLE REVERSE (1932–1998)

Designer: *John Flanagan.* **Weight:** *Silver issue—6.25 grams; clad issue—5.67 grams; silver Proofs—6.25 grams.* **Composition:** *Silver issue—.900 silver, .100 copper (net weight .18084 oz. pure silver); clad issue—outer layers of copper nickel (.750 copper, .250 nickel) bonded to inner core of pure copper; silver Proofs—.900 silver, .100 copper (net weight .18084 oz. pure silver).* **Diameter:** *24.3 mm.* **Edge:** *Reeded.* **Mints:** *Silver issue—Philadelphia, Denver, San Francisco; silver Proofs—San Francisco.*

Circulation Strike   Proof

 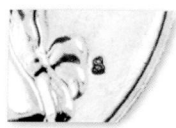

Mintmark location,   Mintmark location,
1932–1964, is   1965 to date, is on
on the reverse,   the obverse, to right
below the eagle.   of the hair ribbon.

Bicentennial variety: Designers: *John Flanagan and Jack L. Ahr.* **Weight:** *Silver issue—5.75 grams; copper-nickel issue—5.67 grams.* **Composition:** *Silver issue—outer layers of .800 silver, .200 copper bonded to inner core of .209 silver, .791 copper (net weight .0739 oz. pure silver); copper-nickel issue—outer layers of .750 copper, .250 nickel bonded to inner core of pure copper.* **Diameter:** *24.3 mm.* **Edge:** *Reeded.*

Bicentennial variety   Bicentennial variety, Proof

History. The Washington quarter, designed by New York sculptor John Flanagan, originally was intended to be a commemorative coin, but it ultimately was produced as a regular circulation issue. The obverse is inspired by a famous bust by Jean Antoine Houdon. Flanagan's initials, JF, are at the base of Washington's neck. The reverse features a modernistic eagle perched on a quiver of arrows, with wings unfolding. In October 1973, the Treasury Department announced an open contest for the selection of suitable designs for the Bicentennial reverses of the quarter, half dollar, and dollar, with $5,000 to be awarded to each winner. Twelve semifinalists were chosen, and from these the symbolic entry of Jack L. Ahr was selected for the quarter reverse. It features a military drummer facing left, with a victory torch encircled by 13 stars at the upper left. Except for the dual dating, "1776–1976," the obverse remained unchanged. Pieces with this dual dating were coined during 1975 and 1976. They were struck for general circulation and included in all the U.S. Mint's offerings of Proof and Uncirculated coin sets. (The grading instructions below are for the regular Eagle Reverse variety.)

Striking and Sharpness. The relief of both sides of the Washington quarter issues from 1932 to 1998 is shallow. Accordingly, any lightness of strike is not easily seen. Nearly all are well struck. On all quarters of 1932 and some of 1934, the motto IN GOD WE TRUST is light, as per the design. It was strengthened in 1934.

Availability. The 1932-D and S are key issues but not rarities. All others are readily available in high grades, but some are scarcer than others. Proof dates available are 1936 to 1942 and 1950 to 1964 (from the Philadelphia Mint) and 1968 to 1998 (from San Francisco). Certain later Proofs are available in clad metal as well as silver strikings. Special Mint Set (SMS) coins were struck in lieu of Proofs from 1965 to 1967; these in some instances closely resemble Proofs. The majority of Proofs made in recent decades are in high levels, PF-66 to 68 or higher.

Note: Values of common-date silver coins have been based on the current bullion price of silver, $17 per ounce, and may vary with the prevailing spot price.

GRADING STANDARDS

MS-60 to 70 (Mint State). *Obverse:* At MS-60, some abrasion and contact marks are evident on the hair above the ear and at the top of the head below E of LIBERTY. At MS-63, abrasion is slight at best, less so for MS-64. An MS-65 coin should display no abrasion or contact marks except under magnification, and MS-66 and higher coins should have none at all. Luster should be full and rich. *Reverse:* Comments apply as for the

1932-S. Graded MS-64.

obverse, except that the eagle's breast and legs are the places to check. On both sides the fields are protected by design elements and do not show contact marks readily.

Illustrated coin: This is a brilliant and lustrous example with excellent eye appeal.

AU-50, 53, 55, 58 (About Uncirculated). *Obverse:* Light wear is seen on the cheek, the high areas of the hair, and the neck. At AU-58, the luster is extensive but incomplete, especially on the higher parts and in the field. At AU-50 and 53, luster is less. *Reverse:* Light wear is seen on the breast, legs, and upper edges of the wings of the eagle. An AU-58 coin has nearly full luster. At AU-50 and 53, there still is significant luster.

1932-D. Graded AU-53.

Illustrated coin: Some of the original luster remains on the obverse of this example, while most of the luster remains on the reverse.

EF-40, 45 (Extremely Fine). *Obverse:* Further wear is seen on the head. Higher-relief details are gone in the hair. The higher-relief parts of the neck show wear, most noticeably just above the date. *Reverse:* Further wear is seen on the eagle. Most breast feathers, not strong to begin with, are worn away.

1940. Graded EF-40.

VF-20, 30 (Very Fine). *Obverse:* Most hair detail is worn away, except above the curls. The delineation between the temple and the edge of the hair is faint. The curl by the ear is worn flat. Tips of the letters in LIBERTY and the date digits touch the rim in some instances. *Reverse:* More details of the eagle are worn away, and the outlines of the feathers in the wing, while nearly all present, are faint. Tips of the letters touch the rim in

1937. Graded VF-20.

some instances on this and lower grades, but this can vary from coin to coin depending on the strength of the rim.

F-12, 15 (Fine). *Obverse:* Most of the hair is worn flat, with no distinction between the face and the beginning of the hair. There is some detail remaining just above and below the curls. *Reverse:* More feathers are worn away. The end of the branch at the left is worn so as to blend into the wing. The edge of the rim is barely visible and in some areas is worn away. (In this and the Very Good grade, opinions concerning the rim vary in the ANA grading standards and in *Photograde*; PCGS is silent on the matter.)

1934, Doubled-Die Obverse. Graded F-12.

VG-8, 10 (Very Good). *Obverse:* Further wear is seen on the head, with most of the upper part of the curls now blending into the hair above. *Reverse:* The rim is worn into the tops of the letters. There is no detail on the leaves. About half of the feathers are outlined, but only faintly.

1935-D. Graded VG-8.

G-4, 6 (Good). *Obverse:* Further wear is seen in all areas. On 1932 and some 1934 coins the IN GOD WE TRUST motto is so worn that some letters are missing. *Reverse:* The rim is worn further into the letters. Fewer details are seen on the eagle's wing. On both sides the coin appears to be "worn flat," with little in relief.

1932-D. Graded G-4.

AG-3 (About Good). *Obverse:* Wear is more extensive, with about half of the letters gone. *Reverse:* Wear is more extensive, with about half of the letters gone. Slight detail remains in the eagle's wings. The mintmark, if any, is very clear.

1942. Graded AG-3.

PF-60 to 70 (Proof). *Obverse and Reverse:* Proofs that are extensively cleaned and have many hairlines, or that are dull and grainy, are lower level, such as PF-60 to 62. These are not widely desired, and represent coins that have been mistreated. Most low-level Proofs are of the 1936 to 1942 dates. With medium hairlines and good reflectivity, assigned grades of PF-63 or 64 are appropriate. PF-66 should have hairlines so delicate that magnification is needed to see them. Above that, a Proof should be free of any hairlines or other problems.

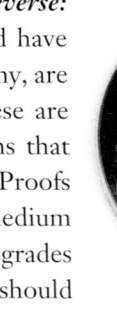

1938. Graded PF-66.

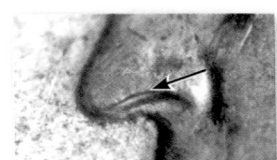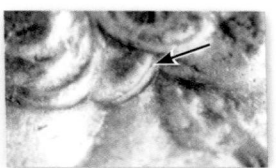

1932, Doubled-Die Obverse
FS-25-1932-101.

	Mintage	Cert	Avg	%MS	VG-8	F-12	VF-20	EF-40	AU-50	MS-60	MS-62	MS-63	MS-65
1932	5,404,000	1,883	62.6	87%	$8	$9	$10	$11	$15	$25	$40	$60	$325
	Auctions: $3,525, MS-66, July 2014; $999, MS-65, August 2014; $6,463, AU-50, November 2013												
1932, DblDie Obv (a)	**(b)**	21	56.2	24%						$350	$400	$500	$800
	Auctions: $235, MS-62, December 2013												
1932D	436,800	3,620	41.6	30%	$175	$190	$250	$300	$400	$1,100	$1,400	$1,750	$10,000
	Auctions: $12,338, MS-65, January 2014; $8,519, MS-65, August 2014; $3,525, MS-64+, October 2014; $1,788, MS-64, November 2014												
1932S	408,000	4,435	48.2	43%	$175	$190	$225	$275	$300	$450	$600	$750	$5,000
	Auctions: $2,585, MS-65, September 2014; $940, MS-64, July 2014; $917, MS-64, October 2014; $705, MS-63, November 2014												

a. The doubling is evident on the earlobe, the nostril, and the braid of hair. **b.** Included in 1932 mintage figure.

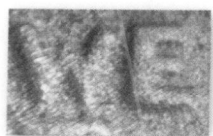

1934, Doubled-Die Obverse
FS-25-1934-101.

1934, Light Motto
FS-25-1934-401.

1934, Heavy Motto
FS-25-1934-403.

	Mintage	Cert	Avg	%MS	VG-8	F-12	VF-20	EF-40	AU-50	MS-60	MS-62	MS-63	MS-65
1934, All kinds	31,912,052												
1934, Doubled-Die Obverse (c)		192	42.1	33%	$75	$85	$200	$300	$600	$1,000	$1,650	$1,900	$4,250
Auctions: $6,463, MS-66, October 2014; $3,055, MS-65, June 2013; $940, MS-62, August 2014; $235, AU-55, August 2014													
1934, Light Motto (d)		297	63.5	90%	$7.50	$7.75	$8	$10	$24	$60	$80	$135	$385
Auctions: $8,813, MS-67, January 2014; $3,173, MS-67, August 2014; $2,879, MS-67, September 2014													
1934, Heavy Motto (e)		58	62.7	79%	$7.50	$7.75	$8	$10	$15	$30	$40	$50	$135
Auctions: $6,463, MS-67, April 2014; $470, MS-66, September 2014; $88, MS-65, August 2014; $118, MS-64, July 2014													
1934D	3,527,200	1,262	61.3	78%	$7.50	$8	$12	$25	$85	$250	$280	$340	$850
Auctions: $14,100, MS-67, June 2013; $1,200, MS-66, August 2014; $505, MS-65, September 2014; $499, MS-65, September 2014													
1935	32,484,000	1,906	64.5	94%	$7.50	$7.75	$8	$9	$10	$22	$30	$35	$135
Auctions: $3,819, MS-67, January 2014; $705, MS-67, July 2014; $3,525, MS-67+, September 2014; $588, MS-67, October 2014													
1935D	5,780,000	1,207	61.8	82%	$7.50	$8	$10	$20	$125	$240	$265	$275	$650
Auctions: $4,700, MS-67, March 2014; $7,050, MS-67+, September 2014; $2,350, MS-67, October 2014													
1935S	5,660,000	1,342	62.7	84%	$7.50	$8	$9	$15	$38	$100	$120	$135	$300
Auctions: $1,528, MS-67, September 2014; $1,528, MS-67, October 2014; $2,820, MS-67, August 2013; $456, MS-66, October 2014													

c. Very strong doubling is visible on the motto, LIBERTY, and the date. **d.** "Notice the considerable weakness in the letters of the motto. In addition, the center point of the W is pointed" (*Cherrypickers' Guide to Rare Die Varieties*, sixth edition, volume II). **e.** The motto has very thick letters, and the central apex of the W is pointed, rising slightly above the other letters.

1937, Doubled-Die Obverse
FS-25-1937-101.

	Mintage	Cert	Avg	%MS	EF-40	AU-50	MS-60	MS-63	MS-65 / PF-64	MS-66 / PF-65	MS-67 / PF-67
1936	41,300,000	1,677	64.7	96%	$8	$10	$25	$35	$120	$200	$550
Auctions: $2,350, MS-67, February 2014; $441, MS-67, July 2014; $382, MS-67, September 2014; $123, MS-66, September 2014											
1936, Proof	3,837	962	64.3						$1,000	$1,250	$9,500
Auctions: $7,638, PF-67, June 2013; $1,939, PF-66, September 2014; $1,763, PF-66, October 2014; $1,087, PF-65, August 2014											
1936D	5,374,000	1,125	60.6	76%	$55	$250	$525	$800	$1,200	$1,900	$8,000
Auctions: $9,400, MS-67, June 2013; $2,115, MS-66+, July 2014; $1,763, MS-66, September 2014; $1,410, MS-66, November 2014											
1936S	3,828,000	1,364	63.9	96%	$15	$50	$120	$140	$325	$650	$3,000
Auctions: $4,994, MS-67+, August 2014; $1,528, MS-67, August 2014; $3,525, MS-67, March 2013; $411, MS-66, August 2014											
1937	19,696,000	1,099	64.5	96%	$8	$12	$25	$35	$90	$200	$900
Auctions: $5,875, MS-67, February 2014; $588, MS-67, August 2014; $940, MS-67, September 2014											
1937, Doubled-Die Obverse (a)	**(b)**	47	27.3	13%	$700	$1,500	$2,450	$3,800	$12,000	$18,000	
Auctions: $1,778, MS-63, April 2013; $188, F-12, November 2014											
1937, Proof	5,542	946	65.1						$370	$475	$1,200
Auctions: $16,450, PF-68, June 2013; $764, PF-67, July 2014; $1,293, PF-67, September 2014; $353, PF-65, October 2014											
1937D	7,189,600	1,145	64.0	95%	$15	$30	$70	$90	$150	$400	$2,750
Auctions: $4,700, MS-67, January 2014; $1,293, MS-67, September 2014; $1,293, MS-67, November 2014											
1937S	1,652,000	1,111	63.4	93%	$35	$95	$150	$250	$400	$800	$3,000
Auctions: $2,115, MS-67, July 2014; $1,645, MS-67, October 2014; $1,293, MS-67, November 2014; $5,581, MS-67, June 2013											

a. Very strong doubling is evident on the motto, LIBERTY, the date, and the end of the braid ribbons. "This variety is considered one of the most important in the series" (*Cherrypickers' Guide to Rare Die Varieties*, sixth edition, volume II). **b.** Included in circulation-strike 1937 mintage figure.

1942-D, Doubled-Die Obverse
FS-25-1942D-101.

1942-D, Doubled-Die Reverse
FS-25-1942D-801.

	Mintage	Cert	Avg	%MS	EF-40	AU-50	MS-60	MS-63	MS-65 / PF-64	MS-66 / PF-65	MS-67 / PF-67
1938	9,472,000	1,061	63.6	91%	$15	$45	$95	$110	$210	$375	$1,650
	Auctions: $3,819, MS-67, June 2014; $823, MS-67, August 2014; $1,293, MS-67, October 2014; $764, MS-67, November 2014										
1938, Proof	8,045	1,219	65.0						$200	$275	$900
	Auctions: $7,050, PF-68, June 2013; $1,645, PF-67, August 2014; $1,116, PF-67, September 2014; $212, PF-66, October 2014										
1938S	2,832,000	1,341	64.2	96%	$20	$55	$105	$140	$230	$375	$1,800
	Auctions: $793, MS-67, September 2014; $705, MS-67, September 2014; $676, MS-67, November 2014; $1,763, MS-67, June 2013										
1939	33,540,000	1,824	65.2	97%	$8	$12	$15	$25	$60	$100	$350
	Auctions: $8,225, MS-68, August 2014; $3,819, MS-68, October 2014; $1,058, MS-67+, September 2014; $2,115, MS-67, August 2013										
1939, Proof	8,795	1,202	65.4						$175	$235	$675
	Auctions: $11,750, PF-68, June 2013; $823, PF-67, July 2014; $646, PF-67, September 2014; $177, PF-66, August 2014										
1939D	7,092,000	1,352	64.7	97%	$11	$20	$40	$50	$115	$185	$1,000
	Auctions: $823, MS-67, August 2014; $470, MS-67, September 2014; $141, MS-66, August 2014; $108, MS-66, November 2014										
1939S	2,628,000	1,111	63.9	93%	$20	$60	$95	$135	$310	$500	$2,800
	Auctions: $1,293, MS-67, August 2014; $1,187, MS-67, September 2014; $4,113, MS-67, February 2013; $353, MS-66+, September 2014										
1940	35,704,000	1,338	65.1	97%	$8	$9	$17	$35	$60	$120	$425
	Auctions: $1,175, MS-67+, July 2014; $940, MS-67, November 2014; $3,055, MS-67, April 2013; $79, MS-66, November 2014										
1940, Proof	11,246	1,456	65.4						$120	$175	$440
	Auctions: $3,819, PF-68, November 2013; $499, PF-67, September 2014; $499, PF-67, October 2014; $123, PF-66, November 2014										
1940D	2,797,600	1,192	64.2	95%	$24	$65	$120	$165	$300	$425	$2,400
	Auctions: $5,288, MS-67, April 2014; $1,058, MS-67, July 2014; $1,116, MS-67+, August 2014; $999, MS-67, September 2014										
1940S	8,244,000	1,177	65.2	97%	$9	$16	$21	$32	$65	$120	$1,000
	Auctions: $1,058, MS-67, September 2014; $529, MS-67, November 2014; $3,067, MS-67, August 2013; $86, MS-66, November 2014										
1941	79,032,000	1,592	65.3	98%	$7.50	$8	$10	$14	$45	$80	$425
	Auctions: $18,800, MS-68, November 2013; $1,528, MS-67+, July 2014; $1,880, MS-67+, August 2014; $306, MS-67, September 2014										
1941, Proof	15,287	1,777	65.4						$100	$140	$440
	Auctions: $14,100, PF-68, June 2013; $377, PF-67, November 2014; $353, PF-67, November 2014; $118, PF-66, September 2014										
1941D	16,714,800	971	64.9	97%	$8	$13	$32	$55	$70	$215	$2,250
	Auctions: $881, MS-67, November 2014; $3,525, MS-67, April 2013; $113, MS-66, September 2014; $123, MS-66, November 2014										
1941S	16,080,000	1,155	64.7	96%	$8	$11	$28	$55	$70	$190	$1,600
	Auctions: $10,281, MS-68, January 2014; $1,880, MS-67, September 2014; $411, MS-67, November 2014; $365, MS-67, November 2014										
1942	102,096,000	1,172	64.8	96%	$7.50	$7	$9	$10	$35	$200	$1,800
	Auctions: $705, MS-67, September 2014; $1,763, MS-67+, November 2014; $3,525, MS-67, November 2013										
1942, Proof	21,123	2,185	65.2						$100	$135	$400
	Auctions: $12,925, PF-68, June 2013; $3,055, PF-67+, September 2014; $341, PF-67, October 2014; $259, PF-67, December 2014										
1942D	17,487,200	1,211	65.2	99%	$8	$10	$17	$20	$40	$200	$925
	Auctions: $3,819, MS-67, January 2014; $306, MS-67, August 2014; $764, MS-67, September 2014; $282, MS-67, October 2014										
1942D, DblDie Obv (c)	**(d)**	51	32.2	8%	$350	$750	$1,800	$4,000	$6,000	$10,500	
	Auctions: $823, MS-64, June 2014; $1,207, AU-55, April 2013; $188, AU-50, August 2014										
1942D, DblDie Rev (e)	**(d)**	20	45.6	40%		$385	$750	$1,250	$2,250	$5,400	
	Auctions: $5,875, MS-66, August 2013										
1942S	19,384,000	1,255	64.1	93%	$10	$20	$70	$115	$175	$375	$1,350
	Auctions: $1,293, MS-67, July 2014; $764, MS-67, September 2014; $4,259, MS-67, April 2013; $2,350, MS-66, September 2014										

c. Doubling is evident, with a very strong spread, on LIBERTY, the date, and the motto. **d.** Included in 1942-D mintage figure. **e.** Doubling on this popular variety is most prominent on the eagle's beak, the arrows, and the branch above the mintmark.

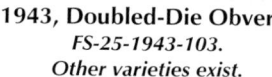

1943, Doubled-Die Obverse
FS-25-1943-103.
Other varieties exist.

1943-S, Doubled-Die Obverse
FS-25-1943S-101.

	Mintage	Cert	Avg	%MS	EF-40	AU-50	MS-60	MS-63	MS-65	MS-66	MS-67
									PF-64	PF-65	PF-67
1943	99,700,000	1,950	65.1	97%	$7.50	$8	$9	$10	$40	$100	$500
	Auctions: $10,281, MS-68, November 2013; $470, MS-67, August 2014; $447, MS-67, September 2014; $206, MS-67, November 2014										
1943, DblDie Obverse (f)	(g)	13	53.9	46%	$300	$500	$1,600	$3,500	$5,500	$8,000	
	Auctions: $30, VF-20, March 2012										
1943D	16,095,600	1,030	65.2	98%	$8	$15	$28	$39	$60	$120	$800
	Auctions: $12,925, MS-68, November 2013; $270, MS-67, August 2014; $3,819, MS-67, September 2014; $103, MS-66, November 2014										
1943S	21,700,000	1,246	65.1	98%	$9	$13	$26	$42	$60	$120	$900
	Auctions: $6,463, MS-68, June 2014; $646, MS-67, September 2014; $382, MS-67, November 2014; $135, MS-66, November 2014										
1943S, DblDie Obv (h)	(i)	120	45.9	49%	$200	$350	$500	$1,000	$2,600	$6,250	$8,250
	Auctions: $7,638, MS-66, November 2013; $1,528, MS-64, November 2014; $499, MS-63, July 2014; $176, AU-53, October 2014										
1944	104,956,000	2,125	65.4	98%	$7.50	$8	$9	$10	$32	$60	$500
	Auctions: $212, MS-67, September 2014; $382, MS-67, November 2014; $270, MS-67, November 2014; $4,406, MS-62, November 2013										
1944D	14,600,800	1,880	65.8	99%	$8	$10	$17	$20	$40	$70	$500
	Auctions: $411, MS-67, August 2014; $382, MS-67, August 2014; $353, MS-67, December 2014; $2,820, MS-67, February 2013										
1944S	12,560,000	1,828	65.7	99%	$8	$10	$14	$20	$35	$60	$525
	Auctions: $7,050, MS-68, November 2013; $558, MS-67, September 2014; $382, MS-67, October 2014; $411, MS-67, November 2014										
1945	74,372,000	1,391	65.1	98%	$7.50	$8	$9	$10	$38	$150	$1,300
	Auctions: $3,819, MS-68, January 2014; $676, MS-67, July 2014; $764, MS-67, August 2014; $646, MS-67, September 2014										
1945D	12,341,600	1,125	65.4	99%	$8	$12	$18	$25	$40	$70	$1,100
	Auctions: $1,645, MS-67, June 2014; $282, MS-67, September 2014; $66, MS-66, November 2014; $56, MS-66, November 2014										
1945S	17,004,001	1,489	65.4	99%	$7.50	$8	$9	$13	$35	$60	$900
	Auctions: $3,525, MS-67, April 2014; $441, MS-67, July 2014; $306, MS-67, August 2014; $282, MS-67, September 2014										
1946	53,436,000	938	65.2	98%	$7	$8	$9	$10	$40	$100	$1,500
	Auctions: $3,055, MS-67, June 2014; $329, MS-67, September 2014; $329, MS-67, November 2014; $90, MS-66, December 2014										
1946D	9,072,800	2,478	65.6	100%	$7.50	$8	$9	$10	$45	$80	$900
	Auctions: $177, MS-67, September 2014; $646, MS-67, November 2014; $881, MS-67, April 2013; $57, MS-66, November 2014										
1946S	4,204,000	5,159	65.6	100%	$7	$8	$9	$10	$40	$60	$400
	Auctions: $9,400, MS-68, April 2014; $588, MS-67+, July 2014; $588, MS-67, September 2014; $282, MS-67, December 2014										
1947	22,556,000	1,480	65.5	99%	$7.50	$8	$11	$19	$42	$80	$550
	Auctions: $3,819, MS-67, March 2014; $329, MS-67, September 2014; $341, MS-67, November 2014; $259, MS-67, November 2014										
1947D	15,338,400	2,466	65.7	100%	$7.50	$8	$11	$17	$40	$60	$275
	Auctions: $2,350, MS-68, August 2014; $212, MS-67, July 2014; $176, MS-67, September 2014; $2,350, MS-67, June 2013										
1947S	5,532,000	4,567	65.7	100%	$7	$8	$9	$15	$35	$55	$265
	Auctions: $247, MS-67, September 2014; $235, MS-67, November 2014; $123, MS-67, November 2014; $1,175, MS-67, August 2013										
1948	35,196,000	2,161	65.5	99%	$7	$8	$9	$10	$35	$60	$425
	Auctions: $2,115, MS-67, April 2014; $282, MS-67, September 2014; $118, MS-67, November 2014; $165, MS-67, December 2014										
1948D	16,766,800	1,466	65.3	99%	$7.50	$8	$13	$18	$55	$100	$800
	Auctions: $1,880, MS-67, February 2014; $282, MS-67, September 2014; $764, MS-67, November 2014; $223, MS-67, November 2014										
1948S	15,960,000	2,493	65.5	99%	$7	$8	$9	$13	$45	$70	$600
	Auctions: $499, MS-67, July 2014; $282, MS-67, July 2014; $270, MS-67, September 2014; $3,290, MS-67, September 2013										

f. Doubling is very strong on the motto, LIBERTY, and the date. **g.** Included in 1943 mintage figure. **h.** Very strong doubling is visible on the motto, LIBERTY, the designer's initials, and the date. "Values for this variety are generally firm, but do change with market conditions and demand fluctuations" (*Cherrypickers' Guide to Rare Die Varieties*, sixth edition, volume II). **i.** Included in 1943-S mintage figure.

1950-D, D Over S
FS-25-1950D-601.
Other varieties exist.

1950-S, S Over D
FS-25-1950S-601.

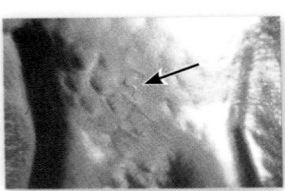

1952, Die Damage, Proof
"Superbird" variety.
FS-25-1952-901.

	Mintage	Cert	Avg	%MS	EF-40	AU-50	MS-60	MS-63	MS-65 / PF-64	MS-66 / PF-65	MS-67 / PF-67
1949	9,312,000	1,324	65.2	98%	$10	$14	$35	$47	$70	$115	$800
	Auctions: $6,463, MS-67, January 2014; $282, MS-67, August 2014; $499, MS-67, September 2014; $259, MS-67, November 2014										
1949D	10,068,400	1,350	65.2	99%	$8	$12	$16	$38	$50	$110	$800
	Auctions: $2,350, MS-67+, September 2014; $3,831, MS-67, September 2013; $188, MS-66, August 2014; $646, MS-66, December 2014										
1950	24,920,126	1,211	65.5	99%	$7	$8	$9	$10	$35	$70	$800
	Auctions: $3,819, MS-67+, August 2014; $529, MS-67, September 2014; $382, MS-67, September 2014; $2,949, MS-67, August 2013										
1950, Proof	51,386	1,674	65.9						$60	$70	$150
	Auctions: $9,988, PF-68Cam, October 2014; $4,406, PF-68Cam, November 2014; $2,820, PF-67Cam, February 2014										
1950D	21,075,600	1,334	64.8	97%	$7	$8	$9	$10	$35	$70	$800
	Auctions: $7,638, MS-68, November 2013; $470, MS-67, August 2014; $353, MS-67, October 2014; $282, MS-67, November 2014										
1950D, D Over S (j)	(k)	2	51.5	0%	$150	$180	$400	$550	$3,000	$12,000	—
	Auctions: $29,375, MS-67, June 2013; $329, MS-61, October 2014; $153, AU-50, August 2014; $129, AU-50, November 2014										
1950S	10,284,004	1,386	64.7	95%	$7.50	$8	$12	$16	$45	$60	$825
	Auctions: $4,113, MS-67, January 2014; $353, MS-67, July 2014; $382, MS-67, October 2014; $329, MS-67, November 2014										
1950S, S Over D (l)	(m)	15	58.3	60%	$150	$250	$350	$500	$1,500	$2,800	$5,000
	Auctions: $16,450, MS-67, September 2013; $217, AU-50, August 2014										
1951	43,448,102	1,434	65.5	99%	$7	$8	$9	$10	$25	$50	$450
	Auctions: $259, MS-67, August 2014; $450, MS-67, September 2014; $282, MS-67, September 2014										
1951, Proof	57,500	1,672	66.0						$55	$65	$125
	Auctions: $1,880, PF-65DCam, July 2014; $1,234, PF-68Cam, November 2014; $7,050, PF-68Cam, August 2013; $764, PF-67Cam, October 2014										
1951D	35,354,800	1,499	65.4	100%	$7	$8	$9	$10	$35	$60	$1,500
	Auctions: $6,463, MS-67, February 2014; $529, MS-67, August 2014; $515, MS-67, September 2014; $212, MS-67, September 2014										
1951S	9,048,000	1,419	65.8	100%	$7.50	$8	$10	$15	$40	$80	$550
	Auctions: $1,528, MS-67+, July 2014; $499, MS-67+, September 2014; $306, MS-67, September 2014; $2,938, MS-67, August 2013										
1952	38,780,093	1,147	65.6	99%	$7.50	$8	$9	$10	$25	$60	$500
	Auctions: $130, MS-67, September 2014; $118, MS-67, November 2014; $92, MS-67, November 2014										
1952, Proof	81,980	1,581	66.2						$40	$45	$110
	Auctions: $8,225, PF-67DCam, January 2014; $2,820, PF-68Cam, November 2014; $881, PF-67Cam, September 2014										
1952, Die Damage, Proof (n)	(o)	(p)							$200	$250	
	Auctions: $3,525, PF-66DCam, April 2014										
1952D	49,795,200	913	65.2	99%	$7	$8	$9	$10	$40	$100	$3,500
	Auctions: $1,998, MS-67, June 2014; $1,763, MS-67, July 2014; $1,175, MS-66, September 2014; $170, MS-66, September 2014										
1952S	13,707,800	1,793	65.8	99%	$7.50	$8	$12	$20	$42	$80	$275
	Auctions: $11,750, MS-68, April 2013; $764, MS-67+, September 2014; $411, MS-67+, November 2014; $165, MS-67, November 2014										

j. The upper left curve of the underlying S is visible west and north of the D mintmark. Most Mint State specimens have brilliant surfaces. **k.** Included in 1950-D mintage figure. **l.** Most Mint State specimens have a frosty luster, rather than the brilliant surface seen on most of this year's Mint State D Over S coins. **m.** Included in 1950-S mintage figure. **n.** "There is an unusual S-shaped mark on the breast of the eagle. The cause of this mark is unknown. The nickname for this well-known variety is, suitably, 'Superbird'!" (*Cherrypickers' Guide to Rare Die Varieties*, sixth edition, volume II). **o.** Included in 1952, Proof, mintage figure. **p.** Included in certified population for 1952, Proof.

	Mintage	Cert	Avg	%MS	EF-40	AU-50	MS-60	MS-63	MS-65	MS-66	MS-67
									PF-64	PF-65	PF-67
1953	18,536,120	928	65.4	99%	$7.50	$8	$9	$10	$40	$80	$600
	Auctions: $212, MS-67, November 2014; $1,410, MS-67, April 2013										
1953, Proof	128,800	2,851	66.7						$40	$45	$80
	Auctions: $4,406, PF-68DCam, November 2014; $6,463, PF-68DCam, March 2013; $588, PF-68Cam, September 2014										
1953D	56,112,400	957	65.0	99%	$7	$8	$9	$10	$35	$100	$1,500
	Auctions: $470, MS-67, September 2014; $2,233, MS-67, June 2013										
1953S	14,016,000	2,372	65.7	100%	$7	$8	$9	$10	$34	$60	$700
	Auctions: $1,293, MS-67, September 2014; $881, MS-67+, November 2014; $176, MS-67, November 2014; $3,055, MS-67, December 2013										
1954	54,412,203	2,031	65.4	99%	$7	$8	$9	$10	$34	$60	$650
	Auctions: $217, MS-67, August 2014; $2,820, MS-67+, September 2014; $223, MS-67, October 2014										
1954, Proof	233,300	3,449	67.0						$15	$25	$60
	Auctions: $12,925, PF-69DCam, November 2014; $999, PF-68DCam, November 2014; $7,050, PF-68DCam, December 2013										
1954D	42,305,500	1,105	65.2	100%	$7	$8	$9	$10	$35	$60	$2,250
	Auctions: $4,113, MS-67, July 2014; $999, MS-67, September 2014; $2,350, MS-67, October 2014										
1954S	11,834,722	4,191	65.6	100%	$7	$8	$9	$10	$36	$60	$750
	Auctions: $4,113, MS-68, January 2014; $270, MS-67, August 2014; $368, MS-67, November 2014; $182, MS-67, November 2014										
1955	18,180,181	2,374	65.4	99%	$7	$8	$9	$10	$27	$60	$950
	Auctions: $441, MS-67, August 2014; $353, MS-67, September 2014; $282, MS-67, October 2014; $823, MS-67, March 2013										
1955, Proof	378,200	4,546	67.3						$15	$25	$50
	Auctions: $1,116, PF-69DCam, November 2014; $1,146, PF-68DCam, October 2014; $2,585, PF-68DCam, April 2013										
1955D	3,182,400	2,698	64.5	100%	$7.50	$8	$9	$10	$60	$400	$2,000
	Auctions: $2,350, MS-66, April 2012										
1956	44,144,000	3,135	65.8	100%	$7	$8	$9	$10	$21	$50	$175
	Auctions: $153, MS-67, November 2013; $54, MS-67, October 2014; $588, MS-64, October 2014; $646, MS-63, September 2014										
1956, Proof	669,384	5,092	67.6						$11	$15	$50
	Auctions: $3,819, PF-69DCam, January 2014; $646, PF-69DCam, November 2014; $135, PF-68DCam, September 2014										
1956D	32,334,500	975	65.4	100%	$7	$8	$9	$10	$27	$60	$2,250
	Auctions: $1,763, MS-67, July 2014; $447, MS-67, July 2014; $3,055, MS-67, August 2013										
1957	46,532,000	2,124	65.7	99%	$7	$8	$9	$10	$27	$50	$175
	Auctions: $1,293, MS-68, January 2014; $2,115, MS-68, September 2014; $70, MS-67, July 2014										
1957, Proof	1,247,952	4,496	67.3						$11	$15	$45
	Auctions: $470, PF-68DCam, November 2014; $1,998, PF-68DCam, April 2013; $376, PF-67DCam, September 2014										
1957D	77,924,160	1,680	65.6	99%	$7	$8	$9	$10	$25	$60	$300
	Auctions: $1,528, MS-68, January 2014; $106, MS-67, November 2014; $47, MS-66, November 2014										
1958	6,360,000	3,878	65.8	100%	$7.50	$8	$9	$10	$20	$50	$140
	Auctions: $92, MS-67, July 2014; $62, MS-67, August 2014; $69, MS-67, November 2014; $217, MS-66, March 2014										
1958, Proof	875,652	3,383	67.1						$11	$15	$40
	Auctions: $529, PF-68DCam, July 2014; $1,528, PF-68DCam, September 2014; $764, PF-68DCam, November 2014										
1958D	78,124,900	2,171	65.7	99%	$7	$8	$9	$10	$25	$50	$335
	Auctions: $411, MS-67, July 2014; $705, MS-67+, September 2014; $259, MS-67, November 2014; $3,525, MS-67, August 2013										
1959	24,384,000	1,579	65.5	100%	$7	$8	$9	$10	$25	$50	$850
	Auctions: $2,233, MS-67, September 2014; $881, MS-67, September 2014; $823, MS-67, November 2014; $999, MS-65, August 2013										
1959, Proof	1,149,291	3,389	67.3						$11	$12	$35
	Auctions: $9,400, PF-69DCam, November 2014; $999, PF-68DCam, April 2014; $881, PF-68DCam, September 2014										
1959, Doubled-Die Obverse, Proof (q)	(r)	78	66.4						$140	$185	
	Auctions: $150, PF-65, February 2012										
1959D	62,054,232	1,355	65.1	99%	$7	$8	$9	$10	$25	$60	$1,350
	Auctions: $1,880, MS-67, October 2014; $8,225, MS-67, February 2013; $16, MS-65, November 2014										

q. Dramatic doubling is evident on all obverse lettering, especially IN GOD WE TRUST. There are at least five different doubled-die obverses for this date; the one featured here is FS-25-1959-101. **r.** Included in 1959, Proof, mintage figure.

	Mintage	Cert	Avg	%MS	EF-40	AU-50	MS-60	MS-63	MS-65	MS-66	MS-67
									PF-64	PF-65	PF-67
1960	29,164,000	1,097	65.4	100%	$7	$8	$9	$10	$20	$80	$950
	Auctions: $1,998, MS-67, July 2014; $738, MS-67, September 2014; $2,820, MS-67, February 2013; $200, MS-66, September 2014										
1960, Proof	1,691,602	4,152	67.0						$10	$11	$30
	Auctions: $2,115, PF-69DCam, September 2014; $764, PF-69DCam, November 2014; $2,174, PF-69DCam, April 2013; $217, PF-68DCam, November 2014										
1960D	63,000,324	808	65.1	99%	$7	$8	$9	$10	$20	$50	$1,900
	Auctions: $2,115, MS-67, April 2014; $92, MS-66, September 2014										
1961	37,036,000	1,055	65.3	100%	$7	$8	$9	$10	$15	$60	$2,400
	Auctions: $3,819, MS-67, April 2014; $50, MS-66, July 2014; $212, MS-66, November 2014										
1961, Proof	3,028,244	5,334	67.2						$10	$11	$30
	Auctions: $1,058, PF-69DCam, September 2014; $235, PF-69DCam, November 2014; $999, PF-69DCam, June 2013; $88, PF-68DCam, November 2014										
1961D	83,656,928	700	64.9	99%	$7	$8	$9	$10	$15	$150	$4,000
	Auctions: $8,225, MS-67, January 2014; $7,638, MS-67, July 2014; $7,638, MS-67, August 2014; $112, MS-66, November 2014										
1962	36,156,000	1,252	65.5	99%	$7	$8	$9	$10	$15	$60	$1,100
	Auctions: $2,585, MS-68, January 2014; $517, MS-67, October 2014; $147, MS-66, September 2014										
1962, Proof	3,218,019	5,300	67.1						$10	$11	$30
	Auctions: $940, PF-69DCam, September 2014; $411, PF-69DCam, November 2014; $823, PF-69DCam, April 2013; $79, PF-68DCam, November 2014										
1962D	127,554,756	707	64.8	98%	$7	$8	$9	$10	$15	$120	$2,000
	Auctions: $9,400, MS-67, July 2014; $1,528, MS-66+, July 2014; $247, MS-66, September 2014; $29, MS-65, November 2014										
1963	74,316,000	1,791	65.4	99%	$7	$8	$9	$10	$15	$60	$1,500
	Auctions: $11,163, MS-67, February 2014; $2,350, MS-67, July 2014; $306, MS-67, October 2014; $2,115, MS-62, September 2014										
1963, Proof	3,075,645	6,357	67.4						$10	$11	$30
	Auctions: $294, PF-69DCam, September 2014; $235, PF-69DCam, September 2014; $223, PF-69DCam, November 2014; $499, PF-69DCam, June 2013										
1963D	135,288,184	729	65.0	98%	$7	$8	$9	$10	$15	$60	$1,750
	Auctions: $1,763, MS-67, August 2014; $2,585, MS-67, October 2014; $15,863, MS-67, November 2013; $329, MS-66, August 2014										
1964	560,390,585	1,688	65.0	98%	$7	$8	$9	$10	$15	$50	$1,000
	Auctions: $1,293, MS-67+, July 2014; $499, MS-67, September 2014; $3,819, MS-67, March 2013; $558, MS-64, October 2014										
1964, Proof	3,950,762	8,299	67.8						$10	$11	$30
	Auctions: $499, PF-69DCam, July 2014; $259, PF-69DCam, November 2014; $940, PF-69DCam, June 2013; $53, PF-68Cam, August 2014										
1964D	704,135,528	1,836	64.8	96%	$7	$8	$9	$10	$15	$50	$650
	Auctions: $4,406, MS-67, April 2014; $3,055, MS-67+, August 2014; $499, MS-67, September 2014; $529, MS-67, October 2014										

1966, Doubled-Die Reverse
FS-25-1966-801.

	Mintage	Cert	Avg	%MS	MS-63	MS-65	MS-66	MS-67
					PF-65	PF-67Cam	PF-68DC	
1965	1,819,717,540	246	64.6	95%	$1	$9	$30	$175
	Auctions: $558, MS-67, September 2014; $14,688, AU-58, June 2014; $588, AU-55, August 2014							
1965, Special Mint Set ‡	2,360,000	2,096	66.8			$12	$375	—
	Auctions: $505, MS-67Cam, January 2014; $588, MS-67Cam, September 2014; $441, MS-67Cam, October 2014							
1966	821,101,500	86	65.0	95%	$1	$7	$30	$120
	Auctions: $259, MS-67, September 2014; $247, MS-67, September 2014; $1,293, MS-62, April 2013							
1966, Doubled-Die Reverse (a)	(b)	2	58.0	50%	$900	$1,400	$2,250	
	Auctions: $920, EF-45, April 2012							
1966, Special Mint Set ‡	2,261,583	2,121	66.9			$12	$135	—
	Auctions: $1,293, MS-68Cam, June 2014; $4,113, MS-68Cam, September 2014; $84, MS-67Cam, November 2014							

‡ Ranked in the *100 Greatest U.S. Modern Coins*. **a.** Very strong doubling is visible on all reverse lettering. Note that this is not the 1966 Special Mint Set issue. **b.** Included in 1966 mintage figure.

1968-S, Doubled-Die Reverse, Proof
FS-25-1968S-801.

1970-D, Doubled-Die Obverse
FS-25-1970D-101.

	Mintage	Cert	Avg	%MS	MS-63	MS-65	MS-66	MS-67
						PF-65	PF-67Cam	PF-68DC
1967	1,524,031,848	121	65.9	98%	$1	$6	$35	$180
	Auctions: $182, MS-67, September 2014; $2,115, MS-65, September 2013; $329, MS-64, July 2014							
1967, Special Mint Set ‡	1,863,344	2,638	67.0			$12	$50	—
	Auctions: $212, MS-68Cam, September 2014; $188, MS-68Cam, August 2013							
1968	220,731,500	210	65.9	99%	$1.25	$8	$25	$100
	Auctions: $9,400, MS-68, September 2013; $159, MS-67, July 2014; $123, MS-67, September 2014							
1968D	101,534,000	419	66.2	100%	$1.10	$6	$15	$55
	Auctions: $123, MS-67, March 2013							
1968S, Proof	3,041,506	877	67.4			$5	$15	$150
	Auctions: $194, PF-64, May 2013							
1968S, Doubled-Die Reverse, Proof (c)	(d)	20	66.0			$165		
	Auctions: $196, PF-66, March 2012							
1969	176,212,000	90	65.0	97%	$3	$10	$35	$300
	Auctions: $135, MS-66, June 2014; $123, MS-66, September 2014							
1969D	114,372,000	375	66.0	99%	$2.50	$10	$25	$40
	Auctions: $1,998, MS-68, July 2014; $3,819, MS-68, November 2013; $72, MS-67, July 2014							
1969S, Proof	2,934,631	1,205	68.1			$5	$15	$100
	Auctions: $617, PF-69DCam, December 2013							
1970	136,420,000	263	65.4	100%	$1	$10	$40	$100
	Auctions: $153, MS-67, August 2014; $441, MS-67, September 2014; $2,115, MS-67, November 2013; $30, MS-66, July 2014							
1970D	417,341,364	773	65.9	99%	$1	$6	$10	$35
	Auctions: $2,926, MS-68, January 2014; $182, AU-55, July 2014							
1970D, Doubled-Die Obverse (e)	(f)	2	59.5	50%	$300	$375	$500	
	Auctions: $2,875, MS-65, January 2012							
1970S, Proof	2,632,810	991	68.0			$5	$15	$125
	Auctions: $705, PF-69DCam, June 2013; $1,175, PF-67Cam, October 2014							
1971	109,284,000	121	64.9	100%	$1	$6	$50	$150
	Auctions: $364, MS-66, June 2014; $123, MS-66, September 2014							
1971D	258,634,428	249	66.0	100%	$1	$6	$20	$100
	Auctions: $4,113, MS-68, September 2013; $86, MS-67, July 2014; $86, MS-67, July 2014; $182, MS-67, September 2014							
1971S, Proof	3,220,733	1,139	67.9			$5	$15	$300
	Auctions: $1,058, PF-69DCam, December 2013							
1972	215,048,000	214	65.8	100%	$1	$6	$25	$175
	Auctions: $588, MS-67, November 2013							
1972D	311,067,732	566	66.2	100%	$1	$6	$20	$30
	Auctions: $3,055, MS-68, January 2014; $259, MS-65, October 2014							
1972S, Proof	3,260,996	752	68.1			$5	$10	$30
	Auctions: $411, PF-65Cam, August 2013							

‡ Ranked in the *100 Greatest U.S. Modern Coins*. **c.** Doubling is evident on all reverse lettering around the rim and the left tips. **d.** Included in 1968-S, Proof, mintage figure. **e.** This extremely rare variety (fewer than a half dozen known) shows very strong doubling on the date, IN GOD WE TRUST, and the ERTY of LIBERTY. **f.** Included in 1970-D mintage figure.

1979-S, Filled S
(Type 1), Proof

1979-S, Clear S
(Type 2), Proof

	Mintage	Cert	Avg	%MS	MS-63	MS-65	MS-66	MS-67
						PF-65	PF-67Cam	PF-68DC
1973	346,924,000	124	65.5	100%	$1	$6	$25	$175
	Auctions: $1,116, MS-67, September 2013							
1973D	232,977,400	139	65.3	100%	$1	$6	$25	$175
	Auctions: $1,410, MS-65, February 2014							
1973S, Proof	2,760,339	386	68.1			$5	$10	$20
	Auctions: $96, PF-67, March 2013							
1974	801,456,000	100	65.2	99%	$1	$5	$15	$80
	Auctions: $382, MS-67, November 2013							
1974D	353,160,300	137	65.6	100%	$1	$7	$25	$75
	Auctions: $1,763, MS-64, September 2013							
1974S, Proof	2,612,568	407	68.1			$5	$10	$20
	Auctions: $7,015, PF-70DCam, April 2012							
1776–1976, Copper-Nickel Clad ‡	809,784,016	443	65.5	99%	$1.25	$6	$15	$35
	Auctions: $306, MS-62, February 2014							
1776–1976D, Copper-Nickel Clad	860,118,839	716	65.5	98%	$1.25	$6	$15	$60
	Auctions: $66, MS-67, March 2013							
1776–1976S, Silver Clad	11,000,000	1,066	66.1	100%	$4	$7	$15	$40
	Auctions: $118, MS-68, April 2014; $78, MS-68, August 2014; $129, MS-68, October 2014							
1776–1976S, Proof, Copper-Nickel Clad	7,059,099	1,657	68.0			$5	$10	$20
	Auctions: $306, PF-70DCam, September 2014; $300, PF-70DCam, September 2014; $441, PF-70DCam, June 2013							
1776–1976S, Proof, Silver Clad	4,000,000	3,140	68.2			$8	$12	$25
	Auctions: $441, PF-70DCam, September 2014; $441, PF-70DCam, September 2014; $441, PF-70DCam, October 2014							
1977	468,556,000	121	65.6	99%	$1	$6	$20	$100
	Auctions: $123, MS-67, September 2014; $79, MS-66, July 2014; $282, MS-66, February 2013							
1977D	256,524,978	93	65.1	99%	$1	$6	$25	$125
	Auctions: $229, MS-67, September 2014							
1977S, Proof	3,251,152	793	68.8			$5	$10	$20
	Auctions: $70, PF-70DCam, August 2014; $103, PF-70DCam, November 2014; $90, PF-70DCam, May 2013							
1978	521,452,000	155	65.5	99%	$1	$6	$20	$100
	Auctions: $294, MS-63, June 2014; $56, MS-62, October 2014; $188, MS-60, November 2014							
1978D	287,373,152	136	65.5	99%	$1	$6	$25	$175
	Auctions: $26, MS-66, August 2014							
1978S, Proof	3,127,781	674	68.7			$5	$10	$16
	Auctions: $61, PF-70DCam, August 2014; $80, PF-70DCam, May 2013							
1979	515,708,000	169	65.9	100%	$1	$6	$25	$125
	Auctions: $411, MS-66, June 2014; $176, MS-64, November 2014							
1979D	489,789,780	135	65.5	100%	$1	$6	$25	$125
	Auctions: $441, MS-67, September 2013							
1979S, Proof, All kinds (g)	3,677,175							
1979S, Type 1 ("Filled" S), Proof		897	68.8			$5	$10	$16
	Auctions: $68, PF-70DCam, August 2014							
1979S, Type 2 ("Clear" S), Proof		884	69.0			$10	$15	$25
	Auctions: $76, PF-70DCam, August 2014; $529, PF-70DCam, September 2014; $72, PF-70DCam, September 2014							

‡ Ranked in the *100 Greatest U.S. Modern Coins*. **g.** The mintmark style was changed during 1979 Proof production, creating two distinctly different types. "The Type 2 is the rare variety, and is easily distinguished from the common Type 1. The Type 1 has a very indistinct blob, whereas the Type 2 shows a well-defined S" (*Cherrypickers' Guide to Rare Die Varieties*, sixth edition, volume II).

1981-S, Rounded S
(Type 1), Proof

1981-S, Flat S
(Type 2), Proof

	Mintage	Cert	Avg	%MS	MS-63	MS-65	MS-66	MS-67
						PF-65	PF-67Cam	PF-68DC
1980P	635,832,000	363	65.9	100%	$1	$6	$18	$85
Auctions: $217, MS-67, September 2014; $382, MS-67, September 2013; $72, MS-64, November 2014								
1980D	518,327,487	147	65.6	100%	$1	$6	$20	$175
Auctions: $1,380, MS-67, February 2007								
1980S, Proof	3,554,806	1,065	68.7			$5	$10	$16
Auctions: $79, PF-70DCam, May 2013								
1981P	601,716,000	242	66.0	100%	$1	$6	$15	$100
Auctions: $176, MS-65, August 2013								
1981D	575,722,833	265	65.6	100%	$1	$6	$15	$150
Auctions: $259, MS-67, September 2013								
1981S, Proof, All kinds (h)	4,063,083							
1981S, Type 1 ("Rounded" S), Proof		1,239	68.7			$4	$8	$16
Auctions: $70, PF-70DCam, May 2013								
1981S, Type 2 ("Flat" S), Proof		790	68.9			$6	$12	$25
Auctions: $705, PF-70DCam, April 2013								
1982P	500,931,000	144	65.5	99%	$7	$30	$60	$240
Auctions: $558, MS-67, November 2014; $16, MS-65, February 2014								
1982D	480,042,788	210	65.5	100%	$5	$18	$60	$100
Auctions: $30, MS-66, March 2013								
1982S, Proof	3,857,479	880	68.9			$4	$8	$16
Auctions: $103, PF-70DCam, May 2014; $56, PF-70DCam, September 2014; $47, PF-70DCam, November 2014								
1983P ‡	673,535,000	685	65.1	99%	$30	$65	$200	$400
Auctions: $74, MS-66, July 2014; $74, MS-66, September 2014								
1983D	617,806,446	213	64.8	97%	$11	$43	$150	$300
Auctions: $1,058, MS-67, June 2014; $108, MS-66, August 2014; $92, MS-66, September 2014								
1983S, Proof	3,279,126	837	68.8			$4	$8	$16
Auctions: $72, PF-70DCam, September 2014; $90, PF-70DCam, August 2013								
1984P	676,545,000	146	65.5	98%	$2	$10	$20	$125
Auctions: $1,058, MS-67, September 2013								
1984D	546,483,064	83	64.7	99%	$2	$12	$65	$300
Auctions: $764, MS-67, September 2013								
1984S, Proof	3,065,110	606	69.0			$4	$8	$16
Auctions: $55, PF-70DCam, August 2014; $80, PF-70DCam, May 2013								
1985P	775,818,962	164	65.6	98%	$2	$15	$25	$100
Auctions: $764, MS-65, June 2014								
1985D	519,962,888	176	65.8	100%	$1	$9	$25	$100
Auctions: $66, MS-66, March 2013								
1985S, Proof	3,362,821	665	69.0			$4	$8	$16
Auctions: $86, PF-70DCam, May 2013								

‡ Ranked in the *100 Greatest U.S. Modern Coins*. **h.** The mintmark style was changed during the 1981 Proof production, creating two distinct types. "The Type 2 is the rare variety, and is not easily distinguished from the common Type 1. For most collectors, the easiest difference to discern on the Type 2 is the flatness on the top curve of the S, which is rounded on the Type 1. Additionally, the surface of the Type 2 mintmark is frosted, and the openings in the loops slightly larger" (*Cherrypickers' Guide to Rare Die Varieties*, sixth edition, volume II).

1989-D, Doubled Mintmark
FS-25-1989D-501.

1990-S, Doubled-Die Obverse, Proof
FS-25-1990S-101.

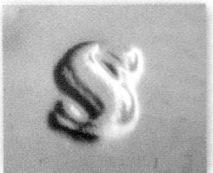

	Mintage	Cert	Avg	%MS	MS-63	MS-65 / PF-65	MS-66 / PF-67Cam	MS-67 / PF-68DC
1986P	551,199,333	156	65.0	99%	$2.50	$12	$30	$125
	Auctions: $103, MS-66, September 2014; $30, MS-66, November 2014; $94, MS-66, March 2013; $129, MS-64, October 2014							
1986D	504,298,660	189	65.7	99%	$6	$18	$25	$100
	Auctions: $104, MS-66, November 2007							
1986S, Proof	3,010,497	578	69.1			$4	$8	$16
	Auctions: $39, PF-70DCam, August 2013							
1987P	582,499,481	102	65.1	100%	$1	$9	$40	$90
	Auctions: $59, MS-66, December 2007							
1987D	655,594,696	119	65.7	100%	$1	$6	$20	$150
	Auctions: $66, MS-66, September 2014							
1987S, Proof	4,227,728	780	69.0			$4	$8	$16
	Auctions: No auction records available.							
1988P	562,052,000	141	65.2	99%	$1.25	$15	$30	$175
	Auctions: $66, MS-66, March 2013							
1988D	596,810,688	115	65.5	100%	$1	$10	$20	$125
	Auctions: $66, MS-66, November 2007							
1988S, Proof	3,262,948	500	69.1			$4	$8	$16
	Auctions: $55, PF-70DCam, August 2013							
1989P	512,868,000	113	65.2	98%	$1	$12	$25	$70
	Auctions: $216, MS-66, August 2009							
1989D	896,535,597	106	65.3	98%	$1	$7	$25	$125
	Auctions: $70, MS-66, March 2013							
1989D, Repunched Mintmark (i)	(j)	0	n/a		$20	$25	$50	
	Auctions: No auction records available.							
1989S, Proof	3,220,194	591	68.9			$4	$8	$16
	Auctions: $79, PF-70DCam, January 2010							
1990P	613,792,000	134	66.0	99%	$1	$10	$20	$100
	Auctions: $282, MS-64, June 2014							
1990D	927,638,181	147	65.9	100%	$1	$10	$20	$125
	Auctions: $646, MS-68, April 2014; $52, MS-67, August 2014							
1990S, Proof	3,299,559	780	69.2			$4	$8	$16
	Auctions: $53, PF-68DCam, April 2013							
1990S, Doubled-Die Obverse, Proof ‡ (k)	(l)	5	68.2			$200	$700	
	Auctions: $4,888, PF-70DCam, April 2012							
1991P	570,968,000	119	66.0	99%	$1	$12	$30	$100
	Auctions: $90, MS-66, November 2007							
1991D	630,966,693	74	65.3	100%	$1	$12	$30	$225
	Auctions: $66, MS-66, March 2013							
1991S, Proof	2,867,787	743	69.3			$4	$8	$16
	Auctions: $69, PF-70DCam, January 2010							

‡ Ranked in the *100 Greatest U.S. Modern Coins*. **i.** The secondary D mintmark is visible west of the primary D. **j.** Included in 1989-D mintage figure. **k.** Very strong doubling is visible on the date and the mintmark, with slightly less dramatic doubling on IN GOD WE TRUST. **l.** Included in 1990-S, Proof, mintage figure.

	Mintage	Cert	Avg	%MS	MS-63 PF-65	MS-65 PF-67Cam	MS-66 PF-67Cam	MS-67 PF-68DC
1992P	384,764,000	106	65.9	100%	$1.50	$16	$35	$225
Auctions: $242, MS-66, February 2008								
1992D	389,777,107	86	65.3	99%	$1	$16	$35	$100
Auctions: $1,763, MS-67, November 2013; $47, MS-66, July 2014								
1992S, Proof	2,858,981	571	69.2			$4	$8	$16
Auctions: $50, PF-70DCam, January 2010								
1992S, Proof, Silver	1,317,579	1,319	69.1			$9	$12	$22
Auctions: $109, PF-70DCam, January 2010								
1993P	639,276,000	154	66.1	97%	$1	$7	$20	$85
Auctions: $86, MS-67, August 2014; $306, MS-64, June 2014								
1993D	645,476,128	130	65.9	98%	$1	$7	$25	$100
Auctions: $59, MS-67, August 2014; $101, MS-66, September 2014; $40, MS-66, March 2013; $36, AU-58, July 2014								
1993S, Proof	2,633,439	573	69.3			$4	$8	$16
Auctions: $58, PF-70DCam, May 2013								
1993S, Proof, Silver	761,353	1,023	69.0			$9	$12	$22
Auctions: $70, PF-70DCam, August 2013								
1994P	825,600,000	119	66.0	100%	$1	$10	$25	$40
Auctions: $70, MS-66, March 2013								
1994D	880,034,110	96	65.0	96%	$1	$10	$30	$150
Auctions: $123, MS-66, September 2014; $212, MS-64, July 2014								
1994S, Proof	2,484,594	525	69.3			$4	$8	$16
Auctions: $69, PF-70DCam, January 2010								
1994S, Proof, Silver	785,329	979	69.0			$9	$14	$25
Auctions: $76, PF-70DCam, September 2014; $96, PF-70DCam, May 2013								
1995P	1,004,336,000	110	66.5	100%	$1.25	$14	$20	$65
Auctions: $129, MS-67, March 2013								
1995D	1,103,216,000	118	66.1	100%	$1	$13	$20	$75
Auctions: $165, MS-67, September 2014								
1995S, Proof	2,117,496	417	69.4			$8	$10	$20
Auctions: $69, PF-70DCam, January 2010								
1995S, Proof, Silver	679,985	1,065	69.0			$9	$14	$25
Auctions: $68, PF-70DCam, September 2014; $69, PF-70DCam, November 2014; $135, PF-70DCam, May 2013								
1996P	925,040,000	196	66.5	100%	$1	$10	$18	$30
Auctions: $441, MS-68, March 2013								
1996D	906,868,000	208	66.3	100%	$1	$10	$20	$40
Auctions: $447, MS-68, March 2013; $165, MS-64, November 2014								
1996S, Proof	1,750,244	491	69.2			$5	$8	$18
Auctions: $84, PF-70DCam, January 2010								
1996S, Proof, Silver	775,021	1,033	69.0			$9	$14	$25
Auctions: $76, PF-70DCam, May 2013								
1997P	595,740,000	96	66.4	100%	$1	$11	$18	$40
Auctions: $15, MS-60, January 2013								
1997D	599,680,000	103	66.1	99%	$1	$12	$18	$40
Auctions: $66, MS-67, March 2013								
1997S, Proof	2,055,000	409	69.4			$5	$8	$18
Auctions: $69, PF-70DCam, January 2010								
1997S, Proof, Silver	741,678	1,084	69.2			$9	$14	$25
Auctions: $89, PF-70DCam, January 2010								

	Mintage	Cert	Avg	%MS	MS-63	MS-65	MS-66	MS-67
						PF-65	PF-67Cam	PF-68DC
1998P	896,268,000	145	66.6	99%	$1	$7	$18	$40
	Auctions: $329, MS-68, June 2014; $364, MS-68, September 2014; $159, MS-64, November 2014							
1998D	821,000,000	131	65.4	97%	$1	$7	$20	$75
	Auctions: $364, MS-67, September 2014; $32, MS-66, June 2014							
1998S, Proof	2,086,507	462	69.5			$6	$8	$18
	Auctions: $9,988, PF-65, August 2014							
1998S, Proof, Silver	878,792	1,252	69.2			$9	$12	$22
	Auctions: $70, PF-70DCam, May 2013							

WASHINGTON, STATE, D.C., AND TERRITORIAL (1999–2009)

Designers: *John Flanagan and others.* **Weight:** *Clad issue—5.67 grams; silver Proofs—6.25 grams.* **Composition:** *Clad issue—Outer layers of copper-nickel (.750 copper, .250 nickel) bonded to inner core of pure copper; silver Proofs—.900 silver, .100 copper (net weight .18084 oz. pure silver).* **Diameter:** *24.3 mm.* **Edge:** *Reeded.* **Mints:** *Clad issue—Philadelphia, Denver, San Francisco; silver Proofs—San Francisco.*

Circulation Strike

Proof

History. In 1999 the U.S. Mint introduced a new program of State quarters (officially called the United States Mint 50 State Quarters® Program). These were released at the rate of five new reverse designs each year, in combination with a restyled obverse, through 2008. Each design honored the state the coin was issued for, and they were released in public celebrations in the order in which the states joined the Union. The coins became very popular, adding millions of Americans to the ranks of everyday coin collectors, and are still widely collected with enthusiasm. In 2009 the Mint released a similar program of quarter dollars for Washington, D.C., and the five U.S. territories. Circulation strikes were made at the Philadelphia and Denver mints, and special silver-content and Proof issues at San Francisco. Each coin combines a modified obverse depicting George Washington, without a date. The reverses are distinctive and bear the date of issue, the date of statehood (for the State quarters), and other design elements. Each state or district/territory selected its own design.

Some State quarters were accidentally made with "disoriented" dies and are valued higher than ordinary pieces. Normal U.S. coins have dies oriented in coin alignment, such that the reverse appears upside down when the coin is flipped from right to left. Values for the rotated-die quarters vary according to the amount of shifting. The most valuable are those that are shifted 180 degrees, so that both sides appear upright when the coin is turned over (called *medal alignment*).

Striking and Sharpness. State quarters can have light striking on the highest area of the obverse. On the reverse there can be weak areas, depending on the design, seemingly more often seen on Denver Mint coins. Some in the State quarter series were struck through grease, obliterating portions of both the obverse (usually) and reverse designs.

Availability. All modern quarters are readily available in high grades. Typical MS coins are MS-63 and 64 with light abrasion. MS-65 and higher coins are in the minority, but enough exist that finding them is no problem. Around MS-68 many issues are scarce, and higher grades are scarcer yet.

Proofs. State and D.C./Territorial quarter dollar Proofs are made in San Francisco. For certain later issues of Washington quarters as well as State, D.C., and Territorial issues, Proofs are available in copper-nickel-clad metal as well as silver strikings. On some Proofs over-polishing of dies eliminated some details, as on part of the WC (for William Cousins) initials on certain 1999 Delaware pieces.

GRADING STANDARDS

MS-60 to 70 (Mint State). *Obverse:* At MS-60, some abrasion and contact marks are evident on the highest-relief parts of the hair and the cheek. At MS-63, abrasion is slight at best, less so at MS-64. An MS-65 coin should display no abrasion or contact marks except under magnification, and MS-66 and higher coins should have none at all. Luster should be full. *Reverse:* Check the highest-relief areas of the design (these differ from coin to coin). Otherwise, comments are as for the obverse.

2006-P, South Dakota. Graded MS-68.

AU-50, 53, 55, 58 (About Uncirculated). *Obverse:* Light wear is seen on the cheek, the high areas of the hair, and the neck. At AU-58, the luster is extensive, but incomplete, especially on the higher parts and in the field. At AU-50 and 53, luster is less. About Uncirculated coins usually lack eye appeal. *Reverse:* Light wear is seen on the higher-relief areas. Otherwise, comments are as for the obverse.

2006-P, Colorado. Graded AU-50.

State, D.C., and Territorial quarter dollars are seldom collected in grades lower than AU-50.

PF-60 to 70 (Proof). *Obverse and Reverse:* These coins are so recent, and as only a few have been cleaned, most approach perfection and can be designated PF-68 to 70, the latter only if no contact marks or other problems can be seen under magnification. A cleaned coin with extensive hairlines would not be collectible for most numismatists and would be classified at a lower level such as PF-60 to 63. Those with lighter hairlines qualify for PF-64 or 65.

2000-S, New Hampshire. Graded PF-70.

| 1999, Delaware | 1999, Pennsylvania | 1999, New Jersey | 1999, Georgia | 1999, Connecticut |

	Mintage	Cert	Avg	%MS	AU-50	MS-63	MS-65 PF-65	MS-66 PF-66DC	MS-67 PF-69DC
1999P, Delaware	373,400,000	1,189	65.9	99%	$0.50	$1.25	$3	$25	$55
Auctions: $1,410, MS-66, April 2013									
1999D, Delaware	401,424,000	1,339	65.9	100%	$0.50	$1.25	$3	$25	$55
Auctions: $529, MS-64, April 2013									
1999S, Delaware, Proof	3,713,359	6,582	69.2				$7	$8	$20
Auctions: $79, PF-70DCam, November 2014; $259, PF-70DCam, June 2013									
1999S, Delaware, Proof, Silver	804,565	12,167	69.0				$30	$35	$50
Auctions: $2,115, PF-70DCam, June 2013									
1999P, Pennsylvania	349,000,000	1,081	66.1	100%	$0.50	$1.25	$3	$25	$55
Auctions: $129, MS-65, February 2013									
1999D, Pennsylvania	358,332,000	968	65.9	100%	$0.50	$1.25	$3	$25	$55
Auctions: $299, MS-68, April 2008									
1999S, Pennsylvania, Proof	3,713,359	6,445	69.2				$7	$8	$20
Auctions: $118, PF-70DCam, May 2013									
1999S, Pennsylvania, Proof, Silver	804,565	11,624	69.1				$30	$35	$50
Auctions: $58, PF-70DCam, November 2014; $423, PF-70DCam, April 2013									
1999P, New Jersey	363,200,000	1,032	66.1	100%	$0.50	$1.25	$3	$25	$55
Auctions: $14, MS-67, April 2008									
1999D, New Jersey	299,028,000	1,166	66.0	100%	$0.50	$1.25	$3	$25	$55
Auctions: $47, MS-67, August 2009									
1999S, New Jersey, Proof	3,713,359	6,452	69.2				$7	$8	$20
Auctions: $182, PF-70DCam, May 2013									
1999S, New Jersey, Proof, Silver	804,565	11,716	69.1				$30	$35	$50
Auctions: $82, PF-70DCam, November 2014; $253, PF-70DCam, June 2013									
1999P, Georgia	451,188,000	1,138	65.7	99%	$0.50	$1.25	$3	$25	$55
Auctions: $69, MS-65, February 2014; $306, MS-62, October 2014									
1999D, Georgia	488,744,000	1,143	65.8	99%	$0.50	$1.25	$3	$25	$55
Auctions: $48, AU-58, May 2013									
1999S, Georgia, Proof	3,713,359	6,485	69.2				$7	$8	$20
Auctions: $101, PF-70DCam, May 2013									
1999S, Georgia, Proof, Silver	804,565	11,790	69.1				$30	$35	$50
Auctions: $159, PF-70DCam, May 2013									
1999P, Connecticut	688,744,000	1,225	65.6	99%	$0.50	$1.25	$3	$25	$55
Auctions: $441, MS-64, February 2014									
1999D, Connecticut	657,880,000	2,249	65.3	100%	$0.50	$1.25	$3	$25	$55
Auctions: $999, MS-64, February 2014									
1999S, Connecticut, Proof	3,713,359	6,522	69.3				$7	$8	$20
Auctions: $85, PF-70DCam, May 2013									
1999S, Connecticut, Proof, Silver	804,565	11,625	69.1				$30	$35	$50
Auctions: $113, PF-70DCam, May 2013									

2000, Massachusetts	2000, Maryland	2000, South Carolina	2000, New Hampshire	2000, Virginia

| | Mintage | Cert | Avg | %MS | AU-50 | MS-63 | MS-65 | MS-66 | MS-67 |
							PF-65	PF-66DC	PF-69DC
2000P, Massachusetts	628,600,000	810	66.2	100%	$0.35	$1	$2	$15	$40
Auctions: $30, MS-68, August 2009									
2000D, Massachusetts	535,184,000	651	66.1	100%	$0.35	$1	$2	$15	$40
Auctions: $79, MS-60, January 2014									
2000S, Massachusetts, Proof	4,020,172	4,541	69.2				$3	$4	$15
Auctions: $127, PF-70DCam, May 2009									
2000S, Massachusetts, Proof, Silver	965,421	9,610	69.2				$8	$10	$20
Auctions: $150, PF-70DCam, August 2009									
2000P, Maryland	678,200,000	622	65.9	99%	$0.35	$1	$2	$15	$40
Auctions: $84, MS-63, February 2014									
2000D, Maryland	556,532,000	635	66.0	100%	$0.35	$1	$2	$15	$40
Auctions: $159, MS-64, November 2013									
2000S, Maryland, Proof	4,020,172	4,445	69.2				$3	$4	$15
Auctions: $138, PF-70DCam, December 2009									
2000S, Maryland, Proof, Silver	965,421	9,742	69.2				$8	$10	$20
Auctions: $144, PF-70DCam, October 2009									
2000P, South Carolina	742,576,000	599	66.1	100%	$0.35	$1	$2	$15	$40
Auctions: $141, MS-67, February 2013									
2000D, South Carolina	566,208,000	739	66.3	100%	$0.35	$1	$2	$15	$40
Auctions: $15, MS-67, March 2009									
2000S, South Carolina, Proof	4,020,172	4,494	69.2				$3	$4	$15
Auctions: $94, PF-70DCam, August 2009									
2000S, South Carolina, Proof, Silver	965,421	9,399	69.2				$8	$10	$20
Auctions: $100, PF-69DCam, February 2013									
2000P, New Hampshire	673,040,000	554	65.6	99%	$0.35	$1	$2	$15	$40
Auctions: $529, MS-66, November 2013; $47, AU-58, July 2014									
2000D, New Hampshire	495,976,000	570	66.0	100%	$0.35	$1	$2	$15	$40
Auctions: $46, MS-62, May 2013									
2000S, New Hampshire, Proof	4,020,172	4,501	69.2				$3	$4	$15
Auctions: $881, PF-69DCam, February 2013									
2000S, New Hampshire, Proof, Silver	965,421	9,390	69.1				$8	$10	$20
Auctions: $144, PF-70DCam, November 2009									
2000P, Virginia	943,000,000	665	66.1	100%	$0.35	$1	$2	$15	$40
Auctions: $130, MS-63, April 2014									
2000D, Virginia	651,616,000	588	66.1	99%	$0.35	$1	$2	$15	$40
Auctions: $112, MS-62, November 2014									
2000S, Virginia, Proof	4,020,172	4,487	69.2				$3	$4	$15
Auctions: $21, PF-70DCam, March 2014									
2000S, Virginia, Proof, Silver	965,421	9,535	69.2				$8	$10	$20
Auctions: $20, PF-69DCam, March 2013									

2001, New York	2001, North Carolina	2001, Rhode Island	2001, Vermont	2001, Kentucky

	Mintage	Cert	Avg	%MS	AU-50	MS-63	MS-65 PF-65	MS-66 PF-66DC	MS-67 PF-69DC
2001P, New York	655,400,000	388	66.1	100%	$0.35	$1	$2	$15	$40
Auctions: $499, MS-65, June 2014									
2001D, New York	619,640,000	461	66.2	100%	$0.35	$1	$2	$15	$40
Auctions: $15, MS-66, August 2009									
2001S, New York, Proof	3,094,140	3,555	69.2				$3	$8	$15
Auctions: $62, PF-70UCam, January 2010									
2001S, New York, Proof, Silver	889,697	7,594	69.2				$10	$15	$20
Auctions: $66, PF-70DCam, April 2013									
2001P, North Carolina	627,600,000	376	66.3	100%	$0.35	$1	$2	$15	$40
Auctions: $558, MS-63, September 2013									
2001D, North Carolina	427,876,000	406	66.3	100%	$0.35	$1	$2	$15	$40
Auctions: $15, MS-66, August 2009									
2001S, North Carolina, Proof	3,094,140	3,647	69.2				$3	$8	$15
Auctions: $55, PF-70DCam, June 2009									
2001S, North Carolina, Proof, Silver	889,697	7,526	69.2				$10	$15	$20
Auctions: $76, PF-70DCam, May 2013									
2001P, Rhode Island	423,000,000	310	66.0	100%	$0.35	$1	$2	$15	$40
Auctions: $86, MS-68, April 2008									
2001D, Rhode Island	447,100,000	360	66.0	100%	$0.35	$1	$1.25	$15	$40
Auctions: $59, MS-64, July 2014									
2001S, Rhode Island, Proof	3,094,140	3,243	69.2				$3	$8	$15
Auctions: $27, PF-70DCam, March 2014									
2001S, Rhode Island, Proof, Silver	889,697	7,604	69.2				$10	$15	$20
Auctions: $58, PF-70DCam, May 2013									
2001P, Vermont	423,400,000	1,871	65.7	100%	$0.35	$1	$2	$15	$40
Auctions: $45, MS-68, April 2008									
2001D, Vermont	459,404,000	373	66.3	100%	$0.35	$1	$2	$15	$40
Auctions: $15, MS-66, October 2009									
2001S, Vermont, Proof	3,094,140	3,420	69.3				$3	$8	$15
Auctions: $21, PF-70DCam, March 2014									
2001S, Vermont, Proof, Silver	889,697	7,658	69.3				$10	$15	$20
Auctions: $66, PF-70DCam, May 2013									
2001P, Kentucky	353,000,000	387	66.3	100%	$0.35	$1.25	$1.50	$16	$40
Auctions: $21, MS-61, August 2013									
2001D, Kentucky	370,564,000	296	66.2	100%	$0.35	$1.10	$1.50	$15	$40
Auctions: $460, MS-68, December 2007									
2001S, Kentucky, Proof	3,094,140	3,280	69.3				$3	$8	$15
Auctions: $130, PF-70DCam, December 2009									
2001S, Kentucky, Proof, Silver	889,697	7,557	69.2				$10	$15	$20
Auctions: $66, PF-70DCam, May 2013									

2002, Tennessee	2002, Ohio	2002, Louisiana	2002, Indiana	2002, Mississippi

	Mintage	Cert	Avg	%MS	AU-50	MS-63	MS-65 PF-65	MS-66 PF-66DC	MS-67 PF-69DC
2002P, Tennessee	361,600,000	300	66.5	100%	$0.75	$1.75	$3	$18	$40
Auctions: $11, MS-66, January 2009									
2002D, Tennessee	286,468,000	303	66.4	100%	$0.75	$1.75	$3	$18	$40
Auctions: $18, MS-68, April 2008									
2002S, Tennessee, Proof	3,084,245	2,870	69.2				$3	$5	$15
Auctions: $89, PF-70DCam, October 2009									
2002S, Tennessee, Proof, Silver	892,229	7,452	69.2				$8	$10	$20
Auctions: $23, PF-69DCam, February 2013									
2002P, Ohio	217,200,000	344	66.7	100%	$0.35	$1	$1.25	$10	$30
Auctions: $15, MS-68, April 2008									
2002D, Ohio	414,832,000	280	66.2	100%	$0.35	$1	$1.25	$10	$30
Auctions: $15, MS-68, April 2008									
2002S, Ohio, Proof	3,084,245	2,853	69.3				$3	$5	$15
Auctions: $99, PF-70DCam, October 2009									
2002S, Ohio, Proof, Silver	892,229	7,547	69.2				$8	$10	$20
Auctions: $35, PF-69DCam, January 2013									
2002P, Louisiana	362,000,000	261	66.7	100%	$0.35	$1	$1.25	$10	$30
Auctions: $31, MS-68, April 2008									
2002D, Louisiana	402,204,000	213	66.3	100%	$0.35	$1	$1.25	$10	$30
Auctions: $25, MS-68, January 2009									
2002S, Louisiana, Proof	3,084,245	2,857	69.2				$3	$5	$15
Auctions: $56, PF-70UCam, February 2010									
2002S, Louisiana, Proof, Silver	892,229	7,267	69.2				$8	$10	$20
Auctions: $150, PF-70DCam, December 2009									
2002P, Indiana	362,600,000	305	66.5	99%	$0.35	$1	$1.25	$10	$30
Auctions: $15, MS-68, April 2008									
2002D, Indiana	327,200,000	239	66.4	100%	$0.35	$1	$1.25	$10	$30
Auctions: $18, MS-68, April 2008									
2002S, Indiana, Proof	3,084,245	2,886	69.2				$3	$5	$15
Auctions: $40, PF-70DCam, October 2009									
2002S, Indiana, Proof, Silver	892,229	7,386	69.2				$8	$10	$20
Auctions: $19, PF-69DCam, January 2013									
2002P, Mississippi	290,000,000	277	66.2	100%	$0.35	$1	$1.25	$10	$30
Auctions: $19, MS-68, April 2008									
2002D, Mississippi	289,600,000	223	66.4	100%	$0.35	$1	$1.25	$10	$30
Auctions: $48, MS-61, May 2013									
2002S, Mississippi, Proof	3,084,245	2,917	69.3				$3	$5	$15
Auctions: $26, PF-70DCam, March 2014									
2002S, Mississippi, Proof, Silver	892,229	7,645	69.2				$8	$10	$20
Auctions: $19, PF-69DCam, January 2013									

2003, Illinois	2003, Alabama	2003, Maine	2003, Missouri	2003, Arkansas

	Mintage	Cert	Avg	%MS	AU-50	MS-63	MS-65 PF-65	MS-66 PF-66DC	MS-67 PF-69DC
2003P, Illinois	225,800,000	252	66.0	100%	$0.50	$1.50	$2	$12	$32
Auctions: $11, MS-67, April 2008									
2003D, Illinois	237,400,000	2,062	65.2	100%	$0.50	$1.50	$2	$12	$32
Auctions: No auction records available.									
2003S, Illinois, Proof	3,408,516	5,579	69.3				$3	$5	$15
Auctions: $62, PF-70UCam, March 2010									
2003S, Illinois, Proof, Silver	1,125,755	8,255	69.2				$8	$9	$20
Auctions: $16, PF-69DCam, January 2013									
2003P, Alabama	225,000,000	270	65.7	100%	$0.35	$1	$1.25	$10	$30
Auctions: $59, MS-67, December 2007									
2003D, Alabama	232,400,000	2,060	65.1	100%	$0.35	$1	$1.25	$10	$30
Auctions: $13, MS-66, April 2006									
2003S, Alabama, Proof	3,408,516	5,673	69.3				$3	$5	$15
Auctions: $47, PF-70DCam, October 2009									
2003S, Alabama, Proof, Silver	1,125,755	8,243	69.2				$8	$9	$20
Auctions: $23, PF-69DCam, February 2013									
2003P, Maine	217,400,000	243	65.8	100%	$0.35	$1	$1.25	$10	$30
Auctions: $17, MS-67, April 2008									
2003D, Maine	231,400,000	2,062	65.2	100%	$0.35	$1	$1.25	$10	$30
Auctions: $1,093, MS-68, December 2007									
2003S, Maine, Proof	3,408,516	5,540	69.2				$3	$5	$15
Auctions: $36, PF-70UCam, March 2010									
2003S, Maine, Proof, Silver	1,125,755	8,143	69.2				$8	$9	$20
Auctions: $45, PF-70DCam, March 2014									
2003P, Missouri	225,000,000	258	65.9	99%	$0.35	$1	$1.25	$10	$30
Auctions: $57, MS-68, April 2008									
2003D, Missouri	228,200,000	2,073	65.2	100%	$0.35	$1	$1.25	$10	$30
Auctions: $57, MS-68, June 2014									
2003S, Missouri, Proof	3,408,516	5,727	69.3				$3	$5	$15
Auctions: $38, PF-70UCam, February 2010									
2003S, Missouri, Proof, Silver	1,125,755	8,242	69.2				$8	$9	$20
Auctions: $17, PF-69DCam, May 2013									
2003P, Arkansas	228,000,000	232	65.8	100%	$0.35	$1	$1.25	$10	$30
Auctions: $74, MS-60, May 2013									
2003D, Arkansas	229,800,000	2,107	65.2	100%	$0.40	$1	$1.25	$10	$30
Auctions: $80, MS-68, March 2013									
2003S, Arkansas, Proof	3,408,516	5,668	69.3				$3	$5	$15
Auctions: $44, PF-70UCam, February 2010									
2003S, Arkansas, Proof, Silver	1,125,755	8,276	69.2				$8	$9	$20
Auctions: $104, PF-70UCam, March 2010									

2004, Michigan	2004, Florida	2004, Texas	2004, Iowa	2004, Wisconsin

	Mintage	Cert	Avg	%MS	AU-50	MS-63	MS-65 / PF-65	MS-66 / PF-66DC	MS-67 / PF-69DC
2004P, Michigan	233,800,000	2,350	65.2	100%	$0.35	$0.75	$1	$10	$30
Auctions: $21, MS-68, April 2008									
2004D, Michigan	225,800,000	398	67.3	100%	$0.35	$0.75	$1	$10	$30
Auctions: $16, MS-68, January 2009									
2004S, Michigan, Proof	2,740,684	3,797	69.3				$3	$5	$15
Auctions: $28, PF-70UCam, January 2010									
2004S, Michigan, Proof, Silver	1,769,786	9,650	69.3				$8	$10	$20
Auctions: $18, PF-69DCam, January 2013									
2004P, Florida	240,200,000	2,338	65.2	100%	$0.35	$0.75	$1	$10	$30
Auctions: $64, MS-68, April 2008									
2004D, Florida	241,600,000	301	66.9	100%	$0.35	$0.75	$1	$10	$30
Auctions: $15, MS-68, April 2008									
2004S, Florida, Proof	2,740,684	3,725	69.3				$3	$5	$15
Auctions: $36, PF-70UCam, December 2009									
2004S, Florida, Proof, Silver	1,769,786	9,475	69.2				$8	$10	$20
Auctions: $24, PF-69DCam, February 2013									
2004P, Texas	278,800,000	2,378	65.2	100%	$0.35	$0.75	$1	$10	$30
Auctions: $115, MS-68, December 2007									
2004D, Texas	263,000,000	314	66.9	100%	$0.35	$0.75	$1	$10	$30
Auctions: $19, MS-68, April 2008									
2004S, Texas, Proof	2,740,684	3,840	69.3				$3	$5	$15
Auctions: $21, PF-70DCam, March 2014									
2004S, Texas, Proof, Silver	1,769,786	9,873	69.3				$8	$10	$20
Auctions: $69, PF-70DCam, October 2009									
2004P, Iowa	213,800,000	2,304	65.1	100%	$0.35	$0.75	$1	$10	$30
Auctions: $25, MS-68, January 2009									
2004D, Iowa	251,400,000	280	66.9	100%	$0.35	$0.75	$1	$10	$30
Auctions: $15, MS-68, April 2008									
2004S, Iowa, Proof	2,740,684	3,873	69.4				$3	$5	$15
Auctions: $79, PF-70DCam, January 2010									
2004S, Iowa, Proof, Silver	1,769,786	9,744	69.3				$8	$10	$20
Auctions: $17, PF-69DCam, February 2013									
2004P, Wisconsin	226,400,000	2,540	65.2	100%	$0.35	$0.75	$1	$10	$30
Auctions: $31, MS-67, April 2008									
2004D, Wisconsin	226,800,000	2,787	65.7	100%	$0.35	$0.75	$1	$10	$30
Auctions: $33, MS-68, April 2008									
2004D, Wisconsin, Extra Leaf High ‡ (a)	(b)	4,698	64.8	96%	$75	$150	$200	$300	$500
Auctions: $705, MS-67, June 2014; $153, MS-65, October 2014; $194, MS-65, November 2014									
2004D, Wisconsin, Extra Leaf Low ‡ (a)	(b)	6,316	64.9	97%	$50	$130	$165	$275	$450
Auctions: $529, MS-67, June 2014; $106, MS-65, October 2014; $92, MS-65, November 2014									
2004S, Wisconsin, Proof	2,740,684	3,872	69.3				$3	$5	$15
Auctions: $56, PF-70DCam, October 2009									
2004S, Wisconsin, Proof, Silver	1,769,786	9,886	69.3				$8	$10	$20
Auctions: $56, PF-70DCam, January 2010									

‡ Ranked in the *100 Greatest U.S. Modern Coins*. **a.** Some 2004-D, Wisconsin, quarters show one of two different die flaws on the reverse, in the shape of an extra leaf on the corn. See page 795 for illustrations. **b.** Included in 2004-D, Wisconsin, mintage figure.

2005, California	2005, Minnesota	2005, Oregon	2005, Kansas	2005, West Virginia

	Mintage	Cert	Avg	%MS	AU-50	MS-63	MS-65 / PF-65	MS-66 / PF-66DC	MS-67 / PF-69DC
2005P, California	257,200,000	450	65.9	100%	$0.30	$0.75	$1.10	$10	$30
Auctions: $2, MS-69 Satin, August 2009									
2005D, California	263,200,000	281	66.2	99%	$0.30	$0.75	$1.10	$10	$30
Auctions: $351, MS-68, December 2007									
2005S, California, Proof	3,262,960	8,574	69.3				$3	$4.50	$15
Auctions: $16, PF-70DCam, March 2014									
2005S, California, Proof, Silver	1,678,649	10,747	69.4				$8	$10	$20
Auctions: $15, PF-69DCam, January 2013									
2005P, Minnesota	239,600,000	363	62.7	95%	$0.30	$0.75	$1	$10	$30
Auctions: $306, MS-65, April 2014									
2005D, Minnesota	248,400,000	171	66.1	99%	$0.30	$0.75	$1	$10	$30
Auctions: $21, MS-69 Satin, December 2008									
2005S, Minnesota, Proof	3,262,960	8,536	69.3				$3	$4.50	$15
Auctions: $40, PF-70UCam, March 2010									
2005S, Minnesota, Proof, Silver	1,678,649	10,529	69.4				$8	$10	$20
Auctions: $33, PF-70DCam, March 2014									
2005P, Oregon	316,200,000	252	65.1	100%	$0.30	$0.75	$1	$10	$30
Auctions: $10, MS-67 Satin, July 2008									
2005D, Oregon	404,000,000	137	66.2	100%	$0.30	$0.75	$1	$10	$30
Auctions: $17, MS-69 Satin, September 2009									
2005S, Oregon, Proof	3,262,960	8,505	69.3				$3	$4.50	$15
Auctions: $59, PF-70DCam, October 2009									
2005S, Oregon, Proof, Silver	1,678,649	10,525	69.4				$8	$10	$20
Auctions: $99, PF-70DCam, October 2009									
2005P, Kansas	263,400,000	322	65.1	98%	$0.30	$0.75	$1	$10	$30
Auctions: $26, MS-69 Satin, March 2010									
2005D, Kansas	300,000,000	226	66.2	100%	$0.30	$0.75	$1	$10	$30
Auctions: $25, MS-69 Satin, January 2009									
2005S, Kansas, Proof	3,262,960	8,558	69.3				$3	$4.50	$15
Auctions: $44, PF-70UCam, February 2010									
2005S, Kansas, Proof, Silver	1,678,649	10,651	69.3				$8	$10	$20
Auctions: $18, PF-69DCam, January 2013									
2005P, West Virginia	365,400,000	299	65.3	100%	$0.30	$0.50	$1	$10	$30
Auctions: $10, MS-67 Satin, July 2008									
2005D, West Virginia	356,200,000	180	66.2	99%	$0.30	$0.75	$1	$10	$30
Auctions: $184, MS-68, April 2008									
2005S, West Virginia, Proof	3,262,960	8,570	69.3				$3	$4.50	$15
Auctions: $26, PF-70UCam, March 2010									
2005S, West Virginia, Proof, Silver	1,678,649	10,649	69.4				$8	$10	$20
Auctions: $38, PF-70UCam, February 2010									

| 2006, Nevada | 2006, Nebraska | 2006, Colorado | 2006, North Dakota | 2006, South Dakota |

	Mintage	Cert	Avg	%MS	AU-50	MS-63	MS-65	MS-66	MS-67
							PF-65	PF-66DC	PF-69DC
2006P, Nevada	277,000,000	273	66.1	100%	$0.30	$0.75	$1	$10	$30
Auctions: $28, MS-68 Satin, August 2009									
2006D, Nevada	312,800,000	356	66.5	100%	$0.30	$0.50	$1	$10	$30
Auctions: $18, MS-69 Satin, August 2009									
2006S, Nevada, Proof	2,882,428	5,823	69.5				$3	$4.50	$15
Auctions: $15, PF-70DCam, May 2013									
2006S, Nevada, Proof, Silver	1,585,008	9,480	69.5				$8	$9	$20
Auctions: $104, PF-70DCam, March 2010									
2006P, Nebraska	318,000,000	141	66.0	100%	$0.30	$0.75	$1	$10	$30
Auctions: $40, MS-69 Satin, June 2008									
2006D, Nebraska	273,000,000	263	66.5	100%	$0.30	$0.75	$1	$10	$30
Auctions: $23, MS-69 Satin, December 2008									
2006S, Nebraska, Proof	2,882,428	5,829	69.4				$3	$4.50	$15
Auctions: $89, PF-70UCam, August 2009									
2006S, Nebraska, Proof, Silver	1,585,008	9,373	69.5				$8	$9	$20
Auctions: $23, PF-70UCam, December 2008									
2006P, Colorado	274,800,000	252	65.9	100%	$0.30	$0.75	$1	$10	$30
Auctions: $32, MS-69 Satin, August 2009									
2006D, Colorado	294,200,000	421	66.4	100%	$0.30	$0.75	$1	$10	$30
Auctions: $11, MS-69 Satin, January 2009									
2006S, Colorado, Proof	2,882,428	5,815	69.4				$3	$4.50	$15
Auctions: $29, PF-70DCam, November 2008									
2006S, Colorado, Proof, Silver	1,585,008	9,464	69.5				$8	$9	$20
Auctions: $36, PF-70UCam, June 2009									
2006P, North Dakota	305,800,000	182	65.8	99%	$0.30	$0.75	$1	$10	$30
Auctions: $148, MS-69 Satin, November 2007									
2006D, North Dakota	359,000,000	260	66.2	100%	$0.30	$0.75	$1	$10	$30
Auctions: $223, MS-65, January 2014									
2006S, North Dakota, Proof	2,882,428	5,828	69.4				$3	$4.50	$15
Auctions: $29, PF-70UCam, December 2008									
2006S, North Dakota, Proof, Silver	1,585,008	9,465	69.5				$8	$9	$20
Auctions: $11, PF-70DCam, October 2008									
2006P, South Dakota	245,000,000	161	66.0	100%	$0.30	$0.75	$1	$10	$30
Auctions: $25, MS-66, June 2013									
2006D, South Dakota	265,800,000	187	66.3	99%	$0.30	$0.50	$1	$10	$30
Auctions: $123, AU-58, July 2014									
2006S, South Dakota, Proof	2,882,428	5,832	69.5				$3	$4.50	$15
Auctions: $69, PF-70DCam, December 2009									
2006S, South Dakota, Proof, Silver	1,585,008	9,458	69.5				$8	$9	$20
Auctions: $66, PF-70UCam, June 2009									

| 2007, Montana | 2007, Washington | 2007, Idaho | 2007, Wyoming | 2007, Utah |

	Mintage	Cert	Avg	%MS	AU-50	MS-63	MS-65 / PF-65	MS-66 / PF-66DC	MS-67 / PF-69DC
2007P, Montana	257,000,000	107	66.1	100%	$0.30	$0.75	$1	$10	$30
Auctions: No auction records available.									
2007D, Montana	256,240,000	153	65.9	99%	$0.30	$0.75	$1	$10	$30
Auctions: No auction records available.									
2007S, Montana, Proof	2,374,778	3,424	69.5				$3	$4.50	$15
Auctions: $15, PF-69DCam, February 2013									
2007S, Montana, Proof, Silver	1,313,481	7,898	69.4				$8	$9	$20
Auctions: $15, PF-69DCam, February 2013									
2007P, Washington	265,200,000	136	66.1	100%	$0.30	$0.75	$1	$10	$30
Auctions: No auction records available.									
2007D, Washington	280,000,000	146	66.0	99%	$0.30	$0.75	$1	$10	$30
Auctions: $24, MS-69 Satin, January 2009									
2007S, Washington, Proof	2,374,778	3,209	69.5				$3	$4.50	$15
Auctions: $19, PF-70DCam, April 2013									
2007S, Washington, Proof, Silver	1,313,481	7,858	69.4				$8	$9	$20
Auctions: $47, PF-70UCam, February 2010									
2007P, Idaho	294,600,000	73	65.8	100%	$0.30	$0.75	$1	$10	$30
Auctions: $123, AU-50, September 2014									
2007D, Idaho	286,800,000	112	66.1	100%	$0.30	$0.75	$1	$10	$30
Auctions: $1,175, MS-66, June 2014; $940, MS-66, September 2014									
2007S, Idaho, Proof	2,374,778	3,225	69.5				$3	$4.50	$15
Auctions: $53, PF-70DCam, October 2009									
2007S, Idaho, Proof, Silver	1,313,481	7,912	69.4				$8	$9	$20
Auctions: $20, PF-69DCam, February 2013									
2007P, Wyoming	243,600,000	56	64.9	100%	$0.30	$0.75	$1	$10	$30
Auctions: No auction records available.									
2007D, Wyoming	320,800,000	127	65.9	99%	$0.30	$0.75	$1	$10	$30
Auctions: $48, AU-55, May 2013									
2007S, Wyoming, Proof	2,374,778	3,151	69.4				$3	$4.50	$15
Auctions: $55, PF-70DCam, June 2014									
2007S, Wyoming, Proof, Silver	1,313,481	7,780	69.3				$8	$9	$20
Auctions: $20, PF-69DCam, February 2013									
2007P, Utah	255,000,000	125	65.6	100%	$0.30	$0.75	$1	$10	$30
Auctions: No auction records available.									
2007D, Utah	253,200,000	190	66.2	100%	$0.30	$0.75	$1	$10	$30
Auctions: No auction records available.									
2007S, Utah, Proof	2,374,778	3,169	69.5				$3	$4.50	$15
Auctions: $84, PF-70DCam, November 2009									
2007S, Utah, Proof, Silver	1,313,481	7,907	69.4				$8	$9	$20
Auctions: $45, PF-70DCam, March 2014									

| 2008, Oklahoma | 2008, New Mexico | 2008, Arizona | 2008, Alaska | 2008, Hawaii |

	Mintage	Cert	Avg	%MS	AU-50	MS-63	MS-65 / PF-65	MS-66 / PF-66DC	MS-67 / PF-69DC
2008P, Oklahoma	222,000,000	65	65.7	98%	$0.30	$0.75	$1	$10	$30
Auctions: No auction records available.									
2008D, Oklahoma	194,600,000	99	66.2	100%	$0.30	$0.75	$1	$10	$30
Auctions: No auction records available.									
2008S, Oklahoma, Proof	2,078,112	3,503	69.5				$3	$5	$18
Auctions: $30, PF-70UCam, March 2010									
2008S, Oklahoma, Proof, Silver	1,192,908	8,284	69.5				$8	$9	$20
Auctions: $45, PF-70UCam, July 2008									
2008P, New Mexico	244,200,000	79	65.3	100%	$0.30	$0.75	$1	$10	$30
Auctions: No auction records available.									
2008D, New Mexico	244,400,000	112	66.3	100%	$0.30	$0.75	$1	$10	$30
Auctions: No auction records available.									
2008S, New Mexico, Proof	2,078,112	3,567	69.4				$3	$5	$18
Auctions: $19, PF-70DCam, March 2014									
2008S, New Mexico, Proof, Silver	1,192,908	8,156	69.5				$8	$9	$20
Auctions: $60, PF-70UCam, November 2008									
2008P, Arizona	244,600,000	119	65.7	100%	$0.30	$0.75	$1	$10	$30
Auctions: No auction records available.									
2008D, Arizona	265,000,000	46	65.8	98%	$0.30	$0.75	$1	$10	$30
Auctions: $1,152, MS-64, February 2013									
2008S, Arizona, Proof	2,078,112	3,648	69.6				$3	$4.50	$15
Auctions: $53, PF-70UCam, March 2010									
2008S, Arizona, Proof, Silver	1,192,908	8,516	69.5				$8	$10	$22
Auctions: $18, PF-69DCam, January 2013									
2008P, Alaska	251,800,000	48	65.3	100%	$0.30	$0.75	$1	$10	$30
Auctions: No auction records available.									
2008D, Alaska	254,000,000	57	65.7	100%	$0.30	$0.75	$1	$10	$30
Auctions: No auction records available.									
2008S, Alaska, Proof	2,078,112	3,483	69.5				$3	$5	$18
Auctions: $40, PF-70UCam, March 2010									
2008S, Alaska, Proof, Silver	1,192,908	8,445	69.5				$8	$10	$22
Auctions: $104, PF-70UCam, March 2010									
2008P, Hawaii	254,000,000	118	65.3	100%	$0.30	$0.50	$1	$10	$30
Auctions: No auction records available.									
2008D, Hawaii	263,600,000	58	65.7	100%	$0.30	$0.75	$1	$10	$30
Auctions: No auction records available.									
2008S, Hawaii, Proof	2,078,112	3,510	69.4				$3	$10	$25
Auctions: $50, PF-70UCam, March 2010									
2008S, Hawaii, Proof, Silver	1,192,908	8,400	69.4				$8	$10	$22
Auctions: $149, PF-70DCam, April 2013									

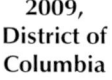

2009, District of Columbia	2009, Puerto Rico	2009, Guam	2009, American Samoa	2009, U.S. Virgin Islands

	Mintage	Cert	Avg	%MS	AU-50	MS-63	MS-65	MS-66	MS-67
							PF-65	PF-66DC	PF-69DC
2009P, District of Columbia	83,600,000	85	66.1	100%	$0.50	$1	$1.50	$10	$30
Auctions: No auction records available.									
2009D, District of Columbia	88,800,000	116	66.4	100%	$0.50	$1	$1.50	$10	$30
Auctions: No auction records available.									
2009S, District of Columbia, Proof	2,113,478	4,148	69.6				$3	$4.50	$15
Auctions: $15, PF-69DCam, November 2013									
2009S, District of Columbia, Proof, Silver	996,548	6,436	69.7				$8	$9	$20
Auctions: No auction records available.									
2009P, Puerto Rico	53,200,000	90	65.9	100%	$0.50	$1	$1.50	$10	$30
Auctions: No auction records available.									
2009D, Puerto Rico	86,000,000	81	66.6	100%	$0.50	$1	$1.50	$10	$30
Auctions: No auction records available.									
2009S, Puerto Rico, Proof	2,113,478	4,132	69.6				$3	$4.50	$15
Auctions: $38, PF-70DCam, February 2010									
2009S, Puerto Rico, Proof, Silver	996,548	6,613	69.7				$8	$9	$20
Auctions: $104, PF-70UCam, March 2010									
2009P, Guam	45,000,000	40	66.1	100%	$0.50	$1	$1.50	$10	$30
Auctions: No auction records available.									
2009D, Guam	42,600,000	63	66.6	100%	$0.50	$1	$1.50	$10	$30
Auctions: No auction records available.									
2009S, Guam, Proof	2,113,478	4,034	69.6				$3	$4.50	$15
Auctions: $15, PF-69DCam, March 2013									
2009S, Guam, Proof, Silver	996,548	6,377	69.7				$8	$9	$20
Auctions: $18, PF-69DCam, January 2013									
2009P, American Samoa	42,600,000	104	66.5	100%	$0.50	$1	$1.50	$10	$30
Auctions: No auction records available.									
2009D, American Samoa	39,600,000	134	67.0	100%	$0.50	$1	$1.50	$10	$30
Auctions: No auction records available.									
2009S, American Samoa, Proof	2,113,478	4,198	69.6				$3	$4.50	$15
Auctions: $16, PF-69DCam, November 2013									
2009S, American Samoa, Proof, Silver	996,548	6,516	69.7				$8	$9	$20
Auctions: $62, PF-70UCam, January 2010									
2009P, U.S. Virgin Islands	41,000,000	65	66.8	100%	$0.75	$1	$1.50	$12	$32
Auctions: No auction records available.									
2009D, U.S. Virgin Islands	41,000,000	68	66.8	100%	$0.75	$1	$1.50	$12	$32
Auctions: No auction records available.									
2009S, U.S. Virgin Islands, Proof	2,113,478	4,173	69.6				$3	$4.50	$15
Auctions: $104, PF-70DCam, March 2010									
2009S, U.S. Virgin Islands, Proof, Silver	996,548	6,489	69.7				$8	$9	$20
Auctions: $60, PF-70UCam, March 2010									

2009,
Northern
Mariana Islands

2004-D, Wisconsin,
Normal Reverse

2004-D, Wisconsin,
Extra Leaf High
FS-25-2004D-WI-5901.

2004-D, Wisconsin,
Extra Leaf Low
FS-25-2004D-WI-5902.

| | Mintage | Cert | Avg | %MS | AU-50 | MS-63 | MS-65 | MS-66 | MS-67 |
							PF-65	PF-66DC	PF-69DC
2009P, Northern Mariana Islands	35,200,000	105	66.7	100%	$0.50	$1	$1.50	$10	$30
Auctions: No auction records available.									
2009D, Northern Mariana Islands	37,600,000	104	66.7	100%	$0.50	$1	$1.50	$10	$30
Auctions: No auction records available.									
2009S, Northern Mariana Islands, Proof	2,113,478	4,175	69.6				$3	$4.50	$15
Auctions: $15, PF-69DCam, January 2013									
2009S, Northern Mariana Islands, Proof, Silver	996,548	6,473	69.7				$8	$9	$20
Auctions: $17, PF-69DCam, November 2013									

WASHINGTON, AMERICA THE BEAUTIFUL™ (2010 TO DATE)

Designers: *John Flanagan and others.* **Weight:** *Clad issue—5.67 grams; silver Proofs—6.25 grams.* **Composition:** *Clad issue—Outer layers of copper-nickel (.750 copper, .250 nickel) bonded to inner core of pure copper; silver Proofs—.900 silver, .100 copper (net weight .18084 oz. pure silver).* **Diameter:** *24.3 mm.* **Edge:** *Reeded.* **Mints:** *Clad issue—Philadelphia, Denver; silver Proofs—San Francisco.*

Circulation Strike

Proof

History. In 2010 the U.S. Mint introduced a new program of quarters honoring national parks and historic sites in each state, the District of Columbia, and the five U.S. territories. It will run through 2021. These are released at the rate of five new reverse designs each year, in combination with the obverse found on the State and D.C./Territorial quarters of previous years. Circulation strikes are made at the Philadelphia and Denver mints, and special silver-content and Proof issues at San Francisco. Each coin combines a modified obverse depicting George Washington, without a date. The reverses are distinctive and bear the date of issue and a special design showcasing a national park in the state, district, or territory. The official title of the series is the America the Beautiful™ Quarters Program; popularly, they are known as National Park quarters.

In 2012, the U.S. Mint introduced a new innovation in the National Park quarters program. For the first time since the 1950s, the San Francisco Mint is being used to produce quarters in a non-Proof format. These Uncirculated coins are made in limited quantities for collectors. They can be purchased directly from the Mint for a premium above their face value, as opposed to being released into circulation like normal quarters. Unlike the Uncirculated S-mintmark Bicentennial quarters dated 1976, which were 40% silver and sold only in sets, the S-mintmark National Park quarters are of normal copper-nickel-clad composition and are sold in bags of 100 and rolls of 40 coins. Thus the 2012-S coins are considered the first circulation-strike quarters made at San Francisco since 1954. The S-mintmark coins have been made of each National Park design from 2012 to date.

Striking and Sharpness. These quarters can have light striking on the highest area of the obverse. On the reverse there can be weak areas, depending on the design, seemingly more often seen on Denver Mint coins.

Availability. All modern quarters are readily available in high grades. Typical MS coins are MS-63 and 64 with light abrasion. MS-65 and higher coins are in the minority, but enough exist that finding them is no problem. Around MS-68 many issues are scarce, and higher grades are scarcer yet. The S-mintmark coins are proportionally scarce compared to Philadelphia and Denver issues, and are not seen in circulation. They are available for direct purchase from the U.S. Mint in their year of issue, and from the secondary market after that.

Proofs. National Park quarter dollar Proofs are made in San Francisco. For certain later issues, Proofs are available in clad metal as well as silver strikings. On some Proofs over-polishing of dies has eliminated some details.

GRADING STANDARDS

MS-60 to 70 (Mint State). *Obverse:* At MS-60, some abrasion and contact marks are evident on the highest-relief parts of the hair and the cheek. At MS-63, abrasion is slight at best, less so at MS-64. An MS-65 coin should display no abrasion or contact marks except under magnification, and MS-66 and higher coins should have none at all. Luster should be full. *Reverse:* Check the highest-relief areas of the design (these differ from coin to coin). Otherwise, comments are as for the obverse.

2010-D, Hot Springs (AR). Graded MS-68.

PF-60 to 70 (Proof). *Obverse and Reverse:* These coins are so recent, and as only a few have been cleaned, most approach perfection and can be designated PF-68 to 70, the latter only if no contact marks or other problems can be seen under magnification. A cleaned coin with extensive hairlines would not be collectible for most numismatists and would be classified at a lower level such as PF-60 to 63. Those with lighter hairlines qualify for PF-64 or 65.

2010-S, Yosemite National Park (CA). Graded PF-70 Deep Cameo.

2010, Hot Springs National Park (Arkansas)	2010, Yellowstone National Park (Wyoming)	2010, Yosemite National Park (California)	2010, Grand Canyon National Park (Arizona)	2010, Mt. Hood National Forest (Oregon)

	Mintage	Cert	Avg	%MS	AU-50	MS-63	MS-65 PF-65	MS-66 PF-66DC	MS-67 PF-69DC
2010P, Hot Springs National Park (AR)	35,600,000	696	66.1	100%	$0.50	$0.75	$1	$10	$30
Auctions: No auction records available.									
2010D, Hot Springs National Park (AR)	34,000,000	1,541	65.6	100%	$0.50	$0.75	$1	$10	$30
Auctions: No auction records available.									
2010S, Hot Springs National Park (AR), Proof	1,401,903	4,041	69.5				$3	$4.50	$15
Auctions: $15, PF-69DCam, January 2013									
2010S, Hot Springs, National Park (AR), Proof, Silver	859,435	11,165	69.6				$8	$9	$20
Auctions: $21, PF-69DCam, February 2013									
2010P, Yellowstone National Park (WY)	33,600,000	433	66.1	100%	$0.50	$0.75	$1	$10	$30
Auctions: No auction records available.									
2010D, Yellowstone National Park (WY)	34,800,000	734	65.8	100%	$0.50	$0.75	$1	$10	$30
Auctions: No auction records available.									
2010S, Yellowstone National Park (WY), Proof	1,402,756	4,081	69.5				$3	$4.50	$15
Auctions: $16, PF-69DCam, March 2013									
2010S, Yellowstone National Park (WY), Proof, Silver	859,435	11,174	69.7				$8	$9	$20
Auctions: $21, PF-69DCam, February 2013									
2010P, Yosemite National Park (CA)	35,200,000	285	66.1	100%	$0.50	$0.75	$1.25	$12	$30
Auctions: No auction records available.									
2010D, Yosemite National Park (CA)	34,800,000	615	66.0	100%	$0.50	$0.75	$1	$10	$30
Auctions: No auction records available.									
2010S, Yosemite National Park (CA), Proof	1,400,215	4,006	69.5				$3	$4.50	$15
Auctions: $17, PF-69DCam, February 2013									
2010S, Yosemite National Park (CA), Proof, Silver	859,435	11,077	69.6				$8	$9	$20
Auctions: $18, PF-69DCam, March 2013									
2010P, Grand Canyon National Park (AZ)	34,800,000	372	66.3	100%	$0.50	$0.75	$1	$10	$30
Auctions: No auction records available.									
2010D, Grand Canyon National Park (AZ)	35,400,000	626	66.1	100%	$0.50	$0.75	$1	$10	$30
Auctions: No auction records available.									
2010S, Grand Canyon National Park (AZ), Proof	1,399,970	3,993	69.5				$3	$4.50	$15
Auctions: $19, PF-69DCam, February 2013									
2010S, Grand Canyon National Park (AZ), Proof, Silver	859,435	11,099	69.6				$8	$9	$20
Auctions: No auction records available.									
2010P, Mt. Hood National Forest (OR)	34,400,000	205	66.1	100%	$0.50	$0.75	$1	$10	$30
Auctions: No auction records available.									
2010D, Mt. Hood National Forest (OR)	34,400,000	408	65.6	100%	$0.50	$0.75	$1	$10	$30
Auctions: No auction records available.									
2010S, Mt. Hood National Forest (OR), Proof	1,397,101	4,008	69.4				$3	$4.50	$15
Auctions: $15, PF-69DCam, February 2013									
2010S, Mt. Hood National Forest (OR), Proof, Silver	859,435	11,272	69.6				$8	$9	$20
Auctions: No auction records available.									

2011, Gettysburg National Military Park (Pennsylvania)	2011, Glacier National Park (Montana)	2011, Olympic National Park (Washington)	2011, Vicksburg National Military Park (Mississippi)	2011, Chickasaw National Recreation Area (Oklahoma)

	Mintage	Cert	Avg	%MS	AU-50	MS-63	MS-65	MS-66	MS-67
							PF-65	PF-66DC	PF-69DC
2011P, Gettysburg National Military Park (PA)	30,800,000	741	66.3	100%	$0.50	$0.75	$1	$10	$30
Auctions: No auction records available.									
2011D, Gettysburg National Military Park (PA)	30,400,000	289	66.5	100%	$0.50	$0.75	$1.25	$12	$30
Auctions: No auction records available.									
2011S, Gettysburg National Military Park (PA), Proof	1,271,553	2,750	69.5				$3	$4.50	$15
Auctions: No auction records available.									
2011S, Gettysburg National Military Park (PA), Proof, Silver	722,076	5,848	69.7				$8	$9	$20
Auctions: No auction records available.									
2011P, Glacier National Park (MT)	30,400,000	270	67.2	100%	$0.50	$0.75	$1	$10	$30
Auctions: No auction records available.									
2011D, Glacier National Park (MT)	31,200,000	438	65.8	100%	$0.50	$0.75	$1	$10	$30
Auctions: No auction records available.									
2011S, Glacier National Park (MT), Proof	1,268,452	2,748	69.6				$3	$4.50	$15
Auctions: No auction records available.									
2011S, Glacier National Park (MT), Proof, Silver	722,076	6,002	69.7				$8	$9	$20
Auctions: No auction records available.									
2011P, Olympic National Park (WA)	30,400,000	293	67.1	100%	$0.50	$0.75	$1	$10	$30
Auctions: No auction records available.									
2011D, Olympic National Park (WA)	30,600,000	543	66.2	100%	$0.50	$0.75	$1	$10	$30
Auctions: No auction records available.									
2011S, Olympic National Park (WA), Proof	1,267,361	2,760	69.6				$3	$4.50	$15
Auctions: No auction records available.									
2011S, Olympic National Park (WA), Proof, Silver	722,076	5,827	69.7				$8	$9	$20
Auctions: No auction records available.									
2011P, Vicksburg National Military Park (MS)	30,800,000	269	66.8	100%	$0.50	$0.75	$1	$10	$30
Auctions: No auction records available.									
2011D, Vicksburg National Military Park (MS)	33,400,000	448	66.3	100%	$0.50	$0.75	$1	$10	$30
Auctions: No auction records available.									
2011S, Vicksburg National Military Park (MS), Proof	1,267,691	2,755	69.5				$3	$4.50	$15
Auctions: No auction records available.									
2011S, Vicksburg National Military Park (MS), Proof, Silver	722,076	5,872	69.7				$8	$9	$20
Auctions: No auction records available.									
2011P, Chickasaw National Recreation Area (OK)	73,800,000	306	67.2	100%	$0.45	$0.50	$1	$10	$30
Auctions: No auction records available.									
2011D, Chickasaw National Recreation Area (OK)	69,400,000	419	66.2	100%	$0.45	$0.50	$1	$10	$30
Auctions: No auction records available.									
2011S, Chickasaw National Recreation Area (OK), Proof	1,266,010	2,743	69.5				$3	$4.50	$15
Auctions: No auction records available.									
2011S, Chickasaw National Recreation Area (OK), Proof, Silver	722,076	5,783	69.6				$8	$9	$20
Auctions: No auction records available.									

2012, El Yunque National Forest (Puerto Rico)	2012, Chaco Culture National Historical Park (New Mexico)	2012, Acadia National Park (Maine)	2012, Hawai'i Volcanoes National Park (Hawaii)	2012, Denali National Park and Preserve (Alaska)

	Mintage	Cert	Avg	%MS	AU-50	MS-63	MS-65 PF-65	MS-66 PF-66DC	MS-67 PF-69DC
2012P, El Yunque National Forest (PR)	25,800,000	598	66.1	100%	$0.50	$0.75	$1	$10	$30
Auctions: No auction records available.									
2012D, El Yunque National Forest (PR)	25,000,000	266	66.7	100%	$0.50	$0.75	$1	$10	$30
Auctions: No auction records available.									
2012S, El Yunque National Forest (PR) (a)	1,679,240	609	66.4	100%		$2	$3	$12	$35
Auctions: No auction records available.									
2012S, El Yunque National Forest (PR), Proof	*1,010,361*	1,954	69.4				$3	$4.50	$15
Auctions: No auction records available.									
2012S, El Yunque National Forest (PR), Proof, Silver	*557,891*	4,721	69.7				$8	$9	$20
Auctions: No auction records available.									
2012P, Chaco Culture National Historical Park (NM)	22,000,000	138	67.2	100%	$0.50	$0.75	$1	$10	$30
Auctions: No auction records available.									
2012D, Chaco Culture National Historical Park (NM)	22,000,000	340	66.2	100%	$0.50	$0.75	$1	$10	$30
Auctions: No auction records available.									
2012S, Chaco Culture National Historical Park (NM) (a)	1,389,020	666	66.5	100%		$2	$3	$12	$35
Auctions: No auction records available.									
2012S, Chaco Culture National Historical Park (NM), Proof	*960,049*	1,913	69.3				$3	$4.50	$15
Auctions: No auction records available.									
2012S, Chaco Culture National Historical Park (NM), Proof, Silver	*557,891*	4,487	69.7				$8	$9	$20
Auctions: No auction records available.									
2012P, Acadia National Park (ME)	24,800,000	338	65.6	100%	$0.50	$0.75	$1	$10	$30
Auctions: No auction records available.									
2012D, Acadia National Park (ME)	21,606,000	105	66.7	100%	$0.50	$0.75	$1	$10	$30
Auctions: No auction records available.									
2012S, Acadia National Park (ME) (a)	1,409,120	664	66.3	100%		$1	$2	$12	$35
Auctions: No auction records available.									
2012S, Acadia National Park (ME), Proof	*960,409*	1,915	69.4				$3	$4.50	$15
Auctions: No auction records available.									
2012S, Acadia National Park (ME), Proof, Silver	*557,891*	4,652	69.7				$8	$9	$20
Auctions: No auction records available.									

a. Not issued for circulation. From 2012 to date, the San Francisco Mint has made Uncirculated S-mintmark quarters of each design in the National Park series. These can be purchased by collectors directly from the U.S. Mint, in bags of 100 or rolls of 40 coins, for a premium above face value.

	Mintage	Cert	Avg	%MS	AU-50	MS-63	MS-65 PF-65	MS-66 PF-66DC	MS-67 PF-69DC
2012P, Hawai'i Volcanoes National Park (HI)	46,200,000	127	67.1	100%	$0.50	$0.50	$1	$10	$30
Auctions: No auction records available.									
2012D, Hawai'i Volcanoes National Park (HI)	78,600,000	392	66.1	100%	$0.45	$0.50	$1	$10	$30
Auctions: No auction records available.									
2012S, Hawai'i Volcanoes National Park (HI) (a)	1,407,520	606	66.3	100%	$0.45	$1	$2	$12	$35
Auctions: No auction records available.									
2012S, Hawai'i Volcanoes National Park (HI), Proof	*961,272*	1,916	69.4				$3	$4.50	$15
Auctions: No auction records available.									
2012S, Hawai'i Volcanoes National Park (HI), Proof, Silver	*557,891*	4,774	69.7				$8	$9	$20
Auctions: No auction records available.									
2012P, Denali National Park and Preserve (AK)	135,400,000	143	67.0	100%	$0.40	$0.50	$1	$10	$30
Auctions: No auction records available.									
2012D, Denali National Park and Preserve (AK)	166,600,000	432	66.2	100%	$0.40	$0.50	$1	$10	$30
Auctions: No auction records available.									
2012S, Denali National Park and Preserve (AK) (a)	1,401,920	454	66.1	100%		$1	$2	$12	$35
Auctions: No auction records available.									
2012S, Denali National Park and Preserve (AK), Proof	*957,856*	1,916	69.3				$3	$4.50	$15
Auctions: No auction records available.									
2012S, Denali National Park and Preserve (AK), Proof, Silver	*557,891*	4,674	69.7				$8	$9	$20
Auctions: No auction records available.									

a. Not issued for circulation. From 2012 to date, the San Francisco Mint has made Uncirculated S-mintmark quarters of each design in the National Park series. These can be purchased by collectors directly from the U.S. Mint, in bags of 100 or rolls of 40 coins, for a premium above face value.

2013, White Mountain National Forest (New Hampshire)	2013, Perry's Victory and International Peace Memorial (Ohio)	2013, Great Basin National Park (Nevada)	2013, Fort McHenry National Monument and Historic Shrine (Maryland)	2013, Mount Rushmore National Memorial (South Dakota)

	Mintage	Cert	Avg	%MS	AU-50	MS-63	MS-65 PF-65	MS-66 PF-66DC	MS-67 PF-69DC
2013P, White Mountain National Forest (NH)	68,800,000	550	66.5	100%	$0.50	$0.75	$1	$10	$30
Auctions: No auction records available.									
2013D, White Mountain National Forest (NH)	107,600,000	312	67.1	100%	$0.50	$0.75	$1	$10	$30
Auctions: No auction records available.									
2013S, White Mountain National Forest (NH) (a)	1,606,900	368	66.5	100%		$2	$3	$12	$35
Auctions: No auction records available.									
2013S, White Mountain National Forest (NH), Proof	*948,364*	1,830	69.5				$3	$4.50	$15
Auctions: No auction records available.									
2013S, White Mountain National Forest (NH), Proof, Silver	*557,647*	4,910	69.7				$8	$9	$20
Auctions: No auction records available.									

a. Not issued for circulation. From 2012 to date, the San Francisco Mint has made Uncirculated S-mintmark quarters of each design in the National Park series. These can be purchased by collectors directly from the U.S. Mint, in bags of 100 or rolls of 40 coins, for a premium above face value.

	Mintage	Cert	Avg	%MS	AU-50	MS-63	MS-65 / PF-65	MS-66 / PF-66DC	MS-67 / PF-69DC
2013P, Perry's Victory and International Peace Memorial (OH)	107,800,000	484	66.6	100%	$0.50	$0.75	$1	$10	$30
Auctions: No auction records available.									
2013D, Perry's Victory and International Peace Memorial (OH)	131,600,000	289	67.2	100%	$0.50	$0.75	$1	$10	$30
Auctions: No auction records available.									
2013S, Perry's Victory and International Peace Memorial (OH) (a)	1,023,640	270	66.4	100%		$1	$2	$12	$35
Auctions: No auction records available.									
2013S, Perry's Victory and International Peace Memorial (OH), Proof	947,055	1,801	69.5				$3	$4.50	$15
Auctions: No auction records available.									
2013S, Perry's Victory and International Peace Memorial (OH), Proof, Silver	557,647	4,793	69.7				$8	$9	$20
Auctions: No auction records available.									
2013P, Great Basin National Park (NV)	122,400,000	221	66.9	100%	$0.50	$0.75	$1	$10	$30
Auctions: No auction records available.									
2013D, Great Basin National Park (NV)	141,400,000	448	66.5	100%	$0.50	$0.75	$1	$10	$30
Auctions: No auction records available.									
2013S, Great Basin National Park (NV) (a)	1,316,500	365	66.9	100%		$1	$2	$12	$35
Auctions: No auction records available.									
2013S, Great Basin National Park (NV), Proof	945,055	1,800	69.5				$3	$4.50	$15
Auctions: No auction records available.									
2013S, Great Basin National Park (NV), Proof, Silver	557,647	4,967	69.7				$8	$9	$20
Auctions: No auction records available.									
2013P, Ft. McHenry National Monument / Historic Shrine (MD)	120,000,000	506	66.5	100%	$0.50	$0.75	$1	$10	$30
Auctions: No auction records available.									
2013D, Ft. McHenry National Monument / Historic Shrine (MD)	151,400,000	294	67.2	100%	$0.50	$0.75	$1	$10	$30
Auctions: No auction records available.									
2013S, Ft. McHenry National Monument / Historic Shrine (MD) (a)	1,313,680	589	67.1	100%		$1	$2	$12	$35
Auctions: No auction records available.									
2013S, Ft. McHenry National Monument / Historic Shrine (MD), Proof	945,414	1,797	69.5				$3	$4.50	$15
Auctions: No auction records available.									
2013S, Ft. McHenry National Monument / Historic Shrine (MD), Proof, Silver	557,647	4,924	69.7				$8	$9	$20
Auctions: No auction records available.									
2013P, Mount Rushmore National Memorial (SD)	231,800,000	196	66.9	100%	$0.50	$0.75	$1	$10	$30
Auctions: No auction records available.									
2013D, Mount Rushmore National Memorial (SD)	272,400,000	445	66.3	100%	$0.50	$0.75	$1	$10	$30
Auctions: No auction records available.									
2013S, Mount Rushmore National Memorial (SD) (a)	1,373,260	513	66.9	100%		$1	$2	$12	$35
Auctions: No auction records available.									
2013S, Mount Rushmore National Memorial (SD), Proof	946,016	1,799	69.5				$3	$4.50	$15
Auctions: No auction records available.									
2013S, Mount Rushmore National Memorial (SD), Proof, Silver	557,647	4,937	69.7				$8	$9	$20
Auctions: No auction records available.									

a. Not issued for circulation. From 2012 to date, the San Francisco Mint has made Uncirculated S-mintmark quarters of each design in the National Park series. These can be purchased by collectors directly from the U.S. Mint, in bags of 100 or rolls of 40 coins, for a premium above face value.

2014, Great Smoky Mountains National Park (Tennessee)	2014, Shenandoah National Park (Virginia)	2014, Arches National Park (Utah)	2014, Great Sand Dunes National Park (Colorado)	2014, Everglades National Park (Florida)

	Mintage	Cert	Avg	%MS	AU-50	MS-63	MS-65 / PF-65	MS-66 / PF-66DC	MS-67 / PF-69DC
2014P, Great Smoky Mountains National Park (TN)	73,200,000	476	66.6	100%	$0.50	$0.75	$1	$10	$30
Auctions: No auction records available.									
2014D, Great Smoky Mountains National Park (TN)	99,400,000	338	67.2	100%	$0.50	$0.75	$1	$10	$30
Auctions: No auction records available.									
2014S, Great Smoky Mountains National Park (TN) (a)	1,326,380	522	66.7	100%		$1	$2	$12	$35
Auctions: No auction records available.									
2014S, Great Smoky Mountains National Park (TN), Proof	790,678	1,750	69.6				$3	$4.50	$15
Auctions: No auction records available.									
2014S, Great Smoky Mountains National Park (TN), Proof, Silver	501,944	3,877	69.7				$8	$9	$20
Auctions: No auction records available.									
2014P, Shenandoah National Park (VA)	112,800,000	412	66.4	100%	$0.50	$0.75	$1	$10	$30
Auctions: No auction records available.									
2014D, Shenandoah National Park (VA)	197,800,000	231	67.4	100%	$0.50	$0.75	$1	$10	$30
Auctions: No auction records available.									
2014S, Shenandoah National Park (VA) (a)	1,237,340	756	66.9	100%		$1	$2	$12	$35
Auctions: No auction records available.									
2014S, Shenandoah National Park (VA), Proof	788,373	1,745	69.6				$3	$4.50	$15
Auctions: No auction records available.									
2014S, Shenandoah National Park (VA), Proof, Silver	501,944	3,878	69.7				$8	$9	$20
Auctions: No auction records available.									
2014P, Arches National Park (UT)	214,200,000	207	67.4	100%	$0.50	$0.75	$1	$10	$30
Auctions: No auction records available.									
2014D, Arches National Park (UT)	251,400,000	232	67.6	100%	$0.50	$0.75	$1	$10	$30
Auctions: No auction records available.									
2014S, Arches National Park (UT) (a)	1,076,740	685	66.8	100%		$2	$3	$12	$35
Auctions: No auction records available.									
2014S, Arches National Park (UT), Proof	786,542	1,748	69.5				$3	$4.50	$15
Auctions: No auction records available.									
2014S, Arches National Park (UT), Proof, Silver	501,944	4,007	69.7				$8	$9	$20
Auctions: No auction records available.									

a. Not issued for circulation. From 2012 to date, the San Francisco Mint has made Uncirculated S-mintmark quarters of each design in the National Park series. These can be purchased by collectors directly from the U.S. Mint, in bags of 100 or rolls of 40 coins, for a premium above face value.

	Mintage	Cert	Avg	%MS	AU-50	MS-63	MS-65 PF-65	MS-66 PF-66DC	MS-67 PF-69DC
2014P, Great Sand Dunes National Park (CO)	159,600,000	161	67.5	100%	$0.50	$0.75	$1	$10	$30
Auctions: No auction records available.									
2014D, Great Sand Dunes National Park (CO)	171,800,000	191	67.7	100%	$0.50	$0.75	$1	$10	$30
Auctions: No auction records available.									
2014S, Great Sand Dunes National Park (CO) (a)	1,040,580	785	67.1	100%		$1	$2	$12	$35
Auctions: No auction records available.									
2014S, Great Sand Dunes National Park (CO), Proof	784,878	1,745	69.6				$3	$4.50	$15
Auctions: No auction records available.									
2014S, Great Sand Dunes National Park (CO), Proof, Silver	501,944	3,873	69.7				$8	$9	$20
Auctions: No auction records available.									
2014P, Everglades National Park (FL)	157,601,200	164	67.3	100%	$0.50	$0.75	$1	$10	$30
Auctions: No auction records available.									
2014D, Everglades National Park (FL)	142,400,000	240	67.7	100%	$0.50	$0.75	$1	$10	$30
Auctions: No auction records available.									
2014S, Everglades National Park (FL) (a)	954,540	0	n/a			$2	$3	$12	$35
Auctions: No auction records available.									
2014S, Everglades National Park (FL), Proof	784,467	1,745	69.6				$3	$4.50	$15
Auctions: No auction records available.									
2014S, Everglades National Park (FL), Proof, Silver	501,944	3,874	69.7				$8	$9	$20
Auctions: No auction records available.									

a. Not issued for circulation. From 2012 to date, the San Francisco Mint has made Uncirculated S-mintmark quarters of each design in the National Park series. These can be purchased by collectors directly from the U.S. Mint, in bags of 100 or rolls of 40 coins, for a premium above face value.

2015,
Homestead
National
Monument of
America (Nebraska)

2015,
Kisatchie
National Forest
(Louisiana)

2015,
Blue Ridge
Parkway
(North Carolina)

2015,
Bombay
Hook National
Wildlife Refuge
(Delaware)

2015,
Saratoga
National
Historical Park
(New York)

	Mintage	Cert	Avg	%MS	AU-50	MS-63	MS-65 PF-65	MS-66 PF-66DC	MS-67 PF-69DC
2015P, Homestead National Monument of America (NE)		0	n/a		$0.50	$0.75	$1	$10	$30
Auctions: No auction records available.									
2015D, Homestead National Monument of America (NE)		0	n/a		$0.50	$0.75	$1	$10	$30
Auctions: No auction records available.									
2015S, Homestead National Monument of America (NE) (a)		0	n/a			$2	$3	$12	$35
Auctions: No auction records available.									
2015S, Homestead National Monument of America (NE), Proof		0	n/a				$3	$4.50	$15
Auctions: No auction records available.									
2015S, Homestead National Monument of America (NE), Proof, Silver		0	n/a				$8	$9	$20
Auctions: No auction records available.									

a. Not issued for circulation. From 2012 to date, the San Francisco Mint has made Uncirculated S-mintmark quarters of each design in the National Park series. These can be purchased by collectors directly from the U.S. Mint, in bags of 100 or rolls of 40 coins, for a premium above face value.

	Mintage	Cert	Avg	%MS	AU-50	MS-63	MS-65	MS-66	MS-67
							PF-65	PF-66DC	PF-69DC
2015P, Kisatchie National Forest (LA)		0	n/a		$0.50	$0.75	$1	$10	$30
Auctions: No auction records available.									
2015D, Kisatchie National Forest (LA)		0	n/a		$0.50	$0.75	$1	$10	$30
Auctions: No auction records available.									
2015S, Kisatchie National Forest (LA) (a)		0	n/a			$2	$3	$12	$35
Auctions: No auction records available.									
2015S, Kisatchie National Forest (LA), Proof		0	n/a				$3	$4.50	$15
Auctions: No auction records available.									
2015S, Kisatchie National Forest (LA), Proof, Silver		0	n/a				$8	$9	$20
Auctions: No auction records available.									
2015P, Blue Ridge Parkway (NC)		0	n/a		$0.50	$0.75	$1	$10	$30
Auctions: No auction records available.									
2015D, Blue Ridge Parkway (NC)		0	n/a		$0.50	$0.75	$1	$10	$30
Auctions: No auction records available.									
2015S, Blue Ridge Parkway (NC) (a)		0	n/a			$2	$3	$12	$35
Auctions: No auction records available.									
2015S, Blue Ridge Parkway (NC), Proof		0	n/a				$3	$4.50	$15
Auctions: No auction records available.									
2015S, Blue Ridge Parkway (NC), Proof, Silver		0	n/a				$8	$9	$20
Auctions: No auction records available.									
2015P, Bombay Hook National Wildlife Refuge (DE)		0	n/a		$0.50	$0.75	$1	$10	$30
Auctions: No auction records available.									
2015D, Bombay Hook National Wildlife Refuge (DE)		0	n/a		$0.50	$0.75	$1	$10	$30
Auctions: No auction records available.									
2015S, Bombay Hook National Wildlife Refuge (DE) (a)		0	n/a			$2	$3	$12	$35
Auctions: No auction records available.									
2015S, Bombay Hook National Wildlife Refuge (DE), Proof		0	n/a				$3	$4.50	$15
Auctions: No auction records available.									
2015S, Bombay Hook National Wildlife Refuge (DE), Proof, Silver		0	n/a				$8	$9	$20
Auctions: No auction records available.									
2015P, Saratoga National Historical Park (NY)		0	n/a		$0.50	$0.75	$1	$10	$30
Auctions: No auction records available.									
2015D, Saratoga National Historical Park (NY)		0	n/a		$0.50	$0.75	$1	$10	$30
Auctions: No auction records available.									
2015S, Saratoga National Historical Park (NY) (a)		0	n/a			$2	$3	$12	$35
Auctions: No auction records available.									
2015S, Saratoga National Historical Park (NY), Proof		0	n/a				$3	$4.50	$15
Auctions: No auction records available.									
2015S, Saratoga National Historical Park (NY), Proof, Silver		0	n/a				$8	$9	$20
Auctions: No auction records available.									

a. Not issued for circulation. From 2012 to date, the San Francisco Mint has made Uncirculated S-mintmark quarters of each design in the National Park series. These can be purchased by collectors directly from the U.S. Mint, in bags of 100 or rolls of 40 coins, for a premium above face value.

Half Dollars
1794 to Date
AN OVERVIEW OF HALF DOLLARS

Many hobbyists consider a collection of half dollars to be one of the most satisfying in the American series. The panorama of designs is extensive, ranging from the early Flowing Hair issues of 1794 and 1795 down to classic 20th-century motifs and the presidential portrait of the present day. The large size of half dollar coins makes them convenient to view and easy to enjoy.

Among the types, the 1794–1795 Flowing Hair half dollar is readily available in circulated grades and rare in Mint State, but at any level is hard to find well struck and without adjustment marks (evidence of where a Mint worker filed an overweight planchet down to proper weight). Most on the market are dated 1795. Careful selection for quality is advised.

The next type, dated 1796–1797 with a Draped Bust obverse and Small Eagle reverse, is the scarcest in the American silver series excepting the 1839 Gobrecht dollar. (However, the latter is available in Proof restrike form, yielding choice and gem examples, so it can be considered in a different category from the circulation-strike 1796–1797 half dollar type.) It might not be possible to be particular, but, finances permitting, a collector should take some time and endeavor to find an example that is sharply struck on both sides. Needle-sharp striking is more of a theory than a practicality, and some compromise in this regard may be necessary.

Half dollars of the 1801–1807 type, with the obverse as preceding but now with the Heraldic Eagle reverse, are plentiful enough in worn grades but somewhat scarce in Mint State. Striking is seldom needle-sharp and ranges from average to very poor. However, there are enough coins in the marketplace that collectors can afford to take their time and seek a sharp strike.

Capped Bust half dollars with a lettered edge, 1807–1836, abound in just about any grade desired. Again, striking is a consideration, and some searching is needed for a high-quality strike. Generally, those in the late 1820s and the 1830s are better struck than are those of earlier dates, the earlier coins being scarcer and more expensive in any event.

The short-lived type of 1836–1837, Capped Bust with a reeded edge and with the denomination spelled as 50 CENTS, is available easily enough through the high-mintage 1837, but most have problems with the quality of striking. Then comes the 1838–1839 type of the same obverse style, its reverse modified with a slightly different eagle and with the denomination as HALF DOL. Generally these are fairly well struck.

Liberty Seated half dollars of the several styles within the series, 1839–1891, admit of no great rarities for the type collector, save for the 1839, No Drapery, in levels of MS-63 and finer. However, among the earlier types in particular, sharply struck pieces are in the minority. Curiously, the most readily available Mint State Liberty Seated half dollars also are the lowest-mintage issues, the dates 1879 and later, as these were recognized as desirable at the time of issue and were widely saved.

Barber half dollars were not popular in their time, and while Proofs exist in proportion to their production figures, few circulation-strike coins were saved by collectors and Mint State examples are quite scarce today. In fact, as a type, a Barber half dollar dated 1900 or later in Mint State is the scarcest of all silver issues of that century. Well-struck MS-63 and better Barber half dollars, with the upper-right corner of the shield and the leg at lower right showing full details, are significantly scarcer than generally realized.

Liberty Walking half dollars, minted from 1916 to 1947, are plentiful in all grades. Again, some attention should be made to striking sharpness, which makes the search become more intense. Fortunately there are countless thousands of MS-63 and finer coins of the 1940s on the market, giving collectors a wide choice. Then come Franklin half dollars, made only from 1948 to 1963, with representative coins easy enough to acquire in about any grade desired. Kennedy half dollars exist in several varieties, all of which are available without any problem. Among these and other modern coins care needs to be taken for value received versus price paid. Modern issues in, for example, MS-65 and 66, selected for quality, are for many collectors preferable to MS-69 or 70 coins offered at a much higher price.

FOR THE COLLECTOR AND INVESTOR: HALF DOLLARS AS A SPECIALTY

Many collectors over the years have pursued half dollars by date, mint, and variety. Except for the series of copper cents, half dollars are the most generally available coins over a nearly continuous span, making them possible to collect for reasonable cost. Also, enough die varieties exist that this can form another focus of interest and importance.

In general, the half dollars of the early era form a concentration in themselves. Die varieties can be attributed by Overton numbers, as listed by Al C. Overton in his immensely popular *Early Half Dollar Die Varieties 1794–1836*. Glenn R. Peterson's book, *The Ultimate Guide to Attributing Bust Half Dollars*, is also useful in this regard. The John Reich Collectors Society (www.jrcs.org) publishes the *John Reich Journal* and serves as a forum for the exchange of information, updates, news about die varieties, and the like.

Among rarities in the early years, the 1796 and 1797 half dollars with the Draped Bust obverse and Small Eagle reverse are perhaps the most famous, needed for variety collections as well as one example for a type set. Variety enthusiasts aspire to get two of 1796—one with 15 stars on the obverse and the other with 16 stars—plus the 1797.

Draped Bust half dollars from 1801 through 1807 have a number of rare die varieties (as listed by Overton), but the basic varieties are easy enough to find. The 1805, 5 Over 4, overdate is particularly popular, as there was no "perfect date" 1804, and this is the closest collectors can come to it.

A vast and interesting field in early American numismatics is that of the Capped Bust half dollar, 1807–1836, with a lettered edge. Several hundred different die combinations exist, and many collectors are active in their pursuit, using the Overton book as a road map. All the major varieties are readily collectible except the 1817, 7 Over 4, overdate, of which only about a half dozen exist. The 1815, 5 Over 2, is considered the key issue among the specific dates (rather than varieties of dates). The majority of these survive in VF grade, not often lower and not often higher either—an interesting situation. During the 1820s vast quantities of these were transferred among banks, not wearing down from as much hand-to-hand circulation

Two famous Americans featured on U.S. half dollars: Benjamin Franklin and President John F. Kennedy.

as they might have otherwise. While many if not most of the varieties listed herein can be obtained in Mint State, most collectors opt for VF or EF, these grades showing the necessary details but also permitting a budget to be stretched to include more varieties, rather than just a few high-grade pieces. Choice and gem examples can be found here and there, and are most plentiful among the later dates.

Among the Capped Bust half dollars of reduced size, 1836–1837, the 1836 is a key date, with fewer than 5,000 believed to have been minted. The next type, 1838 and 1839, Capped Bust, reeded edge, with a modified eagle on the reverse, includes the famous 1838-O rarity, of which only 20 are said to have been struck (per a note published in 1894 in the catalog of the Friesner Collection). These have a proof-like surface. Interestingly, they were not struck until 1839. In the same year, 1839-O half dollars were also struck, to the extensive quantity of 178,976 pieces; they are unusual as the mintmark is on the obverse, an odd placement for the era.

Within the series of Liberty Seated half dollars, collectors generally seek the varieties listed herein, although certain dedicated specialists will consult the *Complete Guide to Liberty Seated Half Dollars*, by Randy Wiley and Bill Bugert—a volume that delineates many interesting features, including the number of different reeds on the edges of certain coins.

Among Liberty Seated half dollars there is just one "impossible" rarity, that being the 1853-O coin without arrows at the date. Only three exist, and each shows extensive wear. At the San Francisco Mint, half dollars were first struck in 1855, and at the Carson City Mint in 1870. Generally, large quantities were minted of most dates and mintmark varieties of Liberty Seated half dollars, making them readily obtainable today. Except for the later dates, 1879 to 1891, Mint State pieces are generally scarce, gems especially so. Many specialists in half dollars belong to the Liberty Seated Collectors Club (LSCC, at www.lsccweb.org) and receive its magazine, *The Gobrecht Journal*.

Proof Liberty Seated halves can be collected by date sequence from 1858 onward. Survivors exist in proportion to their mintage quantities. Generally those before the mid-1870s often are found cleaned or hairlined, and more care is needed in selecting choice examples than is necessary for the later dates.

Barber half dollars were made continuously from 1892 through 1915, in such quantities that today there are no great rarities in the series. However, a number of issues are quite scarce, even in well-worn grades, and in MS-63 and better many are difficult to find. These coins had little honor in the era in which they were issued, and few numismatists saved them. Proofs were made each year from 1892 to 1915 and today can be obtained in proportion to their mintages. However, those of 1914 and 1915 are hard to find with choice, original surfaces—decades ago a collector hoarded these two dates and polished the ones in his possession.

Liberty Walking half dollars are popular to collect by date and mint. Scarce varieties include the 1917-S with obverse mintmark, the three issues of 1921, and the low mintage 1938-D, although the latter is not inordinately expensive. Mint State pieces are most readily available for 1916 and 1917, and then especially so in the 1930s and 1940s. Striking quality can be a problem, particularly for issues of the mid-1920s and also the later dates. For example, with a needle-sharp strike the 1923-S is an extreme rarity. Among later coins the 1940-S and 1941-S often are weakly struck.

Franklin half dollars minted from 1948 through 1963 have been very popular in recent decades. The complete series of dates and mintmarks is short and contains no scarce or rare pieces in higher grades such as MS-63 and MS-64. However, if you consider the element of sharp striking, usually defined as Full Bell Lines (FBL) on the reverse, certain otherwise common dates become elusive. Proofs of most years can also be readily collected.

Kennedy half dollars are easily enough collected, and so many have been made by this time that nearly 200 date-and-mintmark combinations extend from 1964 to present, including a gold version that marks the design's 50th anniversary. The wise collector will select coins that have a meeting point between a high grade such as MS-65 or MS-66 (or equivalent Proofs) and a reasonable price.

FLOWING HAIR (1794–1795)

Designer: *Robert Scot.* **Weight:** *13.48 grams.*
Composition: *.8924 silver, .1076 copper.* **Diameter:** *Approximately 32.5 mm.*
Edge: *FIFTY CENTS OR HALF A DOLLAR with decorations between the words.*

Overton-105.

History. The Flowing Hair design inaugurated the half-dollar denomination. They were immediately popular, as was evident in 1795, when many depositors of silver at the Philadelphia Mint asked for half dollars in return. The same motif was used on half dimes and silver dollars of the same years. Early half dollars have been extensively collected by die varieties, of which many exist for most dates. Valuations given below are in each case for the most readily available variety; scarcer ones, as listed by Overton, generally command higher prices.

Striking and Sharpness. Many have problems of one sort or another, including adjustment marks from the planchet being filed down to proper weight and mushy denticles. On the obverse, check the hair details and the stars. On the reverse, check the breast of the eagle in particular. As with other silver coins of this design, it may not be possible to find a *needle-sharp* example, but with some extensive searching a fairly decent strike can be obtained. Sharp striking and excellent eye appeal add to the value dramatically. However, very few 1794 and 1795 halves are uniformly sharp on both sides.

Availability. Probably 3,500 to 6,000 circulated Flowing Hair half dollars exist. Most are dated 1795, the 1794 being considered a rare date (though not among the great U.S. coin rarities). Typical grades are Good to Fine. EF and AU grades are elusive in regard to the total population. Probably 100 or so could be graded MS (nearly all of them 1795). Unlike half dollars of the 1796–1797 type, none of these are known to have been made with prooflike surfaces.

GRADING STANDARDS

MS-60 to 70 (Mint State). *Obverse:* At MS-60, some abrasion and contact marks are evident, most noticeably on the cheek and in the fields. This denomination, heavier than the half dime of the same design, was more susceptible to contact and other outside influences. A typical half dollar certified at MS-60 or 61 today might well have been designated as About Uncirculated a generation ago. Luster is present, but may be dull or lifeless, and

1795; Overton-110a. Graded MS-63.

interrupted in patches, perhaps as much from old cleaning as from contact the coin may have received. At MS-63, contact marks are very few, and abrasion is present, but not as noticeable. An MS-65 coin has no abrasion, and contact marks are very few. Luster should be full and rich. Higher grades are seldom seen in this type, but are defined in theory by having fewer marks as perfection is approached. *Reverse:* Comments apply as for the obverse, except that abrasion and contact marks are most noticeable on the eagle at the center. This area is often lightly struck, so in all grades do not mistake weak striking for actual wear. Knowledge of specific die varieties is helpful in this regard. The field area is small and is protected by lettering and the wreath, and in any given grade shows fewer marks than on the obverse.

Illustrated coin: This is a well-struck example with superb eye appeal.

AU-50, 53, 55, 58 (About Uncirculated).
Obverse: Light wear is seen on the hair area immediately to the left of the face and above the forehead, on the cheek, and, to a lesser extent, on the top of the neck truncation, more so at AU-50 than at 53 or 55. An AU-58 coin has minimal traces of wear. An AU-50 coin has luster in protected areas among the stars and letters, with little in the open fields or on the portrait. At AU-58, much luster is

1795; O-116. Graded AU-55.

present in the fields but is worn away on the highest parts of the motifs. *Reverse:* Light wear is seen on the eagle's body and the upper part of both wings. On well-struck pieces the details of the wing features are excellent. At AU-50, detail is lost in some feathers in this area. However, striking can play a part, as some coins were weakly struck to begin with. Light wear is seen on the wreath and lettering, but is harder to discern. Luster is the best key to actual wear. This will range from perhaps 20% remaining in protected areas (at AU-50) to nearly full mint bloom (at AU-58), although among certified coins the amounts of luster can vary widely.

Illustrated coin: Significant luster remains in protected areas on this attractive early half dollar.

EF-40, 45 (Extremely Fine). *Obverse:* More wear is evident on the portrait, especially on the hair to the left of and above the forehead, and in the back below the LI of LIBERTY. The tip of the neck truncation shows flatness, and the cheek is worn. Excellent detail remains in low-relief areas of the hair. The stars show wear, as do the date and letters. Luster, if present at all, is minimal and in protected areas. *Reverse:* The eagle shows more

1794; O-101. Graded EF-40.

wear on the body and on the tops of the wings. Interior wing detail is good on most coins (depending on the variety and the striking), and the tail feathers can be discerned. Additional wear is on the wreath and letters, but many details are present. Some luster may be seen in protected areas and if present is slightly more abundant than on the obverse.

Illustrated coin: Note some lightness of the stars at the right and at the reverse center, as struck. The scrape on the reverse below the ribbon knot was mentioned by the cataloger in an auction offering.

VF-20, 30 (Very Fine). *Obverse:* The hair is well worn at VF-20, less so at VF-30, and is most noticeable in the upper part of the head, the area above the level of the eye, and extending to the back. The strands are blended as to be heavy. The cheek shows only slight relief, and the tip of the neck trunca-tion is flat. The stars have more wear, making them appear larger (an optical illusion). Scat-tered marks are common on half dollars at

1795; O-109. Graded VF-20.

this level and below, and should be mentioned if particularly serious. *Reverse:* The body of the eagle shows few if any feathers, while the wings have perhaps a quarter or a third of the feathers visible depend-ing on the strike, with sharper strikes having up to half visible (as PCGS suggests). *Photograde* and the ANA grading standards suggest half of the feathers on all, which may be the case on coins that were well struck to begin with. The leaves lack detail and are in outline form. Scattered, non-disfiguring marks are normal for this and lower grades. Any major defects should be noted separately.

    Illustrated coin: On this variety in this grade, the denticles are especially prominent on each side. Such aspects vary from coin to coin.

F-12, 15 (Fine). *Obverse:* Wear is more extensive than on the preceding, with less hair visible. The ear position can be seen, as can the eye. The cheek is nearly flat, and the stars appear larger. The rim is distinct and most denticles remain visible. *Reverse:* Wear is more extensive. Now, feather details are fewer, mostly remaining on the wing to the left. The wreath and lettering are more worn, and the rim is usually weak in areas, although most denticles can be seen.

1795; O-107. Graded F-12.

VG-8, 10 (Very Good). *Obverse:* The por-trait is mostly seen in outline form, with most hair strands gone save for an area centered behind the neck. The hair tips at the lower left are clear. The eye location is barely dis-cernible. The stars appear larger still and often quite bold, again an illusion. The rim is weak in areas. LIBERTY and the date are readable and usually full, although some let-ters may be weak at their tops. *Reverse:* The

1795; O-109. Graded VG-8.

eagle is mostly an outline, although traces of the separation between the body and the right wing can sometimes be seen. The rim is worn, as are the letters, with some weak, but the motto is readable. On many coins the rim remains fairly prominent.

    Illustrated coin: Note a spot, a tiny edge bruise, and some adjustment marks. A cataloger mentioned that "the top of the obverse is slightly soft due to axial misalignment"—a technical note. On any half dollar of this era, knowledge of the varieties and peculiarities of striking is useful.

G-4, 6 (Good). *Obverse:* Wear is more extensive, and some stars may be missing or only partially visible. The head is an outline, although a few elements of thick hair strands may be seen. The rim is well worn or even missing. LIBERTY is worn, and parts of some letters may be missing, but elements of all should be readable. The date is readable, but worn. *Reverse:* The eagle is flat and discernible in outline form. The wreath is well

1794; O-106. Graded G-6.

worn. Some of the letters may be partly missing. At this level some "averaging" can be done. If the letters are stronger than usual in one area, but some are missing in another area, the coin can still qualify as G-4. Often on this type in lower grades the reverse is more detailed than the obverse.

AG-3 (About Good). *Obverse:* Wear is very extensive. The head is in outline form (perhaps partly blended into the field). LIBERTY is mostly gone. The date, while readable, may be partially worn away. Some stars are missing. *Reverse:* The reverse is well worn, with parts of the wreath and lettering very weak or even missing. The details that remain and those that do not is often dependent on the particular die variety.

1795; O-116. Graded AG-3.

| **1795, Normal Date** | **1795, Recut Date** | **1795, Two Leaves Under Each Wing** | **1795, Three Leaves Under Each Wing** |

	Mintage	Cert	Avg	%MS	AG-3	G-4	VG-8	F-12	VF-20	EF-40	AU-50	AU-55	MS-60
1794	23,464	322	22.2	2%	$2,750	$4,500	$7,750	$12,500	$23,000	$38,000	$75,000	$105,000	$150,000
Auctions: $152,750, MS-61, June 2014; $18,800, VF-30, August 2014; $12,925, VF-20, August 2014; $11,750, VG-10, August 2014													
1795, All kinds (a)	299,680												
1795, Normal Date		1,009	24.4	5%	$650	$1,000	$1,450	$2,750	$3,900	$11,000	$19,000	$25,000	$45,000
Auctions: $129,250, MS-62, November 2013; $3,525, VF-30, August 2014; $1,998, F-12, August 2014; $1,293, F-12, August 2014													
1795, Recut Date		24	23.4	0%	$650	$1,000	$1,450	$2,750	$3,900	$11,000	$20,500	$25,000	$50,000
Auctions: $1,651, F-12, March 2014; $1,645, VG-8, September 2014													
1795, 3 Leaves Under Each Wing		13	27.2	0%	$1,100	$2,200	$3,000	$4,600	$8,500	$20,000	$40,000	$42,000	$65,000
Auctions: $8,519, VF, March 2014													

a. Varieties of 1795 are known with the final S in STATES over a D; with the A in STATES over an E; and with the Y in LIBERTY over a star. All are scarce. Some 1795 half dollars were weight-adjusted by insertion of a silver plug in the center of the blank planchet before the coin was struck.

DRAPED BUST, SMALL EAGLE REVERSE (1796–1797)

Designer: *Robert Scot.* **Weight:** *13.48 grams.*
Composition: *.8924 silver, .1076 copper.* **Diameter:** *Approximately 32.5 mm.*
Edge: *FIFTY CENTS OR HALF A DOLLAR with decorations between words.*

O-101.

History. Robert Scot's Draped Bust design is similar to that used on the half dime, dime, quarter, and silver dollar of this era. In 1796 and 1797 there was little demand for half dollars and the combined mintage for the two years was therefore low. Among design types of U.S. silver coins made in circulation-strike format this is the Holy Grail–a classic rarity, with no common date in the series.

Striking and Sharpness. On the obverse, check the hair details and the stars. On the reverse, first check the breast of the eagle, but examine other areas as well. Also check the denticles on both sides. Look especially for coins that do not have significant adjustment marks (from an overweight planchet being filed down to correct specifications). Coins of this denomination are on average better struck than are half dimes, dimes, quarters (which have reverse problems), and dollars in the Draped Bust suite.

Availability. Examples are rare in any grade—survivors likely number only in the hundreds of coins. MS examples are particularly rare, and when seen are nearly always dated 1796. Some of these have partially prooflike surfaces. Any half dollar of this type has strong market demand.

GRADING STANDARDS

MS-60 to 70 (Mint State). *Obverse:* At MS-60, some abrasion and contact marks are evident, most noticeably on the cheek, the drapery at the shoulder, and the right field. Also check the hair to the left of the forehead. Luster is present, but may be dull or lifeless, and interrupted in patches. At MS-63, contact marks are few, and abrasion is hard to detect, although this type is sometimes graded liberally due to its rarity. An MS-65 coin has

1797; O-101a. Graded MS-66.

no abrasion, and contact marks are so minute as to require magnification. Luster should be full and rich. Coins graded above MS-65 are more theoretical than actual for this type, although some notable pieces have crossed the auction block. These are defined by having fewer marks as perfection is approached. *Reverse:* Comments apply as for the obverse, except that abrasion and contact marks are most noticeable on the eagle at the center, a situation that should be evaluated by considering the original striking (which can be quite sharp, but with many exceptions). The field area is small and is protected by lettering and the wreath, and in any given grade shows fewer marks than on the obverse.

Illustrated coin: This superb gem has prooflike surfaces.

AU-50, 53, 55, 58 (About Uncirculated). *Obverse:* Light wear is seen on the hair area above the ear and extending to the left of the forehead, on the ribbon, and on the drapery at the shoulder, more so at AU-50 than at 53 or 55. An AU-58 coin has minimal traces of wear. An AU-50 coin has luster in protected areas among the stars and letters, with little in the open fields or on the portrait. At AU-58, most luster is present in the fields,

1797; O-101a. Graded AU-50.

but is worn away on the highest parts of the motifs. *Reverse:* Light wear is seen on the eagle's body and the edges of the wings. Light wear is seen on the wreath and lettering. Luster is the best key to actual wear. This ranges from perhaps 20% remaining in protected areas (at AU-50) to nearly full mint bloom (at AU-58).

EF-40, 45 (Extremely Fine). *Obverse:* More wear is evident on the upper hair area, particularly to the left of the forehead and also below LI of LIBERTY, in the ribbon, and on the drapery and bosom. Excellent detail remains in low-relief areas of the hair. The stars show wear as do the date and letters. Luster, if present at all, is minimal and in protected areas. *Reverse:* The eagle shows more wear, this being the focal point to check.

1796, 15 Stars; O-101. Graded EF-40.

Many feathers remain on the interior areas of the wings. Additional wear is on the wreath and letters, but many details are present. Some luster may be seen in protected areas and if present is slightly more abundant than on the obverse.

VF-20, 30 (Very Fine). *Obverse:* The higher-relief areas of hair are well worn at VF-20, less so at VF-30. The drapery and bosom show extensive wear. The stars have more wear. *Reverse:* The body of the eagle shows few if any feathers, while the wings have about half or more of the feathers visible, depending on the strike. The leaves lack most detail and are outlined. Scattered, non-disfiguring marks are normal for this and

1796, 16 Stars; O-103. Graded VF-20.

lower grades; major defects should be noted separately.

F-12, 15 (Fine). *Obverse:* Wear is more extensive than on a Very Fine coin, particularly noticeable on the hair, face, and bosom. The stars appear larger (an optical illusion). About half the hair detail remains, most noticeably behind the neck and shoulder. The rim may be partially worn away and blend into the field, but on many coins it remains intact. *Reverse:* Wear is more extensive. Now, feather details are diminished,

1797; O-101a. Graded F-15.

with fewer than half remaining on the wings. The wreath and lettering are worn further, and the rim is usually weak in areas, but most denticles can be seen.

VG-8, 10 (Very Good). *Obverse:* The portrait is mostly seen in outline form, with most hair strands gone, although there is some definition at the back of the hair and behind the shoulder. The ear is barely discernible and the eye is fairly distinct. The stars appear larger still, again an illusion. The rim is weak in areas, but shows most denticles. LIBERTY and the date are readable and usually full, although some letters may be weak at their

1796, 16 Stars; O-102. Graded VG-10.

tops. *Reverse:* The eagle is mostly an outline, with parts blending into the field (on lighter strikes). The rim is worn, as are the letters, with some weak, but the motto is readable.

G-4, 6 (Good). *Obverse:* Wear is more extensive, and some stars may be partly missing. The head is an outline. The eye is visible only in outline form. The rim is well worn or even missing in areas, but many denticles remain. LIBERTY is worn. The letters and date are weak but fully readable. *Reverse:* The eagle is flat and discernible in outline form, and may be blending into the field. The wreath is well worn. Some of the letters may

1797. Graded G-4.

be partly missing. At this level some "averaging" can be done. If the letters are stronger than usual in one area, but some are missing in another area, the coin can still qualify as G-4.

AG-3 (About Good). *Obverse:* Wear is so extensive that the coin is barely identifiable. The head is in outline form. LIBERTY is mostly gone; same for the stars. The date, while readable, may be partially worn away. *Reverse:* The reverse is well worn, with parts of the wreath and lettering missing. On most coins the reverse shows more wear than the obverse.

1797. Graded AG-3.

1796, 15 Stars   1796, 16 Stars

	Mintage	Cert	Avg	%MS	AG-3	G-4	VG-8	F-12	VF-20	EF-40	AU-50	AU-58	MS-60
1796, 15 Stars †	(a)	18	44.3	39%	$23,000	$34,000	$40,000	$52,000	$70,000	$110,000	$170,000	$220,000	$290,000
Auctions: No auction records available.													
1796, 16 Stars †	(a)	12	33.8	25%	$23,000	$36,500	$43,500	$56,000	$71,000	$110,000	$170,000	$250,000	$305,000
Auctions: $470,000, MS-63, November 2013													
1797, 15 Stars †	3,918	51	28.2	8%	$23,000	$34,000	$40,000	$52,000	$70,000	$110,000	$165,000	$220,000	$290,000
Auctions: $1,292,500, MS-65+, August 2014; $282,000, MS-63, June 2014													

† Ranked in the *100 Greatest U.S. Coins* (fourth edition). **a.** Included in 1797, 15 Stars, mintage figure.

DRAPED BUST, HERALDIC EAGLE REVERSE (1801–1807)

Designer: *Robert Scot.* **Weight:** *13.48 grams.*
Composition: *.8924 silver, .1076 copper.* **Diameter:** *Approximately 32.5 mm.*
Edge: *FIFTY CENTS OR HALF A DOLLAR with decorations between words.*

O-101.

History. The half dollar's Draped Bust, Heraldic Eagle design is similar to that of other silver coins of the era. While dies were prepared for the 1804 half dollar, none were minted in that year, despite Mint reports that state otherwise.

Striking and Sharpness. Most have light striking in one area or another. On the obverse, check the hair details and, in particular, the star centers. On the reverse, check the stars above the eagle, the clouds, the details of the shield, and the eagle's wings. Check the denticles on both sides. Adjustment marks are sometimes seen, from overweight planchets being filed down to correct weight, but not as often as on earlier half dollar types. Typically, the earlier years are better struck; many of 1806 and nearly all of 1807 are poorly struck. Sharp striking and excellent eye appeal add to the value dramatically, this being particularly true for those of 1805 to 1807, which are often weak (particularly 1807).

Availability. Earlier years are scarce in the marketplace, beginning with the elusive 1801 and including the 1802, after which they are more readily available. Some die varieties are scarce. Most MS coins are dated 1806 and 1807, but all are scarce. Finding sharply struck high-grade coins is almost impossible, a goal more than a reality.

GRADING STANDARDS

MS-60 to 70 (Mint State). *Obverse:* At MS-60, some abrasion and contact marks are evident, most noticeably on the cheek, the drapery at the shoulder, and the right field. Luster is present, but may be dull or lifeless, and interrupted in patches. At MS-63, contact marks are very few, and abrasion is hard to detect except under magnification. An MS-65 coin has no abrasion, and contact marks are so minute as to require magnifica-

1803, Large 3; O-101. Graded MS-63.

tion. Luster should be full and rich. Coins grading above MS-65 are more theoretical than actual for this type—but they do exist, and are defined by having fewer marks as perfection is approached. Later years usually have areas of flat striking. *Reverse:* Comments apply as for the obverse, except that abrasion and contact marks are most noticeable on the eagle's neck, the tips of the wing, and the tail. The field area is complex, without much open space, given the stars above the eagle, the arrows and olive branch, and other features. Accordingly, marks are not as noticeable as on the obverse.

Illustrated coin: This is an extraordinary strike with superb eye appeal. A connoisseur might prefer this coin to an MS-65 example with flat striking.

AU-50, 53, 55, 58 (About Uncirculated). *Obverse:* Light wear is seen on the hair area above the ear and extending to left of the forehead, on the ribbon, and on the bosom, more so at AU-50 than at 53 or 55. An AU-58 coin has minimal traces of wear. An AU-50 coin has luster in protected areas among the stars and letters, with little in the open fields or on the portrait. At AU-58, most luster is present in the fields, but is worn away on the

1806, Pointed 6, No Stem; O-109. Graded AU-50.

highest parts of the motifs. *Reverse:* Comments as preceding, except that the eagle's neck, the tips and top of the wings, the clouds, and the tail now show noticeable wear, as do other features. Luster ranges from perhaps 20% remaining in protected areas (at AU-50) to nearly full mint bloom (at AU-58). Often the reverse of this type retains much more luster than the obverse.

Illustrated coin: This example has gray and lilac toning.

EF-40, 45 (Extremely Fine). *Obverse:* More wear is evident on the upper hair area and the ribbon, and on the drapery and bosom. Excellent detail remains in low-relief areas of the hair. The stars show wear, as do the date and letters. Luster, if present at all, is minimal and in protected areas. *Reverse:* Wear is greater than on an About Uncirculated coin, overall. The neck lacks feather detail on its highest points. Feathers have lost some detail

1807; O-105. Graded EF-40.

near the edges of the wings, and some areas of the horizontal lines in the shield may be blended together. Some traces of luster may be seen, more so at EF-45 than at EF-40.

Illustrated coin: Light striking at the obverse center is normal for this die variety.

VF-20, 30 (Very Fine). *Obverse:* The higher-relief areas of hair are well worn at VF-20, less so at VF-30. The drapery on the shoulder and the bosom show extensive wear. The stars have more wear, making them appear larger (an optical illusion seen on most worn silver coins of this era). *Reverse:* Wear is greater, including on the shield and wing feathers. Half to two-thirds of the feathers are visible. Star centers are flat. Other areas have lost detail as well.

1806, 6 Over Inverted 9; O-111a. Graded VF-30.

Illustrated coin: Note the cud break on the reverse rim over the E in UNITED.

F-12, 15 (Fine). *Obverse:* Wear is more extensive than on a Very Fine coin, particularly noticeable on the hair, face, and bosom. The stars appear larger. About half the hair detail remains, most noticeably behind the neck and shoulder, but the fine hair is now combined into thicker tresses. The rim may be partially worn away and blend into the field. *Reverse:* Wear is even more extensive, with the shield and wing feathers being

1805; O-109. Graded F-15.

points to observe. The incuse E PLURIBUS UNUM may have half or more of the letters worn away (depending on striking). The clouds all appear connected. The stars are weak. Parts of the border and lettering may be weak.

VG-8, 10 (Very Good). *Obverse:* The portrait is mostly seen in outline form, with most hair strands gone, although there is some definition at the back of the hair and behind the shoulder. The ear is discernible as is the eye. The stars appear larger still, again an illusion. The rim is weak in areas. LIBERTY and the date are readable and usually full, although some letters may be weak at their tops. *Reverse:* Wear is more extensive. Half

1805, 5 Over 4; O-103. Graded VG-8.

or more of the letters in the motto are worn away. Most feathers are worn away, although separation of some of the lower feathers may be seen. Some stars are faint (depending on the strike). The border blends into the field in areas and some letters are weak.

G-4, 6 (Good). *Obverse:* Wear is more extensive, and some stars may be partly missing. The head is mostly an outline, although some hair strand outlines may be visible on some strikings. The rim is well worn or even missing in areas. LIBERTY is worn, and parts of some letters may be missing, but elements should be readable. The date is readable, but worn. *Reverse:* Wear is more extensive. The upper part of the eagle is flat.

1805; O-111. Graded G-4.

Feathers are noticeable only at the lower edge of the wings, and do not have detail. The upper part of the shield is flat or mostly so (depending on the strike). Only a few letters of the motto can be seen. The rim is worn extensively, and a few letters may be missing.

AG-3 (About Good). *Obverse:* Wear is so extensive that the coin is barely identifiable. The head is in outline form. LIBERTY is mostly gone; same for the stars. The date, while readable, may be partially worn away. *Reverse:* Extensive wear is seen overall, with the rim worn away and some areas worn smooth. The eagle can be discerned in outline form, but not necessarily completely. A few stray motto letters may remain.

1801. Graded AG-3.

	Mintage	Cert	Avg	%MS	G-4	VG-8	F-12	VF-20	EF-40	AU-50	AU-55	MS-60	MS-63
1801	30,289	136	29.0	3%	$800	$1,200	$2,400	$3,500	$6,500	$16,000	$20,500	$50,000	$160,000
	Auctions: $329,000, MS-64, November 2013; $940, G-6, September 2014; $576, G-4, October 2014												
1802	29,890	99	32.1	1%	$750	$1,200	$2,500	$3,500	$7,000	$16,000	$25,000	$60,000	
	Auctions: $70,500, AU-58, August 2013; $3,173, VF-20, August 2014; $2,115, F-15, August 2014												

1803, Small 3

1803, Large 3

1805, 5 Over 4

1805, Normal Date

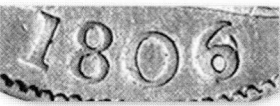
1806, 6 Over 5

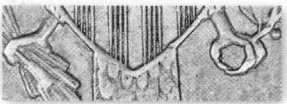
1806, 6 Over Inverted 6

1806, Stem Not
Through Claw

1806, Stem Through Claw

1806, Knobbed-Top 6, Large Stars
With traces of overdate.

1806, Knobbed-Top 6, Small Stars

	Mintage	Cert	Avg	%MS	G-4	VG-8	F-12	VF-20	EF-40	AU-50	AU-55	MS-60	MS-63
1803, All kinds	188,234												
1803, Small 3		37	39.4	3%	$350	$475	$550	$1,000	$2,600	$6,000	$10,000	$21,000	$65,000
Auctions: $49,938, MS-62, June 2014													
1803, Large 3		101	33.4	5%	$325	$425	$500	$900	$2,050	$5,000	$7,000	$16,000	$40,000
Auctions: $88,125, MS-63, August 2013; $999, EF-45, October 2014; $881, EF-40, August 2014; $294, VF-30, August 2014													
1805, All kinds	211,722												
1805, 5 Over 4		102	34.1	2%	$290	$440	$875	$1,600	$3,500	$7,500	$12,750	$30,000	$85,000
Auctions: $152,750, MS-65, November 2013; $3,525, EF-45, August 2014; $3,290, EF-40, August 2014													
1805, Normal Date		380	32.3	2%	$260	$325	$450	$850	$2,250	$5,000	$7,000	$16,000	$35,000
Auctions: $42,594, MS-63, November 2013; $4,113, AU-53, August 2014; $1,528, VF-35, October 2014; $734, VF-25, July 2014													
1806, All kinds	839,576												
1806, 6 Over 5		192	33.6	3%	$265	$350	$450	$900	$2,000	$4,900	$6,150	$10,750	$27,000
Auctions: $21,150, MS-61, November 2013; $881, VF-30, September 2014; $793, VF-25, July 2014; $764, VF-20, July 2014													
1806, 6 Over Inverted 6		63	27.7	2%	$300	$450	$925	$1,450	$3,300	$6,500	$12,000	$18,500	$38,000
Auctions: $28,200, MS-61, November 2013; $999, F-12, September 2014; $940, F-12, August 2014; $999, Fair-2, August 2014													
1806, Knobbed 6, Large Stars (Traces of Overdate)		35	30.0	0%	$250	$300	$400	$700	$2,000	$5,000	$7,000	$10,000	$21,500
Auctions: $2,364, EF-40, August 2013													
1806, Knobbed 6, Small Stars		37	30.1	0%	$250	$300	$400	$700	$2,000	$5,000	$7,000	$11,000	$25,000
Auctions: $2,350, EF-45, January 2014; $435, F-15, July 2014													
1806, Knobbed 6, Stem Not Through Claw		0	n/a		$35,000	$55,000	$85,000	$115,000	$165,000				
Auctions: $126,500, EF-40, January 2009													
1806, Pointed 6, Stem Through Claw		250	33.9	6%	$250	$300	$400	$700	$1,550	$4,500	$5,250	$8,500	$16,750
Auctions: $35,250, MS-64, November 2013; $7,638, AU-53, August 2014; $1,058, VF-35, November 2014; $852, VF-35, November 2014													
1806, Pointed 6, Stem Through Claw, E Over A in STATES		7	19.3	0%	$400	$900	$1,600	$3,200	$7,500	$20,000			
Auctions: No auction records available.													
1806, Pointed 6, Stem Not Through Claw		108	36.4	7%	$250	$300	$400	$700	$2,000	$5,500	$5,750	$9,500	$18,000
Auctions: $12,925, MS-62, November 2013; $3,840, AU-55, August 2014; $1,998, EF-45, August 2014; $441, EF-40, August 2014													
1807	301,076	1,052	34.7	8%	$250	$300	$400	$700	$1,800	$5,000	$5,500	$9,000	$16,250
Auctions: $70,500, MS-65, November 2013; $6,463, AU-58, August 2014; $3,290, AU-53, August 2014; $646, VF-30, November 2014													

CAPPED BUST, LETTERED EDGE (1807–1836)

Designer: *John Reich.* **Weight:** *13.48 grams.*
Composition: *.8924 silver, .1076 copper.* **Diameter:** *Approximately 32.5 mm.*
Edge: *1807–1814—FIFTY CENTS OR HALF A DOLLAR;*
1814–1831—star added between DOLLAR and FIFTY;
1832–1836—vertical lines added between words.

First Style (1807–1808)
O-104.

Remodeled Portrait and Eagle
(1809–1836)
O-109.

Remodeled Portrait and Eagle, Proof
O-103.

History. The Capped Bust design was created by Mint assistant engraver John Reich; the motif was widely used, in several variations, on much of the era's coinage. Reich was the first artist to consistently include the denomination in his designs for U.S. gold and silver coins. The half dollar, minted continuously from 1807 to 1836, except 1816, was the largest silver coin of the realm at the time (silver dollars had not been struck since 1804).

Striking and Sharpness. On the obverse, check the hair and broach details. The stars are often flatly struck on Capped Bust half dollars, much more so than on other denominations. On the reverse, check the motto band and the eagle's head, and the wing to the left, as well as other areas (the neck feathers, often lightly struck on other denominations of Capped Bust silver, are usually fairly sharp on half dollars). The E PLURIBUS UNUM band is often weak in the area left of its center; this does not normally occur on other Capped Bust silver coins. Inspect the denticles on both sides. Generally, later dates are better struck than are earlier ones. Many half dollars have semi-prooflike surfaces, or patches of mirror-like character interspersed with luster. Others can have nearly full prooflike surfaces, with patches of luster being in the minority (and often in the left obverse field); some of these have been mischaracterized as "Proofs." Some issues from the early 1830s have little digs or "bite marks" on the portrait, possibly from some sort of a gadget used to eject them from the press. Unlike the Capped Bust half dime, dime, and quarter dollar, the half dollar is particularly subject to very wide variations in striking quality.

True Proofs have deeply mirrored surfaces. Impostors are often seen, with deeply toned surfaces or with patches of mint luster. This situation is more prevalent with half dollars than with any other Capped Bust denomination. Proceed slowly, and be careful. There are some crushed-lettered-edge ("CLE")

Proofs of the 1833 to 1835 era that are especially beautiful and are more deeply mirrorlike than original issues. Some of these are restrikes (not necessarily an important consideration, but worth mentioning), believed to have been made at the Mint beginning in the spring of 1859.

Availability. Examples of most dates and overdates are easily found in just about any grade desired, from Fine and VF to MS. (As the largest silver coin struck between 1803 and 1836, these half dollars spent much of their time in bags, transferred from bank to bank, rather than wearing down in circulation.) The later years are the most readily available and are also seen in higher average grades. Many die varieties range from scarce to rare. Proofs were made in limited numbers for presentation purposes and for distribution to numismatists.

GRADING STANDARDS

MS-60 to 70 (Mint State). *Obverse:* At MS-60, some abrasion and contact marks are evident, most noticeably on the cheek, the hair below the left part of LIBERTY, the cap, and the front part of the bosom and drapery. These areas also coincide with the highest parts of the coin and are thus susceptible to lightness of strike. Complicating matters is that when an area is lightly struck, and the planchet is not forced into the deepest parts

1827, Square Base 2; O-104. Graded MS-60.

of the die, the *original planchet surface* (which may exhibit scuffing and nicks) is visible. A lightly struck coin can have virtually perfect luster in the fields, deep and rich, and yet appear to be "worn" on the higher parts, due to the lightness of strike. This is a very sophisticated concept and is hard to quantify. In practice, the original planchet surface will usually be considered as wear on the finished coin, which of course is not true. Such grades as high About Uncirculated and low Mint State levels are often assigned to pieces that, if well struck, would be MS-64 and MS-65. As a matter of practicality, but not of logic, you will need to do the same. If a coin has original planchet abrasions, but otherwise is a Gem, those abrasions must be taken into consideration. Apart from this, on well-struck coins in lower Mint State grades, luster is present, but may be dull or lifeless, and interrupted in patches. At MS-63, on a well-struck coin, contact marks are very few, and abrasion is hard to detect except under magnification. A well-struck MS-65 coin has no abrasion, and contact marks are so minute as to require magnification. Luster should be full and rich. Grades above MS-65 are seen now and again and are defined by having fewer marks as perfection is approached. *Reverse:* Comments apply as for the obverse, except that nearly all coins with weak striking on the obverse (so as to reveal original planchet surface) do not show such original surface on the reverse, except perhaps on the motto ribbon. Accordingly, market grading is usually by the obverse only, even if the reverse seems to be in much better preservation. On well-struck coins, abrasion and contact marks are most noticeable on the eagle's head, the top of the wings, the claws, and the flat band that surrounds the incuse motto. The field is mainly protected by design elements and does not show abrasion as much as does the obverse on a given coin.

Illustrated coin: This is an exceptional coin at the low Mint State level.

AU-50, 53, 55, 58 (About Uncirculated). *Obverse:* Light wear is seen on the cheek, the hair below the left part of LIBERTY, the cap, and the front part of the bosom and drapery. Some of this apparent "wear" may be related to the original planchet surface (as noted under Mint State, above), but at the About Uncirculated level the distinction is less important. On a well-struck coin, at AU-58 the luster is extensive except in the open area

1820, Curl Base 2, Small Date; O-103. Graded AU-55.

of the field, especially to the right. At AU-50 and 53, luster remains only in protected areas. *Reverse:* Wear is evident on the eagle's head, the top of the wings, the claws, and the flat band above the eagle. An AU-58 coin has nearly full luster. At AU-50 and 53, there still is significant luster, more than on the obverse.

Illustrated coin: An attractive coin by any measure, this has light toning and ample areas of original luster.

EF-40, 45 (Extremely Fine). *Obverse:* Wear is more extensive, most noticeably on the higher areas of the hair. The cap shows more wear, as does the cheek. Luster, if present, is in protected areas among the star points and close to the portrait. *Reverse:* The wings show wear on the higher areas of the feathers, and some details are lost. The top of the head and the beak are flat. The eagle's claws and the leaves show wear. Luster may be present

1810; O-110. Graded EF-45.

in protected areas, even if there is little or none on the obverse.

Illustrated coin: This coin probably was lightly cleaned years ago so as to give a light silver color, which added some hairlines, but now it has halo toning around the borders that adds attractiveness.

VF-20, 30 (Very Fine). *Obverse:* Wear is more extensive, and most of the hair is combined into thick tresses without delicate features. The curl on the neck is flat. The cap shows significant wear at its top, and the left part of the drapery and bosom is nearly flat. Stars are flat at their centers (even if sharply struck to begin with). *Reverse:* Wear is most evident on the eagle's head, the tops of the wings, and the leaves and claws. Nearly all feathers in the wing remain distinct.

1815, 5 Over 2; O-101. Graded VF-30.

Illustrated coin: The areas of wear appear exaggerated due to the light toning, a feature often observed on half dollars of this date but not as often among other years.

F-12, 15 (Fine). *Obverse:* Wear is more extensive, with much of the hair blended together. The drapery is indistinct on most of its upper edge. The stars are flat at their centers. LIBERTY remains bold. *Reverse:* Wear is more extensive, now with only about half of the feathers remaining on the wings, more on the right wing. The head shows the eye, nostril, and beak but no details. The claws show more wear. Other features are worn as well, but not as noticeable as the key points mentioned.

1827, Square Base 2; O-122. Graded F-12.

VG-8, 10 (Very Good). *Obverse:* The hair is less distinct, with the forehead blended into the hair above. LIBERTY is complete, but may be slightly weak in areas. The stars are flat. The rim is distinct, with most if not all denticles visible. *Reverse:* Feathers are fewer and mostly on the right wing, although sharp strikes can show detail in both wings. Other details are weaker. All lettering remains easily readable.

1831; O-120. Graded VG-8.

Illustrated coin: This coin was cleaned and partially retoned. It is sharply struck on the reverse.

G-4, 6 (Good). *Obverse:* The portrait is mostly in outline, with few interior details discernible. LIBERTY may still be readable or may be partially worn away, depending on the variety. The rim is weak, but distinct in most areas. *Reverse:* The eagle is mostly in outline form, although some feathers can be seen in the right wing. All letters around the border are clear. E PLURIBUS UNUM may be weak. Overall, a typical coin has the reverse in a slightly higher grade than the obverse.

1808. Graded G-4.

AG-3 (About Good). *Obverse:* The portrait is an outline, although some of LIBERTY can still be seen. The rim is worn down, and some stars are blended into it. The date remains clear, but is weak at the bottom (on most but not all). *Reverse:* At this level the reverse shows more wear overall than the obverse, with the rim indistinct in areas and many letters worn away. This is an interesting turnabout from the situation of most G-4 coins.

1824. Graded AG-3.

PF-60 to 70 (Proof). *Obverse and Reverse:* Proofs of this type have confused experts for a long time (as have large copper cents of the same era). Proofs that were extensively cleaned and therefore have many hairlines, or that are dull and grainy, are lower level, such as PF-60 to 62. While any early Proof half dollar will generate interest among collectors, lower levels are not of great interest to specialists unless they are of rare die varieties. With medium

1836; O-108. Graded PF-64 Cameo.

hairlines, an assigned grade of PF-64 may be in order and with relatively few, Gem PF-65. PF-66 should have hairlines so delicate that magnification is needed to see them. Above that, a Proof should be free of such lines. Grading is highly subjective with early Proofs, with eye appeal being a major factor.

1807, Small Stars

1807, Large Stars

1807, Large Stars, 50 Over 20

1807, "Bearded" Liberty

1808, 8 Over 7

	Mintage	Cert	Avg	%MS	G-4	F-12	VF-20	EF-40	AU-50	AU-55	MS-60 / PF-63	MS-63 / PF-64	MS-65 / PF-65
1807, All kinds	750,500												
1807, Small Stars		30	36.9	7%	$140	$450	$850	$2,400	$5,000	$6,000	$9,000	$16,000	$65,000
Auctions: $28,200, MS-61, January 2014; $999, EF-40, August 2014; $123, VG-8, October 2014; $200, G-4, July 2014													
1807, Large Stars		32	40.4	9%	$120	$350	$700	$1,700	$3,500	$5,000	$8,000	$15,000	$85,000
Auctions: $152,750, MS-65, November 2013													
1807, Large Stars, 50 Over 20		133	41.1	5%	$110	$325	$650	$1,400	$2,700	$3,100	$5,750	$10,750	$33,500
Auctions: $28,200, MS-65, June 2014; $734, EF-40, September 2014; $4,700, VF-25, August 2014; $529, VF-20, October 2014													
1807, "Bearded" Liberty (a)		30	32.2	0%	$500	$975	$2,100	$4,000	$9,500	$13,000	$27,500	—	
Auctions: $8,225, VF-30, January 2014													
1808, All kinds	1,368,600												
1808, 8 Over 7		185	42.7	11%	$100	$150	$275	$650	$1,500	$2,000	$4,200	$10,000	
Auctions: $21,150, MS-65, November 2013; $646, EF-45, July 2014; $705, EF-40, July 2014; $388, VF-35, October 2014													
1808		554	42.6	15%	$75	$110	$190	$375	$725	$1,075	$1,900	$4,400	$18,000
Auctions: $52,875, MS-66, November 2013; $282, AU-50, November 2014; $705, EF-45, September 2014; $382, EF-40, October 2014													

a. Also called the Bearded Goddess variety; a die crack gives the illusion of long whiskers growing from Miss Liberty's chin.

1809, xxxx Edge
*Experimental edge has
"xxxx" between the words.*

1809, ||||| Edge
*Experimental edge has
"|||||" between the words.*

1811, (18.11), 11 Over 10
The date is "punctuated" with a period.

1811, Small 8

1811, Large 8

1812, 2 Over 1, Small 8

1812, 2 Over 1, Large 8

**1812, Two Leaves
Below Wing**

**1812, Single Leaf
Below Wing**

	Mintage	Cert	Avg	%MS	G-4	F-12	VF-20	EF-40	AU-50	AU-55	MS-60 PF-63	MS-63 PF-64	MS-65 PF-65
1809, All kinds	1,405,810												
1809, Normal Edge		575	44.4	15%	$75	$110	$190	$375	$900	$1,500	$3,000	$5,500	$19,000
Auctions: $5,170, MS-63, August 2014; $10,575, MS-63, November 2013; $881, MS-60, August 2014; $541, AU-50, October 2014													
1809, xxxx Edge		49	39.0	4%	$90	$135	$230	$475	$1,000	$2,750	$5,000	$7,000	
Auctions: $1,645, AU-50, April 2014; $411, VF-25, July 2014													
1809, IIIII Edge		120	40.7	9%	$90	$135	$230	$475	$950	$1,825	$3,500	$7,300	$22,000
Auctions: $38,188, MS-66, April 2014													
1810	1,276,276	631	44.4	15%	$75	$110	$170	$315	$800	$1,400	$3,500	$5,750	$18,000
Auctions: $64,625, MS-66, November 2013; $705, AU-55, September 2014; $1,410, AU-55, July 2014; $544, AU-53, July 2014													
1811, All kinds	1,203,644												
1811, (18.11), 11 Over 10		117	43.4	12%	$80	$135	$235	$650	$1,400	$2,500	$4,000	$10,000	
Auctions: $6,463, AU-58, January 2014; $364, VF-35, October 2014; $411, VF-25, October 2014													
1811, Small 8		205	45.5	18%	$75	$125	$170	$325	$700	$1,200	$2,500	$4,500	$17,000
Auctions: $94,000, MS-67, June 2013; $999, AU-50, September 2014; $593, AU-50, September 2014; $247, VF-25, October 2014													
1811, Large 8		56	47.0	4%	$75	$125	$170	$325	$675	$900	$1,850	$4,500	$17,250
Auctions: $4,230, MS-64, August 2014; $5,581, MS-63, November 2013; $1,586, AU-58, July 2014; $705, AU-53, September 2014													
1812, All kinds	1,628,059												
1812, 2 Over 1, Small 8		116	45.1	22%	$80	$150	$225	$400	$800	$1,350	$2,900	$5,100	$17,500
Auctions: $22,325, MS-64, November 2013; $1,293, AU-55, July 2014													
1812, 2 Over 1, Large 8		19	34.3	0%	$3,500	$6,000	$10,000	$13,000	$25,000	$35,000	$40,000	—	
Auctions: $14,100, AU-58, August 2013; $8,225, VF-30, August 2014													
1812		937	48.2	28%	$75	$110	$160	$265	$525	$750	$1,750	$3,250	$13,000
Auctions: $44,063, MS-65, November 2013; $441, AU-50, October 2014; $470, EF-45, August 2014; $324, EF-40, October 2014													
1812, Single Leaf Below Wing		2	31.5	0%	$750	$1,300	$2,400	$3,750	$7,000	$12,000	$17,000	$30,000	
Auctions: No auction records available.													

1813, 50 C. Over UNI.

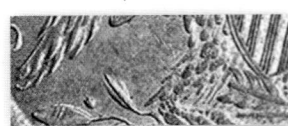

1814, 4 Over 3

1814, E Over A in STATES

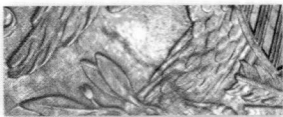

1814, Two Leaves Below Wing

1814, Single Leaf Below Wing

1815, 5 Over 2

1817, 7 Over 3

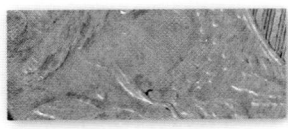

1817, 7 Over 4

1817, Dated 181.7
The date is "punctuated" with a period between the second 1 and the 7.

1817, Two Leaves Below Wing

1817, Single Leaf Below Wing

	Mintage	Cert	Avg	%MS	G-4	F-12	VF-20	EF-40	AU-50	AU-55	MS-60 PF-63	MS-63 PF-64	MS-65 PF-65
1813, All kinds	1,241,903												
1813		607	46.5	19%	$70	$110	$160	$265	$700	$1,000	$2,250	$4,500	$16,000
Auctions: $141,000, MS-67, November 2013; $423, EF-45, October 2014; $412, EF-45, October 2014; $1,293, EF-45, September 2014													
1813, 50 C. Over UNI		71	49.0	23%	$90	$160	$235	$450	$975	$1,500	$2,000	$5,500	
Auctions: $24,675, MS-64, June 2014													
1814, All kinds	1,039,075												
1814, 4 Over 3		104	41.4	13%	$115	$200	$325	$750	$1,750	$2,500	$3,750	$6,500	$19,000
Auctions: $22,325, MS-64, November 2013; $194, Fair-2, October 2014													
1814, E Over A in STATES		27	40.6	7%	$95	$150	$250	$475	$1,500	$2,500	$4,000	$6,000	
Auctions: $4,700, AU-55, January 2014; $505, VF-35, July 2014													
1814		562	48.7	25%	$70	$120	$175	$265	$800	$1,300	$2,500	$4,500	$14,000
Auctions: $22,325, MS-65, November 2013; $3,290, MS-62, August 2014; $705, AU-50, October 2014; $382, EF-45, September 2014													
1814, Single Leaf Below Wing		22	35.3	0%	$80	$125	$225	$550	$1,400	$1,750	$2,850	$5,000	
Auctions: $3,408, AU-50, August 2014; $705, EF-40, November 2013; $159, VF-20, October 2014													
1815, 5 Over 2	47,150	233	44.2	12%	$1,250	$2,200	$3,500	$5,150	$8,500	$13,000	$17,500	$32,000	
Auctions: $117,500, MS-64, November 2013; $4,700, VF-30, August 2014; $2,820, Fair-2, October 2014													
1817, All kinds	1,215,567												
1817, 7 Over 3		151	40.8	15%	$135	$275	$525	$975	$2,500	$3,500	$5,000	$12,500	$42,500
Auctions: $28,200, MS-64, November 2013; $3,290, AU-55, August 2014; $482, VF-20, November 2014; $499, F-15, July 2014													
1817, 7 Over 4 † (b)		2	27.5	0%	$60,000	$150,000	$200,000	$250,000	$350,000				
Auctions: $184,000, VF-20, August 2010													
1817, Dated 181.7		24	45.8	8%	$75	$125	$180	$350	$1,750	$2,500	$3,500	$7,500	$22,000
Auctions: $3,055, AU-58, August 2013; $529, VF-30, July 2014													
1817		532	44.8	17%	$70	$100	$150	$275	$700	$1,100	$2,000	$4,000	$15,500
Auctions: $17,625, MS-65, January 2014; $558, AU-53, September 2014; $382, EF-45, December 2014; $247, EF-45, October 2014													
1817, Single Leaf Below Wing		12	41.5	8%	$95	$135	$190	$475	$1,000	$1,650	$2,750	$4,500	
Auctions: $3,055, AU-55, April 2013													

† Ranked in the *100 Greatest U.S. Coins* (fourth edition). **b.** 8 examples are known.

| 1818, First 8 Small, Second 8 Over 7 | 1818, First 8 Large, Second 8 Over 7 | 1819, Small 9 Over 8 | 1819, Large 9 Over 8 |

| 1820, 20 Over 19, Square Base 2 | 1820, 20 Over 19, Curl Base 2 | 1820, Curl Base, No Knob 2, Small Date | 1820, Square Base, Knob 2, Large Date |

1820, Square Base, No Knob 2, Large Date

1820, Broken Serifs on E's
Compare with normal serifs on 1834, Large Letters, reverse.

	Mintage	Cert	Avg	%MS	G-4	F-12	VF-20	EF-40	AU-50	AU-55	MS-60 PF-63	MS-63 PF-64	MS-65 PF-65
1818, All kinds	1,960,322												
1818, 8 Over 7, Small 8		51	46.7	12%	$90	$130	$160	$375	$950	$1,900	$2,900	$6,500	$18,500
Auctions: $12,338, MS-63, November 2013; $881, AU-53, August 2014; $411, EF-45, July 2014; $499, EF-40, September 2014
1818, 8 Over 7, Large 8		68	43.4	10%	$90	$135	$200	$425	$925	$1,800	$2,900	$6,500	$19,500
Auctions: $7,344, MS-63, November 2013; $999, AU-50, September 2014; $764, EF-40, August 2014
1818		675	47.6	17%	$70	$100	$140	$235	$600	$975	$2,200	$4,000	$13,500
Auctions: $9,988, MS-64, November 2013; $558, MS-60, August 2014; $646, AU-55, October 2014; $529, AU-50, July 2014
1818, Proof	3–5	4	65.5								$50,000	$75,000	$105,000
Auctions: $100,625, PF-65, April 2011
1819, All kinds	2,208,000												
1819, Small 9 Over 8		52	41.2	4%	$75	$120	$160	$275	$550	$750	$1,600	$3,250	$16,000
Auctions: $7,050, MS-63, November 2013; $558, AU-53, September 2014; $235, EF-40, August 2014; $141, VF-20, November 2014
1819, Large 9 Over 8		136	46.2	10%	$80	$140	$200	$300	$750	$1,400	$2,000	$3,600	$16,500
Auctions: $49,938, MS-65, November 2013; $734, AU-53, October 2014; $206, Fair-2, October 2014
1819		487	45.1	18%	$70	$100	$140	$220	$425	$675	$1,500	$3,000	$14,500
Auctions: $18,800, MS-64, April 2014; $852, AU-55, September 2014; $353, EF-45, July 2014; $306, EF-40, October 2014
1820, All kinds	751,122												
1820, 20 Over 19, Square 2		41	42.9	15%	$100	$140	$230	$475	$1,150	$1,875	$2,650	$7,000	$25,000
Auctions: $15,863, MS-63, January 2014; $3,819, AU-58, August 2014; $382, VF-30, July 2014
1820, 20 Over 19, Curl Base 2		56	43.0	5%	$90	$135	$200	$450	$1,100	$1,750	$2,350	$6,000	$18,500
Auctions: $8,225, MS-63, January 2014; $1,880, AU-55, October 2014; $1,058, EF-45, July 2014
1820, Curl Base 2, Small Dt		33	50.5	15%	$85	$130	$170	$340	$1,000	$1,750	$2,000	$5,000	$15,000
Auctions: $10,575, MS-63, November 2013; $881, AU-53, July 2014; $823, EF-45, July 2014
1820, Sq Base Knob 2, Lg Dt		55	49.7	13%	$80	$125	$150	$300	$850	$1,175	$1,550	$3,500	$15,000
Auctions: $18,800, MS-64, January 2014; $1,880, AU-55, October 2014; $1,410, AU-53, August 2014
1820, Sq Base No Knob 2, Large Date		57	46.7	9%	$80	$125	$150	$300	$850	$1,600	$2,000	$5,000	$16,000
Auctions: $61,688, MS-65, June 2014; $1,058, EF-45, July 2014; $470, EF-40, July 2014
1820, Broken Serifs on E's		9	44.1	22%	$475	$800	$1,600	$3,000	$6,000	$6,250	$7,000	$12,000	$40,000
Auctions: $4,888, VF-35, December 2011
1820, Proof	3–5	1	63.0								$50,000	$75,000	$105,000
Auctions: No auction records available.

1822, 2 Over 1

1823, Normal Date

1823, Broken 3

1823, Patched 3

1823, Ugly 3

1824, Normal Date

1824, 4 Over 1

1824, 4 Over
Various Dates
Probably 4 Over 2 Over 0.

1824, 4 Over 4
*4 Over 4 varieties are
easily mistaken for the
scarcer 4 Over 1. Note
the distance between
the 2's and 4's in each.*

	Mintage	Cert	Avg	%MS	G-4	F-12	VF-20	EF-40	AU-50	AU-55	MS-60	MS-63	MS-65
											PF-63	PF-64	PF-65
1821	1,305,797	628	47.9	18%	$70	$100	$130	$225	$650	$800	$1,400	$3,000	$13,000
	Auctions: $15,275, MS-64, November 2013; $646, AU-55, July 2014; $529, AU-53, September 2014; $282, AU-50, November 2014												
1821, Proof	3–5	3	64.0								$50,000	$75,000	$105,000
	Auctions: No auction records available.												
1822, All kinds	1,559,573												
1822		691	49.2	26%	$70	$100	$130	$225	$375	$550	$1,200	$2,850	$14,000
	Auctions: $52,875, MS-66, November 2013; $588, AU-55, November 2014; $529, AU-53, July 2014; $382, AU-50, November 2014												
1822, 2 Over 1		101	49.6	24%	$100	$140	$250	$375	$800	$1,150	$1,600	$3,750	$16,000
	Auctions: $1,410, MS-60, November 2013; $1,645, EF-45, September 2014; $306, VF-30, October 2014												
1822, Proof	3–5	1	64.0								$50,000	$75,000	$105,000
	Auctions: $55,813, PF-64, June 2014												
1823, All kinds	1,694,200												
1823, Broken 3		50	41.6	16%	$80	$135	$225	$550	$1,500	$2,500	$3,750	$7,500	$25,000
	Auctions: $23,500, MS-64, November 2013												
1823, Patched 3		45	51.1	36%	$75	$110	$185	$425	$700	$1,150	$1,500	$3,250	$20,000
	Auctions: $11,750, MS-64, January 2014; $415, EF-40, October 2014												
1823, Ugly 3		22	46.2	18%	$75	$150	$250	$450	$1,000	$2,500	$4,500	$7,500	$18,000
	Auctions: $4,113, AU-55, January 2014												
1823, Normal		838	48.9	23%	$70	$100	$130	$180	$500	$800	$1,250	$2,500	$13,500
	Auctions: $94,000, MS-67, November 2013; $3,290, MS-64, August 2014; $2,115, MS-62, August 2014; $1,410, MS-62, August 2014												
1823, Proof	3–5	1	63.0								$50,000	$75,000	$105,000
	Auctions: $80,500, PF-63, April 2011												
1824, All kinds	3,504,954												
1824, 4 Over Various Dates		57	45.1	11%	$70	$110	$140	$220	$550	$800	$1,550	$3,100	$15,000
	Auctions: $11,163, MS-64, June 2014; $176, VF-20, July 2014												
1824, 4 Over 1		91	49.5	35%	$75	$115	$150	$220	$750	$1,300	$1,700	$3,100	$15,000
	Auctions: $9,400, MS-64, November 2013; $799, AU-53, September 2014; $529, AU-53, September 2014												
1824, 4 Over 4 (c)		142	48.5	20%	$75	$110	$140	$210	$700	$1,200	$1,500	$2,950	$12,000
	Auctions: $19,975, MS-65, November 2013; $852, AU-55, July 2014; $558, AU-50, August 2014; $558, AU-50, July 2014												
1824, Normal		1,044	48.6	24%	$75	$100	$130	$200	$600	$850	$1,150	$2,000	$14,000
	Auctions: $17,625, MS-65, April 2013; $1,763, MS-61, July 2014; $1,763, AU-58, August 2014; $1,059, AU-58, August 2014												

c. 2 varieties.

1827, 7 Over 6

1827, Square Base 2

1827, Curl Base 2

1828, Curl Base, No Knob 2

1828, Curl Base, Knob 2

1828, Square Base 2, Large 8's

1828, Square Base 2, Small 8's

1828, Large Letters

1828, Small Letters

	Mintage	Cert	Avg	%MS	G-4	F-12	VF-20	EF-40	AU-50	AU-55	MS-60 PF-63	MS-63 PF-64	MS-65 PF-65
1825	2,943,166	1,175	51.4	27%	$75	$100	$130	$200	$450	$700	$1,150	$2,000	$12,000
Auctions: $9,694, MS-66, August 2013; $705, AU-58, November 2014; $550, AU-58, October 2014; $793, AU-58, July 2014													
1825, Proof	3–5	1	66.0								$50,000	$75,000	$105,000
Auctions: $32,200, PF-62, May 2008													
1826	4,004,180	1,752	52.0	28%	$75	$100	$130	$200	$400	$525	$1,150	$2,000	$9,500
Auctions: $34,075, MS-66, November 2013; $558, AU-58, November 2014; $823, AU-58, October 2014; $1,821, AU-58, August 2014													
1826, Proof	3–5	2	65.3								$50,000	$75,000	$105,000
Auctions: $76,375, PF-65, September 2013													
1827, All kinds	5,493,400												
1827, 7 Over 6		167	51.4	25%	$80	$120	$160	$240	$525	$600	$1,400	$2,550	$14,000
Auctions: $18,800, MS-65, November 2013; $764, AU-55, October 2014													
1827, Square Base 2		648	49.5	17%	$75	$100	$130	$200	$425	$525	$1,200	$2,100	$10,000
Auctions: $4,994, MS-64, August 2014; $8,813, MS-64, June 2014; $2,468, MS-63, October 2014; $600, AU-58, August 2014													
1827, Curl Base 2		52	50.2	12%	$75	$100	$130	$200	$500	$800	$1,500	$2,500	$10,000
Auctions: $8,813, MS-64, January 2014													
1827, Proof	5–8	3	64.7								$50,000	$75,000	$105,000
Auctions: $21,150, PF-62, September 2013													
1828, All kinds	3,075,200												
1828, Curl Base No Knob 2		73	52.3	22%	$70	$95	$130	$200	$550	$850	$1,200	$2,000	$10,000
Auctions: $15,275, MS-64, November 2013; $1,058, AU-58, October 2014; $329, EF-45, October 2014; $212, EF-45, July 2014													
1828, Curl Base Knob 2		33	52.1	21%	$70	$95	$130	$200	$410	$500	$1,150	$2,000	$10,000
Auctions: $19,975, MS-65, April 2013; $382, AU-58, July 2014													
1828, Square Base 2, Large 8's		45	50.2	13%	$70	$95	$130	$200	$550	$750	$1,150	$2,000	$10,000
Auctions: $32,900, MS-66, November 2013; $306, AU-50, October 2014; $112, EF-45, October 2014													
1828, Square Base 2, Small 8's, Large Letters		316	50.5	17%	$65	$90	$120	$200	$525	$700	$1,150	$2,000	$9,000
Auctions: $9,400, MS-64, November 2013; $170, EF-45, October 2014; $182, EF-40, October 2014; $159, EF-40, October 2014													
1828, Square Base 2, Small 8's and Letters		26	49.8	4%	$75	$105	$150	$250	$600	$750	$1,500	$3,000	$11,000
Auctions: $30,550, MS-65, April 2014; $411, AU-50, July 2014													

1829, 9 Over 7

1830, Small 0

1830, Large 0

1830, Large Letters

Experimental Edge of 1830
Raised segment lines angled to the right.

Experimental Edge of 1830–1831
Raised segment lines angled to the left.

Edge Adopted for Coinage, 1830–1836
Straight vertical lines.

1832, Large Letters Reverse
Note the prominent die crack.

	Mintage	Cert	Avg	%MS	G-4	F-12	VF-20	EF-40	AU-50	AU-55	MS-60 / PF-63	MS-63 / PF-64	MS-65 / PF-65
1829, All kinds	3,712,156												
1829, 9 Over 7		215	52.1	26%	$70	$110	$145	$225	$600	$750	$1,500	$3,500	$18,000
Auctions: $70,500, MS-66, November 2013; $558, AU-53, September 2014; $353, EF-45, July 2014													
1829		981	49.5	25%	$60	$80	$110	$180	$400	$500	$1,000	$2,000	$10,000
Auctions: $18,213, MS-64, November 2013; $427, MS-60, November 2014; 793, AU-58, October 2014; $1,469, AU-58, September 2014													
1829, Large Letters		30	53.3	27%	$65	$90	$120	$200	$400	$550	$1,200	$2,500	$10,500
Auctions: $194, AU-50, September 2013													
1829, Proof	6–9	6	64.3								$40,000	$65,000	$95,000
Auctions: $102,813, PF-64, January 2014													
1830, All kinds	4,764,800												
1830, Small 0		508	48.1	13%	$65	$90	$120	$180	$375	$500	$1,100	$2,100	$10,000
Auctions: $15,863, MS-65, August 2013; $764, AU-58, October 2014; $764, AU-58, September 2014; $485, AU-58, August 2014													
1830, Large 0		123	52.3	18%	$65	$90	$120	$180	$375	$550	$1,000	$2,100	$10,000
Auctions: $41,125, MS-66, November 2013; $588, AU-58, July 2014; $482, AU-55, July 2014; $353, AU-53, July 2014													
1830, Large Letters		11	33.5	9%	$1,400	$2,950	$3,800	$4,800	$9,000	$14,000	$17,500	$22,000	
Auctions: $2,990, VF-35, October 2011													
1830, Proof	3–5	3	64.7								$40,000	$65,000	$95,000
Auctions: $41,400, PF-64, January 2005													
1831	5,873,660	1,766	52.3	27%	$65	$90	$120	$180	$350	$475	$1,050	$2,000	$9,000
Auctions: $11,750, MS-64, November 2013; $1,116, MS-61, October 2014; $499, MS-60, October 2014; $558, AU-58, September 2014													
1831, Proof	3–5	2	64.5								$40,000	$65,000	$95,000
Auctions: $79,313, PF-65, April 2013													
1832, All kinds	4,797,000												
1832		1,600	51.9	25%	$60	$80	$110	$180	$375	$500	$1,000	$2,000	$10,000
Auctions: $6,463, MS-65, October 2014; $7,346, MS-65, November 2013; $1,293, MS-60, November 2014; $411, MS-60, November 2014													
1832, Large Letters		73	50.1	14%	$60	$80	$110	$180	$375	$500	$1,000	$2,000	$10,000
Auctions: $4,406, MS-64, November 2013; $364, AU-55, July 2014; $382, AU-50, August 2014													
1832, Proof	6–9	4	65.3								$40,000	$65,000	$95,000
Auctions: $29,900, PF-63, January 2008													

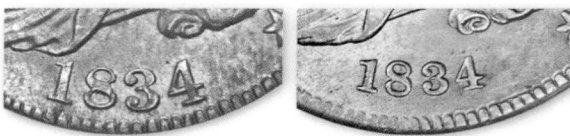

1834, Large Date   **1834, Small Date**   **1834, Large Letters**   **1834, Small Letters**

1836, Over 1336

	Mintage	Cert	Avg	%MS	G-4	F-12	VF-20	EF-40	AU-50	AU-55	MS-60 / PF-63	MS-63 / PF-64	MS-65 / PF-65
1833	5,206,000	1,580	51.5	24%	$60	$80	$110	$180	$375	$500	$1,000	$2,000	$10,000
Auctions: $4,700, MS-64, August 2014; $5,288, MS-64, November 2013; $734, AU-58, October 2014; $705, AU-58, October 2014													
1833, Proof	1–2	2	63.0										
Auctions: No auction records available.													
1833, Crushed Lettered Edge, Proof	3–5	2	64.5								$40,000	$65,000	$95,000
Auctions: No auction records available.													
1834, All kinds	6,412,004												
1834, Large Date and Letters		127	51.0	18%	$60	$80	$110	$180	$375	$500	$1,000	$2,000	$9,000
Auctions: $18,213, MS-65, January 2014; $306, AU-58, October 2014; $441, AU-55, September 2014; $588, AU-55, July 2014													
1834, Large Date, Small Letters		199	50.5	18%	$60	$80	$110	$180	$375	$500	$1,000	$2,000	$9,000
Auctions: $9,988, MS-65, August 2013; $541, AU-58, October 2014; $505, AU-58, October 2014; $382, AU-55, July 2014													
1834, Small Date, Stars, Letters		387	49.9	14%	$60	$80	$110	$180	$350	$475	$1,000	$2,000	$9,000
Auctions: $10,281, MS-65, August 2013; $485, AU-58, November 2014; $541, AU-58, October 2014; $646, AU-58, August 2014													
1834, Proof	8–12	7	64.6								$40,000	$65,000	$95,000
Auctions: $23,710, PF-63, November 2013													
1834, Crushed Lettered Edge, Proof	3–5	2	61.0								$40,000	$65,000	$95,000
Auctions: No auction records available.													
1835	5,352,006	960	50.6	23%	$60	$80	$110	$180	$350	$475	$1,000	$2,000	$9,000
Auctions: $21,150, MS-65, November 2013; $1,351, MS-62, July 2014; $646, AU-58, October 2014; $541, AU-55, October 2014													
1835, Proof	5–8	2	63.0								$40,000	$65,000	$95,000
Auctions: $43,125, PF-64, August 2007													
1835, Crushed Lettered Edge, Proof	3–5	2	65.3								$40,000	$65,000	$95,000
Auctions: No auction records available.													
1836, All kinds	6,545,000												
1836		1,419	50.0	23%	$60	$80	$110	$180	$375	$500	$1,000	$2,000	$9,000
Auctions: $19,975, MS-66, June 2014; $881, MS-60, July 2014; $485, AU-58, October 2014; $852, AU-58, August 2014													
1836, 1836 Over 1336		55	50.0	15%	$80	$100	$130	$225	$475	$700	$1,200	$2,500	$10,000
Auctions: $2,703, MS-64, August 2014; $5,581, MS-64, November 2013; $499, AU-53, July 2014; $194, VF-35, December 2014													
1836, 50 Over 00		47	50.3	19%	$90	$130	$175	$335	$925	$1,350	$2,050	$3,850	
Auctions: $1,645, AU-55, February 2013													
1836, Beaded Border on Reverse (d)		39	45.4	18%	$85	$120	$140	$250	$525	$675	$1,300	$2,400	$9,500
Auctions: $999, AU-58, November 2013; $270, AU-50, November 2014; $147, EF-45, October 2014; $112, EF-40, November 2014													
1836, Lettered Edge, Proof	8–12	5	64.4								$40,000	$65,000	$95,000
Auctions: $96,938, PF-66, November 2013													
1836, 50 Over 00, Proof	3–5	2	64.5								$50,000	$80,000	$115,000
Auctions: $81,937, PF-65, October 2006													

d. The same beaded-border reverse die was used for Proofs of 1833, 1834, and 1835 with the crushed edge lettering; all are very rare.

CAPPED BUST, REEDED EDGE (1836–1839)

Designer: *Christian Gobrecht.* **Weight:** *13.36 grams.* **Composition:** *.900 silver, .100 copper.*
Diameter: *30 mm.* **Edge:** *Reeded.* **Mint:** *Philadelphia.*

Reverse 50 CENTS (1836–1837)   Reverse 50 CENTS, Proof

Reverse HALF DOL. (1838–1839)   Mintmark location is on the obverse, above the date.   Reverse HALF DOL., Proof

History. This half dollar type features a slight restyling of John Reich's Capped Bust design, modified by Christian Gobrecht. It is of smaller diameter than the preceding type, and made with a reeded edge. The reverse is of two variations: the 1836–1837, with 50 CENTS; and the 1838–1839, with HALF DOL.

Striking and Sharpness. The key points for observation are the stars on the obverse. On the reverse, check the border letters and the details of the eagle. The 1839-O nearly always shows die cracks, often extensive (these have no effect on desirability or market value).

Availability. The 1836 is rare. The 1838-O is a famous rarity, and the 1839-O is scarce. The others are easily available in nearly any grade desired, with 1837 being the most common. Proofs are occasionally encountered of the year 1836 and are quite rare. Authentic Proofs of 1837 exist but for all practical purposes are unobtainable. Most 1838-O (a rarity) and a few 1839-O coins have been called branch-mint Proofs.

GRADING STANDARDS

MS-60 to 70 (Mint State). *Obverse and Reverse:* Grading guidelines are the same as for the 1807–1836 type, except on this type the rims are more uniform. On the 1836–1837 dates the reverse rim is generally lower than the obverse, causing the reverse to wear slightly more quickly. On the 1838–1839 type (with slightly different lettering) the wear occurs evenly on both sides, and light striking showing areas of the original planchet on the obverse does not occur here.

1837. Graded MS-62.

Illustrated coin: This example displays light gray toning with a sprinkling of gold over fully lustrous surfaces.

AU-50, 53, 55, 58 (About Uncirculated).
Obverse and Reverse: Grading guidelines are the same as for the 1807–1836 type, except on this type the rims are more uniform. On the 1836–1837 dates the reverse rim is generally lower than the obverse, causing the reverse to wear slightly more quickly. On the 1838–1839 type (with slightly different lettering) the wear occurs evenly on both sides.

1836. Graded AU-53.

EF-40, 45 (Extremely Fine). *Obverse and Reverse:* Grading guidelines are the same as for the 1807–1836 type, except on this type the rims are more uniform. On the 1836–1837 dates the reverse rim is generally lower than the obverse, causing the reverse to wear slightly more quickly. On the 1838–1839 type (with slightly different lettering) the wear occurs evenly on both sides.

1836. Graded EF-40.

VF-20, 30 (Very Fine). *Obverse and Reverse:* Grading guidelines are the same as for the 1807–1836 type, except on this type the rims are more uniform. On the 1836–1837 dates the reverse rim is generally lower than the obverse, causing the reverse to wear slightly more quickly. On the 1838–1839 type (with slightly different lettering) the wear occurs evenly on both sides.

1836. Graded VF-20.

F-12, 15 (Fine). *Obverse and Reverse:* Grading guidelines are the same as for the 1807–1836 type, except on this type the rims are more uniform. On the 1836–1837 dates the reverse rim is generally lower than the obverse, causing the reverse to wear slightly more quickly. On the 1838–1839 type (with slightly different lettering) the wear occurs evenly on both sides.

1839-O. Graded F-15.

VG-8, 10 (Very Good). *Obverse and Reverse:* Grading guidelines are the same as for the 1807–1836 type, except on this type the rims are more uniform. On the 1836–1837 dates the reverse rim is generally lower than the obverse, causing the reverse to wear slightly more quickly. On the 1838–1839 type (with slightly different lettering) the wear occurs evenly on both sides.

1836. Graded VG-10.

G-4, 6 (Good). *Obverse and Reverse:* Grading guidelines are the same as for the 1807–1836 type, except on this type the rims are more uniform. On the 1836–1837 dates the reverse rim is generally lower than the obverse, causing the reverse to wear slightly more quickly. On the 1838–1839 type (with slightly different lettering) the wear occurs evenly on both sides.

1838. Graded G-4.

AG-3 (About Good). *Obverse and Reverse:* Grading guidelines are the same as for the 1807–1836 type, except on this type the rims are more uniform. On the 1836–1837 dates the reverse rim is generally lower than the obverse, causing the reverse to wear slightly more quickly. On the 1838–1839 type (with slightly different lettering) the wear occurs evenly on both sides.

1836. Graded AG-3.

PF-60 to 70 (Proof). *Obverse and Reverse:* Proofs in grades of PF-60 to 62 show extensive hairlines and cloudiness. At PF-63, hairlines are obvious, but the mirrored fields are attractive. PF-64 and 65 coins have fewer hairlines, but they still are obvious when the coin is slowly turned while held at an angle to the light. PF-66 coins require a magnifier to discern hairlines, and higher grades should have no hairlines.

1836. Graded PF-64 Cameo.

1839, Regular Letters Reverse   **1839, Small Letters Reverse**

	Mintage	Cert	Avg	%MS	G-4	F-12	VF-20	EF-40	AU-50	AU-55	MS-60	MS-63	MS-65
											PF-60	PF-63	PF-65
1836	1,200+	207	49.0	18%	$1,000	$1,650	$2,000	$3,250	$5,000	$6,000	$9,000	$19,000	$63,500
Auctions: $38,188, MS-64, October 2014; $52,875, MS-64, November 2013; $8,225, MS-62, October 2014; $8,225, MS-61, August 2014													
1836, Reeded Edge, Proof	10–15	10	63.7								$30,000	$45,000	$90,000
Auctions: $32,900, PF-63, April 2013													
1837	3,629,820	1,371	54.5	38%	$70	$100	$135	$215	$475	$675	$1,200	$2,750	$16,500
Auctions: $25,850, MS-65, October 2014; $15,275, MS-65, October 2014; $23,500, MS-65, August 2013; $4,113, MS-64, November 2014													
1837, Proof	4–6	2	63.5								$30,000	$50,000	$100,000
Auctions: $32,200, PF-62, July 2008													
1838	3,546,000	1,060	53.4	29%	$70	$100	$135	$225	$475	$575	$1,200	$2,400	$20,500
Auctions: $9,400, MS-65, September 2014; $3,819, MS-64, November 2014; $6,463, MS-64, July 2014; $14,100, MS-64, November 2013													
1838, Proof	3–5	0	n/a								$30,000	$50,000	$100,000
Auctions: $129,250, PF-64, April 2014													
1838O, Proof † (a)	20	3	63.7								$375,000	$600,000	
Auctions: $763,750, PF-64, January 2014													
1839	1,392,976	457	52.0	26%	$65	$100	$145	$225	$500	$750	$1,400	$3,100	$30,000
Auctions: $38,188, MS-65, June 2014; $770, AU-58, September 2014; $558, AU-55, September 2014; $441, AU-55, July 2014													
1839, Small Letters Reverse (b)		2	52.5	0%		$40,000	$55,000		$65,000				
Auctions: $50,025, AU-50, January 2010													
1839, Reeded Edge, Proof (c)	n/a	0	n/a								—		
Auctions: No auction records available.													
1839O	116,000	260	48.1	19%	$220	$700	$1,000	$1,750	$2,100	$2,500	$3,500	$6,500	$42,500
Auctions: $129,250, MS-66, June 2014; $3,055, AU-58, August 2014; $3,525, AU-55, November 2014; $3,055, AU-55, October 2014													
1839O, Proof	5–10	5	63.2								$100,000	$150,000	$250,000
Auctions: $92,000, PF-63, March 2012													

† Ranked in the *100 Greatest U.S. Coins* (fourth edition). **a.** The 1838-O, Proof, was the first branch-mint half dollar, though it was not mentioned in the Mint director's report. The New Orleans chief coiner stated that only 20 were struck. **b.** Extremely rare. **c.** Unverified.

LIBERTY SEATED (1839–1891)

Variety 1, No Motto Above Eagle (1839–1853): **Designer:** *Christian Gobrecht.*
Weight: *13.36 grams.* **Composition:** *.900 silver, .100 copper.* **Diameter:** *30.6 mm.*
Edge: *Reeded.* **Mints:** *Philadelphia, New Orleans.*

Mintmark
location is
on the reverse,
below the eagle,
for all varieties.

Variety 1 (1839–1853)　　　　　　　　Variety 1, Proof

Variety 2, Arrows at Date, Rays Around Eagle (1853): **Designer:** *Christian Gobrecht.*
Weight: *12.44 grams.* **Composition:** *.900 silver, .100 copper.* **Diameter:** *30.6 mm.*
Edge: *Reeded.* **Mints:** *Philadelphia, New Orleans.*

Variety 2 (1853)　　　　　　　　Variety 2, Proof

Variety 3, Arrows at Date, No Rays (1854–1855): **Designer:** *Christian Gobrecht.*
Weight: *12.44 grams.* **Composition:** *.900 silver, .100 copper.* **Diameter:** *30.6 mm.*
Edge: *Reeded.* **Mints:** *Philadelphia, New Orleans, San Francisco.*

Variety 3 (1854–1855)　　　　　　　　Variety 3, Proof

Variety 1 Resumed, With Weight Standard of Variety 2 (1856–1866):
Designer: *Christian Gobrecht.* **Weight:** *12.44 grams.* **Composition:** *.900 silver, .100 copper.*
Diameter: *30.6 mm.* **Edge:** *Reeded.* **Mints:** *Philadelphia, New Orleans, San Francisco.*

Variety 1 Resumed, Weight Standard
of Variety 2 (1856–1866)

Variety 1 Resumed, Weight Standard
of Variety 2, Proof

Variety 4, Motto Above Eagle (1866–1873): **Designer:** *Christian Gobrecht.*
Weight: *12.44 grams.* **Composition:** *.900 silver, .100 copper.* **Diameter:** *30.6 mm.*
Edge: *Reeded.* **Mints:** *Philadelphia, San Francisco, Carson City.*

Variety 4 (1866–1873)   Variety 4, Proof

Variety 5, Arrows at Date (1873–1874): **Designer:** *Christian Gobrecht.*
Weight: *12.50 grams.* **Composition:** *.900 silver, .100 copper.* **Diameter:** *30.6 mm.*
Edge: *Reeded.* **Mints:** *Philadelphia, San Francisco, Carson City.*

Variety 5 (1873–1874)   Variety 5, Proof

Variety 4 Resumed, With Weight Standard of Variety 5 (1875–1891): **Designer:** *Christian Gobrecht.*
Weight: *12.50 grams.* **Composition:** *.900 silver, .100 copper.* **Diameter:** *30.6 mm.*
Edge: *Reeded.* **Mints:** *Philadelphia, San Francisco, Carson City.*

Variety 4 Resumed, Weight Standard   Variety 4 Resumed, Weight Standard
of Variety 5 (1875–1891)   of Variety 5, Proof

History. Half dollars of the Liberty Seated type were struck every year from 1839 to 1891. The designs varied slightly over the years, but with the basic obverse and reverse motifs remaining the same (e.g., from 1842 to 1853 the coins bore a modified reverse with large letters in the legend, and in 1846 the date size was enlarged). Large quantities were made until 1879, at which time there was a glut of silver coins in commerce. After that mintages were reduced.

The earliest Liberty Seated half dollars, dated 1839, lacked drapery at Miss Liberty's elbow. In that year Robert Ball Hughes modified Christian Gobrecht's design by adding drapery, a feature that continued for the rest of the series.

Striking and Sharpness. On the obverse, first check the head of Miss Liberty and the star centers. On coins of the Arrows at Date variety, especially 1855, the word LIBERTY tends to wear faster compared to earlier and later varieties. On the reverse, check the eagle at the lower left. Afterward, check all other features. Generally, the higher-mintage issues are the least well struck, and many New Orleans Mint coins can be lightly struck, particularly those of the 1850s. The luster on MS coins usually is very attractive. Resurfaced dies often are prooflike, some with the drapery polished away (as with 1877-S, in particular). Above and beyond issues of strike, the Small Letters coins of 1839 to 1842 have narrower, lower rims that afforded less protection to the central devices of the reverse. In contrast, the No Motto, Large Letters, coins have wider, higher rims that tend to better protect the central devices. Many pre–Civil War dates, particularly of the 1840s, show evidence of extensive die polishing in the fields (especially evident in the open expanses of the obverse). From grades of EF downward, sharpness of strike of the stars and the head does not matter to connoisseurs. Quality is often lacking, with lint marks seen on some issues of the late 1850s and early 1860s. Light striking is occasionally seen on the star centers and the head of Miss Liberty; connoisseurs avoid coins with this detraction, but most buyers will not be aware. Slide marks (usually seen on the right knee) from coin albums can be a problem, more so on Liberty Seated halves than on lower denominations of this design.

Availability. Collecting these coins is a popular pursuit with many enthusiasts. Examples of the higher-mintage dates are readily available, with earlier years being much scarcer than later ones. Most often seen among MS coins are issues from the mid-1870s onward. Circulated coins from well worn through AU can be found of most dates and mintmarks; these are avidly sought. Proofs were made in most years, with production beginning in a particularly significant way in 1858, when an estimated 210 silver sets were sold. Today, Proofs from 1858 through 1891 are readily available.

GRADING STANDARDS

MS-60 to 70 (Mint State). *Obverse:* At MS-60, some abrasion and contact marks are evident, most noticeably on the bosom and thighs and knees. Luster is present, but may be dull or lifeless. At MS-63, contact marks are very few, and abrasion is hard to detect except under magnification. An MS-65 coin has no abrasion, and contact marks are sufficiently minute as to require magnification. Check the knees of Liberty and the right field. Luster

1856-O. Graded MS-63.

should be full and rich. Most Mint State coins of the 1861 to 1865 years, Philadelphia issues, have extensive die striae (from dies not being completely finished); note that these are *raised* (whereas cleaning hairlines are incuse). *Reverse:* Comments as preceding, except that in lower Mint State grades abrasion and contact marks are most noticeable on the eagle's head, neck, and claws, and the top of the wings (harder to see there, however). At MS-65 or higher there are no marks visible to the unaided eye. The field is mainly protected by design elements and does not show abrasion as much as does the obverse on a given coin.

AU-50, 53, 55, 58 (About Uncirculated). *Obverse:* Light wear is seen on the thighs and knees, bosom, and head. At AU-58, the luster is extensive, but incomplete, especially in the right field. At AU-50 and 53, luster is less. *Reverse:* Wear is evident on the eagle's neck, the claws, and the top of the wings. An AU-58 coin has nearly full luster, more so than on the obverse, as the design elements protect the small field areas. At AU-50 and 53, there still are traces of luster.

1841-O. Graded AU-55.

Illustrated coin: Gray toning is evident on this coin. The reverse is lightly struck, a characteristic that should not be mistaken for wear.

EF-40, 45 (Extremely Fine). *Obverse:* Further wear is seen on all areas, especially the thighs and knees, bosom, and head. Little or no luster is seen on most coins. From this grade downward, sharpness of strike of stars and the head does not matter to connoisseurs. *Reverse:* Further wear is evident on the eagle's neck, claws, and wings.

1839, No Drapery From Elbow. Graded EF-40.

VF-20, 30 (Very Fine). *Obverse:* Further wear is seen. Most details of the gown are worn away, except in the lower-relief areas above and to the right of the shield. Hair detail is mostly or completely gone. *Reverse:* Wear is more extensive, with some of the feathers blended together.

1839, No Drapery From Elbow. Graded VF-20.

F-12, 15 (Fine). *Obverse:* The seated figure is well worn, but with some detail above and to the right of the shield. LIBERTY is readable but weak in areas, perhaps with a letter missing (a slightly looser interpretation than the demand for full LIBERTY a generation ago). *Reverse:* Wear is extensive, with about a third to half of the feathers flat or blended with others.

1842-O, Small Date. Graded F-12.

VG-8, 10 (Very Good). *Obverse:* The seated figure is more worn, but some detail can be seen above and to the right of the shield. The shield is discernible, but the upper-right section may be flat and blended into the seated figure. In LIBERTY at least the equivalent of two or three letters (can be a combination of partial letters) must be readable, possibly very weak at VG-8, with a few more visible at VG-10. In the marketplace and among certified coins, parts of

1873-CC, Arrows at Date. Graded VG-8.

two letters seem to be allowed. Per PCGS, "localized weakness may obscure some letters." LIBERTY is *not* an infallible guide: some varieties have the word in low relief on the die, so it wore away slowly. *Reverse:* Further wear has flattened all but a few feathers, and many if not most horizontal lines of the shield are indistinct. The leaves are only in outline form. The rim is visible all around, as are the ends of most denticles.

G-4, 6 (Good). *Obverse:* The seated figure is worn nearly smooth. At G-4 there are no letters in LIBERTY remaining on most (but not all) coins; some coins, especially of the early 1870s, are exceptions. At G-6, traces of one or two can barely be seen and more details can be seen in the figure. *Reverse:* The eagle shows only a few details of the shield and feathers. The rim is worn down, and the tops of the border letters are weak or worn away, although the inscription can still be read.

1873, No Arrows, Open 3. Graded G-6.

AG-3 (About Good). *Obverse:* The seated figure is visible in outline form. Much or all of the rim is worn away. The date remains clear. *Reverse:* The border letters are partially worn away. The eagle is mostly in outline form, but with a few details discernible. The rim is weak or missing.

1873, No Arrows, Open 3. Graded AG-3.

PF-60 to 70 (Proof). *Obverse and Reverse:* Proofs that are extensively cleaned and have many hairlines, or that are dull and grainy, are lower level, such as PF-60 to 62. These are not widely desired, save for the low mintage (in circulation-strike format) years from 1879 to 1891. With medium hairlines and good reflectivity, an assigned grade of PF-64 is appropriate, and with relatively few hairlines, Gem PF-65. In various grades hairlines

1889. Graded PF-65.

are most easily seen in the obverse field. PF-66 should have hairlines so delicate that magnification is needed to see them. Above that, a Proof should be free of such lines.

Illustrated coin: This lovely gem has cameo contrast against mirrored fields.

No Drapery From Elbow (1839)   **Drapery From Elbow (Starting 1839)**

	Mintage	Cert	Avg	%MS	G-4	VG-8	F-12	VF-20	EF-40	AU-50	MS-60 / PF-60	MS-63 / PF-63	MS-65 / PF-65
1839, No Drapery From Elbow	(a)	163	47.2	15%	$45	$120	$400	$600	$1,400	$3,250	$6,500	$30,000	$160,000
	Auctions: $88,125, MS-65, June 2014; $3,672, AU-55, July 2014; $2,585, AU-53, October 2014; $1,645, AU-50, July 2014												
1839, No Drapery, Proof	4–6	6	63.2								$100,000	$135,000	$250,000
	Auctions: $223,250, PF-64, November 2013												
1839, Drapery From Elbow	1,972,400	157	52.5	36%	$42	$55	$65	$100	$175	$290	$625	$2,300	$18,000
	Auctions: $14,100, MS-65, June 2014; $6,463, MS-64, September 2014; $1,880, MS-62, November 2014												
1839, Drapery, Proof	1–2	1	64.0								$115,000	$250,000	
	Auctions: $184,000, PF-64, April 2008												

a. Included in circulation-strike 1839, Drapery From Elbow, mintage figure.

Small Letters in Legend (1839–1841)	1840 (Only), Medium Letters, Large Eagle	Large Letters in Legend (1842–1853)

1842, Small Date   **1842, Medium Date**

	Mintage	Cert	Avg	%MS	G-4	VG-8	F-12	VF-20	EF-40	AU-50	MS-60	MS-63	MS-65
											PF-60	PF-63	PF-65
1840, Medium Letters (b)	(c)	41	41.8	15%	$140	$190	$275	$450	$800	$1,600	$3,750	$7,750	$23,500
Auctions: $55,813, MS-65, April 2014													
1840, Small Letters, Proof	4–8	7	64.0										$100,000
Auctions: $30,550, PF-63, November 2013													
1840O	855,100	98	50.9	32%	$42	$55	$70	$115	$190	$340	$750	$2,500	
Auctions: $36,719, MS-66, October 2014; $5,288, MS-64, August 2014; $10,575, MS-64, August 2013; $212, VF-35, December 2014													
1841	310,000	67	54.8	34%	$42	$60	$95	$150	$275	$450	$1,400	$2,800	$9,000
Auctions: $4,994, MS-64, July 2014; $7,050, MS-64, November 2013; $1,821, MS-62, October 2014; $1,763, MS-62, July 2014													
1841, Proof	4–8	5	64.2								$20,000	$45,000	$85,000
Auctions: $30,550, PF-64, September 2013													
1841O	401,000	105	51.7	30%	$42	$55	$65	$100	$215	$400	$950	$3,500	$19,000
Auctions: $9,283, MS-65, January 2014; $1,058, AU-58, November 2014; $940, AU-58, August 2014; $705, AU-53, August 2014													
1842, Sm Date, Sm Letters	(d)	0	n/a						$4,500	$7,500	$17,500		
Auctions: $99,875, MS-64, June 2014													
1842, Medium Date	2,012,764	133	51.0	23%	$42	$55	$65	$100	$150	$325	$875	$2,100	$7,000
Auctions: $25,850, MS-66, June 2014; $3,055, MS-64, November 2014; $3,290, MS-64, August 2014; $1,528, MS-63, July 2014													
1842, Sm Date, Lg Letters	(d)	55	51.7	25%	$42	$55	$65	$100	$150	$350	$1,175	$3,450	$23,000
Auctions: $21,150, MS-65, April 2014; $4,700, MS-64, September 2014; $529, AU-55, September 2014; $646, AU-53, September 2014													
1842, Sm Date, Lg Ltrs, Proof	4–8	5	64.2								$15,000	$27,500	$60,000
Auctions: $44,063, PF-66, June 2014													
1842O, Sm Date, Sm Letters	203,000	31	36.6	3%	$575	$925	$1,400	$2,350	$4,500	$7,500	$18,500	$39,000	
Auctions: $35,250, MS-62, January 2014; $3,290, EF-40, August 2014; $764, VG-10, November 2014; $823, VG-8, September 2014													
1842O, Med Date, Lg Letters	754,000	59	49.7	31%	$42	$55	$60	$100	$150	$350	$1,100	$4,250	$17,500
Auctions: $28,200, MS-67, June 2014; $558, AU-50, August 2014; $705, AU-50, July 2014; $159, EF-45, September 2014													
1843	3,844,000	202	52.3	32%	$42	$55	$65	$100	$150	$250	$500	$1,200	$7,750
Auctions: $38,188, MS-67, October 2014; $44,063, MS-67, November 2013; $5,434, MS-65, September 2014													
1843, Proof	4–8	3	63.7								$15,000	$27,500	$60,000
Auctions: $70,500, PF-65Cam, August 2013; $44,063, PF-64, October 2014													
1843O	2,268,000	99	51.5	41%	$60	$65	$70	$100	$150	$250	$700	$2,200	$15,000
Auctions: $15,275, MS-66, October 2014; $3,055, MS-63, October 2014; $3,819, MS-63, November 2013													

b. The 1840, Medium Letters, half dollars were struck at the New Orleans Mint from a reverse die of the previous style, without mintmark. **c.** Included in circulation-strike 1840, Small Letters, mintage figure. **d.** Included in 1842, Medium Date, mintage figure.

1846, Medium Date

1844-O, Doubled Date
FS-50-1844o-301.

1846, Tall Date

1846-O, Medium Date

1846-O, Tall Date

1847, 7 Over 6
FS-50-1847-301.

	Mintage	Cert	Avg	%MS	G-4	VG-8	F-12	VF-20	EF-40	AU-50	MS-60 / PF-60	MS-63 / PF-63	MS-65 / PF-65
1844	1,766,000	130	54.8	36%	$42	$55	$65	$100	$150	$225	$500	$1,600	$12,500
Auctions: $5,141, MS-64, June 2014; $441, AU-58, July 2014; $247, AU-55, October 2014; $306, AU-55, September 2014													
1844, Proof	3–6	2	64.0										$125,000
Auctions: $149,500, PF-66Cam, January 2008													
1844O	2,005,000	95	46.9	33%	$42	$55	$70	$110	$175	$300	$900	$2,750	$13,500
Auctions: $4,113, MS-63, November 2014; $3,055, MS-63, August 2013; $823, AU-55, August 2014; $411, EF-45, July 2014													
1844O, Doubled Date (e)	(f)	17	40.9	6%	$600	$800	$1,250	$1,600	$2,750	$6,000	$12,000		
Auctions: $6,463, AU-55, February 2013; $115, VG-8, July 2014; $235, Fair-2, October 2014													
1845	589,000	54	51.3	26%	$60	$70	$80	$120	$240	$400	$1,000	$3,350	$15,000
Auctions: $16,450, MS-64, November 2013; $470, MS-60, October 2014; $505, AU-58, October 2014; $306, AU-55, October 2014													
1845, Proof	3–6	3	65.0								$15,000	$30,000	$67,500
Auctions: $57,500, PF-64, May 2008													
1845O	2,094,000	109	47.4	26%	$42	$55	$65	$100	$150	$235	$725	$2,250	$12,000
Auctions: $3,525, MS-64, August 2014; $8,813, MS-64, August 2013; $153, EF-45, September 2014													
1845O, No Drapery (g)	(h)	17	53.7	24%	$50	$70	$80	$130	$275	$500	$1,400	$4,800	
Auctions: $6,463, MS-64, June 2014													
1846, All kinds	2,210,000												
1846, Medium Date		67	52.6	28%	$42	$50	$55	$85	$150	$400	$800	$1,550	$12,000
Auctions: $16,450, MS-65, November 2013; $4,113, MS-64, October 2014; $1,528, MS-62, August 2014; $676, MS-61, October 2014													
1846, Tall Date		101	53.7	32%	$42	$50	$60	$85	$140	$290	$800	$2,750	
Auctions: $47,000, MS-67, November 2013; $21,150, MS-66, October 2014; $4,847, MS-64, August 2014													
1846, 6 Over Horizontal 6 (i)		38	49.9	21%	$190	$260	$300	$500	$750	$1,500	$3,800	$11,000	$25,000
Auctions: $7,050, MS-62, June 2014													
1846, Med Letters, Proof	15–20	10	63.3								$11,000	$21,000	$50,000
Auctions: $28,200, PF-64, October 2014; $23,500, PF-63, January 2014													
1846O, Medium Date	2,304,000	93	44.5	24%	$42	$50	$55	$85	$140	$300	$1,050	$3,400	$12,000
Auctions: $18,800, MS-65, October 2014; $6,169, MS-64, October 2014; $1,880, MS-62, October 2014; $5,288, MS-62, August 2014													
1846O, Tall Date	(j)	29	37.6	7%	$175	$285	$375	$600	$1,350	$1,900	$6,500	$12,000	
Auctions: $13,513, MS-63, October 2014; $3,819, AU-58, January 2014; $3,408, AU-55, November 2014; $5,728, AU-55, August 2014													
1847, 7 Over 6 (k)	(l)	5	49.8	40%	$1,800	$2,500	$3,250	$4,500	$7,400	$16,000	$30,000		
Auctions: $5,875, AU-50, August 2014; $9,488, EF-45, October 2011; $8,225, VF-35, August 2014													
1847	1,156,000	105	52.8	27%	$42	$50	$65	$85	$185	$250	$500	$1,350	$7,000
Auctions: $1,880, MS-63, August 2014; $38,188, MS-62, November 2013; $229, AU-50, August 2014; $229, EF-45, July 2014													
1847, Proof	15–20	10	63.5								$11,000	$21,000	$50,000
Auctions: $12,338, PF-63, August 2013													
1847O	2,584,000	87	51.1	33%	$50	$65	$70	$90	$195	$300	$800	$2,750	$18,500
Auctions: $5,875, MS-64, August 2014; $8,813, MS-64, August 2013; $1,880, MS-62, August 2014; $558, AU-58, August 2014													

e. This rare variety shows all four numerals protruding from the rock above the primary date. f. Included in 1844-O mintage figure.
g. The drapery is missing because of excessive polishing of the die. h. Included in 1845-O mintage figure. i. This variety can be detected in low grades. j. Included in 1846-O, Medium Date, mintage figure. k. Remains of an underlying 6 are visible below and between the primary 4 and 7. "The overdate might not be evident on later die states" (*Cherrypickers' Guide to Rare Die Varieties*, sixth edition, volume II). l. Included in circulation-strike 1847 mintage figure.

	Mintage	Cert	Avg	%MS	G-4	VG-8	F-12	VF-20	EF-40	AU-50	MS-60	MS-63	MS-65
											PF-60	PF-63	PF-65
1848	580,000	61	55.0	49%	$45	$60	$100	$180	$275	$500	$1,000	$1,750	$7,600
	Auctions: $12,925, MS-65, June 2014; $2,820, MS-64, October 2014; $2,820, MS-62, August 2014; $646, AU-58, November 2014												
1848, Proof	4–8	2	66.0								$13,000	$27,500	$60,000
	Auctions: $34,075, PF-64, June 2014												
1848O	3,180,000	100	49.8	25%	$42	$50	$65	$85	$210	$285	$875	$2,200	$12,000
	Auctions: $25,850, MS-66, June 2014; $1,058, AU-58, October 2014; $1,410, AU-58, September 2014; $499, EF-45, July 2014												
1849	1,252,000	97	55.6	34%	$45	$65	$75	$90	$225	$400	$975	$2,450	$18,000
	Auctions: $15,275, MS-65, November 2013; $5,288, MS-64, October 2014; $2,939, MS-64, October 2014; $3,290, MS-64, August 2014												
1849, Proof	4–8	4	65.0								$13,000	$27,500	$60,000
	Auctions: $38,188, PF-66, October 2014; $70,500, PF-66, January 2014												
1849O	2,310,000	66	51.3	30%	$45	$65	$75	$90	$170	$285	$850	$2,500	$13,500
	Auctions: $15,275, MS-65, October 2014; $28,200, MS-65, August 2013; $1,998, MS-63, August 2014; $1,293, MS-61, October 2014												
1850	227,000	92	54.5	37%	$240	$325	$450	$600	$775	$1,000	$1,800	$4,000	$19,500
	Auctions: $15,275, MS-65, November 2013; $447, Fair-2, October 2014												
1850, Proof	4–8	4	63.8								$13,000	$27,500	$60,000
	Auctions: $20,125, PF-64, July 2009												
1850O	2,456,000	89	55.9	48%	$42	$50	$60	$80	$175	$300	$650	$1,375	$9,000
	Auctions: $25,850, MS-66, August 2013; $3,525, MS-64, November 2014; $2,820, MS-64, October 2014; $999, AU-58, July 2014												
1851	200,750	50	59.0	66%	$750	$850	$1,000	$1,400	$1,750	$2,000	$2,500	$3,900	$13,500
	Auctions: $49,938, MS-66, June 2014; $1,645, EF-45, September 2014; $969, EF-40, July 2014; $881, Fair-2, October 2014												
1851O	402,000	47	55.8	51%	$42	$50	$120	$140	$200	$350	$800	$2,000	$12,000
	Auctions: $41,125, MS-66, June 2014; $3,055, MS-62, August 2014; $541, AU-55, October 2014; $558, AU-53, July 2014												
1852	77,130	73	57.2	55%	$350	$475	$600	$850	$975	$1,400	$2,300	$3,100	$10,000
	Auctions: $12,338, MS-66, October 2014; $15,275, MS-65, August 2013; $2,585, MS-63, August 2014; $1,410, AU-53, July 2014												
1852, Proof	3–6	3	62.7									$35,000	$85,000
	Auctions: $74,750, PF-65, July 2008												
1852O	144,000	42	46.7	14%	$70	$150	$275	$400	$775	$1,400	$3,500	$10,000	$29,500
	Auctions: $36,719, MS-65, October 2014; $15,275, MS-64, August 2013; $246,750, G-6, October 2014; $329, Fair-2, October 2014												
1852O, Proof	2–3	1	62.0									$37,500	
	Auctions: $24,150, PF-62, May 2001												
1853O, Variety 1 † (m)		1	40.0	0%	$200,000	$275,000	$350,000	$500,000					
	Auctions: $368,000, VF-35, October 2006												
1853, Variety 2	3,532,708	1,053	51.1	28%	$42	$50	$65	$110	$265	$550	$1,450	$3,500	$22,000
	Auctions: $42,594, MS-66, August 2014; $76,375, MS-66, April 2013; $21,150, MS-65, October 2014; $10,600, MS-65, August 2014												
1853, Variety 2, Proof	5–10	4	65.0									$60,000	$175,000
	Auctions: $117,500, PF-65, October 2014; $184,000, PF-65, January 2012; $94,000, PF-64, October 2014												
1853O, Variety 2	1,328,000	189	45.6	17%	$50	$60	$80	$160	$350	$750	$2,750	$6,500	$32,000
	Auctions: $21,150, MS-64, October 2014; $7,344, MS-62, August 2013; $1,880, AU-53, October 2014; $823, AU-53, September 2014												
1854	2,982,000	459	53.4	30%	$42	$50	$65	$80	$130	$325	$700	$1,700	$8,400
	Auctions: $4,994, MS-65, August 2014; $5,288, MS-65, November 2013; $823, MS-62, October 2014; $270, MS-60, July 2014												
1854, Proof	15–20	15	64.8								$8,500	$15,000	$40,000
	Auctions: $70,500, PF-67, November 2013												
1854O	5,240,000	676	51.6	33%	$42	$50	$65	$80	$130	$325	$650	$1,700	$8,400
	Auctions: $44,063, MS-67, June 2014; $14,100, MS-66, August 2014; $5,288, MS-65, November 2014; $7,050, MS-65, August 2014												

† Ranked in the *100 Greatest U.S. Coins* (fourth edition). **m.** 4 examples are known.

1855, 1855 Over 854
FS-50-1855-301.

	Mintage	Cert	Avg	%MS	G-4	VG-8	F-12	VF-20	EF-40	AU-50	MS-60 / PF-60	MS-63 / PF-63	MS-65 / PF-65
1855, All kinds	759,500												
1855, 1855 Over 854		52	47.8	27%	$75	$90	$175	$300	$425	$675	$2,250	$4,500	$19,000
Auctions: $15,863, MS-65, August 2013; $353, AU-50, November 2014; $441, AU-50, July 2014; $411, VF-35, December 2014													
1855, Normal Date		140	55.0	40%	$42	$50	$65	$80	$135	$325	$750	$1,750	$11,000
Auctions: $28,200, MS-66, October 2014; $38,188, MS-66, November 2013; $999, MS-61, November 2014; $441, AU-55, July 2014													
1855, 55 Over 54, Proof	1–2	0	n/a								$10,000	$22,000	$60,000
Auctions: $30,550, PF-64, June 2014													
1855, Proof	15–20	8	64.6	100%							$7,500	$15,000	$40,000
Auctions: $41,125, PF-66Cam, June 2014													
1855O	3,688,000	490	53.5	31%	$42	$50	$65	$80	$135	$325	$750	$1,750	$9,500
Auctions: $49,938, MS-67, October 2014; $14,100, MS-66, August 2013; $2,291, MS-64, July 2014; $881, AU-58, November 2014													
1855S	129,950	52	34.5	8%	$350	$550	$850	$1,750	$3,500	$7,600	$24,000	—	
Auctions: $41,125, MS-61, October 2014; $16,450, AU-58, March 2014; $8,225, AU-53, July 2014; $1,146, EF-40, July 2014													
1855S, Proof	2–3	1	65.0								$150,000		
Auctions: $276,000, PF-65, August 2011													
1856	938,000	111	54.0	38%	$42	$50	$65	$85	$130	$225	$500	$1,100	$5,750
Auctions: $5,288, MS-65, August 2013; $646, AU-58, October 2014; $194, AU-53, July 2014; $212, EF-45, July 2014													
1856, Proof	20–30	21	64.4								$4,000	$6,500	$23,000
Auctions: $17,625, PF-65, October 2014; $17,625, PF-65, November 2013													
1856O	2,658,000	254	53.9	44%	$42	$50	$65	$100	$135	$225	$500	$1,100	$6,000
Auctions: $7,638, MS-66, August 2013; $999, MS-62, August 2014; $447, MS-60, September 2014; $529, AU-58, August 2014													
1856S	211,000	33	43.4	12%	$42	$50	$175	$325	$625	$1,275	$4,250	$12,500	
Auctions: $764, MS-60, July 2014; $2,938, AU-55, November 2013; $823, EF-40, October 2014; $499, VF-35, October 2014													
1857	1,988,000	214	53.5	36%	$42	$50	$65	$85	$125	$220	$500	$1,100	$5,250
Auctions: $8,813, MS-66, June 2014; $3,819, MS-65, September 2014; $1,469, MS-64, November 2014; $282, MS-60, July 2014													
1857, Proof	30–50	38	63.7								$3,000	$4,500	$27,500
Auctions: $23,500, PF-66, June 2013													
1857O	818,000	70	49.0	13%	$42	$50	$65	$90	$170	$300	$1,050	$3,500	$12,000
Auctions: $3,819, MS-64, November 2014; $9,400, MS-64, August 2013; $1,293, AU-55, August 2014; $123, AU-50, September 2014													
1857S	158,000	39	47.5	26%	$60	$90	$175	$325	$775	$1,350	$4,850	$20,500	$35,000
Auctions: $61,688, MS-66, June 2014; $400, EF-40, August 2014; $176, VG-8, October 2014													
1858	4,225,700	552	53.3	33%	$42	$50	$65	$85	$125	$225	$450	$1,100	$5,100
Auctions: $17,625, MS-66, October 2014; $7,050, MS-65, August 2013; $588, MS-62, August 2014; $247, MS-60, July 2014													
1858, Proof	300+	55	63.7								$1,400	$2,250	$8,000
Auctions: $25,850, PF-67, June 2014; $7,050, PF-65, August 2014													
1858O	7,294,000	424	49.1	22%	$42	$50	$65	$85	$130	$225	$475	$1,200	$10,000
Auctions: $17,625, MS-66, October 2014; $7,638, MS-65, September 2014; $15,275, MS-65, January 2013; $282, AU-55, November 2014													
1858S	476,000	63	50.7	21%	$45	$55	$70	$120	$260	$440	$1,100	$4,000	$12,000
Auctions: $32,900, MS-66, October 2014; $9,988, MS-65, September 2014; $3,525, MS-63, August 2013; $1,175, AU-58, July 2014													

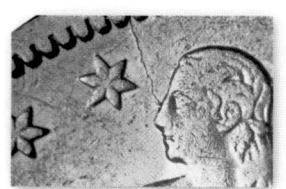

1861-O, Cracked Obverse Die
FS-50-1861o-401.

	Mintage	Cert	Avg	%MS	G-4	VG-8	F-12	VF-20	EF-40	AU-50	MS-60	MS-63	MS-65
											PF-60	PF-63	PF-65
1859	747,200	174	55.6	41%	$42	$50	$65	$85	$120	$250	$500	$1,100	$5,250
	Auctions: $3,525, MS-64, January 2013; $259, MS-60, July 2014; $364, AU-53, July 2014; $176, EF-45, November 2014												
1859, Proof	800	147	63.6								$1,150	$1,600	$7,250
	Auctions: $12,925, PF-67, October 2014; $18,213, PF-66Cam, November 2013; $4,406, PF-64, November 2014												
1859O	2,834,000	204	49.1	23%	$42	$50	$65	$85	$120	$225	$450	$1,275	$7,000
	Auctions: $5,288, MS-65, September 2014; $12,925, MS-65, August 2013; $646, MS-62, November 2014; $1,351, MS-62, August 2014												
1859S	566,000	54	55.5	46%	$45	$55	$70	$105	$225	$350	$1,050	$3,000	$14,500
	Auctions: $7,638, MS-65, February 2013; $588, AU-50, August 2014; $499, AU-50, July 2014; $94, F-15, September 2014												
1860	302,700	77	55.5	42%	$42	$50	$65	$85	$135	$275	$600	$1,100	$5,400
	Auctions: $52,875, MS-67, June 2014; $940, AU-58, July 2014												
1860, Proof	1,000	131	64.0								$800	$1,500	$5,900
	Auctions: $4,700, PF-65, October 2014; $1,998, PF-63, November 2014; $2,350, PF-63, September 2014; $588, PF-61, July 2014												
1860O	1,290,000	232	54.1	42%	$45	$55	$70	$100	$145	$250	$475	$1,300	$6,000
	Auctions: $12,925, MS-66, June 2014; $1,116, MS-63, August 2014; $764, MS-62, August 2014; $793, MS-60, July 2014												
1860S	472,000	66	52.9	38%	$50	$70	$75	$100	$180	$300	$1,000	$3,500	$15,000
	Auctions: $12,925, MS-64, August 2013; $646, AU-55, October 2014; $165, AU-50, November 2014; $212, AU-50, September 2014												
1861	2,887,400	424	56.8	51%	$50	$60	$75	$90	$130	$235	$525	$1,100	$5,250
	Auctions: $10,575, MS-66, October 2014; $17,625, MS-66, August 2013; $3,672, MS-65, November 2014; $1,428, MS-64, August 2014												
1861, Proof	1,000	106	63.7								$750	$1,600	$5,900
	Auctions: $823, PF-61, July 2014												
1861O (n)	2,532,633	267	52.6	42%	$55	$65	$80	$100	$140	$275	$500	$1,100	$5,500
	Auctions: $18,800, MS-66, October 2014; $4,406, MS-64, October 2014; $2,233, MS-64, September 2014; $4,700, MS-64, August 2014												
1861O, Cracked Obv (o)	(p)	28	35.2	4%	$200	$300	$500	$800	$1,500	$2,000	$2,500	—	
	Auctions: $16,450, MS-62, October 2014; $11,750, AU-58, September 2013; $4,700, EF-40, August 2014; $3,525, EF-40, August 2014												
1861S	939,500	92	50.4	34%	$50	$65	$80	$95	$150	$300	$775	$2,350	$13,500
	Auctions: $28,200, MS-66, October 2014; $17,625, MS-65, November 2013; $3,290, MS-64, August 2014; $470, MS-60, August 2014												
1862	253,000	75	54.3	59%	$45	$65	$85	$110	$190	$400	$800	$1,300	$6,000
	Auctions: $28,200, MS-67, April 2013; $3,231, MS-64, August 2014; $558, AU-55, November 2014; $705, AU-53, November 2014												
1862, Proof	550	203	63.7								$750	$1,600	$5,900
	Auctions: $19,388, PF-67, October 2014; $9,694, PF-65Cam, July 2014; $2,233, PF-63Cam, August 2014; $1,529, PF-63, July 2014												
1862S	1,352,000	102	46.1	22%	$45	$60	$75	$85	$150	$275	$750	$2,400	$15,000
	Auctions: $11,163, MS-64, November 2013; $764, AU-55, August 2014; $411, AU-50, July 2014; $200, EF-45, November 2014												
1863	503,200	91	56.9	60%	$45	$60	$75	$90	$155	$315	$800	$1,175	$5,750
	Auctions: $23,500, MS-66, August 2013; $270, VF-30, December 2014; $229, VF-30, July 2014												
1863, Proof	460	131	63.5								$750	$1,600	$5,900
	Auctions: $1,645, PF-63, November 2014; $2,468, PF-63, October 2014; $1,645, PF-63, October 2014; $1,528, PF-63, July 2014												
1863S	916,000	108	55.1	41%	$45	$60	$75	$90	$145	$265	$700	$1,975	$14,000
	Auctions: $9,106, MS-65, June 2014; $1,058, MS-62, September 2014; $999, AU-58, November 2014; $940, AU-58, July 2014												

n. The 1861-O mintage includes 330,000 half dollars struck by the United States government; 1,240,000 struck for the State of Louisiana after it seceded from the Union; and 962,633 struck after Louisiana joined the Confederate States of America. All of these coins were made from federal dies, rendering it impossible to distinguish one from another with but one exception. **o.** In 1861, the New Orleans Mint used a federal obverse die and a Confederate reverse die to strike a handful of Confederate half dollars. That particular obverse die was also paired with a regular federal reverse die to strike some 1861-O half dollars, which today are popular among collectors, especially in higher grades. Their identifying feature is a die crack running from the denticles to the right of the sixth star down to Miss Liberty's nose (and to her shoulder below her jaw). **p.** Included in 1861-O mintage figure.

	Mintage	Cert	Avg	%MS	G-4	VG-8	F-12	VF-20	EF-40	AU-50	MS-60 / PF-60	MS-63 / PF-63	MS-65 / PF-65
1864	379,100	93	57.4	66%	$45	$60	$75	$100	$175	$550	$1,000	$1,600	$8,000
	Auctions: $35,250, MS-67, October 2014; $8,519, MS-65, August 2013; $3,525, MS-64, August 2014; $588, AU-53, July 2014												
1864, Proof	470	161	63.7								$750	$1,600	$5,900
	Auctions: $52,875, PF-66DCam, June 2014; $4,553, PF-65, November 2014; $1,645, PF-63, July 2014												
1864S	658,000	62	44.9	24%	$45	$60	$75	$100	$210	$400	$900	$3,100	$15,000
	Auctions: $19,388, MS-66, October 2014; $3,819, MS-63, August 2013; $2,585, MS-61, August 2014; $364, AU-50, October 2014												
1865	511,400	69	55.3	52%	$45	$60	$75	$100	$235	$375	$900	$1,350	$6,500
	Auctions: $22,325, MS-66, August 2013; $411, AU-50, July 2014; $588, EF-40, July 2014; $505, VF-35, July 2014												
1865, Proof	500	191	64.0								$750	$1,600	$5,900
	Auctions: $35,250, PF-67Cam, October 2014; $13,043, PF-66, November 2014; $7,050, PF-65DCam, August 2014												
1865S	675,000	62	46.1	23%	$45	$60	$75	$100	$210	$500	$1,200	$2,900	$75,000
	Auctions: $9,106, MS-62, August 2013; $2,350, AU-58, September 2014; $940, AU-53, July 2014; $247, EF-45, October 2014												
1866S, Variety 1	60,000	62	28.9	11%	$450	$600	$875	$1,250	$2,300	$3,400	$6,000	$20,000	$65,000
	Auctions: $164,500, MS-67, November 2013; $2,585, EF-45, August 2014; $1,410, VF-35, July 2014; $676, F-12, July 2014												
1866, Variety 4	744,900	101	52.0	51%	$50	$70	$80	$100	$145	$235	$500	$1,350	$5,850
	Auctions: $28,200, MS-67, June 2014; $411, AU-50, July 2014; $329, EF-40, July 2014; $94, VF-35, October 2014												
1866, Variety 4, Proof	725	120	63.7								$750	$1,400	$3,900
	Auctions: $14,100, PF-66Cam, November 2013; $5,581, PF-65Cam, August 2014; $2,115, PF-64Cam, November 2014; $1,058, PF-60, July 2014												
1866, No Motto, Proof † (q)	1	1	62.0										$1,400
	Auctions: No auction records available.												
1866S, Variety 4	994,000	63	48.5	30%	$45	$55	$70	$85	$180	$275	$675	$2,250	$13,000
	Auctions: $14,100, MS-66, June 2014; $969, AU-55, August 2014; $353, AU-53, July 2014; $112, VF-20, November 2014												
1867	449,300	53	51.0	40%	$42	$50	$80	$130	$210	$300	$700	$2,000	$8,000
	Auctions: $55,813, MS-68, October 2014; $3,496, MS-64, August 2013; $282, EF-40, July 2014; $129, Fair-2, October 2014												
1867, Proof	625	173	64.0								$700	$1,500	$4,000
	Auctions: $32,900, PF-67DCam, June 2014; $9,400, PF-67, August 2014; $12,925, PF-66Cam, November 2014; $7,638, PF-66, July 2014												
1867S	1,196,000	83	51.0	30%	$42	$50	$65	$85	$145	$300	$650	$2,300	$12,500
	Auctions: $19,975, MS-66, October 2014; $9,106, MS-65, January 2014; $1,528, MS-61, August 2014; $529, AU-55, August 2014												
1868	417,600	45	52.3	40%	$50	$60	$90	$175	$275	$400	$800	$1,500	$7,000
	Auctions: $4,113, MS-65, April 2013; $200, Fair-2, September 2014												
1868, Proof	600	163	63.8								$750	$1,400	$3,900
	Auctions: $44,063, PF-68, October 2014; $17,625, PF-66Cam, September 2013; $2,820, PF-65, August 2014; $1,058, PF-63, November 2014												
1868S	1,160,000	69	49.1	17%	$45	$50	$65	$85	$145	$250	$650	$1,800	$9,500
	Auctions: $3,525, MS-64, August 2013; $529, AU-53, November 2014; $274, AU-53, October 2014; $382, AU-53, September 2014												
1869	795,300	122	54.0	36%	$42	$50	$65	$85	$145	$250	$525	$1,300	$5,600
	Auctions: $14,100, MS-65, June 2014; $1,880, MS-64, August 2014; $999, MS-63, October 2014; $329, AU-55, October 2014												
1869, Proof	600	152	63.6								$700	$1,500	$3,900
	Auctions: $21,150, PF-67Cam, April 2013; $6,228, PF-66, August 2014; $1,528, PF-63, August 2014; $353, PF-60, November 2014												
1869S	656,000	55	48.8	38%	$42	$50	$65	$85	$165	$300	$825	$2,600	$7,500
	Auctions: $18,800, MS-67, June 2014; $3,290, MS-64, October 2014; $1,998, MS-62, August 2014; $999, AU-58, July 2014												
1870	633,900	74	52.8	38%	$42	$50	$65	$85	$140	$210	$490	$1,150	$6,000
	Auctions: $19,975, MS-67, October 2014; $25,850, MS-67, January 2014; $1,087, MS-62, July 2014; $364, EF-45, July 2014												
1870, Proof	1,000	131	63.3								$700	$1,350	$3,800
	Auctions: $21,150, PF-67, June 2014; $3,672, PF-66, October 2014												
1870CC	54,617	62	27.7	6%	$1,750	$2,750	$4,400	$8,200	$16,000	$32,000	$85,000	—	
	Auctions: $129,250, MS-62, October 2014; $88,125, MS-61, January 2014; $8,225, VF-30, August 2014; $2,468, VG-8, July 2014												
1870S	1,004,000	43	45.5	19%	$42	$50	$65	$90	$170	$325	$1,000	$3,000	$13,000
	Auctions: $55,813, MS-65, October 2014; $67,563, MS-65, January 2014; $7,050, MS-64, October 2014												

† Ranked in the *100 Greatest U.S. Coins* (fourth edition). **q.** Classified as Judd-538 (*United States Pattern Coins*, tenth edition). This fantasy piece was deliberately struck for pharmacist and coin collector Robert Coulton Davis, likely around 1869 or in the early 1870s, along with the No Motto Proof quarter and dollar of the same date.

1873, Close 3   **1873, Open 3**

	Mintage	Cert	Avg	%MS	G-4	VG-8	F-12	VF-20	EF-40	AU-50	MS-60	MS-63	MS-65
											PF-60	PF-63	PF-65
1871	1,203,600	144	54.1	42%	$42	$50	$65	$85	$130	$250	$500	$1,150	$5,350
	Auctions: $4,113, MS-65, August 2013; $1,058, MS-63, August 2014; $646, MS-61, November 2014; $529, AU-58, October 2014												
1871, Proof	960	163	63.3								$700	$1,300	$3,800
	Auctions: $19,975, PF-68, October 2014; $8,930, PF-67Cam, February 2013; $1,645, PF-64, September 2014; $2,115, PF-64, August 2014												
1871CC	153,950	47	29.0	6%	$400	$700	$900	$1,500	$3,200	$5,000	$15,000	$52,500	
	Auctions: $17,038, MS-61, January 2014; $4,406, AU-53, August 2014; $2,585, EF-45, November 2014; $1,998, VF-30, September 2014												
1871S	2,178,000	113	48.8	24%	$45	$50	$65	$85	$120	$250	$600	$1,500	$7,000
	Auctions: $6,463, MS-65, September 2013; $1,500, MS-62, August 2014; $823, AU-58, November 2014; $705, AU-58, August 2014												
1872	880,600	75	52.3	31%	$45	$50	$65	$85	$120	$285	$500	$1,400	$5,500
	Auctions: $21,150, MS-66, June 2014; $160, AU-50, November 2014; $182, EF-40, September 2014												
1872, Proof	950	156	63.3								$750	$1,300	$3,800
	Auctions: $8,813, PF-66DCam, April 2014; $5,758, PF-65Cam, August 2014; $1,998, PF-64Cam, August 2014												
1872CC	257,000	88	30.8	1%	$200	$300	$500	$1,050	$2,500	$4,250	$20,000	$70,000	
	Auctions: $57,281, MS-63, June 2014; $3,055, AU-50, August 2014; $1,410, VF-35, July 2014; $364, VG-10, October 2014												
1872S	580,000	46	49.1	30%	$45	$50	$65	$125	$240	$400	$1,300	$3,000	$13,000
	Auctions: $29,375, MS-67, June 2014; $940, AU-55, August 2014; $588, AU-53, July 2014; $353, AU-50, September 2014												
1873, Close 3, Variety 4	587,000	69	50.1	26%	$45	$55	$70	$110	$175	$300	$620	$1,200	$5,100
	Auctions: $4,700, MS-65, October 2014; $1,645, MS-63, June 2013; $141, AU-55, September 2014												
1873, Open 3, Variety 4	214,200	17	35.6	6%	$3,100	$4,250	$5,500	$6,750	$8,000	$12,000	$21,000	$50,000	
	Auctions: $55,813, MS-61, October 2014; $6,463, EF-35, July 2014; $6,463, VF-35, July 2014; $3,290, VG-8, August 2014												
1873, Variety 4, Proof	600	178	63.8								$750	$1,500	$4,000
	Auctions: $7,638, PF-66, November 2014; $35,250, PF-66, June 2014; $823, PF-62, November 2014; $764, PF-62, November 2014												
1873CC, Variety 4	122,500	43	35.5	16%	$250	$450	$750	$1,350	$2,000	$4,250	$10,000	$40,000	$65,000
	Auctions: $82,250, MS-65, October 2014; $14,100, MS-62, August 2013; $1,586, VF-35, September 2014; $499, VG-8, July 2014												
1873S, Variety 4 (r)	5,000	0	n/a										
	Auctions: No auction records available.												
1873, Variety 5	1,815,200	263	52.1	38%	$45	$50	$65	$100	$230	$425	$950	$1,950	$17,500
	Auctions: $32,900, MS-66, October 2014; $10,575, MS-65, October 2014; $8,225, MS-64, July 2014; $411, AU-55, October 2014												
1873, Variety 5, Proof	500	144	63.8								$1,000	$2,650	$11,000
	Auctions: $12,925, PF-66, September 2014; $12,925, PF-66, June 2014; $3,819, PF-64, August 2014; $999, PF-62, October 2014												
1873CC, Variety 5	214,560	99	40.3	17%	$225	$325	$475	$975	$2,000	$3,750	$7,500	$20,000	$52,000
	Auctions: $42,594, MS-65, March 2014; $30,550, MS-64, October 2014; $4,994, AU-55, August 2014; $940, VF-25, October 2014												
1873S, Variety 5	228,000	44	46.6	20%	$55	$80	$130	$250	$450	$750	$2,500	$6,000	$35,000
	Auctions: $28,200, MS-65, October 2014; $18,800, MS-64, August 2013; $306, VF-30, September 2014; $176, VF-20, October 2014												
1874	2,359,600	344	54.2	44%	$45	$50	$65	$100	$230	$400	$950	$1,875	$17,000
	Auctions: $30,550, MS-66, August 2013; $2,233, MS-63, August 2014; $1,528, MS-63, July 2014; $764, MS-61, August 2014												
1874, Proof	700	210	63.4								$1,000	$2,650	$11,000
	Auctions: $58,750, PF-67, April 2013; $20,563, PF-66, October 2014; $6,463, PF-65, August 2014; $4,700, PF-64Cam, November 2014;												
1874CC	59,000	64	34.5	19%	$700	$1,300	$1,800	$2,400	$4,650	$8,250	$15,000	$28,000	$77,500
	Auctions: $32,900, MS-64, May 2013; $1,821, AU-50, July 2014; $1,293, VG-10, October 2014; $1,410, VG-8, September 2014												
1874S	394,000	53	52.5	45%	$45	$50	$80	$190	$375	$700	$1,700	$3,500	$25,000
	Auctions: $39,656, MS-66, November 2013; $306, AU-50, July 2014; $306, EF-40, October 2014												

r. The 1873-S, No Arrows, half dollar is unknown in any collection.

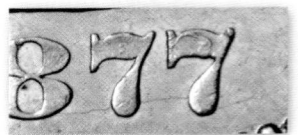

1877, 7 Over 6
FS-50-1877-301.

	Mintage	Cert	Avg	%MS	G-4	VG-8	F-12	VF-20	EF-40	AU-50	MS-60 PF-60	MS-63 PF-63	MS-65 PF-65
1875	6,026,800	351	55.0	52%	$38	$45	$65	$80	$100	$200	$475	$800	$4,000
	Auctions: $7,050, MS-66, June 2014; $1,293, MS-64, November 2014; $1,469, MS-64, July 2014; $1,175, MS-64, July 2014												
1875, Proof	700	131	63.8								$750	$1,300	$3,500
	Auctions: $4,876, PF-65Cam, September 2014; $2,585, PF-65, July 2014; $588, PF-60, July 2014												
1875CC	1,008,000	137	48.5	45%	$55	$85	$120	$150	$250	$375	$900	$2,400	$8,500
	Auctions: $35,250, MS-66, June 2014; $1,645, MS-61, August 2014; $588, AU-55, July 2014; $881, AU-53, August 2014												
1875S	3,200,000	258	59.7	73%	$38	$45	$65	$80	$100	$200	$475	$800	$4,000
	Auctions: $22,325, MS-67, April 2013; $2,851, MS-65, November 2014; $1,293, MS-64, August 2014; $456, MS-61, August 2014												
1876	8,418,000	378	54.6	50%	$38	$45	$65	$80	$100	$185	$475	$750	$4,000
	Auctions: $11,456, MS-67, October 2014; $2,820, MS-65, July 2014; $734, MS-63, October 2014; $705, MS-63, July 2014												
1876, Proof	1,150	210	63.5								$700	$1,300	$3,400
	Auctions: $1,410, PF-64, November 2014; $1,116, PF-62Cam, August 2014; $646, PF-61, September 2014; $999, PF-61, August 2014												
1876CC	1,956,000	191	50.3	46%	$50	$65	$90	$110	$180	$300	$725	$1,500	$5,100
	Auctions: $17,625, MS-66, October 2014; $3,819, MS-65, November 2014; $15,275, MS-65, August 2013; $2,585, MS-64, August 2014												
1876S	4,528,000	199	55.2	52%	$38	$45	$65	$80	$100	$200	$475	$800	$4,000
	Auctions: $8,225, MS-66, October 2014; $3,055, MS-65, August 2013; $294, AU-55, August 2014; $176, AU-50, October 2014												
1877	8,304,000	335	54.5	56%	$38	$45	$65	$80	$100	$200	$475	$800	$4,000
	Auctions: $4,994, MS-66, August 2013; $734, MS-63, August 2014; $382, MS-61, September 2014; $212, AU-55, September 2014												
1877, 7 Over 6 (s)	(t)	0	n/a		$275	$450	$625	$900	$1,350	$3,000	$12,000		
	Auctions: $3,335, MS-62, August 2009												
1877, Proof	510	165	63.5								$700	$1,300	$3,400
	Auctions: $5,875, PF-66Cam, October 2014; $11,163, PF-66Cam, January 2014; $4,259, PF-66, September 2014												
1877CC	1,420,000	228	53.3	63%	$55	$65	$80	$125	$200	$300	$750	$1,300	$4,800
	Auctions: $7,050, MS-66, August 2013; $3,055, MS-64, November 2014; $3,966, MS-64, July 2014; $3,055, MS-64, July 2014												
1877S	5,356,000	471	57.0	59%	$38	$45	$65	$80	$100	$200	$475	$800	$4,000
	Auctions: $12,338, MS-67, November 2013; $6,169, MS-66, July 2014; $1,234, MS-64, November 2014; $1,410, MS-64, October 2014												
1878	1,377,600	98	54.3	51%	$38	$45	$65	$90	$120	$200	$485	$850	$4,250
	Auctions: $21,150, MS-66, June 2014; $646, MS-62, October 2014; $247, MS-60, August 2014; $353, AU-50, July 2014												
1878, Proof	800	229	63.8								$750	$1,300	$3,500
	Auctions: $1,645, PF-64Cam, November 2014; $1,763, PF-64Cam, September 2014; $1,058, PF-63, September 2014; $1,058, PF-63, August 2014												
1878CC	62,000	44	27.5	18%	$700	$1,150	$2,200	$2,500	$3,500	$5,000	$9,000	$22,500	$50,000
	Auctions: $64,625, MS-65, June 2014; $1,763, VG-10, September 2014; $881, G-4, November 2014												
1878S	12,000	13	36.5	46%	$30,000	$40,000	$50,000	$65,000	$67,500	$70,000	$80,000	$120,000	$195,000
	Auctions: $199,750, MS-64, June 2014; $58,750, AU-50, August 2014												
1879	4,800	254	61.0	83%	$275	$315	$365	$415	$525	$675	$850	$1,150	$4,000
	Auctions: $13,513, MS-67, October 2014; $12,925, MS-67, June 2013; $3,819, MS-65, August 2014; $1,645, MS-64, November 2014												
1879, Proof	1,100	316	63.7								$700	$1,300	$3,400
	Auctions: $4,259, PF-66, November 2014; $2,585, PF-65, July 2014; $1,998, PF-64Cam, October 2014; $1,645, PF-64Cam, August 2014												
1880	8,400	104	59.7	79%	$265	$300	$340	$375	$525	$675	$850	$1,150	$4,000
	Auctions: $5,581, MS-66, July 2014; $382, AU-50, November 2014; $458, VF-30, October 2014; $377, G-6, August 2014												
1880, Proof	1,355	371	63.8								$700	$1,300	$3,400
	Auctions: $5,875, PF-66Cam, October 2014; $4,406, PF-66Cam, October 2014; $8,813, PF-66Cam, January 2014; $4,406, PF-66, October 2014												

s. The top portion of a 6 is visible on the upper surface of the last 7. **t.** Included in circulation-strike 1877 mintage figure.

	Mintage	Cert	Avg	%MS	G-4	VG-8	F-12	VF-20	EF-40	AU-50	MS-60	MS-63	MS-65
											PF-60	PF-63	PF-65
1881	10,000	107	58.2	79%	$265	$300	$340	$375	$525	$675	$850	$1,150	$4,250
	Auctions: $9,400, MS-67, June 2014												
1881, Proof	975	322	64.0								$700	$1,300	$3,400
	Auctions: $6,698, PF-67, July 2014; $8,813, PF-66Cam, November 2013; $2,820, PF-65Cam, July 2014; $2,938, PF-65, September 2014												
1882	4,400	73	59.6	78%	$280	$310	$350	$400	$535	$675	$850	$1,150	$4,250
	Auctions: $38,188, MS-68, October 2014; $8,225, MS-67, August 2013; $5,288, MS-66, July 2014; $411, VG-10, October 2014												
1882, Proof	1,100	319	64.1								$750	$1,300	$3,500
	Auctions: $15,275, PF-67Cam, November 2013; $6,463, PF-66DCam, August 2014; $6,169, PF-65DCam, August 2014												
1883	8,000	92	58.0	73%	$280	$310	$350	$400	$535	$675	$850	$1,225	$4,000
	Auctions: $14,100, MS-67, September 2014; $8,813, MS-66, August 2013; $999, MS-63, October 2014; $294, Fair-2, October 2014												
1883, Proof	1,039	326	64.1								$700	$1,300	$3,400
	Auctions: $7,638, PF-67Cam, November 2014; $11,163, PF-67Cam, October 2014; $12,925, PF-67Cam, April 2013												
1884	4,400	93	62.3	90%	$325	$375	$425	$525	$625	$850	$950	$1,225	$4,000
	Auctions: $15,275, MS-67, June 2014; $423, VG-10, October 2014												
1884, Proof	875	228	63.9								$700	$1,300	$3,400
	Auctions: $9,988, PF-67Cam, November 2013; $7,726, PF-66DCam, August 2014; $3,173, PF-66, September 2014; $3,672, PF-66, August 2014												
1885	5,200	72	57.6	74%	$325	$375	$425	$525	$625	$850	$950	$1,300	$4,250
	Auctions: $8,813, MS-67, February 2014; $5,288, MS-66, October 2014; $482, F-15, October 2014												
1885, Proof	930	296	64.1								$700	$1,300	$3,400
	Auctions: $12,925, PF-68, June 2014; $9,988, PF-67, August 2014; $3,290, PF-66, July 2014; $3,290, PF-65Cam, October 2014												
1886	5,000	85	58.6	81%	$400	$475	$575	$700	$800	$875	$975	$1,300	$4,250
	Auctions: $2,115, MS-64, August 2013; $529, AU-50, November 2014; $588, EF-40, September 2014												
1886, Proof	886	241	64.0								$750	$1,300	$3,500
	Auctions: $17,625, PF-68, August 2014; $7,638, PF-67, October 2014; $8,813, PF-67, July 2014; $4,289, PF-66Cam, September 2014												
1887	5,000	111	57.9	76%	$450	$500	$600	$700	$800	$875	$1,000	$1,400	$4,250
	Auctions: $24,675, MS-67, June 2014; $1,116, AU-50, August 2014; $734, EF-40, October 2014												
1887, Proof	710	186	64.2								$750	$1,300	$3,500
	Auctions: $29,375, PF-68DCam, November 2013												
1888	12,001	125	58.3	74%	$250	$300	$350	$400	$475	$650	$800	$1,150	$4,000
	Auctions: $12,925, MS-67, October 2014; $9,988, MS-67, April 2014; $3,819, MS-65, October 2014; $3,525, MS-65, August 2014												
1888, Proof	832	217	63.9								$700	$1,300	$3,400
	Auctions: $5,875, PF-66Cam, November 2014; $1,410, PF-63, October 2014												
1889	12,000	113	57.6	73%	$250	$300	$350	$400	$475	$650	$800	$1,150	$4,000
	Auctions: $8,225, MS-66, June 2013; $4,113, MS-65, September 2014; $1,275, MS-64, November 2014; $388, F-15, October 2014												
1889, Proof	711	194	63.8								$700	$1,300	$3,400
	Auctions: $17,625, PF-67, October 2014; $7,638, PF-66Cam, February 2013; $4,700, PF-66, November 2014; $1,351, PF-63Cam, July 2014												
1890	12,000	94	60.1	82%	$250	$300	$350	$400	$475	$650	$800	$1,150	$4,000
	Auctions: $21,738, MS-68, June 2014; $5,581, MS-66, August 2014; $270, G-4, October 2014												
1890, Proof	590	204	64.4								$700	$1,300	$3,400
	Auctions: $19,975, PF-67DCam, March 2013; $3,525, PF-66Cam, October 2014; $4,301, PF-66, July 2014; $1,293, PF-64Cam, October 2014												
1891	200,000	168	57.8	71%	$50	$65	$100	$125	$150	$225	$450	$775	$4,000
	Auctions: $7,050, MS-66, October 2014; $9,400, MS-66, January 2014; $400, AU-58, October 2014; $153, EF-40, July 2014												
1891, Proof	600	203	64.3								$700	$1,300	$3,400
	Auctions: $8,225, PF-67, September 2014; $3,525, PF-66Cam, November 2014; $10,281, PF-66Cam, November 2013												

BARBER OR LIBERTY HEAD (1892–1915)

Designer: *Charles E. Barber.* **Weight:** *12.50 grams.* **Composition:** *.900 silver, .100 copper.*
Diameter: *30.6 mm.* **Edge:** *Reeded.* **Mints:** *Philadelphia, Denver, New Orleans, San Francisco.*

Mintmark
location is
on the reverse,
below the eagle.

Circulation Strike   Proof

History. Charles E. Barber, chief engraver of the U.S. Mint, crafted the eponymous "Barber" or Liberty Head half dollars along with similarly designed dimes and quarters of the same era. His initial, B, is at the truncation of Miss Liberty's neck. Production of the coins was continuous from 1892 to 1915, stopping a year before the dime and quarter of the same design.

Striking and Sharpness. On the obverse, check Miss Liberty's hair details and other features. On the reverse, the eagle's leg at the lower right and the arrows often are weak, and there can be weakness at the upper right of the shield and the nearby wing area. At EF and below, sharpness of strike on the reverse is not important. Most Proofs are sharply struck, although many are weak on the eagle's leg at the lower right and on certain parts of the arrows and/or the upper-right area of the shield and the nearby wing. The Proofs of 1892 to 1901 usually have cameo contrast between the designs and the mirror fields. Those of 1914 and 1915 are often with extensive hairlines or other problems.

Availability. Most examples seen in the marketplace are well worn. There are no rarities in the Barber half dollar series, although some are scarcer than others. Coins that are Fine or better are much scarcer—in particular the San Francisco Mint issues of 1901, 1904, and 1907. MS coins are available of all dates and mints, but some are very elusive. Proofs exist in proportion to their mintages. Choicer examples tend to be of later dates, similar to other Barber coins.

GRADING STANDARDS

MS-60 to 70 (Mint State). *Obverse:* At MS-60, some abrasion and contact marks are evident, most noticeably on the cheek and the obverse field to the right. Luster is present, but may be dull or lifeless. Many Barber coins have been cleaned, especially of the earlier dates. At MS-63, contact marks are very few; abrasion still is evident but less than at lower levels. Indeed, the cheek of Miss Liberty vir-

1909. Graded MS-62.

tually showcases abrasion. This is even more evident on a half dollar than on lower denominations. An MS-65 coin may have minor abrasion, but contact marks are so minute as to require magnification. Luster should be full and rich. *Reverse:* Comments apply as for the obverse, except that in lower Mint State grades abrasion and contact marks are most noticeable on the head and tail of the eagle and on the tips of the wings. At MS-65 or higher there are no marks visible to the unaided eye. The field is mainly protected by design elements, so the reverse often appears to grade a point or two higher than the obverse.

Illustrated coin: On this example, mottled light-brown toning appears over lustrous surfaces.

AU-50, 53, 55, 58 (About Uncirculated).
Obverse: Light wear is seen on the head, especially on the forward hair under LIBERTY. At AU-58, the luster is extensive but incomplete, especially on the higher parts and in the right field. At AU-50 and 53, luster is less. *Reverse:* Wear is seen on the head and tail of the eagle and on the tips of the wings. At AU-50 and 53, there still is significant luster. An AU-58 coin (as determined by the obverse) can have the reverse appear to be full Mint State.

1915-D. Graded AU-53.

   Illustrated coin: Areas of original Mint luster can be seen on this coin, more so on the reverse than on the obverse.

EF-40, 45 (Extremely Fine). *Obverse:* Further wear is seen on the head. The hair above the forehead lacks most detail. LIBERTY shows wear but still is strong. *Reverse:* Further wear is seen on the head and tail of the eagle and on the tips of the wings, most evident at the left and right extremes of the wings At this level and below, sharpness of strike on the reverse is not important.

1908-S. Graded EF-45.

VF-20, 30 (Very Fine). *Obverse:* The head shows more wear, now with nearly all detail gone in the hair above the forehead. LIBERTY shows wear, but is complete. The leaves on the head all show wear, as does the upper part of the cap. *Reverse:* Wear is more extensive, particularly noticeable on the outer parts of the wings, the head, the shield, and the tail.
   Illustrated coin: This coin is seemingly lightly cleaned.

1897-S. Graded VF-30.

F-12, 15 (Fine). *Obverse:* The head shows extensive wear. LIBERTY, the key place to check, is weak, especially at ER, but is fully readable. The ANA grading standards and *Photograde* adhere to this. PCGS suggests that lightly struck coins "may have letters partially missing." Traditionally, collectors insist on full LIBERTY. *Reverse:* More wear is seen on the reverse, in the places as above. E PLURIBUS UNUM is light, with one to several letters worn away.

1909-O. Graded F-12.

VG-8, 10 (Very Good). *Obverse:* A net of three letters in LIBERTY must be readable. Traditionally LI is clear, and after that there is a partial letter or two. *Reverse:* Further wear has smoothed more than half of the feathers in the wing. The shield is indistinct except for a few traces of interior lines. The motto is partially worn away. The rim is full, and many if not most denticles can be seen.

1915-S. Graded VG-8.

G-4, 6 (Good). *Obverse:* The head is in outline form, with the center flat. Most of the rim is there and all letters and the date are full. *Reverse:* The eagle shows only a few feathers, and only a few scattered letters remain in the motto. The rim may be worn flat in some or all of the area, but the peripheral lettering is clear.

    Illustrated coin: On this coin the obverse is perhaps G-6 and the reverse AG-3. The grade might be averaged as G-4.

1892-O. Graded G-4.

AG-3 (About Good). *Obverse:* The stars and motto are worn, and the border may be indistinct. Distinctness varies at this level. The date is clear. Grading is usually determined by the reverse. *Reverse:* The rim is gone and the letters are partially worn away. The eagle is mostly flat, perhaps with a few hints of feathers. Usually, the obverse appears to be in a slightly higher grade than the reverse.

1896-S. Graded AG-3.

PF-60 to 70 (Proof). *Obverse and Reverse:* Proofs that are extensively cleaned and have many hairlines, or that are dull and grainy, are lower level, such as PF-60 to 62; these are not widely desired. With medium hairlines and good reflectivity, an assigned grade of PF-64 is appropriate. Tiny horizontal lines on Miss Liberty's cheek, known as slide marks, from National and other album slides scuffing the relief of the cheek, are endemic on all Barber

1914. Graded PF-61.

silver coins. With noticeable marks of this type, the highest grade assignable is PF-64. With relatively few hairlines, a rating of PF-65 can be given. PF-66 should have hairlines so delicate that magnification is needed to see them. Above that, a Proof should be free of any hairlines or other problems.

    Illustrated coin: This is an attractive coin at the relatively low PF-61 grade.

1892-O, Normal O **1892-O, Micro O**
FS-50-1892o-501.

	Mintage	Cert	Avg	%MS	G-4	VG-8	F-12	VF-20	EF-40	AU-50	MS-60	MS-63	MS-65
											PF-60	PF-63	PF-65
1892	934,000	957	59.5	75%	$27	$40	$70	$115	$210	$350	$525	$1,000	$2,800
Auctions: $21,150, MS-67, August 2013; $3,290, MS-66, October 2014; $823, MS-62, August 2014; $212, AU-55, October 2014													
1892, Proof	1,245	369	64.3								$800	$1,200	$3,250
Auctions: $10,281, PF-67Cam, September 2013; $3,055, PF-66Cam, November 2014; $2,350, PF-64DCam+, November 2014													
1892O	390,000	386	38.2	38%	$300	$380	$500	$600	$675	$750	$900	$1,600	$3,700
Auctions: $18,800, MS-67, October 2014; $108,688, MS-66, April 2013; $2,585, MS-64+, November 2014; $646, AU-55, October 2014													
1892O, Micro O (a)	(b)	11	30.9	36%	$2,500	$4,250	$5,500	$7,500	$12,000	$18,500	$28,000	$40,000	$80,000
Auctions: $36,014, MS-63, June 2014													
1892S	1,029,028	268	31.0	26%	$235	$340	$400	$500	$575	$700	$950	$2,250	$4,350
Auctions: $11,163, MS-66, June 2014; $3,055, MS-64, August 2014; $1,179, MS-62, September 2014; $515, VF-30, October 2014													
1893	1,826,000	268	55.3	55%	$20	$30	$80	$160	$210	$325	$550	$1,200	$4,300
Auctions: $18,800, MS-67, August 2013; $6,463, MS-66, October 2014; $1,528, MS-64, November 2014; $329, AU-53, October 2014													
1893, Proof	792	279	64.5								$600	$1,200	$3,250
Auctions: $15,863, PF-68, October 2014; $8,813, PF-67Cam, February 2014; $4,113, PF-67, October 2014; $8,636, PF-67, September 2014													
1893O	1,389,000	206	53.6	65%	$35	$70	$130	$220	$350	$425	$700	$1,500	$8,500
Auctions: $11,163, MS-66, October 2014; $1,528, MS-64, October 2014; $3,232, MS-64, June 2014; $306, AU-50, October 2014													
1893S	740,000	212	24.2	20%	$140	$210	$500	$650	$850	$1,350	$1,800	$4,500	$21,500
Auctions: $17,625, MS-65, October 2014; $1,645, MS-60, November 2014; $1,410, AU-55, October 2014; $764, VF-25, October 2014													
1894	1,148,000	205	51.3	60%	$30	$50	$110	$200	$300	$375	$550	$1,100	$3,000
Auctions: $16,450, MS-65, August 2013; $1,263, MS-64, July 2014; $576, MS-63, October 2014; $646, AU-58, September 2014													
1894, Proof	972	316	64.3								$800	$1,200	$3,250
Auctions: $7,050, PF-67Cam, November 2013; $6,169, PF-67, October 2014; $4,406, PF-66, November 2014; $881, PF-62, July 2014													
1894O	2,138,000	185	51.3	61%	$25	$35	$90	$170	$300	$375	$525	$1,000	$5,400
Auctions: $6,169, MS-65, February 2013; $969, MS-64, July 2014													
1894S	4,048,690	218	48.9	52%	$22	$25	$70	$140	$215	$365	$600	$1,500	$8,500
Auctions: $6,463, MS-65, November 2014; $1,763, MS-64, October 2014; $705, MS-62, October 2014; $597, AU-58, July 2014													
1895	1,834,338	190	52.2	58%	$18	$25	$70	$140	$210	$400	$575	$1,000	$3,200
Auctions: $23,500, MS-66, April 2013; $3,819, MS-66, July 2014; $705, AU-58, September 2014; $135, EF-40, November 2014													
1895, Proof	880	349	64.6								$800	$1,200	$3,250
Auctions: $36,719, PF-68Cam, June 2014; $4,700, PF-67, October 2014; $4,406, PF-66, August 2014; $2,100, PF-65, November 2014													
1895O	1,766,000	133	45.3	46%	$40	$60	$130	$180	$260	$385	$625	$1,300	$6,000
Auctions: $32,900, MS-67, June 2014; $4,700, MS-65, August 2014; $940, AU-55, August 2014; $400, EF-45, October 2014													
1895S	1,108,086	180	52.9	68%	$30	$55	$140	$250	$300	$385	$625	$1,400	$6,500
Auctions: $25,850, MS-67, June 2014; $2,233, MS-64, November 2014; $1,058, MS-62, October 2014; $482, EF-40, October 2014													
1896	950,000	119	51.6	59%	$20	$25	$90	$160	$240	$365	$575	$1,000	$5,000
Auctions: $16,450, MS-66, October 2014; $17,625, MS-66, April 2013; $329, EF-45, October 2014; $141, VF-20, November 2014													
1896, Proof	762	268	64.4								$800	$1,200	$3,250
Auctions: $9,988, PF-68, October 2014; $21,150, PF-68, February 2013; $7,931, PF-67Cam+, August 2014; $3,525, PF-66Cam, September 2014													
1896O	924,000	100	27.1	17%	$50	$70	$210	$340	$550	$825	$1,650	$6,500	$20,000
Auctions: $44,063, MS-66+, October 2014; $17,625, MS-64, August 2013; $3,672, EF-45, August 2014; $646, VF-30, October 2014													
1896S	1,140,948	161	28.1	28%	$115	$165	$240	$385	$575	$825	$1,550	$3,700	$9,500
Auctions: $11,750, MS-66, October 2014; $9,400, MS-65, February 2013; $2,820, MS-63, October 2014; $456, VF-25, October 2014													

a. This variety "was created when an O mintmark punch for quarters was used in place of the regular, larger mintmark intended for use on half dollar dies. . . . Many examples show strong strike doubling on reverse" (*Cherrypickers' Guide to Rare Die Varieties*, sixth edition, volume II). **b.** Included in 1892-O mintage figure.

	Mintage	Cert	Avg	%MS	G-4	VG-8	F-12	VF-20	EF-40	AU-50	MS-60 / PF-60	MS-63 / PF-63	MS-65 / PF-65
1897	2,480,000	224	54.7	59%	$20	$22	$45	$95	$200	$360	$550	$925	$3,250
	Auctions: $7,638, MS-66, August 2014; $12,925, MS-66, April 2013; $447, AU-55, October 2014; $135, EF-45, October 2014												
1897, Proof	731	318	64.9								$600	$1,200	$3,250
	Auctions: $27,025, PF-68DCam, November 2013; $9,988, PF-67DCam, November 2014; $4,700, PF-67Cam, November 2014												
1897O	632,000	243	18.5	12%	$160	$230	$500	$750	$1,050	$1,300	$2,000	$4,000	$8,000
	Auctions: $35,250, MS-67, October 2014; $11,899, MS-66, April 2013; $4,406, MS-62, August 2014; $2,585, VF-35, October 2014												
1897S	933,900	228	26.3	25%	$150	$220	$350	$550	$800	$1,000	$1,550	$3,650	$6,600
	Auctions: $6,463, MS-64, August 2013; $2,233, EF-45, October 2014; $1,763, EF-45, July 2014; $223, VG-10, November 2014												
1898	2,956,000	212	52.8	54%	$18	$20	$45	$95	$200	$375	$575	$1,000	$3,200
	Auctions: $18,800, MS-66, January 2014; $2,468, MS-65, October 2014; $441, AU-53, July 2014; $142, EF-40, August 2014												
1898, Proof	735	267	64.9								$600	$1,200	$3,250
	Auctions: $18,800, PF-68Cam, June 2014; $3,290, PF-66Cam, September 2014; $2,585, PF-65Cam, September 2014												
1898O	874,000	115	36.6	32%	$38	$90	$240	$400	$540	$650	$1,200	$3,200	$8,000
	Auctions: $15,863, MS-66, June 2014; $3,067, MS-64, October 2014; $544, VF-30, October 2014; $141, VG-10, August 2014												
1898S	2,358,550	122	43.6	29%	$30	$48	$90	$185	$340	$440	$925	$3,500	$8,850
	Auctions: $12,925, MS-66, August 2013; $4,113, MS-64, August 2014; $364, EF-45, October 2014; $558, EF-45, July 2014												
1899	5,538,000	344	50.7	47%	$18	$20	$45	$95	$200	$375	$575	$1,000	$3,400
	Auctions: $8,813, MS-66+, October 2014; $1,175, MS-64, August 2014; $588, MS-62+, October 2014; $411, AU-58, October 2014												
1899, Proof	846	215	64.5								$800	$1,200	$3,250
	Auctions: $44,063, PF-69, October 2014; $18,800, PF-68Cam, November 2013; $4,847, PF-67, October 2014; $4,122, PF-66Cam, August 2014												
1899O	1,724,000	129	42.9	44%	$25	$35	$80	$165	$275	$350	$675	$1,600	$7,250
	Auctions: $17,625, MS-66, October 2014; $8,813, MS-66, February 2013; $2,585, MS-64, September 2014; $470, MS-60, August 2014												
1899S	1,686,411	117	48.9	40%	$25	$40	$90	$175	$300	$400	$685	$2,150	$5,900
	Auctions: $44,063, MS-68, October 2014; $5,141, MS-66, October 2014; $1,175, MS-62, November 2014; $470, AU-53, November 2014												
1900	4,762,000	346	53.8	58%	$17	$19	$45	$95	$200	$375	$575	$1,000	$3,300
	Auctions: $6,756, MS-66, March 2013; $3,290, MS-65, August 2014; $940, AU-58, November 2014; $141, EF-40, November 2014												
1900, Proof	912	281	64.6								$800	$1,200	$3,250
	Auctions: $22,325, PF-67DCam, January 2014; $3,672, PF-66Cam, November 2014; $2,585, PF-66, October 2014; $3,290, PF-66, August 2014												
1900O	2,744,000	95	42.0	33%	$18	$25	$60	$170	$280	$435	$875	$3,400	$13,000
	Auctions: $11,163, MS-65, April 2013; $823, AU-53, August 2014												
1900S	2,560,322	116	46.4	28%	$17	$19	$45	$100	$210	$375	$650	$2,400	$8,100
	Auctions: $3,450, MS-64, August 2013; $1,880, MS-63, September 2014; $529, AU-55, July 2014; $411, AU-53, October 2014												
1901	4,268,000	305	52.4	47%	$17	$18	$45	$95	$200	$350	$500	$1,000	$3,500
	Auctions: $12,925, MS-66, June 2014; $3,290, MS-65, October 2014; $1,058, MS-64, August 2014; $329, AU-55, August 2014												
1901, Proof	813	273	64.3	99%							$600	$1,200	$3,250
	Auctions: $23,500, PF-68, June 2014; $3,408, PF-66Cam, September 2014; $911, PF-63, November 2014												
1901O	1,124,000	79	45.5	49%	$17	$26	$80	$230	$350	$475	$1,350	$4,850	$13,500
	Auctions: $21,150, MS-66, June 2014; $82, VF-25, October 2014												
1901S	847,044	93	26.7	18%	$32	$55	$165	$350	$700	$1,250	$2,250	$10,000	$15,500
	Auctions: $30,550, MS-67, June 2014; $15,275, MS-66, October 2014; $223, AU-50, November 2014												
1902	4,922,000	266	51.2	45%	$17	$18	$45	$95	$200	$350	$500	$950	$3,400
	Auctions: $4,994, MS-66, October 2014; $3,055, MS-65, April 2014; $306, AU-55, November 2014; $176, EF-45, December 2014												
1902, Proof	777	234	63.9								$600	$1,200	$3,400
	Auctions: $8,813, PF-68, October 2014; $22,325, PF-67Cam, March 2013; $7,638, PF-67, September 2014; $4,700, PF-66Cam, November 2014												
1902O	2,526,000	129	46.6	41%	$17	$20	$55	$105	$220	$400	$775	$3,550	$8,600
	Auctions: $12,925, MS-66, October 2014; $4,113, MS-64, September 2013; $1,939, AU-58, October 2014; $247, EF-40, November 2014												
1902S	1,460,670	76	45.6	47%	$19	$28	$65	$150	$250	$425	$785	$2,800	$7,750
	Auctions: $18,800, MS-67, October 2014; $25,850, MS-67, April 2013; $147, EF-40, October 2014												

	Mintage	Cert	Avg	%MS	G-4	VG-8	F-12	VF-20	EF-40	AU-50	MS-60 PF-60	MS-63 PF-63	MS-65 PF-65
1903	2,278,000	113	50.4	50%	$17	$18	$45	$95	$200	$375	$550	$1,500	$7,200
	Auctions: $8,225, MS-65, May 2013; $529, MS-60, July 2014; $306, AU-55, October 2014; $200, EF-45, November 2014												
1903, Proof	755	256	64.2								$600	$1,200	$3,250
	Auctions: $18,800, PF-67Cam, September 2014; $4,700, PF-67, October 2014; $3,055, PF-67, October 2014; $441, PF-60, November 2014												
1903O	2,100,000	170	51.5	54%	$17	$18	$55	$125	$210	$375	$675	$1,550	$8,000
	Auctions: $12,925, MS-66, August 2013; $84, EF-45, October 2014; $69, VF-20, November 2014												
1903S	1,920,772	116	47.3	55%	$17	$19	$60	$130	$230	$400	$675	$1,700	$4,900
	Auctions: $10,281, MS-66+, October 2014; $3,290, MS-64, June 2014; $1,293, AU-58, July 2014; $940, AU-55, September 2014												
1904	2,992,000	185	51.7	49%	$17	$18	$35	$85	$200	$375	$550	$1,100	$4,100
	Auctions: $15,275, MS-66, June 2014; $3,525, MS-65, October 2014; $353, AU-55, November 2014; $400, AU-55, October 2014												
1904, Proof	670	259	64.1								$600	$1,200	$3,250
	Auctions: $12,925, PF-68, October 2014; $4,113, PF-67, August 2014; $7,050, PF-67, December 2013; $705, PF-62, August 2014												
1904O	1,117,600	84	42.2	29%	$22	$35	$95	$235	$400	$600	$1,250	$3,750	$10,750
	Auctions: $25,850, MS-66, June 2014; $4,406, MS-64, October 2014; $1,586, MS-61, November 2014; $1,293, AU-53, November 2014												
1904S	553,038	166	23.4	12%	$48	$115	$340	$775	$1,500	$2,300	$9,500	$19,500	$39,000
	Auctions: $64,625, MS-66, August 2013; $3,290, EF-40, August 2014; $1,293, VF-30, October 2014; $881, VF-20, October 2014												
1905	662,000	119	48.4	50%	$25	$29	$85	$185	$265	$365	$550	$1,500	$5,350
	Auctions: $15,275, MS-67, October 2014; $6,463, MS-66, August 2014; $1,645, MS-64, September 2014; $382, AU-55, October 2014												
1905, Proof	727	212	64.2								$800	$1,200	$3,250
	Auctions: $24,675, PF-68, October 2014; $12,338, PF-67Cam, November 2013; $4,113, PF-66, August 2014; $411, PF-58, November 2014												
1905O	505,000	122	51.7	69%	$30	$45	$125	$225	$325	$450	$750	$1,650	$3,900
	Auctions: $16,450, MS-67, October 2014; $7,638, MS-66, November 2013; $3,055, AU-55, September 2014; $382, VF-30, October 2014												
1905S	2,494,000	122	42.5	39%	$16	$19	$53	$140	$240	$400	$650	$1,950	$8,500
	Auctions: $7,050, MS-66, October 2014; $9,694, MS-65, August 2013; $499, AU-55, November 2014; $411, EF-45, July 2014												
1906	2,638,000	330	54.4	59%	$16	$17	$45	$95	$200	$375	$550	$1,000	$3,200
	Auctions: $4,406, MS-66, June 2014; $2,115, MS-65, August 2014; $206, AU-50, October 2014; $329, AU-50, July 2014												
1906, Proof	675	257	64.2								$600	$1,200	$3,250
	Auctions: $4,847, PF-67Cam, August 2014; $5,581, PF-67, August 2013; $6,463, PF-66, September 2014; $1,645, PF-64Cam, October 2014												
1906D	4,028,000	264	49.4	48%	$16	$17	$45	$95	$200	$375	$550	$1,000	$3,200
	Auctions: $5,581, MS-66, November 2013; $823, MS-63, October 2014; $176, EF-45, October 2014; $135, VF-35, November 2014												
1906O	2,446,000	115	43.1	38%	$16	$19	$42	$95	$200	$350	$600	$1,400	$5,150
	Auctions: $28,200, MS-67, June 2013; $4,700, MS-65, August 2014; $2,233, MS-64, August 2014												
1906S	1,740,154	123	51.6	54%	$16	$19	$53	$115	$210	$350	$600	$1,350	$4,750
	Auctions: $6,463, MS-66, September 2014; $2,115, MS-64, November 2014; $1,998, MS-64, November 2014; $353, AU-55, August 2014												
1907	2,598,000	297	55.6	66%	$16	$17	$45	$95	$200	$375	$550	$1,000	$3,000
	Auctions: $19,975, MS-66, September 2013; $1,410, MS-64, November 2014; $670, MS-62, October 2014; $529, AU-58, October 2014												
1907, Proof	575	188	64.3								$600	$1,200	$3,250
	Auctions: $18,800, PF-68, June 2014												
1907D	3,856,000	307	51.4	52%	$16	$17	$45	$95	$200	$350	$500	$1,000	$2,950
	Auctions: $25,850, MS-67, April 2013; $2,115, MS-65, September 2014; $441, AU-55, August 2014; $270, AU-53, September 2014												
1907O	3,946,600	269	52.1	59%	$16	$17	$45	$95	$200	$375	$550	$1,000	$3,000
	Auctions: $12,925, MS-67, June 2014; $3,966, MS-66, November 2014; $5,288, MS-66, August 2014; $470, AU-58, July 2014												
1907S	1,250,000	94	37.7	33%	$18	$30	$85	$185	$375	$650	$1,275	$5,700	$11,000
	Auctions: $38,188, MS-67, June 2014; $9,694, MS-65, August 2014; $153, EF-40, October 2014												
1908	1,354,000	175	55.1	65%	$16	$17	$45	$95	$200	$375	$550	$1,000	$3,000
	Auctions: $8,225, MS-66, October 2014; $4,113, MS-66, August 2014; $999, MS-63, September 2014; $148, VF-30, November 2014												
1908, Proof	545	181	64.3								$600	$1,200	$3,250
	Auctions: $9,400, PF-68, October 2014; $4,113, PF-67, September 2014; $5,002, PF-67, April 2013; $4,113, PF-66+, August 2014												
1908D	3,280,000	324	49.4	48%	$16	$17	$45	$95	$200	$375	$550	$1,000	$2,800
	Auctions: $32,900, MS-68, October 2014; $6,169, MS-66+, November 2014; $411, AU-58, October 2014; $112, EF-45, November 2014												
1908O	5,360,000	277	48.7	52%	$16	$17	$45	$95	$200	$350	$500	$1,000	$2,800
	Auctions: $13,000, MS-67, November 2014; $16,450, MS-67, January 2014; $5,581, MS-66, October 2014; $823, MS-62, November 2014												
1908S	1,644,828	92	43.5	50%	$16	$25	$75	$160	$275	$420	$875	$2,400	$5,100
	Auctions: $17,625, MS-67, October 2014; $7,050, MS-66, August 2013; $2,233, MS-64, October 2014; $3,408, MS-64, September 2014												

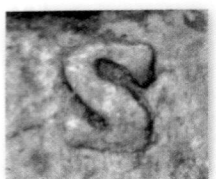

1909-S, Inverted Mintmark
FS-50-1909S-501.

1911-S, Repunched Mintmark
FS-50-1911S-501.

	Mintage	Cert	Avg	%MS	G-4	VG-8	F-12	VF-20	EF-40	AU-50	MS-60 PF-60	MS-63 PF-63	MS-65 PF-65
1909	2,368,000	440	51.5	57%	$16	$17	$45	$95	$200	$375	$550	$1,000	$3,250
	Auctions: $3,819, MS-66, November 2014; $2,468, MS-65, October 2014; $1,234, MS-64, October 2014												
1909, Proof	650	283	64.5								$600	$1,200	$3,250
	Auctions: $15,863, PF-68, December 2013; $4,641, PF-66Cam, November 2014; $5,288, PF-66Cam, July 2014												
1909O	925,400	141	38.2	39%	$18	$22	$65	$175	$375	$650	$1,400	$1,600	$4,200
	Auctions: $4,994, MS-65, August 2013; $1,410, MS-63, October 2014; $764, AU-50, August 2014; $329, VF-35, October 2014												
1909S	1,764,000	135	38.8	36%	$16	$17	$45	$95	$200	$360	$600	$1,250	$4,100
	Auctions: $4,847, MS-66, August 2013; $427, AU-50, July 2014												
1909S, Inverted Mintmark (c)	(d)	0	n/a								$425	$675	$1,550
	Auctions: $4,406, MS-66, November 2014; $206, VF-30, August 2014; $101, F-15, February 2014												
1910	418,000	160	48.4	53%	$20	$30	$95	$175	$320	$410	$600	$1,100	$3,400
	Auctions: $11,163, MS-66, January 2014; $2,820, MS-65, October 2014; $1,528, AU-58, October 2014												
1910, Proof	551	253	64.3								$800	$1,200	$3,250
	Auctions: $14,100, PF-68, August 2013; $4,847, PF-67, July 2014; $4,406, PF-66Cam, September 2014; $477, PF-60, July 2014												
1910S	1,948,000	117	41.9	40%	$18	$20	$35	$95	$200	$375	$650	$2,000	$5,750
	Auctions: $4,700, MS-66, November 2014; $7,638, MS-66, June 2014; $159, AU-50, November 2014; $106, VF-35, August 2014												
1911	1,406,000	313	54.5	62%	$16	$17	$45	$95	$200	$375	$550	$1,000	$2,900
	Auctions: $3,819, MS-66, October 2014; $1,410, MS-64, August 2014; $823, MS-63, September 2014; $427, AU-58, July 2014												
1911, Proof	543	234	64.6								$800	$1,200	$3,250
	Auctions: $11,456, PF-68, October 2014; $10,575, PF-67Cam, November 2013; $3,995, PF-67, October 2014												
1911D	695,080	147	53.2	62%	$16	$17	$45	$95	$200	$350	$500	$1,000	$3,100
	Auctions: $19,975, MS-67, October 2014; $2,585, MS-65, October 2014; $1,028, MS-64, October 2014; $329, AU-55, October 2014												
1911S	1,272,000	100	38.4	34%	$18	$20	$40	$100	$210	$385	$650	$1,500	$5,200
	Auctions: $5,581, MS-66, October 2014; $2,115, MS-64, August 2014; $6,169, AU-58, November 2013												
1911S, Repunched Mintmark (e)	(f)	0	n/a								$475	$750	$1,600	$5,400
	Auctions: $4,888, MS-65, December 2009												
1912	1,550,000	372	54.1	61%	$16	$17	$45	$95	$200	$375	$550	$1,000	$2,900
	Auctions: $2,350, MS-65, June 2014; $1,146, MS-64, September 2014; $823, MS-63, September 2014; $330, AU-53, July 2014												
1912, Proof	700	190	64.1								$800	$1,200	$3,250
	Auctions: $10,575, PF-67Cam, November 2014; $8,813, PF-67, April 2013; $4,113, PF-66, August 2014; $764, PF-62, July 2014												
1912D	2,300,800	530	52.6	58%	$16	$17	$45	$95	$200	$375	$550	$1,000	$2,900
	Auctions: $9,400, MS-66, August 2013; $2,585, MS-65, October 2014; $1,175, MS-64, November 2014; $259, AU-55, October 2014												
1912S	1,370,000	204	43.3	49%	$16	$18	$45	$100	$200	$425	$600	$1,150	$4,100
	Auctions: $5,288, MS-66, June 2014; $764, AU-55, July 2014; $65, EF-40, October 2014												
1913	188,000	376	19.6	14%	$75	$90	$210	$425	$650	$835	$1,150	$1,800	$4,250
	Auctions: $8,813, MS-66, June 2014; $3,290, MS-64+, August 2014; $1,586, MS-62, November 2014; $1,116, EF-45, October 2014												
1913, Proof	627	197	63.7								$700	$1,300	$3,500
	Auctions: $9,400, PF-68, June 2014; $8,519, PF-67, July 2014; $2,585, PF-66, October 2014; $1,528, PF-64, November 2014												
1913D	534,000	265	55.1	58%	$16	$17	$45	$95	$200	$375	$550	$1,000	$4,350
	Auctions: $12,925, MS-66, June 2014; $3,290, MS-65, October 2014; $423, AU-58, October 2014; $212, EF-45, August 2014												
1913S	604,000	142	46.4	55%	$16	$25	$55	$120	$275	$385	$600	$1,350	$3,850
	Auctions: $15,275, MS-66, June 2014; $153, VF-25, October 2014; $153, VF-20, October 2014												

c. The S mintmark was punched into the die upside-down (with the top slightly wider than the base). **d.** Included in 1909-S mintage figure. **e.** The lower serif of the underlying mintmark is visible protruding from the primary serif. **f.** Included in 1911-S mintage figure.

	Mintage	Cert	Avg	%MS	G-4	VG-8	F-12	VF-20	EF-40	AU-50	MS-60 / PF-60	MS-63 / PF-63	MS-65 / PF-65
1914	124,230	436	22.1	19%	$150	$170	$315	$550	$775	$975	$1,350	$1,950	$8,000
	Auctions: $30,550, MS-66+, October 2014; $2,585, MS-64, October 2014; $1,645, AU-55, August 2014; $1,293, AU-53, October 2014												
1914, Proof	380	173	64.5								$800	$1,450	$3,600
	Auctions: $9,694, PF-67, October 2014; $14,688, PF-67, August 2013; $3,349, PF-66, September 2014; $3,173, PF-66, August 2014												
1914S	992,000	178	42.5	45%	$16	$20	$40	$100	$200	$400	$600	$1,150	$4,350
	Auctions: $11,163, MS-66, October 2014; $3,525, MS-65, August 2014; $1,645, MS-64, September 2014; $247, AU-50, November 2014												
1915	138,000	466	16.9	8%	$110	$140	$285	$375	$575	$850	$1,350	$2,250	$5,600
	Auctions: $7,050, MS-65, June 2013; $2,115, MS-63, November 2014; $881, AU-53, July 2014; $411, VF-35, October 2014												
1915, Proof	450	174	64.5								$800	$1,400	$3,600
	Auctions: $22,325, PF-68, December 2013; $3,819, PF-66, November 2014												
1915D	1,170,400	605	55.2	62%	$16	$17	$45	$95	$200	$375	$550	$1,000	$3,200
	Auctions: $5,875, MS-66+, July 2014; $1,175, MS-64, October 2014; $470, MS-61, September 2014; $329, AU-55, November 2014												
1915S	1,604,000	468	51.1	59%	$16	$17	$45	$95	$200	$350	$500	$1,000	$2,800
	Auctions: $8,225, MS-66, February 2013; $940, MS-64, November 2014; $560, MS-62, August 2014; $411, AU-55, July 2014												

LIBERTY WALKING (1916–1947)

Designer: *Adolph A. Weinman.* **Weight:** *12.50 grams.*
Composition: *.900 silver, .100 copper (net weight .36169 oz. pure silver).*
Diameter: *30.6 mm.* **Edge:** *Reeded.* **Mints:** *Philadelphia, Denver, San Francisco.*

Circulation Strike   Proof

Mintmark location, 1916–1917, is on the obverse, below the motto.   Mintmark location, 1917–1947, is on the reverse, below the branch.

History. The Liberty Walking half dollar was designed by Adolph A. Weinman, the sculptor who also created the Mercury or Winged Liberty Head dime. His monogram appears under the tips of the eagle's wing feathers. Mintage was intermittent from 1916 to 1947, with none struck in 1922, 1924, 1925, 1926, 1930, 1931, and 1932. On the 1916 coins and some of the 1917 coins, the mintmark is located on the obverse, below IN GOD WE TRUST. Other coins of 1917, and those through 1947, have the mintmark on the reverse, under the pine branch.

Striking and Sharpness. Most circulation-strike Liberty Walking half dollars are lightly struck. In this respect they are similar to Standing Liberty quarters of the same era. On the obverse, the key points to check are Miss Liberty's left hand, the higher parts and lines in the skirt, and her head; after that, check all other areas. *Very few* coins are sharply struck in these areas, and for some issues sharp strikes might not exist at all. On the reverse, check the breast of the eagle.

Proofs were made beginning in 1936 and continuing through 1942. The entire die was polished (including the figure of Miss Liberty and the eagle), generating coins of low contrast. Proofs are usually fairly well struck. Most Proofs of 1941 are from over-polished dies, with the AW monogram of the designer no longer present. Striking sharpness can vary. Seek coins with full head and left-hand details.

Availability. All dates and mintmarks are readily collectible, although some, such as 1917-S (obverse mintmark), 1919-D, the three issues of 1921, and 1938-D, are scarce. Earlier years are often seen with extensive wear. MS coins are most often seen of the three issues of 1916, the 1917, and those of 1933 to 1947. Collectors saved the issues of the 1940s in large quantities, making the coins common today. As noted, coins with Full Details can range from scarce to extremely rare for certain dates. Half dollars dated 1928-D are counterfeit.

Note: Values of common-date silver coins have been based on the current bullion price of silver, $17 per ounce, and may vary with the prevailing spot price.

GRADING STANDARDS

MS-60 to 70 (Mint State). *Obverse:* At MS-60, some abrasion and contact marks are evident on the higher areas, which are also the areas most likely to be weakly struck. This includes Miss Liberty's left arm, her hand, and the areas of the skirt covering her left leg. The luster may not be complete in those areas on weakly struck coins (even those certified above MS-65)—the *original planchet surface* may be revealed, as it was not smoothed out by strik-

1917. Graded MS-65.

ing. Accordingly, grading is best done by evaluating abrasion as it is observed *in the right field*, plus evaluating the mint luster. Luster may be dull or lifeless at MS-60 to 62, but should have deep frost at MS-63 or better, particularly in the lower-relief areas. At MS-65 or better, it should be full and rich. Sometimes, to compensate for flat striking, certified coins with virtually flawless luster in the fields, evocative of an MS-65 or 66 grade, are called MS-63 or a lower grade. Such coins would seem to offer a lot of value for the money, if the variety is one that is not found with Full Details (1923-S is one of many examples). *Reverse:* Striking is usually better, permitting observation of luster in all areas except the eagle's body, which may be lightly struck. Luster may be dull or lifeless at MS-60 to 62, but should have deep frost at MS-63 or better, particularly in the lower-relief areas. At MS-65 or better, it should be full and rich.

   Illustrated coin: This is a lustrous gem example.

AU-50, 53, 55, 58 (About Uncirculated). *Obverse:* Light wear is seen on the higher-relief areas of Miss Liberty, the vertical area from her head down to the date. At AU-58, the luster in the field is extensive, but is interrupted by friction and light wear. At AU-50 and 53, luster is less. *Reverse:* Wear is most evident on the eagle's breast immediately under the neck feathers, the left leg, and the top of the left wing. Luster is nearly complete at AU-58, but at AU-50 half or more is gone.

1921-S. Graded AU-50.

EF-40, 45 (Extremely Fine). *Obverse:* Wear is more extensive, with the higher parts of Miss Liberty now without detail, and with no skirt lines visible directly over her left leg. Little or no luster is seen. *Reverse:* The eagle shows more wear overall, with the highest parts of the body and left leg worn flat.

1919-S. Graded EF-40.

VF-20, 30 (Very Fine). *Obverse:* Wear is more extensive, and Miss Liberty is worn mostly flat in the line from her head to her left foot. Her skirt is worn, but most lines are seen, except over the leg and to the left and right. The lower part of her cape (to the left of her waist) is worn. *Reverse:* The eagle is worn smooth from the head to the left leg, and the right leg is flat at the top. Most feathers in the wings are delineated, but weak.

1921-S. Graded VF-20.

F-12, 15 (Fine). *Obverse:* Wear is more extensive, now with only a few light lines visible in the skirt. The rays of the sun are weak below the cape, and may be worn away at their tips. *Reverse:* Wear is more extensive, with most details now gone on the eagle's right leg. Delineation of the feathers is less, and most in the upper area and right edge of the left wing are blended together.

1918-S. Graded F-12.

VG-8, 10 (Very Good). *Obverse:* Wear is slightly more extensive, but the rim still is defined all around. The tops of the date numerals are worn and blend slightly into the ground above. *Reverse:* Wear is more extensive. On the left wing only a few feathers are delineated, and on the shoulder of the right wing most detail is gone. Detail in the pine branch is lost and it appears as a clump.

1921-D. Graded VG-8.

G-4, 6 (Good). *Obverse:* Miss Liberty is worn flat, with her head, neck, and arms all blended together. Folds can be seen at the bottom of the skirt, but the lines are worn away. The rim is worn done into the tops of some of the letters. *Reverse:* All areas show more wear. The rim is worn down into the tops of some of the letters, particularly at the top border.

1917-S, Obverse Mintmark. Graded G-4.

AG-3 (About Good). *Obverse:* Wear is more extensive. The sun's rays are nearly all gone, the motto is very light and sometimes incomplete, and the rim is worn down into more of the letters. *Reverse:* Wear is more extensive, with the eagle essentially worn flat. The rim is worn down into more of the letters.

1918. Graded AG-3.

PF-60 to 70 (Proof). *Obverse and Reverse:* Proofs that are extensively cleaned and have many hairlines, or that are dull and grainy, are lower level, such as PF-60 to 62. These are not widely desired, and represent coins that have been mistreated. With medium hairlines and good reflectivity, assigned grades of PF-63 or 64 are appropriate. Tiny horizontal lines on Miss Liberty's leg, known as slide marks, from National and other

1939. Graded PF-65.

album slides scuffing the relief of the cheek, are common; coins with such marks should not be graded higher than PF-64, but sometimes are. With relatively few hairlines and no noticeable slide marks, a rating of PF-65 can be given. PF-66 should have hairlines so delicate that magnification is needed to see them. Above that, a Proof should be free of any hairlines or other problems.

Illustrated coin: This example is a brilliant gem Proof.

	Mintage	Cert	Avg	%MS	G-4	VG-8	F-12	VF-20	EF-40	AU-50	MS-60	MS-63	MS-65
											PF-64	PF-65	PF-67
1916	608,000	1,448	54.4	72%	$50	$55	$90	$160	$225	$265	$350	$550	$1,850
	Auctions: $6,463, MS-67, October 2013; $3,525, MS-66, September 2014; $676, MS-64, October 2014; $306, AU-58, September 2014												
1916D, Obverse Mintmark	1,014,400	1,662	53.6	67%	$50	$60	$85	$135	$215	$240	$360	$600	$2,200
	Auctions: $11,163, MS-67, August 2014; $15,275, MS-67, March 2013; $3,408, MS-66, November 2014; $385, MS-62, November 2014												
1916S, Obverse Mintmark	508,000	928	37.1	43%	$120	$140	$275	$435	$650	$800	$1,200	$2,100	$5,800
	Auctions: $9,988, MS-66, November 2014; $21,150, MS-66, June 2014; $2,585, MS-64, October 2014; $705, AU-50, November 2014												

	Mintage	Cert	Avg	%MS	G-4	VG-8	F-12	VF-20	EF-40	AU-50	MS-60	MS-63	MS-65
											PF-64	PF-65	PF-67
1917	12,292,000	2,147	62.0	84%	$18	$19	$19.50	$21	$40	$70	$150	$210	$900
	Auctions: $8,813, MS-67, October 2013; $1,880, MS-66, September 2014; $382, MS-64, October 2014; $170, MS-62, December 2014												
1917D, Obverse Mintmark	765,400	945	54.1	62%	$25	$35	$80	$150	$240	$325	$600	$1,300	$7,500
	Auctions: $12,404, MS-66, August 2014; $12,925, MS-65, July 2014; $2,706, MS-64+, November 2014; $705, MS-61, October 2014												
1917S, Obverse Mintmark	952,000	527	45.3	44%	$27	$50	$140	$375	$750	$1,300	$2,350	$4,750	$18,000
	Auctions: $30,550, MS-65, August 2013; $6,463, MS-64, September 2014; $4,553, AU-58, July 2014; $499, VF-30, November 2014												
1917D, Reverse Mintmark	1,940,000	568	54.4	52%	$18	$19	$45	$145	$280	$515	$950	$2,200	$16,000
	Auctions: $12,925, MS-65, October 2014; $18,800, MS-65, August 2013; $3,525, MS-64, November 2014; $470, AU-53, October 2014												
1917S, Reverse Mintmark	5,554,000	900	58.8	71%	$18	$19	$20	$35	$70	$170	$425	$2,000	$14,000
	Auctions: $38,188, MS-66, September 2013; $7,050, MS-65, September 2014; $646, MS-61, November 2014; $282, AU-55, October 2014												
1918	6,634,000	779	58.8	70%	$18	$19	$20	$65	$155	$265	$625	$975	$3,400
	Auctions: $17,625, MS-66, October 2014; $4,406, MS-65, November 2014; $999, MS-64, September 2014												
1918D	3,853,040	758	55.6	63%	$18	$19	$38	$100	$250	$475	$1,300	$3,150	$21,500
	Auctions: $30,550, MS-65, August 2013; $4,406, MS-64, October 2014; $1,323, MS-62, September 2014; $881, AU-58, November 2014												
1918S	10,282,000	881	58.0	68%	$18	$19	$20	$35	$80	$200	$525	$2,100	$16,000
	Auctions: $30,550, MS-65, August 2013; $2,350, MS-64, November 2014; $881, MS-62, October 2014; $282, AU-58, November 2014												
1919	962,000	539	45.5	47%	$25	$32	$78	$265	$515	$825	$1,350	$3,500	$6,800
	Auctions: $16,450, MS-66, November 2013; $6,463, MS-65, October 2014; $5,288, MS-64, October 2014; $529, AU-50, November 2014												
1919D	1,165,000	641	44.5	45%	$26	$40	$115	$345	$825	$1,675	$5,900	$17,500	$115,000
	Auctions: $52,875, MS-64, August 2013; $9,988, MS-63, September 2014; $4,994, MS-62, October 2014; $3,525, AU-58, October 2014												
1919S	1,552,000	478	42.3	33%	$20	$30	$85	$275	$815	$1,600	$3,250	$8,750	$18,000
	Auctions: $15,275, MS-65, October 2014; $23,500, MS-65, August 2013; $6,169, MS-62+, August 2014; $3,819, AU-58, July 2014												
1920	6,372,000	829	60.1	76%	$18	$19	$20	$45	$80	$160	$325	$700	$4,400
	Auctions: $3,290, MS-65, November 2014; $881, MS-64, November 2014; $764, MS-62, July 2014; $470, AU-58, August 2014												
1920D	1,551,000	359	46.6	50%	$18	$20	$75	$250	$450	$925	$1,550	$3,850	$16,500
	Auctions: $12,925, MS-65, November 2014; $7,050, MS-64, October 2014; $10,575, MS-64+, September 2014												
1920S	4,624,000	491	53.2	54%	$18	$18.50	$23	$90	$230	$475	$875	$3,000	$13,750
	Auctions: $44,063, MS-66, October 2014; $22,325, MS-65, August 2013; $7,050, MS-64, October 2014; $588, AU-53, December 2014												
1921	246,000	1,114	21.2	17%	$175	$220	$350	$775	$1,700	$2,750	$5,000	$7,750	$20,000
	Auctions: $23,500, MS-65+, October 2014; $29,376, MS-65, April 2014; $8,225, AU-58, August 2014; $2,820, AU-50, October 2014												
1921D	208,000	1,299	18.5	14%	$325	$375	$525	$850	$2,300	$3,300	$5,500	$13,000	$24,000
	Auctions: $32,900, MS-65, August 2013; $11,750, MS-64, November 2014; $7,931, AU-58, August 2014; $2,115, AU-50, October 2014												
1921S	548,000	1,058	21.1	10%	$48	$80	$250	$800	$4,500	$8,300	$14,750	$28,500	$100,000
	Auctions: $108,688, MS-65, August 2013; $38,775, MS-64, November 2014; $15,275, AU-58, August 2014; $1,175, VF-30, October 2014												
1923S	2,178,000	422	50.9	52%	$13	$15	$30	$110	$365	$800	$1,500	$3,700	$14,500
	Auctions: $28,200, MS-66, October 2014; $47,000, MS-66, April 2014; $4,406, MS-62, August 2014; $646, EF-45, October 2014												
1927S	2,392,000	619	58.0	73%	$13	$15	$18	$50	$160	$400	$950	$2,050	$9,000
	Auctions: $28,200, MS-66, October 2013; $4,113, MS-64+, September 2014; $1,645, AU-58, October 2014; $705, AU-53, November 2014												
1928S (a,b)	1,940,000	496	56.1	66%	$13	$15	$19	$75	$180	$435	$950	$2,750	$8,250
	Auctions: $15,275, MS-66, October 2013; $17,038, MS-65+, October 2014; $4,113, MS-64, October 2014; $1,293, AU-58, October 2014												
1929D	1,001,200	852	58.5	63%	$13	$15	$18	$30	$100	$190	$385	$750	$2,700
	Auctions: $5,288, MS-66, October 2014; $10,575, MS-66, April 2014; $1,586, MS-64, September 2014; $764, MS-62, November 2014												
1929S	1,902,000	779	58.4	70%	$13	$15	$18	$35	$115	$230	$410	$900	$2,850
	Auctions: $1,998, MS-65, November 2014; $1,293, MS-64, November 2014; $999, MS-62, July 2014; $247, AU-55, October 2014												
1933S	1,786,000	948	58.3	60%	$13	$15	$18	$20	$60	$240	$635	$1,200	$3,200
	Auctions: $12,925, MS-67, November 2013; $3,231, MS-66, November 2014; $7,638, MS-66, September 2014												
1934	6,964,000	2,411	63.5	91%	$13	$15	$16	$17.50	$19	$26	$75	$110	$400
	Auctions: $6,756, MS-68, June 2014; $3,055, MS-67+, November 2014; $499, MS-66, September 2014; $108, MS-64, November 2014												
1934D (a)	2,361,000	1,344	62.7	89%	$13	$15	$18	$20	$35	$85	$150	$235	$1,400
	Auctions: $1,351, MS-66, November 2014; $3,290, MS-66, November 2013; $282, MS-64, November 2014; $147, AU-58, August 2014												
1934S	3,652,000	877	60.9	73%	$13	$15	$16	$17.50	$30	$90	$325	$800	$3,700
	Auctions: $4,721, MS-66, November 2014; $2,233, MS-65, November 2014; $353, MS-61, November 2014; $259, AU-58, October 2014												

a. Large and small mintmark varieties exist. b. Half dollars dated 1928-D are counterfeit.

1936, Doubled-Die Obverse
FS-50-1936-101.

	Mintage	Cert	Avg	%MS	G-4	VG-8	F-12	VF-20	EF-40	AU-50	MS-60	MS-63	MS-65
											PF-64	PF-65	PF-67
1935	9,162,000	2,410	63.6	93%	$13	$15	$16	$17.50	$19	$25	$45	$80	$260
	Auctions: $2,820, MS-67, October 2014; $7,931, MS-67, November 2013; $441, MS-66, October 2014; $153, MS-64, December 2014												
1935D	3,003,800	988	62.5	88%	$13	$15	$16	$17.50	$30	$65	$140	$300	$2,000
	Auctions: $3,408, MS-66, September 2014; $7,638, MS-66, August 2013; $1,381, MS-65, November 2014; $441, MS-64, July 2014												
1935S	3,854,000	864	62.0	85%	$13	$15	$16	$17.50	$26	$95	$250	$465	$2,800
	Auctions: $41,125, MS-67, March 2013; $2,938, MS-66, November 2014; $646, MS-64, September 2014; $170, AU-58, November 2014												
1936	12,614,000	3,353	64.0	94%	$13	$15	$16	$17.50	$18	$25	$45	$75	$210
	Auctions: $4,818, MS-68, May 2014; $823, MS-67, September 2014; $270, MS-66, December 2014; $84, MS-64, December 2014												
1936, DblDie Obv (c)	(d)	0	n/a		$500	$600							
	Auctions: $940, MS-65, December 2013												
1936, Proof	3,901	1,332	64.7								$2,500	$3,250	$12,500
	Auctions: $5,299, PF-67, August 2014; $18,800, PF-67, March 2013; $3,819, PF-66+, September 2014; $3,655, PF-66, October 2014												
1936D	4,252,400	1,693	63.6	94%	$13	$15	$16	$17.50	$20	$50	$85	$120	$400
	Auctions: $7,638, MS-67+, July 2014; $2,820, MS-67, August 2014; $617, MS-66, October 2014; $141, MS-64, November 2014												
1936S	3,884,000	1,274	63.5	94%	$13	$15	$16	$17.50	$22	$60	$130	$200	$750
	Auctions: $4,179, MS-67, August 2014; $19,975, MS-67, April 2013; $1,293, MS-66, October 2014; $224, MS-64, November 2014												
1937	9,522,000	3,036	63.9	94%	$13	$15	$16	$17.50	$18	$25	$40	$70	$215
	Auctions: $15,275, MS-68, June 2014; $1,058, MS-67, November 2014; $259, MS-66, November 2014; $53, MS-62, November 2014												
1937, Proof	5,728	1,516	65.2								$750	$850	$1,600
	Auctions: $1,293, PF-67, October 2014; $705, PF-66, October 2014; $423, PF-62, November 2014												
1937D	1,676,000	1,155	63.2	90%	$13	$15	$16	$18	$32	$100	$215	$265	$600
	Auctions: $4,406, MS-67, September 2014; $6,169, MS-67, October 2013; $1,293, MS-66+, November 2014; $329, MS-64, December 2014												
1937S	2,090,000	1,223	63.7	94%	$13	$15	$16	$17.50	$25	$60	$165	$210	$625
	Auctions: $3,173, MS-67, November 2014; $19,975, MS-67, June 2014; $940, MS-66+, November 2014; $248, MS-64, November 2014												
1938	4,110,000	2,184	63.5	92%	$13	$15	$16	$18	$20	$45	$70	$160	$300
	Auctions: $1,175, MS-67, November 2014; $2,350, MS-67, June 2014; $441, MS-66, November 2014; $159, MS-64, November 2014												
1938, Proof	8,152	1,825	65.4								$550	$725	$1,300
	Auctions: $7,050, PF-68, November 2014; $5,875, PF-68, October 2014; $705, PF-66, October 2014; $558, PF-66, October 2014												
1938D	491,600	2,658	43.2	43%	$75	$100	$110	$135	$175	$250	$500	$625	$1,450
	Auctions: $7,050, MS-67, November 2014; $19,975, MS-67, January 2014; $1,998, MS-66, September 2014; $793, MS-64, November 2014												
1939	6,812,000	3,604	64.4	94%	$13	$15	$16	$17.50	$18	$26	$40	$65	$155
	Auctions: $9,400, MS-68, July 2014; $499, MS-67, November 2014; $200, MS-66, November 2014; $60, MS-64, November 2014												
1939, Proof	8,808	1,942	65.6								$450	$650	$1,000
	Auctions: $7,638, PF-68, August 2014; $2,820, PF-68, July 2014; $823, PF-67, October 2014; $646, PF-66, October 2014												
1939D	4,267,800	2,860	64.3	96%	$13	$15	$16	$17.50	$18	$25	$43	$75	$180
	Auctions: $3,966, MS-67+, October 2014; $2,298, MS-67, August 2014; $282, MS-66, November 2014; $72, MS-64, November 2014												
1939S	2,552,000	1,933	64.5	96%	$13	$15	$16	$17.50	$26	$70	$140	$180	$300
	Auctions: $1,293, MS-67, November 2014; $6,463, MS-67, April 2013; $411, MS-66, November 2014; $182, MS-64, November 2014												
1940	9,156,000	3,992	64.3	96%	$13	$15	$16	$17.50	$18	$22	$35	$55	$145
	Auctions: $6,463, MS-68, January 2014; $1,293, MS-67+, November 2014; $529, MS-67, November 2014; $200, MS-66, October 2014												
1940, Proof	11,279	2,290	65.4								$450	$575	$900
	Auctions: $2,820, PF-68, November 2014; $1,880, PF-68, October 2014; $646, PF-67, October 2014; $499, PF-66, November 2014												
1940S	4,550,000	2,994	63.9	97%	$13	$15	$16	$17.50	$18	$35	$45	$80	$300
	Auctions: $4,994, MS-67, November 2014; $35,250, MS-67, April 2013; $940, MS-66+, November 2014; $99, MS-64, November 2014												

c. No examples have yet been discovered grading better than Fine. "Extremely strong doubling is evident on the date. Less doubling is evident on IN GOD WE TRUST, the skirt, and some other elements" (*Cherrypickers' Guide to Rare Die Varieties*, sixth edition, volume II). Several varieties exist; this one is FS-50-1936-101. **d.** Included in circulation-strike 1936 mintage figure.

1945, Missing Designer's Initials
FS-50-1945-901.

	Mintage	Cert	Avg	%MS	G-4	VG-8	F-12	VF-20	EF-40	AU-50	MS-60	MS-63	MS-65
											PF-64	PF-65	PF-67
1941	24,192,000	10,774	64.3	95%	$13	$15	$17	$17.50	$18	$22	$35	$55	$150
	Auctions: $3,116, MS-68, September 2014; $7,638, MS-68, April 2013; $499, MS-67, November 2014; $200, MS-66, November 2014												
1941, Proof (e)	15,412	2,585	65.3								$450	$575	$900
	Auctions: $18,213, PF-69, November 2013; $4,700, PF-68, November 2014; $764, PF-67, October 2014; $470, PF-66, October 2014												
1941D	11,248,400	5,748	64.4	96%	$13	$15	$16	$17.50	$18	$22	$38	$65	$160
	Auctions: $12,925, MS-68, December 2013; $646, MS-67, October 2014; $141, MS-66, December 2014; $65, MS-64, November 2014												
1941S	8,098,000	5,673	63.2	92%	$13	$15	$16	$17.50	$18	$26	$75	$120	$850
	Auctions: $28,200, MS-67, April 2013; $1,058, MS-66, November 2014; $212, MS-64, November 2014; $80, MS-62, August 2014												
1942	47,818,000	15,951	63.9	93%	$13	$15	$16	$17.50	$18	$22	$40	$60	$150
	Auctions: $16,450, MS-68, November 2013; $1,058, MS-67, November 2014; $154, MS-66, December 2014; $59, MS-64, November 2014												
1942, Proof	21,120	4,292	65.6								$450	$575	$900
	Auctions: $4,113, PF-68, August 2014; $1,410, PF-68, November 2014; $515, PF-66, December 2014												
1942D	10,973,800	4,187	64.4	96%	$13	$15	$16	$17.50	$18	$20	$40	$75	$215
	Auctions: $4,994, MS-68, November 2013; $705, MS-67, July 2014; $300, MS-66, December 2014; $85, MS-64, November 2014												
1942S (a)	12,708,000	4,417	63.7	96%	$13	$15	$16	$17.50	$18	$22	$40	$80	$425
	Auctions: $47,000, MS-67, April 2013; $1,293, MS-66+, November 2014; $617, MS-66, October 2014; $99, MS-64, November 2014												
1943	53,190,000	15,974	64.0	93%	$13	$15	$16	$17.50	$18	$20	$35	$48	$150
	Auctions: $11,750, MS-68, March 2013; $653, MS-67, November 2014; $165, MS-66, October 2014; $59, MS-64, November 2014												
1943D	11,346,000	4,999	64.7	97%	$13	$15	$16	$17.50	$18	$24	$48	$73	$200
	Auctions: $2,115, MS-67+, September 2014; $600, MS-67, November 2014; $188, MS-66, December 2014; $80, MS-64, November 2014												
1943S	13,450,000	5,090	64.0	97%	$13	$15	$16	$17.50	$18	$25	$42	$60	$300
	Auctions: $4,700, MS-67, October 2014; $1,293, MS-66+, September 2014; $259, MS-66, November 2014; $79, MS-64, November 2014												
1944	28,206,000	9,401	63.9	95%	$13	$15	$16	$17.50	$18	$20	$35	$50	$150
	Auctions: $1,528, MS-67, August 2014; $9,106, MS-67, January 2014; $165, MS-66, December 2014; $62, MS-64, November 2014												
1944D	9,769,000	6,057	64.6	98%	$13	$15	$16	$17.50	$18	$20	$40	$58	$160
	Auctions: $499, MS-67, September 2014; $1,293, MS-67, January 2014; $176, MS-66, November 2014; $65, MS-64, November 2014												
1944S	8,904,000	5,990	63.9	98%	$13	$15	$16	$17.50	$18	$24	$40	$63	$350
	Auctions: $14,100, MS-67, January 2014; $2,820, MS-66+, August 2014; $705, MS-66, September 2014; $89, MS-64, December 2014												
1945	31,502,000	13,022	64.0	96%	$13	$15	$16	$17.50	$18	$20	$35	$50	$150
	Auctions: $4,113, MS-67+, July 2014; $823, MS-67, November 2014; $153, MS-66, December 2014; $64, MS-64, November 2014												
1945, Missing Initials	(f)	15	57.9	73%						$100	$150	$250	
	Auctions: $705, MS-64, January 2014												
1945D	9,966,800	8,714	64.8	98%	$13	$15	$16	$17.50	$18	$20	$35	$55	$150
	Auctions: $16,450, MS-68, January 2014; $3,290, MS-67+, October 2014; $558, MS-67, October 2014; $182, MS-66, October 2014												
1945S	10,156,000	7,273	64.3	99%	$13	$15	$16	$17.50	$18	$24	$35	$55	$160
	Auctions: $5,875, MS-67, October 2014; $23,500, MS-67, March 2013; $617, MS-66+, November 2014; $329, MS-66, November 2014												

a. Large and small mintmark varieties exist. **e.** The variety without the designer's initials was created by the over-polishing of dies.
f. Included in 1945 mintage figure.

 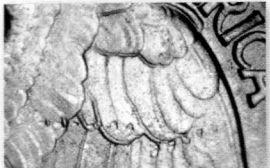  

1946, Doubled-Die Reverse
FS-50-1946-801.

	Mintage	Cert	Avg	%MS	G-4	VG-8	F-12	VF-20	EF-40	AU-50	MS-60	MS-63	MS-65
											PF-64	PF-65	PF-67
1946	12,118,000	6,649	64.0	96%	$13	$15	$16	$17.50	$18	$20	$37	$50	$160
	Auctions: $1,293, MS-67, October 2014; $9,988, MS-67, March 2013; $276, MS-66, December 2014; $74, MS-64, November 2014												
1946, DblDie Rev (g)	(h)	165	51.3	39%	$20	$24	$28	$40	$65	$125	$275	$550	$2,500
	Auctions: $7,050, MS-66, November 2013; $646, MS-64, September 2014; $441, MS-62, November 2014; $194, AU-58, August 2014												
1946D	2,151,000	12,848	64.8	100%	$13	$15	$16	$17.50	$22	$32	$47	$60	$150
	Auctions: $940, MS-67, August 2014; $14,100, MS-67, June 2014; $159, MS-66, December 2014; $72, MS-64, November 2014												
1946S	3,724,000	8,418	64.7	99%	$13	$15	$16	$17.50	$18	$25	$43	$58	$150
	Auctions: $3,055, MS-67, October 2014; $7,638, MS-67, January 2014; $382, MS-66+, December 2014; $200, MS-66, December 2014												
1947	4,094,000	7,288	64.3	98%	$13	$15	$16	$17.50	$18	$25	$48	$60	$160
	Auctions: $1,645, MS-67, October 2014; $15,275, MS-67, April 2013; $382, MS-66+, October 2014; $194, MS-66, October 2014												
1947D	3,900,600	8,172	64.6	99%	$13	$15	$16	$17.50	$18	$30	$45	$60	$150
	Auctions: $1,528, MS-67, October 2014; $7,638, MS-67, August 2013; $353, MS-66, December 2014; $80, MS-64, November 2014												

g. Very strong doubling is visible on E PLURIBUS UNUM, the eagle's wing feathers and left wing, and the branch. **h.** Included in 1946 mintage figure.

FRANKLIN (1948–1963)

Designer: *John R. Sinnock.* **Weight:** *12.50 grams.*
Composition: *.900 silver, .100 copper (net weight .36169 oz. pure silver).*
Diameter: *30.6 mm.* **Edge:** *Reeded.* **Mints:** *Philadelphia, Denver, San Francisco.*

Circulation Strike

Mintmark location is on the reverse, above the beam.

Proof

History. U.S. Mint chief engraver John R. Sinnock developed a motif for a silver half dime in 1942; it was proposed but never adopted for regular coinage. In 1948, the year after Sinnock died, his Franklin half dollar was introduced, its design an adaptation of his earlier half dime motif. The Liberty Bell is similar to that used by Sinnock on the 1926 Sesquicentennial commemorative half dollar modeled from a sketch by John Frederick Lewis. The designs were finished by Sinnock's successor, chief engraver Gilroy Roberts. The coin-collecting community paid little attention to the Franklin half dollar at the time, but today the coins are widely collected.

Striking and Sharpness. Given the indistinct details of the obverse, sharpness of strike usually is ignored. On the reverse, if the bottom lines of the Liberty Bell are complete the coin may be designated as Full Bell Lines (FBL). Virtually all Proofs are well struck.

Availability. All dates and mintmarks are easily available in grades from VF upward. Lower-level MS coins can be unattractive due to contact marks and abrasion, particularly noticeable on the obverse.

High-quality gems are generally inexpensive, although varieties that are rare with FBL can be costly amid much competition in the marketplace. Most collectors seek MS coins. Grades below EF are not widely desired. Proofs were made from 1950 to 1963 and are available today in proportion to their mint-ages. Those with cameo-frosted devices are in the minority and often sell for strong premiums.

Note: Values of common-date silver coins have been based on the current bullion price of silver, $17 per ounce, and may vary with the prevailing spot price.

GRADING STANDARDS

MS-60 to 70 (Mint State). *Obverse:* At MS-60, some abrasion and contact marks are evident on the cheek, on the hair left of the ear, and the neck. At MS-63, abrasion is slight at best, less so for MS-64. An MS-65 coin should display no abrasion or contact marks except under magnification, and MS-66 and higher coins should have none at all. Luster should be full and rich. As details are shallow on this design, the amount and

1951-S. Graded MS-65.

"depth" of luster is important to grading. *Reverse:* General comments apply as for the obverse. The points to check are the bell harness, the words PASS AND STOW on the upper area of the Liberty Bell, and the bottom of the bell.

Illustrated coin: Satiny brilliance is seen on the obverse of this coin, light golden toning on the reverse.

AU-50, 53, 55, 58 (About Uncirculated). *Obverse:* At AU-50, medium wear is evident on the portrait, and most of the luster in the field is gone. At AU-53, wear is less and luster is more extensive. AU-55 and 58 coins show much luster. Wear is noticeable on the portrait and, to a lesser extent, in the field. *Reverse:* At AU-50, medium wear is evident on most of the Liberty Bell, and most of the luster in the field is gone. At AU-53, wear is

1949-D. Graded AU-50.

slightly less. AU-55 and 58 coins show much luster. Light wear is seen on the higher areas of the bell.

EF-40, 45 (Extremely Fine). *Obverse:* Wear is more extensive, and some hair detail (never strong to begin with) is lost. There is no luster. *Reverse:* Wear is seen overall. The inscription on the bell is weak, and the highest parts of the bottom horizontal lines are worn away. There is no luster.

The Franklin half dollar is seldom collected in grades lower than EF-40.

1955. Graded EF-40.

PF-60 to 70 (Proof). *Obverse and Reverse:* Proofs that are extensively cleaned and have many hairlines, or that are dull and grainy, are lower level, such as PF-60 to 62. These are not widely desired, and represent coins that have been mistreated. Fortunately, only a few Proof Franklin half dollars are in this category. With medium hairlines and good reflectivity, assigned grades of PF-63 or 64 are appropriate. PF-66 should have hairlines

1950. Graded PF-65 Cameo.

so delicate that magnification is needed to see them. Above that, a Proof should be free of any hairlines or other problems.

Full Bell Lines

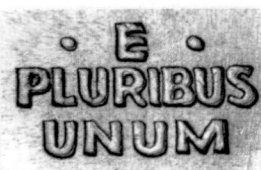

1948, Doubled-Die Reverse
FS-50-1948-801.

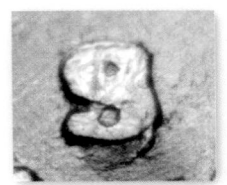

1949-S, Repunched Mintmark
FS-50-1949S-501.

	Mintage	Cert	Avg	%MS	VF-20	EF-40	MS-60	MS-63	MS-64	MS-65	MS-65FBL / PF-64	MS-66 / PF-65	MS-66FBL / PF-65DC
1948	3,006,814	3,857	64.1	97%	$13	$16	$20	$27	$35	$80	$140	$300	$350
Auctions: $5,875, MS-67FBL, August 2014; $823, MS-66FBL+, November 2014; $705, MS-66FBL, September 2014													
1948, Doubled-Die Reverse (a)	(b)	25	64.0	100%				$75	$125	$200	$300	$550	
Auctions: No auction records available.													
1948D	4,028,600	3,620	64.1	98%	$13	$16	$20	$24	$30	$115	$185	$600	$800
Auctions: $1,469, MS-66FBL+, November 2014; $2,820, MS-66FBL, January 2014; $558, MS-66FBL, October 2014													
1949	5,614,000	2,569	63.1	89%	$16	$18	$40	$70	$75	$120	$155	$350	$550
Auctions: $1,410, MS-66FBL+, September 2014; $1,880, MS-66FBL+, July 2014; $353, MS-66FBL, November 2014													
1949D	4,120,600	2,656	63.3	95%	$16	$18	$45	$70	$85	$550	$750	$2,500	$10,000
Auctions: $2,538, MS-66FBL, November 2014; $9,400, MS-66FBL, June 2013; $84, MS-64FBL, December 2014													
1949S	3,744,000	3,059	64.0	95%	$16	$20	$65	$95	$115	$140	$500	$225	$750
Auctions: $8,813, MS-67FBL+, August 2014; $1,763, MS-66FBL+, September 2014; $558, MS-66FBL, October 2014													
1949S, Doubled Mintmark (c)	(d)	6	58.8	50%				$120	$170	$280	$350	$575	
Auctions: $223, MS-65, January 2014													
1950	7,742,123	2,238	63.6	93%	$13	$14	$30	$35	$55	$110	$190	$385	$575
Auctions: $12,925, MS-67FBL, June 2014; $1,293, MS-66FBL+, November 2014; $470, MS-66FBL, November 2014													
1950, Proof	51,386	2,963	64.8								$350	$450	$10,000
Auctions: $8,813, PF-67Cam, April 2013; $2,585, PF-67, November 2014; $3,525, PF-66Cam, November 2014													
1950D	8,031,600	2,315	63.4	95%	$13	$14	$26	$40	$70	$250	$375	$900	$1,350
Auctions: $9,400, MS-66FBL+, November 2014; $1,880, MS-66FBL, November 2014; $16,450, MS-66FBL, September 2013													

a. Doubling is visible on E PLURIBUS UNUM, UNITED, HALF DOLLAR, the dots, and the Liberty Bell's clapper. "There are several similar, yet lesser, DDRs for this date" (*Cherrypickers' Guide to Rare Die Varieties*, sixth edition, volume II). The variety listed and pictured is FS-50-1948-801. **b.** Included in 1948 mintage figure. **c.** The secondary mintmark is visible south of the primary. CONECA lists two other repunched mintmarks for this date; the one illustrated and listed here is FS-50-1949S-501. **d.** Included in 1949-S mintage figure.

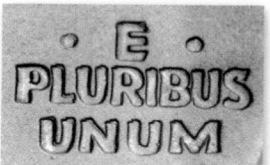

1951-S, Doubled-Die Reverse
FS-50-1951S-801.

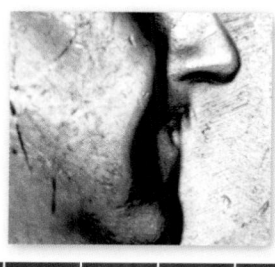

1955, Clashed Obverse Die "Bugs Bunny" variety
FS-50-1955-401.

	Mintage	Cert	Avg	%MS	VF-20	EF-40	MS-60	MS-63	MS-64	MS-65	MS-65FBL / PF-64	MS-66 / PF-65	MS-66FBL / PF-65DC
1951	16,802,102	2,446	63.8	95%	$13	$14	$16	$24	$35	$70	$235	$225	$775
	Auctions: $18,800, MS-67FBL, January 2014; $1,058, MS-66FBL+, September 2014; $1,058, MS-66FBL, October 2014												
1951, Proof	57,500	3,056	64.9								$300	$350	$2,500
	Auctions: $3,819, PF-67Cam, November 2014; $940, PF-67, October 2014; $4,994, PF-66DCam, August 2014												
1951D	9,475,200	1,915	63.6	96%	$13	$14	$30	$45	$70	$150	$250	$650	$1,000
	Auctions: $499, MS-66FBL, October 2014; $2,233, MS-66FBL, January 2014; $129, MS-65FBL, December 2014												
1951S	13,696,000	2,477	64.1	97%	$13	$14	$25	$35	$50	$70	$400	$275	$1,100
	Auctions: $30,550, MS-67FBL, April 2013; $1,763, MS-66FBL+, September 2014; $470, MS-66FBL, November 2014												
1951S, DblDie Rev (e)	(f)	8	64.6	100%			$80	$110	$275	$725	$900		
	Auctions: $188, MS-65, January 2014												
1952	21,192,093	2,537	64.1	96%	$13	$14	$16	$23	$32	$70	$120	$235	$430
	Auctions: $4,994, MS-67FBL, August 2014; $6,345, MS-67FBL, December 2013; $306, MS-66FBL, November 2014												
1952, Proof	81,980	3,472	65.3								$180	$225	$4,500
	Auctions: $11,750, PF-68Cam, April 2014; $4,994, PF-67Cam+, October 2014; $4,994, PF-66DCam, November 2014												
1952D	25,395,600	2,236	63.8	98%	$13	$14	$16	$23	$32	$125	$180	$600	$1,150
	Auctions: $1,087, MS-66FBL, November 2014; $441, MS-66FBL, October 2014; $1,880, MS-66FBL, January 2014												
1952S	5,526,000	2,361	64.5	99%	$15	$17	$50	$70	$80	$100	$750	$225	$2,850
	Auctions: $25,850, MS-67FBL, November 2014; $9,400, MS-66FBL+, August 2014; $14,100, MS-66FBL, February 2014												
1953	2,668,120	1,983	64.0	98%	$13	$14	$16	$25	$40	$105	$635	$475	$2,750
	Auctions: $1,410, MS-66FBL, September 2014; $2,350, MS-66FBL, April 2013; $544, MS-65FBL, November 2014												
1953, Proof	128,800	4,569	65.5								$100	$175	$1,400
	Auctions: $3,055, PF-68Cam, November 2014; $7,638, PF-67DCam, September 2014; $264, PF-67, November 2014												
1953D	20,900,400	2,946	64.0	98%	$13	$14	$16	$23	$38	$110	$175	$550	$725
	Auctions: $19,975, MS-67Cam, June 2014; $1,410, MS-66FBL+, November 2014; $588, MS-66FBL, October 2014												
1953S	4,148,000	4,599	64.8	100%	$13	$14	$25	$35	$48	$70	$25,500	$350	
	Auctions: $2,703, MS-67, November 2014; $153, MS-66, November 2014; $28,200, MS-65FBL, April 2014; $5,875, MS-63FBL, October 2014												
1954	13,188,202	3,869	64.2	99%	$13	$14	$16	$20	$30	$70	$120	$300	$1,100
	Auctions: $2,644, MS-66FBL, January 2014; $235, MS-65FBL, December 2014; $84, MS-65FBL, November 2014												
1954, Proof	233,300	6,200	66.2								$65	$85	$425
	Auctions: $17,626, PF-68DCam, June 2013; $282, PF-68, October 2014; $2,585, PF-67DCam+, November 2014												
1954D	25,445,580	4,645	64.2	99%	$13	$14	$16	$24	$28	$90	$140	$375	$800
	Auctions: $1,998, MS-66FBL+, November 2014; $5,288, MS-66FBL, February 2014; $499, MS-66, August 2014												
1954S	4,993,400	7,490	64.7	100%	$13	$14	$16	$24	$35	$50	$250	$240	$1,050
	Auctions: $3,525, MS-66FBL+, August 2014; $1,293, MS-66FBL, November 2014; $4,994, MS-66FBL, February 2014												
1955	2,498,181	6,660	64.1	99%	$18	$22	$25	$30	$40	$55	$115	$150	$425
	Auctions: $2,644, MS-66FBL+, November 2014; $317, MS-66FBL, August 2014; $123, MS-66, October 2014												
1955, Clashed Obverse Die (g)	(h)	490	63.6	100%			$48	$65	$130	$350	$265	$700	
	Auctions: $423, MS-66FBL, February 2013; $129, MS-64FBL, September 2014; $76, MS-64FBL, September 2014												
1955, Proof	378,200	10,116	66.9								$50	$75	$425
	Auctions: $711, PF-69, October 2014; $3,819, PF-68DCam, November 2014; $499, PF-68Cam, October 2014												

e. Doubling is evident on the eagle's tail feathers and left wing, as well as on E PLURIBUS UNUM. This variety is FS-50-1951S-801.
f. Included in 1951-S mintage figure. **g.** This variety, popularly known as the "Bugs Bunny," has evidence of clash marks that appear as two buckteeth on Benjamin Franklin. **h.** Included in circulation-strike 1955 mintage figure.

1957, Tripled-Die Reverse, Proof
FS-50-1957-801.

1959, Doubled-Die Reverse
FS-50-1959-801.

	Mintage	Cert	Avg	%MS	VF-20	EF-40	MS-60	MS-63	MS-64	MS-65	MS-65FBL / PF-64	MS-66 / PF-65	MS-66FBL / PF-65DC
1956	4,032,000	9,312	64.3	100%	$13	$14	$16	$25	$28	$42	$100	$80	$275
	Auctions: $8,813, MS-67FBL+, August 2014; $3,525, MS-67FBL, November 2014; $129, MS-66FBL, November 2014; $65, MS-66, July 2014												
1956, Proof	669,384	4,655	67.1								$35	$45	$100
	Auctions: $2,350, PF-69DCam, November 2014; $852, PF-69Cam, October 2014; $734, PF-68DCam, September 2014; $79, PF-68, October 2014												
1957	5,114,000	4,245	64.7	100%	$13	$14	$16	$19	$25	$40	$125	$85	$225
	Auctions: $5,581, MS-67FBL+, August 2014; $2,115, MS-67FBL, June 2014; $499, MS-67, October 2014; $176, MS-66FBL, November 2014												
1957, Proof	1,247,952	14,427	67.0								$25	$28	$250
	Auctions: $2,233, PF-69Cam, November 2014; $1,293, PF-68DCam, October 2014; $388, PF-68Cam, November 2014; $101, PF-68, November 2014												
1957, Tripled-Die Reverse, Proof (i)	(j)	4	65.9								$75	$90	$800
	Auctions: No auction records available.												
1957D	19,966,850	4,466	64.4	99%	$13	$14	$16	$19	$23	$40	$75	$85	$375
	Auctions: $4,700, MS-67FBL, November 2014; $1,450, MS-67FBL, September 2014; $1,410, MS-67, August 2014; $259, MS-66FBL, December 2014												
1958	4,042,000	5,985	64.7	99%	$13	$14	$16	$19	$24	$45	$125	$80	$350
	Auctions: $15,275, MS-67FBL, August 2014; $499, MS-67, November 2014; $411, MS-66FBL+, September 2014; $129, MS-66FBL, November 2014												
1958, Proof	875,652	10,397	66.8								$32	$38	$675
	Auctions: $881, PF-69, August 2014; $4,113, PF-68DCam, November 2014; $141, PF-68, November 2014; $1,116, PF-67DCam, October 2014												
1958D	23,962,412	5,732	64.6	99%	$13	$14	$16	$18	$19	$45	$70	$75	$500
	Auctions: $1,821, MS-67FBL, November 2014; $135, MS-66FBL, December 2014; $92, MS-66, July 2014; $55, MS-65FBL, November 2014												
1959	6,200,000	4,199	64.3	99%	$13	$14	$16	$18	$20	$70	$225	$800	$1,750
	Auctions: $7,050, MS-66FBL+, November 2014; $1,293, MS-66FBL, September 2014; $306, MS-66, December 2014; $235, MS-65FBL, December 2014												
1959, Doubled-Die Reverse (k)	(l)	49	63.9	98%				$85	$90	$120	$425	$1,125	
	Auctions: $431, MS-65FBL, March 2011												
1959, Proof	1,149,291	10,822	66.8								$20	$22	$2,000
	Auctions: $3,819, PF-68Cam, November 2014; $7,050, PF-67DCam, February 2013												
1959D	13,053,750	3,967	64.3	99%	$13	$14	$16	$18	$22	$90	$140	$775	$1,050
	Auctions: $2,350, MS-66FBL, November 2014; $646, MS-66FBL, October 2014; $881, MS-66FBL, September 2014; $100, MS-65FBL, December 2014												
1960	6,024,000	3,877	64.2	99%	$13	$14	$16	$18	$19	$100	$225	$550	$2,000
	Auctions: $4,113, MS-66FBL, June 2013; $153, MS-65FBL, November 2014; $194, MS-65FBL, September 2014; $135, MS-65FBL, September 2014												
1960, Proof	1,691,602	13,296	66.8								$20	$22	$100
	Auctions: $17,625, PF-69DCam, April 2013; $2,820, PF-68DCam, November 2014; $282, PF-68Cam, November 2014												
1960, Doubled-Die Obverse, Proof (m)	(n)	67	66.2								$80	$95	$400
	Auctions: $160, PF-67, May 2012												
1960D	18,215,812	3,425	64.0	99%	$13	$14	$16	$18	$28	$200	$425	$900	$4,250
	Auctions: $1,293, MS-66FBL, July 2014; $259, MS-65FBL, December 2014; $102, MS-65, October 2014; $4,113, MS-63, September 2013												

i. A closely tripled image is evident on E PLURIBUS UNUM, portions of UNITED STATES OF AMERICA, and HALF DOLLAR. j. Included in 1957, Proof, mintage figure. k. Strong doubling is evident on the eagle; doubling is also visible on E PLURIBUS UNUM, UNITED, and portions of the Liberty Bell. l. Included in circulation-strike 1959 mintage figure. m. Doubling is visible on LIBERTY, TRUST, and the date. n. Included in 1960, Proof, mintage figure.

1961, Doubled-Die Reverse, Proof
FS-50-1961-801.

	Mintage	Cert	Avg	%MS	VF-20	EF-40	MS-60	MS-63	MS-64	MS-65	MS-65FBL PF-64	MS-66 PF-65	MS-66FBL PF-65DC
1961	8,290,000	4,108	64.2	99%	$13	$14	$16	$18	$25	$75	$900	$600	$5,000
Auctions: $558, MS-65FBL, November 2014; $2,468, MS-65FBL, June 2014; $552, MS-65, December 2014; $141, MS-64FBL, December 2014													
1961, Proof	3,028,244	18,218	66.8								$25	$30	$125
Auctions: $2,938, PF-69Cam, April 2013; $3,290, PF-68DCam, November 2014; $200, PF-67DCam, August 2014; $123, PF-67Cam, August 2014													
1961, Doubled-Die Reverse, Proof (o)	(p)	92	65.6								$2,200	$2,900	
Auctions: $2,350, PF-65, June 2014; $1,880, PF-64, July 2014													
1961D	20,276,442	3,090	64.1	99%	$13	$14	$16	$18	$25	$110	$450	$1,000	$3,000
Auctions: $4,465, MS-66FBL, August 2014; $6,463, MS-66FBL, August 2013; $529, MS-65FBL, November 2014; $106, MS-65, December 2014													
1962	9,714,000	2,895	64.0	99%	$13	$14	$16	$18	$25	$90	$1,750	$750	$11,000
Auctions: $8,225, MS-66FBL, August 2014; $1,410, MS-65FBL, October 2014; $3,819, MS-65FBL, March 2013; $247, MS-64FBL, November 2014													
1962, Proof	3,218,019	23,846	66.8								$20	$27	$60
Auctions: $3,819, PF-69DCam, November 2014; $7,050, PF-69DCam, September 2013; $881, PF-68DCam, September 2014													
1962, Doubled-Die Obverse, Proof (q)	(r)	0	n/a								$25	$30	$150
Auctions: No auction records available.													
1962D	35,473,281	3,749	64.1	99%	$13	$14	$16	$18	$25	$120	$450	$1,000	$3,500
Auctions: $4,230, MS-66FBL, November 2014; $764, MS-66, July 2014; $329, MS-65FBL, November 2014; $6,463, MS-65, April 2014													
1963	22,164,000	10,702	64.3	99%	$13	$14	$16	$18	$19	$40	$1,150	$750	$2,500
Auctions: $28,200, MS-66FBL, July 2014; $411, MS-64FBL, November 2014; $129, MS-64FBL, September 2014; $282, MS-64FBL, August 2014													
1963, Proof	3,075,645	22,987	66.9								$20	$26	$52
Auctions: $7,638, PF-69DCam, November 2014; $764, PF-69Cam, September 2014; $1,645, PF-68DCam+, November 2014													
1963D	67,069,292	8,119	64.1	98%	$13	$14	$16	$18	$19	$45	$175	$350	$1,050
Auctions: $940, MS-66FBL, October 2014; $112, MS-65FBL, December 2014; $106, MS-65FBL, November 2014; $130, MS-65FBL, September 2014													

o. Other reverse doubled dies exist for this date. The variety pictured and listed here (FS-50-1961-801) is by far the most dramatic. Very strong doubling is evident on the reverse lettering. **p.** Included in 1961, Proof, mintage figure. **q.** Doubling is visible on the 62 of the date and on WE TRUST. **r.** Included in 1962, Proof, mintage figure.

KENNEDY (1964 TO DATE)

Designers: *Gilroy Roberts and Frank Gasparro.* **Weight:** *1964, modern silver Proofs, and 2014 silver—12.50 grams; 1965–1970—11.50 grams; 1971 to date—11.34 grams.* **Composition:** *1964 and modern silver Proofs—.900 silver, .100 copper (net weight .36169 oz. pure silver); 1965–1970—outer layers of .800 silver and .200 copper bonded to inner core of .209 silver, .791 copper (net weight .1479 oz. pure silver); 1971 to date—outer layers of copper-nickel (.750 copper, .250 nickel) bonded to inner core of pure copper; 2014 gold—.9999 gold (net weight .75 oz. pure gold).* **Diameter:** *30.6 mm.* **Edge:** *Reeded.* **Mints:** *1964, 1971 to date—Philadelphia, Denver, San Francisco; modern silver Proofs—San Francisco.*

Circulation Strike

Proof

Mintmark location,
1964, is on the
reverse, below the claw
holding the branch.

Mintmark
location, 1968 to date,
is on the obverse,
above the date.

Bicentennial variety: **Designers:** *Gilroy Roberts and Seth Huntington.* **Weight:** *Silver clad—11.50 grams; copper-nickel clad—11.34 grams.* **Composition:** *Silver clad—outer layers of .800 silver, .200 copper bonded to inner core of .209 silver, .791 copper (net weight .14792 oz. pure silver); copper-nickel clad—outer layers of copper-nickel (.750 copper, .250 nickel) bonded to inner core of pure copper.* **Diameter:** *30.6 mm.* **Edge:** *Reeded.*

Bicentennial variety

Bicentennial variety, Proof

50th Anniversary varieties: **Designers:** *Gilroy Roberts and Frank Gasparro.*
Weight: *Gold—23.33 grams; silver Proofs and Unc.—12.50 grams; copper-nickel clad—11.34 grams.*
Composition: *Gold—.9999 gold (net weight .75 oz. pure gold); silver—.900 silver,*
.100 copper (net weight .36169 oz. pure silver); copper-nickel clad—outer layers
of copper-nickel (.750 copper, .250 nickel) bonded to inner core of pure copper.
Diameter: *30.6 mm.* **Edge:** *Reeded.*

50th Anniversary variety, gold

50th Anniversary variety, Uncirculated   50th Anniversary variety,
Enhanced Uncirculated

50th Anniversary variety, Proof   50th Anniversary variety, Reverse Proof

History. Kennedy half dollars, minted from 1964 to date, were struck in 90% silver the first year, then with 40% silver content through 1970, and in later years in copper-nickel (except for special silver issues made for collectors and a gold issue in 2014). The obverse, by Chief Engraver Gilroy Roberts, features a portrait of President John F. Kennedy, while the reverse, by Frank Gasparro, displays a modern version of a heraldic eagle.

The 1976 Bicentennial coin shows Philadelphia's Independence Hall, a design by Seth G. Huntington. The obverse was unchanged except for the dual dating 1776–1976. The Bicentennial half dollars were struck during 1975 and 1976 and were used for general circulation as well as being included in Proof and Uncirculated sets for 1975 and 1976.

The year 2014 brought several special issues to mark the 50th year of the Kennedy half dollar: a .9999 fine gold version containing three-quarters of an ounce of pure gold; a Proof in silver; a Reverse Proof in silver; an Enhanced Uncirculated in silver; and an Uncirculated in silver. These coins are dual-dated 1964–2014 on the obverse. They were offered for sale by the U.S. Mint in a number of packages and options.

Striking and Sharpness. Nearly all are well struck. Check the highest points of the hair on the obverse and the highest details on the reverse.

Availability. All issues are common in high circulated grades as well as MS and Proof.

Proofs and Special Mint Set Coins. Proofs of 1964 were struck at the Philadelphia Mint. Those from 1968 to date have been made in San Francisco. All are easily obtained. Most from the 1970s to date have cameo contrast. Special Mint Set (SMS) coins were struck in lieu of Proofs from 1965 to 1967; in some instances, these closely resemble Proofs. Silver Proofs have been struck in recent years, for Silver Proof sets and for the 2014 50th Anniversary issue (which also includes a Reverse Proof). In 1998, a special Matte Proof silver Kennedy half dollar was struck for inclusion in the Robert F. Kennedy commemorative coin set.

Note: Values of common-date silver coins have been based on the current bullion price of silver, $17 per ounce, and may vary with the prevailing spot price.

GRADING STANDARDS

MS-60 to 70 (Mint State). *Obverse:* At MS-60, some abrasion and contact marks are evident on the cheek, and on the hair to the right of the forehead and temple. At MS-63, abrasion is slight at most, and less so for MS-64. An MS-65 coin should display no abrasion or contact marks except under magnification, and MS-66 and higher coins should have none at all. Luster should be full and rich. *Reverse:* Comments apply as for the

1964. Graded MS-66.

obverse, except that the highest parts of the eagle at the center are the key places to check.

AU-50, 53, 55, 58 (About Uncirculated). *Obverse:* Light wear is seen on the cheek and higher-relief area of the hair below the part, high above the ear. At AU-58, the luster is extensive but incomplete, especially on the higher parts and in the field. At AU-50 and 53, luster is less. *Reverse:* Light wear is seen on the higher parts of the eagle. At AU-50 and 53 there still is significant luster.

1964. Graded AU-55.

EF-40, 45 (Extremely Fine). *Obverse:* Further wear is seen on the head. More details are gone on the higher parts of the hair. *Reverse:* Further wear is seen on the eagle in particular, but also on other areas in high relief (including the leaves, arrowheads, and clouds).

The Kennedy half dollar is seldom collected in grades lower than EF-40.

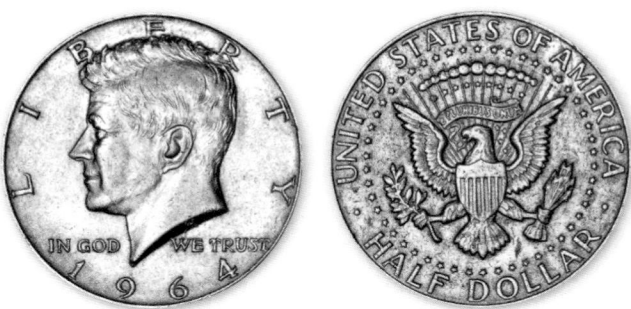

1964. Graded EF-45.

PF-60 to 70 (Proof). *Obverse and Reverse:* Proofs that are extensively cleaned and have many hairlines, or that are dull and grainy, are lower level, such as PF-60 to 62. There are not many of these in the marketplace. With medium hairlines and good reflectivity, assigned grades of PF-63 or 64 are appropriate. With relatively few hairlines a rating of PF-65 can be given. PF-66 should have hairlines so delicate that magnification is needed to see them. Above that, a Proof should be free of any hairlines or other problems.

1964. Graded PF-66.

1964, Doubled-Die Obverse
FS-50-1964-102.

1964, Heavily Accented Hair, Proof
FS-50-1964-401.

1964-D, Doubled-Die Obverse
FS-50-1964D-101.

1964-D, Repunched Mintmark
FS-50-1964D-502.

	Mintage	Cert	Avg	%MS	MS-60	MS-63	MS-65 / PF-65	MS-66 / PF-67Cam	MS-67 / PF-68DC
1964	273,304,004	5,918	64.3	98%	$13	$16	$20	$40	$625
Auctions: $306, MS-66, November 2014; $329, MS-66, July 2014; $270, MS-66, July 2014									
1964, Doubled-Die Obverse (a)	(b)	7	64.4	100%		$35	$65	$250	
Auctions: $21, MS-65, July 2006									
1964, Proof	3,950,762	24,287	67.5				$20	$45	$200
Auctions: $9,400, PF-70, December 2013; $159, PF-69, September 2014; $382, PF-68DCam, November 2014									
1964, Heavily Accented Hair, Proof ‡ (c)	(d)	9,493	66.5				$45	$180	$4,900
Auctions: $999, PF-69, July 2014; $15,128, PF-68DCam, June 2013; $499, PF-67Cam, November 2014									
1964D	156,205,446	3,683	64.2	99%	$13	$15	$20	$40	$800
Auctions: $2,820, MS-67, August 2014; $1,116, MS-67, August 2014; $182, MS-65, July 2014									
1964D, Doubled-Die Obverse (e)	(f)	29	61.9	69%		$45	$70	$150	
Auctions: $60, MS-66, November 2011									
1964D, Repunched Mintmark (g)	(f)	18	63.4	89%		$45	$65	$125	
Auctions: $130, AU-55, June 2010									

‡ Ranked in the *100 Greatest U.S. Modern Coins*. **a.** There are several doubled-die obverses for the 1964 Kennedy half dollar. The one pictured and listed is FS-50-1964-102. **b.** Included in circulation-strike 1964 mintage figure. **c.** This variety "is identifiable by the enhanced hairline in the central area of the hair, just below the part. However, the easiest way to identify the variety is the weak or broken lower left serif of the I (in LIBERTY)" (*Cherrypickers' Guide to Rare Die Varieties*, sixth edition, volume II). **d.** Included in 1964, Proof, mintage figure. **e.** Doubling on this variety is evident on the date, IN GOD WE TRUST, the designer's initials, and LI and TY of LIBERTY. "This is a very popular variety. It is extremely rare above MS-65" (*Cherrypickers' Guide to Rare Die Varieties*, sixth edition, volume II). There are other doubled-die obverses for 1964-D. The one pictured and listed is FS-50-1964D-101. **f.** Included in 1964-D mintage figure. **g.** There are several repunched mintmarks for 1964-D. The one listed is FS-50-1964D-502.

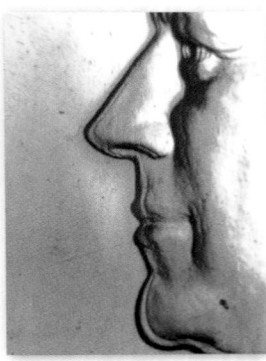
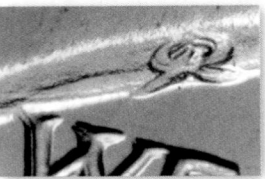

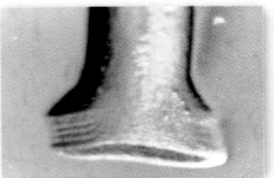

1966, Doubled-Die Obverse, Special Mint Set
FS-50-1966-103.

1967, Quintupled-Die Obverse, Special Mint Set
FS-50-1967-101.

	Mintage	Cert	Avg	%MS	MS-63	MS-65	MS-66	MS-67
						PF-65	PF-67Cam	PF-68DC
1965	65,879,366	356	64.3	96%	$6	$17	$150	$650
Auctions: $259, MS-66, July 2014								
1965, Special Mint Set ‡	2,360,000	8,226	66.6			$11	$175	
Auctions: $118, PF-66Cam, November 2014; $1,998, PF-66DCam, January 2014								
1966	108,984,932	318	63.7	93%	$6	$25	$170	$400
Auctions: No auction records available.								
1966, Special Mint Set ‡	2,261,583	9,547	66.8			$11	$80	
Auctions: $3,055, PF-67DCam, October 2014; $141, PF-67Cam, November 2014								
1966, Special Mint Set, Doubled-Die Obverse (a)	**(b)**	164	66.7	100%		$85	$325	
Auctions: $96, PF-67, July 2014; $74, SP-67, April 2012								
1967	295,046,978	733	64.4	94%	$5	$22	$95	$750
Auctions: $3,525, MS-67, August 2014; $100, MS-66, October 2014; $200, MS-64, September 2013								
1967, Special Mint Set ‡	1,863,344	8,886	66.7			$15	$60	
Auctions: $200, PF-68, September 2014; $734, PF-67DCam, November 2014								
1967, Special Mint Set, Quintupled-Die Obverse (c)	**(d)**	23	66.5			$135	$500	
Auctions: $345, SP-66, February 2012								
1968D	246,951,930	892	64.6	97%	$6	$20	$45	$235
Auctions: $1,410, MS-67, August 2014; $2,585, MS-67, February 2014; $176, MS-66, September 2014								
1968S, Proof	3,041,506	6,029	67.7			$8	$22	$50
Auctions: $259, PF-69DCam, November 2014; $237, PF-69DCam, September 2014								
1969D	129,881,800	1,007	64.5	98%	$5	$25	$225	$1,100
Auctions: $317, MS-66, July 2014								
1969S, Proof	2,934,631	8,982	68.0			$10	$23	$45
Auctions: $224, PF-69DCam, January 2014								
1970D ‡	2,150,000	3,106	64.3	100%	$20	$42	$215	$775
Auctions: $4,113, MS-67, August 2014; $282, MS-66, August 2014; $353, MS-65, August 2014								
1970S, Proof	2,632,810	7,678	68.0			$16	$30	$50
Auctions: $212, PF-69DCam, November 2014; $329, PF-69DCam, June 2013								
1971	155,164,000	149	64.2	95%	$3	$15	$45	$200
Auctions: $170, MS-66, May 2014								
1971D	302,097,424	656	65.0	95%	$3	$10	$22	$70
Auctions: $90, MS-67, July 2014; $1,880, MS-64, April 2013								
1971S, Proof	3,220,733	4,537	68.2			$5	$20	$100
Auctions: $1,821, PF-67, July 2013								

‡ Ranked in the *100 Greatest U.S. Modern Coins*. **a.** There are several doubled-die obverse varieties of the 1966 Special Mint Set half dollar. The one listed is FS-50-1966-103, with strong doubling evident on the profile, IN GOD WE TRUST, the eye, the hair, and the designer's initials. **b.** Included in 1966, Special Mint Set, mintage figure. **c.** "A prominent quintupled (at least) spread is evident on RTY of LIBERTY, with strong multiple images on all obverse lettering and portions of the hair" (*Cherrypickers' Guide to Rare Die Varieties*, sixth edition, volume II). **d.** Included in 1967, Special Mint Set, mintage figure.

1972, Doubled-Die Obverse
FS-50-1972-101.

1972-D, Missing Designer's Initials
FS-50-1972D-901.

	Mintage	Cert	Avg	%MS	MS-63	MS-65	MS-66	MS-67
						PF-65	PF-67Cam	PF-68DC
1972	153,180,000	210	64.8	96%	$2	$15	$50	$290
Auctions: $36, MS-66, July 2014								
1972, Doubled-Die Obverse (e)	(f)	1	58.0	0%	$140	$165	$225	$450
Auctions: $90, AU-50, March 2011								
1972D	141,890,000	351	65.1	97%	$3	$10	$23	$100
Auctions: $129, MS-67, July 2014; $5,288, MS-66, January 2014								
1972D, Missing Initials	(g)	3	56.3	0%	$50	$75	$150	$250
Auctions: $380, EF-45, October 2009								
1972S, Proof	3,260,996	3,063	68.2			$5	$16	$25
Auctions: $92, PF-69DCam, June 2014								
1973	64,964,000	145	64.5	96%	$2	$15	$45	$155
Auctions: $282, MS-67, August 2014; $22, MS-65, September 2008								
1973D	83,171,400	314	65.1	98%	$3	$11	$20	$170
Auctions: $329, MS-67, July 2014								
1973S, Proof	2,760,339	702	68.3			$4	$16	$25
Auctions: $2,350, PF-70DCam, December 2011								
1974	201,596,000	151	64.2	94%	$2	$22	$35	$145
Auctions: $2,350, MS-67, August 2014; $37, MS-66, March 2008								
1974D	79,066,300	225	64.5	93%	$3	$15	$35	$165
Auctions: $382, MS-67, August 2014; $65, MS-65, June 2014								
1974D, Doubled-Die Obverse ‡ (h)	(i)	408	63.8	94%	$40	$100	$200	$450
Auctions: $411, MS-66, July 2014; $135, MS-65, July 2014; $28, MS-63, October 2014								
1974S, Proof	2,612,568	762	68.2			$5	$9	$18
Auctions: $4,406, PF-70DCam, March 2014								
1976	234,308,000	360	64.2	94%	$2	$15	$50	$125
Auctions: $1,998, MS-67, August 2014; $2,350, MS-62, February 2014								
1976D	287,565,248	586	65.1	98%	$3	$15	$25	$375
Auctions: $764, MS-67, August 2014; $165, MS-67, July 2014; $2,585, MS-67, January 2014; $112, MS-65, July 2014								
1976S, Silver Clad	11,000,000	1,191	66.0	100%	$8	$10	$15	$30
Auctions: $217, MS-68, July 2014								
1976S, Proof	7,059,099	1,839	67.8			$5	$13	$18
Auctions: $2,350, PF-70DCam, June 2013								
1976S, Silver Clad, Proof (j)	4,000,000	3,314	68.2			$12	$15	$25
Auctions: $1,528, PF-70DCam, September 2014; $1,058, PF-70DCam, September 2014; $2,115, PF-70DCam, June 2013								
1977	43,598,000	262	65.4	99%	$3	$12	$28	$120
Auctions: $1,116, MS-67, November 2014; $259, MS-67, August 2014; $764, MS-67, June 2014								
1977D	31,449,106	114	64.8	97%	$2	$10	$22	$85
Auctions: $176, MS-67, August 2014; $21, MS-66, August 2007								
1977S, Proof	3,251,152	1,163	68.7			$5	$9	$15
Auctions: $182, PF-70DCam, December 2014; $170, PF-70DCam, November 2014; $194, PF-70DCam, June 2014								

‡ Ranked in the *100 Greatest U.S. Modern Coins*. **e.** Doubling is strongly evident on IN GOD WE TRUST and on the date. This variety is very rare above MS-65. **f.** Included in 1972 mintage figure. **g.** Included in 1972-D mintage figure. **h.** Strong doubling is visible on IN GOD WE TRUST, the date, and LIBERTY. **i.** Included in 1974-D mintage figure. **j.** Mintage figures for 1976-S silver coins are approximate. Many were melted in 1982.

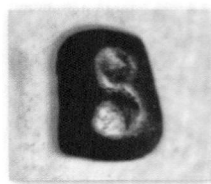

1979-S, Filled S (Type 1), Proof	1979-S, Clear S (Type 2), Proof	1981-S, Rounded S (Type 1), Proof	1981-S, Flat S (Type 2), Proof

	Mintage	Cert	Avg	%MS	MS-63 PF-65	MS-65 PF-67Cam	MS-66 PF-67Cam	MS-67 PF-68DC
1978	14,350,000	212	65.2	99%	$3	$12	$20	$150
Auctions: $411, MS-67, August 2014; $19, MS-66, July 2008								
1978D	13,765,799	141	65.1	100%	$3	$10	$23	$150
Auctions: $881, MS-67, August 2014; $18, MS-66, September 2008								
1978S, Proof	3,127,781	1,323	68.7			$4	$12	$18
Auctions: $147, PF-70DCam, December 2014; $176, PF-70DCam, November 2014; $106, PF-70DCam, November 2014								
1979	68,312,000	243	65.2	98%	$3	$10	$25	$150
Auctions: $423, MS-67, July 2014								
1979D	15,815,422	210	65.1	100%	$2	$12	$25	$160
Auctions: $764, MS-67, August 2014; $11, MS-66, September 2008								
1979S, Proof, All kinds (k)	3,677,175							
1979S, Type 1, Proof		1,843	68.9			$4	$11	$14
Auctions: $200, PF-70DCam, April 2012								
1979S, Type 2, Proof		1,193	68.9			$17	$20	$27
Auctions: $588, PF-70DCam, February 2013								
1980P	44,134,000	197	65.5	99%	$3	$10	$17	$35
Auctions: $129, MS-67, July 2014								
1980D	33,456,449	133	64.8	98%	$2	$13	$55	$145
Auctions: $3,290, MS-68, August 2014; $138, MS-66, September 2008								
1980S, Proof	3,554,806	1,891	68.8			$4	$12	$15
Auctions: $129, PF-70DCam, July 2014; $129, PF-70DCam, August 2013								
1981P	29,544,000	255	65.3	99%	$3	$12	$25	$260
Auctions: No auction records available.								
1981D	27,839,533	100	64.3	98%	$3	$18	$40	$350
Auctions: $1,880, MS-67, August 2014; $50, MS-66, June 2014								
1981S, Proof, All kinds (l)	4,063,083							
1981S, Type 1, Proof		2,119	68.8			$4	$12	$15
Auctions: $259, PF-70DCam, June 2013								
1981S, Type 2, Proof		866	68.8			$25	$29	$33
Auctions: $2,585, PF-70DCam, November 2013								
1982P	10,819,000	166	64.8	97%	$7	$23	$70	$425
Auctions: $2,585, MS-67, August 2014; $382, MS-66, June 2014; $15, MS-64, August 2014								
1982D	13,140,102	206	65.3	99%	$6	$18	$40	$325
Auctions: $999, MS-67, August 2014; $3,290, MS-67, November 2013								
1982S, Proof	3,857,479	1,299	69.0			$5	$12	$15
Auctions: $529, PF-70DCam, June 2013								

k. The mintmark style of 1979-S, Proof, coins was changed during production, resulting in two distinct types. The scarcer, well-defined Type 2 is easily distinguished from the more common blob-like Type 1. l. The mintmark style of the 1981-S, Proof, coins was changed during production, creating two different types. The scarcer Type 2 is not easily distinguished from the common Type 1. Type 2 is flat on the top curve of the S, compared to Type 1, which has a more rounded top. The surface of Type 2 is frosted, and the openings in the loops are slightly larger.

**1988-S, Doubled-Die
Obverse, Proof**
FS-50-1988S-101.

	Mintage	Cert	Avg	%MS	MS-63 / PF-65	MS-65 / PF-67Cam	MS-66 / PF-68DC	MS-67
1983P	34,139,000	103	64.7	94%	$7	$20	$38	$165
Auctions: $147, MS-65, April 2014								
1983D	32,472,244	83	64.8	95%	$7	$15	$30	$330
Auctions: $1,645, MS-67, August 2014; $13, MS-66, October 2008								
1983S, Proof	3,279,126	1,353	69.0			$5	$12	$15
Auctions: $115, PF-70DCam, August 2013								
1984P	26,029,000	184	65.5	99%	$3	$12	$38	$250
Auctions: $1,116, MS-67, August 2014; $98, MS-66, September 2008								
1984D	26,262,158	156	65.1	99%	$3	$17	$40	$350
Auctions: $2,820, MS-67, August 2014; $11, MS-66, September 2008								
1984S, Proof	3,065,110	975	69.0			$6	$12	$15
Auctions: $382, PF-70DCam, June 2013								
1985P	18,706,962	213	66.0	100%	$5	$15	$25	$90
Auctions: $123, MS-67, July 2014								
1985D	19,814,034	281	66.0	100%	$5	$12	$15	$45
Auctions: $159, MS-67, July 2014								
1985S, Proof	3,362,821	1,174	69.0			$5	$12	$15
Auctions: $106, PF-70DCam, August 2013								
1986P	13,107,633	236	66.0	100%	$6	$13	$28	$70
Auctions: $282, MS-67, July 2014								
1986D	15,336,145	344	66.3	100%	$5	$11	$20	$45
Auctions: $57, MS-67, July 2014								
1986S, Proof	3,010,497	875	69.0			$6	$12	$15
Auctions: $108, PF-70DCam, July 2014; $76, PF-70DCam, July 2014								
1987P ‡ (m)	2,890,758	354	65.6	100%	$5	$15	$30	$100
Auctions: $3,290, MS-68, August 2014; $76, MS-67, June 2014								
1987D ‡ (m)	2,890,758	460	65.9	100%	$5	$12	$23	$50
Auctions: $2,585, MS-68, August 2014; $21, MS-67, October 2008								
1987S, Proof	4,227,728	1,440	69.0			$5	$12	$15
Auctions: $96, PF-70DCam, August 2013								
1988P	13,626,000	173	65.8	100%	$5	$15	$28	$90
Auctions: $282, MS-67, July 2014								
1988D	12,000,096	291	66.3	100%	$4	$12	$25	$40
Auctions: $57, MS-67, July 2014								
1988S, Proof	3,262,948	984	69.0			$5	$12	$15
Auctions: $113, PF-70DCam, May 2013								
1988S, Doubled-Die Obverse, Proof (n)	(o)	12	68.8	100%		$110	$160	
Auctions: $260, PF-68UCam, February 2011								

‡ Ranked in the *100 Greatest U.S. Modern Coins*. **m.** Not issued for circulation; included with Mint and Souvenir sets. **n.** Clear doubling is visible on IN GOD WE TRUST, the date, and the mintmark. Some doubling is also evident on LIBERTY and the mintmark. **o.** Included in 1988-S, Proof, mintage figure.

	Mintage	Cert	Avg	%MS	MS-63	MS-65 PF-65	MS-66 PF-67Cam	MS-67 PF-68DC
1989P	24,542,000	233	65.7	99%	$4	$12	$23	$90
	Auctions: $259, MS-67, July 2014							
1989D	23,000,216	258	66.0	100%	$3	$11	$18	$60
	Auctions: $129, MS-67, July 2014							
1989S, Proof	3,220,194	989	69.0			$6	$12	$20
	Auctions: $123, PF-70DCam, May 2013							
1990P	22,278,000	159	65.8	100%	$3	$11	$22	$145
	Auctions: $282, MS-67, August 2014; $76, MS-67, June 2014; $106, MS-65, November 2014							
1990D	20,096,242	192	65.6	100%	$3	$16	$32	$200
	Auctions: $31, MS-66, October 2008							
1990S, Proof	3,299,559	1,148	69.1			$6	$12	$18
	Auctions: $82, PF-70DCam, May 2013							
1991P	14,874,000	196	66.1	100%	$4	$12	$25	$200
	Auctions: $217, MS-67, July 2014							
1991D	15,054,678	228	65.9	100%	$4	$15	$30	$300
	Auctions: $329, MS-67, August 2014; $920, MS-67, September 2008							
1991S, Proof	2,867,787	1,046	69.3			$10	$14	$20
	Auctions: $68, PF-70DCam, July 2013							
1992P	17,628,000	180	66.0	100%	$2	$11	$22	$25
	Auctions: $2,350, MS-68, August 2014; $11, MS-67, October 2008							
1992D	17,000,106	123	66.1	100%	$3	$10	$18	$30
	Auctions: $147, MS-67, August 2014; $30, MS-67, August 2014; $46, MS-67, July 2014							
1992S, Proof	2,858,981	679	69.2			$7	$14	$20
	Auctions: $35, PF-70DCam, May 2013							
1992S, Proof, Silver	1,317,579	1,939	69.1			$17	$20	$25
	Auctions: $92, PF-70DCam, July 2013							
1993P	15,510,000	310	66.5	99%	$3	$11	$20	$40
	Auctions: $58, MS-67, July 2014							
1993D	15,000,006	577	66.0	100%	$3	$10	$22	$60
	Auctions: $2,585, MS-68, August 2014; $11, MS-66, October 2008							
1993S, Proof	2,633,439	739	69.3			$8	$17	$23
	Auctions: $31, PF-70DCam, May 2013							
1993S, Proof, Silver	761,353	1,481	69.1			$30	$33	$37
	Auctions: $99, PF-70DCam, May 2014							
1994P	23,718,000	397	65.8	100%	$3	$10	$20	$55
	Auctions: $2,115, MS-68, August 2014; $10, MS-66, October 2008							
1994D	23,828,110	183	65.9	100%	$3	$10	$20	$75
	Auctions: $364, MS-67, July 2014							
1994S, Proof	2,484,594	661	69.3			$8	$17	$23
	Auctions: $45, PF-70DCam, May 2013							
1994S, Proof, Silver	785,329	1,434	69.1			$30	$33	$35
	Auctions: $206, PF-70DCam, February 2013							
1995P	26,496,000	209	66.2	100%	$3	$10	$17	$40
	Auctions: $55, MS-67, July 2014							
1995D	26,288,000	266	66.2	100%	$3	$10	$20	$50
	Auctions: $2,585, MS-68, August 2014; $13, MS-67, October 2008							
1995S, Proof	2,117,496	609	69.3			$15	$20	$25
	Auctions: $66, PF-70DCam, August 2013							
1995S, Proof, Silver ‡	679,985	1,738	69.1			$38	$40	$45
	Auctions: $135, PF-70DCam, May 2014							

‡ Ranked in the *100 Greatest U.S. Modern Coins.*

	Mintage	Cert	Avg	%MS	MS-63 / PF-65	MS-65 / PF-67Cam	MS-66 / PF-68DC	MS-67
1996P	24,442,000	305	66.2	100%	$3	$10	$17	$35
Auctions: $247, MS-68, July 2014								
1996D	24,744,000	284	66.2	100%	$2	$10	$17	$35
Auctions: $1,293, MS-68, August 2014; $11, MS-67, October 2008								
1996S, Proof	1,750,244	611	69.2			$10	$15	$22
Auctions: $66, PF-70DCam, August 2013								
1996S, Proof, Silver	775,021	1,393	69.0			$30	$35	$40
Auctions: $135, PF-70DCam, August 2013								
1997P	20,882,000	145	66.3	100%	$2	$12	$25	$50
Auctions: $60, MS-67, July 2014								
1997D	19,876,000	245	65.9	100%	$2	$13	$25	$60
Auctions: $646, MS-68, June 2013; $123, MS-67, July 2014								
1997S, Proof	2,055,000	527	69.3			$12	$20	$25
Auctions: $76, PF-70DCam, August 2013								
1997S, Proof, Silver	741,678	1,507	69.2			$30	$40	$50
Auctions: $96, PF-70DCam, August 2013								
1998P	15,646,000	194	66.3	99%	$2	$15	$35	$70
Auctions: $76, MS-67, July 2014								
1998D	15,064,000	181	65.9	99%	$3	$11	$20	$70
Auctions: $62, MS-67, July 2014								
1998S, Proof	2,086,507	580	69.4			$10	$17	$23
Auctions: $56, PF-70DCam, August 2013								
1998S, Proof, Silver	878,792	1,741	69.3			$18	$25	$35
Auctions: $88, PF-70DCam, August 2013								
1998S, Matte Finish Proof, Silver ‡ (p)	62,000	1,993	69.2		$125			
Auctions: $270, PF-70, November 2014; $441, PF-70, July 2014; $113, PF-69, November 2014; $108, PF-69, November 2014								
1999P	8,900,000	214	66.4	100%	$3	$10	$20	$30
Auctions: $2,115, MS-69, June 2013; $823, MS-68, August 2014								
1999D	10,682,000	215	66.2	100%	$2	$10	$16	$23
Auctions: $1,998, MS-68, August 2014; $10, MS-66, October 2008								
1999S, Proof	2,543,401	3,276	69.3			$13	$16	$20
Auctions: $90, PF-70DCam, May 2013								
1999S, Proof, Silver	804,565	5,300	69.1			$25	$30	$32
Auctions: $147, PF-70DCam, August 2013								
2000P	22,600,000	116	66.0	100%	$3	$10	$17	$35
Auctions: $764, MS-68, August 2014; $48, MS-67, October 2008								
2000D	19,466,000	213	66.1	100%	$2	$9	$20	$40
Auctions: $123, MS-67, July 2014								
2000S, Proof	3,082,483	2,580	69.3			$6	$12	$16
Auctions: $58, PF-70DCam, May 2013								
2000S, Proof, Silver	965,421	6,456	69.2			$17	$18	$20
Auctions: $78, PF-70DCam, May 2013								
2001P	21,200,000	382	65.5	100%	$2	$8	$15	$28
Auctions: $90, MS-68, August 2014; $99, MS-68, July 2014								
2001D	19,504,000	427	65.8	100%	$3	$8	$13	$28
Auctions: $247, MS-68, July 2014								
2001S, Proof	2,294,909	1,937	69.3			$8	$10	$13
Auctions: $76, PF-70DCam, May 2013								
2001S, Proof, Silver	889,697	4,687	69.2			$18	$21	$23
Auctions: $90, PF-70DCam, May 2013								

‡ Ranked in the *100 Greatest U.S. Modern Coins.* **p.** Minted for inclusion in the Robert F. Kennedy commemorative set (along with an RFK commemorative dollar).

	Mintage	Cert	Avg	%MS	MS-63	MS-65	MS-66	MS-67
						PF-65	PF-67Cam	PF-68DC
2002P (q)	3,100,000	196	65.6	100%	$3	$8	$15	$30
Auctions: $118, MS-68, July 2014; $182, MS-68, June 2014								
2002D (q)	2,500,000	218	65.8	100%	$3	$9	$20	$40
Auctions: $2,115, MS-69, June 2013								
2002S, Proof	2,319,766	1,952	69.2			$7	$13	$16
Auctions: $60, PF-70DCam, May 2013								
2002S, Proof, Silver	892,229	5,022	69.3			$15	$18	$20
Auctions: $61, PF-70DCam, May 2013								
2003P (q)	2,500,000	260	65.8	100%	$3	$9	$20	$30
Auctions: $59, MS-67, July 2014								
2003D (q)	2,500,000	241	65.8	100%	$2	$8	$16	$25
Auctions: $51, MS-67, July 2014								
2003S, Proof	2,172,684	4,045	69.2			$7	$12	$16
Auctions: $35, PF-70DCam, May 2013								
2003S, Proof, Silver	1,125,755	5,930	69.2			$13	$18	$20
Auctions: $76, PF-70DCam, November 2014; $82, PF-70DCam, May 2014								
2004P (q)	2,900,000	235	66.2	100%	$3	$8	$17	$30
Auctions: $86, MS-67, July 2014								
2004D (q)	2,900,000	378	66.3	100%	$2	$8	$16	$25
Auctions: $423, MS-68, July 2014								
2004S, Proof	1,789,488	1,801	69.2			$13	$17	$24
Auctions: $66, PF-70DCam, August 2013								
2004S, Proof, Silver	1,175,934	5,785	69.2			$20	$22	$23
Auctions: $69, PF-70DCam, January 2013								
2005P (q,r)	3,800,000	229	66.0	100%	$4	$18	$25	$75
Auctions: $42, MS-66, July 2014								
2005D (q,r)	3,500,000	245	66.3	100%	$3	$15	$23	$35
Auctions: $1,116, MS-68, August 2014; $11, MS-66, October 2008								
2005S, Proof	2,275,000	7,055	69.2			$7	$12	$16
Auctions: $66, PF-70DCam, August 2013								
2005S, Proof, Silver	1,069,679	7,172	69.3			$13	$18	$20
Auctions: $74, PF-70DCam, January 2013								
2006P (q,r)	2,400,000	201	66.7	100%	$2	$9	$22	$26
Auctions: $42, MS-69, January 2009; $764, MS-68, August 2014								
2006D (q,r)	2,000,000	190	66.3	100%	$2	$7	$15	$28
Auctions: $82, MS-67, July 2014								
2006S, Proof	2,000,428	2,645	69.3			$7	$12	$16
Auctions: $46, PF-70DCam, August 2013								
2006S, Proof, Silver	1,054,008	4,066	69.4			$15	$18	$20
Auctions: $76, PF-70DCam, August 2013								
2007P (q,r)	2,400,000	164	66.5	100%	$2	$6	$11	$17
Auctions: $270, MS-68, July 2014								
2007D (q,r)	2,400,000	132	66.1	100%	$2	$6	$15	$30
Auctions: $15, MS-69, January 2009								
2007S, Proof	1,702,116	2,831	69.3			$7	$12	$16
Auctions: $64, PF-70DCam, January 2013								
2007S, Proof, Silver	875,050	3,655	69.4			$14	$19	$22
Auctions: $86, PF-70DCam, August 2013								

q. Not issued for circulation. Sold directly to the public in rolls and small bags. **r.** Mint sets issued from 2005 through 2010 have a special satin finish that is somewhat different from the finish on traditional Uncirculated coins.

	Mintage	Cert	Avg	%MS	MS-63	MS-65	MS-66	MS-67
						PF-65	PF-67Cam	PF-68DC
2008P (q,r)	1,700,000	208	66.3	100%	$2	$8	$20	$40
	Auctions: $1,410, MS-68, August 2014; $12, SP-67, April 2012							
2008D (q,r)	1,700,000	101	65.9	100%	$2	$8	$20	$45
	Auctions: $24, MS-66, June 2011							
2008S, Proof	1,405,674	1,772	69.3			$7	$12	$16
	Auctions: $71, PF-70DCam, November 2013							
2008S, Proof, Silver	763,887	3,661	69.4			$15	$20	$23
	Auctions: $66, PF-70DCam, August 2013							
2009P (q,r)	1,900,000	177	66.2	100%	$2	$6	$12	$25
	Auctions: $1,998, MS-68, August 2014; $6, MS-66, November 2011							
2009D (q,r)	1,900,000	131	66.2	100%	$2	$6	$12	$30
	Auctions: $27, MS-66, February 2012							
2009S, Proof	1,482,502	3,588	69.3			$7	$12	$16
	Auctions: $31, PF-70DCam, May 2013							
2009S, Proof, Silver	697,365	4,572	69.3			$17	$18	$20
	Auctions: $41, PF-70DCam, May 2013							
2010P (q,r)	1,800,000	216	66.6	100%	$2	$6	$12	$25
	Auctions: $23, MS-67, July 2014							
2010D (q,r)	1,700,000	151	66.3	100%	$2	$6	$12	$25
	Auctions: $101, MS-67, July 2014							
2010S, Proof	1,103,815	1,284	69.3			$7	$12	$16
	Auctions: $48, PF-70DCam, August 2013							
2010S, Proof, Silver	585,401	4,141	69.6			$17	$18	$20
	Auctions: $48, PF-70DCam, May 2013							
2011P (q)	1,750,000	425	66.7	100%	$2	$6	$12	$25
	Auctions: $229, MS-68, July 2014							
2011D (q)	1,700,000	348	66.5	100%	$2	$6	$12	$25
	Auctions: $1,116, MS-68, August 2014; $1,058, MS-68, August 2014; $33, MS-67, January 2012							
2011S, Proof	*952,881*	2,306	69.4			$7	$12	$16
	Auctions: $21, PF-70UCam, March 2012							
2011S, Proof, Silver	*500,395*	4,918	69.7			$13	$18	$20
	Auctions: $39, PF-70DCam, August 2014; $36, PF-70DCam, April 2012							
2012P (q)	1,800,000	228	66.8	100%	$2	$6	$12	$25
	Auctions: No auction records available.							
2012D (q)	1,700,000	248	66.7	100%	$2	$6	$12	$25
	Auctions: No auction records available.							
2012S, Proof		1,783	69.3			$7	$12	$16
	Auctions: $51, PF-70DCam, May 2013							
2012S, Proof, Silver		1,968	69.6			$13	$18	$20
	Auctions: No auction records available.							
2013P (q)	5,000,000	289	66.9	100%	$2	$6	$12	$25
	Auctions: No auction records available.							
2013D (q)	4,600,000	296	66.9	100%	$2	$6	$12	$25
	Auctions: No auction records available.							
2013S, Proof	*802,460*	1,898	69.3			$7	$12	$16
	Auctions: No auction records available.							
2013S, Proof, Silver	*419,719*	2,230	69.6			$17	$18	$20
	Auctions: No auction records available.							

q. Not issued for circulation. Sold directly to the public in rolls and small bags. **r.** Mint sets issued from 2005 through 2010 have a special satin finish that is somewhat different from the finish on traditional Uncirculated coins.

	Mintage	Cert	Avg	%MS	MS-63 PF-65	MS-65 PF-67Cam	MS-66 PF-67Cam	MS-67 PF-68DC
2014P (q,s)	2,500,000	377	66.8	100%	$2	$6	$12	$25
Auctions: No auction records available.								
2014P, Proof, Silver (t)	188,147	0	n/a				$30	$40
Auctions: No auction records available.								
2014D (q,s)	2,100,000	600	67.3	100%	$2	$6	$12	$25
Auctions: No auction records available.								
2014D, Silver (t)	188,147	0	n/a				$30	$40
Auctions: No auction records available.								
2014S, Enhanced Uncirculated, Silver (t)	188,147	0	n/a				$30	$40
Auctions: No auction records available.								
2014S, Proof	665,100	2,300	69.3			$7	$12	$16
Auctions: No auction records available.								
2014S, Proof, Silver	393,037	3,905	69.6			$17	$18	$20
Auctions: No auction records available.								
2014W, Reverse Proof, Silver (t)	188,147	0	n/a				$30	$40
Auctions: No auction records available.								
2014W, 50th Anniversary, Proof, Gold (u)	69,299	0	n/a					
Auctions: No auction records available.								
2015P (q)					$2	$6	$12	$25
Auctions: No auction records available.								
2015D (q)					$2	$6	$12	$25
Auctions: No auction records available.								
2015S, Proof						$7	$12	$16
Auctions: No auction records available.								
2015S, Proof, Silver						$17	$18	$20
Auctions: No auction records available.								

q. Not issued for circulation. Sold directly to the public in rolls and small bags. **s.** To celebrate the 50th anniversary of the Kennedy half dollar, in 2014 the U.S. Mint issued an Uncirculated two-coin set featuring a Kennedy half dollar from Philadelphia and one from Denver. **t.** Featured in the 2014 half dollar silver-coin collection released by the U.S. Mint to commemorate the 50th anniversary of the Kennedy half dollar. **u.** First gold half dollar offered by the U.S. Mint. It commemorates the 50th anniversary of the first release of the Kennedy half dollar in 1964. Dual-dated 1964–2014.

Silver Dollars
1794–1935

AN OVERVIEW OF SILVER DOLLARS

The silver dollar was authorized by Congress on April 2, 1792, and first coined in 1794. This denomination includes some of the most popular series in American numismatics.

The first coin of the denomination, the Flowing Hair dollar, is easy enough to obtain (given the proper budget) in grades from VF through low Mint State. Striking usually ranges from poor to barely acceptable, and adjustment marks (from an overweight planchet being filed down to correct weight) are often seen. Accordingly, careful examination is needed to find a good example.

The silver dollar with the Draped Bust obverse in combination with the Small Eagle reverse was made from 1795 through 1798, with most examples being dated 1796 or 1797. Today both the 1796 and 1797 exist in about the same numbers. Although mintage figures refer to the quantities produced in the given calendar year, these do not necessarily refer to the dates on the coins themselves, as Mint workers would use coinage dies into the next calendar year. Silver dollars of this type are fairly scarce. Sharpness of strike presents a challenge to the collector, and usually there are weaknesses in details, particularly on the reverse eagle.

The 1798 to 1804 type features a Draped Bust obverse and Heraldic Eagle reverse. Many such coins exist, mostly in grades from VF through lower Mint State levels. Striking can be indifferent, but the population of surviving coins is such that collectors have more to choose from, and can select for quality.

The Gobrecht silver dollars of 1836 (starless obverse, stars on reverse, plain edge) and 1839 (stars on obverse, starless reverse, reeded edge) present a special challenge in the formation of a type set. For quite a few years these were considered by numismatists to be *patterns*, and thus anyone forming a type set of regular-issue U.S. coins did not have to notice them. However, in recent decades, research by R.W. Julian (in particular), Walter Breen, and others, has revealed that the vast majority of 1836 and 1839 silver dollars originally produced were put into circulation at face value. Accordingly, they were coins of the realm at the time, were spent as currency, and are deserving of a place among regular coinage types.

The 1836 Gobrecht dollar is easy enough to find in today's marketplace, although expensive. The original production amounted to 1,600 coins, to which an unknown number of restrikes can be added. The main problem arises with the 1839, made only to the extent of 300 pieces. Those that exist today nearly always have abundant signs of circulation. This is the rarest of all major U.S. coin design types, even outclassing the 1796–1797 half dollar and the 1808 quarter eagle.

In 1840 the regular Liberty Seated dollar made its appearance, with the reverse depicting a perched eagle holding an olive branch and arrows. This style was continued through 1873, with minor modifications over the years; for example, in 1866 the motto IN GOD WE TRUST was added to the reverse. Generally, Liberty Seated dollars can be easily enough found in circulated grades from VF up, as well as low Mint State levels. MS-63 and higher pieces are in the minority, particularly of the 1840–1865 type.

Morgan silver dollars, made by the hundreds of millions from 1878 through 1921, are easily found, with the 1881-S being at once the most common of all varieties existing today in gem condition and also usually seen with sharp strike and nice appearance.

Peace silver dollars of 1921 through 1935 exist in large quantities. Some collectors select the first year of issue, 1921, as a separate type, as the design is in high relief. The 1921 is plentiful in Mint State, but rarely is found sharply struck at the obverse and reverse center. Later Peace dollars with shallow relief abound in MS-63 and finer grades, although strike quality can be a problem.

Yellow Jacket Silver Mining Company at Gold Hill, Nevada. In the 1870s and 1880s, hundreds of silver mines dotted the American West.

The Peace dollar was the last of the United States' circulating .900 fine silver dollars. One final type of dollar coin was produced in the large 38.1 mm format—the Eisenhower dollar, often colloquially called a "silver dollar" even though its regular issues were made of copper and nickel. Since the Eisenhower dollar, U.S. coins of this denomination have been produced in smaller diameters and in base metals. These modern dollars are explored in detail in the next chapter. The U.S. Mint has also produced various *commemorative* silver dollars from 1900 to date, and the one-ounce American Silver Eagle bullion coin has a denomination of one dollar. These coins are covered in the Commemoratives and Bullion sections, respectively.

FOR THE COLLECTOR AND INVESTOR: SILVER DOLLARS AS A SPECIALTY

Generally, silver dollars of the 1794–1803 years are collected by dates and major types.

Although the 1794, of which an estimated 135 or so exist today, is famous and expensive, other varieties are eminently affordable in such grades as VF and EF. Beyond the listings herein there is a rich panorama of die varieties, most extensively delineated in the 1993 two-volume study *Silver Dollars and Trade Dollars of the United States: A Complete Encyclopedia*. This built upon earlier works, including J.W. Haseltine's *Type Table of United States Dollars, Half Dollars and Quarter Dollars*, and, especially, the long-term standard work by M.H. Bolender, *The United States Early Silver Dollars from 1794 to 1803*. In many instances among early dollars the number of aficionados desiring a particularly rare die combination may be even smaller than the population of coins available—with the result that not much premium has to be paid.

The 1804 silver dollar is a study in itself. None were actually produced in the year 1804. Several were made in 1834 as presentation pieces for foreign dignitaries, and even later examples were made for private collectors. Only a handful exist of this classic rarity, the "King of American Coins."

After 1803 it is a long jump to 1836, when silver dollars (of the Gobrecht design) were again struck for circulation. In 1839 more Gobrecht dollars were struck, with the design modified. In addition to the listings in this book are a number of other die combinations, edge and metal varieties, etc., including pieces of the year 1838, most of which are pattern restrikes (studied in *United States Pattern Coins*). These are avidly desired and collected.

Forming a specialized collection of Liberty Seated dollars from 1840 through 1873 has been a pursuit of many collectors over the years. Generally, the Philadelphia Mint dates are available without difficulty, although the 1851 and 1852 are typically acquired as Proof restrikes—originals of both years being prohibitively rare. Most difficult to find in higher grades are coins of the branch mints, including the famous 1870-S, of which only 10 are known to exist and for which no mintage quantity figure was ever listed in official reports. Branch-mint pieces, starting with the 1846-O, were placed into circulation and used extensively. Beginning in 1870, dollars of this type were struck at Carson City; these also are seen with evidence of circulation. The only exceptions to this are certain dollars of 1859-O and 1860-O which turned up in very "baggy" Mint State preservation (showing contact marks from other coins) among Treasury hoards, to the extent of several thousand pieces of both dates combined.

Morgan silver dollars from 1878 through 1921 are one of the most active and popular series in American numismatics. Approximately 100 different major varieties can be collected, although certain unusual varieties (not basic dates and mintmarks) can be dropped from a collection or added as desired. The vast majority of Morgan dollars can be found in Mint State. When these coins were first minted there was little need for them in circulation, and hundreds of millions of coins piled up in Treasury and other vaults. Although many were melted in 1918, enough remained that untold millions exist today in the hands of the public.

Varieties such as the 1881-S are common and are normally seen in high grades with sharp strike, but others with high mintages, the 1886-O and 1896-O being examples, are quite rare in MS-63 and finer, and when seen usually have rather poor eye appeal. Accordingly, quite a bit of discernment is recommended for the savvy collector.

Peace silver dollars, minted from 1921 to 1935, include the High Relief style of 1921, and the shallow-relief motif of 1922 to 1935. A basic set of 24 different dates and mintmarks is easily enough obtained, including in Mint State. The most elusive is the 1934-S.

FLOWING HAIR (1794–1795)

Engraver: *Robert Scot.* **Weight:** *26.96 grams.* **Composition:** *.900 silver,*
.100 copper (net weight 0.78011 oz. pure silver). **Diameter:** *Approximately 39–40 mm.*
Edge: *HUNDRED CENTS ONE DOLLAR OR UNIT with decorations between words.*

Bowers-Borckardt–27, Bolender-5.

History. The first U.S. silver dollars were of the Flowing Hair design. In 1794 only 1,758 were released for circulation (slightly fewer than were struck), and the next year nearly 100 times that amount. These coins were popular in their time and circulated for decades afterward. Many were used in international trade, particularly in the Caribbean.

Striking and Sharpness. On the obverse, check the hair details. It is essential to check the die variety, as certain varieties were struck with very little detail at the center. Accordingly, high-grade examples can appear to be well worn on the hair. Check the star centers, as well. On the reverse, check the breast and wings of the eagle. All 1794 dollars are lightly struck at the lower left of the obverse (often at portions of the date) and to a lesser extent the corresponding part of the reverse. Many coins of both dates have planchet adjustment marks (from overweight blanks being filed down to proper weight before striking), often heavy and sometimes even disfiguring; these are not noted by the certification services. Expect weakness in some areas on dollars of this type; a coin with Full Details on both sides is virtually unheard of. Sharp striking and excellent eye appeal add to the value dramatically. These coins are very difficult to find problem-free, even in MS.

Availability. The 1794 is rare in all grades, with an estimated 125 to 135 known, including a handful in MS. The 1795 is easily available, with an estimated 4,000 to 7,500 still existing, although some die varieties range from scarce to rare. Many if not most have been dipped at one time or another, and many have been retoned, often satisfactorily. The existence of *any* luster is an exception between EF-40 and AU-58. MS coins are quite scarce (perhaps 150 to 250 existing, most dated 1795), especially at MS-63 or above.

Varieties listed herein are those most significant to collectors, but numerous minor variations may be found because each of the early dies was made individually. (Values of varieties not listed in this guide depend on collector interest and demand.) Blanks were weighed before the dollars were struck and overweight pieces were filed to remove excess silver. Coins with old adjustment marks from this filing process may be worth less than the values shown here. Some Flowing Hair dollars were weight-adjusted through insertion of a small (8 mm) silver plug in the center of the blank planchet before the coin was struck.

GRADING STANDARDS

MS-60 to 70 (Mint State). *Obverse:* At MS-60, some abrasion and contact marks are evident, most noticeably on the cheek and in the fields. Luster is present, but may be dull or lifeless, and interrupted in patches. At MS-63, contact marks are very few, and abrasion is light and not obvious. An MS-65 coin has little or, better yet, no abrasion, and contact marks are minute. Luster should be full

**1794; BB-1, Bolender-1. Graded MS-64.
Fully brilliant and highly lustrous.**

and rich. Coins graded above MS-65 are more theoretical than actual for this type—but they do exist, and are defined by having fewer marks as perfection is approached. *Reverse:* Comments apply as for the obverse, except that abrasion and contact marks are most noticeable on the eagle at the center, although most dollars of this type are lightly struck in the higher points of that area. The field area is small and is protected by lettering and the wreath and in any given grade shows fewer marks than on the obverse.

Illustrated coin: Like all 1794 dollars, this coin is weak at the left obverse and the corresponding part of the reverse. Planchet flaws are seen at stars 3 and 5. The center obverse is very well struck.

AU-50, 53, 55, 58 (About Uncirculated). *Obverse:* Light wear is seen on the hair area immediately to the left of the face and neck (except for those flatly struck there), on the cheek, and on the top of the neck truncation, more so at AU-50 than at 53 or 55. An AU-58 coin has minimal traces of wear. An AU-50 coin has luster in protected areas among the stars and letters, with little luster in the open fields or the portrait. Some certified coins have virtually

1795, Two Leaves; BB-21, Bolender-1. Graded AU-58.

no luster, but are considered high quality in other aspects. At AU-58, most luster is partially present in the fields. On any high-grade dollar, luster is often a better key to grading than is the appearance of wear. *Reverse:* Light wear is seen on the eagle's body and the upper edges of the wings. At AU-50, detail is lost for some of the feathers in this area. However, some coins are weak to begin with. Light wear is seen on the wreath and lettering. Again, luster is the best key to actual wear. This ranges from perhaps 20% remaining in protected areas (at AU-50) to two-thirds or more (at AU-58). Generally, the reverse has more luster than the obverse.

Illustrated coin: This coin shows above-average striking sharpness on the obverse.

EF-40, 45 (Extremely Fine). *Obverse:* More wear is evident on the portrait, especially on the hair to the left of the face and neck (again, remember that some varieties were struck with flatness in this area), the cheek, and the tip of the neck truncation. Excellent detail remains in low-relief areas of the hair. The stars show wear, as do the date and letters. Luster, if present at all, is minimal and in protected areas. *Reverse:* The eagle shows more

1795, Three Leaves; BB-26, Bolender-12a. Graded EF-40.

wear, this being the focal point to check. Most or nearly all detail is well defined. These aspects should be reviewed in combination with knowledge of the die variety, to determine the sharpness of the coin when it was first struck. Most silver dollars of this type were flat at the highest area of the center at the time they were made, as this was opposite the highest point of the hair in the press when the coins were struck. Additional wear is on the wreath and letters, but many details are present. Some luster may be seen in protected areas, and if present is slightly more abundant than on the obverse.

Illustrated coin: On the obverse, a massive die crack extends upward through the 7 of the date.

VF-20, 30 (Very Fine). *Obverse:* The hair is well worn at VF-20, less so at VF-30. On well-struck varieties the weakness is in the area left of the temple and cheek. The strands are blended as to be heavy. The cheek shows only slight relief. The stars have more wear, making them appear larger (an optical illusion). *Reverse:* The body of the eagle shows few if any feathers, while the wings have a third to half of the feathers visible, depending on the strike. The leaves

1795, Two Leaves; BB-21, Bolender-1. Graded VF-20.

lack most detail, but veins can be seen on a few. Scattered, non-disfiguring marks are normal for this and lower grades. Any major defects should be noted separately.

Illustrated coin: Light rim bumps should be noted. This coin features attractive medium toning.

F-12, 15 (Fine). *Obverse:* Wear is more extensive than on the preceding, reducing the definition of the thick strands of hair. The cheek has less detail, but the eye is usually well defined. On most coins, the stars appear larger. The rim is distinct in most areas, and many denticles remain visible. *Reverse:* Wear is more extensive. Now, feather details are fewer, mostly remaining on the wing to the left and at the extreme tip of the wing on the

1795, Three Leaves; BB-27, Bolender-5. Graded F-12.

right. As always, the die variety in question can have an influence on this. The wreath and lettering are worn further. The rim is usually complete, with most denticles visible.

Illustrated coin: This variety is flatly struck on the head, and examples in higher grades show no detail at the center. Note the smooth, even wear with some marks.

VG-8, 10 (Very Good). *Obverse:* The portrait is mostly seen in outline form, with most hair strands gone, although some are visible left of the neck, and the tips at the lower left are clear. The eye is distinct. The stars appear larger still, again an illusion. LIBERTY and the date are readable and usually full, although some letters may be weak at their tops. The rim is usually complete, and many denticles can be seen. *Reverse:* The eagle is mostly an

1795, Two Leaves; BB-11, Bolender-3. Graded VG-10.

outline, although some traces of feathers may be seen in the tail and the lower part of the inside of the right wing. The rim is worn, as are the letters, with some weak, but the motto is readable.

Illustrated coin: This coin shows some microscopic granularity overall. It is an interesting variety with a silver plug inserted at the center of the planchet prior to minting, to slightly increase the weight; this feature can barely be seen in outline form.

G-4, 6 (Good). *Obverse:* Wear is more extensive. LIBERTY and the stars are all there, but weak. The head is an outline, although the eye can still be seen. The rim is well worn or even missing. LIBERTY is worn, and parts of some letters may be missing, but elements of all should be readable. The date is readable, but worn. *Reverse:* The eagle is flat and discernible in outline form. The wreath is well worn. Some of the letters

1795, Two Leaves; BB-11, Bolender-1. Graded G-6.

may be partly missing. At this level some "averaging" can be done. If the letters are stronger than usual in one area, but some are missing in another area, the coin can still qualify as G-4.

Illustrated coin: This is an attractive example with smooth, even wear and a few defects.

AG-3 (About Good). *Obverse:* Wear is extensive, but some stars and letters can usually be discerned. The head is in outline form. The date, while readable, may be partially worn away. *Reverse:* The reverse is well worn, with parts of the wreath and lettering missing.

1795, Three Leaves. Graded AG-3.

**1795, Two Leaves
Beneath Each Wing**

**1795, Three Leaves
Beneath Each Wing**

1795, Silver Plug
BB-15, Bolender-7.

	Mintage	Cert	Avg	%MS	AG-3	G-4	VG-8	F-12	VF-20	EF-40	AU-50	MS-60	MS-63
1794 †	1,758	36	38.8	19%	$37,500	$65,000	$95,000	$115,000	$150,000	$275,000	$325,000	$650,000	$1,500,000
Auctions: $305,500, EF-40, January 2014; $223,250, VF-35, August 2014													
1794, Silver Plug (a)	(b)	1	66.0	100%									
Auctions: No auction records available.													
1795, All kinds	160,295												
1795, Two Leaves		211	31.8	6%	$1,100	$1,750	$2,500	$4,350	$5,750	$13,500	$20,000	$70,000	$175,000
Auctions: $25,850, AU-55, August 2013; $4,994, VF-35, August 2014; $5,993, VF-30, August 2014; $3,819, VF-25, October 2014													
1795, Three Leaves		176	34.3	3%	$1,100	$1,750	$2,500	$4,100	$5,500	$12,000	$19,500	$65,000	$160,000
Auctions: $822,500, SP-64, August 2014; $646,250, MS-65, November 2013; $12,925, AU-50, August 2014; $8,813, EF-45, August 2014													
1795, Silver Plug		35	35.6	6%	$1,500	$2,800	$4,750	$8,500	$16,000	$27,500	$47,500	$160,000	
Auctions: $99,875, AU-55, August 2013													

† Ranked in the *100 Greatest U.S. Coins* (fourth edition). **a.** This unique piece, graded SP-66, shows evidence of planchet adjustment marks, as well as traces of a silver plug that was added to bring the coin's weight up to specification. **b.** Included in 1794 mintage figure.

DRAPED BUST, SMALL EAGLE REVERSE (1795–1798)

Designer: *Robert Scot.* **Weight:** *26.96 grams.* **Composition:** *.8924 silver,*
.1076 copper (net weight .77352 oz. pure silver). **Diameter:** *Approximately 39–40 mm.*
Edge: *HUNDRED CENTS ONE DOLLAR OR UNIT with decorations between words.*

BB-51, Bolender-14.

History. The Draped Bust silver dollar with the Small Eagle reverse, inaugurated in 1795, brought the first appearance of this popular obverse portrait—a depiction of Miss Liberty that later was used on other silver denominations as well as copper half cents and cents. The motif was continued into 1798. Production of the Draped Bust silver dollars started at the end of the year on a new mint press that was first used for striking Flowing Hair dollars that summer. Draped Bust dollars circulated widely, especially outside the United States, and in the Caribbean in particular.

Striking and Sharpness. On the obverse, check the highest areas of the hair, the bust line, and the centers of the stars. On the reverse, check the feathers on the eagle's breast and wings. Examine the denticles. Planchet adjustment marks (from the filing down of overweight blanks) are common and should be avoided. Studying die varieties can be helpful for accurate grading. For example, the Small Letters reverse, a long-lived die design used from 1795 to 1798, has shallow relief and is usually seen with a low rim, with the result that its grade is lower than that of the obverse. On some reverse dies the eagle has very little detail. Fairly sharp striking (not necessarily Full Details) and excellent eye appeal add to the value dramatically.

Availability. These silver dollars are readily available as a type, although certain varieties range from scarce to very rare. MS coins are elusive and when seen are usually of the 1795 date, sometimes with prooflike surfaces. Most coins have been dipped and/or retoned, some successfully. These coins acquired marks more readily than did smaller denominations, and such are to be expected (but should be noted along with the grade, if distracting). Careful buying is needed to obtain coins with good eye appeal. Many AU examples are deeply toned and recolored.

The Smithsonian's National Numismatic Collection includes a unique Specimen 1794 dollar, plugged, and a unique Specimen 1797 10 Stars Left, 6 Stars Right, dollar.

GRADING STANDARDS

MS-60 to 70 (Mint State). *Obverse:* At MS-60, some abrasion and contact marks are evident, most noticeably on the cheek, the drapery at the shoulder, and the right field. Luster is present, but may be dull or lifeless, and interrupted in patches. At MS-63, contact marks are few, and abrasion is harder to detect. Many coins listed as Mint State are deeply toned, making it impossible to evaluate abrasion and even light wear; these are best avoided completely. An MS-65 coin has

1796, Small Date, Large Letters;
BB-61, Bolender-2. Graded MS-60.

no abrasion, and contact marks are so minute as to require magnification. Luster should be full and rich. Coins grading above MS-65 are more theoretical than actual for this type—but they do exist, and are defined by having fewer marks as perfection is approached. *Reverse:* Comments apply as for the obverse, except that abrasion and contact marks are most noticeable on the eagle at the center, a situation complicated by the fact that this area was often flatly struck, not only on the famous Small Letters dies used from 1795 to 1798, but on some others as well. Grading is best done by the obverse, then verified by the reverse. In the Mint State category the amount of luster is usually a good key to grading. The field area is small and is protected by lettering and the wreath, and in any given grade shows fewer marks than on the obverse.

Illustrated coin: Note the tiny dig near Miss Liberty's ear. This coin is fairly well struck overall, but with some lightness on the eagle's body and leg on the right. It has excellent eye appeal.

AU-50, 53, 55, 58 (About Uncirculated). *Obverse:* Light wear is seen on the hair area above the ear and extending to left of the forehead, on the ribbon, and on the drapery at the shoulder, more so at AU-50 than at 53 or 55. An AU-58 coin has minimal traces of wear. An AU-50 coin has luster in protected areas among the stars and letters, with little in the open fields or on the portrait. At AU-58, most luster is present in the fields, but is worn away on the highest parts of the

1797, Stars 9x7, Large Letters;
BB-73, Bolender-1. Graded AU-50.

motifs. At this level there are many deeply toned and recolored coins, necessitating caution when buying. *Reverse:* Light wear is seen on the eagle's body (keep in mind this area might be lightly struck) and edges of the wings. Light wear is seen on the wreath and lettering. Luster is the best key to actual wear. This ranges from perhaps 20% remaining in protected areas (at AU-50) to nearly full mint bloom (at AU-58).

Illustrated coin: This coin has some lightness of strike, but is better than average. It has some dings and marks, but these are not immediately obvious; without them, the coin might grade higher. This illustrates the many variables on these large, heavy coins. No single rule fits all.

EF-40, 45 (Extremely Fine). *Obverse:* More wear is evident on the upper hair area and the ribbon, and on the drapery and bosom. Excellent detail remains in low-relief areas of the hair. The stars show wear, as do the date and letters. Luster, if present at all, is minimal and in protected areas. For any and all dollars of this type, knowledge of die variety characteristics is essential to grading. Once again, one rule does not fit all. *Reverse:* The eagle, this being the focal point to check, shows

1796, Small Date, Large Letters;
BB-61, Bolender-4. Graded EF-40.

more wear. On most strikings, the majority of feathers remain on the interior areas of the wings. Additional wear is on the wreath and letters, but many details are present. Some luster may be seen in protected areas and if present is slightly more abundant than on the obverse.

Illustrated coin: Some marks are on the neck and a small pit is above the eagle's beak.

VF-20, 30 (Very Fine). *Obverse:* The higher-relief areas of hair are well worn at VF-20, less so at VF-30. The drapery and bosom show extensive wear, usually resulting in loss of most detail below the neck. The stars have more wear, making them appear larger. *Reverse:* The body of the eagle shows few if any feathers, while the wings have about half of the feathers visible, depending on the strike. The leaves lack most detail and are in outline form. Scattered, non-disfiguring

1797, Stars 9x7, Small Letters;
BB-72, Bolender-2. Graded VF-20.

marks are normal for this and lower grades. Any major defects should be noted separately.

Illustrated coin: This is the particularly famous Small Letters die (one of three Small Letters dies used for this type) first used in 1795 and last used in 1798. Used on 1795 BB-51, later 1796 BB-62, BB-63, and BB-66 now relapped, 1797 BB-72, and 1798 BB-81. The rims are low, and the eagle is in low relief. For coins struck from this particular reverse die, grading must be done by the obverse only.

F-12, 15 (Fine). *Obverse:* Wear is more extensive than on a Very Fine coin, particularly noticeable on the hair, face, and bosom. The stars appear larger. About half the hair detail remains, most noticeably behind the neck and shoulder. The rim shows wear but is complete or nearly so, with most denticles visible. *Reverse:* Wear is more extensive. Now, feather details are diminished, with relatively few remaining on the wings. The wreath and lettering are worn further, and

1796, Large Date, Small Letters;
BB-65, Bolender-5. Graded F-12.

the rim is usually weak in areas, although most denticles can be seen.

Illustrated coin: This is not the long-lived Small Letters die discussed above; this Small Letters die was used only in 1796. It is distinguished by a piece out of the die at the lower right of the reverse.

VG-8, 10 (Very Good). *Obverse:* The portrait is worn further, with much detail lost in the area above the level of the ear, although the curl over the forehead is delineated. There is some definition at the back of the hair and behind the shoulder, with the hair now combined to form thick strands. The ear is discernible, as is the eye. The stars appear larger still, again an illusion. The rim is weak in areas. LIBERTY and the date are readable and usually full. The rim is worn away in

1796, Small Date, Large Letters;
BB-61, Bolender-4. Graded VG-10.

areas, although many denticles can still be discerned. *Reverse:* The eagle is mostly an outline, with parts blending into the field (on lighter strikes). The rim is worn, as are the letters, with some weak, but the motto is readable.

Illustrated coin: Note the vertical scratches on the cheek.

G-4, 6 (Good). *Obverse:* Wear is more extensive, and some stars may be partly missing. The head is an outline. The eye is visible only in outline form. The rim is well worn or even missing in areas. LIBERTY is worn, and parts of some letters may be missing, but elements of all should be readable. The date is readable, but worn. Usually the date is rather bold. *Reverse:* The eagle is flat and discernible in outline form, and may be blending into the field. The wreath is well worn. Some

1797, Stars 9x7, Large Letters;
BB-73, Bolender-1. Graded G-4.

of the letters may be partly missing (for some shallow-relief dies with low rims). At this level some "averaging" can be done. If the letters are stronger than usual in one area, but some are missing in another area, the coin can still qualify as G-4. This general rule is applicable to most other series as well.

Illustrated coin: This is a well-circulated coin with several edge bumps.

AG-3 (About Good). *Obverse:* Wear is very extensive, but most letters and stars should be discernible. The head is in outline form. The date, while readable, may be partially worn away. *Reverse:* The reverse is well worn, with parts of the wreath and lettering missing. At this level, the reverse usually gives much less information than does the obverse.

1796, Large Date, Small Letters;
BB-65, Bolender-5a. Graded AG-3.

1795, Off-Center Bust

1795, Centered Bust

1796, Small Date

1796, Large Date

Small Letters

Large Letters

1797, 10 Stars Left, 6 Right

1797, 9 Stars Left, 7 Right

1798, 15 Stars on Obverse

1798, 13 Stars on Obverse

	Mintage	Cert	Avg	%MS	AG-3	G-4	VG-8	F-12	VF-20	EF-40	AU-50	MS-60	MS-63
1795, All kinds	42,738												
1795, Off-Center Bust		96	39.6	7%	$960	$1,450	$2,150	$3,500	$5,100	$10,750	$15,500	$60,000	$110,000 (a)
Auctions: $910,625, MS-66, November 2013; $30,550, AU-58, August 2014; $12,925, EF-45, August 2014; $4,406, VF-20, October 2014													
1795, Centered Bust		34	38.0	15%	$960	$1,450	$2,150	$3,500	$5,100	$10,750	$16,500	$55,000	$150,000 (b)
Auctions: $17,625, AU-50, March 2013; $7,638, EF-45, August 2014; $7,050, EF-45, August 2014													
1796, All kinds	79,920												
1796, Small Date, Small Letters (c)		27	37.4	4%	$825	$1,550	$2,100	$3,800	$5,500	$10,750	$15,000	$62,500	$150,000
Auctions: $1,175,000, MS-65, April 2013; $4,406, VF-30, August 2014; $3,290, F-12, October 2014													
1796, Small Date, Large Letters		46	38.9	2%	$825	$1,550	$2,100	$3,800	$5,500	$10,750	$15,000	$75,000	$200,000
Auctions: $352,500, MS-63, November 2013; $7,638, EF-45, August 2014; $5,111, VF-30, September 2014													
1796, Large Date, Small Letters		47	33.8	6%	$825	$1,550	$2,100	$3,400	$5,250	$10,500	$15,000	$62,500	$160,000
Auctions: $12,338, AU-50, August 2014; $13,513, AU-50, August 2013; $3,055, VF-20, August 2014													
1797, All kinds	7,776												
1797, 10 Stars Left, 6 Right		105	39.6	6%	$850	$1,550	$2,000	$3,000	$5,000	$10,000	$14,750	$62,000	$125,000 (d)
Auctions: $440,625, MS-64, November 2013; $4,406, VF-25, August 2014													
1797, 9 Stars Left, 7 Right, Large Letters		185	38.0	5%	$850	$1,550	$2,000	$3,100	$6,000	$10,750	$15,300	$63,000	$135,000
Auctions: $381,875, MS-64, November 2013; $5,288, VF-30, August 2014; $2,820, F-12, August 2014													
1797, 9 Stars Left, 7 Right, Small Letters		35	32.5	3%	$1,200	$1,800	$2,750	$3,900	$8,200	$16,250	$32,500	$110,000	
Auctions: $164,500, MS-62, November 2013; $7,638, VF-20, August 2014													
1798, All kinds (e)	327,536												
1798, 15 Stars on Obverse		32	36.6	6%	$1,100	$1,750	$2,650	$3,800	$8,000	$16,000	$24,500	$84,000	$155,000
Auctions: $258,500, MS-63, November 2013; $6,169, VF-35, August 2014; $9,988, VF-25, August 2014													
1798, 13 Stars on Obverse		31	37.5	6%	$1,000	$1,700	$2,100	$3,500	$7,750	$15,000	$19,800	$76,000	
Auctions: $129,250, AU-58, November 2013; $9,106, EF-40, August 2014													

a. Value in MS-64 is $165,000. b. Value in MS-64 is $250,000. c. 3 varieties. d. Value in MS-64 is $165,000. e. The Mint struck 327,536 silver dollars in 1798, but did not record how many of each type (Small Eagle reverse and Heraldic Eagle reverse).

DRAPED BUST, HERALDIC EAGLE REVERSE (1798–1804)

Designer: *Robert Scot.* **Weight:** *26.96 grams.* **Composition:** *.8924 silver, .1076 copper (net weight .77352 oz. pure silver).* **Diameter:** *Approximately 39–40 mm.* **Edge:** *HUNDRED CENTS ONE DOLLAR OR UNIT with decorations between words.*

Circulation Strike
BB-241, Bolender-6.

Proof (Restrike)
BB-302.

History. The design of the silver dollar closely follows that of other silver coins of the era. The two earliest reverse dies of 1798 have five vertical lines in the stripes in the shield. All dollar dies thereafter have four vertical lines. Production of the Draped Bust dollar continued through early 1804, but in that year the coins were struck from earlier-dated dies.

1804 silver dollars were first struck in 1834 from 1804-dated dies prepared at that time. (As a class these can be called *novodels*, rather than *restrikes*, as no originals were ever made in 1804.) The 1804 dollars were produced in Proof format. Later, probably circa 1859, a new reverse die was made up and combined with the earlier 1804 obverse (made in 1834). Those coins made in 1834 and around that time are today known as Class I dollars, whereas those made with a different reverse, beginning in 1859 and continuing perhaps through the 1870s, are known as Class III. An intermediate variety, from the Class III die combination but with a plain instead of lettered edge, is in the Smithsonian Institution's National Numismatic Collection and is known as Class II. All varieties combined comprise 15 different specimens. The 1804 dollar has been called the "King of American Coins" for well over a century and has achieved great fame. Interested numismatists are directed to *The Fantastic 1804 Dollar, Tribute Edition* (2009).

Striking and Sharpness. Very few of these coins have Full Details. On the obverse, check the highest points of the hair, the details of the drapery, and the centers of the stars. On the reverse, check the shield, the eagle, the stars above the eagle, and the clouds. Examine the denticles on both sides. Planchet adjustment marks are often seen, from overweight blanks being filed down to proper specifications, but they usually are lighter than on the earlier silver dollar types. The relief of the dies and the height of the rims can vary, affecting sharpness. Sharp striking and excellent eye appeal add to the value dramatically. Top-grade MS coins, when found, usually are dated 1800.

Availability. This is the most readily available type among the early silver dollars. Most often seen are the dates 1798 and 1799. Many varieties are available in any grade desired, although MS-63 and 65 coins are elusive. Other die varieties are rare at any level. As with other early dollars, connoisseurship is needed to acquire high-quality coins. These silver dollars usually have problems. To evaluate one for the market it is necessary to grade it, determine its quality of striking, and examine the characteristics of its surface. Nearly all have been dipped or cleaned.

Proofs. There were no Proofs coined in the era this type was issued. Years later, in 1834, the U.S. Mint made up new dies with the 1804 date and struck an unknown number of Proofs, perhaps a dozen or so, for inclusion in presentation Proof sets for foreign dignitaries. Today these are called Class I 1804 dollars. Eight examples are known, one of which shows circulation. The finest by far is the Sultan of Muscat coin, which approaches perfection. Circa 1858 or 1859 the Mint prepared a new obverse die dated 1804 and struck an unknown number of examples for private sale to collectors and dealers—the Class III dollars. No records were kept. These were artificially worn to give them the appearance of original dollars struck in 1804.

Sometime between circa 1858 and the 1870s, the Mint prepared new obverse dies dated 1801, 1802, and 1803, and struck Proof dollars for secret sale to the numismatic market. Many if not most were distributed through J.W. Haseltine, a Philadelphia dealer who had close connections with Mint officials. Today these are known as "Proof restrikes." All are rare, the 1801 being particularly so.

Class I 1804 dollars typically show hairlines and light abrasion. Grading is usually very liberal, in view of the fame of this rarity (not that this is logical). Circulated examples of Class I and Class III 1804 dollars have been graded using prefixes such as EF and AU. Proof restrikes of 1801 to 1803 generally survive in much higher grades, PF-64 or finer.

GRADING STANDARDS

MS-60 to 70 (Mint State). *Obverse:* At MS-60, some abrasion and contact marks are evident, most noticeably on the cheek, the drapery, and the right field. Luster is present, but may be dull or lifeless, and interrupted in patches. At MS-63, contact marks are very few, and abrasion is hard to detect except under magnification. Knowledge of the die variety is desirable, but on balance the portraits on this type are usually quite well struck. An MS-65 coin has no abrasion, and

1798, 10 Arrows; BB-108, Bolender-13. Graded MS-63.

contact marks are so minute as to require magnification. Luster should be full and rich. Coins grading above MS-65 are more theoretical than actual for this type—but they do exist and are defined by having fewer marks as perfection is approached. *Reverse:* Comments apply as for the obverse, except that abrasion and contact marks are most noticeable on the eagle's neck, the tips of the wing, and the tail. The field area is complex, without much open space, given the stars above the eagle, the arrows and olive branch, and other features. Accordingly, marks will not be as noticeable as on the obverse.

Illustrated coin: This coin is well struck, essentially problem free, and with superb eye appeal.

AU-50, 53, 55, 58 (About Uncirculated). *Obverse:* Light wear is seen on the hair area above the ear and extending to left of the forehead, on the ribbon, and on the drapery and bosom, more so at AU-50 than at 53 or 55. An AU-58 coin has minimal traces of wear. An AU-50 coin has luster in protected areas among the stars and letters, with little in the open fields or on the portrait. At AU-58, much luster is present in the fields,

1799, Irregular Date, 13-Star Reverse;
BB-152, Bolender-15. Graded AU-50.

but is worn away on the highest parts of the motifs. *Reverse:* Comments as preceding, except that the eagle's neck, the tips and top of the wings, the clouds, and the tail now show noticeable wear, as do other features. Luster ranges from perhaps 20% remaining in protected areas (at AU-50) to nearly full mint bloom (at AU-58). Sometimes the reverse of this type retains much more luster than the obverse, this being dependent on the height of the rim and the depth of the strike (particularly at the center).

Illustrated coin: This is an attractive and problem-free coin.

EF-40, 45 (Extremely Fine). *Obverse:* More wear is evident on the upper hair area and the ribbon, and on the drapery and bosom. The shoulder is a key spot to check for wear. Excellent detail remains in low-relief areas of the hair. The stars show wear, as do the date and letters. Luster, if present at all, is minimal and in protected areas. *Reverse:* Wear is greater than on an AU coin, overall. The neck has lost its feather detail on the highest points. Feathers have lost some detail near the edges of the wings.

1802, Narrow Normal Date; BB-241, Bolender-6. Graded EF-45.

Some traces of luster may be seen, more so at EF-45 than at EF-40.

Illustrated coin: This is an attractive example retaining some mint luster. It has above-average striking sharpness.

VF-20, 30 (Very Fine). *Obverse:* The higher-relief areas of hair are well worn at VF-20, less so at VF-30. The drapery at the shoulder and the bosom show extensive wear. The stars have more wear, making them appear larger (an optical illusion seen on most worn silver coins of this era). *Reverse:* Wear is greater, including on the shield and the wing feathers. Most of the feathers on the wings are clear. The star centers are flat. Other areas have lost detail as well.

1799; BB-157, Bolender-5. Graded VF-20.

Illustrated coin: Some scratches appear on the portrait. This coin was cleaned long ago and now is retoned. It is a typical early dollar at this grade.

F-12, 15 (Fine). *Obverse:* Wear is more extensive than on a Very Fine coin, particularly on the hair, face, and bosom. The stars appear larger. About half the hair detail remains, most noticeably behind the neck and shoulder. The rim may be partially worn away and blend into the field. *Reverse:* Wear is even more extensive, with the shield and wing feathers being points to observe. Half or slightly more of the feathers will remain clear. The incuse E PLURIBUS UNUM

1798, Pointed 9, Close Date; BB-122, Bolender-14. Graded F-12.

may have a few letters worn away. The clouds all seem to be connected except on varieties in which they are spaced apart. The stars are weak. Parts of the border and lettering may be weak.

Illustrated coin: This coin was cleaned long ago. Cleaning and retoning is common on dollars of this era, but often is not noted by the grading services.

VG-8, 10 (Very Good). *Obverse:* The portrait is mostly seen in outline form, with most hair strands gone, although there is some definition at the back of the hair and behind the shoulder. The ear is discernible, as is the eye. The stars appear larger still, again an illusion. The rim is weak in areas. LIBERTY and the date are readable and usually full, although some letters may be weak at their tops. *Reverse:* Wear is more extensive. Half

1799. Graded VG-8.

or more of the letters in the motto are worn away. Most feathers are worn away, although separation of some of the lower feathers may be seen at the edges of the wings. Some stars are faint or missing. The border blends into the field in areas and some letters are weak. As always, a particular die variety can vary in areas of weakness.

G-4, 6 (Good). *Obverse:* Wear is more extensive, and some stars may be partly missing. The head is an outline. The eye is visible only in outline form. The rim is well worn or even missing in areas. LIBERTY is worn, and parts of some letters may be missing, but elements of all should be readable. The date is readable, but worn. *Reverse:* Wear is more extensive. The upper part of the eagle is flat. The feathers are noticeable only at the lower

1799; BB-169, Bolender-21. Graded G-4.

edge of the wings, sometimes incompletely, and do not have detail. The upper part of the shield is mostly flat. Only a few letters of the motto can be seen, if any at all. The rim is worn extensively, and the letters are well worn, but the inscription should be readable.

Illustrated coin: This coin has some marks, but is respectable for the grade.

AG-3 (About Good). *Obverse:* Wear is so extensive that the coin is barely identifiable. The head is in outline form. LIBERTY is mostly gone; same for the stars. The date, while readable, may be partially worn away. *Reverse:* Extensive wear is seen overall, with the rim worn away and some areas worn smooth. The eagle can be discerned in outline form, but not necessarily completely. A few stray motto letters may remain.

1799. Graded AG-3.

PF-60 to 70 (Proof). *Obverse and Reverse:* For lower Proof levels, extensive abrasion is seen in the fields, or even evidence of circulation (the Mickley example of the 1804 Class I, earlier graded as AU-50, was certified as PF-62 by a leading certification service in 2008). Numbers assigned by grading services have been erratic. No rules are known, and grading has not been consistent.

1804, Class I. Proof.

1798, Knob 9

1798, Pointed 9

1798, Pointed 9, Close Date

1798, Pointed 9, Wide Date

Five Vertical Lines in Shield's Stripes

Four Vertical Lines in Shield's Stripes

1798, Pointed 9, 10 Arrows

1798, Pointed 9, 4 Berries

1799, 99 Over 98, 15-Star Reverse

1799, 99 Over 98, 13-Star Reverse

1799, Irregular Date, 15-Star Reverse

1799, Irregular Date, 13-Star Reverse

1799, Irregular Date

1799, Normal Date

1800, Very Wide Date, Low 8

1800, "Dotted Date"

1799, 8 Stars Left, 5 Stars Right

1800, Only 12 Arrows

1800, AMERICAI

	Mintage	Cert	Avg	%MS	G-4	VG-8	F-12	VF-20	EF-40	AU-50	MS-60	MS-63	MS-65
											PF-63	PF-64	PF-65
1798, Knob 9, 5 Vertical Lines	(a)	3	37.8	0%	$900	$1,150	$1,650	$2,800	$4,700	$8,500	$22,000	$70,000	—
Auctions: $10,063, AU-50, September 2011													
1798, Knob 9, 4 Vertical Lines	(a)	9	44.2	22%	$900	$1,150	$1,650	$2,800	$4,700	$8,800	—		
Auctions: $9,775, AU-50, September 2011													
1798, Knob 9, 10 Arrows	(a)	7	35.5	0%	$900	$1,150	$1,650	$2,800	$4,700	$8,800	—		
Auctions: $7,175, AU-53, September 2013													
1798, Pointed 9, Close Date	(a)	147	36.0	3%	$900	$1,150	$1,650	$2,800	$4,700	$8,800	$22,000	$70,000	$165,000
Auctions: $38,188, MS-62, April 2014; $6,463, AU-53, August 2014; $5,302, AU-50, October 2014; $2,350, VF-25, October 2014													
1798, Pointed 9, Wide Date	(a)	160	34.8	6%	$900	$1,150	$1,650	$2,800	$4,700	$8,500	$22,000	$70,000	$165,000
Auctions: $9,988, AU-58, February 2013; $6,463, AU-50, August 2014; $3,819, EF-45, October 2014; $2,115, VF-30, October 2014													
1798, Pointed 9, 5 Vertical Lines	(a)	49	38.0	2%	$900	$1,150	$1,650	$2,800	$4,700	$8,800	$25,000	—	—
Auctions: $8,225, AU-53, September 2013													
1798, Pointed 9, 10 Arrows	(a)	51	32.9	4%	$950	$1,200	$1,750	$3,100	$4,900	$9,250	$23,500	$80,000	—
Auctions: $10,281, AU-55, August 2013; $4,700, EF-45, November 2014; $4,113, EF-45, July 2014													
1798, Pointed 9, 4 Berries	(a)	27	30.4	0%	$900	$1,150	$1,650	$2,800	$4,700	$8,500	$21,500	$67,500	$165,000
Auctions: $2,703, VF-30, July 2014													
1799, All kinds	423,515												
1799, 99 Over 98, 15-Star Reverse (b)		47	43.9	17%	$960	$1,350	$1,800	$2,850	$5,200	$8,700	$23,000	$57,000	—
Auctions: $141,000, MS-64, November 2013; $29,375, MS-62, August 2014; $4,406, EF-45, September 2014													
1799, 99 Over 98, 13-Star Reverse		34	35.9	9%	$950	$1,250	$1,750	$2,700	$4,700	$8,400	$22,400	$56,500	—
Auctions: $852, F-12, November 2014													
1799, Irregular Date, 15-Star Reverse		15	27.9	0%	$950	$1,150	$1,550	$2,550	$4,700	$8,500	$23,000	—	—
Auctions: $3,055, VF-35, September 2013													
1799, Irregular Date, 13-Star Reverse		26	36.9	8%	$950	$1,150	$1,550	$2,550	$4,700	$8,200	$22,000	$56,500	$190,000
Auctions: $99,875, MS-64, August 2013; $2,409, VF-30, October 2014													
1799, Normal Date		1,821	36.3	5%	$900	$1,150	$1,550	$2,550	$4,700	$8,200	$22,400	$56,500	$190,000
Auctions: $822,500, MS-67, November 2013; $6,698, AU-50, September 2014; $4,994, EF-45, August 2014													
1799, 8 Stars Left, 5 Right		30	40.2	7%	$1,000	$1,350	$1,900	$3,100	$5,750	$13,500	$32,500	$92,500	—
Auctions: $41,125, MS-61, November 2013; $646, VG-8, November 2014													
1800, All kinds	220,920												
1800, Very Wide Date, Low 8		20	37.1	0%	$900	$1,100	$1,600	$2,500	$4,600	$8,500	$24,500	$60,000	
Auctions: $11,750, AU-53, January 2014; $8,813, AU-53, August 2014; $1,763, F-15, August 2014													
1800, "Dotted Date" (c)		34	38.5	12%	$900	$1,150	$1,650	$2,600	$5,200	$8,500	$24,500	$59,000	$190,000
Auctions: $11,750, AU-55, August 2014; $9,988, AU-53, August 2013; $2,350, VF-30, October 2014													
1800, Only 12 Arrows		31	39.1	13%	$900	$1,100	$1,600	$2,500	$4,600	$8,500	$24,500	$60,000	—
Auctions: $6,463, AU-50, September 2013; $1,880, VF-25, August 2014													
1800, Normal Dies		806	36.8	2%	$900	$1,100	$1,600	$2,500	$4,600	$8,500	$24,000	$56,500	$190,000
Auctions: $17,625, AU-58, August 2014; $12,925, AU-55, August 2014; $3,525, EF-40, August 2014; $2,585, VF-35, August 2014													
1800, AMERICAI (d)		40	37.2	10%	$900	$1,100	$1,600	$2,500	$4,600	$8,100	$26,500	—	—
Auctions: $223,250, MS-65, November 2013													

Note: The two earliest reverse dies of 1798 have five vertical lines in the stripes in the shield. All dollar dies thereafter have four vertical lines. **a.** The Mint struck 327,536 silver dollars in 1798, but did not record how many of each type (Small Eagle reverse and Heraldic Eagle reverse). **b.** The engraver of the reverse die accidentally engraved 15 stars, instead of the 13 needed to represent the original Colonies. He attempted to cover the two extra stars under the leftmost and rightmost clouds, but their points stick out slightly. **c.** The "dotted" date is the result of die breaks. **d.** A reverse-die flaw resulted in what appears to be a sans-serif letter I after AMERICA. "Perhaps from a punch or from a stray piece of metal during the die making process" (Bowers, *Silver Dollars & Trade Dollars of the United States*).

1802, 2 Over 1, Narrow Date

1802, 2 Over 1, Wide Date

1802, Narrow Normal Date

1802, Wide Normal Date

1803, Small 3

1803, Large 3

	Mintage	Cert	Avg	%MS	G-4	VG-8	F-12	VF-20	EF-40	AU-50	MS-60	MS-63	MS-65
											PF-63	PF-64	PF-65
1801	54,454	291	37.8	4%	$900	$1,100	$1,600	$2,500	$4,900	$8,350	$29,500	$82,500	$250,000
	Auctions: $329,000, MS-65, November 2013; $3,525, EF-40, October 2014												
1801, Restrike, Proof † (e)	*2 known*	1	66.0									$1,500,000	$2,000,000
	Auctions: No auction records available.												
1802, All kinds	41,650												
1802, 2 Over 1, Narrow Date		18	40.6	11%	$950	$1,200	$1,800	$2,600	$5,000	$9,100	$30,000	$68,500	—
	Auctions: $11,750, AU-58, February 2013; $2,820, VF-20, October 2014												
1802, 2 Over 1, Wide Date		31	34.8	6%	$1,000	$1,250	$1,900	$2,700	$5,250	$11,100	$32,000	$71,000	—
	Auctions: $199,750, MS-64, November 2013; $4,113, EF-40, August 2014; $3,290, VF-20, August 2014												
1802, Narrow Normal Date		54	42.4	17%	$950	$1,200	$1,700	$2,500	$4,900	$8,100	$23,500	$68,500	$240,000
	Auctions: $41,125, MS-61, November 2013; $2,233, EF-40, October 2014; $1,293, F-12, October 2014												
1802, Wide Normal Date		7	41.1	0%	$1,000	$1,250	$1,850	$2,800	$5,000	$10,100	$36,000	$76,000	$300,000
	Auctions: $10,869, AU-55, August 2013												
1802, Restrike, Proof † (e)	*4 known*	3	64.0								$500,000	$700,000	$1,000,000
	Auctions: $920,000, PF-65Cam, April 2008												
1803, All kinds	85,634												
1803, Small 3		61	40.1	8%	$1,000	$1,200	$1,800	$2,800	$5,000	$9,000	$27,000	$71,000	—
	Auctions: $117,500, MS-63, November 2013; $2,585, VF-35, October 2014; $2,350, VF-30, August 2014; $999, F-12, July 2014												
1803, Large 3		65	38.0	5%	$1,000	$1,200	$1,800	$2,800	$5,000	$9,000	$27,000	$71,000	—
	Auctions: $705,000, MS-65, November 2013; $6,463, EF-45, August 2014												
1803, Restrike, Proof † (e)	*3 known*	7	65.6								$500,000	$700,000	$1,000,000
	Auctions: $851,875, PF-66, January 2013												

† Ranked in the *100 Greatest U.S. Coins* (fourth edition). **e.** "The Proof silver dollars of 1801, 1802, and 1803 are all extremely rare, valuable, and desirable, although none of them were made anywhere near the dates on the coins, nor do they share any die characteristics with any real silver dollars made from 1801 to 1803" (*100 Greatest U.S. Coins*, fourth edition).

1804 Dollar, Proof **1804, First Reverse, Proof** **1804, Second Reverse, Proof**

Note the position of the words STATES OF in relation to the clouds.

	Mintage	Cert	Avg	%MS	G-4	VG-8	F-12	VF-20	EF-40	AU-50	MS-60	MS-63	MS-65
											PF-63	PF-64	PF-65
1804, First Reverse, Class I, Proof (f)	8 known	6	50.0								$4,000,000	$4,500,000	$6,000,000
Auctions: $3,877,500, PF-62, August 2013													
1804, Second Reverse, Restrike, Class III, Proof (f)	6 known	4	59.3										
Auctions: $2,300,000, PF-58, April 2009; $1,880,000, PF-55, August 2014													
1804, Second Reverse, Restrike, Plain Edge, Class II, Proof (f,g)	1	0	n/a										
Auctions: No auction records available.													
1804, Electrotype of Unique Plain-Edge Specimen (f,h)	4	0	n/a										
Auctions: No auction records available.													

f. The 1804 dollars as a group are ranked among the *100 Greatest U.S. Coins*. **g.** The plain-edge restrike is in the Smithsonian's National Numismatic Collection. **h.** These electrotypes were made by the U.S. Mint.

GOBRECHT (1836–1839)

No Stars on Obverse, Stars on Reverse (1836):
Designer: *Christian Gobrecht.* **Weight:** *26.96 grams.*
Composition: *.8924 silver, .1076 copper (net weight .77352 oz. pure silver).*
Diameter: *39–40 mm.* **Edge:** *Plain.*

No Stars on Obverse, Stars on Reverse

Stars on Obverse, No Stars on Reverse (1838–1839): **Designer:** *Christian Gobrecht.*
Weight: *26.73 grams.* **Composition:** *.900 silver, .100 copper*
(net weight .77345 oz. pure silver). **Diameter:** *39–40 mm.* **Edge:** *Reeded.*

Stars on Obverse, No Stars on Reverse

History. Suspension of silver dollar coinage was lifted in 1831, but it was not until 1835 that steps were taken to resume their production. Late that year, Mint Director R.M. Patterson had engraver Christian Gobrecht prepare a pair of dies based on motifs by Thomas Sully and Titian Peale. The first obverse die, dated 1836, bore the seated figure of Miss Liberty with the inscription C. GOBRECHT F. ("F." for the Latin word *Fecit*, or "made it") in the field above the date. On the reverse die was a large eagle flying left, surrounded by 26 stars and the legend UNITED STATES OF AMERICA • ONE DOLLAR •. It is unknown whether coins were struck from these dies at that time. A new obverse die with Gobrecht's name on the base of Liberty was prepared, and in December 1836, a thousand plain-edged pieces were struck for circulation. These coins weighed 416 grains, the standard enacted in 1792.

The feeder mechanism that was used, apparently designed for coins of half dollar size or smaller, damaged the reverse die's rim. Attempts were made to solve the problem by rotating the reverse die at various times during the striking run, but this only extended the damage to both sides of the rim. The original 1836 issue is thus known in multiple die alignments:

Die Alignment I—head of Liberty opposite DO in DOLLAR; eagle flying upward.

Die Alignment II—head of Liberty opposite ES in STATES; eagle flying upward.

Die Alignment IV—head of Liberty opposite F in OF; eagle flying level.

Original 1836 die orientation using   *Die alignment of original issues*
either "coin" or "medal" turn.   *dated 1838 and 1839.*

Restrikes were made from the late 1850s through the early 1870s. They were struck using the original obverse die and a different reverse die with cracks through NITED STATES O and OLLA, and in a different alignment:

Die Alignment III—head of Liberty opposite N of ONE; eagle flying level.

In January 1837, the standard weight for the dollar was lowered to 412-1/2 grains, and on January 8, 1837, Benjamin Franklin Peale wrote an internal memorandum to Mint Director Patterson noting, among other things, that the new dollar had received much criticism for looking too medallic, rather than like a coin. Peale felt this was due to the "smooth" edge and suggested striking with a segmented, lettered-edge collar like one he had seen in France. In March 1837, the dies of 1836 were used to strike 600 pieces (whether with plain or reeded edge is unknown). According to reports, the results were unsatisfactory and the coins were destroyed—although a single example, with a reeded edge, is known. It is unclear whether it was part of the March striking, from an earlier 1837 striking caused by the Peale memo, or struck at some later period.

Pattern pieces were struck in 1838 using modified dies with Gobrecht's name removed from the base, 13 stars added to the obverse, and the 26 stars removed from the reverse. These were struck in alignment IV using a reeded-edge collar. In 1839, 300 pieces were struck for circulation, also in alignment IV. Both of these were restruck in alignment III and possibly alignment IV in the late 1850s through early 1870s.

Striking and Sharpness. Striking is usually very good. Check the details on Miss Liberty's head and the higher parts of the eagle. Note that the word LIBERTY is raised.

Availability. 1836 Gobrecht dollars are available in grades from so-called Very Fine upward (the coins were struck as Proofs, and worn examples are properly designated as PF-30, PF-40, and so on; however, sometimes they are found graded as Fine, VF, and EF for levels below PF-50). Most in the marketplace range from PF-50 to 62. Most have contact marks. Truly pristine PF-65 and better examples are very elusive. The demand for these coins is intense. For the 1839, circulated grades typically are PF-50 or higher, often with damage. Pristine Proofs are available, but virtually all are restrikes.

GRADING STANDARDS

PF-60 to 70 (Proof). *Obverse and Reverse:* Many Proofs have been extensively cleaned and have many hairlines and dull fields. This is more applicable to 1836 than to 1839. Grades are PF-60 to 61 or 62. With medium hairlines and good reflectivity, an assigned grade of PF-64 is appropriate, and with relatively few hairlines, Gem PF-65. In various grades hairlines are most easily seen in the obverse field. PF-66 should have hairlines so

1839. Graded PF-65.

delicate that magnification is needed to see them. Above that, a Proof should be free of such lines.

Illustrated coin: This is a restrike made at the Mint in or after spring 1859.

PF-50, 53, 55, 58 (Proof). *Obverse:* Light wear is seen on the thighs and knees, bosom, and head. At PF-58, the Proof surface is extensive, but the open fields show abrasion. At PF-50 and 53, most if not all mirror surface is gone and there are scattered marks. *Reverse:* Wear is most evident on the eagle's breast and the top of the wings. Mirror surface ranges from perhaps 60% complete (at PF-58) to none (at PF-50).

1836. Graded PF-58.

Illustrated coin: This original 1836 Gobrecht dollar, of which 1,000 were coined in 1836, is nicely toned and has excellent eye appeal.

PF-40 to 45 (Proof). *Obverse:* Further wear is seen on all areas, especially the thighs and knees, bosom, and head. The center of LIBERTY, which is in relief, is weak. Most at this level and lower are the 1836 issues. *Reverse:* Further wear is evident on the eagle, including the back edge of the closest wing, the top of the farthest wing, and the tail.

1836. Graded PF-45.

PF-20, 25, 30, 35 (Proof). *Obverse:* Further wear is seen. Many details of the gown are worn away, but the lower-relief areas above and to the right of the shield remain well defined. Hair detail is mostly or completely gone. LIBERTY is weak at the center. *Reverse:* Even more wear is evident on the eagle, with only about 60% of the feathers visible.

1836. Graded PF-20.

	Cert	Avg	%MS	PF-20	PF-40	PF-50	PF-60	PF-62	PF-63	PF-64	PF-65
1836. C. GOBRECHT F. on base. Judd-60. Plain edge, no stars on obverse, stars in field on reverse. Die alignment I, ↑↓. Circulation issue. 1,000 struck (a)	140	55.1		$12,500	$15,000	$20,000	$24,500	$30,000	$45,000	$75,000	$150,000
Auctions: $29,900, PF-62, April 2012											
1836. As above. Plain edge. Judd-60. Die alignment II and die alignment IV, ↑↑. Circulation issue struck in 1837. 600 struck (a)	(b)			$13,000	$16,000	$21,000	$25,000	$30,000	$45,000	$75,000	$150,000
Auctions: $16,100, PF-58, March 2012											

a. Originals. Although these are listed in Judd as patterns, they are considered circulation strikes. b. Included in 1836, C. GOBRECHT F. on base, certified population.

	Cert	Avg	%MS	PF-20	PF-40	PF-50	PF-60	PF-62	PF-63	PF-64	PF-65
1838. Obverse stars added around border, reeded edge. Judd-84. Designer's name removed. Reverse eagle flying in plain field. Die alignment IV, ↑↑.	21	62.3					$70,000	$75,000	$80,000	$100,000	$150,000
Auctions: $83,375, PF-64, July 2008											
1839. As above. Reeded edge. Judd-104. Die alignment IV, ↑↑. Circulation issue. 300 struck	47	62.7		$15,000	$17,500	$22,500	$29,000	$38,500	$55,000	$80,000	$150,000
Auctions: $18,975, PF-45, November 2011											

Restrike

	Cert	Avg	%MS	PF-20	PF-40	PF-50	PF-60	PF-62	PF-63	PF-64	PF-65
1836. Name below base; eagle in starry field; plain edge. Judd-58. Die alignment III, ↑↓, and die alignment IV, ↑↑. (a)	10 (b)	64.1		$17,500	$30,000	$70,000	$75,000	$75,500	$100,000	$125,000	$150,000
Auctions: $34,500, PF-63, April 2012											
1836. Name on base; plain edge. Judd 60. Die alignment III, ↑↓. (a,c)	(d)			$15,000	$20,000	$23,500	$26,000	$35,000	$55,000	$90,000	$150,000
Auctions: $18,975, PF-61, September 2010											
1836. C. GOBRECHT F. on base. Judd-61. Reeded edge. No stars on obverse, stars in field on reverse. Die alignment IV, ↑↑. (a)	0	n/a		*(extremely rare)*							
Auctions: $195,000, PF-63, May 2003											
1838. Designer's name removed; reeded edge. Judd-84. Die alignment III, ↑↓, and die alignment IV, ↑↑. (a)	(d)			$25,000	$30,000	$35,000	$47,500	$62,500	$85,000	$125,000	
Auctions: $83,375, PF-64, March 2012											
1839. Designer's name removed; eagle in plain field; reeded edge. Judd-104. Die alignment III, ↑↓, and die alignment IV, ↑↑. (a)	(d)			$20,000	$25,000	$37,500	$42,500	$50,000	$65,000	$100,000	
Auctions: $51,750, PF-64, April 2012											

Note: Restrikes were produced from the late 1850s to the 1870s, and are not official Mint issues. They were all oriented in either die alignment III (coin turn) or die alignment IV (medal turn), with the eagle flying level. Almost all were struck from a cracked reverse die. For detailed analysis of these pieces, consult *United States Pattern Coins*, tenth edition. **a.** Restrikes. Listed in Judd as patterns. **b.** Many originals were certified as restrikes in years past. This figure includes some of these originals. **c.** 30 to 40 are known. **d.** Included in figure for first listing with this Judd number, as the grading services do not consistently distinguish between originals and restrikes.

LIBERTY SEATED (1840–1873)

No Motto (1840–1865): **Designer:** *Christian Gobrecht.* **Weight:** *26.73 grams.*
Composition: *.900 silver, .100 copper (net weight .77344 oz. pure silver).*
Diameter: *38.1 mm.* **Edge:** *Reeded.* **Mints:** *Philadelphia, New Orleans, San Francisco.*

Mintmark location
is on the reverse,
below the eagle,
for all varieties.

No Motto
(1840–1865)

No Motto, Proof

With Motto IN GOD WE TRUST (1866–1873): **Designer:** *Christian Gobrecht.*
Weight: *26.73 grams.* **Composition:** *.900 silver, .100 copper (net weight .77344 oz. pure silver).*
Diameter: *38.1 mm.* **Edge:** *Reeded.* **Mints:** *Philadelphia, Carson City, San Francisco.*

With Motto
IN GOD
WE TRUST
(1866–1873)a

With Motto
IN GOD
WE TRUST,
Proof

History. The Liberty Seated dollar was minted every year from 1840 to 1873, with an obverse design modified from that of the 1839 Gobrecht dollar. On the reverse, the flying eagle of the Gobrecht dollar was replaced with a perched eagle similar to that of contemporary quarter and half dollars. The dollars, minted in modest numbers, circulated in the United States through 1850. In that year the rising value of silver on the international markets brought the cost of minting each coin to more than $1. Production continued for the international, rather than domestic, market, through 1873, when the trade dollar took the Liberty Seated dollar's place.

Striking and Sharpness. On the obverse, check the head of Miss Liberty and the centers of the stars. On the reverse, check the feathers of the eagle. The denticles usually are sharp. Dollars of 1857 usually are weakly struck, but have semi-prooflike surfaces. The word LIBERTY is in a high-relief area on the coin, with the result that it wore away quickly. Therefore this feature cannot be used as the only guide to grading an obverse. From EF downward, strike sharpness in the stars and the head does not matter to connoisseurs. Proof coins were made for all dates. All of 1851 and 1853 are restrikes, as are most of 1852. In 1858 only Proofs were struck, to the extent of an estimated 210 pieces, with no related circulation strikes. Most early dates were restruck at the Mint, augmenting the supply of originals. Nearly all Proofs are very well struck.

Availability. All issues from 1840 to 1850 are available in proportion to their mintages. Those of 1851 to the late 1860s are either scarce or rare in circulated grades, and in MS they range from rare to extremely rare, despite generous mintages in some instances. The later-date coins were shipped to China and later melted. Coins of the 1870s are more readily available, although some are scarce to rare. Today, Proofs from 1858 to 1873 are readily available, but high-quality examples with superb eye appeal are in the minority. Most Proofs prior to 1860 survive only in grades below PF-65 if strict grading is applied.

GRADING STANDARDS

MS-60 to 70 (Mint State). *Obverse:* At MS-60, some abrasion and contact marks are evident, most noticeably on the bosom and thighs and knees. Luster is present, but may be dull or lifeless. At MS-63, contact marks are very few, and abrasion is minimal. An MS-65 coin has no abrasion in the fields (but may have a hint on the knees), and contact marks are trivial. Check the knees of Liberty and the right field. Luster should be full and

1864. Graded MS-65.

rich on later issues, not necessarily so for dates in the 1840s. Most Mint State coins of the 1861 to 1865 years, Philadelphia issues, have extensive die striae (from not completely finishing the die). *Reverse:* Comments apply as for the obverse, except that in lower Mint State grades, abrasion and marks are most noticeable on the eagle's head, the neck, the claws, and the top of the wings (harder to see there, however). At MS-65 or higher, there are no marks visible to the unaided eye. The field is mainly protected by design elements and does not show abrasion as much as does the obverse on a given coin.

    Illustrated coin: The fields show striations from incomplete polishing of the dies, but this does not affect the grade.

AU-50, 53, 55, 58 (About Uncirculated). *Obverse:* Light wear is seen on the thighs and knees, bosom, and head. At AU-58, the luster is extensive but incomplete, especially in the right field. At AU-50 and 53, luster is less. *Reverse:* Wear is visible on the eagle's neck, the claws, and the top of the wings. An AU-58 coin has nearly full luster. At AU-50 and 53, there still are traces of luster.

    Illustrated coin: This is an attractive example with much of the original luster.

1842. Graded AU-58.

EF-40, 45 (Extremely Fine). *Obverse:* Further wear is seen on all areas, especially the thighs and knees, bosom, and head. Little or no luster is seen on most coins. From this grade downward, strike sharpness in the stars and the head does not matter to connoisseurs. *Reverse:* Further wear is evident on the eagle's neck, claws, and the wings, although on well-struck coins nearly all details are sharp.

1846. Graded EF-40.

VF-20, 30 (Very Fine). *Obverse:* Further wear is seen. Many details of the gown are worn away, but the lower-relief areas above and to the right of the shield remain well defined. Hair detail is mostly or completely gone. The word LIBERTY is weak at BE (PCGS allows BER to be missing "on some coins"). *Reverse:* Wear is more extensive, with some feathers blended together, especially on the neck for a typical coin. Detail remains quite good overall.

1854. Graded VF-20.

F-12, 15 (Fine). *Obverse:* The seated figure is well worn, but with some detail above and to the right of the shield. BER in LIBERTY is visible only in part or missing entirely. *Reverse:* Wear is extensive, with about a third to half of the feathers flat or blended with others.

    Illustrated coin: The reverse is stronger than the obverse on this coin.

1872-CC. Graded F-12.

VG-8, 10 (Very Good). *Obverse:* The seated figure is more worn, but some detail can be seen above and to the right of the shield. The shield is discernible, but the upper-right section may be flat and blended into the seated figure. In LIBERTY two or three letters, or a combination totaling that, are readable. *Reverse.* Further wear has flattened half or slightly more of the feathers (depending on the strike). The rim is visible all around, as

1871-CC. Graded VG-8.

are the ends of the denticles. A Very Good Liberty Seated dollar usually has more detail overall than a lower-denomination coin of the same design.

G-4, 6 (Good). *Obverse:* The seated figure is worn nearly smooth. The stars and date are complete, but may be weak toward the periphery. *Reverse:* The eagle shows only a few details of the shield and feathers. The rim is worn down. The tops of the border letters are weak or worn away, although the inscription can still be read.

1850-O. Graded G-6.

AG-3 (About Good). *Obverse:* The seated figure is visible in outline form. Much or all of the rim is worn away. The stars are weak and some may be missing. The date remains clear. *Reverse:* The border letters are partially worn away. The eagle is mostly in outline form, but with a few details discernible. The rim is weak or missing.

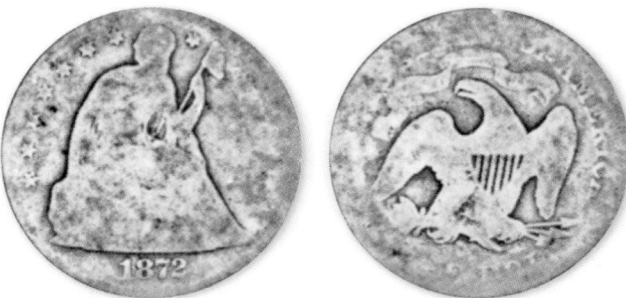

1872. Graded AG-3.

PF-60 to 70 (Proof). *Obverse and Reverse:* Proofs that are extensively cleaned and have many hairlines, or that are dull and grainy, are lower level, such as PF-60 to 62. These are not widely desired, except for use as fillers for the dates (most circulation-strike dollars are rare after 1849 and before 1870). The rarities of 1851, 1852, and 1858 are in demand no matter what the grade. With medium hairlines and good reflectivity, an assigned

1861. Graded PF-63.

grade of PF-64 is appropriate, and with relatively few hairlines, gem PF-65. In various grades hairlines are most easily seen in the obverse field. PF-66 should have hairlines so delicate that magnification is needed to see them. Above that, a Proof should be free of such lines.

   Illustrated coin: The frosty cameo motifs on this example contrast with the deeply mirrored fields.

1851, Original,
High Date

1851, Restrike,
Proof
Date is centered.

1852, Original

1852, Restrike,
Proof

	Mintage	Cert	Avg	%MS	VG-8	F-12	VF-20	EF-40	AU-50	MS-60	MS-63	MS-65
										PF-60	PF-63	PF-65
1840	61,005	268	50.8	26%	$350	$375	$475	$750	$1,300	$4,500	$19,000	$110,000
Auctions: $18,800, MS-63, June 2014; $11,163, MS-62, September 2014; $5,875, MS-61, August 2014; $2,115, AU-55, August 2014												
1840, Proof	*40–60*	27	63.3							$20,000	$29,000	$85,000
Auctions: $85,188, PF-64Cam, April 2013												
1841	173,000	248	50.6	20%	$325	$350	$450	$700	$1,000	$2,650	$8,000	$90,000
Auctions: $30,550, MS-64, February 2014; $35,250, MS-64, October 2014; $3,525, MS-62, August 2014; $588, AU-50, October 2014												
1841, Proof	*10–15*	4	63.0							$25,000	$70,000	$250,000
Auctions: $94,000, PF-64, October 2014; $141,000, PF-64, April 2013												
1842	184,618	562	49.5	14%	$300	$325	$425	$600	$950	$2,400	$5,750	$90,000
Auctions: $12,925, MS-64, August 2013; $1,998, AU-58, October 2014; $1,058, AU-55, July 2014; $1,293, AU-55, August 2014												
1842, Proof	*10–15*	8	63.3							$20,000	$45,000	$125,000
Auctions: $57,281, PF-65, August 2013												
1843	165,100	468	49.1	13%	$300	$325	$425	$600	$950	$2,600	$8,000	$100,000
Auctions: $51,406, MS-64, June 2014; $5,288, MS-63, September 2014; $3,055, MS-62, November 2014; $881, AU-53, August 2014												
1843, Proof	*10–15*	7	63.3							$17,000	$35,000	$110,000
Auctions: $52,875, PF-64, August 2013												
1844	20,000	153	51.9	14%	$300	$350	$425	$800	$1,500	$5,000	$16,000	$100,000
Auctions: $41,125, MS-64, June 2013; $11,750, MS-63, October 2014; $1,733, AU-55, September 2014; $4,113, AU-55, October 2014												
1844, Proof	*10–15*	8	63.9							$15,000	$35,000	$110,000
Auctions: $70,500, PF-65, April 2013; $44,063, PF-64, October 2014												
1845	24,500	173	50.5	11%	$325	$375	$450	$800	$1,500	$9,000	$30,000	$150,000
Auctions: $2,820, AU-58, March 2014; $9,988, AU-58, August 2014; $2,233, AU-55, October 2014; $2,233, AU-55, November 2014												
1845, Proof	*10–15*	11	63.9							$14,000	$30,000	$100,000
Auctions: $141,000, PF-67, August 2013												

	Mintage	Cert	Avg	%MS	VG-8	F-12	VF-20	EF-40	AU-50	MS-60 PF-60	MS-63 PF-63	MS-65 PF-65
1846	110,600	472	51.0	17%	$300	$325	$425	$650	$1,100	$2,500	$6,000	$90,000
	Auctions: $105,750, MS-65, November 2013; $8,225, MS-64, November 2014; $2,233, MS-61, November 2014											
1846, Proof	10–15	13	62.8							$14,000	$30,000	$105,000
	Auctions: $94,000, PF-66, April 2013											
1846O	59,000	171	47.0	12%	$300	$375	$450	$800	$1,400	$7,250	$20,000	$100,000
	Auctions: $35,309, MS-64, November 2014; $17,625, MS-63, June 2014; $2,062, AU-55, October 2014; $1,116, EF-45, August 2014											
1847	140,750	481	51.3	16%	$300	$325	$425	$600	$850	$2,700	$6,900	$90,000
	Auctions: $6,463, MS-64, October 2014; $4,406, MS-63, April 2014; $1,050, AU-58, August 2014; $1,146, AU-55, October 2014											
1847, Proof	10–15	16	63.9							$16,000	$26,000	$65,000
	Auctions: $35,250, PF-65, October 2014; $41,125, PF-65, April 2013											
1848	15,000	86	50.0	12%	$375	$500	$700	$1,100	$1,700	$4,750	$15,000	$115,000
	Auctions: $5,993, MS-61, September 2014; $5,288, AU-58, August 2013; $999, AU-50, November 2014; $1,763, EF-45, August 2014											
1848, Proof	10–15	10	64.2							$16,000	$31,000	$90,000
	Auctions: $117,500, PF-67, August 2013											
1849	62,600	281	53.7	26%	$300	$325	$425	$700	$1,100	$2,600	$7,000	$90,000
	Auctions: $11,163, MS-64, June 2014; $29,375, MS-64+, August 2014; $852, MS-60, September 2014; $1,359, AU-58, October 2014											
1849, Proof	10–15	9	63.9							$19,000	$34,000	$115,000
	Auctions: $129,250, PF-67, April 2013											
1850	7,500	110	54.7	31%	$550	$750	$1,100	$1,800	$2,250	$6,900	$16,000	$90,000
	Auctions: $14,688, MS-63, April 2014; $14,688, MS-63, July 2014; $12,925, MS-63, October 2014; $7,638, MS-61, August 2014											
1850, Proof	20–30	17	64.1							$16,500	$28,000	$65,000
	Auctions: $51,406, PF-66, August 2013; $19,975, PF-64, October 2014											
1850O	40,000	140	44.6	11%	$350	$500	$750	$1,450	$3,200	$13,500	$25,000	$120,000
	Auctions: $105,750, MS-64, August 2013; $28,200, MS-63, October 2014; $11,756, MS-61, November 2014											
1851, Original, High Date † (a)	1,300	26	61.1	73%	$7,500	$10,500	$15,000	$20,000	$27,500	$35,000	$65,000	$140,000
	Auctions: $41,125, MS-60, August 2014; $70,500, AU-58, August 2013											
1851, Restrike, Proof (a)	35–50	18	62.9							$21,000	$31,000	$80,000
	Auctions: $99,875, PF-65Cam, April 2014											
1852, Original † (a)	1,100	19	59.8	68%	$6,000	$10,000	$13,500	$17,500	$27,500	$40,000	$60,000	$140,000
	Auctions: $34,075, AU-58, June 2014; $23,500, AU-50, September 2014											
1852, Original, Proof (a)	20–30	3	64.5							$35,000	$43,500	$77,500
	Auctions: $57,500, PF-65Cam, January 2009											
1852, Restrike, Proof (a)	20–30	13	63.4							$17,500	$30,000	$75,000
	Auctions: $70,500, PF-65, June 2014											
1853	46,110	145	58.4	54%	$350	$450	$650	$1,100	$1,600	$3,200	$7,250	$85,000
	Auctions: $129,250, MS-66, October 2014; $10,575, MS-64, October 2014; $3,819, MS-61, August 2013; $2,233, AU-53, July 2014											
1853, Restrike, Proof (b)	15–20	6	63.8							$21,000	$37,000	$110,000
	Auctions: $99,875, PF-66Cam, October 2014; $152,750, PF-66Cam, August 2013; $105,750, PF-66, October 2014											
1854	33,140	46	55.6	43%	$1,500	$2,500	$3,000	$4,150	$5,500	$9,000	$15,000	$95,000
	Auctions: $4,994, MS-60, September 2014; $9,993, AU-55, March 2014; $4,700, VF-35, July 2014											
1854, Proof	40–60	17	63.8							$13,500	$16,500	$57,500
	Auctions: $49,938, PF-66, April 2013; $15,275, PF-62, August 2014											
1855	26,000	59	53.9	32%	$1,250	$1,500	$2,250	$4,000	$4,750	$7,500	$25,000	$90,000
	Auctions: $141,000, MS-64, June 2014; $7,050, AU-53, July 2014; $5,875, AU-50, October 2014; $3,819, EF-40, August 2014											
1855, Proof	40–60	19	63.9							$12,000	$16,000	$42,500
	Auctions: $45,531, PF-66, August 2013											

† Ranked in the *100 Greatest U.S. Coins* (fourth edition). **a.** Silver dollars of 1851 are found in two formats: originals struck for circulation and Proof restrikes made years later. Silver dollars of 1852 are found in these formats and also as original Proofs. "As part of [Mint Director] James Ross Snowden's restriking activities in 1859, Proof examples of certain rare silver dollars of earlier dates were made, including the 1851 and 1852. For the 1851 dollar, the original die (with four-date digit logotype slanting slightly upward and the date close to the base of Liberty) probably could not be located in 1859. In any event, a different die, not originally used in 1851, with the date horizontal and centered, was employed. Whether this die was created new in 1859 and given an 1851 date, or whether it was made in 1851 and not used at that time, is not known" (*United States Pattern Coins*, tenth edition). **b.** Made at the Mint from postdated dies circa 1862.

	Mintage	Cert	Avg	%MS	VG-8	F-12	VF-20	EF-40	AU-50	MS-60 / PF-60	MS-63 / PF-63	MS-65 / PF-65
1856	63,500	56	53.3	36%	$425	$525	$750	$1,600	$3,500	$5,000	$15,000	$85,000
	Auctions: $14,100, MS-64, October 2014; $6,463, MS-62, September 2014; $5,875, AU-55, June 2014; $1,645, AU-50, August 2014											
1856, Proof	40–60	37	63.7							$6,350	$13,000	$32,500
	Auctions: $30,550, PF-65, October 2014; $27,025, PF-65, April 2013											
1857	94,000	85	58.6	68%	$425	$525	$750	$1,550	$1,900	$3,250	$9,250	$85,000
	Auctions: $99,875, MS-66, January 2014; $16,450, MS-64, September 2014; $2,820, MS-60, November 2014											
1857, Proof	50–70	30	63.9							$7,000	$13,500	$33,500
	Auctions: No auction records available.											
1858, Proof (c)	300	72	62.4							$10,000	$14,000	$38,000
	Auctions: $41,125, PF-66, August 2013; $11,456, PF-63, October 2014; $9,988, PF-62, August 2014											
1859	255,700	76	55.4	43%	$325	$425	$525	$750	$1,225	$2,500	$6,000	$85,000
	Auctions: $15,275, MS-64, June 2014; $1,175, AU-50, November 2014; $529, AU-50, November 2014; $940, EF-45, November 2014											
1859, Proof	800	150	63.9							$2,400	$4,750	$20,000
	Auctions: $4,700, PF-63Cam, July 2014; $82,250, PF-67, August 2013; $22,325, PF-66, October 2014; $4,700, PF-64, October 2014											
1859O	360,000	597	53.7	49%	$300	$325	$425	$600	$850	$2,050	$5,150	$65,000
	Auctions: $41,125, MS-65, June 2014; $2,820, MS-63, August 2014; $3,672, MS-62+, August 2014; $2,115, MS-61, November 2014											
1859S	20,000	138	47.2	17%	$415	$550	$850	$1,700	$3,350	$13,000	$29,000	$130,000
	Auctions: $28,200, MS-63, June 2014; $3,055, AU-53, November 2014; $2,115, AU-50, October 2014; $3,290, AU-50, November 2014											
1860	217,600	115	56.7	51%	$300	$400	$525	$650	$850	$2,100	$5,100	$75,000
	Auctions: $7,638, MS-64, July 2014; $8,225, MS-64, October 2014; $1,645, AU-55, September 2014; $1,116, AU-50, November 2014											
1860, Proof	1,330	156	63.7							$2,400	$4,750	$15,000
	Auctions: $64,625, PF-67, April 2013; $5,728, PF-63, August 2014											
1860O	515,000	880	54.8	55%	$300	$325	$425	$600	$785	$1,900	$3,750	$60,000
	Auctions: $76,375, MS-65+, August 2014; $39,656, MS-65, October 2014; $10,575, MS-64, February 2013; $2,585, MS-63+, July 2014											
1861	77,500	71	56.4	62%	$775	$1,100	$1,400	$2,250	$3,000	$3,450	$5,850	$65,000
	Auctions: $12,338, MS-64, March 2014; $8,225, MS-64, November 2014; $3,819, AU-55, August 2014; $2,468, AU-50, October 2014											
1861, Proof	1,000	101	63.4							$2,400	$4,600	$15,000
	Auctions: $4,994, PF-63Cam+, September 2014; $76,375, PF-66, June 2014											
1862	11,540	90	55.8	64%	$700	$1,100	$1,400	$1,650	$2,650	$3,575	$6,300	$65,000
	Auctions: $31,725, MS-64, June 2014; $12,925, MS-64, November 2014; $3,525, AU-53, August 2014; $3,525, EF-40, November 2014											
1862, Proof	550	167	63.3							$2,400	$4,750	$15,000
	Auctions: $18,800, PF-65DCam, September 2014; $52,875, PF-67Cam, January 2014; $4,406, PF-63Cam, November 2014											
1863	27,200	82	55.1	60%	$800	$1,100	$1,200	$1,600	$2,000	$3,575	$7,000	$65,000
	Auctions: $58,750, MS-65, October 2014; $17,625, MS-64, August 2013; $2,585, AU-55, August 2014; $1,763, AU-50, October 2014											
1863, Proof	460	141	63.2							$2,400	$4,750	$18,000
	Auctions: $129,250, PF-69, April 2013; $9,988, PF-65, August 2014											
1864	30,700	79	49.8	28%	$425	$500	$700	$1,000	$1,600	$3,575	$7,500	$60,000
	Auctions: $5,581, AU-58, August 2014; $3,525, AU-55, February 2013; $1,410, AU-50, September 2014; $1,645, VF-35, October 2014											
1864, Proof	470	155	63.5							$2,400	$4,750	$15,000
	Auctions: $52,875, PF-68, April 2013											
1865 (d)	46,500	75	52.0	39%	$400	$450	$650	$1,600	$2,100	$3,000	$7,500	$80,000
	Auctions: $25,850, MS-64, June 2014; $2,703, AU-55, August 2014; $1,058, AU-50, October 2014; $1,880, EF-40, August 2014											
1865, Proof	500	184	63.9							$2,400	$4,750	$15,000
	Auctions: $16,450, PF-65Cam, October 2014; $30,550, PF-67, February 2013; $3,290, PF-60, July 2014											

c. Proof only. d. There is a common doubled-die reverse variety for 1865, which does not command a premium in today's market. "Doubling is evident only on the U of UNITED. . . . This is probably the most common variety for this date" (*Cherrypickers' Guide to Rare Die Varieties*, sixth edition, volume II).

1869, Repunched Date
FS-S1-1869-302.
Other varieties exist.

	Mintage	Cert	Avg	%MS	VG-8	F-12	VF-20	EF-40	AU-50	MS-60 PF-60	MS-63 PF-63	MS-65 PF-65
1866	48,900	100	52.5	37%	$300	$390	$550	$850	$1,100	$2,300	$5,500	$65,000
Auctions: $79,313, MS-65, October 2014; $1,880, MS-60, March 2014; $2,233, AU-58, August 2014; $881, AU-50, October 2014
1866, Proof	725	237	63.6							$2,100	$3,800	$14,000
Auctions: $44,063, PF-67DCam, April 2013; $22,325, PF-65DCam, October 2014; $2,820, PF-62Cam, September 2014
1866, No Motto, Proof † (e)	2 known	2	64.3								—	
Auctions: No auction records available.
1867	46,900	65	50.9	40%	$300	$365	$525	$850	$1,050	$2,200	$5,300	$70,000
Auctions: $1,645, AU-53, June 2014; $499, EF-40, October 2014; $306, VF-20, October 2014; $317, VF-20, November 2014
1867, Proof	625	217	63.4							$2,100	$3,900	$14,000
Auctions: $23,500, PF-65DCam, April 2014; $11,750, PF-65Cam, August 2014; $4,994, PF-64, July 2014
1868	162,100	102	49.1	18%	$300	$350	$475	$800	$1,150	$2,400	$7,000	$65,000
Auctions: $30,550, MS-64, June 2014; $558, VF-30, July 2014; $499, VF-25, October 2014; $212, VG-8, September 2014
1868, Proof	600	203	63.7							$2,100	$3,800	$14,000
Auctions: $52,875, PF-67DCam, August 2013; $8,813, PF-64, October 2014; $1,763, PF-61, October 2014
1869	423,700	124	51.8	35%	$300	$340	$425	$750	$1,050	$2,300	$5,250	$65,000
Auctions: $76,375, MS-65, October 2014; $9,988, MS-64, June 2014; $4,406, MS-63, September 2014
1869, Repunched Date (f)	(g)	0	n/a						$1,100	$2,750	$7,000	
Auctions: $4,406, MS-62, October 2014
1869, Proof	600	204	63.6							$2,100	$3,800	$14,000
Auctions: $9,988, PF-64DCam, October 2014; $6,463, PF-64Cam, October 2014; $5,875, PF-64Cam, November 2014
1870	415,000	213	49.4	27%	$300	$325	$425	$600	$950	$2,100	$4,750	$55,000
Auctions: $105,750, MS-66, August 2014; $76,375, MS-65, January 2014; $3,819, MS-63, November 2014
1870, Proof	1,000	219	63.3							$2,100	$3,800	$14,000
Auctions: $39,363, PF-67DCam, November 2014; $5,288, PF-64Cam, November 2014; $44,063, PF-66, January 2014
1870CC	11,758	210	41.8	9%	$800	$1,400	$2,250	$4,250	$8,000	$26,000	$40,000	—
Auctions: $117,500, MS-64, October 2014; $70,500, MS-62, January 2014; $14,688, AU-58, August 2014; $7,638, AU-53, October 2014
1870S †	(h)	4	47.0	0%	$200,000	$275,000	$450,000	$650,000	$1,000,000	$1,500,000	—	—
Auctions: $763,750, EF-40, January 2014
1871	1,073,800	700	46.8	22%	$300	$325	$425	$600	$1,050	$2,100	$4,650	$50,000
Auctions: $57,281, MS-65, June 2014; $8,225, MS-64, July 2014; $6,756, MS-64, October 2014; $7,050, MS-63, August 2014
1871, Proof	960	195	63.0							$2,100	$3,800	$14,000
Auctions: $25,850, PF-66DCam, July 2014; $8,225, PF-64DCam, August 2014; $23,500, PF-66Cam, September 2014
1871CC	1,376	47	41.6	9%	$3,500	$4,850	$7,250	$15,000	$24,500	$75,000	$175,000	—
Auctions: $82,250, MS-61, June 2014; $15,428, EF-45, August 2014; $3,525, EF-40, September 2014; $3,290, F-12, July 2014

† Ranked in the *100 Greatest U.S. Coins* (fourth edition). **e.** The 1866, No Motto, dollar is classified as Judd-540 (*United States Pattern Coins*). Two examples of this fantasy piece are known; at least one was deliberately struck for pharmacist and coin collector Robert Coulton Davis, likely around 1869 or in the early 1870s, along with the No Motto Proof quarter and half dollar of the same date. The three-coin set is on display at the American Numismatic Association's Edward C. Rochette Money Museum in Colorado Springs. "A second 1866 'No Motto' silver dollar resurfaced in the 1970s before entering a private Midwestern collection in the early 1980s. After not meeting its auction reserve price in September 2003, the coin was sold privately for nearly a million dollars some time later" (*100 Greatest U.S. Coins*, fourth edition).
f. There are several repunched dates known for 1869. The one listed is FS-S1-1869-302. The top flag of a secondary 1 is evident midway between the primary 1 and the 8. **g.** Included in circulation-strike 1869 mintage figure. **h.** The Mint shows no record of 1870-S dollars being struck, but about a dozen are known to exist. The 1870-S silver dollars may have been struck as mementos of the laying of the cornerstone of the San Francisco Mint (May 25, 1870).

	Mintage	Cert	Avg	%MS	VG-8	F-12	VF-20	EF-40	AU-50	MS-60 PF-60	MS-63 PF-63	MS-65 PF-65
1872	1,105,500	516	44.9	19%	$300	$325	$425	$600	$950	$2,050	$4,950	$50,000
Auctions: $38,188, MS-65, October 2014; $58,750, MS-65, October 2013; $7,050, MS-64, July 2014; $2,115, MS-61, October 2014												
1872, Proof	950	177	63.2							$2,100	$3,850	$14,000
Auctions: $32,900, PF-66Cam, April 2013; $11,750, PF-65+, October 2014												
1872CC	3,150	79	43.6	18%	$3,000	$4,500	$5,000	$8,500	$13,000	$28,000	$100,000	$300,000
Auctions: $111,625, MS-64, October 2014; $44,063, MS-62, April 2014; $35,250, MS-62, August 2014; $27,613, MS-61, September 2014												
1872S	9,000	110	44.0	13%	$500	$675	$950	$1,975	$3,500	$12,000	$37,500	
Auctions: $24,675, MS-63, October 2014; $19,975, MS-62, July 2014; $8,225, MS-61, August 2014												
1873	293,000	169	52.9	41%	$375	$400	$450	$600	$975	$2,100	$4,850	$60,000
Auctions: $52,875, MS-65, July 2014; $1,296, AU-53, October 2014; $431, EF-40, July 2014; $388, VF-35, July 2014												
1873, Proof	600	194	63.4							$2,100	$3,800	$14,000
Auctions: $35,250, PF-66DCam, August 2013; $16,450, PF-65Cam+, August 2014; $3,290, PF-63Cam, August 2014; $5,581, PF-64+, September 2014												
1873CC	2,300	26	43.4	15%	$7,000	$11,000	$18,500	$28,000	$41,500	$115,000	$190,000	$500,000
Auctions: $64,625, AU-55, March 2014; $35,250, EF-45, November 2014; $18,213, VF-25, July 2014; $8,225, F-12, September 2014												
1873S (i)	700	0	n/a									
Auctions: No auction records available.												

i. The 1873-S is unknown in any collection, public or private, despite Mint records indicating that 700 were struck. None have ever been seen.

MORGAN (1878–1921)

Designer: *George T. Morgan.* **Weight:** *26.73 grams.* **Composition:** *.900 silver, .100 copper (net weight .77344 oz. pure silver).* **Diameter:** *38.1 mm.* **Edge:** *Reeded.* **Mints:** *Philadelphia, New Orleans, Carson City, Denver, San Francisco.*

Mintmark location is on the reverse, below the bow.

Circulation Strike

Proof

History. The Morgan dollar, named for English-born designer George T. Morgan, was struck every year from 1878 to 1904, and again in 1921. The coin's production benefited Western silver interests by creating an artificial federal demand for the metal, whose market value had dropped sharply by 1878. Hundreds of millions of the coins, stored in cloth bags of 1,000 each, piled up in government vaults. In the 1900s some were melted, but immense quantities were bought by collectors and investors; today they are the most widely collected of all coins of their era.

Striking and Sharpness. On coins of 1878 to 1900, check the hair above Miss Liberty's ear and, on the reverse, the breast feathers of the eagle. These are weak on many issues, particularly those of the New Orleans Mint. From 1900 to 1904 a new reverse hub was used, and breast feathers, while discernible, are not as sharp. In 1921 new dies were made in lower relief, with certain areas indistinct. Many Morgan dollars have partially or fully prooflike surfaces. These are designated as Prooflike (PL), Deep Prooflike (DPL), or Deep Mirror Prooflike (DMPL). Certification practices can be erratic, and some DMPL-certified coins are not fully mirrored. All prooflike coins tend to emphasize contact marks, with the result that lower MS levels can be unattractive. *A Guide Book of Morgan Silver Dollars* (Bowers) and other references furnish information as to which dates and mintmarks are easily found with Full Details and which usually are weak, as well as the availability of the various levels of prooflike surface.

Proofs were struck from 1878 to 1904, with those of 1878 to 1901 generally having cameo contrast, and 1902 to 1904 having the portrait lightly polished in the die. Some are lightly struck; check the hair above Liberty's ear (in particular), and the eagle's breast feathers. In 1921 many so-called Zerbe Proofs (named thus after numismatic entrepreneur Farran Zerbe), with many microscopic die-finish lines, were made. A very few deeply mirrored 1921 coins were made, called Chapman Proofs (after coin dealer Henry Chapman, who started marketing them shortly after their production). Some Zerbe Proofs have been miscertified as Chapman Proofs.

Availability. All dates and mints of Morgan dollars are available in grades from well worn to MS. Some issues such as certain Carson City coins are rare if worn and common in MS. Other issues such as the 1901 Philadelphia coins are common if worn and are rarities at MS-65. The 1889-CC and 1893-S, and the Proof 1895, are considered to be the key issues. Varieties listed herein are some of those most significant to collectors. Numerous other variations exist, studied in the *Cherrypickers' Guide to Rare Die Varieties* and other specialized texts. Values shown herein are for the most common pieces. Values of varieties not listed in this guide depend on collector interest and demand.

Note: Values of common-date silver coins have been based on the current bullion price of silver, $17 per ounce, and may vary with the prevailing spot price.

GRADING STANDARDS

MS-60 to 70 (Mint State). *Obverse:* At MS-60, some abrasion and contact marks are evident, most noticeably on the cheek and on the hair above the ear. The left field also shows such marks. Luster is present, but may be dull or lifeless. At MS-63, contact marks are extensive but not distracting. Abrasion still is evident, but less than at lower levels. Indeed, the cheek of Miss Liberty showcases abrasion. An MS-65 coin may have minor abrasion, but

1895-O. Graded MS-61.

contact marks are so minute as to require magnification. Luster should be full and rich. Coins with prooflike surfaces such as PL, DPL, and DMPL display abrasion and contact marks much more noticeably than coins with frosty surfaces; in grades below MS-64 many are unattractive. With today's loose and sometimes contradictory interpretations, many at MS-64 appear to have extensive marks as well. *Reverse:* Comments apply as for the obverse, except that in lower Mint State grades abrasion and contact marks are most noticeable on the eagle's breast. At MS-65 or higher there are no marks visible to the unaided eye. The field is mainly protected by design elements, so the reverse often appears to grade a point or two higher than the obverse. A Morgan dollar can have an MS-63 obverse and an MS-65 reverse, as was indeed the nomenclature used prior to the single-number system. A careful cataloger may want to describe each side separately for a particularly valuable or rare Morgan dollar. An example with an MS-63 obverse and an MS-65 reverse should have an overall grade of MS-63, as the obverse is traditionally given prominence.

Illustrated coin: This is a lustrous and attractive example.

AU-50, 53, 55, 58 (About Uncirculated).
Obverse: Light wear is seen on the cheek and, to a lesser extent, on the hair below the coronet. Generally, the hair details mask friction and wear and it is not as easy to notice as on the cheek and in the fields. At AU-58, the luster is extensive, but incomplete, especially on the higher parts and in the left field. At AU-50 and 53, luster is less, but still is present. PL, DPL, and DMPL coins are not widely desired

1889-CC. Graded AU-58.

at these levels, as the marks are too distracting. *Reverse:* Wear is evident on the head, breast, wing tips, and, to a lesser extent, in the field. An AU-58 coin (as determined by the obverse) can have a reverse that appears to be full Mint State. (Incidentally, this is also true of Barber quarter dollars and half dollars.)

Illustrated coin: This is a lustrous example of the rarest Carson City Morgan dollar. As is typical of AU-58 dollars of this design, the reverse appears to be full Mint State, as the field is protected by the design elements.

EF-40, 45 (Extremely Fine). *Obverse:* Further wear is seen on the cheek in particular. The hair near the forehead and temple has flatness in areas, most noticeable above the ear. Some luster can be seen in protected areas on many coins, but is not needed to define the EF-40 and 45 grades. *Reverse:* Further wear is seen on the breast of the eagle (most noticeably), the wing tips, and the leaves.

1879-CC. Graded EF-40.

VF-20, 30 (Very Fine). *Obverse:* The head shows more wear, now with most of the detail gone in the areas adjacent to the forehead and temple. The lower area has most hair fused into large strands. *Reverse:* Wear is more extensive on the breast and on the feathers in the upper area of the wings, especially the right wing, and on the legs. The high area of the leaves has no detail.

1889-CC. Graded VF-20.

F-12, 15 (Fine). *Obverse:* The head shows more wear, with most hair detail gone, and with a large flat area above the ear. Less detail is seen in the lower curls. *Reverse:* More wear is seen on the reverse, with the eagle's breast and legs flat and about a third of the feather detail gone, mostly near the tops of the wings.

1893-S. Graded F-15.

VG-8, 10 (Very Good). *Obverse:* More hair details are gone, especially from the area from the top of the head down to the ear. The details of the lower part of the cap are gone. The rim is weak in areas, and some denticles are worn away. *Reverse:* Further wear has smoothed more than half of the feathers in the wing. The leaves are flat except for the lowest areas. The rim is weak in areas.

1892-CC. Graded VG-8.

G-4, 6 (Good). *Obverse:* The head is in outline form, with most details gone. LIBERTY still is readable. The eye position and lips are discernible. Most of the rim is worn away. *Reverse:* The eagle shows some feathers near the bottom of the wings, but nearly all others are gone. The leaves are seen in outline form. The rim is mostly worn away. Some letters have details toward the border worn away.

The Morgan dollar is seldom collected in grades lower than G-4.

Illustrated coin: Here is a well-worn example of this key issue.

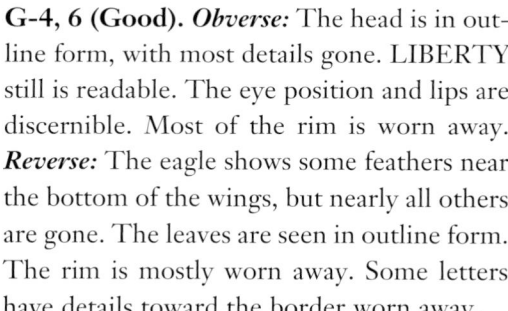

1893-S. Graded G-4.

PF-60 to 70 (Proof). *Obverse and Reverse:* Dull, grainy Proofs, or extensively cleaned ones with many hairlines, are lower level (PF-60 to 62). Only the 1895 is desirable at such low grades. Those with medium hairlines and good reflectivity may grade at about PF-64, and with relatively few hairlines, Gem PF-65. Hairlines are most easily seen in the obverse field. Horizontal slide marks on Miss Liberty's cheek, caused by clear slides on

1898. Graded PF-64.

some coin albums, are common. PF-66 may have hairlines so delicate that magnification is needed to see them. Above that, a Proof should be free of such lines, including slide marks.

First Reverse
Eight tail feathers.

Second Reverse
*Parallel top arrow feather,
concave breast.*

Third Reverse
*Slanted top arrow feather,
convex breast.*

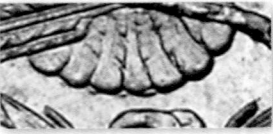

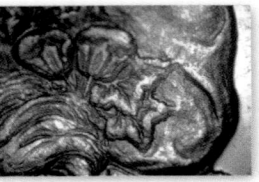

**1878, Doubled
Tail Feathers**
FS-S1-1878-032.

**1878, 8 Feathers,
Obverse Die Gouge**
*The "Wild Eye" variety.
VAM-14.11. FS-S1-1878-014.11.*

1878, 7 Over 8 Tail Feathers, Tripled Leaves
VAM-44. FS-S1-1878-044.

	Mintage	Cert	Avg	%MS	VF-20	EF-40	AU-50	MS-60	MS-63	MS-64	MS-64DMPL / PF-60	MS-65 / PF-63	MS-65DMPL / PF-65
1878, 8 Feathers	749,500	11,376	62.0	94%	$70	$80	$105	$180	$285	$475	$4,850	$1,600	$21,000
Auctions: $306, MS-63PL, October 2014; $294, MS-62PL, September 2014; $212, MS-61PL, November 2014; $9,400, MS-66, June 2013													
1878, 8 Feathers, Obverse Die Gouge (a)	(b)	6	59.5	67%				$8,000	$13,000	$24,000			
Auctions: $16,100, MS-62, August 2011													
1878, 7 Feathers, All kinds	9,759,300												
1878, 7 Over 8, Clear Doubled Feathers	(c)	2,326	61.3	90%	$50	$55	$75	$170	$275	$450	$5,200	$2,300	$16,000
Auctions: $16,450, MS-66DM, April 2014; $1,998, MS-64DM, October 2014; $558, MS-63DM, August 2014; $329, MS-63PL, October 2014													
1878, 7 Over 8, Tripled Leaves (d)	(c)	21	51.9	19%				$5,900	$12,000	$23,000			
Auctions: $8,625, AU-55, January 2012													
1878, 7 Feathers, 2nd Reverse (e)	(c)	13,615	62.4	95%	$45	$48	$50	$80	$150	$250	$2,200	$1,050	$11,000
Auctions: $8,813, MS-65DM, April 2014; $7,050, MS-65DM, October 2014; $558, MS-64PL, November 2014; $382, MS-63DM, November 2014													
1878, 7 Feathers, 3rd Reverse (e)	(c)	5,015	61.8	91%	$45	$48	$50	$100	$200	$490	$5,500	$2,050	$23,000
Auctions: $15,275, MS-66PL, August 2013; $2,585, MS-64DM, August 2014; $294, MS-63PL, October 2014; $165, MS-60PL, September 2014													

a. Two spikes protrude from the front of Liberty's eye. "Fewer than a dozen specimens are known of this Top 100 variety and any sale is a landmark event" (*Cherrypickers' Guide to Rare Die Varieties*, sixth edition, volume II). **b.** Included in circulation-strike 1878, 8 Feathers, mintage figure. **c.** Included in circulation-strike 1878, 7 Feathers, mintage figure. **d.** Called the "King of VAMs" (Van Allen / Mallis varieties), this variety shows three to five weak tail feathers under the seven primary feathers. On the obverse, tripling is evident on the cotton bolls and the leaves, and doubling on LIBERTY. Values are fluid for this popular variety. **e.** The Second Reverse is sometimes known as "Concave Breast" or "Reverse of 1878." The Third Reverse is sometimes known as "Round Breast" or "Reverse of 1879."

1880, 80 Over 79
VAM-6. FS-S1-1880-006.

	Mintage	Cert	Avg	%MS	VF-20	EF-40	AU-50	MS-60	MS-63	MS-64	MS-64DMPL / PF-60	MS-65 / PF-63	MS-65DMPL / PF-65
1878, 8 Feathers, Proof	500	136	64.2								$1,400	$3,500	$7,800
Auctions: $16,450, PF-66Cam, September 2014; $38,188, PF-66Cam, December 2013; $9,400, PF-65, August 2014; $4,406, PF-62, October 2014													
1878, 7 Feathers, 2nd Reverse, Proof	250	102	63.0								$2,750	$3,750	$11,500
Auctions: $32,900, PF-65Cam, January 2014; $4,700, PF-63, October 2014; $6,463, PF-62, September 2014													
1878, 7 Feathers, 3rd Reverse, Proof (e)	(f)	107	63.0								$16,500	$60,000	$200,000
Auctions: $155,250, PF-64, November 2004													
1878CC	2,212,000	23,170	61.1	91%	$120	$140	$170	$300	$475	$600	$2,800	$1,850	$10,000
Auctions: $1,998, MS-64DM, August 2014; $3,290, MS-64DM, October 2014; $1,645, MS-65PL, October 2014; $19,975, MS-66, December 2013													
1878S	9,774,000	42,405	63.2	98%	$45	$47	$48	$65	$95	$120	$2,000	$320	$8,500
Auctions: $1,763, MS-64DM, July 2014; $294, MS-63DM, November 2014; $2,585, MS-66PL, October 2014; $9,988, MS-67, November 2013													
1879	14,806,000	10,922	62.8	95%	$37	$39	$40	$55	$95	$155	$2,100	$825	$15,000
Auctions: $19,975, MS-66DM, April 2014; $84, MS-60DM, September 2014; $6,463, MS-66PL, July 2014; $499, MS-64PL, November 2014													
1879, Proof	1,100	327	64.2								$1,400	$3,100	$6,500
Auctions: $25,850, PF-68Cam, April 2013; $7,050, PF-65Cam, September 2014; $8,225, PF-66, September 2014; $1,586, PF-60, November 2014													
1879CC, CC Over CC	756,000	1,954	50.1	53%	$290	$770	$1,700	$4,000	$6,300	$9,900	$42,000	$40,000	$60,000
Auctions: $22,325, MS-64PL, September 2014; $5,288, MS-62PL, July 2014; $36,719, MS-65, April 2014; $4,700, MS-62, August 2014													
1879CC, Clear CC	(g)	5,331	49.9	58%	$290	$750	$2,200	$4,200	$7,500	$11,000	$25,000	$30,000	$47,500
Auctions: $13,513, MS-64PL, August 2014; $14,100, MS-64PL, November 2014; $8,813, MS-64PL, November 2014; $64,625, MS-66, April 2014													
1879O	2,887,000	8,171	61.4	85%	$40	$42	$47	$90	$250	$600	$4,250	$4,000	$22,000
Auctions: $411, MS-61DM, August 2014; $441, MS-61DM, November 2014; $8,225, MS-65PL, October 2014; $19,975, MS-66, April 2014													
1879O, Proof (h)	4–8	5	64.5										$150,000
Auctions: $176,250, PF-64, August 2013													
1879S, 2nd Reverse	9,110,000	2,100	60.5	82%	$40	$45	$70	$190	$625	$1,500	$8,000	$5,500	$21,000
Auctions: $4,230, MS-66DM, September 2014; $1,645, MS-65DM, August 2014; $558, MS-64DM, November 2014; $8,225, MS-61, April 2013													
1879S, 3rd Reverse	(i)	97,598	64.2	100%	$37	$39	$41	$55	$60	$75	$500	$175	$1,300
Auctions: $12,338, MS-65PL, March 2014; $4,406, MS-65, September 2014; $4,406, MS-65, October 2014; $1,293, MS-64, October 2014													
1880	12,600,000	12,924	62.8	97%	$37	$39	$41	$50	$80	$160	$1,150	$750	$6,900
Auctions: $4,994, MS-65DM, August 2014; $2,703, MS-66, August 2014; $2,820, MS-66, October 2014; $14,100, MS-66, August 2013													
1880, 80 Over 79 (j)	(k)	1	45.0	0%	$37	$39	$55	$100	$850	$675		$3,300	
Auctions: $969, AU-58, December 2013; $176, AU-53, November 2014; $165, EF-45, September 2014													
1880, Proof	1,355	423	64.8								$1,400	$3,000	$6,500
Auctions: $22,325, PF-68Cam, September 2014; $36,719, PF-68Cam, August 2013; $9,988, PF-67Cam, October 2014													

e. The Second Reverse is sometimes known as "Concave Breast" or "Reverse of 1878." The Third Reverse is sometimes known as "Round Breast" or "Reverse of 1879." **f.** Included in 1878, 7 Feathers, Proof, mintage figure. **g.** Included in 1879-CC, CC Over CC, mintage figure. **h.** Some numismatists classify these as Deep Mirror Prooflike circulation strikes, rather than as Proofs. **i.** Included in 1879-S, 2nd Reverse, mintage figure. **j.** Several die varieties exist; values shown are for the most common. **k.** Included in circulation-strike 1880 mintage figure.

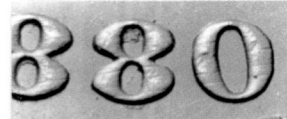

1880-CC, 8 Over High 7
VAM-5. FS-S1-1880CC-005.

1880-CC, 80 Over 79
VAM-4. FS-S1-1880CC-004.

1880-CC, 8 Over Low 7
VAM-6. FS-S1-1880CC-006.

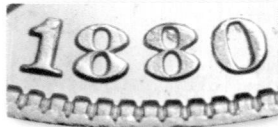

1880-O, 80 Over 79
VAM-4. FS-S1-1880o-004.

1880-O, Die Gouge
The "Hangnail" variety.
VAM-49. FS-S1-1880o-049.

| | Mintage | Cert | Avg | %MS | VF-20 | EF-40 | AU-50 | MS-60 | MS-63 | MS-64 | MS-64DMPL | MS-65 | MS-65DMPL |
											PF-60	PF-63	PF-65
1880CC, All kinds	591,000												
1880CC, 80 Over 79, 2nd Reverse (l)		1,019	63.0	99%	$220	$285	$350	$600	$700	$1,150	$5,000	$2,700	$20,000
Auctions: $7,344, MS-64DM, August 2014; $10,575, MS-66, June 2013; $1,880, MS-65, November 2014; $1,851, MS-65, November 2014													
1880CC, 8 Over 7, 2nd Reverse		949	63.5	100%	$210	$285	$325	$550	$650	$1,050	$5,000	$2,200	$20,000
Auctions: $2,056, MS-65, November 2014; $940, MS-64, July 2014; $940, MS-64, October 2014													
1880CC, 8 Over High 7, 3rd Reverse (m)		526	63.4	100%	$210	$275	$325	$500	$650	$700	$2,450	$1,250	$6,750
Auctions: $705, MS-64PL, November 2014; $564, MS-63PL, July 2014; $22,325, MS-67, August 2013; $2,996, MS-66, August 2014													
1880CC, 8 Over Low 7, 3rd Reverse (n)		423	63.4	99%	$270	$365	$475	$600	$640	$750	$2,700	$1,275	$9,000
Auctions: $529, MS-63PL, October 2014; $8,225, MS-66, January 2013; $596, MS-64, October 2014; $541, MS-64, October 2014													
1880CC, 3rd Reverse	0	n/a			$210	$275	$325	$500	$600	$700	$2,450	$1,200	$9,000
Auctions: $1,645, MS-65PL, September 2014; $881, MS-64PL, August 2014; $881, MS-64PL, November 2014; $12,925, MS-67, April 2013													
1880O, All kinds	5,305,000												
1880O, 80 Over 79 (o)		229	59.1	66%	$37	$39	$48	$150	$625	$2,500	$8,000		
Auctions: $4,700, MS-64, January 2014; $1,175, MS-63, July 2014; $235, AU-55, October 2014; $194, AU-53, October 2014													
1880O		9,305	60.6	76%	$37	$39	$43	$90	$430	$1,800	$7,250	$26,000	$62,500
Auctions: $3,290, MS-64PL, August 2014; $1,880, MS-64PL, November 2014; $329, MS-62PL, November 2014													
1880O, Die Gouge (p)		180	55.6	37%	$200	$450	$900	$2,000	—				
Auctions: $19,975, MS-65, September 2014; $999, MS-64, November 2014; $1,410, MS-64, December 2013; $368, MS-63, November 2014													
1880S, All kinds	8,900,000												
1880S, 80 Over 79		229	59.3	66%	$37	$40	$46	$55	$80	$125	$450	$300	$1,500
Auctions: $1,528, MS-66DM, February 2013; $259, MS-63DM, December 2014; $441, MS-66, September 2014; $1,763, MS-65, August 2014													
1880S, 0 Over 9		754	64.1	100%	$37	$40	$46	$63	$90	$125	$450	$300	$1,500
Auctions: $259, MS-65PL, September 2014; $11,750, MS-68, April 2014; $1,645, MS-67, July 2014; $301, MS-65, July 2014													
1880S		144,103	64.2	100%	$37	$39	$41	$50	$60	$75	$345	$175	$690
Auctions: $1,998, MS-66DM, September 2014; $940, MS-65DM, August 2014; $881, MS-65DM+, September 2014													

l. The top crossbar and diagonal stem of an underlying 79 are clearly seen within the 8. Extensive polishing marks are visible within the 0.
m. An almost complete 7 is visible inside the last 8 of the date. The top edge of the 7 touches the top inside of the 8. n. A complete 7 is visible inside the last 8 of the date. The crossbar of the underlying 7 can be seen in the top loop and the diagonal of the 7 is visible in the lower loop. o. The crossbar of the underlying 7 is visible within the upper loop of the second 8. The 1 and the first 8 are slightly doubled to the right. p. On the reverse of the "Hangnail" variety, a die gouge runs from the bottom of the arrow feather, across the feathers, and out the eagle's rightmost tail feather. On the obverse, the top-left part of the second 8 has a spike.

1881-O, Repunched Mintmark
VAM-5. FS-S1-1881o-005.

1882-O, O Over S
VAM-4. FS-S1-1882o-004.

	Mintage	Cert	Avg	%MS	VF-20	EF-40	AU-50	MS-60	MS-63	MS-64	MS-64DMPL PF-60	MS-65 PF-63	MS-65DMPL PF-65
1881	9,163,000	10,191	63.2	98%	$37	$39	$42	$53	$80	$170	$1,375	$750	$19,500
	Auctions: $382, MS-64PL, November 2014; $200, MS-63PL, September 2014; $15,275, MS-67, April 2014; $28,200, MS-67, November 2014												
1881, Proof	984	260	64.3								$1,400	$3,000	$6,250
	Auctions: $25,850, PF-68Cam, April 2013; $5,581, PF-65Cam, July 2014; $8,813, PF-67, August 2014; $14,100, PF-67, October 2014												
1881CC	296,000	20,120	63.3	99%	$400	$425	$440	$500	$600	$650	$1,200	$950	$3,000
	Auctions: $1,410, MS-64DM, September 2014; $1,001, MS-64DM, October 2014; $529, MS-63DM, October 2014; $28,200, MS-68, April 2014												
1881O	5,708,000	16,205	62.7	95%	$37	$39	$41	$50	$75	$190	$900	$1,400	$18,000
	Auctions: $9,400, MS-65DM, September 2014; $1,645, MS-64DM, September 2014; $1,116, MS-64DM, September 2014												
1881O, Repunched Mintmark (q)	(r)	10	61.5	100%			$80	$110	$250		$1,450	$1,600	
	Auctions: $218, MS-64, March 2012												
1881O, Doubled-Die Obverse (s)	(r)	24	56.0	25%			$175	$400	—	—			
	Auctions: $150, AU-50, September 2011												
1881S	12,760,000	235,632	64.1	100%	$37	$39	$41	$50	$60	$75	$475	$165	$1,000
	Auctions: $881, MS-65DM, August 2014; $435, MS-64DM, October 2014; $311, MS-64DM, October 2014; $12,925, MS-68, April 2014												
1882	11,100,000	17,817	63.2	99%	$37	$39	$41	$50	$70	$120	$1,000	$550	$6,500
	Auctions: $3,466, MS-66PL, November 2014; $767, MS-65PL, November 2014; $306, MS-64PL, October 2014; $11,750, MS-67, April 2014												
1882, Proof	1,100	358	64.2								$1,400	$3,000	$6,250
	Auctions: $5,887, PF-64DCam, August 2014; $8,814, PF-64DCam, October 2014; $24,675, PF-68Cam, August 2013												
1882CC	1,133,000	36,647	63.3	99%	$110	$120	$145	$210	$275	$300	$625	$550	$1,900
	Auctions: $1,763, MS-65DM, September 2014; $2,115, MS-65DM, October 2014; $1,305, MS-64DM, August 2014; $7,638, MS-67, April 2013												
1882O	6,090,000	16,657	62.9	96%	$37	$39	$42	$50	$85	$135	$1,300	$1,500	$5,200
	Auctions: $382, MS-63DM, August 2014; $282, MS-63DM, September 2014; $259, MS-63DM, November 2014; $18,800, MS-67, April 2014												
1882O, O Over S (t)	(u)	3,527	56.9	43%	$50	$70	$120	$235	$775	$2,000	$8,500	$50,000	$62,500
	Auctions: $4,994, MS-64, June 2013; $717, MS-63, September 2014; $270, MS-62, November 2014; $306, MS-62, December 2014												
1882S	9,250,000	75,772	64.2	100%	$37	$39	$41	$50	$70	$85	$950	$200	$3,800
	Auctions: $3,672, MS-65DM, August 2014; $411, MS-64DM, November 2014; $118, MS-62DM, November 2014; $11,163, MS-68, April 2013												
1883	12,290,000	22,057	63.7	99%	$37	$39	$41	$50	$75	$110	$450	$220	$1,600
	Auctions: $529, MS-64DM, October 2014; $223, MS-63DM, July 2014; $150, MS-62DM, October 2014; $11,817, MS-68, April 2014												
1883, Proof	1,039	291	64.1								$1,400	$3,000	$6,200
	Auctions: $11,163, PF-67Cam, November 2014; $170,375, PF-65Cam, August 2013; $4,700, PF-64, October 2014; $1,775, PF-60, November 2014												
1883CC	1,204,000	48,554	63.6	99%	$110	$120	$145	$210	$250	$275	$525	$525	$1,300
	Auctions: $3,819, MS-66DM, September 2014; $3,290, MS-66DM, October 2014; $1,880, MS-66DM, September 2014												
1883O	8,725,000	120,853	63.4	100%	$37	$39	$41	$50	$60	$75	$500	$175	$1,450
	Auctions: $1,410, MS-65DM, August 2014; $441, MS-64DM, November 2014; $212, MS-63DM, November 2014; $5,288, MS-65, April 2014												
1883O, Proof (v)	4–8	2	64.0										$175,000
	Auctions: $270,250, PF-67Cam, April 2013												
1883S	6,250,000	5,213	55.7	35%	$37	$53	$140	$750	$2,500	$6,000	$75,000	$45,000	$125,000
	Auctions: $32,900, MS-65, April 2014; $7,638, MS-64, October 2014; $7,050, MS-64, October 2014; $6,463, MS-64, October 2014												

q. A diagonal image, the remains of one or two additional O mintmark punches, is visible within the primary O. **r.** Included in 1881-O mintage figure. **s.** Clear doubling is evident on the back outside of Liberty's ear **t.** Several varieties exist. **u.** Included in 1882-O mintage figure. **v.** "A numismatic tradition exists, dating back well over a century, that 12 full Proofs were struck of the 1883-O Morgan dollar. And, they may have been, although the differentiation between a cameo DMPL and a 'branch mint Proof' would be difficult to explain" (*A Guide Book of Morgan Silver Dollars*, fourth edition).

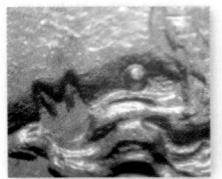 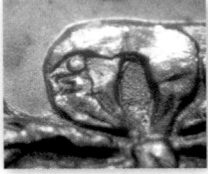

1884, Large Dot
VAM-3. FS-S1-1884-003.

 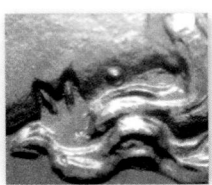

1884, Small Dot
VAM-4. FS-S1-1884-004.

1885, Die Chip
VAM-8. FS-S1-1885-008.

1886, Repunched Date
VAM-20. FS-S1-1886-020.

	Mintage	Cert	Avg	%MS	VF-20	EF-40	AU-50	MS-60	MS-63	MS-64	MS-64DMPL PF-60	MS-65 PF-63	MS-65DMPL PF-65
1884, All kinds	14,070,000												
1884	875	17,097	63.3	98%	$37	$39	$41	$50	$75	$110	$850	$375	$5,000
	Auctions: $3,819, MS-65DM, July 2014; $764, MS-64DM, October 2014; $3,966, MS-67, October 2014; $17,038, MS-67, August 2013												
1884, Large Dot (w)		90	55.1	42%			$55	$85	$250	—			
	Auctions: $80, MS-62, May 2014; $74, AU-55, September 2014												
1884, Small Dot (w)		225	61.8	91%			$65	$90	$350	—			
	Auctions: $170, MS-63, August 2014; $182, MS-63, September 2014; $141, MS-63, September 2014; $259, MS-63, September 2013												
1884, Proof		206	64.4								$1,400	$3,000	$6,200
	Auctions: $32,900, PF-68Cam, April 2013; $3,305, PF-64Cam, August 2014; $2,820, PF-63, August 2014; $940, PF-60, November 2014												
1884CC	1,136,000	56,032	63.6	100%	$140	$150	$160	$210	$230	$250	$550	$525	$1,275
	Auctions: $16,450, MS-67DM, April 2014; $1,058, MS-66, August 2014; $499, MS-65, October 2014; $456, MS-65, October 2014												
1884O	9,730,000	196,116	63.6	100%	$37	$39	$41	$50	$60	$75	$350	$175	$900
	Auctions: $3,534, MS-66DM, June 2014; $823, MS-65DM, August 2014; $588, MS-64DM, September 2014; $734, MS-65DM, October 2014												
1884S	3,200,000	7,319	52.7	6%	$40	$60	$290	$7,200	$35,000	$115,000	$135,000	$235,000	$275,000
	Auctions: $88,125, MS-64, January 2014; $18,800, MS-62, August 2014; $9,988, MS-61, September 2014; $9,988, MS-60, November 2014												
1885	17,787,000	73,759	63.7	100%	$37	$39	$41	$50	$60	$75	$450	$175	$1,000
	Auctions: $7,117, MS-67DM, August 2014; $1,234, MS-65DM, August 2014; $979, MS-65DM, September 2014; $21,150, MS-68, April 2013												
1885, Die Chip (x)	(y)	4	59.8	75%			$70	$95	$550	—			
	Auctions: No auction records available.												
1885, Proof	930	256	64.3								$1,400	$3,000	$6,200
	Auctions: $12,925, PF-66Cam, October 2014; $25,850, PF-67, June 2014; $4,994, PF-66, October 2014												
1885CC	228,000	19,824	63.6	99%	$550	$570	$590	$700	$825	$900	$1,300	$1,200	$2,400
	Auctions: $11,750, MS-66DM, August 2014; $4,177, MS-65DM, September 2014; $1,821, MS-64DM, October 2014												
1885O	9,185,000	193,971	63.7	100%	$37	$39	$41	$50	$60	$75	$450	$175	$1,000
	Auctions: $3,966, MS-66DM, July 2014; $881, MS-65DM, August 2014; $376, MS-64DM, November 2014; $9,988, MS-68, November 2013												
1885S	1,497,000	6,126	61.2	84%	$50	$63	$110	$250	$315	$675	$5,000	$1,800	$45,000
	Auctions: $6,463, MS-66, April 2014; $4,308, MS-66, September 2014; $4,113, MS-66, October 2014; $1,469, MS-65, October 2014												
1886	19,963,000	125,309	63.8	100%	$37	$39	$41	$50	$60	$75	$475	$175	$1,300
	Auctions: $18,800, MS-66DM, July 2014; $1,058, MS-65DM, July 2014; $19,975, MS-68, July 2014												
1886, RPD (z)	(aa)	7	60.3	71%			$2,250	$3,500	$5,750				
	Auctions: $3,819, MS-64, September 2013												
1886, Proof	886	236	64.1								$1,400	$3,000	$6,200
	Auctions: $28,200, PF-68Cam, April 2013; $8,813, PF-67, October 2014; $5,875, PF-66, October 2014; $1,880, PF-62, July 2014												

w. A raised dot, either Large or Small, is visible after the designer's initial and on the reverse ribbon. "These dots varieties are thought to have been used as some sort of identifier" (*Cherrypickers' Guide to Rare Die Varieties*, sixth edition, volume II). **x.** A large, raised die chip is evident below the second 8. **y.** Included in circulation-strike 1885 mintage figure. **z.** Repunching is especially evident in the base of the 1, and the lower loop of the 6. **aa.** Included in circulation-strike 1886 mintage figure.

1887, 7 Over 6
VAM-2.
FS-S1-1887-002.

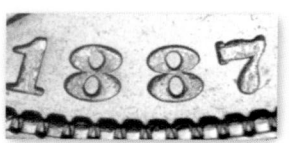

1887-O, 7 Over 6
VAM-3. FS-S1-1887o-003.

**1888-O, Obverse
Die Break**
The "Scarface" variety.
VAM-1B. FS-S1-1888o-001b.

**1888-O, Doubled-Die
Obverse**
The "Hot Lips" variety.
VAM-4. FS-S1-1888o-004.

	Mintage	Cert	Avg	%MS	VF-20	EF-40	AU-50	MS-60	MS-63	MS-64	MS-64DMPL	MS-65	MS-65DMPL
											PF-60	PF-63	PF-65
1886O	10,710,000	5,390	55.9	30%	$39	$45	$75	$900	$3,500	$11,000	$70,000	$185,000	$300,000
Auctions: $152,750, MS-65, January 2014; $7,638, MS-64, October 2014; $3,055, MS-63, September 2014; $3,525, MS-63, October 2014
1886O, Clashed Die (bb)	(cc)	10	52.6	0%				$225	$950	$5,750	—		
Auctions: $3,055, MS-62, April 2014; $1,880, MS-62, November 2014; $940, MS-61, August 2014; $705, AU-58, October 2014
1886S	750,000	4,327	60.2	76%	$78	$105	$150	$350	$500	$850	$8,500	$3,250	$27,000
Auctions: $470, MS-62PL, November 2014; $14,688, MS-67, April 2014; $4,935, MS-66, July 2014; $12,925, MS-66, September 2014
1887, 7 Over 6	(dd)	1,010	62.6	94%	$48	$70	$165	$400	$500	$750	$4,750	$1,800	$26,000
Auctions: $558, MS-63PL, November 2014; $8,225, MS-66, April 2014; $1,410, MS-65, August 2014; $682, MS-64, July 2014
1887	20,290,000	182,062	63.7	100%	$37	$39	$41	$50	$60	$75	$450	$175	$1,000
Auctions: $823, MS-65DM, August 2014; $588, MS-65DM, October 2014; $470, MS-64DM, November 2014; $3,055, MS-67PL, February 2013
1887, Proof	710	214	64.4								$1,400	$3,000	$6,200
Auctions: $11,163, PF-67Cam, April 2013; $3,525, PF-64, November 2014; $2,703, PF-63, July 2014; $2,585, PF-63, October 2014
1887O, 7 Over 6	(ee)	576	60.7	84%	$48	$65	$175	$450	$1,900	$4,800		$27,000	
Auctions: $5,581, MS-64, January 2014; $705, MS-60, October 2014
1887O	11,550,000	9,397	62.3	95%	$37	$42	$55	$70	$150	$400	$1,700	$2,750	$13,500
Auctions: $10,575, MS-65DM, April 2014; $1,645, MS-64DM, October 2014; $382, MS-62DM, November 2014; $705, MS-64PL, September 2014
1887S	1,771,000	6,370	61.3	82%	$40	$45	$50	$135	$300	$750	$7,000	$2,600	$27,500
Auctions: $317, MS-62PL, November 2014; $30,550, MS-67, April 2014; $5,288, MS-66, October 2014; $2,115, MS-65, August 2014
1888	19,183,000	45,166	63.6	99%	$37	$39	$41	$50	$65	$85	$450	$240	$2,400
Auctions: $1,293, MS-65DM, October 2014; $1,763, MS-65DM, November 2014; $306, MS-63DM, September 2014
1888, Proof	833	196	63.9								$1,400	$3,000	$6,200
Auctions: $24,675, PF-66Cam, April 2013
1888O	12,150,000	24,270	62.2	96%	$37	$39	$41	$50	$75	$115	$450	$600	$2,650
Auctions: $705, MS-64DM, July 2014; $247, MS-63DM, August 2014; $1,234, MS-65PL, October 2014; $10,575, MS-67, April 2014
1888O, Obverse Die Break (ff)	(gg)	39	61.3	100%				$2,250	$4,750	$8,650			
Auctions: $14,688, MS-64, December 2013
1888O, Doubled-Die Obverse (hh)	(gg)	767	33.6	1%	$145	$290	$900	$20,000	$30,000	—			
Auctions: $12,925, MS-60, February 2013; $705, AU-53, July 2014; $100, F-15, December 2014
1888S	657,000	4,845	59.0	73%	$175	$185	$205	$315	$500	$1,000	$2,850	$3,500	$15,500
Auctions: $2,585, MS-64DM, September 2014; $823, MS-64PL, November 2014; $611, MS-63PL, November 2014

bb. Clashing of the E of LIBERTY is evident between the eagle's tail feathers and the bow on the wreath. **cc.** Included in 1886-O mintage figure. **dd.** Included in circulation-strike 1887 mintage figure. **ee.** Included in 1887-O mintage figure. **ff.** A major die break runs from the rim between E and P, through the field, and all the way across Liberty's face and neck. This variety is nicknamed "Scarface." **gg.** Included in 1888-O mintage figure. **hh.** Doubling is visible on the lips (especially), nose, eye, chin, entire profile, and part of the hair. This variety is nicknamed "Hot Lips."

1889, Die Break
The *"Bar Wing"* variety.
VAM-22. FS-S1-1889-022.

1889-O, Clashed Die
VAM-1A. FS-S1-1889o-001a.

1890-CC, Die Gouge
The *"Tailbar"* variety.
VAM-4. FS-S1-1890CC-004.

1890-O, Die Gouges
The *"Comet"* variety.
VAM-10. FS-S1-1890o-010.

	Mintage	Cert	Avg	%MS	VF-20	EF-40	AU-50	MS-60	MS-63	MS-64	MS-64DMPL	MS-65	MS-65DMPL
											PF-60	PF-63	PF-65
1889	21,726,000	43,238	63.2	98%	$37	$39	$41	$50	$70	$90	$700	$380	$3,600
Auctions: $705, MS-64DM, September 2014; $282, MS-63DM, July 2014; $106, MS-63PL, September 2014; $14,100, MS-67, April 2013
1889, Die Break (ii)	(jj)	98	58.8	68%				$80	$150	$285	$325	$2,500	
Auctions: $182, MS-63, September 2014; $153, MS-63, December 2013; $89, MS-62, September 2014; $84, MS-61, September 2014
1889, Proof	811	187	64.3								$1,400	$3,000	$6,200
Auctions: $17,038, PF-66Cam, July 2014; $28,200, PF-67, July 2014
1889CC	350,000	4,359	33.9	12%	$1,250	$3,000	$7,000	$24,000	$50,000	$85,000	$75,000	$325,000	$350,000
Auctions: $881,250, MS-68, August 2013; $41,125, MS-63, July 2014; $31,725, MS-63, October 2014; $25,850, MS-61, November 2014
1889O	11,875,000	4,442	60.2	84%	$37	$39	$55	$185	$400	$1,000	$6,500	$7,500	$17,500
Auctions: $499, MS-62PL, July 2014; $306, MS-62PL, October 2014; $17,625, MS-66, January 2014; $4,818, MS-65, July 2014
1889O, Clashed Die (kk)	(ll)	39	36.5	3%			$975	$2,000	—	—			
Auctions: $764, AU-55, March 2014; $282, AU-55, October 2014; $200, VF-30, September 2014
1889S	700,000	6,060	61.0	78%	$60	$75	$105	$275	$375	$675	$5,500	$2,200	$37,500
Auctions: $1,058, MS-64PL, November 2014; $282, MS-61PL, September 2014; $16,450, MS-66, April 2014; $3,525, MS-66, October 2014
1890	16,802,000	16,338	62.8	97%	$37	$39	$43	$53	$95	$175	$2,500	$2,050	$20,000
Auctions: $10,575, MS-65DM, September 2014; $427, MS-63DM, September 2014; $188, MS-63PL, October 2014
1890, Proof	590	228	64.9								$1,400	$3,000	$6,200
Auctions: $88,125, PF-69DCam, April 2013; $12,925, PF-66Cam, July 2014; $4,259, PF-64Cam, November 2014
1890CC	2,309,041	8,057	55.9	75%	$110	$140	$190	$500	$900	$1,500	$2,800	$5,000	$13,750
Auctions: $1,175, MS-63DM, September 2014; $1,293, MS-62DM, July 2014; $969, MS-62DM, July 2014; $45,531, MS-66, February 2013
1890CC, Die Gouge (mm)	(nn)	424	49.4	52%			$650	$1,150	$2,950	—			
Auctions: $8,519, MS-64DM, April 2014; $3,525, MS-62DM, July 2014; $112, VF-20, October 2014
1890O	10,701,000	9,077	62.6	97%	$37	$39	$49	$75	$105	$325	$1,500	$2,500	$9,250
Auctions: $1,880, MS-64DM, September 2014; $15,275, MS-66PL, October 2014; $2,468, MS-65PL, November 2014; $11,750, MS-66, March 2013
1890O, Die Gouges (oo)	(pp)	55	60.7	84%			$65	$90	$260	—		$2,100	
Auctions: $2,585, MS-65, July 2014; $259, MS-64, August 2014; $182, MS-63, September 2014; $118, MS-62, September 2014
1890S	8,230,373	9,029	62.3	92%	$37	$39	$45	$70	$105	$325	$3,200	$1,400	$9,250
Auctions: $1,880, MS-64DM, November 2014; $9,106, MS-66PL, August 2014; $1,528, MS-65PL, September 2014; $8,225, MS-66, April 2014

ii. A die break is visible on the top of the eagle's right wing. This variety is nicknamed the "Bar Wing." Different obverse die pairings exist. **jj.** Included in circulation-strike 1889 mintage figure. **kk.** The E of LIBERTY is visible in the field below the eagle's tail feathers and slightly left of the bow. This variety is extremely rare in Mint State, and unknown above MS-61. **ll.** Included in 1889-O mintage figure. **mm.** A heavy die gouge extends from between the eagle's first tail feather and the lowest arrow feather to the leaves in the wreath below. "This is an extremely popular and highly marketable variety, especially in Mint State" (*Cherrypickers' Guide to Rare Die Varieties*, sixth edition, volume II). This variety is nicknamed the "Tailbar." **nn.** Included in 1890-CC mintage figure. **oo.** Die gouges are evident to the right of the date. This variety is nicknamed the "Comet." **pp.** Included in 1890-O mintage figure.

1891-O, Clashed Die
VAM-1A. FS-S1-1891o-001a.

1891-O, Pitted Reverse Die
VAM-1B. FS-S1-1891o-001b.

	Mintage	Cert	Avg	%MS	VF-20	EF-40	AU-50	MS-60	MS-63	MS-64	MS-64DMPL	MS-65	MS-65DMPL
											PF-60	PF-63	PF-65
1891	8,693,556	6,874	61.7	91%	$38	$40	$45	$75	$220	$900	$6,900	$8,000	$23,000
	Auctions: $14,688, MS-65DM, August 2013; $6,756, MS-64DM, August 2014; $4,555, MS-64DM, October 2014; $499, MS-62DM, August 2014												
1891, Proof	650	220	64.2								$1,400	$3,000	$6,200
	Auctions: $35,250, PF-68Cam, August 2013; $6,463, PF-65Cam, October 2014; $34,075, PF-68, October 2014; $8,225, PF-66, September 2014												
1891CC	1,618,000	10,545	59.8	85%	$110	$140	$190	$450	$750	$1,275	$4,500	$5,000	$32,000
	Auctions: $1,528, MS-63DM, October 2014; $999, MS-62DM, August 2014; $887, MS-62DM, November 2014; $11,163, MS-66, April 2014												
1891O	7,954,529	4,663	60.7	88%	$37	$40	$55	$200	$400	$825	$7,250	$7,500	$36,500
	Auctions: $19,975, MS-66, April 2014; $3,966, MS-65, October 2014; $3,819, MS-65, October 2014; $3,540, MS-65, October 2014												
1891O, Clashed Die (qq)	(rr)	136	37.9	1%			$235	$400	$1,500	—			
	Auctions: $259, AU-53, September 2014; $382, AU-53, December 2013; $79, AU-50, November 2014; $48, F-12, November 2014												
1891O, Pitted Reverse Die (ss)	(rr)	9	52.8	0%			$370		—	—			
	Auctions: $4,700, MS-65, June 2014; $3,055, MS-65, October 2014; $3,290, MS-65, November 2014; $2,585, MS-64, October 2014												
1891S	5,296,000	6,005	62.3	92%	$38	$40	$45	$70	$160	$350	$3,200	$1,750	$20,000
	Auctions: $282, MS-63PL, November 2014; $329, MS-63PL, December 2014; $4,113, MS-66, October 2014; $7,638, MS-66, August 2013												
1892	1,036,000	4,423	60.4	75%	$43	$53	$90	$300	$480	$1,250	$3,400	$5,250	$18,000
	Auctions: $2,375, MS-64DM, October 2014; $485, MS-61PL, July 2014; $5,941, MS-65, October 2014; $8,813, MS-65, April 2013												
1892, Proof	1,245	356	64.4								$1,400	$3,000	$6,200
	Auctions: $35,250, PF-68Cam, August 2013; $7,638, PF-66Cam, July 2014; $3,966, PF-64Cam, July 2014; $4,406, PF-64Cam, October 2014												
1892CC	1,352,000	5,802	56.0	74%	$285	$450	$690	$1,500	$2,400	$3,250	$8,750	$9,000	$36,000
	Auctions: $3,819, MS-63DM, September 2014; $3,966, MS-64PL, July 2014; $3,055, MS-64PL, November 2014; $31,725, MS-66, August 2013												
1892O	2,744,000	5,016	61.1	86%	$40	$48	$70	$290	$425	$1,100	$20,000	$7,500	$50,000
	Auctions: $15,275, MS-65, January 2014; $4,406, MS-65, July 2014; $4,395, MS-65, August 2014; $6,463, MS-65, September 2014												
1892S	1,200,000	3,506	41.2	1%	$140	$300	$1,650	$40,000	$65,000	$115,000	$145,000	$190,000	$250,000
	Auctions: $70,500, MS-63, April 2014; $9,400, AU-58, July 2014; $7,638, AU-55, August 2014; $6,463, AU-55, September 2014												
1893	378,000	4,449	53.0	49%	$225	$275	$400	$725	$1,100	$2,300	$32,500	$8,500	$67,500
	Auctions: $10,575, MS-62PL, August 2014; $44,063, MS-66, August 2014; $8,225, MS-65, April 2014; $18,800, MS-65, November 2014												
1893, Proof	792	241	64.2								$1,400	$3,000	$6,200
	Auctions: $55,813, PF-68Cam, April 2013; $8,813, PF-64, October 2014; $3,290, PF-64, October 2014; $764, AU-50, July 2014												
1893CC	677,000	3,842	42.3	46%	$625	$1,500	$2,400	$5,000	$8,500	$16,000	$46,000	$70,000	$85,000
	Auctions: $141,000, MS-65BMCam, April 2013; $5,581, MS-62PL, September 2014; $19,975, MS-64, August 2014												
1893CC, Proof (tt)	4–8	10	63.8										$175,000
	Auctions: $149,500, PF-65, August 2011												
1893O	300,000	3,016	43.1	22%	$325	$475	$775	$2,850	$6,500	$17,000	$105,000	$200,000	$275,000
	Auctions: $23,500, MS-64PL, January 2014; $7,050, MS-63, November 2014; $4,700, MS-62, August 2014; $4,994, MS-62, September 2014												
1893S † (uu,vv)	100,000	2,750	21.3	1%	$5,200	$9,000	$20,000	$120,000	$225,000	$350,000	$400,000	$650,000	$750,000
	Auctions: $329,000, MS-65, April 2014; $646,250, MS-65, October 2014; $47,000, MS-60, October 2014; $18,800, AU-50, July 2014												

qq. The evidence of a clashed die is visible below the eagle's tail feathers and slightly left of the bow, where the E in LIBERTY has been transferred from the obverse die. **rr.** Included in 1891-O mintage figure. **ss.** Pitting on the reverse is visible around the ONE and on the bottom of the wreath above and between ONE and DOLLAR. This variety is rare in circulated grades, and unknown in Mint State. **tt.** Some numismatists classify these as Deep Mirror Prooflike circulation strikes, rather than as Proofs. **uu.** "All 1893-S Morgan dollars were struck from a single die pairing. Genuine 1893-S silver dollars display a diagonal die scratch in the top of the T in LIBERTY. This diagnostic can be seen even on very low-grade examples" (*100 Greatest U.S. Coins*, fourth edition). **vv.** Beware of altered or otherwise fraudulent mintmarks.

1899-O, Micro O
*VAM-4, 5, 6, 31, and
32. FS-S1-1899o-501.*

	Mintage	Cert	Avg	%MS	VF-20	EF-40	AU-50	MS-60	MS-63	MS-64	MS-64DMPL / PF-60	MS-65 / PF-63	MS-65DMPL / PF-65
1894 (vv)	110,000	3,366	47.6	28%	$1,250	$1,350	$1,700	$3,400	$4,900	$9,500	$60,000	$40,000	$90,000
	Auctions: $39,656, MS-65, December 2013; $16,450, MS-64, August 2014; $15,288, MS-64, September 2014; $10,575, MS-64, October 2014												
1894, Proof	972	339	64.2								$2,850	$4,500	$8,000
	Auctions: $44,063, PF-67Cam, April 2013; $14,100, PF-66Cam, October 2014												
1894O	1,723,000	4,551	51.1	22%	$60	$115	$260	$950	$4,750	$11,500	$29,000	$65,000	$65,000
	Auctions: $44,063, MS-65, August 2013; $8,519, MS-64, July 2014; $8,225, MS-64, September 2014; $8,519, MS-64, November 2014												
1894S	1,260,000	3,162	56.5	66%	$95	$150	$450	$825	$1,200	$2,400	$22,000	$7,000	$35,000
	Auctions: $12,925, MS-66, January 2014; $9,106, MS-65, August 2014; $7,344, MS-65, October 2014; $6,463, MS-65, November 2014												
1895, Proof † (ww)	880	366	62.3								$47,500	$52,500	$75,000
	Auctions: $117,500, PF-68Cam, April 2013; $48,469, PF-64Cam, September 2014; $58,750, PF-64Cam, November 2014												
1895O	450,000	5,093	41.4	3%	$400	$600	$1,200	$14,500	$50,000	$80,000	$140,000	$165,000	$240,000
	Auctions: $82,250, MS-64, February 2013; $16,450, MS-61, August 2014; $4,700, AU-58, September 2014; $11,163, AU-58, October 2014												
1895O, Proof (tt)	2–3	5	64.0				*(extremely rare)*							
	Auctions: $528,750, PF-66, June 2013												
1895S	400,000	2,559	38.4	30%	$900	$1,200	$1,800	$3,900	$6,250	$11,000	$19,500	$26,000	$40,000
	Auctions: $45,531, MS-66, April 2014; $10,575, MS-64, October 2014; $9,988, MS-64, November 2014; $7,050, MS-63, September 2014												
1896	9,976,000	47,486	63.5	99%	$37	$39	$41	$50	$65	$90	$450	$250	$1,200
	Auctions: $9,694, MS-66DM, July 2014; $1,293, MS-65DM, August 2014; $1,116, MS-65DM, November 2014; $11,750, MS-67, September 2013												
1896, Proof	762	273	64.9								$1,400	$3,000	$6,200
	Auctions: $94,000, PF-69DCam, August 2013; $3,672, PF-63DCam, November 2014; $19,975, PF-68, October 2014; $1,528, PF-60, July 2014												
1896O	4,900,000	5,996	54.8	22%	$39	$43	$160	$1,500	$8,000	$42,000	$60,000	$175,000	$200,000
	Auctions: $94,000, MS-65, April 2013; $14,100, MS-63, September 2014; $9,106, MS-63, November 2014; $3,290, MS-62, August 2014												
1896S	5,000,000	1,636	49.6	45%	$70	$220	$775	$2,100	$3,750	$5,750	$57,500	$17,500	$100,000
	Auctions: $38,188, MS-66, April 2014; $18,800, MS-65, August 2014; $12,925, MS-65, November 2014; $6,760, MS-64, October 2014												
1897	2,822,000	16,197	63.4	98%	$37	$39	$41	$50	$65	$90	$500	$350	$3,700
	Auctions: $1,293, MS-64DM, July 2014; $376, MS-64DM, July 2014; $9,400, MS-66PL, June 2014; $6,169, MS-66PL, July 2014												
1897, Proof	731	206	64.5								$1,400	$3,000	$6,200
	Auctions: $35,250, PF-68, April 2014; $2,056, PF-62, September 2014; $881, PF-60, November 2014												
1897O	4,004,000	6,098	55.6	25%	$37	$41	$100	$850	$4,750	$16,500	$37,500	$60,000	$75,000
	Auctions: $3,966, MS-61PL, August 2014; $38,188, MS-65, April 2014; $5,581, MS-63, November 2014; $3,525, MS-62, September 2014												
1897S	5,825,000	7,725	62.9	93%	$37	$39	$45	$85	$140	$175	$800	$625	$2,500
	Auctions: $1,645, MS-66PL, October 2014; $1,528, MS-66PL, November 2014; $7,638, MS-66PL, March 2013; $1,234, MS-65PL, August 2014												
1898	5,884,000	20,668	63.6	98%	$37	$39	$41	$50	$65	$90	$450	$270	$1,300
	Auctions: $4,994, MS-66DM, September 2014; $881, MS-65DM, October 2014; $1,234, MS-66PL, November 2014												
1898, Proof	735	251	64.8								$1,400	$3,000	$6,200
	Auctions: $25,850, PF-67DCam, September 2014; $28,200, PF-67DCam, February 2013; $3,525, PF-64Cam, October 2014												
1898O	4,440,000	68,037	63.9	100%	$37	$39	$41	$50	$60	$80	$365	$175	$1,025
	Auctions: $6,463, MS-66DM, July 2014; $881, MS-65DM, July 2014; $940, MS-65DM, August 2014; $9,400, MS-67, July 2014												
1898S	4,102,000	3,108	59.9	69%	$40	$50	$100	$275	$475	$650	$3,250	$2,400	$13,750
	Auctions: $6,463, MS-64DM, August 2014; $3,966, MS-64DM, September 2014; $458, MS-63PL, July 2014; $5,015, MS-66, August 2013												

† Ranked in the *100 Greatest U.S. Coins* (fourth edition). **tt.** Some numismatists classify these as Deep Mirror Prooflike circulation strikes, rather than as Proofs. **vv.** Beware of altered or otherwise fraudulent mintmarks. **ww.** Mint records indicate that 12,000 1895 Morgan dollars were struck for circulation; however, none have ever been seen. In order to complete their collections, date-by-date collectors are forced to acquire one of the 880 Proofs struck that year, causing much competition for this, "The King of the Morgan Dollars."

**1900-O, Obverse
Die Crack**
VAM-29A. FS-S1-1900o-029a.

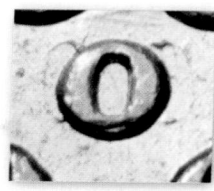

1900-O, O Over CC
Various VAMs.
FS-S1-1900o-501.

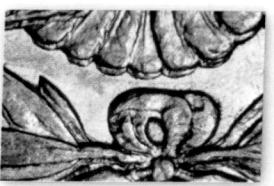

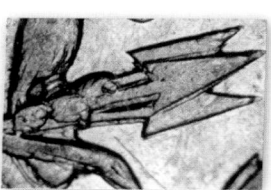

1901, Doubled-Die Reverse
The "Shifted Eagle" variety. VAM-3. FS-S1-1901-003.

	Mintage	Cert	Avg	%MS	VF-20	EF-40	AU-50	MS-60	MS-63	MS-64	MS-64DMPL PF-60	MS-65 PF-63	MS-65DMPL PF-65
1899	330,000	9,611	61.5	88%	$180	$200	$225	$265	$300	$400	$1,200	$925	$2,300
Auctions: $5,875, MS-66DM, April 2014; $368, MS-62DM, September 2014; $940, MS-65PL, November 2014; $764, MS-64PL, July 2014													
1899, Proof	846	225	64.0								$1,400	$3,000	$6,200
Auctions: $44,063, PF-67DCam, April 2013; $8,813, PF-65DCam, September 2014; $5,288, PF-65, August 2014; $764, PF-60, November 2014													
1899O	12,290,000	54,060	63.5	99%	$37	$39	$40	$50	$65	$90	$500	$210	$1,650
Auctions: $529, MS-64DM, September 2014; $17,625, MS-67, January 2014; $3,055, MS-67, October 2014; $1,998, MS-67, November 2014													
1899O, Micro O (xx)	(yy)	430	39.5	5%		$140	$375	$1,000					
Auctions: $49,938, MS-64, January 2014; $94, MS-60, September 2014; $80, EF-45, July 2014													
1899S	2,562,000	2,855	60.6	77%	$48	$65	$140	$380	$500	$825	$3,800	$2,150	$23,000
Auctions: $1,528, MS-65PL, November 2014; $4,994, MS-66, February 2014; $3,055, MS-66, August 2014; $3,525, MS-66, October 2014													
1900	8,830,000	30,636	63.6	98%	$37	$39	$41	$50	$65	$85	$9,000	$190	$40,000
Auctions: $2,115, MS-66PL, October 2014; $9,400, MS-67, January 2014; $5,581, MS-67, October 2014; $4,113, MS-67, October 2014													
1900, Proof	912	269	64.3								$1,400	$3,000	$6,200
Auctions: $27,025, PF-68Cam, August 2013; $7,050, PF-66Cam, October 2014; $8,225, PF-67, October 2014; $1,175, PF-60, July 2014													
1900O	12,590,000	41,285	63.7	99%	$37	$39	$41	$50	$65	$85	$1,100	$190	$5,750
Auctions: $2,115, MS-66PL, November 2014; $250, MS-65PL, November 2014; $153, MS-64PL, August 2014; $4,847, MS-67, August 2013													
1900O, Obverse Die Break (zz)	(aaa)	61	29.8	7%		$700		—	—				
Auctions: $529, AU-55, April 2013; $182, VF-30, August 2014; $165, VF-30, September 2014; $153, EF-40, October 2014													
1900O, O Over CC (bbb)	(aaa)	3,050	59.8	82%	$65	$105	$170	$325	$725	$950	$8,500	$2,100	$19,000
Auctions: $15,275, MS-66, January 2014; $1,939, MS-65, August 2014; $1,763, MS-64, July 2014; $999, MS-64, August 2014													
1900S	3,540,000	3,806	61.0	77%	$40	$48	$90	$300	$400	$650	$19,000	$1,800	$35,000
Auctions: $544, MS-64PL, September 2014; $1,322, MS-64PL, November 2014; $6,463, MS-66, September 2014													
1901 (ccc)	6,962,000	4,653	53.8	15%	$50	$115	$280	$3,000	$15,750	$50,000	$70,000	$475,000	
Auctions: $58,750, MS-64, November 2013; $20,563, MS-63, November 2014; $8,813, MS-62, July 2014; $7,050, MS-62, August 2014													
1901, Doubled-Die Reverse (ddd)	(eee)	104	42.7	2%	$375	$1,100	$1,900	$4,500	—				
Auctions: $41,125, MS-62, August 2013													
1901, Proof	813	279	63.5								$1,650	$3,500	$7,250
Auctions: $38,278, PF-68Cam, April 2013; $8,813, PF-66Cam, August 2014; $4,113, PF-64, October 2014; $2,585, PF-63, October 2014													
1901O	13,320,000	35,797	63.7	100%	$37	$39	$41	$50	$65	$85	$1,200	$200	$8,500
Auctions: $306, MS-63DM, September 2014; $646, MS-65PL, November 2014; $411, MS-65PL, November 2014; $7,075, MS-67, April 2014													
1901S	2,284,000	2,485	59.3	72%	$45	$65	$200	$475	$850	$1,200	$21,000	$3,500	$30,000
Auctions: $4,113, MS-64PL, October 2014; $11,750, MS-66, April 2014; $11,750, MS-66, October 2014; $3,672, MS-65, August 2014													

xx. The O mintmark is smaller than normal; its punch was probably intended for a Barber half dollar. Five different dies are known, all scarce. **yy.** Included in 1899-O mintage figure. **zz.** A die break is visible from the rim through the date to just below the lower point of the bust. This variety is very rare in Mint State. **aaa.** Included in 1900-O mintage figure. **bbb.** An O mintmark was punched into the die over a previously punched CC mintmark. There are at least seven different dies involved; the one pictured is VAM-9. **ccc.** Beware of a fraudulently removed mintmark intended to make a less valuable 1901-O or 1901-S appear to be a 1901 dollar. **ddd.** Doubling is visible on the eagle's tail feathers, and also on IN GOD WE TRUST, as well as on the arrows, wreath, and bow. This variety is nicknamed the "Shifted Eagle." It is very rare in Mint State. **eee.** Included in circulation-strike 1901 mintage figure.

1903-S,
Small S
Mintmark
VAM-2.
FS-S1-1903S-002.

	Mintage	Cert	Avg	%MS	VF-20	EF-40	AU-50	MS-60	MS-63	MS-64	MS-64DMPL / PF-60	MS-65 / PF-63	MS-65DMPL / PF-65
1902	7,994,000	5,665	63.3	96%	$37	$39	$45	$55	$135	$180	$13,000	$475	$20,000
Auctions: $1,645, MS-64PL, November 2014; $4,700, MS-67, October 2014; $4,700, MS-67, November 2013													
1902, Proof	777	231	64.0								$1,400	$3,000	$6,300
Auctions: $6,463, PF-65Cam, September 2014; $23,649, PF-68, April 2013; $9,988, PF-67, July 2014; $8,813, PF-67, October 2014													
1902O	8,636,000	64,692	63.6	100%	$37	$39	$45	$55	$65	$85	$2,800	$200	$13,500
Auctions: $558, MS-65PL, November 2014; $165, MS-64PL, September 2014; $101, MS-63PL, September 2014													
1902S	1,530,000	3,338	58.1	72%	$140	$190	$275	$380	$625	$800	$8,000	$2,750	$14,000
Auctions: $6,816, MS-65PL, April 2013; $6,463, MS-66, September 2014; $6,463, MS-66, October 2014; $2,468, MS-65, October 2014													
1903	4,652,000	11,863	63.4	96%	$50	$55	$65	$78	$90	$120	$7,500	$310	$22,500
Auctions: $2,585, MS-66PL, August 2014; $1,175, MS-65PL, November 2014; $411, MS-64PL, July 2014; $3,525, MS-67, June 2013													
1903, Proof	755	261	64.3								$1,400	$3,000	$6,200
Auctions: $32,900, PF-68Cam, August 2013; $17,625, PF-68, October 2014; $1,763, PF-62, July 2014; $764, PF-60, September 2014													
1903O	4,450,000	7,498	63.1	98%	$340	$350	$365	$415	$450	$475	$1,800	$625	$6,400
Auctions: $5,141, MS-65DM, July 2014; $1,058, MS-65PL, November 2014; $529, MS-64PL, October 2014													
1903S	1,241,000	2,391	34.3	12%	$205	$350	$1,600	$4,250	$6,500	$8,000	$15,000	$11,000	$38,000
Auctions: $16,450, MS-66, April 2014; $15,275, MS-66, September 2014; $14,100, MS-66, October 2014; $12,925, MS-66, October 2014													
1903S, Small S (fff)	(ggg)	125	25.9	1%			$6,400	—	—				
Auctions: $6,756, AU-50, January 2014; $617, VF-35, August 2014; $118, G-6, October 2014													
1904	2,788,000	4,175	62.0	89%	$40	$47	$55	$100	$260	$575	$42,500	$2,850	$60,000
Auctions: $8,813, MS-66, October 2014; $11,163, MS-66, December 2013; $1,763, MS-65, August 2014; $3,055, MS-65, October 2014													
1904, Proof	650	282	63.9								$1,400	$3,000	$6,200
Auctions: $9,400, PF-67, August 2013; $8,813, PF-67, August 2014; $3,525, PF-64, August 2014; $3,055, PF-64, August 2014													
1904O	3,720,000	128,074	63.8	100%	$37	$39	$41	$50	$60	$75	$450	$180	$1,150
Auctions: $1,058, MS-65DM, August 2014; $411, MS-64DM, July 2014; $342, MS-64DM, July 2014; $7,050, MS-67, February 2014													
1904S	2,304,000	1,993	47.3	33%	$80	$200	$500	$2,300	$4,500	$5,250	$13,000	$11,000	$22,000
Auctions: $30,550, MS-66PL, December 2013; $14,688, MS-66, September 2014; $9,400, MS-65, September 2014													
1921	44,690,000	100,867	63.4	99%	$36	$37	$38	$45	$55	$75	$7,750	$160	$11,500
Auctions: $3,525, MS-64DM, November 2014; $259, MS-63PL, September 2014; $176, MS-62PL, September 2014													
1921, Zerbe Proof (hhh)	150–250	71	64.1								$3,500	$5,250	$10,250
Auctions: $35,250, PF-66, January 2014; $18,800, PF-65, September 2014; $9,413, PF-64, October 2014; $9,988, PF-63, September 2014													
1921, Chapman Proof (iii)	25–40	1	66.0								$16,500	—	$75,000
Auctions: $61,688, PF-65, April 2013													
1921D	20,345,000	15,505	63.1	95%	$36	$37	$38	$50	$65	$120	$7,500	$375	$12,000
Auctions: $3,055, MS-64PL, July 2014; $411, MS-63PL, July 2014; $646, MS-63PL, November 2014; $44,063, MS-67, April 2013													
1921S	21,695,000	12,178	62.9	95%	$36	$37	$38	$50	$75	$160	$12,000	$1,200	$30,000
Auctions: $2,585, MS-64PL, July 2014; $5,581, MS-66, July 2014; $5,288, MS-66, August 2014; $14,100, MS-66, April 2013													
1921S, Zerbe Proof (hhh)	1–2	0	n/a										$140,000
Auctions: $117,500, PF-65, August 2013													

fff. The S mintmark is smaller than normal, possibly intended to be punched into a Barber half dollar die. **ggg.** Included in 1903-S mintage figure. **hhh.** "Pieces called Zerbe Proofs are simply circulation strikes with a semi-prooflike character, not as nice as on the earlier-noted [mirrorlike] prooflike pieces, struck from dies that were slightly polished, but that retained countless minute striae and preparation lines. In the view of the writer [Bowers], Zerbe Proofs have no basis in numismatic fact or history, although opinions differ on the subject. It seems highly unlikely that these were produced as Proofs for collectors. If indeed they were furnished to Farran Zerbe, a leading numismatic entrepreneur of the era, it is likely that they were simply regular production pieces. Zerbe had a fine collection and certainly knew what a brilliant Proof should look like, and he never would have accepted such pieces as mirror Proofs" (*A Guide Book of Morgan Silver Dollars*, fourth edition). **iii.** Breen stated that 12 Chapman Proofs were minted (*Walter Breen's Encyclopedia of U.S. and Colonial Proof Coins, 1792– 1977*); Bowers estimates fewer than 30 (*A Guide Book of Morgan Silver Dollars*, fourth edition). These are sometimes called *Chapman Proofs* because Philadelphia coin dealer Henry Chapman advertised them for sale within a few months of their production.

PEACE (1921–1935)

Designer: *Anthony de Francisci.* **Weight:** *26.73 grams.*
Composition: *.900 silver, .100 copper (net weight .77344 oz. pure silver).*
Diameter: *38.1 mm.* **Edge:** *Reeded.* **Mints:** *Philadelphia, Denver, San Francisco.*

Mintmark location is on the reverse, to the left of the tail feathers.

Circulation Strike

Proof

History. In 1921, following the melting of more than 270 million silver dollars as legislated by the Pittman Act of 1918, the U.S. Treasury struck millions more silver dollars of the Morgan type while a new Peace dollar was in development. Sculptor and medalist Anthony de Francisci created the Peace design, originally intended as a commemorative of the end of the hostilities of the Great War. The obverse features a flowing-haired Miss Liberty wearing a spiked tiara, and the reverse an eagle perched before the rising sun. The designer's monogram is located in the field of the coin under the neck of Miss Liberty. Coins of 1921 were struck in high relief; this caused weakness at the centers, so the design was changed to low relief in 1922. The dollars were struck until 1928, then again in 1934 and 1935. Legislation dated August 3, 1964, authorized the coinage of 45 million silver dollars, and 316,076 dollars of the Peace design dated 1964 were struck at the Denver Mint in 1965. Plans for completing this coinage were subsequently abandoned and all of these coins were melted. None were preserved or released for circulation; details are found in *A Guide Book of Peace Dollars* (Burdette).

Striking and Sharpness. Peace dollars of 1921 are always lightly struck at the center of the obverse, with hair detail not showing in an area. The size of this flat spot can vary. For this and other Peace dollars, check the hair detail at the center and, on the reverse, the feathers on the eagle. Many coins are struck from overly used dies, giving a grainy appearance to the fields, particularly the obverse. On many Peace dollars tiny white "milk spots" are seen, left over from when they were struck; these are not as desirable in the marketplace as unspotted coins.

Availability. All dates and mintmarks are readily available. Although some are well worn, they are generally collected in EF and finer grades. MS coins are available for each, with the 1934-S considered to be the key date. San Francisco issues of the 1920s, except for 1926-S, are often heavily bagmarked from coming into contact with other coins during shipment, storage, and other handling. The appearance of luster varies from issue to issue and can be deeply frosty, or—in the instance of Philadelphia Mint coins of 1928, 1934, and 1935—satiny or "creamy."

Proofs. Some Sandblast Proofs were made in 1921 and a limited issue in 1922 in high relief. These are rare today. Seemingly, a few Satin Proofs were also made in 1921. Sandblast Proofs of 1922 have a peculiar whitish surface in most instances, sometimes interrupted by small dark flecks or spots. There are a number of impostors among certified "Proofs."

Note: Values of common-date silver coins have been based on the current bullion price of silver, $17 per ounce, and may vary with the prevailing spot price.

GRADING STANDARDS

MS-60 to 70 (Mint State). *Obverse:* At MS-60, some abrasion and contact marks are evident, most noticeably on the cheek and on the hair to the right of the face and forehead. Luster is present, but may be dull or lifeless. At MS-63, contact marks are extensive but not distracting. Abrasion still is evident, but less than at lower levels. MS-64 coins are slightly finer. Some Peace dollars have whitish "milk spots" in the field; while these are

1921. Graded MS-64.

not caused by handling, but seem to have been from liquid at the mint or in storage, coins with these spots are rarely graded higher than MS-63 or 64. An MS-65 coin may have minor abrasion, but contact marks are so minute as to require magnification. Luster should be full and rich on earlier issues, and either frosty or satiny on later issues, depending on the date and mint. *Reverse:* At MS-60 some abrasion and contact marks are evident, most noticeably on the eagle's shoulder and nearby. Otherwise, comments apply as for the obverse.

Illustrated coin: Note the scattered marks that are practically definitive of the grade. The high relief of this particular year results in light striking at the center; this is normal and not to be mistaken for wear.

AU-50, 53, 55, 58 (About Uncirculated). *Obverse:* Light wear is seen on the cheek and the highest-relief areas of the hair. The neck truncation edge also shows wear. At AU-58, the luster is extensive, but incomplete. At AU-50 and 53, luster is less but still present. *Reverse:* Wear is evident on the eagle's shoulder and back. Otherwise, comments apply as for the obverse.

1934-S. Graded AU-53.

Illustrated coin: This coin shows medium and somewhat mottled toning. Luster is still seen in protected areas.

EF-40, 45 (Extremely Fine). *Obverse:* Further wear is seen on the highest-relief areas of the hair, with many strands now blended together. Some luster can usually be seen in protected areas on many coins, but is not needed to define the EF-40 and 45 grades. *Reverse:* Further wear is seen on the eagle, and the upper 60% of the feathers have most detail gone, except for the delineation of the edges of rows of feathers. PEACE shows light wear.

1928. Graded EF-40.

VF-20, 30 (Very Fine). *Obverse:* More wear shows on the hair, with more tiny strands now blended into heavy strands. *Reverse:* Further wear has resulted in very little feather detail except on the neck and tail. The rock shows wear. PEACE is slightly weak.

1934-D. Graded VF-30.

F-12, 15 (Fine). *Obverse:* Most of the hair is worn flat, with thick strands blended together, interrupted by fewer divisions than on higher grades. The rim is full. *Reverse:* Fewer feather details show. Most of the eagle, except for the tail feathers and some traces of feathers at the neck, is in outline only. The rays between the left side of the eagle and PEACE are weak and some details are worn away.

The Peace dollar is seldom collected in grades lower than F-12.

1921. Graded F-12.

PF-60 to 70 (Proof). *Obverse and Reverse:* Proofs of both types usually display very few handling marks or defects. To qualify as Satin PF-65 or Sandblast PF-65 or finer, contact marks must be microscopic.

1921. Satin Finish Proof.

1921, Line Through L
VAM-3. FS-S1-1921-003.

	Mintage	Cert	Avg	%MS	VF-20	EF-40	AU-50	MS-60	MS-62	MS-63	MS-64 / PF-60	MS-65 / PF-63	MS-66 / PF-65
1921, High Relief	1,006,473	13,879	59.3	77%	$110	$140	$150	$275	$375	$450	$900	$2,100	$7,000
Auctions: $16,450, MS-66, November 2013													
1921, High Relief, Line Through L (a)	(b)	57	59.5	79%			$225	$315	$375	$500	$950	$2,300	
Auctions: $940, MS-63, June 2013													
1921, Satin Finish Proof	*10–20*	17	63.1								$15,000	$30,000	$75,000
Auctions: $32,200, PF-64, July 2009													
1921, Sandblast Finish Proof	*5–8*	3	64.0										$100,000
Auctions: $99,875, PF-66, January 2014; $129,250, PF-64, August 2014													

a. A ray runs through the first L in DOLLAR, instead of behind it. **b.** Included in 1921, High Relief, mintage figure.

1922, Die Break in Field
VAM-1F. FS-S1-1922-001f.

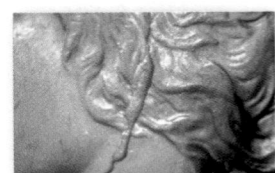

1922, Die Break at Ear
The "Ear Ring" variety.
VAM-2A. FS-S1-1922-002a.

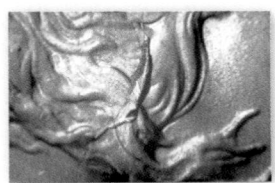

1922, Die Break in Hair
The 1922 "Extra Hair" variety.
VAM-2C. FS-S1-1922-002c.

1922, Die Break on Cheek
The "Scar Cheek" variety.
VAM-5A. FS-S1-1922-005a.

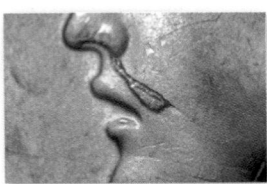

1922, Die Break at Nose
The "Moustache" variety.
VAM-12A. FS-S1-1922-012a.

	Mintage	Cert	Avg	%MS	VF-20	EF-40	AU-50	MS-60	MS-62	MS-63	MS-64 / PF-60	MS-65 / PF-63	MS-66 / PF-65
1922, High Relief (c)	35,401	0	n/a				—						
1922, Normal Relief	51,737,000	181,642	63.6	99%	$30	$32	$36	$41	$45	$50	$65	$160	$675
Auctions: $35,250, MS-67, August 2014; $17,625, MS-67, April 2013; $2,820, MS-66, August 2014; $3,055, MS-66, September 2014													
1922, Die Break in Field (d)	(e)	52	56.3	37%				$400	$800	$1,750	$2,500		
Auctions: $1,528, MS-64, December 2013; $58, AU-55, September 2014													
1922, Die Break at Ear (f)	(e)	54	58.1	50%				$290	$650	$1,400	$2,300		
Auctions: $1,293, MS-63, December 2013													
1922, Die Break in Hair (g)	(e)	207	57.0	52%				$90	$180	$300	$385		
Auctions: $259, MS-64, February 2014; $74, MS-62, October 2014; $69, MS-61, September 2014													
1922, Die Break on Cheek (h)	(e)	34	59.2	68%				$190	$400	$550			
Auctions: $940, MS-65, January 2014; $200, AU-58, September 2014													
1922, Die Break at Nose (i)	(e)	107	58.0	50%				$90	$200	$325	$500	$975	
Auctions: $159, MS-62, September 2014; $65, MS-62, October 2014													
1922, High Relief, Sandblast Finish Proof	10–15	12	64.6										$175,000
Auctions: $329,000, PF-67, January 2014													
1922, Low Relief, Sandblast Finish Proof	3–6	3	65.3										$75,000
Auctions: $35,200, PF-65, November 1988													
1922, Low Relief, Satin Finsih Proof	3–6	2	64.0										$75,000
Auctions: $44,850, PF-60, November 2009													
1922D	15,063,000	6,775	63.2	95%	$32	$33	$37	$42	$50	$80	$150	$625	$2,350
Auctions: $6,463, MS-67, October 2014; $3,525, MS-66, August 2014; $1,998, MS-66, October 2014; $5,875, MS-66, November 2013													
1922S	17,475,000	5,532	62.4	92%	$32	$33	$35	$50	$60	$80	$300	$2,400	$25,000
Auctions: $11,750, MS-66, April 2014; $3,290, MS-65, August 2014; $3,290, MS-65, September 2014													

c. 1 example is known. **d.** A die break is visible in the field above DOLLAR. "This variety has turned out to be much rarer than previously thought, and is very scarce in grades above EF" (*Cherrypickers' Guide to Rare Die Varieties*, sixth edition, volume II). **e.** Included in 1922, Normal Relief, mintage figure. **f.** A major die break near Liberty's ear, dangling down to her neck, gives this variety its nickname, the "Ear Ring." Several die states are known. **g.** An irregular line of raised metal runs along the back of Liberty's hair. This is called the "Extra Hair" variety. Several die states are known. **h.** Liberty's cheek has a raised, almost triangular chunk of metal along a vertical die break. Also, the reverse is lightly tripled. This variety, called the "Scarface," is very scarce in Mint State. **i.** A die break is visible running from Liberty's nose along the top of her mouth. This is known as the "Moustache" variety.

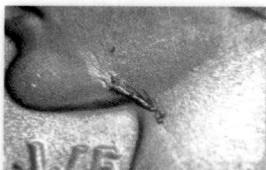

1923, Die Break at Jaw
The "Whisker Jaw" variety.
VAM-1A. FS-S1-1923-001a.

1923, Die Break in Hair
The 1923 "Extra Hair"
variety. VAM-1B.
FS-S1-1923-001b.

1923, Die Break on
O in DOLLAR
The "Tail on O" variety.
VAM-1C. FS-S1-1923-001c.

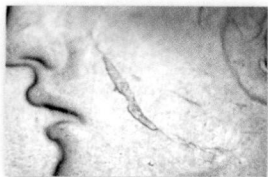

1923, Die Break on Cheek
The "Whisker Cheek" variety.
VAM-1D. FS-S1-1923-001d.

1923, Doubled-Die Obverse
The "Double Tiara" variety. VAM-2. FS-S1-1923-002.

1923-S, Pitted Reverse
VAM-1C. FS-S1-1923S-001c.

1924, Die Break on Wing
The "Broken Wing" variety.
VAM-5A. FS-S1-1924-005a.

	Mintage	Cert	Avg	%MS	VF-20	EF-40	AU-50	MS-60	MS-62	MS-63	MS-64 PF-60	MS-65 PF-63	MS-66 PF-65
1923	30,800,000	277,486	63.8	100%	$30	$32	$35	$41	$45	$50	$65	$150	$625
Auctions: $7,638, MS-67, June 2014; $7,638, MS-67, August 2014; $4,994, MS-67, November 2014; $3,525, MS-66, October 2014													
1923, Die Break at Jaw (j)	(k)	189	61.1	82%			$80	$125	$175	$265	$550		$1,250
Auctions: $999, MS-66, December 2013; $382, MS-65, July 2014; $159, MS-64, September 2014; $223, MS-64, December 2014													
1923, Die Break in Hair (l)	(k)	74	61.4	87%			$125	$200	$300	$400	$600		
Auctions: $223, MS-64, February 2014; $59, MS-64, September 2014; $115, MS-63, August 2014; $84, MS-63, September 2014													
1923, Die Break on O (m)	(k)	62	58.7	73%			$275	$650	$1,150	$1,800			
Auctions: $2,468, MS-65, April 2014													
1923, Die Break on Cheek (n)	(k)	78	59.9	68%			$165	$250	$350	$475	$875		
Auctions: $118, MS-63, October 2014; $259, MS-63, December 2013; $176, MS-62, July 2014; $188, MS-62, October 2014													
1923, DblDie Obverse (o)	(k)	61	61.3	82%			$58	$75	$100	$160	$375		
Auctions: $223, MS-64, April 2014; $62, MS-61, September 2014; $50, AU-58, September 2014; $65, AU-58, November 2014													
1923D	6,811,000	3,335	62.2	90%	$32	$35	$36	$58	$85	$150	$400	$1,300	$4,750
Auctions: $76,375, MS-67, June 2013; $16,450, MS-66+, July 2014; $10,575, MS-66, July 2014; $7,638, MS-66, August 2014													
1923S	19,020,000	5,999	62.2	91%	$32	$35	$38	$45	$70	$90	$500	$6,000	$30,000
Auctions: $5,875, MS-65, August 2014; $3,525, MS-65, September 2014; $1,998, MS-65, November 2014													
1923S, Pitted Reverse (p)	(q)	26	57.6	50%			$125	$250	—	$450	$975		
Auctions: $282, MS-63, December 2013													
1924	11,811,000	42,901	63.8	99%	$30	$32	$37	$41	$45	$50	$65	$150	$650
Auctions: $2,233, MS-67, September 2014; $2,585, MS-67, October 2014; $14,100, MS-67, September 2013													
1924, Die Break on Wing (r)	(s)	48	60.8	77%			$130	$200	$375	$475			
Auctions: $101, MS-63, September 2014; $106, MS-62, August 2014													
1924S	1,728,000	4,018	60.7	74%	$32	$40	$60	$220	$400	$525	$1,400	$9,000	$43,500
Auctions: $4,700, MS-65, July 2014; $6,463, MS-65+, September 2014; $7,638, MS-65, September 2013													

j. A die break bridges Liberty's cheek and jaw. This is the "Whisker Jaw" variety. **k.** Included in 1923 mintage figure. **l.** A significant die break runs diagonally across the strands of Liberty's hair; die breaks may also be visible toward the back of her hair. This variety is nicknamed the 1923 "Extra Hair." **m.** A die break trails from the O of DOLLAR. This variety, called the "Tail on O," is very rare in any grade. **n.** A die break runs down Liberty's cheek toward the junction of the chin and neck. This is the "Whisker Cheek" variety. **o.** Doubling is most evident in the wide spread on the rays of Liberty's tiara, especially those under the BER of LIBERTY. This is the "Double Tiara" variety. **p.** "Pitting runs from the eagle's back tail-feathers, just to the right of the mintmark, upward to the N in ONE. . . . This is the most important Pitted Reverse variety in the Peace dollar series" (*Cherrypickers' Guide to Rare Die Varieties,* sixth edition, volume II). **q.** Included in 1923-S mintage figure. **r.** A dramatic die break runs down and across the entire width of the eagle's back. This is the "Broken Wing" variety. **s.** Included in 1924 mintage figure.

1925, Missing Ray
VAM-5. FS-S1-1925-005.

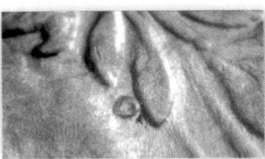

1926-S, Reverse Dot
The "Extra Berry" variety.
VAM-4. FS-S1-1926S-004.

1934-D, Doubled-Die Obverse, Small D
VAM-4. FS-S1-1934D-004.

	Mintage	Cert	Avg	%MS	VF-20	EF-40	AU-50	MS-60	MS-62	MS-63	MS-64 / PF-60	MS-65 / PF-63	MS-66 / PF-65
1925	10,198,000	48,081	63.9	99%	$30	$32	$37	$41	$45	$50	$65	$160	$625
Auctions: $9,106, MS-67, April 2014; $5,875, MS-67, August 2014; $5,581, MS-67, September 2014; $3,290, MS-67, October 2014													
1925, Missing Ray (t)	(u)	79	62.6	90%			$65	$85	$100	$145	$250	$400	
Auctions: $129, MS-64, December 2013; $59, MS-62, September 2014; $47, MS-62, September 2014													
1925S	1,610,000	5,527	61.9	88%	$32	$35	$45	$100	$180	$280	$1,100	$27,500	—
Auctions: $29,375, MS-65, August 2014; $7,638, MS-65, August 2014; $7,298, MS-65, September 2014													
1926	1,939,000	8,566	63.2	97%	$32	$35	$37	$52	$100	$110	$140	$600	$2,100
Auctions: $10,575, MS-66, April 2014; $3,525, MS-66, August 2014; $1,704, MS-66, September 2014; $2,469, MS-65, July 2014													
1926D	2,348,700	3,451	62.3	87%	$32	$35	$40	$80	$140	$190	$425	$1,000	$2,500
Auctions: $2,820, MS-66, August 2014; $1,528, MS-66, September 2014; $1,772, MS-66, November 2014													
1926S	6,980,000	5,696	62.4	90%	$32	$35	$38	$57	$75	$120	$325	$1,100	$4,850
Auctions: $2,820, MS-66, August 2014; $2,468, MS-66, August 2014; $4,553, MS-66, June 2013; $1,293, MS-65, September 2014													
1926S, Reverse Dot (v)	(w)	38	55.7	47%			$55	$90	$140	$200	$360		
Auctions: $823, MS-65, December 2013; $165, MS-64, September 2014; $80, MS-62, August 2014; $61, AU-58, November 2014													
1927	848,000	5,380	62.1	89%	$39	$42	$50	$85	$120	$200	$625	$2,900	$23,000
Auctions: $35,250, MS-66, August 2014; $9,988, MS-65, February 2014; $4,994, MS-65, August 2014													
1927D	1,268,900	3,266	61.0	78%	$39	$45	$75	$200	$250	$380	$1,050	$4,750	$25,000
Auctions: $9,988, MS-65, November 2013; $2,468, MS-64, October 2014; $1,234, MS-64, October 2014													
1927S	866,000	3,801	61.3	82%	$39	$45	$75	$200	$265	$600	$1,300	$9,750	$45,000
Auctions: $17,625, MS-65, April 2014; $3,290, MS-64+, July 2014; $3,819, MS-64+, August 2014; $5,288, MS-64+, October 2014													
1928	360,649	7,030	59.4	69%	$350	$375	$400	$500	$600	$900	$1,300	$4,500	$25,000
Auctions: $30,550, MS-66, November 2014; $21,150, MS-65+, August 2014; $11,163, MS-65+, October 2014													
1928S	1,632,000	5,096	60.7	77%	$39	$48	$65	$200	$300	$525	$1,200	$22,000	—
Auctions: $17,625, MS-65, April 2013; $2,820, MS-64+, July 2014; $2,115, MS-64+, August 2014													
1934	954,057	5,197	62.4	89%	$44	$45	$50	$115	$170	$225	$400	$750	$3,000
Auctions: $11,163, MS-66, June 2014; $4,406, MS-66, July 2014; $3,672, MS-66, August 2014; $3,055, MS-66, September 2014													
1934D (x)	1,569,500	4,786	61.0	78%	$44	$45	$50	$150	$250	$375	$625	$2,100	$4,900
Auctions: $3,819, MS-66, November 2014; $22,325, MS-66, June 2013; $1,998, MS-65, September 2014													
1934D, DblDie Obv, Sm D (y)	(z)	54	56.3	52%	$115	$185	$375	$750	$900	$1,650			
Auctions: $881, MS-62, January 2014; $852, MS-62, September 2014													
1934S	1,011,000	3,563	50.7	35%	$80	$175	$500	$2,000	$2,800	$4,000	$5,250	$9,000	$27,500
Auctions: $23,645, MS-66, April 2014; $23,500, MS-66, October 2014; $5,581, MS-65, October 2014													
1935	1,576,000	6,701	62.7	91%	$44	$45	$50	$85	$90	$125	$270	$775	$2,500
Auctions: $11,163, MS-66, April 2014; $3,819, MS-66, August 2014; $3,290, MS-66, August 2014; $3,055, MS-66, September 2014													
1935S (aa)	1,964,000	3,385	61.2	80%	$44	$50	$88	$275	$350	$460	$675	$1,550	$3,800
Auctions: $4,994, MS-66, August 2014; $4,259, MS-66, October 2014; $4,113, MS-66, October 2014; $39,656, MS-65, April 2013													
1964D (bb)	316,076	0	n/a		*(none known to exist)*								
Auctions: No auction records available.													

t. This variety is the result of a reverse die polished with too much gusto. The partially effaced remains of bold clash marks are evident, but the topmost internal ray is missing. **u.** Included in 1925 mintage figure. **v.** A raised circular dot of metal is visible to the left of the bottom olive leaf. This is nicknamed the "Extra Berry" variety. **w.** Included in 1926-S mintage figure. **x.** Varieties exist with small and large mintmarks. **y.** The obverse shows strong doubling on most letters of IN GOD WE TRUST, the rays on the right, and especially on Liberty's profile. The mintmark is a small D, shaped much like that of the 1920s-era D punches. **z.** Included in 1934-D mintage figure. **aa.** Varieties exist with either three or four rays below ONE. They are valued equally in the marketplace. **bb.** The entire mintage of 1964-D Peace dollars was melted by government order. Deceptive reproductions exist.

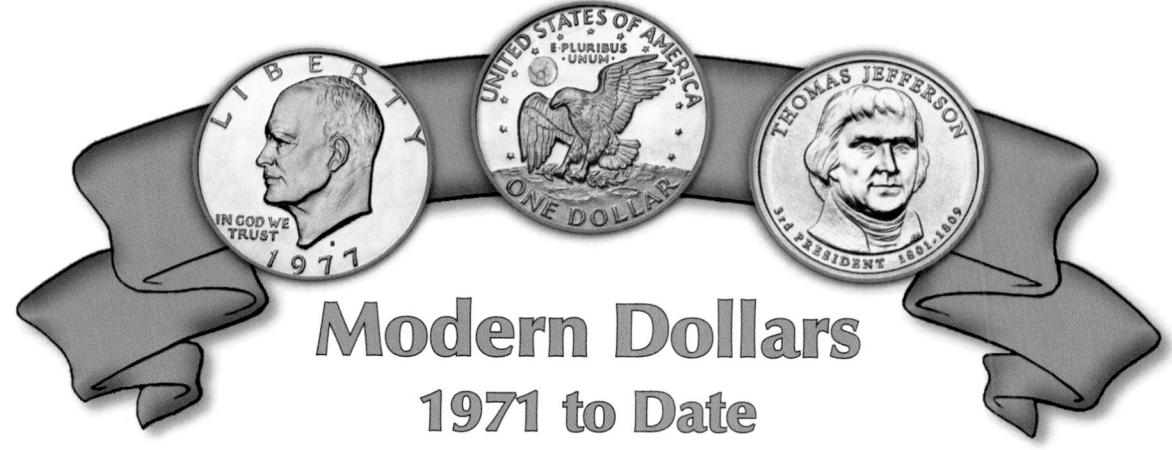

Modern Dollars
1971 to Date

AN OVERVIEW OF MODERN DOLLARS

After the last Peace dollars rolled off the presses at the San Francisco and Philadelphia mints in 1935, there was a long lapse in silver dollar coinage until 1965. In that year the Denver Mint struck Peace dollars dated 1964—the start of production of 45 million coins authorized by legislation of August 3, 1964. This coinage ultimately was stopped after 316,076 of the new Peace dollars were made; they were held back from being released into circulation and melted. It would be another six years before the United States had a new dollar coin, and it would not be silver.

Production of the next dollar started in 1971. The coin was the size of the 20th century's earlier silver dollars, but made in copper-nickel for circulation (and, in much smaller quantities, in .400 fine silver for collectors). Its motifs honor the late President Dwight D. Eisenhower, and the *Apollo 11* spaceflight that had landed the first men on the Moon in 1969.

Silver dollars had long since disappeared from circulation, but there was demand for dollar coins in Las Vegas, Reno, and other centers of legalized gambling. Casinos otherwise had to depend on gaming chips and tokens.

The Eisenhower dollar was minted from 1971 to 1978, with those made in 1975 and 1976 being dual-dated 1776–1976 for the national bicentennial. In 1979 the "Ike" dollar was replaced by a smaller-format coin, the Susan B. Anthony dollar, honoring the famous women's-rights leader. Its reverse design shows an eagle landing on the Moon, similar to that of its predecessor (this design had in turn been based on the official insignia of the *Apollo 11* mission). The Anthony dollar was struck in 1979, 1980, and 1981; then, in 1999 an additional final mintage of more than 40 million coins was produced to meet the needs of the vending-machine industry until distribution of the next year's new-design dollars could begin.

Two famous faces on dollar coins: suffragette Susan B. Anthony and the 34th president of the United States, Dwight D. Eisenhower.

The year 2000 marked the debut of the first of several types of "golden" dollars, so called for the lustrous color of their manganese-brass surfaces. First came the Sacagawea dollar, minted from 2000 to 2008, with its conceptualized portrait of the young Shoshone Native American interpreter and guide who assisted the Lewis and Clark expedition of the early 1800s. A series of Native American dollars, each celebrating a different aspect of Native culture and historical importance, which began in 2009 and is ongoing today, is an offshoot of the Sacagawea dollar. And, since 2007, the golden-dollar format has been the canvas for a series of presidential portrait dollars honoring the nation's chief executives.

FOR THE COLLECTOR AND INVESTOR: MODERN DOLLARS AS A SPECIALTY

Eisenhower dollars, Susan B. Anthony dollars, and the golden dollars of various types are all easily found in today's marketplace. Dealers often have an abundance on hand of every date, mint, and most varieties. Banks sometimes have small quantities of Eisenhower or Anthony dollars. The current series are available directly from the U.S. Mint in collector formats and in rolls and bags of circulation strikes.

Eisenhower dollars are easily obtained in choice Mint State, although some of the coins made for circulation, especially of the earlier years, tend to be blemished with contact marks from jostling other coins during minting, transportation, and storage. Gems can be elusive. The Mint issued many options for collectors, including Proofs and .400 fine silver issues. Specialists look for die varieties including modified features, doubled dies, changes in depth of relief in the design, and other popular anomalies and variations that increase the challenge of building an extensive collection in what is otherwise a fairly short coinage series. Some Denver Mint dollars of 1974 and 1977 are also known to be struck in error, in silver clad composition rather than the intended copper-nickel.

Anthony dollars, too, are easy to assemble into a complete, high-grade collection of dates and mints. Specialists can focus on both varieties of 1979-P (Narrow Rim and Wide Rim), and varieties of S mintmark styles among the Proofs. Even these are common enough to easily acquire. Those seeking a harder challenge can search for the elusive 1980-S, Repunched Mintmark, Proof.

The Sacagawea dollar series includes several uncommon varieties that make an otherwise easy-to-collect type more challenging. The 2000-P coins include popular die varieties as detailed herein. Later dates were struck in smaller quantities and not issued for circulation, but still are readily available in high grades in the numismatic marketplace.

Native American dollars of 2009 to date are readily available in high grades.

The Presidential dollar series includes some error varieties with plain edges, instead of the normal lettered edge. These can be added to a date-and-mintmark collection for reasonable premiums. Otherwise the entire series is readily collectible from the secondary market and, for the current year of issue, in quantity directly from the U.S. Mint.

EISENHOWER (1971–1978)

Designer: *Frank Gasparro.* **Weight:** *Silver issue—24.59 grams; copper-nickel issue—22.68 grams.*
Composition: *Silver issue—40% silver, 60% copper, consisting of outer layers of .800 silver,*
.200 copper bonded to inner core of .209 silver, .791 copper (net weight .3161 oz. pure silver);
copper-nickel issue—outer layers of .750 copper, .250 nickel bonded to inner core of pure copper.
Diameter: *38.1 mm.* **Edge:** *Reeded.* **Mints:** *Philadelphia, Denver, San Francisco.*

Circulation
Strike

Proof

Bicentennial variety: Designers: *Frank Gasparro and Dennis R. Williams.*
Weight: *Silver issue—24.59 grams; copper-nickel issue—22.68 grams.*
Composition: *Silver issue—outer layers of .800 silver, .200 copper bonded
to inner core of .209 silver, .791 copper (net weight .3161 oz. pure silver);
copper-nickel issue—outer layers of .750 copper, .250 nickel bonded to inner core of pure copper.*
Diameter: *38.1 mm.* **Edge:** *Reeded.* **Mints:** *Philadelphia, Denver, San Francisco.*

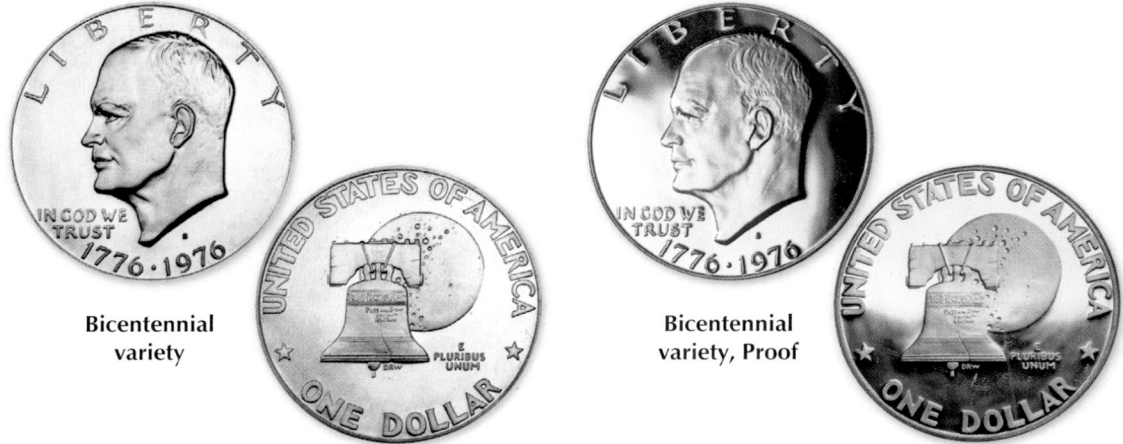

Bicentennial
variety

Bicentennial
variety, Proof

History. Honoring both President Dwight D. Eisenhower and the first landing of man on the Moon, this coin is the work of Chief Engraver Frank Gasparro, whose initials are on the truncation of the president's neck and below the eagle. The reverse is an adaptation of the official *Apollo 11* insignia. Collectors' coins were struck in 40% silver composition and sold by the Mint at a premium, and the circulation issue (for years a staple of the casino trade) was made in copper-nickel.

The dies for the Eisenhower dollar were modified several times by changing the relief, strengthening the design, and making Earth (above the eagle) more clearly defined.

Low-relief (Variety 1) dies, with a flattened Earth and three islands off the coast of Florida, were used for all copper-nickel issues of 1971, Uncirculated silver coins of 1971, and most copper-nickel coins of 1972.

High-relief (Variety 2) dies, with a round Earth and weak or indistinct islands, were used for all Proofs of 1971, all silver issues of 1972, and the reverse of some exceptional and scarce Philadelphia copper-nickel coins of 1972.

Improved high-relief reverse dies (Variety 3) were used for late-1972 Philadelphia copper-nickel coins and for all subsequent issues. Modified high-relief dies were also used on all issues beginning in 1973.

A few 1974-D and 1977-D dollars were made, in error, in silver clad composition.

A special reverse design was selected for the nation's Bicentennial. Nearly a thousand entries were submitted after the Treasury announced an open competition in October 1973. After the field was narrowed down to 12 semifinalists, the judges chose a rendition of the Liberty Bell superimposed on the Moon to appear on the dollar coins. The obverse remained unchanged except for the dual date 1776–1976, which appeared on all dollars made during 1975 and 1976. These dual-dated coins were included in the various offerings of Proof and Uncirculated coins made by the Mint. They were also struck for general circulation. The lettering was slightly modified early in 1975 to produce a more attractive design.

Striking and Sharpness. Striking generally is very good. For circulation strikes, on the obverse check the high parts of the portrait, and on the reverse, the details of the eagle. Nearly all Proofs are well struck and of high quality.

Availability. MS coins are common in the marketplace, although several early varieties are elusive at MS-65 or higher grades. Lower grades are not widely collected. Proofs were made of the various issues (both copper-nickel clad and silver clad from 1971 to 1976; copper-nickel only in 1977 and 1978). All are readily available in the marketplace today.

Note: Values of common-date silver coins have been based on the current bullion price of silver, $17 per ounce, and may vary with the prevailing spot price.

GRADING STANDARDS

MS-60 to 70 (Mint State). *Obverse:* At MS-60, some abrasion and contact marks are evident, most noticeably on the cheek, jaw, and temple. Luster is present, but may be dull or lifeless. At MS-63, contact marks are extensive but not distracting. Abrasion still is evident, but less than at lower levels. MS-64 coins are slightly finer. An MS-65 coin may have minor abrasion, but contact marks are so minute as to require magnification. Luster

1971-S. Graded MS-65.

should be full and rich. *Reverse:* At MS-60, some abrasion and contact marks are evident, most noticeably on the eagle's breast, head, and talons. Otherwise, the same comments apply as for the obverse.

AU-50, 53, 55, 58 (About Uncirculated). *Obverse:* Light wear is seen on the higher-relief areas of the portrait. At AU-58, the luster is extensive, but incomplete. At AU-50 and 53, luster is less but still present. *Reverse:* Further wear is evident on the eagle, particularly the head, breast, talons, and tops of the wings. Otherwise, the same comments apply as for the obverse.

1972. Graded AU-50.

The Eisenhower dollar is seldom collected in grades lower than AU-50.

PF-60 to 70 (Proof). *Obverse and Reverse:* Proofs that are extensively cleaned and have many hairlines, or that are dull and grainy, are lower level, such as PF-60 to 62. There are not many of these in the marketplace. With medium hairlines and good reflectivity, assigned grades of PF-63 or 64 are appropriate. With relatively few hairlines a rating of PF-65 can be given. PF-66 may have hairlines so delicate that magnification is needed

1776–1976, Bicentennial. Graded PF-68.

to see them. Above that, a Proof should be free of any hairlines or other problems.

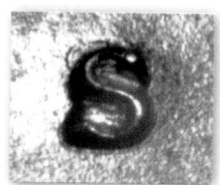

1971-S, Repunched Mintmark, Silver Clad

1971-S, Polished Die, Silver Clad
The "Peg Leg R" variety.

1971-S, Doubled-Die Obverse, Proof

1972-S, Silver Clad, Doubled-Die Obverse, Proof

	Mintage	Cert	Avg	%MS	EF-40	MS-63	MS-65	MS-66
						PF-65	PF-67Cam	PF-68DC
1971, Copper-Nickel Clad ‡	47,799,000	1,370	64.0	97%	$2.25	$6	$120	$1,000
Auctions: $1,645, MS-66, July 2014; $1,410, MS-66, August 2014; $10,281, MS-66+, October 2014							
1971D, Copper-Nickel Clad, Variety 1	68,587,424	2,459	64.8	98%	$3.50	$5	$50	$130
Auctions: $94, MS-66, October 2014; $100, MS-66, November 2014; $165, MS-65, August 2014							
1971D, Copper-Nickel Clad, Variety 2	(a)	0	n/a		$2	$5	$50	$130
Auctions: No auction records available.							
1971S, Silver Clad	6,868,530	2,992	65.2	100%		$13	$20	$75
Auctions: $4,994, MS-67, January 2014; $66, MS-66, August 2014							
1971S, Silver Clad, Repunched Mintmark (b)	(c)	4	65.0	100%			$225	$350
Auctions: $96, MS-65, June 2013							
1971S, Silver Clad, Polished Die (d)	(c)	0	n/a				$125	$250
Auctions: $56, MS-64, January 2010							
1971S, Silver Clad, Proof	4,265,234	4,956	68.1			$14	$15	$25
Auctions: $4,700, PF-70DCam, June 2013; $153, PF-69DCam, November 2014; $44, PF-69DCam, November 2014							
1971S, Silver Clad, DblDie Obv, Proof (e)	(f)	22	67.9			$90	$150	
Auctions: $1,528, PF-68Cam, April 2014							
1972, Copper-Nickel Clad, All kinds	75,890,000							
1972, Copper-Nickel Clad, Variety 1		1,196	64.0	98%	$2	$5	$140	$7,000
Auctions: $823, MS-65, August 2013							
1972, Copper-Nickel Clad, Variety 2 ‡		469	62.3	87%	$7	$80	$1,300	$8,500
Auctions: $4,847, MS-65, January 2014; $485, MS-64+, July 2014; $223, MS-64, October 2014							
1972, Copper-Nickel Clad, Variety 3		927	64.2	98%	$2.50	$5	$125	$900
Auctions: $4,700, MS-66, January 2014; $76, MS-65, August 2014; $84, MS-65, October 2014							
1972D, Copper-Nickel Clad	92,548,511	1,435	64.7	98%	$2	$5	$30	$150
Auctions: $90, MS-66, October 2014; $123, MS-66, November 2014; $79, MS-66, November 2014							
1972S, Silver Clad	2,193,056	4,010	66.5	100%		$13	$15	$20
Auctions: $206, MS-68, January 2014; $135, MS-68, August 2014; $141, MS-68, September 2014							
1972S, Silver Clad, Proof	1,811,631	3,675	68.2			$14	$15	$25
Auctions: $2,820, PF-70DCam, June 2013; $66, PF-69DCam, November 2014							
1972S, Silver Clad, Doubled-Die Obverse, Proof (g)	(h)	13	68.1					—
Auctions: $25, PF-67, March 2008							

‡ Ranked in the *100 Greatest U.S. Modern Coins*. Only issued in Mint sets. **a.** Included in 1971-D, Copper-Nickel Clad, Variety 1, mintage figure. **b.** A secondary S is visible protruding northwest of the primary S. "This is one of fewer than a half dozen RPMs known for the entire series" (*Cherrypickers' Guide to Rare Die Varieties*, sixth edition, volume II). **c.** Included in circulation-strike 1971-S, Silver Clad, mintage figure. **d.** The left leg of the R in LIBERTY was overpolished. This is popularly known as the "Peg Leg R" variety. **e.** Strong doubling is visible on IN GOD WE TRUST, the date, and LIBER of LIBERTY. There are at least two doubled-die obverses for this date (valued similarly); the one listed is FS-S1-1971S-103. "This obverse is also paired with a minor doubled-die reverse" (*Cherrypickers' Guide to Rare Die Varieties*, sixth edition, volume II). **f.** Included in 1971-S, Proof, Silver Clad, mintage figure. **g.** A medium spread of doubling is evident on IN GOD WE TRUST, LIBERTY, and slightly on the date. **h.** Included in 1972-S, Proof, Silver Clad, mintage figure.

1973-S, Silver Clad,
Doubled-Die
Obverse, Proof

	Mintage	Cert	Avg	%MS	EF-40	MS-63	MS-65	MS-66
						PF-65	PF-67Cam	PF-68DC
1973, Copper-Nickel Clad ‡	2,000,056	972	64.4	100%		$13	$65	$750
Auctions: $382, MS-66, November 2014; $999, MS-66, June 2013								
1973D, Copper-Nickel Clad ‡	2,000,000	935	64.5	100%		$13	$50	$275
Auctions: $12,925, MS-67, June 2013								
1973S, Copper-Nickel Clad (i)	**(j)**	0	n/a					
Auctions: No auction records available.								
1973S, Silver Clad	1,883,140	2,746	66.3	100%		$14	$18	$35
Auctions: $247, MS-68, August 2014; $147, MS-68, September 2014; $282, MS-68, August 2013								
1973S, Copper-Nickel Clad, Proof	2,760,339	1,090	68.1			$14	$16	$30
Auctions: $56, PF-69DCam, January 2013								
1973S, Silver Clad, Proof	1,013,646	3,157	68.1			$35	$37	$50
Auctions: $100, PF-69Cam, July 2014; $123, PF-67DCam, January 2014								
1973S, Silver Clad, DblDie Obv, Proof (g)	**(k)**	1	67.0					—
Auctions: No auction records available.								
1974, Copper-Nickel Clad	27,366,000	1,119	64.5	99%	$2	$6	$60	$550
Auctions: $646, MS-66, June 2014; $499, MS-66, July 2014; $3,819, MS-66+, August 2014								
1974D, Copper-Nickel Clad	45,517,000	7,439	65.0	100%	$2	$6	$38	$130
Auctions: $14,100, MS-65, January 2014								
1974S, Silver Clad	1,900,156	3,488	66.4	100%		$13	$20	$25
Auctions: $170, MS-68, August 2014; $259, MS-68, September 2014; $259, MS-68, August 2013								
1974S, Copper-Nickel Clad, Proof	2,612,568	954	68.0			$10	$15	$30
Auctions: $56, PF-69DCam, January 2013								
1974S, Silver Clad, Proof	1,306,579	3,533	68.3			$15	$16	$30
Auctions: $66, PF-68DCam, August 2014; $53, PF-68DCam, August 2014; $47, PF-68DCam, August 2014								
1776–1976, Copper-Nickel Clad, Variety 1	4,019,000	807	64.1	100%	$2	$8	$160	$1,250
Auctions: $7,638, MS-66, October 2014; $200, MS-65, November 2014; $28,200, MS-64, January 2014								
1776–1976, Copper-Nickel Clad, Variety 2	113,318,000	2,905	64.9	99%	$2	$5	$30	$125
Auctions: $112, MS-64, July 2014; $823, MS-63, November 2013								
1776–1976D, Copper-Nickel Clad, Variety 1	21,048,710	1,771	64.8	100%	$2	$5	$50	$185
Auctions: $182, MS-66, July 2014; $223, MS-66, September 2014; $1,410, MS-66, October 2014								
1776–1976D, Copper-Nickel Clad, Variety 2	82,179,564	5,353	65.0	100%	$2	$5	$28	$60
Auctions: $705, MS-66+, August 2014; $48, MS-66, October 2014; $36, MS-66, October 2014								
1776–1976S, Copper-Nickel Clad, Variety 1, Proof ‡	2,845,450	1,182	67.9			$12	$15	$30
Auctions: $141, PF-69DCam, January 2013								
1776–1976S, Copper-Nickel Clad, Variety 2, Proof	4,149,730	1,656	68.1			$8	$12	$30
Auctions: $56, PF-69DCam, January 2013								
1776–1976, Silver Clad, Variety 2		0	n/a					
Auctions: No auction records available.								
1776–1976, Silver Clad, Variety 2, Proof		0	n/a			—		
Auctions: $4,600, PF-70DCam, January 2012								
1776–1976S, Silver Clad, Variety 1	11,000,000	2,547	66.2	100%		$17	$20	$30
Auctions: $999, MS-68, July 2014; $353, MS-68, July 2014; $529, MS-68, August 2014								
1776–1976S, Silver Clad, Variety 1, Proof	4,000,000	4,036	68.1			$19	$20	$35
Auctions: $306, PF-68DCam, July 2014; $46, PF-60, October 2014								

‡ Ranked in the *100 Greatest U.S. Modern Coins.* Only issued in Mint sets. **g.** A medium spread of doubling is evident on IN GOD WE TRUST, LIBERTY, and slightly on the date. **i.** Two reported to exist. **j.** Included in 1973-D, Copper-Nickel Clad, mintage figure. **k.** Included in 1973-S, Proof, Silver Clad, mintage figure.

	Mintage	Cert	Avg	%MS	EF-40	MS-63	MS-65	MS-66
						PF-65	PF-67Cam	PF-68DC
1977, Copper-Nickel Clad	12,596,000	2,417	65.0	100%	$2	$6	$35	$135
	Auctions: $170, MS-66, March 2013							
1977D, Copper-Nickel Clad	32,983,006	15,348	65.1	100%	$2	$6	$35	$170
	Auctions: $4,700, MS-67, April 2013; $69, MS-66, October 2014							
1977S, Copper-Nickel Clad, Proof	3,251,152	1,701	68.4			$10	$15	$25
	Auctions: $60, PF-69DCam, January 2013							
1978, Copper-Nickel Clad	25,702,000	845	64.8	99%	$2	$6	$45	$160
	Auctions: $159, MS-66, October 2014; $212, MS-64, November 2014; $44,063, MS-64, November 2013							
1978D, Copper-Nickel Clad	33,012,890	4,858	65.0	100%	$2	$5.50	$40	$125
	Auctions: $129, MS-66, July 2014; $123, MS-66, November 2014; $200, MS-66, July 2013							
1978S, Copper-Nickel Clad, Proof	3,127,781	1,766	68.5			$10	$15	$25
	Auctions: $44, PF-69DCam, January 2013							

SUSAN B. ANTHONY (1979–1999)

Designer: *Frank Gasparro.* **Weight:** *8.1 grams.*
Composition: *Outer layers of copper-nickel (.750 copper, .250 nickel)*
bonded to inner core of pure copper. **Diameter:** *26.5 mm.*
Edge: *Reeded.* **Mints:** *Philadelphia, Denver, San Francisco.*

Circulation Strike   Proof

History. The Susan B. Anthony dollar was designed by Frank Gasparro, chief engraver of the U.S. Mint, following a congressional mandate. It features a portrait of the famous suffragette, along with an eagle-and-Moon motif reduced from the coin's larger predecessor, the Eisenhower dollar. Legislators hoped that these so-called mini-dollars would be an efficient substitute for paper dollars, which wear much more quickly in circulation. A large mintage in 1979 was followed by smaller quantities in 1980 and 1981, and then a hiatus of almost 20 years. The coins were not popular in circulation, with some members of the public complaining that they were too easily confused with the similarly sized quarter dollar. A final coinage of Anthony dollars was struck in 1999—a stopgap measure to ensure the Treasury's supply of dollar coins before the Sacagawea dollar was launched in 2000.

Striking and Sharpness. Most are well struck, but check the highest areas of both sides.

Availability. Susan B. Anthony dollars are readily available in MS, although those of 1981 are less common than those of 1979 and 1980. Circulated coins are not widely sought by collectors. Proofs were made of all issues and are readily available today.

GRADING STANDARDS

MS-60 to 70 (Mint State). *Obverse:* At MS-60, some abrasion and contact marks are evident, most noticeably on the cheek and upper center of the hair. Luster is present, but may be dull or lifeless. At MS-63, contact marks are extensive but not distracting. Abrasion still is evident, but less than at lower levels. MS-64 coins are slightly finer. An MS-65 coin may have minor abrasion, but contact marks are so minute as to require

1980-D. Graded MS-65.

magnification. Luster should be full and rich. *Reverse:* At MS-60, some abrasion and contact marks are evident, most noticeably on the eagle's breast, head, and talons. Otherwise, the same comments apply as for the obverse.

AU-50, 53, 55, 58 (About Uncirculated). *Obverse:* Light wear is seen on the higher-relief areas of the portrait. At AU-58, the luster is extensive but incomplete. At AU-50 and 53, luster is less but still present. *Reverse:* Further wear is evident on the eagle, particularly the head, breast, talons, and tops of the wings. Otherwise, the same comments apply as for the obverse.

1979-D. Graded AU-50.

The Susan B. Anthony dollar is seldom collected in grades lower than AU-50.

PF-60 to 70 (Proof). *Obverse and Reverse:* Proofs that are extensively cleaned and have many hairlines, or that are dull and grainy, are lower level, such as PF-60 to 62. This comment is more theoretical than practical, as nearly all Proofs have been well kept. With medium hairlines and good reflectivity, assigned grades of PF-63 or 64 are appropriate. With relatively few hairlines a rating of PF-65 can be given. PF-66 may have hair-

1979-S, Type 2. Graded PF-70 Deep Cameo.

lines so delicate that magnification is needed to see them. Above that, all the way to PF-70, a Proof should be free of any hairlines or other problems under strong magnification.

1979-P, Narrow Rim
The "Far Date" variety.

1979-P, Wide Rim
The "Near Date" variety.

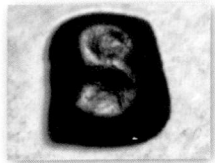   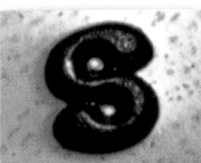 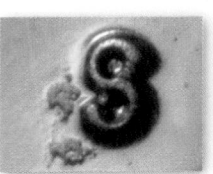

| **1979-S, Filled S (Type 1), Proof** | **1979-S, Clear S (Type 2), Proof** | **1981-S, Rounded S (Type 1), Proof** | **1981-S, Flat S (Type 2), Proof** | **1980-S, Repunched Mintmark, Proof** *FS-C1-1980S-501* |

	Mintage	Cert	Avg	%MS	MS-63	MS-64	MS-65 / PF-65	MS-66 / PF-68DC
1979P, Narrow Rim (a)	360,222,000	609	64.9	97%	$2	$6	$10	$20
Auctions: $15,275, MS-67, January 2014; $529, MS-67, July 2014; $823, MS-67, September 2014								
1979P, Wide Rim ‡ (a)	**(b)**	1,133	64.6	95%	$6	$38	$55	$135
Auctions: $4,406, MS-67, December 2013								
1979D	288,015,744	768	65.3	98%	$2	$7	$12	$25
Auctions: $3,819, MS-68, August 2014; $182, MS-67, August 2014; $118, MS-64, October 2014								
1979S	109,576,000	603	65.4	99%	$2	$6	$10	$20
Auctions: No auction records available.								
1979S, Type 1, Proof (c)	3,677,175	3,917	68.9				$7	$10
Auctions: $112, PF-70DCam, December 2014; $123, PF-70DCam, August 2013								
1979S, Type 2, Proof ‡ (c)	**(d)**	2,312	68.8				$50	$60
Auctions: $282, PF-70DCam, September 2014; $188, PF-70DCam, December 2014; $441, PF-70DCam, March 2013								
1980P	27,610,000	1,018	65.9	100%	$3	$5	$10	$15
Auctions: $1,763, MS-68, June 2014								
1980D	41,628,708	883	65.7	100%	$3	$5	$10	$15
Auctions: $264, MS-67, March 2014; $170, MS-67, August 2014; $79, MS-67, November 2014; $84, MS-67, December 2014								
1980S	20,422,000	755	65.3	100%	$3	$10	$15	$25
Auctions: $470, MS-67, August 2014; $411, MS-67, December 2014								
1980S, Proof	3,554,806	3,726	68.9				$6	$10
Auctions: $80, PF-70DCam, November 2014; $52, PF-70DCam, October 2014; $90, PF-70DCam, August 2013								
1980S, RPM, Proof (e)		0	n/a				—	—
Auctions: No auction records available.								
1981P (f)	3,000,000	759	65.6	100%	$7	$12	$20	$55
Auctions: $165, MS-67, June 2014; $1,116, MS-67, August 2014; $329, MS-67, December 2014								
1981D (f)	3,250,000	898	65.7	100%	$7	$10	$15	$25
Auctions: $382, MS-67, June 2014; $165, MS-67, December 2014								
1981S ‡ (f)	3,492,000	584	64.6	100%	$7	$20	$35	$250
Auctions: $194, MS-66, December 2014; $499, MS-66, December 2013								
1981S, Type 1, Proof	4,063,083	4,359	68.8				$6	$10
Auctions: $94, PF-70DCam, December 2014; $84, PF-70DCam, December 2014; $106, PF-70DCam, May 2013								
1981S, Type 2, Proof ‡	**(g)**	2,207	68.7				$125	$150
Auctions: $646, PF-70DCam, July 2014; $764, PF-70DCam, February 2013; $96, PF-69DCam, August 2014								

‡ Ranked in the *100 Greatest U.S. Modern Coins*. **a.** The obverse design was modified in 1979 to widen the border rim. Late issues of 1979-P and subsequent issues have the wide rim. The 1979-P Wide Rim dollar is nicknamed the "Near Date" because the numerals are closer to the rim. **b.** Included in 1979-P, Narrow Rim, mintage figure. **c.** The S mintmark punch was changed in 1979 to create a clearer mintmark. **d.** Included in 1979-S, Variety 1, Proof, mintage figure. **e.** "The remnants of a previously punched S appear left of the primary S. . . . Very few specimens of this variety have surfaced to date" (*Cherrypickers' Guide to Rare Die Varieties*, sixth edition, volume II). **f.** 1981-P, -D, and -S dollars were issued only in Mint Sets. **g.** Included in 1981-S, Variety 1, Proof, mintage figure.

	Mintage	Cert	Avg	%MS	MS-63	MS-64	MS-65	MS-66
							PF-65	PF-68DC
1999P (h)	29,592,000	656	66.2	100%	$3	$5	$10	$15
	Auctions: $764, MS-64, January 2014; $89, MS-63, November 2014							
1999D (h)	11,776,000	831	66.5	100%	$3	$5	$10	$15
	Auctions: $294, MS-68, June 2014; $235, MS-68, August 2014; $112, MS-68, September 2014; $118, MS-68, December 2014							
1999P, Proof (i)	*750,000*	5,188	69.3				$20	$27.50
	Auctions: $90, PF-70DCam, August 2013							

h. Dies for the 1999 dollars were further modified to strengthen details on the reverse. **i.** The mintage reflects the total for the Proof coins dated 1999, which were sold through 2003.

SACAGAWEA (2000–2008)

Designers: *Glenna Goodacre (obverse), Thomas D. Rogers Sr. (reverse).*
Weight: *8.1 grams.* **Composition:** *Pure copper core with outer layers of manganese brass (.770 copper, .120 zinc, .070 manganese, and .040 nickel).*
Diameter: *26.5 mm.* **Edge:** *Plain.* **Mints:** *Philadelphia, Denver, San Francisco; 22-karat gold experimental specimens dated 2000-W were struck at West Point in 1999.*

Circulation Strike   Proof

History. The Sacagawea dollar was launched in 2000, with a distinctive golden color and a plain edge to distinguish it from other denominations or coins of similar size. (One complaint leveled against the Susan B. Anthony dollar was that it too closely resembled the quarter dollar; both were silvery, with reeded edges, and with only about two millimeters' difference in diameter.) The new coinage alloy and the change in appearance were mandated by the United States Dollar Coin Act of 1997. The core of the coin is pure copper, and the golden outer layer is of manganese brass. The obverse shows a modern artist's conception of Sacagawea, the Shoshone Indian who assisted the Lewis and Clark expedition, and her infant son, Jean Baptiste. (No known contemporary portraits of them exist.) The reverse shows an eagle in flight.

In 1999, about a dozen Sacagawea dollars were struck in 22-karat gold at the West Point Mint, as experimental or presentation pieces. These featured a prototype reverse design with boldly detailed tail feathers on the eagle. The following year, a small number of early circulation strikes from the Philadelphia Mint also featured that same prototype design. These are popularly called "Cheerio" dollars, as the coins were packaged as a promotion in boxes of Cheerios cereal (their unusual nature was not recognized at the time). Today collectors seek them as rare and desirable varieties.

Several distinct finishes can be identified on the Sacagawea dollars as a result of the Mint's attempts to adjust the dies, blanks, strikes, or finishing to produce coins with minimal spotting and better surface color. One group of 5,000 pieces, dated 2000 and with a special finish, was presented to sculptor Glenna Goodacre in payment for the obverse design. These have since entered the numismatic market and command a significant premium.

Another peculiarity in the Sacagawea series is a numismatic mule (a coin made from mismatched dies)—the combination of an undated State quarter obverse and a Sacagawea dollar reverse. Examples of this error are extremely rare.

Striking and Sharpness. Most are very well struck. Weakness sometimes is evident on the higher design points.

Availability. These coins are common in high grades, and are usually collected in MS and Proof.

GRADING STANDARDS

MS-60 to 70 (Mint State). *Obverse:* At MS-60, some abrasion and contact marks are evident, most noticeably on the cheekbone and the drapery near the baby's head. Luster is present, but may be dull or lifeless. At MS-63, contact marks are extensive but not distracting. Abrasion still is evident, but less than at lower levels. MS-64 coins are slightly finer. An MS-65 coin may have minor abrasion, but contact marks are so minute as to require magnification. Luster should be full and rich. *Reverse:* At MS-60, some abrasion and contact marks are evident, most noticeably on the eagle's breast. Otherwise, the same comments apply as for the obverse.

2006-D. Graded MS-65.

AU-50, 53, 55, 58 (About Uncirculated). *Obverse:* Light wear is seen on cheekbone, drapery, and elsewhere. At AU-58, the luster is extensive, but incomplete. At AU-50 and 53, luster is less but still present. *Reverse:* Further wear is evident on the eagle. Otherwise, the same comments apply as for the obverse.

The Sacagawea dollar is seldom collected in grades lower than AU-50.

2000-P. Graded AU-55.

PF-60 to 70 (Proof). *Obverse and Reverse:* Proofs that are extensively cleaned and have many hairlines, or that are dull and grainy, are lower level, such as PF-60 to 62. This comment is more theoretical than practical, as nearly all Proofs have been well kept. With medium hairlines and good reflectivity, assigned grades of PF-63 or 64 are appropriate. With relatively few hairlines a rating of PF-65 can be given. PF-66 may have hairlines so delicate that magnification is needed to see them. Above that, all the way to PF-70, a Proof should be free of any hairlines or other problems under strong magnification.

2002-S. Graded PF-69.

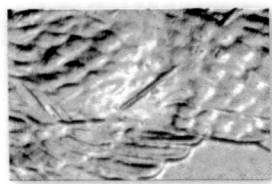
**2000-P, Reverse
Die Aberrations**
The "Speared Eagle" variety.

2000-P, Normal Feathers

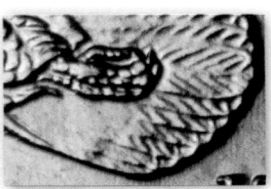
**2000-P, Boldly
Detailed Tail Feathers**

	Mintage	Cert	Avg	%MS	MS-64	MS-65 / PF-65	MS-66 / PF-69DC
2000P	767,140,000	5,897	66.7	100%	$2.50	$5	$12
Auctions: $112, MS-65, July 2014; $9,106, AU-58, June 2013							
2000P, Reverse Die Aberrations (a)	**(b)**	73	67.4	100%		$775	$1,500
Auctions: $2,013, MS-67, January 2012							
2000P, Goodacre Presentation Finish ‡ (c)	5,000	85	66.1	100%	$500	$650	$1,000
Auctions: $5,288, MS-69, April 2013; $823, MS-68, July 2014; $705, MS-68, August 2014; $499, MS-68, August 2014							
2000P, Boldly Detailed Tail Feathers ‡ (d)	5,500	2	64.0	100%		$2,500	$3,000
Auctions: $5,060, MS-66 Plus, March 2012							
2000D	518,916,000	7,134	66.4	100%	$4	$8	$15
Auctions: $57, MS-68, March 2013							
2000S, Proof	4,047,904	15,621	69.1			$12	$25
Auctions: $82, PF-70DCam, April 2013							
2001P	62,468,000	672	67.1	100%	$2	$4	$6
Auctions: $646, MS-69, August 2014; $40, MS-67, August 2014							
2001D	70,939,500	392	65.9	100%	$2	$4	$6
Auctions: $166, MS-68, March 2013							
2001S, Proof	3,183,740	10,870	69.2			$40	$50
Auctions: $72, PF-70DCam, May 2013							
2002P (e)	3,865,610	386	67.1	100%	$2	$4	$6
Auctions: $1,028, MS-69, March 2013							
2002D (e)	3,732,000	353	66.3	100%	$2	$4	$6
Auctions: $229, MS-68, August 2014; $165, MS-68, March 2013							
2002S, Proof	3,211,995	9,121	69.2			$10	$20
Auctions: $41, PF-70DCam, November 2013							
2003P (e)	3,080,000	680	66.7	100%	$3	$5	$6
Auctions: $37, MS-68, July 2008							
2003D (e)	3,080,000	596	66.1	100%	$3	$5	$6
Auctions: $353, MS-68, August 2014; $223, MS-68, March 2013							
2003S, Proof	3,298,439	12,411	69.2			$10	$20
Auctions: $16, PF-69DCam, January 2013							
2004P (e)	2,660,000	556	66.8	100%	$2	$4	$6
Auctions: $71, MS-68, July 2008							
2004D (e)	2,660,000	681	66.6	100%	$2	$4	$6
Auctions: $29, MS-68, March 2013							
2004S, Proof	2,965,422	11,907	69.2			$10	$20
Auctions: $46, PF-70DCam, January 2014; $36, PF-70DCam, October 2014							

‡ Ranked in the *100 Greatest U.S. Modern Coins*. **a.** Two spike-like die aberrations appear through the breast of the eagle. This variety is nicknamed the "Speared Eagle." **b.** Included in 2000-P mintage figure. **c.** A group of 5,000 coins, dated 2000 and with a special finish, were presented to sculptor Glenna Goodacre in payment for the obverse design. **d.** The feathers of the eagle are finely enhanced. This is nicknamed the "Cheerios" variety, as the coins were included as a promotion in boxes of Cheerios cereal. **e.** Not issued for circulation.

	Mintage	Cert	Avg	%MS	MS-64	MS-65 / PF-65	MS-66 / PF-69DC
2005P (e)	2,520,000	350	66.3	100%	$7	$10	$20
Auctions: $26, MS-69 Satin, August 2009							
2005D (e)	2,520,000	593	66.2	100%	$7	$10	$20
Auctions: $529, MS-68, March 2013							
2005S, Proof	3,344,679	17,409	69.2			$10	$15
Auctions: $46, PF-69DCam, March 2014							
2006P (e)	4,900,000	377	66.1	100%	$2	$4	$6
Auctions: $115, MS-69 Satin, July 2008							
2006D (e)	2,800,000	578	65.9	100%	$2	$4	$6
Auctions: $58, MS-67, June 2014							
2006S, Proof	3,054,436	8,337	69.3			$10	$15
Auctions: $17, PF-69DCam, January 2013							
2007P (e)	3,640,000	554	66.7	100%	$3	$5	$6
Auctions: $96, MS-68, August 2014; $74, MS-68, March 2013							
2007D (e)	3,920,000	841	66.5	100%	$3	$5	$6
Auctions: $31, MS-69 Satin, May 2009							
2007S, Proof	2,577,166	8,664	69.2			$10	$15
Auctions: $15, PF-69DCam, January 2013							
2008P (e)	1,820,000	209	66.4	100%	$3	$5	$6
Auctions: $317, MS-68, August 2014; $66, MS-68, March 2013							
2008D (e)	1,820,000	590	66.6	100%	$3	$5	$6
Auctions: $2,115, MS-68, May 2013							
2008S, Proof	2,169,561	6,170	69.2			$10	$15
Auctions: $63, PF-70DCam, March 2013							

e. Not issued for circulation.

NATIVE AMERICAN (2009 TO DATE)

Designers: *Glenna Goodacre (obverse), Norm Nemeth (2009 reverse), Thomas Cleveland (2010 reverse), Richard Masters (2011 reverse), Thomas Cleveland (2012 reverse), Susan Gamble (2013 reverse), Chris Costello (2014 reverse), Ronald D. Sanders (2015 reverse).* **Weight:** *8.1 grams.* **Composition:** *Pure copper core with outer layers of manganese brass (.770 copper, .120 zinc, .070 manganese, and .040 nickel).* **Diameter:** *26.5 mm.* **Edge:** *Lettered.* **Mints:** *Philadelphia, Denver, San Francisco.*

Circulation Strike   **Proof**

History. Since 2009, the reverse of the golden dollar has featured an annually changing design that memorializes Native Americans and, in the words of the authorizing legislation, "the important contributions made by Indian tribes and individual Native Americans to the development [and history] of the United States." The coins are marked (incuse) on their edges with the year of minting, the mintmark, and the legend E PLURIBUS UNUM. The Native American $1 Coin Act also specified that at least 20% of the total mintage of dollar coins in any given year (including Presidential dollars) will be Native American dollars. Production of all dollar coins minted after 2011 has been limited to numismatic sales

(Proofs and other collector formats, and circulation strikes in rolls and bags available directly from the U.S. Mint); none are issued for circulation, as they have proven unpopular in commerce.

The obverse of the Native American dollar coin is a modified version of the Sacagawea dollar, featuring that coin's central portraits (of Sacagawea and Jean Baptiste), and the legends LIBERTY and IN GOD WE TRUST. The date and mintmark, as noted above, are on the coin's edge. Each new reverse design is chosen by the secretary of the Treasury following consultation with the Senate Committee on Indian Affairs, the Congressional Native American Caucus of the House of Representatives, the Commission of Fine Arts, and the National Congress of American Indians. Design proposals are also reviewed by the Citizens Coinage Advisory Committee.

Some error coins have been discovered without edge lettering.

Striking and Sharpness. Most examples are very well struck. Check the higher points of the design.

Availability. Native American dollars are common in high grades, and are usually collected in MS and Proof. Distribution for public circulation has been slow despite Mint efforts such as the $1 Coin Direct Ship program (intended "to make $1 coins readily available to the public, at no additional cost [including shipping], so they can be easily introduced into circulation—particularly by using them for retail transactions, vending, and mass transit"). Proofs have been made each year and are readily available.

GRADING STANDARDS

MS-60 to 70 (Mint State). *Obverse:* At MS-60, some abrasion and contact marks are evident, most noticeably on the cheekbone and the drapery near the baby's head. Luster is present, but may be dull or lifeless. At MS-63, contact marks are extensive but not distracting. Abrasion still is evident, but less than at lower levels. MS-64 coins are slightly finer. An MS-65 coin may have minor abrasion, but contact marks are so minute as to

2009-P, Three Sisters. Graded MS-68.

require magnification. Luster should be full and rich. *Reverse:* At MS-60, some abrasion and contact marks are evident, most noticeably on the eagle's breast. Otherwise, the same comments apply as for the obverse.

Native American dollars are seldom collected in grades lower than MS-60.

PF-60 to 70 (Proof). *Obverse and Reverse:* Proofs that are extensively cleaned and have many hairlines, or that are dull and grainy, are lower level, such as PF-60 to 62. This comment is more theoretical than practical, as nearly all Proofs have been well kept. With medium hairlines and good reflectivity, assigned grades of PF-63 or 64 are appropriate. With relatively few hairlines a rating of PF-65 can be given. PF-66 may have hair-

2009-S, Three Sisters. Graded PF-70 Deep Cameo.

lines so delicate that magnification is needed to see them. Above that, all the way to PF-70, a Proof should be free of any hairlines or other problems under strong magnification.

**Three Sisters
(2009)**

**Great Law of
Peace (2010)**

**Wampanoag
Treaty (2011)**

**Trade Routes
in the 17th
Century (2012)**

**Treaty With the
Delawares (2013)**

| | Mintage | Cert | Avg | %MS | MS-64 | MS-65 | MS-66 |
						PF-65	PF-69DC
2009P, Three Sisters	39,200,000	340	66.1	100%	$3	$5	$6
Auctions: $441, MS-68, June 2014							
2009D, Three Sisters	35,700,000	261	65.3	100%	$3	$5	$6
Auctions: No auction records available.							
2009S, Three Sisters, Proof	2,179,867	9,762	69.3			$10	$15
Auctions: $17, PF-69DCam, January 2013							
2010P, Great Law	32,060,000	462	66.0	100%	$3	$5	$6
Auctions: No auction records available.							
2010D, Great Law	48,720,000	362	65.8	100%	$3	$5	$6
Auctions: $129, MS-67, November 2014; $70, MS-67, November 2014							
2010S, Great Law, Proof	1,689,216	6,151	69.2			$10	$17
Auctions: $26, PF-69DCam, January 2013							
2011P, Wampanoag Treaty	29,400,000	362	66.7	100%	$3	$5	$6
Auctions: No auction records available.							
2011D, Wampanoag Treaty	48,160,000	405	67.0	100%	$3	$5	$6
Auctions: No auction records available.							
2011S, Wampanoag Treaty, Proof	1,453,276	7,722	69.2			$10	$15
Auctions: $17, PF-69DCam, January 2013							
2012P, Trade Routes	2,800,000	222	67.2	100%	$3	$5	$6
Auctions: No auction records available.							
2012D, Trade Routes	3,080,000	1,317	67.4	100%	$3	$5	$6
Auctions: No auction records available.							
2012S, Trade Routes, Proof		4,313	69.3			$10	$15
Auctions: No auction records available.							
2013P, Treaty With the Delawares	1,820,000	323	67.0	100%	$3	$5	$6
Auctions: No auction records available.							
2013D, Treaty With the Delawares	1,820,000	1,146	67.1	100%	$3	$5	$6
Auctions: No auction records available.							
2013S, Treaty With the Delawares, Proof	802,460	4,182	69.5			$10	$15
Auctions: No auction records available.							

Native Hospitality
(2014)

Mohawk
Ironworkers
(2015)

	Mintage	Cert	Avg	%MS	MS-64	MS-65 / PF-65	MS-66 / PF-69DC
2014P, Native Hospitality	3,080,000	201	67.0	100%	$3	$5	$6
Auctions: No auction records available.							
2014D, Native Hospitality	5,600,000	494	67.3	100%	$3	$5	$6
Auctions: No auction records available.							
2014S, Native Hospitality, Proof	665,100	5,700	69.3			$10	$15
Auctions: No auction records available.							
2015P, Mohawk Ironworkers					$3	$5	$6
Auctions: No auction records available.							
2015D, Mohawk Ironworkers					$3	$5	$6
Auctions: No auction records available.							
2015S, Mohawk Ironworkers, Proof						$10	$15
Auctions: No auction records available.							

PRESIDENTIAL (2007–2016)

Designers: *Various (obverse), Don Everhart (reverse).* **Weight:** *8.1 grams.*
Composition: *Pure copper core with outer layers of manganese brass (.770 copper,
.120 zinc, .070 manganese, and .040 nickel.* **Diameter:** *26.5 mm.*
Edge: *Lettered.* **Mints:** *Philadelphia, Denver, San Francisco.*

Obverse Style,
2007–2008,
Circulation Strike
No motto on obverse.

Obverse Style,
2009–2016,
Circulation Strike
*Motto beneath
portrait.*

Common Reverse,
Circulation Strike

Date, Mintmark,
and Mottos
Incused on Edge
*IN GOD WE TRUST
moved to
obverse in 2009.*

Proof

History. Presidential dollars debuted in 2007 and are scheduled for issue at the rate of four designs per year through 2015, with the program's two final coins issued in 2016. The series starts with George Washington and continues in order of office. Living presidents are ineligible, so the program is slated to end with Gerald Ford. Each coin has a common reverse showing the Statue of Liberty. The series began with the date, mintmark, and mottos IN GOD WE TRUST and E PLURIBUS UNUM incused on the edge of the coins; in 2009 IN GOD WE TRUST was moved from the edge to the obverse after some public criticism of the "Godless dollars."

In December 2011, Secretary of the Treasury Timothy Geithner directed that the U.S. Mint suspend minting and issuing circulating Presidential dollars. "Regular circulating demand for the coins will be met through the Federal Reserve Bank's existing inventory of circulating coins minted prior to 2012," the Mint announced. Collector formats, however, have continued to be issued.

Some Presidential dollars were inadvertently struck with the edge lettering missing. A 2009-D, John Tyler, variety has the wrong date, 2010, on the edge.

Striking and Sharpness. These usually are well struck, but check the higher-relief parts of each side.

Availability. Presidential dollars are very common in MS. Most have from a few to many bagmarks, with true MS-65 and better coins in the minority.

GRADING STANDARDS

MS-60 to 70 (Mint State). *Obverse:* At MS-60, some abrasion and contact marks are evident, most noticeably on the highest-relief areas of the portrait, the exact location varying with the president depicted. Luster is present, but may be dull or lifeless. At MS-63, contact marks are extensive but not distracting. Abrasion still is evident, but less than at lower levels. MS-64 coins are slightly finer. An MS-65 coin may have minor abrasion, but

2007-P, Washington. Graded MS-68.

contact marks are so minute as to require magnification. Luster should be full and rich. *Reverse:* At MS-60, some abrasion and contact marks are evident, most noticeably on the cheek and arm. Otherwise, the same comments apply as for the obverse.

AU-50, 53, 55, 58 (About Uncirculated). *Obverse:* Light wear is seen on the portrait, most prominently on the higher-relief areas. At AU-58, the luster is extensive, but incomplete. At AU-50 and 53, luster is less, but still is present. *Reverse:* Further wear is evident on statue. Otherwise, the same comments apply as for the obverse.

Presidential dollars are seldom collected in grades lower than AU-50.

2007-P, Madison. Graded AU-53.

PF-60 to 70 (Proof). *Obverse and Reverse:* Proofs that are extensively cleaned and have many hairlines, or that are dull and grainy, are lower level, such as PF-60 to 62. This comment is more theoretical than practical, as nearly all Proofs have been well kept. With medium hairlines and good reflectivity, assigned grades of PF-63 or 64 are appropriate. With relatively few hairlines a rating of PF-65 can be given. PF-66 may have hair-

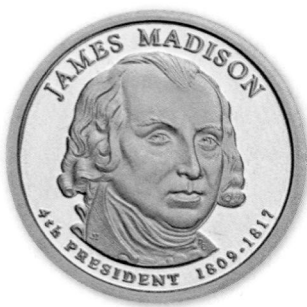

2007-S, Madison. Graded PF-65.

lines so delicate that magnification is needed to see them. Above that, all the way to PF-70, a Proof should be free of any hairlines or other problems under strong magnification.

| 2007, Washington | 2007, J. Adams | 2007, Jefferson | 2007, Madison |

	Mintage	Cert	Avg	%MS	MS-64	MS-65 / PF-65	MS-66 / PF-69DC
2007P, Washington	176,680,000	17,761	65.0	100%	$1.50	$3	$5
Auctions: $42, MS-68 Satin, April 2009							
2007, Washington, Plain Edge ‡ (a)	(b)	43,433	64.7	100%	$30	$45	$80
Auctions: $388, MS-67, June 2014; $66, MS-66, August 2014							
2007D, Washington	163,680,000	14,541	65.1	100%	$1.50	$3	$5
Auctions: $17, MS-65, August 2009							
2007S, Washington, Proof	3,965,989	44,902	69.2			$10	$15
Auctions: $129, PF-70DCam, August 2014; $36, PF-70DCam, December 2009							
2007P, J. Adams	112,420,000	20,104	64.6	100%	$1.50	$2	$5
Auctions: $30, MS-65DCam, January 2013							
2007D, J. Adams	112,140,000	5,845	65.0	100%	$1.50	$3	$5
Auctions: $25, MS-69 Satin, May 2009							
2007S, J. Adams, Proof	3,965,989	44,670	69.2			$10	$15
Auctions: $26, PF-70DCam, December 2009							
2007P, Jefferson	100,800,000	4,956	65.3	100%	$1.50	$3	$5
Auctions: $65, MS-65, October 2009							
2007D, Jefferson	102,810,000	5,646	65.3	100%	$1.50	$2	$5
Auctions: $16, MS-65, August 2009							
2007S, Jefferson, Proof	3,965,989	44,760	69.2			$10	$15
Auctions: $646, PF-69DCam, July 2014							
2007P, Madison	84,560,000	2,657	65.3	100%	$1.50	$3	$5
Auctions: $16, MS-66, August 2009							
2007D, Madison	87,780,000	3,010	65.4	100%	$1.50	$3	$5
Auctions: $15, MS-66, August 2009							
2007S, Madison, Proof	3,965,989	45,024	69.2			$10	$15
Auctions: $30, PF-69DCam, February 2013							

‡ Ranked in the *100 Greatest U.S. Modern Coins*. **a.** Some circulation-strike Washington dollars are known without the normal edge lettering (date, mintmark, IN GOD WE TRUST, and E PLURIBUS UNUM). **b.** Included in 2007-P, Washington, mintage figure.

2008, Monroe	2008, J.Q. Adams	2008, Jackson	2008, Van Buren

	Mintage	Cert	Avg	%MS	MS-64	MS-65	MS-66
						PF-65	PF-69DC
2008P, Monroe	64,260,000	2,182	65.5	100%	$1.50	$3	$5
	Auctions: $11, MS-67, July 2008						
2008D, Monroe	60,230,000	1,792	65.3	100%	$1.50	$3	$5
	Auctions: $11, MS-67, July 2008						
2008S, Monroe, Proof	3,083,940	24,104	69.2			$10	$15
	Auctions: $69, PF-70DCam, March 2010						
2008P, J.Q. Adams	57,540,000	2,525	65.9	100%	$1.50	$3	$5
	Auctions: No auction records available.						
2008D, J.Q. Adams	57,720,000	2,052	65.7	100%	$1.50	$3	$5
	Auctions: No auction records available.						
2008S, J.Q. Adams, Proof	3,083,940	24,111	69.3			$10	$15
	Auctions: $69, PF-70DCam, March 2010						
2008P, Jackson	61,180,000	2,962	65.7	100%	$1.50	$3	$5
	Auctions: $16, MS-67, November 2014						
2008D, Jackson	61,070,000	1,930	65.2	100%	$1.50	$3	$5
	Auctions: No auction records available.						
2008S, Jackson, Proof	3,083,940	24,081	69.2			$10	$15
	Auctions: $59, PF-70DCam, March 2010						
2008P, Van Buren	51,520,000	1,373	65.8	100%	$1.50	$3	$5
	Auctions: No auction records available.						
2008D, Van Buren	50,960,000	931	65.2	100%	$1.50	$3	$5
	Auctions: No auction records available.						
2008S, Van Buren, Proof	3,083,940	24,147	69.3			$10	$15
	Auctions: $15, PF-69DCam, January 2013						

2009, W.H. Harrison	2009, Tyler	2009, Polk	2009, Taylor

	Mintage	Cert	Avg	%MS	MS-64	MS-65	MS-66
						PF-65	PF-69DC
2009P, W.H. Harrison	43,260,000	1,116	65.5	100%	$1.50	$3	$5
	Auctions: No auction records available.						
2009D, W.H. Harrison	55,160,000	1,148	65.2	100%	$1.50	$3	$5
	Auctions: No auction records available.						
2009S, W.H. Harrison, Proof	2,809,452	17,804	69.2			$8	$15
	Auctions: No auction records available.						

	Mintage	Cert	Avg	%MS	MS-64	MS-65 / PF-65	MS-66 / PF-69DC
2009P, Tyler	43,540,000	1,012	65.3	100%	$1.50	$2	$5
Auctions: No auction records available.							
2009D, Tyler	43,540,000	996	65.2	100%	$1.50	$2	$5
Auctions: No auction records available.							
2009D, Tyler, 2010 Edge	(c)	9	65.7	100%	—		
Auctions: $129, MS-66, February 2014; $62, MS-65, November 2014							
2009S, Tyler, Proof	2,809,452	17,774	69.2			$8	$15
Auctions: No auction records available.							
2009P, Polk	46,620,000	1,030	66.0	100%	$1.50	$3	$5
Auctions: No auction records available.							
2009D, Polk	41,720,000	766	65.4	100%	$1.50	$2	$5
Auctions: No auction records available.							
2009S, Polk, Proof	2,809,452	17,781	69.2			$8	$15
Auctions: $127, PF-70DCam, February 2010							
2009P, Taylor	41,580,000	775	65.7	100%	$1.50	$3	$5
Auctions: No auction records available.							
2009D, Taylor	36,680,000	778	65.6	100%	$1.50	$2	$5
Auctions: No auction records available.							
2009S, Taylor, Proof	2,809,452	17,939	69.3			$8	$15
Auctions: $47, PF-70DCam, March 2010							

c. Included in 2009-D, Tyler, mintage figure.

2010, Fillmore   **2010, Pierce**   **2010, Buchanan**   **2010, Lincoln**

	Mintage	Cert	Avg	%MS	MS-64	MS-65 / PF-65	MS-66 / PF-69DC
2010P, Fillmore	37,520,000	860	65.6	100%	$1.50	$3	$5
Auctions: No auction records available.							
2010D, Fillmore	36,960,000	600	65.2	100%	$1.50	$3	$5
Auctions: No auction records available.							
2010S, Fillmore, Proof	2,224,613	15,188	69.2			$8	$15
Auctions: No auction records available.							
2010P, Pierce	38,220,000	758	65.6	100%	$1.50	$3	$5
Auctions: No auction records available.							
2010D, Pierce	38,360,000	688	65.5	100%	$1.50	$3	$5
Auctions: No auction records available.							
2010S, Pierce, Proof	2,224,613	15,135	69.2			$8	$15
Auctions: No auction records available.							
2010P, Buchanan	36,820,000	353	65.6	100%	$1.50	$3	$5
Auctions: No auction records available.							
2010D, Buchanan	36,540,000	492	65.3	100%	$1.50	$3	$5
Auctions: No auction records available.							
2010S, Buchanan, Proof	2,224,613	15,212	69.2			$8	$15
Auctions: No auction records available.							

	Mintage	Cert	Avg	%MS	MS-64	MS-65	MS-66
						PF-65	PF-69DC
2010P, Lincoln	49,000,000	723	65.5	100%	$1.50	$3	$5
Auctions: No auction records available.							
2010D, Lincoln	48,020,000	374	65.2	100%	$1.50	$3	$5
Auctions: No auction records available.							
2010S, Lincoln, Proof	2,224,613	15,916	69.2			$8	$15
Auctions: No auction records available.							

2011, A. Johnson

2011, Grant

2011, Hayes

2011, Garfield

	Mintage	Cert	Avg	%MS	MS-64	MS-65	MS-66
						PF-65	PF-69DC
2011P, A. Johnson	35,560,000	382	66.7	100%	$1.50	$2	$5
Auctions: No auction records available.							
2011D, A. Johnson	37,100,000	371	67.0	100%	$1.50	$3	$5
Auctions: No auction records available.							
2011S, A. Johnson, Proof	1,706,916	8,007	69.2			$8	$15
Auctions: No auction records available.							
2011P, Grant	38,080,000	421	66.8	100%	$1.50	$2	$5
Auctions: No auction records available.							
2011D, Grant	37,940,000	390	67.0	100%	$1.50	$3	$5
Auctions: No auction records available.							
2011S, Grant, Proof	1,706,916	8,070	69.2			$8	$15
Auctions: No auction records available.							
2011P, Hayes	37,660,000	382	66.5	100%	$1.50	$2	$5
Auctions: No auction records available.							
2011D, Hayes	36,820,000	391	67.1	100%	$1.50	$3	$5
Auctions: No auction records available.							
2011S, Hayes, Proof	1,706,916	8,146	69.3			$8	$15
Auctions: No auction records available.							
2011P, Garfield	37,100,000	336	66.4	100%	$1.50	$3	$5
Auctions: No auction records available.							
2011D, Garfield	37,100,000	345	67.0	100%	$2	$3	$5
Auctions: No auction records available.							
2011S, Garfield, Proof	1,706,916	8,140	69.2			$8	$15
Auctions: No auction records available.							

2012, Arthur   **2012, Cleveland, First Term**   **2012, B. Harrison**   **2012, Cleveland, Second Term**

	Mintage	Cert	Avg	%MS	MS-64	MS-65 / PF-65	MS-66 / PF-69DC
2012P, Arthur (d)	6,020,000	694	66.8	100%	$2	$3	$5
Auctions: No auction records available.							
2012D, Arthur (d)	4,060,000	278	67.1	100%	$2	$3	$5
Auctions: No auction records available.							
2012S, Arthur, Proof		4,899	69.3			$9	$15
Auctions: No auction records available.							
2012P, Cleveland, First Term (d)	5,460,000	724	66.7	100%	$2	$3	$5
Auctions: No auction records available.							
2012D, Cleveland, First Term (d)	4,060,000	248	66.9	100%	$2	$3	$5
Auctions: No auction records available.							
2012S, Cleveland, First Term, Proof		4,941	69.3			$9	$15
Auctions: No auction records available.							
2012P, B. Harrison (d)	5,640,000	713	66.6	100%	$2	$3	$5
Auctions: No auction records available.							
2012D, B. Harrison (d)	4,200,000	248	67.1	100%	$2	$3	$5
Auctions: No auction records available.							
2012S, B. Harrison, Proof		4,878	69.3			$9	$15
Auctions: No auction records available.							
2012P, Cleveland, Second Term (d)	10,680,000	678	66.6	100%	$2	$3	$5
Auctions: No auction records available.							
2012D, Cleveland, Second Term (d)	3,920,000	255	67.1	100%	$2	$3	$5
Auctions: No auction records available.							
2012S, Cleveland, Second Term, Proof		4,875	69.3			$9	$15
Auctions: No auction records available.							

d. Not issued for circulation.

2013, McKinley   **2013, T. Roosevelt**   **2013, Taft**   **2013, Wilson**

	Mintage	Cert	Avg	%MS	MS-64	MS-65 / PF-65	MS-66 / PF-69DC
2013P, McKinley (d)	4,760,000	644	67.1	100%	$2	$3	$5
Auctions: No auction records available.							
2013D, McKinley (d)	3,365,100	167	67.0	100%	$2	$3	$5
Auctions: No auction records available.							
2013S, McKinley, Proof	1,068,734	4,961	69.5			$9	$15
Auctions: No auction records available.							

d. Not issued for circulation.

	Mintage	Cert	Avg	%MS	MS-64	MS-65	MS-66
						PF-65	PF-69DC
2013P, T. Roosevelt (d)	5,310,700	886	67.0	100%	$2	$3	$5
Auctions: No auction records available.							
2013D, T. Roosevelt (d)	3,920,000	296	66.7	100%	$2	$3	$5
Auctions: No auction records available.							
2013S, T. Roosevelt, Proof	1,068,734	4,996	69.5			$6	$15
Auctions: No auction records available.							
2013P, Taft (d)	4,760,000	747	67.1	100%	$2	$3	$5
Auctions: No auction records available.							
2013D, Taft (d)	3,360,000	213	67.0	100%	$2	$3	$5
Auctions: No auction records available.							
2013S, Taft, Proof	1,068,734	4,918	69.5			$6	$15
Auctions: No auction records available.							
2013P, Wilson (d)	4,620,000	819	67.3	100%	$2	$3	$5
Auctions: No auction records available.							
2013D, Wilson (d)	3,360,000	198	67.2	100%	$2	$3	$5
Auctions: No auction records available.							
2013S, Wilson, Proof	1,068,734	4,915	69.5			$6	$15
Auctions: No auction records available.							

d. Not issued for circulation.

2014, Harding   **2014, Coolidge**   **2014, Hoover**   **2014, F.D. Roosevelt**

	Mintage	Cert	Avg	%MS	MS-64	MS-65	MS-66
						PF-65	PF-69DC
2014P, Harding (d)	6,160,000	232	66.9	100%	$2	$3	$5
Auctions: No auction records available.							
2014D, Harding (d)	3,780,000	209	67.1	100%	$2	$3	$5
Auctions: No auction records available.							
2014S, Harding, Proof	1,068,734	3,591	69.5			$6	$15
Auctions: No auction records available.							
2014P, Coolidge (d)	4,480,000	277	67.2	100%	$2	$3	$5
Auctions: No auction records available.							
2014D, Coolidge (d)	3,780,000	181	67.3	100%	$2	$3	$5
Auctions: No auction records available.							
2014S, Coolidge, Proof	1,068,734	3,608	69.5			$6	$15
Auctions: No auction records available.							
2014P, Hoover (d)	4,480,000	218	67.0	100%	$2	$3	$5
Auctions: No auction records available.							
2014D, Hoover (d)	3,780,000	190	67.2	100%	$2	$3	$5
Auctions: No auction records available.							
2014S, Hoover, Proof	1,068,734	3,591	69.4			$6	$15
Auctions: No auction records available.							

d. Not issued for circulation.

	Mintage	Cert	Avg	%MS	MS-64	MS-65 PF-65	MS-66 PF-69DC
2014P, F.D. Roosevelt (d)	4,760,000	265	67.1	100%	$2	$3	$5
Auctions: No auction records available.							
2014D, F.D. Roosevelt (d)	3,920,000	153	67.3	100%	$2	$3	$5
Auctions: No auction records available.							
2014S, F.D. Roosevelt, Proof	1,068,734	3,601	69.5			$6	$15
Auctions: No auction records available.							

d. Not issued for circulation.

2015, Truman	**2015, Eisenhower**	**2015, Kennedy**	**2015, L.B. Johnson**

	Mintage	Cert	Avg	%MS	MS-64	MS-65 PF-65	MS-66 PF-69DC
2015P, Truman (d)					$2	$3	$5
Auctions: No auction records available.							
2015D, Truman (d)					$2	$3	$5
Auctions: No auction records available.							
2015S, Truman, Proof						$6	$15
Auctions: No auction records available.							
2015P, Eisenhower (d)					$2	$3	$5
Auctions: No auction records available.							
2015D, Eisenhower (d)					$2	$3	$5
Auctions: No auction records available.							
2015S, Eisenhower, Proof						$6	$15
Auctions: No auction records available.							
2015P, Kennedy (d)					$2	$3	$5
Auctions: No auction records available.							
2015D, Kennedy (d)					$2	$3	$5
Auctions: No auction records available.							
2015S, Kennedy, Proof						$6	$15
Auctions: No auction records available.							
2015P, L.B. Johnson (d)					$2	$3	$5
Auctions: No auction records available.							
2015D, L.B. Johnson (d)					$2	$3	$5
Auctions: No auction records available.							
2015S, L.B. Johnson, Proof						$6	$15
Auctions: No auction records available.							

d. Not issued for circulation.

Trade Dollars
1873–1885

AN OVERVIEW OF TRADE DOLLARS

A new denomination, the silver trade dollar, was authorized by the Coinage Act of 1873. This provided that a coin weighing 420 grains, of .900 fine silver, be struck for use in the export trade. By comparison, contemporary Liberty Seated silver dollars weighed 412.5 grains. Produced in quantity from 1873 through 1878, the trade dollars were a great success, particularly in China, where merchants preferred silver to gold and would not accept paper money of any kind. Coinage would have continued except for passage of the Bland-Allison Act of February 28, 1878, which authorized the government to buy millions of ounces of silver each year and resume the production of standard silver dollars (which had not been minted since 1873). The trade dollar was discontinued forthwith; however, Proof impressions were made for numismatists through 1883, plus a small quantity of Proofs distributed privately in 1884 and 1885, coins of these last two issues being great rarities today.

Choosing a trade dollar for a type set is easy enough to do, the choices being a circulation strike, which requires some connoisseurship, or a Proof, most of which are sharply struck and attractive. Enough exist in both formats that collectors will easily find a nice example, except that MS-65 and better pieces are elusive.

FOR THE COLLECTOR AND INVESTOR: TRADE DOLLARS AS A SPECIALTY

There are two great rarities among trade dollars: the Proof-only 1884, of which just ten are known, and the Proof-only 1885, of which only five are known. Neither was produced openly, and examples were sold for the private profit of Mint officials, going to John W. Haseltine, a Philadelphia dealer who was a favored outlet for such things. The existence of these coins was not generally known to numismatists until 1907–1908, when examples began to appear on the market. As to the mintage figures, the numbers five and ten have no official origin, but are said to represent the number once held by Haseltine. Relatively few numismatists have been able to afford examples of these two dates.

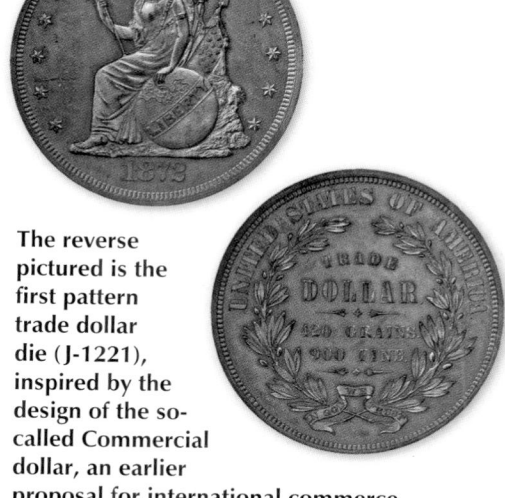

The reverse pictured is the first pattern trade dollar die (J-1221), inspired by the design of the so-called Commercial dollar, an earlier proposal for international commerce.

Beyond the above, a complete collection of trade dollars of the 1873 to 1883 years can be formed with some effort. Proofs were made of each year during this span, and after 1878 *only* Proofs were made, at the Philadelphia Mint, with no branch-mint issues. Proofs had greater appeal than Mint State circulation strikes to collectors of an earlier era, and more were saved, with the result that Proofs of the otherwise common dates 1873 to 1877 are much harder to find today, especially in choice condition.

Circulation strikes were regularly minted from 1873 through 1878, with production greatest at the San Francisco and Carson City mints, these being closest to the Orient, where the coins were used in commerce. Some trade dollars (but not many) went into domestic circulation (they were legal tender until that status was repealed on July 22, 1876). Later, after 1876, they traded widely in the United States but were valued by their silver content, not their face value. In 1878 the 412.5-grain Morgan dollar was worth $1.00 in circulation, while the heavier 420-grain trade dollar was worth only its melt-down value of about $0.90.

Very few of the circulating issues were saved by numismatists, with the result today that assembling a collection in choice or gem Mint State can be a great challenge. The key issue is the 1878-CC, with the lowest mintage by far in the series—scarce in any and all grades. As trade dollars became numismatically popular in the United States, thousands were repatriated from China, often bearing Chinese characters called *chopmarks*, which were applied by bankers and merchants. More often than not the imported coins had been harshly cleaned in China, as the owners thought shiny coins were more desirable. However, many choice and undamaged pieces were imported as well. The pieces with chopmarks are collectible in their own right in view of their historical significance.

Collectors are warned that many modern counterfeit trade dollars lurk in the marketplace.

TRADE DOLLAR (1873–1885)

Designer: *William Barber.* **Weight:** *27.22 grams.*
Composition: *.900 silver, .100 copper (net weight .7874 oz. pure silver).*
Diameter: *38.1 mm.* **Edge:** *Reeded.* **Mints:** *Philadelphia, Carson City, San Francisco.*

Mintmark location is on the reverse, below the fineness.

Circulation Strike

Proof

History. Trade dollars were minted under the Coinage Act of 1873. Containing 420 grains of .900 fine silver, they were heavier than the Liberty Seated dollar (of 412.5 grains). They were made for use in the China export trade and proved to be a great success. Some circulated at par in the United States, until they were demonetized by the Act of July 22, 1876, after which they circulated at their silver value, which was slightly lower than their face value. The Bland-Allison Act of 1878 provided for the new "Morgan" silver dollar, and trade dollars were discontinued, although Proofs continued to be made through 1885. Modifications to the trade dollar design are distinguished as follows.

Reverse 1: With a berry under the eagle's left talon; the lowest arrowhead ends over the 0 in 420. (Used on all coins from all mints in 1873 and 1874, and occasionally in 1875 and 1876.)

Reverse 2: Without an extra berry under the talon; the lowest arrowhead ends over the 2 in 420. (Used occasionally at all mints from 1875 through 1876, and on all coins from all mints 1877 through 1885.)

Obverse 1: The ends of the scroll point to the left; the extended hand has only three fingers. (Used on coins at all mints, 1873 through 1876.)

Obverse 2: The ends of the scroll point downward; the extended hand has four fingers. (Used in combination with Reverse 2 on one variety of 1876-S, and on all coins at all mints from 1877 through 1885.)

Striking and Sharpness. Weakness is often seen. On the obverse, check Miss Liberty's head and the star centers first. On the reverse, check the feathers on the eagle, particularly on the legs. Luster can range from dull to deeply frosty. In EF and lower grades, strike sharpness on the stars and the head does not matter to connoisseurs. Some Proofs are lightly struck on the head and the stars on the obverse and the leg feathers of the eagle on the reverse.

Availability. The 1878-CC is a rarity. Other dates and mintmarks are readily collected in grades from EF to MS. Lower grades are not often seen, for these coins did not circulate for a long time. Many used in China have counterstamps, called *chopmarks*, which are of interest to collectors. On an MS-63 or better coin a chopmark will decrease its value, but on EF and AU coins specialists eagerly seek them. MS coins are mostly in the lower ranges, often with unsatisfactory surfaces. True gems are very scarce. Proofs for collectors were made from 1873 to 1883 in quantity to supply the demand. In addition, a few were secretly made in 1884 and 1885. Most survivors are of high quality today, although gems of the 1873 to 1877 years are much harder to find than are those of 1878 to 1883.

Note: In recent years a flood of modern counterfeit trade dollars, many coming from China, has deluged the market.

GRADING STANDARDS

MS-60 to 70 (Mint State). *Obverse:* At MS-60, some abrasion and contact marks are evident, most noticeably on the left breast, left arm, and left knee. Luster is present, but may be dull or lifeless. Many of these coins are light in color or even brilliant, having been repatriated from China, and have been cleaned to remove sediment and discoloration. At MS-63, contact marks are very few, and abrasion is minimal. An MS-65 coin has

1875-S, Reverse 1. Graded MS-61.

no abrasion in the fields (but may have a hint on the higher parts of the seated figure), and contact marks are trivial. Luster should be full and rich. *Reverse:* Comments apply as for the obverse, except that in lower Mint State grades abrasion and contact marks are most noticeable on the eagle's head, the claws, and the top of the wings. At MS-65 or higher there are no marks visible to the unaided eye. The field is mainly protected by design elements and does not show abrasion as much as does the obverse on a given coin.

Illustrated coin: Some friction in the fields is seen, but much of the original luster remains.

AU-50, 53, 55, 58 (About Uncirculated). *Obverse:* Light wear is seen on the knees, bosom, and head. At AU-58, the luster is extensive but incomplete. At AU-50 and 53, luster is less. *Reverse:* Wear is visible on the eagle's head, the claws, and the top of the wings. An AU-58 coin will have nearly full luster. At AU-50 and 53, there still are traces of luster.

1876, Reverse 2. Graded AU-53.

Illustrated coin: This example shows light, even wear. Most of the luster is gone, except in protected areas, but it has excellent eye appeal for the grade.

EF-40, 45 (Extremely Fine). *Obverse:* Further wear is seen on all areas, especially the head, the left breast, the left arm, the left leg, and the bale on which Miss Liberty is seated. Little or no luster is seen on most coins. From this grade downward, strike sharpness on the stars and the head does not matter to connoisseurs. *Reverse:* Further wear is evident on the eagle's head, legs, claws, and wings, although on well-struck coins nearly all feather details on the wings are sharp.

1876-CC, Reverse 1. Graded EF-40.

VF-20, 30 (Very Fine). *Obverse:* Further wear is seen on the seated figure, although more than half the details of her dress are visible. Details of the wheat sheaf are mostly intact. IN GOD WE TRUST and LIBERTY are clear. *Reverse:* Wear is more extensive; some feathers are blended together, with two-thirds or more still visible.

1877-S. Graded VF-30.

F-12, 15 (Fine). *Obverse:* The seated figure is further worn, with fewer details of the dress visible. Most details in the wheat sheaf are clear. Both mottoes are readable, but some letters may be weak. *Reverse:* Wear is extensive, with about half to nearly two-thirds of the feathers flat or blended with others. The eagle's left leg is mostly flat. Wear is seen on the raised E PLURIBUS UNUM, and one or two letters may be missing.

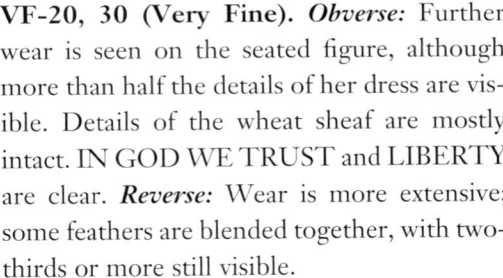

1873-CC. Graded F-12.

The trade dollar is seldom collected in grades lower than F-12.

PF-60 to 70 (Proof). *Obverse and Reverse:* Proofs that are extensively cleaned and have many hairlines, or that are dull and grainy, are lower level, such as PF-60 to 62. These are not widely desired. With medium hairlines and good reflectivity, an assigned grade of PF-64 is appropriate, and with relatively few hairlines, Gem PF-65. In various grades hairlines are most easily seen in the obverse field. PF-66 may have hairlines so delicate that magnification is needed to see them. Above that, a Proof should be free of such lines.

1882. Graded PF-62.

Illustrated coin: This coin has medium-gray toning overall.

Chopmarked Trade Dollar

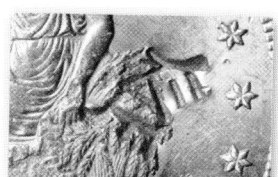

Examples of chopmarks

	Mintage	Cert	Avg	%MS	VG-8	F-12	VF-20	EF-40	AU-50	MS-60	MS-63	MS-64	MS-65
											PF-60	PF-63	PF-65
1873	396,635	164	58.2	68%	$145	$165	$200	$250	$350	$1,050	$3,500	$5,500	$14,500
	Auctions: $12,925, MS-65, April 2014; $11,750, MS-65+, August 2014; $3,819, MS-64, October 2014; $823, MS-60, July 2014												
1873, Proof	865	169	63.2								$1,750	$3,300	$10,000
	Auctions: $4,406, PF-63Cam, August 2014; $28,200, PF-66, June 2014; $11,163, PF-65, August 2014; $2,820, PF-63, October 2014												
1873CC	124,500	127	53.0	28%	$285	$375	$450	$975	$1,700	$10,000	$22,500	$55,000	$110,000
	Auctions: $32,900, MS-63, June 2014; $17,625, MS-63, November 2014; $12,925, MS-62, August 2014; $14,100, MS-62, October 2014												
1873S	703,000	95	59.4	69%	$145	$160	$200	$250	$375	$1,400	$4,000	$5,250	$15,000
	Auctions: $28,200, MS-65, June 2014; $10,575, MS-65, September 2014; $3,525, MS-64, August 2014; $1,763, MS-62, July 2014												

Reverse 1
Arrowheads end over 0;
berry under eagle's left talon.

Reverse 2
Arrowheads end over 2;
no berry under talon.

Obverse 1
Hand has three fingers;
scroll points left.

Obverse 2
Hand has four fingers;
scroll points downward.

1875-S, S Over CC
FS-T1-1875S-501.

	Mintage	Cert	Avg	%MS	VG-8	F-12	VF-20	EF-40	AU-50	MS-60	MS-63	MS-64	MS-65
										PF-60	PF-63	PF-65	
1874	987,100	140	58.2	64%	$145	$160	$200	$250	$350	$1,100	$2,500	$4,500	$15,000
Auctions: $12,044, MS-65, October 2014; $5,288, MS-64, April 2013; $1,293, MS-62, October 2014; $823, AU-58, July 2014													
1874, Proof	700	203	63.3							$1,750	$3,100	$9,000	
Auctions: $3,525, PF-64Cam, August 2014; $3,055, PF-63Cam, August 2014; $2,233, PF-62Cam, October 2014; $7,726, PF-65, June 2013													
1874CC	1,373,200	238	58.1	63%	$280	$365	$425	$600	$775	$3,000	$6,500	$8,500	$32,500
Auctions: $18,800, MS-65, October 2014; $8,813, MS-64, June 2014; $4,704, MS-62, August 2014; $4,409, MS-62, September 2014													
1874S	2,549,000	313	59.6	68%	$140	$160	$185	$245	$325	$1,000	$2,600	$3,500	$15,000
Auctions: $2,820, MS-64, October 2014; $3,055, MS-64, November 2013; $1,998, MS-63, July 2014; $1,821, MS-63, November 2014													
1875	218,200	101	57.8	69%	$240	$375	$450	$575	$875	$2,450	$5,000	$8,000	$17,500
Auctions: $31,725, MS-66, October 2014; $7,050, MS-64, November 2013; $2,468, MS-61, July 2014; $764, AU-50, October 2014													
1875, Reverse 2	(a)	1	64.0	100%	$240	$375	$450	$500	$875	$2,450	$4,650	$9,000	$18,500
Auctions: $4,888, MS-64, April 2012													
1875, Proof	700	222	63.3							$1,750	$3,300	$10,000	
Auctions: $3,525, PF-64Cam, August 2014; $3,290, PF-64Cam, October 2014; $3,055, PF-63Cam, August 2014; $38,188, PF-67, April 2014													
1875CC, All kinds	1,573,700												
1875CC		302	55.7	50%	$265	$350	$400	$500	$750	$2,450	$5,000	$10,000	$35,000
Auctions: $7,050, MS-64, August 2014; $7,050, MS-64, March 2013; $3,525, MS-63, August 2014; $3,055, MS-62, August 2014													
1875CC, Reverse 2		0	n/a		$250	$350	$400	$500	$750	$2,450	$5,000	$10,000	$35,000
Auctions: $1,610, AU-58, January 2012													
1875S, All kinds	4,487,000												
1875S		941	60.4	78%	$140	$155	$165	$235	$300	$975	$2,000	$3,250	$11,000
Auctions: $15,863, MS-65, November 2013; $3,055, MS-64, July 2014; $2,233, MS-64, August 2014; $1,300, MS-63, October 2014													
1875S, Reverse 2		5	61.4	80%	$145	$165	$190	$250	$335	$1,025	$2,350	$3,600	$11,500
Auctions: $69,000, MS-67, January 2012													
1875S, S Over CC (b)		57	58.8	51%	$265	$400	$525	$975	$1,550	$4,350	$12,500	$25,000	$55,000
Auctions: $16,485, MS-63, August 2013; $4,994, MS-62, October 2014; $823, AU-50, October 2014; $823, VF-35, September 2014													

a. Included in circulation-strike 1875 mintage figure. **b.** A weak C from the underlying CC mintmark is visible to the right of the S mintmark.

1876-CC, Doubled-Die Reverse
FS-T1-1876CC-801.

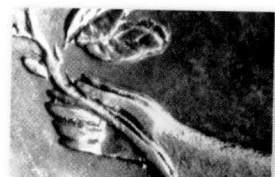

1876-S, Doubled-Die Obverse
FS-T1-1876S-101.

	Mintage	Cert	Avg	%MS	VG-8	F-12	VF-20	EF-40	AU-50	MS-60 PF-60	MS-63 PF-63	MS-64 PF-64	MS-65 PF-65
1876	455,000	436	59.6	77%	$140	$155	$190	$250	$335	$1,050	$2,400	$3,200	$12,000
Auctions: $22,325, MS-66, August 2014; $2,350, MS-64, July 2014; $2,468, MS-64, October 2014													
1876, Obverse 2, Reverse 2 (c)	(d)	0	n/a							—			
Auctions: No auction records available.													
1876, Reverse 2	(d)	1	55.0	0%	$140	$155	$190	$235	$300	$975	$2,250	$3,500	$12,000
Auctions: $2,760, MS-64, April 2012													
1876, Proof	1,150	279	62.9							$1,750	$3,100		$9,000
Auctions: $3,055, PF-63Cam, August 2014; $2,820, PF-63Cam, November 2014; $2,585, PF-62Cam, September 2014; $10,575, PF-65, June 2014													
1876CC, All kinds	509,000												
1876CC		137	55.5	42%	$225	$300	$450	$625	$1,250	$5,750	$25,000	$40,000	$80,000
Auctions: $44,063, MS-64, April 2013; $646, AU-50, September 2014; $499, EF-40, July 2014; $485, VF-30, November 2014													
1876CC, Reverse 1		1	53.0	0%	$245	$325	$485	$690	$1,550	$6,500	$27,500	$40,000	$80,000
Auctions: $3,220, MS-60, February 2006													
1876CC, Doubled-Die Reverse (e)		35	52.2	26%				$850	$1,750	$10,500	—		
Auctions: $2,350, MS-60, February 2014; $382, AU-50, September 2014													
1876S, All kinds	5,227,000												
1876S		813	57.6	59%	$140	$155	$165	$210	$300	$975	$2,000	$3,250	$16,500
Auctions: $2,820, MS-64+, August 2014; $2,938, MS-64, October 2014; $2,585, MS-63, August 2014													
1876S, Doubled-Die Obverse (f)		0	n/a						$1,400	$1,750	$2,200		
Auctions: No auction records available.													
1876S, Reverse 2		3	57.0	0%	$140	$155	$165	$245	$325	$1,000	$2,000	$3,250	$15,000
Auctions: $1,506, MS-63, September 2011													
1876S, Obverse 2, Reverse 2		1	58.0	0%	$165	$200	$225	$250	$375	$1,300	$2,650	$3,700	$15,000
Auctions: $1,495, MS-60 CAC, August 2011													

c. Extremely rare. **d.** Included in circulation-strike 1876 mintage figure. **e.** Doubling is visible on the branches on the right, the eagle's talons, the right wing tip, and the eagle's beak; and is very strong on E PLURIBUS UNUM. Weaker doubling is seen on UNITED STATES OF AMERICA. "Considered by most to be the strongest reverse doubled die in the series, this variety is one of the highlights of the trade dollar varieties and is thought to be extremely rare in grades above AU" (*Cherrypickers' Guide to Rare Die Varieties*, sixth edition, volume II). **f.** Doubling is visible on Liberty's hand, chin, and left foot, and on the olive branch. "This DDO is easily the rarest doubled die in the series, and is considered extremely rare in grades above AU. Most known examples are cleaned. The variety is known as the king of the trade dollar varieties" (*Cherrypickers' Guide to Rare Die Varieties*, sixth edition, volume II).

1877, Doubled-Die Obverse
FS-T1-1877-101.

1877-S, Repunched Date
FS-T1-1877S-301.

1877-S, Doubled-Die Reverse
FS-T1-1877S-801.

1877-S, Doubled-Die Reverse
FS-T1-1877S-802.

1878-S, Doubled-Die Reverse
FS-T1-1878S-801.

	Mintage	Cert	Avg	%MS	VG-8	F-12	VF-20	EF-40	AU-50	MS-60	MS-63 / PF-60	MS-64 / PF-63	MS-65 / PF-65
1877	3,039,200	584	52.7	47%	$140	$155	$165	$200	$300	$1,025	$2,100	$4,000	$17,500
Auctions: $15,275, MS-66, October 2014; $30,550, MS-66, November 2013; $1,028, MS-61, July 2014; $1,293, MS-61, August 2014													
1877, DblDie Obv (g)	(h)	3	40.0	33%				$300	$400	$1,250			
Auctions: No auction records available.													
1877, Proof	510	197	63.5								$1,750	$3,250	$9,000
Auctions: $4,700, PF-63DCam, July 2014; $4,113, PF-64Cam, July 2014; $16,450, PF-66, October 2014; $14,100, PF-65, December 2013													
1877CC	534,000	124	55.5	56%	$265	$350	$450	$675	$825	$2,700	$11,500	$22,000	$60,000
Auctions: $21,150, MS-64, October 2014; $6,463, MS-62, November 2014; $7,931, MS-62, September 2013; $4,700, MS-60, September 2014													
1877S	9,519,000	1,391	55.4	53%	$140	$155	$165	$245	$325	$1,000	$2,050	$3,100	$11,000
Auctions: $25,850, MS-66, November 2013; $6,169, MS-65, October 2014; $3,819, MS-64, July 2014; $6,463, MS-64, October 2014													
1877S, Repunched Date (i)	(j)	0	n/a					$550	$800	$1,600			
Auctions: $250, EF-45, May 2010													
1877S, DblDie Rev (k)	(j)	2	55.0	0%				$300	$425	$1,300			
Auctions: No auction records available.													
1877S, DblDie Rev (l)	(j)	5	52.6	40%				$300	$400	$1,200			
Auctions: $1,323, MS-62, April 2011													
1878		0	n/a					$1,500					
Auctions: No auction records available.													
1878, Proof	900	337	63.7								$1,750	$3,250	$9,000
Auctions: $27,025, PF-66DCam+, August 2014; $31,725, PF-66Cam+, August 2014; $6,756, PF-65Cam, August 2014													
1878CC (m)	97,000	84	49.0	33%	$625	$950	$1,575	$2,850	$6,000	$15,000	$30,000	$60,000	$100,000
Auctions: $25,850, MS-62, April 2013; $18,800, MS-61, August 2014; $10,575, AU-55, July 2014; $3,819, AU-50, September 2014													
1878S	4,162,000	984	52.9	43%	$140	$155	$165	$200	$300	$1,000	$2,200	$3,250	$10,000
Auctions: $49,938, MS-67, April 2013; $10,281, MS-65, July 2014; $12,925, MS-65, August 2014; $9,988, MS-65, November 2014													
1878S, DblDie Rev (n)	(o)	13	53.5	38%				$450	$550	$1,300			
Auctions: $1,000, MS-62, August 2011													

g. Doubling on this rare variety is evident on the wheat stalks, LIBERTY, IN GOD WE TRUST, and stars 11, 12, and 13. **h.** Included in circulation-strike 1877 mintage figure. **i.** A secondary 7 protrudes prominently south from the last 7. **j.** Included in 1877-S mintage figure. **k.** Doubling is visible on E PLURIBUS UNUM, the ribbon, and UNITED STATES OF AMERICA. There are at least two different doubled-die reverses for 1877-S; this one is FS-T1-1877S-801. "Considered a highlight of the trade dollar varieties" (*Cherrypickers' Guide to Rare Die Varieties*, sixth edition, volume II). **l.** Minor doubling is visible on nearly all reverse lettering, especially on 420 GRAINS. This reverse doubled die is more common than the preceding; it is listed as FS-T1-1877S-802. **m.** On July 19, 1878, a quantity of 44,148 trade dollars was melted by the Mint. Many of these may have been 1878-CC. **n.** Strong doubling is visible on the entire lower left of the reverse, on the arrow points and shafts, and on 420 GRAINS; slight doubling is evident on the motto. Rare in AU and higher grades. There are at least two doubled-die reverses for this date; the one listed is FS-T1-1878S-801. **o.** Included in 1878-S mintage figure.

	Mintage	Cert	Avg	%MS	VG-8	F-12	VF-20	EF-40	AU-50	MS-60	MS-63	MS-64	MS-65
											PF-60	PF-63	PF-65
1879, Proof	1,541	555	63.8								$1,750	$3,200	$9,000
Auctions: $16,450, PF-67Cam, October 2014; $49,938, PF-67Cam, April 2013; $3,672, PF-64Cam, August 2014; $4,700, PF-64Cam+, November 2014
1880, Proof	1,987	702	63.6								$1,750	$3,200	$9,000
Auctions: $42,594, PF-68DCam, September 2014; $19,975, PF-67Cam, October 2014; $31,725, PF-67Cam, November 2013
1881, Proof	960	419	63.6								$1,750	$3,200	$9,000
Auctions: $6,463, PF-65Cam, August 2014; $4,406, PF-64Cam, July 2014; $4,113, PF-64Cam, November 2014; $19,975, PF-66, April 2013
1882, Proof	1,097	518	63.9								$1,750	$3,200	$9,000
Auctions: $12,925, PF-66DCam, September 2014; $3,290, PF-64Cam, September 2014; $2,585, PF-63Cam, October 2014
1883, Proof	979	481	63.6								$1,750	$3,200	$9,000
Auctions: $9,400, PF-64DCam, September 2014; $12,338, PF-66Cam, October 2014; $8,225, PF-65Cam, August 2014; $21,150, PF-67, August 2013
1884, Proof † (p)	10	7	64.1									$550,000	$1,000,000
Auctions: $998,750, PF-65, January 2014
1885, Proof † (p)	5	2	62.3									$2,000,000	*$3,000,000*
Auctions: $1,006,250, PF-62, November 2004

† Ranked in the *100 Greatest U.S. Coins* (fourth edition). **p.** Trade dollars of 1884 and 1885 were unknown to the numismatic community until 1907 and 1908. None are listed in the Mint director's report, and numismatists believe that they are not a part of the regular Mint issue but were produced secretly for private sale to collectors.

Gold Dollars
1849–1889

AN OVERVIEW OF GOLD DOLLARS

Coinage of the gold dollar was authorized by the Act of March 3, 1849, after the start of the California Gold Rush.

Although a case could be made for designating the Small Head, Open Wreath, gold dollar as a separate type, it is not generally collected as such. Instead, pieces dated from 1849 through 1854 (whether Open Wreath or Close Wreath) are collectively designated as Type 1. Examples today are readily available in all grades, although truly choice and gem Mint State pieces are in the minority.

In contrast, the Type 2 design, produced at the Philadelphia Mint in part of 1854, and at the Philadelphia, Charlotte, Dahlonega, and New Orleans mints in 1855, and only at the San Francisco Mint in 1856, is a great challenge. Examples are scarcer in all grades than are those of types 1 and 3. Choice and gem coins are especially rare. Striking is a great problem, and while some sharp pieces exist, probably 80% or more have areas of weakness, typically at the 85 (center two digits) of the date, but also often on the headdress and elsewhere. Further, the borders are sometimes imperfect.

Type 3 gold dollars, made from 1856 through 1889, are easier to acquire in nearly any grade desired, including choice and gem Mint State. Most are well struck and in Mint State have excellent eye appeal. Among Type 3 gold dollars the dates from 1879 through 1889 inclusive are most often seen, as these were widely saved by coin dealers and collectors at the time and did not circulate to any appreciable extent. Gold dollar coins also were popular as Christmas gifts in the late 1800s. Some of these have very low mintage figures, making them very appealing to today's collectors.

FOR THE COLLECTOR AND INVESTOR: GOLD DOLLARS AS A SPECIALTY

Forming a specialized collection of gold dollars is a fascinating pursuit, one that has drawn the attention of many numismatists over the years. A complete run of date-and-mintmark issues from 1849 through 1889 includes no impossible rarities, although the 1875, with just 20 Proofs and 400 circulation strikes made, is the key date and can challenge collectors. While the dollars of 1879 through 1889 often have remarkably low mintages, they were saved in quantity, and certain of these dates are easily obtainable (although not necessarily inexpensive).

The branch-mint gold dollars of the early years present a special challenge. Among the Charlotte Mint varieties the 1849 comes with an Open Wreath (of which just five are presently known, with a rumor of a sixth) and with a Close Wreath, the latter being scarce but available. Later Charlotte gold dollars, extending through 1859, range from scarce to rare. The 1857-C is notorious for its poor striking.

Gold dollars were struck at the Dahlonega Mint from 1849 through 1861. In the latter year the facility was under the control of the Confederate States of America, and thus the 1861-D gold dollars, rare in any event, are even more desirable as true Confederate coins. The New Orleans Mint also produced gold dollars, which in general are better struck than those of the Charlotte and Dahlonega mints. From 1854 intermittently to 1860, and then in 1870, gold dollars were struck

A detail of an 1851 land surveyor's drawing of Sutter's Mill on the American River, the site at which the California Gold Rush began in 1848, prompting the creation of the gold dollar.

in San Francisco. These Western issues are usually sharply defined and range from scarce to rare. In particular, choice and gem Mint State pieces are elusive.

LIBERTY HEAD (1849–1854)

Designer: *James B. Longacre.* **Weight:** *1.672 grams.*
Composition: *.900 gold, .100 copper (net weight .04837 oz. pure gold).*
Diameter: *13 mm.* **Edge:** *Reeded.*
Mints: *Philadelphia, Charlotte, Dahlonega, New Orleans, San Francisco.*

Open Wreath Reverse	Close Wreath Reverse	Proof	Mintmark location is on the reverse, below the wreath.

History. U.S. Mint chief engraver James Barton Longacre designed the nation's gold dollars. This first type measured 13 mm in diameter, which proved to be inconvenient, and the two later types were enlarged to 15 mm.

Striking and Sharpness. As a rule, Type 1 gold dollars struck in Philadelphia are sharper than those of the Charlotte and Dahlonega mints. On the obverse, check the highest areas of the hair below the coronet. On the reverse, check the wreath and the central two figures in the date. On both sides check the denticles, which can be mushy or indistinct (particularly on Charlotte and Dahlonega coins, which often have planchet roughness as well).

Availability. All dates and mintmarks are readily collectible, save for the 1849-C Open Wreath variety. MS coins often are found for the Philadelphia issues but can be elusive for the branch mints. Charlotte and Dahlonega coins often have striking problems. The few gold dollars of this type that are less than VF in grade usually are damaged or have problems. Although a few Proofs were coined in the early years, they are for all practical purposes unobtainable. Only about a dozen are known.

GRADING STANDARDS

MS-60 to 70 (Mint State). *Obverse:* At MS-60 to 62, there is abrasion on the hair below the coronet (an area that can be weakly struck as well) and on the cheeks. Marks may be seen. At MS-63, there may be slight abrasion. Luster is irregular. At MS-64, abrasion is less. Luster is rich on most coins, less so on Charlotte and Dahlonega varieties. At MS-65 and above, luster is deep and frosty. At MS-66, and higher, no marks at all are visible without magnification. *Reverse:* On MS-60 to 62 coins, there is abrasion on the 1, the highest parts of the leaves, and the ribbon. Otherwise, the same comments apply as for the obverse.

1854, Close Wreath. Graded MS-62.

    Illustrated coin: Some friction is visible on the portrait and in the fields.

AU-50, 53, 55, 58 (About Uncirculated). *Obverse:* Light wear on the hair below the coronet and the cheek is very noticeable at AU-50, and progressively less at higher levels to AU-58. Luster is minimal at AU-50 and scattered and incomplete at AU-58. Some tiny nicks and contact marks are to be expected and should be mentioned if they are distracting. *Reverse:* Light wear on the 1, the wreath, and the ribbon characterize an AU-50 coin, progressively less at higher levels to AU-58. Otherwise, the same comments apply as for the obverse.

1853-D. Graded AU-58.

    Illustrated coin: Much of the luster remains, especially in protected areas.

EF-40, 45 (Extremely Fine). *Obverse:* Medium wear is seen on the hair below the coronet, extending to near the bun, and on the curls below. Detail is partially gone on the hair to the right of the coronet. Luster is gone on most coins. *Reverse:* Light wear is seen overall, and the highest parts of the leaves are flat. Luster is gone.

1849-C, Close Wreath. Graded EF-45.

VF-20, 30 (Very Fine). *Obverse:* Most hair detail is gone, except in the lower-relief areas and on the lower curls. Star centers are flat. *Reverse:* The wreath and other areas show more wear. Most detail is gone on the higher-relief leaves.

    This gold dollar is seldom collected in grades lower than VF-20.

1851-D. Graded VF-25.

PF-60 to 70 (Proof). *Obverse and Reverse:* PF-60 to 62 coins have extensive hairlines and may have nicks and contact marks. At PF-63, hairlines are prominent, but the mirror surface is very reflective. PF-64 coins have fewer hairlines. At PF-65, hairlines should be minimal and mostly seen only under magnification. One cannot be "choosy" with Proofs of this type, as only a few exist.

1849, Open Wreath. Proof.

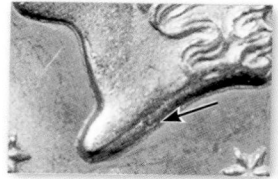
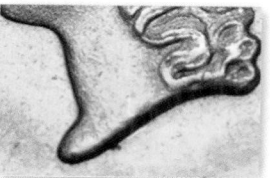

1849, With L   1849, No L

	Mintage	Cert	Avg	%MS	VF-20	EF-40	AU-50	AU-55	AU-58	MS-60	MS-63	MS-64	MS-65
													PF-60
1849, Open Wreath, So-Called Small Head, With L (a)	688,567	925	60.9	74%	$215	$250	$285	$300	$350	$700	$1,450	$2,100	$5,000
Auctions: $61,688, MS-67, September 2014; $1,998, MS-64, August 2014; $2,585, MS-64, November 2014; $79,313, MS-63, April 2014													
1849, Open Wreath, So-Called Small Head, No L (a)	(b)	385	62.2	85%	$250	$300	$375	$400	$500	$750	$1,850	$2,500	$5,500
Auctions: $9,988, MS-65, April 2013; $1,788, MS-64, November 2014; $1,351, MS-63, November 2014; $1,293, MS-62, August 2014													
1849, Open Wreath, So-Called Large Head (a)	(b)	0	n/a					$295	$325	$600	$1,150	$1,850	$5,000
Auctions: $1,495, MS-64, April 2012													
1849, Close Wreath	(b)	485	61.8	83%	$215	$250	$275	$295	$325	$600	$11,250	$1,850	$5,000
Auctions: $11,163, MS-66, February 2013; $3,055, MS-64, August 2014; $1,998, MS-64+, August 2014; $1,880, MS-64+, November 2014													
1849, Open Wreath, So-Called Small Head, No L, Proof (c)	unknown	0	n/a						*(extremely rare)*				
Auctions: No auction records available.													
1849C, Open Wreath (d)	(b)	3	41.0	33%	$250,000	$325,000	$425,000	$500,000	$525,000	$625,000	$850,000		
Auctions: $3,220, AU-58, April 2012													
1849C, Close Wreath	11,634	92	55.7	32%	$1,300	$1,850	$2,800	$3,750	$5,000	$7,500	$16,000	$35,000	
Auctions: $10,281, MS-62, September 2013; $2,820, EF-45, July 2014													
1849D, Open Wreath	21,588	0	n/a		$1,350	$2,000	$2,850	$3,250	$3,750	$5,500	$12,000	$21,500	$55,000
Auctions: $22,325, MS-64, April 2013; $5,288, MS-62, November 2014; $4,414, MS-60, July 2014; $2,585, AU-55, September 2014													
1849O, Open Wreath	215,000	0	n/a		$245	$325	$425	$550	$600	$1,100	$3,500	$6,500	$12,500
Auctions: $11,817, MS-65, November 2014; $11,750, MS-65, November 2014; $7,520, MS-64+, August 2014; $5,581, MS-64, September 2013													

a. It is now well known that the so-called Small Head and Large Head coins are from the same punch.   **b.** Included in 1849, Open Wreath, So-Called Small Head, With L, mintage figure.   **c.** 2 to 3 examples are known.   **d.** This coin is extremely rare.

	Mintage	Cert	Avg	%MS	VF-20	EF-40	AU-50	AU-55	AU-58	MS-60	MS-63	MS-64	MS-65
													PF-60
1850	481,953	529	60.1	68%	$215	$250	$265	$285	$300	$425	$1,100	$2,000	$5,500
	Auctions: $3,819, MS-65, November 2014; $3,408, MS-65, November 2014; $4,700, MS-65, March 2013; $376, MS-61, October 2014												
1850, Proof (e)	unknown	0	n/a										$140,000
	Auctions: No auction records available.												
1850C	6,966	81	54.6	25%	$1,350	$1,750	$2,500	$4,250	$6,000	$8,000	$25,000		
	Auctions: $19,975, MS-63, January 2014; $17,625, MS-63, November 2014; $1,939, EF-45, July 2014												
1850D	8,382	94	53.8	22%	$1,500	$2,000	$3,000	$5,000	$7,250	$11,000	$25,000	$37,500	
	Auctions: $3,204, AU-50, July 2014												
1850O	14,000	190	58.2	43%	$300	$500	$950	$1,350	$2,000	$3,250	$7,000	$12,500	
	Auctions: $2,532, MS-61, April 2012												
1851	3,317,671	4,370	61.1	81%	$215	$250	$265	$275	$290	$350	$650	$1,000	$3,500
	Auctions: $7,050, MS-66, August 2014; $4,700, MS-66, October 2014; $9,400, MS-66, March 2013; $2,820, MS-65, November 2014												
1851C	41,267	386	57.3	35%	$1,250	$1,550	$2,000	$2,250	$2,550	$3,200	$6,250	$12,000	$24,000
	Auctions: $4,994, MS-63, August 2014; $5,613, MS-63, March 2013; $2,585, MS-61, October 2014; $1,968, AU-58, November 2014												
1851D	9,882	137	58.0	41%	$1,500	$1,800	$2,450	$2,750	$3,250	$5,000	$13,500	$22,000	$45,000
	Auctions: $14,688, MS-64, October 2014; $11,163, MS-63, March 2013; $7,138, MS-62, October 2014; $4,113, AU-58, October 2014												
1851O	290,000	907	59.0	50%	$235	$285	$350	$410	$450	$800	$2,250	$4,750	$8,500
	Auctions: $6,463, MS-65, January 2014; $1,645, MS-63, November 2014; $1,116, MS-62, November 2014; $999, MS-62, November 2014												
1852	2,045,351	3,942	61.2	81%	$215	$250	$265	$275	$300	$350	$650	$1,000	$3,500
	Auctions: $5,523, MS-65, July 2014; $3,290, MS-65, August 2014; $4,700, MS-65, September 2014; $999, MS-64+, July 2014												
1852C	9,434	146	57.2	41%	$1,500	$1,850	$2,100	$2,750	$3,000	$4,500	$11,000	$19,500	$30,000
	Auctions: $15,863, MS-64, February 2013; $4,553, MS-62, October 2014; $2,128, AU-55, October 2014; $2,585, AU-53, July 2014												
1852D	6,360	97	56.4	27%	$1,500	$2,000	$2,600	$3,600	$4,750	$8,500	$30,000		
	Auctions: $4,994, AU-55, July 2014												
1852O	140,000	461	56.9	33%	$240	$285	$450	$700	$850	$1,400	$4,000	$10,500	$22,500
	Auctions: $2,820, MS-63, April 2013; $1,763, MS-62, November 2014; $397, AU-55, July 2014; $646, AU-58, November 2014												
1853	4,076,051	10,458	61.2	81%	$215	$250	$265	$275	$300	$350	$650	$1,000	$3,500
	Auctions: $152,750, MS-69, January 2014; $7,050, MS-66, July 2014; $4,994, MS-65, October 2014; $3,966, MS-65+, November 2014												
1853C	11,515	127	57.0	38%	$1,350	$1,600	$2,100	$2,600	$3,500	$5,000	$13,000	$18,500	$40,000
	Auctions: $14,100, MS-64, January 2014; $4,406, MS-62, August 2014; $9,988, MS-62, October 2014; $1,593, EF-40, July 2014												
1853D	6,583	127	57.7	30%	$1,400	$1,850	$2,500	$4,250	$5,500	$8,750	$22,000	$30,000	$45,000
	Auctions: $17,625, MS-63, January 2014; $10,575, MS-62, October 2014; $7,050, MS-62, October 2014; $3,055, AU-55, October 2014												
1853O	290,000	1265	59.6	58%	$235	$255	$335	$425	$450	$825	$2,000	$4,000	$10,000
	Auctions: $25,850, MS-66, October 2014; $7,638, MS-65, October 2014; $3,055, MS-64, November 2014; $2,820, MS-64, April 2013												
1854	855,502	3,715	61.5	86%	$215	$250	$265	$275	$290	$350	$650	$1,000	$3,500
	Auctions: $27,025, MS-67, January 2013; $3,173, MS-65+, November 2014; $1,175, MS-64, August 2014; $881, MS-64, August 2014												
1854, Proof	unknown	0	n/a					*(unique, in the Bass Foundation Collection)*					
	Auctions: No auction records available.												
1854D	2,935	73	56.0	33%	$1,850	$2,450	$4,750	$6,500	$7,750	$11,500	$35,000	$65,000	
	Auctions: $64,625, MS-64, April 2013; $4,113, EF-45, July 2014												
1854S	14,632	145	58.6	40%	$400	$550	$950	$1,150	$1,350	$2,500	$5,750	$13,500	$30,000
	Auctions: $4,113, MS-62, July 2014; $1,293, AU-58, September 2014; $1,116, AU-55, November 2014; $999, AU-53, July 2014												

e. 2 examples are known.

INDIAN PRINCESS HEAD, SMALL HEAD (1854–1856)

Designer: *James B. Longacre.* **Weight:** *1.672 grams.*
Composition: *.900 gold, .100 copper (net weight .04837 oz. pure gold).* **Diameter:** *15 mm.*
Edge: *Reeded.* **Mints:** *Philadelphia, Charlotte, Dahlonega, New Orleans, San Francisco.*

Circulation Strike

Mintmark location is on the reverse, below the wreath.

Proof

History. The Type 2 gold dollar, with the diameter increased from 13 mm to 15 mm, was first made in 1854. The headdress is decorated with *ostrich* plumes, which would not have been used in any genuine Native American headgear. The design proved difficult to strike, leading to its modification in 1856.

Striking and Sharpness. On the obverse, check the highest area of the hair below the coronet and the tips of the feathers. Check the letters. On the reverse, check the ribbon bow knot and in particular the two central digits of the dates. Examine the digits on both sides. Nearly all have problems. This type is often softly struck in the centers, with weak hair detail and the numerals 85 in the date sometimes faint—this should not be confused with wear. The 1855-C and 1855-D coins are often poorly struck and on rough planchets.

Availability. All Type 2 gold dollars are collectible, but the Charlotte and Dahlonega coins are rare. With patience, Full Details coins are available of 1854, 1855, and 1856-S, but virtually impossible to find for the branch-mint issues of 1855. The few gold dollars of this type that are less than VF in grade usually are damaged or have problems. Proofs exist of the 1854 and 1855 issues, but were made in very small quantities.

GRADING STANDARDS

MS-60 to 70 (Mint State). *Obverse:* At MS-60 to 62, there is abrasion on the hair below the band lettered LIBERTY (an area that can be weakly struck as well), on the tips of the feather plumes, and throughout the field. Contact marks may also be seen. At MS-63, there should be only slight abrasions. Luster is irregular. At MS-64, abrasions and marks are less. Luster is rich on most coins, less so on Charlotte and Dahlonega issues. At

1854. Graded MS-61.

MS-65 and above, luster is deep and frosty, with no marks at all visible without magnification at MS-66 and higher. *Reverse:* At MS-60 to 62, there may be abrasions on the 1, on the highest parts of the leaves, on the ribbon knot, and in the field. Otherwise, the same comments apply as for the obverse.

Illustrated coin: Some loss of luster is evident in the fields, but strong luster remains among the letters and in other protected areas. Good eye appeal is elusive for this type.

AU-50, 53, 55, 58 (About Uncirculated).
Obverse: Light wear on the hair below the coronet, the cheek, and the tips of the feather plumes is very noticeable at AU-50, progressively less at higher levels to AU-58. Luster is minimal at AU-50 and scattered and incomplete at AU-58. Some tiny nicks and contact marks are to be expected and should be mentioned if they are distracting. *Reverse:* Light wear on the 1, the wreath, and the ribbon

1855. Graded AU-55.

knot characterize an AU-50 coin, progressively less at higher levels to AU-58. Otherwise, the same comments apply as for the obverse.

Illustrated coin: This coin was lightly struck at the center. Clash marks appear on both sides, most prominent within the wreath on the reverse.

EF-40, 45 (Extremely Fine). *Obverse:*
Medium wear is seen on the hair below the coronet and on the feather plume tips. Detail is partially gone on the hair, although the usual light striking may make this moot. Luster is gone on most coins. *Reverse:* Light wear is seen overall, and the highest parts of the leaves are flat. Luster is gone on most coins.

Illustrated coin: This coin was lightly struck at the centers, but overall has extraordinary quality.

1855-C. Graded EF-40.

VF-20, 30 (Very Fine). *Obverse:* Most hair detail is gone, except at the back of the lower curls. The feather plume ends are flat. *Reverse:* The wreath and other areas show more wear. Most detail is gone on the higher-relief leaves.

This gold dollar is seldom collected in grades lower than VF-20.

Illustrated coin: This coin is well worn, but has an exceptionally bold date, indicating that it must have been a very sharp strike.

1854. Graded VF-25.

PF-60 to 70 (Proof). *Obverse and Reverse:*
PF-60 to 62 coins have extensive hairlines and may have nicks and contact marks. At PF-63, hairlines are prominent, but the mirror surface is very reflective. PF-64 coins have fewer hairlines. At PF-65, hairlines should be minimal and mostly seen only under magnification. There should be no nicks or marks. PF-66 and higher coins have no marks or hairlines visible to the unaided eye.

1854. Graded PF-66.

1854, Doubled-Die Obverse
FS-G1-1854-1101.

	Mintage	Cert	Avg	%MS	VF-20	EF-40	AU-50	AU-55	MS-60	MS-62	MS-63 / PF-63	MS-64 / PF-64	MS-65 / PF-65
1854	783,943	5,743	57.3	29%	$350	$500	$625	$775	$1,700	$3,500	$7,500	$30,000	
Auctions: $49,938, MS-66, February 2013; $4,994, MS-63, August 2014; $4,700, MS-63, August 2014; $3,525, MS-62+, November 2014
1854, Doubled-Die Obverse (a)	**(b)**	12	55.8	8%			$1,100	$2,350	$4,150	$11,500			
Auctions: $3,738, MS-62, December 2011
1854, Proof	*4 known*	5	64.6								$200,000	$300,000	$425,000
Auctions: $218,500, PF-64DCam, March 2009
1855	758,269	5,386	57.3	30%	$350	$500	$625	$775	$1,700	$3,500	$7,500	$30,000	
Auctions: $32,900, MS-65, October 2013; $5,581, MS-63, July 2014; $4,555, MS-63, November 2014; $3,819, MS-62, August 2014
1855, Proof	*unknown*	6	65.0								$165,000	$200,000	$325,000
Auctions: $397,800, PF, September 2013
1855C	9,803	190	51.5	9%	$1,850	$4,000	$8,750	$12,500	$22,500	$35,000			
Auctions: $22,325, MS-61+, September 2014; $22,913, MS, February 2014; $10,575, AU-58, October 2014; $18,800, AU-58, November 2014
1855D	1,811	40	53.6	15%	$8,500	$15,000	$25,000	$27,500	$50,000	$57,500	$95,000		
Auctions: $52,875, EF-45, July 2014
1855O	55,000	490	54.8	14%	$575	$1,000	$1,700	$2,500	$8,000	$14,500	$32,500		
Auctions: $38,188, MS-63, April 2013; $19,975, MS-62, November 2014; $3,848, AU-58, September 2014; $4,406, AU-58, November 2014
1856S	24,600	211	54.5	16%	$950	$1,450	$2,250	$3,250	$8,250	$16,000	$30,000		
Auctions: $52,875, MS-64, February 2013; $1,763, EF-45, July 2014

a. Check for strong doubling on UNITED STATES OF AMERICA, the beads in the headdress, the feathers, and portions of LIBERTY.
b. Included in circulation-strike 1854 mintage figure.

INDIAN PRINCESS HEAD, LARGE HEAD (1856–1889)

Designer: *James B. Longacre.* **Weight:** *1.672 grams.*
Composition: *.900 gold, .100 copper (net weight .04837 oz. pure gold).* **Diameter:** *15 mm.*
Edge: *Reeded.* **Mints:** *Philadelphia, Charlotte, Dahlonega, San Francisco.*

Circulation Strike   **Proof**

History. The design of the Indian Princess Head was modified in 1856. The new Type 3 portrait is larger and in shallower relief. After this change, most (but not all) gold dollars were struck with strong detail. Gold dollars of this type did not circulate extensively after 1861, except in the West. As they did not see heavy use, today most pieces are EF or better. MS coins are readily available, particularly of the dates 1879 through 1889 (during those years the coins were popular among investors and speculators, and many were saved). These gold dollars were very popular with jewelers, who would purchase them at a price of $1.50 for use in a variety of ornaments.

Striking and Sharpness. These dollars usually are well struck, but many exceptions exist. Charlotte and Dahlonega coins are usually weak in areas and can have planchet problems. On all coins, check the hair details on the obverse. The word LIBERTY may be only partially present or missing completely, as the dies were made this way for some issues, particularly in the 1870s; this does not affect their desirability. On the reverse, check the ribbon knot and the two central date numerals. Check the denticles on both sides. Copper stains are sometimes seen on issues of the 1880s due to incomplete mixing of the alloy. Many coins of the 1860s onward have highly prooflike surfaces.

Availability. All Type 3 gold dollars are collectible, but many issues are scarce. Most MS-65 or finer coins are dated from 1879 to 1889. The few gold dollars of this type that are less than VF usually are damaged or have problems. Proofs were made of all years. Most range from rare to very rare, some dates in the 1880s being exceptions. Some later dates have high Proof mintages, but likely many of these coins were sold to the jewelry trade (as the Mint was reluctant to release circulation strikes to this market sector). Such coins were incorporated into jewelry and no longer exist as collectible coins.

GRADING STANDARDS

MS-60 to 70 (Mint State). *Obverse:* At MS-60 to 62, there is abrasion on the hair below the band lettered LIBERTY (an area that can be weakly struck as well), on the tips of the feather plumes, and throughout the field. Contact marks may also be seen. At MS-63, there should be only slight abrasions. Luster is irregular. At MS-64, abrasions and marks are less. Luster is rich on most coins, less so on Charlotte and Dahlonega issues. At

1878. Graded MS-67.

MS-65 and above, luster is deep and frosty, with no marks at all visible without magnification at MS-66 and higher. *Reverse:* At MS-60 to 62, there may be abrasions on the 1, on the highest parts of the leaves, on the ribbon knot, and in the field. Otherwise, the same comments apply as for the obverse.

   Illustrated coin: This exceptionally high-grade coin has superb eye appeal.

AU-50, 53, 55, 58 (About Uncirculated). *Obverse:* Light wear on the hair below the coronet, the cheek, and the tips of the feather plumes is very noticeable at AU-50, progressively less at higher levels to AU-58. Luster is minimal at AU-50 and scattered and incomplete at AU-58. Some tiny nicks and contact marks are to be expected and should be mentioned if they are distracting. *Reverse:* Light wear on the 1, the wreath, and the ribbon

1857-C. Graded AU-58.

knot characterize an AU-50 coin, progressively less at higher levels to AU-58. Otherwise, the same comments apply as for the obverse.

   Illustrated coin: The obverse field is slightly bulged. This coin is lightly struck at the center, unusual for most Type 3 gold dollars, but sometimes seen on Charlotte and Dahlonega varieties. Among 1857-C gold dollars this coin is exceptional. Most have poor striking and/or planchet problems.

EF-40, 45 (Extremely Fine). *Obverse:* Medium wear is seen on the hair below the coronet and on the feather plume tips. Detail is partially gone on the hair, although the usual light striking may make this moot. Luster is gone on most coins. *Reverse:* Light wear is seen overall, and the highest parts of the leaves are flat. Luster is gone on most coins.

1859-S. Graded EF-40.

VF-20, 30 (Very Fine). *Obverse:* Most hair detail is gone, except at the back of the lower curls. The feather plume ends are flat. *Reverse:* The wreath and other areas show more wear. Most detail is gone on the higher-relief leaves.

This gold dollar is seldom collected in grades lower than VF-20.

Illustrated coin: This coin is lightly struck at the center obverse, as well as at the U and IC in the border lettering. It is lightly struck at the center of the reverse.

1859-D. Graded VF-20.

PF-60 to 70 (Proof). *Obverse and Reverse:* PF-60 to 62 coins have extensive hairlines and may have nicks and contact marks. At PF-63, hairlines are prominent, but the mirror surface is very reflective. PF-64 coins have fewer hairlines. At PF-65, hairlines should be minimal and mostly seen only under magnification. There should be no nicks or marks. PF-66 and higher coins have no marks or hairlines visible to the unaided eye.

1884. Graded PF-68.

Illustrated coin: This splendid cameo Proof is one of the finest graded.

	Mintage	Cert	Avg	%MS	VF-20	EF-40	AU-50	AU-55	MS-60	MS-62	MS-63 / PF-63	MS-64 / PF-64	MS-65 / PF-65
1856, All kinds	1,762,936												
1856, Upright 5		316	59.1	50%	$275	$300	$375	$450	$650	$875	$1,500	$2,150	$6,500
Auctions: $2,585, MS-64, June 2013; $764, MS-62, July 2014; $388, AU-58, July 2014; $441, AU-58, October 2014													
1856, Slant 5		1,343	59.4	55%	$245	$250	$265	$285	$575	$675	$950	$1,300	$3,000
Auctions: $5,581, MS-66, March 2014; $1,058, MS-64, July 2014; $705, MS-63, August 2014; $646, MS-63, October 2014													
1856, Slant 5, Proof	unknown	5	66.2								$30,000	$35,000	$65,000
Auctions: $30,550, PF, January 2013													
1856D	1,460	34	55.5	15%	$3,750	$5,750	$8,000	$11,000	$28,500	$42,500	$85,000		
Auctions: $11,750, AU-58, September 2013; $7,050, EF-45, July 2014													

1862, Doubled-Die Obverse
FS-G1-1862-101.

	Mintage	Cert	Avg	%MS	VF-20	EF-40	AU-50	AU-55	MS-60	MS-62	MS-63 PF-63	MS-64 PF-64	MS-65 PF-65
1857	774,789	1,217	60.1	65%	$245	$250	$265	$285	$575	$675	$900	$1,350	$3,500
	Auctions: $3,323, MS-65, March 2014; $3,055, MS-65, November 2014; $823, MS-64, November 2014; $1,058, MS-63, November 2014												
1857, Proof	unknown	6	64.8								$17,500	$20,000	$40,000
	Auctions: $16,100, PF-63Cam, June 2008												
1857C	13,280	138	53.5	7%	$1,350	$1,750	$3,000	$5,250	$11,500	$18,500	$30,000		
	Auctions: $12,925, MS-62, August 2014; $16,450, MS-62, April 2013; $3,055, AU-58, July 2014; $2,585, AU-50, July 2014												
1857D	3,533	92	55.0	13%	$1,500	$2,400	$3,750	$4,850	$10,000	$15,000			
	Auctions: $5,581, AU-58, April 2013; $3,525, AU-53, October 2014; $2,238, EF-45, July 2014												
1857S	10,000	106	54.2	15%	$450	$750	$1,250	$2,000	$5,750	$8,500	$17,500	$40,000	
	Auctions: $2,350, AU-55, July 2014												
1858	117,995	238	60.2	63%	$245	$250	$265	$285	$575	$675	$1,000	$1,500	$4,500
	Auctions: $7,638, MS-66, March 2013; $1,528, MS-64, October 2014; $529, MS-62, November 2014; $382, AU-58, July 2014												
1858, Proof	unknown	14	64.6								$13,500	$15,000	$30,000
	Auctions: $32,900, PF-66Cam+, November 2014; $79,313, PF, March 2014												
1858D	3,477	109	54.9	28%	$1,500	$2,250	$3,750	$4,850	$8,750	$13,000	$19,500	$37,500	$60,000
	Auctions: $7,638, MS-61, December 2013; $1,439, AU-50, September 2014; $1,998, EF-45, July 2014												
1858S	10,000	95	54.0	11%	$385	$675	$1,300	$1,850	$6,000	$9,500	$16,500	$18,500	$30,000
	Auctions: $8,813, MS-62, June 2014; $1,528, AU-55, July 2014; $259, VF-20, November 2014												
1859	168,244	397	60.7	73%	$245	$250	$255	$285	$575	$675	$900	$1,100	$2,500
	Auctions: $4,113, MS-66, October 2013; $999, MS-64, October 2014; $427, MS-62, August 2014; $499, AU-58, July 2014												
1859, Proof	80	13	64.8								$12,000	$14,500	$17,500
	Auctions: $22,325, PF-64, August 2013												
1859C	5,235	78	57.1	29%	$1,400	$2,000	$3,500	$6,500	$10,000	$14,000	$27,500		
	Auctions: $10,575, MS-62, January 2014; $4,113, AU-55, August 2014; $3,290, EF-40, July 2014												
1859D	4,952	111	57.1	30%	$1,600	$2,250	$3,250	$5,000	$8,000	$11,500	$18,500	$3,000	$60,000
	Auctions: $11,750, MS-62, June 2013; $3,290, AU-55, July 2014; $911, AU-50, November 2014												
1859S	15,000	146	52.2	10%	$300	$575	$1,250	$1,900	$5,000	$8,500	$15,000	$22,500	
	Auctions: $6,169, MS-62, February 2013; $1,763, AU-58, November 2014; $3,055, AU-50, July 2014												
1860	36,514	156	61.2	81%	$245	$250	$275	$300	$575	$675	$1,000	$2,000	$5,500
	Auctions: $1,998, MS-64, December 2013; $588, MS-62, October 2014; $353, AU-58, November 2014; $329, AU-53, July 2014												
1860, Proof	154	19	64.8								$8,000	$10,000	$15,000
	Auctions: $27,600, PF-66, January 2012												
1860D	1,566	64	54.8	19%	$3,000	$4,250	$7,500	$9,500	$18,000	$27,500	$50,000	$75,000	
	Auctions: $42,300, MS-64, February 2013; $6,463, EF-40, July 2014												
1860S	13,000	150	56.2	27%	$350	$500	$775	$1,100	$2,650	$4,000	$6,000	$12,500	$27,500
	Auctions: $9,929, MS-64, August 2013; $1,293, AU-58, July 2014; $764, AU-55, August 2014; $470, AU-50, September 2014												
1861	527,150	1384	61.3	84%	$245	$250	$265	$275	$550	$650	$1,000	$1,375	$2,500
	Auctions: $2,820, MS-65, September 2014; $2,820, MS-65, November 2014; $3,525, MS-65, February 2013; $1,528, MS-64, August 2014												
1861, Proof	349	16	64.8								$8,000	$8,500	$13,500
	Auctions: $17,625, PF-65Cam, October 2014												
1861D	1,250	28	58.1	36%	$22,500	$30,000	$40,000	$57,500	$75,000	$85,000	$115,000	$135,000	$185,000
	Auctions: $111,625, MS-63, June 2013; $30,550, EF-45, July 2014												
1862	1,361,355	2,994	61.7	88%	$245	$250	$265	$285	$575	$675	$825	$1,100	$2,500
	Auctions: $5,875, MS-67, July 2013; $1,293, MS-64, July 2014; $1,644, MS-64, November 2014; $1,058, MS-63+, November 2014												
1862, DblDie Obv (a)	**(b)**	15	61.4	80%	$275	$300	$350	$500	$750	$900	$1,350		
	Auctions: $675, MS-62, February 2011												

a. Doubling, visible on the entire obverse, is most evident on the tops of the hair curls and the feathers. **b.** Included in circulation-strike 1862 mintage figure.

	Mintage	Cert	Avg	%MS	VF-20	EF-40	AU-50	AU-55	MS-60	MS-62	MS-63	MS-64	MS-65
											PF-63	PF-64	PF-65
1863	6,200	35	61.7	77%	$1,350	$2,000	$3,250	$4,500	$6,000	$8,750	$10,500	$13,500	$20,000
Auctions: $10,575, MS-64, October 2014; $8,813, MS-63, April 2013; $5,434, AU-55, July 2014													
1863, Proof	50	17	65.1								$9,000	$10,000	$17,500
Auctions: $58,750, PF, February 2013													
1864	5,900	71	61.4	79%	$500	$850	$1,350	$1,750	$2,000	$2,750	$4,000	$5,000	$8,000
Auctions: $58,750, MS-69, January 2014; $705, MS-60, October 2014; $1,293, AU-55, July 2014													
1864, Proof	50	13	64.4								$9,000	$10,000	$15,000
Auctions: $32,200, PF-66UCam, October 2011													
1865	3,725	39	62.7	87%	$600	$900	$1,100	$1,350	$2,000	$2,750	$4,750	$5,600	$8,500
Auctions: $18,213, MS-67, January 2014; $3,055, MS-61, October 2014; $1,116, EF-45, July 2014													
1865, Proof	25	13	65.2								$9,000	$11,500	$16,500
Auctions: $25,300, PF-65, August 2011													
1866	7,100	75	62.4	85%	$400	$500	$750	$900	$1,250	$1,550	$2,150	$3,000	$5,000
Auctions: $29,375, MS-68, July 2014; $617, MS-60, October 2014; $764, AU-53, July 2014													
1866, Proof	30	19	65.4								$9,000	$11,500	$16,500
Auctions: $27,600, PF-67UCam, August 2007													
1867	5,200	76	61.5	72%	$450	$525	$700	$850	$1,200	$1,500	$2,000	$2,750	$5,000
Auctions: $10,281, MS-66, March 2014; $881, AU-58, July 2014; $881, AU-58, November 2014; $427, AU-55, October 2014													
1867, Proof	50	13	63.5								$7,500	$10,000	$15,000
Auctions: $19,975, PF-66Cam, August 2014													
1868	10,500	125	61.1	78%	$285	$425	$525	$625	$1,000	$1,500	$2,000	$2,750	$4,500
Auctions: $21,150, MS-68, August 2013; $881, AU-58, July 2014; $558, AU-55, October 2014													
1868, Proof	25	9	64.5								$7,500	$10,000	$17,500
Auctions: $29,900, PF-66UCam+, August 2011													
1869	5,900	89	61.9	84%	$350	$475	$700	$800	$1,150	$1,600	$2,250	$2,900	$5,500
Auctions: $15,863, MS-67, August 2014; $7,638, MS-66, February 2014; $456, MS-60, October 2014; $999, AU-58, July 2014													
1869, Proof	25	10	64.0								$7,500	$11,500	$17,500
Auctions: $19,975, PF-65Cam, April 2014													
1870	6,300	109	61.7	77%	$325	$450	$675	$750	$1,000	$1,500	$2,000	$2,750	$5,500
Auctions: $22,325, MS-67, January 2014; $8,225, MS-67, October 2014; $646, AU-58, August 2014; $764, AU-55, July 2014													
1870, Proof	35	9	62.6								$7,500	$10,000	$15,000
Auctions: $17,625, PF-64, January 2014													
1870S	3,000	57	60.0	60%	$500	$825	$1,250	$1,650	$2,750	$4,000	$7,000	$11,500	$22,500
Auctions: $18,800, MS-65, April 2014; $1,880, AU-58, July 2014													
1871	3,900	117	62.2	88%	$315	$450	$575	$675	$900	$1,100	$1,900	$2,250	$4,000
Auctions: $9,988, MS-66, April 2013; $823, MS-61, October 2014; $412, MS-60, September 2014; $852, AU-58, July 2014													
1871, Proof	30	4	66.3								$8,000	$10,000	$15,000
Auctions: $27,600, PF-65DCam, November 2011													
1872	3,500	68	60.6	72%	$315	$425	$575	$700	$1,000	$1,350	$2,250	$3,000	$5,000
Auctions: $14,688, MS-68, February 2013; $823, AU-58, July 2014													
1872, Proof	30	15	64.2								$8,000	$11,500	$17,500
Auctions: $4,888, PF-61, March 2011													
1873, Close 3	1,800	119	60.7	72%	$425	$750	$1,100	$1,150	$1,700	$2,500	$4,250	$7,500	$15,000
Auctions: $7,638, MS-64, January 2014; $1,528, MS-62, October 2014; $1,293, MS-61, September 2014; $1,087, AU-58, July 2014													
1873, Open 3	123,300	2,172	61.8	91%	$245	$250	$265	$285	$525	$675	$775	$875	$2,000
Auctions: $11,750, MS-67, April 2013; $1,880, MS-65, November 2014; $999, MS-64, November 2014; $558, MS-63, September 2014													
1873, Close 3, Proof	25	7	63.3								$15,000	$22,500	$32,500
Auctions: $30,550, PF-65, August 2014													
1874	198,800	3846	62.2	94%	$245	$250	$265	$285	$525	$675	$800	$950	$2,250
Auctions: $3,314, MS-67, April 2014; $1,175, MS-65, October 2014; $1,116, MS-65, October 2014; $852, MS-64+, July 2014													
1874, Proof	20	7	64.5								$12,000	$15,000	$24,500
Auctions: $12,650, PF-64UC+, August 2010													

	Mintage	Cert	Avg	%MS	VF-20	EF-40	AU-50	AU-55	MS-60	MS-62	MS-63 / PF-63	MS-64 / PF-64	MS-65 / PF-65
1875	400	32	61.3	81%	$2,750	$4,500	$5,500	$6,500	$8,500	$10,000	$15,000	$20,000	$35,000
	Auctions: $22,325, MS-64, April 2013; $2,820, MS-60, October 2014; $5,875, AU-53, July 2014												
1875, Proof	20	11	64.1								$18,500	$30,000	$45,000
	Auctions: $55,813, PF-66DCam, November 2013												
1876	3,200	139	61.4	78%	$325	$375	$500	$600	$750	$1,000	$1,350	$1,500	$3,500
	Auctions: $16,450, MS-66, April 2013; $940, MS-62, July 2014; $588, AU-55, September 2014; $646, AU-50, October 2014												
1876, Proof	45	16	64.8								$7,000	$11,000	$15,000
	Auctions: $34,075, PF-66DCam, June 2013; $16,450, PF-65DCam, September 2014												
1877	3,900	182	62.2	85%	$300	$375	$525	$600	$800	$1,000	$1,400	$1,550	$3,500
	Auctions: $21,150, MS-68, September 2014; $6,463, MS-65, December 2013; $793, MS-61, July 2014; $353, MS-60, November 2014												
1877, Proof	20	16	64.7								$8,000	$11,000	$15,000
	Auctions: $7,638, PF, February 2014												
1878	3,000	145	61.3	86%	$300	$350	$525	$575	$775	$1,000	$1,350	$1,550	$3,500
	Auctions: $5,900, MS-66, August 2014; $4,142, MS-65, February 2013; $1,175, MS-62, October 2014; $764, MS-61, July 2014												
1878, Proof	20	13	64.3								$7,500	$11,000	$15,000
	Auctions: $19,550, PF-65DCam, January 2012												
1879	3,000	207	63.5	93%	$265	$300	$325	$375	$650	$800	$1,150	$1,300	$2,750
	Auctions: $3,173, MS-66, November 2014; $4,127, MS-66, August 2013; $764, MS-61, October 2014; $529, MS-61, October 2014												
1879, Proof	30	9	64.4								$6,500	$10,500	$15,000
	Auctions: $8,225, PF, August 2013												
1880	1,600	295	65.5	99%	$265	$300	$325	$375	$575	$700	$1,000	$1,150	$2,350
	Auctions: $52,875, MS-69, January 2014; $4,700, MS-67+, October 2014; $3,819, MS-67, October 2014; $2,233, MS-66+, October 2014												
1880, Proof	36	27	64.4								$5,500	$10,500	$12,000
	Auctions: $18,800, PF-65DCam, February 2013												
1881	7,620	382	64.8	97%	$250	$285	$325	$350	$575	$700	$1,000	$1,300	$2,350
	Auctions: $14,100, MS-68, April 2013; $3,290, MS-66, November 2014; $764, MS-63, August 2014; $823, MS-62, July 2014												
1881, Proof	87	27	64.8								$5,750	$8,500	$13,500
	Auctions: $2,820, PF-60, September 2014; $19,975, PF, March 2014												
1882	5,000	208	64.3	97%	$250	$285	$325	$350	$575	$700	$1,000	$1,150	$2,350
	Auctions: $4,406, MS-67, April 2014; $1,469, MS-65, July 2014; $764, MS-63, August 2014; $646, MS-62, July 2014												
1882, Proof	125	36	65.4								$5,000	$8,500	$13,500
	Auctions: $8,813, PF-64DCam, November 2014; $15,275, PF, August 2013												
1883	10,800	498	63.9	96%	$250	$285	$350	$400	$575	$700	$1,200	$1,300	$2,650
	Auctions: $3,819, MS-67, July 2014; $4,994, MS-67+, November 2014; $12,925, MS-67, October 2013; $1,424, MS-65, September 2014												
1883, Proof	207	46	65.0								$5,000	$8,000	$11,500
	Auctions: $9,400, PF-65Cam, February 2013												
1884	5,230	227	63.5	97%	$250	$285	$325	$350	$575	$700	$1,000	$1,150	$2,350
	Auctions: $8,225, MS-68, November 2014; $6,463, MS-67, January 2014; $1,528, MS-65, July 2014; $764, MS-64, October 2014												
1884, Proof	1,006	63	65.3								$5,750	$7,500	$12,500
	Auctions: $29,250, PF, September 2013												
1885	11,156	453	63.7	95%	$250	$285	$325	$350	$575	$700	$1,000	$1,150	$2,350
	Auctions: $3,672, MS-67, November 2014; $3,055, MS-67, January 2013; $1,763, MS-66, November 2014; $831, MS-64, July 2014												
1885, Proof	1,105	113	64.9								$5,000	$6,500	$11,000
	Auctions: $9,400, PF-65Cam, July 2014; $28,200, PF, August 2013												
1886	5,000	312	63.2	97%	$250	$285	$325	$350	$575	$700	$1,000	$1,150	$1,800
	Auctions: $2,115, MS-66, October 2014; $1,645, MS-66, October 2014; $1,528, MS-65, June 2014; $1,116, MS-65, November 2014												
1886, Proof	1,016	72	63.6								$5,000	$6,500	$11,000
	Auctions: $18,800, PF-67Cam, August 2014; $12,925, PF-66Cam, November 2014; $11,163, PF, October 2013												

	Mintage	Cert	Avg	%MS	VF-20	EF-40	AU-50	AU-55	MS-60	MS-62	MS-63	MS-64	MS-65
											PF-63	PF-64	PF-65
1887	7,500	482	63.6	99%	$250	$285	$325	$375	$525	$675	$900	$1,000	$2,000
	Auctions: $2,820, MS-67, October 2014; $1,528, MS-65, August 2014; $4,818, MS-65, August 2013; $999, MS-64, November 2014												
1887, Proof	1,043	62	64.6								$5,750	$7,500	$12,500
	Auctions: $10,575, PF-65DCam, September 2013; $10,288, PF-65Cam+, October 2014												
1888	15,501	732	63.8	98%	$250	$285	$325	$375	$525	$650	$850	$1,000	$2,000
	Auctions: $10,105, MS-68, February 2013; $1,880, MS-66, September 2014; $1,410, MS-65, September 2014; $1,293, MS-65, September 2014												
1888, Proof	1,079	97	64.5								$5,000	$6,500	$10,500
	Auctions: $18,800, PF-66DCam, April 2013												
1889	28,950	1953	64.2	98%	$250	$285	$285	$315	$575	$675	$800	$975	$1,450
	Auctions: $7,931, MS-68, November 2014; $8,108, MS-68, August 2013; $3,525, MS-67, August 2014; $2,820, MS-67, September 2014												
1889, Proof	1,779	35	64.2								$5,000	$6,500	$10,500
	Auctions: $12,925, PF-66Cam, April 2013												

Gold Quarter Eagles ($2.50)
1796–1929

AN OVERVIEW OF GOLD QUARTER EAGLES

The quarter eagle, denominated at one-fourth of an eagle, or $2.50, was authorized by the Act of April 2, 1792. Early types in the series range from rare to very rare. The first, the 1796 without stars on the obverse, Heraldic Eagle motif on the reverse, is a classic, one of the most desired of all pieces needed for a type set, and accordingly expensive. Most examples are in such grades as EF and AU.

Quarter eagles with stars on the obverse and with the Heraldic Eagle reverse were produced from 1796 intermittently through 1807. Today they exist in modest numbers, particularly in grades such as EF and AU, but on an absolute basis are fairly rare.

The standalone 1808 Capped Bust type, by John Reich, of which only 2,710 were minted, is the rarest single type coin in the entire American copper, nickel, silver, and gold series, possibly excepting the 1839 Gobrecht dollar (in a different category, as Proof restrikes were made). Examples of the 1808 can be found in various grades from VF through AU, and only rarely higher.

The next style of quarter eagle, from 1821 through 1827, is scarce, but when seen is usually in grades such as EF, AU, or even the low levels of Mint State. The same can be said for the modified quarter eagle of 1829 through early 1834.

Finally, with the advent of the Classic Head in late 1834, continuing through 1839, quarter eagles become more readily available. Examples can be found in nearly any grade from VF into the lower levels of Mint State. Then come the Liberty Head quarter eagles, minted continuously from 1840 through 1907, in sufficient numbers and for such a long time that it is not difficult to obtain an example to illustrate the type, with choice and gem Mint State coins being plentiful for the dates of the early 20th century.

The last quarter eagles are of the Indian Head type, minted from 1908 through 1929. These pieces are plentiful today, but grading can be difficult, as they were struck in sunken relief and the highest part on the coin is the field (this area was immediately subject to contact marks and wear). Although many opportunities exist in the marketplace, a collector should approach a purchase with care, seeking an example that has frosty, lustrous fields.

FOR THE COLLECTOR AND INVESTOR: GOLD QUARTER EAGLES AS A SPECIALTY

Collecting quarter eagles by dates, mintmarks, and major varieties is a very appealing pursuit. Although many are scarce and rare—this description applies to any variety from 1796 through early 1834—none are truly impossible to obtain. Among the Classic Head issues of 1834–1839, branch-mint coins are especially scarce in higher grades.

Liberty Head quarter eagles, produced continuously from 1840 through 1907, include a number of key issues, such as the famous 1854-S (usually seen in well-circulated grades), the Proof-only 1863 (of which only 30 were struck), and a number of elusive mintmarks. Of particular interest is the 1848 coin with CAL. counterstamped on the reverse, signifying that the coin was made from gold bullion brought to the Philadelphia Mint in a special shipment from California.

CAPPED BUST TO RIGHT (1796–1807)

Designer: *Robert Scot.* **Weight:** *4.37 grams.* **Composition:** *.9167 gold, .0833 silver and copper.*
Diameter: *Approximately 20 mm.* **Edge:** *Reeded.*

No Stars on Obverse (1796)
Bass-Dannreuther–2.

Stars on Obverse (1796–1807)
Bass-Dannreuther–3.

History. The first quarter eagles were struck intermittently during the late 1790s and early 1800s, with consistently small mintages. The earliest issues of 1796 lack obverse stars. They likely circulated domestically, rather than being exported in international trade.

Striking and Sharpness. Most have light striking in one area or another. On the obverse, check the hair details and the stars. On the reverse, check the shield, stars, and clouds. Examine the denticles on both sides. Planchet adjustment marks (from a coin's overweight planchet being filed down to correct specifications) are seen on many coins and are not noted by the certification services. On high-grade coins the luster usually is very attractive. Certain reverse dies of this type were also used to make dimes of the era, which were almost exactly the same diameter.

Availability. Most Capped Bust to Right quarter eagles in the marketplace are EF or AU. MS coins are elusive; when seen, they usually are of later dates.

GRADING STANDARDS

MS-60 to 70 (Mint State). *Obverse:* At MS-60, some abrasion and contact marks are evident, most noticeably on the hair to the left of Miss Liberty's forehead and on the higher-relief areas of the cap. On the No Stars quarter eagles, there is some abrasion in the field—more so than the With Stars coins, on which the field is more protected. Luster is present, but may be dull or lifeless, and

1802, 2 Over 1. Graded MS-61.

interrupted in patches. At MS-63, contact marks are few, and abrasion is very light. An MS-65 coin will have hardly any abrasion, and contact marks are so minute as to require magnification. Luster should be full and rich. Coins grading above MS-65 exist more in theory than in reality for this type—but they do exist, and are defined by having fewer marks as perfection is approached. *Reverse:* Comments apply as for the obverse, except that abrasion and contact marks are most noticeable on the upper part of the eagle and the clouds. The field area is complex; there is not much open space, with stars above the eagle, the arrows and olive branch, and other features. Accordingly, marks are not as noticeable as on the obverse.

Illustrated coin: Some friction appears on the higher areas of this example, but the fields retain nearly full luster, and the coin overall has nice eye appeal.

AU-50, 53, 55, 58 (About Uncirculated).
Obverse: Light wear is seen on the cheek, the hair immediately to the left of the face, and the cap, more so at AU-50 than at 53 or 55. An AU-58 coin has minimal traces of wear. An AU-50 coin has luster in protected areas among the stars and letters, with little in the open fields or on the portrait. At AU-58 most luster is present in the fields, but is worn away on the highest parts of the motifs. The 1796

1796, No Stars; BD-2. Graded AU-58.

No Stars type has less luster in any given grade. *Reverse:* Comments as for Mint State, except that the eagle's neck, the tips and top of the wings, the clouds, and the tail now show noticeable wear, as do other features. Luster ranges from perhaps 40% remaining in protected areas at AU-50 to nearly full mint bloom at AU-58. Often the reverse of this type retains much more luster than does the obverse.

EF-40, 45 (Extremely Fine). *Obverse:* Wear is evident all over the portrait, with some loss of detail in the hair to the left of Miss Liberty's face. Excellent detail remains in low-relief areas of the hair, such as the front curl and the back of the head. The stars show wear, as do the date and letters. Luster, if present at all, is minimal and in protected areas. *Reverse:* Wear is greater than at the About Uncirculated level. The neck lacks feather detail on its

1802; BD-1. Graded EF-45.

highest points. Feathers have lost some detail near the edges of the wings, and some areas of the horizontal lines in the shield may be blended together. Some traces of luster may be seen, more so at EF-45 than at EF-40. Overall, the reverse appears to be in a slightly higher grade than the obverse.

VF-20, 30 (Very Fine). *Obverse:* The higher-relief areas of hair are well worn at VF-20, less so at VF-30. The stars are flat at their centers. *Reverse:* Wear is greater, including on the shield and wing feathers. The star centers are flat. Other areas have lost detail as well. E PLURIBUS UNUM is easy to read.

The Capped Bust to Right quarter eagle is seldom collected in grades lower than VF-20.

1796, With Stars; BD-3. Graded VF-30.

	Mintage	Cert	Avg	%MS	F-12	VF-20	EF-40	AU-50	AU-55	AU-58	MS-60	MS-63	MS-64
1796, No Stars on Obverse	963	34	57.3	35%	$42,500	$65,000	$90,000	$115,000	$135,000	$170,000	$225,000	$500,000	$750,000 **(a)**
Auctions: $64,625, EF-40, August 2014; $94,000, VF-30, December 2013													
1796, Stars on Obverse	432	24	58.4	50%	$35,000	$47,500	$70,000	$95,000	$120,000	$150,000	$200,000	$375,000	$600,000 **(b)**
Auctions: $102,813, AU-58, March 2014; $223,250, AU-58, November 2014													
1797	427	14	48.6	14%	$18,500	$27,500	$40,000	$72,500	$95,000	$100,000	$137,500	$235,000	$375,000
Auctions: $105,750, AU-53, April 2013													

a. Value in MS-65 is $1,600,000. **b.** Value in MS-65 is $1,600,000.

1798, Close Date

1798, Wide Date

1804, 13-Star Reverse

1804, 14-Star Reverse

	Mintage	Cert	Avg	%MS	F-12	VF-20	EF-40	AU-50	AU-55	AU-58	MS-60	MS-63	MS-64
1798, All kinds	1,094												
1798, Close Date		21	54	33%				$30,000	$40,000	$50,000	$67,500	$125,000	
Auctions: $18,800, AU-50, August 2014													
1798, Wide Date		(c)						$30,000	$40,000	$50,000	$67,500	$125,000	
Auctions: $70,500, AU-58, November 2014; $44,063, AU-50, June 2014													
1802	3,035	73	56.8	36%	$6,000	$8,500	$13,000	$17,500	$20,000	$23,500	$32,500	$60,000	$115,000
Auctions: $20,563, AU-58, August 2014; $21,150, AU-58, March 2013; $16,450, AU-50, August 2014; $15,275, EF-45, August 2014													
1804, 13-Star Reverse	(d)	3	51.7	0%	$75,000	$100,000	$125,000	$150,000	$250,000	$600,000			
Auctions: $322,000, AU-58, July 2009													
1804, 14-Star Reverse	3,327	58	53.0	19%	$5,250	$9,000	$14,000	$18,000	$21,000	$23,500	$32,500	$100,000	
Auctions: $44,063, MS-62, April 2014; $70,501, MS-62, November 2014; $21,738, AU-58, November 2014; $19,975, AU-55, August 2014													
1805	1,781	51	55.1	29%	$5,750	$9,500	$14,000	$18,000	$21,000	$23,500	$32,500		
Auctions: $15,275, MS-60, March 2014; $20,563, AU-58, August 2014; $23,500, AU-55, November 2014; $14,100, AU-53, October 2014													
1806, 6 Over 4, 8 Stars Left, 5 Right	1,136	25	53.8	36%	$5,750	$9,500	$14,000	$18,000	$21,000	$23,500	$32,500	$100,000	
Auctions: $30,550, MS-61, June 2014; $22,325, AU-58, August 2014; $21,150, AU-58, August 2014; $20,563, AU-58, October 2014													
1806, 6 Over 5, 7 Stars Left, 6 Right	480	15	57.4	47%	$12,000	$15,000	$20,000	$40,000	$57,500	$65,000	$95,000	$200,000	
Auctions: $67,563, AU-About Uncirculated, February 2014													
1807	6,812	116	55.7	36%	$5,750	$8,500	$13,250	$17,000	$20,000	$23,500	$32,500	$65,000	$115,000 (e)
Auctions: $44,063, MS-62, March 2014; $17,625, AU-55, August 2014; $11,750, AU-50, November 2014													

c. Included in certified population for 1798, Close Date. **d.** Included in 1804, 14-Star Reverse, mintage figure. **e.** Value in MS-65 is $300,000.

CAPPED BUST TO LEFT, LARGE SIZE (1808)

Designer: *John Reich.* **Weight:** *4.37 grams.* **Composition:** *.9167 gold, .0833 silver and copper.* **Diameter:** *Approximately 20 mm.* **Edge:** *Reeded.*

History. John Reich's Capped Bust was an adaptation of the design introduced in 1807 on the half dollar. On the quarter eagle it was used for a single year only, with fewer than 3,000 coins struck, making it the rarest of the major gold coin types (indeed, the rarest of any U.S. coin type).

Striking and Sharpness. All examples are lightly struck on one area or another, particularly the stars and rims. The rims are low and sometimes missing or nearly so (on the obverse), causing quarter eagles of this type to wear more quickly than otherwise might be the case. Sharpness of strike is overlooked by most buyers.

Availability. Examples are rare in any grade. Typical grades are EF and AU. Lower grades are seldom seen, as the coins did not circulate to any great extent. Gold coins of this era were not seen in circulation after 1821, so they did not get a chance to acquire significant wear.

GRADING STANDARDS

MS-60 to 70 (Mint State). *Obverse:* At MS-60, some abrasion and contact marks are seen on the cheek, on the hair below the LIBERTY inscription, and on the highest-relief folds of the cap. Luster is present, but may be dull or lifeless, and interrupted in patches. At MS-63, contact marks are few, and abrasion is very light. Abrasion is even less at MS-64. (Discussion of such high grades in these early coins starts to enter the realm of theory.)

1808; BD-1. Graded MS-63.

Quarter eagles of this type are almost, but not quite, non-existent in a combination of high grade and nice eye appeal. *Reverse:* Comments apply as for the obverse, except that abrasion is most noticeable on the eagle's neck and highest area of the wings.

Illustrated coin: Superbly struck, this coin is a "poster example" with few peers.

AU-50, 53, 55, 58 (About Uncirculated). *Obverse:* Light wear is seen on the cheek and higher-relief areas of the hair and cap. Friction and scattered marks are in the field, ranging from extensive at AU-50 to minimal at AU-58. The low rim affords little protection to the field of this coin, but the stars in relief help. Luster may be seen in protected areas, minimal at AU-50, but less so at AU-58. At AU-58 the field retains some lus-

1808. Graded AU-50.

ter as well. *Reverse:* Comments are as for a Mint State coin, except that the eagle's neck, the top of the wings, the leaves, and the arrowheads now show noticeable wear, as do other features. Luster ranges from perhaps 40% remaining in protected areas at AU-50 to nearly full mint bloom at AU-58. Often the reverse of this type retains much more luster than does the obverse, as on this type the motto, eagle, and lettering protect the surrounding flat areas.

Illustrated coin: Note some lightness of strike.

EF-40, 45 (Extremely Fine). *Obverse:* More wear is seen on the portrait, the hair, the cap, and the drapery near the clasp. Luster is likely to be absent on the obverse due to the low rim. *Reverse:* Wear is more extensive on the eagle, including the top of the wings, the head, the top of the shield, and the claws. Some traces of luster may be seen in protected areas, more so at EF-45 than at EF-40.

1808. Graded EF-40.

VF-20, 30 (Very Fine). *Obverse:* Wear on the portrait has reduced the hair detail, especially to the right of the face and the top of the head, but much can still be seen. *Reverse:* Wear on the eagle is greater, and details of feathers near the shield and near the top of the wings are weak or missing. All other features show wear, but most are fairly sharp. Generally, Capped Bust gold coins at this grade level lack eye appeal.

1808. Graded VF-20.

The Capped Bust to Left, Large Size, quarter eagle is seldom collected in grades lower than VF-20.

Illustrated coin: This is a nice, problem-free example of a lower but very desirable grade for this rare issue.

	Mintage	Cert	Avg	%MS	F-12	VF-20	EF-40	AU-50	AU-55	AU-58	MS-60	MS-62	MS-63	MS-64
1808	2,710	43	54.5	35%	$30,000	$45,000	$60,000	$90,000	$110,000	$120,000	$150,000	$235,000	$375,000	$650,000
	Auctions: $126,900, MS-60, January 2013; $80,781, AU-55, August 2014													

CAPPED HEAD TO LEFT (1821–1834)

Designer: *John Reich.* **Weight:** *4.37 grams.* **Composition:** *.9167 gold, .0833 silver and copper.* **Diameter:** *1821–1827—approximately 20 mm; 1829–1834—approximately 18.2 mm.* **Edge:** *Reeded.*

Circulation Strike
BD-1.

Proof

History. Capped Head to Left quarter eagles dated 1821 through 1827 have a larger diameter and larger letters, dates, and stars than those of 1829 to 1834. The same grading standards apply to both. Gold coins of this type did not circulate in commerce, because their face value was lower than their bullion value. Many legislators, who had the option to draw their pay in specie (silver and gold coinage), took advantage of this fact to sell their salaries at a premium for paper money. Most wear was due to use as pocket pieces, or from minor handling.

Striking and Sharpness. Most Capped Head to Left quarter eagles are well struck. On the obverse, check the hair details (which on the Large Diameter style can be light in areas) and the stars. On the reverse, check the eagle. On both sides inspect the denticles. Fields are often semi-prooflike on higher grades.

Availability. All Capped Head to Left quarter eagles are rare. Grades typically range from EF to MS, with choice examples in the latter category being scarce, and gems being very rare. Proof coins were made on a limited basis for presentation and for sale to numismatists. All Proof examples are exceedingly rare today, and are usually encountered only when great collections are dispersed.

GRADING STANDARDS

MS-60 to 70 (Mint State). *Obverse:* At MS-60, some abrasion and contact marks are seen on the cheek, on the hair below the LIB-ERTY inscription, and on the highest-relief folds of the cap. Luster is present, but may be dull or lifeless, and interrupted in patches. At MS-63, contact marks are few, and abrasion is very light. Abrasion is even less at MS-64. (Discussion of such high grades in these early coins starts to enter the realm of theory.)

1827, BD-1. Graded MS-65.

Quarter eagles of this type are almost, but not quite, non-existent in a combination of high grade and nice eye appeal. *Reverse:* Comments apply as for the obverse, except that abrasion is most noticeable on the eagle's neck and highest area of the wings.

   Illustrated coin: This is a well-struck lustrous gem.

AU-50, 53, 55, 58 (About Uncirculated). *Obverse:* Light wear is seen on the cheek and higher-relief areas of the hair and cap. Friction and scattered marks are in the field, ranging from extensive at AU-50 to minimal at AU-58. The low rim affords little protection to the field of this coin, but the stars in relief help. Luster may be seen in protected areas, minimal at AU-50, but less so at AU-58. At AU-58 the field retains some luster as well.

1833; BD-1. Graded AU-53.

Reverse: Comments are as for a Mint State coin, except that the eagle's neck, the top of the wings, the leaves, and the arrowheads now show noticeable wear, as do other features. Luster ranges from perhaps 40% remaining in protected areas at AU-50 to nearly full mint bloom at AU-58. Often the reverse of this type retains much more luster than does the obverse, as on this type the motto, eagle, and lettering protect the surrounding flat areas.

EF-40, 45 (Extremely Fine). *Obverse:* More wear is seen on the portrait, the hair, the cap, and the drapery near the clasp. Luster is likely to be absent on the obverse due to the low rim. *Reverse:* Wear is more extensive on the eagle, including the top of the wings, the head, the top of the shield, and the claws. Some traces of luster may be seen in protected areas, more so at EF-45 than at EF-40.

1821; BD-1. Graded EF-40.

   The Capped Head to Left quarter eagle is seldom collected in grades lower than EF-40.

PF-60 to 70 (Proof). *Obverse and Reverse:* PF-60 to 62 coins have extensive hairlines and may have nicks and contact marks. At PF-63, hairlines are prominent, but the mirror surface is very reflective. PF-64 coins have fewer hairlines. At PF-65, hairlines should be minimal and mostly seen only under magnification. There should be no nicks or marks. PF-66 and higher coins should have no marks or hairlines visible to the unaided eye.

1824, 4 Over 1. Proof.

	Mintage	Cert	Avg	%MS	F-12	VF-20	EF-40	AU-50	AU-55	AU-58	MS-60	MS-63 / PF-63	MS-65 / PF-64
1821	6,448	20	57.4	40%	$6,750	$9,000	$13,500	$16,000	$17,500	$23,500	$32,500	$75,000	
	Auctions: $44,063, MS-62, March 2014												
1821, Proof	3–5	3	64.7									$275,000	$450,000
	Auctions: $241,500, PF-64Cam, January 2007												
1824, 4 Over 1	2,600	29	56.6	34%	$6,750	$9,500	$14,000	$16,500	$18,750	$25,000	$32,500	$80,000	
	Auctions: $18,800, AU-58, August 2013												
1824, 4 Over 1, Proof	3–5	0	n/a		*(unique, in the Smithsonian's National Numismatic Collection)*								
	Auctions: No auction records available.												
1825	4,434	49	58.8	55%	$6,750	$8,000	$13,000	$15,500	$17,500	$23,500	$30,000	$60,000	
	Auctions: $141,000, MS-65, November 2014; $105,750, MS-64, March 2014; $38,188, MS-62, July 2014; $32,900, MS-61, August 2014												
1825, Proof (a)	*unknown*	0	n/a										
	Auctions: No auction records available.												
1826, 6 Over 6	760	6	56.7	0%	$10,000	$12,500	$17,000	$25,000	$32,500	$40,000	$62,500		
	Auctions: $44,063, AU-58, August 2014; $45,531, AU-55, September 2013; $27,025, AU-55, November 2014												
1826, 6 Over 5, Proof (b)	*unknown*	0	n/a										
	Auctions: No auction records available.												
1827	2,800	23	58.6	65%	$6,500	$9,500	$13,100	$17,500	$20,000	$32,500	$35,000		
	Auctions: $58,750, MS-63, September 2014; $21,150, AU-58, August 2014; $28,200, AU-55, February 2013												
1827, Proof (c)	*unknown*	0	n/a										
	Auctions: No auction records available.												
1829	3,403	43	59.9	63%	$6,000	$7,500	$9,500	$13,000	$17,000	$18,500	$22,500	$35,000	$85,000
	Auctions: $41,125, MS-63, June 2013; $12,925, AU-55, August 2014												
1829, Proof	2–4	0	n/a		*(extremely rare; 2–3 known)*								
	Auctions: No auction records available.												
1830	4,540	44	60.2	52%	$6,000	$7,500	$9,500	$13,000	$17,000	$18,500	$22,500	$35,000	$85,000
	Auctions: $29,375, MS-63, November 2013; $24,675, MS-62, November 2014; $22,913, MS-62, November 2014												
1830, Proof (d)	*unknown*	0	n/a										
	Auctions: No auction records available.												
1831	4,520	64	60.5	69%	$6,000	$7,500	$9,500	$13,000	$17,000	$18,500	$22,500	$35,000	$85,000
	Auctions: $28,200, MS-63, September 2014; $18,800, AU-58, February 2013; $15,863, AU-58, August 2014												
1831, Proof	6–10	3	64.3									$100,000	$150,000
	Auctions: $30,550, PF-60, September 2013												
1832	4,400	41	57.0	41%	$6,000	$7,500	$9,500	$13,000	$17,000	$18,500	$24,000	$35,000	$95,000
	Auctions: $21,150, MS-61, March 2014; $22,913, MS-61, August 2014; $15,275, AU-58, August 2014; $12,338, AU-55, August 2014												
1832, Proof	2–4	0	n/a		*(unique, in the Bass Foundation Collection)*								
	Auctions: No auction records available.												

a. The 1825 quarter eagle might not exist in Proof; see the *Encyclopedia of U.S. Gold Coins, 1795–1933.* **b.** Proofs have been reported, but none have been authenticated. **c.** Proof 1827 quarter eagles almost certainly were made, but none are known to exist. **d.** Examples identified as Proofs are extremely rare, many are impaired, and none have been certified.

	Mintage	Cert	Avg	%MS	F-12	VF-20	EF-40	AU-50	AU-55	AU-58	MS-60	MS-63 PF-63	MS-65 PF-64
1833	4,160	45	59.1	51%	$6,000	$7,500	$9,500	$13,000	$17,000	$18,500	$24,000	$35,000	$95,000
	Auctions: $41,125, MS-63, August 2013; $15,275, AU-58, August 2014												
1833, Proof	2–4	0	n/a		*(extremely rare; 3–4 known)*								
	Auctions: No auction records available.												
1834, With Motto	4,000	9	55.3	22%	$10,000	$15,000	$20,000	$30,000	$40,000	$45,000	$60,000	$125,000	
	Auctions: $19,975, AU-50, November 2014; $64,625, EF-45, August 2014												
1834, With Motto, Proof	4–8	0	n/a		*(extremely rare; 3–5 known)*								
	Auctions: No auction records available.												

CLASSIC HEAD, NO MOTTO ON REVERSE (1834–1839)

Designer: *William Kneass.* **Weight:** *4.18 grams.*
Composition: *.8992 gold, .1008 silver and copper (changed to .900 gold in 1837).*
Diameter: *18.2 mm.* **Edge:** *Reeded.* **Mints:** *Philadelphia, Charlotte, Dahlonega, New Orleans.*

Circulation Strike
Breen-6151.

*Mintmark location
is on the obverse,
above the date.*

Proof

History. Gold quarter eagles had not circulated at face value in the United States since 1821, as the price of bullion necessitated more than $2.50 worth of gold to produce a single coin. Accordingly, they traded at their bullion value. The Act of June 28, 1834, provided lower weights for gold coins, after which the issues (of new designs to differentiate them from the old) circulated effectively. The Classic Head design by William Kneass is an adaptation of the head created by John Reich for the cent of 1808. The reverse illustrates a perched eagle. The motto E PLURIBUS UNUM, seen on earlier gold coins, no longer is present. These coins circulated widely until mid-1861 (for this reason, many show extensive wear). After that, they were hoarded by the public because of financial uncertainty during the Civil War.

Striking and Sharpness. Weakness is often seen on the higher areas of the hair curls. Also check the star centers. On the reverse, check the rims. The denticles usually are well struck.

Availability. Most coins range from VF to AU or lower ranges of MS. Most MS coins are of the first three years. MS-63 to 65 examples are rare. Good eye appeal can be elusive. Proofs were made in small quantities, and today probably only a couple dozen or so survive, most bearing the 1834 date.

GRADING STANDARDS

MS-60 to 70 (Mint State). *Obverse:* At MS-60, some abrasion and contact marks are seen on the portrait, most noticeably on the cheek, as the hair details are complex on this type. Luster is present, but may be dull or lifeless, and interrupted in patches. Many low-level Mint State coins have grainy surfaces. At MS-63, contact marks are few, and abrasion is very light. Abrasion is even less at MS-64. An MS-65 coin has hardly any abrasion, and contact marks are minute. Luster should be full and rich and is often more intense on the

1834. Graded MS-65.

obverse. Grades above MS-65 are defined by having fewer marks as perfection is approached. ***Reverse:*** Comments apply as for the obverse, except that abrasion is most noticeable on the eagle's neck and the highest area of the wings.

Illustrated coin: This coin is especially well struck.

AU-50, 53, 55, 58 (About Uncirculated).

Obverse: Friction is seen on the higher parts, particularly the cheek and hair (under magnification) of Miss Liberty. Friction and scattered marks are in the field, ranging from extensive at AU-50 to minimal at AU-58. Luster may be seen in protected areas, minimal at AU-50 but more visible at AU-58. On an AU-58 coin the field retains some luster as well. ***Reverse:*** Comments as for Mint State,

1837. Graded AU-55.

except that the eagle's neck, the top of the wings, the leaves, and the arrowheads now show noticeable wear, as do other features. Luster ranges from perhaps 40% remaining in protected areas at AU-50 to nearly full mint bloom at AU-58. Often the reverse of this type retains much more luster than does the obverse.

Illustrated coin: The coin has light wear overall, but traces of luster can be seen here and there.

EF-40, 45 (Extremely Fine). ***Obverse:*** Wear

is seen on the portrait overall, with reduction or elimination of some separation of hair strands, especially in the area close to the face. The cheek shows light wear. Luster is minimal or nonexistent at EF-40, and may survive in among the letters of LIBERTY at EF-45. ***Reverse:*** Wear is greater than on an About Uncirculated coin. On most (but not all) coins the eagle's neck lacks some feather detail on its highest points.

1834. Graded EF-40.

Feathers have lost some detail near the edges and tips of the wings. Some areas of the horizontal lines in the shield may be blended together. Some traces of luster may be seen, more so at EF-45 than at EF-40.

Illustrated coin: This coin is well struck.

VF-20, 30 (Very Fine). ***Obverse:*** Wear on

the portrait has reduced the hair detail, especially to the right of the face and the top of the head, but much can still be seen. ***Reverse:*** Wear is greater, including on the shield and wing feathers. Generally, Classic Head gold at this grade level lacks eye appeal.

The Classic Head quarter eagle is seldom collected in grades lower than VF-20.

Illustrated coin: This coin was lightly

1836. Graded VF-30.

cleaned. It is lightly struck at the centers, although at this grade level that is not important.

PF-60 to 70 (Proof). *Obverse and Reverse:* PF-60 to 62 coins have extensive hairlines and may have nicks and contact marks. At PF-63, hairlines are prominent, but the mirror surface is very reflective. PF-64 coins have fewer hairlines. At PF-65, hairlines should be minimal and mostly seen only under magnification. There should be no nicks or marks. PF-66 and higher coins should have no marks or hairlines visible to the unaided eye.

1836. Graded PF-65 Cameo.

1836, Script 8

1836, Block 8

	Mintage	Cert	Avg	%MS	F-12	VF-20	EF-40	AU-50	AU-55	AU-58	MS-60	MS-63	MS-65
											PF-60	PF-63	PF-65
1834, No Motto	112,234	976	56.3	32%	$365	$600	$850	$1,350	$1,650	$2,350	$3,500	$10,000	$42,500
Auctions: $7,947, MS-63, March 2014; $8,813, MS-63, November 2014; $8,225, MS-63, August 2014; $4,700, MS-62, September 2014													
1834, No Motto, Proof	15–25	7	64.3								$35,000	$100,000	$275,000
Auctions: $138,000, PF-64Cam, January 2011													
1835	131,402	305	54.3	30%	$365	$600	$850	$1,350	$1,650	$2,350	$3,800	$12,000	$45,000
Auctions: $9,988, MS-63, November 2014; $3,819, MS-61, August 2014; $2,820, MS-61, August 2014; $3,290, MS-60, March 2014													
1835, Proof	5–8	1	65.0								$35,000	$100,000	$300,000
Auctions: No auction records available.													
1836, All kinds	547,986												
1836, Script 8 (a)		481	51.6	19%	$365	$600	$850	$1,350	$1,650	$2,750	$3,750	$10,000	$40,000
Auctions: $8,225, MS-63, June 2013; $3,760, MS-62, October 2014; $3,290, MS-62, October 2014; $2,820, MS-61, August 2014													
1836, Block 8		428	50.2	15%	$365	$600	$850	$1,350	$1,650	$2,750	$3,750	$10,000	$40,000
Auctions: $10,869, MS-64, September 2014; $7,344, MS-63, June 2013; $4,406, MS-62, August 2014; $3,819, MS-62, August 2014													
1836, Proof	5–8	7	65.1								$35,000	$115,000	$300,000
Auctions: $195,500, PF-64Cam, April 2012													
1837	45,080	266	52.5	20%	$385	$625	$1,200	$2,000	$2,500	$3,500	$5,250	$13,500	$55,000
Auctions: $11,750, MS-63, January 2014; $2,585, MS-60, August 2014; $3,055, AU-58, November 2014; $1,528, AU-50, October 2014													
1837, Proof (b)	3–5	3	65.3								$32,500	$125,000	$350,000
Auctions: No auction records available.													
1838	47,030	277	53.4	23%	$385	$625	$1,000	$1,500	$1,850	$2,750	$4,500	$10,500	$47,500
Auctions: $5,288, MS-62, June 2013; $3,290, MS-61, August 2014; $3,055, MS-61, November 2014; $2,820, MS-60, November 2014													
1838, Proof	2–4	0	n/a		*(unique, in the Bass Foundation Collection)*							
Auctions: No auction records available.													
1838C	7,880	64	55.6	19%	$1,450	$2,500	$3,800	$8,000	$10,500	$15,000	$25,000	$50,000	
Auctions: $7,050, AU-53, August 2014; $2,350, EF-40, January 2014													

Note: So-called 9 Over 8 varieties for Philadelphia, Charlotte, and Denver mints were made from defective punches. **a.** Also known as the "Head of 1835." **b.** Two Proofs of 1837 are known; one is in the Smithsonian's National Numismatic Collection. A third example has been rumored, but its existence is not verified.

	Mintage	Cert	Avg	%MS	F-12	VF-20	EF-40	AU-50	AU-55	AU-58	MS-60	MS-63	MS-65
											PF-60	PF-63	PF-65
1839	27,021	85	52.0	12%	$400	$650	$1,300	$2,250	$2,900	$5,500	$6,500	$19,500	
	Auctions: $28,200, MS-61, August 2013; $6,463, AU-58, August 2014; $2,585, AU-53, November 2014												
1839, Proof (c)	4–6	1	62.0		*(extremely rare)*								
	Auctions: $136,679, PF-62, August 2006												
1839C	18,140	211	52.8	8%	$1,400	$2,350	$3,250	$5,000	$8,000	$16,000	$26,000	$52,500	
	Auctions: $9,106, AU-58, September 2014; $7,931, AU-58, October 2014; $10,575, AU-58, April 2013; $7,344, AU-55, November 2014												
1839D	13,674	111	48.8	11%	$1,500	$2,500	$4,250	$8,500	$10,000	$18,500	$28,500	$50,000	
	Auctions: $105,750, MS-64, January 2013; $19,975, AU-58, November 2014; $8,813, AU-55, August 2014; $6,756, AU-50, August 2014												
1839O	17,781	314	52.9	19%	$650	$950	$1,500	$2,500	$3,800	$6,000	$8,500	$25,000	
	Auctions: $12,925, AU-58, March 2014; $4,700, AU-55, September 2014; $4,113, AU-53, August 2014; $5,288, AU-53, November 2014												

c. Three Proofs of 1839 are reported to exist; only two are presently accounted for.

LIBERTY HEAD (1840–1907)

Designer: *Christian Gobrecht.* **Weight:** *4.18 grams.*
Composition: *.900 gold, .100 copper (net weight .12094 oz. pure gold).* **Diameter:** *18 mm.*
Edge: *Reeded.* **Mints:** *Philadelphia, Charlotte, Dahlonega, New Orleans, San Francisco.*

Circulation Strike

Mintmark location is on the reverse, above the denomination.

Proof

History. The Liberty Head quarter eagle debuted in 1840 and was a workhorse of American commerce for decades, being minted until 1907. Christian Gobrecht's design closely follows those used on half eagles and eagles of the same era.

In 1848, about 230 ounces of gold were sent to Secretary of War William L. Marcy by Colonel R.B. Mason, military governor of California. The gold was turned over to the Philadelphia Mint and made into quarter eagles. The distinguishing mark CAL. was punched above the eagle on the reverse of these coins, while they were in the die. Several pieces with prooflike surfaces are known.

A modified reverse design (with smaller letters and arrowheads) was used on Philadelphia quarter eagles from 1859 through 1907, and on San Francisco issues of 1877, 1878, and 1879. A few Philadelphia Mint pieces were made in 1859, 1860, and 1861 with the old Large Letters reverse design.

Striking and Sharpness. On the obverse, check the highest points of the hair, and the star centers. On the reverse, check the eagle's neck, and the area to the lower left of the shield and the lower part of the eagle. Examine the denticles on both sides. Branch-mint coins struck before the Civil War often are lightly struck in areas and have weak denticles. Often, a certified EF coin from the Dahlonega or Charlotte mint will not appear any sharper than a VF coin from Philadelphia. There are exceptions, and some C and D coins are sharp. The careful study of photographs is useful in acquainting you with the peculiarities of a given date or mint. Most quarter eagles from the 1880s to 1907 are sharp in all areas. Tiny copper staining spots (from improperly mixed alloy) can be a problem. Cameo contrast is the rule for Proofs prior to 1902, when the portrait was polished in the die (a few years later cameo-contrast coins were again made).

Availability. Early dates and mintmarks are generally scarce to rare in MS and very rare in MS-63 to 65 or finer, with only a few exceptions. Coins of Charlotte and Dahlonega (all of which are especially avidly collected) are usually EF or AU, or overgraded low MS. Rarities for the type include 1841, 1854-S, and 1875. Coins of the 1860s onward generally are seen with sharper striking and in higher average grades. Typically, San Francisco quarter eagles are in lower average grades than are those from the Philadelphia Mint, as Philadelphia coins did not circulate at par in the East and Midwest from late December 1861 until December 1878, and thus did not acquire as much wear. MS coins are readily available for the early-1900s years, and usually have outstanding eye appeal. Proofs exist relative to their original mintages; all prior to the 1890s are rare.

Note: Values of common-date gold coins have been based on the current bullion price of gold, $1,200 per ounce, and may vary with the prevailing spot price.

GRADING STANDARDS

MS-60 to 70 (Mint State). *Obverse:* At MS-60, some abrasion and contact marks are evident, most noticeably on the hair to the right of Miss Liberty's forehead, and on the jaw. Luster is present, but may be dull or lifeless, and interrupted in patches. At MS-63, contact marks are few, and abrasion is very light. An MS-65 coin has hardly any abrasion, and contact marks are so minute as to require magnification. Luster should be full and rich.

1859-S. Graded MS-65.

Grades above MS-65 are usually found late in the series and are defined by having fewer marks as perfection is approached. *Reverse:* Comments apply as for the obverse, except that abrasion and contact marks are most noticeable on the eagle's neck and to the lower left of the shield.

    Illustrated coin: Sharply struck, bright, and with abundant luster and great eye appeal, this is a "just right" coin for the connoisseur.

AU-50, 53, 55, 58 (About Uncirculated). *Obverse:* Light wear is seen on the face, the hair to the right of the face, and the highest area of the hair bun, more so at AU-50 than at 53 or 55. An AU-58 coin has minimal traces of wear. An AU-50 coin has luster in protected areas among the stars and letters, with little in the open fields or on the portrait. At AU-58, most luster is present in the fields, but is worn away on the highest parts

1855-D. Graded AU-55.

of the motifs. *Reverse:* Comments apply as for the preceding, except that the eagle shows wear in all of the higher areas, as well as the leaves and arrowheads. Luster ranges from perhaps 40% remaining in protected areas at AU-50 to nearly full mint bloom at AU-58. Often the reverse of this type retains more luster than the obverse.

    Illustrated coin: The example has the bold rims often seen on Dahlonega Mint coins of this denomination.

EF-40, 45 (Extremely Fine). *Obverse:* Wear is evident on all high areas of the portrait, including the hair to the right of the forehead, the tip of the coronet, and the hair bun. The stars show light wear at their centers. Luster, if present at all, is minimal and in protected areas such as between the star points. *Reverse:* Wear is greater than on an AU coin. The eagle's neck is nearly smooth, much detail is lost on the right wing, and there is flatness at the lower left of the shield, and on the leaves and arrowheads. Traces of luster may be seen, more so at EF-45 than at EF-40. Overall, the reverse appears to be in a slightly higher grade than the obverse.

1860-C. Graded EF-40.

Illustrated coin: This is an attractive coin with medium wear.

VF-20, 30 (Very Fine). *Obverse:* The higher-relief areas of hair are worn flat at VF-20, less so at VF-30. The hair to the right of the coronet is merged into heavy strands. The stars are flat at their centers. *Reverse:* Much of the eagle is flat, with less than 50% of the feather detail remaining. The vertical shield stripes, being deeply recessed, remain bold.

1843-O, Small Date, Crosslet 4. Graded VF-20.

The Liberty Head quarter eagle is seldom collected in grades lower than VF-20.

PF-60 to 70 (Proof). *Obverse and Reverse:* PF-60 to 62 coins have extensive hairlines and may have nicks and contact marks. At PF-63, hairlines are prominent, but the mirror surface is very reflective. PF-64 coins have fewer hairlines; PF-65, minimal hairlines mostly seen only under magnification, and no nicks or marks. PF-66 and higher coins should have no marks or hairlines visible to the unaided eye.

1895. Graded PF-66.

Illustrated coin: This is an exceptional gem in rich yellow-orange gold.

	Mintage	Cert	Avg	%MS	VF-20	EF-40	AU-50	AU-55	AU-58	MS-60	MS-62	MS-63 / PF-63
1840	18,859	99	50.1	13%	$350	$900	$2,350	$2,750	$3,500	$6,500	$8,500	$12,500 (a)
Auctions: $2,468, AU-58, April 2013; $1,777, AU-53, October 2014; $1,763, AU-50, September 2014												
1840, Proof	3–6	0	n/a		*(extremely rare; 3 known)*							
Auctions: No auction records available.												
1840C	12,822	134	51.5	11%	$1,500	$2,100	$4,250	$6,500	$7,500	$10,000	$18,500	$27,500
Auctions: $7,638, AU, February 2014; $2,115, EF-45, October 2014												
1840D	3,532	41	48.5	5%	$3,500	$7,500	$11,500	$17,500	$25,000	$35,000	$75,000	
Auctions: $10,575, AU-53, March 2014												
1840O	33,580	108	51.2	14%	$450	$950	$2,000	$2,750	$4,500	$8,500	$16,000	$23,500
Auctions: $14,100, MS-62, April 2014; $9,988, MS-62, November 2014; $7,344, MS-61, October 2014; $270, VF-20, August 2014												

a. Value in MS-64 is $20,000.

1843-C, Small Date, Crosslet 4	1843-C, Large Date, Plain 4	1843-O, Small Date, Crosslet 4	1843-O, Large Date, Plain 4

	Mintage	Cert	Avg	%MS	VF-20	EF-40	AU-50	AU-55	AU-58	MS-60	MS-62	MS-63 / PF-63
1841 (b)	unknown	0	n/a		$65,000	$105,000	$125,000	$150,000	$175,000	$225,000		
	Auctions: $105,800, EF-45, March 2012											
1841, Proof	15–20	5	57.0									$250,000
	Auctions: $149,500, PF-55, April 2012											
1841C	10,281	100	51.4	6%	$1,500	$2,250	$3,250	$5,500	$8,000	$13,000	$25,000	
	Auctions: $28,200, MS-62, March 2014; $5,875, AU-58, November 2014											
1841D	4,164	52	46.4	6%	$2,100	$4,000	$9,000	$12,000	$15,000	$25,000	$40,000	$50,000
	Auctions: $7,638, AU-55, April 2013											
1842	2,823	23	49.7	4%	$1,200	$2,750	$6,000	$8,500	$13,000	$17,500	$35,000	
	Auctions: $15,275, MS-60, January 2014; $7,050, AU-55, July 2014; $3,819, EF-40, November 2014											
1842, Proof	2–3	0	n/a		*(unique, in the Smithsonian's National Numismatic Collection)*							
	Auctions: No auction records available.											
1842C	6,729	59	47.5	5%	$1,750	$3,250	$6,500	$8,000	$12,500	$22,500	$35,000	
	Auctions: $8,813, AU-55, September 2014; $5,581, AU, February 2014											
1842D	4,643	62	48.0	6%	$2,200	$4,250	$8,000	$13,500	$18,500	$30,000	$55,000	
	Auctions: $9,694, AU-55, March 2014; $6,463, AU-53, November 2014											
1842O	19,800	142	48.9	10%	$525	$1,400	$2,500	$4,500	$7,000	$11,000	$15,000	$26,000
	Auctions: $5,288, AU-58, November 2014; $3,290, AU-55, February 2014; $1,763, AU-55, October 2014; $1,293, AU-50, November 2014											
1843	100,546	186	54.3	11%	$360	$450	$800	$900	$1,250	$2,500	$4,250	$6,500 (c)
	Auctions: $1,998, MS-61, January 2014; $631, AU-55, September 2014; $617, AU-53, July 2014; $529, AU-53, October 2014											
1843, Proof	4–8	4	64.0		*(extremely rare; 5–6 known)*							
	Auctions: No auction records available.											
1843C, Small Date, Crosslet 4	2,988	50	51.9	10%	$2,500	$5,250	$7,500	$10,000	$14,000	$24,000	$50,000	
	Auctions: $4,406, MS-63, August 2014; $499, MS-60, July 2014; $646, AU-55, July 2014; $441, AU-55, October 2014											
1843C, Large Date, Plain 4	23,076	194	48.2	9%	$1,400	$2,000	$3,000	$4,500	$5,500	$7,500	$12,500	$20,000
	Auctions: $15,275, MS-63, March 2014; $3,290, MS-60, July 2014; $3,819, AU-58, July 2014; $3,525, AU-55, October 2014											
1843D, Small Date, Crosslet 4	36,209	261	50.0	8%	$1,400	$2,000	$3,000	$4,000	$5,000	$8,000	$16,000	$27,500
	Auctions: $5,875, MS-61, January 2014											
1843O, Small Date, Crosslet 4	288,002	497	53.0	16%	$385	$400	$550	$775	$1,100	$2,000	$3,250	$7,500
	Auctions: $25,850, MS-65, February 2013; $6,500, MS-61, August 2014; $999, AU-53, August 2014; $529, AU-50, September 2014											
1843O, Large Date, Plain 4	76,000	127	54.1	14%	$425	$750	$1,750	$2,750	$4,000	$6,000	$12,500	$20,000
	Auctions: $15,275, MS-62, February 2014											
1844	6,784	53	51.8	9%	$500	$850	$2,000	$3,500	$4,500	$9,500	$13,500	
	Auctions: $15,275, MS-61, January 2014											
1844, Proof	3–6	1	66.0		*(extremely rare; 4–5 known)*							
	Auctions: No auction records available.											
1844C	11,622	118	49.0	11%	$1,375	$2,500	$5,500	$7,000	$9,000	$14,000	$27,500	$40,000
	Auctions: $16,450, MS-62, October 2014; $14,100, MS-61, January 2014; $2,350, AU-50, August 2014											
1844D	17,332	168	52.6	13%	$1,450	$2,500	$3,000	$4,000	$5,000	$7,500	$13,500	$23,500
	Auctions: $17,038, MS-63, April 2014; $2,585, EF-45, August 2014											

b. Values are for circulated Proofs; existence of circulation strikes is unclear. c. Value in MS-64 is $13,500.

	Mintage	Cert	Avg	%MS	VF-20	EF-40	AU-50	AU-55	AU-58	MS-60	MS-62	MS-63
												PF-63
1845	91,051	245	55.7	30%	$360	$385	$550	$650	$850	$1,400	$2,250	$5,000 **(d)**
	Auctions: $18,800, MS-65, January 2014; $14,100, MS-65, October 2014; $7,050, MS-64, October 2014; $3,819, MS-63, November 2014											
1845, Proof	4–8	2	67.3		*(extremely rare; 4–5 known)*							
	Auctions: No auction records available.											
1845D	19,460	157	51.1	6%	$1,450	$2,350	$3,250	$4,250	$7,000	$10,000	$18,500	$35,000
	Auctions: $35,250, MS-63, January 2014											
1845O	4,000	59	50.0	2%	$1,300	$2,600	$5,750	$8,000	$11,000	$22,500	$30,000	$50,000
	Auctions: $5,875, AU-50, January 2014											
1846	21,598	130	55.6	19%	$360	$700	$1,000	$1,500	$2,500	$5,500	$14,000	$23,500
	Auctions: $18,800, MS-63, April 2014; $14,114, MS-63, November 2014; $4,113, MS-61, August 2014; $1,357, AU-58, November 2014											
1846, Proof	4–8	1	64.0		*(extremely rare; 4–5 known)*							
	Auctions: $106,375, PF-64Cam, January 2011											
1846C	4,808	62	50.6	10%	$1,700	$2,750	$7,500	$9,500	$12,500	$17,500	$25,000	$37,500
	Auctions: $15,275, MS-62, April 2014											
1846D	19,303	165	51.4	9%	$1,600	$2,400	$3,250	$4,500	$6,000	$8,500	$13,500	$28,500
	Auctions: $7,638, MS-61, June 2013; $1,528, AU-50, August 2014; $1,293, EF-40, August 2014; $1,293, EF-40, November 2014											
1846D, D Over D	(e)	2	47.5	0%		$2,750	$3,750	$6,500	$9,000	$15,000		
	Auctions: $5,175, AU-55, November 2011											
1846O	62,000	276	51.1	9%	$400	$525	$1,200	$2,000	$3,500	$5,000	$12,000	$18,500
	Auctions: $4,700, MS-61, February 2013; $1,998, AU-58, November 2014											
1847	29,814	119	54.8	17%	$360	$400	$750	$1,250	$2,000	$3,000	$5,000	$8,000
	Auctions: $3,055, MS-61, November 2014; $1,175, AU-58, June 2013											
1847, Proof	2–3	0	n/a		*(unique, in the Smithsonian's National Numismatic Collection)*							
	Auctions: No auction records available.											
1847C	23,226	235	52.2	14%	$1,425	$2,250	$3,000	$4,000	$4,500	$6,000	$8,000	$13,000
	Auctions: $5,581, MS-61, January 2014; $2,820, AU-55, August 2014; $2,350, AU-50, August 2014; $2,186, AU-50, October 2014											
1847D	15,784	160	52.6	13%	$1,550	$2,500	$3,250	$5,250	$5,500	$9,000	$12,500	$24,000
	Auctions: $9,404, MS, February 2014; $2,820, AU-53, August 2014											
1847O	124,000	312	50.0	11%	$385	$475	$1,000	$1,800	$2,750	$4,000	$9,500	$15,000
	Auctions: $9,988, MS-62, January 2014; $10,575, MS-62, August 2014; $2,585, AU-58, November 2014; $411, EF-45, July 2014											

d. Value in MS-64 is $8,500. **e.** Included in 1846-D mintage figure.

1848, CAL. Above Eagle

	Mintage	Cert	Avg	%MS	VF-20	EF-40	AU-50	AU-55	MS-60	MS-62	MS-63	MS-64	MS-65
											PF-60	PF-63	PF-65
1848	6,500	60	55.0	30%	$550	$900	$1,750	$2,500	$5,000	$8,000	$15,000	$25,000	
	Auctions: $2,585, AU-50, February 2014; $823, AU-50, July 2014												
1848, CAL. Above Eagle	1,389	44	57.0	45%	$35,000	$45,000	$52,500	$55,000	$80,000	$115,000	$125,000	$150,000	$200,000
	Auctions: $176,250, MS-64, January 2014; $13,513, AU-50, August 2014												
1848, Proof	3–6	0	n/a		*(extremely rare; 3–4 known)*								
	Auctions: $96,600, PF-64, January 2008												
1848C	16,788	153	50.5	9%	$1,450	$2,500	$3,500	$4,500	$10,000	$17,500	$30,000		
	Auctions: $15,275, MS-62, March 2014												
1848D	13,771	148	53.6	13%	$1,450	$2,500	$3,500	$4,250	$8,000	$13,500	$27,500		
	Auctions: $25,850, MS-63, April 2014												

	Mintage	Cert	Avg	%MS	VF-20	EF-40	AU-50	AU-55	MS-60	MS-62	MS-63 / PF-60	MS-64 / PF-63	MS-65 / PF-65
1849	23,294	130	55.1	17%	$375	$500	$975	$1,250	$2,500	$4,250	$7,500	$14,000	
Auctions: $3,525, MS-62, March 2014; $999, AU-55, July 2014													
1849C	10,220	92	50.8	9%	$1,450	$2,500	$4,500	$7,500	$18,000	$40,000	$60,000		
Auctions: $15,275, MS-61, January 2014; $1,645, AU-50, September 2014; $2,350, EF-45, July 2014													
1849D	10,945	133	53.1	8%	$1,450	$2,500	$3,750	$5,750	$14,000	$25,000	—		
Auctions: $18,800, MS-62, August 2014; $3,202, AU-53, October 2013													
1850	252,923	452	56.5	25%	$360	$380	$400	$500	$1,000	$2,000	$3,250	$7,500	
Auctions: $3,819, MS-63, August 2014; $1,998, MS-62, June 2013; $646, MS-60, November 2014; $529, AU-58, October 2014													
1850, Proof	2–4	0	n/a		*(extremely rare; 1–2 known)*								
Auctions: $41,250, PF-62, June 1995													
1850C	9,148	132	51.4	14%	$1,450	$2,500	$3,500	$4,500	$11,000	$23,500	$32,500		
Auctions: $8,879, MS-61, August 2014; $8,813, MS-61, October 2014; $12,925, MS-60, March 2014													
1850D	12,148	134	52.4	9%	$1,500	$2,750	$3,750	$5,500	$12,500	$27,500	$50,000		
Auctions: $23,500, MS-62, April 2014													
1850O	84,000	322	51.0	3%	$400	$575	$1,250	$1,750	$4,000	$6,000	$15,000		
Auctions: $4,700, MS-61, December 2013; $823, AU-53, July 2014; $1,058, AU-53, October 2014; $764, AU-53, November 2014													
1851	1,372,748	824	59.2	57%	$360	$380	$385	$400	$550	$900	$1,100	$2,250	$5,500
Auctions: $5,875, MS-65, April 2013; $646, MS-62, September 2014; $861, MS-62, October 2014; $353, AU-58, August 2014													
1851C	14,923	103	50.8	15%	$1,450	$2,450	$3,750	$5,000	$9,000	$18,500	$32,500		
Auctions: $28,200, MS-63, October 2013; $1,821, AU-50, September 2014													
1851D	11,264	80	51.0	6%	$1,450	$2,500	$4,000	$5,500	$10,000	$17,500	$35,000	$50,000	
Auctions: $7,638, AU-58, December 2013; $2,115, AU-50, September 2014													
1851O	148,000	432	53.5	10%	$400	$475	$950	$2,000	$4,000	$7,500	$12,500	$23,500	
Auctions: $4,406, MS-61, July 2014; $4,406, MS-61, February 2013; $1,528, AU-58, September 2014; $999, AU-55, November 2014													
1852	1,159,681	1,019	59.9	61%	$360	$380	$385	$400	$550	$850	$1,150	$2,250	$5,000
Auctions: $3,966, MS-65, October 2014; $1,763, MS-64, April 2014; $1,763, MS-64, September 2014; $1,234, MS-63, November 2014													
1852C	9,772	85	52.4	11%	$1,450	$2,500	$3,850	$5,500	$12,000	$25,000	$32,500		
Auctions: $4,994, AU-55, March 2014; $3,349, AU-53, October 2014; $3,055, AU-50, August 2014													
1852D	4,078	56	53.8	13%	$1,850	$3,000	$6,000	$7,500	$15,000	$28,000	$40,000	$65,000	
Auctions: $8,813, AU-53, August 2013													
1852O	140,000	498	52.8	6%	$400	$450	$950	$1,250	$4,500	$8,000	$11,000		
Auctions: $6,169, MS-62, August 2013; $3,672, MS-61, October 2014; $1,998, AU-58, August 2014; $499, EF-45, September 2014													
1853	1,404,668	1,439	59.9	60%	$360	$365	$375	$385	$550	$850	$1,150	$2,250	$5,000
Auctions: $5,288, MS-65, October 2014; $8,519, MS-65, March 2013; $1,410, MS-64, October 2014; $1,293, MS-64, October 2014													
1853D	3,178	48	52.7	15%	$1,800	$3,250	$4,750	$5,500	$15,000	$30,000	$45,000		
Auctions: $25,850, MS-62, January 2014; $12,338, MS-61, October 2014; $13,513, MS-61, November 2014; $4,113, AU-50, July 2014													
1854	596,258	687	59.3	53%	$360	$365	$375	$385	$550	$1,000	$1,200	$2,500	$5,500
Auctions: $5,288, MS-65, August 2014; $5,288, MS-65, August 2014; $8,225, MS-65, April 2013; $1,821, MS-63, August 2014													
1854, Proof	2–4	0	n/a		*(unique, in the Bass Foundation Collection)*								
Auctions: No auction records available.													
1854C	7,295	107	53.9	20%	$1,500	$2,600	$4,350	$5,500	$12,000	$21,000	$37,500		
Auctions: $9,988, MS-61, June 2013; $4,994, AU-58, August 2014; $4,406, AU-55, November 2014													
1854D	1,760	22	48.9	18%	$3,500	$7,500	$12,000	$13,500	$26,000	$40,000	$70,000		
Auctions: $15,275, AU-55, March 2014; $9,467, AU-53, August 2014; $5,875, AU-50, November 2014													
1854O	153,000	496	53.7	8%	$385	$400	$575	$800	$1,500	$4,000	$8,500	$13,500	
Auctions: $14,688, MS-63, April 2013; $4,700, MS-62, August 2014; $4,700, MS-62, November 2014; $709, AU-58, October 2014													
1854S	246	7	35.4	0%	$275,000	$400,000	$500,000	$600,000					
Auctions: $282,000, EF-35, October 2013													

Old Reverse (Pre-1859)   **New Reverse**

	Mintage	Cert	Avg	%MS	VF-20	EF-40	AU-50	AU-55	MS-60	MS-62	MS-63	MS-64	MS-65
											PF-60	PF-63	PF-65
1855	235,480	380	59.6	56%	$360	$365	$375	$385	$550	$1,000	$1,500	$3,000	$6,000
Auctions: $3,290, MS-64, March 2013; $306, AU-58, July 2014; $353, AU-55, August 2014													
1855C	3,677	69	54.6	22%	$1,850	$3,250	$5,500	$10,000	$20,000	$27,500	$40,000		
Auctions: $23,500, MS-62, January 2014													
1855D	1,123	24	53.3	13%	$4,500	$8,000	$14,750	$20,000	$47,500				
Auctions: $25,850, AU-55, July 2014													
1856	384,240	618	59.5	57%	$360	$365	$375	$385	$550	$1,000	$1,200	$3,000	$6,000
Auctions: $951, MS-63, February 2013; $881, MS-60, July 2014; $376, AU-58, July 2014; $329, AU-58, September 2014													
1856, Proof	6–8	0	n/a								$40,000	$75,000	$135,000
Auctions: No auction records available.													
1856C	7,913	85	52.1	14%	$1,500	$2,600	$4,000	$6,500	$11,000	$18,500	$23,500		
Auctions: $6,463, AU-58, April 2013; $3,819, AU-55, October 2014; $1,410, AU-50, October 2014													
1856D	874	16	52.4	25%	$8,000	$12,500	$30,000	$35,000	$90,000				
Auctions: $55,813, AU-58, March 2014													
1856O	21,100	138	53.4	10%	$385	$700	$1,500	$2,000	$7,000	$18,500			
Auctions: $7,050, MS-61, August 2013													
1856S	72,120	194	52.0	14%	$385	$450	$1,200	$1,500	$5,000	$8,000	$11,500	$15,000	$27,500
Auctions: $2,703, AU-58, February 2014; $1,175, AU-58, November 2014; $376, EF-40, July 2014													
1857	214,130	452	59.7	57%	$360	$365	$375	$385	$550	$1,000	$1,500	$3,500	$6,500
Auctions: $4,994, MS-65, April 2013; $1,175, MS-63, November 2014													
1857, Proof	6–8	0	n/a								$35,000	$57,500	$125,000
Auctions: No auction records available.													
1857D	2,364	58	56.4	26%	$1,600	$2,800	$4,000	$5,500	$12,000	$22,000	$30,000		
Auctions: $18,800, MS-62, April 2014; $1,528, AU-50, July 2014; $1,293, AU-50, November 2014													
1857O	34,000	268	55.2	21%	$385	$400	$1,250	$1,850	$4,000	$6,750	$12,500	$20,000	
Auctions: $6,463, MS-62, April 2014; $4,113, MS-61, November 2014; $2,350, AU-58, November 2014; $1,646, AU-55, November 2014													
1857S	69,200	193	52.2	10%	$385	$475	$1,200	$1,850	$6,000	$8,500	$15,000	$25,000	
Auctions: $7,638, MS-62, January 2014; $1,234, AU-55, November 2014; $911, AU-55, November 2014; $317, VF-35, July 2014													
1858	47,377	184	58.4	37%	$375	$390	$450	$550	$1,200	$1,850	$3,000	$5,500	$12,000
Auctions: $3,819, MS, February 2014; $237, EF-45, October 2014													
1858, Proof	6–8	3	65.3								$25,000	$45,000	$115,000
Auctions: $82,250, PF, March 2014													
1858C	9,056	134	54.7	28%	$1,500	$2,250	$3,000	$4,250	$8,000	$15,000	$23,000		
Auctions: $11,163, MS-62, January 2014; $4,113, AU-58, November 2014; $3,525, AU-58, November 2014													
1859, Old Reverse	39,364	125	57.9	34%	$375	$500	$875	$1,200	$3,000	$5,500	$8,000	$12,500	
Auctions: $1,102, AU, February 2014; $456, AU-50, November 2014; $411, EF-40, August 2014													
1859, New Reverse	(a)	44	58.1	18%	$360	$370	$500	$700	$1,200	$2,000	$3,200	$7,500	$10,000
Auctions: $3,290, MS-63, October 2014; $1,998, MS-62, November 2014; $2,879, MS, January 2014													
1859, Proof (b)	80	1	62.0								$15,000	$30,000	$75,000
Auctions: $80,500, PF-66, July 2005													

a. Included in circulation-strike 1859, Old Reverse, mintage figure. **b.** Nearly all 1859 Proofs are of the Old Reverse style.

1862, 2 Over 1

1873, Close 3

1873, Open 3

	Mintage	Cert	Avg	%MS	VF-20	EF-40	AU-50	AU-55	MS-60	MS-62	MS-63 / PF-60	MS-64 / PF-63	MS-65 / PF-65
1859D	2,244	88	54.6	14%	$2,200	$3,250	$4,750	$7,000	$18,000	$37,500			
	Auctions: $3,819, AU-55, October 2014; $7,050, AU, March 2014												
1859S	15,200	87	49.6	10%	$475	$950	$2,000	$3,000	$7,000	$10,000	$16,000		
	Auctions: $4,994, MS-61, April 2014; $4,847, MS-61, August 2014; $3,290, AU-58, October 2014; $2,585, AU-58, July 2014												
1860, Old Reverse	22,563	29	55.7	38%	$1,400	$2,100	$3,000	$4,500	$8,000	$12,000	$14,000		
	Auctions: $6,463, MS-62, April 2013												
1860, New Reverse	(c)	64	59.8	55%	$360	$370	$450	$600	$1,000	$1,600	$2,750		
	Auctions: $1,763, MS-60, August 2013												
1860, Proof (d)	112	9	63.8								$14,000	$22,500	$40,000
	Auctions: $11,550, PF-64Cam, October 1993												
1860C	7,469	109	51.5	10%	$1,650	$2,500	$4,000	$6,500	$14,000	$25,000	$37,500		
	Auctions: $25,850, MS-63, January 2014; $7,638, AU-58, July 2014; $1,586, AU-50, August 2014												
1860S	35,600	117	47.6	9%	$425	$675	$1,150	$1,850	$3,250	$7,000	$13,500		
	Auctions: $6,756, MS-62, August 2013; $317, EF-40, November 2014												
1861, Old Reverse	1,283,788	114	58.4	40%	$525	$1,100	$1,800	$2,350	$4,000	$7,500	$9,000		
	Auctions: $3,819, MS-62, August 2014; $6,345, MS, January 2014; $881, AU-50, September 2014; $646, AU-50, September 2014												
1861, New Reverse	(e)	1,355	59.8	58%	$360	$370	$375	$385	$650	$1,300	$1,800		
	Auctions: $6,169, MS-66, September 2014; $7,638, MS-65, March 2013; $2,585, MS-64, October 2014; $1,645, MS-64, November 2014												
1861, Proof (f)	90	3	65.5								$12,000	$20,000	$40,000
	Auctions: $44,850, PF-65DCam, September 2005												
1861S	24,000	96	46.5	7%	$400	$825	$2,500	$4,000	$7,000	$12,000			
	Auctions: $5,875, AU-58, April 2013												
1862, 2 Over 1	(g)	54	54.5	15%	$1,000	$1,850	$3,000	$4,750	$7,500	$12,500			
	Auctions: $9,400, MS-61, January 2014; $558, AU-50, July 2014												
1862	98,508	180	56.4	32%	$400	$600	$1,000	$1,750	$4,750	$6,000	$11,000	$17,500	
	Auctions: $9,400, MS-63, August 2013; $1,058, MS-60, July 2014; $2,585, AU-58, October 2014; $1,645, AU-53, September 2014												
1862, Proof	35	11	64.7								$12,000	$20,000	$40,000
	Auctions: $46,000, PF-65UCam, February 2007												
1862S	8,000	138	47.3	8%	$1,000	$1,750	$3,000	$5,000	$16,500	$25,000	$35,000		
	Auctions: $23,500, MS-62, January 2014												
1863, Proof (h)	30	7	64.4								$50,000	$75,000	$125,000
	Auctions: $45,531, PF-58, April 2014												
1863S	10,800	76	46.7	11%	$700	$1,350	$3,500	$5,000	$13,000	$20,000	$30,000		
	Auctions: $3,290, EF-45, March 2013												
1864	2,824	8	53.4	25%	$7,500	$15,000	$27,500	$47,500	$75,000				
	Auctions: $48,469, AU-55, March 2014												
1864, Proof	50	15	64.9								$12,000	$25,000	$45,000
	Auctions: $30,550, PF-64Cam, April 2014												
1865	1,520	17	53.5	0%	$4,500	$8,500	$20,000	$27,500	$40,000	$45,000	$60,000		
	Auctions: $15,891, AU-55, June 2013; $4,113, VF-20, November 2014												
1865, Proof	25	13	64.0								$13,500	$20,000	$45,000
	Auctions: $48,875, PF-65UCam, January 2012												
1865S	23,376	94	46.1	5%	$400	$650	$1,250	$2,000	$4,500	$7,500	$11,000		
	Auctions: $1,998, AU-53, March 2014												

c. Included in 1860, Old Reverse, mintage figure. d. All known 1860 Proofs are of the New Reverse style. e. Included in 1861, Old Reverse, mintage figure. f. All 1861 Proofs were struck in the New Reverse style. g. Included in circulation-strike 1862 mintage figure. h. Proof only.

	Mintage	Cert	Avg	%MS	VF-20	EF-40	AU-50	AU-55	MS-60	MS-62	MS-63	MS-64	MS-65
											PF-60	PF-63	PF-65
1866	3,080	35	51.2	17%	$1,150	$3,000	$5,250	$8,000	$12,500	$20,000	$25,000	$35,000	
	Auctions: $7,050, AU-58, February 2013												
1866, Proof	30	13	63.8								$10,000	$17,500	$32,500
	Auctions: $23,500, PF-64Cam, April 2014												
1866S	38,960	185	47.5	5%	$400	$750	$1,700	$3,000	$7,000	$12,000	$20,000		
	Auctions: $16,450, MS-62, January 2014; $2,115, AU-58, October 2014; $329, EF-45, September 2014												
1867	3,200	36	54.7	25%	$400	$650	$1,200	$1,700	$4,500	$6,000	$12,000	$13,500	$35,000
	Auctions: $1,544, AU-55, July 2014; $1,645, AU-55, May 2013												
1867, Proof	50	11	64.1								$10,000	$16,000	$30,000
	Auctions: $18,800, PF-64DCam, October 2014; $99,875, PF, August 2013												
1867S	28,000	162	47.4	6%	$400	$650	$1,250	$1,700	$3,850	$5,000	$12,000	$15,000	
	Auctions: $1,775, AU-58, August 2013; $764, EF-45, August 2014; $411, VF-30, November 2014; $270, VG-8, August 2014												
1868	3,600	141	56.9	21%	$350	$425	$700	$750	$2,000	$3,850	$7,500	$12,000	
	Auctions: $3,290, MS-61, August 2014; $1,998, MS-61, November 2014; $1,998, MS-61, December 2013												
1868, Proof	25	5	63.5								$9,500	$16,500	$35,000
	Auctions: $43,700, PF-65Cam, January 2009												
1868S	34,000	233	51.8	6%	$350	$425	$950	$1,400	$4,000	$6,500	$10,000	$15,000	
	Auctions: $15,275, MS-64, January 2014; $3,819, MS-63, August 2014; $1,528, AU-58, July 2014; $1,058, AU-58, November 2014												
1869	4,320	142	56.7	23%	$350	$425	$700	$1,050	$2,750	$5,000	$8,500		
	Auctions: $19,975, MS-64, August 2014; $9,360, MS-63, June 2014; $4,700, MS-62, November 2014; $3,173, MS-61, November 2014												
1869, Proof	25	18	64.2								$6,500	$14,000	$30,000
	Auctions: $12,650, PF-63, October 2011												
1869S	29,500	218	51.7	8%	$350	$475	$1,000	$1,500	$4,000	$6,000	$8,750	$13,000	
	Auctions: $3,055, MS-61, August 2014; $3,290, MS-61, May 2013; $1,763, AU-58, August 2014; $1,763, AU-58, November 2014												
1870	4,520	86	56.7	20%	$350	$400	$600	$1,250	$3,250	$5,500	$8,000		
	Auctions: $4,994, MS-61, January 2014; $3,408, MS-61, October 2014												
1870, Proof	35	5	63.8								$6,500	$14,000	$30,000
	Auctions: $70,500, PF-66DCam, January 2014												
1870S	16,000	138	51.4	9%	$350	$400	$900	$1,500	$4,000	$6,500	$12,500	$17,500	
	Auctions: $8,225, MS-62, January 2014; $1,528, AU-58, July 2014; $717, AU-53, September 2014; $441, EF-40, November 2014												
1871	5,320	117	56.3	25%	$350	$400	$550	$1,000	$2,000	$2,750	$4,000	$8,000	
	Auctions: $6,463, MS-64, April 2014; $470, AU-50, November 2014												
1871, Proof	30	9	64.4								$6,500	$14,000	$27,500
	Auctions: $19,975, PF-64DCam, August 2014												
1871S	22,000	196	52.6	12%	$350	$400	$550	$1,000	$2,000	$3,000	$4,250	$7,500	$17,500
	Auctions: $7,638, MS-64, November 2014; $911, AU-58, July 2014; $940, AU-58, October 2014; $1,410, AU-55, November 2014												
1872	3,000	68	56.1	18%	$425	$700	$1,100	$2,000	$4,250	$9,000	$13,500	$25,000	
	Auctions: $2,596, AU-58, March 2014												
1872, Proof	30	9	64.9								$6,500	$14,000	$27,500
	Auctions: $34,075, PF-65Cam, March 2013												
1872S	18,000	180	50.8	8%	$350	$400	$950	$1,250	$4,000	$5,500	$10,500	$15,000	
	Auctions: $3,594, MS-61, April 2012												
1873, Close 3	55,200	582	60.0	63%	$350	$375	$400	$425	$600	$1,100	$1,750	$2,750	$5,500
	Auctions: $16,450, MS-66, January 2014; $1,293, MS-64, October 2014; $646, MS-62, July 2014; $529, MS-62, August 2014												
1873, Open 3	122,800	537	61.0	77%	$325	$365	$375	$385	$585	$700	$800	$1,250	$4,500
	Auctions: $5,875, MS-65, February 2014; $4,406, MS-65, August 2014; $1,058, MS-64, November 2014; $558, MS-62, October 2014												
1873, Close 3, Proof	25	11	62.7								$7,500	$14,000	$30,000
	Auctions: $23,500, PF-63Cam, August 2014; $19,388, PF, August 2013												
1873S	27,000	246	50.1	8%	$350	$425	$975	$1,400	$2,300	$4,000	$6,500	$13,500	
	Auctions: $11,163, MS-64, August 2013; $646, AU-55, July 2014; $676, AU-53, July 2014; $558, AU-53, July 2014												

	Mintage	Cert	Avg	%MS	VF-20	EF-40	AU-50	AU-55	MS-60	MS-62	MS-63 / PF-60	MS-64 / PF-63	MS-65 / PF-65
1874	3,920	113	57.0	27%	$350	$400	$650	$1,000	$2,000	$4,500	$6,000	$9,500	$25,000
	Auctions: $3,525, MS-62, August 2013												
1874, Proof	20	10	64.5								$7,500	$15,000	$45,000
	Auctions: $38,188, PF-64DCam, August 2014												
1875	400	30	57.1	20%	$5,000	$7,500	$12,500	$15,000	$35,000	$45,000	$55,000		
	Auctions: $25,850, MS-61, August 2013; $15,275, AU-58, October 2014												
1875, Proof	20	10	63.7								$13,500	$35,000	$60,000
	Auctions: $94,000, PF, October 2013												
1875S	11,600	174	54.2	17%	$350	$400	$650	$1,100	$3,500	$5,000	$7,000	$11,000	
	Auctions: $5,581, MS-63, October 2014; $4,700, MS-62, September 2014; $4,259, MS-62, September 2013; $676, AU-53, August 2014												
1876	4,176	130	54.1	15%	$375	$625	$950	$1,750	$3,000	$4,000	$6,500	$11,000	
	Auctions: $5,581, MS-62, March 2014; $2,585, MS-61, October 2014												
1876, Proof	45	16	64.4								$6,500	$13,500	$30,000
	Auctions: $39,950, PF, January 2013												
1876S	5,000	135	54.1	17%	$350	$525	$950	$1,600	$3,250	$4,500	$8,000		
	Auctions: $8,225, MS-63, January 2014; $2,820, MS-61, August 2014; $1,880, AU-58, October 2014; $1,058, AU-55, November 2014												
1877	1,632	105	56.6	30%	$400	$750	$1,000	$1,250	$3,000	$3,750	$8,500	$15,000	
	Auctions: $4,406, MS-62, April 2014; $3,055, MS-61, August 2014												
1877, Proof	20	6	64.0								$6,500	$13,500	$30,000
	Auctions: $8,050, PF-55, November 2011												
1877S	35,400	389	58.8	47%	$350	$365	$375	$400	$650	$1,500	$2,350	$4,000	$9,000
	Auctions: $9,400, MS-65, December 2013; $764, MS-62, November 2014; $734, MS-61, October 2014; $388, AU-58, November 2014												
1878	286,240	2,307	60.9	75%	$350	$365	$375	$385	$500	$700	$900	$1,300	$2,500
	Auctions: $8,225, MS-66, June 2014; $3,290, MS-66, November 2014; $1,998, MS-65, July 2014; $2,115, MS-65, October 2014												
1878, Proof	20	10	64.4								$6,500	$13,500	$30,000
	Auctions: $50,313, PF-65DCam, April 2012												
1878S	178,000	682	59.4	54%	$350	$365	$375	$385	$525	$1,000	$1,800	$3,500	$12,000
	Auctions: $2,470, MS-64, August 2014; $1,998, MS-64, November 2014; $3,525, MS-64, April 2013; $823, MS-61, July 2014												
1879	88,960	917	60.8	75%	$350	$365	$375	$425	$525	$850	$1,100	$1,500	$3,500
	Auctions: $3,290, MS-65, September 2013; $1,293, MS-64, November 2014; $441, MS-62, October 2014; $414, MS-62, November 2014												
1879, Proof	30	8	65.0								$6,000	$13,000	$30,000
	Auctions: $40,250, PF-67Cam, January 2011												
1879S	43,500	205	53.9	9%	$350	$365	$550	$1,000	$1,750	$3,500	$4,800	$7,500	
	Auctions: $18,800, MS-64, January 2014; $20,001, MS-64, August 2014; $16,450, MS-64, November 2014; $414, AU-55, July 2014												
1880	2,960	143	58.8	47%	$375	$425	$650	$800	$1,500	$2,000	$3,750	$6,000	$12,500
	Auctions: $2,820, MS-62, October 2013; $1,410, AU-58, November 2014												
1880, Proof	36	15	63.3								$6,500	$12,500	$27,500
	Auctions: $3,244, PF-55, January 2011												
1881	640	74	56.8	28%	$2,250	$3,000	$5,000	$6,000	$10,000	$15,000	$25,000	$30,000	
	Auctions: $7,931, MS-60, June 2013; $5,875, AU-58, August 2014; $4,994, AU-50, July 2014												
1881, Proof	51	21	64.1								$6,500	$13,500	$27,500
	Auctions: $34,075, PF-65DCam, August 2013; $14,100, PF-64DCam, July 2014												
1882	4,000	183	59.9	56%	$375	$425	$575	$700	$925	$1,500	$2,750	$4,000	$9,000
	Auctions: $9,400, MS-66, November 2014; $15,275, MS-65, September 2014; $2,703, MS-63, January 2014; $2,585, MS-63, November 2014												
1882, Proof	67	14	65.3								$4,500	$9,500	$22,500
	Auctions: $9,487, PF-64, May 2006												
1883	1,920	81	57.9	37%	$375	$450	$900	$1,000	$1,750	$2,350	$6,500	$6,750	$9,000
	Auctions: $4,994, MS-61, June 2014												
1883, Proof	82	24	64.6								$4,500	$9,500	$22,500
	Auctions: $28,200, PF, March 2014												

1891, Doubled-Die Reverse
FS-G2.5-1891-801.

	Mintage	Cert	Avg	%MS	VF-20	EF-40	AU-50	AU-55	MS-60	MS-62	MS-63	MS-64	MS-65
											PF-60	PF-63	PF-65
1884	1,950	122	60.0	62%	$375	$400	$700	$800	$1,500	$1,900	$3,000	$3,500	$5,000
	Auctions: $2,468, MS-62, June 2014; $1,058, AU-58, August 2014												
1884, Proof	73	26	64.0								$4,500	$9,500	$22,500
	Auctions: $82,250, PF, August 2013												
1885	800	51	58.6	45%	$1,100	$2,000	$2,750	$3,000	$4,750	$5,750	$8,000	$12,000	$20,000
	Auctions: $13,513, MS-63, March 2014; $1,423, AU-50, July 2014												
1885, Proof	87	23	61.5								$5,000	$9,000	$27,500
	Auctions: $56,160, PF, September 2013												
1886	4,000	141	59.6	53%	$375	$400	$550	$600	$1,000	$1,750	$3,000	$7,000	$12,000
	Auctions: $1,528, MS-62, July 2014; $1,763, MS-62, March 2013												
1886, Proof	88	34	62.5								$4,500	$9,500	$22,500
	Auctions: $40,538, PF, August 2013												
1887	6,160	205	60.1	68%	$375	$400	$450	$500	$800	$1,250	$2,750	$4,500	$15,000
	Auctions: $4,700, MS-64, April 2014; $3,290, MS-64, September 2014; $3,290, MS-64, November 2014; $1,880, MS-63, July 2014												
1887, Proof	122	26	64.1								$4,500	$9,500	$22,500
	Auctions: $58,750, PF, August 2013												
1888	16,001	444	62.0	89%	$360	$365	$375	$380	$550	$850	$1,375	$1,475	$5,500
	Auctions: $4,113, MS-65, October 2014; $1,410, MS-64, November 2014; $7,931, MS-63, March 2014; $3,819, MS-63, October 2014												
1888, Proof	97	33	64.4								$4,500	$8,500	$22,500
	Auctions: $25,850, PF-65Cam, February 2013; $6,463, PF-63, November 2014; $5,288, PF-62, August 2014												
1889	17,600	396	61.5	87%	$360	$365	$375	$380	$525	$825	$1,350	$1,425	$5,500
	Auctions: $6,463, MS-65, July 2014; $441, MS-61, August 2014; $341, AU-58, October 2014												
1889, Proof	48	18	65.0								$4,500	$8,500	$22,500
	Auctions: $31,792, PF-65DCam, August 2014												
1890	8,720	217	60.8	69%	$360	$375	$385	$400	$600	$900	$1,350	$2,750	$9,000
	Auctions: $3,819, MS-64, June 2013; $1,293, MS-63, November 2014												
1890, Proof	93	50	64.7								$4,500	$8,500	$20,000
	Auctions: $19,388, PF-65DCam, June 2014; $29,458, PF-65, October 2014												
1891	10,960	311	60.9	76%	$365	$385	$400	$410	$570	$800	$1,150	$1,850	$2,500
	Auctions: $2,233, MS-64, November 2014; $3,055, MS-64, April 2013; $1,234, MS-63, July 2014; $588, MS-61, November 2014												
1891, Doubled-Die Reverse	(i)	0	n/a					$450	$750	$1,100	$1,750		$3,000
	Auctions: $823, MS-63, November 2014												
1891, Proof	80	26	65.5								$4,500	$8,000	$20,000
	Auctions: $30,550, PF, April 2013												
1892	2,440	138	61.2	81%	$365	$400	$475	$525	$900	$1,100	$2,250	$4,000	$8,000
	Auctions: $21,150, MS-67, November 2013; $8,527, MS-66, August 2014; $7,931, MS-66, November 2014; $1,998, MS-63, October 2014												
1892, Proof	105	29	64.5								$4,500	$8,000	$20,000
	Auctions: $111,625, PF, February 2013												
1893	30,000	865	62.3	91%	$360	$365	$375	$380	$550	$800	$1,300	$1,475	$2,250
	Auctions: $11,163, MS-67, March 2014; $6,463, MS-66, September 2014; $3,290, MS-66, November 2014; $1,528, MS-65, November 2014												
1893, Proof	106	39	65.1								$4,500	$7,500	$20,000
	Auctions: $21,150, PF-66DCam, September 2014; $44,063, PF, August 2013												

i. Included in circulation-strike 1891 mintage figure.

	Mintage	Cert	Avg	%MS	VF-20	EF-40	AU-50	AU-55	MS-60	MS-62	MS-63 / PF-60	MS-64 / PF-63	MS-65 / PF-65
1894	4,000	238	61.9	87%	$360	$365	$375	$385	$625	$1,000	$1,500	$1,875	$4,500
Auctions: $4,700, MS-65, October 2014; $2,938, MS-64, September 2014; $4,700, MS, February 2014													
1894, Proof	122	64	64.7								$4,500	$7,500	$20,000
Auctions: $21,150, PF-66DCam, September 2014; $44,063, PF, August 2013													
1895	6,000	255	62.5	92%	$360	$365	$375	$380	$600	$725	$1,100	$1,350	$3,750
Auctions: $8,519, MS-66, March 2013													
1895, Proof	119	67	65.0								$4,500	$7,500	$20,000
Auctions: $23,500, PF-66DCam, January 2014; $28,200, PF-66DCam, August 2014													
1896	19,070	690	62.6	94%	$340	$355	$375	$380	$500	$700	$950	$1,100	$2,500
Auctions: $7,344, MS-67, March 2014; $1,998, MS-65, September 2014; $999, MS-64, July 2014; $1,034, MS-64, December 2014													
1896, Proof	132	64	64.8								$4,500	$7,500	$20,000
Auctions: $3,055, PF-62, November 2014; $21,150, PF, October 2013													
1897	29,768	1,007	62.8	95%	$340	$355	$375	$380	$500	$575	$825	$900	$2,000
Auctions: $5,581, MS-67, September 2013; $1,763, MS-66, October 2014; $1,763, MS-65, July 2014; $2,115, MS-65, October 2014													
1897, Proof	136	81	64.9								$4,500	$7,500	$20,000
Auctions: $27,025, PF, March 2014													
1898	24,000	754	63.2	97%	$325	$340	$350	$370	$475	$575	$775	$850	$2,000
Auctions: $4,113, MS-67, September 2014; $4,113, MS-67, October 2014; $9,400, MS-67, April 2013; $3,290, MS-66, September 2014													
1898, Proof	165	117	64.4								$4,500	$7,500	$20,000
Auctions: $25,850, PF-66DCam, September 2014; $25,850, PF-66DCam, September 2014; $4,700, PF-62Cam, August 2014													
1899	27,200	789	62.9	97%	$325	$340	$350	$370	$475	$575	$650	$750	$1,350
Auctions: $3,525, MS-66, June 2014; $3,672, MS-66, November 2014; $1,645, MS-66, November 2014; $3,290, MS-65, August 2014													
1899, Proof	150	132	64.5								$4,500	$7,500	$20,000
Auctions: $36,425, PF, August 2013													
1900	67,000	1,933	63.0	96%	$325	$340	$350	$370	$475	$575	$650	$750	$1,350
Auctions: $4,406, MS-67, October 2014; $3,055, MS-67, July 2014; $2,820, MS-67, July 2014; $1,645, MS-66, October 2014													
1900, Proof	205	188	63.9								$4,500	$7,500	$17,500
Auctions: $64,625, PF-68DCam, November 2014; $111,625, PF, April 2013													
1901	91,100	2,293	62.9	96%	$325	$340	$350	$370	$475	$575	$650	$750	$1,650
Auctions: $4,700, MS-67, August 2014; $3,672, MS-67, November 2014; $646, MS-64, November 2014; $423, MS-63, October 2014													
1901, Proof	223	127	64.5								$4,500	$7,500	$17,500
Auctions: $28,200, PF-67DCam, October 2014; $11,750, PF-64Cam, September 2014; $4,700, PF-63Cam, August 2014; $42,300, PF, March 2014													
1902	133,540	3,359	63.0	97%	$325	$340	$350	$370	$475	$575	$650	$750	$1,350
Auctions: $12,338, MS-68, February 2013; $3,525, MS-67, July 2014; $2,820, MS-67, August 2014; $3,525, MS-67, October 2014													
1902, Proof	193	96	64.1								$4,500	$7,500	$19,000
Auctions: $7,344, PF-64, October 2014; $5,875, PF-64, November 2014; $8,813, PF-64, December 2013													
1903	201,060	5,868	63.1	96%	$325	$340	$350	$370	$475	$575	$650	$750	$1,350
Auctions: $7,638, MS-67, September 2014; $3,525, MS-67, October 2014; $4,700, MS-67, August 2013; $1,880, MS-66, September 2014													
1903, Proof	197	125	63.2								$4,500	$7,500	$17,500
Auctions: $7,050, PF-64, August 2014; $2,834, PF-62, October 2014; $3,173, PF-62, November 2014; $22,325, PF, August 2013													
1904	160,790	4,451	63.0	96%	$325	$340	$350	$370	$475	$575	$650	$750	$1,650
Auctions: $28,200, MS-68, January 2013; $2,820, MS-67, July 2014; $2,585, MS-67, November 2014; $1,351, MS-66, November 2014													
1904, Proof	170	119	64.1								$4,500	$7,500	$17,500
Auctions: $3,290, PF-62Cam, October 2014; $4,406, PF-63, November 2014; $15,393, PF, August 2013													
1905 (j)	217,800	6,279	63.0	96%	$325	$340	$350	$370	$475	$575	$650	$750	$1,350
Auctions: $16,450, MS-68, June 2014; $4,700, MS-67, November 2014; $1,765, MS-66, November 2014; $1,293, MS-65, October 2014													
1905, Proof	144	117	63.6								$4,500	$7,500	$17,500
Auctions: $8,225, PF-64, October 2014; $8,225, PF-64, December 2013													

j. Pieces dated 1905-S are counterfeit.

	Mintage	Cert	Avg	%MS	VF-20	EF-40	AU-50	AU-55	MS-60	MS-62	MS-63	MS-64	MS-65
											PF-60	PF-63	PF-65
1906	176,330	5,254	63.0	97%	$325	$340	$350	$370	$475	$575	$650	$750	$1,350
	Auctions: $4,406, MS-67, February 2013; $1,645, MS-66, July 2014; $1,234, MS-65, July 2014; $1,116, MS-65, November 2014												
1906, Proof	160	136	64.6								$4,500	$7,500	$17,500
	Auctions: $7,638, PF-64Cam, August 2014; $8,225, PF-64Cam, September 2014; $44,063, PF, August 2013												
1907	336,294	8,806	63.1	97%	$325	$340	$350	$370	$475	$575	$650	$750	$1,350
	Auctions: $3,290, MS-67, October 2014; $3,819, MS-67, November 2014; $4,406, MS-67, June 2013; $1,645, MS-65, July 2014												
1907, Proof	154	106	64.8								$4,500	$7,500	$17,500
	Auctions: $4,700, PF-63Cam, September 2014; $32,900, PF-68, April 2013												

INDIAN HEAD (1908–1929)

Designer: *Bela Lyon Pratt.* **Weight:** *4.18 grams.*
Composition: *.900 gold, .100 copper (net weight .12094 oz. pure gold).*
Diameter: *18 mm.* **Edge:** *Reeded.* **Mints:** *Philadelphia, Denver.*

Circulation Strike | Mintmark is on the reverse, to the left of arrows. | Sandblast Finish Proof | Satin Finish Proof

History. The Indian Head design—used on both the quarter eagle and the half eagle—is unusual in that the lettering and motifs are in sunken relief. (The design sometimes is erroneously described as incuse.) The designer, sculptor Bela Lyon Pratt, was chosen by President Theodore Roosevelt after Augustus Saint-Gaudens died before beginning his own design. Pratt modeled the head on Chief Hollow Horn Bear of the Lakota. The "standing eagle" reverse design was based on the reverse of Saint-Gaudens's Indian Head ten-dollar gold coin of 1907; Pratt was a pupil of the famous sculptor.

Some Americans worried that the sunken designs of the Indian Head quarter eagle would accumulate dirt and germs—an unfounded fear. As the smallest gold denomination of the era, these coins were popular for use as souvenirs and gifts, but they did not circulate as money except in the West.

Striking and Sharpness. The striking quality of Indian Head quarter eagles varies. On many early issues the rims are flat, while on others, including most of the 1920s, they are slightly raised. Some have traces of a wire rim, usually on the reverse. Look for weakness on the high parts of the Indian's bonnet (particularly the garland of flowers) and in the feather details in the headdress. On the reverse, check the feathers on the highest area of the wing, the top of the shoulder. On some issues of the 1911-D, the D mintmark can be weak.

Availability. This design was not popular with collectors, and they saved relatively few of the coins. However, many coins were given as gifts and preserved in high quality. The survival of MS-63 and better coins is a matter of chance, especially for the issues dated from 1909 to 1915. The only scarce issue is 1911-D. Luster can range from deeply frosty to grainy. As the fields are the highest areas of the coin, luster diminished quickly as examples were circulated or jostled with others in bags. The Indian Head quarter eagle is one of the most challenging series for professional graders, and opinions can vary widely.

Proofs. Sandblast (also called Matte) Proofs were made in 1908 and 1911 to 1915, while Satin (also called Roman Finish) Proofs were made in 1909 and 1910. The Sandblast issues are usually somewhat dull, while the Satin Proofs are usually of a light-yellow gold. In their time the Proofs of both styles, made for all gold series, were not popular with numismatists. Today, they are in strong demand. As a class these are significantly more readily available than half eagles of the same date and style of finish.

Most are in grades from PF-63 upward. At lower levels coins can show light contact marks. Some microscopic bright flecks may have been caused by the sandblasting process and, although they do not represent handling, usually result in a coin being assigned a slightly lower grade.

Note: Values of common-date gold coins have been based on the current bullion price of gold, $1,200 per ounce, and may vary with the prevailing spot price.

GRADING STANDARDS

MS-60 to 70 (Mint State). *Obverse:* On MS-60 to 62 coins there is abrasion in the field, this representing the highest part of the coin. Abrasion is also evident on the headdress. Marks and, occasionally, a microscopic pin scratch may be seen. At MS-63, there may be some abrasion and some tiny marks. Luster is irregular. At MS-64, abrasion is less. Luster is rich. At MS-65 and above, luster is deep and frosty. No marks at all are visible

1911-D. Graded MS-64.

without magnification at MS-66 and higher. *Reverse:* At MS-60 to 62, there is abrasion in the field, this representing the highest part of the coin. Abrasion is also evident on the eagle's wing. Otherwise, the same comments apply as for the obverse.

    Illustrated coin: This lustrous example has excellent eye appeal.

AU-50, 53, 55, 58 (About Uncirculated). *Obverse:* Friction on the cheek is very noticeable at AU-50, progressively less at higher levels to AU-58. The headdress shows light wear, most evident on the ribbon above the forehead and on the garland. Luster is minimal at AU-50 and scattered and incomplete at AU-58. Nicks and contact marks are to be expected. *Reverse:* Friction on the wing and neck is very noticeable at AU-50, increasingly

1911-D. Graded AU-55.

less at higher levels to AU-58. Otherwise, the same comments apply as for the obverse.

    Illustrated coin: Much of the original luster remains in the incuse areas but not in the fields, which are the highest points on this design.

EF-40, 45 (Extremely Fine). *Obverse:* Light wear characterizes the portrait and headdress. Luster is gone. Marks and tiny scratches are to be expected, but not distracting. *Reverse:* Light wear is most evident on the eagle's head and wing, although other areas are lightly worn as well. Luster is gone. Marks and tiny scratches are to be expected, but not distracting.

1911-D. Graded EF-40.

VF-20, 30 (Very Fine). *Obverse:* Many details of the ribbon above the forehead and the garland are worn away. Many feather vanes are blended together. The field is dull and has contact marks. *Reverse:* The neck and the upper part of the wing show extensive wear, other areas less so. The field is dull and has contact marks.

The Indian Head quarter eagle is seldom collected in grades lower than VF-20.

PF-60 to 70 (Proof). *Obverse and Reverse:* At PF-60 to 63, there is light abrasion and some contact marks; the lower the grade, the higher the quantity. On Sandblast Proofs these show up as visually unappealing bright spots. At PF-64 and higher levels, marks are fewer, with magnification needed to see any at PF-65. At PF-66, there should be none at all.

Illustrated coin: This is a Sandblast Proof of exceptionally high quality.

1912-S. Graded VF-20.

1913, Sandblast Finish. Graded PF-66.

	Mintage	Cert	Avg	%MS	VF-20	EF-40	AU-50	MS-60	MS-62	MS-63 / PF-60	MS-64 / PF-63	MS-65 / PF-65
1908	564,821	9,345	61.6	84%	$300	$310	$325	$450	$575	$1,000	$1,600	$3,500
	Auctions: $8,225, MS-66, August 2014; $8,460, MS-66, September 2014; $7,050, MS-66, November 2014; $13,806, MS, January 2014											
1908, Sandblast Finish Proof	236	135	65.2							$3,750	$9,500	$25,000
	Auctions: $49,938, PF-68, April 2014; $38,188, PF-66, August 2014; $30,550, PF-66, August 2014											
1909	441,760	7,396	61.3	80%	$300	$310	$325	$450	$600	$1,450	$2,500	$5,000
	Auctions: $14,981, MS-66, September 2013; $4,641, MS-65, September 2014; $5,141, MS-65, October 2014											
1909, Satin Finish Proof	139	46	64.4							$4,000	$9,500	$27,500
	Auctions: $57,500, PF-67, January 2011											
1910	492,000	8,513	61.5	85%	$300	$310	$325	$450	$650	$1,300	$2,350	$4,750
	Auctions: $17,625, MS-66, January 2014; $19,975, MS-66, October 2014; $18,213, MS-66, November 2014											
1910, Satin Finish Proof	682	103	65.2							$4,000	$9,500	$27,500
	Auctions: $27,600, PF-64 Plus, September 2011											
1910, Sandblast Finish Proof (a)	unknown	0	n/a					(unique)				
	Auctions: $47,000, PF-66, August 2014											
1911	704,000	12,839	61.2	82%	$300	$310	$325	$450	$600	$850	$1,500	$6,500
	Auctions: $7,638, MS-65, January 2014; $3,819, MS-65, August 2014; $1,645, MS-64, August 2014; $1,528, MS-64, September 2014											
1911, Sandblast Finish Proof	191	95	65.8							$3,750	$9,500	$25,000
	Auctions: $27,025, PF-66, January 2014											
1911D (b)	55,680	5,142	59.9	59%	$2,850	$4,000	$5,000	$8,000	$11,000	$15,000	$24,000	$60,000
	Auctions: $176,250, MS-66, April 2013; $39,656, MS-65, September 2014; $18,800, MS-64, July 2014; $21,150, MS-64, August 2014											
1911D, Weak D	(c)	203	54.0	3%	$1,500	$2,200	$4,000					
	Auctions: $2,645, AU-55, April 2012											

a. The sole known example is part of a complete 1910 Sandblast Finish Proof gold set. Other examples may exist, but have not yet been confirmed. **b.** Beware of counterfeit and altered pieces. **c.** Included in 1911-D mintage figure.

	Mintage	Cert	Avg	%MS	VF-20	EF-40	AU-50	MS-60	MS-62	MS-63	MS-64	MS-65
										PF-60	PF-63	PF-65
1912	616,000	9,059	60.8	75%	$300	$310	$325	$450	$825	$1,500	$2,750	$11,000
	Auctions: $15,275, MS-65, January 2014; $7,050, MS-64, August 2014; $5,581, MS-64, August 2014; $2,585, AU-58, October 2014											
1912, Sandblast Finish Proof	197	45	65.8							$3,750	$10,000	$25,000
	Auctions: $35,250, PF-66, October 2014; $41,125, PF-66, September 2013											
1913	722,000	12,347	61.2	81%	$300	$310	$325	$475	$675	$950	$1,700	$5,500
	Auctions: $14,100, MS-66, July 2014; $28,200, MS-66, October 2013; $4,994, MS-65, August 2014; $3,531, MS-65, October 2014											
1913, Sandblast Finish Proof	165	55	65.9							$3,750	$9,500	$25,000
	Auctions: $31,050, PF-67, January 2012											
1914	240,000	7,824	60.8	76%	$315	$325	$350	$750	$1,950	$4,750	$8,000	$27,500
	Auctions: $21,150, MS-65, August 2014; $15,275, MS-65, November 2014; $32,900, MS-65, December 2013; $8,813, MS-64, July 2014											
1914, Sandblast Finish Proof	117	74	65.1							$3,750	$10,000	$25,000
	Auctions: $12,650, PF-64, April 2012											
1914D	448,000	10,925	61.3	81%	$300	$310	$325	$475	$775	$1,500	$3,500	$30,000
	Auctions: $19,975, MS-65, August 2014; $19,975, MS-65, November 2014; $25,850, MS-65, August 2013; $3,901, MS-64, October 2014											
1915	606,000	11,652	61.3	83%	$300	$310	$325	$425	$600	$1,000	$1,500	$6,500
	Auctions: $21,738, MS-66, January 2014; $4,113, MS-65, August 2014; $3,290, MS-65, November 2014; $4,406, MS-64, August 2014											
1915, Sandblast Finish Proof	100	41	65.1							$4,000	$12,000	$30,000
	Auctions: $41,688, PF-66, January 2012											
1925D	578,000	20,265	62.3	93%	$300	$310	$325	$425	$500	$650	$750	$1,950
	Auctions: $7,990, MS-66, June 2014; $3,173, MS-65, July 2014; $1,821, MS-65, August 2014; $1,058, MS-64, November 2014											
1926	446,000	18,316	62.3	95%	$300	$310	$325	$425	$500	$650	$750	$1,950
	Auctions: $8,813, MS-66, January 2014; $1,528, MS-65, July 2014; $1,528, MS-65, November 2014; $881, MS-64, October 2014											
1927	388,000	14,999	62.3	95%	$300	$310	$325	$425	$500	$650	$750	$1,950
	Auctions: $11,750, MS-66, March 2013; $2,824, MS-65, September 2014; $969, MS-64, August 2014; $823, MS-63, November 2014											
1928	416,000	16,212	62.4	97%	$300	$310	$325	$425	$500	$650	$750	$1,950
	Auctions: $10,575, MS-66, January 2014; $9,988, MS-66, November 2014; $1,645, MS-65, July 2014; $1,528, MS-65, September 2014											
1929	532,000	19,859	62.4	98%	$300	$310	$325	$425	$500	$650	$900	$4,500
	Auctions: $30,550, MS-66, June 2014; $3,525, MS-65, August 2014; $3,290, MS-65, August 2014; $1,058, MS-64, September 2014											

Three-Dollar Gold Pieces
1854–1889

AN OVERVIEW OF THREE-DOLLAR GOLD PIECES

The three-dollar gold coin denomination was conceived in 1853 and first produced for circulation in 1854. Although there were high hopes for it at the outset, and mintages were generous, the value was redundant given the $2.50 quarter eagle then in circulation. Mintages declined, and although pieces were struck each year through 1889, very few actually circulated after the 1850s.

Although many different three-dollar dates are available at reasonable prices, most numismatists opt to acquire either a circulated or Mint State 1854 (significant as the first year of issue; also, in this year the word DOLLARS is in smaller letters than on later issues) or a Mint State coin from the low-mintage era of 1879–1889. Similar to the situation for gold dollars, although the mintages of these later pieces were low, they were popularly saved at the time, and many more have survived in high quality than might otherwise be the case.

Harry W. Bass Jr. assembled the only complete collection of three-dollar gold pieces. His 1870-S is unique.

FOR THE COLLECTOR AND INVESTOR: THREE-DOLLAR GOLD PIECES AS A SPECIALTY

Collecting three-dollar pieces by date and mint would at first seem to be daunting, but it is less challenging than expected, outside of a handful of pieces. The 1870-S is unique (in the Harry W. Bass Jr. Collection on loan to the American Numismatic Association), the 1875 and 1876 were made only in Proof format to the extent of 20 and 45 pieces respectively, and the 1873 is quite rare. Beyond that, examples of coins in grades such as EF and AU (including some varieties with very low mintages) can be purchased for reasonable prices.

Choice examples can be elusive, this being particularly true of branch-mint issues of the 1854–1860 years. Generally, Mint State Philadelphia pieces are rare after 1855, but then come on the market with frequency for 1861 and later, with dates in the 1860s being scarcer than later issues. Coins of the years 1878 and 1879 were made in larger quantities, with the 1878 in particular being easy to find today, although examples usually are quite bag-marked. The low-mintage three-dollar pieces of 1879 through 1889 were popular at the time of issue, many were saved, and today Mint State pieces exist to a greater extent than would otherwise be the case.

INDIAN PRINCESS HEAD (1854–1889)

Designer: *James B. Longacre.* **Weight:** *5.015 grams.*
Composition: *.900 gold, .100 copper (net weight .14512 oz. pure gold).* **Diameter:** *20.5 mm.*
Edge: *Reeded.* **Mints:** *Philadelphia, Dahlonega, New Orleans, San Francisco.*

Circulation Strike

Mintmark location is on the reverse, below the wreath.

Proof

History. The three-dollar gold coin was designed by U.S. Mint chief engraver James B. Longacre, and first struck in 1854. The quarter eagle and half eagle had already been in use for a long time, and the reason for the creation of this odd new denomination is uncertain, although some numismatists note it could have been used to buy a sheet of current 3¢ postage stamps or a group of 100 silver trimes. After a large initial mintage in 1854, the coins were struck in smaller annual quantities. These coins were more popular on the West Coast, but, even in that region, use of this denomination dropped off sharply by the 1870s.

Striking and Sharpness. Points to observe on the obverse include the tips of the feathers in the headdress, and the hair details below the band inscribed LIBERTY. Focal points on the reverse are the wreath details (especially the vertical division in the ribbon knot), and the two central date numerals. Many of the later issues—particularly those of the early 1880s—are prooflike.

Availability. In circulated grades the issues of 1854 to 1860 survive in approximate proportion to their mintages. MS coins are plentiful for the first-year Philadelphia issue, 1854, but are scarce to rare for other years and for all branch-mint issues. For the 1860s and 1870s most are in grades such as EF, AU, and low MS, except for 1874 and in particular 1878, easily found in MS. Dates from 1879 to 1889 have a higher survival ratio and are mostly in MS, often at MS-65.

Proofs. Proofs were struck of all years. All prior to the 1880s are very rare today, with issues of the 1850s being exceedingly so. Coins of 1875 and 1876 were made only in Proof format, with no related circulation strikes. Most often seen in the marketplace are the higher-mintage Proofs of the 1880s. Some have patches of graininess or hints of non-Proof surface on the obverse, or an aura or "ghosting" near the portrait, an artifact of striking.

GRADING STANDARDS

MS-60 to 70 (Mint State). *Obverse:* On MS-60 to 62 coins there is abrasion on the hair below the band lettered LIBERTY (an area that can be weakly struck as well) and on tips of the feather plumes. At MS-63, there may be slight abrasion. Luster can be irregular. At MS-64, abrasion is less. Luster is rich on most coins, less so on the 1854-D (which is often overgraded). At MS-65 and above,

1879. Graded MS-64.

luster is deep and frosty, with no marks at all visible without magnification at MS-66 and higher. *Reverse:* On MS-60 to 62 coins there is abrasion on the 1, the highest parts of the leaves, and the ribbon knot. Otherwise, the same comments apply as for the obverse.

Illustrated coin: Satiny luster and partial mirror surfaces yield excellent eye appeal.

AU-50, 53, 55, 58 (About Uncirculated). *Obverse:* Light wear on the hair below the coronet, the cheek, and the tips of the feather plumes is very noticeable at AU-50, increasingly less at higher levels to AU-58. Luster is minimal at AU-50 and scattered and incomplete at AU-58. Some tiny nicks and contact marks are to be expected and should be mentioned if they are distracting. *Reverse:* Light wear on the 1, the wreath, and the ribbon knot characterize an AU-50 coin, increasingly less at higher levels to 58. Otherwise, the same comments apply as for the obverse.

1854. Graded AU-55.

Illustrated coin: Most of the original luster is gone, but perhaps 15% remains in the protected areas.

EF-40, 45 (Extremely Fine). *Obverse:* Medium wear is seen on the hair below the coronet and on the feather plume tips. Detail is partially gone on the hair. Luster is gone on most coins. *Reverse:* Light wear is seen overall, and the highest parts of the leaves are flat, but detail remains elsewhere. Luster is gone on most coins.

Illustrated coin: Note the mushy denticles (as seen on all but one specimen of this, the only Dahlonega variety in the series).

1854-D. Graded EF-40.

VF-20, 30 (Very Fine). *Obverse:* Most hair detail is gone, except at the back of the lower curls. The feather plume ends are flat. *Reverse:* The wreath and other areas show more wear. Most detail is gone on the higher-relief leaves.

Three-dollar gold pieces are seldom collected in grades lower than VF-20.

1874. Graded VF-20.

PF-60 to 70 (Proof). *Obverse and Reverse:* PF-60 to 62 coins have extensive hairlines and may have nicks and contact marks. At PF-63, hairlines are prominent, but the mirror surface is very reflective. PF-64 coins have fewer hairlines. At PF-65, hairlines should be minimal and mostly seen only under magnification. There should be no nicks or marks. PF-66 and higher coins should have no marks or hairlines visible to the unaided eye.

1883. Graded PF-65 Cameo.

Illustrated coin: Extensive friction is visible in the fields, but the mirror surface can be seen in protected areas. This is still a desirable example of a date of which only 45 were minted.

| | Mintage | Cert | Avg | %MS | VF-20 | EF-40 | AU-50 | AU-55 | MS-60 | MS-62 | MS-63 | MS-65 |
										PF-60	PF-63	PF-65
1854	138,618	3970	55.6	23%	$825	$1,100	$1,400	$1,500	$2,500	$4,500	$5,000	$20,000
Auctions: $18,800, MS-66, August 2014; $19,975, MS-66, October 2013; $12,338, MS-64+, August 2014; $8,225, MS-64, September 2014
1854, Proof	15–20	7	62.0							$30,000	$95,000	$175,000
Auctions: $164,500, PF-64Cam, November 2013
1854D	1,120	100	51.3	9%	$18,500	$27,500	$37,500	$47,500	$80,000	$175,000		
Auctions: $52,875, EF-35, March 2013
1854O	24,000	797	49.4	3%	$2,000	$3,000	$5,000	$7,500	$27,500	$57,500	$85,000	
Auctions: $25,850, AU-58, January 2014; $7,050, AU-55, November 2014; $4,406, AU-53, August 2014; $4,994, AU-53, October 2014
1855	50,555	1208	54.3	19%	$850	$1,250	$1,600	$1,600	$3,000	$4,500	$7,500	$40,000
Auctions: $10,575, MS-64, August 2014; $8,519, MS-64, November 2014; $15,275, MS-64, August 2013; $3,290, MS-62, August 2014
1855, Proof	4–8	0	n/a							$30,000	$95,000	$200,000
Auctions: $75,900, PF-64Cam, November 2003
1855S	6,600	163	42.7	2%	$1,750	$3,000	$7,000	$10,500	$26,000	$55,000	$95,000	
Auctions: $17,625, AU-58, November 2013; $9,400, AU-55, August 2014; $8,237, AU-55, October 2014; $2,115, EF-40, November 2014
1855S, Proof	unknown	1	64.0									
Auctions: $1,322,500, PF-64Cam, August 2011
1856	26,010	743	55.1	20%	$850	$1,200	$1,500	$1,650	$3,250	$5,750	$7,000	$35,000
Auctions: $35,250, MS-65, January 2013; $4,289, MS-62, September 2014; $2,820, MS-61, September 2014; $2,115, AU-58, October 2014
1856, Proof	8–10	2	63.5							$19,500	$45,000	$100,000
Auctions: $28,750, PF-62Cam, March 2011
1856S (a)	34,500	541	45.9	4%	$1,000	$1,700	$2,750	$4,000	$12,500	$18,000	$32,500	
Auctions: $11,831, MS-61, November 2014; $9,400, MS-61, October 2014; $3,966, AU-55+, November 2014; $12,925, MS-61, March 2013
1857	20,891	615	55.0	19%	$850	$1,200	$1,800	$1,900	$3,500	$7,000	$9,000	$35,000
Auctions: $31,725, MS-65, March 2013; $2,374, MS-61, October 2014; $2,003, AU-58, November 2014; $1,293, AU-55, November 2014
1857, Proof	8–12	1	64.0							$18,000	$30,000	$95,000
Auctions: No auction records available.
1857S	14,000	195	43.6	2%	$1,650	$3,500	$6,000	$9,500	$21,500	$45,000	$65,000	$100,000
Auctions: $12,925, AU-58, November 2014; $6,463, AU-55, April 2013; $3,525, AU-50, September 2014
1858	2,133	104	52.5	9%	$1,300	$3,000	$3,750	$5,000	$12,000	$15,000	$22,500	
Auctions: $7,931, AU-58, August 2013
1858, Proof	8–12	4	64.5							$15,000	$27,500	$85,000
Auctions: $85,188, PF-65Cam, April 2013; $94,000, PF-65, October 2014
1859	15,558	562	55.6	22%	$900	$1,250	$1,750	$1,900	$3,250	$5,750	$8,000	$30,000
Auctions: $38,188, MS-66, June 2013; $10,575, MS-64, July 2014; $9,988, MS-64, August 2014; $9,400, MS-64, September 2014
1859, Proof	80	11	64.6							$8,500	$20,000	$60,000
Auctions: $59,925, PF-65DCam, April 2014
1860 (b)	7,036	318	55.4	24%	$950	$1,300	$1,800	$1,900	$3,500	$6,750	$9,000	$27,500
Auctions: $114,563, MS-67, January 2014; $6,463, MS-63, September 2014; $3,525, MS-61, October 2014; $3,290, AU-58, August 2014
1860, Proof	119	14	64.6							$8,000	$16,000	$55,000
Auctions: $88,125, PF-67Cam, September 2014; $67,563, PF-66Cam, August 2013
1860S	7,000	144	42.1	3%	$1,300	$2,500	$7,000	$11,000	$27,500	$50,000	—	
Auctions: $30,550, MS-61, August 2013; $1,087, VF-20, July 2014
1861	5,959	263	55.4	26%	$1,000	$1,650	$2,500	$3,500	$6,500	$11,000	$11,500	$35,000
Auctions: $9,400, MS-62, November 2013; $7,638, AU-58, July 2014; $5,581, AU-58, November 2014; $2,115, AU-50, August 2014
1861, Proof	113	5	64.8							$8,000	$16,000	$55,000
Auctions: $37,375, PF-64Cam, January 2011
1862	5,750	206	55.0	22%	$1,000	$1,650	$2,500	$3,500	$6,500	$11,000	$12,500	$40,000
Auctions: $8,813, MS-62, April 2013; $4,554, AU-55, August 2014; $3,819, AU-50, October 2014; $646, EF-40, October 2014
1862, Proof	35	9	65.0							$8,000	$16,000	$55,000
Auctions: $74,750, PF-66UCam, August 2009

a. Collectors recognize three mintmark sizes: Large (very rare); Medium (common), and Small (rare). **b.** Of the already low 1860 Philadelphia mintage, 2,592 coins were melted at the Mint.

	Mintage	Cert	Avg	%MS	VF-20	EF-40	AU-50	AU-55	MS-60	MS-62	MS-63	MS-65
										PF-60	PF-63	PF-65
1863	5,000	238	55.6	23%	$1,050	$1,750	$2,650	$4,500	$7,500	$11,000	$13,000	$35,000
	Auctions: $211,500, MS-67, January 2014; $49,938, MS-66, November 2014; $7,638, MS-61, November 2014; $4,847, AU-55, September 2014											
1863, Proof	39	10	63.5							$8,000	$16,000	$50,000
	Auctions: $80,500, PF-66UCam, March 2011											
1864	2,630	154	56.6	29%	$1,200	$2,000	$3,000	$3,850	$6,750	$11,000	$14,000	$37,500
	Auctions: $32,900, MS-65, February 2013; $8,813, MS-61, August 2014; $4,406, AU-55, November 2014											
1864, Proof	50	17	63.4							$8,000	$16,000	$47,500
	Auctions: $48,875, PF-64DCam, April 2012											
1865	1,140	72	56.4	36%	$2,250	$3,500	$7,000	$9,500	$15,000	$20,000	$30,000	$55,000
	Auctions: $70,500, MS-66, January 2014; $3,290, VF-25, November 2014											
1865, Proof	25	8	63.8							$8,500	$20,000	$50,000
	Auctions: $46,000, PF-64Cam, March 2006											
1865, Proof Restrike (c)	5	0	n/a				*(extremely rare)*					
	Auctions: No auction records available.											
1866	4,000	170	55.9	26%	$1,100	$1,500	$2,400	$3,000	$5,250	$7,500	$11,000	$35,000
	Auctions: $13,513, MS-64, February 2013; $7,638, MS-63, November 2014; $2,703, AU-58, August 2014; $3,055, AU-58, November 2014											
1866, Proof	30	9	63.4							$8,000	$16,500	$50,000
	Auctions: $46,000, PF-64DCam, April 2011											
1867	2,600	121	56.5	22%	$1,100	$1,500	$2,400	$3,250	$5,250	$8,500	$13,000	$35,000
	Auctions: $141,000, MS-67, January 2014											
1867, Proof	50	10	62.8							$8,000	$16,500	$50,000
	Auctions: $19,388, PF-63DCam, October 2014; $52,875, PF-66Cam, August 2014; $64,625, PF-66Cam, August 2013											
1868 (d)	4,850	358	56.6	26%	$950	$1,250	$2,000	$2,750	$4,250	$7,500	$10,000	$30,000
	Auctions: $8,879, MS-63, April 2013; $3,819, MS-61, September 2014; $3,525, AU-58, August 2014; $2,352, AU-58, November 2014											
1868, Proof	25	9	64.3							$8,000	$16,500	$50,000
	Auctions: $57,500, PF-65Cam, January 2011											
1869 (d)	2,500	167	54.3	15%	$950	$1,250	$2,200	$2,800	$4,750	$9,000	$12,000	$45,000
	Auctions: $9,988, MS-63, August 2014; $7,050, MS-62, March 2013; $3,819, MS-61, August 2014; $2,820, AU-58, August 2014											
1869, Proof	25	4	64.5							$8,000	$16,500	$50,000
	Auctions: $57,500, PF-65UCam, February 2009											
1870	3,500	276	54.3	13%	$1,000	$1,350	$2,500	$3,000	$5,000	$10,000	$12,500	
	Auctions: $14,688, MS-63, January 2014; $3,525, MS-61, October 2014; $3,290, AU-58, October 2014; $3,055, AU-58, November 2014											
1870, Proof	35	10	62.9							$8,000	$16,500	$50,000
	Auctions: $55,813, PF-64Cam, January 2014											
1870S (e)		0	n/a				*(unique, in the Bass Foundation Collection)*					
	Auctions: $687,500, EF-40, October 1982											
1871	1,300	191	56.9	23%	$1,100	$1,350	$2,250	$3,000	$4,750	$8,500	$12,500	$35,000
	Auctions: $9,400, MS-63, November 2014; $6,463, MS-62, October 2014; $8,813, MS-62, August 2013											
1871, Proof	30	5	62.2							$8,000	$16,500	$55,000
	Auctions: $19,550, PF-63Cam, September 2007											
1872	2,000	196	56.2	22%	$1,100	$1,350	$2,250	$3,000	$4,750	$8,500	$12,500	
	Auctions: $7,638, MS-62, August 2014; $7,050, MS-62, November 2014; $6,463, MS-62, November 2014; $7,344, MS-62, August 2013											
1872, Proof	30	22	62.8							$8,000	$16,500	$47,500
	Auctions: $9,400, MS-62, November 2013; $7,638, AU-58, July 2014; $5,581, AU-58, November 2014; $2,115, AU-50, August 2014											

c. Sometime around 1873, the Mint restruck a small number of 1865 three-dollar pieces using an obverse die of 1872 and a newly created reverse with the date slanting up to the right (previously listed in *United States Pattern Coins* as Judd-440). Two examples are known in gold. Versions were also made in copper (Judd-441) for interested collectors. **d.** Varieties showing traces of possible overdating include 1868, 8 Over 7; 1869, 9 Over 8; and 1878, 8 Over 7. **e.** A second example of the 1870-S is rumored to exist in the cornerstone of the San Francisco Mint, but the precise location of the cornerstone has long been unknown.

	Mintage	Cert	Avg	%MS	VF-20	EF-40	AU-50	AU-55	MS-60	MS-62 / PF-60	MS-63 / PF-63	MS-65 / PF-65
1873, Close 3	(f)	51	56.6	20%	$4,250	$7,500	$13,500	$18,500	$32,500	$37,500	$55,000	
Auctions: $61,688, MS-63, January 2014; $52,875, MS-63, August 2014; $30,550, MS-62, August 2014												
1873, Open 3 (Original), Proof (g)	25	6	64.0							$25,000	$32,500	$70,000
Auctions: $212,750, PF-65DCam, September 2008												
1873, Close 3, Proof	(h)	0	n/a							$25,000	$37,500	$75,000
Auctions: $37,375, PF-61, January 2011												
1874	41,800	2817	56.7	28%	$850	$1,150	$1,400	$1,500	$2,500	$3,500	$5,500	$18,000
Auctions: $9,988, MS-65, October 2014; $12,338, MS-65, September 2013; $4,406, MS-64, October 2014; $2,350, MS-62, October 2014												
1874, Proof	20	9	64.3							$12,500	$28,000	$60,000
Auctions: $54,625, PF-65Cam, January 2012												
1875, Proof (i)	20	7	63.0							$80,000	$150,000	$225,000
Auctions: $218,500, PF-64, January 2012												
1876, Proof (i)	45	29	63.9							$25,000	$45,000	$75,000
Auctions: $76,375, PF-65Cam, June 2013												
1877	1,468	36	56.9	22%	$3,000	$6,000	$13,000	$20,000	$28,500	$35,000	$50,000	
Auctions: $22,325, MS-61, August 2013; $21,150, AU-58, November 2014; $6,463, AU-50, July 2014												
1877, Proof	20	14	63.1							$12,500	$30,000	$55,000
Auctions: $64,400, PF-65DCam, November 2011												
1878 (d)	82,304	5302	59.5	58%	$850	$1,150	$1,400	$1,750	$2,350	$3,000	$4,750	$10,000
Auctions: $25,850, MS-66, January 2014; $20,563, MS-66, August 2014; $12,925, MS-66, August 2014; $12,338, MS-65, September 2014												
1878, Proof	20	8	63.8							$12,500	$27,500	$55,000
Auctions: $877, PF, June 2014												
1879	3,000	401	60.7	66%	$1,000	$1,300	$2,000	$2,750	$3,750	$6,000	$8,000	$20,000
Auctions: $15,863, MS-65, October 2014; $17,038, MS-65, August 2013; $6,463, MS-64+, October 2014; $5,581, MS-63, October 2014												
1879, Proof	30	12	64.7							$10,000	$17,000	$42,500
Auctions: $14,375, PF-63Cam, October 2011												
1880	1,000	123	62.2	89%	$1,200	$2,000	$3,500	$3,850	$5,500	$7,500	$11,000	$25,000
Auctions: $58,750, MS-66, January 2014; $8,225, MS-64, November 2014; $4,465, MS-62, October 2014												
1880, Proof	36	16	64.1							$10,000	$17,000	$42,500
Auctions: $51,113, PF, August 2013												
1881	500	101	57.6	40%	$2,500	$4,500	$7,500	$8,500	$12,000	$15,000	$18,500	
Auctions: $35,250, MS-64, September 2014; $14,100, MS-61, August 2013; $2,233, AU-50, October 2014												
1881, Proof	54	30	64.3							$10,000	$17,000	$42,500
Auctions: $32,200, PF-64Cam, January 2011												
1882	1,500	282	59.3	57%	$1,250	$1,500	$2,350	$3,000	$4,250	$6,750	$10,000	$28,000
Auctions: $105,750, MS-67, January 2014; $7,638, MS-63, July 2014; $3,819, MS-61, July 2014; $1,528, MS-60, August 2014												
1882, Proof	76	34	63.1							$7,500	$13,500	$35,000
Auctions: $38,188, PF-65DCam, September 2014; $28,200, PF-64DCam, March 2014												
1883	900	146	59.0	61%	$1,400	$2,000	$3,000	$3,500	$5,500	$7,500	$10,000	$28,000
Auctions: $8,225, MS-63, November 2014; $7,638, MS-63, November 2014; $5,875, MS-62, September 2014; $10,575, MS, March 2014												
1883, Proof	89	40	64.3							$7,500	$13,500	$35,000
Auctions: $70,500, PF-66Cam+, November 2014; $38,188, PF-65Cam, April 2013												
1884	1,000	53	60.5	68%	$1,500	$2,000	$3,250	$4,000	$5,500	$7,500	$10,000	$28,000
Auctions: $7,931, MS-62, August 2013												
1884, Proof	106	37	64.0							$7,500	$13,500	$35,000
Auctions: $30,550, PF-65DCam, September 2014; $23,500, PF-64DCam, August 2013												

d. Varieties showing traces of possible overdating include 1868, 8 Over 7; 1869, 9 Over 8; and 1878, 8 Over 7. **f.** The mintage figure for the 1873, Close 3, coins is unknown. Research suggests that only Proofs may have been struck (none for circulation), and those perhaps as late as 1879. **g.** Mint records report 25 Proof coins (with no reference to the style, Open or Close, of the number 3 in the date). The actual mintage may be as high as 100 to 1,000 coins. **h.** Included in 1873, Open 3 (Original), Proof, mintage figure. **i.** Proof only.

	Mintage	Cert	Avg	%MS	VF-20	EF-40	AU-50	AU-55	MS-60	MS-62	MS-63	MS-65
										PF-60	PF-63	PF-65
1885	801	149	59.5	56%	$1,650	$2,150	$3,750	$4,500	$6,000	$9,000	$15,000	$35,000
	Auctions: $27,025, MS-64, August 2014; $7,050, MS-62, January 2014; $7,638, MS-62+, August 2014; $6,463, MS-62, November 2014											
1885, Proof	109	53	63.5							$7,500	$13,500	$35,000
	Auctions: $10,281, PF-63, November 2014; $8,813, PF-62, October 2014; $76,050, PF, September 2013											
1886	1,000	157	57.8	43%	$1,500	$1,950	$2,750	$3,750	$5,000	$7,500	$10,500	$35,000
	Auctions: $9,988, MS-63, November 2014; $6,463, MS-62, September 2014; $4,700, MS-61, August 2014; $3,819, AU-58, August 2014											
1886, Proof	142	71	64.0							$7,500	$13,500	$35,000
	Auctions: $38,188, PF-65DCam, April 2013											
1887	6,000	214	60.7	68%	$900	$1,350	$2,000	$2,250	$3,500	$4,750	$10,500	$24,000
	Auctions: $15,275, MS-65, January 2014; $12,338, MS-65, November 2014; $4,406, MS-63, July 2014; $4,259, MS-63, November 2014											
1887, Proof	160	68	63.9							$7,500	$13,500	$35,000
	Auctions: $64,625, PF-67Cam, August 2013											
1888	5,000	511	60.9	73%	$850	$1,150	$1,750	$2,000	$3,000	$4,500	$7,000	$18,000
	Auctions: $19,975, MS-66, September 2014; $10,869, MS-65, August 2014; $19,388, MS, March 2014; $7,050, MS-64+, July 2014											
1888, Proof	291	94	64.2							$7,500	$12,500	$32,500
	Auctions: $38,188, PF-66Cam, November 2013; $15,863, PF-64Cam+, November 2014											
1889	2,300	309	60.6	67%	$850	$1,150	$1,750	$1,650	$2,900	$4,000	$6,000	$13,500
	Auctions: $19,975, MS-66, April 2014; $11,750, MS-65, August 2014; $5,875, MS-64+, November 2014; $6,463, MS-63, October 2014											
1889, Proof	129	51	63.8							$7,500	$12,500	$35,000
	Auctions: $25,850, PF-65Cam, January 2014; $7,050, PF-62, November 2014											

Four-Dollar Gold Pieces
1879–1880

AN OVERVIEW OF FOUR-DOLLAR GOLD PIECES

The four-dollar pattern gold coin, or Stella, is not widely collected, simply because of its rarity. For type-set purposes some numismatists opt to acquire a single example of the only issue readily available, Charles Barber's 1879 Flowing Hair, although these are expensive. However, the Coiled Hair style is a different type, much rarer, and a collector with the means might acquire an example of that design as well.

FOR THE COLLECTOR AND INVESTOR: FOUR-DOLLAR GOLD PIECES AS A SPECIALTY

Over the past century perhaps two dozen numismatists have put together complete sets of one of each gold striking of the 1879 and 1880 Flowing Hair and Coiled Hair Stella, this being made possible by collections being dispersed and sold to others, as it is unlikely that even as many as 20 complete sets could exist at one time.

Charles E. Barber (left), designer of the Flowing Hair Stella, and George T. Morgan (right), designer of the Coiled Hair Stella, sit for an official portrait of Philadelphia Mint employees.

STELLA, FLOWING HAIR AND COILED HAIR (1879–1880)

Designers: *Charles E. Barber (Flowing Hair, and common reverse); George T. Morgan (Coiled Hair).*
Weight: *7.0 grams.* **Composition:** *Approximately .857 gold, .042 silver, .100 copper.*
Diameter: *22 mm.* **Edge:** *Reeded.*

Flowing Hair

Coiled Hair

History. The four-dollar gold Stellas of 1879 and 1880 are Proof-only patterns, not regular issues. However, as they have been listed in popular references for decades, collectors have adopted them into the regular gold series. The obverse inscription notes the coins' metallic content in proportions of gold, silver, and copper in the metric system, intended to facilitate their use in foreign countries, where the value could be quickly determined. The Stella was proposed by John A. Kasson (formerly a U.S. representative from Iowa and chairman of the House Committee on Coinage, Weights, and Measures; in 1879 serving as envoy extraordinary and minister plenipotentiary to Austria-Hungary). Charles E. Barber designed the Flowing Hair type (as well as the reverse common to both types), and George T. Morgan designed the Coiled Hair. Those dated 1879 were struck for congressional examination; popular testimony of the era suggests that the Flowing Hair Stella became a favorite gift for congressmen's lovers in the Washington demimonde. The only issue produced in quantity was the 1879, Flowing Hair. The others were made in secret and sold privately by Mint officers and employees. The Coiled Hair Stella was not generally known to the numismatic community until they were illustrated in *The Numismatist* in the early 20th century. Stellas are cataloged by their Judd numbers, assigned in the standard reference, *United States Pattern Coins.*

Striking and Sharpness. On nearly all examples the high parts of the hair are flat, often with striations. The other areas of the coin are typically well struck. Tiny planchet irregularities are common.

Availability. The 1879 Flowing Hair is often available on the market—usually in PF-61 to 64, although higher-condition examples come on the market with regularity (as do lightly handled and impaired coins). The 1880 Flowing Hair is typically found in PF-63 or higher. Both years of Coiled Hair Stellas are great rarities; typical grades are PF-63 to 65, with a flat strike on the head and with some tiny planchet flaws.

GRADING STANDARDS

PF-60 to 70 (Proof). *Obverse and Reverse:* PF-60 to 62 coins have extensive hairlines and may have nicks and contact marks. At PF-63, hairlines are prominent, but the mirror surface is very reflective. PF-64 coins have fewer hairlines. At PF-65, hairlines should be minimal and mostly seen only under magnification. There should be no nicks or marks. PF-66 and higher coins should have no marks or hairlines visible to the unaided eye.

1879, Flowing Hair; J-1657. Graded PF-62.

Illustrated coin: A nick above the head and some light friction define the grade, but the coin has nice eye appeal overall.

PF-60 to 70 (Proof). *Obverse and Reverse:* PF-60 to 62 coins have extensive hairlines and may have nicks and contact marks. At PF-63, hairlines are prominent, but the mirror surface is very reflective. PF-64 coins have fewer hairlines. At PF-65, hairlines should be minimal and mostly seen only under magnification. There should be no nicks or marks. PF-66 and higher coins should have no marks or hairlines visible to the unaided eye.

1879, Coiled Hair; J-1660. Graded PF-65.

	Mintage	Cert	Avg	%MS	PF-40	PF-50	PF-60	PF-63	PF-64	PF-65	PF-66	PF-67
1879, Flowing Hair, Proof	425+	228	63.9	95%	$80,000	$85,000	$105,000	$150,000	$175,000	$215,000	$250,000	$375,000
	Auctions: $182,125, PF-65, November 2014; $165,675, PF-64, October 2014; $102,813, PF-60, August 2014; $280,800, PF, September 2013											
1879, Coiled Hair, Proof	*12–15 known*	13	65.1	100%			$275,000	$350,000	$500,000	$650,000	$850,000	$1,200,000
	Auctions: $1,041,300, PF, September 2013											
1880, Flowing Hair, Proof	*17–20 known*	20	65.0	100%			$150,000	$225,000	$275,000	$350,000	$450,000	$600,000
	Auctions: $959,400, PF, September 2013											
1880, Coiled Hair, Proof	*8–10 known*	12	65.0	100%			$700,000	$850,000	$100,000	$1,250,000	$1,750,000	$2,500,000
	Auctions: $2,574,000, PF, September 2013											

Note: Many individual high-value rare coins are submitted for certification and grading multiple times over the years, which can inflate the number of certifications above the number of coins actually minted.

Gold Half Eagles ($5)
1795–1929

AN OVERVIEW OF GOLD HALF EAGLES

The half eagle was the first gold coin actually struck for the United States. The five-dollar gold piece was authorized by the Act of April 2, 1792, and the first batch was minted in 1795.

Forming a type set of half eagles is a daunting but achievable challenge—if a collector has the finances and some determination. Examples of the first type, with Capped Bust to Right (conical cap obverse), and with an eagle on a palm branch on the reverse, regularly come up on the market, usually of the date 1795. Typical grades range from EF to lower Mint State levels. Such pieces are scarce, and the demand for them is strong. The next type, the Heraldic Eagle motif, first struck in 1798, but also known from a 1795-dated die used later, was produced through 1807, and is easily enough obtained today. Again, typical grades range from EF to Mint State. MS-63 and better coins are available, but are in the distinct minority.

The short-lived Capped Bust to Left style, 1807–1812, can be found in similar grades, although such pieces did not circulate as extensively, and AU and Mint State levels are the rule, with VF pieces being unusual. Then follows the era of rarities. The Capped Head to Left, stars surrounding head, large diameter, 1813–1829 style is available largely courtesy of the first date of issue, 1813. This is the only date seen with some frequency. When available, examples tend to be choice. The later stretch of this series includes some formidable rarities, among which are the famous 1815 and the even rarer 1822, along with a whole string of other seldom-seen varieties in the 1820s. The same style, but of reduced diameter, 1829–1834, also is rare; examples of the 1830s turn up with some regularity, but these often lack eye appeal. For some reason, half eagles of the early 1830s are often heavily marked and abraded, which is not true at all for coins of the 1820s.

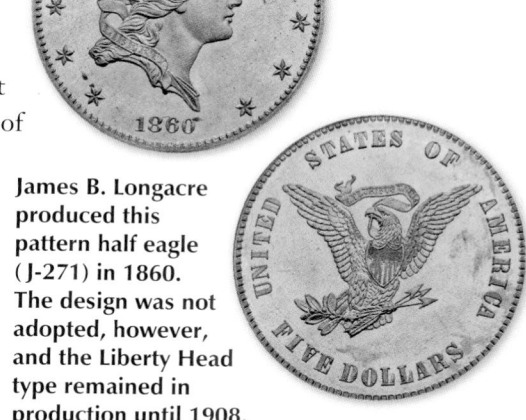

James B. Longacre produced this pattern half eagle (J-271) in 1860. The design was not adopted, however, and the Liberty Head type remained in production until 1908.

Classic Head half eagles, capless and without the motto E PLURIBUS UNUM, first minted in August 1834, are easily enough obtained. Those seen in today's marketplace are usually of the first several dates, and less frequently of 1837 or 1838. Grades range from VF upward, reflecting their extensive use in circulation. Mint State coins can be found on occasion and are scarce. Choice and gem pieces are rare.

With just a few exceptions, Liberty Head half eagles of the 1839–1866 type without the motto IN GOD WE TRUST are very plentiful in worn grades, including certain of the higher-mintage issues from the popular Charlotte and Dahlonega mints (permitting interesting varieties to be added to a type set). Mint State coins are scarce, and when seen are usually in lower levels such as MS-60 and MS-62. Gems of any date are rare. Then follow the Liberty Head pieces with the motto IN GOD WE TRUST on the reverse, 1866 through 1908; the earlier years are mostly encountered in worn grades, the later ones are easy enough to find in Mint State. Proofs were made of all Liberty Head half eagle dates, and today they are generally collectible from about 1860 onward.

With two exceptions (1909-O and 1929), the Indian Head half eagles of 1908 to 1929 are common enough in worn grades as well as low Mint State levels, but true gems, accurately graded and with lustrous, frosty surfaces, are quite rare. The field is the highest area of the coin and thus is quite susceptible to scuffs and marks. Probably the most readily available dates in higher grades are 1908 and 1909, with the 1909-D being plentiful due to a hoard that came on the market a generation ago.

FOR THE COLLECTOR AND INVESTOR: GOLD HALF EAGLES AS A SPECIALTY

While in the annals of American numismatics dozens of old-time numismatists collected half eagles by date (or, less often, by date *and* mint), today rarities are so widely scattered and are so expensive that few collectors can rise to the challenge.

Early half eagles can be collected by dates and basic varieties, and also by die varieties. The year 1795 in particular is rich in the latter, and years ago several scholars described such varieties, beginning with J. Colvin Randall in the 1870s, continuing to William H. Woodin in the early 1900s, then Edgar H. Adams, Thomas Ollive Mabbott, and Walter Breen. In more recent times Robert Miller, Harry W. Bass Jr., John Dannreuther, and others have added their research to the literature.

Among early half eagles there are two unique varieties: the 1797 with a 16-star obverse, and the 1797 with a 15-star obverse, both with the Heraldic Eagle reverse, likely struck in 1798. Of the later 1822, just three are known, two of which are in the National Numismatic Collection at the Smithsonian Institution. Of all early half eagles the 1815 was far and away the most famous during the 19th century. (In the 1880s a publication on the Mint Collection stated that the two highlights there were the 1815 half eagle and the unique 1849 double eagle.) At the time the rarer 1822 was not recognized for its elusive nature. Today an estimated 11 examples of the 1815 half eagles exist, mostly in higher circulated grades, including those in museums. There are only two known of the 1825, 5 Over 4 overdate, but it is not at all famous, probably because it is an overdate variety, not a single date on its own. Half eagles of 1826 through 1829 all are rare, with the 1829 being particularly well known. The latter date includes early pieces with regular diameter and later ones with the diameter reduced. Generally, all half eagles from 1815 through 1834 are scarce, some of them particularly so.

Classic Head half eagles of 1834 to 1838 include the scarce 1838-C and 1838-D, the first of the Charlotte and Dahlonega mints respectively; none are prohibitively rare. Generally, the higher-grade pieces are found toward the beginning of the Classic Head series, especially bearing the date 1834.

Liberty Head half eagles are readily available of most dates and mints from 1839 to 1908, save for the one great rarity, the 1854-S, of which just three are known (one is in the Smithsonian). There is a vast panorama of Charlotte and Dahlonega issues through 1861, most of which were made in fairly large quantities, as this was the highest denomination ever struck at each of these mints (larger-capacity presses were not on hand). Accordingly, they are highly collectible today. Some varieties are scarce, but none are completely out of reach. Typical grades range from VF to EF and AU, occasionally Mint State, though not often MS-63 or higher.

Among San Francisco half eagles most of the early issues are scarce, as such pieces circulated extensively and there was no thought to saving numismatic examples. However, there are not many specialists in the field, and for some varieties it can be said that collectors are harder to find than are the coins themselves, yielding the opportunity to purchase truly rare pieces for significantly less than would otherwise be the case. Carson City half eagles were minted beginning in 1870 and continuing intermittently through 1893. Most of the early issues range from scarce to rare, the 1870-CC being particularly well known in this regard. Proofs of the Liberty Head type are generally collectible from the 1860s onward, with most on the market being of the higher-mintage issues of the 1890s and 1900s.

Among Indian Head half eagles, 1908 to 1929, the 1909-O is the rarest of the early coins, and when seen is usually worn. A choice or gem Mint State 1909-O is an incredible rarity. However, enough worn 1909-O half eagles exist, including many brought from overseas hoards in recent decades, that a piece in VF or so grade presents no problem. Half eagles of 1929, of which just 662,000 were minted, were mostly melted, it seems. A couple hundred or so exist today, nearly all of which are Mint State, but nicked and with bagmarks, MS-60 to 62 or 63. Truly high-quality gems are exceedingly rare.

CAPPED BUST TO RIGHT, SMALL EAGLE REVERSE (1795–1798)

Designer: *Robert Scot.* **Weight:** *8.75 grams.*
Composition: *.9167 gold, .0833 silver and copper.*
Diameter: *Approximately 25 mm.* **Edge:** *Reeded.*

Bass-Dannreuther–2.

History. Half eagles of this style, the first federal gold coins, were introduced in July 1795. The obverse features Miss Liberty wearing a conical cap, a design generally called Capped Bust to Right. The reverse depicts a "small" eagle perched on a palm branch. The same motif was used on contemporary $10 gold coins. No Proofs or presentation strikes were made of this type.

Striking and Sharpness. On the obverse, check the star centers and the hair details. On the reverse, check the feathers of the eagle, particularly on the breast. Examine the denticles on both sides. Adjustment marks (from Mint workers filing down overweight planchets to acceptable standards) often are visible, but are not explicitly noted by the grading services.

Availability. Typical grades range from EF to AU and low MS. MS-63 and better coins are rare; when seen, they usually are of the 1795 date (of which many different die varieties exist). Certain varieties are rare, most famously the 1798 with Small Eagle reverse.

GRADING STANDARDS

MS-60 to 70 (Mint State). *Obverse:* At MS-60, some abrasion and contact marks are evident, most noticeably on the hair to the left of Miss Liberty's forehead and on the higher-relief areas of the cap. Luster is present, but may be dull or lifeless, and interrupted in patches. At MS-63, contact marks are few, and abrasion is very light. An MS-65 coin has hardly any abrasion, and contact marks are so minute as to require magnifica-

1795, S Over D in STATES; BD-6. Graded MS-63.

tion. Luster should be full and rich. Grades above MS-65 for this type are more often theoretical than actual—but they do exist and are defined by having fewer marks as perfection is approached. *Reverse:* Comments apply as for the obverse, except that abrasion and contact marks are most noticeable on the breast and head of the eagle. The field area is mainly protected by the eagle, branch, and lettering.

Illustrated coin: This is the error die with the second S over an erroneous D in STATES (which originally read as STATED).

AU-50, 53, 55, 58 (About Uncirculated). *Obverse:* Light wear is seen on the cheek, the hair immediately to the left of the face, and the cap, more at AU-50 than at 53 or 55. An AU-58 coin has minimal traces of wear. An AU-50 coin has luster in protected areas among the stars and letters, with little in the open fields or on the portrait. At AU-58, most luster is present in the fields but is worn away on the highest parts of the motifs.

1795; BD-7. Graded AU-58.

Reverse: Comments as preceding, except that the eagle shows light wear on the breast and head in particular, but also at the tip of the wing on the left and elsewhere. Luster ranges from perhaps 40% remaining in protected areas (at AU-50) to nearly full mint bloom (at AU-58).

EF-40, 45 (Extremely Fine). *Obverse:* Wear is evident all over the portrait, with some loss of detail in the hair to the left of Miss Liberty's face. Excellent detail remains in low-relief areas of the hair, such as the front curl and at the back of her head. The stars show wear, as do the date and letters. Luster, if present at all, is minimal and in protected areas. *Reverse:* Wear is greater than on an About Uncirculated coin. The breast, neck,

1795; BD-4. Graded EF-40.

and legs of the eagle lack nearly all feather detail. More wear is seen on the edges of the wing. Some traces of luster may be seen, more so at EF-45 than at EF-40.

VF-20, 30 (Very Fine). *Obverse:* The higher-relief areas of hair are well worn at VF-20, less so at VF-30. The stars are flat at their centers. *Reverse:* Wear is greater, the eagle is flat in most areas, and about 40% to 60% of the wing feathers can be seen.

The Capped Bust to Right half eagle with Small Eagle reverse is seldom collected in grades lower than VF-20.

Illustrated coin: While exhibiting typical

1795. Graded VF-20.

wear for a VF-20 coin, this specimen also shows rim damage from having been mounted as jewelry at some point in time.

| | | 1796, 6 Over 5 | | 1797, 15-Star Obverse | | | 1797, 16-Star Obverse | | |

	Mintage	Cert	Avg	%MS	F-12	VF-20	EF-40	AU-50	AU-55	MS-60	MS-62	MS-63	MS-64
1795	8,707	219	55.2	30%	$20,000	$23,500	$30,000	$40,000	$47,500	$70,000	$97,500	$155,000	$250,000 **(a)**
Auctions: $587,500, MS-66★, January 2015; $64,625, MS-61, February 2013; $64,625, AU-58, August 2014; $52,875, AU-58, August 2014													
1795, S Over D in STATES (b)	**(c)**	0	n/a					$42,000	$52,500	$75,000			
Auctions: $345,000, MS-65PL, July 2009													
1796, 6 Over 5	6,196	35	57.0	46%	$20,000	$25,000	$40,000	$60,000	$75,000	$110,000	$145,000	$215,000	$300,000
Auctions: $67,563, AU-58, February 2014; $45,531, AU-55, October 2014; $52,875, AU-53, August 2014; $15,863, EF-40, October 2014													
1797, All kinds	3,609												
1797, 15-Star Obverse		4	56.5	25%	$27,000	$45,000	$65,000	$125,000	$145,000	$245,000			
Auctions: $152,750, AU-53, January 2014													
1797, 16-Star Obverse		6	56.8	17%	$25,000	$40,000	$50,000	$80,000	$135,000	$235,000			
Auctions: $411,250, MS-61, August 2013													
1798, Small Eagle (d)	*unknown*	2	50.0	0%		$375,000	$550,000	$750,000	$900,000	—			
Auctions: No auction records available.													

a. Value in MS-65 is $525,000. **b.** The final S in STATES is punched over an erroneous D. **c.** Included in 1795, Small Eagle, mintage figure. **d.** The reverse of the 1798, Small Eagle, was from a 1795 die. The obverse has an arched die crack or flaw beneath the date. 7 examples are known, and the finest is an AU-55 from the collection of King Farouk of Egypt.

CAPPED BUST TO RIGHT, HERALDIC EAGLE REVERSE (1795–1807)

Designer: *Robert Scot.* **Weight:** *8.75 grams.*
Composition: *.9167 gold, .0833 silver and copper.*
Diameter: *Approximately 25 mm.* **Edge:** *Reeded.*

BD-13.

History. For this type, the obverse design is the same as that of the preceding. The reverse features a heraldic eagle, as used on other silver and gold coins of the era. Some half eagles of the Heraldic Eagle Reverse design are dated 1795, but these were actually struck in 1798, from a leftover obverse coinage die. The *Encyclopedia of U.S. Gold Coins, 1795–1933* notes that "No Proofs were made, but one 1795 half eagle with a Heraldic Eagle reverse has been certified as a Specimen."

Striking and Sharpness. On the obverse, check the star centers and the hair details. On the reverse, check the upper part of the shield, the lower part of the eagle's neck, the eagle's wing, the stars above the eagle, and the clouds. Inspect the denticles on both sides. Adjustment marks (from overweight planchets being filed down to correct standards by Mint workers) can be an aesthetic problem and are not explicitly identified by the grading services.

Availability. Although there are many rare die varieties, as a type this half eagle is plentiful. Typical grades are EF to lower MS. MS-63 and higher coins are seen with some frequency and usually are dated from 1802 to 1807. Sharply struck coins without adjustment marks are in the minority.

GRADING STANDARDS

MS-60 to 70 (Mint State). *Obverse:* At MS-60, some abrasion and contact marks are evident, most noticeably on the hair to the left of Miss Liberty's forehead and on the higher-relief areas of the cap. Luster is present, but may be dull or lifeless, and interrupted in patches. At MS-63, contact marks are few, and abrasion is very light. An MS-65 coin has hardly any abrasion, and contact marks are so minute as to require magnifica-

1802, 2 Over 1. Graded MS-62.

tion. Luster should be full and rich. Grades above MS-65 are not often seen but are defined by having fewer marks as perfection is approached. *Reverse:* Comments apply as for the obverse, except that abrasion and contact marks are most noticeable on the upper part of the eagle and the clouds. The field area is complex, with not much open space, given the stars above the eagle, the arrows and olive branch, and other features. Accordingly, marks are not as noticeable as on the obverse.

Illustrated coin: This is an attractive coin with rich luster. Some friction is visible on the higher points and in the obverse field.

AU-50, 53, 55, 58 (About Uncirculated). *Obverse:* Light wear is seen on the cheek, the hair immediately to the left of the face, and the cap, more at AU-50 than at 53 or 55. An AU-58 coin has minimal traces of wear. An AU-50 coin has luster in protected areas among the stars and letters, with little in the open fields or on the portrait. At AU-58, most luster is present in the fields, but is worn away on the highest parts of the motifs.

1804. Graded AU-58.

Reverse: Comments as preceding, except that the eagle's neck, the tips and top of the wings, the clouds, and the tail now show noticeable wear, as do other features. Luster ranges from perhaps 40% remaining in protected areas (at AU-50) to nearly full mint bloom (at AU-58). Often the reverse of this type retains much more luster than the obverse.

Illustrated coin: An abrasion in the left obverse field keeps this otherwise lustrous and attractive coin below the Mint State level.

EF-40, 45 (Extremely Fine). *Obverse:* Wear is evident all over the portrait, with some loss of detail in the hair to the left of Miss Liberty's face. Excellent detail remains in low-relief areas of the hair, such as the front curl and at the back of her head. The stars show wear, as do the date and letters. Luster, if present at all, is minimal and in protected areas. *Reverse:* Wear is greater than on an About Uncirculated coin. The neck lacks feather detail on its

1804, Small 8 Over Large 8; BD-7. Graded EF-45.

highest points. Feathers have lost some detail near the edges of the wings, and some areas of the horizontal lines in the shield may be blended together. Some traces of luster may be seen, more so at EF-45 than at EF-40. Overall, the reverse appears to be in a slightly higher grade than the obverse.

VF-20, 30 (Very Fine). *Obverse:* The higher-relief areas of hair are well worn at VF-20, less so at VF-30. The stars are flat at their centers. *Reverse:* Wear is greater, including on the shield and wing feathers. The star centers are flat. Other areas have lost detail as well. E PLURIBUS UNUM may be light or worn away in areas.

The Capped Bust to Right half eagle with Heraldic Eagle reverse is seldom collected in grades lower than VF-20.

1798, Large 8, 13-Star Reverse; BD-4. Graded VF-20.

1797, 16-Star Obverse

1797, 15-Star Obverse

1797, 7 Over 5

1798, Small 8

1798, Large 8

1798, 13-Star Reverse

1798, 14-Star Reverse

1799, Small
Reverse Stars

1799, Large
Reverse Stars

	Mintage	Cert	Avg	%MS	F-12	VF-20	EF-40	AU-50	AU-55	MS-60	MS-62	MS-63	MS-64
1795	(a)	19	60.2	68%	$15,000	$22,000	$30,000	$50,000	$60,000	$90,000	$135,000	$185,000	$275,000
Auctions: $15,275, AU-50, January 2014													
1797, 7 Over 5	(a)	4	58.0	25%	$16,000	$27,500	$45,000	$75,000	$115,000	$200,000			
Auctions: $126,500, AU-58, September 2005													
1797, 16-Star Obverse	(a)	0	n/a		*(unique, in Smithsonian's National Numismatic Collection)*								
Auctions: No auction records available.													
1797, 15-Star Obverse	(a)	0	n/a		*(unique, in Smithsonian's National Numismatic Collection)*								
Auctions: No auction records available.													
1798, All kinds	24,867												
1798, Small 8		23	56.2	26%	$5,500	$7,750	$12,500	$18,500	$21,500	$32,500	$47,500	$75,000	
Auctions: $18,800, AU-53, April 2014													
1798, Large 8, 13-Star Reverse		66	53.7	18%	$4,500	$5,750	$9,000	$14,000	$24,500	$50,000			
Auctions: $21,150, AU-55, August 2014; $19,975, AU-55, November 2014; $16,450, AU-53, August 2014; $12,925, AU-50, January 2014													
1798, Large 8, 14-Star Reverse		15	55.9	7%	$4,750	$6,750	$13,000	$25,000	$35,000	$100,000			
Auctions: $32,900, AU-55, August 2014; $25,850, AU-55, October 2014; $25,850, AU, February 2014													
1799, All kinds	7,451												
1799, Small Reverse Stars		10	59.7	50%				$14,000	$18,000	$27,500	$37,500	$65,000	$100,000
Auctions: $47,000, MS-62, February 2013; $19,975, AU-58, August 2014; $13,513, AU-55, September 2014; $4,711, EF-40, August 2014													
1799, Large Reverse Stars		18	58.3	61%				$14,000	$18,000	$27,500	$35,000	$60,000	$90,000
Auctions: $70,500, MS-63, January 2014; $16,450, AU-55, August 2014; $11,750, AU-53, August 2014													

a. The 1795 and 1797 Heraldic Eagle half eagles are thought to have been struck in 1798 and are included in that year's mintage figure of 24,867.

| 1800, Pointed 1 | 1800, Blunt 1 | 1800, 8 Arrows | 1800, 9 Arrows |

1802, 2 Over 1
FS-G5-1802/1-301. | **1803, 3 Over 2** | **1804, Small 8** | **1804, Small 8 Over Large 8**

| 1806, Pointed-Top 6, Stars 8 and 5 | Closeup of Pointed-Top 6 | 1806, Round-Top 6, Stars 7 and 6 | Closeup of Round-Top 6 |

	Mintage	Cert	Avg	%MS	F-12	VF-20	EF-40	AU-50	AU-55	MS-60	MS-62	MS-63	MS-64
1800	37,628	255	56.9	43%	$4,000	$5,000	$7,000	$10,000	$12,000	$15,000	$18,000	$33,500	$75,000
Auctions: $16,100, MS-62, April 2012												
1800, Pointed 1 (b)	(c)	0	n/a							$20,000	$23,000	$27,500	
Auctions: $25,850, MS-63, November 2014; $21,150, MS-62, November 2013; $12,338, MS-61, October 2014												
1800, 9 Arrows (d)	(c)	0	n/a							$16,500	$20,000		
Auctions: No auction records available.												
1802, 2 Over 1	53,176	275	57.6	40%	$4,000	$5,000	$7,000	$10,000	$12,000	$15,000	$18,500	$32,500	$50,000 (e)
Auctions: $58,750, MS-64, January 2014; $47,000, MS-63, August 2014; $16,450, MS-62, October 2014; $11,750, AU-58, September 2014												
1803, 3 Over 2	33,506	314	57.5	45%	$4,000	$5,000	$7,000	$10,000	$12,000	$15,000	$18,500	$32,500	$50,000 (f)
Auctions: $12,925, MS-62, October 2014; $14,100, MS-62, November 2014; $20,563, MS-62, October 2013; $10,575, AU-58, August 2014												
1804, All kinds	30,475												
1804, Small 8		36	60.3	67%	$4,000	$5,000	$7,000	$10,000	$11,500	$15,500	$22,000	$32,500	$60,000
Auctions: $18,800, MS-62, January 2014; $10,575, AU-58, August 2014; $12,925, AU-55, August 2014; $5,875, AU-50, August 2014												
1804, Small 8 Over Large 8 (g)		64	59.4	56%	$4,000	$5,000	$7,000	$10,000	$12,500	$19,500	$25,000	$42,500	$75,000
Auctions: $32,900, MS-63, January 2014; $8,813, AU-53, August 2014; $8,813, AU-53, November 2014; $5,581, AU-50, September 2014												
1805	33,183	184	59.5	60%	$4,000	$5,000	$7,000	$10,000	$11,500	$15,000	$19,000	$32,500	$55,000 (h)
Auctions: $15,275, MS-62, August 2014; $14,688, MS-61, November 2014; $16,450, MS, February 2014; $12,925, AU-58, November 2014												
1806, Pointed-Top 6	9,676	73	57.3	51%	$4,000	$5,000	$7,000	$10,000	$12,000	$16,500	$20,000	$36,500	$60,000 (h)
Auctions: $15,275, MS-61, August 2014; $15,275, MS-60, August 2014; $7,638, EF-45, August 2013												
1806, Rounded-Top 6	54,417	164	58.8	54%	$4,000	$5,000	$7,000	$10,000	$11,500	$15,500	$19,000	$32,500	$50,000 (h)
Auctions: $111,625, MS-65, March 2013; $48,469, MS-64, August 2014; $19,388, MS-62, August 2014; $18,213, MS-62, October 2014												

b. 4 to 6 examples are known. **c.** Included in 1800 mintage figure. **d.** 18 to 25 examples are known. **e.** Value in MS-65 is $135,000.
f. Value in MS-65 is $125,000. **g.** Created when the engraver mistakenly used an 8 punch intended for $10 gold coins, then corrected the error by overpunching with a much smaller 8. **h.** Value in MS-65 is $120,000.

1807, Small Reverse Stars

1807, Large Reverse Stars

	Mintage	Cert	Avg	%MS	F-12	VF-20	EF-40	AU-50	AU-55	MS-60	MS-62	MS-63	MS-64
1807, All kinds	32,488												
1807, Small Reverse Stars		0	n/a					$10,000	$11,500	$15,500	$18,000	$32,500	$50,000
Auctions: $44,563, MS-64, January 2012													
1807, Large Reverse Stars		0	n/a					$10,000	$11,500	$15,500	$18,000	$32,500	$50,000
Auctions: $21,850, MS-63, January 2012													

CAPPED BUST TO LEFT (1807–1812)

Designer: *John Reich.* **Weight:** *8.75 grams.*
Composition: *.9167 gold, .0833 silver and copper.*
Diameter: *Approximately 25 mm.* **Edge:** *Reeded.*

BD-8.

History. This half eagle motif, designed by John Reich and stylistically related to his Capped Bust half dollar of 1807, was used for several years in the early 1800s. Quantities minted were high, and the coins saw wide circulation. No Proof examples were made of this type.

Striking and Sharpness. The striking usually is quite good and is significantly better than on earlier half eagle types. Adjustment marks (from overweight planchets being filed down to acceptable weight) are seen only occasionally. On the obverse, check the star centers and the hair details. On the reverse, check the eagle, particularity at the shield and the lower left. Examine the denticles on both sides.

Availability. After 1821 gold coins of this standard no longer circulated, as their bullion value exceeded their face value. Accordingly, they never sustained extensive wear, and nearly all examples are in EF or higher grades (coins used as pocket pieces or incorporated into jewelry are exceptions). As a type this issue is readily available in grades up to MS-63, although MS-64 and 65 coins are seen on occasion. Most have excellent eye appeal.

GRADING STANDARDS

MS-60 to 70 (Mint State). *Obverse:* At MS-60, some abrasion and contact marks are seen on the cheek, the hair below the LIB-ERTY inscription, and the highest-relief folds of the cap. Luster is present, but may be dull or lifeless, and interrupted in patches. At MS-63, contact marks are few, and abrasion is very light. At MS-64, abrasion is even less. An MS-65 coin has hardly any abrasion, and contact marks are minute. Luster should be

1808. Graded MS-60.

full and rich and is often more intense on the obverse. Grades above MS-65 are defined by having fewer marks as perfection is approached. *Reverse:* Comments apply as for the obverse, except that abrasion is most noticeable on the eagle's neck and the highest area of the wings.

Illustrated coin: This attractive Capped Bust to Left half eagle has nice luster.

AU-50, 53, 55, 58 (About Uncirculated). *Obverse:* Light wear is seen on the cheek and the higher-relief areas of the hair and cap. Friction and scattered marks are in the field, ranging from extensive at AU-50 to minimal at AU-58. Luster may be seen in protected areas, minimal at AU-50 but more evident at AU-58. On an AU-58 coin the field retains some luster as well. *Reverse:* Comments as preceding, except that the eagle's neck, the

1811, Tall 5. Graded AU-58.

top of the wings, the leaves, and the arrowheads now show noticeable wear, as do other features. Luster ranges from perhaps 40% remaining in protected areas (at AU-50) to nearly full mint bloom (at AU-58). Often the reverse of this type retains much more luster than the obverse, as the motto, eagle, and lettering protect the surrounding flat areas.

Illustrated coin: This lustrous example is well struck.

EF-40, 45 (Extremely Fine). *Obverse:* More wear is seen on the portrait, the hair, the cap, and the drapery near the clasp. Luster is minimal or nonexistent at EF-40, and may be slight at EF-45. *Reverse:* Wear is more extensive on the eagle, including the top of the wings, the head, the top of the shield, and the claws. Some traces of luster may be seen, more so at EF-45 than at EF-40.

1807; BD-8. Graded EF-40.

VF-20, 30 (Very Fine). *Obverse:* Wear on the portrait has reduced the hair detail, especially to the right of the face and the top of the head, but much can still be seen. *Reverse:* Wear on the eagle is greater, and details of feathers near the shield and near the top of the wings are weak or missing. All other features show wear, but most are fairly sharp. Generally, Capped Bust gold coins at this grade level lack eye appeal.

1807; BD-8. Graded VF-20.

The Capped Bust to Left half eagle is seldom collected in grades lower than VF-20.

| 1808, 8 Over 7 | 1808, Normal Date | 1809, 9 Over 8 |

| 1810, Small Date | 1810, Large Date |

| Small 5 | Large 5 | Tall 5 |

	Mintage	Cert	Avg	%MS	F-12	VF-20	EF-40	AU-50	AU-55	MS-60	MS-62	MS-63	MS-64
1807	51,605	244	58.6	51%	$3,000	$4,500	$5,500	$8,000	$9,500	$13,500	$15,500	$26,500	$35,500 (a)
Auctions: $76,375, MS-65, April 2013; $19,975, MS-63, October 2014; $11,750, MS-62, August 2014; $12,338, MS-62, November 2014													
1808, All kinds	55,578												
1808, 8 Over 7		47	58.7	57%	$3,250	$5,000	$6,500	$9,000	$11,000	$18,500	$25,000	$35,000	$65,000
Auctions: $24,675, MS-62, August 2014; $19,388, MS-61, June 2014													
1808		177	58.2	53%	$3,000	$4,500	$5,500	$8,000	$9,500	$13,500	$15,500	$28,500	$35,500 (b)
Auctions: $25,850, MS-63, March 2013; $12,925, MS-60, October 2014; $11,750, AU-58, November 2014; $7,638, AU-58, November 2014													
1809, 9 Over 8	33,875	180	58.6	56%	$3,000	$4,500	$5,500	$8,500	$9,000	$13,500	$15,500	$28,500	$50,000
Auctions: $51,406, MS-64, January 2014; $11,750, MS-61, August 2014; $8,001, AU-53, August 2014													
1810, All kinds	100,287												
1810, Small Date, Small 5		6	54.8	33%	$20,000	$40,000	$55,000	$90,000	$110,000				
Auctions: $18,800, AU-50, January 2014													
1810, Small Date, Tall 5		83	57.8	53%	$3,000	$4,500	$5,500	$8,000	$9,500	$14,000	$16,000	$30,000	$55,000
Auctions: $12,925, MS-62, January 2014; $12,925, MS-62, August 2014; $12,925, AU-58, September 2014													
1810, Large Date, Small 5		83	57.7	53%	$30,000	$45,000	$75,000	$90,000	$110,000	$175,000			
Auctions: No auction records available.													
1810, Large Date, Large 5		249	59.3	63%	$3,000	$4,500	$5,500	$8,000	$9,500	$13,500	$15,500	$28,500	$40,000 (c)
Auctions: $32,900, MS-64, January 2014; $18,213, MS-63, September 2014; $11,750, MS-62, November 2014; $8,813, AU-58, August 2014													

a. Value in MS-65 is $100,000. **b.** Value in MS-65 is $127,500. **c.** Value in MS-65 is $100,000.

	Mintage	Cert	Avg	%MS	F-12	VF-20	EF-40	AU-50	AU-55	MS-60	MS-62	MS-63	MS-64
1811, All kinds	99,581												
1811, Small 5		24	56.0	50%	$3,000	$4,500	$5,500	$8,000	$9,500	$13,500	$15,500	$28,500	$40,000 (c)
Auctions: $64,625, MS-64, August 2013; $10,575, MS-61, July 2014; $4,994, MS-60, October 2014; $3,836, AU-50, September 2014													
1811, Tall 5		44	58.8	61%	$3,000	$4,500	$5,500	$8,000	$9,500	$13,500	$15,500	$28,500	$40,000 (c)
Auctions: $76,375, MS-65, August 2013; $9,400, AU-58, August 2014; $1,880, EF-40, July 2014; $3,055, EF-40, September 2014													
1812	58,087	217	59.0	65%	$3,000	$4,500	$5,500	$8,000	$9,500	$13,500	$15,500	$28,500	$40,000
Auctions: $30,550, MS-64, November 2014; $61,688, MS-64, August 2013													

c. Value in MS-65 is $100,000.

CAPPED HEAD TO LEFT (1813–1834)

Designer: *John Reich (design modified by William Kneass in 1829).*
Weight: *8.75 grams.* **Composition:** *.9167 gold, .0833 silver and copper.*
Diameter: *25 mm (reduced to 23.8 mm in 1829).* **Edge:** *Reeded.*

Circulation Strike
BD-1.

Proof
BD-3.

History. Half eagles of the Capped Head to Left design are divided into issues of 1813 to 1829 (with a larger diameter), and issues of 1829 to 1834 (with a smaller diameter, and smaller letters, dates, and stars). Those dated 1813 to 1815 are in bold relief and sometimes collected as a separate variety.

Striking and Sharpness. On the obverse, check the star centers and the hair details (these details are usually less distinct on the 1829–1834 smaller-diameter coins). On the reverse, check the eagle. Most examples are well struck. Adjustment marks (from overweight planchets being filed down to acceptable specifications at the mint) are not often encountered. Proof coins were struck on a limited basis for inclusion in sets and for numismatists. Over the years some prooflike Mint State pieces have been classified as Proofs.

Availability. The 1813 and 1814, 4 Over 3, are seen with some frequency and constitute the main supply available for assembling type sets. Other dates range from very rare to extremely rare, with the 1822 topping the list (just three are known, two of which are in the Smithsonian Institution). As gold coins did not circulate after 1821, issues of 1813 to 1820 are usually seen in high-level AU or in MS, and those of the 1820s in MS. The half eagles of the early 1830s are exceptions; these usually show light wear and are much rarer in high-level MS. All Proofs are exceedingly rare.

GRADING STANDARDS

MS-60 to 70 (Mint State). *Obverse:* At MS-60, some abrasion and contact marks are seen on the cheek, the hair below the LIBERTY inscription, and the highest-relief folds of the cap. Luster is present, but may be dull or lifeless, and interrupted in patches. At MS-63, contact marks are few, and abrasion is very light. At MS-64, abrasion is even less. An MS-65 coin has hardly any abrasion, and

1832, 13 Obverse Stars; BD-1. Graded MS-63.

contact marks are minute. Luster should be full and rich and is often more intense on the obverse. Grades above MS-65 are defined by having fewer marks as perfection is approached. *Reverse:* Comments apply as for the obverse, except that abrasion is most noticeable on the eagle's neck and the highest area of the wings.

AU-50, 53, 55, 58 (About Uncirculated). *Obverse:* Light wear is seen on the cheek and the higher-relief areas of the hair and cap. Friction and scattered marks are in the field, ranging from extensive at AU-50 to minimal at AU-58. Luster may be seen in protected areas, minimal at AU-50 but more evident at AU-58. On an AU-58 coin the field retains some luster as well. *Reverse:* Comments as preceding, except that the eagle's neck, the

1813; BD-1. Graded AU-50.

top of the wings, the leaves, and the arrowheads now show noticeable wear, as do other features. Luster ranges from perhaps 40% remaining in protected areas (at AU-50) to nearly full mint bloom (at AU-58). Often the reverse of this type retains much more luster than the obverse, as the motto, eagle, and lettering protect the surrounding flat areas.

EF-40, 45 (Extremely Fine). *Obverse:* More wear is seen on the portrait, the hair, the cap, and the drapery near the clasp. Luster is minimal or nonexistent at EF-40, and may be slight at EF-45. *Reverse:* Wear is more extensive on the eagle, including the top of the wings, the head, the top of the shield, and the claws. Some traces of luster may be seen, more so at EF-45 than at EF-40.

The Capped Head half eagle is seldom collected in grades lower than EF-40.

1813; BD-1. Graded EF-45.

PF-60 to 70 (Proof). *Obverse and Reverse:* PF-60 to 62 coins have extensive hairlines and may have nicks and contact marks. At PF-63, hairlines are prominent, but the mirror surface is very reflective. PF-64 coins have fewer hairlines. At PF-65, hairlines should be minimal and mostly seen only under magnification. There should be no nicks or marks. PF-66 and higher coins should have no marks or hairlines visible to the unaided eye.

1829, Small Date, Reduced Diameter; BD-2. Proof.

1820, Curved-Base 2

1820, Square-Base 2

1820, Small Letters

1820, Large Letters

	Mintage	Cert	Avg	%MS	F-12	VF-20	EF-40	AU-50	AU-55	MS-60	MS-62	MS-63	MS-64
											PF-63	PF-64	PF-65
1813	95,428	274	58.8	57%	$4,750	$5,750	$7,000	$10,000	$11,000	$15,000	$17,500	$27,500	$40,000 (a)
Auctions: $49,350, MS-64, January 2013; $15,863, MS-62, August 2014; $6,463, MS-60, September 2014; $9,400, AU-55, October 2014													
1814, 4 Over 3	15,454	63	59.8	67%	$5,000	$6,500	$8,500	$11,000	$12,000	$18,500	$25,000	$35,000	$55,000
Auctions: $14,688, AU-58, January 2014; $11,764, AU-55, November 2014													
1815 (b)	635	4	57.8	50%			$175,000	$250,000	$300,000	$450,000	$550,000	$750,000	
Auctions: $460,000, MS-64, January 2009													
1818, All kinds	48,588												
1818		36	59.8	61%	$5,000	$6,000	$7,500	$15,500	$18,500	$25,000	$28,000	$45,000	$75,000 (c)
Auctions: $38,188, MS-62, November 2014; $19,388, MS-62, November 2014; $15,863, AU-50, September 2013													
1818, STATESOF one word		41	60.3	71%	$5,000	$6,000	$7,500	$13,000	$18,000	$25,000	$30,000	$47,500	$75,000
Auctions: $23,500, MS-62, January 2014; $4,994, AU-50, September 2014													
1818, 5D Over 50		6	62.5	100%	$5,000	$6,500	$8,000	$11,000	$15,000	$30,000	$35,000	$70,000	$75,000 (d)
Auctions: $135,125, MS-65, January 2014													
1819, All kinds	51,723												
1819		3	51.7	33%			$50,000	$70,000	$85,000	$115,000			
Auctions: $38,188, AU-50, August 2014													
1819, 5D Over 50		7	55.6	29%			$50,000	$65,000	$80,000	$125,000	$145,000	$200,000	
Auctions: $67,563, AU-55, January 2014													
1820, All kinds	263,806												
1820, Curved-Base 2, Small Letters		1	62.0	100%	$5,250	$7,000	$11,000	$14,000	$20,000	$28,000	$32,500	$47,500	$80,000
Auctions: $172,500, MS-64, January 2012													
1820, Curved-Base 2, Large Letters		1	64.5	100%	$5,000	$6,750	$8,500	$12,500	$17,500	$25,000	$27,500	$37,500	$55,000
Auctions: $19,975, MS-60, January 2014; $11,750, MS-60, September 2014													
1820, Square-Base 2		5	62.2	100%	$5,000	$6,750	$8,000	$10,000	$11,500	$17,500	$24,000	$35,000	$50,000
Auctions: $31,725, MS-63, January 2014													
1820, Square-Base 2, Proof (e)	2–3	1	64.0		(unique, in the Bass Foundation Collection)								
Auctions: No auction records available.													
1821	34,641	6	56.7	50%	$20,000	$30,000	$50,000	$85,000	$125,000	$200,000	$250,000	$375,000	
Auctions: $540,000, MS-63+, January 2015; $141,000, AU-55, January 2014													
1821, Proof (f)	3–5	0	n/a		(extremely rare)								
Auctions: No auction records available.													
1822 (g)	17,796	1	40.0	0%						$5,000,000			
Auctions: No auction records available.													
1822, Proof (h)	unknown	0	n/a		(extremely rare)								
Auctions: No auction records available.													

a. Value in MS-65 is $95,000. **b.** 11 examples are known. **c.** Value in MS-65 is $135,000. **d.** Value in MS-65 is $140,000. **e.** Some experts have questioned the Proof status of this unique piece; the surface of the coin is reflective, but it is not as convincing as other true Proofs of the type. Prior claims that as many as four Proofs exist of this date have not been substantiated. **f.** 2 examples are known. One is in the Harry W. Bass Jr. Foundation Collection, and another is in the Smithsonian's National Numismatic Collection. **g.** 3 examples are known. **h.** 3 examples are known, though the Proof status of these pieces has been questioned.

1825, 5 Over Partial 4

1825, 5 Over 4

1828, 8 Over 7

1829, Large Date
BD-1.

1829, Small Date
BD-2.

	Mintage	Cert	Avg	%MS	F-12	VF-20	EF-40	AU-50	AU-55	MS-60	MS-62 / PF-63	MS-63 / PF-64	MS-64 / PF-65
1823	14,485	25	57.0	48%	$8,500	$10,000	$15,000	$20,000	$25,000	$35,000	$40,000	$65,000	$85,000
Auctions: $82,250, MS-64, January 2014; $29,375, MS-62, August 2014													
1823, Proof (i)	unknown	0	n/a										
Auctions: No auction records available.													
1824	17,340	16	60.4	63%	$15,000	$22,500	$32,000	$40,000	$60,000	$85,000	$92,000	$125,000	$135,000 (j)
Auctions: $199,750, MS-65, January 2014													
1824, Proof (k)	unknown	0	n/a										
Auctions: No auction records available.													
1825, 5 Over Partial 4 (l)	29,060	7	61.4	86%	$14,000	$20,000	$30,000	$37,500	$47,500	$67,500	$85,000	$100,000	$125,000
Auctions: $99,875, MS-61, January 2014													
1825, 5 Over 4 (m)	(n)	2	56.5	50%			$500,000	$675,000					
Auctions: $690,000, AU-50, July 2008													
1825, 5 Over Partial 4, Proof (o)	1–2	0	n/a		(unique, in the Smithsonian's National Numismatic Collection)								
Auctions: No auction records available.													
1826	18,069	7	63.4	100%	$10,000	$15,000	$20,000	$30,000	$40,000	$55,000	$65,000	$85,000	
Auctions: $546,000, MS-66, Jauary 2015; $763,750, MS-66, January 2014													
1826, Proof	2–4	0	n/a		(unique, in the Smithsonian's National Numismatic Collection)								
Auctions: No auction records available.													
1827	24,913	14	62.9	93%	$20,000	$25,000	$30,000	$40,000	$50,000	$65,000	$75,000	$115,000	$150,000
Auctions: $141,000, MS-64, January 2014													
1827, Proof (p)	unknown	0	n/a										
Auctions: No auction records available.													
1828, 8 Over 7 (q)	(r)	3	63.3	100%		$65,000	$85,000	$100,000	$150,000	$250,000	$350,000	$450,000	$650,000
Auctions: $632,500, MS-64, January 2012													
1828	28,029	3	60.7	67%		$45,000	$60,000	$75,000	$100,000	$175,000	$200,000	$300,000	$450,000
Auctions: $499,375, MS-64, April 2013													
1828, Proof	1–2	0	n/a		(unique, in the Smithsonian's National Numismatic Collection)								
Auctions: No auction records available.													
1829, Large Date	57,442	2	66.0	100%							$200,000	$250,000	$400,000
Auctions: No auction records available.													
1829, Large Date, Proof	2–4	0	n/a										$2,000,000
Auctions: No auction records available.													

i. The only auction references for a Proof 1823 half eagle are from 1885 and 1962. Neither coin (assuming they are not the same specimen) has been examined by today's standards to confirm its Proof status. j. Value in MS-65 is $275,000. k. No 1824 Proof half eagles are known to exist, despite previous claims that the Smithsonian's Mint collection specimen (actually an MS-62 circulation strike) is a Proof. l. Sometimes called 1825, 5 Over 1. m. 2 examples are known. n. Included in circulation-strike 1825, 5 Over Partial 4, mintage figure. o. The Smithsonian's example is a PF-67 with a mirrored obverse and frosty reverse. A second example, reported to have resided in King Farouk's collection, has not been confirmed. p. Two purported 1827 Proofs have been revealed to be circulation strikes: the Smithsonian's example is an MS-64, and the Bass example is prooflike. q. 5 examples are known. r. Included in circulation-strike 1828 mintage figure.

Small 5 D.

Large 5 D.

1832, Curved-Base 2,
12-Star Obverse

1832, Curved-Base 2,
13-Star Obverse

1833, Large Date

1833, Small Date

1834, Plain 4

1834, Crosslet 4

	Mintage	Cert	Avg	%MS	F-12	VF-20	EF-40	AU-50	AU-55	MS-60	MS-62	MS-63
										PF-63	PF-64	PF-65
1829, Sm Dt, Reduced Diameter	(a)	2	61.5	100%	$45,000	$75,000	$125,000	$165,000	$225,000	$300,000	$350,000	$500,000
Auctions: $431,250, MS-61, January 2012												
1829, Small Date, Proof (b)	2–4	0	n/a		*(extremely rare)*							
Auctions: No auction records available.												
1830, Small or Large 5 D. (c)	126,351	21	60.0	71%	$20,000	$27,500	$40,000	$45,000	$52,500	$75,000	$80,000	$100,000
Auctions: $73,438, MS-63, January 2014; $47,000, AU-58, August 2014; $41,125, AU-58, October 2014												
1830, Proof (d)	2–4	2	63.5		*(extremely rare)*							
Auctions: No auction records available.												
1831, Small or Large 5 D. (e)	140,594	12	60.7	67%	$20,000	$27,500	$40,000	$45,000	$52,500	$75,000	$80,000	$100,000
Auctions: $82,250, MS-61, January 2014												
1832, Curved-Base 2, 12 Stars (f)	(g)	2	60.5	50%		$300,000	$350,000	$450,000				
Auctions: No auction records available.												
1832, Square-Base 2, 13 Stars	157,487	12	61.8	75%	$20,000	$27,500	$40,000	$45,000	$55,000	$70,000	$75,000	$100,000 (h)
Auctions: $176,250, MS-65, January 2014												
1832, Square-Base 2, 13 Stars, Proof	2–3	0	n/a		*(extremely rare)*							
Auctions: No auction records available.												
1833, Large Date	196,630	1	65.0	100%	$20,000	$27,500	$40,000	$45,000	$52,500	$67,500	$75,000	$100,000 (i)
Auctions: $29,375, AU-50, April 2014												
1833, Small Date (j)	(k)	1	61.0	100%	$20,000	$27,500	$40,000	$45,000	$52,500	$70,000	$100,000	$120,000 (l)
Auctions: $126,500, MS-63 PQ, May 2006												
1833, Proof (m)	4–6	4	61.3		*(extremely rare)*							
Auctions: $977,500, PF-67, January 2005												
1834, All kinds	50,141											
1834, Plain 4		17	58.3	53%	$20,000	$27,500	$37,500	$45,000	$52,500	$85,000	$90,000	$100,000
Auctions: $143,750, MS-65, August 2011												
1834, Crosslet 4		10	58.2	60%	$21,500	$30,000	$40,000	$47,500	$57,000	$85,000	$110,000	$125,000
Auctions: $45,531, AU-55, January 2014												

a. Included in circulation-strike 1829, Large Date, mintage figure (see chart on page 1036). **b.** 2 examples are known. One is in the Harry W. Bass Jr. Foundation Collection, and another of equal quality (PF-66) is in the Smithsonian's National Numismatic Collection. **c.** The 1830, Small 5 D. is slightly rarer than the Large 5 D. Certified population reports are unclear, and auction-lot catalogers typically do not differentiate between the two varieties. **d.** 2 examples are known. One is in the Byron Reed collection at the Durham Museum, Omaha, Nebraska. **e.** The 1831, Small 5 D. is estimated to be three to four times rarer than the Large 5 D. Both are extremely rare. **f.** 5 examples are known. **g.** Included in circulation-strike 1832, Square-Base 2, 13 Stars, mintage figure. **h.** Value in MS-64 is $135,000. **i.** Value in MS-64 is $130,000. **j.** The 1833 Small Date is slightly scarcer than the Large Date. **k.** Included in 1833, Large Date, mintage figure. **l.** Value in MS-64 is $150,000. **m.** 4 or 5 examples are known.

CLASSIC HEAD, NO MOTTO ON REVERSE (1834–1838)

Designer: *William Kneass.* **Weight:** *8.36 grams.*
Composition: *(1834–1836) .8992 gold, .1008 silver and copper; (1837–1838) .900 gold.*
Diameter: *22.5 mm.* **Edge:** *Reeded.* **Mints:** *Philadelphia, Charlotte, Dahlonega.*

Circulation Strike Breen-6518.	*Mintmark location is on the obverse, above the date.*	**Proof**

History. U.S. Mint chief engraver William Kneass based the half eagle's Classic Head design on John Reich's cent of 1808. Minted under the Act of June 28, 1834, the coins' reduced size and weight encouraged circulation over melting or export, and they served American commerce until hoarding became extensive during the Civil War. Accordingly, many show considerable wear.

Striking and Sharpness. On the obverse, weakness is often seen on the higher areas of the hair curls. Also check the star centers. On the reverse, check the rims. The denticles are usually well struck.

Availability. Most coins range from VF to AU or lower grades of MS. Most MS coins are dated 1834. MS-63 and better examples are rare. Good eye appeal can be elusive. Proofs of the Classic Head type were made in small quantities, and today probably only a couple dozen or so survive, most bearing the 1834 date.

GRADING STANDARDS

MS-60 to 70 (Mint State). *Obverse:* At MS-60, some abrasion and contact marks are seen on the portrait, most noticeably on the cheek, as the hair details are complex on this type. Luster is present, but may be dull or lifeless, and interrupted in patches. Many low-level Mint State coins have grainy surfaces. At MS-63, contact marks are few, and abrasion is very light. Abrasion is even less at MS-64. An MS-65 coin will have hardly any

1834, Plain 4. Graded MS-65.

abrasion, and contact marks are minute. Luster should be full and rich and is often more intense on the obverse. Grades above MS-65 are defined by having fewer marks as perfection is approached. *Reverse:* Comments apply as for the obverse, except that abrasion is most noticeable in the field, on the eagle's neck, and on the highest area of the wings. Most Mint State coins in the marketplace are graded liberally, with slight abrasion on both sides of MS-65 coins.

Illustrated coin: This well-struck coin has some light abrasion, most evident in the reverse field.

AU-50, 53, 55, 58 (About Uncirculated).

Obverse: Friction is seen on the higher parts, particularly the cheek and the hair (under magnification) of Miss Liberty. Friction and scattered marks are in the field, ranging from extensive at AU-50 to minimal at AU-58. Luster may be seen in protected areas, minimal at AU-50, more evident at AU-58. On an AU-58 coin the field retains some luster as well. *Reverse:* Comments as preceding, except

1834, Crosslet 4. Graded AU-50.

that the eagle's neck, the top of the wings, the leaves, and the arrowheads now show noticeable wear, as do other features. Luster ranges from perhaps 40% remaining in protected areas (at AU-50) to nearly full mint bloom (at AU-58). Often the reverse of this type retains much more luster than the obverse.

EF-40, 45 (Extremely Fine).

Obverse: Wear is seen on the portrait overall, with reduction or elimination of some separation of hair strands, especially in the area close to the face. The cheek shows light wear. Luster is minimal or nonexistent at EF-40, and may survive in among the letters of LIBERTY at EF-45. *Reverse:* Wear is greater than on an About Uncirculated coin. On most (but not all) coins the neck lacks some feather detail

1837, Script 8. Graded EF-40.

on its highest points. Feathers have lost some detail near the edges and tips of the wings, and some areas of the horizontal lines in the shield may be blended together. Some traces of luster may be seen, more so at EF-45 than at EF-40.

VF-20, 30 (Very Fine).

Obverse: Wear on the portrait has reduced the hair detail, especially to the right of the face and the top of the head, but much can still be seen. *Reverse:* Wear is greater, including on the shield and the wing feathers. Generally, Classic Head gold at this grade level lacks eye appeal.

The Classic Head half eagle is seldom collected in grades lower than VF-20.

1835, Block 8. Graded VF-30.

PF-60 to 70 (Proof). *Obverse and Reverse:* PF-60 to 62 coins have extensive hairlines and may have nicks and contact marks. At PF-63, hairlines are prominent, but the mirror surface is very reflective. PF-64 coins have fewer hairlines. At PF-65, hairlines should be minimal and mostly seen only under magnification. There should be no nicks or marks. PF-66 and higher coins should have no marks or hairlines visible to the unaided eye.

1834, Plain 4. Graded PF-65.

1834, Plain 4   1834, Crosslet 4

	Mintage	Cert	Avg	%MS	VF-20	EF-40	AU-50	AU-55	MS-60	MS-62 / PF-63	MS-63 / PF-64	MS-64 / PF-65
1834, Plain 4 (a)	657,460	2,062	51.4	13%	$675	$800	$1,350	$1,700	$4,500	$7,000	$10,500	$18,500
Auctions: $99,875, MS-65, August 2014; $21,150, MS-64, April 2013; $4,847, MS-61, October 2014; $1,909, AU-58, September 2014												
1834, Crosslet 4	(b)	89	46.8	12%	$2,250	$4,000	$6,000	$9,000	$22,500	$27,500	$55,000	$100,000
Auctions: $22,913, MS-62, April 2013; $9,400, MS-60, July 2014; $45,531, AU-55, January 2014; $6,580, AU-55, July 2014												
1834, Plain 4, Proof	8–12	6	63.2							$95,000	$150,000	$250,000
Auctions: $109,250, PF-63Cam, January 2011												
1835 (a)	371,534	694	51.6	15%	$675	$900	$1,450	$1,800	$4,500	$7,000	$11,500	$25,000
Auctions: $21,150, MS-64, March 2014; $4,406, MS-62, August 2014; $7,050, MS-62, November 2014; $3,819, MS-61, October 2014												
1835, Proof (c)	4–6	1	68.0							$115,000	$175,000	$325,000
Auctions: $690,000, PF-67, January 2005												
1836	553,147	1,159	50.3	12%	$675	$900	$1,450	$1,800	$4,500	$7,000	$11,500	$25,000
Auctions: $16,450, MS-63, February 2013; $4,113, MS-62, August 2014; $2,468, AU-58, August 2014; $6,463, EF-40, October 2014												
1836, Proof (d)	4–6	2	67.3				*(extremely rare)*					
Auctions: No auction records available.												
1837 (a)	207,121	432	50.9	12%	$675	$975	$1,550	$2,000	$4,750	$9,000	$17,000	$35,000
Auctions: $21,738, MS-63, October 2013; $9,400, MS-62, August 2014; $3,525, MS-61, November 2014; $1,763, AU-55, August 2014												
1837, Proof	4–6	0	n/a				*(unique, in the Smithsonian's National Numismatic Collection)*					
Auctions: No auction records available.												
1838	286,588	666	51.8	14%	$375	$975	$1,500	$2,050	$4,500	$7,000	$11,500	$25,000
Auctions: $32,900, MS-64, August 2014; $7,638, MS-62, August 2014; $5,875, MS-62, October 2014; $5,875, MS-62, March 2013												
1838, Proof	2–3	1	65.0				*(unique, in the Bass Foundation Collection)*					
Auctions: No auction records available.												
1838C	17,179	105	44.4	4%	$4,500	$7,250	$12,500	$22,000	$42,500	$62,500	$100,000	
Auctions: $10,575, EF-40, August 2013; $1,645, VF-20, November 2014												
1838D	20,583	133	49.7	8%	$4,000	$7,000	$11,500	$17,000	$32,500	$50,000	$85,000	
Auctions: $21,150, MS-60, January 2014; $21,738, AU-55, August 2014; $1,880, VF-20, November 2014												

a. Varieties have either a script 8 or block-style 8 in the date. (See illustrations of similar quarter eagles on page 994.) **b.** Included in circulation-strike, 1838, Plain 4, mintage figure. **c.** 3 or 4 examples are known. **d.** 3 or 4 examples are known.

LIBERTY HEAD (1839–1908)

Designer: *Christian Gobrecht.* **Weight:** *8.359 grams.*
Composition: *.900 gold, .100 copper (net weight .24187 oz. pure gold).*
Diameter: *(1839–1840) 22.5 mm; (1840–1908) 21.6 mm.* **Edge:** *Reeded.*
Mints: *Philadelphia, Charlotte, Dahlonega, Denver, New Orleans, San Francisco, Carson City.*

Circulation Strike	Mintmark location, 1839, is on the obverse, above the date.	Mintmark location, 1840–1908, is on the reverse, below the eagle.	**Proof**

History. Christian Gobrecht's Liberty Head half eagle design was introduced in 1839. The mintmark (for branch-mint coins) in that year was located on the obverse; for all later issues it was relocated to the reverse. The motto IN GOD WE TRUST was added to the reverse in 1866.

Striking and Sharpness. On the obverse, check the highest points of the hair and the star centers; the reverse, the eagle's neck, the area to the lower left of the shield, and the lower part of the eagle. Generally, the eagle on the $5 coins is better struck than on quarter eagles. Examine the denticles on both sides. Branch-mint coins struck before the Civil War are often lightly struck in areas. San Francisco half eagles are in lower average grades than are those from the Philadelphia Mint, as Philadelphia coins did not circulate at par in the East and Midwest from late December 1861 until December 1878, thus acquiring less wear. Most late 19th- and early 20th-century coins are sharp in all areas; for these issues, tiny copper staining spots (from improperly mixed coinage alloy) can be a problem. Cameo contrast is the rule for Proofs prior to 1902. Beginning that year the portrait was polished in the die, although a few years later cameo-contrast coins were again made.

Availability. Early dates and mintmarks are typically scarce to rare in MS, very rare in MS-63 to MS-65. Charlotte and Dahlonega coins are usually EF or AU, or overgraded as low MS, as seen with quarter eagles. The 1854-S and several varieties in the 1860s and 1870s are rare. Coins from 1880 onward are seen in higher than average grades. Proof coins exist in relation to their original mintages; issues prior to the 1890s are rare.

Note: Values of common-date gold coins have been based on the current bullion price of gold, $1,200 per ounce, and may vary with the prevailing spot price.

GRADING STANDARDS

MS-60 to 70 (Mint State). *Obverse:* At MS-60, some abrasion and contact marks are evident, most noticeably on the hair to the right of Miss Liberty's forehead and on the jaw. Luster is present, but may be dull or lifeless, and interrupted in patches. At MS-63, contact marks are few, and abrasion is very light. An MS-65 coin has only slight abrasion, and contact marks are so minute as to require

1848-C. Graded MS-63.

magnification. Luster should be full and rich. Grades above MS-65 are defined by having fewer marks as perfection is approached. *Reverse:* Comments apply as for the obverse, except that abrasion and contact marks are most noticeable on the eagle's neck and to the lower left of the shield.

Illustrated coin: Friction is seen in the obverse fields amid luster; on the reverse, luster is nearly complete.

AU-50, 53, 55, 58 (About Uncirculated).
Obverse: Light wear is seen on the face, the hair to the right of the face, and the highest area of the hair bun, more so at AU-50 than at 53 or 55. An AU-58 coin has minimal traces of wear. An AU-50 coin has luster in protected areas among the stars and letters, with little in the open fields or on the portrait. At AU-58, most luster is present in the fields, but is worn away on the highest parts

1840. Graded AU-55.

of the motifs. Striking must be taken into consideration, for a lightly struck coin can be About Uncirculated, but be weak in the central areas. *Reverse:* Comments as preceding, except that the eagle shows wear in all of the higher areas, as well as the leaves and arrowheads. From 1866 to 1908 the motto IN GOD WE TRUST helped protect the field, with the result that luster is more extensive on this side in comparison to the obverse. Luster ranges from perhaps 50% remaining in protected areas (at AU-50) to nearly full mint bloom (at AU-58).

EF-40, 45 (Extremely Fine). *Obverse:* Wear is evident on all high areas of the portrait, including the hair to the right of the forehead, the tip of the coronet, the back of the head, and the hair bun. The stars show light wear at their centers (unless protected by a high rim). Luster, if present at all, is minimal and in protected areas such as between the star points. *Reverse:* Wear is greater than on an About Uncirculated coin, and flatness is

1844. Graded EF-40.

seen on the feather ends, the leaves, and elsewhere. Some traces of luster may be seen, more so at EF-45 than at EF-40. Overall, the reverse appears to be in a slightly higher grade than the obverse on coins from 1866 to 1908 (With Motto).

    Illustrated coin: This coin is well struck on both sides.

VF-20, 30 (Very Fine). *Obverse:* The higher-relief areas of hair are worn flat at VF-20, less so at VF-30. The hair to the right of the coronet is merged into heavy strands. The stars are flat at their centers. *Reverse:* Feather detail is mostly worn away on the neck and legs, less so on the wings. The vertical shield stripes, being deeply recessed, remain bold.

1858-C. Graded VF-20.

    The Liberty Head half eagle is seldom collected in grades lower than VF-20.

PF-60 to 70 (Proof). *Obverse and Reverse:* PF-60 to 62 coins have extensive hairlines and may have nicks and contact marks. At PF-63, hairlines are prominent, but the mirror surface is very reflective. PF-64 coins have fewer hairlines. At PF-65, hairlines should be minimal and mostly seen only under magnification. There should be no nicks or marks. PF-66 and higher coins should have no marks or hairlines visible to the unaided eye.

1872. Graded PF-55.

	Mintage	Cert	Avg	%MS	VF-20	EF-40	AU-50	AU-55	MS-60	MS-63	MS-64	MS-65
										PF-63	PF-64	PF-65
1839	118,143	233	51.2	15%	$500	$600	$1,100	$1,200	$3,750	$23,500	$35,000	
	Auctions: $41,125, MS-64, January 2014; $1,058, AU-53, August 2014											
1839, Proof (a)	2–3	1	61.0		*(extremely rare)*							
	Auctions: $184,000, PF-61, January 2010											
1839C	17,205	84	48.8	15%	$2,250	$3,500	$6,000	$9,500	$20,000	$60,000		
	Auctions: $23,500, MS-61, January 2014; $4,406, AU-50, November 2014; $3,290, EF-40, August 2014											
1839D	18,939	107	46.1	4%	$2,750	$4,000	$7,000	$10,000	$23,500			
	Auctions: $9,400, AU-53, September 2013; $2,350, EF-40, November 2014											
1840 (b)	137,382	316	51.3	9%	$5,000	$625	$1,100	$1,600	$3,250	$10,000	$23,000	
	Auctions: $4,994, MS-61, March 2013; $823, AU-53, November 2014; $823, AU-50, August 2014											
1840, Proof	2–3	0	n/a		*(unique, in the Smithsonian's National Numismatic Collection)*							
	Auctions: No auction records available.											
1840C	18,992	88	48.1	10%	$2,250	$3,500	$6,500	$7,000	$20,000	$55,000	$95,000	
	Auctions: $28,200, MS-62, January 2014; $4,994, AU-50, September 2014; $1,645, VF-20, August 2014											
1840D	22,896	67	50.1	18%	$2,250	$3,500	$6,000	$6,750	$14,000	$42,500		
	Auctions: $14,100, MS-61, December 2013; $881, F-12, August 2014											
1840O (b)	40,120	143	51.1	12%	$600	$900	$1,500	$2,400	$9,000	$32,000		
	Auctions: $9,988, MS-61, April 2014; $8,813, MS-61, August 2014; $7,638, MS-61, November 2014; $3,408, AU-58, September 2014											
1841	15,833	66	53.1	29%	$550	$700	$1,250	$1,600	$4,500	$10,250	$17,500	$36,000
	Auctions: $1,763, AU-55, December 2013											
1841, Proof (c)	2–3	1	63.0		*(extremely rare)*							
	Auctions: No auction records available.											
1841C	21,467	84	48.6	8%	$1,850	$2,500	$3,500	$6,000	$12,500	$40,000	$80,000	
	Auctions: $5,581, AU-58, January 2014; $1,705, VF-35, August 2014											
1841D	27,492	99	49.8	22%	$2,000	$2,750	$4,000	$6,500	$12,000	$25,000	$75,000	
	Auctions: $9,988, MS-61, January 2014; $8,578, MS-60, August 2014											
1841O (d)	50	0	n/a									
	Auctions: No auction records available.											

a. 2 or 3 examples are known. **b.** Scarce varieties of the 1840 coins have the fine edge-reeding and wide rims of the 1839 issues. This is referred to as the broad-mill variety. **c.** 2 examples are known. One is in the Smithsonian's National Numismatic Collection; the other is ex Eliasberg Collection. **d.** Official Mint records report 8,350 coins struck at the New Orleans Mint in 1841. However, most—if not all—were actually dated 1840. No 1841-O half eagle has ever appeared on the market.

Small Letters   **Large Letters**

Small Date   **Large Date**

	Mintage	Cert	Avg	%MS	VF-20	EF-40	AU-50	AU-55	MS-60	MS-63 / PF-63	MS-64 / PF-64	MS-65 / PF-65
1842, All kinds	27,578											
1842, Small Letters		24	54.8	21%	$550	$1,000	$3,000	$4,000	$11,000	$22,000	$35,000	$65,000
Auctions: $15,275, MS-62, January 2014												
1842, Large Letters		17	48.9	0%	$725	$1,600	$4,250	$6,500	$13,500	$25,000		
Auctions: $4,113, AU-55, April 2014; $4,700, AU-55, August 2014												
1842, Small Letters, Proof (e)	4–6	1	64.5		*(extremely rare)*							
Auctions: $172,500, PF-64Cam★, January 2009												
1842C, All kinds	27,432											
1842C, Small Date		24	51.4	21%	$7,500	$15,500	$25,000	$30,000	$70,000	$125,000		
Auctions: $49,938, AU-58, January 2014; $49,938, AU-58, July 2014; $13,527, EF-45, November 2014; $15,275, EF-40, August 2014												
1842C, Large Date		112	51.4	13%	$2,000	$2,500	$3,500	$4,750	$13,500	$30,000	$47,500	
Auctions: $25,850, MS-63, September 2013; $11,750, MS-61, November 2014												
1842D, All kinds	59,608											
1842D, Small Date		150	45.8	5%	$2,000	$2,750	$3,750	$5,000	$10,500	$30,000		
Auctions: $16,450, MS-62, April 2014; $3,966, AU-55, September 2014; $2,350, EF-45, July 2014; $999, VF-20, August 2014												
1842D, Large Date		24	44.1	4%	$3,000	$5,500	$11,000	$17,500	$37,500			
Auctions: $7,050, MS-60, January 2014												
1842O	16,400	49	45.1	4%	$1,250	$3,000	$8,000	$12,500	$20,000	$45,000		
Auctions: $7,638, AU-53, January 2014; $646, VF-20, August 2014												
1843	611,205	480	53.8	16%	$550	$575	$600	$650	$1,650	$9,000	$17,000	$37,500
Auctions: $8,813, MS-63, October 2013; $541, AU-55, July 2014; $482, AU-55, November 2014; $529, AU-50, July 2014												
1843, Proof (f)	4–8	4	64.0		*(extremely rare)*							
Auctions: $34,500, PF-58, August 2009												
1843C	44,277	150	45.1	9%	$2,000	$2,500	$4,250	$6,000	$9,500	$26,000	$55,000	
Auctions: $3,525, AU-55, August 2014; $4,994, AU-55, August 2013; $2,820, AU-53, October 2014; $2,838, AU-50, November 2014												
1843D	98,452	206	46.7	8%	$2,000	$2,500	$3,500	$4,500	$9,500	$20,000	$50,000	
Auctions: $19,975, MS-63, April 2013; $2,962, MS-60, July 2014; $4,406, MS-60, November 2014; $5,434, AU-58, September 2014												
1843D, Proof (g)	unknown	1	65.0									—
Auctions: No auction records available.												
1843O, Small Letters	19,075	81	47.7	6%	$850	$1,650	$2,500	$4,500	$17,500	$35,000	$50,000	$65,000
Auctions: $5,875, AU-58, November 2013; $2,585, AU-50, October 2014; $1,116, EF-40, November 2014												
1843O, Large Letters	82,000	101	49.8	16%	$650	$1,250	$2,000	$3,500	$9,500	$25,000	$35,000	
Auctions: $19,975, MS-62, January 2014; $2,585, AU-55, October 2014; $797, EF-40, August 2014												

e. Of the examples known today, one is in the Smithsonian's National Numismatic Collection, and another is ex Pittman Collection.
f. 4 or 5 examples are known. g. One non-circulation example of the 1843-D half eagle, probably a presentation strike of some sort, has been certified by NGC as a Specimen (rated Specimen-65).

1846-D, High
Second D Over D

	Mintage	Cert	Avg	%MS	VF-20	EF-40	AU-50	AU-55	MS-60	MS-63	MS-64	MS-65
										PF-63	PF-64	PF-65
1844	340,330	310	53.7	15%	$550	$575	$600	$650	$1,900	$7,500	$18,000	$55,000
Auctions: $14,100, MS-64, January 2014; $8,813, MS-63, September 2014; $529, AU-55, August 2014; $529, AU-55, September 2014												
1844, Proof (h)	3–5	1	64.0					*(extremely rare)*				
Auctions: No auction records available.												
1844C	23,631	86	46.8	8%	$2,150	$3,000	$4,250	$7,000	$13,000	$30,000		
Auctions: $4,706, AU-53, March 2014; $3,525, AU-53, August 2014												
1844D	88,982	226	47.0	8%	$2,000	$2,750	$3,750	$4,750	$8,500	$25,000	$40,000	
Auctions: $11,163, MS, March 2014; $2,585, EF-45, July 2014; $2,233, EF-40, September 2014; $2,115, EF-40, November 2014												
1844O	364,600	639	50.7	11%	$575	$600	$850	$1,300	$4,000	$12,000	$22,500	$45,000
Auctions: $11,163, MS-63, November 2014; $19,975, MS, February 2014; $1,763, AU-58, August 2014; $1,058, AU-55, September 2014												
1844O, Proof (i)	1	0	n/a					*(unique)*				
Auctions: No auction records available.												
1845	417,099	323	54.1	15%	$550	$575	$600	$700	$2,000	$8,500	$15,000	
Auctions: $6,171, MS, March 2014; $1,175, AU-58, October 2014; $529, EF-45, September 2014; $611, EF-45, October 2014												
1845, Proof (j)	5–8	3	64.7					*(extremely rare)*				
Auctions: $149,500, PF-66UCam, August 2004												
1845D	90,629	281	50.1	8%	$2,000	$2,650	$3,500	$4,500	$10,000	$22,000	$38,000	$85,000
Auctions: $4,700, AU-58, March 2013; $3,408, AU-53, July 2014; $2,820, AU-53, August 2014; $2,233, EF-45, November 2014												
1845O	41,000	136	50.7	13%	$750	$1,000	$2,500	$4,750	$9,750	$22,500		
Auctions: $6,463, AU-58, December 2013												
1846, All kinds	395,942											
1846, Large Date		161	54.6	16%	$550	$575	$700	$900	$2,500	$12,000	$18,500	
Auctions: $12,925, MS-64, April 2014; $5,434, MS-62, September 2014; $588, AU-55, July 2014; $564, AU-55, October 2014												
1846, Small Date		79	54.9	18%	$550	$575	$600	$1,300	$3,000	$13,000	$20,000	
Auctions: $1,528, AU-58, July 2014; $705, AU-53, July 2014; $388, EF-40, July 2014												
1846, Proof (k)	6–10	1	64.0					*(extremely rare)*				
Auctions: $161,000, PF-64Cam, January 2011												
1846C	12,995	68	48.7	10%	$2,000	$2,750	$4,750	$6,500	$13,000	$50,000	$85,000	
Auctions: $10,575, MS-60, January 2014												
1846D, All kinds	80,294											
1846D (l)		115	47.5	3%	$2,150	$2,750	$3,750	$4,750	$12,000			
Auctions: $3,055, AU-53, August 2014; $2,233, AU-50, July 2014; $3,836, EF-45, January 2014; $1,058, EF-40, August 2014												
1846D, High Second D Over D		123	49.5	6%	$2,150	$2,750	$4,000	$5,000	$13,000	$25,000		
Auctions: $21,150, MS-63, January 2014; $2,115, EF-45, August 2014; $1,763, VF-30, July 2014												
1846O	58,000	141	49.7	6%	$675	$1,000	$2,900	$4,500	$10,500	$25,000		
Auctions: $9,400, MS-61, January 2014; $1,293, EF-45, November 2014; $881, EF-40, July 2014; $764, EF-40, August 2014												

h. 2 examples are known. One is in the Smithsonian's National Numismatic Collection; the other is ex Pittman Collection. **i.** This unique coin first sold in 1890; pedigree is ex Seavy, Parmelee, Woodin, Newcomer, Farouk, Kosoff; current location unknown. **j.** 4 or 5 examples are known. **k.** 4 or 5 examples are known. Of the 20 or so Proof sets made in 1846, experts believe only 4 or 5 contained the year's gold coinage. **l.** The 1846-D half eagle with a normal mintmark actually is rarer than the variety with a boldly repunched D Over D mintmark.

| 1847, Top of Extra 7 Very Low at Border FS-G5-1847-301. | 1848-D, D Over D | 1850-C, Normal C | 1850-C, Weak C |

	Mintage	Cert	Avg	%MS	VF-20	EF-40	AU-50	AU-55	MS-60	MS-63	MS-64	MS-65
										PF-63	PF-64	PF-65
1847, All kinds	915,981											
1847		687	55.0	20%	$550	$575	$600	$800	$1,600	$6,500	$15,000	
Auctions: $12,925, MS-64, January 2014; $1,116, MS-61, November 2014; $823, AU-58, November 2014; $605, AU-53, July 2014												
1847, Top of Extra 7 Very Low at Border		166	55.2	16%	$575	$600	$700	$1,100	$2,100	$8,000	$13,000	
Auctions: $3,173, MS-62, October 2013; $1,998, MS-61, November 2014												
1847, Proof	2–3	0	n/a		*(unique, in the Smithsonian's National Numismatic Collection)*							
Auctions: No auction records available.												
1847C	84,151	253	46.3	6%	$2,000	$2,500	$3,500	$4,500	$9,500	$25,000	$35,000	$75,000
Auctions: $4,406, AU-58, April 2014; $2,350, EF-45, July 2014; $1,763, EF-40, August 2014												
1847D	64,405	146	48.1	10%	$2,000	$2,500	$3,500	$4,500	$8,500	$16,000		
Auctions: $3,819, AU-55, February 2014; $1,410, VG-10, July 2014												
1847O	12,000	45	44.9	4%	$2,500	$5,000	$8,000	$13,000	$26,000			
Auctions: $14,100, AU-53, January 2014; $4,113, AU-50, August 2014												
1848	260,775	301	53.7	13%	$550	$575	$600	$850	$1,700	$9,000	$25,000	
Auctions: $1,058, MS-60, April 2013; $573, AU-55, August 2014; $529, AU-55, September 2014; $515, EF-45, July 2014												
1848, Proof (m)	6–10	0	n/a		*(extremely rare)*							
Auctions: No auction records available.												
1848C	64,472	178	46.4	3%	$1,900	$2,500	$3,500	$6,000	$10,000	$25,000		
Auctions: $2,820, AU-53, August 2014; $3,326, EF-45, September 2014; $4,113, EF-45, October 2013; $1,773, EF-40, July 2014												
1848D	47,465	114	48.5	5%	$2,000	$2,500	$3,500	$6,500	$14,000	$40,000	$65,000	
Auctions: $4,113, AU-55, April 2014; $2,241, EF-45, August 2014; $2,115, EF-40, July 2014												
1848D, D Over D	(n)	0	n/a						$9,000	$20,000		
Auctions: $29,900, MS-62, May 2008												
1849	133,070	189	53.2	16%	$550	$575	$700	$850	$2,500	$12,000	$15,000	
Auctions: $2,585, MS-61, August 2014; $5,288, MS-61, April 2013; $911, AU-55, August 2014; $705, AU-53, November 2014												
1849C	64,823	213	49.9	11%	$2,000	$2,500	$3,250	$4,500	$9,500	$22,500	$40,000	
Auctions: $19,975, MS-63, October 2014; $5,875, AU-58, December 2013; $2,115, EF-40, August 2014												
1849D	39,036	131	49.2	5%	$2,000	$2,500	$3,250	$4,500	$9,500	$28,500		
Auctions: $5,288, AU-58, April 2013; $2,585, EF-45, August 2014												
1850	64,491	137	49.8	5%	$550	$575	$1,000	$1,500	$3,000	$15,000	$32,000	$75,000
Auctions: $1,293, AU-58, October 2014; $1,116, AU-58, October 2014; $1,028, AU-55, April 2014; $499, EF-40, August 2014												
1850C	63,591	157	48.4	12%	$1,900	$2,350	$3,250	$4,500	$9,500	$17,000	$37,500	
Auctions: $8,813, MS-61, February 2013; $5,875, AU-58, July 2014; $3,055, AU-55, August 2014; $1,531, AU-50, July 2014												
1850C, Weak C (o)	(p)	35	49.6	11%				$2,500				
Auctions: $3,819, MS-61, August 2014; $1,293, EF-45, July 2014												
1850D	43,984	124	48.3	2%	$2,000	$2,750	$3,500	$5,000	$20,000			
Auctions: $4,553, AU-55, February 2013; $2,115, EF-45, August 2014												

m. 2 examples are known. One is in the Smithsonian's National Numismatic Collection; the other is ex Pittman Collection. **n.** Included in 1848-D mintage figure **o.** Several branch-mint half eagles of the early 1850s can exhibit weak (sometimes very weak or almost invisible) mintmarks; such coins generally trade at deep discounts. **p.** Included in 1850-C mintage figure.

1851-D, Normal D

1851-D, Weak D

1854, Doubled-Die Obverse
FS-G5-1854-101.

1854-C, Normal C

1854-C, Weak C

1854-D, Normal D

1854-D, Weak D

	Mintage	Cert	Avg	%MS	VF-20	EF-40	AU-50	AU-55	MS-60	MS-63	MS-64	MS-65
										PF-63	PF-64	PF-65
1851	377,505	361	55.0	17%	$550	$575	$600	$650	$2,400	$9,000	$23,000	
Auctions: $5,875, MS-63, November 2014; $2,115, MS-61, June 2013; $588, AU-55, July 2014; $611, AU-55, September 2014												
1851C	49,176	135	48.4	9%	$2,000	$2,500	$3,500	$4,750	$11,500	$42,500	$60,000	
Auctions: $30,550, MS-63, April 2013; $1,175, EF-40, August 2014												
1851D	62,710	116	49.5	6%	$2,000	$2,500	$3,750	$5,500	$12,000	$25,000	$45,000	
Auctions: $16,450, MS-62, January 2014												
1851D, Weak D (o)	(q)	9	56.8	44%					$2,500			
Auctions: $2,185, AU-50, July 2009												
1851O	41,000	129	47.7	2%	$800	$1,400	$3,250	$5,500	$9,500	$20,000	$60,000	
Auctions: $11,163, MS-61, October 2014; $6,463, AU-58, June 2013; $3,055, AU-50, July 2014; $999, EF-45, August 2014												
1852	573,901	625	55.3	18%	$525	$550	$575	$600	$1,600	$8,000	$15,000	$27,500
Auctions: $11,750, MS-64, April 2013; $1,880, MS-62, September 2014; $3,525, MS-62, November 2014; $764, AU-55, November 2014												
1852C	72,574	233	49.8	17%	$2,000	$2,500	$3,500	$4,250	$6,000	$18,500	$27,500	
Auctions: $22,325, MS-64, September 2014; $28,200, MS-64, August 2013; $2,585, MS-60, November 2014												
1852D	91,584	249	48.5	7%	$2,000	$2,600	$3,700	$4,500	$9,500	$22,500		
Auctions: $5,875, AU-58, February 2014; $1,351, AU-50, July 2014; $1,528, VF-25, August 2014												
1853	305,770	458	55.0	17%	$550	$575	$600	$600	$1,700	$7,000	$15,000	$60,000
Auctions: $38,188, MS-65, October 2014; $4,113, MS-63, September 2013; $676, AU-58, July 2014; $529, AU-58, August 2014												
1853C	65,571	165	49.7	16%	$2,000	$2,500	$3,500	$4,250	$7,000	$22,500	$50,000	
Auctions: $38,188, MS-64, October 2014; $6,463, MS-61, November 2013; $4,406, AU-58, August 2014; $1,234, EF-40, August 2014												
1853D	89,678	317	51.2	12%	$2,000	$2,600	$3,700	$4,500	$6,500	$16,000	$55,000	
Auctions: $70,500, MS-64, October 2014; $6,169, MS-61, November 2014; $4,700, AU-58, November 2014; $5,581, AU-58, February 2013												
1854	160,675	319	54.7	17%	$550	$575	$600	$900	$2,000	$8,250	$15,000	
Auctions: $9,400, MS-64, June 2013; $1,528, MS-61, August 2014; $1,175, MS-60, September 2014; $881, AU-58, November 2014												
1854, Doubled-Die Obverse	(r)	21	54.3	14%					$1,350	$2,500		
Auctions: $1,998, AU-55, October 2014												
1854, Proof (s)	unknown	0	n/a									
Auctions: No auction records available.												
1854C	39,283	103	49.4	7%	$2,000	$2,500	$3,750	$5,000	$12,000	$30,000		
Auctions: $35,250, MS-63, April 2014; $2,585, AU-55, August 2014												
1854C, Weak C (o)	(t)	36	50.3	17%					$3,000			
Auctions: $12,338, MS-63, January 2014; $4,584, MS-60, September 2014												
1854D	56,413	210	53.3	23%	$2,000	$2,500	$3,500	$4,500	$8,750	$23,500	$42,500	$75,000
Auctions: $8,813, MS-62, June 2013; $7,050, MS-60, August 2014; $4,759, AU-58, September 2014; $5,581, AU-55, August 2014												
1854D, Weak D (o)	(u)	12	49.8	8%					$2,500			
Auctions: $5,581, MS-61, September 2014; $1,998, AU-55, April 2014												

o. Several branch-mint half eagles of the early 1850s can exhibit weak (sometimes very weak or almost invisible) mintmarks; such coins generally trade at deep discounts. **q.** Included in 1851-D mintage figure. **r.** Included in circulation-strike 1854 mintage figure **s.** According to Walter Breen, a complete 1854 Proof set was presented to dignitaries of the sovereign German city of Bremen who visited the Philadelphia Mint. The set resided in Bremen until it disappeared almost 100 years later, during World War II. **t.** Included in 1854-C mintage figure. **u.** Included in 1854-D mintage figure.

	Mintage	Cert	Avg	%MS	VF-20	EF-40	AU-50	AU-55	MS-60	MS-63 / PF-63	MS-64 / PF-64	MS-65 / PF-65
1854O	46,000	157	51.0	6%	$650	$800	$1,500	$2,250	$6,750	$22,500		
Auctions: $8,225, MS-61, August 2013; $499, AU-50, November 2014; $1,175, EF-45, September 2014; $529, VF-25, August 2014											
1854S (v)	268	1	58.0	0%				$3,500,000	—			
Auctions: No auction records available.											
1855	117,098	214	54.3	13%	$525	$550	$575	$600	$1,750	$7,500	$16,000	
Auctions: $1,410, MS-61, August 2013; $470, AU-53, August 2014; $388, AU-53, November 2014											
1855C	39,788	139	50.0	11%	$2,250	$2,600	$3,750	$4,500	$12,500	$42,500	$65,000	
Auctions: $9,694, MS-61, April 2013; $8,225, MS-60, September 2014; $3,290, AU-50, October 2014; $1,998, EF-40, August 2014											
1855D	22,432	86	51.3	7%	$2,000	$2,600	$3,600	$5,500	$15,000	$37,500		
Auctions: $15,275, MS-61, January 2014; $3,819, MS-60, August 2014; $2,820, EF-45, July 2014; $2,820, EF-40, July 2014											
1855O	11,100	55	49.8	5%	$1,000	$2,000	$4,000	$6,000	$17,000			
Auctions: $10,575, AU-58, March 2014; $4,700, AU-50, September 2014; $3,290, AU-50, November 2014											
1855S	61,000	116	48.0	3%	$600	$1,300	$2,500	$4,500	$12,500			
Auctions: $2,115, AU-53, July 2014; $940, AU-50, August 2014; $1,351, EF-45, July 2014											
1856	197,990	337	54.5	12%	$525	$550	$575	$600	$2,000	$10,500	$17,000	$42,500
Auctions: $2,233, MS-61, November 2014; $2,233, MS-61, December 2013; $529, AU-55, August 2014; $499, AU-55, September 2014											
1856C	28,457	128	50.9	10%	$2,000	$2,500	$3,750	$5,000	$15,000	$45,000		
Auctions: $17,625, MS-62, January 2014; $10,575, AU-58, November 2014; $2,703, AU-53, August 2014; $3,055, AU-53, November 2014											
1856D	19,786	105	49.4	12%	$2,000	$2,500	$3,750	$5,500	$10,000	$30,000	$50,000	
Auctions: $12,925, MS-62, January 2014; $1,880, VF-25, July 2014											
1856O	10,000	47	49.2	11%	$1,000	$1,850	$4,250	$6,500	$14,000			
Auctions: $10,575, MS-60, April 2014											
1856S	105,100	147	48.0	5%	$575	$700	$1,250	$2,000	$6,500	$23,500	$38,000	
Auctions: $4,700, AU-58, January 2014; $1,528, AU-55, October 2014; $1,116, AU-55, November 2014; $951, AU-53, July 2014											
1857	98,188	266	55.5	17%	$525	$550	$575	$600	$1,750	$8,000	$16,000	
Auctions: $1,410, MS-61, October 2014; $1,880, MS-61, February 2013; $793, AU-58, July 2014; $793, AU-58, October 2014											
1857, Proof (w)	*3–6*	1	65.0				*(extremely rare)*						
Auctions: $230,000, PF-65Cam, January 2007											
1857C	31,360	164	53.7	16%	$2,000	$2,500	$3,500	$4,500	$7,250	$25,000		
Auctions: $22,325, MS-63, January 2014; $2,820, AU-53, September 2014; $2,115, EF-45, July 2014											
1857D	17,046	93	52.2	14%	$2,000	$2,600	$3,750	$4,750	$10,000	$28,500		
Auctions: $9,988, MS-61, January 2014; $5,581, AU-58, October 2014; $2,056, VF-30, July 2014; $1,586, VF-25, August 2014											
1857O	13,000	83	49.5	4%	$1,000	$1,700	$3,750	$5,500	$12,000	$42,500		
Auctions: $41,125, MS-63, April 2014; $3,672, AU-53, October 2014											
1857S	87,000	110	46.9	5%	$600	$800	$1,500	$2,500	$10,500	$20,000		
Auctions: $3,525, AU-58, June 2014; $881, AU-55, August 2014; $1,528, AU-55, September 2014											
1858	15,136	75	53.7	19%	$550	$575	$750	$1,250	$3,000	$10,500	$14,000	$35,000
Auctions: $52,875, MS-66, April 2013; $9,988, MS-64, July 2014; $1,410, AU-55, August 2014; $823, EF-45, August 2014											
1858, Proof (x)	*4–6*	5	65.8							$75,000	$145,000	$225,000
Auctions: $195,500, PF-66UCam★, March 2006											
1858C	38,856	187	51.4	12%	$2,000	$2,500	$3,750	$4,500	$9,500	$30,000		
Auctions: $9,400, MS-61, August 2013; $3,055, AU-55, August 2014; $1,645, AU-50, July 2014; $2,585, VF-30, August 2014											
1858D	15,362	125	51.8	8%	$2,000	$2,500	$3,750	$4,500	$10,500	$32,500	$45,000	
Auctions: $7,638, MS-61, August 2014; $17,625, MS-61, June 2013											
1858S	18,600	53	47.4	0%	$1,000	$2,600	$5,750	$9,500	$25,000			
Auctions: $7,050, AU-55, March 2014											

v. 3 examples are known. **w.** 2 examples are known. **x.** 4 or 5 examples are known today. One resides in the Smithsonian's National Numismatic Collection, another in the collection of the American Numismatic Society. In recent decades the collections of Eliasberg, Trompeter, and Bass have included examples.

	Mintage	Cert	Avg	%MS	VF-20	EF-40	AU-50	AU-55	MS-60	MS-63	MS-64	MS-65
										PF-63	PF-64	PF-65
1859	16,734	91	50.3	8%	$550	$575	$775	$1,350	$5,500	$11,500		
Auctions: $4,700, AU-58, April 2013; $2,233, AU-55, July 2014; $823, EF-45, August 2014												
1859, Proof	80	4	63.5							$50,000	$85,000	$150,000
Auctions: No auction records available.												
1859C	31,847	150	50.7	8%	$2,000	$2,500	$3,500	$4,750	$11,500	$32,500		
Auctions: $8,225, MS-61, January 2014; $4,113, AU-55, August 2014; $1,645, AU-50, July 2014; $1,469, VF-25, August 2014												
1859D	10,366	111	52.7	12%	$2,000	$2,750	$3,750	$5,000	$12,000	$34,500		
Auctions: $19,975, MS-62, January 2014; $2,938, MS-60, July 2014; $4,553, AU-55, August 2014												
1859S	13,220	33	48.4	6%	$1,500	$3,250	$4,750	$8,500	$22,500			
Auctions: $8,695, AU-58, October 2013; $6,463, AU-53, August 2014												
1860	19,763	109	52.8	7%	$550	$575	$975	$1,350	$3,250	$13,500	$24,000	
Auctions: $4,700, AU-58, January 2014; $2,233, AU-58, August 2014; $646, AU-50, July 2014												
1860, Proof	62	5	64.7							$40,000	$65,000	$100,000
Auctions: $103,500, PF-66Cam★, January 2012												
1860C	14,813	117	53.0	17%	$2,000	$2,750	$4,000	$6,500	$11,000	$27,500	$40,000	
Auctions: $20,124, MS-63, April 2013; $4,113, AU-50, August 2014; $2,585, EF-40, October 2014												
1860D	14,635	132	51.7	13%	$2,250	$3,500	$4,500	$6,750	$13,500	$40,000	$75,000	
Auctions: $14,100, MS-62, March 2014; $4,406, AU-55, August 2014; $2,703, EF-45, August 2014; $4,700, EF-45, September 2014												
1860S	21,200	55	46.2	2%	$1,100	$2,150	$4,750	$7,750	$21,500			
Auctions: $19,975, AU-58, April 2014; $4,994, AU-53, October 2014; $2,585, EF-45, September 2014												
1861	688,084	1,486	56.0	19%	$500	$550	$575	$625	$1,750	$7,500	$11,500	$30,000
Auctions: $32,900, MS-65, January 2014; $2,585, MS-62, August 2014; $1,763, MS-61, October 2014; $999, AU-58, July 2014												
1861, Proof	66	2	65.0							$35,000	$55,000	$87,500
Auctions: No auction records available.												
1861C	6,879	77	50.9	8%	$4,000	$6,500	$10,000	$16,000	$30,000	$100,000		
Auctions: $25,850, MS-61, January 2014; $3,290, AU-50, August 2014												
1861D	1,597	35	53.3	9%	$18,500	$22,500	$35,000	$55,000	$85,000	$150,000		
Auctions: $99,875, MS-62, January 2014												
1861S	18,000	42	43.6	0%	$1,100	$3,500	$6,000	$9,000				
Auctions: $11,163, AU-53, March 2014; $4,259, VF-35, August 2014												
1862	4,430	34	51.7	3%	$1,100	$2,500	$5,000	$8,500	$20,000			
Auctions: $14,702, AU-58, August 2014; $17,625, AU-55, April 2013												
1862, Proof	35	8	64.6							$35,000	$55,000	$87,500
Auctions: $92,000, PF-65UCam, August 2011												
1862S	9,500	44	41.2	5%	$2,500	$4,500	$12,500	$20,000	$40,000			
Auctions: $15,275, AU-53, March 2014; $4,406, VF-25, August 2014												
1863	2,442	18	53.1	11%	$1,500	$4,500	$9,500	$14,000	$25,000			
Auctions: $30,550, AU-58, January 2014												
1863, Proof	30	3	65.5							$35,000	$52,500	$85,000
Auctions: $69,000, PF-64DCam, November 2005												
1863S	17,000	50	41.3	0%	$1,500	$3,750	$9,500	$15,000	$28,500			
Auctions: $16,450, AU-55, March 2014												
1864	4,170	49	52.0	8%	$1,250	$2,000	$5,500	$12,000	$20,000			
Auctions: $12,925, AU-55, January 2014												
1864, Proof	50	17	64.7							$35,000	$50,000	$77,500
Auctions: $103,500, PF-65UCam, October 2011												
1864S	3,888	9	38.8	0%	$10,000	$30,000	$50,000	$60,000				
Auctions: $79,313, EF-45, March 2014												

	Mintage	Cert	Avg	%MS	VF-20	EF-40	AU-50	AU-55	MS-60	MS-63 / PF-63	MS-64 / PF-64	MS-65 / PF-65
1865	1,270	27	53.9	19%	$2,500	$7,500	$15,000	$17,500	$25,000			
Auctions: $17,626, AU-55, August 2014; $18,800, AU-53, January 2014												
1865, Proof	25	13	64.5							$35,000	$50,000	$77,500
Auctions: $86,250, PF-65UCam, April 2012												
1865S	27,612	81	43.3	6%	$1,500	$2,500	$4,500	$7,500	$20,000	$40,000	$60,000	
Auctions: $8,813, AU-55, March 2014; $5,875, EF-45, August 2014												
1866S, No Motto	9,000	54	38.5	0%	$1,700	$3,500	$10,000	$15,000	$30,000			
Auctions: $14,688, AU-58, March 2014; $5,581, AU-50, August 2014; $2,350, VF-20, August 2014												
1866, Motto Above Eagle	6,700	42	53.9	14%	$750	$1,300	$2,750	$4,500	$13,000	$45,000		
Auctions: $34,075, MS-63, February 2013; $3,290, AU-55, August 2014												
1866, Motto Above Eagle, Proof	30	6	61.9							$27,500	$35,000	$60,000
Auctions: $80,500, PF-66UCam★, August 2010												
1866S, Motto Above Eagle	34,920	47	38.5	2%	$925	$2,500	$7,000	$10,000	$25,000			
Auctions: $4,994, AU-50, June 2013; $2,585, EF-45, August 2014; $1,469, VF-30, October 2014												
1867	6,870	53	49.5	2%	$600	$1,250	$3,000	$4,000	$9,500			
Auctions: $16,450, MS-61, September 2014; $8,813, MS-60, January 2014; $881, AU-50, August 2014												
1867, Proof	50	5	63.4							$25,000	$35,000	$60,000
Auctions: $21,150, PF-63Cam, August 2014												
1867S	29,000	80	40.2	0%	$1,100	$2,500	$5,500	$11,000				
Auctions: $5,581, AU, March 2014; $1,293, EF-40, August 2014												
1868	5,700	65	52.5	3%	$600	$1,250	$2,750	$4,500	$10,000			
Auctions: $16,450, MS-61, April 2013; $2,233, AU-50, August 2014												
1868, Proof	25	4	64.0							$25,000	$35,000	$60,000
Auctions: $69,000, PF-64DCam, June 2008												
1868S	52,000	112	44.1	4%	$525	$1,250	$2,750	$4,250	$15,000			
Auctions: $21,150, MS-61, November 2014; $23,500, MS-60, March 2014; $1,645, AU-53, October 2014; $1,827, AU-50, July 2014												
1869	1,760	38	52.6	11%	$950	$2,000	$3,500	$4,500	$12,500	$27,000	$37,500	
Auctions: $9,400, AU-55, April 2014; $2,267, EF-40, August 2014												
1869, Proof	25	5	63.9							$25,000	$35,000	$60,000
Auctions: $69,000, PF-65Cam, April 2012												
1869S	31,000	115	41.4	3%	$575	$1,500	$3,000	$7,000	$20,000			
Auctions: $17,625, MS-61, July 2014; $1,998, EF-45, August 2014												
1870	4,000	54	50.4	0%	$700	$1,500	$2,750	$4,750	$13,500			
Auctions: $7,640, AU-58, September 2014; $8,225, AU-55, January 2014; $1,410, VF-30, October 2014												
1870, Proof	35	2	65.3							$25,000	$35,000	$60,000
Auctions: $82,250, PF-64, January 2014												
1870CC	7,675	42	33.8	2%	$20,000	$27,500	$37,500	$60,000	$115,000			
Auctions: $47,000, AU-53, January 2014												
1870S	17,000	89	39.2	0%	$850	$1,850	$5,500	$9,000	$22,500			
Auctions: $12,925, AU-58, August 2014; $7,696, AU-55, January 2014; $2,115, EF-40, July 2014; $1,116, VF-25, August 2014												
1871	3,200	46	53.2	9%	$750	$1,250	$2,500	$4,750	$10,000			
Auctions: $15,275, MS-61, September 2013; $3,525, AU-55, August 2014; $2,820, AU-53, August 2014												
1871, Proof	30	7	61.4							$25,000	$35,000	$60,000
Auctions: $70,500, PF-65Cam, September 2014												
1871CC	20,770	93	38.5	2%	$3,000	$6,500	$12,500	$22,500	$50,000	$80,000		
Auctions: $48,469, MS-61, April 2013; $2,115, EF-40, July 2014; $5,288, EF-40, September 2014; $3,173, VF-30, August 2014												
1871S	25,000	103	46.2	3%	$525	$900	$2,500	$4,500	$11,500			
Auctions: $35,250, MS-63, August 2014; $25,850, MS-61, March 2014; $2,585, VF-25, August 2014												

1873, Close 3	1873, Open 3

	Mintage	Cert	Avg	%MS	VF-20	EF-40	AU-50	AU-55	MS-60	MS-63 / PF-63	MS-64 / PF-64	MS-65 / PF-65
1872	1,660	26	54.3	15%	$725	$1,350	$2,500	$4,250	$10,500	$17,500	$22,500	
Auctions: $5,434, AU-58, April 2014												
1872, Proof	30	7	62.6							$25,000	$35,000	$60,000
Auctions: $7,188, PF-55, March 2012												
1872CC	16,980	67	35.4	0%	$3,000	$6,750	$13,500	$25,000				
Auctions: $28,200, AU-58, March 2014; $11,764, AU-50, August 2014; $1,175, F-12, November 2014												
1872S	36,400	124	44.1	2%	$575	$800	$2,500	$5,500	$12,000			
Auctions: $3,055, AU-55, October 2014; $1,645, AU-53, October 2014; $2,585, AU-53, February 2013; $2,233, AU-50, July 2014												
1873, Close 3	112,480	295	55.7	25%	$425	$435	$550	$600	$1,100	$6,500	$10,000	$20,000
Auctions: $5,875, MS-64, December 2013; $852, MS-61, September 2014; $470, AU-58, August 2014												
1873, Open 3	112,505	323	56.0	25%	$425	$435	$450	$500	$700	$4,000	$6,500	$12,500
Auctions: $5,875, MS-64, September 2013; $499, MS-61, November 2014; $411, AU-55, August 2014; $317, EF-40, October 2014												
1873, Close 3, Proof	25	11	64.4							$22,500	$35,000	$60,000
Auctions: $24,675, PF-63Cam, August 2014; $12,338, PF-58, January 2014												
1873CC	7,416	30	32.2	3%	$4,500	$11,500	$23,500	$30,000	$65,000	$165,000		
Auctions: $11,750, AU-50, August 2014; $21,150, AU-50, January 2013; $5,581, F-12, August 2014												
1873S	31,000	108	42.4	1%	$600	$1,100	$2,250	$4,250	$18,500			
Auctions: $2,233, AU-55, August 2014; $3,173, AU-53, January 2014; $1,528, AU-50, August 2014												
1874	3,488	57	50.4	9%	$550	$1,000	$2,250	$3,000	$10,000	$22,500		
Auctions: $4,700, AU-58, January 2014; $3,290, AU-55, August 2014												
1874, Proof	20	4	65.8							$27,500	$40,000	$65,000
Auctions: $54,625, PF-65Cam★, August 2011												
1874CC	21,198	128	39.7	1%	$2,000	$3,000	$10,000	$17,000	$35,000			
Auctions: $21,738, AU-58, August 2014; $21,150, AU-55, May 2013; $8,813, AU-53, November 2014; $2,115, VF-30, August 2014												
1874S	16,000	90	41.4	0%	$800	$1,500	$3,500	$6,000				
Auctions: $4,113, AU, March 2014; $400, F-12, September 2014; $646, F-12, August 2014												
1875	200	5	53.6	0%	$75,000	$100,000	$155,000	$215,000				
Auctions: $211,500, AU-55, April 2014												
1875, Proof (y)	20	6	61.2							$125,000	$175,000	$225,000
Auctions: $176,250, PF-65Cam, January 2014												
1875CC	11,828	88	39.3	1%	$2,500	$4,500	$13,500	$18,000	$45,000	$115,000		
Auctions: $17,625, AU-58, January 2014												
1875S	9,000	67	43.0	3%	$775	$2,000	$3,750	$8,000	$18,500			
Auctions: $8,813, AU-58, August 2014; $3,819, AU-55, August 2014; $2,585, AU-50, August 2014; $3,055, AU-50, August 2013												
1876	1,432	24	55.4	17%	$950	$2,000	$3,750	$5,000	$10,000	$18,500	$25,000	$40,000
Auctions: $19,975, MS-63, March 2013												
1876, Proof	45	16	63.9							$20,000	$25,000	$47,500
Auctions: $48,469, PF-65Cam, February 2013												
1876CC	6,887	71	39.5	1%	$2,500	$4,750	$13,500	$18,000	$40,000			
Auctions: $21,150, AU-58, March 2014; $4,113, VF-25, July 2014												
1876S	4,000	21	38.6	5%	$1,150	$3,500	$7,500	$12,000	$30,000			
Auctions: $18,800, AU-58, March 2014												

y. The mintages of only 200 circulation strikes and 20 Proofs for the year 1875 combine to make the Proof a high-demand coin; hence its strong market value.

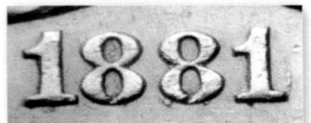 

1881, Final 1 Over 0
FS-G5-1881-301.

1881, Recut 1881 Over 1881
FS-G5-1881-303.

	Mintage	Cert	Avg	%MS	VF-20	EF-40	AU-50	AU-55	MS-60	MS-63	MS-64	MS-65
										PF-63	PF-64	PF-65
1877	1,132	41	53.9	24%	$1,000	$1,800	$3,250	$5,000	$12,500			
	Auctions: $7,638, AU-58, April 2014; $5,288, AU-50, August 2014; $3,525, EF-45, July 2014											
1877, Proof	20	4	65.1							$22,500	$32,500	$57,500
	Auctions: $51,750, PF-63, June 2005											
1877CC	8,680	99	39.8	0%	$1,750	$3,750	$11,500	$13,500	$40,000			
	Auctions: $14,688, AU-55, November 2014; $11,163, AU-53, July 2014; $9,988, AU-53, August 2014; $8,813, AU-50, November 2014											
1877S	26,700	119	44.6	1%	$525	$575	$1,500	$3,750	$6,500	$18,500	$30,000	
	Auctions: $1,116, AU-53, March 2014; $1,293, AU-53, August 2014; $1,175, EF-45, August 2014											
1878	131,720	393	59.1	55%	$400	$425	$435	$500	$600	$1,750	$5,500	$12,000
	Auctions: $8,813, MS-65, September 2013; $3,525, MS-64, August 2014; $411, AU-58, August 2014											
1878, Proof	20	7	64.6							$22,500	$32,500	$57,500
	Auctions: $31,725, PF-63DCam, June 2014											
1878CC	9,054	51	44.4	4%	$4,500	$10,000	$17,500	$30,000	$75,000			
	Auctions: $47,000, AU-58, March 2014											
1878S	144,700	469	56.3	24%	$400	$425	$450	$500	$900	$4,000	$7,000	
	Auctions: $8,225, MS-64, September 2013; $470, MS-61, October 2014; $470, AU-58, July 2014; $427, AU-55, November 2014											
1879	301,920	670	59.3	56%	$400	$425	$435	$450	$600	$2,000	$4,750	$10,000
	Auctions: $6,463, MS-65, September 2014; $4,406, MS-64, September 2014; $3,525, MS-64, October 2014											
1879, Proof	30	8	64.4							$22,500	$30,000	$55,000
	Auctions: $63,250, PF-65Cam, April 2012											
1879CC	17,281	164	45.6	5%	$1,500	$2,500	$3,750	$7,500	$22,500			
	Auctions: $21,150, MS-60, March 2014; $8,813, AU-58, August 2014; $646, VG-8, July 2014; $764, G-6, July 2014											
1879S	426,200	714	57.2	27%	$400	$425	$435	$500	$900	$3,000	$6,000	$20,000
	Auctions: $5,581, MS-64, April 2014; $1,998, MS-63, September 2014; $1,528, MS-63, October 2014; $1,058, MS-62, November 2014											
1880	3,166,400	2,808	60.0	73%	$400	$425	$435	$450	$575	$950	$1,750	$4,500
	Auctions: $4,700, MS-65, April 2014; $3,055, MS-65, August 2014; $3,055, MS-65, August 2014; $1,116, MS-64, August 2014											
1880, Proof	36	7	65.9							$17,500	$30,000	$52,500
	Auctions: $72,702, PF-67Cam, August 2006											
1880CC	51,017	324	46.4	4%	$1,000	$1,350	$2,000	$4,500	$12,000	$40,000		
	Auctions: $11,750, MS-61, January 2014; $3,525, AU-55, August 2014; $3,966, AU-55, October 2014; $1,293, EF-45, July 2014											
1880S	1,348,900	2,153	61.1	84%	$400	$425	$435	$450	$575	$750	$1,750	$6,000
	Auctions: $4,994, MS-65, February 2014; $1,351, MS-64, October 2014; $544, MS-63, August 2014; $823, MS-62, July 2014											
1881, Final 1 Over 0 (z)	(aa)	107	58.3	53%	$550	$700	$850	$1,125	$1,500	$5,000	$10,000	
	Auctions: $2,233, MS-63, January 2014; $646, AU-55, August 2014; $499, EF-40, July 2014											
1881, Recut 1881 Over 1881	(aa)	0	n/a					$535	$625	$1,325		
	Auctions: $705, MS-63, August 2014; $1,528, MS-62, April 2014											
1881	5,708,802	16,162	61.5	92%	$400	$425	$435	$450	$525	$800	$1,350	$4,000
	Auctions: $6,463, MS-66, June 2013; $2,880, MS-65, August 2014; $482, MS-63, October 2014; $470, MS-62, October 2014											
1881, Proof	42	9	65.8							$16,500	$25,000	$40,000
	Auctions: $37,375, PF-65Cam, January 2011											
1881CC	13,886	80	44.9	8%	$1,250	$2,250	$6,500	$11,000	$22,500	$55,000		
	Auctions: $32,900, MS-62, May 2013; $3,055, EF-40, August 2014; $1,763, VF-30, July 2014; $1,293, F-15, August 2014											
1881S	969,000	1,823	61.3	89%	$400	$425	$435	$450	$525	$850	$1,500	$5,000
	Auctions: $3,525, MS-65, November 2013; $1,175, MS-64, August 2014; $999, MS-64, September 2014											

z. The last digit of the date is repunched over the remnants of a zero; this is easily visible with the naked eye, making the 1 Over 0 a popular variety. aa. Included in circulation-strike 1881 mintage figure.

	Mintage	Cert	Avg	%MS	VF-20	EF-40	AU-50	AU-55	MS-60	MS-63 / PF-63	MS-64 / PF-64	MS-65 / PF-65
1882	2,514,520	7,335	61.5	91%	$400	$425	$435	$450	$575	$750	$1,400	$4,000
	Auctions: $7,638, MS-66, August 2013; $441, MS-61, August 2014; $400, AU-58, July 2014; $382, AU-58, September 2014											
1882, Proof	48	12	64.3							$15,500	$25,000	$40,000
	Auctions: $9,085, PF-63Cam, February 2010											
1882CC	82,817	548	51.3	5%	$900	$1,150	$1,750	$3,000	$10,000	$35,000		
	Auctions: $9,400, MS-61, April 2014; $5,288, AU-58, August 2014; $4,994, AU-58, September 2014; $2,703, AU-55, July 2014											
1882S	969,000	2,296	61.6	92%	$400	$425	$435	$450	$575	$750	$1,500	$4,000
	Auctions: $7,344, MS-66, August 2013; $2,820, MS-65, August 2014; $676, MS-63, July 2014; $646, MS-63, August 2014											
1883	233,400	462	60.3	72%	$400	$425	$435	$450	$575	$1,500	$2,350	$12,500
	Auctions: $17,625, MS-67, February 2013; $411, MS-61, October 2014; $411, AU-58, August 2014											
1883, Proof	61	9	64.2							$15,500	$25,000	$40,000
	Auctions: $5,288, PF-55, September 2014											
1883CC	12,598	115	49.8	4%	$850	$1,450	$3,000	$6,000	$18,500	$45,000		
	Auctions: $18,213, MS-61, August 2014; $16,450, AU-58, March 2014											
1883S	83,200	226	58.0	51%	$400	$425	$435	$450	$800	$2,000	$7,000	
	Auctions: $7,050, MS-64, August 2013; $1,410, MS-63, September 2014; $529, MS-61, September 2014; $1,058, AU-53, August 2014											
1884	191,030	445	59.0	58%	$400	$425	$435	$450	$750	$2,100	$3,000	$8,500
	Auctions: $2,468, MS-64, February 2013; $558, MS-62, August 2014; $558, MS-61, August 2014											
1884, Proof	48	8	64.5							$15,500	$25,000	$40,000
	Auctions: $39,100, PF-66UCam, November 2010											
1884CC	16,402	163	49.7	3%	$850	$1,250	$3,250	$6,500	$20,000			
	Auctions: $8,225, AU-58, January 2014; $8,519, AU-58, October 2014; $4,994, AU-55, August 2014											
1884S	177,000	448	59.9	68%	$400	$425	$435	$450	$575	$1,400	$3,500	$10,000
	Auctions: $2,688, MS-64, July 2014; $2,585, MS-64, July 2014; $2,056, MS-64, September 2014; $3,466, MS-64, August 2013											
1885	601,440	1,315	61.3	85%	$400	$425	$435	$450	$575	$900	$1,250	$4,500
	Auctions: $881, MS-64, October 2014; $1,528, MS-64, February 2013; $441, MS-61, August 2014; $329, AU-55, November 2014											
1885, Proof	66	18	64.4							$15,500	$25,000	$40,000
	Auctions: $31,725, PF-65DCam, August 2014											
1885S	1,211,500	4,182	62.0	94%	$400	$425	$435	$450	$575	$700	$1,150	$3,000
	Auctions: $2,938, MS-65, January 2014; $1,998, MS-65, October 2014; $1,880, MS-65, October 2014; $1,590, MS-65, November 2014											
1886	388,360	674	60.1	68%	$400	$425	$435	$450	$575	$750	$1,250	$6,500
	Auctions: $5,288, MS-65, June 2013; $573, MS-63, August 2014; $499, MS-61, July 2014											
1886, Proof	72	12	64.3							$15,500	$25,000	$40,000
	Auctions: $57,281, PF, March 2014											
1886S	3,268,000	8,097	61.4	93%	$400	$425	$435	$450	$575	$750	$1,250	$4,250
	Auctions: $3,525, MS-65, January 2014; $2,115, MS-65, October 2014; $2,468, MS-65, November 2014											
1887, Proof (bb)	87	18	63.3							$65,000	$80,000	$115,000
	Auctions: $54,050, PF, August 2013											
1887S	1,912,000	3,227	61.2	91%	$400	$425	$435	$450	$525	$900	$1,700	$4,750
	Auctions: $4,700, MS-65, June 2014; $646, MS-63, July 2014; $588, MS-63, October 2014; $558, MS-63, October 2014											
1888	18,201	155	59.9	68%	$400	$425	$435	$450	$575	$2,250	$3,500	$7,000
	Auctions: $1,775, MS-63, January 2014; $588, MS-60, August 2014											
1888, Proof	95	18	64.6							$13,500	$20,000	$32,500
	Auctions: $34,500, PF-65DCam, October 2008											
1888S	293,900	339	54.9	22%	$400	$425	$435	$575	$900	$4,000		
	Auctions: $2,350, MS-64, August 2013; $1,116, MS-63, October 2014; $470, AU-53, July 2014; $368, EF-40, August 2014											
1889	7,520	151	58.1	42%	$425	$500	$550	$600	$950	$3,500	$6,500	
	Auctions: $4,406, MS-63, June 2014; $1,763, MS-62, July 2014; $1,175, AU-53, August 2014											
1889, Proof	45	13	64.3							$14,000	$22,500	$35,000
	Auctions: $29,900, PF-65Cam, January 2011											

bb. Proof only.

	Mintage	Cert	Avg	%MS	VF-20	EF-40	AU-50	AU-55	MS-60	MS-63 / PF-63	MS-64 / PF-64	MS-65 / PF-65
1890	4,240	71	55.8	30%	$400	$425	$435	$800	$1,750	$7,000	$8,500	$10,000
	Auctions: $5,581, MS-62, June 2014; $1,000, AU-55, July 2014; $823, AU-50, August 2014											
1890, Proof	88	27	65.1							$14,000	$22,500	$35,000
	Auctions: $24,675, PF-64DCam, January 2014											
1890CC	53,800	612	57.3	48%	$750	$850	$950	$1,100	$1,850	$7,500	$15,000	$45,000
	Auctions: $5,581, MS-63, August 2014; $5,875, MS-63, February 2013; $3,819, MS-62, October 2014; $2,233, MS-61, September 2014											
1891	61,360	363	60.6	79%	$425	$450	$465	$520	$575	$1,700	$3,500	$10,000
	Auctions: $4,700, MS-64, February 2013; $499, MS-61, August 2014; $456, MS-60, July 2014; $382, AU-55, November 2014											
1891, Proof	53	18	65.0							$13,500	$20,000	$32,500
	Auctions: $19,550, PF-64DCam, January 2010											
1891CC	208,000	2,007	58.0	53%	$750	$850	$950	$1,100	$2,750	$4,750	$7,500	$27,500
	Auctions: $3,290, MS-63, July 2014; $3,055, MS-63, August 2014; $4,406, MS-63, April 2013; $2,820, MS-62, July 2014											
1892	753,480	1,981	61.5	92%	$400	$425	$435	$450	$575	$750	$1,400	$3,750
	Auctions: $9,400, MS-67, August 2014; $3,672, MS-65, January 2014; $2,115, MS-65, November 2014; $1,116, MS-64, November 2014											
1892, Proof	92	18	64.5							$13,500	$18,000	$32,500
	Auctions: $6,325, PF-62Cam, December 2011											
1892CC	82,968	729	53.9	20%	$750	$850	$900	$1,200	$2,500	$8,500	$15,000	$30,000
	Auctions: $20,563, MS-64, April 2013; $6,463, MS-63, August 2014; $2,585, MS-60, October 2014; $1,469, AU-58, October 2014											
1892O	10,000	42	57.7	43%	$600	$875	$1,100	$1,500	$2,750	$11,000	$16,000	
	Auctions: $8,225, MS-62, December 2013; $3,290, AU-58, July 2014; $3,290, AU-58, August 2014											
1892S	298,400	430	57.8	44%	$400	$425	$435	$450	$575	$2,850	$4,000	$7,500
	Auctions: $2,350, MS-63, April 2013; $617, MS-62, August 2014; $705, MS-62, October 2014; $593, MS-62, November 2014											
1893	1,528,120	7,391	61.9	96%	$400	$425	$435	$450	$575	$750	$1,000	$2,750
	Auctions: $12,338, MS-67, December 2013; $4,994, MS-66, September 2014; $1,763, MS-65, October 2014; $734, MS-64, October 2014											
1893, Proof	77	20	64.9							$13,500	$18,000	$32,500
	Auctions: $70,500, PF, August 2013											
1893CC	60,000	652	55.5	27%	$750	$850	$1,150	$1,500	$2,750	$8,500	$16,500	$27,500
	Auctions: $21,738, MS-65, November 2014; $30,550, MS-64, November 2014; $7,050, MS-63, April 2014; $5,875, MS-63, August 2014											
1893O	110,000	424	58.8	50%	$425	$450	$550	$650	$1,000	$6,000	$10,000	
	Auctions: $7,638, MS-64, January 2014; $4,113, MS-63, November 2014; $458, AU-58, July 2014; $529, AU-58, August 2014											
1893S	224,000	1,044	61.0	84%	$400	$425	$435	$450	$500	$1,025	$2,750	$8,500
	Auctions: $5,875, MS-65, April 2013; $456, MS-62, August 2014; $441, MS-62, September 2014; $423, MS-62, October 2014											
1894	957,880	3,401	61.7	96%	$400	$425	$435	$450	$500	$650	$1,000	$3,000
	Auctions: $7,638, MS-66, April 2014; $617, MS-63, July 2014; $470, MS-62, August 2014; $499, MS-61, July 2014											
1894, Proof	75	26	64.1							$13,500	$18,500	$32,500
	Auctions: $58,750, PF-67DCam, October 2014; $15,863, PF-64Cam, January 2014											
1894O	16,600	321	57.6	34%	$425	$450	$550	$800	$1,500	$7,000		
	Auctions: $3,525, MS-62, June 2014; $1,888, MS-61, July 2014; $764, MS-61, October 2014; $823, AU-55, November 2014											
1894S	55,900	220	53.1	13%	$400	$425	$435	$900	$2,500	$8,500	$16,000	
	Auctions: $176,250, MS-69, January 2014; $881, AU-58, August 2014											
1895	1,345,855	7,820	61.8	95%	$400	$425	$435	$450	$500	$675	$1,000	$3,250
	Auctions: $7,050, MS-66, November 2014; $2,233, MS-65, August 2014; $2,174, MS-65, August 2014; $2,703, MS-65, August 2013											
1895, Proof	81	26	64.9							$12,500	$18,000	$30,000
	Auctions: $6,233, PF-60, February 2014											
1895S	112,000	312	53.5	8%	$400	$450	$475	$900	$2,100	$5,750	$12,000	$23,000
	Auctions: $2,233, MS-62, August 2014; $1,645, MS-61, June 2013; $823, AU-58, July 2014; $544, AU-58, August 2014											
1896	58,960	474	61.8	93%	$400	$425	$435	$450	$500	$675	$1,000	$3,000
	Auctions: $1,880, MS-64, February 2014; $705, MS-63, July 2014; $382, AU-55, August 2014											
1896, Proof	103	33	64.9							$12,500	$18,000	$30,000
	Auctions: $35,250, PF-65DCam, September 2014											
1896S	155,400	393	54.7	22%	$400	$425	$435	$700	$1,250	$6,000	$8,500	$20,000
	Auctions: $15,275, MS-65, December 2013; $3,008, MS-62, September 2014; $705, MS-61, September 2014; $975, MS-61, October 2014											

1901-S, Final 1 Over 0
FS-G5-1901S-301.

	Mintage	Cert	Avg	%MS	VF-20	EF-40	AU-50	AU-55	MS-60	MS-63	MS-64	MS-65
										PF-63	PF-64	PF-65
1897	867,800	4,056	61.6	92%	$400	$425	$435	$450	$500	$675	$1,000	$3,000
	Auctions: $4,406, MS-65, February 2014; $2,468, MS-65, August 2014; $881, MS-64, September 2014; $823, MS-64, November 2014											
1897, Proof	83	24	64.5							$12,500	$18,000	$30,000
	Auctions: $9,988, PF-63, June 2014											
1897S	354,000	405	56.1	24%	$400	$425	$435	$625	$900	$5,000	$7,500	
	Auctions: $31,725, MS-67, August 2014; $1,645, MS-62, July 2014; $499, MS-61, August 2014; $505, AU-58, July 2014											
1898	633,420	2,366	61.6	93%	$400	$425	$435	$450	$500	$675	$1,600	$3,000
	Auctions: $1,410, MS-64, October 2014; $705, MS-64, October 2014; $1,528, MS-64, March 2013; $646, MS-63, November 2014											
1898, Proof	75	37	64.7							$12,500	$18,000	$30,000
	Auctions: $29,375, PF-65DCam, September 2014											
1898S	1,397,400	653	59.3	68%	$400	$425	$435	$450	$500	$1,100	$2,750	$7,500
	Auctions: $58,889, MS-68, November 2014; $5,434, MS-65, June 2014; $7,050, MS-65, October 2014; $4,406, MS-64, August 2014											
1899	1,710,630	12,625	62.5	98%	$400	$425	$435	$450	$500	$675	$800	$2,750
	Auctions: $9,400, MS-67, September 2013; $3,819, MS-66, October 2014; $2,585, MS-65, July 2014; $764, MS-64, July 2014											
1899, Proof	99	29	64.6							$12,500	$18,000	$30,000
	Auctions: $134,550, PF, September 2013											
1899S	1,545,000	927	59.6	71%	$400	$425	$435	$450	$525	$1,100	$1,750	$8,500
	Auctions: $646, MS-63, November 2014; $564, MS-62, July 2014; $470, MS-62, August 2014; $4,700, MS, March 2014											
1900	1,405,500	15,716	62.1	96%	$400	$425	$435	$450	$500	$675	$800	$2,750
	Auctions: $5,875, MS-66, September 2013; $2,820, MS-65, September 2014; $1,528, MS-65, November 2014; $1,645, MS-64, August 2014											
1900, Proof	230	60	64.2							$12,500	$18,000	$30,000
	Auctions: $35,250, PF-65DCam, September 2013											
1900S	329,000	510	60.2	69%	$400	$425	$435	$450	$500	$1,100	$1,650	$9,500
	Auctions: $1,293, MS-64, March 2013; $705, MS-63, August 2014; $529, MS-62, August 2014											
1901	615,900	5,158	61.9	93%	$400	$425	$435	$450	$500	$675	$800	$2,750
	Auctions: $12,925, MS-67, August 2013; $2,938, MS-66, August 2014; $3,672, MS-66, November 2014; $564, MS-64, October 2014											
1901, Proof	140	43	64.3							$12,500	$18,000	$30,000
	Auctions: $28,200, PF-65DCam, August 2014											
1901S, All kinds	3,648,000											
1901S, Final 1 Over 0		355	60.7	72%	$550	$600	$650	$925	$1,200	$1,500	$2,000	$5,500
	Auctions: $1,763, MS-64, August 2013; $1,116, MS-63, August 2014; $470, MS-62, October 2014; $441, AU-55, August 2014											
1901S		7,199	62.1	92%	$400	$425	$435	$450	$500	$675	$800	$2,750
	Auctions: $25,850, MS-67, August 2013; $7,050, MS-66, July 2014; $1,763, MS-65, October 2014; $2,585, MS-64, August 2014											
1902	172,400	1,432	61.8	94%	$400	$425	$435	$450	$500	$675	$800	$2,750
	Auctions: $30,550, MS-67, July 2014; $2,115, MS-65, November 2014; $564, MS-63, August 2014; $441, MS-62, August 2014											
1902, Proof	162	28	63.3							$12,500	$18,000	$30,000
	Auctions: $12,925, PF-64, April 2013											
1902S	939,000	2,571	62.1	92%	$400	$425	$435	$450	$500	$675	$800	$2,750
	Auctions: $23,500, MS-67, January 2014; $3,525, MS-66, July 2014; $3,055, MS-66, November 2014; $2,820, MS-65, August 2014											
1903	226,870	1,788	61.6	92%	$400	$425	$435	$450	$500	$675	$800	$2,750
	Auctions: $3,290, MS-66, July 2014; $3,819, MS-65, February 2014; $2,644, MS-65, July 2014; $2,820, MS-65, August 2014											
1903, Proof	154	57	64.0							$12,500	$18,000	$30,000
	Auctions: $32,900, PF-65, October 2014; $66,975, PF, March 2014											
1903S	1,855,000	4,244	62.1	92%	$400	$425	$435	$450	$500	$675	$800	$2,750
	Auctions: $12,375, MS-67, September 2013; $1,763, MS-65, November 2014; $705, MS-63, July 2014; $529, MS-63, November 2014											

	Mintage	Cert	Avg	%MS	VF-20	EF-40	AU-50	AU-55	MS-60	MS-63 / PF-63	MS-64 / PF-64	MS-65 / PF-65
1904	392,000	3,882	62.0	95%	$400	$425	$435	$450	$500	$675	$800	$2,750
Auctions: $5,875, MS-66, October 2014; $7,050, MS-66, March 2013; $2,498, MS-65, July 2014; $2,703, MS-65, August 2014												
1904, Proof	136	57	64.0							$12,500	$18,000	$30,000
Auctions: $31,725, PF-66Cam, June 2013												
1904S	97,000	271	57.4	36%	$400	$425	$435	$575	$1,025	$2,750	$4,000	$8,500
Auctions: $4,113, MS-64, April 2013; $2,350, MS-63, October 2014; $1,116, MS-62, July 2014; $881, MS-61, August 2014												
1905	302,200	2,673	61.9	94%	$400	$425	$435	$450	$500	$675	$800	$2,750
Auctions: $12,338, MS-67, August 2013; $4,406, MS-66, November 2014; $3,819, MS-66, November 2014; $1,528, MS-64, October 2014												
1905, Proof	108	34	62.6							$12,500	$18,000	$30,000
Auctions: $23,000, PF-65Cam, October 2010												
1905S	880,700	898	57.4	31%	$400	$425	$435	$450	$675	$1,750	$3,250	$8,000
Auctions: $4,259, MS-64, March 2014; $2,585, MS-64, August 2014; $940, MS-63, October 2014; $1,293, MS-63, November 2014												
1906	348,735	2,766	61.8	93%	$400	$425	$435	$450	$500	$675	$800	$2,750
Auctions: $14,100, MS-67, November 2013; $3,525, MS-65, August 2014; $2,115, MS-65, November 2014; $1,293, MS-64, July 2014												
1906, Proof	85	58	63.8							$12,500	$18,000	$30,000
Auctions: $64,625, PF-66Cam, August 2013												
1906D	320,000	2,624	62.1	94%	$400	$425	$435	$450	$500	$675	$800	$2,850
Auctions: $2,233, MS-65, July 2014; $2,233, MS-65, August 2014; $2,938, MS-65, February 2013; $1,293, MS-64, July 2014												
1906S	598,000	639	60.3	73%	$400	$425	$435	$450	$525	$1,100	$1,750	$4,750
Auctions: $3,525, MS-65, September 2014; $1,469, MS-64, July 2014; $1,528, MS-64, August 2014; $1,880, MS-64, September 2013												
1907	626,100	8,783	62.1	96%	$400	$425	$435	$450	$500	$675	$800	$2,500
Auctions: $10,575, MS-67, June 2014; $823, MS-64, July 2014; $764, MS-64, July 2014; $646, MS-64, August 2014												
1907, Proof	92	40	64.1							$13,000	$18,000	$30,000
Auctions: $24,675, PF-65Cam, April 2014												
1907D	888,000	4,376	62.0	94%	$400	$425	$435	$450	$500	$675	$800	$2,500
Auctions: $2,938, MS-65, April 2014; $1,880, MS-65, July 2014; $1,645, MS-65, October 2014; $764, MS-64, August 2014												
1908	421,874	6,187	62.4	96%	$400	$425	$435	$450	$500	$675	$800	$2,500
Auctions: $51,406, MS-68, April 2014; $11,456, MS-65, September 2014; $8,225, MS-65, November 2014; $2,820, MS-64, November 2014												

INDIAN HEAD (1908–1929)

Designer: *Bela Lyon Pratt.* **Weight:** *8.359 grams.*
Composition: *.900 gold, .100 copper (net weight .24187 oz. pure gold).* **Diameter:** *21.6 mm.*
Edge: *Reeded.* **Mints:** *Philadelphia, Denver, New Orleans, San Francisco.*

Circulation Strike   **Sandblast Finish Proof**   **Satin Finish Proof**

Mintmark location
is on the reverse, to
the left of the arrows.

History. The Indian Head half eagle made its first appearance in 1908; it was minted continuously through 1916, and again in 1929. Its design elements are in sunken relief (sometimes imprecisely called "incuse"), like those of the similar quarter eagle; the mintmark is raised. On most examples the rims are flat, while on others they are slightly raised. These coins saw limited circulation in the West, and were rarely encountered elsewhere.

Striking and Sharpness. Striking quality of Indian Head half eagles varies. Look for weakness on the high parts of the Indian's bonnet and in the feather details in the headdress. On the reverse, check the feathers on the highest area of the wing.

Proofs. Sandblast (also called Matte) Proofs were made in 1908 and from 1911 to 1915, while Satin (also called Roman Finish) Proofs were made in 1909 and 1910. At lower levels, these coins can show light contact marks. Some microscopic bright flecks may be caused by the sandblasting process and, although they do not represent handling, usually result in a coin being assigned a slightly lower grade.

Availability. Indian Head half eagles were not popular with numismatists of the time, who saved very few. Rare issues include the 1909-O, which usually is seen with evidence of circulation (often extensive) and the 1929, most of which are in MS. Luster can range from deeply frosty to grainy. Because the fields are the highest areas of the coin, luster diminished quickly as the coins were circulated or jostled with others in bags. When Proof examples are seen, they are usually in higher Proof grades, PF-64 and above. As a class these half eagles are rarer than quarter eagles of the same date and style of finish.

Note: Values of common-date gold coins have been based on the current bullion price of gold, $1,200 per ounce, and may vary with the prevailing spot price.

GRADING STANDARDS

MS-60 to 70 (Mint State). *Obverse:* At MS-60 to 62, there is abrasion in the field, this representing the highest part of the coin. Abrasion is also evident on the headdress. Marks and, occasionally, a microscopic pin scratch may be seen. At MS-63, there may be some abrasion and some tiny marks. Luster is irregular. At MS-64, abrasion is less. Luster is rich. At MS-65 and above, luster is deep and frosty, with no marks at all visible with-

1911-D. Graded MS-62.

out magnification at MS-66 and higher. *Reverse:* At MS-60 to 62 there is abrasion in the field, this representing the highest part of the coin. Abrasion is also evident on the eagle's wing. Otherwise, the same comments apply as for the obverse.

   Illustrated coin: This example is lustrous and attractive. Most of the luster in the fields (the highest-relief area of this unusual design) is still intact.

AU-50, 53, 55, 58 (About Uncirculated). *Obverse:* Friction on the cheek is very notice-able at AU-50, increasingly less at higher levels to AU-58. The headdress shows light wear, most evident on the ribbon above the forehead and on the garland. Luster is minimal at AU-50 and scattered and incomplete at AU-58. Nicks and contact marks are to be expected. *Reverse:* Friction on the wing and neck is very noticeable at AU-50, increasingly

1911. Graded AU-50.

less noticeable at higher levels to 58. Otherwise, the same comments apply as for the obverse.

EF-40, 45 (Extremely Fine). *Obverse:* Light wear will characterize the portrait and head-dress. Luster is gone. Marks and tiny scratches are to be expected, but not distracting. *Reverse:* Light wear is most evident on the eagle's head and wing, although other areas are lightly worn as well. Luster is gone. Marks and tiny scratches are to be expected, but not distracting.

1909-O. Graded EF-40.

VF-20, 30 (Very Fine). *Obverse:* Many details of the garland and of the ribbon above the forehead are worn away. Many feather vanes are blended together. The field is dull and has contact marks. *Reverse:* The neck and the upper part of the wing show extensive wear, other areas less so. The field is dull and has contact marks.

The Indian Head half eagle is seldom collected in grades lower than VF-20.

1909. Graded VF-25.

Illustrated coin: Some bumps are seen on the top obverse rim and should be mentioned in a description.

PF-60 to 70 (Proof). *Obverse and Reverse:* At PF-60 to 63, there is light abrasion and some contact marks (the lower the grade, the higher the quantity). On Sandblast Proofs these show up as visually unappealing bright spots. At PF-64 and higher levels, marks are fewer, with magnification needed to see any at PF-65. At PF-66, there should be none at all.

Illustrated coin: This is a particularly nice example.

1911, Sandblast Finish. Graded PF-67.

	Mintage	Cert	Avg	%MS	VF-20	EF-40	AU-50	AU-55	AU-58	MS-60	MS-62 / PF-63	MS-63 / PF-64	MS-65 / PF-65
1908	577,845	7,588	61.4	86%	$425	$450	$460	$475	$500	$650	$700	$1,500	$12,500
	Auctions: $35,250, MS-67, September 2013												
1908, Sandblast Finish Proof	167	84	65.2								$13,000	$18,000	$35,000
	Auctions: $152,750, PF, August 2013												
1908D	148,000	2,754	62.3	94%	$425	$450	$460	$475	$500	$650	$700	$1,750	$35,000
	Auctions: $2,368, MS-64, July 2014; $2,820, MS-64, November 2014; $5,170, MS-64, May 2013; $1,645, MS-63, November 2014												
1908S	82,000	520	57.7	44%	$600	$750	$1,000	$1,350	$1,650	$2,750	$5,000	$8,500	$25,000
	Auctions: $47,000, MS-67, August 2014; $47,000, MS-67, November 2013; $17,038, MS-65, July 2014; $2,350, AU-58, August 2014												

	Mintage	Cert	Avg	%MS	VF-20	EF-40	AU-50	AU-55	AU-58	MS-60	MS-62 / PF-63	MS-63 / PF-64	MS-65 / PF-65
1909	627,060	6,863	61.1	83%	$425	$450	$460	$475	$500	$650	$700	$1,700	$13,500
Auctions: $3,819, MS-64, August 2014; $2,585, MS-64, October 2014; $2,938, MS-64, November 2014; $11,163, MS, March 2014													
1909, Satin Finish Proof	78	36	65.3								$14,000	$30,000	$45,000
Auctions: $82,250, PF-67, August 2014; $55,813, PF-66, August 2014; $99,875, PF-66, February 2013													
1909, Sandblast Finish Proof (a)	unknown	1	67										
Auctions: No auction records available.													
1909D	3,423,560	31,531	61.6	87%	$425	$450	$460	$475	$485	$625	$675	$1,100	$10,000
Auctions: $7,638, MS-65, November 2014; $2,585, MS-64, November 2014; $2,233, MS-64, November 2014													
1909O (b)	34,200	967	55.4	14%	$4,500	$6,500	$9,500	$15,000	$24,000	$32,500	$55,000	$95,000	$400,000
Auctions: $646,250, MS-66, January 2014; $18,800, AU-58, September 2014; $17,684, AU-58, November 2014													
1909S	297,200	702	56.8	29%	$450	$500	$525	$600	$750	$1,500	$3,750	$12,500	$55,000
Auctions: $30,550, MS-64, March 2014; $10,011, MS-63, November 2014; $5,288, MS-62, August 2014													
1910	604,000	6,941	60.9	80%	$425	$450	$460	$475	$500	$650	$700	$1,500	$15,000
Auctions: $10,575, MS-65, August 2014; $12,338, MS-65, November 2014; $3,055, MS-64, November 2014													
1910, Satin Finish Proof	250	47	65.3								$13,000	$20,000	$37,500
Auctions: $146,250, PF, September 2013													
1910, Sandblast Finish Proof (c)	unknown	0	n/a										
Auctions: No auction records available.													
1910D	193,600	1,150	60.4	76%	$425	$450	$460	$475	$500	$650	$700	$3,750	$35,000
Auctions: $27,025, MS-65, November 2014; $11,163, MS-64, October 2014; $10,575, MS-64, February 2013													
1910S	770,200	1,495	57.2	28%	$450	$500	$525	$700	$900	$1,750	$3,500	$9,500	$65,000
Auctions: $11,163, MS-63, June 2013; $5,581, MS-62, July 2014; $4,700, MS-62, October 2014; $2,350, MS-61, October 2014													
1911	915,000	10,813	60.7	77%	$425	$450	$460	$475	$500	$650	$700	$1,450	$12,500
Auctions: $9,988, MS-65, August 2014; $23,500, MS-65, August 2013; $2,585, MS-64, July 2014; $2,468, MS-64, August 2014													
1911, Sandblast Finish Proof	139	54	65.7								$13,000	$18,000	$35,000
Auctions: $99,875, PF-67, April 2013													
1911D	72,500	1,386	55.9	15%	$750	$1,000	$1,500	$2,500	$3,500	$10,000	$22,500	$45,000	$225,000
Auctions: $27,025, MS-62, August 2014; $27,025, MS-62, August 2013; $11,750, MS-61, July 2014													
1911S	1,416,000	2,714	57.5	38%	$450	$500	$525	$600	$700	$850	$2,500	$5,750	$35,000
Auctions: $32,900, MS-65, May 2013; $5,288, MS-63, August 2014; $5,875, MS-63, November 2014; $3,290, MS-62, August 2014													
1912	790,000	10,216	60.9	81%	$425	$450	$475	$485	$500	$575	$750	$1,500	$13,500
Auctions: $10,575, MS-65, August 2013; $4,406, MS-64, October 2014; $2,761, MS-64, November 2014; $1,410, MS-63, July 2014													
1912, Sandblast Finish Proof	144	38	66.4								$13,000	$18,000	$35,000
Auctions: $58,750, PF-66, September 2013													
1912S	392,000	1,556	56.2	18%	$450	$500	$525	$700	$950	$2,500	$5,000	$15,000	$150,000
Auctions: $3,294, MS-61, July 2014; $3,290, MS-61, July 2014; $3,525, MS-61, October 2014; $13,513, MS, March 2014													
1913	915,901	11,825	61.0	82%	$425	$450	$460	$475	$500	$650	$700	$1,500	$12,500
Auctions: $9,694, MS-65, February 2014; $3,966, MS-64, July 2014; $3,055, MS-64, November 2014													
1913, Sandblast Finish Proof	99	26	66.2								$13,000	$18,000	$35,000
Auctions: $51,750, PF-67, July 2011													
1913S	408,000	1,870	56.5	22%	$550	$575	$675	$825	$875	$2,500	$7,500	$20,000	$125,000
Auctions: $38,188, MS-64, September 2014; $35,250, MS-64, August 2013; $12,338, MS-63, July 2014													
1914	247,000	2,743	60.8	77%	$425	$450	$460	$475	$500	$650	$700	$1,850	$16,000
Auctions: $21,150, MS-65, February 2013; $3,525, MS-64, September 2014; $2,115, MS-63, July 2014													
1914, Sandblast Finish Proof	125	32	65.8								$13,000	$18,000	$35,000
Auctions: $93,600, PF, September 2013													
1914D	247,000	2,601	60.6	73%	$425	$450	$460	$475	$500	$650	$700	$2,250	$24,000
Auctions: $4,700, MS-64, August 2014; $4,700, MS-64, October 2014; $7,638, MS-64, April 2013; $5,288, MS-63, August 2014													
1914S	263,000	1,474	57.9	36%	$450	$500	$525	$550	$900	$1,750	$4,500	$17,500	$100,000
Auctions: $11,878, MS-63, July 2014; $11,750, MS-63, July 2014; $12,925, MS-63, November 2014; $12,925, MS, March 2014													

a. This unique coin is certified by NGC as PF-67. **b.** Beware spurious "O" mintmark. **c.** This unique coin is part of the unique complete 1910 Sandblast Finish Proof gold set.

	Mintage	Cert	Avg	%MS	VF-20	EF-40	AU-50	AU-55	AU-58	MS-60	MS-62	MS-63	MS-65
											PF-63	PF-64	PF-65
1915 (d)	588,000	6,370	60.9	77%	$425	$450	$460	$475	$500	$650	$700	$1,650	$14,500
	Auctions: $9,988, MS-65, August 2014; $6,463, MS-64, August 2014; $3,290, MS-64, August 2014; $16,450, MS, March 2014												
1915, Sandblast Finish Proof	75	22	65.3								$15,000	$25,000	$45,000
	Auctions: $47,000, PF-66, June 2014												
1915S	164,000	1,300	56.3	22%	$450	$500	$525	$750	$1,050	$2,500	$5,500	$17,000	$120,000
	Auctions: $47,000, MS-64, December 2013; $15,275, MS-63, July 2014; $8,225, MS-62, July 2014; $5,875, MS-62, October 2014												
1916S	240,000	1,989	58.9	49%	$500	$525	$600	$650	$750	$1,000	$2,500	$6,500	$30,000
	Auctions: $18,800, MS-64, November 2013; $7,050, MS-63, July 2014; $5,581, MS-63, November 2014; $4,406, MS-62, July 2014												
1929	662,000	226	62.4	91%	$18,500	$21,000	$25,000	$27,500	$30,000	$35,000	$37,500	$57,500	$105,000
	Auctions: $73,438, MS-64, August 2014; $70,500, MS-64, August 2013; $52,875, MS-63, July 2014; $41,125, MS-62, October 2014												

d. Pieces dated 1915-D are counterfeit.

Gold Eagles ($10)
1795–1933

AN OVERVIEW OF GOLD EAGLES

The ten-dollar gold coin, or *eagle*, was first produced in 1795. Coinage authority for the denomination, including its weight and fineness, had been specified by the Act of April 2, 1792.

The Capped Bust to Right with Small Eagle reverse is the rarest of the early ten-dollar coin types. However, when seen they tend to be in higher grades such as EF, AU, or low levels of Mint State. The Heraldic Eagle reverse issues from 1797 through 1804 are much more readily available and in slightly higher average grade.

The Liberty Head eagles without the motto IN GOD WE TRUST, minted from 1838 through 1865, are elusive in any Mint State grade, although VF and EF pieces are plentiful, and there are enough AU coins to easily satisfy collector demands. Some collectors have considered the 1838 and 1839, 9 Over 8, with the head of Miss Liberty tilted forward in relation to the date, to be a separate type. Eagles with IN GOD WE TRUST on the reverse, produced from 1866 to 1907, are plentiful in high grades, including choice and gem Mint State. Some of these were repatriated from overseas bank vaults beginning in the second half of the 20th century.

The Saint-Gaudens eagles of 1907, of the style with periods between and flanking the words E PLURIBUS UNUM, exist in the Wire Rim and Rounded Rim varieties. These can be collected as a distinct type, or not. Most readily available is the Wire Rim style, of which somewhat more than 400 are likely to exist today, nearly all in Mint State, often choice or gem. These coins were made as regular issues but soon became numismatic delicacies for Treasury officials to distribute as they saw fit. Some were to have gone to museums, but in reality most were secretly filtered out through favored coin dealers. Then comes the 1907–1908 style, without periods, easily available in EF, AU, and lower Mint State levels, although gems are elusive.

The final eagle type, the 1908–1933 style with IN GOD WE TRUST on the reverse, is readily obtained in grades from EF through MS-63. Higher-grade pieces are elusive, and

In 1875 a Liberty Head design—sometimes called the "Sailor Head"—by William Barber was used on a pattern eagle (J-1443, shown; it was also used on a pattern half eagle and a pattern 20-cent piece).

when seen are often dated 1932, a year in which 4,463,000 were struck—more than any other coin in the history of the denomination.

FOR THE COLLECTOR AND INVESTOR: GOLD EAGLES AS A SPECIALTY

Collecting ten-dollar gold coins by die varieties is unusual, as the series includes so many scarce and rare coins. However, unlike other denominations, none is in the "impossible" category, and with some patience a full set of significant varieties, as listed in this book, can be obtained.

The early issues with a Small Eagle reverse, minted from 1795 through 1797, and those with the Heraldic Eagle reverse of 1797 through 1804, can be collected and studied by die varieties, with *United States Ten Dollar Gold Eagles 1795–1804*, by Anthony Teraskza, being one useful guide. *Early U.S. Gold Coin Varieties: A Study of Die States, 1795–1834*, by John W. Dannreuther and Harry W. Bass Jr., offers an abundance of information and enlarged photographs for study. In addition to the regular issues, a few 1804 restrike ten-dollar pieces exist from 1804-dated dies newly created in 1834.

Liberty Head eagles from 1838 through 1866 (without the motto IN GOD WE TRUST) comprise many scarce dates and mintmarks. Years ago the 1858, of which only 2,521 were minted, was highly acclaimed as a landmark issue, but since then the publicity has faded. In any event, although certain date-and-mintmark varieties are rare, the number of numismatists collecting them by date sequence is very small, and thus opportunities exist to acquire very elusive pieces at a much smaller proportionate premium than would be possible in, say, the gold dollar series. No full set of Mint State early eagles has ever been formed; probably none ever will be. EF and AU are typically the grades of choice, with Mint State pieces added when available.

Later Liberty Head eagles of the 1866–1907 style (with the motto IN GOD WE TRUST) include some low-mintage issues, but again these are not impossible to collect. The most famous is the 1875 Philadelphia coin, of which just 100 circulation strikes were made. Although smaller numbers exist for Proof-only mintages, in terms of those made for commerce the 1875 sets a record. The low-mintage 1879-O (1,500 made) and 1883-O (800) also have attracted much attention. Again, these pieces, while rare, are available to the specialist, as there is not a great deal of competition.

Among Indian Head eagles the 1907 With Periods style, Wire Rim, is famous, popular, and rare. Examples come on the market with regularity but are expensive due to the demand they attract. The Rounded Rim style is much rarer and when seen is usually in choice Mint State.

The regular without-periods 1907 and 1908 eagles are easy enough to obtain in Mint State, although gems are elusive. The varieties from 1908 through 1916 include no great rarities, although some are scarcer than others. Not many such pieces were saved at the time they were issued, and, accordingly, gems are elusive. However, grades such as AU and low Mint State will present no problem. Among later eagles, the 1920-S, 1930-S, and 1933 are rarities. In particular the 1920-S is difficult to find in choice and gem Mint State. The 1933 eagle is usually found in Mint State, but is expensive due to the publicity given to it. Readily available at reasonable prices are the 1926 and 1932.

CAPPED BUST TO RIGHT, SMALL EAGLE REVERSE (1795–1797)

Designer: *Robert Scot.* Weight: *17.50 grams.*
Composition: *.9167 gold, .0833 silver and copper.*
Diameter: *Approximately 33 mm.* Edge: *Reeded.*

Bass-Dannreuther–1.

History. Eagles of this style, the first in the denomination, debuted in the autumn of 1795. The obverse features Miss Liberty dressed in a conical cap. The reverse shows a "small" eagle perched on a palm branch and holding a laurel in his beak. The same motif was used on contemporary gold half eagles.

Striking and Sharpness. On the obverse, check the star centers and the hair details. On the reverse, check the feathers of the eagle. In particular, the breast feathers often are weakly struck. Examine the denticles on both sides. Adjustment marks (from a Mint worker filing an overweight planchet down to the correct weight) often are visible, but are not noted by the grading services.

Availability. Typical grades range from EF to AU and low MS. MS-63 and higher coins are rare; when seen, they usually are of the 1795 or 1796 dates. Certain varieties are rare. While no Proofs of this type were made, certain eagles of 1796 have prooflike surfaces and are particularly attractive if in high grades.

GRADING STANDARDS

MS-60 to 70 (Mint State). *Obverse:* At MS-60, some abrasion and contact marks are evident, most noticeably on the hair to the left of Miss Liberty's forehead and on the higher-relief areas of the cap. Luster is present, but may be dull or lifeless, and interrupted in patches. At MS-63, contact marks are few, and abrasion is very light. An MS-65 coin has hardly any abrasion, and contact marks are so minute as to require magnifica-

1795, 13 Leaves; BD-5. Graded MS-63.

tion. Luster should be full and rich. On prooflike coins in any Mint State grade, abrasion and surface marks are much more noticeable. Coins above MS-65 exist more in theory than in reality for this type—but they do exist, and are defined by having fewer marks as perfection is approached. *Reverse:* Comments apply as for the obverse, except that abrasion and contact marks are most noticeable on the breast and head of the eagle. The field area is mainly protected by the eagle, branch, and lettering.

AU-50, 53, 55, 58 (About Uncirculated).
Obverse: Light wear is seen on the cheek, the hair immediately to the left of the face, and the cap, more so at AU-50 than at 53 or 55. An AU-58 coin has minimal traces of wear. An AU-50 coin has luster in protected areas among the stars and letters, with little in the open fields or on the portrait. At AU-58, most luster is present in the fields, but is worn away on the highest parts of the motifs. *Reverse:*

1796. Graded AU-58.

Comments as preceding, except that the eagle shows light wear on the breast and head in particular, but also at the tip of the wing on the left and elsewhere. Luster ranges from perhaps 40% remaining in protected areas (at AU-50) to nearly full mint bloom (at AU-58).

Illustrated coin: This example shows light wear overall, with hints of original luster in protected areas.

EF-40, 45 (Extremely Fine). *Obverse:* Wear is evident all over the portrait, with some loss of detail in the hair to the left of Miss Liberty's face. Excellent detail remains in low-relief areas of the hair, such as the front curl and at the back of her head. The stars show wear, as do the date and letters. Luster, if present at all, is minimal and in protected areas. *Reverse:* Wear is greater than on an About Uncirculated coin. The breast, neck,

1795, 9 Leaves; BD-3. Graded EF-45.

and legs of the eagle lack nearly all feather detail. More wear is seen on the edges of the wing. Some traces of luster may be seen, more so at EF-45 than at EF-40.

VF-20, 30 (Very Fine). *Obverse:* The higher-relief areas of hair are well worn at VF-20, less so at VF-30. The stars are flat at their centers. *Reverse:* Wear is greater, the eagle is flat in most areas, and about 40% to 60% of the wing feathers can be seen.

The Capped Bust to Right eagle coin with Small Eagle reverse is seldom collected in grades lower than VF-20.

1795, 13 Leaves; BD-2. Graded VF-30.

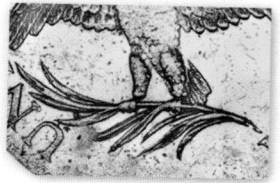

1795, 13 Leaves   **1795, 9 Leaves**

	Mintage	Cert	Avg	%MS	F-12	VF-20	EF-40	AU-50	AU-55	MS-60	MS-62	MS-63
1795, 13 Leaves Below Eagle	5,583	45	55.3	27%	$27,500	$35,000	$47,500	$55,000	$70,000	$110,000	$150,000	$300,000 (a)
Auctions: $881,250, MS-65, August 2014; $675,625, MS-65, August 2013; $152,750, MS-62, November 2014; $49,938, EF-45, August 2014												
1795, 9 Leaves Below Eagle †	(b)	13	56.9	23%	$40,000	$55,000	$77,500	$120,000	$137,500	$250,000	$375,000	$625,000
Auctions: $146,875, EF-45, August 2014; $47,000, EF-40, January 2014												
1796	4,146	67	56.8	25%	$32,500	$42,500	$55,000	$60,000	$70,000	$110,000	$200,000	$350,000
Auctions: $164,500, MS-62, April 2014; $82,250, AU-55, August 2014												
1797, Small Eagle	3,615	28	55.1	32%	$37,500	$55,000	$75,000	$115,000	$130,000	$215,000	$350,000	$425,000
Auctions: $164,500, AU-58, August 2014; $76,375, EF-45, February 2014; $47,000, EF-40, August 2014												

† Ranked in the *100 Greatest U.S. Coins* (fourth edition). **a.** Value in MS-64 is $475,000. **b.** Included in 1795, 13 Leaves Below Eagle, mintage figure.

CAPPED BUST TO RIGHT, HERALDIC EAGLE REVERSE (1797–1804)

Designer: *Robert Scot.* **Weight:** *17.50 grams.*
Composition: *.9167 gold, .0833 silver and copper.*
Diameter: *Approximately 33 mm.* **Edge:** *Reeded.*

Circulation Strike   **Proof**
BD-10.

History. Gold eagles of this type combine the previous obverse style with the Heraldic Eagle—a modification of the Great Seal of the United States—as used on other silver and gold coins of the era. Regarding the Proofs dated 1804: There were no Proofs coined in the era in which this type was issued, and all eagle and silver dollar production was suspended by President Thomas Jefferson in 1804. Years later, in 1834, the Mint made up new dies with the 1804 date (this time featuring a Plain 4 rather than a Crosslet 4) and struck a number of Proofs (the quantity unknown today, but perhaps a dozen or so) for inclusion in presentation Proof sets for foreign dignitaries.

Striking and Sharpness. On the obverse, check the star centers and the hair details. On the reverse, check the upper part of the shield, the lower part of the eagle's neck, the eagle's wing, the stars above the eagle, and the clouds. Inspect the denticles on both sides. Adjustment marks (from where an overweight planchet was filed down to correct specifications) can be problematic; these are not identified by the grading services.

Availability. Mintages of this type were erratic. Eagles of 1797 appear in the market with some regularity, while those of 1798 are rare. Usually seen are the issues of 1799 through 1803. Typical grades range from EF to lower MS. MS-62 and higher coins are seen with some frequency and usually are dated 1799 and later. The 1804 circulation strike is rare in true MS. Sharply struck coins without planchet adjustment marks are in the minority. Only a handful of the aforementioned 1804 Proofs survive today.

GRADING STANDARDS

MS-60 to 70 (Mint State). *Obverse:* At MS-60, some abrasion and contact marks are evident, most noticeably on the hair to the left of Miss Liberty's forehead and on the higher-relief areas of the cap. Luster is present, but may be dull or lifeless, and interrupted in patches. At MS-63, contact marks are few, and abrasion is very light. An MS-65 coin has even less abrasion (most observable in the right field), and contact marks are so

1799, Large Stars; BD-10. Graded MS-65.

minute as to require magnification. Luster should be full and rich. Coins graded above MS-65 are more theoretical than actual for this type—but they do exist, and are defined by having fewer marks as perfection is approached. Large-size eagles are usually graded with slightly less strictness than the lower gold denominations of this type. *Reverse:* Comments apply as for the obverse, except that abrasion and contact marks are most noticeable on the upper part of the eagle and the clouds. The field area is complex, without much open space, given the stars above the eagle, the arrows and olive branch, and other features. Accordingly, marks are not as noticeable as on the obverse.

Illustrated coin: This coin has an exceptionally sharp strike overall, but with some lightness on the eagle's dexter (viewer's left) talon. Note some trivial abrasion in the right obverse field.

AU-50, 53, 55, 58 (About Uncirculated). *Obverse:* Light wear is seen on the cheek, the hair immediately to the left of the face, and the cap, more so at AU-50 than at 53 or 55. An AU-58 coin has minimal traces of wear. An AU-50 coin has luster in protected areas among the stars and letters, with little in the open fields or on the portrait. At AU-58, most luster is present in the fields, but is worn away on the highest parts of the motifs.

1799, Small Stars; BD-7. Graded AU-50.

Reverse: Comments as preceding, except that the eagle's neck, the tips and top of the wings, the clouds, and the tail now show noticeable wear, as do other features. Luster ranges from perhaps 40% remaining in protected areas (at AU-50) to nearly full mint bloom (at AU-58). Often the reverse of this type retains much more luster than the obverse.

Illustrated coin: Note some lightness of strike at the center of the obverse. Significant luster remains.

EF-40, 45 (Extremely Fine). *Obverse:* Wear is evident all over the portrait, with some loss of detail in the hair to the left of Miss Liberty's face. Excellent detail remains in low-relief areas of the hair, such as the front curl and at the back of her head. The stars show wear as do the date and letters. Luster, if present at all, is minimal and in protected areas. *Reverse:* Wear is greater than on the preceding. The neck lacks some feather detail

1801; BD-2. Graded EF-45.

on its highest points. Feathers have lost some detail near the edges of the wings, and some areas of the horizontal lines in the shield may be blended together. Some traces of luster may be seen, more so at EF-45 than at EF-40. Overall, the reverse appears to be in a slightly higher grade than the obverse.

VF-20, 30 (Very Fine). *Obverse:* The higher-relief areas of hair are well worn at VF-20, less so at VF-30. *Reverse:* Wear is greater, including on the shield and wing feathers. The star centers are flat. Other areas have lost detail as well. E PLURIBUS UNUM may be faint in areas, but is usually sharp.

The Capped Bust to Right eagle coin with Heraldic Eagle reverse is seldom collected in grades lower than VF-20.

1799, Small Stars; BD-7. Graded VF-30.

PF-60 to 70 (Proof). *Obverse and Reverse:* PF-60 to 62 coins have extensive hairlines and may have nicks and contact marks. At PF-63, hairlines are prominent, but the mirror surface is very reflective. PF-64 coins have fewer hairlines. At PF-65, hairlines should be minimal and mostly seen only under magnification. There should be no nicks or marks.

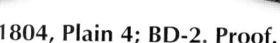

1804, Plain 4; BD-2. Proof.

| 1798, 8 Over 7, 9 Stars Left, 4 Right | 1798, 8 Over 7, 7 Stars Left, 6 Right | 1799, Small Obverse Stars | 1799, Large Obverse Stars |

1803, Small Reverse Stars   1803, Large Reverse Stars

	Mintage	Cert	Avg	%MS	F-12	VF-20	EF-40	AU-50	AU-55	MS-60	MS-62 / PF-63	MS-63 / PF-64	MS-64 / PF-65
1797, Heraldic Eagle	10,940	163	55.9	29%	$12,500	$15,000	$20,000	$27,500	$37,500	$57,500	$95,000	$140,000	$200,000
Auctions: $117,500, MS-63, April 2014; $44,063, MS-61, November 2014; $41,125, AU-58, August 2014; $34,075, AU-58, August 2014													
1798, 8 Over 7, 9 Stars Left, 4 Stars Right †	900	27	56.7	33%	$22,500	$30,000	$40,000	$55,000	$70,000	$145,000	$215,000	$300,000	
Auctions: $176,250, MS-62, April 2014													
1798, 8 Over 7, 7 Stars Left, 6 Stars Right †	842	4	52.5	25%	$40,000	$55,000	$87,500	$160,000	$185,000	$275,000	$350,000		
Auctions: $161,000, AU-55, January 2005; $176,250, AU-50, August 2014													
1799, Small Obverse Stars	37,449	24	55.8	42%	$8,750	$12,500	$16,000	$20,000	$23,500	$32,500	$42,500	$65,000	$135,000
Auctions: $9,988, AU-58, September 2014; $25,850, AU-58, August 2014; $24,675, AU-55, January 2014; $15,275, AU-50, August 2014													
1799, Large Obverse Stars	(a)	23	59.4	61%	$8,750	$12,500	$16,000	$20,000	$23,500	$32,500	$42,500	$65,000	$135,000
Auctions: $32,900, MS-62, October 2014; $19,975, AU-58, August 2014; $16,450, AU-53, November 2014; $17,625, EF-45, February 2013													
1800	5,999	103	57.3	42%	$9,000	$13,000	$16,500	$21,500	$24,500	$35,000	$52,500	$85,000	$140,000
Auctions: $117,500, MS-64, January 2014; $32,900, MS-61, August 2014; $15,275, AU-50, August 2014; $7,638, AU-50, July 2014													
1801	44,344	403	58.7	53%	$8,750	$11,000	$15,000	$18,500	$20,000	$29,000	$38,500	$60,000	$125,000
Auctions: $88,125, MS-64, March 2013; $48,763, MS-63, August 2014; $45,535, MS-63, August 2014; $29,375, MS-61, October 2014													
1803, Small Reverse Stars	15,017	13	55.3	38%	$9,500	$12,000	$16,000	$21,500	$23,500	$36,000	$50,000	$65,000	$135,000
Auctions: $28,200, MS-61, January 2014; $15,875, AU-55, November 2014; $17,625, AU-55, August 2014; $13,513, AU-55, August 2014													
1803, Large Reverse Stars (b)	(c)	7	58.1	43%	$9,500	$12,000	$16,000	$21,500	$23,500	$36,000	$50,000	$65,000	
Auctions: $99,875, MS-64, January 2014; $42,594, MS-62, August 2014; $24,675, AU-53, August 2014													
1804, Crosslet 4	3,757	51	58.9	51%	$20,000	$25,000	$37,500	$50,000	$65,000	$80,000	$100,000	$165,000	
Auctions: $73,438, MS-61, January 2014; $64,625, MS-60, August 2014; $58,750, AU-58, August 2014													
1804, Plain 4, Proof † (d)	5–8	2	65.5								$4,000,000	$4,500,000	$5,000,000
Auctions: $73,438, MS-61, January 2014													

† Ranked in the *100 Greatest U.S. Coins* (fourth edition). **a.** Included in 1799, Small Obverse Stars, mintage figure. **b.** A variety without the tiny 14th star in the cloud is very rare; six or seven examples are known. It does not command a significant premium. **c.** Included in 1803, Small Reverse Stars, mintage figure. **d.** These coins were minted in 1834 (from newly created dies with the date 1804) for presentation sets for foreign dignitaries. Three or four examples are known today.

LIBERTY HEAD (1838–1907)

Designer: *Christian Gobrecht.* **Weight:** *16.718 grams.*
Composition: *.900 gold, .100 copper (net weight: .48375 oz. pure gold).* **Diameter:** *27 mm.*
Edge: *Reeded.* **Mints:** *Philadelphia, Carson City, Denver, New Orleans, San Francisco.*

No Motto Above Eagle (1838–1866)

No Motto Above Eagle, Proof

Motto Above Eagle (1866–1907)

Motto Above Eagle, Proof

History. Production of the gold eagle, suspended after 1804, started up again in 1838 with the Liberty Head design. The coin's weight and diameter was reduced from the specifications of the earlier type. For the first time in the denomination's history, its value, TEN D., was shown. Midway through 1839 the style was modified slightly, including in the letters (made smaller) and in the tilt of Miss Liberty's portrait. In 1866 the motto IN GOD WE TRUST was placed on a banner above the eagle's head.

Striking and Sharpness. On the obverse, check the highest points of the hair and the star centers. On the reverse, check the eagle's neck, and the area to the lower left of the shield and the lower part of the eagle. Examine the denticles on both sides. Branch-mint coins issued before the Civil War often are lightly struck in areas, and some Carson City coins of the early 1870s can have areas of lightness. Most late 19th-century and early 20th-century coins are sharp in all areas. Tiny copper staining spots (from improperly mixed alloy) can be a problem for those issues. Cameo contrast is the rule for Proofs prior to 1902. Beginning that year the portrait was polished in the die, imparting a mirror finish across the entire design, although a few years later cameo-contrast coins were again made.

Availability. Early dates and mintmarks are generally scarce to rare in MS and very rare in MS-63 and better grades, with only a few exceptions. These were workhorse coins in commerce; VF and EF grades are the rule for dates through the 1870s, and for some dates the finest known grade can be AU. In MS, Liberty Head eagles as a type are rarer than either quarter eagles or half eagles of the same design. Indeed, the majority of Mint State examples were only discovered in recent decades, resting in European banks, and some varieties are not known to exist at this level. Eagles of the 1880s onward generally are seen in higher average grades. Proof coins exist in relation to their original mintages, with all issues prior to the 1890s being very rare.

Note: Values of common-date gold coins have been based on the current bullion price of gold, $1,200 per ounce, and may vary with the prevailing spot price.

GRADING STANDARDS

MS-60 to 70 (Mint State). *Obverse:* At MS-60, some abrasion and contact marks are evident, most noticeably on the hair to the right of Miss Liberty's forehead and on the jaw. Luster is present, but may be dull or lifeless, and interrupted in patches. At MS-63, contact marks are few, and abrasion is very light. An MS-65 coin has hardly any abrasion, and contact marks are so minute as to require magnification. Luster should be full and rich.

1880. Graded MS-63.

For most dates, coins graded above MS-65 exist more in theory than in actuality—but they do exist, and are defined by having fewer marks as perfection is approached. *Reverse:* Comments apply as for the obverse, except that abrasion and contact marks are most noticeable on the eagle's neck and to the lower left of the shield.

    Illustrated coin: This coin is brilliant and lustrous with scattered marks in the field, as is typical for this grade.

AU-50, 53, 55, 58 (About Uncirculated). *Obverse:* Light wear is seen on the face, the hair to the right of the face, and the highest area of the hair bun, more so at AU-50 than at 53 or 55. An AU-58 coin has minimal traces of wear. An AU-50 coin has luster in protected areas among the stars and letters, with little in the open fields or on the portrait. At AU-58 most luster is present in the fields, but is worn away on the highest parts

1839, Large Letters, 9 Over 8. Graded AU-53.

of the motifs. *Reverse:* Comments as preceding, except that the eagle shows wear in all of the higher areas, as well as the leaves and arrowheads. Luster ranges from perhaps 40% remaining in protected areas (at AU-50) to nearly full mint bloom (at AU-58). Often the reverse of this type retains more luster than the obverse.

EF-40, 45 (Extremely Fine). *Obverse:* Wear is evident on all high areas of the portrait, including the hair to the right of the forehead, the tip of the coronet, and the hair bun. The stars show light wear at their centers. Luster, if present at all, is minimal and in protected areas such as between the star points. *Reverse:* Wear is greater than on an About Uncirculated coin. On the $10 coins (in contrast to the $2.50 and $5 of the same design),

1868. Graded EF-40.

most of the details on the eagle are sharp. There is flatness on the leaves and arrowheads. Some traces of luster may be seen, more so at EF-45 than at EF-40.

    Illustrated coin: Note the many contact marks on both sides.

VF-20, 30 (Very Fine). *Obverse:* The higher-relief areas of hair are worn flat at VF-20, less so at VF-30. The hair to the right of the coronet is merged into heavy strands. The stars are flat at their centers. *Reverse:* The eagle is worn further, with most neck feathers gone and with the feathers in the wing having flat tips. The branch leaves have little or no detail. The vertical shield stripes, being deeply recessed, remain bold.

1838. Graded VF-25.

The Liberty Head eagle is seldom collected in grades lower than VF-20.

PF-60 to 70 (Proof). *Obverse and Reverse:* PF-60 to 62 coins have extensive hairlines and may have nicks and contact marks. At PF-63, hairlines are prominent, but the mirror surface is very reflective. PF-64 coins have fewer hairlines. At PF-65, hairlines should be minimal and mostly seen only under magnification. There should be no nicks or marks. PF-66 and higher coins should have no marks or hairlines visible to the unaided eye.

1862. Graded PF-65.

Illustrated coin: This is a museum-quality gem, with cameo-contrast motifs and mirror fields.

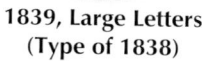

1839, Large Letters (Type of 1838)   **1839, Small Letters (Type of 1840)**

	Mintage	Cert	Avg	%MS	VF-20	EF-40	AU-50	AU-55	AU-58	MS-60	MS-63	MS-65
										PF-63	PF-64	PF-65
1838	7,200	60	48.0	3%	$2,750	$6,000	$13,000	$22,500	$35,000	$45,000	$125,000	
	Auctions: $41,125, AU-58, August 2014; $47,000, AU-58, June 2013; $5,288, VF-25, July 2014											
1838, Proof † (a)	*4–6*	1	65.0		*(extremely rare)*							
	Auctions: $500,000, ChPF, May 1998											
1839, Large Letters (b)	25,801	161	50.4	10%	$1,500	$3,750	$6,500	$10,500	$16,000	$35,000	$85,000	$350,000
	Auctions: $19,975, MS-60, January 2014; $4,847, AU-50, November 2014; $4,994, AU-50, August 2014											
1839, Small Letters	12,447	37	46.9	3%	$1,850	$3,750	$8,500	$20,000	$30,000	$45,000	$135,000	
	Auctions: $47,000, AU-58, February 2014											
1839, Large Letters, Proof (c)	*4–6*	1	67.0		*(extremely rare)*							
	Auctions: $1,610,000, PF-67UCam, January 2007											

† Ranked in the *100 Greatest U.S. Coins* (fourth edition). **a.** 3 examples are known. **b.** The Large Letters style is also known as the "Type of 1838," because of the distinct style of the 1838 Liberty Head motif. The Small Letters style (or "Type of 1840") was used on subsequent issues. **c.** 3 examples are known.

1842, Small Date **1842, Large Date**

	Mintage	Cert	Avg	%MS	VF-20	EF-40	AU-50	AU-55	AU-58	MS-60 / PF-63	MS-63 / PF-64	MS-65 / PF-65
1840	47,338	165	49.1	3%	$1,000	$1,100	$1,550	$2,750	$5,500	$12,000		
Auctions: $35,250, MS-62, August 2014; $3,819, AU-58, October 2014; $6,463, AU-58, January 2014; $2,233, AU-53, September 2014											
1840, Proof (d)	1–2	0	n/a		(unique, in the Smithsonian's National Numismatic Collection)						
Auctions: No auction records available.											
1841	63,131	197	49.9	7%	$1,000	$1,050	$1,250	$2,500	$4,750	$8,000		
Auctions: $9,400, MS-61, February 2014; $1,880, AU-55, November 2014; $764, EF-40, September 2014											
1841, Proof (e)	4–6	1	61.0		(extremely rare)						
Auctions: No auction records available.											
1841O	2,500	50	44.6	0%	$5,500	$13,500	$20,000	$32,500	$45,000			
Auctions: $25,850, AU-53, January 2014; $14,688, AU-50, October 2014											
1842, Small Date	18,623	90	51.0	6%	$1,000	$1,050	$1,800	$3,500	$7,500	$16,000	$40,000	
Auctions: $16,450, MS-61, July 2014; $7,814, AU-58, August 2014											
1842, Large Date	62,884	100	51.2	5%	$1,000	$1,050	$1,650	$2,750	$4,750	$15,000	$35,000	$125,000
Auctions: $2,233, MS-60, January 2014											
1842, Small Date, Proof (f)	2	0	n/a		(extremely rare)						
Auctions: No auction records available.											
1842O	27,400	256	48.3	2%	$1,150	$1,250	$2,750	$8,000	$15,000	$27,500	$75,000	
Auctions: $8,825, AU-55, March 2014; $2,115, AU-50, November 2014; $2,115, EF-45, September 2014; $1,528, EF-45, July 2014											
1843	75,462	177	49.1	2%	$1,000	$1,050	$1,750	$3,500	$5,500	$14,000		
Auctions: $4,700, AU-58, September 2014; $4,113, AU-58, January 2014; $4,113, AU-55, October 2014											
1843, Doubled Die	(g)	0	n/a								
Auctions: No auction records available.											
1843, Proof (h)	6–8	3	62.7		(extremely rare)						
Auctions: No auction records available.											
1843O	175,162	401	49.5	2%	$1,050	$1,100	$1,800	$3,250	$5,500	$12,500		
Auctions: $1,763, AU-55, August 2014; $1,058, AU-50, July 2014; $1,410, EF-45, November 2014; $6,463, VF-30, July 2014											
1844	6,361	38	49.2	5%	$1,200	$2,500	$4,750	$7,500	$9,000	$14,000	$50,000	
Auctions: $24,170, AU-55, January 2014											
1844, Proof (i)	6–8	1	63.0		(extremely rare)						
Auctions: No auction records available.											
1844O	118,700	366	50.8	5%	$1,050	$1,100	$1,850	$3,500	$8,500	$15,000		
Auctions: $7,931, AU-58, June 2013; $5,288, AU-55, November 2014; $1,293, EF-45, November 2014; $1,528, EF-45, September 2014											
1844O, Proof †	1	1	65.0								
Auctions: No auction records available.											
1845	26,153	107	48.7	3%	$1,000	$1,050	$2,000	$2,500	$5,750	$13,500		
Auctions: $4,994, AU-55, April 2013											
1845, Proof (j)	6–8	1	65.0		(extremely rare)						
Auctions: $120,750, PF-64, August 1999											
1845O	47,500	230	49.7	5%	$1,050	$1,150	$2,750	$5,000	$8,500	$15,000	$50,000	
Auctions: $2,820, AU-53, November 2014; $881, AU-50, October 2014; $3,819, AU, March 2014											

† Ranked in the *100 Greatest U.S. Coins* (fourth edition). **d.** While there is only one known example known of this coin, it is possible that other 1840 Proof eagles were made, given that duplicates are known of the quarter eagle and half eagle denominations. **e.** 3 examples are known. **f.** 2 examples are known. **g.** Included in circulation-strike 1843 mintage figure. **h.** 5 examples are known. **i.** 3 or 4 examples are known. **j.** 4 or 5 examples are known.

1846-O, 6 Over 5

1850, Large Date

1850, Small Date

	Mintage	Cert	Avg	%MS	VF-20	EF-40	AU-50	AU-55	AU-58	MS-60 PF-63	MS-63 PF-64	MS-65 PF-65
1846	20,095	92	48.3	4%	$1,050	$1,250	$3,500	$7,500	$11,500	$20,000		
Auctions: $4,994, AU-55, September 2014; $4,406, AU-55, September 2014; $8,225, AU-55, January 2014												
1846, Proof (k)	6–8	1	64.0					*(extremely rare)*				
Auctions: $161,000, PF-64Cam, January 2011												
1846O, All kinds	81,780											
1846O		142	45.9	2%	$1,050	$1,200	$3,200	$6,000	$8,000	$13,500		
Auctions: $2,820, AU-50, January 2014												
1846O, 6 Over 5		8	55.5	0%	$1,100	$1,400	$4,000	$7,500	$10,000	$25,000		
Auctions: $3,525, AU-50, January 2014												
1847	862,258	1,009	52.2	6%	$950	$1,025	$1,075	$1,150	$1,500	$3,500	$21,500	
Auctions: $1,293, AU-58, September 2014; $823, AU-50, September 2014; $8,813, March 2014; $881, EF-45, July 2014												
1847, Proof	1–2	0	n/a				*(unique, in the Smithsonian's National Numismatic Collection)*					
Auctions: No auction records available.												
1847O	571,500	851	50.0	2%	$950	$1,050	$1,150	$1,350	$2,500	$6,000	$21,500	
Auctions: $28,200, MS-63, August 2014; $1,410, AU-58, October 2014; $1,998, AU-58, March 2013; $1,234, AU-55, September 2014												
1848	145,484	353	51.6	7%	$925	$1,000	$1,075	$1,500	$1,850	$4,750	$22,500	
Auctions: $64,625, MS-64, October 2014; $4,994, MS-61, February 2013; $1,028, AU-53, September 2014												
1848, Proof (l)	3–5	1	64.0					*(extremely rare)*				
Auctions: No auction records available.												
1848O	35,850	197	49.6	5%	$1,000	$1,500	$3,200	$6,750	$9,500	$15,000	$35,000	$85,000
Auctions: $64,625, MS-63, January 2014; $2,820, MS-60, October 2014												
1849	653,618	918	50.4	5%	$925	$1,000	$1,075	$1,500	$1,750	$3,250	$13,500	
Auctions: $3,819, MS-61, October 2014; $32,900, MS-64, August 2013; $1,410, AU-58, October 2014; $1,116, AU-55, August 2014												
1849, Recut 1849 Over 849	(m)	32	50.1	6%				$1,250	$2,000			
Auctions: $978, EF-40, May 2011												
1849O	23,900	233	48.4	3%	$1,100	$2,250	$5,000	$6,500	$12,000	$25,000		
Auctions: $5,875, AU-53, October 2013												
1850, All kinds	291,451											
1850, Large Date		423	50.6	5%	$925	$1,000	$1,050	$1,100	$1,750	$4,000	$20,000	
Auctions: $4,406, MS-61, August 2013; $1,586, AU-58, September 2014; $1,410, AU-53, October 2014; $1,234, AU-53, July 2014												
1850, Small Date		132	49.2	4%	$950	$1,100	$2,250	$3,000	$4,500	$8,000	$30,000	
Auctions: $3,819, AU-58, January 2014; $734, AU-50, November 2014; $881, AU-50, October 2014												
1850O	57,500	195	47.5	2%	$1,050	$1,300	$3,500	$5,500	$8,500	$20,000		
Auctions: $6,169, AU-58, November 2014; $18,800, AU-58, August 2014; $4,994, AU-55, October 2013												
1851	176,328	268	52.0	7%	$925	$1,000	$1,050	$1,250	$1,750	$4,000	$26,000	
Auctions: $852, AU-50, September 2014; $881, AU-50, August 2014; $3,819, MS-61, September 2013; $734, VF-30, October 2014												
1851O	263,000	925	50.9	2%	$950	$1,100	$1,600	$2,750	$3,750	$6,500	$27,500	
Auctions: $7,638, MS-61, February 2014; $3,055, AU-58, November 2014; $1,116, AU-55, November 2014												
1852	263,106	602	52.7	6%	$925	$1,000	$1,050	$1,200	$1,500	$5,000		
Auctions: $4,406, MS-61, November 2014; $2,585, AU-58, October 2014; $999, AU-55, October 2014; $4,113, AU-55, June 2013												
1852O	18,000	99	49.8	2%	$1,100	$1,600	$3,750	$7,000	$13,500	$23,500		
Auctions: $3,290, AU-53, November 2014; $18,800, AU, February 2014												

k. 4 examples are known. **l.** 2 examples are known. **m.** Included in circulation-strike 1849 mintage figure.

| 1853, 3 Over 2 | 1854-O, Large Date | 1854-O, Small Date |

	Mintage	Cert	Avg	%MS	VF-20	EF-40	AU-50	AU-55	AU-58	MS-60 / PF-63	MS-63 / PF-64	MS-65 / PF-65
1853, All kinds	201,253											
1853, 3 Over 2		147	52.2	2%	$1,150	$1,500	$1,750	$3,250	$7,500			
Auctions: $5,875, AU-58, October 2014; $4,113, AU-58, July 2014; $4,406, AU-58, January 2014												
1853		622	53.6	6%	$925	$1,000	$1,050	$1,150	$1,500	$3,250	$17,000	
Auctions: $34,075, MS-64, October 2014; $3,819, MS-61, November 2014; $4,553, MS-61, September 2013; $1,028, AU-55, October 2014												
1853O	51,000	245	51.0	2%	$1,000	$1,150	$1,250	$3,000	$6,500	$15,000		
Auctions: $16,450, MS-61, November 2014; $6,463, AU-58, October 2014; $15,275, AU-58, February 2014; $1,293, AU-53, November 2014												
1853O, Proof (n)	*1*	1	61.0									
Auctions: No auction records available.												
1854	54,250	249	52.5	6%	$925	$1,000	$1,050	$1,500	$3,000	$6,500	$27,500	
Auctions: $1,880, AU-58, August 2014; $3,290, AU-58, August 2013; $1,293, AU-55, October 2014												
1854, Proof (o)	*unknown*	1	55.0									
Auctions: No auction records available.												
1854O, Large Date (p)	52,500	155	53.7	10%	$950	$1,100	$1,750	$3,250	$4,500	$10,500		
Auctions: $10,869, MS-60, August 2013; $1,998, AU-53, November 2014												
1854O, Small Date (q)	*(r)*	111	52.9	1%	$950	$1,100	$1,750	$3,250	$4,700	$10,500		
Auctions: $1,821, AU-55, August 2013												
1854S	123,826	463	50.3	2%	$950	$1,050	$1,350	$3,000	$6,500	$12,500		
Auctions: $8,813, AU-58, August 2014; $4,700, AU-58, August 2014; $5,581, AU-58, April 2014; $3,055, AU-55, September 2014												
1855	121,701	536	54.3	10%	$925	$1,000	$1,050	$1,200	$2,250	$4,750	$17,500	
Auctions: $2,350, AU-58, March 2014; $705, AU-50, October 2014												
1855, Proof (s)	*unknown*	0	n/a									
Auctions: No auction records available.												
1855O	18,000	112	49.1	0%	$1,050	$1,800	$5,000	$8,500	$13,500	$25,000		
Auctions: $17,625, AU-58, January 2014												
1855S	9,000	33	48.6	0%	$1,350	$2,250	$5,500	$8,750	$17,500			
Auctions: $17,625, AU-58, March 2014												
1856	60,490	292	53.8	11%	$925	$1,000	$1,050	$1,150	$1,750	$4,000	$15,000	
Auctions: $1,175, AU-58, August 2014; $1,528, AU-58, July 2014; $2,115, AU-58, April 2014; $705, AU-50, October 2014												
1856, Proof (s)	*unknown*	0	n/a									
Auctions: No auction records available.												
1856O	14,500	107	49.8	4%	$1,050	$1,500	$4,250	$8,000	$10,000	$16,500		
Auctions: $4,406, AU-55, January 2014												
1856S	68,000	262	50.1	1%	$925	$1,000	$1,400	$2,500	$5,000	$9,000	$25,000	
Auctions: $9,988, MS-61, April 2014; $3,290, AU-58, November 2014; $2,233, AU-55, September 2014; $3,819, AU-58, July 2014												

n. The 1853-O Proof listed here is not a Proof from a technical standpoint. This unique coin has in the past been called a presentation piece and a branch-mint Proof. "Although the piece does not have the same convincing texture as the 1844-O Proof eagle, it is clearly different from the regular-issue eagles found for the year and mint" (*Encyclopedia of U.S. Gold Coins, 1795–1933*, second edition). **o.** According to Walter Breen, in July 1854 a set of Proof coins was given by the United States to representatives of the sovereign German city of Bremen. Various Proof 1854 gold dollars, quarter eagles, and three-dollar gold pieces have come to light, along with a single gold eagle. **p.** The Large Date variety was made in error, when the diesinker used a date punch for a silver dollar on the much smaller ten-dollar die. **q.** The Small Date variety is scarce in AU. Only 3 or 4 MS examples are known, none finer than MS-60. **r.** Included in 1854-O, Large Date, mintage figure. **s.** No Proof 1855 or 1856 eagles have been confirmed, but Wayte Raymond claimed to have seen one of each some time prior to 1949.

	Mintage	Cert	Avg	%MS	VF-20	EF-40	AU-50	AU-55	AU-58	MS-60	MS-63	MS-65
										PF-63	PF-64	PF-65
1857	16,606	114	51.4	5%	$925	$1,000	$1,950	$3,750	$5,500	$12,000		
Auctions: $4,406, AU-58, April 2014; $1,293, EF-45, September 2014												
1857, Proof	2–3	1	66.0									
Auctions: No auction records available.												
1857O	5,500	59	51.8	0%	$1,600	$2,500	$4,000	$8,500	$15,000			
Auctions: $22,325, AU-58, August 2014; $8,225, AU-55, February 2014												
1857S	26,000	69	47.4	3%	$1,000	$1,250	$2,500	$4,250	$6,500	$11,500	$25,000	
Auctions: $8,225, AU-58, July 2014; $3,378, EF-45, August 2014												
1858 (t)	2,521	32	48.9	6%	$6,000	$7,500	$12,500	$17,500	$27,500	$40,000		
Auctions: $15,275, AU-53, February 2014												
1858, Proof (u)	4–6	2	64.0		*(extremely rare)*							
Auctions: No auction records available.												
1858O	20,000	194	51.6	3%	$1,050	$1,150	$2,000	$3,500	$5,000	$9,500	$32,500	
Auctions: $5,288, AU-58, June 2013; $2,585, AU-55, November 2014												
1858S	11,800	50	50.8	0%	$1,850	$3,250	$5,000	$12,000	$21,500			
Auctions: $15,275, AU-58, April 2013; $3,055, EF-45, November 2014; $2,115, EF-40, November 2014												
1859	16,013	147	50.8	7%	$925	$1,000	$1,300	$2,500	$4,000	$10,000	$50,000	
Auctions: $41,125, MS-62, November 2014; $47,000, MS-62, April 2014												
1859, Proof	80	3	64.3							$75,000	$150,000	$200,000
Auctions: No auction records available.												
1859O	2,300	21	50.6	5%	$5,000	$10,000	$25,000	$37,500	$55,000			
Auctions: $28,200, AU-50, December 2013												
1859S	7,000	37	43.6	3%	$3,000	$7,500	$20,000	$25,000	$35,000	$65,000		
Auctions: $14,100, AU-53, October 2014; $28,200, AU-50, February 2014; $3,290, EF-40, August 2014												
1860	15,055	138	51.9	11%	$925	$1,100	$1,750	$2,700	$3,000	$7,500	$25,000	
Auctions: $70,500, MS-64, February 2013; $1,645, AU-50, September 2014												
1860, Proof	50	5	63.6							$50,000	$80,000	$135,000
Auctions: $142,175, PF-64DCam, April 2014												
1860O	11,100	129	51.4	4%	$1,050	$1,450	$2,500	$5,000	$6,500	$15,000		
Auctions: $8,814, AU-About Uncirculated, March 2014												
1860S	5,000	21	48.0	10%	$3,000	$5,500	$13,000	$25,000	$30,000	$55,000		
Auctions: $28,200, AU-55, March 2014												
1861	113,164	605	54.8	14%	$925	$1,050	$1,100	$2,500	$3,750	$6,000	$20,000	
Auctions: $25,850, MS-63, August 2013; $8,225, MS-62, November 2014; $8,519, MS-62, August 2014; $4,113, AU-58, July 2014												
1861, Proof	69	6	64.2							$45,000	$70,000	$125,000
Auctions: $129,250, PF-64Cam, March 2013												
1861S	15,500	81	49.9	1%	$1,650	$3,000	$8,500	$17,500	$25,000	$45,000		
Auctions: $25,850, AU-58, March 2014; $7,638, AU-53, September 2014												
1862	10,960	87	51.3	13%	$950	$1,200	$2,000	$9,000	$15,000	$17,500	$35,000	
Auctions: $28,200, AU-58, March 2014; $3,672, EF-45, August 2014												
1862, Proof	35	5	64.4							$42,500	$70,000	$125,000
Auctions: $152,750, PF-65DCam, August 2013												
1862S	12,500	45	45.9	0%	$1,750	$3,000	$5,000	$12,500	$22,500	$45,000		
Auctions: $21,150, AU-58, October 2014; $5,581, EF-35, February 2014												
1863	1,218	16	52.0	19%	$6,500	$15,000	$30,000	$50,000	$60,000	$85,000		
Auctions: $49,938, AU-53, January 2014												
1863, Proof	30	12	64.2							$42,500	$70,000	$125,000
Auctions: $299,000, PF-65DCam, August 2011												
1863S	10,000	29	45.1	3%	$3,500	$12,500	$25,000	$30,000	$40,000	$60,000		
Auctions: $32,900, AU-53, February 2014; $15,275, EF-45, October 2014; $5,875, F-12, November 2014												

t. Beware of fraudulently removed mintmark. **u.** 4 or 5 examples are known.

1865-S, 865
Over Inverted 186

	Mintage	Cert	Avg	%MS	VF-20	EF-40	AU-50	AU-55	AU-58	MS-60 / PF-63	MS-63 / PF-64	MS-65 / PF-65
1864	3,530	22	49.8	18%	$3,500	$7,500	$16,500	$27,500	$30,000	$40,000		
Auctions: $41,125, AU-55, October 2014; $28,200, AU-55, January 2014												
1864, Proof	50	17	63.9							$42,500	$70,000	$125,000
Auctions: $138,000, PF-64UCam, October 2011												
1864S	2,500	6	42.5	0%	$30,000	$60,000	$90,000	$150,000				
Auctions: $146,875, AU-53, March 2014												
1865	3,980	32	50.2	3%	$4,000	$7,500	$10,000	$18,500	$25,000	$37,500	$75,000	
Auctions: $15,275, AU-53, October 2014; $18,800, AU-53, January 2014; $13,513, AU-50, October 2014												
1865, Proof	25	13	64.1							$42,500	$70,000	$125,000
Auctions: $528,750, PF, August 2013												
1865S, All kinds	16,700											
1865S		33	39.7	3%	$7,500	$10,000	$15,000	$25,000	$32,000	$55,000		
Auctions: $6,756, F-12, February 2013												
1865S, 865 Over Inverted 186		37	43.2	3%	$6,000	$11,000	$18,500	$20,000	$25,000	$37,500		
Auctions: $18,800, AU-55, October 2014; $27,025, AU-53, March 2014; $14,100, EF-45, October 2014; $1,880, VG-8, August 2014												
1866S, No Motto	8,500	34	46.6	3%	$2,750	$3,750	$12,000	$20,000	$30,000	$55,000		
Auctions: $14,950, EF-45, August 2011												
1866, With Motto	3,750	47	49.5	11%	$1,500	$2,000	$5,000	$9,000	$19,500	$35,000		
Auctions: $14,100, AU-55, September 2013; $7,050, AU-53, November 2014												
1866, Proof	30	9	64.2							$32,500	$50,000	$85,000
Auctions: $66,125, PF-64UCam+★, January 2012												
1866S, With Motto	11,500	36	48.9	0%	$1,500	$3,250	$7,250	$10,000	$17,500			
Auctions: $15,275, AU-58, March 2014; $9,988, AU-55, August 2014												
1867	3,090	62	50.3	2%	$1,500	$2,500	$4,500	$10,000	$20,000	$35,000		
Auctions: $30,550, AU-58, August 2013												
1867, Proof	50	5	64.7							$32,500	$50,000	$85,000
Auctions: $64,625, PF-65Cam, August 2014; $54,344, PF-64Cam, October 2014												
1867S	9,000	33	46.6	0%	$2,350	$5,500	$9,000	$14,500	$22,500			
Auctions: $9,988, AU-53, June 2013												
1868	10,630	147	50.5	3%	$900	$950	$1,700	$3,500	$7,000	$17,500		
Auctions: $15,275, MS-60, June 2013; $4,406, AU-58, October 2014												
1868, Proof	25	4	64.8							$32,500	$50,000	$85,000
Auctions: $24,150, PF-62Cam, June 2005												
1868S	13,500	74	48.4	0%	$1,250	$2,250	$4,000	$5,500	$11,000			
Auctions: $5,875, AU-58, August 2014; $18,213, AU-58, July 2014; $3,290, AU-50, October 2014; $2,115, EF-40, August 2014												
1869	1,830	42	50.2	5%	$1,500	$2,350	$4,750	$11,500	$15,000	$30,000		
Auctions: $14,100, AU-58, August 2013												
1869, Proof	25	8	63.9							$32,500	$50,000	$80,000
Auctions: $161,000, PF-67UCam+★, February 2012												
1869S	6,430	39	47.3	3%	$1,500	$2,350	$4,750	$10,000	$24,000	$32,500		
Auctions: $28,200, AU-58, March 2014; $3,290, EF-45, August 2014												

	Mintage	Cert	Avg	%MS	VF-20	EF-40	AU-50	AU-55	AU-58	MS-60	MS-63	MS-65
										PF-63	PF-64	PF-65
1870	3,990	68	49.1	1%	$950	$1,250	$2,500	$6,000	$11,000	$18,500		
Auctions: $10,575, AU-55, January 2014												
1870, Proof	35	4	64.5							$32,500	$50,000	$80,000
Auctions: $97,750, PF-65UCam, January 2010												
1870CC	5,908	31	41.4	0%	$25,000	$45,000	$75,000	$125,000				
Auctions: $135,125, AU-55, March 2014; $36,719, VF-35, August 2014												
1870S	8,000	60	42.0	0%	$1,100	$2,250	$5,500	$11,000	$15,000	$27,500		
Auctions: $12,925, AU-58, March 2014												
1871	1,790	43	50.2	0%	$1,400	$2,400	$3,750	$8,500	$15,000	$22,500		
Auctions: $15,275, AU-58, September 2013; $9,400, AU-55, August 2014; $3,290, EF-40, August 2014												
1871, Proof	30	5	63.3							$35,000	$50,000	$80,000
Auctions: $76,375, PF-64DCam, August 2013												
1871CC	8,085	71	46.6	3%	$3,250	$7,750	$15,000	$22,500	$32,500	$75,000		
Auctions: $35,250, AU-58, October 2014; $18,213, AU-55, February 2014												
1871S	16,500	90	43.6	0%	$1,200	$1,850	$5,000	$7,500	$12,500			
Auctions: $10,281, AU-58, March 2014; $2,115, AU-50, July 2014												
1872	1,620	26	51.9	4%	$2,150	$3,250	$9,000	$12,000	$17,500	$25,000		
Auctions: $38,188, AU-58, August 2014; $13,513, AU-55, February 2014												
1872, Proof	30	7	64.7							$32,500	$50,000	$80,000
Auctions: $48,875, PF-64DCam, June 2012												
1872CC	4,600	50	43.2	0%	$5,000	$12,000	$25,000	$40,000	$55,000			
Auctions: $47,000, AU, February 2014, $9,988, EF-40, August 2014												
1872S	17,300	145	47.5	1%	$900	$1,050	$1,500	$4,250	$8,500	$17,500		
Auctions: $8,225, AU-58, October 2014; $7,050, AU-58, March 2014												
1873	800	21	50.0	0%	$6,500	$15,000	$20,000	$50,000	$57,500	$75,000		
Auctions: $55,813, AU-55, January 2014; $16,450, EF-40, July 2014												
1873, Proof	25	9	63.8							$37,500	$55,000	$85,000
Auctions: $74,750, PF-65Cam+, February 2012												
1873CC	4,543	34	40.5	0%	$8,000	$15,000	$32,500	$75,000	$100,000			
Auctions: $58,750, AU-53, March 2014												
1873S	12,000	84	43.3	0%	$1,000	$2,250	$4,250	$7,000	$12,000	$20,000		
Auctions: $4,700, AU-53, March 2013												
1874	53,140	330	56.1	20%	$800	$875	$900	$915	$925	$1,600	$7,500	
Auctions: $1,410, MS-61, September 2014; $1,880, MS-61, June 2014; $676, AU-55, July 2014; $999, AU-50, October 2014												
1874, Proof	20	1	62.0							$32,500	$55,000	$85,000
Auctions: $29,500, PF-64Cam, September 2006												
1874CC	16,767	157	42.3	1%	$2,000	$4,000	$8,500	$17,500	$32,500	$50,000	$200,000	
Auctions: $30,550, AU-58, May 2013; $2,585, VF-35, October 2014; $2,585, VF-20, September 2014; $2,350, F-15, August 2014												
1874S	10,000	92	42.5	0%	$1,450	$2,500	$5,000	$7,500	$15,000			
Auctions: $12,338, AU-58, July 2014; $2,644, EF-45, August 2014												
1875	100	7	45.4	0%	$150,000	$185,000	$225,000	$325,000				
Auctions: $211,500, AU-50, February 2014												
1875, Proof	20	4	64.6							$155,000	$200,000	$275,000
Auctions: $164,500, PF-50, January 2014												
1875CC	7,715	71	39.7	3%	$6,000	$10,000	$17,500	$30,000	$38,500	$70,000	$125,000	
Auctions: $8,225, EF-45, February 2014												

	Mintage	Cert	Avg	%MS	VF-20	EF-40	AU-50	AU-55	AU-58	MS-60 / PF-63	MS-63 / PF-64	MS-65 / PF-65
1876	687	21	51.3	5%	$4,500	$9,500	$17,000	$37,500	$60,000	$75,000		
Auctions: $70,500, AU-58, January 2014; $23,500, AU-53, October 2014; $18,800, AU-53, July 2014; $18,800, AU-53, July 2014												
1876, Proof	45	14	63.7							$30,000	$45,000	$75,000
Auctions: $100,625, PF-65Cam, April 2011												
1876CC	4,696	94	41.4	0%	$5,000	$12,000	$18,500	$32,500	$40,000			
Auctions: $14,100, AU-50, October 2013												
1876S	5,000	54	45.1	0%	$1,250	$1,750	$5,500	$10,000	$20,000			
Auctions: $22,325, AU-55, October 2013												
1877	797	30	54.1	0%	$3,000	$5,000	$10,000	$15,000	$20,000	$30,000		
Auctions: $11,163, AU-55, July 2014; $11,163, AU-55, January 2014												
1877, Proof	20	3	64.7							$32,500	$45,000	$75,000
Auctions: $39,100, PF-64Cam, April 2002												
1877CC	3,332	36	39.9	0%	$5,500	$12,500	$22,500	$40,000	$65,000			
Auctions: $10,575, EF-45, April 2014												
1877S	17,000	163	46.7	2%	$850	$900	$1,800	$4,000	$11,000	$25,000		
Auctions: $22,325, MS-61, January 2014; $4,406, AU-55, November 2014; $2,056, AU-53, August 2014; $1,410, EF-40, August 2014												
1878	73,780	360	58.0	45%	$725	$750	$775	$785	$800	$1,100	$6,500	
Auctions: $7,638, MS-64, April 2013; $1,763, MS-62, September 2014; $2,585, MS-62, August 2014; $987, MS-61, September 2014												
1878, Proof	20	4	63.8							$27,500	$45,000	$75,000
Auctions: $25,300, PF-63, August 2011												
1878CC	3,244	45	46.3	2%	$5,500	$9,000	$18,000	$37,500	$55,000	$85,000		
Auctions: $28,200, AU-55, March 2014												
1878S	26,100	215	47.8	2%	$900	$975	$1,750	$2,000	$4,000	$11,500	$25,000	
Auctions: $1,763, AU-55, October 2013; $1,528, AU-55, September 2014; $999, AU-53, November 2014; $646, EF-40, September 2014												
1879	384,740	929	59.0	54%	$725	$750	$775	$785	$800	$1,000	$4,000	
Auctions: $8,225, MS-64, August 2013; $2,480, MS-63, October 2014; $1,293, MS-62, September 2014; $764, AU-58, November 2014												
1879, Proof	30	6	64.8							$25,000	$37,500	$65,000
Auctions: $52,875, PF-65Cam, February 2013												
1879CC	1,762	39	42.7	3%	$10,000	$16,000	$37,500	$42,500	$60,000			
Auctions: $41,125, AU-50, March 2014												
1879O	1,500	46	49.1	2%	$5,000	$12,500	$20,000	$30,000	$55,000	$75,000		
Auctions: $88,125, MS-61, June 2014												
1879S	224,000	458	57.0	26%	$725	$750	$775	$785	$800	$1,150	$7,500	
Auctions: $12,925, MS-64, November 2013; $1,058, MS-61, September 2014; $1,058, MS-61, July 2014; $881, AU-58, November 2014												
1880	1,644,840	2,054	60.0	82%	$725	$750	$775	$785	$800	$950	$2,000	
Auctions: $19,975, MS-65, August 2013; $1,410, MS-63, November 2014; $911, MS-62, October 2014; $999, MS-62, August 2014												
1880, Proof	36	5	64.3							$22,500	$35,000	$60,000
Auctions: $32,200, PF-64, October 1999												
1880CC	11,190	182	50.4	5%	$1,100	$1,350	$2,300	$5,000	$8,000	$17,500		
Auctions: $2,761, AU-53, August 2013; $1,175, EF-40, July 2014												
1880O	9,200	176	51.8	5%	$1,000	$1,150	$2,000	$3,000	$4,500	$10,000		
Auctions: $999, AU-50, September 2014; $2,233, EF-45, August 2014; $4,113, EF-40, June 2014												
1880S	506,250	1,019	60.3	79%	$725	$750	$775	$785	$800	$950	$2,500	
Auctions: $1,939, MS-63, September 2014; $2,233, MS-63, August 2013; $852, MS-62, September 2014												
1881	3,877,220	12,207	61.0	94%	$725	$750	$775	$785	$800	$900	$1,500	$10,000
Auctions: $7,931, MS-64, November 2014; $2,115, MS-64, November 2014; $2,820, MS-64, April 2013; $705, MS-62, October 2014												
1881, Proof	40	5	65.2							$22,500	$32,500	$55,000
Auctions: $56,063, PF-65, October 2011												
1881CC	24,015	335	52.6	14%	$1,000	$1,250	$1,550	$2,750	$4,000	$8,500		
Auctions: $12,925, MS-62, April 2013; $4,259, AU-58, October 2014; $1,116, AU-50, July 2014; $940, EF-40, September 2014												
1881O	8,350	181	52.4	8%	$1,000	$1,250	$1,650	$2,350	$3,800	$8,000		
Auctions: $12,338, MS-60, January 2014												
1881S	970,000	2,443	60.7	90%	$725	$750	$775	$785	$800	$825	$4,000	
Auctions: $705, MS-62, November 2014; $776, MS-62, October 2014; $881, MS-62, August 2014; $999, MS-62, June 2013												

	Mintage	Cert	Avg	%MS	VF-20	EF-40	AU-50	AU-55	AU-58	MS-60	MS-63	MS-65
										PF-63	PF-64	PF-65
1882	2,324,440	13,279	61.2	96%	$725	$750	$775	$785	$800	$825	$1,200	
	Auctions: $1,528, MS-64, November 2014; $3,290, MS-64, January 2014; $831, MS-62, July 2014; $823, AU-55, August 2014											
1882, Proof	40	9	64.2							$20,000	$32,500	$55,000
	Auctions: $43,125, PF-65Cam, October 2009											
1882CC	6,764	147	52.5	3%	$1,100	$1,500	$3,500	$9,500	$15,000	$23,500		
	Auctions: $25,850, MS-60, July 2014											
1882O	10,820	192	52.4	9%	$950	$1,050	$1,500	$2,500	$4,000	$7,500	$45,000	
	Auctions: $30,550, MS-62, January 2014; $2,389, AU-53, September 2014											
1882S	132,000	342	60.6	86%	$725	$750	$775	$785	$800	$825	$3,000	
	Auctions: $28,200, MS-65, November 2014; $14,100, MS-64, April 2014; $2,350, MS-63, July 2014; $1,204, MS-62, October 2014											
1883	208,700	1,315	61.1	95%	$725	$750	$775	$785	$800	$825	$1,600	
	Auctions: $1,250, MS-63, October 2014; $1,880, MS-63, April 2013; $823, MS-62, July 2014											
1883, Proof	40	9	64.4							$20,000	$32,500	$55,000
	Auctions: $8,813, PF-60, July 2014											
1883CC	12,000	328	49.4	4%	$1,250	$1,850	$3,000	$7,500	$15,000	$35,000		
	Auctions: $41,125, MS-61, October 2014; $64,625, MS-61, April 2013; $6,463, AU-55, September 2014; $940, VF-20, July 2014											
1883O	800	21	51.5	5%	$10,000	$25,000	$40,000	$75,000	$100,000	$125,000		
	Auctions: $82,250, AU-58, August 2014; $70,500, AU-55, February 2014; $47,000, AU-50, October 2014; $14,100, AU-50, July 2014											
1883S	38,000	138	56.0	39%	$725	$750	$775	$785	$800	$825	$7,500	
	Auctions: $11,163, MS-63, February 2013; $1,293, MS-61, November 2014; $1,116, MS-61, September 2014; $823, AU-58, November 2014											
1884	76,860	357	58.3	44%	$725	$750	$775	$785	$800	$825	$4,250	
	Auctions: $846, MS-61, July 2014; $823, AU-55, February 2014											
1884, Proof	45	7	64.6							$20,000	$32,500	$55,000
	Auctions: $37,375, PF-64DCam, March 2012											
1884CC	9,925	172	51.6	5%	$1,200	$1,650	$2,750	$5,000	$10,000	$20,000	$55,000	
	Auctions: $17,625, AU-58, February 2014; $2,291, EF-45, July 2014											
1884S	124,250	528	59.4	67%	$725	$750	$775	$785	$800	$825	$4,500	
	Auctions: $4,994, MS-63, July 2014; $4,113, MS-63, July 2014; $1,116, MS-62, October 2014; $764, MS-61, September 2014											
1885	253,462	628	60.5	83%	$725	$750	$775	$785	$800	$825	$3,500	$20,000
	Auctions: $1,528, MS-63, November 2014; $1,880, MS-63, October 2013; $823, MS-60, August 2014											
1885, Proof	65	12	63.5							$20,000	$32,500	$52,500
	Auctions: $57,500, PF-66UCam, January 2012											
1885S	228,000	826	60.7	87%	$725	$750	$775	$785	$800	$825	$1,750	
	Auctions: $5,875, MS-64, August 2014; $4,406, MS-63, August 2013; $705, MS-62, October 2014; $881, MS-62, July 2014											
1886	236,100	632	59.4	64%	$725	$750	$775	$785	$800	$825	$3,000	
	Auctions: $1,998, MS-63, November 2014; $2,820, MS-63, November 2013; $969, MS-62, August 2014; $852, MS-60, August 2014											
1886, Proof	60	14	63.1							$18,500	$32,500	$52,500
	Auctions: $39,656, PF-64DCam, April 2014											
1886S	826,000	2,972	61.3	95%	$725	$750	$775	$785	$800	$825	$1,400	
	Auctions: $4,259, MS-64, August 2014; $1,087, MS-63, August 2014; $646, MS-62, October 2014; $734, MS-62, September 2014											
1887	53,600	280	58.0	45%	$725	$750	$775	$785	$800	$825	$4,500	
	Auctions: $1,410, MS-62, October 2014; $1,792, MS-62, September 2013; $940, MS-61, October 2014; $1,011, MS-61, July 2014											
1887, Proof	80	17	63.9							$18,500	$32,500	$52,500
	Auctions: $64,625, PF-65DCam, April 2014											
1887S	817,000	1,435	60.8	91%	$725	$750	$775	$785	$800	$825	$2,000	
	Auctions: $3,819, MS-64, September 2014; $8,813, MS-64, April 2013; $1,293, MS-63, October 2014; $793, MS-62, July 2014											
1888	132,921	486	58.9	58%	$725	$750	$775	$785	$800	$825	$6,500	
	Auctions: $4,994, MS-63, October 2014; $1,116, MS-62, October 2014; $2,350, MS-62, March 2013; $881, MS-61, September 2014											
1888, Proof	75	11	64.1							$18,500	$32,500	$52,500
	Auctions: $17,250, PF-63DCam, February 2009											
1888O	21,335	623	60.2	81%	$775	$825	$875	$900	$1,000	$1,250	$7,500	
	Auctions: $21,150, MS-64, August 2013; $999, MS-62, October 2014; $1,293, MS-61, July 2014											
1888S	648,700	1,729	60.7	90%	$725	$750	$775	$785	$800	$825	$1,600	
	Auctions: $1,293, MS-63, August 2014; $1,528, MS-63, February 2013; $764, MS-62, November 2014; $823, MS-62, September 2014											

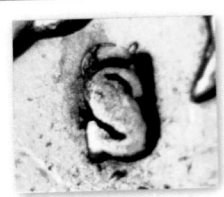

1889-S, Repunched Mintmark
FS-G10-1889S-501.

	Mintage	Cert	Avg	%MS	VF-20	EF-40	AU-50	AU-55	AU-58	MS-60 / PF-63	MS-63 / PF-64	MS-65 / PF-65
1889	4,440	124	58.8	56%	$875	$925	$950	$1,100	$1,250	$2,500	$10,000	
	Auctions: $4,259, MS-61, February 2014; $1,234, MS-60, November 2014; $1,998, AU-58, September 2014											
1889, Proof	45	4	64.4							$18,000	$32,500	$52,500
	Auctions: $23,500, PF-64Cam, August 2014; $4,994, PF-60, April 2013											
1889S	425,400	1,229	60.8	89%	$725	$750	$775	$785	$800	$825	$1,650	
	Auctions: $52,875, MS-65, November 2013; $4,406, MS-64, July 2014; $1,293, MS-63, September 2014; $823, MS-62, August 2014											
1889S, Repunched Mintmark	(v)	1	45.0	0%				$900	$975	$1,025	$1,850	
	Auctions: $1,035, MS-63, August 2006											
1890	57,980	433	59.0	62%	$725	$750	$775	$785	$800	$825	$4,500	$12,500
	Auctions: $2,820, MS-63, July 2014; $4,113, MS-63, June 2013; $1,058, MS-62, November 2014; $1,116, MS-62, September 2014											
1890, Proof	63	24	63.8							$16,500	$25,000	$47,500
	Auctions: $29,900, PF-64UCam, January 2012											
1890CC	17,500	352	56.8	39%	$1,100	$1,200	$1,500	$2,000	$2,750	$4,000	$20,000	
	Auctions: $18,800, MS-63, August 2013; $3,819, AU-58, November 2014; $2,820, AU-58, November 2014; $1,998, AU-55, September 2014											
1891	91,820	697	61.1	95%	$725	$750	$775	$785	$800	$825	$2,500	
	Auctions: $7,344, MS-64, November 2013; $1,998, MS-63, August 2014; $1,410, MS-62, July 2014											
1891, Proof	48	20	64.2							$16,500	$25,000	$47,500
	Auctions: $54,625, PF-65Cam, February 2012											
1891CC	103,732	2,337	58.5	59%	$1,100	$1,200	$1,300	$1,500	$1,750	$2,000	$8,000	
	Auctions: $6,464, MS-63, September 2014; $15,275, MS-63, May 2013; $3,055, MS-62, October 2014; $2,233, MS-61, October 2014											
1892	797,480	8,236	61.4	98%	$725	$750	$775	$785	$800	$825	$1,200	$7,500
	Auctions: $6,756, MS-65, October 2013; $1,028, MS-63, July 2014; $652, MS-62, October 2014; $852, MS-62, August 2014											
1892, Proof	72	12	63.7							$16,500	$25,000	$47,500
	Auctions: $4,406, PF-55, January 2014											
1892CC	40,000	479	52.7	10%	$1,100	$1,250	$1,600	$2,500	$3,500	$5,000	$25,000	
	Auctions: $1,763, AU-53, August 2014; $6,463, MS-61, September 2013											
1892O	28,688	695	60.2	79%	$775	$800	$850	$875	$950	$1,200	$6,000	
	Auctions: $7,931, MS-63, February 2013; $1,763, MS-62, August 2014; $999, MS-61, November 2014; $705, AU-53, October 2014											
1892S	115,500	294	59.4	65%	$725	$750	$775	$785	$800	$825	$2,600	
	Auctions: $5,288, MS-64, September 2014; $7,050, MS-64, August 2014; $3,055, MS-63, April 2014; $852, MS-62, November 2014											
1893	1,840,840	34,342	61.8	99%	$725	$750	$775	$785	$800	$825	$1,000	$5,500
	Auctions: $1,175, MS-64, October 2014; $2,234, MS-64, June 2013; $969, MS-62, August 2014; $677, MS-61, October 2014											
1893, Proof	55	18	63.4							$16,500	$25,000	$47,500
	Auctions: $30,550, PF-64DCam, August 2014; $58,750, PF, March 2014											
1893CC	14,000	223	52.0	7%	$1,150	$1,400	$2,250	$3,750	$5,000	$15,000		
	Auctions: $18,800, MS-61, January 2014; $940, EF-40, September 2014											
1893O	17,000	430	59.7	70%	$775	$800	$850	$950	$975	$1,200	$5,000	
	Auctions: $1,293, MS-61, September 2014; $4,406, AU-58, September 2013											
1893S	141,350	633	60.2	79%	$725	$750	$775	$785	$800	$825	$2,750	
	Auctions: $1,763, MS-63, November 2014; $2,233, MS-63, September 2013; $999, MS-62, September 2014; $940, MS-62, August 2014											

v. Included in 1889-S mintage figure.

	Mintage	Cert	Avg	%MS	VF-20	EF-40	AU-50	AU-55	AU-58	MS-60 / PF-63	MS-63 / PF-64	MS-65 / PF-65
1894	2,470,735	35,819	61.7	99%	$725	$750	$775	$785	$800	$825	$1,000	$8,500
Auctions: $7,931, MS-65, August 2013; $3,525, MS-64, November 2014; $881, MS-62, July 2014; $678, MS-61, October 2014												
1894, Proof	43	11	64.2							$16,500	$25,000	$47,500
Auctions: $105,750, PF-65, January 2014												
1894O	107,500	832	57.4	35%	$750	$800	$850	$900	$975	$1,150	$6,000	
Auctions: $5,288, MS-63, January 2014; $2,115, MS-62, November 2014; $940, AU-58, August 2014; $764, AU-53, August 2014												
1894S	25,000	160	53.9	16%	$750	$775	$950	$1,050	$1,500	$3,000	$14,000	
Auctions: $9,988, MS-61, March 2014; $1,058, AU-55, September 2014												
1895	567,770	11,021	61.7	99%	$725	$750	$775	$785	$800	$825	$1,350	$12,500
Auctions: $11,163, MS-65, August 2013; $964, MS-63, October 2014; $705, MS-62, October 2014; $793, MS-61, July 2014												
1895, Proof	56	18	63.9							$16,000	$25,000	$47,500
Auctions: $51,750, PF-65UCam, January 2012												
1895O	98,000	687	58.9	50%	$750	$775	$850	$875	$925	$1,200	$6,000	
Auctions: $9,400, MS-63, February 2013; $1,234, MS-61, September 2014; $766, MS-60, October 2014; $764, AU-58, October 2014												
1895S	49,000	217	52.4	8%	$900	$950	$975	$1,100	$1,250	$2,000	$8,000	
Auctions: $4,700, MS-62, November 2014; $5,875, MS-62, October 2014; $846, AU-55, September 2014; $1,105, AU-55, August 2013												
1896	76,270	1,401	61.7	99%	$725	$750	$775	$785	$800	$825	$1,400	$12,000
Auctions: $2,115, MS-64, August 2014; $2,585, MS-64, September 2013; $940, MS-63, October 2014; $1,128, MS-63, September 2014												
1896, Proof	78	18	64.1							$16,000	$25,000	$47,500
Auctions: $89,125, PF-66DCam, April 2012; $70,500, PF-66, September 2014												
1896S	123,750	464	54.1	15%	$750	$775	$800	$850	$900	$1,750	$8,000	
Auctions: $6,756, MS-63, December 2013; $1,763, MS-61, November 2014; $881, AU-58, September 2014; $764, AU-53, November 2014												
1897	1,000,090	9,579	61.6	98%	$725	$750	$775	$785	$800	$825	$1,000	$7,500
Auctions: $1,763, MS-64, October 2014; $2,585, MS-64, August 2014; $793, MS-62, July 2014; $653, MS-61, October 2014												
1897, Proof	69	11	64.3							$16,000	$25,000	$47,500
Auctions: $19,975, PF, August 2013												
1897O	42,500	378	58.8	47%	$750	$775	$800	$850	$900	$1,050	$5,000	$25,000
Auctions: $6,169, MS-63, March 2013; $1,293, MS-61, September 2014; $1,880, AU-58, July 2014; $881, AU-55, October 2014												
1897S	234,750	348	57.2	35%	$725	$750	$775	$785	$800	$825	$5,000	$25,000
Auctions: $1,293, MS-62, March 2014; $764, AU-58, October 2014; $823, AU-58, September 2014												
1898	812,130	3,983	61.4	94%	$725	$750	$775	$785	$800	$825	$1,350	$7,500
Auctions: $5,875, MS-65, November 2014; $7,638, MS-65, April 2014; $881, MS-63, November 2014; $705, MS-61, October 2014												
1898, Proof	67	27	65.2							$16,000	$25,000	$47,500
Auctions: $58,750, PF-66DCam, September 2014; $85,188, PF-66DCam, April 2013												
1898S	473,600	438	60.4	86%	$725	$750	$775	$785	$800	$825	$3,500	$12,500
Auctions: $1,645, MS-63, August 2014; $3,290, MS-63, January 2014; $870, MS-61, July 2014												
1899	1,262,219	20,602	62.1	98%	$725	$750	$775	$785	$800	$825	$1,000	$3,500
Auctions: $7,050, MS-65, August 2014; $940, MS-63, August 2014; $823, MS-62, August 2014; $677, MS-61, October 2014												
1899, Proof	86	35	64.6							$15,000	$23,500	$45,000
Auctions: $76,375, PF-67DCam, September 2014; $56,400, PF, March 2014												
1899O	37,047	233	59.3	51%	$750	$775	$800	$850	$900	$1,250	$6,000	
Auctions: $6,463, MS-63, March 2013; $1,763, MS-61, September 2014; $1,293, MS-61, August 2014; $940, AU-55, July 2014												
1899S	841,000	664	60.2	80%	$725	$750	$775	$785	$800	$825	$2,000	$12,000
Auctions: $49,938, MS-67, April 2014; $21,150, MS-64, November 2014; $4,406, MS-64, August 2014; $677, MS-61, October 2014												
1900	293,840	6,455	62.1	99%	$725	$750	$775	$785	$800	$825	$1,000	$4,000
Auctions: $1,058, MS-64, August 2014; $940, MS-63, August 2014; $3,231, MS-65, February 2014												
1900, Proof	120	49	64.6							$15,000	$23,500	$45,000
Auctions: $1,880, PF, February 2014												
1900S	81,000	179	57.9	39%	$725	$750	$775	$785	$800	$825	$5,500	
Auctions: $6,169, MS-63, September 2013; $658, AU-58, November 2014; $705, AU-58, July 2014												

	Mintage	Cert	Avg	%MS	VF-20	EF-40	AU-50	AU-55	AU-58	MS-60 / PF-63	MS-63 / PF-64	MS-65 / PF-65
1901	1,718,740	23,918	62.3	98%	$725	$750	$775	$785	$800	$825	$1,000	$3,250
	Auctions: $8,344, MS-66, September 2014; $8,226, MS-66, April 2014; $2,122, MS-65, October 2014; $2,115, MS-64, November 2014										
1901, Proof	85	45	63.9							$15,000	$23,500	$45,000
	Auctions: $48,875, PF-66Cam, January 2012										
1901O	72,041	423	60.0	68%	$750	$775	$800	$850	$900	$1,250	$3,250	$15,000
	Auctions: $6,169, MS-64, June 2014										
1901S	2,812,750	17,677	62.9	99%	$725	$750	$775	$785	$800	$825	$1,000	$3,250
	Auctions: $3,672, MS-66, November 2014; $4,113, MS-65, October 2014; $1,528, MS-64, August 2014; $7,638, MS, February 2014										
1902	82,400	688	61.1	89%	$725	$750	$775	$785	$800	$825	$2,000	$9,500
	Auctions: $7,344, MS-65, August 2013; $4,700, MS-64, September 2014; $999, MS-62, August 2014										
1902, Proof	113	25	64.0							$15,000	$23,500	$45,000
	Auctions: $61,688, PF-67, February 2013										
1902S	469,500	2,838	62.8	99%	$725	$750	$775	$785	$800	$825	$1,000	$4,000
	Auctions: $8,519, MS-66, February 2014; $1,058, MS-63, September 2014; $1,058, MS-63, August 2014										
1903	125,830	998	61.4	92%	$725	$775	$800	$825	$875	$900	$1,000	$11,000
	Auctions: $1,116, MS-64, October 2014; $6,463, MS-65, January 2014; $1,058, MS-63, October 2014; $1,058, MS-63, August 2014										
1903, Proof	96	43	64.5							$15,000	$23,500	$45,000
	Auctions: $39,950, PF, October 2013										
1903O	112,771	1,118	60.2	73%	$750	$775	$800	$850	$900	$1,200	$3,000	$17,500
	Auctions: $4,406, MS-64, August 2014; $5,288, MS-64, April 2014; $1,234, MS-62, July 2014; $1,011, MS-61, September 2014										
1903S	538,000	911	62.4	92%	$725	$750	$775	$785	$800	$825	$1,350	$3,750
	Auctions: $17,625, MS-67, July 2014; $24,675, MS-67, April 2014; $2,820, MS-65, October 2014; $764, MS-63, October 2014										
1904	161,930	1,131	61.3	92%	$725	$750	$775	$785	$800	$825	$1,500	$8,500
	Auctions: $2,585, MS-64, August 2014; $2,350, MS-64, July 2014; $3,055, MS-64, September 2013; $823, MS-62, August 2014										
1904, Proof	108	36	63.3							$15,000	$23,500	$45,000
	Auctions: $64,625, PF-66Cam, June 2013										
1904O	108,950	631	60.1	70%	$750	$775	$800	$850	$900	$1,200	$3,000	$17,500
	Auctions: $7,344, MS-64, January 2014; $734, AU-55, July 2014; $705, AU-50, October 2014										
1905	200,992	2,242	61.7	94%	$725	$750	$775	$785	$800	$825	$1,000	$5,500
	Auctions: $31,725, MS-67, October 2013; $1,070, MS-64, October 2014; $646, MS-62, October 2014; $677, MS-61, October 2014										
1905, Proof	86	35	63.6							$15,000	$23,500	$45,000
	Auctions: $76,050, PF, September 2013										
1905S	369,250	570	57.0	27%	$725	$750	$775	$785	$800	$825	$5,000	$20,000
	Auctions: $14,100, MS-64, August 2013; $823, MS-61, July 2014; $734, AU-55, September 2014										
1906	165,420	1,474	61.2	91%	$725	$750	$775	$785	$800	$900	$1,900	$9,500
	Auctions: $1,793, MS-64, August 2014; $3,525, MS-64, January 2014; $1,058, MS-63, December 2014; $652, MS-61, October 2014										
1906, Proof	77	35	64.3							$15,000	$23,500	$45,000
	Auctions: $41,125, PF, February 2013										
1906D	981,000	3,751	61.4	91%	$725	$750	$775	$785	$800	$825	$1,000	$6,500
	Auctions: $14,100, MS-66, April 2014; $4,700, MS-65, November 2014; $712, MS-62, September 2014; $940, MS-61, August 2014										
1906O	86,895	349	60.4	70%	$750	$775	$800	$850	$900	$1,100	$4,500	$16,500
	Auctions: $21,150, MS-65, October 2014; $5,875, MS-64, August 2014; $12,925, MS-64, December 2013; $1,175, MS-62, October 2014										
1906S	457,000	560	58.2	45%	$725	$750	$775	$785	$800	$825	$4,000	$16,500
	Auctions: $8,519, MS-64, November 2014; $12,368, MS-64, April 2014; $3,819, MS-63, November 2014; $734, MS-61, July 2014										
1907	1,203,899	23,812	62.0	98%	$725	$750	$775	$785	$800	$825	$1,000	$5,500
	Auctions: $4,994, MS-65, November 2014; $1,068, MS-64, October 2014; $705, MS-62, October 2014; $646, MS-61, November 2014										
1907, Proof	74	53	64.2							$15,000	$23,500	$45,000
	Auctions: $33,638, PF-65Cam, March 2012; $29,375, PF-64Cam, August 2014										
1907D	1,030,000	535	61.4	89%	$725	$750	$775	$785	$800	$825	$1,000	$13,500
	Auctions: $4,700, MS-64, June 2013; $1,821, MS-63, November 2014; $823, MS-61, August 2014										
1907S	210,500	355	58.9	56%	$725	$750	$775	$785	$800	$825	$4,000	$20,000
	Auctions: $9,988, MS-65, March 2014; $964, MS-61, September 2014; $677, AU-58, October 2014										

INDIAN HEAD (1907–1933)

Designer: *Augustus Saint-Gaudens.* **Weight:** *16.718 grams.*
Composition: *.900 gold, .100 copper (net weight: .48375 oz. pure gold).*
Diameter: *27 mm.* **Edge:** *1907–1911—46 raised stars; 1912–1933—48 raised stars.*
Mints: *Philadelphia, Denver, San Francisco.*

No Motto (1907–1908)

*Mintmark location,
1908-D (No Motto),
is on the reverse, at
the tip of the branch.*

*Mintmark location, 1908
(With Motto)–1930,
is on the reverse, to
the left of the arrows.*

With Motto (1908–1933)

With Motto, Sandblast Finish Proof

With Motto, Satin Finish Proof

History. The Indian Head eagle, designed by sculptor Augustus Saint-Gaudens and championed by President Theodore Roosevelt, was struck from 1907 to 1916, and again in intermittent issues through the 1920s and early 1930s. Saint-Gaudens's original design proved impractical to strike and thus was modified slightly by Charles Barber before any large quantities were produced. Not long after (in July 1908), the motto IN GOD WE TRUST was added to the reverse, where it remained to the end of the series. These coins were widely used until 1918, in circulation in the American West and for export.

Striking and Sharpness. On the obverse, check the hair details and the vanes in the feathers. On the reverse, check the shoulder of the eagle. As well-struck coins are available for all varieties, avoid those that are weakly struck. Some examples may exhibit a pink-green color or rust-red "copper spots." Luster varies, but is often deeply frosty. On other coins, particularly from 1910 to 1916, it may be grainy.

Proofs. Sandblast (also called Matte) Proofs were made each year from 1907 through 1915. These have dull surfaces, much like fine-grained sandpaper. Satin (also called Roman Finish) Proofs were made in 1908, 1909, and 1910; they have satiny surfaces and are bright yellow.

Availability. Key rarities in this series are the rolled (or round) rim and wire rim 1907 coins, and the 1920-S, 1930-S, and 1933. Others are generally more readily available. MS-63 and higher coins are generally scarce to rare for the mintmarked issues. The Indian Head eagle is a very popular series. Most such coins in collectors' hands were exported in their time, then brought back to America after World War II. All of the Proofs are rare today.

Note: Values of common-date gold coins have been based on the current bullion price of gold, $1,200 per ounce, and may vary with the prevailing spot price.

GRADING STANDARDS

MS-60 to 70 (Mint State). *Obverse:* At MS-60, some abrasion and contact marks are evident, most noticeably on the hair to the left of Miss Liberty's forehead and in the left field. Luster is present, but may be dull or lifeless, and interrupted in patches. At MS-63, contact marks are few, and abrasion is very light. An MS-65 coin has hardly any abrasion, and contact marks are minute. Luster should be full and rich. Grades above MS-65 are defined by

1907. Graded MS-62.

having fewer marks as perfection is approached. *Reverse:* Comments apply as for the obverse, except that abrasion and contact marks are most noticeable on the front of the left wing and in the left field.

Illustrated coin: This is a brilliant and lustrous example.

AU-50, 53, 55, 58 (About Uncirculated). *Obverse:* Light wear is seen on the cheek, the hair to the right of the face, and the headdress, more so at AU-50 coin than at 53 or 55. An AU-58 coin has minimal traces of wear. An AU-50 coin has luster in protected areas among the stars and in the small field area to the right. At AU-58, most luster is present in the fields but is worn away on the highest parts of the Indian. *Reverse:* Comments as

1908-D. Graded AU-58.

preceding, except that the eagle's left wing, left leg, neck, and leg show light wear. Luster ranges from perhaps 40% (at AU-50) to nearly full mint bloom (at AU-58).

Illustrated coin: With nearly full original luster, this coin has remarkable eye appeal.

EF-40, 45 (Extremely Fine). *Obverse:* More wear is evident on the hair to the right of the face, and the feather vanes lack some details, although most are present. Luster, if present at all, is minimal. *Reverse:* Wear is greater than on the preceding. The front edge of the left wing is worn and blends into the top of the left leg. Some traces of luster may be seen, more so at EF-45 than at EF-40.

1907. Graded EF-40.

VF-20, 30 (Very Fine). *Obverse:* The Indian's forehead blends into the hair to the right. Feather-vane detail is gone except in the lower areas. *Reverse:* Wear is greater on the eagle, with only a few details remaining on the back of the left wing and the tail.

The Indian Head eagle is seldom collected in grades lower than VF-20.

1908-S. Graded VF-25.

PF-60 to 70 (Proof). *Obverse and Reverse:* At PF-60 to 63, there is light abrasion and some contact marks (the lower the grade, the higher the quantity). On Sandblast Proofs these show up as visually unappealing bright spots. At PF-64 and higher levels, marks are fewer, with magnification needed to see any at PF-65. At PF-66, there should be none at all.

1915. Sandblast Finish. Graded PF-65.

				No Periods			Periods				

	Mintage	Cert	Avg	%MS	VF-20	EF-40	AU-50	AU-55	MS-60	MS-62	MS-63	MS-65
									PF-63	PF-64	PF-65
1907, Wire Rim, Periods	500	176	63.3	92%		$24,500	$26,000	$27,000	$30,000	$36,500	$42,500	$70,000
	Auctions: $211,500, MS-67, August 2013; $129,250, MS-66, September 2014; $47,000, MS-64, August 2014											
1907, Rounded Rim, Periods Before and After •E•PLURIBUS•UNUM• † (a)	50	28	62.5	82%		$60,000	$65,000	$75,000	$95,000	$100,000	$150,000	$295,000
	Auctions: $470,000, MS-67, August 2013											
1907, No Periods	239,406	6,146	61.5	83%	$800	$875	$900	$950	$1,150	$2,000	$3,500	$9,500
	Auctions: $176,250, MS-68, August 2013; $13,513, MS-66, September 2014; $1,880, MS-62, July 2014; $2,585, MS-61, August 2014											
1907, Wire Rim, Periods, Plain Edge, Proof (b)	*unknown*	0	n/a									
	Auctions: $359,375, PF-62, August 2010											
1907, Rounded Rim, Periods, Satin Finish Proof	*unknown*	0	n/a					*(extremely rare)*			
	Auctions: $2,185,000, PF-67, January 2011											
1907, Sandblast Finish Proof (c)	*unknown*	0	n/a					*(extremely rare)*			
	Auctions: No auction records available.											

† Ranked in the *100 Greatest U.S. Coins* (fourth edition). **a.** All but 50 of the 31,500 coins were melted at the mint. **b.** According to the *Encyclopedia of U.S. Gold Coins, 1795–1933*, the only confirmed example may be from the Captain North set of 1907 and 1908 gold coins sold by Stack's in the 1970s. **c.** 2 or 3 examples are known.

	Mintage	Cert	Avg	%MS	VF-20	EF-40	AU-50	AU-55	MS-60	MS-62 / PF-63	MS-63 / PF-64	MS-65 / PF-65
1908, No Motto	33,500	673	60.9	75%	$850	$875	$900	$1,000	$1,500	$2,750	$6,000	$17,500
	Auctions: $105,750, MS-67, August 2013; $6,475, MS-64, November 2014; $4,847, MS-63, September 2014; $4,700, MS-63, July 2014											
1908D, No Motto	210,000	872	59.5	52%	$800	$875	$900	$975	$1,250	$2,650	$8,000	$37,500
	Auctions: $82,250, MS-66, August 2013; $7,062, MS-63, November 2014; $5,581, MS-62, August 2014; $4,406, MS-61, July 2014											
1908, With Motto	341,370	4,550	60.9	80%	$725	$750	$775	$785	$1,100	$1,550	$2,600	$13,000
	Auctions: $58,750, MS-68, August 2013; $39,656, MS-67, July 2014; $1,410, MS-62, July 2014; $999, MS-62, July 2014											
1908, With Motto, Sandblast Finish Proof	116	53	65.2							$16,500	$27,500	$50,000
	Auctions: $69,000, PF-66, January 2012; $79,313, PF-65, August 2014											
1908, With Motto, Satin Finish Proof (d)	(e)	2	64.0				*(extremely rare)*					
	Auctions: No auction records available.											
1908D, With Motto	836,500	794	59.3	59%	$725	$825	$850	$875	$1,150	$3,000	$8,000	$27,500
	Auctions: $70,500, MS-67, August 2013; $17,038, MS-64, September 2014; $3,408, MS-62, July 2014; $1,763, MS-61, September 2014											
1908S	59,850	762	54.6	21%	$1,000	$1,150	$1,250	$1,500	$4,000	$8,500	$15,000	$27,500
	Auctions: $182,125, MS-69, August 2013; $7,050, MS-62, November 2014; $7,638, MS-62, September 2014; $5,288, MS-61, July 2014											
1909	184,789	2,157	60.6	75%	$725	$750	$775	$785	$1,100	$1,750	$5,500	$18,500
	Auctions: $28,200, MS-66, August 2013; $14,100, MS-65, August 2014; $1,763, MS-62, July 2014; $1,293, MS-61, July 2014											
1909, Satin Finish Proof	74	0	n/a							$22,500	$35,000	$70,000
	Auctions: $48,875, PF-65, July 2011											
1909, Sandblast Finish Proof (f)	(g)	0	n/a				*(extremely rare)*					
	Auctions: No auction records available.											
1909D	121,540	1,067	59.6	59%	$850	$900	$950	$975	$1,450	$3,000	$8,000	$35,000
	Auctions: $105,750, MS-67, August 2013; $5,875, MS-63, July 2014; $4,406, MS-62, July 2014; $1,410, MS-61, November 2014											
1909S	292,350	829	57.5	35%	$725	$750	$775	$785	$1,250	$4,500	$8,000	$20,000
	Auctions: $64,625, MS-67, August 2013; $14,688, MS-65, October 2014; $7,638, MS-64, July 2014; $3,290, MS-61, July 2014											
1910	318,500	6,374	61.6	89%	$725	$750	$775	$785	$1,000	$1,100	$1,450	$11,500
	Auctions: $44,063, MS-67, August 2013; $16,450, MS-66, November 2014; $1,058, MS-62, October 2014; $911, MS-62, July 2014											
1910, Satin Finish Proof	204	28	63.1							$19,000	$30,000	$60,000
	Auctions: $80,500, PF-67, January 2012											
1910, Sandblast Finish Proof (h)	(i)	1	66.0									
	Auctions: No auction records available.											
1910D	2,356,640	12,398	61.6	90%	$725	$750	$775	$785	$1,000	$1,050	$1,300	$10,500
	Auctions: $52,875, MS-67, August 2013; $18,213, MS-66, November 2014; $1,939, MS-64, September 2014; $940, MS-62, July 2014											
1910S	811,000	1,823	57.2	34%	$725	$750	$775	$785	$1,200	$4,750	$11,500	$60,000
	Auctions: $82,250, MS-66, August 2013; $12,338, MS-64, November 2014; $5,581, MS-62, August 2014; $2,820, MS-61, July 2014											
1911	505,500	10,186	61.6	87%	$725	$750	$775	$785	$925	$1,050	$1,250	$9,500
	Auctions: $94,000, MS-68, August 2013; $14,100, MS-66, August 2014; $2,585, MS-64, August 2014; $1,116, MS-63, November 2014											
1911, Sandblast Finish Proof	95	23	66.3							$16,000	$25,000	$50,000
	Auctions: $152,750, PF-67, November 2013; $74,025, PF-66, October 2014											
1911D	30,100	925	55.1	18%	$1,250	$1,500	$2,200	$3,500	$12,500	$17,500	$45,000	$200,000
	Auctions: $67,563, MS-64, August 2013; $29,375, MS-63, September 2014; $12,338, MS-61, July 2014; $6,463, AU-58, July 2014											
1911S	51,000	360	57.0	29%	$850	$900	$925	$975	$1,750	$7,000	$12,500	$24,000
	Auctions: $44,063, MS-66, August 2013; $11,750, MS-64, July 2014; $6,463, MS-62, August 2014; $4,259, MS-61, July 2014											

d. 3 or 4 examples are known. **e.** Included in 1908, With Motto, Matte Proof, mintage figure. **f.** 2 or 3 examples are known. **g.** Included in 1909, Satin Finish Proof, mintage figure. **h.** The only example known is part of the unique complete 1910 Matte Proof gold set. **i.** Included in 1910, Satin Finish Proof, mintage figure.

	Mintage	Cert	Avg	%MS	VF-20	EF-40	AU-50	AU-55	MS-60	MS-62	MS-63	MS-65
										PF-63	PF-64	PF-65
1912	405,000	6,886	61.3	86%	$725	$750	$775	$785	$925	$1,100	$1,350	$12,500
	Auctions: $12,338, MS-66, October 2014; $23,500, MS-66, August 2013; $2,056, MS-64, July 2014; $969, MS-62, July 2014											
1912, Sandblast Finish Proof	83	21	65.6							$16,000	$25,000	$50,000
	Auctions: $99,875, PF, March 2014											
1912S	300,000	1,144	57.2	28%	$725	$750	$775	$825	$1,250	$5,000	$11,000	$40,000
	Auctions: $64,625, MS-65, August 2013; $14,100, MS-64, July 2014; $3,819, MS-62, October 2014; $3,055, MS-61, July 2014											
1913	442,000	6,094	61.2	83%	$725	$750	$775	$785	$925	$1,100	$1,350	$10,000
	Auctions: $25,851, MS-66, November 2014; $16,450, MS-66, July 2014; $1,028, MS-62, July 2014; $764, MS-60, July 2014											
1913, Sandblast Finish Proof	71	24	65.5							$16,000	$25,000	$50,000
	Auctions: $63,250, PF-66, January 2012											
1913S	66,000	945	55.0	13%	$1,000	$1,100	$1,200	$2,250	$10,000	$15,000	$40,000	$125,000
	Auctions: $44,063, MS-64, August 2013; $22,325, MS-63, November 2014; $30,550, MS-63, July 2014; $8,813, MS-61, July 2014											
1914	151,000	2,258	61.1	82%	$725	$750	$775	$785	$925	$1,050	$2,450	$13,500
	Auctions: $35,250, MS-67, August 2013; $7,638, MS-65, November 2014; $11,163, MS-65, August 2014; $1,528, MS-62, July 2014											
1914, Sandblast Finish Proof	50	32	65.7							$16,000	$25,000	$50,000
	Auctions: $96,938, PF, October 2013											
1914D	343,500	2,801	60.7	75%	$725	$750	$775	$785	$1,000	$1,100	$2,400	$16,500
	Auctions: $30,550, MS-67, August 2013; $4,113, MS-64, August 2014; $940, MS-62, September 2014; $1,058, MS-62, August 2014											
1914S	208,000	1,056	58.4	41%	$725	$775	$800	$900	$1,250	$4,000	$12,000	$32,500
	Auctions: $30,550, MS-65, August 2013; $6,463, MS-63, November 2014; $8,813, MS-63, July 2014; $3,173, MS-61, July 2014											
1915	351,000	4,387	61.1	80%	$725	$750	$775	$785	$900	$1,050	$1,850	$10,000
	Auctions: $30,550, MS-67, August 2013; $7,050, MS-65, November 2014; $4,994, MS-64, July 2014; $1,763, MS-63, July 2014											
1915, Sandblast Finish Proof	75	16	65.7							$20,000	$30,000	$55,000
	Auctions: $94,000, PF, August 2013											
1915S	59,000	443	57.5	28%	$950	$1,000	$1,050	$1,750	$5,000	$10,500	$22,000	$75,000
	Auctions: $99,875, MS-66, August 2013; $55,813, MS-65, September 2014; $11,985, MS-62, November 2014; $8,225, MS-61, July 2014											
1916S	138,500	877	59.2	52%	$950	$985	$1,000	$1,050	$1,500	$4,000	$8,000	$25,000
	Auctions: $111,625, MS-67, August 2013; $7,050, MS-63, July 2014; $3,672, MS-62, July 2014; $2,350, MS-61, September 2014											
1920S	126,500	49	59.5	55%	$16,500	$20,000	$25,000	$30,000	$55,000	$70,000	$110,000	$225,000
	Auctions: $199,750, MS-65, August 2013; $38,188, AU-55, July 2014											
1926	1,014,000	39,929	62.5	99%	$725	$750	$775	$785	$825	$850	$1,000	$3,000
	Auctions: $9,400, MS-66, August 2013; $4,700, MS-65, August 2014; $1,175, MS-63, November 2014; $1,028, MS-62, August 2014											
1930S	96,000	64	63.6	95%	$15,000	$17,500	$22,500	$24,500	$35,000	$40,000	$55,000	$75,000
	Auctions: $85,188, MS-65, September 2014; $70,500, MS-64, March 2014											
1932	4,463,000	59,611	62.9	100%	$725	$750	$775	$785	$825	$850	$1,000	$3,000
	Auctions: $28,200, MS-67, August 2013; $5,875, MS-65, September 2014; $1,410, MS-64, November 2014; $999, MS-62, July 2014											
1933 † (j)	312,500	11	64.4	100%					$275,000	$325,000	$400,000	$600,000
	Auctions: $367,188, MS-64, August 2013											

† Ranked in the *100 Greatest U.S. Coins* (fourth edition). **j.** Nearly all were melted at the mint.

Gold Double Eagles ($20)
1850–1933

AN OVERVIEW OF GOLD DOUBLE EAGLES

Congress authorized the double eagle, or twenty-dollar coin—the largest denomination of all regular U.S. coinage issues—by the Act of March 3, 1849, in response to the huge amounts of gold coming from California.

Double eagles are at once large and impressive to own. Many gold collectors form a type set of the six major double eagle designs (with the 1861 Paquet added as a sub-type if desired). Thanks to overseas hoards repatriated since the 1950s, finding choice and gem Mint State examples is no problem at all for the later types.

The first double eagle type, the Liberty Head of 1850 to 1866 without the motto IN GOD WE TRUST, is generally available in grades from VF up. Mint State pieces were elusive prior to the 1990s, but the market supply was augmented by more than 5,000 pieces—including some gems—found in the discovery of the long-lost treasure ship SS *Central America*. The SS *Brother Jonathan*, lost at sea in 1865, was recovered in the 1990s and yielded hundreds of Mint State 1865-S double eagles, along with some dated 1864 and a few earlier. The wreck of the SS *Republic*, lost in 1865 while on a voyage from New York City to New Orleans and salvaged in 2003, also yielded some very attractive Mint State double eagles of this first Liberty Head type.

The Liberty Head type from 1866 through 1876, with the motto IN GOD WE TRUST above the eagle and with the denomination expressed as TWENTY D., is the rarest in MS-63 and higher grades. Many EF and AU coins have been repatriated from overseas holdings, as have quite a few in such grades as MS-60 through MS-62. However, true gems are hardly ever seen.

Liberty Head double eagles of the 1877–1907 type with the IN GOD WE TRUST motto and with the denomination spelled out as TWENTY DOLLARS are exceedingly plentiful in just about any grade desired, with gems being readily available of certain issues of the early 20th century. While it is easy to obtain a gem of a common date, some collectors of type coins have opted to acquire a coin of special historical interest, such as a Carson City issue.

The famous Saint-Gaudens MCMVII High Relief double eagle of 1907 was saved in quantity by the general public as well as by numismatists, and today it is likely that at least 5,000 to 6,000 exist, representing about half of the mintage. Most of these are in varying degrees of Mint State, with quite a few graded as MS-64 and MS-65. Those in lower grades such as VF and EF often were used for jewelry or were polished, or have other problems. This particular design is a great favorite with collectors, and although the coins are not rarities, they are hardly inexpensive.

The so-called Arabic Numerals 1907–1908 Saint-Gaudens design is available in nearly any grade desired, with MS-60 through MS-63 or MS-64 pieces being plentiful and inexpensive. Double eagles of the final type, 1908–1933, are abundant in any grade desired, with choice and gem coins being plentiful.

FOR THE COLLECTOR AND INVESTOR: GOLD DOUBLE EAGLES AS A SPECIALTY

Collecting double eagles by date and mint is more popular than one might think. Offhand, one might assume that these high denominations, laden with a number of rare dates, would attract few enthusiasts. However, over a long period of years more collectors have specialized in double eagles than have specialized in five-dollar or ten-dollar pieces.

Two particularly notable collections of double eagles by date and mint, from the earliest times to the latest, were formed by Louis E. Eliasberg of Baltimore, and Jeff Browning of Dallas. Both have been dispersed across the auction block. The first was cataloged by Bowers and Ruddy in 1982, and the second was offered by Stack's and Sotheby's in 2001. In addition, dozens of other collections over the years have had large numbers of double eagles, some specializing in the Liberty Head types of 1850–1907, others only with the Saint-Gaudens types from 1907 onward, and others addressing the entire range.

Among rarities in the double eagle series are the 1854-O and 1856-O, each known only to the extent of a few dozen pieces; the 1861 Philadelphia Mint coins with Paquet reverse (two known); the Proof-only issues of 1883, 1884, and 1887; several other low-mintage varieties of this era; the famous Carson City issue of 1870-CC; and various issues from 1920 onward, including 1920-S, 1921, mintmarked coins after 1923, and all dates after 1928. Punctuating these rarities is a number of readily available pieces, including the very common Philadelphia issues from 1922 through 1928 inclusive.

LIBERTY HEAD (1850–1907)

Designer: *James B. Longacre.* **Weight:** *33.436 grams.*
Composition: *.900 gold, .100 copper (net weight: .96750 oz. pure gold).* **Diameter** *34 mm.*
Edge: *Reeded.* **Mints:** *Philadelphia, Carson City, Denver, New Orleans, San Francisco.*

No Motto (1849–1866)

No Motto, Proof

*Mintmark location is on
the reverse, below the eagle.*

With Motto (1866–1907)

With Motto, Proof

History. The twenty-dollar denomination was introduced to circulation in 1850 (after a unique pattern, which currently resides in the Smithsonian's National Numismatic Collection, was minted in 1849). The large new coin was ideal for converting the flood of California gold rush bullion into federal legal tender. U.S. Mint chief engraver James B. Longacre designed the coin. A different reverse, designed by Anthony Paquet with taller letters than Longacre's design, was tested in 1861 but ultimately not used past that date. In 1866 the motto IN GOD WE TRUST was added to the reverse. In 1877 the denomination on the reverse, formerly given as TWENTY D., was changed to TWENTY DOLLARS. The double eagle denomination proved to be very popular, especially for export. By 1933, more than 75 percent of the American gold used to strike coins from the 1850s onward had been used to make double eagles. Oddly, some of the coins of 1850 to 1858 appear to have the word LIBERTY misspelled as LLBERTY.

Striking and Sharpness. On the obverse, check the star centers and the hair details. As made, the hair details are less distinct on many coins of 1859 (when a slight modification was made) through the 1890s, and knowledge of this is important. Later issues usually have exquisite detail. The reverse usually is well struck, but check the eagle and other features. The denticles are sharp on nearly all coins, but should be checked. Proofs were made in all years from 1858 to 1907, and a few were made before then. Proofs of 1902 onward, particularly 1903, have the portrait polished in the die, imparting a mirror finish across the design, and lack the cameo contrast of earlier dates.

Availability. Basic dates and mintmarks are available in proportion to their mintages. Key issues include the 1854-O, 1856-O, 1861 Paquet Reverse, 1861-S Paquet Reverse, 1866 No Motto, 1870-CC, 1879-O, and several Philadelphia Mint dates of the 1880s The vast majority of others are readily collectible. Among early coins, MS examples from about 1854 to 1857 are available, most notably the 1857-S and certain varieties of the 1860s. Most varieties of the 1880s onward, and particularly of the 1890s and 1900s, are easily available in MS, due to the repatriation of millions of coins that had been exported overseas. Proofs dated through the 1870s are all very rare today; those of the 1880s are less so; and those of the 1890s and 1900s are scarce. Many Proofs have been mishandled. Dates that are Proof-only (and those that are very rare in circulation-strike form) are in demand even if impaired. These include 1883, 1884, 1885, 1886, and 1887.

Note: Values of common-date gold coins have been based on the current bullion price of gold, $1,200 per ounce, and may vary with the prevailing spot price.

GRADING STANDARDS

MS-60 to 70 (Mint State). *Obverse:* At MS-60, some abrasion and contact marks are evident, most noticeably on the hair to the right of Miss Liberty's forehead and on the cheek. Luster is present, but may be dull or lifeless, and interrupted in patches. At MS-63, contact marks are few, and abrasion is light. An MS-65 coin has little abrasion, and contact marks are minute. Luster should be full and rich. Grades above MS-65 are defined by

1876-S. Graded MS-64.

having fewer marks as perfection is approached. *Reverse:* Comments apply as for the obverse, except that abrasion and contact marks are most noticeable on eagle's neck, wingtips, and tail.

AU-50, 53, 55, 58 (About Uncirculated).

Obverse: Light wear is seen on the face, the hair to the right of the face, and the highest area of the hair behind the coronet, more so at AU-50 than at 53 or 55. An AU-58 coin has minimal traces of wear. An AU-50 coin has luster in protected areas among the stars and letters, with little in the open fields or on the portrait. At AU-58 most luster is present in the fields, but is worn away on the highest parts of the motifs. *Reverse:* Comments as preceding, except that the eagle and ornaments show wear in all of the higher areas. Luster ranges from perhaps 40% remaining in protected areas (at AU-50) to nearly full mint bloom (at AU-58). Often the reverse of this type retains more luster than the obverse.

1856-S. Graded AU-53.

Illustrated coin: Much of the original luster still remains at this grade level, especially on the reverse.

EF-40, 45 (Extremely Fine). *Obverse:* Wear

is evident on all high areas of the portrait, including the hair to the right of the forehead, the tip of the coronet, and hair behind the coronet. The curl to the right of the neck is flat on its highest-relief area. Luster, if present at all, is minimal and in protected areas such as between the star points. *Reverse:* Wear is greater than on an About Uncirculated coin. The eagle's neck and wingtips show wear, as do the ornaments and rays. Some traces of luster may be seen, more so at EF-45 than at EF-40. Overall, the reverse appears to be in a slightly higher grade than the obverse.

1855-S. Graded EF-45.

VF-20, 30 (Very Fine). *Obverse:* The

higher-relief areas of hair are worn flat at VF-20, less so at VF-30. The hair to the right of the coronet is merged into heavy strands and is flat at the back, as is part of the bow. The curl to the right of the neck is flat. *Reverse:* The eagle shows further wear on the head, the tops of the wings, and the tail. The ornament has flat spots.

The Liberty Head double eagle is seldom collected in grades lower than VF-20.

1857-S. Graded VF-20.

Illustrated coin: Note the small test cut or mark on the top rim.

PF-60 to 70 (Proof). *Obverse and Reverse:* PF-60 to 62 coins have extensive hairlines and may have nicks and contact marks. At PF-63, hairlines are prominent, but the mirror surface is very reflective. PF-64 coins have fewer hairlines. At PF-65, hairlines should be relatively few. These large and heavy coins reveal hairlines more readily than do the lower denominations, mostly seen only under magnification. PF-66 and higher coins should have no marks or hairlines visible to the unaided eye.

Illustrated coin: A beautiful Proof, this is just a few hairlines away from a higher level.

1903. Graded PF-64.

**Value TWENTY D.
(1849–1876)**

**Value TWENTY DOLLARS
(1877–1907)**

1853, So-called 3 Over 2
Note rust under LIBERTY.
FS-G20-1853-301.

	Mintage	Cert	Avg	%MS	VF-20	EF-40	AU-50	AU-55	MS-60	MS-62 / PF-63	MS-63 / PF-64	MS-65 / PF-65
1849, Proof (a)	1	0	n/a		unique; in the Smithsonian's National Numismatic Collection							
	Auctions: No auction records available.											
1850	1,170,261	1,319	50.3	6%	$2,000	$3,200	$5,500	$7,500	$12,000	$36,000	$55,000	$145,000
	Auctions: $51,406, MS-63, April 2014; $32,900, MS-62, August 2014; $32,900, MS-62, October 2014; $31,725, MS-62, November 2014											
1850, Proof (b)	1–2	0	n/a									
	Auctions: No auction records available.											
1850O	141,000	310	47.0	2%	$2,350	$5,750	$14,500	$25,000	$60,000			
	Auctions: $111,625, MS-61, June 2014; $24,675, AU-55, August 2014; $28,200, AU-55, November 2014; $12,925, AU-53, November 2014											
1851	2,087,155	908	51.9	9%	$1,900	$2,300	$2,750	$3,750	$7,500	$17,000	$25,000	
	Auctions: $23,500, MS-63, April 2014; $30,550, MS-63, August 2014; $3,672, MS-60, August 2014; $4,553, AU-58, July 2014											
1851O	315,000	687	49.5	3%	$2,100	$4,250	$7,000	$13,000	$30,000	$55,000	$85,000	
	Auctions: $58,750, MS, February 2014; $17,625, AU-58, August 2014; $16,450, AU-58, August 2014; $15,275, AU-58, November 2014											
1852	2,053,026	1,494	52.2	7%	$1,900	$2,300	$2,900	$3,500	$7,000	$14,000	$18,000	
	Auctions: $18,800, MS-63, January 2014; $11,750, MS-61, August 2014; $7,050, AU-58, August 2014; $4,994, AU-58+, November 2014											
1852O	190,000	581	51.4	4%	$2,500	$4,500	$7,500	$14,500	$35,000	$50,000	$85,000	
	Auctions: $94,000, MS-62, August 2014; $41,125, MS-61, April 2014; $38,188, MS-61, August 2014; $31,725, AU-58, August 2014											
1853, All kinds	1,261,326											
1853, So-called 3 Over 2 (c)		181	52.6	2%	$3,000	$4,500	$7,000	$12,000	$40,000	$75,000		
	Auctions: $17,625, AU-58, April 2014; $28,200, AU-58, August 2014; $28,200, AU-58, October 2014											
1853		1,186	52.6	6%	$1,900	$2,250	$2,750	$3,750	$8,500	$18,000	$30,000	
	Auctions: $152,750, MS-65, August 2014; $15,275, MS-62, October 2014; $12,925, MS-62, October 2014; $14,100, MS-62, August 2013											
1853O	71,000	232	50.0	2%	$2,750	$4,500	$10,500	$14,500	$37,500			
	Auctions: $64,625, MS-61, April 2014; $22,325, AU-55, October 2014; $16,450, AU-53, November 2014; $5,875, AU-50, August 2014											

a. An unknown quantity of Proof 1849 double eagles was struck as patterns; all but two were melted. One (current location unknown) was sent to Treasury secretary W.M. Meredith; the other was placed in the Mint collection in Philadelphia, and transferred with that collection to the Smithsonian in 1923. **b.** Although no examples currently are known, it is likely that a small number of Proof 1850 double eagles were struck. For the years 1851 to 1857, no Proofs are known. **c.** Although overlaid photographs indicate this is not a true overdate, what appear to be remnants of a numeral are visible beneath the 3 in the date. This variety also shows a rust spot underneath the R of LIBERTY.

1854, Small Date   **1854, Large Date**

	Mintage	Cert	Avg	%MS	VF-20	EF-40	AU-50	AU-55	MS-60	MS-62	MS-63	MS-65
										PF-63	PF-64	PF-65
1854, All kinds	757,899											
1854, Small Date		486	52.9	5%	$1,900	$2,250	$2,850	$3,500	$8,500	$18,000	$30,000	
	Auctions: $17,625, MS-62, August 2014; $12,925, MS-61, August 2014; $8,225, MS-60, June 2013; $7,638, AU-58, August 2014											
1854, Large Date		121	53.4	8%	$2,250	$3,500	$7,500	$15,000	$37,500	$55,000	$65,000	
	Auctions: $55,813, MS-61, August 2014; $41,125, MS-61, August 2014; $19,975, AU-58, October 2014; $18,814, AU-58, November 2014											
1854O † (d)	3,250	16	53.1	0%	$140,000	$260,000	$485,000	$500,000				
	Auctions: $440,625, AU-55, April 2014; $329,000, AU-50, August 2014											
1854S	141,468	194	52.7	25%	$3,000	$4,000	$8,500	$11,500	$24,000	$30,000	$37,500	$85,000
	Auctions: $70,500, MS-64, August 2014; $44,063, MS-63, August 2014; $41,125, MS-62, March 2014; $44,063, MS-62, September 2014											
1854S, Proof † (e)	unknown	0	n/a		(unique; in the Smithsonian's National Numismatic Collection)							
	Auctions: No auction records available.											
1855	364,666	353	52.8	5%	$1,900	$2,350	$3,000	$4,500	$13,500	$22,500	$60,000	
	Auctions: $14,688, MS-61, January 2014; $8,225, AU-58, August 2014; $4,406, AU-55+, August 2014; $4,113, AU-55, October 2014											
1855O	8,000	44	50.2	7%	$8,750	$25,000	$47,500	$65,000	$120,000			
	Auctions: $141,000, MS-61, January 2014; $67,563, AU-55, August 2014; $58,750, AU-55, August 2014; $28,200, AU-50, October 2014											
1855S	879,675	875	52.0	4%	$1,900	$2,250	$3,000	$4,500	$7,500	$15,000	$26,000	
	Auctions: $9,988, MS-61, October 2014; $11,750, MS-61, April 2013; $5,581, AU-58, August 2014; $6,463, AU-58, November 2014											
1856	329,878	319	52.4	6%	$1,900	$2,250	$3,000	$5,500	$10,000	$20,000	$30,000	
	Auctions: $41,125, MS-63, August 2014; $10,575, MS-60, July 2014; $5,288, AU-58, November 2014; $3,646, AU-50, July 2014											
1856O † (f)	2,250	8	51.1	0%	$140,000	$275,000	$475,000	$500,000				
	Auctions: $425,938, AU-53, August 2014; $164,500, AU-50, August 2014; $381,875, EF-45, January 2014											
1856O, Proof (g)	unknown	1	63.0									
	Auctions: $1,437,500, SP-63, May 2009											
1856S	1189750	1,035	51.6	5%	$1,900	$2,250	$2,850	$3,500	$7,500	$11,000	$18,750	
	Auctions: $25,850, MS-64, April 2014; $17,038, MS-64, November 2014; $9,400, MS-62, September 2014; $5,891, AU-53, July 2014											
1857	439,375	454	53.4	10%	$1,900	$2,250	$3,250	$4,500	$7,500	$15,000	$37,500	
	Auctions: $47,000, MS-63, August 2013; $30,550, MS-62, August 2014; $17,625, MS-62, November 2014; $12,925, MS-60, August 2014											
1857O	30,000	138	52.4	7%	$2,500	$5,500	$12,000	$22,500	$65,000	$150,000	$200,000	
	Auctions: $176,250, MS-62PL, April 2014; $8,813, AU-50, August 2014											
1857S † (h)	970,500	1,294	55.2	32%	$1,950	$2,250	$2,850	$3,250	$6,000	$7,000	$9,000	$16,500
	Auctions: $32,900, MS-66, August 2013; $5,288, MS-62, August 2014; $5,640, MS-61, August 2014; $5,288, MS-61, August 2014											
1858	211,714	425	52.3	8%	$1,950	$2,250	$3,000	$4,500	$10,000	$35,000	$45,000	
	Auctions: $38,188, MS-62, August 2013; $17,625, MS-61, August 2014; $4,113, AU-55, August 2014; $3,290, AU-53, August 2014											
1858, Proof (i)	unknown	0	n/a		(extremely rare)							
	Auctions: No auction records available.											
1858O	35,250	130	51.0	6%	$3,250	$6,750	$15,000	$27,500	$67,500	$77,500		
	Auctions: $38,188, AU-58, January 2014; $44,063, AU-58, August 2014; $38,188, AU-58, August 2014; $30,550, AU-55, August 2014											
1858S	846,710	883	51.4	3%	$2,000	$2,500	$3,000	$4,000	$11,000	$14,000	$50,000	
	Auctions: $15,275, MS-61, August 2014; $5,875, AU-58, January 2014; $4,406, AU-58, August 2014; $3,525, AU-55, August 2014											

† Ranked in the *100 Greatest U.S. Coins* (fourth edition). **d.** Probably fewer than 35 exist, most in VF and EF. **e.** This unique coin, perhaps more accurately described as a presentation strike than a Proof, was sent to the Mint collection in Philadelphia by San Francisco Mint superintendent Lewis A. Birdsall. It may have been the first coin struck for the year, set aside to recognize the opening of the San Francisco Mint. **f.** Probably fewer than 25 exist, most in VF and EF. **g.** This prooflike presentation strike is unique. **h.** The treasure of the shipwrecked *SS Central America* included thousands of 1857-S double eagles in high grades. Different size mintmark varieties exist; the Large S variety is rarest. **i.** 3 or 4 examples are known.

1861-S, Normal Reverse

1861-S, Paquet Reverse
Note taller letters.

	Mintage	Cert	Avg	%MS	VF-20	EF-40	AU-50	AU-55	MS-60	MS-62 / PF-63	MS-63 / PF-64	MS-65 / PF-65
1859	43,597	125	51.8	6%	$1,900	$4,000	$8,000	$13,000	$30,000	$45,000		
	Auctions: $23,500, AU-58, February 2013; $3,290, AU-50, August 2014											
1859, Proof (j)	80	6	62.8							$250,000	$350,000	$500,000
	Auctions: $210,600, PF, June 2014											
1859O	9,100	59	50.3	2%	$12,500	$27,500	$50,000	$65,000	$130,000			
	Auctions: $28,200, MS-60, August 2014; $76,375, AU-58, August 2014; $54,344, AU-50, January 2014											
1859S	636,445	731	50.7	3%	$1,900	$2,400	$3,000	$5,000	$11,000	$25,000	$55,000	
	Auctions: $30,550, MS-62, August 2014; $22,325, MS-61, April 2014; $18,800, MS-60, August 2014; $7,050, AU-58, August 2014											
1860	577,670	870	53.9	11%	$1,900	$2,250	$2,850	$3,500	$7,500	$12,000	$24,000	
	Auctions: $64,625, MS-64, April 2014; $10,281, MS-62, August 2014; $8,813, MS-61, August 2014; $5,875, AU-58, July 2014											
1860, Proof (k)	59	9	64.3							$110,000	$185,000	$350,000
	Auctions: $367,188, PF-66Cam, August 2014											
1860O	6,600	58	50.2	2%	$12,500	$28,500	$50,000	$65,000				
	Auctions: $55,813, AU-53, April 2014; $55,813, AU-53, August 2014; $41,125, AU-50, August 2014											
1860S	544,950	681	51.1	3%	$1,900	$2,250	$3,000	$4,500	$11,000	$17,500	$35,000	
	Auctions: $25,850, MS-62, August 2014; $14,100, MS-61, January 2014; $5,288, AU-58, August 2014											
1861	2,976,453	3,122	54.3	16%	$1,900	$2,250	$2,850	$3,500	$6,500	$10,000	$20,000	$50,000
	Auctions: $352,500, MS-67, August 2013; $8,813, MS-61, August 2014; $7,403, MS-61, August 2014											
1861, Proof (l)	66	2	64.0							$110,000	$185,000	$325,000
	Auctions: $483,000, PF-67UCam, August 2006											
1861O	17,741	109	48.0	4%	$12,500	$24,000	$50,000	$67,500	$135,000			
	Auctions: $146,875, MS-60, January 2014; $76,375, AU-55, August 2014; $15,275, AU-50, August 2014											
1861S	768,000	837	50.6	3%	$1,900	$2,250	$3,250	$5,000	$13,500	$22,000	$42,500	
	Auctions: $32,900, MS-62, January 2014; $25,850, MS-61, August 2014; $6,756, AU-58, October 2014											
1861, Paquet Rev (Tall Ltrs) † (m)	unknown	1	67.0	100%					$2,000,000			
	Auctions: $1,645,000, MS-61, August 2014											
1861S, Paquet Rev (Tall Ltrs) † (n)	19,250	73	48.6	0%	$37,500	$60,000	$87,500	$140,000				
	Auctions: $223,250, AU-58, April 2014; $64,625, EF-45, August 2014											
1862	92,133	93	52.1	16%	$2,000	$5,750	$12,000	$17,500	$32,500	$42,500	$60,000	
	Auctions: $70,500, MS-62, August 2014; $49,938, MS-62, August 2014; $31,725, AU-58, January 2014											
1862, Proof (o)	35	6	64.2							$100,000	$170,000	$300,000
	Auctions: $381,875, PF-65Cam, April 2014											
1862S	854,173	960	51.2	5%	$1,950	$2,250	$3,200	$5,000	$13,500	$30,000	$50,000	
	Auctions: $34,075, MS-62, April 2014; $17,625, MS-61, August 2014; $18,800, MS-61, October 2014											

† Ranked in the *100 Greatest U.S. Coins* (fourth edition). **j.** 7 or 8 examples are known. **k.** Fewer than 10 examples are known. **l.** 5 or 6 examples are known. **m.** Once thought to be a pattern; now known to have been intended for circulation. 2 examples are known. **n.** Approximately 100 examples are known, most in VF and EF. **o.** Approximately 12 examples are known.

	Mintage	Cert	Avg	%MS	VF-20	EF-40	AU-50	AU-55	MS-60	MS-62	MS-63	MS-65
										PF-63	PF-64	PF-65
1863	142,790	188	52.9	12%	$2,200	$3,000	$6,750	$13,500	$35,000	$42,500	$55,000	
	Auctions: $76,375, MS-62, August 2014; $30,550, AU-58, January 2014; $18,800, AU-55, October 2014; $10,575, AU-50, August 2014											
1863, Proof (p)	30	8	64.3							$100,000	$170,000	$300,000
	Auctions: $381,875, PF-66Cam, August 2014; $345,150, PF, September 2013											
1863S	966,570	1,185	52.0	11%	$1,950	$2,250	$3,000	$3,750	$8,500	$18,500	$32,000	
	Auctions: $29,375, MS-63, April 2014; $22,325, MS-62, August 2014; $12,925, MS-61, August 2014; $5,875, AU-58, November 2014											
1864	204,235	283	52.6	9%	$1,950	$2,500	$6,500	$8,500	$20,000	$50,000	$70,000	
	Auctions: $282,000, MS-65, April 2014; $47,000, MS-62, August 2014; $5,881, AU-50, July 2014; $7,638, AU-50, August 2014											
1864, Proof (q)	50	10	64.5							$100,000	$170,000	$300,000
	Auctions: $199,750, PF-64Cam, April 2014											
1864S	793,660	909	51.4	13%	$1,950	$2,250	$3,000	$4,000	$10,500	$20,000	$40,000	$110,000
	Auctions: $41,125, MS-63, August 2013; $22,325, MS-62, August 2014; $15,275, MS-61, August 2014; $12,925, MS-61, August 2014											
1865	351,175	723	57.1	44%	$1,950	$2,100	$2,850	$4,000	$8,000	$15,000	$25,000	$65,000
	Auctions: $88,125, MS-65, April 2013; $25,850, MS-64, August 2014; $11,765, MS-62, October 2014; $9,988, MS-61, November 2014											
1865, Proof (r)	25	7	64.9							$100,000	$170,000	$300,000
	Auctions: $440,625, PF-66DCam, April 2014											
1865S	1,042,500	1,273	54.0	37%	$1,950	$2,100	$2,850	$3,500	$6,750	$10,000	$16,500	$30,000
	Auctions: $25,850, MS-65, August 2014; $25,850, MS-64, August 2014; $23,500, MS-64, March 2013; $16,450, MS-62, August 2014											
1866S, No Motto	120,000	152	47.3	3%	$4,750	$16,500	$36,500	$65,000	$175,000	$300,000		
	Auctions: $246,750, MS-62, August 2014; $188,000, MS-61, August 2014; $7,638, AU-55, August 2014; $88,125, AU-55, October 2013											

p. Approximately 12 examples are known. **q.** 12 to 15 examples are known. **r.** Fewer than 10 examples are known.

**1866, With Motto,
Doubled-Die Reverse**
FS-G20-1866-801.

	Mintage	Cert	Avg	%MS	VF-20	EF-40	AU-50	AU-55	MS-60	MS-62	MS-63	MS-64
										PF-63	PF-64	PF-65
1866, With Motto	698,745	573	53.5	8%	$1,675	$1,725	$2,500	$4,250	$12,500	$37,500	$75,000	$175,000
	Auctions: $176,250, MS-64DMPL, January 2014; $30,550, MS-62, November 2014; $19,975, MS-61, July 2014; $21,150, MS-61, August 2014											
1866, With Motto, Doubled-Die Reverse	(a)	0	n/a				$4,000	$6,000				
	Auctions: $12,650, MS-61, August 2010											
1866, With Motto, Proof (b)	30	7	64.7							$57,500	$125,000	$200,000
	Auctions: $126,500, PF-64, May 2007											
1866S, With Motto	842,250	746	49.6	3%	$1,675	$1,725	$3,500	$8,000	$20,000	$45,000		
	Auctions: $55,813, MS-62, September 2013; $28,200, MS-61, August 2014; $14,100, AU-58, August 2014; $8,225, AU-55, September 2014											
1867	251,015	375	57.2	43%	$1,600	$1,725	$1,850	$2,750	$7,000	$15,000	$35,000	
	Auctions: $258,500, MS-66, November 2014; $28,200, MS-63, June 2014; $12,352, MS-62, August 2014; $9,694, MS-61, August 2014											
1867, Proof (c)	50	4	64.9							$57,500	$125,000	$200,000
	Auctions: $129,250, PF-64DCam, August 2014; $38,188, PF-61Cam, August 2014											
1867S	920,750	1,091	50.9	2%	$1,600	$1,725	$2,250	$5,000	$18,000	$30,000		
	Auctions: $17,639, AU-58, March 2014; $3,290, AU-55, July 2014; $4,259, AU-55, August 2014; $1,645, EF-45, July 2014											

a. Included in circulation-strike 1866 mintage figure. **b.** Approximately 15 examples are known. **c.** 10 to 12 examples are known.

Open 3   Close 3

	Mintage	Cert	Avg	%MS	VF-20	EF-40	AU-50	AU-55	MS-60	MS-62 / PF-63	MS-63 / PF-64	MS-64 / PF-65
1868	98,575	185	52.1	5%	$1,850	$2,000	$3,000	$7,000	$22,500	$40,000	$60,000	
Auctions: $44,063, MS-62, August 2014; $6,463, AU-55, March 2013; $5,288, AU-53, November 2014; $4,113, EF-45, August 2014												
1868, Proof (d)	25	7	64.4							$65,000	$125,000	$200,000
Auctions: $149,500, PF-64DCam Plus, August 2011												
1868S	837,500	1,372	52.0	3%	$1,600	$1,725	$1,850	$3,750	$16,000	$30,000		
Auctions: $17,038, MS-60, August 2013; $6,463, AU-58, August 2014; $5,875, AU-58, October 2014; $3,290, AU-55, August 2014												
1869	175,130	328	52.9	3%	$1,600	$1,725	$2,000	$3,500	$11,000	$16,000	$27,500	$45,000
Auctions: $108,688, MS-64, January 2014; $99,875, MS-64+, August 2014; $16,450, MS-62, August 2014; $3,525, AU-53, August 2014												
1869, Proof (e)	25	7	65.0							$65,000	$125,000	$200,000
Auctions: $106,375, PF-64DCam, February 2009												
1869S	686,750	1,283	52.4	5%	$1,600	$1,725	$1,775	$4,000	$10,000	$25,000	$42,500	$75,000
Auctions: $22,325, MS-62, December 2013; $15,275, MS-61, August 2014; $12,338, MS-61, November 2014; $5,581, AU-58, August 2014												
1870	155,150	258	53.9	15%	$1,600	$1,725	$2,500	$5,500	$17,500	$25,000	$45,000	
Auctions: $55,813, MS-61, August 2014; $27,025, MS-61, August 2013; $3,819, AU-53, August 2014												
1870, Proof (f)	35	5	65.2							$65,000	$125,000	$200,000
Auctions: $503,100, PF, September 2013												
1870CC † (g)	3,789	34	41.0	0%	$215,000	$275,000	$325,000	$475,000				
Auctions: $411,250, AU-53, March 2014; $58,815, EF-40, August 2014; $188,000, VF-30, October 2014												
1870S	982,000	1,240	52.4	5%	$1,600	$1,725	$1,775	$2,500	$9,000	$25,000	$40,000	
Auctions: $30,550, MS-62, August 2014; $28,200, MS-62, April 2013; $14,100, MS-61, August 2014; $8,225, MS-60, July 2014												
1871	80,120	256	53.7	7%	$1,600	$1,725	$2,500	$4,500	$10,000	$25,000	$40,000	$75,000
Auctions: $44,063, MS-63, August 2014; $2,485, MS-60, September 2014; $5,875, AU-58, January 2014; $4,847, AU-50, August 2014												
1871, Proof (h)	30	6	63.8							$65,000	$125,000	$200,000
Auctions: $26,450, PF-62Cam, August 2004												
1871CC	17,387	177	48.9	3%	$15,000	$23,500	$48,500	$55,000	$100,000			
Auctions: $55,813, AU-55, August 2014; $52,875, AU-53, January 2014; $28,200, EF-45, October 2014												
1871S	928,000	1,479	54.1	9%	$1,600	$1,650	$1,700	$2,250	$5,750	$12,500	$27,500	$50,000
Auctions: $17,625, MS-63, September 2014; $18,800, MS-62, August 2014; $7,346, MS-61, August 2014; $7,666, MS-61, August 2013												
1872	251,850	669	55.4	13%	$1,600	$1,650	$1,700	$2,200	$6,500	$16,000	$35,000	$75,000
Auctions: $28,200, MS-62+, August 2014; $2,350, AU-55, July 2014; $2,233, AU-58, September 2014; $2,233, AU-53, August 2014												
1872, Proof (i)	30	5	63.6							$65,000	$125,000	$200,000
Auctions: $135,125, PF-64, October 2014												
1872CC	26,900	418	49.4	3%	$3,250	$5,000	$11,000	$20,000	$50,000			
Auctions: $61,688, MS-61, January 2014; $21,150, AU-55, October 2014; $15,275, AU-53, August 2014; $8,225, EF-45, November 2014												
1872S	780,000	1,369	54.4	9%	$1,600	$1,650	$1,700	$1,850	$4,750	$13,500	$32,500	
Auctions: $14,100, MS-62, August 2014; $8,225, MS-61, August 2014; $5,993, MS-61, October 2014; $4,994, MS-60, June 2014												
1873, Close 3	1,709,825	354	54.6	12%	$1,600	$1,650	$1,700	$2,000	$4,500	$10,000		
Auctions: $4,700, MS-61, March 2013; $1,528, AU-55, October 2014; $1,998, AU-53, October 2014; $1,469, EF-45, July 2014												
1873, Open 3	(j)	6,985	58.9	54%	$1,600	$1,650	$1,675	$1,750	$2,500	$3,200	$11,500	$38,000
Auctions: $41,125, MS-64, August 2013; $7,050, MS-63, August 2014; $5,581, MS-62, August 2014; $3,819, MS-62, September 2014												
1873, Close 3, Proof (k)	25	7	63.9							$65,000	$125,000	$200,000
Auctions: $230,000, PF-65UCam, April 2011												

† Ranked in the *100 Greatest U.S. Coins* (fourth edition). **d.** Approximately 12 examples are known. **e.** Approximately 12 examples are known. **f.** Approximately 12 examples are known. **g.** An estimated 35 to 50 examples are believed to exist; most are in VF with extensive abrasions. **h.** Fewer than 10 examples are known. **i.** Fewer than 12 examples are known. **j.** Included in circulation-strike 1873, Close 3, mintage figure. **k.** 10 to 12 examples are known.

	Mintage	Cert	Avg	%MS	VF-20	EF-40	AU-50	AU-55	MS-60	MS-62 PF-63	MS-63 PF-64	MS-64 PF-65
1873CC, Close 3	22,410	389	52.1	5%	$4,000	$6,500	$12,500	$20,000	$47,500	$85,000		
Auctions: $58,750, MS-61, August 2014; $41,125, AU-58, March 2014; $32,900, AU-58, August 2014; $19,975, AU-58, August 2014												
1873S, Close 3	1,040,600	1,214	55.5	16%	$1,600	$1,650	$1,675	$1,750	$2,650	$8,000	$27,500	
Auctions: $8,238, MS-62, November 2014; $9,400, MS-62, September 2013; $4,113, MS-61, July 2014; $4,994, MS-61, August 2014												
1873S, Open 3	(l)	750	54.7	11%	$1,600	$1,725	$1,925	$2,750	$10,500			
Auctions: $35,250, MS-62, September 2013; $17,625, MS-61, August 2014; $15,863, MS-61, August 2014; $3,055, AU-58, November 2014												
1874	366,780	951	57.3	28%	$1,600	$1,650	$1,675	$1,700	$3,000	$12,500	$20,000	$55,000
Auctions: $15,275, MS-62, June 2014; $8,225, MS-61, August 2014; $5,581, MS-61, August 2014; $2,233, AU-58+, November 2014												
1874, Proof (m)	20	6	63.8							$75,000	$135,000	$225,000
Auctions: $218,500, PF-64UCam★, January 2012												
1874CC	115,085	1,316	49.0	1%	$3,000	$3,500	$5,500	$9,500	$20,000	$55,000		
Auctions: $64,625, MS-62, April 2014; $38,188, MS-61, August 2014; $12,925, AU-58, August 2014; $12,925, AU-58, November 2014												
1874S	1,214,000	2,818	56.7	22%	$1,600	$1,650	$1,675	$1,700	$3,250	$10,000	$28,500	
Auctions: $28,200, MS-63, January 2014; $7,050, MS-62, September 2014; $7,050, MS-62, October 2014; $6,463, MS-62, November 2014												
1875	295,720	1,358	59.3	59%	$1,600	$1,650	$1,675	$1,700	$2,500	$4,000	$10,000	$40,000
Auctions: $8,813, MS-63, August 2013; $4,113, MS-62, July 2014; $4,113, MS-62, August 2014; $4,406, MS-62+, September 2014												
1875, Proof (n)	20	5	63.8							$100,000	$150,000	$250,000
Auctions: $94,300, PF-63Cam, August 2009												
1875CC	111,151	1,743	53.7	30%	$3,000	$3,250	$3,500	$4,250	$10,000	$23,500	$37,500	$80,000
Auctions: $38,188, MS-63, April 2014; $22,325, MS-62, August 2014; $19,975, MS-62, August 2014; $17,625, MS-62, August 2014												
1875S	1,230,000	3,400	57.3	30%	$1,600	$1,650	$1,675	$1,700	$2,500	$5,500	$18,500	$40,000
Auctions: $15,275, MS-63, April 2014; $12,925, MS-63, October 2014; $4,261, MS-62, July 2014; $8,225, MS-62, August 2014												
1876	583,860	2,265	57.9	37%	$1,600	$1,650	$1,675	$1,700	$2,750	$4,500	$12,000	$45,000
Auctions: $64,625, MS-64, September 2013; $4,113, MS-62, October 2014; $2,291, MS-61, July 2014; $4,259, MS-61, August 2014												
1876, Proof (o)	45	13	63.9							$55,000	$75,000	$115,000
Auctions: $152,750, PF-64DCam, February 2013												
1876CC	138,441	2,034	52.4	13%	$2,750	$3,000	$4,000	$5,500	$11,000	$25,000	$45,000	
Auctions: $22,325, MS-62, April 2014; $18,800, MS-61, August 2014; $16,450, MS-61, August 2014; $11,750, MS-60, November 2014												
1876S	1,597,000	5,280	57.7	34%	$1,600	$1,650	$1,675	$1,700	$2,500	$4,500	$13,000	$40,000
Auctions: $31,725, MS-64, August 2014; $28,200, MS-64, February 2013; $4,700, MS-62+, August 2014; $4,406, MS-62, August 2014												

l. Included in 1873-S, Close 3, mintage figure. **m.** Fewer than 10 examples are known. **n.** 10 to 12 examples are known. **o.** Approximately 15 examples are known.

	Mintage	Cert	Avg	%MS	VF-20	EF-40	AU-50	AU-55	MS-60	MS-62 PF-63	MS-63 PF-64	MS-65 PF-65
1877	397,650	999	59.4	67%	$1,475	$1,500	$1,575	$1,600	$2,100	$4,500	$17,500	
Auctions: $4,700, MS-62, March 2014; $3,819, MS-62, October 2014; $3,290, MS-61, August 2014; $2,585, MS-61, August 2014												
1877, Proof (a)	20	8	63.5							$40,000	$75,000	$125,000
Auctions: $21,150, PF-58, February 2013												
1877CC	42,565	852	49.1	2%	$2,500	$3,500	$5,000	$10,000	$25,000	$60,000		
Auctions: $38,188, MS-61, March 2014; $38,188, MS-61, August 2014; $28,200, MS-61, August 2014; $21,150, AU-58, August 2014												
1877S	1,735,000	2,145	59.0	60%	$1,475	$1,500	$1,575	$1,600	$2,000	$4,500	$16,500	$30,000
Auctions: $5,875, MS-62, August 2014; $5,288, MS-62, August 2014; $8,225, MS-62, April 2013; $2,233, MS-61, July 2014												
1878	543,625	1,567	59.8	70%	$1,475	$1,500	$1,575	$1,600	$2,100	$3,500	$15,000	
Auctions: $11,163, MS-63, August 2014; $10,575, MS-63, November 2014; $14,100, MS-63, April 2013; $4,406, MS-62, November 2014												
1878, Proof (b)	20	8	64.5							$40,000	$65,000	$115,000
Auctions: $69,000, PF-64Cam, April 2011												
1878CC	13,180	331	46.9	2%	$3,000	$5,000	$9,500	$18,500	$40,000	$65,000		
Auctions: $34,075, AU-58, April 2014; $28,200, AU-58, October 2014; $14,100, AU-53, August 2014; $9,106, EF-45, November 2014												
1878S	1,739,000	1,495	58.3	56%	$1,475	$1,500	$1,575	$1,600	$2,000	$6,000	$23,500	
Auctions: $5,875, MS-62, August 2014; $11,163, MS-62, September 2013; $2,115, MS-61, July 2014; $2,350, MS-61, August 2014												

a. 10 to 12 examples are known. **b.** Fewer than 10 examples are known.

	Mintage	Cert	Avg	%MS	VF-20	EF-40	AU-50	AU-55	MS-60	MS-62 / PF-63	MS-63 / PF-64	MS-65 / PF-65
1879	207,600	590	58.3	45%	$1,475	$1,500	$1,575	$1,600	$1,950	$5,500	$20,000	
Auctions: $19,975, MS-63, April 2013; $4,113, MS-61, July 2014; $6,463, MS-61, August 2014; $2,703, MS-61, September 2014												
1879, Proof (c)	30	5	64.1							$40,000	$65,000	$115,000
Auctions: $57,500, PF-64, July 2009												
1879CC	10,708	325	50.0	3%	$3,000	$5,000	$12,000	$25,000	$42,500	$65,000		
Auctions: $28,200, AU-58, August 2014; $24,205, AU-55, May 2013; $11,750, AU-50, November 2014; $10,869, EF-45, November 2014												
1879O	2,325	82	49.5	11%	$15,000	$18,500	$37,500	$60,000	$135,000	$165,000	$200,000	
Auctions: $135,125, MS-60, January 2014; $35,250, AU-50, August 2014												
1879S	1,223,800	1,281	57.4	30%	$1,475	$1,500	$1,575	$1,600	$2,500	$15,000	$42,500	
Auctions: $14,100, MS-62, August 2014; $12,925, MS-62, November 2014; $14,723, MS-62, August 2013; $3,525, AU-58, November 2014												
1880	51,420	356	55.3	15%	$1,475	$1,500	$1,575	$1,600	$4,000	$16,500	$37,500	
Auctions: $23,500, MS-62, August 2014; $14,100, MS-61, April 2013; $1,998, MS-60, November 2014; $1,645, AU-50, August 2014												
1880, Proof (d)	36	4	64.3							$40,000	$65,000	$115,000
Auctions: $217,375, PF-65DCam, August 2014; $235,000, PF, March 2014												
1880S	836,000	865	58.0	38%	$1,475	$1,500	$1,575	$1,600	$1,950	$7,500	$25,000	
Auctions: $42,594, MS-63, March 2013; $10,869, MS-62, August 2014; $3,827, MS-61, July 2014; $2,585, AU-58, July 2014												
1881	2,199	29	53.7	17%	$15,000	$25,000	$40,000	$60,000	$135,000			
Auctions: $152,750, MS-61, April 2014; $61,725, AU-55, August 2014												
1881, Proof (e)	61	7	63.7							$40,000	$75,000	$115,000
Auctions: $172,500, PF-65Cam, January 2011												
1881S	727,000	727	58.7	54%	$1,475	$1,500	$1,575	$1,600	$1,750	$6,500	$22,500	
Auctions: $7,638, MS-62, July 2014; $2,350, MS-61, August 2014; $1,880, AU-58, November 2014; $1,645, AU-55, August 2014												
1882	571	12	54.8	8%	$17,500	$37,500	$70,000	$95,000	$135,000	$150,000	$200,000	
Auctions: $94,000, AU-58, January 2014; $129,250, AU-55, August 2014												
1882, Proof (f)	59	6	63.8							$40,000	$75,000	$115,000
Auctions: $161,000, PF-64Cam, January 2011												
1882CC	39,140	955	53.4	6%	$2,500	$2,750	$3,500	$6,500	$15,000	$25,000		
Auctions: $35,250, MS-62+, August 2014; $30,550, MS-62, August 2014; $23,500, MS-61, August 2014; $24,675, MS-61, April 2013												
1882S	1,125,000	1,370	59.0	61%	$1,475	$1,500	$1,575	$1,600	$2,000	$5,000	$18,500	
Auctions: $3,525, MS-62, October 2014; $8,225, MS-62, September 2013; $2,820, MS-61, August 2014; $3,055, MS-61, November 2014												
1883, Proof (g)	92	13	64.0							$115,000	$150,000	$200,000
Auctions: $282,000, PF-65DCam, January 2014; $158,625, PF-64DCam, August 2014												
1883CC	59,962	1,271	52.6	8%	$2,250	$2,500	$4,000	$6,000	$13,500	$20,000	$40,000	
Auctions: $14,100, MS-61, April 2014; $17,625, MS-61, August 2014; $9,988, AU-58, July 2014; $7,638, AU-58, July 2014												
1883S	1,189,000	2,040	59.8	73%	$1,475	$1,500	$1,575	$1,600	$1,950	$2,300	$8,000	
Auctions: $8,225, MS-63, August 2014; $6,169, MS-63, October 2014; $8,225, MS-63, April 2013; $2,820, MS-62, August 2014												
1884, Proof (h)	71	10	63.2							$110,000	$150,000	$200,000
Auctions: $235,000, PF-65DCam, August 2014; $246,750, PF-66Cam, April 2014												
1884CC	81,139	1,675	54.1	18%	$2,250	$2,500	$3,250	$5,000	$8,500	$20,000	$35,000	
Auctions: $70,500, MS-63, August 2014; $35,838, MS-63, August 2013; $19,975, MS-62, October 2014; $16,450, MS-61, August 2014												
1884S	916,000	2,513	60.6	82%	$1,475	$1,500	$1,575	$1,600	$1,900	$2,500	$6,500	$45,000
Auctions: $12,350, MS-64, November 2014; $4,994, MS-63, July 2014; $4,555, MS-63, August 2014; $6,463, MS-63, August 2013												
1885	751	52	55.7	27%	$12,500	$15,000	$25,000	$47,500	$80,000	$95,000	$145,000	
Auctions: $82,250, MS-62, October 2014; $14,100, MS-60, November 2014; $58,750, AU-58, January 2014; $52,875, AU-55, August 2014												
1885, Proof (i)	77	11	64.1							$42,500	$85,000	$120,000
Auctions: $35,250, PF-61DCam, September 2014												
1885CC	9,450	291	50.8	6%	$3,750	$5,000	$12,500	$19,500	$30,000	$45,000	$75,000	
Auctions: $36,719, MS-61, August 2014; $25,850, AU-58, April 2014; $21,150, AU-55, September 2014; $12,925, AU-53, August 2014												
1885S	683,500	2,198	60.8	87%	$1,475	$1,500	$1,575	$1,600	$1,900	$2,500	$5,500	
Auctions: $12,925, MS-64, April 2013; $4,406, MS-63, July 2014; $4,113, MS-63, August 2014; $5,581, MS-63+, October 2014												

c. 10 to 12 examples are known. d. 10 to 12 examples are known. e. Fewer than 20 examples are known. f. 12 to 15 examples are known. g. Proof only. Approximately 20 examples are known. h. Proof only. Approximately 20 examples are known. i. 15 to 20 examples are known.

1888, Doubled-Die Reverse
FS-G20-1888-801.

	Mintage	Cert	Avg	%MS	VF-20	EF-40	AU-50	AU-55	MS-60	MS-62 PF-63	MS-63 PF-64	MS-65 PF-65
1886	1,000	25	54.7	8%	$22,500	$37,500	$60,000	$75,000	$125,000	$150,000	$195,000	
	Auctions: $129,250, MS-60, January 2014; $111,625, AU-58, August 2014											
1886, Proof (j)	106	18	64.4							$42,500	$75,000	$115,000
	Auctions: $19,975, PF-60, January 2014											
1887, Proof (k)	121	10	65.2							$67,500	$85,000	$125,000
	Auctions: $123,375, PF-65Cam, August 2014; $258,500, PF-66, January 2014											
1887S	283,000	916	60.1	75%	$1,475	$1,500	$1,575	$1,600	$1,900	$5,000	$16,500	
	Auctions: $5,434, MS-62, July 2014; $4,553, MS-62, September 2014; $3,819, MS-62, October 2014; $2,233, MS-61, August 2014											
1888	226,161	1,044	60.0	73%	$1,475	$1,500	$1,575	$1,600	$1,900	$4,000	$11,500	$30,000
	Auctions: $4,700, MS-62, July 2014; $3,290, MS-62+, October 2014; $3,055, MS-62, October 2014; $2,233, MS-61, August 2014											
1888, Doubled-Die Reverse	(l)	16	59.9	75%					$2,750	$3,500		
	Auctions: $3,819, MS-62, April 2013											
1888, Proof (m)	105	19	64.5							$27,500	$45,000	$85,000
	Auctions: $126,500, PF-65DCam, April 2012											
1888S	859,600	2,446	60.8	85%	$1,475	$1,500	$1,575	$1,600	$1,900	$2,500	$5,500	
	Auctions: $8,225, MS-64, October 2014; $13,513, MS-64, April 2013; $4,700, MS-63, July 2014; $4,406, MS-63+, October 2014											
1889	44,070	543	60.6	83%	$1,475	$1,500	$1,575	$1,600	$1,950	$4,000	$17,500	
	Auctions: $4,406, MS-62, August 2014; $3,819, MS-62, August 2014; $4,700, MS-62, April 2013; $2,820, MS-60, August 2014											
1889, Proof (n)	41	9	63.8							$27,500	$45,000	$85,000
	Auctions: $352,500, PF-65, January 2014											
1889CC	30,945	844	52.6	7%	$2,250	$2,500	$4,000	$6,000	$12,500	$25,000	$35,000	
	Auctions: $52,875, MS-63, October 2014; $14,100, MS-60, August 2014; $17,625, MS, February 2014; $9,106, AU-58, November 2014											
1889S	774,700	1,871	60.6	83%	$1,475	$1,500	$1,575	$1,600	$1,950	$2,200	$6,000	
	Auctions: $16,450, MS-64, October 2014; $15,275, MS-64+, October 2014; $15,275, MS-64, April 2013; $4,994, MS-63+, November 2014											
1890	75,940	626	60.5	81%	$1,475	$1,500	$1,575	$1,600	$1,950	$2,300	$12,500	$30,000
	Auctions: $9,106, MS-63, October 2014; $9,988, MS-63, November 2013; $4,700, MS-62, August 2014; $4,113, MS-62, August 2014											
1890, Proof (o)	55	14	65.4							$27,500	$45,000	$85,000
	Auctions: $92,000, PF-65UCam, August 2011											
1890CC	91,209	2,234	53.2	11%	$2,250	$2,500	$2,800	$5,000	$9,500	$20,000	$45,000	
	Auctions: $41,125, MS-63, February 2013; $23,294, MS-62, August 2014; $14,100, MS-61+, November 2014; $11,750, MS-60, August 2014											
1890S	802,750	1,695	60.0	74%	$1,450	$1,500	$1,575	$1,600	$1,900	$2,000	$6,500	
	Auctions: $35,250, MS-65+, October 2014; $12,925, MS-64+, September 2014; $10,575, MS-64, November 2014; $14,100, MS-64, April 2013											
1891	1,390	40	55.4	10%	$8,000	$13,500	$22,500	$50,000	$70,000	$100,000		
	Auctions: $82,250, MS-61, January 2014; $52,875, AU-58, August 2014											
1891, Proof (p)	52	27	63.8							$27,500	$45,000	$85,000
	Auctions: $655,200, PF, September 2013											
1891CC	5,000	236	54.0	16%	$6,000	$10,000	$16,500	$25,000	$35,000	$60,000	$70,000	
	Auctions: $64,625, MS-62, January 2014; $4,406, AU-50, August 2014											
1891S	1,288,125	5,357	61.1	91%	$1,450	$1,500	$1,575	$1,600	$1,900	$1,950	$3,000	
	Auctions: $5,581, MS-64, August 2013; $2,401, MS-63, July 2014; $2,585, MS-63, August 2014; $2,233, MS-62, August 2014											

j. 20 to 25 examples are known. **k.** Proof only. More than 30 examples are known. **l.** Included in circulation-strike 1888 mintage figure. **m.** 20 to 30 examples are known. **n.** 10 to 12 examples are known. **o.** Approximately 15 examples are known. **p.** 20 to 25 examples are known.

	Mintage	Cert	Avg	%MS	VF-20	EF-40	AU-50	AU-55	MS-60	MS-62 / PF-63	MS-63 / PF-64	MS-65 / PF-65
1892	4,430	119	56.3	32%	$3,000	$4,500	$7,500	$9,000	$20,000	$32,500	$50,000	$85,000
Auctions: $38,188, MS-62+, August 2014; $30,550, MS-61, January 2014; $11,788, AU-55, August 2014; $9,400, AU-53, August 2014												
1892, Proof (q)	93	17	64.6							$30,000	$45,000	$85,000
Auctions: $188,000, PF-66DCam, January 2014												
1892CC	27,265	807	54.4	21%	$2,250	$2,650	$4,000	$6,500	$15,000	$30,000	$50,000	
Auctions: $38,188, MS-62, April 2014; $28,200, MS-62, August 2014; $7,075, AU-58, October 2014; $9,400, AU-58, November 2014												
1892S	930,150	4,263	61.1	91%	$1,450	$1,475	$1,485	$1,500	$1,550	$1,600	$4,000	$28,500
Auctions: $20,563, MS-65, November 2014; $30,550, MS-65, August 2013; $14,100, MS-64+, October 2014; $9,988, MS-64+, October 2014												
1893	344,280	5,726	61.6	98%	$1,450	$1,475	$1,485	$1,500	$1,550	$1,600	$2,750	
Auctions: $5,875, MS-64, August 2013; $2,585, MS-63, July 2014; $2,350, MS-63, July 2014; $1,645, MS-62, July 2014												
1893, Proof (r)	59	5	63.5							$27,500	$45,000	$85,000
Auctions: $15,525, PF-60Cam, August 2011												
1893CC	18,402	768	58.0	52%	$2,650	$3,500	$4,500	$7,500	$12,000	$20,000	$45,000	
Auctions: $52,875, MS-63, August 2014; $22,325, MS-62, August 2014; $25,850, MS-62, April 2013; $15,275, MS-61, August 2014												
1893S	996,175	5,026	61.0	92%	$1,450	$1,475	$1,485	$1,500	$1,550	$1,600	$4,000	
Auctions: $6,463, MS-64, October 2014; $4,994, MS-64, November 2014; $12,925, MS-64, April 2013; $3,290, MS-63, July 2014												
1894	1,368,940	14,755	61.4	97%	$1,450	$1,475	$1,485	$1,500	$1,550	$1,600	$2,650	$25,000
Auctions: $4,700, MS-64, January 2014; $5,581, MS-64, August 2014; $5,581, MS-64, November 2014; $2,350, MS-63, October 2014												
1894, Proof (s)	50	13	63.8							$27,500	$45,000	$85,000
Auctions: $54,625, PF-64Cam, January 2005												
1894S	1,048,550	5,456	61.2	93%	$1,450	$1,475	$1,485	$1,500	$1,550	$1,600	$3,000	$22,000
Auctions: $4,700, MS-64+, July 2014; $4,994, MS-64+, November 2014; $6,463, MS-64, August 2013; $2,938, MS-63, August 2014												
1895	1,114,605	21,152	61.7	98%	$1,450	$1,475	$1,485	$1,500	$1,550	$1,600	$2,500	$17,000
Auctions: $5,288, MS-64+, July 2014; $3,055, MS-64+, July 2014; $4,113, MS-64, November 2014; $2,351, MS-63, July 2014												
1895, Proof	51	11	64.2							$27,500	$45,000	$85,000
Auctions: $82,250, PF-65Cam, September 2014												
1895S	1,143,500	6,898	61.3	93%	$1,450	$1,475	$1,485	$1,500	$1,550	$1,600	$2,500	$17,500
Auctions: $3,525, MS-64, August 2014; $4,700, MS-64, October 2014; $5,141, MS-64, August 2013; $3,173, MS-63, July 2014												
1896	792,535	9,887	61.6	97%	$1,450	$1,475	$1,485	$1,500	$1,550	$1,600	$2,250	$17,500
Auctions: $5,288, MS-64, January 2014; $2,350, MS-63, July 2014; $2,233, MS-63, August 2014; $1,821, MS-63, September 2014												
1896, Proof (t)	128	38	63.9							$30,000	$45,000	$85,000
Auctions: $97,750, PF-65DCam, April 2012												
1896S	1,403,925	8,724	61.3	94%	$1,450	$1,475	$1,485	$1,500	$1,550	$1,600	$2,350	$25,000
Auctions: $4,700, MS-64, April 2013; $1,998, MS-63, July 2014; $1,873, MS-63, July 2014; $1,763, MS-62, August 2014												
1897	1,383,175	17,459	61.7	98%	$1,450	$1,475	$1,485	$1,500	$1,550	$1,600	$2,500	$16,000
Auctions: $3,290, MS-64, July 2014; $7,050, MS-64, August 2014; $2,115, MS-64, October 2014; $2,233, MS-63+, August 2014												
1897, Proof (u)	86	22	64.2							$30,000	$45,000	$85,000
Auctions: $73,438, PF-64Cam, August 2014; $30,550, PF-62Cam, April 2013												
1897S	1,470,250	12,320	61.6	95%	$1,450	$1,475	$1,485	$1,500	$1,550	$1,600	$2,600	$16,000
Auctions: $5,288, MS-64, October 2014; $5,875, MS-64, August 2013; $3,290, MS-63, August 2014; $1,645, MS-62, August 2014												
1898	170,395	1,642	61.2	89%	$1,500	$1,600	$1,650	$1,700	$2,750	$3,250	$6,000	
Auctions: $14,100, MS-64, April 2013; $7,050, MS-63, July 2014; $2,585, MS-62, August 2014; $2,350, MS-62+, November 2014												
1898, Proof (v)	75	36	64.1							$30,000	$45,000	$85,000
Auctions: $52,875, PF-64DCam, September 2014; $117,500, PF-65Cam, April 2013												
1898S	2,575,175	21,883	61.7	96%	$1,450	$1,475	$1,485	$1,500	$1,550	$1,600	$2,750	$8,500
Auctions: $10,575, MS-65, September 2013; $2,233, MS-64, November 2014; $1,939, MS-63, August 2014; $1,880, MS-63+, November 2014												

q. Approximately 25 examples are known. r. 15 to 20 examples are known. s. 15 to 20 examples are known. t. 45 to 50 examples are known. u. 20 to 25 examples are known. v. 35 to 40 examples are known.

	Mintage	Cert	Avg	%MS	VF-20	EF-40	AU-50	AU-55	MS-60	MS-62 / PF-63	MS-63 / PF-64	MS-65 / PF-65
1899	1,669,300	23,081	62.0	98%	$1,450	$1,475	$1,485	$1,500	$1,550	$1,600	$2,100	$8,000
	Auctions: $8,519, MS-65, August 2014; $6,463, MS-65, August 2014; $5,581, MS-65, October 2014; $9,400, MS-65, August 2013											
1899, Proof (w)	84	28	64.2							$27,500	$45,000	$85,000
	Auctions: $76,375, PF, March 2014											
1899S	2,010,300	8,978	61.3	91%	$1,450	$1,475	$1,485	$1,500	$1,550	$1,600	$2,750	$17,500
	Auctions: $2,585, MS-64, July 2014; $3,820, MS-64, October 2014; $4,406, MS-64, August 2013; $1,939, MS-63, July 2014											
1900	1,874,460	47,762	62.3	99%	$1,450	$1,475	$1,485	$1,500	$1,550	$1,600	$2,100	$3,750
	Auctions: $6,463, MS-65, January 2014; $4,406, MS-65, August 2014; $4,113, MS-65, November 2014; $3,290, MS-64+, July 2014											
1900, Proof (x)	124	30	64.6							$27,500	$45,000	$85,000
	Auctions: $88,125, PF, March 2014											
1900S	2,459,500	7,392	61.1	92%	$1,450	$1,475	$1,485	$1,500	$1,550	$1,600	$2,750	$24,000
	Auctions: $4,700, MS-64, April 2013; $2,126, MS-63, July 2014; $1,998, MS-63, August 2014; $1,880, MS-61, July 2014											
1901	111,430	4,938	62.9	99%	$1,450	$1,475	$1,485	$1,500	$1,550	$1,600	$1,850	$3,750
	Auctions: $6,463, MS-65, April 2014; $3,525, MS-65, August 2014; $7,638, MS-65+, October 2014; $2,585, MS-64, September 2014											
1901, Proof (y)	96	41	63.0							$27,500	$45,000	$85,000
	Auctions: $68,150, PF, February 2013											
1901S	1,596,000	2,972	61.1	93%	$1,450	$1,475	$1,485	$1,500	$1,550	$1,600	$3,500	$20,000
	Auctions: $16,450, MS-65, April 2013; $5,581, MS-64, October 2014; $3,055, MS-63, July 2014; $1,645, MS-62, August 2014											
1902	31,140	505	60.0	68%	$1,625	$1,675	$1,700	$2,100	$2,500	$3,500	$15,000	
	Auctions: $12,925, MS-63, July 2014; $10,281, MS-63, November 2014; $4,994, MS-62, August 2014; $4,406, MS-62, November 2014											
1902, Proof (z)	114	28	63.1							$27,500	$45,000	$85,000
	Auctions: $9,400, PF-50, January 2014											
1902S	1,753,625	4,372	61.0	94%	$1,450	$1,475	$1,485	$1,500	$1,550	$1,600	$3,500	$23,000
	Auctions: $9,400, MS-64+, November 2014; $11,163, MS-64, April 2013; $4,406, MS-63, July 2014; $1,763, MS-62, August 2014											
1903	287,270	12,224	62.9	100%	$1,625	$1,675	$1,700	$1,725	$1,775	$1,800	$1,850	$3,500
	Auctions: $4,113, MS-65, November 2014; $5,875, MS-65, November 2013; $2,350, MS-64, September 2014; $1,998, MS-64, October 2014											
1903, Proof (aa)	158	39	62.9							$27,500	$45,000	$85,000
	Auctions: $63,450, PF, March 2014											
1903S	954,000	6,282	61.8	98%	$1,450	$1,475	$1,485	$1,500	$1,550	$1,600	$2,100	$11,500
	Auctions: $12,925, MS-65, February 2013; $3,290, MS-64, September 2014; $2,820, MS-64, October 2014; $2,086, MS-63, November 2014											
1904	6,256,699	220,673	62.6	99%	$1,450	$1,475	$1,485	$1,500	$1,550	$1,600	$1,850	$3,500
	Auctions: $5,875, MS-66, August 2014; $5,581, MS-66, September 2014; $10,575, MS-66, February 2013; $4,406, MS-65, September 2014											
1904, Proof (bb)	98	41	63.7							$27,500	$45,000	$85,000
	Auctions: $146,875, PF-67Cam, August 2013											
1904S	5,134,175	24,027	62.4	98%	$1,450	$1,475	$1,485	$1,500	$1,550	$1,600	$2,100	$4,750
	Auctions: $23,500, MS-66, April 2013; $4,406, MS-65, September 2014; $1,880, MS-63, August 2014; $1,645, MS-63, August 2014											
1905	58,919	784	59.3	60%	$1,625	$1,675	$1,700	$1,725	$2,500	$5,000	$15,500	$60,000
	Auctions: $5,875, MS-62, April 2014; $5,581, MS-62, July 2014; $5,581, MS-62, August 2014; $3,055, MS-61, October 2014											
1905, Proof (cc)	92	26	62.9							$27,500	$45,000	$85,000
	Auctions: $10,005, PF-58, January 2012											
1905S	1,813,000	2,285	61.2	89%	$1,450	$1,475	$1,485	$1,500	$1,550	$1,600	$3,750	$20,000
	Auctions: $21,752, MS-65, February 2014; $4,700, MS-64+, October 2014; $3,819, MS-63, July 2014; $3,055, MS-63, October 2014											

w. Fewer than 30 examples are known. **x.** Approximately 50 examples are known. **y.** 40 to 50 examples are known. **z.** Fewer than 50 examples are known. **aa.** 40 to 50 examples are known. **bb.** Approximately 50 examples are known. **cc.** 30 to 40 examples are known.

	Mintage	Cert	Avg	%MS	VF-20	EF-40	AU-50	AU-55	MS-60	MS-62 / PF-63	MS-63 / PF-64	MS-65 / PF-65
1906	69,596	670	60.4	76%	$1,625	$1,675	$1,700	$1,750	$1,800	$3,500	$8,500	$32,500
	Auctions: $8,225, MS-63, July 2014; $6,463, MS-63, July 2014; $7,344, MS-63, August 2014; $3,538, MS-62, November 2014											
1906, Proof (dd)	94	45	63.4							$27,500	$45,000	$85,000
	Auctions: $85,188, PF, August 2013											
1906D	620,250	1,776	61.8	96%	$1,625	$1,675	$1,700	$1,750	$1,800	$3,500	$8,500	$32,500
	Auctions: $4,259, MS-64, October 2014; $3,819, MS-63, July 2014; $2,820, MS-62, August 2014; $6,169, MS, February 2014											
1906D, Proof (ee)	6	0	n/a		*(extremely rare)*							
	Auctions: No auction records available.											
1906S	2,065,750	4,448	61.5	96%	$1,450	$1,475	$1,485	$1,500	$1,550	$1,600	$2,400	$20,000
	Auctions: $4,994, MS-64+, October 2014; $5,141, MS-64+, November 2014; $7,050, MS-64, February 2013; $3,055, MS-63, November 2014											
1907	1,451,786	30,352	61.9	99%	$1,450	$1,475	$1,485	$1,500	$1,550	$1,600	$2,000	$7,500
	Auctions: $8,813, MS-65, June 2013; $3,290, MS-64, October 2014; $2,946, MS-64, November 2014; $1,998, MS-63, July 2014											
1907, Proof (ff)	78	48	63.5							$27,500	$45,000	$85,000
	Auctions: $40,250, PF-64Cam, January 2012											
1907D	842,250	2,208	62.3	96%	$1,450	$1,475	$1,485	$1,500	$1,550	$1,600	$3,250	$8,500
	Auctions: $25,850, MS-66, November 2014; $21,150, MS-66, August 2013; $6,761, MS-65, July 2014; $7,050, MS-65, November 2014											
1907D, Proof (gg)	*unknown*	1	62.0									
	Auctions: $71,875, PF-62, January 2004											
1907S	2,165,800	3,423	61.9	96%	$1,450	$1,475	$1,485	$1,500	$1,550	$1,600	$3,000	$22,500
	Auctions: $24,675, MS-65, July 2014; $4,994, MS-64+, September 2014; $5,875, MS-64+, October 2014; $3,055, MS-63, August 2014											

dd. 45 to 50 examples are known. **ee.** Six 1906-D presentation strikes were made to commemorate the first coinage of double eagles at the Denver Mint. The coins were well documented at the time; however, at present only two are accounted for. **ff.** 25 to 50 examples are known. **gg.** Believed to have once been part of the collection of King Farouk of Egypt; cleaned.

SAINT-GAUDENS, HIGH RELIEF AND ULTRA HIGH RELIEF, MCMVII (1907)

Designer: *Augustus Saint-Gaudens.* **Weight:** *33.436 grams.*
Composition: *.900 gold, .100 copper (net weight: .96750 oz. pure gold).*
Diameter *34 mm.* **Edge:** *E PLURIBUS UNUM with words divided by stars*
(one specimen of the high-relief variety with plain edge is known). **Mint:** *Philadelphia.*

Circulation Strike   Proof, Ultra High Relief Pattern

History. Created by famous artist Augustus Saint-Gaudens under a commission arranged by President Theodore Roosevelt, this double eagle was first made (in pattern form) with ultra high relief, sculptural in its effect, on both sides and the date in Roman numerals. The story of its production is well known and has been described in several books, notably *Renaissance of American Coinage, 1905–1908* (Burdette) and *Striking Change: The Great Artistic Collaboration of Theodore Roosevelt and August Saint-Gaudens* (Moran). After the Ultra High Relief patterns of 1907, a modified High Relief version was developed to facilitate production. Each coin required three blows of the press to strike up properly. Most featured a flat rim (now known as the Flat Rim variety), but planchet metal would occasionally be squeezed up between the collar and the die, resulting in the Wire Rim variety; this can exist around part of or the entire circumference of the coin. The coins were made on a medal press in December 1907 and January 1908, to the extent of fewer than 13,000 pieces. In the meantime, production was under way for low-relief coins, easier to mint in quantities sufficient for commerce—these dated 1907 rather than MCMVII. Today the MCMVII double eagle is a favorite among collectors, and when surveys are taken of beautiful and popular designs (as in *100 Greatest U.S. Coins*, by Garrett and Guth), it always ranks near the top.

Striking and Sharpness. The striking usually is good. Check the left knee of Miss Liberty, which sometimes shows lightness of strike and, most often, shows flatness or wear (sometimes concealed by postmint etching or clever tooling). Check the Capitol at the lower left. On the reverse, check the high points at the top of the eagle. The surface on all is a delicate matte texture, grainy rather than deeply frosty. Under examination the fields show myriad tiny raised curlicues and other die-finish marks. There is no record of any MCMVII double eagles being made as *Proofs*, nor is there any early numismatic record of any being sold as Proofs. Walter Breen in the 1960s made up some guidelines for Proofs, which some graders have adopted. Some homemade "Proofs" have been made by pickling or sandblasting the surface of regular coins—*caveat emptor*.

Availability. Half or more of the original mintage still exist today, as many were saved, and these grade mostly from AU-50 to MS-62. Circulated examples often have been cleaned, polished, or used in jewelry. Higher-grade coins are seen with some frequency, up to MS-65. Overgrading is common.

GRADING STANDARDS

MS-60 to 70 (Mint State). *Obverse:* At MS-60, some abrasion and contact marks are seen on Liberty's chest. The left knee is flat on lower Mint State coins and all circulated coins. Scattered marks and abrasion are in the field. Satiny luster is present, but may be dull or lifeless, and interrupted in patches. Many coins at this level have been cleaned. At MS-63, contact marks are fewer, and abrasion is light, but the knee still has a flat spot. An MS-65 coin

MCMVII (1907), High Relief. Graded MS-63.

has little abrasion and few marks. Grades above MS-65 are defined by having fewer marks as perfection is approached. *Reverse:* Comments apply as for the obverse, except that abrasion and contact marks are most noticeable on the side of the eagle's body and the top of the left wing.

Illustrated coin: This is a splendid choice striking.

AU-50, 53, 55, 58 (About Uncirculated). *Obverse:* Light wear is seen on the chest, the left leg, and the field, more so at AU-50 than at 53 or 55. An AU-58 coin has fewer traces of wear. An AU-50 coin has satiny luster in protected areas among the rays, with little in the open field above. At AU-58, most luster is present. *Reverse:* Comments as preceding, except that the side of the eagle below the front of the wing, the top of the wing, and the field

MCMVII (1907), High Relief. Graded AU-55.

show light wear. Satiny luster ranges from perhaps 40% (at AU-50) to nearly full mint bloom (at AU-58).

EF-40, 45 (Extremely Fine). *Obverse:* Wear is seen on all the higher-relief areas of the standing figure and on the rock at the lower right. Luster is minimal, if present at all. Eye appeal is apt to be lacking. Nearly all Extremely Fine coins have been cleaned. *Reverse:* The eagle shows more wear overall, especially at the bottom and on the tops of the wings.

MCMVII (1907), High Relief. Graded EF-45.

VF-20, 30 (Very Fine). *Obverse:* Most details of the standing figure are flat, her face is incomplete, and the tips of the rays are weak. Eye appeal is usually poor. As these coins did not circulate to any extent, a Very Fine coin was likely carried as a pocket piece. *Reverse:* Wear is greater overall, but most evident on the eagle. Detail is good at the center of the left wing, but worn away in most other areas of the bird.

MCMVII (1907), High Relief. Graded VF-30.

The MCMVII (1907) High Relief double eagle is seldom collected in grades lower than VF-20.

	Mintage	Cert	Avg	%MS	VF-20	EF-40	AU-50	AU-55	MS-60 / PF-63	MS-62 / PF-64	MS-63 / PF-65	MS-65 / PF-67
1907, High Relief, MCMVII, Wire Rim † (a)	12,367	1,330	62.3	91%	$9,750	$11,000	$12,000	$13,000	$15,000	$22,000	$25,000	$47,500
Auctions: $217,375, MS-67, April 2013; $52,875, MS-65, August 2014; $49,938, MS-65, August 2014; $48,469, MS-65, September 2014												
1907, High Relief, MCMVII, Flat Rim †	(b)	546	62.4	86%	$9,750	$11,000	$12,000	$13,500	$15,000	$22,000	$25,000	$50,000
Auctions: $64,625, MS-66, November 2014; $47,000, MS-65, July 2014; $49,938, MS-65, August 2014; $38,188, MS-65, October 2014												
1907, High Relief, MCMVII, Wire or Flat Rim, Proof	unknown	0	n/a						$32,500	$40,000	$75,000	
Auctions: $32,900, PF-64, February 2013												
1907, Ultra High Relief, Plain Edge, Proof	(c)	0	n/a									
Auctions: No auction records available.												
1907, Ultra High Relief, Inverted Edge, Proof	(c)	0	n/a									
Auctions: No auction records available.												
1907, Ultra High Relief, Lettered Edge, Proof †	16–22	3	67.3									$2,250,000
Auctions: $2,115,000, PF-68, January 2015; $1,840,000, PF-68, January 2007												

† Ranked in the *100 Greatest U.S. Coins* (fourth edition). **a.** The Wire Rim and Flat Rim varieties were the result of different collars used in the minting process. The Flat Rim is considered slightly scarcer, but this has not led to large value differentials, as both varieties are very popular among collectors. **b.** Included in 1907, High Relief, MCMVII, Wire Rim, mintage figure. **c.** Included in 1907, Ultra High Relief, Lettered Edge, mintage figure.

Three Valuable Books for Every Stage of Your Hobby

In Pleasure and Profit: 100 Lessons for Building and Selling a Collection of Rare Coins, Robert W. Shipee shares hands-on hobby advice, but his text is also about golf, whisky, friendships, and other good things in life that are attached to the experience of collecting coins. His relaxed, storyteller's wit makes the lessons fun and interesting. Q. David Bowers says, *"Pleasure and Profit is one of the most useful books in American numismatics. It will change your buying strategies."*

320 pages, 6 x 9 inches, full color • $9.95

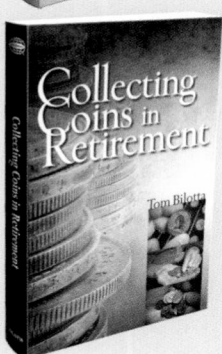

"Coin collecting during retirement poses specialized challenges and opportunities," says numismatist Tom Bilotta. In *Collecting Coins in Retirement*, he covers these issues in depth and guides you toward building your enjoyment of the hobby. In addition to addressing active collectors, he gives valuable real-world advice to inheritors on how to manage the disposition of rare coins and other collectibles. Available June 2015.

288 pages, 6 x 9 inches, full color • $19.95

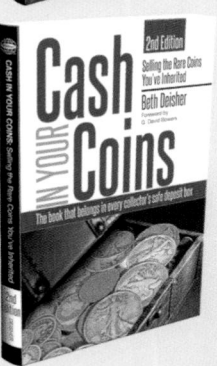

Don't leave your heirs in the dark. *Cash In Your Coins: Selling the Rare Coins You've Inherited* is for anyone who's inherited or found a collection of old coins. How rare are they? What are they worth? Should you sell? Where do you even begin? If you're a coin collector, you want your heirs to make smart, confident decisions—and avoid expensive mistakes! Keep a copy of this book with your collection for the benefit of your loved ones. Updated and expanded 2nd edition.

304 pages, 6 x 9 inches, full color • $9.95

Order individually, or.......
***SPECIAL OFFER* for readers of the**
***Deluxe Edition Red Book*—**
get all three books, a $39.85 value, for just $30 postpaid. Use promo code: 16

.com

Order by phone at 1-866-546-2995, online at Whitman.com, or email customerservice@Whitman.com

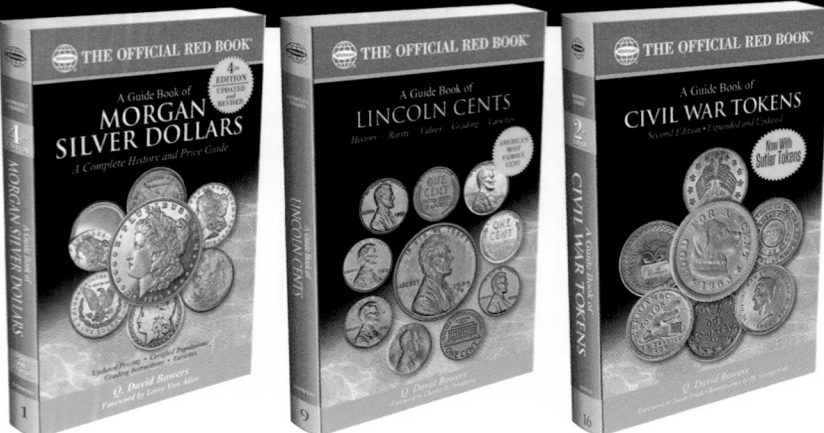

SAINT-GAUDENS, FLAT RELIEF, ARABIC NUMERALS (1907–1933)

Designer: *Augustus Saint-Gaudens.* **Weight:** *33.436 grams.*
Composition: *.900 gold, .100 copper (net weight: .96750 oz. pure gold).*
Diameter: *34 mm.* **Edge:** *E PLURIBUS UNUM with words divided by stars.*
Mints: *Philadelphia, Denver, San Francisco.*

No Motto (1907–1908)

Mintmark location is on the obverse, above the date.

With Motto (1908–1933)   With Motto, Proof

History. In autumn 1907 U.S. Mint chief engraver Charles E. Barber modified Augustus Saint-Gaudens's design by lowering its relief and substituting Arabic (not Roman) numerals. Coins of this type were struck in large quantities from 1907 to 1916 and again from 1920 to 1933. In July 1908 the motto IN GOD WE TRUST was added to the reverse. Coins dated 1907 to 1911 have 46 stars on the obverse; coins of 1912 to 1933 have 48 stars. Sandblast (also called Matte) Proofs were made in 1908 and from 1911 to 1915; Satin (also called Roman Finish) Proofs were made in 1909 and 1910.

The vast majority of these coins were exported. Since World War II millions have been repatriated, supplying most of those in numismatic hands today.

Striking and Sharpness. The details are often light on the obverse. Check the bosom of Miss Liberty, the covering of which tends to be weak on 1907 and, especially, 1908 No Motto coins. Check the Capitol building and its immediate area at the lower left. The reverse usually is well struck, but check the feathers on the eagle and the top of the wings. The Matte Proofs have dull surfaces, much like fine-grained sandpaper, while the Satin Proofs have satiny surfaces and are bright yellow.

Availability. Most dates and mintmarks range from very common to slightly scarce, punctuated with scarce to very rare issues such as 1908-S, 1920-S, 1921, mintmarked coins from 1924 to 1927, and all issues of 1929 to 1933. From their initial mintages, most of the double eagles of the 1920s were returned to the Mint and melted in the 1930s. Some, however, were unofficially saved by Treasury employees. Estimates of the quantities saved range from a few dozen to several hundred thousand, depending on the date; this explains the high values for coins that, judged only by their initial mintages, should otherwise be more common. Probably a million or more MS coins exist of certain dates, most notably 1908 No Motto, 1924, 1925, 1926, and 1928 (especially common). Quality varies, as many have contact marks.

Philadelphia Mint coins from 1922 onward usually are seen with excellent eye appeal. Common varieties are not usually collected in grades below MS. All of the Proofs are rare today.

Note: Values of common-date gold coins have been based on the current bullion price of gold, $1,200 per ounce, and may vary with the prevailing spot price.

Grading Standards

MS-60 to 70 (Mint State). *Obverse:* At MS-60, some abrasion and contact marks are seen on Liberty's chest and left knee, and scattered marks and abrasion are in the field. Luster is present, but may be dull or lifeless, and interrupted in patches. At MS-63, contact marks are fewer, and abrasion is light. An MS-65 coin has little abrasion and few marks, although quality among certified coins can vary. On a conservatively graded coin the lus-

1924. Graded MS-65.

ter should be full and rich. Grades above MS-65 are defined by having fewer marks as perfection is approached. Generally, Mint State coins of 1922 onward are choicer and more attractive than the earlier issues. *Reverse:* Comments apply as for the obverse, except that abrasion and contact marks are most noticeable on the eagle's left wing.

AU-50, 53, 55, 58 (About Uncirculated). *Obverse:* Light wear is seen on the chest, the left knee, the midriff, and across the field, more so at AU-50 than at 53 or 55. An AU-58 coin has minimal traces of wear. An AU-50 coin has luster in protected areas among the rays, with little in the open field above. At AU-58, most luster is present. *Reverse:* Comments as preceding, except that the side of the eagle below the front of the wing, the top of

1909, 9 Over 8. Graded AU-50.

the wing, and the field show light wear. Luster ranges from perhaps 40% (at AU-50) to nearly full mint bloom (at AU-58).

EF-40, 45 (Extremely Fine). *Obverse:* Wear is seen on all the higher-relief areas of the standing figure and on the rock at the lower right. Luster is minimal, if present at all. Eye appeal is apt to be lacking. *Reverse:* The eagle shows more wear overall, especially at the bottom and on the tops of the wings.

1908-S. Graded EF-40.

VF-20, 30 (Very Fine). *Obverse:* Most details of the standing figure are flat, her face is incomplete, and the tips of the rays are weak. Eye appeal is usually poor. *Reverse:* Wear is greater overall, but most evident on the eagle. Detail is good at the center of the left wing, but worn away in most other areas of the bird.

The Saint-Gaudens double eagle is seldom collected in grades lower than VF-20.

PF-60 to 70 (Proof). *Obverse and Reverse:* At PF-60 to 63, there is light abrasion and some contact marks (the lower the grade, the higher the quantity). On Sandblast Proofs these show up as visually unappealing bright spots. At PF-64 and higher levels, marks are fewer, with magnification needed to see any at PF-65. At PF-66, there should be none at all.

1914. Graded VF-20.

1909, Satin Finish. Graded PF-66.

	Mintage	Cert	Avg	%MS	VF-20	EF-40	AU-50	AU-55	MS-60	MS-62 / PF-63	MS-63 / PF-64	MS-65 / PF-65
1907, Arabic Numerals	361,667	10,290	62.7	97%	$1,450	$1,475	$1,485	$1,500	$1,850	$1,875	$2,100	$4,000
Auctions: $47,000, MS-67, April 2013; $15,275, MS-66+, October 2014; $6,169, MS-66, October 2014; $6,169, MS-66, October 2014												
1907, Proof (a)	unknown	0	n/a		*(extremely rare)*							
Auctions: $40,250, PF-64Cam, January 2012												
1908, No Motto	4,271,551	133,706	63.3	100%	$1,450	$1,475	$1,485	$1,500	$1,750	$1,775	$1,875	$2,350
Auctions: $76,375, MS-69, August 2013; $13,513, MS-68, November 2014; $6,463, MS-67, July 2014; $6,463, MS-67, September 2014												
1908D, No Motto	663,750	4,337	62.4	97%	$1,450	$1,475	$1,485	$1,500	$1,700	$1,800	$1,875	$9,500
Auctions: $5,581, MS-65, August 2014; $4,553, MS-65, October 2014; $2,233, MS-64, November 2014; $8,284, MS, February 2014												
1908, With Motto	156,258	2,119	62.1	95%	$1,500	$1,650	$1,700	$1,750	$1,875	$1,900	$2,500	$19,500
Auctions: $10,575, MS-65, August 2013; $3,819, MS-64, July 2014; $3,525, MS-64, September 2014; $2,233, MS-63, July 2014												
1908, With Motto, Sandblast Finish Proof	101	76	65.3							$30,000	$43,500	$72,500
Auctions: $57,500, PF-66+, June 2012												
1908, With Motto, Satin Finish Proof (b)	unknown	0	n/a		*(extremely rare)*							
Auctions: $152,750, PF, August 2013												
1908D, With Motto	349,500	2,215	62.5	93%	$1,450	$1,475	$1,485	$1,500	$1,700	$1,800	$1,850	$5,000
Auctions: $22,325, MS-66, June 2013; $3,850, MS-65, August 2014; $2,585, MS-64, August 2014; $2,585, MS-64, November 2014												
1908S, With Motto	22,000	521	56.1	33%	$2,500	$3,750	$6,000	$7,000	$12,500	$17,500	$24,500	$50,000
Auctions: $21,150, MS-64, August 2014; $22,325, MS-63, February 2014; $17,625, MS-63, November 2014; $14,100, MS-62, July 2014												

a. 2 or 3 examples are known. **b.** 3 or 4 examples are known.

1909, 9 Over 8

	Mintage	Cert	Avg	%MS	VF-20	EF-40	AU-50	AU-55	MS-60	MS-62 / PF-63	MS-63 / PF-64	MS-65 / PF-65
1909, All kinds	161,282											
1909, 9 Over 8 (c)		1,643	59.4	58%	$1,600	$1,650	$1,700	$1,750	$2,250	$3,500	$6,750	$42,000
Auctions: $67,563, MS-65, February 2014; $11,163, MS-64, August 2014; $9,988, MS-64, August 2014; $9,400, MS-64, September 2014												
1909		1,374	60.8	77%	$1,450	$1,475	$1,485	$1,500	$1,700	$2,000	$3,500	$40,000
Auctions: $70,500, MS-66, September 2013; $5,581, MS-64, August 2014; $2,115, MS-63, July 2014; $1,998, MS-62, July 2014												
1909, Satin Finish Proof	67	32	65.4							$28,500	$43,500	$80,000
Auctions: $184,860, PF, September 2013												
1909D	52,500	514	59.9	62%	$1,750	$1,850	$1,900	$1,950	$3,250	$5,000	$8,000	$40,000
Auctions: $64,625, MS-66, November 2014; $8,225, MS-64, August 2014; $7,638, MS-64, October 2014; $11,457, MS-64, March 2013												
1909S	2,774,925	5,709	62.6	96%	$1,450	$1,475	$1,485	$1,500	$1,550	$1,575	$2,000	$4,500
Auctions: $4,113, MS-65, July 2014; $3,966, MS-65, October 2014; $4,113, MS-65, November 2014; $7,344, MS-65, March 2013												
1910	482,000	8,143	62.3	98%	$1,450	$1,475	$1,485	$1,500	$1,550	$1,575	$2,100	$8,500
Auctions: $9,106, MS-65, January 2014; $7,638, MS-65, October 2014; $9,400, MS-65+, November 2014; $1,998, MS-64, August 2014												
1910, Satin Finish Proof	167	0	n/a							$30,000	$43,500	$80,000
Auctions: $76,375, PF-65, August 2014; $56,063, PF-65, June 2012												
1910, Sandblast Finish Proof (d)	unknown	37	65.6				*(unique)*					
Auctions: No auction records available.												
1910D	429,000	6,857	62.9	97%	$1,450	$1,475	$1,485	$1,500	$1,550	$1,575	$1,800	$3,000
Auctions: $10,575, MS-66, March 2013; $3,819, MS-65, August 2014; $3,290, MS-65, October 2014; $2,115, MS-65, November 2014												
1910S	2,128,250	4,318	61.8	90%	$1,450	$1,475	$1,485	$1,500	$1,550	$1,575	$2,000	$7,000
Auctions: $9,694, MS-65, February 2014; $5,875, MS-65, October 2014; $5,993, MS-65, November 2014; $2,585, MS-64, August 2014												
1911	197,250	2,742	61.9	90%	$1,450	$1,475	$1,485	$1,500	$1,700	$1,750	$2,250	$15,000
Auctions: $42,300, MS-66, January 2013; $4,700, MS-65, October 2014; $5,288, MS-64+, October 2014; $4,406, MS-64, November 2014												
1911, Sandblast Finish Proof	100	45	66.1							$27,500	$43,500	$75,000
Auctions: $157,950, PF, September 2013												
1911D	846,500	11,683	63.4	98%	$1,450	$1,475	$1,485	$1,500	$1,550	$1,575	$1,600	$2,350
Auctions: $17,550, MS-67, September 2013; $3,819, MS-66, November 2014; $3,173, MS-65, August 2014; $2,820, MS-65, November 2014												
1911S	775,750	5,368	62.8	97%	$1,450	$1,475	$1,485	$1,500	$1,550	$1,575	$1,600	$5,000
Auctions: $21,150, MS-66+, August 2014; $18,214, MS-66, March 2013; $3,290, MS-65, August 2014; $4,113, MS-65, November 2014												
1912	149,750	2,450	61.5	89%	$1,450	$1,475	$1,485	$1,500	$1,550	$1,575	$1,650	$23,500
Auctions: $21,738, MS-65, August 2014; $21,150, MS-65, October 2014; $19,975, MS-65, March 2013; $7,050, MS-64, July 2014												
1912, Sandblast Finish Proof	74	54	66.0							$30,000	$43,500	$75,000
Auctions: $211,500, PF-67, August 2013												
1913	168,780	2,654	61.4	89%	$1,450	$1,475	$1,485	$1,500	$1,725	$1,900	$2,750	$45,000
Auctions: $48,469, MS-65, February 2014; $4,113, MS-64, August 2014; $3,525, MS-64, October 2014; $2,350, MS-62, August 2014												
1913, Sandblast Finish Proof	58	50	65.4							$27,500	$43,500	$75,000
Auctions: $79,313, PF, August 2013												
1913D	393,500	3,838	62.5	95%	$1,450	$1,475	$1,485	$1,500	$1,550	$1,575	$1,600	$5,500
Auctions: $6,463, MS-65, August 2014; $5,288, MS-65, August 2014; $2,350, MS-64, September 2014; $16,450, MS, February 2014												
1913S	34,000	1,140	61.6	87%	$1,800	$1,850	$1,875	$2,000	$2,350	$3,000	$5,000	$35,000
Auctions: $35,250, MS-65, September 2014; $11,456, MS-64, November 2014; $8,225, MS-64, June 2013; $4,113, MS-63, November 2014												

c. This is one of the few Saint-Gaudens double eagle die varieties that commands a premium over the regular coin. **d.** Part of the unique complete 1910 Sandblast Finish Proof gold set.

1922, Doubled-Die Reverse

	Mintage	Cert	Avg	%MS	VF-20	EF-40	AU-50	AU-55	MS-60	MS-62	MS-63	MS-65
										PF-63	PF-64	PF-65
1914	95,250	1,761	62.0	91%	$1,450	$1,475	$1,485	$1,500	$1,550	$1,800	$3,500	$17,500
	Auctions: $7,638, MS-64, February 2014; $7,050, MS-64+, July 2014; $5,875, MS-64+, September 2014; $3,055, MS-63, August 2014											
1914, Sandblast Finish Proof	70	28	65.5							$30,000	$43,500	$75,000
	Auctions: $60,375, PF-66, June 2012											
1914D	453,000	6,504	63.0	97%	$1,450	$1,475	$1,485	$1,500	$1,550	$1,575	$1,600	$3,250
	Auctions: $8,225, MS-66, June 2014; $7,344, MS-66+, July 2014; $3,879, MS-65, August 2014; $3,827, MS-65, October 2014											
1914S	1,498,000	21,374	63.1	99%	$1,450	$1,475	$1,485	$1,500	$1,550	$1,575	$1,600	$2,400
	Auctions: $4,406, MS-66, September 2014; $9,694, MS-66, March 2013; $2,586, MS-65, August 2014; $3,055, MS-65, September 2014											
1915	152,000	2,256	61.8	89%	$1,450	$1,475	$1,485	$1,500	$1,700	$1,800	$1,850	$25,000
	Auctions: $14,100, MS-65, October 2014; $51,406, MS-65, April 2013; $5,141, MS-64, October 2014; $4,113, MS-64, November 2014											
1915, Sandblast Finish Proof	50	41	64.8							$30,000	$47,500	$85,000
	Auctions: $63,250, PF-66, August 2011											
1915S	567,500	15,829	63.3	99%	$1,450	$1,475	$1,485	$1,500	$1,550	$1,575	$1,600	$2,400
	Auctions: $6,756, MS-66, January 2014; $3,525, MS-66, August 2014; $3,525, MS-66, August 2014; $2,820, MS-65, October 2014											
1916S	796,000	4,250	63.4	97%	$1,450	$1,475	$1,485	$1,500	$1,550	$1,575	$1,600	$3,000
	Auctions: $9,988, MS-66, January 2014; $6,463, MS-66, August 2014; $5,581, MS-66, November 2014; $3,525, MS-65, October 2014											
1920	228,250	6,504	62.1	99%	$1,450	$1,475	$1,485	$1,500	$1,550	$1,575	$1,850	$55,000
	Auctions: $47,000, MS-64, August 2014; $7,344, MS-64+, November 2014; $9,988, MS-64, December 2013; $1,939, MS-63, July 2014											
1920S	558,000	74	60.8	73%	$16,500	$20,000	$25,000	$32,500	$50,000	$75,000	$85,000	$300,000
	Auctions: $111,625, MS-64, August 2014; $55,813, MS-61, February 2014; $30,198, AU-58, August 2014											
1921	528,500	71	59.1	56%	$25,000	$37,500	$55,000	$65,000	$100,000	$125,000	$175,000	$700,000
	Auctions: $164,500, MS-63, January 2014; $105,750, MS-62, August 2014; $99,875, MS-61, October 2014											
1921, Proof † (e)	*unknown*	1	64.0		*(extremely rare)*							
	Auctions: $203,500, PF, 2000; $1,495,000, MS-63, 2006											
1922	1,375,500	53,068	62.6	100%	$1,450	$1,475	$1,485	$1,500	$1,550	$1,575	$1,600	$4,000
	Auctions: $11,163, MS-65, April 2014; $4,406, MS-65, July 2014; $4,230, MS-65, August 2014; $3,538, MS-65, October 2014											
1922, DblDie Rev	**(f)**	4	63.4	100%			$2,000	$2,200	$2,500	$2,750	$3,500	
	Auctions: $2,115, MS-64, December 2013											
1922S	2,658,000	909	62.6	96%	$1,850	$1,900	$2,000	$2,150	$2,650	$3,000	$5,000	$40,000
	Auctions: $45,531, MS-65, September 2014; $5,581, MS-64, August 2014; $3,819, MS-63, August 2014; $28,200, MS, March 2014											
1923	566,000	29,112	62.5	100%	$1,450	$1,475	$1,485	$1,500	$1,550	$1,575	$1,600	$4,000
	Auctions: $9,401, MS-65, January 2014; $4,259, MS-65, July 2014; $3,525, MS-65, August 2014; $2,938, MS-65, October 2014											
1923D	1,702,250	5,974	64.3	100%	$1,450	$1,475	$1,485	$1,500	$1,550	$1,575	$1,600	$2,250
	Auctions: $19,975, MS-67, January 2014; $13,513, MS-67, November 2014; $3,525, MS-66, July 2014; $2,820, MS-66, September 2014											
1924	4,323,500	307,246	63.4	100%	$1,450	$1,475	$1,485	$1,500	$1,550	$1,575	$1,600	$2,000
	Auctions: $19,388, MS-67, January 2014; $3,819, MS-66, September 2014; $3,672, MS-66, September 2014; $3,290, MS-66+, November 2014											
1924D	3,049,500	454	61.9	88%	$2,200	$2,500	$2,750	$3,250	$4,500	$5,500	$8,750	$75,000
	Auctions: $70,500, MS-65, September 2013; $12,925, MS-64, August 2014; $6,169, MS-63, August 2014; $6,463, MS-63, November 2014											
1924S	2,927,500	497	62.5	93%	$2,200	$2,500	$2,750	$3,250	$4,500	$5,500	$10,000	$65,000
	Auctions: $47,000, MS-65, January 2014; $14,100, MS-64, August 2014; $14,100, MS-64, November 2014; $16,450, MS-62, July 2014											

† Ranked in the *100 Greatest U.S. Coins* (fourth edition). **e.** Prior to the first public auction of a 1921 presentation-strike double eagle (a lightly cleaned specimen) in summer 2000, this variety was unknown to the numismatic community at large. That example reportedly was struck in 1921 to celebrate the birth of Joseph Baker, nephew of U.S. Mint director Raymond T. Baker. In 2006 a second example (this one with original, uncleaned surfaces) was discovered and subsequently auctioned. **f.** Included in 1922 mintage figure.

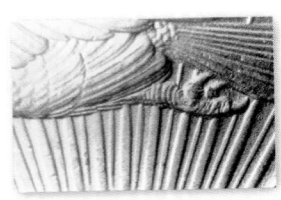

1925, Doubled-Die Reverse

1933 Saint-Gaudens Double Eagle

	Mintage	Cert	Avg	%MS	VF-20	EF-40	AU-50	AU-55	MS-60	MS-62 / PF-63	MS-63 / PF-64	MS-65 / PF-65
1925	2,831,750	52,894	63.2	100%	$1,450	$1,475	$1,485	$1,500	$1,550	$1,575	$1,600	$2,000
Auctions: $9,400, MS-67, November 2014; $13,055, MS-66, January 2014; $4,113, MS-66, November 2014; $2,585, MS-65, September 2014												
1925, Doubled-Die Reverse (g)	(h)	17	64.2	100%				$2,000	$2,500	$2,750	$3,000	$3,500
Auctions: $3,055, MS-65, December 2013												
1925D	2,938,500	317	62.7	98%	$2,600	$3,200	$3,750	$4,250	$5,500	$7,500	$11,000	$75,000
Auctions: $19,975, MS-64, January 2014; $12,925, MS-64, August 2014; $9,694, MS-63, July 2014; $10,575, MS-63, October 2014												
1925S	3,776,500	440	59.2	59%	$2,250	$3,000	$3,750	$5,250	$9,500	$12,000	$16,500	$100,000
Auctions: $16,450, MS-63, July 2014; $9,988, MS-62, August 2014; $8,813, MS-62, August 2014; $5,728, AU-58, November 2014												
1926	816,750	23,532	63.6	100%	$1,450	$1,475	$1,485	$1,500	$1,550	$1,575	$1,600	$2,000
Auctions: $5,288, MS-66, August 2014; $3,819, MS-66, September 2014; $6,522, MS-66, November 2013; $1,939, MS-65, August 2014												
1926D	481,000	112	61.3	89%	$8,000	$12,000	$14,000	$15,500	$17,500	$32,500	$40,000	$150,000
Auctions: $47,000, MS-64, March 2014; $38,188, MS-64+, August 2014; $32,900, MS-64, August 2014; $14,688, MS-62, September 2014												
1926S	2,041,500	693	63.1	97%	$2,150	$2,450	$2,750	$2,950	$3,500	$4,000	$5,500	$32,500
Auctions: $38,188, MS-65, February 2014; $22,325, MS-65, August 2014; $10,575, MS-64, August 2014; $10,575, MS-64+, September 2014												
1927	2,946,750	140,528	63.5	100%	$1,450	$1,475	$1,485	$1,500	$1,550	$1,575	$1,600	$2,000
Auctions: $17,625, MS-67, April 2013; $4,994, MS-66, July 2014; $4,700, MS-66+, August 2014; $2,585, MS-66, October 2014												
1927D †	180,000	5	64.1	80%			$475,000	$550,000	$750,000	$850,000	$1,300,000	$1,600,000
Auctions: $1,997,500, MS-66, January 2014												
1927S	3,107,000	133	61.3	76%			$14,000	$16,000	$26,000	$37,500	$47,500	$110,000
Auctions: $105,750, MS-65, March 2014; $25,850, MS-62, August 2014; $10,575, AU-50, August 2014												
1928	8,816,000	48,939	63.3	100%	$1,450	$1,475	$1,485	$1,500	$1,550	$1,575	$1,600	$2,000
Auctions: $21,150, MS-67, June 2014; $10,575, MS-67+, August 2014; $11,163, MS-67, November 2014; $2,703, MS-66, November 2014												
1929	1,779,750	131	62.6	95%			$13,500	$15,500	$20,000	$30,000	$35,000	$75,000
Auctions: $57,281, MS-65, August 2014; $49,938, MS-63, March 2014; $23,500, MS-62, October 2014; $15,863, MS-60, August 2014												
1930S	74,000	21	64.2	100%			$42,000	$45,000	$65,000	$75,000	$90,000	$175,000
Auctions: $176,382, MS-65, March 2014; $164,500, MS-65, September 2014; $164,500, MS-63, August 2014												
1931	2,938,250	34	64.2	100%			$20,000	$25,000	$34,000	$47,500	$65,000	$80,000
Auctions: $76,375, MS-65, March 2014; $105,751, MS-65, September 2014; $64,625, MS-64, August 2014												
1931D	106,500	42	63.3	98%			$20,000	$25,000	$34,000	$47,500	$65,000	$100,000
Auctions: $129,250, MS-65, September 2014; $99,875, MS-64, January 2014; $64,625, MS-62, August 2014												
1932	1,101,750	70	64.0	100%			$20,000	$25,000	$34,000	$47,500	$65,000	$95,000
Auctions: $108,688, MS-66, March 2014; $99,875, MS-66, August 2014; $94,000, MS-64, August 2014												
1933 † (i)	445,500	0	n/a				(extremely rare)					
Auctions: $7,590,000, Gem BU, July 2002												

† Ranked in the *100 Greatest U.S. Coins* (fourth edition). **g.** Doubling is evident on the eagle's feathers, the rays, and IN GOD WE TRUST. **h.** Included in 1925 mintage figure. **i.** All but a few 1933 double eagles were to have been melted at the mint. Today 13 examples are known to have survived. Only one, said to have previously been in the collection of King Farouk of Egypt, has ever been sold at auction. The federal government has ruled that others are illegal to own privately.

Commemoratives
1892–1954
and 1982 to Date

AN OVERVIEW OF CLASSIC COMMEMORATIVES

Commemorative coins have been popular since the time of ancient Greece and Rome. In the beginning they recorded and honored important events and passed along the news of the day. Today commemorative coins, which are highly esteemed by collectors, have been issued by many modern nations—none of which has surpassed the United States when it comes to these impressive mementoes.

The unique position occupied by commemoratives in the United States coinage is largely due to the fact that, with few exceptions, all commemorative coins have real historical significance. The progress and advance of people in the New World are presented in an interesting and instructive manner on our commemorative coins. Such a record of history artistically presented on U.S. gold, silver, and other memorial issues appeals strongly to the collector who favors the romantic, storytelling side of numismatics. It is the historical features of our commemoratives, in fact, that create interest among many people who would otherwise have little interest in coins, and would not otherwise consider themselves collectors.

Concepts for commemorative issues are reviewed by two committees of Congress: the Committee on Banking, Housing, and Urban Affairs; and the Committee on Banking and Financial Services of the House; as well as by the Citizens Coinage Advisory Committee. Congress is guided to a great extent by the reports of these committees when considering bills authorizing commemorative coins.

These special coins are usually issued either to commemorate events or to help pay for monuments, programs, or celebrations that commemorate historical persons, places, or things. Pre-1982 commemorative coins were offered in most instances by a commission in charge of the event to be commemorated and sold at a premium over face value.

Commemorative coins are popularly collected either by major types or in sets with mintmark varieties. The pieces covered in this section of the *Guide Book of United States Coins, Deluxe Edition*, are those of the "classic" era of U.S. commemoratives, 1892 to 1954. All commemoratives are of the standard weight and fineness of their regular-issue 20th-century gold and silver counterparts, and all are legal tender.

A note about mintages and distribution numbers: Unless otherwise stated, the coinage figures given in each "Distribution" column represent the total released mintage: the total mintage (including assay coins), minus the quantity of unsold coins. In many cases, larger quantities were minted but not all were sold. Unsold coins usually were returned to the mint and melted, although sometimes quantities were placed in circulation at face value. A limited number of Proof strikings or presentation pieces were made for some of the classic commemorative issues.

A note about price performance: It has mostly been in recent decades that the general public has learned about commemorative coins. They have long been popular with coin collectors who enjoy the artistry and history associated with them, as well as the profit to be made from owning these rare pieces. Very few of them ever reached circulation because they were all originally sold above face value, and because they are all so rare. Most of the early issues were of the half dollar denomination, often made in quantities of fewer than 20,000 pieces. This is minuscule when compared to the regular half dollar coins that are made by the millions each year, and still rarely seen in circulation.

At the beginning of 1988, prices of classic commemoratives in MS-65 condition had risen so high that most collectors had to content themselves with pieces in lower grades. Investors continued to apply pressure to the high-quality pieces, driving prices even higher, while the collector community went after coins in grades from AU to MS-63. For several months the pressure from both influences caused prices to rise very rapidly (for all issues and grades) without even taking the price-adjustment breather that usually goes along with such activity.

By 1990, prices dropped to the point that several of the commemoratives began to look like bargains once again. Many of the MS-65 pieces held firm at price levels above the $3,000 mark, but others were still available at under $500 even for coins of similar mintage. Coins in MS-63 or MS-64 were priced at but a fraction of the MS-65 prices, which would seem to make them reasonably priced because the demand for these pieces is universal, and not keyed simply to grade, rarity, or speculator pressure.

Historically, the entire series of commemorative coins has frequently undergone a roller-coaster cycle of price adjustments. These cycles have usually been of short duration, lasting from months to years, with prices always recovering and eventually exceeding previous levels.

See page 1166 for discussion of modern commemorative coins of 1982 to date, page 1254 for pricing of government commemorative sets, and page 1502 for an alphabetical cross-reference list of all commemoratives.

WORLD'S COLUMBIAN EXPOSITION HALF DOLLAR (1892–1893)

Designers: *Charles E. Barber (obverse), George T. Morgan (reverse).* **Weight:** *12.50 grams.*
Composition: *.900 silver, .100 copper (net weight .3617 oz. pure silver).*
Diameter: *30.6 mm.* **Edge:** *Reeded.* **Mint:** *Philadelphia.*

The first U.S. commemorative coin was the Columbian half dollar sold at the World's Columbian Exposition—also known as the Chicago World's Fair—during 1893. The event celebrated the 400th anniversary of Christopher Columbus's arrival in the New World. A great many of the coins remained unsold and a substantial quantity was later released for circulation at face value or melted.

Designs. *Obverse:* Charles Barber's conception of Christopher Columbus, derived from a plaster model by Olin Levi Warner, taken from the explorer's portrait on an 1892 Spanish medal. The medal's portrait was inspired by a statue by Jeronimo Suñel, which itself was from an imagined likeness by Charles Legrand. *Reverse:* A sailing ship atop two globes representing the Old World and the New World. The vessel is from a plaster model by Olin Levi Warner, taken from a model made in Spain of Columbus's flagship, the *Santa Maria.*

Mintage and Melting Data. *Maximum authorized*—5,000,000 (both years combined). *Number minted*—1892: 950,000 (including an unknown number of assay coins; approximately 100 Proofs were struck as well); 1893: 4,052,105 (including 2,105 assay coins). *Number melted*—1893: 2,501,700. *Net distribution*—1892: 950,000; 1893: 1,550,405.

Original Cost and Issuer. Sale price $1. Issued by the Exposition.

Key to Collecting. Both dates are common in all grades through MS-65, and are often available in MS-66 and higher. The typical high-grade coin is lustrous and frosty; some have attractive, original light-blue or iridescent toning. Well-worn examples are very common, as the Treasury Department eventually released large quantities into circulation at face value. Striking usually is good. Some coins can be weak at the center—on the higher areas of the portrait and, on the reverse, in the details of the ship's sails. Most have contact marks from handling and distribution. High-grade 1892 coins typically are better struck than those of 1893. Approximately 100 brilliant Proofs were struck for each date; they vary widely in quality and eye appeal.

First Points of Wear. *Obverse:* The eyebrow, the cheek, and the hair at the back of the forehead. (The hair area sometimes is flatly struck.) *Reverse:* The top of the rear sail, and the right side of the Eastern Hemisphere.

	Distribution	Cert	Avg	%MS	AU-50	MS-60	MS-62	MS-63	MS-64 PF-63	MS-65 PF-64	MS-66 PF-65
1892	950,000	5,512	63.3	95%	$20	$30	$45	$85	$140	$450	$1,050
	Auctions: $9,753, MS-67, November 2014; $14,100, MS-67, September 2014; $35,250, MS-67, August 2013; $2,233, MS-66+, September 2014										
1892, Proof	100	38	64.0						$5,750	$7,000	$13,000
	Auctions: $8,225, PF-65, November 2013										
1893	1,550,405	5,817	62.5	89%	$20	$30	$45	$85	$140	$450	$1,050
	Auctions: $8,225, MS-67, September 2014; $7,050, MS-67, September 2014; $3,084, MS-67, August 2014; $1,410, MS-66+, October 2014										
1893, Proof	3–5	1	63.0								
	Auctions: $15,275, PF-66, January 2014; $5,830, PF-64, September 1993										

Note: Various repunched dates exist for both dates; these command little or no premium in the marketplace. For more information, see the *Cherrypickers' Guide to Rare Die Varieties,* sixth edition, volume II.

WORLD'S COLUMBIAN EXPOSITION ISABELLA QUARTER (1893)

Designer: *Charles E. Barber.* **Weight:** *6.25 grams.* **Composition:** *.900 silver, .100 copper (net weight .18084 oz. pure silver).* **Diameter:** *24.3 mm.* **Edge:** *Reeded.* **Mint:** *Philadelphia.*

In 1893 the Board of Lady Managers of the World's Columbian Exposition (also known as the Chicago World's Fair) petitioned for a souvenir quarter dollar. Authority was granted March 3, 1893, for the coin, which is known as the *Isabella quarter.*

Designs. *Obverse:* Crowned profile portrait of Spain's Queen Isabella, who sponsored Christopher Columbus's voyages to the New World. *Reverse:* A lady kneeling with a distaff and spindle, symbolic of the industry of American women.

Mintage and Melting Data. Authorized on March 3, 1893. *Maximum authorized*—40,000. *Number minted*—40,023 (including 23 assay coins). *Number melted*—15,809. *Net distribution*—24,214.

Original Cost and Issuer. Sale price $1. Issued by the Board of Lady Managers, World's Columbian Exposition.

Key to Collecting. Most examples in the marketplace are in Mint State, including many choice and gem pieces. Most are well struck and show full details, with richly lustrous fields. Connoisseurs avoid darkly toned, stained, and recolored coins. Many lower-grade Mint State examples have marks on Isabella's cheek and on the higher parts of the reverse design. The left obverse field often has marks made from contact with other coins during minting, storage, and distribution. The certification services have classified some coins with mirrored fields as Proofs, although no official records exist for the production of such.

First Points of Wear. *Obverse:* Isabella's cheekbone, and the center of the lower part of the crown. *Reverse:* The strand of wool at the lower-left thigh.

	Distribution	Cert	Avg	%MS	AU-50	MS-60	MS-62	MS-63	MS-64 / PF-63	MS-65 / PF-64	MS-66 / PF-65
1893	24,214	3,659	62.5	89%	$450	$500	$575	$625	$825	$2,700	$5,750
	Auctions: $5,288, MS-67, November 2014; $17,625, MS-67, August 2014; $6,756, MS-67, August 2014; $3,525, MS-66, November 2014										
1893, Proof	*100–105*	46	63.7						$4,750	$7,750	$13,000
	Auctions: $5,288, PF-64, October 2014										

LAFAYETTE DOLLAR (1900)

Designer: *Charles E. Barber.* **Weight:** *26.73 grams.* **Composition:** *.900 silver, .100 copper (net weight .7736 oz. pure silver).* **Diameter:** *38.1 mm.* **Edge:** *Reeded.* **Mint:** *Philadelphia.*

This issue—which was the first commemorative coin of one-dollar denomination, as well as the first authorized U.S. coin to bear a portrait of a U.S. president—commemorated the erection of a statue of Marquis de Lafayette in Paris in connection with the 1900 Paris Exposition (Exposition Universelle).

Designs. *Obverse:* Conjoined portraits of the marquis de Lafayette and George Washington. *Reverse:* Side view of the equestrian statue erected by the youth of the United States in honor of Lafayette. This view was based on an early model of the statue; the final version that was erected in Paris is slightly different.

Mintage and Melting Data. Authorized on March 3, 1899. *Maximum authorized—50,000. Number minted—50,026 (including 26 assay coins). Number melted—14,000. Net distribution—36,026.*

Original Cost and Issuer. Sale price $2. Issued by the Lafayette Memorial Commission through the American Trust & Savings Bank of Chicago.

Key to Collecting. Most surviving examples show evidence of circulation or other mishandling. The typical grade is AU. In Mint State, most are MS-60 to 63, and many are dull or unattractive, having been dipped or cleaned multiple times. Many have marks and dings. Properly graded MS-64 coins are very scarce, and MS-65 or higher gems are very rare, especially if with good eye appeal. Several die varieties exist and are collected by specialists.

Varieties. *Obverse varieties:* (1) Small point on the bust of Washington. The tip of Lafayette's bust is over the top of the L in DOLLAR. The AT in STATES is cut high. (2) The left foot of the final A in AMERICA is recut, and the A in STATES is high. The second S in STATES is repunched (this is diagnostic). (3) The AT in STATES is recut and the final S is low. The letter F in OF and in LAFAYETTE is broken from the lower tip of the crossbar and to the right base extension, and AMERICA is spaced A ME RI C A. The period after OF is close to the A of AMERICA. The tip of Lafayette's vest falls to the right of the top of the first L in DOLLAR. (4) The C in AMERICA is repunched at the inside top (this is diagnostic). The CA in AMERICA is spaced differently from the obverses previously described. *Reverse varieties:* (A) There are 14 long leaves and a long stem. The tip of the lowest leaf is over the 1 in 1900. (B) There are 14 shorter leaves and a short stem. The tip of the lowest leaf is over the space between the 1 and 9 in 1900. (C) There are 14 medium leaves and a short, bent stem. The tip of the lowest leaf is over the 9 in 1900. (D) There are 15 long leaves and a short, bent stem. The tip of the lowest leaf is over the 9 in 1900. (E) The tip of the lowest leaf is over the space to the left of the 1 in 1900.

First Points of Wear. *Obverse:* Washington's cheekbone, and Lafayette's lower hair curl. *Reverse:* The fringe of Lafayette's epaulet, and the horse's blinder and left rear leg bone.

	Distribution	Cert	Avg	%MS	AU-50	MS-60	MS-62	MS-63	MS-64	MS-65	MS-66
1900	36,026	2,531	62.0	88%	$625	$950	$1,200	$1,900	$3,250	$10,000	$19,000

Auctions: $36,719, MS-67, April 2014; $18,800, MS-66, September 2014; $646, MS-61, November 2014; $524, AU-58, October 2014

LOUISIANA PURCHASE EXPOSITION JEFFERSON GOLD DOLLAR (1903)

Designer: *Charles E. Barber (assisted by George T. Morgan).* **Weight:** *1.672 grams.*
Composition: *.900 gold, .100 copper (net weight .04837 oz. pure gold).*
Diameter: *15 mm.* **Edge:** *Reeded.* **Mint:** *Philadelphia.*

The first commemorative U.S. gold coins were authorized for the Louisiana Purchase Exposition, held in St. Louis in 1904. The event commemorated the 100th anniversary of the United States' purchase of the Louisiana Territory from France, an acquisition overseen by President Thomas Jefferson.

Designs. *Obverse:* Bewigged profile portrait of Thomas Jefferson, inspired by an early-1800s medal by John Reich, after Jean-Antoine Houdon's bust. *Reverse:* Inscription and branch.

Mintage and Melting Data. Authorized on June 28, 1902. *Maximum authorized*—250,000 (both types combined). *Number minted*—250,258 (125,000 of each type; including 258 assay coins comprising both types). *Number melted*—215,250 (total for both types; no account was kept of the portraits; 250 assay coins were melted). *Net distribution*—35,000 (estimated at 17,500 of each type).

Original Cost and Issuer. Sale price $3. Issued by the Louisiana Purchase Exposition Company, St. Louis, Missouri (sales through Farran Zerbe). Some were sold as mounted in spoons, brooches, and stick pins; 100 certified Proofs of each design were made, mounted in an opening in a rectangular piece of imprinted cardboard.

Key to Collecting. Market demand is strong, from collectors and investors alike, as most surviving examples are in choice or gem Mint State, with strong eye appeal. Most specimens are very lustrous and frosty. An occasional coin is prooflike. Avoid any with copper stains (from improper mixing of the gold/copper alloy). Proofs enter the market rarely and garner much publicity.

First Points of Wear. *Obverse:* Portrait's cheekbone and sideburn. *Reverse:* Date and denomination.

	Distribution	Cert	Avg	%MS	AU-50	MS-60	MS-62	MS-63	MS-64 PF-63	MS-65 PF-64	MS-66 PF-65
1903	17,500	2,256	63.9	94%	$575	$700	$825	$900	$1,325	$1,850	$2,350
	Auctions: $3,819, MS-67, November 2014; $4,994, MS-67, September 2014; $1,450, MS-66, November 2014; $404, AU-58, November 2014										
1903, Proof (a)	100	31	64.9								
	Auctions: $37,375, PF-67UCam★, January 2012										

a. The first 100 Jefferson gold dollars were struck in brilliant Proof format. True Proofs exhibit deeply mirrored fields and are sharply struck. Many also have frosted devices, giving them a cameo appearance. "Although many of the coins seen today have been certified and lack original packaging, they were originally housed in cardboard holders certifying each coin as having been one of the first 100 impressions from the dies. The original holders are quite interesting, with the coin covered by a small piece of wax paper and a piece of string sealed by dark red wax. The coins are difficult to see behind the wax paper, and the author has seen holders with a circulation-strike example substituted for the Proof piece. Caution should be used when purchasing an example of this extreme rarity" (*Encyclopedia of U.S. Gold Coins, 1795–1933,* second edition).

LOUISIANA PURCHASE EXPOSITION MCKINLEY GOLD DOLLAR (1903)

Designer: *Charles E. Barber (assisted by George T. Morgan).* **Weight:** *1.672 grams.*
Composition: *.900 gold, .100 copper (net weight .04837 oz. pure gold).*
Diameter: *15 mm.* **Edge:** *Reeded.* **Mint:** *Philadelphia.*

President William McKinley—who had been assassinated while in office two years before the Louisiana Purchase Exposition—was remembered on a gold dollar issued alongside the aforementioned coin featuring Thomas Jefferson. Like Jefferson, McKinley oversaw expansion of U.S. territory, with the acquisition of Puerto Rico, Guam, and the Philippines, as well as the annexation of Hawaii.

Designs. *Obverse:* Bareheaded profile portrait of William McKinley, derived from his presidential medal (designed, like this coin, by Charles Barber). *Reverse:* Inscriptions and branch.

Mintage and Melting Data. Authorized on June 28, 1902. *Maximum authorized*—250,000 (both types combined). *Number minted*—250,258 (125,000 of each type; including 258 assay coins comprising both types). *Number melted*—215,250 (total for both types; no account was kept of the portraits; 250 assay coins were melted). *Net distribution*—35,000 (estimated at 17,500 of each type).

Original Cost and Issuer. Sale price $3. Issued by the Louisiana Purchase Exposition Company, St. Louis, Missouri (sales through Farran Zerbe). Some were sold as mounted in spoons, brooches, and stick pins; 100 certified Proofs of each design were made, mounted in an opening in a rectangular piece of imprinted cardboard.

Key to Collecting. Market demand is strong, from collectors and investors alike, as most surviving examples are in choice or gem Mint State, with strong eye appeal. Most specimens are very lustrous and frosty. An occasional coin is prooflike. Avoid any with copper stains (from improper mixing of the gold/copper alloy). Proofs enter the market rarely and garner much publicity.

First Points of Wear. *Obverse:* Portrait's cheekbone and sideburn. *Reverse:* Date and denomination.

	Distribution	Cert	Avg	%MS	AU-50	MS-60	MS-62	MS-63	MS-64	MS-65	MS-66
									PF-63	PF-64	PF-65
1903	17,500	2,116	64.0	96%	$550	$650	$700	$775	$1,050	$1,700	$2,200
	Auctions: $12,925, MS-68, October 2013; $5,728, MS-67+, September 2014; $2,056, MS-67, November 2014; $411, AU-58, November 2014										
1903, Proof (a)	100	27	64.3								
	Auctions: $14,950, PF-65Cam, April 2012										

a. Like the Jefferson issue, the first 100 McKinley gold dollars were struck as Proofs, and packaged as such. "Prooflike circulation strikes are quite common for the issue, and true Proofs can be distinguished by deeply mirrored surfaces and cameo devices. Certification is highly recommended" (*Encyclopedia of U.S. Gold Coins, 1795–1933*, second edition).

LEWIS AND CLARK EXPOSITION GOLD DOLLAR (1904–1905)

Designer: *Charles E. Barber.* **Weight:** *1.672 grams.* **Composition:** *.900 gold, .100 copper (net weight .04837 oz. pure gold).* **Diameter:** *15 mm.* **Edge:** *Reeded.* **Mint:** *Philadelphia.*

A souvenir issue of gold dollars was struck to mark the Lewis and Clark Centennial Exposition, held in Portland, Oregon, in 1905. The sale of these coins financed the erection of a bronze memorial of the Shoshone Indian guide Sacagawea, who assisted in the famous expedition.

Designs. *Obverse:* Bareheaded profile portrait of Meriwether Lewis. *Reverse:* Bareheaded profile portrait of William Clark. These portraits were inspired by works of Charles Willson Peale.

Mintage and Melting Data. Authorized on April 13, 1904. *Maximum authorized*—250,000 (both years combined). *Number minted*—1904: 25,028 (including 28 assay coins); 1905: 35,041 (including 41 assay coins). *Number melted*—1904: 15,003; 1905: 25,000. *Net distribution*—1904: 10,025; 1905: 10,041.

Original Cost and Issuer. Sales price $2 (some at $2.50); many were probably discounted further. Issued by the Lewis and Clark Centennial and American Pacific Exposition and Oriental Fair Company, Portland, Oregon (sales through Farran Zerbe and others).

Key to Collecting. Most surviving examples show evidence of handling. Some exhibit die problems (a rough raised area of irregularity at the denticles). Most range from AU-50 to 58, with an occasional MS-60 to 63. MS-64 coins are scarce, and MS-65 rare. Pristine examples are very rare. Most MS coins have areas of prooflike finish; some are deeply lustrous and frosty. The 1905-dated issue is noticeably scarcer than the 1904.

First Points of Wear. *Obverse:* Lewis's temple. *Reverse:* Clark's temple.

	Distribution	Cert	Avg	%MS	AU-50	MS-60	MS-62	MS-63	MS-64	MS-65	MS-66
									PF-63	PF-64	PF-65
1904	10,025	1,282	63.5	95%	$925	$1,100	$1,275	$1,850	$2,650	$7,750	$10,000
	Auctions: $12,925, MS-67, November 2014; $10,575, MS-67, November 2014; $20,563, MS-67, September 2014; $7,931, MS-66, November 2014										
1904, Proof	2–3	2	63.5								
	Auctions: No auction records available.										
1905	10,041	1,368	62.9	93%	$1,000	$1,375	$1,550	$2,000	$3,500	$10,500	$19,500
	Auctions: $30,550, MS-67, November 2014; $54,344, MS-67, September 2014; $940, MS-61, November 2014; $705, AU-55, November 2014										

PANAMA-PACIFIC EXPOSITION HALF DOLLAR (1915)

Designers: *Charles E. Barber (obverse), George T. Morgan (assisting Barber on reverse).*
Weight: *12.50 grams.* **Composition:** *.900 silver, .100 copper (net weight .3617 oz. pure silver).*
Diameter: *30.6 mm.* **Edge:** *Reeded.* **Mint:** *San Francisco.*

The Panama-Pacific Exposition held in San Francisco in 1915 celebrated the opening of the Panama Canal, as well as the revival of the Bay Area following the 1906 earthquake and fire. Five commemorative coins in four different denominations, including a half dollar, were issued in conjunction with the event.

Designs. *Obverse:* Columbia scattering flowers, alongside a child holding a cornucopia, representing the bounty of the American West; the Golden Gate in the background. *Reverse:* A spread-winged eagle perched on a shield, with branches of oak and olive.

Mintage and Melting Data. Authorized by the Act of January 16, 1915. *Maximum authorized*—200,000. *Number minted*—60,030 (including 30 assay coins). *Number melted*—32,896 (including the 30 assay coins; 29,876 were melted on September 7, 1916 and the balance on October 30, 1916). *Net distribution*—27,134.

Original Cost and Issuer. Sale price $1. Issued by the Coin and Medal Department (Farran Zerbe), Panama-Pacific International Exposition, San Francisco, California (combination offers included a set of four coins, including the buyer's choice of one $50, in a leather case, for $100; and a set of five coins in a copper frame for $200).

Key to Collecting. The half dollar does not have the typical deep mint frost associated with earlier silver issues. Most are satiny in appearance with the high parts in particular having a microscopically grainy finish. Many pieces have an inner line around the perimeter near the rim, a die characteristic. On the reverse of all known coins, the eagle's breast feathers are indistinct, which sometimes gives MS coins the appearance of having light wear. Most surviving coins grade from AU-50 to MS-63.

First Points of Wear. *Obverse:* Columbia's left shoulder. *Reverse:* The eagle's breast.

	Distribution	Cert	Avg	%MS	AU-50	MS-60	MS-62	MS-63	MS-64	MS-65	MS-66
1915S	27,134	2,740	63.5	94%	$500	$550	$650	$775	$1,100	$2,200	$3,500

Auctions: $14,100, MS-67+, August 2014; $5,581, MS-67, November 2014; $7,050, MS-67, August 2014; $470, MS-61, October 2014

PANAMA-PACIFIC EXPOSITION GOLD DOLLAR (1915)

Designer: *Charles Keck.* **Weight:** *1.672 grams.* **Composition:** *.900 gold, .100 copper (net weight .04837 oz. pure gold).* **Diameter:** *15 mm.* **Edge:** *Reeded.* **Mint:** *San Francisco.*

Coin dealer and entrepreneur Farran Zerbe conceived of a program of five different commemorative coins across four denominations (including the gold dollar) in conjunction with the Panama-Pacific Exposition in 1915. The event was held in what eventually constituted a miniature city, whose sculptures and impressive architecture were intended to remind one of Rome or some other distant and romantic place, but which at night was more apt to resemble Coney Island.

Designs. *Obverse:* Capped profile portrait of a Panama Canal laborer. *Reverse:* Two dolphins, symbolizing the Atlantic and Pacific oceans, and legends.

Mintage and Melting Data. Authorized by the Act of January 16, 1915. *Maximum authorized*—25,000. *Number minted*—25,034 (including 34 assay coins). *Number melted*—10,034 (including the 34 assay coins; melted at the San Francisco Mint on October 30, 1916). *Net distribution*—15,000.

Original Cost and Issuer. Sale price $2 (and a few at $2.25). Issued by the Coin and Medal Department (Farran Zerbe), Panama-Pacific International Exposition, San Francisco, California (combination offers included, among others, a set of four coins, with the buyer's choice of one fifty-dollar coin, in a leather case, for $100; and a set of five coins in a copper frame for $200).

Key to Collecting. Most examples are in Mint State. Many exhibit deep mint frost. Friction is common, especially on the obverse.

First Points of Wear. *Obverse:* The peak of the laborer's cap. *Reverse:* The heads of the dolphins, and the denomination.

	Distribution	Cert	Avg	%MS	AU-50	MS-60	MS-62	MS-63	MS-64	MS-65	MS-66
1915S	15,000	3,748	63.7	94%	$600	$635	$660	$750	$975	$1,500	$2,200

Auctions: $8,813, MS-67+, July 2014; $3,819, MS-67, November 2014; $5,434, MS-67, September 2014; $427, AU-58, December 2014

PANAMA-PACIFIC EXPOSITION QUARTER EAGLE (1915)

Designer: *Charles E. Barber (obverse), George T. Morgan (reverse).* **Weight:** *4.18 grams.*
Composition: *.900 gold, .100 copper (net weight .12094 oz. pure gold).*
Diameter: *18 mm.* **Edge:** *Reeded.* **Mint:** *San Francisco.*

The 1915 Panama-Pacific International Exposition—a name chosen to reflect the recently completed Panama Canal, as well as Pacific Ocean commerce—was planned to be the ultimate world's fair. Foreign countries, domestic manufacturers, artists, concessionaires, and others were invited to the 10-month event, which drew an estimated 19 million visitors. This quarter eagle was among the five coins issued to commemorate the celebration.

Designs. *Obverse:* Columbia seated on a hippocampus, holding a caduceus, symbolic of Medicine's triumph over yellow fever in Panama during the canal's construction. *Reverse:* An eagle, standing on a plaque inscribed E PLURIBUS UNUM, with raised wings.

Mintage and Melting Data. Authorized by the Act of January 16, 1915. *Maximum authorized*—10,000. *Number minted*—10,017 (including 17 assay coins). *Number melted*—3,268 (including the 17 assay coins; melted at the San Francisco Mint on October 30, 1916). *Net distribution*—6,749.

Original Cost and Issuer. Sale price $4. Issued by the Coin and Medal Department (Farran Zerbe), Panama-Pacific International Exposition, San Francisco, California (combination offers included, among others, a set of four coins, with the buyer's choice of one fifty-dollar coin, in a leather case, for $100; and a set of five coins in a copper frame for $200).

Key to Collecting. Most grade from AU-55 to MS-63. MS-64 coins are elusive, and MS-65 rare. Most MS pieces show a satiny, sometimes grainy luster.

First Points of Wear. *Obverse:* Columbia's head, breast, and knee. *Reverse:* The torch band and the eagle's leg.

	Distribution	Cert	Avg	%MS	AU-50	MS-60	MS-62	MS-63	MS-64	MS-65	MS-66
									PF-63	PF-64	PF-65
1915S	6,749	2,032	64.6	97%	$1,650	$2,000	$2,800	$4,300	$5,750	$6,750	$7,500
	Auctions: $8,813, MS-67, October 2014; $17,038, MS-67, September 2014; $6,463, MS-66+, November 2014; $2,115, AU-55, November 2014										
1915S, Proof (a)	*unique*	0	n/a								
	Auctions: No auction records available.										

a. This unique Satin Finish Proof resides in the National Numismatic Collection of the Smithsonian Institution.

PANAMA-PACIFIC EXPOSITION FIFTY-DOLLAR GOLD PIECE (1915)

Designer: *Robert Aitken.* **Weight:** *83.59 grams.* **Composition:** *.900 gold, .100 copper (net weight 2.4186 oz. pure gold).* **Diameter:** *43 mm (round), 44.9 mm (octagonal, measured point to point).* **Edge:** *Reeded.* **Mint:** *San Francisco.*

Both round and octagonal $50 gold pieces were struck as part of the series commemorating the Panama-Pacific International Exposition in 1915. These coins, along with the half dollars in the same series, were the first U.S. commemoratives to feature the motto IN GOD WE TRUST.

Designs. Round: *Obverse:* Helmeted profile portrait of Minerva, with shield and armor. *Reverse:* An owl, symbolic of wisdom, vigilant on a pine branch, with pinecones. Octagonal: *Obverse and reverse:* Same as the round coin, but with dolphins in the eight angled exergues on obverse and reverse.

Mintage and Melting Data. Authorized by the Act of January 16, 1915. Round: *Maximum authorized*—Round: 1,500; Octagonal:

1,500. *Number minted* (including 10 assay coins)—Round: 1,510 (including 10 assay coins); Octagonal: 1,509 (including 9 assay coins). *Number melted*—Round: 1,027; Octagonal: 864. *Net distribution*—Round: 483; Octagonal: 645.

Original Cost and Issuer. Round and octagonal: Sale price, each, $100. Coin and Medal Department (Farran Zerbe), Panama-Pacific International Exposition, San Francisco, California. Combination offers included a set of four coins (buyer's choice of one fifty-dollar coin) in a leather case for $100, and a set of five coins in a copper frame for $200, this issued after the Exposition closed.

Key to Collecting. Because such small quantities were issued, these hefty gold commemoratives today are rare in any grade. The round coins trade hands slightly less frequently than the octagonal. Typical grades are MS-63 or 64 for coins kept in an original box or frame over the years, or AU-58 to MS-63 if removed. Coins that have been cleaned or lightly polished exhibit a multitude of tiny hairlines; such pieces are avoided by connoisseurs.

First Points of Wear. *Obverse:* Minerva's cheek. *Reverse:* The owl's upper breast.

	Distribution	Cert	Avg	%MS	AU-50	MS-60	MS-62	MS-63	MS-64	MS-65	MS-66
1915S, Round	483	418	63.4	95%	$48,000	$57,500	$67,500	$90,000	$115,000	$155,000	$230,000
	Auctions: $146,875, MS-66, February 2013; $176,250, MS-65, September 2014; $82,250, MS-62, August 2014										
1915S, Octagonal	645	456	63.1	95%	$50,000	$60,000	$66,500	$82,500	$110,000	$150,000	$220,000
	Auctions: $282,000, MS-67, April 2014; $102,813, MS-64, September 2014; $58,750, MS-61, August 2014										

McKINLEY MEMORIAL GOLD DOLLAR (1916–1917)

Designers: *Charles E. Barber (obverse) and George T. Morgan (reverse).* **Weight:** *1.672 grams.*
Composition: *.900 gold, .100 copper (net weight .04837 oz. pure gold).*
Diameter: *15 mm.* **Edge:** *Reeded.* **Mint:** *Philadelphia.*

The sale of the William McKinley dollars aided in paying for a memorial building at Niles, Ohio, the martyred president's birthplace.

Designs. *Obverse:* Bareheaded profile portrait of William McKinley. *Reverse:* Artist's rendition of the proposed McKinley Birthplace Memorial intended to be erected in Niles, Ohio.

Mintage and Melting Data. Authorized on February 23, 1916. *Maximum authorized*—100,000 (both years combined). *Number minted*—1916: 20,026 (including 26 assay coins); 1917: 10,014 (including 14 assay coins). *Number melted*—1916: 5,000 (estimated); 1917: 5,000 (estimated). *Net distribution*—1916: 15,000 (estimated); 1917: 5,000 (estimated).

Original Cost and Issuer. Sale price $3. Issued by the National McKinley Birthplace Memorial Association, Youngstown, Ohio.

Key to Collecting. The obverse of the 1916 issue often displays friction while its reverse can appear as choice Mint State. Prooflike fields are common. Some are highly prooflike on both sides. The 1917 issue is much harder to find than the 1916; examples usually are in higher grades with rich luster on both sides, and often exhibit a pale yellow color.

First Points of Wear. *Obverse:* McKinley's temple area, and the hair above his ear. *Reverse:* The pillar above the second 1 in the date; and the bottom of the flagpole.

	Distribution	Cert	Avg	%MS	AU-50	MS-60	MS-62	MS-63	MS-64 PF-63	MS-65 PF-64	MS-66 PF-65
1916	*15,000*	2,559	63.8	96%	$500	$580	$625	$675	$800	$1,500	$1,850
	Auctions: $2,585, MS-67, November 2014; $4,259, MS-67, November 2013; $1,704, MS-66, November 2014; $382, AU-55, October 2014										
1916, Proof	*3–6*	1	63.0								
	Auctions: $37,375, PF-63, January 2012										
1917	*5,000*	1,535	63.7	95%	$575	$700	$775	$900	$1,200	$1,875	$2,850
	Auctions: $3,055, MS-67, November 2014; $3,554, MS-67, September 2014; $5,288, MS-67, February 2013; $382, AU-55, October 2014										

ILLINOIS CENTENNIAL HALF DOLLAR (1918)

Designers: *George T. Morgan (obverse) and John R. Sinnock (reverse).* **Weight:** *12.50 grams.*
Composition: *.900 silver, .100 copper (net weight .3617 oz. pure silver).*
Diameter: *30.6 mm.* **Edge:** *Reeded.* **Mint:** *Philadelphia.*

This coin was authorized to commemorate the 100th anniversary of the admission of Illinois into the Union, and was the first souvenir piece for such an event. The head of Abraham Lincoln on the obverse was based on that of a statue of the celebrated president by Andrew O'Connor in Springfield, Illinois.

Designs. *Obverse:* Bareheaded, beardless profile portrait of Abraham Lincoln, facing right.
Reverse: A fierce eagle atop a crag, clutching a shield and carrying a banner; from the Illinois state seal.

Mintage Data. Authorized on June 1, 1918. *Maximum authorized*—100,000. *Number minted*—100,000 (plus 58 assay coins).

Original Cost and Issuer. Sale price $1. Issued by the Illinois Centennial Commission, through various outlets.

Key to Collecting. Examples were struck with deep, frosty finishes, giving Mint State pieces an unusually attractive appearance. The obverse typically shows contact marks or friction on Lincoln's cheek and on other high parts of his portrait. The field typically shows contact marks. The reverse usually grades from one to three points higher than the obverse, due to the protective nature of its complicated design. Most examples are lustrous and frosty, although a few are seen with partially prooflike fields.

First Points of Wear. *Obverse:* The hair above Lincoln's ear. *Reverse:* The eagle's breast. (Note that the breast was sometimes flatly struck; look for differences in texture or color of the metal.)

	Distribution	Cert	Avg	%MS	AU-50	MS-60	MS-62	MS-63	MS-64	MS-65	MS-66
1918	100,058	4,210	64.0	98%	$140	$150	$160	$165	$220	$500	$800
	Auctions: $1,410, MS-67, November 2014; $7,050, MS-67, January 2013; $108, MS-61, November 2014; $88, AU-58, November 2014										

MAINE CENTENNIAL HALF DOLLAR (1920)

Designer: *Anthony de Francisci.* **Weight:** *12.50 grams.* **Composition:** *.900 silver, .100 copper (net weight .3617 oz. pure silver).* **Diameter:** *30.6 mm.* **Edge:** *Reeded.* **Mint:** *Philadelphia.*

Congress authorized the Maine Centennial half dollar on May 10, 1920, to be sold at the centennial celebration at Portland. They were received too late for this event and were sold by the state treasurer for many years.

Designs. *Obverse:* Arms of the state of Maine, with the Latin word DIRIGO ("I Direct"). *Reverse:* The centennial inscription enclosed by a wreath.

Mintage Data. Authorized on May 10, 1920. *Maximum authorized*—100,000. *Number minted*—50,028 (including 28 assay coins).

Original Cost and Issuer. Sale price $1. Issued by the Maine Centennial Commission.

Key to Collecting. Relatively few Maine half dollars were sold to the hobby community; the majority of coins distributed saw careless handling by the general public. Most examples show friction or handling marks on the center of the shield on the obverse. The fields were not completely finished in the dies and always show tiny raised lines or die-finishing marks; at first glance these may appear to be hairlines or scratches, but they have no effect on the grade. Appealing examples in higher Mint State levels are much more elusive than the high mintage might suggest.

First Points of Wear. *Obverse:* The left hand of the scythe holder; the right hand of the anchor holder. (Note that the moose and the pine tree are weakly struck.) *Reverse:* The bow knot.

	Distribution	Cert	Avg	%MS	AU-50	MS-60	MS-62	MS-63	MS-64	MS-65	MS-66
1920	50,028	2,877	64.2	98%	$140	$155	$165	$200	$250	$385	$685

Auctions: $3,820, MS-67, September 2014; $7,050, MS-67, August 2013; $1,116, MS-66+, November 2014; $99, MS-61, November 2014

PILGRIM TERCENTENARY HALF DOLLAR (1920–1921)

Designer: *Cyrus E. Dallin.* **Weight:** *12.50 grams.* **Composition:** *.900 silver, .100 copper (net weight .3617 oz. pure silver).* **Diameter:** *30.6 mm.* **Edge:** *Reeded.* **Mint:** *Philadelphia.*

To commemorate the landing of the Pilgrims at Plymouth, Massachusetts, in 1620, Congress authorized a special half dollar on May 12, 1920. The first issue had no date on the obverse. The coins struck in 1921 show that date in addition to 1620–1920.

Designs. *Obverse:* Artist's conception of a partial standing portrait of Governor William Bradford holding a book. *Reverse:* The *Mayflower* in full sail.

Mintage and Melting Data. Authorized on May 12, 1920. *Maximum authorized*—300,000 (both years combined). *Number minted*—1920: 200,112 (including 112 assay coins); 1921: 100,053 (including 53 assay coins). *Number melted*—1920: 48,000; 1921: 80,000. *Net distribution*—1920: 152,112; 1921: 20,053.

Original Cost and Issuer. Sale price $1. Issued by the Pilgrim Tercentenary Commission.

Key to Collecting. The 1920 issue is common, and the 1921 slightly scarce. Coins grading MS-64 and higher usually have excellent eye appeal, though many exceptions exist. Most coins have scattered contact marks, particularly on the obverse. Nearly all 1921 coins are this way. Many coins (particularly coins which are early impressions from the dies) show tiny raised lines in the obverse field, representing die finish marks; these are not to be confused with hairlines or other evidences of friction (which are recessed).

First Points of Wear. *Obverse:* Cheekbone, hair over ear, and the high areas of Governor Bradford's hat. *Reverse:* The ship's rigging and stern, the crow's nest, and the rim.

	Distribution	Cert	Avg	%MS	AU-50	MS-60	MS-62	MS-63	MS-64	MS-65	MS-66
1920	152,112	4,637	63.8	98%	$85	$110	$115	$120	$125	$250	$650
	Auctions: $1,880, MS-67, November 2014; $2,115, MS-67, August 2014; $7,344, MS-67, February 2014; $646, MS-66+, November 2014										
1921, With Added Date	20,053	2,079	64.3	99%	$170	$200	$220	$230	$265	$400	$850
	Auctions: $2,115, MS-67, September 2014; $4,113, MS-67, August 2013; $3,378, MS-67, July 2014; $881, MS-66, November 2014										

MISSOURI CENTENNIAL HALF DOLLAR (1921)

Designer: *Robert Aitken.* **Weight:** *12.50 grams.* **Composition:** *.900 silver, .100 copper (net weight .3617 oz. pure silver).* **Diameter:** *30.6 mm.* **Edge:** *Reeded.* **Mint:** *Philadelphia.*

The 100th anniversary of the admission of Missouri to the Union was celebrated in the city of Sedalia during August 1921. To mark the occasion, Congress authorized the coinage of a fifty-cent piece.

Designs. *Obverse:* Coonskin-capped profile portrait of a frontiersman. One variety has 2★4 in the field; the other is plain. *Reverse:* Standing figures of a frontiersman and an Indian looking westward, against a starry field; SEDALIA (the location of the Missouri centennial exposition) incused below.

Mintage and Melting Data. Authorized on March 4, 1921. *Maximum authorized*—250,000 (both varieties combined). *Number minted*—50,028 (both varieties combined; including 28 assay coins). *Number melted*—29,600. *Net distribution*—20,428 (estimated; 9,400 for 1921 2★4 and 11,400 for 1921 Plain).

Original Cost and Issuer. Sale price $1. Issued by the Missouri Centennial Committee, through the Sedalia Trust Company.

Key to Collecting. Most grade from AU-55 to MS-63; have friction and contact marks on the higher areas of the design; and are lightly struck at the center of the portrait of Boone on the obverse, and at the torsos of the two figures on the reverse. MS-65 and higher coins with sharply struck centers are rarities.

First Points of Wear. *Obverse:* The hair in back of the ear. *Reverse:* The frontiersman's arm and shoulder.

	Distribution	Cert	Avg	%MS	AU-50	MS-60	MS-62	MS-63	MS-64	MS-65	MS-66
									PF-63	PF-64	PF-65
1921, "2*4" in Field	9,400	1,659	63.8	98%	$650	$775	$800	$1,100	$1,250	$3,500	$9,250
	Auctions: $7,638, MS-66, August 2013										
1921, "2*4" in Field, Matte Proof	1–2	0	n/a								
	Auctions: No auction records available.										
1921, Plain	11,400	1,991	63.4	96%	$445	$625	$750	$900	$1,150	$3,250	$10,000
	Auctions: $8,225, MS-66, October 2014; $3,672, MS-66, October 2014; $12,925, MS-66, August 2013; $159, EF-40, October 2014										

ALABAMA CENTENNIAL HALF DOLLAR (1921)

Designer: *Laura Gardin Fraser.* **Weight:** *12.50 grams.* **Composition:** *.900 silver, .100 copper (net weight .3617 oz. pure silver).* **Diameter:** *30.6 mm.* **Edge:** *Reeded.* **Mint:** *Philadelphia.*

The Alabama half dollars were authorized in 1920 and struck until 1921 for the statehood centennial, which was celebrated in 1919. The coins were offered first during President Warren Harding's visit to Birmingham, October 26, 1921. T.E. Kilby's likeness on the obverse was first instance of a living person's portrait on a United States coin.

Designs. *Obverse:* Conjoined bareheaded profile portraits of William Wyatt Bibb, the first governor of Alabama, and Thomas Kilby, governor at the time of the centennial. *Reverse:* A dynamic eagle perched on a shield, clutching arrows and holding a banner; from the Alabama state seal.

Mintage and Melting Data. Authorized on May 10, 1920. *Maximum authorized*—100,000. *Number minted*—70,044 (including 44 assay coins). *Number melted*—5,000. *Net distribution*—2X2: estimated as 30,000; Plain: estimated as 35,000.

Original Cost and Issuer. Sale price $1. Issued by the Alabama Centennial Commission.

Key to Collecting. Most of these coins were sold to citizens of Alabama, and of those, few were acquired by numismatists. Many are in circulated grades (typical being EF or AU), with most surviving pieces grading MS-63 or less. Those grading MS-65 or finer are rare. Nearly all show friction or contact marks on Governor Kilby's cheek on the obverse, and many are flatly struck on the eagle's left leg and talons on the reverse. These coins were produced carelessly, and many lack sharpness and luster (sharply struck examples are very rare). Nicks and marks from the original planchets are often found on the areas of light striking. The eagle's upper leg is often lightly struck, particularly on the plain variety. The 2X2 coins usually are better struck than the plain variety.

First Points of Wear. *Obverse:* Kirby's forehead and the area to the left of his earlobe. *Reverse:* The eagle's lower neck and the top of its wings.

	Distribution	Cert	Avg	%MS	AU-50	MS-60	MS-62	MS-63	MS-64	MS-65	MS-66
1921, "2X2" in Field	*6,006*	1,674	63.5	95%	$320	$340	$360	$525	$650	$1,400	$3,300
	Auctions: $15,275, MS-67, August 2014; $2,820, MS-66, September 2014; $1,763, MS-66, September 2014; $259, AU-58, September 2014										
1921, Plain	*16,014*	1,961	62.8	91%	$200	$230	$285	$450	$525	$1,300	$2,875
	Auctions: $25,850, MS-67, August 2013; $1,586, MS-66, October 2014; $2,350, MS-66, September 2014; $123, AU-53, August 2014										

GRANT MEMORIAL HALF DOLLAR (1922)

Designer: *Laura Gardin Fraser.* **Weight:** *12.50 grams.* **Composition:** *.900 silver, .100 copper (net weight .3617 oz. pure silver).* **Diameter:** *30.6 mm.* **Edge:** *Reeded.* **Mint:** *Philadelphia.*

This half dollar (along with the Grant Memorial gold dollar) was struck during 1922 as a centenary souvenir of Ulysses S. Grant's birth. The Ulysses S. Grant Centenary Memorial Association originally planned celebrations in Clermont County, Ohio; the construction of community buildings in Georgetown and Bethel; and the laying of a five-mile highway from New Richmond to Point Pleasant in addition to the coins, but the buildings and highway never came to fruition.

Designs. *Obverse:* Bareheaded profile portrait of Ulysses S. Grant in a military coat. One variety has a star above GRANT. *Reverse:* View of the house Grant was born in (Point Pleasant, Ohio), amidst a wooded setting.

Mintage Data. Authorized on February 2, 1922. *Number minted*—With Star: 5,016 (including 16 assay coins); No Star: 5,000. *Net distribution*—10,016 (both varieties combined).

Original Cost and Issuer. Sale price $3 for either variety. Issued by the U.S. Grant Centenary Memorial Commission (mail orders were serviced by Hugh L. Nichols, chairman, Batavia, Ohio).

Key to Collecting. Almost all known specimens are MS-63 to 65 or better. MS-66 and 67 examples are easy to find. Some lower-grade coins show friction on Grant's cheek and hair. Some specimens have dull surfaces; these are avoided by connoisseurs.

First Points of Wear. *Obverse:* Grant's cheekbone and hair. *Reverse:* The leaves of the tree under the U in TRUST.

	Distribution	Cert	Avg	%MS	AU-50	MS-60	MS-62	MS-63	MS-64	MS-65	MS-66
1922, Star in Obverse Field	4,256	1,297	63.6	97%	$975	$1,300	$1,400	$1,800	$3,200	$6,750	$14,000
	Auctions: $21,150, MS-67, January 2014; $10,575, MS-66, November 2014; $4,113, MS-65, November 2014; $764, AU-58, October 2014										
1922, No Star in Obverse Field	67,405	3,507	63.7	97%	$115	$125	$135	$160	$250	$650	$1,000
	Auctions: $4,259, MS-67, November 2014; $2,820, MS-67, November 2014; $9,400, MS-66, April 2013; $106, MS-61, November 2014										

GRANT MEMORIAL GOLD DOLLAR (1922)

Designer: *Laura Gardin Fraser.* **Weight:** *1.672 grams.* **Composition:** *.900 gold, .100 copper (net weight .04837 oz. pure gold).* **Diameter:** *15 mm.* **Edge:** *Reeded.* **Mint:** *Philadelphia.*

The Ulysses S. Grant Centenary Memorial Association, incorporated in 1921, marked the 100th birth anniversary of the Civil War general and U.S. president with this gold dollar (as well as a commemorative half dollar).

Designs. *Obverse:* Bareheaded profile portrait of Ulysses S. Grant in a military coat. One variety has a star above GRANT. *Reverse:* View of the house Grant was born in (Point Pleasant, Ohio), amidst a wooded setting.

Mintage Data. Authorized on February 2, 1922. *Number minted*—With Star: 5,016 (including 16 assay coins); No Star: 5,000. *Net distribution*—10,016 (both varieties combined).

Original Cost and Issuer. Sale price $3 for either type. Issued by the U.S. Grant Centenary Memorial Commission (mail orders were serviced by Hugh L. Nichols, chairman, Batavia, Ohio).

Key to Collecting. Almost all known specimens are MS-63 to 65 or better. MS-66 and 67 examples are easy to find. Some lower-grade coins show friction on Grant's cheek and hair. Some specimens have dull surfaces; these are avoided by connoisseurs.

First Points of Wear. *Obverse:* Grant's cheekbone and hair. *Reverse:* The leaves of the tree under the U in TRUST.

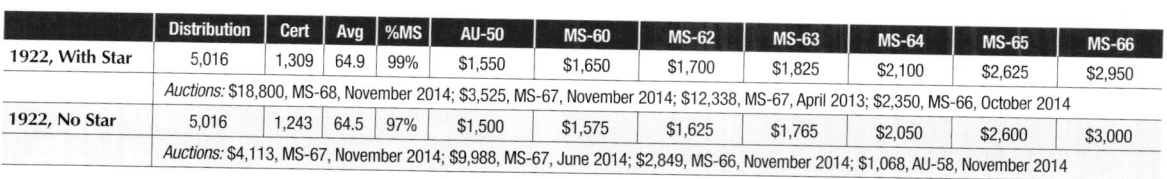

	Distribution	Cert	Avg	%MS	AU-50	MS-60	MS-62	MS-63	MS-64	MS-65	MS-66
1922, With Star	5,016	1,309	64.9	99%	$1,550	$1,650	$1,700	$1,825	$2,100	$2,625	$2,950
	Auctions: $18,800, MS-68, November 2014; $3,525, MS-67, November 2014; $12,338, MS-67, April 2013; $2,350, MS-66, October 2014										
1922, No Star	5,016	1,243	64.5	97%	$1,500	$1,575	$1,625	$1,765	$2,050	$2,600	$3,000
	Auctions: $4,113, MS-67, November 2014; $9,988, MS-67, June 2014; $2,849, MS-66, November 2014; $1,068, AU-58, November 2014										

MONROE DOCTRINE CENTENNIAL HALF DOLLAR (1923)

Designer: *Chester Beach.* **Weight:** *12.50 grams.* **Composition:** *.900 silver, .100 copper (net weight .3617 oz. pure silver).* **Diameter:** *30.6 mm.* **Edge:** *Reeded.* **Mint:** *San Francisco.*

The California film industry promoted this issue in conjunction with a motion-picture exposition held in June 1923. The coin purportedly commemorated the 100th anniversary of the Monroe Doctrine, which warned that European countries that interfered with countries in the Western Hemisphere or established new colonies there would be met with disapproval or worse from the U.S. government.

Designs. *Obverse:* Conjoined bareheaded profile portraits of presidents James Monroe and John Quincy Adams. *Reverse:* Stylized depiction of the continents of North and South America as female figures in the outlines of the two land masses.

Mintage Data. Authorized on January 24, 1923. *Maximum authorized*—300,000. *Number minted*—274,077 (including 77 assay coins). *Net distribution*—274,077.

Original Cost and Issuer. Sale price $1. Issued by the Los Angeles Clearing House, representing backers of the First Annual American Historical Revue and Motion Picture Industry Exposition.

Key to Collecting. Most examples show friction or wear. MS coins are common. Evaluating the numerical grade of MS-60 to 63 coins is difficult because of the design's weak definition. Low-magnification inspection usually shows nicks and graininess at the highest point of the obverse center; these flaws are from the original planchets. Many examples of this coin have been doctored and artificially toned in attempts to earn higher grades upon certification; these are avoided by connoisseurs.

First Points of Wear. *Obverse:* Adams's cheekbone. *Reverse:* The upper figure, underneath CT in DOCTRINE.

	Distribution	Cert	Avg	%MS	AU-50	MS-60	MS-62	MS-63	MS-64	MS-65	MS-66
1923S	274,077	3,632	63.2	96%	$65	$80	$100	$140	$250	$1,600	$4,600

Auctions: $2,633, MS-66, November 2014; $2,585, MS-66, September 2014; $11,750, MS-66, December 2013; $1,998, MS-65, November 2014

HUGUENOT-WALLOON TERCENTENARY HALF DOLLAR (1924)

Designer: *George T. Morgan (with model modifications by James Earle Fraser).*
Weight: *12.50 grams.* **Composition:** *.900 silver, .100 copper (net weight .3617 oz. pure silver).*
Diameter: *30.6 mm.* **Edge:** *Reeded.* **Mint:** *Philadelphia.*

Settling of the Huguenots and Walloons in the New World was the occasion commemorated by this issue. New Netherland, now New York, was founded in 1624 by this group of Dutch colonists. Interestingly, the persons represented on the obverse were not directly concerned with the occasion; both Admiral Gaspard de Coligny and Prince William the Silent were dead long before the settlement.

Designs. *Obverse:* Hat-clad profile portraits representing Admiral Gaspard de Coligny and Prince William the Silent, first stadtholder of the Netherlands. *Reverse:* The ship *Nieuw Nederland* in full sail.

Mintage Data. Authorized on February 26, 1923. *Maximum authorized—300,000. Number minted—142,080 (including 80 assay coins). Net distribution—142,080.*

Original Cost and Issuer. Sale price $1. Issued by the Huguenot-Walloon New Netherland Commission, Inc., and designated outlets.

Key to Collecting. This coin is readily available on the market, with most examples in MS-60 to 63. Those grading MS-64 and 65 are also found quite often; MS-66 coins are scarcer. Relatively few worn pieces exist. Friction and contact marks are sometimes seen on the cheek of Admiral Coligny on the obverse, and on the masts and ship's rigging on the reverse. Many coins have been cleaned or repeatedly dipped. Connoisseurs avoid deeply toned or stained coins, even those certified with high numerical grades. MS coins usually have satiny (rather than deeply lustrous or frosty) surfaces, and may have a gray appearance. High in the reverse field of most coins is a "bright" spot interrupting the luster, from a touch of polish in the die.

First Points of Wear. *Obverse:* Coligny's cheekbone. *Reverse:* The rim near the F in FOUNDING and over RY in TERCENTENARY; the lower part of the highest sail; the center of the ship's stern.

	Distribution	Cert	Avg	%MS	AU-50	MS-60	MS-62	MS-63	MS-64	MS-65	MS-66
1924	142,080	3,250	64.2	99%	$130	$150	$155	$160	$210	$350	$650

Auctions: $2,115, MS-67, November 2014; $1,058, MS-67, August 2014; $499, MS-66, October 2014; $259, MS-66, October 2014

LEXINGTON-CONCORD SESQUICENTENNIAL HALF DOLLAR (1925)

Designer: *Chester Beach.* **Weight:** *12.50 grams.* **Composition:** *.900 silver, .100 copper (net weight .3617 oz. pure silver).* **Diameter:** *30.6 mm.* **Edge:** *Reeded.* **Mint:** *Philadelphia.*

The Battle of Lexington and Concord—fought in 1775 just one day after Paul Revere's famous ride—is commemorated on this coin. Sculptor James Earle Fraser of the Commission of Fine Arts approved Beach's designs, but protested that the local committees had made a poor choice of subject matter.

Designs. *Obverse:* A view of the *Minute Man* statue, by Daniel Chester French, located in Concord, Massachusetts. *Reverse:* Lexington's Old Belfry, whose tolling bell roused the Minute Men to action in 1775.

Mintage and Melting Data. Authorized on January 14, 1925. *Maximum authorized—300,000. Number minted—162,099 (including 99 assay coins). Number melted—86. Net distribution—162,013.*

Original Cost and Issuer. Sale price $1. Issued by the U.S. Lexington-Concord Sesquicentennial Commission, through local banks.

Key to Collecting. Examples are easily found in all grades, with most being in high AU or low MS grades, although eye appeal can vary widely. MS-65 coins are scarce in comparison to those in MS-60 through 64. Some specimens are deeply frosty and lustrous, whereas others have partially prooflike fields.

First Points of Wear. *Obverse:* The thighs of the Minuteman. *Reverse:* The top edge of the belfry.

	Distribution	Cert	Avg	%MS	AU-50	MS-60	MS-62	MS-63	MS-64	MS-65	MS-66
1925	162,013	4,068	63.7	97%	$100	$120	$130	$145	$160	$450	$975

Auctions: $5,288, MS-67, November 2014; $11,880, MS-67, November 2013; $1,176, MS-66+, November 2014; $646, MS-66, November 2014

STONE MOUNTAIN MEMORIAL HALF DOLLAR (1925)

Designer: *Gutzon Borglum.* **Weight:** *12.50 grams.* **Composition:** *.900 silver, .100 copper (net weight .3617 oz. pure silver).* **Diameter:** *30.6 mm.* **Edge:** *Reeded.* **Mint:** *Philadelphia.*

The first of these half dollars were struck at Philadelphia on January 21, 1925, Confederate general Stonewall Jackson's birthday. Funds received from the sale of this large issue were devoted to the expense of carving figures of Confederate leaders and soldiers on Stone Mountain in Georgia. The coin's designer, Gutzon Borglum, was the original sculptor for that project, but left due to differences with the Stone Mountain Confederate Monumental Association. Augustus Lukeman took over in his stead, and the carving was completed and dedicated in 1970; Borglum would meanwhile go on to create the presidents' heads at Mount Rushmore.

Designs. *Obverse:* Equestrian portraits of Civil War generals Robert E. Lee and Thomas "Stonewall" Jackson. *Reverse:* An eagle perched on a cliff with wings in mid-spread.

Mintage and Melting Data. *Maximum authorized—5,000,000. Number minted—2,314,709 (including 4,709 assay coins). Number melted—1,000,000. Net distribution—1,314,709.*

Original Cost and Issuer. Sale price $1. Issued by the Stone Mountain Confederate Monumental Association through many outlets, including promotions involving pieces counterstamped with abbreviations for Southern states.

Key to Collecting. This is the most plentiful commemorative from the 1920s. Examples are easily found in grades ranging from lightly worn through gem Mint State (many with outstanding eye appeal). Circulated coins are also found, as well as those that were counterstamped for special fundraising sales. The typical coin has very lustrous and frosty surfaces, although the reverse field may be somewhat satiny.

First Points of Wear. *Obverse:* Lee's elbow and leg. *Reverse:* The eagle's breast.

	Distribution	Cert	Avg	%MS	AU-50	MS-60	MS-62	MS-63	MS-64	MS-65	MS-66
1925	1,314,709	7,867	63.9	97%	$70	$75	$80	$90	$150	$275	$350

Auctions: $2,585, MS-67, November 2014; $646, MS-67, November 2014; $646, MS-66+, October 2014; $3,819, MS-66, November 2014

CALIFORNIA DIAMOND JUBILEE HALF DOLLAR (1925)

Designer: *Jo Mora.* **Weight:** *12.50 grams.* **Composition:** *.900 silver, .100 copper (net weight .3617 oz. pure silver).* **Diameter:** *30.6 mm.* **Edge:** *Reeded.* **Mint:** *San Francisco.*

The celebration for which these coins were struck marked the 75th anniversary of the admission of California into the Union. Notably, James Earle Fraser of the Commission of Fine Arts criticized Jo Mora's designs at the time. Art historian Cornelius Vermeule, however, called the coin "one of America's greatest works of numismatic art" in his book *Numismatic Art in America.*

Designs. *Obverse:* A rustic miner, squatting to pan for gold. *Reverse:* A grizzly bear, as taken from the California state flag.

Mintage and Melting Data. Authorized on February 24, 1925, part of the act also providing for the 1925 Fort Vancouver and 1927 Vermont half dollars. *Maximum authorized*—300,000. *Number minted*—150,200 (including 200 assay coins). *Number melted*—63,606. *Net distribution*—86,594.

Original Cost and Issuer. Sale price $1. Issued by the San Francisco Citizens' Committee through the San Francisco Clearing House Association and the Los Angeles Clearing House.

Key to Collecting. This coin's design is such that even a small amount of handling produces friction on the shoulder and high parts of the bear, in particular. As a result, most grade in the AU-55 to MS-62 range, and higher-level MS examples are rare. This issue exists in two finishes: frosty/lustrous, and the rarer "chrome-like" or prooflike. The frosty-finish pieces display some lack of die definition of the details. The prooflike pieces have heavily brushed and highly polished dies. Many specimens certified in high grades are toned, sometimes deeply, which can mask evidence of friction. Coins with no traces of friction are rarities.

First Points of Wear. *Obverse:* The folds of the miner's shirt sleeve. *Reverse:* The shoulder of the bear.

	Distribution	Cert	Avg	%MS	AU-50	MS-60	MS-62	MS-63	MS-64	MS-65	MS-66
									PF-63	PF-64	PF-65
1925S	86,594	4,144	64.0	96%	$200	$230	$270	$290	$425	$800	$1,250
	Auctions: $3,055, MS-67, November 2014; $1,998, MS-67, October 2014; $4,700, MS-67, February 2013; $940, MS-66+, September 2014										
1925S, Matte Proof	1–2	1	65.0								
	Auctions: No auction records available.										

FORT VANCOUVER CENTENNIAL HALF DOLLAR (1925)

Designer: *Laura Gardin Fraser.* **Weight:** *12.50 grams.* **Composition:** *.900 silver, .100 copper (net weight .3617 oz. pure silver).* **Diameter:** *30.6 mm.* **Edge:** *Reeded.* **Mint:** *San Francisco.*

The sale of these half dollars at $1 each helped to finance the pageant staged for the celebration of the 100th anniversary of the construction of Fort Vancouver. As part of the publicity, pilot Oakley G. Kelly made a round-trip flight from Vancouver to San Francisco and back again to pick up and deliver the entire issue—which weighed 1,462 pounds.

Designs. *Obverse:* Bareheaded profile portrait of Dr. John McLoughlin, who built Fort Vancouver (Washington) on the Columbia River in 1825. *Reverse:* A pioneer in buckskin with a musket in his hands, with Fort Vancouver in the background.

Mintage and Melting Data. Authorized on February 24, 1925. *Maximum authorized*—300,000. *Number minted* (including 28 assay coins)—50,028. *Number melted*—35,034. *Net distribution*—14,994.

Original Cost and Issuer. Sale price $1. The Fort Vancouver Centennial Corporation, Vancouver, Washington.

Key to Collecting. This coin's design is such that even a small amount of handling produced friction on the higher spots. As a result, higher-level MS examples are rare.

First Points of Wear. *Obverse:* McLoughlin's temple area. *Reverse:* The pioneer's right knee.

| | Distribution | Cert | Avg | %MS | AU-50 | MS-60 | MS-62 | MS-63 | MS-64 | MS-65 | MS-66 |
									PF-63	PF-64	PF-65
1925	14,994	2,236	64.0	97%	$325	$375	$410	$450	$500	$800	$1,100
	Auctions: $4,759, MS-67+, November 2014; $3,672, MS-67, November 2014; $8,225, MS-67, September 2013; $260, MS-61, December 2014
1925, Matte Proof	2–3	0	n/a								
	Auctions: No auction records available.

SESQUICENTENNIAL OF AMERICAN INDEPENDENCE HALF DOLLAR (1926)

Designer: *John R. Sinnock.* **Weight:** *12.50 grams.* **Composition:** *.900 silver, .100 copper (net weight .3617 oz. pure silver).* **Diameter:** *30.6 mm.* **Edge:** *Reeded.* **Mint:** *Philadelphia.*

The 150th anniversary of the signing of the Declaration of Independence was the occasion for an international fair held in Philadelphia in 1926. To help raise funds for financing the fair, special issues of half dollars (as well as quarter eagles, below) were authorized by Congress. The use of Calvin Coolidge's likeness marked the first time a portrait of a president appeared on a coin struck during his own lifetime.

Designs. *Obverse:* Conjoined profile portraits of bewigged George Washington and bareheaded Calvin Coolidge. *Reverse:* The Liberty Bell.

Mintage and Melting Data. Authorized on March 23, 1925. *Maximum authorized*—1,000,000. *Number minted*—1,000,528 (including 528 assay coins). *Number melted*—859,408. *Net distribution*—141,120.

Original Cost and Issuer. Sale price $1. Issued by the National Sesquicentennial Exhibition Association.

Key to Collecting. Accurate grading can be problematic for this coin. Many examples certified at high grades have mottled or deeply toned surfaces that obfuscate examination, and others have been recolored. Most have graininess—marks from the original planchet—on the highest part of the portrait.

First Points of Wear. *Obverse:* Washington's cheekbone. *Reverse:* The area below the lower inscription on the Liberty Bell.

	Distribution	Cert	Avg	%MS	AU-50	MS-60	MS-62	MS-63	MS-64	MS-65	MS-66
1926	141,120	4,366	63.1	96%	$90	$115	$125	$140	$240	$2,450	$25,000
	Auctions: $6,463, MS-66, November 2014; $7,638, MS-66, July 2014; $19,975, MS-66, April 2014; $75, AU-58, October 2014

SESQUICENTENNIAL OF AMERICAN INDEPENDENCE QUARTER EAGLE (1926)

Designer: *John R. Sinnock.* **Weight:** *4.18 grams.* **Composition:** *.900 gold, .100 copper (net weight .12094 oz. pure gold).* **Diameter:** *18 mm.* **Edge:** *Reeded.* **Mint:** *Philadelphia.*

This quarter eagle, along with a related half dollar, was sold to finance the National Sesquicentennial Exposition in Philadelphia (which marked the 150th anniversary of the signing of the Declaration of Independence). Note that though the issuer was known as the National Sesquicentennial *Exhibition* Association, the event was primarily billed with *Exposition* in its name.

Designs. *Obverse:* Miss Liberty standing, holding in one hand a scroll representing the Declaration of Independence and in the other, the Torch of Freedom. *Reverse:* A front view of Independence Hall in Philadelphia.

Mintage and Melting Data. Authorized on March 23, 1925. *Maximum authorized*—200,000. *Number minted*—200,226 (including 226 assay coins). *Number melted*—154,207. *Net distribution*—46,019.

Original Cost and Issuer. Sale price $4. National Sesquicentennial Exhibition Association.

Key to Collecting. Nearly all examples show evidence of handling and contact from careless production at the Mint, and from later indifference by their buyers. Most coins range from AU-55 to MS-62 in grade, and have scattered marks in the fields. MS-65 examples are rare. Well-struck coins are seldom seen. Some pieces show copper stains; connoisseurs avoid these.

First Points of Wear. *Obverse:* The bottom of the scroll held by Liberty. *Reverse:* The area below the top of the tower; and the central portion above the roof.

	Distribution	Cert	Avg	%MS	AU-50	MS-60	MS-62	MS-63	MS-64	MS-65	MS-66
									PF-63	PF-64	PF-65
1926	46,019	7,727	63.1	94%	$450	$465	$525	$775	$1,150	$3,250	$14,000
	Auctions: $5,581, MS-66, November 2014; $9,400, MS-66, April 2013; $356, MS-61, November 2014; $382, AU-58, December 2014										
1926, Matte Proof (a)	*unique*	1	65.0								
	Auctions: No auction records available.										

a. "The coin is unique and displays a matte surface similar to the Proof gold coins of 1908 to 1915. The coin was reportedly from the estate of the designer, John R. Sinnock, who is best known for his Roosevelt dime and Franklin half dollar designs. The piece was in the possession of coin dealer David Bullowa in the 1950s. Another example is rumored by Breen, but the whereabouts or existence of the coin is unknown" (*Encyclopedia of U.S. Gold Coins, 1795–1933*, second edition).

OREGON TRAIL MEMORIAL HALF DOLLAR (1926–1939)

Designers: *James Earle Fraser and Laura Gardin Fraser.* **Weight:** *12.50 grams.*
Composition: *.900 silver, .100 copper (net weight .3617 oz. pure silver).*
Diameter: *30.6 mm.* **Edge:** *Reeded.* **Mints:** *Philadelphia, San Francisco, Denver.*

These coins—the longest-running series of commemoratives—were struck in commemoration of the Oregon Trail and in memory of the pioneers, many of whom lie buried along the famous 2,000-mile highway of history. This was the first commemorative to be struck at more than one Mint facility, and also the first commemorative to be struck at the Denver Mint.

Designs. *Obverse:* A pioneer family in a Conestoga wagon, heading west into the sunset. *Reverse:* A standing Indian with a bow, arm outstretched, and a map of the United States in the background.

Mintage and Melting Data. *Maximum authorized*—6,000,000 (for the entire series from 1926 onward). *Number minted*—1926: 48,030 (including 30 assay coins); 1926-S: 100,055 (including 55 assay coins); 1928: 50,028 (including 28 assay coins); 1933-D: 5,250 (including an unrecorded number of assay coins); 1934-D: 7,006 (including 6 assay coins); 1936: 10,006 (including 6 assay coins); 1936-S: 5,006 (including 6 assay coins); 1937-D: 12,008 (including 8 assay coins); 1938-P: 6,006 (including 6 assay coins); 1938-D: 6,005 (including 5 assay coins); 1938-S: 6,006 (including 6 assay coins). *Number melted*—1926: 75 (defective coins); 1926-S: 17,000; 1928: 44,000; 1933-D: 242 (probably defective coins). *Net distribution*—1926: 47,955; 1926-S: 83,055; 1928: 6,028; 1933-D: 5,008; 1934-D: 7,006; 1936: 10,006; 1936-S: 5,006; 1937-D: 12,008; 1938-P: 6,006; 1938-D: 6,005; 1938-S: 6,006.

Original Cost and Issuer. Sale price $1; later raised. Issued by the Oregon Trail Memorial Association, Inc.; some sold through Scott Stamp & Coin Co., Inc., and some sold through Whitman Centennial, Inc., Walla Walla, Washington. From 1937 onward, distributed solely by the Oregon Trail Memorial Association, Inc.

Key to Collecting. Although most of the later issues have low mintages, they are not rare in the marketplace, because the majority were originally sold to coin collectors and dealers. As a result, most surviving coins are in MS. The quality of the surface finish varies, with earlier issues tending to be frosty and lustrous and later issues (particularly those dated 1938 and 1939) having somewhat grainy or satiny fields. Grading requires care. Look for friction or contact marks on the high points of the Indian and the Conestoga wagon, but, more importantly, check both surfaces carefully for scattered cuts and marks. All three mints had difficulty in striking up the rims properly, causing many rejections. Those deemed acceptable and shipped out usually had full rims, but it is best to check when buying.

First Points of Wear. *Obverse:* The hip of the ox, and high points of the wagon (note that the top rear of the wagon was weakly struck in some years). *Reverse:* The Indian's left thumb and fingers (note that some pieces show flatness on the thumb and first finger, due to a weak strike).

	Distribution	Cert	Avg	%MS	AU-50	MS-60	MS-62	MS-63	MS-64 PF-63	MS-65 PF-64	MS-66 PF-65
1926	47,955	2,100	64.4	98%	$145	$175	$180	$185	$220	$300	$350
	Auctions: $940, MS-67, November 2014; $705, MS-67, August 2014; $5,288, MS-67, August 2013; $223, MS-66, December 2014										
1926, Matte Proof	1–2	1	65.0								
	Auctions: No auction records available.										
1926S	83,055	2,952	64.6	97%	$145	$175	$180	$185	$220	$300	$450
	Auctions: $2,820, MS-68, November 2014; $4,406, MS-68, August 2014; $7,638, MS-68, November 2013; $764, MS-67, November 2014										
1928 (same as 1926)	6,028	1,318	65.3	100%	$215	$235	$250	$275	$300	$340	$460
	Auctions: $646, MS-67, August 2014; $4,113, MS-67, September 2013; $282, MS-66, December 2014; $200, MS-66, October 2014										
1933D	5,008	1,021	65.1	100%	$370	$385	$395	$410	$425	$450	$500
	Auctions: $881, MS-67, August 2014; $1,058, MS-67, July 2014; $5,581, MS-67, June 2013; $470, MS-66+, December 2014										
1934D	7,006	1,305	64.8	100%	$190	$210	$220	$235	$245	$300	$475
	Auctions: $881, MS-67, November 2014; $1,058, MS-67, July 2014; $1,645, MS-67, March 2013; $382, MS-66+, December 2014										
1936	10,006	1,581	65.3	100%	$170	$190	$200	$210	$230	$300	$350
	Auctions: $8,813, MS-68, August 2014; $499, MS-67, November 2014; $375, MS-67, November 2014; $294, MS-66, November 2014										
1936S	5,006	1,105	65.5	100%	$150	$190	$210	$220	$240	$340	$350
	Auctions: $1,763, MS-68, November 2014; $10,575, MS-68, January 2013; $670, MS-67+, October 2014; $425, MS-67, November 2014										
1937D	12,008	2,351	65.9	100%	$180	$200	$210	$225	$255	$300	$350
	Auctions: $863, MS-67+★, June 2012										
1938 (same as 1926)	6,006	1,235	65.4	100%	$145	$175	$185	$200	$220	$310	$410
	Auctions: $10,575, MS-68, January 2014; $482, MS-67, October 2014; $1,528, MS-67, August 2014; $259, MS-66, December 2014										
1938D	6,005	1,406	65.8	100%	$145	$175	$185	$200	$220	$310	$410
	Auctions: $1,586, MS-68, October 2014; $7,931, MS-68, April 2013; $456, MS-67, November 2014; $329, MS-67, October 2014										
1938S	6,006	1,265	65.5	100%	$145	$175	$185	$200	$220	$310	$410
	Auctions: $2,585, MS-68, August 2014; $35,250, MS-68, January 2013; $499, MS-67, December 2014; $405, MS-67, November 2014										
Set of 1938 P-D-S						$520	$570	$620	$670	$975	$1,300
	Auctions: $2,070, MS-67/67/67, February 2012										
1939	3,004	765	65.5	100%	$325	$525	$550	$575	$600	$680	$900
	Auctions: $8,225, MS-68, June 2013; $1,293, MS-67+, October 2014; $852, MS-67, August 2014; $1,410, MS-67, July 2014										
1939D	3,004	801	65.8	100%	$325	$525	$550	$575	$600	$680	$900
	Auctions: $3,055, MS-68, October 2014; $1,410, MS-67, November 2014; $881, MS-67, October 2014; $799, MS-67, September 2014										
1939S	3,005	782	65.5	100%	$325	$525	$550	$575	$600	$680	$900
	Auctions: $5,875, MS-68, February 2013; $1,880, MS-67, August 2014; $1,763, MS-67, July 2014; $705, MS-66+, July 2014										
Set of 1939 P-D-S						$1,650	$1,700	$1,750	$1,825	$2,000	$2,700
	Auctions: $5,175, MS-67/67/67, January 2012										

VERMONT SESQUICENTENNIAL HALF DOLLAR (1927)

Designer: *Charles Keck.* **Weight:** *12.50 grams.* **Composition:** *.900 silver, .100 copper (net weight .3617 oz. pure silver).* **Diameter:** *30.6 mm.* **Edge:** *Reeded.* **Mint:** *Philadelphia.*

This souvenir issue commemorates the 150th anniversary of the Battle of Bennington and the independence of Vermont. Authorized in 1925, it was not coined until 1927. The Vermont Sesquicentennial Commission intended that funds derived would benefit the study of history.

Designs. *Obverse:* Profile portrait of a bewigged Ira Allen. *Reverse:* A catamount walking left.

Mintage and Melting Data. Authorized by the Act of February 24, 1925. *Maximum authorized*—40,000. *Number minted*—40,034 (including 34 assay coins). *Number melted*—11,892. *Net distribution*—28,142.

Original Cost and Issuer. Sale price $1. Issued by the Vermont Sesquicentennial Commission (Bennington Battle Monument and Historical Association).

Key to Collecting. The Vermont half dollar was struck with the highest relief of any commemorative issue to that date. Despite the depth of the work in the dies, nearly all of the coins were struck up properly and show excellent detail. Unfortunately, the height of the obverse portrait encourages evidence of contact at the central points, and nearly all coins show some friction on Allen's cheek. Most are in grades of MS-62 to 64 and are deeply lustrous and frosty. Cleaned examples are often seen—and are avoided by connoisseurs.

First Points of Wear. *Obverse:* Allen's cheek, and the hair above his ear and in the temple area. *Reverse:* The catamount's upper shoulder.

	Distribution	Cert	Avg	%MS	AU-50	MS-60	MS-62	MS-63	MS-64	MS-65	MS-66
1927	28,142	3,056	63.9	98%	$275	$290	$300	$320	$375	$650	$850
	Auctions: $3,525, MS-67, October 2014; $7,344, MS-67, September 2014; $2,233, MS-67, August 2014; $200, MS-61, October 2014										

HAWAIIAN SESQUICENTENNIAL HALF DOLLAR (1928)

Designer: *Juliette M. Fraser.* **Weight:** *12.50 grams.* **Composition:** *.900 silver, .100 copper (net weight .3617 oz. pure silver).* **Diameter:** *30.6 mm.* **Edge:** *Reeded.* **Mint:** *Philadelphia.*

This issue was struck to commemorate the 150th anniversary of the arrival on the Hawaiian Islands of Captain James Cook in 1778. The coin's $2 price was the highest ever for a commemorative half dollar up to that point.

Designs. *Obverse:* Portrait of Captain James Cook. *Reverse:* A Hawaiian chieftain standing with arm outstretched and holding a spear.

Mintage Data. Authorized on March 7, 1928. *Maximum authorized*—10,000. *Number minted*—10,008 (including 8 assay coins and 50 Sandblast Proofs). *Net distribution*—10,008.

Original Cost and Issuer. Sale price $2. Issued by the Captain Cook Sesquicentennial Commission, through the Bank of Hawaii, Ltd.

Key to Collecting. This is the scarcest of classic U.S. commemorative coins. It is elusive in all grades, and highly prized. Most are AU-55 to MS-62 or slightly finer; those grading MS-65 or above are especially difficult to find. Most examples show contact or friction on the higher design areas. Some coins have a somewhat satiny surface, whereas others are lustrous and frosty. Many undipped pieces have a yellowish tint. Beware of coins which have been repeatedly dipped or cleaned. Problem-free examples are rarer even than the low mintage would suggest. Fake "Sandblast Proofs" exist; these are coins dipped in acid.

First Points of Wear. *Obverse:* Cook's cheekbone. *Reverse:* The chieftain's legs; his fingers and the hand holding the spear.

	Distribution	Cert	Avg	%MS	AU-50	MS-60	MS-62	MS-63	MS-64	MS-65	MS-66
									PF-63	PF-64	PF-65
1928	10,008	1,696	63.7	98%	$1,850	$2,600	$2,750	$3,100	$3,300	$5,000	$11,000
	Auctions: $8,225, MS-66, October 2014; $5,288, MS-66, October 2014; $25,850, MS-66, February 2013; $1,645, AU-58, October 2014										
1928, Proof (a)	50	26	64.1						$20,000	$30,000	$50,000
	Auctions: No auction records available.										

a. Sandblast Proof presentation pieces. "Of the production figure, 50 were Sandblast Proofs, made by a special process which imparted a dull, grainy finish to the pieces, similar to that used on certain Mint medals of the era as well as on gold Proof coins circa 1908–1915" (*Guide Book of United States Commemorative Coins*).

MARYLAND TERCENTENARY HALF DOLLAR (1934)

Designer: *Hans Schuler.* **Weight:** *12.50 grams.* **Composition:** *.900 silver, .100 copper (net weight .3617 oz. pure silver).* **Diameter:** *30.6 mm.* **Edge:** *Reeded.* **Mint:** *Philadelphia.*

The 300th anniversary of the founding of the Maryland Colony by Cecil Calvert (known as Lord Baltimore) was the occasion for this special coin. The profits from the sale of this issue were used to finance the celebration in Baltimore during 1934. John Work Garrett, distinguished American diplomat and well-known numismatist, was among the citizens of Maryland who endorsed the commemorative half dollar proposal on behalf of the Maryland Tercentenary Commission of Baltimore.

Designs. *Obverse:* Three-quarter portrait of Cecil Calvert, Lord Baltimore. *Reverse:* The state seal and motto of Maryland.

Mintage Data. Authorized on May 9, 1934. *Maximum authorized*—25,000. *Number minted*—25,015 (including 15 assay coins). *Net distribution*—25,015.

Original Cost and Issuer. Sale price $1. Issued by the Maryland Tercentenary Commission, through various outlets.

Key to Collecting. The coin's field has an unusual "rippled" appearance, similar to a sculptured plaque, so nicks and other marks that would be visible on a coin with flat fields are not as readily noticed. Most examples grade MS-62 to 64. Finer pieces, strictly graded, are elusive. This issue was not handled with care at the time of mintage and distribution, and nearly all show scattered contact marks. Some exist struck from a reverse die broken from the right side of the shield to a point opposite the upper right of the 4 in the date 1634.

First Points of Wear. *Obverse:* Lord Baltimore's nose (the nose usually appears flatly struck; also check the reverse for wear). *Reverse:* The top of the coronet on top of the shield, and the tops of the draperies.

	Distribution	Cert	Avg	%MS	AU-50	MS-60	MS-62	MS-63	MS-64	MS-65	MS-66
									PF-63	PF-64	PF-65
1934	25,015	3,392	64.7	100%	$150	$165	$170	$180	$195	$250	$400
	Auctions: $1,293, MS-67, November 2014; $635, MS-67, November 2014; $64,625, MS-62, November 2013; $101, AU-58, November 2014										
1934, Matte Proof	2–4	2	63.0								
	Auctions: No auction records available.										

TEXAS INDEPENDENCE CENTENNIAL HALF DOLLAR (1934–1938)

Designer: *Pompeo Coppini.* **Weight:** *12.50 grams.*
Composition: *.900 silver, .100 copper (net weight .3617 oz. pure silver).*
Diameter: *30.6 mm.* **Edge:** *Reeded.* **Mints:** *Philadelphia, Denver, San Francisco.*

This issue commemorated the independence of Texas in 1836. Proceeds from the sale of the coin were intended to finance the Centennial Exposition, which was eventually held in Dallas. Sales were lower than expected, but the event was still held and attracted about 7 million visitors.

Designs. *Obverse:* A perched eagle with a large five-pointed star in the background. *Reverse:* The goddess Victory kneeling, with medallions and portraits of General Sam Houston and Stephen Austin, founders of the republic and state of Texas, along with other Texan icons.

Mintage and Melting Data. Authorized on June 15, 1933. *Maximum authorized*—1,500,000 (for the entire series 1934 onward). 1934: *Number minted*—1934: 205,113 (including 113 assay coins); 1935-P: 10,008 (including 8 assay coins); 1935-D: 10,007 (including 7 assay coins); 1935-S: 10,008 (including 8 assay coins); 1936-P: 10,008 (including 8 assay coins); 1936-D: 10,007 (including 7 assay coins); 1936-S: 10,008 (including 8 assay coins); 1937-P: 8,005 (including 5 assay coins); 1937-D: 8,006 (including 6 assay coins); 1937-S: 8,007 (including 7 assay coins); 1938-P: 5,005 (including 5 assay coins); 1938-D: 5,005 (including 5 assay coins); 1938-S: 5,006 (including 6 assay coins). *Number melted*—1934: 143,650; 1935-P: 12 (probably defective coins); 1936-P: 12 (probably defective coins); 1937-P: 1,434; 1937-D: 1,401; 1937-S: 1,370; 1938-P: 1,225; 1938-D: 1,230; 1938-S: 1,192. *Net distribution*—1934: 61,463; 1935-P: 9,996; 1935-D: 10,007; 1935-S: 10,008; 1936-P: 9,996; 1936-D: 10,007; 1936-S: 10,008; 1937-P: 6,571; 1937-D: 6,605; 1937-S: 6,637; 1938-P: 3,780; 1938-D: 3,775; 1938-S: 3,814.

Original Cost and Issuer. Sale price $1; later raised. Issued by the American Legion Texas Centennial Committee, Austin, Texas, from 1934 through 1936; issued by the Texas Memorial Museum Centennial Coin Campaign in 1937 and 1938.

Key to Collecting. The typical example grades MS-64 or 65. Early issues are very lustrous and frosty; those produced toward the end of the series are more satiny.

First Points of Wear. *Obverse:* The eagle's upper breast and upper leg. *Reverse:* The forehead and knee of Victory.

	Distribution	Cert	Avg	%MS	AU-50	MS-60	MS-62	MS-63	MS-64	MS-65	MS-66
1934	61,463	2,422	64.5	98%	$140	$150	$160	$170	$180	$250	$360
	Auctions: $1,293, MS-67, July 2014; $940, MS-67, July 2014; $2,820, MS-67, August 2013; $306, MS-66, December 2014										
1935 (same as 1934)	9,996	1,554	65.6	100%	$140	$150	$160	$170	$180	$250	$360
	Auctions: $11,163, MS-68, September 2013; $382, MS-67, October 2014; $499, MS-67, July 2014; $206, MS-66, December 2014										
1935D	10,007	1,598	65.5	100%	$140	$150	$160	$170	$180	$250	$360
	Auctions: $9,988, MS-68, September 2013; $1,645, MS-67+, September 2014; $441, MS-67, October 2014; $188, MS-66, December 2014										
1935S	10,008	1,337	65.2	100%	$140	$150	$160	$170	$180	$250	$360
	Auctions: $27,025, MS-68, January 2014; $485, MS-67, October 2014; $529, MS-67, August 2014; $235, MS-66, December 2014										
Set of 1935 P-D-S							$450	$465	$480	$540	$800	$1,200
	Auctions: $871, MS-66/66/66, December 2011										

	Distribution	Cert	Avg	%MS	AU-50	MS-60	MS-62	MS-63	MS-64	MS-65	MS-66
1936 (same as 1934)	8,911	1,433	65.4	100%	$140	$150	$160	$170	$180	$250	$360
	Auctions: $4,406, MS-68, September 2013; $482, MS-67, September 2014; $441, MS-67, August 2014; $235, MS-66, November 2014										
1936D	9,039	1,639	65.7	100%	$140	$150	$160	$170	$180	$250	$360
	Auctions: $5,875, MS-68, September 2013; $441, MS-67, November 2014; $2,585, MS-67, July 2014; $259, MS-66, November 2014										
1936S	9,055	1,331	65.3	100%	$140	$150	$160	$170	$180	$250	$360
	Auctions: $1,528, MS-67+, August 2014; $676, MS-67, December 2014; $2,820, MS-67, February 2013; $376, MS-66, November 2014										
Set of 1936 P-D-S					$450	$465	$480	$540	$800	$1,200	
	Auctions: $863, MS-66/66/66, December 2011										
1937 (same as 1934)	6,571	1,168	65.2	100%	$140	$150	$160	$170	$180	$250	$360
	Auctions: $397, MS-67, August 2014; $2,350, MS-67, August 2013; $306, MS-66, November 2014; $247, MS-66, November 2014										
1937D	6,605	1,207	65.4	100%	$140	$150	$160	$170	$180	$250	$360
	Auctions: $19,975, MS-68, September 2013; $411, MS-67, October 2014; $823, MS-67, August 2014; $411, MS-66, December 2014										
1937S	6,637	1,225	65.3	100%	$140	$150	$160	$170	$180	$250	$360
	Auctions: $2,233, MS-67+, November 2014; $558, MS-67, November 2014; $852, MS-67, September 2014; $2,585, MS-67, August 2013										
Set of 1937 P-D-S					$450	$465	$480	$540	$800	$1,200	
	Auctions: $625, MS-66/66/66, April 2012										
1938 (same as 1934)	3,780	830	65.1	100%	$200	$210	$215	$225	$250	$350	$600
	Auctions: $1,645, MS-67, August 2014; $4,406, MS-67, February 2013; $458, MS-66, November 2014; $282, MS-65, December 2014										
1938D	3,775	867	65.4	100%	$200	$210	$215	$225	$250	$350	$600
	Auctions: $32,900, MS-68, August 2013; $1,058, MS-67, August 2014; $911, MS-67, August 2014; $558, MS-66, November 2014										
1938S	3,814	867	65.4	100%	$200	$210	$215	$225	$250	$350	$600
	Auctions: $823, MS-67, September 2014; $1,293, MS-67, August 2014; $3,525, MS-67, January 2014; $470, MS-66, December 2014										
Set of 1938 P-D-S					$650	$700	$800	$900	$1,250	$2,100	
	Auctions: $604, MS-64/65/64, June 2012										

DANIEL BOONE BICENTENNIAL HALF DOLLAR (1934–1938)

Designer: *Augustus Lukeman.* **Weight:** *12.50 grams.*
Composition: *.900 silver, .100 copper (net weight .3617 oz. pure silver).*
Diameter: *30.6 mm.* **Edge:** *Reeded.* **Mints:** *Philadelphia, Denver, San Francisco.*

This coin type, which was minted for five years, was first struck in 1934 to commemorate the 200th anniversary of the birth of Daniel Boone, famous frontiersman, trapper, and explorer. Coinage covered several years, similar to the schedule for the Texas issues; 1934 coins are the only examples with true bicentennial status.

Designs. *Obverse:* Artist's conception of Daniel Boone in a profile portrait. *Reverse:* Standing figures of Boone and Blackfish, war chief of the Chillicothe band of the Shawnee tribe. (In 1935 the date 1934 was added to the reverse design.)

Mintage and Melting Data. Authorized on May 26, 1934 and, with "1934" added to modify the design, on August 26, 1935. *Maximum authorized*—600,000 (for the entire series from 1934 onward). *Number minted*—1934: 10,007 (including 7 assay coins); 1935-P: 10,010 (including 10 assay coins); 1935-D: 5,005 (including 5 assay coins); 1935-S: 5,005 (including 5 assay coins); 1935-P, "Small 1934": 10,008 (including 8 assay coins); 1935-D, "Small 1934": 2,003; 1935-S, "Small 1934": 2,004; 1936-P: 12,012 (including 12 assay coins); 1936-D: 5,005 (including 5 assay coins); 1936-S: 5,006 (including 6 assay coins); 1937-P: 15,010 (including 10 assay coins); 1937-D: 7,506 (including 6 assay coins); 1937-S: 5,006 (including 6 assay coins); 1938-P: 5,005 (including 5 assay coins); 1938-D: 5,005 (including 5 assay coins); 1938-S: 5,006 (including 6 assay coins). *Number melted*—1937-P: 5,200; 1937-D: 5,000; 1937-S: 2,500; 1938-P: 2,905; 1938-D: 2,905; 1938-S: 2,906. *Net distribution*—1934: 10,007; 1935-P: 10,010; 1935-D: 5,005; 1935-S: 5,005; 1935-P, "Small 1934": 10,008 (including 8 assay coins); 1935-D, "Small 1934": 2,003; 1935-S, "Small 1934": 2,004; 1936-P: 12,012; 1936-D: 5,005; 1936-S: 5,006; 1937-P: 9,810; 1937-D: 2,506; 1937-S: 2,506; 1938-P: 2,100; 1938-D: 2,100; 1938-S: 2,100.

Original Cost and Issuer. Sale prices varied by mintmark, from a low of $1.10 per 1935-P coin to a high of $5.15 per 1937-S coin. Issued by Daniel Boone Bicentennial Commission (and its division, the Pioneer National Monument Association), Phoenix Hotel, Lexington, Kentucky (C. Frank Dunn, "sole distributor").

Key to Collecting. Most collectors desire just a single coin to represent the type, but there are enough specialists who want one of each date and mintmark to ensure a ready market whenever the scarcer sets come up for sale. Most surviving coins are in MS, with MS-64 to 66 pieces readily available for most issues. Early issues in the series are characterized by deep frosty mint luster, whereas issues toward the end of the run, particularly 1937 and 1938, often are seen with a satin finish and relatively little luster (because of the methods of die preparation and striking). The 1937-S is very often seen with prooflike surfaces, and the 1938-S occasionally so. In general, the Boone commemoratives were handled carefully at the time of minting and distribution, but scattered contact marks are often visible.

First Points of Wear. *Obverse:* The hair behind Boone's ear. *Reverse:* The left shoulder of the Indian.

	Distribution	Cert	Avg	%MS	AU-50	MS-60	MS-62	MS-63	MS-64	MS-65	MS-66
1934	10,007	1,020	64.8	100%	$130	$135	$140	$150	$165	$270	$385
	Auctions: $558, MS-67, November 2014; $764, MS-67, August 2014; $210, MS-66, December 2014; $282, MS-66, October 2014										
1935	10,010	1,151	64.7	100%	$130	$135	$140	$150	$175	$280	$460
	Auctions: $646, MS-67, October 2014; $793, MS-67, August 2014; $3,055, MS-67, January 2014; $206, MS-66, November 2014										
1935D	5,005	654	64.6	100%	$130	$135	$140	$150	$175	$280	$460
	Auctions: $2,056, MS-67, November 2014; $3,290, MS-67, November 2013; $259, MS-66, November 2014; $282, MS-66, August 2014										
1935S	5,005	825	65.0	100%	$130	$135	$140	$150	$175	$280	$460
	Auctions: $881, MS-67, October 2014; $1,234, MS-67, August 2014; $2,585, MS-67, April 2013; $212, MS-66, November 2014										
Set of 1935 P-D-S					$405	$420	$450	$465	$865	$1,550	
	Auctions: $380, MS-64/64/64, December 2011										
1935, With Small 1934	10,008	1,288	64.9	100%	$130	$140	$145	$155	$175	$285	$410
	Auctions: $1,998, MS-67+, September 2014; $676, MS-67, September 2014; $499, MS-67, August 2014; $294, MS-66, November 2014										
1935D, Same type	2,003	492	65.2	100%	$130	$140	$145	$155	$175	$285	$410
	Auctions: $1,058, MS-67, August 2014; $1,528, MS-66, November 2014; $558, MS-66, September 2014; $317, MS-65, October 2014										
1935S, Same type	2,004	498	64.8	100%	$130	$140	$145	$155	$175	$285	$410
	Auctions: $3,819, MS-67+, September 2014; $1,293, MS-67, August 2014; $7,050, MS-67, January 2014; $646, MS-65, October 2014										
Set of 1935 P-D-S, With Added Date					$900	$955	$1,000	$1,125	$2,025	$3,625	
	Auctions: $925, MS-65/63/64, May 2012										
1936	12,012	1,464	64.8	100%	$130	$135	$140	$150	$175	$285	$385
	Auctions: $25,850, MS-68, April 2013; $364, MS-67, October 2014; $646, MS-67, August 2014; $212, MS-66, November 2014										
1936D	5,005	843	65.0	100%	$130	$135	$140	$150	$175	$285	$385
	Auctions: $940, MS-67, November 2014; $764, MS-67, August 2014; $341, MS-66, December 2014; $200, MS-66, November 2014										
1936S	5,006	888	65.1	100%	$130	$135	$140	$150	$175	$285	$385
	Auctions: $4,553, MS-68, November 2013; $764, MS-67, August 2014; $259, MS-66, August 2014; $170, MS-65, November 2014										
Set of 1936 P-D-S					$405	$420	$450	$465	$865	$1,390	
	Auctions: $920, MS-66/66/66 Plus, November 2011										

	Distribution	Cert	Avg	%MS	AU-50	MS-60	MS-62	MS-63	MS-64	MS-65	MS-66
1937	9,810	1,355	64.9	100%	$130	$135	$140	$150	$175	$285	$385
	Auctions: $9,106, MS-68, October 2014; $499, MS-67, August 2014; $3,290, MS-67, November 2013; $264, MS-66, December 2014										
1937D	2,506	551	64.9	100%	$130	$135	$140	$150	$175	$285	$385
	Auctions: $1,586, MS-67, October 2014; $940, MS-67, October 2014; $3,290, MS-67, March 2013; $435, MS-66, November 2014										
1937S	2,506	675	65.0	100%	$130	$135	$140	$150	$175	$285	$385
	Auctions: $881, MS-67, August 2014; $441, MS-66, November 2014; $764, MS-66, July 2014; $1,175, MS-66, February 2013										
Set of 1937 P-D-S						$875	$895	$930	$990	$1,325	$1,825
	Auctions: $564, MS-66/65/64, November 2011										
1938	2,100	453	64.8	100%	$130	$140	$145	$155	$175	$285	$410
	Auctions: $9,635, MS-67, August 2013; $282, MS-65, September 2014; $247, MS-63, November 2014										
1938D	2,100	482	65.0	100%	$130	$140	$145	$155	$175	$285	$410
	Auctions: $999, MS-67, September 2014; $1,645, MS-67, August 2014; $764, MS-67, August 2014; $176, MS-60, November 2014										
1938S	2,100	485	64.9	100%	$130	$140	$145	$155	$175	$285	$410
	Auctions: $2,115, MS-67, November 2014; $823, MS-67, August 2014; $1,410, MS-67, April 2013; $247, MS-62, November 2014										
Set of 1938 P-D-S						$1,065	$1,150	$1,200	$1,250	$1,640	$3,025
	Auctions: $4,312, MS-66/66/65, September 2011										

CONNECTICUT TERCENTENARY HALF DOLLAR (1935)

Designer: *Henry Kreiss.* **Weight:** *12.50 grams.* **Composition:** *.900 silver, .100 copper (net weight .3617 oz. pure silver).* **Diameter:** *30.6 mm.* **Edge:** *Reeded.* **Mint:** *Philadelphia.*

In commemoration of the 300th anniversary of the founding of the colony of Connecticut, a souvenir half dollar was struck. According to legend, the Royal Charter of the colony was secreted in the Charter Tree (seen on the coin's reverse) during the reign of King James II, who wished to revoke it. The charter was produced after the king's overthrow in 1688, and the colony continued under its protection.

Designs. *Obverse:* A modernistic eagle, standing. *Reverse:* The Charter Oak.

Mintage Data. Authorized on June 21, 1934. *Maximum authorized—25,000. Number minted—25,018* (including 18 assay coins). *Net distribution—25,018.*

Original Cost and Issuer. Sale price $1. Issued by the Connecticut Tercentenary Commission.

Key to Collecting. Most examples survive in upper AU and lower MS grades. Higher-grade coins such as MS-65 are elusive. Friction and/or marks are often obvious on the broad expanse of wing on the obverse, and, in particular, at the ground or baseline of the oak tree on the reverse. Examples that are otherwise lustrous, frosty, and very attractive, often have friction on the wing.

First Points of Wear. *Obverse:* The top of the eagle's wing. *Reverse:* The ground above ON and TI in CONNECTICUT.

	Distribution	Cert	Avg	%MS	AU-50	MS-60	MS-62	MS-63	MS-64	MS-65	MS-66
									PF-63	PF-64	PF-65
1935	25,018	3,459	64.5	99%	$260	$280	$295	$310	$325	$475	$700
	Auctions: $1,116, MS-67, September 2014; $1,293, MS-67, July 2014; $7,638, MS-67, February 2014; $458, MS-66, November 2014										
1935, Matte Proof	*1–2*	1	65.0								
	Auctions: No auction records available.										

Arkansas Centennial Half Dollar (1935–1939)

Designer: *Edward E. Burr.* **Weight:** *12.50 grams.*
Composition: *.900 silver, .100 copper (net weight .3617 oz. pure silver).*
Diameter: *30.6 mm.* **Edge:** *Reeded.* **Mints:** *Philadelphia, Denver, San Francisco.*

This souvenir issue marked the 100th anniversary of the admission of Arkansas into the Union. The 1936 through 1939 issues were the same as those of 1935 except for the dates. The coin's four-year lifespan was intended to maximize profits, and sluggish sales contributed to the crash of the commemorative market and subsequent suspension of commemorative coinage in 1939.

Designs. *Obverse:* An eagle with outstretched wings, stars, and other elements of the Arkansas state seal. *Reverse:* Portraits of a Liberty in a Phrygian cap and an Indian chief of 1836.

Mintage and Melting Data. Authorized on May 14, 1934. *Maximum authorized*—500,000 (for the entire series from 1935 onward). *Number minted* (including 5, 5, and 6 assay coins)—1935-P: 13,012 (including 5 assay coins); 1935-D: 5,505 (including 5 assay coins); 1935-S: 5,506 (including 6 assay coins); 1936-P: 10,010 (including 10 assay coins); 1936-D: 10,010 (including 10 assay coins); 1936-S: 10,012 (including 12 assay coins); 1937-P: 5,505 (including 5 assay coins); 1937-D: 5,505 (including 5 assay coins); 1937-S: 5,506 (including 6 assay coins); 1938-P: 6,006 (including 6 assay coins); 1938-D: 6,005 (including 5 assay coins); 1938-S: 6,006 (including 6 assay coins); 1939-P: 2,140 (including 4 assay coins); 1939-D: 2,104 (including 4 assay coins); 1939-S: 2,105 (including 5 assay coins). *Number melted*—1936-P: 350; 1936-D: 350; 1936-S: 350; 1938-P: 2,850; 1938-D: 2,850; 1938-S: 2,850. *Net distribution*—1935-P: 13,012; 1935-D: 5,505; 1935-S: 5,506; 1936-P: 9,660; 1936-D: 9,660; 1936-S: 9,662; 1937-P: 5,505; 1937-D: 5,505; 1937-S: 5,506; 1938-P: 3,156; 1938-D: 3,155; 1938-S: 3,156; 1939-P: 2,104; 1939-D: 2,104; 1939-S: 2,105.

Original Cost and Issuer. Sale prices varied by mintmark, from a low of $1 per coin to $12 for a set of three. Issued by the Arkansas Centennial Commission in 1935, 1936, 1938, and 1939 (note that dealer B. Max Mehl bought quantities and retailed them at higher prices in 1935). Issued by Stack's of New York City in 1937.

Key to Collecting. The coin sets were produced with a satiny, almost "greasy" finish; even freshly minted coins appeared as if they had been dipped or repeatedly cleaned. Issues of 1937 to 1939 are usually more satisfactory but still are not deeply lustrous. The prominence of the girl's portrait on the center of the obverse renders that part of the coin prone to receiving bagmarks, scuffs, and other evidence of handling. As a result, relatively few pieces have great eye appeal. The obverse area where the ribbon crosses the eagle's breast is often very weak. Some examples are lightly struck on the eagle just behind its head.

First Points of Wear. *Obverse:* The eagle's head and the top of the left wing. *Reverse:* The band of the girl's cap, behind her eye.

	Distribution	Cert	Avg	%MS	AU-50	MS-60	MS-62	MS-63	MS-64 / PF-63	MS-65 / PF-64	MS-66 / PF-65
1935	13,012	1,137	64.4	100%	$100	$105	$110	$115	$125	$175	$350
Auctions: $1,116, MS-67, September 2014; $1,528, MS-67 Plus, July 2014; $400, MS-66, December 2014; $558, MS-66, October 2014											
1935D	5,505	836	64.7	100%	$100	$105	$110	$115	$125	$175	$350
Auctions: $1,175, MS-67, October 2014; $1,528, MS-67, August 2014											
1935S	5,506	834	64.6	100%	$100	$105	$110	$115	$130	$200	$375
Auctions: $1,293, MS-67, October 2014; $940, MS-67, August 2014; $435, MS-66, November 2014; $37,600, MS-64, November 2013											
Set of 1935 P-D-S					$300	$315	$330	$345	$390	$600	$1,200
Auctions: $322, MS-64/64/64 Plus, April 2012											
1936	9,660	965	64.3	100%	$100	$105	$110	$115	$125	$175	$350
Auctions: $3,055, MS-67, November 2014; $4,994, MS-67, June 2013; $764, MS-66, November 2014; $382, MS-66, October 2014											
1936D	9,660	935	64.4	100%	$100	$105	$110	$115	$125	$175	$350
Auctions: $1,351, MS-67, November 2014; $1,704, MS-67, September 2014; $4,406, MS-67, February 2014; $353, MS-66, November 2014											
1936S	9,662	956	64.4	100%	$100	$105	$110	$115	$130	$200	$375
Auctions: $4,406, MS-67, March 2014; $881, MS-66+, September 2014; $411, MS-66, November 2014; $282, MS-66, November 2014											
Set of 1936 P-D-S					$300	$315	$330	$345	$390	$600	$1,200
Auctions: $300, MS-64/64/65, December 2011											
1937	5,505	731	64.3	100%	$100	$105	$110	$115	$130	$200	$350
Auctions: $3,525, MS-67, January 2014; $353, MS-66, November 2014; $329, MS-66, August 2014; $118, MS-64, October 2014											
1937D	5,505	785	64.5	100%	$100	$105	$110	$115	$130	$200	$350
Auctions: $4,700, MS-67+, October 2014; $1,763, MS-67, November 2014; $4,113, MS-67, January 2014; $470, MS-66, November 2014											
1937S	5,506	643	64.2	100%	$100	$105	$110	$115	$130	$200	$350
Auctions: $7,050, MS-67, October 2014; $940, MS-66, October 2014; $3,525, MS-66, April 2014; $646, MS-65, December 2014											
Set of 1937 P-D-S					$300	$315	$330	$345	$390	$700	$1,200
Auctions: $600, MS-65/65/65, January 2012											
1938	3,156	520	64.3	100%	$125	$145	$150	$155	$190	$250	$850
Auctions: $4,994, MS-67, November 2014; $999, MS-66, August 2014; $9,400, MS-66, November 2013; $329, MS-65, November 2014											
1938D	3,155	551	64.4	100%	$125	$145	$150	$155	$190	$425	$950
Auctions: $2,820, MS-67, November 2014; $529, MS-66, October 2014; $1,058, MS-66, August 2014; $394, MS-65, September 2014											
1938S	3,156	498	64.3	100%	$125	$145	$150	$155	$190	$400	$650
Auctions: $1,645, MS-66+, October 2014; $940, MS-66, November 2014; $1,175, MS-66, July 2014; $529, MS-65, November 2014											
Set of 1938 P-D-S					$400	$450	$475	$485	$600	$1,200	$2,750
Auctions: $2,900, MS-66/66/66, April 2012											
Set of 1938 P-D-S, Matte Proof	1–2										
Auctions: No auction records available.											
1939	2,104	430	64.2	100%	$300	$350	$375	$385	$400	$700	$3,000
Auctions: $2,961, MS-66, September 2014; $3,055, MS-66, December 2013; $705, MS-65, August 2014; $940, MS-65, July 2014											
1939D	2,104	451	64.4	100%	$300	$350	$375	$385	$400	$700	$1,000
Auctions: $4,994, MS-67, October 2014; $4,700, MS-66, September 2013; $999, MS-66, October 2014; $646, MS-65, August 2014											
1939S	2,105	489	64.5	100%	$300	$350	$375	$385	$400	$600	$1,100
Auctions: $2,820, MS-67, November 2014; $3,290, MS-67, October 2014; $7,050, MS-67, June 2013; $1,175, MS-66, November 2014											
Set of 1939 P-D-S					$900	$1,100	$1,150	$1,200	$1,300	$2,200	$5,500
Auctions: $1,610, MS-65/65/65, February 2012											

ARKANSAS CENTENNIAL—ROBINSON HALF DOLLAR (1936)

Designers: *Henry Kreiss (obverse) and Edward E. Burr (reverse).* **Weight:** *12.50 grams (net weight .3617 oz. pure silver).* **Composition:** *.900 silver, .100 copper.* **Diameter:** *30.6 mm.* **Edge:** *Reeded.* **Mints:** *Philadelphia, Denver, San Francisco.*

A new reverse design for the Arkansas Centennial coin (see preceding coin) was authorized by the Act of June 26, 1936. Senator Joseph T. Robinson was still living at the time his portrait was used. Note that though it is normally true that portraits appear on the obverse of coins, the side bearing Robinson's likeness is indeed technically the reverse of this coin.

Designs. *Obverse:* An eagle with outstretched wings, stars, and other elements of the Arkansas state seal. *Reverse:* Bareheaded profile portrait of Senator Joseph T. Robinson.

Mintage Data. Authorized on June 26, 1936. *Maximum authorized*—50,000 (minimum 25,000). *Number minted*—25,265 (including 15 assay coins). *Net distribution*—25,265.

Original Cost and Issuer. Sale price $1.85. Issued by Stack's of New York City.

Key to Collecting. Most known coins are in MS, as most or all were originally sold to collectors and coin dealers. Examples are plentiful in the marketplace, usually grading MS-62 to 64. The coins were not handled with care during production, so many have contact marks on Robinson's portrait and elsewhere. Some examples are lightly struck on the eagle, just behind the head.

First Points of Wear. *Obverse:* The eagle's head and the top of the left wing. *Reverse:* Robinson's cheekbone.

	Distribution	Cert	Avg	%MS	AU-50	MS-60	MS-62	MS-63	MS-64	MS-65	MS-66
1936	25,265	2,637	64.3	100%	$140	$160	$170	$190	$215	$300	$500
	Auctions: $1,116, MS-67, November 2014; $2,233, MS-67, April 2014; $270, MS-66, November 2014; $499, MS-66, July 2014										

HUDSON, NEW YORK, SESQUICENTENNIAL HALF DOLLAR (1935)

Designer: *Chester Beach.* **Weight:** *12.50 grams.* **Composition:** *.900 silver, .100 copper (net weight .3617 oz. pure silver).* **Diameter:** *30.6 mm.* **Edge:** *Reeded.* **Mint:** *Philadelphia.*

This souvenir half dollar marked the 150th anniversary of the founding of Hudson, New York, which was named after the explorer Henry Hudson. The area was actually settled in 1662, but not given its permanent name and formally incorporated until 1785. The distribution of these coins was widely criticized, as certain dealers were allowed to purchase large quantities at $1 or less and then resold them at dramatically inflated prices.

Designs. *Obverse:* The ship *Half Moon*, captained by Henry Hudson, in full sail. *Reverse:* The ocean god Neptune seated backward on a whale (derived from the seal of the city of Hudson); in the background, a mermaid blowing a shell.

Mintage Data. Approved May 2, 1935. *Maximum authorized*—10,000. *Number minted*—10,008 (including 8 assay coins). *Net distribution*—10,008.

Original Cost and Issuer. Sale price $1. Issued by the Hudson Sesquicentennial Committee, through the First National Bank & Trust Company of Hudson.

Key to Collecting. Examples are readily available in the marketplace. Note that deep or artificial toning, which can make close inspection impossible, has led some certified coins to certified grades that are higher than they should be. True gems are very rare. These coins were struck at high speed and with little care to preserve their quality; by the time they were originally distributed most pieces showed nicks, contact marks, and other evidence of handling. Most are lustrous and frosty (except on the central devices), and grade in the lower MS levels. MS-62 to 64 are typical. Carefully graded MS-65 coins are scarce, and anything higher is very rare.

First Points of Wear. *Obverse:* The center of the lower middle sail. *Reverse:* The motto on the ribbon, and the figure of Neptune (both of which may also be lightly struck).

	Distribution	Cert	Avg	%MS	AU-50	MS-60	MS-62	MS-63	MS-64	MS-65	MS-66
1935	10,008	1,959	64.0	98%	$750	$825	$900	$1,000	$1,050	$1,400	$2,100

Auctions: $6,463, MS-67, September 2014; $15,275, MS-67, November 2013; $1,175, MS-66, November 2014; $576, AU-58, November 2014

CALIFORNIA PACIFIC INTERNATIONAL EXPOSITION HALF DOLLAR (1935–1936)

Designer: *Robert Aitken.* **Weight:** *12.50 grams.* **Composition:** *.900 silver, .100 copper (net weight .3617 oz. pure silver).* **Diameter:** *30.6 mm.* **Edge:** *Reeded.* **Mints:** *San Francisco, Denver.*

Congress approved the coinage of souvenir half dollars for the California Pacific International Exposition on May 3, 1935. The event—held in San Diego's Balboa Park—was attended by only 4 million people, and interest in the coin was not particularly strong.

Designs. *Obverse:* Minerva seated, holding a spear and shield, with a grizzly bear to her right (from California's state seal). *Reverse:* The Chapel of St. Francis and the California Tower, at the California Pacific International Exposition in San Diego.

Mintage and Melting Data. Originally authorized on May 3, 1935; 1936-D issues authorized on May 6, 1936 (for recoinage of melted 1935-S issues). *Maximum authorized*—1935-S: 250,000; 1936-D: 180,000. *Number minted*—1935-S: 250,132 (including 132 assay coins); 1936-D: 180,092 (including 92 assay coins). *Number melted*—1935-S: 180,000; 1936-D: 150,000. *Net distribution*—1935-S: 70,132; 1936-D: 30,092.

Original Cost and Issuer. Sale prices $1 (1935-S; increased to $3 in 1937; dropped to $2 in 1938) and $1.50 (1936-D; increased to $3 in 1937; reduced to $1 in 1938). Issued by the California Pacific International Exposition Company.

Key to Collecting. Both the 1935-S and 1936-D issues were coined with deeply frosty and lustrous surfaces. The eye appeal usually is excellent. The design made these coins susceptible to bagmarks, and most survivors, even in higher MS grades, show evidence of handling. Minerva, in particular, usually displays some graininess or contact marks, even on coins given high numerical grades. Most coins are deeply lustrous and frosty. On the 1935 San Francisco coins the S mintmark usually is flat, and on the Denver coins the California Tower is often lightly struck at the top.

First Points of Wear. *Obverse:* The bosom and knees of Minerva. *Reverse:* The top right edge of the tower. (The 1936-D was flatly struck in this area; examine the texture of the surface to determine if actual wear exists.)

	Distribution	Cert	Avg	%MS	AU-50	MS-60	MS-62	MS-63	MS-64	MS-65	MS-66
1935S	70,132	4,642	64.9	100%	$105	$110	$115	$120	$125	$140	$200
	Auctions: $2,233, MS-67+, September 2014; $3,525, MS-67, November 2014; $4,994, MS-67, January 2014; $646, MS-67, October 2014										
1936D	30,092	2,714	64.9	100%	$110	$125	$130	$135	$150	$160	$220
	Auctions: $1,410, MS-67, November 2014; $764, MS-67, October 2014; $4,113, MS-67, August 2013; $235, MS-66, November 2014										

OLD SPANISH TRAIL HALF DOLLAR (1935)

Designer: *L.W. Hoffecker.* **Weight:** *12.50 grams.* **Composition:** *.900 silver, .100 copper (net weight .3617 oz. pure silver).* **Diameter:** *30.6 mm.* **Edge:** *Reeded.* **Mint:** *Philadelphia.*

This coin commemorated the 400th anniversary of the overland trek of the Alvar Nuñez Cabeza de Vaca Expedition through the Gulf states in 1535. The coin's designer and distributor, L.W. Hoffecker, is known to have had his hands in many of this era's commemoratives (and the exploitative practices surrounding them).

Designs. *Obverse:* The head of a steer, inspired by the explorer's last name: Cabeza de Vaca translates to "head of cow." *Reverse:* A map of the Southeastern states and a yucca tree.

Mintage Data. Authorized on June 5, 1935. *Maximum authorized*—10,000. *Number minted*—10,008.

Original Cost and Issuer. Sale price $2. Issued by L.W. Hoffecker, trading as the El Paso Museum Coin Committee.

Key to Collecting. These coins were handled with care during their production and shipping—still, most show scattered contact marks. The typical grade is MS-65 and higher. The fields are usually somewhat satiny and gray, not deeply lustrous and frosty.

First Points of Wear. *Obverse:* The top of the cow's head. *Reverse:* The lettering at the top.

	Distribution	Cert	Avg	%MS	AU-50	MS-60	MS-62	MS-63	MS-64	MS-65	MS-66
1935	10,008	1,812	65.0	100%	$1,200	$1,250	$1,275	$1,300	$1,325	$1,500	$1,800
	Auctions: $2,350, MS-67, November 2014; $1,939, MS-67, November 2014; $5,288, MS-67, February 2013; $1,293, MS-66, November 2014										

PROVIDENCE, RHODE ISLAND, TERCENTENARY HALF DOLLAR (1936)

Designers: *Arthur G. Carey and John H. Benson.* **Weight:** *12.50 grams.*
Composition: *.900 silver, .100 copper (net weight .3617 oz. pure silver).*
Diameter: *30.6 mm.* **Edge:** *Reeded.* **Mints:** *Philadelphia, Denver, San Francisco.*

The 300th anniversary of Roger Williams's founding of Providence was the occasion for this special half dollar in 1936. Interestingly, no mention of Providence is to be found on the coin. The distribution of this coin, like that of many other commemoratives of the 1930s, was wrapped in controversy—phony news releases reported that the coin was sold out when it was indeed not, and certain dealers procured large amounts at low prices only to resell for tidy profits.

Designs. *Obverse:* Roger Williams, the founder of Rhode Island, being welcomed by an Indian. *Reverse:* Elements from the Rhode Island state seal, including the anchor of Hope and a shield.

Mintage Data. Authorized on May 2, 1935. *Maximum authorized*—50,000. *Number minted*—1936-P: 20,013 (including 13 assay coins); 1936-D: 15,010 (including 10 assay coins); 1936-S: 15,011 (including 11 assay coins). *Net distribution*—1936-P: 20,013; 1936-D: 15,010; 1936-S: 15,011.

Original Cost and Issuer. Sale price $1. Issued by the Rhode Island and Providence Plantations Tercentenary Committee, Inc.

Key to Collecting. These coins are readily available singly and in sets, with typical grades being MS-63 to 65. Contact marks are common. Higher-level coins, such as MS-66 and 67, are not hard to find, but are elusive in comparison to the lesser-condition pieces. The 1936 (in particular) and 1936-S are sometimes found with prooflike surfaces. Most specimens have a combination of satiny/frosty surface. Many are light gray in color.

First Points of Wear. *Obverse:* The prow of the canoe, and the Indian's right shoulder. *Reverse:* The center of the anchor, and surrounding areas.

	Distribution	Cert	Avg	%MS	AU-50	MS-60	MS-62	MS-63	MS-64	MS-65	MS-66
1936	20,013	2,367	64.7	100%	$100	$110	$115	$120	$130	$175	$250
Auctions: $1,058, MS-67, November 2014; $646, MS-67, November 2014; $1,880, MS-67, April 2013; $159, MS-66, December 2014											
1936D	15,010	1,766	64.7	100%	$100	$110	$115	$120	$130	$175	$250
Auctions: $1,528, MS-67, November 2014; $558, MS-67, November 2014; $1,116, MS-67, October 2014; $270, MS-66, August 2014											
1936S	15,011	1,499	64.6	100%	$100	$110	$115	$120	$130	$175	$250
Auctions: $6,463, MS-67, November 2014; $1,645, MS-67, September 2013; $259, MS-66+, August 2014; $329, MS-66, December 2014											
Set of 1936 P-D-S						$330	$345	$375	$400	$600	$800
Auctions: $2,185, MS-66/66/66, January 2012											

CLEVELAND CENTENNIAL / GREAT LAKES EXPOSITION HALF DOLLAR (1936)

Designer: *Brenda Putnam.* **Weight:** *12.50 grams.* **Composition:** *.900 silver, .100 copper (net weight .3617 oz. pure silver).* **Diameter:** *30.6 mm.* **Edge:** *Reeded.* **Mint:** *Philadelphia.*

A special coinage of fifty-cent pieces was authorized in commemoration of the centennial celebration of Cleveland, Ohio, on the occasion of the Great Lakes Exposition held there in 1936. Numismatic entrepreneur Thomas G. Melish was behind the coins' production and distribution—though he served as the Cleveland Centennial Commemorative Coin Association's treasurer while based in Cincinnati.

Designs. *Obverse:* Bewigged profile portrait of Moses Cleaveland. *Reverse:* A map of the Great Lakes region with nine stars marking various cities, and a compass point at the city of Cleveland.

Mintage Data. Authorized on May 5, 1936. *Maximum authorized*—50,000 (minimum 25,000). *Number minted*—50,030 (including 30 assay coins). *Net distribution*—50,030.

Original Cost and Issuer. Sale prices: one coin for $1.65; two for $1.60 each; three for $1.58 each; five for $1.56 each; ten for $1.55 each; twenty for $1.54 each; fifty for $1.53 each; one hundred for $1.52 each. Issued by the Cleveland Centennial Commemorative Coin Association (Thomas G. Melish, Cincinnati).

Key to Collecting. The Cleveland half dollar is the most readily available issue from 1936—a bumper-crop year for U.S. commemoratives. Nearly all coins are in Mint State, typically from MS-63 to 65, and most are very lustrous and frosty. This issue was not handled with care at the Mint, and scattered contact marks are typically found on both obverse and reverse.

First Points of Wear. *Obverse:* The hair behind Cleaveland's ear. *Reverse:* The top of the compass, and the land (non-lake) areas of the map.

	Distribution	Cert	Avg	%MS	AU-50	MS-60	MS-62	MS-63	MS-64	MS-65	MS-66
1936	50,030	4,738	64.5	100%	$110	$115	$120	$125	$130	$170	$260

Auctions: $705, MS-67, November 2014; $676, MS-67, August 2014; $4,700, MS-67, February 2014; $235, MS-66, December 2014

WISCONSIN TERRITORIAL CENTENNIAL HALF DOLLAR (1936)

Designer: *David Parsons.* **Weight:** *12.50 grams.* **Composition:** *.900 silver, .100 copper (net weight .3617 oz. pure silver).* **Diameter:** *30.6 mm.* **Edge:** *Reeded.* **Mint:** *Philadelphia.*

The 100th anniversary of the Wisconsin territorial government was the occasion for this issue. Benjamin Hawkins, a New York artist, made changes to the original designs by University of Wisconsin student David Parsons so that the piece conformed to technical requirements.

Designs. *Obverse:* A badger on a log, from the state emblem; and arrows representing the Black Hawk War of the 1830s. *Reverse:* A miner's arm holding a pickaxe over a mound of lead ore, derived from Wisconsin's territorial seal.

Mintage Data. Authorized on May 15, 1936. *Minimum authorized*—25,000 (unlimited maximum). *Number minted*—25,015 (including 15 assay coins). *Net distribution*—25,015.

Original Cost and Issuer. Sale price $1.50 plus 7¢ postage for the first coin, 2¢ postage for each additional coin (later sold for $1.25 each in lots of 10 coins, and still later sold for $3 per coin). Issued by the Wisconsin Centennial Coin Committee (also known as the Coinage Committee of the Wisconsin Centennial Commission). Unsold remainders were distributed, into the 1950s, by the State Historical Society.

Key to Collecting. Examples are readily available in the marketplace. Most grade MS-62 to 64—although higher grades are not rare—and are very lustrous and frosty, except for the higher areas of the design (which often have a slightly polished appearance).

First Points of Wear. *Obverse:* The flank and shoulder of the badger. *Reverse:* The miner's hand.

	Distribution	Cert	Avg	%MS	AU-50	MS-60	MS-62	MS-63	MS-64	MS-65	MS-66
1936	25,015	3,848	65.3	100%	$215	$230	$240	$245	$250	$260	$300

Auctions: $1,674, MS-68, November 2014; $4,113, MS-68, July 2014; $940, MS-67+, July 2014; $382, MS-67, November 2014

CINCINNATI MUSIC CENTER HALF DOLLAR (1936)

Designer: *Constance Ortmayer.* **Weight:** *12.50 grams.*
Composition: *.900 silver, .100 copper (net weight .3617 oz. pure silver).*
Diameter: *30.6 mm.* **Edge:** *Reeded.* **Mints:** *Philadelphia, Denver, San Francisco.*

Although the head of Stephen Foster, "America's Troubadour," dominates the obverse of this special issue, the anniversary celebrated bears little to no relation to him. Foster did live in Cincinnati for a time, but never worked in music while there. The coins were supposedly struck to commemorate the 50th anniversary in 1936 of Cincinnati as a center of music, but the issue was really a personal project of numismatist Thomas G. Melish.

Designs. *Obverse:* Bareheaded profile portrait of Stephen Foster, "America's Troubadour." *Reverse:* A woman playing a lyre, personifying Music.

Mintage Data. Authorized on March 31, 1936. *Maximum authorized*—15,000. *Number minted*—1936-P: 5,005 (including 5 assay coins); 1936-D: 5,005 (including 5 assay coins); 1936-S: 5,006 (including 6 assay coins). *Net distribution*—1936-P: 5,005; 1936-D: 5,005; 1936-S: 5,006.

Original Cost and Issuer. Sale price $7.75 per set of three (actually $7.50 plus 25¢ for the display container with cellophane slide front). Issued by the Cincinnati Musical Center Commemorative Coin Association, Ohio (Thomas G. Melish).

Key to Collecting. Nearly all sets of these coins were bought by collectors and investors, thus most still exist in Mint State, primarily MS-63 to 65. Conservatively graded MS-65 and finer pieces are rare. Most coins were carelessly handled at the mints, and nearly all show scattered contact marks. This issue has a somewhat satiny or "greasy" surface, instead of fields with deep luster and frost. Denver Mint coins are typically found in slightly higher grades than their Philadelphia and San Francisco Mint companions.

First Points of Wear. *Obverse:* The hair at Foster's temple. *Reverse:* The left breast, and the skirt, of the female figure.

	Distribution	Cert	Avg	%MS	AU-50	MS-60	MS-62	MS-63	MS-64	MS-65	MS-66
1936	5,005	842	64.4	100%	$285	$300	$310	$325	$380	$500	$900
	Auctions: $7,050, MS-67, October 2014; $7,931, MS-67, February 2014; $499, MS-66, August 2014; $411, MS-65, November 2014										
1936D	5,005	1,219	64.9	100%	$285	$300	$310	$325	$380	$500	$900
	Auctions: $3,525, MS-67+, August 2014; $1,116, MS-67, November 2014; $1,645, MS-67, August 2014; $4,259, MS-67, June 2013										
1936S	5,006	869	64.1	100%	$285	$300	$310	$325	$380	$500	$900
	Auctions: $14,100, MS-67, January 2014; $823, MS-66, October 2014; $764, MS-66, August 2014; $270, AU-58, October 2014										
Set of 1935 P-D-S					$875	$900	$950	$975	$1,200	$1,500	$2,700
	Auctions: $4,198, MS-66/66/66, February 2012										

Long Island Tercentenary Half Dollar (1936)

Designer: *Howard K. Weinman.* **Weight:** *12.50 grams.* **Composition:** *.900 silver, .100 copper (net weight .3617 oz. pure silver).* **Diameter:** *30.6 mm.* **Edge:** *Reeded.* **Mint:** *Philadelphia.*

This souvenir issue was authorized to commemorate the 300th anniversary of the first white settlement on Long Island, which was made at Jamaica Bay by Dutch colonists. This was the first issue for which a date was specified (1936) irrespective of the year minted or issued, as a safeguard against extending the coinage over a period of years. This measure proved effective in preventing many of the profiteering problems that arose with other commemorative issues of the era.

Designs. *Obverse:* Conjoined profile portraits of a Dutch settler and an Algonquin Indian. *Reverse:* A Dutch vessel with full-blown sails.

Mintage and Melting Data. Authorized on April 13, 1936. *Maximum authorized—100,000. Number minted—100,053 (including 53 assay coins). Number melted—18,227. Net distribution—81,826.*

Original Cost and Issuer. Sale price $1. Issued by the Long Island Tercentenary Committee, through various banks and other outlets.

Key to Collecting. These are among the most plentiful survivors from the commemorative issues of the 1930s, and examples grading MS-64 to 66 are readily obtainable. The coins were minted and handled carelessly, and at the time of distribution most showed nicks, bagmarks, and other evidence of contact; these grade from AU-50 to MS-60. Most coins have, as struck, a satiny or slightly "greasy" luster and are not deeply frosty.

First Points of Wear. *Obverse:* The hair and the cheekbone of the Dutch settler. *Reverse:* The center of the lower middle sail.

	Distribution	Cert	Avg	%MS	AU-50	MS-60	MS-62	MS-63	MS-64	MS-65	MS-66
1936	81,826	4,377	64.2	99%	$85	$100	$110	$115	$120	$200	$550
	Auctions: $1,939, MS-67, November 2014; $32,900, MS-67, April 2013; $764, MS-66+, July 2014; $1,586, MS-66, August 2014										

YORK COUNTY, MAINE, TERCENTENARY HALF DOLLAR (1936)

Designer: *Walter H. Rich.* **Weight:** *12.50 grams.* **Composition:** *.900 silver, .100 copper (net weight .3617 oz. pure silver).* **Diameter:** *30.6 mm.* **Edge:** *Reeded.* **Mint:** *Philadelphia.*

A souvenir half dollar was authorized by Congress upon the 300th anniversary of the founding of York County, Maine. While the commemorated event was considered somewhat obscure, the proposing and distributing group—the York County Tercentenary Commemorative Coin Commission, led by ardent numismatist Walter P. Nichols—was lauded for its diligence and proper handling of the release.

Designs. *Obverse:* Brown's Garrison, on the Saco River (site of the original settlement in York County in 1636). *Reverse:* An adaptation of the seal of York County.

Mintage Data. *Maximum authorized*—30,000. *Number minted*—25,015 (including 15 assay coins).

Original Cost and Issuer. Sale price $1.50 ($1.65 postpaid by mail to out-of-state buyers). Issued by the York County Tercentenary Commemorative Coin Commission, York National Bank, Saco, Maine.

Key to Collecting. This issue was well handled at the Mint and in distribution, so most examples are in higher grades and are relatively free of marks. On the reverse, the top of the shield is a key point. Some coins have been brushed and have a myriad of fine hairlines; these can be detected by examining the coin at various angles to the light. MS-64 and 65 coins are readily found in the marketplace.

First Points of Wear. *Obverse:* The mounted sentry near the corner of the fort; the stockade; and the rim of the coin. *Reverse:* The pine tree in the shield; the top-right area of the shield; and the rim.

	Distribution	Cert	Avg	%MS	AU-50	MS-60	MS-62	MS-63	MS-64	MS-65	MS-66
1936	25,015	3,400	65.4	100%	$210	$220	$230	$240	$250	$260	$300
	Auctions: $4,113, MS-68, September 2014; $1,116, MS-68, September 2014; $558, MS-67, November 2014; $2,585, MS-67, February 2013										

BRIDGEPORT, CONNECTICUT, CENTENNIAL HALF DOLLAR (1936)

Designer: *Henry Kreiss.* **Weight:** *12.50 grams.* **Composition:** *.900 silver, .100 copper (net weight .3617 oz. pure silver).* **Diameter:** *30.6 mm.* **Edge:** *Reeded.* **Mint:** *Philadelphia.*

In commemoration of the 100th anniversary of the incorporation of the city of Bridgeport, a special fifty-cent piece was authorized on May 15, 1936. The city—actually originally founded in 1639—served as an important center in the 17th and 18th centuries.

Designs. *Obverse:* Bareheaded profile portrait of P.T. Barnum, Bridgeport's most famous citizen. *Reverse:* An art deco eagle, standing.

Mintage Data. Authorized on May 15, 1936. *Minimum authorized*—25,000 (unlimited maximum). *Number minted*—25,015 (including 15 assay coins). *Net distribution*—25,015.

Original Cost and Issuer. Sale price $2. Issued by Bridgeport Centennial, Inc., through the First National Bank and Trust Co. and other banks.

Key to Collecting. These coins are readily available in the marketplace. Most grade from MS-62 to 64. Many have been cleaned or lightly polished, but pristine MS-65 pieces are readily available. Obvious friction rub and/or marks are often seen. Some coins were struck from dies with lightly polished fields and have a prooflike or partially prooflike appearance in those areas.

First Points of Wear. *Obverse:* Barnum's cheek. *Reverse:* The eagle's wing.

	Distribution	Cert	Avg	%MS	AU-50	MS-60	MS-62	MS-63	MS-64	MS-65	MS-66
1936	25,015	3,035	64.6	100%	$125	$135	$145	$160	$170	$210	$350
	Auctions: $3,525, MS-67, August 2014; $1,116, MS-67, July 2014; $3,819, MS-67, March 2013; $441, MS-66, December 2014										

LYNCHBURG, VIRGINIA, SESQUICENTENNIAL HALF DOLLAR (1936)

Designer: *Charles Keck.* **Weight:** *12.50 grams.* **Composition:** *.900 silver, .100 copper (net weight .3617 oz. pure silver).* **Diameter:** *30.6 mm.* **Edge:** *Reeded.* **Mint:** *Philadelphia.*

The issuance of a charter to the city of Lynchburg in 1786 was commemorated in 1936 by a special coinage of half dollars. Interestingly, Lynchburg native Senator Carter Glass objected to the use of portraits of living persons on coins, but was featured on the issue anyway. It was considered that a portrait of John Lynch—for whom the city was named—would be used, but no such likeness existed.

Designs. *Obverse:* Bareheaded profile portrait of Senator Carter Glass, a native of Lynchburg and former secretary of the Treasury. *Reverse:* A figure of Miss Liberty standing before the old Lynchburg courthouse.

Mintage Data. Authorized on May 28, 1936. *Maximum authorized*—20,000. *Number minted*—20,013 (including 13 assay coins). *Net distribution*—20,013.

Original Cost and Issuer. Sale price $1. Issued by the Lynchburg Sesqui-Centennial Association.

Key to Collecting. Most of these half dollars are in higher grades; MS-65 and 66 examples are readily available in the marketplace. Some show graininess (from striking) on the high areas of the obverse portrait and on the bosom and skirt of Miss Liberty, or show evidences of handling or contact in the same areas. Surfaces are often somewhat satiny, instead of deeply lustrous and frosty. Often the reverse field is semi-prooflike. This issue must have been handled with particular care at the Mint.

First Points of Wear. *Obverse:* The hair above Glass's ear. *Reverse:* The hair of Miss Liberty, the folds of her gown, and her bosom.

	Distribution	Cert	Avg	%MS	AU-50	MS-60	MS-62	MS-63	MS-64	MS-65	MS-66
1936	20,013	2,587	64.8	100%	$230	$250	$260	$270	$290	$325	$425
	Auctions: $1,175, MS-67+, September 2014; $734, MS-67, November 2014; $11,750, MS-67, January 2013; $200, AU-58, October 2014										

ELGIN, ILLINOIS, CENTENNIAL HALF DOLLAR (1936)

Designer: *Trygve Rovelstad.* **Weight:** *12.50 grams.* **Composition:** *.900 silver, .100 copper (net weight .3617 oz. pure silver).* **Diameter:** *30.6 mm.* **Edge:** *Reeded.* **Mint:** *Philadelphia.*

The 100th anniversary of the founding of Elgin, Illinois, was marked by a special issue of half dollars in 1936. The year 1673 (seen on the obverse) bears no relation to the event but refers to the year in which Louis Joliet and Jacques Marquette entered Illinois Territory.

Designs. *Obverse:* The fur-capped profile of a bearded pioneer (a close-up view of the statue depicted on the reverse). *Reverse:* The Pioneer Memorial statuary group, whose creation was financed by the sale of these coins.

Mintage and Melting Data. Authorized on June 16, 1936. *Maximum authorized—25,000. Number minted—25,015 (including 15 assay coins). Number melted—5,000. Net distribution—20,015.*

Original Cost and Issuer. Sale price $1.50. Issued by the Elgin Centennial Monumental Committee, El Paso, Texas (L.W. Hoffecker in charge), through banks in and near Elgin, including the First National Bank of Elgin, the Elgin National Bank, and the Union National Bank.

Key to Collecting. Elgin half dollars are fairly plentiful in today's marketplace. They seem to have been handled with particular care at the time of minting, as most have fewer bagmarks than many other commemoratives of the same era. Typical coins grade MS-64 to 66. The surfaces often have a matte-like appearance (seemingly a combination of a lustrous circulation strike and a Matte Proof) quite different from other commemorative issues of 1936. Some coins are fairly frosty. On many a bright spot is evident on the reverse below the A of AMERICA, the result of an inadvertent polishing on a small area of the die. Chief Engraver John Sinnock made a few Matte Proofs, perhaps as many as 10, by pickling coins in acid at the Mint.

First Points of Wear. *Obverse:* The cheek of the pioneer. *Reverse:* The rifleman's left shoulder. (Note that a lack of detailed facial features is the result of striking, not wear, and that the infant is always weakly struck.)

	Distribution	Cert	Avg	%MS	AU-50	MS-60	MS-62	MS-63	MS-64	MS-65	MS-66
1936	20,015	3,277	65.0	100%	$200	$210	$220	$230	$240	$250	$350

Auctions: $49,938, MS-68, January 2014; $2,115, MS-67+, August 2014; $940, MS-67, November 2014; $120, AU-55, November 2014

ALBANY, NEW YORK, CHARTER HALF DOLLAR (1936)

Designer: *Gertrude K. Lathrop.* **Weight:** *12.50 grams.* **Composition:** *.900 silver, .100 copper (net weight .3617 oz. pure silver).* **Diameter:** *30.6 mm.* **Edge:** *Reeded.* **Mint:** *Philadelphia.*

The 250th anniversary of the granting of a charter to the city of Albany—an event of strictly local significance—was the occasion for this commemorative half dollar. Amusingly, designer Gertrude K. Lathrop kept a live beaver in her studio (courtesy of the state Conservation Department) during her work.

Designs. *Obverse:* A plump beaver gnawing on a maple branch—fauna and flora evocative of Albany and New York State, respectively. *Reverse:* A scene with Albany's first mayor, Peter Schuyler, and his secretary, Robert Livingston, accepting the city's charter in 1686 from Governor Thomas Dongan of New York.

Mintage and Melting Data. Authorized on June 16, 1936. *Maximum authorized*—25,000. *Number minted*—25,013 (including 13 assay coins). *Number melted*—7,342. *Net distribution*—17,671.

Original Cost and Issuer. Sale price $1. Issued by the Albany Dongan Charter Coin Committee.

Key to Collecting. This issue was fairly carefully handled during production and distribution, and most examples are relatively free of marks in the fields. Most specimens are lustrous and frosty, although the frost has satiny aspects. Albany half dollars are readily available on the market. The typical example grades from MS-63 to 65 and has at least minor friction and marks.

First Points of Wear. *Obverse:* The hip of the beaver (nearly all coins show at least minor evidence of contact here). *Reverse:* The sleeve of Dongan (the figure at left).

	Distribution	Cert	Avg	%MS	AU-50	MS-60	MS-62	MS-63	MS-64	MS-65	MS-66
1936	17,671	2,902	64.8	100%	$260	$270	$280	$290	$300	$320	$500

Auctions: $6,815, MS-68, April 2013; $3,672, MS-67+, September 2014; $2,585, MS-67, November 2014; $544, MS-67, October 2014

SAN FRANCISCO–OAKLAND BAY BRIDGE OPENING HALF DOLLAR (1936)

Designer: *Jacques Schnier.* **Weight:** *12.50 grams.* **Composition:** *.900 silver, .100 copper (net weight .3617 oz. pure silver).* **Diameter:** *30.6 mm.* **Edge:** *Reeded.* **Mint:** *San Francisco.*

The opening of the San Francisco Bay Bridge was the occasion for a special souvenir fifty-cent piece. The bear depicted on the obverse was a composite of animals in local zoos.

Designs. *Obverse:* A stylized grizzly bear standing on all fours and facing the viewer. *Reverse:* A fading-to-the-horizon view of the San Francisco–Oakland Bay Bridge and part of San Francisco.

Mintage and Melting Data. Authorized on June 26, 1936. *Maximum authorized*—200,000. *Number minted*—100,055 (including 55 assay coins). *Number melted*—28,631. *Net distribution*—71,424.

Original Cost and Issuer. Sale price $1.50. Issued by the Coin Committee of the San Francisco–Oakland Bay Bridge Celebration.

Key to Collecting. These coins are readily available in today's marketplace, with most grading MS-62 to 64, typically with contact marks on the grizzly bear. The reverse design, being complex with many protective devices, normally appears free of marks, unless viewed at an angle under a strong light. The grade of the reverse for a given coin often is a point or two higher than that of the obverse. The fields of this coin often have a "greasy" appearance, rather than being deeply lustrous and frosty.

First Points of Wear. *Obverse:* The bear's body, in particular the left shoulder. *Reverse:* The clouds.

	Distribution	Cert	Avg	%MS	AU-50	MS-60	MS-62	MS-63	MS-64	MS-65	MS-66
1936S	71,424	3,633	64.6	99%	$150	$155	$160	$165	$180	$200	$450

Auctions: $7,638, MS-68, January 2014; $940, MS-67, November 2014; $1,530, MS-67, August 2014; $113, AU-58, August 2014

COLUMBIA, SOUTH CAROLINA, SESQUICENTENNIAL HALF DOLLAR (1936)

Designer: *A. Wolfe Davidson.* **Weight:** *12.50 grams.*
Composition: *.900 silver, .100 copper (net weight .3617 oz. pure silver).*
Diameter: *30.6 mm.* **Edge:** *Reeded.* **Mints:** *Philadelphia, Denver, San Francisco.*

Souvenir half dollars were authorized to help finance the extensive celebrations marking the sesquicentennial of the founding of Columbia, South Carolina, in 1786. The pieces had not been minted by the time of the actual celebrations, which took place in late March 1936, and only reached collectors (which the Columbia Sesqui-Centennial Commission expressed desire to sell to instead of to dealers) in December.

Designs. *Obverse:* Justice, with sword and scales, standing before the state capitol of 1786 and the capitol of 1936. *Reverse:* A palmetto tree, the state emblem, with stars encircling.

Mintage Data. Authorized on March 18, 1936. *Maximum authorized*—25,000. *Number minted*—1936-P: 9,007; 1936-D: 8,009; 1936-S: 8,007. *Net distribution*—1936-P: 9,007; 1936-D: 8,009; 1936-S: 8,007.

Original Cost and Issuer. Sale price $6.45 per set of three (single coins $2.15 each). Issued by the Columbia Sesqui-Centennial Commission.

Key to Collecting. These coins were widely distributed at the time of issue, and examples are readily obtainable today. Most grade from MS-63 to 65. They were treated carefully in their minting and distribution, so most coins exhibit lustrous surfaces with very few handling marks. Nearly all, however, show friction on the bosom of Justice and, to a lesser extent, on the high areas of the palmetto-tree foliage on the reverse.

First Points of Wear. *Obverse:* The right breast of Justice. *Reverse:* The top of the palmetto tree.

	Distribution	Cert	Avg	%MS	AU-50	MS-60	MS-62	MS-63	MS-64	MS-65	MS-66
1936	9,007	1,535	65.2	100%	$230	$240	$250	$260	$270	$280	$325
	Auctions: $15,275, MS-68, August 2013; $353, MS-67, November 2014; $588, MS-67, October 2014; $270, MS-66, December 2014										
1936D	8,009	1,607	65.7	100%	$230	$240	$250	$260	$270	$280	$325
	Auctions: $4,818, MS-68, September 2013; $881, MS-67+, July 2014; $441, MS-67, October 2014; $223, MS-66, December 2014										
1936S	8,007	1,520	65.4	100%	$230	$240	$250	$260	$270	$280	$325
	Auctions: $3,055, MS-68, September 2014; $2,820, MS-68, September 2013; $306, MS-67, November 2014; $646, MS-67, October 2014										
Set of 1936 P-D-S					$750	$760	$775	$800	$850	$900	$1,050
	Auctions: $690, MS-65/66/65, February 2012										

DELAWARE TERCENTENARY HALF DOLLAR (1936)

Designer: *Carl L. Schmitz.* **Weight:** *12.50 grams.* **Composition:** *.900 silver, .100 copper (net weight .3617 oz. pure silver).* **Diameter:** *30.6 mm.* **Edge:** *Reeded.* **Mint:** *Philadelphia.*

The 300th anniversary of the landing of the Swedes in Delaware was the occasion for a souvenir issue of half dollars—as well as a two-krona coin issued in Sweden. The colonists landed on the spot that is now Wilmington and established a church, which is the oldest Protestant church in the United States still used for worship. Carl L. Schmitz's designs were chosen through a competition. These coins were authorized in 1936 and struck in 1937, but not released until 1938, as the Swedes' arrival was actually in 1638.

Designs. *Obverse:* Old Swedes Church. *Reverse:* The ship *Kalmar Nyckel.*

Mintage and Melting Data. Authorized on May 15, 1936. *Minimum authorized*—25,000 (unlimited maximum). *Number minted*—25,015 (including 15 assay coins). *Number melted*—4,022. *Net distribution*—20,993.

Original Cost and Issuer. Sale price $1.75. Issued by the Delaware Swedish Tercentenary Commission, through the Equitable Trust Company of Wilmington.

Key to Collecting. Most examples in today's marketplace grade MS-64 or 65, though they typically exhibit numerous original planchet nicks and marks. Most coins are very lustrous and frosty.

First Points of Wear. *Obverse:* The roof above the church entrance. (Note that the triangular section at the top of the entrance is weakly struck, giving an appearance of wear.) *Reverse:* The center of the lower middle sail (also often shows graininess and nicks from the original planchet).

	Distribution	Cert	Avg	%MS	AU-50	MS-60	MS-62	MS-63	MS-64	MS-65	MS-66
1936	20,993	2,911	64.7	100%	$250	$265	$270	$280	$300	$325	$450

Auctions: $12,925, MS-67, January 2013; $499, MS-67, November 2014; $1,998, MS-67, October 2014; $382, MS-66, November 2014

BATTLE OF GETTYSBURG ANNIVERSARY HALF DOLLAR (1936)

Designer: *Frank Vittor.* **weight:** *12.50 grams.* **Composition:** *.900 silver, .100 copper (net weight .3617 oz. pure silver).* **Diameter:** *30.6 mm.* **Edge:** *Reeded.* **Mint:** *Philadelphia.*

On June 16, 1936, Congress authorized a coinage of fifty-cent pieces in commemoration of the 75th anniversary of the 1863 Battle of Gettysburg. Similar to the previously mentioned Delaware Tercentenary coins, the coins were authorized two years before the event commemorated, and were minted a year early as well (in 1937). Paul L. Roy, secretary of the Pennsylvania State Commission, desired for the pieces to be struck at multiple mints—so as to sell more expensive sets of three coins, rather than just Philadelphia issues—but no coins were struck in Denver or San Francisco in the end.

Designs. *Obverse:* Uniformed profile portraits of a Union soldier and a Confederate soldier. *Reverse:* Union and Confederate shields separated by a fasces.

Mintage and Melting Data. Authorized on June 16, 1936. *Maximum authorized*—50,000. *Number minted*—50,028 (including 28 assay coins). *Number melted*—23,100. *Net distribution*—26,928.

Original Cost and Issuer. Sale price $1.65. Issued by the Pennsylvania State Commission, Hotel Gettysburg, Gettysburg. The price was later raised to $2.65 for coins offered by the American Legion, Department of Pennsylvania.

Key to Collecting. Examples are fairly plentiful in the marketplace. The typical coin grades from MS-63 to 65, is deeply frosty and lustrous, and shows scattered contact marks, which are most evident on the cheeks of the soldiers on the obverse and, on the reverse, on the two shields (particularly at the top of the Union shield on the left side of the coin).

First Points of Wear. *Obverse:* The cheekbones of each soldier. *Reverse:* The three ribbons on the fasces, and the top of the Union shield.

	Distribution	Cert	Avg	%MS	AU-50	MS-60	MS-62	MS-63	MS-64	MS-65	MS-66
1936	26,928	3,287	64.5	99%	$460	$480	$500	$525	$575	$875	$1,200
	Auctions: $1,939, MS-67★, August 2014; $11,750, MS-67, November 2014; $1,469, MS-67, September 2014; $823, MS-66, November 2014										

NORFOLK, VIRGINIA, BICENTENNIAL HALF DOLLAR (1936)

Designers: *William M. and Marjorie E. Simpson.* **Weight:** *12.50 grams.*
Composition: *.900 silver, .100 copper (net weight .3617 oz. pure silver).*
Diameter: *30.6 mm.* **Edge:** *Reeded.* **Mint:** *Philadelphia.*

To provide funds for the celebration of Norfolk's anniversary of its growth from a township in 1682 to a royal borough in 1736, Congress first passed a law for the striking of medals. The proponents, however, being dissatisfied, finally succeeded in winning authority for half dollars commemorating the 300th anniversary of the original Norfolk land grant and the 200th anniversary of the establishment of the borough. In a strange twist, none of the five dates on these coins actually reflects the year of the coins' actual striking (1937).

Designs. *Obverse:* The seal of the city of Norfolk, Virginia, with a three-masted ship at center. *Reverse:* The city's royal mace, presented by Lieutenant Governor Robert Dinwiddie in 1753.

Mintage and Melting Data. Authorized on June 28, 1937. *Maximum authorized*—25,000. *Number minted*—25,013 (including 13 assay coins). *Number melted*—8,077. *Net distribution*—16,936.

Original Cost and Issuer. Sale price $1.50 locally ($1.65 by mail for the first coin, $1.55 for each additional). Issued by the Norfolk Advertising Board, Norfolk Association of Commerce.

Key to Collecting. Examples are fairly plentiful in today's marketplace, with most in high MS grades. The cluttered nature of the design had a positive effect: all of the lettering served to protect the fields and devices from nicks and marks, with the result that MS-65 and 66 coins are plentiful.

First Points of Wear. *Obverse:* The sails of the ship, especially the lower rear sail. *Reverse:* The area below the crown on the royal mace.

	Distribution	Cert	Avg	%MS	AU-50	MS-60	MS-62	MS-63	MS-64	MS-65	MS-66
1936	16,936	2,731	65.9	100%	$365	$370	$375	$380	$385	$390	$425
	Auctions: $1,410, MS-68, November 2014; $1,880, MS-68, August 2014; $5,288, MS-68, August 2013; $423, MS-67, December 2014										

ROANOKE ISLAND, NORTH CAROLINA, 350TH ANNIVERSARY HALF DOLLAR (1937)

Designer: *William M. Simpson.* **Weight:** *12.50 grams.* **Composition:** *.900 silver, .100 copper (net weight .3617 oz. pure silver).* **Diameter:** *30.6 mm.* **Edge:** *Reeded.* **Mint:** *Philadelphia.*

A celebration was held in Old Fort Raleigh in 1937 to commemorate the 350th anniversary of Sir Walter Raleigh's "Lost Colony" and the birth of Virginia Dare, the first white child born in British North America. Interestingly, Raleigh himself never actually visited America, but only sent ships of colonists who eventually founded a city in his name.

Designs. *Obverse:* Profile portrait of Sir Walter Raleigh in plumed hat and fancy collar. *Reverse:* Ellinor Dare and her baby, Virginia, the first white child born in the Americas to English parents.

Mintage and Melting Data. *Minimum authorized*—25,000 (unlimited maximum). *Number minted*—50,030 (including 30 assay coins). *Number melted*—21,000. *Net distribution*—29,030.

Original Cost and Issuer. Sale price $1.65. Issued by the Roanoke Colony Memorial Association of Manteo.

Key to Collecting. Most of these coins were handled with care during their minting, and today are in high grades. MS-65 pieces are plentiful. Most coins are lustrous and frosty. Partially prooflike pieces are occasionally seen (sometimes offered as "presentation pieces" or "prooflike presentation pieces").

First Points of Wear. *Obverse:* Raleigh's cheek and the brim of his hat. *Reverse:* The head of Ellinor Dare.

	Distribution	Cert	Avg	%MS	AU-50	MS-60	MS-62	MS-63	MS-64	MS-65	MS-66
1937	29,030	3,837	65.1	100%	$185	$190	$200	$210	$220	$230	$250

Auctions: $4,061, MS-68, September 2014; $4,259, MS-68, January 2014; $441, MS-67, December 2014; $147, AU-55, October 2014

BATTLE OF ANTIETAM ANNIVERSARY HALF DOLLAR (1937)

Designer: *William M. Simpson.* **Weight:** *12.50 grams.* **Composition:** *.900 silver, .100 copper (net weight .3617 oz. pure silver).* **Diameter:** *30.6 mm.* **Edge:** *Reeded.* **Mint:** *Philadelphia.*

A souvenir half dollar was struck in 1937 to commemorate the 75th anniversary of the famous Civil War battle to thwart Robert E. Lee's invasion of Maryland. The Battle of Antietam, which took place on September 17, 1862, was one of the bloodiest single-day battles of the war, with more than 23,000 men killed, wounded, or missing.

Designs. *Obverse:* Uniformed profile portraits of generals Robert E. Lee and George B. McClellan, opponent commanders during the Battle of Antietam. *Reverse:* Burnside Bridge, an important tactical objective of the battle.

Mintage and Melting Data. Authorized on June 24, 1937. *Maximum authorized*—50,000. *Number minted*—50,028 (including 28 assay coins). *Number melted*—32,000. *Net distribution*—18,028.

Original Cost and Issuer. Sale price $1.65. Issued by the Washington County Historical Society, Hagerstown, Maryland.

Key to Collecting. Antietam half dollars were handled with care during production. More often seen are scattered small marks, particularly on the upper part of the obverse. Most examples are very lustrous and frosty. MS-65 and finer coins are plentiful in the marketplace.

First Points of Wear. *Obverse:* Lee's cheekbone. *Reverse:* The leaves of the trees; the bridge; and the rim of the coin.

	Distribution	Cert	Avg	%MS	AU-50	MS-60	MS-62	MS-63	MS-64	MS-65	MS-66
1937	18,028	2,649	65.1	100%	$675	$700	$710	$725	$750	$800	$900

Auctions: $4,113, MS-68, July 2014; $8,225, MS-68, January 2014; $2,115, MS-67+, November 2014; $881, MS-67, November 2014

NEW ROCHELLE, NEW YORK, 250TH ANNIVERSARY HALF DOLLAR (1938)

Designer: *Gertrude K. Lathrop.* **Weight:** *12.50 grams.* **Composition:** *.900 silver, .100 copper (net weight .3617 oz. pure silver).* **Diameter:** *30.6 mm.* **Edge:** *Reeded.* **Mint:** *Philadelphia.*

To observe the founding of New Rochelle in 1688 by French Huguenots, a special half dollar was issued in 1938. The title to the land that the Huguenots purchased from John Pell provided that a fattened calf be given away every year on June 20; this is represented the obverse of the coin.

Designs. *Obverse:* John Pell, who sold the French Huguenots the land for New Rochelle, and a fatted calf, an annual provision of the sale. *Reverse:* A fleur-de-lis, adapted from the seal of the city.

Mintage and Melting Data. Authorized on May 5, 1936. *Maximum authorized—25,000. Number minted—25,015 (including 15 assay coins). Number melted—9,749. Net distribution—15,266.*

Original Cost and Issuer. Sale price $2. Issued by the New Rochelle Commemorative Coin Committee, through the First National Bank of New Rochelle, New Rochelle, New York.

Key to Collecting. These half dollars received better-than-average care and handling during the minting and distribution process. The typical coin grades MS-64 or higher. Some examples show very light handling marks, but most are relatively problem-free. Some show areas of graininess or light striking on the high spots of the calf on the obverse, and on the highest area of the iris on the reverse. The majority of pieces have lustrous, frosty surfaces, and a few are prooflike (the latter are sometimes offered as "presentation pieces").

First Points of Wear. *Obverse:* The hip of the calf. *Reverse:* The bulbous part of the fleur-de-lis. (Note that on the central petal the midrib is flatly struck.)

	Distribution	Cert	Avg	%MS	AU-50	MS-60	MS-62	MS-63	MS-64	MS-65	MS-66
									PF-63	PF-64	PF-65
1938	15,266	2,523	65.0	100%	$335	$350	$355	$360	$365	$400	$450

Auctions: $2,820, MS-67+, November 2014; $1,704, MS-67, November 2014; $10,281, MS-66, March 2013; $335, AU-58, October 2014

1938, Proof	1–2	2	61.0								

Auctions: No auction records available.

Iowa Centennial Half Dollar (1946)

Designer: *Adam Pietz.* **Weight:** *12.50 grams.* **Composition:** *.900 silver, .100 copper (net weight .3617 oz. pure silver).* **Diameter:** *30.6 mm.* **Edge:** *Reeded.* **Mint:** *Philadelphia.*

This half dollar, commemorating the 100th anniversary of Iowa's statehood, was sold first to the residents of Iowa and only a small remainder to others. Numismatists of the time, having largely forgotten the deceptions and hucksterism of the 1930s (and also seen the values of previously issued commemoratives rebound from a low point in 1941), were excited to see the first commemorative coin struck in some years. Nearly all of the issue was disposed of quickly, except for 500 that were held back to be distributed in 1996, and another 500 slated for 2046.

Designs. *Obverse:* The Old Stone Capitol building at Iowa City. *Reverse:* An eagle with wings spreading, adapted from the Iowa state seal.

Mintage Data. Authorized on August 7, 1946. *Maximum authorized*—100,000. *Number minted*—100,057 (including 57 assay coins).

Original Cost and Issuer. Sale price $2.50 to in-state buyers, $3 to those out of state. Issued by the Iowa Centennial Committee, Des Moines, Iowa.

Key to Collecting. Most coins are in varying degrees of Mint State, and are lustrous and frosty. MS-63 to 66 are typical grades. The nature of the design, without open field areas, is such that a slight amount of friction and contact is usually not noticeable.

First Points of Wear. *Obverse:* The clouds above the Capitol, and the shafts of the building near the upper-left and upper-right windows. *Reverse:* The back of the eagle's head and neck. (Note that the head sometimes is flatly struck.)

	Distribution	Cert	Avg	%MS	AU-50	MS-60	MS-62	MS-63	MS-64	MS-65	MS-66
1946	100,057	5,848	65.5	100%	$105	$115	$120	$125	$130	$135	$160

Auctions: $1,763, MS-68, October 2014; $9,400, MS-68, January 2013; $558, MS-67+, July 2014; $182, MS-67, December 2014

Booker T. Washington Memorial Half Dollar (1946–1951)

Designer: *Isaac S. Hathaway.* **Weight:** *12.50 grams.*
Composition: *.900 silver, .100 copper (net weight .3617 oz. pure silver).*
Diameter: *30.6 mm.* **Edge:** *Reeded.* **Mints:** *Philadelphia, Denver, San Francisco.*

This commemorative coin was issued to perpetuate the ideals and teachings of African-American educator and presidential advisor Booker T. Washington and to construct memorials to his memory. Issued from all mints, it received wide distribution from the start. Unfortunately, the provision that the coins could be minted over several years led to many of the same problems seen with the Arkansas, Boone, Oregon Trail, and Texas pieces from the prior decade.

Designs. *Obverse:* Bareheaded three-quarters profile portrait of Booker T. Washington. *Reverse:* The Hall of Fame at New York University and a slave cabin.

Mintage Data. Authorized on August 7, 1946. *Maximum authorized*—5,000,000 (for the entire series 1946 onward). *Number minted*—1946-P: 1,000,546 (including 546 assay coins); 1946-D: 200,113 (including 113 assay coins); 1946-S: 500,279 (including 279 assay coins); 1947-P: 100,017 (including 17 assay coins); 1947-D: 100,017 (including 17 assay coins); 1947-S: 100,017 (including 17 assay coins); 1948-P: 20,005 (including 5 assay coins); 1948-D: 20,005 (including 5 assay coins); 1948-S: 20,005 (including 5 assay coins); 1949-P: 12,004 (including 4 assay coins); 1949-D: 12,004 (including 4 assay coins); 1949-S: 12,004 (including 4 assay coins); 1950-P: 12,004 (including 4 assay coins); 1950-D: 12,004 (including 4 assay coins); 1950-S: 512,091 (including 91 assay coins); 1951-P: 510,082 (including 82 assay coins); 1951-D: 12,004 (including 4 assay coins); 1951-S: 12,004 (including 4 assay coins). *Net distribution*—1946-P: 700,546 (estimated); 1946-D: 50,000 (estimated); 1946-S: 500,279 (estimated); 1947-P: 6,000 (estimated); 1947-D: 6,000 (estimated); 1947-S: 6,000 (estimated); 1948-P: 8,005; 1948-D: 8,005; 1948-S: 8,005; 1949-P: 6,004; 1949-D: 6,004; 1949-S: 6,004; 1950-P: 6,004; 1950-D: 6,004; 1950-S: 62,091 (estimated); 1951-P: 210,082 (estimated); 1951-D: 7,004; 1951-S: 7,004.

Original Cost and Issuer. Original sale price $1 per coin for Philadelphia and San Francisco, $1.50 for Denver, plus 10¢ postage per coin. In 1946, issued by the Booker T. Washington Birthplace Memorial Commission, Inc., Rocky Mount, Virginia (Dr. S.J. Phillips in charge); Stack's of New York City; and Bebee Stamp & Coin Company (a.k.a. Bebee's). For later issues, costs and distributors varied.

Key to Collecting. Of all commemorative half dollar issues produced up to this point, the Booker T. Washington half dollars were made with the least amount of care during the coining process at the mints. At the time of release, nearly all were poorly struck on the obverse and were marked with abrasions and nicks. Many have graininess and marks on Washington's cheek, from the original planchet surface that did not strike up fully. Many coins grade from MS-60 to (liberally graded) 65. Some have natural or artificial toning that masks the true condition and facilitates gem certification. Prooflike coins are sometimes seen, including for 1947-S (in particular), 1948-S, 1949, and 1951-S. These are not at all mirror-like, but still have surfaces different from the normal mint frost.

First Points of Wear. *Obverse:* Washington's cheekbone. *Reverse:* The center lettering (FROM SLAVE CABIN TO HALL OF FAME, etc.).

	Distribution	Cert	Avg	%MS	AU-50	MS-60	MS-62	MS-63	MS-64	MS-65	MS-66
1946	700,546	2,682	64.7	99%	$18	$21	$22	$23	$25	$50	$125
	Auctions: $881, MS-67, November 2014; $558, MS-67, October 2014; $2,585, MS-67, February 2014; $86, MS-66, August 2014										
1946D	50,000	1,589	64.8	100%	$18	$21	$22	$23	$25	$50	$125
	Auctions: $4,406, MS-68, November 2014; $1,175, MS-67, October 2014; $764, MS-67, August 2014; $94, MS-66, September 2014										
1946S	500,279	2,264	64.9	99%	$18	$21	$22	$23	$25	$50	$175
	Auctions: $3,525, MS-68, August 2013; $999, MS-67+, November 2014; $1,410, MS-67+, September 2014; $470, MS-67, October 2014										
Set of 1946 P-D-S					$60	$65	$70	$80	$100	$175	$425
	Auctions: $110, MS-65/65/65, May 2012										
1947	6,000	833	64.9	100%	$20	$25	$30	$40	$45	$60	$125
	Auctions: $4,700, MS-67, November 2014; $159, MS-66, December 2014; $212, MS-66, October 2014; $646, MS-66, June 2014										
1947D	6,000	662	65.0	100%	$20	$25	$30	$40	$45	$60	$250
	Auctions: $5,875, MS-67, September 2014; $2,233, MS-67, September 2014; $8,813, MS-67, February 2014; $270, MS-66, August 2014										
1947S	6,000	872	65.1	100%	$20	$25	$30	$40	$45	$60	$300
	Auctions: $1,645, MS-67, October 2014; $2,350, MS-67, September 2014; $3,525, MS-67, August 2013; $147, MS-66, September 2014										
Set of 1947 P-D-S					$60	$65	$70	$80	$100	$175	$675
	Auctions: $196, MS-65/65/65, January 2012										

	Distribution	Cert	Avg	%MS	AU-50	MS-60	MS-62	MS-63	MS-64	MS-65	MS-66
1948	8,005	791	65.2	100%	$20	$25	$30	$40	$45	$60	$175
	Auctions: $2,350, MS-67, April 2014; $194, MS-66, November 2014; $282, MS-66, July 2014; $68, MS-65, August 2014										
1948D	8,005	806	65.2	100%	$20	$25	$30	$40	$45	$60	$275
	Auctions: $823, MS-67, November 2014; $1,058, MS-67, September 2014; $4,406, MS-67, February 2013; $194, MS-66, November 2014										
1948S	8,005	946	65.4	100%	$20	$25	$30	$40	$45	$60	$225
	Auctions: $1,058, MS-67+, September 2014; $1,175, MS-67, October 2014; $2,820, MS-67, February 2013; $270, MS-66+, November 2014										
Set of 1948 P-D-S					$60	$65	$70	$80	$100	$175	$675
	Auctions: $220, MS-66/65/65, June 2012										
1949	6,004	803	65.2	100%	$30	$50	$55	$60	$100	$150	$275
	Auctions: $1,293, MS-67, October 2014; $558, MS-67, September 2014; $3,055, MS-67, March 2013; $184, MS-66+, November 2014										
1949D	6,004	763	65.2	100%	$30	$50	$55	$60	$100	$150	$275
	Auctions: $1,058, MS-67, November 2014; $881, MS-67, November 2014; $4,406, MS-67, February 2014; $153, MS-66, November 2014										
1949S	6,004	829	65.5	100%	$30	$50	$55	$60	$80	$125	$200
	Auctions: $646, MS-67, October 2014; $529, MS-67, September 2014; $1,011, MS-67, March 2013; $165, MS-66, December 2014										
Set of 1949 P-D-S					$100	$150	$175	$200	$280	$425	$725
	Auctions: $320, MS-65/66/66, May 2012										
1950	6,004	594	65.1	100%	$20	$25	$30	$40	$60	$80	$225
	Auctions: $5,875, MS-67, October 2014; $306, MS-66+, November 2014; $382, MS-66+, September 2014; $194, MS-66, November 2014										
1950D	6,004	585	65.1	100%	$20	$25	$30	$40	$60	$80	$350
	Auctions: $2,820, MS-67, October 2014; $1,763, MS-67, October 2014; $7,374, MS-67, February 2013; $470, MS-66+, November 2014										
1950S	62,091	1,237	65.2	100%	$20	$25	$30	$40	$60	$70	$100
	Auctions: $5,581, MS-68, September 2014; $411, MS-67, November 2014; $705, MS-67, August 2014; $3,525, MS-67, April 2014										
Set of 1950 P-D-S					$60	$75	$90	$125	$180	$250	$675
	Auctions: $725, MS-66/66/66, April 2012										
1951	210,082	1,249	64.6	100%	$20	$25	$30	$40	$45	$60	$125
	Auctions: $1,528, MS-67, November 2014; $3,202, MS-67, November 2013; $441, MS-66+, August 2014; $106, MS-66, August 2014										
1951D	7,004	652	65.3	100%	$20	$25	$30	$40	$45	$75	$200
	Auctions: $951, MS-67, November 2014; $764, MS-67, August 2014; $3,819, MS-67, August 2013										
1951S	7,004	761	65.6	100%	$20	$25	$30	$40	$60	$85	$175
	Auctions: $646, MS-67, October 2014; $764, MS-67, August 2014; $1,880, MS-67, August 2013; $135, MS-66, December 2014										
Set of 1951 P-D-S					$60	$75	$90	$120	$150	$225	$500
	Auctions: $475, MS-66/66/66, May 2012										

CARVER / WASHINGTON COMMEMORATIVE HALF DOLLAR (1951–1954)

Designer: *Isaac S. Hathaway.* **Weight:** *12.50 grams.*
Composition: *.900 silver, .100 copper (net weight .3617 oz. pure silver).*
Diameter: *30.6 mm.* **Edge:** *Reeded.* **Mints:** *Philadelphia, Denver, San Francisco.*

Designed by Isaac Scott Hathaway, this coin portrays the conjoined busts of two prominent black Americans. Booker T. Washington was a lecturer, educator, and principal of Tuskegee Institute. He urged training to advance independence and efficiency for his race. George Washington Carver was an agricultural chemist who worked to improve the economy of the American South. He spent part of his life teaching crop improvement and new uses for soybeans, peanuts, sweet potatoes, and cotton waste. Controversy erupted when it came to light that money obtained from the sale of these commemoratives was to be used "to oppose the spread of communism among Negroes in the interest of national defense."

Designs. *Obverse:* Conjoined bareheaded profile portraits of George Washington Carver and Booker T. Washington. *Reverse:* A map of the United States, with legends.

Mintage Data. Signed into law by President Harry S Truman on September 21, 1951. *Maximum authorized*—3,415,631 (total for all issues 1951 onward; consisting of 1,581,631 undistributed Booker T. Washington coins which could be converted into Carver-Washington coins, plus the unused 1,834,000 earlier authorization for Booker T. Washington coins). The following include author's estimates: 1951-P-D-S: *Number minted* (including 18, 4, and 4 assay coins)—110,018; 10,004; 10,004. *Net distribution*—20,018 (estimated); 10,004 (estimated); 10,004 (estimated). 1952-P-D-S: *Number minted* (including 292, 6, and 6 assay coins)—2,006,292; 8,006; 8,006. *Net distribution*—1,106,292 (estimated); 8,006 (estimated); 8,006 (estimated). 1953-P-D-S: *Number minted* (including 3, 3, and 20 assay coins)—8,003; 8,003; 108,020. *Net distribution*—8,003 (estimated); 8,003 (estimated); 88,020 (estimated). 1954-P-D-S: *Number minted* (including 6, 6, and 24 assay coins)—12,006; 12,006; 122,024. *Net distribution*—12,006 (estimated); 12,006 (estimated); 42,024 (estimated).

Original Cost and Issuer. 1951-P-D-S: $10 per set. 1952-P-D-S: $10 per set; many Philadelphia coins were sold at or near face value through banks. 1953-P-D-S: $10 per set; some 1953-S coins were distributed at or near face value (Bebee's prices $9 until January 15, 1952, $10 after that date). 1954-P-D-S: Official sale price: $10 per set; some 1954-S coins were paid out at face value (Bebee's prices for sets $9 until January 20, 1954, $12 after that date). Issued mainly by the Carver-Washington Coin Commission acting for the Booker T. Washington Birthplace Memorial Foundation (Booker Washington Birthplace, Virginia) and the George Washington Carver National Monument Foundation (Diamond, Missouri). Also, for some issues, these dealers: Stack's, Bebee Stamp & Coin Company, Sol Kaplan, and R. Green.

Key to Collecting. Nearly all coins of this issue were handled casually at the mints and also during the distribution process. Most were not fully struck up, with the result that under magnification many tiny nicks and marks can be seen on the higher parts, originating from planchet marks that were not obliterated during the striking process. Many MS examples are available on the market.

First Points of Wear. *Obverse:* Carver's cheekbone. (Note that some pieces were struck poorly in this area; check the reverse also for wear.) *Reverse:* The lettering U.S.A. on the map.

	Distribution	Cert	Avg	%MS	AU-50	MS-60	MS-62	MS-63	MS-64	MS-65	MS-66
1951	20,018	988	64.1	100%	$16	$21	$23	$25	$40	$75	$320
Auctions: $8,225, MS-67, February 2014; $881, MS-66+, November 2014; $764, MS-66, November 2014; $823, MS-66, September 2014											
1951D	10,004	623	64.6	100%	$16	$21	$23	$25	$40	$75	$250
Auctions: $2,585, MS-66+, August 2014; $411, MS-66, December 2014; $881, MS-66, July 2014; $3,290, MS-66, January 2013											
1951S	10,004	810	65.1	100%	$16	$21	$23	$25	$40	$75	$250
Auctions: $3,290, MS-67, August 2014; $8,813, MS-67, March 2013; $353, MS-66+, November 2014; $200, MS-66, November 2014											
Set of 1951 P-D-S					$60	$135	$145	$200	$215	$550	$3,750
Auctions: $140, MS-64/64/64, June 2012											
1952	1,106,292	3,780	64.3	99%	$16	$21	$23	$25	$40	$75	$320
Auctions: $1,528, MS-67, September 2014; $2,174, MS-67, July 2014; $275, MS-66+, November 2014; $150, MS-66, June 2012											
1952D	8,006	497	64.4	100%	$16	$21	$23	$25	$40	$75	$320
Auctions: $940, MS-66, May 2013; $110, MS-65, July 2014; $40, MS-64, November 2014											
1952S	8,006	675	65.1	100%	$16	$21	$23	$25	$40	$75	$320
Auctions: $382, MS-66+, August 2014; $881, MS-66+, July 2014; $282, MS-66, December 2014; $223, MS-66, November 2014											
Set of 1952 P-D-S					$60	$80	$90	$100	$190	$350	$1,500
Auctions: $230, MS-65/65/65, March 2012											

	Distribution	Cert	Avg	%MS	AU-50	MS-60	MS-62	MS-63	MS-64	MS-65	MS-66
1953	8,003	580	64.7	100%	$16	$21	$23	$25	$40	$75	$300
	Auctions: $3,819, MS-67, November 2014; $10,281, MS-67, September 2013; $1,058, MS-66+, July 2014; $306, MS-66, November 2014										
1953D	8,003	464	64.4	100%	$16	$21	$23	$25	$40	$75	$300
	Auctions: $14,100, MS-67, September 2013; $108, MS-65, November 2014; $147, MS-65, July 2014										
1953S	88,020	1,230	64.8	100%	$16	$21	$23	$25	$40	$75	$300
	Auctions: $5,993, MS-67, September 2014; $999, MS-66+, July 2014; $194, MS-66, November 2014; $403, MS-66, June 2012										
Set of 1953 P-D-S					$60	$80	$90	$100	$160	$350	$1,500
	Auctions: $300, MS-65/65/65, May 2012										
1954	12,006	781	64.6	100%	$16	$21	$23	$25	$40	$75	$300
	Auctions: $9,988, MS-67, August 2013; $306, MS-66, October 2014; $1,645, MS-66, August 2014; $382, MS-66, August 2014										
1954D	12,006	694	64.4	100%	$16	$21	$23	$25	$40	$75	$300
	Auctions: $764, MS-66, November 2014; $1,087, MS-66, August 2014; $1,880, MS-66, January 2013; $123, MS-65+, November 2014										
1954S	42,024	1,135	64.6	100%	$16	$21	$23	$25	$40	$75	$300
	Auctions: $212, MS-66, November 2014; $705, MS-66, August 2014; $282, MS-66, July 2014; $38, MS-65, October 2014										
Set of 1954 P-D-S					$60	$80	$90	$100	$160	$300	$1,500
	Auctions: $316, MS-65/65/65, March 2012										

AN OVERVIEW OF MODERN COMMEMORATIVES

No commemorative coins were made by the U.S. Mint from 1955 through 1981. As the years went by, the numismatic community missed having new commemoratives to collect, and many endorsements for events and subjects worthy of the honor were made through letters to congressmen and other officials, which were often reprinted in pages of *The Numismatist*, the *Numismatic Scrapbook Magazine*, *Numismatic News*, and *Coin World*.

Finally, in 1982, the Treasury Department issued the first commemorative coin since 1954—a silver half dollar celebrating the 250th anniversary of the birth of George Washington. This time around, distribution was placed in the hands of the Bureau of the Mint (today called the U.S. Mint) rather than with a commission or private individuals. The profits accrued to the Treasury Department and the U.S. government. The issue was well received in the numismatic community, with more than seven million of the half dollars sold nationwide.

Then came the 1983 and 1984 Los Angeles Olympiad coins, minted in the subject years for the Los Angeles Olympiad held in 1984. These comprised a diverse and somewhat experimental series, with dollars of two different designs and, for the first time, a commemorative ten-dollar gold coin. Sales were satisfactory, and the supply easily met the demand from collectors and investors.

The concept of a surcharge, or built-in fee, was introduced, with a certain amount per coin going to a congressionally designated beneficiary—in the instance of the Olympic coins, the Los Angeles Olympic Organizing Committee. These and related surcharges became controversial with collectors, some of whom resented making involuntary donations when they bought coins. Today the practice continues, though without as much controversy. Surcharges are the spark that has ignited most commemorative programs, as potential recipients of the earmarked profits launch intense lobbying campaigns in Congress.

In 1986 the 100th anniversary of the completion of the Statue of Liberty was commemorated by the issuance of a copper-nickel–clad half dollar (first of its kind in the commemorative series), a silver dollar, and a five-dollar gold coin, with varied motifs, each depicting on the obverse the Statue of Liberty or an element therefrom. Unprecedented millions of coins were sold.

Then followed a lull in commemorative purchases, although the Mint continued to issue coins celebrating more Olympic Games, various national anniversaries, and significant people, places, events, and other subjects. Some years saw four or five or more individual commemorative programs. Some were well received by the hobby community, but sales of most fell far short of projections. In certain cases these low sales would eventually prove beneficial for collectors who placed orders from the Mint. An example is the 1995 five-dollar commemorative honoring baseball star and Civil Rights hero Jackie Robinson. Only 5,174 Uncirculated pieces were sold, creating a modern rarity.

Most modern commemorative coins have seen only modest secondary-market appreciation, if any. Beyond their retail values, however, the coins will always have significant historical, cultural, and sentimental value. The 2001 American Buffalo silver dollar created a sensation with its bold design harkening back to the classic Buffalo nickel of 1913 to 1938; the issue sold out quickly and soon was commanding high premiums in the collector market. It remains popular and valuable today. In 2014, the National Baseball Hall of Fame commemoratives (a three-coin suite in copper-nickel, silver, and gold) captured mainstream-media headlines and national TV news coverage. Other modern commemoratives have honored American inventors and explorers, branches of the U.S. military, Boy Scouts and Girl Scouts, the Civil Rights Act of 1964, and other important themes, continuing a tradition of special coinage dating back to 1892 and giving today's collectors a broad spectrum of issues to study and cherish.

See page 1254 for pricing of government commemorative sets and page 1502 for an alphabetical cross-reference list of all commemoratives.

GEORGE WASHINGTON 250TH ANNIVERSARY OF BIRTH HALF DOLLAR (1982)

Designer: *Elizabeth Jones.* **Weight:** *12.50 grams.*
Composition: *.900 silver, .100 copper (net weight .3617 oz. pure silver).*
Diameter: *30.6 mm.* **Edge:** *Reeded.* **Mints:** *Denver (Uncirculated), San Francisco (Proof).*

This coin, the first commemorative half dollar issued since 1954, celebrated the 250th anniversary of the birth of George Washington. It was also the first 90% silver coin produced by the U.S. Mint since 1964.

Designs. *Obverse:* George Washington on horseback. *Reverse:* Mount Vernon.

Mintage Data. Authorized by Public Law 97-014, signed by President Ronald Reagan on December 23, 1981. *Maximum authorized*—10,000,000. *Number minted*—1982-D: 478,716; 1982-S: 868,326. *Net distribution*—1982-D: 2,210,458 Uncirculated; 1982-S: 4,894,044 Proof.

Original Cost. Sale prices originally $8.50 (Uncirculated) and $10.50 (Proof), later raised to $10 and $12, respectively.

Key to Collecting. Today, Uncirculated 1982-D and Proof 1982-S Washington half dollars are plentiful on the market and are readily available in as-issued condition. They are popular and highly regarded as part of the modern commemorative series.

	Distribution	Cert	Avg	%MS	MS-67	
					PF-67	
1982D	2,210,458	4,420	67.0	100%	$12	
	Auctions: $123, MS-69, June 2014					
1982S, Proof	4,894,044	7,589	69.0		$11	
	Auctions: $110, PF-70, June 2014; $103, PF-70, August 2014; $106, PF-70, November 2014; $100, PF-70, November 2014					

Los Angeles Olympiad Discus Thrower Silver Dollar (1983)

Designer: *Elizabeth Jones.* **Weight:** *26.73 grams.* **Composition:** *.900 silver, .100 copper (net weight .7736 oz. pure silver).* **Diameter:** *38.1 mm.* **Edge:** *Reeded.*
Mints: *Philadelphia, Denver (Uncirculated); San Francisco (Uncirculated and Proof).*

Three distinctive coins were issued to commemorate the 1984 Los Angeles Summer Olympic Games. The 1983 Discus Thrower dollar was the first commemorative silver dollar since the 1900 Lafayette issue.

Designs. *Obverse:* Representation of the traditional Greek discus thrower inspired by the ancient work of the sculptor Myron. *Reverse:* The head and upper body of an American eagle.

Mintage Data. Authorized by Public Law 97-220, signed by President Ronald Reagan on July 22, 1982. *Maximum authorized*—50,000,000 totally for 1983 and 1984. *Number minted*—1983-P: 294,543 Uncirculated; 1983-D: 174,014 Uncirculated; 1983-S: 174,014 Uncirculated and 1,577,025 Proof.

Original Cost. Sale prices $28 (Uncirculated) and $24.95 (Proof, ordered in advance); Proof raised later to $29, and still later to $32. Part of the $10 surcharge per coin went to the U.S. Olympic Committee and the Los Angeles Olympic Organizing Committee.

Key to Collecting. These pieces in both Uncirculated and Proof format can be found today for prices near their issue cost. The vast quantities issued (never mind that 52 million were not sold) made them common. Nearly all surviving coins are in superb gem preservation. Today the aftermarket is supported by coin collectors, not by Olympic sports enthusiasts.

	Distribution	Cert	Avg	%MS	MS-67	
					PF-67	
1983P	294,543	2,056	69.0	100%	$30	
	Auctions: $499, MS-70, September 2014					
1983D	174,014	1,523	69.0	100%	$35	
	Auctions: $7,638, MS-70, April 2013					
1983S	174,014	1,587	69.0	100%	$30	
	Auctions: $8,813, MS-70, April 2013					
1983S, Proof	1,577,025	4,813	69.0		$31	
	Auctions: $1,175, PF-70DCam, April 2014					

LOS ANGELES OLYMPIAD OLYMPIC COLISEUM SILVER DOLLAR (1984)

Designer: *John Mercanti.* **Weight:** *26.73 grams.* **Composition:** *.900 silver, .100 copper
(net weight .7736 oz. pure silver).* **Diameter:** *38.1 mm.* **Edge:** *Reeded.*
Mints: *Philadelphia, Denver (Uncirculated); San Francisco (Uncirculated and Proof).*

This coin became a reality at the insistence of the Los Angeles Olympic Organizing Committee. The semi-nude figures on the obverse created some controversy.

Designs. *Obverse:* Robert Graham's headless torso sculptures at the entrance of the Los Angeles Memorial Coliseum. *Reverse:* Perched eagle looking back over its left wing.

Mintage Data. Authorized by Public Law 97-220, signed by President Ronald Reagan on July 22, 1982. *Maximum authorized*—50,000,000 totally for 1983 and 1984. *Number minted*—1984-P: 217,954 Uncirculated; 1984-D: 116,675 Uncirculated; 1984-S: 116,675 Uncirculated and 1,801,210 Proof.

Original Cost. Sales prices $28 (Uncirculated) and $32 (Proof); Proof later raised to $35. Part of the $10 surcharge per coin went to the U.S. Olympic Committee and the Los Angeles Olympic Organizing Committee.

Key to Collecting. These pieces in both Uncirculated and Proof format can be found today for close to what they cost at the time of issue. The vast quantities issued (never mind that 52 million were not sold) made them common. Nearly all surviving coins are in superb gem preservation. Today, the after-market is supported by coin collectors, not by Olympic sports enthusiasts.

	Distribution	Cert	Avg	%MS	MS-67		
					PF-67		
1984P	217,954	1,598	69.0	100%	$35		
	Auctions: $456, MS-70, September 2014; $705, MS-70, September 2013						
1984D	116,675	1,161	68.9	100%	$40		
	Auctions: $4,994, MS-70, April 2013						
1984S	116,675	1,170	68.9	100%	$40		
	Auctions: $9,400, MS-70, April 2013						
1984S, Proof	1,801,210	4,079	68.9		$31		
	Auctions: $411, PF-70DCam, September 2014; $558, PF-70DCam, April 2013						

Los Angeles Olympiad $10 Gold Coin (1984)

Designer: *John Mercanti.* **Weight:** *16.718 grams.* **Composition:** *.900 gold, .100 copper (net weight .4837 oz. pure gold).* **Diameter:** *27 mm.* **Edge:** *Reeded.*

Mints: *Philadelphia, Denver, San Francisco (Proof); West Point (Uncirculated and Proof).*

This ten-dollar coin was the first commemorative to be struck in gold since the 1926 Sesquicentennial $2.50 gold pieces. Mint engraver John Mercanti based the obverse design on a sketch by James Peed of the Bureau of the Mint's Washington office.

Designs. *Obverse:* Two runners holding aloft the Olympic torch. *Reverse:* Adaptation of the Great Seal of the United States.

Mintage Data. Authorized by Public Law 97-220, signed by President Ronald Reagan on July 22, 1982. *Maximum authorized*—2,000,000. *Number minted*—1984-P: 33,309 Proof; 1984-D: 34,533 Proof; 1984-S: 48,551 Proof; 1984-W: 75,886 Uncirculated and 381,085 Proof.

Original Cost. Sales prices $339 (Uncirculated) and $353 (Proof). Part of the $35 surcharge per coin went to the U.S. Olympic Committee and the Los Angeles Olympic Organizing Committee.

Key to Collecting. These coins are necessarily expensive due to their gold content, but are still quite reasonable. Nearly all surviving coins are in superb gem preservation. Today, the aftermarket is supported by coin collectors, not by Olympic sports enthusiasts.

	Distribution	Cert	Avg	%MS	MS-67
					PF-67
1984W	75,886	1,583	69.3	100%	$800
	Auctions: $764, MS-70, September 2014; $893, MS-70, April 2013; $611, MS-69, October 2014				
1984P, Proof	33,309	1,832	69.0	100%	$750
	Auctions: $823, PF-70DCam, September 2014; $1,763, PF-70DCam, April 2013; $624, PF-69DCam, October 2014				
1984D, Proof	34,533	1,878	69.1	100%	$750
	Auctions: $1,116, PF-70DCam, April 2013; $617, PF-69DCam, October 2014; $611, PF-69DCam, October 2014				
1984S, Proof	48,551	1,789	69.2	100%	$750
	Auctions: $823, PF-70DCam, April 2013; $618, PF-69DCam, October 2014				
1984W, Proof	381,085	5,700	69.1		$750
	Auctions: $693, PF-69DCam, September 2014; $635, PF-69DCam, October 2014; $617, PF-69DCam, November 2014				

Statue of Liberty Centennial Half Dollar (1986)

Designer: *Edgar Z. Steever IV (obverse), Sherl Winter (reverse).* **Weight:** *11.34 grams.* **Composition:** *.9167 copper, .0833 nickel.* **Diameter:** *30.61 mm.* **Edge:** *Reeded.* **Mints:** *Denver (Uncirculated), San Francisco (Proof).*

The 100th anniversary of the dedication of the Statue of Liberty in New York City harbor in 1886 furnished the occasion for the issuance of three different commemorative coins in 1986. The clad half dollar was the first U.S. commemorative issued in copper-nickel format.

Designs. *Obverse:* Ship of immigrants steaming into New York harbor, with the Statue of Liberty greeting them in the foreground and the New York skyline in the distance. *Reverse:* Scene of an immigrant family with their belongings on the threshold of America.

Mintage Data. Authorized by the Act of July 9, 1985. *Maximum authorized*—25,000,000. *Number minted*—1986-D: 928,008 Uncirculated; 1986-S: 6,925,627 Proof.

Original Cost. Sale prices $5 (Uncirculated, pre-order) and $6.50 (Proof, pre-order); Uncirculated later raised to $6, and Proof later raised to $7.50.

Key to Collecting. So many 1986 Statue of Liberty half dollars were issued that the aftermarket affords the possibility of purchasing the coins not much above the original offering price. Nearly all are superb gems.

	Distribution	Cert	Avg	%MS	MS-67 PF-67
1986D	928,008	2,353	69.0	100%	$6
	Auctions: $411, MS-70, April 2013				
1986S, Proof	6,925,627	10,718	69.0		$4
	Auctions: No auction records available.				

STATUE OF LIBERTY CENTENNIAL SILVER DOLLAR (1986)

Designer: *John Mercanti.* **Weight:** *26.73 grams.* **Composition:** *.900 silver, .100 copper (net weight .7736 oz. pure silver).* **Diameter:** *38.1 mm.* **Edge:** *Reeded.* **Mints:** *Philadelphia (Uncirculated), San Francisco (Proof).*

These coins, which are also known as Ellis Island silver dollars, feature an excerpt from Emma Lazarus's poem, *The New Colossus.*

Designs. *Obverse:* Statue of Liberty in the foreground, with the Ellis Island immigration center behind her. *Reverse:* Liberty's torch, along with the words GIVE ME YOUR TIRED, YOUR POOR, YOUR HUDDLED MASSES YEARNING TO BREATHE FREE.

Mintage Data. Authorized by the Act of July 9, 1985. *Maximum authorized*—10,000,000. *Number minted*—1986-P: 723,635 Uncirculated; 1986-S: 6,414,638 Proof.

Original Cost. Sale prices $20.50 (Uncirculated, pre-order) and $22.50 (Proof, pre-order); Uncirculated later raised to $22, and Proof later raised to $24.

Key to Collecting. Nearly all coins of this issue are superb gems.

	Distribution	Cert	Avg	%MS	MS-67 PF-67
1986P	723,635	3,834	69.0	100%	$25
	Auctions: $170, MS-70, January 2013; $27, MS-69, August 2014				
1986S, Proof	6,414,638	12,192	69.0		$23
	Auctions: $141, PF-70DCam, April 2014; $106, PF-70DCam, April 2013; $70, PF-69DCam, August 2014; $188, PF-69DCam, November 2014				

Statue of Liberty Centennial $5 Gold Coin (1986)

Designer: *Elizabeth Jones.* **Weight:** *8.359 grams.* **Composition:** *.900 gold, .100 copper (net weight .242 oz. pure gold).* **Diameter:** *21.6 mm.* **Edge:** *Reeded.* **Mints:** *West Point.*

The designs on these five-dollar gold coins created a sensation in the numismatic community and were widely discussed, and the coin received Krause Publications' Coin of the Year Award. The entire authorization of a half million coins was spoken for—the only complete sellout of any commemorative coin of the 1980s.

Designs. *Obverse:* Face and crown of the Statue of Liberty. *Reverse:* American eagle in flight.

Mintage Data. Authorized by the Act of July 9, 1985. *Maximum authorized*—500,000. *Number minted*— 95,248 Uncirculated and 404,013 Proof.

Original Cost. Sale prices $160 (Uncirculated, pre-order) and $170 (Proof, pre-order); Uncirculated later raised to $165, and Proof later raised to $175.

Key to Collecting. So many 1986 Statue of Liberty commemoratives were issued that the aftermarket affords the possibility of purchasing the coins at prices near bullion value. Nearly all coins of this issue are superb gems.

	Distribution	Cert	Avg	%MS	MS-67 / PF-67
1986W	95,248	3,748	69.5	100%	$365
	Auctions: $353, MS-70, August 2014; $329, MS-70, September 2014; $329, MS-70, November 2014; $441, MS-70, February 2013				
1986W, Proof	404,013	10,546	69.3		$375
	Auctions: $402, PF-70DCam, April 2013; $317, PF-69DCam, August 2014; $329, PF-69DCam, October 2014				

Constitution Bicentennial Silver Dollar (1987)

Designer: *Patricia Lewis Verani.* **Weight:** *26.73 grams.*
Composition: *.900 silver, .100 copper (net weight .7736 oz. pure silver).*
Diameter: *38.1 mm.* **Edge:** *Reeded.* **Mints:** *Philadelphia (Uncirculated), San Francisco (Proof).*

In connection with the 200th anniversary of the U.S. Constitution, observed in 1987, Congress held a competition to design both a silver dollar and a five-dollar gold coin.

Designs. *Obverse:* Quill pen, a sheaf of parchment, and the words WE THE PEOPLE. *Reverse:* Cross-section of Americans from various periods representing various lifestyles.

Mintage Data. Authorized by Public Law 99-582, signed by President Ronald Reagan on October 29, 1986. *Maximum authorized*—1,000,000. *Number minted*—1987-P: 451,629 Uncirculated; 1987-S: 2,747,116 Proof.

Original Cost. Sale prices $22.50 (Uncirculated, pre-issue) and $24 (Proof, pre-issue); Uncirculated later raised to $26, and Proof later raised to $28. A $7 surcharge per coin went toward reducing the national debt.

Key to Collecting. Today, these coins remain inexpensive. Nearly all are superb gems.

	Distribution	Cert	Avg	%MS	MS-67 PF-67
1987P	451,629	3,367	69.1	100%	$25
	Auctions: $90, MS-70, January 2013				
1987S, Proof	2,747,116	5,588	68.9		$23
	Auctions: $115, PF-70DCam, April 2013				

CONSTITUTION BICENTENNIAL $5 GOLD COIN (1987)

Designer: *Marcel Jovine.* **Weight:** *8.359 grams.* **Composition:** *.900 gold, .100 copper (net weight .242 oz. pure gold).* **Diameter:** *21.6 mm.* **Edge:** *Reeded.* **Mint:** *West Point.*

A modernistic design by Marcel Jovine was selected for the five-dollar gold coin honoring the bicentennial of the U.S. Constitution.

Designs. *Obverse:* Stylized eagle holding a massive quill pen. *Reverse:* Large quill pen with nine stars to the left (symbolizing the first colonies to ratify the Constitution) and four to the right (representing the remaining original states).

Mintage Data. Authorized by Public Law 99-582, signed by President Ronald Reagan on October 29, 1986. *Maximum authorized*—1,000,000. *Number minted*—214,225 Uncirculated and 651,659 Proof.

Original Cost. Sale prices $195 (Uncirculated, pre-issue) and $200 (Proof, pre-issue); Uncirculated later raised to $215, and Proof later raised to $225.

Key to Collecting. Nearly all coins of this issue are superb gems.

	Distribution	Cert	Avg	%MS	MS-67 PF-67
1987W	214,225	7,387	69.7	100%	$365
	Auctions: $617, MS-70, September 2014; $558, MS-70, November 2014; $529, MS-70, January 2013; $317, MS-69, September 2014				
1987W, Proof	651,659	16,319	69.5		$375
	Auctions: $364, PF-70DCam, August 2014; $1,116, PF-70DCam, November 2014; $482, PF-70DCam, February 2013				

SEOUL OLYMPIAD SILVER DOLLAR (1988)

Designer: *Patricia Lewis Verani (obverse), Sherl Winter (reverse).* **Weight:** *26.73 grams.*
Composition: *.900 silver, .100 copper (net weight .7736 oz. pure silver).*
Diameter: *38.1 mm.* **Edge:** *Reeded.* **Mints:** *Denver (Uncirculated), San Francisco (Proof).*

The holding of the 1988 Summer Olympic Games in Seoul, Republic of South Korea, furnished the opportunity for the issuance of this silver dollar (as well as a five-dollar gold coin; see next entry).

Designs. *Obverse:* One hand holding an Olympic torch as another hand holds another torch to ignite it. *Reverse:* Olympic rings surrounded by a wreath.

Mintage Data. Authorized by Public Law 100-141, signed by President Ronald Reagan on October 28, 1987. *Maximum authorized*—10,000,000. *Number minted*—1988-D: 191,368 Uncirculated; 1988-S: 1,359,366 Proof.

Original Cost. Sale prices $22 (Uncirculated, pre-issue) and $23 (Proof, pre-issue); Uncirculated later raised to $27, and Proof later raised to $29. The surcharge of $7 per coin went to the U.S. Olympic Committee.

Key to Collecting. These coins are inexpensive. The numismatic market, representing actual buyers and sellers, is not extensive enough to maintain large premiums over the price of hundreds of thousands of coins purchased by the non-numismatic public and then later sold when their novelty passed. Nearly all coins are superb gems.

	Distribution	Cert	Avg	%MS	MS-67 PF-67
1988D	191,368	2,035	69.0	100%	$25
	Auctions: $247, MS-70, September 2014				
1988S, Proof	1,359,366	4,628	68.9		$25
	Auctions: $135, PF-70DCam, September 2014; $141, PF-70DCam, April 2013				

SEOUL OLYMPIAD $5 GOLD COIN (1988)

Designer: *Elizabeth Jones (obverse), Marcel Jovine (reverse).* **Weight:** *8.359 grams.*
Composition: *.900 gold, .100 copper (net weight .242 oz. pure gold).*
Diameter: *21.6 mm.* **Edge:** *Reeded.* **Mint:** *West Point.*

Elizabeth Jones's five-dollar obverse design is considered by many to be the high point of commemorative coinage art of the late 20th century. Some observers suggested that, because the event was not held in the United States, the Seoul Olympics were not an appropriate subject for American coinage; regardless, the gold coin was praised to the skies.

Designs. *Obverse:* Nike, goddess of Victory, wearing a crown of olive leaves. *Reverse:* Stylized Olympic flame.

Mintage Data. Authorized by Public Law 100-141, signed by President Ronald Reagan on October 28, 1987. *Maximum authorized*—1,000,000. *Number minted*—62,913 Uncirculated and 281,465 Proof.

Original Cost. Sale prices $200 (Uncirculated, pre-issue) and $205 (Proof, pre-issue); Uncirculated later raised to $225, and Proof later raised to $235. The surcharge of $35 per coin went to the U.S. Olympic Committee.

Key to Collecting. Examples are readily available today.

	Distribution	Cert	Avg	%MS	MS-67 PF-67
1988W	62,913	2,317	69.5	100%	$375
	Auctions: $306, MS-69, August 2014; $423, MS-69, March 2013				
1988W, Proof	281,465	9,505	69.4		$375
	Auctions: $337, PF-70DCam, September 2014; $441, PF-69DCam, February 2013				

CONGRESS BICENTENNIAL HALF DOLLAR (1989)

Designer: *Patricia Lewis Verani (obverse), William Woodward (reverse).*
Weight: *11.34 grams.* **Composition:** *.9167 copper, .0833 nickel.* **Diameter:** *30.61 mm.*
Edge: *Reeded.* **Mints:** *Denver (Uncirculated), San Francisco (Proof).*

The 200th anniversary of the operation of Congress under the U.S. Constitution was observed in 1989, and a suite of commemorative coins was authorized to observe the bicentennial, among them this copper-nickel half dollar.

Designs. *Obverse:* The head of the *Freedom* statue (erected on top of the Capitol dome in 1863) is shown at the center, with inscriptions around, including LIBERTY in oversize letters at the bottom border. *Reverse:* A distant front view of the Capital is shown, with arcs of stars above and below, with appropriate lettering.

Mintage Data. Authorized by Public Law 100-673, signed by President Ronald Reagan on November 17, 1988. The coins were to be dated 1989 and could be minted through June 30, 1990. *Maximum authorized*—4,000,000. *Number minted*—1989-D: 163,753 Uncirculated; 1989-S: 767,897 Proof.

Original Cost. Sale prices $5 (Uncirculated, pre-issue) and $7 (Proof, pre-issue); Uncirculated later raised to $6, and Proof later raised to $8. The surcharge of $1 per coin went to the Capitol Preservation Fund.

Key to Collecting. Not popular with numismatists in 1989, these coins still languish in the marketplace. Exceptions are coins certified in ultra-high grades. The Uncirculated 1989-D half dollar exists with a misaligned reverse, oriented in the same direction as the obverse, instead of the usual 180 degree separation. These are rare and valuable, but are not widely known. Likely, some remain undiscovered in buyers' hands.

	Distribution	Cert	Avg	%MS	MS-67 PF-67
1984P	217,954	1,598	69.0	100%	$35
	Auctions: $456, MS-70, September 2014; $705, MS-70, September 2013				
1984D	116,675	1,161	68.9	100%	$40
	Auctions: $4,994, MS-70, April 2013				

CONGRESS BICENTENNIAL SILVER DOLLAR (1989)

Designer: *William Woodward.* **Weight:** *26.73 grams.*
Composition: *.900 silver, .100 copper (net weight .7736 oz. pure silver).*
Diameter: *38.1 mm.* **Edge:** *Reeded.* **Mints:** *Denver (Uncirculated), San Francisco (Proof).*

To inaugurate the Congress Bicentennial coins, four coining presses weighing seven tons each were brought from the Philadelphia Mint to the east front of the Capitol building, where in a special ceremony on June 14, 1989, the first silver dollars and five-dollar gold coins were struck (but no half dollars).

Designs. *Obverse:* The statue of *Freedom* full length, with a cloud and rays of glory behind. Lettering around the border. *Reverse:* The mace of the House of Representatives, which is in the House Chamber when that body is in session.

Mintage Data. Authorized by Public Law 100-673, signed by President Ronald Reagan on November 17, 1988. The coins were to be dated 1989 and could be minted through June 30, 1990. *Maximum authorized*—3,000,000. *Number minted*—1989-D: 135,203 Uncirculated; 1989-S: 762,198 Proof.

Original Cost. Sale prices $23 (Uncirculated, pre-issue) and $25 (Proof, pre-issue): Uncirculated later raised to $26, and Proof later raised to $29. Surcharge of $7 per coin went to the Capitol Preservation Fund.

Key to Collecting. Not popular with numismatists in 1989, these coins today can be found for prices close to bullion value. Exceptions are coins certified in ultra-high grades.

	Distribution	Cert	Avg	%MS	MS-67 / PF-67
1989D	135,203	2,394	69.0	100%	$25 (MS-67)
	Auctions: $646, MS-70, September 2014; $940, MS-70, April 2013				
1989S, Proof	762,198	3,607	68.9		$34 (PF-67)
	Auctions: $457, PF-70DCam, May 2013; $42, PF-69DCam, July 2014; $106, PF-69DCam, November 2014; $940, PF-70, March 2013				

CONGRESS BICENTENNIAL $5 GOLD COIN (1989)

Designer: *John Mercanti.* **Weight:** *8.359 grams.* **Composition:** *.900 gold, .100 copper (net weight .242 oz. pure gold).* **Diameter:** *21.6 mm.* **Edge:** *Reeded.* **Mint:** *West Point.*

To diversify the motifs of the three Congress Bicentennial commemorative coins, 11 artists from the private sector were invited to submit designs, as were members of the Mint's Engraving Department staff. The designs for this five-dollar gold coin were praised in the *Annual Report of the Director of the Mint*, 1989, which stated that the obverse displayed "a spectacular rendition of the Capitol dome," while the reverse "center[ed] around a dramatic portrait of the majestic eagle atop the canopy overlooking the Old Senate Chamber."

Designs. *Obverse:* The dome of the Capitol is shown, with lettering around. *Reverse:* The eagle in the old Senate chamber is depicted, with lettering surrounding.

Mintage Data. Authorized by Public Law 100-673, signed by President Ronald Reagan on November 17, 1988. The coins were to be dated 1989 and could be minted through June 30, 1990. *Maximum authorized—1,000,000. Number minted—*46,899 Uncirculated and 164,690 Proof.

Original Cost. Sale prices $185 (Uncirculated, pre-issue) and $195 (Proof, pre-issue); Uncirculated later raised to $200, and Proof later raised to $215. Surcharge of $35 per coin went to the Capitol Preservation Fund.

Key to Collecting. Not popular with numismatists in 1989, these coins today can be purchased in the secondary marketplace for prices close to their bullion value. Exceptions are coins certified in ultra-high grades.

	Distribution	Cert	Avg	%MS	MS-67
					PF-67
1989W	46,899	2,223	69.5	100%	$375
	Auctions: $646, MS-70, September 2014; $400, MS-69, April 2013				
1989W, Proof	164,690	5,450	69.4		$375
	Auctions: $1,116, PF-70DCam, November 2014; $588, PF-67DCam, August 2013				

EISENHOWER CENTENNIAL SILVER DOLLAR (1990)

Designer: *John Mercanti (obverse), Marcel Jovine (reverse).* **Weight:** *26.73 grams.*
Composition: *.900 silver, .100 copper (net weight .7736 oz. pure silver).* **Diameter:** *38.1 mm.*
Edge: *Reeded.* **Mints:** *West Point (Uncirculated), Philadelphia (Proof).*

Five outside artists as well as the artists on the Mint Engraving Department staff were invited to submit designs for this silver dollar. In August 1989, secretary of the Treasury Nicholas F. Brady made the final selections.

This is the only U.S. coin to feature two portraits of the same person on the same side. The reverse shows Eisenhower's retirement residence, identified as EISENHOWER HOME.

Designs. *Obverse:* Profile of President Eisenhower facing right, superimposed over his own left-facing profile as a five-star general. *Reverse:* Eisenhower retirement home at Gettysburg, a national historic site.

Mintage Data. Authorized by Public Law 100-467, signed by President Ronald Reagan on October 3, 1988. *Maximum authorized—4,000,000. Number minted—*1990-W: 241,669 Uncirculated; 1990-P: 1,144,461 Proof.

Original Cost. Sale prices $23 (Uncirculated, pre-issue) and $25 (Proof, pre-issue; Uncirculated later raised to $26, and Proof later raised to $29. Surcharge of $7 per coin went to reduce public debt.

Key to Collecting. Eisenhower Centennial dollars are appreciated as a fine addition to the commemorative series. Examples are plentiful and inexpensive in the marketplace. Nearly all are superb gems.

	Distribution	Cert	Avg	%MS	MS-67
					PF-67
1990W	241,669	2,134	69.1	100%	$25
	Auctions: $206, MS-70, March 2013				
1990P, Proof	1,144,461	3,953	69.0		$28
	Auctions: $135, PF-70DCam, September 2014; $201, PF-70DCam, March 2013; $42, PF-69DCam, July 2014; $35, PF-68DCam, August 2014				

KOREAN WAR MEMORIAL SILVER DOLLAR (1991)

Designer: *John Mercanti (obverse), James Ferrell (reverse).* **Weight:** *26.73 grams.*
Composition: *.900 silver, .100 copper (net weight .7736 oz. pure silver).*
Diameter: *38.1 mm.* **Edge:** *Reeded.* **Mints:** *Denver (Uncirculated), Philadelphia (Proof).*

In the annals of commemoratives, one of the more curious entries is the 1991 silver dollar observing the 38th anniversary of the end of the Korean War, struck to honor those who served there. The 38th anniversary was chosen—rather than the 50th or some other typical anniversary—because, during that war, the 38th degree of latitude on the map defined the division between North and South Korea.

Buyers reacted favorably to the coin, and more than 800,000 were produced.

Designs. *Obverse:* Two F-86 Sabrejet fighter aircraft flying to the right, a helmeted soldier carrying a backpack climbing a hill, and the inscriptions: THIRTY EIGHTH / ANNIVERSARY / COMMEMORATIVE / KOREA / IN GOD WE TRUST / 1953 / 1991. At the bottom of the coin are five Navy ships above the word LIBERTY. *Reverse:* Outline map of North and South Korea, divided. An eagle's head (representing the United States) is depicted to the right. Near the bottom is the symbol of Korea.

Mintage Data. Authorized by Public Law 101-495 of October 31, 1990. *Maximum authorized—1,000,000. Number minted—*1991-D: 213,049 Uncirculated; 1991-P: 618,488 Proof.

Original Cost. Sale prices $23 (Uncirculated, pre-issue) and $28 (Proof, pre-issue); Uncirculated later raised to $26, and Proof later raised to $31. A surcharge of $7 went to fund the Korean War Veterans Memorial.

Key to Collecting. Gem Uncirculated and Proof coins are readily available in the marketplace.

	Distribution	Cert	Avg	%MS	MS-67 PF-67
1991D	213,049	2,245	69.1	100%	$35
	Auctions: $76, MS-70, July 2014; $106, MS-70, January 2013				
1991P, Proof	618,488	2,908	68.9		$26
	Auctions: $382, PF-70DCam, September 2014; $505, PF-70DCam, March 2013				

MOUNT RUSHMORE GOLDEN ANNIVERSARY HALF DOLLAR (1991)

Designer: *Marcel Jovine (obverse), T. James Ferrell (reverse).* **Weight:** *11.34 grams.*
Composition: *.9167 copper, .0833 nickel.* **Diameter:** *30.61 mm.* **Edge:** *Reeded.*
Mints: *Denver (Uncirculated), San Francisco (Proof).*

This half dollar was part of a trio of coins struck to mark the Mount Rushmore National Memorial's 50th anniversary. Surcharges from their sale were divided between the Treasury Department and the Mount Rushmore National Memorial Society of Black Hills, North Dakota, with money going toward restoration work on the landmark.

Designs. *Obverse:* View of Mount Rushmore with rays of the sun behind. *Reverse:* An American bison with the words GOLDEN ANNIVERSARY.

Mintage Data. Authorized by the Mount Rushmore National Memorial Coin Act (Public Law 101-332, July 16, 1990). *Maximum authorized*—2,500,000. *Number minted*—1991-D: 172,754 Uncirculated; 1991-S: 753,257 Proof.

Original Cost. Sale prices $6 (Uncirculated) and $8.50 (Proof); Uncirculated later raised to $7, and Proof later raised to $9.50. Fifty percent of the surcharge of $1 per coin went to the Mount Rushmore National Memorial Society of Black Hills; the balance went to the U.S. Treasury.

Key to Collecting. Examples are easily available today. The coins were carefully struck, with the result that nearly all are superb gems.

	Distribution	Cert	Avg	%MS	MS-67 PF-67
1991D	172,754	1,675	69.1	100%	$15
	Auctions: $306, MS-70, September 2014; $823, MS-70, March 2013				
1991S, Proof	753,257	3,075	69.1		$11
	Auctions: No auction records available.				

MOUNT RUSHMORE GOLDEN ANNIVERSARY SILVER DOLLAR (1991)

Designer: *Marika Somogyi (obverse), Frank Gasparro (reverse).* **Weight:** *26.73 grams.*
Composition: *.900 silver, .100 copper (net weight .7736 oz. pure silver).* **Diameter:** *38.1 mm.*
Edge: *Reeded.* **Mints:** *Philadelphia (Uncirculated), San Francisco (Proof).*

The Mount Rushmore silver dollar displays the traditional portraits of presidents George Washington, Thomas Jefferson, Theodore Roosevelt, and Abraham Lincoln as sculpted on the mountain by Gutzon Borglum. The reverse was by former chief sculptor-engraver of the U.S. Mint Frank Gasparro.

Designs. *Obverse:* View of Mount Rushmore with an olive wreath prominently below. *Reverse:* The Great Seal of the United States, surrounded by a sunburst, above an outline map of the continental part of the United States inscribed SHRINE OF / DEMOCRACY.

Mintage Data. Authorized by the Mount Rushmore National Memorial Coin Act (Public Law 101-332, July 16, 1990). *Maximum authorized*—2,500,000. *Number minted*—1991-P: 133,139 Uncirculated; 1991-S: 738,419 Proof.

Original Cost. Sale prices $23 (Uncirculated, pre-issue) and $28 (Proof, pre-issue); Uncirculated later raised to $28, and Proof later raised to $31. Fifty percent of the surcharge of $7 per coin went to the Mount Rushmore National Memorial Society of Black Hills; the balance went to the U.S. Treasury.

Key to Collecting. Examples are easily available today. The coins were carefully struck, with the result that nearly all are superb gems.

	Distribution	Cert	Avg	%MS	MS-67 PF-67
1991P	133,139	1,770	69.3	100%	$40
	Auctions: $80, MS-70, July 2014; $92, MS-70, January 2013				
1991S, Proof	738,419	3,595	69.0		$38
	Auctions: $194, PF-70DCam, September 2014; $176, PF-70DCam, June 2013; $174, PF-70DCam, February 2013; $53, PF-69DCam, July 2014				

MOUNT RUSHMORE GOLDEN ANNIVERSARY $5 GOLD COIN (1991)

Designer: *John Mercanti (obverse), William Lamb (reverse).* **Weight:** *8.359 grams.*
Composition: *.900 gold, .100 copper (net weight .242 oz. pure gold).*
Diameter: *21.6 mm.* **Edge:** *Reeded.* **Mint:** *West Point.*

The reverse of the five-dollar Mount Rushmore coin consisted solely of lettering, with no emblems or motifs, the first such instance in the history of U.S. commemorative coins.

Designs. *Obverse:* An American eagle flying above the monument with LIBERTY and date in the field. *Reverse:* MOUNT RUSHMORE NATIONAL MEMORIAL in script type.

Mintage Data. Authorized by the Mount Rushmore National Memorial Coin Act (Public Law 101-332, July 16, 1990). *Maximum authorized—* 500,000. *Number minted—*31,959 Uncirculated and 111,991 Proof.

Original Cost. Sale prices $185 (Uncirculated, pre-issue) and $195 (Proof, pre-issue); Uncirculated later raised to $210, and Proof later raised to $225. Fifty percent of the surcharge of $35 per coin went to the Mount Rushmore National Memorial Society of Black Hills; the balance went to the U.S. Treasury.

Key to Collecting. Examples are easily available today. The coins were carefully struck, with the result that nearly all are superb gems.

	Distribution	Cert	Avg	%MS	MS-67
					PF-67
1991W	31,959	1,597	69.6	100%	$375
	Auctions: $653, MS-70, September 2014; $573, MS-70, November 2014; $411, MS-70, June 2013				
1991W, Proof	111,991	4,028	69.4		$375
	Auctions: $456, PF-70DCam, February 2013; $306, PF-69DCam, October 2014				

UNITED SERVICE ORGANIZATIONS SILVER DOLLAR (1991)

Designer: *Robert Lamb (obverse), John Mercanti (reverse).* **Weight:** *26.73 grams.*
Composition: *.900 silver, .100 copper (net weight .7736 oz. pure silver).*
Diameter: *38.1 mm.* **Edge:** *Reeded.* **Mints:** *Denver (Uncirculated), San Francisco (Proof).*

The United Service Organizations is a congressionally chartered nonprofit group that provides services, programs, and live entertainment to U.S. military troops and their families. The 50th anniversary of the USO was commemorated with this silver dollar in 1991.

Designs. *Obverse:* Consists entirely of lettering, except for a banner upon which appears USO. Inscriptions include IN GOD WE TRUST, 50th ANNIVERSARY (in script), USO (on a banner, as noted; with three stars to each side), and LIBERTY 1991. *Reverse:* Illustrates an eagle, facing right, with a ribbon inscribed USO in its beak, perched atop a world globe. An arc of 11 stars is in the space below the globe. The legends include FIFTY YEARS / SERVICE (on the left side of the coin), TO SERVICE / PEOPLE (on the right side of the coin).

Mintage Data. Authorized by Public Law 101-404, October 2, 1990. *Maximum authorized*—1,000,000. *Number minted*—1991-D: 124,958 Uncirculated; 1991-S: 321,275 Proof.

Original Cost. Sale prices $23 (Uncirculated, pre-issue) and $28 (Proof, pre-issue); Uncirculated later raised to $26, and Proof later raised to $31. Fifty percent of the surcharge of $7 per coin went to the USO; the balance went toward reducing the national debt.

Key to Collecting. Mintages were low compared to other recent commemorative silver dollars. Today these coins can be purchased for slightly more than their bullion value.

	Distribution	Cert	Avg	%MS	MS-67 PF-67
1991D	124,958	2,038	69.1	100%	$35
	Auctions: $86, MS-70, July 2014; $92, MS-70, March 2013				
1991S, Proof	321,275	2,215	69.0		$25
	Auctions: $881, PF-70DCam, September 2014; $235, PF-70DCam, September 2014; $382, PF-70DCam, April 2013				

CHRISTOPHER COLUMBUS QUINCENTENARY HALF DOLLAR (1992)

Designer: *T. James Ferrell.* **Weight:** *11.34 grams.* **Composition:** *.9167 copper, .0833 nickel.* **Diameter:** *30.61 mm.* **Edge:** *Reeded.* **Mints:** *Denver (Uncirculated), San Francisco (Proof).*

The 500th anniversary of Christopher Columbus's first trip to the new world was observed in 1992 by a suite of commemoratives, including this clad half dollar. The numismatic tradition fit in nicely with the World's Columbian Exposition coins of a century earlier—the first commemorative half dollars issued in 1892 and 1893.

Designs. *Obverse:* A full-length figure of Columbus walking ashore, with a rowboat and the flagship *Santa Maria* in the background. *Reverse:* The reverse shows Columbus's three ships—the *Nina, Pinta*, and *Santa Maria*.

Mintage Data. Authorized by Public Law 102-281, signed by President George H.W. Bush on May 13, 1992. *Maximum authorized*—6,000,000. *Number minted*—1992-D: 135,702 Uncirculated; 1992-S: 390,154 Proof.

Original Cost. Sale prices $6.50 (Uncirculated, pre-issue) and $8.50 (Proof, pre-issue); Uncirculated later raised to $7.50, and Proof later raised to $9.50. A surcharge of $1 per coin went to the Christopher Columbus Quincentenary Coins and Fellowship Foundation.

Key to Collecting. Examples in the marketplace remain reasonably priced. Nearly all are superb gems.

	Distribution	Cert	Avg	%MS	MS-67 PF-67
1992D	135,702	927	69.2	100%	$12
	Auctions: $86, MS-70, April 2013				
1992S, Proof	390,154	2,479	69.1		$9
	Auctions: No auction records available.				

CHRISTOPHER COLUMBUS QUINCENTENARY SILVER DOLLAR (1992)

Designer: *John Mercanti (obverse), Thomas D. Rogers Sr. (reverse).* **Weight:** *26.73 grams.*
Composition: *.900 silver, .100 copper (net weight .7736 oz. pure silver).*
Diameter: *38.1 mm.* **Edge:** *Reeded.* **Mints:** *Denver (Uncirculated), Philadelphia (Proof).*

Representative Frank Annunzio, a Democrat from Illinois who was prominent in coin legislation for some time, introduced the bill that led to these commemoratives. Interestingly, on the approved sketch for this silver dollar's obverse design, Columbus was depicted holding a telescope—but after it was pointed out that such instrument had not been invented yet in 1492, it was changed to a scroll on the final coin.

Designs. *Obverse:* Columbus standing, holding a flag in his right hand, with a scroll in his left hand, and with a globe on a stand. Three ships are shown in the distance, in a panel at the top border. *Reverse:* A split image is shown, depicting exploration in 1492 at the left, with half of a sailing vessel, and in 1992 at the right, with most of a space shuttle shown in a vertical position, with the earth in the distance.

Mintage Data. Authorized by Public Law 102-281, signed by President George H.W. Bush on May 13, 1992. *Maximum authorized*—4,000,000. *Number minted*—1992-D: 106,949 Uncirculated; 1992-P: 385,241 Proof.

Original Cost. Sale prices $23 (Uncirculated, pre-issue) and $27 (Proof, pre-issue); Uncirculated later raised to $28, and Proof later raised to $31. A surcharge of $7 per coin went to the Christopher Columbus Quincentenary Coins and Fellowship Foundation.

Key to Collecting. Examples in the marketplace remain reasonably priced. Nearly all are superb gems.

	Distribution	Cert	Avg	%MS	MS-67 PF-67
1992D	106,949	1,666	69.2	100%	$40
	Auctions: $86, MS-70, July 2014; $135, MS-70, March 2013				
1992P, Proof	385,241	2,585	69.0		$35
	Auctions: $441, PF-70DCam, September 2014; $418, PF-70DCam, June 2013; $96, PF-70DCam, April 2013				

CHRISTOPHER COLUMBUS QUINCENTENARY $5 GOLD COIN (1992)

Designer: *T. James Ferrell (obverse), Thomas D. Rogers Sr. (reverse).* **Weight:** *8.359 grams.*
Composition: *.900 gold, .100 copper (net weight .242 oz. pure gold).*
Diameter: *21.6 mm.* **Edge:** *Reeded.* **Mint:** *West Point.*

No portrait from the life of Christopher Columbus is known to exist, so the five-dollar gold commemorative features T. James Ferrell's artistic imagining of the explorer's profile.

Designs. *Obverse:* The artist's conception of Columbus's face is shown gazing to the left toward an outline map of the New World. *Reverse:* The crest of the Admiral of the Ocean Sea and a chart dated 1492 are depicted.

Mintage Data. Authorized by Public Law 102-281, signed by President George H.W. Bush on May 13, 1992. *Maximum authorized*—1,000,000. *Number minted*—24,329 Uncirculated and 79,730 Proof.

Original Cost. Sale prices $180 (Uncirculated, pre-issue) and $190 (Proof, pre-issue); Uncirculated later raised to $210, and Proof later raised to $225. A surcharge of $35 per coin went to the Christopher Columbus Quincentenary Coins and Fellowship Foundation.

Key to Collecting. Examples in the marketplace remain reasonably priced. Nearly all are superb gems.

	Distribution	Cert	Avg	%MS	MS-67 PF-67
1992W	24,329	1,300	69.6	100%	$375
	Auctions: $447, MS-70, June 2014; $646, MS-70, September 2014; $317, MS-69, August 2014; $306, MS-69, August 2014				
1992W, Proof	79,730	2,768	69.5		$375
	Auctions: $306, PF-69DCam, August 2014; $435, PF-69DCam, April 2013				

XXV OLYMPIC GAMES HALF DOLLAR (1992)

Designer: *William Cousins (obverse), Steven M. Bieda (reverse).*
Weight: *11.34 grams.* **Composition:** *.9167 copper, .0833 nickel.* **Diameter:** *30.61 mm.*
Edge: *Reeded.* **Mints:** *Philadelphia (Uncirculated), San Francisco (Proof).*

In 1992 the XXV Winter Olympic Games were held in Albertville and Savoie, France, while the Summer Games took place in Barcelona, Spain. Although the events did not take place in the United States, the rationale for a commemorative coin issue was, in part, to raise money to train American athletes. The same line of reasoning had been used for the coins made in connection with the 1988 Olympic Games held in Seoul, South Korea.

Designs. *Obverse:* A pony-tailed female gymnast doing the stretch against a background of stars and stripes. *Reverse:* The Olympic torch and an olive branch, with CITIUS / ALTIUS / FORTIUS nearby in three lines, Latin for "faster, higher, stronger."

Mintage Data. Authorized by the 1992 Olympic Commemorative Coin Act, Public Law 101-406, signed by President George H.W. Bush on October 3, 1990. *Maximum authorized*—6,000,000. *Number minted*—1992-P: 161,607 Uncirculated; 1992-S: 519,645 Proof.

Original Cost. Sale prices $6 (Uncirculated, pre-issue) and $8.50 (Proof, pre-issue); Uncirculated later raised to $7.50, and Proof later raised to $9.50. The surcharge of $1 per coin went to the U.S. Olympic Committee.

Key to Collecting. Examples are easily available today. Nearly all are gems.

	Distribution	Cert	Avg	%MS	MS-67 PF-67
1992P	161,607	1,058	69.3	100%	$12
	Auctions: $59, MS-70, January 2013				
1992S, Proof	519,645	2,462	69.2		$7
	Auctions: No auction records available.				

XXV Olympic Games Silver Dollar (1992)

Designer: *John R. Deecken (obverse), Marcel Jovine (reverse).* **Weight:** *26.73 grams.*
Composition: *.900 silver, .100 copper (net weight .7736 oz. pure silver).* **Diameter:** *38.1 mm.*
Edge: *Lettered (Uncirculated), reeded (Proof).* **Mints:** *Denver (Uncirculated), San Francisco (Proof).*

The image on this coin's obverse fit closely that of Fleer's card showing popular baseball player Nolan Ryan, of the Texas Rangers, but the designer denied there was any connection when queried on the subject by the Treasury Department. The Denver Mint Uncirculated dollars have XXV OLYMPIAD incuse four times around the edge, alternately inverted, on a reeded background; these are the first lettered-edge U.S. coins since the 1933 double eagle.

Designs. *Obverse:* A pitcher is shown about to throw a ball to a batter. *Reverse:* A shield, intertwined Olympic rings, and olive branches make up the main design.

Mintage Data. Authorized by the 1992 Olympic Commemorative Coin Act, Public Law 101-406, signed by President George H.W. Bush on October 3, 1990. *Maximum authorized—4,000,000. Number minted—1992-D: 187,552 Uncirculated; 1992-S: 504,505 Proof.*

Original Cost. Sale prices $24 (Uncirculated, pre-issue) and $28 (Proof, pre-issue); Uncirculated later raised to $28, and Proof later raised to $32. The surcharge of $1 per coin went to the U.S. Olympic Committee.

Key to Collecting. Examples are easily available today. Nearly all are gems.

	Distribution	Cert	Avg	%MS	MS-67 PF-67
1992D	187,552	3,601	69.0	100%	$35
Auctions: $247, MS-70, April 2013					
1992S, Proof	504,505	2,738	69.0		$40
Auctions: $588, PF-70DCam, September 2013; $84, PF-70, February 2013					

XXV Olympic Games $5 Gold Coin (1992)

Designer: *James Sharpe (obverse), James Peed (reverse).* **Weight:** *8.359 grams.*
Composition: *.900 gold, .100 copper (net weight .242 oz. pure gold).*
Diameter: *21.6 mm.* **Edge:** *Reeded.* **Mint:** *West Point.*

The five-dollar entry in the XXV commemorative coin program features a dynamic sprinter against a backdrop of the U.S. flag. Sales were relatively low compared to other recent gold commemoratives.

Designs. *Obverse:* A sprinter running forward with a vertical U.S. flag in the background. *Reverse:* A heraldic eagle with five Olympic rings and USA above.

Mintage Data. Authorized by the 1992 Olympic Commemorative Coin Act, Public Law 101-406, signed by President George H.W. Bush on October 3, 1990. *Maximum authorized—500,000. Number minted—27,732* Uncirculated and 77,313 Proof.

Original Cost. Sale prices $185 (Uncirculated, pre-issue) and $195 (Proof, pre-issue); Uncirculated later raised to $215, and Proof later raised to $230. The surcharge of $35 per coin went to the U.S. Olympic Committee.

Key to Collecting. Examples are easily available today. Nearly all are gems.

	Distribution	Cert	Avg	%MS	MS-67
					PF-67
1992W	27,732	1,543	69.7	100%	$375
	Auctions: $400, MS-70, June 2013; $335, MS-69, July 2014				
1992W, Proof	77,313	3,070	69.5		$375
	Auctions: $206, PF-70DCam, September 2014; $341, PF-70DCam, September 2014; $341, PF-69DCam, July 2014; $435, PF-69DCam, April 2013				

WHITE HOUSE 200TH ANNIVERSARY SILVER DOLLAR (1992)

Designer: *Edgar Z. Steever IV (obverse), Chester Y. Martin (reverse).* **Weight:** *26.73 grams.*
Composition: *.900 silver, .100 copper (net weight .7736 oz. pure silver).*
Diameter: *38.1 mm.* **Edge:** *Reeded.* **Mints:** *Denver (Uncirculated), West Point (Proof).*

This coin is one of few depicting Washington buildings that sold out its full authorized limit. Foliage, two trees, and a fountain were in the original sketch, but were removed at the suggestion of the Fine Arts Commission, yielding a clean and crisp design.

Designs. *Obverse:* The north portico of the White House is shown in a plan view, without shrubbery or background. *Reverse:* James Hoban, architect of the first White House, in a half-length portrait with the original entrance door.

Mintage Data. Authorized by Public Law 102-281, signed by President George H.W. Bush on May 13, 1992. *Maximum authorized—500,000. Number minted—1992-D:* 123,803 Uncirculated; *1992-W:* 375,851 Proof.

Original Cost. Sale prices (pre-issue only) $23 (Uncirculated) and $28 (Proof). The surcharge of $10 per coin went towards the preservation of public rooms within the White House.

Key to Collecting. The White House dollar has remained popular ever since its issuance. Examples are readily available today and are nearly always found in superb gem preservation, as issued.

	Distribution	Cert	Avg	%MS	MS-67
					PF-67
1992D	123,803	1,983	69.2	100%	$35
	Auctions: $108, MS-70, January 2013				
1992W, Proof	375,851	2,799	69.0		$28
	Auctions: $194, PF-70DCam, April 2013				

BILL OF RIGHTS HALF DOLLAR (1993)

Designer: *T. James Ferrell (obverse), Dean McMullen (reverse).* **Weight:** *12.5 grams.*
Composition: *.900 silver, .100 copper.* **Diameter:** *30.6 mm.* **Edge:** *Reeded.*
Mints: *West Point (Uncirculated), San Francisco (Proof).*

This silver half dollar, as well as the silver dollar and five-dollar gold coin issued alongside it, honored James Madison and the Bill of Rights, added to the Constitution in 1789 and intended to give basic rights and freedoms to all Americans. These were the first half dollars to be composed of 90% silver since the George Washington 250th Anniversary of Birth coins in 1982.

Designs. *Obverse:* James Madison seated at a desk, penning the Bill of Rights. Montpelier, Madison's Virginia home, is shown in the distance. *Reverse:* A hand holds a flaming torch, with inscriptions to each side.

Mintage Data. Authorized by Public Law 101-281, part of the White House Commemorative Coin Act, on May 13, 1992. *Maximum authorized*—1,000,000. *Number minted*—1993-W: 193,346 Uncirculated; 1993-S: 586,315 Proof.

Original Cost. Sale prices $9.75 (Uncirculated, pre-issue) and $12.50 (Proof, pre-issue); Uncirculated later increased in $11.50, and Proof later increased to $13.50. The surcharge went to the James Madison Memorial Scholarship Trust Fund.

Key to Collecting. Following the pattern of other commemoratives of the early 1990s, these coins are readily available on the market, typically in superb gem preservation.

	Distribution	Cert	Avg	%MS	MS-67 PF-67
1993W	193,346	1,161	69.2	100%	$20
	Auctions: $82, MS-70, April 2013				
1993S, Proof	586,315	2,679	69.0		$17
	Auctions: $441, PF-70DCam, April 2013; $382, PF-70DCam, April 2013				

BILL OF RIGHTS SILVER DOLLAR (1993)

Designer: *William Krawczewicz (obverse), Dean McMullen (reverse).* **Weight:** *26.73 grams.*
Composition: *.900 silver, .100 copper (net weight .7736 oz. pure silver).*
Diameter: *38.1 mm.* **Edge:** *Reeded.* **Mints:** *Denver (Uncirculated), San Francisco (Proof).*

On June 1, 1992, U.S. Treasurer Catalina Vasquez Villalpando announced a nationwide competition seeking designs for the James Madison / Bill of Rights Commemorative Coin Program, with all entries to be received by August 31. Secretary of the Treasury Nicholas F. Brady selected his favorite motifs from 815 submissions, which were then sent to the Commission of Fine Arts for review.
Many changes were suggested, including simplifying the appearance of Madison's residence, Montpelier.

Designs. *Obverse:* Portrait of James Madison facing right and slightly forward. *Reverse:* Montpelier.

Mintage Data. Authorized by Public Law 101-281, part of the White House Commemorative Coin Act, on May 13, 1992. *Maximum authorized*—900,000. *Number minted*—1993-D: 98,383 Uncirculated; 1993-S: 534,001 Proof.

Original Cost. Sale prices $22 (Uncirculated, pre-issue) and $25 (Proof, pre-issue); Uncirculated later raised to $27, and Proof later raised to $29. The surcharge went to the James Madison Memorial Scholarship Trust Fund.

Key to Collecting. Following the pattern of other commemoratives of the early 1990s, these coins are readily available on the market, typically in superb gem preservation.

	Distribution	Cert	Avg	%MS	MS-67
					PF-67
1993D	98,383	1,339	69.1	100%	$45
	Auctions: $182, MS-70, January 2013				
1993S, Proof	534,001	2,299	68.9		$39
	Auctions: No auction records available.				

BILL OF RIGHTS $5 GOLD COIN (1993)

Designer: *Scott R. Blazek (obverse), Joseph D. Peña (reverse).* **Weight:** *8.359 grams.*
Composition: *.900 gold, .100 copper (net weight .242 oz. pure gold).*
Diameter: *21.6 mm.* **Edge:** *Reeded.* **Mint:** *West Point.*

The coin project that resulted in this five-dollar gold coin (and the related half dollar and silver dollar) was encouraged by the Madison Foundation.

Designs. *Obverse:* Portrait of Madison, waist up, reading the Bill of Rights. *Reverse:* Quotation by Madison with an eagle above and small torch and laurel branch at the border below.

Mintage Data. Authorized by Public Law 101-281, part of the White House Commemorative Coin Act, on May 13, 1992. *Maximum authorized*—300,000. *Number minted*—23,266 Uncirculated and 78,651 Proof.

Original Cost. Sale prices $175 (Uncirculated, pre-issue) and $185 (Proof, pre-issue); Uncirculated later raised to $205, and Proof later raised to $220. The surcharge of $10 per coin went to the James Madison Memorial Scholarship Trust Fund.

Key to Collecting. Following the pattern of other commemoratives of the early 1990s, these coins are readily available on the market, typically in superb gem preservation.

	Distribution	Cert	Avg	%MS	MS-67
					PF-67
1993W	23,266	1,329	69.6	100%	$375
	Auctions: $329, MS-70, August 2014; $652, MS-70, September 2014; $400, MS-69, March 2013				
1993W, Proof	78,651	3,219	69.4		$375
	Auctions: $306, PF-70DCam, November 2014; $435, PF-70DCam, March 2013; $317, PF-69DCam, August 2014; $329, PF-69DCam, October 2014				

50TH ANNIVERSARY OF WORLD WAR II HALF DOLLAR (1991–1995)

Designer: *George Klauba (obverse), Bill J. Leftwich (reverse).* **Weight:** *11.34 grams.*
Composition: *.9167 copper, .0833 nickel.* **Diameter:** *30.61 mm.* **Edge:** *Reeded.* **Mint:** *Philadelphia.*

These half dollars and the other World War II 50th-anniversary coins were issued in 1993 and dated 1991–1995. Despite the importance of the war commemorated, the coins met with a lukewarm response by purchasers.

Designs. *Obverse:* The heads of a soldier, sailor, and airman are shown superimposed on a V (for victory), with a B-17 bomber flying overhead. *Reverse:* An American Marine is shown in action during the takeover of a Japanese-held island in the South Pacific. A carrier-based fighter plane flies overhead.

Mintage Data. Authorized by Public Law 102-414, signed by President William J. Clinton on October 14, 1992. *Maximum authorized*—2,000,000. *Number minted*—197,072 Uncirculated and 317,396 Proof.

Original Cost. Sale prices $8 (Uncirculated, pre-issue) and $9 (Proof, pre-issue); Uncirculated later raised to $9, and Proof later raised to $10. The surcharge of $2 per coin was split between the American Battle Monuments Commission (to aid in the construction of the World War II Monument in the nation's capital) and the Battle of Normandy Foundation (to assist in the erection of a monument in France).

Key to Collecting. Examples are easily enough found in the marketplace today and are nearly always of superb gem quality.

	Distribution	Cert	Avg	%MS	MS-67 PF-67
1991-1995 (1993P)	197,072	1,208	69.1	100%	$18
	Auctions: $165, MS-70Cam, September 2014; $529, MS-70Cam, April 2013; $153, MS-70, June 2013				
1991-1995 (1993P), Proof	317,396	1,964	69.0		$18
	Auctions: No auction records available.				

50TH ANNIVERSARY OF WORLD WAR II SILVER DOLLAR (1991–1995)

Designer: *Thomas D. Rogers Sr.* **Weight:** *26.73 grams.*
Composition: *.900 silver, .100 copper (net weight .7736 oz. pure silver).*
Diameter: *38.1 mm.* **Edge:** *Reeded.* **Mints:** *Denver (Uncirculated), West Point (Proof).*

The designs for these silver dollars and the related half dollars and five-dollar gold coins were the result of a competition. The works of five artists were selected (only one of them, Thomas D. Rogers Sr., being from the Mint staff). It was mandated that the dollar use the Battle of Normandy as a theme.

Designs. *Obverse:* An American soldier is shown as he runs ashore on the beach in Normandy during the D-Day invasion on June 6, 1944, which launched from England to liberate France. *Reverse:* The reverse illustrates the shoulder patch used on a uniform of Dwight D. Eisenhower's Supreme Headquarters Allied Expeditionary Force, with a quotation from Eisenhower.

Mintage Data. Authorized by Public Law 102-414, signed by President William J. Clinton on October 14, 1992. *Maximum authorized*—1,000,000. *Number minted*—1993-D: 107,240 Uncirculated; 1993-W: 342,041 Proof.

Original Cost. Sale prices $23 (Uncirculated, pre-issue) and $27 (Proof, pre-issue); Uncirculated later raised to $28, and Proof later raised to $31. The surcharge of $2 per coin was split between the American Battle Monuments Commission (to aid in the construction of the World War II Monument in the nation's capital) and the Battle of Normandy Foundation (to assist in the erection of a monument in France).

Key to Collecting. Examples are easily enough found in the marketplace today and are nearly always of superb gem quality.

	Distribution	Cert	Avg	%MS	MS-67 PF-67
1991-1995 (1993D)	107,240	1,925	69.3	100%	$45
	Auctions: $86, MS-70, July 2014; $118, MS-70, January 2013				
1991-1995 (1993W), Proof	342,041	3,027	69.0		$42
	Auctions: $206, PF-70DCam, September 2014				

50TH ANNIVERSARY OF WORLD WAR II $5 GOLD COIN (1991–1995)

Designer: *Charles J. Madsen (obverse), Edward Southworth Fisher (reverse).*
Weight: *8.359 grams.* **Composition:** *.900 gold, .100 copper (net weight .242 oz. pure gold).*
Diameter: *21.6 mm.* **Edge:** *Reeded.* **Mint:** *West Point.*

The approval of the American Legion, Veterans of Foreign Wars of the United States, American Veterans of World War, Korea and Vietnam (AMVETS), and the Disabled American Veterans, was required for the designs of all three 50th Anniversary of World War II commemoratives. The five-dollar coin was mandated to reflect the Allied victory in the war.

Designs. *Obverse:* An American soldier holds his rifle and raises his arm to indicate victory. *Reverse:* A large V (for victory) is at the center, with three dots and a dash over it, the Morse code for that letter. Branches are to each side.

Mintage Data. Authorized by Public Law 102-414, signed by President William J. Clinton on October 14, 1992. *Maximum authorized*—300,000. *Number minted*—23,672 Uncirculated and 67,026 Proof.

Original Cost. Sale prices $170 (Uncirculated, pre-issue) and $185 (Proof, pre-issue); Uncirculated later raised to $185, and Proof later raised to $220. The surcharge of $35 per coin was split between the American Battle Monuments Commission (to aid in the construction of the World War II Monument in the nation's capital) and the Battle of Normandy Foundation (to assist in the erection of a monument in France).

Key to Collecting. Examples are easily enough found in the marketplace today and are nearly always of superb gem quality.

	Distribution	Cert	Avg	%MS	MS-67 PF-67
1991-1995 (1993W)	23,672	1,399	69.6	100%	$375
	Auctions: $646, MS-70, September 2014; $411, MS-70, April 2013; $353, MS-69, August 2014				
1991-1995 (1993W), Proof	67,026	2,467	69.3		$435
	Auctions: $458, PF-70DCam, April 2013; $382, PF-70DCam, April 2013; $333, PF-69DCam, August 2014				

THOMAS JEFFERSON SILVER DOLLAR (1993)

Designer: *T. James Ferrell.* **Weight:** *26.73 grams.*
Composition: *.900 silver, .100 copper (net weight .7736 oz. pure silver).*
Diameter: *38.1 mm.* **Edge:** *Reeded.* **Mints:** *Philadelphia (Uncirculated), San Francisco (Proof).*

The 250th anniversary in 1993 of the birth of Thomas Jefferson in 1743 furnished the occasion for a commemorative silver dollar. The obverse portrait was based on an 1805 painting by Gilbert Stuart.

Designs. *Obverse:* Profile bust of President Thomas Jefferson. *Reverse:* Monticello, Jefferson's home.

Mintage Data. Authorized under Public Law 103-186, signed by President William J. Clinton on December 14, 1993. *Maximum authorized*—600,000. *Number minted*—1993-P: 266,927 Uncirculated; 1993-S: 332,891 Proof.

Original Cost. Sale prices $27 (Uncirculated, pre-issue) and $31 (Proof, pre-issue); Uncirculated later raised to $32, and Proof later raised to $35. The surcharge of $10 per coin went to the Jefferson Endowment Fund.

Key to Collecting. Although the Jefferson dollar was a popular sellout in its time, examples are easily found in the numismatic marketplace and are nearly always of superb gem quality. Most in demand, from the enthusiasm of five-cent piece collectors, are the special sets issued with the frosty Uncirculated 1994-P Jefferson nickel.

	Distribution	Cert	Avg	%MS	MS-67 PF-67
1993P	266,927	2,826	69.2	100%	$35
	Auctions: $86, MS-70, January 2013				
1993S, Proof	332,891	2,504	69.0		$25
	Auctions: $400, PF-70DCam, March 2013				

U.S. CAPITOL BICENTENNIAL SILVER DOLLAR (1994)

Designer: *William Cousins (obverse), John Mercanti (reverse).* **Weight:** *26.73 grams.*
Composition: *.900 silver, .100 copper (net weight .7736 oz. pure silver).*
Diameter: *38.1 mm.* **Edge:** *Reeded.* **Mints:** *Denver (Uncirculated), San Francisco (Proof).*

These silver dollars commemorated the 200th anniversary of the U.S. Capitol in Washington, D.C. Although the Federal City, as it was called, was laid out in the 1790s, it was not until 1800 that the federal government relocated there from Philadelphia. In honor of the recently deceased first president, the name was changed to Washington City, or, in popular use, Washington. The Capitol building design represented the work of several architects and artists, among them Benjamin Latrobe, Charles Bulfinch, and Constantino Brumidi.

Designs. *Obverse:* Dome of the Capitol with stars surrounding the *Freedom* statue. *Reverse:* Shield with four American flags, branches, and surmounted by an eagle, a motif based on the center area of a stained-glass window near the House and Senate grand staircases (produced by J. & G. Gibson, of Philadelphia, in 1859 and 1860).

Mintage Data. Authorized by Public Law 103-186, signed by President William J. Clinton on December 14, 1993. *Maximum authorized*—500,000. *Number minted*—1994-D: 68,332 Uncirculated; 1994-S: 279,579 Proof.

Original Cost. Sale prices $32 (Uncirculated, pre-issue) and $36 (Proof, pre-issue; Uncirculated later raised to $37, and Proof later raised to $40. The surcharge of $15 per coin went to the United States Capitol Preservation Commission. A Mint announcement noted that this was to go "for the construction of the Capitol Visitor Center" (itself the subject of a 2001 commemorative dollar).

Key to Collecting. Superb gem Mint State and Proof coins are easily available.

	Distribution	Cert	Avg	%MS	MS-67
					PF-67
1994D	68,332	1,513	69.4	100%	$35
	Auctions: $80, MS-70, July 2014; $101, MS-70, January 2013				
1994S, Proof	279,579	1,742	69.0		$39
	Auctions: $217, PF-70DCam, August 2014; $270, PF-70DCam, September 2014; $294, PF-70DCam, April 2013				

U.S. Prisoner of War Memorial Silver Dollar (1994)

Designer: *Tom Nielsen (obverse), Edgar Z. Steever IV (reverse).* **Weight:** *26.73 grams.*
Composition: *.900 silver, .100 copper (net weight .7736 oz. pure silver).*
Diameter: *38.1 mm.* **Edge:** *Reeded.* **Mint:** *West Point (Uncirculated), Philadelphia (Proof).*

The proposed National Prisoner of War Museum set the stage for the issuance of a silver dollar observing the tribulations of prisoners held by foreign military powers. The obverse designer, Nielsen, was a decorated former prisoner of war employed by the Bureau of Veterans Affairs.

Designs. *Obverse:* An eagle with a chain on one leg flies through a circle of barbed wire, representing flight to freedom. *Reverse:* Plan view, with landscaping, of the proposed National Prisoner of War Museum.

Mintage Data. Authorized by Public Law 103-186, signed by President William J. Clinton on December 14, 1993. *Maximum authorized*—500,000. *Number minted*—1994-W: 54,893 Uncirculated; 1994-P: 224,449 Proof.

Original Cost. Sale prices $27 (Uncirculated, pre-issue) and $31 (Proof, pre-issue); Uncirculated later raised to $32, and Proof later raised to $35. The surcharge of $10 per coin went toward the construction of the museum.

Key to Collecting. The 1994-W dollar is in special demand due to its relatively low mintage. Both varieties are seen with frequency in the marketplace and are nearly always superb gems.

	Distribution	Cert	Avg	%MS	MS-67 PF-67
1994W	54,893	1,820	69.3	100%	$80
	Auctions: $129, MS-70, January 2014; $92, MS-70, July 2014				
1994P, Proof	224,449	2,350	68.9		$45
	Auctions: $1,116, PF-70DCam, September 2014; $999, PF-70DCam, September 2014; $1,763, PF-70DCam, January 2013				

Women in Military Service Memorial Silver Dollar (1994)

Designer: *T. James Ferrell.* **Weight:** *26.73 grams.*
Composition: *.900 silver, .100 copper (net weight .7736 oz. pure silver).*
Diameter: *38.1 mm.* **Edge:** *Reeded.* **Mints:** *West Point (Uncirculated), Philadelphia (Proof).*

These coins were issued to honor women in the military and help fund the Women in Military Service for America Memorial at the ceremonial entrance to Arlington National Cemetery (which became a reality and opened in October 1997 on a 4.2-acre site).

Designs. *Obverse:* Servicewomen from the Army, Marine Corps, Navy, Air Force, and

Coast Guard, with the names of these branches around the border. *Reverse:* A diagonal view of the front of the proposed the Women in Military Service for America Memorial.

Mintage Data. Authorized by Public Law 103-186, signed by President William J. Clinton on December 14, 1993. *Maximum authorized*—500,000. *Number minted*—1994-W: 69,860 Uncirculated; 1994-P: 241,278 Proof.

Original Cost. Sale prices $27 (Uncirculated, pre-issue) and $31 (Proof, pre-issue); Uncirculated later raised to $32, and Proof later raised to $35. The surcharge of $10 per coin went towards the construction of the memorial.

Key to Collecting. Mirroring the situation for other commemoratives of the era, these are easily enough found on the market and are usually in superb gem grades.

	Distribution	Cert	Avg	%MS	MS-67
					PF-67
1994W	69,860	3,180	69.3	100%	$37
	Auctions: $72, MS-70, April 2013				
1994P, Proof	241,278	2,128	68.9		$44
	Auctions: $646, PF-70DCam, April 2013				

VIETNAM VETERANS MEMORIAL SILVER DOLLAR (1994)

Designer: *John Mercanti (obverse), Thomas D. Rogers Sr. (reverse).* **Weight:** *26.73 grams.*
Composition: *.900 silver, .100 copper (net weight .7736 oz. pure silver).*
Diameter: *38.1 mm.* **Edge:** *Reeded.* **Mints:** *West Point (Uncirculated), Philadelphia (Proof).*

In Washington, D.C., the Vietnam Veterans Memorial, often called the Memorial Wall, has been one of the city's prime attractions since it was dedicated in 1984.

Designs. *Obverse:* A hand touching the Wall. In the distance to the right is the Washington Monument. *Reverse:* Three military medals and ribbons surrounded with lettering.

Mintage Data. Authorized by Public Law 103-186, signed by President William J. Clinton on December 14, 1993. *Maximum authorized*—500,000. *Number minted*—1994-W: 57,290 Uncirculated; 1994-P: 227,671 Proof.

Original Cost. Sale prices $27 (Uncirculated) and $31 (Proof); Uncirculated later raised to $32, and Proof later raised to $35. The surcharge of $10 per coin went towards the construction of a visitor's center near the Memorial.

Key to Collecting. Gem specimens are easily available. The aftermarket price for this dollar is stronger than for most others of the early 1990s.

	Distribution	Cert	Avg	%MS	MS-67
					PF-67
1994W	57,290	1,715	69.3	100%	$85
	Auctions: $103, MS-70, July 2014; $141, MS-70, January 2013				
1994P, Proof	227,671	2,906	68.9		$65
	Auctions: $770, PF-70DCam, September 2014; $2,115, PF-70DCam, April 2013				

WORLD CUP TOURNAMENT HALF DOLLAR (1994)

Designer: *Richard T. LaRoche (obverse), Dean McMullen (reverse).* **Weight:** *11.34 grams.*
Composition: *.9167 copper, .0833 nickel.* **Diameter:** *30.61 mm.* **Edge:** *Reeded.*
Mints: *Denver (Uncirculated), Philadelphia (Proof).*

The United States' hosting of the XV FIFA World Cup playoff—the culmination of soccer games among 141 nations—was commemorated with this copper-nickel half dollar, as well as a silver dollar and a five-dollar gold coin.

Designs. *Obverse:* A soccer player in action, on the run with a ball near his feet. *Reverse:* The World Cup USA logo at the center, flanked by branches.

Mintage Data. Authorized by Public Law 102-281, signed by President George H.W. Bush on May 13, 1992. *Maximum authorized*—5,000,000. *Number minted*—1994-D: 168,208 Uncirculated; 1994-P: 609,354 Proof.

Original Cost. Sale prices $8.75 (Uncirculated, pre-issue) and $9.75 (Proof, pre-issue); Uncirculated later raised to $9.50, and Proof later raised to $10.50. The surcharge of $1 per coin went to the World Cup Organizing Committee.

Key to Collecting. The World Cup coins are reasonably priced in the secondary market. Nearly all are superb gems.

	Distribution	Cert	Avg	%MS	MS-67 PF-67
1994D	168,208	913	69.1	100%	$10
	Auctions: $212, MS-70, September 2014				
1994P, Proof	609,354	2,747	69.0		$9
	Auctions: $411, PF-70, September 2014; $558, PF-70, April 2013				

WORLD CUP TOURNAMENT SILVER DOLLAR (1994)

Designer: *Dean McMullen.* **Weight:** *26.73 grams.*
Composition: *.900 silver, .100 copper (net weight .7736 oz. pure silver).*
Diameter: *38.1 mm.* **Edge:** *Reeded.* **Mints:** *Denver (Uncirculated), San Francisco (Proof).*

In terms of mintage goals, this program was one of the greatest failures in the history of American commemorative coinage. The U.S. Mint stated it lost $3.5 million in the effort, noting that there simply were too many commemorative programs in progress, each with excessive mintage expectations. The only winner in the World Cup scenario seemed to be the recipient of the surcharge.

Designs. *Obverse:* Two competing soccer players converge on a soccer ball in play. *Reverse:* The World Cup USA logo at the center, flanked by branches.

Mintage Data. Authorized by Public Law 102-281, signed by President George H.W. Bush on May 13, 1992. *Maximum authorized*—5,000,000. *Number minted*—1994-D: 81,524 Uncirculated; 1994-S: 577,090 Proof.

Original Cost. Sale prices $23 (Uncirculated, pre-issue) and $27 (Proof, pre-issue); Uncirculated later raised to $28, and Proof later raised to $31. The surcharge of $7 per coin went to the World Cup Organizing Committee.

Key to Collecting. The World Cup coins are reasonably priced in the secondary market. Nearly all are superb gems.

	Distribution	Cert	Avg	%MS	MS-67
					PF-67
1994D	81,524	1,234	69.0	100%	$40
	Auctions: $329, MS-70, September 2014; $764, MS-70, April 2013				
1994S, Proof	577,090	2,518	69.0		$39
	Auctions: $170, PF-70DCam, September 2014; $294, PF-70DCam, April 2013				

WORLD CUP TOURNAMENT $5 GOLD COIN (1994)

Designer: *William J. Krawczewicz (obverse), Dean McMullen (reverse).* **Weight:** *8.359 grams.*
Composition: *.900 gold, .100 copper (net weight .242 oz. pure gold).*
Diameter: *21.6 mm.* **Edge:** *Reeded.* **Mint:** *West Point.*

The U.S. Mint's many recent commemoratives had caused buyer fatigue by the time the World Cup Tournament coins came out. Collectors blamed the Mint for creating coins that few people wanted. The complaints should have gone to Congress instead. Faced with so many coins to produce, often with very short deadlines, the Mint simply had no time to call for designs to be submitted from leading artists.

Designs. *Obverse:* The World Cup trophy. *Reverse:* The World Cup USA logo at the center, flanked by branches.

Mintage Data. Authorized by Public Law 102-281, signed by President George H.W. Bush on May 13, 1992. *Maximum authorized*—750,000. *Number minted*—22,447 Uncirculated and 89,614 Proof.

Original Cost. Sale prices $170 (Uncirculated, pre-issue) and $185 (Proof, pre-issue); Uncirculated later raised to $200, and Proof later raised to $220. The surcharge of $35 per coin went to the World Cup Organizing Committee.

Key to Collecting. The World Cup coins are reasonably priced in the secondary market. Nearly all are superb gems.

	Distribution	Cert	Avg	%MS	MS-67
					PF-67
1994W	22,447	1,050	69.5	100%	$400
	Auctions: $382, MS-70, September 2014; $382, MS-70, November 2014; $448, MS-70, April 2013; $306, MS-69, November 2014				
1994W, Proof	89,614	2,112	69.3		$435
	Auctions: $470, PF-70DCam, June 2013; $295, PF-69DCam, October 2014				

XXVI OLYMPIAD BASKETBALL HALF DOLLAR (1995)

Designer: *Clint Hansen (obverse), T. James Ferrell (reverse).* **Weight:** *11.34 grams.*
Composition: *.9167 copper, .0833 nickel.* **Diameter:** *30.61 mm.* **Edge:** *Reeded.* **Mint:** *San Francisco.*

Men's basketball has been an Olympic sport since the 1936 Summer Games in Berlin. The 1996 U.S. team, also known as "Dream Team III," won the gold medal at the Summer Games in Atlanta.

Designs. *Obverse:* Three basketball players. *Reverse:* Symbol of the Atlanta Committee for the Olympic Games superimposed over the Atlantic Ocean as viewed from space.

Mintage Data. Authorized by Public Law 102-390, signed by President George H.W. Bush on October 6, 1992. *Maximum authorized*—2,000,000. *Number minted*—171,001 Uncirculated and 169,655 Proof.

Original Cost. Sale prices $10.50 (Uncirculated, pre-issue) and $11.50 (Proof, pre-issue); Uncirculated later raised to $11.50, and Proof later raised to $12.50. The surcharge per coin went to the Atlanta Olympic Committee.

Key to Collecting. Enough 1995 and 1996 Olympics coins are on the aftermarket that finding designs of choice, or forming a set, will be no problem. The obverse designs are varied, and in total the collection is an excellent representation of this quadrennial worldwide competition.

	Distribution	Cert	Avg	%MS	MS-67
					PF-67
1995S	171,001	1,424	69.3	100%	$20
	Auctions: $118, MS-70, July 2014; $76, MS-70, July 2013				
1995S, Proof	169,655	1,994	69.1		$14
	Auctions: No auction records available.				

XXVI OLYMPIAD BASEBALL HALF DOLLAR (1995)

Designer: *Edgar Z. Steever IV (obverse), T. James Ferrell (reverse).* **Weight:** *11.34 grams.*
Composition: *.9167 copper, .0833 nickel.* **Diameter:** *30.61 mm.* **Edge:** *Reeded.* **Mint:** *San Francisco.*

Baseball was an official Olympic sport at each Summer Games between 1992 and 2008, but was voted out of the 2012 London Olympics and will remain off the docket until at least 2024 following a 2013 International Olympic Committee vote. The team representing Cuba took home the gold medal at the 1996 Atlanta Olympics.

Designs. *Obverse:* Batter at the plate with catcher and umpire. *Reverse:* Symbol of the Atlanta Committee for the Olympic Games superimposed over the Atlantic Ocean as viewed from space.

Mintage Data. Authorized by Public Law 102-390, signed by President George H.W. Bush on October 6, 1992. *Maximum authorized*—2,000,000. *Number minted*—164,605 Uncirculated and 118,087 Proof.

Original Cost. Sale prices $10.50 (Uncirculated, pre-issue) and $11.50 (Proof, pre-issue); Uncirculated later raised to $11.50, and Proof later raised to $12.50. The surcharge per coin went to the Atlanta Olympic Committee.

Key to Collecting. Enough 1995 and 1996 Olympics coins are on the aftermarket that finding designs of choice, or forming a set, will be no problem. The obverse designs are varied, and in total the collection is an excellent representation of this quadrennial worldwide competition.

	Distribution	Cert	Avg	%MS	MS-67 PF-67
1995S	164,605	1,095	69.3	100%	$20
	Auctions: $130, MS-70, April 2013				
1995S, Proof	118,087	1,547	69.1		$18
	Auctions: $329, PF-70DCam, September 2014; $200, PF-70DCam, September 2014				

XXVI OLYMPIAD GYMNASTICS SILVER DOLLAR (1995)

Designer: *James C. Sharpe (obverse), William Krawczewicz (reverse).* **Weight:** *26.73 grams.*
Composition: *.900 silver, .100 copper (net weight .7736 oz. pure silver).*
Diameter: *38.1 mm.* **Edge:** *Reeded.* **Mints:** *Denver (Uncirculated), Philadelphia (Proof).*

The men's gymnastics competition has been held at each Olympic Summer Games since the birth of the modern Olympic movement in 1896. Russia won the gold medal in the team all-around event at the 1996 Games in Atlanta.

Designs. *Obverse:* Men's gymnastics. *Reverse:* Clasped hands of two athletes with torch above.

Mintage Data. Authorized by Public Law 102-390, signed by President George H.W. Bush on October 6, 1992. *Maximum authorized*—750,000. *Number minted*—1995-D: 42,497 Uncirculated; 1995-P: 182,676 Proof.

Original Cost. Sale prices $27.95 (Uncirculated, pre-issue) and $30.95 (Proof, pre-issue); Uncirculated later raised to $31.95, and Proof later raised to $34.95. The surcharge per coin went to the Atlanta Olympic Committee.

Key to Collecting. Enough 1995 and 1996 Olympics coins are on the aftermarket that finding designs of choice, or forming a set, will be no problem. The obverse designs are varied, and in total the collection is an excellent representation of this quadrennial worldwide competition.

	Distribution	Cert	Avg	%MS	MS-67 PF-67
1995D	42,497	1,474	69.2	100%	$50
	Auctions: $90, MS-70, April 2013				
1995P, Proof	182,676	2,094	69.0		$39
	Auctions: No auction records available.				

XXVI Olympiad Track and Field Silver Dollar (1995)

Designer: *John Mercanti (obverse), William Krawczewicz (reverse).* **Weight:** *26.73 grams.*
Composition: *.900 silver, .100 copper (net weight .7736 oz. pure silver).*
Diameter: *38.1 mm.* **Edge:** *Reeded.* **Mints:** *Denver (Uncirculated), Philadelphia (Proof).*

Track and field—grouped with road running and racewalking in the overarching "athletics" category—has been a part of the Olympics from the birth of the modern Games and traces its roots to the ancient Greek Olympics. At the 1996 Summer Games in Atlanta, the United States took home 13 gold medals between its men's and women's track and field teams, easily the most of any nation.

Designs. *Obverse:* Men competing in track and field. *Reverse:* Clasped hands of two athletes with torch above.

Mintage Data. Authorized by Public Law 102-390, signed by President George H.W. Bush on October 6, 1992. *Maximum authorized*—750,000. *Number minted*—1995-D: 24,976 Uncirculated; 1995-P: 136,935 Proof.

Original Cost. Sale prices $27.95 (Uncirculated, pre-issue) and $30.95 (Proof, pre-issue); Uncirculated later raised to $31.95, and Proof later raised to $34.95. The surcharge per coin went to the Atlanta Olympic Committee.

Key to Collecting. Enough 1995 and 1996 Olympics coins are on the aftermarket that finding designs of choice, or forming a set, will be no problem. The obverse designs are varied, and in total the collection is an excellent representation of this quadrennial worldwide competition.

	Distribution	Cert	Avg	%MS	MS-67 PF-67
1995D	24,976	787	69.3	100%	$85
	Auctions: $159, MS-70, July 2014				
1995P, Proof	136,935	1,410	69.0		$40
	Auctions: $411, PF-70DCam, September 2014				

XXVI Olympiad Cycling Silver Dollar (1995)

Designer: *John Mercanti (obverse), William Krawczewicz (reverse).* **Weight:** *26.73 grams.*
Composition: *.900 silver, .100 copper (net weight .7736 oz. pure silver).*
Diameter: *38.1 mm.* **Edge:** *Reeded.* **Mints:** *Denver (Uncirculated), Philadelphia (Proof).*

Part of the Summer Games from the inception of the modern Olympic movement in 1896, cycling has been expanded over the years to include more track races, mountain biking, and BMX racing. France dominated the podium at the 1996 Olympics in Atlanta, taking home the most gold medals (five) and total medals (nine).

Designs. *Obverse:* Men cycling. *Reverse:* Clasped hands of two athletes with torch above.

Mintage Data. Authorized by Public Law 102-390, signed by President George H.W. Bush on October 6, 1992. *Maximum authorized*—750,000. *Number minted*—1995-D: 19,662 Uncirculated; 1995-P: 118,795 Proof.

Original Cost. Sale prices $27.95 (Uncirculated, pre-issue) and $30.95 (Proof, pre-issue); Uncirculated later raised to $31.95, and Proof later raised to $34.95. The surcharge per coin went to the Atlanta Olympic Committee.

Key to Collecting. Enough 1995 and 1996 Olympics coins are on the aftermarket that finding designs of choice, or forming a set, will be no problem. The obverse designs are varied, and in total the collection is an excellent representation of this quadrennial worldwide competition.

	Distribution	Cert	Avg	%MS	MS-67
					PF-67
1995D	19,662	868	69.3	100%	$145
	Auctions: $206, MS-70, July 2014; $200, MS-70, April 2013; $112, MS-69, November 2014				
1995P, Proof	118,795	1,380	69.0		$45
	Auctions: $707, PF-70DCam, September 2014				

PARALYMPICS BLIND RUNNER SILVER DOLLAR (1995)

Designer: *James C. Sharpe (obverse), William Krawczewicz (reverse).* **Weight:** *26.73 grams.*
Composition: *.900 silver, .100 copper (net weight .7736 oz. pure silver).*
Diameter: *38.1 mm.* **Edge:** *Reeded.* **Mints:** *Denver (Uncirculated), Philadelphia (Proof).*

Track and field events (under the umbrella of "athletics") have been a part of the Summer Paralympic Games since 1960. Spanish athletes took home a number of medals in the track events for visually impaired athletes at the 1996 Summer Paralympic Games, including the gold in two of the men's 100-meter dash events (Júlio Requena in the T-10 race, and Juan Antónia Prieto in the T-11 race) and both of the women's 100-meter dash events (Purificación Santamarta in the T-10 race, and Beatríz Mendoza in the T-11 race).

Designs. *Obverse:* Blind runner tethered to a seeing companion in a race. *Reverse:* Clasped hands of two athletes with torch above.

Mintage Data. Authorized by Public Law 102-390, signed by President George H.W. Bush on October 6, 1992. *Maximum authorized*—750,000. *Number minted*—1995-D: 28,649 Uncirculated; 1995-P: 138,337 Proof.

Original Cost. Sale prices $27.95 (Uncirculated, pre-issue) and $30.95 (Proof, pre-issue); Uncirculated later raised to $31.95, and Proof later raised to $34.95. The surcharge per coin went to the Atlanta Olympic Committee.

Key to Collecting. Enough 1995 and 1996 Olympics coins are on the aftermarket that finding designs of choice, or forming a set, will be no problem. The obverse designs are varied, and in total the collection is an excellent representation of this quadrennial worldwide competition.

	Distribution	Cert	Avg	%MS	MS-67 PF-67
1995D	28,649	1,244	69.3	100%	$35
	Auctions: No auction records available.				
1995P, Proof	138,337	1,568	69.0		$44
	Auctions: No auction records available.				

XXVI Olympiad Torch Runner $5 Gold Coin (1995)

Designer: *Frank Gasparro.* **Weight:** *8.359 grams.*
Composition: *.900 gold, .100 copper (net weight .242 oz. pure gold).*
Diameter: *21.6 mm.* **Edge:** *Reeded.* **Mint:** *West Point.*

Whereas the concept of the Olympic flame dates from the ancient Games of ancient Greece, the torch relay has only been a tradition since 1936, when Carl Diem introduced the concept for the Berlin Summer Games. The 1996 Olympic torch relay spanned 112 days, approximately 18,030 miles, and 13,267 torch bearers before ending in Atlanta on July 19, 1996.

Designs. *Obverse:* Olympic runner carrying a torch. *Reverse:* Bald eagle with a banner in its beak with the Olympic Centennial dates 1896–1996.

Mintage Data. Authorized by Public Law 102-390, signed by President George H.W. Bush on October 6, 1992. *Maximum authorized*—175,000. *Number minted*—14,675 Uncirculated and 57,442 Proof.

Original Cost. Sale prices $229 (Uncirculated, pre-issue) and $239 (Proof, pre-issue); Uncirculated later raised to $249, and Proof later raised to $259. The surcharge per coin went to the Atlanta Olympic Committee.

Key to Collecting. Enough 1995 and 1996 Olympics coins are on the aftermarket that finding designs of choice, or forming a set, will be no problem. The obverse designs are varied, and in total the collection is an excellent representation of this quadrennial worldwide competition.

	Distribution	Cert	Avg	%MS	MS-67 PF-67
1995W	14,675	987	69.7	100%	$750
	Auctions: $499, MS-70, September 2014; $499, MS-70, December 2014; $588, MS-70, May 2013; $329, MS-69, September 2014				
1995W, Proof	57,442	1,810	69.3		$375
	Auctions: No auction records available.				

XXVI OLYMPIAD STADIUM $5 GOLD COIN (1995)

Designer: *Marcel Jovine (obverse), Frank Gasparro (reverse).* **Weight:** *8.359 grams.*
Composition: *.900 gold, .100 copper (net weight .242 oz. pure gold).*
Diameter: *21.6 mm.* **Edge:** *Reeded.* **Mint:** *West Point.*

Centennial Olympic Stadium was constructed in Atlanta for the 1996 Summer Games. The 85,000-seat venue hosted the track and field events, as well as the closing ceremony, and then was reconstructed into Turner Field, home of Major League Baseball's Atlanta Braves for two decades.

Designs. *Obverse:* Aerial view of the Olympic Stadium from a distance to the side. *Reverse:* Same as described for the Olympic Torch Runner $5 gold coin.

Mintage Data. Authorized by Public Law 102-390, signed by President George H.W. Bush on October 6, 1992. *Maximum authorized*—175,000. *Number minted*—10,579 Uncirculated and 43,124 Proof.

Original Cost. Sale prices $229 (Uncirculated, pre-issue) and $239 (Proof, pre-issue); Uncirculated later raised to $249, and Proof later raised to $259. The surcharge per coin went to the Atlanta Olympic Committee.

Key to Collecting. Enough 1995 and 1996 Olympics coins are on the aftermarket that finding designs of choice, or forming a set, will be no problem. The obverse designs are varied, and in total the collection is an excellent representation of this quadrennial worldwide competition.

	Distribution	Cert	Avg	%MS	MS-67 PF-67
1995W	10,579	941	69.6	100%	$1,500
	Auctions: $999, MS-70, September 2014; $764, MS-70, October 2014; $1,586, MS-70, May 2013; $646, MS-69, September 2014				
1995W, Proof	43,124	1,811	69.4		$375
	Auctions: $499, PF-70DCam, June 2014; $470, PF-70DCam, June 2014				

XXVI OLYMPIAD SWIMMING HALF DOLLAR (1996)

Designer: *William Krawczewicz (obverse), Malcolm Farley (reverse).* **Weight:** *11.34 grams.*
Composition: *.9167 copper, .0833 nickel.* **Diameter:** *30.61 mm.* **Edge:** *Reeded.* **Mint:** *San Francisco.*

Swimming—an Olympic sport since the modern Games began in 1896—was dominated by U.S. athletes at the 1996 Summer Games in Atlanta. Americans took home a total of 26 medals (more than double the 12 each of Russia and Germany, which come next on the list), and swept all six relay events across the men's and women's competitions.

Designs. *Obverse:* Male swimmer. *Reverse:* Symbols of the Olympic games, including flame, torch, rings, Greek column, and 100 (the latter to observe the 100th anniversary of the modern Olympic games inaugurated with the 1896 Games in Athens).

Mintage Data. Authorized by Public Law 102-390, signed by President George H.W. Bush on October 6, 1992. *Maximum authorized*—3,000,000. *Number minted*—49,533 Uncirculated and 114,315 Proof.

Original Cost. Sale prices $10.50 (Uncirculated, pre-issue) and $11.50 (Proof, pre-issue); Uncirculated later raised to $11.50, and Proof later raised to $12.50. The surcharge per coin went to the Atlanta Olympic Committee.

Key to Collecting. Enough 1995 and 1996 Olympics coins are on the aftermarket that finding designs of choice, or forming a set, will be no problem. The obverse designs are varied, and in total the collection is an excellent representation of this quadrennial worldwide competition.

	Distribution	Cert	Avg	%MS	MS-67
					PF-67
1996S	49,533	839	69.1	100%	$145
Auctions: $499, MS-70, September 2013					
1996S, Proof	114,315	962	69.1		$32
Auctions: No auction records available.					

XXVI Olympiad Soccer Half Dollar (1996)

Designer: *Clint Hansen (obverse), Malcolm Farley (reverse).* **Weight:** *11.34 grams.*
Composition: *.9167 copper, .0833 nickel.* **Diameter:** *30.61 mm.* **Edge:** *Reeded.* **Mint:** *San Francisco.*

Women's soccer debuted as an Olympic sport at the 1996 Summer Games in Atlanta. The host nation's team—featuring such names as Mia Hamm, Brandi Chastain, and Briana Scurry—was victorious in the gold medal game.

Designs. *Obverse:* Women playing soccer. *Reverse:* Symbols of the Olympic games, including flame, torch, rings, Greek column, and 100.

Mintage Data. Authorized by Public Law 102-390, signed by President George H.W. Bush on October 6, 1992. *Maximum authorized*—3,000,000. *Number minted*—52,836 Uncirculated and 112,412 Proof.

Original Cost. Sale prices $10.50 (Uncirculated, pre-issue) and $11.50 (Proof, pre-issue); Uncirculated later raised to $11.50, and Proof later raised to $12.50. The surcharge per coin went to the Atlanta Olympic Committee.

Key to Collecting. Enough 1995 and 1996 Olympics coins are on the aftermarket that finding designs of choice, or forming a set, will be no problem. The obverse designs are varied, and in total the collection is an excellent representation of this quadrennial worldwide competition.

	Distribution	Cert	Avg	%MS	MS-67
					PF-67
1996S	52,836	609	69.3	100%	$130
Auctions: $147, MS-70, July 2014; $170, MS-70, August 2013					
1996S, Proof	112,412	951	69.0		$85
Auctions: $294, PF-70DCam, September 2014					

XXVI OLYMPIAD TENNIS SILVER DOLLAR (1996)

Designer: *James C. Sharpe (obverse), Thomas D. Rogers Sr. (reverse).* **Weight:** *26.73 grams.*
Composition: *.900 silver, .100 copper (net weight .7736 oz. pure silver).*
Diameter: *38.1 mm.* **Edge:** *Reeded.* **Mints:** *Denver (Uncirculated), Philadelphia (Proof).*

Women's tennis was first a part of the Olympics in 1900, and singles competition was regularly held for the Summer Games between 1908 and 1924. Subsequent disputes between the International Lawn Tennis Federation and the International Olympic Committee led to both men's and women's tennis being removed from the Games for more than 60 years, but the sport returned permanently in 1988. U.S. athletes took both the women's singles gold medal (Lindsay Davenport) and women's doubles gold medal (Gigi Fernandez and Mary Joe Fernandez) at the 1996 Games in Atlanta.

Designs. *Obverse:* Woman playing tennis. *Reverse:* Atlanta Committee for the Olympic Games logo with torch and flame.

Mintage Data. Authorized by Public Law 102-390, signed by President George H.W. Bush on October 6, 1992. *Maximum authorized*—1,000,000. *Number minted*—1996-D: 15,983 Uncirculated; 1996-P: 92,016 Proof.

Original Cost. Sale prices $27.95 (Uncirculated, pre-issue) and $30.95 (Proof, pre-issue); Uncirculated later raised to $31.95, and Proof later raised to $34.95. The surcharge per coin went to the Atlanta Olympic Committee.

Key to Collecting. Enough 1995 and 1996 Olympics coins are on the aftermarket that finding designs of choice, or forming a set, will be no problem. The obverse designs are varied, and in total the collection is an excellent representation of this quadrennial worldwide competition.

	Distribution	Cert	Avg	%MS	MS-67
					PF-67
1996D	15,983	737	69.1	100%	$265
	Auctions: $206, MS-70, September 2014; $482, MS-70, April 2013; $170, MS-69, July 2014; $170, MS-69, November 2014				
1996P, Proof	92,016	1,250	68.9		$75
	Auctions: $355, PF-69DCam, November 2014				

XXVI OLYMPIAD ROWING SILVER DOLLAR (1996)

Designer: *Bart Forbes (obverse), Thomas D. Rogers Sr. (reverse).* **Weight:** *26.73 grams.*
Composition: *.900 silver, .100 copper (net weight .7736 oz. pure silver).*
Diameter: *38.1 mm.* **Edge:** *Reeded.* **Mints:** *Denver (Uncirculated), Philadelphia (Proof).*

Rowing has been an official Olympic sport from the first modern Games in 1896, though coincidentally the competition was cancelled for that event due to weather concerns. At the 1996 Summer Olympics in Atlanta, Australia won the most medals (six, two gold).

Designs. *Obverse:* Men rowing. *Reverse:* Atlanta Committee for the Olympic Games logo with torch and flame.

Mintage Data. Authorized by Public Law 102-390, signed by President George H.W. Bush on October 6, 1992. *Maximum authorized*—1,000,000. *Number minted*—1996-D: 16,258 Uncirculated; 1996-P: 151,890 Proof.

Original Cost. Sale prices $27.95 (Uncirculated, pre-issue) and $30.95 (Proof, pre-issue); Uncirculated later raised to $31.95, and Proof later raised to $34.95. The surcharge per coin went to the Atlanta Olympic Committee.

Key to Collecting. Enough 1995 and 1996 Olympics coins are on the aftermarket that finding designs of choice, or forming a set, will be no problem. The obverse designs are varied, and in total the collection is an excellent representation of this quadrennial worldwide competition.

	Distribution	Cert	Avg	%MS	MS-67
					PF-67
1996D	16,258	692	69.2	100%	$265
	Auctions: $382, MS-70, April 2013; $153, MS-69, November 2014; $147, MS-69, November 2014				
1996P, Proof	151,890	1,242	68.9		$68
	Auctions: $6,169, PF-70DCam, September 2014				

XXVI OLYMPIAD HIGH JUMP SILVER DOLLAR (1996)

Designer: *Calvin Massey (obverse), Thomas D. Rogers Sr. (reverse).* **Weight:** *26.73 grams.*
Composition: *.900 silver, .100 copper (net weight .7736 oz. pure silver).*
Diameter: *38.1 mm.* **Edge:** *Reeded.* **Mints:** *Denver (Uncirculated), Philadelphia (Proof).*

High jump has been one of the Olympic track and field program's events since the inaugural modern Games in 1896. At the 1996 Atlanta Olympics, the United States' Charles Austin won the gold medal in the men's competition with a height cleared of 2.39 meters.

Designs. *Obverse:* Athlete doing the "Fosbury Flop" maneuver. *Reverse:* Atlanta Committee for the Olympic Games logo with torch and flame.

Mintage Data. Authorized by Public Law 102-390, signed by President George H.W. Bush on October 6, 1992. *Maximum authorized*—1,000,000. *Number minted*—1996-D: 15,697 Uncirculated; 1996-P: 124,502 Proof.

Original Cost. Sale prices $27.95 (Uncirculated, pre-issue) and $30.95 (Proof, pre-issue); Uncirculated later raised to $31.95, and Proof later raised to $34.95. The surcharge per coin went to the Atlanta Olympic Committee.

Key to Collecting. Enough 1995 and 1996 Olympics coins are on the aftermarket that finding designs of choice, or forming a set, will be no problem. The obverse designs are varied, and in total the collection is an excellent representation of this quadrennial worldwide competition.

	Distribution	Cert	Avg	%MS	MS-67 PF-67
1996D	15,697	678	69.1	100%	$285
	Auctions: $441, MS-70, April 2013; $147, MS-69, July 2014; $165, MS-69, November 2014				
1996P, Proof	124,502	1,291	68.9		$45
	Auctions: No auction records available.				

PARALYMPICS WHEELCHAIR SILVER DOLLAR (1996)

Designer: *James C. Sharpe (obverse), Thomas D. Rogers Sr. (reverse).* **Weight:** *26.73 grams.*
Composition: *.900 silver, .100 copper (net weight .7736 oz. pure silver).*
Diameter: *38.1 mm.* **Edge:** *Reeded.* **Mints:** *Denver (Uncirculated), Philadelphia (Proof).*

Wheelchair racing events have comprised part of the Paralympic track and field program since 1960. Several countries were represented on the podium, though the United States' Shawn Meredith (gold medals in the T-51 400-meter and 800-meter), France's Claude Issorat (gold medals in the T-53 200-meter and 800-meter), and Switzerland's Heinz Frei (gold medals in the T52-53 1,500-meter and 10,000-meter) had particularly strong showings.

Designs. *Obverse:* Athlete in a racing wheelchair competing in a track and field competition. *Reverse:* Atlanta Committee for the Olympic Games logo with torch and flame.

Mintage Data. Authorized by Public Law 102-390, signed by President George H.W. Bush on October 6, 1992. *Maximum authorized*—1,000,000. *Number minted*—1996-D: 14,497 Uncirculated; 1996-P: 84,280 Proof.

Original Cost. Sale prices $27.95 (Uncirculated, pre-issue) and $30.95 (Proof, pre-issue); Uncirculated later raised to $31.95, and Proof later raised to $34.95. The surcharge per coin went to the Atlanta Olympic Committee.

Key to Collecting. Enough 1995 and 1996 Olympics coins are on the aftermarket that finding designs of choice, or forming a set, will be no problem. The obverse designs are varied, and in total the collection is an excellent representation of this quadrennial worldwide competition.

	Distribution	Cert	Avg	%MS	MS-67
					PF-67
1996D	14,497	815	69.2	100%	$265
Auctions: $499, MS-70, April 2013; $153, MS-69, November 2014; $129, MS-69, November 2014					
1996P, Proof	84,280	1,353	69.0		$68
Auctions: No auction records available.					

XXVI Olympiad Flag Bearer $5 Gold Coin (1996)

Designer: *Patricia Lewis Verani (obverse), William Krawczewicz (reverse).*
Weight: *8.359 grams.* **Composition:** *.900 gold, .100 copper (net weight .242 oz. pure gold).*
Diameter: *21.6 mm.* **Edge:** *Reeded.* **Mint:** *West Point.*

For the opening and closing ceremonies of each Olympic Games, each participating nation selects two flagbearers from among its athletes to lead its delegation in the Parade of Nations (opening) and Parade of Flags (closing). Wrestler Bruce Baumgartner served as the United States's flagbearer for the opening ceremony of the 1996 Summer Games, and show jumper Michael Matz was awarded the honor for the closing ceremony.

Designs. *Obverse:* Athlete with a flag followed by a crowd. *Reverse:* Atlanta Committee for the Olympic Games logo within laurel leaves.

Mintage Data. Authorized by Public Law 102-390, signed by President George H.W. Bush on October 6, 1992. *Maximum authorized*—300,000. *Number minted*—9,174 Uncirculated and 32,886 Proof.

Original Cost. Sale prices $229 (Uncirculated, pre-issue) and $239 (Proof, pre-issue); Uncirculated later raised to $249, and Proof later raised to $259. The surcharge per coin went to the Atlanta Olympic Committee.

Key to Collecting. Enough 1995 and 1996 Olympics coins are on the aftermarket that finding designs of choice, or forming a set, will be no problem. The obverse designs are varied, and in total the collection is an excellent representation of this quadrennial worldwide competition.

	Distribution	Cert	Avg	%MS	MS-67
					PF-67
1996W	9,174	695	69.5	100%	$1,500
Auctions: $1,763, MS-70, May 2013; $705, MS-69, August 2014; $532, MS-69, October 2014; $529, MS-69, October 2014					
1996W, Proof	32,886	1,307	69.3		$375
Auctions: No auction records available.					

XXVI OLYMPIAD CAULDRON $5 GOLD COIN (1996)

Designer: *Frank Gasparro (obverse), William Krawczewicz (reverse).*
Weight: *8.359 grams.* **Composition:** *.900 gold, .100 copper (net weight .242 oz. pure gold).*
Diameter: *21.6 mm.* **Edge:** *Reeded.* **Mint:** *West Point.*

The tradition of maintaining an Olympic flame hearkens to the ancient Greek Olympics, during which a fire was kept burning to represent the theft of fire from Zeus by Prometheus. The concept became part of the modern Games in 1928 and now serves as the culmination of the Olympic torch relay. At the 1996 Summer Games in Atlanta, boxing legend and American icon Muhammad Ali (himself a gold medalist at the 1960 Olympics) was the final torch bearer and lit the cauldron.

Designs. *Obverse:* Lighting of the Olympic flame. *Reverse:* Atlanta Committee for the Olympic Games logo within laurel leaves.

Mintage Data. Authorized by Public Law 102-390, signed by President George H.W. Bush on October 6, 1992. *Maximum authorized*—300,000. *Number minted*—9,210 Uncirculated and 38,555 Proof.

Original Cost. Sale prices $229 (Uncirculated, pre-issue) and $239 (Proof, pre-issue); Uncirculated later raised to $249, and Proof later raised to $259. The surcharge per coin went to the Atlanta Olympic Committee.

Key to Collecting. Enough 1995 and 1996 Olympics coins are on the aftermarket that finding designs of choice, or forming a set, will be no problem. The obverse designs are varied, and in total the collection is an excellent representation of this quadrennial worldwide competition.

	Distribution	Cert	Avg	%MS	MS-67 / PF-67
1996W	9,210	786	69.4	100%	MS-67 $1,500
Auctions: $1,763, MS-70, April 2013; $705, MS-69, August 2014; $705, MS-69, September 2014; $705, MS-69, November 2014					
1996W, Proof	38,555	2,215	69.3		PF-67 $375
Auctions: $470, PF-70DCam, September 2014; $341, PF-70DCam, September 2014; $940, PF-70DCam, February 2013					

CIVIL WAR BATTLEFIELD PRESERVATION HALF DOLLAR (1995)

Designer: *Don Troiani (obverse), T. James Ferrell (reverse).* **Weight:** *11.34 grams.*
Composition: *.9167 copper, .0833 nickel.* **Diameter:** *30.61 mm.* **Edge:** *Reeded.* **Mint:** *San Francisco.*

Preserving battlefields associated with the Civil War (1861–1865) formed the topic for a suite of three commemorative coins, including this copper-nickel half dollar.

Designs. *Obverse:* Drummer standing. *Reverse:* Cannon overlooking battlefield with inscription above.

Mintage Data. Authorized by Public Law 102-379. *Maximum authorized*—2,000,000. *Number minted*— 119,520 Uncirculated and 330,002 Proof.

Original Cost. Sale prices $9.50 (Uncirculated, pre-issue) and $10.75 (Proof, pre-issue); Uncirculated later raised to $10.25, and Proof later raised to $11.75. The surcharge of $2 per coin went to the Civil War Trust for the preservation of historically significant battlefields.

Key to Collecting. This coin, as well as those two issued alongside it, are readily available in the marketplace today. Most are superb gems.

	Distribution	Cert	Avg	%MS	MS-67 PF-67
1995S	119,520	965	69.3	100%	$40
	Auctions: $206, MS-70, May 2014; $153, MS-70, July 2014				
1995S, Proof	330,002	1,725	69.0		$32
	Auctions: $188, PF-68DCam, November 2014				

CIVIL WAR BATTLEFIELD PRESERVATION SILVER DOLLAR (1995)

Designer: *Don Troiani (obverse), John Mercanti (reverse).* **Weight:** *26.73 grams.*
Composition: *.900 silver, .100 copper (net weight .7736 oz. pure silver).*
Diameter: *38.1 mm.* **Edge:** *Reeded.* **Mint:** *Philadelphia (Uncirculated), San Francisco (Proof).*

Civil War history attracts millions of followers, and books on the subject are always very popular. While total sales of the Civil War Battlefield Preservation silver dollar didn't approach the million coins authorized, sales of the Proof version were stronger than those of many recent silver dollars.

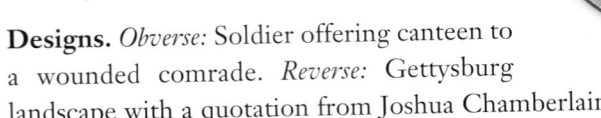
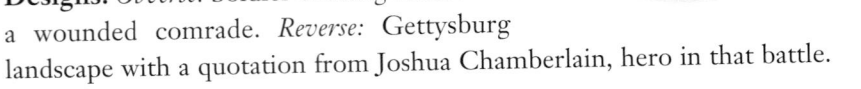

Designs. *Obverse:* Soldier offering canteen to a wounded comrade. *Reverse:* Gettysburg landscape with a quotation from Joshua Chamberlain, hero in that battle.

Mintage Data. Authorized by Public Law 102-379. *Maximum authorized*—1,000,000. *Number minted*— 1995-P: 45,866 Uncirculated; 1995-S: 437,114 Proof.

Original Cost. Sale prices $27 (Uncirculated, pre-issue) and $30 (Proof, pre-issue); Uncirculated later raised to $30, and Proof later raised to $34. The surcharge of $7 per coin went to the Civil War Trust for the preservation of historically significant battlefields.

Key to Collecting. This coin, as well as those two issued alongside it, are readily available in the marketplace today. Most are superb gems.

	Distribution	Cert	Avg	%MS	MS-67 PF-67
1995P	45,866	1,228	69.1	100%	$65
	Auctions: $247, MS-70, April 2013				
1995S, Proof	437,114	3,039	69.0		$50
	Auctions: $435, PF-70DCam, March 2013; $306, PF-70DCam, April 2013				

CIVIL WAR BATTLEFIELD PRESERVATION $5 GOLD COIN (1995)

Designer: *Don Troiani (obverse), Alfred F. Maletsky (reverse).* **Weight:** *8.359 grams.*
Composition: *.900 gold, .100 copper.* **Diameter:** *21.6 mm.* **Edge:** *Reeded.* **Mint:** *West Point.*

Troiani, the designer of this coin's obverse as well as those of the other two Civil War Battlefield Preservation commemoratives, is an artist in the private sector well known for his depictions of battle scenes.

Designs. *Obverse:* Bugler on horseback sounding a call. *Reverse:* Eagle perched on a shield.

Mintage Data. Authorized by Public Law 102-379. *Maximum authorized*—300,000. *Number minted*—12,735 Uncirculated and 55,246 Proof.

Original Cost. Sale prices $180 (Uncirculated, pre-issue) and $195 (Proof, pre-issue); Uncirculated later raised to $190, and Proof later raised to $225. The surcharge of $35 per coin went to the Civil War Trust for the preservation of historically significant battlefields.

Key to Collecting. This coin, as well as those two issued alongside it, are readily available in the marketplace today. Most are superb gems.

	Distribution	Cert	Avg	%MS	MS-67		
					PF-67		
1995W	12,735	796	69.7	100%	$600		
	Auctions: $588, MS-70, January 2014; $881, MS-70, September 2014; $470, MS-70, November 2014; $341, MS-69, November 2014						
1995W, Proof	55,246	1,852	69.3		$435		
	Auctions: $705, PF-70DCam, July 2014; $541, PF-70DCam, July 2014; $300, PF-69DCam, October 2014; $329, PF-69DCam, November 2014						

SPECIAL OLYMPICS WORLD GAMES SILVER DOLLAR (1995)

Designer: *T. James Ferrell from a portrait by Jamie Wyeth (obverse), Thomas D. Rogers Sr. (reverse).*
Weight: *26.73 grams.* **Composition:** *.900 silver, .100 copper (net weight .7736 oz. pure silver).*
Diameter: *38.1 mm.* **Edge:** *Reeded.* **Mints:** *West Point (Uncirculated), Philadelphia (Proof).*

This silver dollar's subject, Eunice Kennedy Shriver, was not only the first living female on U.S. coinage, but also the sister of former president John F. Kennedy and the aunt of Joseph F. Kennedy II, the House representative who sponsored the bill that created the coin. She is credited on the silver dollar as the founder of the Special Olympics.

Designs. *Obverse:* Portrait of Eunice Shriver.
Reverse: Representation of a Special Olympics medal, a rose, and a quotation by Shriver.

Mintage Data. Authorized by Public Law 103-328, signed by President William J. Clinton on September 29, 1994. *Maximum authorized*—800,000. *Number minted*—1995-W: 89,301 Uncirculated; 1995-P: 351,764 Proof.

Original Cost. Sale prices $30 (Uncirculated, pre-issue) and $33 (Proof, pre-issue); Uncirculated later raised to $32, and Proof later raised to $37. The surcharge of $10 per coin went to the Special Olympics to support the 1995 World Summer Games.

Key to Collecting. These coins are plentiful in the marketplace. Most are superb gems.

	Distribution	Cert	Avg	%MS	MS-67 PF-67
1995W	89,301	891	69.2	100%	$40
	Auctions: $135, MS-70, April 2013				
1995P, Proof	351,764	1,397	69.0		$39
	Auctions: $360, PF-70DCam, March 2013				

NATIONAL COMMUNITY SERVICE SILVER DOLLAR (1996)

Designer: *Thomas D. Rogers Sr. from a medal by Augustus Saint-Gaudens (obverse), William C. Cousins (reverse).* **Weight:** *26.73 grams.* **Composition:** *.900 silver, .100 copper (net weight .7736 oz. pure silver).* **Diameter:** *38.1 mm.* **Edge:** *Reeded.* **Mint:** *San Francisco.*

In 1996 the National Community Service dollar was sponsored by Representative Joseph D. Kennedy of Massachusetts, who also sponsored the Special Olympics World Games dollar.

Designs. *Obverse:* Standing figure of Liberty. *Reverse:* SERVICE FOR AMERICA in three lines, with a wreath around, and other lettering at the border.

Mintage Data. Authorized by Public Law 103-328, signed by President William J. Clinton on September 29, 1994. *Maximum authorized*—500,000. *Number minted*—23,500 Uncirculated and 101,543 Proof.

Original Cost. Sale prices $30 (Uncirculated, pre-issue) and $33 (Proof, pre-issue); Uncirculated later raised to $32, and Proof later raised to $37. The surcharge of $10 per coin went to the National Community Service Trust.

Key to Collecting. Uncirculated examples are scarce by virtue of their low mintage, but demand is scarce as well, with the result that they can be purchased easily enough. Both formats are usually seen in superb gem preservation.

	Distribution	Cert	Avg	%MS	MS-67 PF-67
1996S	23,500	1,031	69.3	100%	$125
	Auctions: $153, MS-70, August 2014; $247, MS-70, April 2013; $88, MS-69, July 2014; $86, MS-69, November 2014				
1996S, Proof	101,543	1,964	69.1		$36
	Auctions: $195, PF-70DCam, April 2013				

SMITHSONIAN INSTITUTION 150TH ANNIVERSARY SILVER DOLLAR (1996)

Designer: *Thomas D. Rogers Sr. (obverse), John Mercanti (reverse).* **Weight:** *26.73 grams.*
Composition: *.900 silver, .100 copper (net weight .7736 oz. pure silver).* **Diameter:** *38.1 mm.*
Edge: *Reeded.* **Mints:** *Denver (Uncirculated), Philadelphia (Proof).*

This silver dollar, as well as a five-dollar gold coin, marked the 150th anniversary of Congress establishing the Smithsonian Institution in Washington, D.C., on August 10, 1846. Named for James Smithson—an English scientist whose will funded the entity—the institution quickly became America's national museum.

Designs. *Obverse:* The "Castle" building on the Mall in Washington, the original home of the Smithsonian Institution. Branches to each side. *Reverse:* Goddess of Knowledge sitting on top of a globe. In her left hand she holds a torch, in the right a scroll inscribed ART / HISTORY / SCIENCE. In the field to the right in several lines is FOR THE INCREASE AND DIFFUSION OF KNOWLEDGE.

Mintage Data. Authorized by Public Law 104-96, signed by President William J. Clinton on January 10, 1996. *Maximum authorized—650,000. Number minted—*1996-D: 31,320 Uncirculated; 1996-P: 129,152 Proof.

Original Cost. Sale prices $30 (Uncirculated, pre-issue) and $33 (Proof, pre-issue); Uncirculated later raised to $32, and Proof later raised to $37. The surcharge of $10 per coin went to the Smithsonian Board of Regents.

Key to Collecting. This silver dollar and the five-dollar gold coin issued alongside it have risen in value considerably since their release. Today examples can be found readily in the marketplace and are nearly always superb gems.

	Distribution	Cert	Avg	%MS	MS-67
					PF-67
1996D	31,320	1,015	69.4	100%	$120
	Auctions: $119, MS-70, July 2014; $123, MS-70, April 2013; $65, MS-69, October 2014				
1996P, Proof	129,152	1,798	69.0		$43
	Auctions: $447, PF-70DCam, March 2013				

SMITHSONIAN INSTITUTION 150TH ANNIVERSARY $5 GOLD COIN (1996)

Designer: *Alfred F. Maletsky (obverse), T. James Ferrell (reverse).* **Weight:** *8.359 grams.*
Composition: *.900 gold, .100 copper (net weight .242 oz. pure gold).*
Diameter: *21.6 mm.* **Edge:** *Reeded.* **Mint:** *West Point.*

The U.S. Mint offered the two 1996 Smithsonian commemorative coins via several new options, including the 50,000-set Young Collectors Edition and incorporated in jewelry items.

Designs. *Obverse:* Bust of James Smithson facing left. *Reverse:* Sunburst with SMITHSONIAN below.

Mintage Data. Authorized by Public Law 104-96, signed by President William J. Clinton on January 10, 1996. *Maximum authorized*—100,000. *Number minted*—9,068 Uncirculated and 21,772 Proof.

Original Cost. Sale prices $180 (Uncirculated, pre-issue) and $195 (Proof, pre-issue); Uncirculated later raised to $205, and Proof later raised to $225. The surcharge of $10 per coin went to the Smithsonian Board of Regents.

Key to Collecting. Both Smithsonian Institution 150th Anniversary coins have risen in value considerably since their release. Today examples can be found readily in the marketplace and are nearly always superb gems.

	Distribution	Cert	Avg	%MS	MS-67 PF-67
1996W	9,068	838	69.4	100%	$550
	Auctions: $646, MS-70, September 2014; $617, MS-70, September 2014; $764, MS-70, April 2013; $382, MS-69, August 2014				
1996W, Proof	21,772	1,268	69.2		$410
	Auctions: $588, PF-70DCam, September 2014; $529, PF-70DCam, September 2014; $706, PF-70DCam, April 2013				

U.S. BOTANIC GARDEN SILVER DOLLAR (1997)

Designer: *Edgar Z. Steever IV (obverse), William C. Cousins (reverse).* **Weight:** *26.73 grams.*
Composition: *Silver .900, copper .100 (net weight .7736 oz. pure silver).*
Diameter: *38.1 mm.* **Edge:** *Reeded.* **Mint:** *Philadelphia.*

These coins were purportedly struck to celebrate the 175th anniversary of the United States Botanic Garden (which would have been 1995), but they were dated on one side as 1997. The authorizing legislation that created the coins specified that the French façade of the U.S. Botanic Garden be shown on the obverse and a rose on the reverse.

Designs. *Obverse:* Façade of the United States Botanic Garden in plan view without landscaping. *Reverse:* A rose at the center with a garland of roses above. The inscription below includes the anniversary dates 1820–1995. Note that some listings designate the rose side as the obverse.

Mintage Data. Authorized by Public Law 103-328, signed by President William J. Clinton on September 29, 1994. *Maximum authorized*—500,000. *Number minted*—58,505 Uncirculated and 189,671 Proof.

Original Cost. Sale prices $30 (Uncirculated, pre-issue) and $33 (Proof, pre-issue); Uncirculated later raised to $33, and Proof later raised to $37. The surcharge of $10 per coin went to the National Fund for the Botanic Garden.

Key to Collecting. These coins are readily available on the market today. Nearly all are superb gems. Ironically, the most popular related item is the Mint package containing the 1997-P special-finish Jefferson nickel, the demand coming from collectors of five-cent pieces! Only 25,000 sets were sold. This is *déjà vu* of the 1993 Jefferson dollar offer.

	Distribution	Cert	Avg	%MS	MS-67	
					PF-67	
1997P	58,505	1,502	69.1	100%	$30	
Auctions: $159, MS-70, July 2014; $170, MS-70, April 2013						
1997P, Proof	189,671	1,430	69.0		$42	
Auctions: $306, PF-70DCam, September 2014; $441, PF-70DCam, April 2013						

NATIONAL LAW ENFORCEMENT OFFICERS MEMORIAL SILVER DOLLAR (1997)

Designer: *Alfred F. Maletsky (obverse from a photograph by Larry Ruggieri).* **Weight:** *26.73 grams.* **Composition:** *.900 silver, .100 copper (net weight .7736 oz. pure silver).* **Diameter:** *38.1 mm.* **Edge:** *Reeded.* **Mint:** *Philadelphia.*

The National Law Enforcement Officers Memorial at Judiciary Square in Washington, D.C., dedicated on October 15, 1991, was the subject of this commemorative. The monument honors more than 14,000 men and women who gave their lives in the line of duty.

Designs. *Obverse:* United States Park Police officers Robert Chelsey and Kelcy Stefansson making a rubbing of a fellow officer's name. *Reverse:* Shield with a rose across it, evocative of the sacrifices made by officers.

Mintage Data. Authorized by Public Law 104-329, signed by President William J. Clinton on October 20, 1996. *Maximum authorized*—500,000. *Number minted*—28,575 Uncirculated and 110,428 Proof.

Original Cost. Sale prices $30 (Uncirculated, pre-issue) and $33 (Proof, pre-issue); Uncirculated later raised to $32, and Proof later raised to $37.

Key to Collecting. Once the distribution figures were published, the missed opportunity was realized—collectors saw that these coins would be a modern rarity. The market price rose to a sharp premium, where it remains today. Nearly all coins approach perfection in quality.

	Distribution	Cert	Avg	%MS	MS-67	
					PF-67	
1997P	28,575	778	69.3	100%	$130	
Auctions: $206, MS-70, August 2014; $259, MS-70, May 2013						
1997P, Proof	110,428	1,543	69.0		$72	
Auctions: $243, PF-70DCam, September 2014; $353, PF-70DCam, April 2013						

JACKIE ROBINSON SILVER DOLLAR (1997)

Designer: *Alfred F. Maletsky (obverse), T. James Ferrell (reverse).* **Weight:** *26.73 grams.*
Composition: *.900 silver, .100 copper (net weight .7736 oz. pure silver).*
Diameter: *38.1 mm.* **Edge:** *Reeded.* **Mint:** *San Francisco.*

This silver dollar and a concurrently issued five-dollar gold coin commemorated the 50th anniversary of the first acceptance of a black player in a major league baseball game, Jack ("Jackie") Robinson being the hero. The watershed event took place at Ebbets Field on April 15, 1947.

Designs. *Obverse:* Robinson in game action stealing home plate, evocative of a 1955 World Series play in a contest between the New York Yankees and the Brooklyn Dodgers. *Reverse:* 50th anniversary logotype of the Jackie Robinson Foundation (a motif worn by all Major League Baseball players in the 1997 season) surrounded with lettering of two baseball accomplishments.

Mintage Data. Authorized on October 20, 1996, by Public Law 104-329, part of the United States Commemorative Coin Act of 1996, with a provision tied to Public Law 104-328 (for the Botanic Garden dollar). Coins could be minted for a full year beginning July 1, 1997. *Maximum authorized*—200,000. *Number minted*—30,180 Uncirculated and 110,002 Proof.

Original Cost. Sale prices $30 (Uncirculated, pre-issue) and $33 (Proof, pre-issue); Uncirculated later raised to $32, and Proof later raised to $37. The surcharge of $10 per coin went to the Jackie Robinson Foundation.

Key to Collecting. Although the Jackie Robinson coins were losers in the sales figures of the U.S. Mint, the small quantities issued made both coins winners in the return-on-investment sweepstakes. Today, each of these can be found without a problem, and nearly all are in superb gem preservation.

	Distribution	Cert	Avg	%MS	MS-67 PF-67
1997S	30,180	1,139	69.1	100%	$80
	Auctions: $411, MS-70, October 2014; $682, MS-70, January 2013				
1997S, Proof	110,002	2,005	69.0		$60
	Auctions: $999, PF-70DCam, September 2014; $646, PF-70DCam, September 2013				

JACKIE ROBINSON $5 GOLD COIN (1997)

Designer: *William C. Cousins (obverse), James Peed (reverse).* **Weight:** *8.359 grams.*
Composition: *.900 gold, .100 copper (net weight .242 oz. pure gold).*
Diameter: *21.6 mm.* **Edge:** *Reeded.* **Mint:** *West Point.*

The U.S. Mint's marketing of the Jackie Robinson coins was innovative, as it had been in recent times. One promotion featured a reproduction of a rare baseball trading card, with the distinction of being the first such card ever issued by the U.S. government. But no matter how important Robinson's legacy was, buyers voted with their pocketbooks, and sales were low—making the Uncirculated gold coin a modern rarity.

Designs. *Obverse:* Portrait of Robinson in his later years as a civil-rights and political activist. *Reverse:* Detail of the seam on a baseball, Robinson's 1919–1972 life dates, and the inscription "Life of Courage."

Mintage Data. Authorized on October 20, 1996, by Public Law 104-329, part of the United States Commemorative Coin Act of 1996, with a provision tied to Public Law 104-328 (for the Botanic Garden dollar). Coins could be minted for a full year beginning July 1, 1997. *Maximum authorized*—100,000. *Number minted*—5,174 Uncirculated and 24,072 Proof.

Original Cost. Sale prices $180 (Uncirculated, pre-issue) and $195 (Proof, pre-issue); Uncirculated later raised to $205, and Proof later raised to $225. The surcharge of $35 per coin went to the Jackie Robinson Foundation.

Key to Collecting. The Jackie Robinson five-dollar gold coin takes top honors as the key issue among modern commemoratives. Especially rare and valuable is the Uncirculated version.

	Distribution	Cert	Avg	%MS	MS-67 / PF-67
1997W	5,174	811	69.3	100%	**MS-67** $2,500
	Auctions: $3,643, MS-70, April 2014; $2,820, MS-70, August 2014				
1997W, Proof	24,072	1,465	69.3		**PF-67** $520
	Auctions: $705, PF-70DCam, July 2014; $764, PF-70DCam, August 2014				

FRANKLIN D. ROOSEVELT $5 GOLD COIN (1997)

Designer: *T. James Ferrell (obverse), James Peed (reverse).* **Weight:** *8.359 grams.* **Composition:** *.900 gold, .100 copper (net weight .242 oz. pure gold).* **Diameter:** *21.6 mm.* **Edge:** *Reeded.* **Mint:** *West Point.*

Considering that newly inaugurated President Franklin D. Roosevelt suspended the mintage and paying out of U.S. gold coins in 1933, it was ironic that he should later have a gold coin commemorating his life. The year 1997 does not seem to have been a special anniversary date of any kind, as it was 115 years after his birth, 64 years after his inauguration, and 52 years after his death.

Designs. *Obverse:* Upper torso and head of Roosevelt facing right, based on one of the president's favorite photographs, taken when he was reviewing the U.S. Navy fleet in San Francisco Bay. *Reverse:* Presidential seal displayed at Roosevelt's 1933 inaugural.

Mintage Data. Authorized by Public Law 104-329, signed by President William J. Clinton on October 20, 1996. *Maximum authorized*—100,000. *Number minted*—11,894 Uncirculated and 29,474 Proof.

Original Cost. Sale prices $180 (Uncirculated, pre-issue) and $195 (Proof, pre-issue); Uncirculated later raised to $205, and Proof later raised to $225. A portion of the surcharge of $35 per coin went to the Franklin Delano Roosevelt Memorial Commission.

Key to Collecting. Since the mintages for both Uncirculated and Proof formats were low, their values rose substantially on the aftermarket. Examples are easily available today and are nearly always in superb gem preservation.

	Distribution	Cert	Avg	%MS	MS-67	
					PF-67	
1997W	11,894	838	69.5	100%	$550	
	Auctions: $705, MS-70, August 2014; $611, MS-70, August 2014					
1997W, Proof	29,474	1,718	69.3		$375	
	Auctions: $447, PF-69DCam, March 2013					

BLACK REVOLUTIONARY WAR PATRIOTS SILVER DOLLAR (1998)

Designer: *John Mercanti (obverse), Ed Dwight (reverse).* **Weight:** *26.73 grams.*
Composition: *.900 silver, .100 copper (net weight .7736 oz. pure silver).*
Diameter: *38.1 mm.* **Edge:** *Reeded.* **Mint:** *San Francisco.*

This coin commemorates black Revolutionary War patriots and the 275th anniversary of the birth of Crispus Attucks, the first patriot killed in the infamous Boston Massacre in 1770 (an event predating the Revolutionary War, one among many incidents that inflamed the pro-independence passions of Americans).

Designs. *Obverse:* U.S. Mint engraver John Mercanti's conception of Crispus Attucks. *Reverse:* A black patriot family, a detail from the proposed Black Patriots Memorial.

Mintage Data. Authorized by Public Law 104-329, signed by President William J. Clinton on October 20, 1996. *Maximum authorized*—500,000. *Number minted*—37,210 Uncirculated and 75,070 Proof.

Original Cost. Sale prices $30 (Uncirculated, pre-issue) and $33 (Proof, pre-issue); Uncirculated later raised to $32, and Proof later raised to $37. A portion of the surcharge of $10 per coin went to the Black Revolutionary War Patriots Foundation to fund the construction of the Black Patriots Memorial in Washington, D.C.

Key to Collecting. These coins became highly desirable when the low mintage figures were published. Examples remain valuable today, and deservedly so. Nearly all are superb gems.

	Distribution	Cert	Avg	%MS	MS-67	
					PF-67	
1998S	37,210	1,182	69.2	100%	$120	
	Auctions: $176, MS-70, April 2013					
1998S, Proof	75,070	1,393	69.0		$55	
	Auctions: $353, PF-70DCam, April 2013					

ROBERT F. KENNEDY SILVER DOLLAR (1998)

Designer: *Thomas D. Rogers Sr.* **Weight:** *26.73 grams.*
Composition: *.900 silver, .100 copper (net weight .7736 oz. pure silver).*
Diameter: *38.1 mm.* **Edge:** *Reeded.* **Mint:** *San Francisco.*

These coins marked the 30th anniversary of the death of Robert F. Kennedy, attorney general of the United States appointed by his brother, President John F. Kennedy.

Designs. *Obverse:* Portrait of Robert F. Kennedy. *Reverse:* Eagle perched on a shield with JUSTICE above, Senate seal to lower left.

Mintage Data. Authorized by Public Law 103-328, signed by President William J. Clinton on September 29, 1994. *Maximum authorized*—500,000. *Number minted*—106,422 Uncirculated and 99,020 Proof.

Original Cost. Sale prices $30 (Uncirculated, pre-issue) and $33 (Proof, pre-issue); Uncirculated later raised to $32, and Proof later raised to $37. A portion of the surcharge of $10 per coin went to the Robert F. Kennedy Memorial.

Key to Collecting. Upon their publication the mintage figures were viewed as being attractively low from a numismatic viewpoint. Examples are easily found today and are usually superb gems.

	Distribution	Cert	Avg	%MS	MS-67
					PF-67
1998S	106,422	2,965	69.3	100%	$40
	Auctions: $70, MS-70, July 2014; $129, MS-70, April 2013				
1998S, Proof	99,020	1,449	69.0		$62
	Auctions: $282, PF-70DCam, September 2014; $270, PF-70DCam, September 2014				

DOLLEY MADISON SILVER DOLLAR (1999)

Designer: *Tiffany & Co.* **Weight:** *26.73 grams.*
Composition: *.900 silver, .100 copper (net weight .7736 oz. pure silver).*
Diameter: *38.1 mm.* **Edge:** *Reeded.* **Mint:** *Philadelphia.*

If the myth that Martha Washington was the subject for the 1792 silver half disme is discarded, Dolley Madison, wife of President James Madison, became the first of the first ladies to be depicted on a legal-tender U.S. coin with this silver dollar. The designs by Tiffany & Co. were modeled by T. James Ferrell (obverse) and Thomas D. Rogers Sr. (reverse). Note the T&Co. logo in a flower petal on the obverse and at the base of the trees to the right on the reverse.

Designs. *Obverse:* Portrait of Dolley Madison as depicted near the ice house (in the style of classic pergola) on the grounds of the family estate, Montpelier. A bouquet of cape jasmines is to the left. *Reverse:* Angular view of the front of Montpelier, complete with landscaping.

Mintage Data. Authorized by Public Law 104-329, signed by President William J. Clinton on October 20, 1996. *Maximum authorized*—500,000. *Number minted*—89,104 Uncirculated and 224,403 Proof.

Original Cost. Sale prices $30 (Uncirculated, pre-issue) and $33 (Proof, pre-issue); Uncirculated later raised to $32, and Proof later raised to $37. A portion of the surcharge of $10 per coin went to the National Trust for Historic Preservation.

Key to Collecting. The Dolley Madison dollars have been popular with collectors ever since they were first sold. Examples can be obtained with little effort and are usually superb gems.

	Distribution	Cert	Avg	%MS	MS-67
					PF-67
1999P	89,104	2,137	69.4	100%	$30
Auctions: $90, MS-70, April 2013					
1999P, Proof	224,403	2,541	69.2		$31
Auctions: $106, PF-70DCam, April 2013					

GEORGE WASHINGTON DEATH BICENTENNIAL $5 GOLD COIN (1999)

Designer: *Laura Garden Fraser.* **Weight:** *8.359 grams.*
Composition: *.900 gold, .100 copper (net weight .242 oz. pure gold).*
Diameter: *21.6 mm.* **Edge:** *Reeded.* **Mint:** *West Point.*

The 200th anniversary of George Washington's death was commemorated with this coin. In 1932 Laura Garden Fraser's proposed Washington portrait for the quarter dollar had been rejected in favor of the portrait design by John Flanagan, but it was resurrected for this commemorative gold coin.

Designs. *Obverse:* A portrait of Washington inspired by the bust modeled in 1785 for French sculptor Jean Antoine Houdon. *Reverse:* A perched eagle with feathers widely separated at left and right.

Mintage Data. Authorized on October 20, 1996, by Public Law 104-329, part of the United States Commemorative Coin Act of 1996. *Maximum authorized*—100,000 pieces (both formats combined). *Number minted*—22,511 Uncirculated and 41,693 Proof.

Original Cost. Sale prices $180 (Uncirculated, pre-issue) and $195 (Proof, pre-issue); Uncirculated later raised to $195, and Proof later raised to $225. A portion of the surcharge went to the Mount Vernon Ladies' Association, which cares for Washington's home today.

Key to Collecting. This coin is readily available in any high grade desired.

	Distribution	Cert	Avg	%MS	MS-67
					PF-67
1999W	22,511	1,452	69.5	100%	$425
Auctions: $515, MS-70, August 2014; $764, MS-70, September 2014					
1999W, Proof	41,693	2,012	69.4		$375
Auctions: $705, PF-70DCam, March 2013; $382, PF-69DCam, July 2014					

YELLOWSTONE NATIONAL PARK SILVER DOLLAR (1999)

Designer: *Edgar Z. Steever IV (obverse), William C. Cousins (reverse).* **Weight:** *26.73 grams.*
Composition: *.900 silver, .100 copper (net weight .7736 oz. pure silver).*
Diameter: *38.1 mm.* **Edge:** *Reeded.* **Mint:** *Philadelphia.*

This coin commemorated the 125th anniversary of the establishment of Yellowstone National Park. Technically, it came out and was dated two years later than it should have, as the park was founded in 1872 (and therefore the 125th anniversary would have been in 1997, not 1999).

Designs. *Obverse:* An unidentified geyser (not the famed Old Faithful, for the terrain is different) is shown in action. YELLOWSTONE is above, with other inscriptions to the left center and below, as illustrated. *Reverse:* A bison is shown, facing left. In the background is a mountain range with sun and resplendent rays (an adaptation of the seal of the Department of the Interior).

Mintage Data. Authorized on October 20, 1996, by Public Law 104-329, part of the United States Commemorative Coin Act of 1996. The catch-all legislation authorized seven commemoratives to be issued from 1997 to 1999. *Maximum authorized*—500,000 (both formats combined). *Number minted*—82,563 Uncirculated and 187,595 Proof.

Original Cost. Sale prices $30 (Uncirculated, pre-issue) and $33 (Proof, pre-issue); Uncirculated later raised to $32, and Proof later raised to $37.

Key to Collecting. Easily obtainable in the numismatic marketplace, nearly always in high grades. Investors are attracted to coins certified as MS-70 or PF-70, but few can tell the difference between these and coins at the 69 level. Only a tiny fraction of the mintage has ever been certified.

	Distribution	Cert	Avg	%MS	MS-67 / PF-67
1999P	82,563	1,812	69.3	100%	$45
	Auctions: No auction records available.				
1999P, Proof	187,595	2,135	69.0		$48
	Auctions: No auction records available.				

LIBRARY OF CONGRESS BICENTENNIAL SILVER DOLLAR (2000)

Designer: *Thomas D. Rogers Sr. (obverse), John Mercanti (reverse).* **Weight:** *26.73 grams.*
Composition: *.900 silver, .100 copper (net weight .7736 oz. pure silver).*
Diameter: *38.1 mm.* **Edge:** *Reeded.* **Mint:** *Philadelphia.*

The Library of Congress, located across the street from the U.S. Capitol in Washington, celebrated its 200th anniversary on April 24, 2000; these silver dollars and a ten-dollar bimetallic coin were issued to honor the milestone.

Designs. *Obverse:* An open book, with its spine resting on a closed book, with the torch of the Library of Congress dome behind. *Reverse:* The dome part of the Library of Congress.

Mintage Data. Authorized by Public Law 105-268, signed by President William J. Clinton on October 19, 1996. *Maximum authorized*—500,000. *Number minted*—53,264 Uncirculated and 198,503 Proof.

Original Cost. Sale prices $25 (Uncirculated, pre-issue) and $28 (Proof, pre-issue); Uncirculated later raised to $27, and Proof later raised to $32. A portion of the surcharges went to the Library of Congress Trust Fund Board.

Key to Collecting. The Library of Congress silver dollar (as well as the ten-dollar bimetallic coin issued alongside it) is readily available in the marketplace today, nearly always of the superb gem quality, as issued.

	Distribution	Cert	Avg	%MS	MS-67
					PF-67
2000P	53,264	1,590	69.4	100%	$30
	Auctions: $76, MS-70, July 2014; $108, MS-70, April 2013				
2000P, Proof	198,503	1,896	69.0		$31
	Auctions: $188, PF-70DCam, September 2014; $635, PF-70DCam, April 2013				

LIBRARY OF CONGRESS BICENTENNIAL $10 BIMETALLIC COIN (2000)

Designer: *John Mercanti (obverse), Thomas D. Rogers Sr. (reverse).*
Weight: *16.259 grams.* **Composition:** *.480 gold, .480 platinum, .040 alloy.*
Diameter: *27 mm.* **Edge:** *Reeded.* **Mint:** *West Point.*

This coin was the U.S. Mint's first gold/platinum bimetallic coin. The Library of Congress—the original location of which was burned by the British, but which was resurrected using Thomas Jefferson's personal book collection—is today a repository that includes 18 million books and more than 100 million other items, including periodicals, films, prints, photographs, and recordings.

Designs. *Obverse:* The torch of the Library of Congress dome. *Reverse:* An eagle surrounded by a wreath.

Mintage Data. Authorized by Public Law 105-268, signed by President William J. Clinton on October 19, 1996. *Maximum authorized*—200,000. *Number minted*—7,261 Uncirculated and 27,445 Proof.

Original Cost. Sale prices $380 (Uncirculated, pre-issue) and $395 (Proof, pre-issue); Uncirculated later raised to $405, and Proof later raised to $425. A portion of the surcharges went to the Library of Congress Trust Fund Board.

Key to Collecting. The Library of Congress ten-dollar bimetallic coin (as well as the silver dollar issued alongside it) is readily available in the marketplace today, nearly always of the superb gem quality as issued.

	Distribution	Cert	Avg	%MS	MS-67
					PF-67
2000W	7,261	1,328	69.7	100%	$1,800
	Auctions: $2,362, MS-70, August 2014; $2,350, MS-70, August 2014				
2000W, Proof	27,445	3,008	69.2		$1,075
	Auctions: $1,763, PF-70DCam, January 2014; $1,528, PF-70DCam, August 2014				

LEIF ERICSON MILLENNIUM SILVER DOLLAR (2000)

Designer: *John Mercanti (obverse), T. James Ferrell (reverse).* **Weight:** *26.73 grams.*
Composition: *.900 silver, .100 copper (net weight .7736 oz. pure silver).*
Diameter: *38.1 mm.* **Edge:** *Reeded.* **Mint:** *Philadelphia.*

This silver dollar was issued in cooperation with a foreign government, the Republic of Iceland, which also sponsored its own coin, struck at the Philadelphia Mint (but with no mintmark), a silver 1,000 krónur. Both commemorated the millennium of the year 1000, the approximate departure date of Leif Ericson and his crew from Iceland to the New World.

Designs. *Obverse:* Portrait of Leif Ericson, an artist's conception, as no actual image survives—based on the image used on the Iceland 1 krónur coin. The helmeted head of the explorer is shown facing right. *Reverse:* A Viking long ship with high prow under full sail, FOUNDER OF THE NEW WORLD above, other inscriptions below.

Mintage Data. Authorized under Public Law 106-126. *Maximum authorized*—500,000. *Number minted*—28,150 Uncirculated and 144,748 Proof.

Original Cost. Sale prices $30 (Uncirculated, pre-issue) and $33 (Proof, pre-issue); Uncirculated later raised to $32, and Proof later raised to $37. The surcharge of $10 per coin went to the Leifur Eiriksson Foundation for funding student exchanges between the United States and Iceland.

Key to Collecting. These coins are readily available in the marketplace today.

	Distribution	Cert	Avg	%MS	MS-67 PF-67
2000P	28,150	1,260	69.4	100%	$75
	Auctions: $176, MS-70, July 2014; $212, MS-70, January 2013				
2000P, Proof	144,748	2,122	69.0		$68
	Auctions: $999, PF-70DCam, September 2014; $999, PF-70DCam, April 2013				

AMERICAN BUFFALO SILVER DOLLAR (2001)

Designer: *James Earle Fraser.* **Weight:** *26.73 grams.*
Composition: *.900 silver, .100 copper (net weight .7736 oz. pure silver).*
Diameter: *38.1 mm.* **Edge:** *Reeded.* **Mints:** *Denver (Uncirculated), Philadelphia (Proof).*

James Earle Fraser's design, originally used on nickels from 1913 to 1938, was modified slightly by Mint engravers for this silver dollar. Commonly called the "American Buffalo Commemorative," the coin debuted at the groundbreaking for the Smithsonian Institution's National Museum of the American Indian and was very well received.

Designs. *Obverse:* Portrait of a Native American facing right. *Reverse:* An American bison standing, facing left.

Mintage Data. Authorized by Public Law 106-375, October 27, 2000. *Maximum authorized*—500,000. *Number minted*—2001-D: 227,131 Uncirculated; 2001-P: 272,869 Proof.

Original Cost. Sale prices (pre-issue only) $30 (Uncirculated) and $33 (Proof). The surcharge of $10 per coin went to the National Museum of the American Indian.

Key to Collecting. Both the Uncirculated and Proof of the 2001 American Buffalo were carefully produced to high standards of quality. Nearly all examples today grade at high levels, including MS-70 and PF-70, these ultra-grades commanding a sharp premium for investors. Coins grading 68 or 69 often have little or any real difference in quality and would seem to be the best buys.

	Distribution	Cert	Avg	%MS	MS-67 PF-67
2001D	227,131	14,005	69.1	100%	$190
	Auctions: $270, MS-70, August 2014; $423, MS-70, January 2013				
2001P, Proof	272,869	14,675	69.1		$200
	Auctions: $470, PF-70DCam, February 2014; $435, PF-70DCam, July 2014				

U.S. CAPITOL VISITOR CENTER HALF DOLLAR (2001)

Designer: *Dean McMullen (obverse), Alex Shagin and Marcel Jovine (reverse).* **Weight:** *11.34 grams.* **Composition:** *.9167 copper, .0833 nickel.* **Diameter:** *30.61 mm.* **Edge:** *Reeded.* **Mint:** *Philadelphia.*

In 1991 Congress voted on a Visitor Center to be established near the U.S. Capitol building. This copper-nickel half dollar, as well as a silver dollar and a ten-dollar gold coin, were decided upon to provide the funds through sale surcharges. The center and the coins did not become a reality until more than a decade later, though.

Designs. *Obverse:* The north wing of the original U.S. Capitol (burned by the British in 1814) is shown superimposed on a plan view of the present building. *Reverse:* Within a circle of 16 stars are inscriptions referring to the first meeting of the Senate and House.

Mintage Data. Authorized by Public Law 106-126, signed by President William J. Clinton on December 6, 1999. *Maximum authorized*—750,000. *Number minted*—99,157 Uncirculated and 77,962 Proof.

Original Cost. Sale prices $7.75 (Uncirculated, pre-issue) and $10.75 (Proof, pre-issue); Uncirculated later raised to $8.50, and Proof later raised to $11.50. The $3 surcharge per coin went towards the construction of the Visitor Center.

Key to Collecting. Today, this half dollar is readily available on the market, nearly always in the same gem quality as issued.

	Distribution	Cert	Avg	%MS	MS-67 PF-67
2001P	99,157	3,417	69.5	100%	$20
	Auctions: $153, MS-70, August 2013				
2001P, Proof	77,962	1,333	69.0		$16
	Auctions: No auction records available.				

U.S. Capitol Visitor Center Silver Dollar (2001)

Designer: *Marika Somogyi (obverse), John Mercanti (reverse).* **Weight:** *26.73 grams.*
Composition: *.900 silver, .100 copper (net weight .7736 oz. pure silver).*
Diameter: *38.1 mm.* **Edge:** *Reeded.* **Mint:** *Philadelphia.*

The U.S. Capitol Visitor Center, as first proposed, was to offer free exhibits and films, and it was believed that the center would eliminate lengthy waits to view the Capitol proper. However, presumably many would still want to visit the Capitol itself, and no further plan to eliminate waiting time was presented. After the September 11, 2001, terrorist attack on the World Trade Center in New York City and the Pentagon in the District of Columbia, security at the Capitol was heightened—and the concept of the Visitor Center became even more important.

Designs. *Obverse:* The original Capitol is shown with the date 1800, and a much smaller later Capitol, with the date 2001—a variation on the same theme as used on the half dollar. *Reverse:* An eagle reminiscent of Mint engraver John Mercanti's reverse for the 1986 silver bullion "Eagle" dollar. In the present incarnation, the national bird wears a ribbon lettered U.S. CAPITOL VISITOR CENTER.

Mintage Data. Authorized by Public Law 106-126, signed by President William J. Clinton on December 6, 1999. *Maximum authorized*—500,000. *Number minted*—35,380 Uncirculated and 143,793 Proof.

Original Cost. Sale prices $27 (Uncirculated, pre-issue) and $29 (Proof, pre-issue); Uncirculated later raised to $29, and Proof later raised to $33. The $10 surcharge per coin went towards the construction of the Visitor Center.

Key to Collecting. Today, this silver dollar is readily available on the market, nearly always in the same gem quality as issued.

	Distribution	Cert	Avg	%MS	MS-67 PF-67
2001P	35,380	1,782	69.3	100%	$45
	Auctions: $129, MS-70, April 2013				
2001P, Proof	143,793	2,126	69.0		$45
	Auctions: $294, PF-70DCam, February 2014; $4,113, PF-70DCam, April 2013				

U.S. Capitol Visitor Center $5 Gold Coin (2001)

Designer: *Elizabeth Jones.* **Weight:** *8.359 grams.* **Composition:** *.900 gold, .100 copper*
(net weight .242 oz. pure gold). **Diameter:** *21.6 mm.* **Edge:** *Reeded.* **Mint:** *West Point.*

If there was a potential highlight for what proved to be yet another underperforming commemorative issue—with sales far below projections—it was that Elizabeth Jones, former chief engraver at the Mint, was tapped to do the obverse of the $5 gold coin in the Capitol Visitor Center series. The result might not be a showcase for her remarkable talent, given the nature of the subject, but it rounds out the suite of three commemorative coins with detailed architectural motifs.

Designs. *Obverse:* Section of a Corinthian column. *Reverse:* The 1800 Capitol (interestingly, with slightly different architectural details and proportions than seen on the other coins).

Mintage Data. Authorized by Public Law 106-126, signed by President William J. Clinton on December 6, 1999. *Maximum authorized*—100,000. *Number minted*—6,761 Uncirculated and 27,652 Proof.

Original Cost. Sale prices $175 (Uncirculated, pre-issue) and $177 (Proof, pre-issue); Uncirculated later raised to $200, and Proof later raised to $207. The $35 surcharge per coin went towards the construction of the Visitor Center.

Key to Collecting. Of all the Capitol Visitor Center commemoratives, the Uncirculated five-dollar gold coin is least often seen. After the distribution figure of only 6,761 was released for that coin, buyers clamored to acquire them, and the price rose sharply. Today, it still sells at one of the greatest premiums of any modern commemorative.

	Distribution	Cert	Avg	%MS	MS-67
					PF-67
2001W	6,761	2,018	69.5	100%	$2,000
	Auctions: $1,087, MS-70, July 2014; $1,058, MS-70, August 2014				
2001W, Proof	27,652	1,847	69.4		$375
	Auctions: No auction records available.				

SALT LAKE CITY OLYMPIC WINTER GAMES SILVER DOLLAR (2002)

Designer: *John Mercanti (obverse), Donna Weaver (reverse).* **Weight:** *26.73 grams.*
Composition: *.900 silver, .100 copper (net weight .7736 oz. pure silver).*
Diameter: *38.1 mm.* **Edge:** *Reeded.* **Mint:** *Denver (Uncirculated), Philadelphia (reverse).*

In February 2002, Salt Lake City, Utah, was the focal point for the XIX Olympic Winter Games, a quadrennial event. Congress authorized both this silver dollar and a five-dollar gold coin to commemorate the competition.

Designs. *Obverse:* A stylized geometric figure representing an ice crystal. Five interlocked Olympic rings and inscriptions complete the picture, including XIX OLYMPIC WINTER GAMES. *Reverse:* The skyline of Salt Lake City is shown with exaggerated dimensions, with the rugged Wasatch Mountains in the distance. XIX OLYMPIC GAMES is repeated on the reverse.

Mintage Data. Authorized by Public Law 106-435, the Salt Lake Olympic Winter Games Commemorative Coin Act, signed by President William J. Clinton on November 6, 2000. *Maximum authorized*—400,000. *Number minted*—2002-D: 40,257 Uncirculated; 2002-P: 166,864 Proof.

Original Cost. Sale prices $30 (Uncirculated, pre-issue) and $33 (Proof, pre-issue); Uncirculated were later raised to $32, and Proof were later raised to $37. The surcharge of $10 per coin went to the Salt Lake Organizing Committee for the Olympic Winter Games of 2002 and the United States Olympic Committee.

Key to Collecting. As might be expected, coins encapsulated as MS-70 and PF-70 sell for strong prices to investors and Registry Set compilers. Most collectors are nicely satisfied with 68 and 69 grades, or the normal issue quality, since the coins are little different in actual appearance.

	Distribution	Cert	Avg	%MS	MS-67
					PF-67
2002D	40,257	1,529	69.5	100%	$45
	Auctions: $94, MS-70, January 2013				
2002P, Proof	166,864	2,102	69.1		$39
	Auctions: $217, PF-70DCam, April 2013				

SALT LAKE CITY OLYMPIC WINTER GAMES $5 GOLD COIN (2002)

Designer: *Donna Weaver.* **Weight:** *8.359 grams.*
Composition: *.900 gold, .100 copper (net weight .242 oz. pure gold).*
Diameter: *21.6 mm.* **Edge:** *Reeded.* **Mint:** *West Point.*

The design of the 2002 Olympic Winter Games commemoratives attracted little favorable notice outside of advertising publicity, and, once again, sales were low—all the more surprising, for Olympic coins often attract international buyers.

Designs. *Obverse:* An ice crystal dominates, superimposed over a geometric creation representing "Rhythm of the Land," but not identified. Also appearing are the date and SALT LAKE. *Reverse:* The outline of the Olympic cauldron is shown, with geometric sails above representing flames.

Mintage Data. Authorized by Public Law 106-435, the Salt Lake Olympic Winter Games Commemorative Coin Act, signed by President William J. Clinton on November 6, 2000. *Maximum authorized*—80,000. *Number minted*—10,585 Uncirculated and 32,877 Proof.

Original Cost. Sale prices $180 (Uncirculated, pre-issue) and $195 (Proof, pre-issue); Uncirculated were later raised to $205, and Proof were later raised to $225. The surcharge of $10 per coin went to the Salt Lake Organizing Committee for the Olympic Winter Games of 2002 and the United States Olympic Committee.

Key to Collecting. Although the mintage of the Uncirculated $5 in particular was quite low, there was not much interest in the immediate aftermarket. Coins graded MS-70 and PF-70 sell for strong prices to investors and Registry Set compilers.

	Distribution	Cert	Avg	%MS	MS-67
					PF-67
2002W	10,585	1,175	69.5	100%	$350
	Auctions: $397, MS-70, September 2014; $499, MS-70, August 2013				
2002W, Proof	32,877	1,209	69.5		$375
	Auctions: $108, PF-70DCam, April 2013; $33, PF-69DCam, August 2014				

WEST POINT (U.S. MILITARY ACADEMY) BICENTENNIAL SILVER DOLLAR (2002)

Designer: *T. James Ferrell (obverse), John Mercanti (reverse).* **Weight:** *26.73 grams.*
Composition: *.900 silver, .100 copper (net weight .7736 oz. pure silver).*
Diameter: *38.1 mm.* **Edge:** *Reeded.* **Mint:** *West Point.*

The 200th anniversary of the U.S. Military Academy at West Point, New York, was celebrated with this coin. The Cadet Chapel is shown on the obverse of the dollar.

Designs. *Obverse:* A fine depiction of the Academy color guard in a parade, with Washington Hall and the Cadet Chapel in the distance—and minimum intrusion of lettering—projects this to the forefront of commemorative designs of the era. *Reverse:* The West Point Bicentennial logotype is shown, an adaptation of the Academy seal, showing at the center an ancient Greek helmet with a sword and shield.

Mintage Data. Authorized several years earlier by Public Law 103-328, signed by President William J. Clinton on September 29, 1994. *Maximum authorized*—500,000. *Number minted*—103,201 Uncirculated and 288,293 Proof.

Original Cost. Sale prices $30 (Uncirculated, pre-issue) and $32 (Proof, pre-issue); Uncirculated later raised to $32, and Proof later raised to $37. The surcharge of $10 per coin went to the Association of Graduates.

Key to Collecting. The scenario is familiar: enough coins were struck to satisfy all comers during the period of issue, with the result that there was no unsatisfied demand. Coins certified at the MS-70 level appeal to a special group of buyers and command strong premiums.

	Distribution	Cert	Avg	%MS	MS-67
					PF-67
2002W	103,201	4,425	69.5	100%	$30
	Auctions: No auction records available.				
2002W, Proof	288,293	5,510	69.3		$34
	Auctions: No auction records available.				

FIRST FLIGHT CENTENNIAL HALF DOLLAR (2003)

Designer: *John Mercanti (obverse), Norman E. Nemeth (reverse).* **Weight:** *11.34 grams.*
Composition: *.9167 copper, .0833 nickel.* **Diameter:** *30.61 mm.* **Edge:** *Reeded.* **Mint:** *Philadelphia.*

To celebrate the 100th anniversary of powered aircraft flight by Orville and Wilbur Wright in 1903, Congress authorized a set of 2003-dated commemoratives, including this copper-nickel half dollar.

Designs. *Obverse:* Wright Monument at Kill Devil Hill on the North Carolina seashore. *Reverse:* Wright Flyer biplane in flight.

Mintage Data. Authorized by Public Law 105-124, as an amendment and tag-on to the 50 States Commemorative Coin Program Act (which authorized the State quarters), signed by President William J. Clinton on December 1, 1997. *Maximum authorized*—750,000. *Number minted*—57,122 Uncirculated and 109,710 Proof.

Original Cost. Sale prices $9.75 (Uncirculated, pre-issue) and $12.50 (Proof, pre-issue); Uncirculated later raised to $10.75, and Proof later raised to $13.50. The surcharge of $1 per coin went to the First Flight Centennial Foundation, a private nonprofit group founded in 1995.

Key to Collecting. Values fell after sales concluded. In time, they recovered. Today, all the coins in this set sell for a premium. Superb gems are easily enough found.

	Distribution	Cert	Avg	%MS	MS-67 PF-67
2003P	57,122	2,178	69.5	100%	$18
Auctions: $50, MS-70, April 2013					
2003P, Proof	109,710	2,038	69.1		$17
Auctions: No auction records available.					

FIRST FLIGHT CENTENNIAL SILVER DOLLAR (2003)

Designer: *T. James Ferrell (obverse), Norman E. Nemeth (reverse).* **Weight:** *26.73 grams.*
Composition: *.900 silver, .100 copper (net weight .7736 oz. pure silver).*
Diameter: *38.1 mm.* **Edge:** *Reeded.* **Mint:** *Philadelphia.*

The release of this coin and the two other First Flight Centennial commemoratives with it marked the third straight year that a coin featuring the Wrights' plane was featured on a U.S. coin. In 2001, the North Carolina State quarter had portrayed the Wright Flyer, and the Ohio State quarter did the same in 2002 (though an astronaut was also incorporated).

Designs. *Obverse:* Conjoined portraits of Orville and Wilbur Wright. *Reverse:* The Wright brothers' plane in flight.

Mintage Data. Authorized by Public Law 105-124, as an amendment and tag-on to the 50 States Commemorative Coin Program Act (which authorized the State quarters), signed by President William J. Clinton on December 1, 1997. *Maximum authorized*—500,000. *Number minted*—53,533 Uncirculated and 190,240 Proof.

Original Cost. Sale prices $31 (Uncirculated, pre-issue) and $33 (Proof, pre-issue); Uncirculated later raised to $33, and Proof later raised to $37. The surcharge of $1 per coin went to the First Flight Centennial Foundation, a private nonprofit group founded in 1995.

Key to Collecting. Values fell after sales concluded, but they did recover in time. Today, all the coins in this program sell for a premium. Superb gems are easily enough found.

	Distribution	Cert	Avg	%MS	MS-67 PF-67
2003P	53,533	3,120	69.4	100%	$45
Auctions: $94, MS-70, May 2013					
2003P, Proof	190,240	3,045	69.0		$52
Auctions: $423, PF-70DCam, March 2013; $141, PF-70DCam, April 2013					

FIRST FLIGHT CENTENNIAL $10 GOLD COIN (2003)

Designer: *Donna Weaver (obverse), Norman E. Nemeth (reverse).* **Weight:** *16.718 grams.*
Composition: *.900 gold, .100 copper (net weight .4837 oz. pure gold).*
Diameter: *27 mm.* **Edge:** *Reeded.* **Mint:** *West Point.*

None of the First Flight Centennial commemoratives sold particularly well. The redundancy of the motifs undoubtedly contributed to this: each had the same reverse motif of the Wright brothers' plane, and the two largest denominations each pictured the Wright brothers.

Designs. *Obverse:* Portraits of Orville and Wilbur Wright. *Reverse:* Wright Brothers' plane in flight with an eagle overhead.

Mintage Data. Authorized by Public Law 105-124, as an amendment and tag-on to the 50 States Commemorative Coin Program Act (which authorized the State quarters), signed by President William J. Clinton on December 1, 1997. *Maximum authorized—*100,000. *Number minted—*10,009 Uncirculated and 21,676 Proof.

Original Cost. Sale prices $340 (Uncirculated, pre-issue) and $350 (Proof, pre-issue); Uncirculated later raised to $365, and Proof later raised to $375. The surcharge of $1 per coin went to the First Flight Centennial Foundation, a private nonprofit group founded in 1995.

Key to Collecting. Values fell after sales concluded, but they did recover in time. Today, all the coins in this commemorative program sell for a premium. Superb gems are easily enough found.

	Distribution	Cert	Avg	%MS	MS-67
					PF-67
2003W	10,009	1,887	69.8	100%	$1,000
	Auctions: $821, MS-70, July 2014; $705, MS-70, November 2014				
2003W, Proof	21,676	1,595	69.3		$800
	Auctions: $823, PF-70DCam, July 2014; $1,293, PF-70DCam, April 2013				

THOMAS ALVA EDISON SILVER DOLLAR (2004)

Designer: *Donna Weaver (obverse), John Mercanti (reverse).* **Weight:** *26.73 grams.*
Composition: *.900 silver, .100 copper (net weight .7736 oz. pure silver).*
Diameter: *38.1 mm.* **Edge:** *Reeded.* **Mint:** *Philadelphia.*

The 125th anniversary of the October 21, 1879, demonstration by Thomas Edison of his first successful electric light bulb was the event commemorated with this silver dollar. Despite sales falling far short of the authorized amount, the Edison dollar was well received by collectors. Interestingly, several proposals had earlier been made for commemoratives to be issued in 1997 to observe the 150th anniversary of Edison's February 11, 1847, birth in Milan, Ohio.

Designs. *Obverse:* Waist-up portrait of Edison holding a light bulb in his right hand. *Reverse:* Light bulb of the 1879 style mounted on a base, with arcs surrounding.

Mintage Data. Authorized by Public Law 105-331, signed by President William J. Clinton on December 6, 1999. *Maximum authorized*—500,000. *Number minted*—92,510 Uncirculated and 211,055 Proof.

Original Cost. Sale prices $31 (Uncirculated, pre-issue) and $33 (Proof, pre-issue); Uncirculated later raised to $33, and Proof later raised to $37. The surcharge of $10 per coin was to be divided evenly among the Port Huron (Michigan) Museum of Arts and History, the Edison Birthplace Association, the National Park Service, the Edison Plaza Museum, the Edison Winter Home and Museum, the Edison Institute, the Edison Memorial Tower, and the Hall of Electrical History.

Key to Collecting. Examples are plentiful. Nearly all are superb gems. As was the situation for many other U.S. Mint issues of the period, promoters who had coins encased in certified holders marked MS-70 or PF-70 were able to persuade, or at least imply, to investors (but not to seasoned collectors) that coins of such quality were rarities, and obtained strong prices for them. Smart buyers simply purchased examples remaining in original Mint holders, of which many were just as nice as the "70" coins.

	Distribution	Cert	Avg	%MS	MS-67 PF-67
2004P	92,510	2,765	69.3	100%	$30
	Auctions: $90, MS-70, April 2013				
2004P, Proof	211,055	3,304	69.1		$42
	Auctions: $78, PF-70DCam, July 2014; $141, PF-70DCam, March 2013				

LEWIS AND CLARK BICENTENNIAL SILVER DOLLAR (2004)

Designer: *Donna Weaver.* **Weight:** *26.73 grams.*
Composition: *.900 silver, .100 copper (net weight .7736 oz. pure silver).*
Diameter: *38.1 mm.* **Edge:** *Reeded.* **Mint:** *Philadelphia.*

This was one of the most successful commemorative programs, despite the fact that many events across the nation celebrating the bicentennial were flops. Note that the Lewis and Clark Expedition had previously been commemorated with gold dollars dated 1903 for the Louisiana Purchase Exposition (St. Louis World's Fair held in 1904) and those of 1904 and 1905 for the Lewis and Clark Exposition (Portland, Oregon, 1905).

Designs. *Obverse:* Meriwether Lewis and William Clark standing with a river and foliage in the distance as a separate motif. Lewis holds the barrel end of his rifle in one hand and a journal in the other and is looking at Clark, who is gazing to the distance in the opposite direction. *Reverse:* Copy of the reverse of the Jefferson Indian Peace medal designed by John Reich and presented to Indians on the expedition (the identical motif was also revived for use on one variety of the 2004 Jefferson nickel). Feathers are to the left and right, and 17 stars are above.

Mintage Data. Authorized by Public Law 106-136, signed by President William J. Clinton on December 6, 1999. *Maximum authorized*—500,000. *Number minted*—142,015 Uncirculated and 351,989 Proof.

Original Cost. Sale prices $33 (Uncirculated, pre-issue) and $35 (Proof, pre-issue); Uncirculated later raised to $35, and Proof later raised to $39. Two-thirds of the surcharge of $10 per coin went to the National Council of the Lewis and Clark Bicentennial, while one-third went to the National Park Service for the bicentennial celebration.

Key to Collecting. Superb gem coins are readily available.

	Distribution	Cert	Avg	%MS	MS-67
					PF-67
2004P	142,015	4,058	69.4	100%	$35
Auctions: $90, MS-70, April 2013					
2004P, Proof	351,989	5,526	69.1		$36
Auctions: $88, PF-70DCam, February 2013					

MARINE CORPS 230TH ANNIVERSARY SILVER DOLLAR (2005)

Designer: *Norman E. Nemeth (obverse), Charles L. Vickers (reverse).* **Weight:** *26.73 grams.*
Composition: *.900 silver, .100 copper (net weight .7736 oz. pure silver).*
Diameter: *38.1 mm.* **Edge:** *Reeded.* **Mint:** *Philadelphia.*

The widespread appreciation of the heritage of the Marine Corps plus the fame of the obverse design taken from Joe Rosenthal's photograph of the flag-raising at Iwo Jima, propelled this coin to remarkable success. For the first time in recent memory, pandemonium reigned in the coin market, as prices rose, buyers clamored to find all they could, and most dealers were sold out. Within a year, interest turned to other things, and the prices dropped, but not down to the issue levels.

Designs. *Obverse:* Marines raising the Stars and Stripes over Iwo Jima as shown on the famous photograph by Joe Rosenthal. *Reverse:* Eagle, globe, and anchor emblem of the Marine Corps.

Mintage Data. Authorized under Public Law 108-291, signed by President George W. Bush on August 6, 2004. *Maximum authorized*—500,000, later increased to 600,000. *Number minted*—49,671 Uncirculated and 548,810 Proof.

Original Cost. Sale prices $33 (Uncirculated, pre-issue) and $35 (Proof, pre-issue); Uncirculated later raised to $35, and Proof later raised to $39. The surcharge of $10 per coin went toward the construction of the Marine Corps Heritage Center at the base in Quantico, Virginia.

Key to Collecting. Superb gem coins are readily available.

	Distribution	Cert	Avg	%MS	MS-67
					PF-67
2005P	49,671	11,647	69.6	100%	$48
Auctions: $76, MS-70, July 2014; $62, MS-70, August 2014					
2005P, Proof	548,810	14,046	69.2		$48
Auctions: $165, PF-70DCam, November 2013					

CHIEF JUSTICE JOHN MARSHALL SILVER DOLLAR (2005)

Designer: *John Mercanti (obverse), Donna Weaver (reverse).* **Weight:** *26.73 grams.*
Composition: *.900 silver, .100 copper (net weight .7736 oz. pure silver).*
Diameter: *38.1 mm.* **Edge:** *Reeded.* **Mint:** *Philadelphia.*

Chief Justice John Marshall, who served 34 years in that post in the U.S. Supreme Court, was the subject for this commemorative dollar. Mint engravers submitted designs for the coin, with six depictions of Marshall inspired by a painting by Saint-Mèmin, ten from an oil painting by Rembrandt Peale, and three from a statue by William W. Story. It was John Mercanti's interpretation of the Saint-Mèmin work that was selected.

Designs. *Obverse:* Portrait of Marshall, adapted from a painting made in March 1808 by Charles-Balthazar-Julien Fevret de Saint-Mèmin, of France. *Reverse:* The old Supreme Court Chamber within the Capitol.

Mintage Data. Authorized by Public Law 108-290, signed by President George W. Bush on August 9, 2004. *Maximum authorized*—400,000. *Number minted*—67,096 Uncirculated and 196,753 Proof.

Original Cost. Sale prices $33 (Uncirculated, pre-issue) and $35 (Proof, pre-issue); Uncirculated later raised to $35, and Proof later raised to $39. The surcharge of $10 per coin went to the Supreme Court Historical Society.

Key to Collecting. Superb gem coins are available in the marketplace.

	Distribution	Cert	Avg	%MS	MS-67
					PF-67
2005P	67,096	2,323	69.6	100%	$45
	Auctions: $106, MS-70, January 2013				
2005P, Proof	196,753	3,196	69.3		$35
	Auctions: $86, PF-70DCam, July 2014; $92, PF-70DCam, March 2013				

BENJAMIN FRANKLIN TERCENTENARY SCIENTIST SILVER DOLLAR (2006)

Designer: *Norman E. Nemeth (obverse), Charles L. Vickers (reverse).* **Weight:** *26.73 grams.*
Composition: *.900 silver, .100 copper (net weight .7736 oz. pure silver).*
Diameter: *38.1 mm.* **Edge:** *Reeded.* **Mint:** *Philadelphia.*

Two silver dollars were issued to commemorate the 300th anniversary of Benjamin Franklin's birth. This version celebrated Franklin's scientific accomplishments, which included discoveries in fields from electricity to oceanography to demographics.

Designs. *Obverse:* Franklin standing with a kite on a string, evocative of his experiments with lightning in June 1752. *Reverse:* Franklin's political cartoon, featuring a snake cut apart, titled "Join, or Die," reflecting the sentiment that the colonies should unite during the French and Indian War (and which had nothing to do with perceived offenses by the British, at this early time). This appeared in Franklin's *Pennsylvania Gazette* on May 9, 1754.

Mintage Data. Authorized by Public Law 104-463, the Benjamin Franklin Tercentary Act, and signed by President George W. Bush on December 21, 2004. *Maximum authorized—250,000. Number minted—58,000 Uncirculated, 142,000 Proof.*

Original Cost. Sale prices $33 (Uncirculated, pre-issue) and $35 (Proof, pre-issue); Uncirculated later raised to $35, and Proof later raised to $39. The surcharge of $10 per coin went to the Franklin Institute.

Key to Collecting. Superb gems are easily found in the marketplace.

	Distribution	Cert	Avg	%MS	MS-67
					PF-67
2006P	58,000	7,624	69.7	100%	$40
	Auctions: $76, MS-70, January 2013				
2006P, Proof	142,000	9,811	69.4		$51
	Auctions: No auction records available.				

BENJAMIN FRANKLIN TERCENTENARY
FOUNDING FATHER SILVER DOLLAR (2006)

Designer: *Don Everhart (obverse), Donna Weaver (reverse).* **Weight:** *26.73 grams.*
Composition: *.900 silver, .100 copper (net weight .7736 oz. pure silver).*
Diameter: *38.1 mm.* **Edge:** *Reeded.* **Mint:** *Philadelphia.*

The bill authorizing the issue of this silver dollar and its counterpart (see previous coin) took note of many of his accomplishments, stating he was "the only Founding Father to sign all of our Nation's organizational documents," who printed "official currency for the colonies of Pennsylvania, Delaware, New Jersey and Maryland," and helped design the Great Seal of the United States.

Designs. *Obverse:* Head and shoulders portrait of Franklin facing forward slightly to the viewer's right, with his signature reproduced below. *Reverse:* Copy of a 1776 Continental dollar within a frame of modern lettering. The mottoes on this coin were suggested by Franklin.

Mintage Data. Authorized by Public Law 104-463, the Benjamin Franklin Tercentary Act, and signed by President George W. Bush on December 21, 2004. *Maximum authorized—250,000. Number minted—58,000 Uncirculated, 142,000 Proof.*

Original Cost. Sale prices $33 (Uncirculated, pre-issue) and $35 (Proof, pre-issue); Uncirculated later raised to $35, and Proof later raised to $39. The surcharge of $10 per coin went to the Franklin Institute.

Key to Collecting. Superb gems are easily found in the marketplace.

	Distribution	Cert	Avg	%MS	MS-67
					PF-67
2006P	58,000	8,190	69.8	100%	$45
	Auctions: $90, MS-70, April 2013				
2006P, Proof	142,000	10,072	69.7		$34
	Auctions: $96, PF-70DCam, January 2013; $103, PF-70DCam, April 2013				

SAN FRANCISCO OLD MINT CENTENNIAL SILVER DOLLAR (2006)

Designer: *Sherl J. Winter (obverse), Joseph Menna after George T. Morgan (reverse).*
Weight: *26.73 grams.* **Composition:** *.900 silver, .100 copper (net weight .7736 oz. pure silver).*
Diameter: *38.1 mm.* **Edge:** *Reeded.* **Mint:** *San Francisco.*

This coin and the five-dollar gold coin issued alongside it celebrated the 100th anniversary of the second San Francisco Mint surviving the 1906 Bay Area earthquake and fire.

Designs. *Obverse:* The Second San Francisco Mint as viewed from off the left front corner. *Reverse:* Copy of the reverse of a standard Morgan silver dollar of the era 1878–1921, said to have been taken from a 1904-S.

Mintage Data. Authorized by Public Law 109-230, the San Francisco Old Mint Commemorative Act, signed by President George W. Bush in June 2006. *Maximum authorized*—500,000. *Number minted*—67,100 Uncirculated and 160,870 Proof.

Original Cost. Sale prices $33 (Uncirculated, pre-issue) and $35 (Proof, pre-issue); Uncirculated later raised to $35, and Proof later raised to $39. The surcharge of $10 per coin went to the "San Francisco Museum and Historical Society for rehabilitating the Historic Old Mint as a city museum and an American Coin and Gold Rush Museum."

Key to Collecting. Superb gems are easily found in the marketplace.

	Distribution	Cert	Avg	%MS	MS-67
					PF-67
2006S	67,100	4,510	69.6	100%	$45
	Auctions: $94, MS-70, January 2013				
2006S, Proof	160,870	8,379	69.2		$30
	Auctions: No auction records available.				

SAN FRANCISCO OLD MINT CENTENNIAL $5 GOLD COIN (2006)

Designer: *Charles L. Vickers (obverse), Don Everhart after Christian Gobrecht (reverse).*
Weight: *8.359 grams.* **Composition:** *.900 gold, .100 copper (net weight .242 oz. pure gold).*
Diameter: *21.6 mm.* **Edge:** *Reeded.* **Mint:** *San Francisco.*

The designs of this coin and the corresponding silver dollar both had obverses showing the same subject (albeit from a different view), and reverses being copies of old coinage designs.

Designs. *Obverse:* Front view of the portico of the Second San Francisco Mint, with a portion of the building to each side. Modeled after an 1869 construction drawing by Supervising Architect A.B. Mullet. *Reverse:* Copy of the reverse of the Liberty Head half eagle with motto IN GOD WE TRUST, as regularly used from 1866 to 1907.

Mintage Data. Authorized by Public Law 109-230, the San Francisco Old Mint Commemorative Act, signed by President George W. Bush in June 2006. *Maximum authorized—*100,000. *Number minted—*17,500 Uncirculated and 44,174 Proof.

Original Cost. Sale prices $220 (Uncirculated, pre-issue) and $230 (Proof, pre-issue); Uncirculated later raised to $245, and Proof later raised to $255. The surcharge of $35 per coin went to the "San Francisco Museum and Historical Society for rehabilitating the Historic Old Mint as a city museum and an American Coin and Gold Rush Museum."

Key to Collecting. Superb gems are easily found in the marketplace.

	Distribution	Cert	Avg	%MS	MS-67
					PF-67
2006S	17,500	2,765	69.7	100%	$350
Auctions: $364, MS-70, July 2014; $329, MS-70, October 2014					
2006S, Proof	44,174	3,842	69.5		$375
Auctions: $78, PF-70DCam, July 2014; $96, PF-70DCam, March 2013					

Jamestown 400th Anniversary Silver Dollar (2007)

Designer: *Donna Weaver (obverse), Susan Gamble (reverse).* **Weight:** *26.73 grams.*
Composition: *.900 silver, .100 copper (net weight .7736 oz. pure silver).*
Diameter: *38.1 mm.* **Edge:** *Reeded.* **Mint:** *Philadelphia.*

Note that Jamestown was also honored on the 2000 Virginia State quarter.

Designs. *Obverse:* Captain John Smith is shown with an Indian man and woman. *Reverse:* Three sailing ships are shown, elements already seen from the 2000 State quarter, but differently arranged.

Mintage Data. Authorized by Public Law 108-289, the Jamestown 400th Anniversary Commemorative Coin Act, signed by President George W. Bush on August 6, 2004. *Maximum authorized—*500,000. *Number minted—*81,034 Uncirculated and 260,363 Proof.

Original Cost. Sale prices $33 (Uncirculated, pre-issue) and $35 (Proof, pre-issue); Uncirculated later raised to $35, and Proof later raised to $39. The surcharge of $20 per coin went to fund the public observance of the anniversary.

Key to Collecting. Superb gem coins are readily available.

	Distribution	Cert	Avg	%MS	MS-67
					PF-67
2007P	81,034	7,612	69.6	100%	$40
Auctions: $90, MS-70, April 2013					
2007P, Proof	260,363	10,709	69.5		$35
Auctions: $100, PF-70DCam, April 2013					

JAMESTOWN 400TH ANNIVERSARY $5 GOLD COIN (2007)

Designer: *John Mercanti (obverse), Susan Gamble (reverse).* **Weight:** *8.359 grams.*
Composition: *.900 gold, .100 copper (net weight .242 oz. pure gold).*
Diameter: *21.6 mm.* **Edge:** *Reeded.* **Mint:** *West Point.*

Susan Gamble, who designed the reverse of both this coin and the silver dollar issued alongside it, was a participant in the Mint's Artistic Infusion Program, which was created to bring artists in from the private sector to upgrade the quality of coin designs.

Designs. *Obverse:* Captain John Smith is shown with Indian chief Powhatan, who holds a bag of corn. *Reverse:* Ruins of the old church at Jamestown.

Mintage Data. Authorized by Public Law 108-289, the Jamestown 400th Anniversary Commemorative Coin Act, signed by President George W. Bush on August 6, 2004. *Maximum authorized*—100,000. *Number minted*—18,623 Uncirculated and 47,123 Proof.

Original Cost. Sale prices $33 (Uncirculated, pre-issue) and $35 (Proof, pre-issue); Uncirculated later raised to $35, and Proof later raised to $39. The surcharge of $35 per coin went to fund the public observance of the anniversary.

Key to Collecting. Superb gem coins are readily available.

	Distribution	Cert	Avg	%MS	MS-67 PF-67
2007W	18,623	3,187	69.8	100%	$350
	Auctions: $329, MS-70, October 2014; $329, MS-70, November 2014				
2007W, Proof	47,123	4,067	69.6		$375
	Auctions: $341, PF-70DCam, July 2014; $317, PF-70DCam, August 2014				

LITTLE ROCK CENTRAL HIGH SCHOOL DESEGREGATION SILVER DOLLAR (2007)

Designer: *Richard Masters (obverse), Don Everhart (reverse).* **Weight:** *26.73 grams.*
Composition: *.900 silver, .100 copper (net weight .7736 oz. pure silver).*
Diameter: *38.1 mm.* **Edge:** *Reeded.* **Mint:** *Philadelphia.*

This coin commemorated the 50th anniversary of the desegregation of Little Rock Central High School, which was the result of the landmark U.S. Supreme Court case *Brown v. the Board of Education.*

Designs. *Obverse:* The feet of the "Little Rock Nine" students are shown, escorted by a soldier. *Reverse:* Little Rock Central High School as it appeared in 1957.

Mintage Data. Authorized by Public Law 109-146, the Little Rock Central High School Desegregation 50th Anniversary Commemorative Coin Act, signed by President George W. Bush on December 22, 2005. *Maximum authorized*—500,000. *Number minted*—66,093 Uncirculated and 124,678 Proof.

Original Cost. Sale prices $33 (Uncirculated, pre-issue) and $35 (Proof, pre-issue); Uncirculated later raised to $35, and Proof later raised to $39. The surcharge of $10 per coin went toward improvements at the Little Rock Central High School National Historic Site.

Key to Collecting. Superb gem coins are readily available.

	Distribution	Cert	Avg	%MS	MS-67
					PF-67
2007P	66,093	2,625	69.7	100%	$35
	Auctions: $79, MS-70, October 2014; $90, MS-70, April 2013				
2007P, Proof	124,678	3,017	69.5		$39
	Auctions: $80, PF-70DCam, July 2014; $113, PF-70DCam, April 2013				

BALD EAGLE RECOVERY AND NATIONAL EMBLEM HALF DOLLAR (2008)

Designer: *Susan Gamble (obverse), Donna Weaver (reverse).* **Weight:** *11.34 grams.*
Composition: *.9167 copper, .0833 nickel.* **Diameter:** *30.61 mm.* **Edge:** *Reeded.* **Mint:** *San Francisco.*

This copper-nickel half dollar, as well as the silver dollar and five-dollar gold coin issued alongside it, was issued to commemorate the recovery of the bald eagle species, the 35th anniversary of the Endangered Species Act of 1973, and the removal of the bald eagle from the Endangered Species List.

Designs. *Obverse:* Two eaglets and an egg in a bald eagle nest. *Reverse:* "Challenger," a non-releasable bald eagle in the care of the American Eagle Foundation and the first of his species to be trained to free-fly into major sporting events during the National Anthem.

Mintage Data. Authorized by Public Law 108-486, the Bald Eagle Commemorative Coin Act, signed by President George W. Bush on December 23, 2004. *Maximum authorized*—750,000. *Number minted*—120,180 Uncirculated and 220,577 Proof.

Original Cost. Sale prices $7.95 (Uncirculated, pre-issue) and $9.95 (Proof, pre-issue); Uncirculated later raised to $8.95, and Proof later raised to $10.95. The surcharge of $3 per coin went to the American Eagle Foundation of Tennessee for the purposes of continuing its work to save and protect bald eagles nationally.

Key to Collecting. Superb gem coins are readily available.

	Distribution	Cert	Avg	%MS	MS-67
					PF-67
2008S	120,180	6,771	69.8	100%	$15
	Auctions: $30, MS-70, April 2013				
2008S, Proof	220,577	8,771	69.7		$16
	Auctions: No auction records available.				

BALD EAGLE RECOVERY AND NATIONAL EMBLEM SILVER DOLLAR (2008)

Designer: *Joel Iskowitz (obverse), Jim Licaretz (reverse).* **Weight:** *26.73 grams.*
Composition: *.900 silver, .100 copper (net weight .7736 oz. pure silver).*
Diameter: *38.1 mm.* **Edge:** *Reeded.* **Mint:** *Philadelphia.*

The bald eagle, selected in 1782 by the Second Continental Congress as the national emblem of the United States, was common at the time of the nation's establishment. Through the years, however, poaching, habitat destruction, pesticides, and food-source contamination reduced the number of nesting pairs from approximately 100,000 to just more than 400 in the early 1960s. Fortunately, conservationists have saved the species in the past five decades.

Designs. *Obverse:* Bald eagle in flight, mountains in background. *Reverse:* The Great Seal of the United States used from 1782 to 1841.

Mintage Data. Authorized by Public Law 108-486, the Bald Eagle Commemorative Coin Act, signed by President George W. Bush on December 23, 2004. *Maximum authorized—500,000. Number minted—* 119,204 Uncirculated and 294,601 Proof.

Original Cost. Sale prices $35.95 (Uncirculated, pre-issue) and $39.95 (Proof, pre-issue); Uncirculated later raised to $37.95, and Proof later raised to $43.95. The surcharge of $10 per coin went to the American Eagle Foundation of Tennessee for the purposes of continuing its work to save and protect bald eagles nationally.

Key to Collecting. Superb gem coins are readily available.

	Distribution	Cert	Avg	%MS	MS-67 PF-67
2008P	119,204	9,020	69.7	100%	$30
	Auctions: $90, MS-70, April 2013				
2008P, Proof	294,601	13,391	69.3		$39
	Auctions: $92, PF-70DCam, July 2014; $79, PF-70DCam, July 2014				

BALD EAGLE RECOVERY AND NATIONAL EMBLEM $5 GOLD COIN (2008)

Designer: *Susan Gamble (obverse), Don Everhart (reverse).* **Weight:** *8.359 grams.*
Composition: *.900 gold, .100 copper (net weight .242 oz. pure gold).*
Diameter: *21.6 grams.* **Edge:** *Reeded.* **Mint:** *West Point.*

Government entities, private organizations, and citizens were all part of the bald eagle's recovery from near-extinction in the middle of the 1900s. Bans on certain pesticides, protections granted under the Endangered Species Act of 1973, and captive-breeding and nest-watch programs have been crucial and have led to the removal of the national emblem from the Endangered Species List.

Designs. *Obverse:* Two bald eagles perched on a branch. *Reverse:* The current Great Seal of the United States.

Mintage Data. Authorized by Public Law 108-486, the Bald Eagle Commemorative Coin Act, signed by President George W. Bush on December 23, 2004. *Maximum authorized*—100,000. *Number minted*—15,009 Uncirculated and 59,269 Proof.

Original Cost. Sale prices $284.95 (Uncirculated, pre-issue) and $294.95 (Proof, pre-issue); Uncirculated later raised to $309.95, and Proof later raised to $319.95. The surcharge of $35 per coin went to the American Eagle Foundation of Tennessee for the purposes of continuing its work to save and protect bald eagles nationally.

Key to Collecting. Superb gem coins are readily available.

	Distribution	Cert	Avg	%MS	MS-67 PF-67
2008W	15,009	1,042	69.9	100%	$400
	Auctions: $458, MS-70, January 2013				
2008W, Proof	59,269	1,758	69.8		$375
	Auctions: $442, PF-70DCam, March 2014; $427, PF-70DCam, September 2014				

ABRAHAM LINCOLN BICENTENNIAL SILVER DOLLAR (2009)

Designer: *Justin Kunz (obverse), Phebe Hemphill (reverse).* **Weight:** *26.73 grams.* **Composition:** *.900 silver, .100 copper (net weight .7736 oz. pure silver).* **Diameter:** *38.1 mm.* **Edge:** *Reeded.* **Mint:** *Philadelphia.*

These coins, issued to mark the 200th anniversary of President Abraham Lincoln's birth, were extremely popular with collectors. The 450,000 pieces allocated to individual coin sales sold out after a month. Note that this anniversary was also commemorated with the release of four different reverse designs for the 2009 Lincoln cents.

Designs. *Obverse:* A portrait of Abraham Lincoln in three-quarter view. *Reverse:* The final 43 words of President Lincoln's Gettysburg Address, surrounded by a laurel wreath.

Mintage Data. Authorized Public Law 109-285, the Abraham Lincoln Commemorative Coin Act, signed by President George W. Bush on September 27, 2006. *Maximum authorized*—500,000. *Number minted*—125,000 Uncirculated and 325,000 Proof.

Original Cost. Sale prices $31.95 (Uncirculated, pre-issue) and $37.95 (Proof, pre-issue); Uncirculated later raised to $33.95, and Proof later raised to $41.95. The surcharge of $10 per coin went to the Abraham Lincoln Bicentennial Commission.

Key to Collecting. Superb gem coins are readily available.

	Distribution	Cert	Avg	%MS	MS-67 PF-67
2009P	125,000	10,071	69.8	100%	$35
	Auctions: $96, MS-70, February 2014; $56, MS-70, July 2014				
2009P, Proof	325,000	18,045	69.4		$34
	Auctions: $90, PF-70DCam, August 2014; $353, PF-70DCam, November 2014				

LOUIS BRAILLE BICENTENNIAL SILVER DOLLAR (2009)

Designer: *Joel Iskowitz (obverse), Phebe Hemphill (reverse).* **Weight:** *26.73 grams.*
Composition: *.900 silver, .100 copper (net weight .7736 oz. pure silver).*
Diameter: *38.1 mm.* **Edge:** *Reeded.* **Mint:** *Philadelphia.*

The 200th anniversary of the birth of Louis Braille—the inventor of the eponymous system which is used by the blind to read and write—furnished the occasion for this commemorative. Fittingly, this was the first U.S. coin to feature readable Braille.

Designs. *Obverse:* A forward-facing portrait of Louis Braille. *Reverse:* The word Braille (in Braille code, abbreviated Brl) above a child reading a book in Braille.

Mintage Data. Authorized by Public Law 109-247, the Louis Braille Bicentennial–Braille Literacy Commemorative Coin Act, signed by President George W. Bush on July 27, 2006. *Maximum authorized*—400,000. *Number minted*—82,639 Uncirculated and 135,235 Proof.

Original Cost. Sale prices $31.95 (Uncirculated, pre-issue) and $37.95 (Proof, pre-issue); Uncirculated later raised to $33.95, and Proof later raised to $41.95. The surcharge of $10 per coin went to the National Federation of the Blind.

Key to Collecting. Superb gem coins are readily available.

	Distribution	Cert	Avg	%MS	MS-67 / PF-67
					MS-67
					PF-67
2009P	82,639	3,386	69.5	100%	$35
	Auctions: $90, MS-70, April 2013				
2009P, Proof	135,235	4,366	69.1		$27
	Auctions: $94, PF-70DCam, July 2014; $94, PF-70DCam, April 2013				

AMERICAN VETERANS DISABLED FOR LIFE SILVER DOLLAR (2010)

Designer: *Don Everhart.* **Weight:** *26.73 grams.*
Composition: *.900 silver, .100 copper (net weight .7736 oz. pure silver).*
Diameter: *38.1 mm.* **Edge:** *Reeded.* **Mint:** *West Point.*

This coin honored those members of the U.S. Armed Forces who have made extraordinary personal sacrifices in defense of the country.

Designs. *Obverse:* The legs and boots of three veterans, one of whom is using a pair of crutches. *Reverse:* The words "Take This Moment to Honor Our Disabled Defenders of Freedom," surrounded by a laurel wreath with a forget-me-not (widely known as a symbol for those who fought and became disabled in World War I) at its base.

Mintage Data. Authorized by Public Law 110-277, the American Veterans Disabled for Life Commemorative Coin Act, signed by President George W. Bush on July 17, 2008. *Maximum authorized*—350,000. *Number minted*—78,301 Uncirculated and 202,770 Proof.

Original Cost. Sale prices $33.95 (Uncirculated, pre-issue) and $39.95 (Proof, pre-issue); Uncirculated later raised to $35.95, and Proof later raised to $43.95. The surcharge of $10 per coin went to the Disabled Veterans' LIFE Memorial Foundation for the purpose of constructing the American Veterans' Disabled for Life Memorial in Washington, D.C.

Key to Collecting. Superb gem coins are readily available.

	Distribution	Cert	Avg	%MS	MS-67 / PF-67
2010W	78,301	3,931	69.8	100%	$40
	Auctions: $70, MS-70, May 2013				
2010W, Proof	202,770	4,998	69.7		$31
	Auctions: $42, PF-70DCam, September 2014; $78, PF-70DCam, May 2013				

BOY SCOUTS OF AMERICA CENTENNIAL SILVER DOLLAR (2010)

Designer: *Donna Weaver (obverse), Jim Licaretz from the universal logo of the Boy Scouts of America (reverse).* **Weight:** *26.73 grams.* **Composition:** *.900 silver, .100 copper (net weight .7736 oz. pure silver).* **Diameter:** *38.1 mm.* **Edge:** *Reeded.* **Mint:** *Philadelphia.*

The 100th anniversary of the establishment of the Boy Scouts of America was celebrated with this silver dollar. The design was somewhat controversial due to its inclusion of a female but was specifically requested by the organization itself so as to portray the evolution of the Boy Scouts over time to include all American youth.

Designs. *Obverse:* A Cub Scout, a female member of the Venturer Program, and a Boy Scout saluting. *Reverse:* The universal logo of the Boy Scouts of America, featuring an eagle bearing a shield on a fleur-de-lis.

Mintage Data. Authorized by Public Law 110-363, the Boy Scouts of America Centennial Commemorative Coin Act, signed by President George W. Bush on October 8, 2008. *Maximum authorized*—350,000. *Number minted*—105,020 Uncirculated and 244,693 Proof.

Original Cost. Sale prices $33.95 (Uncirculated, pre-issue) and $39.95 (Proof, pre-issue); Uncirculated later raised to $35.95, and Proof later raised to $43.95. The surcharge of $10 per coin went to the National Boy Scouts of America Foundation; the funds were then meant to be made available to local councils in the form of grants for the extension of Scouting in hard-to-serve areas.

Key to Collecting. Superb gem coins are readily available.

	Distribution	Cert	Avg	%MS	MS-67 / PF-67
2010P	105,020	7,239	69.8	100%	$30
	Auctions: $82, MS-70, March 2013				
2010P, Proof	244,963	8,084	69.4		$49
	Auctions: $82, PF-70DCam, March 2013				

U.S. ARMY HALF DOLLAR (2011)

Designer: *Donna Weaver (obverse), Thomas Cleveland (reverse).* **Weight:** *11.34 grams.*
Composition: *.9167 copper, .0833 nickel.* **Diameter:** *30.61 mm.*
Edge: *Reeded.* **Mints:** *Denver (Uncirculated), San Francisco (Proof).*

This copper-nickel half dollar was one of three commemoratives released in honor of the U.S. Army in 2011, by which time the entity had already defended the nation for 236 years. The reverse design was praised by the Citizens Coinage Advisory Committee (CCAC) and the Commission of Fine Arts.

Designs. *Obverse:* Three scenes split in a "storyboard" fashion (from left to right): a soldier surveying; two servicemen laying a flood wall; the Redstone Army rocket at takeoff. *Reverse:* A Continental with a musket, with 13 stars (representing the first states) in an arc above.

Mintage Data. Authorized by Public Law 110-450, the United States Army Commemorative Coin Act of 2008, signed by President George W. Bush on December 1, 2008. *Maximum authorized*—750,000. *Number minted*—2011-D: 39,442 Uncirculated; 2011-S: 68,332 Proof.

Original Cost. Sale prices $15.95 (Uncirculated, pre-issue) and $17.95 (Proof, pre-issue); Uncirculated later raised to $19.95, and Proof raised to $21.95. The surcharge of $5 went toward the yet-to-be-constructed National Museum of the United States Army.

Key to Collecting. Superb gem coins are readily available.

	Distribution	Cert	Avg	%MS	MS-67 PF-67
2011D	39,442	2,528	69.0	100%	$70
	Auctions: No auction records available.				
2011S, Proof	68,332	2,423	69.5		$36
	Auctions: No auction records available.				

U.S. ARMY SILVER DOLLAR (2011)

Designer: *Richard Masters (obverse), Susan Gamble (reverse).* **Weight:** *26.73 grams.*
Composition: *.900 silver, .100 copper (net weight .7736 oz. pure silver).* **Diameter:** *38.1 mm.*
Edge: *Reeded.* **Mints:** *San Francisco (Uncirculated), Philadelphia (Proof).*

The act authorizing this silver dollar (as well as the related copper-nickel half dollar and five-dollar gold coin) called for the coins to be "emblematic of the traditions, history, and heritage of the U.S. Army and its role in American society from the Colonial period to today."

Designs. *Obverse:* A male and female soldier back-to-back in front of a globe. *Reverse:* The Great Seal of the United States (which appears on Army uniforms) inside a ring that bears the seven core values of the Army (Loyalty, Duty, Respect, Selfless Service, Honor, Integrity, and Personal Courage).

Mintage Data. Authorized by Public Law 110-450, the United States Army Commemorative Coin Act of 2008, signed by President George W. Bush on December 1, 2008. *Maximum authorized*—500,000. *Number minted*—2011-S: 43,512 Uncirculated; 2011-P: 119,829 Proof.

Original Cost. Sale prices $49.95 (Uncirculated, pre-issue) and $54.95 (Proof, pre-issue); Uncirculated later raised to $54.95, and Proof later raised to $59.95. The surcharge of $10 per coin went toward the yet-to-be-constructed National Museum of the United States Army.

Key to Collecting. Superb gem coins are readily available.

	Distribution	Cert	Avg	%MS	MS-67 PF-67
2011S	43,512	2,304	69.7	100%	$55
	Auctions: No auction records available.				
2011P, Proof	119,829	3,805	69.5		$44
	Auctions: $80, PF-70DCam, April 2013				

U.S. ARMY $5 GOLD COIN (2011)

Designer: *Joel Iskowitz (obverse), Joseph Menna from the U.S. Army emblem (reverse).*
Weight: *8.359 grams.* **Composition:** *.900 gold, .100 copper (net weight .242 oz. pure gold).*
Diameter: *21.6 mm.* **Edge:** *Reeded.* **Mints:** *Philadelphia (Uncirculated), West Point (Proof).*

By depicting soldiers from five distinct eras in U.S. history, the obverse of this five-dollar gold coin symbolizes the "continuity of strength and readiness" of the Army.

Designs. *Obverse:* Five U.S. Army soldiers representing various eras (from left to right): Revolutionary War, Civil War, modern era, World War II, and World War I. *Reverse:* The U.S. Army emblem, which features various items representative of home life and war time and the phrase "This We'll Defend" on a banner.

Mintage Data. Authorized by Public Law 110-450, the United States Army Commemorative Coin Act of 2008, signed by President George W. Bush on December 1, 2008. *Maximum authorized*—100,000. *Number minted*—2011-P: 8,052 Uncirculated; 2011-W: 17,148 Proof.

Original Cost. Sale prices $439.95 (Uncirculated, pre-issue) and $449.95 (Proof, pre-issue); Uncirculated later raised to $444.95, and Proof later raised to $454.95. The surcharge of $35 per coin went toward the yet-to-be-constructed National Museum of the United States Army.

Key to Collecting. Superb gem coins are readily available.

	Distribution	Cert	Avg	%MS	MS-67 PF-67
2011P	8,052	420	69.9	100%	$550
	Auctions: $560, MS-70, September 2013				
2011W, Proof	17,148	538	69.8		$455
	Auctions: $353, PF-69DCam, May 2014				

MEDAL OF HONOR SILVER DOLLAR (2011)

Designer: *Jim Licaretz (obverse), Richard Masters (reverse).* **Weight:** *26.73 grams.*
Composition: *.900 silver, .100 copper (net weight .7736 oz. pure silver).*
Diameter: *38.1 mm.* **Edge:** *Reeded.* **Mints:** *San Francisco (Uncirculated), Philadelphia (Proof).*

The 150th anniversary of the creation of the Medal of Honor—the highest award for valor in action in the U.S. Armed Forces—was the impetus for this commemorative silver dollar, as well as a five-dollar gold coin.

Designs. *Obverse:* From left to right, the Medals of Honor of the Army, Navy, and Air Force. *Reverse:* An infantry soldier carrying a wounded soldier to safety on his back.

Mintage Data. Authorized by Public Law 111-91, the Medal of Honor Commemorative Coin Act of 2009, signed by President Barack Obama on November 6, 2009. *Maximum authorized*—500,000. *Number minted*—2011-S: 44,752 Uncirculated; 2011-P: 112,833 Proof.

Original Cost. Sale prices $49.95 (Uncirculated, pre-issue) and $54.95 (Proof, pre-issue); Uncirculated later raised to $54.95, and Proof later raised to $59.95. The surcharge of $10 per coin went to the Congressional Medal of Honor Foundation to help finance its educational, scholarship, and outreach programs.

Key to Collecting. Superb gem coins are readily available.

	Distribution	Cert	Avg	%MS	MS-67 PF-67
2011S	44,752	2,897	69.6	100%	$55
	Auctions: $100, MS-70, April 2013				
2011P, Proof	112,833	2,139	69.3		$55
	Auctions: $123, PF-70DCam, March 2013				

MEDAL OF HONOR $5 GOLD COIN (2011)

Designer: *Joseph Menna (obverse), Joel Iskowitz (reverse).* **Weight:** *8.359 grams.*
Composition: *.900 gold, .100 copper (net weight .242 oz. pure gold).* **Diameter:** *21.6 mm.*
Edge: *Reeded.* **Mints:** *Philadelphia (Uncirculated), West Point (Proof).*

This coin and the silver dollar issued alongside it were created in recognition of the Medal of Honor, the Navy's greatest personal award, first authorized by Congress in 1861. Though counterparts are now given in the Army and Air Force as well, fewer than 3,500 Medals of Honor have ever been awarded to date.

Designs. *Obverse:* The original Medal of Honor, the Navy's highest individual decoration. *Reverse:* Minerva, holding a shield and the U.S. flag on a staff, in front of munitions and a Civil War–era cannon.

Mintage Data. Authorized by Public Law 111-91, the Medal of Honor Commemorative Coin Act of 2009, signed by President Barack Obama on November 6, 2009. *Maximum authorized—100,000. Number minted—2011-P: 8,233 Uncirculated; 2011-W: 17,999 Proof.*

Original Cost. Sale prices $439.95 (Uncirculated, pre-issue) and $449.95 (Proof, pre issue); Uncirculated later raised to $444.95, and Proof later raised to $454.95. The surcharge of $35 per coin went to the Congressional Medal of Honor Foundation to help finance its educational, scholarship, and outreach programs.

Key to Collecting. Superb gem coins are readily available.

	Distribution	Cert	Avg	%MS	MS-67 PF-67
2011P	8,233	471	69.8	100%	$550
	Auctions: $470, MS-70, August 2014; $470, MS-70, November 2014				
2011W, Proof	17,999	496	69.6		$520
	Auctions: $558, PF-70DCam, July 2014; $646, PF-70DCam, November 2014				

INFANTRY SOLDIER SILVER DOLLAR (2012)

Designer: *Joel Iskowitz (obverse), Ronald D. Sanders (reverse).* **Weight:** *26.73 grams.*
Composition: *.900 silver, .100 copper (net weight .7736 oz. pure silver).*
Diameter: *38.1 mm.* **Edge:** *Reeded.* **Mint:** *West Point.*

This coin recognizes the long history and crucial role of the U.S. Army Infantry. The infantry has accounted for more than half of all the Medals of Honor awarded, despite being just one of many branches of the Army.

Designs. *Obverse:* An infantry soldier advancing and motioning for others to follow. *Reverse:* The infantry insignia of two crossed rifles.

Mintage Data. Authorized by Public Law 110-357, the National Infantry Museum and Soldier Center Commemorative Coin Act, signed by President George W. Bush on October 8, 2008. *Maximum authorized—350,000. Number minted—44,352 Uncirculated and 161,218 Proof.*

Original Cost. Sale prices $44.95 (Uncirculated, pre-issue) and $49.95 (Proof, pre-issue); Uncirculated later raised to $49.95, and Proof later raised to $54.95. The surcharge of $10 per coin went to an endowment to support the maintenance of the National Infantry Museum and Solider Center in Columbus, Georgia.

Key to Collecting. Superb gem coins are readily available.

	Distribution	Cert	Avg	%MS	MS-67 PF-67
2012W	44,348	2,012	69.8	100%	$40
	Auctions: $69, MS-70, April 2013				
2012W, Proof	161,151	3,028	69.2		$51
	Auctions: $74, PF-70DCam, April 2013				

STAR-SPANGLED BANNER SILVER DOLLAR (2012)

Designer: *Joel Iskowitz (obverse), William C. Burgard II (reverse).* **Weight:** *26.73 grams.*
Composition: *.900 silver, .100 copper (net weight .7736 oz. pure silver).*
Diameter: *38.1 mm.* **Edge:** *Reeded.* **Mint:** *Philadelphia.*

The 200th anniversary of the War of 1812—particularly the Battle of Baltimore, which is recounted in the U.S. National Anthem—was commemorated with this silver dollar, as well as a five-dollar gold coin issued alongside it.

Designs. *Obverse:* Miss Liberty waving the 15-star version of the U.S. flag with Fort McHenry in the background. *Reverse:* A waving modern U.S. flag.

Mintage Data. Authorized by Public Law 111-232, the Star-Spangled Banner Commemorative Coin Act, signed by President Barack Obama on August 16, 2010. *Maximum authorized*—500,000. *Number minted*—41,686 Uncirculated and 169,065 Proof.

Original Cost. Sale prices $44.95 (Uncirculated, pre-issue) and $49.95 (Proof, pre-issue); Uncirculated later raised to $49.95, and Proof later raised to $54.95. The surcharge of $10 per coin went to the Maryland War of 1812 Bicentennial Commission for the purpose of supporting bicentennial activities, educational outreach activities, and preservation and improvement activities pertaining to the sites and structures relating to the War of 1812.

Key to Collecting. Superb gem coins are readily available.

	Distribution	Cert	Avg	%MS	MS-67 / PF-67
2012P	41,686	2,005	69.8	100%	$50
	Auctions: $94, MS-70, October 2014; $100, MS-70, April 2013				
2012P, Proof	169,065	3,121	69.5		$48
	Auctions: $94, PF-70DCam, April 2013; $153, PF-69DCam, November 2014				

STAR-SPANGLED BANNER $5 GOLD COIN (2012)

Designer: *Donna Weaver (obverse), Richard Masters (reverse).* **Weight:** *8.359 grams.*
Composition: *.900 gold, .100 copper (net weight .242 oz. pure gold).*
Diameter: *21.6 mm.* **Edge:** *Reeded.* **Mint:** *West Point.*

The reverse of this commemorative coin features the first five words of the Star-Spangled Banner in the handwriting of Francis Scott Key, the man who penned it. On September 7, 1814, Key visited the British fleet in the Chesapeake Bay to secure the release of his friend Dr. William Beanes. Key secured Beanes's release, but the two were held by the British during the bombardment of Fort McHenry. It was on the morning of September 14, 1814, that the shelling stopped and Key saw through the smoke the massive American flag, flying above the U.S. fort, that would inspire his song.

Designs. *Obverse:* A naval battle, with a U.S. ship in the foreground and a British vessel in the background. *Reverse:* The words "O say can you see" over an arrangement of 13 stripes and 15 stars, representing the U.S. flag.

Mintage Data. Authorized by Public Law 111-232, the Star-Spangled Banner Commemorative Coin Act, signed by President Barack Obama on August 16, 2010. *Maximum authorized—*100,000. *Number minted—*7,027 Uncirculated and 18,313 Proof.

Original Cost. Sale prices $519.30 (Uncirculated, pre-issue) and $529.30 (Proof, pre-issue); both prices later increased by a base of $5 plus the change in gold market value. The surcharge of $35 per coin went to the Maryland War of 1812 Bicentennial Commission for the purpose of supporting bicentennial activities, educational outreach activities, and preservation and improvement activities pertaining to the sites and structures relating to the War of 1812.

Key to Collecting. Superb gem coins are readily available.

	Distribution	Cert	Avg	%MS	MS-67 PF-67
2012W	7,027	620	69.9	100%	$525
Auctions: $618, MS-70, September 2013					
2012W, Proof	18,313	452	69.8		$475
Auctions: $470, PF-70DCam, April 2014					

GIRL SCOUTS OF THE U.S.A. CENTENNIAL SILVER DOLLAR (2013)

Designer: *Barbara Fox (obverse), Chris Costello (reverse).* **Weight:** *26.73 grams.*
Composition: *.900 silver, .100 copper (net weight .7736 oz. pure silver).*
Diameter: *38.1 mm.* **Edge:** *Reeded.* **Mint:** *West Point.*

This commemorative silver dollar was issued as part of the celebration of the Girl Scouts of the United States of America's 100th anniversary of establishment. The Citizens Coinage Advisory Committee was particularly enthusiastic about this beautiful design.

Designs. *Obverse:* Three Girl Scouts of varying ages and ethnicities. The three girls are meant to reflect the organization's diversity. *Reverse:* The iconic Girl Scouts trefoil symbol.

Mintage Data. Authorized by Public Law 111-86, the 2013 Girl Scouts of the USA Centennial Commemorative Coin Program, signed by President Barack Obama on October 29, 2009. *Maximum authorized—*350,000. *Number minted—*37,463 Uncirculated and 86,354 Proof (figures subject to change as a result of audit).

Original Cost. Sale prices $50.95 (Uncirculated, pre-issue) and $54.95 (Proof, pre-issue); Uncirculated later raised to $55.95, and Proof later raised to $59.95. The surcharge of $10 per coin went to the Girl Scouts of the United States of America.

Key to Collecting. Superb gem coins are readily available.

	Distribution	Cert	Avg	%MS	MS-67		
					PF-67		
2013W	37,463	979	69.9	100%	$50		
	Auctions: No auction records available.						
2013W, Proof	*86,354*	1,733	69.3		$52		
	Auctions: No auction records available.						

5-Star Generals Half Dollar (2013)

Designer: *Phebe Hemphill.* **Weight:** *11.34 grams.* **Composition:** *.9167 copper, .0833 nickel.* **Diameter:** *30.61 mm.* **Edge:** *Reeded.* **Mints:** *Denver (Uncirculated), Philadelphia (Proof).*

The 5-star generals of the U.S. Army—as well as the institution that they each graduated from, the U.S. Army Command and General Staff College—were commemorated with this half dollar, as well as a silver dollar and five-dollar gold coin issued as part of the program.

Designs. *Obverse:* Side-by-side portraits of General Henry "Hap" Arnold and General Omar N. Bradley, 5-star insignia at center.

Reverse: Heraldic crest of Fort Leavenworth, home of the U.S. Army Command and General Staff College.

Mintage Data. Authorized by Public Law 111-262, the 5-Star Generals Commemorative Coin Act, signed by President Barack Obama on October 8, 2010. *Maximum authorized*—750,000. *Number minted*—2013-D: 38,097 Uncirculated; 2013-P: 47,339 Proof (figures subject to change as a result of audit).

Original Cost. Sale prices $16.95 (Uncirculated, pre-issue) and $17.95 (Proof, pre-issue); Uncirculated later raised to $20.95, and Proof later raised to $21.95. The surcharge of $5 per coin went to the Command and General Staff College Foundation.

Key to Collecting. Superb gem coins are readily available.

	Distribution	Cert	Avg	%MS	MS-67		
					PF-67		
2013D	38,097	1,036	69.0	100%	$25		
	Auctions: No auction records available.						
2013P, Proof	*47,339*	2,267	69.4		$30		
	Auctions: No auction records available.						

5-Star Generals Silver Dollar (2013)

Designer: *Richard Masters (obverse), Barbara Fox (reverse).* **Weight:** *26.73 grams.* **Composition:** *.900 silver, .100 copper (net weight .7736 oz. pure silver).* **Diameter:** *38.1 mm.* **Edge:** *Reeded.* **Mints:** *West Point (Uncirculated), Philadelphia (Proof).*

Each of the 5-star generals was given one appearance across this series of three commemoratives. Note that Dwight Eisenhower, who is featured on this silver dollar along with George C. Marshall, had previously appeared on another commemorative silver dollar that marked the centennial of his birth in 1990.

Designs. *Obverse:* Side-by-side portraits of General George C. Marshall and General Dwight D. Eisenhower against a striped background, 5-star insignia at top center. *Reverse:* The Leavenworth Lamp, a symbol of the Command and General Staff College.

Mintage Data. Authorized by Public Law 111-262, the 5-Star Generals Commemorative Coin Act, signed by President Barack Obama on October 8, 2010. *Maximum authorized*—500,000. *Number minted*—2013-W: 34,637 Uncirculated; 2013-P: 69,300 Proof (figures subject to change as a result of audit).

Original Cost. Sale prices $50.95 (Uncirculated, pre-issue) and $54.95 (Proof, pre-issue); Uncirculated later raised to $55.95, and Proof later raised to $59.95. The surcharge of $10 per coin went to the Command and General Staff College Foundation.

Key to Collecting. Superb gem coins are readily available.

	Distribution	Cert	Avg	%MS	MS-67 PF-67
2013W	34,639	1,623	69.9	100%	$60
	Auctions: No auction records available.				
2013P, Proof	69,300	2,620	69.7		$72
	Auctions: No auction records available.				

5-STAR GENERALS $5 GOLD COIN (2013)

Designer: *Ronald D. Sanders (obverse), Barbara Fox (reverse).* **Weight:** *8.359 grams.*
Composition: *.900 gold, .100 copper (net weight .242 oz. pure gold).*
Diameter: *21.6 mm.* **Edge:** *Reeded.* **Mints:** *Philadelphia (Uncirculated), West Point (Proof).*

The Leavenworth Lamp, seen on the reverse of this coin as well as that of the silver dollar in this series, is a symbol of the Command and General Staff College. The institution celebrated its 132nd anniversary in the year these coins were released.

Designs. *Obverse:* A portrait of General Douglas MacArthur and the 5-star insignia to the right. *Reverse:* The Leavenworth Lamp, a symbol of the Command and General Staff College.

Mintage Data. Authorized by Public Law 111-262, the 5-Star Generals Commemorative Coin Act, signed by President Barack Obama on October 8, 2010. *Maximum authorized*—100,000. *Number minted*—2013-P: 5,667 Uncirculated; 2013-W: 15,840 Proof (figures subject to change as a result of audit).

Original Cost. Sale prices $480.50 (Uncirculated, pre-issue) and $485.50 (Proof, pre-issue); both prices later increased by a base of $5 plus the change in gold market value. The surcharge of $35 per coin went to the Command and General Staff College Foundation.

Key to Collecting. Superb gem coins are readily available.

	Distribution	Cert	Avg	%MS	MS-67 PF-67
2013P	5,667	461	69.9	100%	$550
	Auctions: No auction records available.				
2013W, Proof	15,843	507	69.8		$495
	Auctions: $499, PF-70DCam, September 2014				

NATIONAL BASEBALL HALL OF FAME HALF DOLLAR (2014)

Designer: *Cassie McFarland (obverse), Don Everhart (reverse).* **Weight:** *11.34 grams.*
Composition: *.9167 copper, .0833 nickel.* **Diameter:** *30.61 mm.* **Edge:** *Reeded.*
Mints: *Denver (Uncirculated), San Francisco (Proof).*

This half dollar and the silver dollar and five-dollar gold coin issued alongside it were the first "curved" coins to be produced by the U.S. Mint—that is, the obverse is concave, and the reverse is convex. The three commemorated the 75th anniversary of the National Baseball Hall of Fame in Cooperstown, New York.

Designs. *Obverse:* A baseball glove, concave. *Reverse:* A baseball, convex.

Mintage Data. Authorized by Public Law 112-152, the National Baseball Hall of Fame Commemorative Coin Act, signed by President Barack Obama on August 3, 2012. *Maximum authorized*—750,000. *Number minted*—2014-D: 146,816 Uncirculated; 2014-S: 257,173 Proof (as of press time).

Original Cost. Sale prices $18.95 (Uncirculated, pre-issue) and $19.95 (Proof, pre-issue); Uncirculated later raised to $22.95, and Proof later raised to $23.95. The surcharge of $5 per coin went to the National Baseball Hall of Fame.

Key to Collecting. Superb gem coins are readily available.

	Distribution	Cert	Avg	%MS	MS-67 PF-67
2014D	146,816	8,339	69.6	100%	$25
	Auctions: No auction records available.				
2014S, Proof	257,173	33,330	69.6		$29
	Auctions: No auction records available.				

NATIONAL BASEBALL HALL OF FAME SILVER DOLLAR (2014)

Designer: *Cassie McFarland (obverse), Don Everhart (reverse).* **Weight:** *26.73 grams.*
Composition: *.900 silver, .100 copper (net weight .7736 oz. pure silver).*
Diameter: *38.1 mm.* **Edge:** *Reeded.* **Mint:** *Philadelphia.*

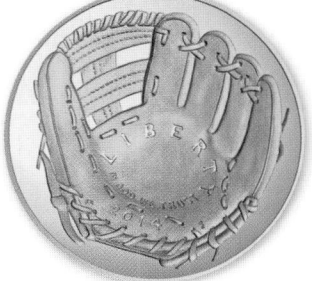 

Coins shaped like this silver dollar (as well as the corresponding half dollar and five-dollar gold coin) had previously been minted by Monnaie de Paris in commemoration of the 2009 International Year of Astronomy. The National Baseball Hall of Fame coins were the first curved issues for the U.S. Mint.

Designs. *Obverse:* A baseball glove, concave. *Reverse:* A baseball, convex.

Mintage Data. Authorized by Public Law 112-152, the National Baseball Hall of Fame Commemorative Coin Act, signed by President Barack Obama on August 3, 2012. *Maximum authorized*—400,000. *Number minted*—131,924 Uncirculated and 268,076 Proof (as of press time).

Original Cost. Sale prices $47.95 (Uncirculated, pre-issue) and $51.95 (Proof, pre-issue); Uncirculated later raised to $52.95, and Proof later raised to $56.95. The surcharge of $10 per coin went to the National Baseball Hall of Fame.

Key to Collecting. Superb gem coins are readily available.

	Distribution	Cert	Avg	%MS	MS-67 / PF-67
2014P	131,924	16,249	69.7	100%	$60
Auctions: No auction records available.					
2014P, Proof	268,076	3,739	69.9		$78
Auctions: No auction records available.					

NATIONAL BASEBALL HALL OF FAME $5 GOLD COIN (2014)

Designer: *Cassie McFarland (obverse), Don Everhart (reverse).* **Weight:** *8.359 grams.*
Composition: *.900 gold, .100 copper (net weight .242 oz. pure gold).*
Diameter: *21.6 mm.* **Edge:** *Reeded.* **Mint:** *West Point.*

The common obverse design for these coins was selected through a national competition, and the Department of the Treasury chose California artist Cassie McFarland's submission after input from the National Baseball Hall of Fame, the U.S. Commission of Fine Arts, and the Citizens Coinage Advisory Committee.

Designs. *Obverse:* A baseball glove, concave.
Reverse: A baseball, convex.

Mintage Data. Authorized by Public Law 112-152, the National Baseball Hall of Fame Commemorative Coin Act, signed by President Barack Obama on August 3, 2012. *Maximum authorized*—50,000. *Number minted*—17,677 Uncirculated and 32,427 Proof (as of press time).

Original Cost. Sale prices $431.90 (Uncirculated, pre-issue) and $436.90 (Proof, pre-issue); Uncirculated later raised to $436.90, and Proof later raised to $441.90. The surcharge of $35 per coin went to the National Baseball Hall of Fame.

Key to Collecting. Superb gem coins are readily available.

	Distribution	Cert	Avg	%MS	MS-67 / PF-67
2014W	17,677	2,282	69.9	100%	$625
Auctions: No auction records available.					
2014W, Proof	32,427	4,130	69.9		$800
Auctions: No auction records available.					

CIVIL RIGHTS ACT OF 1964 SILVER DOLLAR (2014)

Designer: *Justin Kunz (obverse), Donna Weaver (reverse).* **Weight:** *26.73 grams.*
Composition: *.900 silver, .100 copper (net weight .7736 oz. pure silver).*
Diameter: *38.1 mm.* **Edge:** *Reeded.* **Mint:** *Philadelphia.*

This silver dollar commemorated the 50th anniversary of the Civil Rights Act of 1964, which greatly expanded American civil rights protections; outlawed racial segregation in public places and places of public accommodation; and funded federal programs.

Designs. *Obverse:* Three people holding hands at a Civil Rights march; man on left holding sign that reads WE SHALL OVERCOME. *Reverse:* Three intertwined flames representing freedom of education, freedom to vote, and freedom to control one's own destiny. Inspired by a quote by Dr. Martin Luther King Jr.

Mintage Data. Authorized by Public Law 110-451, the Civil Rights Act of 1964 Commemorative Coin Act, signed by President George W. Bush on December 2, 2008. *Maximum authorized—350,000. Number minted—24,720* Uncirculated and 61,992 Proof (as of press time).

Original Cost. Sale prices $44.95 (Uncirculated, pre-issue) and $49.95 (Proof, pre-issue); Uncirculated later raised to $49.95, and Proof later raised to $54.95. The surcharge of $10 per coin went to the United Negro College Fund, which has provided scholarships and internships for minority students for the past 70 years.

Key to Collecting. Superb gem coins are readily available.

	Distribution	Cert	Avg	%MS	MS-67
					PF-67
2014P	24,720	804	69.6	100%	$56
	Auctions: No auction records available.				
2014P, Proof	61,992	944	69.5		$65
	Auctions: No auction records available.				

U.S. MARSHALS SERVICE 225TH ANNIVERSARY HALF DOLLAR (2015)

Designer: *Joel Iskowitz (obverse), Susan Gamble (reverse).* **Weight:** *11.34 grams.*
Composition: *.9167 copper, .0833 nickel.* **Diameter:** *30.61 mm.*
Edge: *Reeded.* **Mints:** *Denver (Uncirculated), San Francisco (Proof).*

The 225th anniversary of the establishment of the U.S. Marshals Service was commemorated with the release of a series including this half dollar as well as a silver dollar and five-dollar gold coin. The actual anniversary—September 24, 2014—was marked with a celebration in Washington, D.C., and the issuance of 35 special preview sets to employees of the Service.

Designs. *Obverse:* An Old West marshal and his horse at left, and a modern marshal in tactical gear at right. *Reverse:* Lady Justice holding scales and the U.S. Marshals Service star and standing over a copy of the Constitution, a stack of books, handcuffs, and a whiskey jug, each representing areas of responsibility of the Service in the past or present.

Mintage Data. Authorized by Public Law 112-104, the United States Marshals Service 225th Anniversary Commemorative Coin Act, signed into law by President Barack Obama on April 2, 2012. *Maximum authorized*—750,000. *Number minted*—To be determined.

Original Cost. Sale prices $13.95 (Uncirculated, pre-issue) and $14.95 (Proof, pre-issue); Uncirculated later raised to $17.95, and Proof later raised to $18.95. The surcharge of $3 per coin is assigned to the U.S. Marshals Museum.

Key to Collecting. Superb gem coins are readily available.

	Distribution	Cert	Avg	%MS	MS-67
					PF-67
2015D		0	n/a		
	Auctions: No auction records available.				
2015S, Proof		0	n/a		
	Auctions: No auction records available.				

U.S. MARSHALS SERVICE 225TH ANNIVERSARY SILVER DOLLAR (2015)

Designer: *Richard Masters (obverse), Frank Morris (reverse).* **Weight:** *26.73 grams.*
Composition: *.900 silver, .100 copper (net weight .7736 oz. pure silver).*
Diameter: *38.1 mm.* **Edge:** *Reeded.* **Mint:** *Philadelphia.*

The first federal law-enforcement officers of the United States, the U.S. Marshals were created under section 27 of the Act of Congress entitled "Chapter XX—An Act to Establish the Judicial Courts of the United States." The original 13 men to serve were confirmed on September 26, 1789.

Designs. *Obverse:* U.S. marshals riding on horseback under the U.S. Marshals Service star. *Reverse:* A U.S. marshal of the frontier era holding a "wanted" poster.

Mintage Data. Authorized by Public Law 112-104, the United States Marshals Service 225th Anniversary Commemorative Coin Act, signed into law by President Barack Obama on April 2, 2012. *Maximum authorized*—500,000. *Number minted*—To be determined.

Original Cost. Sale prices $43.95 (Uncirculated, pre-issue) and $46.95 (Proof, pre-issue): Uncirculated later raised to $48.95, and Proof later raised to $51.95. The surcharge of $10 is assigned to the U.S. Marshals Museum.

Key to Collecting. Superb gem coins are readily available.

	Distribution	Cert	Avg	%MS	MS-67
					PF-67
2015P		0	n/a		
	Auctions: No auction records available.				
2015P, Proof		0	n/a		
	Auctions: No auction records available.				

U.S. Marshals Service 225th Anniversary $5 Gold Coin (2015)

Designer: *Donna Weaver (obverse), Paul C. Balan (reverse).* **Weight:** *8.359 grams.*
Composition: *.900 gold, .100 copper (net weight .242 oz. pure gold).*
Diameter: *21.6 mm.* **Edge:** *Reeded.* **Mint:** *West Point.*

The U.S. Marshals officially became the U.S. Marshals Service in 1969 by order of the Department of Justice. The Service achieved Bureau status in 1974 and today is the primary agency for fugitive operations, as well as protection of officers of the court and court buildings.

Designs. *Obverse:* The U.S. Marshals Service star superimposed on a mountain range. *Reverse:* An eagle, shield on chest, holding a banner and draped flag.

Mintage Data. Authorized by Public Law 112-104, the United States Marshals Service 225th Anniversary Commemorative Coin Act, signed into law by President Barack Obama on April 2, 2012. *Maximum authorized*—100,000. *Number minted*—To be determined.

Original Cost. Sale prices to be determined by the price of gold at time of issuance. The surcharge of $35 per coin is assigned to the U.S. Marshals Museum.

Key to Collecting. Superb gem coins are readily available.

	Distribution	Cert	Avg	%MS	MS-67
					PF-67
2015W		0	n/a		
Auctions: No auction records available.					
2015W, Proof		0	n/a		
Auctions: No auction records available.					

March of Dimes 75th Anniversary Silver Dollar (2015)

Designer: *Paul C. Balan (obverse), Don Everhart (reverse).* **Weight:** *26.73 grams.*
Composition: *.900 silver, .100 copper (net weight .7736 oz. pure silver).*
Diameter: *38.1 mm.* **Edge:** *Reeded.* **Mint:** *To be determined.*

Inspired by his own struggle with polio, President Franklin Delano Roosevelt created the National Foundation for Infantile Paralysis, now known as the March of Dimes, on January 3, 1938. This coin celebrated the organization's 75th anniversary (despite coming out after the actual date of said event) and recognized its accomplishments, which included the funding of research which resulted in Dr. Jonas Salk and Dr. Albert Sabin's polio vaccines.

Designs. *Obverse:* A profile view of President Franklin Delano Roosevelt and Dr. Jonas Salk. *Reverse:* A sleeping baby cradled in its parent's hand.

Mintage Data. Authorized by Public Law 112-209, the March of Dimes Commemorative Coin Act of 2012, signed into law by President Barack Obama on December 18, 2012. *Maximum authorized*—500,000. *Number minted*—To be determined.

Original Cost. Sale prices to be determined. The surcharge of $10 per coin is assigned to the March of Dimes to help finance research, education, and services aimed at improving the health of women, infants, and children.

Key to Collecting. Superb gem coins are readily available.

	Distribution	Cert	Avg	%MS	MS-67 PF-67
2015		0	n/a		
	Auctions: No auction records available.				
2015, Proof		0	n/a		
	Auctions: No auction records available.				

GOVERNMENT COMMEMORATIVE SETS

	Value
(1983–1984) LOS ANGELES OLYMPIAD	
1983 and 1984 Proof dollars	$68
1983 and 1984 6-coin set. One each of 1983 and 1984 dollars, both Proof and Uncirculated gold $10 (a)	$2,050
1983 3-piece collector set. 1983 P, D, and S Uncirculated dollars	$85
1984 3-piece collector set. 1984 P, D, and S Uncirculated dollars	$85
1983 and 1984 gold and silver Uncirculated set. One each of 1983 and 1984 Uncirculated dollar and one 1984 Uncirculated gold $10	$850
1983 and 1984 gold and silver Proof set. One each of 1983 and 1984 Proof dollars and one 1984 Proof gold $10	$975
(1986) STATUE OF LIBERTY	
2-coin set. Proof silver dollar and clad half dollar	$27
3-coin set. Proof silver dollar, clad half dollar, and gold $5	$425
2-coin set. Uncirculated silver dollar and clad half dollar	$35
2-coin set. Uncirculated and Proof gold $5	$750
3-coin set. Uncirculated silver dollar, clad half dollar, and gold $5	$415
6-coin set. One each of Proof and Uncirculated half dollar, silver dollar, and gold $5 (a)	$945
(1987) CONSTITUTION	
2-coin set. Uncirculated silver dollar and gold $5	$450
2-coin set. Proof silver dollar and gold $5	$410
4-coin set. One each of Proof and Uncirculated silver dollar and gold $5 (a)	$830
(1988) SEOUL OLYMPIAD	
2-coin set. Uncirculated silver dollar and gold $5	$420
2-coin set. Proof silver dollar and gold $5	$410
4-coin set. One each of Proof and Uncirculated silver dollar and gold $5 (a)	$830
(1989) CONGRESS	
2-coin set. Proof clad half dollar and silver dollar	$33
3-coin set. Proof clad half dollar, silver dollar, and gold $5	$425
2-coin set. Uncirculated clad half dollar and silver dollar	$40
3-coin set. Uncirculated clad half dollar, silver dollar, and gold $5	$440
6-coin set. One each of Proof and Uncirculated clad half dollar, silver dollar, and gold $5 (a)	$940

a. Packaged in cherrywood box.

	Value
(1991) MOUNT RUSHMORE	
2-coin set. Uncirculated clad half dollar and silver dollar	$58
2-coin set. Proof clad half dollar and silver dollar	$42
3-coin set. Uncirculated clad half dollar, silver dollar, and gold $5	$450
3-coin set. Proof half dollar, silver dollar, and gold $5	$425
6-coin set. One each of Proof and Uncirculated clad half dollar, silver dollar, and gold $5 (a)	$910
(1992) XXV OLYMPIAD	
2-coin set. Uncirculated clad half dollar and silver dollar	$50
2-coin set. Proof clad half dollar and silver dollar	$46
3-coin set. Uncirculated clad half dollar, silver dollar, and gold $5	$450
3-coin set. Proof half dollar, silver dollar, and gold $5	$425
6-coin set. One each of Proof and Uncirculated clad half dollar, silver dollar, and gold $5 (a)	$945
(1992) CHRISTOPHER COLUMBUS	
2-coin set. Uncirculated clad half dollar and silver dollar	$51
2-coin set. Proof clad half dollar and silver dollar	$33
3-coin set. Uncirculated clad half dollar, silver dollar, and gold $5	$450
3-coin set. Proof half dollar, silver dollar, and gold $5	$425
6-coin set. One each of Proof and Uncirculated clad half dollar, silver dollar, and gold $5 (a)	$945
(1993) BILL OF RIGHTS	
2-coin set. Uncirculated silver half dollar and silver dollar	$60
2-coin set. Proof silver half dollar and silver dollar	$47
3-coin set. Uncirculated silver half dollar, silver dollar, and gold $5	$445
3-coin set. Proof half dollar, silver dollar, and gold $5	$425
6-coin set. One each of Proof and Uncirculated silver half dollar, silver dollar, and gold $5 (a)	$945
"Young Collector" set. Silver half dollar	$28
Educational set. Silver half dollar and James Madison medal	$35
Proof silver half dollar and 25-cent stamp	$21
(1993) WORLD WAR II	
2-coin set. Uncirculated clad half dollar and silver dollar	$63
2-coin set. Proof clad half dollar and silver dollar	$46
3-coin set. Uncirculated clad half dollar, silver dollar, and gold $5	$450
3-coin set. Proof clad half dollar, silver dollar, and gold $5	$425
6-coin set. One each of Proof and Uncirculated clad half dollar, silver dollar, and gold $5 (a)	$945
"Young Collector" set. Clad half dollar	$40
Victory Medal set. Uncirculated clad half dollar and reproduction medal	$44
(1993) THOMAS JEFFERSON	
3-piece set (issued in 1994). Silver dollar, Jefferson nickel, and $2 note	$110

a. Packaged in cherrywood box.

	Value
(1994) WORLD CUP SOCCER	
2-coin set. Uncirculated clad half dollar and silver dollar	$50
2-coin set. Proof clad half dollar and silver dollar	$46
3-coin set. Uncirculated clad half dollar, silver dollar, and gold $5	$450
3-coin set. Proof clad half dollar, silver dollar, and gold $5	$425
6-coin set. One each of Proof and Uncirculated clad half dollar, silver dollar, and gold $5 (a)	$945
"Young Collector" set. Uncirculated clad half dollar	$20
"Special Edition" set. Proof clad half dollar and silver dollar	$50
(1994) U.S. VETERANS	
3-coin set. Uncirculated POW, Vietnam, and Women in Military Service silver dollars	$210
3-coin set. Proof POW, Vietnam, and Women in Military Service silver dollars	$105
(1995) SPECIAL OLYMPICS	
2-coin set. Proof Special Olympics silver dollar, 1995S Kennedy half dollar	$150
(1995) CIVIL WAR BATTLEFIELD PRESERVATION	
2-coin set. Uncirculated clad half dollar and silver dollar	$110
2-coin set. Proof clad half dollar and silver dollar	$78
3-coin set. Uncirculated clad half dollar, silver dollar, and gold $5	$790
3-coin set. Proof clad half dollar, silver dollar, and gold $5	$425
6-coin set. One each of Proof and Uncirculated clad half dollar, silver dollar, and gold $5 (a)	$1,065
"Young Collector" set. Uncirculated clad half dollar	$60
2-coin "Union" set. Clad half dollar and silver dollar	$145
3-coin "Union" set. Clad half dollar, silver dollar, and gold $5	$600
(1995-1996) CENTENNIAL OLYMPIC GAMES	
4-coin set #1. Uncirculated half dollar (Basketball), dollars (Gymnastics, Paralympics), gold $5 (Torch Bearer)	$1,000
4-coin set #2. Proof half dollar (Basketball), dollars (Gymnastics, Paralympics), gold $5 (Torch Bearer)	$605
2-coin set #1: Proof silver dollars (Gymnastics, Paralympics)	$91
"Young Collector" set. Uncirculated Basketball half dollar	$38
"Young Collector" set. Uncirculated Baseball half dollar	$38
"Young Collector" set. Uncirculated Swimming half dollar	$195
"Young Collector" set. Uncirculated Soccer half dollar	$175
1995–1996 16-coin Uncirculated set. One each of all Uncirculated coins (a)	$7,950
1995–1996 16-coin Proof set. One each of all Proof coins (a)	$1,820
1995–1996 8-coin Proof silver dollars set	$350
1995–1996 32-coin set. One each of all Uncirculated and Proof coins (a)	$7,500
(1996) NATIONAL COMMUNITY SERVICE	
Proof silver dollar and Saint-Gaudens stamp	$125
(1996) SMITHSONIAN INSTITUTION 150TH ANNIVERSARY	
2-coin set. Proof silver dollar and gold $5	$470
4-coin set. One each of Proof and Uncirculated silver dollar and gold $5 (a)	$900
"Young Collector" set. Proof silver dollar	$100
(1997) U.S. BOTANIC GARDEN	
"Coinage and Currency" set. Uncirculated silver dollar, Jefferson nickel, and $1 note	$260

a. Packaged in cherrywood box.

	Value
(1997) JACKIE ROBINSON	
2-coin set. Proof silver dollar and gold $5	$580
4-coin set. One each of Proof and Uncirculated silver dollar and gold $5 (a)	$3,250
3-piece "Legacy" set. Baseball card, pin, and gold $5 (a)	$675
(1997) FRANKLIN D. ROOSEVELT	
2-coin set. One each of Proof and Uncirculated gold $5	$765
(1997) NATIONAL LAW ENFORCEMENT OFFICERS MEMORIAL	
Insignia set. Silver dollar, lapel pin, and patch	$200
(1998) ROBERT F. KENNEDY	
2-coin set. RFK silver dollar and JFK silver half dollar	$235
2-coin set. Proof and Uncirculated RFK silver dollars	$90
(1998) BLACK REVOLUTIONARY WAR PATRIOTS	
2-coin set. Proof and Uncirculated silver dollars	$150
"Young Collector" set. Uncirculated silver dollar	$150
Black Revolutionary War Patriots set. Silver dollar and four stamps	$150
(1999) DOLLEY MADISON	
2-coin set. Proof and Uncirculated silver dollars	$72
(1999) GEORGE WASHINGTON DEATH	
2-coin set. One each of Proof and Uncirculated gold $5	$780
(1999) YELLOWSTONE NATIONAL PARK	
2-coin set. One each of Proof and Uncirculated silver dollars	$78
(2000) LEIF ERICSON MILENNIUM	
2-coin set. Proof silver dollar and Icelandic 1,000 kronur	$105
(2000) MILENNIUM COIN AND CURRENCY SET	
3-piece set. Uncirculated 2000 Sacagawea dollar; Uncirculated 2000 Silver Eagle; George Washington $1 note, series 1999	$105
(2001) AMERICAN BUFFALO	
2-coin set. One each of Proof and Uncirculated silver dollars	$390
"Coinage and Currency" set. Uncirculated American Buffalo silver dollar, face reprint of 1899 $5 Indian Chief Silver Certificate, 1987 Chief Red Cloud 10¢ stamp, 2001 Bison 21¢ stamp	$235
(2001) U.S. CAPITOL VISITOR CENTER	
3-coin set. Proof clad half dollar, silver dollar, and gold $5	$425
(2002) SALT LAKE OLYMPIC GAMES	
2-coin set. Proof silver dollar and gold $5	$520
4-coin set. One each of Proof and Uncirculated silver dollar and gold $5	$975
(2003) FIRST FLIGHT CENTENNIAL	
3-coin set. Proof clad half dollar, silver dollar, and gold $10	$1,125
(2003) LEGACIES OF FREEDOM	
Uncirculated 2003 $1 American Eagle silver bullion coin and an Uncirculated 2002 £2 Silver Britannia coin	$78
(2004) THOMAS A. EDISON	
Edison set. Uncirculated silver dollar and light bulb	$78
(2004) LEWIS AND CLARK	
Coin and Pouch set. Proof silver dollar and beaded pouch	$200
"Coinage and Currency" set. Uncirculated silver dollar, Sacagawea golden dollar, two 2005 nickels, replica 1901 $10 Bison note, silver-plated Peace Medal replica, three stamps, two booklets	$100

a. Packaged in cherrywood box.

	Value
(2004) WESTWARD JOURNEY NICKEL SERIES	
Westward Journey Nickel Series™ Coin and Medal set. Proof Sacagawea golden dollar, two 2004 Proof nickels, silver-plated Peace Medal replica	$60
(2005) WESTWARD JOURNEY NICKEL SERIES	
Westward Journey Nickel Series™ Coin and Medal set. Proof Sacagawea golden dollar, two 2005 Proof nickels, silver-plated Peace Medal replica	$40
(2005) CHIEF JUSTICE JOHN MARSHALL	
"Coin and Chronicles" set. Uncirculated silver dollar, booklet, BEP intaglio portrait	$68
(2005) AMERICAN LEGACY	
American Legacy Collection. Proof Marine Corps dollar, Proof John Marshall dollar, 11-piece Proof set	$100
(2005) MARINE CORPS 230TH ANNIVERSARY	
Marine Corps Uncirculated silver dollar and stamp set	$95
(2006) BENJAMIN FRANKLIN	
"Coin and Chronicles" set. Uncirculated "Scientist" silver dollar, four stamps, *Poor Richard's Almanack* replica, intaglio print	$75
(2006) AMERICAN LEGACY	
American Legacy Collection. Proof 2006P Benjamin Franklin, Founding Father silver dollar; Proof 2006-S San Francisco Old Mint silver dollar; Proof cent, nickel, dime, quarter, half dollar, and dollar	$90
(2007) AMERICAN LEGACY	
American Legacy Collection. 16 Proof coins for 2007: five state quarters; four Presidential dollars; Jamestown and Little Rock Central High School Desegregation silver dollars; Proof cent, nickel, dime, half dollar, and dollar	$140
(2007) LITTLE ROCK CENTRAL HIGH SCHOOL DESEGREGATION	
Little Rock Coin and Medal set. Proof 2007P silver dollar, bronze medal	$165
(2008) BALD EAGLE	
3-piece set. Proof clad half dollar, silver dollar, and gold $5	$425
Bald Eagle Coin and Medal Set. Uncirculated silver dollar, bronze medal	$73
"Young Collector" set. Uncirculated clad half dollar	$19
(2008) AMERICAN LEGACY	
American Legacy Collection. 15 Proof coins for 2008: cent, nickel, dime, half dollar, and dollar; five state quarters; four Presidential dollars; Bald Eagle dollar	$140
(2009) LOUIS BRAILLE	
Uncirculated silver dollar in tri-folded package	$53
(2009) ABRAHAM LINCOLN COIN AND CHRONICLES	
Four Proof 2009S cents and Abraham Lincoln Proof silver dollar	$150
(2012) STAR-SPANGLED BANNER	
2-coin set. Proof silver dollar and gold $5	$510
(2013) 5-STAR GENERALS	
3-coin set. Proof clad half dollar, silver dollar, and gold $5	$685
Profile Collection. Uncirculated half dollar and silver dollar, replica of 1962 General MacArthur Congressional Gold Medal	$80
(2013) THEODORE ROOSEVELT COIN AND CHRONICLES	
Theodore Roosevelt Proof Presidential dollar; silver Presidential medal; National Wildlife Refuge System Centennial bronze medal; and Roosevelt print	$65
(2013) GIRL SCOUTS OF THE U.S.A.	
"Young Collector" set. Uncirculated silver dollar	$60
(2014) NATIONAL BASEBALL HALL OF FAME	
"Young Collector" set. Uncirculated silver dollar	

Proof and Mint Sets
1936 to Date

AN OVERVIEW OF PROOF AND MINT SETS

PROOF COINS AND SETS

A Proof is a specimen coin struck for presentation, souvenir, exhibition, or numismatic purposes. Before 1968, Proofs were made only at the Philadelphia Mint, except in a few rare instances in which presentation pieces were struck at branch mints. Today Proofs are made at the San Francisco and West Point mints.

The term *Proof* refers not to the condition of a coin, but to its method of manufacture. Regular-production coins (struck for circulation) in Mint State have coruscating, frosty luster; soft details; and minor imperfections. A Proof coin can usually be distinguished by its sharpness of detail, high wire edge, and extremely brilliant, mirrorlike surface. All Proofs are originally sold by the Mint at a premium.

Very few Proof coins were made prior to 1856. Because of their rarity and infrequent sales, they are not all listed in the regular edition of the *Guide Book of United States Coins*. However, here, in the *Deluxe Edition*, you will find them listed individually within their respective denominations.

Frosted Proofs were issued prior to 1936 and starting again in the late 1970s. These have a brilliant, mirrorlike field with contrasting dull or frosted design.

Matte Proofs have a granular, "sandblast" surface instead of the mirror finish. Matte Proof cents, nickels, and gold coins were issued from 1908 to 1916; a few 1921 and 1922 silver dollars and a 1998-S half dollar were also struck in this manner.

Brilliant Proofs have been issued from 1936 to date. These have a uniformly brilliant, mirrorlike surface and sharp, high-relief details.

"Prooflike" coins are occasionally seen. These are examples struck from dies that were lightly polished, often inadvertently during the removal of lines, contact marks, and other marks in the fields. In other instances, such as with certain New Orleans gold coins of the 1850s, the dies were polished in the machine shop of the mint. They are not true Proofs, but may have most of the characteristics of a Proof coin and generally command a premium. Collectors should beware of coins that have been buffed to look like Proofs; magnification will reveal polishing lines and loss of detail.

After a lapse of some 20 years, Proof coins were struck at the Philadelphia Mint from 1936 to 1942, inclusive. During these years the Mint offered Proof coins to collectors for individual sale, rather than in officially packaged sets, as such.

In 1942, when the composition of the five-cent piece was changed from copper-nickel to copper-silver-manganese, there were two Proof types of this denomination available to collectors.

The striking of all Proof coins was temporarily suspended from 1943 through 1949, and again from 1965 through 1967; during the latter period, Special Mint Sets were struck (see page 1268). Proof sets were resumed in 1968.

Sets from 1936 through 1972 included the cent, nickel, dime, quarter, and half dollar; from 1973 through 1981 the dollar was also included, and again from 2000 on. Regular Proof sets issued from 1982 to 1998 contain the cent through the half dollar. Specially packaged Prestige sets containing commemorative coins were sold from 1983 through 1997 at an additional premium. From 1999 to 2009, sets contain five different Statehood or Territorial quarters, and from 2010 to 2021, different National Parks quarters. In 1999 Proof dollars were sold separately. Four-piece Presidential dollar sets have been issued since 2007.

With the recent State and Territorial quarters programs, as well as the ongoing National Park quarters and Presidential dollars programs, the U.S. Mint has offered Proof sets featuring each of the designs issued for a particular year.

From time to time the Mint issues special Proof sets. One recent example is the four-piece 2009-S Lincoln Bicentennial set, which included each of the special cent designs issued that year, but coined in 95% copper (the Lincoln cent's original 1909 alloy).

Collectors are encouraged to consult David W. Lange's *Guide Book of Modern United States Proof Coin Sets* for detailed coverage and illustrations of Proof sets from 1936 to date.

HOW MODERN PROOF COINS ARE MADE

Selected dies are inspected for perfection and are highly polished and cleaned. They are again wiped clean or polished after every 15 to 25 impressions and are replaced frequently to avoid imperfections from wear. Coinage blanks for Proof coins are polished and cleaned to ensure high quality in striking. They are then hand fed into the coinage press one at a time, each blank receiving two or more blows from the dies to bring up sharp, high-relief details. The coinage operation is done at slow speed with extra pressure. Finished Proofs are individually inspected and are handled with gloves or tongs. They also receive a final inspection by packers before being sonically sealed in special plastic cases.

MINT SETS

Official Uncirculated Mint sets are specially packaged by the government for sale to collectors. They contain Uncirculated examples of each year's coins for every denomination issued from each mint. Before 2005, the coins were the same as those normally intended for circulation and were not minted with any special consideration for quality. From 2005 to 2010, however, Mint sets were made with a satin finish rather than the traditional Uncirculated luster. As in the past, coins struck only as Proofs are not included.

Uncirculated Mint sets sold by the Treasury from 1947 through 1958 contained two examples of each regular-issue coin. These were packaged in cardboard holders that did not protect the coins from tarnish. Nicely preserved early sets generally command a 10 to 20% premium above average values. Since 1959, sets have been sealed in protective plastic envelopes.

Privately assembled Mint sets, and Souvenir sets produced for sale at the Philadelphia or Denver mints for special occasions, are valued according to the individual pieces they contain. Only the official, government-packaged full sets are included in the following list. No Mint Sets were produced in 1950, 1982, or 1983, though Souvenir sets were sold in the latter two years (see the final section of this overview).

From time to time the Mint issues special Mint sets. One recent example is the 1996-P-D Mint set, which also included a 1996-W dime (released only in those sets).

SPECIAL MINT SETS

In mid-1964 the Treasury department announced that the Mint would not offer Proof sets or Mint sets the following year. This was prompted by a nationwide shortage of circulating coins, which was wrongly blamed on coin collectors.

In 1966 the San Francisco Assay Office began striking coins dated 1965, for inclusion in so-called United States Special Mint Sets. These were issued in pliofilm packaging similar to that of recent Proof sets. The coins in early 1965 Special Mint Sets are semi-brilliant or satiny (distinctive, but not equal in quality to Proofs); the coins in later 1965 sets feature very brilliant fields (but again not reaching Proof brilliance).

The San Francisco Assay Office started striking 1966-dated coins in August of that year, and its Special Mint Sets were packaged in rigid, sonically sealed plastic holders. The coins were struck once on unpolished planchets, unlike Proof coins (which are struck at least twice on polished planchets). Also unlike Proofs, the SMS coins were allowed to come into contact with each other during their production, which accounts for minor contact marks and abrasions. To achieve a brilliant finish, Mint technicians overpolished the coinage dies. The result was a tradeoff: most of the coins have prooflike brilliance, but many are missing polished-off design details, such as Frank Gasparro's initials on the half dollar.

All 1967-dated coinage was struck in that calendar year. Nearly all SMS coins of 1967 have fully brilliant, prooflike finishes. This brilliance was achieved without overpolishing the dies, resulting in coins that approach the quality of true Proofs. Sales of the 1967 sets were lackluster, however. The popularity of coin collecting had dropped from its peak in 1964. Also, collectors and speculators did not anticipate much secondary-market profit from the sets, which had an issue price of $4.00, compared to $2.10 for a 1964 Proof set. As a result, fewer collectors bought multiples of the 1967 sets, and today they are generally worth more than those of 1965 and 1966.

Similar SMS coins dated 1964 exist as single pieces and in sets. Like the 1965 through 1967 SMS coins, they have a semi-brilliant or satiny finish but are not equal in quality to Proofs. They are referred to as SP (Special Strike) coins and command much higher prices than their regular SMS counterparts.

SOUVENIR SETS

Uncirculated Souvenir sets were packaged and sold in gift shops at the Philadelphia and Denver mints in 1982 and 1983 in place of the "official Mint sets," which were not made in those years. A bronze Mint medal is packaged with each set. Similar sets were also made in other years.

1936 Proof Set
Liberty Walking half dollar, Washington quarter dollar, Mercury or Winged Liberty dime, Buffalo nickel, and Lincoln cent with Wheat Ears reverse.

1938 Proof Set
Buffalo nickel replaced with the new Jefferson nickel.

1950 Proof Set

There was a seven-year hiatus (1943–1949) before Proof sets were issued again after World War II. By 1950 the Liberty Walking half dollar had been replaced by the Franklin half dollar (introduced 1948), and the Mercury dime by the Roosevelt dime (introduced 1946).

1955 Proof Set

Issued in traditional individual envelopes, or in the new pliofilm package (pictured), with a Philadelphia Mint embossed paper seal with a metallic finish.

MODERN PROOF SETS (1936 TO DATE)

	Mintage	Issue Price	Face Value	Current Value
1936	3,837	$1.89	$0.91	$6,750
1937	5,542	$1.89	$0.91	$3,750
1938	8,045	$1.89	$0.91	$1,750
1939	8,795	$1.89	$0.91	$1,700
1940	11,246	$1.89	$0.91	$1,350
1941	15,287	$1.89	$0.91	$1,350
1942, Both nickels	21,120	$1.89	$0.96	$1,300
1942, One nickel	(a)	$1.89	$0.91	$1,200

a. Included in 1942, Both nickels, mintage figure.

	Mintage	Issue Price	Face Value	Current Value
1950	51,386	$2.10	$0.91	$575
1951	57,500	$2.10	$0.91	$600
1952	81,980	$2.10	$0.91	$235
1953	128,800	$2.10	$0.91	$225
1954	233,300	$2.10	$0.91	$115
1955, Box pack	378,200	$2.10	$0.91	$105
1955, Flat pack	(b)	$2.10	$0.91	$125
1956	669,384	$2.10	$0.91	$60
1957	1,247,952	$2.10	$0.91	$25
1958	875,652	$2.10	$0.91	$35
1959	1,149,291	$2.10	$0.91	$35
1960, With Large Date cent	1,691,602	$2.10	$0.91	$35
1960, With Small Date cent	(c)	$2.10	$0.91	$45
1961	3,028,244	$2.10	$0.91	$30
1962	3,218,019	$2.10	$0.91	$30
1963	3,075,645	$2.10	$0.91	$30
1964	3,950,762	$2.10	$0.91	$30
1968S	3,041,506	$5	$0.91	$8
1968S, With No S dime	(d)	$5	$0.91	$16,500
1969S	2,934,631	$5	$0.91	$8
1970S	2,632,810	$5	$0.91	$10
1970S, With Small Date cent	(e)	$5	$0.91	$90
1970S, With No S dime (*estimated mintage: 2,200*)	(e)	$5	$0.91	$900
1971S	3,220,733	$5	$0.91	$5
1971S, With No S nickel (*estimated mintage: 1,655*)	(f)	$5	$0.91	$1,400
1972S	3,260,996	$5	$0.91	$5
1973S	2,760,339	$7	$1.91	$9
1974S	2,612,568	$7	$1.91	$10
1975S, With 1976 quarter, half, and dollar	2,845,450	$7	$1.91	$10
1975S, With No S dime	(g)	$7	$1.91	$275,000
1976S	4,149,730	$7	$1.91	$9
1976S, Silver clad, 3-piece set	3,998,621	$15	$1.75	$31
1977S	3,251,152	$9	$1.91	$8
1978S	3,127,781	$9	$1.91	$8
1979S, Type 1	3,677,175	$9	$1.91	$8
1979S, Type 2	(h)	$9	$1.91	$75
1980S	3,554,806	$10	$1.91	$7
1981S, Type 1	4,063,083	$11	$1.91	$7
1981S, Type 2 (all six coins in set)	(i)	$11	$1.91	$275
1982S	3,857,479	$11	$0.91	$5
1983S	3,138,765	$11	$0.91	$5
1983S, With No S dime	(j)	$11	$0.91	$750
1983S, Prestige set (Olympic dollar)	140,361	$59	$1.91	$50
1984S	2,748,430	$11	$0.91	$6
1984S, Prestige set (Olympic dollar)	316,680	$59	$1.91	$35
1985S	3,362,821	$11	$0.91	$5
1986S	2,411,180	$11	$0.91	$7
1986S, Prestige set (Statue of Liberty half, dollar)	599,317	$48.50	$2.41	35

b. Included in 1955, Box pack, mintage figure. **c.** Included in 1960, With Large Date cent, mintage figure. **d.** Included in 1968-S mintage figure. **e.** Included in 1970-S mintage figure. **f.** Included in 1971-S mintage figure. **g.** Included in 1975-S, With 1976 quarter, half, and dollar, mintage figure. **h.** Included in 1979-S, Type 1, mintage figure. **i.** Included in 1981-S, Type 1, mintage figure. **j.** Included in 1983-S mintage figure.

	Mintage	Issue Price	Face Value	Current Value
1987S	3,792,233	$11	$0.91	$5
1987S, Prestige set (Constitution dollar)	435,495	$45	$1.91	$30
1988S	3,031,287	$11	$0.91	$7
1988S, Prestige set (Olympic dollar)	231,661	$45	$1.91	$35
1989S	3,009,107	$11	$0.91	$7
1989S, Prestige set (Congressional half, dollar)	211,807	$45	$2.41	$35
1990S	2,793,433	$11	$0.91	$7
1990S, With No S cent	3,555	$11	$0.91	$4,750
1990S, With No S cent (Prestige set)	(k)	$45	$1.91	$5,000
1990S, Prestige set (Eisenhower dollar)	506,126	$45	$1.91	$35
1991S	2,610,833	$11	$0.91	$6
1991S, Prestige set (Mt. Rushmore half, dollar)	256,954	$59	$2.41	$45
1992S	2,675,618	$11	$0.91	$6
1992S, Prestige set (Olympic half, dollar)	183,293	$56	$2.41	$50
1992S, Silver	1,009,586	$11	$0.91	$25
1992S, Silver Premier set	308,055	$37	$0.91	$30
1993S	2,409,394	$12.50	$0.91	$6
1993S, Prestige set (Bill of Rights half, dollar)	224,045	$57	$2.41	$60
1993S, Silver	570,213	$21	$0.91	$30
1993S, Silver Premier set	191,140	$37.50	$0.91	$35
1994S	2,308,701	$12.50	$0.91	$6
1994S, Prestige set (World Cup half, dollar)	175,893	$57	$2.41	$45
1994S, Silver	636,009	$21	$0.91	$25
1994S, Silver Premier set	149,320	$37.50	$0.91	$35
1995S	2,010,384	$12.50	$0.91	$13
1995S, Prestige set (Civil War half, dollar)	107,112	$57	$2.41	$85
1995S, Silver	549,878	$21	$0.91	$50
1995S, Silver Premier set	130,107	$37.50	$0.91	$55
1996S	1,695,244	$12.50	$0.91	$7
1996S, Prestige set (Olympic half, dollar)	55,000	$57	$2.41	$300
1996S, Silver	623,655	$21	$0.91	$30
1996S, Silver Premier set	151,366	$37.50	$0.91	$30
1997S	1,975,000	$12.50	$0.91	$10
1997S, Prestige set (Botanic dollar)	80,000	$57	$1.91	$65
1997S, Silver	605,473	$21	$0.91	$35
1997S, Silver Premier set	136,205	$37.50	$0.91	$35
1998S	2,086,507	$12.50	$0.91	$10
1998S, Silver	638,134	$21	$0.91	$30
1998S, Silver Premier set	240,658	$37.50	$0.91	$30
1999S, 9-piece set	2,543,401	$19.95	$1.91	$15
1999S, 5-piece quarter set	1,169,958	$13.95	$1.25	$6
1999S, Silver 9-piece set	804,565	$31.95	$1.91	$115
2000S, 10-piece set	3,082,572	$19.95	$2.91	$8
2000S, 5-piece quarter set	937,600	$13.95	$1.25	$6
2000S, Silver 10-piece set	965,421	$31.95	$2.91	$50
2001S, 10-piece set	2,294,909	$19.95	$2.91	$18
2001S, 5-piece quarter set	799,231	$13.95	$1.25	$8
2001S, Silver 10-piece set	889,697	$31.95	$2.91	$50
2002S, 10-piece set	2,319,766	$19.95	$2.91	$13
2002S, 5-piece quarter set	764,479	$13.95	$1.25	$6
2002S, Silver 10-piece set	892,229	$31.95	$2.91	$35

k. Included in 1990-S mintage figure.

	Mintage	Issue Price	Face Value	Current Value
2003S, 10-piece set	2,172,684	$19.95	$2.91	$10
2003S, 5-piece quarter set	1,235,832	$13.95	$1.25	$4
2003S, Silver 10-piece set	1,125,755	$31.95	$2.91	$38
2004S, 11-piece set	1,789,488	$22.95	$2.96	$12
2004S, 5-piece quarter set	951,196	$15.95	$1.25	$4
2004S, Silver 11-piece set	1,175,934	$37.95	$2.96	$50
2004S, Silver 5-piece quarter set	593,852	$23.95	$1.25	$35
2005S, 11-piece set	2,275,000	$22.95	$2.96	$8
2005S, 5-piece quarter set	987,960	$15.95	$1.25	$4
2005S, Silver 11-piece set	1,069,679	$37.95	$2.96	$45
2005S, Silver 5-piece quarter set	608,970	$23.95	$1.25	$30
2006S, 10-piece set	2,000,428	$22.95	$2.91	$12
2006S, 5-piece quarter set	882,000	$15.95	$1.25	$6
2006S, Silver 10-piece set	1,054,008	$37.95	$2.91	$40
2006S, Silver 5-piece quarter set	531,000	$23.95	$1.25	$35
2007S, 14-piece set	1,702,116	$26.95	$6.91	$18
2007S, 5-piece quarter set	672,662	$13.95	$1.25	$6
2007S, 4-piece Presidential set	1,285,972	$14.95	$4	$10
2007S, Silver 14-piece set	875,050	$44.95	$6.91	$45
2007S, Silver 5-piece quarter set	672,662	$25.95	$1.25	$25
2008S, 14-piece set	1,405,674	$26.95	$6.91	$55
2008S, 5-piece quarter set	672,438	$13.95	$1.25	$50
2008S, 4-piece Presidential set	869,202	$14.95	$4	$15
2008S, Silver 14-piece set	763,887	$44.95	$6.91	$55
2008S, Silver 5-piece quarter set	429,021	$25.95	$1.25	$30
2009S, 18-piece set	1,482,502	$29.95	$7.19	$30
2009S, 6-piece quarter set	630,976	$14.95	$1.50	$8
2009S, 4-piece Presidential set	629,585	$14.95	$4	$12
2009S, Silver 18-piece set	697,365	$52.95	$7.19	$65
2009S, Silver 6-piece quarter set	299,183	$29.95	$1.50	$35
2009S, 4-piece Lincoln Bicentennial set	201,107	$7.95	$0.04	$15
2010S, 14-piece set	1,103,815	$31.95	$6.91	$55
2010S, 5-piece quarter set	276,296	$14.95	$1.25	$25
2010S, 4-piece Presidential set	535,397	$15.95	$4	$20
2010S, Silver 14-piece set	585,401	$56.95	$6.91	$65
2010S, Silver 5-piece quarter set	274,034	$32.95	$1.25	$30
2011S, 14-piece set	1,098,730	$31.95	$6.91	$55
2011S, 5-piece quarter set	152,032	$14.95	$1.25	$20
2011S, 4-piece Presidential set	299,846	$19.95	$4	$30
2011S, Silver 14-piece set	574,103	$67.95	$6.91	$85
2011S, Silver 5-piece quarter set	147,895	$39.95	$1.25	$40
2012S, 14-piece set	792,568	$31.95	$6.91	$115
2012S, 5-piece quarter set	148,420	$14.95	$1.25	$20
2012S, 4-piece Presidential set	249,111	$18.95	$4	$85
2012S, Silver 14-piece set	395,149	$67.95	$6.91	$200
2012S, Silver 8-piece Limited Edition set	44,952	$149.95	$2.85	$200
2012S, Silver 5-piece quarter set	162,397	$41.95	$1.25	$45
2013S, 14-piece set	*802,460*	$31.95	$6.91	$65
2013S, 5-piece quarter set	*128,377*	$14.95	$1.25	$20
2013S, 4-piece Presidential set	*266,677*	$18.95	$4	$60

	Mintage	Issue Price	Face Value	Current Value
2013S, Silver 14-piece set	419,720	$67.95	$6.91	$175
2013S, Silver 8-piece Limited Edition set	47,971	$139.95	$2.85	$185
2013S, Silver 5-piece quarter set	138,451	$41.95	$1.25	$45
2014S, 14-piece set	680,977	$31.95	$6.91	
2014S, 5-piece quarter set	109,423	$14.95	$1.25	
2014S, 4-piece Presidential set	218,976	$18.95	$4	
2014S, Silver 14-piece set	404,665	$67.95	$6.91	
2014S, Silver 5-piece quarter set	111,172	$41.95	$1.25	

UNCIRCULATED MINT SETS (1947 TO DATE)

	Mintage	Issue Price	Face Value	Current Value
1947 P-D-S	5,000	$4.87	$4.46	$2,750
1948 P-D-S	6,000	$4.92	$4.46	$1,650
1949 P-D-S	5,000	$5.45	$4.96	$2,250
1951 P-D-S	8,654	$6.75	$5.46	$1,750
1952 P-D-S	11,499	$6.14	$5.46	$1,600
1953 P-D-S	15,538	$6.14	$5.46	$1,350
1954 P-D-S	25,599	$6.19	$5.46	$700
1955 P-D-S	49,656	$3.57	$2.86	$400
1956 P-D	45,475	$3.34	$2.64	$400
1957 P-D	34,324	$4.40	$3.64	$650
1958 P-D	50,314	$4.43	$3.64	$400
1959 P-D	187,000	$2.40	$1.82	$55
1960 P-D	260,485	$2.40	$1.82	$50
1961 P-D	223,704	$2.40	$1.82	$50
1962 P-D	385,285	$2.40	$1.82	$50
1963 P-D	606,612	$2.40	$1.82	$50
1964 P-D	1,008,108	$2.40	$1.82	$50
1968 P-D-S	2,105,128	$2.50	$1.33	$6
1969 P-D-S	1,817,392	$2.50	$1.33	$6
1970 P-D-S, With Large Date cent	2,038,134	$2.50	$1.33	$18
1970 P-D-S, Small Date cent	(a)	$2.50	$1.33	$65
1971 P-D-S (no Ike dollar)	2,193,396	$3.50	$1.83	$4
1972 P-D-S (no Ike dollar)	2,750,000	$3.50	$1.83	$4
1973 P-D-S	1,767,691	$6	$3.83	$12
1974 P-D-S	1,975,981	$6	$3.83	$7
1975 P-D, With 1976 quarter, half, dollar	1,921,488	$6	$3.82	$8
1976, Silver clad, 3-piece set	4,908,319	$9	$1.75	$20
1976 P-D	1,892,513	$6	$3.82	$8
1977 P-D	2,006,869	$7	$3.82	$8
1978 P-D	2,162,609	$7	$3.82	$8
1979 P-D (b)	2,526,000	$8	$3.82	$6
1980 P-D-S	2,815,066	$9	$4.82	$7
1981 P-D-S	2,908,145	$11	$4.82	$10
1984 P-D	1,832,857	$7	$1.82	$4
1985 P-D	1,710,571	$7	$1.82	$4
1986 P-D	1,153,536	$7	$1.82	$7
1987 P-D	2,890,758	$7	$1.82	$4
1988 P-D	1,646,204	$7	$1.82	$5
1989 P-D	1,987,915	$7	$1.82	$5
1990 P-D	1,809,184	$7	$1.82	$5

a. Included in 1970 P-D-S, With Large Date cent, mintage figure. **b.** S-mint dollar not included.

	Mintage	Issue Price	Face Value	Current Value
1991 P-D	1,352,101	$7	$1.82	$5
1992 P-D	1,500,143	$7	$1.82	$5
1993 P-D	1,297,431	$8	$1.82	$5
1994 P-D	1,234,813	$8	$1.82	$5
1995 P-D	1,038,787	$8	$1.82	$5
1996 P-D, Plus 1996W dime	1,457,949	$8	$1.92	$20
1997 P-D	950,473	$8	$1.82	$7
1998 P-D	1,187,325	$8	$1.82	$5
1999 P-D (18 pieces) (c)	1,243,867	$14.95	$3.82	$8
2000 P-D (20 pieces)	1,490,160	$14.95	$5.82	$10
2001 P-D (20 pieces)	1,116,915	$14.95	$5.82	$10
2002 P-D (20 pieces)	1,139,388	$14.95	$5.82	$10
2003 P-D (20 pieces)	1,001,532	$14.95	$5.82	$11
2004 P-D (22 pieces)	842,507	$16.95	$5.92	$10
2005 P-D (22 pieces)	1,160,000	$16.95	$5.92	$10
2006 P-D (20 pieces)	847,361	$16.95	$5.82	$10
2007 P-D (28 pieces)	895,628	$22.95	$13.82	$18
2008 P-D (28 pieces)	745,464	$22.95	$13.82	$55
2009 P-D (36 pieces)	784,614	$27.95	$14.38	$25
2010 P-D (28 pieces)	583,897	$31.95	$13.82	$25
2011 P-D (28 pieces)	533,529	$31.95	$13.82	$25
2012 P-D (28 pieces)	392,224	$27.95	$13.82	$80
2013 P-D (28 pieces)	376,844	$27.95	$13.82	$35
2014 P-D (28 pieces)	327,969	$27.95	$13.82	

c. Dollar not included.

SPECIAL MINT SETS *(1965–1967)*

	Mintage	Issue Price	Face Value	Current Value
1965	2,360,000	$4	$0.91	$12
1966	2,261,583	$4	$0.91	$11
1967	1,863,344	$4	$0.91	$12

See page 1262 for details on the similar 1964 Special Strike coins. Values for these coins are approximately $13,000 for each denomination.

SOUVENIR SETS *(1982–1983)*

	Issue Price	Face Value	Current Value
1982P	$4	$0.91	$75
1982D	$4	$0.91	$75
1983P	$4	$0.91	$125
1983D	$4	$0.91	$110

POPULAR DIE VARIETIES FROM PROOF AND MINT SETS

As noted in the *Cherrypickers' Guide to Rare Die Varieties,* "Beginning with those modern Mint sets from 1947, and Proof sets from 1950, there are many years of one or the other that are absent of a significant variety. Not all of the known varieties are significant." The following are some popular die varieties from Proof and Mint sets; for more information and additional examples, consult the *Cherrypickers' Guide.*

DIE VARIETIES IN PROOF SETS

Year	Denomination	Variety	Year	Denomination	Variety
1951	5¢	doubled-die obverse	1968-S	10¢	doubled-die obverse
1952	25¢	"Superbird" variety	1968-S	10¢	doubled-die reverse
1953	5¢	doubled-die obverse	1968-S	25¢	doubled-die reverse
1955	5¢	tripled-die reverse	1968-S	50¢	doubled-die obverse
1957	5¢	quadrupled-die obverse	1969-S	25¢	repunched mintmark
1960	1¢	doubled-die obverse **(a)**	1970-S	10¢	No S
1960	10¢	doubled-die reverse	1971-S	5¢	No S
1960	25¢	doubled-die reverse	1975-S	10¢	No S
1961	50¢	doubled-die reverse	1983-S	10¢	No S
1963	10¢	doubled-die reverse	1990-S	1¢	No S

a. Check for both Large Over Small Date, and Small Over Large Date, varieties.

DIE VARIETIES IN MINT SETS

Year	Denomination	Variety	Year	Denomination	Variety
1949	5¢	D/S—over mintmark **(a)**	1970	50¢	D—doubled-die reverse **(d)**
1954	25¢	doubled-die reverse **(b)**	1971	5¢	D/D—repunched mintmark
1960	5¢	(P)—doubled-die obverse **(c)**	1971	10¢	D/D—repunched mintmark
1960	25¢	(P)—doubled-die obverse **(c)**	1971	10¢	D—doubled-die reverse
1961	50¢	D/D—repunched mintmark	1971	50¢	D—doubled-die obverse
1963	10¢	(P)—doubled-die obverse	1971	50¢	D—doubled-die reverse
1963	25¢	(P)—doubled-die obverse	1972	1¢	(P)—doubled-die obverse
1963	25¢	(P)—doubled-die reverse	1972	5¢	D—doubled-die reverse
1963	50¢	(P)—doubled-die obverse	1972	50¢	D—doubled-die reverse
1963	50¢	(P)—doubled-die reverse	1973	50¢	(P)—doubled-die obverse
1968	10¢	(P)—doubled-die obverse	1973	50¢	D—doubled-die obverse
1968	25¢	D—doubled-die reverse	1974	50¢	D—doubled-die obverse
1969	5¢	D/D—repunched mintmark	1981	5¢	D—doubled-die reverse
1969	10¢	D/D—repunched mintmark	1984	50¢	D/D—repunched mintmark
1969	25¢	D/D—repunched mintmark	1987	5¢	D/D—repunched mintmark
1969	50¢	D—doubled-die reverse	1987	10¢	D/D—repunched mintmark
1970	1¢	D/D—repunched mintmark	1989	5¢	D—doubled-die reverse
1970	1¢	D—doubled-die obverse	1989	10¢	P—doubled-die reverse
1970	10¢	D—doubled-die reverse	1989	50¢	D/D—repunched mintmark
1970	25¢	D—doubled-die reverse	1991	5¢	D—doubled-die obverse

a. Although known, most have already been removed from their Mint-packaged sets. **b.** Small Date. **c.** Found in sets labeled as Small Date. **d.** Small Date.

U.S. Mint
Bullion Coins

AN OVERVIEW OF U.S. MINT BULLION COINS

The United States' bullion-coin program was launched in 1986. Since then, American Eagle and other U.S. silver, gold, and platinum coins have provided investors with convenient vehicles to add physical bullion to their investment portfolios, not to mention their value as numismatic collectibles.

In addition to regular investment-grade strikes, the U.S. Mint offers its bullion coins in various collectible formats. Proofs are created in a specialized minting process: a polished coin blank is manually fed into a press fitted with special dies; the blank is struck multiple times "so the softly frosted yet detailed images seem to float above a mirror-like field" (per Mint literature); a white-gloved inspector scrutinizes the coin; and it is then sealed in a protective plastic capsule and mounted in a satin-lined velvet presentation case along with a certificate of authenticity. Members of the public can purchase Proofs directly from the Mint, at fixed prices.

From 2006 to 2012, Burnished (called Uncirculated by the Mint) coins were also sold directly to the public. These coins have the same design as other bullion coins of that year, but are distinguished from regular bullion strikes by a W mintmark (for West Point), and by their distinctive finish (the result of burnished coin blanks). Their blanks were individually fed by hand into specially adapted coining presses. After striking, each Burnished specimen was carefully inspected, encapsulated in plastic, and packaged in a satin-lined velvet presentation case, along with a certificate of authenticity.

In recent years the Mint has also broadened its collectible bullion offerings with Reverse Proof and Enhanced Uncirculated formats. Various bullion coins have been offered in collector sets, as well.

Regular bullion-strike coins are bought in bulk by Mint-authorized purchasers (wholesalers, brokerage companies, precious-metal firms, coin dealers, and participating banks). These authorized purchasers in turn sell them to secondary retailers, who then make them available to the general public. Authorized purchasers are required to meet financial and professional criteria, attested to by an internationally accepted accounting firm. They must be an experienced and established market-maker in bullion coins; provide a liquid two-way market for the coins; be audited annually; have an established and broad retail-customer base for distribution; and have a tangible net worth of $5 million (for American Silver Eagles) or $50 million (for gold and platinum American Eagles). Authorized purchasers of gold must have sold more than 100,000 ounces of gold bullion coins over any 12-month period since 1990. For gold and

Artist John Mercanti created this model of the heraldic eagle, now used as part of the American Silver Eagle reverse design.

platinum, the initial order must be for at least 1,000 ounces, with reorders in increments of 500 ounces. For American Eagles, an authorized purchaser's cost is based on the market value of the bullion, plus a premium to cover minting, distribution, and other overhead expenses. For ASEs, the premium is $1.50 per coin. For gold, the premiums are 3% (for the one-ounce coin), 5% (1/2 ounce), 7% (1/4 ounce), and 9% (1/10 ounce). For platinum: 4% (for the one-ounce coin), 6% (1/2 ounce), 10% (1/4 ounce), and 15% (1/10 ounce).

Note that the U.S. Mint does not release bullion mintage data on a regular basis; the numbers given herein reflect the most recently available official data.

The listed values of uncertified, average Mint State coins have been based on bullion prices of silver ($17 per ounce), gold ($1,200 per ounce), and platinum ($1,400 per ounce).

For more detailed coverage of these coins, readers are directed to *American Silver Eagles: A Guide to the U.S. Bullion Coin Program* (Mercanti), *American Gold and Platinum Eagles: A Guide to the U.S. Bullion Coin Programs* (Moy), and *American Gold and Silver: U.S. Mint Collector and Investor Coins and Medals, Bicentennial to Date* (Tucker).

AMERICAN SILVER EAGLES (1986 TO DATE)

Designers: *Adolph A. Weinman (obverse) and John Mercanti (reverse).*
Weight: *31.101 grams.* **Composition:** *.9993 silver, .0007 copper (net weight 1 oz. pure silver).*
Diameter: *40.6 mm.* **Edge:** *Reeded.* **Mints:** *Philadelphia, San Francisco, West Point.*

Regular Finish

Burnished Finish

Enhanced Uncirculated Finish
This special format incorporates elements with a brilliant mirrored finish, a light frosted finish, and a heavy frosted finish.

Reverse Lettering Style of 1986–2007
Note the lack of spur or stem at bottom right of U.

Reverse Lettering Style of 2008 to Date
Note the spur at bottom right of U.

Proof
Finish

Reverse
Proof Finish

History. The American Silver Eagle (face value $1, actual silver weight one ounce) is a legal-tender bullion coin with weight, content, and purity guaranteed by the federal government. It is the only silver coin allowed in individual retirement accounts (IRAs). The obverse design features Adolph A. Weinman's Liberty Walking, as used on the circulating half dollar of 1916 to 1947. Weinman's initials appear on the hem of Miss Liberty's gown. The reverse design, by John Mercanti, is a rendition of a heraldic eagle.

From 1986 to 1999 all American Silver Eagles were struck at the Philadelphia and San Francisco mints (with the exception of the 1995 West Point Proof). In 2000 they were struck at both Philadelphia (Proofs) and the U.S. Mint's West Point facility (bullion strikes). From 2001 to 2010, West Point was their sole producer (with one exception in 2006), making regular bullion strikes (without mintmarks) and Proof and "Burnished" specimens (with mintmarks). (The exception is the 2006 Reverse Proof, which was struck in Philadelphia.) In 2011, for the 25th anniversary of the American Eagle bullion program, the mints at West Point, San Francisco, and Philadelphia were all put into production to make several collectible formats of the coins. Since 2012, both West Point and San Francisco have minted the American Silver Eagle.

In addition to the individually listed coins, American Silver Eagles were issued in two 2006 "20th Anniversary" sets (see page 1294) and in several other special bullion coin sets (see pages 1276, 1293, and 1294).

Striking and Sharpness. Striking is generally sharp. The key elements to check on the obverse are Miss Liberty's left hand, the higher parts and lines of her skirt, and her head. On the reverse, the eagle's breast is a main focal point.

Availability. The American Silver Eagle is one of the most popular silver-investment vehicles in the world. Between the bullion coins and various collectible formats, more than 340 million have been sold since 1986. The coins are readily available in the numismatic marketplace and from some banks, investment firms, and other non-numismatic channels.

MS-60 to 70 (Mint State). *Obverse and Reverse:* At MS-60, some abrasion and contact marks are evident on the higher design areas (Miss Liberty's left arm, her hand, and the areas of the skirt covering her left leg). Luster may be dull or lifeless at MS-60 to 62, but there should be deep frost at MS-63 and better, particularly in the lower-relief areas. At MS-65 and above, the luster should be full and rich. These guidelines are more academic than practical, as American Silver Eagles are not intended for circulation, and nearly all are in high Mint State grades.

PF-60 to 70 (Proof). *Obverse and Reverse:* Proofs that are extensively cleaned and have many hairlines are lower level, such as PF-60 to 62. Those with fewer hairlines or flaws are deemed PF-63 to 65. (These exist more in theory than actuality, as nearly all Proof ASEs have been maintained in their original high condition by collectors and investors.) Given the quality of modern U.S. Mint products, even PF-66 and 67 are unusually low levels for ASE Proofs.

AMERICAN SILVER EAGLES

	Mintage	MS / PF	MS-69 / PF-69	MS-70 / PF-70
1986 ‡ (a)	5,393,005	$40	$55	$700
	Auctions: $64, MS-69, December 2014; $40, MS-69, November 2014; $646, MS-69, October 2014; $194, MS-69, July 2014			
1986S, Proof	1,446,778	$60	$90	$550
	Auctions: $353, PF-70DCam, December 2014; $411, PF-70DCam, September 2014; $382, PF-70DCam, September 2014			
1987 (a)	11,442,335	$30	$45	$1,650
	Auctions: $7,050, MS-70, April 2013; $44, MS-69, November 2014; $141, MS-60, November 2014; $100, MS-60, November 2014			
1987S, Proof	904,732	$60	$90	$900
	Auctions: $823, PF-70DCam, September 2014; $705, PF-70DCam, September 2014; $663, PF-70DCam, August 2014			
1988 (a)	5,004,646	$30	$45	$1,900
	Auctions: $1,763, MS-70, November 2013; $31, MS-69, November 2014; $28, MS-69, November 2014; $27, MS-69, November 2014			
1988S, Proof	557,370	$60	$93	$550
	Auctions: No auction records available.			
1989 (a)	5,203,327	$30	$50	$1,500
	Auctions: $1,410, MS-70, April 2014; $32, MS-69, November 2014; $36, MS-69, September 2014; $34, MS-69, September 2014			
1989S, Proof	617,694	$60	$90	$325
	Auctions: $353, PF-70DCam, December 2014; $270, PF-70DCam, September 2014; $259, PF-70DCam, September 2014			
1990 (a)	5,840,210	$27	$50	$1,500
	Auctions: $3,819, MS-70, November 2013; $34, MS-69, November 2014; $38, MS-69, September 2014; $34, MS-69, September 2014			
1990S, Proof	695,510	$60	$90	$250
	Auctions: $235, PF-70DCam, December 2014; $135, PF-70DCam, November 2014; $188, PF-70DCam, September 2014			
1991 (a)	7,191,066	$30	$45	—
	Auctions: $4,113, MS-70, November 2013; $31, MS-69, November 2014; $34, MS-69, September 2014; $33, MS-69, September 2014			
1991S, Proof	511,925	$60	$90	$600
	Auctions: $382, PF-70DCam, December 2014; $329, PF-70DCam, October 2014; $306, PF-70DCam, October 2014			
1992 (a)	5,540,068	$30	$50	$1,600
	Auctions: $1,411, MS-70, November 2014; $1,410, MS-70, November 2014; $34, MS-69, November 2014; $38, MS-69, September 2014			
1992S, Proof	498,654	$60	$93	$500
	Auctions: $329, PF-70DCam, December 2014; $341, PF-70DCam, November 2014; $382, PF-70DCam, September 2014			
1993 (a)	6,763,762	$30	$45	$3,200
	Auctions: $4,406, MS-70, October 2014; $3,819, MS-70, November 2013; $31, MS-69, November 2014; $38, MS-69, September 2014			
1993P, Proof	405,913	$120	$140	$3,000
	Auctions: $2,614, PF-70DCam, August 2014; $2,115, PF-70DCam, August 2014; $1,880, PF-70DCam, August 2014; $2,233, PF-70DCam, July 2014			
1994 (a)	4,227,319	$40	$60	$4,000
	Auctions: $11,163, MS-70, November 2013; $47, MS-69, November 2014			
1994P, Proof ‡	372,168	$200	$225	$2,400
	Auctions: $1,763, PF-70DCam, November 2014; $1,645, PF-70DCam, November 2014; $1,763, PF-70DCam, October 2014			
1995 (a)	4,672,051	$40	$55	$1,000
	Auctions: $881, MS-70, November 2013; $39, MS-69, November 2014; $38, MS-69, September 2014			
1995P, Proof	438,511	$90	$110	$460
	Auctions: $259, PF-70DCam, December 2014; $294, PF-70DCam, November 2014; $353, PF-70DCam, September 2014			
1995W, Proof ‡	30,125	$4,200	$4,900	—
	Auctions: $15,275, PF-70DCam, August 2014; $6,586, PF-69DCam, November 2014; $3,525, PF-69DCam, October 2014			
1996 ‡ (a)	3,603,386	$70	$85	—
	Auctions: $9,400, MS-70, March 2014; $74, MS-69, December 2014; $61, MS-69, November 2014; $86, MS-69, October 2014			
1996P, Proof	500,000	$75	$110	$500
	Auctions: $470, PF-70DCam, December 2014; $376, PF-70DCam, November 2014; $353, PF-70DCam, September 2014			

Note: For more information, consult *American Silver Eagles: A Guide to the U.S. Bullion Coin Program*, 2nd edition (Mercanti and Standish). MS values are for uncertified Mint State coins of average quality, in their complete original U.S. Mint packaging. PF values are for uncertified Proof coins of average quality, in their complete original U.S. Mint packaging. ‡ Ranked in the *100 Greatest U.S. Modern Coins*. **a.** Minted at Philadelphia, without mintmark.

	Mintage	MS / PF	MS-69 / PF-69	MS-70 / PF-70
1997 (a)	4,295,004	$33	$50	$2,000
	Auctions: $999, MS-70, November 2013; $36, MS-69, November 2014; $141, MS-69, October 2014; $44, MS-69, September 2014			
1997P, Proof	435,368	$80	$110	$500
	Auctions: $588, PF-70DCam, December 2014; $282, PF-70DCam, November 2014; $247, PF-70DCam, September 2014			
1998 (a)	4,847,549	$30	$49	$1,500
	Auctions: $4,994, MS-70, April 2013; $44, MS-69, December 2014; $35, MS-69, November 2014; $329, MS-68, August 2014			
1998P, Proof	450,000	$70	$95	$250
	Auctions: $188, PF-70DCam, December 2014; $176, PF-70DCam, November 2014; $153, PF-70DCam, November 2014			
1999 (a)	7,408,640	$30	$50	—
	Auctions: $28,200, MS-70, November 2013; $34, MS-69, November 2014; $40, MS-69, September 2014; $36, MS-69, September 2014			
1999P, Proof	549,769	$70	$85	$400
	Auctions: $235, PF-70DCam, December 2014; $317, PF-70DCam, September 2014; $247, PF-70DCam, September 2014			
2000 (b)	9,239,132	$27	$47	$5,600
	Auctions: $10,575, MS-70, March 2013; $34, MS-69, November 2014			
2000P, Proof	600,000	$70	$85	$400
	Auctions: $329, PF-70DCam, December 2014; $282, PF-70DCam, October 2014; $270, PF-70DCam, October 2014			
2001 (b)	9,001,711	$30	$47	$1,000
	Auctions: $3,525, MS-70, April 2013; $32, MS-69, November 2014; $34, MS-69, September 2014; $270, MS-60, November 2014			
2001W, Proof	746,398	$65	$85	$125
	Auctions: $106, PF-70DCam, December 2014; $147, PF-70DCam, November 2014; $113, PF-70DCam, September 2014			
2002 (b)	10,539,026	$27	$40	$250
	Auctions: $235, MS-70, August 2014; $2,350, MS-70, April 2013; $32, MS-69, November 2014			
2002W, Proof	647,342	$65	$85	$125
	Auctions: $147, PF-70DCam, December 2014; $176, PF-70DCam, November 2014; $135, PF-70DCam, September 2014			
2003 (b)	8,495,008	$27	$29	$150
	Auctions: $135, MS-70, August 2014; $34, MS-69, November 2014; $32, MS-69, October 2014; $30, MS-68, November 2014			
2003W, Proof	747,831	$65	$85	$120
	Auctions: $74, PF-70DCam, December 2014; $83, PF-70DCam, November 2014; $76, PF-70DCam, November 2014			
2004 (b)	8,882,754	$27	$29	$125
	Auctions: $188, MS-70, May 2013; $32, MS-69, November 2014			
2004W, Proof	801,602	$65	$85	$100
	Auctions: $86, PF-70DCam, December 2014; $74, PF-70DCam, November 2014; $61, PF-70DCam, September 2014			
2005 (b)	8,891,025	$27	$29	$125
	Auctions: $306, MS-70, December 2014; $212, MS-70, December 2014; $206, MS-70, November 2014; $200, MS-70, November 2014			
2005W, Proof	816,663	$65	$85	$100
	Auctions: $79, PF-70DCam, December 2014; $84, PF-70DCam, November 2014; $84, PF-70DCam, September 2014			
2006 (b)	10,676,522	$27	$29	$125
	Auctions: $96, MS-70, August 2014; $118, MS-70, April 2013; $36, MS-69, December 2014; $31, MS-69, November 2014			
2006W, Burnished (c)	468,020	$100	$115	$185
	Auctions: $165, MS-70, December 2014; $182, MS-70, October 2014; $176, MS-70, July 2014; $135, MS-70, July 2014			
2006W, Proof	1,092,477	$65	$85	$100
	Auctions: $94, PF-70DCam, October 2014; $80, PF-70DCam, September 2014; $118, PF-70DCam, August 2014; $115, PF-70DCam, August 2014			
2006P, Reverse Proof ‡ (d,e)	248,875	$250	$305	$395
	Auctions: $441, PF-70DCam, December 2014; $441, PF-70DCam, September 2014; $382, PF-70DCam, July 2014			

Note: For more information, consult *American Silver Eagles: A Guide to the U.S. Bullion Coin Program*, 2nd edition (Mercanti and Standish). MS values are for uncertified Mint State coins of average quality, in their complete original U.S. Mint packaging. PF values are for uncertified Proof coins of average quality, in their complete original U.S. Mint packaging. ‡ Ranked in the *100 Greatest U.S. Modern Coins*. **a.** Minted at Philadelphia, without mintmark. **b.** Minted at West Point, without mintmark. **c.** In celebration of the 20th anniversary of the Bullion Coinage Program, in 2006 the W mintmark was used on bullion coins produced in sets at West Point. **d.** The 2006-P Reverse Proof coins were issued to mark the 20th anniversary of the Bullion Coinage Program. **e.** Reverse Proofs have brilliant devices, and their background fields are frosted (rather than the typical Proof format of frosted devices and mirror-like backgrounds).

	Mintage	MS / PF	MS-69 / PF-69	MS-70 / PF-70
2007 (b)	9,028,036	$30	$33	$55
Auctions: $306, MS-70, May 2013; $36, MS-69, December 2014				
2007W, Burnished	621,333	$40	$49	$65
Auctions: $94, MS-70, February 2013; $35, MS-69, July 2014				
2007W, Proof	821,759	$65	$80	$95
Auctions: $141, PF-70DCam, December 2014; $76, PF-70DCam, November 2014; $74, PF-70DCam, September 2014				
2008 (b)	20,583,000	$27	$29	$55
Auctions: $70, MS-70, June 2013				
2008W, Burnished	533,757	$70	$85	$100
Auctions: $182, MS-70, August 2013				
2008W, Burnished, Reverse of 2007 ‡ (f)	47,000	$550	$650	$1,000
Auctions: $940, MS-70, October 2014; $764, MS-70, August 2014; $1,645, MS-70, February 2013; $382, MS-69, November 2014				
2008W, Proof	700,979	$75	$85	$100
Auctions: $76, PF-70DCam, December 2014; $74, PF-70DCam, September 2014; $135, PF-70DCam, August 2014				
2009 (b)	30,459,000	$27	$29	$55
Auctions: $108, MS-70, January 2013				
2010 (b)	34,764,500	$27	$29	$55
Auctions: $48, MS-70, November 2014; $47, MS-70, November 2014; $40, MS-70, November 2014; $38, MS-70, November 2014				
2010W, Proof (g)	849,861	$65	$85	$100
Auctions: $92, PF-70DCam, August 2014; $78, PF-70DCam, August 2014; $76, PF-70DCam, August 2014; $70, PF-70DCam, August 2014				
2011 (b,h)	40,020,000	$27	$29	$55
Auctions: $56, MS-70, December 2014; $96, MS-70, April 2013; $44, MS-69, December 2014				
2011W, Burnished	409,776	$50	$69	$125
Auctions: $57, MS-70, September 2014; $212, MS-69, January 2014				
2011W, Proof	947,355	$65	$85	$100
Auctions: $101, PF-70DCam, August 2014; $66, PF-70DCam, August 2014; $54, PF-70DCam, August 2014; $53, PF-70DCam, August 2014				
2011P, Reverse Proof (e)	99,882	$300	$315	$450
Auctions: No auction records available.				
2011S, Burnished	99,882	$275	$285	$300
Auctions: No auction records available.				
2012 (b,h)	33,742,500	$27	$29	$55
Auctions: $153, MS-70, August 2014; $172, MS-70, August 2013				
2012W, Burnished	226,120	$65	$79	$125
Auctions: No auction records available.				
2012W, Proof	877,731	$65	$85	$100
Auctions: No auction records available.				
2012S, Proof	281,792	$60	$85	$110
Auctions: No auction records available.				
2012S, Reverse Proof (e)	224,935	$115	$130	$145
Auctions: $141, PF-70DCam, May 2013				

Note: For more information, consult *American Silver Eagles: A Guide to the U.S. Bullion Coin Program*, 2nd edition (Mercanti and Standish). MS values are for uncertified Mint State coins of average quality, in their complete original U.S. Mint packaging. PF values are for uncertified Proof coins of average quality, in their complete original U.S. Mint packaging. ‡ Ranked in the *100 Greatest U.S. Modern Coins*. **b.** Minted at West Point, without mintmark. **e.** Reverse Proofs have brilliant devices, and their background fields are frosted (rather than the typical Proof format of frosted devices and mirror-like backgrounds). **f.** Reverse dies of 2007 and earlier have a plain U in UNITED. Modified dies of 2008 and later have a small spur at the bottom right of the U. **g.** The U.S. Mint did not strike any Proof American Silver Eagles in 2009. **h.** Minted at San Francisco, without mintmark.

	Mintage	MS / PF	MS-69 / PF-69	MS-70 / PF-70
2013 (b,h)	42,675,000	$27	$29	$55
Auctions: No auction records available.				
2013W, Burnished	221,981	$65	$75	$90
Auctions: No auction records available.				
2013W, Enhanced Uncirculated	235,689	$60	$125	$150
Auctions: No auction records available.				
2013W, Proof	934,331	$65	$75	$95
Auctions: No auction records available.				
2013W, Reverse Proof	235,689	$90	$110	$125
Auctions: No auction records available.				
2013W, Enhanced Finish Proof		$110	$125	$140
Auctions: No auction records available.				
2014 (b,h)	44,006,000	$27	$29	$55
Auctions: No auction records available.				
2014W, Burnished	249,752	$45	$54	$90
Auctions: No auction records available.				
2014W, Proof	757,108	$55	$65	$85
Auctions: No auction records available.				
2015 (b,h)				
Auctions: No auction records available.				
2015W, Proof				
Auctions: No auction records available.				

Note: For more information, consult *American Silver Eagles: A Guide to the U.S. Bullion Coin Program*, 2nd edition (Mercanti and Standish). MS values are for uncertified Mint State coins of average quality, in their complete original U.S. Mint packaging. PF values are for uncertified Proof coins of average quality, in their complete original U.S. Mint packaging. ‡ Ranked in the *100 Greatest U.S. Modern Coins*. **b.** Minted at West Point, without mintmark. **h.** Minted at San Francisco, without mintmark.

AMERICAN SILVER EAGLE COIN SETS

	Uncertified	69	70
2006 20th Anniversary Three-Coin Set. Silver dollars, Uncirculated, Proof, Reverse Proof	$425	$485	$700
Auctions: No auction records available.			
2006W 20th Anniversary 1-oz. Gold- and Silver-Dollar Set. Uncirculated	$1,800	$1,900	$2,100
Auctions: No auction records available.			
2011 25th Anniversary Five-Coin Set	$675	$800	$1,200
Auctions: $92, PF-70, November 2013; $881, PF-69, October 2014			
2012S 75th Anniversary of San Francisco Mint Two-Coin Set. Proof, Reverse Proof	$175	$215	$255
Auctions: $376, PF-70DCam, January 2013			
2013W 75th Anniversary of West Point Depository Two-Coin Set. Reverse Proof, Enhanced Uncirculated	$160	$230	$265
Auctions: $141, PF-70, December 2014; $108, PF-70, December 2014; $101, PF-70, December 2014; $129, PF-70, November 2014			

Note: Uncertified values are for uncertified sets of average quality, in their complete original U.S. Mint packaging. The Proof American Silver Eagle of 1997 is also included in the 1997 Impressions of Liberty set, listed on page 1294.

AMERICA THE BEAUTIFUL 5-OUNCE
SILVER BULLION COINS (2010–2021)

Designers: *various.* **Weight:** *155.517 grams.* **Composition:** *.999 silver, .001 copper*
(net weight 5 oz. pure silver). **Diameter:** *76.2 mm.* **Edge:** *Lettered.* **Mint:** *Philadelphia.*

Bullion
Strike

Specimen
Strike

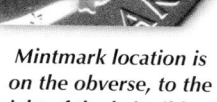

*Mintmark location is
on the obverse, to the
right of the hair ribbon.*

Details of the incused edge markings.

**Details on 2014 Great Smoky Mountains
National Park 5-ounce silver bullion coin (left)
and quarter dollar (right). Note differences
on window, cabin, and grass in foreground.**

History. In conjunction with the National Park quarter dollars, the U.S. Mint issues silver-bullion coins based on each of the "America the Beautiful" program's circulation-strike coins. The coinage dies are cut on a CNC milling machine, bypassing a hubbing operation, which results in finer details than seen on the smaller quarter dollars. The bullion coins are made of .999 fine silver, have a diameter of three inches, weigh five ounces, and carry a face value of 25 cents. The fineness and weight are incused on each coin's edge. The Mint's German-made Gräbener press strikes 22 coins per minute, with two strikes per coin at 450 to 500 metric tons of pressure. In December 2010, the Mint announced it would produce Uncirculated and Specimen versions for collectors.

Striking and Sharpness. Striking is generally sharp.

Availability. The National Park silver bullion coins are distributed through commercial channels similar to those for the Mint's American Silver Eagle coins. Production of the 2010 coins was delayed (finally starting September 21) as the Mint worked out the technical details of striking such a large product. Production and distribution are expected to be smooth, and the Mint anticipates striking up to 500,000 of the coins annually, divided equally between each year's issues, through the program's duration.

MS-65 to 70 (Mint State). *Obverse and Reverse:* At MS-65, some abrasion and contact marks are evident on the higher design areas. Luster may be dull or lifeless at MS-65 to 66, but there should be deep frost at MS-67 and better, particularly in the lower-relief areas. At MS-68 and above, the luster should be full and rich. These guidelines are more academic than practical, as these coins are not intended for circulation, and nearly all are in high Mint State grades.

SP-68 to 70 (Specimen). *Obverse and Reverse:* These pieces should be nearly perfect and with full luster, in their original Mint packaging. Any with imperfections due to careless handling or environmental damage are valued lower.

The U.S. Mint produces the America the Beautiful™ 5-ounce silver coins in bullion and numismatic versions. The bullion version, which lacks the P mintmark, has a brilliant Uncirculated finish and is sold only through dealers. The numismatic version, with the mintmark, has a matte or burnished finish. These coins are designated "Specimens" (SP) by most collectors and grading services. They are sold directly to the public by the Mint.

25¢ AMERICA THE BEAUTIFUL 5-OUNCE SILVER BULLION COINS

	Mintage	MS	MS-69	MS-70
		SP	SP-69	SP-70
2010, Hot Springs National Park	33,000	$135	$170	$350
	Auctions: No auction records available.			
2010P, Hot Springs National Park, Specimen	26,788	$155	$185	$225
	Auctions: $188, SP-68, October 2014			
2010, Yellowstone National Park	33,000	$135	$170	$350
	Auctions: $212, MS-69DM, May 2013			
2010P, Yellowstone National Park, Specimen	26,711	$155	$185	$225
	Auctions: $182, SP-68, October 2014			
2010, Yosemite National Park	33,000	$135	$170	$350
	Auctions: $206, MS-60, March 2013			
2010P, Yosemite National Park, Specimen	26,716	$155	$185	$225
	Auctions: $247, SP-70, January 2014; $176, SP-69, October 2014			
2010, Grand Canyon National Park	33,000	$135	$170	$350
	Auctions: $206, MS-69PL, September 2013			
2010P, Grand Canyon National Park, Specimen	25,967	$155	$185	$225
	Auctions: No auction records available.			

Note: MS values are for uncertified Mint State coins of average quality, in their complete original U.S. Mint packaging. SP values are for uncertified Specimen coins of average quality, in their complete original U.S. Mint packaging.

	Mintage	MS SP	MS-69 SP-69	MS-70 SP-70
2010, Mt. Hood National Forest	33,000	$135	$170	$350
Auctions: No auction records available.				
2010P, Mt. Hood National Forest, Specimen	26,637	$155	$185	$225
Auctions: $308, SP-70, February 2013				
2011, Gettysburg National Military Park	126,700	$120	$155	$350
Auctions: No auction records available.				
2011P, Gettysburg National Military Park, Specimen	24,625	$215	$240	$350
Auctions: $541, SP-70, September 2014; $353, SP-70, February 2013				
2011, Glacier National Park	126,700	$120	$155	$350
Auctions: No auction records available.				
2011P, Glacier National Park, Specimen	20,805	$215	$240	$350
Auctions: $376, SP-70, September 2014; $376, SP-70, February 2013				
2011, Olympic National Park	95,600	$120	$155	$350
Auctions: $165, MS-69DM, December 2014				
2011P, Olympic National Park, Specimen	18,345	$215	$240	$350
Auctions: $400, SP-70, September 2014; $411, SP-70PL, February 2013				
2011, Vicksburg National Military Park	41,200	$120	$155	$350
Auctions: $147, MS-69DM, December 2014				
2011P, Vicksburg National Military Park, Specimen	18,528	$215	$240	$350
Auctions: $341, SP-70, February 2013				
2011, Chickasaw National Recreational Area	31,400	$120	$155	$350
Auctions: $165, MS-69DM, December 2014				
2011P, Chickasaw National Recreational Area, Specimen	16,746	$215	$240	$350
Auctions: $331, SP-70PL, February 2013; $353, SP-70, September 2014				
2012, El Yunque National Forest	21,900	$190	$200	$225
Auctions: $147, MS-69DM, December 2014; $182, MS-69DM, October 2014				
2012P, El Yunque National Forest, Specimen	17,314	$475	$515	$700
Auctions: $364, SP-70, September 2014; $329, SP-70, February 2013				
2012, Chaco Culture National Historical Park	20,000	$190	$200	$225
Auctions: No auction records available.				
2012P, Chaco Culture National Historical Park, Specimen	17,146	$475	$515	$700
Auctions: $341, SP-70, September 2014; $306, SP-70, February 2013				
2012, Acadia National Park	25,400	$190	$200	$225
Auctions: $435, MS-69DM, July 2013				
2012P, Acadia National Park, Specimen	14,978	$525	$575	$875
Auctions: $529, SP-70, September 2014				
2012, Hawai'i Volcanoes National Park	20,000	$190	$200	$225
Auctions: $341, MS-69PL, October 2014; $356, MS-69DM, March 2013				
2012P, Hawai'i Volcanoes National Park, Specimen	14,863	$600	$650	$950
Auctions: $682, SP-70, September 2014				
2012, Denali National Park and Preserve	20,000	$190	$200	$225
Auctions: No auction records available.				
2012P, Denali National Park and Preserve, Specimen	15,225	$475	$515	$700
Auctions: No auction records available.				
2013, White Mountain National Forest	35,000	$125	$135	$160
Auctions: No auction records available.				
2013P, White Mountain National Forest, Specimen	20,530	$160	$190	$230
Auctions: $194, SP-70, December 2014				
2013, Perry's Victory and International Peace Memorial	30,000	$125	$135	$160
Auctions: No auction records available.				
2013P, Perry's Victory and International Peace Memorial, Specimen	17,707	$160	$190	$230
Auctions: No auction records available.				

Note: MS values are for uncertified Mint State coins of average quality, in their complete original U.S. Mint packaging. SP values are for uncertified Specimen coins of average quality, in their complete original U.S. Mint packaging.

	Mintage	MS	MS-69	MS-70
		SP	SP-69	SP-70
2013, Great Basin National Park	30,000	$125	$135	$160
Auctions: No auction records available.				
2013P, Great Basin National Park, Specimen	17,792	$160	$190	$230
Auctions: No auction records available.				
2013, Ft. McHenry Nat'l Mon & Historic Shrine	30,000	$125	$135	$160
Auctions: No auction records available.				
2013P, Ft. McHenry Nat'l Mon & Historic Shrine, Specimen	19,802	$160	$190	$230
Auctions: No auction records available.				
2013, Mount Rushmore National Monument	35,000	$125	$135	$160
Auctions: No auction records available.				
2013P, Mount Rushmore National Monument, Specimen	23,547	$160	$190	$230
Auctions: No auction records available.				
2014, Great Smoky Mountains National Park	33,000	$130	$140	$165
Auctions: No auction records available.				
2014P, Great Smoky Mountains National Park, Specimen	24,710	$160	$190	$230
Auctions: No auction records available.				
2014, Shenandoah National Park	24,400	$130	$140	$165
Auctions: No auction records available.				
2014P, Shenandoah National Park, Specimen	28,276	$160	$190	$230
Auctions: No auction records available.				
2014, Arches National Park	22,000	$130	$140	$165
Auctions: No auction records available.				
2014P, Arches National Park, Specimen	28,183	$160	$190	$230
Auctions: No auction records available.				
2014, Great Sand Dunes National Park	21,900	$130	$140	$165
Auctions: No auction records available.				
2014P, Great Sand Dunes National Park, Specimen	22,262	$160	$190	$230
Auctions: No auction records available.				
2014, Everglades National Park	34,000	$130	$140	$165
Auctions: No auction records available.				
2014P, Everglades National Park, Specimen	19,772	$160	$190	$230
Auctions: No auction records available.				
2015, Homestead National Monument of America				
Auctions: No auction records available.				
2015P, Homestead National Monument of America, Specimen				
Auctions: No auction records available.				
2015, Kisatchie National Forest				
Auctions: No auction records available.				
2015P, Kisatchie National Forest, Specimen				
Auctions: No auction records available.				
2015, Blue Ridge Parkway				
Auctions: No auction records available.				
2015P, Blue Ridge Parkway, Specimen				
Auctions: No auction records available.				
2015, Bombay Hook National Wildlife Refuge				
Auctions: No auction records available.				
2015P, Bombay Hook National Wildlife Refuge, Specimen				
Auctions: No auction records available.				
2015, Saratoga National Historic Park				
Auctions: No auction records available.				
2015P, Saratoga National Historic Park, Specimen				
Auctions: No auction records available.				

Note: MS values are for uncertified Mint State coins of average quality, in their complete original U.S. Mint packaging. SP values are for uncertified Specimen coins of average quality, in their complete original U.S. Mint packaging.

AMERICAN GOLD EAGLES (1986 TO DATE)

Designers: *Augustus Saint-Gaudens (obverse) and Miley Busiek (reverse).*
Weight: *$5 1/10 oz.—3.393 grams; $10 1/4 oz.—8.483 grams; $25 1/2 oz.—16.966 grams;
$50 1 oz.—33.931 grams.* **Composition:** *.9167 gold, .03 silver, .0533 copper.*
Diameter: *$5 1/10 oz.—16.5 mm; $10 1/4 oz.—22 mm; $25 1/2 oz.—27 mm;
$50 1 oz.—32.7 mm.* **Edge:** *Reeded.* **Mints:** *Philadelphia, West Point.*

Regular Finish
Obverse design common to all denominations.

Burnished Finish

Proof Finish

Reverse Proof Finish

*Mintmark location is on the
obverse, below the date.*

History. American Eagle gold bullion coins are made in four denominations: $5 (1/10 ounce pure gold),
$10 (1/4 ounce), $25 (1/2 ounce), and $50 (1 ounce). Each shares the same obverse and reverse designs:
a modified rendition of Augustus Saint-Gaudens's famous Liberty (as depicted on the double eagle of
1907 to 1933), and a "family of eagles" motif by sculptor Miley Tucker-Frost (nee Busiek). From 1986
to 1991 the obverse bore a Roman numeral date, similar to the first Saint-Gaudens double eagles of
1907; this was changed to Arabic dating in 1992. The coins are legal tender—with weight, content, and
purity guaranteed by the federal government—and are produced from gold mined in the United States.
Investors can include them in their individual retirement accounts.

"American Eagles use the durable 22-karat standard established for gold circulating coinage over 350
years ago," notes the U.S. Mint. "They contain their stated amount of pure gold, plus small amounts of
alloy. This creates harder coins that resist scratching and marring, which can diminish resale value."

Since the Bullion Coin Program started in 1986, these gold pieces have been struck in Philadelphia
and West Point, in various formats similar to those of the American Silver Eagles—regular bullion
strikes, Burnished, Proof, and Reverse Proof. Unlike their silver counterparts, none of the American
Gold Eagles have been struck at San Francisco.

In addition to the individual coins listed below, American Eagle gold bullion coins have been issued
in various sets (see pages 1293 and 1294).

Striking and Sharpness. Striking is generally sharp. The key elements to check on the obverse are Liberty's chest and left knee, and the open fields.

Availability. American Gold Eagles are the most popular gold-coin investment vehicle in the United States. The coins are readily available in the numismatic marketplace as well as from participating banks, investment firms, and other non-numismatic channels.

MS-60 to 70 (Mint State). *Obverse and Reverse:* At MS-60, some abrasion and contact marks are evident on the higher design areas (in particular, Miss Liberty's chest and left knee) and the open fields. Luster may be dull or lifeless at MS-60 to 62, but there should be deep frost at MS-63 and better, particularly in the lower-relief areas. At MS-65 and above, the luster should be full and rich. Contact marks and abrasion are less and less evident at higher grades. These guidelines are more academic than practical, as these coins are not intended for circulation, and nearly all are in high Mint State grades.

PF-60 to 70 (Proof). *Obverse and Reverse:* Proofs that are extensively cleaned and have many hairlines are lower level, such as PF-60 to 62. Those with fewer hairlines or flaws are deemed PF-63 to 65. (These exist more in theory than actuality, as nearly all Proof American Eagle gold bullion coins have been maintained in their original high condition by collectors and investors.) Given the quality of modern U.S. Mint products, even PF-66 and 67 are unusually low levels for these Proofs.

$5 1/10-Ounce American Gold Eagles

	Mintage	MS / PF	MS-69 / PF-69	MS-70 / PF-70
$5 MCMLXXXVI (1986)	912,609	$165	$190	$900
		Auctions: $470, MS-70, October 2014; $558, MS-70, September 2014; $142, MS-69, November 2014		
$5 MCMLXXXVII (1987)	580,266	$165	$190	$900
		Auctions: $823, MS-70, October 2014; $999, MS-70, September 2014; $1,293, MS-70, August 2014		
$5 MCMLXXXVIII (1988)	159,500	$175	$230	$4,000
		Auctions: $159, MS-69, October 2014; $147, MS-69, October 2014		
$5 MCMLXXXVIII (1988)P, Proof	143,881	$200	$220	$350
		Auctions: $182, PF-70DCam, November 2014; $294, PF-70DCam, September 2014; $259, PF-70DCam, August 2014		
$5 MCMLXXXIX (1989)	264,790	$165	$190	$3,100
		Auctions: $1,880, MS-70, August 2014; $147, MS-69, October 2014; $141, MS-69, October 2014; $135, MS-69, October 2014		
$5 MCMLXXXIX (1989)P, Proof	84,647	$185	$195	$375
		Auctions: $247, PF-70DCam, November 2014; $317, PF-70DCam, September 2014; $147, PF-69DCam, December 2014		
$5 MCMXC (1990)	210,210	$200	$220	$4,050
		Auctions: $159, MS-69, October 2014; $153, MS-69, October 2014; $141, MS-69, October 2014		
$5 MCMXC (1990)P, Proof	99,349	$185	$195	$375
		Auctions: $235, PF-70DCam, July 2014		
$5 MCMXCI (1991)	165,200	$220	$230	$1,300
		Auctions: $1,293, MS-70, September 2014; $8,519, MS-70, August 2014; $170, MS-69, November 2014		
$5 MCMXCI (1991)P, Proof	70,334	$185	$195	$400
		Auctions: $212, PF-70DCam, October 2014; $194, PF-70DCam, October 2014; $229, PF-70DCam, July 2014		
$5 1992	209,300	$170	$185	$1,375
		Auctions: No auction records available.		
$5 1992P, Proof	64,874	$175	$190	$450
		Auctions: $188, PF-70DCam, October 2014; $212, PF-70DCam, September 2014; $223, PF-70DCam, August 2014		

Note: MS values are for uncertified Mint State coins of average quality, in their complete original U.S. Mint packaging. PF values are for uncertified Proof coins of average quality, in their complete original U.S. Mint packaging.

| | Mintage | MS | MS-69 | MS-70 |
		PF	PF-69	PF-70
$5 1993	210,709	$170	$185	$1,500
	Auctions: No auction records available.			
$5 1993P, Proof	58,649	$175	$200	$475
	Auctions: $235, PF-70DCam, September 2014; $264, PF-70DCam, August 2014			
$5 1994	206,380	$170	$190	$400
	Auctions: $159, MS-68, August 2014			
$5 1994W, Proof	62,849	$175	$190	$450
	Auctions: $217, PF-70DCam, November 2014; $294, PF-70DCam, September 2014; $235, PF-70DCam, September 2014			
$5 1995	223,025	$155	$190	$1,000
	Auctions: $165, MS-69, August 2014			
$5 1995W, Proof	62,667	$175	$190	$450
	Auctions: $282, PF-70DCam, November 2014; $353, PF-70DCam, September 2014; $270, PF-70DCam, July 2014			
$5 1996	401,964	$155	$165	$550
	Auctions: $361, MS-70, July 2014			
$5 1996W, Proof	57,047	$175	$205	$500
	Auctions: $235, PF-70DCam, October 2014; $306, PF-70DCam, September 2014; $235, PF-70DCam, September 2014			
$5 1997	528,266	$155	$165	$350
	Auctions: $329, MS-70, November 2014; $153, MS-69, August 2014			
$5 1997W, Proof	34,977	$175	$210	$750
	Auctions: $294, PF-70DCam, November 2014; $441, PF-70DCam, September 2014; $382, PF-70DCam, August 2014			
$5 1998	1,344,520	$155	$165	$300
	Auctions: $153, MS-70, September 2014			
$5 1998W, Proof	39,395	$175	$200	$450
	Auctions: $212, PF-70DCam, October 2014; $247, PF-70DCam, July 2014			
$5 1999	2,750,338	$155	$165	$275
	Auctions: $194, MS-70, July 2014; $176, MS-70, July 2014; $170, MS-70, July 2014; $165, MS-69, August 2014			
$5 1999W, Unc made from unpolished Proof dies ‡ (a)	14,500	$1,000	$1,100	$3,500
	Auctions: $823, MS-68, October 2014; $705, MS-68, September 2014			
$5 1999W, Proof	48,428	$175	$200	$400
	Auctions: $411, PF-70DCam, October 2014; $223, PF-70DCam, August 2014			
$5 2000	569,153	$155	$170	$450
	Auctions: $147, MS-68, July 2014			
$5 2000W, Proof	49,971	$175	$190	$400
	Auctions: $259, PF-70DCam, October 2014; $206, PF-70DCam, October 2014; $223, PF-70DCam, August 2014			
$5 2001	269,147	$160	$180	$350
	Auctions: $306, MS, October 2014; $282, MS-60, October 2014; $159, MS-69, August 2014			
$5 2001W, Proof	37,530	$175	$210	$400
	Auctions: $529, PF-70DCam, September 2014; $259, PF-70DCam, August 2014			
$5 2002	230,027	$155	$180	$350
	Auctions: No auction records available.			
$5 2002W, Proof	40,864	$175	$190	$400
	Auctions: $223, PF-70DCam, November 2014; $194, PF-70DCam, November 2014; $235, PF-70DCam, October 2014			
$5 2003	245,029	$155	$170	$195
	Auctions: $159, MS-69, August 2014			
$5 2003W, Proof	40,027	$175	$190	$400
	Auctions: $182, PF-70DCam, September 2014; $212, PF-70DCam, August 2014; $188, PF-70DCam, July 2014			

Note: MS values are for uncertified Mint State coins of average quality, in their complete original U.S. Mint packaging. PF values are for uncertified Proof coins of average quality, in their complete original U.S. Mint packaging. ‡ Ranked in the *100 Greatest U.S. Modern Coins.* **a.** Unpolished Proof dies were used to mint some 1999 $5 gold coins, resulting in a regular bullion-strike issue bearing a W mintmark (usually reserved for Proofs). A similar error exists in the $10 (1/4-ounce) series. The mintage listed is an estimate. Other estimates range from 6,000 to 30,000 pieces.

	Mintage	MS / PF	MS-69 / PF-69	MS-70 / PF-70
$5 2004	250,016	$155	$160	$185
Auctions: $147, MS-69, October 2014; $153, MS-69, August 2014; $160, MS-69, July 2014				
$5 2004W, Proof	35,131	$175	$220	$450
Auctions: $188, PF-70DCam, October 2014; $153, PF-69DCam, August 2014; $235, PF-70DCam, July 2014				
$5 2005	300,043	$155	$160	$180
Auctions: $176, MS-70, December 2014				
$5 2005W, Proof	49,265	$175	$215	$350
Auctions: $159, PF-70DCam, December 2014; $176, PF-70DCam, September 2014; $194, PF-70DCam, August 2014				
$5 2006	285,006	$155	$160	$180
Auctions: $159, MS-70, December 2014; $153, MS-70, December 2014; $176, MS-70, October 2014; $159, MS-69, July 2014				
$5 2006W, Burnished	20,643	$210	$215	$255
Auctions: $212, MS-70, October 2014; $182, MS-69, December 2014; $147, MS-69, December 2014; $200, MS-69, November 2014				
$5 2006W, Proof	47,277	$175	$190	$240
Auctions: $194, PF-70DCam, November 2014; $176, PF-70DCam, November 2014; $170, PF-70DCam, September 2014				
$5 2007	190,010	$155	$170	$195
Auctions: No auction records available.				
$5 2007W, Burnished	22,501	$200	$220	$245
Auctions: $200, MS-70, September 2014				
$5 2007W, Proof	58,553	$175	$190	$240
Auctions: $182, PF-70DCam, September 2014; $217, PF-70DCam, July 2014				
$5 2008	305,000	$155	$160	$185
Auctions: No auction records available.				
$5 2008W, Burnished	12,657	$340	$355	$425
Auctions: $353, MS-70, November 2014; $329, MS-70, November 2014				
$5 2008W, Proof	28,116	$175	$190	$275
Auctions: $217, PF-70DCam, August 2014				
$5 2009	270,000	$155	$160	$180
Auctions: No auction records available.				
$5 2010	435,000	$155	$160	$180
Auctions: No auction records available.				
$5 2010W, Proof	54,285	$175	$210	$275
Auctions: $188, PF-70DCam, October 2014				
$5 2011	350,000	$155	$160	$180
Auctions: No auction records available.				
$5 2011W, Proof	42,697	$175	$185	$275
Auctions: No auction records available.				
$5 2012	315,000	$155	$160	$180
Auctions: No auction records available.				
$5 2012W, Proof	20,740	$175	$185	$250
Auctions: $176, PF-70DCam, November 2014; $206, PF-70DCam, July 2014				
$5 2013	535,000	$155	$160	$180
Auctions: No auction records available.				
$5 2013W, Proof	21,879	$175	$185	$235
Auctions: No auction records available.				
$5 2014	565,000	$155	$160	$180
Auctions: No auction records available.				
$5 2014W, Proof	22,692	$175	$195	$225
Auctions: No auction records available.				
$5 2015W, Proof				
Auctions: No auction records available.				

Note: MS values are for uncertified Mint State coins of average quality, in their complete original U.S. Mint packaging. PF values are for uncertified Proof coins of average quality, in their complete original U.S. Mint packaging.

$10 1/4-OUNCE AMERICAN GOLD EAGLES

	Mintage	MS / PF	MS-69 / PF-69	MS-70 / PF-70
$10 MCMLXXXVI (1986)	726,031	$500	$550	$1,850
Auctions: $1,128, MS-70, November 2014; $764, MS-70, November 2014; $1,410, MS-70, October 2014				
$10 MCMLXXXVII (1987)	269,255	$500	$550	$2,000
Auctions: No auction records available.				
$10 MCMLXXXVIII (1988)	49,000	$600	$650	$1,850
Auctions: $3,290, MS-70, August 2014; $3,525, MS-70, July 2014				
$10 MCMLXXXVIII (1988)P, Proof	98,028	$385	$395	$650
Auctions: $499, PF-70DCam, September 2014				
$10 MCMLXXXIX (1989)	81,789	$600	$675	$2,000
Auctions: No auction records available.				
$10 MCMLXXXIX (1989)P, Proof	54,170	$385	$495	$750
Auctions: $544, PF-70DCam, September 2014				
$10 MCMXC (1990)	41,000	$735	$775	$4,000
Auctions: No auction records available.				
$10 MCMXC (1990)P, Proof	62,674	$385	$495	$600
Auctions: $441, PF-70DCam, December 2014				
$10 MCMXCI (1991)	36,100	$735	$775	$2,350
Auctions: $3,819, MS-70, November 2014; $1,293, MS-70, October 2014; $1,410, MS-70, September 2014				
$10 MCMXCI (1991)P, Proof	50,839	$385	$495	$650
Auctions: $427, PF-70DCam, December 2014; $376, PF-70DCam, November 2014; $441, PF-70DCam, September 2014				
$10 1992	59,546	$550	$600	$2,000
Auctions: No auction records available.				
$10 1992P, Proof	46,269	$385	$510	$700
Auctions: $423, PF-70DCam, December 2014; $376, PF-70DCam, November 2014; $427, PF-70DCam, September 2014				
$10 1993	71,864	$550	$600	$2,250
Auctions: $3,290, MS-70, July 2014				
$10 1993P, Proof	46,464	$385	$510	$700
Auctions: No auction records available.				
$10 1994	72,650	$550	$600	$2,050
Auctions: $2,233, MS-70, August 2014				
$10 1994W, Proof	48,172	$385	$425	$650
Auctions: $400, PF-70DCam, December 2014; $388, PF-70DCam, November 2014; $382, PF-70DCam, September 2014				
$10 1995	83,752	$550	$600	$2,000
Auctions: No auction records available.				
$10 1995W, Proof	47,526	$385	$425	$650
Auctions: $376, PF-70DCam, December 2014; $364, PF-70DCam, November 2014; $441, PF-70DCam, September 2014				
$10 1996	60,318	$550	$600	$1,500
Auctions: $1,293, MS-70, October 2014; $1,175, MS-70, September 2014				
$10 1996W, Proof	38,219	$385	$425	$650
Auctions: $411, PF-70DCam, December 2014; $364, PF-70DCam, November 2014; $397, PF-70DCam, September 2014				
$10 1997	108,805	$350	$400	$2,000
Auctions: $411, MS-69, August 2014				
$10 1997W, Proof	29,805	$385	$425	$750
Auctions: $423, PF-70DCam, December 2014; $417, PF-70DCam, November 2014				

Note: MS values are for uncertified Mint State coins of average quality, in their complete original U.S. Mint packaging. PF values are for uncertified Proof coins of average quality, in their complete original U.S. Mint packaging.

	Mintage	MS / PF	MS-69 / PF-69	MS-70 / PF-70
$10 1998	309,829	$350	$400	$2,200
Auctions: No auction records available.				
$10 1998W, Proof	29,503	$385	$425	$750
Auctions: $441, PF-70DCam, December 2014; $400, PF-70DCam, November 2014; $382, PF-70DCam, September 2014				
$10 1999	564,232	$350	$400	$2,500
Auctions: $1,528, MS-70, July 2014				
$10 1999W, Unc made from unpolished Proof dies ‡ (a)	10,000	$1,800	$1,900	$9,500
Auctions: $1,763, MS-69, November 2014; $1,674, MS-69, September 2014; $1,528, MS-68, August 2014				
$10 1999W, Proof	34,417	$385	$425	$700
Auctions: No auction records available.				
$10 2000	128,964	$350	$400	$900
Auctions: $329, MS-69, October 2014; $306, MS-69, October 2014; $364, MS-69, August 2014				
$10 2000W, Proof	36,036	$385	$420	$700
Auctions: $388, PF-70DCam, December 2014				
$10 2001	71,280	$500	$515	$550
Auctions: $558, MS-70, November 2014				
$10 2001W, Proof	25,613	$385	$440	$725
Auctions: No auction records available.				
$10 2002	62,027	$500	$515	$550
Auctions: $499, MS-70, November 2014				
$10 2002W, Proof	29,242	$385	$440	$575
Auctions: $572, PF-70DCam, December 2014; $364, PF-70DCam, November 2014; $368, PF-70DCam, October 2014				
$10 2003	74,029	$350	$400	$550
Auctions: $470, MS-70, October 2014; $306, MS-69, November 2014; $364, MS-69, July 2014				
$10 2003W, Proof	30,292	$385	$440	$575
Auctions: $397, PF-70DCam, November 2014; $364, PF-70DCam, November 2014				
$10 2004	72,014	$350	$400	$550
Auctions: $341, MS-69, July 2014				
$10 2004W, Proof	28,839	$385	$440	$600
Auctions: No auction records available.				
$10 2005	72,015	$350	$400	$500
Auctions: $353, MS-70, November 2014; $382, MS-70, September 2014; $358, MS-69, July 2014; $329, MS-69, July 2014				
$10 2005W, Proof	37,207	$385	$440	$550
Auctions: $400, PF-70DCam, December 2014				
$10 2006	60,004	$350	$400	$550
Auctions: $441, MS-70, December 2014; $382, MS-70, December 2014; $397, MS-70, October 2014; $611, MS-70, July 2014				
$10 2006W, Burnished	15,188	$725	$750	$850
Auctions: $353, MS-69, November 2014				
$10 2006W, Proof	36,127	$385	$440	$550
Auctions: $364, PF-70DCam, November 2014; $330, PF-70DCam, October 2014				
$10 2007	34,004	$500	$525	$700
Auctions: $382, MS-70, November 2014; $391, MS-70, September 2014; $470, MS-70, August 2014				
$10 2007W, Burnished	12,766	$700	$725	$800
Auctions: $588, MS-70, August 2014; $411, MS-69, July 2014				
$10 2007W, Proof	46,189	$385	$420	$500
Auctions: $364, PF-70DCam, November 2014; $176, PF-69DCam, November 2014				

Note: MS values are for uncertified Mint State coins of average quality, in their complete original U.S. Mint packaging. PF values are for uncertified Proof coins of average quality, in their complete original U.S. Mint packaging. ‡ Ranked in the *100 Greatest U.S. Modern Coins*. **a.** Unpolished Proof dies were used to mint some 1999 $10 gold coins, resulting in a regular bullion-strike issue bearing a W mintmark (usually reserved for Proofs). A similar error exists in the $5 (1/10-ounce) series. The mintage listed is an estimate. Other estimates range from 6,000 to 30,000 pieces.

| | Mintage | MS | MS-69 | MS-70 |
		PF	PF-69	PF-70
$10 2008	70,000	$350	$400	$500
Auctions: No auction records available.				
$10 2008W, Burnished	8,883	$1,600	$1,650	$1,750
Auctions: No auction records available.				
$10 2008W, Proof	18,877	$500	$520	$700
Auctions: No auction records available.				
$10 2009	110,000	$350	$380	$475
Auctions: No auction records available.				
$10 2010	86,000	$350	$380	$500
Auctions: No auction records available.				
$10 2010W, Proof	44,507	$385	$445	$550
Auctions: No auction records available.				
$10 2011	80,000	$350	$360	$395
Auctions: No auction records available.				
$10 2011W, Proof	28,782	$385	$420	$525
Auctions: $353, PF-70DCam, November 2014; $370, PF-70DCam, October 2014; $329, PF-70DCam, October 2014				
$10 2012	76,000	$350	$360	$395
Auctions: No auction records available.				
$10 2012W, Proof	13,375	$385	$420	$550
Auctions: $353, PF-70DCam, November 2014				
$10 2013	122,000	$350	$360	$395
Auctions: No auction records available.				
$10 2013W, Proof	12,624	$385	$420	$525
Auctions: No auction records available.				
$10 2014	118,000	$350	$355	$380
Auctions: No auction records available.				
$10 2014W, Proof	14,760	$385	$420	$525
Auctions: No auction records available.				
$10 2015W, Proof				
Auctions: No auction records available.				

Note: MS values are for uncertified Mint State coins of average quality, in their complete original U.S. Mint packaging. PF values are for uncertified Proof coins of average quality, in their complete original U.S. Mint packaging.

$25 1/2-Ounce American Gold Eagles

| | Mintage | MS | MS-69 | MS-70 |
		PF	PF-69	PF-70
$25 MCMLXXXVI (1986)	599,566	$1,000	$1,100	$1,500
Auctions: $1,586, MS-70, October 2014; $1,528, MS-70, October 2014; $1,763, MS-70, July 2014; $799, MS-69, October 2014				
$25 MCMLXXXVII (1987)	131,255	$1,300	$1,450	$2,000
Auctions: No auction records available.				
$25 MCMLXXXVII (1987)P, Proof	143,398	$800	$840	$2,000
Auctions: $1,116, PF-70DCam, September 2014				

Note: MS values are for uncertified Mint State coins of average quality, in their complete original U.S. Mint packaging. PF values are for uncertified Proof coins of average quality, in their complete original U.S. Mint packaging.

	Mintage	MS / PF	MS-69 / PF-69	MS-70 / PF-70
$25 MCMLXXXVIII (1988)	45,000	$1,950	$2,300	$5,500
Auctions: $1,175, MS-65, November 2014; $1,170, MS-65, August 2014				
$25 MCMLXXXVIII (1988)P, Proof	76,528	$800	$970	$1,600
Auctions: No auction records available.				
$25 MCMLXXXIX (1989)	44,829	$2,100	$2,600	$4,500
Auctions: $1,998, MS-69, July 2014; $1,410, MS-64, October 2014; $611, MS-64, October 2014				
$25 MCMLXXXIX (1989)P, Proof	44,798	$800	$1,020	$3,000
Auctions: No auction records available.				
$25 MCMXC (1990)	31,000	$2,450	$2,800	$5,500
Auctions: No auction records available.				
$25 MCMXC (1990)P, Proof	51,636	$750	$1,015	$2,500
Auctions: No auction records available.				
$25 MCMXCI (1991) ‡	24,100	$3,475	$3,850	$5,000
Auctions: $3,525, MS-69, July 2014				
$25 MCMXCI (1991)P, Proof	53,125	$750	$1,015	$1,200
Auctions: $823, PF-70DCam, September 2014				
$25 1992	54,404	$1,500	$1,800	$3,900
Auctions: $3,966, MS-70, July 2014; $1,000, MS-67, October 2014				
$25 1992P, Proof	40,976	$750	$945	$1,300
Auctions: $999, PF-70DCam, September 2014				
$25 1993	73,324	$1,000	$1,300	$3,500
Auctions: $3,055, MS-70, August 2014; $3,819, MS-70, July 2014; $3,290, MS-70, July 2014; $881, MS-69, July 2014				
$25 1993P, Proof	43,819	$750	$1,045	—
Auctions: No auction records available.				
$25 1994	62,400	$1,000	$1,150	$2,000
Auctions: $4,259, MS-70, July 2014; $881, MS-69, July 2014				
$25 1994W, Proof	44,584	$750	$800	$1,250
Auctions: $823, PF-70DCam, September 2014				
$25 1995	53,474	$1,750	$2,000	$5,000
Auctions: $5,875, MS-70, July 2014; $1,410, MS-69, July 2014				
$25 1995W, Proof	45,388	$750	$800	$1,200
Auctions: $676, PF-70DCam, November 2014; $823, PF-70DCam, September 2014; $764, PF-70DCam, September 2014				
$25 1996	39,287	$1,700	$1,850	$4,500
Auctions: $1,645, MS-69, July 2014				
$25 1996W, Proof	35,058	$750	$800	$1,100
Auctions: No auction records available.				
$25 1997	79,605	$1,000	$1,150	$3,300
Auctions: $823, MS-69, July 2014				
$25 1997W, Proof	26,344	$750	$800	$1,200
Auctions: No auction records available.				
$25 1998	169,029	$700	$750	$1,250
Auctions: No auction records available.				
$25 1998W, Proof	25,374	$750	$800	$1,400
Auctions: $823, PF-70DCam, September 2014				
$25 1999	263,013	$1,000	$1,450	$1,700
Auctions: $646, MS-69, November 2014				
$25 1999W, Proof	30,427	$750	$800	$1,100
Auctions: No auction records available.				

Note: MS values are for uncertified Mint State coins of average quality, in their complete original U.S. Mint packaging. PF values are for uncertified Proof coins of average quality, in their complete original U.S. Mint packaging. ‡ Ranked in the *100 Greatest U.S. Modern Coins.*

	Mintage	MS / PF	MS-69 / PF-69	MS-70 / PF-70
$25 2000	79,287	$950	$1,450	$1,700
	Auctions: No auction records available.			
$25 2000W, Proof	32,028	$750	$800	$1,100
	Auctions: $793, PF-70DCam, September 2014			
$25 2001	48,047	$1,500	$1,600	$1,800
	Auctions: $1,763, MS-69, July 2014; $1,410, MS-69, July 2014			
$25 2001W, Proof	23,240	$750	$800	$1,200
	Auctions: $705, PF-70DCam, November 2014			
$25 2002	70,027	$975	$1,025	$1,100
	Auctions: $764, MS-70, November 2014; $1,645, MS-70, August 2014			
$25 2002W, Proof	26,646	$750	$795	$1,200
	Auctions: No auction records available.			
$25 2003	79,029	$700	$750	$900
	Auctions: $705, MS-70, August 2014; $646, MS-69, November 2014			
$25 2003W, Proof	28,270	$750	$795	$1,200
	Auctions: $764, PF-70DCam, November 2014; $793, PF-70DCam, September 2014			
$25 2004	98,040	$700	$725	$900
	Auctions: $764, MS-70, August 2014			
$25 2004W, Proof	27,330	$750	$795	$1,100
	Auctions: No auction records available.			
$25 2005	80,023	$700	$725	$900
	Auctions: No auction records available.			
$25 2005W, Proof	34,311	$750	$795	$1,100
	Auctions: $705, PF-70DCam, September 2014			
$25 2006	66,005	$700	$750	$900
	Auctions: $705, MS-70, October 2014; $764, MS-70, July 2014; $734, MS-69, October 2014			
$25 2006W, Burnished	15,164	$1,100	$1,150	$1,350
	Auctions: $881, MS-70, November 2014; $729, MS-70, November 2014; $646, MS-69, November 2014; $911, MS-69, August 2014			
$25 2006W, Proof	34,322	$750	$795	$950
	Auctions: No auction records available.			
$25 2007	47,002	$1,000	$1,050	$1,150
	Auctions: No auction records available.			
$25 2007W, Burnished	11,455	$1,100	$1,150	$1,400
	Auctions: $776, MS-70, November 2014; $764, MS-69, November 2014			
$25 2007W, Proof	44,025	$750	$820	$900
	Auctions: No auction records available.			
$25 2008	61,000	$700	$750	$870
	Auctions: No auction records available.			
$25 2008W, Burnished	15,682	$1,550	$1,600	$1,800
	Auctions: No auction records available.			
$25 2008W, Proof	22,602	$750	$850	$1,200
	Auctions: No auction records available.			
$25 2009	110,000	$700	$725	$870
	Auctions: No auction records available.			
$25 2010	81,000	$700	$725	$950
	Auctions: $764, MS-70, July 2014; $752, MS-70, July 2014; $720, MS-70, July 2014; $658, MS-70, July 2014			
$25 2010W, Proof	44,527	$750	$795	$950
	Auctions: No auction records available.			

Note: MS values are for uncertified Mint State coins of average quality, in their complete original U.S. Mint packaging. PF values are for uncertified Proof coins of average quality, in their complete original U.S. Mint packaging.

	Mintage	MS	MS-69	MS-70
		PF	PF-69	PF-70
$25 2011	70,000	$700	$725	$870
	Auctions: No auction records available.			
$25 2011W, Proof	26,781	$750	$795	$850
	Auctions: No auction records available.			
$25 2012	71,000	$700	$725	$870
	Auctions: No auction records available.			
$25 2012W, Proof	12,809	$750	$795	$950
	Auctions: $729, PF-70DCam, October 2014			
$25 2013	58,000	$700	$725	$870
	Auctions: No auction records available.			
$25 2013W, Proof	12,570	$750	$795	$1,050
	Auctions: No auction records available.			
$25 2014	46,000	$700	$725	$870
	Auctions: No auction records available.			
$25 2014W, Proof	14,663	$750	$815	$840
	Auctions: No auction records available.			
$25 2015W, Proof				
	Auctions: No auction records available.			

Note: MS values are for uncertified Mint State coins of average quality, in their complete original U.S. Mint packaging. PF values are for uncertified Proof coins of average quality, in their complete original U.S. Mint packaging.

$50 1-OUNCE AMERICAN GOLD EAGLES

	Mintage	MS	MS-69	MS-70
		PF	PF-69	PF-70
$50 MCMLXXXVI (1986)	1,362,650	$1,400	$1,500	$4,500
	Auctions: No auction records available.			
$50 MCMLXXXVI (1986)W, Proof	446,290	$1,550	$1,635	$2,350
	Auctions: $1,645, PF-70DCam, October 2014; $1,763, PF-70DCam, September 2014; $2,174, PF-70DCam, July 2014			
$50 MCMLXXXVII (1987)	1,045,500	$1,400	$1,500	$4,500
	Auctions: $2,115, MS-70, August 2014; $1,351, MS-68, August 2014			
$50 MCMLXXXVII (1987)W, Proof	147,498	$1,550	$1,610	$2,200
	Auctions: $1,645, PF-70DCam, September 2014			
$50 MCMLXXXVIII (1988)	465,000	$1,400	$1,500	$11,000
	Auctions: No auction records available.			
$50 MCMLXXXVIII (1988)W, Proof	87,133	$1,550	$1,750	$2,000
	Auctions: $1,550, PF-70DCam, November 2014; $1,645, PF-70DCam, August 2014			
$50 MCMLXXXIX (1989)	415,790	$1,400	$1,450	—
	Auctions: No auction records available.			
$50 MCMLXXXIX (1989)W, Proof	54,570	$1,550	$1,735	$2,000
	Auctions: $1,704, PF-70DCam, August 2014			

Note: MS values are for uncertified Mint State coins of average quality, in their complete original U.S. Mint packaging. PF values are for uncertified Proof coins of average quality, in their complete original U.S. Mint packaging.

	Mintage	MS PF	MS-69 PF-69	MS-70 PF-70
$50 MCMXC (1990)	373,210	$1,400	$1,450	$5,500
Auctions: No auction records available.				
$50 MCMXC (1990)W, Proof	62,401	$1,550	$1,735	$2,000
Auctions: $1,763, PF-70DCam, September 2014; $1,528, PF-70DCam, September 2014; $1,645, PF-70DCam, August 2014				
$50 MCMXCI (1991)	243,100	$1,400	$1,450	$5,500
Auctions: $1,410, MS-69, October 2014				
$50 MCMXCI (1991)W, Proof	50,411	$1,550	$1,735	$2,600
Auctions: $2,703, PF-70DCam, September 2014; $3,055, PF-70DCam, July 2014				
$50 1992	275,000	$1,400	$1,450	$2,100
Auctions: No auction records available.				
$50 1992W, Proof	44,826	$1,550	$1,735	$3,000
Auctions: $2,115, PF-70DCam, September 2014				
$50 1993	480,192	$1,400	$1,450	$2,600
Auctions: No auction records available.				
$50 1993W, Proof	34,369	$1,550	$1,785	$3,250
Auctions: $2,056, PF-70DCam, July 2014				
$50 1994	221,633	$1,400	$1,450	$6,500
Auctions: No auction records available.				
$50 1994W, Proof	46,674	$1,550	$1,685	$2,100
Auctions: $1,704, PF-70DCam, August 2014				
$50 1995	200,636	$1,400	$1,425	—
Auctions: No auction records available.				
$50 1995W, Proof	46,368	$1,550	$1,685	$2,100
Auctions: $1,775, PF-70DCam, August 2014				
$50 1996	189,148	$1,400	$1,425	—
Auctions: No auction records available.				
$50 1996W, Proof	36,153	$1,550	$1,735	$2,200
Auctions: $1,763, PF-70DCam, September 2014; $1,998, PF-70DCam, July 2014				
$50 1997	664,508	$1,400	$1,450	$3,495
Auctions: No auction records available.				
$50 1997W, Proof	32,999	$1,550	$1,735	$2,250
Auctions: $1,764, PF-70DCam, September 2014; $1,763, PF-70DCam, August 2014				
$50 1998	1,468,530	$1,400	$1,450	$2,300
Auctions: No auction records available.				
$50 1998W, Proof	25,886	$1,550	$1,735	$3,250
Auctions: $2,233, PF-70DCam, September 2014; $1,763, PF-70DCam, August 2014				
$50 1999	1,505,026	$1,400	$1,450	$2,300
Auctions: No auction records available.				
$50 1999W, Proof	31,427	$1,550	$1,685	$2,800
Auctions: $1,998, PF-70DCam, August 2014				
$50 2000	433,319	$1,400	$1,425	$2,500
Auctions: No auction records available.				
$50 2000W, Proof	33,007	$1,550	$1,685	$2,350
Auctions: $1,880, PF-70DCam, August 2014; $1,704, PF-70DCam, August 2014				
$50 2001	143,605	$1,400	$1,450	$3,000
Auctions: $1,351, MS-69, October 2014				
$50 2001W, Proof ‡	24,555	$1,550	$1,800	$4,000
Auctions: $2,174, PF-70DCam, July 2014				

Note: MS values are for uncertified Mint State coins of average quality, in their complete original U.S. Mint packaging. PF values are for uncertified Proof coins of average quality, in their complete original U.S. Mint packaging. ‡ Ranked in the *100 Greatest U.S. Modern Coins*.

	Mintage	MS / PF	MS-69 / PF-69	MS-70 / PF-70
$50 2002	222,029	$1,400	$1,450	$2,800
	Auctions: No auction records available.			
$50 2002W, Proof	27,499	$1,550	$1,635	$2,000
	Auctions: $1,645, PF-70DCam, November 2014; $1,763, PF-70DCam, October 2014; $1,528, PF-70DCam, August 2014			
$50 2003	416,032	$1,400	$1,450	$2,300
	Auctions: No auction records available.			
$50 2003W, Proof	28,344	$1,550	$1,635	$2,000
	Auctions: $1,645, PF-70DCam, August 2014			
$50 2004	417,019	$1,400	$1,450	$2,300
	Auctions: $1,528, MS-70, November 2014			
$50 2004W, Proof	28,215	$1,550	$1,635	$2,000
	Auctions: $1,704, PF-70DCam, August 2014; $1,880, PF-70DCam, July 2014			
$50 2005	356,555	$1,400	$1,450	$1,800
	Auctions: $1,528, MS-70, September 2014			
$50 2005W, Proof	35,246	$1,550	$1,610	$2,150
	Auctions: $1,645, PF-70DCam, August 2014			
$50 2006	237,510	$1,400	$1,450	$1,800
	Auctions: $1,410, MS-70, October 2014; $1,293, MS-69, October 2014			
$50 2006W, Burnished	45,053	$1,625	$1,675	$1,900
	Auctions: $1,410, MS-70, November 2014			
$50 2006W, Proof	47,092	$1,550	$1,610	$1,800
	Auctions: $1,645, PF-70DCam, November 2014; $1,663, PF-70DCam, July 2014			
$50 2006W, Reverse Proof ‡ (a)	9,996	$2,500	$2,750	$3,650
	Auctions: $2,820, PF-70, July 2014			
$50 2007	140,016	$1,400	$1,450	$1,900
	Auctions: No auction records available.			
$50 2007W, Burnished	18,066	$1,700	$1,750	$2,000
	Auctions: No auction records available.			
$50 2007W, Proof	51,810	$1,550	$1,610	$1,800
	Auctions: $1,528, PF-70DCam, September 2014			
$50 2008	710,000	$1,400	$1,450	$1,900
	Auctions: No auction records available.			
$50 2008W, Burnished	11,908	$2,460	$2,520	$2,800
	Auctions: $1,763, MS-70, August 2014			
$50 2008W, Proof	30,237	$1,550	$1,585	$1,900
	Auctions: $1,704, PF-70DCam, August 2014			
$50 2009	1,493,000	$1,400	$1,450	$1,600
	Auctions: $1,469, MS-70, October 2014; $1,998, MS-70, July 2014			
$50 2010	1,125,000	$1,400	$1,450	$1,600
	Auctions: $1,351, MS-70, July 2014			
$50 2010W, Proof	59,480	$1,550	$1,585	$1,700
	Auctions: $1,293, PF-70DCam, November 2014; $1,469, PF-70DCam, September 2014			
$50 2011	857,000	$1,400	$1,450	$1,550
	Auctions: No auction records available.			
$50 2011W, Burnished	8,729	$2,500	$2,600	$2,800
	Auctions: $1,528, MS-70, October 2014; $1,469, MS-69, August 2014; $1,410, MS-69, August 2014			
$50 2011W, Proof	48,306	$1,550	$1,585	$1,800
	Auctions: No auction records available.			

Note: MS values are for uncertified Mint State coins of average quality, in their complete original U.S. Mint packaging. PF values are for uncertified Proof coins of average quality, in their complete original U.S. Mint packaging. ‡ Ranked in the *100 Greatest U.S. Modern Coins*. **a.** The 2006-W Reverse Proof coins were issued to mark the 20th anniversary of the Bullion Coinage Program. They have brilliant devices, and their background fields are frosted (rather than the typical Proof format of frosted devices and mirror-like backgrounds).

	Mintage	MS / PF	MS-69 / PF-69	MS-70 / PF-70
$50 2012	667,000	$1,400	$1,450	$1,600
	Auctions: No auction records available.			
$50 2012W, Burnished	5,829	$2,825	$3,000	$3,300
	Auctions: $1,939, MS-70, November 2014			
$50 2012W, Proof	23,630	$1,550	$1,585	$1,800
	Auctions: $1,410, PF-70DCam, November 2014; $1,880, PF-70DCam, August 2014; $1,528, PF-70DCam, August 2014			
$50 2013	743,500	$1,400	$1,450	$1,600
	Auctions: $1,293, MS-70, October 2014			
$50 2013W, Burnished	7,293	$1,650	$1,700	$2,200
	Auctions: No auction records available.			
$50 2013W, Proof	24,753	$1,550	$1,585	$1,800
	Auctions: $1,410, PF-70, November 2014; $1,351, PF-70, November 2014			
$50 2014	415,000	$1,400	$1,425	$1,550
	Auctions: No auction records available.			
$50 2014W, Burnished		$1,650	$1,675	$1,850
	Auctions: No auction records available.			
$50 2014W, Proof	28,673	$1,550	$1,700	$2,100
	Auctions: No auction records available.			
$50 2015W, Proof				
	Auctions: No auction records available.			

Note: MS values are for uncertified Mint State coins of average quality, in their complete original U.S. Mint packaging. PF values are for uncertified Proof coins of average quality, in their complete original U.S. Mint packaging.

AMERICAN GOLD EAGLE PROOF COIN SETS

	PF	PF-69	PF-70
1987 Gold Set. $50, $25	$2,400	$2,650	$4,200
	Auctions: No auction records available.		
1988 Gold Set. $50, $25, $10, $5	$3,000	$3,050	$5,350
	Auctions: No auction records available.		
1989 Gold Set. $50, $25, $10, $5	$3,000	$3,270	$4,900
	Auctions: No auction records available.		
1990 Gold Set. $50, $25, $10, $5	$3,000	$3,500	$5,500
	Auctions: No auction records available.		
1991 Gold Set. $50, $25, $10, $5	$3,000	$3,350	$4,850
	Auctions: No auction records available.		
1992 Gold Set. $50, $25, $10, $5	$3,000	$3,350	$4,350
	Auctions: No auction records available.		
1993 Gold Set. $50, $25, $10, $5	$3,000	$3,350	$5,050
	Auctions: No auction records available.		
1993 Bicentennial Gold Set. $25, $10, $5, Silver Eagle, and medal (a)	$1,650	$1,750	—
	Auctions: No auction records available.		
1994 Gold Set. $50, $25, $10, $5	$3,000	$3,100	$4,450
	Auctions: No auction records available.		
1995 Gold Set. $50, $25, $10, $5	$3,000	$3,100	$4,400
	Auctions: No auction records available.		
1995 Anniversary Gold Set. $50, $25, $10, $5, and Silver Eagle (b)	$7,750	$8,000	—
	Auctions: No auction records available.		

Note: PF values are for uncertified Proof sets of average quality, in their complete original U.S. Mint packaging. **a.** The 1993 set was issued to commemorate the bicentennial of the first coins struck by the U.S. Mint in Philadelphia. **b.** The 1995 set marked the 10th anniversary of the passage of the Liberty Coin Act, which authorized the nation's new bullion coinage program.

	PF	PF-69	PF-70
1996 Gold Set. $50, $25, $10, $5	$3,000	$3,150	$4,450
Auctions: No auction records available.			
1997 Gold Set. $50, $25, $10, $5	$3,000	$3,150	$4,950
Auctions: No auction records available.			
1997 Impressions of Liberty Set. $100 platinum, $50 gold, Silver Eagle (c)	$3,500	$3,600	$6,000
Auctions: No auction records available.			
1998 Gold Set. $50, $25, $10, $5	$3,000	$3,250	$5,650
Auctions: No auction records available.			
1999 Gold Set. $50, $25, $10, $5	$3,000	$3,100	$5,300
Auctions: No auction records available.			
2000 Gold Set. $50, $25, $10, $5	$3,000	$3,100	$4,550
Auctions: No auction records available.			
2001 Gold Set. $50, $25, $10, $5	$3,000	$3,250	$6,325
Auctions: No auction records available.			
2002 Gold Set. $50, $25, $10, $5	$3,000	$3,050	$4,175
Auctions: No auction records available.			
2003 Gold Set. $50, $25, $10, $5	$3,000	$3,050	$4,175
Auctions: No auction records available.			
2004 Gold Set. $50, $25, $10, $5	$3,000	$3,100	$4,650
Auctions: No auction records available.			
2005 Gold Set. $50, $25, $10, $5	$3,000	$3,050	$4,150
Auctions: No auction records available.			
2006 Gold Set. $50, $25, $10, $5	$3,000	$3,050	$3,550
Auctions: No auction records available.			
2007 Gold Set. $50, $25, $10, $5	$3,000	$3,600	$5,100
Auctions: No auction records available.			
2008 Gold Set. $50, $25, $10, $5	$3,000	$3,250	$3,950
Auctions: No auction records available.			
2010 Gold Set. $50, $25, $10, $5 (d)	$3,000	$3,100	$3,675
Auctions: No auction records available.			
2011 Gold Set. $50, $25, $10, $5	$3,000	$3,100	$3,450
Auctions: No auction records available.			
2012 Gold Set. $50, $25, $10, $5	$3,000	$3,075	$3,550
Auctions: No auction records available.			
2013 Gold Set. $50, $25, $10, $5	$3,000	$3,075	$3,600
Auctions: No auction records available.			
2014 Gold Set. $50, $25, $10, $5	$3,000	$3,100	$3,475
Auctions: No auction records available.			
2015 Gold Set. $50, $25, $10, $5			
Auctions: No auction records available.			

Note: PF values are for uncertified Proof sets of average quality, in their complete original U.S. Mint packaging. **c.** The Impressions of Liberty set was issued in the first year that platinum coins were added to the Mint's bullion offerings. **d.** The U.S. Mint did not issue a 2009 gold set.

2006 American Gold Eagle 20th-Anniversary Coin Sets

	Uncertified	69	70
2006W $50 Gold Set. Uncirculated, Proof, and Reverse Proof	$6,000	$6,250	$7,650
Auctions: No auction records available.			
2006W 1-oz. Gold- and Silver-Dollar Set. Uncirculated	$1,800	$1,900	$2,100
Auctions: No auction records available.			

Note: Uncertified values are for uncertified sets of average quality, in their complete original U.S. Mint packaging.

AMERICAN BUFFALO .9999 FINE GOLD BULLION COINS
(2006 TO DATE)

Designer: *James Earle Fraser.* **Weight:** *$5 1/10 oz.—3.393 grams; $10 1/4 oz.—8.483 grams; $25 1/2 oz.—16.966 grams; $50 1 oz.—31.108 grams.* **Composition:** *.9999 gold.* **Diameter:** *$5 1/10 oz.—16.5 mm; $10 1/4 oz.—22 mm; $25 1/2 oz.—27 mm; $50 1 oz.—32.7 mm.* **Edge:** *Reeded.* **Mint:** *West Point.*

Regular Finish
Obverse design common to all denominations.

Burnished Finish

Proof Finish

Reverse Proof Finish

Mintmark location is on the obverse, behind the neck.

History. American Buffalo gold bullion coins, authorized by Congress in 2005 and produced since 2006, are the first 24-karat (.9999 fine) gold coins made by the U.S. Mint. They are coined, by mandate, of gold derived from newly mined sources in America. They feature an adaptation of James Earle Fraser's iconic Indian Head / Buffalo design, first used on circulating five-cent pieces of 1913 to 1938.

Only 1-ounce ($50 face value) coins were struck in the American Buffalo program's first two years, 2006 and 2007. For 2008, the Mint expanded the coinage to include fractional pieces of 1/2 ounce ($25), 1/4 ounce ($10), and 1/10-ounce ($5), in various finishes, individually and in sets.

The coins are legal tender, with weight, content, and purity guaranteed by the federal government. Investors can include them in some individual retirement accounts. Proofs and Burnished (*Uncirculated,* in the Mint's wording) pieces undergo special production processes, similar to the American Eagle gold-bullion coinage, and can be purchased directly from the Mint. As with other products in the Mint's bullion program, regular bullion-strike pieces are distributed through a network of authorized distributors.

All American Buffalo gold bullion coins (Proofs, Burnished, and regular bullion pieces) are struck at the U.S. Mint's West Point facility.

Striking and Sharpness. Striking is generally sharp.

Availability. American Buffalo .9999 fine gold bullion coins are a popular way to buy and sell 24-karat gold. The coins are readily available in the numismatic marketplace as well as from participating banks, investment firms, and other non-numismatic channels.

MS-60 to 70 (Mint State). *Obverse and reverse:* At MS-60, some abrasion and contact marks are evident on the higher design areas and the open areas of the design. Luster may be dull or lifeless at MS-60 to 62, but there should be deep frost at MS-63 and better, particularly in the lower-relief areas. At MS-65 and above, the luster should be full and rich. Contact marks and abrasion are less and less evident at higher grades. These guidelines are more academic than practical, as these coins are not intended for circulation, and nearly all are in high Mint State grades, as struck.

PF-60 to 70 (Proof). *Obverse and reverse:* Proofs that are extensively cleaned and have many hairlines are lower level, such as PF-60 to 62. Those with fewer hairlines or flaws are deemed PF-63 to 65. (These exist more in theory than actuality, as nearly all Proof American Buffalo gold coins have been maintained in their original high condition by collectors and investors.) Given the quality of modern U.S. Mint products, even PF-66 and 67 are unusually low levels for these Proofs.

AMERICAN BUFFALO .9999 FINE GOLD BULLION COINS

$5 1/10-oz. $10 1/4-oz. $25 1/2-oz.

$50 1-oz.

	Mintage	MS	MS-69	MS-70
		PF	PF-69	PF-70
$5 2008W, Burnished	17,429	$500	$525	$600
	Auctions: $482, MS-70, November 2014; $447, MS-70, November 2014; $588, MS-70, September 2014; $683, MS-70, August 2013			
$5 2008W, Proof	18,884	$600	$625	$700
	Auctions: $8,225, PF-70DCam, July 2014; $752, PF-70DCam, August 2013; $4,847, PF-69DCam, October 2014			
$10 2008W, Burnished ‡	9,949	$1,275	$1,350	$1,450
	Auctions: $999, MS-70, November 2014; $964, MS-70, November 2014; $870, MS-70, November 2014; $1,469, MS-70, February 2013			
$10 2008W, Proof	13,125	$1,500	$1,550	$1,700
	Auctions: $1,704, PF-70DCam, February 2013			
$25 2008W, Burnished	16,908	$1,300	$1,350	$1,650
	Auctions: $1,528, MS-70, February 2013			
$25 2008W, Proof	12,169	$1,650	$1,700	$1,800
	Auctions: $1,293, PF-70DCam, November 2014; $2,115, PF-70DCam, May 2013			
$50 2006	337,012	$1,350	$1,400	$1,550
	Auctions: $1,763, MS-70, April 2013			
$50 2006W, Proof	246,267	$1,450	$1,500	$1,700
	Auctions: $1,528, PF-70DCam, December 2014; $1,586, PF-70DCam, October 2014; $1,498, PF-70DCam, October 2014			

Note: MS values are for uncertified Mint State coins of average quality, in their complete original U.S. Mint packaging. PF values are for uncertified Proof coins of average quality, in their complete original U.S. Mint packaging. ‡ Ranked in the *100 Greatest U.S. Modern Coins.*

	Mintage	MS / PF	MS-69 / PF-69	MS-70 / PF-70
$50 2007	136,503	$1,350	$1,400	$1,550
	Auctions: $1,293, MS-70, October 2014; $1,410, MS-70, July 2014; $1,351, MS-69, October 2014; $1,351, MS-66, September 2014			
$50 2007W, Proof	58,998	$1,450	$1,500	$1,700
	Auctions: $1,469, PF-70DCam, September 2014; $1,416, PF-70DCam, August 2014; $2,056, PF-70DCam, May 2013			
$50 2008	189,500	$1,350	$1,400	$1,550
	Auctions: $1,645, MS-70, November 2014; $1,470, MS-70, July 2014; $1,410, MS-70, July 2014; $1,998, MS-70, September 2013			
$50 2008W, Burnished	9,074	$3,000	$3,050	$3,500
	Auctions: $4,994, MS-70, November 2014; $4,406, MS-70, November 2014; $5,581, MS-70, September 2014			
$50 2008W, Proof ‡	18,863	$3,000	$3,150	$3,500
	Auctions: $5,288, PF-70DCam, November 2014; $4,994, PF-70DCam, April 2014; $2,350, PF-69DCam, October 2014			
$50 2009	200,000	$1,350	$1,400	$1,550
	Auctions: $1,763, MS-70, May 2013			
$50 2009W, Proof	49,306	$1,450	$1,500	$1,700
	Auctions: $1,477, PF-70DCam, August 2014; $1,880, PF-70DCam, September 2013			
$50 2010	209,000	$1,350	$1,400	$1,550
	Auctions: $1,645, MS-70, November 2014; $1,763, MS-70, May 2013			
$50 2010W, Proof	49,263	$1,450	$1,500	$1,700
	Auctions: $1,469, PF-70DCam, August 2014; $1,763, PF-69DCam, December 2013			
$50 2011	174,500	$1,350	$1,400	$1,550
	Auctions: $1,410, MS-70, November 2014; $1,293, MS-70, October 2014; $1,528, MS-70, June 2013			
$50 2011W, Proof	28,683	$1,450	$1,550	$1,750
	Auctions: $1,586, PF-70DCam, August 2014; $1,528, PF-70DCam, August 2014; $2,115, PF-70DCam, May 2013			
$50 2012	132,000	$1,350	$1,400	$1,550
	Auctions: $2,056, MS-70, May 2013			
$50 2012W, Proof	19,715	$1,450	$1,600	$2,200
	Auctions: $1,998, PF-70DCam, October 2014; $2,468, PF-70DCam, April 2013			
$50 2013		$1,350	$1,400	$1,500
	Auctions: $1,998, MS-70, February 2013			
$50 2013W, Proof	18,594	$1,450	$1,600	$2,100
	Auctions: $2,350, PF-70, January 2014			
$50 2013W, Reverse Proof	47,836	$1,700	$1,750	$2,000
	Auctions: No auctions records available.			
$50 2014		$1,350	$1,400	$1,500
	Auctions: No auctions records available.			
$50 2014W, Proof	20,557	$1,590	$1,650	$1,850
	Auctions: No auctions records available.			
$50 2015W, Proof				
	Auctions: No auctions records available.			

Note: MS values are for uncertified Mint State coins of average quality, in their complete original U.S. Mint packaging. PF values are for uncertified Proof coins of average quality, in their complete original U.S. Mint packaging. ‡ Ranked in the *100 Greatest U.S. Modern Coins.*

AMERICAN BUFFALO .9999 FINE GOLD BULLION COIN SETS

	Uncertified	MS-69 / PF-69	MS-70 / PF-70
2008W Four-coin set ($5, $10, $25, $50), Proof	$7,000	$7,400	$8,100
	Auctions: No auction records available.		
2008W Four-coin set ($5, $10, $25, $50), Burnished	$6,500	$6,600	$7,000
	Auctions: No auction records available.		
2008W Double Prosperity set (Unc. $25 American Buffalo gold and $25 American Gold Eagle coins)	$2,850	$2,900	$3,000
	Auctions: No auction records available.		

Note: Uncertified values are for uncertified sets of average quality, in their complete original U.S. Mint packaging.

FIRST SPOUSE $10 GOLD BULLION COINS
(2007 TO DATE)

Designers: *Martha Washington—Joseph Menna (obverse), Susan Gamble (reverse); Abigail Adams—Joseph Menna (obverse), Thomas Cleveland (reverse); Thomas Jefferson's Liberty—Robert Scot / Phebe Hemphill (obverse), Charles Vickers (reverse); Dolley Madison—Don Everhart (obverse), Joel Iskowitz (reverse); Elizabeth Monroe—Joel Iskowitz (obverse), Donna Weaver (reverse); Louisa Adams—Susan Gamble (obverse), Donna Weaver (reverse); Andrew Jackson's Liberty—John Reich (obverse), Justin Kunz (reverse); Martin Van Buren's Liberty—Christian Gobrecht (obverse), Thomas Cleveland (reverse); Anna Harrison—Donna Weaver (obverse), Thomas Cleveland (reverse); Letitia Tyler—Phebe Hemphill (obverse), Susan Gamble (reverse); Julia Tyler—Joel Iskowitz; Sarah Polk—Phebe Hemphill; Margaret Taylor—Phebe Hemphill (obverse), Mary Beth Zeitz (reverse); Abigail Fillmore—Phebe Hemphill (obverse), Susan Gamble (reverse); Jane Pierce—Donna Weaver; James Buchanan's Liberty—Christian Gobrecht (obverse), David Westwood (reverse); Mary Todd Lincoln—Phebe Hemphill (obverse), Joel Iskowitz (reverse); Alice Paul—Susan Gamble (obverse), Phebe Hemphill (reverse); Frances Cleveland, Type 1—Joel Iskowitz (obverse), Barbara Fox (reverse); Caroline Harrison—Frank Morris (obverse), Donna Weaver (reverse); Frances Cleveland, Type 2—Barbara Fox (obverse), Joseph Menna (reverse); Ida McKinley—Susan Gamble (obverse), Donna Weaver (reverse); Edith Roosevelt—Joel Iskowitz (obverse), Chris Costello (reverse); Helen Taft—William C. Burgard (obverse), Richard Masters (reverse); Ellen Wilson—Frank Morris (obverse), Don Everhart (reverse); Edith Wilson—David Westwood (obverse), Joseph Menna (reverse); Florence Harding—Thomas Cleveland (obverse and reverse); Grace Coolidge—Joel Iskowitz (obverse), Frank Morris (reverse); Lou Hoover—Susan Gamble (obverse), Richard Masters (reverse); Eleanor Roosevelt—Chris Costello (obverse and reverse).* **Weight:** *8.483 grams.* **Composition:** *.9999 gold.* **Diameter:** *26.5 mm.* **Edge:** *Reeded.* **Mint:** *West Point.*

Regular Finish
The first coin in the series, featuring Martha Washington.

Mintmark location is on the obverse, below the date.

Proof Finish

History. The U.S. Mint's First Spouse bullion coins are struck in .9999 fine (24-karat) gold. Each weighs one-half ounce and bears a face value of $10. The coins honor the nation's first spouses on the same schedule as the Mint's Presidential dollars program. Each features a portrait on the obverse, and on the reverse a unique design symbolic of the spouse's life and work. In cases where a president held office widowed or unmarried, the coin bears "an obverse image emblematic of Liberty as depicted on a circulating coin of that era and a reverse image emblematic of themes of that president's life." All First Spouse gold bullion coins (Proofs and regular bullion pieces) are struck at the U.S. Mint's West Point facility.

Note that the Mint does not release bullion mintage data on a regular basis; the numbers given herein reflect the most recently available official data.

Striking and Sharpness. Striking is generally sharp.

Availability. These coins are readily available in the numismatic marketplace. They can be purchased by the public, in both bullion-strike and Proof formats, directly from the U.S. Mint. Sales of recent issues have been low, leading to some issues being ranked among the 100 Greatest U.S. Modern Coins.

MS-60 to 70 (Mint State). *Obverse and Reverse:* At MS-60, some abrasion and contact marks are evident on the higher design areas and the open areas of the design. Luster may be dull or lifeless at MS-60 to 62, but there should be deep frost at MS-63 and better, particularly in the lower-relief areas. At MS-65 and above, the luster should be full and rich. Contact marks and abrasion are less and less evident at higher grades. These guidelines are more academic than practical, as these coins are not intended for circulation, and nearly all are in high Mint State grades, as struck.

PF-60 to 70 (Proof). *Obverse and Reverse:* Proofs that are extensively cleaned and have many hairlines are lower level, such as PF-60 to 62. Those with fewer hairlines or flaws are deemed PF-63 to 65. (These exist more in theory than actuality, as nearly all Proof First Spouse gold coins have been maintained in their original high condition by collectors and investors.) Given the quality of modern U.S. Mint products, even PF-66 and 67 are unusually low levels for these Proofs.

First Spouse $10 Gold Bullion Coins

Martha Washington   Abigail Adams   Jefferson's Liberty   Dolley Madison

| | Mintage | MS | MS-69 | MS-70 |
		PF	PF-69	PF-70
$10 2007W, M. Washington	17,661	$750	$765	$800
Auctions: $664, MS-70, August 2014				
$10 2007W, M. Washington, Proof	19,167	$750	$765	$800
Auctions: $646, PF-69DCam, October 2014				
$10 2007W, A. Adams	17,142	$750	$765	$800
Auctions: $764, MS-70, September 2014				
$10 2007W, A. Adams, Proof	17,149	$750	$765	$800
Auctions: $611, PF-69DCam, October 2014				
$10 2007W, Jefferson's Liberty	19,823	$750	$765	$800
Auctions: No auction records available.				
$10 2007W, Jefferson's Liberty, Proof	19,815	$750	$765	$800
Auctions: $705, PF-69DCam, October 2014				
$10 2007W, D. Madison	12,340	$750	$765	$800
Auctions: $705, MS-70, July 2014				
$10 2007W, D. Madison, Proof	17,943	$750	$765	$800
Auctions: $635, PF-69DCam, October 2014				

Note: MS values are for uncertified Mint State coins of average quality, in their complete original U.S. Mint packaging. PF values are for uncertified Proof coins of average quality, in their complete original U.S. Mint packaging.

Elizabeth Monroe   Louisa Adams   Jackson's Liberty   Van Buren's Liberty

	Mintage	MS	MS-69	MS-70
		PF	PF-69	PF-70
$10 2008W, E. Monroe	4,462	$850	$860	$1,050
Auctions: No auction records available.				
$10 2008W, E. Monroe, Proof	7,800	$800	$860	$1,300
Auctions: $544, PF-69DCam, November 2014				
$10 2008W, L. Adams	3,885	$850	$870	$1,050
Auctions: No auction records available.				
$10 2008W, L. Adams, Proof	6,581	$800	$860	$1,300
Auctions: $705, PF-70DCam, September 2014; $588, PF-69DCam, November 2014				
$10 2008W, Jackson's Liberty ‡	4,609	$850	$870	$1,050
Auctions: $1,998, MS-70, August 2014				
$10 2008W, Jackson's Liberty, Proof	7,684	$850	$875	$1,400
Auctions: $1,410, PF-70DCam, August 2014				
$10 2008W, Van Buren's Liberty	3,826	$925	$1,020	$1,100
Auctions: No auction records available.				
$10 2008W, Van Buren's Liberty, Proof	6,807	$1,250	$1,270	$1,600
Auctions: $1,305, PF-70DCam, August 2014; $823, PF-69DCam, July 2014				

Note: MS values are for uncertified Mint State coins of average quality, in their complete original U.S. Mint packaging. PF values are for uncertified Proof coins of average quality, in their complete original U.S. Mint packaging. ‡ Ranked in the *100 Greatest U.S. Modern Coins.*

Anna Harrison   Letitia Tyler   Julia Tyler

Sarah Polk   Margaret Taylor

	Mintage	MS	MS-69	MS-70
		PF	PF-69	PF-70
$10 2009W, A. Harrison	3,645	$1,100	$1,270	$1,350
Auctions: No auction records available.				
$10 2009W, A. Harrison, Proof	6,251	$1,000	$1,020	$1,350
Auctions: $881, PF-70DCam, August 2014				
$10 2009W, L. Tyler	3,240	$1,150	$1,270	$1,350
Auctions: No auction records available.				
$10 2009W, L. Tyler, Proof	5,296	$1,200	$1,220	$1,350
Auctions: $1,528, PF-70DCam, August 2014				
$10 2009W, J. Tyler	3,143	$1,150	$1,270	$1,350
Auctions: $1,998, MS-70, August 2014; $1,410, MS-70, August 2014				
$10 2009W, J. Tyler, Proof	4,844	$1,200	$1,220	$1,350
Auctions: $1,116, PF-70DCam, September 2014				
$10 2009W, S. Polk	3,489	$925	$1,020	$1,400
Auctions: No auction records available.				
$10 2009W, S. Polk, Proof	5,151	$800	$820	$1,000
Auctions: $881, PF-70DCam, August 2014; $752, PF-70DCam, August 2014				
$10 2009W, M. Taylor	3,627	$825	$845	$1,000
Auctions: No auction records available.				
$10 2009W, M. Taylor, Proof	4,936	$800	$820	$1,000
Auctions: $823, PF-70DCam, August 2014; $544, PF-69DCam, November 2014				

Note: MS values are for uncertified Mint State coins of average quality, in their complete original U.S. Mint packaging. PF values are for uncertified Proof coins of average quality, in their complete original U.S. Mint packaging.

| Abigail Fillmore | Jane Pierce | Buchanan's Liberty | Mary Lincoln |

	Mintage	MS	MS-69	MS-70
		PF	PF-69	PF-70
$10 2010W, A. Fillmore	3,482	$950	$1,020	$1,100
Auctions: No auction records available.				
$10 2010W, A. Fillmore, Proof	6,130	$900	$925	$1,025
Auctions: $793, PF-70DCam, August 2014				
$10 2010W, J. Pierce	3,338	$850	$870	$950
Auctions: $734, MS-70, August 2014				
$10 2010W, J. Pierce, Proof	4,775	$1,000	$1,020	$1,200
Auctions: No auction records available.				
$10 2010W, Buchanan's Liberty	5,162	$850	$870	$1,100
Auctions: $969, MS-70, August 2014				
$10 2010W, Buchanan's Liberty, Proof	7,110	$900	$950	$1,200
Auctions: $999, PF-70DCam, August 2014				

Note: MS values are for uncertified Mint State coins of average quality, in their complete original U.S. Mint packaging. PF values are for uncertified Proof coins of average quality, in their complete original U.S. Mint packaging.

| | Mintage | MS | MS-69 | MS-70 |
		PF	PF-69	PF-70
$10 2010W, M. Lincoln	3,695	$850	$870	$1,050
	Auctions: $823, MS-70, October 2014			
$10 2010W, M. Lincoln, Proof	6,861	$900	$920	$1,250
	Auctions: No auction records available.			

Note: MS values are for uncertified Mint State coins of average quality, in their complete original U.S. Mint packaging. PF values are for uncertified Proof coins of average quality, in their complete original U.S. Mint packaging.

| Eliza Johnson | Julia Grant | Lucy Hayes | Lucretia Garfield |

| | Mintage | MS | MS-69 | MS-70 |
		PF	PF-69	PF-70
$10 2011W, E. Johnson	2,905	$875	$920	$1,600
	Auctions: No auction records available.			
$10 2011W, E. Johnson, Proof	3,887	$900	$920	$1,150
	Auctions: No auction records available.			
$10 2011W, J. Grant	2,892	$875	$920	$1,150
	Auctions: $940, MS-70, August 2014			
$10 2011W, J. Grant, Proof	3,943	$900	$920	$1,100
	Auctions: No auction records available.			
$10 2011W, L. Hayes	2,196	$1,200	$1,420	$1,800
	Auctions: $1,822, MS-70, August 2014			
$10 2011W, L. Hayes, Proof	3,868	$900	$920	$1,300
	Auctions: No auction records available.			
$10 2011W, L. Garfield	2,168	$1,200	$1,520	$2,500
	Auctions: No auction records available.			
$10 2011W, L. Garfield, Proof	3,653	$900	$920	$1,200
	Auctions: $823, PF-70DCam, August 2014			

Note: MS values are for uncertified Mint State coins of average quality, in their complete original U.S. Mint packaging. PF values are for uncertified Proof coins of average quality, in their complete original U.S. Mint packaging.

| Alice Paul | Frances Cleveland (Type 1) | Caroline Harrison | Frances Cleveland (Type 2) |

| | Mintage | MS | MS-69 | MS-70 |
		PF	PF-69	PF-70
$10 2012W, Alice Paul	2,798	$800	$815	$850
	Auctions: $881, MS-70, September 2014			
$10 2012W, Alice Paul, Proof	3,505	$875	$900	$1,000
	Auctions: No auction records available.			
$10 2012W, Frances Cleveland, Variety 1	2,454	$800	$815	$850
	Auctions: $705, MS-70, August 2014			
$10 2012W, Frances Cleveland, Variety 1, Proof	3,158	$875	$900	$1,000
	Auctions: No auction records available.			
$10 2012W, Caroline Harrison	2,436	$800	$815	$1,100
	Auctions: $793, MS-70, August 2014; $764, MS-70, August 2014			
$10 2012W, Caroline Harrison, Proof	3,046	$875	$900	$1,000
	Auctions: $1,028, PF-70DCam, August 2014			
$10 2012W, Frances Cleveland, Variety 2	2,425	$800	$815	$850
	Auctions: No auction records available.			
$10 2012W, Frances Cleveland, Variety 2, Proof	3,104	$875	$900	$1,000
	Auctions: No auction records available.			

Note: MS values are for uncertified Mint State coins of average quality, in their complete original U.S. Mint packaging. PF values are for uncertified Proof coins of average quality, in their complete original U.S. Mint packaging.

Ida McKinley   **Edith Roosevelt**   **Helen Taft**

Ellen Wilson   **Edith Wilson**

| | Mintage | MS | MS-69 | MS-70 |
		PF	PF-69	PF-70
$10 2013W, I. McKinley	1,973	$800	$820	$950
	Auctions: No auction records available.			
$10 2013W, I. McKinley, Proof	1,769	$875	$890	$950
	Auctions: No auction records available.			
$10 2013W, E. Roosevelt	1,913	$800	$820	$950
	Auctions: No auction records available.			
$10 2013W, E. Roosevelt, Proof	2,851	$875	$890	$950
	Auctions: No auction records available.			
$10 2013W, H. Taft	1,890	$800	$820	$950
	Auctions: No auction records available.			
$10 2013W, H. Taft, Proof	2,579	$875	$890	$950
	Auctions: No auction records available.			

Note: MS values are for uncertified Mint State coins of average quality, in their complete original U.S. Mint packaging. PF values are for uncertified Proof coins of average quality, in their complete original U.S. Mint packaging.

| | Mintage | MS | MS-69 | MS-70 |
		PF	PF-69	PF-70
$10 2013W, Ellen Wilson	1,880	$800	$820	$950
Auctions: No auction records available.				
$10 2013W, Ellen Wilson, Proof	2,551	$875	$890	$950
Auctions: No auction records available.				
$10 2013W, Edith Wilson	1,881	$800	$820	$950
Auctions: No auction records available.				
$10 2013W, Edith Wilson, Proof	2,452	$875	$890	$950
Auctions: No auction records available.				

Note: MS values are for uncertified Mint State coins of average quality, in their complete original U.S. Mint packaging. PF values are for uncertified Proof coins of average quality, in their complete original U.S. Mint packaging.

| Florence Harding | Grace Coolidge | Lou Hoover | Eleanor Roosevelt |

| | Mintage | MS | MS-69 | MS-70 |
		PF	PF-69	PF-70
$10 2014W, F. Harding	1,489	$800	$815	$950
Auctions: No auction records available.				
$10 2014W, F. Harding, Proof	2,288	$875	$890	$950
Auctions: No auction records available.				
$10 2014W, G. Coolidge	1,426	$800	$815	$950
Auctions: No auction records available.				
$10 2014W, G. Coolidge, Proof	2,196	$875	$890	$950
Auctions: No auction records available.				
$10 2014W, L. Hoover	1,411	$800	$815	$950
Auctions: No auction records available.				
$10 2014W, L. Hoover, Proof	2,025	$875	$890	$950
Auctions: No auction records available.				
$10 2014W, E. Roosevelt	1,590	$800	$815	$950
Auctions: No auction records available.				
$10 2014W, E. Roosevelt, Proof	2,389	$875	$890	$950
Auctions: No auction records available.				

Note: MS values are for uncertified Mint State coins of average quality, in their complete original U.S. Mint packaging. PF values are for uncertified Proof coins of average quality, in their complete original U.S. Mint packaging.

	Mintage	MS	MS-69	MS-70
		PF	PF-69	PF-70
$10 2015W, B. Truman				
Auctions: No auction records available.				
$10 2015W, B. Truman, Proof				
Auctions: No auction records available.				
$10 2015W, M. Eisenhower				
Auctions: No auction records available.				
$10 2015W, M. Eisenhower, Proof				
Auctions: No auction records available.				
$10 2015W, J. Kennedy				
Auctions: No auction records available.				
$10 2015W, J. Kennedy, Proof				
Auctions: No auction records available.				
$10 2015W, Lady Bird Johnson				
Auctions: No auction records available.				
$10 2015W, Lady Bird Johnson, Proof				
Auctions: No auction records available.				

Note: MS values are for uncertified Mint State coins of average quality, in their complete original U.S. Mint packaging. PF values are for uncertified Proof coins of average quality, in their complete original U.S. Mint packaging.

MMIX ULTRA HIGH RELIEF GOLD COIN (2009)

Designer: *Augustus Saint-Gaudens;* **Weight:** *31.101 grams.*
Composition: *.9999 gold (actual gold weight 1 oz.).*
Diameter: *27 mm.* **Edge:** *Lettered.* **Mint:** *Philadelphia.*

MMIX Ultra High Relief Gold Coin
*Photographed at an angle to show the edge (lettered
E PLURIBUS UNUM), the thickness (4 mm), and the depth of relief.*

History. In 2009 the U.S. Mint produced a modern collector's version of the first Saint-Gaudens double eagle. When the original debuted in 1907, the Mint had been unable to strike large quantities for circulation—the ultra high relief design was artistic, but difficult to coin. (It was modified later in 1907 to a lower relief suitable for commercial production.) Just over 100 years later, the 2009 version was a showcase coin: a tangible demonstration of the Mint's 21st-century ability to combine artistry and technology to make an outstanding numismatic treasure.

Like its predecessor, the new coin was dated in Roman numerals (with 2009 as MMIX). The Mint digitally mapped Saint-Gaudens's original plasters and used the results in the die-making process. The date was changed, and four additional stars were inserted, to represent the nation's current 50 states. Augustus Saint-Gaudens's striding Liberty occupied the obverse. On the reverse was his flying eagle, with the addition of IN GOD WE TRUST, a motto not used in the original design. The 2009 version was made in a smaller diameter (27 mm instead of 34), with a thickness of 4 mm, and composed of 24-karat (.9999 fine) gold, thus making it easier to strike and stay true to the ultra high relief design.

As with other bullion products of the U.S. Mint, the coins are legal tender and their weight, content, and purity are guaranteed by the federal government. They were packaged in a fancy mahogany box and sold directly to the public, instead of through a network of distributors.

Note that the Mint does not release bullion mintage data on a regular basis; the number given here reflects the most recently available official data.

Striking and Sharpness. Striking is sharp.

Availability. The coins are available in the numismatic marketplace for a premium above their gold bullion value.

MS-60 to 70 (Mint State). *Obverse and Reverse:* At MS-60, some abrasion and contact marks are evident on the higher design areas and the open areas of the design. Luster may be dull or lifeless at MS-60 to 62, but there should be deep frost at MS-63 and better, particularly in the lower-relief areas. At MS-65 and above, the luster should be full and rich. Contact marks and abrasion are less and less evident at higher grades. These guidelines are more academic than practical, as these coins are not intended for circulation, and presumably all are in high Mint State grades, as struck.

MMIX ULTRA HIGH RELIEF GOLD COIN

	Mintage	MS	MS-69	MS-70
MMIX Ultra High Relief $20 Gold Coin ‡	114,427	$2,300	$2,500	$3,000
	Auctions: $4,700, MS-70PL, August 2014; $6,110, MS-70PL, July 2013; $2,644, MS-70, October 2014			

Note: MS values are for uncertified Mint State coins of average quality, in their complete original U.S. Mint packaging. ‡ Ranked in the *100 Greatest U.S. Modern Coins.*

AMERICAN PLATINUM EAGLES
(1997 TO DATE)

Designers: *John M. Mercanti (obverse), Thomas D. Rogers Sr. (original reverse) (see image captions for other reverse designers).* **Weight:** *$10 1/10 oz.—3.112 grams; $25 1/4 oz.—7.780 grams; $50 1/2 oz.—15.560 grams; $100 1 oz.—31.120 grams.* **Composition:** *.9995 platinum.* **Diameter:** *$10 1/10 oz.—16.5 mm; $25 1/4 oz.—22 mm; $50 1/2 oz.—27 mm; $100 1 oz.—32.7 mm.* **Edge:** *Reeded.* **Mints:** *Philadelphia, West Point.*

Regular Finish

Burnished Finish
Burnished coins of all denominations feature the year's Proof reverse design. Mintmark location varies by design.

Proof Finish
First-year Proof coins featured the original reverse design, which is still in use on bullion strikes. See pages 1312–1316 for illustrations of Proof reverse designs from 1998 to date.

Reverse Proof Finish
Reverse Proofs were only struck in 2007, and only in the $50 1/2-oz. denomination.

Frosted FREEDOM
This variety is seen, very rarely, for 2007 Proof coins of the $25, $50, and $100 denominations.

History. Platinum American Eagles (face values of $10 to $100) are legal-tender bullion coins with weight, content, and purity guaranteed by the federal government. They were added to the U.S. Mint's program of silver and gold bullion coinage in 1997.

In their debut year, Proofs had the same reverse design as regular bullion strikes. Since then, the regular strikes have continued with the 1997 reverse, while the Proofs have featured new reverse designs each year. From 1998 through 2002, these special Proof designs comprised a "Vistas of Liberty" subset, with eagles flying through various American scenes. Since 2003, they have featured patriotic allegories and symbolism. From 2006 to 2008 the reverse designs honored "The Foundations of Democracy"—the nation's legislative branch (2006), executive branch (2007), and judicial branch (2008). In 2009 the Mint introduced a new six-year program of reverse designs, exploring the core concepts of American democracy as embodied in the preamble to the Constitution. The designs—which were based on narratives by John Roberts, chief justice of the United States—began with *To Form a More Perfect Union* (2009), which features four faces representing the nation's diversity, with the hair and clothing interweaving symbolically. The tiny eagle privy mark is from an original coin punch from the Philadelphia Mint's archives. This design is followed by *To Establish Justice* (2010), *To Insure Domestic Tranquility* (2011), *To Provide for the Common Defence* (2012), *To Promote the General Welfare* (2013), and *To Secure the Blessings of Liberty to Ourselves and Our Posterity* (2014).

The Philadelphia Mint strikes regular bullion issues, which are sold to the public by a network of Mint-authorized precious-metal firms, coin dealers, banks, and brokerages. The West Point facility strikes Burnished pieces (called *Uncirculated* by the Mint, and featuring the reverse design of the Proof coins), which are sold directly to collectors. Proofs are also struck at West Point and, like the Burnished coins, are sold by the Mint to the public, without middlemen. Similar to their gold-bullion cousins, the platinum Proofs and Burnished coins bear a W mintmark and are specially packaged in plastic capsules and fancy presentation cases.

In addition to the individual coins listed below, platinum American Eagles were issued in the 1997 "Impressions of Liberty" bullion coin set (see page 1294); in 2007 "10th Anniversary" sets; and in annual platinum-coin sets.

Striking and Sharpness. Striking is generally sharp.

Availability. The platinum American Eagle is one of the most popular platinum-investment vehicles in the world. The coins are readily available in the numismatic marketplace and through some banks, investment firms, and other non-numismatic channels.

MS-60 to 70 (Mint State). *Obverse and Reverse:* At MS-60, some abrasion and contact marks are evident on the higher design areas. Luster may be dull or lifeless at MS-60 to 62, but there should be deep frost at MS-63 and better, particularly in the lower-relief areas. At MS-65 and above, the luster should be full and rich. These guidelines are more academic than practical, as platinum American Eagles are not intended for circulation, and nearly all are in high Mint State grades.

PF-60 to 70 (Proof). *Obverse and Reverse:* Proofs that are extensively cleaned and have many hairlines are lower level, such as PF-60 to 62. Those with fewer hairlines or flaws are deemed PF-63 to 65. (These exist more in theory than actuality, as nearly all Proof American Eagle platinum bullion coins have been maintained in their original high condition by collectors and investors.) Given the quality of modern U.S. Mint products, even PF-66 and 67 are unusually low levels for these Proofs.

$10 1/10-OUNCE AMERICAN PLATINUM EAGLES

	Mintage	MS / PF	MS-69 / PF-69	MS-70 / PF-70
$10 1997	70,250	$160	$185	$1,250
Auctions: $194, MS-69, July 2014; $165, MS-69, July 2014				
$10 1997W, Proof	36,993	$190	$215	$350
Auctions: No auction records available.				
$10 1998	39,525	$160	$185	$950
Auctions: No auction records available.				
$10 1998W, Proof (a)	19,847	$190	$215	$495
Auctions: $206, PF-70DCam, September 2014				
$10 1999	55,955	$160	$185	$800
Auctions: $170, MS-69, August 2014				
$10 1999W, Proof (a)	19,133	$190	$215	$375
Auctions: $235, PF-70DCam, October 2014				
$10 2000	34,027	$160	$185	$400
Auctions: $159, MS-69, August 2014				
$10 2000W, Proof (a)	15,651	$190	$215	$375
Auctions: $176, PF-70DCam, October 2014; $200, PF-70DCam, September 2014; $247, PF-70DCam, July 2014				
$10 2001	52,017	$160	$185	$295
Auctions: $159, MS-69, August 2014				
$10 2001W, Proof (a)	12,174	$190	$215	$425
Auctions: No auction records available.				
$10 2002	23,005	$160	$185	$325
Auctions: No auction records available.				
$10 2002W, Proof (a)	12,365	$190	$215	$400
Auctions: $212, PF-70DCam, October 2014; $170, PF-70DCam, October 2014; $217, PF-70DCam, August 2014				
$10 2003	22,007	$160	$185	$325
Auctions: No auction records available.				
$10 2003W, Proof (a)	9,534	$240	$275	$450
Auctions: $176, PF-69DCam, November 2014				
$10 2004	15,010	$160	$195	$325
Auctions: $411, MS-70, September 2014; $165, MS-69, October 2014				
$10 2004W, Proof (a)	7,161	$400	$420	$650
Auctions: $517, PF-70DCam, August 2014				
$10 2005	14,013	$160	$195	$325
Auctions: $188, MS-70, August 2014				
$10 2005W, Proof (a)	8,104	$260	$275	$600
Auctions: $188, PF-69DCam, November 2014; $165, PF-69DCam, November 2014				
$10 2006	11,001	$160	$195	$395
Auctions: $188, MS-70, August 2014				
$10 2006W, Burnished (a)	3,544	$410	$420	$450
Auctions: No auction records available.				
$10 2006W, Proof (a)	10,205	$190	$225	$450
Auctions: $180, PF-70DCam, August 2014; $153, PF-69DCam, December 2014; $182, PF-69DCam, November 2014				

Note: MS values are for uncertified Mint State coins of average quality, in their complete original U.S. Mint packaging. PF values are for uncertified Proof coins of average quality, in their complete original U.S. Mint packaging. **a.** Burnished and Proof coins from 1998 on featured the designs illustrated on pages 1312–1316.

	Mintage	MS	MS-69	MS-70
		PF	PF-69	PF-70
$10 2007	13,003	$275	$280	$330
	Auctions: No auction records available.			
$10 2007W, Burnished (a)	5,556	$220	$260	$325
	Auctions: $391, MS-70, September 2014			
$10 2007W, Proof (a)	8,176	$190	$220	$365
	Auctions: $441, MS-70DCam, September 2014			
$10 2008	17,000	$160	$195	$295
	Auctions: $282, MS-70, September 2014			
$10 2008W, Burnished (a)	3,706	$335	$355	$450
	Auctions: $411, MS-70, September 2014; $470, MS-70, July 2014			
$10 2008W, Proof (a)	5,138	$400	$425	$700
	Auctions: $329, MS-70DCam, November 2014; $411, MS-70DCam, August 2014			

Note: MS values are for uncertified Mint State coins of average quality, in their complete original U.S. Mint packaging. PF values are for uncertified Proof coins of average quality, in their complete original U.S. Mint packaging. **a.** Burnished and Proof coins from 1998 on featured the designs illustrated on pages 1312–1316.

$25 1/4-Ounce American Platinum Eagles

	Mintage	MS	MS-69	MS-70
		PF	PF-69	PF-70
$25 1997	27,100	$400	$435	$2,200
	Auctions: $2,056, MS-70, September 2014			
$25 1997W, Proof	18,628	$425	$435	$600
	Auctions: $499, PF-70DCam, September 2014			
$25 1998	38,887	$400	$435	$950
	Auctions: No auction records available.			
$25 1998W, Proof (a)	14,873	$425	$435	$495
	Auctions: $529, PF-70DCam, September 2014			
$25 1999	39,734	$400	$435	$2,750
	Auctions: No auction records available.			
$25 1999W, Proof (a)	13,507	$425	$435	$495
	Auctions: $382, PF-70DCam, November 2014; $329, PF-70DCam, November 2014; $470, PF-70DCam, September 2014			
$25 2000	20,054	$400	$435	$800
	Auctions: No auction records available.			
$25 2000W, Proof (a)	11,995	$425	$435	$600
	Auctions: $401, PF-70DCam, November 2014; $329, PF-70DCam, November 2014; $397, PF-70DCam, September 2014			
$25 2001	21,815	$400	$435	$2,300
	Auctions: No auction records available.			
$25 2001W, Proof (a)	8,847	$425	$435	$700
	Auctions: No auction records available.			
$25 2002	27,405	$400	$420	$500
	Auctions: No auction records available.			
$25 2002W, Proof (a)	9,282	$425	$435	$600
	Auctions: $411, PF-70DCam, November 2014; $329, PF-70DCam, November 2014; $423, PF-70DCam, August 2014			

Note: MS values are for uncertified Mint State coins of average quality, in their complete original U.S. Mint packaging. PF values are for uncertified Proof coins of average quality, in their complete original U.S. Mint packaging. **a.** Burnished and Proof coins from 1998 on featured the designs illustrated on pages 1312–1316.

| | Mintage | MS | MS-69 | MS-70 |
		PF	PF-69	PF-70
$25 2003	25,207	$400	$420	$500
	Auctions: No auction records available.			
$25 2003W, Proof (a)	7,044	$425	$435	$750
	Auctions: $329, PF-70DCam, November 2014; $529, PF-70DCam, September 2014; $441, PF-70DCam, September 2014			
$25 2004	18,010	$400	$420	$500
	Auctions: $376, MS-70, October 2014			
$25 2004W, Proof (a)	5,193	$910	$950	$1,150
	Auctions: $573, PF-70DCam, November 2014; $881, PF-70DCam, August 2014; $823, PF-70DCam, July 2014			
$25 2005	12,013	$400	$425	$550
	Auctions: $411, MS-70, September 2014			
$25 2005W, Proof (a)	6,592	$600	$640	$800
	Auctions: $441, PF-70DCam, September 2014			
$25 2006	12,001	$400	$425	$550
	Auctions: No auction records available.			
$25 2006W, Burnished (a)	2,676	$635	$655	$795
	Auctions: $705, MS-70, August 2014			
$25 2006W, Proof (a)	7,813	$425	$435	$750
	Auctions: $376, PF-70DCam, November 2014			
$25 2007	8,402	$400	$425	$550
	Auctions: $382, MS-70, September 2014; $370, MS-69, July 2014			
$25 2007W, Burnished (a)	3,690	$570	$585	$650
	Auctions: $598, MS-70, August 2014			
$25 2007W, Proof (a)	6,017	$425	$435	$750
	Auctions: $411, PF-70DCam, November 2014; $482, PF-70DCam, July 2014			
$25 2007W, Frosted FREEDOM, Proof (a)	21	—		
	Auctions: No auction records available.			
$25 2008	22,800	$400	$415	$550
	Auctions: $353, MS-70, November 2014; $370, MS-70, September 2014			
$25 2008W, Burnished (a)	2,481	$635	$680	$900
	Auctions: No auction records available.			
$25 2008W, Proof (a)	4,153	$735	$750	$950
	Auctions: $764, PF-70DCam, August 2014			

Note: MS values are for uncertified Mint State coins of average quality, in their complete original U.S. Mint packaging. PF values are for uncertified Proof coins of average quality, in their complete original U.S. Mint packaging. **a.** Burnished and Proof coins from 1998 on featured the designs illustrated on pages 1312–1316.

$50 1/2-OUNCE AMERICAN PLATINUM EAGLES

| | Mintage | MS | MS-69 | MS-70 |
		PF	PF-69	PF-70
$50 1997	20,500	$800	$850	$2,250
	Auctions: $870, MS-69, July 2014; $776, MS-69, July 2014			
$50 1997W, Proof	15,431	$850	$875	$1,050
	Auctions: No auction records available.			

Note: MS values are for uncertified Mint State coins of average quality, in their complete original U.S. Mint packaging. PF values are for uncertified Proof coins of average quality, in their complete original U.S. Mint packaging.

	Mintage	MS / PF	MS-69 / PF-69	MS-70 / PF-70
$50 1998	32,415	$800	$850	$3,500
Auctions: No auction records available.				
$50 1998W, Proof (a)	13,836	$850	$875	$1,050
Auctions: $764, PF-70DCam, September 2014				
$50 1999	32,309	$800	$850	$3,500
Auctions: No auction records available.				
$50 1999W, Proof (a)	11,103	$850	$875	$1,050
Auctions: $764, PF-70DCam, September 2014				
$50 2000	18,892	$800	$850	$4,000
Auctions: No auction records available.				
$50 2000W, Proof (a)	11,049	$850	$865	$900
Auctions: $823, MS-70DCam, November 2014; $764, MS-70DCam, September 2014				
$50 2001	12,815	$800	$850	$3,750
Auctions: $795, MS-69, July 2014; $752, MS-69, July 2014				
$50 2001W, Proof (a)	8,254	$850	$865	$1,000
Auctions: No auction records available.				
$50 2002	24,005	$800	$850	$1,700
Auctions: $776, MS-69, August 2014; $752, MS-69, August 2014; $729, MS-69, August 2014				
$50 2002W, Proof (a)	8,772	$850	$865	$1,000
Auctions: $764, PF-70DCam, September 2014; $776, PF-70DCam, August 2014; $752, PF-70DCam, August 2014				
$50 2003	17,409	$800	$825	$1,050
Auctions: $999, MS-70, September 2014; $776, MS-69, August 2014; $752, MS-69, August 2014				
$50 2003W, Proof (a)	7,131	$850	$865	$1,000
Auctions: $793, PF-70DCam, September 2014; $764, PF-70DCam, September 2014				
$50 2004	13,236	$800	$825	$1,050
Auctions: $881, MS-70, September 2014; $823, MS-69, August 2014; $752, MS-69, August 2014				
$50 2004W, Proof (a)	5,063	$1,400	$1,450	$1,650
Auctions: $1,234, PF-70DCam, November 2014; $1,175, PF-70DCam, August 2014				
$50 2005	9,013	$800	$825	$1,050
Auctions: $764, MS-70, September 2014				
$50 2005W, Proof (a)	5,942	$1,150	$1,180	$1,350
Auctions: $823, PF-70DCam, September 2014				
$50 2006	9,602	$800	$825	$1,050
Auctions: $764, MS-70, September 2014				
$50 2006W, Burnished (a)	2,577	$925	$975	$1,250
Auctions: $1,028, MS-70, August 2014				
$50 2006W, Proof (a)	7,649	$850	$875	$1,000
Auctions: $764, PF-70DCam, September 2014				
$50 2007	7,001	$800	$825	$1,000
Auctions: No auction records available.				
$50 2007W, Burnished (a)	3,635	$850	$875	$1,000
Auctions: No auction records available.				
$50 2007W, Proof (a)	25,519	$850	$875	$950
Auctions: $764, PF-70DCam, September 2014; $752, PF-70DCam, August 2014; $881, PF-70DCam, July 2014				
$50 2007W, Reverse Proof (a)	19,583	$900	$930	$1,200
Auctions: $852, MS-70, October 2014; $881, MS-70, September 2014				
$50 2007W, Frosted FREEDOM, Proof (a)	21	$900	$930	$1,200
Auctions: No auction records available.				

Note: MS values are for uncertified Mint State coins of average quality, in their complete original U.S. Mint packaging. PF values are for uncertified Proof coins of average quality, in their complete original U.S. Mint packaging. **a.** Burnished and Proof coins from 1998 on featured the designs illustrated on pages 1312–1316.

| | Mintage | MS | MS-69 | MS-70 |
		PF	PF-69	PF-70
$50 2008	14,000	$800	$825	$940
	Auctions: No auction records available.			
$50 2008W, Burnished ‡ (a)	2,253	$1,200	$1,250	$2,400
	Auctions: $4,406, MS-70, August 2014			
$50 2008W, Proof ‡ (a)	4,020	$1,200	$1,250	$1,500
	Auctions: $3,819, PF-70DCam, August 2014; $1,528, PF-70DCam, August 2014; $1,234, PF-70DCam, August 2014			

Note: MS values are for uncertified Mint State coins of average quality, in their complete original U.S. Mint packaging. PF values are for uncertified Proof coins of average quality, in their complete original U.S. Mint packaging. ‡ Ranked in the *100 Greatest U.S. Modern Coins.* **a.** Burnished and Proof coins from 1998 on featured the designs illustrated on pages 1312–1316.

$100 1-OUNCE AMERICAN PLATINUM EAGLES

Proof Reverse, 1998:
Eagle Over New England.
Vistas of Liberty series.
Designer: John Mercanti.

Proof Reverse, 1999:
Eagle Above
Southeastern Wetlands.
Vistas of Liberty series.
Designer: John Mercanti.

Proof Reverse, 2000:
Eagle Above
America's Heartland.
Vistas of Liberty series.
Designer: Alfred Maletsky.

| | Mintage | MS | MS-69 | MS-70 |
		PF	PF-69	PF-70
$100 1997	56,000	$1,500	$1,550	$9,000
	Auctions: $1,821, MS-69, July 2014			
$100 1997W, Proof	20,851	$1,700	$1,750	$3,400
	Auctions: No auction records available.			
$100 1998	133,002	$1,500	$1,550	$9,000
	Auctions: No auction records available.			
$100 1998W, Proof	14,912	$1,700	$1,750	$2,900
	Auctions: No auction records available.			
$100 1999	56,707	$1,500	$1,550	$10,000
	Auctions: No auction records available.			
$100 1999W, Proof	12,363	$1,700	$1,750	$3,800
	Auctions: $1,998, PF-70DCam, November 2014			
$100 2000	10,003	$1,500	$1,550	$10,000
	Auctions: No auction records available.			
$100 2000W, Proof	12,453	$1,700	$1,750	$3,800
	Auctions: No auction records available.			

Note: MS values are for uncertified Mint State coins of average quality, in their complete original U.S. Mint packaging. PF values are for uncertified Proof coins of average quality, in their complete original U.S. Mint packaging.

Proof Reverse, 2001: Eagle
Above America's Southwest.
Vistas of Liberty series.
Designer: Thomas D. Rogers Sr.

Proof Reverse, 2002:
Eagle Fishing in America's
Northwest. Vistas of Liberty series.
Designer: Alfred Maletsky.

Proof Reverse, 2003.
Designer: Alfred Maletsky.

Proof Reverse, 2004.
Designer: Donna Weaver.

Proof Reverse, 2005.
Designer: Donna Weaver.

Proof Reverse, 2006:
"Legislative Branch."
Designer: Joel Iskowitz.

	Mintage	MS PF	MS-69 PF-69	MS-70 PF-70
$100 2001	14,070	$1,500	$1,550	$10,000
Auctions: No auction records available.				
$100 2001W, Proof	8,969	$1,700	$1,750	$2,900
Auctions: No auction records available.				
$100 2002	11,502	$1,500	$1,550	$7,000
Auctions: No auction records available.				
$100 2002W, Proof	9,834	$1,900	$1,950	$2,900
Auctions: No auction records available.				
$100 2003	8,007	$1,500	$1,550	$3,750
Auctions: No auction records available.				
$100 2003W, Proof	8,246	$1,900	$1,950	$2,900
Auctions: No auction records available.				
$100 2004	7,009	$1,500	$1,550	$2,500
Auctions: No auction records available.				
$100 2004W, Proof	6,007	$2,100	$2,250	$3,500
Auctions: $2,820, PF-70DCam, November 2014				
$100 2005	6,310	$1,500	$1,550	$2,500
Auctions: No auction records available.				
$100 2005W, Proof	6,602	$2,300	$2,450	$3,300
Auctions: $2,350, PF-70DCam, September 2014				
$100 2006	6,000	$1,500	$1,550	$2,100
Auctions: No auction records available.				
$100 2006W, Burnished ‡	3,068	$2,100	$2,125	$2,200
Auctions: No auction records available.				
$100 2006W, Proof	9,152	$1,700	$1,750	$2,500
Auctions: No auction records available.				

Note: MS values are for uncertified Mint State coins of average quality, in their complete original U.S. Mint packaging. PF values are for uncertified Proof coins of average quality, in their complete original U.S. Mint packaging. ‡ Ranked in the *100 Greatest U.S. Modern Coins.*

Proof Reverse, 2007:
"Executive Branch."
Designer: Thomas Cleveland.

Proof Reverse, 2008:
"Judicial Branch."
Designer: Joel Iskowitz.

Proof Reverse, 2009:
"To Form a More
Perfect Union."
Designer: Susan Gamble.

Proof Reverse, 2010:
"To Establish Justice."
Designer: Donna Weaver.

Proof Reverse, 2011:
"To Insure
Domestic Tranquility."
Designer: Joel Iskowitz.

Proof Reverse, 2012:
"To Provide for the
Common Defence."
Designer: Barbara Fox.

	Mintage	MS / PF	MS-69 / PF-69	MS-70 / PF-70
$100 2007	7,202	$1,500	$1,550	$2,100
Auctions: No auction records available.				
$100 2007W, Burnished	4,177	$2,000	$2,025	$2,150
Auctions: No auction records available.				
$100 2007W, Proof	8,363	$1,700	$1,750	$2,500
Auctions: $1,528, PF-70DCam, November 2014; $1,880, PF-70DCam, September 2014; $1,821, PF-70DCam, August 2014				
$100 2007W, Frosted FREEDOM, Proof	12	—		
Auctions: No auction records available.				
$100 2008	21,800	$1,500	$1,525	$1,595
Auctions: No auction records available.				
$100 2008W, Burnished	2,876	$2,200	$2,250	$3,500
Auctions: $3,819, MS-70, August 2014				
$100 2008W, Proof	4,769	$2,700	$2,750	$3,200
Auctions: $2,350, PF-70DCam, August 2014				
$100 2009W, Proof ‡	7,945	$2,100	$2,200	$2,600
Auctions: $1,945, PF-70DCam, October 2014				
$100 2010W, Proof	9,871	$2,000	$2,050	$2,350
Auctions: $1,763, PF-70DCam, October 2014				
$100 2011W, Proof	14,790	$1,700	$1,800	$2,250
Auctions: $1,710, PF-70DCam, October 2014; $1,880, PF-70DCam, September 2014; $1,821, PF-70DCam, August 2014				
$100 2012W, Proof	9,081	$1,700	$1,800	$2,250
Auctions: $1,886, PF-70DCam, October 2014				

Note: MS values are for uncertified Mint State coins of average quality, in their complete original U.S. Mint packaging. PF values are for uncertified Proof coins of average quality, in their complete original U.S. Mint packaging. ‡ Ranked in the *100 Greatest U.S. Modern Coins*.

Proof Reverse, 2013:
"To Promote the
General Welfare."
Designer: Joel Iskowitz.

Proof Reverse, 2014: "To
Secure the Blessings
of Liberty to Ourselves
and Our Posterity."
Designer: Susan Gamble.

| | Mintage | MS | MS-69 | MS-70 |
		PF	PF-69	PF-70
$100 2013W, Proof	5,763	$1,700	$1,800	$2,500
Auctions: No auction records available.				
$100 2014	16,900	$1,500	$1,520	$1,600
Auctions: No auction records available.				
$100 2014W, Proof	4,606	$1,700	$1,750	$2,200
Auctions: No auction records available.				
$100 2015W, Proof				
Auctions: No auction records available.				

Note: MS values are for uncertified Mint State coins of average quality, in their complete original U.S. Mint packaging. PF values are for uncertified Proof coins of average quality, in their complete original U.S. Mint packaging.

AMERICAN PLATINUM EAGLE BULLION COIN SETS

	MS	MS-69	MS-70
1997 Platinum Set. $100, $50, $25, $10	$2,700	$2,815	$14,700
Auctions: No auction records available.			
1998 Platinum Set. $100, $50, $25, $10	$2,700	$2,815	$14,400
Auctions: No auction records available.			
1999 Platinum Set. $100, $50, $25, $10	$2,700	$2,815	$17,050
Auctions: No auction records available.			
2000 Platinum Set. $100, $50, $25, $10	$2,700	$2,815	$15,200
Auctions: No auction records available.			
2001 Platinum Set. $100, $50, $25, $10	$2,700	$2,815	$16,345
Auctions: No auction records available.			
2002 Platinum Set. $100, $50, $25, $10	$2,700	$2,815	$9,525
Auctions: No auction records available.			
2003 Platinum Set. $100, $50, $25, $10	$2,700	$2,815	$5,625
Auctions: No auction records available.			
2004 Platinum Set. $100, $50, $25, $10	$2,700	$2,830	$4,375
Auctions: No auction records available.			
2005 Platinum Set. $100, $50, $25, $10	$2,700	$2,880	$4,425
Auctions: No auction records available.			
2006 Platinum Set. $100, $50, $25, $10	$2,100	$2,280	$4,045
Auctions: No auction records available.			
2007 Platinum Set. $100, $50, $25, $10	$3,750	$4,000	$4,695
Auctions: No auction records available.			
2008 Platinum Set. $100, $50, $25, $10	$2,700	$2,845	$3,380
Auctions: No auction records available.			

Note: MS values are for uncertified Mint State sets of average quality, in their complete original U.S. Mint packaging.

AMERICAN PLATINUM EAGLE PROOF COIN SETS

	PF	PF-69	PF-70
1997W Platinum Set. $100, $50, $25, $10	$3,100	$3,300	$5,550
Auctions: No auction records available.			
1998W Platinum Set. $100, $50, $25, $10	$3,100	$3,300	$5,550
Auctions: No auction records available.			
1999W Platinum Set. $100, $50, $25, $10	$3,100	$3,300	$5,720
Auctions: No auction records available.			
2000W Platinum Set. $100, $50, $25, $10	$3,100	$3,300	$5,675
Auctions: No auction records available.			
2001W Platinum Set. $100, $50, $25, $10	$3,100	$3,300	$5,025
Auctions: No auction records available.			
2002W Platinum Set. $100, $50, $25, $10	$3,100	$3,300	$4,900
Auctions: No auction records available.			
2003W Platinum Set. $100, $50, $25, $10	$3,100	$3,300	$5,100
Auctions: No auction records available.			
2004W Platinum Set. $100, $50, $25, $10	$4,600	$5,070	$6,950
Auctions: No auction records available.			
2005W Platinum Set. $100, $50, $25, $10	$3,800	$4,265	$6,050
Auctions: No auction records available.			
2006W Platinum Set. $100, $50, $25, $10	$3,100	$3,300	$4,700
Auctions: No auction records available.			
2007W Platinum Set. $100, $50, $25, $10	$3,100	$3,300	$4,600
Auctions: No auction records available.			
2008W Platinum Set. $100, $50, $25, $10	$4,600	$4,760	$5,850
Auctions: No auction records available.			

Note: PF values are for uncertified Proof sets of average quality, in their complete original U.S. Mint packaging. The Proof $100 American Platinum Eagle of 1997 is also included in the 1997 Impressions of Liberty set, listed on page 1294.

2007 AMERICAN PLATINUM EAGLE 10TH-ANNIVERSARY PROOF COIN SETS

	PF	PF-69	PF-70
2007 Two-Coin Set (a)	$1,800	$1,845	$2,400
Auctions: $1,528, PF-70, October 2014			

a. This two-coin set, housed in a mahogany-finish hardwood box, includes one half-ounce Proof (with the standard cameo-finish background and frosted design elements) and one half-ounce Reverse Proof (with frosted background fields and mirrored raised elements) dated 2007-W.

Significant U.S. Patterns

Pattern coins are a fascinating part of numismatics that encompass thousands of designs and experimental pieces made by the U.S. Mint to test new motifs, alloys, coin sizes, and other variables. Most were official creations—products of the research-and-development process that takes a coin from congressionally authorized concept to finished pocket change. Some were made in secret, outside the normal day-to-day work of the Mint. The book *United States Pattern Coins*, by J. Hewitt Judd, gives extensive details of the history and characteristics of more than 2,000 different pattern varieties from 1792 to the present era.

Patterns provide students and collectors a chronology of the continuing efforts of engravers and artists to present their work for approval. Throughout the 220-plus years of federal coinage production, concepts meant to improve various aspects of circulating coins have been proposed and given physical form in patterns. In some instances, changes have been prompted by an outcry for higher aesthetics, a call for a more convenient denomination, or a need to overcome striking deficiencies. In many other instances, workers or officials at the Mint simply created special coins for the numismatic trade—often controversial in their time, but enthusiastically collected today. Certain patterns, bearing particular proposed designs or innovations, provided tangible examples for Mint and Treasury Department officials or members of Congress to review and evaluate. If approved and adopted, the pattern design became a familiar regular-issue motif; those that were rejected have become part of American numismatic history.

The patterns listed and illustrated in this section are samples from a much larger group. Such pieces generally include die and hub trials, off-metal Proof strikings of regular issues, and various combinations of dies that were sometimes struck at a later date. Certain well-known members of this extended pattern family historically have been included with regular issues in many popular, general-circulation numismatic reference books. The four-dollar gold Stellas of 1879 and 1880; certain Gobrecht dollars of 1836, 1838, and 1839; the transitional half dimes and dimes of 1859 and 1860; and the Flying Eagle cents of 1856 are examples. No official mintage figures of patterns and related pieces were recorded in most instances, and the number extant of each can usually only be estimated from auction appearances and from those found in museum holdings and important private collections. Although most patterns are very rare, the 2,000-plus distinct varieties make them unexpectedly collectible—not by one of each, but by selected available examples from favorite types or categories. Curiously, the most common of all patterns is the highly sought and expensive 1856, Flying Eagle, cent!

Unlike regular coin issues that were emitted through the usual channels of commerce, and Proofs of regular issues that were struck expressly for sale to collectors, patterns were not intended to be officially sold. Yet as a matter of Mint practice, often against stated policy and law, countless patterns were secretly and unofficially sold and traded to favorite dealers (most notably William K. Idler and his son-in-law John W. Haseltine) and collectors, disseminated to government officials, and occasionally made available to numismatic societies. Not until mid-1885 did an incoming new director of the Mint enforce stringent regulations prohibiting their sale and distribution, although there had been many misleading statements to this effect earlier. In succeeding decades the Mint, while not making patterns available to numismatists, did place certain examples in the Mint Collection, now called the National Numismatic Collection, in the Smithsonian Institution. On other occasions, selected patterns were obtained by Mint and Treasury officials, or otherwise spared from destruction. Today, with the exception of certain cents and five-cent pieces of 1896, all pattern coins dated after 1885 are extremely rare.

The private possession of patterns has not been without its controversy. Most significant was the 1910 seizure by government agents of a parcel containing some 23 pattern pieces belonging to John W. Haseltine, a leading Philadelphia coin dealer with undisclosed private ties to Mint officials. The government asserted that the patterns had been removed from the Mint without authority, and that they remained the property of the United States. Haseltine's attorney successfully used the Mint's pre-1887 policies in his defense, and recovered the patterns a year after their confiscation. This set precedent for ownership, at least for the patterns minted prior to 1887, as all of the pieces in question predated that year. Today pattern coins can be legally held, and, in fact, they were inadvertently made legal tender (as was the earlier demonetized silver trade dollar) by the Coinage Act of 1965.

Among the grandest impressions ever produced at the U.S. Mint are the two varieties of pattern fifty-dollar gold pieces of 1877. Officially titled half unions, these large patterns were created at the request of certain politicians with interests tied to the gold-producing state of California. Specimens were struck in copper, and one of each variety was struck in gold. Both of the gold pieces were purchased around 1908 by numismatist William H. Woodin (who, years later, in 1933, served as President Franklin D. Roosevelt's first secretary of the Treasury). The sellers were John W. Haseltine and Stephen K. Nagy, well known for handling many rarities that few others could obtain from the Mint. The Mint desired to re-obtain the pieces for its own collection, and through a complex trade deal for quantities of other patterns, did so, adding them to the Mint Collection. Now preserved in the Smithsonian Institution, these half unions are regarded as national treasures.

The following resources are recommended for additional information, descriptions, and complete listings:

United States Pattern Coins, 10th edition, J. Hewitt Judd, edited by Q. David Bowers, 2009.

United States Patterns and Related Issues, Andrew W. Pollock III, 1994. (Out of print)

www.harrybassfoundation.org

www.uspatterns.com

Judd-52

J-67

	PF-60	PF-63	PF-65
1836 Two-cent piece (J-52, billon) (a)	$2,500	$4,500	$8,500
Auctions: $8,625, PF-65, January 2009			
1836 Gold dollar (J-67, gold) (b)	$11,000	$17,500	$22,500
Auctions: $24,725, PF-65, November 2010			

a. This proposal for a two-cent coin is one of the earliest collectible patterns. It was designed by Christian Gobrecht. An estimated 21 to 30 examples are known. b. Gobrecht styled the first gold dollar pattern after the familiar "Cap and Rays" design used on Mexican coins, which at the time were legal tender in the United States. An estimated 31 to 75 pieces are known.

J-164

J-177

	PF-60	PF-63	PF-65
1854 Cent (J-164, bronze) (a)	$2,100	$4,000	$6,750
	Auctions: $16,100, PF-67BN, March 2005		
1856 Half cent (J-177, copper-nickel) (b)	$3,100	$5,000	$8,750
	Auctions: $6,038, PF-64, January 2006		

a. Beginning in 1850, the Mint produced patterns for a reduced-weight cent. Among the designs were ring-style, Liberty Head, and Flying Eagle motifs. These experiments culminated with the 1856 Flying Eagle cent. An estimated 31 to 75 examples of J-164 are known. Those with red mint luster are worth more than the values listed here. **b.** Before producing copper-nickel small-size cents in 1856, the Mint experimented with that alloy using half-cent dies. An estimated 31 to 75 examples are known.

J-204

J-239

	PF-60	PF-63	PF-65
1858 Cent (J-204, copper-nickel) (a)	$1,600	$2,500	$4,000
1859 Half dollar (J-239, silver) (b)	$1,500	$2,000	$3,750

a. This pattern cent's flying eagle differs from the one adopted for regular coinage of the one-cent piece. An estimated 31 to 75 pieces are known. **b.** This design proposal for a new half dollar features James Longacre's French Liberty Head design. An estimated 76 to 200 pieces are known.

J-305

	PF-60	PF-63	PF-65
1863 Washington two-cent piece (J-305, copper) (a)	$1,500	$2,250	$4,000

a. Before the two-cent coin was introduced to circulation, two basic designs were considered. If this George Washington portrait design had been adopted, it would have been the first to depict a historical figure. An estimated 76 to 200 pieces are known.

J-349

J-407

J-470

	PF-60	PF-63	PF-65
1863 Eagle (J-349, gold) (a)		$450,000	
1865 Bimetallic two-cent piece (J-407, silver and copper) (b)	$6,000	$11,000	$19,500
1866 Five-cent piece (J-470, nickel) (c)	$1,650	$2,500	$4,500

a. This unique gold eagle features IN GOD WE TRUST on a scroll on the reverse. This feature would not appear on regular eagle coinage until 1866. The obverse is from the regular 1863 die. **b.** This experimental piece is the first "clad" coin. It consists of an irregular and streaky layer of silver fused to copper. The experiment was unsuccessful. An estimated 4 to 6 pieces are known. **c.** Another of George Washington's early pattern appearances was on five-cent pieces of 1866. An estimated 21 to 30 are known.

J-486

J-611

	PF-60	PF-63	PF-65
1866 Lincoln five-cent piece (J-486, nickel) (a)	$5,750	$10,000	$18,000
1868 Cent (J-611, copper) (b)	$20,000	$27,500	$37,500
Auctions: $36,800, PF-66BN, March 2005			

a. A number of pattern nickels were produced in 1866, including one designed to depict the recently assassinated President Abraham Lincoln. An estimated 7 to 12 examples are known. **b.** There is no known reason for the minting of this unusual piece, which mimics the original large cents that had last been made in 1857. There was no intent to resume the coinage of old-style copper "large" cents in 1868. Accordingly, this variety is regarded as a rarity created for collectors. Fewer than 15 examples are believed to exist.

J-1195

J-1235

	PF-60	PF-63	PF-65
1872 Amazonian quarter (J-1195, silver) (a)	$28,000	$50,000	$85,000
Auctions: $80,500, PF-66Cam, January 2009			
1872 Amazonian gold $3 (J-1235, gold) (b)	—	—	$1,250,000

a. Many of the most popular patterns have been given colorful nicknames by collectors in appreciation of their artistry. This design is by Chief Engraver William Barber. An estimated 7 to 12 examples are known. **b.** This unique piece was contained in the Mint's only uniform gold set using the same design from the gold dollar to the double eagle.

J-1373

	PF-60	PF-63	PF-65
1874 Bickford eagle (J-1373, gold) (a)	—	$500,000	$1,250,000

a. Dana Bickford, a New York City manufacturer, proposed a ten-dollar gold coin that would be exchangeable at set rates with other world currencies. Patterns were made, but the idea proved impractical. 2 examples are known.

J-1392

	PF-60	PF-63	PF-65
1875 Sailor Head twenty-cent piece (J-1392, silver) (a)	$3,000	$5,500	$9,500

a. Chief Engraver William Barber's "Sailor Head" is one of the most elegant of several rejected designs for a twenty-cent coin. The same head was used on other patterns, including proposals for trade dollars. An estimated 21 to 30 examples of J-1392 are known.

J-1507

J-1512   J-1528

	PF-60	PF-63	PF-65
1877 Morgan half dollar (J-1507, copper) (a)	$18,000	$29,000	$50,000
1877 Morgan half dollar (J-1512, silver) (b)	$15,000	$28,000	$45,000
1877 Half dollar (J-1528, silver) (c)	$17,000	$33,000	$50,000

a. A year before his famous and eponymous dollar design was adopted for regular coinage, engraver George Morgan's Liberty Head appeared on several varieties of pattern half dollars, all of which are rare today. J-1507 pairs the well-known obverse with an indented shield design. 2 examples are known. **b.** The half dollar pattern cataloged as J-1512 pairs Morgan's "silver dollar style" obverse with a dramatic "Defiant Eagle" reverse. 6 examples are known. **c.** This is one of several 1877 pattern half dollars by Chief Engraver William Barber. 4 are known.

J-1549

	PF-60	PF-63	PF-65
1877 Half union (J-1549, copper) (a)	$100,000	$175,000	$350,000
Auctions: $575,000, PF-67BN, January 2009			

a. This famous fifty-dollar pattern by Chief Engraver William Barber would have been the highest denomination ever issued by the Mint up to that time. The gold impression (J-1548) is unique and resides in the Smithsonian's National Numismatic Collection, but copper specimens (J-1549, which are priced here and are sometimes gilt) occasionally come to the market. Varieties exist with a somewhat larger or smaller head.

J-1590

	PF-60	PF-63	PF-65
1879 Quarter dollar (J-1590, silver) (a)	$7,500	$15,000	$25,000
Auctions: $34,500, PF-68, January 2007			

a. Referred to as the "Washlady" design, this was Charles Barber's first attempt at a uniform silver design. An estimated 13 to 20 examples are known.

J-1609

	PF-60	PF-63	PF-65
1879 Dollar (J-1609, copper) (a)	$25,000	$45,000	$85,000
Auctions: $74,750, PF-66RB, September 2006			

a. The "Schoolgirl" design by George T. Morgan is a widespread favorite among pattern collectors. Examples are rare, with only 7 to 12 known.

J-1643

	PF-60	PF-63	PF-65
1879 Metric double eagle (J-1643, gold) (a)	$325,000	$600,000	$1,000,000

a. James Longacre's Liberty Head design was the same as that used on regular-issue double eagles, but with an added inscription indicating the coin's specifications in metric units. 5 are known.

J-1667   **J-1669**   **J-1673**

	PF-60	PF-63	PF-65
1881 One-cent piece (J-1667, aluminum) (a)	$2,025	$3,780	$6,440
1881 Three-cent piece (J-1669, copper) (a)	$2,000	$3,750	$6,000
1881 Five-cent piece (J-1673, aluminum) (a)	$2,300	$4,800	$9,000

a. These patterns by Chief Engraver Charles Barber represent an attempt at a uniform set of minor coins; if adopted, they would have been struck in nickel for circulation. An estimated 7 to 20 examples are known of each of the illustrated patterns.

J-1698

	PF-60	PF-63	PF-65
1882 Quarter dollar (J-1698, silver) (a)	$17,500	$34,000	$55,000

a. George Morgan's "Shield Earring" design was made in patterns of quarter, half, and dollar denominations. 7 to 12 of the quarter dollar patterns are known.

J-1761   **J-1770**

	PF-60	PF-63	PF-65
1891 Barber quarter (J-1761, silver) (a)	—	—	—
1896 Shield nickel (J-1770, nickel) (b)	$1,500	$2,750	$4,000

a. Charles Barber prepared various pattern dimes, quarters, and half dollars in 1891. The quarter illustrated is similar to the design adopted for regular coinage in 1892. Two pieces are known, both in the Smithsonian's National Numismatic Collection. **b.** In 1896 the Mint struck experimental cents and nickels with similar designs, by Charles Barber. 21 to 30 examples of J-1770 are known.

J-1905

	PF-60	PF-63	PF-65
1907 Indian Head double eagle (J-1905, gold) (a)			*$8,000,000*

a. Designed by Augustus Saint-Gaudens, this pattern is unique and extremely valuable. A variation of the reverse of this design was used on the double eagles struck for circulation from 1907 through 1933.

J-1992

	PF-60	PF-63	PF-65
1916 Liberty Walking half dollar (J-1992, silver) (a)	$60,000	$100,000	$165,000
Auctions: $115,000, PF-65, July 2008			

a. Various pattern Mercury dimes, Standing Liberty quarters, and Liberty Walking half dollars were struck, all dated 1916. All are extremely rare, but a few found their way into circulation.

J-2063

	PF-60	PF-63	PF-65
1942 Experimental cent (J-2051 through J-2069, several metallic and other compositions) (a)	$1,600	$3,000	$5,000

a. Before settling on the zinc-coated steel composition used for the Lincoln cents of 1943, the Mint considered various alternative compositions, including plastics. Most were struck by outside contractors using specially prepared dies provided by the Mint. An estimated 7 to 12 examples are known of most types and colors.

Private and Territorial Gold

The expression *private gold*, used with reference to coins struck outside the United States Mint, is a general term. In the sense that no state or territory had authority to coin money, *private gold* simply refers to those necessity pieces of various shapes, denominations, and degrees of intrinsic worth that were coined by facilities other than official U.S. mints and circulated in isolated areas of the United States by assayers, bankers, and other private individuals and organizations. Some numismatists use the terms *territorial gold* and *state gold* to cover certain issues because they were coined and circulated in a territory or state. While the state of California properly sanctioned the ingots stamped by F.D. Kohler as state assayer, in no instance (except for the Mormon issues of Salt Lake City) were any of the gold pieces struck by authority of any of the territorial governments.

The stamped fifty-dollar and other gold coins, sometimes called *ingots*, but in coin form, were made by Augustus Humbert, the United States Assayer of Gold, but were not receivable at face value for government payments, despite the fact that Humbert was an official agent selected by the Treasury Department. However, such pieces circulated widely in commerce.

Usually, private coins were circulated due to a shortage of regular federal coinage. In the Western states particularly, official money became so scarce that gold itself—the very commodity the pioneers had come so far to acquire—was converted into a local medium of exchange.

Ephraim Brasher's New York doubloons of 1786 and 1787 are also private American gold issues and are described on pages 120 and 121.

TEMPLETON REID
GEORGIA GOLD, 1830

The first private gold coinage in the 19th century was struck by Templeton Reid, a jeweler and gunsmith, in Milledgeville, Georgia, in July 1830. To be closer to the mines he moved some 120 miles northwest to Gainesville, where most of his coins were made. Although their weights were accurate, Reid's assays were not and his coins were slightly short of their claimed value. He was severely attacked in the newspapers by a determined adversary, and soon lost the public's confidence. He closed his mint before the end of October in 1830; his output had amounted to only about 1,600 coins. Denominations struck were $2.50, $5, and $10. All are great rarities today.

	VF	EF	AU
1830 $2.50	$125,000	$175,000	$300,000
1830 $5 (a)	$325,000	$425,000	$575,000

a. 7 examples are known.

	EF	AU
1830 TEN DOLLARS (a)	$675,000	$950,000
(No Date) TEN DOLLARS (b)	$750,000	$1,100,000

a. 6 examples are known. b. 3 examples are known.

CALIFORNIA GOLD, 1849

The enigmatic later issues of Templeton Reid, dated 1849 and marked CALIFORNIA GOLD, were probably made from California gold late in that year when bullion from California arrived in quantity in the East. Reid, who never went to California, was by then a cotton-gin maker in Columbus, Georgia (some 160 miles southwest of his former location of Gainesville), where he would die in 1851. The coins were in denominations of ten and twenty-five dollars. Struck copies of both exist in various metals.

The only example known of the twenty-five–dollar piece was stolen from the cabinet of the U.S. Mint on August 16, 1858. It was never recovered.

1849 TEN DOLLAR CALIFORNIA GOLD	*(unique, in Smithsonian collection)*
1849 TWENTY-FIVE DOLLARS CALIFORNIA GOLD	*(unknown)*

THE BECHTLERS, RUTHERFORD COUNTY, NORTH CAROLINA, 1831–1852

A skilled German metallurgist, Christopher Bechtler, assisted by his son August and his nephew, also named Christopher, operated a private mint in Rutherford County, North Carolina. Rutherford County and other areas in the Piedmont region of North Carolina and Georgia (from the coastal plain to the mountains of north Georgia) were the principal sources of the nation's gold supply from the early 1800s until the California gold strikes in 1848.

The coins minted by the Bechtlers were of only three denominations, but they covered a wide variety of weights and sizes. Rotated dies are common throughout the series. In 1831, the Bechtlers produced the first gold dollar in the United States. (The Philadelphia Mint made patterns in 1836 and struck its first circulating gold dollar in 1849.) Bechtler coins were well accepted by the public and circulated widely in the Southeast without interference from the government.

The legend AUGUST 1. 1834 on several varieties of five-dollar pieces has a special significance. The secretary of the Treasury recommended to the director of the U.S. Mint that gold coins of the reduced weight introduced in 1834 bear the authorization date. This ultimately was not done on federal gold coinage, but the elder Christopher Bechtler evidently acted on the recommendation to avoid potential difficulty with Treasury authorities.

CHRISTOPHER BECHTLER

	VF	EF	AU	Unc.
ONE GOLD DOLLAR N. CAROLINA, 30.G., Star	$2,800	$4,300	$6,750	$15,000
ONE GOLD DOLLAR N. CAROLINA, 28.G Centered, No Star	$4,750	$5,500	$11,500	$26,000
ONE GOLD DOLLAR N. CAROLINA, 28.G High, No Star	$9,000	$15,000	$23,000	$35,000

	VF	EF	AU	Unc.
ONE DOLLAR CAROLINA, 28.G, N Reversed	$2,500	$3,200	$4,750	$8,000
2.50 NORTH CAROLINA, 20 C. Without 75 G.	$27,000	$37,500	$55,000	$115,000

	VF	EF	AU	Unc.
2.50 NORTH CAROLINA, 75 G., 20 C. RUTHERFORD in a Circle. Border of Large Beads	$26,000	$36,000	$52,500	$110,000
2.50 NORTH CAROLINA, 20 C. Without 75 G., CAROLINA above 250 instead of GOLD (a)				—
2.50 NORTH CAROLINA, 20 C. on Obverse, 75 G. and Star on Reverse. Border Finely Serrated	—	—	—	

a. This piece is unique.

	VF	EF	AU	Unc.
2.50 NORTH CAROLINA, 67 G., 21 CARATS	$6,250	$10,500	$15,000	$35,000
2.50 GEORGIA, 64 G., 22 CARATS (Uneven "22")	$6,750	$11,500	$15,500	$30,000
2.50 GEORGIA, 64 G., 22 CARATS (Even "22")	$9,000	$15,000	$22,000	$45,000
2.50 CAROLINA, 70 G., 20 CARATS	$6,500	$11,000	$15,000	$28,000

	VF	EF	AU	Unc.
5 DOLLARS NORTH CAROLINA GOLD, 150 G., 20.CARATS	$27,000	$39,000	$70,000	$120,000
Similar, Without 150.G. (a)		—	—	

a. 1 or 2 examples are known.

CHRISTOPHER BECHTLER, CAROLINA

	VF	EF	AU	Unc.
5 DOLLARS CAROLINA, RUTHERFORD, 140 G., 20 CARATS, Plain Edge	$5,750	$8,250	$12,500	$26,000
5 DOLLARS CAROLINA, RUTHERFORD, 140 G., 20 CARATS, Reeded Edge	$18,000	$30,000	$42,000	$65,000
5 DOLLARS CAROLINA GOLD, RUTHERF., 140 G., 20 CARATS, AUGUST 1, 1834	$10,000	$18,000	$30,000	$50,000
Similar, but "20" Distant From CARATS	$6,250	$10,000	$15,000	$27,500
5 DOLLARS CAROLINA GOLD, 134 G., 21 CARATS, With Star	$5,500	$8,000	$12,000	$24,000

CHRISTOPHER BECHTLER, GEORGIA

	VF	EF	AU	Unc.
5 DOLLARS GEORGIA GOLD, RUTHERFORD, 128 G., 22 CARATS	$8,000	$11,500	$15,000	$32,000
5 DOLLARS GEORGIA GOLD, RUTHERFORD, 128 G:, 22 CARATS, With Colon After G	$15,000	$26,000	$38,500	
5 DOLLARS GEORGIA GOLD, RUTHERF., 128 G., 22 CARATS	$8,000	$11,500	$16,000	$32,000

AUGUST BECHTLER, CAROLINA

	VF	EF	AU	Unc.
1 DOL:, CAROLINA GOLD, 27.G., 21.C	$1,750	$2,400	$3,200	$5,500
5 DOLLARS, CAROLINA GOLD, 134.G:, 21 CARATS	$5,750	$8,750	$15,000	$36,000
5 DOLLARS, CAROLINA GOLD, 134 G:, 21 CARATS, Reverse of C. Bechtler as Shown Above			—	—

	VF	EF	AU	Unc.
5 DOLLARS, CAROLINA GOLD, 128.G., 22 CARATS	$15,000	$18,000	$27,500	$45,000
5 DOLLARS, CAROLINA GOLD, 141.G., 20 CARATS	$12,500	$17,000	$25,000	$40,000

Note: Restrikes in "Proof" of this type using original dies were made about 1920.

NORRIS, GREGG & NORRIS, SAN FRANCISCO, 1849

Collectors consider this piece the first of the California private gold coins. A newspaper account dated May 31, 1849, described a five-dollar gold coin, struck at Benicia City, though with the imprint of San Francisco. It mentioned the private stamp of Norris, Gregg & Norris, the California branch of a New York City plumbing and hardware firm.

	F	VF	EF	AU	Unc.
1849 Half Eagle, Plain Edge	$4,750	$7,000	$12,000	$17,000	$35,000
1849 Half Eagle, Reeded Edge	$4,500	$6,750	$11,000	$16,000	$35,000
1850 Half Eagle, With STOCKTON Beneath Date (a)	—				

a. This unique piece is housed in the Smithsonian's National Numismatic Collection.

MOFFAT & CO., SAN FRANCISCO, 1849–1853

The firm of Moffat & Co. (principals John Little Moffat, Joseph R. Curtis, Philo H. Perry, and Samuel H. Ward) was the most important of the California private coiners. The assay office they conducted became semi-official in character starting in 1851. The successors to this firm, Curtis, Perry, and Ward, later sold their coining facility to the Treasury Department, which in March 1854 reopened it as the branch mint of San Francisco.

In June or July 1849, Moffat & Co. began to issue small, rectangular ingots of gold in response to lack of coin in the locality, in values from $9.43 to $264. The $9.43, $14.25, and $16.00 varieties are the only types known today.

$9.43 Ingot (a)	—
$14.25 Ingot (a)	—
$16.00 Ingot	$175,000

a. This unique piece is housed in the Smithsonian's National Numismatic Collection.

The dies for the five-dollar and ten-dollar Moffat & Co. pieces were cut by a Bavarian engraver, Albrecht Küner, who had moved to the United States in October 1848. On the coronet of Miss Liberty appear the words MOFFAT & CO., instead of the word LIBERTY as in regular U.S. issues.

	F	VF	EF	AU	Unc.
1849 FIVE DOL. (a)	$1,850	$3,000	$4,350	$6,750	$15,000
1850 FIVE DOL. (a)	$1,900	$3,100	$4,500	$7,000	$17,500
1849 TEN DOL.	$3,750	$6,500	$12,500	$22,500	$38,000
1849 TEN D.	$4,000	$7,000	$13,500	$25,000	$45,000

a. Multiple varieties exist.

UNITED STATES ASSAY OFFICE
Augustus Humbert, United States Assayer of Gold, 1851

Augustus Humbert, a New York watchcase maker, was appointed United States assayer by the Treasury Department in 1850 and arrived in California in early 1851. He placed his name and the government stamp on the ingots of gold issued by Moffat & Co., but without the Moffat imprint. The assay office, a provisional government mint, was a temporary expedient to accommodate the Californians until the establishment of a permanent federal branch mint.

The fifty-dollar gold piece was accepted by most banks and merchants as legal tender on a par with standard U.S. gold coins and was known variously as a *slug*, *quintuple eagle*, *five-eagle piece*, or *adobe* (the latter a type of construction brick). It was officially termed an *ingot*.

Lettered-Edge Varieties

  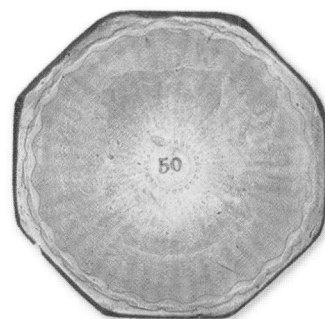

	F	VF	EF	AU	Unc.
1851 50 D C 880 THOUS., No 50 on Reverse. Sunk in Edge: AUGUSTUS HUMBERT UNITED STATES ASSAYER OF GOLD, CALIFORNIA 1851	$22,500	$36,000	$59,000	$85,000	$200,000
Auctions: $546,250, MS-63, August 2010					
1851 50 D C 880 THOUS., Similar to Last Variety, but 50 on Reverse	$30,000	$56,000	$82,500	$150,000	$300,000
1851 50 D C, 887 THOUS., With 50 on Reverse	$26,000	$47,500	$72,500	$110,000	$250,000

Reeded-Edge Varieties

 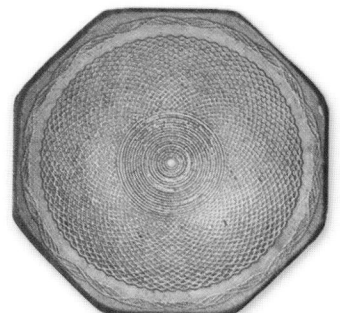

	F	VF	EF	AU	Unc.
1851 FIFTY DOLLS, 880 THOUS., "Target" Reverse	$16,500	$26,500	$40,000	$55,000	$110,000
Auctions: $460,000, MS-65, September 2008					
1851 FIFTY DOLLS, 887 THOUS., "Target" Reverse	$16,500	$26,500	$40,000	$55,000	$110,000
1852 FIFTY DOLLS, 887 THOUS., "Target" Reverse	$17,000	$28,000	$42,000	$57,000	$120,000

MOFFAT-HUMBERT

In 1851, certain issues of the Miners' Bank, Baldwin, Pacific Company, and others were discredited, some unfairly, by newspaper accounts stating they were of reduced gold value. This provided an enhanced opportunity for Moffat and the U.S. Assay Office of Gold. Supplementing privately struck gold pieces and federal issues, coins of almost every nation were being pressed into service by the Californians, but the supply was too small to help to any extent. Moffat & Co. proceeded in January 1852 to issue a new ten-dollar gold piece bearing the stamp MOFFAT & CO.

Close Date   **Wide Date**

	F	VF	EF	AU	Unc.
1852 TEN D. MOFFAT & CO., Close Date	$4,200	$7,000	$15,000	$35,000	$77,500
1852 TEN D. MOFFAT & CO., Wide Date	$4,200	$7,000	$15,000	$35,000	$77,500
Auctions: $940,000, SP-63, January 2014					

1852, Normal Date   **1852, 2 Over 1**

	F	VF	EF	AU	Unc.
1852 TEN DOLS.	$2,750	$4,250	$7,500	$12,000	$27,500
Auctions: $1,057,500, MS-68, April 2013					
1852 TEN DOLS. 1852, 2 Over 1	$2,850	$5,250	$9,500	$16,000	$35,000

	F	VF	EF	AU	Unc.
1852 TWENTY DOLS., 1852, 2 Over 1	$8,000	$13,000	$26,000	$42,500	$140,000
Auctions: $434,500, PF-64, October 1990					

UNITED STATES ASSAY OFFICE OF GOLD, 1852

The firm of Moffat & Co. was dissolved in 1852 and a newly reorganized company known as the United States Assay Office of Gold took over the contract. Principals in the firm were Joseph Curtis, Philo Perry, and Samuel Ward.

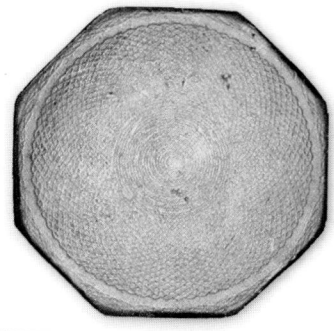

	F	VF	EF	AU	Unc.
1852 FIFTY DOLLS., 887 THOUS.	$17,500	$26,500	$40,000	$55,000	$110,000
1852 FIFTY DOLLS., 900 THOUS.	$18,000	$28,000	$42,000	$57,000	$120,000

	F	VF	EF	AU	Unc.
1852 TEN DOLS., 884 THOUS.	$2,000	$3,500	$5,250	$7,750	$20,000
1853 TEN D., 884 THOUS.	$7,500	$15,000	$27,500	$38,500	$75,000
1853 TEN D., 900 THOUS.	$4,500	$6,500	$10,000	$16,000	$24,000

	F	VF	EF	AU	Unc.
1853 TWENTY D., 884 THOUS.	$7,750	$11,000	$18,000	$30,000	$65,000

	F	VF	EF	AU	Unc.
1853 TWENTY D., 900 THOUS.	$2,250	$3,300	$4,750	$6,500	$13,000

Note: Modern prooflike forgeries exist.

MOFFAT & CO. GOLD, 1853

The last Moffat & Co. issue, an 1853 twenty-dollar piece, is very similar to the U.S. double eagle of that period. It was struck after John L. Moffat retired from the Assay Office. The circumstances of its issue are unclear, but many were coined.

	F	VF	EF	AU	Unc.
1853 TWENTY D.	$4,500	$6,500	$11,000	$17,000	$37,500

J.H. BOWIE, 1849

Joseph H. Bowie joined his cousins in San Francisco in 1849 and possibly produced a limited coinage of gold pieces. A trial piece of the dollar denomination is known in copper, but may never have reached the coinage stage. Little is known about the company or the reason for considering these pieces.

1849 1 DOL., copper pattern	—

CINCINNATI MINING & TRADING CO., 1849

The origin and location of this company are unknown.

	EF	Unc.
1849 FIVE DOLLARS (a)		
1849 TEN DOLLARS (b)	$750,000	—

Note: Beware of spurious specimens cast in base metal with the word TRACING in place of TRADING. **a.** This piece is unique. **b.** 5 examples are known.

MASSACHUSETTS AND CALIFORNIA COMPANY, 1849

This company was organized in Northampton, Massachusetts, in May 1849. Years later fantasy and copy dies were made and coins struck in various metals including gold. Pieces with the denomination spelled as 5D are not genuine.

	VF	EF
1849 FIVE D. (a)	$175,000	$275,000

a. 5 to 7 examples are known.

MINERS' BANK, SAN FRANCISCO, 1849

The institution of Wright & Co., exchange brokers located in Portsmouth Square, San Francisco, was known as the Miners' Bank. The firm issued a ten-dollar gold piece in the autumn of 1849, and it saw wide use in commerce. However, the firm's coinage was ephemeral, and it was dissolved on January 14, 1850. Unlike the gold in most California issues, the gold in these coins was alloyed with copper.

	VF	EF	AU	Unc.
(1849) TEN D.	$18,000	$32,000	$50,000	$110,000

J.S. ORMSBY, SACRAMENTO, 1849

The initials J.S.O., which appear on certain issues of California privately coined gold pieces, represent the firm of J.S. Ormsby & Co., located in Sacramento. They struck five- and ten-dollar denominations, all undated.

	VF
(1849) 5 DOLLS, Plain Edge (a)	—
(1849) 5 DOLLS, Reeded Edge (b)	—
(1849) 10 DOLLS (c)	$450,000

a. This piece may be unique. **b.** This unique piece is housed in the Smithsonian's National Numismatic Collection. **c.** 4 examples are known.

PACIFIC COMPANY, SAN FRANCISCO, 1849

The origin of the Pacific Company is very uncertain. All data regarding the firm are based on conjecture.

Edgar H. Adams wrote that he believed that the coins bearing the stamp of the Pacific Company were produced by the coining firm of Broderick and Kohler. The coins were probably hand struck with the aid of a sledgehammer. Trial pieces exist in silver. All are rarities today.

	EF	AU	Unc.
1849 1 DOLLAR (a)			$300,000
1849 5 DOLLARS (b)	$375,000	$650,000	
Auctions: $763,750, AU-58, April 2014			
1849 10 DOLLARS (c)	$600,000	$700,000	$1,000,000

a. 2 examples are known. **b.** 4 examples are known. **c.** 4 examples are known.

F.D. KOHLER, CALIFORNIA STATE ASSAYER, 1850

The State Assay Office was authorized on April 12, 1850. That year, Governor Peter Burnett appointed to the position of state assayer Frederick D. Kohler, who thereupon sold his assaying business to Baldwin & Co. Kohler served at both the San Francisco and Sacramento offices. The State Assay Offices were discontinued at the time the U.S. Assay Office was established, on February 1, 1851.

Ingots issued ranged from $36.55 to $150. An Extremely Fine specimen sold in the Garrett Sale, 1980, for $200,000. Each is unique.

$36.55 Sacramento	—
$37.31 San Francisco	—
$40.07 San Francisco	—
$45.34 San Francisco	—
$50.00 San Francisco	—
$54.00 San Francisco	—

Note: A $40.07 ingot was stolen from the Mint Cabinet in 1858 and never recovered.

DUBOSQ & COMPANY, SAN FRANCISCO, 1850

Theodore Dubosq Sr., a Philadelphia jeweler, took melting and coining equipment to San Francisco in 1849 and minted five-dollar gold pieces.

	VF
1850 FIVE D. (a)	$275,000
1850 TEN D. (b)	$275,000

a. 3 to 5 examples are known. **b.** 8 to 10 examples are known.

BALDWIN & CO., SAN FRANCISCO, 1850–1851

George C. Baldwin and Thomas S. Holman were in the jewelry business in San Francisco and were known as Baldwin & Co. They were the successors to F.D. Kohler & Co., taking over its machinery and other equipment in May 1850. The firm ceased minting coins in early 1851, at which time newspaper accounts stated that its coins fell short of their stated gold value. The 1850 Vaquero or Horseman ten-dollar design is one of the most famous of the California gold issues.

	F	VF	EF	AU	Unc.
1850 FIVE DOL.	$7,500	$13,000	$25,000	$35,000	$75,000
1850, TEN DOLLARS, Horseman Type	$45,000	$75,000	$125,000	$165,000	$275,000

	F	VF	EF	AU	Unc.
1851 TEN D.	$16,000	$32,500	$48,000	$77,000	$190,000

The Baldwin & Co. twenty-dollar piece was the first of that denomination issued in California. Baldwin coins are believed to have contained about 2% copper alloy.

	EF	Unc.
1851 TWENTY D. (a)	$600,000	—
	Auctions: $646,250, EF-45, April 2014	

a. 4 to 6 examples are known.

SCHULTZ & COMPANY, SAN FRANCISCO, 1851

The firm of Schultz & Co., a brass foundry, was operated by Judge G.W. Schultz and William T. Garratt. The surname is misspelled as SHULTZ on the coins.

	F	VF	EF	AU	Unc.
1851 FIVE D.	$32,500	$57,500	$90,000	$150,000	$350,000

DUNBAR & COMPANY, SAN FRANCISCO, 1851

Edward E. Dunbar operated the California Bank in San Francisco. He later returned to New York City and organized the famous Continental Bank Note Co.

	VF	EF
1851 FIVE D. (a)	$250,000	$425,000

a. 4 to 6 examples are known.

WASS, MOLITOR & CO., SAN FRANCISCO, 1852–1855

The gold-smelting and assaying plant of Wass, Molitor & Co. was operated by two Hungarian patriots exiled after the Revolution of 1848, Count Samu Wass and A.P. Molitor. They maintained an excellent laboratory and complete apparatus for analysis and coinage of gold.

The company struck five-, ten-, twenty-, and fifty-dollar coins. In 1852 they produced a ten-dollar piece similar in design to the five-dollar denomination. The difference is in the reverse legend, which reads: S.M.V. [Standard Mint Value] CALIFORNIA GOLD TEN D.

No pieces were coined in 1853 or 1854, but they brought out the twenty- and fifty-dollar pieces in 1855. A considerable number of the fifty-dollar coins were made. There was a ten-dollar piece issued in 1855 also, with the Liberty Head design and small close date.

Small Head, Rounded Bust

Large Head, Pointed Bust

	F	VF	EF	AU	Unc.
1852 FIVE DOLLARS, Small Head, With Rounded Bust	$5,500	$11,000	$22,500	$40,000	$80,000
1852 FIVE DOLLARS, Large Head, With Pointed Bust	$4,700	$9,500	$18,000	$35,000	$67,500

Large Head

Small Head　　　**Small Date**　　　**1855**

	F	VF	EF	AU	Unc.
1852 TEN D., Large Head	$2,750	$4,500	$8,000	$14,000	$32,500
1852 TEN D., Small Head	$6,200	$8,000	$19,000	$32,000	$80,000
1852 TEN D., Small Close Date	$12,500	$28,000	$47,000	$90,000	
1855 TEN D.	$9,500	$16,000	$22,000	$29,000	$52,500

Large Head　　　　　　　**Small Head**

	F	VF	EF	AU	Unc.
1855 TWENTY DOL., Large Head (a)	—	—	$550,000	—	—
	Auctions: $558,125, AU-53, April 2014				
1855 TWENTY DOL., Small Head	$12,000	$25,000	$35,000	$55,000	$125,000

a. 4 to 6 examples are known. A unique piece with the Large Head obverse and the reverse used on the Small Head coins (which differs in the position of the eagle's left wing) also exists.

	F	VF	EF	AU	Unc.
1855 50 DOLLARS	$25,000	$36,000	$55,000	$85,000	$175,000

KELLOGG & CO., SAN FRANCISCO, 1854–1855

John G. Kellogg went to San Francisco on October 12, 1849, from Auburn, New York. At first he was employed by Moffat & Co., and remained with that organization when control passed to Curtis, Perry, and Ward. When the U.S. Assay Office was discontinued, December 14, 1853, Kellogg became associated with George F. Richter, who had been an assayer in the U.S. Assay Office of Gold. These two set up business as Kellogg & Richter on December 19, 1853.

When the U.S. Assay Office ceased operations, a period ensued during which no private firm was striking gold. The new San Francisco branch mint did not produce coins for some months after Curtis & Perry took the contract for the government (Ward having died). The lack of coin was again keenly felt by businessmen, who petitioned Kellogg & Richter to "supply the vacuum" by issuing private coin. Their plea was soon answered: on February 9, 1854, Kellogg & Co. placed their first twenty-dollar piece in circulation.

The firm dissolved late in 1854 and reorganized as Kellogg & Humbert. The latter partner was Augustus Humbert, for some time identified as U.S. assayer of gold in California. Regardless of the fact that the San Francisco branch mint was then producing coins, Kellogg & Humbert issued twenty-dollar coins in 1855 in a quantity greater than before. On September 12, 1857, hundreds of the firm's rectangular gold ingots in transit to New York City were lost in the sinking of the SS *Central America*. They were the most plentiful of bars aboard the ill-fated ship from several different assayers.

	F	VF	EF	AU	Unc.
1854 TWENTY D.	$3,250	$4,750	$6,500	$9,000	$24,000

The 1855 Kellogg & Co. twenty-dollar piece is similar to that of 1854. The letters on the reverse are larger and the arrows longer on one 1854 variety. There are die varieties of both.

	F	VF	EF	AU	Unc.
1855 TWENTY D.	$3,500	$5,000	$6,750	$9,500	$25,000

In 1855, Ferdinand Grüner cut the dies for a round-format fifty-dollar gold coin for Kellogg & Co., but coinage seems to have been limited to presentation pieces in Proof format. Only 10 to 12 pieces are known to exist. A "commemorative restrike" was made in 2001 using transfer dies made from the original and gold recovered from the SS *Central America*. These pieces have the inscription S.S. CENTRAL AMERICA GOLD, C.H.S. on the reverse ribbon.

	PF
1855 FIFTY DOLLS. (a)	$550,000
Auctions: $763,750, PF-64Cam, April 2014; $747,500, PF-64, January 2007	

a. 13 to 15 examples are known.

OREGON EXCHANGE COMPANY, OREGON CITY, 1849
THE BEAVER COINS OF OREGON

Upon the discovery of gold in California, a great exodus of Oregonians joined in the hunt for the precious metal. Soon, gold seekers returned with their gold dust, which became an accepted medium of exchange. As in other Western areas at that time, the uncertain qualities of the gold and weighing devices tended to irk tradespeople, and petitions were made to the legislature for a standard gold coin issue.

On February 16, 1849, the territorial legislature passed an act providing for a mint and specified five- and ten-dollar gold coins without alloy. Oregon City, the largest city in the territory with a population of about 1,000, was designated as the location for the mint. At the time this act was passed, Oregon had been brought into the United States as a territory by act of Congress. When the new governor arrived on March 2, he declared the coinage act unconstitutional.

The public-spirited people, however, continued to work for a convenient medium of exchange and soon took matters into their own hands by starting a private mint. Eight men of affairs, whose names were Kilborne, Magruder, Taylor, Abernethy, Willson, Rector, Campbell, and Smith, set up the Oregon Exchange Company.

The coins struck were of virgin gold as specified in the original act. Ten-dollar dies were made slightly later.

	F	VF	EF	AU	Unc.
1859 5 D.	$32,000	$48,500	$75,000	$125,000	$250,000

	F	VF	EF	AU	Unc.
1859 TEN.D.	$80,000	$145,000	$270,000	$350,000	—

MORMON GOLD PIECES, SALT LAKE CITY, UTAH, 1849–1860

The first name given to the organized Mormon Territory was the "State of Deseret," the last word meaning "honeybee" in the Book of Mormon. The beehive, which is shown on the reverse of the five-dollar 1860 piece, was a favorite device of the followers of Joseph Smith and Brigham Young. The clasped hands appear on most Mormon coins and exemplify strength in unity. HOLINESS TO THE LORD was an inscription frequently used.

Brigham Young was the instigator of the coinage system and personally supervised the mint, which was housed in a little adobe building in Salt Lake City. The mint was inaugurated late in 1848 as a public convenience and to make a profit for the church. Each coin had substantially less gold than the face value stated.

	F	VF	EF	AU	Unc.
1849 TWO.AND.HALF.DO.	$12,500	$23,000	$35,000	$57,000	$90,000
1849 FIVE.DOLLARS	$9,500	$18,500	$30,000	$42,000	$80,000

	F	VF	EF	AU	Unc.
1849 TEN.DOLLARS	$235,000	$450,000	$550,000	$750,000	$950,000
	Auctions: $705,000, AU-58, April 2014				

	F	VF	EF	AU	Unc.
1849 TWENTY.DOLLARS (a)	$92,500	$175,000	$275,000	$375,000	$525,000
	Auctions: $558,125, MS-62, April 2014				

a. The first coin of the twenty-dollar denomination to be struck in the United States.

	F	VF	EF	AU	Unc.
1850 FIVE DOLLARS	$13,000	$22,000	$34,000	$47,500	$85,000

	F	VF	EF	AU	Unc.
1860 5.D.	$20,000	$32,000	$42,000	$70,000	$90,000

COLORADO GOLD PIECES

CLARK, GRUBER & CO., DENVER, 1860–1861

Clark, Gruber & Co. was a well-known private minting firm in Denver, Colorado, in 1860 and 1861, formed by bankers from Leavenworth, Kansas Territory. In 1862 their operation was purchased by the Treasury Department and thenceforth operated as an assay office.

	F	VF	EF	AU	Unc.
1860 2 1/2 D.	$1,800	$2,750	$4,000	$5,500	$13,500
1860 FIVE D.	$2,100	$3,250	$4,500	$6,250	$14,500

	F	VF	EF	AU	Unc.
1860 TEN D.	$9,000	$14,000	$20,000	$30,000	$55,000
1860 TWENTY D.	$70,000	$135,000	$250,000	$385,000	$650,000
Auctions: $690,000, MS-64, January 2006					

The $2.50 and $5 pieces of 1861 follow closely the designs of the 1860 issues. The main difference is found in the legends. The reverse side now has CLARK GRUBER & CO. DENVER. On the obverse, PIKES PEAK now appears on the coronet of Miss Liberty.

	F	VF	EF	AU	Unc.
1861 2 1/2 D.	$1,900	$3,000	$4,400	$7,500	$14,000
1861 FIVE D.	$2,300	$3,700	$5,750	$10,500	$37,500
1861 TEN D.	$2,400	$4,000	$6,500	$11,000	$28,500

	F	VF	EF	AU	Unc.
1861 TWENTY D.	$20,000	$37,500	$57,500	$95,000	$225,000

JOHN PARSONS & COMPANY, TARRYALL MINES, COLORADO, 1861

Very little is known regarding the mint of John Parsons and Co., although it is reasonably certain that it operated in the South Park section of Park County, Colorado, near the original town of Tarryall, in the summer of 1861.

	VF	EF
(1861) Undated 2 1/2 D. (a)	$200,000	$300,000
(1861) Undated FIVE D. (b)	$275,000	$375,000

a. 6 to 8 examples are known. **b.** 5 or 6 examples are known.

J.J. Conway & Co., Georgia Gulch, Colorado, 1861

Records show that the Conway mint operated for a short while in 1861. As in all gold-mining areas the value of gold dust caused disagreement among the merchants and the miners. The firm of J.J. Conway & Co. solved this difficulty by bringing out its gold pieces in August 1861.

	VF	EF
(1861) Undated 2 1/2 DOLL'S (a)	$155,000	$200,000
(1861) Undated FIVE DOLLARS (b)	$225,000	$300,000

a. 8 to 12 examples are known. **b.** 5 to 8 examples are known.

(1861) Undated TEN DOLLARS (a)	—

a. 3 examples are known.

CALIFORNIA SMALL-DENOMINATION GOLD

There was a scarcity of small coins during the California gold rush. Starting in 1852, quarter, half, and dollar coins were privately minted from native gold to alleviate the shortage. The commercial accept-ability of these hard-to-handle, underweight coins was always limited, but they soon became popular as souvenirs. Early coins contained up to 85% of face value in gold. The amount and quality of gold in the coins soon decreased, and some later issues are merely gold plated.

The Coinage Act of April 22, 1864, made private coinage illegal, but the law was not fully enforced until 1883. In compliance with the law, non-denominated tokens were made, and from 1872 until 1883 both coins and tokens were produced. After 1883, most of the production was tokens. To circumvent the law, and to make them more acceptable, some pieces made after 1881 were backdated to the 1850s or 1860s.

Early issues have Liberty heads; later issues have Indian heads and often are prooflike. Most have a wreath on the reverse, but some have original designs. About 35,000 pieces are believed to exist. Numis-matists have identified more than 570 different varieties, many of them very rare. The quality of strike and edge treatment is inconsistent. Many bear their makers' initials: D, DERI, DERIB, DN, FD, G, GG, GL, H, L, N, or NR. Major denominated coins are listed below; values are for the most common variety of each type. Non-denominated tokens are not included in these listings. They are much less valuable. ***Beware of extremely common modern replicas*** (often having a bear in the design), which have little numismatic value.

The values in the following charts are only for coins made before 1883 with the denomination on the reverse expressed as CENTS, DOL., DOLL., or DOLLAR.

QUARTER DOLLAR, OCTAGONAL

	EF	AU	Unc.
Large Liberty Head / Value and Date in Wreath	$175	$250	$450
Large Liberty Head / Value and Date in Beaded Circle	$175	$275	$470
Large Liberty Head / Value and CAL in Wreath	$175	$230	$350
Small Liberty Head / Value and Date in Wreath	$170	$230	$320
Small Liberty Head / Value and Date in Beaded Circle	$175	$250	$340
Small Liberty Head / Value in Shield, Date in Wreath	$175	$250	$375
Small Liberty Head / Value and CAL in Wreath	$175	$250	$425
Small Liberty Head, date below / Value in Wreath	$175	$230	$320
Large Indian Head / Value in Wreath	$215	$310	$475
Large Indian Head / Value and CAL in Wreath	$200	$280	$450
Small Indian Head / Value and CAL in Wreath	$500	$625	$975
Washington Head 1872 / Value and CAL in Wreath	$775	$1,350	$2,000

QUARTER DOLLAR, ROUND

	EF	AU	Unc.
Liberty Head / Value in Wreath	$150	$250	$425
Large Liberty Head / Value and Date in Wreath	$190	$310	$450
Large Liberty Head / Value and CAL in Wreath	$150	$250	$400
Small Liberty Head / 25 CENTS in Wreath	$320	$500	$800
Small Liberty Head / Value and Date in Wreath	$180	$300	$435
Small Liberty Head / Value in Shield, Date in Wreath	$180	$315	$550
Small Liberty Head / Value and CAL in Wreath	$180	$225	$400
Large Indian Head / Value in Wreath	$350	$520	$825
Large Indian Head / Value and CAL in Wreath	$300	$400	$675
Small Indian Head / Value and CAL in Wreath	$375	$525	$850
Washington Head 1872 / Value and CAL in Wreath	$725	$1,000	$1,600

HALF DOLLAR, OCTAGONAL

	EF	AU	Unc.
Large Liberty Head / Value and Date in Wreath	$300	$370	$690
Large Liberty Head / Value and Date in Beaded Circle	$170	$210	$450
Large Liberty Head / Value and CAL in Wreath	$210	$425	$650
Large Liberty Head / Legend Surrounds Wreath	$400	$600	$1,000
Small Liberty Head / Value and Date in Wreath	$200	$375	$575
Small Liberty Head / Value and CAL in Wreath	$185	$320	$475
Small Liberty Head / Small Eagle With Rays	$1,300	$2,000	$3,250
Small Liberty Head / Large Eagle With Raised Wings	$1,500	$2,200	$3,250
Large Indian Head / Value in Wreath	$210	$400	$675
Large Indian Head / Value and CAL in Wreath	$235	$350	$575
Small Indian Head / Value in Wreath	$250	$425	$700
Small Indian Head / Value and CAL in Wreath	$450	$585	$975

HALF DOLLAR, ROUND

	EF	AU	Unc.
Liberty Head / Value in Wreath	$180	$325	$500
Liberty Head / Value and Date in Wreath	$180	$325	$500
Liberty Head / Value and CAL in Wreath	$225	$350	$575
Liberty Head / CALIFORNIA GOLD Around Wreath	$225	$375	$600
Large Indian Head / Value in Wreath	$210	$325	$525
Large Indian Head / Value and CAL in Wreath	$200	$300	$465
Small Indian Head / Value and CAL in Wreath	$200	$330	$525

DOLLAR, OCTAGONAL

	EF	AU	Unc.
Liberty Head / Value and Date in Wreath	$500	$750	$1,350
Liberty Head / Value and Date in Beaded Circle	$500	$800	$1,500
Liberty Head / Legend Around Wreath	$500	$825	$1,550
Liberty Head / Large Eagle	$2,150	$3,150	$5,250
Large Indian Head / Value in Wreath	$725	$1,150	$2,100
Small Indian Head / Value and CAL in Wreath	$725	$1,150	$2,100

DOLLAR, ROUND

	EF	AU	Unc.
Liberty Head / CALIFORNIA GOLD. Value and Date in Wreath	$1,750	$2,600	$4,500
Liberty Head / Date Beneath Head	$2,300	$3,200	$5,100
Indian Head / Date Beneath Head	$2,000	$3,100	$5,000

COINS OF THE GOLDEN WEST

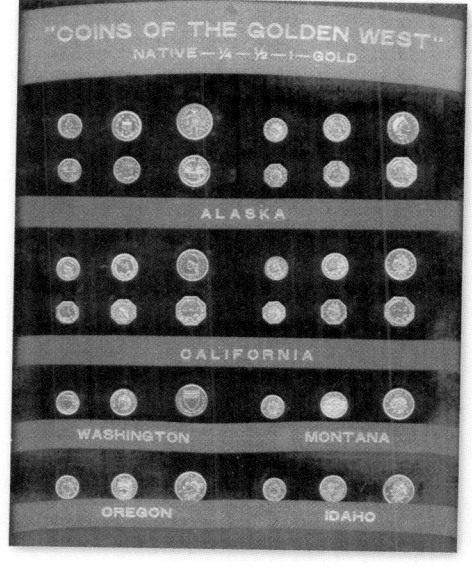

Small souvenir California gold pieces were made by several manufacturers in the early 20th century. A series of 36 pieces, in the size of 25¢, 50¢, and $1 coins, was sold by the M.E. Hart Company of San Francisco to honor Alaska and various Western states. The Hart Company also marketed the official commemorative Panama-Pacific gold coins from the 1915 Exposition and manufactured plush copper cases for them. Similar cases were acquired by Farran Zerbe, who mounted 15 complete sets of what he termed "Coins of the Golden West." Intact, framed 36-piece sets are rare; individual specimens are among the most popular of all souvenir pieces of that era.

	AU	MS-63
Alaska Pinch, 25¢, octagonal, 1902	$350	$650
Alaska Pinch, 50¢, octagonal, 1900	$400	$700
Alaska Pinch, $1, octagonal, 1898	$500	$850
Alaska Pinch, 25¢, round, 1901	$350	$650
Alaska Pinch, 50¢, round, 1899	$400	$700
Alaska Pinch, $1, round, 1897	$500	$850
Alaska Parka, 25¢, round, 1911	$1,200	$1,900
Alaska Parka, 50¢, round, 1911	$1,300	$2,250
Alaska Parka, $1, round, 1911	$1,500	$2,650
Alaska AYPE, 25¢, round, 1909	$175	$300
Alaska AYPE, 50¢, round, 1909	$200	$350
Alaska AYPE, $1, round, 1909	$250	$400
California Minerva, 25¢, octagonal, 1915	$200	$350
California Minerva, 50¢, octagonal, 1915	$250	$400
California Minerva, $1, octagonal, 1915	$300	$500
California Minerva, 25¢, round, 1915	$200	$350
California Minerva, 50¢, round, 1915	$250	$400
California Minerva, $1, round, 1915	$300	$500
California 25¢, octagonal, 1860 or 1902	$500	$1,200
California 50¢, octagonal, 1900	$600	$1,350
California $1, octagonal, 1898	$700	$1,600
California 25¢, round, 1849, 1860, 1871, or 1901	$550	$1,250
California 50¢, round, 1849 or 1899	$650	$1,500
California $1, round, 1849	$800	$1,750
Idaho, 25¢, round, 1914	$650	$1,150
Idaho, 50¢, round, 1914	$750	$1,250
Idaho, $1, round, 1914	$850	$1,500
Montana, 25¢, round, 1914	$650	$1,150
Montana, 50¢, round, 1914	$750	$1,250
Montana, $1, round, 1914	$850	$1,500
Oregon, 25¢, round, 1914	$600	$1,100
Oregon, 50¢, round, 1914	$700	$1,200
Oregon, $1, round, 1914	$800	$1,400
Washington, 25¢, round, 1914	$600	$1,100
Washington, 50¢, round, 1914	$700	$1,200
Washington, $1, round, 1914	$800	$1,400

CALIFORNIA GOLD INGOT BARS

During the Gold Rush era, gold coins, ingots, and "dust" (actually flakes and nuggets) were sent by steamship from San Francisco to other ports, most importantly to New York City and London, where the gold was sold or, in some instances, sent to mints for conversion into coins. The typical procedure in the mid-1850s was to send the gold by steamship from San Francisco to Panama, where it was transported across 48 miles of territory by small water craft and pack animals from 1849 until the Panama Railroad opened in 1855, then loaded aboard another ship at the town of Aspinwall on the Atlantic side. On September 12, 1857, the SS *Central America*, en route from Aspinwall to New York City with more than 475 passengers, over 100 crew members, and an estimated $2.6 million in gold (in an era in which pure gold was valued at $20.67 per ounce) was lost at sea. Miraculously, more than 150 people, including all but one of the women and children, were rescued by passing ships. The *Central America* went to the bottom of the Atlantic Ocean off the Carolina coast.

In the 1980s a group of researchers secured financing to search for the long-lost ship. After much study and many explorations, they discovered the wreck of the *Central America* 7,200 feet below the surface. They used the robotic *Nemo*, a sophisticated device weighing several tons, to photograph the wreck and to carefully bring to the surface many artifacts. A king's ransom in gold ingots was found, along with more than 7,500 coins, the latter mostly consisting of Mint State 1857-S double eagles.

The 500-plus gold ingots furnished a unique opportunity to study specimens that, after conservation, were essentially in the same condition as they had been in 1857. These bore the imprints of five different California assayers, who operated seven offices. With few exceptions, each ingot bears individual stamps, indicating its maker, a serial number, the weight in ounces, the fineness (expressed in thousandths, e.g., .784 indicating 784/1000 pure gold), and the 1857 value in dollars. The smallest bar found was issued by Blake & Co., weighed 4.95 ounces, was .795 fine, and was stamped with a value of $81.34. The largest ingot, dubbed the "Eureka bar," bore the imprint of Kellogg & Humbert, and was stamped with a weight of 933.94 ounces, .903 fine, and a value of $17,433.57.

Blake & Co., Sacramento, California: From December 28, 1855, to May 1858, Blake & Co. was operated by Gorham Blake and W.R. Waters. • 34 ingots recovered. Serial numbers in the 5,100 and 5,200 series. Lowest weight and value: 4.95 ounces, $81.34. Highest weight and value: 157.40 ounces, $2,655.05. These bars have beveled or "dressed" edges and may have seen limited use in California commerce.

Harris, Marchand & Co., Sacramento and Marysville: This firm was founded in Sacramento in 1855 by Harvey Harris and Desiré Marchand, with Charles L. Farrington as the "& Co." The Marysville office was opened in January 1856. Serial numbers in the 6000 series are attributed to Sacramento, comprising 36 bars; a single bar in the 7000 series (7095) is attributed to Marysville. The Marchand bars each have a circular coin-style counterstamp on the face. Lowest weight and value (Sacramento): 9.87 ounces, $158.53. Highest weight and value (Sacramento): 295.20 ounces, $5,351.73. • Unique Marysville bar: 174.04 ounces, $3,389.06.

Henry Hentsch, San Francisco: Hentsch, a Swiss, was an entrepreneur involved in banking, real estate, assaying, and other ventures. In February 1856, he opened an assay office as an annex to his bank. It is likely that many of his ingots were exported to Europe, where he had extensive banking connections. • 33 ingots recovered. Lowest weight and value: 12.52 ounces, $251.82. Highest weight and value: 238.84 ounces, $4,458.35.

Justh & Hunter, San Francisco and Marysville: Emanuel Justh, a Hungarian, was a lithographer in San Francisco in the early 1850s. In 1854 and 1855 he worked as assistant assayer at the San Francisco Mint. Solomon Hillen Hunter came to California from Baltimore. The Justh & Hunter partnership was announced in May 1855. • Although study is continuing, the 60 ingots in the 4000 series are tentatively attributed to San Francisco, and the 26 ingots in the 9000 series are attributed to Marysville. • San Francisco—Lowest weight and value: 5.24 ounces, $92.18. Highest weight and value: 866.19 ounces, $15,971.93. • Marysville—Lowest weight and value: 19.34 ounces, $356.21. Highest weight and value: 464.65 ounces, $8,759.90.

Kellogg & Humbert, San Francisco: John Glover Kellogg and Augustus Humbert, two of the most famous names in the minting of California gold coins, formed the partnership of Kellogg & Humbert in spring 1855. The firm was one of the most active of all California assayers during the mid-1850s. • 346 ingots recovered, constituting the majority of those found. • Lowest weight and value: 5.71 ounces, $101.03. Highest weight and value: 933.94 ounces, $17,433.57.

A selection of gold ingots from the SS *Central America* treasure (with an 1857-S double eagle shown for scale, near lower left). (1) Harris, Marchand & Co., Marysville office, serial number 7095, 174.04 ounces, .942 fine, $3,389.06 (all values as stamped in 1857). (2) Henry Hentsch, San Francisco, serial number 3120, 61.93 ounces, .886 fine, $1,134.26. (3) Kellogg & Humbert, San Francisco, serial number 215, .944 fine, $1,045.96. (4) Blake & Co., Sacramento, 19.30 ounces, .946 fine, $297.42. (5) Another Blake & Co. ingot, serial number 5216, .915 fine, $266.12. (6) Justh & Hunter, Marysville office, serial number 9440, 41.79 ounces, $761.07. (7) Justh & Hunter, San Francisco office, serial number 4243, 51.98 ounces, .916 fine, $984.27. (8) Harris, Marchand & Co., Sacramento office, serial number 6514, 35.33 ounces, .807 fine, $589.38. (9) Harris, Marchand & Co., Sacramento office, serial number 6486, 12.64 ounces, .950 fine, $245.00.

Private Tokens

Privately issued tokens are by no means an American invention. They were common to most capitalist nations in the 1800s (and known even earlier), created and circulated by businessmen and others in periods of economic weakness or uncertainty, during financial panics, depressions, and times of war. Sometimes they were handed out as advertising trinkets or political propaganda pieces; more often they passed as makeshift currency when few real coins were available to make small change. Unlike real coins, which are government-issued as legal tender, tokens are minted by private citizens and companies. Commonly made of metal, usually round in shape, coins and tokens are very similar in appearance, but a token lacks a coin's official status as government-backed currency. Typically it would only have trade value, and then only in the vicinity in which it was issued (if, for example, a local merchant was prepared to redeem it in goods or services).

This section describes several of the more commonly encountered American tokens of the 1800s.

HARD TIMES TOKENS (1832–1844)

Hard Times tokens, as they are called, are pieces of Americana dating from the era of presidents Andrew Jackson and Martin Van Buren. They are mostly the size of a contemporary large copper cent. Privately minted from 1832 to 1844, they display diverse motifs reflecting political campaigns and satire of the era as well as carrying advertisements for merchants, products, and services. For many years these have been a popular specialty within numismatics, helped along with the publication of *Hard Times Tokens* by Lyman H. Low (1899; revised edition, 1906) and later works, continuing to the present day (see the *Guide Book of Hard Times Tokens*, 2015). In 1899 Low commented (adapted) that "the issues commonly called Hard Times tokens . . . had no semblance of authority behind them. They combine the character of political pieces with the catch-words of party cries; of satirical pieces with sarcastic allusions to the sentiments or speeches of the leaders of opposing parties; and in some degree also of necessity pieces, in a time when, to use one of the phrases of the day, 'money was a cash article,' hard to get for daily needs."

Although examples from the earlier 1830s are designated as Hard Times tokens, the true Hard Times period started in a serious way on May 10, 1837, when banks began suspending specie payments and would no longer exchange paper currency for coins. This date is memorialized on some of the token inscriptions. Difficult economic conditions continued through 1843; the first full year of recovery was 1844. From March 1837 to March 1841, President Martin Van Buren vowed to "follow in the steps of my illustrious predecessor," President Andrew Jackson, who had been in office from March 1829 until Van Buren's inauguration. Jackson was perhaps the most controversial president up to that time. His veto in 1832 of the impending (1836) recharter of the Bank of the United States set off a political firestorm, and the flames were fanned when his administration shifted deposits to favored institutions, derisively called "pet banks."

The Jackson era was one of unbridled prosperity. Due to sales of land in the West, the expansion of railroads, and a robust economy, so much money piled up in the Treasury that distributions were made in 1835 to all of the states. Seeking to end wild speculation, Jackson issued the "Specie Circular" on July 11, 1836, mandating that purchases of Western land, often made on credit, by paper money of uncertain worth, or by non-cash means, had to be paid in silver or gold coins. Almost immediately, the land boom settled and prices stabilized. A chill began to spread across the economy, which worsened in early 1837. Finally, many banks ran short of ready cash, causing the specie suspension.

After May 10, 1837, silver and gold coins completely disappeared from circulation. Copper cents remained, but were in short supply. Various diesinkers and others produced a flood of copper tokens. These were sold at discounts to merchants and banks, with $6 for 1,000 tokens being typical. Afterward, they were paid out in commerce and circulated for the value of one cent.

The actions of Jackson, the financial tribulations that many thought he precipitated, and the policies of Van Buren inspired motifs for a class of Hard Times tokens today known as "politicals." Several hundred other varieties were made with the advertisements of merchants, services, and products and are known as "store cards" or "merchants' tokens." Many of these were illustrated with elements such as a shoe, umbrella, comb, coal stove, storefront, hotel, or carriage.

One of the more famous issues depicts a slave kneeling in chains, with the motto "Am I Not a Woman & a Sister?" This token was issued in 1838, when abolition was a major rallying point for many Americans in the North. The curious small-size Feuchtwanger cents of 1837, made in Feuchtwanger's Composition (a type of German silver), were proposed to Congress as a cheap substitute for copper cents, but no congressional action was taken. Lewis Feuchtwanger produced large quantities on his own account and circulated them extensively (see page 1354).

As the political and commercial motifs of Hard Times tokens are so diverse, and reflect the American economy and political scene of their era, numismatists have found them fascinating to collect and study. Although there are major rarities in the series, most of the issues are very affordable. Expanded information concerning more than 500 varieties of Hard Times tokens can be found in Russell Rulau's *Standard Catalog of United States Tokens, 1700–1900* (fourth edition). Collectors and researchers are also encouraged to consult *A Guide Book of Hard Times Tokens* (Bowers). A representative selection is illustrated here.

L1, HT1

L57, HT76

L4, HT6

L56, HT75

	VF	EF	AU
L1, HT1. Andrew Jackson. Copper	$5,750	$9,000	—
L57, HT76. Van Buren, facing left. Brass	$2,500	$3,500	$4,500
L4, HT6. Jackson President of the U.S. Brass	$150	$300	$800
L56, HT75. Van Buren facing left. Copper	$85	$175	$400

L66, HT24

L54, HT81

L55, HT63

L31, HT46

L8, HT9

L18, HT32

L51, HT70

L47, HT66

L60, HT18

L44, HT69

	VF	EF	AU
L66, HT24. Agriculture. Copper	$250	$375	$700
L54, HT81. A Woman & A Sister. Copper	$200	$300	$450
L55, HT63. Loco Foco, 1838. Copper	$60	$175	$300
L31, HT46. Not One Cent, Motto. Copper	$50	$75	$150
L8, HT9. My Victory / Jackson. Copper	$35	$100	$150
L18, HT32. Executive Experiment. Copper	$30	$80	$125
L51, HT70. Roman Firmness. Copper	$40	$75	$150
L47, HT66. Phoenix / May Tenth. Copper	$30	$75	$135
L60, HT18. Ship/Lightning. Copper	$30	$75	$135
L44, HT69. Ship/Jackson. Copper	$30	$90	$150

L59, HT17

L65, HT23

	VF	EF	AU
L59, HT17. Ship / Wreath Border. Copper	$26	$65	$125
L65, HT23. Ship / Liberty Head. Copper	$120	$225	$400

FEUCHTWANGER TOKENS (1837–1864)

Lewis Feuchtwanger, a German-born chemist, moved to the United States in 1829 and settled in New York City. He produced a variety of German silver (an alloy of metals not including any actual silver) consisting of nickel, copper, and some zinc. Feuchtwanger suggested to Congress as early as 1837 that his metal be substituted for copper in U.S. coinage, and he made one-cent and three-cent trial pieces that circulated freely during the coin shortage of 1836 through 1844.

	VF	EF	AU	Unc.
1837 One Cent, Eagle	$130	$210	$300	$500
1837 Three-Cent, New York Coat of Arms	$750	$1,600	$2,750	$5,250
1837 Three-Cent, Eagle	$1,700	$3,600	$5,500	$13,000
1864 Three-Cent, Eagle	$1,300	$2,800	$3,800	$7,500

LESHER REFERENDUM DOLLARS (1900–1901)

Distributed in 1900 and 1901 by Joseph Lesher of Victor, Colorado, these private tokens manufactured in Denver were used in trade to some extent, and stocked by various merchants who redeemed them in goods. Lesher was an Ohio-born Civil War veteran and, after the war, an early pioneer of Colorado's mining fields. His coins, octagonal in shape, were numbered and a blank space left at bottom of 1901 issues, in which were stamped names of businessmen who bought them. All are quite rare; many varieties are extremely rare. Their composition is .950 fine silver (alloyed with copper).

	EF	AU	Unc.
1900 First type, no business name	$3,200	$4,000	$6,500
1900 A.B. Bumstead, with or without scrolls (Victor)	$1,800	$2,400	$3,800
1900 Bank type	$20,000	$32,000	—
1901 Imprint type, no name	$2,000	$3,000	$4,500
1901 Imprint type, Boyd Park. Denver	$2,000	$3,000	$4,600
1901 Imprint type, Slusher. Cripple Creek	$2,500	$3,500	$5,250
1901 Imprint type, Mullen. Victor	$4,000	$6,500	$10,500
1901 Imprint type, Cohen. Victor	$7,000	$11,000	$15,000
1901 Imprint type, Klein. Pueblo	$8,000	$12,500	$18,000
1901 Imprint type, Alexander. Salida	$9,000	$15,000	$21,000
1901 Imprint type, White. Grand Junction	$19,000	$27,000	—
1901 Imprint type, Goodspeeds. Colorado Springs	$32,000	$42,000	—
1901 Imprint type, Nelson. Holdrige, Nebraska	$30,000	$40,000	—
1901 Imprint type, A.W. Clark (Denver) (a)		$40,000	

a. This piece is unique.

CIVIL WAR TOKENS (1860s)

Early Friday morning, April 12, 1861, the Confederate States Army fired shells from 10-inch siege mortars into the Union's Fort Sumter in Charleston Bay, South Carolina, touching off the American Civil War. The ensuing turmoil would bring many changes to America's financial and monetary systems, including a dramatic reworking of the banking structure, federalization of paper money, bold innovations in taxation, tariffs, and land grants, and radical government experiments in new kinds of currency. For the man on the street, one daily noticeable development of the war was the large-scale hoarding of coins, which began in late 1861 and early 1862—people squirreled away first their gold, then silver coins, and finally, as the war dragged on that summer, even small copper-nickel cents. This caused trouble for day-to-day commerce. There were no coins to buy a newspaper or a glass of soda, to get a haircut, or tip a doorman. The situation gave birth to the humble but ubiquitous Civil War token.

Tokens were a familiar sight on the American scene by the time the Civil War was ignited. In fact, Americans had been using tokens as monetary substitutes since the colonial era, during the early days of the new nation, and throughout the 1800s. Two main kinds of tokens entered into American commerce during the war: *patriotics*, so called for their political and nationalistic themes; and *store cards*, or merchant tokens. An estimated 50 million or more were issued—more than two for every man, woman, and child in the Union. Civil War tokens were mostly a Northern phenomenon; not surprising, considering that New York State alone produced four times as much manufacturing as the entire Confederacy at the start of the war. Southerners had to make do with weak government-backed paper money, which quickly depreciated in value; Yankee tradesmen had the industrial base and financial means to produce a hard-money substitute that at least *looked* like money, even if it was backed by nothing more substantial than a local grocery store's promise to accept it at the value of one cent.

Most Civil War tokens were made of copper, some were brass, and rare exceptions were struck in copper-nickel or white metal. In addition to patriotics and store cards, some issuers crafted *numismatic* tokens during the war. These were struck for collectors rather than for day-to-day commerce, and made in the typical alloys as well as (rarely) in silver and other metals. Some were overstruck on dimes or copper-nickel cents.

Many kinds of tokens and medals were issued during the war. This sometimes leads to the question, "What, exactly, counts as a *Civil War token?*" How about the small hard-rubber checks and tickets, in various shapes, of that era? Or encased postage stamps, another small-change substitute of the war years? Or sutler tokens, issued by registered vendors who supplied the Union Army and traveled with the troops? These and more are sometimes collected along with the main body of about 10,000 varieties of store cards and patriotics. There is a long tradition of collecting Civil War tokens, dating back to even before the end of the war, and the hobby community has developed various habits and traditions over the years. Ultimately what to include in a collection is up to the individual collector. The Civil War Token Society (www.cwtsociety.com), the preeminent club for today's collector, suggests that to be "officially" considered a Civil War token, a piece must be between 18 and 25 mm in diameter. (Most of the copper tokens issued to pass as currency during the war were 18 or 19 mm, the size of the federal government's relatively new Flying Eagle and Indian Head cents, introduced in the late 1850s.)

Civil War tokens can be collected by state and by city, by type of issuer (druggist, saloonkeeper, doctor, etc.), or by any number of designs and themes. If you live in New York City and would like to study store cards issued by local shops and businesses, you have hundreds to choose from. You might hail from a small town and still be able to find a Civil War token from where you grew up. In 1863 in Oswego, New York, M.L. Marshall—a general-store seller of the unlikely combination of toys, fancy goods, fishing tackle, and rare coins—issued a cent-sized copper token featuring a fish! Undertakers issued store cards with tiny coffins advertising their services. Booksellers, bootmakers, beer brewers, hat dealers, and hog butchers all pictured their products on small copper tokens. On the patriotic side, Civil War tokens show Abraham Lincoln, various wartime presidential candidates, national heroes, cannons at the ready, unfurled flags, defiant eagles, and soldiers on horseback. They shout out the slogans of the day, warning the South of the strength of THE ARMY & NAVY, urging Americans to STAND BY THE FLAG, and insisting that THE FEDERAL UNION MUST AND SHALL BE PRESERVED.

Many tokens were more or less faithful imitations of the federal copper-nickel Indian Head cent. A few of this type have the word NOT in small letters above the words ONE CENT. For a time the legal status of the Civil War tokens was uncertain. Mint Director James Pollock thought they were illegal; however, there was no law prohibiting the issue of tradesmen's tokens or of private coins not in imitation of U.S. coins. Finally a law was passed April 22, 1864, prohibiting the issue of any one- or two-cent coins, tokens, or devices for use as money, and on June 8 another law was passed that abolished private coinage of every kind. By that summer the government's new bronze Indian Head cents, minted in the tens of millions, were plentiful in circulation.

Today, Civil War tokens as a class are very accessible for collectors. Store-card tokens of Illinois, Massachusetts, Michigan, New York, Ohio, Pennsylvania, and Wisconsin are among those most frequently seen. A collector seeking special challenges will hunt for tokens from Iowa, Kansas, Maryland, and Minnesota—and, on the Confederate side, from Alabama, Louisiana (a counterstamped Indian Head cent), and Tennessee.

Three pieces of advice will serve the beginning collector. First, read the standard reference books, including *Patriotic Civil War Tokens* and *U.S. Civil War Store Cards*, both classics by George and Melvin Fuld, and the *Guide Book of Civil War Tokens*, by Q. David Bowers. These books lay the foundation and offer inspiration for building your own collection. Second, join the Civil War Token Society. This will put you in touch with other collectors who offer mentoring, friendship, and information. Third, visit a coin show and start looking for Civil War tokens in the inventories of the dealers there. Above all, enjoy the hobby and the many paths and byways it can lead you on through this important and turbulent era of American history.

Values shown are for the most common tokens in each composition.

	F	VF	EF	MS-63
Copper or brass	$18	$30	$40	$125
Nickel or German silver	$60	$75	$130	$290
White metal	$80	$125	$150	$275
Copper-nickel	$75	$125	$175	$325
Silver	$200	$300	$500	$1,200

PATRIOTIC CIVIL WAR TOKENS

Patriotic Civil War tokens feature leaders such as Abraham Lincoln; military images such as cannons or ships; and sociopolitical themes popular in the North, such as flags and slogans. Thousands of varieties are known.

	F	VF	AU	MS-63
Lincoln	$35	$70	$150	$300
Monitor	$30	$50	$125	$225
"Wealth of the South" (a)	$200	$400	$600	$1,000
Various common types	$18	$30	$50	$125

a. Dated 1860, but sometimes collected along with Civil War tokens.

CIVIL WAR STORE CARDS

Tradesmen's tokens of the Civil War era are often called store cards. These are typically collected by geographical location or by topic. The Fuld text (see bibliography) catalogs store cards by state, city, merchant, die combination, and metal. Values shown below are for the most common tokens for each state. Tokens from obscure towns or from merchants who issued only a few can be priced into the thousands of dollars and are widely sought.

	F	VF	EF	MS-63
Alabama	$1,500	$3,000	$4,000	$6,500
Connecticut	$10	$30	$50	$125
Washington, D.C.	—	$1,000	$1,400	$2,000
Idaho	$400	$700	$1,300	—
Illinois	$10	$30	$50	$125
Indiana	$10	$30	$50	$135
Iowa	$150	$450	$550	$1,250
Kansas	$900	$2,500	$3,500	$5,500
Kentucky	$50	$125	$200	$350
Louisiana	$2,000	$3,500	$4,500	—
Maine	$50	$100	$175	$275
Maryland	$150	$350	$550	$1,000
Massachusetts	$15	$35	$60	$140
Michigan	$10	$30	$50	$125
Minnesota	$150	$450	$550	$750
Missouri	$40	$100	$150	$250
New Hampshire	$80	$130	$175	$275
New Jersey	$10	$30	$50	$135
New York	$10	$30	$50	$125
Ohio	$10	$30	$50	$125
Pennsylvania	$10	$30	$50	$125
Rhode Island	$10	$30	$50	$135
Tennessee	$300	$650	$1,200	$1,750
Virginia	$250	$500	$1,000	—
West Virginia	$45	$100	$175	$400
Wisconsin	$15	$30	$60	$130
Sutlers' (a)	$185	$375	$500	$700

a. Sutler tokens were issued by registered contractors who operated camp stores that traveled with the military. These were made by coiners who also produced Civil War tokens, including John Stanton, Shubael Childs, and Francis X. Koehler. Each had a denomination, typically 5 cents to 50 cents. Some used on one side a die also used on Civil War tokens.

DC500A-1h   IN190D-3a

	VG	VF	AU	MS-63
DC500a-1h. H.A. Hall, Washington, D.C.	—	$1,000	$1,400	$2,200
IN190D-3a. J.L. & G.F. Rowe, Corunna, IN, 1863	$15	$40	$75	$175

MI865A-1a

MN980A-1a

MO910A-2a

NY630AQ-4a

NY630Z-1a

OH165M-1a

NY630BJ-1a

WI510M-1a

PA750F-1a

WV890D-4a

	VG	VF	AU	MS-63
MI865A-1a, W. Darling, Saranac, MI, 1864	$7,500	$12,000	$15,000	—
MN980A-1a. C. Benson, Druggist, Winona, MN	$300	$700	$900	$1,500
M0910A-4a. Drovers Hotel, St. Louis, MO, 1863	$125	$300	$600	$1,250
NY630AQ-4a. Gustavus Lindenmueller, New York, 1863	$15	$30	$50	$125
NY630Z-1a. Fr. Freise, Undertaker, New York, 1863	$20	$35	$85	$135
OH165M-1a. B.P. Belknp., "Teeth Extracted Without Pain"	$125	$250	$400	$600
NY630BJ-1a. Sanitary Commission, New York, 1864	$400	$850	$1,100	$1,750
WI510M-1a. Goes & Falk Malt House & Brewery, Milwaukee, WI, 1863	$25	$65	$100	$175
PA750F-1a. M.C. Campbell's Dancing Academy, Philadelphia, PA	$20	$35	$50	$130
WV890D-4a. R.C. Graves, News Dealer, Wheeling, WV, 1863	$45	$100	$175	$400

Confederate Issues

The Confederate States of America proclaimed itself in February 1861, a few weeks after Abraham Lincoln was elected president of the United States in November 1860. The newly formed nation based its monetary system on the Confederate dollar. Its paper currency was backed not by hard assets (such as gold) but by the promise to pay the bearer after the war was over—assuming Southern victory and independence. In addition to paper money, the Confederacy also explored creating its own coinage for day-to-day circulation. While this goal never came to fruition, interesting relics remain as testaments to the effort.

CONFEDERATE CENTS

Facts about the creation of the original Confederate cents are shrouded in mystery. However, a plausible storyline has developed based on research and recollections, through telling and retelling over the years. An order to make cents for the Confederacy is said to have been placed with Robert Lovett Jr., an engraver and diesinker of Philadelphia, through Bailey & Co., a jewelry firm of that city. Fearing arrest by the United States government for assisting the enemy, Lovett decided instead to hide the coins and the dies in his cellar. Captain John W. Haseltine, well known for finding numismatic rarities unknown to others, claimed that a bartender had received one of the coins over the counter and sold it to him. Haseltine recognized it as the work of Lovett, called on him, learned that he had struck 12 of the coins, and bought the remaining 11 and the dies. In 1874 Haseltine made restrikes in copper, silver, and gold.

Circa 1961, the dies were copied and additional pieces made by New York City coin dealer Robert Bashlow. These show die cracks and rust marks that distinguish them from earlier examples.

	Mintage	Unc.
		PF
1861 Cent, Original, Copper-Nickel, Unc.	13–16	$130,000
1861 Cent, Haseltine Restrike, Copper, Proof	55	$15,000
1861 Cent, Haseltine Restrike, Gold, Proof	7	$45,000
1861 Cent, Haseltine Restrike, Silver, Proof	12	$12,500

CONFEDERATE HALF DOLLARS

According to records, only four original Confederate half dollars were struck (on a hand press). Regular silver planchets were used, as well as a regular federal obverse die. One of the coins was given to Secretary of the Treasury Christopher G. Memminger, who passed it on to President Jefferson Davis for his approval. Another was given to Professor John L. Riddell of the University of Louisiana. Edward Ames of New Orleans received a third specimen. The last was kept by chief coiner Benjamin F. Taylor. Lack of bullion prevented the Confederacy from coining more pieces.

The Confederate half dollar was unknown to collectors until 1879, when a specimen and its reverse die were found in Taylor's possession in New Orleans. E. Mason Jr., of Philadelphia, purchased both and later sold them to J.W. Scott and Company of New York. J.W. Scott acquired 500 genuine 1861-O half dollars, routed or otherwise smoothed away the reverses, and then restamped them with the Confederate die. Known as restrikes, these usually have slightly flattened obverses. Scott also struck some medals in white metal using the Confederate reverse die and an obverse die bearing this inscription: 4 ORIGINALS STRUCK BY ORDER OF C.S.A. IN NEW ORLEANS 1861 / ******* / REV. SAME AS U.S. (FROM ORIGINAL DIE•SCOTT)

Confederate Reverse   **Scott Obverse**

	Mintage	VF-20	EF-40	Unc.
1861 HALF DOL. (a)	—	—	—	—
Auctions: $632,500, VF, October 2003				
1861 HALF DOL., Restrike	500	$6,500	$7,500	$14,000
1861 Scott Obverse, Confederate Reverse	500	$2,500	$3,750	$5,500

a. 4 examples are known.

Hawaiian and Puerto Rican Issues

Although the following issues of Hawaii and Puerto Rico were not circulating U.S. coins, they have political, artistic, and sentimental connections to the United States. Generations of American numismatists have sought them for their collections.

HAWAIIAN ISSUES

Five official coins were issued for the Kingdom of Hawaii. These include the 1847 cent issued by King Kamehameha III and the 1883 silver dimes, quarters, halves, and dollars of King Kalakaua I. The silver pieces were all designed by U.S. Mint chief engraver Charles E. Barber and struck at the San Francisco Mint. The 1883 eighth-dollar piece is a pattern. The 1881 five-cent piece is an unofficial issue.

The Hawaiian dollar was officially valued equal to the U.S. dollar. After Hawaii became a U.S. territory in 1900, the legal-tender status of these coins was removed and most were withdrawn from circulation and melted.

1847, One Cent

1881, Five Cents
Unofficial issue.

1883, Ten Cents

1883, Eighth Dollar

1883, Quarter Dollar

1883, Half Dollar

1883, Dollar

	Mintage	F-12	VF-20	EF-40	AU-50	MS-60	MS-63
							PF-63
1847 Cent (a)	100,000	$350	$450	$675	$850	$1,100	$2,000
Auctions: $2,585, MS-64BN, August 2014; $3,056, MS-64BN, November 2014; $2,350, MS-63RB, August 2014							
1881 Five Cents		$7,000	$10,000	$15,000	$18,000	$22,000	$30,000
Auctions: $14,688, MS-63, August 2014							
1881 Five Cents, Proof (b)							$7,500
Auctions: $2,185, PF-62, June 2001							
1883 Ten Cents	249,974	$70	$120	$275	$450	$1,200	$2,800
Auctions: $1,528, MS-63, July 2014; $823, MS-62, September 2014; $282, AU-55, September 2014; $206, EF-45, July 2014							
1883 Ten Cents, Proof	26						$13,000
Auctions: $12,690, PF-64, August 2014; $11,750, PF-63, November 2014							
1883 Eighth Dollar, Proof	20						$46,000
Auctions: $8,800, PF-50, July 1994							
1883 Quarter Dollar	499,974	$65	$90	$150	$175	$250	$400
Auctions: $9,400, MS-67, July 2014; $1,293, MS-66, August 2014; $823, MS-65, August 2014; $646, MS-65, August 2014							
1883 Quarter Dollar, Proof	26						$15,000
Auctions: $11,750, PF-62, November 2014							
1883 Half Dollar	699,974	$120	$175	$325	$500	$1,200	$2,800
Auctions: $17,625, MS-66, August 2014; $5,875, MS-65, August 2014; $2,350, MS-64, August 2014; $2,115, MS-64, August 2014							
1883 Half Dollar, Proof	26						$17,000
Auctions: $14,100, PF-63, November 2014							
1883 Dollar	499,974	$350	$450	$700	$1,250	$4,000	$10,000
Auctions: $10,575, MS-64, July 2014; $6,463, MS-63, August 2014; $1,087, AU-55, July 2014; $823, EF-45, August 2014							
1883 Dollar, Proof	26						$35,000
Auctions: $22,325, PF-61, November 2014							

a. Values shown are for the most common of the six known varieties. **b.** All Proofs of the 1881 five-cent coins are later restrikes, circa 1900.

PLANTATION TOKENS

During the 1800s, several private firms issued tokens for use as money in Hawaiian company stores. These are often referred to as Plantation tokens. The unusual denomination of 12-1/2 cents was equivalent to a day's wages in the sugar plantations, and was related to the fractional part of the Spanish eight-reales coin.

(1860) Undated, Waterhouse Token

(1871) Undated, Wailuku Plantation

1880, Wailuku Plantation

1882, Haiku Plantation

1891, Kahului Railroad

	F-12	VF-20	EF-40	AU-50
Waterhouse / Kamehameha IV, ca. 1860	$1,650	$3,200	$4,750	$6,750
Wailuku Plantation, 12-1/2 (cents), (1871), narrow starfish	$750	$2,000	$3,750	$6,000
Similar, broad starfish	$900	$2,250	$4,050	$7,250
Wailuku Plantation, VI (6-1/4 cents), (1871), narrow starfish	$1,800	$4,750	$7,000	$9,500
Similar, broad starfish	$2,100	$5,250	$7,500	$10,500
Wailuku Plantation, 1 Real, 1880	$750	$1,800	$3,500	$8,500
Wailuku Plantation, Half Real, 1880	$2,200	$5,000	$8,000	$11,500
Thomas H. Hobron, 12-1/2 (cents), 1879	$600	$850	$1,200	$1,600
Similar, two stars on both sides	$1,600	$2,800	$5,250	$9,000
Thomas H. Hobron, 25 (cents), 1879 (a)			$45,000	
Haiku Plantation, 1 Rial, 1882	$800	$1,350	$2,000	$2,750
Grove Ranch Plantation, 12-1/2 (cents), 1886	$1,400	$2,600	$4,600	$6,600
Grove Ranch Plantation, 12-1/2 (cents), 1887	$2,250	$4,250	$7,500	$10,000
Kahului Railroad, 10 cents, 1891	$2,000	$3,500	$5,500	$7,500
Kahului Railroad, 15 cents, 1891	$2,000	$3,500	$5,500	$7,500
Kahului Railroad, 20 cents, 1891	$2,000	$3,500	$5,500	$7,500
Kahului Railroad, 25 cents, 1891	$2,000	$3,500	$5,500	$7,500
Kahului Railroad, 35 cents, 1891	$2,000	$3,500	$5,500	$7,500
Kahului Railroad, 75 cents, 1891	$2,000	$3,500	$5,500	$7,500

a. 3 examples are known.

PUERTO RICAN ISSUES

Puerto Rico, the farthest east of the Greater Antilles, lies about 1,000 miles southeast of Florida between the Atlantic Ocean and the Caribbean Sea. Settled by Spain in 1508, the island was ceded to the United States after the Spanish-American War in 1898. Puerto Ricans were granted U.S. citizenship in 1917. Today Puerto Rico is a self-governing territory of the United States with commonwealth status.

The Puerto Rican coins of 1895 and 1896 were minted at the Casa de Moneda de Madrid, in Spain. The peso was struck in .900 fine silver, and the others were .835 fine. The portrait is of King Alfonso XIII, and the arms are of the Bourbons, the royal house of Spain. These coins were in circulation at the time of the Spanish-American War of 1898, which ended with U.S. victory and with Spain's loss of sovereignty over Cuba (along with its cession of the Philippine Islands, Puerto Rico, and Guam to the United States for $20 million). Puerto Rico's Spanish coins continued to circulate after the war.

Collectors of United States coins often include Puerto Rican coins in their collections, even though they are not U.S. issues. After the Spanish-American War, exchange rates were set for these coins relative to the U.S. dollar, and the island transitioned to a dollar-based currency. Today in Puerto Rico the dollar is still popularly referred to as a "peso."

1896, 5 Centavos

1896, 10 Centavos

1895, 20 Centavos

1896, 40 Centavos

1895, One Peso

	Mintage	F-12	VF-20	EF-40	AU-50	Unc.
1896 5 Centavos	600,000	$30	$50	$100	$150	$200
Auctions: $56, EF-45, September 2014						
1896 10 Centavos	700,000	$40	$85	$135	$200	$300
Auctions: $170, AU-55, September 2014; $212, AU-55, January 2014						
1895 20 Centavos	3,350,000	$45	$100	$150	$250	$400
Auctions: No auction records available.						
1896 40 Centavos	725,002	$180	$300	$900	$1,700	$2,900
Auctions: $705, AU-55, January 2015; $352, EF-45, January 2015						
1895 1 Peso	8,500,021	$200	$400	$950	$1,900	$3,250
Auctions: $3,819, MS-63, September 2014; $1,380, AU-55, June 2006						

Philippine Issues

In April 1899, control of the Philippine Islands was officially transferred from Spain to the United States, as a condition of the treaty ending the Spanish-American War. The U.S. military suppressed a Filipino insurgency through 1902, and partway through that struggle, in July 1901, the islands' military government was replaced with a civilian administration led by American judge William Howard Taft. One of its first tasks was to sponsor a new territorial coinage that was compatible with the old Spanish issues, but also legally exchangeable for American money at the rate of two Philippine pesos to the U.S. dollar. The resulting coins—which bear the legend UNITED STATES OF AMERICA but are otherwise quite different in design from regular U.S. coins—today can be found in many American coin collections, having been brought to the States as souvenirs by service members after World War II or otherwise saved. The unusual designs, combined with the legend, have sometimes caused them to be confused with standard federal United States coins.

The coins, introduced in 1903, were designed by Filipino silversmith, sculptor, engraver, and art professor Melecio Figueroa, who had earlier worked for the Spanish *Casa de Moneda*, in Manila. They are sometimes called "Conant coins" or "Conants," after Charles Arthur Conant, an influential American journalist and banking expert who served on the commission that brought about the Philippine Coinage Act of March 2, 1903. "Both in the artistic quality of the designs and in perfection of workmanship, they compare favorably with anything of the kind ever done in America," wrote Secretary of War Elihu Root in his annual report to President Theodore Roosevelt. Figueroa died of tuberculosis on July 30, 1903, age 61, shortly after seeing his coins enter circulation.

Following Spanish custom, the dollar-sized peso was decimally equivalent to 100 centavos. Silver fractions were minted in denominations of fifty, twenty, and ten centavos, and minor coins (in copper-nickel and bronze) included the five-centavo piece, the centavo, and the half centavo.

In addition to the name of the United States, the coins bear the Spanish name for the islands: FILIPINAS. The silver coins feature Miss Liberty standing in a flowing gown, holding in one hand a hammer that she strikes against an anvil, and in the other an olive branch, with the volcanic Mount Mayon (northeast of the capital city of Manila) visible in the background. The minor coinage shows a young Filipino man, barechested and seated at an anvil with a hammer, again with Mount Mayon seen in the distance. The first reverse design, shared across all denominations, shows a U.S. federal shield surmounted by an eagle with outstretched wings, clutching an olive branch in its right talon and a bundle of arrows in its left. This reverse design was changed in 1937 to a new shield emblem derived from the seal of the 1936 Commonwealth.

Dies for the coins were made at the Philadelphia Mint by the U.S. Mint's chief engraver, Charles E. Barber. Mintmarks were added to the dies, as needed, at the branch mints. From 1903 to 1908 the coins were struck at the Philadelphia Mint (with no mintmark) and the San Francisco Mint (with an S mintmark). From

1909 through 1919, they were struck only at San Francisco. In the first part of 1920, one-centavo coins were struck in San Francisco; later in the year a new mint facility, the Mint of the Philippine Islands, was opened in Manila, and from that point into the early 1940s Philippine coins of one, five, ten, twenty, and fifty centavos were struck there. The coins produced at the Manila Mint in 1920, 1921, and 1922 bore no mintmark. No Philippine coins were struck in 1923 or 1924. The Manila Mint reopened in 1925; from then through 1941 its coinage featured an M mintmark. The Denver and San Francisco mints would be used for Philippine coinage in the final years of World War II, when the islands were under Japanese occupation.

Rising silver prices forced reductions in the fineness and weight for each Philippine silver denomination beginning in 1907, and subsequent issues are smaller in diameter. The new, smaller twenty-centavo piece was very close in size to the five-centavo piece (20.0 mm compared to 20.5 mm), resulting in a mismatching of dies for these two denominations in 1918. A small number of error coins were minted from this accidental combination, with some finding their way into circulation (often with the edge crudely reeded to induce them to pass as twenty-centavo coins). A solution was found by reducing the diameter of the five-centavo piece beginning in 1930.

It should be noted that, in addition to normal coins and paper currency, special token money in the form of coins and printed currency was made for use in the Culion Leper Colony. The token coinage saw six issues from 1913 to 1930, some produced at the Manila Mint. The leper colony was set up in May 1906 on the small island of Culion, one of the more than 7,000 islands comprising the Philippines, and the coinage was intended to circulate only there.

In 1935 the United States, responding to popular momentum for independence, approved the establishment of the Commonwealth of the Philippines, with the understanding that full self-governing independence would be recognized after a ten-year transition period. In 1936 a three-piece set of silver commemorative coins was issued to mark the transfer of executive power.

An adaptation of the new commonwealth's seal, introduced on the 1936 commemorative coins, was used for the reverse design of all circulating Philippine issues beginning in 1937. For their obverses, the Commonwealth coins retained the same Figueroa designs as those struck from 1903 to 1936. (A final transitional issue of more than 17 million 1936-dated one-centavo coins was minted using the federal-shield reverse design, rather than the new Commonwealth shield.)

After the bombing of Pearl Harbor, Japanese military forces advanced on the Philippines in late 1941 and early 1942, prompting the civil government to remove much of the Philippine treasury's bullion to the United States. Nearly 16 million pesos' worth of silver remained, mostly in the form of one-peso pieces of 1907 through 1912. These coins were hastily crated and dumped into Manila's Caballo Bay to prevent their capture by Japan. The Japanese occupied the Philippines, learned of the hidden treasure, and managed to recover some of the sunken coins (probably fewer than half a million). After the war, over the course of several years, more than 10 million of the submerged silver pesos were retrieved under the direction of the U.S. Treasury and, later, the Central Bank of the Philippines. Most of them show evidence of prolonged salt-water immersion, with dark corrosion that resists cleaning. This damage to so many coins has added to the scarcity of high-grade pre-war silver pesos.

Later during World War II, in 1944 and 1945, the U.S. Mint struck coins for the Philippines at its Philadelphia, Denver, and San Francisco facilities. These coins were brought over and entered circulation as U.S. and Philippine military forces fought to retake the islands from the Japanese.

After the war, the Commonwealth of the Philippines became an independent republic, on July 4, 1946, as had been scheduled by the Constitution of 1935. Today the Philippine coins of 1903 to 1945, including the set of commemoratives issued in 1936, remain significant mementoes of a colorful and important chapter in U.S. history and numismatics. They are a testament to the close ties and special relationship between the United States of America and the Republic of the Philippines.

PHILIPPINES UNDER U.S. SOVEREIGNTY (1903–1936)

The Philippine Islands were governed under the sovereignty of the United States from 1899 until early 1935. (In the latter year a largely self-governing commonwealth was established, followed by full independence in 1946.) Coinage under U.S. sovereignty began in 1903. There was a final issue of centavos dated 1936, minted in the style of 1903–1934, after which the design of all circulating coins changed to the new Commonwealth style.

BRONZE COINAGE

HALF CENTAVO (1903–1908)

Designer: *Melecio Figueroa.* **Weight:** *2.35 grams.* **Composition:** *.950 copper, .050 tin and zinc.*
Diameter: *17.5 mm.* **Edge:** *Plain.* **Mints:** *Philadelphia.*

History. In 1903 and 1904 the United States minted nearly 18 million half centavos for the Philippines. By March of the latter year, it was obvious that the half centavo was too small a denomination, unneeded in commerce despite the government's attempts to force it into circulation. The recommendation of Governor-General Luke Edward Wright—that the coin be discontinued permanently—was approved, and on April 18, 1904, a new contract was authorized to manufacture one-centavo blanks out of unused half-centavo blanks. In April 1908, Governor-General James Francis Smith received permission to ship 37,827 pesos' worth of stored half centavos (7,565,400 coins) to the San Francisco Mint to be re-coined into one-centavo pieces. Cleared from the Philippine Treasury's vaults, the coins were shipped to California in June 1908, and most of them were melted and made into 1908 centavos.

Striking and Sharpness. Half centavos typically are well struck, except for the 1903 issue, of which some coins may show weak numerals in the date. Reverses sometimes show light flattening of the eagle's wing tips.

Half Centavo, 1903–1908

High Points of Wear. *Obverse Checkpoints:* 1. Figure's left hand. 2. Figure's right hand. 3. Face and frontal hair just above ear. 4. Edge of anvil. *Reverse Checkpoints:* 1. Eagle's wing tips. 2. Eagle's breast feathers. 3. Upper points of shield. 4. Eagle's right leg.

Proofs. The Philadelphia Mint struck small quantities of Proof half centavos for collectors throughout the denomination's existence, for inclusion in Proof sets (except for 1907, when no Proof sets were issued).

	Mintage	EF		MS-60		MS-63	
		PF-60		PF-63		PF-65	
1903	12,084,000	$2.25		$20		$40	
	Auctions: $138, MS-65RD, September 2012; $247, MS-65RB, September 2013; $103, MS-65RB, September 2012						
1903, Proof	2,558	$50		$110		$150	
	Auctions: $447, PF-67RB, October 2014; $282, PF-66RD, October 2014						
1904	5,654,000	$3.50		$25		$60	
	Auctions: $270, MS-65RD, July 2013; $200, MS-65BN, January 2013; $65, MS-64RB, July 2013						
1904, Proof	1,355	$75		$135		$200	
	Auctions: $382, PF-66RB, November 2014						
1905, Proof (a)	471	$175		$250		$500	
	Auctions: $253, PF-64RB, June 2007; $207, PF-62BN, January 2012						
1906, Proof (a)	500	$150		$250		$450	
	Auctions: $323, PF-65BN, January 2012; $374, PF-64RB, June 2007						
1908, Proof (a)	500	$150		$250		$450	
	Auctions: $282, PF-64RB, April 2014; $230, PF-64RB, January 2012						

Note: The half centavo was unpopular in circulation. More than 7,500,000 were withdrawn and melted to be recoined as one-centavo pieces in 1908. **a.** Proof only.

ONE CENTAVO (1903–1936)

Designer: *Melecio Figueroa.* **Weight:** *4.7 grams.* **Composition:** *.950 copper, .050 tin and zinc.* **Diameter:** *24 mm.* **Edge:** *Plain.* **Mints:** *Philadelphia and San Francisco.*

Mintmark location is on the reverse, to the left of the date.

History. Unlike the half centavo, the bronze centavo was a popular workhorse of Philippine commerce from the start of its production. Nearly 38 million coins were minted in the denomination's first three years. In 1920 the centavo was struck for circulation by two different mints (the only year this was the case). San Francisco produced the coins during the first part of 1920; later in the year, the coins were struck at the Manila Mint, after that facility opened. From that point forward all centavos struck under U.S. sovereignty were products of the Manila Mint. Those dated 1920, 1921, and 1922 bear no mintmark identifying their origin. Manila produced no coins (of any denomination) in 1923 and 1924.

Coin collectors, notably educator, writer, and American Numismatic Association member Dr. Gilbert S. Perez, urged Manila Mint officials to include an M mark on their coinage—similar to the way that, for example, San Francisco coins were identified by an S—and this change was made starting with the coinage of 1925.

Coinage of the centavo continued through the late 1920s and early 1930s. U.S. sovereignty was significantly altered in 1935 with the establishment of the Commonwealth of the Philippines, and this change was reflected in all Philippine currency. A final mintage of 1936-dated centavos (17,455,463 pieces) was struck using the federal-shield reverse of the denomination's 1903–1934 coinage. The coin then switched over to the Commonwealth shield design in 1937.

Several centavo die varieties exist to give the specialist a challenge. Among them is the 1918-S, Large S, whose mintmark appears to be the same size and shape of that used on fifty-centavo pieces of the era.

Striking and Sharpness. On the obverse, the figure's right hand (holding the hammer) is almost always found flatly struck. The reverse, especially of later-date centavos, often shows flattening of the eagle's breast and of the left part of the shield. Issues of the Manila Mint, especially of 1920, often are lightly struck. Those of San Francisco typically are better struck, with only occasional light strikes. On centavos of 1929 to 1936, the M mintmark often is nearly unidentifiable as a letter.

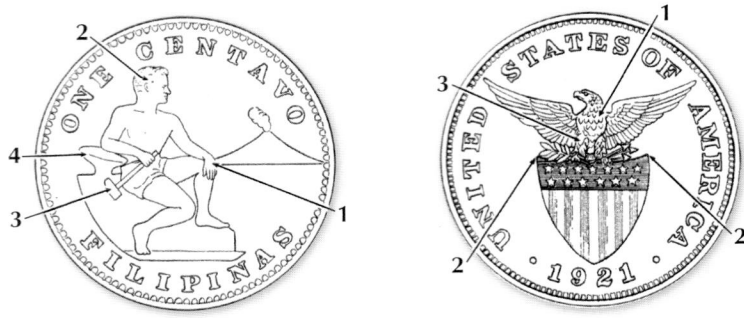

One Centavo, 1903–1936

High Points of Wear. *Obverse Checkpoints:* 1. Figure's left hand. 2. Frontal hair just above ear. 3. Head of hammer. 4. Left part of anvil. *Reverse Checkpoints:* 1. Eagle's breast feathers. 2. Upper points of shield. 3. Eagle's right leg.

Proofs. One-centavo Proofs were struck at the Philadelphia Mint for annual Proof sets in 1903, 1904, 1905, 1906, and 1908. Proof centavos of 1908 bear a date with numerals noticeably larger than those of circulation-strike 1908-S coins.

1908-S, S Over S

| | Mintage | VF | EF | MS-60 | MS-63 |
				PF-60	PF-63
1903	10,790,000	$1.25	$3	$15	$40
Auctions: $247, MS-66BN, January 2014					
1903, Proof	2,558			$60	$120
Auctions: $408, PF-65RB, April 2010					
1904	17,040,400	$1.25	$3	$25	$45
Auctions: No auction records available.					
1904, Proof	1,355			$75	$125
Auctions: $217, PF-65RD, August 2013; $141, PF-64RB, April 2014					
1905	10,000,000	$1.25	$3.50	$30	$45
Auctions: $17, MS-65RB, January 2014					
1905, Proof	471			$175	$275
Auctions: $441, PF-65RB, April 2014; $805, PF-65RB, April 2010; $235, PF-64RD, August 2013					
1906, Proof (a)	500			$150	$250
Auctions: $423, PF-64RD, February 2014					
1908, Proof (a)	500			$150	$275
Auctions: $411, PF-66RD, October 2014; $499, PF-65RB, January 2014					
1908S	2,187,000	$4	$8	$50	$100
Auctions: $141, MS-65RB, April 2014; $129, MS-65RB, February 2014					
1908S, S Over S	(b)	$30	$50	$125	
Auctions: $558, MS-64RB, January 2014					

a. Proof only. b. Included in 1908-S mintage figure.

1918-S, Normal S   **1918-S, Large S**

	Mintage	VF	EF	MS-60	MS-63
1909S	1,737,612	$16	$25	$110	$225
	Auctions: $317, MS-65RB, August 2014; $62, MS-64BN, March 2014				
1910S	2,700,000	$4.50	$8	$50	$60
	Auctions: $118, MS-65RB, April 2014; $80, MS-64RB, April 2014				
1911S	4,803,000	$2.50	$5	$22	$60
	Auctions: $90, MS-65RB, April 2014; $64, MS-64RB, March 2014				
1912S	3,001,000	$7.50	$18	$75	$125
	Auctions: $118, MS-65BN, March 2014; $90, MS-64BN, June 2014				
1913S	5,000,000	$4	$7	$40	$85
	Auctions: $270, MS-65BN, November 2014; $79, MS-63BN, January 2014				
1914S	5,000,500	$3.50	$7	$45	$90
	Auctions: $84, MS-64BN, November 2014; $113, MS-64BN, May 2014				
1915S	2,500,000	$40	$90	$700	$1,500
	Auctions: $805, MS-63BN, June 2011; $647, MS-62BN, January 2014				
1916S	4,330,000	$12.50	$20	$100	$200
	Auctions: $135, MS-64BN, July 2014; $159, MS-63RB, June 2014				
1917S	7,070,000	$4	$10	$75	$150
	Auctions: $176, MS-65RD, February 2014; $53, MS-62BN, September 2014				
1917S, 7 Over 6	(c)	$80	$160	$300	
	Auctions: No auction records available.				
1918S	11,660,000	$4.50	$7.50	$75	$175
	Auctions: $212, MS-65BN, January 2015; $229, MS-64RB, June 2014				
1918S, Large S	(d)	$150	$250	$1,000	$1,900
	Auctions: $306, EF-45, January 2014				
1919S	4,540,000	$4	$8	$75	$160
	Auctions: $110, MS-64BN, June 2014; $128, MS-64BN, January 2014				
1920	3,552,259	$3	$7	$50	$175
	Auctions: $259, MS-65RB, January 2014; $353, MS-65BN, June 2014				
1920S	2,500,000	$8	$20	$125	$225
	Auctions: $236, MS-64BN, January 2014; $90, MS-62BN, March 2014				
1921	7,282,673	$2.50	$5	$35	$65
	Auctions: $153, MS-65RB, January 2014				
1922	3,519,100	$3	$6	$40	$75
	Auctions: $223, MS-65RB, January 2014; $52, MS-64BN, March 2014				
1925M	9,325,000	$2.50	$5	$35	$65
	Auctions: $68, MS-64BN, May 2014				
1926M	9,000,000	$2.50	$5	$30	$65
	Auctions: $89, MS-65BN, January 2015; $30, MS-64RB, March 2014				
1927M	9,279,000	$2.50	$5	$25	$40
	Auctions: $212, MS-66RD, April 2014; $165, MS-66RB, January 2014				
1928M	9,150,000	$2	$5	$30	$65
	Auctions: $75, MS-64RD, April 2014; $50, MS-64RB, May 2014				
1929M	5,657,161	$3	$6	$35	$85
	Auctions: $141, MS-65RD, January 2014; $43, MS-63BN, March 2014				

c. Included in 1917-S mintage figure. **d.** Included in 1918-S mintage figure.

	Mintage	VF	EF	MS-60	MS-63
1930M	5,577,000	$2	$4.50	$35	$60
	Auctions: $69, MS-65BN, January 2014; $75, MS-64RD, August 2014				
1931M	5,659,355	$2.25	$5	$25	$60
	Auctions: $40, MS-65RB, March 2014; $89, MS-65RB, January 2014				
1932M	4,000,000	$3	$6	$50	$75
	Auctions: $112, MS-65RD, April 2014; $95, MS-65RD, January 2014				
1933M	8,392,692	$2	$3	$20	$50
	Auctions: $147, MS-66RD, January 2014; $80, MS-66RB, March 2014				
1934M	3,179,000	$2.50	$4.50	$50	$75
	Auctions: $200, MS-66RD, April 2014; $112, MS-65RB, January 2014				
1936M	17,455,463	$2.50	$4	$35	$65
	Auctions: $37, MS-64BN, March 2014				

COPPER-NICKEL COINAGE

FIVE CENTAVOS (1903–1935)

Designer: *Melecio Figueroa.* **Weight:** *1903–1928, 5 grams; 1930–1935, 4.75 grams.*
Composition: *.750 copper, .250 nickel.* **Diameter:** *1903–1908, 20.5 mm; 1930–1935, 19 mm.*
Edge: *Plain.* **Mints:** *Philadelphia, San Francisco, and Manila.*

Five Centavos, Large Size
(1903–1928, 20.5 mm)

Mintmark location is on the reverse, to the left of the date.

Five Centavos, Reduced Size
(1930–1935, 19 mm)

History. Five-centavo coins were minted under U.S. sovereignty for the Philippines from 1903 to 1935, with several gaps in production over the years. Circulation strikes were made in Philadelphia in 1903 and 1904, then coinage resumed in 1916, this time at the San Francisco Mint. The newly inaugurated Manila Mint took over all five-centavo production starting in 1920, continuing through the end of direct U.S. administration, and under the Commonwealth government beginning in 1937.

The Manila Mint coins of 1920 and 1921 bore no mintmark indicating their producer, a situation noticed by coin collectors of the day. Gilbert S. Perez, superintendent of schools for Tayabas in the Philippines (and a member of the American Numismatic Association), wrote to Assistant Insular Treasurer Salvador Lagdameo in June 1922: "Several members of numismatic societies in Europe and America have made inquiries as to why the Manila mint has no distinctive mint mark. Some do not even know that there is a mint in the Philippine Islands and that the mint is operated by Filipinos." He recommended the letter M be used to identify Manila's coins. Lagdameo replied later that month, thanking Perez and informing him: "It is now being planned that the new dies to be ordered shall contain such mark, and it is hoped that the coins of 1923 and subsequent years will bear the distinctive mint mark suggested by you." Coinage would not resume at the Manila facility until 1925, but from that year forward the mintmark would grace the coins struck in the Philippines.

The diameter of the five-centavo coin was 20.5 mm diameter from 1903 to 1928. This was very close to the 20 mm diameter of the twenty-centavo coin of 1907 to 1929. By 1928 there had been two separate instances where a reverse die of one denomination was "muled" to an obverse of the other. In 1918 this occurred by accident when a small quantity of five-centavo pieces was struck in combination with the reverse die of the twenty centavos (identifiable by its wider shield and a smaller date, compared to the normal five-centavo reverse). This error was known to numismatists by 1922, by which time it was recognized as a scarce variety. The second instance of muling, in 1928, is discussed under twenty-centavo pieces. In 1930, to clearly differentiate the sizes of the coins, the diameter of the five-centavo piece was reduced from 20.5 to 19.0 mm.

Five-centavo coinage under U.S. sovereignty continued to 1935. From 1937 on, the Manila Mint's production of five-centavo coins would use the new Commonwealth shield design on the reverse.

Striking and Sharpness. The obverse of the 1918 and 1919 San Francisco Mint issues often is weakly struck, with considerable loss of detail. The Manila Mint started production in 1920, and many five-centavo coins from that year lack sharpness in the rims and have weak details overall.

Five Centavos, 1903–1928

High Points of Wear. *Obverse Checkpoints:* 1. Figure's right hand. 2. Frontal hair just above ear. 3. Figure's left hand. *Reverse Checkpoints:* 1. Eagle's breast feathers. 2. Eagle's wing tip (to viewer's right). 3. Upper points of shield.

Five Centavos, 1930–1935

High Points of Wear. *Obverse Checkpoints:* 1. Figure's right hand. 2. Frontal hair just above ear. 3. Edge of anvil. *Reverse Checkpoints:* 1. Eagle's breast feathers. 2. Eagle's wing tip (to viewer's right).

Proofs. Five-centavo Proofs were struck at the Philadelphia Mint for annual Proof sets in 1903, 1904, 1905, 1906, and 1908.

	Mintage	VF	EF	MS-60 / PF-60	MS-63 / PF-63
1903	8,910,000	$1.25	$2.50	$18	$30
	Auctions: $247, MS-66, July 2013; $200, MS-65, August 2013; $242, MS-65, December 2012				
1903, Proof	2,558			$75	$130
	Auctions: $270, PF-66, August 2013; $200, PF-65, November 2013				

	Mintage	VF	EF	MS-60 / PF-60	MS-63 / PF-63
1904	1,075,000	$2.50	$4	$20	$40
	Auctions: $82, MS-64, June 2013; $76, MS-64, May 2013				
1904, Proof	1,355			$90	$150
	Auctions: $235, PF-65, August 2013; $153, PF-64, October 2014; $153, PF-64, August 2013				
1905, Proof (a)	471			$200	$300
	Auctions: $952, PF-67, August 2012; $476, PF-65, August 2013; $382, PF-64, August 2013				
1906, Proof (a)	500			$175	$250
	Auctions: $617, PF-66, October 2014; $670, PF-66, August 2013; $400, PF-65, August 2013				
1908, Proof (a)	500			$200	$300
	Auctions: $505, PF-66, October 2014; $969, PF-66, August 2013; $500, PF-66, August 2013				
1916S	300,000	$75	$150	$800	$1,300
	Auctions: $240, MS-62, January 2014; $235, MS-62, February 2014				
1917S	2,300,000	$4	$10	$130	$300
	Auctions: $423, MS-65, April 2014; $447, MS-64, August 2014				
1918S	2,780,000	$8	$14	$130	$300
	Auctions: $306, MS-63, August 2014; $188, MS-62, January 2014				
1918S, Mule (b)	(c)	$550	$1,300	$4,750	$9,750
	Auctions: $881, MS-63, January 2015; $544, VF-30, April 2014				
1919S	1,220,000	$10	$20	$175	$400
	Auctions: $588, MS-64, September 2014; $499, MS-63, January 2014				
1920	1,421,078	$8.50	$35	$175	$300
	Auctions: $141, MS-63, January 2014; $200, MS-63, July 2013				
1921	2,131,529	$10	$20	$110	$200
	Auctions: $212, MS-63, August 2013; $212, MS-63, July 2013; $153, MS-63, August 2014				
1925M	1,000,000	$12	$27	$175	$300
	Auctions: $575, MS-64, November 2011; $217, MS-63, January 2014				
1926M	1,200,000	$6	$18	$120	$200
	Auctions: $112, MS-62, January 2014				
1927M	1,000,000	$6	$13	$85	$150
	Auctions: $259, MS-65, January 2014; $129, MS-64, June 2014				
1928M	1,000,000	$8	$14	$70	$125
	Auctions: $259, MS-65, January 2014; $96, MS-63, June 2014				
1930M	2,905,182	$2.50	$6	$40	$95
	Auctions: $353, MS-65, September 2014; $71, MS-64RD, July 2014; $153, MS-64, August 2013				
1931M	3,476,790	$2.50	$6	$75	$150
	Auctions: $108, MS-64, June 2014; $86, MS-63, June 2014				
1932M	3,955,861	$2	$4	$50	$130
	Auctions: $143, MS-64, June 2014; $65, MS-62, January 2014				
1934M	2,153,729	$3.50	$9	$75	$200
	Auctions: $306, MS-64, September 2014; $170, MS-63, June 2014; $88, MS-63, July 2013				
1934M, Recut 1	(d)	$15	$30	$125	$225
	Auctions: No auction records available.				
1935M	2,754,000	$2.50	$8	$90	$225
	Auctions: $282, MS-64, September 2014; $100, MS-63, January 2014				

a. Proof only. b. Small Date Reverse of twenty centavos. c. Included in 1918-S mintage figure. d. Included in 1934-M mintage figure.

SILVER COINAGE
TEN CENTAVOS (1903–1935)

Designer: *Melecio Figueroa.* **Weight:** *1903–1906, 2.7 grams (.0779 oz. ASW);*
1907–1935, 2 grams (.0482 oz. ASW). **Composition:** *1903–1906, .900 silver, .100 copper;*
1907–1935, .750 silver, .250 copper. **Diameter:** *1903–1906, 17.5 mm; 1907–1935, 16.5 mm.*
Edge: *Reeded.* **Mints:** *Philadelphia, San Francisco, and Manila.*

Ten Centavos, Large Size (1903–1906, 17.5 mm)

Mintmark location is on the reverse, to the left of the date.

Ten Centavos, Reduced Size (1907–1935, 16.5 mm)

History. The Philippine ten-centavo coin was minted from 1903 to 1935, in several facilities and with occasional interruptions in production.

In 1907 the silver ten-centavo coin's fineness was reduced from .900 to .750, and at the same time its diameter was decreased. This was in response to the rising price of silver, with the goal of discouraging exportation and melting of the silver coins. The net effect was nearly 40 percent less silver, by actual weight, in the new ten-centavo piece. The older coins continued to be removed from circulation, and by June 30, 1911, it was reported that only 35 percent of the ten-centavo pieces minted from 1903 to 1906 still remained in the Philippines.

The Manila Mint took over ten-centavo production from San Francisco in 1920. The ten-centavo coins of 1920 and 1921 bear no mintmark identifying them as products of Manila (this was the case for all Philippine coinage of those years, and of 1922). The efforts of Philippine numismatists, including American Numismatic Association member Gilbert S. Perez, encouraged mint officials to add the M mintmark when the facility reopened in 1925 after a two-year hiatus for all coinage.

Ten-centavo production after 1921 consisted of 1 million pieces struck in 1929 and just less than 1.3 million in 1935. The next ten-centavo mintage would be under the Commonwealth, not U.S. sovereignty.

Die varieties include a 1912-S with an S Over S mintmark.

Striking and Sharpness. The ten-centavo coins of 1903 to 1906 generally are well struck, although some show slight weakness of features. Those of 1907 to 1935 also are generally well struck; some obverses may have slight flattening of the hair just above the ear and on the upper part of Miss Liberty. On the reverse, check the eagle's breast feathers for flatness.

Ten Centavos, 1903–1906

High Points of Wear. *Obverse Checkpoints:* 1. Figure's left bosom. 2. Figure's right knee. 3. Figure's left knee. 4. Edge of anvil. *Reverse Checkpoints:* 1. Eagle's breast feathers. 2. Upper points of shield. 3. Eagle's wing tips. 4. Eagle's right leg.

Ten Centavos, 1907–1935

High Points of Wear. *Obverse Checkpoints:* 1. Figure's left thigh. 2. Figure's left bosom. 3. Figure's left hand. *Reverse Checkpoints:* 1. Eagle's breast feathers. 2. Upper points of shield. 3. Eagle's right leg.

Proofs. Ten-centavo Proofs were struck at the Philadelphia Mint for annual Proof sets in 1903, 1904, 1905, 1906, and 1908.

	Mintage	VF	EF	MS-60 / PF-60	MS-63 / PF-63
1903	5,102,658	$4	$5	$35	$75
Auctions: $188, MS-65, January 2015; $100, MS-64, October 2014; $76, MS-64, July 2013					
1903, Proof	2,558			$100	$150
Auctions: $270, PF-65, May 2014; $70, PF-60, June 2013					
1903S	1,200,000	$25	$45	$350	$950
Auctions: $1,645, MS-62, January 2014					
1904	10,000	$20	$35	$80	$140
Auctions: $397, MS-66, September 2014; $223, MS-65, July 2013; $100, MS-64, November 2014					
1904, Proof	1,355			$110	$150
Auctions: $388, PF-66, October 2014; $153, PF-64, October 2014; $88, PF-62, June 2014					
1904S	5,040,000	$4	$7	$55	$130
Auctions: $92, MS-64, June 2014; $59, MS-62, November 2014					
1905, Proof (a)	471			$150	$275
Auctions: $259, PF-63, June 2004; $299, PF-62, April 2011					
1906, Proof (a)	500			$135	$225
Auctions: $470, PF-65, April 2014; $212, PF-61, January 2014					
1907	1,500,781	$4	$5	$50	$135
Auctions: $223, MS-65, April 2014; $188, MS-65, January 2014; $118, MS-65, August 2013					
1907S	4,930,000	$2	$5	$40	$90
Auctions: $170, MS-64, June 2014; $90, MS-63, May 2014					
1908, Proof (a)	500			$150	$200
Auctions: $617, PF-66, October 2014; $353, PF-65, January 2014; $207, PF-63, January 2012					
1908S	3,363,911	$2	$5	$40	$70
Auctions: $306, MS-65, September 2014; $112, MS-64, January 2014					
1909S	312,199	$30	$65	$450	$1,200
Auctions: $752, MS-62, May 2014; $382, MS-61, January 2014					
1911S	1,000,505	$4.50	$12.50	$150	$500
Auctions: $588, MS-63, January 2014					

a. Proof only.

1912-S, S Over S

	Mintage	VF	EF	MS-60 PF-60	MS-63 PF-63
1912S	1,010,000	$4.50	$12	$125	$275
	Auctions: $306, MS-63, April 2014				
1912S, S Over S	(b)		$85	$200	$500
	Auctions: $646, MS-63, September 2014				
1913S	1,360,693	$6	$12	$85	$175
	Auctions: $558, MS-65, September 2014, $270, MS-63, June 2014				
1914S	1,180,000	$7.50	$15	$175	$300
	Auctions: $411, MS-63, May 2014; $374, MS-63, April 2010				
1915S	450,000	$30	$40	$250	$750
	Auctions: $1,234, MS-64, January 2014; $200, AU-58, January 2014				
1917S	5,991,148	$2.50	$5	$55	$125
	Auctions: $247, MS-65, June 2014; $447, MS-64, July 2014				
1918S	8,420,000	$2	$3	$20	$65
	Auctions: $129, MS-65, January 2013; $306, MS-63, July 2014				
1919S	1,630,000	$3	$5	$30	$110
	Auctions: $182, MS-64, June 2014				
1920	520,000	$6	$16	$95	$200
	Auctions: $494, MS-64, June 2014				
1921	3,863,038	$2	$3	$25	$50
	Auctions: $182, MS-65, June 2014; $153, MS-63, July 2014				
1929M	1,000,000	$2	$3	$20	$35
	Auctions: $123, MS-65, June 2014				
1935M	1,280,000	$2	$4	$20	$50
	Auctions: $182, MS-65, June 2014				

b. Included in 1912-S mintage figure.

Twenty Centavos (1903–1929)

Designer: *Melecio Figueroa.* **Weight:** *1903–1906, 5.385 grams (.1558 oz. ASW); 1907–1929, 4 grams (.0964 oz. ASW).* **Composition:** *1903–1906, .900 silver, .100 copper; 1907–1929, .750 silver, .250 copper.* **Diameter:** *1903–1906, 23 mm; 1907–1929, 20 mm.* **Edge:** *Reeded.* **Mints:** *Philadelphia, San Francisco, and Manila.*

Twenty Centavos, Large Size (1903–1906, 23 mm)

Mintmark location is on the reverse, to the left of the date.

Twenty Centavos, Reduced Size (1907–1929, 20 mm)

History. In the early 1900s the rising value of silver was encouraging exportation and melting of the Philippines' silver twenty-centavo coins. As was the case with the ten-centavo piece, in 1907 the diameter of the twenty-centavo coin was reduced and its silver fineness decreased from .900 to .750. The net effect was about 40 percent less silver, by actual weight, in the new smaller coins. Attrition continued to draw the older coins out of circulation and into the melting pot, as their silver value exceeded their face value. A report of June 30, 1911, held that only about 25 percent of the twenty-centavo coins minted from 1903 to 1906 still remained in the Philippines.

Circulation strikes were made at the Philadelphia and San Francisco mints through 1919. In July 1920, a new "Mint of the Philippine Islands," located in Manila, started production. Its output during the period of U.S. sovereignty included twenty-centavo pieces in 1920, 1921, 1928, and 1929. (Production of the coins later continued under the Commonwealth, with a slightly modified design.) The first two years of coinage did not feature a mintmark identifying Manila as the producer of the coins. This was noticed by collectors of Philippine coins; they protested the oversight, and later coinage dies had an M mintmark added.

In 1928 a rush order for twenty-centavo coins was received at the Manila Mint—by that time the only producer of the denomination. Manila had not minted the coins since 1921, and the Philadelphia Mint had not shipped any new reverse dies (which would have featured their 1928 date). Under pressure to produce the coins, workers at the Manila Mint married a regular twenty-centavo obverse die with the 1928-dated reverse die of the five-centavo denomination, which was only .5 mm larger. As a result, the entire mintage of 100,000 1928 twenty centavos consists of these "mule" (mismatched-die) coins. The reverse of the 1928 coins, compared with others of 1907 to 1929, has a narrower shield and a larger date.

Striking and Sharpness. Most twenty centavos of 1903 to 1906 are well struck. The 1904-S usually shows weak striking on Miss Liberty's left bosom, the frontal hair just above her ear, and her left hand. Most of the coins of 1907 to 1929 show flattening of Liberty's hair, sometimes extending into the area of her left bosom and her left hand.

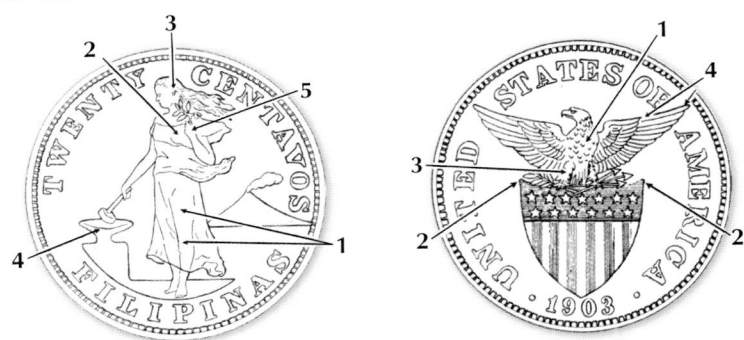

Twenty Centavos, 1903–1906

High Points of Wear. *Obverse Checkpoints:* 1. Figure's left thigh and knee. 2. Figure's left bosom. 3. Figure's left hand. *Reverse Checkpoints:* 1. Eagle's breast feathers. 2. Upper points of shield. 3. Eagle's right leg.

Ten Centavos, 1907–1935

High Points of Wear. *Obverse Checkpoints:* 1. Figure's left thigh. 2. Edge of anvil. 3. Figure's left bosom. 4. Figure's left hand. *Reverse Checkpoints:* 1. Eagle's breast feathers. 2. Eagle's right leg. 3. Upper points of shield.

Proofs. Twenty-centavo Proofs were struck at the Philadelphia Mint for annual Proof sets in 1903, 1904, 1905, 1906, and 1908.

	Mintage	VF	EF	MS-60 / PF-60	MS-63 / PF-63
1903	5,350,231	$5	$8	$45	$100
Auctions: $88, MS-64, July 2014; $86, AU-55, July 2014					
1903, Proof	2,558			$100	$150
Auctions: $482, PF-66, October 2014; $129, PF-63, September 2014; $123, PF-63, September 2014					
1903S	150,080	$35	$85	$600	$1,900
Auctions: $447, AU-58, May 2014					
1904	10,000	$30	$40	$100	$200
Auctions: $529, MS-66, June 2014; $194, MS-64, May 2014; $188, MS-62, January 2015					
1904, Proof	1,355			$110	$175
Auctions: $200, PF-65, July 2014; $153, PF-63, May 2014; $200, PF-61, January 2014					
1904S	2,060,000	$6.50	$11	$100	$200
Auctions: $223, MS-64, January 2015; $211, MS-64, March 2014; $411, MS-63, January 2014					
1905, Proof (a)	471			$225	$375
Auctions: $470, PF-64, January 2013; $282, PF-61, January 2014					
1905S	420,000	$20	$35	$500	$1,250
Auctions: No auction records available.					
1906, Proof (a)	500			$175	$325
Auctions: $541, PF-66, October 2014; $329, PF-62, November 2014; $329, PF-62, October 2014					
1907	1,250,651	$6	$13.50	$200	$450
Auctions: $558, MS-63, September 2014					
1907S	3,165,000	$4	$5.50	$70	$175
Auctions: $374, MS-63, January 2010; $247, MS-62, June 2014					
1908, Proof (a)	500			$175	$325
Auctions: $397, PF-64, January 2014; $299, PF-63, January 2012					
1908S	1,535,000	$4.50	$10	$75	$200
Auctions: $2,233, MS-63, September 2014					
1909S	450,000	$25	$50	$400	$1,500
Auctions: $4,113, MS-64, April 2014; $1,528, MS-64, January 2013					
1910S	500,259	$30	$90	$400	$1,000
Auctions: $3,450, MS-64, April 2012; $2,070, MS-63, April 2012					
1911S	505,000	$25	$40	$300	$900
Auctions: $2,350, MS-64, September 2013					
1912S	750,000	$14	$30	$200	$400
Auctions: $294, MS-63, July 2014					
1913S	795,000	$10	$15	$150	$200
Auctions: $235, MS-63, July 2014; $247, MS-62, June 2014					
1914S	795,000	$12	$40	$250	$450
Auctions: $353, MS-63, January 2014					
1915S	655,000	$20	$65	$600	$1,500
Auctions: $1,116, MS-63, January 2014; $270, AU-58, May 2014					
1916S	1,435,000	$9	$25	$200	$550
Auctions: No auction records available.					
1917S	3,150,655	$3	$7	$75	$200
Auctions: $1,293, MS-66, September 2014; $646, MS-65, September 2014					
1918S	5,560,000	$3	$5	$50	$125
Auctions: $188, MS-64, January 2014; $66, MS-63, June 2014					
1919S	850,000	$5	$15	$125	$225
Auctions: $1,880, MS-66, January 2014; $106, MS-61, November 2014					

a. Proof only.

	Mintage	VF	EF	MS-60	MS-63
1920	1,045,415	$8	$25	$135	$225
	Auctions: $411, MS-63, September 2014				
1921	1,842,631	$3	$5	$70	$100
	Auctions: $79, MS-63, January 2014; $48, AU-58, May 2014				
1928M, Mule (b)	100,000	$25	$70	$900	$1,800
	Auctions: $3,055, MS-65, April 2014; $2,233, MS-64, January 2013				
1929M	1,970,000	$3	$4	$25	$75
	Auctions: $92, MS-64, June 2014; $21, AU-55, May 2014				
1929M, 2 Over 2 Over 2	(c)		$100	$250	$400
	Auctions: No auction records available.				

b. Reverse of 1928 five centavos. **c.** Included in 1929-M mintage figure.

FIFTY CENTAVOS (1903–1921)

Designer: *Melecio Figueroa.* **Weight:** *1903–1906, 13.48 grams (.3900 oz. ASW); 1907–1921, 10 grams (.2411 oz. ASW).* **Composition:** *1903–1906, .900 silver, .100 copper; 1907–1921, .750 silver, .250 copper.* **Diameter:** *1903–1906, 30 mm; 1907–1921, 27 mm.* **Edge:** *Reeded.* **Mints:** *Philadelphia, San Francisco, and Manila.*

Fifty Centavos, Large Size
(1903–1906, 30 mm)

Mintmark location is on the reverse, to the left of the date.

Fifty Centavos, Reduced Size
(1907–1921, 27 mm)

History. After four years of fifty-centavo coinage, in 1907 the denomination's silver fineness was lowered from .900 to .750, and its diameter was reduced by ten percent. This action was in response to rising silver prices. The new smaller coins contained 38 percent less silver, by actual weight, than their 1903–1906 forebears, making them unprofitable to melt for their precious-metal content. Gresham's Law being what it is ("Good money will drive out bad"), the older, heavier silver coins were quickly pulled from circulation; by June 30, 1911, it was officially reported that more than 90 percent of the 1903–1906 coinage had disappeared from the Philippines.

The reduced-size coins of the U.S. sovereignty type were minted from 1907 to 1921. The Manila Mint took over their production from the Philadelphia and San Francisco mints in 1920, using coinage dies shipped from Philadelphia. The fifty centavos was the largest denomination produced at the Manila Mint. Neither the 1920 nor the 1921 coinage featured a mintmark identifying Manila as its producer.

Production of the fifty-centavo denomination would again take place, in 1944 and 1945, in San Francisco, using the Commonwealth design introduced for circulating coins in 1937.

Striking and Sharpness. On fifty-centavo coins of 1903 to 1906, many obverses show slight flattening of the frontal hair just above Miss Liberty's ear. The reverses sometimes show slight flattening of the eagle's breast feathers. On the reverse, a high spot on the shield is the result of an unevenness in striking. The coins of 1907 to 1921 often show notable flatness of strike in Miss Liberty's hair just above her ear, and sometimes on her left hand. A flat strike on the abdomen and left leg should not be mistaken for circulation wear. The reverses are quite unevenly struck; observe the top part of the shield, which has a depressed middle and raised sides. The right side is slightly higher than the left and may show some flattening.

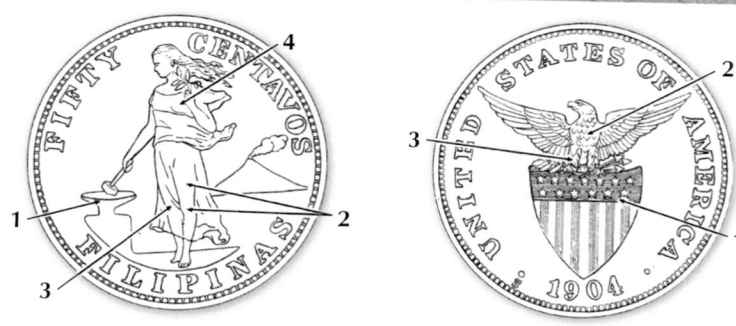

Fifty Centavos, 1903–1906

High Points of Wear. *Obverse Checkpoints:* 1. Edge of anvil. 2. Figure's left thigh and knee. 3. Figure's right knee. 4. Figure's right bosom. *Reverse Checkpoints:* 1. Part of shield just to left of lower-right star. 2. Eagle's breast feathers. 3. Eagle's right leg and claws.

Fifty Centavos, 1907–1921

High Points of Wear. *Obverse Checkpoints:* 1. Figure's left thigh and lower leg. 2. Mid-drapery. 3. Figure's left bosom. 4. Edge of anvil. *Reverse Checkpoints:* 1. Eagle's breast feathers. 2. Eagle's right leg. 3. Part of shield just to left of lower-right star.

Proofs. Fifty-centavo Proofs were struck at the Philadelphia Mint for annual Proof sets in 1903, 1904, 1905, 1906, and 1908. Proofs of 1908 often are found with considerable flatness in the frontal hair above Miss Liberty's hair and sometimes with flatness in her left hand.

| | Mintage | VF | EF | MS-60 | MS-63 |
				PF-60	PF-63
1903	3,099,061	$10	$15	$65	$125
Auctions: $259, MS-64, May 2014; $165, MS-64, September 2013; $129, MS-62, January 2014					
1903, Proof	2,558			$100	$175
Auctions: $734, PF-66, October 2014; $189, PF-64, September 2014; $411, PF-64, January 2014					
1903S (a)			$30,000		
Auctions: No auction records available.					
1904	10,000	$40	$75	$145	$260
Auctions: $1,234, MS-66+, June 2014; $223, MS-63, November 2014; $247, MS-63, May 2014					
1904, Proof	1,355			$125	$250
Auctions: $476, PF-65, September 2012; $247, PF-63, February 2014					
1904S	216,000	$12	$25	$125	$225
Auctions: $881, MS-65, September 2014; $443, MS-64, May 2014					
1905, Proof (b)	471			$275	$425
Auctions: $764, PF-63, January 2015; $411, PF-63, April 2014					
1905S	852,000	$20	$50	$700	$2,100
Auctions: $1,058, MS-62, April 2014; $206, AU-55, June 2014					

a. 2 examples are known. **b.** Proof only.

	Mintage	VF	EF	MS-60 / PF-60	MS-63 / PF-63
1906, Proof (b)	500			$225	$375
		Auctions: $2,820, PF-67, October 2014; $940, PF-65, April 2014; $353, PF-61, November 2014			
1907	1,200,625	$15	$40	$150	$325
		Auctions: $1,763, MS-64, April 2014; $427, MS-62, September 2014			
1907S	2,112,000	$10	$30	$150	$325
		Auctions: $499, MS-63, September 2014; $427, MS-62, September 2014			
1908, Proof (b)	500			$200	$350
		Auctions: $499, PF-64, April 2014; $499, PF-64, January 2014			
1908S	1,601,000	$10	$40	$325	$1,500
		Auctions: $2,820, MS-63, January 2014; $823, MS-62, September 2014			
1909S	528,000	$20	$50	$350	$850
		Auctions: $1,645, MS-64, April 2014; $1,528, MS-63, January 2014			
1917S	674,369	$15	$35	$200	$550
		Auctions: $294, MS-63, January 2014; $411, MS-62, September 2014			
1918S	2,202,000	$7.50	$15	$90	$170
		Auctions: $129, MS-62, June 2014; $176, MS-61, January 2014			
1919S	1,200,000	$7.50	$15	$100	$200
		Auctions: $353, MS-64, July 2014; $129, MS-62, January 2015			
1920	420,000	$7.50	$10	$60	$100
		Auctions: $211, MS-64, January 2014; $212, MS-62, July 2014			
1921	2,316,763	$7.50	$10	$40	$75
		Auctions: $62, MS-63, October 2014; $94, MS-63, July 2014; $82, MS-63, July 2013			

b. Proof only.

One Peso (1903–1912)

Designer: *Melecio Figueroa.* **Weight:** *1903–1906, 26.96 grams (.7800 oz. ASW);* *1907–1912, 20 grams (.5144 oz. ASW).* **Composition:** *1903–1906, .900 silver, .100 copper;* *1907–1912, .800 silver, .200 copper.* **Diameter:** *1903–1906, 38 mm; 1907–1912, 35 mm.* **Edge:** *Reeded.* **Mints:** *Philadelphia and San Francisco.*

Peso, Large Size
(1903–1906, 38 mm)

Peso, Reduced Size
(1907–1912, 35 mm)

Mintmark location is on the reverse, to the left of the date.

History. The Philippine silver peso was struck under U.S. sovereignty from 1903 to 1912. The key date among those struck for circulation is the issue of 1906-S. Although the San Francisco Mint produced more than 200,000 of the coins that year, nearly all of them were held back from circulation. They were instead stored and then later sold as bullion.

By 1906 natural market forces were driving the Philippine silver pesos out of commerce and into the melting pot: the rising price of silver made the coins worth more as precious metal than as legal tender. In 1907 the U.S. Mint responded by lowering the denomination's silver fineness from .900 to .800 and reducing its diameter from 38 mm to 35. The resulting smaller coins had about one-third less silver, by actual weight, than those of 1903 to 1906, guaranteeing that they would stay in circulation. The older coins, meanwhile, were still profitable to pull aside and melt for their silver value. An official report of June 30, 1911, disclosed that less than ten percent of the heavier silver coins still remained in the Philippines.

The new smaller pesos were minted every year from 1907 to 1912, with the San Francisco Mint producing them for commerce and the Philadelphia Mint striking a small quantity of Proofs in 1907 and 1908. Millions of the coins were stored as backing for Silver Certificates (and, later, Treasury Certificates) in circulation in the Philippines. Although the Manila Mint started operations in 1920, the silver peso was never part of its production for circulation.

In December 1941, Imperial Japan, immediately after attacking Pearl Harbor, began a fierce assault on the Philippines. Manila fell on January 2, 1942, and General Douglas MacArthur fell back to the Bataan Peninsula. In late February President Franklin Roosevelt ordered him to leave the Philippines for Australia, prompting the general's famous promise to the Philippine people: "I shall return!" Not long after the fighting erupted it had become apparent that the Japanese would overtake the islands, and early in 1942 the U.S. military dumped crates holding 15,700,000 silver pesos, mostly of 1907–1912 coinage, into the sea near Corregidor, to avoid their seizure. Many millions of these coins were salvaged by the U.S. Treasury and the Central Bank of the Philippines after the war, with all but about five million pieces being reclaimed by 1958. Today a great majority of the salvaged "war pesos" show clear evidence of their prolonged submersion in saltwater. A typical effect is a dark corrosion strongly resistant to any manner of cleaning or conservation.

Striking and Sharpness. The silver pesos of 1903 to 1906 generally have well-struck obverses, but occasionally with some flattening of Miss Liberty's frontal hair above her ear, and sometimes her left bosom and hand. On the reverse, the feathers on the eagle's breast are indistinctly cut, and the wing tips can sometimes be found slightly flatly struck. Of the silver pesos of 1907 to 1912, some but not all exhibit flattened frontal hair, and sometimes a flattened left hand. On the reverse, the eagle's breast feathers are not clearly defined. On some examples the reverses are quite unevenly struck; check the top part of the shield, which has a depressed middle and raised sides, and the right side, which is slightly higher than the left and may show some flattening.

One Peso, 1903–1906

High Points of Wear. *Obverse Checkpoints:* 1. Figure's upper-left leg and knee. 2. Figure's right knee. 3. Figure's left bosom. 4. Frontal hair just above ear. *Reverse Checkpoints:* 1. Eagle's breast feathers. 2. Eagle's right leg. 3. Eagle's wing tips.

One Peso, 1907–1912

High Points of Wear. *Obverse Checkpoints:* 1. Figure's upper-left leg and knee. 2. Figure's lower-left leg. 3. Figure's left hand. 4. Frontal hair just above ear. *Reverse Checkpoints:* 1. Eagle's breast feathers. 2. Eagle's right leg.

Proofs. Proof pesos were struck at the Philadelphia Mint for annual Proof sets in 1903, 1904, 1905, 1906, and 1908. Unlike the smaller denominations, Proof pesos of 1907 also are known—but only to the extent of two examples.

1905-S, Curved Serif on "1"   1905-S, Straight Serif on "1"

	Mintage	VF	EF	MS-60 PF-60	MS-63 PF-63
1903	2,788,901	$35	$40	$190	$550
	Auctions: $552, MS-63, October 2014				
1903, Proof	2,558			$200	$350
	Auctions: $3,525, PF-67, October 2014; $200, PF-62, September 2014				
1903S	11,361,000	$28	$35	$130	$250
	Auctions: $690, MS-63, March 2011; $188, MS-60, January 2014				
1904	11,355	$80	$125	$250	$500
	Auctions: $705, MS-64, January 2014; $329, MS-63, August 2013				
1904, Proof	1,355			$250	$450
	Auctions: $3,525, PF-67, October 2014; $3,290, PF-67, October 2014; $881, PF-64, September 2014				
1904S	6,600,000	$30	$40	$175	$375
	Auctions: $440, MS-63, September 2014; $188, MS-62, January 2015				
1905, Proof (a)	471			$750	$1,500
	Auctions: $11,163, PF-67, January 2013; $911, PF-63, October 2014				
1905S, Curved Serif on "1"	6,056,000	$35	$50	$325	$750
	Auctions: $764, MS-61, January 2014				
1905S, Straight Serif on "1"	(b)	$50	$70	$875	$2,500
	Auctions: $3,819, MS-63, September 2014				
1906, Proof (a)	500			$700	$1,200
	Auctions: $3,819, PF-67, October 2014; $3,525, PF-67, October 2014; $1,880, PF-63, April 2014				
1906S	201,000	$1,400	$2,700	$17,500	$32,500
	Auctions: $7,050, AU-55, October 2014; $7,638, AU-55, April 2014				

Note: Philippine silver pesos of 1907–1912 that were corroded from submersion in Caballo Bay during World War II are worth considerably less than their problem-free counterparts, but are avidly collected for their historical value. **a.** Proof only. **b.** Included in 1905-S, Curved Serif on "1," mintage figure.

	Mintage	VF	EF	MS-60	MS-63
				PF-60	PF-63
1907, Proof (a,c)					$160,000
	Auctions: No auction records available.				
1907S	10,278,000	$16	$22	$90	$200
	Auctions: $940, MS-64, October 2014; $188, MS-62, December 2014; $112, MS-60, January 2014				
1908, Proof (a)	500			$650	$1,000
	Auctions: $1,763, PF-64, January 2015; $940, PF-64, August 2014; $999, PF-64, January 2014				
1908S	20,954,944	$16	$22	$90	$200
	Auctions: $852, MS-64, January 2015; $705, MS-64, September 2014				
1909S	7,578,000	$18	$24	$125	$300
	Auctions: $1,058, MS-64, October 2014; $235, MS-62, January 2014				
1909S, S Over S	(d)		$90	$150	$500
	Auctions: No auction records available.				
1910S	3,153,559	$23	$35	$225	$450
	Auctions: $489, MS-63, January 2010				
1911S	463,000	$40	$75	$750	$4,250
	Auctions: No auction records available.				
1912S	680,000	$50	$80	$2,000	$5,000
	Auctions: $9,988, MS-63, October 2014; $5,875, MS-61, April 2014; $999, AU-58, April 2014				

Note: Philippine silver pesos of 1907–1912 that were corroded from submersion in Caballo Bay during World War II are worth considerably less than their problem-free counterparts, but are avidly collected for their historical value. **a.** Proof only. **c.** 2 examples are known. **d.** Included in 1909-S mintage figure.

MANILA MINT OPENING MEDAL (1920)

Designer: *Clifford Hewitt.* **Composition:** *bronze; silver; gold.*
Diameter: *38 mm.* **Edge:** *Plain.* **Mint:** *Manila.*

Bronze

Silver

Gold

History. During U.S. sovereignty, much of the civilian government of the Philippines was administered by the Bureau of Insular Affairs, part of the War Department. Most heads or secretaries of Philippine government departments were appointed by the U.S. governor general, with the advice and consent of the Philippine Senate. In 1919, the chief of the Bureau of the Insular Treasury (part of the Department of Finance) was Insular Treasurer Albert P. Fitzsimmons, formerly a mayor of Tecumseh, Nebraska, and member of the municipal board of Manila. Fitzsimmons, a surgeon who had served in the U.S. Army Medical Corps in Cuba and the Philippines, was active in civil affairs, and had been in charge of U.S. government bond issues in the Philippines during the Great War. On May 20, 1919, he was named director ad interim of the Mint of the Philippine Islands, which was then being organized.

The genesis of this new mint started on February 8, 1918, when the Philippine Legislature passed an appropriations bill for construction of its machinery. The war in Europe was interfering with shipments from the San Francisco Mint, where Philippine coinage was produced, and a local mint was seen as more expedient and economical. In addition, a mint in Manila would serve the United States' goal of preparing the Philippines for its own governance and infrastructure.

The mint was built in Manila in the Intendencia Building, which also housed the offices and hall of the Senate, and the offices and vaults of the Philippine Treasury. Its machinery was designed and built in Philadelphia under the supervision of U.S. Mint chief mechanical engineer Clifford Hewitt, who also oversaw its installation in Manila. The facility was opened, with formalities and machine demonstrations, on July 15, 1920. The fanfare included the production of an official commemorative medal, the first example of which was struck by Speaker of the House of Representatives Sergio Osmeña.

The medal has since come to be popularly known as the "Wilson Dollar" (despite not being a legal-tender coin), because of its size and its bold profile portrait of Woodrow Wilson on the obverse, surrounded by the legend PRESIDENT OF THE UNITED STATES. The reverse features the ancient Roman goddess Juno Moneta guiding a youth—representing the fledgling mint staff of the Philippines—in the art of coining. She holds a pair of metallurgical scales. The reverse legend is TO COMMEMORATE THE OPENING OF THE MINT / MANILA P.I., along with the date, 1920. The medal was designed by Hewitt, the mint's supervising engineer from Philadelphia. Its dies were made by U.S. Mint chief engraver George T. Morgan, whose initial, M, appears on the obverse on President Wilson's breast and on the reverse above the goddess's sandal.

The issue was limited to 2,200 silver medals (2,000 of which were struck on the first day), sold to the public at $1 apiece; and 3,700 in bronze, sold for 50¢. In addition, at least five gold specimens were reportedly struck. These included one for presentation to President Wilson and one for U.S. Secretary of War Newton Baker. The other gold medals remained in the Philippines and were lost during World War II. Of the medals unsold and still held by the Treasury in the early 1940s, some or all were dumped into Caballo Bay in April 1942 along with millions of silver pesos, to keep them from the approaching Japanese forces. The invaders learned of the coins and in May attempted to recover the sunken silver coins using the labor of Filipino divers. Although skilled divers, the Filipinos were not experienced in deep-sea diving, and the coins were at the bottom of the bay, 120 feet below the surface. After three deaths the Filipinos refused to participate in further recovery efforts. The Japanese then forced U.S. prisoners of war who were experienced deep-sea divers to recover the sunken treasure. The American divers conspired to salvage only small quantities of the sunken treasure. They repeatedly sabotaged the recovery process, and smuggled a significant number of recovered silver coins to the Philippine guerrillas. Only about 2 to 3 percent of the dumped coinage was recovered before the Japanese ceased recovery operations. Following the war the United States brought up much of the coinage that had been dumped into the sea. Many of the recovered silver and bronze Wilson dollars in grades VF through AU bear evidence of saltwater corrosion.

The Manila Mint Opening medal is popular with collectors of Philippine coins and of American medals. It is often cataloged as a *so-called dollar*, a classification of historic dollar-sized souvenir medals, some of which were struck by the U.S. Mint and some produced privately. The Manila Mint Opening medal is valued for its unique connections to the United States and to American numismatics.

	Mintage	VF-20	EF-40	AU-50	MS-60	MS-63	MS-65
Manila Mint medal, 1920, bronze	3,700	$35	$80	$235	$785	$1,350	$4,500
Manila Mint medal, 1920, silver	2,200	$85	$250	$525	$875	$1,850	$3,200

Note: VF, EF, and AU examples in bronze and silver often show signs of saltwater corrosion. The values above are for problem-free examples.

	Mintage	AU-55	MS-62
Manila Mint medal, 1920, gold	5	$44,000	$75,000

COMMONWEALTH ISSUES FOR CIRCULATION (1937–1945)

The Philippine Islands were largely self-governed, as a commonwealth of the United States, from 1935 until full independence was recognized in 1946. Coinage under the Commonwealth began with three commemorative coins in 1936 (see next section). Circulating issues were minted from 1937 to 1941 (in Manila) and in 1944 and 1945 (in Philadelphia, Denver, and San Francisco).

The Commonwealth coinage retained the obverse motifs designed by Melecio Figueroa and used on the coinage of 1903 to 1936. Its new reverse design featured a shield derived from the official seal of the government of the Philippines, with three stars symbolizing Luzon, Mindanao, and the Visayas, the islands' three main geographical regions. In the oval set in the shield's center is a modification of the colonial coat of arms of the City of Manila: a fortress tower above with a heraldic crowned *morse* or sea-lion (half dolphin, half lion) below. An eagle with outstretched wings surmounts the entirety of the shield design, and beneath is a scroll with the legend COMMONWEALTH OF THE PHILIPPINES.

World War II forced the Commonwealth government to operate in exile during the Japanese occupation of 1942 to 1945. A pro-Japan puppet government was set up in Manila in 1943; it issued no coins of its own, and in fact during the Japanese occupation many coins were gathered from circulation to be melted and remade into Japanese coins. Barter and low-denomination emergency paper money took their place in day-to-day commerce. (Much of the money used in the Philippines during World War II consisted of hastily printed "guerrilla" currency.) The United States military knew of the local need for circulating coins, and the U.S. and Philippine governments included new coinage in the plans to liberate the islands. The U.S. Treasury Department used its Philadelphia, San Francisco, and Denver mints to produce brass, copper-nickel-zinc, and silver coins in 1944 and 1945, to be shipped to the Philippines during and after the liberation.

BRONZE AND BRASS COINAGE
ONE CENTAVO (1937–1944)

Designer: *Melecio Figueroa (obverse).* **Weight:** *5.3 grams.*
Composition: *.950 copper, .050 tin and zinc (except for 1944-S: .950 copper, .050 zinc).*
Diameter: *24 mm.* **Edge:** *Plain.* **Mints:** *San Francisco and Manila.*

Bronze Alloy (1937–1941)

Mintmark location is on the reverse, to the left of the date.

Brass Alloy (1944)

History. The Manila Mint struck one-centavo coins for the Commonwealth of the Philippines every year from 1937 through 1941. This production was brought to an end by the Japanese invasion that started in December 1941, immediately after the bombing of Pearl Harbor. Part of the United States–Commonwealth plan to retake the islands included the San Francisco Mint's 1944 striking of 58 million one-centavo coins—a quantity greater than all of Manila's centavo output since 1937. Like the federal Lincoln cents of 1944 to 1946, these coins were made of *brass* rather than bronze—their alloy was derived in part from recycled cartridge cases, and their composition included copper and zinc, but no tin (a vital war material). The coins were transported to the islands to enter circulation as U.S. and Philippine military forces fought back the Japanese invaders. This would be the final mintage of centavos until the Republic of the Philippines, created on July 4, 1946, resumed the denomination's production in 1958.

The centavo was a popular coin that saw widespread circulation. As a result, many of the coins today are found with signs of wear or damage, exacerbated by corrosion and toning encouraged by the islands' tropical climate.

Striking and Sharpness. Well-struck examples are uncommon. Obverses of the Commonwealth centavos usually have very flat or depressed strikes in the left shoulder of the seated figure, and part of the face and chest. His right hand is better struck than in the coins struck under U.S. sovereignty. The left side of the anvil's edge is slightly rounded. On the reverse, many Uncirculated coins have flatness on the lower and central sections of the coat of arms, and some of most of the words COMMONWEALTH OF THE PHILIPPINES are unreadable.

On a perfectly struck coin, the eagle surmounting the Commonwealth shield would have a pattern of feathers visible on its breast; this level of detail is rarely evident, with the breast instead appearing smooth or flat.

Many 1937-M centavos have a barely readable mintmark. Issues of 1938 to 1941 used a narrow M mintmark, rather than a square version of the letter, resulting in better legibility.

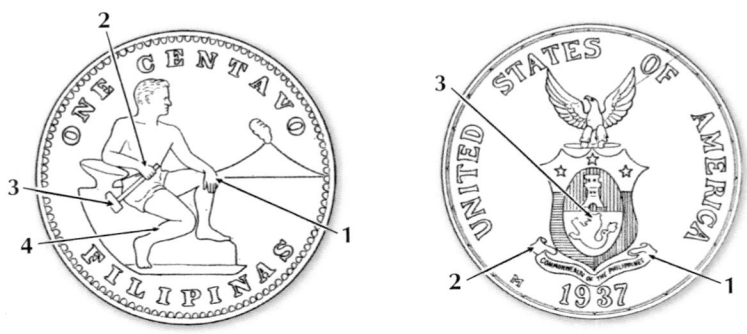

One Centavo, 1937–1944

High Points of Wear. *Obverse Checkpoints:* 1. Figure's left hand. 2. Figure's right hand. 3. Head of hammer. 4. Figure's right calf. *Reverse Checkpoints:* 1. Inner-right fold of ribbon. 2. Outer-left fold of ribbon. 3. Center of coat of arms.

	Mintage	VF	EF	MS-60	MS-63
1937M	15,790,492	$2	$3	$20	$40
	Auctions: No auction records available.				
1938M	10,000,000	$1.50	$2.50	$15	$35
	Auctions: $66, MS-65RB, March 2014; $94, MS-64RB, January 2014				
1939M	6,500,000	$2.50	$3.50	$17.50	$40
	Auctions: $223, MS-66RD, April 2014				

	Mintage	VF	EF	MS-60	MS-63
1940M	4,000,000	$1.25	$3	$12	$30
	Auctions: $50, MS-65RB, May 2014; $30, MS-64RD, March 2014				
1941M	5,000,000	$1.25	$3.50	$18	$35
	Auctions: $59, MS-65RD, March 2014				
1944S	58,000,000	$0.25	$0.50	$2	$7
	Auctions: $32, MS-65RD, March 2014				

COPPER-NICKEL AND COPPER-NICKEL-ZINC COINAGE
FIVE CENTAVOS (1937–1945)

Designer: *Melecio Figueroa (obverse).* **Weight:** *1937–1941, 4.8 grams; 1944–1945, 4.92 grams.*
Composition: *1937–1941, .750 copper, .250 nickel; 1944–1945, .650 copper, .230 zinc, .120 nickel.*
Diameter: *19 mm.* **Edge:** *Plain.* **Mints:** *Manila, Philadelphia, and San Francisco.*

Copper-Nickel
(1937–1941)

Mintmark location is on the reverse, to the left of the date (Manila and San Francisco issues only; Philadelphia issues have no mintmark).

Copper-Nickel-Zinc
(1944–1945)

Manila mintmark style of 1937 and 1941 (wide, with midpoint not extending to baseline).

Manila mintmark style of 1938 (narrow, with midpoint extending to baseline).

History. The Manila Mint switched its coinage of five-centavo pieces to the Commonwealth reverse design in 1937. Production of the coins increased in 1938, then skipped two years. The 1941 output would be Manila's last for the type; the Japanese invasion at year's end stopped all of its coinage.

Philippine commerce was starved for coins during the war. As part of the broader strategy for liberating the Philippines from Japanese occupation, the U.S. Treasury Department swung its mints into production of five-centavo coins in 1944 (Philadelphia and San Francisco) and 1945 (San Francisco alone). This effort dwarfed that of the Commonwealth's late-1930s coinage, producing in those two years more than ten times the combined output of 1937, 1938, and 1941. In order to help save copper and nickel for military use, the U.S. Mint reduced the proportions of those metals in the five-centavo coinage, making up for them with the addition of zinc. This substitution saved more than 4.2 million pounds of nickel and 3.2 million pounds of copper for the war effort. The Philadelphia and San Francisco coins were shipped to the islands during the combined American-Filipino military operations against Japan.

Striking and Sharpness. Most pre-war five-centavo coins are poorly struck. On the obverse, the seated figure's left hand is flat, and the left shoulder can be as well. The left side of the pedestal and the right side of Mount Mayon can be poorly detailed. The obverse rim typically lacks sharpness. On the reverse, the ribbon usually is flat, with its wording partially or completely illegible, and the coat of arms can lack detail especially at the top-left side. On a perfectly struck coin, the eagle surmounting the Commonwealth shield would have a pattern of feathers visible on its breast; this level of detail is rarely evident, with the breast instead appearing smooth or flat.

The mintmark style of 1937 and 1941—a wide M, with the middle point not descending to the letter's baseline—usually did not strike clearly, making it difficult to read. The mintmark style of 1938 was narrower, with the middle point descending to the base, and typically is more legible.

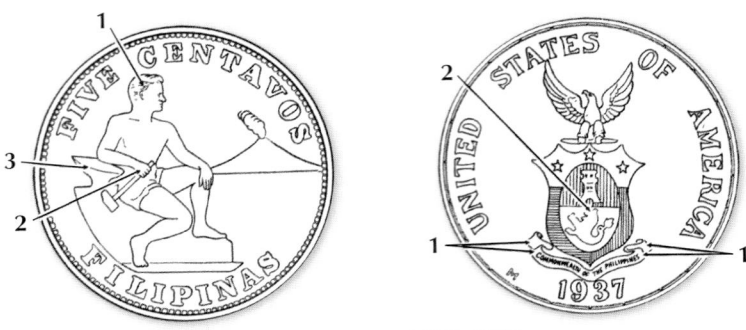

Five Centavos, 1937–1945

High Points of Wear. *Obverse Checkpoints:* 1. Frontal hair just above ear. 2. Figure's right hand. 3. Edge of anvil. ***Reverse Checkpoints:*** 1. Inner and outer folds of ribbon. 2. Center of coat of arms.

	Mintage	VF	EF	MS-60	MS-63
1937M	2,493,872	$5	$7	$50	$110
	Auctions: $188, MS-65, September 2013				
1938M	4,000,000	$1	$2.25	$20	$65
	Auctions: $92, MS-65, July 2014; $112, MS-65, September 2013				
1941M	2,750,000	$3	$8	$55	$140
	Auctions: $282, MS-65, January 2014; $88, MS-64, September 2013				
1944 (a)	21,198,000	$0.50	$1	$2	$3
	Auctions: $46, MS-65, June 2013; $29, MS-64, April 2013				
1944S (a)	14,040,000	$0.25	$0.50	$1	$2
	Auctions: $165, MS-67, September 2013; $200, MS-67, August 2013; $188, MS-67, August 2013				
1945S (a)	72,796,000	$0.25	$0.50	$1	$2
	Auctions: No auction records available.				

a. Copper-nickel-zinc alloy.

SILVER COINAGE
TEN CENTAVOS (1937–1945)

Designer: *Melecio Figueroa.* **Weight:** *2 grams (.0482 oz. ASW).* **Composition:** *.750 silver, .250 copper.* **Diameter:** *16.5 mm.* **Edge:** *Reeded.* **Mints:** *Denver and Manila.*

Mintmark location is on the reverse, to the left of the date.

History. As with its production of other denominations, the Manila Mint under Commonwealth governance struck ten-centavo coins in 1937 and 1938, followed by a hiatus of two years, and a final coinage in 1941. Normal mint functions were interrupted in 1941 when Imperial Japan invaded the Philippines as part of its war with the United States. The Japanese puppet government of 1943–1945 would not produce any of its own coins, and the Manila Mint, damaged by bombing during the Japanese assault, was later used as part of the invaders' defensive fortifications on the Pasig River.

Japan's wartime exportation of Philippine coins resulted in scarcity of coinage in day-to-day commerce. The U.S. Treasury geared up the Denver Mint for a massive production of Philippine ten-centavo coins in 1944 and 1945, to be shipped overseas and enter circulation as American and Philippine troops liberated the islands. The 1945 coinage was particularly heavy: more than 130 million ten-centavo coins, compared to the Denver Mint's production of just over 40 million Mercury dimes that year. This large mintage of silver coins continued to circulate in the Philippines into the 1960s.

Striking and Sharpness. Well-struck examples of the Commonwealth ten-centavo coin are unusual. Part of Miss Liberty's bust is nearly always flatly struck, especially along the left side. The hair and left arm may also be poorly struck. On the reverse, the coat of arms usually lacks detail, and COMMONWEALTH OF THE PHILIPPINES, on the ribbon, often is only partly legible. On a perfectly struck coin, the eagle surmounting the Commonwealth shield would have a pattern of feathers visible on its breast; this level of detail is rarely evident, with the breast instead appearing smooth or flat.

The Denver coinage of 1944 and 1945 often is weakly struck on the obverse, with loss of detail. The reverse typically is weakly struck on the ribbon, with indistinct lettering.

The mintmark style of 1937 and 1941—a wide M, with the middle point not descending to the letter's baseline—usually did not strike clearly, making it difficult to read. The mintmark style of 1938 was narrower, with the middle point descending to the base, and typically is more legible.

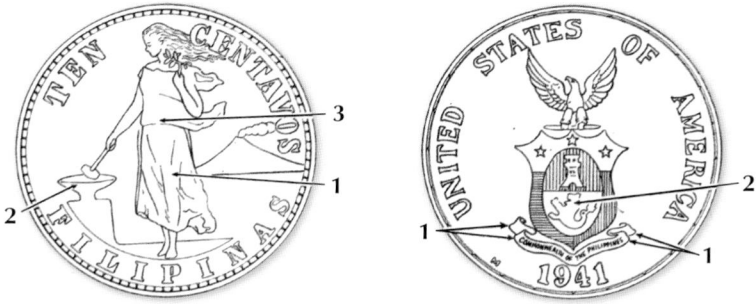

Ten Centavos, 1937–1945

High Points of Wear. *Obverse Checkpoints:* 1. Figure's left leg. 2. Edge of anvil. 3. Mid-drapery area. *Reverse Checkpoints:* 1. Inner and outer folds of ribbon. 2. Center of coat of arms.

	Mintage	VF	EF	MS-60	MS-63
1937M	3,500,000	$2.25	$3.50	$25	$50
	Auctions: $500, MS-67, January 2013				
1938M	*3,750,000*	$1.75	$2.25	$10	$20
	Auctions: $36, MS-63, August 2009				
1941M	*2,500,000*	$1.75	$2.50	$10	$15
	Auctions: $36, MS-65, August 2009				
1944D	31,592,000	$1.25	$2	$2.50	$5
	Auctions: No auction records available.				
1945D	137,208,000	$1.25	$2	$2.50	$5
	Auctions: No auction records available.				
1945D, D Over D	(a)	$8.50	$15	$30	$50
	Auctions: $470, AU-50, April 2014				

a. Included in 1945-D mintage figure.

TWENTY CENTAVOS (1937–1945)

Designer: *Melecio Figueroa (obverse).* **Weight:** *4 grams (.0964 oz. ASW).*
Composition: *.750 silver, .250 copper.* **Diameter:** *20 mm.*
Edge: *Reeded.* **Mints:** *Denver and Manila.*

*Mintmark location is on the
reverse, to the left of the date.*

History. The twenty-centavo piece was the largest circulating coin struck by the Commonwealth of the Philippines at the Manila Mint. Production commenced in 1937 and 1938, followed by a hiatus of two year, and a final year of output in 1941 before Japan's December invasion put a halt to all coinage. During their occupation, the Japanese pulled many twenty-centavo pieces out of circulation and melted them as raw material for new imperial coins.

Anticipating driving the Japanese military out of the islands, the United States and Commonwealth governments planned an impressive production of coinage for the Philippines in 1944 and 1945. The Denver Mint was the source for twenty-centavo pieces, and its output was immense, in 1945 exceeding even the Philadelphia Mint's production of Washington quarters for domestic use. 111 million of the coins were shipped overseas to accompany the U.S. military as Americans and Filipinos fought to liberate the islands. The need was great, as legal-tender coins had largely disappeared from circulation. Most day-to-day commerce was transacted with small-denomination scrip notes and paper money issued by guerrilla military units, local governments, or anti-Japanese military and civilian currency boards.

Striking and Sharpness. Well-struck twenty-centavo Commonwealth coins are a challenge to locate. Nearly all obverses have flattened hair on Miss Liberty's head. On the reverse, the coat of arms usually lacks detail, and COMMONWEALTH OF THE PHILIPPINES, on the ribbon, often is only partly legible. The Denver coins typically lack sharp details on the obverse and have the same reverse weakness as earlier Manila issues.

On a perfectly struck coin, the eagle surmounting the Commonwealth shield would have a pattern of feathers visible on its breast; this level of detail is rarely evident, with the breast instead appearing smooth or flat.

The mintmark style of 1937 and 1941—a wide M, with the middle point not descending to the letter's baseline—usually did not strike clearly, making it difficult to read. The mintmark style of 1938 was narrower, with the middle point descending to the base, and typically is more legible.

Twenty Centavos, 1937–1945

High Points of Wear. *Obverse Checkpoints:* 1. Figure's left thigh and knee. 2. Figure's left hand. 3. Edge of anvil. *Reverse Checkpoints:* 1. Inner folds of ribbon. 2. Center of coat of arms.

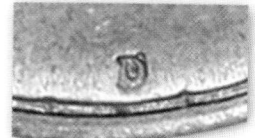

1944-D, D Over S

	Mintage	VF	EF	MS-60	MS-63
1937M	2,665,000	$3	$5	$35	$50
	Auctions: No auction records available.				
1938M	3,000,000	$3	$3.50	$15	$30
	Auctions: $40, MS-64, August 2009; $32, MS-64, August 2009				
1941M	1,500,000	$3	$3.50	$12.50	$20
	Auctions: No auction records available.				
1944D	28,596,000	$1	$2.75	$3	$5
	Auctions: No auction records available.				
1944D, D Over S	(a)	$7.50	$10	$25	$50
	Auctions: $403, MS-66, January 2010				
1945D	82,804,000	$1	$2.75	$3	$5
	Auctions: No auction records available.				

a. Included in 1944-D mintage figure.

FIFTY CENTAVOS (1944–1945)

Designer: *Melecio Figueroa.* **Weight:** *10 grams (.2411 oz. ASW).*
Composition: *.750 silver, .250 copper.* **Diameter:** *27 mm.*
Edge: *Reeded.* **Mint:** *San Francisco.*

Mintmark location is on the
reverse, to the left of the date.

History. No fifty-centavo coins were struck at the Manila Mint for the Commonwealth of the Philippines. The denomination's first issue was a wartime production of the San Francisco Mint, in 1944, to the extent of some 19 million coins, or double that facility's production of Liberty Walking half dollars for the year. This was followed by a similar mintage in 1945. These coins were intended to enter circulation after being shipped overseas with the U.S. military during the liberation of the Philippines from Imperial Japan's 1942–1945 occupation. They were readily accepted in the coin-starved wartime economy and continued to circulate in the islands into the 1960s.

Striking and Sharpness. Many Commonwealth fifty-centavo coins are lightly struck, but they typically show flattening less severe than that of the 1907–1921 issues struck under U.S. sovereignty. On the reverse, the coat of arms usually is weakly struck, with COMMONWEALTH OF THE PHILIPPINES rarely completely legible. On a perfectly struck coin, the eagle surmounting the Commonwealth shield would have a pattern of feathers visible on its breast; this level of detail is rarely evident, with the breast instead appearing smooth or flat.

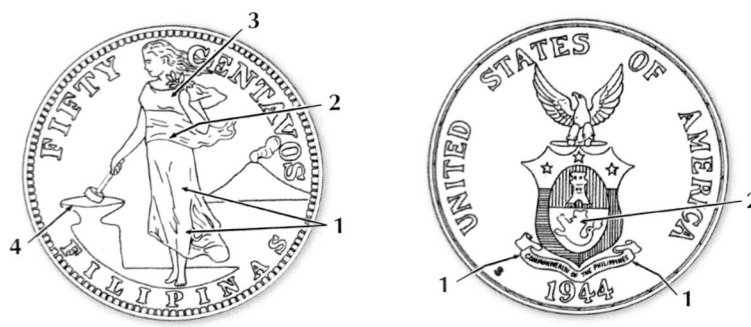

Fifty Centavos, 1944–1945

High Points of Wear. *Obverse Checkpoints:* 1. Figure's left thigh and lower leg. 2. Mid-drapery area. 3. Figure's left bosom. 4. Edge of anvil. *Reverse Checkpoints:* 1. Inner folds of ribbon. 2. Center of coat of arms.

1945-S, S Over S

	Mintage	VF	EF	MS-60	MS-63
1944S	19,187,000	$7	$8	$10	$15
	Auctions: $44, MS-64, March 2013				
1945S	18,120,000	$7	$8	$10	$15
	Auctions: $100, MS-66, January 2014				
1945S, S Over S	(a)	$12	$30	$80	$180
	Auctions: $306, MS-66, May 2014				

a. Included in 1945-S mintage figure.

COMMONWEALTH COMMEMORATIVE ISSUES

The American territory of the Philippines was governed by the U.S. military from 1899 to mid-1901. Its executive branch was managed by the Bureau of Insular Affairs (part of the War Department) from mid-1901 to 1935. In the latter year the Philippines' status was changed to that of a commonwealth—a type of organized but unincorporated dependent territory, self-governed (except in defense and foreign policy) under a constitution of its own adoption, whose right of self-government would not be unilaterally withdrawn by Congress. This was a step in the direction of complete independence, scheduled to be recognized after an additional ten years of "nation building."

To celebrate this transfer of government, the Manila Mint in 1936 produced a set of three silver commemorative coins—one of the fifty-centavo denomination, and two of the one-peso. These were designed by Ambrosio Morales, professor of sculpture at the University of the Philippines School of Fine Arts.

The fifty-centavo coin and one of the set's pesos feature busts of Philippine president Manuel L. Quezon and the last U.S. governor-general, Frank Murphy, who served (largely ceremonially) as the first U.S. high commissioner to the Commonwealth of the Philippines. On the fifty-centavo piece the two men face each other with the rising sun between them; on the peso, they appear jugate (in conjoined profile portraits). The other peso has busts of Quezon and U.S. president Franklin D. Roosevelt. This was a rare instance of a living American president appearing on a coin, the only precedent being the 1926 Sesquicentennial commemorative half dollar, which showed President Calvin Coolidge.

On each of the three coins appears the date November 15, 1935, when the new commonwealth's government was inaugurated on the steps of the Legislative Building in Manila, witnessed by 300,000 people in attendance.

The set's issue price was $3.13, or about 2.5 times the coins' face value expressed in U.S. dollars. Commemorative coins were popular in the United States at the time, but still these sets sold poorly, and thousands remained within the Philippine Treasury at the onset of World War II. In early 1942 many if not all of the remainders were crated and thrown into Caballo Bay, to keep them (along with millions of older silver pesos) from being captured by the approaching forces of Imperial Japan. Today many of the coins are found with corrosion caused by their long exposure to saltwater before being salvaged.

FIFTY CENTAVOS (1936)

Designer: *Ambrosio Morales (obverse).* **Weight:** *10 grams (.2411 oz. ASW).*
Composition: *.750 silver, .250 copper.* **Diameter:** *27.5 mm.* **Edge:** *Reeded.* **Mint:** *Manila.*

Striking and Sharpness. This issue typically is found well struck.

	Mintage	VF	EF	MS-60	MS-63
1936M, Silver fifty centavos	20,000	$25	$50	$110	$175
	Auctions: $206, MS-64, January 2014; $112, MS-63, December 2014				

ONE PESO (1936)

Designer: *Ambrosio Morales (obverse).* **Weight:** *20 grams (.5144 oz. ASW).*
Composition: *.800 silver, .200 copper.* **Diameter:** *35 mm.* **Edge:** *Reeded.* **Mint:** *Manila.*

One Peso, Busts of Murphy and Quezon   One Peso, Busts of Roosevelt and Quezon

Striking and Sharpness. Sharply struck gems of the Murphy/Quezon peso can be a challenge to locate. Weak strike is evident on the reverse in particular, where the sea-lion can be softly detailed. On some pieces, tiny bubbles resulting from improper fabrication of the planchet can be observed among the letters surrounding the rim.

The Roosevelt/Quezon peso typically is found well struck.

	Mintage	VF	EF	MS-60	MS-63
1936M, Silver one peso, busts of Murphy and Quezon	10,000	$60	$85	$200	$250
	Auctions: $940, MS-66, October 2014; $764, MS-66, October 2014				
1936M, Silver one peso, busts of Roosevelt and Quezon	10,000	$60	$85	$200	$250
	Auctions: $359, MS-65, August 2013; $329, MS-65, January 2013				

Alaska Tokens

ALASKA RURAL REHABILITATION
CORPORATION TOKENS OF 1935

Before the Roosevelt Administration's dramatic New Deal response to the Great Depression, it was the states themselves, rather than the federal government, that organized and funded the relief of their citizens in need. This changed with the Federal Emergency Relief Act of 1933, by which Congress appropriated $250 million for states to use in their relief efforts, with the same amount funded for federal programs. Other relief acts would follow. The states were to use their 1933 FERA grant money "to aid in meeting the costs of furnishing relief and in relieving the hardship and suffering caused by unemployment in the form of money, service, materials, and/or commodities to provide the necessities of life to persons in need as a result of the present emergency, and/or their dependents, whether resident, transient, or homeless," as well as to "aid in assisting cooperative and self-help associations for the barter of goods and services."

Americans living in cities benefited from direct relief grants as well as employment in work-relief projects. Those in rural areas, however, had a stronger need for *rehabilitation* programs rather than relief as such. In April 1934 a special Rural Rehabilitation Division was set up. This helped establish rural camps where people made homeless by the Depression could find shelter and assistance until conditions improved. Nonprofits called *rural rehabilitation corporations* were devised to carry this effort forward. One function of the corporations was to buy large expanses of farmland to divide into 40- or 60-acre plots. These would be mortgaged to displaced farm families who agreed to develop and farm the land in exchange for low-interest loans and other assistance. One community developed under this plan was the Matanuska Valley Colony at Palmer, about 45 miles northeast of Anchorage, in the territory of Alaska. For the Alaska program some 203 families were recruited from Michigan, Minnesota, and Wisconsin. Those states were targeted not only because they had a very high percentage of displaced farmers on social-assistance relief, but also because their cold-weather climates were similar to Alaska's.

A suite of (undated) 1935 tokens was issued by the U.S. government for the use of the Midwesterners who relocated to the colonization project. These aluminum and brass tokens (nicknamed "bingles") would supply the settlers with much-needed federal aid, being paid out for work at the rate of 50¢ per hour. In theory this wage payment in tokens, rather than regular coinage, would also discourage the workers from spending their money unwisely, as the bingles were redeemable only at Alaska Rural Rehabilitation Corporation stores. In addition to use as wages, the tokens were issued based on immediate need and according to the size of the family. A family of two would receive a monthly allowance of $45; a family of three, $55; a family of four, $75; and a family of five, $85. The bingles were in use only about six months, during the winter of 1935 and 1936. The colony's managers were unable to restrict their use to the purchase of necessities in corporation-run stores—other merchants, including the local saloon, realized they could also accept them as currency. Eventually the tokens were recalled and redeemed for regular U.S. money. Practically all of the circulated tokens were destroyed after redemption.

Of the $23,000 face value minted, about $18,000 worth of tokens were issued in the months they were in active use. The unissued tokens were later made into souvenir sets for collectors. Some 250 complete sets were thus preserved in unused condition, in addition to about 100 "short" sets consisting of the one-cent, five-cent, and ten-cent pieces.

Each token is similar in size to the corresponding U.S. coin of the same denomination (one cent through ten dollars), with the exception of the one-cent piece, which is octagonal. The design is the same on both sides of each denomination.

Even after leaving hardship in the Midwest, and even with this federal aid, the Alaska colonists faced ongoing challenges. Potatoes and other crops were successfully grown, but the farming seasons were short, markets were far away, and the expense of shipping was high. More than half of the Alaska colonists left the Matanuska Valley within five years, and thirty years later only twenty of the original families were still farming there. Still, the New Deal colony helped the Matanuska Valley to slowly grow into Alaska's most productive agricultural region.

For more information on these and other Alaska-related coins and tokens, see *Alaska's Coinage Through the Years,* by Maurice Gould, Kenneth Bressett, and Kaye and Nancy Dethridge.

ALUMINUM

	Mintage	EF	Unc.
One Cent	5,000	$100	$185
Five Cents	5,000	$100	$185
Ten Cents	5,000	$100	$185
Twenty-Five Cents	3,000	$150	$275
Fifty Cents	2,500	$150	$275
One Dollar	2,500	$250	$325

BRASS

	Mintage	EF	Unc.
Five Dollars	1,000	$250	$375
Ten Dollars	1,000	$275	$450

APPENDIX A
Misstrikes and Errors

With the production of millions of coins each year, it is natural that a few abnormal pieces escape inspection and are inadvertently released for circulation, usually in original bags or rolls of new coins. These are not considered regular issues because they were not made intentionally. They are all eagerly sought by collectors for the information they shed on minting techniques, and as a variation from normal date and mint series collecting.

MISSTRUCK COINS AND ERROR PIECES

Nearly every misstruck or error coin is unique in some way, and prices may vary from coin to coin. They may all be classified in general groups related to the kinds of errors or manufacturing malfunctions involved. Collectors value these pieces according to the scarcity of each kind of error for each type of coin. Non-collectors usually view them as curios, and often believe that they must be worth much more than normal coins because they look so strange. In reality, the value assigned to various types of errors by collectors and dealers reflects both supply and demand, and is based on recurring transactions between willing buyers and sellers.

The following listings show current average values for the most frequently encountered kinds of error coins. In each case, the values shown are for coins that are unmarred by serious marks or scratches, and in Uncirculated condition for modern issues, and Extremely Fine condition for obsolete types. Exceptions are valued higher or lower. Error coins of rare-date issues generally do not command a premium beyond their normal values. In most cases each of these coins is unique in some respect and must be valued according to its individual appearance, quality, and eye appeal.

There are many other kinds of errors and misstruck coins beyond those listed in this guide book. Some are more valuable, and others less valuable, than the most popular pieces that are listed here as examples of what this interesting field contains. The pieces illustrated are general examples of the types described.

Early in 2002 the mints changed their production methods to a new system designed to eliminate deformed planchets, off-center strikes, and similar errors. They also changed the delivery system of bulk coinage, and no longer shipped loose coins in sewn bags to be counted and wrapped by banks or counting rooms, where error coins were often found and sold to collectors. Under the new system, coins are packaged in large quantities and go directly to automated counters that filter out deformed coins. The result has been that very few error coins have entered the market since late 2002, and almost none after that date. The values shown in these listings are for pre-2002 coins; those dated after that, with but a few exceptions, are valued considerably higher.

For additional details and information about these coins, the following books are recommended:

Margolis, Arnold, and Fred Weinberg. *The Error Coin Encyclopedia* (4th ed.). 2004.

Herbert, Alan. *Official Price Guide to Minting Varieties and Errors.* New York, 1991.

Fivaz, Bill, and J.T. Stanton. *The Cherrypickers' Guide to Rare Die Varieties.* Atlanta, GA, updated regularly.

The coins discussed in this section must not be confused with others that have been mutilated or damaged after leaving the mint. Examples of such pieces include coins that have been scratched, hammered, engraved, impressed, acid etched, or plated by individuals to simulate something other than a normal coin. Those pieces have no numismatic value, and can only be considered as altered coins not suitable for a collection.

TYPES OF ERROR COINS

Clipped Planchet—**An incomplete coin, missing 10 to 25% of the metal.** Incomplete planchets result from accidents when the steel rods used to punch out blanks from the metal strip overlap a portion of the strip already punched. There are curved, straight, ragged, incomplete, and elliptical clips. Values may be greater or less depending on the nature and size of the clip. Coins with more than one clip usually command higher values.

Multiple Strike—**A coin with at least one additional image from being struck again off center.** Value increases with the number of strikes. These minting errors occur when a finished coin goes back into the press and is struck again with the same dies. The presence of a date can bring a higher value.

No Rim   **With Rim**

Blank or Planchet—**A blank disc of metal intended for coinage but not struck with dies.** In the process of preparation for coinage, the blanks are first punched from a strip of metal and then milled to upset the rim. In most instances, first-process pieces (blanks without upset rims) are slightly more valuable than the finished planchets. Values shown are for the most common pieces.

Defective Die—**A coin showing raised metal from a large die crack, or small rim break.** Coins that show evidence of light die cracks, polishing, or very minor die damage are generally of little or no value. Prices shown here are for coins with very noticeable, raised die-crack lines, or those for which the die broke away, producing an unstruck area known as a *cud*.

Off Center—**A coin that has been struck out of collar and incorrectly centered, with part of the design missing.** Values are for coins with approximately 10 to 20% of design missing from obsolete coins, or 20 to 60% missing from modern coins. These are misstruck coins that were made when the planchet did not enter the coinage press properly. Coins that are struck only slightly off center, with none of the design missing, are called broadstrikes (see the next category). Those with nearly all of the impression missing are generally worth more, but those with a readable date and mint are the most valuable.

Broadstrike—**A coin that was struck outside the retaining collar.** When coins are struck without being contained in the collar die, they spread out larger than normal pieces. All denominations have a plain edge.

Lamination—**A flaw whereby a fragment of metal has peeled off the coin's surface.** This defect occurs when a foreign substance, such as gas oxides or dirt, becomes trapped in the strip as it is rolled out to the proper thickness. Lamination flaws may be missing or still attached to the coin's surface. Minor flaws may only decrease a coin's value, while a clad coin that is missing the full surface of one or both sides is worth more than the values listed here.

Brockage—**A mirror image of the design impressed on the opposite side of the same coin.** These errors are caused when a struck coin remains on either die after striking, and impresses its image into the next blank planchet as it is struck, leaving a negative or mirror image. Off-center and partial brockage coins are worth less than those with full impression. Coins with negative impressions on both sides are usually mutilated pieces made outside the mint by the pressing together of coins.

Wrong Planchet—**A coin struck on a planchet intended for another denomination or of the wrong metal.** Examples of these are cents struck on dime planchets, nickels on cent planchets, or quarters on dime planchets. Values vary depending on the type of error involved. Those struck on coins of a different denomination that were previously struck normally are of much greater value. A similar kind of error occurs when a coin is struck on a planchet of the correct denomination but wrong metal. One famous example is the 1943 cent struck in bronze (pictured), rather than in that year's new steel composition. (Fewer than three dozen are thought to exist.) Such errors presumably occur when an older planchet is mixed in with the normal supply of planchets and goes through the minting process.

MINT-CANCELED COINS

In mid-2003, the U.S. Mint acquired machines to eliminate security concerns and the cost associated with providing Mint police escorts to private vendors for the melting of scrap, substandard struck coins, planchets, and blanks. Under high pressure, the rollers and blades of these machines cancel the coins and blanks in a manner similar in appearance to the surface of a waffle, and they are popularly known by that term. This process has effectively kept most misstruck coins produced after 2003 from becoming available to collectors. Waffled examples are known for all six 2003-dated coin denominations, from the Lincoln cent through the Sacagawea dollar. The Mint has not objected to these pieces' trading in the open market because they are not considered coins with legal tender status.

MISSTRUCK AND ERROR PIECES

	Clipped Planchet	Multiple Strike	Blank, No Raised Rim	Planchet, Raised Rim	Defective Die	Off Center	Broadstrike	Lamination	Brockage
Large Cent	$60	$1,000	$200	$350	$25	$600	$100	$25	$1,100
Indian Head 1¢	$15	$600	—	—	$25	$150	$60	$15	$400
Lincoln 1¢ (95% Copper)	$3	$65	$4	$3	$12	$12	$8	$3	$35
Steel 1¢	$30	$250	$30	$40	$15	$60	$35	$15	$200
Lincoln 1¢ (Zinc)	$4	$35	$3	$2	$15	$8	$5	$15	$40
Liberty 5¢	$20	$700	—	$250	$35	$200	$110	$25	$450
Buffalo 5¢	$20	$2,500	—	$350	$40	$500	$300	$35	$850
Jefferson 5¢	$3	$50	$15	$10	$15	$12	$10	$15	$40
Wartime 5¢	$10	$400	$400	$350	$25	$175	$70	$15	$200
Barber 10¢	$50	$750	—	—	$75	$300	$85	$15	$400
Mercury 10¢	$20	$800	—	—	$35	$175	$55	$15	$275
Roosevelt 10¢ (Silver)	$12	$250	$50	$40	$35	$150	$45	$12	$100
Roosevelt 10¢ (Clad)	$3	$65	$3	$4	$15	$10	$10	$16	$40

	Clipped Planchet	Multiple Strike	Blank, No Raised Rim	Planchet, Raised Rim	Defective Die	Off Center	Broadstrike	Lamination	Brockage
Washington 25¢ (Silver)	$20	$400	$175	$150	$25	$350	$200	$15	$300
Washington 25¢ (Clad)	$5	$150	$7	$5	$12	$70	$20	$25	$50
Bicentennial 25¢	$35	$350	—	—	$65	$150	$50	$50	$250
State 25¢	$20	$500	—	—	$25	$100	$40	$400	$350
Franklin 50¢	$40	$1,800	—	—	$150	$1,800	$500	$25	$750
Kennedy 50¢ (40% Silver)	$25	$1,000	$185	$135	$70	$450	$200	$40	$450
Kennedy 50¢ (Clad)	$20	$600	$135	$100	$50	$250	$75	$25	$300
Bicentennial 50¢	$45	$700	—	—	$90	$300	$95	$40	$650
Silver $1	$50	$5,000	$1,750	$1,600	$950	$2,500	$1,000	$50	—
Eisenhower $1	$40	$1,200	$175	$100	$500	$600	$150	$50	$950
Bicentennial $1	$60	$2,000	—	—	$750	$850	$200	$50	$1,250
Anthony $1	$25	$600	$160	$120	$100	$275	$75	$30	$300
Sacagawea $1	$85	$1,800	$275	$85	$50	$1,500	$300	$50	$500

WRONG PLANCHETS

	Zinc 1¢	Copper 1¢	Steel 1¢	5¢	Silver 10¢	Copper-Nickel Clad 10¢	Silver 25¢	Copper-Nickel Clad 25¢	Copper-Nickel Clad 50¢
Indian Head 1¢	(a)	—	(a)	(a)	$8,500	(a)	(a)	(a)	(a)
Lincoln 1¢	—	—	—	(a)	$1,000	$350	(a)	(a)	(a)
Buffalo 5¢	(a)	$4,000	(a)	—	$5,000	(a)	(a)	(a)	(a)
Jefferson 5¢	$300	$275	$2,500	—	$450	$375	(a)	(a)	(a)
Wartime 5¢	(a)	$2,500	$3,500	—	$2,000	(a)	(a)	(a)	(a)
Washington 25¢ (Silver)	(a)	$950	$7,000	$500	$1,800	—	—	—	(a)
Washington 25¢ (Clad)	—	$750	(a)	$225	—	$350	—	—	(a)
Bicentennial 25¢	(a)	$3,000	(a)	$2,500	—	$3,500	—	—	(a)
State 25¢ (b)	—	$4,500	(a)	$750	(a)	$4,000	(a)	—	(a)
Walking Liberty 50¢	(a)	—	—	—	—	(a)	$25,000	(a)	(a)
Franklin 50¢	(a)	$5,000	(a)	$5,000	$6,000	(a)	$1,500	(a)	(a)
Kennedy 50¢ (c)	(a)	$3,000	(a)	$1,250	—	$2,000	—	$650	—
Bicentennial 50¢	(a)	$4,000	(a)	$2,750	—	—	—	$1,200	—
Eisenhower $1	(a)	$12,500	(a)	$9,500	—	$11,000	—	$6,000	$2,750
Anthony $1	(a)	$3,500	(a)	$5,000	(a)	—	—	$1,000	(a)
Sacagawea $1	$10,000	(a)	(a)	$10,000	(a)	$10,000	(a)	$3,000	(a)

Note: Coins struck over other coins of different denominations are usually valued three to five times higher than these prices. Coins made from mismatched dies (State quarter obverse combined with Sacagawea dollar reverse) are extremely rare. **a.** Not possible. **b.** Values for State quarter errors vary with each type and state, and are generally much higher than for other quarters. **c.** The Kennedy fifty-cent piece struck on an Anthony one-dollar planchet is very rare.

A GALLERY OF SIGNIFICANT U.S. MINT ERROR COINS

Every high-production manufacturing facility makes a certain percentage of "factory irregulars." The U.S. Mint—which for decades has produced billions of coins annually—is no exception. Today's Mint, though, has cutting-edge machinery and quality-control procedures that keep errors and misstruck coins to a minimum. When such coins *do* come into being, the Mint's sophisticated safeguards (such as riddlers that filter aside odd-shaped coins) prevent nearly all of them from leaving its facilities. Over the course of its 220-plus years of making and issuing coins, however, the Mint has produced some amazing and unusual coins that have made their way into collectors' hands. This gallery highlights a selection of collectible, significant, and valuable errors and misstruck coins.

Some early U.S. Mint coins might appear to be misstrikes when in fact they simply illustrate the standard operating procedures of the time. For example, many 1795 and 1797 half cents show faint evidence of the design of Talbot, Allum & Lee tokens. These are not highly prized double-denominations, but rather regular federal coins intentionally struck on planchets made from cut-down tokens. Other examples exist, such as "spoiled" (misstruck) large cents salvaged and cut down into planchets for half cents.

The introduction of steam-driven coining presses in the 1830s ushered in what today's collector might consider a golden age of misstruck coins. Two competing factors were at work: improved minting techniques and quality control helped curb (or at least catch) most errors and misstrikes, but dramatically increasing mintages naturally led to a greater quantity of such mistakes.

The 1900s and 2000s saw continuing modernization of the mints and a gradual conversion from older presses to new higher-speed presses, eventually capable of striking up to 750 coins per minute. In addition to their speed, today's presses strike coins horizontally, allowing highly efficient and consistently accurate production. As discussed earlier, major misstrikes and coinage errors from 2002 to the present are very rare. Currently, only a handful of new significant pieces enter the market each year.

Error and misstruck coins are a growing specialty in the rare-coin market. Their appeal and value lie in their rarity, their unusual appearance, and the insight they provide into the minting process. When major specimens appear at auction, they bring excitement and active bidding. While no misstrike or error coin has yet sold for a million dollars, several have sold for six-figure sums.

This gallery illustrates a variety of such pieces not typically seen. Some of the featured coins reside in museums or other permanent collections. Each is a classic representation of its type (e.g., wrong planchet or double strike). In many cases, they are unique; for the rest, only a few such pieces are known. The valuations are approximate, based on recent sales and market conditions. For misstruck and error coins, the grade, type, and eye appeal are important factors in market pricing.

Special credit is due to Nicholas P. Brown, David J. Camire, and Fred Weinberg, authors of *100 Greatest U.S. Error Coins*, for contributing to this feature.

1904 Lewis and Clark Exposition gold dollar (partial collar with reverse brockage). This specimen, part of the Smithsonian's National Numismatic Collection, is unique among commemorative gold coinage. It was created when a struck coin failed to fully eject from the press. A new planchet entered and came to rest partially atop the coin; when they were struck together, a reverse image was transferred to the error coin. The obstruction also prevented the planchet from being fully enclosed by the collar. *Value:* $25,000 or more.

1943 Lincoln cent struck over a struck 1943 Mercury dime (double denomination). This piece is unique for the date, and one of only a handful known in silver for the series. It occurred when 1943-dated cent dies struck a 1943 dime instead of a steel cent planchet. *Value:* $16,000 or more.

1999-P Anthony dollar struck on a 2000 Sacagawea planchet (wrong planchet–transitional). About six examples of this kind are known, most acquired from Mint rolls and bags. During transitions in a coin series (e.g., in metal content or design), wrong planchets may accidentally be used in production. This transitional error shows a "golden dollar" planchet that was used to strike an Anthony dollar. *Value:* $16,000 or more.

1863 Indian Head cent (obverse capped die). This dramatic piece is unique for the date and the series. The coin was struck multiple times by the obverse die against a planchet that rested atop the reverse die. Since the planchet was not properly seated in the collar, the force of the strike spread the planchet (cracking it in the process) until it was larger than a quarter dollar. *Value:* $55,000 or more.

1906 Indian Head cent struck on a quarter eagle planchet (wrong planchet). This error is unique for the date, and one of perhaps four known in the series. Somehow a gold quarter-eagle planchet made its way into the coining chamber for cent production. Some theorize that this and similar specimens were intentionally struck, but most show light to moderate wear that suggests they entered circulation. *Value:* $150,000 or more.

1860 Liberty Seated quarter struck on a cent planchet (wrong planchet). This specimen is unique for the date and the series. Its bright bronze color (from the copper-nickel Indian Head cent planchet) and Mint State grade give it great visual appeal. *Value:* $50,000 or more.

1837 Capped Bust half dollar struck on a struck large cent (double denomination). This misstrike is unique for the date and the series. It was made when the steam press had been in use for half dollars only a little more than a year. The coin appears to have circulated for a while before being placed into a collection. Much detail still shows from both strikes. *Value:* $50,000 or more.

Peace dollar struck on a Standing Liberty quarter planchet (wrong planchet). This error is unique for the date and the series. Judging from its Mint State grade, it was probably placed into a collection after being found in a bag or roll of coins. *Value:* $75,000 or more.

   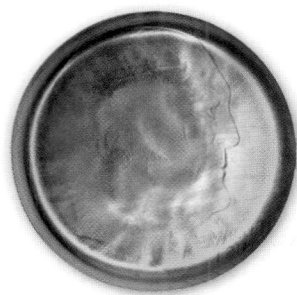

1909 Indian Head cent struck on a struck 1906 Barber dime (double denomination). This piece is unique for the date and the series. Considerable detail shows from both strikes. *Value:* $25,000 or more.

1976-D Eisenhower dollar (obverse die cap). This specimen is unique for the date, and one of only a couple known in the series. It occurred when a struck coin adhered to the die, essentially becoming a die itself. Each subsequent strike caused the planchet to bend around the die, forming a deep, bottle cap–shaped coin. *Value:* $25,000 or more.

1976-D Washington quarter (double strike). A few such specimens are known, in varying degrees of off-center double striking. This misstrike has a second strike 40% off center from the first, and is die-struck on both sides. *Value:* $2,750 or more.

1923 Peace dollar (double strike). This misstrike is unique for the date and the series. Apparently the coin was struck about 45% off center, then repositioned and struck a second time, centered normally. *Value:* $75,000 or more.

1977 Jefferson nickel struck on a 1976 Lincoln cent (double denomination–dual date). Two examples of this error are known for the date, among a half dozen in the series. Both dates are clearly visible. *Value:* $8,000 or more.

(1976 or 1977) Lincoln cent struck off center on a Philippine five-sentimos planchet (wrong planchet–multiple error). This error is unique for the series as an off center; several are known struck on center. The Philadelphia Mint struck almost 99 million five-sentimo coins for the Philippines in 1976, and more than 1 million in 1977. Only a few U.S. coins are known accidentally struck on their planchets. *Value:* $2,750 or more.

(1960) Jefferson nickel struck on a 1960 Peruvian five-centavos coin (double denomination–dual country). This error is unique for the date and the series. Interestingly, Mint records do not indicate any coins of Peru were struck at the Philadelphia Mint in 1960. *Value:* $10,000 or more.

Lincoln cent struck off center on a Roosevelt dime (double denomination–off center). Only a few off-center double denominations are known for this series. This is a full dime that was struck off-center by cent dies. *Value:* $5,500 or more.

1943 Lincoln cent struck on a bronze planchet (wrong planchet–transitional). About a dozen of these well-known errors have been confirmed. They came about when bronze planchets left over from 1942 cent production were mixed with the regular 1943 steel planchets. All but one were found in circulation. This error was voted among the *100 Greatest U.S. Coins* (Garrett and Guth). *Value:* $100,000 or more.

(2000) Washington quarter obverse muled with a Sacagawea dollar reverse (mule). About two dozen of these dramatic errors are known to have been struck at Philadelphia, in three die pairings. They have received nationwide publicity in the mainstream press. *Value:* $100,000 or more.

APPENDIX B

Collectible Red and Blue Books

The book you are reading is the *Deluxe Edition* of a classic hobby reference, the *Guide Book of United States Coins*, popularly known as the "Red Book." More than 23 million copies of the Red Book have been sold since 1946, making it one of the best-selling nonfiction titles in American publishing history. By 1959 more than 100,000 copies were being printed annually. The 1965 (18th) edition, published in 1964, reached a peak of 1,200,000 copies. That year the Red Book was ranked fifth on the list of best-selling nonfiction—ahead of Dale Carnegie's classic *How to Win Friends and Influence People* (at number 6) and John F. Kennedy's *Profiles in Courage* (at number 9).

The idea for the Red Book started in the 1940s with R.S. Yeoman. Employed by Whitman Publishing Company (part of Western Publishing), Yeoman at first created the "Blue Book" (official title, the *Handbook of United States Coins With Premium List*), which gave hobbyists an overview of American coinage and a detailed guide to the prices that dealers were paying for collectible coins. The first edition was published in 1942. Yeoman saw that collectors wanted even more information, and he began compiling data and records for an expanded *retail* version of the Blue Book (showing how much a collector could expect to pay a dealer for coins). After World War II ended, Yeoman and his team introduced the new volume, the *Guide Book of United States Coins*, soon nicknamed the Red Book because of its distinctive cover color.

Numismatist Kenneth E. Bressett joined the Red Book in 1956 as a freelance editor. He has continued to work on the annually published book, and other Whitman projects, ever since. He took a full-time editorial position with Whitman Publishing in 1959, and assumed full editorship of the Red Book in 1975. Today Bressett serves as the Red Book's senior editor, assisted by research editor Q. David Bowers, valuations editor Jeff Garrett, and a panel of more than 100 coin dealers, researchers, and other specialists.

THE RED BOOK AS A COLLECTIBLE

The *Guide Book of United States Coins* holds the record as the longest-running annual retail coin-price guide. It has passed its 65th anniversary, and collectors seem to be almost as interested in assembling sets of old Red Books as of old coins. The demand for old Red Books has created a solid market. Some who collect these old editions maintain reference libraries of all kinds of coin publications. To them, having one of each edition is essential, because that is the way old books are collected. Others are speculators who believe that the value of old editions will go up as interest and demand increase. Many people who save old Red Books do so to maintain a record of coin prices going back further than any other source.

Following price trends in old Red Books is a good indicator of how well individual coins are doing in comparison to each other. The price information published in each year is an average of what collectors are paying for each coin. It is a valuable benchmark, showing how prices have gone up or down over the years. Information like this often gives investors an edge in predicting what the future may hold.

Old Red Books are also a handy resource on collecting trends. They show graphically how grading has changed over the years, what new coins have been discovered and added to the listings, and which areas are growing in popularity. Studying these old books can be educational as well as nostalgic. It's great fun to see what your favorite coins sold for 15 or 25 years ago or more—and a bit frustrating to realize what might have been if we had only bought the right coins at the right time in years past.

Many collectors have asked about the quantities printed of each edition. That information has never been published, and now no company records exist specifying how many were made. The original author, R.S. Yeoman, told inquirers that the first press run in November 1946 was for 9,000 copies. In February 1947 an additional 9,000 copies were printed to satisfy the unexpected demand.

There was a slight but notable difference that can be used to differentiate between the first and second printings. The wording in the first printing at the bottom of page 135 reads, "which probably accounts for the scarcity of *this* date." Those last few words were changed to "the scarcity of *1903 O*" in the second printing.

The second edition had a press run of 22,000. The printing of each edition thereafter gradually increased, with the highest number ever being reached with the 18th edition, dated 1965 and published in 1964. At the top of a booming coin market, a whopping 1,200,000 copies were produced. Since that time the numbers have decreased, but the Red Book still maintains a record of being the world's largest-selling coin publication each year.

In some years a very limited number of Red Books were made for use by price contributors. Those were interleaved with blank pages. No more than 50 copies were ever made for any one year. Perhaps fewer than 20 were made in the first few years. Three of these of the first edition, and one of the second edition, are currently known. Their value is now in four figures. Those made in the 1960s sell for about $300–$500 today.

There are other unusual Red Books that command exceptional prices. One of the most popular is the 1987 special edition that was made for, and distributed only to, people who attended the 1986 American Numismatic Association banquet in Milwaukee. Only 500 of those were printed with a special commemorative cover.

Error books are also popular with collectors. The most common is one with double-stamped printing on the cover. The second most frequently seen are those with an upside-down cover. Probably the best known of the error books is the 1963 16th edition with a missing page. For some uncanny reason, page 239 is duplicated in some of those books, and page 237 is missing. The error was corrected on most of the printing.

The terminology used to describe book condition differs from that utilized in grading coins. A "Very Fine" book is one that is nearly new, with minimal signs of use. Early editions of the Red Book are rarely if ever found in anything approaching "New" condition. Exceptionally well-preserved older editions command a substantial premium and are in great demand. Nice used copies that are still clean and in good shape, but slightly worn from use, are also desirable. Only the early editions are worth a premium in badly worn condition.

For a more detailed history and edition-by-edition study of the Red Book, see Frank J. Colletti's *A Guide Book of The Official Red Book of United States Coins* (Whitman, 2009).

VALUATION GUIDE FOR PAST EDITIONS OF THE RED BOOK
CLASSIC HARDCOVER BINDING
See page 1411 for special editions in the classic hardcover binding.

Year/Edition	Issue Price	VG	F	VF	New
1947 (1st ed.), 1st Printing	$1.50	$350	$650	$1,000	$1,700 (a)
1947 (1st ed.), 2nd Printing	$1.50	$300	$600	$900	$1,600 (a)
1948 (2nd ed.)	$1.50	$80	$150	$225	$350 (a)
1949 (3rd ed.)	$1.50	$80	$150	$350	$500 (a)
1951/52 (4th ed.)	$1.50	$55	$110	$175	$225 (a)
1952/53 (5th ed.)	$1.50	$150	$300	$450	$1,500 (a)
1953/54 (6th ed.)	$1.75	$45	$65	$100	$150
1954/55 (7th ed.)	$1.75	$40	$50	$100	$120
1955 (8th ed.)	$1.75	$30	$45	$90	$115
1956 (9th ed.)	$1.75	$25	$35	$60	$110
1957 (10th ed.)	$1.75	$15	$20	$35	$50
1958 (11th ed.)	$1.75		$8	$12	$25
1959 (12th ed.)	$1.75		$8	$12	$25
1960 (13th ed.)	$1.75		$7	$9	$20
1961 (14th ed.)	$1.75		$4	$6	$17
1962 (15th ed.)	$1.75		$4	$6	$10
1963 (16th ed.)	$1.75		$4	$6	$10
1964 (17th ed.)	$1.75		$4	$5	$7
1965 (18th ed.)	$1.75		$3	$4	$7
1966 (19th ed.)	$1.75		$3	$4	$7
1967 (20th ed.)	$1.75		$3	$5	$8
1968 (21st ed.)	$2		$3	$5	$10
1969 (22nd ed.)	$2		$3	$5	$10
1970 (23rd ed.)	$2.50		$3	$6	$11
1971 (24th ed.)	$2.50		$3	$4	$7
1972 (25th ed.)	$2.50		$5	$8	$10
1973 (26th ed.)	$2.50		$4	$5	$7
1974 (27th ed.)	$2.50		$3	$4	$7
1975 (28th ed.)	$3			$4	$6
1976 (29th ed.)	$3.95			$4	$7
1977 (30th ed.)	$3.95			$4	$6
1978 (31st ed.)	$3.95			$4	$6
1979 (32nd ed.)	$3.95			$4	$7
1980 (33rd ed.)	$3.95			$4	$9
1981 (34th ed.)	$4.95			$2	$5
1982 (35th ed.)	$4.95			$2	$5
1983 (36th ed.)	$5.95			$2	$5
1984 (37th ed.)	$5.95			$2	$5
1985 (38th ed.)	$5.95			$2	$5
1986 (39th ed.)	$5.95			$2	$5
1987 (40th ed.)	$6.95			$2	$5
1988 (41st ed.)	$6.95			$2	$5
1989 (42nd ed.)	$6.95			$3	$7
1990 (43rd ed.)	$7.95			$2	$6
1991 (44th ed.)	$8.95			$2	$5
1992 (45th ed.)	$8.95			$2	$5

Note: Values are for unsigned books. Those signed by R.S. Yeoman are worth substantially more. **a.** Values are for books in Near Mint condition, as truly New copies are effectively nonexistent.

Year/Edition	Issue Price	VG	F	VF	New
1993 (46th ed.)	$9.95			$2	$5
1994 (47th ed.)	$9.95			$1	$4
1995 (48th ed.)	$10.95			$1	$4
1996 (49th ed.)	$10.95			$1	$4
1997 (50th ed.)	$11.95			$1	$4
1998 (51st ed.)	$11.95				$3
1999 (52nd ed.)	$11.95				$3
2000 (53rd ed.)	$12.95				$3
2001 (54th ed.)	$13.95				$3
2002 (55th ed.)	$14.95				$3
2003 (56th ed.)	$15.95				$2
2004 (57th ed.)	$15.95				$2
2005 (58th ed.)	$15.95				$2
2006 (59th ed.)	$16.95				$3
2007 (60th ed.)	$16.95				$3
2008 (61st ed.)	$16.95				$3
2009 (62nd ed.)	$16.95				$3
2010 (63rd ed.)	$16.95				$3
2011 (64th ed.)	$16.95				$2
2012 (65th ed.)	$16.95				$2
2013 (66th ed.)	$16.95				$2
2014 (67th ed.)	$16.95				$2
2015 (68th ed.)	$16.95				
2016 (69th ed.)	$16.95				

Note: Values are for unsigned books. Those signed by R.S. Yeoman are worth substantially more.

SOFTCOVERS (1993–2007)

The first softcover (trade paperback) Red Book was the 1993 (46th) edition. The softcover binding was offered (alongside other formats) in the 1993, 1994, 1995, and 1996 editions; again in the 1998 edition; and from 2003 through 2007. All are fairly common and easily collectible today. Values in New condition range from $2 up to $3–$4 for the earlier editions.

SPIRALBOUND SOFTCOVERS (1997 TO DATE)

The first spiralbound softcover Red Book was the 1997 (50th) edition. The spiralbound softcover format was next available in the 1999 edition, and it has been an annually offered format every edition since then. Today the spiralbound softcovers all are easily collectible. The 1997 edition is worth $4 in New condition, and later editions are valued around $2.

SPIRALBOUND HARDCOVERS (2008 TO DATE)

The first spiralbound hardcover Red Book was the 2008 (61st) edition. The format has been available (alongside other formats) every edition since. All spiralbound hardcovers are readily available to collectors, and are valued from $2 to $4.

JOURNAL EDITION (2009)

The large-sized Journal Edition, featuring a three-ring binder, color-coded tabbed dividers, and removable pages, was issued only for the 2009 (62nd) edition. Today it is valued at $5 in VF and $30 in New condition.

LARGE PRINT EDITIONS (2010 TO DATE)

The oversized Large Print format of the Red Book has been offered annually since the 2010 (63rd) edition. All editions are readily available to collectors and are valued at $5 in New condition.

LEATHER LIMITED EDITIONS (2005 TO DATE)

Year/Edition	Print Run	Issue Price	New
2005 (58th ed.)	3,000	$69.95	$75
2006 (59th ed.)	3,000	$69.95	$75
2007 (60th ed.)	3,000	$69.95	$100
2007 1947 Tribute Edition	500	$49.95	$135
2008 (61st ed.)	3,000	$69.95	$60
2008 (61st ed.), Numismatic Literary Guild (a)	135 (b)		$1,000
2008 (61st ed.), American Numismatic Society (c)	250 (b)		$750
2009 (62nd ed.)	3,000	$69.95	$75
2010 (63rd ed.)	1,500	$69.95	$75
2011 (64th ed.)	1,500	$69.95	$75
2012 (65th ed.)	1,000	$69.95	$80
2013 (66th ed.)	1,000	$69.95	$75
2014 (67th ed.)	1,000	$69.95	$75
2015 (68th ed.)	500	$99.95	$100
2016 (69th ed.)	500	$99.95	$100

a. One hundred thirty-five imprinted copies of the 2008 leather Limited Edition were created. Of these, 125 were distributed to members of the NLG at its 2007 literary awards ceremony; the remaining 10 were distributed from Whitman Publishing headquarters in Atlanta. **b.** Included in total print-run quantity. **c.** Two hundred fifty copies of the 2008 leather Limited Edition were issued with a special bookplate honoring the 150th anniversary of the ANS. They were distributed to attendees of the January 2008 celebratory banquet in New York.

SPECIAL EDITIONS

Year/Edition	Print Run	Issue Price	VF	New
1987 (40th ed.), American Numismatic Association 95th Anniversary	500		$700	$1,400
1992 (45th ed.), American Numismatic Association 100th Anniversary	600		$150	$250
1997 (50th ed.), Red Book 50th Anniversary	1,200	$24.95	$50	$100
2002 (55th ed.), American Numismatic Association "Target 2001"	500	$100	$50	$100
2002 (55th ed.), SS Central America		$35	$25	$35
2005 (58th ed.), FUN (Florida United Numismatists) 50th Anniversary	1,100		$45	$100
2007 (60th ed.), American Numismatic Association 115th Anniversary	500		$50	$125
2007 (60th ed.), Michigan State Numismatic Society 50th Anniversary	500		$50	$125
2007 (1st ed.), 1947 Tribute Edition		$17.95	$5	$20
2008 (61st ed.), ANA Milwaukee World's Fair of Money	1,080		$30	$50
2008 (61st ed.), Stack's Rare Coins			$4	$18
2010 (63rd ed.), Hardcover, Philadelphia Expo (a)		$24.95	$18	$35
2011 (64th ed.), Boston Numismatic Society		$85	$50	$85
2012 (65th ed.), American Numismatic Association		$35	$30	$100
2013 (66th ed.), American Numismatic Society (b)	250		$75	$250
2015 (68th ed.), Central States Numismatic Society	500	$15		
2016 (69th ed.) American Numismatic Association 125th Anniversary				

a. Two thousand and nine copies of a special 2010 hardcover edition were made for distribution to dealers at the premiere Whitman Coin and Collectibles Philadelphia Expo (September 2009). Extra copies were sold at $50 apiece with proceeds benefiting the National Federation for the Blind. **b.** Two hundred fifty copies of the 2013 hardcover were issued with a special bookplate honoring ANS Trustees' Award recipient (and Red Book research contributor) Roger Siboni.

THE BLUE BOOK AS A COLLECTIBLE

The precursor to the Red Book was the *Handbook of United States Coins With Premium List*, popularly known as the "Blue Book." Its mastermind was R.S. Yeoman, who had been hired by Western Publishing as a commercial artist in 1932. He distributed Western's Whitman line of "penny boards" to coin collectors, promoting them through department stores, along with children's books and games. He eventually arranged for Whitman to expand the line into other denominations, giving them the reputation of a numismatic endeavor rather than a "game" of filling holes with missing coins. He also developed these flat boards into a line of popular folders.

Yeoman began to compile coin-mintage data and market values to aid collectors. This research grew into the Blue Book: now collectors had a coin-by-coin guide to the average prices dealers would pay for U.S. coins. The first two editions were both published in 1942.

In the first edition of the Red Book, Whitman Publishing would describe the Blue Book as "a low-priced standard reference book of United States coins and kindred issues" for which there had been "a long-felt need among American collectors."

The Blue Book has been published annually (except in 1944 and 1950) since its debut. Past editions offer valuable information about the hobby of yesteryear as well as developments in numismatic research and the marketplace. Old Blue Books are collectible; most editions after the 12th can be found for a few dollars in VF or better condition. Major variants were produced for the third, fourth, and ninth editions, including perhaps the only "overdate" books in American numismatic publishing. Either to conserve the previous years' covers or to correct an error in binding, the cloth on some third-edition covers was overstamped "Fourth Edition," and a number of eighth-edition covers were overstamped "Ninth Edition." The third edition was produced in several shades of blue ranging from light to dark. Some copies of the fourth edition were also produced in black cloth—the only time the Blue Book was bound in other than blue.

VALUATION GUIDE FOR SELECT PAST EDITIONS OF THE BLUE BOOK

Edition	Date (a)		VF	New
	Title Page	Copyright		
1st	1942	1942	$100	$460
2nd	1943	1942	$45	$75
3rd	1944	1943	$35	$85
4th	none	1945	$40	$85
5th	none	1946	$20	$35
6th	1948	1947	$15	$30
7th	1949	1948	$12	$25
8th	1950	1949	$10	$20
9th	1952	1951	$5	$10
10th	1953	1952	$5	$8
11th	1954	1953	$3	$7
12th	1955	1954	$3	$7

a. During its early years of production, the Blue Book's date presentation was not standardized. Full information is given here to aid in precise identification of early editions.

APPENDIX C
Bullion Values

These charts show the bullion values of silver and gold U.S. coins. These are intrinsic values and do not reflect any numismatic premium a coin might have. The weight listed under each denomination is its actual silver weight (ASW) or actual gold weight (AGW).

In recent years, the bullion price of silver has fluctuated considerably. You can use the following chart to determine the approximate bullion value of many 19th- and 20th-century silver coins at various price levels—or you can calculate the approximate value by multiplying the current spot price of silver by the ASW for each coin, as indicated. Dealers generally purchase common silver coins at around 15% below bullion value, and sell them at around 15% above bullion value.

Nearly all U.S. gold coins have an additional premium value beyond their bullion content, and thus are not subject to minor bullion-price variations. The premium amount is not necessarily tied to the bullion price of gold, but is usually determined by supply and demand levels in the numismatic marketplace. Because these factors can vary significantly, there is no reliable formula for calculating "percentage below and above bullion" prices that would remain accurate over time. The gold chart lists bullion values based on AGW only; consult a coin dealer to ascertain current buy and sell prices.

BULLION VALUES OF SILVER COINS

Silver Price Per Ounce	Wartime Nickel .05626 oz.	Dime .07234 oz.	Quarter .18084 oz.	Half Dollar .36169 oz.	Silver Clad Half Dollar .14792 oz.	Silver Dollar .77344 oz.
$10	$0.56	$0.72	$1.81	$3.62	$1.48	$7.73
11	0.62	0.80	1.99	3.98	1.63	8.51
12	0.68	0.87	2.17	4.34	1.78	9.28
13	0.73	0.94	2.35	4.70	1.92	9.28
14	0.79	1.01	2.53	5.06	2.07	10.83
15	0.84	1.09	2.71	5.43	2.22	11.60
16	0.90	1.16	2.89	5.79	2.37	12.38
17	0.96	1.23	3.07	6.15	2.51	13.15
18	1.01	1.30	3.26	6.51	2.66	13.92
19	1.07	1.37	3.44	6.87	2.81	14.70
20	1.13	1.45	3.62	7.23	2.96	15.47
21	1.18	1.52	3.80	7.60	3.11	16.24
22	1.24	1.59	3.98	7.96	3.25	17.02
23	1.29	1.66	4.16	8.32	3.40	17.79

Silver Price Per Ounce	Wartime Nickel .05626 oz.	Dime .07234 oz.	Quarter .18084 oz.	Half Dollar .36169 oz.	Silver Clad Half Dollar .14792 oz.	Silver Dollar .77344 oz.
$24	$1.35	$1.74	$4.34	$8.68	$3.55	$18.56
25	1.41	1.81	4.52	9.04	3.70	19.34
26	1.46	1.88	4.70	9.40	3.85	20.11
27	1.52	1.95	4.88	9.77	3.99	20.88
28	1.58	2.03	5.06	10.13	4.14	21.66
29	1.63	2.10	5.24	10.49	4.29	22.43
30	1.69	2.17	5.43	10.85	4.44	23.20
31	1.74	2.24	5.61	11.21	4.59	23.98
32	1.80	2.31	5.79	11.57	4.73	24.75
33	1.86	2.39	5.97	11.94	4.88	25.52
34	1.91	2.46	6.15	12.30	5.03	26.30
35	1.97	2.53	6.33	12.66	5.18	27.07
36	2.03	2.60	6.51	13.02	5.33	27.84
37	2.08	2.68	6.69	13.38	5.47	28.62

BULLION VALUES OF GOLD COINS

Gold Price Per Ounce	$5.00 Liberty Head 1839–1908 Indian Head 1908–1929 .24187 oz.	$10.00 Liberty Head 1838–1907 Indian Head 1907–1933 .48375 oz.	$20.00 1849–1933 .96750 oz.
$900	$217.68	$435.38	$870.75
925	223.73	447.47	894.94
950	229.78	459.56	919.13
975	235.82	471.66	943.31
1,000	241.87	483.75	967.50
1,025	247.92	495.84	991.69
1,050	253.96	507.94	1,015.88
1,075	260.01	520.03	1,040.06
1,100	266.06	532.12	1,064.25
1,125	272.10	544.22	1,088.44
1,150	278.15	556.31	1,112.63
1,175	284.20	568.41	1,136.81
1,200	290.24	580.50	1,161.00
1,225	296.29	592.59	1,185.19
1,250	302.34	604.69	1,209.38
1,275	308.38	616.78	1,233.56
1,300	314.43	628.88	1,257.75
1,325	320.48	640.97	1,281.94
1,350	326.52	653.06	1,306.13
1,375	332.57	665.16	1,330.31
1,400	338.62	677.25	1,354.50
1,425	344.66	689.34	1,378.69
1,450	350.71	701.44	1,402.88
1,475	356.76	713.53	1,427.06
1,500	362.81	725.63	1,451.25
1,525	368.85	737.72	1,475.44
1,550	374.90	749.81	1,499.63
1,575	380.95	761.91	1,523.81
1,600	386.99	774.00	1,548.00

Note: The U.S. bullion coins first issued in 1986 are unlike the older regular issues. They contain the following amounts of pure metal: silver $1, 1 oz.; gold $50, 1 oz.; gold $25, 1/2 oz.; gold $10, 1/4 oz.; gold $5, 1/10 oz.

Gold Price Per Ounce	$5.00 Liberty Head 1839–1908 Indian Head 1908–1929 .24187 oz.	$10.00 Liberty Head 1838–1907 Indian Head 1907–1933 .48375 oz.	$20.00 1849–1933 .96750 oz.
$1,825	$441.41	$882.84	$1,765.69
1,850	447.46	894.94	1,789.88
1,875	453.51	907.03	1,814.06
1,900	459.55	919.13	1,838.25
1,925	465.60	931.22	1,862.44
1,950	471.65	943.31	1,886.63
1,975	477.69	955.41	1,910.81

Note: The U.S. bullion coins first issued in 1986 are unlike the older regular issues. They contain the following amounts of pure metal: silver $1, 1 oz.; gold $50, 1 oz.; gold $25, 1/2 oz.; gold $10, 1/4 oz.; gold $5, 1/10 oz.

APPENDIX D

Top 250 U.S. Coin Prices Realized at Auction

Rank	Price	Coin	Grade	Firm	Date
1	$10,016,875	$1(s), 1794 **(A)**	PCGS SP-66	Stack's Bowers	January 2013
2	$7,590,020	$20, 1933	Gem BU	Soth/Stack's	July 2002
3	$4,582,500	Prefed, 1787, Brasher dbln, EB on Wing	NGC MS-63	Hertage	January 2014
4	$4,140,000	$1(s), 1804, Class I	PCGS PF-68	B&M	August 1999
5	$3,877,500	$1(s), 1804, Class I	PCGS PF-62	Heritage	August 2013
6	$3,737,500	5¢, 1913, Liberty Head **(B)**	NGC PF-64	Heritage	January 2010
7	$3,737,500	$1(s), 1804, Class I	NGC PF-62	Heritage	April 2008
8	$3,290,000	5¢, 1913, Liberty Head **(B)**	NGC PF-64	Heritage	January 2014
9	$3,172,500	5¢, 1913, Liberty Head	PCGS PF-63	Heritage	April 2013
10	$2,990,000	Prefed, 1787, Brasher, EB on Breast **(C)**	NGC EF-45	Heritage	January 2005
11	$2,990,000	$20, MCMVII, Ultra HR, LE **(D)**	PCGS PF-69	Heritage	November 2005
12	$2,760,000	$20, MCMVII, Ultra HR, LE **(D)**	PCGS PF-69	Stack's Bowers	June 2012
13	$2,585,000	Pattern 1¢, 1792, Birch Cent, LE, J-4	NGC MS-65RB	Heritage	January 2015
14	$2,574,000	$4, 1880, Coiled Hair **(E)**	NGC PF-67Cam	Bonhams	September 2013
15	$2,415,000	Prefed, 1787, Brasher, EB on Wing	NGC AU-55	Heritage	January 2005
16	$2,350,000	1¢, 1793, Chain AMERICA, S-4	PCGS MS-66BN	Heritage	January 2015
17	$2,300,000	$1(s), 1804, Class III	PCGS PF-58	Heritage	April 2009
18	$2,232,500	Pattern 25¢, 1792, copper, J-12	NGC MS-63BN	Heritage	January 2015
19	$2,185,000	$10, 1907, Rounded Rim	NGC Satin PF-67	Heritage	January 2011
20	$2,115,000	$20, MCMVII, Ultra HR, LE	PCGS PF-68	Heritage	January 2015
21	$1,997,500	Pattern 1¢, 1792, Silver Center, J-1	PCGS MS-64BN	Heritage	August 2014
22	$1,997,500	$20, 1927-D	NGC MS-66	Heritage	January 2014
23	$1,897,500	$20, 1927-D **(F)**	PCGS MS-67	Heritage	November 2005
24	$1,880,000	$1(s), 1804, Class III	NGC PF-55	Stack's Bowers	August 2014
25	$1,840,000	10¢, 1873-CC, No Arrows	PCGS MS-65	Stack's Bowers	August 2012
26	$1,840,000	5¢, 1913, Liberty Head	NGC PF-66	Superior	March 2008
27	$1,840,000	$20, MCMVII, Ultra HR, LE	PCGS PF-68	Heritage	January 2007
28	$1,840,000	$1(s), 1804, Class I **(G)**	PCGS PF-64	Stack's	October 2000
29	$1,815,000	$1(s), 1804, Class I	PF-63	B&M/Stack's	April 1997
30	$1,725,000	$2.50, 1796, No Stars **(H)**	PCGS MS-65	Heritage	January 2008
31	$1,725,000	$10, 1920-S	PCGS MS-67	Heritage	March 2007
32	$1,645,000	$20, 1861, Paquet Reverse **(I)**	PCGS MS-61	Heritage	August 2014

Rank	Price	Coin	Grade	Firm	Date
33	$1,610,000	$10, 1839/8, Type of 1838, Lg Letters **(J)**	NGC PF-67UCam	Heritage	January 2007
34	$1,610,000	$20, 1861, Paquet Reverse **(I)**	PCGS MS-61	Heritage	August 2006
35	$1,552,500	10¢, 1894-S	PCGS PF-64	Stack's	October 2007
36	$1,527,500	Prefed, 1776, Cont. $1 Silver, N-3D	NGC MS-62	Heritage	January 2015
37	$1,527,500	Prefed, 1776, Cont. $1 Silver, N-1C	NGC EF-40	Heritage	January 2015
38	$1,527,500	25¢, 1796, B-2	NGC MS-67+	Heritage	November 2013
39	$1,495,000	$20, 1927-D	PCGS MS-66	Heritage	January 2010
40	$1,495,000	$20, 1921	PCGS MS-63	B&M	August 2006
41	$1,485,000	5¢, 1913, Liberty Head	Gem PF-66	B&M/Stack's	May 1996
42	$1,437,500	$20, 1856-O	NGC SP-63	Heritage	May 2009
43	$1,410,000	Prefed, 1776, Cont. $1 Silver, N-3D	NGC MS-63	Heritage	May 2014
44	$1,410,000	Pattern 1¢, 1792, Silver Center, J-1	NGC MS-63+ BN	Heritage	May 2014
45	$1,410,000	Pattern half disme, 1792, J-7 **(K)**	PCGS SP-67	Heritage	January 2013
46	$1,380,000	$5, 1829, Large Date	PCGS PF-64	Heritage	January 2012
47	$1,380,000	1¢, 1793, Chain AMERICA, S-4	PCGS MS-65BN	Heritage	January 2012
48	$1,380,000	50¢, 1797, O-101a **(L)**	NGC MS-66	Stack's	July 2008
49	$1,380,000	$2.50, 1796, No Stars **(H)**	PCGS MS-65	Stack's (ANR)	June 2005
50	$1,322,500	$3, 1855-S	NGC PF-64Cam	Heritage	August 2011
51	$1,322,500	Pattern half disme, 1792, J-7 **(K)**	PCGS SP-67	Heritage	April 2006
52	$1,322,500	$20, 1927-D	NGC MS-65	Heritage	January 2006
53	$1,322,500	10¢, 1894-S	NGC PF-66	DLRC	March 2005
54	$1,292,500	Pattern half disme, 1792, J-7 **(K)**	PCGS SP-67	Heritage	August 2014
55	$1,292,500	50¢, 1797, O-101a	PCGS MS-65+	Heritage	August 2014
56	$1,265,000	Pattern $10, 1874, Bickford, J-1373	PCGS PF-65DCam	Heritage	January 2010
57	$1,265,000	1¢, 1795, Reeded Edge, S-79 **(M)**	PCGS VG-10	Goldberg	September 2009
58	$1,265,000	$1(s), 1795, Flowing Hair, B-7, BB-18	V Ch Gem MS	Bullowa	December 2005
59	$1,210,000	$20, MCMVII, Ultra HR, LE **(N)**	PCGS PF-67	Goldberg	May 1999
60	$1,207,500	$1(s), 1794	NGC MS-64	B&M	August 2010
61	$1,207,500	$1(s), 1866, No Motto	NGC PF-63	Stack's (ANR)	January 2005
62	$1,207,500	$1(s), 1804, Class III **(O)**	PCGS PF-58	B&M	July 2003
63	$1,175,000	Prefed, 1783, quint, T-II, Nova Const.	PCGS AU-53	Heritage	April 2013
64	$1,175,000	$1(s), 1796, Sm Dt, Sm Ltrs, B-2,BB-63	NGC MS-65	Heritage	April 2013
65	$1,150,000	1/2¢, 1794, C-7	PCGS MS-67RB	Goldberg	January 2014
66	$1,150,000	Pattern 1¢, 1792, Silver Center, J-1	PCGS MS-61BN	Heritage	April 2012
67	$1,150,000	$1(s), 1794	NGC MS-64	Stack's (ANR)	June 2005
68	$1,145,625	Pattern half disme, 1792, J-7	NGC MS-68	Stack's Bowers	January 2013
69	$1,121,250	1/2¢, 1811, C-1	PCGS MS-66RB	Goldberg	January 2014
70	$1,092,500	$20, 1921	PCGS MS-66	Heritage	November 2005
71	$1,092,500	$1(s), 1870-S	BU PL	Stack's	May 2003
72	$1,057,500	Pattern disme, 1792, copper, J-11	NGC MS-64RB	Heritage	January 2015
73	$1,057,500	Terr, 1852, Humbert, $10, K-10	NGC MS-68	Heritage	April 2013
74	$1,057,500	$20, MCMVII, Ultra HR, LE of 06	PCGS PF-58	Heritage	August 2012
75	$1,041,300	$4, 1879, Coiled Hair **(P)**	NGC PF-67Cam	Bonhams	September 2013
76	$1,035,000	10¢, 1894-S	PCGS PF-65	Heritage	January 2005
77	$1,012,000	$20, 1921 **(Q)**	PCGS MS-65 PQ	Goldberg	September 2007
78	$1,006,250	$2.50, 1796, Stars, Bass-3003, BD-3 (R)	NGC MS-65	Heritage	January 2008
79	$1,006,250	$1 Trade, 1885	NGC PF-62	DLRC	November 2004
80	$998,750	Pattern disme, 1792, J-9	NGC AU-50	Heritage	January 2015
81	$998,750	$1 Trade, 1884	PCGS PF-65	Heritage	January 2014
82	$998,750	1¢, 1793, Chain, S-2	PCGS MS-65BN	Stack's Bowers	January 2013
83	$990,000	$1(s), 1804, Class I **(G)**	Choice Proof	Rarcoa	July 1989
84	$977,500	1¢, 1799, S-189	NGC MS-62BN	Goldberg	September 2009

Rank	Price	Coin	Grade	Firm	Date
85	$977,500	$4, 1880, Coiled Hair (E)	NGC PF-66Cam	Heritage	January 2005
86	$977,500	$5, 1833, Large Date	PCGS PF-67	Heritage	January 2005
87	$966,000	50¢, 1797, O-101a (L)	NGC MS-66	Stack's (ANR)	March 2004
88	$962,500	5¢, 1913, Liberty Head	Proof	Stack's	October 1993
89	$959,400	$4, 1880, Flowing Hair	NGC PF-67	Bonhams	September 2013
90	$948,750	Terr., 1852, Moffat & Co., $10, Wide Date, K-9	PCGS SP-67	Stack's (ANR)	August 2006
91	$940,000	Terr., 1852, Moffat & Co., $10, Wide Date, K-9	PCGS SP-63	Heritage	January 2014
92	$920,000	1/2¢, 1793, C-4	PCGS MS-66BN	Goldberg	January 2014
93	$920,000	$1(s), 1802, Restrike	PCGS PF-65Cam	Heritage	April 2008
94	$920,000	$20, 1907, Small Edge Letters	PCGS PF-68	Heritage	November 2005
95	$920,000	$1 Trade, 1885	NGC PF-61	Stack's	May 2003
96	$910,625	$1(s), 1795, Draped, Off-Ctr, B-14, BB-51	NGC MS-66+	Heritage	November 2013
97	$907,500	$1 Trade, 1885	Gem PF-65	B&M/Stack's	April 1997
98	$891,250	1/2¢, 1796, No Pole, C-1	PCGS MS-65BN	Goldberg	January 2014
99	$891,250	10¢, 1873-CC, No Arrows (S)	NGC MS-65	B&M	July 2004
100	$881,250	Confed, 1861, Original 50¢	NGC PF-30	Heritage	January 2015
101	$881,250	25¢, 1796, B-1	PCGS SP-66	Heritage	August 2014
102	$881,250	$10, 1795, BD-5	PCGS MS-65	Heritage	August 2014
103	$881,250	10¢, 1796, JR-1	PCGS MS-67	Heritage	June 2014
104	$881,250	$1(s), 1889-CC (T)	PCGS MS-68	Stack's Bowers	August 2013
105	$881,250	1¢, 1794, Head of 93, S-18b	PCGS MS-64BN	Stack's Bowers	January 2013
106	$874,000	$1(s), 1804, Class III (O)	PCGS PF-58	B&M	November 2001
107	$862,500	1¢, 1793, Strawberry Leaf, NC-3	NGC F-12	Stack's	January 2009
108	$862,500	Pattern $4, 1879, Quintuple Stella, J-1643, P-1843	PCGS PF-62	Heritage	January 2007
109	$862,500	$2.50, 1796, Stars, Bass-3003, BD-3 (R)	NGC MS-65	Heritage	January 2007
110	$851,875	$4, 1879, Coiled Hair	PCGS PF-66	Heritage	January 2014
111	$851,875	$1(s), 1803, Restrike	PCGS PF-66	Heritage	January 2013
112	$851,875	$1(s), 1802, Restrike	PCGS PF-65Cam	Heritage	August 2012
113	$825,000	$20, MCMVII, Ultra HR, LE	Proof	Sotheby's	December 1996
114	$824,850	Pattern half disme, 1792, copper, J-8	NGC AU-55	Heritage	January 2015
115	$822,500	$1(s), 1795, Flowing Hair, B-2, BB-20	NGC SP-64	Stack's Bowers	August 2014
116	$822,500	$1(s), 1799, B-5, BB-157	NGC MS-67	Heritage	November 2013
117	$822,500	Pattern 1¢, 1792, Silver Center, J-1 (U)	NGC MS-61+ BN	Heritage	April 2013
118	$805,000	$1(s), 1870-S	NGC EF-40	Heritage	April 2008
119	$805,000	$20, 1921	PCGS MS-65	Heritage	November 2005
120	$793,125	10¢, 1796, JR-6	PCGS MS-68	Heritage	August 2014
121	$793,125	Pattern half disme, 1792, J-7	PCGS MS-66	Stack's Bowers	August 2013
122	$763,750	Terr, 1849, Pacific Company, $5, K-1	PCGS AU-58	Heritage	April 2014
123	$763,750	Terr, 1855, Kellogg & Co., $50	PCGS PF-64Cam	Heritage	April 2014
124	$763,750	50¢, 1838-O	NGC PF-64	Heritage	January 2014
125	$763,750	$1(s), 1870-S	PCGS EF-40	Heritage	January 2014
126	$763,750	$5, 1826, BD-2 (V)	PCGS MS-66	Heritage	January 2014
127	$747,500	1¢, 1793, Chain, S-3	NGC MS-66BN	Stack's Bowers	August 2012
128	$747,500	$20, 1921	PCGS MS-66	Heritage	January 2012
129	$747,500	Terr, 1855, Kellogg & Co., $50	PCGS PF-64	Heritage	January 2007
130	$747,500	$1(s), 1794	NGC MS-61	Heritage	June 2005
131	$734,375	50¢, 1838-O	PCGS PF-64	Heritage	January 2013
132	$725,000	Prefed, 1787, Brasher, EB on Wing	MS-63	B&R	November 1979
133	$718,750	1/2¢, 1793, C-3	PCGS MS-65BN	Goldberg	January 2014
134	$718,750	1/2¢, 1796, With Pole, C-2	PCGS MS-65+ RB	Goldberg	January 2014
135	$718,750	$10, 1933	Unc.	Stack's	October 2004
136	$705,698	$1(s), 1870-S	VF-25	B&M	February 2008

Rank	Price	Coin	Grade	Firm	Date
137	$705,000	Pattern 1¢, 1792, Silver Center, J-1 (U)	NGC MS-61+ BN	Heritage	September 2014
138	$705,000	Prefed, 1783, Nova Const., PE Bit, W-1820	NGC AU-55	Heritage	May 2014
139	$705,000	Terr, 1849, Morman, $10, K-3	NGC AU-58	Heritage	April 2014
140	$705,000	$1(s), 1803, Large 3, B-6, BB-255	NGC MS-65+	Heritage	November 2013
141	$690,300	$5, 1836	NGC PF-67UCam	Bonhams	September 2013
142	$690,000	$5, 1909-O (T)	PCGS MS-66	Heritage	January 2011
143	$690,000	1¢, 1796, Liberty Cap, S-84	PCGS MS-66RB	Goldberg	September 2008
144	$690,000	Pattern disme, 1792, copper, RE, J-10 (W)	NGC PF-62BN	Heritage	July 2008
145	$690,000	$5, 1825 Over 4	NGC AU-50	Heritage	July 2008
146	$690,000	$20, MCMVII, Ultra HR, LE of 06	NGC PF-58	Stack's	July 2008
147	$690,000	Terr, 1860, Clark, Gruber & Co., $20	NGC MS-64	Heritage	January 2006
148	$690,000	Prefed, 1742 (1786), Lima Brasher	NGC EF-40	Heritage	January 2005
149	$690,000	$5, 1835	PCGS PF-67	Heritage	January 2005
150	$690,000	$1(g), 1849-C, Open Wreath	NGC MS-63 PL	DLRC	July 2004
151	$690,000	$20, MCMVII, Ultra HR, LE	Proof	Soth/Stack's	October 2001
152	$690,000	$10, 1839/8, Type of 1838, Lg Letters (J)	NGC PF-67	Goldberg	September 1999
153	$687,500	$3, 1870-S	EF-40	B&R	October 1982
154	$687,500	$5, 1822	VF-30 / EF-40	B&R	October 1982
155	$675,525	$10, 1795, BD-5	NGC MS-65	Heritage	August 2013
156	$672,750	$1(s), 1803, Restrike	PF-66	B&M	February 2007
157	$661,250	1¢, 1804, S-266c	PCGS MS-63BN	Goldberg	September 2009
158	$661,250	1/2 dime, 1870-S	NGC MS-63 PL	B&M	July 2004
159	$660,000	$20, MCMVII, Ultra HR, LE (N)	PF-67	B&M	January 1997
160	$660,000	$20, 1861, Paquet Reverse	MS-67	B&M	November 1988
161	$655,500	$4, 1879, Coiled Hair (P)	NGC PF-67Cam	Heritage	January 2005
162	$655,200	$20, 1891	NGC PF-68UC	Bonhams	September 2013
163	$646,250	$1(s), 1893-S	PCGS MS-65	Legend	October 2014
164	$646,250	Prefed, (1652), NE 6 Pence, N-1-A, S-1-A	NGC AU-58	Heritage	May 2014
165	$646,250	Terr, 1851, Baldwin & Co., $20, K-5	PCGS EF-45	Heritage	April 2014
166	$646,250	1¢, 1795, Reeded Edge, S-79 (M)	PCGS VG-10	Heritage	January 2014
167	$646,250	$5, 1909-O (T)	PCGS MS-66	Heritage	January 2014
168	$646,250	$1(s), 1795, 3 Leaves, B-5, BB-27	NGC MS-65	Heritage	November 2013
169	$646,250	$4, 1879, Coiled Hair	PCGS PF-64Cam	Stack's Bowers	May 2013
170	$632,500	$5, 1828 Over 7	NGC MS-64	Heritage	January 2012
171	$632,500	$1(s), 1870-S	PCGS EF-40	B&M	August 2010
172	$632,500	10¢, 1804, 14 Star Reverse, JR-2	NGC AU-58	Heritage	July 2008
173	$632,500	1¢, 1793, Liberty Cap, S-13, B-20	PCGS AU-55	Heritage	February 2008
174	$632,500	1¢, 1794, Starred Reverse, S-48, B-38	PCGS AU-50	Heritage	February 2008
175	$632,500	50¢, 1838-O	PCGS PF-63 BM	Heritage	February 2008
176	$632,500	Prefed, 1652, Willow Tree Threepence, N-1A	VF	Stack's	October 2005
177	$632,500	50¢, 1838-O	PCGS PF-64 BM	Heritage	June 2005
178	$632,500	Confed, 1861, Original 50¢	VF	Stack's	October 2003
179	$632,500	10¢, 1873-CC, No Arrows (S)	PCGS MS-64	Heritage	April 1999
180	$625,000	Prefed, 1787, Brasher, EB on Breast (C)	VF	B&R	March 1981
181	$618,125	$4, 1880, Coiled Hair	NGC PF-63	Superior	July 2005
182	$605,000	$2.50, 1796, No Stars	Choice BU	Stack's	November 1995
183	$603,750	1/2¢, 1852, Large Berries	PCGS PF-65RD	Goldberg	January 2014
184	$603,750	$20, 1854-O	PCGS AU-55	Heritage	October 2008
185	$603,750	Pattern 1¢, 1792, No Silver Center, J-2	PCGS VF-30	Heritage	January 2008
186	$603,750	$1 Trade, 1884	PCGS PF-65	Heritage	November 2005
187	$587,500	$5, 1795, Small Eagle, BD-1	NGC MS-66	Heritage	January 2015
188	$587,500	Pattern disme, 1792, copper, RE, J-10 (W)	NGC PF-62BN	Heritage	October 2012

Rank	Price	Coin	Grade	Firm	Date
189	$587,500	$20, 1921 (Q)	PCGS MS-65	Heritage	August 2012
190	$586,500	$5, 1795, Small Eagle, BD-1	PCGS MS-65	Stack's	June 2008
191	$583,000	$5, 1795, Small Eagle	NGC MS-65 PL	Bullowa	January 2007
192	$577,500	$20, 1927-D	PCGS MS-65	Akers	May 1998
193	$577,500	$1(s), 1794	Gem BU	Stack's	November 1995
194	$576,150	$20, 1856-O	NGC AU-58	Heritage	October 2008
195	$575,000	$20, 1920-S	PCGS MS-66	Heritage	January 2012
196	$575,000	$1(s), 1794	PCGS AU-58 PQ	Goldberg	May 2011
197	$575,000	$4, 1880, Coiled Hair	NGC PF-62	Heritage	January 2009
198	$575,000	Pattern $50, 1877, copper, J-1549	NGC PF-67BN	Heritage	January 2009
199	$575,000	$1(s), 1895-O	PCGS MS-67	Heritage	November 2005
200	$575,000	$20, MCMVII, HR, WR (X)	PCGS MS-69	Heritage	November 2005
201	$575,000	$20, 1927-D	NGC MS-62	DLRC	July 2004
202	$573,300	$20, MCMVII, HR, WR	NGC PF-69	Bonhams	September 2013
203	$564,000	Pattern 1¢, 1792, Birch Cent, LE, J-5	NGC MS-61BN	Heritage	January 2015
204	$564,000	$5, 1826, BD-2 (V)	PCGS MS-66	Heritage	January 2015
205	$564,000	20¢, 1876-CC	PCGS MS-65	Stack's Bowers	January 2013
206	$558,125	Terr, 1849, Morman, $20, K-4	NGC MS-62	Heritage	April 2014
207	$558,125	Terr, 1855, Wass, Molitor & Co., $20, Lg Head	NGC AU-53	Heritage	April 2014
208	$558,125	1¢, 1793, Wreath, S-9	PCGS MS-69BN	Stack's Bowers	January 2013
209	$552,000	$10, 1933	PCGS MS-65	Heritage	January 2008
210	$552,000	$1(s), 1870-S	VF-20	Stack's	October 2007
211	$550,000	$10, 1838	Ch Proof	Akers	May 1998
212	$550,000	10¢, 1873-CC, No Arrows (S)	Gem MS-65	B&M/Stack's	May 1996
213	$550,000	25¢, 1901-S	NGC MS-68	Superior	May 1990
214	$546,250	Prefed, 1776, Cont. $1, pewter, N-3D	NGC MS-67	Heritage	January 2012
215	$546,250	$1(s), 1893-S	NGC MS-67	Heritage	August 2011
216	$546,250	Terr, 1851, Humb't, $50, 880 Thous., No 50 on Rev	PCGS MS-63	Heritage	August 2010
217	$546,250	$4, 1880, Coiled Hair	NGC PF-62	Heritage	July 2009
218	$546,250	$10, 1795, 13 Leaves, BD-1, T-1	PCGS MS-64	Stack's	July 2008
219	$546,250	$10, 1933	PCGS MS-65	Heritage	January 2007
220	$546,250	$20, MCMVII, HR, WR (X)	PCGS MS-69	Heritage	January 2007
221	$542,800	$20, 1856-O	NGC SP-63	Heritage	June 2004
222	$540,500	$5, 1821, BD-1	PCGS MS-63+	Goldberg	January 2014
223	$534,750	$20, MCMVII, HR, FR	NGC PF-69	Heritage	November 2005
224	$531,875	$1(s), 1889-CC	PCGS MS-68	Heritage	January 2009
225	$529,000	Pattern $1, 1838, copper, J-87, P-96	PCGS PF-63RB	Stack's	January 2008
226	$529,000	$1(s), 1889-CC	PCGS MS-68	B&M	January 2001
227	$528,750	1¢, 1793, Wreath, S-9	PCGS MS-66+ BN	Heritage	August 2014
228	$528,750	Pattern half disme, 1792, J-7	PCGS MS-65	Heritage	January 2014
229	$528,750	$10, 1865	PCGS PF-66+ DCam	Stack's Bowers	August 2013
230	$528,750	$1(s), 1895-O, Vam-3	NGC PF-66Cam	Heritage	June 2013
231	$528,750	Pattern half disme, 1792, J-7	PCGS MS-64	Heritage	January 2013
232	$522,500	$20, 1927-D (F)	Gem BU	Stack's	March 1991
233	$517,500	$10, 1933	PCGS MS-65 PQ	Goldberg	February 2009
234	$517,500	$2.50, 1808, BD-1	PCGS MS-63	Stack's	November 2008
235	$517,500	25¢, 1839, No Drapery	NGC PF-65	Heritage	April 2008
236	$517,500	$20, MCMVII, HR, WR (X)	PCGS MS-69	Heritage	March 2008
237	$517,500	$10, 1933	PCGS MS-65	Heritage	November 2005
238	$517,500	$20, 1920-S	PCGS MS-66	Heritage	November 2005
239	$517,000	50¢, 1797, O-102a	Gem BU	Stack's	November 1995
240	$510,600	$1 Trade, 1884	PCGS PF-67	Goldberg	October 2000

Rank	Price	Coin	Grade	Firm	Date
241	$506,000	1¢, 1794, Liberty Cap, Bisected Obv, S-14	PCGS AU-53	Goldberg	September 2009
242	$506,000	$10, 1795, 13 Leaves, T-1	PCGS MS-65	B&M	July 2003
243	$506,000	1/2¢, 1796, No Pole	MS-65RB PL	B&M/Stack's	May 1996
244	$506,000	$1(s), 1794 (A)	PCGS MS-65	Superior	May 1991
245	$503,125	$1(s), 1794	NGC MS-61	Heritage	April 2009
246	$503,125	$1(s), 1870-S	PCGS EF-40	Heritage	April 2009
247	$503,125	Pattern half disme, 1792, J-7, P-7	PCGS MS-63	Heritage	January 2008
248	$503,100	$20, 1870	NGC PF-67UC	Bonhams	September 2013
249	$500,000	Terr, 1851, Humbert, $50	Proof	B&R	March 1980
250	$499,375	Pattern disme, 1792, Reeded Edge, J-10, P-11	NGC AU-55	Heritage	May 2014

KEY

Price: The sale price of the coin, including the appropriate buyer's fee.

Coin: The denomination/classification, date, and description of the coin, along with pertinent catalog or reference numbers. B = Baker (for pre-federal), Bolender (for silver dollars), Breen (for gold), or Browning (for quarter dollars); BB = Bowers/Borckardt; BD = Bass-Dannreuther; Confed = Confederate States of America issue; dbln = doubloon; HR = High Relief; J = Judd; JR = John Reich Society; LE = Lettered Edge; N = Newman; NC = Non-Collectible; O = Overton; P = Pollock; Pattern = a pattern, experimental, or trial piece; Prefed = pre-federal issue; S = Sheldon; T = Taraskza; Terr = territorial issue; VAM = Van Allen–Mallis. Letters in parentheses, **(A)** through **(X)**, denote instances in which multiple sales of the same coin rank within the Top 250.

Grade: The grade of the coin, plus the name of the grading firm (if independently graded). BM = branch mint; NGC = Numismatic Guaranty Corporation of America; PCGS = Professional Coin Grading Service; PQ = premium quality.

Firm: The auction firm (or firms) that sold the coin. ANR = American Numismatic Rarities; B&R = Bowers & Ruddy; DLRC = David Lawrence Rare Coins; Soth = Sotheby's; Stack's Bowers = Stack's Bowers Galleries (name under which Stack's and B&M merged in 2010; also encompasses the merger of Stack's and ANR in 2006).

Date: The month and year of the auction.

Auction records compiled and edited by P. Scott Rubin.

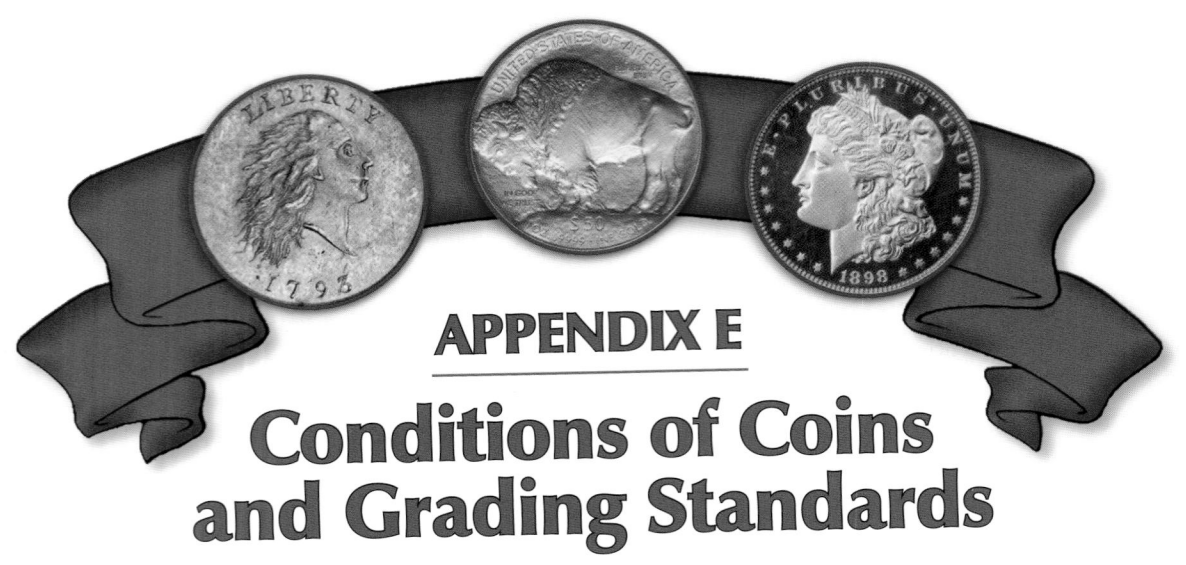

APPENDIX E

Conditions of Coins and Grading Standards

ESSENTIAL ELEMENTS OF THE AMERICAN NUMISMATIC ASSOCIATION GRADING STANDARDS

Proof—A specially made coin distinguished by sharpness of detail and usually with a brilliant, mirrorlike surface. *Proof* refers to the method of manufacture and is not a grade. The term implies superior condition unless otherwise noted.

Gem Proof (PF-65)—Surfaces are brilliant, with no noticeable blemishes or flaws. A few scattered, barely noticeable marks or hairlines.

Choice Proof (PF-63)—Surfaces are reflective, with only a few blemishes in secondary focal places. No major flaws.

Proof (PF-60)—Surfaces may have several contact marks, hairlines, or light rubs. Luster may be dull and eye appeal lacking.

Mint State—The terms *Mint State (MS)* and *Uncirculated (Unc.)* are interchangeable and refer to coins showing no trace of wear from circulation. Such coins may vary slightly because of minor surface imperfections, as described in the following subdivisions:

Perfect Uncirculated (MS-70)—Perfect new condition, showing no trace of wear. The finest quality possible, with no evidence of scratches, handling, or contact with other coins. Very few circulation-issue coins are ever found in this condition.

Gem Uncirculated (MS-65)—An above-average Uncirculated coin that may be brilliant or lightly toned and that has very few contact marks on the surface or rim.

Choice Uncirculated (MS-63)—A coin with some distracting contact marks or blemishes in prime focal areas. Luster may be impaired.

Uncirculated (MS-60)—A coin that has no trace of wear, but which may show a number of marks from contact with other coins during minting, storage, or transportation, and whose surface may be spotted or lack some luster.

Choice About Uncirculated (AU-55)—Evidence of friction on high points of design. Most of the mint luster remains.

About Uncirculated (AU-50)—Traces of light wear on many of the high points. At least half of the mint luster is still present.

Choice Extremely Fine (EF-45)—Light overall wear on the highest points. All design details are very sharp. Some of the mint luster is evident.

Extremely Fine (EF-40)—Light wear on the design throughout, but all features are sharp and well defined. Traces of luster may show.

Choice Very Fine (VF-30)—Light, even wear on the surface and highest parts of the design. All lettering and major features are sharp.

Very Fine (VF-20)—Moderate wear on design high points. All major details are clear.

Fine (F-12)—Moderate to considerable even wear. The entire design is bold with an overall pleasing appearance.

Very Good (VG-8)—Well worn with main features clear and bold, although rather flat.

Good (G-4)—Heavily worn, with the design visible but faint in areas. Many details are flat.

About Good (AG-3)—Very heavily worn with portions of the lettering, date, and legend worn smooth. The date may be barely readable.

Important: Undamaged coins are worth more than bent, corroded, scratched, holed, nicked, stained, or mutilated ones. Flawless Uncirculated coins are generally worth more than values quoted in this book. Slightly worn coins ("sliders") that have been cleaned and conditioned ("buffed") to simulate Uncirculated luster are worth considerably less than perfect pieces.

Unlike damage inflicted after striking, manufacturing defects do not always lessen values. Examples include colonial coins with planchet flaws or weakly struck designs; early silver or gold coins with weight-adjustment "file marks" (parallel cuts made on the planchet prior to striking); and coins with "lint marks" (surface marks due to the presence of dust or other foreign matter during striking).

Note that while grading *standards* strive to be precise, interpretations are subjective and can vary among collectors, dealers, and certification services.

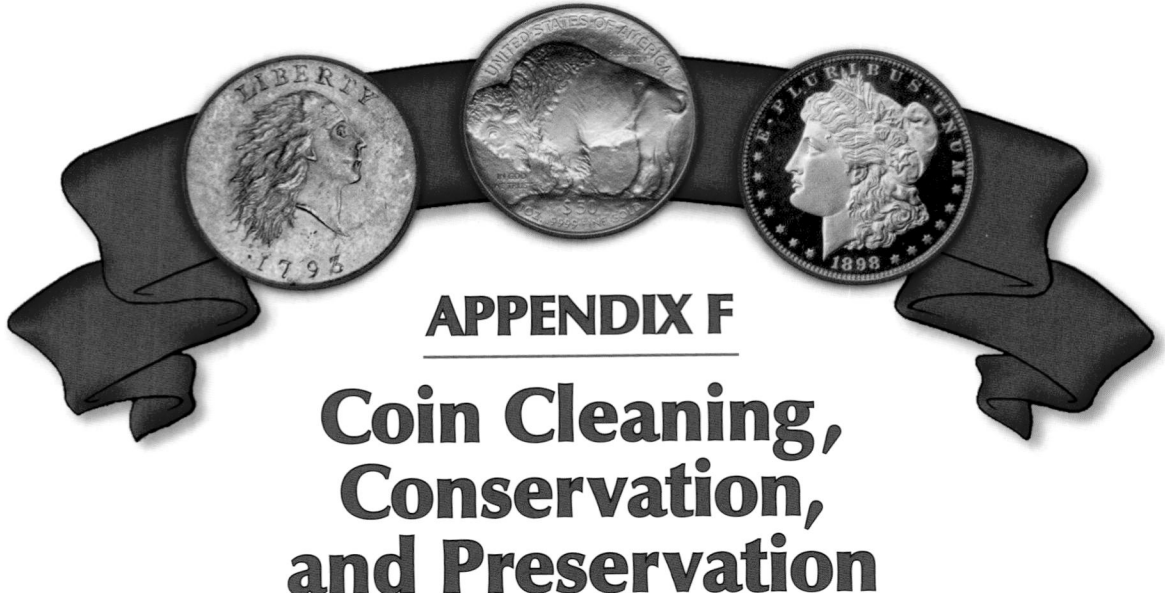

APPENDIX F

Coin Cleaning, Conservation, and Preservation

There is a common misconception among collectors that because coins are durable enough to circulate for decades, they are also resistant to most types of mishandling. In fact, the metal surfaces of coins record their history of treatment exceptionally well—for better or worse. On the positive side, for example, the patina of a coin can reveal if it resided in an old collection, because some types of storage albums impart distinctive toning patterns that develop gradually over many years.

Unfortunately, an examination of a coin's surface just as readily reveals if it has been mistreated. A coin can have dark stains, thick residues, or fingerprints—undesirable consequences of mishandling that negatively affect value. As a further detriment, many coins suffer even more severe and irreversible damage as a result of amateur efforts to save them or improve their appearance. Once a coin exhibits hairlines, impaired luster, or changes in color, or develops corrosion from inadequate neutralization, its surface will always bear evidence.

In today's marketplace, for example, most old copper, nickel, silver, and gold Proof coins are less than superb gem grade—that is, less than Proof-66. The vast majority has tiny hairlines visible under magnification, and Proofs in the 60 to 63 range are apt to have many. When they left the mint, the coins had no hairlines at all. How did the hairlines happen? From improper cleaning. Similarly, most brilliant silver coins

This 1881-S Morgan dollar shows toning from its contact with the environment—the bag it was transported in, the other coins it touched, the very air that surrounded it. "A relatively common date with a not-so-common display of toning" is how it was described at auction. Many collectors find such natural displays of color attractive. Others might be tempted to dip such a coin to make it brilliant and white. "Coin doctors" try to imitate such toning through artificial means like baking and chemical applications.

Old fingerprints add some mystery to these Braided Hair large cents—could they be Abraham Lincoln's?—but they detract from the coins' value.

dated before 1900 are "white" because they've been cleaned (certain Treasury-hoard Morgan dollars being exceptions); perhaps 90 percent of all pre-federal (colonial) coins and tokens have been cleaned; and all high-grade ancient coins have been cleaned at one point or another.

This appendix explains the philosophy about coin cleaning that was prevalent from the mid-1800s until just a generation or two ago. It discusses old methods of cleaning that are discouraged today because of the harm they do to coins. It looks at modern methods of professional conservation. And it offers advice on how to clean coins yourself, in the rare instances that this is advisable.

EARLY ATTITUDES TOWARD CLEANING

The numismatic hobby in America commenced on a large scale in 1857 and 1858, when the discontinuation of the large copper cent prompted many people to try to find as many dates as possible. Since that boom more than 150 years ago, there has been the philosophy that "brilliant is best."

An improperly cleaned Capped Bust half dollar.

Accordingly, a silver coin (in particular) with natural toning (perhaps brown, perhaps golden, perhaps iridescent, perhaps somewhat spotted) was a candidate to be brightened by using acid, silver polish, or some other substance. This did the trick, and the result was a brilliant coin. However, nature and chemistry being what they are, the typical coin retoned over a period of time, as it was subjected to various influences

WHY COINS CHANGE IN APPEARANCE

Coins are most often produced in copper, nickel, silver, or gold. All of these metals are derived from ores that are smelted from a mineral state (which is relatively stable) to a crystalline solid or a metal state (which is somewhat unstable). Virtually all coinage metals are a mixture of more than one elemental metal. These alloys are mixed in order to attain desired coinage characteristics such as color, intrinsic value, and durability.

A coin's survival and state of preservation are influenced by its environment. The interaction of both organic and synthetic elements with the coin's metallic composition can alter its surface in a variety of ways. Coins produced during the last couple of centuries commonly have debris particles, residues, and other potentially corrosive elements on their surfaces. Such particles often are found stuck in the recesses of design features. Over time, they can develop severe spots of active corrosion.

Other harmful surface conditions result from handling and storage. Even the most careful handling enables contaminants on your fingers to be transferred to your coins. Oils and salts are continuously secreted through the skin and will be transferred to the coin, along with many other potentially harmful substances that adhered to the skin through contact with other items. To avoid putting very noticeable and often irremovable fingerprints on the fields of a coin, collectors emphasize handling coins by their edges—but even this allows residues to transfer. Sometimes this is seen on early copper coins, where the obverse and reverse display an attractive brown color while the rim has a slightly lighter and pink coloration from contact with fingertips. In more extreme examples, the obverse and reverse may appear to be in Very Good condition, while small green spots of corrosion are visible on the edge and rim.

such as dampness, warmth, fumes with sulfur (from home heating, industrial residue in the air, etc.), and careless handling. The coin would be sent back to the polish and chemicals, and again it would be bright.

While today this sounds unusual, perhaps even improbable, the scenario was very much the case generations ago. In August 1903, *The Numismatist* included this comment from Farran Zerbe, who had just viewed the Mint Collection in Philadelphia:

> I found many of the silver Proof coins of late years partially covered with a white coating. On inquiry I learned that an over zealous attendant during the last vacation months when the numismatic room was closed took it on himself to clean the tarnished coins, purchase some metal polish at a department store, and proceeded with his cleaning operation. Later a coating of white appeared on the coins, which was now slowly disappearing.
>
> I expressed my displeasure at this improper treatment of Proof coins, and the custodian explained, "That is nothing. I have been here eight years and they have been cleaned three or four times in my time."

Zerbe speculated that should this cleaning continue, in the future one would have nothing left except plain planchets and badly worn coins!

In 1921, one of America's leading collectors, J. Sanford Saltus, was in a hotel room, using potassium cyanide—a lethal liquid—to clean silver coins. He was found dead shortly afterward. The presence of a glass of ginger ale on the table suggested he mistook one for the other. Even so, for many years the advice to use cyanide to clean coins continued.

In the 1950s James F. Kelly, a leading Dayton, Ohio, dealer, suggested that potassium cyanide, if very carefully used, would remove signs of friction from the higher parts of silver coins that were graded About Uncirculated, giving them an appearance of full Mint State.

In the meantime, in *The Numismatist*, *The Numismatic Scrapbook Magazine*, and elsewhere, products were offered to brighten coins. In one instance, a compound plus a wire brush was said to be very effective on copper coins.

During this era, American dealers found that coins that were toned, even very attractively, met with very few buyers. The operative term of the day was "BU," for Brilliant Uncirculated. A Morgan silver dollar, a commemorative half dollar, or some other coin, if toned, would be rejected by buyers nine times out of ten.

Dipping in a jewelry- or silver-cleaning liquid was very popular. Baking soda might be applied to the surface of a coin and rubbed vigorously to remove stubborn stains. The latter process imparted tiny hairlines. Coins toned, and then were cleaned again, creating more hairlines.

Collectors got into the game also when they found that a bright coin would sell readily, but a toned coin wouldn't. Again, this mostly applied to silver. Gold, an inert metal, but with 10% copper as alloy, tended to tone very slowly, and relatively few gold coins were dipped or brightened. Copper coins were a different story. Dip used for silver coins would instantly brighten a Lincoln or Indian Head cent that had some brown toning. (For a while it would look as good as new, so to speak. However, the dipping had its own problems.) Sometimes gentle heat, such as from a lightbulb, was applied to add toning. If all went well, and the copper cent was kept in a plastic holder, it might remain attractive. On the other hand, if there was the slightest residue of leftover dip, or other contaminants, the result eventually would be staining and blotching, making the coin less attractive than it was to begin with.

The leading grading services have been trapped a number of times on this, by certifying copper coins as "RD" (red) in gem (65 and higher) categories, only to find that a later buyer ended up with a coin that had developed spots. Accordingly, guarantees concerning the stability of copper coins have been revised. The grading services make no comment as to whether a coin has been cleaned or not.

The secret that is not a secret is that any Proof coin on the market today that has hairlines in the field—and virtually all of them do that are graded below Proof-66, as well as many that are graded higher—have been cleaned at one time by using friction. When the coins were minted the hairlines weren't there. Curiously, this fact is very difficult to find in print, and most collectors are not aware of it. Many readers of the *Professional Edition* will learn this information about coins for the first time. In a broader view, in other areas of collecting and connoisseurship (such as antiquities, Old Masters paintings, and historical documents), cleaning, good and bad, is often discussed. Not so in numismatics.

CHANGING PHILOSOPHIES

The mindset for "brilliant is best" began to change—although slowly—in the 1960s and 1970s. New Netherlands Coin Company, a leading New York City dealer at the time, offered many coins at auction, suggesting that attractive toning was an asset, and often describing it in detail. Lester Merkin, another leading dealer, did likewise.

John J. Ford Jr., the co-owner of New Netherlands, gave this commentary in the 1950s in an issue of the firm's magazine, *Numisma*:

> There are as many "expert" ways to clean coins as there are coin dealers. We suggest you read Dr. Sheldon's comments in his book [*Early American Cents*, 1949, the standard reference on large copper cents of the 1793–1814 years; succeeded by *Penny Whimsy*, 1958], and talk to older, experienced collectors. Well toned coins, strictly
>
> Uncirculated or Proof and without blemishes, are valued more highly by us than the usually found "cleaned" silver examples. It is almost inevitable that a really old silver coin which has so-called brilliance must have been meticulously cleaned so as to seem so. The aluminum pan with baking soda in solution, often used for cleaning silverware, is good for ordinary dull tarnish and is probably the commonest method, as well as one of the safest. . . .
>
> For my money, "expert cleaning" leaves the coin looking as if it *had not been touched*. In this light, we suggest coins with an even and attractively colored toning be left alone, as it will for a long time protect them against less desirable tarnish.
>
> Abrasives of any sort are dangerous. Jeweler's rouge is to be avoided; it is simply iron oxide (rust) ground to fine powder, and its action is simply scouring. . . .
>
> Proofs are no different from other coins, except they show the results of sloppy cleaning more easily. We do not retouch 99% of the material we handle, except for an occasional brushing, or the judicious use of a little mineral oil. To sum it up, it is much better to leave "improving" to the other fellow, as well as the "expert" designation in this field of endeavor.

THE GARRETT COLLECTION

In 1979 came the first of four auction offerings of the Garrett Collection, put on the market by The Johns Hopkins University. This cabinet had been gathered, beginning in the 1870s, by T. Harrison Garrett, an heir to the Baltimore and Ohio Railroad fortune. After his untimely death in a boating accident in 1888, the collection remained dormant and later passed to his son, John Work Garrett. The latter was an ardent numismatist who picked up the traces from his father, and made significant additions to his collection. The thought of cleaning or brightening a coin did not enter his mind. In 1942 Garrett died, and the collection was willed to the university. Then, in the 1970s, it was deaccessioned, as it had been stored in a subterranean bank vault for years, not accessible for scholarship or anything else. The funds from its sale were needed elsewhere. The firm of Bowers and Ruddy cataloged and described each coin, nearly all of which were attractively toned, reflecting the connoisseurship of the past owners. The prices realized amazed the hobby, with many pieces bringing double or triple current values, or even more. From that point forward, attractive toning was in style, and the practice of dipping and brightening of coins lessened.

During all of this time, knowledgeable dealers carefully conserved gold, silver, and copper by removing "vault grime," dirt, grease, and other distractions through the use of inert chemicals, without friction. In many instances acetone—a powerful solvent (which must be used carefully and with ventilation)—helped. Ammonia was useful as well (but tended to give copper coins an iridescent color), and the use of plain soap and water could be advantageous. Meanwhile, as some coins were being conserved, some others (in the distinct minority) were being artificially toned to increase their marketability, and still others were being dipped.

COIN STORAGE

In an effort to minimize the handling of coins, manufacturers have created a wide variety of storage devices for hobbyists. Over the years hundreds of different products, ranging from flips and envelopes to books and boxes, have been sold to help collectors store and manage their collections. The earliest versions were not without problems. Many holders contained sulfur, polyvinyl chloride (PVC), and a variety of other potential contaminants. In recent decades, manufacturers have become better informed and more responsible, and we have seen the development of much safer storage products. Nevertheless, not all collectors and dealers seek out these coin-friendly products, and many hobbyists have not removed their coins from the old and potentially hazardous holders.

Coins from improper holders are seen every day in the marketplace. PVC contamination is one of the more commonly seen problems resulting from bad coin holders. In many cases PVC "goo" has corroded into the surfaces of the coin.

Even if coin-friendly holders are used, the surrounding environment can still adversely affect a coin's condition by facilitating corrosion or tarnish. An attractive pattern of colors on a coin is called *toning*. When unattractive, this same condition is called *tarnish* or *spots*. And when very dark it often is called *environmental damage*. Tarnish is a form of oxidation and is primarily caused by hydrogen sulfide and carbonyl sulfide. Tarnish can result from direct contact with reactive elements, or through vapors.

Some common tarnish-causing elements are wool, silk, felt, dyed fabrics, paper, cardboard, wood, and wood products, to name just a few. In short, traces of tarnish-causing elements can be found all around the house and office, and even in the clothes we wear. While people are not able to smell sulfur until it reaches unhealthy levels, coins are many times more sensitive. Add fluctuations in temperature and humidity, and the speed and effect of the tarnish-causing materials is increased.

Coins displaying the effects of these hazards are prevalent in the marketplace. Their appearance may vary considerably, but it is generally unappealing and can worsen over time. The difficulty most dealers and collectors experience when attempting to conserve their coins is that they lack the technical expertise, appropriate materials, and, more importantly, experience and training. The results of amateur attempts to address these problems are also easy to find in the many improperly cleaned or "problem" coins that display hairlines, scratches, impaired luster, or unnatural color.

THE *PHOTOGRADE* COMMENTARY AND ADVICE

Photograde, written by James F. Ruddy and published in 1970, contained this advice (excerpted):

Many products for cleaning coins are available on the market, and in some instances the representation is made that the use of such products will enhance a coin's value. At one time a "kit" was offered, consisting of a brass wire brush in combination with a cleaning solution. The statement was made that by using the kit an "ugly" old copper coin could be transformed to a brilliant, and thus desirable piece. Left unstated was the fact that most experienced collectors of copper coins would not have touched the resultant coin with a 10-foot pole!

Although many other examples and quotations could be given concerning the harm done by cleaning coins, human nature being what it is, you may be tempted to try your hand at the cleaning process. If you do, consider the subject carefully. Probably for every one coin "improved" by cleaning, 10 or more have had their values lessened.

Cleaning, when necessary, should be done only with nickel, silver, and gold coins in top grades. To clean such pieces in grades less than About Uncirculated will produce an unnatural appearance that is not acceptable to most collectors. The cleaning of copper and bronze coins in any condition should be avoided unless it is necessary to remove an unsightly carbon spot or fingerprint. In all instances, practice cleaning methods with low-value coins, so if you ruin them, they can simply be spent!

To clean a high-grade nickel, silver, or gold coin, use only a clear liquid "dip," not a paste, powder, or polish. Pour some dip, full strength, into a pliable plastic dish. Completely immerse the coin in the liquid. Do not leave the coin in the liquid longer than a few seconds. Immediately rinse the coin thoroughly under running cold water. Pat (do not rub) the coin dry with a soft absorbent cloth; a terry cloth towel is ideal. Holding the coin in your fingers and using a cotton swab may result in uneven cleaning. For copper coins, if you must experiment with them, use a mixture of half "dip" and half cold water.

In lieu of rinsing the coin for a long period of time under running cold water, the "dip" can be neutralized somewhat by immersing the coin, after dipping, in water in which a generous amount of baking soda has been dissolved. Swish the coin around in the water, remove it, and then hold it under running cold water. After drying the coin with a soft absorbent cloth, be sure there is no moisture adhering to the surfaces. It is a good idea to allow the coin to remain exposed to the open atmosphere for an hour or more before encasing it in an airtight holder. Trace amounts of "dip" adhering to a coin's surface will eventually tarnish or corrode the coin.

The "dip" acts on the coin's surface by removing the tarnish and, at the same time, minute parts of the coin's metal. If a silver coin is dipped repeatedly, it will take on a dull, gray appearance. Under magnification, the mirror surface of a Proof coin will be seen to be finely etched, resulting in a cloudy surface which cannot be corrected.

In the cleaning of a coin, never use any substance which requires friction. To be avoided are jeweler's rouge, silver-cleaning paste, baking soda, salt, or any similar substances. These substances clean coins by forcibly removing metal from the surface. The result will be a coin showing many hairlines. The application of a cleaning paste to a Proof coin can reduce its value to a tiny fraction of what would have been otherwise.

It is sometimes desirable on circulated coins, Uncirculated coins, and Proofs as well, to remove a light film of dirt, grease, or PVC residue (the latter from storing coins in plastic holders which over a period of time exude a substance which forms a greenish coating on coins). Residues from tape, spots of glue, and other substances are sometimes found on coin surfaces and need to be removed. A commercial solvent, acetone (a chemical available at drug stores), usually will do the trick. Acetone is highly flammable and gives off fumes which should not be inhaled. Use acetone only in an open area, well ventilated, and away from spark or flame. Do not treat acetone casually.

The removal of dirt, grit, and other verdigris, which sometimes accumulates on the surface of a coin, particularly one which has been in circulation for many years, can be done by using an ultrasonic cleaning machine in combination with a solution which does not change the surface coloration. Jewelers commonly use such devices to clean dirty rings, bracelets, and the like.

Cleaning with acetone or by ultrasonic methods is different from dipping, for the latter methods simply remove dirt or residue without affecting the toning or coloration of a coin. In general, dipping and cleaning to change the color of a coin's surface is undesirable; removing dirt and residue is desirable.

CLEANING COPPER AND BRONZE COINS

Having given you ample warning, but with the realization that on occasion cleaning can be desirable, we now discuss cleaning of various coins.

The "dipping" or chemical cleaning of copper and bronze coins is to be avoided. The only exceptions, and such exceptions are rare, are coins which have unsightly fingerprints, blotches, or areas of oxidation. Cleaning by dipping, following the procedure outlined earlier, will result in the surface becoming bright yellow or orange, an unnatural hue quite unlike a normal uncleaned coin. As such, a piece then becomes a candidate for judicious retoning. Under no circumstances should a *worn* copper or bronze coin be dipped or chemically cleaned, for the result will be a bright and unnatural color. Worn copper coins in their natural state are toned varying shades from black to light brown; this natural toning is destroyed by dipping.

Dirt, green PVC goo, grease, and other substances adhering to the surface of a coin can be removed by acetone (be sure to use it in a well-ventilated area, away from flame), or in some instances simply by the application of soap and water. A bath in a cleaning solution (but not a solution which will remove toning) in a jeweler's ultrasonic cleaner may likewise be desirable. None of these methods will remove toning or change the basic surface color.

A key-date 1914-D Lincoln cent, before and after professional conservation. The unattractive toning has been lightened, and environmental damage from polyvinyl chloride (PVC) removed.

After dirt has been removed from the surface of a copper coin, it can be given a glossy surface by brushing it carefully with a No. 4 jeweler's camelhair brush (a method employed by many collectors of early half cents and large cents), or by gentle rubbing with a soft cloth lightly treated with mineral oil.

CLEANING NICKEL COINS

What we call "nickel" coins are primarily copper. For example, nickel three-cent pieces minted from 1865 to 1889 and nickel five-cent pieces produced beginning in 1866 are composed of three parts copper and one part nickel.

If a nickel coin displays unsightly toning blotches, oxidation areas, or fingerprints, the surface can sometimes be made brilliant by immersing in a liquid "dip."

Nickel coins are more chemically active than silver or gold, so it becomes even more critical to neutralize the "dip" by immersing the coins in cold running water for a long period of time, and then drying each piece thoroughly. Failure to do this will result in the coin acquiring

Graded as having Very Good details, but corroded and at some point improperly cleaned, this key-date 1885 Liberty Head nickel sold in 2009 for about half of what an original, uncleaned VG-8 specimen would bring.

unsightly brown blotches within a matter of weeks. If a nickel coin is dipped more than two or three times, it will become cloudy and soon will have a "cleaned" appearance. As is true with copper and bronze coins, the typical nickel coin is best left uncleaned.

Grease, PVC goo, and dirt on nickel coins can be removed by the judicious application of acetone (again we mention that this substance must be used carefully, in a well-ventilated area and away from flame), by ultrasonic cleaning, or by soap and water. Done correctly, none of these processes is harmful to the coin, and such treatment is recommended in indicated cases.

CLEANING SILVER COINS

Think twice, and then think again, before immersing any silver coin in "dip," for it is often the case that attractively toned coins are worth more than brilliant ones. Dipping of silver coins is recommended only to remove unsightly or blotchy spotting, fingerprints, or oxidation. In these instances, use silver "dip" following the methods outlined earlier. If a silver coin has a very deep surface tarnish—deep gray or even coal black—the removal of this tarnish or toning will usually result in a cloudy, etched surface. Cleaning a heavily toned silver coin usually has unfavorable results.

In 2008 this improperly cleaned 1871-CC Liberty Seated dollar sold for about half of what an original specimen in the same grade (Fine-15) would have brought. "Dipped long ago then improperly rinsed afterward," noted its auction description, "leaving deep brown and umber stains behind—anyone who remembers the dipping craze of the late '70s will know exactly the hue of the stains we write about."

In instances in which a silver coin has surface dirt, PVC goo, or other residue, the judicious application of the dangerous substance acetone (note the safety precautions mentioned earlier), or the use of a jeweler's ultrasonic bath, or the application of soap and water, can have favorable results and is recommended.

CLEANING GOLD COINS

Of all metals used in U.S. coinage—copper, nickel, steel, zinc, silver, gold, and others—gold is the most inert. In general, gold coins retain their brilliance for many decades, even centuries. As most U.S. gold coins consist of nine parts gold and one part copper, the copper alloy will cause a light toning over a period of time, so that early pieces often obtain a warm rosy or golden appearance. This is desirable and should not be changed.

The use of a "dip" on gold coins will make the surface brilliant—sometimes brassy—in appearance, which for very early pieces is not desirable. Dipping rarely removes copper-colored spots or staining occasionally seen on gold coins (the result of an imperfect alloy mixture). For such copper stains, professional conservators use a heat treatment that is quite efficient but should not be attempted by others.

Surface film, dirt, and grease can be removed from gold coins with acetone (note the safety precautions mentioned earlier), a jeweler's ultrasonic bath, or soap and water. Ammonia, carefully applied to a gold coin's surface, can remove a film which sometimes is seen on higher-grade pieces, including Proofs. In all instances, avoid rubbing or the use of friction as this will generate undesirable hairlines.

EXPERT PROFESSIONAL CONSERVATION OF COINS

Today, in the early 21st century, careful conservation by experts continues. The greatest American numismatic treasure ever found included gold coins recovered in the 1980s from the SS *Central America* (lost at sea off the coast of North Carolina on February 12, 1857). These were brought up from a depth of 7,200 feet. Many pieces had become encrusted with stains, iron that had been dissolved from the ship's mechanisms, coral, and other substances. Highly skilled scientists who assisted in the recovery of the ship set up a conservation laboratory to carefully dissolve these substances. They used separate baths, but no friction or acids. Their work revealed double eagles, for example, which were as brilliant and lustrous as the day they were made, without any hairlines or problems. In spite of wide recognition in the press, the conservators would not reveal their methods. This was for good reason, as improper use and experimenting could certainly result in damage.

An 1896 gold quarter eagle, before and after professional conservation. In its stained and dirty state, such a coin might be sold for its bullion content alone. Professionally conserved to an eye-pleasing Mint State, its value increases to 10 times that amount.

About the same time, recovered gold coins from the SS *Brother Jonathan* (lost at sea on July 30, 1865), were carefully conserved by a laboratory in California. Then, in 2002, the wreck of the SS *Republic* (lost at sea October 18, 1865) was found. Many of the recovered coins were conserved with great success. Shipwreck-recovered coins in silver (a chemically active metal) often were etched or corroded by the seawater. Even with the coral and other substances removed, they still showed the effects of immersion. Marketing terms such as *saltwater effect* were devised, and added to the holders of such coins.

ATTITUDES IN TODAY'S MARKETPLACE

In the numismatic marketplace the words "cleaned" and "dipped" are rarely heard. "Conserved" is acceptable, due to the great publicity given to the SS *Central America* and later discoveries, and advances made in professional numismatic conservation.

Artificial toning or re-toning is not mentioned either, although it is widely practiced. Various methods have been used including frying coins in a pan, subjecting them to iodine fumes, gently heating them, placing them in old cardboard holders or fast-food napkins (which contain residual sulfur), and adding rainbow toning through various chemical interactions. Such artificially induced toning may be "pretty" at first, but the tarnish can alter and become ugly over time.

THE IMPORTANCE OF CONSERVATION

Professional numismatic conservation has grown out of the need to rescue coins from detrimental surface problems and to preserve our numismatic heritage, while also providing hobbyists with a safe alternative to cleaning coins on their own. While professional conservation may be relatively new to numismatics, other cultural and historical artifacts have been routinely conserved for a very long time. Conservation is a very specialized field, and conservators usually focus on one type of artifact or conservation method. This specialization is necessary because they must possess tremendous knowledge of the item they are conserving. They must be experts in evaluating the composition, production, and condition of the item in order to be able to master the complexities of treating it to produce successful and consistent results. This specialization, along with extensive hands-on experience, can lead the conservator to sound judgments during evaluation and subsequent conservation. There are professional conservation services that specialize in numismatics.

HOW NUMISMATIC CONSERVATION WORKS

In professional numismatic conservation, before any procedure is undertaken, a careful and thorough evaluation of the coin is made. During this detailed analysis, the evaluator assesses the condition of the coin's underlying surfaces, identifies the surface problems, and determines what, if any, treatment will be most beneficial in removing or reducing the contamination and stabilizing the coin to limit further deterioration. The coin's method of manufacture, age, composition, and grade are especially important, because they influence which procedure will be most effective in producing results of the highest standards.

Since the evaluation process is every bit as important as the procedure undertaken, the evaluator has to have seen hundreds of thousands of coins. He must understand their production and the subtleties of their luster patterns, color, and originality.

Unlike with other conservation specialties, the third-party–certified grading system used in numismatics makes the job of the evaluator very difficult. When reviewing a certified coin the evaluator must determine if it will maintain its current grade after conservation. Even though the procedure only removes foreign material from the coin, these materials might conceal minor marks that affect the grade once the coin's true surfaces are visible again. This is a very important consideration, especially when only very slight differences in luster brilliance can mean the difference between a coin grading MS-68 or MS-67.

Having the most experienced evaluators and foremost conservation experts working in unison ensures results of the highest caliber, while reducing the risk of a coin not maintaining its current grade. In many cases, when all of the elements work well together, coins can and do increase in grade, as their original surfaces become visible and unimpeded by residues.

After the specimen has been evaluated and a procedure is prescribed, the coin is conserved in a laboratory setting specifically designed and equipped to ensure consistency and quality of results. Through the systematic application of chemicals and solvents, the conservator is able to reduce or remove the detrimental surface conditions while protecting the integrity of the coin's surfaces. In some cases, several different treatments may be used to address several different contaminants. In addition to removing foreign materials, the procedure also neutralizes the coin's surface, ensuring longer-term stability.

Professional conservators use inert solvents. A coin is introduced into a liquid that will dissolve surface contaminants and suspend them in solution. The coin can be removed from the solution and then rinsed and stabilized for reevaluation and assessment. Oftentimes proper conservation will involve a multi-step process, and very dilute solvents are used under precise temperature to control the rate of reaction. Because these treatments are prescribed and performed by experienced numismatists, it's possible to halt or arrest the conservation process as soon as a desired result has been achieved.

The most important difference between numismatic conservation and many other conservation specialties is in regard to the restoration of the object. In other fields it is acceptable to strip down the item and its outermost original surfaces and then restore it by rebuilding its surfaces before applying preservative materials. For obvious reasons this is not acceptable in numismatic conservation, where the principle goal is to remove detrimental foreign materials and protect the originality of the specimen's surface. No materials are ever added to a coin's surface during professional numismatic conservation.

One of the more dramatic situations involves the coins of the late King Farouk of Egypt. For many years, especially in the period from the late 1930s until he was deposed by a military junta in 1952, the king amassed a great collection of copper, silver, and gold coins. All of his silver and copper coins were cleaned with friction, using silver polish. They were then lacquered. The sale of Farouk's collection took place in Cairo in early 1954, and the coins were dispersed, with many American coins returning to the United States. Included were vast holdings of rare, sometimes unique, patterns. Dealers and collectors removed the lacquer, and in some instances endeavored to retone the coins, but without much success. The auction of certain pattern coins in the Harry W. Bass Jr. Collection in 1999 contained a number of Farouk pieces that had not been touched—with the copper being bright orange. After being sold, certain of these went to coin conservators and were given attractive brown finishes, of a mahogany or chestnut color. The leading certification services encapsulated them with sometimes high Proof grades, with no mention that they had been cleaned. The coins had been improved in appearance, and most people would agree that they are more attractive and more desirable now than before. However, if a detailed explanation were given about retoning them, they might not be marketable.

Similarly, if just about any brilliant 19th-century Proof coin were described as, for example, "Proof-63, brilliant, once cleaned and now with hairlines," it would not be readily saleable. Accordingly, such aspects are rarely mentioned. However, they exist, and the detailed discussion of them here is simply to make you aware of the different processes and possibilities.

Picking up on the commentary in *Photograde*, good advice today is to *not* clean any coin you have. Possible exceptions include the careful use of soap and water, or (for nickel, silver, and gold coins) acetone. Cleaning can improve a coin, but it also can damage it, and over a long period of years more have been harmed than have been benefited. Besides, a dipped or cleaned coin is apt to retone. If the coin is valuable, a professional numismatic conservation service should be consulted as to costs and advisability. Alternatively, a trained, skilled dealer might be able to help.

A coin not "improved" today can always, if advisable, be treated at a later date.

APPENDIX G

COUNTERFEIT COINS IN TODAY'S MARKET

MODERN CHINESE COUNTERFEIT COINS: A CLASSIFICATION SYSTEM

The production and ownership of copies or replicas of U.S. coinage, regardless of their quality or metal content, is not prohibited by law. The Hobby Protection Act of 1973 requires a reproduction to be clearly marked on one side with the word COPY, incused (not in raised lettering). There are many reputable manufacturers of replica coins in the United States and around the world; examples of their products are frequently seen advertised on television, in print media, and even in numismatic publications.

Unfortunately there are modern counterfeit coins in today's marketplace that do not abide by the Hobby Protection Act. Many of these fakes are crude, underweight, and obviously not genuine. Others, however, are deceptive enough to fool even a longtime student of numismatics.

An experienced coin collector who finds, for example, a raw (uncertified) 1893-S Morgan dollar, in a circulated grade such as Extremely Fine, will examine the coin—feeling the heft of its silver, observing the bag marks from 19th-century travel from mint to bank, seeing the evidence of its circulation through the Old West, inspecting the tiny devices that contain a century and more of dirt and grime. After this visual inspection, the collector might perform some basic analyses, finding that the coin weighs the proper 26.7 grams, measures exactly 38.1 mm in diameter, and has the specific gravity (10.34) of a .900 fine silver dollar. Given these reassurances, it might be difficult to convince even the experienced collector that this "coin" is actually a level D-4 counterfeit, manufactured two weeks ago in China.

There are Chinese counterfeiters who admit they produce 100,000 fake coins per month—exceeding the volume of legitimate coins struck by many small nations. These counterfeits are in compliance with Chinese law as long as they are dated before 1949, the year the People's Republic of China was founded. Unlike the United States, China does not require replicas or copies to be marked as such.

On December 19, 2014, President Barack Obama signed into law the Collectible Coin Protection Act, which strengthens the 1973 Hobby Protection Act by, among other things, allowing faster response by law enforcers, making seizure easier, and expanding legal remedies available to those harmed by the sale of counterfeit coins. What follows is a discussion of, and a classification system for, replicas that are not in compliance with the Hobby Protection Act—those that have the greatest potential to deceive collectors.

FACTORS AFFECTING THE QUALITY OF A COUNTERFEIT COIN

Several factors blend together to establish the quality of a counterfeit coin and thus its ability to defraud unsuspecting collectors or even expert numismatists.

PLANCHETS

The planchet is a blank metal disk with upset rims, intended to be struck by dies to produce a coin. Often the planchet is the most difficult item for a counterfeiter to obtain—at least with specifications accurate enough to create a convincing replica. To deceive a buyer, a counterfeit's planchet must be of the proper diameter, thickness, weight, and metal composition. Since governmental mints maintain a high degree of planchet accuracy, the counterfeiter's task can be challenging. (Currently only about 1 planchet in 100 is accurate enough to create a level D-4 counterfeit.)

DIES, HAMMER, ANVIL, AND COLLAR

Three dies are necessary to produce a coin: the anvil die, the hammer die, and the collar die. The accuracy of this combination is crucial to high-quality counterfeit production.

Production of coinage dies has been problematic for centuries. High-quality steel is necessary to produce a working die. Early counterfeiters, after obtaining tool steel, would cut dies by hand; later, they would fabricate dies by spark erosion, impact methods, one-to-one transfer methods, and casting. Each of these techniques was fraught with problems. The counterfeiter's solution came with the advent of desktop computers controlling metal-cutting lasers.

PROBLEMS WITH HAND-CUT DIES

Crude design details

Quality limited to the engraver's abilities

Numerous design errors

Frequent letter transposition or spelling errors

PROBLEMS WITH DIES MADE BY ONE-TO-ONE DIE TRANSFER

Lack of detail

Odd color and texture on the counterfeit's surface

Tool marks

Repeating depressions

PROBLEMS WITH DIES MADE BY SPARK EROSION

Granular surface or prooflike surface with granular devices

Slightly lower relief than authentic coins

Lack of fine detail

Prooflike edges on coins that should have plain edges

PROBLEMS WITH IMPACTED DIES

Mushy perimeter details, with sharp central details

Incorrect square rims

PROBLEMS WITH CAST DIES

Mushy details

Low-detail relief

Incorrect rims

PROBLEMS WITH COMPUTER-ENHANCED LASER-CUT DIES

Few physical problems, but expensive

High-quality dies cost $2,000 to $3,000 per three-die set

Lower-quality dies cost $250 to $500 per three-die set

COIN PRESS AND STRIKING EQUIPMENT

The equipment necessary to establish a counterfeit-coin production facility is readily available and affordable. Both new and used equipment is available through Internet sales and from major suppliers. Some modifications, performed by a master machinist, are required before production can commence.

According to the U.S. Customs and Border Protection Agency, about 80% of all counterfeit goods seized at U.S. ports were created in China. The International Intellectual Property Alliance reports that China produces more counterfeits than all other countries combined. One of the major producers of modern Chinese counterfeit coins is Mr. L—, owner and operator of an established factory in Fujian Province. Mr. L—'s coin presses were at one time in operation at a U.S. mint, and in the early 1900s were sent to the mint in Shanghai, China. In the mid-1950s the presses and ancillary equipment, being obsolete for China's modern coining needs, were sold off as scrap and ended up in the counterfeiters' shops of Fujian. In short, Mr. L—'s counterfeit coins are struck on original U.S. Mint coin presses and at the identical strike pressures as the original coins.

POST-STRIKE COIN ENHANCEMENT OR TREATMENT ("COIN DOCTORING")

Post-production artificial enhancement is designed to alter the "just-struck" appearance of the counterfeit, to deceive a potential buyer into believing the item is genuine. Many methods exist, and Chinese counterfeiters have become masters of this deceitful art. "Coins" can be produced with a cameo Proof appearance, or altered to a grade of About Good. This coin doctoring combines artistry, advanced chemistry, and mechanics to artificially create the appearance of years of circulation. Alterations and treatments include:

pre-strike planchet damage

purposefully designed die and mechanical imperfections (e.g., clashed dies, cuds, excess grease)

planchet imperfections

rim damage

surface stains

toning

scratches

jewelry mounting

any conceivable change that will deceive the buyer into believing the counterfeit is genuine

THE D-1 TO D-4 CLASSIFICATION SYSTEM

This system is not a set of coin-grading standards along the same lines as Dr. William Sheldon's 70-point scale for early large cents, or the Official American Numismatic Association Grading Standards for United States Coins. It is, rather, designed as a method to accurately describe the quality of modern counterfeits and their dies, by providing universal standards for their analysis.

Special thanks to Gregory V. DuBay for contributing this classification system.

"COIN" CHARACTERISTICS: LEVEL D-1

Relief is low, flatly struck

Metal composition is wrong for the coin type

Dimensions are rarely within mint tolerances

Weight is below standard for the coin type

Specific gravity is incorrect for the coin type

Surface is granular

Designs are damaged by excessive grease or other surface die problems

Design and devices are fuzzy

Coloration is odd

Edge design often is incorrect for the coin type

Rims usually are sharp, square

Die pairing often is inconsistent with the coin type

Post-strike enhancement is rare

Mottoes are incomplete or missing

Die flaws are obvious

"COIN" CHARACTERISTICS: LEVEL D-2

Central and peripheral designs are in low relief

Metal composition is wrong for the coin type

Rims are square and prooflike

Specific gravity is incorrect for the coin type

Surface is granular

Devices are soft and incomplete

Mottoes are incomplete in portions

Edge design or reed count often is incorrect for the coin type

Post-strike enhancement is often evident

Die flaws are often seen

Often sold in pre-packaged sets

"COIN" CHARACTERISTICS: LEVEL D-3

Physical characteristics are close to mint tolerances

Metal composition often is correct for the coin type, but trace elements might not be accurate on surface analysis

Specific gravity is close to accurate for the coin's metal composition

Surfaces are mostly free of die flaws

Edge design is correct for the coin type

Rims are rounded to appear as a circulation strike

Inscriptions are complete, but may have weak areas

Post-strike enhancement is common

Wear and damage (simulated to appear to be caused by circulation) is common

Stars often are weak and lack central details

Purposeful planchet imperfections are often evident

Central details usually are clear and distinct

Peripheral details are somewhat weak or mushy, unless the dies are of high quality and have been dished to enhance metal flow

"COIN" CHARACTERISTICS: LEVEL D-4

Metallic content is accurate to mint tolerance

Weight, diameter, and thickness meet mint specifications

Striking pressure was equal to original mint specifications

Multiple striking to achieve full detail is common

Edge treatment is correct for the coin type: square for Proofs and rounded for circulation strikes

Edge design is correct for the year and coin type

Specific gravity is accurate for the coin's metal composition

Reed count is accurate for the coin type

Upper circulated grades are most common, the "coins" having been treated to reduce their newly minted appearance

Post-strike enhancement is advanced; artificial coloration, wear, scratches, graffiti, and circulation damage are standard

Pre-strike planchet damage is often seen

Surfaces are free of non-standard die defects

Die defects typically used as diagnostic features on genuine coins are reproduced

DIE CHARACTERISTICS: LEVEL D-1

Die steel often is of poor quality

Dies often are recycled with design elements of the previous coin type

Die surfaces are flat

Coin design elements are in low relief

Very few fine details are present

Mottoes, initials, and mintmarks are incomplete or absent

Die blemishes are common

Die damage, such as clash marks, is seen

Die surface is granular or poorly polished

Rust and die neglect often are evident

Diameter is not within mint tolerance

DIE CHARACTERISTICS: LEVEL D-2

Die surfaces are flat

Design elements are in low relief

All major details are present, but some are weak

Stars are flat, lacking central detail

Surfaces have been lightly polished to remove defects

Small details (e.g., initials and mintmarks) often are missing

Die defects from mishandling often are evident

Hand engraving of fine details is typical

Granular surfaces are notable upon magnification

DIE CHARACTERISTICS: LEVEL D-3

Steel used for die fabrication is of high quality

Design and devices are deeply cut

Small details (e.g., designer initials and mintmarks) usually are weak or absent

Dies are highly polished and well finished, with only slight granulation

Surfaces are flat or only slightly dished

Dies show signs of hand engraving to enhance fine details

Diameter is within mint tolerance

DIE CHARACTERISTICS: LEVEL D-4

Steel used for die fabrication is of the highest quality

Engraving is deep, with attention paid to fine details

Dies are heavily polished, to remove any tooling marks

Surfaces are dished to enhance metal flow during the strike

Diameter is precisely to mint specifications

GALLERY OF COUNTERFEIT COINAGE DIES

A Level D-1 counterfeit Liberty Head eagle die.

A Level D-4 counterfeit Liberty Walking half dollar die.
Note the die breaks from extended use.

Level D-4 counterfeit Buffalo nickel dies.

Level D-2 counterfeit trade dollar die.

Level D-3 counterfeit Liberty Seated dollar die.

Level D-1 counterfeit Morgan dollar die.

Level D-2 counterfeit Morgan dollar die.

SPECIFICATIONS AND TOLERANCES FOR U.S. COINS

HALF CENTS

Dates	Weight (Grams)	Tolerance	Weight (Grains)	Tolerance	Diameter (mm)	Composition (%)	Specific Gravity
1793–1795	6.739		104.000		23.50*	Pure copper	8.92
1795–1837	5.443		84.000		23.50*	Pure copper	8.92
1837–1857	5.443	0.227	84.000	3.50	23.50*	Pure copper	8.92

* Unofficial data.

LARGE CENTS

Dates	Weight (Grams)	Tolerance	Weight (Grains)	Tolerance	Diameter (mm)	Composition (%)	Specific Gravity
1793–1795	13.478		208.000		28.50*	Pure copper	8.92
1795–1837	10.886		168.000		28.50*	Pure copper	8.92
1837–1857	10.886	0.454	168.000	7.00	28.50*	Pure copper	8.92

* Unofficial data.

SMALL CENTS

Dates	Weight (Grams)	Tolerance	Weight (Grains)	Tolerance	Diameter (mm)	Composition (%)	Specific Gravity
1856–1864	4.666	0.259	72.000	4.00	19.30*	88 copper, 12 nickel	8.92
1864–1873	3.110	0.259	48.000	4.00	19.05	95 copper, 5 zinc and tin	8.84
1873–1942	3.110	0.130	48.000	2.00	19.05	95 copper, 5 zinc and tin	8.84
1943	2.689	0.130	41.500	2.00	19.05	Zinc–platinumated steel	7.80
	2.754		42.500**				
1944–1946	3.110	0.130	48.000	2.00	19.05	95 copper, 5 zinc	8.83
1947–1962	3.110	0.130	48.000	2.00	19.05	95 copper, 5 zinc and tin	8.84
1962–1982	3.110	0.130	48.000	2.00	19.05	95 copper, 5 zinc	8.83
1982 to Date	2.500	0.100	38.581	1.54	19.05	97.5 zinc, 2.5 copper***	7.17

* Unofficial data. ** Cents struck on steel planchets produced in 1942 weigh 41.5 grains. Those struck on planchets produced later in 1943 weigh 42.5 grams. *** Planchet composed of 99.2% zinc and 0.8% copper, plated with pure copper.

TWO-CENT PIECES

Dates	Weight (Grams)	Tolerance	Weight (Grains)	Tolerance	Diameter (mm)	Composition (%)	Specific Gravity
1864–1873	6.221	0.259	96.000	4.00	23.00*	95 copper, 5 zinc and tin	8.84

* Unofficial data.

SILVER THREE-CENT PIECES

Dates	Weight (Grams)	Tolerance	Weight (Grains)	Tolerance	Diameter (mm)	Composition (%)	Specific Gravity
1851–1853	0.802	0.032	12.375	0.50	14.00*	75 silver, 25 copper	10.11
1854–1873	0.746	0.032	11.520	0.50	14.00*	90 silver, 10 copper	10.34

* Unofficial data.

NICKEL THREE-CENT PIECES

Dates	Weight (Grams)	Tolerance	Weight (Grains)	Tolerance	Diameter (mm)	Composition (%)	Specific Gravity
1865–1873	1.944	0.259	30.000	4.00	17.90*	75 copper, 25 nickel	8.92
1873–1889	1.944	0.130	30.000	2.00	17.90*	75 copper, 25 nickel	8.92

* Unofficial data.

COPPER-NICKEL FIVE-CENT PIECES

Dates	Weight (Grams)	Tolerance	Weight (Grains)	Tolerance	Diameter (mm)	Composition (%)	Specific Gravity
1866–1873	5.000	0.130	77.162	2.00	20.50*	75 copper, 25 nickel	8.92
1873–1883	5.000	0.194	77.162	3.00	20.50*	75 copper, 25 nickel	8.92
1883–1942	5.000	0.194	77.162	3.00	21.21	75 copper, 25 nickel	8.92
1942–1945	5.000	0.194	77.162	3.00	21.21	56 copper, 35 silver, 9 manganese	9.25*
1946 to Date	5.000	0.194	77.162	3.00	21.21	75 copper, 25 nickel	8.92

* Unofficial data.

HALF DIMES

Dates	Weight (Grams)	Tolerance	Weight (Grains)	Tolerance	Diameter (mm)	Composition (%)	Specific Gravity
1794–1795	1.348		20.800		16.50*	90 silver, 10 copper	10.34
1795–1805	1.348		20.800		16.50*	89.2427 silver, 10.7572 copper	10.32
1829–1837	1.348		20.800		15.50*	89.2427 silver, 10.7572 copper	10.32
1837–1853	1.336	0.032	20.625	0.50	15.50*	90 silver, 10 copper	10.34
1853–1873	1.244	0.032	19.200	0.50	15.50*	90 silver, 10 copper	10.34

* Unofficial data.

DIMES

Dates	Weight (Grams)	Tolerance	Weight (Grains)	Tolerance	Diameter (mm)	Composition (%)	Specific Gravity
1796–1828	2.696		41.600		18.80*	89.2427 silver, 10.7572 copper	10.32
1828–1837	2.696		41.600		17.90*	89.2427 silver, 10.7572 copper	10.32
1837–1853	2.673	0.032	41.250	0.50	17.90*	90 silver, 10 copper	10.34
1853–1873	2.488	0.032	38.400	0.50	17.90*	90 silver, 10 copper	10.34
1873–1964	2.500	0.097	38.581	1.50	17.91	90 silver, 10 copper	10.34
1965 to Date	2.268	0.091	35.000	1.40	17.91	75 copper, 25 nickel, on pure copper	8.92

* Unofficial data.

TWENTY-CENT PIECES

Dates	Weight (Grams)	Tolerance	Weight (Grains)	Tolerance	Diameter (mm)	Composition (%)	Specific Gravity
1875–1878	5.000	0.097	77.162	1.50	22.50*	90 silver, 10 copper	10.34

* Unofficial data.

QUARTER DOLLARS

Dates	Weight (Grams)	Tolerance	Weight (Grains)	Tolerance	Diameter (mm)	Composition (%)	Specific Gravity
1796–1828	6.739		104.000		27.00*	89.2427 silver, 10.7572 copper	10.32
1831–1837	6.739		104.000		24.26*	89.2427 silver, 10.7572 copper	10.32
1837–1853	6.682	0.065	103.125	1.00	24.26*	90 silver, 10 copper	10.34
1853–1873	6.221	0.065	96.000	1.00	24.26*	90 silver, 10 copper	10.34
1873–1947	6.250	0.097	96.452	1.50	24.26	90 silver, 10 copper	10.34
1947–1964	6.250	0.194	96.452	3.00	24.26	90 silver, 10 copper	10.34
1965 to Date	5.670	0.227	87.500	3.50	24.26	75 copper, 25 nickel, on pure copper	8.92
1976	5.750	0.200	88.736	3.09	24.26	40 silver clad**	9.53

* Unofficial data. ** Layers of .800 silver, .200 copper bonded to a core of .215 silver, .785 copper.

HALF DOLLARS

Dates	Weight (Grams)	Tolerance	Weight (Grains)	Tolerance	Diameter (mm)	Composition (%)	Specific Gravity
1794–1795	13.478		208.000		32.50*	90 silver, 10 copper	10.34
1796–1836	13.478		208.000		32.50*	89.2427 silver, 10.7572 copper	10.32
1836–1853	13.365	0.097	206.250	1.50	30.61*	90 silver, 10 copper	10.34
1853–1873	12.441	0.097	192.000	1.50	30.61*	90 silver, 10 copper	10.34
1873–1947	12.500	0.097	192.904	1.50	30.61	90 silver, 10 copper	10.34
1947–1964	12.500	0.259	192.904	4.00	30.61	90 silver, 10 copper	10.34
1965–1970	11.500	0.400	177.472	6.17	30.61	40 silver clad****	9.53
1971 to Date	11.340	0.454	175.000	7.00	30.61	75 copper, 25 nickel, on pure copper	8.92
1976	11.500	0.400	177.472	6.17	30.61	40 silver clad**	9.53

* Unofficial data. ** Layers of .800 silver, .200 copper bonded to a core of .215 silver, .785 copper.

SILVER AND RELATED DOLLARS

Dates	Weight (Grams)	Tolerance	Weight (Grains)	Tolerance	Diameter (mm)	Composition (%)	Specific Gravity
1794–1795	26.956		416.000		39.50*	90 silver, 10 copper	10.34
1796–1803	26.956		416.000		39.50*	89.2427 silver, 10.7572 copper	10.32
1840–1935	26.730	0.097	412.500	1.50	38.10	90 silver, 10 copper	10.34
1971–1978	22.680	0.907	350.000	14.00	38.10	75 copper, 25 nickel, on pure copper	8.92
1971–1976	24.592	0.984	379.512	15.18	38.10	40 silver clad**	9.53
1979–1999	8.100	0.300	125.000	5.00	26.50	75 copper, 25 nickel, on pure copper	8.92
2000 to Date	5.670	n/a	87.500	n/a	26.50	77 copper, 12 zinc, 7 manganese, 4 nickel, on pure copper	

* Unofficial data. ** Layers of .800 silver, .200 copper bonded to a core of .215 silver, .785 copper.

TRADE DOLLARS

Dates	Weight (Grams)	Tolerance	Weight (Grains)	Tolerance	Diameter (mm)	Composition (%)	Specific Gravity
1873–1883	27.216	0.097	420.000	1.50	38.10	90 silver, 10 copper	10.34

GOLD DOLLARS

Dates	Weight (Grams)	Tolerance	Weight (Grains)	Tolerance	Diameter (mm)	Composition (%)	Specific Gravity
1849–1854	1.672	0.016	25.800	0.25	13.00*	90 gold, 10 copper and silver	17.16
1854–1873	1.672	0.016	25.800	0.25	14.86*	90 gold, 10 copper and silver	17.16
1873–1889	1.672	0.016	25.800	0.25	14.86*	90 gold, 10 copper	17.16

* Unofficial data.

QUARTER EAGLES

Dates	Weight (Grams)	Tolerance	Weight (Grains)	Tolerance	Diameter (mm)	Composition (%)	Specific Gravity
1796–1808	4.374		67.500		20.00*	91.667 gold, 8.333 copper and silver	17.45
1821–1827	4.374		67.500		18.50*	91.667 gold, 8.333 copper and silver	17.45
1829–1834	4.374		67.500		18.20*	91.667 gold, 8.333 copper and silver	17.45
1834–1836	4.180	0.008	64.500	0.13	18.20*	89.225 gold, 10.775 copper and silver	17.14
1837–1839	4.180	0.008	64.500	0.25	18.20*	90 gold, 10 copper and silver	17.16
1840–1873	4.180	0.008	64.500	0.25	17.78*	90 gold, 10 copper and silver	17.16
1873–1929	4.180	0.008	64.500	0.25	17.78*	90 gold, 10 copper	17.16

* Unofficial data.

THREE-DOLLAR GOLD PIECES

Dates	Weight (Grams)	Tolerance	Weight (Grains)	Tolerance	Diameter (mm)	Composition (%)	Specific Gravity
1854–1873	5.015		77.400		20.63*	90 gold, 10 copper and silver	17.16
1873–1889	5.015	0.016	77.400	0.25	20.63*	90 gold, 10 copper	17.16

* Unofficial data.

HALF EAGLES

Dates	Weight (Grams)	Tolerance	Weight (Grains)	Tolerance	Diameter (mm)	Composition (%)	Specific Gravity
1795–1829	8.748		135.000		25.00*	91.667 gold, 8.333 copper and silver	17.45
1829–1834	8.748		135.000		22.50*	91.667 gold, 8.333 copper and silver	17.45
1834–1836	8.359	0.017	129.000	0.26	22.50*	89.225 gold, 10.775 copper and silver	17.14
1837–1840	8.359	0.016	129.000	0.25	22.50*	90 gold, 10 copper and silver	17.16
1840–1849	8.359	0.016	129.000	0.25	21.54*	90 gold, 10 copper and silver	17.16
1849–1873	8.359	0.032	129.000	0.50	21.54*	90 gold, 10 copper and silver	17.16
1873–1929	8.359	0.016	129.000	0.25	21.54*	90 gold, 10 copper	17.16

* Unofficial data.

EAGLES

Dates	Weight (Grams)	Tolerance	Weight (Grains)	Tolerance	Diameter (mm)	Composition (%)	Specific Gravity
1795–1804	17.496		270.000		33.00*	91.667 gold, 8.333 copper and silver	17.45
1838–1849	16.718	0.016	258.000	0.25	27.00*	90 gold, 10 copper and silver	17.16
1849–1873	16.718	0.032	258.000	0.50	27.00*	90 gold, 10 copper and silver	17.16
1873–1933	16.718	0.032	258.000	0.50	27.00*	90 gold, 10 copper	17.16

* Unofficial data.

DOUBLE EAGLES

Dates	Weight (Grams)	Tolerance	Weight (Grains)	Tolerance	Diameter (mm)	Composition (%)	Specific Gravity
1850–1873	33.436	0.032	516.000	0.50	34.29	90 gold, 10 copper and silver	17.16
1873–1933	33.436	0.032	516.000	0.50	34.29	90 gold, 10 copper	17.16

AMERICAN EAGLE BULLION COINS

Denomination	Weight (Grams)	Tolerance	Weight (Grains)	Composition (%)	Weight (Ounces)
$1 one-ounce	31.103	1.00000	40.1	99.9 silver	1.000 silver
$5 tenth-ounce	3.393	0.10910	16.5	91.67 gold, 3.0 silver, 5.33 copper	0.100 gold, 0.003 silver, 0.006 copper
$10 tenth-ounce	3.112	0.10005	16.5	99.95 platinum	0.100 platinum
$10 quarter-ounce	8.483	0.27270	22.0	91.67 gold, 3.0 silver, 5.33 copper	0.250 gold, 0.008 silver, 0.015 copper
$25 quarter-ounce	7.780	0.25010	22.0	99.95 platinum	0.250 platinum
$25 half-ounce	16.966	0.54550	27.0	91.67 gold, 3.0 silver, 5.33 copper	0.500 gold, 0.016 silver, 0.029 copper
$50 half-ounce	15.560	0.50030	27.0	99.95 platinum	0.500 platinum
$50 one-ounce	33.931	1.09100	32.7	91.67 gold, 3.0 silver, 5.33 copper	1.000 gold, 0.033 silver, 0.058 copper
$100 one-ounce	31.120	1.00050	32.7	99.95 platinum	1.000 platinum

THE HOBBY PROTECTION ACT

[Code of Federal Regulations]
[Title 16, Volume 1, Parts 0 to 999]
[Revised as of January 1, 1998]
From the U.S. Government Printing Office via GPO Access
[CITE: 16CFR304]

TITLE 16—COMMERCIAL PRACTICES
CHAPTER I—FEDERAL TRADE COMMISSION

PART 304—RULES AND REGULATIONS UNDER THE HOBBY PROTECTION ACT—Table of Contents

Sec.
304.1 Terms defined.
304.2 General requirement.
304.3 Applicability.
304.4 Application of other law or regulation.
304.5 Marking requirements for imitation political items.
304.6 Marking requirements for imitation numismatic items.

Authority: 15 U.S.C. 2101 et seq.

Source: 40 FR 5496, Feb. 6, 1975, unless otherwise noted.

Sec. 304.1 Terms defined.

(a) Act means the Hobby Protection Act (approved November 29, 1973; Pub. L. 93-167, 87 Stat. 686, (15 U.S.C. 2101 et seq.)).

(b) Commerce has the same meanings as such term has under the Federal Trade Commission Act.

(c) Commission means the Federal Trade Commission.

(d) Imitation numismatic item means an item which purports to be, but in fact is not, an original numismatic item or which is a reproduction, copy, or counterfeit of an original numismatic item. Such term includes an original numismatic item which has been altered or modified in such a manner that it could reasonably purport to be an original numismatic item other than the one which was altered or modified. The term shall not include any re-issue or re-strike of any original numismatic item by the United States or any foreign government.

(e) Imitation political item means an item which purports to be, but in fact is not, an original political item, or which is a reproduction, copy or counterfeit of an original item.

(f) Original numismatic item means anything which has been a part of a coinage or issue which has been used in exchange or has been used to commemorate a person, object, place, or event. Such term includes coins, tokens, paper money, and commemorative medals.

(g) Original political item means any political button, poster, literature, sticker, or any advertisement produced for use in any political cause.

(h) Person means any individual, group, association, partnership, or any other business entity.

(i) Regulations means any or all regulations prescribed by the Federal Trade Commission pursuant to the Act.

(j) United States means the States, the District of Columbia, and the Commonwealth of Puerto Rico.

(k) Diameter of a reproduction means the length of the longest possible straight line connecting two points on the perimeter of the reproduction. [40 FR 5496, Feb. 6, 1975, as amended at 53 FR 38942, Oct. 4, 1988]

Sec. 304.2 General requirement.

Imitation political or numismatic items subject to the Act shall be marked in conformity with the requirements of the Act and the regulations promulgated thereunder. Any violation of these regulations shall constitute a violation of the Act and of the Federal Trade Commission Act.

Sec. 304.3 Applicability.

Any person engaged in the manufacturing, or importation into the United States for introduction into or distribution in commerce, of imitation political or imitation numismatic items shall be subject to the requirements of the Act and the regulations promulgated thereunder.

Sec. 304.4 Application of other law or regulation.

The provisions of these regulations are in addition to, and not in substitution for or limitation of, the provisions of any other law or regulation of the United States (including the existing statutes and regulations prohibiting the reproduction of genuine currency) or of the law or regulation of any State.

Sec. 304.5 Marking requirements for imitation political items.

(a) An imitation political item which is manufactured in the United States, or imported into the United States for introduction into or distribution in commerce, shall be plainly and permanently marked with the calendar year in which such item was manufactured.

(b) The calendar year shall be marked upon the item legibly, conspicuously and nondeceptively, and in accordance with the further requirements of these regulations.

(1) The calendar year shall appear in arabic numerals, shall be based upon the Gregorian calendar and shall consist of four digits.

(2) The calendar year shall be marked on either the obverse or the reverse surface of the item. It shall not be marked on the edge of the item.

(3) An imitation political item of incusable material shall be incused with the calendar year in sans-serif numerals. Each numeral shall have a vertical dimension of not less than two millimeters (2.0 mm) and a minimum depth of three-tenths of one millimeter (0.3 mm) or one-half (1/2) the thickness of the reproduction, whichever is the lesser. The minimum total horizontal dimension for the four numerals composing the calendar year shall be six millimeters (6.0 mm).

(4) An imitation political button, poster, literature, sticker, or advertisement composed of nonincusable material shall be imprinted with the calendar year in sans-serif numerals. Each numeral shall have a vertical dimension of not less than two millimeters (2.0 mm). The minimum total horizontal dimension of the four numerals composing the calendar year shall be six millimeters (6.0 mm).

Sec. 304.6 Marking requirements for imitation numismatic items.

(a) An imitation numismatic item which is manufactured in the United States, or imported into the United States for introduction into or distribution in commerce, shall be plainly and permanently marked "COPY".

(b) The word "COPY" shall be marked upon the item legibly, conspicuously, and nondeceptively, and in accordance with the further requirements of these regulations.

(1) The word "COPY" shall appear in capital letters, in the English language.

(2) The word "COPY" shall be marked on either the obverse or the reverse surface of the item. It shall not be marked on the edge of the item.

[40 FR 5496, Feb. 6, 1975, as amended at 53 FR 38942, Oct. 4, 1988]

ADVICE FOR AVOIDING COUNTERFEIT COINS

Coin collectors occasionally find counterfeit coins, or coins that have been altered or changed so that they appear to be something other than what they really are. Any coin that does not seem to fit the description of similar pieces listed in this guide book should be looked upon with suspicion. Experienced coin dealers can usually tell quickly whether a coin is genuine, and an ethical dealer would never knowingly sell spurious coins to a collector. Coins found in circulation or bought from a nonprofessional source should be examined carefully.

The risk of purchasing a spurious coin can be minimized through the use of common sense and an elementary knowledge of the techniques used by counterfeiters. It is well to keep in mind that the more popular a coin is among collectors and the public, the more likely it is that counterfeits and replicas will abound. Until recently, collector coins valued at under $100 were rarely replicated because of the high cost of making such items. The same was true of counterfeits made to deceive the public. Few counterfeit coins were made because it was more profitable for the fakers to print paper money. Today, however, counterfeiters in Asia and elsewhere create fakes of a surprising variety of coins, most notably silver dollar types, but also smaller denominations and gold.

Different Types

Replicas

Reproductions of famous and historical coins have been distributed for decades by marketing firms and souvenir vendors. These pieces are often tucked away by the original recipients as curios, and later are found in old furniture by others who believe they have discovered objects of great value. Most replicas are poorly made by the casting method, and are virtually worthless. They can sometimes be identified by a seam that runs around the edge of the piece where the two halves of the casting mold were joined together. Genuine specimens of extremely rare or valuable coins are almost never found in unlikely places.

Counterfeits

For many centuries, counterfeiters have produced base-metal forgeries of gold and silver coins to deceive the public in the normal course of trade. These pieces are usually crudely made and easily detected on close examination. Crudely cast counterfeit copies of older coins are the most prevalent. These can usually be detected by the casting bubbles or pimples that can be seen with low-power magnification. Pieces struck from handmade dies are more deceptive, but the engravings do not match those of genuine Mint products.

More recently, as coin collecting has gained popularity and rare coin prices have risen, "numismatic" counterfeits have become more common. The majority of these are die-struck gold coin counterfeits that have been mass produced overseas since 1950. Forgeries exist of most U.S. gold coins dated between 1870 and 1933, as well as all issues of the gold dollar and three-dollar gold piece. Most of these are very well made, as they were intended to pass the close scrutiny of collectors. Fewer gold coins of earlier dates have been counterfeited, but false 1799 ten-dollar gold pieces and 1811 five-dollar coins have been made. Gold coins in less than Extremely Fine condition are seldom counterfeited.

Silver dollars dated 1804, Lafayette dollars, several of the low-mintage commemorative half dollars, and the 1795 half dimes have been forged in quantity. Minor-coin forgeries made in recent years are the 1909-S V.D.B., 1914-D and 1955 doubled-die Lincoln cents, 1877 Indian Head cents, 1856 Flying Eagle cents, and, on a much smaller scale, a variety of dates of half cents and large cents. 19th-century copies of colonial coins are also sometimes encountered.

ALTERATIONS

Coins are occasionally altered by the addition, removal, or change of a design feature (such as a mint-mark or date digit) or by the polishing, sandblasting, acid etching, toning, or plating of the surface of a genuine piece. Changes of this sort are usually done to deceive collectors. Among U.S. gold coins, only the 1927-D double eagle is commonly found with an added mintmark. On $2.50 and $5 gold coins, 1839 through 1856, New Orleans O mintmarks have been altered to C (for Charlotte, North Carolina) in a few instances.

Over a century ago, five-dollar gold pieces were imitated by gold plating 1883 Liberty Head five-cent coins without the word CENTS on the reverse. Other coins commonly created fraudulently through alteration include the 1799 large cent and the 1909-S, 1909-S V.D.B., 1914-D, 1922 "plain," and 1943 "copper" cents. The 1913 Liberty Head nickel has been extensively replicated by alteration of 1903 and 1912 nickels. Scarce, high-grade Denver and San Francisco Buffalo nickels of the 1920s; 1916-D and 1942 Over 1941 dimes; 1918 Over 1917-S quarters; 1932-D and -S quarters; and 1804 silver dollars have all been made by the alteration of genuine coins of other dates or mints.

DETECTION

The best way to detect counterfeit coins is to compare suspected pieces with others of the same issue. Carefully check size, color, luster, weight, edge devices, and design details. Replicas generally have less detail than their genuine counterparts when studied under magnification. Modern struck counterfeits made to deceive collectors are an exception to this rule. Any questionable gold coin should be referred to an expert for verification.

Cast forgeries are usually poorly made and of incorrect weight. Base metal is often used in place of gold or silver, and the coins are lightweight and often incorrect in color and luster. Deceptive cast pieces have been made using real metal content and modern dental techniques, but these too usually vary in quality and color.

Detection of alterations sometimes involves comparative examination of the suspected areas of a coin (usually mintmarks and date digits) at magnification ranging from 10x to 40x.

Coins of exceptional rarity or value should never be purchased without a written guarantee of authenticity. Professional authentication of rare coins for a fee is available with the services offered by commercial grading services, and by some coin dealers.

In the *United States Gold Counterfeit Detection Guide*, author Bill Fivaz writes, "A surprisingly large number of the United States gold pieces currently on the market are counterfeit. . . . Many of these counterfeit pieces have been produced overseas, and they usually contain gold of the proper weight and fineness." Fivaz offers several rules of thumb for identifying counterfeit gold coins, some of which are summarized here:

Weak, fat, mushy letters and devices. These often reveal a coin to be counterfeit. Authentic pieces should be sharp and crisp.

Weak, fat letters on a counterfeit quarter eagle.

Repeating depressions. A depression that appears in the same place (often the fields) on several coins of the same series/date/mintmark likely is the result of contact marks that were on a genuine coin used to create a counterfeit die. "These should always be suspect," writes Fivaz, "especially when they are of the same texture as the rest of the field and have soft, rounded edges."

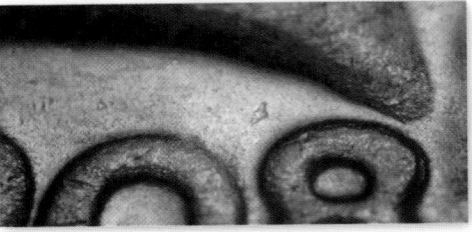

Depression on a counterfeit gold eagle.

Tool marks. Many counterfeit Indian Head quarter eagles and half eagles have worm-like, raised tooling marks—often at the back of the Indian's neck or above the necklace. These come from the counterfeiter's attempts to finesse a false die.

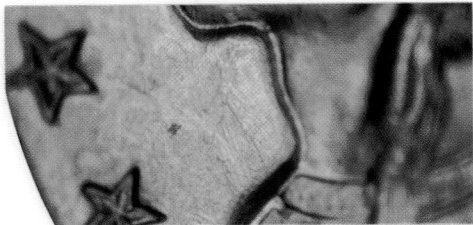

Tool marks on a counterfeit Indian Head quarter eagle.

Spikes. "In most cases," writes Fivaz, "these tool marks running from the dentils on a coin are a good indication that it is not a genuine piece. However, this characteristic should not be used exclusively."

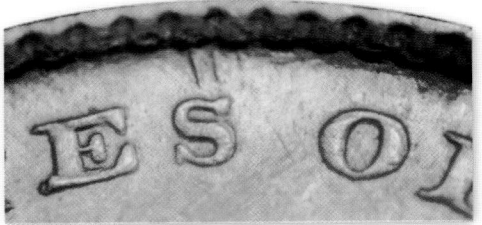

Spikes on a counterfeit gold coin.

Sunken letters or numbers. If the centers of a coin's letters or numbers appear to be depressed or concave, it is probably a counterfeit. Counterfeit 1811 Capped Bust half eagles are commonly found with this diagnostic.

**Sunken date numerals on a
counterfeit Capped Bust half eagle.**

Irregular edge. Irregular, uneven, or coarse reeding can reveal a coin to be a counterfeit. Also, test marks on the edge can be a tipoff, indicating that someone else, in the past, questioned the coin's authenticity.

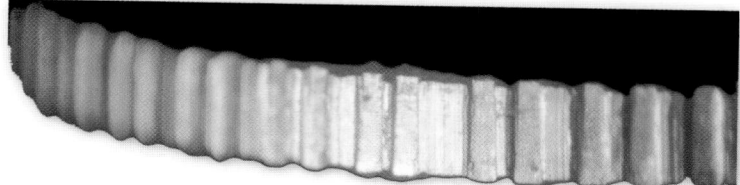

Irregular reeding on a counterfeit gold dollar.

Bubbles. Surface bubbles are the telltale sign of a cast counterfeit. Typically also the details will be very weak and ill-defined, and the color incorrect.

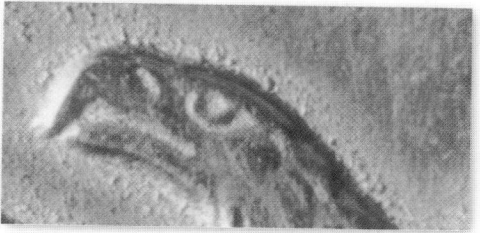

Bubbles on a counterfeit quarter eagle.

Color. Experienced collectors and gold-specialist dealers can usually tell, even at arm's length, if a coin is of the proper color for its date and mint. For example, branch-mint gold coins struck in Dahlonega and New Orleans often have a greenish hue, while those made in Charlotte usually have a reddish color.

"Spinning." Fivaz notes that some counterfeit Indian Head half eagles may "spin" when placed flat on a hard surface, due to one side being cup-shaped.

Mintmark. It is estimated that nearly 90% of counterfeit Liberty Head gold coins are Philadelphia fakes (with no mintmark).

It is essential to study as many authentic coins as possible in the series you wish to collect. Examine slabbed coins and note the crispness of their letters, numbers, and devices, their color and luster, and their surface qualities. Education is crucial to wise collecting and investing. The American Numismatic Association offers a Counterfeit Detection Course at its annual Summer Seminar, as well as other educational opportunities at its shows. Hobby periodicals report on counterfeit coins, as well. The more you learn, the better equipped you will be to identify fraudulent coins that are less than they seem.

APPENDIX H

Treasures Between the Pages

This appreciation of numismatic literature is taken from
Ken Bressett's foreword of **Lost and Found Coin Hoards and Treasures.**

Do not think of this as simply another book with stories about coins to be added to your shelf for future reference. It is far more than that. This, you will learn, is more like a gateway to the study and appreciation of the legacy of numismatic history. The data herein will transport you to places and times that are the genesis of the treasures we now hold in our collections, enhancing our appreciation of them. That is what a proper book should do for the reader. That is why books are of such critical importance to the understanding and enjoying of our hobby.

President Thomas Jefferson, in a letter to John Adams in 1815, said, "I cannot live without books; but fewer will suffice where amusement, and not use, is the only future object." He was right on target then, and his words still resonate with truth. Books on any subject are meant to be used as well as enjoyed. Jefferson's library at one time contained over 6,500 volumes that were acquired over a 50 year period of careful selection. They included works on such diverse subjects as history, mathematics, sciences, ethics, law, politics, religion, literature, and fine arts. He drew his ideas, inspiration, knowledge, and pleasure from the information found in his books, and he commented on how he turned to reading as a welcome escape from the daily tedium of business affairs.

Not everyone can hope to build a library such as Jefferson's, but fortunately for us today we have public lending libraries and a number of new resources like the Internet, where almost unlimited information can be had at the touch of a button. Those of us who have targeted interests, such as numismatics, have been blessed with a plethora of fine literature on nearly every phase of the hobby. Yet if those books are not being used, we are missing out on the very essence of why so many people enjoy the beauty and allure of coins.

When I contemplated writing this, I first took a book from my shelf for inspiration. It was no special book, just the first one that caught my eye. It wasn't until much later, and with four other books by my side, that I went back to my mission. I had been drawn away by jumping from one book to another while exploring coin after coin in a quest to learn more about a subject that I had not taken time to fully investigate in the past. For over an hour I was once again totally absorbed in my favorite pastime. All cares of the world or other distractions were completely overlooked. It was book time: a time to regenerate enthusiasm and slake my thirst for appreciating the beauty and lore of numismatics.

Yes, I am a bibliophile. That is to say, someone who loves books. A bibliophile may be, but is not necessarily, a book collector. The classic bibliophile is one who loves to read, admire, and collect books, quite often to the point of amassing a large and specialized collection. And I am not alone. According to Arthur Minters, "the private collecting of books was a fashion indulged in even by many ancient Romans, including Cicero and Atticus."

Over the years several people have asked me to name my favorite numismatic book. When I glance about my shelves with thousands of volumes I find it nearly impossible to single out just one, but when pressed on the issue I usually name *Coins of the World* by R.A.G. Carson. It is probably the book most often referred to by me for guidance and inspiration. It is not some weighty tome full of dry statistics; not a colorful picture book; not a list of prices. This is another 'gateway' book that leads me down numerous pathways to savor and explore the fascinating history of coins and money from the most ancient to the present.

Now, you may find it odd that I did not mention a more ubiquitous book or something closer to my heart like *A Guide Book of United States Coins.* Many have used this as their introduction to the world of coins and have found it to be a bountiful source of useful information on their nation's money from beginning to present. Yes, I too use it often, but I never forget the lesson projected in the Spanish milled dollar that has always been shown at the beginning of the "Introduction to United States Coins" in the regular edition. In case you have never thought about it, check the motto on those Spanish pillars. It says PLUS ULTRA, which means *more beyond*. The words apply to more than just the Spanish Empire at that time, or even our own country's coinage that grew from those beginnings. It is an inspiration to go beyond the world of information in this book—and all others.

The obverse of a Spanish milled dollar, whose columns are inscribed PLUS ULTRA.

No collector can fully appreciate his coins without learning all there is to know about them. While my personal library is large, I haven't read them all—at least not cover-to-cover. That is because many are references that are used only when I need to look something up for verification or additional information. I do, however, have a pretty good working knowledge of what is in each of them and where to find them. There are also a few that I read and reread for pure entertainment. *Lost and Found Coin Hoards and Treasures*, by Q. David Bowers, is one of those kinds of books that will never grow old. One that you will use over and over again and still find it a passage to extended or forgotten adventures.

As Sara Nelson says in *So Many Books, So Little Time*, "Reading's ability to beam you up to a different world is a good part of the reason why people like me do it in the first place—because dollar for dollar, hour per hour, it's the most expedient way to get from our proscribed little 'here' to an imagined, intriguing there."

The value of numismatic reference books cannot be overstated if one desires to fully enjoy the hobby or engage in any activity related to understanding, buying, selling, or simply knowing the history of these tiny objects of art, beauty, and commercial necessity. Choose your topic, field of interest, or the coins that you like best. There are numerous books on just about every subject from the most ancient beginnings of commerce to the most recent developments in special designs and finishes on coins from nations around the globe.

Helen E. Haines is quoted as saying: "From every book invisible threads reach out to other books; and as the mind comes to use and control those threads the whole panorama of the world's life, past and present, becomes constantly more varied and interesting, while at the same time the mind's own powers of reflection and judgment are exercised and strengthened."

Author Q. David Bowers and I have occasionally discussed and contemplated the growing trend toward e-book publications and their merits. The advancement of available information presented this way should be admired and appreciated by all. Yet there is always the question of whether electronic publications will ever replace the printed book. Neither of us can imagine that ever happening. How can anything surpass the look, feel, or smell of a freshly printed book; or the anticipation of opening it and seeing for the first time a new adventure nearby? Who would give up the pleasure of nodding off while reading, only to awake with book in hand and reread those last couple of paragraphs? Will there ever be a society without books? Of course not. I imagine that three thousand years ago, when writing was first invented and inscribed on clay tablets, some wag must have wondered if speaking would someday go out of style.

There has never been a time when so many numismatic references have been available to collectors and students. They seem to appear almost weekly, covering topics never before explored in depth in the past. The quality and quantity of new publications is astounding. To quote Toni Morrison, "If there's a book you really want to read but it hasn't been written yet, then you must write it"; and this seems to have been taken to heart now that it is quite possible through the advent of self-publishing.

Thomas Jefferson spent his life surrounded by books. For him, books were "a necessary of life." We should all take inspiration from him to respect, use, and enjoy the vast world of books that are available to all through libraries like that of the American Numismatic Society, the free lending library of the American Numismatic Association, and the many publications that are now available online and without charge.

As the noted author Heinrich Mann wrote, "A house without books is like a room without windows." Let this book now be a window to your world of numismatics and an inspiration to explore all the avenues it will open for you.

Ken Bressett, 2014
Colorado Springs, Colorado

Kenneth Bressett has actively promoted the study and hobby of numismatics for over 50 years. His published works on the subject cover a wide range of topics and extend from short articles to standard reference books on such diverse areas as ancient coins, paper money, and British and U.S. coins.

Throughout his career he has worked as an author, editor, and publisher of books and products for coin collectors. He has also taught the subject of numismatics to hundreds of students through courses at Colorado College and other locations.

APPENDIX I

Dynamics of the Rare-Coin Market

The science of coins and medals is as old as antiquity itself. There is probably no other branch of collecting so ancient and honorable, or that has received the attention of the students of all ages, as that of coin collecting. . . . If there are "sermons in stones," etc., what eloquence and learning must be stored up in these bits of metal? If they could only talk, what strange stories would they tell?

—Dr. Geo. F. Heath, November 1889

This essay is adapted from chapter 3 of Q. David Bowers's
Expert's Guide to Collecting and Investing in Rare Coins.

MEASURING THE MARKET

COUNTING THE PARTICIPANTS

What is the nature of the rare-coin market today? How many people are involved? How many of them are casual collectors? How many are serious? How many dealers are there? Precise figures are elusive. In April 1986, *The Numismatist* carried this:

> On the average, Americans have nearly a thousand pennies around their homes, according to the latest Epcot Poll, a special survey conducted by Walt Disney World on behalf of the United States Mint. The poll revealed that of approximately 12,000 visitors to the popular Florida attraction, 33% of adults and nearly 50% of children collect coins in general. More than 33% of adults reported having more than $10 worth of pennies at home; 50% of adults use pennies daily; and 40% of adults and 60% of children save pennies. Of all U.S. coins, quarter dollars are most used and half dollars are least used.
>
> Regarding coin collecting among adults, 21% said they collect as a hobby, 12% as an investment; of the juniors surveyed, 27% collect as a hobby, 19% as an investment. The Epcot Poll is a daily activity at Epcot's Center's Electronic Forum and is conducted in association with the market research firm of ASK Associates, Inc. The January 14–February 10 coin survey sampled 10,532 U.S. adults and 1,462 youngsters.

While visitors to Walt Disney World no doubt have more disposable income than do 12,000 people selected at random from all across the American population, these figures are nonetheless impressive.

Jay Johnson, who served as director of the Mint at the turn of the 21st century, including when the Sacagawea "golden dollars" were making news headlines, said in the year 2000 that 130,000,000 people collected coins. This number included citizens who might casually save a newly minted 1999 quarter of the Delaware motif with horse and rider on the reverse, or the 2000 New Hampshire quarter with the

Old Man of the Mountain and the motto "Live Free or Die," as well as those who might set aside one of the Sacagawea dollars. Billions of Kennedy half dollars have been struck in our generation, and yet I can go shopping for a year without receiving one in change. Where have they all gone? Probably to some of those 130 million collectors.

Coins are interesting to just about everyone. Time was when Mint directors stayed in their office in Washington, D.C. That changed in the 1960s when Director Eva Adams became a frequently seen figure at coin conventions and was even a participant in skits put on by the Numismatic Literary Guild. Her successors have followed suit, and recently retired Director Henrietta Holsman Fore was a much appreciated visitor to coin shows and other events, always willing to listen to collectors and to share ideas.

According to Beth Deisher, at the time editor of *Coin World*, in 2002 the total paid circulation for the seven major national numismatic periodicals (*Coin World*; *COINage*; *Coins*; *Coin Prices*; *Numismatic News*; *World Coin News*; and *The Numismatist*) was just under 250,000. She extrapolated, taking into account such factors as duplication (one person subscribing to multiple periodicals) and pass-along (subscribers sharing their periodicals with friends) to arrive at a "coin hobby core" of about 445,000 people who read these publications on a regular basis. "Radiating out from the core are probably two to three times as many people who spend serious time and money on coins, but who for whatever reason do not obtain information regularly from hobby publications. Many, based on the activity we see on the Internet and cable television, are no doubt depending on the electronic world for information." This would suggest a population, at that time, of about 1.3 to 1.8 million serious collectors.

Figures can be bandied about with reckless abandon, and in the everyday news there is no lack of charts, tallies, estimates, surveys, and the like, relating to business, political favorites, consumer preferences, and more. However, as one wag said, 37% of all estimates are just made up!

Anyway, the numismatic numbers mentioned here are a combination of my guesses and those of people I have consulted.

At the California State Fair some time ago, Dwight Manley and others in the California Gold Marketing Group set up the "Ship of Gold" exhibit for the public to see, and an estimated 700,000 people came to appreciate and to gawk and wonder at the gold coins and ingots on display—all found in the wreck of the SS *Central America* lost at sea on September 12, 1857. My own involvement in this exhibit will forever remain one of my fondest memories. Still, it might not be correct to say that all 700,000 people who spent time seeing these coins had a numismatic interest or were potential collectors.

More recently, at the Tucson Gem and Mineral Show (an annual event that draws worldwide attendance), thousands of people waited in line over a period of several days to view the treasures. For the first time in this event's 50-year history, crowd-control procedures had to be put in place—not necessary at earlier shows, even when the Hope Diamond and Fabergé eggs were featured! How many viewers became numismatists?

What about the 1,500,000 people who waited their turn at the Smithsonian Institution a generation ago to view the gem coins of the Eliasberg Collection? How many were collectors then? How many became numismatists after they were inspired by the exhibit? Or the thousands of Americans who scrambled to line up and buy the 2014 National Baseball Hall of Fame commemoratives, and the 2014 gold Kennedy half dollar—were they simply looking to grab the latest headline-making coins, with no deeper interest in the hobby? Or will some of them branch out into Buffalo nickels and Morgan dollars?

A CLOSER VIEW

Narrowing the focus somewhat, there have been upward of 2,000,000 buyers on the U.S. Mint mailing list in recent years. Such people have laid out their hard-earned dollars to acquire Proof sets, commemoratives, and other modern Mint products.

It is likely that many hobbyists have walked into local or regional coin shows publicized in newspapers, radio, and television, and, perhaps, have bought a coin or two, perhaps an old silver dollar or a Proof set from the year they were born, but may never buy anything else.

This happens even with truly rare coins. In the 1970s, a Chicago resident read something I wrote about the famous 1894-S Barber dime, of which only 24 were struck and of which fewer than a dozen are known today. He simply had to have one, never mind that it cost the best part of $100,000. This became the only coin in his "collection." In another instance, a couple years ago a real-estate broker saw me on one of the documentaries about the SS *Central America* treasure (produced for the History Channel, or perhaps it was the Discovery Channel or a network news feature)—the finding of the coins attracted wide attention and was widely covered by most networks. He determined that owning a brilliant Mint State 1857-S double eagle, one of about 5,400 such coins found in the shipwreck, would be very satisfying. He bought one, at which time I mentioned that he might enjoy the magazines and catalogs that would be coming his way from our company. At that point he said that he was not a coin collector and did not intend to become one, and that this single coin was all he wanted. I suppose that it is fair to include the buyer of the 1894-S dime and also the owner of the 1857-S $20 as part of the community of collectors, whether they want to be or not.

On the other end of the scale, I read of a tavern-keeper who found Buffalo nickels (minted 1913 to 1938) to be interesting. In the 1940s and 1950s many were still in circulation. Each time he took one in payment he tossed it behind the back bar, eventually "collecting" thousands of them. I suppose he was a collector, too.

Although not all active collectors buy a copy of *A Guide Book of United States Coins* every year, and some who do buy the book are not collectors at all, it is worth noting that today this is among the best-selling American nonfiction titles of all time. In one record year more than a million copies were sold!

Putting all of this together, it may be fair to estimate that at least 2,000,000 people in the United States are interested enough to buy an occasional book on the subject, or to order coins now and then from the U.S. Mint—in other words, to pay a premium for coins and information, or to seriously and systematically extract interesting pieces from circulation.

CORE COLLECTORS

Narrowing the focus a bit further, I estimate that upward of 250,000 people subscribe to one or another of the numismatic publications (*Coin World, Numismatic News, COINage, Coins* magazine, the *Coin Dealer Newsletter*, etc.), belong to coin clubs, are customers of established rare-coin dealers, and attend local, regional, and national coin shows at least on an occasional basis, buying from several to many old coins (opposed to modern Mint products) for their collections. Actually, as the annual sales of the *Guide Book* are considerably higher than 250,000, I believe that there are 250,000 to 500,000 core collectors.

Offhand, one might think that just about every truly serious advanced collector belongs to the American Numismatic Association (membership currently around 28,000), but this is not the case. When I was president of the ANA (1983 to 1985), I occasionally gave talks to various clubs. Once in New Britain, Connecticut, I met with a very active group, a roomful of enthusiasts, and asked a few questions. Seeking a show of hands to see how many belonged to the ANA, I found that, of the more than 100 people present, fewer than 10 indicated their membership. Then I asked how many people subscribed to *Coin World*, saw perhaps a couple dozen hands, then to *Numismatic News*, and saw about 10 or so. I then asked how many people subscribed to both *Coin World* and *Numismatic News* and scarcely any collectors indicated they doubled up.

In 2004, at the ANA's summer convention (usually the biggest coin show of the year), nearly 14,000 people registered, including more than 1,000 dealers and their assistants who staffed more than 500 tables, plus many dealers who did not set up. Perhaps the count was about 2,000 to 3,000 dealers plus

11,000 to 12,000 collectors and potential collectors. Among these visitors were many with just a casual interest, or with no interest at all yet, but eager to learn (such as a troop of Boy Scouts I saw come into the room). Others came armed with checking-account balances sufficient to buy Proof double eagles or high-grade colonial coins, among other notable rarities.

The Professional Numismatists Guild (PNG) has about 300 members, these generally representing the larger-volume dealers in *rare* coins. There are other important dealers who do not belong to the PNG for one reason or another, or who have never applied, including quite a few leading specialists in numismatic items other than coins—such as tokens, medals, paper money, and books. At a regional coin show I saw more than 50 dealers set up, and only one belonged to the PNG. A few years ago Chet Krause, founder of *Numismatic News*, told me it was his estimate that there were 6,000 rare-coin dealers in the United States, many of them dealing on a casual or part-time basis.

By the way, I like to think of numismatics as a hobby, a pleasant pastime, and rare-coin dealing as a combined art and profession. However, quite a few in the field insist on calling it an *industry*, probably because *hobby* sounds casual, and *industry* sounds like a big deal. Perhaps one of these days, neurologists and sculptors will want to call themselves industrialists. Who knows?

SMALL NUMBERS THAT COUNT!

Cutting to an even tighter number, how many people actually registered to bid on two of the most valuable rare coins ever auctioned? Consider the finest-known 1804 silver dollar (of which 15 exist, some in museums), which I cataloged for the Childs family and auctioned in 1999 for more than $4 million. Then there's the 1933 double eagle cataloged by David E. Tripp and sold by Sotheby's and Stack's in the summer of 2002 for $7.6 million. In each instance, about a dozen people were registered and had their credit approved to bid into the millions. At both events there were many others who attended and simply watched—adding to the excitement.

For these two rarities it did not matter whether there were 130,000,000 collectors in America (Mint director Johnson's earlier quoted estimate), or 500,000 advanced or serious collectors, or any other number. All it took in each instance was *two* people who desired the coin and were able to pay the price!

This reminds me of a sale we held back in 1974 of the Stanislas Herstal Collection, the finest offering of coins of Poland to cross the auction block in many years. The cataloging was done by Karl Stephens (who later went on to conduct his own business), and it fell to me to write some of the background and introduction as well as the publicity and advertising. In the same catalog, many superb U.S. coins from other consignors were also featured.

The American coins did very well and played to a full house of enthusiastic bidders. Lots of excitement, many bidder hands in the air, many different buyers. Then came the Herstal Collection part of the sale, and the gallery emptied. Only a handful of bidders remained! *Woe is me*, I thought. Bravely, I carried on with feigned enthusiasm.

The auctioneer began to cry out the numbers from the podium. Immediately, all bets were off, presale estimates became meaningless, and excitement prevailed! The several active bidders, scattered here and there in the otherwise vacant room, must have been the world's most enthusiastic buyers of Polish coins, long starving for such an opportunity. When the dust settled, the entire collection brought nearly *five times* what we had anticipated!

Not long ago, American Numismatic Rarities and Stack's conducted a joint auction at the MidAmerica Coin Expo in Chicago, via shared space in the same catalog (in addition, Stack's had a separate catalog for the Ford Collection items). Staffers from both organizations worked very hard for several days, and each company did very well. When all was over we all enjoyed a memorable dinner at Carlucci's Restaurant nearby.

We had every good reason to celebrate, as many records had been set. However, one part of the event was rather lightly attended—the offering of Hard Times tokens (privately issued in the 1830s and early 1840s) formed over a long period of time by John J. Ford Jr. At the time such tokens were a rather arcane specialty, and not many people knew about them at all (for today's hobby community it's a different scenario). However, despite the empty chairs, at that part of the sale, tokens expected to bring $1,000 often sold for several times that figure, and more than a million dollars was realized! It was a replay of the Herstal Collection scenario—large numbers of bidders are not nearly as important as a small group of really serious buyers.

COLLECTING QUIETLY

After becoming involved in the hobby, many if not most serious collectors concentrate on doing business with just one or two dealers. Although some numismatists are gregarious, attend conventions and auctions, and enjoy socializing, others do not.

I recall a father-and-son team who bought coins from me for a long time, then in 1965 auctioned them under the name of the Century Collection. They tapped me and Jim Ruddy (my partner at that time) to be their eyes and ears, and, so far as I know, never attended a coin show or auction in person. They did read extensively and had a library with all of the basics. However, from a distance they were very active bidders at most of the important auctions of the era. For example, in the March 1961 sale of the Edwin M. Hydeman Collection, conducted by Abe Kosoff, I bought for them the 1894-S dime, paying $29,000. Today, the same coin would be worth in the $1,000,000 to $1,500,000 range, but a few years earlier, in 1957, I had bought another one for just $5,750. (It is tempting to pause and just talk about prices, but I will continue on track.) I believe my company was the sole supplier of rare coins to this father-and-son team's marvelous collection.

This desire for remaining in the background reminds me of another incident. On December 10, 1960, at Stack's, the Fairbanks Collection crossed the block. Lot 576 was a nice example of the rare 1804 silver dollar, and presale estimates suggested it would bring $15,000 to $20,000. Ambassador R. Henry Norweb accompanied me to the sale, having instructed me to bid on his behalf to and beyond $25,000, as he wanted to purchase it as a birthday present for his wife, Emery May, one of the most dedicated collectors of all time. The ambassador wanted to remain anonymous. And he did. From the back of the room he watched as I bid the coin up to close to $30,000, then yielded to a representative of Samuel Wolfson, who later told me he would have paid *any* price to get it.

Buying items through trusted dealers is a common practice in other areas of pursuit. My fine friend since childhood, Ken Rendell, was given the commission to build a personal library of historical and literary volumes for Bill Gates, founder of Microsoft. Gates commissioned Rendell alone to accomplish this, as he was assured of expertise, good coverage of the market, and a wide selection of opportunities.

COUNTING THE MONEY

In contemplating the dynamics of the rare-coin market, there is no public accounting required of dealers, auctioneers, and others involved. We do know that the U.S. Mint has sold hundreds of millions of dollars' worth of Proof coins, commemoratives, sets, bullion Eagles, and other coins in recent years. However, beyond that, much is conjecture. No statistics are kept by collectors' or dealers' organizations (or by any government agency) on their activities.

Coin sales can be divided into auctions and outright sales, the latter being wholesale or retail.

In the auction area, ranging from important collections and rarities offered by a half dozen or so leading firms, to everyday action on eBay and elsewhere, sales run well over $1 billion annually. Factor in the many coins sold by dealers, coin offerings on television, telemarketing firms, dealers in bulk gold coins for investment, and others, and that figure probably extends into multiple billions of dollars. To this can be added the yearly sales of current coins by the Mint. Some years have higher volume than do others, but these sales estimates are probably on target as an average.

In the rare-coin market there is no dealer monopoly or oligopoly, no cartel. Prices float freely depending upon supply and demand. The business is conducted by dealers who began business yesterday along with people who have been in the profession for decades.

While there are numerous large companies, particularly in the auction and investment sales fields, there are also many one-person and modest-size operations that enjoy excellent business and fine reputations. At a recent convention I had nice conversations with Tony Terranova, Julian Leidman, and Ken Goldman, each individual proprietors. These professionals have done a large amount of business with me for a long time, and with good results for all concerned. I rather imagine that if I were to ask Tony, Julian, or Ken if they would like to add a staff of a dozen people to help them, they would say no. They like it the way it is. On the other hand, David M. Sundman, a personal friend for a long time, is the main owner of Littleton Coin Company, which employs more than 300 people and conducts business from a 65,000-square-foot building—the largest such operation in the world. Littleton's trade is mainly in lower-value coins and supplies, just as important to the market as are the activities of, for example, Laura Sperber, who recently sold a 1913 Liberty Head nickel for well over a million dollars.

A review of the roster of the PNG will quickly confirm this. The majority of members are on their own or work with just a small staff. Such dealers go about their business quietly and add to the overall sales numbers of the numismatic field, but the extent of their activity cannot be measured.

In addition to established professionals, there are many part-timers in that group of 6,000 dealers estimated by Chet Krause. Once, I received a letter from a seller whose stationery included the notation "A.F.D." after his name. I asked what this meant, and the explanation was "After-Five Dealer." When he returned home from work at five in the afternoon, he then started selling coins to mail-order customers!

Many dealers specialize in a narrow area, such as tokens, Morgan silver dollars, or modern Proof coins with frosted cameo contrast. Other dealers reach out to the investment community, attend "hard money" seminars and the like, and reach those who enjoy owning gold and silver (the two most popular metals), but do not want to become numismatists. Still others sell modern coin books and supplies, while some deal only in out-of-print numismatic literature.

While most rare-coin dealers concentrate on numismatics, either generally or in a specialty, some art auction houses such as Christie's and Sotheby's occasionally sell coins and paper money. Some other firms, well known in numismatics, also sell sports memorabilia, posters, autographs, comic books, and the like.

INVESTMENT MONEY

Every so often there is a big influx of investment money into numismatics, as in 1988 and 1989 when many Wall Streeters decided buying coins instead of stocks was a great thing to do. Several brokerage firms, including Merrill Lynch and Kidder Peabody, got into the act. A big hoopla resulted, "Wall Street money" poured into the hobby, and prices of so-called investment-grade coins (being mostly silver and gold in grades of MS-65 and higher, and in certified holders) skyrocketed. Limited partnerships and rare-coin funds were set up and took in millions of dollars. The bubble burst. After a while most investors disappeared, headed for greener pastures, perhaps including the dot-com stocks that were all the rage in the 1990s—until they too crashed, in 2000.

I can only speculate, but coin-market sales rose to perhaps $1 billion or more during the Wall Street fever. When the newcomers exited, prices of certain "investment-quality" coins plummeted, but the rest of the market—comprising the majority of trading activity—did just fine.

Perhaps coin-market sales figures, not knowable, are not as important as the knowledge that year after year, decade after decade, many people have enjoyed the hobby of coin collecting. Today, it is a well-established field, with many buyers and sellers, ample available information, and a good track record of long-term price performance.

NEWCOMERS AND OLD-TIMERS

THE COIN BUG

As to the length of time the typical collector remains involved with the hobby, I asked several dealers and publishers about this, and three years was about average. This is for someone who comes in, discovers coins, becomes serious about the hobby, buys intensely, then runs out of money, or interest, or both. The late R.W. McLachlan called such a collector a *comet*—appearing from nowhere, blazing brightly, then disappearing.

A lot of day-trippers come into the hobby, and first-year nonrenewals and drop-out rates often exceed 50 percent with publications and coin clubs. Perhaps this is a natural weeding-out. However, once people collect for a few years, chances are good they will remain in the hobby for the rest of their lives.

Once you are bitten by the "coin bug," as it is sometimes called, there is no cure! You may well have this marvelous affliction for the rest of your life.

A LIFETIME PURSUIT

I can think of no better example of longevity in the hobby than the Rittenhouse Society. In the 1950s, while in high school, and, later, at Pennsylvania State University, I spent a great deal of time studying the history of United States coins, checking into die varieties of state and colonial coins, trying to find out about the enigmatic Machin's Mills (a private coining facility in Newburgh, New York), and otherwise tracking down obscure information. At the time, relatively few others were interested in numismatic research.

A bunch of us concerned with such matters got together, had informal meetings and discussions, and called ourselves the Rittenhouse Society, after the first director of the Mint, David Rittenhouse, a scholar, artist, and philosopher. A few years later, in 1960, we wrote something on paper, not a charter or anything so formal, but at least a listing of names and addresses. The original or founding members included D. Wayne ("Dick") Johnson, Kenneth W. Rendell, Grover Criswell, Kenneth E. Bressett, George Fuld, Walter Breen, and me. Today, as I write these words in 2015, each and every member is still very active—collecting, reading, writing, and enjoying other hobby pursuits—except for three who have passed away, Criswell, Fuld, and Breen. I wonder if any other group has commanded such attention from its original membership for such a long time?

This was among the first special-interest groups in American numismatics. Not long afterward other niche groups were formed, including the Society of Paper Money Collectors (SPMC) and the Token and Medal Society (TAMS). Today, there are at least a couple dozen such societies, and I belong to perhaps half of them.

Apparently, the Rittenhouse Society example of sustained interest is hardly unique. About ten years ago, in *Numismatic News*, editor Dave Harper reported survey findings showing that 43% of his readers have been collecting for 40 years or more.

NEWCOMERS IMPORTANT

While old-time collectors are enjoyable to talk with, much of the dynamics in the marketplace comes from newcomers with fresh-faced enthusiasm and excitement. No doubt newcomers spend more money on average each year than old-timers do, a boon to the economics of our hobby.

My favorite type of new collector is someone—anyone—who has a sincere interest in numismatics. Of course, eventually spending significant sums on rare coins is desirable for the bottom line of my business, but it is true that quite a few collectors who keep in touch with me spend very little. However, they contribute a great deal to my enjoyment of the hobby, by communicating on research and sharing experiences.

I could tell quite a few stories about people who began in a modest way, then went on to become highly important in the field. Robert A. ("Bob") Vlack commenced in the 1950s by ordering from me a "starter collection" of old Connecticut copper cents, 1785 to 1788, became enthralled with the purchase, learned more, and the rest is history. Not long afterward, he jumped feet-first into research, and within a year or two he wrote a *book* on colonial coins. At one ANA convention Bob showed me his *latest* book, on French colonial issues.

For a number of years I taught the "All About Coins" class at Colorado College in Colorado Springs, part of the ANA Summer Seminar. Usually, most of my students were newcomers. At least two of them, both teenagers when they attended, found the week-long immersion in rare coins sufficiently interesting that they decided then and there to become professional numismatists! One was Dwight Manley, who a few years ago headed the sale of the SS *Central America* treasure and, among other things, has owned such rarities as the finest known 1913 Liberty Head nickel (the Eliasberg specimen) and an 1804 silver dollar. The other was Kerry Wetterstrom, who today is one of the leading dealers in ancient Greek and Roman coins and for many years was editor of the *Celator*, a highly acclaimed magazine.

One of my favorite Summer Seminar stories involves Mrs. M.W., a lady who enrolled in my class but warned me at the beginning of the first day, "I do not collect coins and am not interested in them. I came on the trip just to keep my husband company. Do not call on me or ask any questions. I will be in the back row, reading and knitting." What happened probably surprised her, and it certainly surprised me: I don't think a page was turned or a piece of yarn was handled. At the end of the week she said, "I enjoyed every minute. Now I know why my husband is so excited about coin collecting."

"Bert" Bressett, wife of Ken, came to my "All About Coins" class one year, liked it a lot, and the next year came back to take it all over again. This was fine, as each year I changed the course somewhat, and there were always new things to talk about.

Another newcomer in the early 1980s was Liz Arlin, who had just graduated from secretarial school and landed her very first job with me. This was during the time I was president of the ANA, giving her firsthand experience at dealing with everything from convention planning, to budgets, to growth of the collecting hobby, to resolving disputes—you name it, and it probably crossed Liz's desk! She became so interested that she learned about coin grading, market values, and other skills, after which she decided to become a professional dealer in her own right. She went on, with her husband Miles Coggan (a distant relative of the late dealer B. Max Mehl, by the way), to operate the Boston firm of J.J. Teaparty & Co., with notable success.

Newcomers are indeed important—especially those who are bitten by the coin bug and stay with the hobby. May more keep coming, and may the bug keep biting!

EASY COME, EASY GO—OR PERHAPS STAY!

In contrast with newcomers who develop a deep interest, some are here today and gone tomorrow. Frequently, a big spender will come onto the scene with a splash, determined to build a fine collection quickly. Some who can afford it will even go after "trophy coins," such as an 1879 Flowing Hair $4 gold Stella, an MCMVII High Relief $20, or even an 1804 silver dollar. Most such coins have done well for their uneducated but wealthy buyers, simply because as the market rises, classic issues rise with it. However, with knowledge, even trophy coins can be bought to better advantage. While I always give this advice, and the reminder that one should learn about coins before jumping into the field too deeply, not everyone wants to hear it.

Some such buyers prove to be a flash in the pan, easy come and easy go. Others decide to stay. I recall a bidder, previously unknown to me, who spent several hundred thousand dollars on a trophy coin in one of our sales. *Afterward*, he bought his first book on coins. Soon, he learned how to pronounce *numismatist*, and became one!

In another instance, a gentleman bought a spectacular collection of pattern coins from me, then asked me to track down a book on the subject (by Edgar H. Adams and William H. Woodin; this was in the 1950s, before the popular book on the same subject by Dr. J. Hewitt Judd was published). This man was in the financial accounting business. He liked coins so much that he decided to become a dealer, which he did, with some success.

GETTING COMFORTABLE

I am not suggesting that when you discover coins you sit down in an armchair and do nothing but read before making any purchases. Indeed, it is normal to get your feet wet, and even to jump into the numismatic water. This is true in many other fields as well. I bought my first music box and *then* decided to learn about what I had bought (eventually making this one of my collecting specialties). Ditto when I bought my first Currier & Ives print, *The Clipper Ship Dreadnought off Tuskar Light*, although, unlike with music boxes, my interest in these prints has remained at the casual level.

Probably most collectors begin by buying an interesting silver dollar through a television marketing program, or by ordering items from the U.S. Mint, or perhaps by visiting a coin dealer. A California man bought a large and expensive group of 100 bullion-type gold coins from a telemarketer, turned a nice profit in a rising market, then got acquainted with dealers in rare coins and set about collecting $20 gold double eagles by date and mintmark. Eventually, his collection was of such importance that several auctioneers each did headstands trying to land his consignment.

Fascination with coins is generated quickly—choice and beautiful specimens can have that effect! If you spend a few thousand dollars or even more to get started, you are in good company.

With a bunch of interesting coins at your elbow, *then* there may be time for you to read, to snuggle into an overstuffed chair and get comfortable. The *book you're reading now* beckons with all of its information, and beyond that, *Walter Breen's Complete Encyclopedia of U.S. and Colonial Coins* is a gold mine of technical information. In recent years, books on nearly every major U.S. coin type have been published for those who wish to dig deeper. Study them and you will know as much as most experts.

When I was a teenager I loved coins, but could not afford most of those that I desired. I could afford books, and much of my budget was spent in that direction. Since then I have said many times that if I could not replace my library, I would not trade it for its weight in gold!

It is likely that if you begin your interest in coins by buying a few pieces that catch your eye, then along the way browse through some books, attend a coin show or two, sign up for some dealers' catalogs, and subscribe to a numismatic newspaper—all the while conserving your budget—the coin bug will take a nip. Then, in the sunset years of your life, you will have a wonderful asset: the rare-coin hobby. With some good planning, careful buying, and good fortune, your favorite pastime may well be your most profitable investment as well. Other treasures are those that money cannot buy—the memories of nice experiences and many fine friends.

Such are the dynamics of the numismatic market—a hobby or an industry if you prefer—with many collectors and dealers buying, selling, and appreciating the pleasures and possibilities of coins, tokens, medals, and paper money.

APPENDIX J

Predicting the Rare-Coin Market

This is the age of collections, and the spirit of gathering together and classifying is abroad. It shows itself in the gigantic museums, the vast art and antiquarian collections, and the great libraries that grace the capitals and literary centers of the world, that have become the Meccas of so many pilgrims today. . . . There is nothing you can collect that will represent so much, if properly selected, or will cost so little, if properly bought, as a variety of fifty, one or two hundred coins.

—*Dr. Geo. F. Heath, September 1888*

This essay is adapted from chapter 13 of Q. David Bowers's
Expert's Guide to Collecting and Investing in Rare Coins.

THE PAST IS PROLOGUE

Rather than gazing into a crystal ball or reading tea leaves to predict the future of numismatics and the coin market, I have always tried to rely on common sense, plus a knowledge of coin-collecting history in combination with economic trends and human psychology.

In 1964, when I wrote the first study on coin-market cycles, I drew from the past—some of it from my own experience from 1952 onward, the rest from history. Today, some 50 years after that study, there have been several well-defined cycles in the investment market for rare coins. I say *investment* market, for, with few exceptions, niches and specialties in numismatics are immune to cycles. Such items as obsolete paper money of Maine, copper coins of Vermont from 1785 through 1788, die varieties of 1795 half dollars, copper-nickel cent patterns of 1858, and even Mint State Barber coins of 1892 through 1916, exist in relatively small numbers—there are not enough cards in the deck or pieces on the board to allow many players to participate.

Preferences have been different for each boom period in the coin-investment market. Here are some of the buyer values that defined "investment-quality" coins in the run-up of the late 1980s (the "Wall Street money" boom):

- *High grades:* MS-65, Proof-65, or finer.
- *Gold or silver:* These are "precious metals," and as such they make investment even more attractive.

- *Ease of understanding:* Or, more accurately, *apparent* ease—such as a grade on a certified holder that instantly tells you "everything" you need to know, except the price. No need even to look at the coin—just buy it, sight unseen.

- *Ease of pricing:* Prices must be easily available in sheets and elsewhere—no research needed.

- *Ready availability:* There has to be plenty of "product" so you can buy immediately—no waiting until next week or next month. (Which is no problem with common-date gold, most coins minted since 1934, most Proof coins from 1936 to date, etc.)

- *Dazzling action and hype:* Lots of enthusiastic comments in dealer ads, suggestions that this is where the action is, that the coins are gems, or rare, or just the things collectors would die for, and on and on.

- *A new definition of "rare":* It is not important that millions of a desired coin exist, so long as few have been certified. To us (we investors, that is) such coins are *rare*. Make that *Rare*, with a capital *R*. And don't you forget it!

- *Irrelevance of history:* Facts—including that a coin might be common, or that it is selling for $1,000 now but could be bought for $300 five years ago, or that only 10 have been certified in this grade now but 100 might be in the future—must at all costs be ignored or dismissed as stupid and irrelevant. Obviously, anyone who is a naysayer is completely out of touch with market reality. Learning is for the birds. Besides, books cost money and take time to read. Why bother with such effort?

These buyer values that dictated "investment-quality" characteristics in the late 1980s enticed many newcomers to invest millions of dollars. Of course, the coins were and still are of high quality. It is just that the market for them at the time was not based upon *true numismatic demand*.

The coins themselves don't change. They are as collectible as ever. However, their market prices do change, and if you are a smart buyer, you can build a higher-quality collection and at lower cost than anyone who simply has money, but knows little.

As to coin investors who don't want to learn anything, but who have a lot of money, all serious collectors owe them a debt of gratitude—for buying all of those coins, including lots of real dogs that connoisseurs don't want! This helps sustain the general market. The headline "Baggy Generic Morgans Up" in the *Certified Coin Dealer Newsletter* (September 24, 2004) reflects this—noting that bagmarked common dollars were in strong demand. I doubt if even a *single person* who reads this book and takes my advice to heart would want a "baggy generic" dollar for his or her collection.

What has happened in the past will undoubtedly be prologue to the future, plus there will be some events and evolutions that we cannot envision. However, *numismatic common sense*, a guiding precept of this book, will not go out of style!

WHEN SHOULD I START?

"The best time to plant a tree is 20 years ago. The second-best time is now." So goes an old proverb.

In 1971 the coin market was so-so in activity, not in the doldrums, but not hot, either. Collectors were collecting, dealers were dealing, but not many investors were investing.

For the *Forecaster*, an investment newsletter published by John Kamin, I wrote a piece about coin investment, picking a 1902 Proof Barber half dollar as a miscellaneous but good example of a rare coin. I was quite familiar with such coins. When I first started my business, they were worth $7 to $10, this being for a gem, as you could find gems if you looked for them. All Proofs were $7 to $10—some having nicks, others being superb—it made no difference. Only 777 Proofs were made, and thus the term *rare* seemed applicable back then, as it still does.

Over the years, the price rose, and although I did not profit from this, as I simply bought and sold them (as I still do), anyone who bought a 1902 Proof in 1953 was pleased in 1963 that it had appreciated in value to become worth $80. By 1971, when I wrote my *Forecaster* article, the price had gone up further. I posed this question:

> Will the 1902 Proof half dollar, a coin which might cost $180 today, be a good investment for the future? After all, quite a bit of profit has already been made by others on the coins—by people who bought them when they were cheaper 10 years ago. This is a logical and reasonable question to ask.
>
> Perhaps the quickest way to answer would be to say that 10 years ago isn't now, and we must concern ourselves with the present, not the past. Valuable objects in any field—Rembrandt paintings, antiques, etc.—have a history of price appreciation over the years. Waiting to buy them for the prices of 10 or 20 years ago is not realistic. So long as the trend of our economy is inflationary, prices seem to be headed for an ever-upward spiral. Coins have shared in this spiral and will continue to do so.
>
> Today [remember, this was written in 1971] the number of available 1902 Proof half dollars combined with the number of people desiring them, have set the price at approximately $180. Again we remind our readers that we have picked the 1902 Proof half dollar merely as an example. The reasoning applies to many coins in the United States series.

I have no way of knowing how many, if any, readers of the *Forecaster* rushed out to buy Proof Barber half dollars. It turned out that $180 was a great value. Today a beautiful gem would cost more than $4,000, which, for the 1902, is low in its market cycle—during the silver and gold mania of 1980, one could have been sold (and some *were* sold) for $15,000.

This prompts me to mention that *collectors* seldom buy "investment-quality" coins at market peaks—it is the *investors* who do all the buying. Usually, when coins that are not basically rare experience an abnormal run-up in price or a much-hyped buying fad sets in, collectors keep their checkbooks in their pockets and collect items in other series. However, they often *sell* into market peaks—which, of course, is a good thing to do!

While investors will continue to come and go, *collectors* will be around for a long time. Such are the foundations of the art and science of collecting and enjoying coins, tokens, medals, and paper money.

STRENGTH FOR THE FUTURE

As I see it, numismatics will be a dynamic hobby for a long time to come. The advantages, including the following, seem to be in place, ready for *you*.

Many Participants. The hobby has hundreds of thousands of serious participants and millions of casual dabblers. There are enough people involved that just about any specialty within numismatics, from obscure to obvious, has a sizeable contingent.

New and Exciting Coin Issues. The program of continuing coinage in the United States by the Treasury Department and the U.S. Mint will bring to us more National Park quarters, plus commemoratives and other interesting issues. Some might be controversial, others might seem illogical, but they will be there to collect. As each new variety is introduced, whether it be a distinctive topic on the back of a quarter for Texas or American Samoa, or a new alloy or new design for another circulating denomination, more people will take notice and become interested. On a similar note, in the allied field of paper money, the continuing parade of issues by the 12 different Federal Reserve districts, plus signature combinations, plus a fascination with collecting plate numbers and serial numbers, seems to assure new faces in that area.

Eager Buyers With Money to Spend. There is a lot of money in the market (no pun intended), and when collections are bought and sold, there is a lot of activity. This denotes strength, and is far different from a field that comprises just a handful of enthusiasts. There are more dealers, more market sites (including those on the Internet), more people active in selling coins than ever before. This means more choices when you buy and more options when you sell.

Interest Added by Research and Study. Numismatic research and study, once the focal point of just a few dozen people in the hobby, has become widespread, resulting in a delightful panorama of interesting historical facts, die varieties, and other things being publicized. Such activities lend their own brand of enthusiasm.

Universal Fondness for Money. *Money* is a popular subject, doesn't seem to go out of style, and attracts the interest of just about everyone. I know from my own experiences in television, including on the Discovery Channel, the History Channel, and the major networks, that certain features regarding gold coins or sunken treasures or related things seem to have everlasting interest—and can be run again and again. As time goes on, new treasure ships will be found on the ocean floor, a scarce piece of paper money will come to light in a bank vault in Montana, and the Mint will produce weird varieties (such as the combination Washington quarter and Sacagawea dollar that excited the nation in the year 2000). All of these factors will keep numismatics in the limelight. Societies, special-interest groups, and others will remain active and proliferate. The American Numismatic Society and American Numismatic Association are both long established and offer many services. Coin clubs and societies with interests in areas as diverse as out-of-print books and Indian Head cents will continue to attract members, and other meeting places will be developed, including connections on the Internet. Technology is always advancing.

Availability of Useful Information. Good numismatic publications, as well as information in electronic media, will be developed and will be available inexpensively, enabling numismatists to have a wonderful world of useful information at their fingertips, quickly and inexpensively. To this can be added the Internet as an information source. If you would like to know about the biography of David Rittenhouse, the first director of the Mint, a Web search will probably give you about all you need for a basic speech at your local coin-club meeting. I purchased for $45 a CD-ROM with all the back issues of the *Colonial Newsletter*, in searchable format—a combination of low cost and versatility not dreamed of a generation ago. Soon, the entire numismatic world will be at your fingertips, or so it seems likely.

Ease of Storing and Displaying. Coins, tokens, medals, and paper money are easy to store, and a valuable collection can be housed in a bank vault. Also, their small size makes them easy to ship from place to place safely and conveniently. Moreover, the coin market is scarcely local, but is national for all American series, and international for series beyond that. If in New Hampshire I have a VF-20 example of the curious 1794 large copper cent, variety Sheldon-48, known as the "Starred Reverse," with 94 tiny five-pointed stars around the rim, and I offer it for sale, the chances are that it will be sold to a buyer in some distant place—perhaps someone in Seattle who will request it by air shipment and have it available for examination the next day, or perhaps someone in Salt Lake City or Fort Lauderdale. Moreover, through the use of electronic and other images, as well as a grading interpretation that we all understand (more or less), we all have the same score card. Indeed, if I tell John Doe in Seattle that I have a Sheldon-48 cent in VF-20 grade, "with medium brown surfaces, very lightly porous on the obverse, rather smooth on the reverse, well struck, with all of the 94 stars visible, and without any serious edge dings, nicks, or scrapes," a transaction can probably be made without the buyer's even seeing the coin! In many other areas of investment interest, such as paintings, antique automobiles, and real estate, such ease is not possible.

Good Times in the Offing. Coin people are enjoyable to know, and coin events are fun to attend. The pleasures of numismatics can enrich your life, whether you begin as a youngster or are in your retirement years. Lucky *you*! To the preceding can be added the opportunity of being a "smart buyer" in the marketplace, which I hope you will become! As you already know, this is somewhat of a sport, a game—using knowledge to find sharply struck coins, or pieces of unusual quality, or items of exceptional value, while your competitors in the marketplace are unaware.

IN THEIR WORDS

In the future, as in the past, the life of numismatics will be in the people who participate. Coins by themselves are not numismatics. Thousands of gold double eagles on the sea floor in the wreck of the SS *Central America* are not numismatics, nor are a thousand bags of 1903-O dollars stored in a Philadelphia Mint vault, nor is a 1955 Doubled Die cent resting undiscovered in a child's piggybank in Brookhaven, Georgia.

People are needed to make coins, tokens, medals, and paper money interesting, to turn them into a hobby, to make them a focus of personal enjoyment and, possibly, financial security.

In connection with my book *The Expert's Guide to Collecting and Investing in Rare Coins* I invited two numismatists, one of each gender, one new to the hobby and the other an old-timer, to share their thoughts on the significance of the hobby to them.

ROBIN WELLS

Robin Wells, a lady who for the first time visited an ANA convention on August 2004 in Pittsburgh, stopped by to say hello at my bourse table and to have me sign a copy of my *Guide Book of Morgan Silver Dollars*. She really enjoys the hobby, she said. At the same time, Daniel Carr, designer of three State quarters, was chatting with me about that coin program and how interesting it was. After Mrs. Wells returned home she sent this commentary:

> As a child I enjoyed the time spent with my father poring over his coin collection and filling holes in his albums from pocket change. Isn't that how so many of us have started out? The years progressed and my interest in this with him waxed and waned as I grew up and began a life of my own.
>
> The launch of the State quarters served to reignite that flame of interest in my father as well as in me, helping us reestablish a connection that brought back many warm memories from my youth in a small town in Wisconsin. Unfortunately he passed away last year, a loss to his family and all who knew him. I know he loved his new collection of quarters. Like many others I am diligently working on filling my State quarter album, not only for myself but as a tribute to and in memory of him, and as a thank-you for opening my eyes to this great hobby.
>
> The State quarters and other coins I have collected have brought many pleasures, indeed gifts, to my life. I have a newfound interest and appreciation of our country's history. I've been sharing the hobby with my son, a first grader, and have seen his eyes light up with excitement every time he fills another hole in his album. I have also enjoyed meeting many people and making some wonderful friends along the way. "Coin people" have a special warmth and kindness, and it is very impressive that at the convention everyone was so willing to share information and give suggestions.
>
> Being a relative newcomer to the more serious side of numismatics, I find myself doing all that I can to increase my knowledge of the hobby and the history that it so grandly represents. I subscribe to various periodicals and publications as well as adhering to the wise advice of "buying the book before the coin." However, I've found that some of the best knowledge that I've acquired has come from attending shows, both large and small. No amount of reading and researching can compare to actually studying the objects of my desire up close. The ANA convention was my first large show. I am in awe at the

wealth of information available at these functions and the willingness of collectors to share it. From viewing various exhibits to attending lectures in my areas of interest, there seems to be no end to the knowledge and information available to anyone willing to take the time to pursue it. All of this is in addition to the stunning merchandise available at every turn. Anyone lucky enough to be able to attend a show of this magnitude will be faced with the same dilemma that I had: What to do first? Fill my brain with knowledge or empty my wallet?

We all have our own special stories of what piqued our interest in coins and how we got started on this road of collecting, some simple, many sentimental, but all meaningful to ourselves. For me, the knowledge and excitement gained from attending the recent ANA show was truly priceless, and an experience that I will never forget. It is something that every collector from the seasoned veteran to the youngest "newbie" should experience, so as to feel more educated and excited than ever about numismatics. I look forward to learning more about coins and meeting more fine people.

CLIFFORD MISHLER

To give all of the numismatic accomplishments of Cliff Mishler would require an entire chapter, and even then it would be only a summary. During his career, which is still in progress, he has shared with Chet Krause the management of Krause Publications, publisher of *Numismatic News*, *Coins* magazine, and many reference books, some of the best of which have Cliff's name on the cover.

Here is his contribution, with his suggested title, "A Collector by Accident; an Advocate by Conviction."

Many of the acquaintances I have made through the years, outside the hobby community, have inquired about how and why I became a coin collector, what it is about the hobby that caused me to become a lifelong collector, and why I chose to pursue the discipline as a career. The answer is both quite simple and rather detailed. Hopefully, what follows digests a comprehensible and motivating overview of those developments into the space available.

The beginning came during the summer of 1950, as I was nearing my 11th birthday. I had moved into a new community and met a new friend, who happened to share an interest in the collecting of postally cancelled stamps with his mother, and who was eager to have me join in that interest. That idea did not take root, but in scanning the contents of a publication they were subscribing to, an advertisement offering *coins* on approval sparked an ember of inquisitiveness.

Among the coins included in the selection that reached me a few days after I sent away a dime—for 10 pieces of obsolete World War II currency promised with that first approval selection—in a 3¢ stamped envelope, was a quite worn copper coin from a faraway place, Zanzibar, that immediately captured my fascination. I had to have it, as it appeared to my uninitiated mind to be more than 750 years old—a bargain at any price, or I thought—although I learned not too long after acquiring it that what had appeared to me to be a crudely rendered Christian date of 1199 was really the Mohammedan-era date of 1299 rendered in Arabic numerals, or 1882 by Christian reckoning!

It was the mysterious connotations of that coin, I'm convinced, that caused me to become a coin collector. First came the purchase of a few more coins of various origins from similar approval selections. Then, the saving of U.S. coins culled from circulation and pressed into the die-cut holes of the then-ubiquitous Whitman blue folders became my focus. Initially, that obsolete WWII currency broadcast little appeal to me. Rather, I discovered a hobby shop where I could buy a few coins, the two or three times a year that I got there, that eluded me in my searches of pocket change and bank-wrapped rolls of U.S. coins. By the time I graduated from high school I was even buying coins at auction.

Along the way, however, the diversity offered by the numismatic discipline was blossoming for me. I soon became actively interested in paper money, principally of foreign origins—that obsolete WWII currency that I had initially given short shrift resurfaced, along with a small olive-drab pouch of paper money and coins my father had carried home from his service time in the South Pacific theater—while the fascinating prospects offered up by pursuit of tokens and medals, now collectively known as *exonumia*, unfolded before me as well.

As my fascination and commitment grew, I was on the receiving end of much encouragement, most particularly from my parents, along with my many relatives and teachers and the kids I grew up with. This encouragement was embodied in many forms. There was the patronizing and fiscal support provided by my parents. There was the respect I was accorded by my peers for the specialized knowledge I gained. There was the deferential treatment accorded by teachers in calling upon me to share my blossoming outside world in the classroom.

Educationally, development of an ongoing interest in coin collecting was undoubtedly a godsend to me. While I had developed an abiding interest in the subjects of history, math, and spelling at an early age, I'm certain that I became a much more interested and skilled student of those subjects, along with geography, politics, economics, and English, than would have otherwise been the case as my schooling rolled into junior high and high school. And, while my personal artistic capabilities were and remain very minimal, I believe I also became more appreciative of artistic expression than would have otherwise been the case.

I have found that through the years my appreciation for each of these disciplines has been unabated, with virtual equilibrium in appeal. Invariably, when reading a news story or feature item, or becoming engaged in a discussion with anyone about anyplace in the world, I find myself unconsciously creating a tie to my knowledge of the coins or paper money of that place. Not infrequently, this causes me to seek out a numismatic reference or an encyclopedic reference to seek greater detail on some historical, geographical, or monetary fact that surfaces as a consequence of the experience.

As time passed and my inquisitiveness became a flame, I also came to recognize and appreciate the attributes of numismatic items as storehouses of wealth. I've always acquired my collectible coins and related objects, first and foremost, for what they represent and what they are: historical relics that preserve the economic and cultural histories of their issuers, gathered systematically by succeeding generations. And the beautiful thing about a collection is that its form is something the individual can control as to both scope and quality. Acquired and assembled intelligently and with long-term objectives, they provide fiscal preservation, at the same time they are providing aesthetic and acquisitional satisfactions to the dispositions of the owner.

Eventually, of course, I progressed beyond merely collecting and enjoying, to studying and learning the history and heritage of what I was collecting. That's a natural and beneficial transition experienced by most of those who are bitten by the collecting bug, but for me, that was just the beginning. As I learned, my instincts motivated me to a predisposition to share the knowledge I'd gained. Knowledge can be gained from many sources and shared in many ways, including exhibiting, speaking, and organizational involvement, but for me the primary vehicles of both input and output became the written word.

The coin-collecting discipline had garnered my dedication to ongoing pursuit by the time I was passing from schooldays to adulthood. After casting about for a time seeking direction to my life, doing some writing about the objects of my pursuits, engaging in some self-publishing, creating a few commercial products, and becoming involved at the organizational level, the opportunity to embark upon a career in the hobby community presented itself. I jumped at that opportunity. The pursuit of my interests soon became an obsession, and I have never looked back, so to speak, as the ever-changing visage of the hobby community has bloomed before me.

Numismatics (coin collecting) is a hobby community that is multifaceted. Its pursuit can be casual or serious, inexpensively or extravagantly focused, by individuals from all age groups and stations in life. I have always found the audience mix to be most appealing, as everyone from train conductors to doctors, sanitation engineers to professors, and from innumerable other stations in life, gather to exchange their views, knowledge, and treasures. Most importantly, perhaps, while no two are cut from the same bolt of cloth, just as no two collections are the same, they blend into a seemingly seamless montage of interests and objectives.

For me, it doesn't matter if I'm admiring my latest nondescript stickered dollar acquisition, my high-quality and valuable historic 1792 silver half disme, or that well-worn, once-mysterious 1882 Zanzibar one-pysa coin—each conjures up in my mind its own distinctive and compelling heritage and history that motivated me to make the acquisition. Rather, it's the coin from Zanzibar that got me started so long ago, that's perhaps worth no more in today's market than what I paid for it at the time. It is also that example of the first U.S. coin (the 1792 half disme) that I acquired almost 50 years later, which has certainly grown appreciably in value. To these can be added the many thousands of items of varied descriptions that I have added to my accumulations over more than half a century of enjoying my immersion in the hobby community. I cherish each and every one for what they have added to my life's experience, in knowledge and value alike.

While I became a coin collector by accident many years ago, I'm proud to be an advocate for the hobby community by conviction today. I am firmly convinced that exposure enhances the individual's comprehension and appreciation of, and ongoing homage to, educational opportunities. Beyond that, it provides a degree of personal satisfaction where achievement and accomplishment are concerned. Then, there are the benefits gained from personal interaction by communication, in clubs and at shows. In addition, it can be financially beneficial. Most importantly, however, it can provide temporary liberation and refreshment of the mind from lifestyles both mundane and hectic.

It seems to me that with people who, like Robin Wells, come into the hobby with fresh-faced enthusiasm, and those who, like Cliff Mishler, have been in the hobby for decades but with "appreciation unabated" today, numismatics has a secure future!

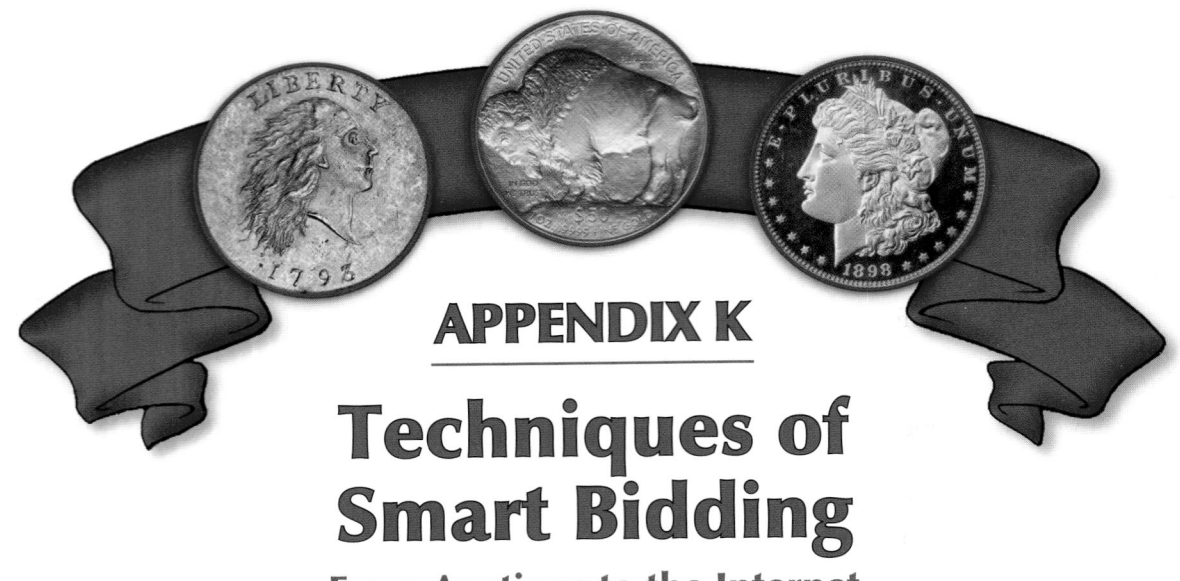

APPENDIX K

Techniques of Smart Bidding
From Auctions to the Internet

If a collector is reasonable and businesslike in his relations with any well-established dealer he will usually be fairly treated and will find it more to his interest in the end to pay a dealer commission for his services and judgment than to enter the lists himself and challenge the jealousy and opposition of the whole trade or profession.

—Augustus G. Heaton, commenting on having a dealer as a representative at a sale, November 1894

This essay is adapted from Q. David Bowers's
Expert's Guide to Collecting and Investing in Rare Coins.

AUCTIONS: AN INSIDE VIEW

Buying a coin in a private transaction, such as at a coin show, over the counter from a dealer, or through the mail, offers you the opportunity to contemplate, consider, and contemplate some more. You can ask questions, view the coin again after you hear the answers to your questions, and in other ways make a leisurely and informed purchase. Often, you can obtain a specimen on approval and view it over a period of a day or two.

This is not necessarily so when you buy coins at auction. Often, a split-second decision is needed during the heat of competitive bidding. To buy effectively in an auction, you need another set of guidelines—actually, two sets: one for sales conducted by professional numismatists (let's call them "professional auctions," just for illustration) and the other for the proliferation of auctions held on the Internet and elsewhere by people who are not in the trade ("casual auctions").

Certain practices and procedures apply to both professional and casual auctions. Having been in the professional auction business since the 1950s, and having attended countless events held by others, I've seen just about everything! Moreover, as past president of both the Professional Numismatists Guild (PNG) and the American Numismatic Association (ANA), I've witnessed many auction-related problems brought to the attention of these organizations. Furthermore, I have been an expert witness in arbitrations and disputes.

Before proceeding, I hasten to mention that participating in an auction or a mail-bid sale can be great fun and a very effective way to acquire desirable numismatic items. However, a degree of awareness is called for, and that is what I hope to share with you here.

TERMS OF SALE

FAKES

Just about every professional seller has terms of sale. In the instance of a printed catalog, they can be multiple pages in length and contain many paragraphs, usually carefully prepared by legal counsel. It is important for you to read the fine print. One auctioneer may permit the return of a coin, if it is found to be fake, within a specified short time, and another might not allow a return at all—selling coins "as-is." In certain sales of confiscated, abandoned, and other coins by a local, state, or federal government agency, the items are offered as-is. Buy something and you own it, no matter whether it's phony or authentic.

That said, most professional auctions conducted by numismatic firms do permit returns if a coin is proved to be fake. *Proved* is an important word; your neighbor's or brother-in-law's opinion that it's a fake probably won't mean much when you inform the auction house. Instead, a specified procedure must be followed, or judgment passed by a mutually agreed-upon authority—hopefully, as outlined in the terms of sale.

For many casual sales of coins on the Internet, either no terms are posted, or the venue host has general rules not specific to coins. Often an item is pictured, and if you buy it, you own it. It may be illegal to sell a fake coin, but if you buy one on the Internet from someone a thousand miles away, you are apt to lose everything with little recourse against the seller. Auction-site hosts may allow you to post complaints or "feedback," but if you paid $2,000 for a "rare colonial" that proves to be worthless, there is little actual help to get your money back. You can hire an attorney, but by the time the case is investigated your bill will likely be more than $2,000. If you contact a distant chamber of commerce, or the Better Business Bureau, or a law-enforcement agency, the chances are still slight that you will make a significant recovery.

Be sure the seller has good, verifiable credentials.

While your chances of buying an out-and-out fake from an established, professional rare-coin firm are small, it does happen. Usually, if the fake is obvious (which sometimes happens, as large companies run a lot of items through their sales, and many consigned items are cataloged by clerks or other non-experts), a refund is forthcoming—and quickly. If the questioned coin appears to be genuine to the auctioneer and his or her staff, but you and your consultants believe it to be fake, the matter may be arbitrated, or another procedure may be followed. Again, read the terms of sale.

On Internet purchases, you have great exposure if the seller is not a recognized professional with numismatic expertise. Read the terms of sale carefully, but if you have the slightest question about an item offered, or if it seems to be too good to be true, either don't bid or make arrangements to have the coin examined by a professional (if the seller will allow this and if there is time to do so).

PRICES AND MINIMUMS

Nearly all auction offerings by professionals are subject to minimum bids, usually not disclosed in the catalog or Internet offering. However, the terms of sale usually make note of the practice. On Internet and other offerings by casual sellers, this may not be specified, but minimum bids are still used.

There are several reasons for having minimum bids. A licensed auctioneer, a professional numismatist, or a country seller of antiques is supposed to have a responsibility and obligation to both the owner and the buyer. If Widow Jones consigns a $1,000 currency note, Series of 1928, to Auctioneer Smith, the auctioneer cannot, or at least should not, offer it for sale and quickly sell it for $800. There would seem to me to be a responsibility to deliver at least *face value* after charges and commissions! Widow Jones could have spent the bill for face value, so her expectation is to realize more than that.

In such a circumstance, it would be perfectly reasonable for Auctioneer Smith to have a reserve of, say, $1,100, for starters. In this way, if it sells, he makes a few dollars and so does Widow Jones.

In other instances, consignors request or negotiate reserves with the auctioneer. "I have an 1879 Flowing Hair Stella, and you can put it in your next sale, but I want to reserve it at $100,000." The auctioneer contemplates the coin, and if he feels it can sell for an attractive advance over $100,000, will probably accept it. The reserve will likely not be printed in the catalog. The bidding may open at, say, $80,000, to get some "action" going, but until it crosses the $100,000 mark, the house or "book" will also be bidding. In other instances, an agent or representative of the auctioneer (*shill* is the nasty word for this) will be in the audience, unidentified, and will be bidding for the house. In still other instances the auctioneer may make an arrangement with a dealer friend who will run the reserve bids (while giving the appearance that the person is bidding on his or her own account).

Sometimes a sale is advertised as "unreserved" or "absolute." I am not aware that either term has specific legal meaning, at least not universally. I have bid in "unreserved" sales after being told, for example, "Bidding on lot 335 will commence at $2,000." That, to me, is a reserve!

To summarize, the terms of sale might specify that reserves are on some or all lots. However, if this is not stated, there may be reserves anyway.

The endgame is simple: reserve or no reserve, bid only what a coin is actually worth.

LOT INSPECTION

Most public sales allow the items to be inspected before the bidding. I say "most," as I have seen a few government and law-authority sales, not auctions conducted by recognized numismatic auctioneers, in which sealed boxes, bags, or tubes of coins are offered sight unseen, in the manner that unclaimed luggage is sometimes sold. However, you are not apt to encounter such a situation.

Most terms of sale in a printed catalog allow for in-person inspection before the sale (usually through a setup in which you can sit down at a table in a firm's home office or in a room near the sale itself) and, under security precautions, inspect the lots one at a time. Some professional numismatic firms allow inspection by mail for established clients. Casual auctioneers, such as an auctioneer of antiques who advertises that some coins will be sold at a forthcoming event, usually won't allow mail inspection. In fact, many casual auctioneers consider anyone who asks questions from a distance, instead of simply coming to the sale, to be a pest.

In any event, if you attend a sale in person, regardless of whether you have availed yourself of the opportunity to inspect the items, sales to floor bidders are usually final. The only exception is if a coin is found to be a fake and rescinding the sale is allowed. If an auction starts at 7:00 in the evening, and you come to the lot-viewing area at 4:00 p.m. and find there is a long wait, or that time for inspection is over, that's your problem, not that of the auction house.

If you attend the sale and buy a coin described as a gorgeous gem and, after you buy it, you find it's ugly as a toad, again, that's your problem.

In short, if you attend a sale, allow sufficient time in advance to inspect each and every lot you bid on.

As to bidding on the Internet, there are few rules. It can be really wild out there! Many if not most casual sellers picture the items, this being the complete situation—no detailed descriptions, no commentary, no anything—just a picture. If a coin is certified by a recognized, leading service of good reputation, this may help.

If you contemplate bidding on the Internet, and the seller is not a recognized professional who describes items with expertise, ask questions (most sites have a method for this) before bidding. In any event, be careful.

BUYER'S FEES

Beginning in a strong way in the 1980s and almost universally applied now, numismatic auction houses add a "buyer's fee" to the hammer price or basic sale price of a coin. Some call this a "buyer's *penalty*," and in the numismatic trade, the term *juice* is sometimes used.

In the United States, the typical buyer's fee is 15% or 17.5%. However, higher or lower fees can be charged. Some auctioneers charge no fee at all. The fee procedure will be listed in the terms of sale.

With a 15% buyer's fee, a coin that an auctioneer sells for $1,000—the so-called hammer price—will appear on your bill as $1,150. A coin that is sold for $300 will be billed as $345. A coin that is sold for $100,000 will actually cost you $115,000.

It is not unusual for a newcomer to grouse about the buyer's fee, in absence of understanding it. If a buyer's fee is charged, to me, it makes no difference. I simply figure it in when bidding. If I want to pay no more than the total amount of $1,000 for a coin, I stop bidding around the $875 level. With some experience, it is easy enough to do mental calculations, even if a sale moves quickly.

The hammer price is 86.96% (we'll say 87%) of the total price when 15% is added. You can use a pocket calculator to figure this out at a sale—or at home, if you bid by mail or on the Internet. (Remember always to check the terms of sale, of course—many Internet sales by private individuals do not involve buyer's fees.) If you want to pay $2,000, and no more, for a nice 1955 Doubled-Die Lincoln cent, then bid 87% of this price, or $1,740. If you win it for your full bid, your bill will be at $1,740 plus 15%, or $2,001.

OTHER TERMS OF SALE

Read each and every paragraph in the terms of sale. Other text might include information about sales taxes. In some states and cities, taxes are charged against coin-auction purchases, possibly for the entire amount, although there may be exceptions. If you are buying for resale and have a valid resale permit, you may be exempt. Sometimes, when lots are shipped out of state, there is an exemption, other times not.

It may be that gold coins are exempt from taxation, but numismatic books might not be. There are hundreds of different twists and turns in sales-tax laws and regulations. If in doubt, ask the auctioneer, who should know.

Are the items illustrated in the catalog or on the Internet the actual items being sold, or are the photographs simply "representative"? The terms of sale should tell you. If not, ask.

Many, if not most, terms of sale state that catalog descriptions notwithstanding, no guarantees, representations, and so on are made concerning the grades of coins, their attributions, their values, their potential for resale, their quality, or their merchantability. So there! Said simply, any coin, token, medal, or piece of currency is what it is—not necessarily conforming to its presale description.

Procedures for bidding by mail, or by telephone, or by Internet, or by in-person attendance may vary. Sometimes mail bids have to be received a day or so before the sale begins, and requirements are in place for email bids as well. In other instances, real-time bidding is allowed by telephone or the Internet. Read such terms carefully.

Some auction houses allow a "maximum expenditure" or "one-lot-only" option, again explained in the terms of sale.

Under a maximum-expenditure arrangement, you can state your budget for the sale (say, $10,000), and the auction house will run your bids until you have spent that much, after which all further bids will be canceled. Remember that the sale is conducted in the order of listing, and if you spend your $10,000 by the time that lot 600 comes up, and lot 600 sells for a low price, you won't have the possibility of buying it.

Under a one-lot-only arrangement, if a sale has eight 1881-S dollars in MS-65 grade or three MCMVII (1907) High Relief double eagles in MS-63, and you want just one of each, the auction house may allow you to bid on all of them, but in sequence as they are offered. As soon as you buy one, later bids on similar lots are canceled, even if the later-offered coins are just as nice and sell for cheaper prices.

What if you place a bid by mail or on the Internet, and then want to change or cancel it? What if you want to pay for your lots over a period of time? What about packing and shipping costs? Insurance in transit? Policies vary, and again the terms of sale will provide the answer. On very small purchases, postage and handling can be a large proportion of the transaction. I once bought a $4 postcard on the Internet and was charged an additional $6 postage and handling. On the Internet, it is often the case that such charges are not stated in advance. *Handling* has various meanings when it comes to costs.

Many other opportunities, restrictions, and provisions apply. While printed catalogs and some Web sites will list terms of sale in detail, there are other auction venues in which the provisions can be just as strict, or for which there may be interesting opportunities, but they will not be easy to find. In such instances, ask before you bid.

In all instances, when you bid in a sale, be prepared to buy! This might seem obvious, but now and again someone will send in $10,000 in bids on a string of coins, then get an invoice for $9,760, and say, "I was not expecting to actually buy that much." If you bid on $10,000 worth of coins you might not get a thing. On the other hand, you might spend the full amount!

Terms of sale are usually subject to modification at the time of sale, such as by comments of the auctioneer or late postings on the Internet. The right is usually reserved to withdraw any item for sale without notice (the reasons can be many, such as a vague title, insistence by the consignor, changing market conditions, etc.). Entire sales can be canceled without notice—and in today's world of various problems in large cities and elsewhere, this is a real consideration. A few years back, a leading rare-coin firm (not active today) offered a collection for auction, then canceled the sale when someone stepped up to buy the entire holding for outright cash. If you plan to travel any distance, verify the sale in advance if you can.

Sometimes an auctioneer will have amenities and services to offer alongside the sale itself—such as contacts for preferential hotel rates, suggestions for restaurants, or even a presale reception or mid-sale buffet or dinner.

AUCTIONEERS' POLICIES: ESTIMATES

Some auction listings have estimates. The terms of sale will probably state that the estimates are just that—*estimates*—and that at the actual sale, higher or lower prices may prevail for a given item. In other instances, the auctioneer will use the estimates for his or her starting bids. In a recent sale of paper money, a well-known auction firm routinely opened every item at 60% of the low estimate figure, unless a higher bid had been received beforehand. Accordingly, a piece of currency estimated at $1,000 to $1,500 opened at $600.

Sometimes states or localities will have rules concerning estimates and opening bids. An example may be that in no instance can a reserve bid be higher than the highest estimate printed for a lot. Under such a rule, a coin with a printed estimate of $2,000 to $3,000 cannot have a reserve bid over $3,000. This means that if someone bids at least $3,000, an actual sale will take place. However, such rules are in place in only a few areas. If you ever want to immerse yourself in almost continuous commentary about auctions and Internet sales (nearly all concerning antiques, art, and non-numismatic material), the monthly *Maine Antique Digest*, published in Waldoboro, Maine, is extremely enlightening and informative. I've been a regular reader for years. Don't let the *Maine* part of the title fool you; it covers the entire country.

As a long-time participant in many auction sales, from coins to antiques and beyond, I have concluded that there are at least three different "classes" of estimates. The auctioneer's policy in this regard is not disclosed in the catalog, so you have to figure the situation out for yourself.

To illustrate, I'll use a rare 1877 Indian Head cent, a hypothetical specimen certified by one of the major third-party grading firms in a grade for which, if I were buying it for stock, I would pay $2,500; if I were offering it for sale I would ask $3,000. The coin is well struck and of nice appearance. So, the real value is $2,500 to $3,000. At a well-conducted auction sale the coin would likely sell for about $3,000. (I'm ignoring the 15% buyer's fee to simplify the illustration.)

The following are some types of estimates, the reasons some auctioneers use them, and what you should do in each case.

LOWBALL ESTIMATE: *$1,000 TO $1,500*

Reasons for Use. It seems that this will be a grand auction to participate in. Wow! I *might* be able to buy a $3,000 Indian Head cent for just $1,000. It must be so, or it would not be printed as an estimate. At least the *possibility* exists. I'll rearrange my schedule so I can attend.

For the auction house, the lowball estimate makes the firm "look good." Coin periodicals and advertisements will trumpet: "Coin brings way over estimate! Wow!" An estate attorney or an heir who consigns, but is not conversant with values, will be delighted to see how spectacularly the firm has performed, even if the coin sleeps at $2,000 because hardly anyone participated! If it brings its real value (say, $3,000), he or she will be on cloud nine. In the field of antiques this is the rule, not the exception. Antique music boxes (a passion of mine) are nearly always lowballed.

Strategy for Bidding. Figure what the coin is worth before you submit your bid or make travel plans. Realize that the rarity of the 1877 cent is well known, that the bid price in the *Certified Coin Dealer Newsletter* is $2,500, and the chances the coin will sell at the estimate are like a snowball in you-know-where. If you want the coin, be prepared to pay $2,500 to $3,000 (less an allowance to take care of the buyer's fee).

Negatives. The auction house loses credibility with knowledgeable bidders, even if it makes naïve consignors happy. The auction itself and lot viewing may be congested with bargain hunters who take up time and space, but who don't buy anything when the sale takes place. Those who travel to attend the sale, expecting to gobble up bargains, will be disappointed that everything sold for such "strong prices" that they were not able to buy.

EXPERT ESTIMATE: *$2,500 TO $3,200*

Reasons for Use. The auction house trades primarily with collectors, dealers, museums, investors, and others who are proven buyers and who have knowledge. Such buyers know that they can rely upon the estimates to be at least in the ballpark. Chances are good that if asked, an auction representative can discuss or defend the estimate.

Strategy for Bidding. The estimate can be relied upon. If you want the coin only if "the price is right" and there is no urgency, bid $2,500 to $2,800 and you might get it. If it is a dandy coin with nice appearance, and it is on your want list, bid $3,000 to $3,500, and you might take it home.

Negatives. If it brings "only" $2,800, a naïve consignor may feel that the coin was sold for too little. If the auction house wants a larger attendance—never mind that some will be bargain hunters who do not buy—there will be fewer on hand when estimates are realistic.

GRANDSTAND ESTIMATE: *$5,000 TO $7,000*

Reasons for Use. This "grandstand" or "come-on" estimate is common in country fairs, huckstering, and the like. "Who'll start this chair at $500? Well, how about $200?" In coins it is less common. The purpose is to put an artificially high price so that those attending the sale will feel they are getting a bargain if they buy that 1877 cent for "only" $4,000! This often works if there are pigeons or patsies attracted to the sale, but it does not sit well with knowledgeable numismatists. Accordingly, grandstand estimates are rare among sales held by professional numismatists. However, they are very common in Internet offerings. Greedy consignors may be delighted that a coin is estimated at $5,000 to $7,000, when other auction houses "appraised" the coin for much less!

Strategy for Bidding. Bid what the coin is really worth.

Negatives. The consignor will be disappointed, even if such a coin brings full market value—say, $3,200. The auction house will not care, as that consignor is history—the estate collection (or whatever) has been sold, and no future business is in the offing. Knowledgeable numismatic buyers may be turned off by the whole thing and not attend or otherwise participate in the sale. They will also think that the firm conducting the sale has a staff with few experts on board, or else that they are a bunch of promoters, or both.

Notes

HALF CENTS

1. Ron Manley, "Original Mintages of 1797 and 1800 Half Cents," *Penny-Wise*, July 15, 2000.

2. Listed as a grocer on Gouverneur Street, corner of Front Street, in contemporary directories. R.W. Julian could find no record of any shipment being made to Cilley in the treasurer's ledger, but that is not conclusive, as acknowledgements were not given to all orders (personal communication to Q. David Bowers, March 2, 2009).

3. Although the book bore Snowden's name as author, likely most of the text was prepared by William Ewing Dubois and George Bull (curator of the Mint Cabinet).

4. After Cohen's passing, his daughter Debby handled his numismatic estate and consigned his collection of half cents to Superior Galleries, where it was sold on February 2, 1992.

5. Bill Eckberg, communication to Q. David Bowers, March 2, 2009.

6. Greg A. Silvis, "An Interview with R. 'Tett' Tettenhorst" *Penny-Wise*, January 2006.

7. Estimate of Jim McGuigan, April 20, 2009.

8. Ronald P. Manley, *Half Cent Die State Book 1793–1857*, 1998, p. 36.

9. *Ibid.*, p. 30.

10. Bill Eckberg, communication to Q. David Bowers, March 2, 2009.

11. R. Tettenhorst, letter to Q. David Bowers, March 16, 2009.

12. *Ibid.*

13. *Ibid.*

14. Frank H. Stewart, *History of the First United States Mint*, 1924, p. 115.

15. *Hobbies* magazine, February 1932. The Detroit collector was Howard R. Newcomb.

16. This crossed the block for $506,000 in 1996, setting the record for *any* copper coin sold up to that point in time.

17. R. Tettenhorst, letter to Q. David Bowers, March 16, 2009.

18. Estimate of Jim McGuigan, April 20, 2009.

19. *American Journal of Numismatics,* June 1866.

20. *Numisgraphics,* 1876, p. 42.

21. R. Tettenhorst, letter to Q. David Bowers, March 16, 2009.

22. Ronald P. Manley, *Half Cent Die State Book 1793–1857*, p. 81.

23. Description (which varies in the literature) suggested by R. Tettenhorst, letter to Q. David Bowers, March 16, 2009.

24. Adapted from Q. David Bowers, *American Coin Treasures and Hoards*, Bowers & Merena Galleries, 1997.

25. Communication to Q. David Bowers, March 8, 2009.

26. Estimate of Jim McGuigan, April 20, 2009.

27. *Walter Breen's Encyclopedia of United States Half Cents 1793–1857*, American Institute of Numismatic Research, 1983, p. 223.

28. From research by Craig Sholley.

29. R. Tettenhorst, letter to Q. David Bowers, March 16, 2008.

30. Only two were known to Walter Breen. Ronald P. Manley, correspondence with Q. David Bowers, February 23, 2009: "EAC member Ed Fuhrman has discovered 4 or more specimens of this 'variety' unattributed on eBay."

31. *Walter Breen's Encyclopedia of United States Half Cents 1793–1857*, p. 252.

32. *Walter Breen's Complete Encyclopedia of U.S. and Colonial Coins*, Doubleday, 1988, pp. 165–166, gives the name *Henry Chapman* and the 200 estimate. Alternatively, *Walter Breen's Encyclopedia of United States Half Cents 1793–1857*, p. 276, places the number as "many hundreds" and gives the name *Chapman brothers*.

33. The pedigree of this piece is notable: The reverse was used in 1916 to illustrate the Gilbert text on half cents. Later it was part of the sale of the F.R. Alvord Collection; S.H. Chapman, June 9, 1924, Lot 131, where it realized $6, a strong price at the time.

34. Ronald P. Manley, *Half Cent Die State Book 1793–1857*, p. 196, citing Bill Weber's discovery reported in *Penny-Wise* No. 4, 1987.

35. Craig Sholley, research in the National Archives, also noted in *Walter Breen's Encyclopedia of United States Half Cents 1793–1857*.

36. Correspondence between Ronald P. Manley and Q. David Bowers, February 23, 2009.

37. John Dannreuther, correspondence with Q. David Bowers, February 24, 2009.

38. See Bill Eckberg, "The 1809 C5 Over What," *Penny-Wise*, November 2006; also communication to Q. David Bowers, February 25, 2009.

39. R.W. Julian from Mint records (communication to Q. David Bowers, March 8, 2009).

40. *American Numismatical Manual of the Currency or Money of the Aborigines, and Colonial, State, and United States Coins: With Historical and Descriptive Notices of Each Coin or Series*, p. 213.

41. Estimate per Jim McGuigan, April 20, 2009.

42. Boyd's obituary, by Elston G. Bradfield, appeared in *The Numismatist*, October 1958, p. 1180. He died on September 7, 1958, at the age of 71.

43. Conversation between John J. Ford Jr. and Q. David Bowers, June 27, 1996.

44. Walter H. Breen, "Survey of American Coin Hoards," *The Numismatist*, January 1952, modified by his comments in the same journal, October 1952, p. 1010 (pointing out inaccuracies in the Chapman account, this new information having been gained by Breen from old-time numismatist John F. Jones, who had known and visited Collins); *Walter Breen's Complete Encyclopedia of U.S. and Colonial Coins*, p. 169.

45. R.W. Julian from Mint documents in the National Archives.

46. R. Tettenhorst, letter, March 16, 2009, describing a coin in his collection.

47. R.W. Julian from Mint documents in the National Archives.

48. *Walter Breen's Encyclopedia of United States Half Cents 1793–1857*, p. 338.

49. *Walter Breen's Complete Encyclopedia of U.S. and Colonial Coins*, p. 171; also personal recollection of Q. David Bowers concerning the availability of the coins in the 1950s.

50. *Walter Breen's Encyclopedia of United States Half Cents 1793–1857*, p. 338.

51. *Walter Breen's Complete Encyclopedia of U.S. and Colonial Coins*, p. 171; also personal recollection of Q. David Bowers concerning the availability of the coins in the 1950s.

52. *Walter Breen's Encyclopedia of United States Half Cents 1793–1857*, p. 338.

53. Recollection of Q. David Bowers, who was given her "want list."

54. Robert Schonwalter, *Penny-Wise*, whole number 111, November 15, 1885.

55. Eavenson had been collecting since at least 1894 (listed as new member 221 in *The Numismatist*, October 1894; at that time he worked for the Denver & Rio Grande Railroad and lived in Denver; moving to Eckart, Colorado in 1903). Eavenson's sale had a long run of Proof sets and also included a rare 1838-O half dollar.

56. *Walter Breen's Complete Encyclopedia of U.S. and Colonial Coins* spread the word about Gies. On p. 323 he related, concerning Barber dimes, that he "obtained rolls of all of them;" on p. 358 he credited Gies with having rolls of all Barber quarter dollars; on p. 410 he said the same thing about Barber halves. William Pukall and Wayte Raymond were also credited with having most or all Barber coins in roll form, also a highly unlikely scenario.

57. Ford, conversation with Q. David Bowers, June 27, 1996; Ford worked for Stack's, New York City, circa 1941–1942 and saw the Gies coins at that time.

58. Bill Eckberg, communication to Q. David Bowers, March 3, 2009.

59. Putnam-Woodward connection courtesy of Karl Moulton, letter, September 10, 1996, with enclosures.

60. Coins were first struck in Carson City in 1870; first reviewed by the Assay Commission in 1871. In 1863 (the year for which coins were being reviewed by the Assay Commission in 1864) there were two active mints, Philadelphia and San Francisco.

61. Certain information is from Francis Pessolano-Filos, *The Assay Medals, the Assay Commissions, 1841, 1977*, pp. 155, 159, 162, and 168.

62. Those stored at the Mint were melted by spring 1857, per an account of Director James Ross Snowden in *A Description of Ancient and Modern Coins in the Cabinet of the Mint of the United States.* Philadelphia: J.B. Lippincott, 1860 (this excellent book was mostly researched and written by George Bull, who was then curator of the Mint Cabinet, and William Ewing DuBois).

63. Citation suggested by Bob Vail. Copy of Woodward's sale catalog furnished by Karl Moulton.

64. Charles French, conversation with Q. David Bowers.

65. For several years in the 1950s and early 1960s Q. David Bowers and partner James F. Ruddy bought every 1856 they could find, after determining that although they were priced about the same as other dates of this period, they were much scarcer in the marketplace.

66. Craig Sholley, letter to Q. David Bowers, January 18, 2001. Also, early in 1857 large copper cents were paid out to the extent of 100,000 coins, again until February 28.

67. A small number of 1857 half cents have a depression in the right obverse field below the hair bun. This struck-through error was first described by Mark Borckardt in the May 1976 issue of *Penny-Wise*.

LARGE CENTS

1. A reference to the new small-size Flying Eagle cent launched in May 1857.

2. 1858 essay provided by Anthony Bongiovanni Jr. As a student, Ingersoll must have made diligent inquiry in an era in which no general numismatic texts were available, probably consulting various *Annual Reports of the Director of the Mint* to learn about distribution patterns of cents. Ingersoll later became treasurer of the Academy of Music, Haverhill, Massachusetts, a popular entertainment venue from the early 1880s onward. Thanks also to Dennis Tucker and David Sundman for information.

3. Breen died in 1993, and Borckardt organized his notes and helped with the publication in 2000. As this was a "Breen book," the considerable research of others, including that of Borckardt and modern contributors to *Penny-Wise*, was not added.

4. Silver coins in the form of 1792 half dismes were struck in July at the home of John Harper, before the Mint cornerstone was laid, and soon reached circulation. The first gold coins would not be delivered until summer 1795.

5. "The Mint Investigation of 1795," *Numismatic Scrapbook Magazine*, July 1961.

6. In the present cross-references below, "Crosby" is spelled out in full, to avoid confusion with other "C" authors such as S. Hudson Chapman and Roger S. Cohen Jr., although both described copper coins other than 1793 cents.

7. The estimated mintages of 1793 Chain cents are by Mark Borckardt, contribution to the Eliasberg Collection catalog, 1996; based on a distribution of an estimated 1,000 examples surviving across all five varieties.

8. Stetson, born in 1832, lived in Quincy, MA, and enjoyed hoarding cents of his birth date.

9. "The Mint Investigation of 1795," *Numismatic Scrapbook Magazine*, July 1961.

10. "The Strawberry Leaf Cent. A Reappraisal," essay in *America's Large Cent*, Coinage of the Americas Conference, American Numismatic Society, 1998.

11. Jim Neiswinter, communication to Q. David Bowers, March 30, 2009.

12. As written by Charles Davis, Armand Champa Library III, Lot 2566.

13. Jim Neiswinter, in "Reverses Revisited: S-63 Is the Reworked S-13," *Penny-Wise*, July 2006, presented photographic overlays demonstrating that the reverse of S-13 of 1793 was reworked to create S-63 of 1794.

14. Jim Neiswinter, communication to Q. David Bowers, March 30, 2009.

15. Denis Loring, communication to Q. David Bowers, March 6, 2009, contributed to these comments.

16. From the catalog, *The Celebrated John W. Adams Collection*, 1982, Also, Carl W.A. Carlson, "Garrett, Raymond and the Ellsworth Collection," 1991.

17. Incorrectly plated in the Breen *Encyclopedia*.

18. Steigerwalt, "1794 cents," *The Numismatist*, July 1906, as cited in *Walter Breen's Encyclopedia of Early United States Cents 1793–1814*, Bowers and Merena Galleries, 2000, p. 149.

19. S. Hudson Chapman, *The United States Cents of the Year 1794*, 1926, p. 20. S.H. was born in 1857, Henry in 1859. In 1877 they were both in the employ of Philadelphia dealer J.W. Haseltine.

20. Harry E. Salyards, communication to Q. David Bowers, February 7, 2009.

21. *Ibid.*

22. Pete Smith, in "Observations on the Starred Reverse Cent," *Penny-Wise*, January 15, 1989, debunked an earlier-published theory by Walter Breen that the reverse die for S-48 was used earlier for S-63, by using photographic overlays.

23. Jim Neiswinter, in "Reverses Revisited: S-63 Is the Reworked S-13," *Penny-Wise*, July 2006, presented photographic overlays demonstrating that the reverse of S-13 of 1793 was reworked to create S-63 of 1794.

24. Harry E. Salyards, M.D., communication, February 7, 2009.

25. Not a correct statement; the standard remained the same as 1793.

26. An error. The number of one-cent pieces minted with the 1794 date is not known with certainty, but it is far short of 12+ million. The *Guide Book of U.S. Coins* suggests 918,521, while *Walter Breen's Complete Encyclopedia of U.S. and Colonial Coins* states that 807,500 were made.

27. R.W. Julian, "The Harper Cents," *Numismatic Scrapbook Magazine*, September 1964.

28. Harper had a previous relationship with the Mint. In 1792, incoming equipment for the Mint, then planned, later under construction, had been set up in Harper's coach house in Philadelphia on Sixth Street above Chestnut, opposite Jayne Street. A press made by Mint mechanic Adam Eckfeldt was used to strike certain coins there (per *The Historical Magazine*, September 1861). Other accounts suggest Harper's *cellar*.

29. *Walter Breen's Encyclopedia of Early United States Cents 1793–1814*, p. 63.

30. *Ibid.*, p. 257.

31. Frank H. Stewart, *History of the First United States Mint*, 1924, p. 71.

32. Denis Loring, communication to Q. David Bowers, March 6, 2009.

33. Walter H. Breen, "A Survey of American Coin Hoards," *The Numismatist*, January 1952.

34. William H. Sheldon, *Penny Whimsy*, p. 189.

35. *The Numismatist*, August 1917.

36. From Q. David Bowers's 1997 book, *American Coin Treasures and Hoards*, which includes a long list of Nichols Find citations.

37. *Penny Whimsy*, p. 179.

38. Incorrectly plated in the Breen *Encyclopedia*.

39. Mark Borckardt, letter to the editor of *Numismatic News*, November 27, 2007. Among specialists not everyone agrees that the misstruck *half cent* should qualify as a *cent* of this variety and be included in the population.

40. *Walter Breen's Encyclopedia of Early United States Cents 1793–1814*, p. 365.

41. Frank H. Stewart, *History of the First United States Mint*, p. 72.

42. Details are in *Penny-Wise*, May 15, 1985, and in *Walter Breen's Encyclopedia of Early United States Cents 1793–1814*, p. 424.

43. Harry E. Salyards, communication to Q. David Bowers, March 17, 2009.

44. *Ibid.*

45. *Ibid.*

46. *Penny-Wise*, November 15, 1968.

47. Harry E. Salyards, communication to Q. David Bowers, March 17, 2009.

48. Harry E. Salyards, communication to Q. David Bowers, March 18, 2009.

49. *Ibid.*

50. Bill Maryott, "Die Varieties, Die Stages, Die States, and the Theory Behind Coining," *Penny-Wise*, March 2009, calls these die *stages*, as the die was reworked after heating and annealing.

51. *Ibid.*

52. *Ibid.*

53. Harry E. Salyards, communication, March 18, 2009.

54. *Ibid.*

55. Bill Maryott, "Die Varieties, Die Stages, Die States, and the Theory Behind Coining," *Penny-Wise*, March 2009, calls these die *stages*, as the die was reworked after heating and annealing.

56. For example, the 1791 Liverpool Halfpenny has the edge lettered PAYABLE IN ANGLESEY LONDON OR LIVERPOOL X.

57. Incorrectly plated in the Breen *Encyclopedia*.

58. Harry E. Salyards, communication to Q. David Bowers, March 18, 2009.

59. Text of this comment from Craig Sholley, February 15, 2009.

60. Obituary of Henry C. Hines, *The Numismatist*, February 1949. The cent was described as "Uncirculated."

61. Suggestion by Craig Sholley, communication to Q. David Bowers, February 15, 2009.

62. Harry E. Salyards, communication, March 18, 2009.

63. Craig Sholley states (communication to Q. David Bowers, March 8, 2009) that during the War of 1812 the price of copper soared to 80¢ per pound, or about twice the face value of copper coins!

64. Mickley, recollection in the *American Journal of Numismatics*, June 1868.

65. *Ibid.*, p. 24.

66. The Abbey 1799 cent was sold as part of the Louis E. Eliasberg, Sr., Collection, May 1996, Lot 510; various pedigree information was related in the catalog, including a chronology from John J. Ford Jr., February 17, 1953 (in which was stated that the coin was purchased by Abbey from a dealer named Rogers on Fulton Street for $25, circa 1844–1846, and was retained by Abbey until he sold it in a private transaction in 1856). After the Eliasberg sale, some corrections to the pedigree were made. • In 1875, Abbey, in South Orange, New Jersey, published a small sheet offering large cents for sale, unrelated to the famous 1799.

67. American Journal of Numismatics, January 1891. The January 1, 1882, issue of *Frank Leslie's Illustrated Newspaper* includes his biography, on the occasion of Abbott having been recently elected mayor of Boston.

68. *Penny-Wise*, September 15, 1968.

69. Harry E. Salyards, communication to Q. David Bowers, March 18, 2009.

70. *Ibid.*

71. Bill Maryott, "Die Varieties, Die Stages, Die States, and the Theory Behind Coining," *Penny-Wise*, March 2009, calls these die *stages*, as the die was reworked after heating and annealing.

72. *Ibid.*

73. *Ibid.*

74. *Ibid.*

75. The "perfect die" mentioned in the Breen *Encyclopedia* as having been discovered by Tom Warfield in 1951 seems to be fictitious, a case of Breen mis-remembering. In any event, no such perfect die has ever been seen by specialists such as Jack H. Robinson and Harry E. Salyards (per note to Q. David Bowers, March 20, 2009).

76. Bill Maryott, "Die Varieties, Die Stages, Die States, and the Theory Behind Coining," *Penny-Wise*, March 2009, calls these die *stages*, as the die was reworked after heating and annealing.

77. *Ibid.*

78. *Penny Whimsy*, p. 13.

79. This grade description would be impossible to translate into today's terms.

80. R.W. Julian, communication to Q. David Bowers, March 8, 2009.

81. Congress moved from Philadelphia to Washington in 1800 and thus was not "almost next door" in 1802 or 1803.

82. Bill Maryott, "Die Varieties, Die Stages, Die States, and the Theory Behind Coining,"

Penny-Wise, March 2009, calls these die *stages*, as the die was reworked after heating and annealing.

83. Craig Sholley, communication to Q. David Bowers, February 15, 2009.

84. Denis Loring, communication to Q. David Bowers, March 6, 2009. Also see Bill Noyes, *et al.*, *The Official Condition Census for U.S. Large Cents 1793–1839*, which uses "EAC standards," in which the top two are listed as AU-50, followed by EF listings.

85. *Mason's Coin and Stamp Collectors' Magazine*, March 1869.

86. In the early 1970s Q. David Bowers assisted the Secret Service in the identification of fake 1877, 1909-S, and certain other coins. The counterfeiter was found, and claimed that he used genuine coins as a base and then added metal to them. The Secret Service dropped the case as it could not determine that, legally, these were counterfeits. They were not willing to share any further information. Jack Beymer identified other suspected fakes, including the 1809 cent.

87. Other examples include the 1922 "plain" cent struck from a worn, filled 1922-D die; the 1937-D 3-Legged Buffalo nickel; and the 1800 AMERICAI silver dollar.

88. Per notes by Mark Borckardt in the Eliasberg Collection catalog, 1996.

89. Citation furnished by Bob Vail.

90. G.M. Davison, The Traveller's Guide Throughout the Middle and Northern States, and the Provinces of Canada, Saratoga Springs, New York, 1834, p. 69.

91. Annals of Congress, 14th Congress [convened in 1815], First Session, p. 694.

92. Vattemare's work, never printed in English (although a Spanish edition was published in 1904), was based upon the cabinet of the Bibliothéque Nationale in Paris, not upon cabinets he had observed during his travels in the United States, although American coins were discussed.

93. R.W. Julian, "The Philadelphia Mint and Coinage of 1814–1816," American Numismatic Association Centennial Anthology, 1991.

94. However, in most modern references and citations the 1816 is included; e.g., John D. Wright, The Cent Book, 1992, p. 4, concerning 1816 Newcomb-2: "Possibly a few thousand Mint State examples survive from the Randall Hoard circa 1867."

95. R.W. Julian, "The Philadelphia Mint and Coinage of 1814–1816," American Numismatic Association Centennial Anthology, 1991.

96. Another variety, N-8, has slight traces of a "mouse" in the later obverse die state.

97. Comments to Q. David Bowers during the preparation of this manuscript.

98. John D. Wright, *The Cent Book*, 1992, pp. 81–82. James L. Halperin, letter to the Q. David Bowers, July 1, 1996. New England Rare Coin Auctions, October 1981 Long Beach Sale, lots 58–64. The "brightest," graded as MS-64 RD (the plate coin in this text), the Naftzger coin, was sold as Lot 116 by Larry and Ira Goldberg in the Naftzger sale of February 2009.

99. And offered for sale by New Netherlands Coin Company, privately, after Raymond's death (personal recollection of Q. David Bowers).

100. *Mason's Coin and Stamp Collectors' Magazine*, March 1869.

101. Recollection of Oscar G. Schilke to Q. David Bowers, circa 1959.

102. To list all such instances of wide discrepancies would involve a lot of space. Occasional mentions, as here, are simply to remind readers that opinions can differ dramatically, and to use great care when paying strong premiums for coins that have exceptionally high grades attached.

103. R.W. Julian, "U.S. Half Cent Thrives Despite Second Rate Treatment," *Numismatic Scrapbook Magazine*, October 1972.

104. In the 1950s, when it was possible to buy wholesale lots of cents by the thousands and sort them, this was the variety most often encountered from its era. Typically, these lots had scarce dates (but not varieties) and EF or finer coins had been picked out beforehand.

105. Denis Loring, communication to Q. David Bowers, April 26, 2009.

106. For descriptions of these see John R. Grellman Jr., *The Die Varieties of United States Large Cents 1840–1857*, 2001. Variations in digit alignment for the Large Date coins are also described.

107. John R. Grellman Jr., in *The Die Varieties of United States Large Cents 1840–1857*, debunks Breen "Proofs" (Proof coin *Encyclopedia*) for N-2 and 5, and questions N-8.

108. John R. Grellman Jr., *Ibid.*, debunks certain other Breen-listed "Proofs."

109. Denis Loring, communication, March 25, 2009.

110. John R. Grellman Jr., *The Die Varieties of United States Large Cents 1840–1857*.

111. From R.W. Julian, "New York Coiners Plague Hobby with Bogus 1848, 1849 Cents," *Numismatic Scrapbook Magazine*, June 24, 1972, who gives many more details.

112. John R. Grellman Jr., *The Die Varieties of United States Large Cents 1840–1857*.

113. Communication to Q. David Bowers, April 26, 2009. PCGS has certified an N-30 as Proof-64.

114. Denis Loring, communications with Q. David Bowers, March 25 and April 26, 2009. Other "Proofs" of this year have turned out to be circulation strikes.

115. *Walter Breen's Complete Encyclopedia of U.S. and Colonial Coins*, p. 211; also personal recollection of Q. David Bowers concerning the availability of the coins in the 1950s. These comments are not otherwise confirmed.

116. Denis W. Loring, communication to Q. David Bowers, April 26, 2009.

117. Craig Sholley, communication to Q. David Bowers, January 18, 2001.

118. Denis Loring, communication to Q. David Bowers, March 25, 2009.

DYNAMICS OF THE RARE-COIN MARKET

1. *Coin World*, "Numbers Confirm Coin Hobby Core," November 18, 2002.

2. Citation suggested by John Kraljevich.

3. Issue of December 14, 2004.

Glossary

Over the years coin collectors have developed a special jargon to describe their coins. The following list includes terms that are used frequently by coin collectors or that have a special meaning other than their ordinary dictionary definitions. You will find them useful when you want to discuss or describe your coins.

alloy—A combination of two or more metals.

altered date—A false date on a coin; a date altered to make a coin appear to be one of a rarer or more valuable issue.

bag mark—A surface mark, usually a small nick, acquired by a coin through contact with others in a mint bag.

billon—A low-grade alloy of silver (usually less than 50%) mixed with another metal, typically copper.

blank—The formed piece of metal on which a coin design will be stamped.

bronze—An alloy of copper, zinc, and tin.

bullion—Uncoined gold or silver in the form of bars, ingots, or plate.

cast coins—Coins that are made by pouring molten metal into a mold, instead of in the usual manner of striking blanks with dies.

cent—One one-hundredth of the standard monetary unit. Also known as a *centavo*, *centimo*, or *centesimo* in some Central American and South American countries; *centime* in France and various former colonies in Africa; and other variations.

certified coin—A coin that has been graded, authenticated, and encapsulated in plastic by an independent (neither buyer nor seller) grading service.

cherrypicker—A collector who finds scarce and unusual coins by carefully searching through unattributed items in old accumulations or dealers' stocks.

circulation strike—An Uncirculated coin intended for eventual use in commerce, as opposed to a Proof coin.

clad coinage—Issues of the United States dimes, quarters, halves, and some dollars made since 1965. Each coin has a center core of pure copper and a layer of copper-nickel or silver on both sides.

collar—The outer ring, or die chamber, that holds a blank in place in the coinage press while the coin is impressed by the obverse and reverse dies.

contact marks—Minor abrasions on an Uncirculated coin, made by contact with other coins in a bag or roll.

countermark—A stamp or mark impressed on a coin to verify its use by another government or to indicate revaluation.

crack-out—A coin that has been removed from a grading service holder.

crown—Any dollar-size coin (c. 38 mm in diameter) in general, often struck in silver; specifically, one from the United Kingdom and some Commonwealth countries.

cud—An area of raised metal at the rim of a coin where a portion of the die broke off, leaving a void in the design.

designer—The artist who creates a coin's design. An engraver is the person who cuts a design into a coinage die.

die—A piece of metal engraved with a design and used for stamping coins.

die crack—A fine, raised line on a coin, caused by a broken die.

die defect—An imperfection on a coin, caused by a damaged die.

die variety—Any minor alteration in the basic design of a coin.

dipped, dipping—Refers to chemical cleaning of a coin to remove oxidation or foreign matter.

double eagle—The United States twenty-dollar gold coin.

doubled die—A die that has been given two misaligned impressions from a hub; also, a coin made from such a die.

doubloon—Popular name for a Spanish gold coin originally valued at $16.

eagle—A United States ten-dollar gold coin; also refers to U.S. silver, gold, and platinum bullion pieces made from 1986 to the present.

edge—Periphery of a coin, often with reeding, lettering, or other decoration.

electrotype—A reproduction of a coin or medal made by the electrodeposition process. Electrotypes are frequently used in museum displays.

electrum—A naturally occurring mixture of gold and silver. Some of the world's first coins were made of this alloy.

encapsulated coins—Coins that have been authenticated, graded, and sealed in plastic by a professional service.

engrailed edge—A coin edge marked with small curved notches.

engraver—The person who engraves or sculpts a model for use in translating to a coin die.

error—A mismade coin not intended for circulation.

exergue—That portion of a coin beneath the main design, often separated from it by a line, and typically bearing the date.

field—The background portion of a coin's surface not used for a design or inscription.

filler—A coin in worn condition but rare enough to be included in a collection.

fineness—The purity of gold, silver, or any other precious metal, expressed in terms of one thousand parts. A coin of 90% pure silver is expressed as .900 fine.

flan—A blank piece of metal in the size and shape of a coin; also called a *planchet*.

gem—A coin of exceptionally high quality, typically considered MS-65 or PF-65 or better.

gripped edge—An edge with irregularly spaced notches.

half eagle—The United States five-dollar gold coin minted from 1795 to 1929.

hub—A positive-image punch to impress the coin's design into a die for coinage.

incuse—The design of a coin that has been impressed below the coin's surface. A design raised above the coin's surface is in relief.

inscription—The legend or lettering on a coin.

intrinsic value—Bullion or "melt" value of the actual precious metal in a numismatic item.

investment grade—Promotional term; generally, a coin in grade MS-65 or better.

junk silver—Common-date silver coins taken from circulation; worth only bullion value.

key coin—One of the scarcer or more valuable coins in a series.

laureate—Head crowned with a laurel wreath.

legal tender—Money that is officially issued and recognized for redemption by an authorized agency or government.

legend—A principal inscription on a coin.

lettered edge—The edge of a coin bearing an inscription, found on some foreign and some older United States coins, modern Presidential dollars, and the MMIX Ultra High Relief gold coin.

luster—The brilliant or "frosty" surface quality of an Uncirculated (Mint State) coin.

milled edge—The raised rim around the outer surface of a coin, not to be confused with the reeded or serrated narrow edge of a coin.

mint error—Any mismade or defective coin produced by a mint.

mint luster—Shiny "frost" or brilliance on the surface of an Uncirculated or Mint State coin.

mintmark—A small letter or other mark on a coin, indicating the mint at which it was struck.

Mint set—A set of Uncirculated coins packaged and sold by the Mint. Each set contains one of each of the coins made for circulation at each of the mints that year.

motto—An inspirational word or phrase used on a coin.

mule—A coin struck from two dies not originally intended to be used together.

obverse—The front or face side of a coin.

overdate—Date made by superimposing one or more numerals on a previously dated die.

overgraded—A coin in poorer condition than stated.

overstrike—An impression made with new dies on a previously struck coin.

patina—The green or brown surface film found on ancient copper and bronze coins, caused by oxidation over a long period of time.

pattern—Experimental or trial coin, generally of a new design, denomination, or metal.

pedigree—The record of previous owners of a rare coin.

planchet—The blank piece of metal on which a coin design is stamped.

Proof—Coins struck for collectors by the Mint using specially polished dies and planchets.

Proof set—A set of each of the Proof coins made during a given year, packaged by the Mint and sold to collectors.

quarter eagle—The United States $2.50 gold coin.

raw—A coin that has not been encapsulated by an independent grading service.

reeded edge—The edge of a coin with grooved lines that run vertically around its perimeter, as seen on modern United States silver and clad coins.

regula—The bar separating the numerator and the denominator in a fraction.

relief—Any part of a coin's design that is raised above the coin's field is said to be in relief. The opposite of relief is incuse, meaning sunk into the field.

restrike—A coin struck from genuine dies at a later date than the original issue.

reverse—The back side of a coin.

rim—The raised portion of a coin that protects the design from wear.

round—A round one-ounce silver medal or bullion piece.

series—A set of one coin of each year of a specific design and denomination issued from each mint. For example, Lincoln cents from 1909 to 1959.

slab—A hard plastic case containing a coin that has been graded and encapsulated by a professional service.

spot price—The daily quoted market value of precious metals in bullion form.

token—A privately issued piece, typically with an exchange value for goods or services, but not an official government coin.

trade dollar—Silver dollar issued especially for trade with a foreign country. In the United States, trade dollars were first issued in 1873 to stimulate commerce with the Orient. Many other countries have also issued trade dollars.

truncation—The sharply cut-off bottom edge of a bust or portrait.

type—A series of coins defined by a shared distinguishing design, composition, denomination, and other elements. For example, Barber dimes or Franklin half dollars.

type set—A collection consisting of one representative coin of each type, of a particular series or period.

Uncirculated—A circulation-strike coin that has never been used in commerce, and has retained its original surface and luster; also called Mint State.

unique—An item of which only one specimen is known to exist.

variety—A coin's design that sets it apart from the normal issue of that type.

wheaties—Lincoln cents with the wheat ears reverse, issued from 1909 to 1958.

year set—A set of coins for any given year, consisting of one of each denomination issued that year.

Bibliography

COLONIAL ISSUES

Bowers, Q. David. *Whitman Encyclopedia of Colonial and Early American Coins*. Atlanta, GA, 2009.

Breen, Walter. *Walter Breen's Complete Encyclopedia of U.S. and Colonial Coins*. New York, NY, 1988.

Carlotto, Tony. *The Copper Coins of Vermont*. Chelsea, MI, 1998.

Crosby, S.S. *The Early Coins of America*. Boston, 1875. Reprint, 1945, 1965, 1974, and 1983.

Demling, Michael. *New Jersey Coppers*. 2011.

Kessler, Alan. *The Fugio Cents*. Newtonville, MA, 1976.

Maris, Edward. *A Historic Sketch of the Coins of New Jersey*. Philadelphia, 1881. Reprint, 1965, 1974, and 1987.

Martin, Syd. *The Hibernia Coinage of William Wood (1722–1724)*. 2007.

Martin, Syd. *The Rosa Americana Coinage of William Wood*. Ann Arbor, MI, 2011.

Miller, Henry C., and Ryder Hillyer. *The State Coinages of New England*. New York, NY, 1920.

Nelson, Philip. *The Coinage of William Wood, 1722–1733*. London, 1903. Reprint, 1959.

Newman, Eric P. *Coinage for Colonial Virginia*. New York, NY, 1956.

Newman, Eric P. *The United States Fugio Copper Coinage of 1787*. Ypsilanti, MI, 2007.

Newman, Eric P., and Richard G. Doty. *Studies on Money in Early America*. New York, NY, 1976.

Noe, Sydney P. *The New England and Willow Tree Coinage of Massachusetts*. New York, NY, 1943; *The Oak Tree Coinage of Massachusetts*. New York, NY, 1947; and *The Pine Tree Coinage of Massachusetts*. New York, NY, 1952. Combined reprint as *The Silver Coins of Massachusetts*. New York, NY, 1973.

Noyes, William C. *United States Large Cents, 1816–1857*. Ypsilanti, MI, 2012.

Rulau, Russell, and George Fuld. *Medallic Portraits of Washington*. Iola, WI, 1999.

Salmon, Christopher J. *The Silver Coins of Massachusetts*. New York, NY, 2010.

Vlack, Robert. *An Illustrated Catalogue of the French Billon Coinage in the Americas*. Boston, NY, 2004.

HALF CENTS

Bowers, Q. David. *A Guide Book of Half Cents and Large Cents*. Atlanta, GA, 2015.

Breen, Walter. *Walter Breen's Encyclopedia of United States Half Cents 1793–1857*. South Gate, CA, 1983.

Cohen, Roger S., Jr. *American Half Cents—The "Little Half Sisters"* (2nd ed.). 1982.

Eckberg, William, Robert Fagaly, Dennis Fuoss, and Raymond Williams. *Grading Guide for Early American Copper Coins*. Heath, OH, 2014.

Fivaz, Bill, and J.T. Stanton. *The Cherrypickers' Guide to Rare Die Varieties* (6th ed., vol. I). Atlanta, GA, 2015.

Frossard, Édouard. *United States Cents and Half Cents Issued Between the Years of 1793 and 1857*. Irvington, NY, 1879.

Manley, Ronald P. *The Half Cent Die State Book, 1793–1857*. United States, 1998.

Robinson, Jack H. *Copper Quotes by Robinson* (20th ed.). 2011.

LARGE CENTS

Bowers, Q. David. *A Guide Book of Half Cents and Large Cents.* Atlanta, GA, 2015.

Breen, Walter. *Walter Breen's Encyclopedia of Early United States Cents, 1793–1814.* Wolfeboro, NH, 2001.

Eckberg, William, Robert Fagaly, Dennis Fuoss, and Raymond Williams. *Grading Guide for Early American Copper Coins.* Heath, OH, 2014.

Fivaz, Bill, and J.T. Stanton. *The Cherrypickers' Guide to Rare Die Varieties* (6th ed., vol. I). Atlanta, GA, 2015.

Frossard, Édouard. *United States Cents and Half Cents Issued Between the Years of 1793 and 1857.* Irvington, NY, 1879.

Grellman, J.R. *Attribution Guide for United States Large Cents, 1840–1857* (3rd ed.). Bloomington, MN, 2002.

Newcomb, H.R. *United States Copper Cents, 1816–1857.* New York, NY, 1944. Reprint, 1983.

Noyes, William C. *United States Large Cents, 1793–1794.* Ypsilanti, MI, 2006.

Noyes, William C. *United States Large Cents, 1793–1814.* Bloomington, MN, 1991.

Noyes, William C. *United States Large Cents, 1795–1797.* Ypsilanti, MI, 2007.

Noyes, William C. *United States Large Cents, 1816–1839.* Bloomington, MN, 1991.

Penny-Wise. Official publication of Early American Coppers, Inc.

Robinson, Jack H. *Copper Quotes by Robinson* (20th ed.). 2011.

Sheldon, William H. *Penny Whimsy (1793–1814).* New York, NY, 1958. Reprint, 1965 and 1976.

Wright, John D. *The Cent Book, 1816–1839.* Bloomington, MN, 1992.

SMALL CENTS

Bowers, Q. David. *A Buyer's and Enthusiast's Guide to Flying Eagle and Indian Head Cents.* Wolfeboro, NH, 1996.

Bowers, Q. David. *A Guide Book of Lincoln Cents.* Atlanta, GA, 2008.

Fivaz, Bill, and J.T. Stanton. *The Cherrypickers' Guide to Rare Die Varieties* (6th ed., vol. I). Atlanta, GA, 2015.

Lange, David W. *The Complete Guide to Lincoln Cents.* Wolfeboro, NH, 1996.

Snow, Richard. *Flying Eagle and Indian Cent Attribution Guide, 1856–1909* (2nd ed.). Tuscon, AZ, 2010.

Snow, Richard. *A Guide Book of Flying Eagle and Indian Head Cents* (2nd ed.). Atlanta, GA, 2009.

Steve, Larry, and Kevin Flynn. *Flying Eagle and Indian Cent Die Varieties.* Jarretteville, MD, 1995.

Taylor, Sol. *The Standard Guide to the Lincoln Cent.* Anaheim, CA, 1999.

Wexler, John, and Kevin Flynn. *The Authoritative Reference on Lincoln Cents.* Rancocas, NJ, 1996.

TWO-CENT PIECES

Fivaz, Bill, and J.T. Stanton. *The Cherrypickers' Guide to Rare Die Varieties* (6th ed., vol. I). Atlanta, GA, 2015.

Flynn, Kevin. *Getting Your Two Cents Worth.* Rancocas, NJ, 1994.

Leone, Frank. *Longacre's Two Cent Piece Die Varieties and Errors.* College Point, NY, 1991.

NICKEL FIVE-CENT PIECES

Bowers, Q. David. *A Guide Book of Buffalo and Jefferson Nickels.* Atlanta, GA, 2007.

Bowers, Q. David. *A Guide Book of Shield and Liberty Head Nickels.* Atlanta, GA, 2006.

Fivaz, Bill, and J.T. Stanton. *The Cherrypickers' Guide to Rare Die Varieties* (6th ed., vol. I). Atlanta, GA, 2015.

Fletcher, Edward L., Jr. *The Shield Five Cent Series.* Ormond Beach, FL, 1994.

Lange, David W. *The Complete Guide to Buffalo Nickels.* Virginia Beach, VA, 2006.

Nagengast, Bernard. *The Jefferson Nickel Analyst* (2nd ed.). Sidney, OH, 1979.

Peters, Gloria, and Cynthia Mahon. *The Complete Guide to Shield and Liberty Head Nickels.* Virginia Beach, VA, 1995.

Wescott, Michael. *The United States Nickel Five-Cent Piece.* Wolfeboro, NH, 1991.

HALF DISMES

Judd, J. Hewitt. *United States Pattern Coins* (10th ed.), edited by Q. David Bowers. Atlanta, GA, 2009.

Logan, Russell, and John McCloskey. *Federal Half Dimes, 1792–1837.* Manchester, MI, 1998.

Newlin, H.P. *The Early Half-Dimes of the United States.* Philadelphia, PA, 1883. Reprint, 1933.

Valentine, D.W. *The United States Half Dimes.* New York, NY, 1931. Reprint, 1975.

HALF DIMES

Blythe, Al. *The Complete Guide to Liberty Seated Half Dimes.* Virginia Beach, VA, 1992.

Breen, Walter. *United States Half Dimes: A Supplement.* New York, NY, 1958.

Fivaz, Bill, and J.T. Stanton. *The Cherrypickers' Guide to Rare Die Varieties* (5th ed., vol. II). Atlanta, GA, 2012.

Logan, Russell, and John McCloskey. *Federal Half Dimes, 1792–1837.* Manchester, MI, 1998.

Newlin, Harold P. *The Early Half-Dimes of the United States.* Philadelphia, PA, 1883. Reprint, 1933.

Valentine, D.W. *The United States Half Dimes.* New York, NY, 1931. Reprint, 1975.

DIMES

Ahwash, Kamal M. *Encyclopedia of United States Liberty Seated Dimes, 1837–1891.* Kamal Press, 1977.

Bowers, Q. David. *A Guide Book of Barber Silver Coins.* Atlanta, GA, 2015.

Bowers, Q. David. *A Guide Book of Mercury Dimes, Standing Liberty Quarters, and Liberty Walking Half Dollars.* Atlanta, GA, 2015.

Davis, David, Russell Logan, Allen Lovejoy, John McCloskey, and William Subjack. *Early United States Dimes, 1796–1837.* Ypsilanti, MI, 1984.

Fivaz, Bill, and J.T. Stanton. *The Cherrypickers' Guide to Rare Die Varieties* (5th ed., vol. II). Atlanta, GA, 2012.

Flynn, Kevin. *The 1894-S Dime: A Mystery Unraveled.* Rancocas, NJ, 2005.

Flynn, Kevin. *The Authoritative Reference on Roosevelt Dimes.* Brooklyn, NY, 2001.

Greer, Brian. *The Complete Guide to Liberty Seated Dimes.* Virginia Beach, VA, 2005.

Lange, David W. *The Complete Guide to Mercury Dimes* (2nd ed.). Virginia Beach, VA, 2005.

Lawrence, David. *The Complete Guide to Barber Dimes.* Virginia Beach, VA, 1991.

TWENTY-CENT PIECES

Brunner, Lane J., and John M. Frost. *Double Dimes: The United States Twenty-Cent Piece.* Hanover, PA, 2014.

Flynn, Kevin. *The Authoritative Reference on Twenty Cents.* Lumberton, NJ, 2013.

QUARTER DOLLARS

Bowers, Q. David. *A Guide Book of Barber Silver Coins.* Atlanta, GA, 2015.

Bowers, Q. David. *A Guide Book of Mercury Dimes, Standing Liberty Quarters, and Liberty Walking Half Dollars.* Atlanta, GA, 2015.

Bowers, Q. David. *A Guide Book of Washington and State Quarters.* Atlanta, GA, 2006.

Bressett, Kenneth. *The Official Whitman Statehood Quarters Collector's Handbook.* New York, NY, 2000.

Briggs, Larry. *The Comprehensive Encyclopedia of United States Seated Quarters.* Lima, OH, 1991.

Browning, Ard W. *The Early Quarter Dollars of the United States, 1796–1838.* New York, NY, 1925. Reprint, 1992.

Cline, J.H. *Standing Liberty Quarters* (4th ed.). 2007.

Duphorne, R. *The Early Quarter Dollars of the United States.* 1975.

Fivaz, Bill, and J.T. Stanton. *The Cherrypickers' Guide to Rare Die Varieties* (5th ed., vol. II). Atlanta, GA, 2012.

Haseltine, J.W. *Type Table of United States Dollars, Half Dollars and Quarter Dollars.* Philadelphia, PA, 1881. Reprint, 1927 and 1968.

Kelman, Keith N. *Standing Liberty Quarters.* 1976.

Lawrence, David. *The Complete Guide to Barber Quarters.* Virginia Beach, VA, 1989.

Rea, Rory, Flenn Peterson, Bradley Karoleff, and John Kovach. *Early Quarter Dollars of the U.S. Mint, 1796–1838.* 2010.

Tompkins, Steve M. *Early United States Quarters, 1796–1838.* Sequim, WA, 2010.

HALF DOLLARS

Bowers, Q. David. *A Guide Book of Barber Silver Coins.* Atlanta, GA, 2015.

Bowers, Q. David. *A Guide Book of Mercury Dimes, Standing Liberty Quarters, and Liberty Walking Half Dollars.* Atlanta, GA, 2015.

Fivaz, Bill, and J.T. Stanton. *The Cherrypickers' Guide to Rare Die Varieties* (5th ed., vol. II). Atlanta, GA, 2012.

Flynn, Kevin. *The Authoritative Reference on Barber Half Dollars.* Brooklyn, NY, 2005.

Fox, Bruce. *The Complete Guide to Walking Liberty Half Dollars.* Virginia Beach, VA, 1993.

Haseltine, J.W. *Type Table of United States Dollars, Half Dollars and Quarter Dollars.* Philadelphia, PA, 1881. Reprint, 1927 and 1968.

Lawrence, David. *The Complete Guide to Barber Halves.* Virginia Beach, VA, 1991.

Overton, Al C. *Early Half Dollar Die Varieties, 1794–1836* (3rd ed.), edited by Donald Parsley, 1990. Colorado Springs, CO, 1967.

Peterson, Glenn R. *The Ultimate Guide to Attributing Bust Half Dollars.* Rocky River, OH, 2000.

Tomaska, Rick. *A Guide Book of Franklin and Kennedy Half Dollars* (2nd ed.). Atlanta, GA, 2012.

Wiley, Randy, and Bill Bugert. *The Complete Guide to Liberty Seated Half Dollars.* Virginia Beach, VA, 1993.

SILVER DOLLARS

Bolender, M.H. *The United States Early Silver Dollars From 1794 to 1803* (5th ed.). Iola, WI, 1987.

Bowers, Q. David. *The Encyclopedia of United States Silver Dollars, 1794–1804.* Irvine, CA, 2013.

Bowers, Q. David. *The Rare Silver Dollars Dated 1804.* Wolfeboro, NH, 1999.

Bowers, Q. David. *Silver Dollars and Trade Dollars of the United States: A Complete Encyclopedia.* Wolfeboro, NH, 1993.

Bowers, Q. David. *A Guide Book of Morgan Silver Dollars* (4th ed.). Atlanta, GA, 2012.

Burdette, Roger W. *A Guide Book of Peace Dollars* (2nd ed.). Atlanta, GA, 2012.

Fey, Michael S., and Jeff Oxman. *The Top 100 Morgan Dollar Varieties.* Morris Planes, NJ, 1997.

Fivaz, Bill, and J.T. Stanton. *The Cherrypickers' Guide to Rare Die Varieties* (5th ed., vol. II). Atlanta, GA, 2012.

Haseltine, J.W. *Type Table of United States Dollars, Half Dollars and Quarter Dollars.* Philadelphia, PA, 1881. Reprint, 1927 and 1968.

Judd, J. Hewitt. *United States Pattern Coins* (10th ed.), edited by Q. David Bowers. Atlanta, GA, 2009.

Logies, Martin A. *The Flowing Hair Silver Dollars of 1794.* 2004.

Newman, Eric P., and Kenneth E. Bressett. *The Fantastic 1804 Dollar, Tribute Edition.* Atlanta, GA, 2009.

Standish, Michael "Miles," and John B. Love. *Morgan Dollar: America's Love Affair With a Legendary Coin.* Atlanta, GA, 2014.

Van Allen, Leroy C., and A. George Mallis. *Comprehensive Catalogue and Encyclopedia of U.S. Morgan and Peace Silver Dollars.* New York, NY, 1997.

TRADE DOLLARS

Bowers, Q. David. *Silver Dollars and Trade Dollars of the United States: A Complete Encyclopedia.* Wolfeboro, NH, 1993.

Fivaz, Bill, and J.T. Stanton. *The Cherrypickers' Guide to Rare Die Varieties* (5th ed., vol. II). Atlanta, GA, 2012.

Willem, John M. *The United States Trade Dollar* (2nd ed.). Racine, WI, 1965.

MODERN DOLLARS

Bowers, Q. David. *Silver Dollars and Trade Dollars of the United States: A Complete Encyclopedia.* Wolfeboro, NH, 1993.

Fivaz, Bill, and J.T. Stanton. *The Cherrypickers' Guide to Rare Die Varieties* (5th ed., vol. II). Atlanta, GA, 2012.

Judd, J. Hewitt. *United States Pattern Coins* (10th ed.), edited by Q. David Bowers. Atlanta, GA, 2009.

GOLD DOLLARS

Akers, David W. *Gold Dollars (and Other Gold Denominations)*. Englewood, OH, 1975–1982.

Bowers, Q. David. *A Guide Book of Gold Dollars* (2nd ed.). Atlanta, GA, 2011.

Bowers, Q. David. *United States Gold Coins: An Illustrated History*. Wolfeboro, NH, 1982.

Breen, Walter. *Major Varieties of U.S. Gold Dollars (and Other Gold Denominations)*. Chicago, IL, 1964.

Fivaz, Bill. *United States Gold Counterfeit Detection Guide*. Atlanta, GA, 2005.

Fivaz, Bill, and J.T. Stanton. *The Cherrypickers' Guide to Rare Die Varieties* (5th ed., vol. II). Atlanta, GA, 2012.

Garrett, Jeff, and Ron Guth. *Encyclopedia of U.S. Gold Coins, 1795–1933* (2nd ed.). Atlanta, GA, 2008.

GOLD QUARTER EAGLES

Akers, David W. *Gold Dollars (and Other Gold Denominations)*. Englewood, OH, 1975–1982.

Bowers, Q. David. *United States Gold Coins: An Illustrated History*. Wolfeboro, NH, 1982.

Breen, Walter. *Major Varieties of U.S. Gold Dollars (and Other Gold Denominations)*. Chicago, IL, 1964.

Dannreuther, John W., and Harry W. Bass. *Early U.S. Gold Coin Varieties*. Atlanta, GA, 2006.

Fivaz, Bill. *United States Gold Counterfeit Detection Guide*. Atlanta, GA, 2005.

Fivaz, Bill, and J.T. Stanton. *The Cherrypickers' Guide to Rare Die Varieties* (5th ed., vol. II). Atlanta, GA, 2012.

Garrett, Jeff, and Ron Guth. *Encyclopedia of U.S. Gold Coins, 1795–1933* (2nd ed.). Atlanta, GA, 2008.

THREE-DOLLAR GOLD PIECES

Akers, David W. *Gold Dollars (and Other Gold Denominations)*. Englewood, OH, 1975–1982.

Bowers, Q. David. *United States Gold Coins: An Illustrated History*. Wolfeboro, NH, 1982.

Bowers, Q. David, and Douglas Winter. *United States $3 Gold Pieces, 1854–1889*. Wolfeboro, NH, 2005.

Breen, Walter. *Major Varieties of U.S. Gold Dollars (and Other Gold Denominations)*. Chicago, IL, 1964.

Fivaz, Bill. *United States Gold Counterfeit Detection Guide*. Atlanta, GA, 2005.

Fivaz, Bill, and J.T. Stanton. *The Cherrypickers' Guide to Rare Die Varieties* (5th ed., vol. II). Atlanta, GA, 2012.

Garrett, Jeff, and Ron Guth. *Encyclopedia of U.S. Gold Coins, 1795–1933* (2nd ed.). Atlanta, GA, 2008.

FOUR-DOLLAR GOLD PIECES

Akers, David W. *Gold Dollars (and Other Gold Denominations)*. Englewood, OH, 1975–1982.

Bowers, Q. David. *United States Gold Coins: An Illustrated History*. Wolfeboro, NH, 1982.

Breen, Walter. *Major Varieties of U.S. Gold Dollars (and Other Gold Denominations)*. Chicago, IL, 1964.

Garrett, Jeff, and Ron Guth. *Encyclopedia of U.S. Gold Coins, 1795–1933* (2nd ed.). Atlanta, GA, 2008.

Judd, J. Hewitt. *United States Pattern Coins* (10th ed.), edited by Q. David Bowers. Atlanta, GA, 2009.

GOLD HALF EAGLES

Akers, David W. *Gold Dollars (and Other Gold Denominations)*. Englewood, OH, 1975–1982.

Bowers, Q. David. *United States Gold Coins: An Illustrated History*. Wolfeboro, NH, 1982.

Breen, Walter. *Major Varieties of U.S. Gold Dollars (and Other Gold Denominations)*. Chicago, IL, 1964.

Dannreuther, John W., and Harry W. Bass. *Early U.S. Gold Coin Varieties*. Atlanta, GA, 2006.

Fivaz, Bill. *United States Gold Counterfeit Detection Guide*. Atlanta, GA, 2005.

Fivaz, Bill, and J.T. Stanton. *The Cherrypickers' Guide to Rare Die Varieties* (5th ed., vol. II). Atlanta, GA, 2012.

Garrett, Jeff, and Ron Guth. *Encyclopedia of U.S. Gold Coins, 1795–1933* (2nd ed.). Atlanta, GA, 2008.

Miller, Robert W., Sr. *United States Half Eagle Gold Coins, 1795–1834*. 1997.

GOLD EAGLES

Akers, David W. *Gold Dollars (and Other Gold Denominations)*. Englewood, OH, 1975–1982.

Bowers, Q. David. *United States Gold Coins: An Illustrated History*. Wolfeboro, NH, 1982.

Breen, Walter. *Major Varieties of U.S. Gold Dollars (and Other Gold Denominations)*. Chicago, IL, 1964.

Dannreuther, John W., and Harry W. Bass. *Early U.S. Gold Coin Varieties*. Atlanta, GA, 2006.

Fivaz, Bill. *United States Gold Counterfeit Detection Guide*. Atlanta, GA, 2005.

Fivaz, Bill, and J.T. Stanton. *The Cherrypickers' Guide to Rare Die Varieties* (5th ed., vol. II). Atlanta, GA, 2012.

Garrett, Jeff, and Ron Guth. *Encyclopedia of U.S. Gold Coins, 1795–1933* (2nd ed.). Atlanta, GA, 2008.

Teraskza, Anthony. *United States Ten Dollar Gold Eagles, 1795–1804*.

GOLD DOUBLE EAGLES

Akers, David W. *Gold Dollars (and Other Gold Denominations)*. Englewood, OH, 1975–1982.

Bowers, Q. David. *A Guide Book of Double Eagle Gold Coins*. Atlanta, GA, 2004.

Bowers, Q. David. *United States Gold Coins: An Illustrated History*. Wolfeboro, NH, 1982.

Bowers, Q. David. *U.S. Liberty Head $20 Double Eagles: The Gilded Age of Coinage*. Irvine, CA, 2014.

Fivaz, Bill. *United States Gold Counterfeit Detection Guide*. Atlanta, GA, 2005.

Fivaz, Bill, and J.T. Stanton. *The Cherrypickers' Guide to Rare Die Varieties* (5th ed., vol. II). Atlanta, GA, 2012.

Garrett, Jeff, and Ron Guth. *Encyclopedia of U.S. Gold Coins, 1795–1933* (2nd ed.). Atlanta, GA, 2008.

Moran, Michael. *Striking Change: The Great Artistic Collaboration of Theodore Roosevelt and Augustus Saint-Gaudens*. Atlanta, GA, 2008.

COMMEMORATIVES

Bowers, Q. David. *A Guide Book of United States Commemorative Coins*. Atlanta, GA, 2008.

Bullowa, David M. *The Commemorative Coinage of the United States, 1892–1938*. New York, NY, 1938.

Fivaz, Bill, and J.T. Stanton. *The Cherrypickers' Guide to Rare Die Varieties* (5th ed., vol. II). Atlanta, GA, 2012.

Flynn, Kevin. *The Authoritative Reference on Commemorative Coins, 1892–1954*. Roswell, GA, 2008.

Mosher, Stuart. *The Commemorative Coinage of the United States, 1892–1938*. New York, NY, 1940.

Slabaugh, Arlie. *United States Commemorative Coinage*. Racine, WI, 1975.

Swiatek, Anthony. *Encyclopedia of the Commemorative Coins of the United States*. Chicago, IL, 2012.

Swiatek, Anthony, and Walter Breen. *The Encyclopedia of United States Silver and Gold Commemorative Coins, 1892–1954*. New York, NY, 1981.

Taxay, Don. *An Illustrated History of U.S. Commemorative Coinage*. New York, NY, 1967.

PROOF AND MINT SETS

Lange, David W. *A Guide Book of Modern United States Proof Coin Sets* (2nd ed.). Atlanta, GA, 2010.

U.S. MINT BULLION COINS

Mercanti, John M., and Michael Standish. *American Silver Eagles: A Guide to the U.S. Bullion Coin Program* (2nd ed.). Atlanta, GA, 2013.

Moy, Edmund. *American Gold and Platinum Eagles: A Guide to the U.S. Bullion Coin Programs*. Atlanta, GA, 2013.

Tucker, Dennis. *American Gold and Silver: U.S. Mint Collector and Investor Coins and Medals, Bicentennial to Date*. Atlanta, GA, 2015.

TOKENS AND MEDALS

Bowers, Q. David. *A Guide Book of Civil War Tokens* (2nd ed.). Atlanta, GA, 2015.

Bowers, Q. David. *A Guide Book of Hard Times Tokens*. Atlanta, GA, 2015.

Fuld, George, and Melvin Fuld. *Patriotic Civil War Tokens*. Ypsilanti, MI, 1982.

Fuld, George, and Melvin Fuld. *U.S. Civil War Store Cards* (3rd ed.). 2015.

Gould, Maurice, Kenneth Bressett, and Kaye and Nancy Dethridge. *Alaska's Coinage Through the Years*. Racine, WI, 1960.

Jaeger, Katherine. *A Guide Book of United States Tokens and Medals*. Atlanta, GA, 2008.

Jaeger, Katherine, and Q. David Bowers. *100 Greatest American Medals and Tokens*. Atlanta, GA, 2007.

Rulau, Russell. *Standard Catalog of United States Tokens, 1700–1900*. Iola, WI, 1997.

PATTERNS

Judd, J. Hewitt. *United States Pattern Coins* (10th ed.), edited by Q. David Bowers. Atlanta, GA, 2008.

PRIVATE AND TERRITORIAL GOLD

Adams, Edgar H. *Official Premium Lists of Private and Territorial Gold Coins*. Brooklyn, NY, 1909.

Adams, Edgar H. *Private Gold Coinage of California, 1849–1855*. Brooklyn, NY, 1913.

Bowers, Q. David. *A California Gold Rush History Featuring Treasure from the S.S.* Central America. Wolfeboro, NH, 2001.

Bowers, Q. David. *The History of United States Coinage as Illustrated by the Garrett Collection*. Los Angeles, CA, 1979.

Breen, Walter, and Ronald Gillio. *California Pioneer Fractional Gold* (2nd ed.). Santa Barbara, CA, 1983.

Clifford, Henry H. "Pioneer Gold Coinage in the West—1848–1861," reprint from *The Westerners Brand Book—Book Nine*. Los Angeles, CA, 1961.

Griffin, Clarence. *The Bechtlers and Bechtler Coinage and Gold Mining in North Carolina, 1814–1830*. Spindale, NC, 1929.

Kagin, Donald H. *Private Gold Coins and Patterns of the United States*. New York, NY, 1981.

Lee, Kenneth W. *California Gold—Dollars, Half Dollars, Quarter Dollars*. Santa Ana, CA, 1979.

Owens, Dan. *California Coiners and Assayers*. Wolfeboro, NH, and New York, NY, 2000.

Seymour, Dexter C. "The 1830 Coinage of Templeton Reid." *American Numismatic Society Museum Notes 22*. New York, NY, 1977.

WORLD ISSUES

Allen, Lyman L. *U.S. Philippine Coins*. Oakland Park, FL: Lyman Allen Numismatic Services, 1998.

Haxby, James. *A Guide Book of Canadian Coins and Tokens*. Atlanta, GA, 2012.

Medcalf, Donald, and Ronald Russell. *Hawaiian Money Standard Catalog* (2nd ed.). Mill Creek, WA, 1991.

Perez, Gilbert S. *The Mint of the Philippine Islands*. New York, NY, 1921.

Shafer, Neil. *United States Territorial Coinage for the Philippine Islands*. 1961.

TYPE COINS

Bowers, Q. David. *A Guide Book of United States Type Coins* (2nd ed.). Atlanta, GA, 2008.

Garrett, Jeff, and Ron Guth. *100 Greatest U.S. Coins* (3rd ed.). Atlanta, GA, 2008.

Guth, Ron, and Jeff Garrett. *United States Coinage: A Study by Type*. Atlanta, GA, 2005.

MISSTRIKES AND ERRORS

Colletti, Frank J. *A Guide Book of the Official Red Book of United States Coins*. Atlanta, GA, 2009.

Fivaz, Bill, and J.T. Stanton. *The Cherrypickers' Guide to Rare Die Varieties* (6th ed., vol. I). Atlanta, GA, 2015.

Fivaz, Bill, and J.T. Stanton. *The Cherrypickers' Guide to Rare Die Varieties* (5th ed., vol. II). Atlanta, GA, 2012.

Herbert, Alan. *Official Price Guide to Minting Varieties and Errors*. New York, NY, 1991.

Margolis, Arnold, and Fred Weinberg. *The Error Coin Encyclopedia* (4th ed.). 1991.

COIN CLEANING, CONSERVATION, AND PRESERVATION

White, Weimar W. *Coin Chemistry, Including Preservation and Cleaning* (3rd ed.). Victor, NY, 2012.

Index

General Index

abbreviations, used in this book, 17

A.C. Gies Hoard, 244, 245, 362

African Head copper, 117

Alaska Rural Rehabilitation Corporation, 1396, 1397

Alaska, coinage of, 14, 1396, 1397

Albany Church pennies, 132

altered coins, 23, 24, 349, 391, 430, 435, 531, 541, 609, 700, 927, 928, 1009, 1399

America the Beautiful™ bullion, 1277

America the Beautiful™ quarter dollars, 795

American Buffalo bullion coinage, 1295

American Gold Eagle (AGE), 1281–1294

American Numismatic Association (ANA), 13, 19, 21, 915, 1011, 1369, 1372, 1375, 1408, 1411, 1422, 1438, 1451, 1454, 1457, 1462, 1467–1469, 1472, 1483

grading standards of, 19, 265, 266, 277, 336, 537, 550, 570, 691, 699, 722, 755, 769, 810, 851, 1422

American Plantations tokens, 97

American Platinum Eagle (APE), 1306–1316

American Silver Eagle (ASE), 24, 1271–1276

ANACS, 19

Anthony dollars, 86, 938, 943–946, 1404

Articles of Confederation, 48, 54, 56, 130

Atlee, James F., 113, 123, 124

auction prices, top 250 U.S., 1416

Auctori Plebis tokens, 131

authentication, 23, 24, 146, 437, 765, 1449

Baltimore Find, 31

Bailey, John, 113, 121, 123, 125

Baldwin & Co., 66

Baltimore, Lord, 42, 95

Bank of New York hoard, 29

bank notes, national, 63, 73, 80, 82

bank notes, private, 63, 64, 72

Bar coppers, 131

Barber, Charles E., 76, 78, 83, 535, 697, 724–726, 753, 754, 756, 806, 807, 850, 852, 918, 929, 930, 1018, 1019, 1083, 1107, 1114–1121, 1123, 1322, 1323, 1362, 1366

Barber, William, 720, 721, 962, 1061, 1320–1322

Barnum, P.T., 1153, 1154

Barry, Standish, 120, 132

barter system, 40, 42, 44, 46, 56

Bechtler, August, 65, 70

Bechtler, Christopher, 65, 70

Bechtler gold, 65, 70

Bermuda (Sommer Islands), 90, 91

Bicentennial coinage, 82, 87, 88, 550, 561–564, 724, 726, 767, 796, 870, 871, 937, 939, 940,

1141, 1142, 1159, 1172, 1173, 1175, 1176, 1191, 1218–1220, 1226, 1229, 1230, 1238, 1239, 1245, 1246, 1261, 1266, 1271, 1293, 1402

billon coinage, 109

bimetallism, 75

Birch cent, 150, 151

Birch, Robert, 58, 59, 150, 627

Bishop, Samuel, 117

bit, 147, 153

Bland-Allison Act, 28, 74, 961, 962

blanks, 36, 61, 98, 109, 229, 392, 427, 461, 462, 885, 886, 890, 896, 946, 1261, 1270, 1368, 1399, 1401, 1485

Blue Books

collectible, 1407

See also Handbook of United States Coins

Boudinot, Elias, 61, 62, 320, 328, 353

Boulton and Watt, 134

branch mints, 22, 69, 70, 72–74, 576, 588, 690, 884, 971, 1259, 1330, 1331, 1340, 1366, 1421, 1451

Brasher, Ephraim, 52, 120, 121, 123, 125

Brasher doubloons, 52, 120, 121, 125

Breen, Walter, 13, 65, 105, 155, 156, 253, 593, 608, 734, 883, 930, 992, 1022, 1038, 1047, 1074, 1103, 1135, 1421, 1461, 1463

Alphabetical Index of Dates for Commemoratives

See also "Government Commemorative Sets" on page 1254.

*See also "Government Commemorative Sets" on page 1254.